U. S. DEPARTMENT
STATES RELAT
A. C. TRUE, DIRECTOR

EXPERIMENT STATION RECORD

VOLUME XXXVII

JULY–DECEMBER, 1917

WASHINGTON
GOVERNMENT PRINTING OFFICE
1918

U. S. DEPARTMENT OF AGRICULTURE.

Scientific Bureaus.

WEATHER BUREAU—C. F. Marvin, *Chief.*
BUREAU OF ANIMAL INDUSTRY—J. R. Mohler, *Chief.*
BUREAU OF PLANT INDUSTRY—W. A. Taylor, *Chief.*
FOREST SERVICE—H. S. Graves, *Forester.*
BUREAU OF SOILS—Milton Whitney, *Chief.*
BUREAU OF CHEMISTRY—C. L. Alsberg, *Chief.*
BUREAU OF CROP ESTIMATES—L. M. Estabrook, *Statistician.*
BUREAU OF ENTOMOLOGY—L. O. Howard, *Entomologist.*
BUREAU OF BIOLOGICAL SURVEY—E. W. Nelson, *Chief.*
OFFICE OF PUBLIC ROADS AND RURAL ENGINEERING—L. W. Page, *Director.*
BUREAU OF MARKETS—C. J. Brand, *Chief.*

STATES RELATIONS SERVICE—A. C. True, *Director.*
OFFICE OF EXPERIMENT STATIONS—E. W. Allen, *Chief.*

THE AGRICULTURAL EXPERIMENT STATIONS.

ALABAMA—
College Station: *Auburn;* J. F. Duggar.[1]
Canebrake Station: *Uniontown;* J. M. Burgess.[1]
Tuskegee Station: *Tuskegee Institute;* G. W. Carver.[1]
ALASKA—*Sitka:* C. C. Georgeson.[2]
ARIZONA—*Tucson:* ———.[1]
ARKANSAS—*Fayetteville:* M. Nelson.[1]
CALIFORNIA—*Berkeley:* T. F. Hunt.[1]
COLORADO—*Fort Collins:* C. P. Gillette.[1]
CONNECTICUT—
State Station: *New Haven;* }
Storrs Station: *Storrs;* } E. H. Jenkins.[1]
DELAWARE—*Newark:* H. Hayward.[1]
FLORIDA—*Gainesville:* P. H. Rolfs.[1]
GEORGIA—*Experiment:* J. D. Price.[1]
GUAM—*Island of Guam:* C. W. Edwards.[2]
HAWAII—]
Federal Station: *Honolulu;* J. M. Westgate.[2]
Sugar Planters' Station: *Honolulu;* H. P. Agee[1].
IDAHO—*Moscow:* J. S. Jones.[1]
ILLINOIS—*Urbana:* E. Davenport.[1]
INDIANA—*La Fayette:* C. G. Woodbury.[1]
IOWA—*Ames:* C. F. Curtiss.[1]
KANSAS—*Manhattan:* W. M. Jardine.[1]
KENTUCKY—*Lexington:* T. P. Cooper.[1]
LOUISIANA—
State Station: *University Station, Baton Rouge;* }
Sugar Station: *Audubon Park, New Orleans;* } W. R. Dodson.[1]
North La. Station: *Calhoun;* }
Rice Station: *Crowley;* }
MAINE—*Orono:* C. D. Woods.[1]
MARYLAND—*College Park:* H. J. Patterson.[1]
MASSACHUSETTS—*Amherst:* W. P. Brooks.[1]
MICHIGAN—*East Lansing:* R. S. Shaw.[1]
MINNESOTA—*University Farm, St. Paul:* R. W. Thatcher.[1]
MISSISSIPPI—*Agricultural College:* E. R. Lloyd.[1]

MISSOURI—
College Station: *Columbia;* F. B. Mumford.[1]
Fruit Station: *Mountain Grove;* Paul Evans.[1]
MONTANA—*Bozeman:* F. B. Linfield.[1]
NEBRASKA—*Lincoln:* E. A. Burnett.[1]
NEVADA—*Reno:* S. B. Doten.[1]
NEW HAMPSHIRE—*Durham:* J. C. Kendall.[1]
NEW JERSEY—*New Brunswick:* J. G. Lipman.[1]
NEW MEXICO—*State College:* Fabian García.[1]
NEW YORK—
State Station: *Geneva;* W. H. Jordan.[1]
Cornell Station: *Ithaca;* A. R. Mann.[1]
NORTH CAROLINA—*Raleigh* and *West Raleigh;* B. W. Kilgore.[1]
NORTH DAKOTA—*Agricultural College:* L. Van Es.[4]
OHIO—*Wooster:* C. E. Thorne.[1]
OKLAHOMA—*Stillwater:* H. G. Knight.[1]
OREGON—*Corvallis:* A. B. Cordley.[1]
PENNSYLVANIA—
State College: R. L. Watts.[1]
State College: Institute of Animal Nutrition: H. P. Armsby.[1]
PORTO RICO—
Federal Station: *Mayaguez;* D. W. May.[2]
Insular Station: *Rio Piedras;* E. Colón.[1]
RHODE ISLAND—*Kingston:* B. L. Hartwell.[1]
SOUTH CAROLINA—*Clemson College:* H. W. Barre.[1]
SOUTH DAKOTA—*Brookings:* J. W. Wilson.[1]
TENNESSEE—*Knoxville:* H. A. Morgan.[1]
TEXAS—*College Station:* B. Youngblood.[1]
UTAH—*Logan:* F. S. Harris.[1]
VERMONT—*Burlington:* J. L. Hills.[1]
VIRGINIA—
Blacksburg: A. W. Drinkard, jr.[1]
Norfolk: Truck Station; T. C. Johnson.[1]
WASHINGTON—*Pullman:* Geo. Severance.[4]
WEST VIRGINIA—*Morgantown:* J. L. Coulter.[1]
WISCONSIN—*Madison:* H. L. Russell.[1]
WYOMING—*Laramie:* A. D. Faville.[1]

---

[1] Director. [2] Agronomist in charge. [3] Animal husbandman in charge. [4] Acting director.

II

ISBN 978-1-5282-3137-4
PIBN 10927492

1 MONTH OF
FREE
READING

at

www.ForgottenBooks.com

By purchasing this book you are eligible for one month membership to ForgottenBooks.com, giving you unlimited access to our entire collection of over 1,000,000 titles via our web site and mobile apps.

To claim your free month visit:
www.forgottenbooks.com/free927492

English
Français
Deutsche
Italiano
Español
Português

www.forgottenbooks.com

Mythology Photography **Fiction**
Fishing Christianity **Art** Cooking
Essays Buddhism Freemasonry
Medicine **Biology** Music **Ancient
Egypt** Evolution Carpentry Physics
Dance Geology **Mathematics** Fitness
Shakespeare **Folklore** Yoga Marketing
Confidence Immortality Biographies
Poetry **Psychology** Witchcraft
Electronics Chemistry History **Law**
Accounting **Philosophy** Anthropology
Alchemy Drama Quantum Mechanics
Atheism Sexual Health **Ancient History**
Entrepreneurship Languages Sport
Paleontology Needlework Islam
Metaphysics Investment Archaeology
Parenting Statistics Criminology
Motivational

EXPERIMENT STATION RECORD.

Editor: E. W. ALLEN, Ph. D., *Chief, Office of Experiment Stations.*
Assistant Editor: H. L. KNIGHT.

EDITORIAL DEPARTMENTS.

Agricultural Chemistry and Agrotechny—E. H. NOLLAU.

Meteorology Soils, and Fertilizers {W. H. BEAL.
R. W. TRULLINGER.

Agricultural Botany, Bacteriology, and Plant Pathology {W. H. EVANS, Ph. D.
W. E. BOYD.

Field Crops {J. I. SCHULTE
J. D. LUCKETT.

Horticulture and Forestry—E. J. GLASSON.

Economic Zoology and Entomology—W. A. HOOKER, D. V. M.

Foods and Human Nutrition {C. F. LANGWORTHY, Ph. D., D. Sc.
H. L. LANG.

Zootechny, Dairying, and Dairy Farming {D. W. MAY.
M. D. MOORE.

Veterinary Medicine {W. A. HOOKER.
E. H. NOLLAU.

Rural Engineering—R. W. TRULLINGER.

Rural Economics—E. MERRITT.

Agricultural Education {C. H. LANE.
M. T. SPETHMANN.

Indexes—M. D. MOORE.

CONTENTS OF VOLUME XXXVII.

EDITORIAL NOTES.

Page.
The response of the experiment stations to the present emergency............. 1
The adjustment of theory and practice to war conditions....................... 4
Adequate station administration.. 101
Some tendencies under deficient administration............................. 105
The Federal food production act.. 301
Research and the research worker in relation to national affairs................ 401
The development of American technical agricultural journals................ 405
The Thirty-first Annual Convention of the Association of American Agricultural Colleges and Experiment Stations.................................. 601
Attendance at the agricultural colleges as affected by the war................ 701

STATION PUBLICATIONS ABSTRACTED.

ALABAMA COLLEGE STATION:
    Bulletin 193, February, 1917.. 233
    Bulletin 194, February, 1917.. 234
    Circular 35, February, 1917... 599
    Circular 36, April, 1917.. 682

ALABAMA TUSKEGEE STATION: Page.
    Bulletin 34, April, 1917.................................... 364
ARIZONA STATION:
    Bulletin 78, October 20, 1916............................. 209
ARKANSAS STATION:
    Bulletin 129, June, 1917.................................. 642
    Bulletin 130, March, 1917................................ 536
    Bulletin 131, March, 1917................................ 502
    Bulletin 132, 1917....................................... 881
    Bulletin 133, April, 1917................................ 678
    Bulletin 134, May, 1917.................................. 744
CALIFORNIA STATION:
    Bulletin 277, March, 1917................................ 236
    Bulletin 278, April, 1917................................ 338
    Bulletin 279, May, 1917.................................. 483
    Bulletin 280, May, 1917.................................. 586
    Bulletin 281, July, 1917................................. 757
    Circular 160, March, 1917................................ 143
    Circular 161, March, 1917................................ 139
    Circular 162, March, 1917................................ 182
    Circular 163, April, 1917................................ 289
    Circular 164, April, 1917................................ 447
    Circular 165, May, 1917.................................. 443
    Circular 166, August, 1917............................... 888
    Bean Culture... 641
    Observations on the Recent Agricultural Inquiry in California.......... 697
COLORADO STATION:
    Bulletin 219, July, 1916................................. 11, 38
    Bulletin 220, January, 1917.............................. 37
    Bulletin 221, January, 1917.............................. 41
    Bulletin 222, February, 1917............................. 43
    Bulletin 223, February, 1917............................. 241
    Bulletin 224, February, 1917............................. 209
    Bulletin 225, February, 1917............................. 286
    Bulletin 226, March, 1917................................ 232, 248
    Bulletin 227, April, 1917................................ 437
    Bulletin 228, April, 1917................................ 586
    Bulletin 229, May, 1917.................................. 690
    Bulletin 232, June, 1917................................. 646
    Bulletin 233, June, 1917................................. 661
    Twenty-ninth Annual Report, 1916........................ 599
CONNECTICUT STATE STATION:
    Bulletin 192, January, 1917.............................. 231
    Bulletin 193, March, 1917................................ 232, 234
    Bulletin 194, July, 1917................................. 813
    Bulletin 195, July, 1917................................. 848
    Bulletin of Information 7, April, 1917................... 290
    Annual Report, 1916, pt. 2............................... 254
    Annual Report, 1916, pt. 3............................... 268
    Annual Report, 1916, pt. 4............................... 863
CONNECTICUT STORRS STATION:
    Bulletin 88, October, 1916............................... 383
    Bulletin 89, February, 1917.............................. 368
    Bulletin 90, February, 1917.............................. 684

DELAWARE STATION: Page.
    Bulletin 117, March, 1917...   644
FLORIDA STATION:
    Bulletin 134, April, 1917...   356
    Bulletin 135, April, 1917...   313
    Bulletin 136, April, 1917...   453
    Bulletin 137, June, 1917..   656
    Bulletin 138, June, 1917..   644
    Annual Report, 1916..................... 635, 649, 651, 652, 656, 659, 683, 684, 699
GEORGIA STATION:
    Bulletin 125, February, 1917..   65
    Circular 75, January, 1917..   35
    Circular 76, February, 1917...   44
    Twenty-ninth Annual Report, 1916......................... 23, 28, 40, 48, 95
GUAM STATION:
    Report, 1916.. 728, 742, 767, 778. 796
HAWAII STATION:
    Bulletin 43, May 7, 1917..   320
    Annual Report, 1916.................... 116, 131, 132, 142, 144, 155, 165, 168, 195
HAWAIIAN SUGAR PLANTERS' STATION:
    Division of Agriculture and Chemistry Bulletin 45, 1917...................   515
IDAHO STATION:
    Bulletin 88, May, 1916..   39
    Bulletin 89, May, 1916..   67
    Bulletin 90, June, 1916...   75
    Bulletin 91, December, 1916...   87
    Bulletin 92 (Annual Report, 1916), December, 1916.........................   16,
                                    20, 29, 30, 37, 57, 66, 68, 70, 75, 95
    Bulletin 93, January, 1917..   640
    Bulletin 94, January, 1917..   639
    Bulletin 95, January, 1917..   640
    Bulletin 96, January, 1917..   676
    Bulletin 97, February, 1917...   646
    Bulletin 98, February, 1917...   647
    Circular 3, May, 1916...   271
    Circular 4, January, 1917...   244
ILLINOIS STATION:
    Bulletin 185 (abstract), February, 1916...................................   647
    Bulletin 196, February, 1917..   449
    Bulletin 197, March, 1917...   471
    Bulletin 198, April, 1917...   438
    Bulletin 199, May, 1917...   684
    Bulletin 200, May, 1917...   677
    Bulletin 201, June, 1917..   641
    Bulletin 202, July, 1917..   819
    Circular 193, April, 1917...   214
    Circular 194, April, 1917...   242
    Circular 195, April, 1917...   273
    Circular 196, April, 1917...   474
    Circular 197, May, 1917...   594
    Circular 198, May, 1917...   543
    Circular 199, June, 1917..   696
    Circular 200, June, 1917..   645

ILLINOIS STATION—Continued.   Page.
    Circular 201, June, 1917... 642
    Circular 202, June, 1917... 683
    Circular 203, August, 1917... 882
    Soil Report 15, March, 1917.. 514
    Soil Report 16, May, 1917.. 720
    Twenty-ninth Annual Report, 1916... 297

INDIANA STATION:
    Bulletin 178, popular ed., November, 1914.................................... 270
    Bulletin 179, popular ed., November, 1914.................................... 270
    Bulletin 197, December, 1916... 239
    Bulletin 198, March, 1917.. 214
    Bulletin 199, April, 1917.. 724
    Circular 58, January, 1917... 169
    Circular 59, March, 1917... 343
    Circular 60, March, 1917... 378
    Circular 61, April, 1917... 360
    Circular 62, July, 1917.. 882

IOWA STATION:
    Bulletin 151 (abridged ed.), December, 1915..................................   24
    Bulletin 166 (abridged ed.), July, 1916......................................   90
    Bulletin 169, March, 1917.. 854
    Bulletin 170, March, 1917.. 548
    Bulletin 171, July, 1917... 753
    Research Bulletin 34, July, 1916... 119
    Research Bulletin 35, July, 1916... 126
    Research Bulletin 36, July, 1916... 120
    Research Bulletin 37, November. 1916... 633
    Research Bulletin 38, January, 1917.. 686
    Circular 34, May, 1917... 474
    Circular 35, April, 1917... 552
    Circular 36, July, 1917.. 788
    Circular 37, July, 1917.. 736
    Soil Survey Report 1, January, 1917.. 211
    Annual Report, 1916... 30, 40, 66, 70, 95

KANSAS STATION:
    Bulletin 215, November, 1916... 560
    Bulletin 216, April, 1917.. 696
    Bulletin 217, May, 1917.. 671
    Inspection Bulletin 1, December. 1915.. 270
    Circular 56, June, 1916.. 373
    Circular 57, October, 1916... 368
    Circular 58, January, 1917... 451
    Circular 59, January, 1917... 376
    Circular 60, March, 1917... 368
    Inspection Circular 2, December, 1916.. 868
    Inspection Circular 3, October, 1916... 324
    Inspection Circular 4, March 1, 1917... 324

KENTUCKY STATION:
    Circular 13...   48
    Circular 14, March, 1917... 342

LOUISIANA STATIONS:
    Twenty-ninth Annual Report, 1916......................... 509, 529, 568, 572, 599

MAINE STATION: Page.
    Bulletin 257, December, 1916.................................. 314, 370, 371, 396
    Bulletin 258, January, 1917.. 395
    Bulletin 259, February, 1917... 663
    Bulletin 260, March, 1917........................... 628, 635, 647, 676, 680, 699
    Official Inspection 81, January, 1917................................... 40
    Official Inspection 82, February, 1917.................................. 570
    Document 522, February, 1916... 538
    Document 523, March, 1916.. 544
    Document 531, December, 1916... 533

MARYLAND STATION:
    Bulletin 198, October, 1916.. 340
    Bulletin 199, December, 1916... 320
    Bulletin 200, January, 1917.. 332
    Bulletin 201, February, 1917... 442
    Bulletin 202, February, 1917... 540
    Bulletin 203, March, 1917.. 541
    Bulletin 204, March, 1917.. 645
    Bulletin 205, April, 1917.. 660
    Bulletin 206, April, 1917.. 667
    Bulletin 207, May, 1917.. 648
    Bulletin 208, June, 1917... 856
    Twenty-eighth Annual Report, 1915...................................... 599
    Twenty-ninth Annual Report, 1916....................................... 599

MASSACHUSETTS STATION:
    Bulletin 172, March, 1917.. 342
    Meteorological Bulletins 339–340, March–April, 1917.................... 116
    Meteorological Bulletins 341–342, May–June, 1917...................... 619
    Meteorological Bulletins 343–344, July–August, 1917.................... 807

MICHIGAN STATION:
    Bulletin 277, December, 1916... 474
    Bulletin 278, December, 1916... 524
    Special Bulletin 80, May, 1917... 742
    Circular 33, July, 1917.. 724

MINNESOTA STATION:
    Bulletin 165, March, 1917.. 446
    Twenty-fourth Annual Report, 1916.. 217, 226, 228, 229, 240, 241, 270, 271, 289, 297
    Report Crookston Substation, 1910–1916....... 210, 226, 241, 268, 270, 286, 289, 297
    Report Duluth Substation, 1915.................................. 270, 271, 298
    Report Duluth Substation, 1916............................ 228, 269, 271, 286, 298
    Report Morris Substation, 1915... 229, 298

MISSISSIPPI STATION:
    Bulletin 178, December, 1916... 334

MISSOURI STATION:
    Bulletin 144, February, 1917... 69, 90
    Bulletin 145, February, 1917... 428
    Bulletin 146, March, 1917.. 428
    Bulletin 147 (Annual Report, 1916), June, 1917......................... 718,
                      728, 730, 743, 749, 754, 756, 760, 768, 779, 789, 796
    Research Bulletin 26, November, 1916................................... 71
    Research Bulletin 27, December, 1916................................... 72
    Circular 82, June, 1917.. 774

Montana Station: Page.
    Bulletin 111, October, 1916... 290
    Bulletin 112, December, 1916... 255
    Bulletin 113, December, 1916... 238
    Bulletin 114, December, 1916... 241
    Bulletin 115, January, 1917.. 283
Nebraska Station:
    Bulletin 158, February 15, 1917.. 544
    Bulletin 159, April 10, 1917... 678
    Research Bulletin 10, April 10, 1917... 447
    Circular 1, June 30, 1917.. 887
    Circular 2, March 10, 1917... 384
    Circular 3, May 5, 1917.. 591
Nevada Station:
    Bulletin 85, December, 1916.. 183
    Bulletin 86, April, 1917... 435
    Bulletin 87, April, 1917... 442
    Bulletin 88, April, 1917... 436
    Annual Report, 1916... 16, 30, 32, 78, 95
New Jersey Stations:
    Bulletin 299... 259
    Bulletin 300, June 1, 1916... 260
    Bulletin 301, October 2, 1916.. 243
    Bulletin 302, November 1, 1916... 239
    Bulletin 303, December 12, 1916.. 219
    Bulletin 304, January 22, 1917... 429
    Bulletin 305, January 6, 1917.. 425
    Bulletin 306, October 17, 1916... 664
    Bulletin 307, February 7, 1917... 665
    Circular 63, January 30, 1917.. 251
    Circular 64, February 15, 1917... 490
    Circular 65, March 7, 1917... 466
    Circular 66, March 25, 1917.. 645
    Circular 67, March 15, 1917.. 629
    Circular 68, April 4, 1917... 653
    Circular 69, April 18, 1917.. 642
    Circular 70, April 18, 1917.. 642
    Circular 71, April 25, 1917.. 654
    Circular 72, April 25, 1917.. 645
    Circular 73, May 1, 1917... 684
    Circular 74, May 10, 1917.. 767
    Circulars 75-79, May 10, 1917.. 744
    Hints to Poultrymen, vol. 5, No. 1, October, 1916............................ 71
    Hints to Poultrymen, vol. 5, No. 2, November, 1916........................... 71
    Hints to Poultrymen, vol. 5, No. 3, December, 1916........................... 82
    Hints to Poultrymen, vol. 5, N . 4, January, 1917............................ 71
    Hints to Poultrymen, vol. 5, o. 5, February, 1917............................ 71
    Hints to Poultrymen, vol. 5, o. 6, March, 1917.............................. 71
    Hints to Poultrymen, vol. 5, o. 7, April, 1917.............................. 280
    Hints to Poultrymen, vol. 5, o. 8, May, 1917................................ 368
    Hints to Poultrymen, vol. 5, . 9, June, 1917................................ 573
    Hints to Poultrymen, vol. 5, o. 10, July, 1917.............................. 774
    Hints to Poultrymen, vol. 5, No. 11, August, 1917........................... 872
    Hints to Poultrymen, vol. 5, No. 12, September, 1917........................ 871

NEW MEXICO STATION: Page.
    Bulletin 104, 1917.. 328
    Bulletin 105, March, 1917.. 343
    Bulletin 106, April, 1917.. 465
    Bulletin 107, May, 1917.. 644
    Twenty-seventh Annual Report, 1916.................... 32, 40, 52, 57, 68, 75, 95

NEW YORK CORNELL STATION:
    Bulletin 387, March, 1917.. 454
    Bulletin 388, April, 1917.. 464
    Bulletin 389, April, 1917.. 475
    Twenty-ninth Annual Report, 1916.. 298

NEW YORK STATE STATION:
    Bulletin 426, October, 1916.. 350
    Bulletin 427, December, 1916... 343
    Bulletin 428, December, 1916... 396
    Bulletin 429, February, 1917... 570, 575
    Bulletin 429, popular ed., February, 1917................................ 576
    Bulletin 430, March, 1917.. 523
    Bulletin 431, March, 1917.. 561
    Bulletin 432, April, 1917.. 544
    Bulletin 432, popular ed., April, 1917................................... 545
    Bulletin 433, April, 1917.. 655
    Technical Bulletin 56, December, 1916.................................... 359
    Technical Bulletin 57, January, 1917..................................... 516
    Technical Bulletin 58, March, 1917....................................... 516
    Technical Bulletin 59, March, 1917....................................... 516
    Technical Bulletin 60, March, 1917 517
    Technical Bulletin 61, March, 1917....................................... 521
    Technical Bulletin 62, May, 1917... 616

NORTH CAROLINA STATION:
    Bulletin 237, April, 1917.. 541
    Technical Bulletin 12, January, 1917..................................... 449
    Technical Bulletin 13, January, 1917..................................... 666
    Circular 35, May, 1917... 445
    Thirty-ninth Annual Report, 1916... 625,
                            636, 674, 676, 679, 681, 682, 689, 690, 691, 699

NORTH DAKOTA STATION:
    Bulletin 120, January, 1917.. 362
    Bulletin 121, January, 1917.. 720
    Bulletin 122, June, 1917... 863
    Special Bulletin, vol. 4, No. 11, February–March, 1917 63
    Special Bulletin, vol. 4, No. 12, April, 1917........................ 468, 488
    Special Bulletin, vol. 4, No. 13, May, 1917 570
    Special Bulletin, vol. 4, No. 14, June–July, 1917........................ 863
    Circular 16, March, 1917 492

OHIO STATION:
    Bulletin 306, December, 1916 124
    Bulletin 307, January, 1917 159
    Bulletin 308, January, 1917 169
    Bulletin 309, January, 1917 143
    Bulletin 310, February, 1917 258
    Bulletin 311, March, 1917.. 258
    Bulletin 312, March, 1917.. 235
    Bulletin 313, March, 1917.. 241

WASHINGTON STATION—Continued.
  Western Washington Station Monthly Bulletin, vol. 5—   Page.
    No. 1, April, 1917..   96
    No. 2, May, 1917..   491
    No. 3, June, 1917... 566, 591, 599
    No. 4, July, 1917...   699
    No. 5, August, 1917...   895
WEST VIRGINIA STATION:
    Bulletin 162, January, 1917.....................................   448
    Bulletin 163, November, 1916....................................   190
    Bulletin 164, March, 1917.......................................   344
    Inspection Bulletin 5, February, 1917...........................   127
WISCONSIN STATION:
    Bulletin 277, February, 1917....................................   37
    Bulletin 278, January, 1917.....................................   90
    Bulletin 279, April, 1917.......................................   324
    Bulletin 280, April, 1917.......................................   442
    Bulletin 281, June, 1917..   471
WYOMING STATION:
    Bulletin 111, December, 1916....................................   334
    Bulletin 112, January, 1917.....................................   780
    Bulletin 113, March, 1917.......................................   788
    Twenty-sixth Annual Report, 1916........................... 314, 374, 396

UNITED STATES DEPARTMENT OF AGRICULTURE PUBLICATIONS
ABSTRACTED.

Annual Reports, 1916... 277, 289, 297
Journal of Agricultural Research:
  Volume 8—
    No. 11, March 12, 1917.. 50, 59
    No. 12, March 19, 1917.. 49, 77
  Volume 9—
    No. 1, April 2, 1917.. 154, 160, 181
    No. 2, April 9, 1917..   117
    No. 3, April 16, 1917...   222
    No. 4, April 23, 1917... 281, 282
    No. 5, April 30, 1917... 318, 380
    No. 6, May 7, 1917.. 352, 381
    No. 7, May 14, 1917... 318, 353
    No. 8, May 21, 1917... 422, 456
    No. 9, May 28, 1917... 421, 429
    No. 10, June 4, 1917..   564
    No. 11, June 11, 1917....................................... 536, 559, 583
    No. 12, June 18, 1917....................................... 653, 654, 672
  Volume 10—
    No. 1, July 2, 1917...................................... 637, 653, 660, 663
    No. 2, July 9, 1917.................................. 612, 658, 661, 673, 676
    No. 3, July 16, 1917.. 623, 686
    No. 4, July 23, 1917.................................... 753, 754, 759, 766
    No. 5, July 30, 1917.. 785, 787
    No. 6, August 6, 1917..................................... 709, 738, 764
    No. 7, August 13, 1917................................... 809, 812, 848, 885
    No. 8, August 20, 1917.. 808, 857

Bulletin 389, Public Road Mileage and Revenues in the Central, Mountain, and Page.
Pacific States, 1914...   288
Bulletin 390, Public Road Mileage and Revenues in the United States, 1914..   289
Bulletin 458, Handling and Marketing Durango Cotton in the Imperial Valley,
J. G. Martin and G. C. White..   37
Bulletin 460, The Pine Trees of the Rocky Mountain Region, G. B. Sudworth.   346
Bulletin 475, Reforestation on the National Forests, C. R. Tillotson..........   348
Bulletin 476, A Study of Cotton Market Conditions in North Carolina with a view
to Their Improvement, O. J. McConnell and W. R. Camp...................   36
Bulletin 477, Marketing and Distribution of Strawberries in 1915, O. W.
Schleussner and J. C. Gilbert...   43
Bulletin 479, Nursery Practice on the National Forests, C. R. Tillotson.......   348
Bulletin 480, Solid-stream Spraying against the Gipsy Moth and the Brown-tail
Moth in New England, L. H. Worthley....:................................   563
Bulletin 481, The Status and Value of Farm Woodlots in the Eastern United
States, E. H. Frothingham..   245
Bulletin 484, Control of the Gipsy Moth by Forest Management, G. E. Clement
and W. Munro...   55
Bulletin 491, The Melon Fly in Hawaii, E. A. Back and C. E. Pemberton.....   566
Bulletin 497, Tests of Western Yellow Pine Car Sills, Joists, and Small Clear
Pieces, C. W. Zimmerman..   89
Bulletin 502, The Drainage of Irrigated Shale Land, D. G. Miller and L. T.
Jessup..   86
Bulletin 504, The Theory of Correlation as Applied to Farm Survey Data on
Fattening Baby Beef, H. R. Tolley..   269
Bulletin 506, Production of Lumber, Lath, and Shingles in 1915 and Lumber
in 1914, J. C. Nellis..   148
Bulletin 510, Timber Storage Conditions in the Eastern and Southern States
with Reference to Decay Problems, C. J. Humphrey......................   349
Bulletin 511, Farm Practice in the Cultivation of Cotton, H. R. Cates........   36
Bulletin 512, Prevention of the Erosion of Farm Lands by Terracing, C. E.
Ramser...   87
Bulletin 520, A System of Accounts for Cotton Warehouses, R. L. Newton and
J. R. Humphrey..   594
Bulletin 521, Courses in Secondary Agriculture for Southern Schools (First
and Second Years), H. P. Barrows.......................................   395
Bulletin 522, Characteristics and Quality of Montana-grown Wheat, L. M.
Thomas...   361
Bulletin 523, Utilization of Ash, W. D. Sterrett.............................   548
Bulletin 524, Detection of Lime Used as a Neutralizer in Dairy Products, H. J.
Wichmann..   313
Bulletin 525, Experiments in the Determination of the Digestibility of Millets,
C. F. Langworthy and A. D. Holmes.....................................   364
Bulletin 527, Some Exercises in Farm Handicraft for Rural Schools, H. O.
Sampson...   699
Bulletin 528, Seasonal Distribution of Farm Labor in Chester County, Pa.,
G. A. Billings..   390
Bulletin 529, Validity of the Survey Method of Research, W. J. Spillman....   389
Bulletin 530, The Organization and Management of a Farmers' Mutual Fire
Insurance Company, V. N. Valgren......................................   391
Bulletin 531, Rhizopus Rot of Strawberries in Transit, N. E. Stevens and
R. B. Wilcox..   351
Bulletin 532, The Expansion and Contraction of Concrete and Concrete Roads,
A. T. Goldbeck and F. H. Jackson, jr....................................   884

Page.

Bulletin 533, Extension of Cotton Production in California, O. F. Cook....... 335
Bulletin 534, Apple Blotch and Its Control, J. W. Roberts.................. 654
Bulletin 535, The Horse-radish Flea-beetle: Its Life History and Distribution, F. H. Chittenden and N. F. Howard..................................... 566
Bulletin 537, The Results of Physical Tests of Road-building Rock in 1916, Including All Compression Tests, P. Hubbard and F. H. Jackson, jr........ 386
Bulletin 538, Shrimp: Handling, Transportation, and Uses, E. D. Clark, L. MacNaughton, and Mary E. Pennington.................................. 863
Bulletin 539, The Lesser Cornstalk Borer, P. Luginbill and G. G. Ainslie...... 851
Bulletin 540, A First-year Course in Home Economics for Southern Agricultural Schools, Louise Stanley..................................... 894
Bulletin 542, The Pollination of the Mango, W. Popenoe..................... 835
Bulletin 543, Control of Peach Bacterial Spot in Southern Orchards, J. W. Roberts.. 842
Bulletin 545, Important Range Plants: Their Life History and Forage Value, A. W. Sampson.. 818
Bulletin 546, Effect of Fall Irrigation on Crop Yields at Belle Fourche, S. Dak., F. D. Farrell and B. Aune... 822
Bulletin 547, Cooperative Purchasing and Marketing Organizations among Farmers in the United States, O. B. Jesness and W. H. Kerr.............. 888
Bulletin 548, The Business of Ten Dairy Farms in the Blue-grass Region of Kentucky, J. H. Arnold.. 873
Bulletin 549, Crossties Purchased and Treated in 1915, A. M. McCreight...... 838
Bulletin 550, Control of the Grape-berry Moth in the Erie-Chautauqua Grape Belt, D. Isely.. 852
Bulletin 551, Variation in the Chemical Composition of Soils, W. O. Robinson, L. A. Steinkoenig, and W. H. Fry...................................... 811
Bulletin 552, The Seasoning of Wood, H. S. Betts.......................... 886
Bulletin 553, The Chicken Mite: Its Life History and Habits, H. P. Wood.... 859
Bulletin 556, Mechanical Properties of Woods Grown in the United States, J. A. Newlin and T. R. C. Wilson....................................... 885
Bulletin 557, A Comparison of Several Classes of American Wheats and a Consideration of Some Factors Influencing Quality, L. M. Thomas.............. 860
Bulletin 558, Marketing Grain at Country Points, G. Livingston and K. B. Seeds... 889
Bulletin 559, Accounting Records for Country Creameries, J. R. Humphrey and G. A. Nahstoll.. 875
Bulletin 560, Cost of Keeping Farm Horses and Cost of Horse Labor, M. R. Cooper... 867
Bulletin 561, Feed Cost of Egg Production.—Results of Three Years' Experiments at the Government Poultry Farm, H. M. Lamon and A. R. Lee...... 871
Farmers' Bulletin 788, The Windbreak as a Farm Asset, C. G. Bates.......... 46
Farmers' Bulletin 793, Foxtail Millet: Its Culture and Utilization in the United States, H. N. Vinall... 37
Farmers' Bulletin 794, Citrus-fruit Improvement, A. D. Shamel............. 144
Farmers' Bulletin 795, The Domestic Silver Fox, N. Dearborn............... 156
Farmers' Bulletin 796, Some Common Edible and Poisonous Mushrooms, Flora W. Patterson and Vera K. Charles..................................... 263
Farmers' Bulletin 797, Sweet Clover: Growing the Crop, H. S. Coe.......... 540
Farmers' Bulletin 798, The Sheep Tick and Its Eradication by Dipping, M. Imes... 357
Farmers' Bulletin 799, Carbon Disulphid as an Insecticide, W. E. Hinds..... 559
Farmers' Bulletin 800, Grains for the Dry Lands of Central Oregon, L. R. Breithaupt... 333

Farmers' Bulletin 801, Mites and Lice on Poultry, F. C. Bishopp and H. P.   Page.
   Wood.. 357
Farmers' Bulletin 802, Classification of American Upland Cotton, D. E. Earle
   and F. Taylor.. 830
Farmers' Bulletin 803, Horse-breeding Suggestions for Farmers, H. H. Reese.. 368
Farmers' Bulletin 804, Aphids Injurious to Orchard Fruits, Currant, Goose-
   berry, and Grape, A. L. Quaintance and A. C. Baker...................... 358
Farmers' Bulletin 805, The Drainage of Irrigated Farms, R. A. Hart......... 587
Farmers' Bulletin 806, Standard Varieties of Chickens.—I, The American
   Class, R. R. Slocum... 368
Farmers' Bulletin 807, Bread and Bread Making in the Home, Caroline L.
   Hunt and Hannah L. Wessling... 364
Farmers' Bulletin 808, How to Select Foods.—I, What the Body Needs, Caro-
   line L. Hunt and Helen W. Atwater..................................... 364
Farmers' Bulletin 809, Marketing Live Stock in the South, S. W. Doty...... 390
Farmers' Bulletin 810, Equipment for Farm Sheep Raising, V. O. McWhorter.. 388
Farmers' Bulletin 811, The Production of Baby Beef, S. H. Ray............. 367
Farmers' Bulletin 812, How Live Stock is Handled in the Blue-grass Region
   of Kentucky, J. H. Arnold... 471
Farmers' Bulletin 813, Construction and Use of Farm Weirs, V. M. Cone...... 882
Farmers' Bulletin 814, Bermuda Grass, S. M. Tracy........................ 440
Farmers' Bulletin 815, Organization, Financing, and Administration of Drain-
   age Districts, H. S. Yohe... 883
Farmers' Bulletin 816, Minor Articles of Farm Equipment, H. N. Humphrey
   and A. P. Yerkes... 491
Farmers' Bulletin 817, How to Select Foods.—II, Cereal Foods, Caroline L.
   Hunt and Helen W. Atwater... 668
Farmers' Bulletin 818, The Small Vegetable Garden........................ 447
Farmers' Bulletin 819, The Tobacco Budworm and Its Control in the Southern
   Tobacco Districts, A. C. Morgan and F. L. McDonough.................... 663
Farmers' Bulletin 820, Sweet Clover: Utilization, H. S. Coe................. 444
Farmers' Bulletin 821, Watermelon Diseases, W. A. Orton.................. 554
Farmers' Bulletin 822, Live-stock Classifications at County Fairs, S. H. Ray. 598
Farmers' Bulletin 823, Sugar-beet Sirup, C. O. Townsend and H. C. Gore..... 511
Farmers' Bulletin 824, How to Select Foods.—III, Foods Rich in Protein,
   Caroline L. Hunt and Helen W. Atwater................................. 864
Farmers' Bulletin 825, Pit Silos, T. P. Metcalfe and G. A. Scott............. 789
Farmers' Bulletin 827, Shallu or "Egyptian Wheat," B. E. Rothgeb.......... 740
Weekly News Letter, vol. 5, No. 16, November 21, 1917...................... 670
Yearbook, 1916.................................. 511, 520, 521, 522, 537, 540, 542, 543,
     547, 556, 558, 559, 563, 572, 573, 574, 577, 585, 589, 592, 593, 594, 595, 598, 599
OFFICE OF THE SECRETARY:
   Circular 73, Automobile Registrations, Licenses, and Revenues in the
     United States, 1916.. 590
   Office of Farm Management Circular 2, Plan for Handling the Farm Labor
     Problem.. 790
BUREAU OF ANIMAL INDUSTRY:
   Service and Regulatory Announcement 116............................. 81
   How to Use Skim Milk.. 669
   Milk as a Food... 669
   Simple Directions for Making Cottage Cheese on the Farm.............. 686
   Ways to Use Cottage Cheese.. 669
   The Manufacture of Cottage Cheese in Creameries and Milk Plants....... 686
   The Food Value of American Cheese................................... 669
   Buttermilk as a Food Drink... 669

BUREAU OF CROP ESTIMATES:
Monthly Crop Report, Volume 3—   Page.
  No. 3, March, 1917... 92
  No. 4, April, 1917... 191
  No. 5, May, 1917.. 392
  No. 6, June, 1917... 697
  No. 7, July, 1917... 697
  No. 8, August, 1917.. 891

BUREAU OF ENTOMOLOGY:
Some Timely Suggestions for the Owners of Woodlots in New England,
  F. H. Mosher and G. E. Clement...................................... 451

BUREAU OF PLANT INDUSTRY:
Inventory of Seeds and Plants Imported, January 1 to March 31, 1914.... 819
Inventory of Seeds and Plants Imported, April 1 to June 30, 1914........ 819
Inventory of Seeds and Plants Imported, July 1 to September 30, 1914.. 819
A Lister Attachment for a Cotton Planter, S. H. Hastings................ 90

BUREAU OF SOILS:
Field Operations, 1914—
  Soil Survey in Alabama, Barbour County, H. C. Smith, N. E. Bell,
    and J. F. Stroud... 621
Field Operations, 1915—
  Soil Survey in California, Healdsburg Area, E. B. Watson, W. C. Dean,
    C. J. Zinn, and R. L. Pendleton................................. 810
  Soil Survey in Delaware, New Castle County, T. M. Morrison, W. B.
    Seward, and O. I. Snapp.. 211
  Soil Survey in Idaho, Latah County, J. H. Agee, G. W. Graves. and
    C. B. Mickelwaite.. 21
  Soil Survey in Indiana, Wells County, W. E. Tharp and W. E. Wiley.. 21
  Soil Survey in Iowa, Clinton County, H. W. Hawker and F. B. Howe.. 514
  Soil Survey in Iowa, Van Buren County, C. Lounsbury and H.W. Reid. 21
  Soil Survey in Kansas, Cowley County, E. C. and R. H. Hall and B. W.
    Tillman.. 419
  Soil Survey in Maine, Cumberland County, C. Van Duyne and M.
    W. Beck.. 810
  Soil Survey in Mississippi, Chickasaw County, E. M. Jones and C. S.
    Waldrop.. 621
  Soil Survey in Missouri, Buchanan County, B. W. Tillman and C. E.
    Deardorff.. 122
  Soil Survey in Nebraska. Polk County, J. M. Snyder and T. E. Kokjer. 122
  Soil Survey in Nebraska, Richardson County, A. H. Meyer, P. H.
    Stewart. and C. W. Watson..................................... 211
  Soil Survey in Nebraska, Washington County, L. V. Davis and H. C.
    Mortlock... 22
  Soil Survey in New Jersey, Camden Area, A. L. Patrick. C. C. Engle,
    and L. L. Lee.. 123
  Soil Survey in New York, Schoharie County, E. T. Maxon and G. L.
    Fuller... 514
  Soil Survey in North Carolina, Anson County, E. S. Vanatta and F. N.
    McDowell.. 621
  Soil Survey in North Carolina, Davidson County, R. B. Hardison and
    L. L. Brinkey.. 22
  Soil Survey in Ohio, Hamilton County, A. L. Goodman, E. R. Allen,
    and S. W. Phillips... 212

BUREAU OF SOILS—Continued.
  Field Operations, 1915—Continued.

    Soil Survey in Pennsylvania, Blair County, J. O. Veatch, H. P. **Page.**
      Young, and H. P. Cooper... 123
    Soil Survey in Virginia, Fairfax and Alexandria Counties, W. T.
      Carter, jr., and C. K. Yingling, jr................................. 514
    Soil Survey in West Virginia, Lewis and Gilmer Counties, W. J. Lati-
      mer.. 22

STATES RELATIONS SERVICE:
  Syllabus 24, Illustrated Lecture on Leguminous Forage Crops for the South,
    C. V. Piper and H. B. Hendrick...................................... 194
  Syllabus 25, Illustrated Lecture on Leguminous Forage Crops for the
    North, C. V. Piper and H. B. Hendrick............................... 194
  Syllabus 26, Illustrated Lecture on Sweet Potatoes: Culture and Storage,
    H. M. Conolly.. 297
  Syllabus 27, Illustrated Lecture on the Farm Vegetable Garden, H. C.
    Thompson and H. M. Conolly....................................... 297
  Syllabus 28, Illustrated Lecture on Practical Improvement of Farm
    Grounds, F. L. Mulford and H. M. Conolly........................... 396
  Syllabus 29, Illustrated Lecture on Public-road Improvement........... 598

OFFICE OF MARKETS AND RURAL ORGANIZATION:
  Document 4, Preliminary report on apple-packing houses in the Northwest,
    W. M. Scott and W. B. Alwood...................................... 648

WEATHER BUREAU:
  National Weather and Crop Bulletin 7, 1917........................... 315
  National Weather and Crop Bulletin 8, 1917........................... 316
  National Weather and Crop Bulletin 9, 1917........................... 316
  National Weather and Crop Bulletin 10, 1917.......................... 317
  National Weather and Crop Bulletin 11, 1917.......................... 316
  U. S. Monthly Weather Review—
    Volume 45—
      Nos. 1–2, Jannary–February, 1917........................... 114, 115
      Nos. 3–4, March–April, 1917................................ 512, 513
      Nos. 5–6, May–June, 1917.................................. 807, 808
      Supplement 5.. 116
      Supplement 6.. 314
      Supplement 7.. 807
    Climatological Data—
    Volume 3—
      No. 13, 1916.. 314
    Volume 4—
      Nos. 1–2, January–February, 1917........................... 116
      Nos. 3–4, March–April, 1917................................ 619

SCIENTIFIC CONTRIBUTIONS.[1]

Adams, F., Irrigation of Orchards.. 143
Ainslie, C. N., Construction of the Cocoon of Praon........................... 856
Ainslie, C. N., Life History of *Phalonia spartinana*......................... 358
Ainslie, G. G., Crambid Moths and Light..................................... 259
Albright, A. R., Method for Examination of Methyl Salicylate................. 415
Aldrich, J. M., Sarcophaga and Allies in North America...................... 160

---

[1] Printed in scientific and technical publications outside the Department.

49002°—18——2

Page.

Allard, H. A., Effect of Environmental Conditions on Tobacco Plants........   224
Ashe, W. W., Some Problems in Appalachian Timber Appraisal..............   46
Ayers, S. H., Cook, L. B., and Clemmer, P. W., Significance of Colon Bacilli in
    Milk...   874
Back, E. A., The Mediterranean Fruit Fly.....................................   565
Bailey, V., A New Subspecies of Meadow Mouse from Wyoming..............   846
Baker, A. C., Eastern Aphids, New or Little-known, II.......................   850
Baker, A. C., Some Sensory Structures in the Aphididæ......................   850
Baker, A. C., Synopsis of the Genus Saltusaphis...............................   157
Balcom, R. W., The Volatile Reducing Substance in Cider Vinegar...........   112
Banks, N., New Mites, Mostly Economic......................................   860
Banks, N., Greene, C. T., McAtee, W. L., and Shannon, R. C., District of
    Columbia Diptera: Syrphidæ..   57
Bassett, C. E., Extent and Possibilities of Cooperative Marketing............   796
Bates, C. G., Biology of Lodgepole Pine as Revealed by Behavior of Its Seed..   244
Bates, C. G., Forest Succession in Central Rocky Mountains..................   451
Bates, C. G., Rôle of Light in Natural and Artificial Reforestation............   45
Beckett, S. H., and Robertson, R. D., Economical Irrigation of Alfalfa in Sacra-
    mento Valley..   586
Benson, O. H., and Betts, G. H., Agriculture and the Farming Business......   290
Berry, S., Determining the Quality of Standing Timber......................   243
Berry, S., Volume of Western Yellow Pine Logs from an Actual Mill Tally....   451
Bigelow, W. D., and Dunbar, P. B., Acid Content of Fruits...................   714
Bird, H. S., Important Factors in the Successful Cold Storage of Apples........   833
Bishopp, F. C., Insect Control about Abattoirs and Packing Houses..........   560
Boncquet, P. A., and Stahl, C. F., Wild Vegetation as a Source of Curly-top
    Infection of Sugar Beets..   847
Bonsteel, J. A., Control Factors in Agricultural Development................   189
Branch, G. V., Cooperative Organization.....................................   143
Brooks, F. E., Two Destructive Grape Insects of the Appalachian Region.....   58
Brown, F. W., Fertilizers and Industrial Wastes.............................   630
Brown, H. H., Inflammability of Carbonaceous Dusts.......................   109
Brown, H. H., and Clement, J. K., Inflammability of Carbonaceous Dusts in
    Atmospheres of Low Oxygen Content......................................   410
Buckley, J. S., and Shippen, L. P., Relation of Anaerobic Organisms to Forage
    Poisoning...   179
Bunzel, H. H., Mode of Action of the Oxidases.............................   326
Bunzel, H. H., Oxidase Activity of Plant Juices and Their Hydrogen Ion
    Concentrations.. 9, 429
Bunzel, H. H., Relative Oxidase Activity of Different Organs of the Same
    Plant...   326
Bunzel, H. H., and Hasselbring, H., Supposed Action of Potassium Perman-
    ganate with Plant Peroxidases...   726
Burgess, A. F., and Griffin, E. L., New Tree Banding Material for Control of
    Gipsy Moth..   258
Burke, H. E., A Buprestid Household Insect (Chrysophana placida)...........   854
Burke, H. E., Some Western Buprestidæ......................................   566
Burr, W. W., Cultivation to Conserve Soil Moisture.........................   437
Busck, A., Perisierola emigrata, a Parasite of the Pink Bollworm.............   667
Bushnell, T. M., and Erni, C. P., Soil Survey of White County [Indiana].....   21
Bushnell, T. M., Smies, E. H., Watkins, W. I., Anderson, A. C., Thomas, M.,
    Stebbins, M. E., Doneghue, R. C., and Ince, J. W., Soil Survey of Dickey
    County, North Dakota..   720

Page.

Cance, A. E., Functions of a State Bureau of Markets......................... 888
Chace, E. M., Maturity Standard for Washington Navel Orange............... 345
Chace, E. M., Standards of Maturity for the Washington Navel Orange....... 649
Chernoff, L. H., Viehoever, A., and Johns, C. O., A Saponin from *Yucca filamentosa*.. 9
Chilcott, E. C., Dry-land Agriculture Investigations in the Great Plains Area.. 437
Chittenden, F. H., The Two-banded Fungus Beetle......................... 567
Clapp, E. H., The Correlation of American Forest Research.................... 44
Clark, E. D., and Almy, L. H., Chemical Changes in Shucked Oysters under Refrigeration... 311
Clark, W. B., A Sampling Press... 711
Clark, W. M., On the Formation of "Eyes" in Emmental Cheese............. 875
Clark, W. M., and Lubs, H. A., Improved Chemical Methods for Differentiating Bacteria of the Coli-aerogenes Family..................................... 506
Clark, W. M., and Lubs, H. A., The Colorimetric Determination of Hydrogen Ion Concentration and Its Applications in Bacteriology.................... 506
Cole, F. R., Osten Sacken's Group "Poecilanthrax," with Descriptions of New Species.. 565
Collins, C. W., Determining Wind Dispersion of the Gipsy Moth and Other Insects... 254
Cone, V. M., Divisors (for the Measurement of Irrigation Water)............. 586
Cook, O. F., and Cook, Alice C., Polar Bear Cacti........................... 434
Corbett, L. C., Variety Testing... 240
Crawley, H., Zoological Position of the Sarcosporidia....................... 53
Crosby, D. J., Present Relation of Farmers' Institutes and Extension Schools.. 796
Crossman, S. S., Some Methods of Colonizing Imported Parasites............... 257
Currie, J. N., Citric Acid Fermentation of *Aspergillus niger*.................... 613
Dachnowski, A. P., Agricultural Possibilities of Ohio Peat Soils.............. 212
Dachnowski, A. P., Formation and Characteristics of Massachusetts Peat Lands and Some of Their Uses.. 810
Davidson, W. M., Little-known Western Plant Lice, II...................... 562
Davidson, W. M., The Reddish-brown Plum Aphis (*Rhopalosiphum nymphex*).. 562
Davidson, W. M., *Typha latifolia* as a Summer Host of Injurious Insects...... 461
Dearing, C., Muscadine Grape Breeding..................................... 544
Dilla, F. M., Belle Fourche Reservoir as a Bird Reservation and Refuge...... 355
Dille, F. M., The Minidoka National Bird Reservation, Idaho................ 355
Dorset, M., and Henley, R. R., Preparation and Use of Agglutinin from Beans.. 81
DuBois, C., Latest Devices in Protection Work............................... 348
Dyar, H. G., A New Noctuid from Brazil................................... 564
Dyar, H. G., A New Phycitid from the Bahamas............................ 564
Dyar, H. G., A Note on Cysthene... 564
Dyar, H. G., Miscellaneous New American Lepidoptera..................... 564
Dyar, H. G., Notes on North American Nymphulinæ....................... 564
Dyar, H. G., Notes on North American Pyraustinæ......................... 564
Dyar, H. G., Notes on North American Schœnobiinæ....................... 564
Dyar, H. G., Seven New Crambids from the United States................... 564
Dyar, H. G., Seven New Pyralids from British Guiana...................... 564
Dyar, H. G., The Barnes and McDunnough "List"......................... 563
Dyar, H. G., The Mosquitoes of the Mountains of California................. 564
Dyar, H. G., Three New North American Phycitinæ......................... 564
Dyar, H. G., and Knab, F., Bromelicolous Anopheles....................... 565
Dyer, D. C., New Method of Steam Distillation for Determination of Volatile Fatty Acids... 13

Page.

Eichhorn, A., Vesicular Stomatitis in Cattle.................................... 81
Evans, Alice C., Numbers of *Bacterium abortus* var. *lipolytious* Which May Be
    Found in Milk.. 173
Evans, M. W., Some Effects of Legumes on Associated Nonlegumes........... 438
Evans, M. W., The Flowering Habits of Timothy............................. 140
Evenson, O. L., Correction Required in Applying the Babcock Formula to
    Estimation of Total Solids in Evaporated Milk............................. 508
Fetherolf, J. M., Aspen as a Permanent Forest Type......................... 837
Fisher, W. S., A New Species of Agrilus from California.................... 566
Fisher, W. S., A New Species of Xylotrechus............................... 566
Fortier, S., Duty of Water in Irrigation.................................... 185
Fortier, S., The Farmers' Part in Irrigation Development.................... 281
Fortier, S., Use of Water in Irrigation.................................... 185
Foster, W. D., A Further Note on Polyradiate Cestodes..................... 361
Foster, W. D., Two New Cases of Polyradiate Cestodes, with Summary of Cases
    Already Known.. 361
Fox, H., Field Notes on Virginia Orthoptera............................... 461
Frothingham, E. H., Ecology and Silviculture in Southern Appalachians....... 45
Fuller, A. V., Simple Improvised Apparatus for Hydrogen Sulphid Precipita-
    tion under Pressure.. 712
Gallagher, B., Epithelioma Contagiosum of Quail........................... 83
Gallagher, B., Fowl Cholera and other Immunization Experiments............ 83
Gardiner, R. F., and Shorey, E. C., Action of Solutions of Ammonium Sulphate
    on Muscovite.. 505
Gibson, E. H., A New Species of Corythucha from the Northwest............. 849
Gibson, E. H., Additions to the List of Missouri Cicadellidæ................ 157
Gibson, E. H., Three New Species of Jassoidea from Missouri................ 157
Gibson, E. H., Two New Species of Dicyphus from Porto Rico................ 561
Gilbert, J. C., The Federal Office of Markets and Rural Organization......... 888
Gillespie, L. J., and Walters, E. H., Possibilities and Limitations of the Duclaux
    Method for Estimation of Volatile Acids................................... 803
Girard, J. W., Forest Service Stumpage Appraisals.......................... 838
Girault, A. A., A Chalcid Parasite of the Pink Bollworm.................... 569
Girault, A. A., A New Genus of Omphaline Eulophidæ from North America... 162
Girault, A. A., A New West Indian Chalcid Fly............................. 667
Girault, A. A., Australian Hymenoptera Chalcidoidea....................... 855
Girault, A. A., Chalcid Flies, Chiefly from California...................... 467
Girault, A. A., Descriptions of Various Chalcidoid Hymenoptera, with Obser-
    vations... 467
Girault, A. A., New Australian Chalcid Flies,............................. 569
Girault, A. A., New Chalcid Flies from Maryland, II....................... 766
Girault, A. A., New Javanese Chalcidoid Hymenoptera...................... 59
Girault, A. A., North American Species of Habrocytus (Chalcid Flies)....... 162
Girault, A. A., Occurrence of the Genus Monobæus in North America........ 667
Girault, A. A., Occurrence of the Genus Parachrysocharis in the United States 570
Girault, A. A., Some New Australian Chalcid Flies, Mostly of the Family En-
    cyrtidæ... 569
Girault, A. A., Some Parasites of Sugar-cane Insects in Java, with Descrip-
    tions of New Hymenoptera Chalcidoidea.................................... 667
Girault, A. A., Three New Chalcid Flies from California.................... 360
Glaser, R. W., Growth of Insect Blood Cells in Vitro...................... 759
Glaser, R. W., and Chapman, J. W., Nature of Polyhedral Bodies Found in
    Insects... 253
Goddard, L. H., Results of Farm Management Demonstration Work.......... 389

Page.

Goldbeck, A. T., Causes of Cracks in Cement-concrete Pavements............   88
Goldman, E. A., New Mammals from North and Middle America.............   757
Goldman, E. A., Two New Pocket Mice from Wyoming......................   758
Goss, B. C., Adsorption of Tin by Proteins and Solution of Tin by Canned
    Foods..   12
Graves, H. S., Practical Reforestation..   836
Gruse, W. A., and Acree, S. F., Reactions of Ions and Molecules of Acids,
    Bases, and Salts..   201
Hall, M. C., Synoptical Key to the Adult Tænioid Cestodes of Some Carnivores.   82
Hall, M. C., and Foster, W. D., Oil of Chenopodium and Chloroform as Anthel-
    mintics.—Preliminary Note..   578
Hall, R. C., Timber Estimating in Southern Appalachians...................   46
Hanzlik, E. J., Fuller, F. S., and Erickson, E. C., Breakage, Defect, and Waste
    in Douglas Fir...   651
Hartman, B. G., and Tolman, L. M., Vinegar Investigation.—Changes That
    Cider Undergoes during Fermentation and Storage and Its Subsequent Con-
    version into Vinegar in Rotating Generators...............................   716
Hawley, L. F., Discontinuous Extraction Processes............................   803
Hedgcock, G. G., and Hunt, N. R., *Dothichiza populea* in the United States..   354
Heidemann, O., Two New Species of Lace Bugs.............................   563
Henshaw, H. W., Friends of Our Forests.....................................   846
Hitchcock, A. S., Taxonomic Botany and the Washington Botanist...........   435
Hoagland, R., Quantitative Estimation of Dextrose in Muscular Tissue......   617
Hoagland, R., and Mansfield, C. M., Function of Muscular Tissue in Urea
    Formation..   802
Hoagland, R., and Mansfield, C. M., Glycolytic Properties of Muscular Tissue..   802
Hood, J. D., A New Sericothrips from Africa................................   849
Hood, J. D., Annotated List of Thysanoptera of Plummer's Island, Md........   561
Hood, S. C., Factors Causing Variation in Yield in Florida Camphor Tree.....   346
Hood, S. C., Possibility of Commercial Production of Lemon-grass Oil in the
    United States...   546
Horton, J. R., Some Weather-proof Bands for Use against Ants.............   59
Howard, L. O., A New Aphis-feeding Aphelinus............................   766
Howard, L. O., The Carriage of Disease by Insects.........................   848
Howard, L. O., Dyar, H. G., and Knab, F., Mosquitoes of North and Central
    America and West Indies..   762
Howell, A. H., Description of a New Ground Squirrel from Wyoming.........   758
Hubbard, W. S., Identification of Emodin-bearing Drugs...................   509
Hudson, C. S., Acetyl Derivatives of the Sugars...........................   201
Hudson, C. S., Phenylhydrazids of Certain Acids of the Sugar Group.........   201
Hudson, C. S., and Dale, J. K., Forms of *d*-Glucose and Their Mutarotation...   109
Hudson, C. S., and Harding, T. S., Preparation of Xylose...................   410
Hudson, C. S., and Johnson, J. M., Rotatory Powers of Some New Derivatives
    Gentiobiose...   502
Hudson, C. S., and Sawyer, H. L., Preparation of Pure Crystalline Mannose..   201
Hudson, C. S., and Yanovsky, E., Indirect Measurements of the Rotatory Powers
    of Some Sugars..   410
Hunter, W. D., The Pink Bollworm..   358
Hyslop, J. A., Notes on an Introduced Weevil (*Ceutorhynchus marginatus*)....   568
Jackson, H. H. T., A New Shrew from Nova Scotia..........................   753
Jayne, S. O., Duty of Water...   231
Johns, C. O., and Brewster, J. F., Kafirin, an Alcohol-soluble Protein from
    Andropogon sorghum..   8
Johns, C. O., and Jones, D. B., The Proteins of the Peanut, *Arachis hypogæa*..   468

Page.

Johns, C. O., and Jones, D. B., The Proteins of the Peanut.—I, Arachin and
Conarachin... 8
Johns, C. O., and Jones, D. B., The Proteins of the Peanut.—II, Distribution
of Basic Nitrogen in Arachin and Conarachin.............................. 501
Jones, D. B., and Johns, C. O., Some Proteins from the Jack Bean, *Canavalia
ensiformis*... 8
Judd, R. C., and Acree, S. F., A Method of Producing Crude Wood Creosote
from Hardwood Tar... 114
Keister, J. T., Application of the Cryoscopic Method for Determining Added
Water in Milk... 804
Kelly, E. O. G., The Green Bug (*Toxoptera graminum*) Outbreak of 1916...... 561
Kempton, J. H., Lobed Leaves in Maize.................................... 136
Knab, F., On Some North American Species of Microdon..................... 766
Kress, O., and McNaughton, G. C., Further Studies on the Ives Tint Photo-
meter... 110
Kress, O., and Silverstein, P., Influence of Humidity on Paper............ 109
La Forge, F. B., *d*-Mannoketoheptose, a New Sugar from the Avocado........ 9
La Forge, F. B., and Hudson, C. S., Sedoheptose, a New Sugar from *Sedum
spectabile*, I... 502
La Rue, C. D., and Bartlett, H. H., Matroclinic Inheritance in Mutation
Crosses of *Œnothera reynoldsii*.. 724
Lamb, G. N., Marketing Farm Woodlot Products in Maine.................... 838
Lane, C. H., Home Project at an Agricultural School...................... 795
Lane, C. H., and Crosby, D. J., District Agricultural Schools of Georgia...... 193
Lathrop, E. C., A Simple Device for the Washing of Precipitates........... 503
Lathrop, E. C., Generation of Aldehydes by *Fusarium cubense*............. 843
Lathrop, E. C., Organic Nitrogen Compounds of Soils and Fertilizers........ 216
Le Clerc, J. A., and Bailey, L. H., Composition of Grain Sorghum Kernels.... 539
Long, W. H., Æcial Stage of *Coleosporium ribicola*....................... 354
McAtee, W. L., How Birds' Stomachs Are Examined.......................... 355
McDonnell, C. C., and Graham, J. J. T., Decomposition of Dilead Arsenate by
Water... 802
McDonnell, C. C., and Smith, C. M., Arsenates of Lead.—III, Basic Arsenates.. 410
McIndoo, N. E., Recognition among Insects................................ 459
McIndoo, N. E., Sense Organs on Mouth Parts of the Honeybee.............. 360
McKay, A. W., Preventing Frost Damage in Transit........................ 649
McMurran, S. M., Notes on Pecan Diseases................................ 756
McMurran, S. M., Winterkilling, Sun Scald, or Sour Sap of Pecans.......... 755
Mangam, A. W., and Acree, S. F., Preparation of Beta Glucose............. 410
Marlatt, C. L., Losses Caused by Imported Tree and Plant Pests........... 559
Marsh, C. D., Potassium Permanganate as an Antidote for the Effects of Poison-
ous Plants.. 688
Martin, O. B., Mass Instruction through Group Training................... 596
Mathewson, E. H., and Moss, E. G., Tobacco Culture in North Carolina...... 541
Meigs, E. B., and Blatherwick, N. R., Calcium and Phosphorus in Blood of
Lactating Cows.. 308
Melvin, A. D., Are Uniform Regulations Feasible for Diseases of Animals?.... 77
Merritt, E., Economic Factors to be Considered in Connection with the Project
for Extension Work among Farm Women...................................... 699
Mohler, J. R., American Veterinary Medical Association.—Report of Com-
mittee on Diseases.. 274
Mohler, J. R., An Outbreak of Vesicular Stomatitis...................... 81
Mohler, J. R., Shipping Fever of Horses................................. 182
Monahan, A. C., and Lane, C. H., Agricultural Education................. 392

Page.

Morrison, H., Nearctic Hymenoptera of the Genus Bracon.................... 360
Mundell, J. E., and Smith, H. G., Dry Farming in Eastern New Mexico...... 328
Munger, T. T., Problem of Making Volume Tables for Use on National Forests.. 450
Murphy, L. S., Seeding Habits of Spruce in Competition with Its Associates.. 45
Myers, P. R., An American Species of the Hymenopterous Genus Wesmælia
 of Foerster.. 855
Nelson, E. K., Gingerol and Paradol.. 612
Oakleaf, H. B., Douglas Fir Shipbuilding................................... 452
Oberholser, H. C., Description of a New Genus of Anatidæ................... 758
Oberholser, H. C., Description of a New Sialia from Mexico.................. 846
Oberholser, H. C., Diagnosis of a New Laniine Family of Passeriformes...... 846
Oberholser, H. C., Mutanda Ornithologica, I, II............................ 758
Obst, Maud M., Bile Compared with Lactose Bouillon for Determining *Bacil-
lus coli*... 188
Page, L. W., Policy and Program in Road Construction under the Federal Aid
 Law.. 89
Palmer, T. S., Deer Flat National Bird Reservation, Idaho.................... 355
Patten, H. E., and Mains, G. H., Apparatus for the Purification of Mercury... 503
Patten, H. E., and Mains, G. H., Carbonation Studies.—I, A Mechanical Stirrer
 for Carbonation Direct in the Bottle................................... 716
Pemberton, C. E., and Willard, H. F., Parasitism of the Larvæ of the Mediter-
ranean Fruit Fly in Hawaii during 1916.................................... 856
Pennington, Mary E., Hepburn, J. S., St. John, E. Q., and Witmer, E., Influ-
ence of Temperatures Above Freezing on Flesh of Fowl.................... 62
Pennington, Mary E., Hepburn, J. S., St. John, E. Q., and Witmer, E., Influ-
ence of Temperatures Below Freezing on Flesh of Fowl 62
Phelps, I. K., and Palmer, H. E., Estimation of Butyric Acid in Biological
 Products, I... 206
Phillips, E. F., Outdoor Wintering [of Bees]............................... 360
Phillips, E. F., Results of Apiary Inspection............................... 263
Phillips, W. J., Report on Isosoma Investigations.......................... 263
Pieper, E. J., Acree, S. F., and Humphrey, C. J., Chemical Composition of the
 Higher Fractions of Maple-wood Creosote............................... 502
Pieper, E. J., Acree, S. F., and Humphrey, C. J., Toxicity to a Wood-destroying
Fungus of Maple-wood Creosote and of Some of Its Constituents and Deriva-
tives, together with a Comparison with Beechwood Creosote.............. 502
Pierce, W. D., Notes on a Southern Trip.................................... 560
Pierce, W. D., Studies of Weevils with Descriptions of New Genera and Species. 58
Piper, C. V., Grasses in Relation to Dry Farming........................... 437
Piper, C. V., and Oakley, R. A., Turf for Golf Courses...................... 146
Pittier, H., New or Noteworthy Plants from Colombia and Central America, VI. 819
Pittier, H., The Middle American Species of Lonchocarpus.................. 819
Popenoe, W., The Avocado in Florida and Other Lands...................... 144
Pritchard, F. J., Morphological Characters and Saccharin Content of Sugar
 Beets.. 28
Pritchard, F. J., Recent Investigations in Sugar-beet Breeding.............. 442
Ransom, B. H., Parasites of Food Animals Transmissible to Man............ 355
Ransom, B. H., and Hall, M. C., Further Note on the Life History of *Gongy-
lonema scutatum*.. 577
Reed, W. G., The Coefficient of Correlation................................ 621
Reeve, C. S., and Lewis, R. H., Effects of Exposure on Some Fluid Bitumens. 711
Reeves, G. I., The Alfalfa Weevil Investigation............................ 262
Ricker, P. L., A Valuable Unpublished Work on Pomology.................... 41
Ricker, P. L., New Names in Amygdalus.................................... 220

Page.

Robertson, R. D., Irrigation of Rice in California.............................. 483
Rockwood, L. P., An Aphis Parasite Feeding at Puncture Holes Made by the
    Ovipositor.. 856
Rohwer, S. A., A Nearctic Species of Dolichurus............................. 569
Rohwer, S. A., Collection of Hymenoptera (Mostly from California) Made by
    W. M. Giffard.. 855
Rohwer, S. A., *Diprion simile* in North America............................. 568
Rohwer, S. A., Two Bethylid Parasites of the Pink Bollworm................. 569
Rohwer, S. A., Two New Species of Macrophya............................... 667
Ross, W. H., Extraction of Potash from Silicate Rocks, II.................... 427
Round, L. A., Fermentation of Sauerkraut................................... 165
Round, L. A., Normal Fermentation of Sauerkraut........................... 208
Round, L. A., and Coppersmith, S. C., Sauerkraut Industry of the United
    States... 806
Salant, W., and Mitchell, C. W., Influence of Heavy Metals on Isloated
    Intestine.. 266
Salant, W., Mitchell, C. W., and Schwartze, E. W., Action of Succinate,
    Malate, Tartrate, and Citrate on Intestine................................ 471
Salant, W., and Schwartze, E. W., Action of Xanthin and Methyl Xanthins on
    Isolated Intestine... 471
Sasscer, E. R., Foreign Insect Pests Collected on Imported Nursery Stock in
    1916.. 257
Scammell, H. B., New Method of Controlling the Black-head Fireworm....... 56
Scheffer, T. H., The Pocket Gopher and Destructive Habits.................. 355
Schorger, A. W., Chemistry of Wood.. 502
Schorger, A. W., Chemistry of Wood.—III, Mannan Content of Gymnosperms.. 710
Schorger, A. W., Oleoresin of Douglas Fir................................... 411
Schroeder, E. C., Control and Prevention of Infectious Diseases of Cattle...... 583
Schroeder, J. P., Automatic Suction Attachment for an Ordinary Pipette..... 503
Schroeder, J. P., Fertilizer Value of City Wastes.—II, Garbage Tankage....... 723
Schwartz, B., Serum Therapy for Trichinosis............................... 784
Schwarz, E. A., Ants Protecting Acacia Trees in Central America............ 568
Scott, L. B., Comparative Merits of California Avocado Varieties............. 345
Shamel, A. D., A Bud Variation of Euonymus............................... 145
Shamel, A. D., A Bud Variation of Pittosporum............................. 546
Shamel, A. D., A Lemon Bud Variation..................................... 345
Shamel, A. D., Sampling Tubes for Manure, Alfalfa, or Other Organic Materials. 711
Shamel, A. D., Variation in Artichokes...................................... 342
Shear, C. L., Spoilage of Cranberries After Picking.......................... 745
Shorey, E. C., and Fry, W. H., Influence of Calcite Inclusions on Determination
    of Organic Carbon in Soils.. 505
Show, S. B., Effect of Depth of Covering Seed on Germination and Quality of
    Stock... 451
Sievers, A. F., Further Notes on Germination of Belladonna Seed............. 545
Sievers, A. F., Rubber from *Eucommia ulmoides*........................... 417
Skinner, J. J., and Beattie, J. H., Influence of Fertilizers and Soil Amendments
    on Acidity.. 23
Smith, E. F., Further Evidence as to the Relation between Crown Gall and
    Cancer.. 245
Smith, H. E., Notes on New England Tachinidæ, with Description of One New
    Genus and Two New Species... 763
Smith, H. K., and Acree, S. F., Commercial Beech-wood Creosote............ 114
Smith, W. S. A., Utilization of Waste on the Farms......................... 389
Snyder, T. E., Horse Flies as a Pest in Southern Florida..................... 565

Page.

Spaulding, P., Notes on *Cronartium comptoniæ*, III. 845
Spillman, W. J., Biology and the Nation's Food. 263
Spillman, W. J., The Farmer's Response to Economic Forces. 389
Stedman, J. M., Statistics of Farmers' Institutes in United States, 1915-16.... 796
Sterrett, W. D., Marketing Woodlot Products in Tennessee. 548
Stevens, N. E., Influence of Climatic Factors on Development of *Endothia parasitica*. 557
Stevens, N. E., Influence of Temperature on Growth of *Endothia parasitica*.... 557
Stevens, N. E., Method for Studying Humidity Relations of Fungi in Culture. 549
Stuart, W., Growing Potatoes under Irrigation for Profit. 830
Summers, J. N. [Parasite Work in Maine]. 459
Taylor, A. E., Control of Food Supplies in Blockaded Germany. 166
Thompson, C. W., Rural Surveys. 592
Thompson, C. W., The Federal Farm Loan Act. 291
Thompson, H. C., Peanut Growing in the Cotton Belt. 442
Thomson, E. H., Gaining a Foothold on the Land. 389
Townsend, C. H. T., Head and Throat Bots of American Game Animals....... 565
Townsend, C. H. T., New Genera and Species of American Muscoid Diptera.. 764
Townsend, C. H. T., Recent Questioning of the Transmission of Verruga by Phlebotomus. 358
Townsend, C. H. T., Synoptic Revision of the Cuterebridæ, with Synonymic Notes and Description of One New Species. 565
Townsend, C. H. T., The Stages in the Asexual Cycle of the Organism of Verruga Peruviana. 460
Townsend, C. H. T., Two New Genera of African Muscoidea. 359
Townsend, C. O., Present Status of Sugar-beet Seed Industry in the United States. 540
True, A. C., Relation of the Smith-Lever Funds to Farmers' Institutes....... 796
Urbahns, T. D., Destroy the Grasshoppers. 561
Van Dine, D. L., Relation of Malaria to Crop Production. 57
Vosbury, E. D., Avocado Varieties in Florida. 345
Vrooman, C., Work of the U. S. Department of Agriculture. 796
Waite, M. B., Additional Suggestions on Treatment of Hazel Blight. 755
Walters, E. H., Isolation of Parahydroxybenzoic Acid from Soil. 709
Ward, A. R., Suppuration in Cattle and Swine Caused by *Bacterium pyogenes*.. 276
Weir, J. R., Control of Mistletoe in the Northwest. 458
Wetmore, A., Birds of Culebra Island, Porto Rico. 355
Wetmore, A., New Honey Eater from the Marianne Islands. 758
White, E. C., and Acree, S. F., Quinone-phenolate Theory of Indicators...... 409
Wilcox, A. M., Rearing Insects for Experimental Purposes and Life History Work. 758
Willett, G., East Park Bird Reservation, California. 355
Willett, G., Salt River National Bird Reservation, Arizona. 355
Williams, R. R., Chemical Nature of the Vitamins, III. 411
Winslow, C. P., Grouping of Ties for Treatment. 748
Winslow, C. P., and Thelen, R., The Purchase of Pulpwood. 452
Wise, L. E., Simplified Microcombustion Method for Determination of Carbon and Hydrogen. 803
Woglum, R. S., Fruit Injury during Fumigation of Citrus Trees. 634
Woglum, R. S., Mealy Bug Control. 158
Wright, S., Color Inheritance in Mammals. 866
Yarnell, D. L., Farm Drainage in Virginia. 384
Yothers, W. W., Some Reasons for Spraying Citrus Trees in Florida. 460
Zon, R., Some Problems in Light as a Factor of Forest Growth. 45

U. S. DEPARTMENT OF AGRICULTURE
STATES RELATIONS SERVICE
A. C. TRUE, DIRECTOR

Vol. 37   JULY, 1917   No. 1

EXPERIMENT
STATION
RECORD

WASHINGTON
GOVERNMENT PRINTING OFFICE
1917

U. S. DEPARTMENT OF AGRICULTURE.

Scientific Bureaus.

WEATHER BUREAU—C. F. Marvin, *Chief.*
BUREAU OF ANIMAL INDUSTRY—A. D. Melvin, *Chief.*
BUREAU OF PLANT INDUSTRY—W. A. Taylor, *Chief.*
FOREST SERVICE—H. S. Graves, *Forester.*
BUREAU OF SOILS—Milton Whitney, *Chief.*
BUREAU OF CHEMISTRY—C. L. Alsberg, *Chief.*
BUREAU OF CROP ESTIMATES—L. M. Estabrook, *Statistician.*
BUREAU OF ENTOMOLOGY—L. O. Howard, *Entomologist.*
BUREAU OF BIOLOGICAL SURVEY—E. W. Nelson, *Chief.*
OFFICE OF PUBLIC ROADS AND RURAL ENGINEERING—L. W. Page, *Director.*
BUREAU OF MARKETS—C. J. Brand, *Chief.*

STATES RELATIONS SERVICE—A. C. True, *Director.*
OFFICE OF EXPERIMENT STATIONS—E. W. Allen, *Chief.*

THE AGRICULTURAL EXPERIMENT STATIONS.

ALABAMA—
  College Station: *Auburn;* J. F. Duggar.[1]
  Canebrake Station: *Uniontown;* F. R. Curtis.[1]
  Tuskegee Station; *Tuskegee Institute;* G. W.
    Carver.[1]
ALASKA—*Sitka;* C. C. Georgeson.[2]
ARIZONA—*Tucson;* R. H. Forbes.[1]
ARKANSAS—*Fayetteville;* M. Nelson.[1]
CALIFORNIA—*Berkeley;* T. F. Hunt.[1]
COLORADO—*Fort Collins;* C. P. Gillette.[1]
CONNECTICUT—
  State Station: *New Haven;*   } E. H. Jenkins.[1]
  Storrs Station: *Storrs;*   }
DELAWARE—*Newark;* H. Hayward.[1]
FLORIDA—*Gainesville;* P. H. Rolfs.[1]
GEORGIA—*Experiment;* J. D. Price.[1]
GUAM—*Island of Guam;* C. W. Edwards.[2]
HAWAII—
  Federal Station: *Honolulu;* J. M. Westgate.[2]
  Sugar Planters' Station: *Honolulu;* H. P. Agee.[2]
IDAHO—*Moscow;* J. S. Jones.[1]
ILLINOIS—*Urbana;* E. Davenport.[1]
INDIANA—*La Fayette;* A. Goss.[1]
IOWA—*Ames;* C. F. Curtiss.[1]
KANSAS—*Manhattan;* W. M. Jardine.[1]
KENTUCKY—*Lexington;* A. M. Peter.[4]
LOUISIANA—
  State Station: *Baton Rouge;*   }
  Sugar Station: *Audubon Park,*   } W. R. Dodson.[1]
    New Orleans;   }
  North La. Station: *Calhoun;*   }
MAINE—*Orono;* C. D. Woods.[1]
MARYLAND—*College Park;* H. J. Patterson.[1]
MASSACHUSETTS—*Amherst;* W. P. Brooks.[1]
MICHIGAN—*East Lansing;* R. S. Shaw.[1]
MINNESOTA—*University Farm, St. Paul;*——.
MISSISSIPPI—*Agricultural College;* E. R. Lloyd.[1]
MISSOURI—
  College Station: *Columbia;* F. B. Mumford.[1]
  Fruit Station: *Mountain Grove;* Paul Evans.[1]

MONTANA—*Bozeman;* F. B. Linfield.[1]
NEBRASKA—*Lincoln;* E. A. Burnett.[1]
NEVADA—*Reno;* S. B. Doten.[1]
NEW HAMPSHIRE—*Durham;* J. C. Kendall.[1]
NEW JERSEY—*New Brunswick;* J. G. Lipman.[1]
NEW MEXICO—*State College;* Fabian Garcia.
NEW YORK—
  State Station: *Geneva;* W. H. Jordan.[1]
  Cornell Station: *Ithaca;* A. R. Mann.[4]
NORTH CAROLINA—
  College Station: *West Raleigh;* } B. W. Kilgore.[2]
  State Station: *Raleigh;*   }
NORTH DAKOTA—*Agricultural College;* T. P.
  Cooper.[1]
OHIO—*Wooster;* C. E. Thorne.[1]
OKLAHOMA—*Stillwater;* W. L. Carlyle.[1]
OREGON—*Corvallis;* A. B. Cordley.[1]
PENNSYLVANIA—
  State College: R. L. Watts.[1]
  State College: Institute of Animal Nutrition;
    H. P. Armsby.[1]
PORTO RICO—
  Federal Station: *Mayaguez;* D. W. May.[2]
  Insular Station: *Rio Piedras;* W. V. Tower.[1]
RHODE ISLAND—*Kingston;* B. L. Hartwell.[1]
SOUTH CAROLINA—*Clemson College;* H. W. Barre.[1]
SOUTH DAKOTA—*Brookings;* J. W. Wilson.[1]
TENNESSEE—*Knoxville;* H. A. Morgan.[1]
TEXAS—*College Station;* B. Youngblood.[1]
UTAH—*Logan;* F. S. Harris.[1]
VERMONT—*Burlington;* J. L. Hills.[1]
VIRGINIA—
  Blacksburg; A. W. Drinkard, jr.[1]
  Norfolk; Truck Station; T. C. Johnson.[2]
WASHINGTON—*Pullman;* Geo. Severance.[2]
WEST VIRGINIA—*Morgantown;* J. L. Coulter.[1]
WISCONSIN—*Madison;* H. L. Russell.[1]
WYOMING—*Laramie;* H. G. Knight.[1]

[1] Director.   [2] Agronomist in charge.   [3] Animal husbandman in charge.   [4] Acting director.

EXPERIMENT STATION RECORD.

Editor: E. W. ALLEN, Ph. D., *Chief, Office of Experiment Stations.*
Assistant Editor: H. L. KNIGHT.

EDITORIAL DEPARTMENTS.

Agricultural Chemistry and Agrotechny—E. H. NOLLAU.
Meteorology, Soils, and Fertilizers{W. H. BEAL.
R. W. TRULLINGER.
Agricultural Botany, Bacteriology, and Plant Pathology{W. H. EVANS, Ph. D.
W. E. BOYD.
Field Crops{J. I. SCHULTE.
J. D. LUCKETT.
Horticulture and Forestry—E. J. GLASSON.
Economic Zoology and Entomology—W. A. HOOKER, D. V. M.
Foods and Human Nutrition{C. F. LANGWORTHY, Ph. D., D. Sc.
H. L. LANG.
Zootechny, Dairying, and Dairy Farming{M. D. MOORE.
Veterinary Medicine{W. A. HOOKER.
E. H. NOLLAU.
Rural Engineering—R. W. TRULLINGER.
Rural Economics—E. MERRITT.
Agricultural Education{C. H. LANE.
M. T. SPETHMANN.
Indexes—M. D. MOORE.

CONTENTS OF VOL. 37, NO. 1.

Page.

Editorial notes:
The response of the experiment stations..................................... 1
The adjustment of theory and practice to war conditions................. 4
Recent work in agricultural science... 8
Notes... 97

SUBJECT LIST OF ABSTRACTS.

AGRICULTURAL CHEMISTRY—AGROTECHNY.

Kafirin, protein from *Andropogon sorghum*, Johns and Brewster.............. 8
Some proteins from the jack bean, *Canavalia ensiformis*, Jones and Johns...... 8
The proteins of the peanut.—I, Arachin and conarachin, Johns and Jones..... 8
The proteins of the colostrum and milk of the cow, Crowther and Raistrick.... 8
Protein copper compounds, Osborne and Leavenworth......................... 8
d–Mannoketoheptose, a new sugar from the avocado, La Forge................. 9
A saponin from *Yucca filamentosa*, Chernoff, Viehoever, and Johns........... 9
Oxidase activity of plant juices and hydrogen ion concentrations, Bunzell.. 9
The sampling of fertilizers, Lodge... 9
Influence of carbohydrates on accuracy of Van Slyke method, Hart and Sure.. 10
Estimation of mixtures of four or more carbohydrates, Wilson and Atkins.... 10
[Method for analysis of wheat grain, plants, and straw], Headden 11
New qualitative test and colorimetric method for estimation of vanillin, Estes .. 12
Summary of the composition of the wines of current consumption, Filaudeau.. 12
Adsorption of tin by proteins and the solution of tin by canned foods, Goss.. 12
The detection of added water in milk in India, Leather....................... 13

Page.

Nature of the reducing substances precipitated by lead subacetate, Pellet....   13
Notes upon oil testing, Gill...   13
Color tests for oils.—Palm oil, Gill...   13
New method of steam distillation for volatile fatty acids, Dyer...............   13
[Examination of lulu kernels and lulu oil (shea butter) from Uganda]..........   14
Estimating general turbidity of fluid suspensions, Dreyer and Gardner.........   14
The estimation of amino-acid nitrogen in blood, Bock.........................   14
Concentration and rotatory power of solutions of nicotin, Tingle and Ferguson.   14
New method for determination of nicotin in tobacco, Tingle and Ferguson.....   14
Sirups for canning and preserving, McNair....................................   15
The manufacture of apple jelly, Truelle.......................................   15

METEOROLOGY.

The quantitative study of climatic factors in relation to plant life, Adams.....   15
World-wide changes of temperature, Brooks....................................   15
Improved methods in hygrometry, Shaw..   16
Department of meteorology..   16
[Meteorological summary]...   16
New England snowfall, Brooks...   16
Meteorology, Flammarion..   16
Climatology of 1915, Flammarion..   16
The rainfall of Java, Wallis...   16

SOILS—FERTILIZERS.

Biological changes in soil during storage, Allison.............................   17
A method for determining volume weight of soils in field condition, Shaw.....   18
Soil valuation and soil investigation, Remy...................................   18
The capacity of the soil to absorb and hold water, Rindell....................   18
Dynamics of soluble phosphoric acid in the soil...............................   18
Solubility of manganese compounds in the soil, Masoui........................   18
Soil bacteriology, Hutchinson...   19
Studies of north Idaho soils, Putnam..   20
Organic matter of the soil.—III. Production of humus from manures, Gortner.   20
The loess soils of Nebraska portion of transition region, VI, Alway et al.......   20
Soil survey of Latah County, Idaho, Agee et al................................   21
Soil survey of Wells County, Indiana, Tharp and Wiley........................   21
Soil survey of White County [Indiana], Bushnell and Erni.....................   21
Soil survey of Van Buren County, Iowa, Lounsbury and Reid...................   21
Soil survey of Washington County, Nebraska, Davis and Mortlock.............   22
Soil survey of Davidson County, North Carolina, Hardison and Brinkley......   22
Soil survey of Lewis and Gilmer Counties, West Virginia, Latimer............   22
Arable soils, Charron...   22
Stable manure, Temple..   23
Absorption and washing out of nitrogen from nitrates, van Harreveld-Lako....   23
Lime nitrogen as a fertilizer, Milo..   23
Residual effect of phosphatic manures on green crops.........................   23
Influence of fertilizers and soil amendments on acidity, Skinner and Beattie ..   23
The rotary kiln for lime burning—descriptive and comparative, Jones.........   24
Soil acidity and the liming of Iowa soils, Brown..............................   24
Fertilizer analyses, McDonnell..   24

AGRICULTURAL BOTANY.

The progressive development of the wheat kernel.............................   24
Translocation of protein reserves in corn seedling, Pettibone and Kennedy.....   24
Relation of amid nitrogen to nitrogen metabolism of pea, Sure and Tottingham.   24
Release of oxygen during reduction of nitrates in green plants, Molliard......   25
Cytological formation of anthocyanin in living plants, Mirande...............   25
Selective permeability: Absorption by Hordeum vulgare, Brown and Tinker...   25
Some photochemical experiments with pure chlorophyll, Jörgensen and Kidd.   26
Aeriferous tissue in willow galls, Cosens and Sinclair........................   26
Determining the transpiring power of plant surfaces, Livingston and Shreve..   26
Germinability tests with seeds of Lepidium sativum, Lesage..................   26
Influence of medium on orientation of secondary terrestrial roots, Holman.....   27

Page.

The growth of forest tree roots, McDougall.. 27
The toxicity of bog water, Rigg.. 27
Experimental cultures of plants on the seashore, Daniel.............................. 27
Establishment of varieties in Coleus by selection of somatic variations, Stout.. 27
Mutation in *Matthiola annua*, a "Mendelizing" species, Frost................. 28
Morphological characters and saccharin content of sugar beets, Pritchard..... 28
Anomalies in *Beta vulgaris*, Munerati and Zapparoli............................. 28
Green manures and manuring in the Tropics, de Sornay, trans. by Flattely... 28

FIELD CROPS.

[Report of field crop work at the Georgia Experiment Station], McClelland... 28
[Report of field crop work], Ray, Eklof, Peterson, and Graves................ 29
[Report of field crop work at the Aberdeen substation], Aicher............... 30
[Report of field crop work]... 30
Irrigation experiments with alfalfa, sugar beets, potatoes, and wheat......... 30
Variety testing and crop improvement... 32
[Report of field crop work]... 32
Farm crops.. 32
Alfalfa fertilizers, Brown... 33
Phosphorus and potassium requirements of barley plant during growth, Pember. 34
Report on corn and cotton varieties, 1916, McClelland.......................... 35
Farm practice in the cultivation of cotton, Cates................................... 36
A study of cotton market conditions in North Carolina, McConnell and Camp.. 36
Handling and marketing Durango cotton in Imperial Valley, Martin and White. 37
Foxtail millet.—Its culture and utilization in the United States, Vinall...... 37
Potato growing in Colorado, Sandsten... 37
[Field experiments with potatoes at the Jerome substation], Dewey.......... 37
The management of tobacco soils, Johnson... 37
A study of Colorado wheat, III, Headden.. 38
Dry-farmed and irrigated wheat, Jones. Colver, Kelly, and Hays............. 39
Commercial agricultural seeds, 1916, Woods....................................... 40

HORTICULTURE.

[Report of the] department of horticulture, Stuckey............................. 40
[Some results of horticultural work]... 40
[Report on horticultural investigations].. 40
[Report of the] division of horticulture.. 40
Hotbeds and cold frames, Limbocker... 41
[Experiments with tomatoes and cucumbers]....................................... 41
Fruit growing for amateurs, Thomas and Gardner................................ 41
Fruit varieties for Maine, Brown.. 41
A valuable unpublished work on pomology, Ricker.............................. 41
The pruning manual, Bailey.. 41
Pruning problems in the Hood River Valley, Brown............................. 41
Influence of commercial fertilizer on bearing apple tree, Lewis and Brown.... 41
Experimental dusting and spraying of peaches, Chase.......................... 42
What the experiment station peach orchard has cost and produced, McCue... 42
Experimental investigations of the plum (*Prunus domestica*), I, Feruglio..... 42
Strawberry growing, Fletcher.. 42
The forcing of strawberries, Kinnison.. 43
Marketing and distribution of strawberries in 1915, Schleussner and Gilbert.... 43
Behavior of the root system of various graft stocks, Ravaz...................... 43
Oil percentage in different varieties of olives, Laffer........................... 43
Citrus fertilization experiments in Porto Rico, Kinman......................... 43
Some profitable and unprofitable coffee lands, McClelland...................... 43
What tea planters can and must do for selection, Stuart......................... 43
Investigations on tea fermentation, Bosscha and Brzesowsky.................. 44
Report on varieties of pecans at the Georgia Station, Stuckey................. 44
Breeding for atropin, Arny... 44
Planting the home grounds, McFarland.. 44
Decorative shrubs and trees, Wolf.. 44
How to grow chrysanthemums, Clayton... 44

FORESTRY.

Page.
The correlation of American forest research, Clapp............................   44
Sixteenth annual report of the State Board of Forestry, 1916, Gladden.........   44
Report of the department of forestry of Pennsylvania for 1914–15, Conklin....   45
Report of the committee on forests, Leavitt...................................   45
Forest administration in Northwest Frontier Province for 1915–16, Parnell....   45
Progress report of forest administration in Baluchistan for 1915–16, Mulraj.....   45
Ecology and silviculture in the southern Appalachians, Frothingham...........   45
Reforesting Pennsylvania's waste land.—What and how to plant, Conklin....   45
Silvicultural problems on forest reserves, Fernow............................   45
Some problems in light as a factor of forest growth, Zon.....................   45
The rôle of light in natural and artificial reforestation, Bates..................   45
Seeding habits of spruce in competition with its associates, Murphy..........   45
Practical method of preventing damping-off of coniferous seedlings, Scott.....   46
The windbreak as a farm asset, Bates...   46
Timber estimating in the southern Appalachians, Hall.........................   46
Some problems in Appalachian timber appraisal, Ashe.........................   46
Rôle of microscope in identification of "timbers of commerce," Bailey.......   46

DISEASES OF PLANTS.

[Report of the division of botany.—Bacteriology and pathology]...............   46
[Plant diseases in 1915]..   47
Plant protection, Stebler...   47
Studies in tropical teratology, Costerus and Smith...........................   47
Studies in the physiology of parasitism, II, Blackman and Welsford..........   47
Studies in the physiology of parasitism, III, Brown..........................   47
Osmotic pressure of tissue fluids of Loranthaceæ, Harris and Lawrence.......   47
The fungicidal properties of certain spra fluids, Eyre and Salmon...........   47
The effect of covering winter crops, Hiltner.................................   48
Notes on some diseases of collards, Higgins..................................   48
A new sweet corn disease in Kentucky, Garman...............................   48
Dissemination of the angular leaf spot of cotton, Faulwetter..................   49
Peanut wilt caused by *Sclerotium rolfsii*, McClintock.........................   49
The Verticillium disease of the potato, Pethybridge..........................   49
Potato spraying experiments for the control of early blight, Jack.............   50
Does it pay to spray potatoes in southern Rhodesia? Jack.....................   50
Weather injury to rice in 1915 in Italy, Marcarelli...........................   50
Fusarium blight, or wilt disease, of the soy bean, Cromwell..................   50
Black rot of tobacco, Preissecker...   51
Suggestions for control of more serious plant diseases at Hood River, Childs....   51
Diseases of the apple, pear, and quince, Orton...............................   51
The oak fungus disease of fruit trees, Horne..................................   51
The relation of the height of fruit to apple scab infection, Childs.............   51
Blister canker control, Vasey...   51
[Notes on some plant diseases]...   52
Diseases of the brambles and methods of controlling them, Orton.............   52
Direct bearer grapevines in relation to disease, Dalmasso and Sutto...........   52
The pink disease of cacao, Rorer..   52
Tea roots, Tunstall...   52
Ustulina zonata, a fungus affecting *Hevea brasiliensis*, Sharples.................   52
Cryptogamic diseases of forest trees, Guinier................................   53

ECONOMIC ZOOLOGY—ENTOMOLOGY.

Bird friends.—A complete bird book for Americans, Trafton   53
How to make friends with birds, Ladd..   53
The birds of Britain: Their distribution and habits, Evans...................   53
The zoological position of the Sarcosporidia, Crawley........................   53
Microtechnical methods for studying certain insects in situ, Brown...........   53
Studies on gregarines, Watson..   53
[Cranberry insects], Franklin..   53
The rôle of insects as carriers of fire blight, Gossard........................   53
Summary of the season's experiments with the newer insecticides, Houser.....   53
Analyses of some more recent and older pest remedies, Miller.................   53
Fly poisons, Phelps and Stevenson..   53

Page.

Suggestions for control of more serious insect pests at Hood River, Childs...... 54
[Report of the] division of zoology and entomology.......................... 54
Annual report on the entomological laboratory for 1914, Anderson............. 54
List of Egyptian insects in collection of Ministry of Agriculture, Storey...... 54
The fauna of British India, edited by Shipley and Marshall.................... 54
The coulee cricket [*Peranabrus scabricollis*], Melander and Yothers........... 54
Results of work against the locust in Uruguay, Sundberg et al................. 55
The pear thrips in British Columbia and its control, Cameron and Treherne... 55
The tomato and bean bug (*Nezara viridula*), Froggatt........................ 55
The Helopeltis question, especially in connection with cacao, Roepke....... 55
The maple aphis and its dimorphic larva, Bunnett........................... 55
Scale insects and their control, Cotton.................................... 55
Mimicry in butterflies, Punnett... 55
The bollworm in Egypt, Dudgeon... 55
Control of the gipsy moth by forest management............................. 55
Control of the fruit tree leaf roller in the Hood River Valley, Childs......... 56
A new method of controlling the black-head fireworm, Scammell............. 56
Life cycle of *Tortrix viridana*, Sich...................................... 57
[Codling moth investigations].. 57
Spraying for codling moth, Vincent et al................................... 57
Life history of some Japanese Lepidoptera, Nagano.......................... 57
District of Columbia Diptera: Syrphidæ, Banks et al........................ 57
The relation of malaria to crop production, Van Dine....................... 57
Mosquitoes and man again, Ludlow.. 57
Delphastus catalinæ, a valuable enemy of white flies, Smith and Branigan..... 58
Two destructive grape insects of the Appalachian region, Brooks............ 58
Life history and feeding records of a series of Coccinellidæ, Clausen.......... 58
Studies of weevils with descriptions of new genera and species, Pierce......... 58
Nosema apis in Victoria, Beuhne.. 58
Spore-forming bacteria of the apiary, McCray.............................. 59
Some weather-proof bands for use against ants, Horton..................... 59
New Javanese chalcidoid Hymenoptera, Girault............................. 59
Some chalcidoid parasites of the seeds of Myrtaceæ, da Costa Lima........... 59
Observations on the insect parasites of some Coccidæ, I, Imms............... 59

FOODS—HUMAN NUTRITION.

The use of cotton seed as food, Osborne and Mendel......................... 60
Nature of the dietary deficiencies of the oat kernel, McCollum et al.......... 61
Influence of temperatures above freezing on flesh of fowl, Pennington et al.... 62
Influence of temperatures below freezing on flesh of fowl, Pennington et al..... 62
A study of good fishes, Clark and Almy.................................... 63
The grayfish.—Try it... 63
Tenth report of chemical department of Indiana Laboratory of Hygiene, Barnard 63
Annual report of the food and drug commissioner, Fricke.................... 63
[Food and drug inspection in North Dakota], Ladd and Johnson............... 63
California pure foods and drugs acts....................................... 63
The dairy and food laws of the State of Michigan........................... 63
Manual for Army bakers, 1916... 63
Economical dishes for wartime, George..................................... 63
The rural school luncheon... 64
Studies in carbohydrate metabolism, XIV–XX, McDanell and Underhill...... 64
A chemical study of prolonged inanition, Swain............................. 64
The regulation of the calcium excretion in the dog, Givens.................. 64
The active constituent of the thyroid, Kendall.............................. 65
The use of the pancreatic vitamin in cases of malnutrition, Eddy............ 65

ANIMAL PRODUCTION.

Associative digestibility of corn silage and cottonseed meal, II, Ewing et al... 65
Animal husbandry experiments... 66
[Animal husbandry studies], Iddings and Hickman.......................... 66
Lamb and sheep feeding experiments, Iddings.............................. 67
[Live stock experiments].. 68
[Grazing experiments with pigs].. 68
[Feeding experiments with pigs].. 69
Self-feeders for fattening swine, Weaver................................... 69

Page.
[Poultry husbandry studies], Moore..................................... 70
[Poultry experiments]... 70
Mating and early hatching, Aubry...................................... 71
Colony brooding, Aubry.. 71
Preparing birds for exhibition, Irvin................................. 71
The Vineland international egg laying and breeding contest, Lewis...... 71
Our State department of poultry husbandry, Lewis...................... 71

DAIRY FARMING—DAIRYING.

The nutrients required to develop the bovine fetus, Eckles............ 71
Effects of feeding cottonseed products on the butter, Eckles and Palmer...... 72
Silage feeding.. 75
[Feeding experiments with dairy cows]................................. 75
[Machine milking versus hand milking], Ellington..................... 75
Creamery records, Holmes.. 75

VETERINARY MEDICINE.

Veterinary therapeutics, Hoare.. 76
Biology, general and medical, McFarland............................... 76
Microbiology, Marshall et al.. 76
Applied immunology, Thomas and Ivy.................................... 76
The cause of anaphylaxis and the nature of the antibodies, Danysz..... 76
Analysis of the anaphylactic and immune reactions, Manwaring and Kusama.. 76
Disappearance of agglutinin from anaphylactic and normal animals, Hempl... 76
The antigenic properties of β-nucleoproteins, Wells................... 77
Transformation of pseudoglobulin into euglobulin, Berg............... 77
Weyl's handbook of hygiene: Meat inspection, edited by Fraenken....... 77
Are uniform regulations feasible for diseases of animals? Melvin...... 77
Department of veterinary science and bacteriology.................... 78
Annual report on the Punjab Veterinary College for 1915–16, Pease et al...... 78
Complement fixation in abortions of women, Williams and Kolmer........ 78
Action of rabbit-blood serum in the complement-fixation test, Huddleson..... 79
Resistance of anthrax bacillus to sodium chlorid solution, Bordoli.... 79
Human anthrax.—An outbreak among tannery workers, Brown and Simpson.. 79
Report on foot-and-mouth disease from 1912–1916, Van Hoek............ 79
Second report of special committee for detection of glanders, Ackerman et al... 79
Rinderpest in swine, Boynton... 79
The treatment of tetanus with cicutin hydrobromid, Rocton............ 79
The ophthalmic tuberculin test for diagnosis of bovine tuberculosis, Bergman. 80
Bovine tuberculosis and milk for children, Regner.................... 80
Box elder poisoning, Bond.. 80
Malignant catarrhal fever of cattle in Kansas, Goss.................. 80
Bovine onchocerciasis in South America, Piettre..................... 80
Bovine sarcosporidiosis, Franco and Borges.......................... 81
Vesicular stomatitis in cattle, Eichhorn............................ 81
An outbreak of vesicular stomatitis, Mohler......................... 81
Note on preparation and use of agglutinin from beans, Dorset and Henley.... 81
Pseudotuberculosis in swine, Chaussé................................ 82
The treatment of surgical foot lesions in the horse with sugar, Bimbi....... 82
Notes on the occurrence of equine sporotrichosis in Montana, Meyer.... 82
The clinical importance of verminous aneurism of the horse, Folmer....... 82
Larvæ of Gastrophilus equi and hæmorrhoidalis and infectious anemia, Favero.. 82
A synoptical key to the adult tænioid cestodes of some carnivores, Hall...... 82
The value of post-mortem examinations, Thompson..................... 82
Comparison of Bacterium pullorum and B. sanguinarium, Rettger and Koser.. 82
Fowl cholera and other immunization experiments, Gallagher.......... 83
Epithelioma contagiosum of quail, Gallagher......................... 83

RURAL ENGINEERING.

Fifteenth annual report of the Reclamation Service, 1915–16, Davis........ 84
Seventh biennial report of the State engineer of North Dakota, Bliss........ 84
Surface water supply of Pacific slope Basins in California, 1914 84
Surface water supply of Missouri River Basin, 1914.................... 84
Surface water supply of Hudson Bay and upper Mississippi River Basins, 1915.. 84
Second report on the water powers of Alabama, Hall................... 84
Profile surveys of rivers in Wisconsin............................... 84
The economical use of irrigation water, Powers...................... 84

Page.

The drainage of irrigated shale land, Miller and Jessup..................... 86
Rural sanitation in the Tropics, Watson...................................... 86
Treatment of sewage by aeration in the presence of activated sludge, Bartow.. 87
Methods of clearing logged-off land, Shattuck............................... 87
Prevention of the erosion of farm lands by terracing, Ramser................ 87
The causes of cracks in cement-concrete pavements, Goldbeck............... 88
Policy and program in road construction under the Federal Aid Law, Page.. 89
Good roads and community life in Iowa, Brindley and Dodds................ 89
Tests of pine car sills, joists, and small clear pieces, Zimmerman............ 89
A lister attachment for a cotton planter, Hastings.......................... 90
Mechanical unloading of cane, Tönjes....................................... 90
Modern farm buildings, Hopkins.. 90
Dairy buildings... 90
Community hog houses, Davidson, Evvard, and Kaiser...................... 90
Building a self-feeder [for swine], Lehmann................................. 90

RURAL ECONOMICS.

The country church; an economic and social force, Galpin.................. 90
Living conditions in rural Alabama, Hobdy................................. 91
Wages of farm help [in Iowa]... 91
[Conditions among rural laborers in Finland in 1901], Gebhard............. 91
Rate sheet essential in long-time and short-time farm loans, Bennett......... 91
The Federal Farm Loan Act, Bulkley....................................... 91
The working of credit banks in the Netherland East Indies, Alting.......... 91
Annual report on cooperative societies in the Bombay Presidency, 1916....... 91
A municipally owned and operated abattoir, McCuistion.................... 91
Market survey of the City of Atlanta, Ga., Montgomery...................... 91
Report on the storage and handling of wheat in bulk in Victoria............ 91
Comments on the report on the bulk handling system of wheat in Victoria.... 92
Monthly crop report.. 92
[Extent of crops grown on reclamation projects]............................ 92
Annual statistics of Chile... 92
Agricultural situation in Corrèze [France] before the war, Berthault.......... 92
[Increasing the agricultural production of Italy], Lissone................... 92
[Agriculture and live stock in Sweden]..................................... 93
[Agricultural statistics of Norway]... 93
[Agricultural statistics of Finland, 1910]................................... 93

AGRICULTURAL EDUCATION.

[The teaching of rural sociology], Sanderson................................ 93
The value of home economics in our schools, Ray.......................... 93
The school garden as regarded and carried on in the different provinces...... 93
Proceedings of the [Ill.] high school conference, 1915, edited by Hollister.... 93
Notes on agricultural instruction in Spain, Gorria.......................... 93
The story of corn and the westward migration, Brooks...................... 94
Vegetable gardening, Carris and Tompson.................................. 94
Productive feeding of farm animals, Woll.................................. 94
Judging farm animals, Plumb.. 94
Dairy farming, Eckles and Warren... 94
A laboratory manual of foods and cookery, Matteson and Newlands........... 94
A rural arithmetic, Madden and Turner.................................... 95
The school garden: How to establish it, Magnan............................ 95
Gardening for the schools of Saskatchewan................................. 95

MISCELLANEOUS.

Twenty-ninth Annual Report of Georgia Station, 1916...................... 95
Annual Report of Idaho Station, 1916...................................... 95
Annual Report of Iowa Station, 1916....................................... 95
Annual Report of Nevada Station, 1916.................................... 95
Twenty-seventh Annual Report of New Mexico Station, 1916................ 95
Report of the Hood River, Oreg., Branch Experiment Station, 1916........... 96
Twenty-sixth Annual Report of Washington Station, 1916................... 96
Publications of the experiment station of Rhode Island..................... 96
Monthly bulletin of the Western Washington Substation.................... 96

LIST OF EXPERIMENT STATION AND DEPARTMENT PUBLICATIONS REVIEWED.

Stations in the United States.

	Page.
Colorado Station:	
Bul. 219, July, 1916............	11, 38
Bul. 220, Jan., 1917............	37
Bul. 221, Jan., 1917............	41
Bul. 222, Feb., 1917............	43
Georgia Station:	
Bul. 125, Feb., 1917.........	65
Circ. 75, Jan., 1917............	35
Circ. 76, Feb., 1917............	44
Twenty-ninth An. Rpt. 1916..	23, 28
	40, 48, 95
Idaho Station:	
Bul. 88, May, 1916............	39
Bul. 89, May, 1916............	67
Bul. 90, June, 1916............	75
Bul. 91, Dec., 1916..........	87
Bul. 92 (An. Rpt. 1916), Dec.,	
1916........................	16, 20
29, 30, 37, 57, 66, 68, 70, 75, 95	
Iowa Station:	
Bul. 151 (abridged ed.), Dec.,	
1915........................	24
Bul. 166 (abridged ed.), July,	
1916........................	90
An. Rpt. 1916................	30, 40
	66, 70, 95
Kentucky Station:	
Circ. 13......................	48
Maine Station:	
Off. Insp. 81, Jan., 1917......	40
Missouri Station:	
Bul. 144, Feb., 1917............	69, 90
Research Bul. 26, Nov., 1916..	71
Research Bul. 27, Dec., 1916..	72
Nevada Station:	
An. Rpt. 1916................	16, 30
	32, 78, 95
New Jersey Stations:	
Hints to Poultrymen, vol. 5—	
No. 1, Oct., 1916.........	71
No. 2, Nov., 1916.........	71
No. 3, Dec., 1916........	82
No. 4, Jan., 1917..........	71
No. 5, Feb., 1917........	71
No. 6, Mar., 1917.........	71
New Mexico Station:	
Twenty-seventh An. Rpt. 1916	32, 40
	52, 57, 68, 75, 95
North Dakota Station:	
Spec. Bul., vol. 4, No. 11,	
Feb.–Mar., 1917............	63

*Stations in the United States—*Contd.

	Page.
Oregon Station:	
Bul. 140, Jan., 1917............	84
Bul. 141, Feb., 1917............	33, 41
	51, 54, 56, 96
Porto Rico Station:	
Bul. 18 (Spanish ed.), Mar. 26,	
1917.......................	43
Bul. 21, Mar. 15, 1917........	43
Porto Rico Board of Agriculture	
Station:	
Circ. 9, 1917.................	55
Circ. 9 (Spanish ed.), 1917....	55
Rhode Island Station:	
Bul. 169, Jan., 1917............	34
Bul. 169, Sup., 1917............	96
Washington Station:	
Bul. 136 (Twenty-sixth An.	
Rpt. 1916), Jan., 1917.....	24, 32
	40, 46, 54, 69, 75, 96
Bul. 137, Jan., 1917...........	54
West Wash. Sta., Mo. Bul.—	
Vol. 4, No. 12, Mar., 1917..	96
Vol. 5, No. 1, Apr., 1917..	96
Wisconsin Station:	
Bul. 277, Feb., 1917.........	37
Bul. 278, Jan., 1917............	90

U. S. Department of Agriculture.

Jour. Agr. Research, vol. 8:	
No. 11, Mar. 12, 1917........	50, 59
No. 12, Mar. 19, 1917........	49, 77
Bul. 458, Handling and Marketing	
Durango Cotton in the Imperial	
Valley, J. G. Martin and G. C.	
White......................	37
Bul. 476, A Study of Cotton Market	
Conditions in North Carolina	
with a View to Their Improve-	
ment, O. J. McConnell and	
W. R. Camp..................	36
Bul. 477, Marketing and Distribu-	
tion of Strawberries in 1915, O. W.	
Schleussner and J. C. Gilbert...	43
Bul. 484, Control of the Gipsy Moth	
by Forest Management, G. E.	
Clement and W. Munro........	55
Bul. 497, Tests of Western Yellow	
Pine Car Sills, Joists, and Small	
Clear Pieces, C. W. Zimmerman.	89
Bul. 502, The Drainage of Irrigated	
Shale Land, D. G. Miller, and	
L. T. Jessup..................	86

U. S. Department of Agriculture—Contd.

Page.

Bul. 511, Farm Practice in the Cultivation of Cotton, H. R. Cates..   36

Bul. 512, Prevention of the Erosion of Farm Lands by Terracing, C. E. Ramser....................   87

Farmers' Bul. 788, The Windbreak As a Farm Asset, C. G. Bates...   46

Farmers' Bul. 793, Foxtail Millet— Its Culture and Utilization in the United States, H. N. Vinall....   37

Bureau of Animal Industry: Serv. and Regulatory Announcement 116.............   81

Bureau of Crop Estimates: Mo. Crop Rpt., vol. 3, No. 3, Mar., 1917...................   92

Bureau of Plant Industry: A Lister Attachment for a Cotton Planter, S. H. Hastings..   90

Bureau of Soils: Field Operations, 1915—

Soil Survey of Latah County, Idaho, J. H. Agee, G. W. Graves, and C. B. Mickelwaite......   21

Soil Survey of Wells County, Indiana, W. E. Tharp and W. E. Wiley.   21

Soil Survey of Van Buren County, Iowa, C. Lounsbury and H. W. Reid..   21

Soil Survey of Washington County, Nebraska, L. V. Davis and H. C. Mortlock...................   22

Soil Survey of Davidson County, North Carolina, R. B. Hardison and L. L. Brinkey   22

Soil Survey of Lewis and Gilmer Counties, West Virginia, W. J. Latimer.   22

Scientific Contributions: [1]

Kafirin, an Alcohol-soluble Protein from Andropogon Sorghum, C. O. Johns and J. F. Brewster..............   8

Some Proteins from the Jack Bean, *Canavalia ensiformis*, D. B. Jones and C. O. Johns......................   8

The Proteins of the Peanut.— I, Arachin and Conarachin, C. O. Johns and D. B. Jones......................   8

d–Mannoketoheptose, a New Sugar from the Avocado, F. B. La Forge..............   9

A Saponin from *Yucca filamentosa*, L. H. Chernoff, A. Viehoever and C. O. Johns....................   9

U. S. Department of Agriculture—Contd.

Page.

Scientific Contributions—Contd.

The Oxidase Activity of Plant Juices and Their Hydrogen Ion Concentrations, H. H. Bunzell....................   9

Absorption of Tin by Proteins and the Solution of Tin by Canned Foods, B. C. Goss..   12

New Method of Steam Distillation for Determination of Volatile Fatty Acids, D. C. Dyer......................   13

Soil Survey of White County [Indiana], T. M. Bushnell and C. P. Erni..............   21

Influence of Fertilizers and Soil Amendments on Acidity, J. J. Skinner and J. H. Beattie......................   23

Morphological Characters and Saccharin Content of Sugar Beets, F. J. Pritchard......   28

A Valuable Unpublished Work on Pomology, P. L. Ricker..   41

The Correlation of American Forest Research, E. H. Clapp......................   44

Ecology and Silviculture in the Southern Appalachians, E. H. Frothingham.........   45

Some Problems in Light as a Factor of Forest Growth, R. Zon......................   45

The Rôle of Light in Natural and Artificial Reforestation, C. G. Bates.................   45

Seeding Habits of Spruce in Competition with Its Associates, L. S. Murphy........   45

Timber Estimating in the Southern Appalachians, R. C. Hall......................   46

Some Problems in Appalachian Timber Appraisal, W. W. Ashe...............   46

The Zoological Position of the Sarcosporidia, H. Crawley..   53

A New Method of Controlling the Black-head Fireworm, H. B. Scammell............   56

District of Columbia Diptera: Syrphidæ, N. Banks et al...   57

The Relation of Malaria to Crop Production, D. L. Van Dine......................   57

Two Destructive Grape Insects of the Appalachiau Region, F. E. Brooks......   58

Studies of Weevils with Descriptions of New Genera and Species, W. D. Pierce......   58

[1] Printed in scientific and technical publications outside the Department.

U. S. Department of Agriculture—Contd.

Scientific Contributions—Contd.

Page.

Some Weather-proof Bands for Use Against Ants, J. R. Horton.................... 59

New Javanese Chalcidoid Hymenoptera, A. A. Girault... 59

Influence of Temperatures above Freezing on Flesh of Fowl, M[ary] E. Pennington et al....................... 62

Influence of Temperatures below Freezing on Flesh of Fowl, M[ary] E. Pennington et al....................... 62

Are Uniform Regulations Feasible for Diseases of Animals? A. D. Melvin.............. 77

Vesicular Stomatitis in Cattle, A. Eichhorn................ 81

An Outbreak of Vesicular Stomatitis, J. R. Mohler.... 81

U. S. Department of Agriculture—Contd.

Scientific Contributions—Contd.

Page.

Note on Preparation and Use of Agglutinin from Beans, M. Dorset and R. R. Henley 81

A Synoptical Key to the Adult Tænioid Cestodes of Some Carnivores, M. C. Hall...... 82

Fowl Cholera and Other Immunization Experiments, B. Gallagher.................. 83

Epithelioma contagiosum of Quail, B. Gallagher....... 83

The Causes of Cracks in Cement-concrete Pavements A. T. Goldbeck............. 88

Policy and Program in Road Construction Under the Federal Aid Law, L. W. Page...................... 89

EXPERIMENT STATION RECORD.

Vol. 37.   July, 1917.   No. 1.

The response of men of science to the needs of the hour has been one of the striking features in the preparation for war. They have exhibited not only a desire for service but also a quick appreciation of what needed to be done and of the present dependence of a successful outcome upon the aid of science in many directions. It is doubtful if this exhibition has been paralleled in any other country or at any other time. We have had, of course, the example of European countries to suggest this dependence and point out directions in which the services of men of science were needed, and we have had the stimulating influence of nearly three years of war to arouse men to action. And fortunately we have had both the men and the institutions. The latter, especially, have felt the call very keenly. The institutions of the whole country have come forward with a splendid spirit of service, and represent a breadth and resourcefulness which already are recognized as a powerful asset.

In this prompt response the land-grant colleges have stood out conspicuously. They have shown that they were not only willing but ready. They have realized the occasion as their great opportunity, as it was their duty under their Federal charter. Their initiative and leadership have been a striking illustration of the value of these institutions to the country, and of the kind of training they offer. Students have gone from the classroom to the officers' training camps and into various forms of agricultural service in such numbers as to reduce the attendance to one-third or a quarter or even less; and many of the colleges cut their spring terms short to release students and faculty. The agricultural extension service has become a chief reliance and assumed paramount importance in stimulating production, locating supplies, and giving personal aid and instruction to farmers, amateur gardeners, boys' and girls' clubs, and women of the town and country.

And back of it all, the experiment stations have continued their quiet but effective work, shaping it where necessary to the present emergency, speeding it up in other cases, and in general making their results and practical suggestions the basis of action by the public. Because their efforts often keep them in the background where their work lies, and does not bring them so prominently into evidence as the teacher who is before the public, they should not be overlooked or their vital importance forgotten. It is in very large measure their work which has made it possible to meet promptly the present emergency, by building upon the teachings of investigation and experiment throughout the whole gamut of agricultural production, protection, utilization, and preservation. We can hardly comprehend how different the task would have been twenty-five years ago. There is hardly a phase, even a local one, which their work has not touched and is not now being realized upon.

But this does not mean that we have touched bottom in all there is to know or all there is need to know to meet a sudden crisis. The foresight and insight, the resources and ingenuity, of the experiment stations and all agencies for research should be drawn upon as they never have been before. It will rest largely with them to anticipate the needs for dependable information and to forestall these needs by setting the necessary studies in operation. This means working close to the ground, with a keen eye to the emergency and the measures for meeting it. Never was it more important for the experiment station forces to be alert to the whole agricultural situation, to see with the eyes of experts, and weigh suggestion on the broad basis of relationships as well as of necessity.

It is gratifying to learn definitely, through word received from a considerable number of the stations, that they are fully alive to the situation and have already set their plans in motion. In a number of cases the directors are occupying prominent positions on the State councils of defense, and in others the stations are cooperating actively with these councils in agricultural matters and food supply. At several of the agricultural colleges and experiment stations war emergency committees have been formed to review the projects in hand and outline suggestions regarding special emergency investigations. To a notable extent such studies of more immediate importance have been started, replacing in some degree those which can be postponed until a later time. Thus a majority of the stations already are operating more or less under a war-time program.

In addition to these new undertakings, it is interesting to note the large amount of work in progress before the declaration of war which fits well into the new program. This is shown by a review of the stations' projects and an examination of their work in the field. It emphasizes anew the practical character of their studies and demonstrates their place in the present emergency.

For example, one of the measures advocated to increase food production is the more extensive cultivation of legumes, like soy bean, velvet bean, and the peanut, to be used either as pasturage, for ensiling with corn, or for grinding as stock feed. This gives quite a variety of products, especially when there is added the residues from oil extraction, the value, utilization and effect of which products have not been well known. The stations in the South have anticipated the need for such information, and during the past year especially have made many field and feeding experiments of various kinds.

It was found, for example, that peanuts and soy beans make a soft pork and lard, and that hogs fed extensively on these products are of less value to the packinghouses. Numerous experiments show the extent to which these materials may be fed, the amount of other feeds necessary to harden the pork, and the period over which they must be fed to accomplish this. Already probably sufficient data are on hand to answer many of these leading questions if they could be brought together and digested.

The increase of pork production is advised as an important means of maintaining meat supply. Successions of forage crops for pasturing hogs throughout the year have been worked upon at several of the stations, which give relatively cheap products. Waste products, especially those on farms, will need to be utilized to a larger extent to piece out and economize the feed supply. This has been a subject of much experimentation, in all parts of the country. The ordinary materials include such as corn stalks, cotton stalks, straw, waste hay, and aftergrowth in cultivated fields. The wintering in good condition, at one station, of a lot of fifty-eight steers on the hay cut from a corn stalk field containing pea vines, Johnson grass, crab grass, etc., which grew up after the corn had been pulled, emphasizes the possibility of utilizing to advantage roughage which would otherwise be practically wasted. Experiments with steers and with sheep on dry-land feeds show how far these materials may be relied upon, and in the case of sheep demonstrate the advantage to farmers of having a sufficient number to eat up the roughage and waste instead of keeping them all on the range.

No less than ten different stations have lately been working on various aspects of the conservation, handling, and most efficient use of barnyard manure—a subject of prime importance at a time when there is a shortage of fertilizers and difficulty in securing potash. That so many stations still regard the subject as a fruitful one for study is strong indication of the possibilities for constructive work outside the field of propaganda and demonstration. Indeed, there is not yet full agreement on the theory of the beneficial action of this material, or how it may be further extended.

Increase of the acre-yield of wheat is one of the direct ways of increasing the volume of production. The means for this have been the subject of continued study and experiment the country over, the larger application of which has awaited just such conditions as the

present affords. The working of these results into the practice of
wheat growing is not altogether a matter of bulletins and propaganda. The Ohio Station recognizes this in its call to farmers to
attend its "wheat field meetings," and join in the slogan "Sixty
million bushels of wheat for Ohio in 1918." Its circular says: "For
a third of a century the Ohio Experiment Station has been preparing for this emergency, and its wheat fields, scattered over the State
as they are, are in condition to show both what to avoid and what to
do in order to produce a maximum crop of wheat on Ohio soil."

Another station has just completed an extensive study of the rice
weevil and the method of preventing the immense injury it does to
corn stored on farms. This control is based on simple, practicable
methods of harvesting and storing the crop, which it is confidently
asserted would save some three million dollars' worth of corn in
Alabama alone. The ensiling of the fodder would help to keep down
the weevil and at the same time add further to the value of the crop.

Illustrations could be multiplied without end. The important
thing is that the results should be put out promptly, and preferably
summarized so that they will be more readily available to extension
workers and farmers over a wide area.

With a view to stimulating experiment and investigation along
the lines of the present need, the Agriculture Committee of the
National Research Council has undertaken to formulate suggestions
and serve as an agency in arranging for cooperation or coordinated
effort. This committee is a representative one, covering in a general ·
way the whole field of agricultural investigation, and will be assisted
by the Office of Experiment Stations in inaugurating its plans.

From the relation of the National Research Council to the Council
of National Defense, it is in position to view broadly the special needs
of investigation and offer suggestions for work which will be timely.
Through this Office the cooperation of the experiment stations in
this undertaking has been invited, and they will be asked to partici-
pate in conducting specific inquiries.

It will be clear that the occasion offers unusual opportunity for
cooperation among the experiment stations, which will be one of the
chief agencies in providing new information at this time. The situation also makes extremely desirable a larger measure of coordination of effort than ordinarily exists. Concerted action on topics
which are urgent will be more effective and yield quicker returns
than isolated individual effort conducted without knowledge of a
general plan.

Information as to emergency investigations already in progress at
different stations will prevent an unnecessary amount of duplication
and thus serve to conserve effort; and on the other hand, suggestions

as to subjects upon which investigation is deemed necessary will enable participation in a constructive plan aimed to advance the common cause. Such suggestions coming from a central committee in close contact with the Council of National Defense will naturally carry an unusual appeal.

In a new sense the present problem of agricultural production is a national one, in which the whole country and even the Allies of Europe are deeply concerned. Hence the measures to accomplish that end justify an unusual measure of coordination, which may extend properly to the investigation conducted at the experiment stations. Never was it more important to demonstrate the capacity of station workers to unite for cooperative or coordinated effort and their willingness to subordinate the individual in measures for the common good.

The research workers and experimenters are to agricultural production what the information service and the strategic branch are to the military forces. An effective dash can be made on what we already know, but in any protracted contest new information and new resources will often be needed to meet the requirements, and especially to adapt what we know to war-time conditions. The latter are so different and in a sense abnormal as to warrant practices not ordinarily employed, and require special experiments to be made. Continued warfare naturally tends to make agricultural production less effective because of the drains it makes on men, on live stock, on supplies like seed, fertilizers, and spray material, and the increasing difficulties of distribution. If our live stock is to remain undepleted, except through the intelligent weeding out of the drones, weaklings, and unproductive individuals, there must be provision for using more of the waste of farms, growing leguminous feeds without displacing the cereal acreage, an economy of protein, and a utilization of feeds of all kinds to the best possible advantage.

In time of stress there is less warrant for the outlay of feed to produce ideal fattening or a high degree of finish in meat animals. From the large amount of experimental data secured by a number of the stations, in the Central West especially, it ought to be possible to deduce simple, cheap methods for meat production suited to the needs of the hour, even though they give less fancy products.

To a certain extent the potash question is an emergency problem, as are others connected with the provision of necessary fertilizing materials. But the solution of the potash problem lies in determining the economy of potash and where the actual necessity for it lies in agriculture, as well as in increasing the supplies.

At this time, especially, there is the large question of how to cut down hand work and increase the man power so as to make it more productive in the face of labor shortage. The tractor problems are not all solved, either in their mechanical or economic aspects, and there is still opportunity for the agricultural engineer to point out the place of these machines and their weaknesses.

The furnishing of a billion bushels of wheat and other cereals to the European Allies, as is estimated to be required, will call for a large saving in the consumption of cereals and corn in this country. This will have to be effected by the partial substitution of corn for wheat as human food, and a corresponding saving in the corn fed to live stock. The latter ordinarily represents over three-fourths of the entire corn crop. To accomplish this saving of corn and still feed the same live stock will call for the use of other feeds in its place.

How far this chain of readjustment may reach is illustrated, for example, by the simple case of a proposal to save for feed the large amounts of wheat bran now used in the process of making tin plate. The bran is employed to take up the excess of oil applied to the plate to prevent corrosion, and this use renders it unfit for feed. An effort has been started to substitute ground peanut hulls for this purpose, the provision of which will involve an adjustment of practice at some of the oil mills handling peanuts.

The large underlying questions connected with meeting the present demand on American agriculture furnish the problems for the experiment stations. Many of these are relatively elementary and to a certain extent local, some of them verging on experimental demonstration, while others involve more extended and profound inquiry. The wisdom or feasibility of undertaking such inquiries may be questioned by some on the score of time; but if there is time and it is feasible to build a large fleet of vessels for transporting the world's commerce, there is time and it is expedient to set in motion a body of inquiry and experiment specially suggested by the wartime needs of agriculture. This inquiry, like the ships, will be useful and will be needed even though peace should come before they are completed.

The emergency provides a special opportunity for effecting radical and farreaching changes in our agriculture based on experimental knowledge, which it would otherwise require many years to bring about. It is well, therefore, to plan carefully, with the agricultural conditions and the need of permanent as well as temporary improvement clearly in mind. And the program made need not be dependent wholly on the time element as measured by the probable duration of the war. Never has there been such an opportunity to secure the acceptance of sound practical science in agriculture; and beyond helping to save the day through increased production, the experiment stations may aid in bringing about many radical changes in the art which will be of permanent character.

It is hardly necessary to caution that the attempt to meet emergency conditions should not result in the abandonment of fundamental investigations already in progress and which would suffer from interruption. It is highly important to protect our institutions and machinery for research. The war has dealt a severe blow to those of Europe and greatly interfered with the progress of scientific work. Many of the workers of outstanding ability have taken part in the conflict and sacrificed their lives to it. The progress of agricultural investigation, along with other branches, has thus been handicapped to a degree which will long be felt.

The foreign literature relating to agricultural research has very materially diminished, and much of what remains has taken on a war emergency flavor. The publications of this Department and the experiment stations, on the other hand, have greatly increased in volume. Our literature has been made use of in meeting the crisis abroad, and our work will find application there later. It may be one of America's responsibilities to keep alive the lines of research in agriculture which were sprouted on European soil, and to add to the store the product of new fundamental inquiries which by reason of dealing with the principles of science will have world-wide application.

102477°—17——2

RECENT WORK IN AGRICULTURAL SCIENCE.

AGRICULTURAL CHEMISTRY—AGROTECHNY.

Kafirin, an alcohol-soluble protein from Kafir, Andropogon sorghum, C. O. JOHNS and J. F. BREWSTER (*Jour. Biol. Chem., 28 (1916), No. 1, pp. 59–65*).—The authors have isolated from Kafir corn seeds a new alcohol-soluble (kafirin) protein which constitutes more than one-half of the protein of the seed. The new protein is similar to zein in its ultimate composition, but differs in physical properties. Analysis showed it to contain both tryptophan and lysin. The experimental data are described in detail.

Some proteins from the jack bean, Canavalia ensiformis, D. B. JONES and C. O. JOHNS (*Jour. Biol. Chem., 28 (1916), No. 1, pp. 67–75*).—Two globulins, canavalin and concanavalin, and an albumin similar to legumelin have been isolated from the bean. The percentage distribution of nitrogen in the albumin was as follows: Humin, 0.23; amid, 1.16; basic, 3.73; and nonbasic, 11.18. In canavalin the following percentage distribution was obtained: Humin, 0.28; amid, 1.41; basic, 3.17; and nonbasic, 11.55.

The proteins of the peanut, Arachis hypogæ.—I, The globulins arachin and conarachin, C. O. JOHNS and D. B. JONES (*Jour. Biol. Chem., 28 (1916), No. 1, pp. 77–87*).—Two globulins. designated by the authors as arachin and conarachin, have been isolated from the peanut. Arachin was found to contain 0.4 per cent sulphur and 4.96 per cent basic nitrogen; conarachin, 1.09 per cent sulphur and 6.55 per cent basic nitrogen. the latter being the highest percentage of basic nitrogen recorded for any seed protein.

From the analytical results it is deemed probable that peanut press cake will prove to be of value in supplementing food products made from cereals and other seeds deficient in basic amino acids. It is indicated that feeding experiments to determine the nutritive value of combinations of peanut proteins with other proteins are in progress

A comparative study of the proteins of the colostrum and milk of the cow and their relations to serum proteins, C. CROWTHER and H. RAISTRICK (*Biochem. Jour., 10 (1916), No. 3. pp. 434–452*).—Detailed analytical data obtained by the application of the Van Slyke procedure (E. S. R., 26, p. 22) to the proteins of cow colostrum and cow's milk show that caseinogen, total lactoglobulin, and lactalbumin are sharply differentiated, distinct proteins and have respectively the same compositions whether prepared from colostrum or normal milk. Eulactoglobulin and pseudolactoglobulin are identical so far as the protein part of their molecule is concerned. The presence of the globulin in very small quantities in milk was proved.

Lactoglobulin from either colostrum or milk was found to be very closely allied to and probably identical with serum globulin from ox blood. Lactalbumin from either colostrum or milk, however, was found to be very different in composition from the serum albumin of ox blood.

Protein copper compounds, T. B. OSBORNE and C. S. LEAVENWORTH (*Jour. Biol. Chem., 28 (1916), No. 1, pp. 109–123*).—The authors report in detail the

8

results of experiments on the preparation of copper compounds of edestin and gliadin. The probable structure of these complex compounds and the significance of such data as submitted are briefly discussed.

d-Mannoketoheptose, a new sugar from the avocado, F. B. LA FORGE (*Jour. Biol. Chem.*, 28 (1917), No. 2, pp. 511–522).—The isolation of the sugar and its chemical properties are described in detail.

A saponin from Yucca filamentosa, L. H. CHERNOFF, A. VIEHOEVER, and C. O. JOHNS (*Jour. Biol. Chem.*, 28 (1917), No. 2, pp. 437–443).—A new saponin ($C_{24}H_{40}O_{14}$) has been isolated from the root stock of *Y. filamentosa*, a yield of the crude saponin of about 6 per cent being obtained. The material is soluble in water, alcohol, phenol, and glacial acetic acid, but can not be precipitated from aqueous solution by neutral or basic lead acetate and barium hydroxid. No cholesterol compound could be prepared. Hemolysis of rabbit blood was observed after 15 minutes in the saponin solution at 37° C.

Hydrolysis yielded a sapogenin which crystallized in regular, fine needles, melting at 175°. The molecular weight of this material was approximately 255. It was soluble in alcohol, phenol, and glacial acetic acid, but not in alkali or dilute acids. The crystals of this material showed practically no hemolytic action. A sugar identified as glucose was also obtained on hydrolysis. The evidence indicated that glucuronic acid is formed during the hydrolysis.

The saponin is located as a brownish amorphous mass in the fibro-vascular bundles in the roots and leaf bases.

The relationship existing between the oxidase activity of plant juices and their hydrogen ion concentrations, with a note on the cause of oxidase activity in plant tissues, H. H. BUNZELL (*Jour. Biol. Chem.*, 28 (1916), No. 1, pp. 315–333, figs. 3).—Experimental data on the oxidase activity of potato peel powder (1915); potato peel powder (1916); potato sprouts; scaled tulip tree buds and tulip tree leaves (1916); tulip tree leaves (1915); magnolia leaves and flower petals (1915); and magnolia leaves, flower petals, and stamens from these flowers (1916) under varying hydrogen ion concentrations are reported in detail and the results discussed.

The results corroborate in a quantitative way the findings of earlier investigators on the inhibition of oxidase activity by acids. For the potato material the inhibiting hydrogen ion concentration ranged from 3.55 to 3.7. For the tulip tree material (scaled buds, scales, or leaves) the range was between 2.3 and 2.8. In the magnolia the range was from 2.45 to 3.05. These results seem to indicate " that the sensitiveness to acidity of all the oxidase factors throughout the same plant is approximately uniform; moreover, since different specimens of the same genus collected at different times of the year were used, it would indicate also that the acid sensitiveness figure is a rather fixed number, characteristic for any particular genus. It would even seem that the acid sensitiveness constant is the same or nearly the same for different genera (tulip tree and magnolia) of the same family (Magnoliaceæ)."

The material responsible for the phenomena of oxidase activity thus appeared to be identical in closely related plants.

The experiments are considered not to be exhaustive. See also a previous note by Reed (E. S. R., 36, p. 503).

The sampling of fertilizers, F. S. LODGE (*Jour. Indus. and Engin. Chem.*, 9 (1917), No. 2, pp. 167–169, fig. 1).—This is a general discussion of the various types of samplers used throughout the country in the control of fertilizing materials. The lack of uniformity in samplers and the difficulty of securing a representative sample by most of the samplers used is pointed out.

The sampler considered to meet all conditions best is one which was designed at the Indiana Experiment Station, and consists of two telescoping slotted brass tubes terminating in a solid pointed end. The sampler can be inserted to the full length of the bag before any material can enter the sample chamber. As representative a sample of the material as is practically possible is thus obtained.

The necessity of drafting standard methods for sampling fertilizers and the recognition of such methods as official is indicated.

The influence of carbohydrates on the accuracy of the Van Slyke method in the hydrolysis of casein, E. B. HART and B. SURE (*Jour. Biol. Chem., 28* (1916), No. 1, pp. 241-249).—Experimental data obtained from hydrolysis and amino-acid nitrogen distribution determination according to the Van Slyke procedure (E. S. R., 26, p. 22) for pure casein and casein with dextrose, sucrose, starch, and xylan, respectively, are reported in tabular form.

The results indicate that the presence of these carbohydrates during the hydrolysis brings about a total redistribution of the amino acids, varying with the nature of the carbohydrate employed. Marked changes were especially apparent in the hexone bases and a decided loss of nonamino nitrogen occurred in the presence of xylan.

The authors conclude from the results of Gortner (E. S. R., 36, p. 108) and the present results submitted that the method of direct hydrolysis for the estimation of amino acids in feeding stuffs by Van Slyke's method is inapplicable, and that the results so secured will be inaccurate. The use of factors is deemed to be impossible because of the variation of the nature and quantity of the carbohydrates in feeding stuffs, and because of this variation the results obtained are not even of comparative value.

It is further concluded that " in the present unsatisfactory status of the methods for estimating the amino acids in the complex protein-carbohydrate mixture of feeding stuffs the only reliable procedure for obtaining an insight into the nutritive worth of the proteins in such a mixture will be the biological one."

Methods for the estimation of mixtures of four or more carbohydrates, involving oxidation with bromin, EDITH G. WILSON and W. R. G. ATKINS (*Biochem. Jour., 10* (1916), No. 3, pp. 504-521, fig. 1).—Analytical data submitted and discussed show that glucose and maltose are quantitatively oxidized by bromin at room temperature when allowed to stand in a saturated solution. Fructose is not oxidized at all or only to a very small extent by bromin under these conditions. In the presence of tenth-normal sulphuric acid there is slight loss of fructose in 66 hours at room temperature.

For the analysis of a mixture of sucrose, maltose, glucose, and fructose the following scheme is described : The sucrose is determined by polarization and reduction before and after treatment with invertase. The resulting mixture of reducing sugars is treated with bromin under standard conditions of acidity and temperature, by which the aldehydic sugars, glucose and maltose, are oxidized. The ketonic sugar remains behind. The reducing power of the solution may then be taken as due to fructose alone. The rotations due to the fructose and sucrose are then allowed for in the initially determined rotation. This gives the rotation due to glucose and maltose. The reduction due to fructose is subtracted from the initial reduction, which thus gives the reduction due to glucose and maltose. From these data equations can be constructed for determining the amounts of the two remaining sugars.

It is indicated that the addition of dilute alkali to a solution of glucose, fructose, or maltose produces a large temporary increase in its reducing power. The necessity of keeping solutions neutral or very faintly acid in analytical work is obvious. Some indication has been obtained of the formation of a compound between sodium hydroxid and glucose from a study of the electrical conductivity of such a mixture.

An attempt to modify Barfoed's solution for quantitative work was unsuccessful.

[Methods for analysis of wheat grain, plants, and straw], W. P. HEADDEN (*Colorado Sta. Bul. 219 (1916), pp. 124–127*).—The following procedures were used in the study noted on page 38.

For oxidizing the wheat grain 25-gm. samples were treated with concentrated nitric acid in separate portions of from 15 to 20 cc. The material foams strongly and care must be taken that none is lost during the oxidation. Silica dishes were used, but it was found that small flakes sometimes broke off and were weighed as silica. The amount, however, was usually extremely small and negligible. When 50 cc. of nitric acid had been added the residue was evaporated to a gummy mass and charred over a free flame, and finally heated in the muffler. To remove the small portion of carbon remaining the mass was treated with aqua regia, the solution evaporated to dryness, the residue treated with hydrochloric acid, and filtered. The filter which contained the residual carbon and silica was returned to the dish, burned, and treated as before. In the solution of the ash, the iron, calcium and magnesium were precipitated as phosphates, the iron weighed as phosphate, the calcium as oxid, and the magnesium as pyrophosphate.

The filtrate which contained the alkalis was concentrated and acidulated with hydrochloric acid if necessary, an excess of ferric chlorid was added, and then ammonia in excess to precipitate the ferric oxid and with it the phosphoric acid. The precipitate was filtered off, washed, dissolved in hydrochloric acid, and again reprecipitated. The united filtrates contained the alkalis as chlorids and were treated in the usual manner.

The chlorin was determined in a separate 10-gm. sample which was dissolved in a mixture of nitric acid and silver nitrate. When completely dissolved, water was added, which increased the bulk of the white flocculent precipitate of silver chlorid. It was filtered off, washed, the mass mixed with a mixture of potassium nitrate and sodium carbonate, transferred to a nickel dish containing 2 or 3 gm. of the nitrate-carbonate mixture, the mass covered with the mixture, and heated until completely fused. The fused material was dissolved in water and the usual determination for chlorin followed.

The phosphorus was determined in a 10-gm. sample which was dissolved in concentrated nitric acid, after which 1.5 gm. of magnesium oxid was added and the whole evaporated to a brown, gummy mass, and ignited. The cooled mass was treated with dilute nitric acid, evaporated again, and the combustion completed. It was then dissolved in nitric acid, evaporated with sulphuric acid to separate silica, and the phosphoric acid precipitated as molybdate and finally weighed as magnesium pyrophosphate.

The sulphur was determined in a manner similar to the phosphorus determination, except that ordinary gas could not be used during the oxidation.

The manganese was determined colorimetrically and the samples oxidized and ashed by means of nitric acid as in the other procedures. The combustion was completed in the muffler and the residue taken up with sulphuric acid and filtered. The solution should contain about 5 per cent sulphuric acid. A few milligrams of silver sulphate and a few grams of ammonium persulphate were added and the solution heated until the color had developed completely.

Some difficulties were experienced in determining the ash of the wheat plant and wheat straw. For the ash determination 10 gm. of the ground straw or plant was thoroughly charred and extracted three times with boiling water.

The carbon was then burned out as completely as possible, again thoroughly extracted with water, and the residue finally ignited and weighed as insoluble ash.

For the analysis proper 100 gm. of the ground straw was taken and treated as noted above. The charred mass was extracted, however, with hydrochloric acid and after filtration the carbon burned out as far as possible, and the residue again extracted with hydrochloric acid and then ignited and considered as pure silica. The hydrochloric acid extracts were evaporated to dryness to separate the soluble silicic acid, and the weight of the silicic acid thus obtained added to the insoluble silica to obtain the total silica. The hydrochloric acid solution was made up to 250 cc. and aliquots taken for further determinations by the procedures used for the wheat grain. The phosphorus was determined in a separate 25 gm. sample which was treated with nitric acid and magnesium oxid. The thoroughly burned mass was dissolved in nitric acid and a few cubic centimeters of concentrated sulphuric acid added, and evaporated until sulphuric acid fumes were given off, after which the dish was placed in a hot-air oven and kept at 160° C., or higher, to allow the separation of the silicic acid. The phosphoric acid was then determined by the usual procedure of precipitation by ammonium molybdate, and finally weighed as magnesium pyrophosphate. If necessary, the silicic acid could be removed by hydrofluoric acid before the addition of the magnesium oxid.

The sulphur was determined in the same manner as in the wheat grain. The same procedure was also used for the determination of manganese, except that the silica was removed by concentrated hydrofluoric acid.

A new qualitative test and colorimetric method for the estimation of vanillin, C. ESTES (*Jour. Indus. and Engin. Chem., 9 (1917), No. 2, pp. 142–144*).—After some preliminary experimentation the author devised a procedure for the determination of vanillin which depends on the production of a violet to violet-red color when a solution of vanillin is treated with an acid solution of mercuric nitrate.

The procedure as applied to alcoholic extracts is as follows: To 5 cc. of the extract in a 50-cc. graduated flask, 6 cc. of water and 1.5 cc. of the acid mercuric nitrate reagent are added. The standard is made up at the same time with 5 cc. of the standard vanillin solution, 0.5 cc. of the reagent, and 6 cc. of water. The two flasks are placed in boiling water for 20 minutes. They are then taken out, rapidly cooled, made up to the mark, filtered, and the colors compared.

For nonalcoholic extracts the standard is prepared in the same way as for alcoholic extracts, and the only change in the preparation of the unknown is the quantity of reagent used, 1 cc. having been found to give the maximum intensity of color.

Analytical data submitted indicate that the results obtained on commercial vanilla extracts agree very closely with those from the gravimetric procedure.

Summary of the composition of the wines of current consumption, G. FILAUDEAU (*Ann. Falsif., 9 (1916), No. 96, pp. 347–413*).—These pages contain detailed tabular analytical data of the various wines of the harvest of 1915, together with comments on the data.

Adsorption of tin by proteins and its relation to the solution of tin by canned foods, B. C. Goss (*Jour. Indus. and Engin. Chem., 9 (1917), No. 2, pp. 144–148*).—The work reported shows that "the solution of tin by canned foods is neither dependent upon, nor proportional to, the acidity alone, and, also, that in the foods of relatively slight acidity which dissolve large amounts of tin the greater part of the tin is in the form of an insoluble and stable complex." The data indicate that the phenomena are due to adsorption, and that the tin, after being dissolved from the lining of the can, is continually removed from solution by the proteins, carbohydrates, and other highly porous solid phases in contact with the solution. The theory in regard to the adsorption of the tin ions is discussed.

The seeds of red cherries, black cherries, black raspberries, strawberries, and tomatoes were found to have adsorbed quantities of tin far in excess of the tin found in solution. The physiological significance of this adsorption of the tin by the seeds is indicated, since the seeds are usually eliminated intact. It is also noted that "it would appear that the amount of soluble tin salts, rather than the total tin present in a can of food, should be limited, since it is the part of the tin adsorbed which determines the physiological action."

The detection of added water in milk in India, J. W. LEATHER (*Agr. Research Inst. Pusa Bul. 57 (1915), pp. 7*).—Using the procedure described by Beckmann (E. S. R., 6, p. 611), with some slight modifications, the author determined the freezing point of milks of Indian cows and buffaloes, and from the data has evolved a formula for determining the percentage of added water by this procedure. A table showing the percentage of added water corresponding to the freezing point of the sample, ranging from $-0.542°$ to $-0.247°$ C., is included.

The nature of the reducing substances precipitated by lead subacetate in the defecation of impure sugar solutions, H. PELLET (*Ann. Chim. Analyt., 21 (1916), No. 11, pp. 217-223*).—The author briefly reviews previous studies of the precipitate produced by defecation with lead subacetate, and from the results, together with his own experience, concludes that its use is unsatisfactory.

The use of normal lead acetate (30 per cent solution) and the removal of the excess lead with a saturated solution of sodium carbonate is recommended as being entirely satisfactory for defecation in the determination of reducing sugars in cane products, foods, diabetic urine, etc.

Notes upon oil testing, A. H. GILL (*Jour. Indus. and Engin. Chem., 9 (1917), No. 2, p. 136*).—A test for oils by salting out their soaps is described, and some analytical data, expressed in grams of sodium chlorid per gram of oil, for several oils, a sample of oleomargarin, and a sample of butter are submitted. A test for gelatinous matter in linseed oils and its use are also described.

Color tests for oils.—Palm oil, A. H. GILL (*Jour. Indus. and Engin. Chem., 9 (1917), No. 2, pp. 136-139*).—The Halphen and Becchi tests for cottonseed oil, the Baudouin test for sesame oil, the Liebermann-Storch test for rosin oil, and the Crampton-Simons test for palm oil are briefly discussed and some analytical data on the Crampton-Simons test submitted.

From the data the test is considered to be no longer available for use in connection with the testing of oleomargarin (to determine the presence of palm oil) because of its unreliability, due to the difficulty in interpretation. The test is one for carotin rather than palm oil and may be given by butter, oleo oil, or sesame oil, ingredients ordinarily found in oleomargarin. As commouly applied, it is also untrustworthy on account of the presence of interfering oils, as sesame, which are not washed out.

The work reported is considered preliminary and the subject is being further studied.

A new method of steam distillation for the determination of the volatile fatty acids, including a series of colorimetric qualitative reactions for their identification, D. C. DYER (*Jour. Biol. Chem., 28 (1917), No. 2, pp. 445-473, pl. 1, fig. 1*).—A method of steam distillation for the determination of volatile fatty acids, which depends on the maintenance of the aqueous solution containing the acids at a constant volume throughout the course of the distillation, is described. The distilling constants of the individual volatile fatty acids have been determined and are represented graphically by straight lines on a logarithmic chart, while the distilling variables of mixtures are indicated by curved lines. The calculations necessary for determining the amounts of the various acids in a mixture are described in detail.

Some qualitative tests for the identification of various acids in a mixture, together with a simple and convenient apparatus for maintaining a constant volume during the distillation, are described in detail.

[**Examination of lulu kernels and lulu oil (shea butter) from Uganda**] (*Ann. Rpt. Dept. Agr. Uganda, 1916, pp. 59–61*).—Analytical data of a sample of lulu kernels and of two samples of butter made from the oil of the kernels are submitted.

A general method of estimating the general turbidity or opacity of fluid suspensions including bacterial emulsions, G. Dreyer and A. D. Gardner (*Biochem. Jour., 10 (1916), No. 3, pp. 399–407, fig. 1*).—A simple and accurate method for measuring the turbidity of two fluids and its special application to the standardization of agglutinable cultures is described in detail. The procedure is indicated as being applicable to all chemical and biological investigations which require turbidity measurements.

The estimation of amino-acid nitrogen in blood, J. C. Bock (*Jour. Biol. Chem., 28 (1917), No. 2, pp. 357–368*).—Experimental data submitted indicate that the use of alcohol as a protein precipitant in the determination of amino nitrogen in blood, as recommended by Van Slyke and Meyer,[1] is undesirable. A comparative study indicates that the use of trichloroacetic acid as introduced by Greenwald[2] is very serviceable, and a slight modification of the procedure is described. Coagulation of the blood at boiling temperature in a weakly acid solution was found not to increase the filtrate nitrogen provided the traces of protein which escaped coagulation were properly removed.

Factors connecting the concentration and the optical rotatory power of aqueous solutions of nicotin, A. Tingle and A. A. Ferguson (*Proc. and Trans. Roy. Soc. Canada, 3. ser., 10 (1916), Sect. III, pp. 19–25*).—Experimental data on the influence of dilution on the rotatory power of aqueous nicotin solutions, the effect of free alkali and alkali salts on the rotatory power of nicotin solutions, effect of evaporation in the presence of sulphuric acid, and the preparation of pure nicotin are reported.

The results show that for concentrations between 4 per cent and 0.37 per cent the rotatory power of an aqueous solution of nicotin is strictly proportional to its concentration. Repeated evaporation with sulphuric acid in small excess did not cause any change in the rotatory power of nicotin, nor did the presence of free caustic alkali or salts of the alkaline metals cause any change in the rotatory power of such solutions. The rotatory power of nicotin in water was found to be such that. examined in a 200 mm. tube, 1 gm. of nicotin in 100 cc. of solution would give a negative rotation of 4.5 divisions on the Ventzke sugar scale, or conversely a negative rotation of 1 division would correspond to 0.2198 gm. of nicotin in 100 cc.

A new method for the determination of nicotin in tobacco, A. Tingle and A. A. Ferguson (*Proc. and Trans. Roy. Soc. Canada, 3. ser., 10 (1916), Sect. III, pp. 27–51*).—A polarimetric method which depends on the assumptions that the rotatory power of a solution of nicotin in water is not changed by the presence of alkalis or salts of alkalis in the solution. that the acid solutions of nicotin sulphate may be evaporated without either loss by vaporization

---

[1] Jour. Biol. Chem., 12 (1912), No. 3, pp. 399–410.
[2] Jour. Biol. Chem., 21 (1915), No. 1, pp. 61–68.

or racemization, and that the rotatory power of an aqueous solution of nicotin containing 3 per cent of the base or less is proportional to its concentration, is proposed.

The procedure described consists of distilling the nicotin with barium hydroxid by a current of steam, acidifying the distillate with sulphuric acid, and then evaporating to about 50 cc. volume. The concentrated solution is made to volume and then made strongly alkaline with concentrated KOH followed by a few drops of barium hydroxid. This last addition is not essential, but tends to clarify the solution when any turbidity is developed. The liquid is again made to volume, the precipitate allowed to settle, and, after filtering the supernatant liquid, the filtrate is examined in a polarimeter. The calculations for the amount of nicotin present from the polarimetric readings are described.

A slightly modified procedure in which the distillate is not acidified, but extracted with chloroform and the chloroform extracts treated with sulphuric acid in a separatory funnel is also described. After heating to expel the dissolved chloroform the solution is made alkaline with KOH and the filtrate then examined polarimetrically.

The method yields higher results and is considered to be more accurate than the Kissling procedure, which is official.

Sirups for canning and preserving, J. B. McNair (*Jour. Indus. and Engin. Chem., 9 (1917), No. 2, pp. 151-153, fig. 1*).—Tables showing number of the gallons of water or ounces of sugar per gallon of sirup required to change a sirup from a given degree Brix to another given degree Brix at 17° C., changes in volume (in parts per 10,000) of sirups at different temperatures, and the correction for the readings of Balling's saccharimeter on account of temperature are submitted and their use described.

The value of such data in connection with the preparation of fruit jellies is indicated.

The manufacture of apple jelly, A. Truelle (*Vie Agr. et Rurale, 6 (1916), No. 46, pp. 357-361, figs. 2*).—This is a general discussion of English methods of preparation, together with the results of some original experiments by the author.

A table giving the grams of acid (as malic), tannin, and pectin in 100 cc. of the juice of 50 varieties of apples is included.

METEOROLOGY.

The quantitative study of climatic factors in relation to plant life, J. Adams (*Proc. and Trans. Roy. Soc. Canada, 3. ser., 10 (1916), Sect. IV, pp. 105-123*).—This article discusses the relations of temperature, light, precipitation, evaporation, and wind to plant growth at various places in Canada and makes certain general deductions as to such relationships.

World-wide changes of temperature, C. F. Brooks (*Sci. Amer. Sup., 83 (1917), No. 2152, pp. 194, 195; Geogr. Rev., 2 (1916), No. 4, pp. 249-255*).—This article deals primarily with the possibility of seasonal forecasts. It is stated that "the weather in widely separated parts of the earth is correlated because of the extensive control of the large belts and centers of atmospheric action. . . . These are subsequent, however, to changes in the sun's radiation, which produce immediate, world-wide pressure alterations. Any possibilities for widespread seasonal forecasts must rest, therefore, first on an ability to forecast solar changes and, second, on a knowledge of the immediate and subsequent atmospheric effects of such variations."

Improved methods in hygrometry, A. N. SHAW (*Proc. and Trans. Roy. Soc. Canada, 3. ser., 10 (1916)*, Sect. *III*, pp. *85–92*, pl. *1*).—This paper describes "experiments with several hygrometers of simple construction which apparently give results of accuracy greater than that given by the instruments in common use." These included a modification of Rideal and Hannah's absorption hygrometer (E. S. R., 34, p. 208), a simple weighing hygrometer, and two electrical methods. The advantages and disadvantages of these methods as compared with the limitations of hygrometric methods in general use are discussed.

Department of meteorology (*Nevada Sta. Rpt. 1916*, pp. *47–49, fig. 1*).— Brief notes are given regarding the work on snow surveying as a means of forecasting water supplies and temperature surveys in the Truckee-Carson Project in western Nevada. It is stated that "a method for the economical and accurate measurement of snow seems now to have been attained in the method of seasonal percentage, which involves the maintenance of a few fixed courses in typical parts of the watershed as a basis for computing the relation of the annual snow cover to normal."

[Meteorological summary] (*Idaho Sta. Bul. 92 (1916)*, pp. *61–63*).—Tabular summaries are given of observations on temperature and precipitation at the station at Moscow and the substations at Aberdeen, Gooding, Jerome, and Sandpoint.

New England snowfall, C. F. BROOKS (*Geogr. Rev., 3 (1917), No. 3, pp. 222–240, figs. 20*).—The conditions of temperature, precipitation, and direction of wind, which are the three important factors controlling snowfall, are discussed in some detail. It is stated that as a result of the fact that some of the strongest cyclones pass through the south or southeastern part of New England, "this section from time to time experiences extraordinary snowstorms, a great characteristic of the climate of New England."

Meteorology, C. FLAMMARION (*Ann. Astron. et Mét.* [*Paris*], *53 (1917)*, pp. *255–288*).—Observations at Paris and nearby points on temperature since 1699 and on rainfall since 1689 are summarized, the observations being brought up to 1916.

Climatology of 1915, C. FLAMMARION (*Ann. Astron. et Mét.* [*Paris*], *53 (1917)*, pp. *387–412, figs. 8*).—The conditions of atmospheric pressure, temperature of the air and soil, rainfall, cloudiness, etc., with special reference to the region of Juvisy and the environs of Paris, are summarized. A short note on the relation of cannonading to rainfall is included, the author concluding that observations in connection with the recent military operations in Europe indicate no connection whatever between the two.

The rainfall of Java, B. C. WALLIS (*Scot. Geogr. Mag., 33 (1917), No. 3, pp. 108–119, figs. 7*).—This article reports a study of the distribution of rainfall in Java, with reference to both time and place.

This study showed that "the mountain axis of Java forces the winds to maintain two distinct surface movements, one to the north and the other to the south of the island; the northern coastal lowlands receive, therefore, a different type of rainfall from those of the southern coast. Along the northern coast, out of a total precipitation of about 80 in., during the driest month only about one thirty-second (i. e., 2.5 in.) of the annual fall is precipitated, while during the wettest months at least one-fifth of the precipitation occurs. The ratio of rainfall intensity is thus roughly 1:6. The southern lowlands are relatively wet when the northern lowlands are dry, and vice versa. They receive more rain annually, and the ratio of rainfall intensity is not greater than 1:3.

"The equipluves . . . tend to run parallel to the contours. Consequently, the elevated axis is usually an area of intermediate character with a more intense rainfall on one slope and a less intense rainfall upon the other. This fact is of considerable importance, since it suggests a kind of seesaw arrangement. Most rain is actually precipitated upon the elevated land. When the rainfall tendency comes from the north more water is precipitated on the northern lowlands than on those of the south, but most water falls on the mountain slopes although it does not register so high a pluviometric coefficient. The dry slopes are those which have what may be termed the 'sunny aspect,' i, e., which have the more nearly vertical radiations from the sun. Since the action of the wind is largely frictional, along the slopes rather than up them, neither the west monsoon nor the 'east monsoon' affects the whole island equally. . . .

"The results of this inquiry suggest that in tropical areas wind direction is not a prime cause of rainfall intensity as distinguished from rainfall quantity; but they also suggest that the direction of high mountains serves to restrain the influence of the great factor in producing rainfall intensity. Now these two statements appear to be contradictory, but the cases of Java and Mauritius show that the rainfall cause which is restrained by the mountains is working either in the opposite direction or at right angles to the direction of the prevailing wind."

A short bibliography of literature relating to the subject is given.

SOILS—FERTILIZERS.

Biological changes in soil during storage, F. E. ALLISON (*Soil Sci., 3* (*1917*), *No. 1, pp. 37–62, figs. 12*).—Experiments conducted at Rutgers College to determine how long fresh soil samples may be kept in the laboratory without being appreciably altered in their biological properties are reported. The soils used were shaley loam, gravelly loam, sandy loam, and clay, part being collected in summer and part in winter. In general the work consisted of a study of the bacterial changes from the standpoints of numbers and physiological activity.

It was found that "soils change biologically to a very marked extent during storage in the laboratory, and the rate of change depends largely upon the temperature of the soil when sampled. A change in numbers of bacteria in two hours amounted to as much as 30 to 40 per cent in some soils during the winter months. There is a decided tendency for the ammonification of dried blood and peptone to vary as the numbers of bacteria vary; and for the ammonia production from cottonseed meal to go hand in hand with the numbers of fungi. In the winter there is a diminution in bacterial numbers and usually in ammonification until the end of one week and this is followed by a steady increase. In the summer the decrease in numbers and ammonia production from peptone and dried blood proceeds more slowly and continues for at least two months. To the very end of this experiment the point had not been reached where ammonification ceased to decrease.

"From the data presented . . . it may be said that in order to obtain reliable results during the winter months it is necessary to pour plates for bacterial counts and start all ammonification experiments immediately on bringing the soil sample into the warm laboratory. During the summer months it is desirable to pour plates soon after taking the sample, but this is not as essential as during the colder months. Ammonification experiments need not be started with such haste. During the first ten days the variations in ammonification were almost within the limits of experimental error.

"Air-drying caused a decided decrease in numbers of bacteria except in the case of the Penn loam during the winter months. The decrease was much less marked for fungi than for bacteria. Air-drying had very little effect on the ammonification of dried blood and cottonseed meal, but caused a pronounced diminution in ammonia production from peptone in solution. Nitrogen-fixation results were very little affected."

Six references to literature bearing on the subject are appended.

A method for determining the volume weight of soils in field condition, C. F. Shaw (*Jour. Amer. Soc. Agron.*, *9 (1917)*, *No. 1, pp. 38–42*).—The paraffin immersion method used by Brown et al. in previous work (E. S. R., 25, p. 820) is described.

Soil valuation and soil investigation, T. Remy (*Landw. Jahrb.*, *49 (1916)*, *No. 1, pp. 147–158*).—This is a general discussion of important factors in soil investigation and valuation.

The capacity of the soil to absorb and hold water, A. Rindell (*Om Jordens Förmåga att Upptaga och Kvarhålla Vatten. Helsingfors: Kejserliga Senatens Tryckeri*, *1915, pp. 34, figs. 8*).—This paper deals with the absorptive powers of different soils for water, with special reference to the transportation of nutritive substances in solution by water.

Dynamics of soluble phosphoric acid in the soil (*Otchet Bezenchuk. Selsk. Khoz. Opytn. Sta.*, *5 (1914), pp. 89–100*).—Investigations on the solubility of the phosphoric acid in different fallow soils at different times of the year are reported.

The results are taken to indicate that the amount of phosphoric acid extracted from the soil by water, weak acid, or weak alkali does not indicate the amount of soil phosphoric acid soluble in these substances, but rather indicates the dissolving power of the soil solution for soil phosphoric acid. Soil extracts obtained from different parts of the same field showed about the same dissolving powers for soil phosphates. It is concluded that the process of mobilization of phosphoric acid in soil is insignificant. It is thought further that the importance of any particular method of culture as influencing the condition of soil phosphoric acid can not be determined on the basis of present data.

The alkaline reaction produced by acids in soils in relation to plant nutrition.—II, Solubility of manganese compounds in the soil, G. Masoni (*Staz. Sper. Agr. Ital.*, *49 (1916)*, *No. 2, pp. 132–149; abs. in Internat. Inst. Agr. [Rome], Internat. Rev. Sci. and Pract. Agr.*, *7 (1916)*, *No. 6, pp. 799, 800; Jour. Soc. Chem. Indus.*, *35 (1916)*, *No. 23, pp. 1227, 1228; Chem. Abs.*, *11 (1917)*, *No. 2, p. 181*).—Continuing previous work (E. S. R., 34, p. 720), experiments are reported on the action of tenth-normal solutions of hydrochloric, nitric, sulphuric, phosphoric, formic, acetic, oxalic, succinic, malic, tartaric, and citric acids on manganese compounds (1) in common soils, (2) in mixtures of pure calcium carbonate with manganous oxid, mangano-manganic oxid, manganese dioxid, manganese carbonate, and manganese sulphate, and (3) in a mixture of common soils with manganese sulphate or dioxid. From 25 to 50 gm. of the earth or mixture used were treated with 50 to 100 cc. of the acid solution, the whole was thoroughly shaken, and, after the appearance of an alkaline reaction, the mixture was filtered and the filtrate tested for manganese.

In the experiments with soil it was found that the so-called oxyacids alone threw manganese into solution in large amounts in spite of the alkaline reaction produced. Citric and malic acids were especially active.

In the experiments with pure calcium carbonate and oxids of manganese the ability of lime to prevent the retention of manganese in solution was demonstrated. The oxid of manganese behaved rather differently from the other oxids, giving a comparatively strong manganese reaction in the filtered liquid even with acids other than oxyacids.

With manganese carbonate much smaller quantities of manganese were obtained in solution, even under the action of oxyacids. In the tests with manganese sulphate, quantities of the salt corresponding to 2, 5, and 50 mg. of manganese were used with 15 gm. of calcium carbonate. With the smallest quantity of manganese, whatever the acid used relatively large amounts of manganese passed into solution eight hours from the beginning of acid action. These amounts were largest with citric and malic acids. With 5 and 50 mg. of manganese a strong manganese reaction was found even after 36 and 48 hours.

"Experiments with manganese sulphate and dioxid mixed with earth proved that for small quantities of sulphate (2 mg. of manganese to 50 mg. of earth) the treatment with citric and malic acids alone increased the quantity of manganese passing into solution, while for relatively large quantities (50 mg. of manganese to 50 gm. of earth) the increase in dissolved manganese was marked on treatment with any acid; and that for dioxid there was no increase of the manganese dissolved except on treatment with citric and malic acids."

These results are taken to indicate that compounds of manganese naturally contained in the soil behave in a way similar to that of iron compounds as regards their solubility in acids when lime is in excesss. "The markedly greater capacity of oxyacids for retaining these elements in solution, in spite of the excess of OH occasioned by the acids themselves, is therefore likewise confirmed with regard to the manganese in the soil."

Soil bacteriology, C. M. HUTCHINSON (*Rpt. Agr. Research Inst. and Col. Pusa, 1915–16, pp. 86–89*).—Continuing the work of the previous year (E. S. R., 35, p. 626), "a series of field experimental plats under wheat demonstrated the production of infertility in soil containing nitrogenous organic matter (oil cake) as a consequence of semianaerobic conditions artificially induced by water-logging. This infertility did not occur to the same extent when ammonium sulphate was substituted for cake, nor did the effect of the water-logging become apparent until the roots of the plants had gone down some inches to that level in the soil which oxidation consequent on the cultivation had failed to reach. Parallel plats with barley illustrated this effect more markedly than those with wheat. . . .

"Laboratory work on nitrification and on the growth of seedlings in water and soil cultures demonstrated the possibility of separating substances from certain bacterial cultures, from decomposing organic matter, and from anaerobically incubated soil whose toxicity to nitrifiers, and in greater concentration to seedling plants, was demonstrable under these conditions."

Observations were made on the interference with the growth of seedlings resulting from the bacterial invasion of the unexhausted and still attached seed, and the consequent absorption by the plant of toxic bacterial by-products showed that this invasion occurred most readily in water-logged soil and more especially in the presence of bacteria derived from anaerobically incubated soils of high organic matter content. Copper sulphate was found to neutralize most of the toxic bodies obtained in this way, and seeds treated with this salt were found to be immunized to some extent, although not entirely or invariably, against this action.

It was further found that the presence of nitrites in soils is not alone due to the reduction of nitrates already formed, but that in many of the soils examined in the laboratory nitrites accumulate to some extent before nitrate formation becomes evident, even under conditions apparently favorable to nitrification. The concentration of nitrites required to injure various field crops in soils was found in no case to be so great as that required in water cultures. "Weekly borings and nitrate determinations throughout the year were made in three sets of duplicate plats under grass, . . . wheat and maize, and fallow. . . .

Only in the last of these was there any accumulation of nitrate in the first foot of soil, a much smaller amount occurring in the cropped soil and only very small quantities under grass."

Studies of north Idaho soils, J. J. Putnam (*Idaho Sta. Bul. 92* (*1916*), *p. 9*).—Ammonification and nitrification studies of two soils, similar to timber soils, showed that "both with ammonium sulphate and blood as the source of nitrogen the presence of 1 per cent of calcium carbonate greatly increases the activity of the nitrifying organisms. The presence of 5 per cent of sawdust greatly lessens the activity of the nitrifying organisms even when calcium carbonate is present. With blood as a source of nitrogen the presence of sawdust greatly lessens the activity of the ammonifying organisms. When 2.5 per cent of sawdust was used, 36.72 per cent of the nitrogen was transformed into ammonia. When the amount of sawdust was increased to 5 per cent, only 27.84 per cent of the nitrogen was transformed to ammonia."

The organic matter of the soil.—III, On the production of humus from manures, R. A. Gortner (*Soil Sci., 3* (*1917*), *No. 1, pp. 1–8*).—In continuation of work previously noted (E. S. R., 36, p. 815), experiments conducted at the Minnesota Experiment Station are reported on the increase of ammonia-soluble humus brought about by adding powdered silk waste, powdered wool, flour, and alfalfa meal to moist subsoil at respective rates of 500, 460, 50, and 200 gm. per 7,500 gm. of subsoil, and allowing the mixture to undergo natural "humification." Carbon, nitrogen, and humus were determined in the original mixture and in the final product after remaining in a moist condition in the greenhouse for one year.

It was found that there was a decided loss of organic carbon from all of the samples, ranging from a minimum loss of 18.4 per cent to a maximum of 55 per cent of the carbon originally present. There was likewise a loss of nitrogen, but this loss was not proportional to the loss of organic carbon, ranging from 5 to 26.5 per cent of the nitrogen originally present. There was a loss of humus, the material dissolved from the leached soil by 4 per cent NH_4OH, and this loss appeared to be directly proportional to the loss of nitrogen. In three of the four experiments no significant change was apparent in the materials extracted by 4 per cent NH_4OH from the unleached soil. In the remaining experiment there was a loss of 60 per cent of the original materials.

"These experiments furnish no evidence that an increase of soil humus is brought about by a specific humification. On the contrary all the evidence is directly opposed to such a conclusion, and it appears altogether probable that the maximum amount of ammonia-soluble material is present in a soil immediately after a green manuring crop has been plowed under and before the humifying bacteria or fungi begin their work."

Eight references to literature bearing on the subject are appended.

The loess soils of the Nebraska portion of the transition region.—VI, The relative "rawness" of the subsoils, F. J. Alway, G. R. McDole, and C. O. Rost (*Soil Sci., 3* (*1917*), *No. 1, pp. 9–36. pls. 9, figs. 4*).—Pot experiments conducted at the Minnesota Experiment Station with loess surface soils, described in previous reports (E. S. R., 36, p. 421), and with the corresponding subsoils from the second to the sixth foot, using corn, beans, clover, and alfalfa to determine the relative "rawness" or infertility of the subsoils, are reported.

It was found that the soils evidenced no rawness toward the inoculated legumes. "Eight successive crops of alfalfa gave almost as heavy yields on the subsoils from the eastern half of Nebraska as on the corresponding surface soils.

"From field observations on the loess soils of eastern Nebraska it is evident that the deep subsoils at depths of even 20 to 30 ft., both when the surface of these is simply exposed by grading operations and when such excavated material is piled up, are not 'raw' toward inoculated legumes, although very unproductive with nonleguminous crops. In the case of alfalfa they produce practically as satisfactory crops as the adjacent surface soils. After such exposed subsoils have for a period of years been devoted to the production of alfalfa hay it appears that they may be planted to nonleguminous crops with satisfactory returns.

"There is a distinct increase in the nitrogen content of the surface portion of such exposed subsoils, it being much greater when the land is devoted to alfalfa. Even in this case, however, it has by no means attained that of the surrounding surface soils by the time its productivity for nonleguminous crops appears to have been restored. At depths below the plowed area, however, there appears to be no greater gain in nitrogen in the land devoted to alfalfa.

"A field with ordinary surface soil devoted to the production of alfalfa hay for thirteen years showed no distinct enrichment in nitrogen in the subsoil of the second to sixth foot. . . .

"The loess subsoils of the semiarid part, as well as those of the more humid half, of the Nebraska portion of the transition region show, in the matter of rawness, a behavior intermediate between that of arid subsoils and that of the humid subsoils of the eastern and southern United States and of western Europe, with inoculated legumes resembling the former, but with nonleguminous plants, the latter."

Twenty references to literature bearing on the subject are appended.

Soil survey of Latah County, Idaho, J. H. AGEE, G. W. GRAVES, and C. B. MICKELWAITE (*U. S. Dept. Agr., Advance Sheets Field Operations Bur. Soils, 1915, pp. 24, pls. 3, figs. 2, map 1*).—This survey, made in cooperation with the Idaho Experiment Station, deals with the soils of an area of 582,400 acres in the west-central part of northern Idaho. "The western and southern parts of the county are rolling prairie, while the extreme eastern and northern parts are mountainous. The south-central part has been dissected by swift-flowing streams. . . . Drainage is well established over the whole county."

The soils are of residual, eolian, and alluvial origin. Including rough mountainous land and rough stony land, nine soil types of six series are mapped, of which the Palouse silt loam, Helmer silt loam, and rough mountainous land cover 33.7, 25.7, and 22.5 per cent of the area, respectively.

Soil survey of Wells County, Indiana, W. E. THARP and W. E. WILEY (*U. S. Dept. Agr., Advance Sheets Field Operations Bur. Soils, 1915, pp. 29, fig. 1, map 1*).—This survey, made in cooperation with the Indiana Department of Geology, deals with the soils of an area of 233,600 acres in northeastern Indiana, the topography of which is undulating to rolling. The natural drainage varies with the topography from poor to good. The surface formation throughout the county is a glacial deposit of the late Wisconsin ice invasion.

Including muck and meadow, eight soil types of six series are mapped, of which the Crosby silty clay loam, Clyde silty clay loam, and Miami silty clay loam cover 38.9, 30.2, and 25.7 per cent of the area, respectively.

Soil survey of White County [Indiana], T. M. BUSHNELL and C. P. ERNI (*Ind. Dept. Geol. and Nat. Resources Ann. Rpt., 40 (1915), pp. 109–155, pl. 1*).— This survey has been noted from another source (E. S. R., 36, p. 812).

Soil survey of Van Buren County, Iowa, C. LOUNSBURY and H. W. REID (*U. S. Dept. Agr., Advance Sheets Field Operations Bur. Soils, 1915, pp. 32, fig. 1. map 1*).—This survey, made in cooperation with the Iowa Experiment Station, deals with the soils of an area of 308,480 acres in southern Iowa, the surface of which consists of a broad, level plain dissected by southeast-wardly flowing streams. Fairly good drainage is said to prevail over most of the county. "There is some deficiency on the broad plateau level in the northeastern part where drainage ways have not yet become thoroughly established."

The soils of the county are of glacial, loessial, and alluvial origin. "The greater part of the county is covered with glacial drift over which lies a thin mantle of loess, and these formations give rise to the upland soils. The alluvial soils include both stream-bottom and terrace or second-bottom types." Fourteen soil types of nine series are mapped, of which the Memphis silt loam and an eroded phase cover 42.4 per cent of the area and the Grundy silt loam 36.7 per cent.

Soil survey of Washington County, Nebraska, L. V. Davis and H. C. Mortlock (*U. S. Dept. Agr., Advance Sheets Field Operations Bur. Soils, 1915. pp. 38, fig. 1, map 1*).—This survey, made in cooperation with the Nebraska Soil Survey, deals with the soils of an area of 243,200 acres on the central eastern border of Nebraska. "Physiographically, the county is an old loessial plain, now dissected by dendritic drainage systems. It may be divided into two main topographic divisions, the uplands and the lowlands. Most of the upland consists of undulating to broken land developed by erosion from the old loessial plain. The lowlands consist mainly of first bottoms or alluvial flood plains, but also include flat to undulating terraces or second bottoms. . . . The surface drainage is everywhere good."

The soils are of glacial, loessial, and alluvial origin. Including river wash, 14 soil types of seven series are mapped, of which the Marshall silt loam covers 63.5 per cent of the area.

Soil survey of Davidson County, North Carolina, R. B. Hardison and L. L. Brinkley (*U. S. Dept. Agr., Advance Sheets Field Operations Bur. Soils, 1915. pp. 39, fig. 1, map 1*).—This survey, made in cooperation with the North Carolina Department of Agriculture, deals with the soils of an area of 370,560 acres in west-central North Carolina, the topography of which is prevailingly rolling to steeply rolling or badly broken. becoming semimountainous in the southern part. "Many small perennial streams, spring branches, and intermittent streams make up a well-developed drainage system, which reaches all parts of the county. All the first-bottom land along the streams is subject to overflows of short duration."

The soils of the area are of residual and alluvial origin. Twenty-two soil types of 11 series are mapped, of which the Cecil sandy loam. Georgeville silt loam. Alamance silt loam. and Durham sandy loam cover 16.8, 14.4, 9.5, and 8.1 per cent of the area, respectively.

Soil survey of Lewis and Gilmer Counties, West Virginia, W. J. Latimer (*U. S. Dept. Agr., Advance Sheets Field Operations Bur. Soils. 1915. pp. 34. fig. 1, map 1*).—This survey. made in cooperation with the West Virginia Geological Survey, deals with the soils of an area of 469,120 acres in central West Virginia which lies wholly within the Appalachian Mountain and Plateau Province. The topography in general is steep and broken. Many small streams and spring branches reach well back into the uplands and furnish all sections of the area with good drainage outlets. Owing to the steep topography, the runoff is rapid and drainage is excessive.

The soils of the area are divided naturally into upland or residual soils, terrace, and bottom soils. Including rough stony land, nine soil types of six series are mapped, of which the Dekalb silt loam, Meigs clay loam, and Upshur silty clay loam cover 36.1, 29.7, and 22.6 per cent of the area, respectively.

Arable soils, A. T. Charron (*Rpt. Min. Agr. Prov. Quebec. 1916. pp. 104–112*).—Analyses of 26 samples of arable soils representative of different parts of Quebec are reported and discussed. Acidity was evident in about three-fourths of the samples.

Stable manure, J. C. TEMPLE (*Georgia Sta. Rpt. 1916, p. 11*).—Experiments on the influence of stable manure on soil bacteria showed that the increase of bacteria in soils receiving sterilized stable manure and finely cut green oats was greater than in soil receiving unsterilized manure. "The character of the soil's microflora is sometimes greatly changed by the addition of these organic materials. Two soils have been studied in which Actinomyces made up from 79 to 90 per cent of the colonies developing on agar plates. The addition of manure caused a big increase in number of the colonies, but the increase was due entirely to the multiplication of the true bacteria. The bacterial complexes from the soil receiving the unsterilized manure showed much the highest cellulose-dissolving power."

The absorption and washing out of nitrogen from fertilization with nitrates, C. H. VAN HARREVELD-LAKO (*Arch. Suikerindus. Nederland. Indië, 24 (1916), No. 7, pp. 207–213; Meded. Proefstat. Java-Suikerindus., 6 (1916), No. 3, pp. 45–51*).—This is a review of work by others, the results of which are taken to indicate that nitrates are readily leached out of very pervious soils, and that in tropical soils especially ammonia fertilizers are preferable. See also a previous note by the author (E. S. R., 36, p. 219).

Lime nitrogen as a fertilizer, C. J. MILO (*Arch. Suikerindus. Nederland. Indië, 24 (1916), Nos. 19, pp. 709–743, pl. 1; fig. 1; 20, pp. 749–796*).—This article deals with the physical and chemical properties of lime nitrogen and reports the general results of experiments on its use as a nitrogenous fertilizer on Java sugar-cane soils. A list of 49 references to literature on the subject is appended.

Residual effect of phosphatic manures on green crops in the year following that of application (*Indian Tea Assoc., Sci. Dept. Quart. Jour., No. 3 (1916), pp. 95–102*).—Continuing previous experiments (E. S. R., 35, p. 428) on comparative tests of superphosphate, bones, phosphatic slag, and a proprietary basic phosphate with green crops, including sunn hemp, cowpeas, *Sesbania aculeata*, and *Tephrosia candida*, it was observed that the different phosphates showed the same order of relative efficiency in the second year as in the first after application, the differences, however, being much less marked. The results obtained with the superphosphate were so much better than with the other phosphates tested that the conclusion is reached that "the use of the less rapidly available forms of phosphate is only justified if these forms are very much cheaper per unit of phosphoric acid."

Influence of fertilizers and soil amendments on soil acidity, J. J. SKINNER and J. H. BEATTIE (*Jour. Amer. Soc. Agron., 9 (1917), No. 1, pp. 25–35*).—"In an experiment growing wheat, rye, clover, timothy, corn, cowpeas, and potatoes, conducted on a heavy silty clay loam at Arlington, Va., calcium sulphate, ferrous sulphate, manganese sulphate, potassium sulphate, and potassium sulphid added singly to the soil annually for five years increased its acidity.

"Magnesium carbonate decreased the acidity of the soil. Soil fertilized with sodium nitrate was less acid than the untreated soil or soil fertilized with acid phosphate or potassium sulphate. Acid phosphate fertilization increased the acidity of the soil, but not as much so as potassium sulphate.

"Organic materials affected the soil differently as to causing acidity. Starch caused increased acidity; stable manure slightly increased acidity, which was still greater with manure leached of its soluble organic and inorganic substances. The leachings from manure produced less acidity than the untreated soil and less than the whole manure or leached manure. The nature of the

102477°—17——3

decomposition of the organic material in the soil and the character of the life processes in the soil affects the influence of such substances on soil acidity."

The rotary kiln for lime burning—descriptive and comparative, J. G. Jones (*Nat. Lime Manfrs. Assoc. Bul. 15 (1914), pp. 16*).—The rotary type of kiln for lime burning is described. In a comparison with the vertical kiln it is stated that the rotary kiln has the advantage of better and more uniform burning of the lime.

Soil acidity and the liming of Iowa soils, P. E. Brown (*Iowa Sta. Bul. 151, abridged ed. (1915), pp. 22, fig. 1*).—An abridged edition (E. S. R., 32, p. 212).

Fertilizer analyses, H. B. McDonnell (*Md. Agr. Col. Quart., No. 73 (1916), pp. 30*).—This report contains the results of actual and guarantied analyses of 687 samples of fertilizers and fertilizing materials collected for inspection in Maryland from February to June, 1916, inclusive, together with a brief discussion of lime in mixed fertilizers as a drier and filler.

AGRICULTURAL BOTANY.

The progressive development of the wheat kernel (*Washington Sta. Bul. 136 (1917), pp. 25, 26*).—A summarized report is given on studies in which it is stated that inorganic materials are high in the young plant, the largest amount of potassium nitrate occurring in the root and stem just before the formation of the spike, after which time it gradually decreases. Free magnesium falls to a minimum during the formation of the aleurone, while free phosphate rises rapidly to a maximum during the development of the sporogenous tissue, falling to a minimum after the development of the sex cells. Asparagin is considered a very important nutritive substance for growth and it was found together with fructose in all young growing regions. Pectic substances on the stigma are considered especially important in reducing the absorption of water by pollen grains.

From fertilization of the egg to the mature grain, there is a constant translocation of nutrient materials to the growing embryo from the leaves and glumes, these including fructose, glucose, asparagin, arginin, histidin, and leucin. Any excess sugar is at once condensed into starch. Excess asparagin and amino acids remain as such in the endosperm cells until desiccation of the grain begins. Aside from aleurone and protoplasm, in the endosperm just before ripening of the grain are found asparagin, arginin, histidin, and some leucin, but no glutamin. On desiccation of the grain, protein appears in the storage cells and the amino acids and most of the asparagin disappear. The formation of storage protein in wheat is believed to be a condensation process that takes place on dessication of the kernel.

Translocation of seed protein reserves in the growing corn seedling, C. J. V. Pettibone and Cornelia Kennedy (*Jour. Biol. Chem., 26 (1916), No. 2, pp. 519-525, figs. 2*).—The authors describe studies claimed to show that amino acids are present in the flowing sap of corn seedlings. The fact that these compounds are always present in the seed, rootlet, and plumule, coupled with the demonstrated migration of nitrogen, is held to indicate that the transportation of reserve building proteins of the seed occurs in a manner analogous to the transportation of protein food supplies in the animal organism. It is proposed to investigate further certain phenomena suggesting that a portion of the nitrogen may be transported in the form of soluble protein or protein hydrolytic products of the peptid type.

The relation of amid nitrogen to the nitrogen metabolism of the pea plant, B. Sure and W. E. Tottingham (*Jour. Biol. Chem., 26 (1916), No. 2, pp. 535-548, figs. 3*).—The purpose of this investigation was to determine whether during germination there is a distinct relation between the disappearance of amino acids and the accumulation of amids, as determined by methods which are described and claimed to be more strictly quantitative than those formerly employed. The investigation consisted in following the changes of the total and water-soluble nitrogen, and the various compounds of the latter, in the etiolated pea plant, which lent itself readily to this purpose and to the methods which are described.

It is stated that in the shoot the percentage of total nitrogen more than doubled in 26 days, but only in cases in which carbohydrate decomposition exceeded protein disintegration. This fact supposedly indicates that during the early stages of growth rapid carbohydrate catabolism occurs in the shoot.

Total nitrogen decreased in the cotyledon, and during early growth α-amino acids accumulated in the cotyledon more than in the shoot. Catabolism is therefore thought to be the predominant type of change in protein material during germination. Water-soluble nitrogen showed a nearly constant proportion to the total nitrogen except in the first stage of growth, when it accumulated considerably. Ammonia, only traces of which occurred in the seed, accumulated during germination. Its fluctuations roughly paralleled those of amid nitrogen, but it decreased in the shoot. Amid nitrogen increased in the shoot throughout all stages of germination, but not so considerably as reported by previous investigators.

Since amids accumulated while carbohydrates and ammonia decreased, it is suggested that the former may have been produced synthetically from the latter compounds. The α-amino acids accumulated rapidly, especially in the cotyledon, during early growth, but later they decreased in the shoot and disappeared from the cotyledon. The accumulation of amids simultaneously with the decrease of the α-amino acids and ammonia in the shoot is considered to indicate that α-amino acids serve for amid production in the nitrogen metabolism of the etiolated pea plant.

The release of oxygen separated during the reduction of nitrates in green plants, M. MOLLIARD (*Compt. Rend. Acad. Sci.* [Paris], *163* (*1916*), *No. 15, pp. 371–373*).—A study of the behavior of radish grown under controlled conditions as regards space and nutritive medium is described. The results appear to indicate that for the fixation of one atom of nitrogen there was a corresponding disengagement of two atoms of oxygen.

Observations on the cytological formation of anthocyanin in living plants, M. MIRANDE (*Compt. Rend. Acad. Sci.* [Paris], *163* (*1916*), *No. 15, pp. 368–371*).—The author has extended to lower plants the studies regarding the mitochondrial origin of anthocyanin, which had been pursued among higher plants by Guilliermond (E. S. R., 35, p. 523), employing for this purpose *Azolla filiculoides*, which lends itself readily to direct observation in this connection.

He states that he has been able to obtain fresh evidences of the mitochondrial origin of anthocyanin pigment. In case of *A. filiculoides*, anthocyanin is secreted by granular mitochondria, which in due time emigrating from the central vacuole of the cell become impregnated with a phenol compound which gradually develops anthocyanin pigment. In cases of extreme reddening the anthocyanin is dissolved in the vacuole.

Selective permeability: The absorption of phenol and other solutions by the seeds of Hordeum vulgare, A. J. BROWN and F. TINKER (*Proc. Roy. Soc.* [*London*], *Ser. B, 89* (*1916*), *No. B 617, pp. 373–379, figs. 2*).—Previous study (E. S. R., 34, p. 626) on the absorption of aqueous solutions by barley seeds has related mainly to the phenomena attending diffusion of the solvent through the semipermeable seed covering, which is permeable also to certain classes of contained solutes (as phenols and fatty acids), behaving, in fact, rather as a selectively permeable membrane. **The authors have now** studied more particularly the entrance of these solutes into the seeds, together with water, in the hope of throwing some light on the physical causes governing selective permeability. A preliminary investigation having shown that phenol and anilin solutions enter the seeds in higher concentrations than the solutions in which they are immersed, quantitative experiments were made employing variously concentrated solutions of anilin, phenol, and acetic acid.

The results are presented in tabular and graphical form with discussion. Pure acetic acid was not absorbed by dry seeds.

The relation between the concentration of various inside solutions and the amount absorbed at equilibrium was also studied, and the results have been tabulated. The various forces involved are discussed.

Some photochemical experiments with pure chlorophyll and their bearing on theories of carbon assimilation, I. JÖRGENSEN and F. KIDD (*Proc. Roy. Soc.* [*London*], *Ser. B, 89* (*1916*), *No. B 617, pp. 342–361, figs. 2*).—The authors have examined certain photochemical reactions of chlorophyll observed and hypotheses advanced by previous investigators as a basis for theories of carbon assimilation. Pure chlorophyll was employed in this work as a sol, with water as a dispersion medium, and this sol, in contact with different gases in closed vessels, was exposed to light.

In nitrogen no change occurred in the chromogen complex of the chlorophyll molecule. In carbon dioxid (which here behaved in solution as any other weak acid) phæophytin was produced, but no further change took place in the chromogen complex and formaldehyde was not formed. In oxygen a yellowing, attributed to phæophytin, was observable, and this was followed by a bleaching, the latter development being accelerated and the former omitted when alkali was added. Formaldehyde was produced gradually at first, but more rapidly after bleaching was completed, increasing to a maximum and then diminishing, while acidity increased throughout. It is suggested that formaldehyde arises mainly from the phytol, which is presumably split off from the chlorophyll molecule under light and oxygen.

Aeriferous tissue in willow galls, A. COSENS and T. A. SINCLAIR (*Bot. Gaz., 62* (*1916*), *No. 3, pp 210–225, pls. 3, figs. 5*).—The failure of all attempts by varying environment to develop or increase the aeriferous tissue where found in certain portions of insect galls is considered to prove that they are heritable tissues. The reinstatement in a gall of vestigial characters of the plant is considered to have an important bearing on the question of gall formation. It is claimed that there is no authentic instance of any organ or tissue in a gall that is new, ontogenetically or phylogentically. to the host in question.

Improvements in the method for determining the transpiring power of plant surfaces by hygrometric paper, B. E. LIVINGSTON and EDITH B. SHREVE (*Plant World, 19* (*1916*), *No. 10. pp. 287–309*).—The authors have given in considerable detail the results of several years of work on improvements which are claimed to render field tests of the transpiring power of plants much less arduous and more precise than was formerly the case. These improvements relate to the elimination of repeated field tests over the standard evaporating surface, the substitution therefor of a thermometer reading and a simple arithmetical calculation, the introduction of composite paper slips including two permanent color standards and the use of small desiccators for keeping the slips dry and at air temperature until a test is to be made, improvements in the standard evaporating surface, and a more uniform cobalt chlorid paper than any previously employed.

Germinability tests with seeds of **Lepidium sativum under** diverse conditions, P. LESAGE (*Compt. Rend. Acad. Sci.* [*Paris*], *163* (*1916*), *No. 18, pp. 486–*

489).—Employing the potash test previously mentioned (E. S. R., 25, p. 222) for determining germinability or its absence, the author has experimented with seeds of pepper cress in alcoholic or in saline solutions, in petroleum ether or in ordinary ether, in moist air and in oxygenated water. He has detailed the results of the several tests, with some references to observations previously made by himself (E. S. R., 27, p. 330) and by Demoussy (E. S. R., 36, p. 29).

Influence of the medium upon the orientation of secondary terrestrial roots, R. M. HOLMAN (*Amer. Jour. Bot., 3 (1916), No. 8, pp. 407–414, figs. 3*).— The results arrived at by the study, previously noted (E. S. R., 35, p. 223; 36, p. 129), of the primary roots of *Vicia faba, Lupinus albus,* and *Pisum sativum* suggested the question as to whether or not the secondary roots of these species show any relation between geotropic behavior and medium, such as exists in primary roots. The author has carried out a series of experiments, chiefly with *V. faba,* in the course of which a striking parallel was noted between the behavior of primary roots and secondary roots of the first order, the media used being air as nearly as possible saturated with water, uniformly moist sawdust, and fine garden earth. The results are described in detail.

The growth of forest tree roots, W. B. McDOUGALL (*Amer. Jour. Bot., 3 (1916), No. 7, pp. 384–392*).—A series of systematic observations, by means of two methods described, on growing roots of *Quercus alba, Tilia americana, Carya laciniosa,* and *Acer saccharinum,* are considered to show that the root growth of forest trees corresponds to the warm period during which absorption can go on. Any possible resting period in summer is deemed due to scarcity of water and not to any inherent tendency of the plants toward periodicity in growth.

The toxicity of bog water, G. M. RIGG (*Amer. Jour. Bot., 3 (1916), No. 8, pp. 436, 437*).—A brief statement is given regarding data obtained from studies on waters taken from sphagnum bogs of the Puget Sound region and Alaska, in relation to the injurious effect of such waters on certain plants (in this case Tradescantia cuttings). The author considers these data to warrant the suggestion that its content of colloidal matters is a large factor in the toxicity of this water to certain plants.

Experimental cultures of plants on the seashore, L. DANIEL (*Compt. Rend. Acad. Sci. [Paris], 163 (1916), No. 18, pp. 483–486*).—During fifteen years of experiments with various plants which had been taken from Rennes to Erquy and there grown under exposure to spray and intermittent wetting with sea water, no change of real significance or permanence occurred, so far as could be detected. Any differences due to abundant or deficient water supply showed a tendency to disappear quickly when the plants were returned to their former environment.

The establishment of varieties in Coleus by the selection of somatic variations, A. B. STOUT (*Carnegie Inst. Washington Pub. 218 (1915), pp. 80, pls. 4, figs. 4*).—The author reports that a single variety of Coleus propagated vegetatively by cuttings in two main clones has shown gradual fluctuations and sudden mutations, giving a total of 16 distinct and characteristically different color patterns. The results indicate that slight variations, arising either as sudden mutations or as gradual fluctuations, can perpetuate themselves. It is claimed that bud variations in Coleus are common, give numerous different types which may be vegetatively constant from the first or can be made so by selection, show development of certain types more commonly than others, produce reversions to parental types, give development of different degrees of variability among sister clones, and exhibit spontaneous changes in the fundamental color characters and in the cellular and tissue processes resulting in color patterns. The results of the investigation indicate that in Coleus asexual and sexual reproduction are not fundamentally different in respect to the extent and range of variation.

A bibliography of literature pertaining to the subject is given.

Mutation in Matthiola annua, a "Mendelizing" species, H. B. Frost (*Amer. Jour. Bot., 3 (1916), No. 7, pp. 377–383, figs. 3*).—The author states that six or seven of the series of types noted previously (E. S. R., 28, p. 439) as having sprung from *M. annua* have reproduced themselves in progeny tests, some through several generations, though only the early (few-noded) type has proved to be evidently homozygous. A brief characterization is given of eight of the mutant types, including all that have proved to be hereditary.

The mutant individuals are considered to be not extracted pure recessives but heterozygous dominants, and (since they have occurred many times in cultures from selfed parents) not due to combination of complementary factors by cross-fertilization. They are considered to be due to definite changes in the germ plasm distinct from the shiftings which result from ordinary Mendelian phenomena.

Correlations between morphological characters and the saccharin content of sugar beets. F. J. Pritchard (*Amer. Jour. Bot., 3 (1916), No. 7, pp. 361–576, figs. 8*).—Extensive statistical data obtained from a study of beets are said to show correlation coefficients between root weight and sugar percentage of -0.253, -0.258, -0.254, -0.257, and -0.499; between weight of root and quantity of sugar, 0.920. Correlation between percentage and quantity of sugar in roots of 35 gm. range in weight was nearly perfect, being 0.93, 0.96, and 0.99, but no such correlation appeared in roots of miscellaneous sizes. Correlation was slight or absent between other qualities noted.

Anomalies in Beta vulgaris, O. Munerati and T. V. Zapparoli (*Atti R. Accad. Lincei, Rend. Cl. Sci. Fis., Mat. e Nat., 5. ser., 25 (1916), I, No. 12, pp. 816–822, figs. 6*).—This is a progress report on the continuation of studies previously noted (E. S. R., 35, p. 436). Morphological deviations, which have proved to be much more frequent than formerly appeared, are reported on as regards the portions of the plant involved, and certain correlations have been observed.

Green manures and manuring in the Tropics, including an account of the economic value of Leguminosæ as sources of foodstuffs, vegetable oils, etc., P. de Sornay, trans. by F. W. Flattely (*London: John Bale, Sons & Danielsson, Ltd., 1916, pp. XVI+466, figs. 74*).—In this translation from Les Plantes Tropicales Alimentaires et Industrielles de la Famille des Légumineuses, the author, after summarizing investigations and theories regarding the fixation of free atmospheric nitrogen by leguminous plants, describes about 40 species that are more or less extensively grown in the Tropics as green-manure crops, as well as for forage and other purposes. Comparisons are drawn between several common species as to their relative values in rotation experiments. Chapters are devoted to the presence of manganese and prussic acid in leguminous plants, a description of the principal starches they contain, their uses in agriculture and various arts, insect and fungus pests, etc. Much of the information is derived from reports of experiments conducted in various countries, but the author adds much original matter from his own investigations at the agricultural station of the island of Mauritius.

FIELD CROPS.

[Report of field crop work at the Georgia Experiment Station], O. K. Mc-Clelland (*Georgia Sta. Rpt. 1916, pp. 7–9, 28–31*).—Fertilizer tests with corn showed an increase of 13.4 per cent when fertilizer was applied around the corn instead of under it. In testing the amount of fertilizer to apply to corn, 1,000-lb. applications resulted in the highest yield, 27.9 bu. per acre, as compared with 18.9 bu. on the check plat and from 20.5 to 25.5 bu. from 200- to 1,200-lb. applications. A yield of only slightly more than 8 bu. per acre of corn was realized from a field in which velvet beans were sown with the corn. In a comparison of basic slag with acid phosphate the yield with the latter was 23.2 bu., with the former 22.5 bu., and the check 20 bu. per acre.

Fertilizer experiments with cotton showed a gradual increase in the yields of seed cotton with increasing amounts of fertilizers, the increase over the check varying from about 22 per cent with a 200-lb. to 50 per cent with a 1,200-lb. application. There was no material difference in yields of cotton when fertilized with either basic slag or acid phosphate. A comparison of early with late thinning of cotton gave increased yields in favor of the latter method of 26 lbs. of seed cotton per acre for the Trice variety and 28 lbs. for the Sunbeam variety.

Top-dressing small grains with nitrate of soda gave slightly better results than the use of sulphate of ammonia, both being superior to cottonseed meal. The latter, however, doubled the yield of oats. In preparing for oats after peas double disking was followed by a yield of 44 bu., deep plowing by one of 53 bu., and shallow plowing by one of 55 bu. per acre.

Brief notes are given on Sudan, para, teff, Giant Bermuda, rescue, redtop, and Kikuyu grasses. Rescue grass is reported as the best winter grass.

In experiments with leguminous plants, seeding tests with alfalfa showed no difference in stand by different times or depths of plowing, manured or unmanured, with lime plowed under or left on top of plowed land, or with different rates of seeding. There was a difference with different amounts of limestone applied per acre, 1 ton proving insufficient to overcome the soil acidity while slight difference was realized between 2- and 3-ton applications. Analyses of roots and stubble of crimson clover showed a nitrogen residue of 46 lbs. per acre.

Studies of the water requirement of cotton have been continued. An apparent regularity in the blooming of the cotton plant has been observed in that the time between horizontal blooms was double that between vertical blooms, a given bloom opening on the same day as the one on the second branch above but one node nearer the central stalk of the plant. The period of greatest moisture requirement was found to be from the middle of July to late August.

Observations on the germination of cotton seed sown after turning under a green manure crop are reported for purposes of comparing field conditions with those observed by Fred (E. S. R., 35, p. 24) under greenhouse conditions. It was concluded that there is some injury to germination (from 0.7 to 5.1 per cent) from the use of a green manure crop, but that the difference in field plantings is not sufficient to militate against the use of such a crop. The observations indirectly showed a benefit from the early planting of the green manure crop in the fall to afford sufficient growth to make early spring plowing permissible.

[Report of field crop work], G. S. RAY, C. M. EKLOF, P. P. PETERSON, and G. W. GRAVES (Idaho Sta. Bul. 92 (1916), pp. 19–22, 30–34, figs. 4).—This reports the continuation of field crop work previously noted (E. S. R., 34, p. 734).

Variety tests are noted with winter and spring varieties of wheat, oats, barley, rye, field peas, and corn. The leading varieties and their respective yields were as follows: Red Russian winter wheat 59.7, Jenkins Club spring wheat 72, Tennessee Winter barley 47.9, with the 4-year average for white winter barley 67.1; Hannchen spring barley; Colorado 37 spring oats 168.7 (all winter oats winterkilled); Invincible winter rye 58.9; and Amraoti field peas 53.3 bu. per acre. Minnesota 13 was the only corn variety to mature seed. Idaho White Dent produced 15.8 tons of silage per acre when cut in the glazed stage. The best silage production from Rustler White Dent with different planting methods was 16.1 tons, secured from rows 30 in. apart and hills 3 ft. 8 in. apart.

A seeding of 90 lbs. of field peas and 32 lbs. of oats gave the highest yield of hay, 4.6 tons, in a comparison of different rates of seeding. In cultural tests with field peas the highest yield, 70.5 bu. per acre, was secured from broadcasted seed plowed under.

In crop rotation experiments on Palouse silt loam a yield of 76.1 bu. of wheat was secured after potatoes as compared with a yield of 25.3 bu. after oats, 29.8 bu. after wheat, 48.4 bu. after corn, 51.2 bu. after peas, and 63.1 bu. after fallow. Fertilizer experiments on this soil showed an apparent average increase in yield of oats due to fertilizers added in 1915 of 19.8 bu. for nitrogen, 2.5 bu. for potash, and a 2.4-bu. loss for phosphorus. Similar tests with wheat were deemed inconclusive because of smut.

[Report of field crop work at the Aberdeen substation], L. C. AICHER (*Idaho Sta. Bul. 92 (1916), pp. 36-42, figs. 3*).—This reports a continuation of work previously noted (E. S. R., 34, p. 734), including cultural tests with clovers, sugar beets (seed), peas, alfalfa, wheat, and potatoes, and variety tests with wheat, oats, barley, potatoes, and field peas, etc.

In the potato culture work a yield of 520 bu. per acre was obtained from a plat planted with the stem ends only of 3-oz. seed cut in half.

[Report of field crop work] (*Iowa Sta. Rpt. 1916, pp. 22, 23, 29*).—Cooperative trials with Iowa 103 and Iowa 105 oats, originated at the station, show an approximate increase of 5 bu. per acre over common varieties. The winter wheat variety has exhibited great hardiness under conditions that resulted in severe winterkilling with most commercial varieties. This variety has also been grown in Minnesota and North and South Dakota, the winterkilling in these regions being reported as about 5 per cent.

The Ames scarifying machine is reported as having increased the germinability of various clover seed, especially sweet clover, to over 90 per cent. when in many cases previous to treatment germination was not over 20 per cent.

In pollination studies with clover and alfalfa, conducted in cooperation with the U. S. Department of Agriculture, it was found that moisture conditions were a determining factor in the setting of red clover seed, as little fertilization occured when the flowers were wet. In July the interval between pollination and fertilization was about 18 hours, and in October from 35 to 50 hours. The bumblebee is found an efficient pollinator of red clover, while the honeybee is occasionally so. The clover cross-pollinating machine and hand-pollinating brushes were not satisfactory.

J. N. Martin found that the setting of the seed pods in alfalfa is dependent upon the proper functioning of the pollen and that germination of the pollen is dependent upon the moisture supply. If the supply of soil and atmospheric moisture is above or below the optimum, germination is inhibited. Blasting of the seed is due to the arrested development of the embryo caused either by pathological conditions or the inability of the plant to furnish the required moisture.

Irrigation experiments with alfalfa, sugar beets, potatoes, and wheat (*Nevada Sta. Rpt. 1916, pp. 30-34*).—Experiments similar to those previously noted (E. S. R., 36, p. 35) were continued during the season of 1915.

Alfalfa was given 6-, 9-, and 12-in. applications of water before and at the time the plants showed need of water by the dark green color of the foliage and when the plants had suffered for water as indicated by the dark green color of the foliage and drooping leaves. The results show that alfalfa can not be allowed to reach the wilting stage without materially decreasing the yield of hay. Where the plants were never allowed to show need of water the yield was higher with a 6-in. than with a 9-in. application, but slightly lower than with the 12-in. application. The greatest total yield was had at the expense of yield per acre-foot of water and of quality of hay, the latter being due to the large proportion of coarse stems to leaves. A gradual decrease in yield was noted with the same applications of water applied as the wilting stage advances. Alfalfa responded better than wheat, potatoes, and sugar beets to heavy applications of water, but not so well as did clover the previous year.

Potato yields were seriously affected by dry rot, but comparative results for 1914 and 1915 indicate that light applications of water are preferable under all conditions. Very little difference in yield is shown, however, where the crop receives four, six, or eight 3-in. applications. Where the plants wilted before irrigation a second growth was made, resulting in lowered starch content. Plats receiving over 24 in. of water produced very scabby potatoes.

The average results with sugar beets for 1914 and 1915 indicate that plants irrigated after having wilted and failed to revive at night will not produce a profitable crop. Only slight variations in yield were realized from 2-, 4-, and 6-in. applications, or from total applications of 12-, 18-, and 24-in., this being partly attributed to the lateral diffusion of moisture from one plat to another. The sugar content was not materially affected by the stage of wilting or depth of application. The purity of the juice varied with the stage of wilting, being greatest in beets which received 6-in. applications after the plants wilted down and failed to revive at night. The beets in this plat produced 5.36 tons per acre, while the highest-yielding plat produced 11.8 tons.

The wheat experiments were altered in that 3-, 5-, and 7-in. applications were made instead of 3-, 4.5-, and 6-in. applications, as previously, the stages of growth remaining the same. The plats were harvested from August 9 to 17, those receiving the least total irrigation, when an irrigation at the milk stage was omitted, attaining maturity first. The three highest yields were obtained from plats receiving four 7-in. applications, that on which the irrigation at the 5-leaf stage was omitted, being first with 34.7 bu. per acre, with that on which the irrigation at the boot stage was omitted second, and that on which the irrigation at the dough stage was omitted third. With the omission of irrigations at the 5-leaf and dough and the milk and dough stages, the yields were 28.5 and 27.8 bu. per acre, respectively, and a marked decrease in yield was noted on all other plats where two irrigations were omitted. With a 7-in. application at each stage of growth a yield of 24.2 bu. per acre was obtained. The yield obtained with four 7-in. applications when the irrigation at the milk stage was omitted was 27 per cent less than the highest yield, 11 per cent less than when the irrigation at the boot stage was omitted, 6 per cent less than when the irrigation at the dough stage was omitted, and 8 per cent more than when the irrigation at the bloom stage was omitted, thus indicating that the bloom and milk stages are critical periods in the irrigation of the wheat crop.

With only two irrigations the yields were lower in all cases, but the 6-in. application before heading and the 12-in. application after heading produced the greatest yield, 27 bu. per acre. Nine- and 12-in. irrigations before heading provided an excess of water over that utilized by the crop, as shown by decreased yields amounting to 39 and 40 per cent. respectively.

In a comparison of 3- and 7-in. applications, 83 per cent of the results were strongly in favor of the 7-in. applications, with an average increase in yields of 28.7 per cent and a maximum increase of 87.6 per cent where one irrigation at the boot stage was omitted. Where irrigations were omitted at the 5-leaf and bloom stages, boot and bloom stages, boot and milk stages, and bloom and milk stages, the 3-in. applications are about as effective as twice that amount in supplying the water requirements of the crop, but the omission of these applications greatly decreased the yield, 19.9 bu. being the highest production in any of the last four instances.

The minimum soil moisture content for the first 2 ft. was 11.6 per cent before the irrigation at the milk stage and where two irrigations were omitted at the boot and bloom stages, and the maximum 16.5 per cent where irrigations at the 5-leaf and dough stages were omitted. Only 1.5 per cent maximum average difference down to 6 ft. was realized between 3- and 7-in. applications where two irrigations were omitted. When one irrigation was omitted the variation in moisture content between 3- and 7-in. applications was greater. The 7-in. applications at the first foot showed an increase of 14.8 per cent over that of the 3-in. applications, a 10 per cent increase for the second foot, a 12 per cent increase for the third foot, and a 3 per cent loss for the fourth foot.

Variety testing and crop improvement (*Nevada Sta. Rpt. 1916, pp. 34–37, figs. 2*).—Variety and selection tests are reported with wheat, oats, barley, corn and sorghum (for silage), field peas and beans, millets, potatoes, and field beets.

[Report of field crop work] (*New Mexico Sta. Rpt., 1916, pp. 34–49, figs. 3*).— Potato experiments for 1916 included plantings receiving stable manure, level and ridge cultivation, cultivation by the Greeley system, 10- and 5-in. winter irrigations, no winter irrigation, no summer irrigation, no winter or summer irrigation, and 1, 2, and 3 summer irrigations. The rainfall amounted to 1.89 in. The highest plat yield was secured where the Greeley system of cultivation had been practiced and where 3 summer irrigations but no winter irrigation had occurred. The second highest yield was obtained from a plat receiving the level cultivation, 2 summer irrigations, and 1 10-in. winter irrigation. Both plats were manured.

Of 11 varieties of sorghum tested for silage, sumac sorghum gave the highest yield, 14.3 tons of green forage per acre, and White Durra the lowest, with 3.2 tons per acre.

In cultural and variety tests with corn, Mexican June sown with a planter and with irrigation preceding planting gave the highest yield, 52.4 bu. per acre. The lowest yield, 11.7 bu., was secured with Hickory King under the same conditions.

Sudan grass seeded in rows gave a total yield of 7,428 lbs. as compared with 6,261 lbs. on a plat seeded broadcast, and required an average of 284 lbs. less water in the production of dry matter.

Sugar beet tests included a study of spring and fall planting dates, involving a comparison of spring and fall planting, a comparison of the furrow method of irrigation with the flooding method, and a comparison of irrigating before and after planting. Beets planted in January were ready to harvest in July and tested 14 per cent sugar with about 85 per cent purity.

A study is being made of the duty of water, with special reference to alfalfa production. In the season of 1915–16 five cuttings of alfalfa were secured, averaging 6 tons per acre with an average duty of water of 40 acre-inches.

Farm crops (*Washington Sta. Bul. 136 (1917), pp. 10–19, 29, 30, fig. 1*).— This reports the work of the 1915 season and the plantings for 1916.

In inheritance studies the F_2 generation of hybrid seed from true spring varieties of barley when seeded in the spring produced 18.75 per cent of winter plants and 81.75 per cent of spring plants.

The following varieties yielded best for their respective crops for two years: Winter wheat, Triplet, 49.37 bu.; spring wheat, Chul × Bluestem, 32.79 bu.; oats, Abundance; winter barley, Tapp, 64.1 bu.; spring barley, Blue Barley, 64.77 bu.; and field peas, Canada, 28.5 bu. (one year).

Variety tests at Ritzville under a 12-in. rainfall and summer fallowed ground were continued in 1915. Hybrid 143 gave the highest yield of winter wheat varieties, 54.4 bu.; Early Baart, of spring wheat varieties, 52.6 bu.; Blue Barley, of the barleys, 82.5 bu.; and Sixty Day, of the oats, 76.25 bu.

Environmental tests conducted in cooperation with the U. S. Department of Agriculture were continued.

Rotation and cultural experiments extending over a period of 15 years indicate that the plat growing corn and winter wheat in alternate years has given the greatest total yield of grain for 15 years and ranked among the highest in yield of winter wheat in 1915 (45 bu. per acre). The plat giving the highest wheat yield in 1915 (46 bu. per acre) was on a 5-year rotation of clover and timothy, 1911 and 1912; oats and peas (10 tons of manure per acre), 1913; corn, 1914; and wheat, 1915. The plats in rotation gave larger yields in general than those growing wheat continuously, either annually or in alternation with summer fallow.

Approximately 2,000 nitrogen determinations were made of different varieties of wheat grown under different conditions. The spring wheats grown at Pullman were high in nitrogen content, the lowest percentage, 2.41, being found in Red Chaff and the highest, 3.15, in Little Club. Among the winter wheats Jones Winter Fife was lowest, with 2.11 per cent, and Turkey × Bluestem Hybrid highest, with 3.03 per cent. The highest average nitrogen content, 2.82 per cent, occurred in wheat grown on summer fallow, while the lowest, 1.62 per cent, occurred in wheat grown on ground used for the production of wheat hay the previous year. Following summer fallow the nitrogen content diminshed in order after the following crops: Potatoes, carrots, beets, beans, and peas.

Alfalfa fertilizers, G. G. Brown (*Oregon Sta. Bul. 141 (1917), pp. 55, 56*).— Field experiments at Hood River to determine the relative influence of land plaster (gypsum) and flowers of sulphur on alfalfa are briefly reported.

A 100-lb. application of land plaster to unthrifty plants was followed by a total yield of 7,522 lbs. of cured hay per acre, as compared with a yield of 2,104 lbs. on the untreated plat. Doubling the treatment resulted in a total yield of only 5,660 lbs. In this experiment an application of air-slaked lime, followed by a 100-lb. application of land plaster after the first cutting, resulted in greatly increased vigor and a total yield considerably in excess of the untreated plat.

An application of 16.6 lbs. of sulphur (the sulphur equivalent of 100 lbs. of land plaster) was followed by a total yield of 7,650 lbs. of cured hay per acre, or 890 lbs. in excess of that for the check plat. With a 200-lb. applica- tion of sulphur 9,880 lbs. of hay was produced. Land plaster applied at the rate of 100 lbs. per acre in this series showed a total yield of 11,300 lbs. of hay per acre. A gain of 400 lbs. of hay per acre per cutting was obtained following a 200-lb. application of land plaster, 100 lbs. applied in March and 100 lbs. applied after the first cutting.

Another series of experiments on which data for the first two cuttings only were secured showed a total yield of 6,500 lbs. per acre following a 200-lb.

application of sulphur and 8,300 lbs. following a 100-lb. application of land plaster.

Air-slaked lime and nitrate of soda were also tested, but failed to give increased yields.

It is recommended that sulphur be applied not later than January or February, while land plaster should be applied early in March.

Studies by means of both pot and solution culture of the phosphorus and potassium requirements of the barley plant during its different periods of growth, F. R. PEMBER (*Rhode Island Sta. Bul. 169 (1917), pp. 50, pls. 2, figs. 3*).—Investigations are reported to determine the actual requirements of the barley plant for potassium and phosphorus during different periods of growth and where most of the conditions essential to growth were under control. The experiments include (1) those with plants grown in sand or soil and (2) those with barley grown in solutions.

The first group of experiments included four tests of varying applications of potassium and phosphorus applied at different periods in the growth of barley grown in sand, a study of the relation of vigor of growth of the young plants to the percentage of phosphorus contained in the seed, and a comparative study of oats grown in sunken pots out of doors.

Tests for the potassium requirement of the barley plant grown in sand were not continued after the first experiment because of the large growth the plants were capable of making when no potassium was added. Where little or no potassium was added, the plants showed spots or flecks of brown on the oldest leaves, the discoloration being greatest when no potassium was added. Plants grown without the addition of phosphorus were darker green and showed considerable purple in their stalks and leaves.

In the sand experiments the weight of dry straw, or straw and roots, was practically the same whether all of the phosphorus was added at the beginning in three equal applications, or one-third at the beginning and one-third at the end of the second period, or two-thirds at the beginning and one-third at the end of the second period. In the third experiment the amount of seed produced was much greater where phosphorus had been received in three equal applications, while in the fourth experiment plants having the full phosphorus application at the beginning produced the most seed.

Selected barley seed varied in the percentage of phosphorus contained, but the weight of the entire dry plants grown from similar seeds bore no relation to the amount contained. Plants grown for 19 days from planting with a full phosphorus application at their disposal were not markedly larger than those having only a one-third application of phosphorus, but the amount of phosphorus recovered from the former was more than twice that recovered from the latter. In the fourth experiment, the amount of phosphorus recovered from the plants harvested at the end of the second period was much the same whether the full phosphorus application was made at the beginning, or one-third at the beginning of both the first and second periods. The best recovery of phosphorus by the barley plants grown in sand was about 89 per cent of the amount added.

Oat plants grown in 1909 in soil receiving the full phosphorus application before planting were larger and recovered more phosphorus than those which had three equal applications, but the latter produced a larger amount of seed. In the season of 1910 these differences were negligible. The best recovery of phosphorus by the oat plant was one-fifteenth of the amount added.

The second group of experiments dealt with the actual requirements of the barley plant for potassium and phosphorus during its different periods of growth in solutions. Studies were made of the phosphorus absorption during fortnightly periods; the effect of different cultural methods, of boron and manganese, and of varying the relation of the potassium, nitrogen, and phosphorus; applications of potassium and phosphorus made according to certain curves; the stage of growth at which the minimum phosphorus is best utilized; the ability of barley plants to utilize phosphorus if it is mainly withheld until the last four weeks of growth; and the necessary amount of phosphorus for the optimum growth of the barley plant. The results of these investigations are briefly summarized as follows:

Ten plants receiving an average of 13 mg. of P_2O_5 per week for the first 10 weeks absorbed nearly all of it, while plants receiving the maximum amount of phosphorus absorbed about 30 mg. P_2O_5 per week from the third to the sixth week, inclusive. The small application of phosphorus was sufficient for the needs of the plants but the percentage of phosphorus recovered was much increased by the largest application. Plants receiving minimum amounts of phosphorus the first eight weeks of growth were noticeably handicapped in size and in color of stems and leaves, while those receiving liberal amounts of phosphorus during the next four weeks made a liberal growth and appeared perfectly normal at harvest. The minimum phosphorus requirement for 10 plants producing the optimum amount of seed was about 75 mg. of P_2O_5.

Plants grown in cultures and receiving 80 mg. of K_2O_5 did not mature seed, were limp, and showed a marked spotting of stems and leaves. The amount of potassium recovered from the seed showed little variation regardless of the amount of potassium applied, while the amount recovered from the seed-free plants was markedly influenced by the amount added.

The amount of potassium, nitrogen, or phosphorus absorbed by the plants was greatly influenced by the relation of the other nutrients. Changes in cultural methods, that is, aerating the solutions daily, keeping a piece of fresh charcoal in the solutions, or lowering the temperature of the solutions in summer weather, had no noticeable influence on plant growth. Titrations of certain composite samples of the residual solutions showed slight variations from the neutral point. In the quantity used in these tests, the addition of boron or manganese to the culture medium had no apparent effect upon the growth of the plants.

Results of tests made for potassium and phosphorus in distilled water, in which plants were allowed to remain for one to two weeks after they attained their growth, did not substantiate the belief that either element was freely given off by way of the roots at maturity.

Report on corn and cotton varieties, 1916, C. K. McClelland (*Georgia Sta. Circ. 75 (1917), pp. 8*).—This reports the results of variety tests with corn and cotton for 1916 and is a continuation of work previously noted (E. S. R., 35, p. 830).

Fifteen varieties of corn were tested. Scott Marlboro and Steinheimer Marlboro gave the highest yields of 22 and 21 bu., respectively, while Rockdale gave the lowest yield of 12.6 bu. per acre. Nearly all of the varieties were the prolific two-eared type.

Of 28 cotton varieties tested, Wanamaker Big Boll, with a yield of 1,575 lbs., and Smith Piedmont Big Boll, with a yield of 1,550 lbs. of seed cotton per acre, were the leading varieties. Forty-nine per cent of the bolls of the former and 60 per cent of those of the latter were open by the second picking, October 6. Blackshear Wilt-Resistant Lee, with a yield of 960 lbs., was the lowest yielding variety. The Cleveland types of cotton, which have led in variety tests 8 out of the last 11 years, are considered the best all-around varieties for the middle Piedmont region. These varieties yielded from 1,310 to 1,420 lbs. of seed cotton per acre this past year.

The Cleveland, Sunbeam, Triumph, Cook, and other similar types are recommended for use as weevil-resistant varieties, due to their high yielding qualities and in the event that early maturity can be developed. Covington-Toole, Tri-Cook, Dix-afifi, and Lewis No. 63 are recommended for sandy soils as being early enough for weevil and wilt resistant.

Farm practice in the cultivation of cotton, H. R. CATES (*U. S. Dept. Agr. Bul. 511 (1917), pp. 62, figs. 20*).—Extensive studies of cultural practices with cotton are reported, giving tabulated data secured from a survey of 25 or more farms in each of 19 representative areas of the cotton belt. Complete farm records were secured, showing in detail the tillage practices and farm conditions. The data are summarized and discussed, but no attempt made " to recommend any certain methods for cultivating cotton."

In summarizing these studies the author indicates that the yields of cotton are governed largely by climatic conditions, the inherent fertility of the soil, the quantity of commercial fertilizers used, and the character of the tillage given. Cotton yields are directly related to the amount of tillage given after planting. Furthermore, the kind of tillage given and the implements used are determined largely by economic conditions, topography, soil type, and custom. The amount of tillage depends chiefly upon the kind and number of weeds, economic conditions, and the prevailing weather.

A study of cotton market conditions in North Carolina with a view to their improvement, O. J. McCONNELL and W. R. CAMP (*U. S. Dept. Agr. Bul. 476 (1917), pp. 18, fig. 1*).—Investigations are described made for the purpose of ascertaining the value to the cotton producer of a knowledge of the class of his cotton before sale and to determine whether this information could be furnished to producers by disinterested parties with practical results. A detailed study of local conditions affecting cotton marketing was made in the eastern part of North Carolina during the season of 1914–15 and embracing all cotton-producing sections of the State during 1915–16.

Data are presented showing the character of the cotton produced, the relative merits of certain primary markets in North Carolina, and a comparison of prices received for classed cotton with those received for unclassed cotton.

The cotton samples graded and stapled during the period of this study showed an average grade of slightly above Middling. The use of more modern gins, especially in the Coastal Plain section, would raise the average grade in the State.

Marketing conditions on the whole were better in the Piedmont than in the Coastal Plain section, the grading and stapling of individual bales being given more consideration.

Account sales were at a higher rate than cash sales on coinciding dates and the range in prices for credit sales greater than for cash sales. As a rule, however, the gain is compensated by the higher price charged for the goods represented by the account.

It is estimated that the average producer who knew the class of his cotton profited about $1.15 per bale, and it is suggested that counties producing 5,000 or more bales would profit by employing a county classer as provided for by the State grading-law.

The relative value of different grades and lengths of staple was more nearly approximated in the sale of classed cotton than in the sale of unclassed cotton. This should stimulate the producer to exercise more careful selection of varieties and more care in handling the product. Producers selling in lots of 10 or more bales received 88 cts. to $1.45 per bale more than those selling one or two bales, indicating the economic value of pooling or selling organizations.

Handling and marketing Durango cotton in the Imperial Valley, J. G. MARTIN and G. C. WHITE (*U. S. Dept. Agr. Bul. 458 (1917), pp. 22, figs. 6*).— This reports studies of the marking, tagging, and sampling of the bales, concentrating the cotton into small lots of a few bales each, and into minimum carload lots for compression, undertaken by the Office of Markets and Rural Organization in cooperation with the Imperial Valley Long-Staple Cotton Growers' Association to assist the growers of Durango long-staple cotton in the Imperial Valley in the handling, classing, and marketing of their product. The studies also afforded an opportunity for studying the field conditions under which Durango cotton is produced and to inspect the methods of picking, handling, and storing of the seed cotton on the farm, the methods of hauling cotton to the gins, its subsequent ginning and baling, and its handling and storage in the yards. Inquiries were also made to determine the advisability of marketing Durango cotton directly to the spinning mills at prices equal to those obtained by growers of staple cotton in the Mississippi Delta and elsewhere.

A brief discussion is given of the transportation facilities and rates for all classes of cotton grown in the Imperial Valley.

Foxtail millet.—Its culture and utilization in the United States, H. N. VINALL (*U. S. Dept. Agr., Farmers' Bul. 793 (1917), pp. 28, figs. 10*).—This is a general discussion of the kinds, production, and utilization of millets grown in the United States.

A comparison of varieties, based on data compiled from experiment station tests in various sections of the country, indicates that the German and Hungarian millets are best adapted to humid regions, with the Kursk and Common for the dry northwestern plains. Analyses reported show that the feeding value of the hay of foxtail millet is approximately the same as that of timothy, although injury has resulted from a continuous ration of millet hay for horses.

These millets are utilized chiefly as a catch crop in the United States, and are especially valuable in the semiarid regions because of their short growing season. They are reported as being remarkably free from plant diseases.

Potato growing in Colorado, E. P. SANDSTEN (*Colorado Sta. Bul. 220 (1917), pp. 3–29, pl. 1, figs. 7*).—This is a general discussion of the cultural methods and field practices employed in potato production in Colorado, including data on potato diseases.

[Field experiments with potatoes at the Jerome substation], G. W. DEWEY (*Idaho Sta. Bul. 92 (1916), pp. 55–57*).—Irrigation and cultural experiments with potatoes are reported. The latter included the testing of greened *v.* ungreened seed, foreign *v.* homegrown seed, mature *v.* immature seed, and cut *v.* whole seed.

Greened Idaho Rural seed produced 41.1 bu., or 17.9 per cent, per acre more than the ungreened. Greened Netted Gem produced 19 bu., or 10.8 per cent, more than the ungreened. Seed exchanged with the Greeley (Colo.) substation outyielded the home-grown seed at Jerome by 25.6 bu. (Idaho Rural variety) and 18 bu. at Greeley (Netted Gem variety). Plants from immature seed developed 4.8 per cent of curly dwarf, while those from mature seed developed 37.6 per cent. Idaho Rural grown from immature seed yielded 59.7 bu., or 16.7 per cent, more per acre than that grown from mature seed, while with the Peoples variety the immature seed yielded 88.7 bu., or 29.5 per cent, more than the mature seed.

One hundred potato varieties were introduced from South America and grown during the 1916 season, but only two are to be tested further.

The management of tobacco soils, J. JOHNSON (*Wisconsin Sta. Bul. 277 (1917), pp. 2–29, figs. 12*).—This is a general discussion of the preparation and cultivation of tobacco soils, with special reference to the maintenance of soil fertility. The decreased yield and quality of tobacco grown on "sick" soils, due to the presence of the root rot disease (*Thielavia basicola*), is emphasized and control measures recommended.

A study of Colorado wheat, III, W. P. HEADDEN (*Colorado Sta. Bul. 219 (1916), pp. 3–131*).—In continuation of previous work (E. S. R., 35, p. 832), the author presents data relative to the composition of Colorado wheats in general, and the results of studies of the effects of fertilizers, of water, and of climate upon the composition of wheat. Defiance, Red Fife, and Kubanka wheats grown in the seasons of 1913, 1914, and 1915 under known conditions form the basis for the analytical results obtained.

The results served to show that Colorado wheats contain large percentages of nitrogen and of true gluten. The ratio of gliadin nitrogen to glutenin nitrogen falls well within the limits accepted for good flours. On the other hand, some samples were low in nitrogen but had a fair gliadin-glutenin ratio. Samples grown under dry-farm conditions were not found to be superior to those grown under irrigation.

The factors which determine the wheat crop are given as distribution of rainfall rather than quantity, the degree of cloudiness, resistance of the plant to rust, the stage of development of the plant when attacked, temperature, and soil fertility.

The character of the wheat grain is deemed much more easily influenced by soil fertility than is generally supposed, and the individual plant food elements exercise specific influences upon its composition. The nitric nitrogen in the soil affects the growth of the plant, increasing the nitrogen content of both the plant and the seed. Nitric nitrogen also influences the composition and character of the grain, producing the characteristic "hard" wheat. These characters are believed to have a deeper significance in the plant metabolism than the production of an increase of a few tenths of one per cent in the nitrogen content of the berry. The mineral constituents contained in the berry are influenced by the amount of nitric nitrogen available to the plant, as are those in the plant itself, but in the latter instance to a different extent and not necessarily in the same direction as in the berry. Furthermore, nitric nitrogen produces a soft, weak straw, causing lodging both from a production of a heavy growth of leaves and elongation of the upper parts of the plant and from a weakness in the lower nodes. It also greatly increases susceptibility to rust, probably by furnishing a better nutrient and because of the softened condition of the plant. Organic nitrogen in farmyard manure does not produce these results, except as it is converted into nitric nitrogen, the rate of which process depends upon the nitrifying power of the individual soils.

The investigations with potassium indicate that that element has no positive effect on the quantity of starch produced. Potassium has a tendency, however, to suppress the nitrogen content of the berry, and it suppresses that of the plant, particularly in the stems and leaves, throughout its growing period, but does not appear to suppress that of the head. Potassium stimulated growth at a certain stage of development, but the plants on the other plats attained the same degree of development a few days later. It apparently increases yellow berry.

Phosphorus has produced no definite effect. The phosphorus in the berry was depressed by nitric nitrogen but was not affected by potassium.

Manganese was uniformly present.

The amount of irrigation water applied may increase yields but has practically no effect upon the composition of the crop. The leaching effect of irrigation water on the nitrates is not sufficient to affect the nitrogen content of the plant if applied two months after the use of the nitrates. Frequent light rains, together with heavy dews, produce different effects from irrigation. The time of rainfall and weather conditions following are of great but indirect importance, depending upon the development of rust.

Just before maturity, the plant transfers its substance to the berries and the effect of rust is to inhibit this transfer. Rust causes a marked depression in the protein content of the wheat, even if the crop is well developed at the time of attack. Rust also increases the percentage of crude fiber in the wheat by preventing the filling out of the berries.

There exists an optimum ratio between nitric nitrogen and available potassium in the soil. If potassium predominates, yellow berry is produced, while, if nitric nitrogen predominates, soft, weak plants and small, flinty, and often shrunken berries result.

In regard to crushing strength, Colorado wheats range from semihard to hard. The general composition of these wheats is above the average but undergoes considerable variation due to soil and other immediate causes, but not as a rule to climatic conditions.

Nitrogen fixation proceeds rapidly enough, in the soils studied, to furnish an amount of nitrogen sufficient to become an important factor in these problems. Furthermore, nitrification proceeds rapidly enough to more than quintuple in five months the nitrate nitrogen in the soil at harvest time.

The analytical methods employed by the author are abstracted on page 11.

Dry-farmed and irrigated wheat, J. S. JONES, C. W. COLVER, AMY KELLY, and ELIZABETH HAYS (*Idaho Sta. Bul. 88* (*1916*), *pp. 18*).—This reports analytical and baking tests with samples of dry-farmed and irrigated wheat grown in southern Idaho during 1912, 1913, and 1914, for a comparison of the quality of wheat so produced and as supplementary to work previously noted (E. S. R., 27, p. 266).

From an analysis of the mill products of 79 samples of dry-farmed wheat and 60 samples of irrigated wheat, two things are outstanding in the Bluestem and Turkey Red varieties, the two varieties which seem to be most commonly grown on both dry and irrigated farms. These are (1) the lower yield of flour from the soft wheat, and (2) the lack of any decided difference between dry-farmed and irrigated Bluestem and dry-farmed and irrigated Turkey Red in the percentage of flour obtained. The average gain in milling for all dry-farmed samples was 1.17 per cent and for all irrigated samples 1.12 per cent.

Additional data are presented showing the weights per bushel and per thousand kernels for all wheat samples, together with the percentages of moisture, ash, ether extract, and protein for all wheat and flour samples and the percentages of gluten (wet and dry) and of gliadin for all flour samples. In a comparison of Bluestem and Turkey Red samples the irrigated samples are slightly heavier in weight per bushel, while in weight per thousand kernels the difference is more pronounced, especially in Turkey Red. The moisture, ash, and ether extract of both wheat and flour show no differences that would serve to identify them with the system of farming under which they were produced. There was an average difference between the flours of dry-farmed and irrigated Bluestem of only 0.38 per cent of protein, 2.35 per cent of wet gluten, and 1.06 per cent of dry gluten, while those of the average dry-farmed and irrigated Turkey Red wheats show a difference of 2.79 per cent protein, 9 per cent wet gluten, and 2.24 per cent dry gluten, all differences being in favor of the dry-farmed samples. The ratio of wet to dry gluten in both dry-farmed and irrigated Bluestem is 2.9, in dry-farmed Turkey Red 3.2, and in irrigated Turkey Red 3. Since the relative strength of flours is believed to be indicated by the relative amounts of water their glutens absorb, flour from dry-farmed Turkey Red would by this test be slightly superior to that from irrigated Turkey Red.

The dry-farmed samples were higher in weight per bushel by 0.4 lb., in protein of grain by 1.8 per cent and of flour by 1.47 per cent, in wet gluten by 2.86 per cent, and in dry gluten by 1.68 per cent, and lower in weight per thousand kernels by 1.68 gm. The ratio of wet to dry gluten was 2.8 and 2.9, respectively.

The results of the baking tests are reported in tabular form, showing the amount of water absorbed per 340 gm. of flour, the weight and volume of baked loaf, and the score obtained on the various points considered. Dry-farmed Bluestem produced higher-scoring loaves than irrigated Bluestem, while irrigated Turkey Red produced higher-scoring loaves than dry-farmed Turkey Red. The product of varieties grown under irrigation only scored 3.4 points higher than that from varieties grown under dry-farm conditions only. The average score of all loaves (71) representing all dry-farmed samples was 0.7 point lower than that of all loaves (51) representing all irrigated samples.

It is concluded that, from the standpoint of home baking, insistence for brands of flour milled from the better varieties would do more to raise the flour standards of the State than discrimination in favor of either dry-farmed or irrigated products. Moreover, these results indicate that large differences in gluten percentages are not sharply reflected in results secured from different flours under home-baking conditions. These conclusions are in accord with those arrived at previously.

Commercial agricultural seeds, 1916, C. D. Woods (*Maine Sta. Off. Insp. 81 (1917), pp. 28*).—Tables are given showing the results of the 1916 seed inspection, together with a list of the weed seeds found.

HORTICULTURE.

[Report of the] department of horticulture, H. P. STUCKEY (*Georgia Sta. Rpt. 1916, pp. 16–18*).—A brief progress report on horticultural work for the year, including some records of peach trees planted in the spring of 1914 and receiving different fertilizer treatments during 1915 and 1916.

[Some results of horticultural work] (*Iowa Sta. Rpt. 1916, pp. 32–34*).—A popular summary of results secured from horticultural work conducted under the direction of the Iowa Station, including results of grape pruning and apple spraying tests.

[Report on horticultural investigations] (*New Mexico Sta. Rpt. 1916, pp. 27–31*).—A brief progress report on the station's various horticultural projects.

A table is given showing the results of pear pollination work for the year. Experimental grafts of apple scions on pear stocks have apparently made strong unions. In case of the Delicious apple the fruit grown on pear stocks holds on the branches much better than that grown on apple stocks.

One noticeable feature of the fertilizer experiment with peach trees, which was completed during the year, was the material decline of trees heavily fertilized with barnyard manure. Previously the growth of these trees had been vigorous although the fruit was inferior in quality and color. The fruit during the past year was too small to pick and the manured trees were attacked by chlorosis more severely than the unfertilized trees.

[Report of the] division of horticulture (*Washington Sta. Bul. 136 (1917), pp. 42–44*).—Tests were made in some 50 orchards, part of which were given clean tillage and part planted to alfalfa or red clover for three years or more to ascertain whether the alkali content of the soil is appreciably modified by growing these crops. Analyses secured indicate that the alkali content of the soil to a depth of 2 ft. was reduced only 0.002 per cent and that the humus and volatile content of the soil was increased only 0.03 per cent in the cover crop orchards. Observations relative to the relation of winter injury to rosette indicate that winter injury of the trunk and larger limbs does not as a rule occur in rosetted orchards but is most frequent in those free from that trouble.

Work upon the relation of soil moisture to the keeping quality of Jonathan and Rome Beauty apples showed very little difference in the date of ripening upon plats which received 12, 9, and 6.6 per cent of water, respectively. The large-sized fruits of any variety ripened first regardless of the moisture conditions.

A study of orchard cover crops has shown that peas and vetch produce a slightly better physical condition of the soil than such crops as oats, wheat, and rye. In some experiments in the renovation of prune orchards in Clarke County it has been found that great improvement in the production and quality of prunes was secured by the use of lime and nitrogen fertilizers.

In connection with a variety test of potatoes it was found that the character of the seed storage has much to do with the stand of plants produced.

Hotbeds and cold frames, T. F. LIMBOCKER (*Colorado Sta. Bul. 221 (1917), pp. 8, figs. 4*).—Popular directions are given for the construction and management of hotbeds and cold frames.

[Experiments with tomatoes and cucumbers] (*Expt. and Research Sta., Waltham Cross, Ann. Rpt., 2 (1916), pp. 7–28*).—The results are given for one season of fertilizer, management, and cultural experiments with tomatoes and cucumbers in the greenhouses at the Experimental and Research Station of the Nursery and Market Garden Industries' Development Society, Limited, Waltham Cross, Herts, England.

Fruit growing for amateurs, H. H. THOMAS and J. GARDNER (*London and New York: Cassell & Co., Ltd., 1916, pp. VII+152, figs. 129*).—A popular treatise on the culture, management, and home conservation of orchard and small fruits.

Fruit varieties for Maine, B. S. BROWN (*Univ. Maine Ext. Bul. 111 (1917), pp. 19*).—This comprises a varietal list of orchard and small fruits recommended for planting in Maine.

A valuable unpublished work on pomology, P. L. RICKER (*Science, n. scr., 44 (1916), No. 1124, pp. 62–64*).—The author here announces the donation by the grandchildren of Elizabeth (Coxe) McMurtrie to the library of the U. S. Department of Agriculture of a bound collection of colored drawings of the fruits that were illustrated by woodcuts in A View of the Cultivation of Fruit Trees of America, published in 1817 by William Coxe. The drawings are accompanied by the bound manuscript upon which the published work was based, to which have been added numerous notes intended for a second edition.

The pruning manual, L. H. BAILEY (*New York: The Macmillan Co., 1916, 18. ed., rev., pp. XIII+407, figs. 381*).—The present edition of this work (E. S. R., 11, p. 152) has been revised to include the results of recent investigations on the subject of pruning. The author points out, however, that very few of the pruning experiments in different places are really comparable with each other, and do not warrant the relinquishment of much of the traditional practice which is often the result of accumulated experience.

Pruning problems in the Hood River Valley, G. G. BROWN (*Oregon Sta. Bul. 141 (1917), pp. 48–54, figs. 2*).—A discussion of pruning practices with special reference to the Hood River Valley and based upon pruning investigations conducted at the Oregon Station. ·

Influence of commercial fertilizer upon the bearing apple tree, C. I. LEWIS and G. G. BROWN (*Oregon Sta. Bul. 141 (1917), pp. 37–47, figs. 2*).—In the previous report (E. S. R., 35, p. 540), it was pointed out as a result of two seasons' experiments that nitrate of soda had a decidedly beneficial effect upon the vigor and production of devitalized apple trees. In the present paper the results of previous experiments are summarized and additional data are given on these experiments, together with the results secured from two more orchards treated with the nitrate in 1916. No fertilizer was applied in 1916 to the orchards receiving nitrate in 1914 and 1915. In one of the orchards a crop of clover was turned under and in the other alfalfa and clover were allowed to grow.

The observations for the season indicate that the invigorating influence of nitrate of soda has continued into 1916 and gives good promise for the following season. Beneficial results from nitrates were also secured on the orchards treated for the first time in 1916. The results of the experiments as a whole indicate that nitrate of soda is valuable as a means of rapidly renewing the vigor and production of devitalized apple trees. It is pointed out, however, that the beneficial effects of shade or cover crops in restoring nitrogen and humus should be understood. In case of unsatisfactory growth nitrate of soda in small quantities might be found useful in rotation with shade crops.

Experimental dusting and spraying of peaches, W. W. CHASE (*Ga. Bd. Ent. Circ. 21 (1917), pp. 14, pls. 4*).—This circular summarizes the results of three seasons' experiments in dusting peaches with lead arsenate and sulphur preparations, conducted by the Georgia State Board of Entomology.

The use of dust mixtures has resulted in almost perfect control of peach scab, brown rot, and curculio; good coloring of fruit; thorough and uniform distribution of material; saving of time, labor, teams, and initial cost of equipment as compared with liquid spraying; independence of water; and little deterioration of dusting mechanism and none of material. The dusting method has a tendency to burn leaves, defoliate the trees, and crack or check the flesh of the fruit when applied too heavily. This is more marked when the application is closely followed by rain. It is suggested that the use of improved machinery, better methods of application, accurate regulation of output, and modification of formulas may reduce this type of injury to negligible quantities.

What the experiment station peach orchard has cost and what it has produced, C. A. McCUE (*Del. Farmer, 4 (1916), No. 2, pp. 25–28, fig. 1*).—A popular summary of the subject matter in Bulletin 113 of the Delaware Station (E. S. R., 36, p. 42).

Experimental investigations of the plum (Prunus domestica).—I, Agri-cultural chemical statistics and the composition of the fruit, D. FEBUGLIO (*R. Lab. Chim. Agr. Udine, Ric. Sper. e Attiv. Spiegata, 4 (1911–1914), pp. 99–110, pls. 2*).—This is the first of a series of notes dealing with the plum and its culture. It gives a brief review relative to the importance of the plum industry in Europe, particularly in Italy, together with analytic data showing the physical and chemical composition of the fruit, as well as the chemical composition of the seed, foliage, annual shoots, and the estimated amount of various plant foods annually removed by plum trees.

Strawberry growing, S. W. FLETCHER (*New York: The Macmillan Co., 1917, pp. XXII+325, pls. 24, figs. 23*).—The aim of the present work is to reflect modern commercial practice in North America. The successive chapters discuss locations, sites, and soils; planting; rotations, manuring, and fertilizing; tillage and irrigation; training the plant; mulching; pollination; packages; picking and packing; marketing; cost of production, yields, and profits; propagation and renewal; everbearing varieties, forcing and other special methods of culture; insects, diseases, and frost; varieties; and statistics on acreage, production, and value.

The forcing of strawberries, FLORENCE I. KINNISON (*Colorado Sta. Bul. 222* (*1917*), *pp. 8, figs. 2*).—The forcing experiment with strawberries, here described, was conducted with the view of studying the cultural methods and the best varieties for forcing.

Marshall and Glen Mary proved to be the best two varieties for forcing, the former being used as a pollenizer for the latter. New crowns produced a heavier yield and larger and better berries than old ones. It is concluded that forcing strawberries can be made profitable with the berries selling at 25 cts. a half a pint.

Marketing and distribution of strawberries in 1915, O. W. SCHLEUSSNER and J. C. GILBERT (*U. S. Dept. Agr. Bul. 477* (*1917*), *pp. 32, pls. 4, figs. 10*).—A review of the 1915 strawberry season in the United States, based upon observations made by the authors at shipping points and by members of the staff working in the markets. The subject matter is presented under the general headings of methods employed in dealing with strawberry pickers; cooperative associations; sales methods commonly employed; transportation; a study of the Louisiana district; extent, length, and volume of movement from all districts; comparison of prices received for strawberries on important markets; average quality of strawberries shipped; distribution of strawberries in 1915; and total strawberry shipments in 1915. In addition to tabular data given, the distribution and total strawberry shipments from various sections is illustrated by charts.

Behavior of the root system of various graft stocks, L. RAVAZ (*Prog. Agr. et Vit. (Ed. l'Est-Centre), 38* (*1917*), *No. 10, p. 227*).—The author gives some tabular data showing the average number and size of roots of various American grape stocks used in vineyard reconstitution. In certain stocks it is observed that the number of roots is always few but they are generally large and long, whereas in other stocks the roots are very numerous, small, and short.

Oil percentage in different varieties of olives, H. E. LAFFER (*Jour. Dept. Agr. So. Aust., 20* (*1917*), *No. 7, pp. 548, 549*).—Analyses for one season are given showing the oil percentage in 13 different varieties of olives growing at the Roseworthy Agricultural College. The oil content of the fresh olives ranged from 11.51 to 27.29 per cent.

Citrus fertilization experiments in Porto Rico, C. F. KINMAN (*Porto Rico Sta. Bul. 18* (*1917*), *Spanish Ed., pp. 34, pls. 2, figs. 2*).—The English edition of this bulletin has been previously noted (E. S. R., 33, p. 241).

Some profitable and unprofitable coffee lands, T. B. McCLELLAND (*Porto Rico Sta. Bul. 21* (*1917*), *pp. 13, pls. 2, figs. 5*).—This bulletin, which is based upon studies of Porto Rican coffee soils extending over a number of years, gives specific instances in which coffee is being grown on lands suited for coffee culture and on lands unsuited for coffee culture, together with information relative to the selection of good coffee lands and the improvement of poor lands when they are to be used for growing coffee. It is pointed out, however, that many of these poorer soils should be devoted to pasture or forests or some other crop for which the land may be better adapted.

What tea planters can and must do for selection, C. P. C. STUART (*Dept. Landb., Nijv. en Handel [Dutch East Indies], Meded. Proefstat. Thee, No. 48* (*1916*), *pp. 22*).—The author reviews the work of the Buitenzorg tea station in the development of improved strains of tea, and outlines practical selection investigations which must be conducted by the planters in order to render the selection work of practical value.

Investigations on the process of tea fermentation as conducted in the Malabar Laboratory, K. A. R. Bosscha and A. Brzesowsky (*Dept. Landb., Nijv. en Handel [Dutch East Indies], Meded. Proefstat. Thee, No. 47 (1916), pp. 40, pl. 1, figs. 10*).—An account is given of investigations relative to the various microorganisms occurring on tea leaves and the fermentation of tea with and without the presence of these microorganisms. A bibliography of cited literature is given.

The authors conclude in substance that although the process of tea fermentation progresses hand in hand with the development of micro-organisms on the tea leaves it is independent of the presence of these micro-organisms. Fermentation does not progress successfully above a certain critical temperature. The present experiments indicate this temperature to be from 43 to 43.5° C. (109.4 to 110.3° F.). Likewise, fermentation will not take place in an atmosphere deprived of oxygen. The experiments do not show, however, whether fermentation is brought about by the action of the ferment present in the tea or by oxidation of the constituents of the tea through the oxygen of the atmosphere.

Report on varieties of pecans for 1914, 1915, and 1916 at the Georgia Experiment Station, H. P. Stuckey (*Georgia Sta. Circ. 76 (1917), pp. 5*).—In continuation of previous records on the varieties of pecans grown at the station orchard (E. S. R., 34, p. 151), this circular records the behavior of the trees during the years 1914, 1915, and 1916.

Breeding for atropin, L. W. Arny (*Jour. Heredity, 8 (1917), No. 4, pp. 164–167, fig. 1*).—Preliminary observations on F_1 belladonna seedlings suggest that size of plant at the harvest period in connection with color of stem may be an index to the relative atropin content of the plant. In the present work high-yielding plants were small, with light stems, and low-yielding plants were large and vigorous, with dark stems. Observations are to be continued on selected F_2 plants.

Planting the home grounds, J. H. McFarland (*Harrisburg, Penn.: The Countryside Press, 1915, pp. 70, figs. 29*).—A popular treatise on planning and planting the home grounds, including lists of plants recommended for various purposes.

Decorative shrubs and trees, E. L. Wolf (*Dekoratirnye Kustarniki i Derev'ia dlia Sadov i Parkov. Petrograd: A. F. Derrien, 1915, pp. XI+462, pl. 1, figs. 203*).—A treatise on the selection, planting, and care of ornamental trees and shrubs, including lists of varieties recommended for different purposes.

How to grow chrysanthemums, J. Clayton (*London: The Cable Printing and Publishing Co., Ltd. [1917], pp. 4+97, pls. 4*).—A practical guide for beginners, giving details for growing chrysanthemums in the greenhouse and in the open.

FORESTRY.

The correlation of American forest research, E. H. Clapp (*Jour. Forestry, 15 (1917), No. 2, pp. 165–175*).—In this paper the author gives a general summary of research investigations of the Forest Service of the U. S. Department of Agriculture and calls attention to research work being conducted by certain States and private foresters and to the importance of securing correlation of the forest research work carried on by all agencies in the United States.

Sixteenth annual report of the State Board of Forestry, 1916, E. A. Gladden (*Ann. Rpt. Ind. Bd. Forestry, 16 (1916), pp. 217+V, figs. 107*).—In addition to a report on activities on the State forest reservation, descriptive lists are given of native trees found on the State forest reserve and native trees of

Indiana planted in the park at the reserve, together with a general list of trees and shrubs in the park. Some miscellaneous papers dealing with woodlot problems and forest planting are also included.

Report of the department of forestry of the State of Pennsylvania for the years 1914–15, R. S. CONKLIN (*Rpt. Penn. Dept. Forestry, 1914–15, pp. 247, pls. 17*).—A report of the department of forestry for the years 1914 and 1915, reviewing forest protection work, development work and operations on the State forests and nurseries, lumbering operations, timber sales, surveys, etc.

Report of the committee on forests, C. LEAVITT (*Com. Conserv. Canada Rpt., 7 (1916), pp. 41–52, pls. 2*).—A short résumé of recent activities in forestry and fire protection in Canada.

Progress report on forest administration in the Northwest Frontier Province for the year 1915–16, R. PARNELL (*Rpt. Forest Admin. North-West Frontier Prov., 1915–16, pp. 3+II+18+XXV*).—The usual progress report on the administration of the State forests in the Northwest Frontier Province, including a financial statement for the year 1915–16. All important data relative to alterations in forest areas, forest surveys, working plans, forest protection, miscellaneous work, revenues, expenditures, etc., are appended in tabular form.

Progress report of forest administration in Baluchistan for 1915–16, MULRAJ (*Rpt. Forest Admin. Baluchistan, 1915–16, pp. II+28*).—A report similar to the above relative to the administration of the State forests in Baluchistan for the year 1915–16.

Ecology and silviculture in the southern Appalachians: Old cuttings as a guide to future practice, E. H. FROTHINGHAM (*Jour. Forestry, 15 (1917), No. 3, pp. 343–349*).—A paper on this subject presented at the New York meeting of the Ecological Society, December 28, 1916.

Reforesting Pennsylvania's waste land.—What and how to plant, W. G. CONKLIN (*Penn. Dept. Forestry Bul. 15 (1916), pp. 34, pls. 19*).—This bulletin contains practical suggestions for reforesting waste lands in Pennsylvania, based upon operations on the State forests.

Silvicultural problems on forest reserves, B. E. FERNOW (*Com. Conserv. Canada Rpt., 7 (1916), pp. 66–74*).—This paper reviews a number of the difficulties that are encountered in practicing the art of producing forest trees, with special reference to conditions in Canada.

Some problems in light as a factor of forest growth, R. ZON (*Jour. Forestry, 15 (1917), No. 2, pp. 225–232*).—In this paper the author calls attention to important phases in the study of light that deserve particular consideration by the forester, and outlines tests for determining the effect of soil fertility upon shade endurance of forest trees and the effect of heat upon the tolerance of forest trees.

The rôle of light in natural and artificial reforestation, C. G. BATES (*Jour. Forestry, 15 (1917), No. 2, pp. 233–239*).—The author briefly reviews the literature of the subject, and reaches the conclusion that "if we are to obtain a solution of the problems which are conceived in the terms 'tolerance' and 'intolerance,' and if we would give quantitative expression to the requirements of the various species of light we must consider this factor in its full meaning of radiant energy; we must consider the physical value of radiant energy rather than its chemical value; and finally we must determine its effective physical value in combination with the heat of the air rather than its theoretical physical value."

Seeding habits of spruce as a factor in the competition of spruce with its associates, L. S. MURPHY (*Plant World, 20 (1917), No. 3, pp. 87±90*).—A short contribution on this subject, based on observations made in the fall of 1910 and the spring of 1911 and offered with the view of calling attention to a promising field of research.

A practical method of preventing the damping-off of coniferous seedlings, C. A. Scott (*Jour. Forestry, 15 (1917), No. 2, pp. 192–196, pls. 2*).—The author here describes a practical method of sterilizing forest nursery seed beds with high pressure steam to reduce the loss of evergreen seedlings by damping-off. This method was recently developed with successful results at the Kansas Experiment Station.

The windbreak as a farm asset, C. G. Bates (*U. S. Dept. Agr., Farmers' Bul. 788 (1917), pp. 15, figs. 8*).—This publication discusses windbreaks with special reference to their use in protecting the fields and farm buildings from the force of the wind, including planting instructions and kinds of trees recommended for planting in different sections. Estimates are also given of financial returns per acre to be expected from various kinds of windbreaks.

To determine the total effect, whether beneficial or injurious, of windbreaks on crop yields a number of crop measurements were made in Nebraska, Kansas, Iowa, and Minnesota. The measurements as a whole indicate that with ordinary field crops the farmer may count on a benefit from windbreak protection which will make the loss of the area occupied by the trees negligible.

Timber estimating in the southern Appalachians, R. C. Hall (*Jour. Forestry, 15 (1917), No. 3, pp. 310–321*).—In this paper the author discusses methods employed in estimating timber and approving forest lands for purchase under the so-called Weeks Law, together with new adaptations which have proved especially valuable.

Some problems in Appalachian timber appraisal, W. W. Ashe (*Jour. Forestry, 15 (1917), No. 3, pp. 322–334*).—A paper somewhat similar to the above discussing problems in timber appraisal work peculiar to the Appalachian forests.

The rôle of the microscope in the identification and classification of the " timbers of commerce," I. W. Bailey (*Jour. Forestry, 15 (1917), No. 2, pp. 176–191, pls. 3, figs. 2*).—In this paper the author concludes that anatomical keys for distinguishing woods as constructed by botanists and microscopists have failed to receive the recognition and extended use that have commonly been predicted for them. Two important reasons for this failure, as here discussed, are limitations to the use of anatomical keys in the lumber business and variability of anatomical characters. A careful study of some of the supposedly most reliable diagnostic criteria, such as the distribution of wood parenchyma, form and structure of the rays, type of pitting, etc., indicates very clearly that these characters may fluctuate considerably, not only in certain families, genera, and species, but also in different parts of a single tree.

DISEASES OF PLANTS.

[Report of the division of botany.—Bacteriology and pathology] (*Washington Sta. Bul. 136 (1917), pp. 19–25, figs. 3*).—A progress report is given of some of the more important investigations being carried on by the division of botany. Among these are studies of tomato blight, previous notes of which have been given (E. S. R., 36, p. 350); identification of fungus diseases; investigations of fire blight, an account of which has already been noted (E. S. R., 35, p. 848); and wheat smut, also previously noted (E. S. R., 34, p. 644).

In connection with the wheat smut investigations, two sources of infection have been discovered, the first from spores adhering to the wheat grain and infecting at the time of sprouting, the second from the spores which settle upon summer fallow ground during the thrashing season. In the prevention of this disease, for the first method of infection soaking the seed in copper sulphate or formaldehyde solution is recommended, and for the second method of infection either early sowing of wheat before the thrashing season has begun or late sowing after the smut spores scattered over the soil have germinated. In these investigations an automatic sprinkler has been devised and perfected by the station for use in connection with thrashing outfits.

[Plant diseases in 1915] (*Phytopath. Lab.* "*Willie Commelin Scholten*" *Jaarver. 1915, pp. 18*).—The report on plant diseases and investigations deals with injuries to fruit trees due to Hymenomycetes, anthracnose of flax, narcissus diseases, Botrytis on flowers, potato mosaic, and *Rhizoctonia* (*Hypochnus*) *solani* on potato.

Plant protection, F. G. STEBLER (*Landw. Jahrb. Schweiz, 30 (1916), No. 1, pp. 20–23*).—This is a very condensed account dealing with the spring condition of cereals; diseases and protection of cereals, potatoes, beets, and legumes; and various wild plants, or weeds, as noted at the Zurich Experiment Station.

Studies in tropical teratology, J. C. COSTERUS and J. J. SMITH (*Ann. Jard. Bot. Buitenzorg, 2. ser., 14 (1916), pt. 2, pp. 83–94, pls. 5*).—The authors have here described a number of monstrosities, including witches' broom, as observed in plants representing a wide range of classification, the specimens examined having been from Buitenzorg.

Studies in the physiology of parasitism.—II, Infection by Botrytis cinerea, V. H. BLACKMAN and E. J. WELSFORD (*Ann. Bot. [London], 30 (1916), No. 119, pp. 389–398, pl. 1, figs. 2*).—This is in continuation of the series of contributions begun by Brown (E. S. R., 34, p. 847).

Vicia faba was studied regarding its capacity for infection by *B. cinerea.* Infection was readily accomplished when the leaf surface was moistened with turnip juice. The germ tube soon develops a mucilaginous layer by which it appears to be so firmly anchored to the cuticle that its tip can bend in and penetrate the cuticle with a peglike outgrowth, apparently by mechanical pressure alone. No swelling or other change in the cuticle or in the underlying epidermal layers prior to penetration has been observed, but as soon as the cuticular layer is passed a swelling of the subcuticular layer occurs, showing enzym action. Penetration of the cuticle by the germ tube was not preceded by death of epidermal cells, but swelling of the latter preceded the disorganization of the protoplast. No microscopic evidence was found for the secretion of a special toxic substance other than the enzym for dissolving the cell wall.

Studies in the physiology of parasitism.—III, On the relation between the "infection drop" and the underlying host tissue, W. BROWN (*Ann. Bot. [London], 30 (1916), No. 119, pp. 399–406*).—It is stated that the results of this purely physiological study, as here detailed, are in exact agreement with the results of the microscopical study, as above noted, by Blackman and Welsford.

On the osmotic pressure of the tissue fluids of Jamaican Loranthaceæ parasitic on various hosts, J. A. HARRIS and J. V. LAWRENCE (*Amer. Jour. Bot., 3 (1916), No. 8, pp. 438–455, figs. 2*).—Data gathered from a study of materials obtained in 1915 near Cinchona, in the Blue Mountains of Jamaica, employing seven species of Loranthaceæ in three genera parasitic on nineteen species of host, are presented. The authors claim that stem sap from the leafless species of Dendrophthora has a lower osmotic pressure than that from leaf tissue of Phoradendron or Phthirusa, also that the osmotic pressure of the sap from the chlorophyll-bearing tissue of the parasite is almost always greater than in that from the mature leaves of the host.

The fungicidal properties of certain spray fluids, J. V. EYRE and E. S. SALMON (*Jour. Agr. Sci. [England], 7 (1916), No. 4, pp. 473–507*).—In the hope of ascertaining to what particular factor the fungicidal value of alkaline sulphid solutions should be attributed, the authors carried out a study during 1914 and 1915 with powdery mildews (Erysiphaceæ), the materials and methods of which are discussed in detail.

Such fungicides as liver of sulphur and ammonium sulphid when used against powdery mildews require some such substance as soft soap to insure adequate wetting of the foliage by the spray. Liver of sulphur was not effective when used at concentrations below 0.6 to 0.8 per cent. Yellow ammonium sulphid proved to be efficacious against hop mildew in the greenhouse and against American gooseberry mildew in the open. Unlike lime sulphur it leaves no disfiguring deposit, and at definite fungicidal strength it does not scorch the foliage. Iron sulphid at 0.6 per cent quickly destroys hop mildew. When so made as to contain a trace of ammonium sulphid, it is in a condition in which it can be reduced to a line spray and is harmless.

Free alkali is not the determining fungicidal factor in alkaline sulphid solutions, nor is the proportion of sulphid sulphur present an index of their fungicidal value. Apparently the polysulphids in yellow ammonium sulphid act fungicidally as such, and not by virtue of the sulphur deposited when they decompose.

The effect of covering winter crops, L. HILTNER (*Prakt. Bl. Pflanzenbau u. Schutz, n. scr., 14 (1916), No. 1, pp. 3–10*).—A report is given of experiments conducted in 1914–15 to determine the effect of mechanical winter covering of cereals on the development of Fusarium diseases. Most of the experiments were carried out with winter rye, although winter wheat and clover were also tested. Seed treated with formaldehyde and untreated seed were employed, the mechanical coverings being straw, manure, various chemical fertilizers, etc. The results for rye are tabulated, marked varietal differences due to the treatment being noted. In practically every instance the harvest was greatest from the treated seed.

The general conclusion drawn from the experiments is that any form of covering, even snow when the ground is unfrozen, is injurious when Fusariums are present, as it produces conditions favorable for the development of the fungus.

Notes on some diseases of collards, B. B. HIGGINS (*Georgia Sta. Rpt. 1916, pp. 21–27, figs. 6*).—Attention is called to black mold of collards due to *Alternaria brassicæ,* which is said to have been very destructive during several years. The fungus attacks the more tender parts of the plant, causing their destruction, and in many instances it is associated with soft rot bacteria which enter through the fungus lesions. As a result of observations, it was suspected that the harlequin bug plays an important part in the spread of the disease and this suspicion was confirmed by investigations carried on in 1916. In connection with the study of the rôle of this insect in spreading the disease, an investigation was made to determine whether the fungus entered through insect punctures, but all the evidence obtained seemed to indicate that the germ tube of the fungus entered through the stomata of the plant. For the control of this disease, one or two applications of Bordeaux mixture are recommended, though no experiments in control have been undertaken. The destruction of harlequin bugs is also considered important.

In addition to the above disease, *Sclerotinia libertiana* also attacks collards, considerable damage being done, especially to young plants.

A new sweet corn disease in Kentucky, H. GARMAN (*Kentucky Sta. Circ. 13, pp. 4, fig. 1*).—A description is given of a destructive bacterial disease attacking sweet corn, first noted at the Kentucky Station in June, 1916. The disease is considered the same as that previously described by Stewart (E. S. R., 9, p. 1056). In addition to the usual characteristics of this disease, the author describes a soft rot occurring at the base of the cornstalk, which is thought to be due probably to the admission of other bacteria. Since the disease is known to be conveyed with the seed corn, the importance of obtaining seed from non-infested regions is pointed out.

Dissemination of the angular leaf spot of cotton, R. C. FAULWETTER (*U. S. Dept. Agr., Jour. Agr. Research, 8 (1917), No. 12, pp. 457–475, pl. 1, fig. 1*).— The author presents data obtained during the summer of 1916 at the South Carolina Experiment Station on the dissemination of the angular leaf spot of cotton. He also suggests that the factors recognized as concerned in the dissemination of this disease may also have an important bearing on the spread of other diseases.

Studies were made of insect carriers, seed-borne infection, winds, etc., in relation to this disease, and the author concludes that much of its spread, under the conditions of his experiments, was due to the carrying of bacteria from infected plants by wind-blown rain. This conclusion is largely drawn from observations on the dissemination of the disease from inoculated plants following two severe storms in July, in which high winds were accompanied by heavy rains. The spread of the disease from the artificially inoculated plants was determined to be in the direction of the prevailing winds during these storm periods. Insects are considered as playing a very unimportant rôle, while seed dissemination aside from its primary infection is not believed to be important.

Peanut wilt caused by Sclerotium rolfsii, J. A. McCLINTOCK (*U. S. Dept. Agr., Jour. Agr. Research, 8 (1917),· No. 12, pp. 441–448, pls. 2*).—An account is given of observations and investigations conducted at the Virginia Truck Experiment Station to determine the cause and methods of control of the wilt disease of peanuts first observed at the station in the summer of 1915.

The disease appears under field conditions when the plants are from one to two months old and continues to develop throughout the season. The fungus attacks the shoots at or near the surface of the soil, killing the invaded tissues. Wilted plants have been observed scattered over the entire area of each plat, indicating that the causal organism is well distributed. Isolation and inoculation experiments have shown the pathogenicity of the causal organism and established its identity as *S. rolfsii.*

In a test of six varieties of peanuts and one of the so-called hog goober (*Voandzeia subterranea*) marked differences were observed in susceptibility to fungus attack. The variety Valencia appeared most susceptible, while Virginia Runner, African, and *V. subterranea* were found practically immune to *S. rolfsii.* Investigations have shown that the fungus retains its vitality in the soil for at least three years, and as a consequence the planting of resistant varieties is recommended rather than attempting to rid the soil of the pest by rotation.

In connection with the growing of peanuts, crimson clover is said to be commouly used as a winter cover crop. This plant did not suffer attack· by *S. rolfsii* so far as observations during the seasons of 1915 and 1916 showed.

The Verticillium disease of the potato, G. H. PETHYBRIDGE (*Sci. Proc. Roy. Dublin Soc., n. ser., 15 (1916), No. 7, pp. 63–92, pls. 2; abs. in Roy. Bot. Gard. Kew. Bul. Misc. Inform., No. 4 (1916), pp. 110–112*).—Reporting a more prolonged and more detailed study of the Verticillium disease than the one previously noted (E. S. R., 34, p. 443), the author describes the general symptoms as those of a process of gradual desiccation, resulting in the more or less premature death of the plant. The mycelium of *V. albo-atrum* is found in the wood vessels of all parts of affected plants, passing into the corresponding vessels of growing tubers and thence into the young plants arising from such tubers when used for seed. The disease is not strictly localized at or near the heel end of the tuber, as formerly supposed. The fungus grows well as a saprophyte. The disease is reproduced on infecting sound plants with pure cultures. It is considered advisable to remove this disease from the category of those usually designated by such terms as leaf roll and curl, since the Verticillium disease is regarded as a specific type of those in which the mycelium affects the wood vessels and for which the term hadromycosis is suggested.

The disease does not appear to be very common or destructive in the British Isles at present. Preventive measures include rotation and use of seed known to be free from infection.

Potato spraying experiments for the control of early blight (Alternaria solani), R. W. JACK (*Rhodesia Agr. Jour., 10 (1913), No. 6, pp. 852-862, pl. 1*).—A preliminary account is given of the methods and results of spraying tests for control of early blight, the only leaf disease of potatoes prevalent in this territory at the time of the report.

The author states that the disease may be treated profitably with a 4½ : 4½ : 50 Bordeaux mixture, if commenced when the plants are from 4 to 6 in. high (but not when the disease has become apparent on the leaves), three or four sprayings giving good results, but seven weekly sprayings being preferable. Not less than 75 gal. per acre should be employed. Knapsack pumps with copper tanks have been found suitable to local conditions. An arsenical may be added for insects if desired.

Does it pay to spray potatoes in southern Rhodesia? R. W. JACK (*Rhodesia Agr. Jour., 13 (1916), No. 3, pp. 354-360, pls. 2*).—In a progress report of work continued for three years following that above noted, it is stated that *Alternaria solani*, while not usually severe on early crops grown on irrigated ground, causes losses sometimes amounting to 50 per cent on ground depending on rainfall alone if not properly sprayed. The work herein reported, which dealt with the fairly resistant variety Up-to-Date, is said to show that the employment of a 4 : 4 : 40 Bordeaux mixture, begun early and repeated weekly, is profitable to growers in localities where the disease is prevalent.

Weather injury to rice in 1915 in Italy, B. MARCARELLI (*Gior. Risicolt., 5 (1915), No. 13, pp. 212-216, fig. 1; abs. in Internat. Inst. Agr. [Rome], Mo. Bul. Agr. Intel. and Plant Diseases, 6 (1915), No. 9, p. 1253*).—A period of cool, moist weather from May 27 to June 4, 1915, was associated with an unusually severe chlorosis, sometimes death of the foliage, of rice plants and weakness of the stalk, these conditions being only in part relieved by the return of more favorable weather. *Puccinia oryzæ*, though found on the foliage in numerous cases, was regarded as only secondary in its attack, which was supposedly induced by the condition of lowered vitality in the rice plants.

Fusarium blight, or wilt disease, of the soy bean, R. O. CROMWELL (*U. S. Dept. Agr., Jour. Agr. Research, 8 (1917), No. 11, pp. 421-440, pl. 1, fig. 1*).— In a contribution from the North Carolina Experiment Station, the author describes a disease of soy beans due to *F. tracheiphilum* and gives the results of investigations to determine the parasitism of this species of Fusarium and the relationship of the species on the soy bean to that causing a wilt disease of cowpeas.

The disease on the soy bean is characterized by a chlorosis and shedding of the leaves or leaflets, followed by the death of the plants. It has been observed in several localities in North Carolina on soils infected with cowpea wilt. Cultural and morphological studies, as well as reciprocal inoculation experiments, have shown that the two diseases are caused by the same species of Fusarium. Infection is thought to occur through the roots, but the presence of nematodes does not appear to increase the percentage of blight. The character of the soil is considered to influence the amount of infection, the largest proportion of diseased plants occurring on coarse, sandy soils.

Black rot of tobacco, K. PREISSECKER (*Fachl. Mitt. Österr. Tabakregie, 15 (1915), No. 4, pp. 113-116, figs. 4*).—This is a brief discussion of the disease attacking stored tobacco due to *Sterigmatocystis nigra (Aspergillus niger)*. The accounts given by Rapaics (E. S. R., 30, p. 450) and others are referred to.

Suggestions for the control of the more serious plant diseases occurring at Hood River, L. CHILDS (*Oregon Sta. Bul. 141 (1917), pp. 28-32*).—Based upon experiments carried on in this region, directions are given for the spraying of apple, pear, and peach trees for the control of the more important diseases to which they are subject.

Diseases of the apple, pear, and quince, C. R. ORTON (*Proc. State Hort. Assoc. Penn., 57 (1916), pp. 45-52, pls. 4*).—The author has limited the discussion in this paper to diseases of orchard fruits not treated in the communication previously noted (E. S. R., 35, p. 351). The several diseases are dealt with alphabetically in connection with their hosts.

The oak fungus disease of fruit trees, W. T. HORNE (*Proc. Fruit Growers' Conv. Cal., 47 (1915), pp. 208-215*).—This is a report on experiences with, also a discussion of, the oak fungus and wood decay of fruit trees.

It is stated that English walnut budded about a foot above the ground on California black walnut is safe from the oak fungus. Isolation trenches, if kept open and disinfected, are successful in checking the spread of the infection by means of rhizomorphs. The fungus goes down several feet. The effects of carbon bisulphid in the soil are variously reported, depending apparently on soil conditions.

Wood decay of fruit trees appears to be more widely destructive in this region than the oak fungus, as it affects wild growths abundantly. Unlike the oak fungus, it can not enter except through a break made in the bark. The fruiting bodies, after being dry all the summer, may give off infecting spores within 24 hours after being moistened. The fungus works in the wood chiefly or exclusively. Wounds should be painted before being wet, and they should be kept covered with paint or other reliable disinfectants, among which corrosive sublimate is considered to be one of the best. It is thought that apples and walnuts, carefully protected from disease, may live 100 years.

Observations on the relation of the height of fruit to apple scab infection, L. CHILDS (*Oregon Sta. Bul. 141 (1917), pp. 5-17, figs. 6*).—While engaged in some experiments on apple scab, the author observed that the fruits near the top of the trees were usually much more scabby than those produced nearer the ground. In following up this observation, several orchards were examined as to the actual conditions existing at harvest in certain trees that had been carefully sprayed.

It was found that at least one-fourth of the crop in case of most of the trees was produced at a height of 15 ft. or more, and at least one-half of this amount was found to be scabby, while lower and poorer quality fruit possessed a very slight scab infection. On smaller trees sprayed in exactly the same manner as the above, much better results were obtained. Under the conditions prevailing in the Hood River region during the spraying season, the average wind velocity is said to be too great for good spraying at a height of more than 22 or 23 ft. On this account, it is recommended that a tower be used in spraying and that long, out-of-the-way limbs be cut back.

Blister canker control, H. E. VASEY (*Nebr. Hort., 6 (1916), No. 7, pp. 1-3*).— Stating that apple blister canker is to be found in fully 96 or 97 per cent of the orchards in Nebraska, the author discusses practical means of control. These include acquaintance with the disease, skillful scraping and pruning of the cankered limbs, disinfecting and covering of wounds, and careful observation of all trees for at least two years after the completion of the above treatment.

[Notes on some plant diseases] (*New Mexico Sta. Rpt. 1916, pp. 25, 26*).— In continuation of investigations on the chlorosis of pear trees (E. S. R., 32, p. 641), it is stated that trees treated with ferrous sulphate in 1914–15 showed some benefit from plugging the salt in holes bored in the trees. Where young pear trees were sprayed in 1915 with a 1 per cent solution of ferrous sulphate, they continued to show in 1916 the same yellow color exhibited in the previous year.

It is stated that pear blight was more serious in 1915 than in any season previously noted.

Diseases of the brambles and methods of controlling them, C. R. ORTON (*Proc. State Hort. Assoc. Penn., 57 (1916), pp. 66–71, pls. 3*).—This is a discussion of various diseases of blackberry, raspberry, and dewberry, with recommendations regarding measures for their control.

Direct bearer grapevines in relation to disease, G. DALMASSO and S. SUTTO (*Rivista [Conegliano], 5. ser., 21 (1915), No. 15, pp. 337–341; abs. in Internat. Inst. Agr. [Rome], Mo. Bul. Agr. Intel. and Plant Diseases, 6 (1915), No. 9, pp. 1257–1259*).—Examination of direct bearer vines in July, 1915, at the Royal College of Enology at Conegliano showed that in spite of the unfavorable season none of the vines were attacked by Peronospora or by Oidium. Some showed melanose (*Septoria ampelina*), some anthracnose (*Glœosporium ampelophagum*). A number of varieties are reported upon in detail as regards the presence or absence of the several diseases under observation, a gratifying degree of resistance being apparent in most instances.

The pink disease of cacao, J. B. ROREER (*Bul. Dept. Agr. Trinidad and Tobago, 15 (1916), No. 3, pp. 86–89, pl. 1*).—From reports of studies or observations in several parts of the world, the conclusion is reached that the pink disease, whether in the East or in the West, is caused by the same fungus, *Corticium salmonicolor*. The disease as it occurs in very characteristic form on cacao is described. In the East, the fungus has been found on 141 different species of plants.

Careful removal of all affected portions is said to be effective where its occurrence is sporadic. In case of old trees or where many are affected, good results are obtained by treating with tar on the first appearance of the symptoms in each case.

Tea roots, A. C. TUNSTALL (*Indian Tea Assoc. [Pamphlet] 1 (1916), pp. 22, pls. 5, figs. 11*).—This pamphlet discusses first the characters and behavior of healthy tea roots and, second, some root diseases, their transmission, their identification, and general plans for their treatment. The disease fungi mentioned include Diplodia, Rosellinia, *Hymenochæte noxia, Fomes lucidus, Ustulina zonata,* and *Thyridaria tarda.*

Ustulina zonata, a fungus affecting Hevea brasiliensis, A. SHARPLES (*Dept. Agr. Fed. Malay States Bul. 25 (1916), pp. 27, pls. 10*).—It is stated that during the past two years the fungus *U. zonata* has become an important factor in the Federated Malay States. It is the cause of a collar and root disease which develops typically in rubber trees over 10 years of age but has been found in trees aged from 5 to 8 years. The trouble was noted by the author in 1913, but evidence recently obtained suggests that it has been present in this region for several years, perhaps since 1907. The typical dry rot produced by *U. zonata* is said to be unmistakable, the wood in advanced cases crumbling readily on slight pressure. Control measures consist in thoroughly cleaning out the portions of the tree that have been cut away during the process of clearing and thinning and in such sanitation measures as giving early attention to wounds arising from different causes.

Cryptogamic diseases of forest trees, P. GUINIER (*Vie Agr. et Rurale, 6 (1916), No. 45, pp. 334–338, figs. 6*).—Briefly discussing types of fungus tree diseases, circumstances favoring their development, and measures for their control in forest areas, some of which are said to show deterioration as regards both the quantity and the quality of growth produced, the author holds that remedial measures, to be practically preventive, must look to the prevention of disease by the improvement of living conditions for the trees.

ECONOMIC ZOOLOGY—ENTOMOLOGY.

Bird friends.—A complete bird book for Americans, G. H. TRAFTON (*Boston: Houghton Mifflin Co., 1916, pp. XVIII+330, pls. 30, figs. 7*).—A popular work relating to the value of birds, their enemies, attraction and protection, and study in schools.

How to make friends with birds, N. M. LADD (*Garden City, N. Y.: Doubleday, Page & Co., 1916, pp. 10–228, figs. 165*).—A small pocket guide.

The birds of Britain: Their distribution and habits, A. H. EVANS (*London: Cambridge University Press, 1916, pp. XII+275, figs. 94*).—A short handbook which includes the results of the most recent observations of British birds.

The zoological position of the Sarcosporidia, H. CRAWLEY (*Proc. Acad. Nat. Sci. Phila., 68 (1916), pt. 3, pp. 379–388*).

Microtechnical methods for studying certain plant-sucking insects in situ, K. B. BROWN (*Science, n. ser., 44 (1916), No. 1143, pp. 758, 759*).—The author describes methods which he has made use of for determining the relation of certain sucking insects to their host plants.

Studies on gregarines, MINNIE E. WATSON (*Ill. Biol. Monographs, 2 (1916), No. 3, pp. 258, pls. 15*).—This work includes descriptions of 21 new species and a synopsis of the eugregarine records from the Myriapoda, Coleoptera, and Orthoptera of the world.

[Cranberry insects], H. J. FRANKLIN (*Ann. Rpt. Cape Cod Cranberry Growers' Assoc., 28 (1915), pp. 19–31*).—Substantially noted from another source (E. S. R., 36, p. 54).

The rôle of insects as carriers of fire blight, H. A. GOSSARD (*Ohio State Hort. Soc. Ann. Rpt., 49 (1916), pp. 73–83*).—The observations here reported, relating to the honeybee, have been largely noted (E. S. R., 35, p. 662).

Summary of the season's experiments with the newer insecticides, J. S. HOUSER (*Ohio State Hort. Soc. Ann. Rpt., 49 (1916), pp. 49–56*).—A summary of the work at the Ohio Experiment Station from which the author concludes that the home-boiled, dilute lime-sulphur wash, the commercial concentrated lime-sulphur wash (1:7), and the soluble oils (usually 1:15) are standard remedies for the San José scale and will control it if properly applied. The soluble oils, used at the strength of 1:15, controlled the elm bark louse, the elm Aspidiotus, the tulip tree lecanium, the pit-making oak scale, the scurfy scale of the honey locust, the Putnam scale, the oak kermes, and the obscure scale.

Analyses of some more recent and older pest remedies, M. R. MILLER (*Mo. Bul. Com. Hort. Cal., 6 (1917), No. 1, pp. 23–26*).—This paper reports upon analyses made of newer remedies and of those in regard to which there appears to be doubt as to their composition.

Fly poisons.—Studies on sodium salicylate, a new muscicide, and on the use of formaldehyde, E. B. PHELPS and A. F. STEVENSON (*Pub. Health Rpts. [U. S.], 31 (1916), No. 44, pp. 3033–3035*).—The authors find that a 1 per cent solution of sodium salicylate is slightly less efficient than formaldehyde, but that it possesses certain marked advantages, especially for household use. The best results with formaldehyde were obtained from a solution containing 1 per cent of the formaldehyde, or 2.5 per cent of the 40 per cent solution.

Suggestions for the control of the more serious insect pests occurring at Hood River, L. CHILDS (*Oregon Sta. Bul. 141 (1917), pp. 33, 34*).—These notes relate to the leaf-roller, brown aphis, woolly apple aphis, green apple aphis, codling moth, pear leaf blister mite, and San José scale.

[Report of the] division of zoology and entomology (*Washington Sta. Bul. 136 (1917), pp. 35–42, figs. 8*).—Brief reference is made to the occurrence of and work with the coulee cricket (*Peranabrus scabricollis*), noted below.

Work with the strawberry root weevil (*Otiorhynchus ovatus*) has been carried on under a special appropriation made by the commissioners of Benton County, where it has appeared in the Kennewick region and rendered acres of berry fields worthless. In the course of the work, which was based principally on soil fumigation, numerous materials were tested. Carbon disulphid is the only material that has given promise of practical value, and this only when applied under a cover, such as oil cloth, canvas, etc.

Brief reference is made to the continuation of work on progressive immunity of insects, an account of which has been previously noted (E. S. R., 34, p. 551). A discussion of the physiological effects of endoparasitism in aphids is also included.

Annual report on the entomological laboratory for the year ended March 31, 1914, T. J. ANDERSON (*Dept. Agr. Brit. East Africa Ann. Rpt. 1913–14, pp. 52–83*).—This is the report of the work of the year with the more important insects, particularly with the coconut beetle (*Oryctes monoceros*).

List of Egyptian insects in the collection of the Ministry of Agriculture, G. STOREY (*Min. Agr. Egypt, Tech. and Sci. Serv. Bul. 5 (1916), pp. V+50*).—Of the 154 families represented in the list here presented about 100 are said to include species of economic interest.

The fauna of British India, including Ceylon and Burma, edited by A. E. SHIPLEY and G. A. K. MARSHALL (*London: Taylor & Francis, 1916, vol. 6, pp VIII+248, figs. 177*).—This volume of the work previously noted (E. S. R., 25, p. 557), is an appendix to the Homoptera, by W. L. Distant, and describes 348 species of which many are new.

The coulee cricket [Peranabrus scabricollis], A. L. MELANDER and M. A. YOTHERS (*Washington Sta. Bul. 137 (1917), pp. 56, figs. 37*).—The first part of this bulletin (pp. 5–35), by A. L. Melander, consists of a general discussion and photographs; the second part (pp. 36–50), by M. A. Yothers, consists of miscellaneous notes on the biology of the coulee cricket (*P. scabricollis*), a brief account relating to the control of which has been previously noted (E. S. R., 35, p. 756).

This cricket has been a source of injury in Washington State since 1899, when outbreaks were first observed by C. V. Piper. It occurs sporadically in restricted localities in the Big Bend country of central Washington, where immense migratory hordes destroy whatever vegetation grows in their pathway. It breeds in nonarable areas characterized by the presence of scabland sage brush (*Artemisia rigida*), among the fallen leaves of which the newly hatched crickets secure protection in early spring. During the first four of its seven stages the cricket feeds in the breeding grounds and at the fifth instar it begins moving in bands and spreads over miles of country. The eggs are deposited singly during the migration whenever the insects come to a favorable location, usually at the base of grass stems, each female averaging about 50 eggs. This cricket is practically omnivorous. It is marked cannabalistic, attacking and devouring weakened individuals throughout its life cycle.

The parasite *Sparaison pilosum* has been reared from its egg and *Calosoma zimmermanni, Cyrtopogon maculosis*, and species of ants have been observed as predatory on small crickets. The crickets are more easily reached and killed when young before they have spread from the restricted breeding grounds. At this time spraying with a 5 to 10 per cent kerosene emulsion, the use of fresh horse manure containing 2 per cent of an arsenical as a poisoned bait, and burning with straw or with an insecticidal blast torch are practical. Migratory crickets may be checked by vertical walled ditches containing deeper pitfalls dug across their path, since through massing in the pits, they quickly smother out each other's lives. Fencing of 1 by 8 in. boards joined end to end on edge and furnished with frequent pitfalls is sometimes employed in place of ditching.

Results of work against the locust in Uruguay, R. SUNDBERG ET AL. (*Defensa Agr. [Uruguay] Mem., 1915, pp. 154, figs. 19*).—A report upon locust control work in 1914–15.

The pear thrips in British Columbia and its control, A. E. CAMERON and R. C. TREHERNE (*Agr. Gaz. Canada, 3 (1916), No. 11, pp. 946–952, figs. 4*).— This paper reports upon observations of this pest in British Columbia, where it was first discovered in April, 1915, as recorded by Hewitt.[1] It has been found in that Province throughout the district lying between Victoria and Sidney in the Saanich Peninsula, being more or less uniformly distributed within this area. It has also been found at Duncan and is thought to occur at Nanaima. Quite satisfactory results were obtained from spraying.

The tomato and bean bug (Nezara viridula), W. W. FROGGATT (*Agr. Gaz. N. S. Wales, 27 (1916), No. 9, pp. 649, 650, pl. 1*).—This bug, which first appeared on tomato plants in the neighborhood of Sydney some five years ago, has increased in numbers during the last two years and become a pest of the fruits and foliage of the tomato, the foliage and young pods of French beans and potato plants.

The Helopeltis question, especially in connection with cacao, W. ROEPKE (*Meded. Proefstat. Midden-Java, No. 21 (1916), pp. 40+III; abs. in Rev. Appl. Ent., Ser. A, 4 (1916), No. 11, pp. 442–444*).—A discussion of *Helopeltis antonii* and *H. theivora*, including their economic status, biology, natural enemies, and control measures.

The maple aphis and its dimorphic larva, E. J. BUNNETT (*Proc. So. London Ent. and Nat. Hist. Soc., 1915–16, pp. 21–24, pl. 1*).—Reports observations of the biology and anatomy of *Chaitophorus aceris*.

Scale insects and their control, R. T. COTTON (*Porto Rico Bd. Agr. Expt. Sta. Circ. 9 (1917), pp. 7; Spanish Ed., pp. 7*).—A brief popular account.

Mimicry in butterflies, R. C. PUNNETT (*London: Cambridge University Press, 1915, pp. VIII+188, pls. 16, figs. 8*).—A popular work.

The bollworm in Egypt, G. C. DUDGEON (*Trans. 3. Internat. Cong. Trop. Agr. 1914, vol. 1, pp. 399–432, pls. 2*).—This extended account of the biology, economic status, natural enemies, and control measures for the Egyptian bollworm (*Earias insulana*) includes much data relating to its immature stages taken from a contribution by F. C. Willcocks published in 1905.[2] See also another note (E. S. R., 30, p. 252). A colored plate of the several forms of the adult after Storey (E. S. R., 32, p. 152) is included.

Control of the gipsy moth by forest management (*U. S. Dept. Agr. Bul. 484 (1917), pp. 54, pl. 1*).—This bulletin consists of two parts.

---

[1] Agr. Gaz. Canada, 2 (1915), No. 8, pp. 734–737.
[2] Yearbook Khediv. Agr. Soc., Cairo, 1905, pp. 57–91.

I. *The gipsy moth in woods*, by G. E. Clement (pp. 1–16).—The subject is dealt with under the headings of behavior of the gipsy moth in the woods, composition and condition of woods in infested territory, feeding habits of gipsy moth caterpillars, precautions needed, application of food plant data to individual species, other measures in need of attention, and recommendations. A plan of procedure for woodland owners who wish to improve and protect their woods is suggested.

II. *Management of typical woodlots infested with the gipsy moth in the white pine region*, by W. Munro (pp. 17–54).—In this second paper an attempt is made to coordinate the results of food plant experiments with known principles of forest management and with economic conditions in the infested region with a view to determining the extent to which forest management may be relied upon in the control of the moth. The subject is dealt with under the headings of susceptibility to gipsy moth attack as a basis of management, other factors in management for moth control, some controlling factors in management, trees which control, typical stands, and conclusions.

Each lot and each combination of species presents a problem in which the controlling factors are site, soil, location, market, species present, their value and relative proportion, the degree of infestation, and the cost of labor.

A map of the forest regions of New England showing their relation to the region infested by the gipsy moth, July 1, 1916, is attached.

Further observations on the control of the fruit tree leaf roller in the Hood River Valley, L. CHILDS (*Oregon Sta. Bul. 141 (1917), pp. 18–27*).—In further work with this insect (*Archips argyrospila*) (E. S. R., 34, p. 552; 35, p. 551), it was found that fair, settled weather for several days following spraying is the most important factor in the destruction of its eggs. A continued rainfall for four days following spraying was found to destroy the effectiveness of the miscible oil. Emulsions made from eastern or paraffin-base oils spread better than the western or asphaltum-base oils. The addition of 1 to 2 gal. of liquid soap to 100 gal. of emulsion greatly increased the spreading properties of the spray. "Oil sprays do not 'set' with the rapidity of other applications used in the apple orchard. Oil which could be removed by rains has been found on the trees as long as a week after application—it must be considered active while in this form. The other orchard sprays set within two to eight hours and effectiveness from that time on is only slightly reduced by continued rains."

In trapping work, as many as 600 leaf roller moths were caught during a single night by a Tungsten electric light trap. Of these 95 per cent were males, 3 per cent spent females, and 2 per cent female moths containing eggs.

"Miscible oils used at the rate of 6:100 during 1915 and 1916, though causing considerable foliage injury when used after the fruit buds begin to show, have not injured these buds in numbers sufficient to reduce the crop or to cause any injury to the tree other than slightly retarding its development. In both years a very high percentage of the eggs was destroyed when the oils were applied at this time. Oils applied late can usually be applied during a period of warm settled weather."

A new method of controlling the black-head fireworm, H. B. SCAMMELL (*Proc. Amer. Cranberry Growers' Assoc., 47 (1916), pp. 8–12*).—In the control of *Rhopobota vacciniana* the author recommends that the winter flowage be withdrawn about May 10 in an effort to bunch the hatching of the fireworm eggs. Nicotin sulphate should be applied at the rate of 200 gal. of spray per acre at each application, the first application to be made about May 20, followed in five days by a second application. Where there is more than a scattering of the second brood worms, a third application should be made when the majority of the eggs have hatched, or about the end of the first week in July. The following formula to make 200 gal. of the 40 per cent nicotin sulphate spray is recommended: Dissolve 8 lbs. of fish-oil soap in a small amount of water, add the dissolved soap to nearly the required amount of water in the spray tank, and then add 1 qt. of nicotin sulphate diluted with the remainder of the water.

Life cycle of Tortrix viridana, A. SICH (*Proc. So. London Ent. and Nat. Hist. Soc., 1915–16, pp. 15–20*).—The studies here reported relate to a leaf roller enemy of the oak in England.

[Codling moth investigations] (*New Mexico Sta. Rpt. 1916, pp. 31–34*).— This is a brief report of results of observations of the life history and habits of this pest in New Mexico, together with codling moth spraying schedules for 1916.

Spraying for codling moth, C. C. VINCENT, W. C. EDMUNDSON, G. J. DOWN· ING, and E. P. TAYLOR (*Idaho Sta. Bul. 92 (1916), pp. 25–27*).—This is a brief report of progress on spraying work with the codling moth commenced three years ago with a view to determining the relative efficiency of one, two, and three applications of arsenate of lead and for the purpose of comparing the efficiency in the control of the codling moth of two well-known brands of powdered arsenate of lead. The results obtained from spraying for three years are reported in tabular form. It is believed that either brand of material properly applied will prove satisfactory.

"The first or calyx spray should be applied when from 80 to 90 per cent of the petals have fallen, or work should begin in time to complete the first spray before the calyx lobes have closed. . . . The second spray should be applied about three weeks after the first. . . . To determine the time for the application of a third spray the trees should be banded about the middle of June. The spray should be given 20 days after the first larvæ come down under the bands. Trap or breeding cages may also be employed to determine the exact time for the application of the third spray. It should be applied when the first moths appear.

"The number of applications will depend on the infestation the previous year, the variety of the fruit, the infestation in neighboring orchards, effectiveness of early sprays, and seasonal conditions. The early calyx spray, however, is the most important. If this and other early brood sprays are neglected or improperly applied when the worms are bad, no amount of spraying late in the season will save the crop."

Life history of some Japanese Lepidoptera containing new genera and species, K. NAGANO (*Bul. Nawa Ent. Lab. [Japan] No. 1 (1916), pp. 27+[102], pls. 9*).—This bulletin gives descriptions of the immature stages of 31 species of Lepidoptera, together with colored illustrations of the larvæ and drawings illustrating the structure of the several stages. Three genera are erected and one species and one variety described as new to science.

District of Columbia Diptera: Syrphidæ, N. BANKS, C. T. GREENE, W. L. MCATEE, and R. C. SHANNON (*Proc. Biol. Soc. Wash., 29 (1916), pp. 173–203*).— One hundred and thirty-six species and two varieties are recorded from the District of Columbia.

The relation of malaria to crop production, D. L. VAN DINE (*Sci. Mo., 3 (1916), No. 5, pp. 431–439, figs. 2*).—This paper is based upon investigations conducted since 1913 by the Bureau of Entomology of the U. S. Department of Agriculture in the South, particularly in Madison Parish, La., a report of which work has been previously noted (E. S. R., 33, p. 255), together with data obtained from the Office of Farm Management of the Department.

Mosquitoes and man again, C. S. LUDLOW (*Science, n. ser., 44 (1916), No. 1144, pp. 788–790*).—A continuation of the discussion previously noted (E. S. R., 36, p. 552).

On Delphastus catalinæ, a valuable ladybird enemy of the white flies. H. S. SMITH and E. J. BRANIGAN (*Mo. Bul. Com. Hort. Cal., 5 (1916), No. 12, pp. 448–450, figs. 4*).—*D. catalinæ*, which was first observed during the summer of 1915 feeding upon a heavy infestation of *Aleyrodes kelloggi* on Catalina cherry at Pasadena, Cal., has been found to be largely confined in its food habits to white flies. The species has since been introduced into Florida, where it is thought that it will prove of considerable value.

Two destructive grape insects of the Appalachian region, F. E. BROOKS (*Off. Rpt. Sess. Internat. Cong. Vit., 1915, pp. 237–248, figs. 10*).—This paper relates to the grape curculio and the grape root borer, accounts of which by the author have been previously noted (E. S. R., 18, p. 61; 19, p. 962).

It is stated that the grape curculio is the most destructive insect attacking the fruit of the grape in many parts of the Appalachian region and also in some sections of the Mississippi Valley, causing in some localities a loss of 100 per cent of the crop on unprotected vines. The species is also recorded as occurring in destructive numbers in certain parts of Kentucky, Ohio, Illinois, Missouri, and Arkansas. The grape root borer is said to be especially destructive in certain localities in the Appalachian region, the most severe injury to grapevines having been reported from West Virginia and Kentucky.

Life history and feeding records of a series of California Coccinellidæ, C. P. CLAUSEN (*Univ. Cal. Pubs., Ent., 1 (1916), No. 6, pp. 251–299*).—The studies here presented were conducted during the spring and summer of 1913 at Sacramento and during 1914 at Berkeley and Riverside.

"The life history of an aphid-feeding coccinellid under normal summer conditions in California, based upon the results secured from eight species, may be given as 27 days, divided as follows: Egg stage, 5 days; first larval stage, 5 days; second, 3 days; third, 3 days; fourth, 6 days; and the pupal stage, 5 days.

"The number of aphids eaten by the larvæ of the different species is in proportion to the size of the individuals. The above, to a limited extent, may be said to be true in the case of the adults also. Temperature and humidity are very strong contributing factors in the development and behavior of the various species.

"The number of eggs to be expected under normal field conditions will vary from 200 to 500, or occasionally more, and extending over a period of from 4 to 8 weeks where the female has lived the full adult life under optimum conditions. The period intervening between emergence and mating is 1 to 3 days, and from mating to oviposition, 8 to 11 days, thus giving a period of from 10 to 15 days after emergence before oviposition may be expected. Oviposition normally takes place daily, with occasional exceptions. Only one fertilization is necessary during the life of the female, fertile eggs having been produced in one instance 55 days after mating."

Studies of weevils (Rhynchophora) with descriptions of new genera and species, W. D. PIERCE (*Proc. U. S. Nat. Mus., 51 (1916), pp. 461–473, figs. 2*).—The author erects three new families, five new subfamilies, one new tribe, and one new genus, and describes two new species, namely, *Leiomerus granicollis* from specimens found alive in cassava stems from Brazil at Washington, D. C.; and *Eisonyx* (*Eumononycha*) *picipes* from a specimen collected in a strawberry field at Nashville, Tenn. The latter has also been collected at Nashville from aster roots.

Nosema apis in Victoria, F. R. BEUHNE (*Jour. Dept. Agr. Victoria, 14 (1916), No. 10, pp. 629–632*).—Though widely distributed in Australia *N. apis* appears to be merely an occasional inhabitant of the alimentary canal of the

bee. Losses are said to occur only after seasons of drought and no fresh outbreaks of the disease follow the restocking with bees of defunct hives.

Spore-forming bacteria of the apiary, A. H. McCRAY (*U. S. Dept. Agr.,
Jour. Agr. Research, 8 (1917), No. 11, pp. 399–420, pls. 2, figs. 6*).—The first
part of this paper consists of descriptions and comparisons of *Bacillus mesentericus, B. vulgatus,* and *B. orpheus,* three of the five spore-bearing species occurring commonly about the apiary, *B. alvei* and *B. larvæ* having previously
been considered by White (E. S. R., 18, p. 561). Reference is first made to the
statement of Lambotte in 1902 that foul brood of bees can be produced by
feeding them cultures of *B. mesentericus vulgatus* grown upon a special medium
prepared from the juices of bee larvæ, and also that by the use of this special
medium *B. alvei* arises as a special variety of the above-mentioned bacillus
and produces, on feeding, tissue changes characteristic of the disease (E. S. R.,
14, p. 678).

The second part of the paper consists of a report on inoculation experiments.
The author finds that mistakes in the identification of these spore-forming
bacteria might well be made, especially without knowledge of their occurrence,
and that many of the earlier investigators of bee diseases confused these
species. The author's studies of *B. vulgatus, B. mesentericus,* and *B. alvei*
led him to conclude that the biological differences of the three species are too
great to warrant expecting the transformation from one to another in any
short period of time. " Even if it is granted that Lambotte fed pure cultures
of *B. alvei,* his results would not agree with those of present-day investigators
of bee diseases, since *B. alvei* has not been found to produce disease in bees
upon repeated inoculations."

A list of 19 references to the literature is included.

Some weather-proof bands for use against ants, J. R. HORTON (*Mo. Bul.
Com. Hort. Cal., 5 (1916), No. 11, pp. 419–421*).—This paper describes the best
formulas for banding mixtures that were developed in the course of a series of
experiments in which some 20 combinations were tested.

A mixture consisting of corrosive sublimate, which has a repellent and toxic
action, and commercial tree-sticky, at the rate 1 : 6, has been found to give the
best consistency, no ants crossing and no spreading or renewal being needed
for a period of three months. The softness of the mercuric tree-sticky band
was equally well maintained by substituting flowers of sulphur for the mercury salt.

New Javanese chalcidoid Hymenoptera, A. A. GIRAULT (*Proc. U. S. Nat.
Mus., 51 (1916), pp. 479–485*).—Two genera, ten species, and one variety are
here described as new to science, among which are *Cheiloneuromyia javensis,
Cristatithorax latiscapus, Coccophagus javæ, Asemantoideus dubius, Epitetras-
tichus lecanii,* and *Epitrastichus ibseni,* all reared from the green scale at
Salatiga, Java.

Some chalcidoid parasites of the seeds of Myrtaceæ, A. DA COSTA LIMA
(*Arch. Mus. Nac. Rio de Janeiro, 19 (1916), pp. 193–203, pls. 2*).—This paper
includes descriptions of three seed chalcids that attack guava (*Psidium* spp.)
in Brazil, namely, *Syntomaspis myrtacearum* n. sp. *Prodecatoma* sp., and
Eurytoma sp.

Observations on the insect parasites of some Coccidæ.—I, On Aphelinus
mytilaspidis, a chalcid parasite of the mussel scale (Lepidosaphes ulmi),
A. D. IMMS (*Quart. Jour. Micros. Sci. [London], n. ser., 61 (1916), No. 243, pp.
217–274, pls. 2, figs. 5*).—This paper deals at length with the life history, bionomics, and economic status of *A. mytilaspidis,* a parasite of the oyster-shell
scale (*L. ulmi*) as observed in England.

There are two generations a year, parthenogenesis apparently being the usual method of reproduction. The adults of the first generation appear in greatest frequency between the third week in June and the middle of July, and of the second generation between the middle of August and the first week in September. The efficiency of this parasite is said to be far below that of the most effective insecticides, due primarily to four factors, namely, its extremely limited powers of migration, its relatively low fecundity, its marked susceptibility to the influence of unfavorable climatic conditions, and the effects of the second annual generation of parasitism being only partial and incomplete.

A list of 33 references to the literature is included.

FOODS—HUMAN NUTRITION.

The use of cotton seed as food, T. B. OSBORNE and L. B. MENDEL (*Jour. Biol. Chem., 29 (1917), No. 2, pp. 289-317, figs. 5*).—This paper reports data compiled from experiments with laboratory animals (rats) which were fed cottonseed products of various descriptions. The following facts were established as results of these experiments:

Cottonseed kernels were found to be unsatisfactory for nutrition. All of the animals receiving this product in the ration died within two weeks. The samples of cottonseed meal and flour tested were found to be valuable foods for growing rats, both when used as a sole source of protein in the diet and when used in smaller quantity to supplement their less efficient protein concentrates.

The injurious substances in the kernels can be removed by extraction with ether and, according to other investigators, by extraction with carbon bisulphid, chloroform, benzene, or alcohol, but not with petroleum ether or gasoline. The ether-soluble material is deleterious, either because it contains some toxic ingredients or else because it renders the food so unpalatable that the animals refuse to eat it. Foods containing cottonseed oil prepared by cold pressing or the crude unbleached commercial oil prepared by hot pressing were eaten without detriment by the rats.

"By treatment with steam under suitable conditions the kernels lose their deleterious effect on rats. The variations in the results of feeding different samples of cottonseed meal, which have been reported, may be due to differences in the mode of heating which the products have experienced in their preparation."

With regard to the question as to whether cottonseed injury in the feeding of domestic animals can be classed with the deficiency diseases, the authors state that it is possible that food mixtures lacking some of the now recognized essential ingredients of an adequate diet have been employed in the past. Experiments with rats which were grown successfully on cottonseed rations excluded the probability that there is ordinarily any lack of the water-soluble vitamin. There is no definite information that the quota of inorganic salts furnished in agricultural products is always sufficient.

The authors have "induced young rats to double their weight at a normal rate of growth on a food mixture containing nothing except cottonseed meal, starch, and lard. The deleterious effects of unheated cottonseed kernels can not be denied. Whether the reputed detrimental effect after feeding some of the commercial cottonseed meals is associated with a failure to destroy a deleterious constituent—as has been indicated above—or is attributable to unsuitable methods of feeding in some cases is still debatable. The treatment of the cotton seed so as at least to render it harmless now seems to lie within the range of ready possibilities."

The nature of the dietary deficiencies of the oat kernel, E. V. McCollum, N. Simmonds, and W. Pitz (*Jour. Biol. Chem.*, 29 (*1917*), *No. 2, pp. 341–354, figs. 9*).—This paper reports data obtained in feeding experiments with laboratory animals regarding the supplementary relations between the oat kernel and isolated food factors. The results of these experiments may be summarized briefly as follows:

The proteins of the oat kernel seem to be of poorer quality than those of the maize or wheat kernel. With all other dietary factors properly adjusted, 9 per cent of oat protein served to induce a small amount of growth at the beginning of the experiments, but cessation of growth followed after about one month and thereafter the animal remained stationary in weight or declined. Casein does not appear to supplement the proteins of the oat kernel satisfactorily and the addition of this to oat proteins does not induce growth at the maximum rate, as does the combination of casein with wheat protein or with maize protein. Combinations of gelatin and oat proteins in about equal proportions proved to be superior to casein and oat protein combinations.

" The unidentified dietary factor fat-soluble A is present in very small amount in the oat kernel. It is not possible to supplement the oat kernel with inorganic salts and purified protein so as to induce growth beyond the third month. The inclusion of butter fat or some other substance which supplies the unknown A prevents the failure at this point, just as it does in experiments where the ration consists of purified protein, salts, carbohydrates, and an extract which furnishes the dietary factor B.

" The whole oat kernel, with the hulls removed in the laboratory by coarse grinding and fanning, will not induce any growth in young rats. A mixture of hulled oats or rolled oats with 5 per cent of butter fat induces very slow increase in body weight for at least 125 days.

" The oat kernel, like unpolished rice, wheat, wheat germ, maize kernel, alfalfa leaves, cabbage, and clover leaves, contains a liberal supply of the water-soluble B, the preparations of which induce relief from polyneuritis. . . .

" The addition of any single dietary component as protein, inorganic salts, or fat-soluble A does not supplement the oat kernel so as to induce appreciable growth. The addition of two dietary factors to the oat kernel serves to induce. good growth during the first 60 days when one of the additions is a suitable salt mixture. Without modifying the inorganic content of the ration when this is derived solely from the oat kernel . . . rats have not made any marked increase in body weight. When the oat kernel is fed supplemented by but two dietary factors there is always early failure with loss of weight and death following the brief period of growth. . . .

" The oat kernel, like the wheat kernel, appears to cause injury to the animals when their diet is of such a character as to lower their vitality. It is not necessary to assume the presence of something toxic in the oat kernel to account for the injury which results from the presence of a high content of oats in a monotonous food mixture taken over a considerable period. Oats produce feces of a pasty character which makes their elimination difficult, and in all probability tend to debilitate the animal. . . .

" When the oat kernel is supplemented with casein, a suitable salt mixture, and butter fat, growth may proceed to the normal adult size at the normal rate in some animals, but in general growth is slower than the normal rate. . . . The authors have been able to secure reproduction with these rations in but a single instance, and the young survided but one day."

Further investigations on this subject are in progress.

The influence of temperatures above freezing on the changes in chemical composition, bacterial content, and histological structure of the flesh of the common fowl, M[ARY] E. PENNINGTON, J. S. HEPBURN, E. Q. ST. JOHN, and E. WITMER (*Jour. Biol. Chem.*, 29 (1917), No. 2, pp. XXXI, XXXII).—The animal heat was removed from freshly killed chickens by storage at about 0° C. for 24 hours. Some of the birds were then analyzed as "freshly killed chickens." One lot was stored at the average temperature of 23.9° C. for a period of four days at the maximum; another in a household refrigerator at a temperature of 7.2 to 12.8° C. for a period of seven days at the maximum; and a third lot at a temperature of 0° C. for a period of three weeks at the maximum. Analyses of birds from each of these lots showed that while the total nitrogen content of the muscle remained unchanged the partition of the nitrogen underwent changes in all three cases.

"At all three temperatures of holding the amino acid and basic nitrogen increased at the expense of the protein nitrogen, usually in a progressive manner. The most striking change in the fat constants was an increase in the acid value, which became progressively greater as the period of holding lengthened. Both the formation of amino acid and basic nitrogen and the increase in the acid value of the fat occurred most rapidly at the temperature of the room, least rapidly at that of the chill room. . . . The bacteria, which grow under aerobic conditions, increased in both the muscles and the skin at all three temperatures of holding. The increase was enormous in the chickens kept in the room and was less marked, though distinct, in those kept in the refrigerator and in the chill room. The increase usually became greater as the period of holding lengthened."

Changes were also noted in the histological structure of the animals in all cases, these changes depending both on the temperature and the time of holding.

"The changes which occurred during holding in the chill room for three weeks were about equal to those occurring during holding in the house refrigerator for five to seven days. The changes which took place during holding in the house refrigerator for five days were less than those taking place during holding in the room for two days."

The influence of temperatures below freezing on the changes in chemical composition, bacterial content, and histological structure of the flesh of the common fowl, M[ARY] E. PENNINGTON, J. S. HEPBURN, E. Q. ST. JOHN, and E. WITMER (*Jour. Biol. Chem.*, 29 (1917), No. 2, pp. XXXIII, XXXIV).—This paper presents a brief report of chemical, bacteriological, and histological studies of chickens which, after having been frozen hard, were stored at temperatures varying from —9 to —13° C. for periods as long as two years.

Analyses and organoleptic tests showed that no loss of food value occurred while the chickens were in the freezer, and the birds were still wholesome and nutritious, the only appreciable changes being a loss in flavor after holding for a priod longer than nine months. The muscular tissue showed a progressive loss of water while the chickens were held in the freezer. The total nitrogen of the muscle remained unchanged, but changes occurred in the partition of the nitrogen which indicated the occurrence of a slow but distinct proteolysis. The hydrolysis of the fat and the digestion of the protein occurred much less rapidly than in the case of birds held at temperatures above freezing. These chemical changes were believed to be due to an enzymatic rather than to a bacteriologic cause. Certain characteristic changes took place in the histological structure of the cells of the muscle, nerves, and blood vessels.

"The changes here recorded were most marked after the normal commercial period of freezer storage had been exceeded. . . . The changes in chemical composition during holding in the freezer for one year were about equal to the changes which occurred during holding in the chill room for three weeks."

A study of food fishes. The complete analysis of 20 common food fishes, with especial reference to a seasonal variation in composition, E. D. CLARK and L. H. ALMY (*Jour. Biol. Chem., 29 (1917), No. 2, p. XXII*).—In general, little variation was found in the amount of nitrogenous and ash constituents. The amount of fat varied considerably and depended upon the season, age of the fish, and relation to the time of spawning and feeding. With migratory fish, such as shad, bluefish, weakfish, and mackerel, the fat content varied from less than 0.5 to over 16 per cent, while typical bottom fish, like cod, haddock, and flounders, had a minimum amount of fat which varied but slightly as compared with the surface and migratory species.

The grayfish.—Try it (*U. S. Dept. Com., Bur. Fisheries Econ. Circ. 22 (1916), pp. 8, fig. 1*).—This circular describes the grayfish (commonly known as dogfish) and discusses its food value.

Grayfish is said to have been eaten for some time on the shores of the Mediterraneau and in northern Europe, and the Bureau of Fisheries recommends that it be used for food purposes in this country. It is said to be excellent when eaten fresh, canned, salted and dried, or smoked. The circular contains a number of recipes for its preparation.

Tenth annual report of the chemical department of the [Indiana State] Laboratory of Hygiene, H. E. BARNARD (*Ind. Bd. Health, Ann. Rpt. Chem. Div. Lab. Hyg., 10 (1915), pp. 85*).—The work of the laboratory during the year ended September 30, 1915, is reviewed. This included analyses of 652 samples of different foods, of which 481 were found to conform to existing standards of composition and labeling. The work also included the examination of 246 samples of drugs and patent medicines and the sanitary inspection of a large number of food establishments, including canneries.

Annual report of the food and drug commissioner, F. H. FRICKE (*Ann. Rpt. Food and Drug Comr., Missouri, 1916, pp. 45, pls. 5*).—This report covers the work of the food and drug department for the year ended December 31, 1916. This included the examination of a large number of samples of miscellaneous food products, the inspection of miscellaneous food establishments, etc.

[Food and drug inspection in North Dakota], E. F. LADD and ALMA K. JOHNSON (*North Dakota Sta. Spec. Bul., 4 (1917), No. 11, pp. 259–330, figs. 3*).— This bulletin contains a report on The Composition of Canned Corn, by R. E. Remington, including a large number of analyses; the results of the examination of 35 samples of tincture of iodin, by Matty Jongeward; and the results of the sanitary inspection of a large number of groceries, restaurants, hotels, slaughterhouses, etc.

California pure foods and drugs acts, food sanitation act, cold storage act (*[Sacramento], Cal.: State, 1916, pp. 160*).—The texts are given of the acts as amended to 1915, with rules and regulations for their enforcement, standards of purity, etc.

The dairy and food laws of the State of Michigan (*Lansing, Mich.: State, 1915, pp. 201*).—This is a compilation of the texts of the laws and digests of court decisions relating thereto.

Manual for army bakers, 1916 (*War Dept. [U. S.], Doc. 563 (1917), pp. 123, pl. 1, figs. 20*).—This book contains information regarding the nature, care, and storage of different food materials, recipes for the preparation of bread, and general information regarding post and field bakeries and baking equipment.

Economical dishes for wartime, FLORENCE A. GEORGE (*Birmingham [England]: Cornish Brothers, Ltd., 1916, pp. 48*).—A compilation of recipes.

The rural school luncheon (*Regina, Canada: Govt., 1916, pp. 40, pl. 1, figs. 9*).—This pamphlet, which was issued by the Department of Education, Saskatchewan, as Household Science Circular No. 1, contains information regarding the equipment and supplies to be furnished by the school board and the duties of the teacher and the mothers, and gives recipes and directions for the preparation of the luncheon.

Studies in carbohydrate metabolism, **XIV–XX**, LOUISE McDANELL and F. P. UNDERHILL (*Jour. Biol. Chem., 29 (1917), No. 2, pp. 227–232; 233–243; 245–250; 251–254, fig. 1; 255–263; 265–272, fig. 1; 273–280*).—Seven articles are here presented.

XIV. *The influence of alkali administration upon blood sugar content in relation to the acid-base-producing properties of the diet.*—The data here reported indicate that the injection of sodium carbonate is as ineffective in altering the blood sugar content of normal laboratory animals (rabbits) when maintained either upon acid-forming or base-forming diets as is the case with animals receiving a mixed diet.

XV. *The influence of acid-forming and base-forming diets upon blood sugar content.*—Experiments with normal laboratory animals (rabbits) showed that the blood sugar content was not changed by variations in the acid-base content of the diet which were sufficient to cause a marked change in the hydrogen ion concentration of the urine.

XVI. *The relation of epinephrine glycosuria to dosage and to the character of the diet.*—The following conclusions are drawn in part from the data reported:

With a sufficient quantity of food, laboratory animals (rabbits) maintained upon a mixed diet excreted larger amounts of sugar after epinephrine administration than when maintained upon either an acid-producing diet or one yielding a basic ash. During a base-forming diet a somewhat larger output of sugar occurs after injection of epinephrine than is the case under similar conditions with an acid-producing diet. It is possible that there is a greater glycogen storage upon a base-producing diet than upon a diet yielding acid ash.

XVII. *Further experiments upon the influence of the intravenous injection of sodium carbonate upon epinephrine hyperglycemia and glycosuria.*

XVIII. *The relation of diet to the glycogen content of the liver.*—Studies of the influence of the diet upon the glycogen content of the liver were carried out with normal laboratory animals (rabbits).

It was found that a base-forming diet is somewhat more efficient in the formation of glycogen than an acid-producing diet. These results are in agreement with those of other investigators, who have found that an excess of alkali contributes to the accumulation of glycogen. However, it was also demonstrated that a large storage of glycogen may take place upon an acid-forming diet when sufficient food is ingested.

XIX. *The influence of the intravenous injection of sodium carbonate upon the hyperglycemia and glycosuria following the subcutaneous administraion of glucose.*

XX. *New experiments upon the mechanism of salt glycosuria.*

A chemical study of prolonged inanition, R. E. SWAIN (*Jour. Biol. Chem., 29 (1917), No. 2, p. XXXV*).—This is a brief report of observations on a 30-year-old man, who subjected himself to a starvation period of 60 days.

Preliminary observations on the regulation of the calcium excretion in the dog, M. H. GIVENS (*Jour. Biol. Chem., 29 (1917), No. 2, p. XXIV*).—In a laboratory animal (dog) maintained in nitrogenous equilibrium for 60 days, negative calcium balance was brought about by a diet of meat, lard, and cracker meal. The substitution for cracker meal, on the basis of nitrogen and calorie equivalent, of dried skim milk and sucrose resulted in an approach toward a calcium balance. No effect was produced on the calcium output by the addition of sodium bicarbonate to either of these diets. The addition of hydrochloric acid to the meat-cracker diet produced a prompt increase in the excretion of calcium by way of the kidneys, and the addition of the acid to the dried-skim-milk diet produced an increased urinary excretion of calcium, though not at the expense of the fecal output.

The active constituent of the thyroid: Its isolation, chemical properties, and physiological action, E. C. KENDALL (*Jour. Biol. Chem., 29 (1917), No. 2, pp. XXIX, XXX*).—The active constituent separates in microscopic needles. It may be precipitated as free base or in salt form. Its chemical properties depend upon the degree of purification and the presence of other substances, and its physiological activity depends upon the amount administered and the susceptibility of the individual.

The use of pancreatic vitamin in cases of malnutrition, W. H. EDDY (*Jour. Biol. Chem., 29 (1917), No. 2, pp. XVI, XVII*).—A report of a preliminary study which suggests the possibility of stimulating assimilation by the artificial feeding of pancreatic vitamins.

ANIMAL PRODUCTION.

The associative digestibility of corn silage and cottonseed meal in steer rations, II, P. V. EWING, C. A. WELLS, and F. H. SMITH (*Georgia Sta. Bul. 125 (1917), pp. 149–164, fig. 1*).—This is the second progress report of an investigation at the station on the associative action of feeds, or the influence of one ingredient of a ration on the digestibility of the nutrients of the other ingredient (E. S. R., 34, p. 169). The feeds used were silage made from corn from which the ears had been removed, and screened choice cottonseed meal. Of the six rations involved in the experiments two were silage alone, two silage and cottonseed meal, and two cottonseed meal alone. Only one of the two rations of cottonseed meal gave satisfactory digestive trials. High-grade two-year-old Shorthorn steers were used.

In the digestive trials, which lasted ten days each, the feces composite only were collected. An improved form of feces duct, which is described, was used. The feces sample was divided into three fractional parts by a method which is described, one fraction being assumed to represent the corn silage residue. Data are tabulated showing the feed schedule, analyses of feeds used, a general summary of the digestion trials, analyses of the different fractional parts of the feces, the utilization of the nutrients consumed, and gains and losses in digestibility due to food combination.

In general, it was found that with the feeds used there were no appreciable differences in the digestibilities of the nitrogen and fats as a result of the combination of the two feeds. When silage and cottonseed meal were fed together in the proportion of 3.4 : 1, the digestibility of the total dry matter was 4.62 per cent below the theoretical standard; and when these feeds were combined in the proportion of 7.7 : 1 the digestibility of the total dry matter exceeded the theoretical standard by 1.1 per cent. There was an appreciable gain in digestibility of the ash and nitrogen-free extract in both rations in which the feeds were combined, but an appreciable loss in the digestibility of crude fiber. In attempting to ascertain the cause of these gains and losses of digestibility by an examination of the fractions of the feces, it was concluded that a steer macerates his food approximately four times as well when fed silage alone as when fed silage and cottonseed meal in the proportion of 3.4 : 1, and twice as well when fed silage alone as when fed the mixture in the proportion of 7.7 : 1. The digestibility of the dry matter and crude fiber of silage seemed to be proportionate to the extent or completeness of maceration or physical disintegration. The feeding of silage and cottonseed meal in combination apparently increased the digestibility of total ash in the cottonseed meal.

It is stated that " heavy cottonseed meal feeding tends to lower the nutritive value of the silage fed along with it and the most economically used rations are those containing a maximum amount of silage with a minimum amount of cottonseed meal. The nutrients of cottonseed meal and silage are not digested in the same proportions when fed alone and in combinations."

Animal husbandry experiments (*Iowa Sta. Rpt. 1916, pp. 25, 26*).—In fattening experiments with 2-year-old steers, rations of silage with about one-fourth to one-half of a full ration of corn returned from $2 to $6 more profit per head than when the steers were hand-fed or self-fed. The results of four years' cooperative beef cattle experiments in Monona County indicate that baby beef can be profitably raised and fed out on the average Iowa farm under present conditions.

The results of an experiment in which a Shorthorn bull and Galloway cows were originally crossed and their offspring intercrossed indicate that " the white color of the Shorthorn type is due to the lack of a factor E for extension, which is present in colored cattle. The extension factor óperates on both black and red pigment. There is another type of white in cattle which does not involve the loss of the extension factor. The previously assumed allelomorphic nature of red and black, and also of horned and polled, is demonstrated. In regard to its bearing on farm practice, the experiment shows that breeders of polled cattle may introduce superior horned animals into their breeding herds without danger of seriously losing ground."

[Animal husbandry studies], E. J. IDDINGS and C. W. HICKMAN (*Idaho Sta. Bul. 92 (1916), pp. 4–7*).—Continuing the work in sheep breeding and management (E. S. R.. 34, p. 767), information was obtained on the yield and composition of milk of the different breeds in the test. The following table gives a summary of these data together with five years' weights of fleece and three years' birth weights of lambs. lambing percentages, and average daily gains of lambs to three months of age.

Results of tests in sheep breeding and management.

Breed.	Weight of fleece.	Birth weight of lambs.	Lambing percentage.	Daily gain per lamb.	Daily milk yield per ewe.	Milk fat.	Total milk solids.
	Pounds.	*Pounds.*		*Pounds.*	*Pounds.*	*Per cent.*	*Per cent.*
Rambouillet......	14.1	8.3	147	0.45	2.32	8.82	14.66
Hampshire.......	7.8	9.4	173	.61	2.38	6.64	11.98
Shropshire........	11.2	8.2	154	.49	1.65	9.02	14.86
Southdown.......	7.3	7.1	116	.39	1.22	8.60	14.61
Cotswold.........	15.1	7.0	142	.45	2.46	8.62	14.98

No adequate explanation has thus far been found for differences noted in the growth of lambs.

Silage from peas and oats and from wheat and vetch was used with satisfactory results in maintaining beef cattle during the winter. It was found that silage from either of these mixtures readily replaced corn silage for milk production.

The results of hogging off 3.88 acres of Canada field peas are summarized in the following table:

Results in tests of hogging off field peas.

Lot.	Area in acres.	Number of pigs.	Average initial weight per head.	Days on test.	Average gain.		Net profit per acre. (Pork 8 cents per pound.)
					Per head daily.	Per acre.	
			Pounds.		*Pounds.*	*Pounds.*	
1................	0.82	14	88.6	28	1.16	553	$44.24
2................	.84	26	81.7	21	1.45	940	54.44
3................	.70	16	125.0	21	1.32	631	50.48
4................	1.52	18	160.0	35	1.09	450	36.00

The pigs in lot 2 were fed, in addition to the peas, rolled barley at the rate of 2 lbs. per 100 lbs. of live weight, or a total of 1,162 lbs. This barley was charged at the rate of $30 per ton. The plat on which lot 4 grazed was sown with a mixture of 80 lbs. of field peas and 20 lbs. of wheat per acre.

In tests of nitrogenous supplements for barley for pigs during the winter of 1915–16, chopped alfalfa showed a relatively high feeding value. Tankage produced relatively cheap and the largest gains.

Lamb and sheep feeding experiments, E. J. IDDINGS (*Idaho Sta. Bul. 89 (1916), pp. 3–14, figs. 3*).—In continuation of work already noted (E. S. R., 29, p. 870), results are reported of feeding experiments completed in 1914 with 511 lambs and 223 ewes and wethers at Caldwell, and 27 lambs at Moscow.

At Caldwell the tests were conducted in open lots, the pens being so arranged as to permit little exercise. The lambs were divided into three lots of approximately 170 each and fed for 109 days. The lambs in lot 1 received alfalfa hay ad libitum and a grain mixture of corn and barley (1:3). They were started on ¼ lb. of grain per head daily, which was increased to 1.5 lbs. These lambs made an average daily gain of 0.28 lb. per head at a feed cost of 6.14 cts. per pound of gain, and returned a profit, after deducting all expenses, of 59 cts. per head. The lambs in lot 2 were fed alfalfa hay alone for the first month of the test and then were given a grain mixture which averaged 60 per cent of barley, 33 per cent of corn, and 7 per cent of oats. They made an average daily gain of 0.24 lb. per head at a feed cost of 5.85 cts. per pound of gain and a net profit of 70 cts. per head. The lambs in lot 3 were fed alfalfa hay and grain throughout the test. For the first 25 days the grain consisted of barley and oats (3:1), and thereafter of barley alone. The lambs in this lot gained an average of 0.28 lb. per head daily at a feed cost of 5.58 cts. per pound of gain and a net profit of 77 cts. per lamb.

The ewes and wethers were fed for 128 days a ration of cut mixed grain hay and whole alfalfa hay. After about two months they were also fed a grain ration of oats, which was changed after a few days to a mixture of ground barley, ground wheat, and ground corn (1:1:1). They made an average daily gain of 0.14 lb. per head at a feed cost of 8.62 cts. per pound of gain and a net profit of 8 cts. per head. In these experiments the following values per ton for hay were realized after deducting all expenses: For lambs, lot 1 $10.53, lot 2 $12.42, and lot 3 $12.47, and for ewes and wethers $6.40. The prices charged for feeds were alfalfa hay $5 and cut hay $6 per ton; barley and oats $1 per hundredweight, with 10 cts. for grinding; corn $1.40 per hundredweight, with 10 cts. for cracking; and ground wheat $1.20 per hundredweight.

In the Moscow experiment 27 farm grown lambs, averaging about 101 lbs. each, were fed for 55 days under shelter. The nine lambs in lot 1 were fed mixed hay and a mixture of barley and field peas (3:1). They made an average daily gain of 0.281 lb. per head, at a feed cost of 9.07 cts. per pound of gain. The nine lambs in lot 2 were fed mixed hay and a mixture of barley and bran (3:1). They made an average daily gain of 0.274 lb. per head. at a feed cost of 8.5 cts. per pound of gain. The nine lambs in lot 3 were fed mixed hay and a mixture of barley and linseed cake (3:1). They gained an average of 0.318 lb. per head daily at a feed cost of 8.71 cts. per pound of gain. All the lambs received alfalfa hay during the last eight days of the test. The grain mixtures were fed either ground or rolled. The lambs were bought at 5 cts. per pound and sold for 6 cts. Each lot returned a profit, the average for the three lots being 41 cts. per head. The charges per ton for feeds in this experiment were hay $8, barley $24, bran $20, linseed cake $42, and field peas $30.

Suggestions are given for feeding range lambs.

[Live-stock experiments] (*New Mexico Sta. Rpt. 1916*), *pp. 51–55*).—In an experiment with four lots of seven pigs each in which lot 1 was fed all the concentrates the pigs would eat within a reasonable time, lots 2 and 4 a concentrate ration at the rate of 2 lbs. per 100 lbs. live weight, and lot 3 1 lb. of a concentrate and 8 lbs. of skim milk per 100 lbs., all of the lots having access to good alfalfa pasture, the results were favorable to lots 2 and 4. However, these pigs required an additional feeding period on a full ration to fit them for market.

In a test with two lots of 16 pigs each on alfalfa hay, one lot fed a full ration of ground milo maize and a small quantity of skim milk was ready for market 30 days earlier than the other lot which received a limited amount of these supplements. In another test with pigs on alfalfa hay, one lot was fed a mixture of milo maize and mesquite beans (2:1), and the other lot had a full ration of ground milo maize. The results indicate that with pork at 10 cts. per pound, milo maize $1.50 per 100 lbs., and alfalfa hay 50 cts. per 100 lbs., mesquite beans are worth $1.30 per 100 lbs. Some difficulty was experienced in getting the beans properly ground for the pigs. This was best accomplished by grinding the beans and the grain together in the proportions wanted.

Data from feeding experiments at the Tucumcari dry-land substation indicate that good results may be obtained in feeding range steers wholly on dry-land crops.

[Grazing experiments with pigs] (*Idaho Sta. Bul. 92 (1916), pp. 46, 47, 53, 54, fig. 1*).—In tests at the Caldwell substation, reported by O. D. Center and C. B. Hampson, three sows and 19 pigs were placed on 1 acre of alfalfa pasture on May 18, 1915. On June 5 three sows and 14 pigs were added to the lot. This drove was insufficient to keep the alfalfa pasture closely grazed, and on June 27 588 lbs. of cured alfalfa hay was harvested from the acre. The animals were fed 25 lbs. of barley and 140 lbs. of skim milk daily. By August 11 these sows and pigs had gained 1,211 lbs. The pigs were then grazed on 1 acre of peas for 19 days, receiving in addition 11 lbs. of soaked barley and 20 lbs. of skim milk daily, and gained 155 lbs. on this acre. On August 30 they were turned on a second acre of peas and grazed for 13 days, and on September 11 on an acre of peas and wheat in combination for 17 days. The barley and skim milk were continued in the same quantity. The pigs gained 429 and 447 lbs. on these acres, respectively.

At the Gooding substation, in work reported by J. S. Welch, 21 young pigs on one-half acre of alfalfa, supplemented by 3,284 lbs. of grain and 1,878 lbs. of skim milk, made a gain of 1,362 lbs. in 131 days. In hogging off experiments, five pigs grazed on 0.238 acre of peas for 27 days and produced gains at the rate of 496 lbs. per acre. On a plat of 0.23 acre of peas and wheat five pigs grazed for 39 days, making gains at the rate of 565 lbs. per acre. On 0.216

acre of horse beans planted too late for high yields, five pigs grazed for 20 days and gained at the rate of 394 lbs. per acre.

[Feeding experiments with pigs] (*Washington Sta. Bul. 136 (1917), pp. 8, 9*).—In an experiment with newly weaned pigs, 73 head were divided into three lots and placed in a dry lot, pea and oat pasture, and alfalfa pasture, respectively. In addition each group received a ration of 95 per cent of rolled barley and 5 per cent of commercial pig meal for 24 days, and thereafter a ration of 92 per cent of rolled barley and 8 per cent of tankage. On changing the dry lot to tankage the gains were practically doubled and the amount of concentrates required per pound of gain reduced from 5.5 to 3.93 lbs. The change to tankage increased the gains of the pea and oat pasture group from 0.35 to 0.69 lb. per head daily, and decreased the concentrates from 4.09 to 3.26 lbs. per pound of gain. The alfalfa pasture group gained 0.31 lb. per head daily on the pig meal and 0.836 lb. on tankage. The amount of concentrates required per pound of gain by this lot was 5.24 lbs. on the pig meal and 3.73 lbs. on tankage.

A group of pigs that had been wintered around straw stacks and in stubble fields with no grain and a group that had been fed a growing ration through the winter were subsequently finished on rolled barley and shorts (3:1). The poor wintering had not destroyed the ability of the pigs to grow and fatten, but had limited their capacity for food consumption and delayed their finishing.

In a comparison of wheat *v.* barley, for fattening barrows, it required 4.47 lbs. of wheat, or 5.52 lbs. of barley, to produce a pound of gain.

Twelve pigs on alfalfa pasture with a supplemental ration of 90 per cent of rolled barley and 10 per cent of tankage in a self-feeder, and 100 lbs. of skim milk daily for 74 days, produced gains at 5.5 cts. per pound, not considering the value of the pasture.

Self-feeders for fattening. swine, L. A. WEAVER (*Missouri Sta. Bul. 144 (1917), pp. 3-17, figs. 2*).—Some of the results of experiments at the station on the value and limitations of self-feeders for swine are given in the following table:

Self-feeding v. hand-feeding of pigs.

Lot No.	Ration.	Number of pigs.	Average initial weight.	Duration of test.	Average daily gain per head.	Feed per pound of gain.	
						Amount.	Cost.
			Lbs.	Days.	Lbs.	Lbs.	Cents.
1	Corn and tankage (12:1)—(self-fed).	7	112.0	56	1.97	4.00	6.40
2	Corn and tankage (12:1)—(hand-fed).............	7	112.0	56	1.98	4.18	6.68
3	Corn, shorts, and tankage (self-fed).	10	77.4	60	1.69	4.19	5.75
4	Corn, shorts, and tankage (8:2:1)—(hand-fed).............	10	77.4	60	1.51	4.04	5.66
5	Corn, shorts, and tankage (self-fed).	10	137.7	42	2.00	3.63	5.07
6	Corn and tankage (self-fed)........	10	136.4	42	1.77	3.50	5.05
7	Corn and tankage(12:1)—(hand-fed)	12	150.2	42	1.76	4.07	5.73
8	Corn and tankage (self-fed)........	10	122.2	60	1.62	4.61	6.43
9	Corn and tankage (12:1)—(hand-fed).............	10	119.8	60	1.54	4.62	6.56
10	Corn, shorts, and tankage (self-fed).	10	121.0	60	1.80	4.55	6.31
11	Corn, shorts, and tankage (8:2:1)—(hand-fed).............	10	122.7	60	1.68	4.38	6.35
12	Corn, shorts, and tankage (self-fed).	8	39.93	112	1.05	3.84	....
13	Corn, shorts, and tankage (9:3:1)—(hand-fed).............	8	39.91	112	.95	3.65	....

In addition to the above rations the animals had access to a mixture of copperas, Glaubers salts, common salt, sal soda, and sulphur. The pigs of lots 12 and 13 were grazed on rape pasture, which furnished abundant forage throughout the test. In the other experiments the pigs were fed on dry lots. In all the tests, except with lots 1 and 2, the feeds in the self-feeders were unmixed. The proportions in which the unmixed feeds were consumed from self-feeders were as follows:

Lot 3, corn, shorts, and tankage (17.5 : 5.6 : 1) ; lot 5, corn, shorts, and tankage (18.5 : 8.1 : 1) ; lot 6, corn and tankage (8.9 : 1) ; lot 8, corn and tankage (17.1 : 1) ; lot 10, corn, shorts, and tankage (20.66 : 3.93 : 1) ; and lot 12, corn, shorts, and tankage (11.6 : 0.23 : 1).

The cost of gains in these experiments was figured on the basis of 75 cts. per bushel for corn, $1.40 per 100 lbs. for shorts, and $2.50 per 100 lbs. for tankage.

The author states that while these results do not warrant definite conclusions they indicate that "fattening hogs fed with a self-feeder gain more rapidly than when hand-fed in the usual manner. There is no difference in the economy of gain which can be accredited to the method of feeding. . . . When each feed is placed in a separate feeder the hogs will choose the different feeds, so that the gain will be both rapid and relatively economical. This will perhaps be true only when each feed is supplied in abundance. . . .

"It is apparent that the advantage which the self-feeder method will have in any specific instance over hand-feeding, in regard to rate of gain, will depend to a large degree upon the ability of the person doing the hand-feeding to feed so that the hogs will consume a maximum amount of feed. In practically all cases, when the self-fed hogs gained more rapidly than those which were hand-fed, they also consumed more feed. In a similar manner the relative efficiency of the self-fed ration, and the same feeds hand-fed, will depend upon the ability of the feeder to combine properly the feeds used."

[Poultry husbandry studies], P. Moore (*Idaho Sta. Bul. 92 (1916), pp. 28-30*).—Four pens of 25 White Leghorn pullets each received the following rations for one year: Pen IV a grain ration of peas, wheat, and corn (10 : 14 : 6), and a mash of bran, shorts, corn meal, wheat meal, pea meal, linseed meal, and charcoal (3 : 3 : 1 : 1 : 1 : 6 : 1), the nutritive ratio being 1 : 4.2; pen V a grain ration of corn and wheat (6 : 10), and a mash of bran, shorts, corn meal, wheat meal, beef scrap, and charcoal (2 : 1 : 1 : 1 : 3 : 1), with a nutritive ratio of 1 : 4.2; pen VI the same as pen IV, except that the grain ration was in the ratio of 1 : 10 : 5, and the mash three parts of linseed meal to one part each of the other ingredients, the nutritive ratio being 1 : 5.5; and pen VII the same as pen V, except that the mash ingredients were in the ratio of 2 : 2.5 : 1 : 1 : 1.5 : 1, and the nutritive ratio 1 : 5.5. During the year pen V produced 55.8 per cent more eggs than pen IV, 51.1 per cent more eggs than pen VI, and 35.2 per cent more eggs than pen VII. The percentage of eggs under 2 oz. in pen IV was 46.5, in pen V 15.2, in pen VI 41.9, and in pen VII 17.5.

[Poultry experiments] (*Iowa Sta. Rpt. 1916, pp. 27, 28*).—Feeding experiments carried on at the station indicate that corn is equal, pound for pound, if not superior, to wheat as the basis of a ration for feeding both growing and laying stock. Corn gave results superior to wheat as a food for laying stock during warm weather. To obtain satisfactory results in feeding both wheat and corn, it was found necessary to use some animal food, such as high-grade tankage, meat meal, or skim milk, and also to supplement the grain with mineral food rich in lime and phosphate, such as bone meal.

Experiments indicate that capon production is profitable with the larger breeds of general purpose fowls. Capons produced a net profit of from 25 to 40 per cent more than cockerels.

In experiments with nest eggs of various kinds, it was found that hens prefer to lay in nests provided with the natural egg.

Mating and early hatching, V. G. Aubby (*New Jersey Stas. Hints to Poultrymen*, *5* (*1917*), *No. 4, pp. 4*).—Brief directions are given for selecting and mating fowls for increased egg production, together with an outline of the advantages of early hatching.

Colony brooding, V. G. Aubby (*New Jersey Stas. Hints to Poultrymen*, *5* (*1917*), *No. 6, pp. 4*).—Brief directions are given for the artificial brooding of chicks by the colony plan.

Preparing birds for exhibition, R. F. Irvin (*New Jersey Stas. Hints to Poultrymen*, *5* (*1916*), *No. 1, pp. 4*).—Brief directions are given for selecting, conditioning, training, washing and cleaning, and shipping poultry for exhibition.

The Vineland international egg laying and breeding contest, H. R. Lewis (*New Jersey Stas. Hints to Poultrymen*, *5* (*1916*), *No. 2, pp. 4*).—This circular briefly describes the three-year international egg laying and breeding contest being conducted at Vineland, N. J., and points out ways by which the poultrymen of the State may follow the results of the contest.

Our state department of poultry husbandry, its organization and activities, H. R. Lewis (*New Jersey Stas. Hints to Poultrymen, 5* (*1917*), *No. 5, pp. 4*).—A brief outline is given.

DAIRY FARMING—DAIRYING.

The nutrients required to develop the bovine fetus, C. H. Eckles (*Missouri Sta. Research Bul. 26* (*1916*), *pp. 3–36, figs. 4*).—The author reviews investigations by others upon the utilization of food by mammals for the development of the fetus and reports experiments with cows from which it is concluded that a cow can produce a fetus on the same ration that will maintain her when dry and farrow, or that the amount of nutrients necessary to develop the bovine fetus is so small that it can not be measured by ordinary methods of experimentation.

Four cows were kept during the entire period of gestation on a ration found by six months' trial to be only sufficient to maintain them at uniform weight when not pregnant and not producing milk. These cows developed calves of normal size on this ration, and one cow weighed 48 lbs. more after the calf was dropped than when bred and the other weighed only 17 lbs. less. This result was confirmed by two additional cows, the feeding of which was regulated during gestation by that required to maintain a dry farrow cow at uniform weight. One of the Jersey cows developed a normal fetus while receiving less than a maintenance ration during the period of gestation.

The author states that these results may be due to one or more of three possible factors—(1) better use of feed during gestation, (2) decreased maintenance during pregnancy, and (3) small amount of dry matter in fetus. Conclusions with reference to these factors are summarized as follows:

" While the data taken are not very satisfactory, the indications are that the coefficient of digestibility is not changed by pregnancy. The data do not make it possible to conclude definitely that the maintenance of the animals is decreased by pregnancy, but it is thought this is probable and could be accounted for by the animal being quieter when in this condition. The data show that the amount of dry matter contained in the fetus and its accompanying fluid and membranes is very small. The small feed requirement necessary to supply the dry matter of the fetus, together with the amniotic fluid and placenta, is either too small to be measured on account of the length of time represented or it is offset by the saving due to decreased maintenance.

"Four Jersey calves analyzed at birth contained an average of 73.09 per cent of water. Data available indicate that breed is not a factor influencing the composition of the new-born calves. The amniotic fluid weighs about 30 lbs. and contains approximately 95 per cent water. The placenta weighs about 18 lbs., of which approximately 85 per cent is water. A Jersey cow produces a total of only 15 or 20 lbs. and a Holstein 20 or 25 lbs. of dry matter in the fetus and its accompanying fluid and membranes. On the dry-matter basis a Jersey calf at birth is equivalent to from 110 to 170 lbs. of Jersey milk. In the Holstein breed the calf at birth will contain as much dry matter as from 200 to 275 lbs. of Holstein milk.

"Using [one of the Jersey cows] as typical of all, it is shown that she produced during one year 1,263 lbs. of dry matter in her milk. During this time 2,828 therms of energy were available in her ration for this milk production in excess of maintenance. Her calf with placenta and amniotic fluid contained approximately 24 lbs. of dry matter, or 1.9 per cent as much dry matter as in her milk for one year. If the calorific value of the solids in the fetus are considered equivalent pound for pound to that of the solids in the milk it would appear by calculation that this cow would require 1.9 per cent as much energy as was used for her milk production, or 47.7 therms. The actual energy in the fetus and its accompanying fluid and membranes calculated from the weights and composition was 56.4 therms, a figure surprisingly close to the calculated requirement of 47.7 therms.

"All the data available indicate that the weight of a calf at birth is not ordinarily influenced by the ration received by the mother during gestation. This is especially true with reference to the energy value of the ration, but may not hold good when the ration has been decidedly deficient in some constituent for a long period."

The data are tabulated and discussed in detail, and feed and weight records during pregnancy for each animal are shown by graphs.

Effects of feeding cottonseed products on the composition and properties of butter, C. H. Eckles and L. S. Palmer (*Missouri Sta. Research Bul. 27* (*1916*), *pp. 3–44, figs. 3*).—The investigations reported in this bulletin were confined chiefly to a study of the effects that the feeding of cottonseed products exerts on the physical and chemical constants of milk fat and on the standing-up quality of butter and its keeping and market qualities. Studies were also made on the cause of the effects, as well as several minor studies, such as the persistence of the effects and the typical characteristics of butter produced where cottonseed products are fed according to the ordinary practice in the South. The investigations of other workers in this field are reviewed, and results secured by them are tabulated with respect to the effect of the character of the roughage and the amount of cottonseed products fed upon the milk fat and butter.

In studying different phases of this subject at the station, 23 experiments were conducted in which 43 pure-bred animals of the university herd were used. There were 177 periods usually lasting about two weeks, in which samples were taken, and 2,033 chemical determinations and experimental observations were made, each in duplicate and frequently in triplicate. Of the great amount of data collected only those are reported which have a bearing upon the influence of feeding cottonseed products on the composition and properties of butter.

To test the effect of the oil in cottonseed products fed, eight cows were divided into four lots of two each and fed a basal ration of timothy hay and corn stover and a grain mixture of corn, bran, and linseed meal (4:2:1) in sufficient quantity to meet the demands of the Armsby standard. In addition, lot 1 was fed enough cottonseed meal to furnish 0.4, 0.6, and 0.8 lb. of oil per head daily during different periods of the experiment, lot 2 enough cottonseed meats, i. e., the kernel of the seed from which the oil had not been pressed, to furnish the same amounts of oil as were fed lot 1 during the corresponding periods, and lot 3 was fed 0.4, 0.6, and 0.8 lb. of unrefined cottonseed oil per head daily in the respective periods. Lot 4 was later carried through an experiment identical with the cottonseed meal lot. An examination of the effects of these rations on the physical and chemical constants of the milk fat showed that the character of the effects was similar for each lot of cows. This was manifested by a marked drop in the saponification value and the Reichert-Meissl number and a marked increase in the iodin value and melting point. The data secured indicate that the effects on the constitution of milk fat which accompany the feeding of cottonseed meal are due to the oil in the meal. There was, however, some evidence that less pronounced effects were secured when the oil was fed in the cottonseed meal than when it was added directly to a ration containing no cottonseed meal, especially when not more than 4 lbs. of cottonseed meal was fed daily. In studying the standing-up quality of the butter small cakes of butter 3 cm. square and 1 cm. thick were placed in a water-jacketed oven and the temperature gradually raised a degree or two at a time until the cake of butter lost its shape. Temperatures were maintained at each point for one-half to three-quarters of an hour. In general the basal ration samples lost their shape at from 32 to 35° C., while all the samples during the feeding of meal, meats, and oil withstood a temperature of from 40 to 43°. The maximum effects in almost every case were secured when 6 lbs. of meal, or its equivalent of oil, was fed.

In a study made of the influence of the character of roughage on the effect of cottonseed feeding, two experiments were conducted in which timothy hay was the sole roughage, three cows being used in the first experiment and two in the second. Each animal consumed from 12 to 15 lbs. of hay daily in addition to the above grain mixture. In each experiment a basal period of from two to three weeks was followed by a period of three weeks in which 4 lbs. of the grain mixture of each animal was replaced by 4 lbs. of cottonseed meal. Averaging the results of the two experiments, it was found that there was a drop in the saponification value and Reichert-Meissl number and an increase in the iodin value and melting point of the milk fat during the cottonseed meal periods. With regard to the standing-up quality of the butter, it was found that the basal ration butter lost its shape at about 34°, and the cottonseed meal ration butter at from 40 to 41°. The butter made during the feeding of cottonseed meal was inferior in market quality and superior in keeping quality to that made during the basal period.

In three experiments with individual cows, alfalfa hay was fed with the above grain mixture. In certain periods of these experiments different amounts of cottonseed meal replaced equal quantities by weight of the grain mixture. It was found that the fat constants were very similar with like amounts of meal and that they were very similar to those obtained when the same amount of meal was fed with timothy hay or timothy hay and corn stover.

Cottonseed meal was fed with alfalfa hay and corn silage to two lots of seven and eight cows each. One lot was fed for 62 days a daily basal ration of from 30 to 45 lbs. of silage, from 7 to 11 lbs. of alfalfa hay, and from 6 to 11 lbs. of the usual grain mixture. The other lot was fed the same ration in a first and fifth period. During the three intervening periods the grain mixture was replaced pound for pound with 2, 4, and 6 lbs. of cottonseed meal, respectively. It was found that there was a striking lack of effect on the physical and chemical constants of the milk fat when cottonseed meal was fed with these supplements. The only difference noted was an increase of 1.6° in melting point when the basal ration was changed to 6 lbs. of meal. Some effects on the butter due to the feeding of cottonseed meal were noted in this test, but these were not sufficient to detract from its market value. The basal ration butter lost its shape usually between 29 and 30°, while this was increased to 33° during the feeding of 4 lbs. of cottonseed meal and to 34.5° during the feeding of 6 lbs. of meal. Butter made during the feeding of cottonseed meal was decidedly superior in keeping quality as compared with the basal ration butter, and the larger the amount of cottonseed meal fed the better the keeping quality of the butter.

In order to investigate further the relation of roughage to the effects of cottonseed meal feeding, two lots of three cows each were fed for six consecutive periods, the first and sixth being basal periods and the others experimental. One lot received 0.6 lb. of crude cottonseed oil per cow in addition to the usual grain mixture in each of the experimental periods. The roughage was the same for each lot in the same period, but varied for the different periods. The results of this experiment confirmed those of the previous experiments, that silage feeding has a marked influence on the effects of adding cottonseed oil to the ration. It was also found that this influence was practically as great when from 20 to 25 lbs. of silage was fed as when from 30 to 40 lbs. was fed. Data from lot 2, which received no cottonseed oil, indicate that this result is due to the effect which silage itself exerts upon the milk fat constants. Moreover, the effect of silage on the fat constants is in the opposite direction to that resulting from cottonseed meal or cottonseed oil feeding. From this the authors conclude that corn silage contains a specific substance which counteracts the effects of feeding cottonseed products. The nature of this counteracting material is being investigated. There was practically no difference in the composition of the milk fat due to the feeding of different dry feed rations in this experiment.

Several preliminary experiments were carried on in which cottonseed meal was fed with pasture, but omitted since the milk fat was clearly affected by underfeeding in the periods when no cottonseed meal was fed. In order to prevent underfeeding when animals were turned to pasture, an experiment was conducted with four lots of two cows each in which an ample grain ration supplemented mature pasture. Three of the lots received cottonseed products during their pasture period as a part of the grain mixture. The fourth lot received no cottonseed products. A fifth lot of two cows was fed 110 lbs. of green alfalfa per head daily during this experiment. The cottonseed products consisted of from 1 to 3 lbs. of cottonseed meal per head for the different lots plus an amount of crude cottonseed oil equal to the amount of oil in the cottonseed meal fed. The milk fat produced by the lot fed the usual grain mixture on blue grass pasture and by the lot fed green alfalfa was of similar composition. The principal change in the milk fat of these two lots due to the change from dry feed to pasture or green alfalfa was a decrease in the saponification value and melting point. The milk fat of the lots fed cottonseed products showed a marked decrease in the volatile fatty acids which resulted in a higher melting point. This was more or less proportional to the quantity of cottonseed products fed. With reference to the standing-up quality of the butter, it was found that when the cows were changed from the basal ration to pasture or green alfalfa there was a softening effect on the butter. However, when cottonseed products were fed on pasture there was a marked improvement in the standing-up quality of the butter as compared with butter from pasture rations containing no cottonseed products. When 0.6 lb. of cottonseed oil was fed the butter had a standing-up temperature of 38°. The butter from the lots fed cottonseed products showed decidedly better keeping qualities than that from the other lots.

Two cows were placed upon the usual grain mixture, plus a little gluten meal for one cow, and timothy hay. After about a month 4 lbs. of cottonseed meal was substituted for 4 lbs. of the grain mixture for each cow and continued for 70 days. The meal was then increased to 5 lbs. for 30 days and to 6 lbs. for a final 30-day period. An examination of the physical and chemical constants of the milk fat of these cows throughout the test and of the keeping qualities and other characteristics of butter from these cows and from two herds of cows in Georgia, one of which had been fed cottonseed meal for six months and the other cottonseed for from four to six months, showed that the effects of feeding cottonseed products persist as long as such feeding is continued.

The results of the experiments are discussed and their practical application pointed out. It is stated that "the feeding of large quantities of cottonseed meal and whole cottonseed, as still practiced in many localities in the South, must be considerably modified if the butter industry of that part of the country is to attain its proper place in the butter industry of the nation. The use of the whole seed as a feed for dairy cattle is to be strongly discouraged on account of its excessive oil content." However, "the results indicate that 1 to 1.5 lbs. of whole seed, or 2 to 3 lbs. of cottonseed meal added to the ration of cows on fresh pasture will exert a decided improvement on the quality of the butter. Such a practice would also be of value in preventing the underfeeding which cows frequently suffer, often with serious results upon the milk flow, when first turned to pasture."

A list of the literature cited is included.

Silage feeding (*Washington Sta. Bul. 136 (1917), p. 10*).—In a progress report of experiments with four kinds of silage for dairy cows, it is stated that pea and oat silage compared favorably with corn silage, keeping in excellent condition and being relished and eaten as readily as corn by the cows. Wheat silage was slightly inferior to corn silage, both from the standpoint of milk production and the way the feed was relished by the cow. Clover silage fed in comparison with the other silage feeds showed little or no difference in its effect upon production. Cows failed to eat it quite so well at first, but upon becoming accustomed to it apparently ate it with as much relish as the corn silage.

[Feeding experiments with dairy cows] (*New Mexico Sta. Rpt. 1916, p. 55*).—A medium concentrate ration for dairy cows on average irrigated pasture did not prove profitable. The results of an experiment in the winter of 1915–16 favored the use of corn silage in a limited way to replace alfalfa hay for dairy cows.

[Machine milking versus hand milking], E. V. ELLINGTON (*Idaho Sta. Bul. 92 (1916), p. 17*).—In tests of a mechanical milker with the university herd for eight months of one lactation period, it was found that with the same amount of labor necessary to milk the cows by hand they could be milked three times daily with the milking machine, with a resulting average increase in the milk flow of 22 per cent. One Holstein cow that was difficult to milk produced in eight months in 1916, with the mechanical milker, 11,795 lbs. of milk, containing 360 lbs. of fat. During similar periods on hand milking she gave, in 1915, 8,001.5 lbs. of milk, containing 274 lbs. of fat, and in 1914, 8,500 lbs. of milk, containing 336 lbs. of fat. It is stated that with hard-milking cows the milking machine apparently lengthens the lactation period.

Creamery records, O. W. HOLMES (*Idaho Sta. Bul. 90 (1916), pp. 20*).—This bulletin outlines and explains in detail the use of a proposed system of records for creameries. The forms illustrated and explained include a daily cream receiving sheet, route or station report, patron's cream statement and check, sales slip, ledger sales sheet, cash record sheet for cashbook, daily sales record, daily make record, butter maker's report, monthly butter fat and overrun report, expense record, monthly inventory, check tag for cans and ice cream packers, and retail milk route report.

VETERINARY MEDICINE.

Veterinary therapeutics, E. W. HOARE (*Chicago: Alexander Eger, 1916, 3. ed., pp. XXIV+943*).—The first of the three parts of this work (pp. 1-199) consists of a discussion of the diagnosis and general symptoms of disease; the care, management, and nursing of sick animals; the actions and uses of drugs; prescribing and administration of medicines; and veterinary pharmacy. The second part (pp. 200–556) is devoted to materia medica; and the third part (pp. 559–912) to special therapeutics. Numerous formulas are given in an appendix (pp. 864-906).

Biology, general and medical, J. McFARLAND (*Philadelphia and London: W. B. Saunders Co., 1916, 3. ed., rev., pp. 457, pls. 3, figs. 151*).—The third edition of the work previously noted (E. S. R., 24, p. 584). The subject matter has been corrected and some additions made to bring the material to date.

Microbiology, C. E. MARSHALL ET AL. (*Philadelphia: P. Blakiston's Son & Co., 1917, 2. ed., rev. and enl., pp. XXIV+900, pl. 1, figs. 183*).—This is the second edition of the work previously noted (E. S. R., 26, p. 372). The chapters originally by J. L. Todd have been revised by E. E. Tyzzer. A chapter on intestinal microbiology by W. J. MacNeal and one on microbial diseases of insects by Zae Northrup have been added.

Applied immunology, B. A. THOMAS and R. H. IVY (*Philadelphia and London: J. B. Lippincott Co., 1916, 2. ed., rev., pp. XVII+364, pls. 26, figs. 451*).—This is the second edition of the work previously noted (E. S. R., 34, p. 275). A number of additions and some new material have been incorporated.

The cause of anaphylaxis and the nature of the antibodies, J. DANYSZ (*Compt. Rend. Acad. Sci. [Paris], 163 (1916), No. 26, pp. 985–989*).—Experiments are reported which show that the antigens do not appear to be directly assimilable, but by their introduction produce substances which later transform them to assimilable products. This change consists of the formation of a precipitate which in nonfatal cases is again dissolved. It is indicated that the formation of the embolus in the blood vessel produces the symptoms of anaphylaxis and brings about the shock. The substance formed on the introduction of the antigen appears to be of the nature of a precipitin.

Analysis of the anaphylactic and immune reactions by means of the isolated guinea pig lungs, W. H. MANWARING and Y. KUSAMA (*Jour. Immunol., 2 (1917), No. 2, pp. 157–165, fig. 1*).—Experimental data submitted show that three essential factors are involved in anaphylactic and immune reactions studied by the perfusion method, viz. cellular hypersensitiveness, or the anaphylactic response of the hypersensitive fixed pulmonary tissues; humoral anaphylaxis, or the chemical response (anaphylatoxin formation) of the anaphylactic blood; and humoral immunity, or the inhibiting or protecting action of the immune blood.

The immune guinea pig, from the data obtained, shows a seemingly paradoxical phenomenon, the coexistence of a fixed cellular hypersensitiveness and a humoral immunity.

The disappearance of agglutinin from the blood of anaphylactic and normal animals, HILDA HEMPL (*Jour. Immunol., 2 (1917), No. 2, pp. 141–145*).—Guinea pigs weighing between 400 and 450 gm. were sensitized with

0.004 cc. of rabbit serum given subcutaneously. Twenty-one days later 0.2 cc. of coli-agglutinating rabbit serum was given intracardially. The sensitized animal displayed moderate anaphylactic symptoms, while the control did not react. Samples of blood were taken from the hearts of both control and experimental animals five minutes and two hours after injection and the agglutinin titer determined. The blood of the sensitized animal showed an agglutinin content higher than that of the control animal five minutes after reinjection, and a lower content than that of the control two hours later.

It is concluded in general that "a foreign serum disappears more quickly from the blood of an animal sensitized to that serum than from that of a normal animal. It disappears more quickly from the blood of highly reacting animals than from that of slightly reacting animals." The individual variation and the need of results from a large number of animals to give definite conclusions is indicated.

The antigenic properties of β-nucleoproteins, H. G. WELLS (*Jour. Biol. Chem., 28 (1916), No. 1, pp. 11–16*).—The results of the study reported are summarized as follows:

The so-called β-nucleoproteins obtained from various tissues by extracting with boiling water possess definite antigenic properties demonstrable by the anaphylaxis reaction. As there are but few known proteins that retain their antigenic capacity after boiling, this observation may indicate something as to the nature of the protein complex of β-nucleoproteins. The proteins of α-nucleoproteins are, on the contrary, very susceptible to chemical and physical changes. β-Nucleoproteins from beef pancreas, beef spleen, and pig pancreas seem to be similar but not identical, as far as can be determined by the anaphylaxis reaction.

See also a previous note (E. S. R., 32 p. 179).

Transformation of pseudoglobulin into euglobulin, W. N. BERG (*U. S. Dept. Agr., Jour. Agr. Research, 8 (1917), No. 12, pp. 449–456*).—As indicated by Banzhaf,[1] the author presents evidence of a transformation of pseudoglobulin into euglobulin from data obtained in the concentration of anthrax, diphtheria, and tetanus sera when the sera were heated at 60° C. in the presence of 30 per cent saturated ammonium sulphate. It is noted that the amounts transformed were considerable in some instances, while in one case the amount was so small as to indicate that there was no transformation at all.

The experimental technique used was that described by Eichhorn, Berg, and Kelser (E. S. R., 36, p. 577).

The failure of Homer (E. S. R., 35, p. 680) to observe any transformation of pseudoglobulin into euglobulin is considered by the author as probably due to the use of analytical technique that was not delicate enough to detect such slight transformation, and to errors incidental to the handling of large amounts of serum mixtures.

Weyl's handbook of hygiene: Meat inspection, edited by C. FRAENKEN (*Weyl's Handbuch der Hygiene: Fleishbeschau. Leipsig: Johann Ambrosius Barth, 2. ed., Lieferung 23 (1915), pp. IX–227, figs. 33*).—In this part of the 8-volume Handbook of Hygiene meat inspection is dealt with by R. Edelmann. A work by the author on the subject has previously been noted (E. S. R., 35, p. 879).

Are uniform regulations feasible among the different American countries for the prevention of the introduction and dissemination of diseases of animals? A. D. MELVIN (*Jour. Amer. Vet. Med. Assoc., 50 (1916), No. 3, pp. 361–366*).—This is an abstract of a paper in which the author calls attention to the

---

[1] Collected Studies Bur. Lab. Dept. Health N. Y. City, 7 (1912–13), pp. 114–116.

desirability of entering into some kind of cooperation for the exchange of information with regard to contagious diseases of animals, and so far as practicable of adopting uniform regulations for preventing the spread of such diseases. It is pointed out that certain fundamentals should and doubtless could be followed, although the different conditions in different countries will probably make an absolutely uniform set of regulations for all American countries impractical.

Papers on the subject by J. Besnard, chief of the National Veterinary Service, Chile; R. Munoz Jimenez, of Uruguay; and F. Etchegoyen, of Cuba, are included.

Department of veterinary science and bacteriology (*Nevada Sta. Rpt. 1916, pp. 38–44, fig. 1*).—Investigational work with equine anemia was suspended through the scarcity of material for study in eastern Nevada. Investigations have shown that on some ranches anthrax and hemorrhagic septicemia occur simultaneously, evidence of double infection having been found in two animals.

Work on the separation of the active principle of hog-cholera serum by fractional precipitation is noted as having been successful.

Continuing the work on contagious epithelioma (E. S. R., 35, p. 885), results were obtained which appeared to indicate that the immunity conferred by vaccination without subsequent exposure is of comparatively brief duration. Experiments are being conducted to determine the duration of the immunity conferred by vaccination and that acquired through a natural attack of the disease. It is indicated, however, that too much dependence should not be placed upon vaccination as a preventive measure when exposure does not follow within a brief period of time. An attempt has been made to improve the vaccine by eliminating other bacteria in order to prevent secondary infections. Some experiments are reported in which the vaccine treatment was only moderately successful. The lesions in these birds were characteristic but the symptoms were chiefly catarrhal. A careful bacteriological study showed that the principal cause of the disease was a mixed bacterial infection. It is indicated that while the experiments are far from conclusive they emphasize the need of further study of secondary bacterial infections, and that the vaccine must probably be of a mixed type rather than absolutely free from other organisms as attempted in the improved technique for its preparation.

Experiments in the immunization of fowls affected with chicken cholera by vaccination followed by inoculation to determine the degree of immunity conferred by the intramuscular inoculation of fully virulent cultures were not successful. It is noted, however, that the clinical results indicate that a degree of immunity sufficient to protect birds against a natural infection is thus conferred. It is deemed probable that the method will eventually prove satisfactory from a clinical point of view, even if the birds treated are unable to resist artificial infection.

Annual report on the Punjab Veterinary College, Civil Veterinary Department, Punjab, and the Government Cattle Farm, Hissar, for the year 1915–16, H. T. Pease, J. Farmer, and R. Branford (*Ann. Rpt. Punjab Vet. Col. and Civ. Vet. Dept., 1915–16, pp. II+2+17+XVII*).—The usual annual report (E. S. R., 35, p. 483).

Complement fixation in abortions of women, with special reference to the Bacillus abortus and the B. abortivo-equinus, P. F. Williams and J. A. Kolmer (*Amer. Jour. Obstet., 75 (1917), No. 2, pp. 193–203*).—Complement fixation reactions with polyvalent antigens of *B. abortus* (Bang) and *B. abortivo-equinus* and the sera of 50 women aborting in the early months of pregnancy yielded negative results. These organisms were thus apparently not etiological factors in the cases reported.

It is indicated that "since the bacillus of epidemic abortion of cows has been found in milk it is advisable to subject aborting cows to rigid bacteriological and immunological tests for the bacilli before permitting the distribution and consumption of their milk, although it has not been definitely proved that the *B. abortus* is capable of producing abortion in women."

The specific and nonspecific action of rabbit blood serum in the complement-fixation test, I. F. HUDDLESON (*Jour. Immunol., 2 (1917), No. 2, pp. 147-156*).—Experiments by the author at the Michigan Experiment Station, to determine whether rabbits would become infected and show *Bacillus abortus* antibodies in their blood as a result of ingesting milk reacting positively to the agglutination and complement-fixation tests, are reported in detailed tabular form and briefly discussed.

It is concluded that the data do not furnish sufficient evidence to condemn naturally infected milk as dangerous to rabbits by ingestion, since it shows no pathogenic action and no antigenic action. A nonspecific absorption of complement was found to take place in the presence of inactivated rabbit blood serum and a bacterial antigen of *B. abortus*. No explanation of this nonspecific peculiarity of rabbit blood serum is offered.

Resistance of the anthrax bacillus to the action of sodium chlorid solution, J. B. BORDOLI (*Rev. Hig. y Sanidad Vet. [Spain], 6 (1917), No. 10, pp. 747-751*).—Experimental data are submitted which show that anthrax bacilli are not affected by a 10 per cent solution of sodium chlorid, even when in contact with the solution for more than a month. Guinea pigs injected with a suspension of the organisms which had been in contact with the sodium chlorid solution developed symptoms and died in two days with anthrax.

Human anthrax.—Report of an outbreak among tannery workers, W. H. BROWN and C. E. SIMPSON (*Jour. Amer. Med. Assoc., 68 (1917), No. 8, pp. 608, 609*).—Twenty-five cases of human anthrax which were reported within a period of four months are noted. The clinical histories of twenty of these cases which appeared to have been infected from a common source, namely, three tanneries located in adjoining towns, are given in tabular form.

The data are briefly discussed and recommendations for the control and treatment of the disease submitted.

Report on foot-and-mouth disease from 1912–1916, P. VAN HOEK (*Dept. Landb. Nijv. en Handel [Netherlands], Verslag. en Meded. Dir. Landb., No. 4 (1916), pp. 165, pls. 19*).—This is a detailed report of the occurrence of and control work with foot-and-mouth disease in the Netherlands from 1912 to 1916 and in other countries since 1911.

Second report of the special committee for the detection of glanders, E. B. ACKERMAN ET AL. (*Jour. Amer. Vet. Med. Assoc., 50 (1917), No. 6, pp. 747-757*).—This report, by a committee of the American Veterinary Medical Association, considers the cause, susceptibility, period of incubation, modes of infection, symptoms, and the various diagnostic tests for glanders and recommends in general that uniform measures for the control and eradication of the disease by the sanitary officers of various States and Provinces be adopted. See also a previous note (E. S. R., 29, p. 499).

Rinderpest in swine, with experiments upon transmission from cattle and carabao to swine and vice versa, W. H. BOYNTON (*Philippine Agr. Rev. [English Ed.], 9 (1916), No. 4, pp. 288-336, pls. 2, figs. 10*).—The data submitted show that cattle, carabao, and pigs vary but slightly in susceptibility to rinderpest. It appears that the disease can be transmitted practically as readily from one type of animal to the other as among their individual kind.

The treatment of tetanus with cicutin hydrobromid, ROCTON (*Rec. Méd. Vét., 92 (1916), No. 23, pp. 684-686*).—A case is reported in which the injection of cicutin hydrobromid into a mare which had already manifested general symptoms of tetanus yielded excellent results.

A contribution to the ophthalmic tuberculin test for the diagnosis of bovine tuberculosis, A. M. BERGMAN (*Ztschr. Infektionskrank. u. Hyg. Haustiere, 17 (1915), No. 1–2, pp. 37–67, pls. 3*).—Tabulated experimental data are reported and discussed.

A tuberculin consisting of 92 per cent of a bovine strain and 8 per cent of a human strain with 40 per cent glycerin was found to yield excellent results. Of 107 animals tested, 87 were tuberculous and 20 nontuberculous. Of the tuberculous animals, 70 reacted positively, 11 were doubtful, and 6 negative. Of the 20 nontuberculous animals, one reacted positively. A second test on the same eye yielded identical results. From the results thus obtained the ophthalmic test is considered to be the most preferable diagnostic test, especially in cases where the animals have been previously sensitized. In the first tuberculin test a sympathetic reaction in the untreated eye was obtained in about 4 per cent of the positive reactions.

A previous sensitization is considered to be of value not only in yielding a more distinct second reaction but also in bringing about an earlier response after instillation of the tuberculin. Repeated instillations of tuberculin at intervals of from one to three days were found to cause a decrease in susceptibility after four instillations. The reaction was evident very early, but also disappeared early, in some cases five hours after the instillation. The ability of the eye to become accustomed to repeated treatment of tuberculin is considered not to be of any practical significance.

Bovine tuberculosis and milk for children, G. REGNÉR (*Deut. Vrtljschr. Öffentl. Gsndhtspflege, 47 (1915), No. 1; abs. in Internat. Centbl. Gesam. Tuberkulose Forsch., 10 (1916), No. 6, p. 166*).—The author concludes that human tuberculosis is transmitted chiefly from individual to individual, but the disease may also be transmitted by bovines with open tuberculosis, especially udder infections. In such cases milk is the carrier of the infection, and the infection in most cases takes place in childhood. In a campaign against the disease measures against the transmission of the disease from individual to individual must be devised and all possibilities of infection from bovine sources eliminated. Only milk from tuberculosis-free animals should be used for children. The usual hygienic measures in connection with the use of milk must also be strictly observed.

Box elder poisoning. H. G. BOND (*Vet. Alumni Quart. [Ohio State Univ.], 4 (1916), No. 3, pp. 111, 112*).—This is a report of the poisoning of cows through feeding on the leaves and seed pods of box elder, which resulted fatally in three of the four animals affected.

Malignant catarrhal fever of cattle in Kansas, L. W. Goss (*Vet. Alumni Quart. [Ohio State Univ.], 4 (1916), No. 1, pp. 4–6*).—This reports upon studies made of cases of this disease during an outbreak which took place in the fall of 1916.

Bovine onchocerciasis in South America, PIETTRE (*Bul. Soc. Cent. Méd. Vét., 92 (1916), No. 14, pp. 202, 203*).—It is stated that an Onchocerca which resembles *O. gibsoni*, although differing to some extent, has been found to occur frequently in cattle slaughtered in South America. At the Frigorifico La Negra in Argentina 70 per cent of the cattle show extensive lesions on the cervical ligament and 25 per cent localizations on the external face of the great trochanter. At the Frigorifico Uruguaya in Uruguay 90 per cent show cervical lesions and 18 per cent lesions on the trochanter. The localization of this Onchocerca is quite different from the type occurring in France.

The parasite is longer than the European form, females reaching 70 cm. in length, and the lesions are more serious than those produced by the French form. The extensive congestion may give rise to the formation of large pockets in the inflamed connective tissue and frequently to encysted purulent collections.

Bovine sarcosporidiosis, E. E. FRANCO and I. BORGES (*Arq. Inst. Bact. Camara Pestana, 4 (1916), No. 3, pp. 269–289, pls. 11*).—Six cases of this affection in cattle from the Province of Alemtejo, Portugal, were found to be caused by a species belonging to the new genus Besnoitia, namely, *B. besnoiti.* The lesions in the form of spherical yellowish granules from 0.25 to 0.4 mm. in diameter were present, especially in the superficial aponeuroses and in the subcutaneous tissue. In generalized infections they occurred in the connective tissue of all parts of the body, head, trunk, and limbs, but were most numerous on the thighs and flanks. A detailed report is given of microscopical studies.

A list of 12 references to the literature is included.

Vesicular stomatitis in cattle, A. EICHHORN (*Amer. Jour. Vet. Med., 12 (1917), No. 3, pp. 162, 170*).—An account given by the author at the twentieth annual meeing of the U. S. Live Stock Sanitary Association at Chicago, Ill., in December, 1916, of the recent outbreak of this affection detected at Kansas City. The author found the manifestations in the mouth to resemble those of foot-and-mouth disease so closely that the differentiation was only possible through inoculation tests.

"The transmission of the disease to horses from cattle and the failure to transmit it to pigs, of course, would practically eliminate foot-and-mouth disease; but other things also substantiate a negative diagnosis as far as foot-and-mouth disease is concerned. Not a single case did we observe with foot lesions, either in the originally infected animals or in the exposed cattle. . . . Temperatures were taken of about 100 animals, and in not a single instance did we observe a temperature over 103° F. . . .

"As far as the etiology of the disease is concerned nothing definite has yet been developed."

An outbreak of vesicular stomatitis, J. R. MOHLER (*U. S. Dept. Agr., Bur. Anim. Indus. Serv. and Regulatory Announcement 116 (1917), pp. 105–107; Jour. Amer. Vet. Med. Assoc., 50 (1917), No. 6, pp. 667–670*).—This is a brief account of the outbreak of vesicular stomatitis that took place during the fall of 1916, a report of which by Eichhorn is noted above.

A note on the preparation and use of agglutinin from beans, M. DORSET and R. R. HENLEY (*Jour. Amer. Vet. Med. Assoc., 50 (1917), No. 6, pp. 699–702*).—The following improved procedure for preparing the bean extract used to secure a clear serum in hog-cholera work, as previously noted by the authors (E. S. R., 35, p. 488), is described:

The beans commonly known as the "Wisconsin pea bean" have been found to yield the most satisfactory results. Other varieties may prove satisfactory, but appear to be distinctly lower in agglutinative power. The dry beans should be finely ground, so that about 70 per cent will pass through a 20-mesh sieve.

To 20 gm. of the bean meal 100 cc. of physiological salt solution, containing 0.5 per cent crystallized phenol and heated to 60° C., is added. The mixture is thoroughly stirred and placed for about one hour in a water bath, the temperature of which is maintained at 69 to 70°. When the extraction is completed the entire contents of the flask containing the bean meal is poured into a cheesecloth bag and the residue thoroughly pressed. The liquid obtained, while still hot, is mixed with powdered infusorial earth in the proportion of about 2 gm. to 100 cc. of the extract. The mixture is then poured on a folded filter, the first runnings returned to the funnel, and again passed through the filter. Before use the materials should be passed through a bacteria-proof filter.

In agglutinating the corpuscles in the defibrinated blood, as previously described, the authors have found the use of a saturated sodium chlorid solution more satisfactory than the use of solid sodium chlorid.

Pseudotuberculosis in swine, caseous adenitis, and visceral pseudotubercles, P. CHAUSSÉ (*Rec. Méd. Vét., 92 (1916), No. 23, pp. 679–682, fig. 1*).— The author reports and discusses five observations and points out that the differentiation of such cases from true tuberculosis is not always an easy one. The characteristics of the nodules form the basis for the differentiation. The cause of the disease has not been determined. The bacillus of Koch, however, was not found in the nodules. The importance of the differentiation of the disease from true tuberculosis is emphasized.

The treatment of surgical foot lesions in the horse with sugar, P. BIMBI (*Mod. Zooiatro, Parte Sci., 27 (1916), No. 4, pp. 109–116; abs. in Internat. Inst. Bedeutung des Aneurysma Verminosum Equi. Inaug. Diss., Univ. Bern, 1914*). The author reports the treatment of six cases of foot injury in horses with sugar, the results of which confirm those obtained by Bussano, previously noted (E. S. R., 36, p. 178). The use of sugar as a dressing promotes the rapid formation of both the soft and horny tissue of the foot to a greater degree than the other dressings commonly employed.

Notes on the occurrence of equine sporotrichosis in Montana and the "blastomycotic" form of Sporotrichum schencki-beurmanni, K. F. MEYER (*Proc. Soc. Expt. Biol. and Med., 14 (1916), No. 1, pp. 23, 24*).—The author records the occurrence of sporotrichosis endemically in Montana.

A contribution to the knowledge of the clinical importance of verminous aneurism of the horse, C. J. FOLMER (*Beitrag zur Kenntnis der Klinischen Bedeutung des Aneurysma VerminosumEqui. Inaug. Diss., Univ. Bern, 1914*).— *pp. 127+IV, pls. 16*).—The author first reviews the literature on the subject in connection with a bibliography of 37 titles which is appended, and then deals with studies made of *Sclerostomum bidentatum* and its effect upon the horse. Fifteen cases which resulted fatally are reported upon at length.

The larvæ of Gastrophilus equi and G. hæmorrhoidalis and infectious anemia of the horse, F. FAVERO (*Nuovo Ercolani, 21 (1916), Nos. 1, pp. 4–7; 2, pp. 17–21; abs. in Rev. Appl. Ent., Ser. B, 5 (1917), No. 2, p. 27*).—The author reports upon work the results of which he considers to disprove the findings of the Seyderhelms, previously noted (E. S. R., 35. p. 80), as regards the importance of oestrid larvæ in the etiology of infectious anemia of the horse.

A synoptical key to the adult tæniod cestodes of the dog, cat, and some related carnivores, M. C. HALL (*Jour. Amer. Vet. Med. Assoc., 50 (1916), No. 3, pp. 356–360*).

The value of post-mortem examinations, W. C. THOMPSON (*New Jersey Stas. Hints to Poultrymen, 5 (1916), No. 3, pp. 4*).—In addition to brief directions for the examination of sick and dead birds, this contains a chart showing causes, symptoms, and prevention and treatment of the more common diseases of poultry.

A comparative study of Bacterium pullorum and B. sanguinarium, L. F. RETTGER and S. A. KOSER (*Jour. Med. Research, 35 (1917), No. 3, pp. 443–458*).— This is a report of a systematic study made with a view to determining the possible identity or exact relationship of the organisms of bacillary white diarrhea and fowl typhoid.

"Despite the several characters which the two organisms have in common, and particularly the serological reactions, *B. pullorum* and *B. sanguinarium* constitute two separate and distinct types, and each bears a specific relationship to the disease with which it has been associated in the past, namely, bacillary white diarrhea or fowl typhoid.

"*B. pullorum* differs from *B. sanguinarium* in several important respects, aside from morphology. Dextrin, maltose, and dulcite are attacked by the latter with the production of acid, but no gas. *B. pullorum*, on the other hand, produces no visible change in media containing these agents except slight alkali production. *B. pullorum* acts upon dextrose and mannite with the evolution of appreciable amounts of gas, while the fowl typhoid bacillus, whether recently isolated or artificially cultivated for many years, does not produce gas in any of the carbohydrate media. Furthermore, prolonged cultivation of *B. pullorum* in the laboratory does not cause this organism to lose its power of producing gas in dextrose and mannite broth.

"The methyl red test applied to cultures grown in one per cent maltose bouillon was found to furnish a practical method of distinguishing between the two types of bacteria, *B. sanguinarium* being methyl red positive and *B. pullorum* negative.

"While both organisms are pathogenic to fowls of all ages in experimental inoculation, *B. pullorum* manifests itself only as the cause of natural epidemic infection in young chicks. On the other hand, *B. sanguinarium* attacks fowls of different ages, although it is of relatively little, if indeed any, significance as the cause of epidemic disease in very young chicks."

Fowl cholera and other hemorrhagic septicemia immunization experiments, B. GALLAGHER (*Jour. Amer. Vet. Med. Assoc., 50 (1917), No. 6, pp. 708–728*).— Tabulated experimental immunization data are reported and discussed.

In the experiments an attempt was made to produce immunity to hemorrhagic septicemia by employing as the immunizing agent living organisms of a strain of fowl cholera bacilli nonvirulent for fowls. In one case a mixture of killed organisms of both virulent and nonvirulent strains of fowl cholera bacilli was used. Fowls, rabbits, guinea pigs, and white rats were selected for test animals, and virulent strains of *Bacillus avisepticus, B. bovisepticus, B. suisepticus*, and *B. ovisepticus* were used for determining the degree of resistance required.

It is concluded in general that no noticeable resistance is conferred on fowls by the use of killed fowl cholera bacilli as immunizing agents. One strain of fowl cholera organisms conferred a marked resistance to a highly virulent strain of the same bacillus. The immunity, however, was found not to be absolute, since dilutions of from 0.01 to 1 cc. of a virulent culture are usually fatal in fowls, rabbits, and guinea pigs. The same strain also conferred a fair degree of immunity on rabbits against certain strains of *B. bovisepticus* and complete immunity to a virulent strain of *B. suisepticus*.

It is indicated that "there is an unknown factor at work in natural fowl cholera outbreaks, since such outbreaks, if due to the fowl cholera bacillus alone, would be easily produced by feeding a virulent culture to susceptible birds. We have failed to produce any symptoms of cholera by feeding several highly virulent strains of fowl cholera organisms."

Epithelioma contagiosum of quail, B. GALLAGHER (*Jour. Amer. Vet. Med. Assoc., 50 (1916), No. 3, pp. 366–369*).—The author reports upon an outbreak of bird pox or avian diphtheria at Kansas City among quail received from Mexico during January, 1916, principally for the purpose of stocking game preserves. Eighty-five per cent of some 400 birds under observation succumbed in a period of five weeks. It is stated that there was no indication of the disease during the ten days that the birds were held in quarantine at a point on the border.

RURAL ENGINEERING.

Fifteenth annual report of the Reclamation Service, 1915–16, A. P. DAVIS (*Ann. Rpt. Reclamation Serv.* [*U. S.*], *15 (1916), pp. 806, fig. 1*).—This report relates in particular to the work completed and in progress during the fiscal year ended June 30, 1916, but in addition contains a brief history of construction and engineering features from the beginning of the enterprise in order that its methods, progress, and results may be more readily understood.

Seventh biennial report of the State engineer to the governor of North Dakota for the biennial period ending June 30, 1916, J. W. BLISS (*Bien. Rpt. State Engin. N. Dak., 7 (1915–16), pp. 162, pls. 26*).—This report of work and expenditures includes data on roads and bridges, measurements of flow of streams of the State, and mining.

Surface water supply of Pacific slope basins in California, 1914 (*U. S. Geol. Survey, Water-Supply Paper 391 (1917), pp. 9–334+XXXVI, pls. 2*).— This report, prepared in cooperation with the State of California, contains the results of measurements of flow made on Pacific coast drainage basins in California, together with a list of gauging stations and publications relating to water resources.

Surface water supply of Missouri River Basin, 1914 (*U. S. Geol. Survey, Water-Supply Paper 386 (1917), pp. 7–220+XLI, pls. 3*).—This report, prepared in cooperation with the States of Colorado, Montana, Nebraska, and South Dakota, presents the results of measurements of flow made on the Missouri River and tributary basins during 1914. Additional sections are included on steam-gauging stations and a list of publications relating to water resources.

Surface water supply of Hudson Bay and upper Mississippi River Basins, 1915 (*U. S. Geol. Survey, Water-Supply Paper 405 (1917), pp. 7–215+XXX, pls. 4*).—This report, prepared in cooperation with the States of Minnesota, Wisconsin, Iowa, and Illinois, contains the results of measurements of flow made on the Hudson Bay and upper Mississippi drainage basins, together with an appendix of gauging stations and a list of publications relating to water resources.

Second report on the water powers of Alabama, B. M. and M. R. HALL (*Geol. Survey Ala. Bul. 17 (1916), pp. 448, pls. 19, figs. 4*).—This is a second report on the water powers of Alabama, giving the results of measurements of flow made on the Apalachicola, Choctawhatchee, Escambia, and Mobile River basins, together with river profiles and miscellaneous information.

Profile surveys of rivers in Wisconsin (*U. S. Geol. Survey, Water-Supply Paper 417 (1917), pp. 16, pls. 32*).—This report, prepared under the direction of W. H. Herron and in cooperation with the State of Wisconsin, describes the general features of natural drainage in Wisconsin and gives plans and profiles resulting from river surveys of the Peshtigo, Chippewa, Black, and Wisconsin River basins.

The economical use of irrigation water, W. L. POWERS (*Oregon Sta. Bul. 140 (1917), pp. 3–79, figs. 15*).—This is a preliminary report of experiments with different volumes of water applied to the chief soils and crops of Oregon during 1915–16, made under a cooperative agreement between the station and the Division of Irrigation Investigations of the U. S. Department of Agriculture. The soils studied ranged from clay loam to coarse sand.

"In Powder Valley, the maximum yield of potatoes was obtained with 7.79 in., of barley with 16.3 in., and of timothy with 30.55 in. In Wallowa Valley grain yielded highest with 12 in., and alfalfa showed little increase with amounts ranging from 18 to 33 in. In Deschutes Valley grain yielded best with 8 to 17 in., and meadows with 26 in. The most crop per unit of water with native meadows on central Oregon marshes was obtained with from 10 to 12 in., and the maximum yield with an average of about 18 in. depth an acre. These meadows can be greatly improved in productiveness and a higher efficiency from irrigation water secured by seeding in tame grasses and clovers. On sandy upland at Paisley, the most economical yield was received with from 11.16 to 18 in., and the maximum yield with from 32 to 34 in. The best yield on black sage land in Harney Valley was secured from 6 in. on grain, 8 in. on peas, and 18 in. on alfalfa. In Goose Lake Valley the depth giving maximum yield was 7.5 in. for potatoes, 9 to 16 in. for grain, and 18 in. for alfalfa. In Rogue River Valley 10 in. depth gave the maximum yield of sugar beets, and 6 in. the maximum yield of corn." Results secured in the Willamette Valley from several crops with different amounts of water and the effect of crop rotation and manure in lowering the amount of water required are also reported. "A close relation was found between irrigation, fluctuations in the water table, the substrata, and concentration of alkali on different flat areas."

With reference to the effect of soil texture on the economical use of irrigation water, it was found that "the coarser soils generally have a low water requirement and a comparatively low amount of surface area, pore space, organic matter, and are apt to be medium in fertility. The light, frequent irrigations required on these soils necessitate more waste and it is impracticable to use as small an amount of water on these soils as on the soils of finer texture.

"The kind of crop affects the amount of water required. Alfalfa and other meadow crops are requiring relatively large amounts of water, grain and field peas but medium amounts, and cultivated crops, such as potatoes, still less.

"The altitude and accompanying climatic conditions affect the irrigation requirements. . . . In general for the same soils and crops where 3 ft. depth is needed per season up to 2,000 ft. elevation, 2 ft. is a reasonable amount at 3,000 ft. elevation, and 1.5 ft. for each season is a reasonable amount for elevation of 4,000 ft. or more. Drying or other effects of the weather are intensified at the lower altitudes.

"Soil fertility is one of the most important factors affecting irrigation requirements. . . . Frequently, applying the simple fertilizer needed has saved from a quarter to one-half the total irrigation or doubled the returns for each unit of water where fertilizer was applied. This is especially true on the lighter types of soil.

"The time of irrigation affects greatly the efficiency of the water applied, since irrigation . . . is worth more when applied just at the right time. . . . The amount applied at each irrigation will affect the economical use of water or irrigation requirement. . . . Coarse-textured soils or those with gravelly substrata should have a distribution system that will permit or supply comparatively light and frequent applications which can be retained in the soil without percolation loss. The frequency of irrigation is related to the time and amount for each irrigation. Irrigation should only be applied when the moisture content drops to near the wilting point for the particular soil and crop, and in sufficient amount to fill it up to the excess point in all cases except where flood irrigation in the early spring is necessary to retain as much water as possible in the soil reservoir. This would be true in the absence of artificial storage for summer irrigation. . . .

"The head and length of run should be such that the plat irrigated can be covered by the time the irrigation has wet up the root zone of the crops. A high head forces over the land rapidly and is necessary in flood irrigation or in irrigating loose soils. The longer length of run gives more time for soaking during irrigation on the heavier textured soils. Longer runs can be used on more sloping land and shorter runs with a higher head should be used on the flatter lands in order to cover the land without waste. . . . It is important for the irrigated farm to have a moderate proportion of cultivated crops. . . . Small, direct ditches which carry the water to the point of application will save water as compared with broad, shallow ones, which expose the water to evaporation and percolation loss."

A further cooperative study of the relation of proper irrigation to bacterial count is reported by T. D. Beckwith. It was found "that the bacterial counts vary with soil moisture. . . . Irrigation, by increasing the amount of soil moisture, stimulates bacterial growth."

The drainage of irrigated shale land, D. G. MILLER and L. T. JESSUP (*U. S. Dept. Agr. Bul. 502 (1917), pp. 40, pls. 9, figs. 12*).—This bulletin contains information on the drainage of those irrigated lands of the Rocky Mountain States that are underlain by shale.

"Outcroppings of shale and lands immediately underlain by shale . . . are found in northern New Mexico, in southeastern Arizona, in large areas of Colorado, in the eastern portion of Utah, in the extreme eastern part of Idaho, in Wyoming, Montana, and in the western parts of Nebraska and the Dakotas." Three different ways by which the movement of seepage water takes place in shale are "(1) over the top of the undisturbed and impervious strata, (2) between the layers, and (3) through joints, faults, and cleavage planes. . . . The source of the seepage water is deep percolation, resulting from irrigation and from seepage losses from canals and laterals. . . .

"The drainage of shale lands can not be accomplished by ordinary methods of drainage, due to the movement of the water through the shale under pressure and also to the extreme retentiveness of the overlying adobe soil. The three essential factors for successful drainage of shale lands are (1) proper location of drains, (2) sufficient depth, and (3) relief wells. Drains must be so located as to tap the contributing shale features, such as ridges, points, knolls, etc. . . . The amount of shale reached and the amount of water developed are augmented by increasing the depth of the drains. These depths never should be less than 6 ft., and generally depths of 7 and 8 ft. and greater are essential to success.

"A system of drainage in many of the shales will be incomplete and unsuccessful without relief wells. The area of influence of relief wells is small; this necessitates that they be closely spaced—in many cases 5 or 6 to 100 ft. of trench. The most efficient depth for the wells has been found to range from 6 to 20 ft. below the bottom of the tile drain. The major portion of the water developed by most of the drainage systems in shale comes from the relief wells. A diameter of 2 in. has been found to be sufficient for the relief wells, and in most of the shales they have been installed with the soil auger. Frequently, however, hard strata require the use of a churn drill.

"For trenches in shale ranging from 6 to 7 ft. in depth, and with labor at 25 cts. per hour, unit costs for excavating, laying tile, and back filling, together with the cost of installing the relief wells, have ranged from 12 to 25 cts. per linear foot of trench. This does not include the cost of any material for the drains. The acreage costs of drainage of the lands referred to in this bulletin have ranged from $13 to $100 per acre for the area actually affected."

Rural sanitation in the Tropics, M. WATSON (*London: John Murray, 1915, pp. XVI+320, pls. 45, figs. 2*).—This book deals with swamp and soil drainage and oiling as antimalarial measures, tropical water supplies, sewage disposal, and general rural sanitation as practiced in British Malaya, Italy, India, Sumatra, Hongkong, and the Philippine Islands, Panama, British Guiana, and Barbados.

The destruction of mosquitoes and their breeding places and the provision of clean and adequate supplies of drinking water seem to have been the greatest of the problems encountered by the author in his work in tropical rural sanitation.

The treatment of sewage by aeration in the presence of activated sludge, E. Bartow (*Trans. Amer. Inst. Chem. Engin.*, 8 (*1915*), *pp. 119–131, figs. 6*).— This is a general review of the experience of the author and others.

Methods of clearing logged-off land, C. H. Shattuck (*Idaho Sta. Bul. 91* (*1916*), *pp. 59, figs. 40*).—Tests of methods of clearing logged-off lands in Idaho are reported.

It was found that methods employing explosives cost from $35 to $150 per acre and frequently required much leveling. Such methods were found to take out stumps completely, break up hardpan, and bring land into cultivation quickly. On the other hand the cost was found to be prohibitive for the poorer farmers and the fertility of the soil was frequently injured by clay, sand, rock, and gravel brought to the surface.

Charpitting was found to cost from $10 to $75 per acre and was one of the cheapest methods, as it required no apparatus. Charpitting was not a success in sandy soil, however, and required constant attention and much labor. Burning from the center of the stump by boring cost about the same as charpitting and required less labor and care. Burning from the center by sawing the stump off and skidding it up generally cost less than charpitting and required less care than charpitting or burning from the center by boring. Another advantage of this method is that the fire is kept going by gravity. The general advantages of burning methods were found to be that little capital and only a small amount of inexpensive apparatus are needed, less leveling is required than by the use of explosives, and much débris is disposed of.

Methods employing hoods on outside charpitting, bored stumps, and sawed off stumps cost slightly more than straight charpitting. Such methods were found to require less work and care after the stump was fired and if a condenser was used part of the by-products could be saved.

Methods employing stump pullers on cracked stumps, small stumps, and on small standing timber generally cost more than charpitting and required more equipment. Less leveling was required, the cost of powder was reduced where stumps were cracked, and fewer snags and roots were left than by burning. Methods employing donkey and traction engines on small trees, small stumps, and cracked stumps generally cost much more than charpitting and required skilled operators and expensive machinery. These methods were found, however, to work rapidly in young standing timber or on small stocks of heavy stumps. Little leveling was required, the cost of powder was reduced, and few snags and stumps were left in the soil. Another advantage was that the stumps were piled, preparatory to burning.

Methods employing pasturage were found to be the cheapest of all methods and the best of all methods where time is not an important factor.

Prevention of the erosion of farm lands by terracing, C. E. Ramser (*U. S. Dept. Agr. Bul. 512* (*1917*), *pp. 40, pls. 9, figs. 18*).—This bulletin is based upon the results of surveys, observation, and a study of terraced fields in the best terraced sections of the country, and deals with terracing as a means of preventing the erosion of hillside land, describing the different types of terraces, pointing out the applicability of each to the various kinds of soil and topography and discussing the principles of terrace design.

"The terraces in use in this country are of two general classes, the bench terrace and the ridge terrace. . . . The disadvantages of the bench terrace are that it can not be crossed by modern farm machinery; the banks can not be cultivated, while each bench must be cultivated as a separate field; weeds and objectionable grasses which grow on the banks tend to sow the entire field. It is best adapted to slopes too steep to permit the use of any form of cultivated terrace, but it can not be recommended for use on slopes exceeding 20 per cent.

"The narrow-base level-ridge terrace . . . is cheap to construct and easy to maintain. However, . . . considerable land is lost to cultivation and the growth of weeds and grasses on the embankments tends to seed the entire field. . . . Outside of these objections, the narrow-base level-ridge terrace, where heavily sodded, renders satisfactory service on pervious soils and slopes not greater than 8 per cent.

"The broad-base level-ridge terrace . . . has all the advantages of the latter terrace with the added one that no land is lost to cultivation. . . . It is best adapted to use on open, pervious soils on slopes not exceeding 15 per cent, but under proper conditions of design, construction, and maintenance can be used on any soil and on slopes somewhat greater than 15 per cent. . . .

"The broad-base graded-ridge terrace (the Mangum terrace) . . . not only can be cultivated but it can be crossed at any angle with large farm machinery. Its broad base and flat embankment slopes render it less liable to damage by the flowing water than is the case with the narrow-base type. The grade may be either uniform or variable, but both practice and theory indicate the variable-graded terrace to be superior to the uniform-graded type. The graded terrace is adapted particularly for use on impervious and worn-out soils, and on shallow open soils with an impervious foundation. . . .

"By the selection and proper construction of suitable types of terraces erosion can be controlled on slopes up to 20 per cent or even more. Instances were found where erosion was controlled by the use of terraces on land which had a slope of 30 per cent. However, slopes steeper than 20 per cent usually can be devoted more profitably to grasses or timber than to cultivated crops.

"Of all types of terraces, the use of the broad-base level-ridge terrace is recommended wherever conditions will permit. This type, supplemented with efficient tile drains, offers the most ideal method of preventing soil erosion on any type of soil."

The causes of cracks in cement-concrete pavements, A. T. GOLDBECK (*West. Engin., 8 (1917), No. 2, pp. 59–62*).—The causes of cracking in concrete roads are classified as (1) expansion and contraction due to changes in temperature and moisture content, (2) nonuniform bearing under the slab due to frost action, lack of homogeneity in the sub-base and moisture expansion and shrinkage of the sub-base, and (3) bending resulting from heavy loads and impact.

Tests to determine the amount of friction that can act at the sub-base of a concrete road when the slab expands and contracts, made by sliding 6 in. by 2 ft. by 2 ft. concrete slabs along previously prepared sub-bases, gave the results shown in the following table:

Frictional resistance of concrete on various sub-bases.

Kind of base.	Movement.	Force.	Coefficient.	Movement.	Force.	Coefficient.	Movement.	Force.	Coefficient.
	Inches.	*Pounds.*		*Inches.*	*Pounds.*		*Inches.*	*Pounds.*	
Level clay	0.001	480	0.55	0.01	1,130	1.30	0.05	1,800	2.07
Uneven clay	.001	500	.57	.01	1,120	1.29	.05	1,800	2.07
Loam	.001	300	.34	.01	1,030	1.18	.05	1,800	2.07
Level sand	.001	600	.69	.01	1,080	1.24	.05	1,200	1.38
½-inch gravel	.001	450	.52	.01	960	1.10	.05	1,100	1.26
½-inch broken stone	.001	380	.44	.01	800	.92	.05	950	1.09
3-inch broken stone	.001	1,060	1.84	.01	1,550	1.78	.05	1,900	2.18

In tests of the effects of change in moisture content "specimens were made of 1:2:4 and 1:3:6 concrete of very wet and very dry consistency. Several days after hardening they were immersed in water and extensometer readings were made on them at frequent intervals. As long as they were wet they remained expanded, with a maximum expansion of 0.0001 in. per inch of length. After six months they were removed from the water and allowed to dry in the warm, dry air of the laboratory. They immediately began to contract, reaching an ultimate contraction of 0.0008 in. per inch of length."

Policy and program of Government in road construction under the new Federal Aid Law, L. W. Page (*Good Roads, 51 (1917), No. 7, pp. 116–118*).— This is a brief discussion of important features of the law.

Good roads and community life in Iowa, J. E. Brindley and J. S. Dodds (*Iowa Engin. Expt. Sta. Bul. 39 (1917), pp. 31, pls. 5, figs. 4*).—This bulletin presents the results of a study of good roads and community life in five typical counties of Iowa, together with a detailed statistical tabulation of what is termed strictly rural traffic. The points in question were (1) the proper distribution of taxes for the construction and maintenance of roads, including culverts and bridges, (2) the cost of marketing agricultural products under the varying conditions presented by a State like Iowa, and (3) the educational and social, as contrasted with the purely economic, value of properly constructed and well maintained public highways.

It is concluded that "the proper distribution of taxes for roads and bridges in a given State is necessarily determined by topography, density and character of traffic, nature of local and commonwealth government with particular reference to the revenue system of each, the density of population and the distribution of the same both from a rural and urban standpoint, the progress of rural organization service, and numerous other considerations."

A survey of the number of farm homes located on different road systems in the several counties showed "that about four-fifths of all the farmhouses considered are located on secondary or township roads. This fact tends to show why there is opposition to spending a relatively high percentage of the highway budget on a small mileage of main-traveled roads. . . . The house miles even of strictly rural traffic reveal the necessity of relatively greater expenditure on the country road system. In Story, Marion, and Carroll Counties it appears that 12, 15.2, and 15 per cent of the roads carry 27.6, 33.9, and 38.8 per cent, respectively, of the rural traffic as already defined, which means that the density of the traffic on township roads is much less than on the county roads. . . . Approximately four-fifths of the Iowa farmers live on the township road system, and also about one-third of the farmers are directly connected with city roads and need not use the county road system for market hauling. To the former transportation costs are determined largely by the condition of the secondary roads, while to the latter no direct benefit would be obtained from the hard surfacing of what are now classed as primary roads."

Tests of western yellow pine car sills, joists, and small clear pieces, C. W. Zimmerman (*U. S. Dept. Agr. Bul. 497 (1917), pp. 16, pls. 2, figs. 4*).—Tests of the mechanical properties of western yellow pine, with special reference to its use as a structural material, are reported. The following conclusions are drawn:

"The strength values of structural timbers are influenced considerably by the defects found in them. These values vary according to the grades in the green material, but the increase in strength from air seasoning is not uniform and does not vary with the grades. Seasoning greatly increases the strength of the wood, the increase being greater and more uniform in small, clear sticks than in structural timbers, owing to the development of defects in the latter. Lowering the moisture content of yellow pine causes it to become more brittle.

"Western yellow pine is a lighter wood than the other western lumber species, weighing approximately 26.9 lbs. per cubic foot, oven dry, in structural sizes. The dry weight of clear wood readily suggests its strength or weakness, but this factor alone can not be depended upon to indicate comparative strength when structural forms of various grades are taken into consideration, owing to the presence of defects which have an important influence on their strength."

A table comparing the strengths of various western species, based on tests of small clear specimens, is given. In addition to the results of tests on western yellow pine there are included average values derived from similar tests on material from five trees from each of four other localities.

A lister attachment for a cotton planter, S. H. HASTINGS (*U. S. Dept. Agr., Bur. Plant Indus.* [Circ.], 1917, pp. 3, fig. 1).—This circular describes and diagrammatically illustrates a lister attachment to a cotton planter in the nature of a modified sweep, the purpose of which is to push away the dry surface soil. A hole is drilled through each shoe about half an inch from the top and about 7 in. from the rear. Two pieces of 2 by 4 in. lumber, 17 in. long, with one side beveled so that when the two are placed one on either side of the shoe they will just clear the wheel, complete the attachment.

Mechanical unloading of cane, C. J. TÖNJES (*Arch. Suikerindus. Nederland. Indië, 24 (1916), No. 39, pp. 1518–1561, pls. 18, figs. 17*).—This is a description of the principles of operation and the mechanical details of unloading and conveying machinery and apparatus for sugar cane.

Modern farm buildings, A. HOPKINS (*New York: Robert M. McBride & Co., 1916, pp. 206, pls. 31, figs. 77*).—It is the purpose of this book to give suggestions "for the most approved ways of designing the cow barn, dairy, horse barn, hay barn, sheepcote, piggery, manure pit, chicken house, root cellar, ice house, and other buildings of the farm group, on practical, sanitary, and artistic lines."

Dairy buildings (*Bien. Rpt. State Dairy Bur.* [Cal.], 11 (1915–16), pp. 16–37, figs. 22).—A number of plans for milking sheds are given.

Community hog houses, J. B. DAVIDSON, J. M. EVVARD, and W. G. KAISER (*Iowa Sta. Bul. 166, abridged ed. (1916), pp. 40, figs. 29*).—An abridged edition of Bulletin 166, previously noted (E. S. R., 35, p. 587).

Building a self-feeder [for swine], E. W. LEHMANN (*Missouri Sta. Bul. 144 (1917), pp. 18–22, figs. 4*).—Plans and specifications for a one-way and a two-way self-feeder for hogs are given.

RURAL ECONOMICS.

The country church; an economic and social force, C. J. GALPIN (*Wisconsin Sta. Bul. 278 (1917), pp. 48, figs. 16*).—The author points out that:

"Farmers go to church in the open country churches in which 95 per cent of the membership are from farm families; in hamlet churches where 75 per cent of the members are from the farm; in village churches where 50 per cent of the members are from the farm; and in small city churches where the farm membership is but 15 per cent. The open country and hamlet churches have the best chance in a farm population that is not shifting about from place to place. A large compact parish, a single church in the parish, and a regular pastor or priest living in the parish are social conditions of strong country and hamlet churches. . . .

"Agriculture is a party to the rural church problem for the reason that in the national struggle to unite farmers into successful producing and business groups the rural parish is a force whose pull is felt by local agriculture. . . .

"A joint commission from the national religious bodies could formulate the principles upon which to reparish the rural districts so as to give every farm family a chance to belong to a strong church. . . . Some examples of farmers' churches in Wisconsin [which] show how churches and their religious leaders are cooperating with a progressive agriculture in rural social development " are cited.

A brief account of the life of Rev. John Frederick Oberlin is appended.

Living conditions in rural Alabama, J. B. HOBDY (*Montgomery, Ala.: Brown Printing Co., 1915, pp. 27*).—The information given in this report was gathered by a questionnaire sent to 402 high-school pupils, and relates to the work of the wife and children on the farm and in the home, and the extent of modern conveniences, recreation, and sanitary conditions.

Wages of farm help [in Iowa] ([*Bien.*] *Rpt. Bur. Labor Statis. Iowa, 17 (1915-16), pp. 119-122*).—Statistical data are given showing by counties the average monthly wages paid during the summer and winter months for 1915, with comparative data for earlier years.

[Conditions among rural laborers in Finland in 1901], H. GEBHARD (*Statis. Undersökn. Soc. Ekon. Förhdl. Finland, No. 5 (1916), pp. X+211*).—In this report are discussed the conditions of the homes, the amount of land possessed by the laborers, and the number of live stock. Extensive data are included showing conditions in various regions.

Rate sheet essential in long time and short time farm loans, R. L. BENNETT (*Tex. Agr. Col. Ext. Serv. Bul. B-28 (1916), pp. 8, figs. 2*).—The author points out the essentials of safe farming, gives a sample rate sheet, and calls attention to the relation between the cost of securing a loan based upon a single crop system of farming compared with the cost under a diversified system which attempts to produce food and feed for the farm.

The Federal Farm Loan Act, R. J. BULKLEY (*Jour. Polit. Econ., 25 (1917), No. 2, pp. 129-147*).—The author gives the history of the various bills introduced in Congress regarding rural credit, describes their striking features, and discusses the provisions of the Federal Farm Loan Act as finally passed.

The working of credit banks in the Netherland East Indies, H. C. ALTING (*Trans. 3. Internat. Cong. Trop. Agr. 1914, vol. 1, pp. 109-124*).—The author describes the different types of credit institutions, the organization for promotion and supervision, and the attitude of the native population.

Annual report on the working of cooperative societies in the Bombay Presidency, 1916 (*Ann. Rpt. Work. Coop. Socs. Bombay Pres., 1915-16, pp. 6+39+3*).—This report continues data previously noted (E. S. R., 35, p. 589).

A municipally owned and operated abattoir, E. H. McCUISTION (*Texas Dept. Agr. Bul. 51 (1916), pp. 14, figs. 3*).—The author discusses the method of organization and operation, and describes the construction and plan of the abattoir, as well as the inspection service.

Market survey of the City of Atlanta, Georgia, J. A. MONTGOMERY (*Atlanta, Ga.: State Dept. Agr., 1915, pp. 57, pl. 1*).—The author discusses the quantity and sources of products handled, marketing conditions, cold storage facilities, standards in use, and agencies available for improving the marketing of agricultural products.

Report on the storage and handling of wheat in bulk in Victoria (*Melbourne: Govt., 1916, pp. 78, pls. 20, figs. 2*).—Among the conclusions reached by John S. Metcalf Co., Limited, in their study of the bulk handling of wheat are the following:

" The rail and ocean freights on the bags is an important and unnecessary loss. Any supposed extra value of bagged wheat abroad is more than offset

by the extra cost of handling such wheat at the importing point. . . . It offers
no encouragement to the farmer to grow the best wheat possible as would a
system offering a premium for quality. . . .

"Unloading farmers' wagons, loading and unloading railway trucks, and
loading and unloading of ocean vessels would be very much quicker under the
bulk than under the bag system. . . . The saving in time of loading and
unloading vessels should result in lower freight rates, even if any possible extra
costs for preparing vessels or for insurance should tentatively be considered
operative for a time. . . .

"The present large waste of wheat from weather and vermin damage, leakage, and rebagging can be prevented by the bulk system. . . . The bulk system
offers a better method of financing . . ., will provide cheaper means of cleaning
wheat, will save the freight on rubbish now shipped abroad, and the cleaned
wheat will obtain higher prices in Europe. . . .

"A system built and operated by the Government is recommended, with the
farmers adequately represented in its control. Inspection, weighing, elevator
operation in general, and marketing, should be under supervision of a grain
commission."

Comments of the Victorian Railways Commissioners on the report on the
bulk handling system of wheat in Victoria (*Melbourne: Govt., 1916, pp. 7*).—
These comments are made on the report in the abstract given above.

Monthly crop report (*U. S. Dept. Agr., Mo. Crop Rpt., 3 (1917), No. 3, pp.
21-28*).—In this report are contained the usual data regarding the estimated
farm value of important crops and range of prices of agricultural products at
important markets. Data are also given concerning the farm stocks on hand
March 1 and the shipments out of the counties where grown of wheat, oats,
corn, and barley, and concerning farm wages of male labor per month, per day
at harvest time, and per day at other than harvest time, with and without
board. Special reports are given concerning Florida and California crops, the
shortage in 1916 in the world's potato crops, frost damage March 4, 1917, in
Texas and California, monthly farm marketings and exports of wheat, the
effect of the cold wave February 1 to 6 on truck crops in Florida, and other data.

A special investigation is reported regarding the use of firewood on farms.
It was found that the total amount used was 81,875,000 cords valued at $225,-
426,000. The average number of cords per farm was 12.5 and the average
value $34.35.

[Extent of crops grown on reclamation projects] (*Ann. Rpt. Reclamation
Serv. [U. S.], 15 (1915-16), pp. 681-695*).—These pages give data as to the
acreage, average yield, and value of crops grown on the individual reclamation
projects.

Annual statistics of Chile (*An. Estad. Chile, 10 (1913-14), pp. 8+195, pls.
14; 10 (1914-15), pp. 308*).—These volumes continue data previously noted
(E. S. R., 32, p. 689), adding data for 1913-14 and 1914-15.

The agricultural situation in the Department of Corrèze [France] before
the war, P. BERTHAULT (*Ann. Sci. Agron., 4. ser., 5 (1916), Nos. 1-6, pp. 157-
206, pl. 1, figs. 12*).—After discussing the condition of the soil, climate, means
of communication, sizes of farms, and rural population, the author calls attention to the use of land, extent of crops, and live stock production under war
conditions.

[Increasing the agricultural production of Italy], S. LISSONE (*Ann. R.
Accad. Agr. Torino, 58 (1915), pp. 77-115*).—The author gives the extent of
agricultural production from 1909 to 1914 and the number of live stock, and
points out the causes for the scarcity of certain agricultural products. He believes that this scarcity is due to the lack of knowledge of the best agricultural

practice and the lack of capital. He advocates the establishment of experimental and agricultural educational institutions, an increase of capital, and a better application of labor.

[Agriculture and live stock in Sweden] (*Sveriges Off. Statis., Jordbr. och Boskapsskötsel, 1913, pp. VIII+160*).—This report gives by minor subdivisions data as to the area and production of the principal crops, the number of live stock, and the number of agricultural enterprises.

[Agricultural statistics of Norway] (*Aarsber. Offentl. Foranst. Landbr. Fremme, 1915, I, pp. 90; 1916, I, pp. 88*).—These reports continue the data previously noted (E. S. R., 33, p. 193), adding data for 1915 and 1916.

[Agricultural statistics of Finland, 1910] (*Finlands Off. Statis., III, No. 9, pt. 1 (1916), pp. 327*).—Statistical data are given for minor subdivisions showing the area devoted to different agricultural purposes, the classification of farms by the area of cultivated land, and the extent of those farms devoted to the principal crops. The number of agricultural machines are given for all farms and for the farms classified by sizes.

AGRICULTURAL EDUCATION.

[The teaching of rural sociology], D. SANDERSON (*Amer. Jour. Sociol., 22 (1917), No. 4, pp. 433–460*).—The author has gathered information by means of a questionnaire as to the content of the courses of instruction in rural sociology, the relation of the courses to the other departments of the institution, and their extent.

The value of home economics in our schools, FRANCES RAY (*Proc. and Addresses N. C. Teachers' Assembly, 32 (1915), pp. 205–211*).—The author discusses the educational, cultural, social, and vocational values of home economics and its correlation with other school subjects.

The school garden as regarded and carried on in the different provinces (*Canada Dept. Agr. Pamphlet 4 (1916), pp. 64, figs. 33*).—A series of articles on school gardening in Canada, previously noted (E. S. R., 33, p. 897; 34, pp. 92, 93; 35, p. 594).

Proceedings of the [Illinois] high school conference, 1915, edited by H. A. HOLLISTER (*Univ. Ill. Bul., 13 (1916), No. 21, pp. 78–95, 173–193*).—The following papers presented before the agricultural and domestic science sections of this conference are included: Requirements for University Entrance Units in Agriculture; The Use of the Home Farm as a Laboratory for Secondary School Agriculture; Vocational Opportunities in Scientific Agriculture; The Home Course as Taught in the High School; and Problems in High School Sewing. Reports of the committee on agricultural textbooks and reference libraries and of the executive committee of the domestic science section embodying suggestions for teaching various subjects are also given.

The agricultural section recommended to the faculty of the College of Agriculture of the University of Illinois that schools be credited in agriculture up to four units for specific subjects, such as agronomy, animal husbandry, horticulture, etc., providing the work is approved by the high-school visitor. It was the opinion of the section that instead of the one-year general course in agriculture specific courses of not less than one semester's length in single phases of agricultural work should be given.

Notes on agricultural instruction in Spain, H. GORRIA (*Rev. Inst. Agr. Catalán San Isidro, 65 (1916), No. 18, pp. 277+282*).—This is a brief survey of the facilities for agricultural instruction in Spain, including The School for Agricultural Engineers in Madrid; the Provincial Higher Agricultural School at Barcelona; schools of agriculture with theoretical and practical instruction, practical farm schools, the school of viticulture and enology, and the school of aviculture; general argicultural, ampelographical, enological, pomological, sericultural, irrigation, olive culture, enotechnical, rice, seed control, vegetable pathology, dairy, and agricultural machinery testing stations; the acclimatization garden; provincial demonstration and experiment fields and laboratories, and provincial district· agricultural experts; the Catalán Agricultural Institute of San Isidro (an agricultural society organized more than 60 'years ago), which offers annually courses in agricultural chemistry, etc.; and publications.

The story of corn and the westward migration, E. C. BROOKS (*Chicago and London: Rand McNally and Co., 1916, pp. IX+308, pl. 1, figs. 114*).—This book treats of the struggle of the human race for food; food as a factor in civilization; the origin of corn, and the effect of its discovery on the world's food supply; the opening and settling of the great corn country and connecting it with the world; the economic value of corn; changes in the cultivation, harvesting, and marketing of grain; farmers' demonstration work and the corn-club movement; varieties of corn; and the most important corn products. This is a companion book to The Story of Cotton (E. S. R., 29, p. 738), and may be used with it as a course in elementary economic history for the last year of the grammar school or the first year of the high school.

Vegetable gardening, L. H. CARRIS and H. F. TOMPSON (*N. J. Dept. Pub. Instr., El. Agr. Leaflet, 4 (1916), pp. 27*).—Instructions are given for pursuing the project of vegetable gardening, which may be conducted as (1) school gardening, in which the ground may be used either wholly for the cultivation of one vegetable, as a general kitchen garden, or for individual plats; and (2) individual and partnership home gardening. Correlations with other school subjects and references to literature are suggested.

Productive feeding of farm animals, F. W. WOLL (*Philadelphia and London: J. B. Lippincott Co., 1916, pp. XII+385, pl. 1, figs. 105*).—In this second edition of this text, previously noted (E. S. R., 33, p. 696) a few minor changes and corrections have been made, and a chapter on Feeding Poultry, by *J. E. Dougherty,* has been added.

Judging farm animals, C. S. PLUMB (*New York: Orange Judd Co., 1916, pp. XI+590, pl. 1, figs. 299*).—The author presents a study of animal form and function in general and of horses, cattle, sheep, and swine in particular. An appendix contains rules governing live-stock judging contests, boys' stock judging contests, the students' contest in judging dairy cattle at the National Dairy Show in 1916, and age classification in the show ring. The volume is intended to serve the stockman but more especially the student.

Dairy farming, C. H. ECKLES and G. F. WARREN (*New York: The Macmillan Co., 1916, pp. XV+309, pl. 1, figs. 78*).—This book, which is adapted for use in schools and colleges, is the first of a series of texts to be known as The Farm Series, each of which is to discuss the phases of its subject that are of most importance to the farmer. This text deals with the importance of the dairy industry, breeds of cattle, selection, improvement, management, feeding, and common ailments of dairy cattle, the dairy barn, milk and its products, conditions affecting the development of dairying, systems of farming on dairy farms, methods of renting dairy farms, cost of production and methods of marketing, and other important factors for success in dairy farming. From three to five recitations and two laboratory periods a week are recommended as usually desirable.

A laboratory manual of foods and cookery, EMMA B. MATTESON and ETHEL M. NEWLANDS (*New York: The Macmillan Co., 1916, pp. XI+325, figs. 5*).—In this laboratory manual a considerable number of experiments are given under each topic to afford a knowledge of the leading characteristics of each kind of food, furnish a basis for the discussion of the procedures used in cookery, and give a grasp of the principles involved that will enable the student to work without recipes or to develop her own. Thoroughly tested recipes, a considerable number of score cards for judging the finished products, illustrative calculations of nutritive values of typical cooked foods, and references to literature are included.

A rural arithmetic, I. A. MADDEN and E. A. TURNER (*Boston: Houghton Mifflin Co., 1916, pp. XV+258, figs. 30*).—The problems in this text are based on rural activities, such as the mathematical phases of farm crops, fertilizers, feeding of live stock, household economy, fencing, building and construction, silos, and horticulture. Two chapters are devoted to business forms and farm accounts, and about one-fourth of the book to a systematic review of the fundamental principles of arithmetic. It is intended for the seventh and eighth grades of rural schools and for secondary schools offering courses in agriculture.

The school garden: How to establish it, practical instructions and directions, J. C. MAGNAN (*Min. Agr. Prov. Quebec Bul. 12 (1915), pp. 24, pls. 7, figs. 6*).—This bulletin contains directions for establishing school-garden work and reasons for teaching agriculture in the elementary school.

Gardening for the schools of Saskatchewan (*Regina: Dept. Ed., 1915. pp. 41, pls. 12*).—This publication discusses the desirability of school gardening instruction, defines horticulture, and gives detailed directions for school-garden work.

MISCELLANEOUS.

Twenty-ninth Annual Report of Georgia Station, 1916 (*Georgia Sta. Rpt. 1916, pp. 31, figs. 6*).—This contains the organization list, reports by the president of the board of directors and the acting director of the station on its work during the year, a financial statement for the fiscal year ended June 30, 1916, and two special articles, which, together with the experimental work reported in the acting director's report, are abstracted elsewhere in this issue.

Annual Report of Idaho Station, 1916 (*Idaho Sta. Bul. 92 (1916), pp. 71, figs. 9*).—This contains the organization list, reports by the director and heads of departments, the experimental features of which are for the most part abstracted elsewhere in this issue, and a financial statement for the main station for the fiscal year ended June 30, 1916, and for the substations for the period from December 1, 1914, to December 31, 1916.

Annual Report of Iowa Station, 1916 (*Iowa Sta. Rpt. 1916, pp. 36*).—This contains the organization list and a report by the director of the work of the station, including a financial statement for the fiscal year ended June 30, 1916. The experimental work recorded is for the most part abstracted elsewhere in this issue.

Annual Report of Nevada Station, 1916 (*Nevada Sta. Rpt. 1916, pp. 56, figs. 8*).—This contains the organization list, a report of the director on the work of the station, departmental reports, the experimental work in which is for the most part abstracted elsewhere in this issue, a list of the publications of the year, and a financial statement for the fiscal year ended June 30, 1916.

Twenty-seventh Annual Report of New Mexico Station, 1916 (*New Mexico Sta. Rpt. 1916, pp. 64, figs. 4*).—This contains the organization list, a report of the director on the work, publications, and exchanges of the station, including reports of heads of departments, and a financial statement for the Federal funds for the year ended June 30, 1916. The experimental features are for the most part abstracted elsewhere in this issue.

Report of the Hood River, Oregon, Branch Experiment Station, 1916 (*Oregon Sta. Bul. 141 (1917), pp. 56, figs. 10*).—A report is given of the work of the year, the experimental features recorded being for the most part abstracted elsewhere in this issue.

Twenty-sixth Annual Report of Washington Station, 1916 (*Washington Sta. Bul. 136 (1917), pp. 66, figs. 17*).—This contains the organization list, a report on the work and publications of the station during the year, and a financial statement for the fiscal year ended June 30, 1916. The experimental work reported is for the most part abstracted elsewhere in this issue.

Publications of the work of the agricultural experiment station of the Rhode Island State College (*Rhode Island Sta. Bul. 169, Sup. (1917), pp. VIII*).—Lists are given of the annual reports and bulletins of the station since its establishment, and of contributions by members of its staff to scientific journals since 1909.

Monthly bulletin of the Western Washington Substation (*Washington Sta., West. Wash. Sta., Mo. Bul., 4 (1917), No. 12, pp. 20, figs. 2; 5 (1917), No. 1, pp. 16*).—These numbers contain brief articles on the following subjects:

Vol. 4, No. 12.—Peas and Vetches in Western Washington, by E. B. Stookey; Care and Management of Baby Chicks, by Mr. and Mrs. George R. Shoup; Spraying Program for 1917, by A. Frank; and Tanning Mole Skins.

Vol. 5, No. 1.—Poisoning by Water Hemlock, by S. B. Nelson; Benefits from Cow-testing Associations, by O. E. Gibson; Soiling Crops, by H. L. Blanchard; Burning Stumps in Place, by I. D. Charlton; Cereals in Western Washington, by E. B. Stookey; The Spring Moult, by Mrs. Geo. R. Shoup; and Plant Clean Potato Seed, by A. Frank.

NOTES.

Alabama Stations.—Frank R. Curtis, county agent of Marengo County, has been appointed director of the Canebrake Station. L. H. Moore, the former director, is to continue as assistant director, and Director J. F. Duggar of the College Station will act as advisory director in the experimental work.

Arkansas University and Station.—J. Lee Hewitt, head of the department of plant pathology since 1909, resigned June 1 to take up State inspection work for the newly established State plant board. Dr. J. A. Elliott, associate plant pathologist of the Delaware College and Station, has been appointed to succeed him, beginning July 1. G. W. Hervey has resigned as assistant in animal husbandry, and has been succeeded by S. R. Stout.

Connecticut College.—The college closed May 11, as only 20 of the 200 students registered still remained, the others having engaged in various forms of military and agricultural service.

Purdue University and Station.—C. G. Woodbury, horticulturist, has been appointed director of the station beginning September 1. J. D. Harper, assistant in crops in the extension work, has become county agent for Laporte County.

Maine University.—By May 9, 420 students had withdrawn from the institution for war service, about half for work on farms.

Maryland College.—Special short courses in practical farm work are being offered to women, beginning June 4.

Massachusetts College and Station.—Despite the general policy of stringent economy, the State legislature appropriated $40,000 to enlarge the power plant, $33,000 additional for new equipment, $17,500 additional for running expenses to meet the increased costs of labor and supplies, and $10,000 for maintenance and improvement of the market garden substation at Lexington.

Because of the war conditions, the elaborate celebration of the fiftieth anniversary of the opening of the college, planned for next October, has been postponed.

Missouri University.—University students who enlisted for national service in connection with the war have been given credit for the current semester with a grade based on the quality of the work being done at the time of enlistment. More than 550 students have availed themselves of this opportunity for service. The university has also placed at the disposal of the Government any technical equipment and apparatus that can be of use. Members of the teaching staff who take up work with the Government are to be granted leave of absence during the period of such service.

Recent appointments include L. L. Alexander as extension assistant in farm crops, Winona Windsor as extension assistant in home economics, W. W. Langston as county agent for Butler County, and E. J. Trosper as district agricultural agent for northeastern Missouri. R. A. Kinnaird has been promoted from extension instructor to extension assistant professor of soils. Charles G. Carpenter, assistant in horticulture, has resigned.

Nevada University and Station.—The State has organized a committee on food resources, of which Dean C. S. Knight of the College of Agriculture is chairman and Director S. B. Doten of the station, secretary.

New Hampshire College.—By May 14 about 230 students had left to work on farms.

New Jersey College and Stations.—Recent appointments include William H. Hamilton as assistant State leader in farm demonstration, R. F. Poole as research assistant in plant pathology, and Louis Schwartz, as assistant chemist. Frank O. Fitts, assistant chemist, and Miss Nevada S. Evans, assistant seed analyst, have resigned.

Cornell University and Station.—Dr. A. W. Gilbert, professor of plant breeding, who has been on leave of absence for graduate work in rural economics at Harvard University, has resigned and accepted an appointment with the Boston Chamber of Commerce. Donald K. Tressler, assistant in agricultural chemistry, has resigned to accept a position with the Bureau of Soils of the U. S. Department of Agriculture.

Ohio State University and Station.—Following a faculty ruling permitting students to withdraw from the university with full credit to take positions on farms, approximately 600 students have left for this purpose. Of these 414 are from the college of agriculture and the remainder chiefly from the arts college.

An additional experiment farm is to be located in Belmont County in the near future.

Oregon College and Station.—The forty-eighth annual commencement was held June 4, 281 graduates receiving degrees. There were also 101 absent on military or civil duty connected with the war, who were graduated in absentia.

A grain grading course for farmers and wheat dealers was held under the auspices of the farm crops department June 7 to 14. The purpose was to acquaint growers and others interested with the new Federal grain standardization rules and afford training in classifying and grading northwestern grains.

E. L. Westover, a graduate of the Kansas College with experience in the organization of breeding associations in Minnesota and Wisconsin, has been appointed cooperative extension specialist in dairy husbandry, vice W. A. Barr resigned to become a county agent in Arizona. D. E. Richards, foreman of the college live stock farm, has been appointed instructor in animal husbandry. R. I. Scoville, of the dairy department, and Geo. F. Moznette, of the department of entomology, have resigned to accept appointments with the U. S. Department of Agriculture. John T. Bregger of the Michigan College, and Frank H. Lathrop, of the Ohio State University, have been appointed teaching fellow in botany and research assistant in entomology, respectively. It is reported that over 60 members of the faculty have resigned to accept positions in other institutions or in the Federal service during the present college year.

Pennsylvania College and Station.—Harold Williamson, herdsman for three years, was killed in France recently while serving with a Canadian regiment. P. S. Baker, assistant agronomist, resigned April 1; A. A. Hansen, instructor in botany, May 1; G. A. Meckstroth, assistant in botany, June 1; and I. J. Bibby, instructor in dairy husbandry, June 21. Recent appointments effective July 1 include C. G. McBride as assistant professor of agricultural extension, C. F. Preston as assistant professor of farm organization extension, and Miss Edna B. MacNaughton and Miss Aurelia B. Potts, as instructors in home economics extension. J. S. Owens has been appointed assistant in experimental agronomy, effective June 13.

Porto Rico Insular Station.—On March 3, under the provisions of the new organic act for Porto Rico, the Board of Commissioners of Agriculture was dissolved and the management of the station passed into the hands of the Department of Agriculture and Labor, of which Manuel Camuñas is commissioner.

Rhode Island College.—By May 8 approximately half the students had left the college for agricultural work. The college is cultivating about 300 acres of additional land.

South Dakota Station.—As a result of experiments conducted by the department of chemistry during the past 20 years, it is expected that sugar beet factories will soon be established in both the eastern and the western part of the State. Information from western South Dakota, where sugar beets are being raised on a large scale, shows that the price of land has greatly increased. The loss of so many sugar factories in Belgium and France is reported as stimulating efforts to produce more sugar in this country.

In an experiment to determine the best time to cut corn for the silo, steers fed an exclusive ration of the silage, cut at four different periods, gained during 148 days over 2 lbs. per head daily. In an experiment in breeding sheep, the wool from half-blood Siberians or half-blood fat rump sheep brought as much in the market as wool from the pure-bred Down breeds.

Texas College and Station.—Provision has been made by the legislature for establishing a third junior agricultural college, to be known as the Northeast Texas Agricultural College. An appropriation of $250,000 has been made for its establishment and maintenance. The board of directors of the State A. and M. College is given control over the institution.

State appropriations have also been made for the station and substations aggregating $225,095.34 for the year beginnng September 1, and $181,270.40 for the following year.

Utah College and Station.—Recent appointments include·Dr. M. C. Merrill as professor of horticulture and horticulturist, Bervard Nichols as assistant in plant pathology, J. H. Wittwer and Horace Argyle as agricultural demonstrators for Uinta and San Juan counties respectively, and L. M. Price as assistant demonstrator for Weber County. George Stewart has been made assistant professor of agronomy in the college and assistant agronomist of the station, and H. R. Hagan, assistant professor of zoology and entomology in the college and associate entomologist in the station. W. E. Goodspeed, assistant horticulturist, has resigned to engage in commercial work.

Vermont University.—Following a general exodus for war service, only about 15 students were left by May 14 in the agricultural courses.

Virginia Station.—A. A. Ingham, assistant horticulturist, died June 13.

Washington Station.—Geo. Severance, agriculturist, was appointed acting director May 1. C. A. Thompson has been appointed assistant in soils and assigned to the dry land substation at Lind. O. E. Barbee has been appointed assistant in farm crops. C. B. Sprague resigned May 1 as assistant horticulturist to accept the position of county agriculturist of Kitsap County.

Wisconsin University and Station.—Dr. E. V. McCullom, professor of agricultural chemistry and agricultural chemist, has been appointed professor of biological chemistry at the new school of hygiene and public health at the Johns Hopkins University. Miss Nina Simmonds and Walter Pitz, assistants, have also accepted appointments in the same institution.

The recent death is noted of Carl D. Livingston, assistant professor of agricultural engineering. Professor Livingston was a 1914 graduate of the University of Washington, with a year's graduate work in agricultural engineering at the Ohio State University. His service at the University of Wisconsin began in 1915 at the forest products research laboratory. His work in the college of agriculture had dealt especially with tests of land clearing methods and apparatus.

Wyoming University.—Dean H. G. Knight has been made chairman of the State Council for National Defense, organized April 17. Every county in the

State has a county council, and the increased land placed under plow is estimated at about 20 per cent.

Philipppine College of Agriculture.—A bill appropriating 125,000 pesos ($62,500) for the establishment of an experiment station in connection with the college was passed by the House of Representatives at its last session, but reached the Senate too late for action. An appropriation was made for the completion of a series of students' houses near the new site of the forest school.

Beginning with April, 1918, the requirements for entrance to the 6-year course of the college of agriculture have been raised to include two years of high-school work. New forestry courses leading to a degree in forestry have also been announced.

Changes in Canadian Agricultural Institutions.—Dr. C. Gordon Hewitt has been appointed by the Canadian Government consulting zoologist in addition to his previous duties as Dominion entomologist and chief of the entomological branch of the Department of Agriculture. His new duties will be of an advisory nature in matters relating to the protection of birds and mammals and the treatment of noxious species.

G. H. Cutler, professor of cereal husbandry in the University of Saskatchewan, has been appointed to a corresponding position in the department of field husbandry of the University of Alberta, beginning July 1.

F. S. Jacobs, professor of animal husbandry at the Manitoba Agricultural College, has resigned to take up farming in Alberta.

Necrology.—Professor Emil von Behring, widely known for his studies in bacteriology and immunology, died April 5. Professor von Behring was born in 1854 and received his professional education at the Army Medical College, Berlin, obtaining the doctor's degree in 1878. In 1898 he was appointed assistant in the Institute of Hygiene at Berlin and in 1891 in Koch's Institute for Infectious Diseases. He was made professor in 1894 and appointed to the chair of hygiene in the University of Halle, and in the following year he became professor and director of the Institute of Hygiene at Marburg. He was best known as the discoverer of diphtheria antitoxin, but had also worked extensively on tuberculosis and other diseases.

T. Wilson, inspector of Indian orchards in the entomological branch of the Canadian Department of Agriculture, was fatally burned in a hotel in British Columbia, March 6. He had been notably successful in stimulating interest in fruit growing and horticulture among the Indians, as well as in promoting entomological and botanical work in the region.

Lieut. H. N. Thompson, weeds and seeds commissioner in the Saskatchewan Department of Agriculture, was killed in action at Vimy Ridge, France. J. A. P. Arden, of the Sidney, B. C., substation, has also been killed in action.

Miscellaneous.—M. D. Butler and B. C. Sibley, of the Oregon Agricultural College, have been appointed extension specialists in the Nicaragua Department of Agriculture. Their work is to consist mainly of field demonstrations and the introduction of promising crops.

Nature announces that publication of the *Kew Bulletin* has been suspended under an order deferring, because of the shortage of paper and other considerations, the issue of all Government publications not deemed essential.

The Agricultural Institute at Alnarp, Sweden, is planning to erect a building to cost about $20,000, for studies in heredity under the direction of H. Nilsson Ehle, recently appointed professor at Lund.

According to a recent number of *School and Society*, Victor E. Rector has been elected professor of agriculture at the University of South Carolina.

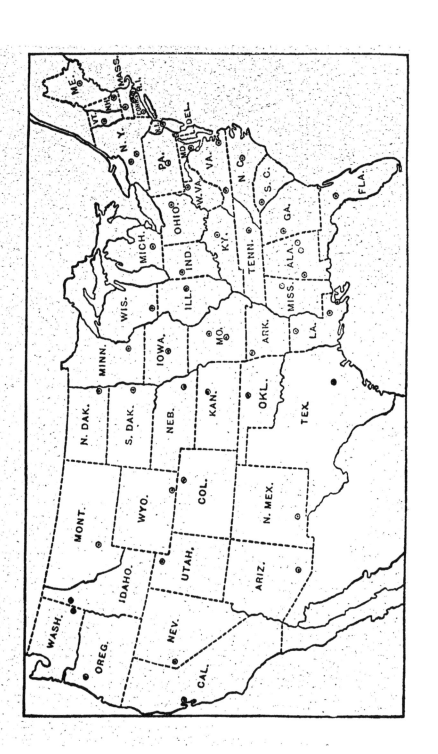

U. S. DEPARTMENT OF AGRICULTURE
STATES RELATIONS SERVICE
A. C. TRUE, DIRECTOR

Vol. 37   AUGUST, 1917   No. 2

EXPERIMENT STATION RECORD

WASHINGTON
GOVERNMENT PRINTING OFFICE
1917

U. S. DEPARTMENT OF AGRICULTURE.

Scientific Bureaus.

WEATHER BUREAU—C. F. Marvin, *Chief.*
BUREAU OF ANIMAL INDUSTRY—A. D. Melvin, *Chief.*
BUREAU OF PLANT INDUSTRY—W. A. Taylor, *Chief.*
FOREST SERVICE—H. S. Graves, *Forester.*
BUREAU OF SOILS—Milton Whitney, *Chief.*
BUREAU OF CHEMISTRY—C. L. Alsberg, *Chief.*
BUREAU OF CROP ESTIMATES—L. M. Estabrook, *Statistician.*
BUREAU OF ENTOMOLOGY—L. O. Howard, *Entomologist.*
BUREAU OF BIOLOGICAL SURVEY—E. W. Nelson, *Chief.*
OFFICE OF PUBLIC ROADS AND RURAL ENGINEERING—L. W. Page, *Director.*
BUREAU OF MARKETS—C. J. Brand, *Chief.*

STATES RELATIONS SERVICE—A. C. True, *Director.*
OFFICE OF EXPERIMENT STATIONS—E. W. Allen, *Chief.*

THE AGRICULTURAL EXPERIMENT STATIONS.

ALABAMA—
  College Station: *Auburn:* J. F. Duggar.[1]
  Canebrake Station: *Uniontown:* F. R. Curtis.
  Tuskegee Station: *Tuskegee Institute;* G. W. Carver.[1]
ALASKA—*Sitka:* C. C. Georgeson.[2]
ARIZONA—*Tucson:* R. H. Forbes.[1]
ARKANSAS—*Fayetteville:* M. Nelson.[1]
CALIFORNIA—*Berkeley:* T. F. Hunt.[1]
COLORADO—*Fort Collins:* C. P. Gillette.[1]
CONNECTICUT—
  State Station: *New Haven;*⎫E. H. Jenkins.[1]
  Storrs Station: *Storrs:*⎭
DELAWARE—*Newark:* H. Hayward.[1]
FLORIDA—*Gainesville:* P. H. Rolfs.[1]
GEORGIA—*Experiment:* J. D. Price.[1]
GUAM—*Island of Guam:* C. W. Edwards.[2]
HAWAII—
  Federal Station: *Honolulu:* J. M. Westgate.[2]
  Sugar Planters' Station: *Honolulu:* H. P. Agee.
IDAHO—*Moscow:* J. S. Jones.[1]
ILLINOIS—*Urbana:* E. Davenport.[1]
INDIANA—*Lafayette:* A. Goss.[1]
IOWA—*Ames:* C. F. Curtiss.[1]
KANSAS—*Manhattan:* W. M. Jardine.[1]
KENTUCKY—*Lexington:* A. M. Peter.[4]
LOUISIANA—
  State Station: *Baton Rouge;*⎫
  Sugar Station: *Audubon Park,*⎬W. R. Dodson.[1]
    New Orleans;   ⎪
  North La. Station: *Calhoun;*⎭
MAINE—*Orono:* C. D. Woods.[1]
MARYLAND—*College Park:* H. J. Patterson.[1]
MASSACHUSETTS—*Amherst:* W. P. Brooks.[1]
MICHIGAN—*East Lansing:* R. S. Shaw.[1]
MINNESOTA—*University Farm, St. Paul:* R. W. Thatcher.[1]
MISSISSIPPI—*Agricultural College:* E. R. Lloyd.[1]
MISSOURI—
  College Station: *Columbia;* F. B. Mumford.[1]
  Fruit Station: *Mountain Grove;* Paul Evans.[1]

MONTANA—*Bozeman:* F. B. Linfield.[1]
NEBRASKA—*Lincoln:* E. A. Burnett.[1]
NEVADA—*Reno:* S. B. Doten.[1]
NEW HAMPSHIRE—*Durham:* J. C. Kendall.[1]
NEW JERSEY—*New Brunswick:* J. G. Lipman.
NEW MEXICO—*State College:* Fabian Garcia.[1]
NEW YORK—
  State Station: *Geneva;* W. H. Jordan.[1]
  Cornell Station: *Ithaca;* A. R. Mann.[4]
NORTH CAROLINA—
  College Station: *West Raleigh;*⎫B. W. Kilgore.[1]
  State Station: *Raleigh;*   ⎭
NORTH DAKOTA—*Agricultural College:* T. P. Cooper.[1]
OHIO—*Wooster:* C. E. Thorne.[1]
OKLAHOMA—*Stillwater:* W. L. Carlyle.[1]
OREGON—*Corvallis:* A. B. Cordley.[1]
PENNSYLVANIA—
  State College: R. L. Watts.[1]
  State College: Institute of Animal Nutrition. H. P. Armsby.[1]
PORTO RICO—Federal Station: *Mayaguez:* D. W. May.[2]
RHODE ISLAND—*Kingston:* B. L. Hartwell.[1]
SOUTH CAROLINA—*Clemson College:* H. W. Barre.[1]
SOUTH DAKOTA—*Brookings:* J. W. Wilson.[1]
TENNESSEE—*Knoxville:* H. A. Morgan.[1]
TEXAS—*College Station:* B. Youngblood.[1]
UTAH—*Logan:* F. S. Harris.[1]
VERMONT—*Burlington:* J. L. Hills.[1]
VIRGINIA—
  Blacksburg: A. W. Drinkard, jr.[1]
  Norfolk: Truck Station; T. C. Johnson.[1]
WASHINGTON—*Pullman:* Geo. Severance.[4]
WEST VIRGINIA—*Morgantown:* J. L. Coulter.[1]
WISCONSIN—*Madison:* H. L. Russell.[1]
WYOMING—*Laramie:* H. G. Knight.[1]

[1] Director.   [2] Agronomist in charge.   [3] Animal husbandman in charge.   [4] Acting director.

EXPERIMENT STATION RECORD.

Editor: E. W. ALLEN, Ph. D., *Chief, Office of Experiment Stations.*
Assistant Editor: H. L. KNIGHT.

EDITORIAL DEPARTMENTS.

Agricultural Chemistry and Agrotechny—E. H. NOLLAU.
Meteorology, Soils, and Fertilizers{W. H. BEAL.
                                     {R. W. TRULLINGER.
Agricultural Botany, Bacteriology, and Plant Pathology{W. H. EVANS, Ph. D.
                                                       {W. E. BOYD.
Field Crops{J. I. SCHULTE.
           {J. D. LUCKETT.
Horticulture and Forestry—E. J. GLASSON.
Economic Zoology and Entomology—W. A. HOOKER, D. V. M.
Foods and Human Nutrition{C. F. LANGWORTHY, Ph. D., D. Sc.
                          {H. L. LANG.
Zootechny, Dairying, and Dairy Farming{M. D. MOORE.
Veterinary Medicine{W. A. HOOKER.
                   {E. H. NOLLAU.
Rural Engineering—R. W. TRULLINGER.
Rural Economics—E. MERRITT.
Agricultural Education{C. H. LANE.
                      {M. T. SPETHMANN.
Indexes—M. D. MOORE.

CONTENTS OF VOL. 37, NO. 2.

	Page.
Editorial notes:	
Adequate station administration	101
Some tendencies under deficient administration	105
Recent work in agricultural science	108
Notes	196

SUBJECT LIST OF ABSTRACTS.

AGRICULTURAL CHEMISTRY—AGROTECHNY.

A textbook of organic chemistry, McCollum	108
The synthesis of protein substances, Verkade	108
The phytic acid of the wheat kernel and some of its salts, Boutwell	108
Studies on the forms of d-glucose and their mutarotation, Hudson and Dale	109
Influence of amino acids on action of alkali on glucose, Waterman	109
Notes on some fatty oils, Uchida	109
Effect of anesthetics and frosting on *Sorghum vulgare*, Willaman	109
The chemical composition of the placenta, Fenger	109
Influence of humidity on paper, Kress and Silverstein	109
Inflammability of carbonaceous dusts, Brown	109
The chemistry of wood decay.—I, Introductory, Rose and Lisse	109
Tyrosinase, a mixture of two enzyms, Folpmers	110
An efficient desiccator, Pratt	110

Page.

A simple gas generator, Fernandez... 110
A new direct reading refractometer with uniformly divided scale, Moffit...... 110
Further studies on the Ives tint photometer, Kress and McNaughton......... 110
Determination of carbon dioxid in carbonates by diminished pressure, Zinn... 110
The Penfield test for carbon, Mixter and Haigh.............................. 110
The volumetric determination of tin, Hallett............................... 110
On the determination of potassium as perchlorate, Baxter and Kobayashi..... 110
The use of methylene blue in chemical analysis, Monnier.................... 111
The phenoldisulphonic acid method for nitrates in soils, Davis.............. 111
The detection and estimation of small amounts of methyl alcohol, Elvove..... 111
Cellulose, Cross, Bevan, and Beadle.. 112
A quantitative method for the determination of arginin in protein, Jansen...... 112
Red peppers, Boyles.. 112
Vinegar: Its manufacture and examination, Mitchell........................ 112
The volatile reducing substance in cider vinegar, Balcom................... 112
The analysis of Peruvian bark, Commelin................................... 113
Determination of the various forms of nitrogen in forage plants, Passerini...... 113
The estimation of hydrocyanic acid in *Sorghum vulgare*, Willaman........... 113
Relation of the fat in milk to the solids-not-fat, Brown and Ekroth.......... 113
The detection of preservatives and coloring matter in milk, Kolthoff......... 113
A new method for the analysis of rancid fats and oils, Issoglio.............. 114
[Report of the analysis of various samples]................................ 114
Fruit drying, Allen.. 114
Sulphitation in white sugar manufacture, Maxwell.......................... 114
A study of commercial beech wood creosote, Smith and Acree............... 114
A method of producing crude wood creosote from hardwood tar, Judd and Acree. 114

METEOROLOGY.

Relation of weather to amount of cotton ginned during certain periods, Kincer. 114
Monthly Weather Review.. 115
Climatological data for the United States by sections....................... 116
Meteorological records... 116
Meteorological observations at Massachusetts Station, Ostrander and Saunders. 116
Free-air data at Drexel aerological station: January–March, 1916............. 116
Ammonia in dew... 116

SOILS—FERTILIZERS.

Water content of soil and composition of soil solution, McCool and Millar...... 116
Water-retaining capacity of soil and hygroscopic coefficient, Alway and McDole. 117
Investigations on the acidity of acid mineral soils, Osugi and Uetsuki......... 118
The sulphur content of some typical Kansas soils, Swanson and Miller........ 119
Studies in sulfofication, Brown and Johnson................................ 119
Nitrous nitrogen in irrigated soils, Greaves, Stewart, and Hirst.............. 120
Influence of humus-forming materials on bacterial activities, Brown and Allison. 120
Organic matter of soil.—IV, Data on humus-phosphoric acid, Gortner and Shaw. 121
Soil survey of Buchanan County, Missouri, Tillman and Deardorff............ 122
Soil survey of Polk County, Nebraska, Snyder and Kokjer................... 122
Soil survey of the Camden area, New Jersey, Patrick et al.................... 123
Soil survey of Blair County, Pennsylvania, Veatch et al..................... 123
Summary of results of cane-culture tests in Java, I–III, Geerts.............. 123
The solubility of mineral phosphates in citric acid, II, Robertson........... 124
Liming and lime requirement of soil, Ames and Schollenberger.............. 124
Effect of manganese on ammonification and nitrification, Brown and Minges.. 126
Fertilizer analyses, McDonnell et al 127
Commercial fertilizers, 1916, Hite and Kunst.............................. 127

AGRICULTURAL BOTANY.

The morphology of the monocotyledonous embryo, Worsdell................. 127
Further experiments on correlation of growth in *Bryophyllum calycinum*, Loeb. 127
Cambial activity in certain horticultural plants, Knudson................... 127
The epidermal cells of roots, Roberts...................................... 128
New determinations of permeability, Brooks................................ 128
Studies on exosmosis, Brooks.. 128
Rôle of osmotic pressure of soil solution in culture of wheat, Tulaïkov......... 128

Page.

The structure of the bordered pits of conifers, Bailey........................ 128
Relation of transpiration to assimilation in steppe plants, Iljin............... 129
Recent developments in the study of endotrophic mycorrhiza, Rayner....... 129
Studies in the physiology of fungi.—I, Nitrogen fixation, Duggar and Davis... 129
Studies in the physiology of fungi.—II, *Lenzites sepiaria*, Zeller.............. 129
The mitochondrial origin of rhodoxanthin, Moreau.........?.................. 129
Distribution and rôle of arsenic and manganese in plants, Jadin and Astruc... 130
Specific action of barium, Osterhout....................................... 130
The plant as an index of smoke pollution, Crowther and Ruston............. 130
Teratology in iris flowers, Armitage.. 130
New dimorphic mutants of the Œnotheras, De Vries......................... 131
Sterility as result of hybridization and condition of pollen in Rubus, Hoar... 131

FIELD CROPS.

Report of the agronomy division, Sahr...................................... 131
Report of [field crop work at] the Glenwood substation, Thompson........... 132
The possible Wayne County farm, Thorne................................... 132
The residual effect of fertilizers and manure, Thorne....................... 133
Effect of soluble nitrogenous salts on nodule formation, Fred and Graul....... 133
Seeding small grains, Williams... 134
[Field crops]... 134
[Field crops]... 134
The cultivation of dry land, Escobar....................................... 134
Field culture tests on peaty soils in 1915, Von Feilitzen.................... 134
[Culture experiments on moor soils at Flahult and Torestorp], Von Feilitzen... 134
Time of sowing and harvesting forage crops on lowland moor soil, Lende-Njaa. 135
Botanical composition of a 20-year-old moorland meadow, Mentz............ 135
The culture of Bengal grass, teosinte, and Sudan grass, Schimmel............ 136
Wild fodder grasses, Burns... 136
Carrots and turnips as catch crops, Vendelmans............................ 136
Bean culture, Strausz.. 136
Early studies in selection of *Trifolium incarnatum* and medicagos, De Cillis... 136
Improvement of red clover, Beverley....................................... 136
The relation of ear characters of corn to yield, Cunningham.................. 136
Lobed leaves in maize, Kempton... 136
Report on corn pollination, IV, Fisher..................................... 137
Delbridge cotton-seed calculator, Delbridge................................ 137
Methi as a fodder crop in the Nasik district, Athalye........................ 137
Continuous oat culture on a highly nitrogenous moor soil, Von Feilitzen....... 137
Arachis hypogæa, Dudgeon.. 138
Potato fertilizers, Johnson... 138
The effect of removing the tops on the bearing of potatoes, Schlumberger...... 138
[Potato varieties]... 138
Potatoes in California, Gilmore.. 139
Potato growing in Washington, I, Morris.................................... 139
Branching-headed rye grass, Green... 139
Botanical description of some varieties of Java and other canes, Fawcett...... 139
Varieties of sugar cane.—Results of five years' experiments, Rosenfeld........ 139
The planting of sugar cane in single and double rows, Cross.................. 139
Comparison of planting thin canes with canes of ordinary size, Cross.......... 139
Trials with thinning sugar cane in the row, Cross............................ 139
Suggestions relative to the cultivation of sugar cane in Tucumán, Wale....... 139
A study of the adsali cane, Padhye... 139
Japanese sugar cane as a forage crop, Leidigh, McNess, and Laude............ 140
Sweet clover, Lutts... 140
The flowering habits of timothy, Evans.................................... 140
On the improvement of Red Olona, Venino................................. 141
The roots of zacaton and their exploitation, Martinez........................ 141
Correlation phenomena in the physical properties of grain, Akemine......... 141
Combating plant diseases by means of careful seed selection, Henning........ 141
Twelfth report of Canadian Seed Growers' Association, 1916.................. 141
Conversion of fern land into grass, Cockayne............................... 142
Goat's rue (*Galega officinalis*), Cockayne................................. 142
[Field crops], Hoffmann et al.. 142

HORTICULTURE.

Page.

Report of the horticultural division, Higgins................................. 142
[New fruit trees, ornamentals, and other plants], Hansen..................... 142
Notes on novelties and plants not well known, Buck........................... 143
Calendar for the treatment of plant diseases and insect pests, Green et al...... 143
Winter sprays: Lime-sulphur spray and crude oil emulsions, Melander......... 143
Cabbage and cauliflower culture, Sprague.................................... 143
Celery culture, Allen... 143
Lettuce growing in California, Rogers.. 143
Growing tomatoes on stakes, Green... 143
Forms of some Philippine fruits, De Leon y German........................... 143
Irrigation of orchards, Adams.. 143
The Maryland apple grading and packing law, Symons and Shaw.............. 143
Cooperative organization, Branch.. 143
North American varieties of the strawberry, Fletcher......................... 143
Viticultural and enological experiments at Paarl during 1915–16, Perold...... 144
California's grape industry... 144
Culture of the olive on the southern shore of the Crimea, Wolf et al.......... 144
Maintenance of fertility of pineapple fields, Krauss.......................... 144
Station work for the avocado, Webber.. 144
Varieties of the avocado, Popenoe.. 144
The avocado in Florida and other lands, Popenoe............................. 144
Citrus fruit improvement: How to secure and use performance records, Shamel. 144
Records and accounts for citrus groves, Vaile................................ 144
[Coconuts, rubber, coffee, and cacao], Harrison.............................. 144
Experiments in manuring of cacao, Bamber and Corlett....................... 144
Culture of the pistachio tree on the southern shore of the Crimea, Kalaïda..... 145
The cultivation and drying of medicinal plants, Holmes....................... 145
One hundred flowers, Haverstick... 145
The book of the peony, Harding.. 145
The American rose annual, edited by McFarland.............................. 145
A bud variation of Euonymus, Shamel.. 145
Aristocrats of the garden, Wilson... 145
Garden guide.—The amateur gardener's handbook, edited by Dick............ 145
Back-yard gardening for business men, Best.................................. 145
Street and park trees for Wisconsin communities, Castle...................... 145
Turf for golf courses, Piper and Oakley....................................... 146

FORESTRY.

Report of the superintendent of forestry, Judd............................... 146
Report of the forest nurseryman, Haughs..................................... 146
Report of forest department of Madras Presidency for 1916, Cowley-Brown, et al. 146
Report on forest administration in Bihar and Orissa for 1915–16, Haines....... 146
Report on forest administration in Ajmer-Merwara for 1915–16, Hukam Chand. 146
Forest administration in Assam for 1915–16, Tottenham and Blunt............ 146
Report of forest administration in the Punjab for the year 1915–16, McIntosh.. 146
Tree planting in eastern Washington, Morris.................................. 146
Ornamental windbreaks, Bontrager... 147
Investigation on the optimum limit of intensity of thinnings, Mer............ 147
Toxic atrophy, Woodruffe-Peacock... 147
The forests of Quebec, Bedard... 147
Notes on some North American conifers based on leaf characters, Durrell..... 147
The tulip poplar (*Liriodendron tulipifera*), Taylor......................... 147
Mode of occurrence of latex vessels in *Hevea brasiliensis*, Bryce and Campbell.. 147
Tapping experiments at Gunong Angsi, Spring and Bunting.................. 147
"Tarwad" bark as a tanning agent, Limaye................................... 147
Production of lumber, lath, and shingles in 1915 and lumber in 1911, Nellis... 148
Forest industries... 148

DISEASES OF PLANTS.

Additional notes on Philippine plant diseases, Baker......................... 148
Some Phycomycetous diseases in the Philippines, Mendiola and Espino...... 148
Plant diseases and other injuries, Brick...................................... 148
The genus Meliola in Porto Rico, Stevens.................................... 149
Specialization of parasitic fungi, particularly of cereal rusts, Montemartini.... 149

Page.

Some Septorias of wheat, Grove... 149
Smut of wheat, Devoto.. 149
Some bacterial diseases of vegetables found in Ontario, Jones................. 149
Club root of crucifers and its control, Werth................................ 150
A new host of *Ascochyta hortorum*, Gabotto.................................. 150
Controlling cabbage yellows, Green and Humbert..., ... 150
Potato diseases, Heald... 150
Important potato diseases and their control, Schander........................ 150
Osmotic pressure of cell sap in relation to mosaic disease, Sprecher......... 150
Tomato fruit diseases, Waters.. 150
Manual of fruit diseases, Hesler and Whetzel................................. 151
Bitter pit, McAlpine... 151
The Illinois canker, or the blister canker of the apple tree, Lewis.......... 151
Apparent relation between aphids and fire blight, Merrill.................... 151
Ripe rot of stone fruits, Mansfield.. 151
Grape downy mildew in Algarve, Judice.. 151
Vine mildew in Piedmont, Italy, in 1915, Martinotti.......................... 152
Treatment of downy mildew, Convergne and Trouchaud-Verdier................... 152
Treatment of Oïdium, Capus... 152
Fog and grape diseases, Larue.. 152
[Treatments for grape troubles], Causse...................................... 152
The effect of asphyxiating gases on grapevines at the battle front, Viala.... 153
The effects of asphyxiating gas on vines, Cordonnier and Richez-Péchon....... 153
Effects of gases from aeroplane bombs, Cordonnier............................ 153
Citrus blast, a new disease in California, Coit.............................. 153
Citrus blast, a new disease, Hodgson... 153
A new bacterial citrus disease, Lee.. 154
The cause of June drop of navel oranges, Coit and Hodgson.................... 154
Spraying for ripe rot of the plantain fruit, Dastur......................... 154
[Notes on some pineapple diseases], Johnson.................................. 155
Rusts of cultivated trees and their treatment with lime-sulphur, Savastano... 155
Carnation leaf spot in Italy, Turconi.. 155
Sweet-pea diseases and their control, Taubenhaus............................. 155
Oak mildew, Schoevers.. 155
White pine blister rust, Duff.. 155

ECONOMIC ZOOLOGY—ENTOMOLOGY.

Animal micrology, Guyer.. 155
Notes on some animal parasites in British Guiana, Bodkin and Cleare, jr...... 155
More minor horrors, Shipley.. 156
The domesticated silver fox, Dearborn.. 156
Habits and food of the roadrunner in California, Bryant...................... 156
Insect behavior as a factor in applied entomology, Hewitt.................... 156
Theories of hibernation, Rasmussen... 156
Simple apparatus for insect photography, Walden.............................. 156
Eighth annual report of Quebec Society for Protection of Plants, 1915–16..... 156
The principal insect pests and plant diseases, Huard......................... 157
Garden and truck crop insect pests, Sanborn.................................. 157
Potato insects, Yothers.. 157
South American crickets, Gryllotalpoidea and Achetoidea, Bruner.............. 157
Notes on black apple leaf hopper (*Idiocerus fitchi*), Brittain and Saunders....... 157
Additions to the list of Missouri Cicadellidæ, Gibson........................ 157
Three new species of Jassoidea from Missouri, Gibson......................... 157
The bay flea louse, *Trioza alacris*, as a new pest in New Jersey, Weiss...... 157
Relation between aphids and fire blight (*Bacillus amylovorus*), Merrill...... 157
Synopsis of the genus Saltusaphis, Baker..................................... 157
The California species of Myzus, with description of a new species, Shinji.... 158
Mealy bug control, Woglum.. 158
A list of the Coccidæ of Porto Rico, Jones................................... 158
A new scale insect affecting sugar cane in New Guinea, Rutherford............ 158
The development of the silk glands in the chief races of silkworms, Bucci.... 158
Genetic studies on the silkworm, Tanaka...................................... 158
The Lepidoptera of the Isle of Pines, Holland................................ 158
Hyponomeuta species and their control in Sweden, Tullgren................... 158
An outbreak of the eight-spotted forester in New Haven, Conn., Lowry........ 158
Notes on the peach-tree borer (*Sanninoidea exitiosa*), Becker............... 158

Page.

The peach-tree borer: Life, history, habits, and control measures, King....... 159
The lesser peach-tree borer (*Synanthedon pictipes*), King...................... 159
The head capsule and mouth parts of Diptera, Peterson....................... 159
The response of the house fly to certain foods, Richardson.................... 159
Biological note on *Rhacodineura antiqua* (not *Ceromasia rufipes*), Pantel......... 160
Sarcophaga and allies in North America, Aldrich.............................. 160
Sheep maggot flies, II, Froggatt... 160
Fruit flies of the genus Dacus occurring in India, Burma, and Ceylon, Bezzi... 160
Wheat sheath miner, Seamans.. 160
The control of the round-headed apple-tree borer, Becker..................... 161
[Banana weevil borer in Jamaica].. 161
A new weevil attacking pineapples in Jamaica, Marshall...................... 161
Pineapples: New weevil injury in Above Rocks District....................... 162
The pineapple black weevil, Newell... 162
Diseases of the honeybee, Bahr... 162
The habit of leaf oviposition among the parasitic Hymenoptera, Smith......... 162
A new genus of omphaline Eulophidæ from North America, Girault............ 162
The North American species of Habrocytus (chalcid flies), Girault............ 162
Notes on coccid-infesting Chalcidoidea, I, Waterston......................... 162
Search for melon fly parasites, Fullaway...................................... 162
A new species of Amphrophora from California, Shinji......................... 163
The mites attacking wild and cultivated plants in Sweden, Trägårdh.......... 163
Ascaris canis and *felis.*—A taxonomic and a cytological comparison, Walton.... 163
On the life cycle of some cestodes, Joyeux................................... 163

FOODS—HUMAN NUTRITION.

Dietary deficiencies of the white bean, *Phaseolus vulgaris*, McCollum et al.... 163
Corn as a source of protein and ash for growing animals, Hogan............... 164
The soy bean in nutrition, Balland... 164
The chemistry of bread making, Grant.. 165
The bread-fed man, Snyder... 165
The sablefish [or] black cod, Moore.. 165
Nutritive value of margarin and butter substitutes, Drummond and Halliburton. 165
The edible canna, Johnson... 165
Caramels, McGill... 165
Fermentation of sauerkraut, Round... 165
The fermentation of sauerkraut, Round....................................... 165
Botulism, Dickson.. 165
Report of division of food and drugs, Lythgoe................................ 165
Sixteenth Report of Minnesota State Dairy and Food Commissioner, Farrell.... 166
What to feed the children, Mendenhall and Daniels........................... 166
Manual for Army cooks, 1916... 166
Report of Mayor Mitchel's committee on food supply, Perkins................. 166
The control of food supplies in blockaded Germany, Taylor................... 166
Food values in Belgium, Snyder.. 166
The physiology of food and economy in diet, Bayliss......................... 166
The desire for food in man, Denton... 166
Supplementary dietary relationships among our natural foodstuffs, McCollum.. 166
[Progress in] physiological chemistry, Hopkins............................... 166
Elimination of certain urinary constituents during brief fasts, Neuwirth...... 167
Proteose intoxications and injury of body protein, I, II, Whipple et al........ 167
Metabolism in gout, Bain... 167

ANIMAL PRODUCTION.

Digestibility of sugars, starches, and pentosans of roughages, Fraps............ 168
Chemical composition of fodder plants of the Province of Samara............. 168
Low-grade cottonseed meal.—Warning to purchasers, Perkins and Grady...... 168
Hydrocyanic acid in cassava, Johnson.. 168
Stallion enrollment.—VI, Report for 1916, McCartney....................... 169
Stallion registration and licenses for the year 1916, Carlyle et al.............. 169

DAIRY FARMING—DAIRYING.

The mineral metabolism of the milch cow; second paper, Forbes, Beegle, et al.. 169
Feeds for dairy cows, Jarnagin and Goodwin................................. 171
[Feeding cows with subcutaneous matter of skins for tanning], Gerlach......... 171

Page.

Dairy cattle feeding and management, Larson and Putney................... 172
Dairy farming, Michels... 172
Dairying in Denmark, Dunne... 172
Kerry and Dexter cattle as producers of milk and butter fat, Plumb.......... 172
A score card for dairy cows, Woodward..................................... 172
Relation between quantity of milk formed and obtained in milking, Zwart.... 172
Influence of parturition on the milk and milk fat, Eckles and Palmer........ 172
Effect of extracts of certain endocrine glands on amount of milk, D'Alfonso.. 173
Numbers of *Bacterium abortus* var. *lipolyticus* found in milk, Evans........ 173
Milk and its hygienic relations, Lane-Claypon.............................. 174
City milk supply, Parker... 174
Milk, sanitary and otherwise, Waddell..................................... 174
Oxygenated milk, Grulee... 174
Chemical quality of New York City market milk, Brown and Ekroth.......... 175
A note on the milk supply of Bangalore, Aiyer............................. 175
A survey of dairy score cards, North....................................... 175
The Babcock test, and testing problems, Troy.............................. 175
How to make creamery butter on the farm, McLaughlin..................... 175
Pepsin in cheese making, Stevenson.. 175
Is the ripening of cheese influenced by its fat content? van Dam........... 175
The judicial problem of Camembert, Marre................................. 176
The "cracking" of Edam cheese, Boekhout and de Vries.................... 176

VETERINARY MEDICINE.

A textbook of the principles and practice of veterinary medicine, White..... 176
Comparative resistance of bacteria and tissue cells to antiseptics, Lambert... 176
The prophylaxis of the infection of war wounds, Vincent.................... 176
The treatment of wounds in war by magnesium sulphate, Morison and Tulloch.. 176
Platelets and the coagulation of the blood, Ducceschi...................... 177
The separation of serum into coagulative and noncoagulative fractions, Hess.. 177
Studies on anaphylaxis (antianaphylaxis), Thomsen........................ 178
Anaplasmosis, Finzi and Campus... 178
Vitamins, amino acids, and other factors involved in meningococcus, Lloyd... 178
Relation of anaerobic organisms to forage poisoning, Buckley and Shippen.. 179
Pulmonary strongylosis, Herms and Freeborn.............................. 179
Anthrax (charbon), Dalrymple... 179
Anthrax as an occupational disease, Andrews.............................. 179
Vaccinations against hemorrhagic septicemia, Hardenbergh and Boerner, jr.... 179
Transmission of pneumonic and septicemic plague, Eberson and Wu Lien Teh.. 180
A digest of the insect transmission of disease in the Orient, Mitzmain........ 180
The complement-fixation test in the diagnosis of tuberculosis, Craig......... 180
Biochemistry of loss of power of tubercle "bacillus" to stain, Miller......... 180
Isolation of tubercle bacilli from sputum and their type, Chung Yik Wang.... 180
An investigation of human bone and joint tuberculosis, Griffith............ 181
Some facts about abortion disease, Schroeder and Cotton................... 181
Etiology of worm nests in cattle due to *Onchocerca gibsoni*, II, Cleland et al.. 181
Shipping fever of horses, Mohler.. 182
Vesicular stomatitis contagiosa, Gregg et al............................... 182
So-called staggers in horses caused by ingestion of *Pteris aquilina*, Hadwen... 182
A splenic abscess, secondary to invasion by *Spiroptera megastoma*, Dickenson.. 182
Bacillary white diarrhea and coccidiosis of chicks, Beach.................. 182
The use of bacterins in the control of fowl cholera, Mack and Records........ 183
The case of Trichomonas, Hadley.. 183

RURAL ENGINEERING.

Irrigation enterprise in the United States: Introductory paper, Grunsky..... 183
Present condition of irrigation in Argentina, Wauters...................... 183
Irrigation in Spain: Distribution systems, methods, and appliances, Stevens.. 183
Irrigation in Spain: Regulations controlling the use of water, Stevens........ 183
Italian irrigation, Luiggi.. 183
Irrigation in Libia, Luiggi.. 184
The distribution of water in irrigation in Australia, Mead.................. 184
Recent developments of irrigation in India, Nethersole.................... 184
Economic advisability of irrigation, Newell................................ 184
The utilization of ground waters by pumping for irrigation, Smith.......... 185
Distribution systems, methods, and appliances in irrigation, Dennis et al.... 185

Page.
Duty of water in irrigation, Fortier... 185
Use of water in irrigation, Fortier.. 185
Irrigation studies, Ontario and Covina [California], Vaile...................... .186
Drainage as a correlative of irrigation, Elliott................................ 186
Flood control for Pecatonica River... 186
Tests indicate drain tile beddings increase strength........................... 187
Report of stream measurements, 1915, Peters, Sauder, et al..................... 187
Water supply, Mason.. 187
Makawao waterworks for rural supply, Cox....................................... 187
A simple method of water analysis, Thresh...................................... 187
Direct microscopical counting of bacteria in water, Nelson..................... 187
Bile compared with lactose bouillon for determining *Bacillus coli*, Obst...... 188
Septic tank, Hart and Jones.. 188
Report of joint committee on Federal aid in the construction of post roads..... 188
Highway traffic analysis and traffic census procedure, Connell................. 188
A standard of carbureter performance, Berry.................................... 188
Rural electric service profitable in Wisconsin................................. 189
Wet weather dryers for hay, Hitier... 189

RURAL ECONOMICS.

The economic history of American agriculture as a field for study, Schmidt.. 189
Control factors in agricultural development, Bonsteel......................... 189
Country planning, Waugh... 189
The Torrens Land Transfer Act of Nebraska, Browne............................ 190
The Land-Title Registration Act of the State of New York..................... 190
Land settlement in California... 190
Report of commission on land colonization and rural credits of California.... 190
Settlement on land in England and Wales of discharged sailors and soldiers... 190
Agricultural Argentina, Pickell... 190
[Farming and farm labor conditions in North Carolina]........................ 190
Labor required for growing crops in West Virginia, Johnson and Dadisman... 190
Women agricultural workers in Germany... 191
Second annual report of the cooperative organization branch, 1915–16, Thomson. 191
Monthly crop report... 191
Ohio agricultural statistics, 1915–16... 191
[Agricultural statistics for the United Kingdom, 1901–1915].................. 191
[Agricultural statistics of Spain].. 191
Agriculture and live stock in Sweden]... 191
[Agricultural statistics of Java and Madura].................................. 191

AGRICULTURAL EDUCATION.

[Agricultural and home economics instruction]................................. 192
Agriculture and the public schools, Dennis.................................... 192
Vocational secondary education.. 192
Vocational agricultural education, Dennis..................................... 192
Agricultural education in Virginia and the Virginia Military Institute, Wise... 192
The district agricultural schools of Georgia, Lane and Crosby................ 193
Seventh report of district agricultural schools of Georgia, Stewart.......... 193
Ninth annual report of the inspector of high schools, Edwards................ 193
Agricultural and horticultural officials, institutions, and associations..... 193
High-school courses in agriculture, Dadisman and Wilson...................... 194
Illustrated lecture on leguminous forage crops for South, Piper and Hendrick.. 194
Illustrated lecture on leguminous forage crops for North, Piper and Hendrick.. 194
Types and market classes of live stock, Vaughan.............................. 194
[Nature study and elementary agriculture in Georgia]......................... 194
Class projects for agriculture students, Welles.............................. 194
Home projects in agriculture for Michigan high schools, French............... 194
Practical arts below the seventh grade.. 194

MISCELLANEOUS.

Report of Hawaii Station, 1916.. 195
Annual Report of South Dakota Station, 1916.................................. 195
First Annual Report of the Adams Branch Experiment Station, 1916, McCall.. 195
Monthly Bulletin of the Ohio Agricultural Experiment Station................. 195

LIST OF EXPERIMENT STATION AND DEPARTMENT PUBLICATIONS REVIEWED.

Stations in the United States.

California Station: Page.
  Circ. 160, Mar., 1917........... 143
  Circ. 161, Mar., 1917........... 139
  Circ. 162, Mar., 1917........... 182
Hawaii Federal Station:
  An. Rpt. 1916................. 116,
    131, 132, 142, 144, 155, 165, 168, 195
Indiana Station:
  Circ. 58, Jan., 1917........... 169
Iowa Station:
  Research Bul. 34, July, 1916.. 119
  Research Bul. 35, July, 1916.. 126
  Research Bul. 36, July, 1916.. 120
Massachusetts Station:
  Met. Buls. 339–340, Mar.–Apr.,
    1917....................... 116
Nevada Station:
  Bul. 85 Dec., 1916............ 183
Ohio Station:
  Bul. 306, Dec., 1916.......... 124
  Bul. 307, Jan., 1917.......... 159
  Bul. 308, Jan., 1917.......... 169
  Bul. 309, Jan., 1917.......... 143
  Mo. Bul., vol. 2—
    No. 1, Jan., 1917........ 159, 195
    No. 2, Feb., 1917.......... 133,
      140, 147, 150, 168, 195
    No. 3, Mar., 1917...........132,
      134, 143, 147, 195
Oklahoma Station:
  Circ. 42, Jan., 1917.......... 169
South Dakota:
  An. Rpt. 1916.............. 142, 195
Texas Station:
  Bul. 195, Aug., 1916.......... 140
  Bul. 196, Aug., 1916.......... 168
Virginia Station:
  Tech. Bul. 11, Aug., 1916..... 143
Virginia Truck Station:
  Bul. 21, Oct. 1, 1916.......... 138
Washington Station:
  Bul. 138, Feb., 1917.......... 195
  Popular Bul. 106, Feb., 1917.. 139,
    150, 157
  Popular Bul. 107, Feb., 1917.. 143
  Popular Bul. 108, Mar. 10, 1917. 146
  Popular Bul. 109, Mar. 13, 1917. 143
  Popular Bul. 110, Mar. 14, 1917. 143
  Popular Bul. 111, Mar. 18, 1917. 136
West Virginia Station:
  Bul. 163, Nov., 1916.......... 190
  Insp. Bul. 5, Feb., 1917...... 127

U. S. Department of Agriculture.

Jour. Agr. Research, vol. 9:   Page.
  No. 1, Apr. 2, 1917...... 154, 160, 181
  No. 2, Apr. 9, 1917............ 117
Bul. 506, Production of Lumber,
  Lath, and Shingles in 1915 and
  Lumber in 1914, J. C. Nellis.... 148
Farmers' Bul. 794, Citrus-fruit Im-
  provement, A. D. Shamel....... 144
Farmers' Bul. 795, The Domes-
  ticated Silver Fox, N. Dear-
  born.......................... 156
Bureau of Crop Estimates:
  Mo. Crop Rpt., vol. 3, No. 4,
    Apr., 1917................. 191
Bureau of Soils:
  Field Operations, 1915—
    Soil Survey in Buchanan
      County, Missouri, B. W.
      Tillman and C. E. Dear-
      dorff.................... 122
    Soil Survey of Polk
      County, Nebraska, J. M.
      Snyder and T. E.
      Kokjer................. 122
    Soil Survey of the Camden
      Area, New Jersey, A. L.
      Patrick, C. C. Engle,
      and L. L. Lee.......... 123
    Soil Survey of Blair
      County, Pennsylvania,
      J. O. Veatch, H. P.
      Young, and H. P.
      Cooper................. 123
States Relations Service:
  Syllabus 24, Illustrated Lec-
    ture on Leguminous For-
    age Crops for the South,
    C. V. Piper and H. B. Hen-
    drick...................... 194
  Syllabus 25, Illustrated Lec-
    ture on Leguminous For-
    age Crops for the North,
    C. V. Piper and H. B. Hen-
    drick...................... 194
Weather Bureau:
  Mo. Weather Rev., vol. 45,
    Nos. 1-2, Jan.–Feb., 1917...
  Mo. Weather Rev., Sup. 5..... 114,
    115, 116
  Climat. Data, vol. 4, Nos. 1-2, 116
    Jan.–Feb., 1917............. 116

U. S. Department of Agriculture—Con.

Scientific Contributions:[1]   Page.

Studies on the Forms of d-
Glucose and Their Mutaro-
tation, C. S. Hudson and
J. K. Dale...................   109
Influence of Humidity on Pa-
per, O. Kress and P. Silver-
stein........................   109
Inflammability of Carbona-
ceous Dusts, H. H. Brown..   109
Further Studies on the Ives
Tint Photometer, O. Kress
and G. C. McNaughton....   110
The Volatile Reducing Sub-
stance in Cider Vinegar,
R. W. Balcom..............   112
A Study of Commercial Beech
Wood Creosote, H. K. Smith
and S. F. Acree...........   114
A Method of Producing Crude
Wood Creosote from Hard-
wood Tar, R. C. Judd and
S. F. Acree...............   114
Lobed Leaves in Maize, J. H.
Kempton..................   136
The Flowering Habits of Tim-
othy, M. W. Evans.......   140
Irrigation of Orchards, F.
Adams....................   143
Cooperative Organization, G.
V. Branch................   143
The Avocado in Florida and
Other Lands, W. Popenoe..   144
A Bud Variation of Euonymus,
A. D. Shamel.............   145
Turf for Golf Courses, C. V.
Piper and R. A. Oakley...   146
Additions to the List of Mis-
souri Cicadellidæ, E. H.
Gibson...................   157
Three New Species of Jassoidea
from Missouri, E. H. Gibson.   157

U. S. Department of Agriculture—Con.

Scientific Contributions—Con.   Page.

Synopsis of the Genus Saltusa-
phis, A. C. Baker...........   157
Mealy Bug Control, R. S.
Woglum..................   158
Sarcophaga and Allies in North
America, J. M. Aldrich.....   160
A New Genus of Omphaline
Eulophidæ from North
America, A. A. Girault.....   162
The North American Species
of Habrocytus (chalcid flies),
A. A. Girault..............   162
Fermentation of Sauerkraut,
L. A. Round..............   165
The Fermentation of Sauer-
kraut, L. A. Round........   165
The Control of Food Supplies
in Blockaded Germany, A. E.
Taylor...................   166
Numbers of *Bacterium abortus*
var. *Lipolyticus* Which May
Be Found in Milk, Alice C.
Evans....................   173
Relation of Anærobic Organ-
isms to Forage Poisoning,
J. S. Buckley and L. P.
Shippen..................   179
Shipping Fever of Horses, J.
R. Mohler................   182
Duty of Water in Irrigation,
S. Fortier................   185
Use of Water in Irrigation, S.
Fortier...................   185
Bile Compared with Lactose
Bouillon for Determining
Bacillus coli, Maud M. Obst.   188
Control Factors in Agricultu-
ral Development, J. A.
Bonsteel.................   189
The District Agricultural
Schools of Georgia, C. H.
Lane and D. J. Crosby.....   193

[1] Printed in scientific and technical publications outside the Department.

EXPERIMENT STATION RECORD.

VOL. 37.   AUGUST, 1917.   No. 2.

The responsibilities of the administrative officers of our agricultural institutions have been brought out in a new light by the entrance of the country into war. The new and unprecedented demands have imposed a heavy tax upon the organizations of these institutions and tested the provision which had been made for handling the various phases of the agricultural work. The experience has developed the broad field which these administrative officers are attempting to cover through their own personal efforts in a manner to raise anew the question whether sufficient provision has generally been made in the administrative machinery to insure strength and elasticity and bring the best results.

Manifestly no organization could fully provide against such an unusual contingency, but the more complete the organization the better the added strain may be distributed. The special demand upon these institutions has just begun, and their opportunity will not close with the war. Hence the question of strengthening the organization where necessary is a pertinent one at this time.

An important step in the direction of progress was made with the grouping of the various forms of agricultural activity in the universities and colleges, differentiating them and their forces, and bringing all into a well-knit organization. This provided more definitely for centralized administration and established relationships and responsibilities more clearly. But in the provision for the administrative machinery the process often stopped short of the ideal, probably for reasons of expediency, and in the growth of the institutions it has not caught up with the original plan.

As a result, the general administrative officers in normal times are directing such a variety of important enterprises, constantly becoming more complicated, that only the things of most pressing importance can be gone into thoroughly. This is the case with any large organization; the chief officer can deal only with the larger questions of policy and practice, and must maintain his contact with the various features through associates. But unless provision is made for these in such an institution, many things of real importance to

101

the welfare of the different enterprises are likely to be passed over with slight consideration or study of all their bearings.

The overworked condition of many of the administrative officers started far back of the war, and is a direct result of the growth which has been taking place. The system of organization had frequently stopped short of the actual needs as they developed with this growth; and when to the usual routine of duties were added calls to exercise active leadership in the agricultural affairs of the State on a war footing, the difficulties of the situation naturally became manifest. There was no shirking, but a ready assumption of the new responsibilities and of an amount of personal work which in some cases can not be maintained indefinitely.

In the history of these colleges the experiment station was usually the first group to be definitely organized and have a responsible head. The station was recognized as representing a definite line of endeavor, with a force of workers and special facilities to meet its needs, methods of its own, and problems and a clientele different from those of the instruction departments.

Hence the provision of an organization and an administrative officer seemed wholly logical, and the office and duties of director became generally recognized. Gradually it was separated from the office of president of the college, wherever it had been combined with that office; and the efficient development of the stations was in large measure the result of the guiding hand of the directors. A good station and a good director usually went hand in hand; and the successful director studied the problems both of his constituents and of his workers.

Events therefore justified the provision of an administrative head to supply leadership to the station, and confirmed the view of the necessity for administration of its funds and its work if the greatest economy and usefulness were to result. Although our station work has changed much in character, and the efficiency of the station staff has increased greatly, the importance of maintaining a station organization, with adequate attention to its affairs and a general supervision of its work and relations, has remained unchanged.

The establishment of the office of dean in the colleges and universities often carried with it the abolition of the directorship of the experiment station as a separate and distinct office. Frequently the mantle of dean fell upon the director of the station, as one who had distinguished himself for administration and perhaps stood nominally at the head of the agricultural work of the college. The situation in the early days was such that the station received a large share of his attention. But in the majority of institutions the duties of this dual officer have greatly changed.

Steady growth of the instruction side of the college, the large development of the experiment station, unprecedented appropriations for wider expansion of the whole institution, and finally the organization of extension work on a novel scale, have increased the working staff many fold and made the duties of administration fully equal to those of the large independent colleges. Indeed, the responsibilities and the internal and external relationships of the dean and director in our larger institutions are now often more exacting than those of president of many of the colleges. It is little wonder then that the dual position of dean and director has made it difficult or impossible to give the attention to the station work which it formerly received, unless special provision is made for assistance.

Nor is this overburdened condition confined to the institutions having this combined officer. Where the position of director is retained, he often has manifold duties outside of that office, and may serve as nominal head of all the agricultural work, or as head of an independent department of the college, or even as director of extension work. His relationships to the agricultural interests and to the people of the State, like those of the dean, often make large demands upon his time. Hence it frequently happens that the director of the station is much more than the responsible head of the research department of the college, and needs to have his office carefully organized to discharge his functions.

The present situation in respect to the office and duties of those in charge of the stations is shown in the following analysis.

In twenty-four institutions the office of dean of agriculture and director of the experiment station is combined in a single person. In other words, the dean or head of all the agricultural work in the institution is likewise director of the experiment station, and there is no separate officer or associate to look especially after the latter's affairs. In six States the dean and director of the station is also director of agricultural extension, an office sufficiently engrossing in most instances to warrant a separate head; and in eight cases the dual officer serves as head of an important subject matter department in the institution. In one instance the combined dean and director acts as State leader of county agents, and in at least three others he has additional duties of an exacting nature.

In twenty-six institutions the director of the station is an independent officer, reporting directly to the head of the institution. In five of these cases he is likewise director of agricultural extension, and in several of the remaining cases he is in charge of a division in the college having both teaching and investigation. In several instances the overworked condition of these dual officers and its effect upon the efficiency of administration have already been recognized, and steps are under way to relieve the situation. In others the desirability of such relief is indicated.

While the congested administrative situation is a result of the general growth of the agricultural affairs of the college, the inauguration of extension work is often a large factor. This has brought a new set of problems and has added materially to the administrative burden upon the dean and director, even though his office is organized with a competent extension director. It has broadened the external relations through cooperation, and being in an evolutionary stage without precedent to guide action, it has required careful study and many important decisions.

This new activity has had the natural effect of taking away from the experiment station a considerable measure of the thoughtful planning and consideration it previously enjoyed. Indeed, this has been one of the most noticeable effects of the extension work upon the experiment station. Theoretically, the station work has been undergoing something of an adjustment to fit it into its new place, but with so much to divert attention to other channels it has rarely been possible to give it more than secondary consideration. One dean and director, who was also director of extension, recently stated that the extension business had probably occupied nearly or quite three-quarters of his time.

This is the fault of no one, least of all of the heavily burdened officers who are trying to meet the demands of their growing work; but it is a condition which seems not to be adequately realized.

In many ways the station work is most liable to neglect or inadequate supervision if the administrative head of the college is overburdened. The station work, being in the hands of capable experts and of a nature which requires time rather than constant direction, will usually run smoothly for an indefinite period, with little likelihood of friction or difficulties which call for action. The result of any neglect it suffers is largely a cumulative one, likely to be reflected in the general internal condition, in the program of operations, and a laxity in publication, which in turn affect its highest efficiency.

To afford anything more than a quite general supervision of the experiment station and its activities under present conditions will usually require some special provision for it, such as an associate who stands between the dean's office and the various departments of the station. Unless this is done, there is danger that there will not be an intimate contact with the station affairs and that many matters which are vital to the welfare of the station, but in themselves may not be sufficiently insistent to command attention, will be allowed to drift or the situation result in an increasing degree of independence. In only a quite limited number of cases has such special provision been made. The dean may have an executive clerk who looks out for correspondence, the handling of requisitions and bills, follows up the budget, keeps track of manuscripts for publication, and similar routine matters, but in only two or three instances has a technical associate been provided to maintain a contact with the workers, give the station coherence, follow its needs, and aid in shaping its course as a distinct branch of the institution.

One evidence of deficient administration and inadequate attention is the tendency for the work of a station to become in a certain sense stereotyped. Lines or projects which have been established are allowed to continue from year to year for a long time without critical examination as to their actual progress or the promise they offer of successful outcome. In some cases there may be a failure of the leaders to give the data and the experiments the critical, thoughtful study from year to year that is needed—a failure to measure the actual progress from one season or one stage to another, or to ascertain whether the method of procedure which is followed is proving adequate to the original purpose and the need. This may result in mainly routine procedure, lacking the vital force of research. For, as has been said, "neither logic without observation, nor observation without logic, can move one step in the formation of science."

There are some indications that we are mainly marking time in certain lines of investigation, and especially in some of the projects, because the end of the resources has apparently been reached for the time being. Some things can not be successfully attacked or worked out because the necessary stage of scientific knowledge has not yet been reached. A new inspiration or, in some cases, another set of postulates is needed to rid the work of being superficial and ineffective. There is a failure to acknowledge such limitations or to be guided by the weaknesses of the undertaking. Projects whose plan and method are apparently not competent, and which are not being strengthened by new features or by a division of the problem, are continued from year to year in a hope that the accumulation of data without change may eventually shed some light. This is one of the first evidences of lack of critical supervision, or of lack of time on the part of the leader to examine his results and his method critically.

Such activity is unproductive because it is unprogressive in plan and unconstructive in results. The first essential of research is a theory, an hypothesis on which a plan of attack is devised and a method worked out. If the theory does not prove sound or the method adequate, new ones need to be devised. There is a waste of time and funds unless there is an effort to determine, to the best of the investigator's judgment, whether the theory and the method are proving adequate and enabling progress. The excuse that data are being accumulated is not sound unless it seems reasonably clear that the added data are marking progress and that the process is not leading around in a circle.

Investigation is a serious business. It requires hard study in outlining the problem as well as in its conduct. The separate experiments comprising it are only means to an end, which are of relatively little account in themselves unless they meet the needs and are assimilated in the general plan. The kind of study demanded requires time for concentration and an intensity which makes a man sweat. It is a searching inquiry.

It not infrequently happens that station workers left to themselves stray outside the economic field, far beyond the bounds of an agricultural experiment station. They fail to keep the natural limitations of their problem in view, or, becoming engrossed with special scientific aspects, are led far beyond the needs of the problem itself, and neglect to return to it until much time and expense have been diverted. It is as though a botantist studying a plant disease and finding a class of uneconomic plants which also served as hosts, should allow himself to be led away into an exhaustive study of the structure and taxonomy, etc., of these hosts, far beyond the particular relationships of these to his problem. No narrow view of science is implied in the maintenance of reasonable boundaries to the function and field of an experiment station. But it is frequently a matter which calls for the discriminating attention of the administrative officer.

Then again the general program of work needs thoughtful and studious consideration to make the station's course one of progress and suited to the special needs. Each station ought to have a fairly definite plan, varied as conditions may require. The revision of this plan, the checking of work which has reached its conclusion or become unproductive, and the introduction of new features can only be done by a general officer and usually requires considerable study.

New projects need consideration from the standpoint of expediency and their relations to the general program, as well as their other merits. They should be practicable in that the end sought seems promising of attainment. The method of procedure should be sound and competent to the purpose, as viewed from the standpoint of the existing stage of science, and it should be evident that advantage has been taken of all available information on the subject. The fact that many of the station investigators are young and with relatively limited experience makes such an examination especially helpful. There is evidence, however, that new projects are not always subjected to such close, discriminating scrutiny.

Again, inadequate supervision may result in long delay in publishing results or in making progress reports. Many workers are prone to take up new lines of work instead of using the time to digest and publish what they have already acquired. This is the explanation why practical results of importance sometimes remain for a long time unprinted. Unfortunately a considerable amount of our station work is behind in publication, much of it still in the form of the original notes. Hence, when a demand like the present comes, with a need for all available data and results having a practical value, the work of compilation must be speeded up and conclusions made ready for application. To guard against unnecessary delay in publication and see that the product of station work is promptly placed before the public is a matter to which the director may well give systematic attention.

Our agriculture is more and more drifting into a condition where the highest efficiency will be required. This is evident from the increase in population, the higher price of land, the deficiency of soils, the need for vigilance in controlling or evading diseases and insect pests, the increasing problems of economical meat production, and so on throughout the whole range of the agricultural industry. There is every reason, therefore, for maintaining our agricultural investigation upon a high plane of efficiency, a process which requires not alone well trained men but effective administration.

Efficiency is a term so overworked and misused that it has lost some of its force as applied to scientific institutions. Whether or not we like the term as employed by investigating bodies, it is an end which must be striven for intelligently. We are now contending with a nation which exemplifies this trait to a high degree, and which shows how far its course in agriculture as well as in other things has been shaped toward attaining it. Our investigation will need to be as efficient as it can be made after the war, as well as to meet present needs. This suggests a kind of administration which gives direction to the work as a whole and counsel in individual cases, encourages deliberation, and exercises restraint where necessary.

RECENT WORK IN AGRICULTURAL SCIENCE.

AGRICULTURAL CHEMISTRY—AGROTECHNY.

A text-book of organic chemistry, E. V. McCollum (*New York: The Macmillan Co., 1916, pp. XIII+426, figs. 25*).—In this volume the effort of the author has been to select, for the purposes of illustration of a class of compounds, such compounds as are of biological importance and interest rather than of technical or synthetical.

The synthesis of protein substances, P. E. Verkade (*Chem. Weekbl., 14 (1917), No. 3, pp. 89–104*).—This is a general discussion of protein substances, including the synthesis and analysis of the material and of intermediate products.

The phytic acid of the wheat kernel and some of its salts, P. W. Boutwell (*Jour. Amer. Chem. Soc., 39 (1917), No. 3, pp. 491–503*).—This paper consists of two parts.

In part I (pp. 491–499), the work on phytic acid is reviewed, and the lack of uniformity in the results of the analysis of the acid and its salts which have been previously published indicated.

Phytin free from inorganic phosphates has been prepared both from wheat bran and wheat embryo by precipitation from a boiling acetic acid solution. The product obtained was a crystalline calcium-magnesium salt, insoluble in water. It did not agree in composition with any simple calcium-magnesium salt of inosit hexaphosphoric acid, and is indicated as representing a new compound from wheat not previously described. The free acid has been separated from this preparation and differs from the sample previously described in that it is a solid substance readily undergoing spontaneous decomposition during drying in vacuum.

Crystalline barium salts have been prepared from the phytin obtained both from the wheat embryo and the wheat bran by the new procedure. "The barium salt crystallized from the cold dilute hydrochloric solution agrees in composition with an equi-molecular mixture of the tri- and tetra-barium salts of inosit hexaphosphoric acid. The barium salts crystallized from the dilute hydrochloric acid solution on boiling do not agree in composition with any salts of inosit hexaphosphoric acid, but with a mixed salt consisting of two molecules of tri-barium inosit hexaphosphate and one molecule of tri-barium inosit tetraphosphate." It is indicated that "phytin exists in the wheat kernel as salts of inosit phosphoric acid, and that phytic acid is an ester of inosit and phosphoric acid."

II. *Concerning the phytase of wheat bran and wheat embryo* (pp. 499–503).— "In hydrochloric acid of 0.2 per cent concentration the hydrolysis effected by the enzym in wheat bran as indicated by the production of inorganic phosphoric acid is inhibited, and is only about one-third as great as in the ease of 0.1 per cent hydrochloric acid, the concentration of acid in which the enzym exhibits its maximum activity." Dry heat was found to increase the amount of inorganic phosphorus extracted from the wheat bran, without apparently destroying the enzym. Formaldehyde had no effect on the activity of the phytase. The phytin-splitting enzym was found in the wheat embryo. The maximum activity was evident in the presence of 0.1 per cent hydrochloric acid, but was inhibited by 0.2 per cent hydrochloric acid. The enzym is practically destroyed by 0.4 per cent acid.

See also previous notes by Clarke (E. S. R., 32, p. 16) and Anderson (E. S. R., 31, p. 707; 33, p. 11).

Studies on the forms of d-glucose and their mutarotation, C. S. HUDSON and J. K. DALE (Jour. Amer. Chem. Soc., 39 (1917), No. 2, pp. 320–328).

The influence of amino-acetic acid and α-amino propionic acid on the action of alkali on glucose, H. I. WATERMAN (Chem. Weekbl., 14 (1917), No. 4, pp. 119–124).—Analytical data submitted and discussed show that the influence of alanin on the action of alkali on glucose as regards the change in polarimetric readings is similar to that exhibited by glycocoll. For equal weights of the materials the action of alanin, however, is not so marked.

It is indicated that the reactions involved are being further studied and will be published in a future contribution.

Notes on some fatty oils, S. UCHIDA (Jour. Soc. Chem. Indus., 35 (1916), No. 21, pp. 1089–1093).—These pages give data relative to the yield and physical and chemical constants of the oils of Para rubber tree seed (Hevea brasiliensis), shiromoji seed (Lindera triloba), Calophyllum inophyllum, Hernandia seed (Hernandia peltata), hakuunboku seed (Styrax obassia), akebi seed (Akebia quinata), kuromoji seed (L. serica), aburachan seed (L. præcox), magnolia fruit, magnolia flesh, magnolia seed (Magnolia hypoleuca), and tea seed (Thea chinensis).

The effect of anesthetics and of frosting on the cyanogenetic compounds of Sorghum vulgare, J. J. WILLAMAN (Jour. Biol. Chem., 29 (1917), No. 1, pp. 37–45).—Sorghum leaves exposed to chloroform, ether, and alcohol vapors yielded more hydrocyanic acid, both glucosidic and nonglucosidic, than the normal leaves. The anesthetics thus apparently appeared to stimulate both the hydrolytic and the synthetic action of the glucosidic enzyms. This case is considered as a demonstrated enzym synthesis in vivo.

"Enzym powder prepared from chloroformed leaves was about twenty-five times as active toward amygdalin as the powder from untreated leaves. Frosting also causes an increased yield of both glucosidic and nonglucosidic hydrocyanic acid. This is partly due to a rupturing of the cells, and partly to disturbed enzym equilibrium."

The chemical composition of the placenta, F. FENGER (Jour. Biol. Chem., 29 (1917), No. 1, pp. 19–23).—Analytical data of the fresh tissue and the desiccated fat-free material of the two portions of the placenta of a cow are reported in detailed tabular form and discussed. The data show that the constituents of the uterine placenta in general remain comparatively uniform throughout gestation, while the fetal placenta varies considerably at the different stages of pregnancy.

Some observations on the influence of humidity on the physical constants of paper, O. KRESS and P. SILVERSTEIN (Jour. Indus. and Engin. Chem., 9 (1917), No. 3, pp. 277–282, figs. 3).

Inflammability of carbonaceous dusts, H. H. BROWN (Jour. Indus. and Engin. Chem., 9 (1917), No. 3, pp. 269–275, figs. 7).

The chemistry of wood decay.—I, Introductory, R. E. ROSE and M. W. LISSE (Jour. Indus. and Engin. Chem., 9 (1917), No. 3, pp. 284–287).—Detailed analytical data of samples of sound, partially decayed, and totally decayed heartwood of Douglas fir are submitted and briefly discussed.

The data show that the progress of decay may be readily followed by chemical methods, and that even a comparative cellulose determination might serve to detect incipient decay, since in the cases studied decay was accompanied by a very rapid fall in cellulose content. The lignin was found to be far more resistant to decay than cellulose.

The value of a study of the process and products of decay in relation to studies on the composition of the organic substances in soil is indicated.

Tyrosinase, a mixture of two enzyms, T. FOLPMERS (*Chem. Weekbl., 13 (1916), No. 48, pp. 1282–1289*).—The author reviews the literature on the products of tyrosinase action, and submits some experimental data which substantiate the contention that the reaction consists of a deaminization (by oxidation) and then a further oxidation.

An efficient desiccator, L. S. PRATT (*Jour. Amer. Chem. Soc., 39 (1917), No. 2, pp. 271–273, fig. 1*).—The construction and use of the apparatus is described in detail. The advantages claimed for this type of desiccator are simplicity of construction and operation, rapidity of desiccation, adaptability to vacuum desiccation, and adaptability to desiccation at elevated temperatures.

A simple gas generator, R. O. FERNANDEZ (*Jour. Amer. Chem. Soc., 39 (1917), No. 2, p. 271, fig. 1*).—A simple apparatus which is indicated as yielding satisfactory results is described by a diagram.

A new direct reading refractometer with uniformly divided scale, G. W. MOFFITT (*Jour. Indus. and Engin. Chem., 9 (1917), No. 3, pp. 305–309, figs. 4*).—The theory, construction, and manipulation of a new form of apparatus are described in detail.

Further studies on a numerical expression for color as given by the Ives tint photometer, O. KRESS and G. C. McNAUGHTON (*Jour. Indus. and Engin. Chem., 9 (1917), No. 3, pp. 282–284, fig. 1*).—See also a previous note (E. S. R., 36, p. 207).

Determination of carbon dioxid in carbonates by diminished pressure, J. B. ZINN (*Jour. Amer. Chem. Soc., 39 (1917), No. 2, p. 270*).—The author recommends the use of an 8-liter aspirating bottle instead of the usual suction pump as being more satisfactory and yielding excellent results in this determination.

The Penfield test for carbon, W. G. MIXTER and F. L. HAIGH (*Jour. Amer. Chem. Soc., 39 (1917), No. 3, pp. 374, 375, figs. 3*).—The application of the well-known reaction for determining carbon and carbonates, which consists of heating a mixture of the sample with lead chromate in a small horizontal tube, near the open end of which is placed a drop of barium hydroxid solution, is described. In a determination of the delicacy of the test, using a mixture of silicon carbid and aluminum oxid, 0.01 mg. silicon carbid (containing 0.003 mg. carbon) was found to give an unquestionable reaction. It is indicated that the reaction could undoubtedly be made more delicate by using a minute drop of barium hydroxid solution and observing the result with a microscope.

The volumetric determination of tin, R. L. HALLETT (*Jour. Soc. Chem. Indus., 35 (1916), No. 21, pp. 1087–1089*).—This is a general review and discussion of the procedures for the determination of tin. A bibliography of 40 references to the literature cited is appended.

On the determination of potassium as perchlorate, G. P. BAXTER and M. KOBAYASHI (*Jour. Amer. Chem. Soc., 39 (1917), No. 2, pp. 249–252*).—From solubility and analytical data reported the authors submit, as recommendations for the determination of potassium as perchlorate in the presence of sodium, the use of absolute alcohol for washing, the use of a low temperature in washing (0° C.), and the use of a platinum-sponge crucible. The value of the use of a washing liquid saturated with potassium perchlorate, as previously suggested, is indorsed, as well as the solution and recrystallization of the precipitate in the presence of rather large amounts of sodium salts.

The use of methylene blue in chemical analysis and its special application for the determination of perchlorates in Chile saltpeter, A. MONNIER (*Ann. Chim. Analyt.*, 22 (*1917*), *No. 1, pp. 1–6*).—The author has found that in dilute solutions iodids, perchlorates, persulphates, bichromates, permanganates, ferricyanids, metavanadates, molybdates, and tungstates give a precipitate with a solution of methylene blue. For the distinction of ferricyanids from ferrocyanids, iodids in iodates and periodates, persulphates in the presence of other sulphur acids, and perchlorates in chlorates or other acids of chlorin the reactions are characteristic. A colorimetric procedure for the determination of perchlorate in saltpeter which depends on the production of a violet precipitate with a bronze fluorescence is described in detail. The effect of the presence of iodids in the Chile saltpeter, which can easily be removed as silver iodid, is noted. The other salts present in crude saltpeter are without effect on the production of the color.

Studies on the phenoldisulphonic acid method for determining nitrates in soils, C. W. DAVIS (*Jour. Indus. and Engin. Chem.*, 9 (*1917*), *No. 3, pp. 290–295*).—The author studied the various factors which had previously been found to influence the accuracy of the results obtained by the phenoldisulphonic acid procedure and found that ammonia fumes did not affect the results of the determination. Light was found to affect the color material, so that the readings to influence the accuracy of the results obtained by the phenoldisulphonic acid acid had no effect on the results, nor did the temperature of the solution at the time the alkali is added to develop color show any variation in results except at freezing temperature, when a loss of 4 per cent resulted. Potassium chlorid added just before and just after the developing of the color by potassium hydroxid produced no loss of nitrates. With the use of uniform amounts of phenoldisulphonic acid (2 cc.) the maximum loss of nitrates was 30 per cent. When proportional amounts of the reagent were used (2 cc. for each 0.025 mg.) the maximum loss was reduced to 10 per cent.

A modified procedure in which the loss of nitrates is prevented by keeping the solution alkaline during evaporation is described. The addition of two drops of hydrochloric acid in a solution containing 25 parts per million of nitrates caused a loss of all nitrates. By keeping the solution alkaline during evaporation there was no loss even in the presence of chlorids, sulphates, and carbonates. Potassium alum may be used as a flocculent in preparing the soil solution without a loss of nitrates.

The work of Lipman and Sharp (E. S. R., 28, p. 610) was checked up and similar results obtained.

A bibliography of 35 references to the literature cited is included.

A note on the detection and estimation of small amounts of methyl alcohol, E. ELVOVE (*Jour. Indus. and Engin. Chem.*, 9 (*1917*), *No. 3, pp. 295–297*).—In a study of the application of Denigès test [1] for methyl alcohol to its colorimetric estimation the author found that by reducing the proportion of ethyl alcohol from 10 per cent, as recommended by Simmonds,[2] to 0.5 per cent the accuracy of the method was markedly increased.

For preparing the reagent the following procedure was found to yield the best results: Two-tenths gm. finely powdered fuchsin is dissolved in 120 cc. hot water and cooled to room temperature. Two gm. of anhydrous sodium sulphite dissolved in 20 cc. of water is added to the fuchsin solution, after which 2 cc. hydrochloric acid (specific gravity 1.19) is added and the whole diluted to

[1] Compt. Rend. Acad. Sci. [Paris], 150 (1910), No. 13, pp. 832–834.
[2] Analyst, 37 (1912), No. 430, pp. 16–18.

200 cc. with water. After standing for about an hour this solution is ready for use. A solution kept in a closed container for six weeks was found to be as reliable at the end of that time as a freshly prepared solution.

When formaldehyde is present in the solution to be tested it should be accurately determined and the same amount used in the standards.

Cellulose, C. F. Cross, E. J. Bevan, and C. Beadle (*London and New York: Longmans, Green & Co., 1916, new ed., XVII+328, pls. 14*).—This edition is in the main a reprint of the former edition with a small portion of the text rewritten and the addition of an appendix which includes an account of the more important recent contributions. The subject as a whole treats of the chemistry of the structural elements of plants with reference to their natural history and industrial uses, and is divided into three parts, the typical cellulose and the cellulose group, compound celluloses, and experimental and applied chemistry.

A quantitative method for the determination of arginin in proteins, B. C. P. Jansen (*Chem. Weekbl., 14 (1917), No. 4, pp. 125–129*).—A new method is proposed which consists of hydrolyzing a suitable sample of protein with hydrochloric acid (specific gravity 1.19), removing as much of the excess hydrochloric acid as possible by evaporation, and neutralizing the hydrolyzate with alkali until slightly alkaline to litmus or neutral to neutral red. Aliquot portions are then treated simultaneously with solutions of arginase and urease for about 24 hours, after which time the ammonia from the ammonium carbonate formed is liberated by a saturated solution of potassium carbonate and distilled by aeration into standard acid. A blank determination is made with an aliquot and urease alone to determine the presence and amount of urea in the hydrolyzate. One molecule of arginin yields one molecule of ornithin and urea, so that the amount of arginin originally present is readily calculated from the amount of ammonia obtained.

The method is considered to yield more accurate results than the procedure of boiling the hydrolyzate with alkali as described by Van Slyke (E. S. R., 26, p. 22).

The preparation of the arginase from the fresh liver of a dog or cat is described in detail.

Red peppers, F. M. Boyles (*Jour. Indus. and Engin. Chem., 9 (1917), No. 3, pp. 301, 302*).—Analytical data of a number of samples of South Carolina capsicum, Bombay capsicum, Japan capsicum, Mombasa chilies, and miscellaneous capsicums and chilies are reported in tabular form. The data include total ash, insoluble ash, fiber, total ether extract, and volatile and nonvolatile ether extract.

It is indicated that the present standards for red peppers (E. S. R., 18, p. 459) are in need of revision and the following is submitted: Total ash 7.5 per cent, hydrochloric acid-insoluble ash 1 per cent, nonvolatile ether extract 14 per cent, and crude fiber 29 per cent.

Vinegar: Its manufacture and examination, C. A. Mitchell (*London: Charles Griffin & Co., Ltd., 1916, pp. XVI+201, pls. 5, figs. 49*).—This volume discusses the subject in detail under the general topics of historical introduction, theories of acetic fermentation, acetic bacteria, chemical reactions in acetification, acetic acid, preparation and acetification of the gyle, treatment of the crude vinegar, methods of examination, and characteristics of different vinegars. Appendixes contain British import duties on vinegar and acetic acid and French duties on vinegar.

The volatile reducing substance in cider vinegar, R. W. Balcom (*Jour. Amer. Chem. Soc., 39 (1917), No. 2, pp. 309–315*).—The author has shown that the volatile reducing substances in cider vinegar consist largely, if not wholly, of acetylmethyl-carbinol and that this substance is a normal constituent of the vinegar.

The experimental procedures used in the investigation are described in detail.

The analysis of Peruvian bark, J. W. COMMELIN (*Meded. Kina Proefstat.* [*Dutch East Indies*], *No. 1 (1912), pp. 38*).—This pamphlet describes and discusses in detail procedures for the determination of moisture, total alkaloids, quinin, and cinchonidin. Simplicity of methods was the aim, since they were to be used in cultural experiments. Formulas for calculating the quantity of total alkaloids and cinchonidin are included, together with correction tables for polarimetric readings, etc.

The determination of the various forms of nitrogen in forage plants, N. PASSERINI (*Ann. Chim. Appl.* [*Rome*], *6 (1916), No. 5–8, pp. 162–164*).—The author describes a procedure by which the forms of nitrogen in the hydrolyzed sample are determined as nuclein nitrogen, amino acid nitrogen, ammonia nitrogen, and preformed amid nitrogen. The procedure consists essentially of determining the pure protein according to the procedure of Kellner in a 1 gm. sample. In another 5 gm. hydrolyzed sample, after treating according to Kellner's method, the copper is removed with hydrogen sulphid and the ammonia determined in an aliquot of the filtrate. The nonhydrolyzable nitrogen, considered to be nuclein, is then determined in the residue. The amino acid nitrogen is determined by subtracting the sum of the ammonia and nonhydrolyzable nitrogen from the total protein nitrogen.

A table showing the distribution of nitrogen in whole wheat, wheat bran, wheat flour, maize, beans, and vetch is submitted.

The estimation of hydrocyanic acid and the probable form in which it occurs in Sorghum vulgare, J. J. WILLAMAN (*Jour. Biol. Chem., 29 (1917), No. 1, pp. 25–36*).—The author, at the Minnesota Experiment Station, considers the methods in general use for the determination of hydrocyanic acid in plant tissues of questionable accuracy because of the difficulty of obtaining complete hydrolysis of the glucosids by means of acids and because of the retention of the cyanid from distillation by the tissues involved.

Analytical data show that the hydrolysis of durrin, the glucosid in sorghum, is best accomplished by autolysis, the reaction taking place rapidly at 45° C. " Retention of hydrocyanic acid by the tissues during distillation can not be prevented by the presence of tartaric acid, nor can it appreciably be lessened by distilling under reduced pressure." Hydrocyanic acid occurs in *S. vulgare* in two forms, as a glucosid and as a nonglucosid, the nature of which is yet unknown. The nonglucosidic form is considered to be probably responsible for the poisoning of stock. This form can be distinguished from the glucosidic by grinding the leaves in the presence of 5 per cent tartaric acid to prevent any enzym action and then distilling.

Relation of the fat in milk to the solids-not-fat, L. P. BROWN and C. V. EKROTH (*Jour. Indus. and Engin. Chem., 9 (1917), No. 3, pp. 297–299, fig. 1*).— The authors have devised a zone chart from the figures for percentage fat and percentage solids-not-fat of a large number of published analyses of milk. The chart shows the approximate chemical composition of normal milk and is intended as a guide in fixing legal standards and also in detecting adulteration.

It is indicated that " a milk standard having regard only for the total solids is illogical. Most of the legal milk standards in force in the several States of the Union as well as that of the Federal Government are unbalanced and, therefore, incapable of enforcement."

The detection of preservatives and coloring matter in milk, I. M. KOLT-HOFF (*Pharm. Weekbl., 53 (1916), No. 48, pp. 1609–1618*).—The author briefly reviews the preservatives and coloring matters commonly used and the procedures for their detection by the official Dutch methods.

A considerably shorter scheme for routine examination is proposed, in which formalin is detected by phenol sulphonic acid, hydrogen peroxid by vanadic acid in sulphuric acid, and carbonate by the difference in acidity before and after heating. The coloring matters are determined by the usual tests. An outline for the detection of salicylic, benzoic, and boric acids and fluorids in the ether extract of milk is also submitted.

A new method for the analysis of rancid fats and oils, G. Issoglio (*Ann. Chim. Appl. [Rome], 6 (1916), No. 1-2, pp. 1-18*).—Rancidity and its detection in oils and fats is briefly reviewed, and a new procedure by which a new constant called the oxidation number is determined is described. This constant is represented by the milligrams of oxygen necessary to oxidize the volatile organic material obtained by steam distillation from 100 gm. of the sample. The material is oxidized with standard permanganate and the excess permanganate titrated against oxalic acid.

Analytical data showing the oxidation number, acid index, and iodin number of a number of pure and rancid olive oils, three samples of peanut oil, two each of sesame and soy-bean oil, rape-seed oil, cottonseed oil, butter, vegetable butters, oleomargarin, and some animal fats are submitted. For pure edible oils the constant was found generally to range from 3 to 10. For rancid fats it was much higher, a value of 15 being an indication of slight rancidity or some change in the material. The new constant proposed is considered to be of value in evaluating oils, and should be determined with the other constants in the usual examination of oils.

[Report of the analysis of various samples] (*Dept. Landb., Nijr. en Handel [Netherlands], Verslag. en Meded. Dir. Landb., No. 5 (1916), pp. 52-59*).—These pages contain brief notes on the analysis of various samples of soil, plant products, water, dairy products, insecticides, fungicides, and fertilizers.

Fruit drying, W. J. Allen (*Agr. Gaz. N. S. Wales, 28 (1917), No. 1, pp. 13-29, figs. 7*).—These pages describe procedures for the curing and drying of apricots, peaches, nectarines, prunes, apples, pears, figs, raisins, sultanas, and currants as practiced in New South Wales.

Sulphitation in white sugar manufacture, F. Maxwell (*London: Norman Rodger, 1916, pp. XII+72, pls. 3, figs. 8*).—This is a general discussion of the subject under the following topics: Sulphur, its origin, preparation, and properties; sulphurous acid, its preparation, chemical properties, and action; generating plants for sulphurous acid gas and sulphitation vessels for juice and sirup; the control of the sulphurous acid gas generating station; analysis of the sulphurous acid gas; action of sulphurous acid on juices; principles of the application of sulphitation to juice; sulphitation of the sirup and of molasses; the sulphitation process in practice; processes adopted by the leading white sugar countries; and a general summary.

A study of commercial beech wood creosote, H. K. Smith and S. F. Acree (*Jour. Indus. and Engin. Chem., 9 (1917), No. 3, pp. 275, 276*).

A method of producing crude wood creosote from hardwood tar, R. O. Judd and S. F. Acree (*Jour. Indus. and Engin. Chem., 9 (1917), No. 3, pp. 276, 277*).

METEOROLOGY.

Relation of weather to the amount of cotton ginned during certain periods, J. B. Kincer (*U. S. Mo. Weather Rev., 45 (1917), No. 1, pp. 6-10, figs. 2*).—Data regarding cotton ginned, as related to temperature and fair days during the 11-year period 1905-1915, are presented in tables and diagrams.

The conclusion is reached that "a forecast of the size of the cotton crop, based on the ginning reports, has a much greater value when consideration is given to the influencing weather factors. . . . than when the reports alone are considered. For example, if temperatures during the critical months of growth be high and thus conduce to a rapid advancement and early maturity of the crop, and in addition the weather be favorable for picking during the period covered by a given early ginning report, say September 1 to September 25, it may be safely considered that the percentage of the total crop ginned during the period will be much in excess of the average and the final yield less than that apparently indicated by the actual amount ginned to that date. . . .

"If, however, these modifying weather influences work in opposition and thus largely neutralize each other then the amount ginned, whether above or below the average, gives a better direct indication as to whether the final yield will also show values above or below the average than in the other case. Furthermore if the temperature conditions were unfavorable for early maturity and the percentage of fair days during the ginning period small, it may be safely assumed that the final yield will be larger than apparently indicated by the actual amount ginned.

"In studying early ginning reports in connection with the two modifying weather factors under discussion, it must be borne in mind that temperature has the dominating influence and should be given greater weight, but later, say for the period from September 25 to October 18, the amount of fair weather during the period itself takes precedence. . . .

"The fact that favorable temperatures during the early growing season are also conducive to comparatively large yields, as well as to early maturity of the crop, should likewise be considered, and it might also be noted that early maturity, in effect, postpones the date of first killing frost in fall by an equal number of days represented by the earliness of the crop and thus reduces the chance of damage from this source."

Monthly Weather Review (*U. S. Mo. Weather Rev., 45 (1917), Nos. 1, pp. 1–46, pls. 10, figs. 2; 2, pp. 47–90, pls. 10, figs. 3*).—In addition to weather forecasts, river and flood observations, and seismological reports for January and February, 1917; lists of additions to the Weather Bureau Library and of recent papers on meteorology and seismology; notes on the weather of the months; solar and sky radiation measurements at Washington, D. C., during January and February, 1917; condensed climatological summaries; and the usual climatological tables and charts, these numbers contain the following articles:

No. 1.—Notes on the Horizontal Rainbow, by S. Nakamura; Demonstration of Horizontal and Intersecting Rainbows, by K. Otobe; Aurora of August 26, 1916, Observed at Hessel, Mich., by F. E. Nipher; Relation of Weather to the Amount of Cotton Ginned during Certain Periods (illus.), by J. B. Kincer (see p. 114); Grasshoppers at Sea, by W. E. Hurd; National Meteorological Service of Colombia; Another "Dark Day of May 19, 1780"? Classification of the Hydrometeors, II, by G. Hellmann; Notes and Comments on Hellmann's Classification of Hydrometeors; Alternate Deposition of Rauhreif and Ranheis (illus.), by W. R. Blair; and Ammonia in Dew (see p. 116).

No. 2.—The Smoke Cloud and the High Haze of 1916, by H. H. Kimball; Free-air Data in the Hawaiian Islands, July, 1915, by W. E. Ellis; Weather Bureau Exhibit at the First Pan American Aeronautic Exposition (illus.), by W. R. Gregg; Sound Areas of the Explosion at East London, January 19, 1917, by C. Davison; Parhelic Circle with Two Pairs of Parhelia at Fargo, N. Dak.; Competency of Wind in Land Depletion, by C. R. Keyes; Reduction of Air Temperatures at Swedish Stations to a True Mean, by N. Ekholm; Formation of Winter Stratus, Depth of Northeast Wind, by D. Manning; Atmospheric Circulation and the Weather in Argentina, by H. H. Clayton; The Argentine Meteorological Service; and Report of the Meteorological Station at Berkeley, Cal., for the Year Ending June 30, 1915 (illus.), by W. G. Reed.

Climatological data for the United States by sections (*U. S. Dept. Agr., Weather Bur. Climat. Data, 4 (1917), Nos. 1, pp. 238, pls. 2, figs. 4; pp. 246, pls. 2, figs. 7).*—These volumes contain brief summaries and detailed tabular statements of climatological data for each State for January and February, 1917, respectively.

Meteorological records (*Hawaii Sta. Rpt. 1916, p. 43*).—Monthly summaries of observations from January 1 to June 30, 1916, on temperature, precipitation, and rainy and clear days at the Glenwood substation, Hawaii, are tabulated.

Meteorological observations at the Massachusetts Agricultural Experiment Station, J. E. OSTRANDER and W. P. SAUNDERS (*Massachusetts Sta. Met. Buls. 339–340 (1917), pp. 4 each*).—Summaries of observations at Amherst, Mass., on pressure, temperature, humidity, precipitation, wind, sunshine, cloudiness, and casual phenomena during March and April, 1917, are presented. The data are briefly discussed in general notes on the weather of each month.

Free-air data at Drexel aerological station: January, February, and March, 1916 (*U. S. Mo. Weather Rev., Sup. 5 (1917), pp. 59, pls. 3*).—The results of 138 free-air observations at Drexel, Nebr., by means of kites are reported in detail. "The means of the highest points reached with the kites are 2.722 meters above sea level in January, 2.809 in February, 2,631 in March, and 2,731 for the period."

Ammonia in dew (*Met. Off. [Gt. Brit.] Circ. 7 (1916), p. 4; U. S. Mo. Weather Rev., 45 (1917), No. 1, p. 19*).—Samples of dew collected on glass plates 12 in. square exposed 1 ft. above the ground over grass land in fine weather from September 23 to December 6, 1914, and within one hour of sunrise, showed no nitrates, traces of chlorids, and a comparatively large proportion of ammonia, namely, 7.5 and 5 parts by weight in 1,000,000, respectively.

SOILS—FERTILIZERS.

The water content of the soil and the composition and concentration of the soil solution as indicated by the freezing-point lowerings of the roots and tops of plans, M. M. McCOOL and C. E. MILLAR (*Soil Sci., 3 (1917), No. 2, pp. 113–138*).—This paper, prepared at the Michigan Experiment Station, presents the principal results of greenhouse and field studies on the concentration and composition of the soil solution, the water content of soils, and the rate of water movement in soils as measured by the freezing point lowerings of the roots and leaves of plants. Several different soils and plants were used.

It was found that "consistent determinations of the freezing-point depression of plant tissue may be obtained by inserting the thermometer directly into material triturated in the freezing tube. Results with material repeatedly reduced to the point of solidification, repeatedly frozen at low temperatures, and material frozen at low temperatures and macerated or triturated were essentially the same as those obtained by direct freezing of the triturated material.

"The freezing-point depression of sap expressed under great pressure from the aerial portion of the plants studied, previously frozen at low temperatures, was practically the same as that of the material frozen directly, but greater if the pressure is not so great. The freezing-point depressions of the juice expressed from roots frozen at low temperatures were not consistent. It was found necessary to take samples of vegetable material for freezing-point work at the same time of day or else protect the plants from light and retard transpiration, since the freezing-point depression of the leaves was found to increase from morning till noon and decrease again in the evening. It appeared that this change was due to the products of photosynthesis, as well as to the moisture content of the material which decreased from morning till noon and increased again in the evening.

. "The concentration of the solution in which roots of Canada field pea and wheat are grown is indicated by the freezing-point lowerings of the root tissues, but on the other hand only rather wide variations are indicated by the freezing-point lowerings of the tops. Changes in the concentration of the soil solution induced by the addition of salts may be detected by determining the freezing-point lowerings of the roots of the plants growing therein. It was found that the tops of the plants are far less sensitive to changes in the concentration of the soil solution.

"The moisture content of soils is closely correlated with the freezing-point lowerings of the roots of the plants in contact with them, due in part at least to changes in the concentration of the soil solution so induced, but again the tops of the plants studied, under both greenhouse and field conditions, prove to be far less sensitive to soil moisture changes, at least until the critical water content is approached. The indications are that the soil solution and the root sap of plants approach each other in concentration at or near the critical (low) water content of the soil. The freezing-point lowering of a given crop growing in widely different soils of high water content were found to differ but slightly. On the other hand, different crops growing on the same soil, under similar conditions, vary appreciably in this respect. The field studies show that crops may be subjected to sudden and very wide variations in the concentration of the soil solution during the growing season."

Twenty-eight references to literature bearing on the subject are appended.

Relation of the water-retaining capacity of a soil to its hygroscopic coefficient, F. J. ALWAY and G. R. McDOLE (*U. S. Dept. Agr., Jour Agr. Research,* 9 (1917), No. 2, pp. 27–71, figs. 4).—Laboratory experiments conducted at the Nebraska Experiment Station with uniform columns of soil of known hygroscopic coefficient and moisture content are reported. The 13 soils used ranged in texture from a coarse sand to a silt loam, with hygroscopic coefficients of 0.6 and 13.3, respectively.

"Five of the loams, placed in capillary connection with the natural subsoil mass, saturated with water, and allowed to stand protected from surface evaporation for several months, lost water until the amount retained bore a close relation to the hygroscopic coefficient, being from 2.1 to 3.1 times this value, according to the particular soil. When a layer of coarse sand or gravel separated the column of loam from the natural subsoil mass or interrupted it, the downward movement of the water in the soil above this layer was much delayed. Where the column consisted of successive 2-in. layers of loams differing widely in texture, the order of their arrangement exerted no influence upon their final water content.

"Soil columns 30 to 36 in. long, while protected from all loss of moisture at the sides and bottom, were freely exposed to evaporation at the surface for periods varying from a few weeks to half a year. The moisture content, originally uniform and lying between 2 and 3 times the hygroscopic coefficient, fell until it reached, at depths below the first foot, an almost constant minimum with the ratio 1.9 : 2.2.

" Employing 2-ft. columns of 12 different loams, each with an initial moisture content approximately equal to its hygroscopic coefficient, enough water was added to raise the average moisture content of the column to 1.5 times the hygroscopic coefficient, the water being applied in one experiment to the top and in another to the base of the column. After the cylinders had stood for three or four months fully protected from evaporation the distribution of moisture, with regard to the surface to which it had been applied, was found to be the same in both experiments. The maximum distance through which an effect was shown was about 2 ft., but in most cases much less. The maximum final ratio of moisture content to hygroscopic coefficient was found in the section adjacent to the surface of application, where it lay between 1.7 and 2.4. The ratio, while falling within these limits, is not a constant, it not being the same for all the soils that have the same hygroscopic coefficient.

" The water-retaining capacity of the loams, as determined by laboratory experiments, was found to bear a somewhat closer relation to the moisture equivalent than to the hygroscopic coefficient, the ratio varying between 0.8 and 1.2.

" Coarse sands exhibited a behavior very different from that of the loams. The ratio in the surface 6-in. section, even three months after 1 in. of water had been applied to the surface, was as high as 6 or 7, while in the second foot it was only 1. The field studies on coarse sands showed as high a final ratio as was observed in the laboratory experiments. The very limited studies on fine sands indicate that these occupy a position intermediate between the loams and the coarse sands, the ratio of the water-retaining capacity to the hygroscopic coefficient rising as the latter value falls.

" Field studies show that when loams, after rains sufficiently heavy to moisten them thoroughly, are protected from losses by evaporation and transpiration, they lose water by downward movement until the ratio of moisture content to hygroscopic coefficient lies between 1.8 and about 2.5, and accordingly on the uplands of dry-land regions this is the ratio to be expected in the deeper subsoil—the portion below the range of plant roots.

" A comparatively abrupt transition from the moistened soil to the thoroughly exhausted underlying layers, with ratios of 2:2.5 and 1:1.1, respectively, is found even several months after liberal rains have fallen, if the subsoil to a considerable depth had previously been exhausted of available water. The moisture of the deeper subsoil will be able to move upward only so slowly and through such a short distance in a single season that it will be at most of no practical benefit to annual crops. To make use of any portion of the precipitation which penetrates beyond the reach of the roots of annual crops it will be necessary to follow such crops at intervals by deep-rooting perennials."

Twenty-five references to literature bearing on the subject are appended.

Investigations on the acidity of acid mineral soils, I. S. Osugi and T. Uetsuki (Ber. Ōhara Inst. Landw. Forsch., 1 (1916), No. 1, pp. 27–52, fig. 1).— On the assumption that the acidity of acid soils is intimately related to their alumina content, the authors conducted experiments in which it was found that when the bases of soils disappear as a result of active weathering and decomposition certain colloidal substances are formed in the soils which actively absorb bases. When such soils are then treated with salt solutions acids are set free. It was found that the alumina in soils is easily dissolved out by hydrochloric acid but not by acetic acid. Therefore, considerable alumina was found in the filtrate of a potassium chlorid solution of the soil but only a little in the filtrate of a potassium acetate solution of the soil. It is thought that other factors also influence the difference in the intensity of the acidity of the two filtrates, and that the action of the acids set free by adsorption of bases is important in this connection.

It is concluded best, therefore, to consider an acid soil as one not saturated with bases.

The sulphur content of some typical Kansas soils, and the loss of sulphur due to cultivation, C. O. Swanson and R. W. Miller (*Soil Sci., 3 (1917), No. 2, pp. 139–148*).—Studies of the sulphur content of eleven samples of typical Kansas soils made at the Kansas Experiment Station are reported. The soils are loams, silt loams, and silty clay loams. Five were from fields in the native sod and six from fields in cultivation for from 30 to 40 years.

The results " show that the percentage loss of sulphur from cultivated soils is proportionately equal to that of organic matter. It has also been shown that the loss of sulphur due to the amount taken up by the crop is insignificant as compared with the total amount which has disappeared from the soil. This means that the sulfofication has been in excess of the needs of the crop and the sulphates produced have leached out of the ground. As measured by crop requirements, sulfofication has been much more rapid than nitrification."

It is further concluded that the loss of sulphur from soil may be a very important factor in the loss of productivity. "Whether or not sulphur is at present a limiting element in the production of crops on Kansas soils, it is apparent that the supply of this essential element is closely related to the supply of organic matter. . . . It would seem that sulphur would become a limiting factor sooner than phosphorus unless sulphur is made available more rapidly than phosphorus. This, however, would not affect the ultimate supply."

Sixteen references to literature bearing on the subject are appended.

Studies in sulfofication, P. E. Brown and H. W. Johnson (*Iowa Sta. Research Bul. 34 (1916), pp. 3–24*).—Continuing previous work (E. S. R., 34, p. 19), experiments on the relative effects of gypsum, acid phosphate, rock phosphate alone and with gypsum, and monocalcium phosphate, on sulfofication and on ammonification and the yields of oats in pots are reported. The soil used was a black loam, high in organic matter and of basic reaction.

It was found that " the sulphate content of the soil varied only slightly from one sampling to the next. There were no sudden or striking changes in the amount of sulphates present in soil kept fallow in the greenhouse. The sulphate content of soils in the field is subject to the same influences as the nitrate content, but the effects are probably much less pronounced.

" Calcium sulphate, monocalcium phosphate, acid phosphate, rock phosphate, and rock phosphate plus gypsum increased the sulfofying power of the soil. The sulphate alone and phosphates alone had greater effects than combinations of the two materials as in acid phosphate. All the materials used increased the ammonifying power of the soil, but the differences between the effects of the various substances were not pronounced. The rock phosphate had less effect, however, than the other materials. The sulfofication tests and ammonification tests did not always run parallel, although very similar effects of the materials used, on the two processes, were noted. The phosphorus fertilizers, except monocalcium phosphate, increased the yield of oats on the soil, the acid phosphate to a greater extent than the rock phosphate. The sulphate had no effect on the crop yield. . . .

" The crop yields, sulfofication, and ammonification results were not always parallel. In general, it appeared that on this soil increases in sulfofication were not necessarily parallel with increases in yields. The ammonification results were not conclusive but indicate that materials supplying plant food constituents which are lacking in the soil may be of double value because of increases in the production of other plant food constituents in an available form."

Further studies on sulfofication in five soils of varying texture and composition showed that "in the use of the free-sulphur-fresh-soil method for testing the sulfofying power of soils, the incubation period should be 14 days at room temperature to give the most conclusive results. Ten days' incubation gave the relative sulfofying powers of soils quite accurately, but the differences were much more distinctive for the longer period.

"Calcium sulphate in ordinary applications had no detrimental effect on sulfofication, but very large applications might decrease the rate of oxidation of sulphur. Calcium carbonate in ordinary applications on acid soils increased sulfofication considerably and even in excessive amounts affected sulphur oxidation favorably. Magnesium carbonate in small amounts increased sulfofication, but in large amounts depressed it even below that in the same soil with its acidity unneutralized. Magnesium carbonate and calcium carbonate in combination exerted a beneficial influence on sulfofication when used in small amounts. Larger applications, however, depressed the oxidation of sulphur. The effects of the combined materials were less than that of the calcium carbonate alone."

Nitrous nitrogen in irrigated soils, J. E. GREAVES, R. STEWART, and C. T. HIRST (Soil Sci., 3 (1917), No. 2, pp. 149–154, pl. 1).—This paper, prepared at the Utah Experiment Station, reports a study of the nitrous nitrogen content of soils made in connection with studies of the influence of irrigation water on the movement and production of nitrates in irrigated soils (E. S. R., 27, p. 418).

"The data reported represent some 800 determinations of the nitrous nitrogen of a calcareous soil without crop, cropped to alfalfa, to oats and alfalfa, to oats, to potatoes, and to sugar beets. The water applied to the soil varied from none to 37.5 in. per acre yearly.

"The nitrous nitrogen content of the soil was very low and was about evenly distributed throughout the 10 ft. The total quantity found in an acre of soil to a depth of 10 ft. varied from a trace . . . up to 17 lbs. per acre.

"No relationship was found to exist between the nitrous nitrogen and the nitric nitrogen content of the soil. The application of irrigation water had no appreciable influence upon the nitrous nitrogen content of the soil, [but] there was a slight seasonal variation. . . . In the alfalfa and the oat soils it was highest in the spring and decreased toward fall, while in the potato and the corn soils it was lowest in spring and increased toward fall. In the fallow the nitrous nitrogen was highest in midsummer. The greatest quantity of nitrous nitrogen was found in the alfalfa soil during the spring, while the least was found under the oats during midsummer. The application of manure to the soil had no appreciable influence upon the nitrous nitrogen content of the soil."

Influence of humus forming materials of different nitrogen-carbon ratios on bacterial activities, P. E. BROWN and F. E. ALLISON (Iowa Sta. Research Bul. 36 (1916), pp. 3–30).—Pot experiments on the influence of materials of narrow and wide nitrogen-carbon ratio on the bacterial activities in Miami sandy loam soil, low in organic matter, are reported.

It was found that "applications of the common humus-forming materials in maximum amounts for farm conditions and in a dried condition increased ammonification, nitrification, and azofication to a considerable extent. Horse manure, cow manure, and rotted manure gave the greatest effect on ammonification in most cases, although timothy hay surpassed the horse manure and cow manure in the extent of its effect in several instances. The oats, straw, and corn stover gave a smaller effect than the manures, and the legume hays, clover, and cowpeas showed the least effect on ammonification of any of the materials used. Increases in ammonification due to the applications of humus-forming materials were independent of the nitrogen-carbon ratio of the materials added and were probably dependent on the chemical composition of the substances. . . .

"The dried-blood fresh-soil method gave better results for ammonification than the casein fresh-soil method. The latter gave better duplicate results, but the differences between different soils were not nearly so pronounced. Some further modification of the casein method seems necessary for its general use.

"Nitrification was increased in much the same way as ammonification, by the various organic materials. The leguminous green manures exerted, however, somewhat greater effects than the manures, and also more influence than the nonlegumes. These results were the opposite of those secured with ammonification, but the differences were not great enough to permit of definite conclusions. Increases in nitrification brought about by the various materials were apparently independent of the nitrogen-carbon ratio in the substances. Indications of a greater effect of materials of a narrower ratio over those of a wide ratio can not be considered conclusive.

"Nonsymbiotic nitrogen fixation was favored by manure to a large extent. Straw, stover, and nonleguminous hays had almost as great an effect as the manures, and the leguminous hays had the least effect of any of the materials used. The nitrogen-carbon ratio of the materials employed were of little or no significance in indicating their effects on azofication. There were indications, however, that nonlegumes and straws might increase azofication in soils to a large enough extent to make their use more profitable than that of legumes, which add nitrogen to the soil but are somewhat more expensive to use. . . .

"Dextrose gave better results in the azofication experiments than mannit and may, therefore, be substituted for the more expensive material. There was little similarity between the effects of the different organic materials on the different bacterial processes. . . .

"The manures and legumes increased the first crop of oats, except in the case of the horse manure, which apparently exerted an injurious effect on the crop in its early stages of growth. . . . The substances with wide nitrogen-carbon ratio decreased the crop yield while those of narrow ratios gave increases. The nitrogen factor was evidently very important on this soil.

"'The nitrogen-carbon ratio of the organic materials did seem to be of importance in determining the influence on the first crop of oats. . . . The influence of the various substances applied to the soils was noted on a second crop of oats, but the relative effects were different. The nonlegumes had as great an influence as the legumes, and hence previous conclusions are confirmed that with the use of the former materials sufficient time must be allowed to elapse for azofication to occur if as beneficial effects are to be secured as with legumes. The nitrogen-carbon ratio of the materials applied to the soil did not seem to be of as much importance in determining the effect on the second crop of oats as in the case of the first crop."

The organic matter of the soil.—IV, Some data on humus-phosphoric acid, R. A. GORTNER and W. M. SHAW (*Soil Sci.*, *3* (*1917*), No. *2*, pp. *99–111*).— Studies of the phosphoric acid in the humus of soils described in previous reports of this series (E. S. R., 37, p. 20) are reported. These included the determination of the phosphoric acid content of the ammonia extracts of the soils, of peats, and of unchanged vegetable materials both before and after leaching the samples with 1 per cent hydrochloric acid.

It was found that " ammonium hydroxid in 4 per cent concentration will, in certain soil types, extract more phosphoric acid from the air-dry soil than will 1 per cent hydrochloric acid, and in only one sample of eight different soil types did hydrochloric acid extract appreciably more phosphoric acid than did the ammonia. There appears to be no relation between the amounts of phosphoric acid extracted by ammonia from the unleached soil and that extracted after leaching with 1 per cent hydrochloric acid, although in both instances there is usually a greater quantity of phosphoric acid extracted by the ammonia than is extracted by the acid. The amounts of humus-phosphoric acid present in the eight soil types studied when compared with the known fertility of these soil types do not support the theory that a high humus-phosphoric acid content is a necessary factor in soil fertility. . . .

" There is no relationship detectable between the total nitrogen content of the soil and the phosphoric acid extracted by the different treatments. The· amount of ' humus ash ' present in an ammonia extract is extremely variable, even when the extractions have been carried out under identical working conditions. A minimum of 6.7 per cent and a maximum of 32.6 per cent of ash were found in the ' humus ' extracted from the eight mineral soil types studied. Such a wide divergence can be accounted for only by the presence of considerable amounts of clay or absorbed mineral materials. . . .

" The ' humification ' of vegetable materials in contact with a mineral soil for an entire year did not increase the humus-phosphoric acid over that contained in the original subsoil. The phosphoric acid present in the ammonia extract of soils can not be correlated either with the amount of organic matter present or with the known fertility of the soil type. Inasmuch as this phosphoric acid does not represent a definite chemical entity, there appears to be no valid reason why determinations of humus-phosphoric acid should be made. It is pointed out that the conclusions drawn in regard to colloidal absorption of phosphoric acid apply with equal force to determinations of humus-potash, that in all probability organically bound potash does not occur in the soil in appreciable amounts."

Twenty-four references to literature bearing on the subject are appended.

Soil survey of Buchanan County, Missouri, B. W. TILLMAN and C. E. DEARDORFF (U. S. Dept. Agr., Advance Sheets Field Operations Bur. Soils, 1915, pp. 46, fig. 1, map 1).—This survey, made in cooperation with the Missouri Experiment Station, deals with the soils of an area of 258,560 acres in northwestern Missouri, which is divided into upland and level flood plain. The upland ranges from hilly to rolling and undulating, and is thoroughly, and in places excessively, drained. The bottom land drainage is generally imperfect. The soils of the county are of loessial, glacial, residual, and alluvial origin.

Including marsh, 15 soil types of 10 series are mapped, of which the Knox silt loam, Marshall silt loam, and Wabash silt loam cover 33.6, 32.6, and 11.8 per cent of the area, respectively.

Soil survey of Polk County, Nebraska, J. M. SNYDER and T. E. KOKJER (U. S. Dept. Agr., Advance Sheets Field Operations Bur. Soils, 1915, pp. 30, fig. 1, map 1).—This survey, made in cooperation with the Nebraska Soil Survey, deals with the soils of an area of 275,200 acres in east-central Nebraska.

"About two-thirds of the county consists of uplands of the loess plain and has a flat to undulating topography. On the north there is an abrupt break from this upland, and a strip of roughly rolling land intervenes between it and the broad valley of the Platte River. The alluvial lands of the valley are generally level or undulating, with local surface inequalities." The upland soils are of loessial origin.

Including riverwash, 16 soil types of 11 series are mapped, of which the Grundy silt loam, a dark brown prairie soil with heavy subsoil, covers 62.9 per cent of the area and is considered the most important soil type in the county.

Soil survey of the Camden area, New Jersey, A. L. PATRICK, C. C. ENGLE, and L. L. LEE (*U. S. Dept. Agr., Advance Sheets Field Operations Bur. Soils, 1915, pp. 45, pls. 5, figs. 3, map 1*).—This survey, made in cooperation with the New Jersey Geological Survey and Agricultural Experiment Station, deals with the soils of an area of 449,280 acres in the Coastal Plain in southern New Jersey, the topography of which is level to gently rolling. Drainage is effected by numerous small streams. The soils of the area are derived from beds of unconsolidated sand, sandy clay, gravel, greensand, and marly clay.

Including riverwash and tidal marsh, 26 soil types of 10 series are mapped, of which the Sassafras sandy loam and sand cover 19.1 and 14.1 per cent of the area, respectively. The Sassafras and Collington series cover the greater part of the area.

Soil survey of Blair County, Pennsylvania, J. O. VEATCH, H. P. YOUNG, and H. P. COOPER (*U. S. Dept. Agr., Advance Sheets Field Operations Bur. Soils, 1915, pp. 48, fig. 1, map 1*).—This survey, made in cooperation with the Pennsylvania College and Station, deals with the soils of a well-drained area of 341,760 acres in south-central Pennsylvania, the topography of which is in general mountainous and hilly.

The soils of the county are of residual, alluvial, and colluvial origin. Including rough stony land, 23 soil types of 13 series are mapped. "The Dekalb soils are most widely distributed, covering about 29.3 per cent of the area of the county." The most extensive soil type is, however, rough stony land, covering 17.7 per cent of the area, followed in order by the Dekalb stony loam 15.4 per cent, and Upshur stony loam 12.2 per cent.

Summary of results of cane culture tests in Java, I–III, J. M. GEERTS (*Meded. Proefstat. Java-Suikerindus., 5 (1915), No. 21, pp. 593–607; 6 (1916), Nos. 6, pp. 139–203, figs. 4; 9, pp. 233–305, figs. 5; Arch. Suikerindus. Nederland. Indië, 23 (1915), No. 52, pp. 1965–1979; 24 (1916), Nos. 14, pp. 473–537, figs. 4; 25, pp. 929–1001, figs. 5*).—In part 1 of this series of papers on sugar cane experiments in Java the author presents a general outline of the methods and aims of experimental work with sugar cane, with special reference to fertilizers.

In part 2, comparative studies of ammonium sulphate and boengkil, an organic nitrogenous fertilizer made of crushed oil-containing seeds, as nitrogenous fertilizers for cane are reported.

In general, the better results were obtained with ammonium sulphate. When a part of the sulphate was replaced by boengkil the results were more favorable than when boengkil was used alone. Better results were obtained on light soils with boengkil than on heavy soils. With a fertilization of light soil with boengkil furnishing an amount of nitrogen equivalent to 124 lbs. of ammonium sulphate the crop yield decreased about 1 per cent. Fertilization with boengkil was more expensive than with ammonium sulphate.

In part 3, dealing with 41 comparative tests of ammonium sulphate and sodium nitrate on cane, it was found that with reference to yield the advantage lay with the ammonium sulphate to an average amount of 0.73 per cent for cane and 0.24 per cent for sugar. In the 21 tests made on light soil the yields obtained with ammonium sulphate were 1.75 per cent greater for cane and 1.1 per cent greater for sugar. In the remaining 20 tests, made on heavy soil, greater yields were obtained with sodium nitrate to the amount of 0.33 per cent for cane and

0.6 per cent for sugar. No injurious influence of the sodium nitrate on the soil structure was observed.

The greatest difficulty encountered in the use of sodium nitrate was the ease with which it is leached out of the soil. It is considered probable that on heavy soils there was some loss of sodium nitrate through denitrification. For this reason it is considered inadvisable to use stable manure with sodium nitrate on heavy soils. In five tests on light soil the use of stable manure with sodium nitrate or ammonium sulphate had no such injurious results.

In four tests on soil rich in lime, ammonium sulphate gave better results than sodium nitrate. In two tests in which molasses was used with ammonium sulphate and with sodium nitrate, good results were obtained in the former case but not in the latter. In four tests on light and four tests on heavy soils, it was found that ammonium sulphate can be partially replaced by sodium nitrate with profit.

It is considered, therefore, that the advisability of using sodium nitrate as a substitute for ammonium sulphate on Java cane soils will depend mainly on the cost or scarcity of the ammonium sulphate and the cost of sodium nitrate.

The solubility of mineral phosphates in citric acid, II, G. S. ROBERTSON (*Jour. Soc. Chem. Indus., 35 (1916), No. 4, pp. 217-220; Chem. News, 114 (1916), No. 2978, pp. 295-298*).—Continuing previous work (E. S. R., 33, p. 313), experiments with Makatea Island, Florida pebble, and Algerian, Gafsa, Tunisian, and Belgian phosphates are reported, which led to the conclusions "that mineral phosphates are completely soluble in 2 per cent citric acid if a sufficient number of extracts are made. In the majority of the rock phosphates examined five extracts removed from 90 to 100 per cent of the phosphoric acid present.

"Even a small amount of free lime or calcium carbonate decreases substantially the solubility of mineral phosphates as judged by the citric acid test. When a large amount of calcium carbonate or free lime is present, the citric acid test, as commonly practiced, is a test for lime and not for phosphates. It is important in this respect to distinguish between free lime and calcium carbonate and lime actually entering into the composition of the phosphate. The higher the percentage of lime actually entering into the phosphate compound, the higher the citric solubility of the phosphate. Fineness of grinding affects the total citric solubility of the mineral phosphates (judged by five extracts) to the extent of approximately 10 per cent decrease for each of the gradients—passes '100,' refuses '100,' refuses '60,' and refuses '30' sieve. With one exception, calcining produces a marked decrease in the citric solubility of mineral phosphates. The longer the calcining continues, the more insoluble does the phosphate become."

The results as a whole are taken to indicate the worthlessness of the citric acid test as a means of judging the relative fertilizing values of phosphatic manures. Mineral phosphates are considered as valuable as a source of phosphoric acid for plants as basic slag.

Liming and lime requirement of soil, J. W. AMES and C. J. SCHOLLENBERGER (*Ohio Sta. Bul. 306 (1916). pp. 281-306, figs. 5*).—The work of others bearing on the subject is briefly reviewed, and data obtained from several years' study of fertility plats under various conditions of liming and treatment and the results of certain pot experiments are reviewed and summarized.

It was found that "the chemical composition and mechanical condition of lime materials are probably of primary importance in relation to speed of reaction with soil, rate of loss, and usefulness as soil amendments. The comparatively small amounts of carbonate residual from applications of various lime materials after relatively brief periods indicate that the speed of reaction with soil of commercial lime materials is of a high order. From data obtained for a silt loam soil quite deficient in basic material and receiving different amounts of ground limestone under normal conditions, it can be considered that under similar conditions 70 per cent of the calcium supplied by a moderate application of limestone—say 2 tons per acre—will have left the carbonate form within a year. From heavy applications—6 to 13 tons per acre—the percentage of calcium and magnesium combining with the soil and the proportion carried downward and lost are less when referred to the total amount applied, but, expressed as pounds per acre, the quantities are really greater than those from smaller applications. . . .

" With regard to the effect of fertilizer treatment upon carbonates residual from applications, it was found that ammonium sulphate was capable of accelerating the decomposition of carbonates, and is the only fertilizer in common use the effects of which in this direction are unmistakably apparent. In distinction from ammonium sulphate, a physiologically acid salt, sodium nitrate, a physiologically alkaline salt, appears to have a general tendency toward the conservation of carbonates."

Manure appeared to exert an influence toward the conservation of carbonates. Of the bases added and not accounted for by the presence of carbonates, a considerable proportion was retained by the first 12 in. of soil. The unfertilized plats retained much less than the average of the fertilized. The differences in amounts of bases retained in forms other than carbonate by the fertilized plats were not great. The soil of the lime extension plats to which were applied 6 and 13 tons of limestone per acre with and without manure retained more calcium and magnesium in the first 12 in. than the soils from five-year rotation plats, although not by any means a proportionate amount. The bases retained were mainly in the first 8 in., but increases were apparent as deep as the samples were taken (24 in.). The manure appeared to have caused increased fixation of calcium by the soil and to have had a tendency toward equalizing its distribution in the several depths sampled. Leaching was the most important source of loss of carbonates and basic calcium.

Very coarse limestone (1/3 to 1/20 in.) is probably of little value unless applied in excessive amounts. In general, dolomitic stone ground to different degrees of fineness and applied to the soil suffered a less degree of decomposition than corresponding applications of a higher calcium stone. Crop yields from small plats gave no consistent indications of superiority for either form of stone. Soils containing water-soluble acid constituents in determinable quantity were rarely encountered.

" The litmus paper test, when carefully conducted and intelligently interpreted, is probably as good as any chemical test for the determination of the soil's need of lime. All the lime requirement methods tried indicated marked differences between limed and unlimed soil of the same character and treatment, and all, except the Veitch method, loss in bases due to a long period of cultivation.

" The data available indicate that the vacuum method is the best adapted of the procedures tested for use as a quantitative method in studying the relations between the soil and its supply of bases. There is no evidence that any of the lime requirement methods tested furnishes reliable indications as to the optimum rate of application for field practice. For the several soils investigated, there was found to be an approximately quantitative relationship between the bases soluble in fifth-normal nitric acid (excluding carbonates) and differences in lime requirement by the vacuum method.

"Acidity of soil, as the term is usually employed, is a negative property; that is, due to qualities inherent in all soils, but manifested only by those deficient in basic constituents. Too much empnasis has been laid upon soil acidity, and the more important theme, soil basicity, has been neglected.

"Calcium and magnesium are retained in the soil mainly as silicates, possibly partly in combination with organic matter.

"Field tests show that the yields of clover on plats treated with acid phosphate have been less than on plats where bone meal and basic slag were used as carriers of phosphorus. The evidence obtained by laboratory studies, however, does not indicate that acid phosphate has any important influence toward the depletion of the soil's supply of bases; effects due to the acid nature of this fertilizer are insignificant when compared with those attributable to the use of ammonium sulphate.

"Dried and green crop residues mixed with soil did not increase its lime requirement as determined in the laboratory. Field observations and tests made do not indicate that organic matter furnished by green crops causes acidity in soil. A mulch of fermenting material (apple pomace) caused the lime requirement of the soil beneath to be increased. Sawdust similarly used had little effect.

"Pot experiments indicate that the base of various silicates, including blast-furnace slag, may be of benefit to crop growth.

"Lime requirement determinations on samples taken at various depths of a limed soil indicate that the effect of lime applied is perceptible to a depth of 24 in. or more.

"Unusual weather conditions to which the soil may have been exposed in the field have had no great effect upon the lime requirement as determined in the laboratory."

Effect of some manganese salts on ammonification and nitrification, P. E. Brown and G. A. Minges (*Iowa Sta. Research Bul. 35 (1916), pp. 3-22*).--Experiments on the effects of manganese sulphate, manganese chlorid, manganese nitrate, and manganous oxid in varying amounts on the ammonification of dried blood and the nitrification of ammonium sulphate in a clay-loam soil are reported.

It was found that "manganese chlorid, in applications greater than 2,000 lbs. per acre, depressed both ammonification and nitrification, the depression increasing as the size of the application was increased until a point was reached at which both processes ceased. With smaller amounts of the chlorid the effects on the two processes were not identical, but tended in the same direction. Thus the applications of 100 and 200 lbs. per acre gave increases which were slight in the case of ammonification, but quite distinct in the case of nitrification. With amounts greater than 200 lbs. per acre and less than 2,000 lbs., however, ammonification was depressed while no appreciable depression was apparent on nitrification.

"Manganese sulphate, when applied to the soil at the rate of 100 lbs. per acre, increased appreciably both ammonification and nitrification. In amounts greater than 100 lbs. per acre and less than 2,000 lbs., ammonification was increased, but to a less extent than with the 100-lb. application, but with nitrification no gains nor depressions were found with these amounts. In applications equal to or greater than 2,000 lbs. per acre nitrification and ammonification were depressed by manganese sulphate, the depression increasing with the size of the application.

"Manganse nitrate added to the soil at the rate of 500 lbs. per acre, or in greater amounts, depressed both ammonification and nitrification, the depression increasing as the size of the application was increased. Manganous oxid, when applied to the soil at the rate of 2,000 lbs. per acre or in larger quantities, depressed both ammonification and nitrification, the depression becoming greater as the size of the addition was increased."

It is concluded that "if manganese salts in small quantities increase crop yields on a soil, that increase may be due in part at least to a beneficial effect on ammonification and nitrification with a consequently greater production of available plant food. On the other hand, if manganese salts when applied to the soil restrict crop growth, that restriction may be due in part to a depression of bacterial activity."

Fertilizer analyses, H. B. McDonnell et al. (*Md. Agr. Col. Quart., No. 75 (1917), pp. [31]*).—This contains the results of actual and guaranteed analyses of 505 samples of fertilizers and fertilizing materials offered for sale in Maryland from August, 1916, to January, 1917, inclusive, together with the text of the Maryland fertilizer law.

Commercial fertilizers, 1916, B. H. Hite and F. B. Kunst (*West Virginia Sta. Insp. Bul. 5 (1917), pp. 3–85*).—This bulletin contains the results of actual and guaranteed analyses of 477 samples of fertilizers and fertilizing materials offered for sale in West Virginia during 1916.

AGRICULTURAL BOTANY.

The morphology of the monocotyledonous embryo and of that of the grass in particular, W. C. Worsdell (*Ann. Bot. [London], 30 (1916), No. 120, pp. 509–524, figs. 10*).—The author, concluding a study of *Zea mays, Hordeum vulgare,* and other monocotyledonous plants, states that the scutellum is the lamina of the cotyledon, corresponding to that of the foliage leaf in grass. The part of the cotyledon which corresponds to the sheath of the foliage leaf becomes obscured after the early stage of its development. The coleoptile appears to be that part of the cotyledon which is represented in the foliage leaf by the ligule. The epiblast is that part of the cotyledon corresponding to the auricles of the base of the lamina of the foliage leaf in certain grasses.

The cotyledon of the grasses differs in no essential, however, from that of other monocotyledons. The mesocotyl is the elongated primary node. The position of the cotyledon is terminal in all monocotyledons, being the continuation of the hypocotyl. The balance of development of the cotyledonary lamina and sheath may vary in favor of the latter in certain cases and stages. In certain instances the sheath may develop into a second cotyledon, this character being novel and progressive instead of ancestral and reversionary.

Further experiments on correlation of growth in Bryophyllum calycinum, J. Loeb (*Bot. Gaz., 62 (1916), No. 4, pp. 293–302, figs. 17*).—Further observations (E. S. R., 34, p. 730) under varied conditions are reported. These show that there is in a detached leaf, or pair of leaves, and adjacent portions of a cutting of Bryophyllum, a suction (this term serving as a symbol to denote the direction of the flow of materials) associated with the growth of a marginal or axial bud, which inhibits growth in neighboring portions. The experiments show that a vigorous growth in the notches of a leaf may act as a center of suction which may prevent the flow of sap to the cortex, and thus inhibit growth there if the suction by the stem, or in this case the cortex, is not so strong.

Cambial activity in certain horticultural plants, L. Knudson (*Bul. Torrey Bot. Club, 43 (1916), No. 10, pp. 533–537*).—Recording in tabular form studies regarding the season of cambial activity in woody plants, the author states that cambial activity began in the peach at the time of the opening of the buds. This is contrasted with the result of observations on the larch, grape, and apple. Observations on other trees are also noted. No evidence was obtained to show that the formation of phloëm continued later than that of xylem.

The epidermal cells of roots, EDITH A. ROBERTS (*Bot. Gaz., 62 (1916), No. 6, pp. 488–506, figs. 17*).—This attempt to determine the varying factors within and without the epidermal cell of the root and their reciprocal relations was prompted by the fact that frequently the presence or the absence of root hairs is used as an indicator of changed external conditions.

It is stated, as the result of study with various plants, that the formation of a root hair is first indicated by the swelling of the outer wall of the epidermal cell. This is due to the fact that the physical resistance of the wall is overcome by the osmotic pressure within the wall, continued swelling and growth occurring in a region of comparatively slight resistance which has no apparent relation to the position of the nucleus. The wall of the root hair is composed of an inner cellulose membrane and an outer membrane of calcium pectate, soil particles being held to the layer by pectin mucilage, these facts accounting supposedly for the high absorbing efficiency of the root hairs.

New determinations of permeability, S. C. BROOKS (*Proc. Nat. Acad. Sci., 2 (1916), No. 10, pp. 569–574, figs. 6*).—The author reports determinations of permeability of plant tissues by a new method claimed to be independent of methods or improvements thereof, as previously employed. The results are said to agree in showing that living protoplasm is normally permeable to the salts employed, but that salts in solution may alter permeability. Some (as sodium chlorid) cause an increase, others (chlorids of calcium, lanthanum, and cerium) a decrease followed by an increase, the permeability remaining normal in a balanced solution.

Studies on exosmosis, S. C. BROOKS (*Amer. Jour. Bot., 3 (1916), No. 9, pp. 483–492, figs. 4*).—The author has made a study on the tendency of osmotically active substances to diffuse out of the cell in the course of experiments where turgidity or osmotic pressure is used as a criterion of permeability. Strips from scapes of dandelion were used in experiments in which the exosmosis of electrolytes into distilled water from such strips was determined after their treatment with distilled water or solutions of the chlorids of sodium, calcium, or cerium.

It was found that sodium salts increase, while calcium salts decrease, the rate of exosmosis of other electrolytes from the protoplasm of *Taraxacum officinale*. It is possible to prepare a solution such that, when it is used at a concentration isotonic with the protoplasm, it causes no perceptible alteration in the permeability of the plasma membrane.

The rôle of osmotic pressure of a soil solution in the culture of wheat, N. M. TULAĬKOV (TOULAIKOFF) (*Zhur. Opytn. Agron. (Jour. Agr. Expt.), 17 (1916), No. 2, pp. 122–164, figs. 9*).—The osmotic pressure of the soil solution is considered of great importance in the development of wheat, manifesting itself at germination and at every other important period in the life of the plant. Some particulars are given regarding observed modifications of the relations between the grain and the stalk produced. These may be made to deviate considerably from the normal or observed tendency in the direction of a desired optimum.

The structure of the bordered pits of conifers and its bearing upon the tension hypothesis of the ascent of sap in plants, I. W. BAILEY (*Bot. Gaz., 62 (1916), No. 2, pp. 133–142, pl. 1, figs. 2; abs. in Jour. Roy. Micros. Soc. No. 6 (1916), p. 572*).—The author claims to have shown that in case of Larix and Sequoia the pit membranes are supplied with perforations of various forms, generally elongated, and of sizes varying from 0.5μ to 3μ, but the detailed structure of which is obscured by the overhanging and thickened pit borders. It is stated that aqueous solutions containing fine particles can be passed through the membranes of the bordered pits of sapwood from the stems of these and other conifers, also that gases can be readily forced through bordered pits thoroughly saturated with sap. The surface tension of sap in the pit membranes can in some cases, it is claimed, be overcome by pressures of less than 3 atmospheres. This is thought to disprove the tension hypothesis, according to which a tension of from 5 to 20 atmospheres is required to maintain continuous columus of water in trees.

Relation of transpiration to assimilation in steppe plants, V. S. ILJIN (*Jour. Ecology, 4 (1916), No. 2, pp. 65-82*).—The author, reporting in considerable detail on another phase of the work previously noted (E. S. R., 33, p. 628), claims that the experiments herein described show simply that we may expect to find in drought-resistant plants a more economical evaporation of water.

Recent developments in the study of endotrophic mycorrhiza, M. C. RAYNER (*New Phytol., 15 (1916), No. 8, pp. 161-175*).—This is a review of recent studies and views on endotrophic mycorrhiza and a discussion of their bearing on current conceptions of the physiology of the relationship and of their significance in experimental ecology.

The view held by the author is that the phenomenon of mycorrhiza in plants is only an expression of the warfare waged continually by all organisms against parasitic invasion of their tissues. The flowering plant possessing mycorrhiza not only has checked the invading fungus, but has turned the invasion to its own advantage.

Studies in the physiology of the fungi.—I, Nitrogen fixation, B. M. DUGGAR and A. R. DAVIS (*Ann. Missouri Bot. Gard., 3 (1916), No. 4, pp. 413-437*).—This is the first report of a series of several studies now in progress on the physiology of the fungi. Tabular details are given of the results obtained from a study of nitrogen fixation. This was not established for *Aspergillus niger, Macrosporium commune, Penicillium digitatum, P. expansum*, and *Glomerella gossypii*, but cultures of *Phoma betæ* on mangel and on sugar beet decoction with sugar showed a nitrogen gain, which is considered to prove definitely that nitrogen fixation occurs. Comparative studies of Azotobacter strains indicate the usual relatively large fixation of nitrogen by that organism.

Studies in the physiology of the fungi.—II, Lenzites sepiaria, with special reference to enzym activity, S. M. ZELLER (*Ann. Missouri Bot. Gard., 3 (1916), No. 4, pp. 439-512, pls. 2*).—This article, continuing the series indicated above, is an account with discussion of studies on the wood-destroying fungus, *L. sepiaria*, as regards the behavior of this fungus when grown in pure cultures on selected media. The fungus grows well on 50 per cent resin by weight (which is said to be a proportion greater than that found in any coniferous wood), and growth is not entirely inhibited by 85 per cent resin.

The metabolism of the fungus was studied through the agency of enzym action, and this study is reported in some detail. A comparative study of enzyms found in the sporophores and mycelium indicated that the important metabolic processes are carried on chiefly in the vegetative organs in the case of diastase, invertase, tannase, and cellulase, while the oxidases show greater activity in the sporophores.

The mitochondrial origin of rhodoxanthin, F. MOREAU (*Bul. Soc. Bot. France, 62 (1915), No. 4-6, pp. 158-160*).—Discussing observations made by himself and other investigators, the author claims that rhodoxanthin may originate in a plastid or in a chondriosome without passing through a chlorophyll stage. It is thought that mitochondria and plastids may fix certain substances which they select from the protoplasm. These they transform later into products, which may themselves be transitory or final, by means of modifications in which the phenomena of oxidation and reduction play a leading or at least an important part.

The presence, distribution, and rôle of arsenic and manganese in plants, F. JADIN and A. ASTRUC (*Rev. Sci.* [*Paris*], *54* (*1916*), *II, No. 19, pp. 589–593*).— Summarizing the more general results of recent and former investigations (E. S. R., 32, p. 628), the authors state that all the organs of all plants analyzed by them showed the presence of both arsenic and manganese. The former was present in rather small proportion in a number of plants named, and the latter in larger proportion in a few. The chlorophylliferous portions generally contained more than the subterranean parts, and the content of the leaves varied sensibly with age.

No preponderant influence is exerted by the soil content of arsenic or manganese on the percentage of those substances found in the plants, which take what they require, even, if necessary, through the medium of the plants on which they are parasitic. Vegetable foods constitute, if not the only source, at least one of the most important of the sources of the manganese and arsenic normally found in animal tissues.

The authors conclude that arsenic and manganese are of the greatest importance in the vegetable cell, the former exerting an influence comparable to that of phosphorus, the second favoring the oxygen reactions in the plant.

Specific action of barium, W. J. V. OSTERHOUT (*Amer. Jour. Bot., 3* (*1916*), *No. 9, pp. 481, 482*).—The author briefly describes experiments with Spirogyra in which the chloroplasts were characteristically contracted toward the center of the cells when the filaments were subjected to 0.0001 molecular solution of barium chlorid. This action is considered specific for barium, no other salt examined producing this effect at such dilutions.

The plant as an index of smoke pollution, C. CROWTHER and A. G. RUSTON (*Abs. in Rpt. Brit. Assoc. Adv. Sci., 85* (*1915*), *p. 780*).—The results are reported of experiments and observations during several years on the types of vegetation injured by smoke, the general appearance of plants so injured, and the specific effects of smoke on plants.

The authors state that where smoke is excessive trees and shrubs make only a stunted growth. Bulbous and seed-bearing plants are sensitive to smoke, conifers particularly so. Hawthorn barely persists in such areas, leguminous plants rapidly disappear, and coarse grasses and weeds monopolize meadows and lawns, while rhubarb is very little or not at all affected, and elder grows successfully in such regions.

Destruction of buds and young shoots is noticeable. Characteristic discoloration of leaves occurs and the leaves fall earlier than normally. Colors are weakened, blues and reds tending to white and bronzes to pale yellow, and certain definiteness of correlation appears between depth of tinting and smoke pollution. The choking of stomata by soot particles has been observed to occur. Crop yields are lowered by excess of smoke, and development of root structures is found to be retarded. A relatively high content of chlorin, of arsenic, and especially of sulphur in nonprotein forms in plants is observable.

Seeds in smoke-polluted areas show decrease as regards size, weight, germination capacity, and germination energy. Inhibitory effects upon enzym activity have been demonstrated by comparative measurements of the activity of oxidase, catalase, lipase, and emulsin.

Teratology in iris flowers, ELEANORA ARMITAGE (*Gard. Chron., 3. ser., 60* (*1916*), *No. 1557, p. 203*).—Abnormalities relating to the number, shape, arrangement or fusion of floral parts are noted as occurring in different species and varieties of iris.

New dimorphic mutants of the Œnotheras, H. DeVries (*Bot. Gaz.*, 62 (1916), *No. 4, pp. 249–280, figs. 5*).—A study has been made of the genetic behavior of *Œ. scintillans, Œ. cana, Œ. pallescens, Œ. lactuca*, and *Œ. liquida*, mutants of *Œ. lamarckiana*. Each of these in every generation, under ordinary circumstances, splits into nearly equal groups of the mutant type and of the parent type, the *Œ. lamarckiana* offspring being nearly constant in their progeny. Besides the two main types each usually produces a relatively high percentage of other mutants. The parental types appear on an average in about 40 per cent (on very strong biennials as much as 97 per cent), the other 60 per cent (or less) being *Œ. lamarckiana* mutants, these figures varying with cultures or with individuals. Dimorphic mutants of this type also occur in allied species of the biennis group. In dimorphic mutants the special characters are inherited through the ovules, but not, so far as known, through the pollen, which appears like that of pure *Œ. lamarckiana*.

The dimorphic mutants constitute a group in which the hereditary phenomena are evidently independent of the external visible characters of the special members of the group, but are assumed to have the same intrinsic causes in the different cases.

Sterility as the result of hybridization and the condition of pollen in Rubus, C. S. Hoar (*Bot. Gaz.*, 62 (1916), *No. 5, pp. 370–388, pls. 3*).—The author gives a brief review of previous work and information regarding pollen sterility and related phenomena, with an account of work done by himself in 1915 on some 40 species of Rubus, from which mature pollen grains were obtained for utilization in study by a method which is described. He also details the percentages obtained of pollen found to be sterile in different degrees in many of the species.

It is stated that pollen sterility is a common character throughout the entire genus. This is thought to typify a condition prevailing in many angiosperms, among which are found many forms appearing as natural hybrids between distinct species and exhibiting more or less blending of characters rather than Mendelian segregation. Rubus hybrids formed between distinct species are almost entirely sterile, while crosses of closely related and supposedly more compatible varieties may give almost no indication of a hybrid origin.

FIELD CROPS.

Report of the agronomy division, C. A. Sahr (*Hawaii Sta. Rpt. 1916, pp. 26–31, pls. 2*).—This reports a continuation of work previously noted (E. S. R., 35, p. 527).

The 1916 spring rice crop on the nonaerated plat fell 51 per cent below the yield of the same plat in 1915, but outyielded the aerated plat by 490 lbs. of rice paddy, or 18.7 per cent.

Early Rose outyielded Burbank and American Wonder in potato variety tests at the Tantalus substation (elevation 1,000 ft.). In culinary tests of these varieties the Burbank proved superior in mealiness and flavor.

Cultural trials of *Phaseolus aconitifolius, Crotalaria candicans, Desmodium hirtum*, and several clovers are briefly noted. The average yields of green forage per acre for the red clovers were as follows: Red clover from Switzerland (S. P. I. No. 37939) 8.55 tons, ordinary red clover (F. C. I. No. 1472) 8.45, Swiss Rummellee clover or apitrefle (S. P. I. No. 37937) 2.1, and red clover from Switzerland (S. P. I. No. 37938) 1.8 tons. Alsike clover gave a yield of 6.15 tons per acre. Ordinary white clover (S. P. I. No. 34930) made appreciably more growth than wild white (S. P. I. No. 38579) and Ladino white (F. C. I. No. 1482). *Trifolium striatum* (F. C. I. No. 1450) succumbed to drought in the summer of 1915, while *T. dubium*, replanted in April, 1915, produced a good stand and was maturing seed in July, 1916.

Tests of five varieties of winter rye, two of oats, and one of winter barley for grain and forage were begun in December, 1915. Mexican winter was the only rye variety headed out at the time of this report. The results of the oat tests indicated yields of from 13 to 22 bu. Winter barley failed to head out. A second planting of five varieties each of oats, barley, and rye, and three varieties of wheat was made in March, 1916. Fulghum oats was the first variety to head out, with Smyrna the first barley variety.

Kafir corn, milo maize, and feterita were grown in connection with Sugar Drip sorghum for a comparison of yields of grain and forage. The yields of grain per acre were 66.5, 436, 235, and 689 lbs., and of forage per acre, 6, 4.52, 6.65, and 11.27 tons, respectively. Tests of other grain sorghums are noted.

New long-period tests for yields of forage were begun in August, 1915, with nonsaccharin sorghum No. 309 and Japanese cane. The latter was propagated partly by division of the roots and partly by cuttings of the cane. The first cutting for forage was made December 29, and the estimated acre yield of the stand from cuttings totaled 2 tons more than that from the division of roots.

Andropogon nodosum, A. sericeus, A. saccharoides, Tricholaena rosea, and Giant Bermuda grass are listed as the best five drought-resistant pasture grasses for low and medium elevations. Brief notes are given on numerous other grasses and of a test of rape.

Spraying Japanese nut grass with arsenite of soda when the grass is in full bloom continued to be the most effective control measure. Plowing with a disk plow at intervals of four or five weeks during exceedingly dry periods greatly reduced the vitality of the tubers.

Report of [field crop work at] the Glenwood substation, J. B. Thompson (*Hawaii Sta. Rpt. 1916, pp. 40–42, pl. 1*).—*Paspalum dilatatum* has been subjected to a number of field tests in an effort to obtain a suitable forage crop for dairy cattle to supplement *Commelina nudiflora* and *Panicum barbinode* by producing a heavy winter growth. *Paspalum dilatatum* having been associated with stock poisoning in the Southern States (E. S. R., 34, p. 676), extreme precautionary measures are deemed necessary in introducing the plant into the dairy regions.

Volunteer plants of California bur clover were observed to make a rank and rapid growth between December and April, and trial plantings of this crop will be made during the coming winter season.

Edible canna (*Canna edulis*) was planted in December, 1914, in an attempt to secure a local product suitable for hog feed. A yield at the rate of approximately 31.5 tons per acre was harvested in January, 1916. Further tests of this crop are in progress. A portion of the harvested crop stored in ordinary bags showed practically no loss from decay for a period of three months. The chemical composition of the fleshy rhizome is said to be closely comparable to that of the Irish potato.

Jerusalem artichokes (*Helianthus tuberosus*) were also grown as a hog feed, and yielded at the rate of approximately 11 tons per acre from a stand estimated at only 33⅓ per cent at the time of harvest. The artichoke was completely ruined by a moldlike fungus when stored in bags, although roots remaining in the ground were in a perfect state of preservation over two months after the bulk of the crop was harvested.

The possible Wayne County farm, C. E. Thorne (*Mo. Bul. Ohio Sta., 2 (1917), No. 3, pp. 96–98*).—Comparing statistics of acreage and yield on the average Wayne County farm and on the experiment station farm at Wooster, it was found that on an area of 46.3 acres the average Wayne County farmer produced annually crops valued at $764, while on an area of 40 acres of representative soil at Wooster the value of the same crops had amounted to $1,251 per annum. The additional expenditures for fertilizers, lime, and labor are estimated at $197, which is thus returned with a dividend of $287, or 140 per cent.

It is concluded that by reducing the acreage in crops and concentrating time and energy on a smaller area of the best land, two-thirds of the area now cultivated in the county might be made to produce all that is now grown within the county, and at a saving in labor which would more than pay for the fertilizers required.

The residual effect of fertilizers and manure, C. E. THORNE (*Mo. Bul. Ohio Sta., 2 (1917), No. 2, pp. 48–50*).—Supplementing a report previously noted (E. S. R., 36, p. 829), average results obtained in crop-rotation experiments extending over a period of 23 years show that from one-third to one-half the total effect of fertilizers and manure is carried forward to the crops following the one receiving the treatment. The results are summarized in the following table:

Residual effect of fertilizers and manure.

			Increase per acre.			
	Period of experimentation.	Treatment and crop to which applied.	Weight.		Value.	
Rotation.			Fertilized crops.	Residuary crops.	Fertilized crops.	Residuary crops.
	Years.		*Per cent.*	*Per cent.*	*Per cent.*	*Per cent.*
Corn, oats, wheat, clover, and timothy.	23	Chemical fertilizer applied to wheat.	51	49	56	44
Do....................	23	Chemical fertilizer applied to wheat and corn.	65	35	73	27
Do....................	23	Manure applied to wheat and corn.	52	48	64	36
Corn, wheat, and clover...	18	Manure applied to corn..	47	53	55	45
Tobacco, wheat, and clover.	14	Fertilizers and manure applied to tobacco.	....	....	70	30

The effect of soluble nitrogenous salts on nodule formation, E. B. FRED and E. J. GRAUL (*Jour. Amer. Soc. Agron., 8 (1916), No. 5, pp. 316–328*).—This paper gives the results of some investigations of soluble nitrogenous salts and their effect on nodule formation. The plan of the experimental work included the following points of investigation: (1) The effect of ammonium nitrate on nodule formation in sand, (2) the effect of calcium nitrate on nodule formation in a mixture of soil and sand, (3) the effect of sodium nitrate and ammonium sulphate on alfalfa and crimson clover in Miami silt loam, and (4) the effect of accumulated nitrates in various soils on nodule formation.

From the data secured it seems evident that under field conditions nitrates rarely, if ever, occur in amounts sufficient to prohibit nodule formation. It is probable, however, that the percentage gain of nitrogen in legumes is injured by the presence of soluble nitrogen. The nitrogen assimilating power of legumes in the presence of soluble salts appears to depend upon many factors, such as the physical, chemical, and biological composition of the soil, species of plant, etc. An abundant moisture supply may be beneficial to nodule formation in two ways, (1) water is necessary for the normal function of the plant and bacteria, and (2) water tends to leach out the soluble nitrogen. As a general conclusion it may be said that, in order to secure a maximum growth as well as a maximum gain of nitrogen from legumes, a small amount of soluble nitrogen is beneficial while large amounts are detrimental.

A brief bibliography is given at the end of the article.

Seeding small grains, C. G. WILLIAMS (*Mo. Bul. Ohio Sta., 2 (1917), No. 3, pp. 76, 77*).—Limited seeding experiments are reported with 8-in. and 4-in. grain drills.

An average of two years' tests with oats shows yields of 49.19 and 45.48 bu. of grain and 3,020 and 3,080 lbs. of straw per acre for the 8-in. and 4-in. drills, respectively. In tests with wheat in 1915, using a 6.5 and 4.5 pk. rate of seeding, the respective yields for the 8-in. and 4-in. drills were 28.71 and 28.37 bu. of grain and 3,247 and 3,487 lbs. of straw.

[Field crops] (*Rev. Indus. y Agr. Tucumán 7 (1916), No. 1-2, pp. 5-59, figs. 16*).—Extensive notes are given on sugar cane culture, together with brief notes on maize, sorghum, cowpeas, and peanuts, in the Province of Tucumán.

[Field crops] (*Jaarb. Dept. Landb. Nijv. en Handel Nederland, Indië, 1914, pp. VI+331, pls. 16*).—This is a general administrative report of the work conducted at the various experimental centers of the Dutch East Indies.

The cultivation of dry land, R. ESCOBAR (*Estac. Agr. Expt. Ciudad Juárez, Chihuahua, Bol. 47 (1914), pp. 97, pls. 26*).—This is an extensive publication upon dry land farming in Mexico. The meteorological and soil conditions are discussed in detail. Implements for dry land cultivation are described and illustrated. Brief notes are given on a number of crops recommended for growing in these regions, the most important of which are sorghum, beans, corn, wheat, cotton, potatoes, peanuts, alfalfa, sweet potatoes, and canaigre.

Field culture tests on peaty soils in 1915, H. VON FEILITZEN (*Svenska Mosskulturför. Tidskr., 30 (1916), No. 3, pp. 221-235*).—The experiments here described were conducted in different sections of Sweden.

The use of lime on various kinds of peaty soils gave quite diverse results, due to varying soil conditions. Where the soil was well supplied with lime, further lime applications remained without effect. In a test on soil with an insufficient lime content the influence of lime applications was still observable seven years later.

Yearly applications of fertilizer on pasture lands of this type were found much more profitable than applications made from time to time. While the best results on all fields were not secured from the same application, it was found in general that it was best to use 100 or 200 kg. of superphosphate, or 300 kg. of Thomas slag, together with 100 or 200 kg. of potash salt per hectare. The residual effect of nitrate of soda on grassland, even on soil of high nitrogen content, was quite marked, which is considered as possibly due to insufficient nitrification of the soil under ordinary conditions. Barnyard manure used for oats also showed residual effects in one section, while in another it was practically without effect after the first year. The increase in the yields of root crops from the use of barnyard manure and fertilizers, which was considerable, seemed to be determined by the excess of commercial fertilizers over barnyard manure.

The two varieties of oats giving the best results in this connection were Gold Rain and Victory. The yield of green forage was generally quite satisfactory, while the yield of root crops was under the average. Of three varieties of rape Munich proved the best. The yields of grass were also satisfactory where frost did not interfere.

[Culture experiments on moor soils at Flahult and Torestorp, Sweden], H. VON FEILITZEN (*Svenska Mosskulturför. Tidskr., 29 (1915), No. 6, pp. 441-473, figs. 4; 30 (1916), Nos. 1, pp. 51-72; 2, pp. 119-159, figs. 6*).—The results of experiments here described showed that the beneficial effect of mixing sand with the surface of insufficiently decayed moor soil was still discernible four years later, and that the treatment had paid for itself with the third harvest. The use of sand on moor or peat soils, either by working the sand into the surface or covering the soils, also gave generally good results. Lime applied to this type of land affected different crops quite differently, the greatest increases in yield apparently due to the treatment being secured with flax and rape followed by barley, red clover, and horse beans.

Fertilizer experiments on low, peaty soil showed a residual effect of barnyard manure the third year after its application and also indicated the greater value of spring application as compared with fall application. Liquid manure applied on moor soil meadows in quantities furnishing approximately 23.4 kg. of nitrogen per hectare (20.8 lb. per acre) increased the yield of hay 1,306 kg. per hectare. Analyses of the liquid manure made at different times brought out a definite relation between its specific gravity and its nitrogen content and consequent manurial effect.

Nitrate of soda and sulphate of ammonia, used in growing rape on a sandy soil, gave practically equal results. Common salt applied in addition to the sulphate of ammonia remained without effect. On a good, peaty soil different quantities of nitrogenous fertilizers gave no increase, while of the phosphatic materials tested Thomas slag proved most effective and superphosphate and bone meal were of about equal value. Of different potash fertilizers 20 per cent potash salt gave a slightly higher increase than kainit, or 37 per cent potash salt, but the dry matter content was highest in the crop grown with the last-mentioned substance and lowest in the crop receiving the kainit. When increasing amounts of the different plant food sources were used it was found that nitrogenous fertilizers in no case paid for themselves, while among the applications of phosphorus the use of 120 kg. of phosphoric acid, equivalent to about 600 kg. of superphosphate, per hectare was most economical and in the potash series the use of 150 kg. of potash, or about 400 kg. of 37 per cent potash salt, gave the highest return.

Of different crops tested for a number of years in this connection, the following varieties gave the best yield: Petkus, Swedish Gray, and Midsummer rye; Plymage and Svanhals barley; Gold Rain, Dala, and Brown Moor oats; Sand, Glenoe, and Solo field peas; Gertrude, Lucia, Moor Rose, and Jewel potatoes; and Bortfeld rape. Notes are also given on drainage experiments and the culture of potatoes.

Time of sowing and harvesting green forage crops on lowland moor soil, J. LENDE-NJAA (*Meddel. Norske Myrselsk.*, *14* (*1916*), *No. 3, pp. 85–108*).—Oats and peas were sown in the proportion of 2:1 by weight on May 1, 15, and 30, and harvested at the beginning of blossoming, 15 days later, and when the oats were mature. The results secured, together with the chemical composition of the material harvested at the different stages of growth, are tabulated in detail and discussed.

The results indicated in general that a mixture of oats and peas for green forage, in order to make the heaviest and best growth, should be sown as early as possible. The best time of harvesting was 'found to be about two weeks after the oats began blossoming. The quantity of green forage continued to increase after this period, but the increase did not compensate for the loss in quality which was quite evident in the latest sowings.

Botanical composition of a 20-year-old moorland meadow, A. MENTZ (*Hedeselsk. Tidsskr.*, *No. 10* (*1916*), *pp. 127–134*).—The method of seeding this meadow in 1895 is described, together with the fertilizer treatment given during the period. The seed mixture used per töndeland (1.36 acres) was as follows: Red clover 3 lbs., alsike clover 5 lbs., white clover 2 lbs., Italian rye grass 2 lbs., timothy 5 lbs., meadow foxtail 8 lbs., orchard grass 2 lbs., and rough-stalked meadow grass 3 lbs. After 20 years the flora of the meadow was composed of 22.56 per cent of cultivated grasses, 44.97 per cent of wild grasses, 16.43 per cent of leguminous plants, and 12.95 per cent of weeds.

The culture of Bengal grass, teosinte, and Sudan grass, E. Schimmel (*Teysmannia, 27 (1916), No. 3, pp. 169–191, figs. 5*).—Rather detailed notes are given on the cultivation and yield of Bengal grass, together with brief notes on teosinte and Sudan grass.

Wild fodder grasses, W. Burns (*Dept. Agr. Bombay, Ann. Rpt. Expt. Work Ganeshkhind Bot. Gard., 1914–15, pp. 29–31*).—A list of 32 wild fodder grasses native to the Poona District, India, is given, together with brief notes on the yields and dates of harvesting.

Carrots and turnips as catch crops, H. Vendelmans (*Jour. Bd. Agr. [London], 23 (1916), No. 4, pp. 366, 367*).—This is a brief note on the use of carrots and turnips as a catch crop after wheat in Belgium. The carrots are sown broadcast in the wheat just before it heads out, and thus become well established before the wheat is harvested. The turnips are sown immediately after the wheat harvest.

Bean culture, A. L. Strausz (*Washington Sta. Popular Bul. 111 (1917), pp. 4*).—A popular treatise on the climatic and soil requirements, culture, and harvesting of beans.

Early studies in the selection of Trifolium incarnatum and of the medicagos, E. de Cillis (*Ann. R. Scuola Sup. Agr. Portici, 2. ser., 12 (1914), pp. 721–726*).—This is a brief review of the early improvement of crimson clover and certain of the medicagos, with special reference to their cultivation for forage.

Improvement of red clover, J. Beverley (*Jour. Agr. [New Zeal.], 12 (1916), No. 4, pp. 293, 294, fig. 1*).—This is a brief note on a red clover single-plant selection, five years old, in August, 1915. Two hundred and seventy flowering-stem growths have been removed from the parent plant and set out in 3-ft. rows. The parent plant gives a large kidney-shaped good-colored seed. About 1,000 seedlings have been grown as single plants. Four per cent of the seedlings have white flowers.

The relation of ear characters of corn to yield, C. C. Cunningham (*Jour. Amer. Soc. Agron., 8 (1916), No. 3, pp. 188–196*).—This paper is a discussion of some investigations conducted at the Kansas Experiment Station as to the relation of certain ear characters of corn to yield. A brief review of the literature bearing directly on the subject is also given. The data presented were compiled from ear-to-row tests and include the relations to yield of length of ear, circumference of ear, filling out of tips, rounding out of butts, indentation, percentage of grain, and number of rows. The varieties used in the test were Boone County White, Reid Yellow Dent, Hildreth Yellow Dent, Kansas Sunflower, Hogue Yellow Dent, McAuley White Dent, Legal Tender, Leaming, and Pride of Saline.

The data presented indicate that certain ear characters have been over-emphasized as to their worth as related to yield, while other characters have been emphasized that may actually tend to decrease yield. Considerably more information is deemed necessary before drawing definite conclusions, especially in regard to those characters whose correlation with yielding capacity may vary with soil and climatic conditions.

Lobed leaves in maize, J. H. Kempton (*Jour. Heredity, 7 (1916), No. 11, pp. 508–510, fig. 1*).—Early in 1911 an abnormality was observed in a Russian variety of maize and later was found on all of 90 varieties planted that season at Lanham, Md. This abnormality consisted of a pronounced lobing of the leaves, but the lobes were not mere tears, as was evident from the fact that the margins of the lobes, like those of all normal leaves, were beset with long brittle hairs and a double row of short saw-like teeth directed toward the apex of the leaf. That this abnormality was not a local phenomenon was revealed by observations made by Blaringhem in France and Gernert in Illinois.

The cause of lobing was not fully understood until dissecting some very small lateral branches of Euchlæna, it was noticed that several shoots were prevented from unfurling by having the margins of one of the leaf blades firmly held together with lobes. By examining smaller shoots the stage was finally reached where the lobes were just being formed. It was at once evident that the lobes were formed by the margins of the leaf blades cutting each other where they crossed in unfurling.

"The forcing of the inside margin of the leaf against the outside margin results in the inside margin being cut, but at the same time the outside margin also receives a slight cut through which the lobe on the inside margin grows. As this lobe grows it cuts up into the outside margin, which accounts for the small back cut sometimes found on one margin of the more perfect specimens."

The slight rupture of the tissue, which is extremely tender, results in the separated cells developing independently of the remainder of the leaf blade. "The fact that the two margins of the same leaf mutually rupture each other accounts for the lobes being most often found in pairs one on each side of the leaf."

Report on corn pollination, IV, M. L. FISHER (*Proc. Ind. Acad. Sci., 1914, pp. 207, 208*).—This is the fourth and last report on some studies of cross pollinating corn (E. S. R., 30, p. 635), and deals with a cross of sweet (male) and Reid Yellow Dent (female).

"In the third year two types of sweet corn were distinguishable, one a large ear with whitish kernels and white cobs like the original Stowell Evergreen, and the other a smaller ear with yellowish kernels and red cobs." The quality of the corn when cooked was excellent, the yellow-kernel, red-cob type being slightly sweeter and also earlier maturing

In the season of 1913 three plantings were made, two of the white-kernel, white-cob type in local gardens and the third of both types in the trial gardens of a commercial seedsman at Detroit, Mich. The Detroit tests were reported on as follows:

"The salient features of our reports are to the effect that neither of your selections seem as yet well enough fixed in type to be ready for presentation. Both show a large percentage of reversion to plain parent stock. They are both late and half of the ears in our trial were irregularly and poorly filled. Quality seems excellent, but the color of the red cob shows badly in cooking. From a seedsman's standpoint we do not believe the strains to be as yet of any value."

Sufficient seed is still on hand for further trials and it is hoped that a successful and fixed variety may yet be established.

Delbridge cotton seed calculator, C. L. DELBRIDGE (*St. Louis: The Delbridge Co., 1916, pp. 129*).—This is a table for calculating the value of any amount of cotton seed within the limits of $30.25 and $60 per ton.

Methi as a fodder crop in the Nasik District, M. G. ATHALYE (*Poona Agr. Col. Mag., 7 (1916) No. 4, pp. 226, 227*).—Brief notes are given on the production of methi as a green fodder crop in India. This crop is frequently used to prepare ground for sugar cane or onions, and is usually grown under well irrigation.

Disadvantage of continuous oat culture on a highly nitrogenous moor soil, H. VON FEILITZEN (*Svenska Mosskulturför. Tidskr., 30 (1916), No. 3, pp. 269–273, fig. 1*).—The results of experiments here described indicated that on good moor soil with sufficient nitrogen oats grown in rotation will give much higher yields than when grown continuously, provided any lacking plant food is supplied. Under continuous culture it was found that the land could not be kept free from weeds, which hindered the development of the crop. It is recommended that land in a very weedy condition should be kept in bare fallow for a year before crop culture is attempted.

Arachis hypogæa, G. C. DUDGEON (*Min. Agr. Egypt, Agr. Prod. No. 2a (1916), pp. 24, pl. 1*).—This is a detailed discussion of the production and uses of the peanut in Egypt. A botanical description of the more common varieties is given, together with a comprehensive review of the history of the crop. Preparation of the seed bed, cultivation, and harvesting are discussed in turn for both upper and lower Egypt.

Statistics are given on the yield of nuts and fodder.

Potato fertilizers, T. C. JOHNSON (*Virginia Truck Sta. Bul. 21 (1916), pp. 429-452, figs. 4*).—Truck crop potato fertilizer experiments conducted at the Virginia Truck Station and the Tasley (Accomac County) substation are reported. The plan of the experiments included the application of commercial fertilizers at the rate of 1,600 lbs. per acre, containing varying proportions of nitrogen, phosphoric acid, and potash. To determine the relative effects of the fertilizer on early, midseason, and late production one-third of each plat at Norfolk was harvested June 14, shortly after the blossoms had fallen, the second third June 22, and the last third July 3, at which time the vines were practically mature. The first harvest at Tasley was June 27-28, the second July 7, and the third July 17. Tabulated data show the yields of each plat for each harvest, together with the percentage increase or decrease.

The largest acre yields were obtained with a mixture containing the equivalent of 5 per cent of ammonia, 6 per cent of phosphoric acid, and 5 per cent of potash at both Norfolk (first and second harvests) and Tasley. A mixture equivalent to 9 per cent of ammonia, 6 per cent of phosphoric acid, and 5 per cent of potash resulted in the highest yield for the third harvest at Norfolk. Excellent results at both Norfolk and Tasley, based on percentage increase, were obtained with a 7 : 8 : 5 mixture.

The tests indicate that where the soil has received heavy applications of organic matter a fertilizer containing an equivalent of 5 per cent of ammonia should be satisfactory, but that a soil deficient in organic matter would give better results with one containing 7 per cent. At least 8 per cent of phosphoric acid should be used, better results being secured with this amount in all cases than with smaller quantities. Mixtures containing 3 and 5 per cent potash showed very satisfactory results, while those containing 7 and 10 per cent were not satisfactory at the first and second harvests, the excess of potash evidently delaying maturity.

The effect of removing the tops on the bearing of potatoes, O. SCHLUM-BERGER (*Mitt. K. Biol. Anst. Land u. Forstw., No. 15 (1914), pp. 11-13*).—In case of potatoes planted April 15 and deprived of their tops at different dates, it was found that the number of tubers produced was slightly lowered by removal of the tops July 21, and much more by their removal June 20. The total weight of the tubers was considerably reduced in both cases, particularly the latter.

[Potato varieties] (*Agr. Gaz. Canada, 3 (1916), No. 4, p. 372*).—Potato varieties found to be best adapted at each of 11 experimental centers in Canada are listed. Prominent among the early varieties are Early Ohio, Early Rose, and Irish Cobbler, and among the medium or late varieties, Carman No. 1 and Green Mountain.

Potatoes in California, J. W. GILMORE (*California Sta. Circ. 161 (1917), pp. 8*).—This is a general discussion of potato production in California, including cultural directions. The average cost of the preparation of the land and the growing of the crop, exclusive of harvesting, is estimated at approximately $28.75 per acre.

Potato growing in Washington, I, O. M. MORRIS (*Washington Sta. Popular Bul. 106 (1917), pp. 3–14*).—This is a brief general discussion of potato growing under Washington conditions.

Branching-headed rye grass, A. W. GREEN (*Jour. Agr. [New Zeal.], 12 (1916), No. 2, pp. 122–124, fig. 1*).—Some brief notes are given on branching in the heads of rye grass. The author states that seldom more than 10 per cent of the progeny of branched individuals possessed similar characters. The plants possessing branched heads were more vigorous than normal plants.

The botanical description of some varieties of Java and other canes, G. L. FAWCETT (*Rev. Indus. y Agr. Tucuman, 6 (1916), No. 12, pp. 509–523, figs. 3*).—Several varieties of sugar cane are described, and a key devised for their identification.

Varieties of sugar cane.—The result of five years' experiments, A. H. ROSENFELD (*Rev. Indus. y Agr. Tucuman, 6 (1915), No. 6, pp. 231–278*).—This is an extended report of five years of variety testing of sugar cane in Tucuman. A large number of varieties were compared as regards the comparative yielding ability of native and foreign varieties, the highest sugar-producing varieties, the varieties most resistant to insects and diseases, the varieties best adapted to temperature changes, and the varieties which furnish more and better fuel.

Two Java varieties, designated as Java 36 and Java 213, and Barbados 3277 are recommended most highly as the result of these trials.

The planting of sugar cane in single and double rows, W. E. CROSS (*Rev. Indus. y Agr. Tucuman, 7 (1916), No. 4, pp. 127–132*).—Some notes are given on tests begun by A. H. Rosenfeld on the planting of sugar cane in single and double rows. The results obtained indicate consistently higher yields where the cane was planted in double rows.

A comparison of planting thin canes with canes of ordinary size, W. E. CROSS (*Rev. Indus. y Agr. Tucuman, 7 (1916), No. 4, pp. 160, 161*).—Brief notes are given on experiments begun by A. H. Rosenfeld to compare the planting of sugar cane in the usual manner with the planting of thin canes.

The results obtained indicate that the use of thin canes slightly increased the yield. An average of 28,619 kg. per hectare (12.7 tons per acre) was obtained from the common method and 29,267 kg. from planting thin canes.

Trials with thinning sugar cane in the row, W. E. CROSS (*Rev. Indus. y Agr. Tucuman, 7 (1916), No. 4, pp. 145, 146*).—This reports the continuation of work begun in 1911 by A. H. Rosenfeld and J. A. Hall, and previously noted (E. Ś. R., 31, p. 42). After five consecutive years the results show that the average yield for the five-year period without thinning has been 35,440 kg. per hectare (15.8 tons per acre), as compared with 31,967 kg. when the cane was thinned.

Suggestions relative to the cultivation of sugar cane in Tucuman, J. H. WALE (*Rev. Indus. y Agr. Tucuman, 6 (1915), No. 5, pp. 185–188*).—This is a general discussion of the cultivation of sugar cane in Tucuman, with special reference to planting.

A study of the adsali cane, R. G. PADHYE (*Poona Agr. Col. Mag., 7 (1915), No. 1, pp. 60–66, pl. 1*).—Some notes are given on the production of ' adsali' cane, or " 18-months " cane, in India. This practice is followed to delay the harvesting of the cane until after the monsoon period. Analyses of the juice show

105033°—No. 2—17——4

that the purity of adsali cane, if standing, is higher than 90 per cent, and if lodged, from 80 to 85 per cent. Although the cane deteriorates in hot weather, a regular increase in the purity of the juice takes place as the monsoon sets in, especially in the lower and middle portions of the cane.

Japanese sugar cane as a forage crop, A. H. LEIDIGH, G. T. McNESS, and H. H. LAUDE (*Texas Sta. Bul. 195 (1916), pp. 3-28, figs. 7*).—The adaptation of Japanese sugar cane to the Gulf coast region of Texas and its production and use as a forage crop are discussed.

Observations of the crop under adverse weather conditions indicate that it possesses remarkable yielding qualities under such conditions; that it can grow on damp, undrained soils and resist floods better than any of the crops commonly grown in that region; and that it is decidedly resistant to frost. As a forage crop it is reported as producing a succulent feed at less cost in that region than sorghum or corn silage and comparing favorably with these crops in the feeding value of its green fodder. Comparative analyses indicate that the cane is lower in protein content than green sorghum or sorghum hay, Johnson grass, or Sudan grass hay, but its high sugar content, cheapness, and succulence make it valuable as the basis of a ration balanced by the use of cottonseed meal, peanut hay, or some other nitrogenous feed.

Depth-of-plowing and rate-of-seeding tests indicate that the highest yields are obtained from plowing to a depth of from 12 to 14 in., and that thick plantings (3,000 to 4,000 lbs. of seed canes per acre) are preferable. Although the yield of forage probably decreases considerably after the first season, with proper care the crop may be grown several years without replanting.

Sweet clover, F. M. LUTTS (*Mo. Bul. Ohio Sta., 2 (1917), No. 2, pp. 45-47, fig. 1*).—This briefly notes a test with sweet clover, at the Paulding County experiment farm, in comparison with red clover and mammoth clover as a crop to follow oats and be plowed under in the fall for the succeeding corn crop. The superior root development of sweet clover, especially in time of drought, is emphasized.

The flowering habits of timothy, M. W. EVANS (*Jour. Amer. Soc. Agron., 8 (1916), No. 5, pp. 299-309, pl. 1*).—This paper gives the results of observations on the flowering habits of timothy, made during the blooming period in 1912, 1913, 1914, and 1915, at the Timothy-Breeding Station, New London, Ohio, which is conducted cooperatively by the United States Department of Agriculture and the Ohio Experiment Station. Special attention was given to the time of blooming, length of the blooming period, how and at what time of day the flowers open, the conditions under which they open most readily, the color of various parts of the flower and the general color effect of meadows, and other phases of the blooming process. The observations may be briefly summarized as follows:

When timothy blooms the anthers emerge first and then the stigmas. Anthers do not dehisce until the stigmas of the same flower have been exposed for some time. The flowers on the upper portion of the spike bloom first, with those lower down coming into bloom on succeeding days. The flowers on a single spike may bloom from 6 to 16 days. The period of bloom in northern Ohio extends from June 16 or 20 to July 12 or 15, although the bulk of the blooming is from June 24 or 26 to July 3 or 5. The greatest number of flowers bloom from midnight until sunrise.

The number of flowers that bloom each day, as well as the time of blooming, are affected by climatic conditions, especially temperature. Clear weather and a minimum temperature of 60° F. are most favorable. Timothy was not observed blooming when the temperature during the preceding 24 hours was as low as 50°. Timothy cut during the blooming period will bloom 12 hours or more after cutting, providing that the hay has not wilted.

The color of timothy bloom varies greatly, due chiefly to the changes in the color of the anther and the anther sack and the variations in the number of flowers that bloom on different days. When weather conditions are favorable, timothy blooming may be regarded as a continuous process to the end of the blooming period, and the so-called "first" and "second" bloom, or the "blue" and "gray" bloom, are misnomers.

On the improvement of Red Olona, P. VENINO (*Ann. Ist. Agr.* [*Milan*], *12* (*1913–14*), *pp. 109, 110*).—This is a brief note on the improvement of Red Olona wheat through selection since 1910.

The roots of zacaton and their exploitation, I. R. MARTINEZ (*La Raiz de Zacaton y su Explotacion. Mexico: Govt., 1914, pp. 26 pls. 12*).—Three varieties of zacaton are described and illustrated, namely, *Festuca amplissima*, *Muehlembergia gracilis*, and *Epicampes stricta*. The fiber is extracted by means of a macerating machine, bleached with sulphurous acid, and classified according to length and color. Directions and regulations are given regarding the exploiting of the product.

Correlation phenomena in the physical properties of grain and their practical significance, M. AKEMINE (*Jour. Col. Agr. Tohoku Imp. Univ., 7 (1916), No. 2, pp. 101–127*).—This article is a discussion of some investigations dealing with the correlations existing between certain of the physical properties of the seed of rice, barley, wheat, and naked barley as to absolute weight and (1) length, breadth, or thickness, (2) volume, (3) size of the embryo, and (4) specific gravity. The author summarizes his conclusions as follows:

In whole ripe seed the correlation between absolute weight and length or breadth is significant. In the same seeds a correlation between the absolute weight and thickness is very slight, but in unripe seed such a correlation exists. In whole ripe seed the correlation between absolute weight and the volume is very significant. In the same seed a significant correlation exists between absolute weight and the size of the embryo except in hulled rice, in which case the correlation is negligible—for what reason is not yet clear.

There is no correlation between absolute weight and specific gravity, and a sorting method based on specific gravity can only be applied to the separating of ripe, whole or dry seed from unripe, broken or wet seed. Seed sorting based on the absolute weight by means of air currents is a theoretical certainty, but further improvement must be made in regulating the strength of the air current.

A brief bibliography is given at the end of the article.

The possibility of combating plant diseases by means of careful seed selection, E. HENNING (*K. Landtbr. Akad. Handl. och Tidskr., 55 (1916), No. 4, pp. 282–300, fig. 1*).—This is a paper presented before the Royal Agricultural Academy of Sweden reviewing the history of seed control work, together with the results of the more important investigations conducted from time to time to increase the accuracy and reliability of seed testing. It is also pointed out how various factors, especially the influences of plant diseases, may affect the results of seed growth by reducing the viability below that indicated by the seed examination.

Twelfth annual report of the Canadian Seed Growers' Association for the year ending March 31, 1916 (*Canad. Seed Growers' Assoc. Ann. Rpt., 12 (1916), pp. 32*).—A list of the operating members is given which includes the kind and variety of crops grown and the number of years the seed is known to have been selected.

Conversion of fern-land into grass, A. H. Cockayne (*Jour. Agr.* [*New Zeal.*], *12 (1916), No. 6, pp. 421-439, figs. 9*).—This article discusses in some detail the suppression of the fern as a weed in New Zealand by the seeding of fern land to pasture grasses. The following grass mixture is recommended: Cocksfoot 8 lbs., *Danthonia pilosa* 5 lbs., *Poa pratensis* 3 lbs., Chewings fescue 5 lbs., crested dogstail 2 lbs., *P. nemoralis* 2 lbs., white clover 1 lb., and *Lotus angustissimus* 0.5 lb., a total of 26.5 lbs., to which should be added a few pounds of Italian rye grass for quick results.

Goat's rue (Galega officinalis), A. H. Cockayne (*Jour. Agr.* [*New Zeal.*], *12 (1916), No. 2, pp. 125-130, fig. 1*).—This is a botanical and popular description of goat's rue (*G. officinalis*), which has lately been added to the schedule of "noxious" plants under the Noxious Weeds Act of New Zealand. Notes are given on its cultural habits and methods of control.

[Field crops], M. Hoffmann et al. (*Jahresber. Landw., 29 (1914), pp. 72-179*).—German literature on the subject of field crops is classified and reviewed in the usual manner.

HORTICULTURE.

Report of the horticultural division, J. E. Higgins (*Hawaii Sta. Rpt. 1916, pp. 13-21, pls. 2*).—The horticultural work was continued largely along lines previously noted (E. S. R., 35, p. 538).

With the view of securing improved commercial varieties of pineapples for Hawaii preliminary work in breeding and selection, both among cultivated varieties and seedling forms, was started. The station is collecting varieties grown in different parts of the world, and a number of local seedlings are also being grown. Satisfactory methods, here described, have been devised for the germination of pineapple seeds and the growing of the young seedlings beyond the critical period.

The cooperative experiments with the litchi were continued. Over 1,000 seeds were successfully shipped from Hawaii to Florida in slightly moist sphagnum moss, wrapped in waxed paper surrounded by corrugated strawboard. The water added to the moss equaled half the weight of the dry moss. A disease of litchi leaves similar to the erinose disease of the grape and which has been named litchi erinose was under observation and treatment. The injury is caused by an undescribed Eriophyes species of mite and can be controlled by spraying the trees several times with nicotin sulphate and whale-oil soap mixed at the rate of 10 oz. of nicotin sulphate and 1.75 lbs. of whale-oil soap to 50 gal. of water. The treatment is more effective if the seriously damaged leaves are removed before spraying. The longan tree, a related species, was not infested with this mite although surrounded by infested litchi trees.

In the breeding work with avocados and mangos a number of apparent crosses were secured during the season. The technique thus far developed in cross-pollinating mangos is described. Breeding work with papayas was continued with the view of securing a pure elongata strain as well as further data on the determination of sex and the combining of desired characters. Seventy-two supposed seedling crosses of the Chinese wood oil nut (*Aleurites fordii*) and the Hawaiian kukui nut (*A. moluccana*) are under observation.

Notes are given on the condition of the station orchards and miscellaneous plantings at the Tantalus substation.

[New fruit trees, ornamentals, and other plants], N. E. Hansen (*South Dakota Sta. Rpt. 1916, pp. 22-26*).—This comprises brief descriptions of some new trees and plants sent out by the station for trial in the spring of 1916. The list includes the Ivan and Dolgo crab apples; Sereda, Adno, and Hibkee apples; some seedling plums; a Turkestan radish and Siberian muskmelons and watermelons found by the author; Siberian forms of almond, buckthorn, and Lavatera; *Rosa rugosa;* Manitoba hazelnut; and New Ulm black walnut.

Attention is called to the value of Siberian and Hybrid Siberian crab apples as important stocks for insuring freedom from root killing. In the station orchard the Wealthy apple has borne abundantly on the Siberian stock.

Notes on novelties and plants not well known, F. E. Buck (*Ann. Rpt. Hort. Socs. Ont., 11 (1916), pp. 95, 96*).—Brief descriptive notes are given on flowers and plants grown in the test plats of the Central Experimental Farm for the first time during the season of 1916.

Calendar for the treatment of plant diseases and insect pests, W. J. Green, A. D. Selby, and H. A. Gossard (*Ohio Sta. Bul. 309 (1917), pp. 485-516, figs. 3*).—A revised edition of Bulletin 232, previously noted (E. S. R., 26, p. 539).

Winter sprays: Lime-sulphur spray and crude oil emulsions, A. L. Melander (*Washington Sta. Popular Bul. 107 (1917), pp. 12*).—A revised edition of Popular Bulletin 64 of the station, previously noted (E. S. R., 31, p. 740).

Cabbage and cauliflower culture, C. B. Sprague (*Washington Sta. Popular Bul. 110 (1917), pp. 4*).—A popular treatise on the climatic and soil requirements, culture, harvesting, and storage of cabbage and cauliflower.

Celery culture, F. W. Allen (*Washington Sta. Popular Bul. 109 (1917), pp. 4*).—A treatise similar to the above.

Lettuce growing in California, S. S. Rogers (*California Sta. Circ. 160 (1917), pp. 16, figs. 11*).—This circular discusses the classification of lettuce, importance of the industry in California, lettuce growing districts in California, cost of production, yields, profits, cultural requirements, harvesting, packing, varieties, and crop troubles.

Growing tomatoes on stakes: .Advantages, increased profits, and proper methods of culture, S. N. Green (*Mo. Bul. Ohio Sta., 2 (1917), No. 3, pp. 91-95, figs. 2*).—This paper presents some data based on information secured from practical growers, as well as on tests conducted by the station, showing the proper methods of growing tomatoes on stakes, together with the advantages and increased profits therefrom.

Forms of some Philippine fruits, J. de Leon y German (*Philippine Agr. and Forester, 5 (1916), No. 8, pp. 251-283, figs. 16*).—In the present study the author aims to show the importance of improving varieties of fruits by the selection of the best native forms and propagating them vegetatively. Various native varieties of fruits are here described.

Irrigation of orchards, F. Adams (*Cal. Citrogr., 2 (1917), No. 7, pp. 2, 3, figs. 2*).—A paper on this subject read at the Citrus Institute, Riverside, Cal.

The Maryland apple grading and packing law, T. B. Symons and S. B. Shaw (*Md. Agr. Ext. Serv. Bul. 1 (1916), pp. 23, figs. 10*).—This bulletin gives the text of the Maryland apple grading and packing law, calls attention to similar laws enacted by other States and by the Federal Government, explains the requirements of the law, and gives suggestions relative to harvesting, grading, and packing apples.

Cooperative organization, G. V. Branch (*Ann. Rpt. State Hort. Maine, 5 (1915) pp. 35-43*).—An address to the apple growers of Maine in which the author points out the benefits of cooperative organization in marketing.

North American varieties of the strawberry, S. W. Fletcher (*Virginia Sta. Tech. Bul. 11 (1916), pp. 3-126, figs. 19*).—This bulletin, which comprises a descriptive list of 1,879 varieties of strawberries, includes all varieties that have originated in North America so far as can be discovered from an extensive review of the literature of the subject. A bibliography of North American literature on the strawberry, exclusive of articles on injurious insects and diseases, is also given.

Some viticultural and enological experiments conducted at the Paarl Viticultural Experiment Station during 1915–16, A. I. PEROLD (*Union So. Africa Dept. Agr.* [*Pub.*], *21* (*1916*), *pp. 13*).—This briefly summarizes the results of pruning, training, thinning, and other experiments with table grapes, as well as some experiments in wine making, conducted at the Paarl Viticultural Experiment Station during 1915–16.

California's grape industry (*Cal. Bd. Vit. Comrs. Bul. 8* (*1917*), *pp. 24*).— A statistical review of the grape industry of California for the year 1916. During the year a total of 10,741 cars of grapes were shipped to points outside of the State. The estimated raisin production for the year was 126,000 tons. About 478,197 tons of grapes were used in the production of wine and brandy.

The culture of the olive (Olea europaea) on the southern shore of the Crimea, E. V. WOLF, F. K. KALAÏDA, and G. A. PLOTNITSKIĬ (*Bot. Kab. i Bot. Sad Imp. Nikitsk. Sada* [*Pub.*] *No. 1* (*1916*), *pp. 24, figs. 9*).—Some results are given of experimental tests in propagating and planting olives and the extraction of oil from various species.

Maintenance of fertility of pineapple fields, F. G. KRAUSS (*Hawaii Sta. Rpt. 1916, pp. 36–38*).—An account is given of cooperative demonstration experiments being conducted on the plantation of the Haiku Fruit and Packing Company for the purpose of testing the accumulative renovating power of green-manuring legumes.

Station work for the avocado, H. J. WEBBER (*Rpt. Cal. Avocado Assoc., 1915, pp. 69–72*).—This paper comprises a brief statement of investigations with avocados being conducted under the direction of the Citrus Experiment Station.

Varieties of the avocado, F. O. POPENOE (*Rpt. Cal. Avocado Assoc., 1915, pp. 44–69*).—Previously noted from another source (E. S. R., 35, p. 448).

The avocado in Florida and other lands, W. POPENOE (*Rpt. Cal. Avocado Assoc., 1915, pp. 29–42*).—In this paper the author gives a general account of avocado culture and the importance of the industry in Florida and the West Indies.

Citrus fruit improvement: How to secure and use tree performance records, A. D. SHAMEL (*U. S. Dept. Agr., Farmers' Bul. 794* (*1917*), *pp. 16, figs. 4*).— This publication is based upon the results obtained in bud selection experiments in California citrus groves which have been under way since 1909 (E. S. R., 36, pp. 141, 537). It describes the methods that have been found effective and practical in locating the desirable and undesirable trees in groves and for transforming the latter when found.

Records and accounts for citrus groves, R. S. VAILE (*Cal. Citrogr., 2* (*1917*), *No. 7, pp. 7, 8, figs. 2*).—A discussion of cost accounting with special reference to citrus groves in southern California.

[Coconuts, rubber, coffee, and cacao], J. B. HARRISON (*Rpt. Dept. Sci. and Agr. Brit. Guiana, 1914–15, pp. 15–21*).—A brief statistical review of the above-named crops, including the progress made in cultural experiments at the Georgetown Botanic Gardens and at the Onderneeming Farm.

Experiments in manuring of cacao, M. K. BAMBER and D. S. CORLETT (*Dept. Agr. Ceylon Bul. 26* (*1916*), *pp. 9*).—The results are given of manurial experiments with cacao in which the trees were continuously manured during the period from 1902 to 1911, inclusive, but since which period manures have been withheld.

The principal feature of the experiment was the permanent beneficial effect of castor pomace, which, during the 10-year manurial period, had been applied annually at the rate of 833 lbs. per acre, containing 50 lbs. of nitrogen. This plat gave poor results for some years during the application, but later it steadily increased from the twelfth to the first place, which it has held for the last two years it received no manure. A new series of manurial experiments started in 1915 is here outlined.

Culture of the pistachio tree (Pistacia vera) on the southern shore of the Crimea, F. K. KALAÏDA (*Bot. Kab. i Bot. Sad Imp. Nikitsk. Sada* [*Pub.*] *No. 2 (1916), pp. 22, pls. 8, figs. 2*).—Directions are given for propagating and growing the pistachio tree, based upon experience in the Imperial orchard at Nikitsky.

The cultivation and drying of medicinal plants, E. M. HOLMES (*Sevenoaks, England: Author, 1916, pp. 15*).—A lecture on this subject embracing the results of the author's observations and experience for a number of years in the cultivation of medicinal plants.

One hundred flowers, H. HAVERSTICK (*Hershey, Penn.: Hershey Press, 1917, pp. 91, figs. 16*).—In this work the author describes and gives directions for growing 100 decorative flowers and plants, including old-time favorites and the best of the new ones, the subject matter being based upon personal observation and experience.

The book of the peony, MRS. E. HARDING (*Philadelphia and London: J. B. Lippincott Co., 1917, pp. 259, pls. 43, figs. 8*).—A treatise on the peony, discussing its mythology, ancient and modern history, best varieties and their characteristics, methods of extending the period of bloom, purchasing peonies, where to plant and how to prepare the soil, planting and cultivation, and propagation. Chapters are also devoted to the history, description, cultivation, propagation, and best varieties of tree peonies.

The American rose annual, edited by J. H. McFARLAND (*Harrisburg, Penn.: American Rose Society, 1917, pp. 161, pls. 10, figs. 7*).—This annual comprises numerous articles by various authorities on roses dealing with the following subjects: The use of the rose in the landscape, the literature of the rose, the American rose advance, methods of rose growing, rose importations, how to conduct an amateur rose show, the rose all over America, the enemies of the rose, cut-flower rose growing, a partial list of roses introduced in America, and the work of the American Rose Society.

A bud variation of Euonymus, A. D. SHAMEL (*Jour. Heredity, 8 (1917) No. 5, pp. 218–220, figs. 2*).—The author calls attention to a variegated form of *E. japonicus* as an illustration of a valuable cultivated variety produced through the propagation of bud variations, the variegated form being a bud variation of the green form.

Aristocrats of the garden, E. H. WILSON (*Garden City, N. Y.: Doubleday, Page & Co., 1917, pp. VII+312, pls. 16*).—This work comprises a series of articles on ornamental plants previously noted (E. S. R., 35, pp. 345, 450).

Garden guide.—The amateur gardener's handbook, edited by J. H. DICK (*New York: A. T. De La Mare Co., 1917, pp. 255, figs. 173*).—A compilation of information relative to planning, planting, and maintaining the home grounds, the suburban garden, and the city lot, including lists of plants for various purposes, together with chapters on garden furniture and accessories.

Back yard gardening for business men, T. R. BEST (*New York: Street & Smith, 1917, pp. 125, figs. 2*).—A popular treatise discussing opportunities in the back yard and giving directions for growing the more important vegetables.

Street and park trees for Wisconsin communities, M. A. CASTLE (*Wis. Conserv. Com. Bul. 2 (1916), pp. 54, figs. 32*).—A compilation of material dealing with the planting and care of street and park trees, including lists of trees and shrubs for planting in different situations.

Turf for golf courses, C. V. PIPER and R. A. OAKLEY (*New York: The Macmillan Co., 1917, pp. XVII+262, pls. 20, figs. 50*).—A treatise on growing turf for golf courses, the successive chapters of which discuss soils for turf grasses; fertilizers; manures, composts, and other humus materials; lime and its use; the important turf plants; how to distinguish different kinds of turf; the turf grasses for different purposes; the making of the turf; subsequent care; weeds and their control; animal pests; turf machinery; experimental work on golf courses; and personal experiences.

FORESTRY.

Report of the superintendent of forestry, C. S. JUDD ([*Bien.*] *Rpt. Bd. Comrs. Agr. and Forestry Hawaii, 1915–16, pp. 23–48, pls. 8*).—A report for the calendar years 1915 and 1916 relative to the work of forest protection, operations on the Government reserves and nurseries, private planting work, and miscellaneous activities.

During the past biennial period two more forest reserves have been added to the general forest-reserve system, making a total of 39, with a total area of 798,344 acres, of which 546,352 acres is Government land.

Report of the forest nurseryman, D. HAUGHS ([*Bien.*] *Rpt. Bd. Comrs. Agr. and Forestry Hawaii, 1915–16, pp. 54–59*).—A report for the years 1915 and 1916 relative to collection and exchange of seed, trees distributed from the Government nurseries, and miscellaneous work.

Annual administration report of the forest department of the Madras Presidency for the twelve months ended June 30, 1916, F. L. C. COWLEY-BROWN, H. B. BRYANT, P. M. LUSHINGTON. H. A. LATHAM, ET AL. (*Ann. Admin. Rpt. Forest Dept. Madras, 1916, pp. 73+LIX+16*).—The usual progress report relative to the administration of the State forests in the Northern, Central, Southern, and Western Circles of the Madras Presidency, including a financial statement for the year ended June 30, 1916. All important data relative to alterations in forest areas, working plans, surveys, miscellaneous work, yields in major and minor forest products, revenues, expenditures, etc., are appended in tabular form.

Annual progress report on forest administration in the Province of Bihar and Orissa for the year 1915–16, H. H. HAINES (*Ann. Rpt. Forest Admin. Bihar and Orissa, 1915–16, pp. II+56+4*).—A report similar to the above relative to the administration of the State forests of the Province of Bihar and Orissa.

Annual report on the forest administration in Ajmer-Merwara for the year 1915–16, HUKAM CHAND (*Ann. Rpt. Forest Admin. Ajmer-Merwara, 1915–16, pp. 3+29*).—A report similar to the above relative to the administration of the State forests of Ajmer-Merwara.

Progress report of forest administration in the Province of Assam for the year 1915–16, W. F. L. TOTTENHAM and A. W. BLUNT (*Rpt. Forest Admin. Assam, 1915–16 pp. 2+24+55+3, pl. 1*).—A report similar to the above relative to the administration of the State forests of Assam.

Progress report of forest administration in the Punjab for the year 1915–16, R. McINTOSH (*Rpt. Forest Admin. Punjab, 1915–16, pp. [12]+14+LXVII, pl. 1*).—A report similar to the above relative to the administration of the State forests of the Punjab.

Tree planting in eastern Washington, O. M. MORRIS (*Washington Sta. Popular Bul. 108 (1917), pp. 4*).—Practical directions are given for planting trees, including a descriptive list of varieties recommended for eastern Washlugton.

Ornamental windbreaks.—Evergreens are grouped with small trees and flowering shrubs, W. E. BONTRAGER (*Mo. Bul. Ohio Sta.*, 2 (1917), No. 3, pp. 82–84, fig. 1).—This paper presents suggestions relative to the use of ornamental trees in the development of windbreaks for protecting orchards, gardens, barnyards, etc.

Investigation on the optimum limit of intensity of thinnings, E. MER (*Rev. Eaux et Forêts*, 55 (1917), Nos. 2, pp. 33–43; 3, pp. 65–72).—In continuation of previous papers (E. S. R., 36, p. 345) the author gives the results secured from thinnings of different intensities in some selected fir stands that were thinned in 1886 and in 1899.

Toxic atrophy, E. A. WOODRUFFE-PEACOCK (*Quart. Jour. Forestry*, 11 (1917), No. 2, pp. 88–93).—In this paper the author presents his views relative to toxic atrophy as an important factor in the failure of species to reproduce themselves in woodlands.

The forests of Quebec, A. BEDARD (*Statis. Year Book Prov. Quebec, 1916*, pp. 414–428).—A short description of the three forest zones in Quebec, including some statistical and economic considerations.

Notes on some North American conifers based on leaf characters, L. W. DURRELL (*Proc. Iowa Acad. Sci.*, 23 (1916), pp. 519–582, figs. 117).—The author here presents a series of drawings, with descriptive text, of the leaf characters of the arboreal conifers of North America bearing needle leaves, except Pinus. The characters of the same species were found to be constant even though the specimens came from widely separated localities.

The tulip poplar (Liriodendron tulipifera).—A forest tree of important commercial value for Ohio, A. E. TAYLOR (*Mo. Bul. Ohio Sta.*, 2 (1917), No. 2, pp. 51–58, figs. 4).—An account of the tulip poplar with reference to its characteristics, soil and light requirements, commercial value, and silvical management.

On the mode of occurrence of latex vessels in Hevea brasiliensis, G. BRYCE and L. E. CAMPBELL (*Dept. Agr. Ceylon Bul. 30* (1917), pp. 22).—The authors here record a study of the distribution and mode of occurrence of latex vessels as observed in a number of untapped trees at the Peradeniya Experiment Station, as well as in trees growing on plantations in several different districts of Ceylon.

Tapping experiments at Gunong Angsi, F. G. SPRING and B. BUNTING (*Agr. Bul. Fed. Malay States*, 5 (1917), No. 4, pp. 111–123).—In continuation of previous work (E. S. R., 30, p. 535) the results of the third season are given on tapping experiments with rubber to determine the relative yields from adjacent and opposite quarters with both daily and alternate tapping.

The results thus far secured indicate that the yield from adjacent quarters of the tree (double V cuts) is approximately 18 per cent greater than that from opposite quarters of the tree. The daily tapping of adjacent quarters gave 26 per cent more rubber than opposite quarters, while on alternate-day tapping the difference in favor of adjacent quarters was only 9.5 per cent. Opposite quarters not only gave much poorer total yields and higher percentages of scrap rubber than adjacent quarters but had the disadvantage of having two distinct tapping areas which makes the system much more difficult both as regards tapping and supervision.

"Tarwad" bark as a tanning agent, D. B. LIMAYE (*Ranade Indus. and Econ. Inst., Poona, Bul. 1* (1916), pp. 18).—An account of the "tarwad" bark, the product of the perennial shrub *Cassia auriculata*, with reference to its use for tanning purposes in India. Analysis of tannin content and methods of collecting the bark are also given.

Production of lumber, lath, and shingles in 1915 and lumber in 1914, J. C. Nellis (*U. S. Dept. Agr. Bul. 506 (1917), pp. 45, pls. 2, figs. 4*).—This bulletin gives detailed statistics on the production of lumber, lath, and shingles in 1915 with comparisons for previous years. The data given include production, by classes of mills, by States, and by kinds of wood. Reports from 16,815 mills showed an aggregate timber cut for 1915 of 31,241,735,000 ft. b. m., from which it is estimated that the total lumber cut of the country was approximately 38,000,000,000 ft. b. m.

Forest industries (*Statis. Year Book Prov. Quebec, 1916, pp. 429–443*).—A statistical survey of the forest products of Quebec for 1915, including comparative data for 1914. An article on the manufacture of wood pulp, by G. C. Piché, is also included.

DISEASES OF PLANTS.

Additional notes on Philippine plant diseases, C. F. Baker (*Philippine Agr. and Forester, 5 (1916), No. 3, pp. 73–78*).—Since the publication of the review of plant diseases previously noted (E. S. R., 32, p. 749), considerable work has been done in this direction by the author and, in collaboration with him, by Rehm, Sydow, Saccardo, and Diedicke, in the determination of parasitic fungi. A number of these are considered as new to science and are named herein, without technical descriptions, in connection with the host plants. These forms include the new varieties *Phomopsis palmicola arecæ* on *Areca catechu* and *Mycogone cervina theobromæ* and *Nectria bainii hypoleuca* on *Theobroma cacao;* the new species *Phyllosticta insularum* on *Annona muricata, Exosporium pulchellum* and *Anthostomella arecæ* on *Areca catechu, Phomotospora migrans* on *Arenga saccharifera, Diatrypella barleriæ* on *Barleria cristata, Physalospora guignardioides* on *Canavalia gladiata, Zignoella nobilis* on *Citrus nobilis, Exosporium durum* and *Chætosphæria eximia* on *Cocos nucifera, Phyllosticta euchlænæ* on *Euchlæna luxurians, Diplodia crebra* on *Musa sapientum, Oospora oryzetorum, Phyllosticta glumarum, Ophiobolus oryzinus, Sordaria oryzeti*, and *Coniosporium oryzinum* on *Oryza sativa, Pionnotes capillacea* on *Persea gratissima, Pezizella ombrophilacea* and *Aschersonia parænsis* on *Psidium guajara, Diplodina degenerans* on *Solanum melongena, Physalospora affinis* and *Botryosphæria minuscula* on *Theobroma cacao, Macrophoma trichosanthis* on *Trichosanthes anguina, Vermicularia xanthosomatis* on *Xanthosoma sagittifolium*, and *Helminthosporium curvulum, Clasterosporium maydicum, Broomella zeæ*, and *Acerbia maydis* on *Zea mays;* and the new genera and species *Bakerophoma sacchari* on *Saccharum officinarum* and *Discothecium bakeri* on *Trichosanthes anguina.*

Some Phycomycetous diseases of cultivated plants in the Philippines, N. Mendiola and R. B. Espino (*Philippine Agr. and Forester, 5 (1916), No. 3, pp. 65–72, figs. 2*).—It has been found that *Phytophthora faberi* (*P. theobromæ*) is the cause of a pod disease of cacao and a fruit disease of papaya, and it is thought that it may develop on other plants in this region. Though the primary agent in the above-mentioned cases, it is quickly followed by other fungi, commonly by Lasiodiplodia.

P. colocasiæ was found and studied on leaves of gabi (*Colocasia antiquorum*) at Anos, Los Baños. *Pythium debaryanum* has been noted in the Philippines as causing a damping-off in seedlings of lettuce, tomato, and other vegetables, also in tobacco plants.

Plant diseases and other injuries, C. Brick (*Hamburg Bot. Staatsinst., Ber. Abt. Pflanzenschutz, 16 (1913–14), pp. 9–21*).—This deals with diseases, animal enemies, and other harmful agencies affecting various plants in domestic and colonial German territory, also in some neighboring countries or foreign lands. The results are briefly indicated of tests with several proprietary or standard fungicidal preparations.

The genus Meliola in Porto Rico, F. L. STEVENS (*Ill. Biol. Monographs, 2 (1916), No. 4, pp. 473–554, pls. 5*).—The author has described material collected in Porto Rico during 1912, 1913, and 1915. This has been arranged in 95 species and 6 varieties of Meliola parasitic on 171 different hosts, 146 of which are said to be new to Porto Rico for Meliola.

Specialization of parasitic fungi, particularly of the cereal rusts, L. MONTE-MARTINI (*Riv. Patol. Veg., 8 (1916), Nos. 2, pp. 33–44; 6–7, pp. 145–158*).—The author, besides giving a bibliographic discussion of this subject, describes a number of his own investigations.

He concludes that parasitic fungi are extremely sensitive to the chemical composition of the nutritive medium on which they live, and under its influence easily acquire characters of adaptation which attain to a certain fixity. In consequence fungi may become unable to flourish on species different from that to which they have accustomed themselves, and even on other portions of the same plant which they inhabit, or in different developmental stages or other conditions of such plant or organ. This unfitness may manifest itself in differences of germinability or of virulence of the spores originating in different situations.

In grain rusts, or at least in *Puccinia rubigo-vera* of rye, which has been made the object of special study by the author, it is stated that these may pass from one to another species of fall or spring wheat and oats, infection varying in an irregular manner even within a single species and a given stage. This matter is further complicated by atmospheric conditions and the influence thereof upon sensitivity to attack as well as upon the infecting bodies. It is thought that temporary adaptation and differences or parallelism of development in both host and parasite may explain what are considered real specializations.

Some septorias of wheat, W. B. GROVE (*Gard. Chron., 3. ser., 60 (1916), Nos. 1556, p. 194, figs. 3; 1557, p. 210, fig. 1*).—The author gives the results of comparing a number of Septorias on wheat sent from west Australia by F. Stoward with some collected in England by J. W. Ellis or by himself.

Practical or complete identity appeared in several cases, some apparent differences arising from such causes as different positions of the fungus on the host plant or age of the different portions attacked. *S. nodorum* is thus apparently identical with *S. glumarum*. A specimen causing a dry blight in west Australia is apparently identical with *S. graminum* in England, though in some respects another specimen approached *S. ophioides* and may prove to be identical therewith. Other forms or modifications are described, in particular *S. graminum crassipes*. *S. bromi* and *S. bromi brachypodii* are thought to belong to the same species, which is probably widespread, and *S. tritici* is probably a closely allied form.

Smut of wheat, F. E. DEVOTO (*Min. Agr. Nac. [Buenos Aires], Dir. Gen. Enseñanza e Invest. Agr. [Pub.] No. 53 (1916), pp. 7–12, figs. 5*).—This is a discussion of the development, effects, and treatments of the wheat smuts *Tilletia tritici* and *T. lævis*, with directions for the preparation of Bordeaux mixture, which appears to be in common use in this region.

Some bacterial diseases of vegetables found in Ontario, D. H. JONES (*Ontario Dept. Agr. Bul. 240 (1916), pp. 24, figs. 31*).—This bulletin deals with bacterial diseases according to the four general types of change they induce in the host, namely, soft rots, wilts, cankers or blights, and galls.

The cause of bacterial soft rot of various fleshy vegetables, considered as practically one and the same organism, has been discussed under the various names *Bacillus carotovorus, B. oleraceæ, B. melonis, B. aroideæ,* and *Pseudomonas destructans.* Soft rots of potato are associated with *B. solanisaprus* and a Fusariam, black leg with *B. phytophthorus* and with a Rhizoctonia. Bacterial wilt of crucifers, also called black rot of cabbage, or brown rot, is associated with P. *campestris,* and bacterial wilt of cucurbits with *B. tracheiphilus.* Bean blight, or bacteriosis, is associated with P. *phaseoli,* which organism appears to be, as regards morphological and cultural characteristics, practically identical with P. *campestris.* It is not, however, pathogenic for cabbage or cauliflower, while P. *campestris* is pathogenic for most crucifers but not for legumes.

Club root of crucifers and its control, E. WERTH (*K. Biol. Anst. Land u. Forstw. Flugbl., 56 (1916), pp. 3, fig. 1*).—This circular deals with *Plasmodiophora brassicæ,* its persistence in spore form in the soil, its infection of subsequent crops, and its effective control.

Excess of soil water, deficiency of lime, use of one-sided fertilizers, too long a succession of cruciferous crops, and the presence of wild crucifers in fields are among the conditions favoring the perpetuation of the club root organism. Rigid inspection of plantlets, judicious rotation of crops, improvement of physical and chemical conditions in the soil (especially deep plowing with a liberal use of lime), and disinfection of the soil with 5 liters per square meter (4.4 qts. per square yard) of a 2 to 3 per cent solution of formalin are among the measures recommended.

A new host of Ascochyta hortorum, L. GABOTTO (*Riv. Patol. Veg., 8 (1916), No. 2, pp. 45, 46*).—The author records a fungus, supposed to be *A. hortorum,* as causing an external spotting and an internal rot of artichoke.

Controlling cabbage yellows, S. N. GREEN and J. G. HUMBERT (*Mo. Bul. Ohio Sta., 2 (1917), No. 2, pp. 37–40, fig. 1*).—An account is given of experiments begun in 1911 to develop by careful selection strains of cabbage resistant to the yellows disease caused by *Fusarium conglutinans.* As a result of these experiments, several resistant strains of a commercial variety of cabbage have been developed.

Potato diseases, F. D. HEALD (*Washington Sta. Popular Bul. 106 (1917), pp. 15–94, figs. 26*).—After a discussion of the loss due to potato diseases, some of their causes, and methods of prevention and control, the author describes nonparasitic diseases, due to unfavorable environment and chemical treatment, and those transmitted by seed, the cause of which is unknown, and parasitic diseases due to bacteria, slime molds, and fungi.

Important potato diseases and their control, R. SCHANDER (*Arb. Gesell. Förd. Baues u. Verwend. Kartoffeln, No. 4 (1915), pp. 90, figs. 19*).—This is a synthetic review, chiefly from a practical standpoint, of the principal potato diseases prevalent in Germany, including nematode attack, their effects, and their control.

The osmotic pressure of cell sap in relation to tobacco plants affected with mosaic disease, A. SPRECHER (*Ann. Jard. Bot. Buitenzorg, 2. ser., 14 (1916), pt. 2, pp. 112–128*).—The author, describing a series of studies, states that tobacco plants affected with mosaic disease show practically the same freezing point and osmotic pressure as normal plants. The former, however, show lower molecular weights in the substances dissolved in the cell sap, this fact being supposedly connected with a small content in organic, and a large content in mineral, substances.

Tomato fruit diseases, R. WATERS (*Jour. Agr. [New Zeal.], 12 (1916), No. 3, pp. 198–201, figs. 4*).—Notes are given of tomato black rot due to *Macrosporium tomato,* probably identical with *M. solani;* circular white patch, supposedly induced by unfavorable weather conditions; and premature softening, which it is thought may prove to be the incipient stages of the circular white patch condition.

Manual of fruit diseases, L. R. HESLER and H. H. WHETZEL (*New York: The Macmillan Co., 1917, pp. XX+462, figs. 126*).—The authors give popular descriptions, together with suggestions for control, of bacterial and fungus diseases, as well as those of unknown causation, of the apple, apricot, blackberry, cherry, cranberry, currant, gooseberry, grape, peach, pear, plum, quince, raspberry, and strawberry. The various diseases are treated in the order of their usual economic importance. A chapter is devoted to the importance of the preparation of some of the more common copper and sulphur fungicides. The information given is designed for fruit growers and embraces the results of recent investigations.

Bitter pit, D. McALPINE (*Fruit World Austral., 17 (1916), No. 1, pp. 2, 3, 5, 7, figs. 2*).—The author discusses bitter pit control as regards fruit on the tree, in storage, and in transit, also the influence of resistant stocks.

The trouble is worse on main branches and spurs thereof than on laterals and their spurs, on pruned than on unpruned laterals, on trees bearing a few large fruits than on those bearing many small ones, on trees with large than on those with small bearing surface, on rank than on less profuse growths, and on trees having very abundant or irregular water supply and faulty transpiration. Drainage, cultivation, manuring, and in general maintenance of good conditions are considered important means of prevention and regulation. It has been found that in apples kept at 30 to 32° F. in storage or transit the development of bitter pit and ripening are practically arrested. Breeding of resistant varieties is regarded as a possibility.

The Illinois canker, or the blister canker of the apple tree, D. E. LEWIS (*Trans. Kans. State Hort. Soc., 33 (1914–15), pp. 175–178*).—Observations are summarized on blister canker (*Nummularia discreta*), said to have been present in Kansas for more than 15 years and very destructive during some years during some of the latter part of that period (owing to the weakening effect of drought). The author outlines the development and the effects of the attack, and the control measures favored, which consist in selection of resistant varieties (some of which are named), and in aeration and general sanitation.

Notes on an apparent relation between aphids and fire blight (Bacillus amylovorus), J. H. MERRILL (*Trans. Kans. State Hort. Soc., 33 (1914–15), p. 71*).—Observations carried on since 1913 in Doniphan County by the department of entomology of the Kansas Experiment Station are said to have shown that where aphids are kept down by spraying with black leaf 40, the percentage of attack by fire blight (*B. amylovorus*) is greatly diminished and in some cases is practically zero. Comparatively few aphids were found in orchards which had received a thorough dormant spraying with lime-sulphur.

Ripe rot of stone fruits, A. B. MANSFIELD (*Jour. Agr. [New Zeal.], 12 (1916), No. 3, pp. 214–216, figs. 2*).—It is stated that in the Auckland districts the loss in stone fruits due to ripe rot (*Monilia fructigena*) has recently been considerable. The term ripe rot is preferred to that of brown rot, the latter being deemed more appropriate to a similar disease of apples and similar fruits.

Grape downy mildew in Algarve, P. P. M. JUDICE (*Bol. Assoc. Cent. Agr. Portuguesa, 18 (1916), Nos. 3, pp. 81–90; 4, pp. 126–137*).—This is an account of observations carried out in the Province of Algarve during a number of years on the intensity of mildew attack in connection with meteorological conditions.

It is stated that the attacks in this region have usually been of comparatively slight intensity, varying from year to year and with the locality in the same year. Some localities never have suffered from mildew attack, so that while three or more treatments are considered as technically advisable, these are not always justifiable from an economic standpoint. It is stated that in case of much rainfall in spring a preventive treatment applied on the first indications of an outbreak, and followed up as found necessary, is sufficient to control the mildew. In those localities where severe attacks appear annually, with rare exceptions, preventive treatment under competent scientific advice is considered necessary.

Vine mildew in Piedmont, Italy, in 1915, F. MARTINOTTI (*Gior. Vin. Ital., 41 (1915), No. 30, pp. 613–615; abs. in Internat. Inst. Agr. [Rome], Mo. Bul. Agr. Intel. and Plant Diseases, 6 (1915), No. 9, p. 1261*).—It is stated that downy mildew, while showing variations with the locality and the portion of the plant attacked, caused considerable losses in the vineyards of Piedmont in 1915. This was owing partly to rainy or damp weather and imperfect treatment of the bunches, partly to lack of timeliness in spraying, and partly to the poor quality of the sprays, as shown by analysis of samples of the materials employed.

Treatment of downy mildew, A. CONVERGNE and L. TROUCHAUD-VERDIER (*Rev. Vit., 45 (1916), No. 1149, pp. 9–11*).—The authors have summarized the principal conclusions arrived at regarding the treatment of downy mildew as instituted in 1915 by the Agricultural Society of Gard.

It is stated that the crop returns were usually to be gauged by the amount of copper in the sprays applied to the vines. Small proprietors obtained relatively good results on account of the timeliness, thoroughness, and frequency of the applications in such cases. Adherence and a sufficiency of copper content proved to be important factors when washing rains were prevalent, 2 per cent of copper being usually sufficient in such a period. Comparable results were given by Bordeaux, Burgundy, and verdigris solutions when properly prepared.

Sprays owe their immediate action to the presence of copper which is immediately soluble, and the efficiency of any spray depends upon its persistence in soluble form on the leaf surface. The question as to how a spray can be prepared that is both immediately effective and durable is not regarded as having been solved. Powders have been used with good effect after spraying, when applied before the surface become dry, but such treatments are regarded as complementary only. The minimum of sprayings required in normal years is about two, one about May 20 and the other about June 10, or just before and just after the flowering period. Circumstances will vary the requirements in this respect as in others.

Treatment of Oïdium, J. CAPUS (*Rev. Vit., 45 (1916), No. 1149, pp. 8, 9*).—Experimentation has shown that grapevines when shielded from direct precipitation are largely protected from downy mildew and black rot, but may be severely attacked by Oïdium. Treatment with powdered sulphur, while only preventive in cases of the first two of these diseases, is also in a measure curative in case of Oidium, and decidedly so when the treatment is employed in clear, warm weather, soon after the outbreak of the disease.

Fog and grape diseases, P. LARUE (*Rev. Vit., 44 (1916), No. 1145, pp. 411, 412*).—Fog is said to increase infection, particularly of grape downy mildew, by favoring the adherence of the infecting bodies to surfaces rendered less resistant or more favorable to their development.

[Treatments for grape troubles], P. CAUSSE (*Rev. Vit., 44 (1916), No. 1145, pp. 409–411*).—Besides giving a brief discussion of the hot-water treatment for insects, the author states that he considers basic Bordeaux mixture preferable for the treatment of grape downy mildew. Good results have been obtained by treating vines showing court-noné with tar applied to wounds on the stock. The growth was at first backward and the vines looked sickly, but later they attained normal color, growth, and yield.

The effect of asphyxiating gases on grapevines at the battle front, P. VIALA (*Compt. Rend. Acad. Agr. France, 2 (1916), No. 20, pp. 558–561; Rev. Vit., 44 (1916), No. 1146, pp. 424, 425*).—An account is given of the effects upon vegetation, particularly upon grapevines, of exposure to the fumes released by the explosion of aeroplane bombs dropped in raids during the latter part of April, 1916.

Severe injury was caused, which, it was found, could be duplicated by subjecting the vines to chlorin fumes or by sprinkling them with Javelle water. In case of outdoor plants on dry areas, discoloration was not so evident as where dew was present, but the growth was temporarily checked after absorbing the injurious gases. Injury to the other plants varied with the stage of their vegetative advancement. Rye and other cereals were affected.

The effects of asphyxiating gas on vines, A. CORDONNIER and RICHEZ-PÉCHON (*Rev. Vit., 44 (1916), No. 1148, pp. 459–461*).—This contains a few particulars, in addition to those reported above by Viala, of observations made on forms of injury to plants by fumes from aeroplane bombs.

Effects of gases from aeroplane bombs, A. CORDONNIER (*Bul. Soc. Path. Veg. France, 3 (1916), No. 1, pp. 32, 33*).—This is a brief account of the occurrences and results above noted.

Citrus blast, a new disease in California, J. E. COIT (*Univ. Cal. Jour. Agr., 3 (1916), No. 6, pp. 234, 235, figs. 2*).—A brief account is given of a new citrus disease which was first observed by the author in the spring of 1914 on an old seedling orange tree near Oroville, Cal. Later in the same summer, the disease was found in a number of commercial orchards in the northern districts of that State.

The disease is characterized by an apparent infection which takes place nearly always at the joint between the petiole or leaf stalk and the leaf blade. The leaf blade soon dies and the disease progresses downward to the twig, involving the bark and killing it in a circular area from $\frac{1}{4}$ to $\frac{1}{2}$ in. in diameter. When the twigs are small, girdling often results and the twig dies back to the point of infection. Large twigs and limbs seem to have a certain degree of resistance, the disease being confined to new growth and limbs not over 1 in. in diameter. Badly infected trees are said to be filled with dead brush from girdled twigs, and the dead twigs and leaves soon become covered with fungi. The disease does its chief damage by killing the fruiting brush and greatly reducing the bearing area of the tree.

As a result of preliminary investigations, citrus blast is believed to be due to bacteria.

Citrus blast, a new disease, R. W. HODGSON (*Pacific Rural Press, 92 (1916), No. 6, p. 124*).—An account is given of investigations carried on in 1915 on the newly recognized bacterial disease of citrus occurring in northern California, which, according to the author, was first observed in 1912.

Infection is apparently confined to the new spring growth and occurs chiefly at the junction of the petiole and blade of the leaf. It also occurs at the tips of the very young leaves and tender shoots. When once established, the disease is said to progress rapidly down the shoot toward the older wood, but only the new tender growth is affected. Young shoots are often killed back to the older wood, including a portion of the bark about the base of the infected shoots, and it is not uncommon to find branches several feet long with every node infected. Upon infection the leaves are said to turn pale yellow, then to darken in spots and wilt, and later to shrivel and dry, though still hanging to the shoot.

The disease appears to spread with remarkable rapidity, only a few days of favorable weather conditions being required for serious damage. As the dry season approaches it is retarded, and in midsummer it seems to be entirely quiescent. The organism, which is a bacterium, does not appear to be able to penetrate into the wood, and in some cases the cambium is not killed. Where trees contain a large amount of weak growth in the interior this is badly attacked and the bark rots away, leaving the interior of the tree full of dead, white twigs which are very resistant to further decay.

Some experiments are said to have been begun for the control of this disease, employing the methods used in pear blight control in California.

A new bacterial citrus disease, H. A. LEE (*U. S. Dept. Agr., Jour. Agr. Research, 9 (1917), No. 1, pp. 1–8, pls. 3*).—In a contribution from the California Experiment Station the author describes a new disease of citrus trees which is endemic to the citrus regions of northern and central California, previous accounts of this disease having been noted above.

In the author's investigations, sections of fresh, diseased material showed a bacterial organism present en masse. The organism has been isolated and the disease produced by inoculation experiments. A technical description of the organism, *Bacterium citrarefaciens* n. sp., is given and its morphological and physiological characters are detailed at some length.

The cause of June drop of navel oranges, J. E. COIT and R. W. HODGSON (*Univ. Cal. Jour. Agr., 4 (1916), No. 1, pp. 8–10, 27–29, figs. 5*).—The authors give a brief preliminary report of studies on the shedding of young fruits by orange trees in spring, which was excessive in 1916 despite good conditions as regards both weather and soil.

The dropped fruits in practically every test developed Alternaria, the cause of black rot. This fungus, the spores of which are deposited on the stigma in some way not yet determined, grows down to the base of the orange, infecting the portions of the old mutilated style which are left between the main fruit and the diminutive secondary fruit which pushes up through it to form the so-called navel. Valencia oranges, in which the old style breaks away clean, do not suffer from black rot or from excessive June drop.

The resistance of the fruit restrains for some time the development of the fungus and the fruit may reach its maturity and ripen without developing outwardly the black rot, though infected with Alternaria. Experiment shows that when transpiration is rapid, as in dry weather or districts, water is drawn back from the fruits by the leaves. The enzyms produced by the fungus probably poison and weaken the leaf and other cell tissues of the plant, in particular causing the formation of a cork layer and lending to the fall of the fruit. It is suggested that the navel-end splits occurring in fruits in the interior valleys may also be due to Alternaria.

Experiments looking to the control of June drop are under way and the distribution of the fungus also seems to require further investigation.

Spraying for ripe rot of the plantain fruit, J. F. DASTUR (*Agr. Jour. India, 11 (1916), No. 2, pp. 142–149, figs. 2*).—It is stated that ripe rot (*Glœosporium musarum*) of the plantain, while affecting chiefly stored fruits, may also appear on young fruits, generally near the distal end, supposedly arising in most cases from early infection at the style. Although spores germinated in water do not survive desiccation, some of those remaining in the ascervuli may germinate after nine months.

Experiments for three years on a restricted scale appear to show that spraying only when the fruit is picked, or even after it is half grown, is useless, but Burgundy mixture used monthly is found to control the disease. However, as this tends to leave bluish specks on freshly sprayed fruits, the last spraying is more satisfactorily done with ammoniacal copper carbonate.

This keeps the fruit clean and free from bluish spots, although if used several times it spots the fruits at points where they are in contact. Cutting back must be careful and destruction of diseased parts must be thorough in order to avoid the saprophytic preservation of the fungus. The fruit must be carefully handled in order to avoid injury.

[Notes on some pineapple diseases], M. O. JOHNSON (*Hawaii Sta. Rpt. 1916, pp. 23, 24*).—A brief account is given of an investigation of a serious disease of pineapples known as the Kauai wilt. This is rather definitely associated with a certain type of soil, and it is thought, from a lack of lime in the ash of diseased plants, that the trouble may be in some way connected with soil acidity. Pot and field experiments have been begun to determine the effect of liming on this wilt.

A brief account is also given of the yellowing of pineapples on manganese soil, a more detailed report of which has been noted (E. S. R., 36, p. 850).

Rusts of cultivated trees and their treatment with lime-sulphur, L. SAVASTANO (*R. Staz. Sper. Agrum. e Frutticol. Acireale, Bol. 25 (1916), pp. 10*).— This bulletin gives a résumé of some results of observation and experimentation during 1912 to 1916, in connection with rusts of cultivated trees, including their characters, causal organisms, favoring conditions, spread, and treatments.

Carnation leaf spot in Italy, M. TURCONI (*Riv. Patol. Veg., 8 (1916), No. 1, pp. 1–4*).—A carnation disease was observed in Italy in 1915, due to a fungus, which, from the morphological characters of its mycelium and fructifications, appeared to be *Alternaria dianthi*.

Sweet pea diseases and their control, J. J. TAUBENHAUS (*Trans. Mass. Hort. Soc., 1916, pt. 1, pp. 131–143*).—The author discusses the results of investigations dealing with root rot (*Corticum vagum*) of the sweet pea, Fusarium wilt (*F. lathyri*), stem or collar rot (*Sclerotinia libertiana*), Thielavia root rot (*T. basicola*), root knot or nematode disease (*Heterodera radicicola*), mosaic (unknown as to causation), powdery mildew (*Microsphera alni*), anthracnose (*Glomerella rufomaculans*), streak (*Bacillus lathyri*), physiological troubles ascribed mainly to soil conditions, certain insects which wound or weaken the plants or carry spores, bringing about infection, and control methods.

Oak mildew, T. A. C. SCHOEVERS (*Tijdschr. Plantenziekten, 22 (1916), No. 2–4, pp. 84–93*).—This is chiefly a discussion of contributions, more particularly that of Neger (E. S. R., 33, p. 745), on the classification and host relationships of the fungus causing oak mildew. This organism is considered distinct from that causing gooseberry mildew.

White pine blister rust, J. S. DUFF (*Rpt. Min. Agr. Ontario, 1915, p. 22*).— It is stated that early in 1915 an outbreak of white pine blister rust was reported to the department and, as a result, the importation of five-leaved pines into Canada from Europe and the sale of such pines was for the present prohibited. A survey gave evidences of the disease in the counties of Brant, Durham, Halton, Kent, Lincoln, Wellington, and Wentworth.

ECONOMIC ZOOLOGY—ENTOMOLOGY.

Animal micrology, M. F. GUYER (*Chicago: Univ. of Chicago Press, 1917, rev. ed., pp. XI+289, figs. 74*).—This consists of practical exercises in zoological microtechnique.

Notes on some animal parasites in British Guiana, G. E. BODKIN and L. D. CLEARE, JR. (*Bul. Ent. Research, 7 (1916), No. 2, pp. 179–190, pl. 1 figs. 3*).— Notes are given on the more important animal parasites occurring in British Guiana.

More minor horrors, A. E. SHIPLEY (*London: Smith, Elder & Co., 1916, pp. XIV+163, figs. 50*).—This sequel to the volume previously noted (E. S. R., 34, p. 251) deals with cockroaches, the bot or warble fly, the malaria and yellow fever mosquitoes, the biscuit weevil (*Anobium paniceum*), the fig moth (*Ephestia cautella*), the stable fly, rats, and the field mouse (*Apodemus sylvaticus*).

The domesticated silver fox, N. DEARBORN (*U. S. Dept. Agr., Farmers' Bul. 795 (1917), pp. 32, figs. 22*).—This bulletin is based upon Department Bulletin 301, previously noted (E. S. R., 34, p. 180), and supersedes Farmers' Bulletin 328 (E. S. R., 20, p. 350).

Habits and food of the roadrunner in California, H. C. BRYANT (*Univ. Cal. Pubs., Zool., 17 (1916), No. 5, pp. 21–58, pls. 4, figs. 2*).—In a study of the roadrunner (*Geococcyx californianus*) the author has examined the contents of 84 stomachs of birds collected in southern California in 1911 and 1912 during every month of the year except March, and here reports at length upon the results.

The examinations showed that practically 90 per cent of the total food was made up of animal matter and that slightly less than 10 per cent was of vegetable material, nearly all of the latter consisting of the fruit and seeds of the sour-berry (*Rhus integrifolia*). Of the insects and certain vertebrates which composed the animal food 18.2 per cent were beetles, 36.82 per cent grasshoppers and crickets, 7 per cent cutworms and caterpillars, 5 per cent cicadas and other hemipterous insects, 4.24 per cent ants, bees, and wasps, and 3.67 per cent scorpions, 3.73 per cent lizards, 1.56 per cent birds, 1 per cent a tiny cotton-tail rabbit, and 2.38 per cent two different species of wild mice.

The results seem to substantiate rather than alter published statements regarding the food of the roadrunner, little evidence having been obtained that it is detrimental to man's interests. The roadrunner never turns its attention to any sort of cultivated crops, but rather feeds upon insect and rodent pests which attack such crops, and destroys the hairy caterpillars, not commonly attacked by other birds.

The paper includes a review of the literature in connection with a list of 40 titles.

Insect behavior as a factor in applied entomology, C. G. HEWITT (*Jour. Econ. Ent., 10 (1917), No. 1, pp. 81–94*).—The annual address of the president of the American Association of Economic Entomologists.

Theories of hibernation, A. T. RASMUSSEN (*Amer. Nat., 50 (1916), No. 598, pp. 609–625*).—A general summary with references to the literature, of which a list of 83 titles is included.

Simple apparatus for insect photography, B. H. WALDEN (*Jour. Econ. Ent., 10 (1917), No. 1, pp. 25–30, pl. 1*).—The author gives a brief description of simple photographic apparatus and methods for field and laboratory work used in the entomological department of the Connecticut State Experiment Station.

Eighth annual report of the Quebec Society for the Protection of Plants from Insects and Fungus Diseases, 1915–16 (*Ann. Rpt. Quebec Soc. Protec. Plants [etc.], 8 (1915–16), pp. 116, figs. 30*).—Among the more important entomological papers presented in this, the usual annual report (E. S. R., 34, p. 250), are the following: Some Aspects of Insect Behavior, by W. Lochhead (pp. 12–23); Apple Plant Lice and Their Control, by R. Matheson (pp. 24–41); The Chrysopa or Golden-eyed Fly, by J. C. Chapais (pp. 50, 51); Grasshoppers and Their Control, by A. Gibson (pp. 52–57); Insect Notes, 1915, by E. M. DuPorte (pp. 73–77); Three Injurious Acridians of Nova Scotia, by C. B. Gooderham (pp. 89–91); and Insect Pests of Cereal Crops of Quebec, by W. Lochhead (pp. 101–115).

The principal insect pests and plant diseases, V. A. HUARD (*Min. Agr. Prov. Quebec Bul. 23 (1916), pp. 75, figs. 78).*—This paper, which is in the French language, consists in large part of accounts of the more important insect pests of the Province.

Garden and truck crop insect pests, C. E. SANBORN (*Okla. Agr. Col., Ext. Div. Circ. 41 (1916), pp. 76, figs. 78).*—This is a popular account of the more important insect enemies of truck and garden crops in Oklahoma.

Potato insects, M. A. YOTHERS (*Washington Sta. Popular Bul. 106 (1917), pp. 96–123, figs. 17).*—This is a brief descriptive account of the more important insect enemies of the potato in Washington, with directions for their control. Those mentioned as affecting the foliage are the apple leaf-hopper, blister beetles (*Epicauta maculata* and *E. oregona*), the Colorado potato beetle, cutworms, grasshoppers, the potato aphis (*Macrosiphum solanifolii*), and the tobacco worm. The insects, etc., which affect the tubers include the sand cricket (*Stenopelmatus* sp.), wireworms, and eelworms (*Heterodera* spp.). Those which affect both foliage and tubers are the potato flea beetle (*Epitrix subscrinita*), the potato tuber worm, and the twelve-spotted cucumber beetles (*Diabrotica soror, D. 12-punctata,* and *D. 12-punctata tenella*).

South American crickets, Gryllotalpoidea, and Achetoidea, L. BRUNER (*Ann. Carnegie Mus., 10 (1916), No. 3–4, pp. 344–428).*—This paper contains descriptions of a number of apparently new forms.

Notes on the black apple leaf hopper (Idiocerus fitchi), W. H. BRITTAIN and L. G. SAUNDERS (*Canad. Ent., 49 (1917), No. 5, pp. 149–153, pl. 1).*—This leaf hopper, originally described from New York State, apparently occurs quite generally throughout the northeastern United States and Canada and is said to be very common throughout the Annapolis Valley of Nova Scotia. While considered by many farmers a pest of some importance, observations indicate that the injuries attributed to it have largely been brought about by other causes.

Technical descriptions of its several stages and brief notes on its life history are given.

Additions to the list of Missouri Cicadellidæ, E. H. GIBSON (*Canad. Ent., 49 (1917), No. 2, pp. 75, 76).*—Supplementary to the paper previously noted (E. S. R., 35, p. 463).

Three new species of Jassoidea from Missouri, E. H. GIBSON (*Canad. Ent., 49 (1917), No. 5, pp. 183, 184).*—The three new species here described supplement the lists of Jassoidea occurring in Missouri noted above.

The bay flea louse, Trioza alacris, as a new pest in New Jersey, H. B. WEISS (*Canad. Ent., 49 (1917), No. 2, pp. 73–75).*—This psyllid has been present in several greenhouses in New Jersey for the past several years, but not until recently has it increased sufficiently to disfigure seriously its host plant, *Laurus nobilis.*

Further data on the relation between aphids and fire blight (Bacillus amylovorus), J. H. MERRILL (*Jour. Econ. Ent., 10 (1917), No. 1, pp. 45–47, pl. 1).*—In further observations (E. S. R., 34, p. 452), the author finds blight to develop only in the tender succulent growth on the twigs. By hatching from eggs laid in blight cankers the aphids come in contact with the fire blight organisms, and can and do inoculate trees with the bacteria of fire blight. It appears that the amount of fire blight infection in an orchard may be materially decreased by destroying all of the aphids which may appear there.

Synopsis of the genus Saltusaphis, A. C. BAKER (*Canad. Ent., 49 (1917), No. 1, pp. 1–9, pls. 2, figs. 17).*—Five members of this genus which live on sedges and in marshy localities are recognized as occurring in America, three of which are here described as new.

The California species of **Myzus**, with the description of a new species, G. O. SHINJI (*Canad. Ent., 49 (1917), No. 2, pp. 49-51, fig. 1*).—Seven species of this important genus are recognized from California, of which one (*Myzus godetiæ*) is described as new to science.

Mealy bug control, R. S. WOGLUM (*Cal. Citrogr., 2 (1917), No. 4, pp. 4, 5, figs. 3*).—This is a report of an address delivered before the Lemon Men's Club, at Alhambra, Cal., on January 3, 1917. The effect of fumigation on the citrus mealy bug, sprays effective against it, and important natural enemies, the interrelation of ants to mealy-bug infestation, etc., are discussed.

A list of the Coccidæ of Porto Rico, T. H. JONES (*Jour. Bd. Comrs. Agr. P. R., 1 (1917), No. 1, pp. 1-16*).—This is an annotated list of 50 species of the Coccidæ recorded from Porto Rico. A bibliography of 25 titles is included.

A new scale insect affecting sugar cane in New Guinea, A. RUTHERFORD (*Proc. Linn. Soc. N. S. Wales, 41 (1916), pt. 2, pp. 215, 216*).—Under the name *Aulacaspis major* the author describes a new coccid occurring on the stems of sugar cane in New Guinea.

The development of the silk glands in the chief races of silkworms and in their first crosses, from the point of view of the quality and length of the reelable silk from each cocoon, P. BUCCI (*Staz. Sper. Agr. Ital., 48 (1915), No. 12, pp. 841-888; abs. in Internat. Inst. Agr. [Rome], Internat. Rev. Sci. and Pract. Agr., 7 (1916), No. 2, pp. 261-265*).—Experiments repeated during 1914 and 1915 led to the conclusion that the weight of the adult worm in the nine races studied varies from 6,000 to 8,000 times that of the silkworm at the time of emergence from the egg. The lengths of the thread and the reelable silk of some of the races and hybrids are given. In each of the races studied the ratio between the average length of the reservoir and the average total length of a cocoon is always greater than 1 : 2.5. There is a correlation between the average weight of an adult silkworm, the average length of the silk gland, the absolute weight of the reelable silk of a single gland, and the average length of the reelable silk.

Genetic studies on the silkworm, Y. TANAKA (*Jour. Col. Agr. Tohoku Imp. Univ., 7 (1916), No. 3, pp. 129-255, pls. 6, figs. 8*).—A report of experiments carried on from 1910 to 1915 which relate particularly to the larval characters. A bibliography of 108 titles is included.

The Lepidoptera of the Isle of Pines, being a list of the species collected on the island by J. L. Graf and G. A. Link, sr., in 1910 and 1912-13, W. J. HOLLAND (*Ann. Carnegie Mus., 10 (1916), No. 3-4, pp. 487-518, pl. 1*).—An annotated list of 109 species.

Hyponomeuta species and their control in Sweden, A. TULLGREN (*Meddel. Centralanst. Försöksv. Jordbruksområdet, No. 110 (1915), pp. 23, figs. 16; abs. in Internat. Inst. Agr. [Rome], Internat. Rev. Sci. and Pract. Agr., 7 (1916), No. 2, pp. 316, 317*).—*Hyponomeuta cronymellus* is said to be most widely distributed in Sweden, where it has appeared in recent years on *Prunus padus* in such numbers as to cause serious injury. *H. malinellus, H. padellus,* and *H. cognatellus* are less common and never very injurious.

An outbreak of the eight-spotted forester, **Alypia** octomaculata, in New Haven, Connecticut, Q. S. LOWRY (*Jour. Econ. Ent., 10 (1917), No. 1, pp. 47, 48*).—The author records an outbreak of this pest on grape at New Haven, Conn., in 1916.

Notes on the peach-tree borer (Sanninoidea exitiosa), G. G. BECKER (*Jour. Econ. Ent., 10 (1917), No. 1, pp. 49-59, fig. 1*).—These notes relate largely to the pupation, emergence, and habits of the moth in Arkansas.

The peach tree borer: Life history, habits, injuries, and control measures, J. L. KING (*Mo. Bul. Ohio Sta.*, *2* (*1917*), *No. 1, pp. 23–28, figs. 2*).—This brief summarized account of the peach borer includes a diagram which graphically illustrates its life cycle in Ohio, month by month.

The lesser peach tree borer (Synanthedon pictipes), J. L. KING (*Ohio Sta. Bul. 307* (*1917*), *pp. 399–448, figs. 21*).—The lesser peach tree borer is a native insect, first recorded from Pennsylvania in 1868, which is quite generally distributed throughout the eastern half of the United States. The native food plants consist of wild cherry, wild plum, knots of black-knot, and the Juneberry; its cultivated food plants include the peach, plum, and cherry. It prefers the peach and may be easily confused with the common peach tree borer, though in the field it may be recognized through its habit of working, as a rule, above the soil level on the trunks and branches of the tree.

"Complete life history studies show that the winter is passed in all stages of larval development except the first. The moths emerge in May, June, and July. The egg-laying period corresponds closely to the time the adults are on the wing. In Ohio, the early hatched larvæ from the spring brood may complete their growth and give rise to a partial second generation, or summer brood. The adults of the second generation are on the wing from July to September. The larvæ from this brood of moths pass the winter as very small larvæ."

Serious injury by this species seems to be locally distributed. In Ohio the older peach-growing district of the Ottawa County peninsula and Catawba Island is very generally infested. Control measures consist in avoiding all mechanical injuries as scraping or barking during cultivation, improper pruning, or careless thinning or harvesting of the fruit. Timely and systematic digging out of the larvæ in the late fall and again in late May or early June is recommended. Sprays and repellent washes have proved of little or no value as a control.

A bibliography of 53 titles is included.

The head capsule and mouth parts of Diptera, A. PETERSON (*Ill. Biol. Monogr.*, *3* (*1916*), *No. 2, pp. 112, pls. 25*).—This report of anatomical studies is profusely illustrated by pen drawings.

The response of the house fly to certain foods and their fermentation products, C. H. RICHARDSON (*Jour. Econ. Ent.*, *10* (*1917*), *No. 1, pp. 102–109*).—The experiments here reported, which relate to solutions of known chemical compounds found in certain foods or their fermentation products which are eagerly sought by house flies, form a part of a larger project on the response of the house fly to environmental factors undertaken by the New Jersey Experiment Stations, accounts of which have been previously noted (E. S. R., 36, pp. 156, 460). The following conclusions are drawn from these experiments:

"Glucose, fructose, maltose, lactose, sucrose, starch, and dextrin were not very attractive to house flies. Lactose and dextrin caught the largest number of flies, starch the least. Sucrose was consistently a poor bait. Four per cent amylic alcohol gave better results than ethyl alcohol, or acetic acid in 4 or 10 per cent concentrations, and better than 10 per cent amylic alcohol. Four per cent ethyl alcohol was better than 10 per cent, 10 per cent acetic acid gave better results than 4 per cent. Succinic and lactic acids showed some attractive qualities in two experiments. Maltose, lactose, sucrose, and dextrin in 4 per cent solutions of amylic alcohol, ethyl alcohol, and acetic acid were more frequently visited by house flies than the corresponding aqueous solutions. Maltose and dextrin solutions were more effective than lactose or sucrose.

The order of response to the alcohols and acetic acid containing carbohydrate was the same as that for the aqueous solutions of these compounds.

"Crude gluten from wheat flour was not attractive. The water-soluble portion with or without starch in suspension was decidedly attractive. Several experiments with milk indicate that fat-free caseinogen is attractive, while butter fat is not. Experiments indicate that aqueous solutions of wheat flour and molasses to which sodium arsenite and amylic alcohol are added have considerable value as poisoned baits for house flies."

Biological note on Rhacodineura antiqua (not Ceromasia rufipes), a tachinid parasite of earwigs, J. PANTEL (*Bul. Soc. Ent. France, No. 8 (1916), pp. 150–154; abs. in Rev. Appl. Ent., Ser. A, 4 (1916), No. 8, p. 324*).—It is pointed out that in the previous papers on the habits of *R. antiqua* the author has incorrectly recorded it under the name *C. rufipes*. The species was first described by Rodzianko from south Russia, where it was observed to live singly in young forms of *Forficula tomis*. The adults have been obtained in Portugal and Holland. In the present paper the author considers its life history and habits.

Sarcophaga and allies in North America, J. M. ALDRICH (*Lafayette, Ind.: The Thomas Say Foundation, Ent. Soc. Amer., 1916, pp. 311, pls. 16; rev. in Science, n. scr., 45 (1917), No. 1158, pp. 240, 241*).—In this work the author describes 145 species and varieties belonging to 16 genera, of which 9 genera, 95 species, and 6 varieties are described as new. The genitalia of 138 are figured.

Sheep maggot flies, II, W. W. and J. L. FROGGATT (*Dept. Agr. N. S. Wales, Farmers' Bul. 110 (1916), pp. 30, figs. 8*).—This second paper (E. S. R., 34, p. 64) consists of a report of work carried out in the New England District during 1914–15 at the Government Sheep Fly Experiment Station.

On the fruit flies of the genus Dacus occurring in India, Burma, and Ceylon, M. BEZZI (*Bul. Ent. Research, 7 (1916), No. 2, pp. 99–121*).—Twenty-six species of Dacinæ representing nine genera are noted of which one genus, eight species, and one variety are described as new. See also a previous note (E. S. R., 35, p. 259.)

Wheat sheath miner, H. L. SEAMANS (*U. S. Dept. Agr., Jour. Agr. Research, 9 (1917), No. 1, pp. 17–25, fig. 1*).—This is a report of investigations carried on at the Montana Experiment Station.

During the investigations in 1915 of wheat plants supposed to be infested with the greater wheat stem maggot (*Meromyza americana*), a whitish larva was found associated with the greenish larva of *M. americana*. This proved to be *Cerodonta femoralis*, concerning which very little has previously been known, and further investigations have shown that it was largely responsible for the damage to the wheat plants. Records of its occurrence indicate that the species is generally distributed in the Northwest and infests winter wheat, spring wheat, oats, and timothy. Technical descriptions are given of its several life stages.

The injury caused by the wheat sheath miner appears to be identical with that of the stem maggot until the leaves are examined. It is stated that in each case the larva enters the leaf sheath by mining down from the point in the leaf where the egg was deposited. If the injury is due to *C. femoralis* the mine in the leaf is narrow, clean cut, and almost straight, while if it is done by *M. americana* it is broad and irregular with indistinct edges. While *M. americana* enters the stem and eats out the central stalk, usually cutting it off above the first node, *C. femoralis* confines its attack to mining up and down the leaf sheath and sometimes girdling the stem without completely cutting it off.

Whether it girdles the stem or not, the injuries caused by mining in the sheath appear to be sufficient to kill the stalk. Some farmers estimated that their yields in winter wheat were cut down at least 25 per cent in the season of 1915, while in 1916 a field of spring wheat was visited which by actual count showed 95 per cent of the plants to have been injured by this insect. Some of the plants had only one culm injured while others had lost two or three. An adjoining field of oats is said to have had 12 per cent of its plants infested.

There is also said to be a slight amount of injury done to the plants, just before blossoming, by the second brood of larvæ. This injury is only to the leaves and probably has little or no effect on the yield as the central stalk does not appear to be injured.

In observations made at Bozeman the incubation period of the egg was found to be about six days under insectary conditions. Upon hatching out, the larva immediately starts mining down the leaf toward the stalk, eventually ending in the leaf sheath at the crown of the plant or at the first node. On reaching the base of the leaf sheath it feeds up and down the sheath and sometimes around the stalk. The length of the larval period is said to vary with climatic conditions, some of the larvæ pupating at the end of 10 days while others take as long as 20 days. The pupal period lasted about 25 days under insectary conditions. The adult flies appear about May 20 and lay eggs in wheat seedlings until about June 10. The flies of the second brood emerged in the insectary about July 16 and lived until August 5. The third generation of flies began to emerge September 7. The next generation is believed to hibernate as pupæ and produce the first brood of flies the following spring.

Two hymenopterous parasites were reared from puparia of *C. femoralis*, namely, a new braconid of the genus Dacnusa and the chalcidid *Cyrtogaster occidentalis*, but these do not occur in sufficient numbers to be effective agents in control. While control measures have not been tested, it is thought that a large percentage of the pests can be destroyed by scattering the straw over the field and burning the stubble as well as the grass borders surrounding the field. Where this is not practicable, the stubble can be plowed under about 6 in. and harrowed just after removing the crop or before planting the spring crop. It is also thought that the late seeding of winter wheat, after a thorough destruction of volunteer wheat and grass, will help much in control.

The control of the round-headed apple tree borer, G. G. BECKER (*Jour. Econ. Ent., 10 (1917), No. 1, pp. 66–71*).—The author's investigations in Arkansas have led to the conclusion that the protection afforded by white lead is not commensurate with the returns. Pruning compound is worthless as a borer protector, paper wrappers and wooden veneers, from first observations, appear to be impracticable, the cost of screening is too great, and the efficiency of asphaltum against the borer is not worth the risk of injury to the trees. Worming the trees during the months of August and in early September is deemed the most practical as well as the cheapest method for controlling the borer.

[Banana weevil borer in Jamaica] (*Jour. Jamaica Agr. Soc., 20 (1916), Nos. 4, pp. 129–132, 145, 146; 5, pp. 168, 169; 12, pp. 478–481*).—These papers relate to the banana weevil (*Cosmopolites sordida*) in Jamaica, an account of which by Ballou has been previously noted (E. S. R., 36, p. 158).

A new weevil attacking pineapples in Jamaica, G. A. K. MARSHALL (*Bul. Ent. Research, 7 (1916), No. 2, pp. 197, 198, fig. 1*).—Under the name *Metamasius ritchiei* the author describes a large black weevil which was found doing serious damage to pineapples in Jamaica. It is stated that this weevil made its appearance in the Above Rocks District, Jamaica, about four years ago and grew steadily worse until 1916, when it is estimated 75 per cent of the pines were lost.

The plants seem to be attacked at various points. Sometimes the root stock is bored, or again the fruit stalk is hollowed out and collapses. A favorite place of attack is the junction of the fruit and stalk, when the larva proceeds into the fruit and riddles it, or the heart may be attacked before the pineapple has shot above the leaves.

Another weevil occurring in pineapples, namely, *M. sericeus*, appears to be secondary, it being attracted from the surrounding bananas by the decaying pines killed by *M. ritchiei*.

Pineapples: New weevil injury in Above Rocks District (*Jour. Jamaica Agr. Soc., 20 (1916), No. 8, pp. 316–318*).—This paper gives an account of the injury to pineapples caused by *Metamasius ritchiei* above noted.

The pineapple black weevil, W. NEWELL (*Quart. Bul. Plant Bd. Fla., 1 (1917), No. 2, pp. 47–50, fig. 1*).—A brief account of the pest (*Metamasius ritchiei*) above noted in which the author calls attention to the danger of introducing it into Florida.

Diseases of the honeybee, L. BAHR (*Meddel. K. Vet.· og Landbohöjskoles Serumlab., No. 37 (1915), pp. 109, pls. 2, figs. 6*).—Following an account of the bacteria which normally occur in the hive, the author gives summarized accounts of the various diseases, etc., of the honeybee.

The habit of leaf oviposition among the parasitic Hymenoptera, H. S. SMITH (*Science, n. ser., 44 (1916), No. 1148, pp. 925, 926*).—The observations here reported relate to *Perilampus hyalinus*, a hyperparasite of the fall webworm, and are in continuation of those previously noted (E. S. R., 27, p. 261).

In connection with observations of this species, which was occasionally reared at Sacramento, Cal., from Chrysopa cocoons, the author secured several adult female Perilampus hovering about oleanders infested with *Aphis nerii* and fed upon by Chrysopa. The author has found that the eggs are deposited on the leaf, thus establishing beyond doubt the habit of leaf oviposition among parasitic Hymenoptera. The eggs are numerous, one female having deposited 52 in a single day. They hatch in from seven to ten days, and the first-stage larva, which is of the planidium type, is active at first, crawling rapidly about, but later attaches itself to the leaf by the caudal end, then standing out at right angles to the surface, where it awaits the approach of the Chrysopa larva, to which it attaches.

A new genus of omphaline Eulophidæ from North America, A. A. GIRAULT (*Entomologist, 49 (1916), No. 642, pp. 249, 250*).—*Miromphalomyia perilampoides* n. g. and n. sp. is described from Arizona.

The North American species of Habrocytus (chalcid flies), A. A. GIRAULT (*Canad. Ent., 49 1917, No. 5, pp. 178–182*).—A table based upon the females is given of ten species of Habrocytus recognized as occurring in the United States, and six species and one variety are described as new.

Notes on coccid-infesting Chalcidoidea, I, J. WATERSTON (*Bul. Ent. Research, 7 (1916), No. 2, pp. 137–144, figs. 3*).—*Diversinervus silvestrii* reared from *Lecanium viride* on coffee in Mauritius and *Coccophagus acanthosceles* from the body of *Lecanium* sp., Singapore, Straits Settlements, are described as new.

Search for melon fly parasites, D. T. FULLAWAY (*Hawaii. Forester and Agr., 13 (1916), No. 8, pp. 303–306*).—The author reports upon a trip made to Singapore, Java, and India in search of parasites of the melon fly. The parasite discovered, *Opius fletcheri*, was found to occur in all three localities, particularly in India, from whence it has been introduced by the author into the Hawaiian Islands.

During the course of several months spent in the Philippine Islands rearing the parasites, the author's attention was called to the heavy parasitism of the corn leafhopper. An attempt made to introduce these parasites into Hawaii failed.

A new species of Amphrophora from California, G. O. SHINJI (*Canad. Ent.*, *49 (1917), No. 2, pp. 51, 52, fig. 1*).—*Amphrophora cicutæ* reared from wild and cultivated blackberry is described as new to science.

A contribution to the knowledge of the mites attacking wild and cultivated plants in Sweden, I. TRÄGÅRDH (*Meddel. Centralanst. Försöksv. Jordbruksområdet, No. 109 (1915), pp. 60, figs. 20; abs. in Internat. Inst. Agr. [Rome], Internat. Rev. Sci. and Pract. Agr., 7 (1916), No. 3, pp. 463, 464*).— This account relates to various species of Neotetranychus, Paratetranychus, and Tetranychus which are a source of injury in Sweden.

Ascaris canis and Ascaris felis.—A taxonomic and a cytological comparison, A. C. WALTON (*Biol. Bul. Mar. Biol. Lab. Woods Hole, 31 (1916), No. 5, pp. 364–372, pl. 1, figs. 6*).—The most important points brought out in the study are summarized as follows:

"Material used is same as recognized European forms of *A. canis* and *A. felis.* *A. canis* shows 18 chromosomes for the haploid number, 12 di-tetrad autosomes, and 6 tetrad idiosomes. These 6 tetrad idiosomes form a heterosome group of the X-type. There are two types of second spermatocytes and spermatids found, one type having 12 autosomes and 6 idiosomes, the other type having but the 12 autosomes. In *A. felis* there are 9 chromosomes in the primary spermatocytes, 8 autosomes, and one large heterochromosome composed of unequal parts. This is in agreement with Edwards. *A. canis* and *A. felis* are morphologically and cytologically two different species, not varieties of the same species. Chromosomes of true *A. canis* do not agree in form or number with those described by Marcus for his so-called *A. canis.*"

On the life cycle of some cestodes, C. JOYEUX (*Bul. Soc. Path. Exot., 9 (1916), No. 8, pp. 578–583*).—An account of the life cycles of three cestodes, namely, *Dipylidium caninum, Hymenolepis diminuta,* and *H. nana siebold,* for which insects play the rôle of intermediate hosts.

FOODS—HUMAN NUTRITION.

The dietary deficiencies of the white bean, Phaseolus vulgaris, E. V. McCOLLUM, M. SIMMONDS, and W. PITZ (*Jour. Biol. Chem., 29 (1917), No. 3, pp. 521–536, pl. 1, figs. 9*).—This paper presents the results of experiments in which laboratory animals (rats) were fed the white bean as the principal constituent of the diet and also the bean supplemented in various ways with purified food factors. The following facts were brought out in these experiments:

There was a high mortality and pronounced stunting of growth in animals fed a ration which contained 19.8 per cent of proteins, all derived from the bean. The addition of 3 per cent of casein improved noticeably the condition of the animals, but this is attributed by the authors to the casein itself rather than to any marked increase in the value of the beans through the supplying of a particular amino acid present in very small amount in bean proteins and plentiful in casein.

A high content of beans in the diet apparently had an injurious effect on the rats. Animals fed a ration containing 45 per cent of beans were better nourished than others receiving a ration which contained 70 per cent of beans, each ration containing 9 per cent of casein. Animals receiving a ration containing 50 per cent of beans with 4 per cent of casein were better nourished than another lot, the ration of which contained 86.3 per cent of beans and 3 per cent of casein. Two possible explanations of this are offered. One is that the beans contain some unknown chemical complex which is harmful when ingested in large amounts, but the more plausible is that the rats are mechanically injured by the distention of the digestive tract, due to the fermentation of the hemicelluloses contained in the beans.

The white bean appeared to be even poorer in its content in the dietary factor "fat-soluble A" than are the cereal grains. It was found that the inorganic content of the bean is not of the character which supports growth. The bean was found to contain an abundance of the unidentified diet factor "fat-soluble B," and 25 per cent of beans in the diet, as the sole source of this factor, supported completion of growth and repetition of reproduction.

The authors state that their experiments furnish conclusive evidence that the entire protein mixture of the bean is of low value, although further inquiry must be made to show which amino acid is the limiting factor, and that the bean proteins are decidedly inferior to those of meat, milk, eggs, and the cereal grains (wheat, maize, oat, and rice kernels) which they have studied. It is pointed out that the frequent recommendation for the substitution of legumes as a class for the apparently more expensive sources of protein, such as meat, milk, and eggs, may be misleading and that, owing to the extensive fermentation of the carbohydrates of beans, this legume should not form a principal part in a relatively monotonous diet such as is furnished the inmates of many institutions in this country.

From the data of these and earlier experiments on the feeding of the cereal grains the general conclusion is drawn that "the great problem in practical dietetics and in animal production lies not in securing enough of the unidentified chemical complex associated with the causation of polyneuritis ('water-soluble B') but in securing a satisfactory adjustment among (1) the digestion products of the proteins of the diet (amino acids), (2) an adequate supply of the 'fat-soluble A,' and (3) more important even than a high biologic value of the protein mixture of the ration, a content of the essential inorganic elements suitable in amounts and proportions."

Extensive experience in feeding natural food substances restricted to a single source has shown that the character of the inorganic content of the food mixture, if fed monotonously, constitutes a factor of the greatest importance in influencing the growth and well-being. Furthermore, as small amounts as 15 per cent of wheat kernel, 3 per cent of wheat germ, or 25 per cent of thoroughly cooked beans will supply an ample amount of all of the unidentified food essentials except that supplied by butter fat ("fat-soluble A").

The authors state that the tendency to regard scurvy, pellagra, rickets, and other types of malnutrition as being due to the lack of a specific chemical complex in the diet lacks convincing experimental proof. "Any diet containing a moderate content of a wholesome natural food will not be lacking in the 'water-soluble B'."

Corn as a source of protein and ash for growing animals, A. G. Hogan (*Jour. Biol. Chem., 29 (1917), No. 3, pp. 485-493, figs. 3*).—These experiments constitute an extension of earlier work by the author (E. S. R., 36, p. 158). The object was to determine specifically what inorganic elements in the ash of the corn and what amino acids in its proteins are deficient in quantity and thus constitute limiting factors when the corn kernel is used as an exclusive diet. The experiments were conducted with laboratory animals (usually rats).

From the data reported the author concluded that the most important mineral deficiency of corn is calcium, and that tryptophan is the first and lysin the second limiting factor in the proteins of the corn kernel.

The soy bean in nutrition, Balland (*Compt. Rend. Acad. Sci. [Paris], 164 (1917), No. 7, pp. 300-302*).—Descriptions and analyses are given of some soy-bean products used in France. Among those used in the army are canned raw soy beans, canned soy-bean soup, whole beans, soy-bean flour, and war bread and biscuit made with soy-bean and wheat flours.

The chemistry of bread making, J. GRANT (*New York: Longmans, Green & Co., 1917, 2. ed., pp. VI+230, pls. 4, figs. 35*).—The earlier edition of this book has been noted (E. S. R., 31, p. 657).

The bread-fed man, H. SNYDER (*Northwest. Miller, 110 (1917), No. 4, pp. 239, 240, 265*).—This paper discusses the relative cost of bread as a food, and summarizes considerable information regarding the nutritive value of bread.

The sablefish [or] black cod, H. F. MOORE (*U. S. Dept. Com., Bur. Fisheries Econ. Circ. 23 (1917), p. 6, fig. 1*).—A popular treatise on the food value of the sablefish, in which are included recipes for its preparation for the table.

The nutritive value of margarin and butter substitutes, J. C. DRUMMOND and W. D. HALLIBURTON (*Jour. Physiol., 51 (1917), No. 1-2, pp. VIII-X*).—This is a preliminary report of an investigation of the nutritive value of various commercial edible fats, data being here reported regarding margarin.

The authors state that their experiments with oleo-oil margarins have confirmed the results of other investigators and have shown these fats to be "quite able to replace butter in satisfying the nutritive requirements of the young rat." With reference to the vegetable-oil margarins, they state that their experiments thus far have shown that margarins prepared with a basis of coconut fat are not equal in nutritive value to butter or oleo-oil margarins.

Included in this study was a heterogeneous collection of butter substitutes which consisted of a basal vegetable fat with which was incorporated a greater or less proportion of crushed, dried nuts. The nutritive value of these products was found to vary considerably. One composed of the basal vegetable fat and dried walnuts was entirely unable to replace butter, while another preparation made from the same basal fat and crushed coconut fiber had a high nutritive value.

Two preparations, one apparently a deodorized coconut oil and the other probably a hydrogenated cottonseed product, were also examined. Both were found to be free from the fat-soluble accessory food substances.

The edible canna, M. O. JOHNSON (*Hawaii Sta. Rpt. 1916, p. 25*).—Analyses are reported of two samples of rootstalks of the edible canna (*Canna edulis*).

Caramels, A. McGILL (*Lab. Inland Rev. Dept. Canada Bul. 365 (1917), pp. 13*).—This bulletin reports the results of an examination of 110 samples of caramels. Of these 51 were found to contain paraffin in amounts varying from 1 to 7 per cent by weight.

Fermentation of sauerkraut, L. A. ROUND (*Amer. Grocer, 95 (1916), No. 7, p. 55*).—In this address the author outlines the conditions necessary for the successful fermentation of sauerkraut.

The fermentation of sauerkraut, L. A. ROUND (*Canner, 42 (1916), No. 9, p. 116*).—This contains essentially the same information as that noted above.

Botulism, E. C. DICKSON (*Proc. Soc. Expt. Biol. and Med., 14 (1916), No. 2, pp. 47, 48*).—In extension of earlier work (E. S. R., 33, p. 866) on the growth of *Bacillus botulinus* in vegetable medium, the author has found that corn and apricots are also suitable for the development of the toxin of the organism.

Report of division of food and drugs, H. C. LYTHGOE (*Ann. Rpt. Dept. Health Mass., 1 (1915), pp. 433-534*).—This report covers the work of the division for the year ended November 30, 1915, which included the inspection of slaughtering, dairy inspection, and the chemical examination of a large number of samples of milk, miscellaneous foods for adulteration, foods held in cold storage, drugs, poisons, etc. A list of legal actions taken and food confiscations is given. As an appendix is added a report by L. I. Nurenberg on dairy products presented to the thirty-second convention of the Association of Official Agricultural Chemists at Washington, D. C., November 15, 1915.

Sixteenth biennial report of the Minnesota State Dairy and Food Commissioner, J. J. FARRELL (*Bien. Rpt. Minn. State Dairy and Food Comr., 16* (*1915–16*), *pp. 114, figs. 3*).—This publication reviews the work of the dairy and food division for the two years ended July 31, 1916. It also includes the results of the analyses of a large number of miscellaneous food products, reports of sanitary inspections, etc.

What to feed the children, DOROTHY R. MENDENHALL and AMY L. DANIELS (*Wis. Col. Agr. Ext. Serv. Circ. 69* (*1917*), *pp. 10, figs. 5*).—Suggestions are given for the feeding of healthy infants and young children.

Manual for army cooks, 1916 (*War Dept.* [*U. S.*], *Doc. 564* (*1917*), *pp. 270, pls. 3, figs. 33*).—The first chapter of this manual contains definitions of a great number of culinary terms and later chapters are devoted to a consideration of the garrison ration, meat and fish, elementary principles of cooking and nutrition, management of the company mess, field cooking, and messing on railroad trains and transports. The manual contains descriptions of various types of cooking utensils and field and other cooking ranges, and a large number of recipes.

Reports of the executive committee of Mayor Mitchel's Committee on Food Supply, G. W. PERKINS (*New York:* [*City*], *1914, pp. 20*).—This is a preliminary report on the increase in price of foods, which is attributed to four important factors, namely, " the present and anticipated foreign demand for . . . [United States] domestic foodstuffs for future shipment; the heavy buying of household supplies by housewives against future needs; the holding back by the producer; and the stocking up by local storekeepers and village storekeepers—the latter class having made unusually heavy demands on the producers and wholesalers throughout the country."

The control of food supplies in blockaded Germany, A. E. TAYLOR (*Saturday Even. Post, 189* (*1917*), *Nos. 34, pp. 7, 8, 56, 59, 61, 64, 65, figs. 2; 35, pp. 18–20, 35, 37, 38, 41, 43, 46, 47, figs. 9; 36, pp. 25, 26, 49, 50, 53, 55 figs. 7*).—This article gives an account of the measures developed by the German Government to combat the shortage of food resulting from the blockade and other phases of the war.

Food values in Belgium, H. SNYDER (*Northwest. Miller, 110* (*1917*), *No. 2, pp. 96, 117*).—This is a review of a pamphlet by R. Smith, which presents data regarding the foods used, their cost and nutritive value, and the distribution of supplies in the work of the Commission for Relief in Belgium.

The physiology of food and economy in diet, W. M. BAYLISS (*London: Longmans, Green & Co., 1917, pp. VIII+107*).—The first chapter of this book considers briefly the problem of food as a whole. Later chapters are devoted to the uses of food, the quantity of food required, accessory food factors, digestibility, value of cooking, characteristics of certain articles of the diet, possibilities of economy, etc. A list of references concludes the publication.

The desire for food in man, MINNA C. DENTON (*Sci. Mo., 3* (*1916*), *No. 6, pp. 557–568*).—The author analyzes, on the basis of recent experimental data, hunger and appetite, which are considered to be distinctly different motives in the desire for food.

The supplemental dietary relationships among our natural foodstuffs, E. V. McCOLLUM (*N. Y. Med. Jour., 105* (*1917*), *No. 4, pp. 167, 168*).—This is a summary of a lecture in which the author reviews briefly the results of his experiments which have been noted in full from their original sources.

[Progress in] physiological chemistry, F. G. HOPKINS (*Ann. Rpts. Prog. Chem.* [*London*], *13* (*1916*), *pp. 195–218*).—A summary and digest of experimental data contributed to the field of physiological chemistry during 1916. This includes the subjects of coagulation of the blood, anaphylaxis, hydrolysis of proteins, the importance of individual amino acids in nutrition, residual nitrogen of the blood, sugar of the blood, and renal permeability.

The hourly elimination of certain urinary constituents during brief fasts, I. NEUWIRTH (*Jour. Biol. Chem., 29 (1917), No. 3, pp. 477–484*).—The data here presented form a part of a contemplated study of the influence of various agents (chiefly foodstuffs) upon the elimination of certain urinary constituents, especially uric acid. The subject of the experiments was a normal male.

In experiments in which the quantity of the water ingested was low there was a marked fall in the uric acid output during the morning hours, followed by a more gradual decline during the afternoon. There was also an unmistakable relationship, within certain limits, between urinary volume and uric acid excretion. When a constant and fairly liberal quantity of water was ingested the excretion of uric acid was somewhat more regular than in experiments where the water intake was low or irregular.

The relation between uric acid elimination and the creatinin output was not quite so definite as that between uric acid and the total nitrogen. In a general way the creatinin elimination also paralleled the total nitrogen, but this relation was not so constant as for the uric acid. The experiments here reported showed that for short fasts the creatinin output may show marked hourly variations.

Proteose intoxications and injury of body protein.—I, II, G. H. WHIPPLE, J. V. COOKE, and T. STEARNS (*Jour. Expt. Med., 25 (1917), No. 3, pp. 461–477, fig. 1; 479–494, fig. 1*).—Two papers are presented.

I. *The metabolism of fasting dogs following proteose injection.*—The experiments here reported were carried out upon laboratory animals (dogs). The results of the observations may be summarized in part as follows:

The nitrogen elimination curve in a fasting dog, after proteose injection, showed a great rise in total urinary nitrogen. The apex of the curve generally fell during the second 24-hour period following the injection and might increase more than 100 per cent above the mean base-line nitrogen level. It did not fall promptly to normal, but declined slowly in three to five days or more toward the original base line.

II. *The metabolism of dogs with duodenal obstruction and isolated loops of intestine.*—These experiments indicated that dogs with isolated loops of small intestine showed evidences of intoxication. The total nitrogen elimination rose greatly above the normal minimum of the fasting period in the preceding experiments, indicating that the intoxication was associated with great destruction of body protein. The authors assume that the intoxications are associated with a definite proteose intoxication which is capable of initiating and continuing a profound injury of tissue protein, one indication of this protein inqury being this great rise in total nitrogen elimination.

Metabolism in gout, W. BAIN (*Lancet [London], 1917, I, No. 13, pp. 494, 495*).—Observations on four cases of gout showed that the excretion of calcium in the the urine was lower than exhibited normally. However, as is usually the case, most of the calcium was excreted in the feces.

The administration of calcium chlorid to individuals kept on a fixed diet caused a slight retention of nitrogen but did not affect the phosphorus metabolism. "The effect on total calcium metabolism was not constant. In one case a small negative calcium balance was transformed into a small positive one; in the other the positive calcium balance was reduced. In both cases the urinary calcium was not affected."

ANIMAL PRODUCTION.

Digestibility of sugars, starches, and pentosans of roughages, G. S. FRAPS (*Texas Sta. Bul. 196 (1916), pp. 5–56*).—The investigations here reported pertain to the digestibility of the sugars, starches, and pentosans of the feeding stuffs used in experiments already noted (E. S. R., 27, p. 668). Tabulated data show the percentage composition of these constituents, their digestibilty, and the composition and digestibility of the substances obtained by boiling in dilute acid and alkali.

The results of digestion experiments with sheep are given in the following table:

Coefficients of digestibility of the sugars, starches, and pentosans of Texas feeds.

Kind of feeding stuff.	Monosaccharids.	Disaccharids.	Starch.	Soluble pentosans.	Reducing sugar from hemicellulose.	Material rendered insoluble by acids.	Soluble residue.	Nitrogen-free extract.		
								Soluble.	Insoluble.	Total.
	Per ct.	*Per ct.*	*Per ct.*	*Per ct.*	*Per ct.*	*Per ct.*	*Per ct.*	*Per ct.*	*Per ct.*	*Per ct.*
Alfalfa hay	98.5	98.2	93.8	75.7	61.6	8.59	74.7	71.6	77.1	65.0
Bermuda hay	98.4	98.7	92.9	55.5	....	....	....	59.8	43.6	50.2
Bur clover.........	98.7	82.9	82.4	85.4	64.0	70.3	92.2	85.1	45.8	75.9
Buffalo grass......	98.8	98.1	91.0	65.4	0.0	91.9	28.2	62.9	55.2	58.0
Corn shucks........	97.8	98.7	92.7	80.9	70.8	0.0	52.1	63.1	56.5	60.6
Cowpea hay	90.1	99.1	....	....	....	....	....	....	....	65.3
Guam grass........	98.8	98.5	68.4	60.2	0.0	4.5	69.2	63.4	51.7	53.8
Johnson grass hay...	98.6	89.8	38.9	65.7	67.5	11.1	37.6	49.1	52.1	52.3
Do..............	94.5	98.3	85.2	76.0	0.0	18.8	61.5	64.6	57.7	61.0
Kafir corn fodder....	99.4	99.1	93.7	80.1	0.0	3.3	77.3	78.4	55.0	69.4
Millett.............	95.9	83.6	71.5	84.3	91.9	7.1	.04	67.3	45.1	59.3
Oat hay............	99.4	69.9	99.1	73.2	14.7	6.2	0.0	56.1	69.3	66.8
Peanut hay	97.2	97.9	99.5	88.4	0.0	92.2	87.9	91.7	3.3	74.3
Para grass.........	93.7	99.6	....	49.7	17.9	....	....	....	37.5	46.9
Rice straw (Japan)..	97.5	99.7	95.9	23.6	46.7	0.0	53.4	46.9	42.6	45.0
Rice straw (Honduras).............	88.6	56.2	65.5	51.7	71.4	0.0	67.5	51.8	43.6	47.3
Sorghum hay........	99.7	95.5	79.1	71.3	0.0	4.9	....	67.3	62.9	65.0
Vetch hay...........	95.7	98.2	91.2	71.0	64.2	79.8	54.0	65.8	62.7	74.5

Chemical composition of fodder plants of the Province of Samara (*Otchet Bezenchuk. Selsk. Khoz. Opytn. Sta. 5 (1914), pp. 101–127*).—Experiments covering a period of several years to determine the feeding value from the chemical composition of a number of fodder plants are reported. The analytical data are submitted in tabular form.

The general conclusion drawn is that the hays from the steppe have as high a nutritive value and are as valuable for feeding stuffs as the hays from other sections.

Low-grade cottonseed meal.—Warning sounded to purchasers of feeding stuffs, A. E. PERKINS and R. I. GRADY (*Mo. Bul. Ohio Sta., 2 (1917), No. 2, pp. 41–45*).—Attention is called to the prevalence of inferior cottonseed meal on the market during 1916, and the need is pointed out for a better State law for the control of feeding stuffs. Results are given of chemical and mechanical analyses of samples of two lots of cottonseed meal bought by the station. Both of these lots fell below guaranty, and one contained from 40 to 60 per cent of a material thought to be cottonseed hull bran.

Hydrocyanic acid in cassava, M. O. JOHNSON (*Hawaii Sta. Rpt. (1916), pp. 24, 25*).—Determinations were made of hydrocyanic acid in " bitter " and " sweet " cassava. The percentage of hydrocyanic acid in the samples tested varied from

0.006 to 0.025 in whole roots, from 0.007 to 0.021 in peeled roots, and from 0.015 to 0.042 in the peel of roots. In samples of the waste from cassava roots used in the manufacture of starch there was found to be 0.003 per cent of hydrocyanic acid in the waste from whole roots and 0.0008 per cent in the waste from peeled roots. These results indicate that cassava waste, if boiled before feeding, is safe for use as a hog feed. The author cautions against the use of cassava itself, however, for feeding unless the finely-divided roots are thoroughly boiled with two or three changes of water.

Stallion enrollment.—VI, Report of stallion enrollment work for the year 1916, with lists of stallions and jacks enrolled, H. E. McCARTNEY (*Indiana Sta. Circ. 58 (1917), pp. 182, figs. 25*).—This reviews the work of the stallion enrollment board of the State during the year, gives facsimile reproductions of the certificates of registry recognized by the State stallion enrollment law, and lists the stallions and jacks enrolled in the State by breeds and counties.

Stallion registration and licenses for the year 1916, W. L. CARLYLE, L. L. LEWIS, and W. L. FOWLER (*Oklahoma Sta. Circ. 42 (1917), pp. XVIII+105*).—This first annual report of the Oklahoma State Live Stock Registry Board contains the text of the State live stock registration law and rules and regulations adopted by the board for its enforcement, and gives lists by breeds and counties of the stallions and jacks licensed in the State during 1916.

DAIRY FARMING—DAIRYING.

The mineral metabolism of the milch cow; second paper, E. B. FORBES, F. M. BEEGLE, ET AL. (*Ohio Sta. Bul. 308 (1917), pp. 451–481*).—The objects of the experiments reported in this bulletin, in continuation of those already noted (E. S. R., 35, p. 481), were to learn whether mineral equilibrium can be maintained on rations containing the maximum amounts of mineral nutriment obtainable in common practical feeds; to determine the effects of large additions to these rations of calcium, magnesium, and phosphorus in supplemental form, as inorganic salts; and to ascertain the reason for the limited utilization of the mineral nutrients during ordinarily liberal food consumption.

Six Holstein cows were used in collection periods of 20 days, separated by ten-day intervals on the ration of the collection period to follow. The cows were all in their second, third, or fourth period of lactation. None was bred during this experiment. They were fed and milked four times daily at six-hour intervals. The milk yield varied from 38.7 to 58.35 lbs. per head daily.

In order to supply maximum amounts of calcium, magnesium, and phosphorus, the rations were based on a leguminous roughage (either clover or alfalfa hay), corn silage, cottonseed meal, linseed meal, and wheat bran. Corn meal was used as the principal source of carbohydrate. During the first period of the experiments the variable portion of the rations was the roughage—three cows receiving alfalfa hay and three clover hay. During the second period three of the cows received a double portion of salt. The rations were further varied during this period by giving calcium carbonate to two cows and bone flour to two cows.

Detailed tabular data are given of the average daily feeds consumed, milk produced, and live weights of cows; percentage composition and weight of constituents of feeds and milk; weight of constituents of urine and feces; daily intake and balances of minerals and nitrogen; minerals in daily rations computed to normal solutions; utilization and elimination of nitrogen; coefficients of digestibility of rations; and distribution of the outgo of elements among milk, urine, and feces.

"The prevailing belief that all animals which receive leafy forage as a considerable part of the ration consume and digest an abundance of mineral nutriment is shown not to be true in relation to cows during ordinarily liberal milk production. With rations of common practical foods, especially chosen to provide maximum supplies of the mineral nutrients, all calcium, magnesium, and phosphorus balances were negative, as in the previous year's work. With large increases in the calcium, magnesium, and phosphorus contents of these rations, through increased amounts of food consumed and through the addition to the rations of large amounts of calcium carbonate and bone flour, all calcium balauces and all but one magnesium balance remained negative, but the phosphorus balances became positive. This work presents satisfactory evidence that in the selective improvement of milch cows we encounter limited capacities to digest calcium magnesium, and phosphorus, and inability to maintain their body stores of these elements before any such limitations are apparent in their ability to digest and to utilize the organic nutrients. . . .

"Doubling the usual sodium chlorid allowance did not improve the retention of calcium, magnesium, and phosphorus. Twenty-eight gm. (1 oz.) of salt per head and day, with a ration of common foods, provides enough sodium for cows producing 45 lbs. of milk per day. An allowance of 1 to 2 oz. of salt per head and day, in accord with the amount of milk produced, will cover all sodium requirements. Rations containing enough sodium to meet the cow's needs commonly contain a larger proportionate supply of chlorin.

"Enough potassium seems to have been supplied by all the rations studied. A deficiency of potassium in normal rations, therefore, seems unlikely.

"The various circumstances which determine the path of outgo of absorbed nutrients are commonly without corresponding effect on the retention of these elements in the body. In some cases nearly all the sodium of the excreta was in the urine, while in others it was nearly all in the feces. The same may be said of chlorin. The elimination of sodium and chlorin in the urine is increased by high intake of these elements, by constipation, and by high water intake. Potassium in cows is commonly excreted in much larger proportion in the urine than in the feces, but in rations characterized by predominance of acid minerals, potassium was eliminated more largely in the feces.

"Calcium is excreted by cows almost wholly in the feces, but a predominance of acid minerals in the ration may cause slight increase in urinary calcium. Magnesium always exceeds calcium in the urine, but is contained in the feces in amounts usually about four times as great as in the urine.

"The excretion of phosphorus is characterized by much the same proportionate distribution as the excretion of calcium, except that urinary phosphorus may be much increased by general physiologic disturbance. Sulphur is normally excreted in the feces, in quantities three or four times as great as in the urine, but with high sulphur intake the urinary sulphur may equal the feces sulphur.

"There were no noticeable effects of the foodstuffs or the mineral supplements (sodium chlorid, calcium carbonate, or bone flour) on the amount or composition of the milk.

"Such variations in the balance of acid and basic mineral elements as occur in normal cow rations do not affect the retention of the mineral elements in unmistakable ways. Evidence was obtained showing that negative balances of the mineral nutrients may signify either deficient intake of the same or the throwing off of previously absorbed stores in the face of continued superabundant supplies. Either positive or negative balances may signify, under certain circumstances, only comparatively unimportant fluctuations in extensive reserves.

"The nitrogen compounds of rations containing alfalfa hay are more digestible than the nitrogen compounds of rations containing clover hay; they are more completely absorbed from the intestine, but are more largely eliminated in the urine. The greater digestibility of the alfalfa nitrogen, therefore, seems not to signify corresponding nutritive superiority. The percentages of utilization of the nitrogen compounds of rations containing clover and of those containing alfalfa were the same.

"The deficient utilization of the minerals by cows . . . has practical bearings in the malnutrition of the bones of cattle, which is not uncommon after seasons of drought and overstocking of pastures, particularly in regions of unfertile, sandy soils or soils of granitic origin, especially if these be worn through long cropping with deficient fertilization. Further practical bearings are probably seen in the rather common failure of cows to breed after a season of forced milk production; also in the failure of many cows fed for high production to maintain high records during consecutive periods of lactation; perhaps also as a contributory cause in the usual shrinkage of milk flow, with advance in the period of lactation. . . . Thus far, under no circumstances, have we been able to cause calcium storage or to maintain calcium equilibrium."

Feeds for dairy cows, M. P. JARNAGIN and O. T. GOODWIN (*Ga. State Col. Agr. Circ. 45 (1917), pp. 8, figs. 2*).—The rations used in the experiments here reported consisted of a maximum and minimum feed of sorghum and Kafir-corn silage and a minimum and maximum feed of mixed concentrates, with a check ration of silage and cottonseed meal. Twelve cows were divided into three lots of four cows each and fed by the reversal system for 90 days in 30-day periods, so that each group received each of the rations for 30 days.

On a ration of 36 lbs. of silage and 6 lbs. of cottonseed meal per head daily, the cows lost an average of 5 lbs. each in weight during the 90 days, and produced 6,829.9 lbs. of milk and 335.99 lbs. of butter at a feed cost of $49.35. On a ration of 36 lbs. of silage, 7 lbs. of peavine hay, and 5 lbs. of a mixture of cottonseed meal, wheat bran, and corn-and-cob meal (4:3:3), the cows produced 6,820.7 lbs. of milk and 327.84 lbs. of butter at a feed cost of $61.20. Each cow lost an average of 9 lbs. in weight during the 90 days on this ration. On a ration of 12 lbs. of silage, 10 lbs. of hay, and 10 lbs. of the above grain mixture, the cows produced 7,078.5 lbs. of milk and 341.14 lbs. of butter at a feed cost of $79.92. On this ration they lost in weight an average of 5.5 lbs. each during the 90 days. The prices per ton charged for feeds were for cottonseed meal $27.50, wheat bran $30, corn-and-cob meal $23, hay $14, and silage $3.

[Feeding cows with the subcutaneous matter of skins intended for tanning], GERLACH (*Deut. Landw. Presse, 43 (1916), No. 26, p. 229; abs. in Internat. Inst. Agr. [Rome], Internat. Rev. Sci. and Pract. Agr., 7 (1916). No., 7, p. 996*).—Feeding experiments are reported with a subcutaneous material, glue leather—i. e., leather cuttings containing gelatinous matter and consisting, according to the author's analysis, of 14.72 per cent of water, 55.77 per cent of protein, 12.35 per cent of fat, and 10.06 per cent of mineral matter. Nine milch cows between the second and third months of lactation were fed by the reversal system for 63 days, the basal ration consisting of chopped forage, hay, beet-leaf silage, mangels, potatoes, wheat bran, and lupines with the bitter taste removed. In addition, one group received 3 kg. of linseed meal and the other 1.5 kg. of glue leather per head daily.

The animals at once took to the latter ration. The milk secretion was 10 per cent less during the first period and a little greater during the second period in the glue-leather group than in the linseed-meal group. The milk was a little richer in fat during both periods in the glue-leather group.

Dairy cattle feeding and management, C. W. LARSON and F. S. PUTNEY (*New York: John Wiley & Sons, 1917, pp. XX+471, figs. 128*).—This book, which is intended for students and others interested in dairy cattle feeding and management, has been prepared by the authors primarily to meet the need of a textbook to broaden the field of the ordinary lecture course. A brief bibliography follows each lecture and the appendix gives suggested practicum exercises.

Dairy farming, J. MICHELS (*Peebles, Wis.: Author, 1916, 8. ed. rev., pp. 300, figs. 89*).—This is a revised and enlarged edition of this text and reference book for dairy students and farmers (E. S. R., 26, p. 574).

Dairying in Denmark, J. J. DUNNE (*Better Business, 2 (1917), No. 2, pp. 127–162, figs. 2*).—This review of the organization of the dairy industry of Denmark deals especially with the establishment and growth of cooperative creameries, butter shows, and the use of the statutory trademark for Danish butter.

Kerry and Dexter cattle as producers of milk and butter fat, C. S. PLUMB (*Amer. Kerry and Dexter Cattle Club Bul. 6 (1917), pp. 5–16. figs. 11*).—Milk and milk fat records of Kerry and Dexter cows in America and England and notes on the weight of Dexter cattle are given.

The highest year's records reported in America are for Kerry cows 6,103.9 lbs. of milk containing 269.8 lbs. of fat and for Dexter cows 9,046 lbs. of milk testing 4.26 per cent fat. The Dexter cow Bognut of Waddington, in the Ohio State University herd, produced in 1913 6,261 lbs. of milk, the percentage of fat ranging from 4 to 5.6.

A score card for dairy cows, E. G. WOODWARD (*Breeder's Gaz., 71 (1917), No. 5, pp. 210, 212, fig. 1*).—Some of the defects of the breed score card for dairy cows are noted. A score card is given which has been prepared with a view to pointing out without too much detail the relation between the appearance of the cow and her various functions which are essential to production.

Relation between the quantity of milk formed and that obtained in milking, S. G. ZWART (*Ztschr. Fleisch u. Milchhyg. 26 (1916), Nos. 15. pp. 231–234; 16, pp. 246–250; abs. in Internat. Inst. Agr. [Rome], Internat. Rev. Sci. and Pract. Agr., 7 (1916), No. 8. pp. 1139–1141*).—The author reviews the literature and reports results of experiments on the relation of the quantity of milk formed and that obtained during the process of milking.

The experimental results failed to confirm the theory that the greater portion of the milk is formed during the interval between milkings. In reference to the theory that milk is chiefly formed during milking. it was repeatedly possible to inject into the udder all the milk and in some cases twice the quantity of milk previously drawn from the udder. From results obtained in attempts to determine by exact measurement the quantity of milk formed in the udder, the author concludes that, while there is great variation in normal cows in good condition of lactation, on the average the quantities of milk formed during the period of rest and during milking by hand are equal.

The influence of parturition on the composition and properties of the milk and milk fat of the cow, C. H. ECKLES and L. S. PALMER (*Jour. Biol. Chem., 27 (1916), No. 2, pp. 313–326*).—In this paper, contributed from the Missouri Experiment Station, data collected in cooperation with the Dairy Division of the U. S. Department of Agriculture are presented on the effects of parturition on the composition of colostrum milk and milk fat as influenced (1) by milking the cow up to the time of parturition and (2) by the length of the period the cow is dry before parturition. The general characteristics of colostrum milk are discussed and shown in tabular form, minimum, maximum, and average values of the various constituents being given as found by various investigators.

In studying the effects of continuous milking on the composition of the colostrum milk analyses were made of the milk and milk fat of three pure-bred Jersey cows for a suitable length of time before and after parturition. The length of time since the last paturition was normal for each animal. The character of the rations was not identical, but was uniform for each cow throughout the experiment. It was found that parturition failed to exert the usual depressing influence on the percentage of lactose in each of the three cases, although the lactose content was somewhat below normal in the milk of two of the cows. In regard to casein no effect was noticed in the case of two cows, but there was a high casein percentage for the other cow. The composition of the milk fat was uniformly unaffected by parturition. Very abnormal fat constants followed parturition in the case of one cow, but the fat showed the same abnormalities in even more striking degree for several days before parturition. The most uniform effect of parturition was upon the albumin and globulin or heat-coagulable proteins of the milk. The percentages of these proteins increased very materially up to the time of parturition, reaching a maximum in the first milk drawn after parturition. However, the actual proportion of the total milk represented by albumin and globulin in the case of these three cows was far below the minimum value for heat-coagulable proteins of normal colostrum.

To secure data on the influence of the length of time the cow is dry on the composition of colostrum and milk fat, complete analyses were made of the milk and milk fat of four cows for the first two or three milkings following parturition. These cows had been dry for from 19 to 83 days. In the case of each of the animals the first milk was drawn within a few hours after parturition.

It was found that the abnormalities in composition of colostrum milk are in direct relation to the length of the period of dryness. All the colostrum samples showed a composition more or less characteristic of the first milk drawn after parturition, but this was particularly striking in the case of the cow which was dry 83 days. The percentage of total solids, protein, casein, heat-coagulable proteins, and ash was abnormally high in each case, while the percentage of lactose and fat was abnormally low. However, in the case of the cow dry 19 days, the milk was much less abnormal in composition, although it showed a protein, casein, and heat-coagulable protein content considerably above normal. The fat content of the colostrum milk of the cow which was dry 19 days was 4.43 per cent, which was slightly below normal for this cow. The colostrum milk of the cow that had been dry 83 days contained only 1.3 per cent of fat. The results of this experiment indicate that the length of the period of dryness had little if any effect upon the composition of the colostrum fat. In each case the fat showed the composition characteristic of colostrum fat, having a low saponification and Reichert-Meissl value and high melting point. The iodin value of the fats analyzed did not show the extremely high figure usually characteristic of colostrum fat.

Preliminary research upon the effect of extracts of certain endocrine glands upon the amount of milk produced by cows and goats, C. D'ALFONSO (*Indus. Latt. e Zootec.*, *14* (*1916*), *Nos. 15, pp. 215, 216; 16–17, pp. 234, 235; 18, pp. 253, 254; 19, pp. 268 269; 20, pp. 286, 287; 21, pp. 302, 303, 305; 22, p. 316; 24, pp. 350, 351; [15] (1917), No. 1, pp. 7, 9*).—This is a report of studies of the effect of the injection of extracts of the ovaries, testes, adrenal glands, thyroid glands, hypophyses, and mammary glands upon milk production in cows and goats.

The large numbers of Bacterium abortus var. lipolyticus which may be found in milk, ALICE C. EVANS (*Jour. Bact.*, *2* (*1917*), *No. 2, pp. 185, 186*).— By the use of methods described in an earlier paper. (E. S. R., 35, p. 674), *B.*

abortus developed in 17 out of 23 samples of milk plated on one dairy farm. In the milk of one cow there were 112,000 of these organisms per cubic centimeter. If the milk of the 23 cows on this farm had been mixed there would have been about 7,000 *B. abortus* per cubic centimeter, or approximately 28 per cent of the total number of bacteria. Detailed studies of cultures from 11 of the samples indicated that nine of them were *B. abortus* var. *lipolyticus* and two resembled the cultures from pathological material.

Milk and its hygienic relations, JANET E. LANE-CLAYPON (*New York & London: Longmans. Green & Co., 1916, pp. VIII+348, pls. 8, figs. 21*).—In this book the author presents a survey of investigations directly related to the hygienic and nutritional aspects of milk. The different phases of the subject treated include the general composition, organic and inorganic constituents, biological properties, and cellular content of milk; breast feeding; the nutritive value of raw and boiled milk for the young of the same and different species; raw and boiled cow's milk for infants; dried milk for infants; Barlow's disease and rickets in relation to heated milk; changes in milk during heating; pathogenic organisms in milk, with notes on milk-borne epidemics; sources of milk contamination; sanitary milk production; bacteria commonly found in milk and their thermal death points; pasteurization of milk; and pathogenic bacteria in butter and cheese. Appendixes deal with the development of the mammary function, the subsequent development of the organism in relation to the method of feeding in early life, the preservation of human milk, a comparison of mother's and boiled cow's milk for infants, milk depots of England, desiccation of milk, grading of milk, and destruction of bacteria in milk without the application of heat. Each chapter is prefaced with a popular summary and is followed by a bibliography.

City milk supply, H. N. PARKER (*New York: McGraw-Hill Book Co., 1917. pp. XI+493. figs. 63*).—This book treats of milk and its production, transportation, and delivery to city milk consumers, and of the methods of control adopted to insure its purity. An extensive bibliography of the literature cited is given at the end of each chapter.

Milk, sanitary and otherwise, J. WADDELL (*Sci. Mo., 4 (1917), No. 2, pp. 155-164*).—This is a general account of the composition, sanitary production, and use of milk; the changes taking place during the fermentation, pasteurization, and digestion of milk; and the production and use of certified milk for infants.

Oxygenated milk, C. G. GRULEE (*N. Y. Med. Jour., 104 (1916), No. 23, pp. 1092-1094. figs. 3*).—A report is given of an experiment at the Presbyterian Hospital in Chicago on the treatment of milk by hydrogen peroxid by a process, which is described. similar to the Budde process (E. S. R., 14, p. 1009).

Bacteriological examinations indicated that the oxygenated milk was sterile. except in one instance when there were approximately 100,000 streptococci per cubic centimeter. whereas in the raw milk before treatment there were 3,250,000 bacteria per cubic centimeter. Raw milk was inoculated with known virulent strains of hemolytic streptococci and typhoid and diphtheria bacilli, and treated with hydrogen peroxid. Plated cultures of this milk remained sterile during 72 hours of incubation, while blood agar plates of the same milk previons to oxidation contained from 2,500,000 to 3,000,000 bacteria per cubic centimeter.

The chemical changes in milk due to oxidation were not definitely studied. It is stated, however, that no gross changes have been noted. The rising of cream and digestive processes, such as coagulation with rennin and the usual digestion with pepsin, occur as in raw or cooked milk. It was impossible to prepare buttermilk from oxygenated milk. During the use of this milk for over a year in the infants' and children's wards and throughout the hospital, nothing developed which has been ascribed to a deleterious influence of the oxygenated milk.

Chemical quality of New York City market milk, L. P. Brown and C. V. Ekroth (*Jour. Indus. and Engin. Chem., 9 (1917), No. 3, pp. 299–301, figs. 3*).—This is a general discussion of data collected from various sources and having a direct bearing on the subject. The need of placing chemical standards for milk on a more rational basis is emphasized.

A note on the milk supply of Bangalore, A. K. Y. N. Aiyer (*Dept. Agr. Mysore, Gen. Ser., Bul. 7 (1916), pp. 11, pls. 7*).—The author describes the present condition of the milk supply of the city of Bangalore, gives the fat contents of a number of samples of various grades of street milk, tabulates the milk and fat yields of Mysore cows, and suggests methods for the improvement of the local breed and the production of crossbreeds of dairy cattle and buffaloes for supplying the city milk trade.

A survey of dairy score cards, C. E. North (*Amer. Jour. Pub. Health, 7 (1917), No. 1, pp. 25–39*).—Brief notes on the history, application, and general uses of dairy score cards are given, together with a careful consideration of their value, particularly as affecting the character of municipal milk supplies.

In the author's opinion the three essentials upon which clean milk production depends are proper milking, cooling, and sterilizing. "If we assume that dairy cows and dairy employees are free from disease, sanitary milk of the highest type can be produced by a strict adherence to simple but standard methods for carrying out the three above-mentioned operations." A new type of dairy score card, based upon these essentials, is presented.

The Babcock test, and testing problems, H. C. Troy (*Cornell Reading Course for Farm, No. 118 (1916), pp. 117–144, pl. 1, figs. 14*).—Directions are given for the use of the Babcock test in determining the fat content of milk, cream, skim milk, and buttermilk, together with practical problems relating thereto and notes on the use of the Babcock test in rural schools.

How to make creamery butter on the farm, W. J. and Mrs. McLaughlin (*Owatonna, Minn.: Minnetonna Co., 1916, pp. 110, pls. 7, figs. 11*).—A revised edition of this manual (E. S. R., 33, p. 577).

Pepsin in cheese making, C. Stevenson (*Jour. Agr. [New Zeal.], 14 (1917), No. 1, pp. 32–34*).—In experiments at Taranaki, by the dairy division of the Commonwealth, milk arriving at a cheese factory was divided equally into three vats. The milk in vat 1 was coagulated with pepsin, vat 2 with a mixture of pepsin and rennet, and vat 3 with rennet only. The pepsin was used at the rate of 2.5 dr. per 1,000 lbs. of milk, and the rennet at the rate of 3.5 oz. per 1,000 lbs. of milk.

The curd in vats 2 and 3 was ready for cutting in 30 minutes, while that in vat 1 required 10 minutes longer to firm sufficiently for cutting. No difference was observed between the curds of any of the vats as regards the development of acidity or otherwise during the whole process of manufacture, and the yield of cheese from each vat was practically the same. The loss of fat in the whey of the vat in which only pepsin was used showed a slight increase as compared with the other two vats. Fifteen weeks after manufacture no difference was noted between the cheese made with pepsin and that made with rennet.

Directions are given for the use of pepsin for cheese making.

Is the ripening of cheese influenced by its fat content? W. van Dam (*Verslag. Landbouwk. Onderzoek. Rijkslandbouwproefstat. [Netherlands], No. 20 (1917), pp. 21–26*).—The work of Jensen on the influence of fat on the ripening of cheese (E. S. R., 17, p. 1010) is critically discussed. The conclusions drawn from the results of the work are considered not to be well founded.

From the study with Edam cheese reported it is concluded that independent of the amount of paracasein present the digestion (ripening) proceeds slowly until a definite concentration of split products is reached. This explains the fact of a larger percentage digestion of cheese material in a sample rich in fat than in a sample poor in fat. The stimulating action of the fat on the casein could not be determined.

The judicial problem of Camembert, F. MABRE (*Le Problème Juridique du Camembert. Paris: Editions Scientifiques Francaises [1915], pp. 141*).—In addition to notes on the history, manufacture, composition, definition, and fat content of Camembert cheese, this book deals with the legal status of this cheese in France.

The " cracking " of Edam cheese, F. W. J. BOEKHOUT and J. J. O. DE VRIES (*Verslag. Landbouwk. Onderzoek. Rijkslandbouwproefstat. [Netherlands], No. 20 (1917), pp. 71–78, pl. 1*).—The results of the study reported indicate that the use of saltpeter has very little effect in preventing the cracking of Edam cheese when *Bacillus coli communis* and *B. lactis aerogenes* are present with the butyric acid bacteria. The former organisms destroy the preservative before it can suppress the development of the butyric acid organisms.

VETERINARY MEDICINE.

A text-book of the principles and practice of veterinary medicine, D. S. WHITE (*Philadelphia: Lea & Febiger, 1917, pp. 484*).—This work, prepared for use as a textbook by students of veterinary medicine, is based upon the author's personal experience for over 20 years as a teacher of veterinary students.

The comparative resistance of bacteria and human tissue cells to certain common antiseptics, R. A. LAMBERT (*Jour. Expt. Med., 24 (1916), No. 6, pp. 683–688*).—This material has been previously noted from another source (E. S. R., 36, p. 177).

The prophylaxis of the infection of war wounds.—A comparative study of various antiseptics, H. VINCENT (*Compt. Rend. Acad. Sci. [Paris], 164 (1917), No. 3, pp. 153–156*).—The antiseptic and germicidal value of sodium fluorid, sodium formate, zinc chlorid, calcium hypochlorite, boric acid, sodium borate, copper sulphate, ferrous sulphate, potassium permanganate, and iodoform was studied by noting the action of the substances on a bouillon culture of *Bacillus perfringens*.

All the substances except boric acid and sodium borate were found to be very active. Copper sulphate yielded excellent results. Sodium fluorid was also found to possess excellent germicidal properties, but possessed a certain toxicity. The most satisfactory antiseptic used was a mixture of 10 parts of fresh calcium hypochlorite and 90 parts of crystallized boric acid in aqueous solution. This antiseptic was also found to possess hemostatic properties.

The treatment of wounds in war by magnesium sulphate, A. E. MORISON and W. J. TULLOCH (*Jour. Roy. Army Med. Corps. 27 (1916), No. 4, pp. 375–398, pls. 2*).—" From the first series of experiments it appears that magnesium sulphate exhibits to a greater degree than do the other salts investigated the desirable property of interfering with the digestive activity of pus. This statement is made with reservation as the experimental methods that one is forced to employ are open to certain criticisms, and I suggest that the rate of epithelialization of the wounds treated would give a truer index of the property than does experimental investigation.

" Magnesium sulphate has not so markedly inhibitory an action on phago-cytosis as one would expect, and, therefore, even if it be absorbed to a slight extent, it would not have a deleterious influence on the process, while salt, being more readily absorbed, might well interfere with this function of the leucocytes.

"Experimental work in physical chemistry and pharmacology points to magnesium sulphate as the least absorbable of the readily soluble salts, while clinical evidence—absence of pain, etc.—points in the same direction. By virtue of the nonabsorption of magnesium sulphate the granulations produced are more compact than when a more readily absorbable salt is employed. The magnesium ion has a markedly inhibitory action on the growth of streptococci and *Bacillus coli*, and a slightly inhibitory effect on the growth of *B. pyocyaneus*. It has, however, no easily demonstrable influence in the concentrations examined on the growth of staphylococci, or on the diphtheroids investigated."

Platelets and the coagulation of the blood, V. DUCCESCHI (*Arch. Ital. Biol., 64 (1915), No. 3, pp. 341–353*).—In the study reported the addition of cocaine (2.5 per cent solution) to frog blood immediately after being drawn prevented its coagulation. It retarded the coagulation time about 24 hours in chicken blood and from 1 to 2 hours in dog's blood.

In equal amounts the cocaine prevents the agglutinating phenomenon of the platelets in frog and chicken blood and also arrests the morphological modifications which ordinarily occur. The same effect, although not so marked, is observed with dog blood. In cases where coagulation results even after the addition of the cocaine a marked retraction in the clot was observed.

From the results it is concluded that the first phase of the coagulation of the blood consists of an active reaction of the platelets (agglutination, adhesion to the surface contacts, and morphological modifications), and a mechanical and chemical stimulation caused by contact with the normal cardiovascular surfaces and the presence of the thrombokinase, stimulations which are ordinarily the cause of coagulation. This first phase of the coagulation appears to be paralyzed completely or partially by cocaine, which also retards the coagulation.

The separation of serum into coagulative and noncoagulative fractions, A. F. HESS (*Jour. Expt. Med., 24 (1916), No. 6, pp. 701–708*).—The coagulative principle of blood serum was found to be closely associated with the euglobulin fraction. A hemostatic containing about 2 per cent protein, which is more potent than the whole serum, has been prepared by the following procedure: The serum was saturated in the cold with pure crystals of sodium chlorid, filtered, and a small amount of chloroform added to the precipitate, which was then dialyzed for about a week. The dialyzate was taken up with Ringer's solution, and 0.3 per cent tricresol added. This solution was then filtered through a Berkefeld filter and bottled in 20-cc. vials.

The preparation has been employed in various manifestations of intractable hemorrhage, and has yielded most satisfactory results. When injected intravenously the euglobulin fraction is preferable, since a much smaller amount of foreign protein is introduced. It is also more quickly absorbed from the subcutaneous tissues.

While the exact way in which the substance exerts its coagulative effect on the blood was not determined "it would seem, in view of the fact that euglobulin is found in the normal blood, that it should be regarded as a physiologic coagulant, and its mode of action in these tests as merely an intensification of the normal clotting processes." Other globulins examined (egg and edestin from hemp seed) showed no coagulative power. That the coagulative effect of the euglobulin fraction was not due to a counteraction of antithrombin was evident from experiments in which the material was only partly able to overcome the inhibitory effect of hirudin.

Studies on anaphylaxis (antianaphylaxis), O. Thomsen (*Overs. K. Danske Vidensk. Selsk. Forhandl., No. 5 (1915), pp. 363–413, figs. 3*).—In the experiments reported sterilized horse serum was used as antigen in all cases and guinea pigs as the experimental animals. The sensitizing dose was given subcutaneously, the reinjection intravenously.

Animals sensitized on the same day and with the same dose, and thus considered to belong to the same group, reacted in a similar way as regards sensibility. Some differences, however, were observed between various groups of animals, although the dose was the same. The reason for this phenomenon is considered to depend in all probability on the season of the year and its effect on the production of the anaphylatoxin.

Sensitization was not found to remain unchanged indefinitely, as has been previously stated, but, while maintained in the beginning, a gradual decrease was observed. The guinea pigs reacted more and more weakly as they grew older. Very young animals (a few days old) are considered to produce a different antisubstance than those several months old (weighing from 300 to 500 gm.). Fully grown animals (from 800 to 900 gm.) appear to yield very weak antisubstances.

Antianaphylaxis is deemed subject to three phenomena: (1) The destruction of anaphylatoxin, (2) the prevention of the reaction between antigen and antisubstance, and (3) the reduction of the effect of the anaphylatoxin. The disappearance of the anaphylatoxin was found to depend to a great degree on the existing degree of sensibility. This has been determined by passive sensitization. Sensibility was found to rise very slowly with the increase of material used. The desensitizing influence of a sublethal dose of antigen was found to vary greatly, depending on the degree of the existing sensibility. Narcotics, peptones, urine, etc. were found to act as antisubstances by decreasing the rapidity of the reaction between antigen and antibody, in which case a larger dose of antigen was needed to produce shock. The effect of these substances was found to be much greater on weakly sensitized than on strongly sensitized animals.

Anaplasmosis.—The significance of intracorpuscular bodies, marginal points, and anaplasms found in the blood of sheep from Sardinia and Piedmont, G. Finzi and A. Campus (*Nuovo Ercolani, 21 (1916), Nos. 30–31, pp. 493–500; 34–35, pp. 557–571; 22 (1917), No. 1–2, pp. 2–8; abs. in Trop. Vet. Bul., 5 (1917), No. 1, pp. 3–5*).—The greater part of this work consists of a survey of the literature dealing with the subject of anaplasms.

On vitamins, amino acids, and other chemical factors involved in the growth of the meningococcus, Dorothy J. Lloyd (*Jour. Path. and Bact., 21 (1916), No. 1, pp. 113–130*).—The study reported shows that the primary cultivation of the meningococcus in vitro is only possible in the presence of certain accessory growth factors present in blood, serum, milk, and other animal fluids, and probably also in vegetable tissues. These accessory factors were found to be moderately thermostable, soluble in water and alcohol, and rapidly adsorbed by filter paper but not by glass wool. "There is a relationship of the inverse order between the amount of amino acid present in the medium and the amount of vitamin required to stimulate the growth of laboratory strains, and it is therefore suggested that the action of the accessory growth factors is to increase the reaction velocity of the proteolytic metabolism of the meningococcus."

After isolation from the body the organism was observed to develop a change in its metabolism so that it became increasingly independent of the growth accessories in the medium, old strains requiring no additional vitamin supply if an abundant supply of free amino acids was present. It is deemed probable that the main food requirements of the meningococcus are the amino acids.

Preliminary report on the relation of anaerobic organisms to forage poisoning, J. S. BUCKLEY and L. P. SHIPPEN (*Jour. Amer. Vet. Med. Assoc., 50* (*1917*), *No. 7, pp. 809–816*).—The resemblance of this disease in the horse to that of botulism or sausage poisoning in man led the authors to conduct experimental work with *Bacillus botulinus.*

Experiments with a strain of this organism isolated from cheese showed it to possess intense toxin-producing powers. *B. botulinus* grown in modified Rideal-Walker broth produced death in both small laboratory animals and horses and donkeys. When grown in a medium containing dextrose instead of lactose, under strict anaerobic conditions, it was fully as potent to produce death in both small laboratory animals and horses and donkeys as when grown in the modified Rideal-Walker broth.

"While the few symptoms exhibited by the donkey and horses that succumbed greatly resemble some of the characteristic symptoms of forage poisoning, and while the post-mortem findings are yet more characteristic of this disease, it will require further research to establish a definite relationship to the natural or spontaneous so-called forage poisoning. Certain it is that *B. botulinus* is capable of producing a form of forage poisoning should conditions exist in nature for the development of the organism and the elaboration of its toxin as on pastures or in masses of feed material. We can see no good reason why such a development may not take place. Symbiosis is probably the rule rather than the exception in the development of anaerobes in nature."

Pulmonary strongylosis, W. B. HERMS and S. B. FREEBORN (*Jour. Amer. Vet. Med. Assoc., 50* (*1917*), *No. 7, pp. 862–868*).—This has been substantially noted from another source (E. S. R., 35, p. 182).

Anthrax (charbon), W. H. DALRYMPLE (*Jour. Amer. Vet. Med. Assoc., 50* (*1917*), *No. 7, pp. 831–846, figs. 5*).—This paper, which was presented at the meeting of the Mississippi Veterinary Medical Association at Clarksdale, Miss., in January, 1917, relates particularly to the control and the possible eradication of anthrax. Data relating to the transmission of anthrax infection by insects, as based upon investigations by H. Morris at the Louisiana Experiment Stations, are briefly summarized.

Anthrax as an occupational disease, J. B. ANDREWS (*U. S. Dept. Labor, Bur. Labor Statis. Bul. 205* (*1917*), *pp. 155, pls. 11*).—Though anthrax is primarily a disease of animals, such as cattle and sheep, from which it is transmitted to man in a number of industrial pursuits, the present work deals with it particularly as affecting man.

Vaccinations against hemorrhagic septicemia, II, J. B. HARDENBERGH and F. BOERNER, JR. (*Jour. Amer. Vet. Med. Assoc., 50* (*1917*), *No. 7, pp. 868–876*).—Continuing the work previously noted (E. S. R., 35, p. 77), the authors have used the hemorrhagic septicemia vaccine in field work with promising results.

No standard animal test has been found for the vaccine other than that it is virulent for rabbits and guinea pigs, but not for sheep or calves. "Twenty-two recoveries among 23 vaccinated steers with but 12 recoveries among 25 native cattle on pasture seems to indicate a therapeutic value for the vaccine in chronic cases of hemorrhagic septicemia taking the form of pneumonia." Death within one week following vaccination of a few apparently healthy animals appears to indicate that sufficient immunity for protection is not developed within that time. It is indicated that the use of an antiserum simultaneously with a vaccine may eliminate such losses.

The work is being continued.

Transmission of pneumonic and septicemic plague among marmots, F. EBERSON and WU LIEN TEH (*Jour. Infect. Diseases, 20 (1917), No. 2, pp. 170–179*).—In two series of experiments a total of 38 marmots was exposed to plague, resulting in the death of 23.

"Of the marmots placed in contact with marmots which had received inoculation by inhalation, 52.6 per cent developed pulmonary plague and died on an average within from four to six days. Early infectivity on the part of the inoculated animals and a short incubation period characterize the transmission.

"Pulmonary plague can be transmitted readily to the small marmot (*Spermophilus citellus*), and these animals are capable, in turn, of transmitting the same disease through the respiratory passages.

"Septicemic plague can be developed in marmots very easily as a result of respiratory infection, and also by direct subcutaneous inoculation with small amounts of culture. The marmot can take plague by way of the alimentary tract and can spread the disease by feeding on plague-infected carcasses. The microscopic lesions observed in these cases are characteristic."

A digest of the insect transmission of disease in the Orient with especial reference to the experimental conveyance of Trypanosoma evansi, M. B. MITZMAIN (*New Orleans Med. and Surg. Jour., 69 (1916), No. 6, pp. 416–424*).— This summary is based upon the author's experience in the Philippines, reports relating to which have been previously noted (E. S. R., 30, p. 780; 31, p. 777).

The complement-fixation test in the diagnosis of tuberculosis, C. F. CRAIG (*Jour. Amer. Med. Assoc., 68 (1917), No. 10, pp. 773–776*).—The recent work on the complement-fixation test in tuberculosis is reviewed.

Continued observations by the author have led him to conclude that the complement-fixation test is the most valuable diagnostic method that has as yet been devised for the early recognition of the disease and the best index of its activity. A positive reaction with the test is considered to indicate the presence of an active tuberculous focus, and as long as the reaction remains positive the patient should not be considered cured. While a single negative result with the test can not indicate a cure or absence of the disease, repeated negative results extended over a considerable period of time should be sufficient evidence that the infection is cured or that the disease is not present, especially in instances in which the diagnosis is doubtful.

Some experimental data are reported and discussed.

On the biochemistry of the loss of power of the tubercle "bacillus" to stain with carbol fuchsin, A. H. MILLER (*Jour. Path. and Bact., 21 (1916), No. 1, pp. 41–46, pl. 1*).—From the study reported the variations encountered in the staining power of the tubercle bacillus with carbol fuchsin which has been grown on sperm and olive oil media depend upon the production of free oleic acid in the interior of the rod. This acid is considered to be formed by the round granules or spores of the organism.

The experimental procedures are described in detail.

Isolation of tubercle bacilli from sputum and determination of their type, CHUNG YIK WANG (*Jour. Path. and Bact., 21 (1916), No. 1, pp. 14–22, pl. 1*).— Of 29 strains of the tubercle bacilli isolated from sputum, 28 produced in the rabbit either no tuberculosis or a form similar to that produced by the bacilli of the human type. The remaining culture showed the well-marked characteristics of the "bovine" type and possessed a high virulence for rabbits.

A table showing the work on the subject by various investigators up to the present time is included. In 998 cases examined the human type was found in 991 instances, the bovine in 4, and 3 of the cases were mixed.

A bibliography of 21 references to the literature is appended.

An investigation of human bone and joint tuberculosis, A. S. GRIFFITH (*Jour. Path. and Bact., 21 (1916), No. 1, pp. 54–77*).—Of 155 cases of human bone and joint tuberculosis examined, 14 cases yielded negative results, 1 case was of multiple abscesses in the muscles, 4 cases were joint tuberculosis, in which cases the cultures were not isolated from the joint lesions but from tuberculous foci in other parts of the body, and in 136 cases cultures of tuberele bacilli were obtained from tuberculous bone or joint lesions. Of these cases 107 yielded human strains, 24 bovine, and 5 were atypical. The detailed clinical data and bacteriological results of the cases are reported in tabular form. The bacteriological characteristics of the tubercle bacilli isolated are discussed, and tabulated experimental data relative to experiments on the subcutaneous inoculation of rabbits with cultures isolated from various sources are reported.

The relative prevalence of human and bovine infection in bone and joint tuberculosis in different countries and at various age periods is discussed in some detail. The intimate connection between human and bovine tuberculosis and the danger to human beings, especially in childhood, of the consumption of living tubercle bacilli is emphasized. See also a previous note (E. S. R., 35, p. 576).

Some facts about abortion disease, E. C. SCHROEDER and W. E. COTTON (*U. S. Dept. Agr., Jour. Agr. Research, 9 (1917), No. 1, pp. 9–16*).—The data here presented have largely been noted from another source (E. S. R., 36, p. 881). The subject is dealt with under the headings of characteristics of the abortion bacillus, production of seemingly normal calves by infected cows, experimental infection introduced through the teat, the udder as a positive channel of infection, possibility of infection through the bull, and relation of the abortion bacillus to the embryo or fetus. The conclusions drawn are as follows:

" To prevent the further spread of abortion disease, owners of uninfected cattle should be instructed to have careful agglutination tests for abortion disease made of all cattle they propose to introduce into their herds; and owners of infected herds should be taught that aborted fetuses, also the afterbirth and discharge from the vaginas of infected cows, are infected with abortion bacilli and must therefore be disposed of with care. •

" The treatment of individual cows which have aborted or failed to clean properly after parturition must be left largely to the good judgment of the practicing veterinarian. If the uterus is given a proper chance to heal after it has been damaged by an abortion or a retained afterbirth, the abortion bacilli in it need occasion little worry, as they will rapidly disappear of their own accord, and it is very questionable whether reparative processes are not retarded rather than facilitated by douching with germicidal solutions which are strong enough to kill bacteria in a reasonable length of time, or the length of time during which they may remain undiluted in the uterus. Douching is no doubt good practice, but it is desirable that there be a flooding out, a washing out, a real physical cleaning of the uterus; and this can best be done with solutions which are healing rather than germicidal, soothing, and not irritating."

Further investigations into the etiology of worm' nests in cattle due to Onchocerca gibsoni, II, J. B. CLELAND, S. DODD, and E. W. FERGUSON (*Melbourne, Aust.: Govt. [1917], pp. 41*).—This communication gives the details of investigations carried on from 1913 to the end of October, 1915, in continuation of those previously noted (E. S. R., 32, p. 377), together with the deductions drawn. The authors summarize the results obtained and the views which they now hold in regard to the transmission of *O. gibsoni* as follows:

" Conveyance of *O. gibsoni* from one bovine to another in the open is still taking place at Milson Island. Experiments with large numbers of Stomoxys, under conditions in which transference of Onchocerca might be expected to take place, supposing this insect to be the vector, failed to convey infection. This renders it apparently unlikely that *S. calcitrans* is the vector. Similar experiments of a less satisfactory nature with mosquitoes failed to convey infection. Transmission by mosquitoes can not, however, as yet be ruled out of court. A control calf protected in a fly- and mosquito-proof cage failed to become infected with Onchocerca. A calf, penned in an earthen floored cage, in the open, level with the ground, and exposed to the attacks of mosquitoes, Stomoxys, and tabanids showed the presence of a worm nest. In one of the stock animals examined, an arrested 'traveling' worm, 2.5 to 3 in. long, was found in a delicate fibrous tunnel. Circumstantial evidence appears to indicate that a tabanid may be the vector, which is supported to some extent by the apparent distribution of worm nests and of tabanids in Australia. Worm nests are more common in local cattle in the Sydney and Newcastle districts than was anticipated."

Shipping fever of horses, J. R. MOHLER (*Jour. Amer. Vet. Med. Assoc., 50* (*1917*), *No. 7, pp. 817–823*).—This paper, presented at the meeting of the American Veterinary Medical Association held at Detroit, Mich., in August, 1916, has been substantially noted (E. S. R., 36, p. 85).

Vesicular stomatitis contagiosa, J. GREGG, F. X. McGUIRE, G. J. GLOVER, A. GILLESPIE, and G. GREGORY (*Amer. Jour. Vet. Med., 12* (*1917*), *No. 4, pp. 221, 222*).—This account of the disease is based upon observations during the last four months of several thousand cases in horses and mules at the remount hospitals at Newport News, Va. The authors describe it as a contagious, febrile disease affecting horses and mules, with the principal pathological changes confined to the tongue, buccal mucous membrane, lips, and occasionally the nose. A large gram-positive micrococcus was obtained in pure culture by withdrawing the material, under aseptic conditions, from unruptured vesicles occurring chiefly on the tongue. One attack appears to render an immunity.

So-called staggers in horses caused by the ingestion of Pteris aquilina, the common bracken, S. HADWEN (*Jour. Amer. Vet. Med. Assoc., 50* (*1917*), *No. 6, pp. 702–704*).—The death of many horses during January and February, 1916, from what farmers have commonly known as staggers led to an investigation. It appears that cases of this disease may be found in every country district along the banks of the Fraser River and on Vancouver Island. The author's experiments show that it can be reproduced by feeding bracken fern in both winter and summer, and the designation "bracken poisoning" is proposed for the affection.

A case of splenic abscess, secondary to invasion of the stomach wall of a horse by Spiroptera megastoma, C. G. DICKENSON (*Vet. Jour., 73* (*1917*), *No. 502, pp. 14, 15*).—The case here reported is said to be the first to come to the author's attention in which a splenic abscess has been found as a secondary infection.

Bacillary white diarrhea or fatal septicemia of chicks and coccidiosis or coccidial enteritis of chicks, J. R. BEACH (*California Sta. Circ. 162* (*1917*), *pp. 8*).—It is stated that in California coccidiosis is very prevalent while outbreaks of bacillary white diarrhea are comparatively infrequent. In none of the outbreaks of coccidiosis investigated by the station have there been any symptoms or history which might be confused with those of bacillary white diarrhea. In the present paper the author deals with the two diseases separately and attempts to describe them in such a manner as to avoid any confusion regarding their identity.

The use of bacterins in the control of fowl cholera, W. B. MACK and E. RECORDS (*Nevada Sta. Bul. 85 (1916), pp. 3-29*).—Eleven strains of *Bacterium avisepticum* isolated from outbreaks of fowl cholera in Nevada were found to possess a comparatively low degree of virulence for chickens in laboratory tests. " No strain behaved uniformly as to the time required to kill when inoculated into chickens; some birds failed to succumb to inoculation. The virulence for chickens could not be maintained by frequent passages through either rabbits or chickens; and no strain could be depended upon to kill by oral administration."

The bacterin was prepared by growing cultures of *B. avisepticum* on agar for 48 hours, washing with normal salt solution, and diluting to a content of 500,000,000 bacteria per cubic centimeter, or by growing in neutral plain bouillon. The organisms were killed by the addition of from 0.5 to 0.9 per cent phenol.

Three subcutaneous inoculations of the bacterin failed to immunize chickens against subsequent subcutaneous or intramuscular inoculations of the virulent organism. In 15 out of 16 lots of fowls in 14 flocks the use of the bacterin produced sufficient resistance to check promptly outbreaks of fowl cholera, although in one lot there was a recurrence requiring three treatments. The treatment of the other lot resulted in complete failure.

No apparent difference was observed in the use of homologous or heterologous strains of the organism in the bacterins. The use of a stock bacterin containing several strains appears to be satisfactory. It is indicated that " the value of a protective method must be judged by clinical rather than by experimental results."

The cultural characteristics, variation in virulence, and both laboratory and field inoculation data are submitted in tabular form.

The case of Trichomonas, P. [B.] HADLEY (*Amer. Nat., 51 (1917), No. 604, pp. 209-224, figs. 12*).—Substantially noted from another source (E. S. R., 36, p. 483).

RURAL ENGINEERING.

Irrigation enterprise in the United States: Introductory paper, C. E. GRUNSKY (*Trans. Internat. Engin. Cong., 1915, Waterways and Irrig., pp. 342-370*).—This paper outlines the various ways in which irrigation enterprises have been handled and constructed by landowners; by private owners, usually corporations, for profit; under the Desert Land Act; under the Carey Act; under the U. S. Reclamation Act; and under State irrigation district laws. Irrigation statistics and a bibliography are appended.

Present condition of irrigation in Argentina, C. WAUTERS (*Trans. Internat. Engin. Cong., 1915, Waterways and Irrig., pp. 672-687*).—This paper deals mainly with the legal, administrative, and economic phases of irrigation in Argentina.

Irrigation in Spain: Distribution systems, methods, and appliances, J. C. STEVENS (*Trans. Internat. Engin. Cong., 1915, Waterways and Irrig., pp. 643-656, figs. 4*).—This is a brief general description of distribution systems, methods, and appliances.

Irrigation in Spain: Regulations controlling the use of water, metering water for irrigation, and methods of charging, J. C. STEVENS (*Trans. Internat. Engin. Cong., 1915, Waterways and Irrig., pp. 657-671*).—This paper deals with the regulations controlling the use of water, metering water for irrigation, and methods of charging.

Italian irrigation, L. LUIGGI (*Trans. Internat. Engin. Cong., 1915, Waterways and Irrig., pp. 530-582, figs. 35*).—The author, in dealing with irrigation in Italy, concludes that " irrigation is decidedly most beneficial to the farmer.

Besides acting as an insurance against failure of crops in bad years, it generally doubles or more than doubles the normal crops, or it permits of the cultivation of crops of higher commercial value. It represents also a very important factor of progress for the district in which it is applied. But it is not equally beneficial for the corporations that carry out the irrigation works, because generally many years are required before all the water can be disposed of and thus there is a dead loss for a period of about 20 years, or even more, during which the State must grant some subsidy. . . . It is only just that the State should either carry out these works at its own expense or grant some substantial financial help to encourage irrigation projects."

A bibliography is included.

Irrigation in Libia, L. Luiggi (*Trans. Internat. Engin. Cong., 1915, Waterways and Irrig., pp. 583–590, figs. 4*).—This is a brief general description of irrigation as practiced in Libia. It is stated that the future of Libia depends on the development of agriculture aided by irrigation.

The distribution of water in irrigation in Australia, E. Mead (*Trans. Internat. Engin. Cong., 1915, Waterways and Irrig., pp. 611–642, pl. 1, figs. 7*).—The purpose of this paper is to describe the methods employed and the results obtained in distributing water for irrigation in Australia, special reference being made to water measurement devices.

Recent developments of irrigation in India, M. Nethersole (*Trans. Internat. Engin. Cong., 1915, Waterways and Irrig., pp. 591–610, pls. 4*).—This article enumerates the natural factors dominating irrigation progress in India, and describes irrigation methods and some of the more important irrigation works. Of the 220,000,000 acres annually cultivated in India, it is stated that about 41,000,000 are irrigated.

"The development of irrigation in [the decade ended with 1912], measured by the difference in the first and last totals, is about 25 per cent, while measured by the increase in the average for the last five years over that of the first five years of the period it is about 20 per cent. . . . The classification of the 41,000,000 acres irrigated in 1912 is approximately as follows: From government canals 42, private canals 5, tanks 13, wells 25, and other sources 15 per cent. . . .

"Irrigation from wells ranks in area and importance next to irrigation from government works. Irrigation wells are wholly the private property of the landowners, but construction is encouraged by the grant of temporary advances from public funds to the owners, which advances with interest at 4 per cent are recoverable by easy installments. The government further assists this class of irrigation by the loan to the owners of boring plants and the services of expert borers, both to make preliminary tests of the subsoil supply and to improve the supply in existing wells by tapping deeper water-bearing strata."

Economic advisability of irrigation, F. H. Newell (*Trans. Internat. Engin. Cong., 1915, Waterways and Irrig., pp. 371–397*).—It is pointed out in this paper that "irrigation is of prime economic importance to the community, State, and nation by enabling a complete agricultural development of the arid lands and by insuring immunity from loss by drought on other lands, thus making possible intensive cultivation and a maximum annual crop production. The material benefits to the community are not measured by the crop production alone, but by the stimulation of other industries, such as stock raising, mining, manufacturing, and transportation. A still greater benefit to the nation, rising far above material wealth, is that coming from the increase of an intelligent and prosperous rural population, who are not merely producers of food for other people, but who, living in the open, contribute most largely to the best elements of citizenship.

"The stagnation which now prevails in irrigation development is due to lack of proper recognition by engineers and investors of the fundamental economic conditions governing the profits of the individual irrigator, and can be relieved only when these conditions are more fully recognized and used as guides in future projects."

The utilization of ground waters by pumping for irrigation, G. E. P. Smith (*Trans. Internat. Engin. Cong., 1915, Waterways and Irrig., pp. 414–457, figs. 7*).—This paper has been previously noted from another source (E. S. R., 35, p. 787).

Distribution systems, methods, and appliances in irrigation, J. S. Dennis, H. B. Muckleston, and R. S. Stockton (*Trans. Internat. Engin. Cong., 1915, Waterways and Irrig., pp. 398–413*).—This paper consists of a discussion of the factors making for success in an irrigation system, which are enumerated as (1) a sufficient water supply, (2) good construction, and (3) a well organized system for transporting and delivering water to the settler. General features of design, construction, and maintenance of distribution systems are described. It is concluded "that the most important part of the distribution system is the farmer who is to use it. If the man is not successful, the project is a failure."

Duty of water in irrigation, S. Fortier (*Trans. Internat. Engin. Cong., 1915, Waterways and Irrig., pp. 458–509, figs. 3*).—The author discusses the legal, administrative, economic, and agricultural phases of duty of water in irrigation. The discussion is confined to the practice and conditions prevailing throughout the irrigated districts of the United States, and consists largely of a review and summary of the important features of investigations previously reported, especially those conducted under the author's supervision by the Irrigation Investigations of the U. S. Department of Agriculture.

Use of water in irrigation, S. Fortier (*New York: McGraw-Hill Book Co., 1916, 2. ed., pp. XVI+325, pls. 12, figs. 77*).—This is the second edition of this book (E. S. R., 32, p. 389) in which "the typographical and other minor errors of the first edition have been corrected, the article on the measurement of water revised and enlarged, and a new article added on sewage irrigation." The most important change in the revision consists in the addition of a new chapter on the use of water in foreign countries, including irrigation in Italy, Spain, France, Russia, Egypt, South Africa, India, Java, Japan, the Philippine Islands, Australia, western Canada, the Hawaiian Islands, Argentina, northern Brazil, Colombia, Peru, and Siam.

The article on sewage irrigation deals with experience, especially in southern California. In one case at Redlands "the sewage is conducted through the farm lands in underground sewer pipe and delivered to the fields through a modern hydrant system. The soil is a light sandy loam, naturally well drained. but not extremely absorbent. The principal crop irrigated is orange trees, which receive from 3 to 6 in. of sewage at intervals of 30 days, with the exception of the dormant season when the sewage is used on barley and oat land for its fertilizing value. Furrow irrigation is the only system of application used on all crops, and cultivation follows as closely as possible after irrigation. . . . The success of the Redlands disposal is principally due to the efficient system of distribution, the farm management of the sewage used, the very favorable natural conditions, and sufficient land."

In another case at Santa Ana "the raw sewage is distributed through a system of concrete pipe lines and valves to lands upon which sugar beets are grown. The soils vary from a heavy loam to a very light sandy loam. Two irrigations are used during the growth of a crop on the heavy lands, while as high as six are applied on the sandy lands during growth." Sterile sandy lands have been built up with Santa Ana sewage by applications of approximately 8 in. every 30 days for two years before planting to sugar beets to maintain the fertility. It is estimated in this case that "sewage irrigation increases the yield of beets 3 to 4 tons per acre over clear-water irrigation. . . .

"The sewage farm should be considered as a large receiving bed and a part of the purification system, upon portions of which the sewage is intermittently spread and where purifying takes place through the action of the soil bacteria and sunlight. For this reason an efficient distribution system on the farm is as important as any part of the plant. Every small stream of sewage should be under absolute control and a rotation of irrigation followed which will not overload any portion of the land and hinder the purification processes or the growth of crops. The bacteria dangerous to health may be destroyed by chemical treatment of the effluent from septic tanks, but this should not be necessary if proper precaution is taken to prevent the sewage getting into drinking water or coming into contact with vegetables which are to be eaten without cooking. . . .

"One of the chief causes of failure in sewage irrigation in the United States is the lack of proper irrigation construction and management on the farm. Open ditches still unfortunately prevail on sewage farms. These ditches are the greatest source of offensive odors due to the dangerous accumulations of putrefying matters which collect wherever there are weeds, pockets, or dead ends. Seepage from earthen ditches is apt to be large in porous soils and dangerous to the public health. The continuous control of sewage in ditches and an efficient division into irrigation units can best be obtained with a pipe and hydrant system. . . . The management of the sewage irrigated farm is a vital and serious problem upon which the success of the project depends."

Irrigation studies, Ontario and Covina [California], R. S. VAILE (*Cal. Citrogr., 2 (1917), No. 5, pp. 9, 10, figs. 3*).—Irrigation experiments with citrus orchards on comparatively open gravelly soil with a very pervious subsoil of coarse gravel at from 3 to 8 ft. are reported. The following conclusions were drawn as to economic methods of irrigation on these soils:

"Irrigation districts should be so far reorganized as to accommodate more frequent delivery of water to users. It is somewhat doubtful if more total water may be used to advantage provided the interval is reduced, although the data submitted does not entirely establish this point. Neither is it clear that 15 days is necessarily the correct interval. . . . Shorter furrows should be provided as rapidly as economic conditions justify."

It is further considered advisable to mulch the lower few rows of trees to prevent run-off and conserve moisture at that point.

Drainage as a correlative of irrigation, C. G. ELLIOTT (*Trans. Internat. Engin. Cong., 1915, Waterways and Irrig., pp. 510–529, figs. 7*).—It is the purpose of this paper to correlate the practices of irrigation and drainage "and, particularly, to show the methods of draining wet lands under irrigation as now successfully practiced in this country." Special attention is given to the work of the Drainage Investigations of the U. S. Department of Agriculture along this line, as formerly conducted under the supervision of the author.

Flood control for Pecatonica River (*Ill. Rivers and Lakes Com. Bul. 18 (1916), pp. 33, pls. 2, figs. 22*).—This bulletin is compiled from the results of investigations made by the Illinois Rivers and Lakes Commission and the U. S. Geological Survey into the flood conditions of the Pecatonica Valley.

It is concluded "that the river, in its natural state, spreads out over the whole valley during flood periods, and the tendency is toward a general increase of flood height and property damage due to the silting up of the channel and the encroachments of civilization. The benefits to be derived from a general project designed to prevent the inundation of the bottom lands of the valley as a whole would not, at the present time, be commensurate with the cost of such work, but the annual damage sustained at Freeport and vicinity is sufficient to warrant the outlay necessary to protect that city against a flood flow of 21,000 cu. ft. per second, or nearly 25 per cent greater than that of March 28, 1916. This protection can best be accomplished by providing channel area sufficient to carry a flood of 21,000 cu. ft. per second with a slope of approximately 0.5 ft. per mile . . . and where necessary constructing levees to protect the low sections against overflow. The required cross section can be most economically obtained by constructing an auxiliary channel."

Tests indicate drain tile beddings increase strength (*Engin. Rec., 75 (1917), No. 12, pp. 459, 460*).—This is an abstract of a paper presented by W. J. Schlick before the American Concrete Pipe Association, in which tests made at the Iowa Engineering Experiment Station are reported. These consisted of bedding 24-in. drain and sewer tile in shallow trenches and then loading them through a standard upper sand bedding. It was found that an increase in strength of 25 per cent may be obtained by careful earth bedding and as much as 90 per cent by certain forms of concrete bedding, especially in solid soils.

Report of hydrometric surveys (stream measurements), 1915, F. H. PETERS, P. M. SAUDER, ET AL. (*Dept. Int. Canada, Irrig. Branch Rpt. Hydromet. Surveys, 1915, pp. V+590, pls. 13, figs. 10*).—This report presents the results of measurements of flow made on streams, irrigation ditches, and canals in Alberta and Saskatchewan during 1915.

Water supply, W. P. MASON (*New York: John Wiley & Sons, 1916, 4. ed., rev., pp. X+528, pl. 1, figs. 129; rev. in Engin. News, 76 (1916), No. 25, p. 1181; Amer. Jour. Pub. Health, 7 (1917), No. 2, p. 197*).—This book contains chapters on drinking water and disease; artificial purification of water; natural purification of water; rain, ice, and snow; river and stream water; stored water; ground water; deep-seated water; quantity of per capita daily supply; and action of water upon metals. Appendixes are included on analyses of sea waters, rights and duties regarding the pollution of streams, and typhoid fever contracted from drinking polluted water decided to be " an accident."

In the chapter on drinking water, considerable space is devoted to the distribution of typhoid fever and factors operating in its transmission. Newly developed methods of water purification, particularly processes aiming at disinfection, are considered, as are also certain recently discovered factors influencing natural purification in streams and stored waters. The use of chlorin, ozone, ultra-violet light, and copper sulphate receive a good deal of attention, and considerable space is also devoted to a discussion of various phases of the pollution of drinking water supplies and the care of watersheds.

Makawao waterworks for rural supply, J. B. Cox (*Engin. News, 77 (1917), No. 8, pp. 310–312, figs. 2*).—This is a description of a county water supply for a rural district in Hawaii, which is maintained under tropical conditions.

A simple method of water analysis, J. C. THRESH (*London: J. & A. Churchill, 1915, 8. ed., pp. 69*).—This book describes methods and equipment necessary for simple chemical analysis of water and describes the chlorin method of water purification, especially for residential or camp supplies.

Direct microscopical counting of bacteria in water, B. E. NELSON (*Jour. Amer. Chem. Soc., 39 (1917), No. 3, pp. 515–523, fig. 1*).—Experiments are reported, from which it is concluded that " direct microscopical counts of bacteria in water may be made in from 20 to 40 minutes and allow of the examination of other microorganisms at the same time."

It was found that "these counts are fully more accurate than those by the plate method, although not directly comparable with them. The centrifugal method of concentrating the bacteria after 'flocking' is the most rapid, but is less efficient and accurate than filtration. The morphological character of the organisms themselves, rather than the appearance of their growth, is considered in judging their possible general characteristics. These total counts are in no sense intended to supersede the specific cultural and other tests for *Bacillus coli* or other individual groups of organisms."

Bile compared with lactose bouillon for determining the presence of Bacillus coli in water, MAUD M. OBST (*Jour. Bact.*, 1 (1916), No. 1, pp. 73–79).— Experiments are reported in which it was found that lactose bouillon used as a substitute for lactose peptone ox-bile permitted the development of about twice as many *B. coli* from 191 samples of water as the bile medium.

"The bile was never used later than a week after collection. It was sterilized upon receipt and stored during this period at a temperature of 1° C. It was enriched with 1 per cent lactose and 1 per cent peptone and tubed in Dunham tubes. The lactose bouillon was made from neutral nutrient broth prepared with 0.5 per cent Liebig's meat extract, 1 per cent peptone, and 1 per cent lactose. . . .

"Lactose bouillon cost less in money and labor. The difficulty of obtaining pure, fresh bile puts it almost out of the reach of many workers. The stored bile proved to show progressive deterioration. Lactose bouillon can be prepared when desired and can be made more uniform. It need contain no precipitate to clog the inner tube or to affect the activity of the organism."

Septic tank, L. C. HART and G. C. JONES (*Ga. State Col. Agr. Circ. 41* (1917), pp. 7, figs. 5).—This circular briefly describes and illustrates a septic tank made of 24-in. terra cotta pipe. A tile absorption area for final disposal is recommended.

Report of the joint committee on Federal aid in the construction of post roads (*U. S. House Representatives, 63. Cong., 3. Sess., Doc. 1510 (1915), pp. 317, pls. 3*).—This is the first report of the joint committee on Federal aid in the construction of post roads. It contains the following chapters:

Importance of good roads and Federal aid; desirability of congressional control; review of committee's work; data from foreign countries; data from the several States; tonnage transported over rural roads; rural free delivery roads; special transportation rates on material for road improvement; comparative statistics bearing upon Federal aid apportionment; statistics of wealth, debt, highway expenditures, etc.; comparative statistics on cost of road construction; the old Cumberland Road; instruction in highway and bridge engineering; synopsis of good-roads bills introduced in the Sixty-third Congress; and record on congressional action.

Two final chapters give a table showing comparative statistics on road systems of foreign countries and a bibliography. A financial statement is appended.

Highway traffic analysis and traffic census procedure, W. H. CONNELL. (*West. Engin., 8 (1917), No. 3, pp. 96–102, figs. 4*).—This article outlines the procedure in the collection, classification, analysis, and application of traffic census data in their relations to the planning of a highway, the design and maintenance of pavements, the cleaning of highways, and traffic regulations.

A standard of carbureter performance, O. C. BERRY (*Gas Engine, 19 (1917), No. 4, pp. 196–200, figs. 5*).—Tests on the proper carburetion of petroleum fuels, conducted at Purdue University, are reported.

It is concluded that "a wide range of mixtures of gasoline vapor and air can be used in an engine to give regular firing in all of the cylinders. At half-load and mid-speed on an automobile engine any mixture between 0.055 and 0.155 lb. of gasoline per pound of dry air can be fired, and practically full power will be developed between the limits of 0.065 and 0.115 lb. The highest power will be developed with a mixture of about 0.08, while the best efficiency will accompany the theoretically perfect mixture of 0.0671 lb.

"A change of engine speed apparently does not affect the mixture at which the best power or the best efficiency will be realized, or the ability of the engine to use the leaner mixture, but at the higher speeds a smaller amount of excess gasoline can be used successfully. A change of load does not noticeably affect the points of highest power or efficiency, but at the higher loads a wider range of extreme mixtures can be used. The engine can run idle with as wide a range of mixtures as it can when pulling a good load."

Rural electric service profitable in Wisconsin (*Elect. World, 69 (1917), No. 12, pp. 565, 566*).—This is an abstract of a report by F. C. Babson before the Wisconsin Electrical Association, in which the findings and opinions of the 1916 committee on rural electrical service were summarized as follows:

"(1) The construction of purely rural-service lines is not ordinarily warranted unless the saturation of service is such that a reasonable return on the added investment and sale of energy may be shown. (2) Rural-service consumers on transmission lines of not over 6,600 volts connecting towns or villages are ordinarily profitable if a suitable minimum charge is made. (3) A suitable minimum charge to cover the higher cost of service for rural consumers should be made, variously estimated at from $2 to $3 per month. (4) A low second step in the energy rate should be provided so as to encourage a sufficient use of the service by the farmer to make it practical and attractive."

Wet weather dryers for hay, H. HITIER (*Jour. Agr. Prat., n. ser., 29 (1916), No. 17, pp. 289, 290, fig. 1*).—A device is described and illustrated to be used as a framework upon which to stack hay in damp weather so that it will dry properly.

RURAL ECONOMICS.

The economic history of American agriculture as a field for study, L. B. SCHMIDT (*Miss. Valley Hist. Rev., 3 (1916), No. 1, pp. 39–49*).—The author points out that this phase of history has not hitherto received the attention at the hands of historians which its importance merits. He has attempted to define the economic history of agriculture as a field for study and to review some of the reasons why special attention should be directed to this field, and suggests some of the more important problems which this field offers for investigation.

Control factors in agricultural development, J. A. BONSTEEL (*Univ. Cal. Jour. Agr., 4 (1917), No. 6, pp. 183, 184, 201*).—The author has classified the different factors influencing agricultural production under the head of climate, soil, markets, and human efficiency. He points out that the first two factors are reasonably constant and unchangeable while the other two are purely artificial and change rapidly. He points out some of the adjustments which are necessary in farming for it to keep up with changes in the marketing conditions and in the efficiency of the farming population.

Country planning, E. A. WAUGH (*Amer. Civic Assoc. [Pub.], 2 ser., No. 8 (1916), pp. 13*).—The author points out some of the problems to be solved in country planning, as well as methods of meeting them and organizing the rural communities. He also outlines the purposes, problems, and methods in detail.

The Torrens Land Transfer Act of Nebraska, T. A. Browne (*Nebr.* [*Univ.*] *Hist. and Polit. Sci. Ser. Bul. 10 (1916), pp. 60, pl. 1, figs. 5*).—The bulletin gives a brief historical sketch and detailed description of the Nebraska Torrens law, and arguments for and against the system as a permanent provision. The author also calls attention to the provisions of the Torrens law in the different States and compares it with other systems of land transfer. A bibliography is appended.

The Land-Title Registration Act of the State of New York (*Albany, N. Y.: State, 1916, 2. ed., pp. 87*).—This booklet gives, in convenient form, the land title registration statutes of New York, and a statement of the aim and methods of the Torrens system as adopted and available to landowners in New York State. The complete text of the statutes is included, as well as an introduction by D. Viele and J. C. Beacher.

Land settlement in California (*Trans. Commonwealth Club Cal., 11 (1916), No. 8, pp. 369-465*).—In this report are included papers by F. Adams on land settlement, by E. Mead on colonization in California, by R. L. Adams on financial considerations of California agriculture. and by E. E. Cox on farm tenantry in California. These papers are accompanied by a discussion.

Report of the commission on land colonization and rural credits of the State of California (*Sacramento, Cal.: State, 1916, pp. 87*).—This report contains a discussion of land colonization conditions in California, the methods of land settlement enterprises, the condition of settlers in colonies recently established, and the problem of tenantry and farm labor, together with a discussion of the methods and policy of land colonization in other countries.

The commission advises that there should be State supervision of settlement, to provide that adequate attention be given to water supplies and drainage in irrigated areas, that the land be suited for the purpose for which it is being sold, and that there be no misrepresentation in the advertising. It is also suggested that from 20 to 30 years be allowed to pay for the land, and that, after the initial payment, no further payments on principal be required for the first two years. The contract should, however, stipulate the character of the improvements which must be made. It also recommends that the payments on the land be on the amortization system and the amount of annual or semiannual payments be equal throughout the entire period.

Minutes of evidence taken before the departmental committee appointed by the president of the Board of Agriculture and Fisheries to consider the settlement and employment on the land in England and Wales of discharged sailors and soldiers (*Dept. Com. Land Settlement Sailors and Soldiers* [*London*], *Minutes of Evidence, 1916, pp. IV+399*).—The minutes of evidence discussed in the report previously noted (E. S. R., 36, p. 290).

Agricultural Argentina, J. R. Pickell (*Chicago: J. Rosenbaum Grain Co., [1917], pp. 124, figs. 50*).—The author has set forth his observations of the people, methods of producing and distributing agricultural products, and rural housing conditions.

[Farming and farm labor conditions in North Carolina] (*Ann. Rpt. Dept. Labor and Print. N. C., 30 (1916). pp. 16-29*).—These pages continue the data previously noted (E. S. R., 35, p. 589), adding data for 1916.

Amount and cost of labor required for growing crops in West Virginia, O. M. Johnson and A. J. Dadisman (*West Virginia Sta. Bul. 163 (1916), pp. 3-11, fig. 1*).—The data upon which this study is based was obtained by visiting farmers in 12 counties in different parts of West Virginia. From 15 to 30 records on each crop were taken in each county. The amount and cost of labor have been summarized as follows

Amount and cost of labor in growing crops in West Virginia.

Kind o crop.	Yield per acre.	Man days.	Horse days.	Total cost.
Corn	40.4 bushels	5.71	4.20	$12.86
Wheat	18.4 bushels	2.31	3.36	6.83
Oats	31.6 bushels	2.29	2.84	6.28
Hay	1.27 tons	.81	.71	1.91
Potatoes	154.6 bushels	10.17	8.24	23.49
Buckwheat	24.8 bushels	2.91	2.98	7.34
Tobacco	985 pounds	37.76	5.31	61.95

With the exception of hay the cost refers to the expense of growing and harvesting. In the case of hay it refers simply to the expense of harvesting. The man labor has been valued at 15 cts. per hour and horse labor at 10 cts. per hour for ten-hour days.

Women agricultural workers in Germany *(Dept. Agr. and Tech. Instr. Ireland Jour., 17 (1917), No. 2, pp. 225–241).*—This article describes the extent of the employment of women in agriculture, the type of farm work performed, social conditions among women agricultural workers, wages, and special education and organizations for their benefit.

Second annual report of the cooperative organization branch, 1915–16, W. W. THOMSON *(Saskatchewan Dept. Agr., Ann. Rpt. Coop. Organ. Branch, 2 (1915–16), pp. 30).*—This report gives, for the Province of Saskatchewan, a list of the cooperative organizations, together with the extent of their business; also a brief description of the special accomplishments of the various types of associations during the year.

Monthly crop report *(U. S. Dept. Agr., Mo. Crop Rpt., 3 (1917), No. 4, pp. 29–36, fig. 1).*—This number contains the usual data regarding the estimated value of important products and the range of products at important markets. Data are also given concerning the condition of farm animals on April 1 and the estimated loss during the year, the condition of winter wheat and rye, and the preliminary estimates on the early cabbage, strawberry, and potato crops. There are likewise special reports on the portion of the total corn crop that is of marketable quality, the estimated value per acre of farm lands with and without improvements, the apple production and value by varieties, number of gas tractors in commission on farms, and a comparison of the increase in population, the production of 12 of the leading crops, the per capita production, and other data.

Ohio agricultural statistics, 1915–16 *(Ohio Agr. Statis., 1915–16, pp. 75).*—This report continues the information previously noted (E. S. R., 35, p. 497).

[Agricultural statistics for the United Kingdom, 1901–1915] *(Statis. Abs. United Kingdom, 1901–1915, pp. 308–321).*—These pages continue the information previously noted (E. S. R., 34, p. 792).

[Agricultural statistics of Spain] *(Bol. Agr. Téc. y Econ., 9 (1917), No. 97, pp. 24–43).*—These pages contain data showing by minor geographic divisions the production of principal crops for 1916, with comparative data for earlier years.

[Agriculture and live stock in Sweden] *(Sveriges Off. Statis., Jordbr. och Boskapsskötsel, 1914, pp. IV+38; 1915, pp. IV+38).*—These reports continue the information previously noted (E. S. R., 37, p. 93).

[Agricultural statistics of Java and Madura] *(Jaarc. Konink. Nederlanden, Koloniën, 1914, pp. 70–82).*—This report continues the data previously noted (E. S. R., 36, p. 594) adding data for 1914.

AGRICULTURAL EDUCATION.

[Agricultural and home economics instruction] (*Nat. Soc. Prom. Indus. Ed. Bul. 22 (1916), pp. 173-195, 212-225, 271-277, 291-324*).—The following papers, presented at the 1916 meeting of the National Society for the Promotion of Industrial Education, are included: Home Economics Training as Related to Vocational Work, by Abby Marlatt and Lilla Frich, respectively; Vocational Significance of Domestic Art in the Schools, by Carrie L. Wilkerson; The Training of the Teacher of Household Arts for the Vocational School, by Anna M. Cooley; Business of Home-Making, by Mrs. Harvey M. Hickok; Significance of the Survey to the Vocational Training of Girls in Minneapolis, by Elizabeth Fish; Shop Methods and the Utilization of Product [at the Manhattan Trade School for Girls], by Violet Coen; Trade Extension and Part-time Courses for Girls in New York City, by Florence M. Marshall; Provision for Commercial Experience During the Period of Training [by the Womens' Educational and Industrial Union, Boston], by Antoinette Roof; Apprentice Teacher Training [in Agriculture], by G. A. Works; The Status of Teacher-Training for Agriculture in the United States, by A. C. Monahan; The Home Project as the Center *v.* the Home Project as the Outgrowth of Agricultural Instruction, by C. G. Selvig, previously noted (E. S. R., 35, p. 298); and Plans and Records of Home Project Instruction, by L. S. Hawkins.

Agriculture and the public schools, L. H. DENNIS (*Ann. Rpt. Penn. Dept. Agr., 21 (1915), pp. 249-263*).—This is an illustrated lecture, in which the author discusses the problem of the agricultural leader and the three different types of secondary schools of agriculture, viz, the congressional district and the county agricultural schools and the agricultural department in an existing high school. He finds that the advantages of the latter are chiefly that it is near to the homes of the pupils, and it is not necessary to purchase and operate a school farm. The school farm is objected to mainly because it is very apt to be run under conditions that are not natural, so that the experience gained on such a farm does not always compare favorably with that gained in home-project work. "Descriptive notes are given on work at individual schools in explanation of lantern slides shown.

Vocational secondary education (*U. S. Bur. Ed. Bul. 21 (1916), pp. 163*).— This report was prepared by the committee on vocational education of the National Education Association with the object of assisting the average superintendent of schools in a community of ordinary size in introducing such work, where needed, into his home school system. The report deals with the history and development, definitions, analysis, and illustrative examples of vocational secondary education, including agricultural and home economics education, types of vocational secondary schools, some ways in which vocational education may be introduced, methods of organization, proper methods of financing, problems, etc. A digest of laws of States that provide State aid for a more or less State-wide system of education is appended.

Vocational agricultural education, L. H. DENNIS (*Ann. Rpt. Penn. Dept. Agr., 21 (1915), pp. 429-445*).—Notes accompanying an illustrated lecture to show what Pennsylvania is doing along the lines of vocational education in the secondary schools of the rural districts are presented.

A special report to the board of visitors of the Virginia Military Institute on the history of agricultural education in Virginia and the Virginia Military Institute as a school of agriculture, including a sketch of the physical survey of Virginia by the School of Applied Science, J. C. WISE ([*Lexington*], *Va.: Author, 1914, pp. 34*).—The author reviews the history of agricultural education in Virginia, including an account of the establishment and development of agricultural instruction at the Virginia Military Institute, at Lexington, followed by the founding of the Hampton Normal and Agricultural School for colored students and the Virginia Agricultural and Mechanical College at Blacksburg.

The district agricultural schools of Georgia, C. H. LANE and D. J. CROSBY (*U. S. Bur. Ed. Bul. 44 (1916), pp. 32*).—The authors give a brief history of the establishment of the district agricultural schools of Georgia, detailed descriptions of (1) the school plant and equipment of a typical school, with brief notes on special features of the other schools, and (2) the course in agriculture and domestic science. Statistical data with reference to enrollment of students, farms, farm crops, and animals of the various schools, a financial statement for 1911–12, and the text of the act creating the schools are appended.

Seventh annual report of **the eleven district agricultural** schools of Georgia, J. S. STEWART (*Bul. Ga. State Col. Agr., No. 109 (1916), pp. 36*).—This bulletin contains the minutes of the fifth annual meeting of the principals of the district agricultural schools, held April 28, 1916, the organization lists of the schools, reports of improvements and special features for the year at each school, the new curriculum adopted in May, 1915, the revised course of study for 1916–17, a suggested daily schedule, an account of the first Georgia District Agricultural School Contest, held at the Georgia State College of Agriculture April 28 and 29, 1916, the text of the act creating the schools, and statistical data on the value of farm products, repairs, salaries, value of the plant, attendance, farm acreages, and equipment:

The State appropriation for each of these schools for 1916–17 was $15,000, an increase of $5,000 over previous appropriations. Arrangements had been made with the college of agriculture to place a county agent or congressional district agent at each of these schools. Seven of the schools had teacher training departments, and the others reported that they would introduce such courses in September, 1916.

Ninth annual report of the inspector of high schools, E. R. EDWARDS (*Ann. Rpt. Insp. State High Schools [N. Dak.], 9 (1916), pp. 75, pls. 5*).—This report includes, among other information, statistical data on the enrollment, equipment, salaries of instructors, etc., with reference to agriculture and domestic science and art in North Dakota schools.

The agricultural enrollment in the high schools nearly doubled since the previous year, yet included only 16.2 per cent of the total enrollment. There were 1,420 students taking at least one unit of agricultural work as against 689 in 1914–15; 7 schools gave 2 units and 3 each gave 3 and 4 units. The 2 county agricultural and training schools had an enrollment of 110 and 24, respectively. The 5 State high schools with agricultural departments had a total enrollment of 176 in agriculture as against 133 in the previous year, and 118 in cooking and 151 in sewing.

Special equipment for instruction in agriculture was reported by 55 high schools. Of the first-class schools one reported such equipment valued at $5,500 and another at $500. The 5 schools with agricultural departments have an average agricultural equipment of $830 each, and the other 48 schools an average of $47.52.

List of agricultural and horticultural officials, institutions, and associations (*Dept. Landb., Nijv. en Handel [Netherlands], Verslag. en Meded. Dir. Landb., No. 2 (1916), pp. 128*).—This is the official organization list of the Direction of Agriculture of the Department of Agriculture, Industry, and Commerce, including higher and secondary agricultural education and research institutions, agricultural and horticultural winter schools and courses, itinerant instructors, and associations in the Netherlands in 1916.

High-school courses in Agriculture, S. H. DADISMAN and G. M. WILSON (*Iowa State Col., Schools Circ. 5 (1916), pp. 56*).—This bulletin outlines a four-year course in agriculture for high schools comprising instruction in farm animals for one year, in farm crops, horticulture, poultry, and farm management one-half year each, in farm mechanics two-fifths of a year, and in soils three-fifths of a year. A suggestive schedule for one, two, three, and four year courses, laboratory and field exercises and home products, and references to helpful literature are included. It is stated that the outlines have been prepared to assist the high-school teachers of Iowa in organizing agricultural instruction on a thoroughly practical basis.

Illustrated lecture on leguminous forage crops for the South, C. V. PIPER and H. B. HENDRICK (*U. S. Dept. Agr., States Relat. Serv. Syllabus 24 (1917), pp. 16*).—The authors discuss the distinguishing characteristics of the leguminous plants, the function of root nodules and nodule bacteria, inoculation, the relation of legunes to cropping systems, commendable cropping systems, the utilization of leguminous crops, legumes as green manures, and the principal leguminous crops for the South. A list of fifty lantern slides to illustrate the syllabus is appended.

Illustrated lecture on leguminous forage crops for the North, C. V. PIPER and H. B. HENDRICK (*U. S. Dept. Agr., States Rel. Serr. Syllabus 25 (1917), pp. 18*).—This syllabus corresponds in treatment to that for the South, noted above, but deals with the principal leguminous crops for the North. A list of 45 lantern slides to illustrate the lecture is appended.

Types and market classes of live stock, H. W. VAUGHAN (*Columbus, Ohio: R. G. Adams and Co., 1916, pp. 448, pl. 1, figs. 117*).—This text consists of a study of the types, carcasses, breeding for market and other purposes, markets, and products of cattle, sheep, swine, and horses. The arrangement of the subject matter corresponds to the order usually followed in teaching, but may be varied, as the study of each class of animals is complete in itself. A loose-leaf edition of the text has been used at the beginning of the work in animal husbandry at the Ohio State University during the past three years.

[Nature study and elementary agriculture in Georgia] (In *Manual Ga. Teachers, 1916, pp. 168–202, figs. 3*).—This manual includes the following articles: (1) Nature Study and Agriculture, by R. J. H. DeLoach, which discusses the objects and results of nature study and its relation to agriculture, and the true conception of agriculture as a subject to be taught in the common schools, end outlines practical lessons in nature study; (2) School Clubs, by M. L. Duggan and supervisors, giving directions for the organization and work of boys' and girls' clubs; and (3) Easy Experiments in Agriculture.

Class projects for agriculture students, W. S. WELLES (*River Falls, Wis.: State Normal School, 1916, pp. 19*).—Class projects are outlined in weeds and seed inspection, marketing, agricultural pedagogy, economic entomology, agricultural biology, feeds and feeding, field crops, farm management, dairying, farm mechanics, soils, and animal husbandry.

Home projects in agriculture for Michigan high schools and school credits, W. H. FRENCH (*Mich. Agr. Col., Dept. Agr. Ed. Bul. 17 (1916), pp. 15, fig. 1*).—The author discusses suitable home projects for students in agriculture in public high schools and offers suggestions and recommendations with reference to proper school credit for such project work.

Practical arts below the seventh grade (*[Indianapolis]: State Supt. Pub. Instr., 1916–17, pp. 35*).—This is an outline in agriculture, domestic science, and industrial arts, including suggestions for practical work and correlation with other school subjects, for the first six grades of the Indiana public schools. A suggestive list of books for reference in practical arts work is included.

MISCELLANEOUS.

Report of Hawaii Station, 1916 (*Hawaii Sta. Rpt. 1916, pp. 46, pls. 6*).—This contains the organization list, a summary by the agronomist in charge as to the work of the year, and reports of the divisions of horticulture, chemistry, plant pathology, agronomy, extension, and Territorial marketing, and of the Glenwood substation. The experimental work recorded is for the most part abstracted elsewhere in this issue.

Annual Report of South Dakota Station, 1916 (*South Dakota Sta. Rpt. 1916, pp. 27*).—This contains a report by the director on the organization, work, and publications of the station, a financial statement for the fiscal year ended June 30, 1916, and departmental reports, of which a portion of that of the horticulturist is abstracted on page 142 of this issue.

First Annual Report of the Adams Branch Experiment Station, 1916, M. A. M'CALL (*Washington Sta. Bul. 138, pp. 16, figs. 9*).—This contains a report of the superintendent of this substation for the fiscal year ended June 30, 1916, including a description of the projects initiated.

Monthly Bulletin of the Ohio Agricultural Experiment Station (*Mo. Bul. Ohio Sta., 2 (1917), Nos. 1, pp. 34, figs. 5; 2, pp. 37–68, figs. 10; 3, pp. 71–102, figs. 6*).—These numbers contain, in addition to several articles abstracted elsewhere in this issue and miscellaneous notes, the following:

No. 1.—The Wheatfield in Winter.—Improvement by Use of Manure, Commercial Fertilizers and Lime, by C. E. Thorne; Corn and Oats for Work Horses.—A Comparison of Their Efficiency and Economy in Feeding, by B. E. Carmichael, adapted from Bulletin 195 (E. S. R., 20, p. 470) ; The Field Bean.— A Promising Crop for Many Ohio Farms, by S. N. Green; White Snakeroot a Poisonous Plant.—Trembles in Animals and Milk Sickness in Man Often Fatal, by A. D. Selby; Composition of Limestone.—The Relative Merits of Magnesian and Nonmagnesian Forms, by J. W. Ames and C. J. Schollenberger, an extract from Bulletin 306 (abstracted on page 124) ; Selling Woodlot Products.— Advantages Secured through Cooperative Marketing, by J. W. Calland, an extract from Bulletin 302 (E. S. R., 36, p. 244) ; The Feeding Situation.—Suggestions for Computing Winter Rations for Dairy Cows, by C. C. Hayden; and Farm-management Field Studies.—A Reconnaissance Conducted in Butler Township, Knox County, by C. W. Montgomery.

No. 2.—Mineral Requirements of Milch Cows.—Heavy Milk Production Involves Loss of Minerals from Body, by E. B. Forbes, an abstract of Bulletin 308, noted on page 169; Boys' and Girls' Club Work.—County-agent Demonstration in Butler Township, Knox County, by C. W. Montgomery.

No. 3.—Range Versus Confinement for Laying Hens.—Profits Materially Increased under Range Conditions, by W. J. Buss, an abstract of a portion of Bulletin 291 (E. S. R., 35, p. 171) ; Fire Blight.—Timely Suggestions for Its Control, by R. C. Walton; Cutworms.—Their Habits, Characteristics, and Means of Control, by H. A. Gossard; and Arlington Timothy.—New Variety Being Sent from Experiment Station.

NOTES.

Connecticut State Station.—The general assembly has appropriated $28,000 for the construction of a central heating plant and added $2,500 per year to the maintenance appropriation of the station. Other appropriations for the biennium include $12,000 for the State entomologist, $40,000 for the suppression of gipsy and brown-tail moths and nursery inspection, $1,500 for bee diseases, $10,000 for the elimination of mosquito breeding, $15,000 for the control of white pine blister rust, $5,000 for the State forester, $5,000 for the purchase of forest land, and $9,000 for the fire-warden service.

Florida Station.—Recent appointments effective July 1 include Miss Mildred Nothnagel, Ph. D., as assistant plant physiologist. Arthur M. Smith as assistant chemist, and C. W. Long as laboratory assistant in animal husbandry.

Hawaii College.—D. L. Crawford, of Pomona College, has been appointed professor of entomology beginning in September.

Purdue University and Station.—O. F. Hunziker, chief of the dairy department, who has been on leave of absence for a year to study commercial butter making, has resigned to continue in commercial work.

Iowa College.—Paul R. Lisher, associate professor of animal husbandry, has resigned to become county adviser for the Will County (Illinois) Farm Bureau.

Kansas College and Station.—The station, assisted by the Office of Cereal Investigations, U. S. Department of Agriculture, has made a complete survey of Kansas to determine the location of pure seed of the hard red winter varieties of wheat. A circular giving the names of the farmers and elevator men having the seed for sale is being prepared to place in the hands of farmers and organizations in counties where the entire wheat crop was winter killed and the seed will be needed.

The staff of the department of entomology and Federal entomologists are being organized to control the Hessian fly in counties where it promises to injure the wheat crop in 1918. The early and thorough plowing under of wheat stubble, elimination of volunteer wheat in fields later, and planting after the fly-free date are the recommendations being made. These practices, however, are advisable in order to obtain maximum yields, regardless of Hessian fly infestation.

Chas. A. Scott, professor of forestry, forester of the station, and State forester, has resigned to engage in commercial work. Ralph Kenney, assistant professor of crops, has resigned to accept a commercial position in Paraguay.

Dr. Geo. M. Potter, veterinary inspector of the Bureau of Animal Industry of the U. S. Department of Agriculture, has been appointed specialist in veterinary medicine in the extension division and entered upon his duties about May 1. His work deals especially with hog cholera and contagious abortion.

Appointments to fellowships in the division of agriculture for the ensuing year include Jay L. Lush of the Kansas College in animal genetics, Levi J. Horlacker of Purdue University in animal production, W. P. Tuttle of the Kentucky University in soils, and W. H. Stacy of the Iowa College in crops.

Louisiana Stations.—W. L. Owen, bacteriologist of the Sugar Station since 1908, has resigned effective October 1, to take charge of the research department of a large sirup and molasses canning industry in New Orleans.

Michigan College and Station.—Ezra Levin has been appointed muck crop specialist with headquarters at Kalamazoo. His time is to be divided between research and extension work.

Minnesota University and Station.—A chair of comparative pathology and bacteriology has been established in the veterinary division, to which Dr. Clifford P. Fitch, assistant professor of pathology and bacteriology in the New York State Veterinary College, has been appointed beginning August 1. Dr. Fitch will also become chairman of the veterinary division of the animal industry group, succeeding Dr. M. H. Reynolds, who will be in charge of veterinary sanitation.

Philip A. Anderson, instructor in animal husbandry, has been appointed in charge of a new section of meats in the animal industry group. Alice L. Edwards has been appointed assistant professor of nutrition beginning August 1.

John T. Stewart, chief of the division of agricultural engineering, has been granted leave of absence to accept a commission in the engineering corps of the U. S. Army. Louise Jensen has resigned as mycologist of the station and has been succeeded by F. Jean MacInnis of the Illinois Station. Phil C. Bing of the Wisconsin University and Station has succeeded L. G. Hood as assistant editor. Mildreth J. Haggard has resigned as assistant chemist in animal nutrition.

Nebraska University and Station.—The contract has been let for the agricultural engineering building at a cost of $132,450.

The department of animal husbandry is experimenting with various crops for hog and sheep pastures. Rape, cane, sweet clover, and oats are being compared with the blue grass and alfalfa.

New Hampshire College.—Ralph D. Hetzel, director of the extension service of the Oregon College, has been appointed president beginning about August 15.

New Jersey College and Stations.—W. J. Carson, professor of dairy husbandry and dairy husbandman, L. S. Riford, instructor in dairy husbandry and assistant in the State Station, Thurlow C. Nelson, biologist in charge of oyster investigations, and Howard F. Huber, extension specialist in horticulture, have resigned. Wm. M. Regan has been appointed dairy husbandman, and Willes B. Combs, assistant dairy husbandman. Other appointments include J. T. Barlow as research assistant in plant physiology, Miss Jessie G. Fiske as assistant seed analyst, C. S. Clarkson as assistant chemist, D. A. Coleman, Ph. D., as assistant agronomist, and H. M. Biekart as florist.

New York State Station.—A. J. Flume, assistant chemist, has resigned to take up commercial work and is succeeded by Walter L. Kulp, formerly assistant in bacteriology at the Michigan College and recently engaged in bacteriological work in connection with hospitals in Boston, Mass.

Oregon College.—A bequest estimated at from $25,000 to $40,000 has been made to the college by the late J. T. Apperson, a member of the board of regents since its establishment, for use as a permanent loan fund to students working their way through college.

Pennsylvania College and Station.—Recent changes in title and promotions include the following: As professor, A. W. Cowell, landscape art; as associate professors, C. E. Myers, plant breeding, and C. F. Noll and J. W. White, experimental agronomy; as assistant professors, C. R. Anderson, forestry, S. I. Bechdel, dairy husbandry, J. R. Bechtel, vegetable gardening, A. F. Mason, horticultural extension, L. O. Overholts, Ph.D., botany, E. I. Wilde, floriculture, F. N. Fagan, pomology, and C. L. Goodling, farm management (and superintendent of farms); and as instructors, H. P. Cooper and D. C. Wimer, agronomy, L. P. McCann, animal husbandry, R. S. Spray, botany, J. S. Gardner, plant breeding, and L. D. Jesseman and A. F. Yeager, pomology. E. R. Hitchner has resigned as instructor in bacteriology, effective July 1, and Paul Gerlaugh, as instructor in animal husbandry, effective August 1.

W. W. Farnham has been appointed instructor in landscape gardening, beginning March 19. Miss Etta J. McCoy, Miss Elsie Noble, Miss Edith Hershey, and Miss Jeanette Bliss have been appointed instructors in home economics extension, beginning June 25, and Miss Mary V. Dick, beginning July 1.

Tennessee University and Station.—A bond issue of $1,000,000 has been authorized by the State legislature for buildings and other improvements, supplemented by the proceeds of a half mill tax, estimated to produce about $836,000 per annum at present and to be used for maintenance. About $100,000 may be used for the construction of buildings at a substation in middle Tennessee, to be located on land provided by the county securing the institution. Provision will also be made for a large central administration building, a building for the College of Agriculture, an auditorium, and other buildings.

As the result of unanticipated findings in the lysimeter studies on lime and magnesia, begun in July 1914, the problem of sulphur conservation is to be taken up. This involves an additional equipment of 22 lysimeter tanks of the hillside equipment type, previously described (E. S. R., 32, p. 719).

W. A. Holding has been appointed assistant chemist.

Utah Station.—An experimental dry farm to investigate problems of high altitude has been established at Widtsoe in Garfield County.

Tracy H. Abel, M. S., has been appointed assistant horticulturist, and A. O. Larson, B. S., assistant entomologist.

West Virginia University and Station.—The recent legislature granted an additional $75,000 for the agricultural building, thus making it possible to complete the entire structure during the summer and fall, whereas otherwise an important segment would have been left uncompleted. The legislature also appropriated $20,000 for buildings on the new farms, and made a small increase for operating expenses and a special emergency appropriation of $10,000 to meet · the abnormally high prices of apparatus, chemicals, etc.

Wisconsin University and Station.—Special exercises were held during Commencement in recognition of the twenty-fifth anniversary of the conferring of the Ph.D. degree upon Dean Russell and his completion of 24 years of service at the university. In connection with the occasion, a compilation of the published results of the bacteriological work carried on during this period, aggregating some 2,000 pages, was presented to him.

Wyoming University and Station.—Dr. C. A. Duniway has resigned as president to become president of Colorado College, Colorado Springs. Dean H. G. Knight was granted the degree of doctor of philosophy by the University of Illinois in June. T. S. Parsons, agronomist, has been given a year's leave of absence for graduate work at the University of Wisconsin. W. A. Albrecht has been appointed acting agronomist for the year, and Joe Robinson has been appointed assistant agronomist. P. T. Meyers has resigned to become county agent for Campbell County.

Federal Board for Vocational Education.—Nominations to complete the membership of this board were transmitted to the Senate by President Wilson on June 29. The nominees include Arthur E. Holder of Iowa as a representative of the labor interests for a term of three years, Charles A. Greathouse of Indiana as a representative of the agricultural interests for a term of two years, and James Phinney Munroe of·Massachusetts as a representative of the manufacturing and commercial interests for a term of one year. These appointments were confirmed by the Senate July 17.

Agricultural and Home Economics Instruction in Utah.—An act of the 1917 legislature of Utah creates the positions of State supervisor of agricultural and industrial education and State supervisor of home economics education for the high and district schools of the State. The State leader in junior vocational work at the Utah College is designated for the former position, and the State leader for junior vocational work for girls for the latter. Appointees to these positions must be 25 years of age or over, have at least a B. S. degree in agriculture or home economics, respectively, understand the practical side of agriculture and home economics, and possess the qualifications prescribed by the State board of education. The duties of these supervisors will be to systematize the teaching of agriculture, mechanic arts, and home economics in these schools, suggesting the courses particularly suited to the individual students and to the communities in which the schools are located and the best methods of teaching the principles underlying agricultural, industrial, and home economics work in the school room and laboratory, and the practical work to be done at home. They are to visit each county school district in the State at least once a year, and do their work under the supervision of the board of education and in cooperation with the Utah college and State normal school of the University of Utah. Their salaries will be paid by the college as leaders of vocational work.

The legislature also accepted the benefits of the Federal act for the promotion of vocational education. It designated the State Board of Education as the agency to cooperate with the Federal board in the administration of the provisions of the act, and the State treasurer as the custodian of the funds. An appropriation of $12,500 was made for the biennium ending March 31, 1919.

Forest Ranger Course for the Southern Appalachians.—The Lincoln Memorial University at Harrogate, near Cumberland Gap, Tenn., has recently organized a department of forestry for the purpose of furnishing a training suitable to the needs of farmers and other owners of woodland, and which will equip boys as rangers in Government, State, and private employ.

The course will cover one year of 12 months, divided into four terms of three months each. Each term is made a unit in itself, and aims to give a definite knowledge about some one phase of the practical work. The course will include the elements of forestry (fundamental needs and purposes, the relation of forests to water resources, the effect of forest destruction, the benefits to the community in maintaining forests in a productive condition, etc.), forest botany, elementary field surveying, forest protection, timber cruising and mapping, logging and scaling, manufacturing and marketing of products, silviculture, forest improvements, and elementary land law.

The greater part of the instruction will be given in the forest or in connecnection with practical field problems. As a forest laboratory the university has secured a timber tract of 2,080 acres extending along the Cumberland Mountains from Cumberland Gap east into Virginia. This tract contains many thousand feet of merchantable timber, a large part of which is mature and will be cut as soon as possible.

Mobilizing Massachusetts Boys for Farm Labor.—A subcommittee of the Massachusetts public safety committee is endeavoring to mobilize the school boys of the State for farm service. It is planned that those under 16 years of age are to stay in their local communities and work on community or home gardens, while those 16 years or older are asked to enlist for farm work outside their own communities when needed.

A distinctive badge and certificates of honorary discharge are among the forms of recognition contemplated. Arrangements have also been made with the Massachusetts Agricultural and Tufts colleges, Boston University, and the Massachusetts Institute of Technology, whereby these institutions have agreed to accept for a trial period without entrance examination such boys as present an honorary discharge from this service, had satisfactory school records at the time of leaving, and are recommended by their principals.

The existing school organization is being utilized, as far as possible, in conducting the enterprise and supplying the necessary supervision. Up to June 1, about 500 boys from 16 to 18 years of age had been released from high schools and State-aided vocational agricultural schools and departments for the work, while several hundred others were working while living at home or were to be released June 10. Nine camps for housing the boys had been established, with three others under way.

New Journals.—The experiment stations in the Netherlands Indies are issuing a journal, *Archief voor de Rubbercultuur in Nederlandsch-Indië*, the first number of which appeared in February, 1917. This journal is to include all of the stations' articles on rubber and will supersede the various bulletins and pamphlets previously publishing such articles. Although the articles will be written in Dutch, extensive abstracts or summaries in English treating all important points will be added. The committee of editors is composed of the directors and scientific officers of the experiment stations.

The *Journal of Soil Improvement* is being issued monthly as the official publication of the Wisconsin Soil Improvement Association. The initial number consists mainly of several short articles by members of the staff of the Wisconsin University and Station on various phases of soil improvement.

Madroño is being published at irregular intervals as the journal of the California Botanical Society. The initial numbers contain a number of original articles on various botanical phases.

Miscellaneous.—A grant of $625,000 has been made from the Development Fund as a loan for the development of sugar beet growing and sugar manufacture in England. An estate of 5,600 acres has been acquired at Kelham, near Newark, where a factory will be erected. The enterprise is to be under the management of the British Sugar Beet Growers Society, Ltd., an organization not trading for profit, and an ultimate expenditure of $2,500,000 is contemplated.

Following a suggestion from the Council of the Royal Horticultural Society, the University of London has established a degree of bachelor of science in horticulture. The university has also under consideration the recognition of the society's school and research station at Wisley as a school of the university.

Charles F. Baker, professor of agronomy in the University of the Philippines, has been granted a year's leave of absence to accept a temporary appointment as assistant director of the botanical gardens at Singapore, in charge of experimental work in tropical agronomy.

An act of the Wyoming State Legislature, approved February 1, 1917, provides for the establishment of normal training departments in the graded high schools of the State, and requires, among other subjects, the teaching of agriculture.

○

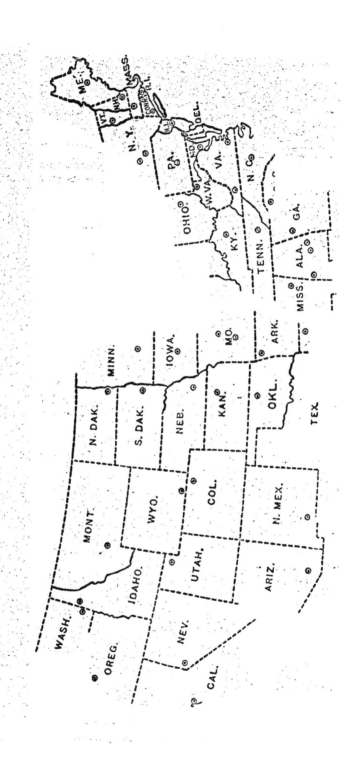

Issued September 5, 1917.

U. S. DEPARTMENT OF AGRICULTURE

STATES RELATIONS SERVICE

A. C. TRUE, DIRECTOR

Vol. 37   ABSTRACT NUMBER   No. 3

EXPERIMENT STATION RECORD

WASHINGTON

GOVERNMENT PRINTING OFFICE

1917

EXPERIMENT STATION RECORD.

Editor: E. W. ALLEN, Ph. D., *Chief, Office of Experiment Stations.*
Assistant Editor: H. L. KNIGHT.

EDITORIAL DEPARTMENTS.

Agricultural Chemistry and Agrotechny—E. H. NÓLLAU.

Meteorology, Soils, and Fertilizers {W. H. BEAL.
R. W. TRULLINGER.

Agricultural Botany, Bacteriology, and Plant Pathology {W. H. EVANS, Ph. D.
W. E. BOYD.

Field Crops {J. I. SCHULTE.
J. D. LUCKETT.

Horticulture and Forestry—E. J. GLASSON.

Economic Zoology and Entomology—W. A. HOOKER, D. V. M.

Foods and Human Nutrition {C. F. LANGWORTHY, Ph. D., D. Sc.
H. L. LANG.

Zootechny, Dairying, and Dairy Farming {M. D. MOORE.

Veterinary Medicine {W. A. HOOKER.
E. H. NOLLAU.

Rural Engineering—R. W. TRULLINGER.

Rural Economics—E. MERRITT.

Agricultural Education {C. H. LANE.
M. T. SPETHMANN.

Indexes—M. D. MOORE.

CONTENTS OF VOL. 37, NO. 3.

	Page.
Recent work in agricultural science	201
Notes	299

SUBJECT LIST OF ABSTRACTS.

AGRICULTURAL CHEMISTRY—AGROTECHNY.

The preparation of pure crystalline mannose, Hudson and Sawyer	201
The acetyl derivatives of the sugars, Hudson	201
The phenylhydrazids of certain acids of the sugar group, Hudson	201
Reactions of ions and molecules of acids, bases, and salts, Gruse and Acree	201
Concerning the failure to detect ornithin in plants, Kizel (Kiesel)	201
Decomposition of pyroracemic acid by dead plants, Palladin et al	201
Reductase and carboxylase in decomposition of lactic acid, Palladin et al	202
Decomposition of lactic acid by killed yeast, Palladin and Sabinin	202
Formation of carbon dioxid by dead yeast, Palladin and Lovchinovskaia	203
On reductase of plants, Palladin, Platishenskiu, and Elladi	203
The action of peroxidase on chlorophyll, Liubimenko	203
Effect of reaction of medium on activity of inulase of *Aspergillus niger*, Kizel	203
Studies of arginase and urease in plants, Kizel (Kiesel)	204
Effect of medium on proteolytic enzyms of plants, Palladin	204
Some auxoamylases, Rockwood	204

Page.
Quantitative microscopy, Wallis.. 205
An improved method of determining solubility, Hendrixson................... 205
Preparation of sulphurous acid, Hart.. 205
An improved nephelometer-colorimeter, Kober.............................. 205
The iodometric determination of sulphur dioxid and the sulphites, Ferguson.. 205
Estimation of butyric acid in biological products, I, Phelps and Palmer...... 206
Thiobarbituric acid as a qualitative reagent for ketchexose, Plaisance......... 206
Nitrogen in amino form as determined by formol titration, Swanson and Tague. 206
The amino-acid nitrogen content of the blood of various species, Bock........ 206
A rapid method for determining calcium in blood and milk, Lyman.......... 207
[Note on the Duclaux method].. 207
The detection of small amounts of oxalic acid in wine, Besson................. 207
Researches on the ultrafiltration of milk, Borrino 207
Method for determining diastatic activity of germinated grain, Nowak........ 208
The soluble carbohydrate content of feeding stuffs, van Kampen............. 208
Cane juice clarification, Hines... 208
Normal fermentation of sauerkraut, Round................................... 208

METEOROLOGY.

Relation of weather to crops and varieties adapted to Arizona conditions...... 209
Native vegetation and climate of Colorado in relation to agriculture, Robbins.. 209
Weather conditions, 1911–1916.. 210

SOILS—FERTILIZERS.

Soil survey of New Castle County, Delaware, Morrison et al................... 211
Analyses of soils of Habersham County, Worsham, jr., et al................... 211
Bremer County soils, Stevenson, Brown, and Howe........................... 211
Soil survey of Richardson County, Nebraska, Meyer et al.................... 211
Soil Survey of Hamilton County, Ohio, Goodman et al....................... 212
Agricultural possibilities of Ohio peat soils, Dachnowski..................... 212
Study of the vine growing soils of Vevey [Switzerland], Anken.............. 212
The soils of Southern Rhodesia and their origin, Maufe...................... 212
The soil mulch, Call and Sewell... 212
Lime-requirement methods and the soil's content of bases, Schollenberger.... 212
Effect of some acids and alkalis on soil bacteria in the soil solution, Gruzit.... 213
Investigations in soil protozoa and soil sterilization, Kopeloff and Coleman.... 213
The ecological significance of soil aeration, Cannon and Free.................. 213
Reclaiming the waste, Graham... 214
Summaries of soil fertility investigations, Wiancko and Jones................. 214
Why Illinois produces only half a crop, Hopkins.............................. 214
Live stock and the maintenance of organic matter in the soil, Fippin.......... 215
The manual of manures, Vendelmans... 215
Fertilizers and their supply in war time, Voelcker............................ 215
Artificial manures for crops in western India, Mann and Paranjpe............. 215
[Fertilizer experiments], Liechti.. 216
Standardization of humus used for fertilizer, Hoff............................ 216
The organic nitrogen compounds of soils and fertilizers, Lathrop............. 216
Sources of nitrogen compounds in the United States, Gilbert................. 217
The nitrate industry, Cuevas... 217
When are summer crops to be fertilized with lime nitrogen? Wagner.......... 217
Fertilizer experiments, Alway.. 217
Phosphate rock, Stone... 217
Potash in agriculture, Aston... 218
The volatilization of potash from cement materials, Anderson and Nestell..... 218
Growing crops without potash in 1916, Woods............................... 218
Lime in agriculture, Felder.. 218
Forms of agricultural lime and their application, Fearnow.................... 218
The relation of lime to agriculture, Broughton............................... 218
The question of lime fertilization, Liechti and Trunninger.................... 219
Decomposition and utilization of limestone in soil, Ames and Schollenberger.. 219
The fertilizing value of wastes from the hemp industry, Draghetti........... 219
[Fertilizers, season 1915–16], Ross... 219
Analyses of commercial fertilizers, ground bone, and lime, Cathcart et al...... 219
Analyses of fertilizers and cottonseed meal, Kilgore et al.................... 220
List of fertilizer and lime manufacturers and importers..................... 220

AGRICULTURAL BOTANY.

Page.

Plant physiology as horticultural theory, Molisch............................. 220
Applied and economic botany, Kraemer.. 220
Canaigre, a quick-growing tannin plant for acclimatization in France, Piédallu. 220
New names in Amygdalus, Ricker... 220
Studies in the nomenclature and classification of bacteria, Buchanan.......... 220
Note on the classification of some lactose-fermenting bacteria, Levine.......... 220
The preparation of culture media from whole blood, Kelser..................... 220
The development of Azotobacter, Cauda.. 221
The oxygen requirements of biological soil processes, Murray................... 221
Depression of freezing point in triturated tissues, Hibbard and Harrington..... 221
Glandular hairs on roots, Haberlandt.. 222
Absorption of nutrients as affected by number of roots, Gile and Carrero...... 222
The excretion of acids by roots, Haas... 222
Leaf epidermis and light perception, Haberlandt............................... 222
Chemical organization of the assimilatory apparatus, Willstätter and Stoll...... 222
Assimilation of organic nitrogen by Zea mays, Brigham........................ 223
Catalytic action of potassium nitrate in alcoholic fermentation, Molliard....... 223
Stimulation and injury to plants by acids, Onodera............................ 224
Frost and alterations in leaves of trees, Arnaud............................... 224
Effect of environmental conditions on tobacco pla s, Allard................... 224
The shedding of flower buds in cotton, Harland.. .nt......................... 224
On the genetics of crinkled dwarf rogues in Sea Island cotton, I, Harland..... 224
Partial sterility of Nicotiana hybrids, II, Goodspeed and Ayres................ 225
Partial sterility of Nicotiana hybrids, III, Goodspeed and Kendall............. 225

FIELD CROPS.

[Report of field crops work at the Minnesota Station]........................ 226
[Report of field crops work at the Crookston substation]..................... 226, 228
[Report of field crops work at the Duluth substation]........................ 228
[Report of field crops work at the Grand Rapids substation].................. 228
[Report of field crops work at the Morris substation]........................ 229
[The Woburn field experiments, 1915], Voelcker............................. 229
Cultivation and utilization of sunflower, niger, and safflower seed............. 230
Pasture problems, Stapledon and Jenkin..................................... 230
Observations on alfalfa, Jenkins... 231
Beans in Colorado, Kezer.. 232
Clover and clover hay, Howard.. 232
Corn problems.—Varieties; time, manner, and rate of planting, Gearhart....... 232
How much plant food does a corn crop take from an acre? Jenkins et al....... 233
Corn variety tests for 1915, Winters, Garren, and White...................... 233
Egyptian maize (Zea mays), Dudgeon and Bolland........................... 233
Fique (Furcræa gigantea) 233
Culture and manufacture of flax for fiber and seed in Oregon, Thorne......... 233
Indian hemp fiber (Crotalaria juncea), D'Lima............................... 233
[The composition of mangels], Gimingham................................... 233
Great millet (Sorghum vulgare) and berseem (Trifolium alexandrinum), Bolland 233
Peanuts.—Tests of varieties and fertilizers, Duggar et al...................... 233
Growing peanuts in Alabama, Duggar et al................................... 234
A note on the inheritance of certain stem characters in sorghum, Hilson....... 234
Tests of soy beans in 1916, Jenkins, Street, and Hubbell..................... 234
Soy beans.—Their culture and use, Williams and Park....................... 235
Sudan grass, Madson and Kennedy... 236
Report of the plant breeder, Cowgill.. 236
The value of crop rotation in practical cane culture, Rosenfeld................ 237
Some sugar-cane experiments in Travancore, Pillai........................... 237
Washington wheats.—Their classification and identification, Alvord........... 237
The wheat field in April.—Top-dressing with fertilizers, Thorne............... 238
The saving of irrigation water in wheat growing, Howard...................... 238
Third annual report of the State grain laboratory of Montana, Atkinson et al... 238
Results of seed inspection, 1915 and 1916, Helyar et al....................... 239
Weeds in the Government of Novgorod, Malzew.............................. 239
Broom rape.. 239
Red sorrel and its control (Rumex acetosella), Pipal.......................... 239

HORTICULTURE.

Page.

Proceedings of the American Society for Horticultural Science, 1916........... 239
[Report of the] division of horticulture... 240
[Report of horticultural investigations at the Crookston substation]............. 241
[Horticultural work at the Crookston substation]............................... 241
Report of the work of the horticultural substation, Whipple.................... 241
A fruit survey of Mesa County, Sandsten, Limbocker, and McGinty........... 241
Fruits, trees, and shrubs recommended for northern Minnesota, McCall....... 241
Dependable fruits, Green et al... 241
Annual report of the Fruit Experiment Station, Shillong, 1916, Holder........ 242
Pruning, Clement and Reeves... 242
Apple breeding at the university experiment station, Crandall............... 242
Field experiments in spraying apple orchards in 1916, Gunderson and Brock.. 242
Dominion experimental orchard work, Blair................................... 242
The culture of small fruits on irrigated sandy land, Allen................... 243
Fruiting habits of budded trees of the different avocado varieties, Barber.... 243
Cultural experiments with the filbert in the East, McGlennon................ 243
Analyses of insecticides and fungicides for 1916, Cathcart and Willis.......... 243

FORESTRY.

The training of a forester, Pinchot.. 243
The theory and practice of working plans, Recknagel.......................... 243
Determining the quality of standing timber, Berry............................ 243
Forest tree planting camps, Illick... 243
Eleventh report of the forest commissioner of Maine, 1916, Mace.............. 243
The conservation law as amended to 1916..................................... 244
Report of the forestry branch... 244
Fifty years of forest administration in Bashahr, Glover....................... 244
Notes on the forests of Algeria, Marc... 244
A discussion of Australian forestry, Hutchins................................ 244
Correlation between the light and soil requirements of a species, Coventry... 244
The biology of lodgepole pine as revealed by the behavior of its seed, Bates.. 244
The Mexican and Central American species of Ficus, Standley................. 244
Forest and shade trees and basket willows for planting in Idaho, Shattuck... 244
Status and value of farm woodlots in the eastern United States, Frothingham.. 245
Canadian woods for structural timbers, Lee................................... 245
Forest products of Canada, 1913, 1914, and 1915, Lewis et al.................. 245
Recent industrial and economic development of Indian forest products,
    Pearson... 245

DISEASES OF PLANTS.

The susceptibility of cultivated plants to diseases and pests, Keuchenius..... 245
Studies in the physiology of parasitism, Brown.............................. 245
A study of Glœosporium, Krüger.. 245
Further evidence as to the relation between crown gall and cancer, Smith... 245
Report of the pathologist, Stevenson... 246
[Reports on plant diseases in Switzerland, 1913–14], Müller-Thurgau et al.... 246
Fungus parasites in Kharkov and adjacent provinces, Potebnfa............... 246
Diseases and pests of cultivated plants in Dutch East Indies, 1915, van Hall.. 246
Control measures against plant diseases and injurious insects, van Hall et al.. 247
Tests of new fungicides, Riehm... 247
Tests of fungicides with cereal diseases, Riehm.............................. 247
Overwintering of stinking smut in soil, Appel and Riehm.................... 247
Diseases and pests of rice, Rutgers... 247
Treatment of loose smut of wheat and barley, Appel and Riehm.............. 247
A wheat disease caused by Dilophospora graminis, Mangin................... 247
[Wheat rust in New Zealand], Waters... 247
Stalk disease of wheat, Foex.. 248
Diseases of beans, Sackett.. 248
Control of clubroot of crucifers, Appel and Schlumberger................... 248
Phoma disease in crucifers, Laubert... 248
Corynespora melonis, Krüger.. 248
Flax blight, Arnaud.. 248
The dying out of pepper vines in the Dutch East Indies, II, Rutgers.......... 248
Potato diseases in the Dutch East Indies, Westerdijk......................... 249

Page.

Experiments for control of potato canker, Werth................................ 249
Potato leaf roll in France, Foex.. 249
Potato leaf roll, Appel and Schlumberger..................................... 249
Chlorosis of beets, Arnaud... 249
Crown gall of sugar beets, Peters.. 249
Sweet potato diseases, McClintock... 249
Sclerotium disease of tobacco, Westerdijk.................................... 249
The parasitism of Coryneum on trees and shrubs, Arnaud...................... 250
Hail effects on trees, Arnaud.. 250
Behavior of apple canker in two grafts differing in susceptibility, Dangeard.. 250
A new Oospora on pear, Mangin... 250
Biological observations on pear rust, Trotter................................ 250
Disease of apricots in the Rhone Valley, Chifflot and Massonnat............. 250
Some observations on witches' brooms of cherries, Schmitz................... 250
Biology of *Exoascus deformans* and preventive treatment, Peglion.......... 250
Substitute for self-boiled lime-sulphur and other sprays for peaches, Gillam... 251
A new canker disease of Prunus caused by *Valsa japonica* n. sp., Hemmi...... 251
Dieback in currant, Appel and Werth... 251
Peronospora in 1915, and its control, Marescalchi........................... 251
Treatment of Peronospora during 1915, D'Albaretto.......................... 251
The germination of the winter spores of *Plasmopara viticola*, Ravaz and Verge.. 252
The present status of the coconut bud rot disease, Johnston................. 252
Fungi parasitic on the tea plant in northeast India, V, VI, Tunstall......... 252
Tumors on *Chrysanthemum frutescens*, Laubert.............................. 252
Canker of oleander, Hariot.. 252
A new fungus parasitic on Ceara rubber trees, Vincens...................... 252
Diseases of *Hevea brasiliensis* in the Amazon Valley, I, II, Vincens....... 252
Diseases of Hevea in Ceylon, Petch.. 253
The effects of asphyxiating gases on forest vegetation, Döé................ 253
A beech disease due to *Nectria ditissima*, Guinier........................ 253
Galls on juniper, Hariot.. 253
Peridermium strobi on Swiss pine, Werth.................................. 253
Dry rot, Groom.. 253

ENTOMOLOGY.

The nature of the polyhedral bodies found in insects, Glaser and Chapman.... 253
Influence of atmospheric humidity on insect metabolism, Headlee............ 254
Determining wind dispersion of the gipsy moth and other insects, Collins..... 254
A method for the study of underground insects, McColloch................... 254
Report of the State entomologist of Connecticut, 1916, Britton.............. 254
Fourteenth annual report of the State entomologist of Montana, Cooley....... 255
Notes on several insects not heretofore recorded from New Jersey, Weiss....... 255
Report of the entomologist, Wolcott... 255
Report on tobacco and vegetable insects, Cotton............................ 256
Foreign insect pests collected on imported nursery stock in 1916, Sasscer...... 257
Some methods of colonizing imported parasites, Crossman.................... 257
Efficiency and economy in grasshopper control, Ball........................ 257
The seventeen-year locust in western New York, Hadley, jr., and Matheson.. 257
Biological and systematic notes on British Thysanoptera, Williams........... 257
The green soldier bug (*Nezara hilaris*), Whitmarsh....................... 258
Mercurial ointment, an effective control of hen lice, Lamson, jr........... 258
Distribution of Ohio broods of periodical cicada, Gossard................. 258
Aphid eggs in Texas (Lat. 30°, 30'), Yingling.............................. 258
New tree banding material for control of gipsy moth, Burgess and Griffin..... 258
Present status of the gipsy and brown-tail moths in Connecticut, Davis....... 259
Crambid moths and light, Ainslie... 259
"Side injury" and codling moth control, Felt............................... 259
Recent antimosquito work in Connecticut, Britton.......................... 259
Influence of salinity on development of mosquito larvæ, Chidester.......... 259
Biological study of important fish enemies of salt-marsh mosquitoes, Chidester. 260
Results of ten years of experimental wheat sowing to escape Hessian fly, Dean. 260
Wind as a factor in the dispersion of the Hessian fly, McColloch........... 260
The protection of dairy cattle from flies, Cory........................... 260
The radish maggot and screening, Parrott.................................. 261
Analysis of white grubs and May beetles and its economic application, Davis.. 261
The spinach carrion beetle (*Silpha bituberosa*), Cooley.................. 261

Page.
The striped cucumber beetle, Gossard.. 261
Egg-laying habits of *Diprion simile*, Zappe.................................... 261
Notes on the bean weevil (*Acanthoscelides [Bruchus] obtectus*), Manter......... 262
The alfalfa weevil investigation, Reeves.. 262
The clover weevil in Iowa, Webster.. 262
The plum curculio, Goodwin.. 262
Lime as an insecticide, Metcalf... 262
Problems of bee inspection, Pellett... 262
The results of apiary inspection, Phillips...................................... 263
Some new and practical methods for the control of European foul brood, Carr.... 263
Report on Isosoma investigations, Phillips...................................... 263

FOODS—HUMAN NUTRITION.

Biology and the Nation's food, Spillman... 263
Bread of the future and measures taken for its utilization, Schribaux.......... 263
On the rations of bread in the Army... 263
Some common edible and poisonous mushrooms, Patterson and Charles............... 263
Concerning copper in tomatoes, Carles... 263
Food economics at agricultural school, Minnesota University.................... 264
Food [of the Labrador Eskimo], Hawkes... 264
The food supply of the United Kingdom... 264
Great Britain's measures for control of food, Williams......................... 264
Growth of rats on diets of isolated food substances, Osborne and Mendel........ 264
The supplementary dietary relationship between leaf and seed, McCollum et al.   264
Feeding experiments with deficiencies in amino-acid supply, Ackroyd and
    Hopkins... 265
Influence of heavy metals on the isolated intestine, Salant and Mitchell....... 266
The respiratory process in muscle, Fletcher and Hopkins........................ 266
Clinical calorimetry, XIX–XXV... 266

ANIMAL PRODUCTION.

Commercial feeding stuffs, Street et al... 268
[Animal husbandry work at the Crookston substation]............................ 268
[Feeding experiments with beef cattle, brood sows, and work horses]............ 269
Theory of correlation as applied to farm-survey data on baby beef, Tolley...... 269
Steer feeding.—X, Winter steer feeding, 1913–14, Skinner and King.............. 270
Sheep feeding.—IV, Fattening western lambs, 1913–14, Skinner and King.......... 270
[Feeding experiments with pigs in Minnesota]................................... 270
The fall litter of pigs, Dietrich.. 270
[Clover pasture for hogs].. 270
[Report of the] Kansas State live stock registry board......................... 270
Feeding for egg production, Moore... 271
Poultry feeding test, home-grown versus purchased feeds........................ 271

DAIRY FARMING—DAIRYING.

The dairy industry in Argentina, Berges... 271
Net value of pasturage.. 271
[Pasturing experiments with cows at the Duluth substation]..................... 271
[Record of dairy herd at the Grand Rapids substation].......................... 271
Studies in milk secretion, I, II, Hammond and Hawk............................. 272
On the fat of Egyptian buffalo milk, Hogan and Griffiths-Jones................. 272
Variations in human milk during the first 11 days after parturition, Hammett.. 273
A new defect in milk caused by *Bacterium lactis aerogenes*, Duggeli........... 273
An epidemic of septic sore throat due to milk, Rosenow and Hess................ 273
Septic sore throat, Henika and Thompson.. 273
Spring conditions affecting the cream producer, Ruehe.......................... 273
Manufacture and composition of Bulgarian cheeses, Zlataroff.................... 273
Rennet substitutes.. 273

VETERINARY MEDICINE.

American Veterinary Medical Association.—Report on diseases, Mohler............. 274
Report of State Live Stock Sanitary Commission of Michigan, Dunphy and
    Hallman... 274

                                                                                            Page.
Report of civil veterinary department in Baluchistan for 1915–16, Cattell.....   274
Report of civil veterinary department, Madras Presidency, for 1914–15.......   274
Studies in pneumonia.—II, Determining bactericidal action, Kolmer et al....   274
The differentiation of the paratyphoid-enteritidis group, I, Jordan............   275
The enzyms of the tubercle bacillus, Corper and Sweany....................   275
The immune reaction to tuberculous infection, Weil.........,.............   275
Treatment of experimental tuberculosis by taurin, Takeoka..................   275
Suppuration in cattle and swine caused by *Bacterium pyogenes*, Ward..........   276
The diastase in the saliva of the ox, Palmer...............................   276
Diagnosis of infectious abortion of cattle, I, Reichel and Harkins.............   276
Formalin in the treatment of mastitis, Frost................................   277
Eradication of the cattle tick in Argentina, Ayerza, Sivori, et al.............   277
A fatal parasitic infestation in cattle and goats, Boynton and Wharton........   277
Louping-ill, Stockman...   277
Roundworms of sheep, Ransom...   277
The influence of partial thyroidectomy in pigs, Palmer......................   278
Fetal athyrosis.—The iodin requirement of the pregnant sow, Smith..........   278
Spirochetes of digestive tract of swine and relation to hog cholera, Bekensky..   279
Swine fever, Powley..   279
A granulomatous affection of the horse—habronemic granulomata, Bull.......   279
Sclerostome parasites of the horse in England, II, Boulenger..................   280
Parasitic occurrence of *Eimeria stiedæ* in the liver of the dog, Guillebeau......   280
Chick troubles, Thompson..   280
Apparent recovery of a hen infected with bacillary white diarrhea, Horton....   280
The part played by the goblet cells in protozoan infections, Hadley...........   280
Eimeria avium: A morphological study, Hadley and Amison..................   280
Coccidia in subepithelial infections of the intestines of birds, Hadley..........   280
Another occurrence of *Dioctophyme renale* in the abdominal cavity, Riley.....   281

                                RURAL ENGINEERING.

Proceedings of meetings of Washington Irrigation Institute....................   281
Flow through submerged rectangular orifices with modified contractions, Cone..   281
The Venturi flume, Cone...   282
Investigations of irrigation pumping plants, Murdock.......................   283
Growth of moss in irrigation canals, Salt River Project, Halton...............   285
Control of moss, weeds, and willows on Minidoka Project, Dibble and Parry...   285
Drainage..   286
By-products of land clearing...   286
The soil saving dam, Baker..   286
Bacteriological study of the water supply of Denver, Colo., Sackett...........   286
The activated sludge process of sewage purification, Ardern..................   286
Sewage disposal for village and rural homes, Nichols.........................   286
Designs for privies, Messer..   287
Hydroelectric power, I, Lyndon..   287
Screening and washing gravel for country road construction, McKay...........   288
Tests on corrugated metal culverts...   288
Road mileage and revenues in Central, Mountain, and Pacific States, 1914.....   288
Public road mileage and revenues in the United States, 1914: A summary.....   289
Maine State Highway Commission..   289
Building a farm poultry house in northwestern Minnesota, Brown.............   289
Poultry management...   289

                                RURAL ECONOMICS.

Food supply of the United States, Houston..................................   289
Fundamental considerations affecting food supply of United States, Hunt.....   289
Mobilization for food production, Davenport................................   290
"Universal military service" for farmers, Jenkins............................   290
The redistribution of the labor now employed in producing war supplies, Lund.   290
The land problem and rural welfare, Vogt...................................   290
Two dimensions of productivity, Taylor.....................................   290
Agriculture and the farming business, Benson and Betts......................   290
Profits in farming on irrigated areas in Gallatin Valley, Mont., Currier........   290
The Federal Farm Loan Act, Thompson.....................................   291
Report on cooperative societies in Bengal for 1915–16, Mitra..................   291
Agriculture in Oxfordshire, Orr..   291

Page.

Crop conditions and harvest field needs...................................... 291
[Agricultural statistics of British Guiana], Harrison......................... 291
Return of prices of crops, live stock, and other Irish agricultural products.... 291
Agricultural statistics of Finland for 1910................................... 291
Prices of cattle and meat in Russia, Koremblit............................... 292
Live stock statistics of [Egypt, Spain, Morocco and Tunis].................. 292

AGRICULTURAL EDUCATION.

State higher educational institutions of Iowa................................ 292
Agricultural education in the high and common schools of the State, Hawkins.. 293
Report of elementary agricultural education for British Columbia, Gibson.... 293
Report of elementary agricultural education for British Columbia, Gibson.... 293
Special grants, regulations, and organization................................ 293
The general direction of agricultural instructions, Amadeo................... 294
Agricultural and rural extension schools in Ireland, Monahan................ 294
Agricultural education and live stock improvement in Wales, 1913–1915, Jones. 294
Report on the agricultural and housekeeping schools for 1914–15............. 294
Report of the Department of Agriculture [of Finland] for 1914............... 295
Agricultural yearbook for 1917, edited by Larsen........................... 295
Instruction in agriculture and gardening in elementary schools............... 295
Course in agriculture for grade XI... 295
Instructions with reference to school and home gardening.................... 295
Home and school gardening, McLarty et al.................................. 295
School and home gardening for elementary schools in Oregon, Evans, jr....... 296
Possibilities of school-directed home gardening in Richmond, Ind............ 296
Supervised home project work, Smith....................................... 296
Supplementary lessons in West Virginia agriculture.......................... 296
Illustrated lecture on sweet potatoes: Culture and storage, Conolly........... 297
Illustrated lecture on the farm vegetable garden, Thompson and Conolly...... 297
Agricultural arithmetic, Shutts and Weir.................................... 297
Illustrative fair exhibits, Lutts.. 297

MISCELLANEOUS.

Annual Reports of the Department of Agriculture, 1916...................... 297
Twenty-ninth Annual Report of Illinois Station, 1916........................ 297
Twenty-fourth Annual Report of Minnesota Station, 1916.................... 297
Report of the superintendent, Northwest Experiment Station, 1910–1916...... 297
Reports of Northeast Experiment Station, Duluth, 1915 and 1916............. 298
Report of West Central substation, Morris, 1915............................ 298
Twenty-ninth Annual Report of New York Cornell Station, 1916.............. 298
Report of the Porto Rico Insular Station, 1915–16.......................... 298
Monthly Bulletin of the Ohio Experiment Station........................... 298

LIST OF EXPERIMENT STATION AND DEPARTMENT PUBLICATIONS REVIEWED.

Stations in the United States.

	Page.
Alabama College Station:	
Bul. 193, Feb., 1917............	233
Bul. 194, Feb., 1917............	234
Arizona Station:	
Bul. 78, Oct. 20, 1916.........	209
California Station:	
Bul. 277, Mar., 1917...........	236
Circ. 163, Apr., 1917...........	289
Colorado Station:	
Bul. 223, Feb., 1917............	241
Bul. 224, Feb., 1917	209
Bul. 225, Feb., 1917............	286
Bul. 226, Mar., 1917........ 232,	248
Connecticut State Station:	
Bul. 192, Jan., 1917............	231
Bul. 193, Mar., 1917........ 232,	234
Bul. Inform. 7, Apr., 1917....	290
An. Rpt. 1916, pt. 2............	254
An. Rpt. 1916, pt. 3............	268
Idaho Station:	
Circ. 3, May, 1916..............	271
Circ. 4, Jan., 1917.............	244
Illinois Station:	
Circ. 193, Apr., 1917...........	214
Circ. 194, Apr., 1917...........	242
Circ. 195, Apr., 1917...........	273
Twenty-ninth An. Rpt., 1916.	297
Indiana Station:	
Bul. 178, popular ed., Nov., 1914.........................	270
Bul. 179, popular ed., Nov., 1914.........................	270
Bul. 197, Dec., 1916.........	239
Bul. 198, Mar., 1917...........	214
Iowa Station:	
Soil Survey Rpt. 1, Jan., 1917.	211
Kansas Station:	
Insp. Bul. 1, Dec., 1915......	270
Minnesota Station:	
Twenty-fourth An. Rpt., 1916.	217,
226,228,229,240,241,270,271,289,297	
Rpt. Crookston Substa., 1910–1916.........................	210,
226, 241, 268, 270, 286, 289, 297	
Rpt. Duluth Substa., 1915.. 270,	298
Rpt. Duluth Substa., 1916....	228,
269, 271, 286, 298	
Rpt. Morris Substa., 1915... 229,	298
Montana Station:	
Bul. 111, Oct., 1916..........	290
Bul. 112, Dec., 1916...........	255
Bul. 113, Dec., 1916...........	238
Bul. 114, Dec., 1916...........	241
Bul. 115, Jan., 1917...........	283

Stations in the United States—Continued.

	Page.
New Jersey Stations:	
Bul. 299........................	259
Bul. 300, June 1, 1916.........	260
Bul. 301, Oct. 2, 1916..........	243
Bul. 302, Nov. 1, 1916........	239
Bul. 303, Dec. 12, 1916.......	219
Circ. 63, Jan. 30, 1917.........	251
Hints to Poultrymen, vol. 5, No. 7, Apr., 1917...........	280
New York Cornell Station:	
Twenty-ninth An. Rpt., 1916.	298
Ohio Station:	
Bul. 310, Feb., 1917..........	258
Bul. 311, Mar., 1917..........	258
Bul. 312, Mar., 1917..........	235
Bul. 313, Mar., 1917...........	241
Mo. Bul., vol. 2, No. 4, Apr., 1917.......................	219,
232, 238, 261, 262, 298	
Illus. Fair Exhibits, Feb., 1917.........................	297
Oregon Station:	
Bul. 142, Mar., 1917..........	243
Porto Rico Insular Station:	
An. Rpt., 1916.................	298
Virginia Truck Station:	
Bul. 22, Jan. 1, 1917...........	249

U. S. Department of Agriculture.

An. Rpts., 1916............. 277,289,297	
Jour. Agr. Research, vol. 9:	
No. 3, Apr. 16, 1917...........	222
No. 4, Apr. 23, 1917...... 281,282	
Bul. 389, Public Road Mileage and Revenues in the Central, Mountain, and Pacific States, 1914.............................	288
Bul. 390, Public Road Mileage and Revenues in the United States, 1914.............................	289
Bul. 481, The Status and Value of Farm Woodlots in the Eastern United States, E. H. Frothingham..............................	245
Bul. 504, The Theory of Correlation As Applied to Farm-survey Data on Fattening Baby Beef, H. R. Tolley..............................	269
Farmers' Bul. 796, Some Common Edible and Poisonous Mushrooms, Flora W. Patterson and Vera K. Charles................	263

U. S. Department of Agriculture—Con.

Bureau of Soils: Page.
  Field Operations, 1915—
    Soil Survey of New Castle
      County, Del., T. M. Mor-
      rison, W. B. Seward,
      and O. I. Snapp........   211
    Soil Survey of Richardson
      County, Nebr., A. H.
      Meyer, P. H. Stewart,
      and C. W. Watson......   211
    Soil Survey of Hamilton
      County, Ohio, A. L.
      Goodman, E. R. Allen,
      and S. W. Phillips.....   212
States Relations Service:
  Syllabus 26, Illustrated Lec-
    ture on Sweet Potatoes:
    Culture and Storage, H. M.
    Conolly....................   297
  Syllabus 27, Illustrated Lec-
    ture on the Farm Vegetable
    Garden, H. C. Thompson
    and H. M. Conolly.........   297
Scientific Contributions: [1]
  The Preparation of Pure Crys-
    talline Mannose, C. S. Hud-
    son and H. L. Sawyer......   201
  The Acetyl Derivatives of the
    Sugars, C. S. Hudson.......   201
  The Phenylh drazids of Cer-
    tain Acidsy of the Sugar
    Group, C. S. Hudson.......   201
  Reactions of Ions and Mole-
    cules of Acids, Bases, and
    Salts, W. A. Gruse and S. F.
    Acree......................   201
  Estimation of Butyric Acid in
    Biological Products, I. I. K.
    Phelps and H. E. Palmer..   206
  Normal Fermentation of Sauer-
    kraut, L. A. Round.......   208
  Agricultural Possibilities of
    Ohio Peat Soils, A. Dach-
    nowski....................   212
  The Organic Nitrogen Com-
    pounds of Soils and Fer-
    tilizers, E. C. Lathrop......   216
  New Names in Amygdalus,
    P. L. Ricker..............   220
  Effect of Environmental Con-
    ditions on Tobacco Plants,
    H. A. Allard...............   224
  Variety Testing, L. C. Corbett.   240
  Determining the Quality of
    Standing Timber, S. Berry..   243

U. S. Department of Agriculture—Con.

Scientific Contributions—Con.   Page.
  The Biology of Lodgepole Pine
    as Revealed by the Behavior
    of Its Seed, C. G. Bates....   244
  Further Evidence as to the
    Relation Between Crown
    Gall and Cancer, E. F.
    Smith......................   245
  The Nature of the Polyhedral
    Bodies Found in Insects,
    R. W. Glaser and J. W.
    Chapman...................   253
  Determining Wind Dispersion
    of the Gipsy Moth and Other
    Insects, C. W. Collins......   254
  Foreign Insect Pests Collected
    on Imported Nursery Stock
    in 1916, E. R. Sasscer......   257
  Some Methods of Colonizing
    Imported Parasites, S. S.
    Crossman...................   257
  New Tree Banding Material
    for Control of Gipsy Moth,
    A. F. Burgess and E. L.
    Griffin....................   258
  Crambid Moths and Light,
    G. G. Ainslie...............   259
  The Alfalfa Weevil Investiga-
    tion, G. I. Reeves.........   262
  The Results of Apiary Inspec-
    tion, E. F. Phillips.........   263
  Report on Isosoma Investiga-
    tions, W. J. Phillips........   263
  Biology and the Nation's Food,
    W. J. Spillman............   263
  Influence of Heavy Metals on
    the Isolated Intestine, W.
    Salant and C. W. Mitchell..   266
  American Veterinary Medical
    Association.—Report of Com-
    mittee on Diseases, J. R.
    Mohler.....................   274
  Suppuration in Cattle and
    Swine Caused by *Bacterium
    pyogenes*, A. R. Ward......   276
  The Farmer's Part in Irriga-
    tion Development, S. For-
    tier.......................   281
  Duty of Water, S. O. Jayne..   281
  Agriculture and the Farming
    Business, O. H. Benson and
    G. H. Betts................   290
  The Federal Farm Loan Act,
    C. W. Thompson...........   291

[1] Printed in scientific and technical publications outside the Department.

RECENT WORK IN AGRICULTURAL SCIENCE.

AGRICULTURAL CHEMISTRY—AGROTECHNY.

The preparation of pure crystalline mannose and a study of its mutarotation, C. S. HUDSON and H. L. SAWYER (*Jour. Amer. Chem. Soc., 39 (1917), No. 3, pp. 470–478*).—A method of crystallizing mannose directly and in large yield from the products of acid hydrolysis of vegetable ivory (the endosperm of the seed of the tagua palm, *Phytelephas macrocarpa*) has been devised and is described in detail. The rate of mutarotation of an aqueous solution was carefully studied, the results indicating that it is similar to that of other aldose and ketose sugars and is caused by a balanced reaction between α-mannose and β-mannose.

The acetyl derivatives of the sugars, C. S. HUDSON (*Jour. Indus. and Engin. Chem., 8 (1916), No. 4, pp. 380–382*).—An address delivered at the presentation of the Nichols medal to the author, March 10, 1916.

A relation between the chemical constitution and the optical rotatory power of the phenylhydrazids of certain acids of the sugar group, C. S. HUDSON (*Jour. Amer. Chem. Soc., 39 (1917), No. 3, pp. 462–470*).

The reactions of both the ions and the molecules of acids, bases, and salts; the inversion of menthone by sodium, potassium, and lithium ethylates, W. A. GRUSE and S. F. ACREE (*Jour. Amer. Chem. Soc., 39 (1917), No. 3, pp. 376–388, figs. 3*).

Concerning the failure to detect ornithin in plants, A. KIZEL (KIESEL) (*Izv. Imp. Akad. Nauk (Bul. Acad. Imp. Sci. Petrograd), 6. ser., 1915, No. 15, pp. 1661–1665*).—The author considers previous failures to detect ornithin in plants to be due to the lack of proper conditions for successful analyses. Experiments were conducted with ornithin obtained from arginin from edestin of hempseed by the action of arginase from liver and from wheat sprouts. From the results of the experiments it is concluded that the following conditions are necessary for the best precipitation of ornithin by phosphotungstic acid: More concentrated solutions of ornithin; a large excess of phosphotungstic acid to reduce the solubility of the precipitated ornithin; increased acidity of the solution during precipitation; washing of the precipitate with phosphotungstic acid or a mixture of phosphotungstic and sulphuric acids, rather than with 5 per cent sulphuric acid alone; and allowing the precipitate to stand for some time before filtration, as the precipitate forms very slowly.

Decomposition of pyroracemic acid by dead plants in the presence of a hydrogen acceptor, V. I. PALLADIN, E. I. LOVCHINOVSKAÎÂ, and A. I. ALEKSÎÊEV (*Izv. Imp. Akad. Nauk (Bul. Acad. Imp. Sci. Petrograd), 6. ser., 1915, No. 7, pp. 589–600*).—In earlier work the authors have studied the influence exerted by hydrogen acceptors on alcoholic fermentation and respiration of plants, as well as on the decomposition of individual organic compounds in the course of these processes. Pyroracemic acid appeared among the decomposition products in both cases. In the work submitted the effect of the addition of methylene blue on the process of decomposition of pyroracemic acid resulting in the formation of acetaldehyde and carbon dioxid was determined.

In general, it is concluded that methylene blue retards the decomposition of potassium pyroracemate by old yeast and the sprouts of wheat, especially during the first hours of the reaction. A slight stimulation, however, was observed with pea seeds. The formation of acids takes place along with the activity of carboxylase. Methylene blue is considered to take up the hydrogen of water and thus favor the accumulation of acids through the remaining oxygen.

Activity of reductase and carboxylase in decomposition of lactic acid by yeasts, V. I. PALLADIN, D. A. SABININ, and E. I. LOVCHINOVSKAÍA (*Izv. Imp. Akad. Nauk (Bul. Acad. Imp. Sci Petrograd), 6. ser., 1915, No. 8, pp. 701-718).*—The results of the investigation reported are summarized as follows:

The decomposition of potassium lactate by dead yeast in the presence of methylene blue leads to a splitting off of carbon dioxid with the production of acetaldehyde. Theoretically, one-half of the carbon dioxid should be in the free state and the other combined as potassium carbonate, but in reality a much larger quantity of carbon dioxid is given off. If the decomposition of potassium lactate by dead yeast takes place in a current of air oxygen is energetically absorbed and the ratio $\frac{CO_2}{O_2}$ approaches unity.

The decomposition of lactic acid by yeasts in the presence of a hydrogen acceptor consists of, first, the separation of hydrogen by reductase with the production of pyroracemic acid and, secondly, the splitting off of carbon dioxid from the pyroracemic acid through the action of carboxylase, with the production of acetaldehyde. Since pyroracemic acid is considered to be an intermediate product of alcoholic fermentation, its production from lactic acid is considered to offer new proof that lactic acid is an intermediate product of alcoholic fermentation.

Decomposition of lactic acid by killed yeast, V. I. PALLADIN (W. PALLADIN) and D. A. SABININ (*Izv. Imp. Akad. Nauk (Bul. Acad. Imp. Sci. Petrograd), 6. ser., 1916, No. 3, pp. 187-194; Biochem. Jour., 10 (1916), No. 2, pp. 183-196).*—The authors endeavored to determine under what conditions the decomposition of lactic acid would produce alcohol instead of acetaldehyde. Methylene blue as ordinarily used for a hydrogen receptor was replaced by pyroracemic acid which, when decomposed by carboxylase, yields acetaldehyde. The data submitted, while not considered to prove conclusively that lactic acid is the intermediate product of alcoholic fermentation, are indicated as showing that alcohol does not present the result of decomposition but the product of reduction of acetaldehyde by removing the hydrogen from one of the intermediate products of the decomposition of glucose.

Investigations on the significance of hydrogen in alcoholic fermentation and respiration have shown that on the reductions depend the anaerobic oxidations. During the formation of the intermediate products in the molecule of glucose the hydrogen and not the oxygen is displaced. The chemical processes of alcoholic fermentation and respiration can not be explained by reactions of decomposition alone, as the hydrogen is displaced not only within the confines of one molecule but also passes from one molecule into another. Points in favor of the theory that lactic acid is an intermediate product in alcoholic fermentation are discussed.

The effect of alcohol and methylene blue on the formation of carbon dioxid by dead yeast, V. I. PALLADIN and E. I. LOVCHINOVSKAÍA (*Izv. Imp. Akad. Nauk (Bul. Acad. Imp. Sci. Petrograd), 6. ser., 1916, No. 4, pp. 253–256*).—Experiments are reported, the purpose of which was to determine whether or not those plants which are able to oxidize alcohol under normal conditions may do so in the presence of a hydrogen acceptor with the formation of carbon dioxid.

The results obtained in general were negative. Preparations containing alcohol and methylene blue sometimes produced slightly more carbon dioxid than mixtures with alcohol alone. This small increase is attributed to the stimulation of the process of fermentation by the methylene blue.

On reductase of plants, V. I. PALLADIN, P. G. PLATISHENSKIĬ, and E. V. ÉLLADI (*Izv. Imp. Akad. Nauk (Bul. Acad. Imp. Sci. Petrograd), 6. ser., 1915, No. 4, pp. 309–326, fig. 1*).—It is indicated that the process of reduction in living organisms is of much more general occurrence than any other enzymic process, and that a thorough knowledge of its mode of action is especially important for the correct conception of the process of respiration. Experiments carried on with seeds and sprouts of peas, wheat sprouts, and several preparations of yeast are described in detail. The progress of reduction was determined by comparison with control solutions of methylene blue.

Soaking was found to accelerate reduction in pea seeds considerably. An acceleration was also noted in pea sprouts, especially on the addition of potassium bicarbonate. It is considered to be quite possible that germination is accompanied by an increase in the amount of reductase.

Extracted yeast reduced methylene blue less easily than nonextracted. The reductase activity was paralyzed by autolysis. Boiled taka-diastase was found to act as a coezym, while the unboiled exerted no influence. Peroxidase inhibited the action of reductase.

Water was found indispensable for the activity of the enzym, while glycerin, pyridin, alcohol, and formamid retarded its activity. Potassium hydroxid in moderate quantities greatly stimulated reduction, but in larger amounts retarded it. The action of calcium hydroxid was the reverse of that of potassium hydroxid, while magnesium oxid exerted a stimulative action. The presence of reductase in commercial diastase, taka-diastase, and emulsin was not determined with certainty.

It is indicated that the course of reduction depends on the amount of reductase and the substance to be oxidized, as well as on the amount of the hydrogen acceptor (substance to be reduced).

The action of peroxidase on chlorophyll, V. LĬUBIMENKO (*Izv. Imp. Akad. Nauk (Bul. Acad. Imp. Sci. Petrograd), 6. ser., 1915, No. 11, pp. 1159–1170*).— The author notes a recently discovered enzym of green plants, provisionally named antioxidase, which paralyzes the oxidizing activity of peroxidase and thus protects chlorophyll from decomposition in the course of the process of assimilation. The action of the antioxidase ceases immediately on the addition of antiseptics which destroy the new enzym, and rapid decomposition of chlorophyll follows.

The effect of the reaction of the medium on the activity of inulase of Aspergillus niger, A. KIZEL (KIESEL) (*Izv. Imp. Akad. Nauk (Bul. Acad. Imp. Sci. Petrograd), 6. ser., 1915, No. 11, pp. 1077–1092, figs. 3*).—The action of inulase extracted from the mycelium of *A. niger* on inulin obtained from dahlia roots was tested in the presence of sulphuric, hydrochloric, phosphoric, and acetic acids, sodium nitrate, disodium phosphate, disodium citrate, monosodium phosphate, and monosodium citrate.

A slight increase of the activity of inulase was noted in the presence of the acids, while a great activation was afforded by the acid salts, especially disodium citrate and monosodium phosphate. Alkaline salts, on the contrary, appeared to exert a harmful effect on the activity of the enzym.

Studies of arginase and urease in plants, A. KIZEL (KIESEL) (*Izv. Imp. Akad. Nauk (Bul. Acad. Imp. Sci. Petrograd), 6. ser., 1915, No. 13, pp. 1337–1364*).—Confirming earlier findings the author ascertained the presence of arginase and urease in *Aspergillus niger*, and also established the occurrence of the enzyms in ergot on *Secale cornutum*, in vetch (*Vicia sativa*), and in ripe fruits of *Angelica silvestris*, as well as the presence of urease in etiolated sprouts of the white lupine. In previous work the existence of arginase in the sprouts of the white lupine and both arginase and urease in meadow mushrooms had been established.

The enzyms of *A. niger* were found not to split guanidin tetramethylenamin, although there was a partial cleavage of tetramethylendiguanidin with the formation of guanidin tetramethylenamin. The enzyms found in ergot, meadow mushrooms, and vetch do not decompose either of these reagents. In the work with the enzyms of the ergot, guanidin also remained unchanged. In some experiments with the white lupine and red clover (*Trifolium pratense*), in which only tetramethylendiguanidin was used, no cleavage of the reagent was observed.

The experimental procedures used and the data obtained are described in detail.

Effect of medium on proteolytic enzyms of plants, V. I. PALLADIN (*Izv. Imp. Akad. Nauk (Bul. Acad. Imp. Sci. Petrograd), 6. ser., 1916, No. 7, pp. 527–538*).— Since proteolytic enzyms affect the activity of other enzyms, particularly the oxidases, the author attempted to determine experimentally substances which would check the action of the proteolytic enzyms but would not at the same time be harmful to the oxidative enzyms. Preparations of yeast and wheat sprouts served as experimental material, and sucrose, glycerin, ethylenglycol, pyroracemic acid, formalin, and sodium chlorid were tested as inhibitors.

Corroborative evidence was obtained in regard to the poisonous action of formalin on the proteolytic enzyms of yeast. A 1 per cent solution of pyroracemic acid neutralized by potassium hydroxid exerted practically no influence. The other substances were found to divide themselves into two groups, electrolytes and nonelectrolytes. Nonelectrolytes retarded the action of proteolytic enzyms in a manner proportionate to their concentration, while weak solutions of the electrolytes stimulated the action of proteolytic enzyms. A strong solution of sodium chlorid slightly inhibited the action, but in a much less degree than any of the nonelectrolytes.

It is concluded that the introduction of the harmless nonelectrolytes which arrest the action of proteolytic enzyms should have a beneficial effect on the action of the enzyms in alcoholic fermentation. Notwithstanding the fact that zymase may also be affected by nonelectrolytes, the formation of carbon dioxid is increased with the increase of concentration of these substances until an optimum of concentration is reached. Beyond this the nonelectrolytes may entirely inhibit the action of zymase.

Some auxoamylases, E. W. ROCKWOOD (*Abs. in Proc. Iowa Acad. Sci., 23 (1916), pp. 37–39*).—The author designates nitrogenous substances (particularly those containing an NH₂ group) which stimulate the activity of amylases as auxoamylases. In the work reported glycin, tyrosin, hippuric acid, anthranilic acid, and asparagin were found to be active, while sulphanilic acid and acid amids like urea, acetamid, and propionamid were inactive.

The effect of the amino acids as produced by digestive proteolysis on the amylolytic enzyms is indicated. The work is being continued.

Quantitative microscopy, T. E. WALLIS (*Analyst, 41 (1916), No. 489, pp. 357–375, fig. 1*).—The author points out the common errors in the microscopical examination for adulteration, and describes a method of general applicability which obviates the usual sources of error. As a standard for comparison in the new procedure, the author uses a suspension of lycopodium spores.

An improved method of determining solubility, W. S. HENDRIXSON (*Proc. Iowa Acad. Sci., 23 (1916), pp. 31–34, figs. 2*).—A simple procedure for determining solubility, in which the solution is stirred by air which has been previously saturated with moisture at the temperature for which it is desired to determine the solubility, is described in detail. This saturation of the air compensates for the usual unavoidable loss by evaporation when the stirring is accomplished by air. The apparatus was used in connection with solubility determinations of acid sodium and acid potassium phthalates, which have been proposed by the author as standards in acidimetry and alkalimetry (E. S. R., 34, p. 408).

Preparation of sulphurous acid, E. HART (*Jour. Amer. Chem. Soc., 39 (1917), No. 3, p. 376*).—For the preparation of small amounts of sulphurous acid for the laboratory the author recommends the warming of fuming sulphuric acid containing 30 per cent SO_3 with sulphur. Lump sulphur in not too large amount should be used. It dissolves in the acid and forms a blue solution from which, on warming, SO_2 mixed with some SO_3 is given off. If SO_3 is objectionable, the gas obtained can be absorbed, and the resulting solution boiled to obtain the SO_2. The acid which remains is still fit for most uses. The value of the procedure, in view of the saving in copper, is considerable.

An improved nephelometer-colorimeter, P. A. KOBER (*Jour. Biol. Chem., 29 (1917), No. 2, pp. 155–168, figs. 9*).—The construction and manipulation of the new instrument, together with a simple and convenient lamp and lamp house, are described in detail. Advantages claimed for the new apparatus are a screw arrangement for changing the heights of the liquids, and, therefore, the elimination of lost motion inherent in racks and pinions; the elimination of dark cloth curtains; black one-piece glass plungers; fused one-piece nephelometric and colorimetric cups; and a convenient eye support.

The iodometric determination of sulphur dioxid and the sulphites, J. B. FERGUSON (*Jour. Amer. Chem. Soc., 39 (1917), No. 3, pp. 364–373*).—The author briefly reviews the methods which have been used, and points out a number of sources of error.

For the very accurate determination of large or small amounts of sulphur dioxid the excess iodin method is recommended. When carbon dioxid and sulphur dioxid are to be determined in the same sample the sulphite method can be used to advantage. For the most accurate results it is indicated that the following conditions must be observed:

"The gas sample must not come in contact with even a trace of moisture prior to its reaching the absorbent. The analyzing apparatus must be free from all rubber connectors when exact analyses of mixtures containing 10 per cent or more of sulphur dioxid are desired. For very accurate work it would be better to dispense with them entirely, although this source of error for mixtures containing less than 3 per cent of sulphur dioxid may be neglected. Mixtures of sulphur dioxid and air when dry do not react appreciably, but when moist a slow oxidation takes place. For this reason it is impossible to recover from a moist container, even by pumping, the initial amount of sulphur dioxid if the gas mixture has been in the container for any great length of time."

For the analysis of such soluble sulphites as anhydrous sodium sulphite the solution of the solid salt directly in an excess of an iodin solution containing sufficient hydrochloric acid and the determination of the excess iodin with thiosulphate is recommended. This procedure eliminates several sources of error, due to oxidation of the salt by agents other than the iodin solution.

The separation and estimation of butyric acid in biological products, I, I. K. PHELPS and H. E. PALMER (*Jour. Biol. Chem., 29 (1917), No. 2, pp. 199–205*).—A method for the separation of butyric acid from formic and acetic acids by treating their barium salts with an excess of quinin sulphate, extracting the quinin butyrate with carbon tetrachlorid, crystallizing, weighing, and identifying it by its melting point is described.

A table showing the melting point and approximate solubility in carbon tetrachlorid of the quinin salts of formic, acetic, propionic, butyric, and sulphuric acids is submitted. The solubilities of the propionate and butyrate are so nearly the same that only a partial separation can be effected. The difference in the solubilities of the formate and propionate is, however, so much greater that their separation is effected easily.

Thiobarbituric acid as a qualitative reagent for ketohexose, G. P. PLAISANCE (*Jour. Biol. Chem., 29 (1917), No. 2, pp. 207, 208*).—The author, at the Iowa Experiment Station, recommends the use of thiobarbituric acid as a test for ketohexoses as follows:

The sample to be tested is treated in a test tube with sufficient hydrochloric acid and water to bring the acid concentration to 12 per cent. The mixture is then heated to boiling, cooled under the tap, and a few drops of thiobarbituric acid solution (in 12 per cent hydrochloric acid) added. If a ketohexose was originally present an orange-colored precipitate forms on standing; if only aldoses were present the solution may become yellow but no precipitate results. It is indicated that barbituric acid can not be used in place of the thiobarbituric acid, as the condensation product is much more soluble.

Nitrogen in amino form as determined by formol titration, in relation to some other factors measuring quality in wheat flour, C. O. SWANSON and E. L. TAGUE (*Jour. Amer. Chem. Soc., 39 (1917), No. 3, pp. 482–491, figs. 5*).—The authors, at the Kansas Experiment Station, have shown " that a comparatively large amount of nitrogen in amino form, as determined by the method of precipitation with phosphotungstic acid, is an indication of certain undesirable qualities in flour. These qualties in sound flour are of the same kind as those denoted by ash and acidity. Nitrogen in amino form, as measured by formol titration, is valuable together with the determination of ash and acidity in measuring quality in flour."

It is indicated, however, that titrable nitrogen is more uniformly distributed in the wheat kernel than are the materials which determine the amount of ash and acidity. In clear and low-grade flours, therefore, as compared with patent and straight flours made from the same wheat, the increase in titrable nitrogen is not proportional to the increase in ash or acidity.

Data relative to the ash, acidity, formol titration, and total nitrogen in 10-gm. samples of mill streams, commercial patent flours, commercial straight flours, commercial clear flours, and commercial low-grade flours are submitted. They show that the lower grades of flour, such as the clear and low-grade, made from sound wheat, do not contain nitrogenous substances measured by formol titration in as large a proportion as ash and acidity.

See also previous notes (E. S. R., 30, p. 555; 33, p. 160.)

The amino-acid nitrogen content of the blood of various species, J. C. BOCK (*Jour. Biol. Chem., 29 (1917), No. 2, pp. 191–198*).—Tabulated analytical data of the amino-acid nitrogen per 100 cc. of ox, calf, sheep, pig, cat, dog, chicken, duck, turkey, goose, human, and placental blood, and a number of pathological specimens of human blood, and in the whole blood, plasma, and corpuscles of the calf, goose, chicken, and ox, are submitted, together with a detailed procedure for the determination of amino acids in blood. See also a previous note (E. S. R., 37, p. 14).

A rapid method for determining calcium in blood and milk, H. LYMAN (*Jour. Biol. Chem., 29 (1917), No. 2, pp. 169–178*).—Applying the principles previously used for determining calcium in urine and feces (E. S. R., 34, p. 508), a slightly modified procedure is described for determining calcium in blood and milk. The method is simple and rapid and yields results accurate to within less than 1 per cent.

For the preparation of the calcium soap a reagent prepared as follows was used: Four gm. of stearic acid and 0.5 gm. of oleic acid are dissolved in 400 cc. of hot alcohol, 20 gm. of ammonium carbonate dissolved in 100 cc. of hot water is added, and the mixture is allowed to boil for a few moments. It is cooled and 400 cc. of alcohol, 100 cc. of water, and 2 cc. of ammonium hydroxid (specific gravity 0.9) are added, and then filtered. This solution should be perfectly clear and if well stoppered will keep indefinitely. Before using, this solution should be tested in the nephelometer for impurities. Since the introduction of 0.002 mg. of calcium in the course of the determination would result in an error of 1 per cent the importance of having reagents absolutely free from calcium is emphasized.

[Note on the Duclaux method] (*Dept. Landb., Nijv. en Handel [Netherlands], Verslag. en Meded. Dir. Landb., No. 5 (1916), p. 12*).—The importance of maintaining at 110 cc. the volume of the mixture being distilled after the removal of the 10 cc. fractions, especially where a mixture of several acids is being distilled, is pointed out.

The detection of small amounts of oxalic acid in wine, A. A. BESSON (*Schweiz. Apoth. Ztg., 55 (1917), No. 7, pp. 81–85*).—The author has thoroughly studied the method of Kreis and Baragiola,[1] which consists of treating 50 cc. of the sample in the cold with 2.5 cc. of a 5 per cent calcium chlorid solution, 2.5 cc. acetic acid, and 5 cc. of a cold saturated solution of sodium acetate, allowing it to stand for 24 hours, and then centrifugalizing and examining the residue obtained. It is indicated that 0.01 per cent of oxalic acid can easily be detected by this procedure.

The results of the study show that the concentration of the reagents has a great influence not only on the crystal form of the precipitated oxalate but also on the delicacy of the test. A reagent consisting of a solution of 20 gm. of pure crystallized calcium chlorid in 250 cc. water to which 250 cc. of acetic acid and 500 cc. of a cold saturated solution of sodium acetate are added has been found to yield excellent results. Ten cc. of this reagent is used for a 50 cc. sample of the wine.

In the course of the study it was observed that in the samples containing oxalic acid, even in amounts as small as 0.01 per cent, there was no growth of mold, indicating the preservative action of the acid, at least in respect to molds. Certain samples which originally gave positive tests for oxalic acid yielded negative tests after several weeks. The oxalic acid thus appears to be destroyed in time. No explanation is given for this phenomenon.

Researches on the ultrafiltration of milk, A. BOBBINO (*Arch. Ital. Biol., 64 (1915), No. 3, pp. 417–425*).—After having experienced some difficulty in the ultrafiltration of milk through collodion membranes the author obtained a clear

---

[1] Schweiz. Apoth. Ztg., 53 (1915), No. 29, pp. 397–400.

filtrate by passing the centrifugalized milk through an alundum filter. About 250 cc. of clear filtrate was obtained in two hours by this procedure.

Comparative analytical data relative to the specific gravity, electrical conductivity, freezing point, protein, lactose, ash (soluble and insoluble), chlorin, calcium, and phosphorus of the whole milk and filtrate (cow and human), and the probable combinations between the casein, calcium, and phosphorus in the residue from the filtrate of cow's milk are submitted in tabular form. It is concluded that in human milk as well as in cow's milk the lactose is not combined with the protein. A part of the calcium and phosphorus exists free in a dissociable form. The calcium forms, not alone with the casein but also with the phosphoric acid and probably other anions, certain combinations which as yet have not been determined. These are retained by the filter and are probably to be regarded as nondissociable combinations, for the most part colloidal. In cow's milk a calcium-casein combination containing 2.4 per cent calcium oxid was determined.

In human milk the quantity of calcium and phosphorus in inorganic combination is relatively larger than that in cow's milk, representing more than one-half of the total calcium and phosphorus. In cow's milk the quantity represents less than one-third of the total.

A rapid and exact method for determining the diastatic activity of germinated grain, C. A. Nowak (*Pure Products, 13 (1917), No. 3, pp. 128–131*).— The author describes in detail a rapid modified procedure which is considered to yield reliable results.

The soluble carbohydrate content of feeding stuffs as a guide in determining quality, G. B. Van Kampen (*Cultura, 27 (1915), No. 324, pp. 241–256*).— The author briefly indicates that the results of a chemical and microscopical examination of feeding stuffs do not always yield the desired information in regard to the quality of the material.

The literature on the soluble and insoluble carbohydrates in normal and abnormal press cakes is reviewed. A procedure for determining soluble sugars polarimetrically before and after inversion is described and some experimental data submitted and discussed. While the data are considered to be only preliminary and it is deemed hardly possible to define any definite limits for sugar content of normal and abnormal samples because of the small amount of data available, the following percentage contents of sugar (calculated as sucrose) are considered normal for samples of first-grade material: Coconut cake, 17.5; soy bean cake, 13; peanut cake, 12; cottonseed meal, 7; linseed meal, 5; palm nut cake, 3.5; and sesame cake, 3.

Cane juice clarification, C. W. Hines (*Philippine Agr. Rev. [English Ed.], 9 (1916), No. 4, pp. 339–347*).—This is a general discussion of the common clarifiers used in cane sugar manufacture, as well as some special trade clarifiers.

Normal fermentation of sauerkraut, L. A. Round (*Jour. Bact., 1 (1916), No. 1, p. 108*).—The author has studied the fermentation of sauerkraut in two factories, in the first making microscopical and chemical examinations and in the second a bacteriological study.

It was found that bacteria alone were concerned with the fermentation proper. Wherever air came in contact with the material, as at the top of the vat, yeasts grew rapidly and produced a heavy foul-smelling scum which destroyed the acid. A vat just being filled showed the presence of 5,000,000 organisms per cubic centimeter, 80 per cent of which fermented glucose and the remaining 20 per cent being mainly yeasts. The rate of growth of bacteria and the rapidity of fermentation were found to vary directly with the temperature, being much slower in cold than in warm weather. After reaching a maximum, the number of bacteria gradually decreased until at the end of five weeks between 4,000,000 and 10,000,000 viable organisms were present.

Vats showing abnormal fermentation contained a different class of organisms. Bad fermentations in properly salted vats were found to be due to the growth of unfavorable organisms during the first few days before the normal acid flora had been able to establish itself and produce sufficient acid to stop decomposition. A slight increase in temperature was found in the course of normal fermentation.

METEOROLOGY.

Relation of weather to crops and varieties adapted to Arizona conditions (*Arizona Sta. Bul. 78 (1916), pp. 45–118, pl. 1, fig. 1*).—"This publication is a thorough revision of Bulletin 61 (E. S. R., 22, p. 418). The arrangement and much of the body of the publication are essentially the same, but considerable new matter has been added, and information concerning the various crops and their adaptability to different parts of the State has been revised in accordance with new developments and the added experience of the past several years. This information has been secured from records which have been accumulating at the experiment station farms, and from personal visits and correspondence of the different members of the station staff throughout the State."

The records upon which the bulletin is based have now covered a period of 18 years. The bulletin deals briefly with methods of keeping weather records; factors influencing results; general effects of temperature, direct sunshine, and aridity and rainfall; and more in detail with varieties of crops which have proved most suitable to different sections of the State, arranged alphabetically for convenient reference and also with reference to the months in which they should be planted and when they mature.

Native vegetation and climate of Colorado in their relation to agriculture, W. W. ROBBINS (*Colorado Sta. Bul. 224 (1917), pp. 3–56, pls. 4, figs. 16*).—"This bulletin is an outgrowth of a number of years of observation and study of the native vegetation of Colorado in its relation to climate and to agriculture" supplemented by a reconnoissance survey especially of the west middle portion of the State during the summer of 1916, which was undertaken "for the purpose of testing conclusions arrived at and finding new relations."

In this study little consideration has been given "to the question of the value of native plant life as an indicator of the local physical conditions of the environment. Such detailed study, however, is of much practical importance, and it is planned to engage in such a study later. But the attempt here is to point out the broader relations between our large native plant associations and the principal climatic factors under which they are growing, and to show their relation, in a very general way, to Colorado agriculture." Data, original and compiled, on temperature of the surface of the plant, air, and soil, with different altitudes, slopes, and other conditions; length of frostless season and effects of frosts and freezes; amount and distribution of precipitation under varying conditions; humidity; and sunshine, are presented and discussed.

"The following large communities of Colorado native plants, with their climatic and agricultural relations, are discussed: (1) Grass-steppe or short-grassland (Great Plains); (2) shrub-steppe—sagebrush, greasewood, rabbitbrush, etc.; (3) chaparral or brushland (thicket)—oakbrush, buckbrush, willow thicket, chokeberry, thornapple, mountain mahogany, etc.; (4) coniferous woodland—pinyon pine and juniper woodland; (5) coniferous forests—(a) yellow pine-Douglas fir forest, (b) white fir forest, (c) lodgepole pine forest, (d) Engelmann spruce-balsam fir forest."

The grass-steppe is stated to be "a vegetative response to a low, infrequent rainfall, the greater percentage (approximately 75 per cent) of which comes during the growing season, and about 60 per cent of which is during the four months, June, July, August, and September." The average annual temperature for the steppe area ranges from 45 to 56° F. The relative humidity is generally low, from about 50 to 55 per cent. The grass-steppe is indicative of temperature conditions favorable to a varied agriculture when sufficient moisture is supplied.

The shrub-steppe, which is scattered throughout the entire intermountain area, and occupies nearly 25 per cent of the area of the State, is as a rule representative of good general farming and orchard lands. The most important and by far the most extensive vegetation of the shrub-steppe is sagebrush, which is the characteristic type of vegetation of the well-drained, nonalkaline arid districts of western Colorado. Types of shrub-steppe vegetation of secondary importance are greasewood and rabbitbrush, which cover the larger part of San Luis Valley and limited areas in other parts of the State. Greasewood is not indicative of any particular set of climatic factors, but is a response to local soil conditions. It is, however, almost always an indication of a high water table and consequently of soil rich in alkali. "The round-leaved saltbush (*Atriplex confertifolia*), sometimes along with greasewood (*Sarcobatus vermiculatus*), and common Grayia (*Grayia spinosa*), is found chiefly on alkaline flats in western Colorado, especially in the lower valleys. Extensive and typical areas of this association are found in the lower Snake River Valley. The soil it occupies is usually fine-grained, the surface layers dry, and the soil below the first and second foot quite high in salt content. Salt sage or small saltbush (*Atriplex nuttalli*) is another plant of alkaline flats."

Scrub oak forms the most extensive growth of chaparral or brushland and grows under a wide range of climatic conditions as found between 4,000 and 9,000 ft. It is frequently associated with buckbrush, and both usually occupy deep rich soil. Scrub oak forms are seldom found above the limit of successful growth of alfalfa, potatoes, small grains, strawberries, hardy can fruits, and the hardy vegetables.

The pinyon pine-juniper woodland zone is confined to a region of which the mean annual precipitation is uniformly under 15 in. It is an index "of temperature conditions which permit the growth of all but the tenderest fruits, all the small grains, flax, sugar beets, potatoes, alfalfa, and the garden vegetables, excluding melons. In the lower part of the belt peaches, sweet cherries, melons, and other tender crops yield bountifully. Much valuable orchard land of Colorado is cleared pinyon pine-juniper soil."

Yellow-pine forests seldom show typical development in areas having less than 15 in. of precipitation annually. Its altitude ranges approximately from 6,000 to 8,000 ft. in northern Colorado and 7,000 to 9,000 ft. in southern Colorado. A large percentage of the area of growth of this plant is so steep and stony as to be economically adapted only to grazing and timber growing. Yellow-pine forest indicates temperature conditions favorable to the maturing usually of wheat, oats, barley, and rye, and is well suited to alfalfa, potatoes, and the hardier vegetables, cane fruits, and strawberries.

"Lodgepole pine, as a strongly developed plant association, indicates temperature conditions too low for the maturing of the small cereals, for the profitable growth of alfalfa, potatoes, peas, and any but the most hardy vegetables." The same is true of the white-fir forest zone. Engelmann fir occupies a region of nonagricultural climatic conditions.

Weather conditions, 1911-1916 (*Minnesota Sta., Rpt. Crookton Substa., 1910-1916, pp. 14-19*).—Tables are given which show the precipitation by months and the dates of the latest killing frost in the spring and the earliest in the fall at Crookston, Minn., from 1897 to October 1, 1916, and summaries of observations on temperature, precipitation, clear and cloudy days, and prevailing winds during the same period. The average date of the earliest killing frost was September 24, the average growing period being 127 days.

SOILS—FERTILIZERS.

Soil survey of New Castle County, Delaware, T. M. MORRISON, W. D. SEWARD, and O. I. SNAPP (*U. S. Dept. Agr., Advance Sheets Field Operations Bur. Soils, 1915, pp. 34, fig. 1, map 1*).—This survey, made in cooperation with the Delaware Experiment Station, deals with the soils of an area of 278,400 acres in northern Delaware, two-thirds of which lie in the Coastal Plain and one-third in the Piedmont Plateau. The surface includes a smooth to rolling plain in which drainage is not yet thoroughly established, and a well-drained and deeply dissected plateau.

Including tidal marsh and meadow, 16 soil types of six series are mapped, of which the Sassafras silt loam and loam and the Chester loam cover 26.5, 12.4, and 11.9 per cent of the area, respectively.

Analyses of soils of Habersham County, W. A. WORSHAM, JR., D. D. LONG, L. M. CARTER, and M. W. LOWRY (*Bul. Ga. State Col. Agr., No. 114 (1917), pp. 40, figs. 5*).—This report is intended to supplement the physical survey of the soils of the county made in cooperation with the Bureau of Soils of the U. S. Department of Agriculture, and contains data on the chemical composition of both the surface soil and subsoil of the various soil types found in the county.

"Taking the average of all soils of the county, analyses show the plant food content to be as follows: Nitrogen, 0.0425 per cent; phosphoric acid, 0.0616; and potash, 1.0126. Nitrogen and phosphoric acid are relatively low in the average soil of the county. Nitrogen is lowest, and, without doubt, the limiting factor of crop production."

Bremer County soils, W. H. STEVENSON, P. E. BROWN, and F. B. HOWE (*Iowa Sta. Soil Survey Rpt. 1 (1917), pp. 48, pl. 1, figs. 11*).—This is the first of a series of reports on the soils of Iowa, and supplements the survey made in cooperation with the Bureau of Soils of the U. S. Department of Agriculture (E. S. R., 32, p. 317).

Analyses of samples of the soils taken at depths of 6¾ in., 6¾ to 20 in., and 20 to 40 in., are reported. "These results, as a whole, show that the soils of Bremer County are not so richly supplied with necessary plant food as to assure abundant crop growth continuously. . . . In general the application of phosphorus, the increase of humus and of nitrogen, and the addition of limestone are needed to make the soils of the county permanently fertile. Other essential elements are apparently present in sufficient amounts for many years to come."

General information regarding the principles of permanent soil fertility and the results of greenhouse tests of some of the prevailing soil types of the county are included.

Soil survey of Richardson County, Nebraska, A. H. MEYER, P. H. STEWART, and C. W. WATSON (*U. S. Dept. Agr., Advance Sheets Field Operations Bur. Soils, 1915, pp. 36, fig. 1, map 1*).—This survey, made in cooperation with the University of Nebraska, deals with the soils of an area of 348,800 acres in southeastern Nebraska, the topography of which is in general rolling. The surface drainage is considered to be adequate. The county lies almost entirely within the glacial and loessial region, with only a small area belonging to the river flood plain province.

The soils include upland, terrace, and first bottom soils. Including river wash and rough stony land, 14 soil types of nine series are mapped, of which the Carrington silt loam, Wabash silt loam, and Marshall silt loam cover 46.5, 19.6, and 16.5 per cent of the area, respectively.

Soil survey of Hamilton County, Ohio, A. L. GOODMAN, E. R. ALLEN, and S. W. PHILLIPS (*U. S. Dept. Agr., Advance Sheets Field Operations Bur. Soils, 1915, pp. 39, fig. 1, map 1*).—This survey, made in cooperation with the Ohio Experiment Station, deals with the soils of an area of 260,480 acres in southwestern Ohio, the topography of which ranges from level or nearly flat to hilly, ridgy, and rough. Drainage in general is said to be well established.

The soils consist of upland, terrace, and bottom land. "The soil-forming material is complex in origin as well as in mode of accumulation. It is partly glacial drift or till, partly residual material left in the decay of limestone and calcareous shales, partly a smooth, silty material whose origin is not thoroughly understood, and partly alluvium." Seventeen soil types of ten series are mapped, of which the Cincinnati silt loam and the Fairmont silty clay loam cover 38 and 24.8 per cent of the area, respectively.

Agricultural possibilities of Ohio peat soils, A. DACHNOWSKI (*Jour. Amer. Peat Soc., 9 (1916), No. 1, pp. 10-21*).—This is a report of rather general observations on the necessary fertility treatment of Ohio peat soils, including cultivation, liming, fertilization, drainage, and cropping. It is concluded that "the essential objects are, aside from more effective organization, an increase in smaller farms, a greater use of fibrous soils for pasture, meadow, or general livestock farming, and more intensive farming and greater specialization upon the better, suitable types of peat and muck."

Study of the vine-growing soils of Vevey [Switzerland], I. ANKEN (*Ann. Sci. Agron., 4. ser., 5 (1916), No. 1-6, pp. 1-156, pls. 3, figs. 4*).—This is the report of a survey of the geology, origin, mineralogy, and mechanical, physical, and chemical composition of the vine soils of the district of Vevey on the northern shore of Lake Geneva in Switzerland.

The soils of Southern Rhodesia and their origin, H. B. MAUFE (*Rhodesia Agr. Jour., 14 (1917), No. 1, pp. 8-23*).—The soils of Southern Rhodesia are discussed as red clay, granite, sandy, and black soil, and mechanical analyses of samples of the last three are given. It is stated that the soils of the regions are mainly the result of the decomposition of rocks and that clayey matter consisting of hydrated aluminum silicates is the chief product of that decomposition.

The soil mulch, L. E. CALL and M. C. SEWELL (*Jour. Amer. Soc. Agron., 9 (1917), No. 2, pp. 49-61*).—Experiments conducted at the Kansas Experiment Station, in which moisture determinations were made to a depth of several feet on cultivated and uncultivated, uncropped areas, kept free from weeds, are reported.

The results are taken to indicate that "a cultivated soil is no more effective than a bare uncultivated soil in preventing evaporation. Cultivation conserves soil moisture by the elimination of weeds and by preventing run-off. The development of nitrates may be as extensive without cultivation as with cultivation."

Relation between indications of several lime-requirement methods and the soil's content of bases, C. J. SCHOLLENBERGER (*Soil Sci., 3 (1917), No. 3, pp. 279-288, figs. 3*).—Laboratory experiments conducted at the Ohio Experiment Station on two soils well supplied with basic material other than carbonates and data obtained from analyses of soil from the 5-year rotation fertility experiment plats at the station are reported. The soils were neutral clay loam deficient in organic matter, alkaline black clay, and acid silt loam.

"Experiments upon acid-extracted and washed soils and upon field-treated soils demonstrate that the vacuum method is, of the number studied, the most nearly quantitative method which is at the same time universally applicable.

The idea of determining the percentage of total lime requirement satisfied is offered as a means of comparing the condition of basicity of different soils and as an aid in the solution of other soil problems. The limited amount of experimental data available indicates that there may be some relation between the percentage of total lime requirement satisfied and the reaction of the soil to litmus, carbonates being practically absent. Crop yields in pot experiments have not indicated that an application of precipitated calcium carbonate, according to the indications of the vacuum method, which is considered to represent saturation with calcium, is harmful in other than exceptional cases."

Four references to literature bearing on the subject are appended.

The effect of some acids and alkalis on soil bacteria in the soil solution, O. M. GRUZIT (*Soil Sci., 3 (1917), No. 3, pp. 289–295, figs. 2*).—This is an abstract of a thesis, in which experiments conducted at the Michigan Agricultural College on solutions extracted from rich, sandy loam and sandy soils are reported.

"The solutions were adjusted to various degrees of reaction with N/100 sodium hydroxid and hydrochloric acid, methyl red being used as an indicator for titration, and 10-cc. quantities were placed in 100 gm. of pure sterile quartz sand. The moisture content of the cultures was adjusted about every ten days. The counts of bacteria in the soil solution were made upon sodium asparaginate agar after seven days of incubation at a temperature varying between 19 and 23° C."

It was found that "the development of the general flora of the soil bacteria from sand and sandy loam soils, when studied in the soil solution of sand cultures, was retarded if the reaction of the medium had a higher OH-ion concentration than N/1,000. The development of soil bacteria was inhibited when the reaction of the medium became neutral. The H-ion concentration of N/1,200 hydrochloric and sulphuric acids was germicidal to about 99.2 per cent of soil bacteria. . . . With H-ion concentration of N/2,164 the rate of multiplication of soil bacteria from sandy loam corresponded to the rate of destruction so that there was no change in the total number of bacteria. The H-ion concentration of N/2,840 inhibited the growth of 43 per cent of soil bacteria when compared with the growth of soil bacteria in the medium with N/412 OH-ion concentration. The reaction of alkaline cultures was gradually neutralized and later became acid. When the 'toxic limit' of acids toward Indian corn seedlings was compared with the toxic limit of about the same concentration of the same acids on the general flora of the soil bacteria from sand and sandy loam soils, the soil bacteria were injured to the extent of 43 per cent."

Twenty references to literature bearing on the subject are appended.

A review of investigations in soil protozoa and soil sterilization, N. KOPELOFF and D. A. COLEMAN (*Soil Sci., 3 (1917), No. 3, pp. 197–269*).—This paper is intended to be a survey of the subject to date and includes a list of 337 references to literature bearing on the subject.

The ecological significance of soil aeration, W. A. CANNON and E. E. FREE (*Science, n. ser., 45 (1917), No. 1156, pp. 178–180*).—Experiments conducted by the Carnegie Institution of Washington and Johns Hopkins University are reported, which show "that different species of plants may differ markedly in their response to variations in the composition of the soil atmosphere, and hence to changes in soil aeration. The effects of diminution of oxygen are manifest and the results with Opuntia indicate a direct and specific effect of carbon dioxid in addition to the effect of the dilution of the oxygen."

It is pointed out that "although deficiency in aeration has frequently been suggested as an agricultural difficulty, or as the reason why certain species do not grow upon soils of heavy texture, it does not appear that this suggestion has had any exact experimental basis. Nor does it seem to have been appreciated that different species may have great differences in the oxygen requirement of their roots and widely variant responses to differences in soil aeration, responses which appear to be quite as specific and significant as the responses to temperature and to available water which form the present basis of ecological classification."

Reclaiming the waste, P. A. GRAHAM (*London: Country Life, Ltd.; New York: Charles Scribner's Sons, 1916, pp. XIII+175; rev. in Country Life [London], 41 (1917), No. 1050, pp. 149, 150*).—This book is a number of the so-called "Increased Productivity Series." Its object is "to direct attention to the vast possibilities of waste land reclamation in Great Britain and Ireland." It contains the following chapters:

The urgency of land reclamation; reclaiming a Norfolk heath (March 9, 1916); reclaiming a Norfolk heath—four months' progress (July 12, 1916); the weeds of a Norfolk heath, by Brenchley; how to hold reclaimed waste; nowt but bracken and fuzz; how much reclaimable waste is there; sand dunes and coast erosion; poverty bottom—a lesson from downland; reclamation of waste land in Holland; reclamation in Holland—a colonial minister's experience; making farms out of moorland; fish ponds and reclamation; reclamation in Belgium, by H. Vendelmans; a war of timber; afforestation of peat bogs and sand dunes, by A. Henry; planting on the South Downs, by Somerville; reclaiming the pit bank; labor and reclamation; forestry and reclamation; and the industrialization of land in France, by Sonchon.

The apparent main purpose of this book is to outline ways and means of meeting war-time conditions in England.

Summaries of soil fertility investigations, A. T. WIANCKO and S. C. JONES (*Indiana Sta. Bul. 198 (1917), pp. 3–20*).—This bulletin presents in a condensed form the principal results obtained up to the present time from the use of lime, legumes, manure, and various commercial fertilizers upon seven outlying experiment fields and upon one of the older series of plats on the university farm.

Excluding two fields which have been under treatment only one year, the following results have been secured from the principal treatments: With ground limestone the profits have ranged from $3.31 to $18.34 per acre per rotation, and with manure from $1.62 to $4.45 per ton per rotation. On limed land mixed fertilizers have been used at a profit in all cases. At North Vernon (Jennings Co.) and Worthington (Greene Co.), where fertilizers were applied to wheat on manured land, good wheat increases were secured with a 200-lb. application of a fertilizer carrying 2 per cent nitrogen, 8 per cent phosphoric acid, and 4 per cent potash following corn, which had received 6 tons of manure and 200 lbs. of acid phosphate per acre.

Rock phosphate without manure has yielded profitable returns at Scottsburg (Scott Co.) and Wanatah (Laporte Co.). With manure it has been profitable at North Vernon and Worthington, while at Scottsburg and South Bend (St. Joseph Co.) it has been used at a loss. Acid phosphate, with or without manure, has shown large profits in all cases, and per dollar invested has been the most profitable fertilizer treatment either alone, with lime, or with both lime and manure.

Clover in place of timothy in rotation with corn and wheat has increased the value of the rotation by $8.07 at North Vernon and $7.80 at Worthington, where no fertilizer was used. On fertilized land the legume has increased the value of the rotation by $12.50 and $5.08, respectively, after paying for the fertilizer.

Why Illinois produces only half a crop, C. G. HOPKINS (*Illinois Sta. Circ. 193 (1917), pp. 3–16*).—In this address before the Illinois State Farmers' Institute, at Streator, February 21, 1917, the author analyzes the Illinois crop yields and reviews experimental data relative to increased yields due to improved soil fertility methods.

It is concluded that both the average acre-yields and the average acre-values of the most common Illinois crops (corn, oats, wheat, and clover) on the most common Illinois soil can be doubled by the adoption of better crop rotations, including a more liberal use of legumes, with a return of more organic manures, together with a systematic application of limestone and phosphorus in the form of raw rock phosphate but without commercial potassium or commercial nitrogen.

Live stock and the maintenance of organic matter in the soil, E. O. FIPPIN (*Jour. Amer. Soc. Agron., 9 (1917), No. 3, pp. 97–105, fig. 1).*—This is a review and summary of the results of work by others at several of the State experiment stations, from which the following conclusions are drawn:

" The higher plants are able to use organized carbonaceous foods, both nitrogenous and nonnitrogenous. Carbonaceous food conserves energy in the process of growth of the crop and makes possible a larger total growth in a given time. The organic matter in the soil is the direct source of the carbonaceous material used by the plant. Any process that permits the destruction of organic matter that might find its way into the soil is likely to be poor economy.

"Animals destroy from half to nine-tenths of the organic matter in the feed consumed. It is burned up in the body processes and expended as energy. A further large loss occurs in the handling of the manure.

" It is entirely possible to maintain the organic matter in the soil without animal husbandry. On very poor soils, animal husbandry may be bad practice. It may be justified by large profits from the animal products by means of which the loss of organic matter can be made up from other sources."

The manual of manures, H. VENDELMANS (*London: Country Life; New York: Charles Scribner's Sons, 1916, pp. XVI+164, figs. 6).*—This is a number of the so-called " Increased Productivity Series," and its purpose is to give practical information on manures and fertilizers and their proper uses. A discussion of manures in general is followed by specific information regarding nitrogenous, chemical, phosphatic, and potassic manures, ashes and soot, magnesia and silica, and organic manures of different kinds. Materials for soil improvement, including lime-containing compounds, are also discussed, and final sections deal with auximones and the quantities of manures to be used per acre.

The text of the English fertilizers and feeding-stuffs act is also given.

Fertilizers and their supply in war time, J. A. VOELCKER (*Jour. Roy. Soc. Arts, 65 (1917), No. 3356, pp. 324–337).*—The purpose of this paper is to summarize the present general agricultural requirements in England in regard to fertilizers as consisting in the supply of superphosphate and basic slag as phosphatic manures and of ammonium sulphate as the nitrogenous one. " The supply of these three is all essential, and if farmers are to meet successfully the demands now made on them, it is all important that they should be put in the way of obtaining an adequate and ready supply of these."

Artificial manures.—Experiments on their value for crops in western India, H. H. MANN and S. R. PARANJPE (*Dept. Agr. Bombay Bul. 76 (1915), pp. 55).*—This bulletin gives the results of a number of fertilizer experiments with various crops in western India, where commercial fertilizers have not proved popular heretofore. The crops were divided into field crops, which included tobacco, potatoes, wheat, cotton, and sugar cane, and garden crops, which included chillies, onions, alfalfa, and bananas.

A general conclusion which seems applicable to all districts alike is that where irrigation is not practiced an application of commercial fertilizers is not so profitable as the fertilizing methods already in practice. The use of acid phosphate on the black soils of western India gives good results, providing there is a considerable quantity of organic matter present in the soil.

[Fertilizer experiments], P. LIECHTI (*Landw. Jahrb. Schweiz, 30 (1916), No. 5, pp. 506–508*).—Mixing liquid manure with peat dust was found not to prevent the escape of ammonia from the liquid manure.

Experiments with oats on an acid sandy loam soil, to compare samples of lime nitrogen from five different sources ,showed that in one case the effect of the lime nitrogen was injurious. Analyses of samples of this lime nitrogen showed the presence of appreciable quantities of dicyandiamid, which is thought to explain the injurious action.

Incomplete experiments with urea on oats are also reported.

Standardization of humus used for fertilizer, J. H. HOFF (*Jour. Amer. Soc., 10 (1917), No. 1, pp. 18–22*).—It is the author's opinion, based on a review of work by himself and others. that the important factors in properly judging the manurial value of muck and peat are (1) natural productivity, (2) reaction and freedom from excess moisture, (3) whether high in nitrogen and whether the other fertility elements are properly balanced and proper bacterial flora prevail, and (4) solubility.

The organic nitrogen compounds of soils and fertilizers, E. C. LATHROP (*Jour. Franklin Inst., 183 (1917), Nos. 2, pp. 169–206; 3. pp. 303–321; 4. pp. 465–498*).—This article summarizes the results of investigations, partly reported elsewhere (E. S. R., 32. p. 217; 36. p. 25), which were undertaken to determine the origin. chemical composition. biochemical changes, and distribution of organic nitrogenous substances in the soils. as well as the action and availability of the nitrogen of soils, peats. and organic fertilizers. The investigations of others. as well as of the author. are reviewed. and an extensive bibliography of the subject is given. The studies were made with a large number of soils from widely different regions. The methods employed are fully described.

The author concludes that "histidin. hypoxanthin, cystosin, xanthin. nucleic acid, creatinin, cyanuric acid, or its isomer cyamelid. may be considered to be organic nitrogenous constituents commonly occurring in soils. Arginin. lysin. adenin, cholin, [and] trimethylamin may be considered at the present time to be nitrogenous constituents unusual to soils, inasmuch as they occur infrequently in soils. These compounds may either not be normally formed by the processes of change taking place in the soil or if they are formed they are probably very quickly changed into other compounds, for example, arginin into ornithin and urea or adenin into hypoxanthin."

Studies were made of the nitrogenous compounds of natural and processed organic fertilizers. In the first nitrogen was found to be present in the form of ammonia, melanin, cystin, arginin, histidin, lysin. monoamino compounds, and nonamino compounds. In the second there were found arginin, histidin, lysin, leucin, tryosin, guanin, and hypoxanthin. The conclusion was reached that "the process by which the nitrogen of certain trade wastes, such as hair, leather, garbage, etc., is made more available is recognized as a process of partial hydrolysis of the complex proteins contained in such materials resulting in ammonia, amino acids, etc., all of which are more readily available than the original protein materials. This hydrolysis is almost complete, the nitrogenous compounds formed being principally the primary products of protein hydrolysis, together with a small amount of proteose-like compound which has not been fully decomposed. . . . The more extended and final the hydrolysis the more available the nitrogen of the compounds formed, since, as has been shown, the final products of hydrolysis are utilized by the plants as such and are at the same time more readily changed into ammonia by soil organisms than are the intermediate compounds produced by partial hydrolysis."

Sources of nitrogen compounds in the United States, C. G. GILBERT (*U. S. Senate, 64. Cong., 1. Sess., Doc. 471 (1916), pp. 11; abs. in Nature [London], 98 (1917), No. 2466, pp. 431, 432*).—This is an article on the natural occurrence of nitrogen and its adaptability to use, especially as a fertilizer. In summarizing the situation it is stated that "the evolution of a practicable process for the oxidation of by-product ammonia to render present resources available, with the development of an atmospheric nitrogen fixation output by the cyanamid process carefully timed to meet growing demands following a reduction in the retail price of nitrogenous fertilizer, would appear to be the desirable governmental procedure as being the one least liable to disastrous consequences."

The nitrate industry, E. CUEVAS (*New York: W. S. Myers, 1916, pp. 61, pls. 3, figs. 4*).—This is a paper presented at the second Pan American Congress at Washington, D. C. It gives a brief history of the Chilean nitrate fields and describes in detail the character and composition of the nitrate deposits as well as the methods of mining and preparing the material for industrial purposes.

The author is of the opinion that the deposits are capable of supplying the needs of the world for at least 300 years. It is suggested that as a matter of national preparedness, from both the military and the purely agricultural standpoint, the United States should proceed at once to buy and store large quantities of the nitrate.

In an introductory note by the publisher, attention is called to the fact that "the Central Empires of Europe imported from Chile in the five years ended December 31, 1914, an unheard of tonnage of nitrate of soda, amounting to about 5,000,000 tons. The area of the Central Empires is hardly greater than the combined areas of California and Texas. These empires imported more than all the rest of Europe for the period named. It is not improbable that a very great amount of this 5,000,000 tons is still held in reserve in Germany, and it is privately reported that no Chilean nitrate is to be permitted to be used in agriculture for some time to come."

When are summer crops to be fertilized with lime nitrogen? P. WAGNER (*Deut. Landw. Presse, 43 (1916), Nos. 18, pp. 149, 150; 19, pp. 158, 159*).—Data relating to the time of fertilizing summer crops with lime nitrogen, obtained from numerous experiments carried on at different stations, are reported.

It is concluded that it is not necessary to apply lime nitrogen to loam and clay soils previous to seeding time. On heavy soil the ground should be worked with a harrow as early as possible and lime nitrogen applied and thoroughly mixed with the soil just prior to seeding. Better results were obtained by applying all the lime nitrogen just prior to seeding than by applying a part as a top-dressing.

Fertilizer experiments (*Minnesota Sta. Rpt. 1916, pp. 58, 59*).—The results of several years' fertilizer experiments at the different Minnesota experiment farms are taken to indicate "that the experiment station is not justified in recommending the use of phosphates in general farming operations in this State."

Phosphate rock, R. W. STONE (*U. S. Geol. Survey Bul. 666–J [1917], pp. 4*).—This is a brief review of the phosphate rock resources of the United States and includes data on production. It is stated that the total output for 1916 was 1,980,000 tons, valued at $5,897,000.

Potash in agriculture, B. C. Aston (*Jour. Agr.* [*New Zeal.*], *11* (1915), *No. 4, pp. 283-295, figs. 3; 13* (1916), *No. 6, pp. 446-454*).—This is a review of the natural sources of potash in New Zealand, from which it is concluded "that only for special crops, such as potatoes, garden crops, mangels, and a few other potash-loving crops, are New Zealand soils immediately in need of potash manuring, and it is with these crops and with reclaimed swamps deficient in potash that experiments might be instituted to determine whether the deficiency may be economically supplied by resources available in the Dominion. Researches having as their object the extraction of potash with a view to its export might well give place to others having a greater prospect of economic success."

The volatilization of potash from cement materials, E. Anderson and R. J. Nestell (*Jour. Indus. and Engin. Chem., 9* (1917), *No. 3, pp. 253-261, figs. 13*).—

The results of an extended series of investigations on potash volatilization from silicate mixtures are reported, which are taken to indicate that "the potash in any cement material can all be volatilized. The determining factors in this reaction are temperature and the length of time exposure of the cement material to the temperature and gas volume prevailing. The lower limit of temperature for potash volatilization is 1,100° C., and the rate of volatilization increases rapidly with the temperature.

" The presence of chlorids, particularly calcium chlorid, increases the velocity of the volatilization, while sulphates decrease this rate. Because of the formation of sulphates, sulphur dioxid in the furnace gases retards the volatilization. Sodium is driven off nearly as easily as is the potassium.

" In the kiln, besides the factors of time and temperature, the size of the clinker also affects the volatilization rate. The smaller the clinker the better the volatilization of potash from it.

"Although the potash in any cement mix can be driven off, the rate of expulsion at any given temperature varies for different materials, and is probably dependent on the mineralogical character of the potash-bearing component of the cement material."

Growing crops without potash in 1916, C. D. Woods (*Agr. of Maine, 1915, pp. 293-307*).—This paper is a reprint of that previously noted (E. S. R., 35, p. 325).

Lime in agriculture, E. A. Felder (*S. C. Dept. Agr., Com. and Indus., Bul. 59* (1917), *pp. 75, figs. 2*).—This bulletin is intended to be a complete treatise on the subject, discussing the varied forms of agricultural lime and their uses, sources of supply, and the relative values of limestone, shell lime, calcined marl, and noncaustic, dried phosphomarl in South Carolina agriculture. It is stated that liming is the greatest need of South Carolina agriculture and that marl is the greatest undeveloped asset of the State in this respect. Special attention is given to the intelligent use of lime.

Forms of agricultural lime and their application, M. L. Fearnow (*Nat. Lime Manfrs. Assoc., Agr. Bul. 3* (1917), *pp. 16*).—This pamphlet deals with ground limestone, quicklime, and hydrated lime with reference to their advantages and disadvantages for agricultural use, pointing out especially the conditions under which each may best be used.

The relation of lime to agriculture, L. B. Broughton (*Md. Agr. Ext. Serv. Bul. 2* (1916), *pp. 25-56*).—This bulletin discusses different lime-bearing compounds and their physical, chemical, and biological effects on soil, and summarizes the results of experiments at the Maryland Experiment Station on the effect of lime in increasing crop production.

The summarized results are taken to indicate that "physically even a small amount of lime carbonate by its solubility in the carbonated soil water will act beneficially in causing the flocculation of clay and in the subsequent conservation of the flocculent or tilth condition, by acting as a light cement holding the soil crumbs together when the capillary water has evaporated, thus favoring the penetration of both water and air, and of the roots themselves. Among the most important chemical effects are, by neutralizing the soil acidity, the maintenance of fertility is raised; by maintaining the proper degree of moisture and warmth bacterial life is enhanced, especially that of nitrification, also the development and activity of root bacteria of legumes and other nitrogen-gathering bacteria; the rendering available, directly or indirectly, of relatively small percentages of plant food, notably phosphoric acid and potash."

The text of the Maryland lime-grinding bill is included.

The question of lime fertilization, P. LIECHTI and E. TRUNNINGER (*Landw. Jahrb. Schweiz, 30 (1916), No. 5, pp. 480–488, figs. 2*).—Experiments on the influence of liming on soil fertility are reported, and the conclusion drawn that more attention should be given to the size of the grains of calcium carbonate used for fertilizing purposes. It is thought that the use of the finest ground calcium carbonate is not justified in all cases, but that coarse calcium carbonate should be used where experience has shown that the soil fertility is injured by excessive liming or by a liming which is quickly effective. It is believed that by the use of coarser ground lime a more uniform distribution on the soil can be obtained, and that more can be used without injuring soil fertility.

Liming the land.—Decomposition and utilization of limestone in soil, J. W. AMES and C. J. SCHOLLENBERGER (*Mo. Bul. Ohio Sta., 2 (1917), No. 4, pp. 121–124*).—This is a review of experience at the station, the results of which are thought to "furnish conclusive evidence and emphasize the fact that the larger part of light and moderate applications of ground limestone, when applied to a soil in need of lime and similar to the silt loam at the station, decomposes within a year. Even at the end of five years, however, traces remain; this may be due to the superior resistance of the larger particles contained in the ground limestone. Other experiments have shown that limestone screenings ($\frac{1}{8}$ to $\frac{1}{4}$ in.) are very slowly decomposed, indicating that they have but slight value unless applied in excessive amounts.

"The data indicate that although there is a considerable loss of bases when limestone is applied to the soil at any rate, such loss is excessively large when the rate of application greatly exceeds the amount which can be absorbed by the soil.

"Small or moderate applications frequently repeated would probably pay better in the final analysis than large applications at less frequent intervals."

The fertilizing value of wastes from the hemp industry, A. DRAGHETTI (*Staz. Sper. Agr. Ital., 49 (1916), No. 5–6, pp. 324–333*).—This is a brief description of the hemp treating process and a review of different analyses of the waste liquors and materials from the process.

[Fertilizers, season 1915–16], B. B. ROSS (*Ala. Dept. Agr. Bul., 7 (1916), No. 75, pp. 96*).—This bulletin reports the results of actual and guaranteed analyses of 466 samples of fertilizers and fertilizing materials offered for sale in Alabama during the fiscal year ended September 30, 1916, together with general information on the classification of fertilizer materials and formulas for home mixtures, the text of the Alabama fertilizer law, and a list of concerns licensed to sell fertilizers in the States during the year.

Analyses of commercial fertilizers, ground bone, and agricultural lime, C. S. CATHCART ET AL. (*New Jersey Stas. Bul. 303 (1916), pp. 5–52*).—Supplementing previous work (E. S. R., 36, p. 429), this bulletin contains the results of actual and guaranteed analyses of 283 samples of fertilizers and fertilizing materials, 43 samples of ground bone, and 35 samples of agricultural lime collected for inspection in New Jersey during 1916, together with a list of brands registered for sale.

Analyses of fertilizers and cottonseed meal, B. W. KILGORE ET AL. (*Bul. N. C. Dept. Agr., 37 (1916), No. 10, pp. 86*).—This report contains the results of actual and guaranteed analyses of 1,371 samples of fertilizers and fertilizing materials and 187 samples of cottonseed meal collected for inspection in North Carolina during the fall of 1915 and the spring of 1916.

List of fertilizer and lime manufacturers and importers (*Penn. Dept. Agr. Bul. 289 (1917), pp. 47*).—This bulletin gives the texts of the Pennsylvania fertilizer, bone, and lime laws, and a list of fertilizer manufacturers and brands of fertilizers licensed for sale during 1917.

AGRICULTURAL BOTANY.

Plant physiology as horticultural theory, H. MOLISCH (*Pflanzenphysiologie als Theorie der Gärtnerei. Jena: Gustav Fischer, 1916, pp. X+305, figs. 128*).— The seven sections of this book, which is intended primarily for horticulturists, deal principally with plant nutrition, respiration, growth, freezing and frost killing, reproduction, germination of seeds, and variability, inheritance, and plant breeding.

Applied and economic botany, H. KRAEMER (*Philadelphia: Author, 1916. 2. ed., pp. VIII+822, pls. 2, figs. 420*).—In the present edition (E. S. R., 33. p. 27), the text has been revised, bringing the work up to date. Among the portions added are a glossary and a concise statement regarding the nature and properties of vitamins.

Canaigre, a quick-growing tannin plant for acclimatization in France, A. PIÉDALLU (*Compt. Rend. Acad. Sci. [Paris], 163 (1916), No. 20, pp. 575, 576*).—This is a discussion of canaigre (*Rumex hymenosepalus*) as a rapidly growing and abundant source of tannin to take the place of the oak and chestnut trees destroyed by military activities in portions of France.

New names in Amygdalus, P. L. RICKER (*Proc. Biol. Soc. Wash., 30 (1917), pp. 17, 18*).—It has been considered necessary, in accordance with present usage, to make several transfers from Prunus to Amygdalus. A list is given of such recent transfers, resulting in 14 species of Amygdalus.

Studies in the nomenclature and classification of bacteria. The problem of bacterial nomenclature, R. E. BUCHANAN (*Jour. Bact., 1 (1916), No. 6, pp. 591–596*).—The author expresses the view that the present time is propitious for the careful formulation of general rules of bacteriological nomenclature and of a general scheme of bacterial classification. Regarding this work several suggestions are offered.

Preliminary note on the classification of some lactose-fermenting bacteria, M. LEVINE (*Jour. Bact., 1 (1916), No. 6, pp. 619–621*).—A key is given which is said to be the result of a study of 333 lactose-fermenting organisms isolated from soil, sewage, and animal sources. The subdivisions proposed are not based upon single characters but upon differences in groups of characters. The names employed are considered as tentative only.

The preparation of culture media from whole blood, R. A. KELSER (*Jour. Bact., 1 (1916), No. 6, pp. 615–617*).—Describing the method employed in the preparation of a whole blood culture medium, said to be more easily and quickly prepared than ordinary beef infusion and to be inexpensive and well adapted to organisms which do not thrive well on ordinary culture media, the author states that this can practically replace the more difficult preparation serum agar. A concentrated extract from blood, which was still further reduced by evaporation, proved satisfactory as a culture medium.

The development of Azotobacter, A. CAUDA (*Staz. Sper. Agr. Ital., 49 (1916), No. 2, pp. 125–131*).—Details are given of a study during several years of Azotobacter, as regards its morphology, its relationships, and its physiology as influenced by salts of phosphoric acid, by calcium carbonate, by magnesium and nitrogen compounds, by humus and various other soils, and by association with other organisms.

The soils which are rich, well worked, and provided with humus and mineral fertilizers, prove to be those in which the development of Azotobacter is most active. This fact agrees with the observed results obtained from practice on well-managed farms.

The oxygen requirements of biological soil processes, T. J. MURRAY (*Jour. Bact., 1 (1916), No. 6, pp. 597–614*).—In the work here detailed, which was planned to test the relative influence of aerobic and anaerobic conditions on some fundamental processes due to the agency of soil bacteria, the author found that denitrification goes on under aerobic and anaerobic conditions, being little affected by either. Denitrification proceeds better in solutions than in soils, nitrogen being lost in the greenhouse type of soil used but not in either a silt loam or a clay hillside soil.

Depression of the freezing point in triturated plant tissues and the magnitude of this depression as related to soil moisture, R. P. HIBBARD and O. E. HARRINGTON (*Physiol. Researches, 1 (1916), No. 10, pp. 441–458*).—This paper deals with the freezing-point lowering that characterizes the pulpy mass formed by grinding plant tissues, and presents evidence that this lowering is as valuable a criterion for comparing osmotic concentrations of the tissues as is the corresponding index for the expressed juice. The material was first subjected to a preliminary freezing, to render the cell membranes more readily permeable to dissolved materials, after which it was thoroughly triturated. The pulp thus prepared was placed in the cryoscopic apparatus and its freezing-point depression determined just as is usually done with the sap expressed from such pulps. Beckmann's freezing point apparatus was employed.

It was found that this method of testing the pulp without pressing gave concordant results when different samples of the same pulp were tested. In a series of duplicate tests the greatest plus or minus variation between two lowerings that one might expect to be alike was only 0.5 per cent; usually it was less than this. Comparisons of the depressions obtained from tests of plant pulps with those from tests of the expressed juices of the same pulps showed that the two values obtained in these two ways were practically identical, providing that the process of pressing had been very thorough. The agreement was usually within much less than 1 per cent.

The materials employed in these tests were potato tubers, cabbage leaves (from the head), apples, lemons, oranges, grapefruit, onion bulbs, and the tops and roots of maize plants grown in pot cultures. In the case of the maize plants the pots were furnished with autoirrigators, so arranged that six different degrees of soil moisture were practically maintained, in as many different cultures. It was found that the triturated tops showed depressions of from 1.835° C. (culture with mean soil moisture of 31 per cent on dry weight) to 2.204° (culture with soil moisture of 11 per cent), and that the ground roots showed corresponding depressions of from 0.492 to 0.995°. The root material thus had a much lower depression (and consequently a much lower osmotic concentration) than the top material. The depression of the freezing point was found to increase, for both tops and roots, as the moisture content of the soil in which the plants grew decreased, from culture to culture in the series. The order of magnitudes was the same for both roots and tops, being the reverse of the order for soil moisture content.

A list of 27 references to literature bearing on the subject is appended together with an author index.

Glandular hairs on roots, G. HABERLANDT (*Sitzber. K. Preuss. Akad. Wiss., 1915, XII, pp. 222–226, figs. 6*).—The author gives a preliminary report of the occurrence, structure, etc., of multicellular glandular hairs. These were discovered to exist in greater or less abundance on nearly all the rootlets from 2 to 8 mm. in length, springing, with adventitious buds, from marginal leaf notches of *Bryophyllum calycinum* kept in a glass in the laboratory. The various forms are described and discussed.

Absorption of nutrients as affected by the number of roots supplied with the nutrient, P. L. GILE and J. O. CARRERO (*U. S. Dept. Agr., Jour. Agr. Research, 9 (1917), No. 3, pp. 73–95, figs. 2*).—In a contribution from the Porto Rico Experiment Station, the authors give a report on tests conducted in water cultures to see whether a plant could absorb a maximum amount of one mineral element which was supplied to only part of the roots if all other essential elements were supplied to all the roots. The plants were grown with their roots divided between two flasks, one of which contained a complete nutrient solution and the other a nutrient solution lacking one element, and the absorption of nitrogen with rice and corn and of phosphorus, potassium, and iron with rice was tested.

The results show that, under the conditions of the experiments, the plant is not able to absorb a maximum amount of the element, and the fewer the number of roots supplied with the element, the smaller the amount absorbed. This is found to apply when the total amount of the element supplied is equal to or in excess of the needs of the plant. With nitrogen and phosphorus, the total amount of the element absorbed by plants with half their roots in the complete solution was equal to 0.76 of that absorbed by plants with all their roots in a complete solution. The similar figure for potassium and iron was 0.66. An increase in concentration of the element in question in the complete solution did not appreciably alter the results. The amount of the element absorbed per gram of roots increased greatly as the number of roots in the complete solution was diminished.

Attention is called to the bearing of these results on the method of applying fertilizers.

The excretion of acids by roots, A. R. HAAS (*Proc. Nat. Acad. Sci., 2 (1916), No. 10, pp. 561–566*).—Controlled experiments with sweet corn seedlings grown in water culture indicated that no acids other than carbon dioxid were excreted by the roots. The increase in the alkalinity shown by one culture in quartz in seven days is thought to indicate the presence of some dead cells not visible. Distilled water into which only the roots of wheat seedlings extended showed a very slight increase in alkalinity when the roots had decayed, but when the screen, seeds, and roots were in water a slightly greater increase in alkalinity was noticed.

Leaf epidermis and light perception, G. HABERLANDT (*Sitzber. K. Preuss. Akad. Wiss., 1916, XXXII, pp. 672–687*).—This is mainly a discussion of contributions by other investigators as bearing upon the author's theory regarding the sensitivity to light of foliar organs. According to this view, structural peculiarities in the cells near the upper side of the leaf cause differences in illumination, and thus serve as a means of detecting the direction of the incidental light ray.

The chemical organization of the assimilatory apparatus, R. WILLSTÄTTER and A. STOLL (*Sitzber. K. Preuss. Akad. Wiss., 1915, XX, pp. 322–346, fig. 1*).— Several series of tests with flowers having foliage of different colors are detailed. The fact that assimilation supposedly requires the presence of both chlorophyll and an enzym is considered to indicate that these factors work together in that process. Chlorophyll supposedly forms a dissociable compound with carbon dioxid. The absorption capacity of green, dry, and powdered leaves for carbon dioxid was studied under different conditions and the results are described. It is considered possible that carbamino compounds may be formed from amino or albuminous compounds. The absorbing substance is supposed to act as an accumulator effecting, or favoring, condensation of carbon dioxid.

Assimilation of organic nitrogen by Zea mays and the influence of Bacillus subtilis on such assimilation, R. O. BRIGHAM (*Soil Sci., 3 (1917), No. 2, pp. 155–195, pls. 2, figs. 2*).—This work was carried out in order to ascertain whether higher plants can utilize organic nitrogen directly without the agency of micro-organisms, to determine the relative importance of the compounds used, and to show how the utilization of organic compounds by plants is affected by the action of a bacterium known to be able to decompose such compounds with the production of ammonia. The work includes experiments on the influence of different nitrogenous compounds, in sterile or inoculated cultures, upon the growth of seedlings of two varieties of Indian corn.

It is stated that *Z. mays* uses asparagin, casein, cottonseed meal, hemoglobin, linseed meal, uric acid, peptone, guanin, alanin, urea, creatin, malt, and glycocoll, these organic nitrogenous substances being named in order of their availability. Guanidin carbonate, guanidin nitrate, diphenylamin, caffein, and benzamid are unfavorable to the growth of *Z. mays.* Guanin is toxic to popcorn but not to dent corn.

Organic substances found to be directly available, but to produce better growth when acted upon by *B. subtilis* were peptone, guanin, alanin, linseed meal, cottonseed meal, casein, hemoglobin, and urea, the last showing this effect only with popcorn. The action of *B. subtilis* did not increase the availability of urea (by dent corn), sodium nitrate, asparagin, ammonium sulphate, uric acid, malt, creatin, glycocoll, and those compounds which were toxic.

Substances found to be better than sodium nitrate in case of dent corn were cottonseed meal, linseed meal, casein, hemoglobin, uric acid, and asparagin. Urea, peptone, guanin, alanin, and creatin, though available, were not better than sodium nitrate. Guanin was toxic to popcorn but available to dent corn. The compounds of the benzene ring were found to be exceedingly toxic to the plants tested.

Ammonium sulphate is said to be a far better source of nitrogen for dent corn than is sodium nitrate, being surpassed only by casein and asparagin. Generally speaking, organic compounds of high complexity are better after ammonification, those of low complexity not being improved thereby. It is thought that nitrification following ammonification would be detrimental. The simpler method of measuring growth by length of leaves gave results very nearly parallel to those obtained by determining the dry weight.

The catalytic action of potassium nitrate in the alcoholic fermentation produced by Sterigmatocystis nigra, M. MOLLIARD (*Compt. Rend. Acad. Sci. [Paris], 163 (1916), No. 20, pp. 570–572*).—Alcoholic fermentation ascribed to *S. nigra* in a nutritive solution, following a 0.2 per cent addition of potassium nitrate, was 3.3 times as active as that produced by the addition of the same quantity of ammonium chlorid. The optimum for the former solution was reached at a concentration of 0.4 per cent, as contrasted with a concentration of approximately 5 per cent required for the optimum fermentation with yeast which has been reported by some other investigators.

Stimulation and injury to plants by acids, I. ONODERA (*Ber. Ōhara Inst. Landw. Forsch., 1 (1916), No. 1, pp. 53–110, pls. 2*).—Having made a study of the effects of acids on the germination and growth of several cereals and legumes, the results of which are tabulated, the author states that lactic acid is almost harmless to growth. Formic acid stimulates germination in barley, but hinders growth in rice and clover. The effects of hydrochloric acid were decided, but it was surpassed, as regards root injury, by butyric acid. Nitric acid was generally less injurious than the other acids tested, favoring considerably, in dilute concentrations, both germination and growth in rice. Hydrochloric and sulphuric acids strongly stimulated germination and growth, but tended to kill the seedlings eventually.

Acids in moderate concentrations generally tend to produce stimulation, also hastening the attainment of maturity in the plant. Longitudinal growth is more particularly encouraged by acids than is growth in thickness. The increase of growth of plants in dilute acids generally continues longer in the leaves than in the roots.

The various acids are classified according to their injurious effects on plants.

Frost and alterations in leaves of trees, G. ARNAUD (*Bul. Soc. Path. Veg. France, 1 (1914), No. 1, pp. 21–25, figs. 2*).—A study was made of a leaf injury of chestnuts in Paris, which had been ascribed to the influence of tar. The author considers it due to cold weather in spring, in some cases accompanying or conditioning attacks of certain fungi on the leaves.

Effect of environmental conditions upon the number of leaves and the character of the inflorescence of tobacco plants, H. A. ALLARD (*Amer. Jour. Bot., 3 (1916), No. 9, pp. 493–501, pls. 4*).—In a study of very severely stunted tobacco plants it was found that the average number of nodes produced above the cotyledons, exclusive of the branches of the terminal whorl, remained constant under all conditions, but that the size of the inflorescence was reduced by unfavorable conditions. Extreme stunting may result in suppression of the branches of the terminal whorl, the inflorescence being reduced to the terminal bloom.

The shedding of flower buds in cotton, S. C. HARLAND (*West Indian Bul., 16 (1916), No. 1, pp. 72–78*).—The author has studied the shedding of buds by cotton to test the truth of the statement that if West Indian native cottons be sown out of season they will refuse to bloom until the proper flowering time, November to May.

It is stated that West Indian native and Seredo cottons from Brazil exhibited periodicity, normally producing no flowers during a period extending roughly from June to September. Such types as upland and Sea Island showed no such periodicity.

Shedding was not greatly influenced by root conditions or rainfall. It was shown by the F_1 generation of a cross between Sea Island and West Indian native cotton, the presence of the habit being thus dominant to its absence in this cross. The F_1 progeny of upland and West Indian native cotton did not shed their buds, the absence of the habit being dominant in this case.

A correlation is suggested between resistance to cotton leaf blister-mite (*Eriophyes gossypii*) and periodicity in flowering.

On the genetics of crinkled dwarf rogues in Sea Island cotton, I, S. C. HARLAND (*West Indian Bul., 16 (1916), No. 1, pp. 82–84, fig. 1*).—The author noticed in 1915 in a plat of Sea Island cotton made up of the progeny of single plant selections since 1910, certain rogue plants showing reduction in size of all the vegetative parts and in the seed weight, also crinkling, mosaic, and raggedness of edges in the leaves, extreme development of the sympodial habit, and a tendency to excessive boll shedding amounting to complete sterility in some plants. He has succeeded in growing a few plants from self-fertilized seeds, all of which proved to be rogues, while in case of seeds not self-fertilized the majority of the plants were rogues.

A large number of crosses were made between rogues and Sea Island cotton, the characters of the latter being completely dominant to those of the former. Later, one of the rogues threw off some of the rogue characters. It is thought that the rogue may be considered as a retrogressive mutation due to the loss of a single factor, the deficiency in the proportion of rogues being explained as due to their weakness and liability to early attack by angular leaf spot disease and by mole crickets. Further work in this connection is considered necessary.

On the partial sterility of Nicotiana hybrids made with N. sylvestris as a parent, II, T. H. GOODSPEED and A. H. AYRES (*Univ. Cal. Pubs. Bot.*, 5 (1916), No. 9, pp. 273-292, pl. 1).—Having continued the investigations previously noted (E. S. R. 29, p. 320), the authors state that the F_1 hybrids between *N. tabacum* varieties and *N. sylvestris* produce very little pollen of normal appearance, while the anther cells show, almost exclusively, shriveled, functionless grains. The apparently normal F_1 pollen did not germinate in its own stigmatic secretion, in that of the parents, or in any one of a great variety of artificial germinating fluids. The pollen of the parents germinated readily in the stigmatic secretion of the F_1 flowers.

The evidence is considered to oppose the view that specific chemical substances play an important rôle in determining whether or not pollen will germinate, and certain results of tests made on germination and growth reaction are deemed to be the effect of the reagents upon the swelling of cell colloids. The absciss-layer formation is the cause of the fall of flower and fruit, and the stimulus thereto is nonfertilization. Fall of flowers and fruits can be retarded by lowering the total concentration of available mineral materials or nutrients, variations in individual constituents being ineffective.

A few normally matured ovules capable of fertilization are produced in F_1 flowers, and a little viable seed is formed after pollination with the normal pollen of the parents. Back crosses are difficult to make in the field, but plants under conditions of low nutrition retained their flowers longer and back crosses were usually successful, though no increase of fertilizable ovules resulted from this more favorable condition for successful back crossing. Grafts between the F_1 hybrid and its parent *N. tabacum macrophylla* resulted in pollen similar to that from the same plants grown on their own roots, but the flowers and fruits were better retained in the former case.

On the partial sterility of Nicotiana hybrids made with N. sylvestris as a parent, III, T. H. GOODSPEED and J. N. KENDALL (*Univ. Cal. Pubs. Bot.*, 5 (1916), No. 10, pp. 293-299).—Continuing the work noted above, the present paper gives the results of experiments to ascertain the mode of abscission of flowers and fruits on the F_1 species of Nicotiana hybrids. These studies are considered to yield further evidence regarding the relation between successful pollination and fertilization on the one hand, and abscission of flowers and fruits on the other. The general problem and the literature of abscission are to be dealt with later in a more extended discussion.

It is stated that in *N. tabacum*, *N. sylvestris*, and other hybrids, also in *N. langsdorffii*, the abscission zone is to be found at the base of the pedicel. A conspicuous grooved ridge, or ring, of tissue stands out around the base of the pedicel in Nicotiana species, which may indicate the position of motor tissue or of a node. The position of the absciss-layer is independent of this groove, being usually distant from it 5 to 7 cell layers. Abscission appears to take place in any portion of the abscission zone distal to the groove, starting in the cortical tissues just beneath the epidermis on the ventral side and extending around the cortex. There is neither indication of cell division in the tissue involved nor evidence of alteration of cell walls by dissolution of the middle lamellæ or elongation and softening of the entire wall. The separation of the cells appears to be due mainly to increased turgor. Contact may persist until some mechanical agency, as a slight shaking or tapping, breaks the epidermis and the few tracheal elements which may remain intact. The number of cells actually concerned in the process of abscission is greater in the hybrids mentioned than in the parental species, and the same is true of automatic as contrasted with spontaneous abscission.

FIELD CROPS.

[Report of field crops work at the Minnesota Station] (*Minnesota Sta. Rpt. 1916, pp. 38–42*).—Additional data on the cost of tobacco growing are reported. The estimated cost per acre was $36.53, as compared with $24.25 previously reported, due chiefly to adverse weather conditions necessitating extra hand labor. The yield averaged 1,280.51 lbs. per acre, selling at an average price of 7.5 cts. per pound, and graded as filler.

Selection tests are reported with winter and spring wheat and with oats, as well as cultural studies with alfalfa, Sudan grass, and sweet clover.

The results of crop rotation experiments show increased yields of 13.7 per cent for corn, 14.95 per cent for oats, and 30.98 per cent for wheat, secured in a 4-year rotation of oats, wheat, clover, and corn, as compared with continuous cropping. In the same rotation increases in net gains per acre, as compared with continuous cropping, were for corn 21.4 per cent and for wheat 72.3 per cent.

Corn yields on land plowed in the fall and early spring were practically equal. The growing of oats and the securing of a stand of clover and timothy on spring-plowed land was not so satisfactory as on fall-plowed land or on double-disked corn land.

[Report of field crops work at the Crookston substation] (*Minnesota Sta., Rpt. Crookston Substa., 1910–1916, pp. 27–70, 81, 82*).—Cultural, variety, fertilizer, and rotation tests are reported, together with brief notes on corn-breeding work and methods of weed eradication.

Rate-of-seeding tests have been conducted with corn, oats, barley, spring and winter wheat, and winter rye. The winter cereals have not proved satisfactory, owing to excessive winterkilling, while tests with spring-sown grain have failed to give conclusive results and will be continued.

Tests of different methods for protecting winter wheat were begun in 1911 but failed to give very satisfactory results until 1916. Wheat sown on corn left uncut yielded 43.5 bu. in 1912 and 32.1 bu. in 1916. Wheat sown on corn stubble and covered with 1 ton of straw per acre yielded 28.8 bu. in 1916. The tests with straw covering are to be continued.

Trials of seeding alfalfa and red and sweet clover with wheat and oats at different rates as nurse crops, and with no nurse crop, were begun in 1915. With a nurse crop, in 1915, a stand of 60 per cent and low vigor resulted without any apparent difference between the rates of seeding, while without a nurse crop, a 100 per cent stand and excellent vigor were secured. The 1916 results were rather contradictory, due to the relatively short and less rank growth of the nurse crops. Field tests with alfalfa to determine the relative importance of various factors in their influence upon the growth of the crop indicated that they rank as follows: No nurse crop, manure, inoculation, and lime.

Other cultural projects which are briefly noted include tests of subsoiling, deep plowing, and packing the seed bed, a comparison of tractor and horse plowing and disking, date of plowing, and disking stubble tests. Final conclusions are not yet drawn.

In variety tests with oats, 1911–1916, the seven highest-yielding varieties, Danish Trifolium, King Oscar, Improved American, Canadian 429, Golden Beauty, Swedish Victory, and Early Everett averaged over 55 bu. per acre. Early Champion, Kischener, Big Four, New Zealand, and Swedish Select, the five lowest-yielding varieties, averaged under 45 bu. per acre.

Swanhals barley, with an average yield of 40.1 bu., was first of the two-rowed types, with Gutecon lowest with a yield of 24.6 bu. The highest-yielding six-rowed type was a Russian variety, which yielded 44 bu. per acre, with the lowest yield from Eagle No. 913, 21.82 bu.

With wheat, the three highest-yielding varieties, Minnesota No. 951, Marquis, and Kubanka, averaged over 24 bu. per acre. The four lowest-yielding varieties, Minnesota No. 169, Rysting, Powers, and Eames, averaged from 15 to 18 bu.

Field tests with millet, field peas, soy beans, clover, and alfalfa have continued for a period of 20 years to determine the adaptability of these crops to northwestern Minnesota. Variety tests were begun in 1913. The highest yield of forage was secured from Early Amber cane, 10,757 lbs. per acre, in 1916, with Sudan grass second with a yield of 7,454 lbs. Southern German millet gave a four-year average yield of 7,394.25 lbs. Blue Scotch No. 1436 field pea gave the highest average yield, 13 bu., of the varieties tested.

In 1915, 12 varieties of grasses, 4 of legumes, and 7 combinations of grasses and legumes were seeded separately and harvested for the first time in 1916. Of the grasses sown alone, the highest yield was secured from meadow fescue, 6,780 lbs. per acre. Sweet clover, with a yield of 6,380 lbs., was highest for the legumes. The highest yielding combination consisted of 10 lbs. *Bromus inermis*, 6 lbs. tall meadow oat grass, 2 lbs. white clover, and 4 lbs. alfalfa, and gave a yield of 6,660 lbs. per acre.

In corn variety tests, Northwestern Dent gave the highest grain yields for the two years reported, 1914 and 1916, with 46.87 and 38.4 bu., respectively.

Tests with flax for fiber, conducted in cooperation with the Office of Fiber Investigations, U. S. Department of Agriculture, in an effort to develop strains of fiber flax adapted to northwestern Minnesota, are reported. Hemp has been successfully grown for fiber at the station.

The following are the highest average yields per acre secured in crop-rotation tests from 1911 to 1916, inclusive: Wheat, 22.84 bu. in the three-year rotation, with a yield of 16.25 bu. for continuous wheat; oats, 57.7 bu. for the seven-year rotation, with a yield of 53.8 bu. for oats grown continuously (two-year average); barley, 43.3 bu. for continuous barley (two-year average) and 39.03 bu. for the seven-year rotation; flax, 15.73 bu. in the seven-year rotation; corn, 39.83 bu. in the seven-year rotation, with a yield of 34.33 bu. when grown continuously; potatoes, 98.2 bu. in the four-year rotation (two-year average) without manure, fertilizer, or legume; and hay, first year, 4,765 lbs. in the seven-year rotation, and second year, 1,918 lbs. in the five-year rotation.

Data are presented showing the results of commercial fertilizer tests with and without manure for crops grown in rotation for 1914, 1915, and 1916. No definite conclusions have been drawn.

Eradication of quack grass has been accomplished through severe bare fallow, followed by corn.

A number of potato variety tests are reported. Early Ohio is deemed the best market variety for this region, while Irish Cobbler is a high yielder and

the best early white potato tested. Carmen No. 1, Green Mountain, and Carmen No. 3 are considered the best late varieties. In cultural tests to determine the size of seed pieces, the double eye and quarter sizes have given the highest yields per pound of seed. A planting rate of 16 bu. per acre gave an average yield of 140.25 bu. as compared with a yield of 78.26 bu. from a 10-bu. planting rate. Hill-selected seed gave an average yield of 184.92 bu. per acre, as compared with a yield of 134 bu. from cellar-selected seed, 64.75 bu. from field run, ·
88.72 bu. from run-out seed, 136.15 bu. from tuber-unit selection, 75.4 from little field-run stock, and 144.6 bu. from little-selected stock. Tests with various treatments for seed potatoes and spraying tests for tuber and leaf diseases and insect pests are also reported.

Twenty-four varieties of rutabagas, mangels, carrots, and stock turnips have been tested. The highest-yielding varieties were the White Half Sugar mangels, 24.86 tons; Sweet Russian rutabagas, 488.6 bu.; Cowhorn turnip, 504 bu.; and Mastodon carrots, 355 bu. per acre.

[Report of field crops work at the Crookston substation] (*Minnesota Sta. Rpt. 1916, pp. 68–70, 72*).—Field crops work for 1915, as noted above, is briefly reviewed.

[Report of field crops work at the Duluth substation] (*Minnesota Sta., Rpt. Duluth Substa., 1916, pp. 5, 6, 7, 9; abs. in Minnesota Sta. Rpt. 1916, pp. 79, 80*).—In variety tests the average oat yield for the season was 42.5 bu. per acre and the time required for maturity from 93 days for Sixty Day oats to 113 days for the White Russian side oats. The early-maturing strains are considered the best yielders. The average barley yield was 20 bu. per acre, with Minnesota No. 105, a 6-rowed variety, highest. The 2-rowed barley, Princess, required 93 days to ripen, while all others required 87 days. The Alaska variety of peas is recommended because of its early maturity (84 days). Minnesota No. 95 required 112 days. Twenty-two varieties of corn were tested, the following giving the most promise for fodder: Minnesota No. 13, Northwestern Dent, Longfellow, and King Philip Flint.

Flax sown June 1 matured in 101 days. Rutabagas planted in May were harvested the middle of October, little difference being noted between three standard varieties.

Fertilizer tests under a 3-year rotation plan, using rock phosphate manure and acid phosphate, are reported. The crops grown were potatoes and rutabagas.

Three methods of seeding grass on cut-over land were compared. Harrowing with a spring-toothed harrow before and after seeding proved more satisfactory than harrowing before seeding, and this in turn was superior to harrowing after seeding.

[Report of field crops work at the **Grand Rapids** substation (*Minnesota Sta. Rpt. 1916, pp. 75, 76, 77*).—The crop yields secured in 1915 and the projects in progress are briefly noted.   •

The average yield for all oats was 76.9 bu. and the average of 13 varieties, 91.7 bu., with Sixty Day highest with 110.6 bu. The wheat average was 26.9 bu. per acre. The average of 13 varieties was 26.6 bu., with Prelude highest with 30.6 bu., followed by Marquis with 30.5 bu., and Haynes Bluestem with 30.3 bu.

The average barley yield was 42.6 bu. per acre, with an average for 10 varieties of 54.6 bu. O. A. C. No. 21 gave the highest yield, 63.9 bu. for the 6-rowed varieties, and Champion of Vermont, 55.6 bu. for the 2-rowed varieties.

Average yields were secured of corn for silage 3.4 tons; potatoes, 136.6 bu.; clover and timothy (first cutting), 2.42 tons; and rutabagas (topped), 24.47 tons per acre. Potato trials indicated homegrown seed to be superior to imported seed. Meadow fescue showed promise as a grass crop for either hay or pasture on muskeg.

[Report of field crops work at the Morris substation] (*Minnesota Sta., Rpt. Morris Substa., 1915, pp. 5–12, figs. 3; abs. in Minnesota Sta. Rpt. 1916, pp. 73, 74*).—Field experiments at the West Central substation at Morris for 1915 were confined to crop rotations, fertilizer tests, and variety and seeding trials with the farm crops common to western Minnesota.

A four-year rotation of corn, wheat, oats, and clover is being grown with 18 plats in each crop each year. These plats receive six different treatments, including no fertilizer, rock phosphate alone, acid phosphate alone, manure alone, rock phosphate with manure, and acid phosphate with manure. Two seasons' crops have been harvested and the results tabulated, but thus far have not shown sufficiently increased yields over the untreated plats to pay the cost of applying the fertilizer.

Yields of 21 strains and varieties of alfalfa being tested in nursery rows are reported. The Grimm, Baltic, and Imported Turkestan varieties appear to be sufficiently hardy to withstand the winters of this locality.

Alsike clover has proved satisfactory on wet lands.

Yields of 9 varieties of corn tested which failed to mature fully, 7 varieties of spring wheat tested for rust resistance, and 3 varieties of barley damaged by storms, are reported.

Of 7 varieties of oats tested the yields varied from 64.2 to 100.5 bu. per acre. Improved Ligowa gave the highest yield with the least lodging. Marrowfat peas yielded 24.3 bu. per acre, as compared with 9.5 bu. from Early Alaska.

[The Woburn field experiments, 1915], J. A. VOELCKER (*Woburn Expt. Sta. Rpt., 1915, pp. 1–15, 20–29; Jour. Roy. Agr. Soc. England, 76 (1915), pp. 317–330, 334–344*).—In continuation of work previously reported (E. S. R., 35, p. 30), this deals with the season of 1915, which was marked by heavy rainfall during the winter and a prolonged drought in the summer.

In the wheat experiments the plat receiving farmyard manure gave the highest yield, 24.4 bu. per acre, together with the most straw. The plat receiving rape dust gave the second highest yield, 23.2 bu., while the average of the two unfertilized plats was 12.9 bu. With mineral manures alone the yield was about 1 bu. less per acre than on the unmanured plats, but there was rather more straw. Ammonium sulphate used alone was unsuccessful, but upon the addition of lime increased yields were obtained. Nitrate of soda showed, on the whole, better results than sulphate of ammonia, probably due to the dry season. The use of phosphates produced 1 bu. more per acre than the use of potassium sulphate. The highest quality of wheat was obtained from the nitrate of soda plats, that from the farmyard manure plat being graded as only moderate.

In order to determine whether flax is a soil-exhausting crop wheat was sown on two adjoining fields, from one of which flax and the other oats had just been removed. The yield after flax was just double that after oats.

In the barley experiments, determinations showed a higher moisture content on the nitrate of soda plats than on the ammonium sulphate plats. The highest barley yield, 27.3 bu., was obtained from the plat receiving farmyard manure, while the plat receiving mineral manures and 1 ton of lime in 1915 was second, with 19.1 bu. The average for the untreated plats was 10.2 bu. The use of ammonium sulphate alone gave no crop, and when used with lime inferior yields were obtained, but when mineral manures were added an increased yield resulted. Sodium nitrate alone gave poor results, although increased yields were obtained when used in conjunction with mineral manures.

The yield was smaller by 2.2 bu. per acre after the use of potash than with phosphates, and the quality of the barley was reported as poor. Variety tests with barley were continued, Chevalier yielding 13 bu. more than Tystofte and 19 bu. more than Svalöf, but its quality being inferior to that of the other two.

Rotation experiments to study the unexhausted manurial value of grain (barley, oats, and chaff) and cake (linseed cake, cottonseed cake, and chaff), when fed to sheep as a supplement to the roots in the rotation, showed tentatively that the corn-fed plat gave slightly higher yields in the subsequent crops.

Tests were continued with clover and grass mixtures, the best yields of hay being obtained from a mixture including " wild " white clover. Variety tests with alfalfa laid down in 1911 show the best results with Russian (Europe) and with Province second.

Mangels were grown beside sugar-beet plats, and it was observed that the beets required approximately three times the labor that the mangels did in harvesting. It was also ascertained that, due to the large amount of earth retained, the beets lost 32 per cent in washing, while the mangels lost only 9 per cent.

In pasture improvement the farmyard manure plat gave the highest returns, but was inferior in quality, while the plat receiving 10 cwt. of basic slag and 1 cwt. of potassium sulphate gave the best all-round results. In testing the varieties of lime best for grassland, Buxton lime showed the highest yield. Lump lime and ground chalk gave better results than ground lime and ground limestone.

In tests instituted in 1913, plats alternately mown and grazed gave the highest yields of hay and left an aftermath of superior quality.

Cultivation and utilization of sunflower, niger, and safflower seed (*Bul. Imp. Inst.* [*So. Kensington*], *14* (*1916*), *No. 1, pp. 88–101*).—Brief notes are given on the cultivation, harvesting, and utilization of the seed of sunflower (*Helianthus annuus*), niger-seed plant (*Guizotia abyssinica*), and safflower (*Carthamus tinctorius*) in South Africa.

The entire sunflower plant produces silage of fair quality. The stalks alone are often used for fuel and the ash, which is high in potash, as a fertilizer. The seed of all three plants is used for oil extraction, and the seed cake resulting as a concentrate.

Pasture problems.—Indigenous plants in relation to habitat and sown species, R. G. STAPLETON and T. J. JENKIN (*Jour. Agr. Sci.* [*England*], *8* (*1916*), *No. 1, pp. 26–64*).—This paper continues work previously noted (E. S. R., 33, p. 227), and attempts to trace (1) the relationship that exists between the several indigenous plants that contribute to the herbage ·of definite types of grassland, (2) the progressive changes that occur on fields, down to grass for a varying number of years, belonging to these types, (3) the competitive interaction between sown and indigenous species, and (4) the contrast in effect on the herbage of continual mowing and continual grazing.

The types of grassland investigated are divided into two groups, the natural and the seminatural. By natural types are meant those pastures which historical evidence shows never to have been extensively under the plow or manured and which, if broken or manured at some remote period, have completely reverted to type. By seminatural types are meant those pastures which of certainty have been under the plow and, at all events, manured during the rotation previous to reverting to grass. The seminatural types are further classified as the tended and untended. The tended are those pastures which have been down to grass about 20 to 50 years, receiving periodic if but slight dressings of manure and probably sown in the first instance with rye grasses and clovers only or with loft sweepings. The untended are those which have been plowed and probably manured from 50 to 100 years ago and then, after yielding crops for some seasons, allowed to revert to grass without any sowing (with the possible exception of loft sweepings) and have so remained ever since without any further manuring in most cases.

Plants which colonize natural grasslands are called primary indigenous species, and those which come in without being sown and contribute largely to the herbage on seminatural grasslands are designated as secondary indigenous species. Plants that come in alone but which disappear as the field approaches the seminatural are called tertiary indigenous species, and are to be dealt with in a subsequent paper. Plants which are indigenous in a district but do not contribute to the flora of a well-marked type of grassland are called locally exotic, and those not indigenous in a district exotic. These classifications and distinctions are deemed applicable to all districts and type of grasslands.

Considerable space is devoted to a discussion of the composition of the herbage on the various pasture lands observed and on the stabilization of grasslands. The behavior of the chief plants found on all the types of grassland studied is also discussed under a separate heading for each individual species. The general conclusions may be summarized as follows:

The number of primary species on most types is not considerable and they are usually late in making their appearance in fields put down to grass after a long period of rotation. Primary species which come in early are frequently weeds of arable land, such as *Poa trivialis, Festuca rubra*, and *Agrostis vulgaris*.

As regards the relation of primary and secondary species to their commercial and sown counterparts, commercial seed may not appreciably hasten the appearance or add to the quantity of the desired plant. This is especially true of the fine-leaved fescues and even of *Trifolium repens*. Phosphatic manures often prove to be sufficient to hasten the appearance of the indigenous plants.

Commercial seed may produce a great bulk of the required plant and only after several years will the plant attain its normal development, indicating that the final plant is the indigenous counterpart of the sown species. Commercial seeding is ecnomically justified in such cases. Commercial seed may also hasten the appearance of the desired species, but there is a risk of the sown plant interfering with the development of the definitely lasting indigenous species; this is more a matter of local importance. The spontaneous appearance of primary and secondary species on land long under rotation when put down to grass may be due to the following: (a) Many species remain as arable weeds; (b) the seeds of many species may be wind borne; (c) seeds may be introduced as impurities in sown seed; and (d) the seeds of a great many species are evidently capable of lying dormant in the soil for long periods.

In addition to the conclusions given above, certain generalizations are presented regarding experimental work on grassland and the whole problem and economics of putting land down to grass. A bibliography of 20 references is given at the end of the paper.

Observations on alfalfa, E. H. JENKINS (*Connecticut State Sta. Bul. 192* (*1917*), *pp. 12*).—Limited observations of four years of alfalfa growing with the Grimm, Sand Lucerne, Kansas-grown, Provence, Utah-grown, and Turkestan strains are briefly noted. Grimm gave the highest average yield for the 4-year period, 4.39 tons per acre, on limed soil. The lowest average yield, 3.4 tons, was secured from the Turkestan variety. These two varieties suffered least from winterkilling, while the Sand Lucerne and Provence suffered slightly, and the Utah- and Kansas-grown strains the most.

The determined cost of plowing, seed bed preparation, liming, and fertilizing (basic slag, acid phosphate, and muriate of potash) amounted to $53.91 per acre. The estimated cost of seeding and inoculating, spreading fertilizer, and cutting, curing, and hauling the crop (4 tons per year for four years, at $2 per ton) brought the total cost of production for four years to $95.91 per acre.

Beans in Colorado, A. KEZER (*Colorado Sta. Bul. 226 (1917), pp. 3-20, figs. 6*).—Detailed directions are given for preparing the seed bed, planting, cultivating, harvesting, threshing, and marketing the bean crop in Colorado. It is estimated that the acreage planted to beans increased 81 per cent in 1916 over that planted in 1914 and 1915, and that the total yield increased 41 per cent in the same period.

It is stated that Pinto beans, the chief Colorado market variety, average from 300 to 800 lbs. per acre under dry-farming conditions and may yield 1,800 lbs. Under irrigation this variety will average from 1,200 to 2,000 lbs. and may yield 3,000 lbs. or more. The bean straw will average on dry land from one-half to three-quarters ton per acre.

Systematic rotation of beans is urged as a disease-control measure. Wheat following beans on dry land is reported as yielding as well as after the usual summer fallow in most seasons.

The cost of bean production on dry land has been found to average from $5 to $8 per acre and on irrigated land from $9 to $15. These estimates are exclusive of machinery costs, interest on land, cost of irrigation, ditch upkeep, and rentals.

Clover and clover hay, A. and GABRIELLE L. C. HOWARD (*Agr. Jour. India, 11 (1916), No. 1, pp. 71-78*).—Notes are given on the value and production of Persian clover or shaftal (*Trifolium resupinatum*) in the Quetta Valley, India. Its adaptability to local conditions and the excellent quality of hay obtained under arid conditions have contributed largely to its successful production.

Corn problems.—Choice of varieties; time, manner, and rate of planting, C. A. GEARHART (*Mo. Bul. Ohio Sta., 2 (1917), No. 4, pp. 104-109, figs. 5*).—Brief recommendations are made regarding the choice of varieties and the time, manner, and rate of planting corn.

In date-of-planting tests at Wooster the periods of May 4 to 10 and May 14 to 17 gave the highest yields, 64.22 and 64.36 bu. per acre, respectively, for an 8-year average, while corn planted April 24 to 29 outyielded that planted May 25 to 28 and June 2 to 6. The last two named planting periods produced 26.15 and 38.36 per cent nubbins, respectively, while the other planting periods were comparatively uniform, giving about 17 per cent nubbins. The early-planted corn was also more mature than that planted later, the moisture content at the time of husking varying from 25.85 per cent for the first planting to 36.4 per cent for the last.

Corn drilled rather than planted in hills, with plants 12 in. apart, gave the highest 3-year average yield of grain, 46.88 bu. per acre, and of stover, 2,827 lbs. It is stated, however, that the methods of cultivation and harvesting will determine to a large extent the method of planting to be employed.

In rate-of-planting tests the yields from the four- and five-plant rates were the highest, 64.34 and 62.6 bu. per acre for an 11-year average, respectively, but with a percentage of nubbins of 30.2 and 41.2, respectively. The three-plant rate was deemed the most satisfactory where corn is to be husked. The yield of the latter was 60.95 bu. of shelled corn per acre, with 21.4 per cent nubbins. Where the crop is to be fed from the shock the thicker rates of planting are preferable.

How much plant food does a corn crop take from an acre? E. H. JENKINS, J. P. STREET, and C. D. HUBBELL (*Connecticut State Sta. Bul. 193 (1917), pp. 11, 12*).—From nine series of tests with husking and silage corn at different experiment stations the average amounts of nitrogen, phosphoric acid, and potash removed by the crop were 87.5, 42, and 67.1 lbs per acre, respectively. Six tests at Mt. Carmel gave for a 15-ton silage crop an average of 88 lbs. of nitrogen, 37 lbs. of phosphoric acid, and 100 lbs. of potash. Several crops of husking corn, grown elsewhere in Connecticut and calculated at 75 bu. per acre, gave an average of 92 lbs. of nitrogen, 34 lbs. of phosphoric acid, and 74 lbs. of potash.

It is estimated that by careful conservation of the manure returned from feeding 30 tons of silage approximately 50 lbs. of nitrogen, from 25 to 30 lbs. of phosphoric acid, and from 45 to 50 lbs. of potash may be regained regardless of any fertilizing ingredients in the litter or fermenting organic matter which might serve as a soil amendment or plant-food solvent.

Corn variety tests for 1915, R. Y. WINTERS, G. M. GARREN, and B. WHITE (*Bul. N. C. Dept. Agr., 37 (1916), No. 4, pp. 5-21*).—Tests of 24 varieties of corn at six experimental farms in North Carolina are reported and compared with the average results of previous tests.

The 2-eared prolific varieties yielded best, except in the extreme western part of the State, where Boone County White, a 1-eared variety, gave the highest yield in a series of five tests. It is recommended that the best 2-eared varieties be improved by selecting for increased yield of grain per stalk rather than a larger number of ears per stalk. For production of silage the 2-eared and more prolific varieties have given a higher yield of dry matter and more food value per acre than the 1-eared varieties.

Egyptian maize (Zea mays), G. C. DUDGEON and B. G. C. BOLLAND (*Min. Agr. Egypt, Tech. and Sci. Serv. Bul. 9 (1916), pp. 5*).—This is a progress report of variety tests with corn at the Gheezeh Experimental Farm in an effort to isolate and describe the varieties grown. Brief notes are also given on the production of the crop in Egypt.

Fique (Furcræa gigantea) (*Roy. Bot. Gard. Kew, Bul. Misc. Inform., No. 7 (1916), pp. 169, 170, pl. 1*).—This is a brief note on fique in Colombia, including an enumeration by M. T. Dawe of the principal uses to which the fiber is put.

The culture and manufacture of flax for fiber and seed with special reference to the industry in Oregon, J. F. THORNE (*Univ. Oreg. Bul., n. ser., 13 (1916), No. 13, pp. 70, figs. 5*).—This is a compilation of data and expert opinions on the establishment of the flax industry in Oregon, made by the School of Commerce of the University of Oregon at the request of the Flax Committee of the Portland Chamber of Commerce. It discusses the climatic conditions and advantages of Oregon for flax production, and, in addition, the demand, freights, markets, prices, profits, and conditions of the flax industry in foreign countries.

Indian hemp fiber (Crotalaria juncea), C. D'LIMA (*Agr. Jour. India, 11 (1916), No. 1, pp. 31-41*).—This is a general discussion of the hemp situation in India from a commercial standpoint.

[The composition of mangels], C. T. GIMINGHAM (*Univ. Bristol, Ann. Rpt. Agr. and Hort. Research Sta., 1915, pp. 114-119*).—Analyses of six varieties of mangels grown at each of eight experimental centers are reported.

Great millet (Sorghum vulgare) and berseem (Trifolium alexandrinum), B. G. C. BOLLAND (*Min. Agr. Egypt. Tech. and Sci. Serv. Bul. 8 (1916), pp. 5*).— A progress report of work conducted with millets in 1915 in an effort to isolate and describe the individual varieties grown at the Gheezeh Experimental Farm. Tests with four strains of berseem are also reported.

Peanuts.—Tests of varieties and fertilizers, J. F. DUGGAR, E. F. CAUTHEN, J. T. WILLIAMSON, and O. H. SELLERS (*Alabama Col. Sta. Bul. 193 (1917), pp. 3-32, pls. 4*).—Variety tests covering a period of five years and fertilizer tests extending over six years in different parts of the State are reported.

The average yield of unshelled peanuts obtained in the variety tests ranged from 871 lbs. for the McGovern variety to 1,244 lbs. for Red Spanish. The average percentage of shelled nuts varied from 39.3 for Jumbo to 75.1 for White Spanish. The heaviest unshelled peanuts were the Tennessee Red (246 pods to the pound) and the lightest White Spanish (461 pods to the pound). Based on the average percentage of sound nuts and the oil content of each variety, the varieties, arranged according to pounds of oil produced per ton, are as follows: White Spanish 702 lbs., Red Spanish 693, Valencia 572, McGovern 548, Tennessee Red 527, North Carolina Runner 524, Virginia Runner 493, and Jumbo 354 lbs.

Brief directions are given for preparing the seed bed, planting, cultivating, and harvesting the crop. The largest yields were obtained from plantings made between May 1 and June 15.

Chemical analysis of peanut straw showed 10.72 per cent water, 10.69 protein, 1.66 fat, 29.5 crude fiber, 41.39 carbohydrates, 6.03 ash, 1.2 potash, and 0.5 per cent phosphoric acid.

From tests made to study the residual effect of peanuts on the succeeding crops, as compared with corn, it was concluded that the peanut crop harvested in the usual way for seed does not improve the soil for succeeding crops. From complete fertilizer tests it was concluded that acid phosphate at the rate of 200 to 300 lbs. per acre produced profitable increases in yields on sandy and other well-adapted soils. Potash, as kainit, at the rate of 100 and 200 lbs. per acre was not always profitable except on a few infertile, sandy soils. Slacked lime at the rate of 600 lbs. per acre gave profitable increases on sandy soil. Cottonseed meal as a nitrogenous fertilizer was not profitable.

The average yield of peanut straw from four experiments varied from 2,316 lbs. for North Carolina Runner to 1,234 lbs. for Virginia Bunch per acre. The average percentage of dry, unhulled peanuts to the weight of the whole plant ranged from 32 for North Carolina Runner to 39 for Red Spanish.

Growing peanuts in Alabama, J. F. DUGGAR, E. F. CAUTHEN, J. T. WILLIAMSON, and O. H. SELLERS (*Alabama Col. Sta. Bul. 194 (1917), pp. 35–48*).—A popular edition of the above.

A note on the inheritance of certain stem characters in sorghum, G. R. HILSON (*Agr. Jour. India, 11 (1916), No. 2, pp. 150–155, pl. 1*).—Observations of some selected strains of sorghum in the Madras Presidency led to the conclusion that all of these strains could be placed in one or the other of two groups, according to the appearance of the midrib of the leaf. One group is composed of all plants in which the midrib appears as an opaque white band running the entire length of the leaf, while the other group includes those plants in which the midrib in the lower leaves is marked by dull white, generally broken bands never extending across the full width of the midrib and rarely to the end of the leaf, while the upper leaves are entirely devoid of any white marking.

Repeated tests have led to the conclusion that a grayish midrib indicates a stem rich in sugar, while a white midrib shows a pithy, insipid stem. With these characteristics in mind a number of breeding experiments were conducted with the following results: (1) The character of the green stem in sorghum can be readily diagnosed from the appearance of the midrib of the leaf, and (2) in breeding tests the pithy, insipid character of the stem behaves as a simple dominant to the sweet-stalked character.

Tests of soy beans in 1916, E. H. JENKINS, J. P. STREET, and C. D. HUBBELL (*Connecticut State Sta. Bul. 195 (1917), pp. 3–10*).—Continuing work previously noted (E. S. R., 35, p. 532), the yield and composition of 17 varieties of soy beans are reported. The range in time of maturity in 1916 was from

105 to 127 days; in yield of green forage from 7,362 to 13,590 lbs. per acre, with an average of 9,839 lbs.; in yield of dry matter from 1,992 to 3,325 lbs., with an average of 2,600 lbs.; and in protein from 3.2 to 6.6 per cent, with an average of 4.6 per cent.

Of 12 varieties of soy beans tested for three years the Wilson has produced the highest amount of dry matter per year, 3,329 lbs., with the Mongol variety last, 2,406 lbs. Both varieties required an average of 122 days to attain maturity.

Exclusive of roots the crops of the last three years contained per acre 3,637 lbs. of organic matter, 111 lbs. of nitrogen, 20 lbs. of phosphoric acid, and 79 lbs. of potash.

The Whippoorwill and Brahman varieties of cowpeas were tested, yielding 2,542 and 2,160 lbs. of organic matter and 54 and 50 lbs. of nitrogen per acre, respectively. The average composition of the dry matter of soy beans and cowpeas grown at Mt. Carmel during 1916 is compared in tabular form.

Soy bean growing is briefly discussed and the uses of the crop in Connecticut outlined as follows: Sowing as a catch crop following winterkilled grain or clover or a poor spring seeding, from the first of May to the middle of June; as a late summer soiling crop for cattle; as a silage crop grown either with or without corn and cut into the silo—about 3 tons of corn to one of soy beans; as a green manure; and as a seed crop.

Soy beans.—Their culture and use, C. G. WILLIAMS and J. B. PARK (*Ohio Sta. Bul. 312 (1917), pp. 579–600, figs. 4*).—Soy-bean production in Ohio is discussed in detail.

In rate-of-seeding tests 3 pk. of medium-sized soy beans (Medium Green variety), sown in rows 28 in. apart, has usually given the best results for seed production. A seeding of 8 pk. per acre drilled solid gave a smaller yield of seed, but a higher yield of total forage.

Twenty-five varieties and pure-line strains are briefly described, and the results of variety tests in yields of grain and straw and the pounds of straw per bushel of grain are reported in tabular form. The five leading varieties in order of rank were: Ohio 9016, Ohio 7496, Elton (Chestnut), Ito San 17268, and Shinto. The five lowest yielders were Sable, Cloud, Yosho, Mikado, and Taha. The yield in grain per acre for the five-year average, 1911–1916, inclusive, varied from 14.01 bu. for the Sable variety to 29.22 bu. for Ohio 9016. The high-yielding varieties showed a low proportion of straw to grain, ranging from 72 to 97 lbs. of straw per bushel of grain, with an average of 81 lbs., whereas in the five low-yielding varieties the range was from 106 to 164 lbs., with an average of 133 lbs. The total average yield of straw, however, in the two classes varied only 177 lbs. per acre.

Results obtained with a few varieties tested at the experimental farms located in Clermont, Hamilton, Washington, Paulding, and Trumbull counties are also reported.

Tests with ten varieties of soy beans for hay have been conducted at Wooster for five years. The Medium Green variety has given the highest average yield, 5,402 lbs. per acre, with the Mammoth Yellow lowest, with 3,814 lbs. Medium Green is deemed better adapted for hay production than for grain because of its tendency to shatter.

Limited observations have been made of the effect of soy beans upon subsequent crops in the rotation. Fifty rotations are in progress, and 24 wheat plats were harvested in 1916. Ten of these plats followed corn, 6 soy beans, 5 potatoes, and 3 oats. The average yield of wheat following soy beans was 10.3 bu. greater than that following corn, 1.27 bu. greater than that following oats, and 0.34 bu. greater than that following potatoes.

The uses of soy beans for human and animal food and for such special products as soy-bean meal and soy-bean oil are discussed. Charts are presented showing the relative value of soy beans and several common food materials.

Sudan grass, B. A. MADSON and P. B. KENNEDY (*California Sta. Bul. 277* (*1917*), *pp. 195–224, figs. 5*).—The field practices and cultural methods employed in the production of Sudan grass, both for hay and seed, in California are discussed. Date, rate, and method-of-seeding tests for hay production and method-of-seeding tests for seed production, carried on in cooperation with the U. S. Department of Agriculture, are for 1913, 1914, 1915, and 1916.

The average yield of cured hay varied from 1.8 to 5.9 tons per acre on dry land and 3.9 to 6.7 tons on irrigated land. The average yield of seed is estimated at from 600 to 800 lbs. per acre. For hay production seedings of from 10 to 15 lbs. in rather narrow rows (18 in.) seemed to give the best results, although heavier seedings sown broadcast, drilled, or in wider rows gave good results, depending largely upon the available moisture supply. Seeding should not be done until all danger of frost is passed and the soil has become thoroughly warm. From 75 to 80 days after seeding are required to secure the first cutting, about 45 days more for the second, and 50 days more for the third. A seed crop can be produced in from 95 to 100 days.

Analyses are reported of various hay crops for a comparison with Sudan grass and indicate that due to the large production of dry matter (6,367.7 lbs. per acre for a 3-year average) this crop is superior to the usual cereal and grass hays in the amount of food constituents produced per acre, although it can not compete with alfalfa.

It is recommended that Sudan grass be grown in rotation following a spring crop, such as grain or spring pasture, which could be removed by the first to the middle of July.

The method for distinguishing the seed of Johnson grass and Sudan grass devised by Hillman (E. S. R., 35, p. 834), is noted.

Report of the plant breeder, H. B. COWGILL (*Rpt. Bd. Comrs. Agr. P. R., 4* (*1914–15*), *pp. 22–33; 5* (*1915–16*), *pp. 16–20, 21–34*).—This reports the continuation of work at the Porto Rico Insular Station with sugar cane (E. S. R., 33, p. 532) for the years of 1914–15 and 1915–16.

The propagation of seedling canes and a rigid selection and careful choice of parent varieties has been continued. Several attempts at cross-pollinating cane varieties are reported with a considerable degree of success. The methods employed in 1914–15 included planting a pollen-sterile variety to the leeward of a pollen-fertile variety which blooms at the same time and tying together the tassels of the varieties to be crossed before the florets of either had opened. The pollen-sterile variety used in the first case was the Otaheite and the pollen-fertile parent B 347. In the second case Crystalina (the pollen-sterile parent) and D 109 were the varieties used. Sixteen hundred seedlings were produced by the latter method and 1,745 seedlings obtained from open cross-pollination were planted in the field in 1915–1916. Of the last-named group 80 plants were selected as of superior quality. The results of the crosses and the value of different varieties as parents are discussed.

A list of the cane varieties grown most extensively on the island is given and their relative importance discussed. Striped cane, Otaheite, and Crystalina take rank in the order named with regard to the area occupied by each. The value of numerous imported varieties, as indicated by actual field observations, is also discussed.

Tests of 25 varieties of cane are reported for 1914–15, showing the yields of plant cane and first and second ratoons, with an analysis of the juice for the first two crops. Seeley Seedling gave the best results, considering the quality of the juices and the weight of the cane produced. Twenty varieties of recently introduced cane were tested for the first time during 1914–15, and the test continued in 1915–16. Among these varieties the most promising were B 1809, B 7245, B 6292, B 3859, B 3405, and B 3747, all giving higher yields than Crystalina or Otaheite, the check varieties.

Thirteen leguminous cover crops were tested in 1914–15, and the results are presented in tabular form with regard to germination of the seed, habit of growth, length of growing season, amount of seed produced, and resistance to insect and disease pests.

The average yield of cane from all unfertilized plats in 1914–15 was 8.17 tons per acre as compared with an average yield of 22.46 tons for the plats receiving a complete fertilizer. The highest yield, 26.6 tons, was secured from the plat receiving 120 lbs. phosphoric acid, 60 lbs. nitrogen, and 60 lbs. potash. These results are in agreement with those obtained in the two previous years, and in general were confirmed in 1915–16, when the highest yield, 20.75 tons, was obtained from a double application of a complete fertilizer. All the fertilizer experiments indicated the need of abundant phosphoric acid applications on these soils,, while potash and nitrogen fertilization is evidently of secondary importance.

Further fertilizer experiments were conducted in 1915–16 in cooperation with local growers on sandy clay and clay soils. The results are reported in tabular form. All combinations of fertilizers gave good returns for the money invested.

An application of 4 tons of lime per acre made in 1912 was followed by increased yields of cane of 4.98, 14.78, and 12.1 tons for 1913, 1914, and 1915, respectively.

A comparison of cultivation by hoes and by cultivator was made in 1915–16. Plats receiving four hoeings gave an acre yield of 27.02 tons, at a labor cost of $10.41, while plats receiving five cultivations gave a yield of 25.03 tons, at a labor cost of $8.41.

A demonstration of the value of crop rotation in practical cane culture, A. H. ROSENFELD (*Sugar [Chicago], 18 (1916), No. 9, pp. 463, 464*).—This is a popular discussion of crop rotation experiments with sugar cane conducted by the author while the director of the experimental work in Tucumán, Argentina. Continuous cropping with sugar cane is compared with cane following one year of cowpeas, corn, and alfalfa, respectively.

Remarkable increases in yield are reported. In a 3-year period, the highest gains were made after alfalfa, although the gains after corn were twice the average for the Province. The plats planted to cane after alfalfa showed an average annual gain of 3.5 tons per acre, the cane being superior in average stalk weight and slightly richer in juice than that following corn.

Some sugar cane experiments in Travancore, N. K. PILLAI (*Agr. Jour. India, 11 (1916), No. 1, pp. 79–81*).—In experiments with sugar cane conducted during the 1914–15 season, the ridge and furrow system of planting seemed superior to planting in pits, the common practice in Travancore. Thin planting (5,000 sets per acre) was better than thick planting (10,000 sets or more). The application of a complete fertilizer was more profitable than that of ashes alone, as is the usual practice.

Washington wheats.—Their classification and identification, E. D. ALVORD (*Wash. Agr., 9 (1916), No. 8, pp. 217–219, figs. 2*).—A popular classification of 20 of the more common varieties of Washington wheats, based upon (1) head characteristics, and (2) kernel characteristics, each classification being complete in itself.

The wheat field in April.—Top-dressing with fertilizers may often be profitable, C. E. Thorne (*Mo. Bul. Ohio Sta., 2 (1917), No. 4, pp. 110–112, fig. 1*).—The wheat yields obtained at Wooster, Strongsville, Germantown, and Carpenter from fertilized and unfertilized plats in 3- and 5-year rotations and for good and bad seasons are tabulated.

An average increase in yield of 40 per cent at Wooster and 50 per cent at the substations was obtained in good seasons from applications of phosphorus and potassium. In bad seasons the increase was from 109 to nearly 200 per cent of the unfertilized yield. A further increase in the number of bushels was realized from applications of nitrogen, but the percentage of the unfertilized yields was smaller in good than in bad seasons.

With nitrate of soda selling at 3 cts. a pound or less, wheat at $1 per bushel returned the cost of the nitrate in good seasons in all tests except at Strongsville. In bad seasons, however, wheat failed to return the cost of the nitrate at both Strongsville and Germantown. At the present price of nitrate (3.5 to 4 cts. per pound) wheat must bring more than $1 a bushel to justify its use. The nitrate was in all cases preceded by a fall application of acid phosphate; otherwise the crop increase has never paid the cost of the nitrate.

For wheat fields not fertilized in the fall a top-dressing of approximately 200 lbs. of of acid phosphate and 50 lbs. of nitrate of soda in April is recommended. Sulphate of ammonia may be substituted for nitrate of soda, although its action is slower than that of the nitrate.

The saving of irrigation water in wheat growing, A. and Gabrielle L. C. Howard (*Agr. Jour. India, 11 (1916), No. 1, pp. 14–30*).—Wheat growing under irrigation in the Quetta Valley, India, is discussed with special reference to the conservation of irrigation water. The fundamental principles of water saving are formulated as follows: (1) Irrigation water should be spread over the largest possible area, as was demonstrated by Widtsoe (E. S. R., 32, p. 784). (2) Heavy waterings reduce the proportion of grain to total crop, causing an increase in the length and weight of straw. (3) The growing period of wheat is lengthened by heavy watering, thus delaying maturity, a very undesirable condition in the Quetta Valley, owing to the rapid rise in temperature and hot, dry, westerly winds. (4) When the water supply is limited the root development of the wheat crop will be deeper, provided the seed bed has been properly prepared. (5) Soil moisture must be preserved by the maintenance of a surface mulch of dry soil, accomplished by shallow harrowing.

Experiments on a somewhat extensive scale are reported in growing wheat with the natural moisture only and with a single irrigation. The yield without irrigation was approximately 28.8 bu. per acre. The single irrigation was applied in September, prior to sowing in October, and showed an increase of 5.8 bu. per acre over the yield obtained from fields receiving 7 irrigations. In addition to the increased yield, much earlier maturity was secured, together with a full development of the chaff color, rarely seen in the native-grown wheat.

Third annual report of the State grain laboratory of Montana, A. Atkinson, B. W. Whitlock, and E. W. Jahnke (*Montana Sta. Bul. 113 (1916), pp. 77–100, figs. 21*).—The work for the year ended September 30, 1916, is reported, including purity and germination tests of 5,035 samples, a study of the seed value of frosted wheat, and a study of the germinability of seeds at different periods after harvesting.

The weed seed content of samples of alfalfa, clover, timothy, and sweet clover is reported as having greatly increased.

The average field germination of frosted and unfrosted wheat was 75 and 78 per cent, respectively, while the average number of heads per row was 1,525 for the frosted wheat and 1,509 for the unfrosted wheat. The grain weight per row was 1,457 and 1,375 gm., respectively.

Germination tests of samples of winter and spring wheat, oats, and barley taken one week, one month, and two months after threshing indicate that germination improves greatly a few weeks after threshing.

Twenty-one of the worst weeds encountered in Montana are briefly described and illustrated.

Results of seed inspection, 1915 and 1916, J. P. HELYAR ET AL. (*New Jersey Stas. Bul. 302 (1916), pp. 3–23*).—Continuing work previously noted (E. S. R., 34, p. 832), the author states that during the past two years more attention has been paid to the analysis of vegetable seeds offered for sale in bulk on the New Jersey markets. Analyses of official samples for 1915 include red clover, alfalfa, crimson clover, cowpeas, Canadian field peas, beans, lima beans, sweet corn, peas, radishes, tomatoes, turnips, cucumbers, and cabbages.

The 1916 analysis was confined entirely to vegetable seeds, except for crimson clover seed investigations. A comparison of the analyses of 29 crimson clover samples showed a variation in germination percentage of from 24.5 to 92.5 per cent.

Weeds in the Government of Novgorod, A. MALZEW (*Trudy Büro Prikl. Bot. (Bul. Appl. Bot.), 9 (1916), No. 4, pp. 137–174*).—The weeds found in winter rye, spring oats, barley, flax, potatoes, and cabbage in the Government of Novgorod are discussed, those peculiar to each crop listed separately, and all the weeds identified (81 in number) listed alphabetically and briefly described. It is pointed out that only about 12 of these weeds are serious pests and that as a rule the annuals are more noxious than the perennials.

Broom rape (*Jour. Bd. Agr. [London], 23 (1916), No. 5, pp. 478–481, fig. 1*).— This is a note on the parasitic weed broom rape (*Orobanche minor*), which was unusually prevalent in English clover fields during the summer of 1916. The life history of the plant is briefly outlined, together with preventive and control measures.

Red sorrel and its control (Rumex acetosella), F. J. PIPAL (*Indiana Sta. Bul. 197 (1916), pp. 28, figs. 16*).—Red sorrel is described and measures for its control outlined.

An abundance of red sorrel in a field is held to indicate soil acidity, insufficient organic matter or mineral plant food, or inadequate drainage. Pot tests with several types of soils indicated that correction of such unfavorable conditions will stimulate clover production and check the growth of the sorrel, although lime was not found to have harmful effects on the growth of the plant itself.

Other tests indicated that eradication of the weed may be effected by one or more applications in the form of a fine spray of a 20 per cent solution of sulphate of iron or of full strength orchard heating oil. For badly infested fields cultivation or grazing with sheep is recommended, and it is pointed out that pending eradication sorrel may be cut and utilized for feed.

HORTICULTURE.

Proceedings of the American Society for Horticultural Science, 1916 (*Proc. Amer. Soc. Hort. Sci., 13 (1916), pp. 162, pls. 3, figs. 6*).—In addition to the routine business report, the following papers presented at the annual meeting of the society, held in New York City, December 28 and 29, 1916, are given: Methods of Work in Pruning Investigations, by C. H. Connors (pp. 14–17); Monographic Studies with Flowers, by A. C. Beal (pp. 17–22); Gardenia

4066°—No. 3—17——4

Studies, by C. H. Connors (pp. 22–30) ; What Science Has Done and Will Do for Floriculture, by E. A. White (pp. 30–40) ; The Inheritance and Permanence of Clonal Varieties, by M. J. Dorsey (pp. 41–71) ; Experiments in Bud Selection with the Apple and Violet at Geneva, by R. D. Anthony and J. W. Wellington (pp. 71–76) ; Improvement of Vegetable Varieties by Selection, by R. Wellington (pp. 77–80) ; Variety Testing, by L. C. Corbett (pp. 80–84) ; Variety Testing at the Dominion Experimental Farms, and What Has Been Accomplished by It, by W. T. Macoun (pp. 85–90) ; Methods for the Study of Vegetable Varieties and Strains, by P. Work (pp. 91–95) ; Factors Influencing the Abscission of Flowers and Partially Developed Fruits of the Apple, by A. J. Heinicke (pp. 95–103) ; Horticulture as a Science and as an Art, by M. A. Blake (pp. 103–106) ; Influence of Nitrogen in Western Orchards, by C. I. Lewis (pp. 107–110) ; Report of the Committee on Research and Experimentation: Part I, by L. H. Bailey, Part II, Research and Experimentation, by W. L. Howard, Part III, How to Lay Out an Experiment in Horticulture, by H. J. Webber, and Part IV, Fundamental Training Required for the Successful Undertaking of Research, by W. T. Macoun (pp. 110–120) ; and Report of Committee on Graduate Courses, by M. J. Dorsey (pp. 120–128).

A list is given of horticultural projects being conducted at institutions with which members of the society are connected.

[Report of the] division of horticulture (*Minnesota Sta. Rpt. 1916, pp. 49–54*).—In the sterility studies with fruits the results with the strawberry indicate that where good pollen is produced in the cultivated varieties the plants are self-fertile. Studies conducted under tent and in the greenhouse show that a number of Burbank-Wolf plum crosses, as well as the Burbank plum, the sand cherry, and the Compass cherry, are self-sterile. Some of the hybrids of these fruits were intersterile. Self-sterility did not appear to be due to aborted pollen or defective nuclei. Studies were made of the flowers of five species of maples. The pollen of the partially suppressed anthers of the functionally pistillate flowers were found to be normal in all five species, but the flowers were self-sterile because dehiscence does not take place in this type of anther.

Of the hardy seedlings at the fruit breeding farm, Minnesota No. 4 raspberry is considered promising as it has sustained no winter injury in the last four seasons. At Deerwood it was not injured by a temperature of —49° F. when left uncovered.

A test of ten varieties of Minnesota apples with reference to their value for cider and vinegar making showed that the apples are relatively low in sugar content but that vinegar of standard grade can be obtained within five months by pressing if kept in reasonably warm quarters.

A study of the most desirable time of the year for pruning apples and plums indicates thus far that success depends more on careful pruning than on the season in which the pruning is done.

Results of the potato investigations at the stations show conclusively that the improvement of seed by any kind of selection is an impossibility when the seed has been affected with curly dwarf. Tests made of potato seedlings and varieties showed in all cases that new stock is superior in productiveness and vigor to the old stock grown for one or more years in the station grounds.

Among the results secured in breeding various vegetables a pure line of Red Globe onion gives promise of being a valuable acquisition, owing to its good keeping quality. The work with squashes indicates the possibility of isolating and fixing a desirable commercial type of the Hubbard squash. In the tomato experiments marked increases in yield were obtained from some of the crosses, and it is believed certain combinations will prove valuable, owing to their earliness, smoothness, and productiveness.

Observations of various hedge plants on the station grounds indicate that the best plants for clipped hedges are buckthorn, *Cotoneaster acutifolia*, and Alpine currant. Hackberry and *Viburnum lantana* have been used with good results under some conditions.

[Report of horticultural investigations at the Crookston substation] (*Minnesota Sta., Rpt. Crookston Substa., 1910–1916, pp. 70–81*).—Tabular data are given showing the number and kinds of fruit trees and shrubs, as well as ornamental trees and shrubs planted at the Crookston substation chiefly during the period 1910–1916, including the number alive in 1916. Much injury and death among the plantings was caused by soil alkali, sun scald, freezing in the fall, and winter injury. The yields secured from variety tests of vegetables during the period of 1911–1916 are also reported, including notes on the best varieties.

[Horticultural work at the Crookston substation] (*Minnesota Sta. Rpt. 1916, pp. 70, 71*).—Notes are given on hardiness, variety, and cultural tests in 1915–16 of windbreak and ornamental trees and shrubs, orchard and small fruits, and vegetables, conducted at the Crookston substation, as noted above.

Report of the work of the horticultural substation, O. B. WHIPPLE (*Montana Sta. Bul. 114 (1916), pp. 101–123, figs. 8*).—A progress report on orchard culture and variety tests started at the substation in 1908.

The results of cultural experiments taken as a whole show the detrimental effect of continuous clean tillage as maintained during the period 1908–1916, inclusive, and the beneficial effects of leguminous cover crops in building up the fertility of the soil. The variety tests included apples, apricots, cherries, pears, peaches, plums, and walnuts. Notes are given on the behavior and adaptability of different varieties to western Montana conditions.

A fruit survey of Mesa County, E. P. SANDSTEN, T. F. LIMBOCKER, and R. A. McGINTY (*Colorado Sta. Bul. 223 (1917), pp. 3–52, figs. 12*).—The survey here reported was conducted during the summer and fall of 1915. The area surveyed included the portion of Grand Valley, about 75,000 acres in extent, which was irrigated previous to the opening of the Government ditch in 1915. The information secured pertains to various cultural practices, the extent to which they are used, areas in different kinds of fruits, varieties grown, yields, costs, culture, etc. In presenting the results suggestions are given relative to improvement in cultural operations.

The results show that there are nearly 16,000 acres of orchard in the valley, of which 10,000 are apples, 3,000 peaches, 2,400 pears, and the remainder plums, apricots, and cherries. Fewer than one-third of the fruit trees in the Grand Valley are over 12 years old. The orchards as a rule were found to be too small to be profitable, the average size being slightly below 9 acres. The authors recommend that more land be devoted to general farming, stock raising, and dairying, and that the average fruit grower include other crops besides fruit. It is estimated that more than 2,500 acres of orchard have been pulled out during the last five years. The estimated average cost of production per box of fruit laid down at the shipping station is for apples 61.2 cts., pears 60.5 cts., and peaches 31.2 cts.

Fruits, trees, and shrubs recommended for northern Minnesota, T. M. Mc-CALL (*Minnesota Sta., Rpt. Crookston Substa., 1910–1916, pp. 88–91*).—The varieties given are listed in order of adaptability as shown by work at the Northwest Substation at Crookston and results obtained by growers in different parts of northern Minnesota.

Dependable fruits: Apples, pears, plums, peaches, cherries, small fruits, W. J. GREEN, P. THAYER, and J. B. KEIL (*Ohio Sta. Bul. 313 (1917), pp. 603–614, pl. 1*).—This bulletin includes varietal lists prepared by the station of apples, pears, plums, peaches, cherries, and small fruits recommended for culture in Ohio. The selection of the varieties here suggested for culture is based upon experience covering 25 years in the station orchard, in orchards of cooperators, and on observation and study of horticultural problems in various sections of the State.

Annual report of the Fruit Experiment Station, Shillong, for the year ended June 30, 1916, C. H. HOLDER (*Ann. Rpt. Agr. Expt. Stas. Assam. 1916, pp. 64–85*).—Tabular data are given showing the number and kinds of orchard and small fruits in the station nurseries and orchards.

Pruning, F. M. CLEMENT and F. S. REEVES (*Ontario Dept. Agr. Bul. 248 (1917), pp. 36, figs. 78*).—A practical treatise on methods of pruning fruit trees, vines, and bushes.

Apple breeding at the university experiment station, C. S. CRANDALL (*Trans. Ill. Hort. Soc., n. ser., 50 (1916), pp. 444–451*).—A popular summary of progress made in apple breeding investigations which have been under way at the Illinois Experiment Station since 1907.

One phase of the work comprises an attempt to determine whether varieties of apples are affected through propagation from selected buds. The results secured indicate in brief that just as good trees are grown from small buds as from large buds, and there is no evidence that it makes any difference from which location on the tree or shoot the bud may be taken. Buds from water sprouts are equal to buds from top terminal shoots.

Field experiments in spraying apple orchards in 1916, A. J. GUNDERSON and W. S. BROCK (*Illinois Sta. Circ. 194 (1917), pp. 3–15*).—The experiments here summarized were conducted to determine the relative values of Bordeaux and lime-sulphur in the control of apple blotch, the relative merits of dust and liquid spraying in the control of insects and fungi, and the value of the cluster-bud spray in the control of scab. A more detailed account will appear in a later publication.

Although Bordeaux caused some russeting of the fruit and a small amount of foliage injury, it proved superior to lime-sulphur as a spray for blotch, probably because of its greater adhesiveness. It was thus effective over a longer period of time than lime-sulphur. Dust mixtures were less efficient than the liquid sprays in the control of fungi, but apparently controlled the codling moth and curculio equally as well as the liquid sprays. The prebloom or cluster bud spray was valueless in the control of scab where the infection was not present the preceding season. Bordeaux applied just before the bloom was no more efficient than lime-sulphur arsenate of lead in the control of apple scab. On one plat where arsenate of lead was used alone throughout the season scab infection was reduced materially.

Based on results of the experiments, spray schedules are given for different sections of Illinois, together with formulas and methods of preparation.

Dominion experimental orchard work, W. S. BLAIR (*Ann. Rpt. Fruit Growers' Assoc. Nova Scotia, 1917, pp. 132–159*).—The results are given of cooperative spraying experiments conducted under the direction of the Kentville station in 1916.

The investigations as a whole show that four regular lime-sulphur arsenate sprays, the first of which is applied when the buds have burst and the leaves are partly open, the second when the blossom clusters have separated and before the petals have opened, the third when 90 per cent of the petals have fallen, and the fourth about ten days after the third spray, are necessary for the best control of apple scab. If three applications only can be made, a thorough application should be given midway between the time for the first and second sprays. If only two applications can be made, the one before and the one after the blossoms will give the best results.

In view of the less serious injury from burning, lime-sulphur lead arsenate was more satisfactory than other sulphur lead arsenate sprays and Bordeaux lead arsenate sprays. The kind of nozzle was not a factor in causing foliage injury, provided an equal amount of spray was applied. A heavy application of lime-sulphur lead arsenate is liable to cause foliage injury, whereas the regular application will cause very slight, if any, injury.

In order to avoid the injury from the drench spray of the combined nicotin sulphate and lime-sulphur lead arsenate used for the green apple worm, it seems necessary to reduce considerably the strength of the lime-sulphur solution. Lime-sulphur weaker than the standard 1.008 or 1:37 is not so effective for scab control.

The culture of small fruits on irrigated sandy land, R. W. ALLEN (*Oregon Sta. Bul. 142 (1917), pp. 3–14, figs. 2*).—The results of varietal and cultural experiments with strawberries, together with variety tests of currants, gooseberries, dewberries, raspberries, and blackberries, conducted at the Umatilla substation are here briefly stated, and cultural directions are given for growing small fruits based on the substation's work.

Fruiting habits of budded trees of the different avocado varieties, T. U. BARBER (*Rpt. Cal. Avocada Assoc., 1916, pp. 98–103 fig. 1*).—A list is given of varieties of budded avocada trees which are fruiting in California and the age that they started to bear, together with a discussion of different characteristics of growth. The data given are based upon reports from members of the California Avocada Association.

Cultural experiments with the filbert in the East, J. S. McGLENNON (*Amer. Nut Jour., 6 (1917), No. 5, p. 71*).—A brief statement of results secured in propagating and growing filberts during the past three seasons, including a list of varieties grown.

Analyses of materials sold as insecticides and fungicides for 1916, C. S. CATHCART and R. L. WILLIS (*New Jersey Stas. Bul. 301 (1916), pp. 5–16*).—The results are given of analyses of various samples of Paris green, lead arsenate, lime-sulphur, Bordeau mixture, and miscellaneous materials inspected by the station during the year 1916.

FORESTRY.

The training of a forester, G. PINCHOT (*Philadelphia and London: J. B. Lippincott Co., 1917, 3. ed., rev., pp. 157, pls. 8*).—In the present edition of this work (E. S. R., 30, p. 742) the facts and figures have been revised throughout and brought up to date, and a new chapter containing some essential information about American forests has been added.

The theory and practice of working plans, A. B. RECKNAGEL (*New York: John Wiley & Sons, 1917, 2. ed., rev., pp. XIV+265, pls. 6, figs. 8*).—The present edition of this work (E. S. R., 28, p. 644) has been thoroughly revised to embody the recent developments in forest organization.

Determining the quality of standing timber, S. BERRY (*Jour. Forestry, 15 (1917), No. 4, pp. 438–441*).—An account of methods of determining the value of stands involved in stumpage appraisals as used in District 5 of the Forest Service of the U. S. Department of Agriculture.

Forest tree planting camps, J. S. ILLICK (*Jour. Forestry, 15 (1917), No. 4, pp. 394–409*).—In this article the author describes the methods employed by the Pennsylvania forest department in the establishment and operation of tree planting camps.

Eleventh report of the forest commissioner of the State of Maine, 1916, F. E. MACE (*Rpt. Forest Comr. Maine, 11 (1916), pp. 157, pls. 13, fig. 1*).—This report embraces various forest activities in Maine during 1915 and 1916, including work of forest protection, forest extension and improvements, and forest education. A statement by G. B. Posey of the U. S. Department of Agriculture relative to the extent and distribution of the white-pine blister rust in Maine is also included.

The conservation law as amended to the close of the regular session of 1916 (*Albany, N. Y.: State, 1916, pp. 409*).—This comprises the conservation law of the State of New York dealing with the administration of lands, forests, and parks, fish and game, waters, and the State reservation at Saratoga Springs.

Report of the forestry branch (*Rpt. Min. Lands, Forests and Mines, Ontario, 1916, pp. 146–151, pl. 1*).—A brief report on forestry nursery work, white pine blister rust inspection, and railway fire protection in Ontario for the year ended October 31, 1916.

Fifty years of forest administration in Bashahr, H. M. GLOVER (*Indian Forester, 41 (1915), No. 11, pp. 398–407, pls. 4; 42 (1916), No. 3, pp. 119–129, pls. 2*).—In the present article the author considers the general effects of regular management during the last 50 years on the forests of Bashahr State, India, and the way in which the development of the forests has reacted on the prosperity of the State.

Notes on the forests of Algeria, MARC (*Notes sur les Forêts de l'Algérie. Algiers: Gouvt. Gén. Algérie, Div. Forêts, 1916, pp. 333, pls. 15*).—This work comprises as a whole a report on the past and present status of forestry in Algeria. The subject matter is presented under the following general headings: Forest revenues, the cork harvest, the forests and the transportation tariffs, forest activities from 1902 to 1914, forest fires in Algeria, measures taken in favor of the natives, lands withdrawn from the forest reserve from 1892 to 1915, and the accessory functions of the forest service in Algeria.

A discussion of Australian forestry, with special reference to forestry in western Australia, the necessity of an Australian forest policy, and notices of organized forestry in other parts of the world, together with appendixes relating to forestry in New Zealand, forestry in South Africa, and control of the rabbit pest, D. E. HUTCHINS (*Perth, Aust.: Govt., 1916, pp. XXIII+434, pls. 17*).—The present discussion embraces the results of a survey of forestry and forest conditions in Australia conducted under the auspices of the government of western Australia. Although special consideration is given to the forests of western Australia, the subject matter deals also with forestry in all the States of the Commonwealth and New Zealand.

Correlation between the light and soil requirements of a species for its natural regeneration, B. O. COVENTRY (*Indian Forester, 43 (1917), No. 4, pp. 186–194*).—A discussion of this subject with special reference to Indian species of trees. The principal species are here classified with reference to both light and soil requirements.

The biology of lodgepole pine as revealed by the behavior of its seed, C. G. BATES (*Jour. Forestry, 15 (1917), No. 4, pp. 410–416*).—The author briefly reviews the nature and results of seed production, extraction, and germination tests with lodgepole pine conducted by the Forest Service of the U. S. Department of Agriculture, and presents some deductions based on these experiments relative to the biology of lodgepole pine.

The Mexican and Central American species of Ficus, P. C. STANDLEY (*U. S. Nat. Mus., Contrib. Nat. Herbarium, 20 (1917), pt. 1, pp. VIII+35*).—This comprises a systematic description of the Mexican and Central American species of Ficus. Forty-one species are here enumerated, of which only two are common to the West Indies and Central America.

Forest and shade trees and basket willows recommended for planting in Idaho, C. H. SHATTUCK (*Idaho Sta. Circ. 4 (1917), pp. 4*).—A descriptive list of trees recommended for various planting purposes in Idaho, including a price list of trees which the department of forestry of the station is prepared to furnish the residents of the State.

The status and value of farm woodlots in the eastern United States, E. H. FROTHINGHAM (*U. S. Dept. Agr. Bul. 481 (1917), pp. 43, pl. 1, figs. 2*).—The purpose of this bulletin is to show as nearly as can be done from available census statistics what the relation of the woodlot has been to the agricultural development of different parts of the East, what the tendencies appear to be, and, in general, what value the woodlot actually has to the Nation, the rural community, and the individual farm. The subject matter is presented under the general headings of woodlots of the Eastern States, how the growth of farming has affected the woodlot, amount and quality of woodlot timber, what the woodlot promises for the future, and the woodlot as a farm resource. In addition to considerable tabular data maps are given showing the proportion of woodland to total farm land in different sections of the East and the actual farm woodland area in the United States in 1910 by counties.

Canadian woods for structural timbers, H. N. LEE (*Dept. Int. Canada, Forestry Branch Bul. 59 (1917), pp. 44, figs. 22*).—This bulletin gives a sketch of the forest resources of Canada and discusses the qualities that affect the usefulness of timber for structural purposes. Descriptions are then given of the chief Canadian species suitable for this purpose and comparisons, tables, and charts relating to mechanical and physical tests. The bulletin concludes with a short discussion of the grading of timber.

Forest products of Canada, 1913, 1914, and 1915, R. G. LEWIS ET AL. (*Dept. Int. Canada, Forestry Branch Buls. 52 (1915), pp. 79, pls. 2, figs. 5; 57 (1916), pp. 82, pls. 3, figs. 7; 58 (1917), pp. 72, pl. 1, figs. 8*).—These comprise statistical reports for the years 1913, 1914, and 1915, respectively, relative to the use of lumber, lath and shingles, pulpwood, poles, and crossties throughout the Dominion. The production is given both by Provinces and by kinds of wood.

The recent industrial and economic development of Indian forest products, R. S. PEARSON (*Jour. Roy. Soc. Arts, 65 (1917), No. 3366, pp. 487–493*).—A paper on this subject read before the Indian section of the Royal Society of Arts in April, 1917.

DISEASES OF PLANTS.

The susceptibility of cultivated plants to diseases and pests, P. E. KEUCHENIUS (*Teysmannia, 27 (1916), No. 1–2, pp. 65–77*).—This is a somewhat general discussion, with illustrative examples, of the several degrees of parasitism of economic plants, namely, infections induced by weakness, injury, or true parasitic activity of the attacking organism with the circumstances favorable thereto, as virulence, stage of development of host or parasite, physical conditions, and specializations.

Studies in the physiology of parasitism, W. BROWN (*Jour. Bd. Agr. [London], 23 (1916), No. 5, pp. 474–478*).—This is a summary of work done and results obtained by the author and by Blackman and Welsford as previously noted (E. S. R., 37, p. 47).

A study of Glœosporium, KRÜGER (*Mitt. K. Biol. Anst. Land u. Forstw., No. 15 (1914), pp. 15, 16*).—A brief review is given of a few species (with their hosts) of Glœosporium, of which Colletotrichum is treated as a subgenus.

Further evidence as to the relation between crown gall and cancer, E. F. SMITH (*Proc. Nat. Acad. Sci., 2 (1916), No. 8, pp. 444–448*).—Previous opinions are reviewed regarding cancer in animals and crown gall in plants. The author states that if inoculations with *Bacterium tumefaciens* are made in regions not previously known to contain totipotent cells such as supposedly originate tumors on inoculation in the neighborhood of dormant buds, tumors are produced too numerously to be explained as due to the development of embryonic "cell rests" or what are conceived to be fragments displaced from the embryo in early stages of growth and remaining dormant amid other tissues. It is claimed that embryomas are the results of specific tissue responses to the stimulus of a specific schizomycete, taking the embryoma form if a complex anlage containing totipotent or nearly totipotent cells is involved. The conclusion is regarded as almost unavoidable that cancer is due to a parasite and that, as shown in case of plants, this parasite may be found to give rise to the most diverse forms of the abnormality.

Report of the pathologist, J. A. Stevenson (*Rpt. Bd. Comrs. Agr. P. R., 5 (1915–16), pp. 35–74*).—In addition to an account of routine work of the laboratory, the author gives descriptions of citrus and sugar cane diseases observed in Porto Rico. Notes are also given on a number of minor diseases, among them root knot of various ornamental and other plants, trunk rot of *Ficus nitida* due to *Nummularia bulliardii*, a root rot of avocado caused by an undetermined fungus probably of the Nummularia group, together with notes on entomogenous fungi.

[Reports on botany and plant diseases in Switzerland, 1913–14], H. Mül-ler-Thurgau et al. (*Landw. Jahrb. Schweiz, 29 (1915), No. 5, pp. 476–484, 503–522, 574, 575, 578, 579, 593, 594*).—The sections here noted relate to observations and experiments in connection with various phases of botany and plant parasitism, including disease resistance and injury by nematodes as well as by other animal pests.

Notes are given on a number of rather common parasites observed on various economic plants, the information being grouped according to whether the hosts are orchard, garden, or ornamental plants. There are also brief accounts of special studies on sugar in floral leaves; acetaldehyde formation in orchard fruits; hydrofluoric acid injury to grapes; cases of Phytophthora disease; control of *Pseudopeziza tracheiphila* on grapevines; Gnomonia on cherry leaves; control of *Oïdium euonymi japonicæ;* a dieback of young plum trees probably due to root fungi; injury to ornamental plants by *Aphelenchus ormerodis* and *Tylenchus dipsaci;* and control of grape Peronospora, leaf roll of grape, and *Sphærella fragariæ* on strawberry.

Fungus parasites of the higher plants in the region of Kharkov and adjacent provinces, A. A. Potebnia (*Kharkov. Oblast. Selsk. Khoz. Opytn. Sta., Fitopatol. Otd., No. 1 (1916), pp. 121–251, figs. 21*).—In continuation of a previous report (E. S. R., 35, p. 453) an account is given of the ascomycetous parasites up to and including in part the Erysiphaceæ.

Of the Exoasceæ, species of Taphrina (in which the author includes the members of Exoascus) are found on a large number of hosts in four different families. Among Discomycetes, species of Sclerotinia and Pseudopeziza appear to be most prevalent. Particular attention is called to the occurrence of a little-known parasite, *Phacidiella discolor*, found on pear, apple, and *Pyrus paradisiaca*. This fungus causes serious trouble, however, only in case of apple, killing the bark on the trees and thus producing large wounds.

Diseases and pests of cultivated plants in the Dutch East Indies in 1915, C. J. J. van Hall (*Dept. Landb., Nijv. en Handel [Dutch East Indies], Meded. Lab. Plantenziekten, No. 20 (1916), pp. 47*).—An account is given of diseases and animal enemies affecting a large number of orchard, garden, forest, and field plants in Java during the year, with control measures employed or recommended, together with a list of phytopathological literature which appeared in 1915 relating to the Dutch East Indies.

Control measures against plant diseases and injurious insects, C. J. J. VAN HALL, A. A. L. RUTGERS, and K. W. DAMMERMAN (*Dept. Landb., Nijv. en Handel* [*Dutch East Indies*], *Meded. Lab. Plantenziekten, No. 17 (1915), pp. 42, figs. 20*).—This is a discussion of a large number of preparations, with devices and appliances for their employment, for the control of diseases and animal enemies of various plants in Java.

Tests of new fungicides, E. RIEHM (*Mitt. K. Biol. Anst. Land u. Forstw., No. 15 (1914), pp. 7, 8*).—The results are detailed of tests, principally with new mercury preparations offered as means of combating cereal diseases, particularly *Tilletia tritici* on wheat and *Helminthosporium gramineum* on barley.

Tests of fungicides with cereal diseases, E. RIEHM (*Mitt. K. Biol. Anst. Land u. Forstw., No. 16 (1916), pp. 8, 9*).—The experiments noted above have been continued. The tests with mercury chlorophenol against *Helminthosporium gramineum* are said to have proved the adequacy of this fungicide in this connection. Chinosol proved less effective at safe concentrations. Mercury chlorophenol at 0.2 per cent concentration applied to seed grain for 10 minutes, or at 0.1 per cent for 15 minutes, controlled stinking smut as completely as did formaldehyde, copper sulphate, or corrosive sublimate, but it appeared to be ineffective against loose smut of barley.

Overwintering of stinking smut in soil, O. APPEL and E. RIEHM (*Mitt. K. Biol. Anst. Land u. Forstw., No. 15 (1914), p. 6*).—Spores of stinking smut in samples of soil from various localities could not be made to germinate in spring by any means employed.

Diseases and pests of rice, A. A. L. RUTGERS (*Teysmannia, 27 (1916), No. 6, pp. 313–342*).—Influences discussed as local causes of loss to rice interests include root rot (soil conditions), head rot (climate or weather), *Tilletia horrida, Ustilaginoidea virens, Sclerotium rolfsii*, fungus leaf spotting, and various insects and birds.

Treatment of loose smut of wheat and barley, O. APPEL and E. RIEHM (*Mitt. K. Biol. Anst. Land u. Forstw., No. 15 (1914), pp. 5, 6*).—After two hours in hot water and two more in moist air, wheat seed infected with loose smut showed a degree of infection amounting to 1 per cent. Complete freedom from infection was obtained by treating infected wheat or barley seed with 0.1 per cent corrosive sublimate for one hour, also by use of the combined treatment consisting of four hours in water at 25 to 30° C. and 10 minutes at 50 to 52°, likewise by use of the treatment in which barley seed are kept in water at 45° for two hours.

A wheat disease caused by Dilophospora graminis, L. MANGIN (*Bul. Soc. Path. Veg. France, 1 (1914) No. 1, pp. 55–77, pl. 1*).—An account is given of the destructive effects on wheat of *D. graminis. Dilophia graminis* and *Mastigosporium album*, supposed to be other forms or stages of this fungus, are more or less common in wild grains, which may thus become sources of infection for wheat and perhaps oats, if not other crops.

[Wheat rust in New Zealand], R. WATERS (*Jour. Agr.* [*New Zeal.*], *13 (1916), No. 1, pp. 41–46, fig. 1*).—Wheat rust, though present to some extent every season in New Zealand, is rarely widespread and severe, but a period of exceptional severity in this respect was experienced in the neighborhood of Greenfield, Bruce County, South Otago, where yields were so greatly reduced as to be worthless in some cases. Volunteer oat plants in some badly rusted wheat fields showed practically no signs of rust.

Barberry is rare in many parts of New Zealand and it is not known to bear the fungus producing the æcidiospores of the wheat rust fungus, the usual mode of overwintering possibly being omitted in this case. It is believed that the summer spores infect the volunteer plants and autumn crops and that the spores produced thereon infect the spring crops. The Greenfield outbreak is thought to have originated from a crop planted in autumn.

The relation of weather to the development locally of the fungus is discussed, as are also subordinate related factors and some proposed methods of treatment, which include destruction of all aftermath and self-sown grain with avoidance of autumn and late spring sowing and of heavy nitrogen fertilizing.

Stalk disease of wheat, E. Foex (*Bul. Soc. Path. Veg. France, 1 (1914), No. 1, pp. 26–30, pl. 1*).—A brief discussion is given of foot disease of cereals, said to be due principally to *Ophiobolus graminis*, which works around the base of the stalk, and to *Leptosphæria herpotrichoides*, appearing higher on the stem, around which it also works its way more gradually. *O. herpotrichus* has been observed to cause stem weakening in cereals, as has also *Cercosporella herpotrichoides*, which has been considered a conidial form of Leptosphæria. Germination tests with these fungi are discussed.

Diseases of beans, W. G. Sackett (*Colorado Sta. Bul. 226 (1917), pp. 21–31, figs. 6*).—Descriptions are given of a number of diseases of beans known to occur in Colorado, with suggestions for their control.

Among the more troublesome diseases are bacterial blight (*Pseudomonas phaseoli*), pod spot or anthracnose (*Colletotrichum lindemuthianum*), bean rust due to *Uromyces appendiculatus*, and a new disease to which the name bean streak has been given. The last disease was first observed in Colorado in the summer of 1916. It attacks stems, leaves, and pods, producing symptoms similar to those present in plants affected with bacterial blight. On the pods rusty, orange-brown discolorations later appear. The leaves are destroyed and the plants become defoliated before the crops mature. The cause and methods of control are being further investigated.

Control of clubroot of crucifers, O. Appel and O. Schlumberger (*Mitt. K. Biol. Anst. Land u. Forstw., No. 15 (1914), pp. 13–15*).—Among the more favorable results tabulated as obtained from tests of preparations for reducing infection of cruciferous crops by *Plasmodiophora brassicæ* in the soil, those given by 2 or 3 per cent formalin and those by certain proprietary preparations were almost equal in value.

Phoma disease in crucifers, R. Laubert (*Mitt. K. Biol. Anst. Land u. Forstw., No. 16 (1916), pp. 10–12, fig. 1*).—It is considered probable that the same species of Phoma causes the more or less similar diseases of different cruciferous plants noted during recent years at points in Holland, France, Germany, Australia, and North America.

Corynespora melonis, Krüger (*Mitt. K. Biol. Anst. Land u. Forstw., No. 15 (1914), pp. 16, 17*).—*C. melonis*, the cause of leaf scorch of cucumbers, said to cause loss in England, Holland, and Germany, is briefly described and discussed as to effects and dispersal, with suggestions regarding seed disinfection.

Flax blight, G. Arnaud (*Bul. Soc. Path. Veg. France, 1 (1914), No. 1, pp. 38–41, fig. 1*).—*Asterocystis radicis* is said to cause a blight of cultivated flax in Flanders by attacking the roots and lowering water absorption. The intracellular behavior of the fungus is described. Alkalis seem to favor, acids to hinder, its development. Fungicides are difficult of application. Rotation of crops is recommended, though the parasite attacks also a number of common crops, which are named.

Studies in the dying out of pepper vines in the Dutch East Indies.—II, **Pepper culture on Banka**, A. A. L. Rutgers (*Dept. Landb., Nijv. en Handel [Dutch East Indies], Meded. Lab. Plantenziekten, No. 19 (1916), pp. 56, pls. 17*).—This contribution, in continuation of one previously noted (E. S. R., 35, p. 349), besides giving a brief history of pepper culture and its forms and characteristics on the island of Banka, deals briefly with such drawbacks as unsuitable soil and animal and plant parasites, including nematodes (*Heterodera radicicola*) and an unnamed cobweb fungus on the leaves.

Potato diseases in the Dutch East Indies, JOHANNA WESTERDIJK (*Teysmannia, 27 (1916), No. 1-2, pp. 1-15, pl. 1*).—This is a discussion of potato varieties, culture, and diseases with related protective measures. The diseases include *Phytophthora infestans, Macrosporium solani*, leaf roll, a leaf rust, and a root fungus.

Experiments for control of potato canker, E. WERTH (*Mitt. K. Biol. Anst. Land u. Forstw., No. 16 (1916), pp. 9, 10*).—Experiments with sulphur on the potato varieties Wohltmann, Silesia, and Industry gave a lowering of canker infection amounting to less than one-third, accompanied by a decrease of more than three-fourths in yield. Tests for resistance showed less than 10 per cent susceptibility in Kaiserkrone, Richter Imperator, Fürstenkrone, Gertrud, Schnellert, and Paulsen July.

Potato leaf roll in France, E. FOEX (*Bul. Soc. Path. Veg. France, 1 (1914), No. 1, pp. 42-48*).—Potato leaf roll is said to attack severely several varieties of potato in the canton of Orchies in northern France.

Potato leaf roll, O. APPEL and O. SCHLUMBERGER (*Mitt. K. Biol. Anst. Land u. Forstw., No. 15 (1914), pp. 8-11, fig. 1*).—The authors continue to report on the study of potato leaf roll previously noted (E. S. R., 27, p. 247; 28, p. 52; 31, p. 52; 34, p. 443). The results obtained by planting the diseased stock from different sources on various soils were not consistent throughout. Improvement was noted in some cases, while in others the leaf roll appeared later in the season.

Chlorosis of beets, G. ARNAUD (*Bul. Soc. Path. Veg. France, 2 (1915), No. 2, pp. 123, 124*).—Describing the foliar discoloration in sugar beets previously noted by Berthault (E. S. R., 35, p. 350) and by Miège (E. S. R., 36, p. 543), the author states that the trouble was somewhat general in the north of France during 1915. It is thought that the phenomenon is related causally to the prevalence of *Cercospora beticola, Uromyces betæ, Phoma tabifica*, and leaf aphids, in connection with lack of water, cultivation, and fertilizers, and with late seeding.

Crown gall of sugar beets, PETERS (*Mitt. K. Biol. Anst. Land u. Forstw., No. 16 (1916), pp. 12, 13, fig. 1*).—In 1912, beets penetrated to a depth of 2 to 3 cm. with a needle which had been dipped in cultures of *Bacillus tumefaciens* showed partial, or doubtful, results. On repeating the tests the next year, however, and using also shallower penetration (0.5 to 1 cm.), a high percentage of the plants so treated developed crown gall, while the controls were free from enlargements.

Sweet potato diseases, J. A. MCCLINTOCK (*Virginia Truck Sta. Bul. 22 (1917), pp. 455-486, figs. 14*).—Popular accounts are given of diseases of the sweet potato, with suggestions for their control.

The diseases are classified according to the part of the plant involved as those of the above-ground parts, those of the roots, and those of both vines and roots. For the control of many of the diseases, and especially of the more destructive of those affecting both vine and roots, the author recommends careful selection of seed tubers, their treatment with corrosive sublimate solution, and planting in seed beds in which clean sand has been substituted for soil. The cuttings should afterwards be planted in soil that is known to be not infected or where sweet potatoes have not been planted for several years.

Sclerotium disease of tobacco, JOHANNA WESTERDIJK (*Meded. Deli-Proefstat. Medan, 10 (1916), No. 2, pp. 30-40, pls. 2*).—A study of a disease of young tobacco, carried on at the Deli Station, is said to indicate that the trouble is due to *S. rolfsii*, which flourishes on wild Crotalaria and probably on various other legumes which may be found growing with tobacco.

The parasitism of Coryneum on trees and shrubs, G. ARNAUD (*Bul. Soc. Path. Veg. France, 2 (1915), No. 1, pp. 64–70, figs. 3*).—This is a bibliographical discussion of several species of Coryneum on different hosts named in relation with several other fungus forms.

Hail effects on trees, G. ARNAUD (*Bul. Soc. Path. Veg. France, 2 (1915), No. 2, pp. 121, 122, pl. 1*).—Injuries, particularly to young trees, due to hail driven by strong wind in May, 1915, and observed in July and in October of that year, are described, and resemblances and differences are noted between such injury and the characteristic effects of fungi, in particular *Nectria ditissima.*

Behavior of apple canker in two grafts differing in susceptibility on the same stock, P. A. DANGEARD (*Bul. Soc. Path. Veg. France, 2 (1915), No. 2, pp. 127, 128*).—A case is noted in which two varieties of apple, one very susceptible to Nectria and usually developing canker, and the other ordinarily very resistant thereto, were grafted on the same stock. The resulting growths both showed canker, the originally resistant one, however, in lesser degree. After the removal of the more susceptible half, the new growths on the other portion were free from Nectria.

A new Oospora on pear, L. MANGIN (*Bul. Soc. Path. Veg. France, 3 (1916), No. 1, pp. 9–11, figs. 2*).—A brief account is given of a fungus attacking pear leaves and branches. It is considered a new species and described under the name *O. piricola*

Biological observations on pear rust, A. TROTTER (*Riv. Patol. Veg., 8 (1916), No. 3, pp. 65–76*).—A study of pear rust (*Roestelia cancellata*), carried out near Avellino, has convinced the author that normally the fungus can not winter in that host but that its persistence from year to year in a given locality requires the presence of an alternate host. *Juniperus sabina* is noted as sustaining such relation in this locality, though several other junipers are known to harbor the fungus.

Disease of apricots in the Rhone Valley, J. CHIFFLOT and MASSONNAT (*Bul. Soc. Path. Veg. France, 2 (1915), No. 2, pp. 117–120*).—This has been previously noted (E. S. R., 35, p. 249).

Some observations on witches' brooms of cherries, H. SCHMITZ (*Plant World, 19 (1916), No. 8, pp. 239–242*).—The author, noting the results of observations and tests made in the course of a microchemical study of witches' brooms of cultivated cherries due to *Exoascus cerasi*, holds these results to sustain the claims that witches' brooms elaborate much or all of the food materials needed for their own growth. The increased amount of stored food and resulting high osmotic pressure may account for the prolonged and rapid growth of the diseased parts. The fungus disturbs the normal periodicity of the affected region. Chlorophyll is only masked by the red color in the leaves on the broom. The red color is due to acidity in the leaves, which acidity may itself be due either to the hydrolytic influence of the fungus on the stored material or on the cell walls, or to an influence exerted by the fungus in prolonging the embryonic condition of the leaves and twigs, since even the leaves of the brooms lose their red color upon becoming fully mature.

The biology of Exoascus deformans and preventive treatment of peach leaf curl, V. PEGLION (*Staz. Sper. Agr. Ital., 49 (1916), No. 3–4, pp. 200–218; abs. in Riv. Patol. Veg., 8 (1916), No. 3, pp. 88, 89*).—The important means of preservation and transmission of *E. deformans*, the peach leaf curl parasite, is said to be the ascospores, the effectiveness of these depending largely upon atmospheric conditions. The fungus is best controlled during the winter rest of the trees by employing a spray made up of 2 per cent copper sulphate, 1 per cent lime, and 0.2 per cent ammonium chlorid.

A substitute for self-boiled lime-sulphur and other summer sprays for peaches, L. G. GILLAM (*New Jersey Stas. Circ. 63 (1917), pp. 2–4*).—Directions are given for the preparation of a summer spray for peaches to be used as a substitute for self-boiled lime-sulphur. This fungicide is composed of 8 lbs. fine sulphur, 4 lbs. hydrated lime, and 1½ oz. ground glue dissolved in 3 gal. water, the whole diluted with water to make 50 gal. In the preparation of the spray the dry sulphur and lime should be mixed, then thoroughly incorporated with the glue solution before the addition of the water.

A test of this fungicide proved its value for preventing scab and brown rot without injury to the trees.

On a new canker disease of Prunus yedoensis, P. mume, and other species caused by Valsa japonica n. sp., T. HEMMI (*Jour. Col. Agr. Tohoku Imp. Univ., 7 (1916), No. 4, pp. 257–319, pls. 4*).—An account is given of a study on a disease first noticed in Sapporo in 1913 and at present limited to Hokkaido. It is common on P. yedoensis, P. sachalinensis, and P. mume, and is found also on P. persica and other species of Prunus. The trouble is said to be due to a new species of fungus of the subgenus Euvalsa, which has been named V. japonica. It may simply cause a canker or else a girdling disease of a different type on the branches.

In the saprophytic condition V. japonica seems almost omnivorous. As a parasite it attacks its host most readily through old wounds having a layer of dead cells. Gummosis always develops as a result of the invasion.

Treatment with copper sulphate and sodium carbonate appears to be ineffective. Corrosive sublimate at from 0.05 to 0.1 per cent is the most effective fungicide employed in this connection.

Dieback in currant, O. APPEL and E. WERTH (*Mitt. K. Biol. Anst. Land u. Forstw., No. 16 (1916), pp. 13, 14*).—A dieback of currant bushes, extending from a center and increasing the second year (resistance differing with varieties), is ascribed to Plowrightia ribesia. Somewhat different from this fungus as to mode of development, but resembling each other in some ways, are dieback diseases ascribed respectively to Botrytis cinerea and to Pleonectria berolinensis, to both of which all varieties appear to be about equally susceptible.

Peronospora in 1915, and its control, A. MARESCALCHI (*Ann. R. Accad. Agr. Torino, 58 (1915), pp. 349–357, figs. 7; abs. in Riv. Patol. Veg., 8 (1916), No. 3, pp. 81, 82*).—The very violent outbreaks of downy mildew occurring May 24 and 25, June 4 and 5, and June 27 and 28, with one of lesser violence May 10 to 12, are said to be closely connected with the high temperature, humidity, and cloudiness which were common in 1915, but not so closely with the actual amount of precipitation. The author points out the necessity for the early and effective dissemination of information regarding the imminence of mildew attack and the necessity for timely sprayng.

Treatment of Peronospora during 1915, E. C. D'ALBARETTO (*Ann. R. Accad. Agr. Torino, 58 (1915), pp. 304–312*).—Giving an account, with discussion, of experiences in connection with the unusually violent grape downy mildew outbreaks of 1915, the author states that while in some cases from 10 to 20 sprayings were ineffective as regards control, five sprayings with the ordinary copper solutions controlled the mildew with a great saving of materials and labor. The precise observance of the prescribed manner and times of spraying is thought to be essential to success in dealing with grape downy mildew and to be sufficient even in years of unusually unfavorable conditions.

The germination of the winter spores of Plasmopara viticola, L. RAVAZ and G. VERGE (*Bul. Soc. Path. Veg. France, 1* (1914), No. 1, pp. 51–54).—This is a summary of the development and existing state of knowledge regarding the autumn, winter, and spring behavior of P. *viticola* on *Vitis vinifera*.

The present status of the coconut bud rot disease, J. R. JOHNSTON (*Habana: 1916, June, pp. 8, fig. 1*).—The author states that coconut bud rot is an internal disease of the terminal bud. This fact precludes the employment of pruning except in the initial state (which it is practically impossible to determine), and also the external use of germicides. The slow growth of the tree, moreover, practically prevents the employment of breeding for resistant varieties.

In Cuba, for which somewhat complete records have been obtained and summarized herein, the disease was destructive as early as 1886. It is also said to have been reported as causing, or as having caused, loss in British Guiana, Jamaica, Trinidad, the Cayman Islands, and the lesser Antilles, but its presence is denied or doubted in some other localities which are mentioned.

Fungi parasitic on the tea plant in northeast India, V, VI, A. C. TUNSTALL (*Indian Tea Assoc., Sci. Dept. Quart. Jour., 1915, Nos. 1, pp. 12–16; 3, pp. 53–56*).—Continuing the series of reports previously noted (E. S. R., 33, p. 650), the author states that *Exobasidium vexans*, the cause of blister blight, attacks leaves and stems and, in general, only young succulent growths of tea plants and no jungle plants so far as known. The spores die after two or three days and the fungus a little later. It is thought, therefore, that the fungus has no dormant stage. On many tea gardens in Assam the disease dies out spontaneously. In the hilly districts, bushes in damp, shady places may show the blisters at any time of the year. Under favoring conditions, the disease may spread with great rapidity.

Fomes lucidus is a common cause of root disease in tea bushes. *Pestalozzia palmarum* causes a gray blight of alder leaves and is sometimes found on the stems. The fungus is common in the jungle on both dead leaves and living plants, but it does little harm so long as the plants are healthy. A dieback of weakened plants is due to at least one species of Gloeosporium. A closely similar disease ascribed to *Colletotrichum camelliæ* is prevented by sprays and soil improvement. Internal root disease is ascribed to various species of Diplodia, the commonest being *Botryodiplodia theobromæ*, a fuller report of which is to be given later.

Tumors on Chrysanthemum frutescens, R. LAUBERT (*Mitt. K. Biol. Anst. Land u. Forstw., No. 15 (1914), p. 17*).—The author notes the occurrence on *C. frutescens chrysaster*, near Berlin, of enlargements or outgrowths similar to those designated in America as crown gall, and supposedly due to infection with *Bacterium tumefaciens*.

Canker of oleander, P. HARIOT (*Bul. Soc. Path. Veg. France, 2 (1915), No. 1, pp. 38–40, fig. 1*).—Briefly describing a disease of oleander, which is said to attack any organ thereof, causing enlargements which are described, the author mentions approvingly the views of Tonelli, who supposed the trouble to be of bacterial causation and to be favored as to transmission by the activity of insects (E. S. R., 29, p. 156).

A new fungus parasitic on Ceara rubber trees, F. VINCENS (*Bul. Soc. Path. Veg. France, 3 (1916), No. 1, pp. 22–25, figs. 6*).—A brief account is given of a disease of *Manihot glaziovii* observed in 1913 north of the bay of Rio Janerio. The causal fungus, which is considered to be a new species, is described as *Haplographium manihoticola*.

Diseases of Hevea brasiliensis in the Amazon Valley.—I, Leaf diseases, II, Trunk diseases, F. VINCENS (*Bul. Soc. Path. Veg. France, 2 (1915), No. 1, pp. 11–27, 54–63, pls. 3, figs. 7*).—Fungi noted in connection with diseases or abnormalities of *H. brasiliensis* include forms more or less reliably identified with *Dothidella ulei, Fusicladium macrosporum, Phyllachora huberi, Aposphæria ulei, Colletotrichum (Glæosporium) heveæ, Pestalozzia palmarum,* and *Phyllosticta* sp., besides the supposedly new species *Scolecotrichum heveæ, Fusarium heveæ, Zygosporium paraense, Cercospora heveæ,* and *Meliola heveæ,* some of the above being compared with other forms.

Trunk and branch diseases mentioned in the second article as of considerable importance include those caused by *Fusicladium macrosporum* and *G. alborubrum.* Organisms of less importance are *Cephaleuros virescens, Botryodiplodia theobromæ,* a *Corticium,* and a *Microthyrium.*

Diseases of Hevea in Ceylon, T. Petch (*Trans. 3. Internat. Cong. Trop. Agr. 1914, vol. 1, pp. 596–607*).—A preliminary abstract summarizing the principal points in this paper has been noted previously (E. S. R., 34, p. 849).

The effects of asphyxiating gases on forest vegetation, F. Döé (*Rev. Eaux et Forêts, 54 (1916), No. 7, pp. 192–195; abs. in Forestry Quart., 14 (1916), No. 4, p. 748*).—Giving a brief account of the results of gas attacks in the Champagne in October, 1915, the author states that while grapevines, cruciferous garden crops, and deciduous forest trees were not seriously injured, ornamental plants were severely damaged. Conifers showed the injurious effects in a yellowing and shedding of leaves, recovery from which had become apparent, in some cases at least, by May 15, 1916.

A beech disease due to Nectria ditissima, M. Guinier (*Bul. Soc. Path. Veg. France, 2 (1915), No. 2, pp. 91–92*).—The author records, supposedly for the first time, a mode of attack by *N. ditissima,* in which the fungus starts on a young branch and kills the tissues for a certain distance, thus causing the death of the portion beyond.

Galls on juniper, P. Hariot (*Bul. Soc. Path. Veg. France, 2 (1915), No. 1, pp. 8–10, fig. 1*).—A description is given of a juniper gall associated with a fungus which is thought to be *Ceratostoma juniperinum,* hitherto unknown in France.

Peridermium strobi on Swiss pine, E. Werth (*Mitt. K. Biol. Anst. Land u. Forstw., No. 16 (1916), pp. 14, 15*).—A disease causing blister rust on Swiss pine was tested as to its ability to attack Ribes. Experiments proved successful in those cases in which the infected Ribes plant was kept under a bell glass. The fungus is therefore considered to be identical with *P. strobi.*

Dry rot, P. Groom (*Jour. Bd. Agr. [London], 23 (1916), No. 5, pp. 465–474, figs. 12*).—A brief discussion is given of *Merulius lacrymans, Coniophora cerebella,* and *Polyporus vaporarius,* including conditions favorable to infection and development and measures for control of the dry rot fungi, which are said to cause immense losses annually in the United Kingdom.

ENTOMOLOGY.

The nature of the polyhedral bodies found in insects, R. W. Glaser and J. W. Chapman (*Biol. Bul. Marine Biol. Lab., Woods Hole, 30 (1916), No. 5, pp. 367–390, pls. 3*).—The authors' investigations of the nature of polyhedral bodies carried on in connection with the work previously noted (E. S. R., 33, p. 856) have been summarized as follows:

"Polyhedral bodies are found in many different species of lepidopterous larvæ. The bodies are specific for a certain type of disease. The polyhedra vary in size in the different species. There exists a striking similarity in shape between the polyhedra found in different species. The polyhedra are structurally complicated. They arise in the nuclei of certain tissue cells. Cytoplasmic inclusions are found in certain diseases of higher animals. Nuclear inclusions have not been known previously. The polyhedra are nucleoprotein crystal-like degeneration products and not organisms. The polyhedra contain iron and phosphorus. On dissolving polyhedra in alkali and after dialyzing away the alkali and evaporating the protein solution crystals are obtained which simulate the original polyhedra."

A bibliography of 23 titles is included.

Some facts relative to the influence of atmospheric humidity on insect metabolism, T. J. HEADLEE (*Jour. Econ. Ent., 10 (1917), No. 1, pp. 31–38*).— The author's studies indicate that the speed of metabolism in the pupæ of both the bean weevil and the Angoumois grain moth varies inversely with the atmospheric humidity. In the adult of the former it varies with, while in the adult of the latter it varies inversely with, the humidity. In the egg stage the speed of metabolism varies inversely with the humidity, but in the larvæ and in the life cycle as a whole it varies with the humidity. It was found that reproduction of the bean weevil in tightly closed jars can be prevented by the introduction of sufficient concentrated sulphuric acid to keep the atmospheric humidity low.

Methods used in determining wind dispersion of the gipsy moth and some other insects, C. W. COLLINS (*Jour. Econ. Ent., 10 (1917), No. 1, pp. 170–177, pls. 2*).—"Additional data [E. S. R., 33, p. 653] have been collected on long-distance wind dispersion of gipsy moth larvæ; namely, across Cape Cod Bay off the coast of Massachusetts. The direction of the wind, recorded at the time taken and previously, indicated the source of infestation to be from 19 to 30 miles distant on the mainland. Frequent examinations of the screens and close data kept on movements and direction of the winds were necessary to make these records of value.

"Screens used in the cranberry bog experiments and placed horizontally over the vines were well adapted to catch the drop of small larvæ floating over such areas, while the upright wire and cloth screens proved better for securing long distance spread.

"The recording of three extra lepidopterous species and possibly a fourth being carried by the wind in the larval stage suggests some possibilities for investigation with others along this line."

A method for the study of underground insects, J. W. McCOLLOCH (*Jour. Econ. Ent., 10 (1917), No. 1, pp. 183–188, fig. 1*).—The author has found that the use of a 6-foot excavation in the ground, the sides of which are boarded up or cemented and a roof added, permits the rearing of subterranean insects at a fairly constant temperature. The fact that the daily range of temperature is small makes it possible to hold it at any desired degree for some time. The conditions in the cave have appeared to approximate those that would be encountered in the field by the subterranean forms studied.

Sixteenth report of the State entomologist of Connecticut for the year 1916, W. E. BRITTON (*Connecticut State Sta. Rpt. 1916, pt. 2, pp. VII+65–146, pls. 16, figs. 3*).—Following a report of nursery and apiary inspection, work with the gipsy and brown-tail moths is discussed. An account is next given of the turnip aphis (*Aphis pseudobrassicæ*) which was widely destructive during the year in Connecticut. Brief reference is made to the control of aphids in fields of seed beets in which it is stated that blackleaf 40 proved a satisfactory remedy. General accounts are given of the white-marked tussock moth and the rose chafer.

Experiments in controlling the striped cucumber beetle and the squash borer are briefly described by W. E. Britton and Q. S. Lowry (pp. 116–118). The striped beetle was more abundant than has ever been observed elsewhere and ruined nearly all plants notwithstanding various treatments that were applied. The greatest benefit obtained in control measures with the squash borer was followed by the combined treatments of cutting out the borers and covering the vines with soil.

An outbreak of the eight-spotted forester (*Alypia octomaculata*) at New Haven in which grapes and the Virginia creeper were defoliated is reported upon by Q. S. Lowry (pp. 118–122), as previously noted (E. S. R., 37, p. 158). Arsenate of lead at the rate of 3 lbs. to 50 gal. of water was found to be very effective, one spraying being sufficient in most cases. The pine tip moth (*Pinipestis zimmermani*) was reared from material collected in several counties and apparently occurs throughout the State. The parallel spittle insect on pine (*Aphrophora parallela*), reported upon by B. H. Walden (pp. 125, 126), is said to have been quite abundant in the forest plantations at Rainbow during the past two or three seasons. Antimosquito work in Connecticut during 1916 is reported upon by W. E. Britton and B. H. Walden (pp. 126–138). The entomological features of 1916 are briefly referred to.

The work concludes with accounts of miscellaneous insects of which mention may be made of a scale on azalea (*Eriococcus azaleæ*), the European elm case bearer (*Coleophora limosipennella*), another spruce gall aphid in Connecticut (*Chermes coolegi*) infesting the Colorado blue spruce at Hartford, injury by silverfish (*Thermobia domestica*), a scolytid beetle (*Xyleborus dispar*) which tunnels in the trunk of sugar maple, the walnut caterpillar (*Datana integerrima*) which was prevalent during the year, the tarnished plant bug injuring tobacco, the greenhouse leaf tyer (*Phlyctænia ferrugalis*) which damaged snapdragons, geranium, and cineraria at Norwalk in January, a flea-beetle (*Œdionychis sexamaculata*) found at Middlebury feeding on ash, white grubs injuring California privet, the grapevine sawfly (*Erythraspides pygmæus*), *Euclemensia bassettella*, a microlepidopteran reared from a coccid thought to be *Kermes sassceri*, termites injuring shotgun cartridges, the girdling of hardwood twigs by *Vespa crabro*, the hickory gall aphid (*Phylloxera caryæcaulis*), and the grapevine tomato gall (*Lasioptera vitis*).

Fourteenth annual report of the State entomologist of Montana, R. A. COOLEY (*Montana Sta. Bul. 112 (1916), pp. 53–76, fig. 1*).—The first part of this report consists of brief notes on the occurrence of the more important insect pests of 1916. This is followed by a review of the principal State interests in entomology in 1916, including the occurrence of and quarantine work against the alfalfa weevil, army cutworm, wheat sheath miner (*Cerodonta femoralis*), sugar-beet root louse (*Pemphigus betæ*), lesser clover leaf weevil (*Phytonomus nigrirostris*), spinose ear tick (*Ornithodoros megnini*), and foul brood of bees. Notes on the More Common Mosquitoes of Montana, by J. R. Parker (pp. 69–75) follow.

Notes on several insects not heretofore recorded from New Jersey, H. B. WEISS (*Jour. Econ. Ent., 10 (1917), No. 1, p. 224*).—The sawflies *Janus abbreviatus* and *Diprion simile* are recorded as occurring at several points in New Jersey. The columbine leaf miner (*Phytomyza aquilegiæ*) is a local pest of columbine at several points in the State, and a large roach (*Blaberus discoidalis*) has been found several times in greenhouses, having been introduced on orchids imported from South America.

Report of the entomologist, G. N. WOLCOTT (*Rpt. Bd. Comrs. Agr. P. R., 5 (1915–16), pp. 75–85, pl. 1*).—This is a brief summary of the activities of the year, including inspection and quarantine work, citrus insect, tobacco insect, and sugar-cane insect investigations. Analyses of sugar cane free from and infested by *Diatraea saccharalis* are included.

Report on tobacco and vegetable insects, R. T. COTTON (*Rpt. Bd. Comrs. Agr. P. R., 5* (*1915–16*), *pp. 86–99, figs. 3*).—Particular attention was given to flea-beetles, of which four species, namely, *Epitrix cucumeris*, *Systena basalis*, *E. parvula*, and *E. fuscata*, attack tobacco, ranking in importance in the order named. The eggs of these beetles are deposited about the roots of the plants, upon which the larvæ feed, and the leaves are attacked by the adults.

E. cucumeris, unlike the other species of the genus, is present throughout the year and does a great deal of damage. Its eggs hatch in 5 days, the larvæ feed from 20 to 35 days, and 6 days are passed as a pupa. *E. parvula*, which is the third in importance, usually causes injury during dry spells. Its eggs hatch in 5 days and the larvæ feed for from 15 to 25 days, the pupal stage lasting for a period of 6 days. *E. fuscata*, which is occasionally found doing damage to tobacco, is very similar in its habits to *E. cucumeris*.

S. basalis, the largest of the flea-beetles that attack tobacco, is present in great numbers throughout the year. Its eggs hatch in 12 days, from 20 to 35 days are passed in the larval stage, and 9 days in the pupal stage. Preventive measures include the destruction of weeds and bushes that grow near tobacco fields. The seed beds and the young plants in the field should be kept dusted with a mixture consisting of 3 per cent Paris green and 97 per cent corn flour or leached wood ashes. Diplumbic arsenate of lead when used as a spray at the rate of 3 to 4 lbs. per 100 gal. of water also gives good results. When used as a dust it should be applied with at least an equal amount of dry wood ashes.

In reporting upon vegetable insects the author estimates that there is a 20 per cent annual loss due to their ravages. Two of the more abundant and destructive pests were studied, namely the chrysomelid beetles *Cerotoma ruficornis* and *Diabrotica graminea*. *C. ruficornis* feeds upon beans and cowpeas and when abundant strips the leaves to their veins and midribs. The damage is not confined to the beetles alone, for the larvæ which live in the soil around the roots of the beans, feed on the roots and nodules and make furrows in the subterranean portion of the stem. The eggs, which are laid in the soil upon the roots of the host plant, hatch in 8 days, the larvæ feed for a period of from 25 to 30 days before pupating, and from 5 to 8 days are passed in the pupal stage. The methods of control consist in the collection of the beetles as they first appear and spraying with a mixture of Bordeaux and arsenate of lead at the rate of 3 lbs. of the latter to 50 gal. of spray.

D. graminea is a source of injury to all kinds of truck crops, breeding as it does continuously throughout the year. The principal damage is done by the adult beetles, which feed on the foliage and flowers of the tender young plants; the larvæ feed on the roots of a number of plants, which they may seriously weaken. The eggs are deposited in the soil about the base of the plant and hatch in 8 days. The larvæ, which feed for a period averaging 22 days, generally attack the roots from the outside, but occasionally bore into the tissues of the plant at the crown. From 6 to 9 days are passed in the pupal state. The entire life cycle from egg to adult requires at least 36 days.

The sweet potato root borer (*Cylas formicarius*) has become a bad pest in Porto Rico only in the district near Fajardo known as "Las Cabezas," although present in small numbers in many parts of the island. The sweet potato scarabee (*Cryptorhynchus batatæ*) has also done considerable damage to sweet potatoes in Porto Rico.

"Experiments with plant lice and lace bugs on peppers, eggplant, and cucumbers showed that blackleaf 40 applied at the rate of 1 fluid ounce to 8 gal. of water plus 0.5 lb. of whale-oil soap gave perfect control. Arsenate of lead applied at the rate of 2.5 lbs. to 50 gal. of water gave excellent results in the control of the leaf-feeding larvæ of the moth *Xylomeges sunia* and the leaf-eating beetles *C. ruficornis* and *D. graminca*. Further experiments with the 'changa' showed that almost perfect control may be obtained by surrounding the young plants when they are planted out in the field with a ring of the Paris green and flour mixture. This mixture consists of 3 per cent Paris green and 97 per cent of a flour high in gluten."

Important foreign insect pests collected on imported nursery stock in 1916, E. R. SASSCER (*Jour. Econ. Ent., 10 (1917), No. 1, pp. 219-223*).—A summary of the more important results of Federal inspection work.

Some methods of colonizing imported parasites and determining their increase and spread, S. S. CROSSMAN (*Jour. Econ. Ent., 10 (1917), No. 1, pp. 177-183, fig. 1*).—The author describes the methods made use of at the Gipsy Moth Laboratory of the Bureau of Entomology of the U. S. Department of Agriculture.

Efficiency and economy in grasshopper control, E. D. BALL (*Jour. Econ. Ent., 10 (1917), No. 1, pp. 135-139, fig. 1*).—The author describes a grasshopper catching machine which is efficient, inexpensive, and when once built is always ready for immediate use. The details of its construction have been given in a bulletin previously noted (E. S. R., 33, p. 59). The machine takes 24 ft. at a sweep, and 40 acres can be covered in a day.

The seventeen-year locust in western New York, C. H. HADLEY, JR. and R. MATHESON (*Jour. Econ. Ent., 10 (1917), No. 1, pp. 38-41*).—The authors record the occurrence of this insect during the summer of 1916.

Biological and systematic notes on British Thysanoptera, C. B. WILLIAMS (*Entomologist, 49 (1916), Nos. 641, pp. 221-227, fig. 1; 642, pp. 243-245; 643, pp. 275-284*).—The author's studies have led to the conclusion that the American pear thrips (*Tæniothrips pyri*) is no other than *T. inconsequens*, a species which has been known to occur in England for nearly 100 years, and which does not usually cause much injury in Europe. The author considers it practically certain that the species was introduced into California from Europe in the larval or pupal stage in the soil attached to the roots of fruit trees. Its spread from there to other parts of the United States, and recently into Canada, may have been by the same means, or by the rapid transference of adults by railway trains, etc., or it is possible that a fresh introduction from Europe might have occurred. Its distribution as now known includes Bohemia, Italy, England, the United States, and Canada.

In further notes on the pea thrips *Kakothrips pisivora* (E. S. R., 34, p. 450), it is stated that during 1915 the damage which it caused was more severe than ever before noticed. "By June 25 first and second stage larvæ were abundant in all the flowers and on the pods, and by July 5, when nearly all the larvæ were large, over 60 per cent of all the pods were more or less severely damaged by them. In nearly all cases the pods nearest the base of the plants, that is the earlier ones, were almost undamaged, while those near the top were so severely attacked that in many cases the flower dried up without setting any pod, while those pods which did start were small, deformed, and contained no seed at all.

"Most of the larvæ were feeding quite openly on the pods, only a few being hidden by the remains of the flower, and specimens examined during the night were found to be as active then as during the daytime. At this stage it would be possible to kill a large percentage by spraying. On July 7 there was an extremely heavy, almost tropical rainstorm, yet immediately after it quite a large number of larvæ were still feeding openly on the pods, chiefly on the lower surfaces. In the first fortnight in July nearly all the larvæ descended, but a few fed ones were found on till the end of July."

Notes on its natural enemies and host plants are included.

Four new species representing the genera Seriocothrips, Heliothrips, Thrips, and Haplothrips are described.

The green soldier bug (Nezara hilaris), R. D. WHITMARSH (*Ohio Sta. Bul. 310 (1917), pp. 519–552, figs. 16*).—This is a detailed report of studies of *N. hilaris*, which is recorded for the first time as causing serious damage in the Northern States, although previously reported as a pest of peaches in Georgia and of oranges in Florida. It was first noticed as a serious pest of peaches in the Northern States in 1911, when it did considerable damage along the shores of Lake Erie, especially in the vicinity of Gypsum and Port Clinton, Ohio. Attention is called to the fact that it is widely distributed in the northeastern United States and Canada, where it is quite a general feeder.

There is but one brood, the greater part of the year including the winter months being passed in the adult stage. In Ohio the eggs commence to hatch the second week in June, from which time the several stages appear until about the middle of October, when the greater part become adult. The nymphs hatch out in about 7 days, and from 49 to 75 days are required for the young to pass through the five instars before becoming adult. The young nymphs of the first instar are gregarious in their habits, but upon molting the first time lose this tendency, separating in all directions in search of food.

"Fruit when badly punctured by these insects is entirely unsalable, while fruit showing but slight injury must be placed in a lower grade. It is entirely possible that one bug from the time of hatching until harvest is capable of injuring several bushels of fruit. In badly infested orchards it was not uncommon to note an average loss of at least 3 bu. per tree. Besides the actual loss one must take into consideration the amount of extra labor involved in sorting the damaged fruit."

While a proctotrypid egg parasite, probably *Trissoleus euschisti*, is of considerable importance in checking the green soldier bug, weather conditions are a dominating factor in suppressing it.

Mercurial ointment, an effective control of hen lice, G. H. LAMSON, JR. (*Jour. Econ. Ent., 10 (1917), No. 1, pp. 71–74*).—Substantially noted from another source (E. S. R., 35, p. 183).

Distribution of the Ohio broods of periodical cicada with reference to soil, H. A. GOSSARD (*Ohio Sta. Bul. 311 (1917), pp. 555–577, figs. 15*).—This is a report of studies which have led the author to conclude that a definite relation exists between the distribution of the cicada broods in Ohio and the soil areas in which they occur. The subject is taken up under the headings of comparative description of soils, possible ecological factors, theories of brood formation, etc.

Aphid eggs in Texas (Lat. 30° 30'), H. C. YINGLING (*Jour. Econ. Ent., 10 (1917), No. 1. pp. 223, 224*).—The author records the deposition of eggs in Texas in December on a dogwood stem (*Cornus asperifolia*) by what is thought to be *Schizoneura corni*.

A new tree banding material for the control of the gipsy moth, A. F. BURGESS and E. L. GRIFFIN (*Jour. Econ. Ent., 10 (1917), No. 1, pp. 131–135, pls. 2*).—Following tests of Raupenleim applied by means of a gun manufactured for such use, the Bureau of Entomology has conducted investigations in cooperation with the Bureau of Chemistry of the U. S. Department of Agriculture which have led to the preparation of a quite satisfactory banding material. This consists of a high boiling neutral coal-tar oil having a density of about 1.15 at 20° C., a soft coal-tar pitch, rosin oil of the grade known as first-run "Kidney" oil, and ordinary commercial quicklime, directions for the preparation of which are given. This material is considerably cheaper than any successful banding material now on the market.

"Pound for pound the tree-banding material will cover about two-thirds as many lineal feet as tree tanglefoot, but as the trees do not have to be scraped before applying the former band, the labor is reduced, so that a large saving is made by using this material. The bands remain on the trees during the winter and can be moistened with turpentine in the spring so that they will be effective for two seasons."

The present status of the gipsy and brown-tail moths in Connecticut, I. W. Davis (*Jour. Econ. Ent., 10 (1917), No. 1, pp. 193-195*).—A brief review of the present status of these pests in Connecticut.

Crambid moths and light, G. G. Ainslie (*Jour. Econ. Ent., 10 (1917), No. 1, pp. 114-123. figs. 2*).—This study is based upon collections made at light at Nashville, Tenn., during the summer of 1915. At least 14 species of Crambinæ were found to occur at that place, although the greater bulk of the material consisted of *Crambus teterrellus,* a very common and widely distributed species on which the data presented are based and to which the conclusions drawn directly apply. The author has been unable to determine what meteorological condition determines their attraction to light, but finds that it does not depend on temperature.

The studies have led to the conclusion that, so far at least as this species is concerned and very probably with all crambids, neither trap lights nor poisoned baits can be used successfully under normal conditions to reduce the number of these very common and secretly injurious insects.

"Side injury" and codling moth control, E. P. Felt (*Jour. Econ. Ent., 10 (1917), No. 1, pp. 60-66*).—The term "side injury" is limited in this paper to the characteristic blemish produced by late-hatching codling moth larvæ entering the smooth side of the apple, running just under the skin a circular gallery with a radius of about $\frac{1}{8}$ in. and then in a few days deserting this initial point of injury and usually migrating to the blossom end. This blemish, which is frequently marked by a red or reddish-brown discoloration, was the cause of serious loss in western New York in 1915, as high as 20 per cent of such injury often being found in sprayed orchards. The experimental work of 1916, here reported upon, is in continuation of that of 1915, previously noted (E. S. R., 36, p. 855).

The variation in the percentage of wormy apples appears to be affected more by the size of the crop than the number of sprayings, and there is a fairly constant ratio between the total wormy fruit and the apples showing side injury. "Generally speaking, the development of side injury is conditioned upon the deposition of numerous eggs after the apples have become an inch or so in diameter and smooth enough so as not to repel the parent moth. We are satisfied that by far the greater benefit comes from the spraying just after blossoming, and that the side injury is in general proportional to the infestation of the orchard."

Recent antimosquito work in Connecticut, W. E. Britton (*Jour. Econ. Ent., 10 (1917), No. 1, pp. 109-111*).—A brief statement of the work carried on in Connecticut. See also the work noted on page 255.

The influence of salinity on the development of certain species of mosquito larvæ and its bearing on the problem of the distribution of species, F. E. Chidester (*New Jersey Stas. Bul. 299 [1916], pp. 3-16, figs. 6*).—From field records and laboratory experiments it is concluded that the distribution of the two dominant species of the salt-marsh mosquitoes in New Jersey is in part dependent on the salinity of the water. The fresher waters seem to bring out the brown salt-marsh mosquito (*Aedes cantator*), while the marsh pools with slightly higher salinity seem to be more favorable for the development of *A. sollicitans.*

Aside from its value as a means of bringing fish to the pools and providing means of quickly draining some areas, ditching is of importance in bringing salt water to increase the salinity of permanent pools, thus rendering them salt enough in some cases to retard and in some cases to check completely the development of the mosquitoes. It is suggested that there is a possibility that the incoming tide may drown the mosquito larvæ by the rise and fall of its waves as they advance.

See also a previous note (E. S. R., 36, p. 255).

A biological study of the more important of the fish enemies of the salt-marsh mosquitoes, F. E. CHIDESTER (*New Jersey Stas. Bul. 300 (1916), pp. 3–16, pl. 1, figs. 2).*—This is a report of studies commenced September 19, 1914, and carried on for more than a year.

The barred killifish (*Fundulus heteroclitus*) was found to be the greatest natural enemy of the salt-marsh mosquito and also to eat many green-head flies. "*F. heteroclitus* captures larvæ, pupæ, and adults of the mosquito, eating as many as 50 a day and killing many more. The vast hordes of fishes which migrate to the shallows and even into almost fresh water render the species especially formidable. The number of enemies of the mosquito which are eaten by *F. heteroclitus* is negligible and is more than compensated for by the great preponderance of mosquitoes in the diet of the fish. The ease with which Fundulus may be artificially fertilized and the remarkable vigor and resistance of the young embryos make the stocking of pools and streams with this species a simple matter."

A list of 19 references to the literature relating to the subject is appended.

Results of ten years of experimental wheat sowing to escape the Hessian fly, G. A. DEAN (*Jour. Econ. Ent., 10 (1917), No. 1, pp. 146–162, fig. 1).*—This is a summary of work conducted at the Kansas Experiment Station, much of which is presented in tabular form. In that State the most important steps in the control of the Hessian fly are (1) early, deep plowing of the stubble, (2) proper preparation of the seed bed, (3) destruction of all volunteer wheat, (4) delay in sowing until the fly-free date, and (5) cooperation.

Wind as a factor in the dispersion of the Hessian fly, J. W. McCOLLOCH (*Jour. Econ. Ent., 10 (1917), No. 1, pp. 162–170, fig. 1).*—This deals with observations made at the Kansas Experiment Station which show that wind is an important factor in the distribution of the Hessian fly. At the place where many of the observations were made the flies were being carried up over the hills and into the wheat fields lying on the other side in the Blue River Valley. The fact that the flies were uninjured on reaching the screens would indicate that they could be carried much greater distances. The relatively large number of illes caught on the small screen area at 2 miles is indicative of the possible magnitude of their flights.

This work shows that cooperation must be practiced over large areas and that the individual grower can not be promised immunity from injury even if he does prepare a good seed bed and plants late. All stubble fields and volunteer wheat fields must be plowed under early in the fall, as they are the greatest sources of infestation.

The protection of dairy cattle from flies, E. N. CORY (*Jour. Econ. Ent., 10 (1917), No. 1, pp. 111–114).*—Several complaints that butter made at the Maryland Experiment Station was very perceptibly tainted with the coal-tar odor where proprietary coal-tar products had been used in protecting cattle from flies led to the preparation of a pine-tar creosote emulsion which left no such taint. This was made by dissolving ½ lb. of caustic soda, 98 per cent pure, in a known quantity of water for every gallon of pine-tar creosote, and then diluting with cold water to the desired strength.

In tests made of 1 to 5 per cent emulsions it was found that the 3 and 5 per cent emulsions killed all flies that were thoroughly wetted. The 3 per cent emulsion was the most effective minimum strength, its protection being fully effective for one day, and there was considerable protection afforded for two and even three days. The cost of spraying was less than 0.5 ct. per cow per application.

The radish maggot and screening, P. J. PARROTT (*Jour. Econ. Ent., 10* (*1917*), *No. 1, pp. 79–81*).—Experiments carried on at the New York State Station for the past three years show that, as with the seedlings of late cabbage (E. S. R., 35, p. 855), satisfactory results may be obtained from screening beds for the protection of radishes. Cheesecloth when properly attached affords complete protection from root maggots and according to the fineness of the mesh reduces to a more or less extent injuries by the flea-beetle, both of which pests when abundant may destroy as well as retard growth.

A chemical feeding analysis of white grubs and May beetles (Lachnosterna) and its economic application, J. J. DAVIS (*Jour. Econ. Ent., 10* (*1917*), *No. 1, pp. 41–44*).—The advantages of pasturing hogs on grub-infested land are summarized as "eradication of grubs which might otherwise destroy the crops planted on the ground; value of the grubs as hog feed, which is comparable with feeds costing $25 to $35 per ton; and value of the manure distributed over the land, which has a money value, according to the experts of the Federal Bureau of Animal Industry, of $3.29 per ton."

The spinach carrion beetle (Silpha bituberosa), R. A. COOLEY (*Jour. Econ. Ent., 10* (*1917*), *No. 1, pp. 94–102, pl. 1*).—This little-known pest has at times been very abundant and injurious to sugar beets in the Yellowstone Valley of Montana.

The injuries by both the larvæ and adults take place mainly early in May, while the plants are still very small and before the work of blocking and thinning has been done. In Montana it is a source of injury to the sugar beet only, but has been reported by Fletcher (E. S. R., 10, p. 866) as also injuring spinach, squash, pumpkin, etc. Both adults and larvæ have been found to feed upon *Monolepis nuttalliana* and *Solanum triflorum*, and the adults only on alfalfa. It occurs from northern Kansas northward to Alberta and Saskatchewan, but does not appear west of the main divide of the Rocky Mountains except in the State of Idaho.

At Bozeman, Mont., there is but one brood per year, and the winter is passed by the adults buried in the soil. The eggs are laid, preferably in moist soil, as deep as 2 in., oviposition occurring as early as March 15 and the number laid by an individual in confinement running as high as 75, with an average of 39. The incubation period was found to vary from 3 to 6, with an average of 4.76 days, and the larval period from 20 to 33 days. The larvæ prefer to feed during the night and remain in hiding in the soil during the day. Both the adults and larvæ feed from the edges of the leaves and injured plants present a characteristic appearance. When full grown the larvæ burrow into the soil to a depth of from 1 to 2 in. and construct an oval cell in which to pupate. The period in the soil is about 25 days and the pupal period about 18 days.

In control work, poisoned-bran mash, prepared by the usual formula, scattered among the weeds near the beet fields where the insects were present in great numbers resulted in nearly complete destruction of them.

The striped cucumber beetle, H. A. GOSSARD (*Mo. Bul. Ohio Sta., 2* (*1917*), *No. 4, pp. 117–120, fig. 1*).—A popular summary of information on this pest.

Egg-laying habits of Diprion simile, M. P. ZAPPE (*Jour. Econ. Ent., 10* (*1917*), *No. 1, pp. 188–190*).—The author reports upon oviposition observations of this European sawfly, which was first discovered in Connecticut in August, 1914, as previously noted (E. S. R., 35, p. 53).

In captivity eggs were laid on five species of five-needle pines, on six species of two-needle pines, and on one species of three-needle pines. As many as 128 eggs are deposited by a single female, usually being placed in needles of the previous year's growth, if any are present.

Notes on the bean weevil (Acanthoscelides [Bruchus] obtectus), J. A. MANTER (Jour. Econ. Ent., 10 (1917), No. 1, pp. 190–193).—A summarized account of the biology of this pest and means for its control.

The alfalfa weevil investigation, G. I. REEVES (Jour. Econ. Ent., 10 (1917), No. 1, pp. 123–131).—In reporting upon the results of investigations of the alfalfa weevil by the Bureau of Entomology of the U. S. Department of Agriculture, it is stated that five practical control measures have been developed, namely, flooding with sediment, spraying with arsenical poisons, pasturing, harrowing the stubble, and colonizing with parasites. While none of these measures is entirely perfected and not all are equally valuable, they are all useful and all are in actual use.

The clover weevil in Iowa, R. L. WEBSTER (Jour. Econ. Ent., 10 (1917), No. 1, p. 225).—Records indicate that the clover weevil (Hypera punctata) occurs all through southern Iowa and probably most of eastern Iowa.

The plum curculio, W. H. GOODWIN (Mo. Bul. Ohio Sta., 2 (1917), No. 4. pp. 113–116, figs. 4).—A brief summary of information relating to the curculio. It is stated that during the last three seasons arsenate of lead paste at the rate of 2 to 3 lbs., with 2 : 3 : 50 Bordeaux and 2 lbs. of soft soap, was used successfully under the author's direction for preventing the injuries caused by the curculio, with no injury to the fruit or foliage.

Lime as an insecticide, Z. P. METCALF (Jour. Econ. Ent., 10 (1917), No. 1, pp. 74–78, pls. 2).—This paper relates to work at the North Carolina Experiment Station with the bean weevil and cowpea weevil in cowpeas being saved for seed.

Cowpeas were treated late in September, 1913. and left until the following spring, when they were examined. Those treated with air-slaked lime at the rate of one part to four parts of peas gave a germination of 71 per cent; those with air-slaked lime, one part to eight parts of peas, gave a germination of 48 per cent; those with crude carbolic acid at the rate of one-half and one pint per bushel gave 21 per cent germination; those with kerosene at the rate of one-half and one pint per bushel, 21.5 per cent germination; and those with carbon bisulphid, at from 15 to 30 lbs. to 1,000 cu. ft. of space, 17.5 per cent germination.

The favorable results obtained with air-slaked lime resulted in the further experiments, here reported. These have led to the recommendation that cowpeas be stored in air-slaked lime at the rate of one part lime to two parts peas by weight, at least until something cheaper and more effective can be devised for the average farmer.   •

In a discussion of this paper which follows, W. E. Hinds states that in a series of experiments at the Alabama College Station in which several varieties of dry cowpeas were submerged in liquid carbon bisulphid for periods ranging approximately from one minute to 1,000 hours, absolutely perfect germination resulted in all cases. Tests made have shown the reported differences in germination to be due to the varying percentage of moisture at the time of the experiment.

Problems of bee inspection, F. C. PELLETT (Jour. Econ. Ent., 10 (1917), No. 1, pp. 200–203).—A discussion of the problems that must be solved by the bee inspector.

The results of apiary inspection, E. F. Phillips (*Jour. Econ. Ent., 10* (*1917*), *No. 1, pp. 204–210*).—A discussion of results obtained from the inspection of apiaries since the first inspection law was passed by Wisconsin in 1897.

Some new and practical methods for the control of European foul brood, E. G. Carr (*Jour. Econ. Ent., 10* (*1917*), *No. 1, pp. 197–200*).—A strong colony, cessation of brood rearing in the diseased combs for a time, and good Italian stock are the three principles involved in the treatment of European foul brood without destroying the combs.

Report on Isosoma investigations, W. J. Phillips (*Jour. Econ. Ent., 10* (*1917*), *No. 1, pp. 139–146, pls. 2*).—This is a review of the present status of Isosoma work as conducted by the Cereal and Forage Insect Investigations division of the Bureau of Entomolgy of the U. S. Department of Agriculture.

It is stated that the injury caused by *Isosoma vaginicolum*, described by Doane in a paper previously noted (E. S. R., 36, p. 59), agrees entirely with that noted in the Eastern States, and apparently is due to the same species. Up to the present time no species has been induced to breed on any other plant than its own particular host. One of the most promising measures in the control of *I. tritici* at present in some of the Eastern States is to plow under wheat stubble as soon after harvest as is possible, prepare a fine seed bed, and sow the clover and grass in August or September instead of seeding in the wheat in the spring.

FOODS—HUMAN NUTRITION.

Biology and the nation's food, W. J. Spillman (*Sci. Mo., 4* (*1917*), *No. 3, pp. 220–225*).—In this paper the author discusses certain biological problems, such as increasing the acre yield of crops and increasing the production of livestock, in their relation to the future food supply.

Bread of the future and measures taken for its utilization, Schribaux (*Compt. Rend. Acad. Agr. France, 3* (*1917*), *No. 14, pp. 407–409*).—Data are reported regarding the use of barley, buckwheat, and corn in supplementing the wheat supply.

It has been found possible to make a satisfactory bread by mixing 80 per cent of wheat flour and 20 per cent of barley flour. On the contrary, the mixture of buckwheat flour with that of wheat makes a dough of poor consistency on account of the decreased quantity of gluten, and fermentation is slow and irregular. The baking in this case must be done at a lower temperature than when wheat alone is used, if a hard, crusty bread is to be avoided. The proportion of barley used may be as high as 30 per cent, but not more than 20 per cent of buckwheat can be used with good results.

On the rations of bread in the army (*Compt. Rend. Acad. Agr. France, 3* (*1917*), *No. 12, pp. 352, 353*).—It is maintained that there is a large amount of waste in the bread supply of the French Army. This is due to the soiling of the bread in transportation and handling and to the fact that the hard-baked bread or biscuit is often wasted by soldiers who have bad teeth.

Some common edible and poisonous mushrooms, Flora W. Patterson and Vera K. Charles (*U. S. Dept. Agr., Farmers' Bul. 796* (*1917*), *pp. 24, figs. 23*).—This contains information regarding the structure of mushrooms and gives descriptions of different mushrooms and miscellaneous fungi. Precautionary measures in the selection of mushrooms for food and recipes for the canning and drying of mushrooms and their preparation for the table are included.

Concerning copper in tomatoes, P. Carles (*Rev. Sci.* [Paris], *55* (*1917*), *No. 6, p. 183*).—According to the author, copper has been found in fresh tomatoes and in other fresh vegetables, but not in sufficient quantity to endanger health.

Food economics at agricultural school, Minnesota University (*Hotel Mo.*, *25 (1917), No. 290, pp. 40–45, figs. 5*).—It is stated that this institution is able to serve abundant, well-planned meals to its students at a cost of 21 cents per person per day for food materials. This is made possible by careful planning, by purchasing in quantity when prices are low, and by the use of specially planned cold-storage houses, detailed plans of which are given. Fruits and vegetables are put up in their season for winter use and bread is made from cleaned whole-wheat berries which have been ground in the coffee mill at the school. Only good cream or butter is used on the table. The cost quoted was for January, 1917.

Food [of the Labrador Eskimo], E. W. HAWKES (*Canada Dept. Mines, Geol. Survey Mem. 91 (1916), pp. 29–36*).—This article gives an account of the food habits of the people and describes the methods of preparation of the foods. The diet consists largely of game (seal, walrus, whale, and reindeer), fish, eggs of wild birds, herbs, and berries.

The food supply of the United Kingdom (*Jour. Bd. Agr.* [*London*], *23 (1917), No. 11, pp. 1046–1052*).—This is a brief report of a survey made by a committee of the Royal Society appointed by the Board of Trade to study the food supply of the United Kingdom. It contains data regarding the food supply before the war, the food supply in 1916, and possible methods of economizing the available food supply.

Great Britain's measures for control of food, P. C. WILLIAMS (*U. S. Dept. Com., Com. Rpts., No. 101 (1917), pp. 407–410*).—A brief review of the efforts of the British Government to insure the conservation, economical distribution, and increased production of foodstuffs.

The growth of rats upon diets of isolated food substances, T. B. OSBORNE and L. B. MENDEL (*Biochem. Jour., 10 (1916), No. 4, pp. 534–538*).—In this paper the authors call attention to the fact that in an article by McCollum (E. S. R., 35, p. 472) the facts reported were essentially in harmony with their own experience in the study of the growth of white rats fed upon mixtures of isolated food substances. The results of their experiments upon certain phases of the problem are reviewed and discussed in their relation to the results of other investigators in order to make clear that their own views are not at variance with those of some other investigators in this field at the present time.

The supplementary dietary relationship between leaf and seed as contrasted with combinations of seed with seed, E. V. McCOLLUM, N. SIMMONDS, and W. PITZ (*Jour. Biol. Chem., 30 (1917), No. 1, pp. 13–32, figs. 14*).—Earlier work of the authors has demonstrated the close resemblance of wheat, maize, and oat kernels in their dietary properties, namely, the relatively poor quality of the proteins, poor content and composition of the inorganic portion of each seed, and the inadequate supply of fat-soluble A.

The present paper presents further data regarding the lines on which successful nutrition is to be attained when the diet is derived solely from vegetable sources, the discussion being limited to the results obtained with combinations of seeds from several sources and of seeds with the alfalfa leaf. Feeding experiments have shown that the nutritive requirements for rats and swine are essentially the same and that neither species can grow satisfactorily when restricted to one of the cereal grains, although both respond in much the same way with growth and reproduction to specific modifications of the diet when restricted as to source.

The authors have been unable to make up a ration derived solely from the seeds of plants which would support normal nutrition through the growing period even though from 2 to 5 seeds of widely different varieties were employed. However, results of a very different character were secured when simple combinations of leaf and seed were fed as monotonous diets. It has been found that with wheat, oats, and maize in equal proportions both salts and fat-soluble A must be added to the ration before growth can take place, and that "it is difficult if not impossible to obtain even a moderate amount of growth over an extended period on a diet restricted to the seeds of plants."

Satisfactory protein mixtures can be had from seed mixtures, and experiments have shown also that certain seeds, such as flaxseed and millet, contain the fat-soluble A in fairly liberal amounts. "Since the water-soluble B is everywhere abundant in the seeds the cause of failure to secure growth on seed mixtures is seen to lie in the amount and character of the inorganic moiety. . . . Of the seven most important seeds from the standpoint of human nutrition and animal production only cotton seed and flaxseed contain a high total inorganic content, and in both cases the ash is very poor in three important elements, sodium, calcium, and chlorin. Since a pronounced deficiency of these elements is characteristic of all other seeds as well, no combinations of seeds will supply these elements in satisfactory amounts."

The necessary inorganic supplements may be secured in some localities through the drinking water, which would enable the animals in those localities to grow on a ration restricted to seeds.

"The leaf is distinctly different from the seed in its dietary properties in two respects: Its total inorganic content is very high, and it is especially rich in both sodium and calcium, both of which are deficient in the seeds generally. In addition the leaf of the plant is several times richer in fat-soluble A than are the wheat, oat, and maize kernels. Certain seeds approximate the value of the leaf in this substance. Hempseed is distinctly better than those just named, but flaxseed and millet seed are still richer than hempseed and may readily be incorporated in the diet in amount sufficient to meet the needs of an animal for the fat-soluble A during growth."

Feeding experiments with deficiencies in the amino-acid supply: Arginin and histidin as possible precursors of purins, H. ACKROYD and F. G. HOPKINS (*Biochem. Jour., 10 (1916), No. 4, pp. 551–576, figs. 6*).—This paper reports the results of a large number of experiments with laboratory animals (rats). The data obtained may be summarized briefly as follows:

Removal of arginin and histidin from the diet of rats which had been previously growing on a complete amino-acid mixture resulted in a rapid loss of body weight. Restoration of the missing diamino acids to the diet resulted in renewing growth.

Restoration of arginin alone or histidin alone resulted in no loss of weight and in some cases in growth. Nutritional equilibrium was possible in the absence of one of these related protein constituents, although not in the absence of both. A reason suggested for this is that each one of them can in metabolism be converted into the other. When arginin and histidin were both removed from the food the amount of allantoin in the urine was much decreased, but when they were replaced the excretion returned to normal. The decrease was very much less when either one of these diamino acids was present alone.

When tryptophan was removed from the food no decrease of allantoin occurred, although nutritional failure was even greater than when arginin and histidin were withheld. No decrease of allantoin excretion was observed when the animals were losing weight as the result of the absence of vitamins from the diet.

In view of these results the authors suggest that arginin and histidin play a special part in purin metabolism, probably constituting the most readily available raw material for the synthesis of the purin ring in the animal body.

The influence of heavy metals on the isolated intestine, W. Salant and C. W. Mitchell (*Amer. Jour. Physiol.*, *39* (1916), *No. 4, pp. 355–374, figs. 14*).

The respiratory process in muscle and the nature of muscular motion, W. M. Fletcher and F. G. Hopkins (*Proc. Roy. Soc.* [*London*], *Ser. B, 89* (1917), *No. B 619, pp. 444–467, figs. 8*).—This lecture deals with the intra-molecular oxygen and the theory of "inogen," the effects of oxygen upon muscle, lactic acid in muscle, and the heat production of muscle. From a consideration of all the data presented, the authors bring out the fact that the actual chemical changes which underlie the contraction, fatigue, and recovery of muscle are relatively simple and that the chemical changes themselves are not complex or obscure, the complexity being found only in the condition under which they occur. A bibliography is appended.

Clinical calorimetry, **XIX–XXV** (*Arch. Int. Med.*, *19* (1917), *No. 5, pp. 823–957*).—Seven articles are presented.

XIX. *The basal metabolism of old men*, by J. C. Aub and E. F. DuBois (pp. 823–831, figs. 2).—The subjects of these experiments were from 77 to 83 years old and were in good health, considering their ages. The average basal heat production, as determined by calorimeter experiments, was found to be 35.1 calories per square meter of body surface per hour, which is 12 per cent below the average for men between the ages of 20 and 50. The results obtained by direct and indirect calorimetry agreed closely and the respiratory quotients were all within normal limits.

XX. *The effect of caffein on the heat production*, by J. H. Means, J. C. Aub, E. F. DuBois, and G. F. Soderstrom (pp. 832–839, fig. 1).—The authors review the literature regarding the effect of caffein on metabolism and report the results of calorimeter experiments on four normal men. After a preliminary period and one or two hours' observation of the subjects' normal basal metab-olism, the caffein was ingested in the form of the pure alkaloid dissolved in pure water. Studies were made of the basal metabolism after the ingestion of caffein, of the respiratory quotient, of the elimination of water from the skin and lungs, of the elimination of nitrogen, and of the pulse rate. The results of the investigation are summarized as follows:

"An increase of from 7 to 23 per cent in the basal metabolism was found in four normal subjects after receiving from 8 to 10 grains of caffein alkaloid (8.6 mg. per kilogram of body weight). After taking the drug there was no significant change in the pulse rate, in the respiratory quotient, in the pro-portions of the various foodstuffs metabolized, or in the percentage of heat lost in the vaporization of water. The independent methods of direct and indirect calorimetry gave results which agreed within 1 per cent."

XXI. *The basal metabolism of dwarfs and legless men with observations on the specific dynamic action of protein*, by J. C. Aub, E. F. DuBois, and G. F. Soderstrom (pp. 840–864, figs. 8).—This paper reports the results of calori-metric observations upon five dwarfs, two legless men, and six normal (male) controls. The results are summarized as follows:

"The legless men and the dwarfs with apparently normal endocrine systems showed, in relation to their surface area, the same level of metabolism as normal men. The law of surface area holds good for men of unusual body shape.

"The dwarfs with involvement of the ductless glands and symptoms of cretinism showed a marked reduction in metabolism below the average found in normal cases, as has been reported by other authorities.

"Following the ingestion of large quantities of meat, the excretion of urinary nitrogen during the earlier hours is not an accurate index of the protein metabolism. The sulphur excretion is more rapid than the nitrogen excretion.

"The stimulation of metabolism following a large amount of meat is almost at its height two hours after the meal is eaten. The extra heat produced may amount to three-quarters of the calories in the protein metabolized, and may lead to an increase of 46 per cent above the level of the basal heat production.

"The specific dynamic action of a meal containing 24 gm. of nitrogen in the form of meat was larger in the case of a legless man and of an achondroplastic dwarf with very small arms and legs and normal trunk than in the cases of three normal controls of greater weight and greater surface area. This indicates that the intensity of the specific dynamic action is not proportional to the mass of the musculature. The true explanation of the results can not be given in the light of present knowledge. Various possible explanations come naturally to mind, such, for example, as a greater concentration of amino acids in the blood flowing to the muscles, or the presence of a liver, which, in proportion to the size of the organism, is relatively larger than the normal."

XXII. *The respiratory metabolism in nephritis*, by J. C. Aub, E. F. Du Bois, and G. F. Soderstrom (pp. 865–889).—This paper reports the results of studies, in the respiration calorimeter, of 10 individuals suffering from nephritis. The following are quotations from the author's summary:

"In most of the patients with greatly increased blood pressure the metabolism was higher than in the other nephritics with lower blood pressures. Most of the patients with marked dyspnea showed some increase in metabolism. . . .

"The respiratory quotients are all within normal limits, showing that nephritics derive their energy from very much the same proportions of the various foodstuffs as do normal men. . . .

"The normal quotients found in patients with low carbon dioxid combining capacity of the plasma prove that nephritic acidosis is not caused by difficulty in oxidizing carbohydrates."

XXIII. *The effect of Roentgen-ray and radium therapy on the metabolism of a patient with lymphatic leukemia*, by J. B. Murphy, J. H. Means, and J. C. Aub (pp. 890–907, figs. 3).

XXIV. *Metabolism in three unusual cases of diabetes*, by F. C. Gephart, J. C. Aub, E. F. Du Bois, G. Lusk, and G. F. Soderstrom (pp. 908–930).

XXV. *The water elimination through skin and respiratory passages in health and disease*, by G. F. Soderstrom and E. F. Du Bois (pp. 931–957). As a result of these experiments the authors state that the technique of determining the water eliminated from the skin and respiratory passages of the subject in a respiration chamber is exceedingly difficult for the following reasons: Moisture will be deposited on the contents of the chamber if the humidity of the air in the chamber rises, and water will be removed which was not eliminated by the subject in the experimental period if the relative humidity of the air in the chamber falls. Over 300 experiments were made with the Sage calorimeter at an air temperature of 22 to 25° C. and a relative humidity between 30 and 50 per cent. For purposes of comparison, all experiments were excluded in which the relative humidity changed more than 10 per cent during the observation period. A table is given showing the water vaporization of different groups of subjects studied under different conditions of growth, temperature, and ventilation.

"Normal men 20 to 50 years old under the standard conditions excrete on an average 29 gm. water an hour (about 700 gm. a day) through skin and air passages, losing in this manner 24 per cent of the total heat produced. Few normal men depart more than one-tenth from this figure. All the results on groups of patients are compared with this standard figure of 24 per cent ±0.1. Boys 12 to 13 years old give figures close to the upper limit and very old men lose almost the same percentage of calories in vaporization. **Dwarfs** and legless men are also close to the normal average. Cretinoid dwarfs show diminished water elimination. Typhoid patients with a rising temperature also have a decreased water output; those with a falling temperature lose an increased percentage of calories in vaporization. The water output in convalescence is low.

"Some patients with hyperthyroidism have a decreased water output; most of them lose the normal percentage of calories in vaporization. Some lose much more than normals in this manner. In pernicious anemia the water of vaporization is not affected. Cardiac and nephritic patients on the whole give figures close to the normal. There is a slight increase in dyspneic patients. Edema seems to have no effect on the water output through the skin. The results in diabetes show great variations. The average figure, however, is about the same as that obtained in normals.

"In conclusion it may be said that the output of water is very little affected in disease. When the heat production is increased the body responds and dissipates the usual percentage of calories in the vaporization of water. When it is necessary to get rid of unusual amounts of heat the percentage lost in vaporization is increased."

ANIMAL PRODUCTION.

Commercial feeding stuffs, J. P. STREET ET AL. (*Connecticut State Sta. Rpt. 1916, pt. 3, pp. 147–184*).—This is a report of the State feed inspection, including analyses of cottonseed meal, linseed meal, wheat bran, wheat middlings, red dog flour, rye middlings, buckwheat middlings, corn gluten meal, corn gluten feed, hominy feed, dried brewers' grains, malt sprouts, dried distillers' grains, dried beet pulp, meat scrap, tankage, bone, coconut meal, salvage wheat, cracked corn, alfalfa meal, beans, bread crumbs, and mixed, proprietary, and poultry feeds.

[Animal husbandry work at the Crookston substation] (*Minnesota Sta., Rpt. Crookston Substa., 1910–1916, pp. 83–87*).—In an experiment during the winter of 1913–14 beef cattle were maintained in prime condition in a straw shed. In this test dry shock corn was equal to corn silage as a supplement to millet and timothy hay and ground oats and barley. There was some waste from unconsumed cornstalks, whereas all the silage was eaten. Difficulty was experienced in feeding silage out of doors in cold weather.

In a test during the winter of 1913–14 it was found that sheep did not relish warm water.

Ground flaxseed was compared with tankage as a protein supplement to barley, corn, and oats for pigs. The tankage proved distinctly superior to the flaxseed, and the results indicated that the latter is not a practical feed for swine.

Wet-mash feeding was compared with dry-mash feeding for laying hens in the winter of 1913–14. The wet-marsh lot laid slightly more eggs at a smaller cost per dozen than the dry-mash lot. In later years, however, the dry-mash method gave better results at a less labor expenditure than the other method. Wet mash proved superior to dry mash for young chicks, especially during the first week of the chick's life. In a fattening test with three-months-old cockerels, Barred Plymouth Rock cockerels gained 2 lbs. each in three weeks as compared with 1.16 lbs. for Leghorn cockerels.

The results of egg preservation experiments in 1913 showed that a solution of sodium silicate and water (1:5) is unnecessarily strong, a dilution of 1:10 giving the best results. Eggs stored in limewater (1 lb. of lime to 5 gal. of water) kept in excellent condition, except that the bottom layer of eggs had a slight flavor of lime. Similar results were secured in tests in 1915. In 1915 eggs packed in boxes in powdered peàt and in common salt evaporated considerably in 6.5 months' storage, and the flavor was only fairly good.

[Feeding experiments with beef cattle, brood sows, and work horses] (*Minnesota Sta., Rpt. Duluth Substa., 1916, pp. 7-9, 10, 11*).—In 1916 young beef animals were pastured without extra feed on range a part of which was tame grass pasture. Three of the yearlings were on grass 49 days and seven 127 days. They made an average daily gain of 1.59 lbs. per head.

Brood sows on pasture from June to September, inclusive, slightly increased in weight when receiving ⅓ lb. of grain per 100 lbs. live weight, whereas before and after the pasture period they consumed 1 lb. of grain per 100 lbs. live weight.

Six work horses were pastured at night on stump-land pasture from June to August, inclusive. During the three months the night pasture resulted in a saving of 12 lbs. of hay and 1 lb. of grain per head daily.

In a test of a self-feeder for pigs on a ration of tankage shorts, ground barley, and skim milk, 13 pigs made an average daily gain from June 15 to October 15 of 118 lbs. per head at cost for grain of $4.69 and a profit of $11.80.

A feeding trial with a litter of fall pigs is also noted.

The theory of correlation as applied to farm-survey data on fattening baby beef, H. R. TOLLEY (*U. S. Dept. Agr. Bul. 504 (1917), pp. 14*).—This bulletin gives the results of an experiment in applying the theory of correlation to the study of some of the data obtained by the Office of Farm Management in a survey of corn-belt farms upon which baby beef was being fattened for market, the details of which have already been noted (E. S. R., 35, p. 668). The factors here considered are the profit or loss per head, the weight, value per 100 lbs., value of feed consumed per head, cost at weaning time, and date of sale. Coefficients of correlation were computed and tabulated for every pair of these factors and used as a measure of the relationship existing between them.

The author concludes that "data such as those obtained by farm management surveys can be analyzed very thoroughly by the use of the correlation coefficients. It is generally known before the analysis is attempted which factors are causal and which resultant, and consequently there should be very little difficulty in interpreting the coefficients correctly. The coefficients of net correlation afford a very good means of determining the net effect of each of several factors bearing upon a result, or of eliminating the effect of other factors when it is desired to find the true relationship existing between any two.

"Although it is not possible to give a definite concrete meaning to correlation coefficients, they are very concise relative measures of the degree of relationship existing between the factors being studied. They therefore give the investigator a single index which will show what, by the ordinary tabular method, it takes a whole table to show. While properly constructed tables will show whether or not any relationship exists between factors, it is a difficult matter to determine which of two causes, say, has the greater effect on the result, and it is impossible, without a large number of records and a great amount of sorting and tabulation, to separate all the factors being considered in a study and find the effect that each one would have had if the others had not been present, or if they had been constant throughout the investigation.

"If the gross coefficients of correlation between every pair of factors have been determined, it is possible to find these relationships by simply substituting in the formula for determining a net coefficient from the gross coefficients, without any further reference to the records themselves. This method should be especially useful if only a limited number of records or observations are available, for it does away with the necessity of sorting into many groups, with the consequent falling off in the reliability of the averages obtained."

The analysis of the data on fattening baby beef animals indicates that "for the herds considered, the cost of producing the calves and carrying them until weaning time was by far the most important factor in determining the profit. There was no connection between the cost at weaning time and any of the other factors, for the calves which were produced cheaply were seemingly just as good feeders and brought just as good a price per pound as the more expensive ones. The weight at which the calves were sold and the date of sale had very little effect on the profit, except for the fact that in the two years of the records the price was higher in the latter part of the summer, at the time when the heavier calves were put on the market. The calves which consumed the heaviest ration sold at higher prices than the others, but did not return a correspondingly greater profit, as the advanced price scarcely offset the extra value of feed consumed."

Steer feeding.—X, Winter steer feeding, 1913–14, J. H. SKINNER and F. G. KING (*Indiana Sta. Bul. 178 (1914), pop. ed., pp. 8*).—A brief summary of experiments already noted (E. S. R., 33, p. 371).

Sheep feeding.—IV, Fattening western lambs, 1913–14, J. H. SKINNER and F. G. KING (*Indiana Sta. Bul. 179 (1914), pop. ed., pp. 8*).—A brief summary of experiments already noted (E. S. R., 33, p. 374).

[Feeding experiments with pigs in Minnesota] (*Minnesota Sta. Rpt. 1916, pp. 45, 72*).—In a comparison of hand feeding with self feeding, 100 pigs in ten lots were fed solely on grain rations consisting of various mixtures of shelled corn, shorts, tankage, ground barley, and linseed meal. In every case the self-fed pigs made larger daily gains than those fed twice daily by hand.

Rape pasture supplemented with 2, 3, and 4 per cent shelled-corn rations gave average daily gains per pig of 0.61, 0.81, and 0.93 lbs., respectively. Valuing corn at 75 cts. a bushel, and pasture at $10 an acre, the actual feed cost per pound of gain was 4.6, 4.46, and 4.81 cts., respectively.

Results at the Crookston substation are noted on page 268 and below.

The fall litter of pigs, W. DIETRICH (*Minnesota Sta., Rpt. Crookston Substa., 1910–1916, pp. 93–95; Minnesota Sta. Rpt. 1916, p. 72*).—Suggestions are given for the successful raising of fall pigs under northern Minnesota conditions.

Twelve pigs born about September 1, 1915, were weaned and put on feed November 22 and fed until the following May. The rations consisted of barley, oats, and tankage, to which corn was added at the beginning of the eleventh week, and a little rye during the last week of the test.

In addition to the above feeds and water these pigs had a small quantity of a 1 per cent solution of concentrated lye, and were also given access to ground limestone and bone meal. At eight months these pigs averaged 255 lbs. each. They required 5.42 lbs. of feed per pound of gain.

[Clover pasture for hogs] (*Minnesota Sta., Rpt. Duluth Substa., 1915, pp. 5, 6*).—In a feeding test with three sows during July and August, it was found that dry brood sows may be maintained on good clover pasture with practically no grain if they are mature, but that a light grain ration is desirable if they are growing.

[Report of the] Kansas state live stock registry board (*Kansas Sta. Insp. Bul. 1 (1915), pp. 239*).—This gives data as to the effect of the stallion license law on the horse-breeding industry of the State, a report of the sixth annual meeting of the Kansas Horse Breeders' Association, a summary of the results secured at the Kansas Station in experiments upon developing draft colts (E. S. R., 36, p. 172), and lists by counties and breeds of stallions licensed in the State during 1915.

Feeding for egg production, P. Moore (*Idaho Sta. Circ. 3 (1916), pp. 6*).— Results are given of a feeding experiment which began November 1, 1914, and ended October 31, 1915, with three pens of 30 White Leghorn pullets each. The following rations were fed: Pen 1, a scratch feed of wheat, oats, and barley (15:2:2), and no mash; pen 2, a scratch feed of wheat, peas, oats, barley, Kafir corn, millet, sunflower seed, and buckwheat (12:2:3:2:1:1:.5:05:1), and a dry mash of bran, shorts, corn meal, wheat meal, fish-meat meal, and charcoal (2:2:1:1:2:1); and pen 3, the same as pen 2 except that corn was substituted for peas in the scratch mixture, and the proportion of oats and barley slightly decreased. All the fowls were given green feed in some form throughout the year.

The fowls in pen 1 failed to keep in flesh, and those in pen 3 maintained more uniform weights than those in pen 2, indicating that corn is essential in a well-balanced poultry ration. During the year pen 1 laid 739 eggs, 66½ per cent of which were under 2 oz. in weight; pen 2 laid 3,486 eggs, 5.5 per cent of which were under 2 oz.; and pen 3 laid 3,938 eggs, 6⅝ per cent of which were under 2 oz.

Notes are given on balancing poultry rations.

Poultry feeding test, home-grown versus purchased feeds (*Minnesota Sta., Rpt. Duluth Substa., 1916, p. 11; abs. in Minnesota Sta. Rpt. 1916, p. 79*).—Two pens of 40 White Leghorn hens each were fed during January, February, and March, 1916. In addition to other feeds the hens in the purchased-feeds lot received corn and meat scrap and those in the home-grown-feeds lot, barley, milk, and peas. The former lot laid 476 eggs and the latter 499 eggs within the three months.

DAIRY FARMING—DAIRYING.

The dairy industry in Argentina, P. Berges (*An. Soc. Rural Argentine, 50 (1916), No. 2, pp. 81–131, figs. 21; abs. in Internat. Inst. Agr. [Rome], Internat. Rev. Sci. and Pract. Agr., 7 (1916), No. 9, pp. 1357–1362*).—The author treats of the present state of the dairy industry of Argentina, sanitary inspection of milk and butter, testing of milk intended for human consumption and butter making, economic returns of the dairy industry, a comparison of the dairy industry of Argentina with that of other countries, and plans for the development of the dairy industry in Argentina.

Net value of pasturage (*Minnesota Sta., Rpt. Duluth Substa., 1915, pp. 7, 8*).—Five acres of pasture land seeded after clearing maintained an average of three cows and two heifers for 30 days the first year after seeding, during which time the total returns of beef and milk fat amounted to $5.33 per acre. It is estimated that this pasture land gave a total return of $10 per acre for the whole season.

[Pasturing experiments with cows at the Duluth substation] (*Minnesota Sta., Rpt. Duluth Substa., 1916, p. 7*).—Continuing the work noted above, 4 cows were pastured on the same 5-acre tract for 137 days in the summer of 1916, receiving in addition 1 lb. of grain to each 4 lbs. of milk produced. During this time the cows produced 497.83 lbs. of milk fat. Valuing the milk fat at 33 cts. per pound and the grain fed at $25.95, the pasture was worth $13.83 per acre for the season.

[Record of dairy herd at the Grand Rapids substation] (*Minnesota Sta. Rpt. 1916, pp. 75, 76*).—Data are tabulated showing the results of five years' work in breeding up a herd of common cows by the use of pure-bred Guernsey sires.

It is noted that the average annual milk production per cow increased from 5,300.9 lbs. in 1911 to 5,721.2 lbs. in 1915. During this time the average fat content of the milk increased from 4.27 to 4.9 per cent, and the annual milk-fat production per cow from 226.6 to 279.8 lbs.

Studies in milk secretion, I, II, J. HAMMOND and J. C. HAWK (*Jour. Agr. Sci.* [*England*], 8 (*1917*), *No. 2, pp. 139–153, figs. 2*).—Two articles are presented.

I. *The effect of nutrition on yield and composition* (pp. 139–146).—Using well-fed goats, a study was made of changes in the yield and composition of the milk which followed a sudden change in nutrition. The changes in nutrition were brought about by the administration of phlorizin, together with the control of the food supply.

When food was withheld from goats for a short time and then an abundant supply given them, the amount of milk and fat secreted was decreased and the percentage of fat increased, due to the lowering of the plane of nutrition. When food was withheld, phlorizin injected, and a few days afterwards a plentiful supply of food given, results similar to those above, yet much more marked, were secured. The return to normal production was very gradual, indicating that phlorizin has a rather long-continued action. In two cases out of the three, the fat percentages at the end of the experiment was below that at the beginning, although the milk yield had not returned to normal. In a third series of experiments phlorizin was injected into goats under normal conditions of feeding. There was great variation in the effects on different individuals, the results indicating that it was the goats in the poorest state of nutrition that showed a diminution in milk yield as a result of the injection of phlorizin.

II. *The relation of the glands of internal secretion to milk production* (pp. 147–153).—The effect of pituitary extract on the milk flow of animals under conditions of reduced nutrition was studied. Goats were injected with 1 cc. of pituitary extract per head daily during a period of sudden change from a high to a low condition of nutrition. This change was brought about by withholding food or by the injection of phlorizin as in the experiments noted above.

The results indicate that the amount of milk produced by the action of pituitary extract varies with the state of nutrition. It was found that the variation in yield as a result of pituitary injections was not so great as the normal daily variations. The percentage of fat in the milk produced within half an hour after the injection of pituitary extract rises with the fall in nutrition, as it does in the case of normal milk.

A study was made of the effect of the injection of adrenalin into lactating goats. In these tests an average of 6 cc. of a 1:1,000 solution of adrenalin chlorid was injected into each goat on alternate days after the morning milking, the goats being milked again after an interval of half an hour. On the other days sterilized water was injected in place of the adrenalin. The injection of the adrenalin had no immediate effect on the amount of milk secreted, but there was a secondary effect causing a decrease in the amount of milk produced for a day following the injection. The percentage of fat in the milk was increased, but the amount of fat was somewhat decreased following the injection of adrenalin.

The results of these experiments indicate that the rate of milk flow is very susceptible to changes in the sugar metabolism of the animal.

On the fat of Egyptian buffalo milk, G. HOGAN and E. GRIFFITHS-JONES (*Dept. Pub. Health* [*Egypt*], *Hyg. Inst. Pub. 5* (*1916*), *pp. 3*).—Analyses are given of 69 samples of buffalo milk fat, each sample being representative of the mixed milk of a complete milking of five or six buffaloes.

The maximum figures obtained were Reichert-Meissl value 37, Polenske value 2.8, saponification value 235, Hübl's iodin value 39.7, and butyro-refrae-tometer reading at 40° C. 44. The corresponding minimum figures were 24.5, 1, 218, 23, and 40.4, and the average, 31.2, 1.5, 229, 31.4, and 42.5, respectively.

Variations in the composition of human milk during the first eleven days after parturition, F. S. HAMMETT (*Jour. Biol. Chem., 29 (1917), No. 2, pp. 381-390*).—A study is reported of variations observed in the chemical composition of human milk during the first 11 days after parturition. The milk production of eight women was studied.

There was an increase in the amount of fat and lactose during the period, while there was a falling off in the production of protein. It is stated that the protein mechanism is apparently the best regulated, and is less dependent upon the factors controlling the fat and lactose production than they are on each other. For the single constituents there was found to be a production plane uniform for the individual subject. This plane of production is apparently fixed for the individual, independent of the plane of nutrition, and dependent upon the individuality. An increase or decrease in the lactose production was usually accompanied by a change in the opposite direction in the percentage of fat and protein.

A bibliography is included.

A new defect in milk caused by Bacterium lactis aerogenes, M. DUGGELI (*Ztschr. Gärungsphysiol., 5 (1916), No. 5, pp. 321-340; abs. in Internat. Inst. Agr. [Rome], Internat. Rev. Sci. and Pract. Agr., 7 (1916), No. 9, pp. 1363, 1364*).—Attempts were made to discover the cause of a bitter taste and typical rancid smell in bottled milk produced under sanitary conditions in a herd of 36 cows. No bitter substance could be discovered in the milk, but it was found that the defect was due to one cow with a diseased udder. A bacterium belonging to the group *B. lactis aerogenes*, and thought to be the cause of the defect in question, was isolated from specimens of the mixed milk. This bacterium gave rise to an abnormal smell and taste, possessed the property of making glucose bouillon very ropy, and prevented the coagulation of milk in the presence of *B. güntheri.* It lost the characteristic taste and smell when cultivated on lactose agar, but these reappeared in part when the organism was cultivated in a suitable medium.

An epidemic of septic sore throat due to milk, E. C. ROSENOW and C. L. V. HESS (*Jour. Amer. Med. Assoc., 68 (1917), No. 18, pp. 1305-1307, fig. 1*).—An account is given of an outbreak of severe sore throat in Galesville, Wis., involving about 200 persons, the cause of which was traced to three cows on one farm, affected with mastitis.

Septic sore throat, G. W. HENIKA and I. F. THOMPSON (*Jour. Amer. Med. Assoc., 68 (1917), No. 18, pp. 1307-1309, fig. 1*).—This is an epidemiologic study of the milk-born epidemic noted above.

Spring conditions affecting the cream producer, H. A. RUEHE (*Illinois Sta. Circ. 195 (1917), pp. 4, fig. 1*).—Suggestions are given for overcoming some of the more common troubles that affect the production of high-grade cream under spring conditions.

Manufacture and composition of Bulgarian cheeses, A. S. ZLATAROFF (*Ztschr. Untersuch. Nahr. u. Genussmtl., 31 (1916), No. 12, pp. 387-394; abs. in Internat. Inst. Agr. [Rome], Internat. Rev. Sci. and Pract. Agr., 7 (1916), No. 9, pp. 1364-1367*).—A description is given of Bulgarian and Kaschkawal cheeses, which, it is stated, make up the bulk of the total output of cheese in Bulgaria. Information is included on the importance of cheese making in Bulgaria.

Rennet substitutes (*N. Y. Produce Rev. and Amer. Cream., 43 (1917), No. 22, pp. 906, 908, 909*).—A brief symposium is given on the use of rennet substitutes in cheese making. Results of cheese making experiments at the Finch dairy station in Ontario, Canada, in which several commercial brands of pepsin and rennet were tested, and notes on the use of pepsin in cheese making are summarized by J. A. Ruddick and G. H. Barr. In these experiments the pepsin cheese was found to be as good in texture and slightly better in flavor after nine months' storage than that made from rennet. The relative value and milk-coagulating power of the various brands tested are tabulated.

VETERINARY MEDICINE.

American Veterinary Medical Association.—Report of committee on diseases, J. R. MOHLER (*Jour. Amer. Vet. Med. Assoc., 50 (1917); No. 7, pp. 895–904*).—This report consists of a brief statement regarding the status of the more important diseases which threaten the live-stock industry of the United States, including hemorrhagic septicemia, hog cholera, foot-and-mouth disease, dourine, tuberculosis, swamp fever, contagious abortion, and influenza.

Sixteenth biennial report of the State Live Stock Sanitary Commission of Michigan for the years 1915 and 1916, G. W. DUNPHY and E. T. HALLMAN (*Bien. Rpt. State Live Stock Sanit. Com. Mich., 16 (1915–16), pp. 31, pls. 4*).—This report deals with the work of the years 1915 and 1916 including the occurrence of and control measures against tuberculosis, hog cholera, contagious abortion, hemorrhagic septicemia, rabies, and anthrax.

Annual administration report of the civil veterinary department in Baluchistan for the official year 1915–16, J. G. CATTELL (*Ann. Admin. Rpt. Civ. Vet. Dept. Baluchistan, 1915–16, pp. 16*).—This report deals with veterinary instruction, treatment of disease, including the occurrence of and work with the contagious diseases of animals during the year, breeding operations, etc.

Annual administration report of the civil veterinary department, Madras Presidency, for 1914–15 (*Ann. Admin. Rpt. Civ. Vet. Dept. Madras. 1914–15, pp. 26, pl. 1*).—This report includes accounts of the occurrence and treatment of diseases of live stock in the Madras Presidency during 1914–15.

Studies in pneumonia.—II. Various methods of determining the bactericidal action of substances in vitro and their relation to the chemotherapy of bacterial infections, J. A. KOLMER, S. SOLIS-COHEN, and G. D. HEIST (*Jour. Infect. Diseases, 20 (1917), No. 3, pp. 293–312*).—The authors have carefully studied, and modified in some instances, the Rideal-Walker and Hygienic Laboratory methods, the centrifuge method, pipette method, combined in-vitro-vivo method, antiseptic method, and plating method.

It is concluded in general that in-vitro bactericidal tests are probably of value in chemotherapeutic studies, this being based on the general observation that substances most parasiticidal in vitro also show this quality in marked degree in vivo. " In-vitro tests should be conducted when possible with the microparasite causing the malady under study, as the object of chemotherapy should be the production not only of polybacteriotropic and polyprotozootropic chemicals but also of monotropic substances for a definite microparasite. In the absence of a pure culture of the particular microparasite under study, a closely allied species may be used. . . . It is highly important to adopt a definite technique and adhere to it in every detail in conducting these tests, because different methods yield varying results, depending mainly on whether the substance excels as a bactericide (killing quickly in high concentration, but losing rapidly in bactericidal power in low concentration) or as an antiseptic (retaining bactericidal power to a better extent in low concentration)."

The procedures are described in detail, discussed, and some experimental data submitted. See also a previous note by Kolmer, Schamberg, and Raiziss (E. S. R., 36, p. 679).

The differentiation of the paratyphoid-enteritidis group, I, E. O. JORDAN (*Jour. Infect. Diseases, 20 (1917), No. 4, pp. 457–483*).—The cultures of bacilli belonging to the paratyphoid-enteritidis group that were examined by the author and are here considered fall into four subdivisions, namely, *Bacillus paratyphosus* A, *B. paratyphosus* B, *B. suipestifer*, and *B. enteritidis.*

The enzyms of the tubercle bacillus, H. J. CORPER and H. C. SWEANY (*Jour. Biol. Chem., 29 (1917), No. 2, pp. XXI, XXII*).—It is noted that tubercle bacilli, both human and bovine, possess autolytic enzyms, as is indicated by the liberation at incubator temperature of noncoagulable nitrogen and amino-acid α-nitrogen after the organisms have beeen killed by toluene and chloroform. The bacilli themselves, or autolyzates therefrom, also possess a trypsin-like enzym capable of cleaving proteins in alkaline solution, a weak pepsin-like⁻ enzym active in acid solution, an erepsin-like enzym capable of cleaving peptone in acid solution, a nuclease which acts on nucleic acid, and a urease. No starch-hydrolyzing or saccharose-inverting enzyms or enzyms capable of digesting elastic tissue prepared from lamb's lung or connective tissue prepared from tubercles could be demonstrated by the methods used for detecting these enzyms. It is indicated that the demonstration of the latter enzyms must be by indirect methods, and the results are therefore not conclusive.

The immune reaction to tuberculous infection, R. WEIL (*Jour. Amer. Med. Assoc., 68 (1917), No. 13, pp. 972, 973, figs. 2*).—From some data obtained by suspending the uterus from a sensitized animal in Locke's solution and determining the effect of the antigenic substance on its muscular contractions, the author indicates that "it is clear that these antibodies must be considered to be cellular or 'sessile,' since it is only on this theory that the response of the isolated organ can be explained. It is not to be supposed that the uterine cells are the only ones of the body which contain the specific antibodies. In fact, it is highly probable that many, if not all, of the tissues of the body are similarly altered by tuberculous infection. . . . If this be the case, it seems highly probable that the various types of altered reaction, . . . whether local or general, are to be explained on the basis of cellular sensitization to the agent of the disease and to its products. The details of the mechanism of these reactions, as well as of the partial immunity of the infected animal, will perhaps be found to correspond to analogous conditions in general anaphylaxis."

The treatment of experimental tuberculosis in guinea pigs and rabbits by taurin, alone and in combination with gold chlorid and sodium oleate, M. TAKEOKA (*Jour. Infect. Diseases, 20 (1917), No. 4, pp. 442–456*).—Experimental data of a study of the curative value of taurin alone or in combination with a colloidal mixture of sodium gold chlorid and sodium oleate in experimental tuberculosis in guinea pigs and rabbits are reported. The guinea pigs were infected with either bovine or human strains of the organisms, the results being similar in both cases.

In general the control animals died before any of the treated animals, and whereas the controls lost weight almost uniformly, the treated animals gained. The majority of the treated animals were killed for observation many days after the controls had died, and the contrast in the extent of visible tuberculosis was marked. While the process was found to be advanced in the controls, it was arrested and in some instances apparently cured in the treated animals.

Rabbits were infected with intraperitoneal or intravenous injections of the bovine strain. The treatment was carried out by intravenous injections of taurin alone, the results being similar but even more marked than in the experiments with guinea pigs. Histologic examination of the organs in treated animals showed arrested tubercles, absence of caseation, disappearance of the tubercle bacilli and lesions, and evidence of repair by connective-tissue in growth. The controls showed advancing lesions, caseation, and numerous bacilli. A number of the treated animals showed slight evidences of tuberculosis, but in no inconsiderable number were the tissues essentially normal microscopically.

Suppuration in cattle and swine caused by Bacterium pyogenes, A. R. WARD (*Cornell Vet.*, 7 (1917), No. 1, pp. 29–42, pl. 2).—This discussion of the general characteristics of the lesions and of those found in swine and in cattle is based upon investigations and an extensive review of the literature in connection with a list of 15 references appended.

"*Bacillus pyogenes* differs from the common pyogenic organisms in that it possesses the peculiarity, under certain conditions, of stimulating the proliferation of connective tissue to form tumor-like masses similar to granulation tissue, and of subsequently inducing the necrotic changes leading to the formation of an abscess within the newly formed tissue. This type of suppuration as a consequence of the preliminary tissue proliferation follows a slow chronic course. In this peculiarity the development of the lesions of *B. pyogenes* bears a general resemblance to the changes occurring in tuberculosis and in actinomycosis."

B. pyogenes is deemed undoubtedly the most common suppurative organism affecting swine. Abscesses caused by it may develop in all parenchymatous visceral organs, the walls of the gastro-intestinal canal, the musculature, and the subcutis. It is also said to be quite as important in cattle as in swine.

The diastase in the saliva of the ox, C. C. PALMER (*Vet. Alumni Quart.* [*Ohio State Univ.*], 4 (1916), No. 2, pp. 44–52).—Previously noted from another source (E. S. R., 36, p. 82).

The diagnosis of infectious abortion of cattle (Bang's disease) with special reference to the intradermal abortin test.—I, Review of Bang's disease, J. REICHEL and M. J. HARKINS (*Jour. Amer. Vet. Med. Assoc.*, 50 (1917), No. 7, pp. 847–862, figs. 4).—This is a general discussion of the subject with regard to history, symptoms, bacteriological examinations (microscopic and cultural), and biological tests (serological and diagnostic reagents), together with detailed tabulated data on the use of the "abortin" test as introduced by the British commission (E. S. R., 22, p. 584) and also tested by Meyer and Hardenbergh (E. S. R., 31, p. 380).

The abortin used was prepared by removing from six to eight strains of *Bacillus abortus*, which were grown in Blake bottles of neutral glycerin agar at 37° C. until their maximum growth was obtained, with sterile physiological salt solution, collecting as one mixture, heating to 60° for one hour, and centrifugalizing. The killed bacteria were then once more washed with physiological salt solution and the emulsion shaken up in a mechanical mixer with a definite amount of the saline and filtered through four thicknesses of sterile cheesecloth. The filtrate was so diluted that each cubic centimeter included approximately 5,000,000,000 bacteria, cultured for sterility and preserved with 0.5 per cent phenol. It was applied in the test in a manner similar to the intradermal tuberculin test as used by Haring and Bell (E. S. R., 30, p. 883).

It is indicated that the intradermal test is hardly destined to assist in establishing a diagnosis, as far as the individual animal is concerned, but as an aid in determining whether or not the infection actually exists in a herd it is a valuable test for the practicing veterinarian. "As much can be said for a positive reaction in the test as a positive reaction in any of the serological tests, and when the history of the herd is such as to arouse the suspicion that

Bang's disease may exist, then positive reaction with the intradermal abortin test in several animals would show that the suspicion is well founded, whereas uniformly negative results would tend to indicate that the infection was not present.

"Outside of clinical observations, including the history of the herd and deductions made of material aborted, the veterinarian must rely on the results of tests that include laboratory procedures, the results of which as a rule are very difficult to interpret. . . . When the results of the bacteriological or serological tests are available the results of the intradermal abortin test can be used as additional confirmation, and if circumstances prevail where bacteriological or serological tests can not be made then the intradermal abortin test can serve as an additional means or procedure open to the veterinarian in practice."

Formalin in the treatment of mastitis, J. N. FROST (*Jour. Amer. Vet. Med. Assoc., 51 (1917), No. 1, pp. 85–88*).—The author reports having obtained gratifying results from the administration of formalin by mouth in the treatment of infectious mastitis. In his experiments 25 cc. of formalin given to a cow undiluted in capsules twice daily for two weeks failed to produce ill effects in any way, either by loss of appetite, constipation, or emaciation. Fifty cc. was also given at one time without ill effect. Five cases of mastitis cured by this treatment are reported.

When one dram of formalin was given faint traces could be found in the milk in 24 hours. When 25 cc. was given three hours after water and seven hours after milking it was found in the milk two hours afterwards and continued to be present for 48 hours.

Eradication of the cattle tick in Argentina, A. AYERZA, F. SIVORI ET AL. (*An. Soc. Rural Argentina, 50 (1916), No. 6, pp. 582–584*).—A plan for the eradication of the cattle tick in Argentina, prepared by a commission appointed by the Minister of Agriculture, is presented.

Notes on a fatal parasitic infestation in a herd of cattle and goats in the Province of Ambos Camarines, W. H. BOYNTON and L. D. WHARTON (*Philippine Agr. Rev. [English Ed.], 9 (1916), No. 4, pp. 348–353*).—This paper reports upon the occurrence in the Province of Ambos Camarines of helminths in cattle and goats which had succumbed to their attack. The helminths dealt with are *Bunostomum phlebotomum, Œsophagostomum columbianum, Œsophagostomum* sp., *Hæmonchus contortus, Trichuris ovis, Filaria labiato-papillosa,* nematode species, and *Paramphistomum* sp.

Louping-ill, S. STOCKMAN (*Jour. Compar. Path. and Ther., 29 (1916), No. 3, pp. 244–264*).—This article, which deals particularly with the possibility of the transmission of this disease by ticks, includes reports of experiments in which the tick theory was tested.

"The experimental evidence so far is against the view that louping-ill is a disease carried by ticks. There still remains to be tested by direct experiment, however, the possibility of ticks acquiring infection when sucking as larvæ, remaining noninfective in the nymphal stage, and developing infectivity when adults."

The author concludes that until the experiments now being carried out have been completed it will be unwise to conclude that louping-ill is not a tick-borne disease.

Roundworms of sheep, B. H. RANSOM (*U. S. Dept. Agr. Rpts. 1916, pp. 127–130*).—During 1915 nematode experiments were made at Vienna, Va., with approximately 100 ewes and lambs separated into four lots. The first lot was kept continuously on the same pasture from May to September. The second lot was kept on a double pasture from May to September, grazing alternately two weeks in each of the two parts. The animals in the third lot were grazed separately and moved every week to fresh ground or ground not recently grazed, but were allowed together at noontime and night, when they were together in a barn with slat floors which was cleaned and disinfected at least once a week. The fourth lot was moved once a week from May to September to fresh pasture and was kept together most of the time, the ewes occasionally being separated from the lambs and grazed on infested pasture when the available fresh pasture was limited.

At least five lambs from each of the lots were killed and examined in September or later, but no material difference was observed in the degree of stomach worm infestation in the various lots. A great reduction in the number of stomach worms present occurred in all of the lots after November 1, as a rule only a comparatively few individual worms being found instead of the usual thousands found in the lambs or ewes examined earlier.

With reference to hookworms, nodular worms, lungworms, and tapeworms, there was no important difference between the first and second lots. The lambs of the third lot showed hookworms in only one case and then only two specimens. They had few and in some cases no nodular worms or worm nodules, no tapeworms, and no lungworms. The lambs in lot 4 also had comparatively few hookworms, nodular worms, and worm nodules, only one having lungworms and none tapeworms.

These experiments apparently indicate that the plan followed as to change of pastures can not be depended upon to control parasitic infestation in lambs, especially in the case of the stomach worm, although, on the other hand, it appeared that a change of pasture every week during the season from May 1 to September 1 kept down the infestation of lambs with hookworms, nodular worms, lungworms, and tapeworms to a very small amount. It thus appears that these parasites can be more easily controlled than the stomach worm by a system of pasture rotation. " The probable meaning of the presence of only a few stomach worms in sheep during the winter following a summer in which they were comparatively numerous in other sheep of the same flock is that the average length of life of the adult stomach worm is not more than a few weeks or months; in brief, that the stomach worm is essentially a short-lived parasite."

The influence of partial thyroidectomy in pigs, C. C. PALMER (*Amer. Jour. Physiol.*, *42* (*1917*), *No. 4, pp. 572–581, fig. 1*).—The results of a study by the author at the Veterinary Research Laboratories of the Minnesota Experiment Station show that the extirpation of the main thyroid gland in young pigs does not induce cretinism, at least within a period of nearly one year. A slight retardation of growth was observed, but the operated pigs otherwise acted similarly to the controls except that they showed a marked lowered resistance to infection. A marked hypertrophy of the accessory thyroid tissue was observed on post-mortem examination of the thyroidectomized pigs.

It is indicated that "the main thyroid gland plays an important part in the normal body resistance to infection, and when this structure is removed the accessory thyroids can not completely compensate. In pigs a degree of hypothyroidism not sufficient to lead to marked changes in physical appearance of the animal lowers the resistance to infection to quite a degree, and impairs the functions of reproduction."

Fetal athyrosis.—A study of the iodin requirement of the pregnant sow, G. E. SMITH, with the cooperation of H. WELCH (*Jour. Biol. Chem.*, *29* (*1917*), *No. 2, pp. 215–225*).—The authors, at the Montana Experiment Station, have studied the condition of the birth of hairless and otherwise defective pigs which has been reported from western North Dakota and South Dakota, Washington, Minnesota, and western Canada.

The affected pigs when born are of full size and occasionally larger than normal. They are, however, strikingly weak and low in vitality, although born of apparently normal sows. Except for a few hairs on the nose and a few around the eyes, the skin is smooth, shiny, and bald. This hairless condition is, however, very variable. The skin, particularly around the shoulders, is thick and feels pulpy, but on incision no fluid escapes, although it appears edematous. The hoofs are thin-walled, short, brittle, and in an undeveloped condition. The thyroid is dark red and sometimes almost black, and histological examination shows a uniform hyperplasia and a distention of the blood vessels. Chemical examination of the thyroids showed the iodin content to be extremely low in comparison with normal glands. In general, the iodin content of a diseased gland was found to vary inversely with the hairlessness of the animal. The glands of the affected pigs also showed a large accumulation of iron. The data are presented in tabular form.

Pregnant sows in the affected districts which were fed potassium iodid and desiccated sheep thyroid in the last four or five weeks before farrowing gave birth to strong and vigorous young, while the young of the control animals were weak, dull, and lacked vitality. The significance of the iodin feeding is discussed.

It is concluded in general that an iodin deficiency during the gestation period causes a lack of function and hyperplasia of the fetal thyroid, resulting in an arrested development of the fetus. "If more iodin were fed to the pregnant animals in large sections of this continent, especially during the winter months, the young that they produce would be more healthy and more vigorous and the large number of weak and defective young animals that are produced annually would be greatly reduced. Fetal athyrosis presents strong evidence that there is a direct relation between the physiologically active constituents of the thyroid and growth of the epidermal appendages. An abundant secretion of the fetal thyroid, during the later stages of the intrauterine life, is essential for the normal development of the fetus."

The spirochetes of the digestive tract of swine and their relation to hog cholera, P. BEKENSKY (Rec. Méd. Vét., 92 (1916), No. 19, pp. 545–552).—The author has examined the intestinal tract of 100 hogs at an abattoir and found spirochetes in 58 per cent of the cases. The spirochetes were found not only in animals affected with hog cholera but also in animals affected with other diseases. It is indicated that in hog cholera these organisms might provoke a secondary infection (as is often the case in infectious diseases), but that the disease is fundamentally due to the invisible microorganism. The data obtained are discussed in some detail.

Swine fever, J. O. POWLEY (Vet. Rec., 29 (1917), No. 1497, pp. 383–390).—This is a general discussion of the subject under the topics of history, etiology, semeiology, post-mortem appearances, diagnosis, methods of infection, treatment, efficacy of serum, and a brief account of the preparation of serum.

A granulomatous affection of the horse—habronemic granulomata (cutaneous habronemiasis of Railliet), L. B. BULL (Jour. Compar. Path. and Ther., 29 (1916), No. 3, pp. 187–199, figs. 5).—"The granulomatous condition found on the penis and sheath, and infrequently in other situations, has the same etiology as summer sores. The parasite associated with the condition is a larval nematode of the genus Habronema. This parasite is accidental, and probably can not maintain its life for longer than four weeks. The parasite is almost certainly carried by a biting fly, and is accidentally inoculated during the feeding operations of the fly. The tissue reaction following the introduction of the parasite leads to a tumor presenting a characteristic macroscopic and microscopic appearance. The affection known as swamp cancer in the Northern Territory of Australia is almost certainly a variation of the same condition.

"Prophylaxis should be in the direction of (1) ridding horses of the adult forms of the genus Habronema which are located in the stomach, and (2) in the destruction of feces which bear the embryos and which act as a breeding ground for flies. Complete excision of the lesion before it has become inoperable is the only treatment to be advised."

Sclerostome parasites of the horse in England.—II, New species of the genus Cylichnostomum, C. L. BOULENGER (*Parasitology, 9 (1917), No. 2, pp. 203–212, figs. 5*).—This second part of the paper previously noted (E. S. R., 36, p. 280) consists of descriptions of three new species of the genus Cylichnostomum.

Parasitic occurrence of Eimeria stiedæ in the liver of the dog, A. GUILLEBEAU (*Schweiz. Arch. Tierheilk., 58 (1916), No. 11, pp. 596–602, figs. 6; abs. in Rec. Méd. Vét., 93 (1917), No. 1–2, pp. 71–73; Trop. Vet. Bul., 5 (1917), No. 1, pp. 5, 6*).—The author describes two cases of the occurrence of *E. stiedæ* in the liver of dogs, 10 and 13 years old, respectively, in which great enlargement of the abdominal cavity was the most marked symptom during life. Coccidiosis of the liver, although common in rabbits, is said to be very rarely found in the pig or dog.

Chick troubles, W. C. THOMPSON (*New Jersey Stas. Hints to Poultrymen, 5 (1917), No. 7, pp. 4*).—This circular discusses a few of the more common chick troubles, especially those that usually appear when chicks are brooded in large colonies.

Apparent recovery of a hen infected with bacillary white diarrhea as determined by the macroscopic agglutination test, G. D. HORTON (*Jour. Bact., 1 (1916), No. 6, pp. 625, 626*).—The author reports upon the recovery of a Bantam hen, indicating the possibility of recovery or the throwing off of ovarian infection.

The part played by the goblet cells in protozoan infections of the intestinal tract, P. B. HADLEY (*Jour. Med. Research, 36 (1917), No. 1, pp. 79–86, pl. 1*).—"The present paper presents observations which demonstrate that, in the case of the flagellate protozoan, Trichomonas, the cause of an acute malady of several species of birds, notably the turkey (blackhead), the avenue of invasion of the subepithelial tissues is the goblet or chalice (gland) cells located in the fundus of the crypts of Lieberkühn. It is suggested that the passage of the parasites through these cells is not inadvertent, but due to a natural invasive power present in the motile flagellate trophozoite which accomplishes the infection of the deeper tissues."

Eimeria avium: A morphological study, P. B. HADLEY and ELIZABETH E. AMISON (*Arch. Protistenk., 23 (1911), No. 1–2, pp. 7–50, pls. 2*).—Following an introduction and historical résumé the authors discuss the material, methods, and technique and the life cycle of the coccidium and the infectious process; and give a detailed description of the several stages of the coccidium, namely, the mature cyst, sporoblasts, sporozoites, schizonts, merozoites, macrogametes, microgametocytes, and microgametes.

A list of 37 references to the literature is included.

Coccidia in subepithelial infections of the intestines of birds, P. B. HADLEY (*Jour. Bact., 2 (1917), No. 1, pp. 73–78*).—This is a brief report of studies of coccidia now in progress, in continuation of investigations above noted, in which the author considers in a preliminary way the bearing of certain of the observations upon the problem as discussed by Smith (E. S. R., 35, p. 684).

"Although the full significance of the presence of merozoites and of other stages of *Eimeria avium* in subepithelial regions of the intestines can not yet be grasped, their frequency of occurrence there and their freedom from all appearances of degenerative changes lead us to assume that this phenomenon marks an ordinary phase of the normal infective process; and that so far as the coccidia are concerned, we must, as the writer pointed out some years ago, abandon the view that they are exclusive parasites of epithelial cells in the sense that they must occupy epithelial cells to complete their normal development."

Another case of the occurrence of the giant nematode, Dioctophyme renale, in the abdominal cavity, and data bearing upon the theory of entry via the genito-urinary tract, W. A. RILEY (*Cornell Vet., 7 (1917), No. 1, pp. 43–45*).—The data here presented supplement the account previously noted (E. S. R., 36, p. 86).

RURAL ENGINEERING.

Proceedings of the second, third, and fourth annual meetings of the Washington Irrigation Institution, December, 1914, January, 1916, and November, 1916 (*Proc. Wash. Irrig. Inst., 2 (1914), pp. 163, fig. 1; 3 (1916), pp. 214, fig. 1; 4 (1916), pp. 141, figs. 3*).—These proceedings contain, respectively, the following special articles bearing on irrigation engineering:

Second meeting.—Experience with Canal Lining, by E. M. Chandler; Canal Lining Experience, by J. G. Heinz; Plant Growth in Canals, by F. C. Lee; Methods of Water Delivery, Rotation, and Size of Head, by M. Chase; Operation of the State Drainage Law, by W. B. Bridgman and J. O. Greenway; The Use of Electric Power in Pumping Water for Irrigation, by H. D. Hanford; Discussion of Drainage and Reclamation of Alkali Land, by H. E. Nicolai; Hydrated Lime in Irrigation Work, by C. D. Smith; Economy, Durability, and Efficiency of Water Distribution Systems, by A. B. Fosseen; Vitrified Clay Pipe for Irrigation and Drainage, by W. M. Watt; Irrigation District Laws, by C. B. Graves; The State College and Irrigation, by E. A. Bryan; The Farmer's Part in Irrigation Development, by S. Fortier; The Use of Metallic Flumes and Pipes in Irrigation Development, by G. L. Hess; and Duty of Water, by S. O. Jayne. Articles on Plaster Concrete Lining for Canals and Laterals, by C. Casteel; and Experience with Wood Stave, Concrete, and Steel Pipe, by E. M. Chandler, are appended.

Third meeting.—Irrigation Conditions, by E. F. Benson; Maintenance and Construction of Metal Flumes, by W. B. Armstrong; Uses of Concrete in Irrigation Development, by C. N. Reitze; Irrigation Pumping by Means of Electric Pumping, by G. Longmuir; Irrigation Pumping, Other Methods, by S. B. Hill; Wood Pipe, Its Uses and Limitations, by T. A. Noble; and Conflicting Interests in Water Legislation, by W. F. Allison. Descriptions of irrigation projects in the State are included.

Fourth meeting.—Method and Time of Applying Water, by O. L. Waller; Wood and Thin Metal Pipe, by T. A. Noble; Light Iron Pipes, by C. Casteel; The Value of Irrigation to the State, by M. Chase; Metal Flumes, by W. B. Armstrong; Metal Flumes as Canal Lining, by E. M. Chandler; The Agricultural Duty of Water, by J. C. Wheelon; Drainage, by G. Severance; Wooden Flumes, by W. F. Allison; Oil-Burning Engines, by J. B. Frem; and Cement Lining of Canals, by C. Casteel.

Flow through submerged rectangular orifices with modified contractions, V. M. CONE (*U. S. Dept. Agr., Jour. Agr. Research, 9 (1917), No. 4, pp. 97–114, figs. 13*).—Experiments conducted at the Colorado Experiment Station in cooperation with the Office of Public Roads and Rural Engineering of the U. S. Department of Agriculture are reported, which consisted of 317 observations, with 60 different combinations of sizes of orifices, sharp and thick edges, with and without gate guides, with and without small bottom contraction, with different depths of water in the channel of approach, and with different end contractions in the channel of approach and recession.

The results of the experiments are summarized and a consolidation of the expressions for the exponent and coefficient values of the head, h, "gives the general formula for the discharge through submerged rectangular orifices placed according to the conditions which have been taken as the standard:

$$Q=\left(_{(4.8+0.1d)a}^{(0.02d+0.99)}\right)_h\left(0.495d+0.06d-\frac{7.26a}{A}\right)$$

in which $Q=$ the discharge in second-feet; $d=$ depths of orifice in feet; $a=$ area of orifice in square feet; $A=$ area of cross section of water in channel of approach in square feet; and $h=$ the difference in feet between the water levels upstream and downstream from the orifice."

The agreement of the discharge formula with the experimental data is shown to be within a mean of approximately 0.5 per cent, with a few individual exceptions, which are more than 1 per cent off.

The standard conditions are taken as follows:

"The total length of the orifice box is 16 ft., 10 ft. of which forms the channel of approach. Wings set at an angle of 90° are attached to the sides of the upstream end of the orifice box. The floor of the box is level throughout and at the same elevation as the bottom of the canal. The box should be set in the center line of the canal, so as to allow the water to enter the box in straight lines. The sides are parallel and are placed apart a distance equal to the length of the orifice plus 2 ft.

"Orifices of all sizes have end-contraction distances of 1 ft. The orifice must have sharp sides and top, and no bottom contraction. . . . The orifice must be placed with its greatest dimension horizontal. If it is desirable to use an orifice with bottom contraction, or with wood sides and top, or with gate guides and gate, the discharge tables may be corrected in accordance with the data given. . . .

"The elevations of the water levels in the channels of approach and recession should be taken in separate stilling boxes, one connection being 5 ft. upstream and the other 1.5 ft. downstream from the plane of the orifice. The connections should be through the side of the orifice box about 0.5 ft. above the floor line."

A few supplemental experiments are also reported.

The Venturi flume, V. M. CONE (*U. S. Dept. Agr., Jour. Agr. Research, 9* (1917), *No. 4, pp. 115–129, pls. 4, figs. 8*).—"The purpose of this article is to present the fundamental plans and results of preliminary experiments on a new type of device, called the 'Venturi flume,' for measuring water in open channels."

The flume "consists essentially of a flume with a converging and a diverging section and short 'throat' section between them. The floor, which is level, is placed at the elevation of the bottom of the channel in which it is set. . . .

"The action of this device depends upon an adaptation or extension of Venturi's principle to the flow of a liquid in an open channel. As water passes through the flume there is a slight surface slope in the converging section, a rather sudden depression in the 'throat' section, and a rise in the diverging section. The actual loss of head is small. The determination of the flow depends upon the velocity and wetted cross-sectional area at two points in the flume, and two gage readings, therefore, are necessary."

From the experimental data the formula for discharge through the V-notch Venturi flume is as follows:

$$Q = 6.68 H_b^2 [(H_d - 0.14 H_a + 0.02)^2 + 0.01 H_a + 0.56] \sqrt{1 - \frac{\dfrac{H_d}{H_b^4}}{(2\frac{2}{3} + H_a)^2 H_a^2}}$$

In this formula Q=the discharge in second-feet; H_a=the head at the gage in the upstream section; H_b=the head at the throat section; and $H_d = H_a - H_b$.

"The discharge through the Venturi flume with trapezoidal cross section, having side slopes of 1:1 in a plane normal to the axis of the flume and with a bottom throat width of 6 in., is represented by the following equation, which was derived in a manner similar to that given for the V-notch Venturi flume:

$$Q = \left[\frac{[(H_d - 0.09 H_a - 0.005)^2 + 0.001 H_a + 0.274]}{0.30} \right] (\tfrac{1}{2} + H_b) H_b \sqrt{1 - \frac{\dfrac{2g H_d}{(\frac{1}{2} + H_b)^2 H_b^2}}{\frac{1^1}{b} + H_a) H_a^2}}$$

"The Venturi flume is not an exact measuring device, but it is thought to be sufficiently accurate to meet usual practical needs, especially such as are encountered in irrigation practice in the West. Although experiments have been made only on the smaller sizes of Venturi flumes, it seems reasonable to expect that structures built according to the general plans will be applicable to the measurement of streams of considerable size with an accuracy compatible with field requirements. The Venturi flume seems to fulfill the conditions of being free of trouble from sand, silt, or floating trash; requires little loss of head for making the measurement; is a structure that is simple to build, easy to operate, and has a comparatively low cost; and is free from error in measurement due to aquatic growth or other changes in the channel, provided the floor of the flume is not below the grade of the channel."

Investigations of irrigation pumping plants, H. E. MURDOCK (*Montana Sta. Bul. 115 (1917), pp. 125–148, figs. 6*).—Field and laboratory tests of pumping outfits, consisting of various combinations of engines and pumps for different heads, are reported. The results of the laboratory tests are summarized in the following table:

Summary of results of laboratory tests.

Kind of engine.	Kind of pump.	Engine, rated horse-power.	Engine speed (revolutions per minute).	Pump speed (revolutions per minute).	Discharge of pump per second.	Lift.	Fuel per foot acre-foot.	Lubricating oil per foot acre-foot.
					Cu. ft.	Feet.	Galls.	Galls.
Gasoline.......	Plunger............	¾	....	....	0.0540	10.0	0.940	0.224
Do........	do........	¾	....	....	.0540	25.0	.573	.224
Do........	do........	4	....	....	.0191	50.0	3.120	.253
Do........	do........	4	....	....	.0679	50.0	1.050	.071
Do........	do........	1	....	....	.0550	8.2	3.480	....
Do........	do........	1	....	....	.0570	8.2	3.740	....
Do........	do........	1	....	....	.0580	8.2	2.510	....
Do........	Central 3-inch horizontal...	4	385	342	.3447	10.0	.938	.070
Do........	do........	4	600	393	.6000	10.0	.848	.040
Do........	do........	5	284	392	.6000	10.0	.704	.040
Do........	do........	5	318	548	.6000	25.0	.674	.016
Do........	do........	45	274	548	.6000	25.0	1.528	.064
Do........	do........	45	272	1,055	.6000	50.0	.916	.064
Do........	Central 5-inch vertical...	5	424	676	1.2760	10.0	1.180	.019
Do........	do........	5	366	726	1.5000	10.0	.703	.016
Do........	do........	45	315	876	1.5000	25.0	.974	.026
Do........	do........	45	325	1,135	1.5000	50.0	.604	.013
Do........	Central 7-inch vertical.....	45	314	336	3.0000	10.0	1.220	.027
Do........	do........	45	300	462	3.0000	25.0	.623	.011
Do........	do........	45	306	602	3.0000	50.0	.424	.011
Kerosene.......	Plunger............	1	....	....	.0600	8.2	2.720	....
Do........	Central 3-inch horizontal...	45	272	1,055	.6000	50.0	1.052	.040
Do........	Central 5-inch vertical.....	5	366	726	1.5000	10.0	....	....
Do........	do........	45	315	876	1.5000	25.0	.944	.026
Do........	do........	45	325	1,135	1.5000	50.0	.590	.013
Do........	Central 7-inch vertical.....	45	300	462	3.0000	25.0	.625	.011
Do........	do........	45	306	602	3.0000	50.0	.416	.011
							Lbs.	
Steam, using coal.	Central 3-inch horizontal...	36	214	548	.6000	25.0	70.000	.024
Do........	do........	36	255	1,055	.6000	50.0	65.400	.024
Do........	Central 5-inch vertical.....	75	228	1,135	1.5000	50.0	28.500	.010
Do........	Central 7-inch vertical.....	75	212	462	3.0000	25.0	28.300	.008
Do........	do........	75	212	602	3.0000	50.0	20.200	.008

The results of field tests are summarized in the following table:

Summary of field tests on horizontal centrifugal pumps.

Kind of plant.	Kind of fuel.	Engine rated horse-power.	Engine speed (revolutions per minute).	Diameter of discharge pipe.	Pump speed (revolutions per minute).	Discharge of pump per second.	Lift.	Fuel cost per unit.	Fuel per foot acre-foot.	Lubricating oil per foot acre-foot.
				Inches.		Cu. ft.	Feet.		Lbs.	Galls.
Steam engine....	Lignite...	75	170	6	370	2.33	12.65	$3.00	103.00	0.02460
Do............	do.....	75	236	6	332	3.06	37.60	3.00	40.10	.01870
Do............	Coal...	75	236	6	332	3.06	37.60	5.00	30.00	.01870
Do............	do.....	65	205	18	257	15.12	14.23	4.00	37.80	.00433
Do............	do.....	65	220	18	276	19.73	14.45	4.00	32.60	.00258
Do............	do.....	65		18						
Do............	do.....	65	219	18	275	20.23	14.50	4.00	26.20	.00172
Do............	do.....	65		18						
Do............	do.....	65	....	18	Normal.	....	14.47	4.00	30.00	.00215
Do............	do.....	65		18						
Do............	do.....	65	237	18	298	25.00	14.77	4.00	30.50	.00200
									Galls.	
Gasoline engine..	Gasoline.	12	130	6	251	1.60	4.60	.16	1.38	....
Do............	do.....	12	135	6	264	1.45	4.35	.16	1.54	.09000
Do............	do.....	12								
Do............	do.....	12	128	6	248	1.61	4.50	.16	1.41	....
Do............	do.....	12	127	6	247	1.65	4.42	.16	1.45	....
Do............	do.....	15	230	6	373	2.72	12.00	.16	.75	....
Do............	do.....	8	289	8	274	.97	11.50	.19	.755	.04900
Do............	do.....	8	291	8	278	1.17	11.50	.19	.540	.03400
Kerosene engine..	Kerosene.	20	233	10	280	5.56	10.00	.11	.573	.00900

Brake and water horsepower and efficiency tests of three centrifugal pumps are reported in the following table:

Brake and water horsepower and efficiency of centrifugal pumps.

Kind of pump.	Head on pump.	Discharge per second.	Brake horse-power.	Water horse-power.	Effi-ciency.
	Feet.	*Cubic feet.*			*Per cent.*
3-in. horizontal centrifugal............................	10	0.6	1.859	0.68	36.6
Do...	25	.6	3.580	1.70	47.5
Do...	50	.6	6.700	3.40	50.7
5-in. vertical (submerged).............................	10	1.5	3.456	1.70	49.2
Do...	25	1.5	7.840	4.25	54.2
Do...	50	1.5	14.480	8.50	58.7
7-in. vertical centrifugal (submerged)................	10	3.0	7.800	3.40	43.6
Do...	25	3.0	13.370	8.50	63.6
Do...	50	3.0	23.840	17.00	71.3

Growth of moss in irrigation canals, Salt River Project, A. J. HALTOM (*Reclam. Rec.* [*U. S.*], 8 (*1917*), No. 4, pp. 191, 192).—Studies of the growths of moss which obstruct the flow in the wide, shallow, low-velocity canals of the project led to the following conclusions:

"Moss does not grow in canals of high velocity. Neither does it flourish in canals that have uniform grades, but canals of uneven grades which contain low spots are very favorable for healthy growth. Moss does not grow in the absence of sunlight. It does not grow in canals with water depth of more than 5 ft. It flourishes best in canals with a silt bottom because the silt furnishes an excellent medium for root development. It obtains its healthiest growth in clear water. Muddy water retards but does not completely stop its growth."

The best results in experiments on control "were obtained with an Acme harrow. This machine was used with such satisfactory results that it is highly recommended for the removal of moss under conditions similar to those on this project."

Control of moss, weeds, and willows on the Minidoka Project, B. DIBBLE and T. W. PARRY (*Reclam. Rec.* [*U. S.*], 8 (*1917*), No. 4, pp. 192, 193, fig. 1).— In experiments on the control of moss and weeds on the project during June "the only method which was found successful in clearing the moss from the larger canals was by cutting with the Ziemsen submarine saw.

"This saw consists of a flexible band of steel with hooked teeth on both edges. It can be obtained in any length, and the weights to hold it to the bottom are adjusted to fit the canal. It is operated at an angle of about 30° with the cross section of the canal, the crew always working upstream. The rate of progress is from 6 to 12 in. at each double stroke and from 0.25 to 1 mile per day can be cut with each saw. The long streamers of moss when cut rise to the surface and float down to the next bridge or check, where they are thrown out by men with pitchforks. . . .

"Where it can be done the cheapest and most effective method of cleaning the canal is to shut the water out entirely and let the ditch dry in the sun. Five to seven days' exposure is necessary ordinarily to kill the moss. This method kills the growth, but does not destroy the bulb. . . .

"During the 1916 season 260 miles of cleaning were done. The total cost of this work was $4,200, making the cost per mile a fraction over $16. The average cost per mile of the different methods is about as follows: Sawing $22, chaining late in the season $8, cutting with scythes in laterals $11, and spring-tooth harrow in laterals $9. . . .

"Willows are cut by men with grubbing hoes and brush scythes. Men equipped with grubbing hoes go ahead for cutting out larger willows, and men with scythes follow and cut the remainder."

Drainage (*Minnesota Sta., Rpt. Crookston Substa., 1910–1916, pp. 20–27, figs. 3*).—This is a brief report on a seven years' test of a tile drainage system at the Northwest Substation at Crookston, Minn. The soil is a dark, sticky clay loam with a heavy compact bluish gray clay subsoil.

"Tile drainage is limited in operation to the period after the frost is out above them. This makes shallow surface ditches necessary for early spring drainage. Observations have emphasized the necessity of supplementing tile drains with surface ditches during the entire growing season in order to secure the best results. . . . The drainage system has been found to be of the greatest service. The two detailed inspections which have been made, in 1912 and 1916, showed the tile in as good condition as in other localities."

By-products of land clearing (*Minnesota Sta., Rpt. Duluth Substa., 1916, pp. 9, 10*).—The receipts per acre for lumber, cordwood, and fence posts were found to be $62.08, with a total cost for clearing up to the stumping stage of $57.39 per acre.

The soil saving dam, W. H. BAKER (*Univ. Missouri Agr. Ext. Serv. Circ. 14 (1917), pp. 4, figs. 3*).—This circular describes and illustrates the construction of dams the purpose of which is to hasten the filling up of washed ditches on farms by preventing the sudden run-off of storm water.

A comparative bacteriological study of the water supply of the city and county of Denver, Colo., W. G. SACKETT (*Colorado Sta. Bul. 225 (1917), pp. 3–14, pls. 4, figs. 2*).—This bulletin describes the water supply system of the city and county of Denver, Colo., and the methods of purification in use and reports comparative bacteriological tests of samples of the purified water made by four different experimenters, of which the author reported for the Colorado Station.

In these tests the results from the four sources were very uniform. Attention is called "to the excellent and safe condition of the filtered and treated waters as shown by the low gelatin and agar counts and by the total absence of *Bacillus coli* from the main supply, complying in all respects with the standard adopted by the Public Health Service of the U. S. Treasury Department."

Data on the prevalence of typhoid in the city and county of Denver and the text of the ordinance protecting the watershed are also given.

The activated sludge process of sewage purification, E. ARDERN (*Jour. Soc. Chem. Indus., 36 (1917), No. 2, pp. 65–68; Surveyor, 51 (1917), No. 1314, pp. 298–300*).—Further studies on the activated sludge process (E. S. R., 34, p. 888), including experiments on the effect of trade effluents on the process, are reported.

It was found "that, contrary to the opinion formed as the result of earlier experiments when working with a strong trade sewage, the maintenance of the activity of the sludge is not dependent on the stage to which nitrification is carried. When dealing with a sewage free from inhibitory trade effluents no appreciable loss of efficiency need be anticipated in this country [England] during the winter months. While the problem of disposal of the sludge remains to be fully developed, it would certainly appear from known data that the cost of dewatering and drying will be more than repaid by the value of the resultant dried sludge."

Sewage disposal for village and rural homes, C. S. NICHOLS (*Iowa Engin. Expt. Sta. Bul. 41 (1916), pp. 29, figs. 10, pls. 3*).—It is the purpose of this bulletin to correct dangerous misconceptions recently published about septic tanks, to point out the general principles covering the proper disposal of household wastes, and to illustrate some practical designs for sewage-disposal plants for construction by the average householder which are the results of experiments at the engineering experiment station.

It is pointed out that "septic tanks are only water-tight cesspools provided with an overflow. . . . A septic tank is only a receiving tank for the sewage in which the solid material is settled out and allowed to remain for 'septic' (i. e., bacterial) action. Experience has shown that certain provisions as to size, shape, and structural details will facilitate the proper operation of such a tank, although septic action will take place in any receptacle which will retain sufficient liquid to cover the solid material and exclude light and air. . . . The liquid escaping from such tanks, whether through a tile overflow from a tight tank or through the porous soil or rock seams of a 'leaching' (not water-tight) cesspool, is extremely foul, and is dangerous to life and health."

The two fundamental principles of sewage disposal are said to embody two distinct, supplementary, and equally necessary treatments, as follows: "(1) Septic action, in a properly arranged, water-tight, covered, masonry tank for removing, retaining, and decomposing the solid material contained in the sewage; and (2) filtration and consequent oxidation and nitrification, by means of a properly arranged and maintained area of porous material through which the effluent from the tank is filtered and subjected to bacterial action.

"In general, it may be said that only approximately one-third of the necessary purification takes place in the tank. The degree of further purification will depend upon the type of filter chosen, its construction, care, and operation."

As a current breaker, it was found in the experiments that an ordinary box 12 by 12 by 12 in., open at the top, bolted to the end of the wall of the tank, and receiving directly the downward discharge of the inlet pipe through an elbow on the end, is effective. An upward sand filter at the outlet was found to minimize the passing on of sediment due to disturbance to the filter bed.

With reference to filters, "experimentation has shown that a bed of $\frac{1}{2}$-in. pebbles, with ample provision for its aeration and the even distribution of sewage in small quantities over its surface will do good work and discharge an effluent comparatively free from offensive materials. With such beds it is necessary that very special precautions be exercised to insure thorough aeration so that the purifying agencies may have a constant supply of oxygen." Intermittent sand filters are also discussed.

"The size of the dosing chamber is made such that the quantity of sewage discharged will flood the bed to a depth of only about $\frac{1}{2}$ in., this being repeated from two to four times during 24 hours."

Diagrammatic illustrations of three plants designed at the station are presented.

Designs for privies, R. MESSER (*Amer. Jour. Pub. Health, 7 (1917), No. 2, pp. 190–196, figs. 5*).—The author briefly describes and illustrates several well-known types of so-called sanitary privies and points out the advantages and disadvantages of each. It is believed "that some modification of the L. R. S. wet closet is the most satisfactory that has yet been suggested, and, furthermore, the additional expense of building is more than offset by permanency and small cost of maintenance. That the problem is far from being satisfactorily solved is clearly evident."

Hydroelectric power.—I, Hydraulic development and equipment; II, Electrical equipment and transmission, L. LYNDON (*New York: McGraw-Hill Book Co., 1916, vols. 1, pp. VII+499, pl. 1, figs. 234; 2, pp. VII+360, figs. 194*).—This work is in two volumes. It is the author's purpose "to produce a work for the guidance of engineers in the practical design of hydroelectric plants which would have the characteristics of accuracy, clearness, and completeness. Scientific discussions of various hypotheses and theories have been omitted except in cases where their incorporation in the text has been essential to the understanding of the subjects treated. . . . A number of new and original formulas appear, for the first time, here. Among these may be mentioned the exact formulas for solid dams and for the magnitude and location of the resultants of forces acting on dams."

Volume 1 contains the following chapters: General conditions, flow in streams, weirs and orifices, power variation and storage, artificial waterways, pipe lines and penstocks, dams, movable crests for dams, headworks, water wheels, speed regulation of water wheels and abnormal penstock pressures, and a set of mathematical tables. Volume 2 contains the following chapters: Alternating current generators, transformers, switchboards, cranes, design and testing of power stations, fires and cables, insulators, pole and tower lines, electric circuits, calculation of transmission lines, deflection and mechanical stresses in transmission lines, line protection and accessories, and substations.

Methods and cost of screening and washing gravel for country road construction, A. A. McKay (*Engin. and Contract.*, 47 (1917), No. 14, pp. 318, 319).—This is a description of methods of obtaining gravel of extra good quality from low-grade gravel in Calhoun County, Mich.

Tests on corrugated metal culverts (*Technol. Expt. Sta. [Univ. Me.] Bul. 2 (1916), No. 1, pp. 15, figs. 2*).—Tests of the physical characteristics, crushing strengths, amount of zinc coating, and acid tests of 13 galvanized corrugated metal pipes are reported, the results being summarized in the following table:

Tests of corrugated metal pipes.

Type.	Weight per foot.	Gage.	Inside diameter.	Character of assembly.	Crushing load per linear foot.	Zinc per square foot.	Acid test.
			Inches.		Pounds.	Ounces.	
Lap joint, riveted........	10.7	51+	11¾	Good....	4,800 good.....	2.10 O. K......	High.
Do.................	9.0	16	11½	Good....	3,870 fair......	2.56 high......	High.
Do.................	9.7	16—	11⅝	Good....	4,470 good.....	1.62 O. K......	Poor.
Do.................	10.7	16—	12¼	Good....	5,940 good [1]....	2.34 high......	Good.
Do.................	7.0	18	11	Poor....	3,280 fair [3]....	1.42 low........	Poor.
Smooth bottom, bolted..	7.6	{ 18— / 16 }	10	Good....	10,920 high.....	{ 1.58 O. K....... / 1.82 O. K.......	Poor. / Fair.
Do.................	8.1	{ 18 / 18+ }	11½	Good....	5,410 good [4]....	{ 1.84 O. K....... / 1.52 O. K.......	Fair. / Good.
Butt joint, clamped......	10.0	16	12	Good....	....	1.72 O. K......	Poor.
Do.................	9.0	16+	10½	Good....	4,750 good.....	1.32 low........	Fair.
Butt joint, wired........	8.1	18+	11½	Poor....	3,120 fair [4]....	1.66 O. K......	Fair.
Do.................		19—				2.00 O. K......	High.
Butt joint, bolted flange.	10.8	{ 15 / 17 }	12⅝	Poor....	1,800 poor [5]....	{ 1.84 O. K....... / 3.66 high.......	Poor. / Fair.
Do.................	10.4	{ 16 / 17 }	12½	Poor....	1,670 poor.....	....	....

[1] Reinforced at one end.
[3] Failed on account of rivets pulling out.
[4] Failed soon because top was merely wired to bottom.
[4] Loading slightly eccentric, hastening failure.
[5] Very scaly.

Public road mileage and revenues in the Central, Mountain, and Pacific States, 1914 (*U. S. Dept. Agr. Bul. 389 (1917), pp. 56+LXXV, fig. 1*).—This report, prepared jointly by the Division of Road Economics of the Office of Public Roads and Rural Engineering and State collaborators, is a compilation showing mileage of improved and unimproved roads, sources and amounts of road revenues, and bonds issued and outstanding in the States of Arizona,

California, Colorado, Idaho, Illinois, Indiana, Iowa, Kansas, Michigan, Minnesota, Missouri, Montana, Nebraska, Nevada, New Mexico, North Dakota, Ohio, Oregon, South Dakota, Utah, Washington, Wisconsin, and Wyoming. A description is also given of the systems of road administration, fiscal management, and other factors affecting road improvement in each State.

Public road mileage and revenues in the United States, 1914: A summary (*U. S. Dept. Agr. Bul. 390 (1917), pp. 11, fig. 1*).—This is a summary, prepared jointly by the Office of Public Roads and Rural Engineering and State collaborators and based upon Bulletins 386, 387, 388, and 389, showing for each State the total and surfaced mileage of public roads at the close of 1914, revenues for roads and bridges in 1914, State and local road and bridge bonds outstanding January 1, 1915, and other related data.

Maine State Highway Commission ([*Augusta, Me.: State, 1915*], pp. 64+20).—This pamphlet gives the texts of the laws of Maine relating to the laying out, construction, and maintenance of highways under the supervision of the State highway commission, including the law of the road. A section is appended on an act to establish a State highway commission and to provide for an issue of State highway bonds.

Building a farm poultry house in northwestern Minnesota, C. E. BROWN (*Minnesota Sta., Rpt. Crookston Substa., 1910–1916, pp. 97–102, figs. 6*).—This is a brief outline of the essentials of poultry-house construction for northern latitudes, including plans showing certain structural details.

Poultry management (*Minnesota Sta. Rpt. 1916, pp. 78, 79*).—A study of the comparative values of glass and muslin screening in poultry-house construction showed that the average temperature was lower for the muslin front than for the glass front at 7 a. m., 1 p. m., and 7 p. m. Observations were made from January 12 to March 31, inclusive.

RURAL ECONOMICS.

Food supply of the United States, D. F. HOUSTON (*U. S. Dept. Agr. Rpts. 1916, pp. 10–13*).—It is pointed out that within the period 1889–1915, inclusive, the population of the Nation has increased 26,000,000, or 33 per cent, but that, notwithstanding this very rapid increase in population, the per capita production of fish, cereals, potatoes, and vegetables has remained approximately the same, or has increased slightly. The per capita production of meat and dairy products, which constituted 37 per cent of the average diet, has not kept pace with the increase in population. The activities of the Department have taken two important directions to increase the supply, that is, by checking and eliminating disease and parasites, and by increasing and improving stock raising by extending the industry where conditions are favorable and by pointing out the way to better breeding and feeding. With all the agencies now available for improving agriculture, there is said to be reason for optimism as to the ability of the Nation, not only to supply itself with food, but increasingly to meet the needs of the world.

Some fundamental considerations affecting the food supply of the United States, T. F. HUNT (*California Sta. Circ. 163 (1917), pp. 3–13, fig. 1*).—On this memorandum prepared for the committee on resources and food supply of the State Council of Defense, the author points out that the Nation can not be starved as long as there is an abundance of corn and cotton. It is not deemed advisable to attempt to control food production by legal or military means, nor is admonition necessary to the farmer to grow materials so long as he understands which are likely, in the long run, to bring him the best returns for his labor. Attention is called to the possible need of financing the farmer and conserving the labor supply.

Mobilization for food production, E. Davenport (*Urbana: Univ. Ill., 1917, pp. 4*).—The author outlines a scheme to provide farm labor to increase the food supply through the enlistment of certain groups of men and boys for food production and their mobilization at training camp farms. He maintains that limiting the food of the people is wholly unnecessary if reasonable attention is given to the business of production and the present farm labor supply is adequately increased.

"Universal military service" for farmers, E. H. Jenkins (*Connecticut Sta. Bul. Inform. 7 (1917), pp. 4*).—The author maintains that the place for the farmer who has tillable land and expert knowledge and machinery to make it produce food is not in the training camp but in the field. He considers it better to fit and plant all of the land which it seems possible to handle, with the present expectation of summer help, at a risk of loss of part of the crop, rather than through fear to plant only that which there is a certainty to be harvested.

The redistribution of the labor now employed in producing war supplies, H. H. Lund (*Amer. Econ. Rev., 7 (1917), No. 1, Sup., pp. 238-250*).—The author describes the methods used and results obtained by the Forward-to-the-Land League in placing city men on farms.

The land problem and rural welfare, P. L. Vogt (*Amer. Econ. Rev., 7 (1917), No. 1, Sup., pp. 91-101*).—"The most hopeful solution appears to be the control of tenantry through the exercise of the taxing power. If the tax were so adjusted as to give a strong inducement to the prospective absentee landlord to dispose of his land to the prospective tenant, much of the speculative holding of land would be quickly eliminated and prices of land to prospective purchasers would much more nearly equal their productive value. The inducement to transfer investment from land to other forms of property would work no great hardship to the owner, because under the rural credit law land mortgage bonds would be available as well as other types of securities the absentee ownership of which does not bring such serious difficulties in business management as does the absentee ownership of land."

Two dimensions of productivity, H. C. Taylor (*Amer. Econ. Rev., 7 (1917), No. 1, Sup., pp. 49-57*).—The author discusses the significance of capacity and efficiency as they relate to productivity, and the problem of land ownership on the part of the farmer. He illustrates his discussions by making comparisons of the results obtained by a study of 51 farms in Barron County, Wis., and the efficiency and capacity of a number of cows where detailed records have been kept.

Agriculture and the farming business, O. H. Benson and G. H. Betts (*Indianapolis: The Bobbs-Merrill Co., 1917, pp. [16]+778, figs. 263*).—This book attempts to bring together in one simple, nontechnical volume, the practical scientific information related directly to the every day problem of the farm and home. Among the topics studied are the organization of farm business, methods of growing and harvesting crops, types of soil, live stock, the farm home and its management, farm machinery, and education for farm life.

Profits in farming on irrigated areas in the Gallatin Valley, Mont., E. L. Currier (*Montana Sta. Bul. 111 (1916), pp. 52, fig. 2*).—This bulletin gives the results of a farm-management survey made during the summer of 1914.

It was found that the average farm labor income on the farms studied was $555. As the amount of capital increased, the labor income increased correspondingly. Farms which had a large percentage of their capital tied up in real estate did not do so well as those that reserved an amount sufficient to adequately equip and operate their farms.

Farmers whose land was valued at $100 an acre made better labor income than those with either higher or lower valuations. Farmers who sold a large percentage of their marketable crops had a better labor income than those who reserved a considerable portion for feed and seed, and farmers receiving a little less than one-third of their receipts from stock have a much better labor income than those who received either more or less from that source. The most favorable crop and stock relation seems to be attained on farms that have stock enough to utilize all cheap feeds and waste products but not so much as to require any considerable proportion of their feed to consist of products that have a high market value.

Tenants in this region receive a somewhat better labor income than do farm owners. The tenants are running a larger business and utilizing their land to better advantage than are those farmers that own their land. Tenants could improve their condditions by securing more and better live stock and owners could improve theirs by increasing the size of their business and using their land to fuller capacity.

The Federal Farm Loan Act, C. W. Thompson (Amer. Econ. Rev., 7 (1917), No. 1, Sup., pp. 115–131).—This paper discusses briefly the causes and steps leading up to the enactment of the Federal Farm Loan Act of 1916, the apparent intent of Congress in providing for two distinct farm mortgage bonding systems, the provisions for safeguarding the proper granting of farm mortgage credit, the means adopted for a form of security that will find ready access to the investment market, and the more important benefits that may be reasonably expected as a result of this system.

Report on the working of the cooperative societies in Bengal for the year 1915–16, J. M. Mitra (Rpt. Work Coop. Socs. Bengal, 1915–16, pp. 9+ 16+XIX).—This report continues the data previously noted (E. S. R., 36, p. 593), by adding data for a later year.

Agriculture in Oxfordshire, J. Orr (Oxford, England: The Clarendon Press, 1916, pp. XII+239, pls. 29, figs. 11).—The author describes the types of farming carried on in the different regions in Oxfordshire, and discusses the administration of the land, the management of farm labor, soils, crops, and live stock. The book contains a chapter on soils by C. G. T. Morison.

Crop condition and harvest field needs (Nebr. Dept. Labor Bul. 33 (1916), pp. 28, fig. 1).—This report contains data for the various counties in Nebraska, showing the acreage, average yield, total production of important crops, and demand for extra labor and wages during the previous year.

[Agricultural statistics of British Guiana], J. B. Harrison (Rpt. Dept. Sci. and Agr. Brit. Guiana, 1915, Apr.–Dec., pp. 22–24).—This report continues the data previously noted (E. S. R., 35, p. 795), adding statistics for a later year.

Return of prices of crops, live stock, and other Irish agricultural products (Dept. Agr. and Tech. Instr. Ireland, Agr. Statis. 1915, pp. 38, pls. 16, figs. 1).—This report adds to that previously noted (E. S. R., 33, p. 894) data for 1915.

Agricultural statistics of Finland for 1910 (Finland Off. Statis., III, No. 9, pt. 1 (1916), pp. VI+327).—This report contains data showing by minor subdivisions the area cultivated and not cultivated, the area devoted to different agricultural purposes and to individual crops and pastures, the number of farms by sizes and tenure, and the distribution of land among different agricultural uses on farms by sizes, together with data relating to agricultural machinery.

Prices of cattle and meat in Russia, A. ÎÀ. KOBENBLIT (*Kharkov. Obshch. Selsk. Khoz., Oblast. Kom. Peresmotru Russ.-Germ. Torg, Dogov., No. 8 (1915), pp. 84*).—This report gives the monthly and yearly prices for 1903–1912 at Moscow and Petrograd for various classes of meat and cattle.

Live stock statistics [of Egypt, Spain, Morocco and Tunis] (*Internat. Inst. Agr. Rome, Internat. Crop Rpt. and Agr. Statis., 8 (1917), No. 3, pp. 183–185*).— These pages give the number of live stock, by classes, for 1916, with comparative data for earlier years.

AGRICULTURAL EDUCATION.

State higher educational institutions of Iowa (*U. S. Bur. Ed. Bul. 19 (1916), pp. 223, figs. 45*).—This is a report of a survey of the State higher educational institutions of Iowa, made under the direction of the U. S. Commissioner of Education for the Iowa State Board of Education. Among the findings of the survey committee summarized in recommendations are the following:

The adoption of the principle of "major and service lines of work" at the three State institutions; the creation of an annual conference consisting of members of faculties of the institutions and the State board of education, to adjust questions of overlapping not automatically determined by the establishment of major lines for each institution; the readjustment of the work in engineering at the State University of Iowa and the Iowa State College of Agriculture and Mechanic Arts, through a vertical division of work, assigning some branches of engineering to one institution and some to the other; the encouragement of the development of graduate work at the State university and agricultural college along the major lines of the institutions; the exercise of greater care by the graduate division of the agricultural college in admitting students from other institutions to graduate standing; the creation of a standing committee on graduate work to consist of members of the State board of education and of the institutions giving graduate work, the latter to be elected by the graduate faculties; the strict enforcement by the State board of education of the principle that departments of liberal arts and sciences at the agricultural college shall be simply service departments, especially the revision of the work offered in the departments of economic science, geology, physics, and mathematics, to conform to this principle; the abandonment of courses in chemistry at the agricultural college which neither contribute to the major lines of that institution nor reinforce the work of the experiment stations; the revision of the requirements for the degree of bachelor of science in the division of industrial science to render it impossible to secure the degree except on completion of industrial and professional courses (in contradistinction to liberal arts courses) equal in amount to those required in technical curricula; the strict application of the principle of the major lines of work to the development of the extension enterprises of the three State institutions; the establishment of a conference on extension work, composed of members of the board of education and extension officers of the three institutions, to discuss projects; the imposition of no external limitations upon facilities offered at the three institutions for giving work for the training of teachers in home economics, agriculture, and manual training until the present force of teachers in the State schools is equipped to meet the obligations imposed by the State law; but thereafter the delimitation of work in psychology and education at the agricultural college to the amount requisite to meet the requirements of the first-class State certificate; the development at the university of home economics as a service department, the establishment of special lines of work for the training of hospital dietitians, and the avoidance of courses that duplicate the work at the agricultural college in the preparation of high school teachers; the provision in the near future at the agricultural college of enlarged accommodations for the department of home economics, of opportunities for preparation in institutional and cafeterial management, and of special courses for the preparation of trade and industrial school teachers; the improvement of the accommodations provided for work in home economics at the State Teachers College, and the organization of the department under a single head; the abandonment by the agricultural college of noncollegiate work except for limited short winter, or summer courses for special groups of students and the establishment of corresponding work in selected high schools throughout the State under the direction of the agricultural college; the general reduction of the number of one and two hour courses, especially in elementary work and in the first half of the college year, and of the number of small classes of 10 or under; and the inclusion of the president of the agricultural college in the membership of the board of educational examiners and the inclusion of the presidents of the State higher institutions ex officio in the membership of the State board of education, without power to vote.

Agricultural education in the high schools and common schools of the State, L. S. HAWKINS (*N. Y. Dept. Agr. Bul. 81 (1916), pp. 1844–1853, pls. 11*).—The author briefly explains how the State of New York encourages agricultural instruction in its schools and gives a general description of the agricultural work, particularly the home project work, being done in the 61 high schools and 3 consolidated rural schools that have taken advantage of State aid for agricultural instruction.

Report of the director of elementary agricultural education for the Province of British Columbia, 1914–15, J. W. GIBSON (*Ann. Rpt. Pub. Schools Brit. Columbia, 44 (1914–15), pp. A74–A85, pls. 4*).—This is the first annual report on elementary agricultural education in the Province of British Columbia. It deals with the author's view of agricultural education in the schools, summer schools in rural science for public and high school teachers, including outlines of courses, and with the organization of the first class in high-school agriculture and of an extension class in agriculture in connection therewith for young men not attending school.

Report of the director of elementary agricultural education for the Province of British Columbia, 1915–16, J. W. GIBSON (*Ann. Rpt. Pub. Schools Brit. Columbia, 45 (1915–16), pp. A54–A71, pls. 10*).—This is a report on the history and development of agricultural teaching in British Columbia, progress of the school home gardening movement under the direction of the education department, school-ground improvement, agricultural instruction in high schools with district supervision, including an outline of the two-year course of study by months, and extension high school classes in agriculture for young men and boys over 15 years of age who are not in attendance at school. Plans of school gardens are included.

In 1915, of 100 schools with gardens, 80 qualified for the department grant. In these 80 schools the gardening work was conducted by 115 teachers with approximately 2,500 children. The total grant to the school boards on account of school garden expenditures in 1915 was $4,052.11 and to teachers, as bonus grants, $1,765.00. In 1916, 145 schools with gardens and 6,563 pupils took part in the work.

Special grants, regulations, and organization (*Dept. Ed. Alberta, Tech. Ed. Bul. 1, pp. 6*).—This bulletin contains the regulations pertaining to the payment of grants for instruction in science, agriculture, and school gardening,

manual training, household science and art, etc., and to the training and
certification of teachers of these subjects.

For instruction in science, agriculture, and school gardening in rural and
village school districts an annual grant is made to the school board equal to
50 per cent of its expenditure for approved improvements and maintenance
of school gardens, and not exceeding $15 for approved equipment, with an
annual grant of $25 to the teacher. In any school district including a town
or city in which fewer than 30 teachers are employed in instruction in science,
agriculture, and related school gardening in grades 7 to 11, inclusive, or all
of such grades as may be represented in such schools, a similar grant of 50
per cent is made to the board, a maximum grant of $75 for equipment, and
$50 to the teacher for full-time service. In a similar district in which at
least 30 teachers are employed in the agricultural course of grade 11 the
annual grant to the board is 50 per cent of its expenditure on approved improvements and maintenance of the necessary garden and experimental plats
and for equipment, $75.

The general direction of agricultural instruction, T. AMADEO (*Min. Agr.
Argentina, Mem. Cong. Nac., 1914. pp. 91–101*).—This is a report on the object,
work, equipment, and improvements of the agricultural schools and on extension activities in Argentina in 1914.

Agricultural and rural extension schools in Ireland, A. C. MONAHAN (*U. S.
Bur. Ed. Bul. 41 (1916), pp. 38, pls. 10*).—This bulletin contains a brief account of the administration of public education in Ireland through the Commissioners of National Education, the Intermediate Board of Commissioners, and
the Department of Agriculture and Technical Instruction for Ireland, together
with information concerning the organization of the department and a brief
outline of its activities. Descriptions of the principal types of agricultural
schools are included.

In progression from the lower to the higher, there are for men three agricultural station schools or farm apprenticeship institutions and three other
agricultural schools, the Albert Agricultural College, which is a farm-practice
school giving a one-year course, and the Royal College of Science, with a four-
year course, similar to the standard State colleges of agriculture in this country.
For women there are nine rural schools of domestic science, the Munster Institute, the Ulster Dairy Institute, the Training School for Lace Teachers, and the
Irish Training School of Domestic Economy for the training of teachers.
Itinerant instruction in agriculture, through county instructors or agricultural
agents, comprises schemes of instruction in poultry keeping and butter making,
horticulture and bee keeping, and general instruction in farming in congested
districts. There are also rural extension schools or winter classes in agriculture, and, for girls, in poultry keeping and butter making; and, through the
division of technical instruction, rural extension schools in household arts, home
industries, and farm carpentry.

Agricultural education and live stock improvement in Wales, 1913–1915,
C. B. JONES (*Bd. Agr. and Fisheries [London], Rpt. Agr. Comr. Wales, 1913–
1915, pp. 39*).—This is the report of the agricultural commissioner for Wales
for the years 1912–13 to 1914–15. It deals mainly with the progress made in
agricultural education, both in regard to the agricultural departments of the
colleges and the farm institute scheme in the counties, and live-stock improvement. A summary of the report has been previously noted (E. S. R., 36, p. 495).

Report on the agricultural and housekeeping schools for 1914–15 (*Aarsber. Offentl. Foranst. Landbr. Fremme, 1915, II, pp. VIII+339*).—Detailed
reports are given on the faculty, students, equipment, instruction, farm work,

and receipts and expenditures of the agricultural and housekeeping schools in Norway.

Report of the Department of Agriculture [of Finland] for 1914 (*Landtbr. Styr. Meddel. [Finland], No. 105 (1914), pp. 165*).—This is a comprehensive report on the activities of the department, through its education and research institutions, societies, and experts, for the advancement of Finnish agriculture.

Agricultural yearbook for 1917, edited by H. C. LARSEN (*Landökonom. Aarbog [Copenhagen], 18 (1917), pp. 135*).—This is the annual directory of public institutions and associations for the advancement of Danish agriculture in its various branches. A list of periodicals published in Denmark is appended.

Bulletin relating to instruction in agriculture and gardening in elementary schools (*Edmonton, Alberta: Dept. Ed., pp. 125, pl. 1, figs. 30*).—This bulletin contains a schedule of grants to the school board and teacher for instruction in science, agriculture, and school gardening, an outline of the course in agriculture and gardening required in the seventh and eighth grades, and detailed suggestions to teachers regarding the method of teaching the subjects of soils and plants, including textbook work, practical exercises, and school and home gardening. Nature study and elementary gardening are required in grades 1 to 6, inclusive, in all schools, and agriculture is an examination subject in grade 11.

Course in agriculture for grade XI (*Edmonton, Alberta: Dept. Ed., 1915, pp. 9*).—This is an outline of a course in agriculture for grade 11 of the Alberta high schools, on which the 1916 examination was based.

Instructions to teachers and school boards with reference to school and home gardening (*Brit. Columbia Dept. Ed. Circ. 4 (rev. and enl.) (1917), pp. 15*).—This circular contains instructions to teachers and school boards with reference to school and home-garden plans; projects involving experimental work in the variety and condition of seed, prevention of disease, selection, methods of seeding and cultivation, and fertilizers; supplementary home projects where pupils find it difficult or impossible to have home gardens; and competitions and care of school gardens during the summer holidays. A statement concerning grants to school boards toward approved school gardens and home gardening or related home projects, as well as teachers' bonus grants, is included.

Home and school gardening, J. E. MCLARTY ET AL. (*Agr. Gaz. Canada, 4 (1917), No. 3, pp. 220–231, figs. 3*).—This is a series of articles on the relative educational value of school and home gardens, based on the experience with these two forms of gardens of the officials in charge of this work in Prince Edward Island, Nova Scotia, New Brunswick, Quebec, Ontario, Manitoba, Saskatchewan, Alberta, and British Columbia.

In Prince Edward Island it is agreed that under ideal conditions the location of the garden at the school is the more satisfactory. However, the Department of Education is encouraging home gardens at least until a system of consolidated schools is established. In Nova Scotia school gardens are a failure, but home gardens are popular. In New Brunswick, Quebec, southern Saskatchewan, and Alberta it is found that class-room instruction, the observation, demonstration and investigation of the school garden (as the laboratory), and the home garden or project (the practical field) which is the natural outgrowth of these two features, are all necessary in an adequate plan for effective instruction in practical agriculture. In northern Saskatchewan the relative value of the two kinds of gardens has not been demonstrated, but the director of school agriculture is of the opinion that for the earlier grades, school gardening, and for the higher grades, a combination of school and home gardens with the latter predominating in the final year, would appear almost ideal. In British Columbia the school garden is found to have important advantages over the home garden, but home gardening is deemed best suited to pupils of grades 7 and 8 or form 4. In other words, school gardening, which is more the broadly educational in its bearing, is the logical antecedent of home gardening, which is rather narrower in its scope and which as a rule makes larger demands upon the individual pupil.

Attention is called to the danger becoming apparent in Canada of regarding home gardening and related agricultural home projects as a preparation upon the part of pupils for the holding of a large and sensational school fair, the success of which is too apt to be estimated in the number of entries and the size of the crowd, whereas it should be only an incident in the year's work to arouse an interest among the people and the children themselves. Scores to be taken into consideration in awarding prizes at school fairs to overcome the tendency of making the winning of distinction the chief incentive of the work are also discussed.

School and home gardening for elementary schools in Oregon, M. O. EVANS, JR. (*Oreg. Agr. Col. Bul. 176, pp. 23, figs. 22*).—The author offers suggestions on the organization and cultivation of school and home gardens for elementary schools in Oregon.

Educative and economic possibilities of school-directed home gardening in Richmond, Ind., J. L. RANDALL (*U. S. Bur. Ed. Bul. 6 (1917), pp. 25, pls. 4*).—This bulletin contains a report of a study, made in cooperation with the Indiana vocational education survey, of the possibilities of home gardening directed by the public schools in the city of Richmond, Ind.

It is recommended that the Board of Education of Richmond establish a complete department of home gardening under the direction of the public schools within the next three years. The aims should be to train many people to produce their own vegetables and small fruit foods, and to carry out other avocational home projects which may have economic value to the people of the city. A vocational agricultural course should be given for high school students from the country and for those of the city who wish to take up farming as a life work. The course should be given by a teacher with theoretical and practical training in agriculture, who should be employed for twelve months and should also be the general home garden supervisor, giving one-half of his time to the high school work.

Supervised home project work, Z. M. SMITH (*Dept. Pub. Instr. [Ind.], Ed. Pubs., Bul. 19 (1917), pp. 44, figs. 24*).—This is a report on the project work in Indiana during the past year, including the larger purpose of this work, the income and profit, how the results were accomplished, and the value of close supervision and of county agents as supervisors. Suggestions are offered on organization for home project work and school credit for such work. A suggested list of projects, outlines of projects, a basis of awards for use in annual exhibit contests, and a list of references to literature for use in home project and club work are included.

Supplementary lessons in West Virginia agriculture (*Morgantown: W. Va. Univ. [1916, pp. 157, figs. 35]*).—This is a bound collection of all the boys' corn, potato, pig, and poultry club, and girls' tomato, strawberry, and raspberry club instruction sheets, accompanied by directions to teachers on the use of the sheets in making the instruction in agriculture in the rural schools of the State more practical and concrete. Suggestions for correlations with other school subjects are included.

Illustrated lecture on sweet potatoes: Culture and storage, H. M. CONOLLY (*U. S. Dept. Agr., States Relat. Serv. Syllabus 26 (1917), pp. 22*).—This syllabus deals with the raising of sweet potatoes, including a discussion of soils, rotations, propagation of plants, manures and fertilizers, preparation of the soil, planting, harvesting, storage, diseases, varieties, marketing, cost of production, and sweet potatoes as a feed for live stock. A list of 51 lantern slides to illustrate the syllabus is included.

Illustrated lecture on the farm vegetable garden, H. C. THOMPSON and H. M. CONOLLY (*U. S. Dept. Agr., States Relat. Serv. Syllabus 27 (1917), pp. 15*).—In this syllabus, prepared in cooperation with the Bureau of Plant Industry, the authors briefly discuss reasons for establishing a vegetable garden, its location, soil and plan, seed, methods of planting, establishing the garden, cultivation, irrigation, control of insects and diseases, special practices, etc. A list of 50 lantern slides to illustrate the syllabus is appended.

Agricultural arithmetic, G. C. SHUTTS and W. W. WEIR (*St. Paul, Minn.: Webb Publishing Co., 1916, pp. 255+10, figs. 54*).—Part 1 of this book is devoted to a review of the processes of arithmetic. Part 2 is an application of arithmetic to farm experiences, including problems dealing with farm crops and animals, feeds and feeding, the dairy, the soil, fertilizers, farm management and measurements, orchard and garden, household economy and human feeding, etc.

Illustrative fair exhibits, F. M. LUTTS (*Ohio Sta. [Pub.], 1917, Feb., pp. 27, figs. 27*).—This gives the earlier history of the illustrative fair exhibits of the Ohio Station; brief descriptions of the State fair exhibit and of the county fair exhibits, the latter representing nine station departments; information with reference to exhibit assignments, publicity, memorandum of understanding between the station and fair association, and the bill of material; and a summary of fair exhibit work in 1916.

MISCELLANEOUS.

Annual Reports of the Department of Agriculture, 1916 (*U. S. Dept. Agr. Rpts. 1916, pp. VI+451*).—This contains the reports of the Secretary and heads of bureaus and other administrative officers. The various reports are also issued as separates. Sections dealing with roundworms of sheep and the food supply of the United States are abstracted on pages 277 and 289 of this issue.

Twenty-ninth Annual Report of Illinois Station, 1916 (*Illinois Sta. Rpt. 1916, pp. 18*).—This contains the organization list, a financial statement for the fiscal year ended June 30, 1916, brief notes as to the principal lines of work, a note commemorative of the work of the late Dr. T. J. Burrill, and a list of the publications of the year.

Twenty-fourth Annual Report of Minnesota Station, 1916 (*Minnesota Sta. Rpt. 1916, pp. 83*).—This contains the organization list, a financial statement for the Federal funds for the fiscal year ended June 30, 1916, and for the State funds for the fiscal year ended July 31, 1916, and a report of the director summarizing the work of the station and its substations. The experimental work recorded is for the most part abstracted elsewhere in this issue.

Report of the superintendent, Northwest Experiment Station, 1910–1916 (*Minnesota Sta., Rpt. Crookston Substa., 1910–1916, pp. 102, pl. 1, figs. 14*).—This contains the organization list and a report of the superintendent of the substation from 1911 to 1916, including several special articles by members of the staff. The experimental work reported is for the most part abstracted elsewhere in this issue.

Reports of **Northeast Demonstration Farm and Experiment Station, Duluth, 1915 and 1916** (*Minnesota Sta., Rpts. Duluth Substa., 1915, pp. 11, fig. 1; 1916, pp. 12*).—These are reports of the work of the respective years. The experimental work reported is for the most part abstracted elsewhere in this issue.

Report of **West Central substation, Morris, 1915** (*Minnesota Sta., Rpt. Morris Substa., 1915, pp. 15, figs. 3*).—This is a report of the work of the year. The experimental work with field crops is abstracted on page 229 of this issue.

Twenty-ninth Annual Report of New York Cornell Station, 1916 (*New York Cornell Sta. Rpt. 1916, pp. LXXXVIII+832, pls. 41, figs. 145*).—This contains the organization list, reports of the director of the station and heads of departments, and reprints of Bulletins 362–377 and Circular 32, previously noted.

Report of the Porto Rico Insular Station, 1915–16 (*Rpt. Bd. Comrs. Agr. P. R., 5 (1915–16), pp. 101, pl. 1, figs. 3*).—This contains the organization list, a report by the director for the fiscal year 1915–16, and departmental reports, the experimental features of which are for the most part abstracted elsewhere in this issue. Analyses of soils are also included.

Monthly Bulletin of the Ohio Experiment Station (*Mo. Bul. Ohio Sta., 2 (1917), No. 4, pp. 103–137, figs. 15*).—This contains several articles abstracted elsewhere in this issue, together with the following: Post Timbers, by J. J. Crumley, an abstract of Bulletin 219 (E. S. R., 24, p. 644); Soil Bacteria, by E. R. Allen; and notes.

NOTES.

Alabama Canebrake Station.—A canning demonstration was held at the station July 20, in cooperation with the State extension forces. The total attendance for the day was about two hundred.

Iowa College and Station.—George M. Turpin, head of the poultry section, resigned June 30 to engage in practical poultry work, and has been succeeded by H. A. Bittenbender, formerly in extension work at the college.

Kansas Station.—A cooperative study to determine the value of sweet clover as a pasture crop for dairy cows has been begun by the departments of agronomy and dairy husbandry.

S. J. Pearce, a 1917 graduate of the University of Nebraska, began work July 1 at Herington as field dairy bacteriologist for the station in connection with a study in cream grading in progress at that point, in cooperation with the Dairy Division of the U. S. Department of Agriculture. M. W. Kirkpatrick, formerly superintendent of the Dodge City substation, has been appointed superintendent of the Tribune substation to succeed C. E. Cassel, resigned.

Minnesota University.—The university stock barn erected in 1886 was entirely destroyed by fire July 18, causing an estimated loss of about $40,000. All live stock was saved, but a considerable amount of machinery and supplies was consumed. The cause is thought to have been a spark from a motor in the feed-grinding room.

Montana Station.—Ray S. Jones, assistant chemist, resigned May 1 to join the U. S. Officers Reserve Corps. He has been granted leave of absence until the end of the war.

Cornell University.—Dr. V. A. Moore, director of the New York State Veterinary College, has been appointed major in the Veterinary Corps of the U. S. Army.

New York State Station.—Substantial progress is being made in the construction of the new $100,000 administration building, auditorium, and museum, although it is regarded as doubtful whether it will be ready for occupancy before the summer of 1918.

Irving Rouse of Rochester and C. Fred Boshart of Lowville have been appointed to the board of control, vice Thomas Newbold and William H. Manning. J. F. Barker, agronomist, has resigned to accept a position in charge of extension work in agronomy at the Ohio State University, and will be succeeded by R. C. Collison, associate chemist, on September 1. Mr. Collison has also been granted a year's leave of absence for study, beginning with the next college year. W. W. Baer, assistant chemist, has entered the U. S. Naval Service.

Oregon College and Station.—A horticultural products building is being erected to aid in solving some of the many problems of food preservation confronting the department of horticulture. Many types of drying and canning equipment will be installed, including a modern evaporator of commercial capacity.

Dean A. B. Cordley has been elected chairman of the State Lime Board, which is to obtain lime for the use of farmers.

Porto Rico Federal Station.—The Porto Rico legislature, at its last session, appropriated $1,000,000 for aid in the growing of food crops and an extensive campaign is under way. About forty rural teachers are actively engaged in all sections of the island and a great many seeds of economic crops have been bought and distributed. Cane planters have been induced to plant or to allow their laborers to grow beans in the young cane, so that whereas last year over $800,000 worth of beans was imported, beans have already been produced for export.

Rhode Island Station.—Howard A. Johns, a 1917 graduate of the Pennsylvania College, has been appointed assistant in chemistry beginning July 1.

South Carolina College and Station.—The animal husbandry and dairying division has been separated into divisions of dairying and animal husbandry. R. L. Shields continues as chief of the animal husbandry division and W. W. Fitzpatrick, dairy expert in extension work, has been appointed chief of the division of dairying.

G. M. Armstrong has been appointed instructor in botany in the college and assistant in the station. A new position of research assistant has been established in the division of horticulture.

Tennessee University.—H. D. Tate has been succeeded by W. A. Schoenfeld as assistant director of the division of extension, and he in turn by C. E. Brehm as specialist in marketing.

Utah College and Station.—Plans have been completed for the new dairy building and are under way for some new feeding sheds for experimental work with steers. Dr. C. E. Davis has resigned as assistant professor of chemistry to accept a position as research chemist with a commercial firm.

Virginia College and Station.—E. R. Hodgson, associate agronomist, has resigned to become specialist in agronomy in the extension division and has been succeeded by T. K. Wolfe, the assistant agronomist. G. S. Ralston has been appointed field horticulturist, to have charge of the several experimental orchards in the State.

Wyoming University and Station.—W. A. Albrecht, of the Missouri University and Station, has been appointed associate agronomist and acting head of the department of agronomy, beginning July 1.

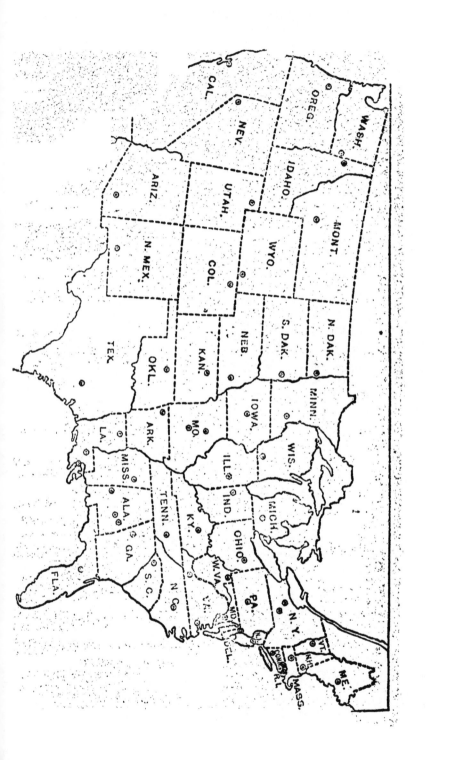

U. S. DEPARTMENT OF AGRICULTURE

STATES RELATIONS SERVICE

A. C. TRUE, DIRECTOR

Vol. 37   SEPTEMBER, 1917   No. 4

EXPERIMENT
STATION
RECORD

WASHINGTON
GOVERNMENT PRINTING OFFICE
1917

U. S. DEPARTMENT OF AGRICULTURE.

Scientific Bureaus.

WEATHER BUREAU—C. F. Marvin, *Chief.*
BUREAU OF ANIMAL INDUSTRY—A. D. Melvin, *Chief.*
BUREAU OF PLANT INDUSTRY—W. A. Taylor, *Chief.*
FOREST SERVICE—H. S. Graves, *Forester.*
BUREAU OF SOILS—Milton Whitney, *Chief.*
BUREAU OF CHEMISTRY—C. L. Alsberg, *Chief.*
BUREAU OF CROP ESTIMATES—L. M. Estabrook, *Statistician.*
BUREAU OF ENTOMOLOGY—L. O. Howard, *Entomologist.*
BUREAU OF BIOLOGICAL SURVEY—E. W. Nelson, *Chief.*
OFFICE OF PUBLIC ROADS AND RURAL ENGINEERING—L. W. Page, *Director.*
BUREAU OF MARKETS—C. J. Brand, *Chief.*

———

STATES RELATIONS SERVICE—A. C. True, *Director.*
OFFICE OF EXPERIMENT STATIONS—E. W. Allen, *Chief.*

———

THE AGRICULTURAL EXPERIMENT STATIONS.

ALABAMA—
College Station: *Auburn;* J. F. Duggar.[1]
Canebrake Station: *Uniontown;* F. R. Curtis.[1]
Tuskegee Station: *Tuskegee Institute;* G. W. Carver.[1]
ALASKA—*Sitka:* C. C. Georgeson.[2]
ARIZONA—*Tucson:* R. H. Forbes.[1]
ARKANSAS—*Fayetteville:* M. Nelson.[1]
CALIFORNIA—*Berkeley:* T. F. Hunt.[1]
COLORADO—*Fort Collins:* C. P. Gillette.[1]
CONNECTICUT—
State Station: *New Haven;*
Storrs Station: *Storrs;* } E. H. Jenkins.[1]
DELAWARE—*Newark:* H. Hayward.[1]
FLORIDA—*Gainesville:* P. H. Rolfs.[1]
GEORGIA—*Experiment:* J. D. Price.[1]
GUAM—*Island of Guam:* C. W. Edwards.[2]
HAWAII—
Federal Station: *Honolulu;* J. M. Westgate.[2]
Sugar Planters' Station: *Honolulu;* H. P. Agee.
IDAHO—*Moscow:* J. S. Jones.[1]
ILLINOIS—*Urbana:* E. Davenport.[1]
INDIANA—*La Fayette:* C. G. Woodbury.[1]
IOWA—*Ames:* C. F. Curtiss.[1]
KANSAS—*Manhattan:* W. M. Jardine.[1]
KENTUCKY—*Lexington:* A. M. Peter.[4]
LOUISIANA—
State Station: *Baton Rouge;*
Sugar Station: *Audubon Park,* } W. R. Dodson.[1]
New Orleans;
North La. Station: *Calhoun;*
MAINE—*Orono:* C. D. Woods.[1]
MARYLAND—*College Park:* H. J. Patterson.[1]
MASSACHUSETTS—*Amherst:* W. P. Brooks.[1]
MICHIGAN—*East Lansing:* R. S. Shaw.[1]
MINNESOTA—*University Farm, St. Paul:* R. W. Thatcher.[1]
MISSISSIPPI—*Agricultural College:* E. R. Lloyd.[1]

MISSOURI—
College Station: *Columbia;* F. B. Mumford.[1]
Fruit Station: *Mountain Grove;* Paul Evans.[1]
MONTANA—*Bozeman:* F. B. Linfield.[1]
NEBRASKA—*Lincoln:* E. A. Burnett.[1]
NEVADA—*Reno:* S. B. Doten.[1]
NEW HAMPSHIRE—*Durham:* J. C. Kendall.[1]
NEW JERSEY—*New Brunswick:* J. G. Lipman.[1]
NEW MEXICO—*State College:* Fabian Garcia.[1]
NEW YORK—
State Station: *Geneva;* W. H. Jordan.[1]
Cornell Station: *Ithaca;* A. R. Mann.[1]
NORTH CAROLINA—
College Station: *West Raleigh;*
State Station: *Raleigh;* } B. W. Kilgore.[1]
NORTH DAKOTA—*Agricultural College:* T. P. Cooper.[1]
OHIO—*Wooster:* C. E. Thorne.[1]
OKLAHOMA—*Stillwater:* W. L. Carlyle.[1]
OREGON—*Corvallis:* A. B. Cordley.[1]
PENNSYLVANIA—
State College: R. L. Watts.[1]
State College: Institute of Animal Nutrition; H. P. Armsby.[1]
PORTO RICO—*Mayaguez;* D. W. May.[3]
RHODE ISLAND—*Kingston:* B. L. Hartwell.[1]
SOUTH CAROLINA—*Clemson College:* H. W. Barre.[1]
SOUTH DAKOTA—*Brookings:* J. W. Wilson.[1]
TENNESSEE—*Knoxville:* H. A. Morgan.[1]
TEXAS—*College Station:* B. Youngblood.[1]
UTAH—*Logan:* F. S. Harris.[1]
VERMONT—*Burlington:* J. L. Hills.[1]
VIRGINIA—
Blacksburg: A. W. Drinkard, jr.[1]
Norfolk: Truck Station; T. C. Johnson.[3]
WASHINGTON—*Pullman:* Geo. Severance.[4]
WEST VIRGINIA—*Morgantown:* J. L. Coulter.[1]
WISCONSIN—*Madison:* H. L. Russell.[1]
WYOMING—*Laramie:* H. G. Knight.[1]

———

[1] Director. [2] Agronomist in charge. [3] Animal husbandman in charge. [4] Acting director.

EXPERIMENT STATION RECORD.

Editor: E. W. ALLEN, PH. D., *Chief, Office of Experiment Stations.*
Assistant Editor: H. L. KNIGHT.

EDITORIAL DEPARTMENTS.

Agricultural Chemistry and Agrotechny—E. H. NOLLAU.

Meteorology, Soils, and Fertilizers {W. H. BEAL.
R. W. TRULLINGER,

Agricultural Botany, Bacteriology, and Plant Pathology {W. H. EVANS, Ph. D.
W. E. BOYD.

Field Crops {J. I. SCHULTE.
J. D. LUCKETT.

Horticulture and Forestry—E. J. GLASSON.

Economic Zoology and Entomology—W. A. HOOKER, D. V. M.

Foods and Human Nutrition {C. F. LANGWORTHY, Ph. D., D. Sc.
H. L. LANG.

Zootechny, Dairying, and Dairy Farming {————
M. D. MOORE.

Veterinary Medicine {W. A. HOOKER.
E. H. NOLLAU.

Rural Engineering—R. W. TRULLINGER.

Rural Economics—E. MERRITT.

Agricultural Education {C. H. LANE.
M. T. SPETHMANN.

Indexes—M. D. MOORE.

CONTENTS OF VOL. 37, NO. 4.

	Page.
Editorial notes:	
The Federal Food Production Act	301
Recent work in agricultural science	308
Notes	397

SUBJECT LISTS OF ABSTRACTS.

AGRICULTURAL CHEMISTRY—AGROTECHNY.

Method for separation of "fat-soluble A" from butter fat, McCollum et al	308
Antineuritic substances from egg yolk, Steenbock	308
Adenin and guanin in cows' milk, Voegtlin and Sherwin	308
Calcium and phosphorus in blood of lactating cows, Meigs and Blatherwick	308
The distribution of esterases in the animal body, Porter	308
The nonspecificity of animal and vegetable reductase, Bach	309
The composition of adipocere, Ruttan and Marshall	309
The isolation of stachydrin from alfalfa hay, Steenbock	309
The pectic substances of plants, Schryver and Haynes	309
The acids of fruit wines, Baragiola	310
Tartaric acid contents of grape musts and young wines, Baragiola and Schuppli	310
Investigations on the camphors of Mauritius	310
Standard methods of chemical analysis, edited by Scott	310
Report of Swiss Agricultural Chemical Institute at Bern for 1915, Liechti	311
Standard methods for the examination of water and sewage	311
Applications of a new reagent for separation of ammonia, I, Folin and Bell	311
Chemical changes in shucked oysters under refrigeration, Clark and Almy	311

Page.

Determination of peanut oil in mixtures with olive oil, Biazzo and Vigdorcik.. 312
Determination of colza oil in mixtures with olive oil, Biazzo and Vigdorcik... 312
Determination of theobromin and caffein in cocoa and chocolate, Savini...... 312
Detection of lime used as a neutralizer in dairy products, Wichmann......... 313
The determination of sugar in gummy substances, Savini.................... 313
Quantitative determination of minute amounts of sugar by α-naphthol, Blake.. 313
Utilization of cull citrus fruits in Florida, McDermott.................... 313
Action of ultraviolet rays on alcoholic fermentation, de Fazi.................. 314
Value of household remedies for vinegar disease in wine, Baragiloa and Braun. 314

METEOROLOGY.

Climatological data for the United States by sections........................ 314
Meteorological observations, Stevens....................................... 314
Meteorological summary, Brown.. 314
Relative humidities and vapor pressures over the United States, Day......... 314
Average rainfall, May and June... 315
A safe method proposed for estimating minimum rainfall, Wells.............. 315
Effect of a late spring upon crop yields...................................... 316
Safe dates for planting corn.. 316
Weather and cotton.. 316
Safe date for planting potatoes... 317

SOIL—FERTILIZERS.

Special crop soils [of New York], Fippin..................................... 317
Peat moors in the coast regions of southern German East Africa, Janensch..... 317
Recent studies on nitrification in soils, Sarachaga........................... 318
Fixation of ammonia in soils, McBeth....................................... 318
Relation of soil nitrogen to nutrition of citrus plants, McBeth................. 318
Tests on the disinfection of soil, Miége..................................... 319
Chemical studies of legumes as green manures in Hawaii, Thompson.......... 320
Tests of manure, fertilizer, and crimson clover for vegetable crops, White..... 320
Experiments with nitrogenous fertilizers, Îakushkin (Jakouchkine)............ 321
Preparation of dried blood in the army slaughterhouses, Ranc................. 321
The atmospheric nitrogen industry, Tobiansky D'Altoff...................... 321
The displacement of potash by ammonium nitrate, Zavaritskiĭ (Zavaritzki).... 321
Potash fertilizer salts, van Stolk... 322
Potash: Economic sources in South Australia, Winterbottom................. 322
Pumping potash from Nebraska lakes, Crawford............................. 322
Artificial zeolite as a source of potash for plants, Smirnov................... 322
Remarks and technical tests on the preparation of superphosphates, Aita..... 322
The composition of some Thomas meals, van Raaij.......................... 323
Assimilation of phosphoric acid from phosphorites by cereals, Îakushkin....... 323
Assimilation of phosphoric acid of phosphorite by plants, Chirikov (Tchirikov).. 323
The value of diphosphate, Îakushkin (Jakouchkine) 323
Solubility of difficultly soluble phosphates in citric acid, Aita................ 323
Influence of calcium carbonate on solution of iron phosphate, Semushkin...... 324
Analyses of inspection samples of fertilizers, 1915–16, Willard and Wiley..... 324
Analyses of inspection samples of fertilizers, fall 1916, Willard and Wiley..... 324
Fertilizers sold in Wisconsin, Strowd....................................... 224

AGRICULTURAL BOTANY.

Method of ascertaining mechanism of growth of dormant buds, Loeb.......... 324
Influence of the leaf upon root formation and geotropic curvature, Loeb...... 325
The spontaneous negative geotropism of roots, Mameli and Cattaneo........ 325
Behavior of certain gels useful as to action of plants, MacDougal and Spoehr.. 325
Effect of continuously supplying water to plants by capillarity, Daniel....... 325
A study of permeability by the method of tissue tension, Brooks.............. 326
Similarity in the effects of potassium cyanid and of ether, Osterhout.......... 326
The mode of action of the oxidases, Bunzel................................. 326
Relative oxidase activity of different organs of the same plant, Bunzel........ 326
A comparative study of winter and summer leaves of various herbs, Stober... 327
Local and temporary autumnal symbiosis, Montemartini..................... 327
The penetration of foreign substances introduced into trees, Rankin.......... 327
The injurious effects of tarvia fumes on vegetation, Chivers................... 327

Page.

Imperfection of pollen and mutability in the genus Rosa, Cole............... 228
Œnothera lamarckiana velutina, de Vries...................................... 228
The cowhage and related species, Piper....................................... 328

FIELD CROPS.

Dry farming in eastern New Mexico, Mundell and Smith...................... 328
Progress report of Substation No. 3, Angleton, Tex., 1909–1914, Winters...... 329
Progress report, Texas Substation No. 6, Denton, Tex., 1909–1914, Cory...... 330
Progress report of Substation No. 12, Chillicothe, Tex., 1905–1914, Edwards... 331
Inheritance in wheat, barley, and oat hybrids, Gaines........................ 332
Winter oats, barley, spelt, and emmer, Schmitz.............................. 332
Grains for the dry lands of central Oregon, Breithaupt...................... 333
Grasses used in binding the shifting sands of southern Italy, Borzì.......... 333
Permanent pastures on lowland moors, Freckmann........................... 333
Green manuring in India, Dobbs... 334
Color variation in seed crops of cultivated legumes, Galang.................. 334
Alfalfa in Wyoming, Parsons... 334
Barley in Washington, Schafer and Gaines.................................... 334
Corn experiments in 1915, Fedorov... 334
Cotton experiments, 1916.. 334
Extension of cotton production in California, Cook........................... 335
Cotton species indigenous to Italian Somaliland, Mattei..................... 336
Tests and selections of mungo beans, San Miguel............................ 336
Experiments with the overhead electrical discharge in 1915, Jorgensen........ 336
Contribution to the study of Panicum miliaceum, Belov...................... 336
Field pea production, Schafer and Gaines.................................... 337
The value of immature potato tubers as seed, Hutchinson.................... 337
Fertilizing the potato crop, Thorne.. 337
Potato growing, Green... 338
Potato growing in the loess area of the southwest, Zaporozhenko............. 338
Fertilization of rice, Balangue y Rulloda.................................... 338
Grain sorghums, Madson... 338
Sugar-beet plantations in the peasant husbandry, Novinskiĭ.................. 339
[Sugar cane], Agee... 339
Further observations on the cultivation of Helianthus annuus, Tropea........ 339
Fertilizer tests with tobacco varieties, Palafox y de la Cuesta............... 339
Variability of tobacco in cultures on the college farm, Cagurangan........... 339
Production of tobacco under shade in the Philippines, Paguirigan y Amalingan. 339
Tobacco.—The production of light-colored pipe and cigarette leaf, Tregenna.. 340
Wheat, Schmitz.. 340
Effect of soil moisture content on wheat production, Harris and Maughan..... 340
Gluten formation in the wheat kernel, Olson................................. 341
Spraying of charlock in corn... 342

HORTICULTURE.

Horticultural laws of the State of Washington................................ 342
Luther Burbank, his methods and discoveries, edited by Whitson and Williams. 342
The garden, Shaw.. 342
The home garden in Kentucky, Adams.. 342
Variation in artichokes, Shamel.. 342
Experiments in keeping asparagus after cutting, Morse....................... 342
New Mexico beans, Garcia... 343
Report of the Taliparamba Agricultural Station for 1913–14, Sampson........ 343
Report of the Taliparamba Agricultural Station for 1914–15, Sampson........ 343
Report of Taliparamba Agricultural Station for 1915–16, Ramasastrulu Nayudu. 343
The tomato as a farm crop for the canning factory, Reed..................... 343
[Vegetable seed production at Vineland, Ontario]............................ 343
New or noteworthy fruits, V, Hedrick....................................... 343
Variety testing at the Dominion Experimental Farms, Macoun................ 343
Varieties of fruit in the Province of Starkenburg............................ 343
Studies in fruit bud formation, Magness..................................... 343
The freezing of fruit buds, West and Edlefsen............................... 344
Pruning fruit trees, Alderman and Auchter.................................. 344
The Taylor system of pruning, Taylor.. 344
Influence of pruning upon the fruit spur system of the apple, Gardner........ 344

Page.
The influence of commercial fertilizers on bearing apple orchards, Brown.....   344
The selection and hybridization of American vines in Italy, Patanè..........   344
Comparative merits of California avocado varieties, Scott....................   345
Avocado varieties in Florida, Vosbury.......................................   345
Report on cacao manurial experiments at Djati-Roenggo, Peelen and de Jong.   345
The culture of citrus plants in Cuba, Cunliffe and van Hermann..............   345
A lemon bud variation, Shamel...   345
Maturity standard for Washington navel, Chace...............................   345
A practical guide to coconut planting, Munro and Brown......................   345
The genus Annona in the Hawaiian Islands, MacCaughey.......................   345
Cultivation of the papaya, Cunliffe...   345
South American markets for fresh fruits, Fischer............................   345
Making nuts in five years, Littlepage.......................................   345
Gladiolus studies.—III, Varieties of the garden gladiolus, Hottes...........   345
The culture of garden roses, Beal...   346
Sweet peas up-to-date, Kerr...   346
Milady's house plants, Palmer...   346
Putnam's garden handbook, Croy...   346
The joyous art of gardening, Duncan...   346
"Know your city" trees, Bannwart..   346

FORESTRY.

Trees worth knowing, Rogers...   346
Bud and twig key to deciduous trees in United States, Sponsler..............   346
The pine trees of the Rocky Mountain region, Sudworth.......................   346
Note on the forests of Java and Madoera of the Dutch East Indies, Milward...   346
Factors causing variation in yield in Florida camphor tree, Hood............   346
The rubber industry, edited by Torrey and Manders..........................   347
A practical tapping experiment conducted on scientific principles, de Jong...   347
Scientific tapping experiments with Hevea brasiliensis, de Jong.............   347
Investigations of the quality of plantation rubber..........................   347
Influence of rubber content of latex on inner qualities of rubber, de Vries....   347
Influence of amount of acetic acid on inner qualities of rubber, de Vries......   347
Sugar as a coagulant for crepe rubber, de Vries.............................   348
Reforestation on the National Forests, Tillotson...........................   348
Nursery practice on the National Forests, Tillotson.........................   348
Latest devices in protection work, DuBois..................................   348
Annual report of the National Forest Reservation Commission for 1916........   348
Report of the State forester, Schaaf..   348
First annual report of the State forester, Foster et al.....................   348
Forest administration of the Central Provinces for 1915–16, Forteath et al......   348
Organization and activities of the Chinese forest service, Sherfesee...........   348
Timber storage conditions in the Eastern and Southern States, Humphrey.....   349

DISEASES OF PLANTS.

Report of the mycologist, Bunting...   349
Parasitic diseases of cultivated plants, Renacco............................   349
Black mold of onions, Van Pelt...   349
Investigations on potato diseases (seventh report), Pethybridge.............   350
Cork, drought spot, and related diseases of the apple, Mix..................   350
Rhizopus rot of strawberries in transit, Stevens and Wilcox.................   351
Control of American gooseberry mildew by spraying, Petherbridge and Cole...   351
Mysterious vine disease, Jeffrey..   352
The gray root fungus of Cinchona, Rant.....................................   352
Control of black spot and brown spot in citrus, Darnell-Smith...............   352
Composition of citrus leaves at various stages of mottling, Jensen..........   352
Relation of nitrogen to mottle-leaf, McBeth................................   353
A new species of Endothia, Bruner..   353
Rose diseases, Massey..   353
A disease of Clivia under glass, Arnaud.....................................   353
An Alternaria on Sonchus, Elliott..   353
[Cucurbitaria pithyophila on Scotch pine in Scotland], M'Intosh.............   353
Canker of Scotch pine caused by Dasyscypha subtilissima, Borthwick and Wilson.   354
The æcial stage of Coleosporium ribicola, Long.............................   354
Dothichiza populea in the United States, Hedgcock and Hunt.................   354

ECONOMIC ZOOLOGY—ENTOMOLOGY.

Page.

The parasites of food animals transmissible to man, Ransom.................... 355
Concerning the pocket gopher and destructive habits, Scheffer................. 355
New monostome trematode parasitic in muskrat, with key to parasites, Barker.. 355
Belle Fourche reservoir as a bird reservation, Dille................. 355
The Salt River national bird reservation, Arizona, Willett.................... 355
East Park bird reservation, California, Willett................................ 355
The Deer Flat national bird reservation, Idaho, Palmer....................... 355
The Minidoka national bird reservation, Idaho, Dille.......................... 355
The birds of Culebra Island, Porto Rico, Wetmore............................. 355
How birds' stomachs are examined, McAtee.................................... 355
The technique of experimentation in agricultural entomology, I, Emeliānov.. 355
The longevity of some insects in captivity, Labitte........................... 355
Precipitation in relation to insect prevalence and distribution, Criddle........ 355
Resistance of larvæ of Cossus and Carpocapsa to cold, Gueylard and Portier... 356
Insects attacking stored wheat in the Punjab, Barnes and Grove.............. 356
Florida truck and garden insects, Watson..................................... 356
Insects injurious to timber in Sweden, Kemner................................ 356
Report of first expedition to South America, 1913, Strong et al................ 356
Report of the Kansas State Entomological Commission for 1915 and 1916....... 357
Report of work done during year ended June 30, 1916, Dutt................... 357
Reports of the microbiologist, Nicholls....................................... 357
Notes on Argentine, Patagonian, and Cape Horn Muridæ, Thomas............. 357
The sheep tick and its eradication by dipping, Imes........................... 357
The destruction of locusts in Colombia by dipterous parasites, Dawe........... 357
The cacao thrips, Hutson.. 357
Mites and lice on poultry, Bishopp and Wood................................. 357
A contribution to the study of kala-azar, Cornwall and La Frenais............. 357
Notes on a froghopper attacking sugar cane in Surinam, Williams.............. 358
Aphids injurious to orchard fruits, etc., Quaintance and Baker................. 358
The San José scale, Paddock... 358
Some new scale insects of Japan, Kuwana.................................... 358
A scale enemy of the vine in Uruguay, Schurmann............................ 358
Introduction of *Diaspis pentagona* and its control in Argentina, Gallardo...... 358
The pink bollworm, Hunter.. 358
The life of the caterpillar, Fabre, trans. by Teixeira de Mattos................. 358
A few notes on the life history of *Phalonia spartinana*, Ainslie................. 358
Recent questioning of the transmission of verruga by Phlebotomus, Townsend.. 358
Studies in flies: II, Structures other than genitalia, Awati.................... 358
Two new genera of African Muscoidea, Townsend............................. 359
The lantana seed fly, Jepson... 359
Plagiodera versicolora.—An imported pest, Weiss and Dickerson.............. 359
Scientific annihilation of the tobacco beetle, Skerrett........................ 359
Report of the South Carolina Boll Weevil Commission, Riggs.................. 359
On some Curculionidæ which live in bamboo stems, da Costa Lima............ 359
The leaf weevil (*Polydrusus impressifrons*), Parrott and Glasgow.............. 359
Bees for the farmer, Troop and Price.. 360
Outdoor wintering [of bees], Phillips... 360
The sense organs on the mouth parts of the honeybee, McIndoo............... 360
Contribution to the etiology of infectious diarrhea of bees, Serbinov.......... 360
Connection of *Nosema apis* with Isle of Wight disease in hive bees, Anderson.. 360
Observations bearing on Isle of Wight disease, Anderson and Rennie......... 360
Three new chalcid flies from California, Girault.............................. 360
Monograph of the nearctic Hymenoptera of the genus Bracon, Morrison....... 360
Signiphora merceti n. sp., Malenotti... 360
Gonatocerus mexicanus, a mymarid parasitic in *Draeculacephala mollipes*, Swezey. 360
The ticks which attack domestic animals in Russian Turkestan, Yakimoff.... 360
Parasitism of *Rhipicephalus sanguineus* by *Hunterellus hookeri*, da Costa Lima.. 360
Occurrence of tropical fowl mite (*Liponyssus bursa*) in Australia, Hirst....... 360
The structure and life history of *Nosema bombycis*, Kudo..................... 361
Larval forms of heteroxenous nematode parasites, Seurat..................... 361
Two new cases of polyradiate cestodes, with summary of cases known, Foster.. 361
Polyradiate cestodes, Barker.. 361
A further note on polyradiate cestodes, Foster............................... 361

FOODS—HUMAN NUTRITION.

Characteristics and quality of Montana-grown wheat, Thomas................. 361
The capacity of wheat and mill products for moisture, Stockham.............. 362

                                                                    Page.
The composition of rice and its by-products, Fraps...................... 363
Determination of the digestibility of millets, Langworthy and Holmes....... 364
Bread and bread making in the home, Hunt and Wessling.................. 364
Forty-three ways to save the wild plum crop, Carver.................... 364
How to select foods.—I, What the body needs, Hunt and Atwater........... 364
Effect of starvation of catalase content of tissues, Burge and Neill........... 365

ANIMAL PRODUCTION.

Some neglected factors underlying the stock breeding industry, Pearl..... 365
Steer-feeding experiments, Tombave, Severson, and Gerlaugh................ 365
Feeding baby beeves, Burns.. 366
The production of baby beef, Ray.................................. 367
Peanut meal and ground-whole pressed peanuts for hogs, Burk............. 367
Horse-breeding suggestions for farmers, Reese....................... 368
Growing draft colts, McCampbell................................. 368
Chicken management on the farm, Sherwood et al..................... 368
Standard varieties of chickens.—I, The American class, Slocum.............. 368
The capon, Aubry... 368
Fifth annual international egg-laying contest, Kirkpatrick and Card.......... 368
Breeding for egg production.—I, Annual and total production, Ball et al..... 369
The separate inheritance of plumage pattern and pigmentation, Pearl........ 370
Effect of continued administration of certain poisons to fowl, Pearl.......... 370
Physiology of reproduction in the domestic fowl.—XVI, Double eggs, Curtis.. 371

DAIRY FARMING—DAIRYING.

Report of special milk board of Massachusetts State Department of Health.... 372
The feeding of dairy cows on pasture, Berry........................ 372
A good bull's influence upon three generations, Dunne.................. 373
The yield and composition of cows' milk during lactation, Berry............ 373
Notes on modern dairy chemistry, van Dam........................ 373
Cream production and grading in Kansas, Hine...................... 373
Changes in composition of Cheddar cheese during ripening, Berry........... 373
Paying for milk in cheese making, Troy............................ 374

VETERINARY MEDICINE.

Report of Oregon State Live Stock Sanitary Board for 1916, Lytle et al....... 374
Report of the parasitologist, Scott................................ 374
[Report of the] division of animal industry, Nörgaard.................. 374
Animal diseases in Russian Turkestan caused by parasites, Yakimoff et al.... 374
Development of Ascaris lumbricoides and A. suilla in rat and mouse, Stewart.. 374
Spirochæta morsus muris n. sp., the cause of rat-bite fever, II, Futaki et al.... 375
Experimental rat-bite fever, Ishiwara, Ohtawara, and Tamura............... 365
Toxic action of copper compounds of amino acids on protozoa, Shaw-Mackenzie. 375
The action of digitalis in pneumonia, Cohn and Jamieson.................. 375
Studies on the blood proteins, II, Hurwitz and Whipple.................. 375
The mechanism of the agglutination reaction, Priestley.................. 376
Factors limiting the extent of the concentration of antitoxic sera, Homer...... 376
The effects of serum treated with pararabin, Zunz and Mohilevith........... 376
Report on two new methods of preventing blackleg, Schoenleber et al........ 376
Some considerations on the new dual theory of Carrion's disease, Arce........ 377
Gaseous gangrene.—Bacillus œdematous, Weinberg and Séguin.............. 377
The reversible precipitation in glanderous serum, Belin.................. 377
Culture of the causative organism of epizootic lymphangitis, Boquet and Négre. 377
Treatment of epizootic lymphangitis by potassium iodid, Cartier............ 377
Pseudotuberculosis in guinea pigs, Van Saceghem..................... 377
Pseudotuberculosis in a South American horse, Bringard.................. 378
Tuberculosis, Craig and Clink.................................... 378
The infection of tuberculosis through air expired during coughing, Chaussé... 378
Delayed or "latent" tuberculous infection, Delépine.................... 378
Types of tubercle bacilli in cervical and axillary gland tuberculosis, Griffith.. 378
Bovine tuberculosis in the horse, Fröhner........................... 378
Possibility of developing an experimental chemotherapy of tuberculosis, Lewis. 379
Eradicating bovine tuberculosis, Pew.............................. 379
Sterility of cattle and methods of treatment, Albrechtsen................ 379
Prevention and treatment of hemorrhagic septicemia of cattle, Brandenburg.. 379

Page.

Diseases of new-born calves and recommendations for control, Williams....... 379
Anaphylaxis in cattle and sheep, Hadwen and Bruce....................... 379
The etiology of bradsot or braxy, Jensen.................................... 380
A tick-borne gastroenteritis of sheep and goats, Montgomery.................. 380
Morphology of normal pigs' blood, Palmer.................................. 380
Effects of exercise and sun on pigs, Palmer................................. 381
The etiology of hog cholera.—Preliminary report, Proescher and Seil......... 382
Pathology and treatment of pernicious and infectious anemia of horse, III, Ries. 382
Vaccination against infectious arthritis of foals, Hardenbergh............... 382
Bacillary white diarrhea of young chicks, VI, Rettger et al.................. 383
Enterohepatitis or blackhead in turkeys, Higgins........................... 383
Field experiments bearing on transmission of blackhead in turkeys, Smith.... 383
Coccidia in sparrows and their relation to blackhead, Smith and Smillie...... 384

RURAL ENGINEERING.

Report of the superintendent of public works, Hawaii, Forbes............... 384
Surface water supply of New Mexico, 1915, French......................... 384
Surface water supply of lower Columbia River and Pacific drainage basins, 1914. 384
Pump irrigation in Nebraska, Brackett and Sjogren......................... 384
Irrigation of the Chéliff Plain in the department of Oran [Algiers], Vielle...... 384
Farm drainage in Virginia, Yarnell.. 384
[Land drainage in] Ontario, Spry.. 385
Institutional sewage plants, Mebus.. 385
New stump burner for logged-off lands requires no blower, Allison........... 385
Report of board of road commissioners of Wayne County [Mich.], 1916........ 385
First report of commissioner of highways [of Oklahoma], 1915, Noble......... 385
Second annual report of the State engineer [of Oklahoma], 1916, Cunningham. 385
Annual report on highway improvement, Ontario, 1914, McLean.............. 385
Laws of Iowa relating to roads and highways passed in 1915, Elliott.......... 386
Cost of engineering an extensive county road system, Davidson.............. 386
Physical tests of road-building rock in 1916, Hubbard and Jackson, jr........ 386
Material specifications.. 386
United States Government specification for Portland cement................. 386
Creosoting bridge stringers and ties without loss in strength, Goss............ 386
Timber framing, Dewell... 386
Elementary primer of electricity for light and power customers.............. 387
Performance of two successful windmill generating plants, Culver............ 387
Electric heating, Wilcox.. 387
More tractor evidence.. 387
Equipment for the farm and the farmstead, Ramsower...................... 388
Equipment for farm sheep raising, McWhorter............................. 388
Municipal piggeries, Bridges.. 388
Pit, semipit, and bank silos, Chase.. 388
Poultry house construction, Ekblaw....................................... 389

RURAL ECONOMICS.

[Report of sixth annual meeting of American Farm Management Association].. 389
Validity of the survey method of research, Spillman......................... 389
Agriculture and preparedness, Myrick...................................... 389
The relation of p d i to consumption, duToit............................ 389
Solving the food problem, Soule... 390
Plantation farming in the United States.................................... 390
Farms for sale or rent in New York, 1917, Larmon.......................... 390
Land settlement, Turnor.. 390
Causes or rural migration, Simonot.. 390
Seasonal distribution of farm labor in Chester County, Pa., Billings........... 390
Marketing live stock in the South: Suggestions for improvement, Doty....... 390
Report of territorial marketing division of Hawaii, 1916, Longley.............. 391
Market distribution of poultry products, Benjamin.......................... 391
Marketing, Adams.. 391
Marketing and farm credits... 391
Suggestions from America for cooperative selling, Ashby.................... 391
Organization of farmers' mutual fire insurance company, Valgren............ 391
[Cooperation in Switzerland].. 392
Monthly crop report.. 392

Page.

Trade and commerce in agricultural products in Chicago, 1916].............. 392
The agricultural output of Great Britain.................................... 392
Returns of produce of crops in England and Wales, Anstruther.............. 392
Acreage and live stock returns of Scotland, Ramsay........................ 392
[Agricultural statistics of Denmark]....................................... 392

AGRICULTURAL EDUCATION.

Agricultural education, Monahan and Lane................................... 392
Rural and agricultural education at the Panama-Pacific Exposition, Foght.... 393
Work of the Bureau of Education for the natives of Alaska, 1914–15.......... 392
Home economics, Calvin and Lyford... 393
Elementary agricultural instruction, Smits................................. 394
Report of the commissioner of industrial and vocational education, Snyder.... 394
Schools of agriculture, mechanic arts, and homemaking, Hawkins............. 394
Rural education associations and their activities.......................... 394
Problems of a department of poultry husbandry at a secondary school, Banta.. 394
How can we attain greater efficiency in laboratory instruction? Irvin......... 395
Gardening in elementary city schools, Jarvis............................... 395
A course in nature study and agriculture, Skilling......................... 395
Courses in secondary agriculture for southern schools, Barrows.............. 395
Suggested experiments in elementary plant physiology, Pennington........... 395
Farm spies, Conradi and Thomas.. 395
Food study, Wellman... 396
Illustrated lecture on farm grounds, Mulford and Conolly................... 396

MISCELLANEOUS.

Abstracts of papers not included in bulletins, finances, meteorology, index.... 396
Director's report for 1916, Jordan... 396
Twenty,sixth Annual Report of Wyoming Station, 1916..................... 396
Monthly Bulletin of the Ohio Experiment Station.......................... 396

LIST OF EXPERIMENT STATION AND DEPARTMENT PUBLICATIONS REVIEWED.

Stations in the United States.

Alabama Tuskegee Station: Page.
   Bul. 34, Apr., 1917........... 364
California Station:
   Bul. 278, Apr., 1917.......... 338
Connecticut Storrs Station:
   Bul. 88, Oct., 1916........... 383
   Bul. 89, Feb., 1917........... 368
Florida Station:
   Bul. 134, Apr., 1917.......... 356
   Bul. 135, Apr., 1917.......... 313
Hawaii Federal Station:
   Bul. 43, May 7, 1917.......... 320
Indiana Station:
   Circ. 59, Mar., 1917.......... 243
   Circ. 60, Mar., 1917.......... 378
   Circ. 61, Apr., 1917.......... 360
Kansas Station:
   Circ. 56, June, 1916.......... 373
   Circ. 57, Oct., 1916.......... 368
   Circ. 59, Jan., 1917.......... 376
   Circ. 60, Mar., 1917.......... 368
   Insp. Circ. 3, Oct., 1916...... 324
   Insp. Circ. 4, Mar. 1, 1917.... 324
Kentucky Station:
   Cir. 14, Mar., 1917........... 342
Maine Station:
   Bul. 257, Dec., 1916.314, 370, 371, 396
   Bul. 258, Jan., 1917.......... 395
Maryland Station:
   Bul. 198, Oct., 1916.......... 340
   Bul. 199, Dec., 1916.......... 320
   Bul. 200, Jan., 1917.......... 332
Massachusetts Station:
   Bul. 172, Mar., 1917.......... 342
Mississippi Station:
   Bul. 178, Dec., 1916.......... 334
Nebraska Station:
   Circ. 2, Mar. 10, 1917........ 384
New Jersey Stations:
   Hints to Poultrymen, vol. 5,
    No. 8, May, 1917........... 368
New Mexico Station:
   Bul. 104, 1917............... 328
   Bul. 105, Mar., 1917.......... 343
New York State Station:
   Bul. 426, Oct., 1916.......... 350
   Bul. 427, Dec., 1916.......... 343
   Bul. 428, Dec., 1916.......... 396
   Tech. Bul. 56, Dec., 1916.... 359
North Dakota Station:
   Bul. 120, Jan., 1917.......... 362

Stations in the United States—Contd.

Ohio Station: Page.
   Mo. Bul., vol. 2, No. 5, May,
    1917............ 337, 338, 394, 396
Pennsylvania Station:
   Bul. 145, Apr., 1917.......... 365
Texas Station:
   Bul. 191, June, 1916.......... 363
   Bul. 197, Nov., 1916.......... 329
   Bul. 198, Nov., 1916.......... 366
   Bul. 199, Dec., 1916.......... 330
   Bul. 201, Dec., 1916.......... 367
   Bul. 202, Dec., 1916.......... 331
   Circ. 18, Dec., 1916.......... 358
Utah Station:
   Bul. 148, Dec., 1916.......... 369
   Bul. 151, Feb., 1917.......... 344
   Bul. 152, Feb., 1917.......... 340
Washington Station:
   Bul. 135, Mar., 1917.......... 332
   Bul. 140, Mar., 1917.......... 337
   Bul. 141, Mar., 1917.......... 334
   Bul. 142, Mar., 1917.......... 341
West Virginia Station:
   Bul. 164, Mar., 1917.......... 344
Wisconsin Station:
   Bul. 279, Apr., 1917.......... 324
Wyoming Station:
   Bul. 111, Dec., 1916.......... 334
   Twenty-sixth An. Rpt., 1916.. 314, 374, 396

U. S. Department of Agriculture.

Jour. Agr. Research, vol. 9:
   No. 5, Apr. 30, 1917......... 318, 380
   No. 6, May 7, 1917.......... 352, 381
   No. 7, May 14, 1917......... 318, 353
Bul. 460, The Pine Trees of the
   Rocky Mountain Region, G. B.
   Sudworth...................... 346
Bul. 475, Reforestation on the
   National Forests, C. R. Tillotson 348
Bul. 479, Nursery Practice on the
   National Forests, C. R. Tillotson 348
Bul. 510, Timber Storage Condi-
   tions in the Eastern and South-
   ern States with Reference to
   Decay Problems, C. J. Humph-
   rey........................... 349
Bul. 521, Courses in Secondary
   Agriculture for Southern Schools
   (First and Second Years), H. P.
   Barrows....................... 395

U. S. Department of Agriculture—Contd.

Page.

Bul. 522, Characteristics and Quality of Montana-grown Wheat, L. M. Thomas.................. 361

Bul. 524, Dectection of Lime Used as a Neutralizer in Dairy Products, H. J. Wichmann.......... 313

Bul. 525, Experiments in the Determination of the Digestibility of Millets, C. F. Langworthy and A. D. Holmes.................. 364

Bul. 528, Seasonal Distribution of Farm Labor in Chester County, Pa., G. A. Billings............. 390

Bul. 529, Validity of the Survey Method of Research, W. J. Spillman.......................... 389

Bul. 530, The Organization and Management of a Farmers' Mutual Fire Insurance Company, V. N. Valgren.................. 391

Bul. 531, Rhizopus Rot of Strawberries in Transit, N. E. Stevens and R. B. Wilcox............. 351

Bul. 533, Extension of Cotton Production in California, O. F. Cook 335

Bul. 537, The Results of Physical Tests of Road-building Rock in 1916, Including All Compression Tests, P. Hubbard and F. H. Jackson, jr.................... 386

Farmers' Bul. 798, The Sheep Tick and Its Eradication by Dipping, M. Imes...................... 357

Farmers' Bul. 800, Grains for the Dry Lands of Central Oregon, L. R. Breitbaupt.............. 333

Farmers' Bul. 801, Mites and Lice on Poultry, F. C. Bishopp and H. P. Wood.................... 357

Farmers' Bul. 803, Horse-breeding Suggestions for Farmers, H. H. Reese........................ 368

Farmers' Bul. 804, Aphids Injurious to Orchard Fruits, Currant, Gooseberry, and Grape, A. L. Quaintance and A. C. Baker.... 358

Farmers' Bul. 806, Standard Varieties of Chickens.—I, The American Class, R. R. Slocum....... 368

Farmers' Bul. 807, Bread and Bread Making in the Home, Caroline L. Hunt and Hannah L. Wessling.................... 364

Farmers' Bul. 808, How to Select Foods.—I, What the Body Needs, Caroline L. Hunt and Helen W. Atwater.............. 364

Farmers' Bul. 809, Marketing Live Stock in the South, S. W. Doty.. 390

Farmers' Bul. 810, Equipment for Farm Sheep Raising, V. O. McWhorter...................... 388

Farmers' Bul. 811, The Production of Baby Beef, S. H. Ray........ 367

U. S. Department of Agriculture—Contd.

Page.

Bureau of Crop Estimates:
Mo. Crop Rpt., vol. 3, No. 5, May, 1917.................. 392

States Relations Service:
Syllabus 28, Illustrated Lecture on Practical Improvement of Farm Grounds, F. L. Mulford and H. M. Conolly.. 396

Weather Bureau:
Nat. Weather and Crop Bul. 7, 1917...................... 315
Nat. Weather and Crop Bul. 8, 1917...................... 316
Nat. Weather and Crop Bul. 9, 1917...................... 316
Nat. Weather and Crop Bul. 10, 1917...................... 317
Nat. Weather and Crop Bul. 11, 1917...................... 316
Mo. Weather Rev., Sup. 6.... 314
Climat. Data, vol. 3, No. 13, 1916...................... 314

Scientific Contributions: [a]
Calcium and Phosphorus in Blood of Lactating Cows, E. B. Meigs and N. R. Blatherwick.............. 308
Chemical Changes in Shucked Oysters under Refrigeration, E. D. Clark and L. H. Almy. 311
The Mode of Action of the Oxidases, H. H. Bunzel.... 326
Relative Oxidase Activity of Different Organs of the Same Plant, H. H. Bunzel....... 326
Dry Farming in Eastern New Mexico, J. E. Mundell and H. G. Smith.............. 328
Variation in Artichokes, A. D. Shamel.................... 342
Comparative Merits of California Avocado Varieties, L. B. Scott...................... 345
Avocado Varieties in Florida, E. D. Vosbury............ 345
A Lemon Bud Variation, A. D. Shamel.................... 345
Maturity Standard for Washington Navel, E. M. Chace.. 345
Factors Causing Variation in Yield in Florida Camphor Tree, S. C. Hood.......... 346
Latest Devices in Protection Work, C. DuBois.......... 348
The Æcial Stage of *Coleosporium ribicola*, W. H. Long... 354
Dothichiza populea in the United States, G. G. Hedgcock and N. R. Hunt....... 354
The Parasites of Food Animals Transmissible to Man, B. H. Ransom.................... 355
Concerning the Pocket Gopher and Destructive Habits, T. H. Scheffer................ 355

[a] Printed in scientific and technical publications outside the Departments.

U. S. Department of Agriculture—Contd.

Page.

Scientific Contributions—Contd.

Belle Fourche Reservoir As a
Bird Reservation and Refuge
F. M. Dille................   355
The Salt River National Bird
Reservation, Arizona, G.
Willett....................   355
East Park Bird Reservation,
California, G. Willett......   355
The Deer Flat National Bird
Reservation, Idaho, T. S.
Palmer....................   355
The Minidoka National Bird
Reservation, Idaho, F. M.
Dille......................   355
The Birds of Culebra Islands,
Porto Rico, A. Wetmore....   355
How Birds' Stomachs are Ex-
amined, W. L. McAtee....
The Pink Bollworm, W. D.
Hunter....................   355
A Few Notes on the Life His-
tory of *Phalonia spartinana*,
C. N. Ainslie..............   358
Recent Questioning of the
Transmission of Verruga by
Phlebotomus, C. H. T. Town-
send......................   358
Two New Genera of African
Muscoidea, C. H. T. Town-
send   359

U. S. Department of Agriculture—Contd.

Page.

Scientific contributions—Contd.

Outdoor Wintering [of Bees],
E. F. Phillips.............   360
The Sense Organs on the Mouth
Parts of the Honeybee, N. E.
McIndoo...................   360
Three New Chalcid Flies from
California, A. A. Girault....   360
Monograph of the Nearctic Hy-
menoptera of the Genus
Bracon, H. Morrison.......   360
Two New Cases of Polyradiate
Cestodes, with Summary of
Cases Already Known, W. D.
Foster   361
A further Note on Polyradiate
Cestodes, W. D. Foster.....   361
Farm Drainage in Virginia,
D. L. Yarnell.............   384
Utilization of Waste on the
Farms, W. S. A. Smith.....   389
Results of Farm Management
Demonstration Work, L. H.
Goddard   389
Gaining a Foothold on the
Land, E. H. Thomson   389
The Farmer's Response to
Economic Forces, W. J. Spill-
man.....................   389
Agricultural Education, A. C.
Monahan and C. H. Lane....   392

EXPERIMENT STATION RECORD.

VOL. 37.　　　　　　SEPTEMBER, 1917.　　　　　　No. 4.

The passage of the Federal Food Production Act has added to the list of war measures an enactment of direct interest to agriculture. It constitutes a tangible recognition by Congress of the exceptional importance attached to the maintenance of an ample food supply as a strategic phase of the present conflict, and of the consequent need of fostering production on the farm and conservation in the home through Federal aid to an extent never before attempted. It materially increases the funds at the disposal of the Federal Department of Agriculture and enlarges its powers and functions in a number of directions during the national emergency.

The responsibility resting upon the agricultural interests of the country to develop food production was pointed out by President Wilson soon after the outbreak of hostilities. In his address to the American people of April 15, the President said:

"The supreme need of our own Nation and for the nations with which we are cooperating is an abundance of supplies and especially of foodstuffs. The importance of an adequate food supply, especially for the present year, is superlative. Without abundant food, alike for the armies and the peoples now at war, the whole great enterprise upon which we have embarked will break down and fail. The world's food reserves are low. Not only during the present emergency but for some time after peace shall have come both our own people and a large proportion of the people of Europe must rely upon the harvests in America. Upon the farmers of this country, therefore, in large measure rests the fate of the war and the fate of the nations."

An agricultural mobilization of huge proportions followed the declaration of a state of war. The resources of the Federal Department of Agriculture, the agricultural colleges and experiment stations, and many other agencies were concentrated so far as possible upon the emergency situation with a view to rendering all possible assistance. The campaign to increase production which followed has been without precedent in its magnitude and comprehensiveness, its resourcefulness, and its spirit of intelligent leadership and service. The results have already demonstrated in convincing fashion what important assets these institutions have become in the Nation's resources, as well as some of their potentialities for the days still to come.

The activities of the Department of Agriculture, which is administered mainly on a basis of annual appropriations, are at all times quite closely prescribed in advance by the terms of existing legislation. When the United States entered the war, routine appropriation acts had already been adopted covering its work up to June 30, 1918. This legislation had of course been framed when the Nation was still at peace, so that the passage of emergency legislation became necessary to meet the altered conditions.

A number of measures designed to supplement the resources of the Department were introduced into Congress, among them the act under review. This law was passed by the House of Representatives May 28, and with numerous amendments by the Senate June 2. It was hoped that the measure would become law prior to the beginning of the new fiscal year on July 1, but it was not until August 2 that it was reported from conference, and it was on August 10 that it was signed by President Wilson. On the same day was signed the so-called Food Control Act, an entirely separate measure having to do chiefly with the regulation of the distribution of foods, feeds, fuel including fuel oil and natural gas, and fertilizer and fertilizer ingredients, tools, utensils, implements, machinery, and equipment required for the actual production of foods, feeds, and fuel. This measure is likewise intimately related to agriculture, but it is not administered by the Department of Agriculture and no editorial discussion of it is here attempted. A description of its main provisions may be found elsewhere in this issue (p. 399).

The Food Production Act, as stated in its opening section, is " for the purpose of more effectually providing for the national security and defense and carrying on the war with Germany by gathering authoritative information concerning the food supply, by increasing production, by preventing waste of the food supply, by regulating the distribution thereof, and by such other means and methods as are hereinafter provided." It is thus primarily a war measure. Its duration is restricted to the termination of the national emergency resulting from the existing state of war, as determined by the President, but not later than the beginning of the next fiscal year after the ending of the war. During this period certain functions of the Government are enlarged and extended, and the President is authorized to direct any agency or organization of the Government to cooperate with the Secretary of Agriculture in carrying out the purposes of the act and to coordinate their activities so as to avoid any preventable loss or duplication of work. In addition, the Secretary is authorized "to cooperate with such State and local officials, and with such public and private agencies or persons, as he finds necessary."

The appropriations contained in the act are made for the period ending June 30, 1918. They thus supplement those carried in previous appropriations for this period, a summary of which has already appeared in these columns.[1]

The aggregate amount carried by the act is $11,346,400. This is not a large sum as compared with many of the emergency appropriations. The Food Control Act, for instance, appropriates $162,500,000, of which $10,000,000 is placed at the disposal of the President for the purchase and sale of nitrate of soda under certain conditions for agricultural production. None the less, it represents a total substantially equivalent to that carried in the regular appropriation act for the Department for the fiscal year 1908, and is larger than that for any earlier year. It increases the total funds for the Department's work to $55,160,513, of which $26,579,113 is carried in routine appropriation acts, and $17,235,000 as permanent and indefinite appropriations, chiefly under the Federal-aid Road Act, the meat-inspection provision, and the Extension Act. As compared with the preceding fiscal year, this constitutes a net increase of $20,007,661.

The principal items of expenditure authorized are for educational and demonstration work, food surveys, marketing and distribution studies and advice, the procuring and sale of seeds, aiding in the supply of farm labor, stimulating live stock production, combating insect pests and plant and animal diseases, and promoting the conservation and utilization of plant and animal products. Most of the projects provided for will be an extension of present activities on a larger scale, but some will represent new undertakings.

The largest single appropriation is $4,348,400 for increasing food production and promoting the conservation of food by extension teaching and demonstration through country, district, and urban Federal funds for these purposes, the annual appropriations to the States Relations Service for cooperative demonstration work for the year aggregating $1,237,800 and the appropriations under the Extension Act $2,080,000. It is expected to use the increased funds largely for county agents, home demonstration, and boys' and girls' club work.

Plans have been made to expand immediately the cooperative extension work of the Department and the State agricultural colleges by a large increase in the number of county agricultural agents and home demonstration agents. Approximately fourteen hundred men and five hundred women are at present employed, and the number

[1] E. S. R., 36, p. 401.

to be added will depend in large degree upon the number of trained men and women available. The plans formulated contemplate the extension of the male county agent work to all rural counties of the Union in which there is a need for it, and the placing of an additional agent in some of the larger counties already organized. They also contemplate a considerable increase in the number of women agents engaged in extension activities, including the placing of these agents in the larger towns and cities for the first time. The use of urban agents is deemed especially desirable because of the importance attached in the present crisis to the conservation and efficient utilization of foods. These agents will work mainly in cooperation with existing organizations of women, stimulating the production of garden truck, poultry, and other products by women and children, as well as the promotion of economy in the purchase and use of food and methods of food conservation by canning, drying. etc.

The States Relations Service will also seek to enlarge materially the enrollment of young people in the boys' and girls' clubs, which are devoted to increasing agricultural production and conserving the food supply. Opportunity for additional assistance is likewise afforded to the Office of Home Economics, which plans to work out problems in the efficient utilization of various foods and prepare popular bulletins on diet and food conservation.

The funds at the disposal of the Bureau of Markets, which receives $1,718,575 in the current appropriation act, will be more than doubled by the emergency appropriation, which provides $2,522,000 for work along this line. The Secretary of Agriculture, with the approval of the President, is given very broad authority to ascertain conditions relating to food and agricultural supplies. This contemplates not only data as to the demand, the supply, consumption, costs, and prices of food, but also the basic facts relating to the ownership, production, transportation, manufacture, storage, and distribution of foods. The authority applies likewise to food materials, feeds, seeds, fertilizers, agricultural implements and machinery, and indeed to any article required in connection with the production, distribution, or utilization of food.

A quick survey carried on chiefly by the Bureaus of Markets, Crop Estimates, and Chemistry, and the States Relations Service as to the existing food situation is projected, and a system of monthly reports and, if needed, additional surveys are also under consideration. The object will be to ascertain as accurately as possible the status of the country's food and feed supply from the farm to the consumer, including data as to the normal consumption, as a basis for rational production and conservation. Additional legal authority is given for obtaining the necessary information, and wilful failure to supply this is made a misdemeanor punishable by fine or imprisonment or both.

Provision is made for further extending the market news service of the Department to include grain, hay, seeds, and dairy and poultry products, and to supply additional information as to the marketing, movement, and distribution of perishable products. Steps to decrease waste of food in storage or during transit and sale are also contemplated, such as the working out of improved methods of packing and handling. The Department is empowered to examine and certify to shippers the condition as to soundness of fruits, vegetables, and other food products when received at important central markets designated by the Secretary of Agriculture, and it is provided that these certificates will be received as prima facie evidence in the courts. It is anticipated that this inspection service, among other benefits, will tend to inspire confidence in the minds of producers and so increase shipments of perishable commodities.

An appropriation of $885,000 is made for additional work relating to the meat supply. Enlarged production of hogs and poultry is the special object to be sought, since these are the two live-stock products capable of most rapid increase. The pig and poultry clubs are to be further developed and specialists added in the principal States. The further development of dairying and the better utilization of dairy products are also to be fostered. Efforts will likewise be made to increase animal production indirectly by extending the campaign against animal diseases and pests, especially hog cholera, the cattle tick, and tuberculosis.

For the combating of insect pests and plant diseases and the conservation and utilization of plant products $441,000 is appropriated. Special efforts are to be made to disseminate knowledge of methods of insect and plant disease prevention and control through demonstrations, the supplying of specialists in case of serious outbreaks, and in similar ways. One phase of the entomological work to receive increased attention is that dealing with insect infestations of stored products, a separate division for which has been recently established in the Bureau of Entomology. Black rust of wheat, grain smut, and the diseases of potatoes, beans, and truck crops are to receive special prominence in the Bureau of Plant Industry, which will also seek to stimulate conservation of food products by demonstrating proper methods of storing such crops as may be kept in common storage, by improving the methods of storage, and otherwise.

In order to overcome a possible shortage of seed in localized areas, authority is given the Department, whenever an acute need arises

5750°—17—No. 4——2

in such areas for seeds of food or feed crops, to purchase seeds or contract with persons to grow them, and to sell the seed to farmers for cash at the cost price plus the expense of packing and transportation. An appropriation of $2,500,000 is made for this work, which may be used as a revolving fund until June 30, 1918.

An allotment of $650,000 is made for miscellaneous purposes. Among these an item of special interest is that of aiding agencies in the various States in supplying farm labor. For some time the Office of Farm Management has been cooperating with the Federal Department of Labor in endeavoring to bring about better organization of the labor remaining on farms and to call into service available labor which heretofore has not been fully or regularly utilized in farming operations. Representatives have been detailed to cooperate with the State officials in charge of labor matters, the agricultural colleges, county agents, and county or local labor committees or representatives. The increased funds now made available will enable the extension of this undertaking.

Provision is made for enlarging the informational work of the Department, including the distribution of large editions of emergency leaflets, posters, and the like. Additional work in crop estimating is also provided, both for assisting in the nation-wide food survey already referred to and for an enlarged service along lines previously in progress.

The enormous increase in the amount of administrative work of the Department in recent years is recognized in the authorization for the appointment by the President, subject to confirmation by the Senate, of two additional Assistant Secretaries of Agriculture. Under this provision, Prof. Clarence Ousley, director of the extension service of the A. & M. College of Texas, and President Raymond A. Pearson of the Iowa State College have been appointed to these positions.

Appended to the act are three sections affecting existing permanent legislation. One of these amends the Meat Inspection Act of 1890, by authorizing, under certain restrictions and at the discretion of the Secretary of Agriculture, the admission for immediate slaughter at points of entry below the southern cattle quarantine line of tick-infested cattle otherwise free from disease. The purpose of this amendment is to increase the meat supply through importations of live cattle from Mexico, South and Central America, and the islands of the Gulf of Mexico and the Caribbean Sea.

An amendment to the Enlarged Homestead Act of 1910 increases from 320,000 to 1,000,000 acres the amount of land available for entry in Idaho and renders less rigorous certain requirements for residence thereon. Under the third amendment, the Secretary of the Interior is authorized at his discretion to suspend certain residence requirements of the Reclamation Act with reference to the supplying of irrigation water.

The Food Production Act thus provides for the rendering of assistance by the Department of Agriculture on a larger scale and along lines of broader scope than ever before. Despite the fact that the bill did not become a law until the crop season of 1917 was past its zenith, and other difficulties inherent in the rapid organization of so great an expansion of work, a comprehensive program has been formulated and the increased activities provided are being vigorously undertaken. It is believed that if the campaign projected is successful, and the American people respond as expected, a marked contribution will have been made to the national efficiency and economy. Moreover, the results should be of assitance not only in the existing emergency but should possess considerable residual value of permanent advantage to the Nation.

RECENT WORK IN AGRICULTURAL SCIENCE.

AGRICULTURAL CHEMISTRY—AGROTECHNY.

A method for the separation of the dietary essential, "fat-soluble **A**," from butter fat, E. V. McCollum, Nina Simmonds, and H. Steenbock (*Jour. Biol. Chem.*, 29 (1917), No. 2, p. XXVI).—The authors, at the Wisconsin Experiment Station, conducted feeding experiments in which milk fat which had been melted and thoroughly agitated with 20 successive portions of water was used. After this treatment it was found to be no longer effective in producing growth when fed with suitably constituted diets. Change to unwashed milk fat was followed by a prompt resumption of growth.

Antineuritic substances from egg yolk, H. Steenbock (*Jour. Biol. Chem.*, 29 (1917), No. 2, p. XXVII).—The author, at the Wisconsin Experiment Station, notes the preparation of an acetone-soluble fraction from egg yolk which in small doses by intraperitoneal injection was able to cure a pigeon suffering from polyneuritis. The antineuritic substance was found to be stable to concentrated hydrochloric acid at 98° C. and to concentrated alkalis at room temperature, but was readily destroyed by dilute alkalis at boiling temperature. It was incompletely precipitated by phosphotungstic acid. It is indicated that it was not adenin.

Adenin and guanin in cows' milk, C. Voegtlin and C. P. Sherwin (*Jour. Biol. Chem.*, 29 (1917), No. 2, p. VI).—From 100 liters of a mixed sample of cows' milk the authors isolated 500 mg. of adenin and 100 mg. of guanin by means of silver precipitation of the protein-free residue.

Calcium and phosphorus in the blood of lactating cows, E. B. Meigs and N. R. Blatherwick (*Jour. Biol. Chem.*, 29 (1917), No. 2, pp. XI, XII).—Calcium, nitrogen, total phosphorus, and lipoid and inorganic phosphorus have been determined in the blood and plasma of cows and heifers of various ages on various rations and at various stages of pregnancy and lactation.

The calcium content of cow's plasma was found to be surprisingly constant, the highest figure obtained being 0.0114 per cent and the lowest, 0.0086 per cent. The results indicate that the amount is not appreciably altered by pregnancy, lactation, or considerable changes in diet.

The total, lipoid, and inorganic phosphorus contents of normal plasma were found to be extremely variable. The total phosphorus varied from 0.0085 to 0.0178 per cent; the lipoid, from a little less than 0.002 to a little over 0.008 per cent; and the inorganic, from about 0.004 to 0.008 per cent. In general the variations of inorganic phosphorus appeared to depend to some extent on the amount of grain fed. No tabulated data are submitted.

The distribution of esterases in the animal body, Agnes E. Porter (*Biochem. Jour.*, 10 (1916), No. 4, pp. 523–533).—Fat- and wax-splitting ferments were found to be widely distributed among the organs of man, ox, sheep, goat, pig, cat, rabbit, and guinea pig. Butyrinase and lecithase were present in all of the organs examined. Olein lipase was also commonly present, but often only as a mere trace. It appeared to be strongest in pig's pancreas but

308

was also active in the pancreas of other species, in the liver and in the thymus, and to a lesser degree in the lymphatic glands, ox suprarenals and thyroid, cat kidney, and pig lung. Tristearin was also frequently found. Wax-splitting enzyms were found in ox, sheep, and pig pancreas, human, ox, pig, cat, and rabbit liver, thymus, and lymphatic glands, ox and sheep thyroid, or suprarenals, human skin, and cat and human kidney.

"The distribution of esterases in the body appears to have some relation to resistance to tubercle. The cat, which is very little susceptible to tubercle, is well provided with esterases throughout its organs. The sheep, although less well-provided for than the susceptible pig in other regions, possesses very active lymphatic glands. The susceptible guinea pig has the chief part of its lipase in the form of butyrinase and olein lipase, and is deficient in higher esterases. The lungs in all species were found very poor in these ferments. The more resistant liver showed active lipolytic properties."

The experimental procedures used and the data obtained are described and submitted in detail.

The nonspecificity of animal and vegetable reductase, A. Bach (Compt. Rend. Acad. Sci. [Paris], 164 (1917), No. 5, pp. 248, 249).—From data obtained in a study with 14 different aldehydes in the reduction of nitrate by reductase (of milk and potato) in the presence of an aldehyde the author concludes that the specificity of the reducing ferment is functional and not structural. The specificity is considered to depend on a determined chemical function and not on any geometrical configuration.

The composition of adipocere, R. F. Ruttan and M. J. Marshall (Jour. Biol. Chem., 29 (1917), No. 2, pp. 319–327).—The following percentage composition of a sample of adipocere found near Rockburn, Quebec, is reported: Palmitic acid, 67.52; stearic acid, 3.3; oleic acid, 5.24; l-hydroxy stearic acid, 9.48; θ-hydroxy stearic acid, 6.32; stearin and palmitin, 1.21; olein, 0.16; unsaponified matter, 0.87; calcium soaps, 4.41; protein, 0.665; ash, 0.578; humus and undetermined, 0.247. The physical and chemical constants of the ether-soluble matter found were specific gravity at 100° C., 0.8436; refractive index at 65°, 1.436; melting point, 60 to 63°; acid value, 201.7; saponification value, 207; iodin value, 6.04; and acetyl value, 34.75.

The data are discussed.

The isolation of stachydrin from alfalfa hay, H. Steenbock (Jour. Biol. Chem., 29 (1917), No. 2, p. XXVII).—The author at the Wisconsin Experiment Station notes the isolation of l-stachydrin in a pure form and as the hydrochlorid from the phosphotungstic acid fraction of the water-soluble constituents of alfalfa hay. It was identified by the preparation of the picrate, chloroplatinate, aurate, methyl ester, and methyl ester chloroaurate, all of which were found to be characteristic. It is indicated that "the Kossel and Van Slyke methods when applied directly to alfalfa hay nitrogen give erroneous values for the diamino acids, the error in the first case falling upon the lysin fraction and in the second case upon the histidin fraction."

The pectic substances of plants.—Preliminary communication, S. B. Schryver and Dorothy Haynes (Biochem. Jour., 10 (1916), No. 4, pp. 539–547).—A procedure for the preparation of the pectic substances of plants which consists essentially of extracting the residue, obtained after expressing the juice, with a warm 0.5 per cent ammonium oxalate solution and precipitation with alcohol is described in detail. The substance so obtained was acidic in character, soluble in water, and designated by the authors as pectinogen. It was purified, usually in small quantities, by dissolving in water to make a 3 to 4 per cent solution, centrifugalizing, and precipitating the clear fluid by alcohol. The precipitate was filtered, washed, air dried, and obtained in the form of a granular white powder. The largest amount of this preparation was obtained from turnips, but preparations were also obtained from strawberries, apples, and rhubarb stems.

An alkaline solution of the pectinogen kept at room temperature was readily converted into another substance of acidic character which could be precipitated from alkaline solutions by acids as a gel insoluble in water. This substance has been designated as pectin. It is insoluble in water and the solution of its sodium salt gives a gelatinous precipitate with calcium chlorid.

The analyses of the pectins obtained from the various sources agree well with the formula $C_{17}H_{24}O_{16}$. On distillation with hydrochloric acid the pectinogin yielded furfural in such quantity as to indicate the presence of one pentose group in each complex of 17 carbon atoms. It is indicated that the results obtained show that "there is a single pectin, which is a complex built up by the combination of a pentose group with another group containing twelve carbon atoms. There is no evidence that it is a carbohydrate, but it appears to be an acid sui generis."

The acids of fruit wines, W. J. BARAGIOLA (*Landw. Jahrb. Schweiz, 30* (1916), No. 5, pp. 441–454).—This is a general discussion of the subject, together with some experimental data on the decrease in total acidity with increasing ripeness of the fruit; the decrease of tannic acid with increasing ripeness in the juice pressed from crushed, coarsely ground, and very finely ground fruit; the variation of the amount of tannic acid in the juice from the peel, flesh, and core of pears; and the decrease of tannic acid in the juice from fruit which had been exposed to the air and had consequently undergone some oxidative changes brought about by the oxidases.

The author points out the errors which are likely to arise in drawing conclusions from data obtained from grape wines and applied in the preparation of fruit wines. A complete analysis of a cider is submitted.

It is concluded that in the case of berry wines the acidity of the young wines remains fairly constant because of the large amount of tartaric acid present. The sour taste of grape wine is first markedly influenced by the other organic acids after the greater part of the tartaric acid has been removed. The reverse is the case in fruit wines, where the individual acids in the young wines exercise a marked influence on the general character of the product.

Tartaric acid content of grape musts and young wines, W. J. BARAGIOLA and O. SCHUPPLI (*Landw. Jahrb. Schweiz, 30* (1916), No. 5, pp. 455–479).—Detailed analytical data relative to the total acidity, tartaric acid content, and percentage of tartaric acid of the total acidity of musts prepared at the Swiss experiment station at Wüdenswil, musts from the private experimental fields in the Canton of Zurich, and a number of wines which were made in 1914 are submitted and briefly discussed.

Investigations on the camphors of Mauritius (*Dept. Agr. Mauritius, Sci. Ser., Bul. 4 (1916)*, [*English Ed.*], pp. 14).—The results of a number of distillation experiments preliminary to a reforestation of certain parts of the island have shown that the existing camphors yield no solid camphor on distillation. The small amount of camphor present is readily dissolved in the oil and not easily separated therefrom.

Standard methods of chemical analysis, edited by W. W. SCOTT (*New York: D. Van Nostrand Co., 1917, pp. XXXI+864, pls. 3, figs. 142*).—As stated in the preface, this volume is a compilation of carefully selected methods of technical analysis that have proved of practical value to the professional chemist. The methods are described in sufficient detail to be easily carried out, but lengthy theoretical discussions have been avoided in order to include a large amount of information in a compact, accessible form.

The material is grouped under three major divisions, (1) quantitative determination of the elements, (2) special subjects, and (3) tables and useful data. In the chapters on the elements the subject matter is treated in a general way under the headings of physical properties, detection, estimation, preparation and solution of the samples, separations, and gravimetric and volumetric methods.

Report of the work of the Swiss Agricultural Chemical Institute at Bern (Liebefeld) for the year 1915, P. LIECHTI (*Landw. Jahrb. Schweiz, 30 (1916),* No. 5, pp. 489–508).—This report contains the results of the fertilizer and feeding stuff control work and brief notes on some projects being carried on, chiefly in connection with fertilizers.

Standard methods for the examination of water and sewage (*Boston: Amer. Pub. Health Assoc., 1917, 3. ed., pp. XVI+115, fig. 1*).—This is a revision of the methods by committees of the American Public Health Association and the American Chemical Society and referees of the Association of Official Agricultural Chemists. It includes chemical, microscopical, and bacteriological procedures and a chemical and bacteriological bibliography.

Applications of a new reagent for the separation of ammonia.—I, The colorimetric determination of ammonia in urine, O. FOLIN and R. D. BELL (*Jour. Biol. Chem., 29 (1917), No. 2, pp. 329–335*).—On account of the impossibility of obtaining the charcoal used in the method described by Folin and Denis (E. S. R., 36, p. 316), and for which no substitute could be found, the authors have modified the procedure for nitrogen determination by direct nesslerization. The material used in the procedure is a synthetic mineral, an "aluminate silicate," which possesses the peculiar absorptive properties characteristic of some natural zeolites. The crude product is sold under the trade name "permutit."

The modified procedure is as follows: Two gm. of the powder is transferred to a 200-cc. volumetric flask, 5 cc. of water added and, with an Ostwald pipette, 1 or 2 cc. of undiluted or, with a 5-cc. pipette, 5 cc. of diluted urine introduced. The added sample is rinsed down with a little water and the mixture gently but continuously shaken for five minutes. The powder is rinsed to the bottom of the flask with water, and the supernatant liquid decanted. Water is added once more and decanted. A little water is now added to the powder, 5 cc. of 10 per cent sodium hydroxid introduced, the liquid agitated, and water added until the flask is about three-fourths full. It is then shaken for a few seconds, 10 cc. of Nessler's reagent added, the liquid thoroughly mixed, and allowed to stand for 10 minutes or as much longer as may be convenient. It is then filled to the mark with water, mixed, and compared with the standard in the colorimeter.

Experimental data submitted indicate the accuracy of the method.

A note on certain chemical changes in shucked oysters under refrigeration, and methods of detecting these changes, E. D. CLARK and L. H. ALMY (*Jour. Biol. Chem., 29 (1917), No. 2, pp. XXIII, XXIV*).—Preliminary experiments showed that freshly shucked oysters standing at temperatures above the freezing point yielded regularly increasing percentages of ammoniacal nitrogen by aeration, amino-acid nitrogen, and reducing substances.

Larger scale studies were made to simulate commercial practices in the handling and transporting of oysters, in which samples were held at different temperatures for various periods of time up to 15 days. During storage the ammoniacal nitrogen showed the most marked increases, but the low temperature of 34° F. had a great inhibiting effect on the production of ammonia. Amino-acid nitrogen and a reducing substance, which is indicated as probably being sugar, did not show increases of the same magnitude as ammonia.

The amino-acid nitrogen was determined by Van Slyke's gasometric procedure and by Sörensen's formol titration method, and the reducing substances by Benedict's quantitative method for sugar.

It is indicated that, "as is the case with all perishable substances, decomposition in oysters is not prevented by low temperatures but is merely retarded, especially at temperatures near the freezing point."

The determination of peanut oil in mixtures with olive oil, R. Biazzo and S. Vigdorcik (*Ann. Chim. Appl. [Rome], 6 (1916), No. 9–12, pp. 179–185*).—Methods which have been proposed for the determination of peanut oil in mixtures are briefly reviewed.

The method proposed by the author consists of treating the fatty acids obtained from the oil in 200 cc. of ether with 50 cc. of a 30 per cent lead acetate solution. The lead soaps of the liquid fatty acids dissolve in the ether, while the insoluble soaps of the solid acids form an intermediate layer between the aqueous solution and the ether. The clear ethereal solution is decanted through a dry filter, the residue washed with ether, transferred to the filter, and again washed. It is then transferred to a separatory funnel with 200 cc. of ether, the fatty acids liberated with hydrochloric acid, the ethereal layer separated, washed with water, the ether distilled, and the residue dried and finally tested for arachidic acid by the usual tests.

The determination of colza oil in mixtures with olive oil, R. Biazzo and S. Vigdorcik (*Ann. Chim. Appl. [Rome], 6 (1916), No. 9–12, pp. 185–195*).—Earlier work on the subject is reviewed.

The method proposed by the author depends on the concentration of erucic acid, its conversion into behenic acid, and the identification of the latter. The fatty acids from 20 cc. of the oil are dissolved in 180 cc. of anhydrous acetone, the solution heated to boiling, and treated with 20 cc. normal potassium hydroxid. The precipitated acid potassium soaps are filtered off, washed with acetone, dissolved in water, decomposed with hydrochloric acid, and the fatty acids extracted by ether. The ethereal solution is shaken with lead acetate, and the insoluble lead soaps treated for the determination of arachidic acid as noted above. The soluble lead soaps are decomposed with hydrochloric acid, the free acids separated, and then hydrogenated in the presence of palladium catalyzer. The hydrogenated acids are fractionally crystallized and their melting point determined.

On the determination of theobromin and caffein in cocoa and chocolate, G. Savini (*Ann. Chim. Appl. [Rome], 6 (1916), No. 9–12, pp. 247–250*).—In the procedure described 12 gm. of the pulverized sample is treated with 70 cc. of petroleum ether in a 500-cc. flask and heated on the water bath for 10 minutes. The liquid is then decanted and the operation repeated with two portions of the solvent.

The defatted material is transferred to a flask and boiled for about one hour with 5 cc. of 10 per cent sulphuric acid and about 250 cc. of water. During the heating the contents are occasionally shaken, and finally made up to volume (300 cc.) at about 30° C. and filtered. Two hundred and fifty cc. of the filtrate (corresponding to 10 gm. of the original substance) is evaporated in a porcelain dish after the addition of magnesia to make the mixture alkaline and 10 gm. of fine sand. When the mass attains a sirupy consistency and about 8 to 10 gm. of magnesia have been added it is allowed to cool, pulverized in the mortar, and extracted with chloroform to which 0.25 cc. of concentrated ammonium hydroxid has been added. The extraction is repeated several times until about 500 cc. of chloroform has been used. The solvent is then removed by distillation. The residue obtained is of sufficient purity to be weighed directly. The procedure is indicated as being easy to manipulate and to be applicable to a variety of substances.

Some analytical data submitted indicate the accuracy of the procedure.

Detection of lime used as a neutralizer in dairy products, H. J. WICHMANN (*U. S. Dept. Agr. Bul. 524 (1917), pp. 22*).—From an analytical study of the calcium oxid in cream, the total ash and the salt-free (sodium-chlorid-free) ash, 25 per cent calcium oxid in the salt-free ash was found to be a good maximum standard. If the calcium oxid percentage is below 25 it is considered that the butter may be classed as made from unlimed cream, while samples with calcium oxid percentages between 25 and 28 in a salt-free ash should be considered suspicious. In cases of doubt as to the possibilities of the presence of large amounts of calcium sulphate in the salt used, a sulphate determination should be made and the proper correction applied. The effect of calcium chlorid, magnesium chlorid, and sodium sulphate which might be present in the salt used was studied, and the amounts ordinarily present found to have no effect.

The use of lime in renovating old storage butter is noted and briefly discussed.

Analytical data of the ash of a number of creams before liming, of butter made from unneutralized cream, of salted and unsalted butters made from unneutralized cream, and of unlimed and limed dairy products are submitted.

The determination of sugar in gummy substances, G. SAVINI (*Ann. Chim. Appl. [Rome], 6 (1916), No. 9–12, pp. 250–255*).—In the examination of gummy substances the results obtained by Fehling's solution were higher than those obtained by the optical procedure (Clerget's formula). During the inversion in the presence of gum appreciable amounts of dextrorotatory material were found to be formed, which caused the discordant results. This was obviated by defecating the sample with basic lead acetate and 95 per cent alcohol. An aliquot from the defecated material is evaporated to remove the alcohol, the residue dissolved in water, and the excess lead removed with alum. The clear filtrate is then treated in the usual manner.

Some analytical data are submitted.

The quantitative determination of minute amounts of sugar by α-naphthol and the estimation of entrainment losses, A. F. BLAKE (*Internat. Sugar. Jour., 19 (1917), No. 217, pp. 26–28, fig. 1*).—The following procedure is described:

Five cc. of the solution to be tested is placed in a perfectly clean vial and five drops of a 20 per cent solution of α-naphthol in pure alcohol, together with 10 cc. of concentrated sulphuric acid, are carefully added. The mixture, which becomes very hot, is immediately stirred with a glass rod. In the presence of sugar a purple-red color develops, the intensity being proportionate to the amount of sugar present. After two minutes the color of the solution in the vial is compared with that of a standard prepared in the same manner as the unknown sample.

It is indicated that the error in developing and matching the colors is about 20 per cent. The reaction is not specific, but it is noted that the impurities which might be present do not introduce a great error. The presence of iron interferes somewhat by producing a peculiar coloration.

The test is of special value in determining entrainment losses.

The utilization of cull citrus fruits in Florida, F. A. McDERMOTT, summarized by S. S. WALKER (*Florida Sta. Bul. 135 (1917), pp. 129–144*).—The results of the investigation show that both orange and grapefruit juice can be preserved in the original condition at least for 18 months and probably indefinitely by pasteurization in the absence of air. After proper clarification, the juice may be concentrated by vacuum evaporation to about 20 per cent of its original volume. The concentrated product, flavored with orange extract, can be packed and preserved in the same way as the fresh juice. The reduction of the juices to a dry material, while possible, is considered hardly to be commercially practicable.

A flavoring oil can be prepared from the peel of the Florida orange by distillation with steam at reduced pressure. The colorless oil so obtained, colored by means of the pigment present in the thin outer peel of the orange, is entirely suitable for marketing. Grapefruit peel was found to contain a similar oil, but in such small amounts that its production would not be profitable.

It is indicated that the juice of decayed fruits, drops, etc., after being sterilized can be fermented for the production of alcohol and the residue used for producing citric acid. The residue from the pulp after the removal of the juice is considered to be suitable for use as stock food. The waste seeds, ground peel, etc., are practically valueless.

The action of ultraviolet rays on the alcoholic fermentation of India fig must, ROMOLO and REMO DE FAZI (*Ann. Chim. Appl.* [*Rome*], 6 (*1916*), *No. 9–12, pp. 221–246, figs. 13*).—The fermentation of fig must by *Saccharomyces opuntiæ* was found to be more vigorous through the action of ultraviolet rays if the time of exposure to the rays was limited. Prolonged exposure caused a gradual diminution of the action of the organism. In the ordinary fermentation of the fig must a heavy film forms on the surface which gradually increases as the fermentation proceeds. No trace of such a film was evident, however, where the fermentation took place under the influence of ultraviolet rays.

Data are submitted in detailed tabular and graphical form and discussed.

The value of supposed household remedies for vinegar disease in wine, W. J. BARAGIOLA and F. BRAUN (*Landw. Jahrb. Schweiz, 30 (1916), No. 5, pp. 509–525*).—Data obtained in a study of the value of veal, carrots, and charcoal as remedies for vinegar disease in wine are reported in tabular form and discussed. The authors strongly advise against the use of these materials, as results indicate that they are of no value in curing the disease.

METEOROLOGY.

Climatological data for the United States by sections (*U. S. Dept. Agr., Weather Bur. Climat. Data, 3 (1916), No. 13, pp. 389, pls. 2, figs. 51*).—Summaries and detailed tabulated statements of climatological data for the year 1916 are given for each State.

Meteorological observations, J. S. STEVENS (*Maine Sta. Bul. 257 (1916), pp. 357, 358*).—A monthly and annual summary of observations at the University of Maine on temperature, precipitation, cloudiness, and wind movement during 1916 is given. The mean temperature for the year was 44.83° F., as compared with an average of 42.77° for 48 years; the total precipitation was 41.2 in., the snowfall 115 in., the number of clear days 213, the number of cloudy days 101, and the total movement of wind 49,818 miles.

Meteorological summary, F. BROWN (*Wyoming Sta. Rpt. 1916, pp. 95–98*).— Monthly summaries are given of observations at Laramie, Wyo., during 1915 on temperature, pressure, precipitation, humidity, sunshine, and wind movement. The highest temperature was 84° F., July 14; the lowest —14°, January 16. The total precipitation was 12.92 in. The highest relative humidity was 100 per cent, January 5; the lowest, 27 per cent, July 12. The greatest velocity of wind was 43 miles per hour, November 19. The first killing frost was October 3.

Relative humidities and vapor pressures over the United States, P. C. DAY (*U. S. Mo. Weather Rev., Sup. 6 (1917), pp. 61, pls. 34, figs. 6*).—Detailed data are given in tables, charts, and diagrams, and are briefly discussed under the following heads: Source, amount, and distribution of atmospheric water vapor; influence of atmospheric water vapor on climate; terms "absolute" and "relative" humidity; moist and dry climates; measurements of atmospheric moisture; statistical data available; diurnal changes, annual march, and seasonal variations in relative humidity; absolute humidity; and saturation deficit. Data from recording hair hygrometers for a period of about five years are reported and discussed.

Average rainfall, May and June (*U. S. Dept. Agr., Nat. Weather and Crop Bul. 7 (1917), pp. 2, 3, 7, fig. 1*).—A chart is given which shows the average rainfall for the period from May 1 to June 30, inclusive, for the 20 years 1895 to 1914. This shows that "the heaviest rainfall during these two months is over the Florida Peninsula, where it reaches between 13 and 14 in. In the lower Mississippi Valley the rainfall is over 10 in. at a number of points, and the chart indicates that there are quite large areas in the Great Plains States where the fall during May and June averages over 9 in., and that this amount is exceeded at a few points in the east-central part of the country. The least rainfall is in southern California and southwestern Arizona, where it is less than 0.5 in. Over most of the region west of the Rocky Mountains the fall averages less than 3 inches.

"In most of the eastern part of the country, except in southern Florida, the annual rainfall is well distributed throughout each month of the twelve. Over the Great Plains region there is much more precipitation during the summer months than falls in winter time. In eastern North Dakota and central South Dakota 80 per cent of the annual precipitation falls during the period from April 1 to September 30, and over a large part of the Great Plains States from western Texas northward to Montana and western Wisconsin, 70 per cent of the annual fall comes between the above-mentioned dates. On the Pacific coast, on the other hand, the rainy season is in the winter time, and very little precipitation occurs from June to October, during most seasons."

A safe method proposed for estimating minimum rainfall, J. P. WELLS (*Engin. News, 77 (1917), No. 13, pp. 502–504, fig. 1*).—The author presents the results of his studies of all the long-time rainfall records of the U. S. Weather Bureau up to 1909 and tabulates the mean, maximum, and minimum annual precipitations. The relations between these records, as calculated, are called maximum-minimum, maximum-mean, and minimum-mean rainfall factors. It is considered essential to have some safe method of determining the minimum rainfall that will occur during a long period of years in order to estimate conservatively minimum run-off conditions. From these studies, it is concluded that the minimum-mean factors afford a safe basis for estimating minimum rainfall.

"In hydraulic investigations it is often the case that only short records of precipitation are available and it is desirable to know what the minimum rainfall for a long period of years would be. If the minimum-mean factor for the locality is known, at least an approximate estimate of the minimum rainfall can be made." The following formula is proposed: "$X = M \frac{(LS)}{L'}$," in which X=required minimum rainfall, M=minimum-mean factor for the district, L=mean rainfall for entire period at adjacent station which has a long record, L'=mean rainfall at adjacent station during the period in which the records were taken at the station which has a short record, and S=the mean rainfall at the station which has a short record. By averaging the results obtained in the above way from a number of adjacent stations with long records, a safe estimate of the minimum rainfall can be made.

"The results obtained from using the factors 1/2 for 110 years and 2/3 for 50 years are conservative for eastern United States. These factors, however, should not be used for the western part of the country, for they are shown to be much less west of the Mississippi River."

Effect of a late spring upon crop yields (*U. S. Dept. Agr., Nat. Weather and Crop Bul. 11 (1917), pp. 2, 3, 5, figs. 4*).—Diagrams are given which show the fallacy of the belief that a late spring is usually followed by a poor crop season, especially as applied to corn, oats, and cotton.

Safe dates for planting corn (*U. S. Dept. Agr., Nat. Weather and Crop Bul. 8 (1917), pp. 2, 3*).—It is stated that the average date of beginning corn planting in the United States varies from February 1 in the extreme South to the latter half of May in the extreme North. The average number of days necessary for maturity of the crop varies from 120 days or slightly less in the North to 150 days or slightly more in the Gulf States. In the corn-belt region the growing period varies from about 130 days in Kansas to 140 days in the Ohio Valley, the period varying, however, with the variety of corn, soil, prevailing temperature, moisture, etc.

"The average date of the first killing frost in the fall east of the Rocky Mountain region varies from about the middle of September in extreme northern districts to December 1 at some distance from the Gulf coast. From Nebraska and Iowa eastward to northern Ohio the first killing frost in the fall is observed on the average between October 1 and 11. From Kansas and Missouri eastward to the Appalachian Mountains the frost date varies between October 11 and 21. In Oklahoma these dates are between October 21 and November 11, while in central and eastern Texas they vary between November 11 and November 25. Eastward across the Southern States from Oklahoma and Texas the variation from the dates recorded in those States is largely a matter of topography. Between the Appalachian Mountains and the Atlantic coast the dates vary from November 1 to 11 in the South; October 21 and November 1 in central districts; and October 11 to 21 farther north. In northern New England and central New York State frost frequently occurs before the middle of September."

The number of days from June 1 to the average first killing frost in the fall varies from 100 to 120 in the extreme North to 120 to 140 in the principal corn-growing region, and from 150 to 170 in the Gulf States.

The above figures show that there are few sections of the country east of the one-hundredth meridian where corn may not safely be planted any time during May, with the expectation that it will mature before the average fall frost date. "In some sections of the central part of the country, and in many districts in the South, corn may be planted until near the close of June, with the expectation that it will mature sufficiently to escape damage from frost nine years out of ten."

Weather and cotton (*U. S. Dept. Agr., Nat. Weather and Crop Bul. 9 (1917), p. 3*).—From a review of the data bearing on this subject, it is concluded that "in general, the most favorable weather conditions for cotton are warm and comparatively dry weather during May and June and moderate rainfall during the succeeding three months. The most unfavorable are cool and wet weather during the former period and dry and hot during the latter. It is especially harmful for May and June to be cool and wet, as this greatly retards growth and final maturity, and also prevents proper cultivation. For best results thorough cultivation is especially important, owing to the length of the time between the final chopping-out period and the maturity of the last fruit, and the resulting tendency of the fields to become grassy.

"Subnormal rainfall during the months of July and August is more frequently harmful in the western portion of the belt than in the central and eastern portions, owing to the normally greater amounts received in the latter districts. In general, the yield of cotton is largely affected by the rainfall during the months of July and August, especially the latter, but in the central and eastern portions of the belt temperature and moisture conditions during the early period of growth are of scarcely less importance. The amount of rainfall during the latter part of the growing season, particularly in September, is also of special significance, as this largely determines the amount of the top crop, which plays an important part in the total yield."

Safe date for planting potatoes (*U. S. Dept. Agr., Nat. Weather and Crop Bul. 10 (1917), p. 3*).—It is stated that the potato is "a cool weather crop, and the largest yields in the United States are in the northern tier of States and the Rocky Mountain region, where the mean annual temperature is between 40 and 50° and where the July temperature does not average over 70° F.

The planting of early potatoes progresses from south to north in the Eastern States in close correlation with the spring temperature of 45°, and is usually nearly one month earlier than the average date of the last killing frost in the spring. The total number of days from planting to harvesting of early potatoes is about 100 in the Central States; 90 in the Southeastern, North Cenral, and Pacific Coast States; and 70 to 90 in the Lake States. The planting of the northern commercial crop becomes general about April 11 in the southern portion of the States running westward from Virginia to Kansas and extreme western Texas, and then extends northward to slightly later than June 1 in extreme northern Ohio, central Michigan, and central Wisconsin.

"Taking the length of the growing period and the first killing frost in the fall into consideration, potatoes should be planted by the first of June in the central and upper Missouri Valley and eastern Rocky Mountain slope, and by June 15 in most districts from the lower Missouri and upper Mississippi Valley eastward to the Atlantic coast in order to thoroughly mature before the average date of killing frost."

SOILS—FERTILIZERS.

Special crop soils [of New York], E. O. FIPPIN (*Cornell Countryman, 14 (1917), No. 7, pp. 568–571, 598, figs. 2*).—The so-called general purpose soils of New York, including the light sandy and gravelly soils, heavy clay, and muck soils are discussed.

"The most prominent of these three groups of soil is the muck. . . . Through the central part of the State beds of marl commonly occur under the muck. . . . The smaller and deeper areas of muck are generally the safest for cropping purposes."

Peat moors in the coast regions of southern German East Africa, W. JANENSCH (*Arch. Biontol., 3 (1914), No. 3, pp. 263–276, pls. 2, figs. 2*).—This is a report on the origin, formation, and physical and chemical composition of peat moor soils of the Lukuledi and Mbenkuru regions of German East Africa.

Analyses of the ashes and dry substance of samples of the peat from four different localities are reported, showing the potash content to vary from 0.97 to 2.91 per cent in the ash and from 0.22 to 1.3 per cent in the dry matter, the phosphoric acid from 0.41 to 1.34 per cent in the ash and from 0.1 to 0.31 in the dry matter, and the organic matter from 55.24 to 76.91 per cent. The nitrogen content of the organic matter varied from 2.46 to 3.38 per cent. The lime content is considered to be in general relatively lower than that of European peats, being on the average about 9.62 per cent.

Recent studies on nitrification in soils, J. U. SABACHAGA (*Bol. Min. Agr.* [*Argentina*], 20 (1916), No. 9–12, pp. 719–728).—This is a review of recent work by the author and others bearing on the subject, in which several different types of organisms were studied.

It is concluded that nitrites are not normally found in a fertile soil, that the reduction of nitrates is always brought about by a certain class of bacteria, and that there are certain conditions of soil favorable to the reduction of nitrates. It was found that none of the organisms examined possesses a nitrifying power comparable to that of the organisms in soil. The total studies appeared to demonstrate that with isolated species only a small amount of nitric or nitrous acid was obtained in solutions.

Fixation of ammonia in soils, I. G. McBETH (*U. S. Dept. Agr.*, Jour. *Agr. Research*, 9 (1917), No. 5, pp. 141–155, fig. 1).—Experiments on the fixation of ammonia by soils, conducted in cooperation with the California Citrus substation at Riverside, are reported.

It was found that "many semiarid subsoils have the property of fixing large quantities of ammonia. Much of the ammonia fixed can not be removed by the ordinary methods for determining the ammonia content of the soils. Extracting the soil with 10 per cent hydrochloric acid gives approximately the same quantity of ammonia as distilling the soils with magnesium oxid. Anions apparently have little or no influence on the fixation of ammonia by soils. The ammoniacal nitrogen removed from duplicate samples of soil extracted with 10 per cent acid gives remarkably consistent results, while duplicate samples of soil distilled at atmospheric pressure with magnesium oxid frequently fail to give a satisfactory agreement. A large percentage of the ammonia added to semiarid soils and subsoils can not be recovered by boiling the soil with excessive amounts of caustic solutions. Boiling soils with 10 per cent hydrochloric acid removes practically all of the ammoniacal nitrogen from one soil studied, but less than 75 per cent was recovered from another soil.

"The fixation of ammonia by semiarid soils increases with depth. In this regard semiarid soils appear to differ from humid soils. The addition of ammonum salts in a concentrated solution results in greater fixation than when the same amount is added in a dilute solution. The fixation of ammonia by soils increases with the temperature. The fixation of ammonia by a soil is most rapid during the first few minutes, but the fixation process appears to continue for several days. Heating a soil for six hours at temperatures of 200° C. or above reduces its power of fixing ammonia.

"When small amounts of ammonium salts are added, the percentage of ammonia fixed remains constant. If increasing amounts of ammonia are added, a point is reached at which the percentage fixation becomes less, but the absolute fixation may continue to increase.

"Aluminum, iron, and potassium salts added to soils prior to the addition of ammonia reduce the ammonia-fixing power of the soils very decidedly. Calcium, magnesium, and sodium salts added to the semiarid soils prior to the addition of the ammonia have little effect on the ammonia-fixing power of semi-arid soils. The anions of aluminum, iron, potassium, calcium, sodium, or magnesium salts apparently have no influence on the action of these salts in reducing the ammonia-fixing power of semi-arid soils.

"In semiarid soils the quantity of calcium brought into solution by ammonium chlorid increases with depth; when extracted with aluminum, sodium, or magnesium chlorid, the calcium brought into solution does not increase with the depth."

Relation of the transformation and distribution of soil nitrogen to the nutrition of citrus plants, I. G. McBETH (*U. S. Dept. Agr.*, Jour. *Agr. Research*,

9 (1917), No. 7, pp. 183–252, figs. 19).—Experiments conducted in cooperation with the California Citrus Substation at Riverside are reported.

It was found that "semiarid soils frequently fail to nitrify dried blood when added in 1 per cent quantities, but invariably nitrify blood when added in amounts not greater than are ordinarily applied under the field conditions. The addition of dried blood to semiarid soils in 1 per cent quantities frequently caused large amounts of ammonia to accumulate in the soil. The addition of dried blood or other nitrogenous substances applied as fertilizers caused no marked increase in the ammonia content of the soils. When 1 per cent of dried blood is added to semiarid soils, as much as 50 per cent of the nitrogen added may be lost during an incubation period of six weeks. As the soils frequently give off a strong ammoniacal odor, it is believed that this loss is due, in a large measure at least, to the volatilization of ammonia. Ammonification or nitrification studies on semiarid soils in which 1 per cent of dried blood is added are of questionable value and may lead to erroneous conclusions.

"Green manures, especially the legume varieties, nitrify very rapidly. As much as 50 per cent of the nitrogen contained in green plant tissues may be converted into nitrates in 30 days. Green manures furnish a valuable source of energy for the nonsymbiotic nitrogen-fixing organisms.

"The furrow system of irrigation frequently causes a very unsatisfactory distribution of the soil nitrates. In many citrus groves more than two-thirds of the nitric nitrogen in the upper 4 ft. of soil is found in the surface 6 in., in which, because of the frequent cultivation, few feeding roots are found. The furrow system of irrigation frequently causes the formation of niter spots. Surface scrapings from these spots in heavily fertilized groves may contain as much as 1 per cent of nitrogen as nitrates. The brown color which characterizes the niter spots is probably due to a number of factors, but it is believed that the deliquescent character of the calcium nitrate is important in this regard. Where the furrow system of irrigation is employed, the fertilizing materials should be plowed down somewhat deeper than the land is cultivated. The feeding roots will then have an opportunity to assimilate the food as it is rendered available, whereas, if it is formed within the cultivated zone, the irrigation will tend to carry it farther away from the roots.

"Much nitric nitrogen is lost from citrus lands by leaching. The most effective means of preventing this loss is by growing a winter cover crop.

"Basin irrigation or overhead irrigation gives a more satisfactory distribution of soil nitrates than the furrow system. The basin system of irrigation seems to give greatest promise when combined with a mulching system. However, the rapidity with which organic materials rich in nitrogen decay would seem to make it inadvisable to maintain a constant mulch with these materials, as the nitrates produced will probably be far in excess of the needs of the tree, and much loss will result."

Conclusions as to mottle-leaf are noted on page —.

Fourteen references to literature bearing on the subject are appended.

Tests on the disinfection of soil, MIÈGE (*Compt. Rend. Acad. Sci.* [*Paris*], *164 (1917), No. 9, pp. 362–365).*—Two series of experiments on field, garden, and greenhouse soils with potatoes, buckwheat, tomatoes, kidney beans, carrots, leeks, cucumbers, and carnations are reported. The materials used were toluene, carbon bisulphid, lysol, potassium permanganate, copper sulphate, formalin, sulphur, calcium hypochlorite, charcoal, and oxygenated water.

It was found that treatment of the soil with these substances had a favorable influence on the different vegetables on different soils. This favorable influence was found to be specific with reference to the chemical substance used for certain plants. Thus, in the greenhouse toluene and carbon bisulphid had the best influence on tomatoes. These results are thought to justify the conclusion that the treatment of soils with antiseptics is, on the whole, beneficial.

Chemical studies of the efficiency of legumes as green manures in Hawaii, ALICE R. THOMPSON (*Hawaii Sta. Bul. 43 (1917), pp. 26*).—The results of the first year's experiments to determine the comparative values for soil improvement of 32 different varieties of legumes on a rich brown calcareous soil from the station grounds and a red, apparently acid, soil low in phosphate and lime from Kunia are reported.

It was found that " the nitrate content of soils in which legumes are growing is low as compared with unplanted check soils, owing possibly to absorption of nitrates by the roots of the growing plants. Where a large amount of leguminous growth is turned under to decompose, the nitrate content of the soil usually is greatly increased.

"Legumes grown on station soil usually showed a higher percentage of nitrogen in the water-free material than those grown on Kunia soil. Liming in a few cases increased the nitrogen content and the nodule development of legumes on Kunia soil. The nitrogen content of the above-ground parts of legumes, although more variable than that of roots, was also usually greater, especially on the station soil, where only the velvet bean and German lupine gave the same value for plant and roots, owing possibly to the large bunches of nodules on their roots. . . .

" In calculations of nitrogen in the entire legume plant on a water-free basis the plants grown on Kunia soil again appear deficient in this element. Liming increased the nitrogen content of the entire plant in case of the jack bean and cowpea, but not of the velvet bean. The crotalarias contained the most nitrogen on both a fresh and water-free basis. As green manure, *Sesbania ægyptiaca* and the velvet bean might be used successfully on Kunia soil if a lime dressing is employed.

" The results of analyses indicate that the nitrogen of leguminous plants is gained through atmospheric assimilation and not from the soil.

"When a legume is to be grown for turning under the roots only, the percentage of nitrogen in the roots and the weight of roots per acre should be considered. The varieties which gave the heaviest yield of root nitrogen per pot were the cowpea, velvet bean, jack bean, Mauritius bean, alfalfa, *Indigofera anil*, and *Phaseolus semierectus* grown on station soil.

" From the results obtained in beaker experiments, it appears that one-fifth of the total nitrate nitrogen of cowpeas is converted into soluble ammonia and nitrate salts in three weeks' time. In pot experiments, where the conditions more nearly represented those in the field, in the station soil pots one-half the nitrogen decomposing cowpeas and jack beans was lost through weathering. In Kunia soil a loss of nitrogen was also observed in case of these legumes and also of velvet beans and soy beans, which showed no loss from weathering in station soil, probably because of their later maturity and consequently shorter period of weathering. It appears that in the field, with heavy rains or irrigation, considerable loss of nitrogen probably results through the leaching of soluble ammonia compounds and nitrates from decomposing legumes. It would be advisable, therefore, to follow the turning under of leguminous crops in field soil by the growth of a crop which would utilize the soluble nitrates and ammonia salts formed from the nitrogen of the legumes before they are lost by drainage."

Tests of the value of stable manure, commercial fertilizer, and crimson clover for vegetable crops, T. H. WHITE (*Maryland Sta. Bul. 199 (1916), pp. 93–106*).—Experiments begun in 1904 to determine the comparative lasting qualities of stable manure, animal refuse fertilizers, and chemical fertilizers when used on garden crops are reported. The soil was a silt clay loam underlain with yellow clay and was used in five one-fortieth-acre plats.

It was found "that stable manure is cheaper than fertilizer, even at the high price of $2 per ton. Commercial fertilizers, both of mineral and animal origin, will permanently improve the soil. Such large amounts as 20 tons of manure and a ton and a half of fertilizer were more than could be applied annually with a profit to the crops grown. The residual effects from both the fertilizers and the manure yielded a good profit. The most remarkable gain in the 12 years was in the season of 1915, when 800 lbs. of highgrade fertilizer was applied for tomatoes. This fertilizer, costing $13.50, made a gain of $60 per acre."

Experiments begun in 1913 on the use of crimson clover as a green manure for tomatoes on silty clay loam and clay loam soils are also reported. In one experiment crimson clover was plowed under before blossoming and when mature. In the second experiment the clover was cut when in bloom and fed to cattle and the manure returned to the soil and clover was also plowed under when mature.

In the first experiment it was found that on the average the early plowed plat of crimson clover gave the best results. In the second experiment the largest yield was obtained on the plat from which the clover was fed to cattle.

Experiments with nitrogenous fertilizers, I. ÎAKUSHKIN (I. V. JAKOUCHKINE) (*Iz Rezul't. Veget. Opytov Lab. Rabot (Rec. Trav. Lab. Agron.), Moskov. Selsk. Khoz. Inst., 10 (1914), pp. 137–144; Izv. Moskov. Selsk. Khoz. Inst. (Ann. Inst. Agron. Moscou), 22 (1916), No. 1, pp. 137–144*).—Experiments are reported which showed favorable results from the use not only of ammonium sulphate but also of ground horn and castor bean pomace. Poor results were obtained with fish fertilizer, its effectiveness being only from 40 to 50 per cent of that of sodium nitrate. The nitrogen of manure gave higher results when peat instead of straw was used as litter.

Preparation of dried blood in the army slaughterhouses, A. RANC (*Compt. Red. Acad. Agr. France, 3 (1917), No. 15, pp. 428–431*).—The quantity of blood which may be collected from the army slaughterhouses for use as a fertilizer is considerable, as the average amount is estimated at 10 kg. (22 lbs.) of blood for each animal. The manufacture of coagulated blood under ordinary conditions is relative simple. A method for collecting the dried blood in the war zone is described in detail. The classical method of preparation of dried blood with the use of ferric sulphate may be used in all the army slaughterhouses, whatever may be their installation. The process is important because of the great quantity of fertilizer which it produces.

The atmospheric nitrogen industry, A. TOBIANSKY D'ALTOFF (*L'Industrie de l'Azote Atmosphérique. Paris: H. Dunod & E. Pinat, 1914, pp. 16*).—This is a discussion of the subject in general and of several processes for the fixation of atmospheric nitrogen in particular.

The displacement of potash by ammonium nitrate, V. N. ZAVARITSKÏĬ (V. N. ZAVARITZKI) (*Iz Rezul.t. Veget. Opytov Lab. Rabot (Rec. Trav. Lab. Agron.), Moskov. Selsk. Khoz. Inst., 10 (1914), pp. 132–136; Izv. Moskov. Selsk. Khoz. Inst. (Ann. Inst. Agron. Moscou), 22 (1916), No. 1, pp. 132–136*).—Ammonium nitrate was found to be more effective than ammonium chlorid in displacing potash from such substances as biotite and similar silicates. The nitrate extracted from biotite appreciable amounts of potash, giving results confirming those obtained in culture experiments in showing that a considerable amount of the potash of this substance is available to plants.

Potash fertilizer salts, D. VAN STOLK (*Verslag. Landbouwk. Onderzoek. Rijkslandbouwproefstat.* [*Netherlands*], No. 20 (1917), pp. 35–42).—Analyses and tests of 20 per cent potash salts obtained by Holland from Germany after the outbreak of the European war are reported. While consisting principally of sodium and potassium chlorids the 20 per cent salt contained also mixtures of other materials in greater or less quantities. Some samples contained as high as 50 per cent carnallite, others greater quantities of kieserite.

Potash: An investigation into its economic sources in South Australia, D. C. WINTERBOTTOM (*So. Aust. Dept. Chem. Bul. 2 (1916), pp. 7–29*).—This report deals with the natural potash resources of Australia, including seaweed, ash of land plants, wool scour, sea water, alunite, beet sugar residues, and feldspar. It is concluded that "the sources which present the most promising possibilities seem to be the recovery from wool scouring and the development of the alunite deposits."

Simple tests for potash are described.

Pumping potash from Nebraska lakes, R. P. CRAWFORD (*Engin. and Min. Jour., 103 (1917), No. 18, pp. 777, 778, figs. 6*).—This is a brief description of the extraction of potash from the brines of Nebraska lakes. An analysis of salts from lake water at Hoffland, Nebr., showed a content of potassium oxid of 27.35 per cent.

Artificial zeolite as a source of potash for plants, A. I. SMIRNOV (*Iz Rezul't. Veget. Opytov Lab. Rabot (Rec. Trav. Lab. Agron.), Moskov. Selsk. Khoz. Inst., 10 (1914), pp. 115–131, figs. 2; Izv. Moskov. Selsk. Khoz. Inst. (Ann. Inst. Agron. Moscou), 22 (1916), No. 1, pp. 115–131, figs. 2*).—Using the method of "isolated nutrition" described by Prianischnikow (E. S. R., 30, p. 215), it was found that artificial zeolite prepared by the method of Gans but not in contact with other nutritive substances was practically ineffective as a source of potash. When, however, it was mixed with other nutritive salts excellent results were obtained and a nearly normal crop was secured. Slightly better results were obtained with a mixture of phosphorite and zeolite than with zeolite alone in the case of barley, but in the case of buckwheat no advantage from the mixture was observed.

Remarks and technical tests on the preparation of superphosphates, A. AITA (*Ann. Chim. Appl.* [*Rome*], 6 (1916), No. 9–10, 11–12, pp. 195–220, figs. 7; abs. in *Chem. Abs.*, 11 (1917), No. 6, p. 682).—Experiments with different rock phosphates, including Florida land pebble, Gafsa, and Constantine phosphates, are reported, the purpose of which was to determine the best conditions for treating phosphorites in order to obtain superphosphates of the greatest solubility and of the best physical state for application to soils. A description of the mechanical and chemical processes involved is given. Tables show analyses of the phosphates, weights of sulphuric acid used, and percentages of soluble and insoluble phosphoric acid obtained.

It was found that for land pebble phosphate from 98 to 100 kg. of acid (53° B.) is required per 100 kg. of the rock meal, for the Gafsa phosphate 86 to 90 kg. of acid, and for Constantine phosphate 96 to 99 kg. of acid of 53 to 54° B. provided the water content of the phosphate does not exceed 4 per cent. Definite results in this respect could not be obtained for other phosphorites.

The water content of the superphosphate is related on one hand to the water content of the mineral phosphate and on the other to the concentration of the acid and degree of heat used during treatment. With acid of 53 to 54° B. a product containing from 13 to 14 per cent of water was obtained with pebble phosphate, and 13 to 15 per cent water with Gafsa and Constantine phosphate. With acid of 52° B. the products contained 15 to 16 per cent water for pebble and 15 to 17 per cent water for Gafsa and Constantine phosphates.

The composition of some Thomas meals, C. J. VAN RAAIJ (*Verslag. Landbouwk. Onderzoek. Rijkslandbouwproefstat. [Netherlands], No. 20 (1917), pp. 27–34).*—Analyses and tests of samples of Thomas meal imported into Holland after the outbreak of the European war are reported. They are divided into those containing from 7 to 8 per cent of phosphoric acid, considered low-grade, and those containing 15 to 19 per cent. A characteristic of both types of meal was a high content of silica, which is attributed to the addition of sand during manufacture to increase the citrate solubility. The contents of alumina, magnesia, and calcium oxid were somewhat above normal in the low-grade meals and they also contained considerable iron. These constituents were present in normal quantities in the higher-grade meals.

The higher-grade meals are considered to be by-products of processes similar to the Thomas process, and their chemical composition should not interfere appreciably with their agricultural value. The use of low-grade meals, on the other hand, is considered uneconomical, especially on account of their high iron content.

The assimilation of phosphoric acid from phosphorites by cereals, I. V. ÎAKUSHKIN (*Iz Rezul't. Veget. Opytov Lab. Rabot (Rec. Trav. Lab. Agron.), Moskov. Selsk. Khoz. Inst., 10 (1914), pp. 66–84, figs. 6; Izv. Moskov. Selsk. Khoz. Inst. (Ann. Inst. Agron. Moscou), 22 (1916), No. 1, pp. 66–84, figs. 6).*—Tests of certain Russian phosphorites on wheat in sand cultures showed that these phosphorites were from 60 to 70 per cent as effective as superphosphate. From 10 to 15 per cent of the phosphoric acid was soluble in alkaline ammonium citrate which dissolves only traces of phosphoric acid from ordinary phosphorites.

The assimilation of phosphoric acid of phosporite by plants under different conditions of nutrition, F. V. CHIRIKOV (T. V. TCHIRIKOV) (*Iz. Rezul't. Veget. Opytov Lab. Rabot (Rec. Trav. Lab. Agron.), Moskov. Selsk. Khoz. Inst., 10 (1914), pp. 149–171, figs. 4; Izv. Moskov. Selsk. Khoz. Inst. (Ann. Inst. Agron. Moscou), 22 (1916), No. 1, pp. 149–171, figs. 4).*—Experiments are reported which showed that *Spergula arvensis, Trifolium resupinatum, Vicia faba,* and *Onobrychis sativa* grown with phosphorite contained appreciable amounts of phosphoric acid, while *Andropogon sorghum, Panicum germanicum, Zea mays,* and *Camelina sativa* showed little power of assimilation of phosphorite. The yields of cereals were greater with small amounts of lime in solution than with large. The plants which utilized the phosphorites best appeared least sensitive to changes in the composition of the nutritive solution.

The value of diphosphate, I. V. ÎAKUSHKIN (J. V. JAKOUCHKINE) (*Iz Rezul't. Veget. Opytov Lab. Rabot (Rec. Trav. Lab. Agron.), Moskov. Selsk. Khoz. Inst., 10 (1914), pp. 51–65, figs. 6; Izv. Moskov. Selsk. Khoz. Inst. (Ann. Inst. Agron. Moscou), 22 (1916), No. 1, pp. 51–65, figs. 6).*—It is pointed out that the phosphoric acid of precipitated phosphate (diphosphate) is much more soluble in water than that of Thomas slag. Experiments are reported which show that on the rich black soils of southern Russia the precipitated phosphate is equal, and in some cases superior, to superphosphate for millet and sugar beets.

Causes influencing the solubility of difficultly soluble phosphates in citric acid, A. AITA (*Ann. Chim. Appl. [Rome], 6 (1916), No. 3–4, pp. 119–131, fig. 1).*—Continuing studies previously reported (E. S. R., 36, p. 626), experiments on the influence of salts of manganese, iron, aluminum, and magnesium in mineral phosphates and phosphatic slags on the solubility of the phosphoric acid therein are reported.

It was found that the secondary constituents of phosphatic slag may be divided into two groups, (1) those which interfere with the solubility in citric acid of the phosphoric acid, such as lime, silicates, and manganese, and (2) those which favorably influence the solubility of the phosphoric acid, such as the sulphates of aluminum and iron. It is thought that the salts of iron and aluminum when present act in neutralizing the effect of those compounds which retard the solubility.

It is concluded that phosphatic slags contain tricalcium phosphate the same as do mineral phosphates, and that their high degree of solubility in citric acid may be attributed to the specific action of the iron and aluminum ions present as secondary constituents. It is further concluded that variations in the solubility of phosphatic slag are due to variations in the content of the secondary constituents.

The influence of calcium carbonate on the solution of iron phosphate in acetic acid and its availability to plants, V. V. SEMUSHKIN (SEMOUCH-KINE) (*Iz Rezul't. Veget. Opytov Lab. Rabot (Rec. Trav. Lab. Agron.), Moskov. Selsk. Khoz. Inst., 10 (1914), pp. 85–103; Izv. Moskov. Selsk. Khoz. Inst. (Ann. Inst. Agron. Moscou). 22 (1916), No. 1, pp. 85–103*).—The addition of calcium carbonate to iron phosphate was found to reduce its solubility in acetic acid and to reduce its effectiveness as a food for plants grown in pots. Calcium nitrate produced no such effect on the solubility in acetic acid but produced analogous effects in pot experiments. Magnesium carbonate acted like calcium carbonate but to a less degree. Sodium carbonate increased the solubility of the phosphoric acid. The effect of ammonium nitrate varied at different periods of growth. The addition of calcium carbonate in this case increased growth during the first period and gave a larger yield.

Analyses of inspection samples of fertilizers, 1915–16, J. T. WILLARD and R. C. WILEY (*Kansas Sta. Insp. Circ. 3 (1916), pp. 17*).—This circular contains the results of actual and guarantied analyses of 76 samples of fertilizers and fertilizing materials collected for inspection in Kansas during 1915–16, together with financial statements relating to such work and the text of the Kansas fertilizer law.

Analyses of inspection samples of fertilizers, fall 1916, J. T. WILLARD and R. C. WILEY (*Kansas Sta. Insp. Circ. 4 (1917), pp. 11*).—This circular contains the results of actual and guarantied analyses of 57 samples of fertilizers and fertilizing materials collected for inspection in Kansas during the fall of 1916, together with a list of Kansas fertilizer dealers.

Fertilizers sold in Wisconsin, W. H. STROWD (*Wisconsin Sta. Bul. 279 (1917), pp. 13, fig. 1*).—This bulletin gives general information on the purchase and use of commercial and other fertilizers and fertilizing materials, with special reference to Wisconsin conditions, and reports the results of actual and guarantied analyses of 49 samples of fertilizers and fertilizing materials collected for inspection in the State during 1916. It is stated that in Wisconsin most of the commercial fertilizers are used in sections where truck and cash crops predominate, the largest amounts being used in Milwaukee, Racine, and Kenosha Counties in the extreme southeastern part.

AGRICULTURAL BOTANY.

A quantitative method of ascertaining the mechanism of growth and of inhibition of growth of dormant buds, J. LOEB (*Science, n. ser., 45 (1917), No. 1166, pp. 436–439*).—Studies are reported on the development of the dormant buds in the leaves of *Bryophyllum calycinum*.

Leaves of equal size and from the same node were found to produce, in the same time and under identical conditions, equal masses of young shoots. From experiments with two sets of leaves, one with the centers cut out, the other intact, it was found that the production of shoots is in proportion to the mass of the leaves themselves. The investigation here reported leads to the assumption that the growth of dormant buds is determined by and is in proportion to the quantity of a certain material available for the buds. The author does not discuss the nature of the substances which cause the growth of buds, but he points out the fact that leaves form no shoots or very few if kept in the dark. This is believed to indicate that the material from which the new shoots are produced in a leaf is itself to a large extent a direct product of or is dependent upon the assimilatory activity of the leaf.

Influence of the leaf upon root formation and geotropic curvature in the stem of Bryophyllum calycinum and the possibility of a hormone theory of these processes, J. LOEB (*Bot. Gaz., 63 (1917), No. 1, pp. 25–50, figs. 30*).—In studies previously noted (E. S. R., 37, p. 127), which showed that substances (water or solutes) may be drawn away from the leaves to accelerate organ formation in the stem but that if not so removed, they will accelerate root and shoot growth in the leaf notches, it was observed also that the leaf has an accelerating influence upon the geotropic curvature of the stem itself. The present article notes a number of studies by the author on the influence in this connection of such factors as the presence, absence, or position of leaves; splitting, decortication, or notching of the stem; and combinations of these factors on the degree of geotropic bending.

It appears that in *B. calycinum*, the substances which induce root formation tend to collect on the lower side of a stem placed horizontally, although roots may appear also in notches on the upper side under conditions to be discussed in a later paper. Leafless stems curve and form roots much more slowly than do those having one or more leaves. The position and number of the leaves influence in certain ways the geotropic curvature. Generally it appears that each leaf sends shoot-forming substances toward the apex and root-forming substances toward the base of the stem. The probable significance of these and other observed facts is discussed.

The spontaneous negative geotropism of roots, EVA MAMELI and ELIGIA CATTANEO (*Separate from Atti Ist. Bot. R. Univ. Pavia, 2. ser., 17 [1916], pp. 12*).—Concluding a study of negative geotropism and related phenomena observable in *Helianthus annuus* and in some other plants, the authors state that in spontaneous negative geotropism the root cap becomes shorter and more obtuse than in case of roots positively geotropic. It presents an evident arrest of development with complete absence of starch in that portion during that stage, although starch appears in the stage immediately preceding a new orientation of the rootlet consequent upon the development of diageotropism or positive geotropism. In such case the starch is always found in the physically inferior part of the cell.

The behavior of certain gels useful in the interpretation of the action of plants, D. T. MACDOUGAL and H. A. SPOEHR (*Science, n. ser., 45 (1917), No. 1168, pp. 484–488*).—The authors claim that the systematic endeavor to construct a colloidal mixture which would display some of the fundamental physical properties of protoplasm of plants has resulted in finding that a mixture of substances of two of the three more important groups of constituents, carbohydrates, and proteins, shows the imbibitional behavior of tissues and tracts of protoplasts of the plant. The differential action of such colloidal masses in distilled water and acid and alkaline solutions is said to yield many striking parallels with growth.

The effect of continuously supplying water to plants by capillarity, L. DANIEL (*Compt. Rend. Acad. Sci. [Paris], 163 (1916), No. 19, pp. 525–527*).—Several garden plants supplied with water permitted to percolate continuously, but very slowly as evaporated by the plant, through cotton or wool to the roots, were found to utilize water much better and more economically than did plants watered in the ordinary way. They also showed modifications as to growth and qualities which suggest the profitable employment of apparatus by which a known quantity of water can be furnished as the needs of the plant may require.

A study of permeability by the method of tissue tension, S. C. BROOKS (*Amer. Jour. Bot., 3 (1916). No. 10, pp. 562–570, figs. 3*).—It is claimed that the permeability of the protoplasm of *Taraxacum officinale* remains practically normal in a balanced mixture consisting of sea water and calcium chlorid, such that the ratio of univalent to bivalent cations is about 70 : 15. Salts of univalent cations cause a great increase, those of bivalent or trivalent cations a great decrease, in permeability. Saccharose permeates protoplasm rapidly, affecting permeability as a univalent cation.

Similarity in the effects of potassium cyanid and of ether, W. J. V. OSTER-HOUT (*Bot. Gaz., 63 (1917), No. 1, pp. 77–80, fig. 1*).—As relating to the evidence obtained by the author (E. S. R., 28, p. 732) that typical anesthetics temporarily decrease permeability, instead of increasing it as claimed by Krebau (E. S. R., 34, p. 333), the author has carried out experiments on the permeability of the tissues of *Laminaria agardhii*. This was measured by determining electrical resistance in the manner described in an article previously noted (E. S. R., 26, p. 823), in order to ascertain the manner in which permeability is affected by potassium cyanid, which not only acts as an anesthetic but markedly inhibits oxidation.

In tissue placed in sea water to which had been added potassium cyanid so as to give molecular concentrations ranging from 0.002 to 0.381 no such temporary increase of permeability was observed as described by Krebau. Experiments demonstrated that there is a temporary decrease of permeability instead of a temporary increase. Whenever the permeability began to increase, it continued to increase steadily until the tissue was dead.

The fact that potassium cyanid resembles typical anesthetics such as ether and chloroform in producing a temporary decrease in permeability does not, in the opinion of the author, show that anesthesia is a form of asphyxiation. It is considered probable that the decrease of permeability and the anesthesia produced by potassium cyanid are related to its effect on oxidation.

The mode of action of the oxidases, H. H. BUNZEL (*Jour. Biol. Chem., 24 (1916), No. 2, pp. 91–102*).—The results of studies by the author on the oxidase activity (this term being preferred, for reasons stated, to concentrations of oxidases) in different portions of various plants are presented and discussed. They are considered to show that in the work under discussion several factors were operative, each exerting either an augmenting or a depressing effect on the end result. The presence of reductases and the concentration of hydrogen ions are thought to affect the results, but the nature of their action is not yet clear.

The relative oxidase activity of different organs of the same plant, H. H. BUNZEL (*Jour. Biol. Chem.. 24 (1916), No. 2. pp. 103–110, figs. 5; abs. in Jour. Chem. Soc. [London], 109 (1916), No. 643, 1, p. 357*).—The author has used in this work the oxidase unit as employed in that previously noted (E. S. R., 27, p. 9) and defined in this article as an oxidase solution of such strength that 1 liter will bring about the consumption by pyrogallol of 8 gm. of oxygen, or the equivalent of 1 gm. of hydrogen.

The results, as shown in tabular and graphical form, of experiments with potato leaves and tubers, onion leaves and bulbs, tulip tree leaves and buds, and spinach leaves and roots, show a marked parallelism between the oxidase activities of different parts in the potato, tulip tree, and sugar beet. The onion showed no oxidase activity in either leaves or roots, and the graphs for these parts in spinach were entirely at variance, so far as appearances indicate. Each plant apparently has its characteristic relationships.

The results of this work are considered to indicate that the capacity of the plant to oxidize the various compounds employed is characteristic of the particular plant, but that it varies in intensity, and in this respect only, in the different parts of the same plant, showing a distinct and characteristic type of metabolism for each plant. It remains to be investigated to what extent plants of the same genus or species resemble each other in their metabolism.

A comparative study of winter and summer leaves of various herbs, J. P. STOBER (*Bot. Gaz., 63 (1917), No. 2, pp. 89–109*).—Summarizing the findings and conclusions of a study carried out with numerous plants collected near Chicago or in eastern Pennsylvania, the author states that typical rosette leaves in shaded and protected situations are on the whole decidedly more mesophytic than are stem leaves, which are exceeded as regards xerophytism by winter leaves on stolons or runners.

Local and temporary autumnal symbiosis, L. MONTEMARTINI (*Separate from Atti Ist. Bot. R. Univ. Pavia, 2. ser., 17 [1916], pp. 7*).—The author, having observed cases in which the portions of leaves of *Acer platanoides* which were parasitized by *Uncinula aceris* remained green while other parts went through the regular autumnal changes, and cases of similar behavior in *Corylus avellana* attacked by *Phyllactinia suffulta*, has made a study of maple leaves during a period nearly coincident with the first half of November.

It was found that the dry matter of the leaf was greater in the parasitized areas than outside them during this period, especially during the middle portion. The ratio of ash content to dry substances was somewhat less during that period in both green and yellow portions of the leaves. From these and other facts it is concluded that these cases may represent a temporary symbiosis, due to a diminution of virulence of the parasite and to a variation in the resistance of the host during this period owing to the effects of external conditions then prevalent.

The penetration of foreign substances introduced into trees, W. H. RANKIN (*Phytopathology, 7 (1917), No. 1, pp. 5–13, fig. 1*).—Experiments are reported upon in which chestnut trees from 2.5 to 9 in. in diameter were fed solutions of lithium nitrate, a modification of the Shevyrev method being employed (E. S. R., 15, p. 60).

An examination of cross sections of the trunks of the trees showed that lithium nitrate, under the method employed, penetrates to all places in the tree where there is active translocation of food materials; that is, to all parts of the bark and sapwood above and below the point of feeding. Complete penetration of the heartwood was obtained in trees of less than 3 in. in diameter. In trees of greater diameter the process of penetration was slow and did not seemingly follow any definite rule.

The injurious effects of tarvia fumes on vegetation, A. H. CHIVERS (*Phytopathology, 7 (1917), No. 1, pp. 32–36*).—Following up observations of the effect of tarvia fumes on growing plants where at least 20 species and many varieties were injuriously affected (E. S. R., 35, p. 734), the author presents data secured from laboratory investigations which confirm the previous conclusions.

Experiments conducted under controlled conditions showed that the injury was due in large part to the volatile substances, which condensed in the form of an oily coating on the surfaces of the plants. The injury is considered due to the action of fumes on the aerial parts of plants, its amount varying with the distance from the escaping fumes, the temperature of the melting tar, the age of the plant structures, and the species used.

Imperfection of pollen and mutability in the genus Rosa, RUTH D. COLE (*Bot. Gaz., 63 (1917), No. 2, pp. 110–123, pls. 3*).—A study of all obtainable species of Rosa carried out by the author during the winter of 1915–16 is said to have shown that these species are characterized by great variability and by a large proportion of abortive pollen. From this it is inferred that these species are largely of hybrid origin, due to contamination in nature, and hence that the mutability of the species of this genus can not properly be used in support of the mutation hypothesis.

Œnothera lamarckiana velutina, H. DE VRIES (*Bot. Gaz., 63 (1917), No. 1, pp. 1–24, pl. 1*).—Observations during several years of cultures from Œnothera mutations having tended to show that such mutation phenomena are far more complex than they were formerly assumed to be, the author is now giving attention to the question whether the characters of Œnothera mutants and hybrids are single or built up of a greater or less number of theoretically independent units. *Œ. lamarckiana velutina* has been chosen for this work on account of its alleged freedom from specific admixtures. A number of crosses were made in 1915, but this article gives chiefly a description of the mutant itself and of those hybridizations which give proof of its right to the name it bears.

A study of this new mutant shows the existence of at least two recessive characters in *Œ. lamarckiana*, namely, the bubbles of the leaf blade and the presence of typical empty seeds.

The cowhage and related species, C. V. PIPER (*Proc. Biol. Soc. Wash., 30 (1917), pp. 51–62*).—In connection with investigations of the Florida velvet bean and other cultivated forms of velvet bean, the author has made a study of various related species characterized by having stinging hairs on the calyx and pods. The species of Stizolobium which are distinguished from Mucuna by well defined characteristics are grouped under two subgenera. The name for the well-known stinging-haired species should be *S. pruriens*. *S. pruritum* is described as a new combination with several varieties, and *S. microspermum*, *S. venulosum*, and *S. forbesii* are described as new species. *S. hirsutum* is the name given for the species formerly known as *M. hirsuta*.

FIELD CROPS.

Dry farming in eastern New Mexico, J. E. MUNDELL and H. G. SMITH (*New Mexico Sta. Bul. 104 (1917), pp. 61, figs. 15*).—This is a popular discussion of general crop conditions and methods of farming in the dry-land area of eastern New Mexico for the purpose of furnishing information to present and prospective settlers. The information is based upon extensive observations of dry-farming methods in eastern New Mexico and other dry-farming districts and on results obtained in experiments conducted by the Office of Dry Land Agriculture, of the U. S. Department of Agriculture, at the dry-land field station, Tucumcari, N. Mex.

In addition to a discussion of the general factors to be considered in dry-land agriculture, such as the limiting factors encountered, the cultural practices employed, the most suitable crops, etc., considerable crop and climatological data secured at the field station are presented and discussed. The average annual precipitation at Tucumcari for a 12-year period was 16.21 in., over 70 per cent of which fell between April 1 and October 1. The average evaporation from a free water surface for the 4-year period 1913 to 1916, inclusive, was

54.003 in. for the 6-month period from April 1 to October 1. The total evaporation varied from 49.92 in. in 1914 to 58.901 in. in 1916.

The crop data show the yields per acre of milo maize, Kafir corn, sorgho, broom corn, Sudan grass, millet, cowpeas, beans, cotton, corn, winter wheat, winter rye, spring wheat, oats, and barley under various cultural conditions. From the results obtained it has been concluded that summer fallowing and subsoiling are relatively unprofitable, while fall and spring plowing and listing are deemed to be the methods best adapted for use in preparing the land.

Tests with sorghum planted in rows 8, 16, 24, 32, and 44 in. part, respectively, conducted during 1914, 1915, and 1916 gave the highest yields with planting widths of 24, 32, and 44 in.

Date-of-planting tests with Mexican June corn gave the best results with plantings between May 1 and June 10. Tests with Dwarf Milo gave the best results with plantings made between May 10 and June 10.

Tabulated data are presented showing the effect of the previous crop on the yields of the several crops listed above, obtained on land cropped continuously and on land where systematic rotation has been practiced.

Variety tests begun in 1912 are reported for grain sorghums, forage sorghums, millets, cowpeas ,broom corn, beans, cotton, corn, peanuts, and potatoes.

Progress report of Substation No. 3, Angleton, Tex., 1909–1914, N. E. WINTERS (*Texas Sta. Bul. 197 (1916), pp. 3–20, figs. 4*).—Varietal, rotation, and cultural tests with corn, cowpeas, and oats, and field tests with leguminous forage crops, sorghum for forage, Japanese sugar cane, Sudan grass, and dasheens are reported for the seasons of 1913 and 1914.

The Strawberry, Thomas, and Chisholm corn varieties gave the highest yields based on a 2-year average, 27.78, 27.3, and 26.21 bu. per acre, respectively. The lowest-yielding variety was Collier Excelsior, with 18.24 bu. The highest average yield, 18.36 bu., in seeding-rate tests was secured from rows 3 ft. apart, with the stalks 2 ft. apart in the row, giving 7,260 plants per acre. Different row widths, with various distributions of the plants in the row, showed practically no variation in yields so long as the total stand remained constant. On sowing cowpeas in 1913 between the corn rows when the corn was beginning to tassel, a yield of 20.32 bu. of corn was obtained, as compared with a yield of 17.1 bu. in 1914 from corn grown alone. A comparison of planting dates for the cowpeas indicated that plantings made with the corn in full tassel gave increased yields of corn over earlier plantings. A rotation of cotton, cowpeas for seed, corn, and oats, with cowpeas plowed under as a green manure, showed increased corn yields of 2.27 bu. in 1913 and 9.94 bu. in 1914 over corn grown continuously.

Oats were grown for hay only, Rust Proof, with a yield of 968 lbs., and Appler, with 836 lbs. of cured hay per acre, giving the best results. Frazier Red Rust Proof gave the lowest yield, 678 lbs., while Virginia Gray Winter failed entirely, due to rust. The quality of 100-Bushel Oats was superior to that of all other varieties, the yield being 682 lbs. of hay. Oats grown in rotation in 1914 produced 1,235 lbs. of cured hay per acre, while only 528 lbs. was secured from oats grown continuously.

Based on a 2-year average yield of cowpeas for seed and forage, New Era with 18.89 bu., Whippoorwill with 17 bu., and Groit with 14.88 bu. per acre, gave the highest yields of seed, with Blackeye lowest with only 2.77 bu. For hay production the Iron variety was first, with a yield of 2,571 lbs. of cured hay per acre, Groit second with a yield of 2,270 lbs., and Red Ripper lowest with 1,210 lbs. Seeding rates of 6, 12, and 18 lbs. per acre for hay production in 1913 showed yields of 2,640, 3,300, and 3,685 lbs. of cured hay, respectively. The results obtained with cowpeas grown in rotation, as compared with continuous cropping, show very little difference both in yield of grain and forage for 1913 and 1914.

In seeding-rate tests with sorghum for forage, the highest average yield, 16,742 lbs. per acre, was secured from a seeding rate of 8 pk. per acre in close drills, but a 2 pk. rate gave an average yield of 16,740 lbs. Plants sown in 3-ft. rows, 1 in. apart in the row, and cultivated, gave an average yield of 16,026 lbs., the highest for seedings in cultivated rows.

Harvests of Japanese sugar cane secured September 10, December 4, and December 16, 1914, yielded 23,200, 51,030, and 39,820 lbs. of green forage per acre, respectively.

Method-of-seeding tests with Sudan grass showed average yields of 4,266, 6,124, and 5,302 lbs. of cured hay per acre for seedings in 3-ft. rows, 18-in. rows, and close drills, respectively. Sudan grass is considered valuable chiefly as a summer grazing crop, as sorghum is preferred for hay in this section and Japanese sugar cane gives higher yields of green forage than either sorghum or Sudan grass. Sudan grass does not produce seed on account of the prevalence of the sorghum midge.

Dasheens are reported as giving promise for the future.

Progress report, Texas Substation No. 6, Denton, Tex., 1909–1914, V. L. CORY (*Texas Sta. Bul. 199 (1916), pp. 3–18, figs. 3*).—Variety tests with wheat, barley, oats, rye, corn, cowpeas, and peanuts, and cultural and field tests with wheat, emmer, spelt, cotton, miscellaneous legumes, and Sudan grass, are reported for the crop years 1910–1914, inclusive.

Twenty-one winter wheat varieties have been tested, including 8 hard red, 7 soft bearded, and 6 soft beardless varieties. Defiance and Bacska, with 3-year average yields of 27.04 and 24.93 bu. per acre, respectively, were the leading hard red wheats. The durum and spring wheats have not proved of much value.

Eight varieties of winter barley and 6 of spring barley were tested. A comparison of the average yields of 4 varieties grown both as winter and spring varieties in 1912 and 1913, showed a decreased yield of 6.08 bu. per acre from spring seeding. The highest-yielding winter variety was White Smyrna, with 32.65 bu., and the lowest, Hooded barley, with 11.21 bu. These two varieties also gave the highest and lowest yields when grown as spring varieties, with yields of 18.22 and 12.03 bu., respectively.

Red Rust Proof oats is the standard variety for the section, both for fall and spring planting. Sixty-Day, Burt, and Ninety-Day are deemed excellent varieties for late seeding and for dry seasons. No appreciable advantage has been gained by fall seeding as compared with spring seeding.

Comparative tests of Tennessee Winter barley, Red Rust Proof oats, Red Winter spelt, and Black Winter emmer for 1912, 1913, and 1914 have shown average yields of grain of 1,541, 1,355, 1,074, and 887 lbs. per acre, respectively.

Three rye varieties were tested and gave practically identical results. Rye is not considered of great value for this region.

A comparison of early and late plowing and of deep and shallow plowing of stubble land for wheat showed yields of 32.62 bu. for deep, early plowing as compared with 20.41 bu. for shallow, late plowing. Cultivation of the soil after plowing the wheat was followed by a yield of 32.62 bu. as compared with 17.41 bu. from land not cultivated. Corn land plowed in preparation for wheat yielded 28.08 bu. per acre with wheat drilled in and 25.5 bu. with wheat broadcasted. Disking and drilling in the wheat gave 25.25 bu., broadcasting 20 bu., and drilling wheat in without any preparation 18.66 bu.

In corn variety tests Surcropper has given the best results, with June corns good varieties for late seeding.

The Early Buff variety of cowpea has given the highest yields of seed, with New Era, Blackeye, Iron, and Brabham also reported as satisfactory.

Spanish, Virginia, and Tennessee Red peanuts yielded an average of 476, 460, and 105 lbs. of seed, and 3,890, 4,350, and 850 lbs. of hay, respectively.

None of the legumes tested has proved especially well suited to local conditions.

Tests with Sudan grass for forage showed a total yield of 4,575 lbs. per acre when sown April 30 in 36-in. rows. Sudan grass is considered a valuable hay and pasture grass for this section.

Progress report of Substation No. 12, Chillicothe, Tex., 1905–1914, R. W. EDWARDS (*Texas Sta. Bul. 202 (1916), pp. 3–30, figs. 13*).—Forage-crop work conducted in cooperation with the Office of Forage Crop Investigations, U. S. Department of Agriculture, is reported for the 10-year period of 1905 to 1914. The field experiments include variety and date- and rate-of-planting tests with sorghums, date-, rate-, and method-of-seeding tests with Sudan grass for hay, and variety tests with alfalfa.

Meteorological data for 1906–1914 show a mean annual rainfall of 25.03 in. The maximum annual precipitation was 32.47 in. in 1908, and the minimum 14.19 in. in 1910.

Kafirs have outyielded milos in both forage and grain in favorable seasons, but in poor growing seasons milo maize and feterita were both more productive than Kafir corn. The latter yielded 2.1 tons of forage and 10.3 bu. of grain as compared with 1.68 tons of forage and 15 bu. of grain for milo maize for an 8-year average, 1907–1914. Drought resistance in Kafir corn was evidently secured at a sacrifice in yield in good seasons, since the most drought-resistant strains did not respond to abundant moisture in the same proportion as did many of the common or standard varieties.

Selection F. C. I. No. 811 of dwarf feterita proved earlier, more dwarf and uniform in height, and produced higher yields at Chillicothe than the original S. P. I. No. 19517. Kaoliang proved to be of relatively little importance for this region.

Amber (saccharin) sorghums were early maturing and produced a good quality of hay when sown broadcast or in close drills. Sumac or red top sorghums gave larger yields than the ambers, but, unless planted thickly, produced rather coarse hay. Honey and gooseneck sorghums proved suitable for sirup making and for silage, but produced inferior hay.

The grain sorghums have produced the best yields of grain and forage when planted from April 15 to May 15 for seed, and from June 15 to July 1 for forage, with the plants from 4 to 8 in. apart in the row. The sorghums have produced the best quality and quantity of forage with plants from 2 to 4 in. apart in the row. Seedings of 75 lbs. per acre for sumac and 45 lbs. for red amber in close drills have given the best hay yields.

Sudan grass seeded at the rate of 15 lbs. per acre in close drills produced 1.51 tons of hay per acre in 1913 and 5.57 tons in 1914. Medium early plantings, April 3 to May 4, gave the largest number of cuttings, and an average yield of about 5.19 tons in 1914. About the same yields but a better quality of hay was secured from seedings in close drills over those in cultivated rows. Considerably more seed was produced in cultivated rows than in drilled plats.

Of the millets tested Turkestan was the highest yielder and produced a good quality of hay. The millets are considered inferior to Sudan grass for hay purposes.

Early Buff, Brabham, Iron, Groit, New Era, and Red Ripper are all considered excellent cowpea varieties, especially suited for use as annual leguminous crops for rotations. Chiquita, Mammoth, Cloud, and Jet for forage, and Haber-landt for seed production, proved to be good soy-bean varieties. All soy beans suffered from rabbit depredations.

Kansas, Wyoming, and Algeria alfalfas have produced good yields. A comparison of close drilling with cultivated rows 42 in. apart gave a yield of 2.25 tons per acre for the former method and 1.31 tons for the latter in 1914. Artificial inoculation is not recommended for this region.

About 50 varieties of vetches were tested, but none proved suitable for the locality.

Sunflowers have been tested extensively but were not considered profitable, due to their susceptibility to insect attack.

Inheritance in wheat, barley, and oat hybrids, E. F. GAINES (*Washington Sta. Bul. 135 (1917), pp. 3–61, figs. 9*).—Extensive hybridization studies are reported with 6 wheat, 7 barley, and 9 oat varieties, the standard commercial varieties of Washington being used wherever the proper combinations could be obtained.

The following characters were studied: Wheat—beards *v.* no beards, long head *v.* club head, and white grain *v.* red grain; barley—beards *v.* hoods, bald *v.* covered grain, 6-row *v.* 2-row heads, and winter *v.* spring types; and oats— white *v.* black grain color, side *v.* tree type of panicle, and hulled *v.* hull-less character. The results of the hybridization are discussed in detail and considerable tabulated data presented, showing the hybrid composition and relative frequency of the characters studied in the F_2 and F_3 generations.

While many of the observations recorded are corroborative of work published in America and Europe, other results were secured which are briefly summarized below.

The following characters segregated as simple allelomorphs in the F_2 generation: Beardless wheat was dominant over bearded, and club head over long head; hooded barley was dominant over bearded, covered over bald, and 2-row over 6-row; and black oats were dominant over white. The remaining characters were produced by multiple factors, or were irregular in inheritance.

In the bearded and beardless wheat hybrids, the F_1 was intermediate and could be segregated in the F_2. The heterozygote of the bearded and hooded barley crosses could not be so segregated, and large numbers carried into the F_4 failed to produce modified types of these characters.

Two different crosses of spring barleys produced winter plants in the ratio of 3:13 in the F_2 generation.

One variety of white hulless oats produced black oats when crossed with white hulled varieties. Hullessness prevented the development of glume color in the parent and hybrids of all the crosses tested. Crosses of side and tree oats produced intermediate types which bred true in subsequent generations. The percentage of hulled plants in the F_2 of crosses between hulled and hulless oats approached a simple Mendelian recessive, but there was great irregularity between the true hulless and heterozygous types, with an excess of heterozygotes in most cases.

Winter oats, barley, spelt, and emmer, N. SCHMITZ (*Maryland Sta. Bul. 200 (1917), pp. 107–130, figs. 8*).—Variety tests with winter oats, winter barley, spelt, and emmer since 1907 are reported and the production of the crops discussed.

Dewey, Bicknell, and Culberson, with average yields of 51.23, 49.89, and 49.49 bu., respectively, for the period of 1908–1914, inclusive, were the leading oat varieties tested. The lowest-yielding variety was Boswell, with 22.66 bu. Further data show the percentage of winterkilling, average date of ripening, and average height of plants for the varieties tested. In extensive tests over the State, Culberson and Winter Turf proved a little more hardy than Bicknell and were also better adapted to light, sandy soils of medium to poor fertility and are considered best for Maryland conditions. The Culberson, Bicknell, Winter Turf, Dewey, and Red Rust Proof varieties are briefly described.

The two leading barley varieties were Mammoth Winter, with an average yield of 34.64 bu., and Maryland Winter, with 34.59 bu. Tennessee Winter, yielding 30.43 bu., is recommended together with the two varieties named above because of its ready availability on the market.

Five varieties of spelt and 3 of emmer were tested. Alstroum spelt yielded an average of 63.23 bu., but contained 40 per cent hulls to grain. Black Winter emmer yielded 34.43 bu.

The total weight of grain produced per acre of the highest yielding variety of wheat, oats, barley, spelt, and emmer was as follows: Bearded Purple Straw wheat 2,412.2 lbs., Dewey oats 1,639.4 lbs., Mammoth Winter barley 1,662.5 lbs., Alstronum spelt 1,896.9 lbs., and Black Winter emmer 1,032.9 lbs.

Grains for the dry lands of central Oregon, L. R. BREITHAUPT (*U. S. Dept. Agr. Farmers' Bul. 800 (1917), pp. 2–22, figs. 6*).—The production of small grains on the nonirrigated lands of central and southeastern Oregon at elevations of from 4,000 to 5,000 ft. is discussed. The information presented is based partly upon the results of three years' experiments conducted in cooperation with the Oregon Experiment Station, at the Harney substation at Burns, and applies only where the rainfall, summer frost, and winter cold are average and where the nature, depth, and alkali content of the soil are favorable for crop production.

The important cereal crops for the region as a whole are winter and spring wheat, winter and spring rye, spring oats, and spring barley. Flax, field peas, and dry-land alfalfa are important but are not yet fully established. Minor crops include emmer, spelt, rape, sweet clover, root crops, and potatoes. Crops which have proved to be rather definitely unadapted to the average conditions are corn, millet, sorghum, beans, buckwheat, and cultivated grasses.

Grasses used in binding the shifting sands of southern Italy, A. BORZI (*Bol. R. Giard. Colon. Palermo, 2 (1916), No. 4, pp. 189–213, figs. 6; abs. in Internat. Inst. Agr. [Rome], Internat. Rev. Sci. and Pract. Agr., 7 (1916), No. 5, pp. 646, 647*).—The problems encountered in finding suitable grasses to bind the shifting sands of southern Italy are reviewed, and *Saccharum spontaneum* described in detail and its value for this purpose discussed at some length. *Cynodon dactylon* is mentioned as being of value in this region, together with several other less common grasses.

Permanent pastures on lowland moors, W. FRECKMANN (*Mitt. Ver. Förd. Moorkultur Deut. Reiche, 34 (1916), Nos. 1, pp. 7–11; 2, pp. 24–32*).—This is a general discussion of the management of permanent pastures on low-lying moor lands. The division of the pasture into separate units, thus allowing alternate grazing, is recommended and the recommendation supported by experimental data.

A comparison of results obtained from pasturing young stock continuously on the same pasture, and alternating the pasture as indicated above, showed an increase of 80.78 marks per hectare (about $7.79 per acre) in favor of the latter method. Other arguments advanced in favor of this system are that the forage in the pasture is more fully utilized, the vigor of the animals is increased, the care of the pasture is made easier through a better distribution of the manure and the use of the roller after the animals are removed, and the alternate removal of the crop of the permanent pasture, as secured by this system, has (with not too frequent repetition) a favorable influence on the pasture flora.

Some study has been made of fertilizing permanent lowland moor pastures with commercial fertilizers, indicating that good results may be expected.

Green manuring in India, A. C. Dobbs (*Agr. Research Inst. Pusa Bul. 56 (1915), pp. 55, pls. 7, figs. 2*).—This is a comprehensive discussion of the theory and practice of green manuring as applied to agricultural conditions in India, consisting chiefly of a compilation of data from various sources.

Color variation in seed crops of cultivated legumes, F. G. Galang (*Philippine Agr. and Forester, 5 (1916), No. 3, pp. 79–101*).—This is a preliminary report of an attempt at simple selection with certain legumes, based on seed color. The crops used were as follows: *Vigna sinensis* (three varieties), *Glycine hispida*, *Cyamopsis psoraleoides*, *Phaseolus calcaratus*, *P. lunatus*, *Psophocarpus tetragonolobus* (two varieties), *Dolichos biflorus*, *Centrosema plumieri*, and *Cajanus cajan*. The color of the original seed planted is described in detail for each variety, and the color variations obtained from the different colored seeds of the different varieties are tabulated and discussed for each group of seeds, but no definite conclusions are drawn.

Alfalfa in Wyoming, T. S. Parsons (*Wyoming Sta. Bul. 111 (1916), pp. 19–55, figs. 6*).—The field practices employed in the production of alfalfa in Wyoming are discussed in detail, and variety and cultural tests for 1911 to 1915, inclusive, are reported.

The field experiments for each year of the five-year period are outlined and the results briefly summarized. Grimm alfalfa gave an average yield of 5.25 tons per acre for the 5-year period, leading all other varieties in yield, hardiness, and earliness of maturity. Broadcasting gave as good results as drilling the seed. Summer fallow put the soil in the best condition for alfalfa. An average hay yield of 1 ton per acre was obtained the first year when a nurse crop was used. No advantage was gained from liming or from inoculation on the experimental plats at Laramie. A seeding rate of 10 lbs. per acre was found ample in all cases, and one irrigation per cutting was usually sufficient. A well-packed seed bed with a loose surface, good seed, and sufficient moisture to insure germination are deemed to be the essential factors for successful alfalfa growing under conditions similar to those on the station farm.

Barley in Washington, E. G. Schafer and E. F. Gaines (*Washington Sta. Bul. 141 (1917), pp. 3–12, figs. 5*).—Comparative observations of winter and spring wheat, spring oats, and winter and spring barley for 1914, 1915, and 1916 indicate that spring barley produces the heaviest yields, while winter barley matures 12 days before winter wheat, 20 days before spring oats, 23 days before spring wheat, and 10 days before spring barley. The short growing season renders the crop well adapted to high altitudes.

Sixteen barley varieties are briefly described and the results of nursery and field tests reported. The covered six-rowed bearded varieties proved more productive than the naked six-rowed hooded varieties.

Corn experiments in 1915, P. R. Fedorov (*Bezenchuk. Selsk. Khoz. Opytn. Sta. No. 75 (1916), pp. 6*).—Experiments for the past two years show that the local (Samara) varieties of corn yield the higher in dry seasons, mature better, contain smaller percentages of water, and keep better than varieties imported from warmer and more humid regions. The latter, however, give higher yields in seasons with high humidity.

Cotton experiments, 1916 (*Mississippi Sta. Bul. 178 (1916), pp. 3–40, figs. 3*).—Suggestions for cotton culture in different parts of Mississippi are presented and the results of cotton experiments conducted at the Mississippi Station and the Holly Springs and Delta substations reported as heretofore (E. S. R., 34, p. 830).

In variety tests at the main station Express–350, with a yield of 674 lbs. of seed cotton per acre, and Express–341 and Foster–120, with yields of 672 lbs. each, were the leading varieties. Holdon, with a yield of 187 lbs., was lowest. The medium early big boll varieties Wannamaker-Cleveland, Cleveland Big Boll, and Miller are recommended for the hill portion of the State, due to good qualities exhibited in tests extending over a number of years.

At the Holly Springs substation, on valley land Trice, with a yield of 1,872 lbs. per acre, and Express–350, with 1,827 lbs., were best. Holdon, with a yield of 995 lbs., was lowest. On hill land Wannamaker-Cleveland was first, with 860 lbs., and Sproull Big Boll lowest with 600 lbs. Wannamaker-Cleveland, Trice, Express, and Unknown are recommended for the valley land of this district.

Results of variety tests at the Delta substation showed Lone Star–132 and Express–350, with yields of 992 and 961 lbs. per acre, respectively, to be first, with Holdon lowest with a yield of 292 lbs. Express, Allen Unknown, and Foster–120 are recommended as good varieties for the Delta district.

Further tabulated data show the variety averages from the three localities, the rank of varieties grown for the last six years on a basis of the money value per acre at each, the average length of certain varieties grown for six years, and the quantity of cotton ginned annually per county in Mississippi from 1907 to 1916.

Variety selections and individual selections of hybrids at the main station are reported in an effort to secure wilt-resistant strains and strains that could be grown profitably under boll-weevil conditions. Covington-Toole has given good results under wilt conditions but matures too late for regions badly infested with weevil. Wannamaker-Cleveland is reported as being an earlier-maturing strain and as also possessing good wilt-resistant qualities.

Spacing tests were conducted with varying results. At the main station the best yields were secured from rows 3 ft. apart, with 12 in. between plants in the row, while at the Holly Springs substation 3.5 ft. between rows gave the best yields. Conflicting results were secured at the Delta substation, but in every case the thinned rows outyielded the unthinned rows. Extensive tests of the single-stalk method of cotton culture were conducted at the main station and results obtained comparable with those of Cook (E. S. R., 31, p. 433), Meade (E. S. R., 33, p. 730), and others.

Methods for the development and maintenance of good cotton varieties are briefly outlined and the danger of deterioration of cotton seed at the public gin emphasized.

Extension of cotton production in California, O. F. Cook (*U. S. Dept. Agr. Bul. 533 (1917), pp. 16*).—This bulletin discusses the possible development of the cotton industry in California, with special reference to the long-staple types of cotton.

A brief history of cotton growing in California is given. Recent demonstrations have been made in the Imperial Valley and the Colorado Valley in extreme southern California, but the San Joaquin and other northern valleys contain much larger areas of irrigated and readily irrigable land available for cotton production.

Experimental plantings indicate that the Egyptian type can be grown in the southern part of the San Joaquin Valley, while in the northern parts Durango, or other long-staple Upland varieties, are more likely to succeed.

The labor requirements and other economic phases of cotton production are discussed. The author believes that the cost of labor is not so much a limiting factor as the scarcity, but also believes that the less acute demands made by the cotton crop render it well adapted for use in a practical cropping system of diversified agriculture.

It is urged that any undertaking to establish the cotton industry in these regions be a community undertaking with a strongly centralized organization, similar to that existing among the fruit growers, for the control of the gins and oil mills, marketing of the crop, and dissemination of information relative to the production of the crop.

Cotton species indigenous to Italian Somaliland, G. E. MATTEI (*Bol. R. Giard. Colon. Palermo, 2 (1916), No. 4, pp. 221-224, fig. 1; abs. in Internat. Inst. Agr. [Rome], Internat. Rev. Sci. and Pract. Agr., 7 (1916), No. 5, p. 683*).—Two varieties of cotton said to be indigenous to Italian Somaliland are described by the author. The varieties are *Gossypium paolii* and *G. benadirense*. A brief summary of other species of Gossypium previously described as native to this region is given.

Tests and selections of mungo beans, L. A. SAN MIGUEL (*Philippine Agr. and Forester, 5 (1916), No. 5, pp. 164-179*).—Variety tests of mungo beans, Phaseolus sp., in the Philippines are reported, and the species found there are classified and described. Fertilizer tests were also conducted indicating that this crop thrives best with no fertilization, or with the addition of ashes alone.

Experiments with the overhead electrical discharge in 1915, I. JORGENSEN (*Jour. Bd. Agr. [London], 23 (1916), No. 7, pp. 671, 672*).—This is a brief note on the effect of overhead electrical discharges on a crop of oats in 1915. The experiments were conducted by Miss E. C. Dudgeon, and are a continuation of work previously noted (E. S. R., 30, p. 827). The crop was grown on two 1.5-acre plats lying side by side, one plat receiving the electrical discharge and the other serving as a "control." The two plats were separated by a well-earthed wire screen which reached to a height of 3 ft. above the level of the charged network. The screen greatly reduced the amount of discharge reaching the nonelectrified area, but did not do away with leakage altogether. The discharge occurred for 557 hours during 108 days, or an average of about 5 hours per day.

The season was droughty and the soil light, but from the early stages the growth of the crop on the electrified area showed a superiority to that on the "control" area. An increase of 30 per cent in grain and 58 per cent in straw over the nonelectrified crop was obtained.

Contribution to the study of Panicum miliaceum, S. A. BELOV (*Bezenchuk. Selsk. Khoz. Opytn. Sta., No. 73 (1916), pp. 333-352, figs. 9*).—This is a further contribution to botanical studies of the group Panicoideæ, with particular reference to flowering phenomena (E. S. R., 32, p. 727).

Observations are reported which indicate a close connection between the opening of the flowers and the meteorological conditions. The flower glumes were not observed to open on cloudy days having a high humidity. With high temperatures and low humidity on bright days flowering began at about 8 a. m., the flowers remaining open from 15 to 20 minutes. On days with similar temperature and moisture conditions, but with clouded skies, the flowers remained open about 25 minutes. Moderate heating of the flower with the sun's rays by means of a lens caused flowering to occur at 7 a. m. An excessive use of the lens, however, did not cause flowering, and after 11 a. m. acted negatively on flowers ready to open. Maximum flowering was observed from 10 to 11 a. m., diminishing rapidly from 12 to 12.30 p. m. Under intermediate conditions, even in the mean phase of flowering, flowering has been much more rarely observed than on bright warm days.

The anthers are reported as being even more sensible to changes in the external conditions.

The germination of the pollen on the stigma was accomplished 30 minutes after the closing of the flowers.

Notes are given on the color of the panicle and on the structure of the inflorescence and of the flower.

Field pea production, E. G. SCHAFER and E. F. GAINES (*Washington Sta. Bul. 140 (1917), pp. 3–16, pl. 1, figs. 2*).—The production and utilization of field peas are briefly discussed, and seven varieties described and comparative tests reported. The Bangalia variety has produced the largest yields for a four-year average, 31.8 bu. per acre.

The value of immature potato tubers as seed, H. P. HUTCHINSON (*Jour. Bd. Agr. [London], 23 (1916), No. 6, pp. 529–539*).—This is a general discussion of experimental work relating to the use of immature potato tubers for seed.

It is concluded that immature seed is superior because (1) in using immature tubers for seed the largest tubers of the most productive plants will naturally be selected, thus resulting in increased yields, or, at least, in maintaining previous yields. (2) The cortex of immature tubers is thinner than that of mature tubers, thus lessening the check on the imbibition of water from without, which is necessary during the early stages of growth. (3) The amount and availability of the reserve plant food material may be greater in the immature tubers than in the mature ones. (4) The length of time of storage may materially affect the amount and form of plant food material, which would favor immature tubers due to the longer period of storage to which they are subjected. The use of immature tubers for seed also promotes earliness, vigor, and an ability to form tubers under adverse seasonal conditions.

Directions are given for procuring and storing immature tubers.

Fertilizing the potato crop, C. E. THORNE (*Mo. Bul. Ohio Sta., 2 (1917), No. 5, pp. 142–146, fig. 1*).—The results of fertilizer experiments at the station with potatoes and wheat in a 3-year rotation of potatoes, wheat, and clover, extending over a 23-year period, are summarized and discussed.

An 1,100-lb. application for each 3-year period, carrying 50 lbs. of nitrogen, 30 lbs. of phosphorus, and 123 lbs. of potassium, half the nitrogen and two-thirds each of the phosphorus and potassium being applied to the potatoes and the remainder to the wheat, resulted in an average production of 190 bu. of potatoes per acre for the first 12 years and 159 for the remaining 11 years, while the wheat yields were 37.3 and 38.5 bu., respectively. When the total application was made on the potatoes the average yields were 187 and 155 bu. for the potatoes and 36 and 37 bu. for the wheat, respectively.

Applications of 8 tons of yard manure to the potatoes, with no further treatment for wheat, resulted in yields of 188 and 159 bu. per acre of potatoes and 30.3 and 33.8 bu. of wheat. Applying the manure to the wheat instead of the potatoes resulted in potato yields of 175 and 129 bu. and wheat yields of 30.4 and 36.8 bu., respectively. Applications of 16 tons of yard manure all applied to wheat resulted in yields of 192 and 175 bu. of potatoes and 34 and 37.5 bu. of wheat. In total effectiveness the 16-ton manure application exceeded the 1,100 lbs. of fertilizer by from $3 to $4 per acre for the first period and by from $4 to $7 for the second period.

Land left continuously without fertilizer or manure yielded at the rate of 166 bu. of potatoes per acre for the first period and 103 bu. the second period, the 63-bu. decrease being attributed largely to the growing of potatoes at too frequent intervals on the same land. It is recommended, therefore, that potatoes be planted on a good clover sod on land on which potatoes have not been grown for five or six years; that from 12 to 16 tons of manure be plowed under and supplemented with 300 lbs. of acid phosphate applied broadcast; and that if manure is scarce 4 or 5 tons supplemented with 400 lbs. of acid phosphate and 100 lbs. of nitrate of soda be used.

Potato growing, S. N. GREEN (*Mo. Bul. Ohio Sta.*, **2** (*1917*), *No. 5, pp. 147–152, figs. 2*).—The factors tending toward larger yields of potatoes under more intensive cultural methods are discussed. The seeding of small tubers (less than 2 oz.) gave an increase of 5.7 bu. per acre over the check (cut pieces of 2 oz.) as compared with an increase of 17.5 bu. from large (more than 6 oz.) tubers. This indicates that potato culls can be profitably utilized for seed, although their continued selection for seed is not recommended. The use of potato eyes only for seed is considered practicable under intensive cultural methods.

The yields from seven different planting dates ranging from May 17 to June 30 are compared with those of plantings made May 10 as a check. The May 17 planting gave an increase of 12.4 bu. per acre, while each succeeding planting gave decreased yields as compared with the checks ranging from 4.5 bu. for the plantings of May 24 to 44.8 bu. for those of June 30. Where late plantings were unavoidable the yields were greatly increased by exposing the bud end of the seed stock to a partial light, allowing short, green sprouts to develop. Plantings on June 30 from such seed yielded only 4.3 bu. less than plantings made May 10.

The 2-year average yields of marketable tubers of 41 varieties grown at Wooster and considered suitable for intensive culture are reported in tabular form. The average yields varied from 71.9 bu. for Eureka Extra Early, a Cobbler type, to 287.1 bu. for Livingston, a Rose type.

Potato growing in the loess area of the southwest, A. P. ZAPOROZHENKO (*Kiev. Agron. Obshch., Trudy Kom. Izuch. Khoz. Iugo-Zapad. Kraĩã, 4* (*1915*), *pp. 1–118*).—This is a detailed study of potato growing in the loess area of southwestern Russia. The cost of production has been determined in detail for a number of individual producers, and the results indicate a considerable lack of uniformity in the cultivation of the crop. The author concludes that the present type of potato culture in this region is not dependent on soil conditions and that it can be materially altered.

Fertilization of rice, C. BALANGUE Y RULLODA (*Philippine Agr. and Forester, 5* (*1916*), *No. 5, pp. 144–158*).—Fertilizer trials are reported with upland and lowland rice at three centers in the Philippines, using wood, grass, and rice ashes; stable manure; acid phosphate; ammonium sulphate, and lime. The results obtained from the various fields are reported in tabular form and discussed. Simple systems of fertilization of both upland and lowland rice were found profitable. Stable manure proved to be the best of the locally available fertilizers, with ashes next, and a combination of stable manure and ashes giving good results. Liming increased production, especially on the " old " fields.

Grain sorghums, B. A. MADSON (*California Sta. Bul. 278* (*1917*), *pp. 227–250, figs. 6*).—The adaptation, production, and value of the grain sorghums in California are discussed in detail.

Variety tests for grain production were conducted at Davis from 1913 to 1916, inclusive, with 6 varieties of durras, 6 of Kafir corn, 4 of kaoliangs, and 1 of shallu. The highest average yield per acre was obtained from Dwarf milo maize, 3,575 lbs. Of the Kafir corns, Dwarf Blackbull was first with 1,962 lbs., and of the kaoliangs Brown with 2,962 lbs. Shallu averaged 3,542 lbs.

The highest average yield of both grain and stalk for 1914 and 1915, of the seven kinds most suitable for forage purposes, was secured from Blackhull White Kafir corn, 16.06 tons per acre, with feterita lowest, with 7.01 tons.

The best results were obtained from plantings made between April 10 and 20, with the planting rate varying from 4 to 7 lbs. per acre, depending upon conditions.

The composition of 5 varieties of durras, 3 of Kafir corn, 4 of kaoliang, and 1 of shallu grown in 1914 is reported in tubular form and compared with similar analyses of corn and barley. It is concluded that grain sorghums fed either as grain fodder or silage are but slightly inferior to corn in feeding value.

Second-growth sorghums may develop stock poisoning properties, but first crops seldom do, if ever, while the dried forage is entirely free from any harmful substances.

Sugar beet plantations in the peasant husbandry, M. Novinskiĭ (*Kiev. Agron. Obshch., Trudy Kom. Izuch. Khoz. Iugo-Zapad. Kraîa, 3 (1915), pp. 5–40*).—The author advocates the cultivation of sugar beets among the peasants of these southwestern Provinces of Russia, since the supply of land is limited, and they could by this means eliminate the 3-year rotation system and at the same time improve the land by the deep and careful cultivation that sugar beets demand. Cooperation among the large planters, sugar factories, and peasant growers is urged. Projects of agreements to be made between the beet producers and the sugar factories are submitted. It is pointed out that sugar beet culture would also aid the peasant in the feeding of his cattle.

[Sugar cane], H. P. Agee (*Hawaii. Sugar Planters' Sta. Rpt. Expt. Sta. Com., 1916, pp. 19–25*).—The results from the Waipio experiments with sugar cane, together with various plantation experiments dealing with fertilizer and variety tests, are reported, and the field experiments now in progress are listed.

Further observations on the cultivation of Helianthus annuus, C. Tropea (*Bol. R. Giard. Colon. Palermo, 2 (1916), No. 4, pp. 214–220; abs. in Internat. Inst. Agr. [Rome], Internat. Rev. Sci. and Pract. Agr., 7 (1916), No. 5, pp. 686, 687*).—This is a brief report of some tests with varieties of Russian sunflowers producing white seed, black seed, and variegated colored seed, the plants being classified entirely according to color of seed.

Fertilizer tests with tobacco varieties on college soils, G. Palafox y de la Cuesta (*Philippine Agr. and Forester, 5 (1916), No. 2, pp. 50–59*).—A series of fertilizer trials with five varieties of tobacco in the Philippines is reported.

All the varieties used responded creditably in height, vigor, and yield to fertilizer treatment. The largest gains were realized from the use of stable manure alone and legumes alone. From an economic standpoint green manuring with cowpeas and the use of stable manure was the cheapest source of material for obtaining increased production. Applications of commercial fertilizers by large growers are recommended.

Variability of tobacco in cultures on the college farm, A. B. Cagubangan (*Philippine Agr. and Forester, 5 (1916), No. 2, pp. 60–64*).—This is a summarized report of work conducted at the Philippine College of Agriculture to study the variations in leaves and habits of growth of the Texas Cuban, Lowland Turkish, Connecticut Havana, and Tirona Hybrid tobaccos grown on the college farm, and to determine what forms in each variety are most desirable for selection. The conclusions arrived at from these studies are regarded as thus far of rather local importance.

The production of cigar wrapper tobacco under shade in the Philippines, D. B. Paguirigan y Amalingan (*Philippine Agr. and Forester, 5 (1916), No. 2, pp. 39–49*).—In these experiments, the native varieties Cagayan and Tirona Hybrid and the acclimatized foreign varieties—Turkish Lowland, Vuelta Abajo, Sumatra, and Texas Cuban—were grown both in the open and under shade.

The native varieties gave the best results, the leaves produced under shade being classified as almost " ideal " in quality for wrapper purposes. The burning qualities of Cagayan, Sumatra, and Tirona Hybrid were improved when shaded, while the other varieties showed no response to shading. The length of the leaves and height of the plants was considerably increased by shading, but the weight of the unshaded leaves was the greater.

General recommendations are made for tobacco culture in the Philippines.

Tobacco.—The production of light-colored pipe and cigarette leaf, C. J. Tregenna (*Dept. Agr. N. S. Wales, Farmers' Bul. 106 (1915), pp. 14*).—This is a general discussion of the production of tobacco in New South Wales.

Wheat, N. Schmitz (*Maryland Sta. Bul. 193 (1916), pp. 59–94, figs. 11*).— The field practices employed in the production of wheat in Maryland are discussed at some length, and variety tests conducted in cooperation with the U. S. Department of Agriculture, extending over the period of 1908 to 1916, inclusive, are reported. The tabulated data show the annual and average yields per acre of grain and straw for the 24 varieties remaining in the test through 1916. Further data show the yields of 78 varieties which have been discarded from time to time since 1908. Descriptions are included of several varieties.

The highest average yield for the 9-year period was obtained from Bearded Purple Straw, 29.87 bu. of grain and 1.77 tons of straw per acre. China, Dietz Longberry, Currell Prolific, and Mammoth Red followed in the order named, with average yields of grain of 29.66, 29.37, 29.27, and 28.94 bu., respectively. The lowest average yield was secured from Miracle, 20.09 bu., in a 5-year test, seeded at the rate of 2 pk. per acre.

The more common diseases and insect pests of wheat are briefly described and control measures are recommended.

The effect of soil moisture content on certain factors in wheat production, F. S. Harrs and H. J. Maughan (*Utah Sta. Bul. 152 (1917), pp. 3–15, figs. 15*).— Supplementary to work previously noted (E. S. R., 32, p. 814; 36, p. 234), experiments are reported on the water requirements of wheat conducted during 1913, 1914, and 1915 in large tanks, previously described (E. S. R., 22, p. 425.).

The life of the wheat plant was divided into three periods, as follows: From planting to the five-leaf stage, from the five-leaf stage to the boot stage, and from the boot stage to maturity. The results of the experiments are presented in 15 figures, the lower part of which represent the average moisture content of the soil during each of the three periods in the growth of the crop. The effects of the moisture treatments are noted on yield of grain, weight of straw, yield of dry matter, number of kernels produced, weight of 100 kernels, number of heads produced, length of heads, number of kernels per head, weight of grain per head, amount of tillering, height of plants, date of maturity, and evaporation and transpiration of water. The moisture treatments for the different periods varied from 7.5 to 35 per cent (saturation) of the soil.

The highest yield of grain was obtained on the soil having about 20 per cent moisture throughout the season. The wheat plant seems especially sensitive to soil moisture conditions during the period immediately preceding the boot stage.

The evaporation and transpiration from a soil producing a large crop was greater than from a free-water surface, but there was a greater loss from the water surface than from the soil producing only a small crop. The importance of favorable soil moisture conditions to good wheat yields is apparent, the yield being more than 20 times as great with proper soil moisture conditions as with unfavorable conditions. Excessive soil moisture was as detrimental to good yields as a lack of sufficient soil moisture.

Gluten formation in the wheat kernel, G. A. OLSON (*Washington Sta. Bul. 142 (1917), pp. 3–19*).—After briefly reviewing previous work, the author presents data which tend to show the formation of gluten in the wheat kernel to be due to the synthetic activity of an enzym. The experiments included a study of the effect of temperature on the formation of gluten in Jones Winter Fife and Red Russian wheat in 1914, and in Red Russian and Turkey Red X Bluestem (Washington No. 536) in 1915, of the various forms of nitrogen groups separated from the flour of the 1914 crop, of the effect of heating for various lengths of time on the formation of gluten in Marquis wheat in 1915, and of the amino nitrogen in Red Russian wheat in 1915. The wheat samples were selected in an early stage of development to determine whether or not gluten was present as such or developed in the kernel as a final product of protein synthesis. The wheat was desiccated at varying temperatures and under varying conditions, including air-drying at room temperature, heating in vacuum pans, and heating in an oil bath.

Positive evidence that gluten was formed within the kernel and not translocated as such from other regions of the plant was obtained in the 1914 experiments. Fife wheat air-dried at a room temperature of 20° C. showed 24.2 per cent wet gluten and 10 per cent dry gluten, while that heated at from 50 to 60° showed only 1.4 and 0.7 per cent, respectively. Samples collected six days later than those noted above and air-dried at 20° showed 27.3 per cent wet and 11 per cent dry gluten. These larger yields are attributed to the translocation or formation of additional material out of which gluten was formed. A temperature range from 30 to 35° under reduced pressure did not materially affect the transformation, the percentages of wet and dry gluten being 22.5 and 9.6 respectively, while with a temperature of 40° or over the percentage was reduced 50 per cent or more. Comparable results were obtained with Red Russian wheat.

In an effort to determine whether or not the protein materials in the kernel were affected by different temperatures the separation of the protein groups was made by the author's method (E. S. R., 31, p. 208). The results obtained indicate that the synthesis of the more complex nitrogenous substances was not complete at the time of harvest, and that the samples heated to a temperature which suppressed the transformation of the materials into gluten contained the largest amounts of amid nitrogen. Since these samples were exposed to relatively high temperatures under reduced pressure it would be expected that under normal pressure the destructive temperatures would be considerably lower.

The 1915 experiments conducted in an oil bath obviated reduced pressures and, in addition to the 1914 observations, moisture determinations were made on all samples. Red Russian wheat air-dried at room temperature showed 23.5 per cent wet and 10.4 per cent dry gluten. Samples containing 65 per cent moisture failed to yield any gluten when heated as low as 40° for 30 minutes. With a reduction in the moisture content some gluten was formed. Samples heated at 50° for 30 minutes after 66 hours desiccation and having 44.73 per cent moisture yielded 13.3 per cent wet and 6.6 per cent dry gluten.

While enzyms that will cause the formation of gluten have not been isolated, the author believes them to be the active agent. Gluten formation is inhibited by heating to relatively low temperatures, 40 to 45°, and desiccation accelerates gluten formation through the concentration of a solution of the materials upon which the enzym acts. The enzym may be present in the kernel from a very early stage but not functional until the soluble nitrogenous materials in the kernel have became concentrated through a rapid translocation from the leaves, and through desiccation.

The results obtained from Washington wheat No. 536 indicated that the wheat was too nearly matured for a satisfactory study of enzymatic action, but further confirmed the results noted above regarding the formation of gluten in the presence of considerable moisture. A comparison of the temperature effects obtained for the first day of harvest showed that heating to 35° was as effective in inhibiting gluten formation as was heating to 50 or 55°, indicating that a temperature of 35° is destructive to the gluten-forming enzym.

Samples of Marquis spring wheat were subjected to temperatures of from 40 to 50° for periods of 5, 10, 20, and 30 minutes, but further observations are considered necessary before attempting to establish the relationship of temperature and moisture content of grain to gluten formation.

Wheat subjected immediately to temperatures ranging from 40 to 55° showed more nitrogen in the amino form than wheat heated to 50° after intervals of 24, 48, and 66 hours.

Spraying of charlock in corn (*Univ. Col. No. Wales, Bangor, Dept. Agr.* [*Pub.*] 7 (*1915*), pp. 2–6).—Cooperative spraying tests at numerous centers in North Wales for the eradication of charlock in corn are reported. A 4 per cent solution of copper sulphate is recommended, applied as a fine spray when the weed is in full bloom.

HORTICULTURE.

Horticultural laws of the State of Washington (*Olympia, Wash.: State,* *1915, pp. 32*).—The text of the laws enacted in 1915 is given.

Luther Burbank, his methods and discoveries and their practical application, edited by J. Whitson and R. J. and H. S. Williams (*New York and London: Luther Burbank Press, 1914, vols. 4–9. pp. 308, pls. 105 each; 1915, vols.* *10–12, pp. 308, pls. 105 each*).—The first three volumes of this work have been noted (E. S. R., 32, p. 143).

The garden, S. B. Shaw (*Md. Agr. Ext. Serv. Bul. 3 (1917), pp. 57–67, figs. 4*).—A popular bulletin on vegetable gardening including directions for the use of spray materials in small quantities.

The home garden in Kentucky, C. S. Adams (*Kentucky Sta. Circ. 14 (1917),* *pp. 9–59, figs. 19*).—A practical treatise on vegetable gardening, including a discussion of the general principles and directions for growing the more important vegetables.

Variation in artichokes, A. D. Shamel (*Jour. Heredity, 8 (1917), No. 7, pp.* *306–309, figs. 2*).—The author points out and illustrates instances of variation in the plants and flower heads of globe artichokes, and suggests the opportunity for improving these plants through bud selection.

Experiments in keeping asparagus after cutting, F. W. Morse (*Massachu-* *setts Sta. Bul. 172 (1917), pp. 297–307*).—The author conducted a number of experiments to determine the changes which take place in asparagus when stored under different conditions from the time when it is cut in the field until it is ready to be cooked. Data are given showing the weight when fresh as well as the loss in weight of dry matter and total sugars from dry matter after storage.

The results show in substance that asparagus stalks will become limp even when on ice unless their butts are in water or some other means are taken to reduce the evaporation to the lowest point. Even when the butts are placed in water there is loss, both in dry matter and total sugars from dry matter. This loss is greater under room temperatures than under refrigeration. The weight of stalks placed in water under room temperature increased more than those placed in water under refrigeration. By placing the stalks under refrigeration in a close atmosphere it was found possible to hold asparagus for a week with very little deterioration in quality. The temperature should be as low as 45° F. if possible in order to check plant growth. The usual methods of keeping asparagus at summer temperatures cause rapid deterioration in quality.

Although experiments on a commercial scale have not been tried, the present experiment led to the suggestion that the asparagus be cooled as soon as possible after cutting. The stalks may be laid loosely in boxes, placed on ice in the ice house, and covered with canvas to maintain a low temperature and reduce the circulation of air.

New Mexico beans, F. GARCIA (*New Mexico Sta. Bul. 105 (1917), pp. 56, figs. 15*).—A treatise on bean culture, including notes on varieties adapted for New Mexico conditions, and analyses showing the protein content of various types. Reports by various county agents relative to local methods of culture in several counties of the State are appended.

Report of the experimental work of the Taliparamba Agricultural Station for 1913–14, H. C. SAMPSON (*Dept. Agr. Madras, Rpt. Taliparamba Agr. Sta., 1913–14, pp. 13*).—Data are given on manurial experiments with peppers conducted at the station for a number of years, together with an account of the local agriculture in the neighborhood of the station.

Report of the work of the Taliparamba Agricultural Station for 1914–15, H. C. SAMPSON (*Dept. Agr. Madras, Rpt. Taliparamba Agr. Sta., 1914–15, pp. 11*).—A report on pepper fertilizer experiments similar to the above for 1914–15.

Report of the work of the Taliparamba Agricultural Station for 1915–16, K. RAMASASTRULU NAYUDU (*Dept. Agr. Madras, Rpt. Taliparamba Agr. Sta., 1915–16, pp. 12*).—A report on pepper fertilizer experiments similar to the above for 1915–16.

The tomato as a farm crop for the canning factory, H. J. REED (*Indiana Sta. Circ. 59 (1917), pp. 28, figs. 13*).—This circular is based on investigations by the station previously reported (E. S. R., 29, p. 434; 30, p. 738), supplemented by further field studies. It deals particularly with the culture of tomatoes with reference to their sale to canning factories.

[Vegetable seed production at Vineland, Ont.] (*Agr. Gaz. Canada, 4 (1917), No. 5, pp. 397, 398*).—A brief statement of progress made in the home production of vegetable seed at the Horticultural Experiment Station at Vineland, Ont. Tests made by growers in 1916 of seed produced in 1915 indicate that germination in the home seed of a number of vegetables was in most cases 20 per cent or better than that of other seed.

New or noteworthy fruits, V, U. P. HEDRICK (*New York State Sta. Bul. 427 (1916), pp. 523–529, pls. 5*).—This is the fifth of a series of bulletins (E. S. R., 35, p. 36) dealing with new or noteworthy fruits under observation at the station. The present bulletin describes and illustrates the J. H. Hale and Pearson peaches, Drap d'Or plum, Empire raspberry, and Good Luck strawberry.

Variety testing at the Dominion Experimental Farms, and what has been accomplished by it, W. T. MACOUN (*Agr. Gaz. Canada, 4 (1917), No. 5, pp. 349–354*).—A popular review of results secured from long-continued variety tests of orchard and small fruits at the Canadian Experimental Farms.

Varieties of fruit in the Province of Starkenburg (*Arb. Landw. Kammer Hesse, No. 19 (1915), pp. 64, pls. 30*).—This comprises a list of varieties of orchard and small fruits recommended for culture in the Province of Starkenburg, Hesse. A number of the more important varieties are illustrated by colored plates.

Studies in fruit bud formation, J. R. MAGNESS (*Ann. Rpt. Oreg. State Hort. Soc., 8 (1916), pp. 98–105*).—A paper on this subject, with a discussion following, based upon the author's investigations previously noted (E. S. R., 36, p. 237).

The freezing of fruit buds, F. L. WEST and N. E. EDLEFSEN (*Utah Sta. Bul. 151 (1917), pp. 3-24, figs. 6*).—This bulletin reports methods used by the authors in conducting freezing studies of detached branches and also of whole trees. The results obtained on between 5,000 and 6,000 buds of apples, peaches, cherries, and prunes are reported and the literature on the subject is reviewed.

In addition to improving the methods of freezing buds in the laboratory an equipment was devised for freezing branches without removing them from the tree. It was also found that the whole tree could be frozen under natural conditions by surrounding it with a tank of ice and salt. The factors that enter into the problem are thus satisfactorily controlled and accurately determined. Frost damage can be measured by the injured buds and also by the yield of fruit in the fall.

The investigation shows that the fruit buds in the same orchard do not have a uniform freezing point. An orchard can usually stand two or three freezes without losing more than half of its buds, thus leaving enough buds for a normal fruit crop.

Data are given on some preliminary studies with Jonathan apples and Elberta peaches. The results show in general that the further developed the buds are the more sensitive they are to frost. There is a range of at least 5° F. between the temperature at which only about 5 per cent of the buds are damaged and the temperature that will kill all of them. With Jonathan apples in full bloom, 28.5° caused no damage and 24° killed about half of the blossoms. The following temperatures will kill about 50 per cent of Elberta peach buds in various stages of development: When they are slightly swollen, 14°; when well swollen, 18°; when they are showing pink, 24°; when they are in full bloom, 25°; and when the fruit is setting, 28°. In the case of Double Nattie cherries 29° caused no damage when the fruit was setting but 24° killed practically all of them. Prune buds are slightly hardier than those of the other kinds of fruit tested.

Pruning fruit trees, W. H. ALDERMAN and E. C. AUCHTER (*West Virginia Sta. Bul. 164 (1917), pp. 3-40, figs. 33*).—The purpose of this bulletin is to present simple and practical directions for pruning based upon the most recent information available. In addition to a discussion of the general principles of pruning directions are given for pruning and training the apple, peach, cherry, plum, pear, and quince at the time of planting and in subsequent years. Some of the data secured in the station's recent experiments in pruning apple trees (E. S. R., 36, p. 535) are also included.

The Taylor system of pruning, A. TAYLOR (*San Jose, Cal.: Eaton & Co., 1917, pp. 79, pl. 1, figs. 38*).—A treatise on pruning fruit trees with special reference to California conditions, based on the author's experience extending over a period of 25 years.

The influence of pruning upon the fruit spur system of the apple, V. R. GARDNER (*Ann. Rpt. Oreg. State Hort. Soc., 8 (1916), pp. 66-72*).—A popular discussion of this subject, based upon the author's investigations previously noted (E. S. R., 36, p. 237).

The influence of commercial fertilizers on bearing apple orchards, G. G. BROWN (*Ann. Rpt. Oreg. State Hort. Soc., 8 (1916), pp. 36-41*).—A popular summary of the author's investigations, previously noted (E. S. R., 37, p. 41).

The selection and hybridization of American vines in Italy, G. PATANÈ (*Internat. Inst. Agr. [Rome], Internat. Rev. Sci. and Pract. Agr., 7 (1916), No. 10, pp. 1393-1404*).—An account of the results secured with American species of grapes in the reconstitution of phylloxera-infested vineyards in Italy.

Comparative merits of California avocado varieties, L. B. Scott (*Cal. Citrogr., 2 (1917), No. 8, pp. 2–4, figs. 4*).—An address delivered before the California Avocado Association.

Based on their performance records the author is of the opinion that the number of varieties for commercial plantings should be greatly reduced. Of a great number of varieties under observation only nine, the Sharpless, Fuerte, Surprise, Spinks, Taft, Monroe, Lyon, Blakeman, and Dickinson, appear to approach the requirements of an ideal avocado.

Avocado varieties in Florida, E. D. Vosbury (*Cal. Citrogr., 2 (1917), No. 8, p. 5, fig. 1*).—A brief discussion relative to the adaptability of different avocado varieties to Florida conditions.

Report on cacao manurial experiments at Djati-Roenggo during the years 1912, 1913, and 1914, J. R. C. Peelen and A. W. K. de Jong (*Meded. Proefstat. Midden-Java, No. 24 (1917), pp. 8, pl. 1*).—The experiments here reported show that the use of stable manure resulted in only slight increases in yield, whereas the use of a combination of stable manure and superphosphate resulted in increased yields of from 40 to 50 per cent over the check plats.

The culture of citrus plants in Cuba, R. S. Cunliffe and H. A. van Hermann (*Estac. Expt. Agron. Cuba Bol. 32 (1916), pp. 62, pls. 44*).—A treatise on citrus fruits with reference to soil and climatic requirements, methods of propagation, fertilization, culture, varieties, insect pests and diseases, methods of harvesting, marketing, and citrus products.

A lemon bud variation, A. D. Shamel (*Jour. Heredity, 8 (1917), No. 6, p. 284, fig. 1*).—The author here describes and illustrates a navel lemon produced by a normal tree bearing, except for this specimen, normal fruits.

Maturity standard for Washington navel, E. M. Chace (*Cal. Citrogr., 2 (1917), No. 9, pp. 7, 17, fig. 1*).—A popular review of the work of the Bureau of Chemistry of the U. S. Department of Agriculture in the development of maturity standards for oranges, including a discussion of the effect of the different proposed standards.

A practical guide to coconut planting, R. W. Munro and L. C. Brown (*London: John Bale, Sons & Danielsson, Ltd., 1916, pp. XX+186, pls. 103*).—This work comprises an enlargement of the junior author's bulletin on the subject written in 1910 (E. S. R., 24, p. 40).

The genus Annona in the Hawaiian Islands, V. MacCaughey (*Torreya, 17 (1917), No. 5, pp. 69–77*).—A brief account of the adaptation of different members of the custard-apple genus that have been introduced into Hawaii.

Cultivation of the papaya, R. S. Cunliffe (*Agriculture [Cuba], 1 (1917), No. 4, pp. 12–27, figs. 12*).—Methods of propagating and growing papayas are described, including an account of the collection and preparation of papain from the fruit.

South American markets for fresh fruits, W. Fischer (*U. S. Dept. Com., Bur. Foreign and Dom. Com., Spec. Agents Ser., No. 131 (1917), pp. 163, pls. 7*).—This report reviews fully the native fruit industry in Brazil, Argentina, Uruguay, Paraguay, Peru, and Chile, and discusses the development of the foreign fresh-fruit trade in those countries, with special reference to the possibility of opening new markets for the United States.

Making nuts in five years, T. P. Littlepage (*Amer. Nut Jour., 6 (1917), No. 6, p. 87*).—In this brief note the author reports the development of catkins on 3-year-old Busseron, Greenriver, and Major pecans growing in Maryland, indicating the probability of the trees bearing fruit at the age of 4 or 5 years.

Gladiolus studies.—III, Varieties of the garden gladiolus, A. C. Hottes (*N. Y. State Col. Agr., Cornell Ext. Bul. 11 (1916), pp. 275–451, pl. 1, figs. 31*).—

In continuation of previous studies (E. S. R., 36, p. 643), this bulletin describes most of the varieties of gladiolus received for trial on the grounds of the Cornell University department of floriculture in cooperation with the American Gladiolus Society. The descriptions are preceded by an account of the methods used in testing and describing the varieties.

The culture of garden roses, A. C. BEAL (*Cornell Reading Course for the Farm, No. 121 (1917), pp. 189–215, figs. 17*).—A popular treatise on rose culture.

Sweet peas up-to-date, G. W. KERR (*Philadelphia: W. Atlee Burpee & Co., 1917, rev. ed., pp. 100, figs. 16*).—In addition to cultural directions a descriptive list is given of all varieties of sweet peas, as far as known, introduced up to 1917.

Milady's house plants, F. E. PALMER (*New York: A. T. De La Mare Co., Inc., 1917, pp. 176, figs. 96*).—A popular treatise on the selection, culture, and care of various house plants.

Putnam's garden handbook, MAE S. CROY (*New York: G. P. Putnam's Sons, 1917, pp. V+359*).—A popular manual of ornamental gardening.

The joyous art of gardening, FRANCES DUNCAN (*New York: Charles Scribner's Sons, 1917, pp. XIII+239, pls. 8, figs. 54*).—A popular treatise on the planning and planting of home grounds, designed especially for the amateur gardener.

"Know your city" trees, C. BANNWART (*Newark, N. J.: Newark Shade Tree Com., 1916, pp. 20, figs. 14*).—This comprises a directory of the noteworthy trees of Newark, N. J., with special reference to those of historic and special botanic interest.

FORESTRY.

Trees worth knowing, JULIA E. ROGERS (*Garden City, N. Y.: Doubleday, Page & Co., 1917, pp. XXIII+291, pls. 48*).—This comprises popular descriptive accounts of the principal trees of the United States. The trees are grouped as nut trees, water-loving trees, trees with showy flowers and fruits, wild relatives of our orchard trees, the pod-bearing trees, desiduous trees with winged seeds, the cone-bearing evergreens, and the palms.

A bud and twig key to the more important broadleaf deciduous trees in the United States, O. L. SPONSLER (*Ann. Arbor, Mich.: George Wahr, 1916, rev. ed., pp. 26, figs. 8*).—About 85 species of the more important broadleaf deciduous trees, including the more important forest trees, as well as a few of the smaller trees and more common exotics, are given in the key.

The pine trees of the Rocky Mountain region, G. B. SUDWORTH (*U. S. Dept. Agr. Bul. 460 (1917), pp. 46, pls. 42*).—Supplementing a previous bulletin dealing with cypress and juniper trees (E. S. R., 33, p. 343), this bulletin comprises descriptions and illustrations of the distinguishing characteristics of all of the pine trees that inhabit the Rocky Mountain region. Graphic illustrations of the range of these trees and discussions of their forest habits are also included.

Note on the forests of Java and Madoera of the Dutch East Indies, R. C. MILWARD (*Calcutta: Govt., 1915, pp. 8, pls. 5*).—The note deals chiefly with the extent, silvical management, exploitation, yields, and revenues of teak forests in Java and Madoera.

Factors causing variation in the yield of camphor in the Florida camphor tree, S. C. HOOD (*Jour. Indus. and Engin. Chem., 9 (1917), No. 6, pp. 552–555*).—The present paper is based on observations on camphor trees growing under various conditions in Florida during the years 1907 to 1912, at which time the author was on the scientific staff of the Bureau of Plant Industry of the U. S. Department of Agriculture. The paper presents the more important results having a direct bearing on the methods of commercial production of camphor.

The rubber industry, edited by J. Torrey and A. S. Manders (*London: Internat. Rubber & Allied Trades Ex., Ltd., [1917], pp. 516, pl. 1, figs. 34*).— This book comprises as a whole the official report of the Fourth International Rubber Congress, held in London in 1914. In addition to the papers dealing with various phases of the rubber industry and the discussions thereon, numerous papers and discussions dealing with fibers, cotton, oils, etc., together with the principal papers read at the rubber congress held in New York in 1912 and a report of the proceedings of the Fourth International Rubber and Allied Industries Exhibition held in London in 1914, are also given.

A practical tapping experiment conducted on scientific principles, A. W. K. DE JONG (*Teysmannia, 28 (1917), No. 1, pp. 30–32*).—The results are given of comparative tests of a number of methods of tapping rubber that have been conducted for a period of three and one-half years.

Scientific tapping experiments with Hevea brasiliensis, A. W. K. DE JONO (*Dept. Landb., Nijv. en Handel [Dutch East Indies], Meded. Agr. Chem. Lab., No. 14 (1916), pp. 26, figs. 14*).—Two sets of experiments are reported. In one set various systems of tapping were compared on the same tree. In the other set the various systems of tapping compared were used on different trees.

Investigations of the quality of plantation rubber conducted under the Ceylon rubber research scheme (*Bul. Imp. Inst. [So. Kensington], 14 (1916), No. 4, pp. 495–566*).—The investigations recorded in the present article were conducted under the auspices of the government of Ceylon in conjunction with some of the principal planting companies of the island and with the Imperial Institute. They deal with the effect upon the mechanical properties of the vulcanized rubber of different methods of coagulation, the addition of various substances to the latex in order to retard coagulation, the form of the rubber, the method of drying, "overworking" freshly coagulated rubber in the washing machine, various methods of smoking, drying sheet rubber under tension, rolling up wet and dry sheet rubber, with and without tension, the conversion of wet and dry crepe rubber into block, and separating the rubber from the latex in successive portions.

The influence of the rubber content of latex on the inner qualities of the rubber, O. DE VRIES (*Arch. Rubbercult. Nederland. Indië, 1 (1917), No. 1, pp. 25–34*).—Several experiments were made to determine what effect the dilution of latex has on the inner qualities of rubber. The tensile strength showed no difference, except in the case of a very diluted latex which gave a lower tensile strength. The viscosity was diminished slightly by dilution and the rate of cure in an appreciable degree. In view of the differences in rate of cure noted, it is held to be desirable to dilute the latex to a standard rubber content in order to obtain rubber of uniform qualities.

Influence of the amount of acetic acid on the inner qualities of the rubber, O. DE VRIES (*Arch. Rubbercult. Nederland. Indië, 1 (1917), No. 1, pp. 35–41*).— As a result of experiments conducted in part by the author and in part by P. Arens and N. L. Swart it was found that for quantities of acetic acid ranging from the minimum to four times as much the tensile strength of the rubber shows no difference. The slope or type of rubber remained the same in all experiments in which the rubber was prepared as crepe, although in one experiment with smoked sheet rubber the type was sligthly less when using a double quantity of acetic acid. The viscosity increased slightly with increasing quantities of acetic acid. When four times the minimum quantity of acetic acid was used the rate of cure diminished to the extent of 10 minutes in 135.

It is concluded in brief that the small variations in amount of acetic acid used in actual practice can not be the cause of lack of uniformity in the rubber.

Sugar as a coagulant for crepe rubber, O. DE VRIES (*Arch. Rubbercult. Nederland, Indië, 1 (1917), No. 1, pp. 5–16*).—As a result of experiments conducted in part by the author and in part by N. L. Swart and A. J. Ultée the conclusion is reached that the difference between rubber coagulated by acetic acid and by sugar is insignificant. Such difficulties as arise in the practice of sugar coagulation can be overcome, and it is believed that sugar might possibly be the coagulant most fitted to replace acetic acid if necessary.

Reforestation on the National Forests, C. R. TILLOTSON (*U. S. Dept. Agr. Bul. 475 (1917), pp. 63, pls. 12, figs. 4*).—The present bulletin is based partially on Forest Service Bulletin 98 (E. S. R., 26, p. 241), which it supersedes, and partially on more recent results secured in the reforestation work of the U. S. Forest Service as a whole.

Nursery practice on the National Forests, C. R. TILLOTSON (*U. S. Dept. Agr. Bul. 479 (1917), pp. 86, pls. 22, figs. 6*).—This bulletin presents the results of the study and experience of many different members of the Forest Service. The subject matter is presented under the headings of factors influencing selection of a nursery site, size and arrangement of nursery, outfit, nursery operations, removal of planting stock from the nursery, diseases and injuries in the nursery, fertilizers, and costs of operations.

Latest devices in protection work, C. DuBois (Proc. *Forest Indus. Conf., West. Forestry and Conserv. Assoc., 1916, p. 13*).—A popular discussion of improvements in methods, equipment, and appliances employed in forest fire protection work.

The annual report of the National Forest Reservation Commission for the fiscal year ended June 30, 1916 (*U. S. Senate, 64. Cong., 2. Sess., Doc. 643 (1916), pp. 10*).—A report relative to the acquisition of lands for the protection of watersheds of navigable streams in the White Mountains and southern Appalachians during the fiscal year ended June 30, 1916. At this time 1,329,038 acres of land had been approved for purchase and 706,974.5 acres of land actually acquired at an average price of $5.52 per acre.

Report of the State forester, M. SCHAAF (*Bien. Rpt. Pub. Domain Com. Mich., 1915–16, pp. 87–129, figs. 14*).—A progress report on State forest activities in Michigan covering the period from January 1, 1915, to June 30, 1916, including a brief description of the State forests, results secured from forest fire protection, nursery work, planting operations, etc.

First annual report of the State forester, J. H. FOSTER ET AL. (*Bul. Agr. and Mech. Col. Tex., 3. ser., 3 (1917), No. 3, pp. 16*).—A brief statement of progress made along the lines of forest protection, assistance rendered to private owners, educational work in forestry, and investigations, with suggested plans for improving the forestry work in Texas.

Report on the forest administration of the Central Provinces for the year 1915–16, H. H. FORTEATH, C. B. SMALES, and F. TRAFFORD (*Rpt. Forest Admin. Cent. Prov. [India], 1915–16, pp. 3+29+49+XCVI*).—This is the usual report relative to the administration and management of the State forests of the Northern, Southern, and Berar Circles, including a financial statement for the year.

All important data relative to alterations in forest areas, forest protection, forest surveys, miscellaneous work, yields in major and minor forest products, revenues, expenditures, etc., are appended in tabular form.

Organization and activities of the Chinese forest service, F. SHFRFESEX (*Indian Forester, 43 (1917), No. 5, pp. 205–221*).—An account of the organization and functions of the six divisions into which the Chinese forest service is organized.

Timber storage conditions in the Eastern and Southern States with reference to decay problems, C. J. HUMPHREY (*U. S. Dept. Agr. Bul. 510 (1917), pp. 42, pls. 10, figs. 41*).—This bulletin embraces the results of a survey of timber storage conditions in the Eastern and Southern States, conducted with the view of securing data for a study of the effective control of decay in building timber. The subject matter is presented under the general headings of cause of decay in timber, handling timber at sawmills, location of mills and its relation to decay, quality of stock with reference to decay, condition of storage sheds at mills, condition of storage yards at mills, handling timber at retail yards, fungi which rot stored lumber, wood preservatives in the lumberyard, and branding structural timber. A number of suggestions are given relative to the improvement of lumber storage conditions by modifying the present insanitary practices.

DISEASES OF PLANTS.

Report of the mycologist, R. H. BUNTING (*Govt. Gold Coast, Rpt. Agr. Dept., 1915, pp. 21–25*).—It appears that the yield of the cacao trees on the old established farms is decreasing, and that this is due largely to the increase of cacao diseases. Pod rot (*Phytophthora faberi*, frequently associated with *Diplodia cacaoicola*) is considered as the most widespread and destructive of these diseases. A fungus resembling *Colletotrichum cradwickii* may be responsible for enormous loss from the withering of the young pods. Of somewhat less importance are the thread blights, *Marasmius scandens* and *M. equicrinis*. Important root diseases of cacao are due to *Polyporus lignosus* (*Fomes semitostus*), *Hymenochœte noxia*, and a species of Rosellinia. Numerous cases of die-back appear to be related only secondarily to fungi.

The most serious diseases of Hevea are due to root parasites, *P. lignosus*, *H. noxia*, *Sphœrostilbe repens*, and a Rosellinia killing rubber trees at various points.

Other diseases noted, or suspected, are an undetermined mildew of *Coffea liberica;* brown rot (*H. noxia*) of *C. stenophylla;* white thread (*M. scandens*) on *Coffea* sp., soursop, and cola; *Cercospora personata* on peanut; bleeding disease (probably *Thielaviopsis ethaceticus*) of coconut; *S. repens* on jak fruit; *P. lignosus* on camphor, cassava, *Combretum* sp., and *Irvingia* sp.; *Corticium* sp. on *Ficus elastica;* and coffee-leaf disease (*Hemileia vastatrix*) on *Strophanthus hispidus*.

Parasitic diseases of cultivated plants, R. RENACCO (*An. Soc. Cient. Argentina, 81 (1916), No. 1–2, pp. 62–70*).—A list is given, with a systematic arrangement according to relationships, of about 35 fungi parasitic on economic plants as observed, mostly during the latter part of 1914, in a portion of the Province of Buenos Aires.

Black mold of onions, W. VAN PELT (*Mo. Bul. Ohio Sta., 2 (1917), No. 5, pp. 152–156, fig. 1*).—A popular account is given of a new fungus disease which is said to cause serious damage in storage houses. The cause of the trouble is *Aspergillus niger*, the presence of which is indicated by the occurrence of small circular spots scattered over the onion, generally about the upper half. As the areas develop, there is formed a large diseased mass which often involves the greater part of the onion. The outer layers of the bulb become wrinkled, dry, and practically worthless. This condition, however, is rarely found except in storage. As a rule white varieties are most subject to infection, although the disease has been found on red ones as well.

Examination of samples of onion seed showed the presence of spores, and experiments in applying formalin to the affected seed proved that this fungicide will control the trouble. It is recommended that the fungicide be applied by the drip method which is used for the prevention of onion smut. No efficient method has been determined for the treatment of onion sets, but experiments along this line are in progress.

Investigations on potato diseases (seventh report), G. H. PETHYBRIDGE (*Dept. Agr. and Tech. Instr. Ireland Jour.*, 16 (1916), No. 4, pp. 564–596, pls. 12).—The special investigations on potato diseases, which were started in 1909 at Clifden, Ireland, and since reported on from time to time (E. S. R., 34, p. 443), were continued during 1915, and the results are here described in considerable detail.

Phytophthora infestans appeared very late in 1915, supposedly on account of the fine dry weather which prevailed after planting until the end of June, and after that time supposedly on account of the scarcity of infecting spores. From the work already done, it is thought that in favorable seasons, at least, the use of 1 per cent Bordeaux or Burgundy mixture is about as effective as is the 2 per cent application. Tests with a fungicidal powder showed this to be inferior to the ordinary sprays. Burgundy mixture gave slightly greater freedom from blight than Bordeaux mixture, but a somewhat lighter yield of tubers. It is considered better to spray several times at comparatively short intervals with a relatively weak mixture than a few times with a strong one. The names and relative ranks of varieties tested for resistance are detailed. Outbreaks appear to originate only from the planting of diseased potato tubers in which the fungus lives over from one season to the next.

Stalk, or Sclerotium, disease (*Sclerotinia sclerotiorum*) was less severe than in any of the five or six previous seasons. Infection occurs first on one or more of the older, yellowing leaves and then passes directly to the stalk. Abnormally early planting, in some localities, is thought to favor the disease. Two sprayings with lime-sulphur or with milk of lime decreased the attack and increased the yield. Attention is called to recent findings that this fungus has no Botrytis stage, as formerly held.

Botrytis cinerea was studied under favorable conditions as it developed, unmasked by blight, in July and the early part of August, and its characters, habits, and effects are detailed. It is regarded as not definitely proved that *B. cinerea* is the conidial stage of *S. fuckeliana*. The usual sprays have little or no effect upon this disease, but it is resisted by the same varieties which are resistant to blight.

Verticillium alboatrum has thus far been observed at three places in Ireland. It spreads from the infected mother tubers into the young stalks, and practically any part of the plant, if left, will contaminate the soil. Heating tubers for five hours from 41 to 45.5° C. does not kill the fungus nor does it injure the tubers.

Hypochnus (*Rhizoctonia*) *solani* was studied, and it is concluded that under the conditions employed this fungus does not cause a rot of potato tubers.

Work has been done with other diseases, some of which is still incomplete. Notes given in this connection refer to *Spongospora subterranea, Spondylocladium atrovirens, Fusarium cœruleum,* and *P. erythroseptica.*

Cork, drought spot, and related diseases of the apple, A. J. MIX (*New York State Sta. Bul. 426 (1916), pp. 473–522, pls. 12; abs., pp. 8, figs. 9*).—A description is given of two little known diseases which were observed in the Champlain Valley, New York. Both are nonparasitic in nature and may be different types of the same disease. They are considered closely related to the well-known fruit pit or stippen disease. The names drought spot and cork are proposed for them. Associated with the drought spot are abnormal conditions of the twigs and foliage, and it is proposed that these be designated drought dieback and drought rosette.

Cork is said to affect chiefly the Fameuse variety. In addition to occurring in New York, it is also known to be present in Ontario and New South Wales. The drought spot has been reported from Maine and Virginia, while a closely related trouble is said to occur in the Pacific Northwest. Rosette has been reported from Colorado, California, and Idaho, and both rosette and dieback occur in the irrigated sections of Washington and Oregon. It is claimed that in the Champlain Valley certain orchards and even individual trees are more affected than others.

In infected trees, cork is evident late in June as dead brown spots beneath the skin of the fruit or around the core. Later the fruit becomes distorted and knobby, and brown corky spots are said to occur throughout the flesh. Drought spot occurs in early June and fresh stages may develop throughout the summer if the weather continues dry. Superficial or sunken dead brown spots show in the skin of the fruit and dead brown areas may occur in the flesh beneath. In later stages, the apples become cracked and deformed. The internal spots of both diseases are in close proximity to branches of the vascular system.

Die-back associated with drought spot is characterized by the death of the twigs from the tips backward. The dead twig may be replaced by a healthy lateral from the base, but often there is found near the base of the twig a rosette-like cluster of dwarfed leaves. This appearance and one in which a compact cluster of similarly dwarfed leaves crowns a long, bare twig have been included under the name rosette.

From field observations it appears that these diseases may occur on the best types of soil and under conditions of careful culture. Poor moisture supply seems to be connected with their occurrence, and a drought accompanied by high, dry winds appears to bring on a large amount of the diseases. It is said that these troubles may appear to a limited extent in a rainy season when lack of moisture can not be considered their sole cause. This is believed, however, to be the predisposing factor, though other as yet unknown factors may be operative.

Conservation of soil moisture and even distribution of moisture throughout the season are thought to be the only satisfactory methods of control.

Rhizopus rot of strawberries in transit, N. E. STEVENS and R. B. WILCOX (*U. S. Dept. Agr. Bul. 531 (1917), pp. 22, fig. 1*).—In continuation of previous investigations (E. S. R., 35, p. 458), the authors give an account of field and laboratory studies of the rot of strawberries due to *R. nigricans*, with special reference to the relation of the disease to packing house and shipping problems. This fungus is said to cause serious deterioration of strawberries during transit, the fruit softening and collapsing with the liberation of much juice, but it has not been found of primary importance as a cause of field rot, as it usually develops in the berries some time after they are picked. Conditions of shipping have been found to influence the development of the disease, the growth of the fungus increasing rapidly at temperatures above 50° F.

In some packing houses the berries are washed; and if they are packed without drying, the evaporation of the water, by cooling the berries, seems to retard the development of rot; but if they are dried before packing, especially by exposure to direct sunlight, the amount of decay is usually greatly increased. It is believed that proper cooling and refrigeration of the berries from the time they are picked until they are marketed will reduce the losses from this rot.

The control of American gooseberry mildew by spraying, F. R. PETHER-BRIDGE and A. C. COLE (*Jour. Bd. Agr. [London], 23 (1916), No. 8, pp. 750–*

755).—Observations during recent years, on the fruit plantations of the eastern counties, have shown that American gooseberry mildew has been reduced, and in some places almost eradicated, by growers who have subjected their bushes to a thorough tipping (cutting off and burning the diseased shoots), followed by two or three thorough sprayings with lime-sulphur during the growing season. The authors therefore undertook these experiments to ascertain how much the disease could be reduced in a single season by spraying alone, employing for this purpose the variety Whinham Industry, on the plats used by Brooks, Petherbridge, and Spinks, as previously noted (E. S. R., 34, p. 846). The hand pumps used gave a pressure of 60 lbs. per square inch and carried swivel nozzles set to spray almost vertically.

The results show that 2.5 per cent lime-sulphur is, in certain seasons, capable of reducing the American gooseberry mildew attack on the berries to less than 1 per cent even in case of a susceptible variety badly affected previously. The first spraying should be applied before the primary outbreak in the spring, preferably the first week in April. Two more sprayings, three or four weeks apart, should also be given. In 1916, the first week in May proved to be the most suitable time for a single spraying.

Thorough spraying reduces to a marked extent the disease on the shoots. Tipping, as carried out commercially, is of little value on a thoroughly infested plantation in such a season as the one in question.

Mysterious vine disease, J. W. JEFFREY (*Mo. Bul. Com. Hort. Cal., 5 (1916), No. 11, pp. 416, 417).*—A peculiar grapevine trouble has appeared in several districts of California for each of the last three seasons. The vines start with apparently normal vigor in spring but lose their leaves in midsummer, and show later only a small, sickly leaf at each axil, the fruit meanwhile withering away in an immature condition. Although weakened the second season, the vines may not die until the third season. No variety is immune, so far as known. The trouble appears to be independent of soil and irrigation, though a decay of the roots seems to precede the final death of the plants.

The gray root fungus of cinchona, A. RANT (*Bul. Jard. Bot. Buitenzorg, 2. ser., No. 22 (1916), pp. 23, pls. 3).*—An account is given of observation and experimentation on a gray root fungus on cinchona, which has been observed to attack also a considerable number of other plants named. The organism, which appears to be transmitted through both soil and air, is considered as genetically related to Graphium.

Control of black spot and brown spot in citrus, G. P. DARNELL-SMITH (*Agr. Gaz. N. S. Wales, 27 (1916), No. 12, p. 844).*—Black spot (*Phoma citricarpa*) of oranges and brown spot (*Colletotrichum glœosporioides*) of oranges and mandarins have been dealt with during four years by O. Brooks at Erina, and the results are briefly set forth.

Of the spraying solutions tested, potassium sulphid and copper sulphate were dropped after the first year, and formalin and lime-sulphur after the third year, leaving Bordeaux mixture alone to be tested the fourth year. This preparation, at first used at a strength of 6 lbs. of copper sulphate with 4 lbs. of lime in 50 gals. of water, can, according to subsequent tests, be reduced to half that strength, or less, with complete safety. The lime should be freshly burnt and the mixture applied as soon as made, the application to be preceded by a thorough pruning of all dead or diseased wood.

Composition of citrus leaves at various stages of mottling, C. A. JENSEN (*U. S. Dept. Agr., Jour. Agr. Research, 9 (1917), No. 6, pp. 157–166).*—In experiments carried on at the California Citrus substation at Riverside, the author undertook to determine whether mottled citrus leaves show a deficiency of the mineral elements directly affecting chlorophyll formation.

From a comparison of the average percentages of the inorganic elements in healthy leaves and leaves in medium stages of mottling, data were obtained which are considered not to show that the initial mottling could be accounted for by deficiency in the transfer of the iron, calcium, magnesium, and phosphoric acid from the conducting system of the leaf stem and midrib to the mesophyll tissue. On the other hand sharply localized yellow areas in old orange leaves contained less of these elements than the adjoining green areas, but whether this relation obtained in the initial stages of mottling was not determined. In very badly mottled leaves there was found in general an increase in the percentage of these elements in the conducting tissues, including the leaf stems, indicating difficulty in their transfer to the mesophyll tissues, probably because the leaf had become functionless.

Relation of nitrogen to mottle-leaf, I. G. McBeth (*U. S. Dept. Agr.*, Jour. *Agr. Research, 9 (1917), No. 7, pp. 248-250*).—In investigations carried on by the author in cooperation with the California Citrus substation, Riverside, and noted on page 352, in which a study was made of factors influencing nitrification and the forces controlling the distribution of nitric nitrogen as related to the nutrition of citrus trees, much attention was given to the production and distribution of ammonia and nitrate and their possible relation to mottling, a serious trouble of oranges and other citrus trees. Mottled orange leaves were found to have a higher moisture content and in general a higher nitrogen content than healthy leaves of the same age from the same tree. Extreme mottling is frequently found associated with high nitrate content, but the correlation is said to be by no means an invariable one.

A new species of Endothia, S. C. Bruner (*Mycologia, 8 (1916), No. 5, pp. 239-242, pl. 1*).—An account is given of a study by the author of a fungus said to be common as a saprophyte or parasite on several species of Eucalyptus, and saprophytic on mango (*Mangifera indica*), in the vicinity of Santiago, Cuba. The fungus is an Endothia, somewhat resembling *E. radicalis*, but as a result of studies by the author it is considered as a new species and has received the name *E. havanensis*. The pycnidial stage has been observed on *Persea gratissima* and *Spondias mombin*. The fungus is thought to be of Cuban origin.

Rose diseases, L. M. Massey (*Amer. Florist, 47 (1916), No. 1489, pp. 1148, 1149*).—An extensive investigation of rose diseases was undertaken in 1916 by the department of plant pathology of Cornell University in connection with the American Rose Society. The preliminary survey shows that on both indoor and outdoor plants, powdery mildew and black spot are more common than other diseases, and the results of studies on these troubles are to be published later. Two varieties are affected with a root or crown rot, which is described. Other rose diseases are crown gall, Phyllosticta leaf spot, besides other leaf spots, and cane diseases of unknown causation.

A disease of Clivia under glass, G. Arnaud (*Bul. Soc. Path. Veg. France 1 (1914), No. 1, pp. 36, 37, fig. 1*).—A disease of Clivia in the greenhouse is described as due to the fungus *Colletotrichum cliviæ*.

An Alternaria on Sonchus, J. A. Elliott (*Bot. Gaz., 62 (1916), No. 5, pp. 414-416, fig. 1*).—A fungus said to cause a spot on leaves of *S. asper*, near Madison, Wis., and also on *Lactuca canadensis*, is reported as having been sent in by J. J. Davis, who has described the fungus as a new species under the name *A. sonchi*.

[Cucurbitaria pithyophila on Scotch pine in Scotland], C. M'Intosh (*Trans. Roy. Scot. Arbor. Soc., 29 (1915), pt. 2, pp. 209, 210; abs. in Internat. Inst. Agr. [Rome], Mo. Bul. Agr. Intel. and Plant Diseases, 6 (1915), No. 11, pp. 1539, 1540*).—A fungus parasitic on stems and branches of Scotch pine, noted near

Inver in 1907 and elsewhere later, attacking trees from 30 to 40 years old or older, has recently been found in a considerable number of felled trees, the fruiting body being present in many instances. The affected trees are suspected to have been grown from foreign seed.

The parasite may girdle and kill the branch, around which may form a fascicle of twigs resembling a witches' broom, or it may form a patch on one side, resulting in swellings and contortions and flooding the wood with resin. The effects are said to resemble those produced by *Peridermium pini corticola* (*Cronartium sp.*).

The canker of the Scotch pine caused by **Dasyscypha subtilissima**, A. W. BORTHWICK and M. WILSON (*Trans. Roy. Scot. Arbor. Soc., 29 (1915), pt. 2, pp. 184–187, pl. 1; abs. in Internat. Inst. Agr. [Rome], Mo. Bul. Agr. Intel. and Plant Diseases, 6 (1915), No. 11, pp. 1540, 1541*).—An account is given of observations made on a cankerous affection of Scotch pine as noted in the case of a specimen sent from Carmichael, in Lanarkshire. The fungus *D. subtilissima*, which has been previously known elsewhere as a saprophyte on P. *sylvestris*, is compared with *D. willkommii*, which it resembles in some respects, notably in the cankers produced (in case of the latter fungus, on larch). *D. subtillissima* is known to occur on several host species, and may be able to pass from one to the other. Experiments have been instituted to determine whether the larch can be infected by the fungus from the Scotch pine.

The æcial stage of Coleosporium ribicola, W. H. LONG (*Mycologia, 8 (1916), No. 6, pp. 309–311*).—The author has found a Peridermium on needles of piñou (*Pinus edulis*) near which *Ribes leptanthum* was growing, and has successfully inoculated the latter with æciospores of the fungus. He obtained a Coleosporium which proved to be identical in all its characters with *C. ribicola*. This is considered to prove that the fungus on piñon is the æcial stage of *C. ribicola* and that it should be called *P. ribicola*, a technical description thereof being given.

The fungus is found early in the spring at an elevation of about 7,500 ft. The coleosporial stage occurs also at much lower elevations on Ribes, supposedly reaching these points by successive infection of Ribes plants throughout the summer months by the urediniospores.

Dothichiza populea in the United States, G. G. HEDGCOCK and N. R. HUNT (*Mycologia, 8 (1916), No. 6, pp. 300–308, pls. 2*).—Many reports having been received during the spring of 1916 of a serious blight of newly transplanted black poplars (*Populus nigra*) and Canada poplars (*P. deltoides*), a study was made of a fungus found, usually alone, in connection therewith. This proved to be morphologically identical with *D. populea*.

From earlier accounts it appears that this fungus has been imported, though not very recently, from Europe. The parasite attacks the trunk, limbs, and twigs of both of these poplars, causing cankers primarily. Trees, after becoming well established in the soil, may show marked resistance to the fungus. The fungus spreads most rapidly in trees recently transplanted or in those heeled in for early spring planting, but transplanted trees may become badly diseased from fresh infections between October and the following May.

D. populea is said to be the most rapidly growing of the canker-producing fungi known to the authors. Pycnospores spread the disease to adjacent trees, being carried by the wind, and perhaps also, while in the sticky stage or condition, by insects or birds. Eradication of diseased stock is the only control measure recommended.

ECONOMIC ZOOLOGY—ENTOMOLOGY.

The parasites of food animals transmissible to man, B. H. RANSOM (*Ann. Rpt. Proc. Missouri Valley Pub. Health Assoc., 1 (1915), pp. 45–49*).—An address given in September, 1915, at the annual meeting of the Missouri Valley Public Health Association.

Concerning the pocket gopher and destructive habits, T. H. SCHEFFER (*Better Fruit, 10 (1916), No. 10, pp. 7, 8, figs. 5*).

A new monostome trematode parasitic in the muskrat, with a key to the parasites of the American muskrat, F. D. BARKER (*Trans. Amer. Micros. Soc., 35 (1916), No. 3, pp. 175–184, pl. 1*).—The author describes a small monostone trematode taken in large numbers from the intestine of an American muskrat from Lake Chisago, Minn., which represents the new genus and species *Nudacotyle novicia*.

Belle Fourche reservoir as a bird reservation and refuge for migratory waterfowl, F. M. DILLE (*Reclam. Rec. [U. S.], 7 (1916), No. 6, pp. 267–269, figs. 2*).—This description of the reservation includes a discussion of fall and spring migration, with notes on some conspicuous birds.

The Salt River national bird reservation, Arizona, G. WILLETT (*Reclam. Rec. [U. S.], 7 (1916), No. 7, pp. 315, 316, figs. 2*).—A brief description of this reservation, including a list of the fowl which frequent it.

East Park bird reservation, California, G. WILLETT (*Reclam. Rec. [U. S.], 8 (1917), No. 1, pp. 33, 34, fig. 1*).—A brief description of this reservation, with notes on the birds, made during the course of two visits, one in April, 1914, and the other in March, 1915.

The Deer Flat national bird reservation, Idaho, T. S. PALMER (*Reclam. Rec. [U. S.], 7 (1916), No. 5, pp. 221–223, fig. 1*).—This description of the reservation includes an account of the location, birds on the reservation, how the birds are protected, and the opportunity for development.

The Minidoka national bird reservation, Idaho, F. M. DILLE (*Reclam. Rec. [U. S.], 7 (1916), No. 12, pp. 564, 565, figs. 3*).—A brief description of the bird reservation adjoining the reservoir on the Minidoka project.

The birds of Culebra Island, Porto Rico, A. WETMORE (*Auk, 34 (1917), No. 1, pp. 51–62*).—This paper, which is based upon observations on Culebra Island from April 4 to 22, includes a discussion of the physical features, general conditions, and bird life on the island, together with a list of 14 species of birds observed on Louis Peña Island on April 11, and of 19 forms observed on Culebrita Island on April 15. The greater part of the paper is taken up by an annotated list of 54 forms of birds found on Culebra Island. Some of the data are included in the paper previously noted (E. S. R., 35, p. 155).

How birds' stomachs are examined, W. L. MCATEE (*Bul. Amer. Game Protec. Assoc., 6 (1917), No. 1, pp. 3, 4, figs. 4*).

The technique of experimentation in agricultural entomology.—I, Thermostats and hygrographs, I. V. EMELÎÂNOV (*Kharkov. Oblast. Selsk. Khoz. Opytn. Sta., Ent. Otd., No. 1 (1915), pp. 55, figs. 22*).—This first paper discusses methods of determination of temperature and moisture.

The longevity of some insects in captivity, A. LABITTE (*Bul. Mus. Nat. Hist. Nat. [Paris], No. 2 (1916), pp. 105–113; abs. in Rev. Appl. Ent., Ser. A, 5 (1917), No. 1, pp. 20, 21*).—This paper, which relates to the Coleoptera, records observations made of the average length of life in days of both sexes of 50 forms and the maximum period of existence of 48 species.

Precipitation in relation to insect prevalence and distribution, N. CRIDDLE (*Canad. Ent., 49 (1917), No. 3, pp. 77–80*).—In this paper the author calls attention to a few instances in which humidity, chiefly in the form of rain or snow, has been and is instrumental in either aiding or curtailing the spread of insects over the country, particularly in the prairie Provinces of Canada.

Investigations on the resistance of the larvæ of Cossus and Carpocapsa to cold, MLLE. F. GUEYLARD and P. PORTIER (*Compt. Rend. Soc. Biol.* [Paris], 79 (1916), No. 15, pp. 774–777).—The authors conclude that the larva of *Cossus cossus* is able to resist a complete freezing of all its organs and tissues and that freezing may be repeated a considerable number of times without its tissues being altered. A rapid rise of temperature, from —15° to 30° C., (from 5° to 86° F.), did not cause the death of the caterpillar or appear to alter its tissues. This resistance to cold results from an adaptation during the winter months only.

The reactions of the larva of the codling moth appear to be quite similar.

The insects attacking stored wheat in the Punjab, and the methods of combating them, including a chapter on the chemistry of respiration, J. H. BARNES and A. J. GROVE (*Mem. Dept. Agr. India, Chem. Ser., 4* (1916), No. 6, pp. VI+165–284, pls. 5, figs. 12; abs. in Ent. Mo. Mag., 3. ser., 3 (1917), No. 28, pp. 88–90).—The several chapters of this memoir, based upon investigations first commenced in 1911, deal, respectively, with the life history of the principal insects infesting wheat in the Punjab, chemical experiments, respiration, effect of moisture and dryness on the rice weevil, *Attagenus undulatus*, and *Rhizopertha dominica*.

The insects found in stored wheat consist of eight species of Coleoptera and one of Lepidoptera. Only three of these are actively responsible for damage to the wheat, namely, the dermestid *A. undulatus*, the bostrychid *R. dominica*, and the rice weevil. Of the other species, *Læmophloeus* sp. is found only ou floury frass and grains already damaged by other insects. *Tribolium castaneum* was proved by experiment unable to live on sound grains, and is strictly a flour beetle rather than a wheat beetle, as is *Latheticus oryzae*. *Alphitobius piceus* appears to be merely a scavenger and not to attack the grain, and the granary weevil is rarely found. The Angoumois grain moth was observed in only one district. The life histories of these insects are dealt with and illustrated in colored plates.

The senior author is largely responsible for the chemical and physical studies and the mechanical and remedial work and the junior author for the entomological phases.

Florida truck and garden insects, J. R. WATSON (*Florida Sta. Bul. 134* (1917), pp. 35–127, figs. 57).—This is a summary of information in which particular attention is given to control measures.

Insects injurious to timber in Sweden, N. A. KEMNER (*Meddel. Centralanst. Försöksv. Jordbruksområdet, No. 108* (1915), pp. 45, figs. 33; abs. in Internat. Inst. Agr. [Rome], Internat. Rev. Sci. and Pract. Agr., 7 (1916), No. 3, pp. 465, 466).—The insects that are particularly injurious to timber in Sweden belong to the family Anobiidæ. A list is given of their important natural enemies and recommendations as to control measures.

Report of first expedition to South America, 1913, R. P. STRONG, E. E. TYZZER, C. T. BRUES, A. W. SELLARDS, and J. C. GASTIABURU (*Cambridge: Harvard School Trop. Med., 1915, pp. XIV+220, pls. 49, figs. 9*).—The main part of this work relates to Oroya fever and to verruga peruviana, which the authors consider to be separate diseases. The investigations of Townsend on insect transmission of verruga peruviana, previously noted (E. S. R., 35, p. 258), are also discussed. Chapters on entomological investigations at Matucana; uta; sanitary conditions, prevailing diseases, and entomological investigations at Guayaquil; investigations of the blood and clinical and pathological studies of yellow fever; and Linguatulida from crocodiles follow.

Papers on A New Linguatulid from Ecuador, by W. M. Wheeler; Some Flies of the Family Phoridæ Obtained by the Expedition, with Notes on a Species Possibly Associated with External Myiasis in Man, by C. T. Brues; Notes on Peruvian Mosquitoes and Mosquito Literature, by F. Knab; Heteroptera from the West Coast of South America, by J. R. de la Torre Bueno; and a list of the bees obtained by the expedition, by T. D. A. Cockerell, are appended to the report.

Report of the Kansas State Entomological Commission for 1915 and 1916 (*Rpt. Kans. State Ent. Com., 1915–16, pp. 15*).—This report consists of two parts. The first by G. A. Dean covers inspection of nurseries and imported nursery stock, work with the San José scale, and the location and suppression of foul brood in the north half of the State. The second part, by S. J. Hunter, deals with nursery, Federal, and apiary inspection and work with the San José scale in the south half of the State.

Annual report of work done in the entomological section during the year ended June 30, 1916, H. L. DUTT (*Rpt. Dept. Agr. Bihar and Orissa, 1915–16, pp. 10–12*).—This reports upon the occurrence of the more important insect pests of the year.

Reports of the microbiologist, H. M. NICHOLLS (*Agr. and Stock Dept. Tasmania Rpt., 1913–14, pp. 28, 29; 1914–15, pp. 5, 6; 1915–16, pp. 18–20*).—Brief accounts are given of the occurrence of the more important insect pests of the three years.

Notes on Argentine, Patagonian, and Cape Horn Muridæ, O. THOMAS (*Ann. and Mag. Nat. Hist., 8. ser., 17 (1916), No. 98, pp. 182–187*).—Five forms are described as new.

The sheep tick and its eradication by dipping, M. IMES (*U. S. Dept. Agr., Farmers' Bul. 798 (1917), pp. 31, figs. 15*).—An account is given of the life history and habits of the sheep tick or ked (*Melophagus ovinus*) and means for its control, in which it is pointed out that the only practical way of destroying it is by dipping the sheep. Two dippings about 25 days apart are necessary, since the first dipping may not destroy the eggs. Lime-sulphur-arsenic dip is said to be the most effective. Plans are given for wooden and cement sheep dipping vats.

The destruction of locusts in Colombia by dipterous parasites, M. T. DAWE (*Rev. Agr. [Colombia], 2 (1916), No. 3, pp. 143–150; abs. in Rev. Appl. Ent., Ser. A, 4 (1916), No. 10, p. 410*).—A brief account is given of two sarcophagids found to be parasitic on locusts (*Schistocerca paranensis*) at two localities in Colombia, namely, *Sarcophaga caridei* and a species of doubtful identity. The various methods used in combating locusts are reviewed, and a list is given of the locust parasites recorded from various parts of the world.

The cacao thrips, J. C. HUTSON (*Agr. News [Barbados], 16 (1917), No. 385, pp. 26, 27*).—This is a brief general account of *Heliothrips rubrocinctus*, studied by the author during a recent visit to Grenada.

Mites and lice on poultry, F. C. BISHOPP and H. P. WOOD (*U. S. Dept. Agr., Farmers' Bul. 801 (1917), pp. 26, figs. 14*).—This is a popular summary of information on the common mites and lice, in which particular consideration is given to means for their control.

A contribution to the study of kala-azar, J. W. CORNWALL and H. M. LA FRENAIS (*Indian Jour. Med. Research, 3 (1916), No. 4, pp. 698–724, pls. 3; 4 (1916), No. 1, pp. 105–119, pl. 1*).—The authors' provisional conclusions are that "*Cimex rotundatus* can not transmit either kala-azar or oriental sore by biting. Viable forms of *Leishmania donovani* and *L. tropica* are not passed in the feces of *C. rotundatus*. *Conorhinus rubrofasciatus* is not concerned in the transmission of kala-azar."

Notes on a froghopper attacking sugar cane at Marienburg Estate, Surinam, C. B. WILLIAMS (*Bul. Ent. Research, 7 (1917), No. 3, pp. 271, 272*).—The author's observations indicate that *Tomaspis tristis* may become a serious pest of sugar cane in Surinam.

Aphids injurious to orchard fruits, currant, gooseberry, and grape, A. L. QUAINTANCE and A. C. BAKER (*U. S. Dept. Agr., Farmers' Bul. 804 (1917), pp. 42, figs. 30*).—A practical summary of information, including control measures.

The San José scale, F. B. PADDOCK (*Texas Sta. Circ. 18 (1916), pp. 3–11, figs. 3*).—A brief summary of information on the San José scale and its control.

Some new scale insects of Japan, S. I. KUWANA (*Annot. Zool. Japonenses, 9 (1916), pt. 2, pp. 145–152, pl. 1*).—One genus (Nipponorthezia) and seven species are described as new.

A scale enemy of the vine in Uruguay, G. SCHURMANN (*Rev. Asoc. Rural Uruguay, 44 (1915), No. 8, pp. 481–483, fig. 1; abs. in Rev. Appl. Ent., Ser. A, 4 (1916), No. 8, p. 351*).—*Pulvinaria vitis* appeared in Uruguay for the first time in 1914 and has become a source of serious injury to vineyards.

The introduction of Diaspis pentagona and its control in Argentina, A. GALLARDO (*An. Zool. Aplicada, 3 (1916), No. 1, pp. 33–50; abs. in Rev. Appl. Ent., Ser. A, 4 (1916), No. 11, p. 467*).—A review of the history of the introduction of the West Indian peach scale into Argentina and its control there by *Prospaltella berlesei*.

The pink bollworm, W. D. HUNTER (*Science, n. ser., 45 (1917), No. 1160, pp. 293, 294*).—Following a brief reference to the occurrence of *Gelechia gossypiella* in Mexico and to the inspection work being carried on by the U. S. Department of Agriculture with a view to preventing its introduction into this country, the author records its recent introduction into Brazil in cotton seed from Egypt. It is stated that a careful survey of the cotton belt in Brazil early in 1914 failed to detect its presence there, although late in 1916 during another trip made over the same territory it was found generally and thoroughly established and so numerous that the yields of certain fields were reduced by 50 per cent.

The life of the caterpillar, J. H. FABRE, trans. by A. TEIXEIRA DE MATTOS (*New York: Dodd, Mead & Co., 1916, pp. 376*).—This, the sixth volume of the collected edition of the author's entomological works (E. S. R., 35, p. 468) contains all his essays on butterflies and moths, or their caterpillars.

A few notes on the life history of Phalonia spartinana, C. N. AINSLIE (*Canad. Ent., 49 (1917), No. 3, pp. 93–96, pl. 1*).—The larva of this lepidopteran (P. *spartinana*) lives on *Spartina michauxiana*.

Recent questioning of the transmission of verruga by Phlebotomus, C. H. T. TOWNSEND (*Bul. Ent. Research, 6 (1916), No. 4, pp. 409–411*).—The author here answers the objections raised by Strong et al. in their report noted on page 356.

It is pointed out that the author's conclusion that P. *verrucarum* is the vective agent of verruga is based upon nearly two years' experience with the bloodsucking fauna of the Rimac verruga zone in Peru. Papers relating to the subject by him have been previously noted (E. S. R., 35, p. 258).

Studies in flies.—Contributions to the study of specific differences in the genus Musca: II, Structures other than genitalia, P. R. AWATI (*Indian Jour. Med. Research, 4 (1916), No. 1, pp. 123–139, figs. 10*).—This third paper (E. S. R., 35, p. 856) deals with structures of the head, thorax, and abdomen.

Two new genera of African Muscoidea, C. H. T. TOWNSEND (*Ann. and Mag. Nat. Hist., 8. ser., 17 (1916), No. 98, pp. 174–176*).—The genera Congochrysosoma and Ocypteromima, together with the genotype of each, are described as new.

The lantana seed fly, F. P. JEPSON (*Dept. Agr. Fiji Pamphlet 31 (1916), p. 1; abs. in Rev. Appl. Ent., Ser. A, 4 (1916), No. 12, p. 529*).—An agromyzid introduced from Hawaii into Fiji is now so thoroughly established that it is not possible to find *Lantana camara* within several miles of Suva which is not attacked.

Plagiodera versicolora.—An imported poplar and willow pest, H. B. WEISS and E. L. DICKERSON (*Canad. Ent., 49 (1917), No. 3, pp. 104–109, pl. 1*).—This imported chrysomelid has been observed by the authors in New Jersey for the past three years, appearing in greatest numbers at Irvington in a nursery on poplar and at South Paterson on willow. Observations relating to its biology are reported.

Scientific annihilation of the tobacco beetle, R. G. SKERRETT (*Sci. Amer., 115 (1916), No. 15, pp. 319, 336, fig. 1; abs. in Rev. Appl. Ent., Ser. A, 5 (1917), No. 1, p. 3*).—A description of an X-ray apparatus made practical use of in the destruction of the cigarette beetle, an account of which by Runner has been previously noted (E. S. R., 35, p. 554).

Report of the South Carolina Boll Weevil Commission, W. M. RIGGS (*Clemson Agr. Col. S. C., Farmers' Reading Course Bul. 20 [1916], pp. 24, figs. 2; U. S. Senate 64. Cong., 2. Sess., Doc. 701 (1917), pp. 20, figs. 2*).—This is a report of a commission which made a trip of inspection through the boll-weevil infested territory. It includes a report of a meeting held at Brookhaven, Miss., on October 7, 1916, a brief account of the life history of the boll weevil, a comparison of the conditions in Louisiana and South Carolina as related to the boll-weevil problem in the latter State, effects of the boll weevil on cotton production, oil mills, ginneries, etc., changes in agricultural methods due to the boll weevil, and raising cotton under boll-weevil conditions.

On some Curculionidæ which live in bamboo stems, A. DA COSTA LIMA (*Mem. Inst. Oswaldo Cruz, 8 (1916), No. 1, pp. 41–43*).—This supplementary paper (E. S. R., 33, p. 658) refers to *Rhinastus pertusus* in *Chusquea gaudichaudii*, *Desmosomus longipes*, and *Astyage punctulata* n. sp., in *Mcrostachys clausseni mollior*.

The leaf weevil (Polydrusus impressifrons), P. J. PARROTT and H. GLASGOW (*New York State Sta. Tech. Bul. 56 (1916), pp. 3–24, pls. 8, figs. 6*).—*P. impressifrons*, an important European bud and leaf-eating beetle of which a preliminary account has been noted (E. S. R., 36, p. 859), was first discovered in western New York in 1906, where it occurs in several counties and in certain localities has become very abundant, particularly in nurseries. It feeds on a large variety of plants, particularly upon willows, poplars, and birches. It is a source of injury through nibbling the developing buds of budded and grafted stock and attacking the foliage and succulent tissues, as stems of newly-unfolded leaves and stalks of terminal growth. The gouging of tender tissues is not infrequently attended by severing of leaves and destruction of tips of shoots.

The adults, which are light metallic green in color, emerge from the ground during May and early June and oviposition soon commences. The eggs are deposited under the loosened bark on dead stubs or about wounds due to pruning or scars in the bark resulting from hail injury or attacks by insects, and hatch in about 11 or 12 days. Upon hatching out the larvæ enter the earth and live on the roots of plants. Pupation occurs in the spring.

A new braconid of the genus Diospilus, a description of which by A. B. Gahan under the name *Diospilus polydrusi* is appended (pp. 23, 24), has been quite abundant and during recent years apparently has been exerting an important repressive action on its host. Protection from the beetle can be obtained through the use of arsenicals at standard strengths.

Bees for the farmer, J. Troop and W. A. Price (*Indiana Sta. Circ. 61 (1917), pp. 20, figs. 10*).—This is a popular summary of information for the beekeeper.

Outdoor wintering [of bees], E. F. Phillips (*Iowa Yearbook Agr., 16 (1915), pp. 564–572*).—Substantially noted from another source (E. S. R., 34, p. 158).

The sense organs on the mouth parts of the honeybee, N. E. McIndoo (*Smithsn. Misc. Collect., 65 (1916), No. 14, pp. 55, figs. 10*).

Contribution to the etiology of infectious diarrhea of bees caused by Bacterium coli apium n. sp. and Proteus alveicola n. sp., I. L. Serbinov (*Zhur. Mikrobiol., 2 (1915), No. 1–2, pp. 19–44, pls. 2. fig. 1*).—The author describes a new form of diarrhea which has occurred in the spring for a number of years among bees on the south coast of the Gulf of Finland, near Oranienbaum. Two new bacteria considered to be causative organisms of the disease are described. The disease develops rapidly and becomes epidemic, the bees become weakened, and death follows frequently in convulsions.

The connection of Nosema apis with Isle of Wight disease in hive bees.— Remarks on the evidence submitted in the Board of Agriculture reports of 1912 and 1913, J. Anderson (*Proc. Roy. Phys. Soc., Edinburgh, 20 (1916), No. 1, pp. 16–22; abs. in Rev. Appl. Ent., Ser. A, 4 (1916), No. 11, p. 462*).—The author's observations do not entirely support the view that *N. apis* is the cause of Isle of Wight disease.

Observations and experiments bearing on Isle of Wight disease in hive bees, J. Anderson and J. Rennie (*Proc. Roy. Phys. Soc., Edinburgh, 20 (1916), No. 1, pp. 23–61, pl. 1; abs. in Rev. Appl. Ent., Ser. A, 4 (1916), No. 11, pp. 462, 463*).—The observations here reported support those above noted.

Three new chalcid flies from California, A. A. Girault (*Jour. Ent. and Zool., 8 (1916), No. 3, pp. 119–122*).

Monograph of the nearctic Hymenoptera of the genus Bracon, H. Morrison (*Proc. U. S. Nat. Museum, 52 (1917), pp. 305–343, pls. 4*).—The author recognizes 12 forms, of which 9 are described as new.

Signiphora merceti n. sp., E. Malenotti (*Redia, 12 (1916), No. 1, pp. 181, 182; abs. in Rev. Appl. Ent., Ser. A, 4 (1916), No. 11, p. 483*).—This new chalcidid was reared from *Chrysomphalus dictyospermi* in Spain.

Gonatocerus mexicanus, a mymarid parasitic in the eggs of Draeculacephala mollipes in Hawaii, O. H. Swezey (*Proc. Hawaii. Ent. Soc. 3 (1915), No. 3, p. 146*).—This is said to be the first record of the establishment of *G. mexicanus* in Hawaii, the introduction of which from Chapultepec, Mex., was attempted by Koebele in 1908 (E. S. R., 27, p. 554).

The ticks which attack domestic animals in Russian Turkestan, W. L. Yakimoff (*Bul. Soc. Path. Exot., 10 (1917), No. 4. pp. 298–301*).—A summary of information relating to the Ixodidæ infesting domestic animals in Russian Turkestan.

Parasitism of Rhipicephalus sanguineus in Rio Janeiro by Hunterellus hookeri, A. da Costa Lima (*Rev. Vet. e Zootech., 5 (1915), No. 4. pp. 201–203, pl. 1*).—The author records the parasitism of nymphs of the brown dog tick by *H. hookeri* in Brazil.

On the occurrence of the tropical fowl mite (Liponyssus bursa) in Australia, and a new instance of its attacking man, S. Hirst (*Ann. and Mag. Nat. Hist., 8. ser., 18 (1916), No. 104, pp. 243, 244*).—A widely distributed gamasid mite parasitic on domestic fowl, previously described by the author as *Leiognathus morsitans* (E. S. R., 35, p. 263), is now thought to be the same species as that described by Berlese, from specimens collected at Buenos Aires, under the name *Liponyssus bursa*. Another instance of its attack upon man is recorded. The author suggests that the wide distribution of *L. bursa* may be due to its being carried about by the starling.

It is stated that the European fowl mite (*Dermanyssus gallinæ*) apparently does not thrive in tropical and subtropical countries.

Contributions to the study of parasitic protozoa.—I, On the structure and life history of Nosema bombycis, R. KUDO (*Bul. Imp. Sericult. Expt. Sta. Japan, 1 (1916), No. 1, pp. 31–51, pls. 2*).—This first paper dealing with the structure and life history of the causative organism of pebrine in the silkworm includes a bibliography of 43 titles.

Contribution to the study of larval forms of heteroxenous nematode parasites, L. G. SEURAT (*Bul. Sci. France et Belg., 49 (1916), No. 4, pp. 297–377, figs. 14*).—This paper, dealing with the Spiruridæ and Acuariidæ, includes a catalogue and a 12-page bibliography of the literature relating to the subject.

Two new cases of polyradiate cestodes, with a summary of the cases already known, W. D. FOSTER (*Jour. Parasitology, 2 (1915), No. 1, pp. 7–19, figs. 4*).—In reviewing the literature the author finds that altogether 44 cases of polyradiate cestodes, including larvæ, have been reported, in all but two of which the adult forms were triradiate. The fact that the greater number of these cases are triradiate forms of *Tænia saginata*, although several species are represented, is thought to be due to the greater chances for observation of this species.

A feeding experiment with triradiate proglottids of *T. pisiformis* tended to show that in this species perfectly normal cysticerci may result from abnormal adults.

Polyradiate cestodes, F. D. BARKER (*Science, n. ser., 43 (1916), No. 1101, pp. 170, 171*).—The author calls attention to a paper [1] which gives descriptions of two new species of polyradiate cestodes not referred to in the paper above noted. It was based upon a study of four perfect and entire specimens of *Tænia serrata*, i. e., *T. pisiformis*, and three perfect specimens of *T. serialis* from dogs at Lincoln, Nebr.

A further note on polyradiate cestodes, W. D. FOSTER (*Science, n. ser., 44 (1916), No. 1133, pp. 388, 389*).—A further discussion of the subject in which the author replies to the paper above noted.

FOODS—HUMAN NUTRITION.

Characteristics and quality of Montana-grown wheat, L. M. THOMAS (*U. S. Dept. Agr. Bul. 522 (1917), pp. 34, pls. 2, figs. 17*).—This bulletin contains information regarding the varieties and types of wheat grown in Montana and their grading, together with a discussion of wheat quality, color of flour and bread, water absorption, loaf volume, and texture. It also reports the results of a number of baking tests with Montana wheat and gives data regarding the correlation of physical characters and milling quality and a comparison of the wheats of Montana with those grown in other sections.

In conclusion the author states that five distinct classes of wheat are produced in Montana, which may be designated as hard spring, hard winter, western red, western white, and durum. " The two first-named classes are of about the same milling quality, except that the spring wheat is decidedly superior in baking strength. The wheats of these two classes also resemble each other closely in physical characteristics and composition; both are best suited for the production of a bread flour.

---

[1] Science, n. ser., 31 (1910), No. 804, p. 837.

"The flour from the western red and western white wheat is very low in strength and absorption and has the general characteristics of other soft-wheat flours. The flour is best adapted for the production of crackers and pastry products. The bread produced from this wheat is very close-textured and heavy.

"Durum wheat is decidedly different from the wheat of any other class. Although generally yielding a high percentage of flour, the flour is usually very creamy or yellow in color and consequently receives a low score for color. In spite of the fact that the flour contains a very high percentage of crude protein, it falls between the hard winter and western red wheats in baking strength. In water absorption the flour is slightly superior to that of all other classes. The flour from this wheat is not popular for bread-making purposes on account of its creamy color, but it is especially adapted for the manufacture of macaroni and similar products."

A table is given showing the average of results of all baking tests of each of the five classes of Montana wheat.

The capacity of wheat and mill products for moisture, W. L. STOCKHAM (*North Dakota Sta. Bul. 120 (1917), pp. 97-131, figs. 12*).—This bulletin reports the results of an extended study of the absorption of water vapor and water in the liquid state by wheat and wheat products. The results of the study may be summarized as follows:

"The capacity or amount of water required to make a mixture of a given consistency of water and colloidal material is greatest when the component parts are in a state of equilibrium with each other.

"The capacity of wheat and its products for atmospheric moisture and water increases as the physical equilibrium between the component particles is approached. Wheat has a higher moisture capacity than any of its products. . . . Starch prepared from patent flour has a higher capacity for atmospheric moisture than that from clear flour.

"The capacity of wheat for atmospheric moisture is greater at 0° C. than at higher temperatures, diminishing with increase in temperature. Above 60° it is dependent upon chemical changes which in turn are dependent upon the amount of moisture available. With the humidity zero the capacity is zero regardless of the temperature. At the saturation point between 0 and 40° C. the theoretical limits are only one-third to one-half reached because of secondary changes produced by enzyms, bacteria, and molds.

"Previously sprouted wheat absorbs both water and water vapor more rapidly than wheat in the natural state. It reaches its maximum sooner but does not reach as high a maximum as the normal wheat. Wheat products have a more rapid rate of adjustment to modified moisture conditions than wheat and are more subject to secondary changes.

"Germination does not take place from water absorbed from the atmosphere (condensation excluded).

"The rate of change of the moisture content of wheat in the atmosphere or in water becomes slower as the maximum limits are approached. . . .

"The absorptive capacity of the wheat varies inversely as the water-absorbing power of the flour produced from the same wheat, and as a rule inversely to the protein content. The durums are similar to hard red spring wheat samples of the same protein content in rate and quantity of water absorbed. . . . The absorptive capacity varies with the protein content of flours of the same grade. This relation is not so marked between different flour grades. . . .

"Sprouted wheat flour has on the average a 2 per cent lower absorption than that from the same wheat in the natural state. Both normal and sprouted wheat flour increase in absorptive capacity during storage; in some instances as much as 3 or 4 per cent. . . .

" The proportion of water in gluten is slightly higher under conditions which give it the greatest freedom during its formation, i. e., with higher temperature, or with more water at its disposal. Approximately 180 per cent of water is absorbed by gluten, and once it is formed it retains practically a constant amount of water at all temperatures below its decomposing point.

" The absorption of a starch gluten mixture is less than the sum of the absorption of the two taken separately.

" By hydrolysis starch has its capacity for water doubled. By dextrinization it is markedly decreased.

" By baking or by decomposition gluten has its capacity for water decreased. Baked gluten does not vary in water capacity with change in temperature.

" The maximum staleness of bread occurs when the ratio of water present in the bread to the capacity of the starch is least, or the fresher the bread the more nearly satisfied with water are its starch particles, and with a given moisture content this satisfaction would vary with the temperature changes inversely as the absorptive capacity of either starch, hydrolyzed starch, or bread.

" The capacity for moisture of the inner portion of the bread indicates that practically all of the starch is hydrolyzed during the baking process. That of the crust is less, indicating some dextrinization.

" The higher the starch content of a flour the more water would it require in proportion to its capacity to produce a loaf of a given apparent freshness."

The composition of rice and its by-products, G. S. FRAPS (*Texas Sta. Bul. 191 (1916), pp. 41*).—This bulletin reports the analysis of different varieties of rice and the various intermediate products of milling and discusses the composition, food, and feeding value of rice and rice by-products. A description is also given of the milling process. From the data here reported the following conclusions are drawn:

Milling rice gives it a whiter and more attractive appearance and partly removes phosphoric acid, potash, vitamins, and other constituents. White or milled rice has a different taste and better cooking quality than does the unmilled or brown rice.

" Chicken feed, or rough rice screenings, contains chiefly weed seeds, broken rice, and dirt, and is variable in composition. So-called stone bran is the sifting from rice hulls and rice and consists largely of rice hulls, with some rice bran, germ, and broken rice. Stone bran from Blue Rose rice contains more fat and more fiber on an average than that from Honduras rice. Rice hulls also get into rice bran with the so-called chits. Huller bran, or rice bran removed by the huller, is rich in protein and fat and is practically free from hulls. Rice hulls have a very low feeding value, but there is no evidence that they are actually poisonous or injurious to animals.

" The rice bran on the market consists of a mixture of huller bran, cone bran, and stone bran. The addition of hulls, immature rice, inferior stone bran, excessive amounts of stone bran, chicken feed, dust, or any other milling by-product, is an adulteration."

Tables are given showing the composition and feeding value of rice bran and rice polish. These two products compare favorably with corn. A method is also given for calculating the hull content of rice from the fiber content. The author states that the production coefficients of rice by-products vary with the grade, as does the productive value and the digestible protein.

Rice bran and rice huller bran contain large percentages of fat, but the extraction of this fat commercially has not been successful. A table is given showing the mineral and sugar contents of rice and its by-products.

"Dust from rough rice contains much dirt and hulls, and its presence in a feed is highly objectionable. Light rice consists chiefly of hulls, and the addition of light rice or the grindings from it to rice bran is an adulteration. Rice hull ashes consist mostly of silica and have an average fertilizer valuation of $1.38 per ton."

Experiments in the determination of the digestibility of millets, C. F. LANGWORTHY and A. D. HOLMES (*U. S. Dept. Agr. Bul. 525 (1917), pp. 11*).— This paper reports the results of a study of the digestibility of common millet (*Setaria italica*) and proso (*Panicum miliaceum*). The methods employed in this investigation were similar to those used in an earlier study of the digestibility of the grain sorghums (E. S. R., 36, p. 660).

The millets were eaten in the form of a bread, which was added to a basal ration low in protein and consisting of potato, orange, and sugar. Five normal young men served as the subjects of the experiment. Since millets do not contain gluten, they are not suitable for making leavened bread when used alone, but may be used for making unleavened bread and may be prepared for the table in ways similar to the grain sorghums and corn meal. The amount of the protein supplied by the ration averaged less than 50 gm. per day, due to the low protein content of the bread prepared from millets.

The breads made from bolted millet and proso meal did not show a high digestibility for protein in these experiments, the values being 35.8 per cent for millet protein and 41.2 per cent for proso protein.

No marked difference was noticed in the flavor of the millet and proso breads. A decorticated millet made into a mush was found to give a product of pleasing flavor, but a sufficient quantity was not obtained for a study of its digestibility.

The carbohydrates of millet and proso were found in these experiments to be as well utilized by the subjects as are those of the more common cereals, the coefficients of digestibility being 95.7 per cent for millet and 96.2 per cent for proso.

The general conclusion is drawn that "while the millets would contribute somewhat to the protein of the diet, they would be decidedly more important as a source of carbohydrates than of protein. In this they resemble such grains as the sorghums more closely than they do wheat or rye, which are important sources of both protein and carbohydrates."

Bread and bread making in the home, CAROLINE L. HUNT and HANNAH L. WESSLING (*U. S. Dept. Agr., Farmers' Bul. 807 (1917), pp. 26, figs. 3*).—This deals with the importance of bread in the diet, the qualities of good bread, and the principal requirements of bread making. Under the last head are included choice of materials and utensils; cleanliness; proportions of ingredients; measuring, mixing, and molding; and the care of the dough at various stages and care of the finished product. Recipes are given for making wheat bread by different methods, and for biscuits, rolls, and potato, wheat, rye, corn, and other breads. Suggestions for the judging of bread and a discussion of the food value of bread and its place in the diet are included.

Forty-three ways to save the wild plum crop, G. W. CARVER (*Alabama Tuskegee Sta. Bul. 34 (1917), pp. 12*).—A compilation of recipes.

How to select foods.—I, What the body needs, CAROLINE L. HUNT and HELEN W. ATWATER (*U. S. Dept. Agr., Farmers' Bul. 808 (1917), pp. 14, figs. 2*).—This is a popular statement of what the body needs to obtain from its food for tissue building, maintenance in good working order, and energy for its work. In general, it shows how different food materials meet these requirements and groups them according to their uses in the body, as follows: Foods depended on for mineral matters, vegetable acids, and body-regulating substances; for protein; for starch; for sugar; and for fat. One of the principles suggested for the planning of economical meals is that ·by remembering these groups and having them all suitably represented in the daily diet the housekeeper can easily plan attractive meals which meet the needs of the family without the wasting of money or material.

The effect of starvation on the catalase content of the tissues, W. E. BURGE and A. J. NEILL (*Amer. Jour. Physiol., 43 (1917), No. 1, pp. 58–61*).—Data are submitted which show that during starvation the catalase content of the heart (rabbit) remains normally high, while that of the fat and skeletal muscles is greatly decreased.

From the results it is concluded that the heart is not autolyzed during starvation, "because oxidation in this organ remains normally intense and thus provides for this oxidation of the autolyzing enzyms and the maintenance of the normal balance between oxidation and autolysis. On the other hand the fat and skeletal muscles are autolyzed during starvation, because of the decreased oxidation which leaves the autolytic enzyms free to digest these tissues."

ANIMAL PRODUCTION.

Some commonly neglected factors underlying the stock breeding industry, R. PEARL (*Maine Sta. Bul. 258 (1917), pp. 28, fig. 1*).—In addition to an outline of the importance of the live-stock breeding industry as a business (E. S. R., 35, p. 772), the author discusses a number of factors which make for success in the business of breeding, including the test of progeny and its implications, continuity of purpose in breeding, the superiority of the pure bred, and the importance of the man himself in the successful breeding enterprise.

Steer feeding experiments, W. H. TOMHAVE, B. O. SEVERSON, and P. GERLAUGH (*Pennsylvania Sta. Bul. 145 (1917), pp. 3–20, figs. 3*).—Summarized results are given of feeding experiments with steers conducted during the three winters 1913–14 to 1915–16, inclusive. The work of 1913–14 has already been noted (E. S. R., 32, p. 864). The six lots of 12 steers each were mostly two-year olds, and averaged about 900 lbs. at the beginning of the tests. The feeds used and some of the results secured during the two periods of 56 and 84 days, respectively, of each test are given in the following table:

Three-year summary of steer-feeding experiments.

Lot.	Period.	Average daily feed per steer.									Average daily gain per steer.	Dry matter per pound of gain.	Cost per pound of gain.	Average returns from pork produced.
		Wheat bran.	Cottonseed meal.	Ear corn.	Corn and cob meal.	Shelled corn.	Corn stover.	Corn silage.	Alfalfa hay.	Mixed hay.				
		Lbs.	Lbs.	Lbs.	Lbs.	Lbs.	Lbs.	Lbs.	Lbs.	Lbs.	Lbs.	Lbs.	Cts.	
I	1	3.14	.....	9.60	.....	.....	3.22	.....	.....	8.63	1.68	12.28	11.94	} $6.19
	2	4.14	.....	.....	12.45	.....	2.68	.....	.....	8.46	1.97	12.32	12.40	
II	1	.....	2.22	.....	.....	.....	.....	53.69	.....	.....	2.23	8.20	5.84	} 22.09
	2	.....	2.72	.....	.....	11.15	.....	29.53	.....	.....	1.89	11.41	12.54	
III	1	.....	.....	.....	.....	.....	.....	47.13	4.61	.....	1.71	10.50	6.77	} 18.42
	2	.....	.....	.....	.....	11.04	.....	25.70	5.11	.....	1.85	12.74	11.62	
IV	1	.....	2.11	.....	.....	.....	.....	21.15	.....	10.79	1.64	10.76	8.59	} 25.44
	2	.....	2.65	.....	.....	10.97	.....	19.93	.....	5.69	2.01	11.44	12.61	
V[1]	1	.....	2.28	.....	.....	.....	.....	37.58	4.36	.....	1.65	10.66	8.29	} 19.98
	2	.....	2.69	.....	.....	10.38	.....	21.36	4.78	.....	1.96	11.64	12.72	
V[2]	1	.....	2.17	2.88	.....	.....	.....	19.93	.....	8.73	2.01	9.32	7.59	} 45.65
	2	.....	2.48	.....	.....	11.92	.....	19.93	.....	4.66	2.19	11.19	11.65	
VI[3]	1	.....	2.14	.....	.....	.....	.....	62.59	.....	.....	2.48	7.14	5.88	} 0.29
	2	.....	3.56	.....	.....	.....	.....	66.66	.....	.....	1.79	10.86	9.89	

[1] 1913–14 only.   [2] 1914–15 only.   [3] 1915–16 only.

The authors interpret the results as indicating that "the common Pennsylvania ration of corn-and-cob meal, wheat bran, mixed hay, and corn stover, fed during the entire 140-day period, did not improve the finish nor value of the cattle, and it proved to be more expensive than any of the rations which contained silage as roughage only, or roughage and cottonseed meal in the early part of the feeding period, and whose combinations were supplemented with corn in the latter part; also when corn silage and cottonseed meal were fed during the entire period. Corn silage proved to be the most desirable roughage. A ration with a limited amount of corn silage supplemented with mixed hay was not so economical nor so satisfactory a roughage ration as one containing silage as a sole roughage. . . .

"A ration of corn silage and alfalfa hay as a source of protein during the first 56 days of the feeding period, supplemented with corn the balance of a 140-day period, was the cheapest daily ration, but it did not produce sufficient gains and finish.

"Wheat bran at $25 per ton is not so desirable a source of protein as cottonseed meal at $32.66 per ton, or alfalfa hay at $15 per ton.

"The results from comparing alfalfa hay and cottonseed meal as a source of protein, in a ration of corn silage as roughage, supplemented with corn during the last three months of a five-month feeding period, indicate that cottonseed meal is a superior source of protein on account of producing a more rapid finish on the cattle, which will thus command a higher selling price on the market.

"The margin necessary between the buying and selling prices is reduced by hogs following cattle in the feed lots, especially when whole grain is fed.

"Corn silage fed to the limit of appetite and supplemented with 2.5 lbs. of cottonseed meal per head daily the first three months, and 3.5 lbs. per head daily the last two months, proved to be the most economical ration. Cattle thus fed were valued within 5 cts. per 100 lbs. of cattle receiving, during the last 84 days, corn in addition to silage and cottonseed meal.

"The returns per steer, after paying for the feed consumed, were in direct proportion to the amount of silage consumed. The lots receiving the largest amount of silage alone and silage supplemented with cottonseed meal gave the best returns per steer.

"Five lbs. of alfalfa hay per day, in addition to 2.5 lbs. of cottonseed meal as a source of protein, was not found economical. . . .

"The manure produced was figured as being sufficient to pay for the bedding and labor required to take care of the cattle."

Feeding baby beeves, J. C. BURNS (*Texas Sta. Bul. 198 (1916), pp. 5-21, figs. 8*).—The objects of the experiments reported were to study the production of baby beef in general; to compare cottonseed meal, cold pressed cottonseed, and peanut meal for supplementing a ration composed of ground milo maize, corn, or sorghum silage, and Sudan grass hay; and to compare the feeding values of Sudan grass hay and cottonseed hulls.

Four lots of 12 high-grade Aberdeen-Angus steer calves were used. Before the experiment was begun the calves were fed together on a ration consisting of cold pressed cottonseed, ground milo maize, corn silage, and Sudan grass hay. In the experiment proper lot 1 was fed the above ration; lot 2, peanut meal, ground milo maize, corn silage, and Sudan grass hay; lot 3, cold pressed cottonseed, ground milo maize, corn silage, and Sudan grass hay; and lot 4, cottonseed meal, ground milo maize, corn silage, and cottonseed hulls. The actual feeding experiment covered a period of 201 days. Sorghum silage replaced corn silage for the last 51 days of the test and a small quantity of blackstrap molasses was fed to all the lots as an appetizer for 11 days during the latter part of the experiment, the average daily allowance being 0.59 lb. per head. Pigs followed all lots.

At the close of the experiment very little difference in the gains of the four lots was observed, the average daily gains being 1.62, 1.52, 1.57, and 1.55 lbs. per head, respectively. Considerable advantage was found in having hogs follow the calves. The dressing percentages of the different lots of calves were practically the same, and little difference in the quality of carcasses was observed.

The calculations pertaining to the financial results of the experiment are based on the following costs per ton of the feeding stuffs used: Cottonseed meal, $35; peanut meal (hulls included), $28; cold pressed cottonseed, $24; milo maize chops, $23.80; corn silage, $3.50; sorghum silage, $3.50; Sudan grass hay, $10; cottonseed hulls, $10; blackstrap molasses, at 16.25 cts. a gallon, $27. Based on the selling prices of $9.50 per 100 lbs. for lots 1 and 3, $9.41 for lot 2, and $9.43 for lot 4, peanut meal (hulls included) was worth only $21.40 per ton and cold pressed cottonseed only $22.80 per ton, with cottonseed meal at $35 per ton, while cottonseed hulls were worth only $5.34 per ton with Sudan grass hay at $10 per ton.

Detailed data are submitted in tabular form and discussed.

The production of baby beef, S. H. RAY (*U. S. Dept. Agr., Farmers' Bul. 811 (1917), pp. 22, figs. 8*).—This discusses the various phases of the production of baby beef for market, including the breeds and type of cows, bulls, and calves suitable for baby-beef production, the management and feeding of the breeding herd, calf management and feeding, and hogs following baby beeves.

Peanut meal and ground whole pressed peanuts for hogs, L. B. BURK (*Texas Sta. Bul. 201 (1916), pp. 3-9*).—The object of the experiments reported was to determine the value of both peanut meal and ground whole pressed peanuts when used as a supplement to milo maize chop in a ration for feeding hogs; to compare peanut meal and ground whole pressed peanuts with meat meal and cottonseed meal as supplements to milo maize chop; to compare a narrow peanut meal, milo maize ration with a similar balanced ration; to compare both rations with a ration of milo maize chop when fed alone; and to study the effects of peanut meal and ground whole pressed peanuts on the quality of the pork and lard.

Six lots, consisting of 10 each of pure-bred Duroc-Jersey hogs were fed the following rations for 77 days: Lot 1, milo maize chop alone; lot 2, milo maize chop 6 lbs., cottonseed meal 1 lb.; lot 3, milo maize chop 10 lbs., meat meal 1 lb.; lot 4, milo maize chop 7 lbs., peanut meal (without hull) 1 lb.; lot 5, milo maize chop 2.5 lbs., ground whole pressed peanuts 1 lb.; lot 6, milo maize chop 1 lb., peanut meal (without hull) 1 lb. The hogs were fed twice each day for two weeks, and after this they received all the feed they would clean up.

At the close of the experiment the animals were satisfactorily firm. Detailed results of the experiment and a financial statement are submitted in tabular form.

The average daily gains per head were 0.727, 1.26, 1.18, 1.21, 1.228, and 1.424 lbs., respectively. Lot 1, although producing a profit, was unsatisfactory when compared with the other lots, lot 2 returning 85, lot 3 70, lot 5 77, lot 4 81, and lot 6 105 per cent greater profits. The hogs of lot 2, although receiving an average of 0.75 lb. of cottonseed meal for the entire period of the experiment, showed no indications of cottonseed meal poisoning. Lot 6 produced the fastest and most economical gains of any of the lots. Although half of the ration fed to this lot was peanut meal, the pork was found to be firm.

After the animals were slaughtered various samples were taken from a medium sized and well-nourished hog of each lot, and the melting point and iodin number determined. The data are submitted in tabular form. A wide variation in the melting point was observed. With the exception of the back fat of lots 1 and 3 and the flank fat of lot 4, the melting points of all the samples of lots 1, 3, 4, 5, and 6 were found to be rather low and close together. The samples taken from lot 2 showed a much higher melting point. It is noted that this indicates "that cottonseed meal does have a hardening quality when fed in a balanced ration with milo maize chop." The samples of leaf fat in general showed a much higher melting point than the samples of fat taken from the back, shoulder, and flank.

Horse-breeding suggestions for farmers, H. H. REESE (*U. S. Dept. Agr., Farmers' Bul. 803 (1917), pp. 21, figs. 10*).—A general discussion, under the topics of profit in breeding farm mares, selecting breeding and working mares, uniformity of the mares, soundness, selecting a stallion, mating considerations, feeding and management of mares in foal, abortions, approaching parturition, parturition, care of the foal, feeding after foaling, raising the orphan foal, and feeding and management of young horses.

Growing draft colts, C. W. McCAMPBELL (*Kansas Sta. Circ. 57 (1916), pp. 16, figs. 8*).—A reprint of the article previously noted (E. S. R., 36, p. 172).

Chicken management on the farm, R. M. SHERWOOD, W. A. LIPPINCOTT, F. E. MUSSEHL, N. L. HARRIS, and F. E. MIXA (*Kansas Sta. Circ. 60 (1917), pp. 23, figs. 13*).—This circular gives full general directions on the selection of stock, the farm breeding stock, selection and care of eggs for hatching, incubation, brooding, feeding, housing, and marketing poultry products.

Standard varieties of chickens.—I, The American class, R. R. SLOCUM (*U. S. Dept. Agr., Farmers' Bul. 806 (1917), pp. 18, figs. 13*).—A general description of the Plymouth Rock, Wyandotte, Java, Dominique, Rhode Island Red, and Buckeye breeds.

The capon, V. G. AUBRY (*New Jersey Stas., Hints to Poultrymen, 5 (1917), No. 8, pp. 4*).—A brief discussion of caponizing and the care and marketing of capons.

Fifth annual international egg-laying contest, W. F. KIRKPATRICK and L. E. CARD (*Connecticut Storrs Sta. Bul. 89 (1917), pp. 255–301, figs. 21*).—A brief discussion is made of the growth of egg-laying competitions in the United States, and a detailed report is given of the fifth contest at the Storrs Station.

It is noted that the mash and grain mixtures used in the earlier contests (E. S. R., 36, p. 570) were made up of no less than 14 different feeds in various proportions, whereas the simplified formulas used in this contest necessitated the use of only eight ingredients, and these were, with two exceptions, mixed equal parts by weight.

The average annual egg yield per hen in the first four contests was 151.5 eggs. In the fifth contest, on the simpler rations, the hens averaged 162 eggs each for the year.

The scratch feed consisted of wheat and cracked corn (1:1). The dry mash was made up of wheat bran, corn meal, ground oats, flour middlings, fish scrap, and beef scrap (2:2:2:2:1:1).

The number of hens in the four principal breeds and their average pen scores at the opening of the contest were as follows: White Leghorns, 350 hens, score 91.8 per cent; Rhode Island Reds, 210, 87.2 per cent; Wyandottes, 170, 90 per cent; and Plymouth Rocks, 170, 88.1 per cent, respectively.

All the pens taken together laid 4,667 unrecorded eggs, or 2.88 per cent of the total egg yield.

Practically all of the 1,000 birds in the contest received the agglutination test for bacillary white diarrhea. Twenty-eight birds in 14 pens reacted positively to the test. In 4 of these 14 pens there were, respectively, 3, 4, 5, and 6 reactors. The average individual egg yield of these 4 infected pens was 130 eggs.

There was a loss by death during the contest of 10.4 per cent of the hens. About one-third of the deaths were due to various disorders of the reproductive system, and one-fourth to hypertrophied or enlarged livers.

In this contest the Plymouth Rock eggs averaged 26.4 oz. per dozen, the Rhode Island Red eggs 24.4 oz., the White Leghorn eggs 23.8 oz., the Wyandotte eggs 23.5 oz., and the remaining breeds 24.3 oz. The average weight of all eggs was 24.3 oz. per dozen. The number of eggs laid per month varied from 5,291 in November to 19,986 during May. The average value of all the eggs was 34.54 cts. per dozen, and the highest gross receipts for eggs was made in August.

The percentages of broody hens averaged from 13.6 for the White Leghorns to 65.6 for the Rhode Island Reds, the average for all the breeds being 39.3. The average number of days lost by each broody hen was 52.8. It is estimated that the combined loss in egg yield in this contest due to the 887 broody periods was 688.5 dozen eggs, worth $237.81.

Tabulated data show the amount and cost of feed consumed, the number of eggs produced with their average weight and total value, and the returns above feed cost for each pen in the contest. The average amount of feed consumed for all breeds was 4.48 lbs. for each pound of eggs laid, or 6.81 lbs. for each dozen. The cost of feed (including grit, shell, and charcoal) per dozen eggs produced was 12.7 cts. for the Leghorns, 13.2 cts. for the Wyandottes, 15.1 cts. for the Rhode Island Reds, 15.5 cts. for the Plymouth Rocks, and an average of 14 cts. for all breeds. The cost data are based on a hundredweight valuation of $1.93 for mash, $2.11 for grain, $0.75 for grit and oyster shells, and $2 for charcoal. The cost of green food is estimated at 10 cts. per bird.

The text of the rules and regulations governing the contest, together with general information and suggestions, is included.

Breeding for egg production.—I, A study of annual and total production, E. D. BALL, B. ALDER, and A. D. EGBERT (*Utah Sta. Bul. 148 (1916), pp. 3–60, figs. 12*).—Continuing previous work (E. S. R., 32, p. 73), this bulletin reports the results of a study of eight years' records of a flock of White Leghorn hens, with a similar study on the production of each successive flock of the unselected descendants.

From the data collected it is concluded that " the production of unselected White Leghorns varies widely in different years as influenced by the environment, but from all available records averages about 130 for the first year, 120 for the second, and less than 110 for the third, drops to about 85 in the fourth, and falls about 10 eggs a year after this up to the eighth year. Selected flocks have averaged 160 in America and 190 in Australia. The American record corresponds closely to the average of the upper one-half of the unselected flocks and indicates that the selection has been able to eliminate the lower half."

The first-year production of a flock of White Leghorns is considered to be no indication of their total production. If the first year's production is high, the second will be low, and vice versa. The total production in three years, however, will in all cases be about the same. " If the first year record of a flock is high, selection of the high layers will materially improve the later production of the flock. If the first record is low, there will be little value in selection, as even the lowest producer will make a second-year record above the general average. The three-year average is in all cases a much more reliable indication of productivity."

From the data at hand the average life of a White Leghorn appears to be about six years. The average production of the fourth year is equal to the average total production given for the United States. In general, the average total production is above 500 eggs and the maximum possible production above 1,000 eggs.

A list of 40 references to the cited literature is appended.

The separate inheritance of plumage pattern and pigmentation in Plymouth Rocks, R. PEARL (*Pract. Husb. Maine, 6 (1916), No. 2, pp. 567, 568; abs. in Maine Sta. Bul. 257 (1916), p. 354*).—Experiments at the Maine Station are referred to, in continuation of those already noted (E. S. R., 23, p. 674), the results of which are said to indicate that pattern and pigmentation are distinct unit characters in Barred Plymouth Rock fowls. A brief report is also given of crossing experiments with White Plymouth Rock and Cornish Indian Game fowls, the results of which throw light on the probable nature of the mutation by which the White Plymouth Rock variety was produced, and indicate that White Rocks carry the factor for the barred pattern but lack the hereditary determiner for pigment.

On the effect of continued administration of certain poisons to the domestic fowl, with special reference to the progeny, R. PEARL (*Proc. Amer. Phil. Soc., 55 (1916), pp. 243-258; Proc. Nat. Acad. Sci., 2 (1916), 7, pp. 380-384; abs. in Maine Sta. Bul. 257 (1916), pp. 352-354*).—In the investigation here reported, which has a bearing on the general problem of the origin and causation of new, heritable variations, the method pursued was that of exposing systematically the germ cells of an animal to something unusual or abnormal in the surrounding conditions and then analyzing the results as shown in the offspring. The specific problems with which the investigation dealt are (1) whether the continued administration of certain narcotic poisons to the domestic fowl induces precise and specific changes in the germinal material such as to lead to new, heritable, somatic variations; (2) whether, if there is no specific effect, there is a general effect upon the germinal material; (3) the effects in general upon the soma of the treated individual of the continued administration of such poisons; and (4) whether the somatic effects upon the treated individuals are of a sort to give any clue to the probable origin or mechanism of the germinal changes.

The foundation stock used in these experiments came from pedigreed strains of two breeds of poultry—Black Hamburgs and Barred Plymouth Rocks. Both of the strains used had been so long pedigree-bred and used in such a variety of Mendelian experiments by the author that their genetic behavior under ordinary circumstances was fairly well known. Furthermore, the results of crossing these two breeds reciprocally have been thoroughly studied.

Three poisons were used in the work, namely, ether, methyl alcohol, and ethyl alcohol. These substances were administered to the birds daily by the inhalation method.

It is noted that "the egg production of the treated birds and the untreated controls was entirely normal in respect of its seasonal distribution, as well as in regard to its amount. There has been no significant difference in the egg production of the treated birds and their untreated control sisters, either in the total average number of eggs produced per bird nor in the seasonal distribution of this production. The only conclusion which can be drawn from the statistically insignificant differences which appear between treated and control birds is that the inhalation treatment has not affected the egg production of the birds either favorably or adversely."

"Regarding the offspring the results show that out of 12 different characters for which we have exact quantitative data the offspring of treated parents taken as a group are superior to the offspring of untreated parents in eight characters. The offspring of untreated parents are superior to those of the treated in respect of but two characters, and these are characters which are quite highly correlated with each other and really should be counted as but one single character. Finally with respect to two character groups there is no difference between the treated and the untreated."

The author interprets the results of the investigation as showing that "(1) there is no evidence that specific germinal changes have been induced by the treatment, at least in those germ cells which produced zygotes; and (2) there is no evidence that the germ cells which produced zygotes have in any respect been injured or deleteriously affected."

Studies on the physiology of reproduction in the domestic fowl.—XVI, Double eggs, MAYNIE R. CURTIS (*Biol. Bul. Mar. Biol. Lab. Woods Hole, 31* (*1916*), *No. 3, pp. 181–212, pls. 3, figs. 7; abs. in Maine Sta. Bul. 257* (*1916*), *pp. 348–351*).—Double or inclosed eggs which were laid or found partly formed within the oviduct at autopsy are described and their formation discussed from a physiological standpoint. The specimens described are classified, according to their general structure, into double eggs with the inclosing egg a normal egg and the inclosed egg also normal or the inclosed egg a dwarf egg, and double eggs in which the inclosing egg does not contain a yolk but is simply a set of egg envelopes containing a normal egg or a dwarf egg.

In all the specimens examined the yolk was contained in the blunt end and the inclosed egg in the pointed end. Although one specimen has been described in which the yolk was found in the pointed and the inclosed egg in the blunt end of the inclosing egg, the accuracy of the observation is indicated as being doubtful.

The results of the study show that "a membrane-covered or hard-shelled normal or dwarf egg may be returned up the duct and may either meet its successor and return with it, becoming inclosed in a common set of egg envelopes, or not meeting its successor it may again be forced through the duct stimulating the secretion of a set of egg envelopes around itself.

"The number of egg envelopes common to the inclosed egg and the yolk of the inclosing egg or the number of egg envelopes which surround the inclosed egg when the inclosing egg has no yolk depends apparently on the level of the duct at which the inclosed egg resumes its normal direction toward the cloaca.

"The inclosed egg is usually forced up the duct without turning on its axis, but occasionally the poles are reversed. A similar reversal of poles sometimes occurs in normal laying, and it seems probable that in both cases this turning takes place in the uterus when the first powerful contractions of the uterus brings the outwardly directed end of the egg slightly above the opening from the shell gland into the vagina and tangentially against the curved caudo-dorsal angle of the uterus.

"The inclosed egg usually precedes its successor through the duct, and therefore usually lies in the pointed or anterior end of the inclosing egg, while the yolk of the inclosing egg lies in the blunt or posterior end. . . .

"A hard-shelled egg uncovered by membrane or albumin is sometimes found in the body cavity or upper oviduct, while a hard-shelled egg inclosed within another egg is not usually immediately surrounded by an egg membrane. It would, therefore, seem that the egg does not cause the secretion of egg envelopes around itself on its way up the duct. Since, in the case of a double-yolked egg, a second yolk closely following the first does stimulate the secretion of the successive envelopes, it does not seem probable that the failure of the duct to form envelopes around the returning egg is due to exhaustion of the glands. . . .

"The double egg results from a modification of the normal processes of egg formation due chiefly to a reversal in the direction of the egg after it has received its membrane or its membrane and shell. This backward movement must cease before the egg is expelled from the funnel mouth, and the movement in the normal direction must be resumed. If the backward movement sets in before the egg receives its membrane but stops before it is expelled from the funnel mouth and if the normal direction is then resumed, the result will be a normal egg with a large percentage of albumin or, in case the returned egg meets its successor, a double-yolked egg."

A double egg is deemed to be the result "of a combination of normal and abnormal processes which, when combined in other proportions, result in other abnormal phenomena of egg production."

DAIRY FARMING—DAIRYING.

Report of the special milk board of the Massachusetts State Department of Health (*Boston: State, 1916, pp. 358, pl. 1, figs. 7*).—This is the report of the special board of the State health department appointed in 1915 to investigate the status of milk production, distribution, and inspection, and the relation thereof to the health of the State. The report deals with the history and development of the present milk controversy in the State, together with summaries of proposed laws and present State laws relating to milk; statements from various persons and interests concerned in the milk question; data on the production, processing, and marketing of milk; the present official control of the milk supply of the State; the relation between cow's milk and public health; the grading of milk; and experiences of other localities. Appendixes give forms of and replies to various questionnaires and letters used in collecting data for the report, an abstract of milk-borne epidemics in the State during the past decade, effect of pasteurization on the chemical content of milk, status of local milk inspection, statistics of milk transportation into Boston, etc.

The feeding of dairy cows on pasture, R. A. BERRY (*West of Scot. Agr. Col. Bul. 76 (1916), pp. 15–48*).—This is a detailed report of experiments conducted during 1912–1914 at several centers in the West of Scotland, the object of which was to ascertain the advantage or disadvantage of supplying extra feed to cows during the grazing season. In the experiments proper 224 cows were employed. In each test two lots, generally of 8 cows each, were pastured for three months from the middle of July. In addition one of the lots in each test was fed 2 lbs. per head daily for the first month and 4 lbs. during the second and third months of a mixture of decorticated cottonseed cake and soy bean cake.

Averaging the results secured during the three years it was found that the milk production of the lot fed concentrates was increased 1.9 per cent during the first month, 2.8 during the second month, and 4 per cent during the third month over that of the other lot. The average rise in the percentage of fat during the course of the experiment was more pronounced for the cows fed grass only than for those on concentrates. Apparently this was due to the action of the extra feeding in prolonging the lactation period. Valuing milk at 8d. per gallon the increase per cow due to feeding concentrates was 11s. 9d., and the cost of extra feed consumed per cow was £1 1s. 10d., making a deficit of 10s. per cow, of which 7s. 4d. is credited for the residual manurial value of the cakes.

A good bull's influence upon three generations, J. J. DUNNE (*Hoard's Dairyman, 53 (1917), No. 12, pp. 518, 519*).—For the purpose of showing the value of cow-testing records, production records are given of the offspring of a number of bulls in one family in Denmark, indicating in general that the influence of these sires was good.

The fat content of the milk of the offspring was almost always increased, and in many cases the amount of milk was increased, as compared with their dams. It is stated that " when the average milk yield and fat percentage of a herd are lower than those inherited by the bull from his dam and granddams, the offspring resulting therefrom will be found to have, in the majority of cases, more milk and a higher fat percentage than their dams. On the other hand, when the milk and fat records of a herd average higher than those inherited by the bull, the opposite is generally the case."

The yield and composition of cows' milk during lactation, R. A. BERRY (*West of Scot. Agr. Col. Bul. 76 (1916), pp. 49–73, figs. 6*).—The author gives results of a preliminary study of the effects of individuality on the changes in the yield and composition of milk during lactation as shown in the case of three cows.

The effect of advance in lactation on milk yield followed much the same order of variation in the case of two of the cows, but differed greatly in the third. Data from the milk records of a large number of cows show that the milk yield generally rises for the first two months after calving, after which it falls more or less regularly until the end of the lactation period. These milk records also show that the fat content of the milk generally falls in the second month after calving, followed by a gradual rise thereafter. With one of the three cows under observation the fat content of the milk showed little variation throughout the lactation period. Apart from the normal effects due to advance in lactation, the fat content of the milk of the other two cows was appreciably influenced by change of environment and feed. Other changes in the milk and milk fat of the three cows due to advance in lactation are discussed.

Notes on modern dairy chemistry, W. VAN DAM (*Opstellen over Moderne Zuivelchemie. The Hague: Alg. Nederland. Zuivelbond, 1916, pp. 180, figs. 12*).—This volume discusses the true acidity of milk and its effect on curdling; the antiseptic action of the acidity of whey used for feeding; the influence of the hydrogen ion concentration on the growth and destruction of colon and typhoid bacilli; the action of microbial lipase in relation to the true acidity of dairy products; erroneous ideas in regard to the acidity of cheese mass; acidity of the curds of Edam and Emmental cheese and its significance; relation of acidity to cheese ripening; the influence of temperature on the physical condition of the milk fat; the preparation of Edam cheese, using pepsin in place of rennin; and closely related topics.

Cream production and grading in Kansas, G. S. HINE (*Kansas Sta. Circ. 56 (1916), pp. 4, fig. 1*).—Brief essentials are outlined.

The changes in the composition of Cheddar cheese during the process of ripening, R. A. BERRY (*West of Scot. Agr. Col. Bul. 76 (1916), pp. 74–78*).—The Cheddar cheese used in this preliminary experiment was made from milk in which a pure culture of *Streptococcus lacticus* was used as a starter.

Due to a continuous loss of water the total nitrogen showed a gradual increase from the beginning to the end of the ripening period. The water-soluble compounds rose from about 3 per cent of the total nitrogen in the green cheese to 37 per cent by the ninth month, when the experiment ended. There was also a small but persistent rise in the amount of the ammonium compounds. No trace of sugar was found after the second or third month of ripening. The acidity, expressed in terms of lactic acid, rose from 0.94 per cent in the green cheese to 2.05 per cent in the fifth month, after which it gradually decreased to 1.75 per cent in the ninth month. The moisture decreased from 35.6 per cent in the green cheese to 32.1 per cent at the end of the test. During the nine months' curing there was a loss in weight of about 7 per cent.

Paying for milk in cheese making, H. C. TROY (*Hoard's Dairyman, 53 (1917), No. 15, pp. 647, 648*).—The author gives data indicating that when the increased energy value of cheeses made from milk of higher fat content is taken into consideration, payment for milk on the fat percentage basis is equitable.

VETERINARY MEDICINE.

Second biennial report of the Oregon State Live Stock Sanitary Board for the year ended November 30, 1916, W. H. LYTLE ET AL. (*Bien. Rpt. Oreg. Live Stock Sanit. Bd., 2 (1915–16), pp. 127, figs. 18*).—The three parts of this report deal, respectively, with finances and legislation, the occurrence of and work with infectious diseases of live stock, etc., particularly tuberculosis, contagious abortion, and hog cholera, and a report of the Board of Sheep Commissioners, dealing especially with the occurrence of sheep diseases.

Report of the parasitologist, J. W. SCOTT (*Wyoming Sta. Rpt. 1916, pp. 88–91*).—In reporting upon the transmission of swamp fever in horses, in continuation of work previously noted (E. S. R., 32, p. 754), it is stated that circumstantial evidence points very strongly to the stable fly as one of the agents implicated in its transmission, and that transmission experiments with mosquitoes have given negative results.

Feeding experiments with *Tænia (Moniezia) expansa* have failed to produce infestation in lambs. Further work with *Thysanosoma actinioides* has helped to substantiate the conclusion that standing water, or at least a swampy area, is a necessary condition for infestation. The work with *Sarcocystis tenella* shows that lambs may become infested with this sarcocystid by eating grass and certain kinds of insects.

[Report of the] division of animal industry, V. A. NÖRGAARD ([*Bien.*] *Rpt. Bd. Comrs. Agr. and Forestry Hawaii, 1915–16, pp. 119–165, pls. 12*).—In the main part of this report the author and L. N. Case report upon the occurrence of and work with diseases of live stock, particularly hog cholera and bovine tuberculosis. The report of the live-stock inspector, J. Richard (pp. 138–143), and the reports of four deputy territorial veterinarians are appended.

Animal diseases in Russian Turkestan caused by endoglobular parasites. W. L. YAKIMOFF ET AL. (*Bul. Soc. Path. Exot., 10 (1917), No. 4, pp. 302–311*).—This article deals with the piroplasmoses, theilerioses, nuttallioses, and anaplasmoses.

On the development of Ascaris lumbricoides and A. suilla in the rat and mouse, F. H. STEWART (*Parasitology, 9 (1917), No. 2, pp. 213–227, pl. 1, figs. 9*).—It has been found that when eggs of *A. lumbricoides* or *A. suilla* containing mature embryos gain entrance to the alimentary canal of the sewer rat (*Mus decumanus*) or the mouse (*M. musculus*) they hatch. A certain proportion of the larvæ thus liberated escape in the feces where under suitable circumstances they live for at least three days, but probably ultimately succumb. The majority of the larvæ gain entrance into the body of the host, some animals showing signs of illness as soon as the second day after infection.

" Larvæ are found in the lungs and liver of the host not later than four days after infection and possibly as early as two days. . . . Larvæ are not found in the liver after the fifth day from infection. They are found in the bronchi about the seventh day and in the trachea on the eighth day. No larvæ are found in any portion of the lung on the ninth day after infection. Dead larvæ have been found in the stomach and rectum on the ninth day after the last infection." The route by which the larvæ reach the lungs, liver, etc., is either by boring through the wall of the stomach or intestine and entering a mesenteric venule or by traveling up the bile duct.

Spirochæta morsus muris n. sp., the cause of rat-bite fever, II, K. Futaki, I. Takaki, T. Taniguchi, and S. Osumi (*Jour. Expt. Med.*, 25 (1917), *No. 1*, *pp. 33–44, pls. 3, fig. 1*).—In this second paper (E. S. R., 35, p. 783), the authors record five additional cases in each of which a spirochete has been found. In two of the patients examined the spirochete was taken in the circulating blood derived from a vein or the punctured skin.

"The organism is not present in the blood of all rats, and there is no relation between the species of the rat and the ratio of infection. We have never found the spirochete in healthy guinea pigs or mice. By permitting a rat infected with the spirochete to bite a guinea pig, the latter develops the disease. We have succeeded in cultivating the spirochete in Shimamine's medium.

"Among the spirochetes described in the literature or discovered in the blood of rats and mice there may be some resembling our spirochete, but none of the descriptions agree with it fully. Hence, we have named our organism *Spirochæta morsus muris* and regard it as belonging to the Spironemacea of the nature of treponema. . . .

"The spirochete can be detected in about 3 per cent of house rats. These facts enable us to identify the cause of the disease."

Experimental rat-bite fever, K. Ishiwara, T. Ohtawara, and K. Tamura (*Jour. Expt. Med.*, 25 (1917), *No. 1*, *pp. 45–64, pls. 2, figs. 6*).—Spirochetes have always appeared in the peripheral blood when a mouse or white rat was inoculated, although no other symptoms developed.

"Spirochetes disappear from the blood of the animals as a result of the injection of salvarsan, thus indicating that the spirochete is arsenotropic."

Toxic action of copper compounds of amino acids on protozoa, J. A. Shaw-Mackenzie (*Jour. Physiol.*, 51 (1917), *No. 1–2, pp. III, IV*).—Investigations show the copper compounds of organic acids to possess a high toxicity for protozoa.

The action of digitalis in pneumonia, A. E. Cohn and R. A. Jamieson (*Jour. Expt. Med.*, 25 (1917), *No. 1, pp. 65–81, pl. 1*).—"Digitalis acts during the febrile period of pneumonia. It produces a beneficial, possibly a life-saving effect in cases of auricular irregularity (fibrillation and flutter). Whatever beneficial action it has on the function of the normally beating nonfebrile heart may be expected from its use in the febrile heart in pneumonia."

A bibliography of 23 titles is appended.

Studies on the blood proteins.—II, The albumin-globulin ratio in experimental intoxications and infections, S. H. Hurwitz and G. H. Whipple (*Jour. Expt. Med.*, 25 (1917), *No. 2, pp. 231–253, figs. 3*).—Continuing the work previously noted (E. S. R., 36, p. 778), the authors have found that "the intoxication which develops as the result of a simple obstruction or a closed intestinal loop is accompanied by definite changes in the coagulable proteins of the blood serum. These changes consist essentially in an alteration in the normal albumin-globulin ratio; the globulin fraction is greatly increased and at times the normal relation of the two fractions may show a complete inversion."

The infections and intoxications produced by inflammatory irritants were accompanied by a rise in the blood globulins. It is indicated that this suggests that tissue disintegration with absorption of toxic products is responsible for the changes noted, and that bacterial invasion is important only in so far as it gives rise to toxic substances. The most marked increase in globulin content of the blood serum was found in animals which showed some of the complications met with in loop animals, as rupture of the loop and peritonitis. The globulin increase was especially rapid and large in the latter condition. This reaction is deemed to be of diagnostic value in acute infections.

The experimental data are submitted in tabular and graphical form and discussed.

The mechanism of the agglutination reaction, H. PRIESTLEY (*Jour. Hyg.* [*Cambridge*], *15 (1917), No. 4, pp. 485–504*).—From the study reported the author concludes that the agglutination and precipitin reactions are probably essentially the same in nature. " The agglutination of bacteria by specific sera is probably due to the formation of altered serum protein in and around the bacteria and the subsequent flocculation by electrolytes of this altered protein and the bacteria. This altered protein is probably altered serum globulin, and possibly other altered serum proteins."

The inhibition phenomenon exhibited on heating an agglutinating serum was found to resemble closely the inhibition by acids and alkalis. The inactivation of an agglutinating serum by heating and the production of " zones of inactivation " are deemed probably due to the formation of inhibitory substances rather than to the destruction of the agglutinin.

The data are reported in detail and discussed.

On factors limiting the extent of the concentration of antitoxic sera by the fractional precipitation methods at present employed, ANNIE HOMER (*Jour. Hyg.* [*Cambridge*], *15 (1917), No. 4, pp. 580–590*).—Detailed tabular experimental data submitted show that a product containing not more than 20 per cent of protein and having a potency eight or ten times that of the original serum can be obtained where the pooled antidiphtheritic sera have a unitage not greater than 500 and where the heat denaturation is about 40 per cent.

It is noted that with the methods at present employed for the concentration of an antitoxic serum for therapeutic use, a concentration of more than 22,500 units of antitoxin per gram of protein can not be obtained.

See also previous notes (E. S. R., 35, p. 680; 36, p. 178).

The effects of serum treated with pararabin, E. ZUNZ and C. MOHILEVITH (*Jour. Expt. Med., 25 (1917), No. 2, pp. 211–229*).—Horse serum treated with pararabin (a portion of the carbohydrate of agar practically free from nitrogen), as previously noted by Zunz and Gelat (E. S. R., 36, p. 575), produced the same results as when treated with agar.

A preliminary report on two new methods of preventing blackleg by means of an antiblackleg serum and an aggressin, F. S. SCHOENLEBER, T. P. HASLAM, and O. M. FRANKLIN (*Kansas Sta. Circ. 59 (1917), pp. 7*).—The authors describe the preparation of a highly potent antiblackleg serum from the horse. The serum was found to be curative for calves in the early stages of the disease. The passive immunity produced, however, is of short duration, and in order to produce an active immunity of a certain degree virus pellets are administered a few days after the serum treatment.

The edematous fluid sterilized by filtration through a Berkefeld N filter in doses of from 8 to 15 cc. possessed a strong immunizing power and was found sufficient to protect calves against doses lethal for nonvaccinated animals.

The vaccine has been found to yield excellent results in field treatment in doses of 5 cc., producing in calves six months of age or older sufficient immunity to protect them for the remainder of their susceptible period.

Some considerations on the new dual theory of Carrion's disease, J. AROE (*Crón. Méd.* [Peru], *33* (1916), *No. 641, p. 377; abs. in Jour. Amer. Med. Assoc., 68 (1917), No. 4, p. 318*).—The author's long years of experience in Peru have confirmed more and more the view that Peruvian verruga and Oroya fever are the benign and the malignant forms of one and the same disease. He has failed to find any proof of the zooparasitic nature of the inclusions in the red corpuscles referred to in the report by Strong et al. noted on page 356 as *Bartonella bacilliformis.*

Gaseous gangrene.—Bacillus œdematous and antiedematous serum, M. WEINBERG and P. SÉGUIN (*Compt. Rend. Acad. Sci.* [Paris], *164* (1917), *No. 9, pp. 365-368*).—The organism *B. œdematous,* isolated from a number of cases of gaseous gangrene, was found to be highly pathogenic. A highly antitoxic and prophylactic serum was prepared by the injection of the organism into a horse. This antiserum was found to yield excellent results in the treatment of gaseous gangrene caused by *B. œdematous* in removing the focus of the gangrene.

The reversible precipitation in glanderous serum, M. BELIN (*Compt. Rend. Soc. Biol.* [Paris], *79* (1916), *No. 20, pp. 1095-1098*).—The author notes the formation of a precipitate on heating the serum from a glanderous horse. The precipitate appears at 47° C. and increases in amount rapidly until the temperature reaches about 55°, at which point the serum is very turbid. Further heating to about 60 to 61° dissolves the precipitate completely if the heating be rapid enough. If this solution temperature is attained rapidly enough and the material then placed in cold water a reprecipitation takes place. It is indicated that the substance precipitated is not a globulin but an albumin.

The serum in contact with the clot or preserved alone in a test tube forms a precipitate as well as the serum preserved with an antiseptic.

The reaction was not found to be uniform. A general parallelism was, however, noted between the intensity of mallein reactions and the amount of precipitation. The positive reversible precipitation reaction is considered to indicate an unpromising prognosis in glanders. The injection of mallein was found not to influence the reaction in any way.

The culture of the causative organism of epizootic lymphangitis, A. BOQUET and L. NÉGRE (*Bul. Soc. Path. Exot., 10* (1917), *No. 4, pp. 274-276*).— The authors' studies indicate that the causative organism of epizootic lymphangitis belongs to the genus Endomyces.

Treatment of epizootic lymphangitis by potassium iodid, J. CARTIER (*Rec. Méd. Vét., 92* (1916), *No. 21, pp. 614-618; abs. in Vet. Rev., 1* (1917), *No. 2, pp. 131, 132*).—In the treatment of epizootic lymphangitis the author has found potassium iodid to give satisfactory results when administered in doses of from 12 to 20 gm. daily. It was found desirable to divide the daily dose and also to interrupt the course of treatment by periods of from seven to ten days during which the drug is not given. Seven cases are reported upon.

Pseudotuberculosis in guinea pigs, R. VAN SACEGHEM (*Compt. Rend. Soc. Biol.* [Paris], *79* (1917), *No. 17, pp. 908, 909*).—The author notes an outbreak of pseudotuberculosis in guinea pigs which were used in a study on the treatment of trypanosomiasis in animals. The symptoms of the disease, together with the post-mortem findings, are described.

An organism which could not be distinguished morphologically from the plague bacillus was isolated from the tubercles which were found at autopsy. On being injected into normal animals the organism reproduced the disease. A vaccine made by heating a bouillon culture of the organism at 60° C. for two hours and injected subcutaneously in doses of 1 cc. protected the animals against a subsequent subcutaneous injection of the virulent organism.

The possibility of preparing a vaccine against human plague from the organism isolated is indicated.

Pseudotuberculosis in a South American horse, BRINGARD (*Rec. Méd. Vét., 93 (1917), No. 1-2, pp. 33, 34*).—The symptoms, treatment, and post-mortem findings of a case observed at a military depot are reported.

Tuberculosis, R. A. CRAIG and C. H. CLINK (*Indiana Sta. Circ. 60 (1917), pp. 8, figs. 7*).—This circular discusses the subject under the topics of occurrence, symptoms, effect on the different body organs, tuberculin testing used in detecting tuberculosis, and controlling tuberculosis in cattle and hogs.

The infection of tuberculosis through air expired during coughing, P. CHAUSSÉ (*Ann. Inst. Pasteur, 30 (1916), No. 11, pp. 613-641, figs. 2*).—Experimental data are submitted and discussed in detail, together with a description of the procedure and apparatus used in the study.

It is concluded in general that the possibility of infection through air expired during coughing is definitely established by the results obtained. The infection depends on the direct inhalation of the fine droplets formed during coughing from the saliva and sputum. The extreme infectivity of tuberculosis is indicated and the great need for a rational prophylactic campaign emphasized.

Contribution to the study of delayed or " latent " tuberculous infection. S. DELÉPINE (*Ann. Inst. Pasteur, 30 (1916), No. 11, pp. 600-612*).—Inoculation experiments with guinea pigs, using artificially and naturally infected tuberculous milk, are reported and discussed.

Untreated (control) and treated milk (to various temperatures) was used for the injections. The animals which received the untreated milk developed extensive tuberculous lesions at the seat of inoculation in two weeks, while animals treated with a much larger dose of the same tuberculous product, previously heated, developed only slight lesions at the seat of inoculation in the course of 11 weeks. The postmortem findings were similar to the lesions developed at the seat of inoculation.

Tubercle bacilli were found still living and capable of a modified pathogenic action after being kept for nearly 500 days in milk. It is indicated that this "supports the view that under certain circumstances tubercle bacilli are still infective after remaining dormant for a considerable period of time."

Post-mortem and other experimental data are submitted in tabular form.

Types of tubercle bacilli in cervical and axillary gland tuberculosis, A. S. GRIFFITH (*Lancet [London], 1917, I, No. 6, pp. 216-218*).—Continuing previous work, the author reports the bacteriological examination of material from 52 persons suffering from enlarged cervical or axillary lymphatic glands. The material examined consisted of glands removed by surgical operations and pus aspirated from the abscesses or collected from the dressings of the lesions.

The material from 35 cases produced tuberculosis in guinea pigs, and cultures of the tubercle bacilli were isolated either directly from the original material or through the test animals. Fifteen of the 35 strains were of standard bovine type, 17 of the human type, and 3 atypical. Two of the atypical cultures were obtained from cervical glands, while the third was derived from an intramuscular abscess in a patient also suffering from tuberculosis of the cervical glands.

The experimental results of the three atypical cases are reported in detail, together with a general tabulated summary of statistical data of previous work and that here reported. See also a previous note (E. S. R., 35, p. 576).

Bovine tuberculosis in the horse, E. FRÖHNER (*Monatsh. Prakt. Tierheilk., 26 (1914), No. 1-2, pp. 5-10*).—The clinical data and post-mortem findings of a case are reported in detail.

Observations bearing on the possibility of developing an experimental chemotherapy of tuberculosis, P. A. LEWIS (*Bul. Johns Hopkins Hosp.*, 28 (*1917*), *No. 313, pp. 120–125*).—This is a general discussion of the subject, together with experimental data on the disinfectant action of phenol, resorcin, and several organic dyes on the tubercle bacillus. The tubercle bacillus was found to be considerably more susceptible to the action of disinfectants than is ordinarily considered.

Eradicating bovine tuberculosis, W. H. PEW (*Breeder's Gaz.*, 71 (*1917*), *No. 19, pp.·968, 970*).—The author reports upon the successful eradication of tuberculosis from the Iowa Agricultural College herd by means of the "modified Bang system," suggested by E. C. Schroeder of the U. S. Department of Agriculture as a possible method for managing a reacting herd with the least cost and minimum loss.

The cows were maintained absolutely in quarantine, kept in the open winter and summer, and fed in the open. The calves were dropped in the quarantine pasture and permitted to remain with their dams until weaning time, which was from 6 to 11 months of age. They were then tested, retested in from 60 to 90 days, and then taken to the clean herd. Of 21 calves tested that were dropped in quarantine from 1908 to 1914 and permitted to nurse their dams until weaning time 18 passed the test and 3 reacted. At the time the quarantine herd was discontinued in 1915, only two animals were left, the others having died or were sold.

The results tend to show that it is not necessary to discard reacting animals and that calves can be kept with cows in open conditions with a fair degree of safety. Whenever it is found that a cow under this system produces two calves in succession that are reactors at weaning time, it may be suspected that this cow is a contaminating factor through the udder, which is probably affected.

Sterility of cattle and methods of treatment, J. ALBRECHTSEN (*Cornell Vet.*, 7 (*1917*), *No. 2, pp. 57–110*).—This account, a translation from the Danish, deals with the subject at length under the headings of treatment of sterility, diseases of the uterus, diseases of the ovaries, cystic degeneration of the ovaries, diseases of the vagina, and results.

Prevention and treatment of hemorrhagic septicemia of cattle by the use of bacterial vaccine made from the causative agent, T. O. BRANDENBURG (*Jour. Amer. Vet. Med. Assoc.*, 51 (*1917*), *No. 1, p. 93*).—The use of a vaccine in a number of cases is noted. From the results the author considers the vaccine to be "an absolute preventive if properly used and curative in all cases which are not advanced."

Two injections about eight days apart are considered necessary to establish a positive protection. Younger animals were found to be more susceptible to the disease and also to treatment than older animals.

Diseases of new-born calves and outline of recommendations for control, W. L. WILLIAMS (*Cornell Vet.*, 7 (*1917*), *No. 2, pp. 110–134*).—This article, prepared by the author in cooperation with the Bureau of Animal Industry of the U. S. Department of Agriculture, is part of an extensive report upon investigations of contagious abortion of cattle to be published in the annual report of the New York State Veterinary College.

Anaphylaxis in cattle and sheep, produced by the larvæ of Hypoderma bovis, H. lineatum, and Œstrus ovis, S. HADWEN and E. A. BRUCE (*Jour. Amer. Vet. Med. Assoc.*, 51 (*1917*), *No. 1, pp. 15–44, figs. 15*).—Experiments are reported in which anaphylaxis was produced in cattle, sheep, rabbits, and guinea pigs with extracts of the larvæ of *H. lineatum*, *H. bovis*, and *O. ovis*.

The reactions could be induced by crushing and returning an extract of an animal's own larvæ into the jugular vein, showing that larvæ living in the animals make them receptive.

Natural cases of anaphylaxis were observed where injury had ruptured the larvæ subcutaneously, liberating the contents in sufficient quantity to produce shock. Immunity lasting for varying periods was observed in animals which recovered from the reaction. Eye and other local reactions were obtained with extracts of the larvæ applied to the mucous membranes. The reaction was specific in cattle for extracts of Hypoderma, and in a horse for Gastrophilus.

The symptoms produced were those previously noted (E. S. R., 36, p. 478), which work is also included in this paper.

The etiology of bradsot or braxy, C. O. JENSEN (*Ztschr. Infektionskrank. u. Hyg. Haustiere, 17 (1915), No. 1–2, pp. 1–18, pls. 4; abs. in Jour. Compar. Path. and Ther., 29 (1916), No. 2, pp. 179–181*).—After reviewing recent literature relating to the etiology of bradsot, the author reports upon the results of investigations, including the details of ten cases, conducted with a view to demonstrating that the so-called bacillus of braxy is more than an agonal invader.

In all cases the typical lesions of braxy were present in the fourth stomach, and the braxy bacillus was demonstrated in pure culture in the altered parts of the mucous membrane and in the infiltrated submucous tissue. Since the pathological changes in the abomasum are characteristic of a primary infection which closely resembles malignant edema, and the bacilli which occur in the wall of the abomasum and later in the blood when inoculated into sheep produce characteristic lesions which closely resemble those observed in malignant edema, there can be no reasonable doubt as to the causal connection of the bacillus with bradsot.

On a tick-borne gastroenteritis of sheep and goats occurring in British East Africa, E. MONTGOMERY (*Jour. Compar. Path. and Ther., 30 (1917), No. 1, pp. 28–57, figs. 6*).—Hemorrhagic gastroenteritis of sheep and goats appears to be epizootic in British East Africa, principally in the Kikuyu region. Grade and pure-bred sheep are more resistant than native sheep, in which the mortality is about 70 per cent of those attacked.

The disease is carried by the brown tick (*Rhipicephalus appendiculatus*) and possibly by other ticks. Ticks which as nymphs have fed upon affected sheep convey the infection after arriving at the adult stage. It is possible that the larvæ from adults which have fed on sick animals may also transmit the disease.

No success has yet been obtained from different methods of preventive inoculation, the most favorable measure appearing to be that of attenuating the virulence of the disease for sheep by passing the virus for several generations through the more resistant goat. The eradication of ticks capable of carrying the disease forms the basis of preventive measures.

Morphology of normal pigs' blood, C. C. PALMER (*U. S. Dept. Agr., Jour. Agr. Research, 9 (1917), No. 5, pp. 131–140*).—The author at the Minnesota Experiment Station reports the examination of the blood of 25 normal pigs between the ages of 2 and 42 days. The average number of erythrocytes was 3,855,000 per cubic millimeter, and 13,500 leucocytes per cubic millimeter. The average clotting time was 64 seconds, specific gravity 1.024, and hemoglobin percentage 56.8. The differential count of the leucocytes yielded the following percentages: Lymphocytes, 63.25; polymorphs, 32.14; mononuclears, 2.63; eosinophils, 1.28; and mast cells, 0.24.

Twenty-five examinations of the blood of pigs weighing in the neighborhood of 100 lbs. showed the average number of erythrocytes per cubic millimeter to be 6,215,000, and the average number of leucocytes, 18,000. The average clotting time was found to be 57.6 seconds, specific gravity 1.062, and hemoglobin percentage 79.4. The differential leucocyte count yielded lymphocytes 55.21, polymorphs 39.79, mononuclears 0.79, eosinophils 3.42, and mast cells 0.79 per cent.

A detailed description of the various classes of leucocytes observed in the investigation is submitted. The average differential counts in male and female animals were found to be about the same, and also the counts by various workers to be fairly uniform. The number of erythrocytes was found to vary under different conditions, and to be higher in an animal in good condition than in an animal of the same age in poor condition.

Effects of muscular exercise and the heat of the sun on the blood and body temperature of normal pigs, C. C. PALMER (*U. S. Dept. Agr., Jour. Agr. Research, 9 (1917), No. 6, pp. 167–182, figs. 2*).—This report of investigations at the Minnesota Experiment Station has been summarized by the author as follows:

"Blood examinations in normal resting pigs, covering a period of 24 hours, may be quite uniform; but in some animals there is marked variation throughout the period. . . . Results based on only one or a few experiments may lead to wrong conclusions, owing to the variability in the blood of pigs."

"Observations made upon a number of animals lead to the conclusion that muscular exercise does not cause an increase of red corpuscles in the peripheral circulation of the pig. . . . Evidence given by work with the pig tends to confirm the theory of perspiration being responsible for the increase in the number of red corpuscles following muscular exercise in man.

"Muscular exercise in the pig is usually followed by a leucocytosis. This leucocytosis is probably the result of muscular exercise forcing leucocytes into the general circulation from the tissues. Muscular exercise leads to marked changes in the differential counts. The mononuclear elements are decreased, and the polymorphonuclear elements are increased. The height of the curve is reached several hours after exercise, and the normal proportions do not return for many hours.

"Exposure to the sun causes similar changes in the differential curve. These changes under both conditions are the result of increased rate of aging of the leucocytes, the cells becoming older faster than young cells are being produced. Muscular exercise and heat of the sun lead to a marked increase in body temperature. Body temperature changes are more pronounced in fat pigs than lean ones, but even in pigs weighing from 75 to 100 lbs. marked changes are likely to occur.

"Increased atmospheric temperature and increased percentage of humidity lead to increased body temperature.

"Blood examinations of pigs which are to be used for clinical records should be taken from animals which have been confined in a small cool pen for at least 24 hours, and better, 48 hours. The animals must be kept absolutely quiet and not worried. Feeding and watering should be regular. The daily blood examinations should be made at the same time on each day.

"Temperature records which are to be used for clinical records should be taken from pigs kept in a cool, shady pen. The animals should not be exercised or worried when the temperatures are taken. If the animals are chased around the pen in endeavoring to obtain the temperature, the last temperatures taken may show a marked rise. For tuberculin work where the temperatures are used it would be best to keep them confined in a crate throughout the test.

" The condition of the animal (amount of fat), the temperature of the atmosphere, and the percentage of humidity are factors which should be considered in determining the normal temperature of the pig."

The etiology of hog cholera.—Preliminary report, F. Proescher and H. A. Seil (*Jour. Amer. Vet. Med. Assoc., 51 (1917), No. 1, pp. 64–69, pls. 2*).—-The authors prepared smears from the blood of 6 pigs in the advanced stages of hog cholera and from the blood of 28 pigs artificially infected with virus. All the animals were examined post-mortem and the characteristic lesions of the disease established.

The smears, after being fixed, were thoroughly washed and then stained in a 1 per cent aqueous solution of methylene azure containing 1 per cent of phenol and finally mounted in paraffin or cedar oils. The general blood pictures are described in detail.

In all the preparations a very small diplococcus uniformly less than 0.2 μ in size was found. They were stained either a deep blue or a metachromatic violet. The micro-organisms were also found in the urine of three pigs artificially infected with hog-cholera virus.

The close resemblance of the changes in the blood picture in hog cholera to those of typhus fever is pointed out and briefly discussed.

The artificial cultivation of the organism observed in the smears and a histological study of the changes taking place in the blood vessels of animals affected with cholera are in progress.

On the pathology and treatment of pernicious and infectious anemia of the horse, III, J. N. Ries (*Rec. Méd. Vét., 92 (1916), No. 1-2, pp. 14–20*).—It is concluded that the pernicious anemia of Lorraine and adjacent territory is a gastrophilic anemia in the great majority of cases.

Vaccination against infectious arthritis of foals due to Bacillus abortus equi, J. B. Hardenbergh (*Mo. Bul. State Live Stock Sanit. Bd. [Penn.], 1 (1916), No. 2, pp. 16, pls. 3; Jour. Amer. Vet. Med. Assoc., 50 (1916), No. 3, pp. 331–349, figs. 6*).—A number of cases in an outbreak of infectious arthritis in foals are reported in detail. The organism causing the outbreak was found to belong to a subgroup of the paratyphoid-enteritidis group which has been isolated by various investigators.

The complement-fixation and agglutination tests are deemed reliable for determining the extent of the infection in the stable, but the best results are obtained by repeating the tests at intervals of from three to four weeks. "Animals giving an agglutination reaction of 1:500 or over, with no complement-fixation reaction, should be watched and retested in three weeks. Immune bodies in some cases disappear rapidly."

One ophthalmic test with a purified "abortin" is considered to be of no value in determining infected animals. The possibility of using a different preparation of abortin or a retest as yielding more satisfactory results is indicated. Two or three injections of from 50,000,000 to 100,000,000 organisms, followed by more if necessary, are considered to be much better than numerous injections of small amounts.

" The fact that all of the colts, either infected or later developing affections of the joints, gave marked local reactions to the bacterin may indicate such a preparation to be of diagnostic value when injected or rather vaccinating foals against joint evil, which do not at the time give serum reactions. Vaccination of exposed foals with a specific bacterin appears to confer some immunity to the disease, and may also have some curative properties, as 7 out of 10 foals, either thoroughly exposed to the infection or badly infected, failed to develop or completely recovered from a severe attack of infectious arthritis. Owing to the fact that we were unable to try the vaccine on a large number of animals experimentally, we hesitate to base our conclusions too strongly on results obtained, and they should be confirmed."

Tabulated data of complement-fixation tests and complement-fixation, agglutination, and ophthalmic reactions, together with some other data, are submitted.

Bacillary white diarrhea of young chicks.—VI, Second progress report on the elimination of infected breeding stock, L. F. RETTGER, W. F. KIRKPATRICK, and R. E. JONES (*Connecticut Storrs Sta. Bul. 88 (1916), pp. 247–254*).—A brief summary is first given of the more significant data obtained in a systematic campaign against bacillary white diarrhea in Connecticut, inaugurated in June, 1914, a detailed report on the methods and results of which for the first year has been previously noted (E. S. R., 35, p. 184).

During the second year (1915–16), in which the agglutination test was applied to 7,799 fowls in 78 flocks, of which 25 flocks failed to react and were regarded as free from ovarian infection, the average percentage of infection was 8.2 as compared with 10.24 for the previous year. As before, ovarian infection was again less prevalent in the White Leghorn than in the heavier breeds, only 3.4 per cent of 2,870 Leghorns examined being infected while the average for 3,178 Plymouth Rocks, Wyandottes, and Rhode Island Reds was 11.45, and for a single lot of Orpingtons 31.7 per cent.

While the elimination of reacting hens from breeding stock has a far-reaching influence on the health and condition of the future chicks the work has shown that a single set of agglutination tests and the elimination of reactors is not an absolute guaranty that the flock is entirely rid of ovarian infection. Single tests have, however, on numerous occasions sufficed to stamp out completely the infection from the breeding stock and the results thus far obtained are said to have been very gratifying. Many tested and nonreacting flocks of almost all breeds have been located in the State, so that buyers of eggs for hatching and day-old chicks should have no trouble in procuring stock which has a thoroughly clean known record.

A simplification of the technique employed in testing has made possible the reduction of the cost of the agglutination test in all but small flocks. Instead of making two transfers of the blood serum as was formerly done, 0.03 cc. of the serum in the original blood tube is introduced directly into 3 cc. of the test blood in which the final observations are made.

A summary of the work of the first two years of the campaign shows that 9.3 per cent of 21,317 hens and 2.1 per cent of 1,037 males tested were found infected.

Enterohepatitis or blackhead in turkeys, C. H. HIGGINS (*Jour. Amer. Assoc. Instr. and Invest. Poultry Husb., 3 (1917), No. 8, pp. 57, 58*).—The data here presented have been substantially noted from another source (E. S. R., 36, p. 384).

Some field experiments bearing on the transmission of blackhead in turkeys, T. SMITH (*Jour. Expt. Med., 25 (1917), No. 3, pp. 405–414*).—The author's experiments show that healthy turkeys may be raised from the eggs of infected flocks when all older turkeys and poultry are kept away and the ground has not been used before, there being no evidence favoring the theory that the protozoan parasite can be transmitted in the egg. In these experiments all the turkeys remained well until August 14, the end of the hen exposure test, when they were 12 weeks and 4 days old. The first death occurred 2 weeks after the beginning of exposure to actual disease, when they were more than

14 weeks old. Hens from a blackhead farm and from a farm free from turkeys did not convey the disease to the incubator turkeys on uninfected land.

It is concluded that the infection is either not transmitted at all or only under exceptional conditions by turkeys in the early acute stage. It is considered as probably carried and shed by those birds which have successfully passed through an attack.

Note on coccidia in sparrows and their assumed relation to blackhead in turkeys, T. SMITH and E. W. SMILLIE (*Jour. Expt. Med.*, *25* (*1917*), *No. 3*, *pp. 415–420*).—This is a report of an investigation carried on in connection with those above noted.

" Of 54 sparrows examined in or near Princeton, coccidia were found in 43, or 80 per cent. Most of the negative cases were encountered in November and December. In the summer and fall practically all were infected. These figures agree closely with Hadley's [E. S. R., 26, p. 187] who found 79 per cent infected from May to December. Cultures of feces on agar showed that, at least in this locality, the infecting species belongs to the genus Isospora or Diplospora and not to Eimeria."

RURAL ENGINEERING.

Report of the superintendent of public works, Hawaii, C. R. FORBES (*Rpt. Supt. Pub. Works Hawaii, 1916, pp. 87, figs. 15*).—This report contains sections on road construction, drainage, reclamation, and sanitation projects in the islands.

Surface water supply of New Mexico, 1915, J. A. FRENCH (*Santa Fe, N. Mex.: State Engin. Dept., 1915, pp. 149*).—This report gives the results of measurements of flow made on streams in New Mexico during 1915, and the results of studies of evaporation from water surfaces made near Deming and Farmington, N. Mex.

Surface water supply of lower Columbia River and Pacific drainage basins in Oregon, 1914 (*U. S. Geol. Survey, Water-Supply Paper 394 (1917), pp. 7–180+XLIX, pls. 2*).—This report, prepared in cooperation with the States of Oregon and Washington, presents the results of measurements of flow made on streams in the lower Columbia River basin and on the Cowlitz, Rogue, Umpqua, Wilson, and Nehalem River basins during 1914.

The usual appendix on stream-gaging stations and publications relating to water resources is included.

Pump irrigation in Nebraska, E. E. BRACKETT and O. W. SJOGREN (*Nebraska Sta. Circ. 2 (1917), pp. 28, figs. 21*).—This bulletin gives data on the design, installation, and cost of irrigation pumping plants including wells, with special reference to Nebraska conditions, and is based on a study of the installation and operation of pumping plants in Nebraska and other States.

A bibliography of 14 references is included.

Note on the irrigation of the Chéliff plain in the department of Oran [Algiers], VIELLE (*Ann. Ponts et Chaussées, 9. ser., 35 (1916), pt. 1, No. 5, pp. 166–187, figs. 7*).—This report deals with the general engineering features involved in the irrigation of an area of about 25,000 hectares (about 61,750 acres) in an Algerian dependency.

Farm drainage in Virginia, D. L. YARNELL (*Dept. Agr. and Immigr. Va., Farmers' Bul. 26, pp. 30, figs. 11*).—The purpose of this bulletin is to give definite information regarding methods of removing excess moisture from wet soils, with particular reference to Virginia conditions. The most space is devoted to the planning, construction, and cost of tile drains. Two brief sections deal with the reclamation of tidal marshes and the Virginia drainage law. Fourteen references to literature bearing on the subject are appended.

[Land drainage in] Ontario, J. R. SPBY (*Agr. Gaz. Canada, 4 (1917), No. 3, pp. 190, 191*).—Experimental tile drainage of five plats of loam soil in Ontario, Canada, was found to increase the yields of wheat, oats, barley, and hay on the average in 1916 by an amount worth $12.44 per acre, which exceeded one-third the total cost of the drainage system. On clay soils the average increase was less, being $4.61 per acre. No increase due to drainage of heavy clay soils was obtained during 1914, 1915, or 1916.

Institutional sewage plants, C. F. MEBUS (*Amer. Jour. Pub. Health, 7 (1917), No. 5, pp. 296–298*).—The general requirements for the proper operation of institutional plants for the purification and disposal of sewage are outlined.

New stump burner for logged-off lands requires no blower, L. W. ALLISON (*Engin. Rec., 75 (1917), No. 13, pp. 495, 496, fig. 1*).—A new stump burner is described and illustrated.

"In contrast with the closed type of hood burner, this stump burner consists of a metal housing with various apertures for particular service, with smoke pipe connection at the top. It is constructed in sections to provide for any class of service, covering both large and small stumps.

"By the use of movable draft pipes arranged around and near the base of the burner, it eliminates the necessity for any blower or other artificial draft device, the required draft being brought about by natural conditions and hood construction, and in a highly efficient manner for the service designed. While this burner operates more slowly through the use of natural draft, demanding greater periods of time for stump consumption, the operating cost is reduced to a minimum, the primary expense being that of labor and attendance, which is low when a number of burners are in operation on the same land at the same time. . . . Recent tests on Washington timber lands show that this type of stump burner will consume stumps from 3 to 5 ft. in diameter, together with roots within the range of the burner, in a period of 24 hours, while larger stumps from 6 to 7 ft. are burned in 30 or 40 hours."

Tenth annual report of the board of county road commissioners of Wayne County [Mich.], 1916 (*Ann. Rpt. Bd. Road Comrs. Wayne Co. [Mich.], 10 (1916), pp. 87, pl. 1, figs. 79*).—This reports the work and expenditures of the board of road commissioners of Wayne Co., Mich., on road construction, especially concrete roads, for the year ended September 30, 1916.

First annual report of the commissioner of highways [of Oklahoma], 1915, G. B. NOBLE (*Ann. Rpt. Comr. Highways Okla., 1 (1915), pp. 19, pl. 1*).—This is a report, in manuscript, of the work and expenditures of the office of the commissioner of highways of Oklahoma on the construction, maintenance, and cost of highways in the State for the year ended December 31, 1915.

Second annual report of the state engineer [of Oklahoma], 1916, M. L. CUNNINGHAM (*Ann. Rpt. State Engin. Okla., 2 (1916), pp. 26*).—This is a mimeographed report of the work and expenditures of the Oklahoma State engineer's office pertaining to the construction, cost, and maintenance of highways in the State during the fiscal year 1915–16 and for the calendar year 1916 up to December 1.

Annual report on highway improvement, Ontario, 1914, W. A. McLEAN (*Ann. Rpt. Highway Improv. Ontario, 1914, pp. 223, figs. 68*).—This report has special reference to the work of road and bridge construction carried on by the several counties of the Province of Ontario during the year 1914. It includes appendixes on county road inspection, testing of materials, nonasphaltic road oils, and traffic census statistics.

5750°—17——No. 4——7

Laws of Iowa relating to roads and highways passed by the thirty-sixth general assembly, 1915, LOLA S. ELLIOTT (*Des Moines, Iowa: State, 1915, pp. 28*).—The text of the laws is given.

Cost of engineering an extensive county road system, W. C. DAVIDSON (*Engin. Rec., 75 (1917), No. 13, pp. 498, 499*).—This article is a description of the items charged to engineering in the cost of construction of a road system in Texas consisting of 5 miles of concrete, 63 miles of water-bound macadam, and 110 miles of gravel construction and entailing the building of 488 bridges and culverts. The total cost amounted to $1,075,000, of which 4.58 per cent was for engineering.

The results of physical tests of road building rock in 1916, including all compression tests, P. HUBBARD and F. H. JACKSON, JR. (*U. S. Dept. Agr. Bul. 537 (1917), pp. 23, fig. 1*).—This bulletin supplements Bulletin 370 (E. S. R., 35, p. 685) and reports the results of the more common physical tests, including crushing, of 396 samples of road-building rock examined by the Office of Public Roads and Rural Engineering during 1916, as well as a complete record of all crushing-strength tests made by the Office up to January 1, 1917.

Material specifications (*Ohio Highway Dept., Material Specifica. 5 (1916), pp. 80, figs. 9*).—Specifications for Portland Cement, paving block, stone and slag, gravel and sand, nonbituminous binders, bituminous materials, creosoted timber, oils and paints, steel and iron, and pipe, as prepared by the Ohio highway department, are presented, together with outlines of methods of testing.

United States Government specification for Portland cement (*U. S. Dept. Com., Bur. Standards Circ. 33, 3. ed. (1917), pp. 43, figs. 10*).—This specification is the result of several years' work of a joint conference representing the U. S. Government, the American Society of Civil Engineers, and the American Society for Testing Materials. It was adopted by the U. S. Government and by the American Society for Testing Materials, to become effective January 1, 1917.

Creosoting Douglas fir bridge stringers and ties without loss in strength, O. P. M. Goss (*Seattle, Wash.: Assoc. Creosot. Cos. of the Pacific Coast, 1916, pp. 27, figs. 11*).—This circular briefly describes Douglas fir as a structural timber, and discusses particularly a method of effectively creosoting structural forms without loss in strength. This consists essentially of boiling the timber in cresote oil under a vacuum of from 24 to 27 in.

Results of strength tests on bridge stringers and ties and of spike-pulling tests are also reported, giving information which in general should be of interest to engineers responsible for the efficient use of structural timber.

Timber framing, H. D. DEWELL (*West. Engin., 7 (1916), Nos. 6, pp. 209–216, figs. 2; 7, pp. 251–256, figs. 10; 8, pp. 289–298, figs. 11; 9, pp. 339–346, figs. 9; 10] pp. 385–393, figs. 13; 11, pp. 416–424, figs. 11; 12, pp. 455–461, figs. 11; 8 (1917), Nos. 1, pp. 9–17, figs. 7; 2, pp. 52–56, figs. 7; 4, pp. 132–142, figs. 7*).— This is a series of ten articles on the design and construction of timber-frame structures.

Part 1 summarizes specifications for grading timber in use on the Pacific coast and discusses working-unit stresses and ultimate strengths of main members. Part 2 deals with washers and pin-connected joints and gives experimental data regarding their strength. Part 3 discusses the design of timber connections using nails, screws, lag screws, and bolts, and summarizes related experimental data. Part 4 deals with end joints of timber trusses and gives detailed computations and drawings for eight different types of joint. Part 5 discusses the complete design of intermediate joints in trusses, of tension splices, and of compression splices. Part 6 dicusses compression chords and struts, including laminated members, timber-tension members, tension rods, and bracing trusses. Part 7 discusses the complete design of timber trusses, both of the simple and lattice type. Part 8 deals with timber columns, column connections, and joist hangers. The use of mill construction for reducing the fire risk in timber structures is also considered. Part 9 deals with timber foundations, including anchorages for columns. Part 10 discusses miscellaneous structures, including flumes, head frames, and tank towers, and also considers wind stresses and the preparation of working drawings. General specifications for timber buildings of the mill-building type are also given.

Elementary primer of electricity for light and power customers (*Salem, Oreg.: Univ. Oreg., 1916, pp. 95, pl. 1, figs. 8*).—This bulletin gives general information for the nontechnical reader regarding electricity and its use, and deals in some detail with the use of electricity in the home and on the farm, with special reference to Oregon conditions. A final section deals with the relation of the hydroelectric power resources to the prospective industrial development of Oregon.

Performance of two successful windmill generating plants, F. S. Culver (*Elect. World, 69 (1917), No. 8, pp. 367–369, figs. 7*).—This article states the considerations on which the selection of the equipment for the two plants was based, describes features of the arrangements employed, and gives the results of tests of the plants showing their ability to utilize a wide range of wind velocities.

The results of tests of the chain-driven and geared types of plant showed "that with a wind velocity of 22 miles per hour the charging rate of the geared plant had nearly reached a maximum, while with the chain-driven plant the charging current was increasing almost directly with the wind velocity. This action is due to the difference in adjustment of the differential windings of the generators. In the first case nearly the entire winding was effective, while in the other it was nearly all cut out of circuit. Thus, by adjusting the amount of the differential winding in circuit the peak charging current can be easily controlled. Another interesting fact is the low wind velocity at which the generator will charge the storage battery, current being furnished with a wind velocity of only 10 miles per hour."

Electric heating, E. A. Wilcox (*San Francisco: Technical Publishing Co., 1916, pp. [VI]+286, figs. 192*).—This is a semitechnical presentation of the different uses of electric heat, in which the advantages and disadvantages of various kinds of heating loads are compared and several types of heating devices explained. Data are given on the relative operating costs of electric and fuel-heated apparatus, together with suggestions regarding approved methods of installing and using domestic and commercial ranges, bake ovens, water heaters, and industrial heating devices.

More tractor evidence (*Amer. Thresherman, 19 (1917), No. 11, pp. 17–19*).—Tabulated data covering the operations of 59 large tractors and 37 small tractors for the past year are reported and compared with similar data for the two previous years.

Fifteen of the large tractors used gasoline and 44 used either kerosene or distillate. Among the smaller machines, 27 used gasoline and only 10 reported the use of kerosene. In the cases of 42 of the large tractors and of 30 of the small tractors, operation was cheaper than by use of horses.

"As regards tractor sentiment, 40 owners of large tractors report local sentiment favorable, as against 31 two years ago. In 12 communities the replies are unfavorable, while in the remaining 7 they either do not reply or are undecided. Out of the 37 owners of small machines, 33 reported favorable sentiment last year and only 30 this year."

The relation of horsepower to work done is shown in the following table:

Relation of horsepower to work in farm tractors.

Rating of tractors.	Area plowed in 10 hours.	Rating of tractors.	Area plowed in 10 hours.
HORSEPOWER.	*Acres.*	HORSEPOWER.	*Acres.*
5–12	6.30	15–30	11.80
8–16	6.60	25–45	19.20
10–20	7.70	35–60	21.00
12–25	9.00	40–50	25.75

Equipment for the farm and the farmstead, H. C. RAMSOWER (*New York and London: Ginn & Co., 1917, pp. XII+523, figs. 543*).—This is a semitechnical treatise on the subject, which contains the following chapters: Some principles of mechanics, transmission of power, materials of construction, cement and concrete, laying out the farm, farm fences, farm building, the farmhouse, lighting the farm home, sources of farm water supply, the pumping and piping of water, pumps and their operation, windmills, the hydraulic ram, power from streams, water-supply systems, sewage disposal for farm homes, the plow, tillage tools, seeding machinery, manure spreaders, haying machinery, grain binders, corn harvesters, wagons, miscellaneous tools and machines, gasoline and oil engines, and rope and its uses.

Equipment for farm sheep raising, V. O. MCWHORTER (*U. S. Dept. Agr., Farmers' Bul. 810 (1917), pp 27, figs. 37*).—"The object of this publication is to furnish a practical guide for the equipping of farms for sheep raising. Wide differences in climatic conditions render it impracticable to suggest a particular type of building for all sections; therefore a number of types of barns and sheds are presented."

"Equipment for raising sheep on farms need not be expensive. In mild latitudes little housing is needed, and the main need is for fencing and pastures of sufficient number and size to allow frequent changing of flocks to fresh ground to insure health. Where winters are longer and more severe, buildings and sheds are necessary to furnish protection from storms, though no special provisions are needed for warmth. Dryness, good ventilation, and freedom from drafts are the first requisites of buildings for sheep. Convenience in feeding and shepherding must also be held in mind in locating and planning such buildings or sheds. Small flocks can be cared for in sections of barns having stabling or feed storage for other stock, but with a flock of, say, 100 ewes separate buildings are desirable. The interior arrangement of these buildings should be such as to require a minimum of labor and the least possible moving of the ewes in doing the feeding and caring for them during the lambing season. A building of this type can also be utilized for fattening purchased lambs to be disposed of before lambing begins in the regular farm flock. A good supply of feed racks, grain troughs, etc., can be provided at small expense and will save labor and prevent waste of feed."

Fencing, crates, feed racks, and miscellaneous equipment are also described.

Municipal piggeries, O. A. BRIDGES (*Surveyor, 51 (1917), No. 1315, pp. 322, 323, figs. 4*).—This article gives plans and a brief description of hog houses for municipal use, these being advocated as a war-time measure in England.

Pit, semipit, and bank silos, L. W. CHASE (*Nebr. Col. Agr., Ext. Serv. Bul. 39 (1917), pp. 16, figs. 19*).—This bulletin gives information on the construction and cost of pit, semipit, and bank silos in Nebraska. It is stated that the bank silo is the most convenient and most expensive, while the pit silo is the cheapest and least convenient.

Poultry house construction, K. J. T. EKBLAW (*Nat. Lumber Manfrs. Assoc., Trade Ext. Dept. Farm Bul. 5 (1916), pp. 21, figs. 8*).—This bulletin deals with the general requirements, construction, and equipment of poultry houses, and includes several diagrammatic illustrations.

RURAL ECONOMICS.

[Report of the sixth annual meeting of the American Farm Management Association] (*Amer. Farm Management Assoc. Rpt., 6 (1915), pp. 91, pl. 1, figs. 4*).—Among the papers presented at this meeting were the following: What the Future Holds in Farm Management, by A. Boss; Land Credits and Land Settlements, by T. F. Hunt; Utilization of Waste on the Farms, by W. S. A. Smith; Results of Farm Management Demonstration Work, by L. H. Goddard; Gaining a Foothold on the Land, by E. H. Thomson; Farm Management Summer Practice Courses, by R. L. Adams; The Practical Application of Farm Management Principles, by H. W. Jeffers; The Farmer's Response to Economic Forces, by W. J. Spillman; and Farm Management Investigations in Minnesota, by F. W. Peck.

Validity of the survey method of research, W. J. SPILLMAN (*U. S. Dept. Agr. Bul. 529 (1917), pp. 15*).—The author cites numerous comparisons of farmers' estimates with actual records, and states that "our studies lead to the conclusion that errors in the farmer's knowledge of the details of his business and of the work he does are in every way comparable to the departures from the true means in field plat experimental work, and that they distribute themselves about the true values in approximately the same manner. The fact that the survey method of investigation gives data sufficient to permit the law of averages to eliminate plus errors by the occurrence of similar minus errors, while plat experiments ordinarily do not do this, appears to justify the statement that the survey method is a more reliable means of arriving at those facts to which it is applicable than the field plat experimental method. It appears, in fact, to occupy a place intermediate between plat experiments on the one hand, where variations in other factors than that under observation occur and are not adequately eliminated, and laboratory studies on the other hand, in which variations in other factors are largely prevented. These variations due to factors other than that studied do occur in using the survey method, but the amount of data obtained by this method is sufficient to permit the elimination of such variations by the operation of the law of averages."

Agriculture and preparedness, H. MYRICK (*New York: Orange Judd Co., 1917, pp. 67*).—Among the various means that may be used to put agriculture on a better basis are suggested easier means of distributing agricultural products, increased use of the Federal Farm Loan Act, a provision for short-time credit, the stimulating of saving and thrift among the American people, and the securing of an abundant labor supply through the revision of our immigration laws.

he relation of production to consumption, P. J. DUTOIT (*So. African Jour. Sci., 13 (1916), No. 4, pp. 132–139*).—The author points out that the condition of both the consumer and producer can be improved by an enlargement of the consuming power as well as the producing power. This can proceed in South Africa along three lines, namely, (1) natural increase of population, (2) increase of, or new, demand beyond their boundaries, and (3) stimulation of the wants of the native population.

Solving the food problem, A. M. Soule (*Ga. State Col. Agr. Bul. 124 (1917),* pp. 13).—The author has indicated the quantity of food necessary to maintain an adult and an average family, the acreage of crops and the number of animals necessary to produce this food, and the best methods of planting the various crops.

Plantation farming in the United States (*Bur. of the Census* [*U. S.*], *Plantation Farming in U. S., 1916, pp. 40, figs. 37*).—The Bureau of the Census has defined a plantation as a "continuous tract of land of considerable area under the general supervision or control of a single individual or firm, all or a part of such tract being divided into at least five smaller tracts, which are leased to tenants." This report gives details regarding the number of such plantations, the total and improved acreage, and the value of land and buildings. Special data are also given for the Southern States, covering altogether 325 counties.

Farms for sale or rent in New York, 1917, C. W. Larmon (*N. Y. Dept. Agr. Bul. 90 (1917), pp. 179, pls. 63*).—This bulletin brings up to date for 1917 the list previously noted (E. S. R., 35, p 589).

Land settlement, C. Turnor (In *Labor, Finance, and the War, London: Sir Isaac Pitman & Sons, Ltd., [1916], pp. 329–342*).—The author points out that to increase the output of food Great Britain must raise the standard of cultivation of all the average farmers, guarantee a remunerative price for home-grown food, check as far as possible great fluctuations in prices, improve marketing conditions by organization, lay it down as essential to the safety and welfare of the country that certain definite quantities of the chief articles of food must be produced at home, and increase the agricultural population by securing to the laborer a reasonable living wage, providing a sufficient supply of good cottages, and making village life more attractive. With these considerations as a basis, he advises the creation of a land-settlement board to control all settlement in the United Kingdom, and provide that small holdings should be placed on reclaimed land, land bought in open market or acquired when existing tenants give up their farms, land taken from excessively large farms, and land so situated near new plantations that the new settler would be provided with a dual occupation as forester and cultivator.

Causes of rural migration, J. Simonot (*Vie Agr. et Rurale, 7 (1917), No. 13, pp. 217–221*).—Among the causes mentioned are the limiting of the size of the family because of the size of the income and housing conditions. It is suggested that improvement could be obtained through agricultural instruction and the breaking up of the larger sized farms.

Seasonal distribution of farm labor in Chester County, Pa., G. A. Billings (*U. S. Dept. Agr. Bul. 528 (1917), pp. 29, figs. 3*).—The region studied for this investigation "includes the region already covered by a farm-management survey made by this Department (E. S. R., 34, p. 592), and, in addition, areas outside of this area having similar agricultural conditions." The farmers selected were 165 who received more than the average net income. A description is given of the periods of performing the various field operations in connection with the more important farm crops, with data showing the various operations with the usual crew of men and horses, acres covered in a 10-hour day, as well as days per acre. With these data as a basis, the author outlines how a typical farm may be reorganized to make a more efficient utilization of its horse and man labor.

Marketing live stock in the South: Suggestions for improvement, S. W. Doty (*U. S. Dept. Agr., Farmers' Bul. 809 (1917), pp. 16*).—The author reports that the prevailing methods of marketing live stock in Tennessee, North Carolina, South Carolina, Georgia, Florida, Louisiana, Mississippi, Alabama, and Arkansas are as follows:

Relative use of various methods of marketing live stock in the nine Southeastern States.

Kind of live stock.	Sold to local butchers. on foot.	Sold as farm-dressed carcasses.	Sold to local dealer-shippers for shipment to market.	Shipped by owners in car lots.	Miscellaneous.
	Per cent.	*Per cent.*	*Per cent.*	*Per cent.*	*Per cent.*
Cattle	38	9	36	7	10
Calves	50	6	35	....	9
Sheep	43	12	30	....	15
Hogs	54	16	17	7	6

The author describes the various marketing systems that are being used in the South, such as the local marketing of stock on foot, cooperative live-stock shipping associations, Tennessee lamb and wool marketing clubs, the cattle-sales system of South Carolina, the marketing of farm-cured meats, the establishment of ice plants to facilitate the storing and marketing of meats, and the public abattoir. He points out that the farmer should study the requirements of the market in order that he may make his offerings in the best form.

Report of the superintendent of the territorial marketing division to the governor of the Territory of Hawaii, for the period ending December 31, 1916, A. T. LONGLEY (*Honolulu: Mercantile Printing Co., Ltd., 1917, pp. 15*).— The author reports the amount of business done by the Hawaii Marketing Division and new work undertaken during the year, and makes recommendations for the expansion of the marketing equipment.

Market distribution of poultry products, E. W. BENJAMIN (*N. Y. Dept. Agr. Bul. 86 (1916), pp. 2380-2386*).—The author outlines methods that may be used in organizing farmers for the sale of their poultry, as gained from his experience with the Poultry Producers Association of Ithaca, N. Y.

Marketing, B. ADAMS (*N. Y. Dept. Agr. Bul. 86 (1916), pp. 2311-2320*).— The author believes that marketing of farm products could be carried on to better advantage by a thorough understanding of the consumer's desires, the standardization of the products, and better organization at the producer's end.

Marketing and farm credits (*Nat. Conf. Marketing and Farm Credits, 4 (1916), pp. XII+546*).—This is the report of the fourth National Conference on Marketing and Farm Credits, held at Chicago, December 4-9, 1916. It contains papers on the subjects of the Federal Farm Loan Act and personal credit land settlement and immigration, marketing of live stock, marketing of grain and cheese, and the organization of agriculture.

Suggestions from America for cooperative selling, A. W. ASHBY (*Jour. Bd. Agr. [London], 22 (1915), No. 3, pp. 201-210, pl. 1, figs. 2*).—The author discusses the marketing organizations, and packing, marking, use of brand, and advertising as practiced by the various agricultural organizations in the United States.

The organization and management of a farmers' mutual fire insurance company, V. N. VALGREN (*U. S. Dept. Agr. Bul. 530 (1917), pp. 34, fig. 2*).— The author discusses the ideal purpose of such a company, the business territory, the membership and voters' privileges, the officers, methods of conducting the inspection, the form and terms of policy, the liability of the company and of the insured, fees and assessments, etc. He also includes model articles of incorporation, and suggestions for organization and business forms.

[Cooperation in Switzerland] (*Pubs. Sec. Paysans Suisses, No. 55 (1916), pp. 95*).—This is the nineteenth annual report of the Swiss Agricultural Society (E. S. R., 33, p. 394).

Monthly crop report (*U. S. Dept. Agr., Mo. Crop Rpt., 3 (1917). No. 5, pp. 37–44*).—This report contains the usual statistical data relating to the summary of farm prices, crop conditions on May 1 for winter wheat, rye, and hay, and the condition of spring pasture, spring plowing, and spring planting, the estimated farm value of important products, and the range of prices of agricultural products at important markets. It also contains special articles regarding the efficiency of agricultural workers in the United States and European countries, yearly summaries of world production of important crops, materials used to make alcoholic liquors in the United States, export of food products, index numbers of prices of meat animals, and index number of the combined price of 10 important crops. There is also a special report on commercial acreage and production of strawberries, the honeybee. crop conditions in California and Florida, production of maple sugar and sirup, beet-sugar production, and the 1916 Louisiana sugar crop, as well as miscellaneous data.

[Trade and commerce in agricultural products in Chicago, 1916] (*Ann. Rpt. Bd. Trade Chicago, 59 (1916), pp. XXXV+194+141*).—This report continues data previously noted (E. S. R., 35, p. 497), adding data for the following year.

The agricultural output of Great Britain (*London: Bd. Agr. and Fisheries, 1912, pp. 62*).—This is the report made by the Board of Agriculture and Fisheries in connection with the Census of Production Act of 1906. relating to the total output of agricultural land, the number of persons engaged, and the motive power employed. The discussion in this report is amplified by a large number of statistical tables, giving data in detail regarding the items mentioned.

Returns of produce of crops in England and Wales, A. W. ANSTRUTHER (*Bd. Agr. and Fisheries [London], Agr. Statis., 51 (1916), No. 2. pp. 37–59*).— This publication continues data previously noted (E. S. R., 35, p. 893).

Acreage and live stock returns of Scotland, J. M. RAMSAY (*Agr. Statis. Scotland, 4 (1915), pt. 1, pp. 55*).—This report continues data previously noted (E. S. R., 35, p. 497).

[Agricultural statistics of Denmark] (*Statis. Aarbog. Danmark, 21 (1916), pp. 40–62*).—This yearbook contains information along the lines previously noted (E. S. R., 34, p. 792), adding data for the crop year 1916.

AGRICULTURAL EDUCATION.

Agricultural education, A. C. MONAHAN and C. H. LANE (*Rpt. Comr. Ed. [U. S.], 1915–16, I, pp. 237–258*).—This is a review of progress in agricultural instruction in secondary schools; a discussion of the question of the administration of boys' and girls' agricultural club work in the various States, i. e., whether as a function of the State department of education or of the State agricultural college, and if in the college, whether in the department of agricultural extension teaching or in the department of agricultural education; A State System of Agricultural Education, by K. L. Butterfield, previously noted (E. S. R., 36, p. 93); agricultural education at meetings of the year; educational work of the U. S. Department of Agriculture through its States relations Service and the Forest Service; and the principal developments of agricultural education in foreign countries.

According to the report, 2,175 high schools are teaching agriculture to a total of 41,055 boys and girls. Of these schools, 19 were established before 1901, 33 from 1901 to 1905, 413 from 1906 to 1910, and the remainder since 1910. The teaching of agriculture as an informational subject is reported by 1,521 high schools, and as a vocational subject by 506. Of 2,254 persons teaching agriculture, 1,021 have special training in the subject, varying from a four-year agricultural course to a summer course. School land for instructional purposes is used by 392 schools, 337 schools are teaching through the home-project method, 416 give classroom instruction only, and 1,064 give classroom instruction with laboratory exercises and observation of neighboring farms.

There are also 68 special secondary schools supported in whole or in part by the State, with a total cost of maintenance of $766,000, and a total of 416 teachers, and 1,079 elementary and 6,301 secondary pupils. Special schools of agriculture are maintained in connection with ten of the State colleges of agriculture on the college campus, and agricultural courses of secondary grade are given to special students in 20 other State colleges of agriculture.

Rural and agricultural education at the Panama-Pacific International Exposition, H. W. Foght (U. S. Bur. Ed. Bul. 2 (1916), pp. 112, figs. 82).—This bulletin deals with the educational exhibits at the Panama-Pacific Exposition of 1915, which were prepared to indicate recent progress in rural life and education. It discusses (1) government exhibits illustrating the organization and work of the U. S. Bureau of Education, the proposed plan of Federal aid for vocational education, progress in negro education, the promotion of school health, rural school progress by means of miniatures of school grounds and buildings, organization of agricultural education in the United States, and the activities of State agricultural colleges and experiment stations; (2) State educational exhibits, illustrating the improvement of the one-teacher school through standardization and vitalization of school activities by means of industrial club work, the establishment of effective farm community schools by means of school consolidation and organization of rural high schools, and the organization of State wide, State aided agricultural extension work through special schools and special agricultural projects; (3) rural education in the territories and insular possessions; and (4) exhibits of public and private agencies. The exhibit material consisted of mounted graphic charts, maps, photographs, transparencies, samples, specimens, miniature models, publications, stereomotographs, moving pictures, and moving hexagonal cylinders.

Report on the work of the Bureau of Education for the natives of Alaska, 1914-15 (U. S. Bur. Ed. Bul. 47 (1916), pp. 85, pls. 18).—This bulletin contains, among other material, reports by teachers in the public schools under the control of the Federal Government, including notes on instruction in gardening, cooking, sewing, laundering, hygiene, sanitation, etc.

Home economics, HENRIETTA W. CALVIN and CARRIE A. LYFORD (Rpt. Comr. Ed. [U. S.], 1915-16, I, pp. 271-288).—This annual review deals with the importance of home economics in recent educational surveys, home economics instruction in colleges, universities, normal schools, and public schools, the conference of home economics teachers employed in land-grant colleges, cafeterias and lunch rooms, hot lunches in rural schools, practice cottages, home economics in colored schools, home economics associations, and extension teaching.

The authors find that while there has been a steady increase in the number of schools offering instruction in home economics and in the length of courses, the most marked advance has been in the type of course offered, in the standards of instruction that have been established, and in the effort to relate the instruction to home life and conditions. In their opinion, schools of education and systems of city supervision are going to be the most potent factors in the development of educational methods in home economics, while colleges and universities are developing the subject matter in its scientific and economic relationship, strengthening their teacher-training courses, and installing courses for the preparation of extension teachers.

Elementary agricultural instruction, M. B. SMITS (*Teysmannia, 27 (1916), No. 9–10, pp. 524–549*).—The author briefly discusses the organization of agricultural instruction in Holland, Hungary, South Africa, Argentina, Ceylon, German East Africa, the Philippines, and the Dutch East Indies, with suggestions for the improvement of that in the country last named.

Report of the commissioner of industrial and vocational education, E. R. SNYDER (*[Bien] Rpt. Comr. Indus. and Vocational Ed. Cal., 1915–16, pp. 98*).—This report contains statistical data with reference to courses in manual and industrial arts, household arts, commercial training, and agriculture. This includes the date of introduction of the course, its length, and the grades to which it is open, the experience and certification of the teachers, practical work, subjects of instruction, and the character of the course (whether prevocational, preparatory, cultural or disciplinary, vocational, or strictly supplementary to a vocation) in California day high schools, intermediate day schools with a ninth grade, secondary evening schools, elementary city schools with grades above the sixth, and elementary rural schools with six or more teachers. The statistics are discussed, and suggestions and recommendations presented.

Schools of agriculture, mechanic arts, and home making, L. S. HAWKINS (*Univ. State N. Y. Bul. 626 (1916), pp. 27, pls. 5, figs. 6*).—Information is given with reference to the two types of schools of agriculture, mechanic arts, and home making, in New York, including the procedure in organizing them, qualifications of teachers, curriculums and courses of study, summer work for the teacher of agriculture, the use of land (including project work), and rooms and equipment, in accordance with the vocational education law, the text of which is given, and the rules and regulations of the University of the State of New York.

Rural education associations and their activities (*Saskatchewan Dept. Ed., School Agr. Circ. 7 (1917), pp. 16*).—This circular contains a history of the movement, the chief object of which is to arose public interest in rural life generally and agricultural education particularly; suggestions for work of an association, including the organization of boys' and girls' agricultural and home economics clubs, of projects for school garden work and competitions, of boy scout troops and girl guide troops who undertake nature study work, and of school fairs and social service work; a constitution for the organization of an association; and a list of associations, with a summary of their activities. There are at present 40 rural education associations in Saskatchewan.

Some problems in the organization and administration of a department of poultry husbandry at a secondary school of agriculture, L. BANTA (*Jour. Amer. Assoc. Instr. and Invest. Poultry Husb., 3 (1917), No. 6, pp. 41–45*).—The author points out a few of the problems that have come up for solution during a year of instruction in poultry husbandry at a secondary school. They include the task of defining the scope and limitations of this work, the equipment, the extent of experimentation and of elective, specialized courses in addition to the usual fundamental and elementary ones, pedagogical training of college-trained instructors, lack of interest in some localities, lack of sufficient fundamental scientific preparation on the part of students, the pedagogical importance of the lecture and recitation, entrance requirements, practical experience of students, college entrance credit, etc.

How we can attain greater efficiency in laboratory instruction? R. F. Irvin (*Jour. Amer. Assoc. Instr. and Invest. Poultry Husb., 3 (1917), No. 6, pp. 45–47*).—In discussing the problems involved in laboratory instruction in poultry husbandry in the college, the author suggests that each course should first be outlined in syllabus form, lecture, recitation, and laboratory exercises being correlated. This should be followed by a standard laboratory plan or laboratory exercise sheet, which should include as essential features the title of the exercise, object of the exercise, apparatus and equipment needed, method of procedure, leading questions, and conclusions. It is claimed that laboratory instruction on such an organized basis would enable the instructor to utilize every minute of the laboratory period to the best advantage. Suggested outlines are given of model laboratory sheets on a study of the 60-hour embryo and the sticking and dry picking of market poultry.

Gardening in elementary city schools, C. D. Jarvis (*U. S. Bur. Ed. Bul. 40 (1916), pp. 74, pls. 3, figs. 4*).—In this bulletin the author attempts to show briefly how productive gardening contributes to the needs of the school, as in democratizing education, supplying a long-felt need in vocational guidance and a substitute for hurtful child labor, developing thrift and industry, furnishing recreation, improving health and morals, uniting the home and the school, etc. He discusses the kinds of gardens, their control, instruction, supervision, and financing, and outlines a suggestive program for the promotion of gardening by schools employing the home garden method in its broadest sense. This includes gardening on the school grounds where it forms a part of the home garden system and where the individual plats are regarded as home gardens or independent projects. The program includes a preliminary survey, procuring land, the selection of crops, planning the garden, outside and classroom instruction, disposing of the crop, keeping records, and means of arousing and maintaining interest.

A course in nature study and agriculture, W. T. Skilling (*Bul. State Normal School, San Diego, Cal., 3 (1915), No. 3, pp. 8*).—This is an outline of the course in nature study and agriculture, with suggestions for work in the model and training school, of the State Normal School at San Diego, Cal.

Courses in secondary agriculture for southern schools (first and second years), H. P. Barrows (*U. S. Dept. Agr. Bul. 521 (1917), pp. 53*).—These outlines, covering work in agriculture for the first two years of a 4-year course, have been prepared to meet a demand for a more uniform standard in agicultural instruction in secondary schools in the South. They are based on work in nature study and a general course in elementary agriculture in the graded or rural school. The outline for the first year covers lessons and practical exercises in soils and field crops, and for the second year, lessons and practicums in animal husbandry. Suggestions for home projects, equipment, distribution of time and credit, etc., and lists of texts and references are included.

Suggested experiments in elementary plant physiology, L. H. Pennington (*Syracuse Univ. [Pubs.], 17 (1917), No. 30, pp. 46*).—This is a series of laboratory experiments and exercises to illustrate the fundamental scientific facts and theories underlying elementary plant physiology, arranged especially for students in forestry at the New York State College of Forestry.

Farm spies, A. F. Conradi and W. A. Thomas (*New York: The Macmillan Co., 1916, pp. XI+165, figs. 67*).—This book deals with the facts concerning the life history and habits of the boll weevil, the black billbug and budworm of corn, the black corn weevil, grasshoppers, chinch bugs, the cotton root louse, and the larger cornstalk borer, and methods of controlling them. It is written in story form for boys and girls.

Food study, MABEL T. WELLMAN (*Boston: Little, Brown and Co., 1917, pp. XXIV+324, pls. 8, figs. 38*).—This text in home economics for high schools consists of a study of the principles involved in cooking, the economic and dietary value of foodstuffs, their care and preservation, the origin of various food plants, and the manufacture of food products. The instruction given from an inductive standpoint consists of classroom cooking and experiments. Food requirements for adults, tables of height and weight and of fuel values, and a list of supplementary laboratory lessons are appended.

Illustrated lecture on practical improvement of farm grounds, F. L. MULFORD and H. M. CONOLLY (*U. S. Dept. Agr., States Relat. Serv. Syllabus 28 (1917), pp. 13*).—Suggestions are given with reference to the location, exposure, and type of house; location of barns; the size, arrangement, and care of grounds; walks and drives; entrances; the lawn; plan of the grounds; and where, what, when, and how to plant, and cost of planting, in order to make the farm-home grounds attractive and interesting. A list of 51 lantern slides to illustrate the syllabus and a brief list of references to literature on the subject are appended.

MISCELLANEOUS.

Abstracts of papers not included in bulletins, finances, metereology, index (*Maine Sta. Bul. 257 (1916), pp. 343-367+XII*).—This contains the organization list of the station; abstracts of 6 papers published elsewhere and previously noted, and abstracts of 3 papers noted elsewhere in this issue; meteorological observations noted on page 314; a financial statement for the fiscal year ended June 30, 1916; an index to Bulletins 246 to 257, inclusive, which collectively constitute the thirty-second report of the station; and announcements as to the work, publications, and equipment of the station.

Director's report for 1916, W. H. JORDAN (*New York State Sta. Bul. 428 (1916), pp. 529-558*).—This contains the organization list and a review of the work and publications of the station during the year.

Twenty-sixth Annual Report of Wyoming Station, 1916 (*Wyoming Sta. Rpt. 1916, pp. 61-100*).—This contains the organization list, a financial statement for the fiscal year ended June 30, 1916, reports of the acting director and heads of departments, of which that of the parasitologist is abstracted on page 374 of this issue, and meteorological observations noted on page 314.

Monthly Bulletin of the Ohio Experiment Station (*Mo. Bul. Ohio Sta., 2 (1917), No. 5, pp. 137-171, figs. 11*).—This contains several articles abstracted elsewhere in this issue, together with the following: The Soy-bean crop, by C. G. Williams, adapted from Bulletin 312 (E. S. R., 37, p. 235); The Lesser Peach Tree Borer, by J. L. King, an abstract of Bulletin 307 (E. S. R., 37, p. 159); More Corn to the Acre, by C. E. Thorne; and Notes.

NOTES.

Delaware College and Station.—Wolf Hall, the new $280,000 building which will house all the activities of the agricultural department and temporarily the college departments of chemistry and biology, is practically completed and will be occupied in September.

Frank A. Hays, Ph. D. (Iowa State College, 1917), has been appointed assistant professor of animal husbandry. Mark L. Nichols, assistant professor of agronomy and assistant agronomist, and Raymond R. Pailthorp, assistant professor of horticulture and assistant horticulturist, have been transferred entirely from station to college work.

Idaho University and Station.—Appropriations made by the last legislature for the station for the present biennium are as follows: For the further study of insect pests troublesome to alfalfa and clover seed producers, $4,000; for emergency calls in the investigation of plant diseases, insect pests, and soil troubles, $1,200; for soil survey work in cooperation with the Bureau of Soils, U. S. Department of Agriculture, $1,200; for the erection of additional greenhouses, $4,500; and for tile-draining a portion of the university farm and fencing the farm, $2,500. In addition, the Aberdeen substation received $5,000, that at Caldwell $7,800, and that at Sandpoint $5,000.

The segregation of 160 acres of State lands was authorized for use in a study of problems concerned with high altitude agriculture. A substation, to be known as the high altitude substation, is to be established in a region whose altitude is 6,000 feet or more. An appropriation of $3,500 is made for the biennium, and the citizens of the community in which it is located are obligated to raise a amount for the erection of buildings.

The irrigation work of the station has been transferred from Gooding to Caldwell. This transfer was made necessary by the approaching expiration of the lease under which the Gooding substation has been operated since 1909, and the resignation of Superintendent J. S. Welch, who is now connected with the Maori Agricultural College of New Zealand.

From a State appropriation made for the erection of new buildings at the university, the State Board of Education has authorized the use of $25,000 for the erection of a new horse barn, hog and sheep barns, and a seed house. The completion of the south wing of the university administration building and the erection of an annex to the engineering building have also been authorized.

Dr. Ernest H. Lindley, professor of philosophy at the University of Indiana since 1902, has been appointed president, succeeding Dr. M. A. Brannon, who became president of Beloit College on July 1. Dr. C. H. Shattuck, professor of forestry and forester, resigned June 30. Dr. A. R. Hahner, instructor in veterinary science, resigned last April and has been succeeded temporarily by Dr. H. C. Luce. Other appointments include H. W. Hulbert as instructor and assistant in farm crops, and A. C. Baltzer as instructor in dairy husbandry and assistant dairy husbandman.

397

New members of the governing board include William Healy of Boise, J. A. Lippincott of Idaho City, and J. A. Keefer of Shoshone.

Kentucky University and Station.—Dr. Robert Graham, professor of veterinary science and head of the department of diseases of live stock in the station, has been appointed professor of animal pathology and chief of animal pathology in the Illinois University and Station. Dr. C. D. Bohannan, associate professor of agricultural economics, R. C. Dabney, connected with the inspection of bakery sanitation, R. B. Taylor, assistant chemist in the fertilizer department, and J. T. Milligan, in charge of the egg laying contest, have resigned.

Minnesota University and Station.—A modern structure is to replace in the near future the old stock barn which was recently burned. This building will be of reinforced concrete and hollow tile, with the upper portion of frame and stucco. A new seed house is also to be erected.

R. W. Thatcher has been appointed dean of the department of agriculture and director of the station. Dr. E. M. Freeman has been appointed dean of the college of agriculture within the department.

Dr. R. A. Gortner, associate professor of biochemistry, has been appointed professor in this subject and chief of the division in the college and station. R. A. Dutcher, assistant professor of agricultural chemistry at the Oregon College, and C. A. Morrow, professor of chemistry in the Nebraska Wesleyan University, have been appointed assistant professors of agricultural biochemistry, effective September 15. S. D. Wilkins and V. C. Crowl have been appointed assistants in the division of animal nutrition; A. J. Wuertz, assistant in agricultural biochemistry, and J. E. Chapman, assistant in soils.

C. W. Howard, associate professor of economic entomology and assistant entomologist, has resigned to become professor of biology in Canton Christian College, China. W. F. Lusk, assistant professor of agricultural education, has accepted a similar appointment in Cornell University, and John Parker a position in agronomy in the Kansas College. Miss Ferne Peck, instructor in agricultural botany and seed analyst, has been appointed State seed analyst in Nebraska, and has been succeeded by A. H. Larson.

Leave of absence for six months has been granted to Miss Josephine T. Berry, chief of the division of home economics, to become assistant director of vocational education and director of home economics work with the Federal Vocational Education Board, and for one year to Miss Grace I. Williams, assistant professor of home economics, for graduate study. Miss Anna E. Bayha and Miss Olive N. Tuttle have resigned as instructors in home economics.

W. L. Oswald, assistant professor of agricultural botany and assistant botanist and plant pathologist, has accepted an appointment with the Bureau of Markets of the U. S. Department of Agriculture to assist in a survey of the seed situation. Francis Jager, chief of the division of apiculture, has been appointed a member of the Red Cross mission to Serbia. Miss Alice McFeely has been appointed assistant editor of station bulletins.

At Crookston, T. R. Sewall, superintendent of buildings and grounds, and Mrs. T. R. Sewall, instructor in domestic science, resigned July 31. Miss Hazel Rockwood, a 1917 graduate of the college, has been appointed instructor in home economics, and A. M. Folker instructor in farm engineering and superintendent of buildings and grounds.

Missouri University and Station.—A new position has been established in the extension work, known as the woman county home demonstration agent. Demonstrations are to be conducted cooperatively by the agricultural extension service, the U. S. Department of Agriculture, and the county. Each county is required to appropriate not less than $500 for the support of the agent, while the university will contribute not more than $750 a year for salary and maintenance.

Leaves of absence have been granted Howard Hackedorn, assistant professor of animal husbandry, and C. R. Moulton, assistant professor of agricultural chemistry, for a year's graduate work, and to E. M. McDonald, assistant professor of farm crops, who has entered a reserve officers' training camp. Resignations have been accepted of Roy Hastings, assistant in agricultural extension; Thomas M. Olson, agricultural agent for Butler County; Chester Pollock, dairy cattle herdsman; Walter E. Thrun, assistant in agricultural chemistry; and Willis B. Combs, assistant in dairy husbandry.

Recent appointments include the following: Carl Marsh, dairy cattle herdsman; J. A. Machliss, assistant in soil survey; L. W. Morley, assistant in dairy husbandry; Paul M. Robinett, assistant in horticulture; Sarah Pettit, superintendent of women's county home demonstration work; Edward A. Livesay, assistant county agent leader; John T. Stinson, assistant in agricultural extension; E. Roy Keller, assistant in boys' and girls' club work; Mary E. Robinson, extension instructor in home economics; and Dr. F. W. Caldwell, extension assistant professor of veterinary science.

North Dakota College.—H. L. White, professor of physiological chemistry and toxicology, has been appointed professor of biological chemistry in the college of physicians and surgeons of the University of Southern California.

Oklahoma College and Station.—The station has recently completed a modern two-story grain storage house. The upper story will be used for laboratory work in plant breeding, seed selection, etc. The lower floor has six rooms, three of them designed for storage rooms for small grains and equipped with special appliances for fumigation, and the remainder are designed for a general receiving and work room, a machine room for the graders, ginners, etc., and a general storage room, respectively.

The station reports the resignation of Dr. C. K. Francis, chemist, B. A. Ahrens, poultry husbandman and head of the poultry department, Henry L. Thomson, head of the farm engineering department, and W. L. Fowler, animal husbandman and head of the animal husbandry department. Harry Embleton has been appointed professor of poultry husbandry and poultryman, and Dr. Wallace Macfarlane has been transferred from assistant agronomist to station chemist. Dr. L. L. Lewis, veterinarian and bacteriologist of the station and dean of the veterinary school, has been granted six months' leave of absence on account of ill health.

Oregon College and Station.—Roy R. Graves, professor of dairying and dairyman, has resigned to accept a position with the Dairy Division of the U. S. Department of Agriculture. A. F. Kerr, of the Forest Service, has been appointed instructor of forestry. O. D. Center, director of extension of the University of Idaho, has been appointed director of extension to succeed R. D. Hetzel, whose resignation has been previously noted.

Wyoming University.—Dr. Aven Nelson, professor of botany, has been appointed acting president.

Federal Food Control Act.—This elaborate war measure was signed by President Wilson, August 10. Its object is expressed in the opening section as " to assure an adequate supply and equitable distribution, and to facilitate the movement, of foods, feeds, fuel including fuel oil and natural gas, and fertilizer and fertilizer ingredients, tools, utensils, implements, machinery, and equipment required for the actual production of foods, feeds, and fuel, hereafter in this act called necessaries; to prevent, locally or generally, scarcity, monopolization, hoarding, injurious speculation, manipulations, and private controls, affecting such supply, distribution, and movement; and to establish and maintain governmental control of such necessaries during the war."

The act confers greatly extended powers upon the President during the existence of a state of war and imposes drastic penalities for violation of its provisions. Many of these powers deal with the control and distribution of food as well as a number of other commodities. In administering the act, the President is authorized to use any Department or agency of the Government, as well as to establish and work with other agencies. The enforcement of the provisions relating to the control and distribution of foods has been entrusted by him to Herbert Hoover, appointed Food Administrator.

Among practices specifically prohibited in the act are the wilful destruction of necessaries for the purpose of enhancing the price or restricting the supply, conspiring to restrict their production or manufacture for the same purposes, and to hold or attempt to monopolize necessaries as defined in the act. A system of licensing various operations is authorized when deemed essential, and the President under certain conditions may seize factories, packinghouses, or other plants and operate them. He may requisition foods, feeds, fuels, and other supplies needed by the Army or Navy, and may purchase, store, and sell to the public wheat, flour, meal, beans, and potatoes, as well as procure nitrate of soda to sell at cost if the emergency requires it and it is possible to secure the material. In an emergency requiring stimulation of wheat production, he may fix a minimum guarantied price. For the crop of 1918 this guaranty is made absolute until May 1, 1919, and is fixed at not less than $2.00 per bushel for No. 1 northern spring wheat or its equivalent at the principal interior markets.

The use of foods, fruits, food materials, or feeds for the production of distilled spirits for beverage purposes is prohibited after September 8, 1917. The President is also empowered to restrict or prohibit the use of these materials for the production of malt or vinous liquors if deemed essential to the food supply or the national security and defense.

An appropriation of $152,500,000 is provided for the enforcement of the act, with $10,000,000 additional for the purchase of nitrate of soda.

Food Training Camps at Agricultural Fairs.—A recent article in *Breeder's Gazette* outlines plans adopted by the American Association of Fairs and Expositions for cooperating with the Government in conserving the food supply through emergency food conservation exhibits and demonstrations. These plans include the use of standardized exhibits dealing especially with wheat substitutes, the conservation of fats and milk, and the home canning, drying, etc., of fruits and vegetables. The boys' and girls' clubs are expected to furnish demonstrations of these and other desirable practices, and the U. S. Department of Agriculture, the Food Administration, and the Council of National Defense are among the many agencies actively cooperating.

O

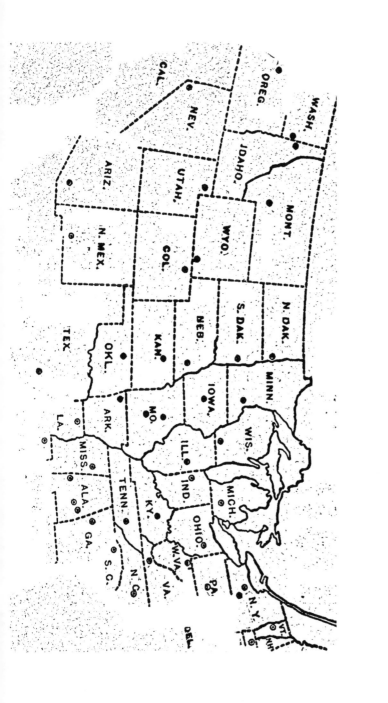

U. S. DEPARTMENT OF AGRICULTURE
STATES RELATIONS SERVICE
A. C. TRUE, DIRECTOR

Vol. 37   OCTOBER, 1917   No. 5

EXPERIMENT STATION RECORD

WASHINGTON
GOVERNMENT PRINTING OFFICE
1917

U. S. DEPARTMENT OF AGRICULTURE.

Scientific Bureaus.

WEATHER BUREAU—C. F. Marvin, *Chief.*
BUREAU OF ANIMAL INDUSTRY—A. D. Melvin, *Chief.*
BUREAU OF PLANT INDUSTRY—W. A. Taylor, *Chief.*
FOREST SERVICE—H. S. Graves, *Forester.*
BUREAU OF SOILS—Milton Whitney, *Chief.*
BUREAU OF CHEMISTRY—C. L. Alsberg, *Chief.*
BUREAU OF CROP ESTIMATES—L. M. Estabrook, *Statistician.*
BUREAU OF ENTOMOLOGY—L. O. Howard, *Entomologist.*
BUREAU OF BIOLOGICAL SURVEY—E. W. Nelson, *Chief.*
OFFICE OF PUBLIC ROADS AND RURAL ENGINEERING—L. W. Page, *Director.*
BUREAU OF MARKETS—C. J. Brand, *Chief.*

STATES RELATIONS SERVICE—A. C. True, *Director.*
OFFICE OF EXPERIMENT STATIONS—E. W. Allen, *Chief.*

THE AGRICULTURAL EXPERIMENT STATIONS.

ALABAMA—
  College Station: *Auburn;* J. F. Duggar.[1]
  Canebrake Station: *Uniontown;* F. R. Curtis.[1]
  Tuskegee Station: *Tuskegee Institute;* G. W. Carver.[1]
ALASKA—*Sitka:* C. C. Georgeson.[2]
ARIZONA—*Tucson:* R. H. Forbes.[1]
ARKANSAS—*Fayetteville:* M. Nelson.[1]
CALIFORNIA—*Berkeley:* T. F. Hunt.[1]
COLORADO—*Fort Collins:* C. P. Gillette.[1]
CONNECTICUT—
  State Station: *New Haven;* } E. H. Jenkins.[1]
  Storrs Station: *Storrs;* }
DELAWARE—*Newark:* H. Hayward.[1]
FLORIDA—*Gainesville:* P. H. Rolfs.[1]
GEORGIA—*Experiment:* J. D. Price.[1]
GUAM—*Island of Guam:* C. W. Edwards.[4]
HAWAII—
  Federal Station: *Honolulu;* J. M. Westgate.[2]
  Sugar Planters' Station: *Honolulu;* H. P. Agee.[1]
IDAHO—*Moscow:* J. S. Jones.[1]
ILLINOIS—*Urbana:* E. Davenport.[1]
INDIANA—*Lafayette:* C. G. Woodbury.[1]
IOWA—*Ames:* C. F. Curtiss.[1]
KANSAS—*Manhattan:* W. M. Jardine.[1]
KENTUCKY—*Lexington:* A. M. Peter.[4]
LOUISIANA—
  State Station: *Baton Rouge;* }
  Sugar Station: *Audubon Park,* } W. R. Dodson.[1]
    New Orleans; }
  North La. Station: *Calhoun;* }
MAINE—*Orono:* C. D. Woods.[1]
MARYLAND—*College Park:* H. J. Patterson.[1]
MASSACHUSETTS—*Amherst:* W. P. Brooks.[1]
MICHIGAN—*East Lansing:* R. S. Shaw.[1]
MINNESOTA—*University Farm, St. Paul:* R. W. Thatcher.[1]
MISSISSIPPI—*Agricultural College:* E. R. Lloyd.[1]

MISSOURI—
  College Station: *Columbia;* F. B. Mumford.[1]
  Fruit Station: *Mountain Grove;* Paul Evans.[1]
MONTANA—*Bozeman:* F. B. Linfield.[1]
NEBRASKA—*Lincoln:* E. A. Burnett.[1]
NEVADA—*Reno:* S. B. Doten.[1]
NEW HAMPSHIRE—*Durham:* J. C. Kendall.[1]
NEW JERSEY—*New Brunswick:* J. G. Lipman.[1]
NEW MEXICO—*State College:* Fabian Garcia.[1]
NEW YORK—
  State Station: *Geneva;* W. H. Jordan.[1]
  Cornell Station: *Ithaca;* A. R. Mann.[1]
NORTH CAROLINA—
  College Station: *West Raleigh;* } B. W. Kilgore.[1]
  State Station: *Raleigh;* }
NORTH DAKOTA—*Agricultural College:* T. P. Cooper.[1]
OHIO—*Wooster:* C. E. Thorne.[1]
OKLAHOMA—*Stillwater:* W. L. Carlyle.[1]
OREGON—*Corvallis:* A. B. Cordley.[1]
PENNSYLVANIA—
  State College: R. L. Watts.[1]
  State College: Institute of Animal Nutrition; H. P. Armsby.[1]
PORTO RICO—*Mayaguez;* D. W. May.[2]
RHODE ISLAND—*Kingston:* B. L. Hartwell.[1]
SOUTH CAROLINA—*Clemson College:* H. W. Barre.[1]
SOUTH DAKOTA—*Brookings:* J. W. Wilson.[1]
TENNESSEE—*Knoxville:* H. A. Morgan.[1]
TEXAS—*College Station:* B. Youngblood.[1]
UTAH—*Logan:* F. S. Harris.[1]
VERMONT—*Burlington:* J. L. Hills.[1]
VIRGINIA—
  Blacksburg: A. W. Drinkard, jr.[1]
  Norfolk: Truck Station; T. C. Johnson.[1]
WASHINGTON—*Pullman:* Geo. Severance.[1]
WEST VIRGINIA—*Morgantown:* J. L. Coulter.[1]
WISCONSIN—*Madison:* H. L. Russell.[1]
WYOMING—*Laramie:* H. G. Knight.[1]

[1] *Director.* [2] *Agronomist in charge.* [3] *Animal husbandman in charge.* [4] *Acting director.*

EXPERIMENT STATION RECORD.

Editor: E. W. ALLEN, Ph. D., *Chief, Office of Experiment Stations.*
Assistant Editor: H. L. KNIGHT.

EDITORIAL DEPARTMENTS.

Agricultural Chemistry and Agrotechny—E. H. NOLLAU.
Meteorology, Soils, and Fertilizers{W. H. BEAL.
                                     {R. W. TRULLINGER.
Agricultural Botany, Bacteriology, and Plant Patholog {W. H. EVANS, Ph. D.
                                                       {W. E. BOYD.
Field Crops{J. I. SCHULTE.
           {J. D. LUCKETT.
Horticulture and Forestry—E. J. GLASSON.
Economic Zoology and Entomology—W. A. HOOKER, D. V. M.
Foods and Human Nutrition{C. F. LANGWORTHY, Ph. D., D. Sc.
                          {H. L. LANG.
Zootechny, Dairying, and Dairy Farming{M. D. MOORE.
Veterinary Medicine{W. A. HOOKER.
                    {E. H. NOLLAU.
Rural Engineering—R. W. TRULLINGER.
Rural Economics—E. MERRITT.
Agricultural Education{C. H. LANE.
                       {M. T. SPETHMANN.
Indexes—M. D. MOORE.

CONTENTS OF VOL. 37, NO. 5.

Page.
Editorial notes:
  Research and the research worker in relation to National affairs........ 401
  The development of American technical agricultural journals........... 405
Recent work in agricultural science... 409
Notes... 496

SUBJECT LIST OF ABSTRACTS.

AGRICULTURAL CHEMISTRY—AGROTECHNY.

Annual reports on progress of chemistry for 1916, edited by Cain et al........ 409
Pervaporation, perstillation, and percrystallization, Kober................... 409
On the quinone-phenolate theory of indicators, White and Acree.............. 409
Reducing matter extractable from filter paper, McBride and Scherrer......... 409
Preparation of hydrochloroplatinic acid, Rudnick and Cooke............... 409
The arsenates of lead.—III, Basic arsenates, McDonnell and Smith........... 410
Indirect measurements of rotatory powers of sugars, Hudson and Yanovsky... 410
The preparation of beta glucose, Mangam and Acree......................... 410
The preparation of xylose, Hudson and Harding............................. 410
On the cleavage in starch grains, Reuss................................... 410
Determination of gelatinization temperatures of starches, Dox and Roark, jr.... 410
Inflammability of carbonaceous dusts, Brown and Clement................... 410
Hydrolysis of the soluble protein of Swede turnips, Williams 410

Page.
Experimental investigations of the plum, II, Feruglio and Bernardis..........   410
Tobacco seed oil, Cohen...   411
The oleoresin of Douglas fir, Schorger................................   411
The oxidase of *Rhus diversiloba*, McNair.............................   411
Achroodextrinase, Effront...   411
The chemical nature of the vitamins, III, Williams....................   411
Titration of magnesium, Bruckmiller...................................   412
A study of the volumetric or Pemberton method for phosphoric acid, Shuey....   412
Determination of ammonium sulphate, Schouten-Ilcken and Tuinzing.......   412
Determination of nitrogen in lime nitrogen, Berkhout et al.............   413
The Duclaux method for estimation of volatile fatty acids, Upson et al........   413
A note on the Duclaux method for volatile fatty acids, Lamb..............   413
The Duclaux method, Boekhout and De Vries.............................   414
The systematic extraction of aqueous solutions with ether, Pinnow........   414
Determination of added water in meats and sausages, Baumann and Grossfeld..   414
The alkalinity of cocoa, Arpin..   414
The determination of the alkalinity of cocoa, Rocques.................   414
Moisture determination in spices and similar products, Scholl and Strohecker..   414
Determination of ammonia in wine and its significance, Baragiola and Godet...   414
The determination of ammonia in wine, Baragiola and Schuppli..........   415
A method for the examination of methyl salicylate, Albright...........   415
A study of certain ferments.—I, Reductases, Lee and Mellon............   415
Characteristic milk powder forms, Griebel............................   415
The method for the determination of fat in cheese, Brodrick-Pittard..........   416
The microscopic examination of colza and rape seed cake, Ezendam..........   416
The chemical examination of rape seed press cake, van Kampen..............   416
Cider and the cider industry in England, Warcollier et al.................   416
Washing fruits and vegetables, Bitting...............................   416
Beet molasses: Its composition and utilization, Osborn..................   416
Preparation of acid coagulants, and their effect on rubber, Eaton and Whitby.   416
Notes on the rubber from *Eucommia ulmoides*, Sievers..................   417
The artificial drying of tobacco, De Vries...........................   417

METEOROLOGY.

A new system of weather prediction, Paresce..............................   417
Normal anomalies of the mean annual temperature variation, Arctowski......   417
Effect of short period variations of solar radiation on atmosphere, Clayton.....   417
The influence of intense and prolonged cannonading on rainfall, Deslandres...   418
Does violent cannonading induce rainfall? Sebert.......................   418
Influence of climatic conditions on composition of plant oils, Pigulevski......   418
The past winter, Harding..   418

SOILS—FERTILIZERS.

Soil moisture and plant succession, Fuller................................   418
Evaporation and soil moisture in forests and cultivated fields, Groves.........   418
Tobacco soils and the tobaccos grown thereon, Cohen......................   419
Soil survey of Cowley County, Kansas, Hall and Tillman...................   419
Mecklenburg County soils, agriculture, and industries, Williams et al..........   419
Lime requirements of some acid soils, Conner............................   420
Study of soil containing residual limestone, Noyes.......................   420
Character of soils in area devastated by Soufrière of St. Vincent, Tempany.....   420
The "gall patches" in Antigua soils, Tempany............................   421
Sterilization and fatigue of soil......................................   421
Influence of crop, season, and water on bacterial activities, Greaves et al......   421
The behavior of legume bacteria in acid and alkaline media, Salter..........   422
Effect of decomposing organic matter on certain constituents of soil, Jensen....   422
Conversion of soluble into insoluble phosphoric acid in the soil, Skalkij......   423
The gases of swamp rice soils, IV, Harrison and Subramania Aiyer............   424
Maintaining the nitrogen supply of the soil, Blair.......................   425
Fertilizers and increased production, Shutt.............................   425
Is the recovery of the nitrogen in sewage sludge practicable? Copeland......   425
Report on humogen, Russell..   426
Grape cake as a fertilizer, Roos.......................................   426
Comparison of four nitrogenous materials, Bonomi and Margreth.............   426

Page.

The action of superphosphate in tests in 1913, Geerts......................... 426
The extraction of potash from silicate rocks, II, Ross......................... 427
Potash from Canadian feldspar, Benham................................... 427
Report on wood and plant ashes as a source of potash, Berry.................. 427
[Liming and manurial experiments]...................................... 427
The effect of fineness of division of pulverized limestone, Kopeloff............ 428
Limestones of Michigan, Smith.. 428
Agricultural lime, Miller and Krusekopf................................... 428
Tabulated analyses of agricultural lime................................... 428
Inspection of commercial fertilizers, 1916, Trowbridge...................... 428
[Commercial fertilizer analyses]... 429
Fertilizer registrations for 1917, Cathcart................................ 429

AGRICULTURAL BOTANY.

Periodicity in transpiration, Wilkie....................................... 429
Comparison of the hourly evaporation rate of atmometers and free water surfaces
    with the transpiration rate of *Medicago sativa*, Briggs and Shantz.......... 429
Oxidase activity of plant juices and hydrogen ion concentrations, Bunzel..... 429
Evidence of action of oxidases within the growing plant, Kastle and Buckner.. 430
Occurrence and significance of flavone derivatives in plants, Shibata et al..... 430
The acidity of plant cells as shown by natural indicators, Haas............... 430
Germination of seeds of *Lepidium sativum* in solutions of electrolytes, Lesage. 431
The influence of different media on the histology of roots, Wilkie............. 431
The permeability of living cells to acids and alkalies, Haas.................. 431
Salt antagonism in gelatin, Fenn... 431
Similarity in the behavior of protoplasm and gelatin, Fenn.................. 431
Tolerance of fresh water by marine plants, Osterhout........................ 431
Copper in the flora of a copper-tailing region, Bateman and Wells............. 432
Models to illustrate segregation and combination, Chibber.................. 432
The probable error of a Mendelian class frequency, Pearl.................... 432
Note on the inheritance of crossability, Backhouse......................... 432
The results of hybridization in Salix, Ikeno............................... 432
Evolution by means of hybridization, Lotsy................................ 432
The bearing of some general biological facts on bud variation, East........... 433
Mendelian factor difference *v*. reaction system contrasts, Goodspeed and Clausen. 433
Œnothera mutants with diminutive chromosomes, Lutz...................... 433
Root cuttings, chimeras, and sports, Bateson.............................. 434
Faciation in *Pharbitis hederacea*, Yamaguchi............................. 434
Plant succession.—An analysis of the development of vegetation, Clements... 434
Polar bear cacti, Cook.. 434
Vegetation of the *Pinus tæda* belt of Virginia and the Carolinas, Harper....... 435
Meadow vegetation in the montane region of northern Colorado, Reed........ 435
Taxonomic botany and the Washington botanist, Hitchcock.................. 435

FIELD CROPS.

Forage and root crops, Knight... 435
Field crops for late planting, Knight...................................... 436
[Field crops]... 436
[Field crops], Nobbs.. 436
[Field experiments], De Jong and van Rossem............................. 436
[Field crops]... 436
[Registration of varieties], Montgomery, Williams, and Hayes............... 437
[Field crops]... 437
[Field crops]... 437
Dry farming in Colorado, Kezer... 437
Grasses under drought conditions at Hawkesbury Agricultural College, Kerle.. 437
Artificial reseeding of range lands, Sampson.............................. 437
Cereal experiments, Tonnelier... 438
Seed grain inspection and crop reports, 1915–16, Garland.................... 438
Some effects of legumes on associated nonlegumes, Evans................... 438
Soy beans and cowpeas in Illinois, Burlison and Allyn...................... 438
The dry-matter content of field-cured and green forage, Arny............... 439
Alfalfa in Kansas, Doyle et al... 439
[Alfalfa], Graber and Johnson... 440

Page.

Bermuda grass, Tracy... 440
Irrigation and manuring studies.—II, Effect on corn, Harris and Pittman..... 440
Cotton production and distribution, 1915–16............................... 441
Cotton in Brazil, Coelho de Souza.. 441
Cotton varieties in Brazil, Green.. 441
Third report on the improvement of indigo in Bihar, Howard................. 441
Peanut growing in the cotton belt, Thompson............................... 442
Home potato patches, Knight.. 442
Potato growing in Wisconsin, Milward....................................... 442
Rice growing in New South Wales.. 442
Soy beans, Schmitz... 442
Some recent investigations in sugar beet breeding, Pritchard.............. 442
Fundamentals of sugar beet culture under California conditions, Adams...... 443
Russian sugar beet seed, Palmer.. 443
[Sugar cane varieties], Jeswiet.. 443
Notes on fallowing in sugar cane cultivation, Ledeboer.................... 443
Lodging in sugar cane, and its prevention, Douglas......................... 443
Lodging in sugar cane and its prevention, Houtman......................... 444
[Sugar cane].. 444
The relation of applied science to sugar production in Hawaii, Agee et al..... 444
Sweet clover: Utilization, Coe... 444
[Tobacco], Argerio... 445
Tobacco culture in Albania, Baldacci....................................... 445
Velvet beans: How to grow and use, Williams............................... 445
Spring wheats, Biffen.. 445
A new hybrid yellow wheat, Gaudot.. 445
On growing two white-straw crops in succession, Russell................... 445
Agriculture and the wheat supply, Russell.................................. 445
The wheats of Baluchistan, Khorassan, and the Kurram Valley, Howard..... 446
Third annual seed laboratory report, 1915–16, Oswald...................... 446
Seed impurities, Cockayne.. 446
Weeds on arable land and their suppression, Brenchley..................... 446
Weed control with pulverized kainit, Lindeman............................. 446

HORTICULTURE.

The persistence of lawn and other grasses, Hartwell and Damon............. 446
The small vegetable garden... 447
Small fruit culture in California, Hendrickson............................. 447
Spraying experiments in Nebraska, Cooper.................................. 447
Five years' investigations in apple thinning, Auchter..................... 448
Inheritance of sex in *Vitis rotundifolia*, Detjen........................ 449
Breeding southern grapes, Detjen... 449
The use of commercial fertilizers in growing roses, Muncie................ 449

FORESTRY.

Proceedings of the Southern Forestry Congress, 1916........................ 450
Tree growth and climate in the United States, Woodward.................... 450
Laws of tall-tree growth investigated mathematically, Bohannan............ 450
The problem of making volume tables for use on the National Forests, Munger 450
Site determination, classification, and application, Watson................ 450
Volume of western yellow pine logs from an actual mill tally, Berry........ 451
The Swiss method of regulating the cut in practice, Guise................. 451
Effect of depth of covering seed on germination and quality of stock, Show... 451
A study of reforested chestnut cut-over land, Richards.................... 451
Forest succession in the central Rocky Mountains, Bates................... 451
The woodlot, Scott... 451
Suggestions for owners of woodlots in New England, Mosher and Clement..... 451
Tree planting needed in Texas, Foster and Krausz.......................... 452
Report of committee on forestry, Thurston et al........................... 452
Douglas fir shipbuilding, Oakleaf.. 452
Brazilian woods: Their utilization for the manufacture of wood pulp........ 452
The purchase of pulpwood.—Some suggestions, Winslow and Thelen........... 452

DISEASES OF PLANTS.

Page.

Fungus and bacterial diseases, Nowell.. 452
Annual report of the mycologist for the year 1913-14, Dowson................ 453
Annual report of the mycologist for the year ending March 31, 1915, Dowson.. 453
The treatment of fungus diseases by spraying, Salmon and Eyre............... 453
Control of root knot by calcium cyanamid and other means, Watsou.......... 453
Rosellinia root diseases in the Lesser Antilles, Nowell...................... 454
Observations on a new disease in cotton, Patel.............................. 454
Studies on clubroot of cruciferous plants, Chupp.........................·... 454
Bitter pit investigation, McAlpine... 455
Xylaria root rot of apple, Wolf and Cromwell............................... 456
[Brown rot of plum and apple].. 457
Further studies of the orange rusts of Rubus in the United States, Kunkel.... 457
Note on a Botrytis disease of fig trees, Brierley............................ 457
The "band" disease of betel-nut palms in the Konkan, Gokhble et al........ 457
An epidemic of rust on mint, Chivers....................................... 457
[Lophodermium pinastri and Phacidium infestans on pine], Lagerberg.......... 458
The pine blister disease.. 458
Recent study of pod disease and canker in Hevea, Rutgers................... 458
Root disease of plantation rubber due to Poria hypolaterita, Belgrave......... 458
Some suggestions on the control of mistletoe in the Northwest, Weir......... 458

ENTOMOLOGY.

Recognition among insects, McIndoo... 459
Proceedings of the Entomological Society of British Columbia................ 459
Seventh annual report of the State entomologist, Gillette and List........... 459
[Parasite work in Maine], Summers... 459
Report of the economic zoologist, Surface.................................. 459
[Insect pests], Surface.. 459
[Report of the] division of entomology, Scholl.............................. 459
[Report of entomological work], Agee...................................... 459
Insect pests [in the West Indies during 1915], Ballou...................... 460
[Insect pests in St. Vincent].. 460
[Insects of economic importance in South America]......................... 460
[Insects of economic importance in South America]......................... 460
[Insects and insect control in Germany].................................... 460
Report of the entomological laboratory for 1915, Anderson................... 460
Some reasons for spraying citrus trees in Florida, Yothers................... 460
Typha latifolia as a summer host of injurious insects, Davidson.............. 461
Hackberry insects and their control, Paddock............................... 461
Contribution to a study of the toxins of spiders, Lévy...................... 461
The genera and species of Mallophaga, Harrison............................ 461
Field notes on Virginia Orthoptera, Fox.................................... 461
Fourth campaign against locusts (Schistocerca peregrina) in Algeria, Béguet... 461
The fungus on cacao thrips, Nowell.. 461
Cost of spraying for pear thrips in British Columbia, Cameron et al.......... 462
The green apple bug in Nova Scotia, Brittain............................... 462
The spiny citrus white fly.—A potential pest of citrus trees, Hutson.......... 462
The spiny citrus white fly and means for its control in Cuba................. 462
On the supposed varieties of Chrysomphalus dictyospermi, Malenotti.......... 462
The codling moth and its control in the Western Province, Pettey............. 463
Statistics on the production of silk in France and elsewhere................. 463
The meadow foxtail midge, Cockayne....................................... 463
Anopheline mosquitoes.—Their distribution and infection, Mitzmain.......... 463
Is mosquito or man the winter carrier of malaria organisms? Mitzmain....... 463
Muscicides and other fly-destroying agencies, Phelps and Stevenson.......... 464
The limitations of kerosene as a larvicide, Macfie........................... 464
Observations on the distribution of warble flies in Ohio, Mote............... 464
The poplar and willow borer (Cryptorhynchus lapathi), Matheson.............. 464
Evidence that bark borers are able to kill healthy fir trees, Welander......... 465
The bean beetle (Epilachna corrupta), Merrill............................... 465
1916 tests of sulphur-arsenical dusts against strawberry weevil, Headlée........ 466
Further trial of sulphur-arsenate of lead dust, Headlee...................... 467
Method of cockchafer control used in Germany, Escherich................... 467
Descriptions of various chalcidoid Hymenoptera with observations, Girault... 467

Page.
Notes on chalcid flies, chiefly from California, Girault........................ 467
Notes on coccid-infesting Chalcidoidea, II, Waterston........................ 467
Annual reports of the State bee inspector for 1915 and 1916, Pellett.......... 467
The question of denatured sugar for the feeding of honeybees, Zarin......... 467
Beauveria peteloti n. sp., a parasite of Hymenoptera, Vincens............... 467

FOODS—HUMAN NUTRITION.

The effect of high temperatures on the nutritive value of foods, Hogan........ 467
Bread making, McDonald.. 468
The proteins of the peanut, *Arachis hypogæa*, Johns and Jones................ 468
[Examination of milk, ice, oysters, ice cream, and catsup], Stokes............ 468
[Report of State Food and Drug Commissioner], Caspari, jr., and Penniman.... 468
[Pure food topics and drug inspection], Ladd and Johnson.................... 468
Food and efficiency, Tracy.. 469
Food, fuel for the human engine, Fisk.. 469
Food values and the selection of a nutritious and economical diet, Soule...... 469
Diet lists, compiled by Carter.. 469
Reports of the [Massachusetts] Commission on Cost of Living, Luce et al...... 469
Government control of food supplies in France............................... 469
Diet, body condition, and energy production, Anderson and Lusk........... 469
Influence of protein intake on excretion of creatin in man, Denis and Minot... 469
Inhibition of digestion of proteins by absorbed tin, Goss..................... 470
Ingestion of coffee, tea, and caffein and uric acid, Mendel and Wardell....... 470
Action of xanthin and methyl xanthins on intestine, Salant and Schwartze... 471
Action of succinate, malate, tartrate, and citrate on intestine, Salant et al.... 471

ANIMAL PRODUCTION.

How feed inspection helps the farmer, Strowd............................... 471
How to feed live stock successfully, Willson.................................. 471
How live stock is handled in the blue-grass region of Kentucky, Arnold....... 471
A study of the rate and economy of gains of fattening steers, Mumford et al... 471
Information for horse breeders, Lewis and Shuler........................... 473
Preserving eggs for the home, Alder... 473

DAIRY FARMING—DAIRYING.

Selecting dairy bulls by performance, Carroll................................ 473
Cow testing associations, Clark.. 474
Feeding dairy cattle, McCandlish... 474
Studies in the cost of market milk production, Anderson and Riddell......... 474
Clarification of milk, McInerney... 475
Pasteurization of cream, Larsen et al.. 476

VETERINARY MEDICINE.

Eighth biennial report of the State veterinarian of California, Keane.......... 477
Report of the bureau of veterinary science, Dawson et al.................... 477
Fifth annual report of the commissioner of animal industry, Howard......... 477
Live stock sanitation, Graves.. 477
Proceedings of the Wisconsin Veterinary Medical Association............... 477
Report of State veterinary of Wyoming for 1913 and 1914, Davis............ 477
Report of State veterinarian of Wyoming, for 1914 to 1916, French.......... 477
Progress in veterinary work [in India]....................................... 477
Chlor-antiseptics, Eakins.. 477
Treatment of wounds with serum Guillaume and Bittner................... 477
Mechanism of the serum reactions, Dean................................... 477
Influence of serum upon the staining of bacteria in suspensions, Fleisher...... 478
On the cause of negative tissue transplantation, III, Albanese............... 478
The origin of the proteolytic ferments of the blood, Sloan................... 478
Origin of proteolytic ferments.—II, Character of certain ferments, Sloan...... 478
Desiccated anthrax antigen for immunization purposes, Ferry............... 479
Special report on foot-and-mouth disease in Virginia, Ferneyhough.......... 479
Johne's disease.—The reactions of animals to "Johuin," M'Fadyean et al..... 479
A new Italian method for antirabic treatment, Fermi....................... 480

                                                                                    Page.
Rinderpest.—Preparation of antiserum, Shilston.............................. 480
The piroplasmoses and means for their prevention and control, Alessandrini... 480
The pathogenic action of Ixodidæ, Parodi..................................... 481
Application of the complement-fixation test to tuberculosis, Burns et al...... 481
Complement fixation in tuberculosis with "partial antigens," Woods et al. ... 481
Influence of certain organic substances on the tubercle bacillus, Lewis....... 481
Typhoid vaccine on tuberculous guinea pigs, Baldwin and L'Esperance...... 481
The presence of the tubercle bacillus in butter, Marchisotti................... 481
Tuberculosis in the goat, Moussu... 481
Age determination of cattle in different countries........................... 482
Health herd book for breeders of pure-bred cattle, Moore.................... 482
A rational and successful method of preventing abortion in cattle, Peters...... 482
Abortion in dairy cattle, Williams.. 482
A report upon an outbreak of stomatitis contagiosa, Gibbs................... 482
A new variety of Nocardia bovis, Actinomyces lanfranchii, Sani............... 482
Sheep poisoned by western goldenrod (Solidago spectabilis), Lockett.......... 482
The kidney worm of swine (Stephanurus dentatus), Luaces.................... 482
"Piroplasmosis," "equine malaria," Stoute.................................. 483
Parasites of the dog in Michigan, Hall....................................... 483
Trichina spiralis in the polar bear, Fox...................................... 483
Mortality statistics of fifth national egg-laying contest, Missouri, Horton...... 483
Fermenting properties of Bacterium pullorum and B. sanguinarium, Goldberg. 483
Is Leucocytozoon anatis the cause of a new disease in ducks? Wickware....... 483

                              RURAL ENGINEERING.

Irrigation of rice in California, Robertson.................................... 483
Annual irrigation revenue report of the Government of Bengal for 1915–16..... 484
River discharge, Hoyt and Grover.. 484
Geology and water resources of Nevada, Meinzer............................ 484
Ground water in San Simon Valley, Arizona and New Mexico, Schwennesen... 485
Report [of the California] State water problems conference.................... 486
Ditch flow found quickly and accurately with new portable weir, Fuller...... 486
Determining daily discharge of canals affected by check control, Humphrey... 486
The turbidity of water, Rado and Trelles..................................... 486
Silt observations at Yuma gauging station, compiled by Lawson.. 486
Sluicing silt to reduce canal leakage, Barnes................................. 487
Modern practice in wood-stave pipe design, Partridge........................ 487
Analyses of Fargo city water supply, Hulbert................................ 488
Investigations on the filtration of drinking water, I, Kisskalt................. 488
New process for chemical sterilization of drinking water in the field, Rhein.... 488
The manner of action of biological sewage purification media, Messerschmidt.. 488
A new type of trickling filter, Nasmith....................................... 488
Brushwood as a medium for sewage filters, Phelps........................... 489
Regulations respecting highways, 1916, Macdiarmid......................... 489
Intelligent use of road oil reduces maintenance, Agg......................... 490
Colorimetric test for organic impurities in sands, Abrams and Harder.......... 490
Effect of water on the strength of concrete, Abrams.......................... 490
Bearings for agricultural machinery, Page.................................... 490
Review of mechanical cultivation, Ringelmann............................... 490
A press for the Georgia carrier, Blake and Haines............................ 490
The drying of potatoes, Dantin.. 491
Some details in the construction of wooden hoop silos, Charlton............. 491
Housing of chickens, Dryden.. 491

                               RURAL ECONOMICS.

A theory of rural attitudes, Bernard... 491
Farm organization, balance between crops and stock, etc., Livermore......... 491
Minor articles of farm equipment, Humphrey and Yerkes.................... 491
Food preparedness, Seager and Chaddock.................................... 491
A farm census of New York State.. 491
Redistribution of farm land in France, Cabaussel............................ 491
The Torrens system, Massie... 492
Agricultural labor, Ponsonby... 492
[Agricultural wages in Sweden, 1915], Richert............................... 492

Page.
The Federal Farm Loan Act and the farmer, Bomberger...................... 492
Oregon rural credits primer, Macpherson...................................... 492
Organizing cooperative associations, Boyle.................................... 492
[Bulk handling of wheat in the Inland Empire], Hegardt..................... 492
Statistical information relating to stocks, cotton, grain, etc., 1916............ 492
[Livestock statistics of Sweden]... 492
Statistics of live stock for 1916 [in Rhodesia], Nobbs and Eyles.............. 492
[Agriculture in Japan].. 492

AGRICULTURAL EDUCATION.

Agricultural education, Tisserand... 493
Report of the acting secretary for agriculture for 1914–15, Holm.............. 493
[Agricultural instruction in the Philippine Islands], Foreman et al............ 494
Agriculture in the high school, Goddard and James........................... 494
[Agricultural and home economics instruction in New Hampshire], Whitcher.. 494
Suggestive outlines of industrial courses for consolidated and rural schools..... 494
Organization of a collegiate department in poultry husbandry, Lewis......... 495

LIST OF EXPERIMENT STATION AND DEPARTMENT PUBLICATIONS REVIEWED.

Stations in the United States.

Rhode Island Station: Page.

California Station: Page.
 Bul. 279, May, 1917.......... 483
 Circ. 164, Apr., 1917......... 447
 Circ. 165, May, 1917......... 443
Colorado Station:
 Bul. 227, Apr., 1917.......... 439
Florida Station:
 Bul. 136, Apr., 1917.......... 453
Illinois Station:
 Bul. 196, Feb., 1917......... 449
 Bul. 197, Mar., 1917.......... 471
 Bul. 198, Apr., 1917......... 438
 Circ. 196, Apr., 1917......... 474
Iowa Station:
 Circ. 34, May, 1917.......... 474
Kansas Station:
 Circ. 58, Jan., 1917........... 451
Maryland Station:
 Bul. 201, Feb., 1917......... 442
Michigan Station:
 Bul. 277, Dec., 1916......... 474
Minnesota Station:
 Bul. 165, Mar., 1917.......... 446
Missouri Station:
 Bul. 145, Feb., 1917......... 428
 Bul. 146, Mar., 1917.......... 428
Nebraska Station:
 Research Bul. 10, Apr. 10, 1917 447
Nevada Station:
 Bul. 86, Apr., 1917........... 435
 Bul. 87, Apr., 1917........... 442
 Bul. 88, Apr., 1917........... 436
New Jersey Stations:
 Bul. 304, Jan. 22, 1917....... 429
 Bul. 305, Jan. 6, 1917........ 425
 Circ. 64, Feb. 15, 1917....... 490
 Circ. 65, Mar. 7, 1917........ 466
New Mexico Station:
 Bul. 106, Apr., 1917.......... 465
New York Cornell Station:
 Bul. 387, Mar., 1917.......... 454
 Bul. 388, Apr., 1917.......... 464
 Bul. 389, Apr., 1917.......... 475
North Carolina Station:
 Tech. Bul. 12, Jan., 1917...... 449
 Circ. 35, May, 1917.......... 445
North Dakota Station:
 Spec. Bul., vol. 4, No. 12,
  Apr., 1917................. 468, 488
 Circ. 16, Mar., 1917.......... 492
Oklahoma Station:
 Circ. 43, Apr., 1917.......... 473

Stations in the United States—Continued.

Rhode Island Station: Page.
 Bul. 170, Apr., 1917.......... 446
South Dakota Station:
 Bul. 171, Nov., 1916......... 476
Tennessee Station:
 Bul. 116, Dec., 1916......... 471
Utah Station:
 Bul. 153, Apr., 1917.......... 473
 Bul. 154, Apr., 1917.......... 440
 Circ. 25, Apr., 1917.......... 473
Washington Station:
 West. Wash. Sta., Mo. Bul.,
  vol. 5, No. 2, May, 1917 491
West Virginia Station:
 Bul. 162, Jan., 1917........... 448
Wisconsin Station:
 Bul. 280, Apr., 1917.......... 442
 Bul. 281, June, 1917.......... 471

U. S. Department of Agriculture.

Jour. Agr. Research, vol. 9:
 No. 8, May 21, 1917......... 422, 456
 No. 9, May 28, 1917......... 421, 429
Farmers' Bul. 812, How Live Stock
 is Handled in the Bluegrass
 Region of Kentucky, J. H.
 Arnold........................ 471
Farmers' Bul. 814, Bermuda Grass,
 S. M. Tracy.................... 440
Farmers' Bul. 816, Minor Articles
 of Farm Equipment, H. N.
 Humphrey and A. P. Yerkes... 491
Farmers' Bul. 818, The Small
 Vegetable Garden.............. 447
Farmers' Bul. 820, Sweet Clover:
 Utilization, H. S. Coe.......... 444
Bureau of Entomology:
 Some Timely Suggestions for
  the Owners of Woodlots in
  New England, F. H. Mosher
  and G. E. Clement......... 451
Bureau of Soils:
 Field Operations, 1915—
  Soil Survey of Cowley
   County, Kans., E. C.
   Hall, R. H. Hall, and
   B. W. Tillman.......... 419
Scientific Contributions:[1]
 On the Quinone-phenolate
  Theory of Indicators, E. C.
  White and S. F. Acree...... 409

---

[1] Printed in scientific and technical publications outside the Department.

U. S. Department of Agriculture—Contd.

Scientific Contributions—Contd.   Page.

The Arsenates of Lead.—III,
Basic Arsenates, C. C.
McDonnell and C. M. Smith.   410
Indirect Measurements of the
Rotatory Powers of Some
Sugars, C. S. Hudson and
E. Yanovsky..............   410
The Preparation of Beta Glu-
cose, A. W. Mangam and
S. F. Acree...............   410
The Preparation of Xylose,
C. S. Hudson and T. S.
Harding...................   410
Inflammability of Carbonace-
ous Dusts, H. H. Brown and
J. K. Clement.............   410
The Oleoresin of Douglas Fir,
A. W. Schorger...........   411
The Chemical Nature of the
Vitamins, III, R. R. Wil-
liams....................   411
A Method for the Examination
of Methyl Salicylate, A. R.
Albright..................   415
Notes on the Rubber from
Eucommia ulmoides, A. F.
Sievers...................   417
The Extraction of Potash from
Silicate Rocks, II, W. H.
Ross.....................   427
Oxidase Activity of Plant
Juices and Hydrogen Ion
Concentrations, H. H. Bun-
zel......................   429
Polar Bear Cacti, O. F. Cook
and Alice C. Cook.........   434
Taxonomic Botany and the
Washington Botanist, A. S.
Hitchcock.................   435
Grasses in Relation to Dry
Farming, C. V. Piper......   437
Cultivation to Conserve Soil
Moisture, W. W. Burr......   437
Dry-land Agriculture Investi-
gations in the Great Plains
Area, E. C. Chilcott.......   437
Some Effects of Legumes on
Associated Nonlegumes, M.
W. Evans.................   438
Peanut Growing in the Cotton
Belt, H. C. Thompson......   442
Some Recent Investigations in
Sugar Beet Breeding, F. J.
Pritchard.................   442
The Problem of Making Vol-
ume Tables for Use on the
National Forests, T. T.
Munger...................   450

U. S. Department of Agriculture—Contd.

Scientific Contributions—Contd.   Page.

Volume of Western Yellow
Pine Logs from an Actual
Mill Tally, S. Berry........   451
Effect of Depth of Covering
Seed on Germination and
Quality of Stock, S. B. Show   451
Forest Succession in the Cen-
tral Rocky Mountains, C. G.
Bates....................   451
Douglas Fir Ship Building,
H. B. Oakleaf.............   452
The Purchase of Pulpwood.—
Some Suggestions, C. P.
Winslow and R. Thelen....   452
Some Suggestions on the Con-
trol of Mistletoe in the North-
west, J. R. Weir..........   458
Recognition Among Insects, N.
E. McIndoo...............   459
[Parasite Work in Maine], J. N.
Summers..................   459
Simuliidæ of Northern Chile,
F. Knab..................   460
Résumé of Work in Peru on
Phlebotomus verrucarum and
Its Agency in the Trans-
mission of Verruga, C. H.
T. Townsend.............   460
Discovery and Interpretation
of the Stages in the Asexual
Cycle of the Organism of
Verruga Peruviana, C. H. T.
Townsend................   460
Some Reasons for Spraying
Citrus Trees in Florida, W.W.
Yothers..................   460
Typha latifolia as a Summer
Host of Injurious Insects,
W. M. Davidson..........   461
Field Notes on Virginia Or-
thoptera, H. Fox..........   461
Descriptions of Various Chal-
cidoid Hymenoptera, with
Observations, A. A. Girault.   467
Notes on Chalcid Flies, Chiefly
from California, A. A.
Girault..................   467
The Proteins of the Peanut,
Arachis hypogæa, C. O. Johns
and D. B. Jones...........   468
Action of Xanthin and Methyl
Xanthins on Isolated Intes-
tine, W. Salant and E. W.
Schwartze...............   471
Action of Succinate, Malate,
Tartrate, and Citrate on
Intestine, W. Salant et al...   471
Irrigation of Rice in California,
R. D. Robertson..........   483

EXPERIMENT STATION RECORD.

Vol. 37.   October, 1917.   No. 5.

The great importance to the national welfare of research and education in agriculture has been given striking illustration at this time. It has been made apparent that the foundation of our present agricultural preparedness—the thing which makes it possible to invoke and stimulate more intensive and more highly effective production, is the existence of a vast fund of reliable information resting on a sound scientific basis. It is the product of research and experiment, seconded by teaching to inculcate it and make it more broadly known. It is seen that this foundation was being laid in the past decades by long and patient effort, and in large measure is now ready for use at the time it is needed. The result is a tribute to the agencies concerned. The time has brought enlarged recognition of their services and their inherent possibilities.

In this country, as well as in the warring countries of Europe, the present emergency has forced home as nothing else could, the dependence of power and resourcefulness upon the progress of science through investigation, and the development of men and institutions for it. Research in general has been given a great impetus and a new understanding. Its indispensability to the national welfare as a means of progress has been vastly emphasized, and its place will continue to be magnified after the war.

Everyone familiar with the process by which knowledge is advanced realizes that it is a relatively slow operation and can rarely be hurried. The general public has not always understood this. The actually new and fundamental facts which can be worked out in time to serve a sudden emergency are quite limited, but with a broad scientific basis of facts and principles to draw upon, profitable suggestion may become fertile in devising improvements and economies of various kinds which are effective in meeting special conditions. This is now being done in agriculture and is the large contribution of science in aiding the present situation.

The lesson has been taught that research can not be carried on spasmodically under stress of temporary emergency, but must go forward continuously, year in and year out, from generation to

401

generation. And it must be surrounded by conditions in which it will best thrive, without the handicap of being expected to produce something every day of immediate market value or application.

The existence of the necessary organization and facilities for systematic investigation is one of the outstanding advantages which the agricultural industry enjoys; and the opportunity for their exercise with enlarged freedom is increasing far more rapidly than could have been anticipated. Education is of course largely responsible for this broadened view—the kind of instruction that comes not only through the colleges and the schools, but through the intimate contact of the county agent, the agricultural press and popular literature which now find as interesting features in agricultural progress as in other human subjects.

The effect of these things upon the public mind and upon the industry of farming is very pronounced. Already the latter is being recognized as an industry in which intelligence based on wide knowledge is quite as essential as muscle and brawn.

A recent writer calls attention to the remark of Prof. Joseph Le Conte, made long ago, that each of the great professions first attained high standing when it was taught as such in universities. The professional men turned out under such teaching are no longer quacks but have a real command of the fundamental principles in their chosen field. Any profession has standing in so far as its fundamental principles have been developed and applied. To retain standing a profession must be continuously increasing its stock of knowledge of fundamental principles through research.

How applicable this is to agriculture—to the industry of farming and all that goes with it—will be fully apparent from its very modern history. A more striking illustration of change and development on the basis of knowledge and understanding could hardly be found; and the real significance of it is rapidly dawning, even though we are as yet little more than at the beginning. More and more the need is now understood for "the constant flow of new knowledge derived from the everlasting questioning of nature by trained men, whose eagerness is for the answer and the truth regardless of the immediate commercial value of that truth and answer." If the aim is right the practical value will follow surely enough and the result may be given deeper importance.

To insure this flow of knowledge which will give deeper insight and to maintain the standards which will mean steady advancement, there is still need for more men for research in agriculture—for men who know the aspect and significance of research and understand its methods and possibilities. This need results both from the growth in opportunity and the advance in grade of our agricultural inquiry. It is evidenced by the difficulty experienced by this Department and the experiment stations in finding properly qualified people for their work.

If there is to be steady progress, advanced workers need to be produced at a faster rate than formerly. More of the suitable minds and temperaments need to be drawn into it. The provision of research scholarships and graduate fellowships has done considerable to direct men to this field and to afford opportunity for them to acquire the essential broad and rigid training. Such men as are now largely required can not be prepared over night, and hence the plans must be laid with foresight.

"We must welcome the inventive wonder but not wait for him to happen." The vast majority of that class are handicapped by lack of opportunity for learning the foundations of the sciences they are attempting to short circuit. Their spirit of research and patience in application to an idea are worthy of the investigator, but their deficiency lies in the fundamental knowledge which would avoid futile efforts and usually make their work better rewarded. The things that can be discovered by chance or even by earnest but insufficiently trained and informed effort have in very large measure been found out. The surface has been well skimmed. This was properly the first step, but it is now necessary to dig deep for the new knowledge.

The potential research worker is not an essentially distinct type, although he may possess certain qualities requisite to success. Contrary to the usual saying, he is probably less born than made. An eminent biologist has ventured the assertion that about two-fifths of the greatness of a man is born in him and three-fifths made. This leaves much for his environment and education.

In commenting on this subject, Dr. P. G. Nutting has made some interesting remarks as reported in a recent address. "Some writers," he says, "have spoken of the investigator as a rare individual, to be sifted out from educational institutions with great care for a particular line of work. My personal opinion is that a large percentage of the men students are fitted for research work if properly started along the right line. The investigator should have a mind at once fertile and well trained. His mind should be teeming with new ideas, but he should possess unerring judgment to reject those which are not logical or promising. . . . Fertility of mind is not so much an inborn quality of the mind itself as of the training and association which that mind has had."

He defines the best preparation for the investigator to be "a thorough grounding in the fundamental principles of his science—physics, chemistry, or whatever it may be. If he has this thorough knowledge of fundamental principles it is safe to say that in any properly organized research laboratory, with the proper leadership and companions, such a student will have many times as many useful

ideas as he can himself possibly follow up with research. Hardly
any one who has completed advanced work in a science can read,
say an abstract journal, without thinking of many problems which
he would like to investigate."

The leaders of research " have not only a taste for research and
logical minds to analyze clearly and attack problems with thorough
scientific knowledge, but have a knowledge of the principles of research, getting the most out of their own minds, avoiding side issues,
cooperating with their colleagues, and putting their most valuable
results in permanent, readily available form. Research is one of the
youngest of the professions and one with a promising future, but
let no one enter it without thorough knowledge or a full understanding of its aims and methods."

And again he says, in speaking of the incentive to do the best that
is in a man—to live up to his possibilities: "A great many students
enter research because their favorite professors have made reputa-
tions in research or because their friends and colleagues are doing
such work. Incentive by contact covers the psychology of getting
started at the line of work you wish to become interested in. It is
well known that the work itself produces a reaction on one's mind
which makes it much easier to continue the work. . . . Incentive
by contract to put forth our best efforts comes from putting ourselves
under obligation to produce certain results," that is, the setting or
acceptance of a task and undertaking to accomplish it.

This "incentive by contract," it may be noted, finds familiar illustration in station research in the project system so largely employed,
and is one of the important advantages of it. The project outline
is an attempt to block out on paper a definite line of inquiry, to
answer a specific question or add a step toward the solution of a
problem. Having formulated this undertaking and set his hand
and mind to it, there is larger obligation and incentive for the investigator to accomplish the purpose as far as possible. It has become a venture on which his scientific reputation and ability may be
gaged. This and the desire for accomplishment should be an incite-
ment to hold to the main issue, refusing to follow side lines which develop; and it is also an added argument for the analysis of broad
problems and the framing of projects within reasonable scope, so
that the end may be promising of attainment.

Too broad and comprehensive projects reflect laudable ambition
but point to inadequate realization of practicability and usual limitations. The large things often seem more attractive and worth
while to the worker of limited experience and outlook, but to be
practicable of attainment and bring credit to the investigator the
project of definiteness and limited scope has proved to be far more
promising in agriculture. Some large projects which have been

under way ever since the Adams fund came are still very far from
solution and are seen to be more intricate and less feasible in their
entirety as knowledge advances. To abandon them is looked upon
as an admission of weakness or of bad judgment, and so they may be
continued after their defects have become apparent.

This is no argument against the project system but it is a sign
for caution, which happily is finding expression in the newer undertakings.

The establishment and successful maintenance of a considerable
number of technical agricultural journals in this country is a development of the past decade of much importance to agricultural research. It reflects in a striking manner the growth of agricultural
investigation and the substantial support now available for periodical literature of this sort. It has increased materially the channels
open for the publication of agricultural research, assembled many
of the most important studies in the various specialized fields, and
in other ways done much to unite workers and foster their interests.

The advantages of an American periodical devoted to agricultural science were foreseen by a number of teachers and investigators at a comparatively early date. In 1884 a meeting was held at
the U. S. Department of Agriculture for the express purpose of considering the establishment of a journal of scientific agriculture. It
was announced at this meeting that about forty of the leading agricultural workers of the period, among them Brewer, Johnson,
Atwater, and Hilgard, had agreed to become contributors and that
a guarantee fund had been secured to provide the necessary financial
support, but the project was abandoned for the time being because
of failure to secure an editor.

Advocacy of a journal continued, however, and in January, 1887,
appeared the initial number of a monthly known as *Agricultural
Science*. This was a private enterprise with Prof. Charles S. Plumb,
then of the New York State Station, as editor and publisher. It
constituted the first journal to be devoted to agricultural science
not only in this country but in the English language. It also ante-
dated by several weeks the passage of the Hatch Act, and by two
years the establishment of *Experiment Station Record*.

The purposes of the new publication were set forth in its editorial
columns as follows: "To publish original work, the results of experiments conducted in the promotion of agricultural science in
America, either by individuals or otherwise; to disseminate knowledge relating to agricultural research, as obtained from researches
carried on in Europe or other portions of the globe, that students
and investigators may have the opportunity to learn of the work
and results of co-laborers in the field; that students of agriculture,

in all its branches, may have a medium through which a free interchange of ideas may be brought about; that the field of agricultural research, so rapidly developing in America, may have a journal that will serve as a chronicler of work past, present, and to come, so as to form a valuable record of progress in agriculture; that agricultural science may be represented in one journal having no commercial or selfish motives, whose only effort shall be to uphold and promote investigation and research, and raise the standard of the field and its workers."

The publication of *Agricultural Science* continued with some vicissitudes and changes for eight years. In 1892 the management was assumed by Dr. Wm. Frear of the Pennsylvania State College with a corps of associates from various agricultural colleges, this Department, and elsewhere, and in 1894 it became the organ of the Society for the Promotion of Agricultural Science. Its final issue, that of December, 1894, appeared in June of the following year.

During its existence a considerable amount of experimental work was reported in its columns. Much space was also given to abstracts of agricultural literature, although this feature was less extensively developed than in the *Record*. The journal also contained reports of scientific meetings and other news notes of interest, and afforded opportunity for the discussion of current questions.

In spite of the unique position thus occupied by *Agricultural Science*, it appears that among the principal difficulties encountered in its publication was a lack of suitable material. This situation had indeed been predicted by *Science*, which in a review of the new journal expressed the opinion that one of the greatest handicaps would prove to be "a paucity of original investigations." Although a considerable body of research was steadily developing, this prophecy came true in so far as the material it was desired to publish outside the station and Department series was concerned, and there was also difficulty in obtaining the necessary financial support.

Following the suspension of *Agricultural Science*, station workers found themselves for many years restricted in the publication of their technical work to the regular bulletin series and the journals of general science. Much material was also sent abroad, many papers even appearing in German periodicals, notably *Centralblatt für Bakteriologie, Parasitenkunde, und Infektionskrankheiten.* With the advent of the *Journal of Agricultural Science* in England, in 1905, numerous American contributions were submitted to that periodical, but owing to a congestion of material and the limited number of issues, long delays of publication were entailed.

In 1908 the first of the American journals to be devoted to a single division of agricultural science began publication. This was the *Journal of Economic Entomology*, issued bi-monthly and now completing its tenth volume. This journal was first financed through a stock company composed of members of the Association of Economic Entomologists, but in a few years was taken over completely by that association. The *Journal of Home Economics* was established by the American Home Economics Association in 1909, the *American Breeders' Magazine*, subsequently the *Journal of Heredity*, by the American Breeders' Association in 1910, and *Phytopathology* by the American Phytopathological Society in 1911. Of more recent date may be mentioned the *Journal of the Society of Agronomy*, which in 1913 replaced the Annual Proceedings of the American Society of Agronomy, the *Journal of the American Association of Poultry Instructors* starting in 1914, the *Journal of the Association of Official Agricultural Chemists* beginning in 1915, *Soil Science* founded by Rutgers College in 1916, and the *Journal of Dairy Science* published by the American Society of Dairy Science beginning with the current year.

Nearly all of these journals, it will be noted, are under the management of a corresponding society. In addition to providing for the publication of an increasing amount of original research, they afford a convenient medium for the printing of the societies' proceedings and otherwise serve to keep members in closer touch with matters of interest and promote the welfare of their respective divisions of science.

The establishment of the *Journal of Agricultural Research* by the U. S. Department of Agriculture in 1913, followed by the opening of its columns to contributions from the stations in 1914 under a cooperative arrangement with the Association of American Agricultural Colleges and Experiment Stations, should also be referred to. Unlike the topical journals, this publication is, of course, not restricted to a single phase of agricultural science. The large and steadily increasing number of contributions available for its use is evidenced in part by the change, two years ago, from monthly to weekly issues, attesting the amount and high grade of research now at hand from agricultural institutions in this country.

Meanwhile the stations have, of course, presented the results of much of their technical work in bulletin form, both in the regular series and in technical series, and workers have continued to employ the journals of general science, such as the *Journal of the American Chemical Society*, the *Journal of Biological Chemistry*, the *Journal of Bacteriology*, and the numerous botanical journals. Likewise workers in this Department have in recent years availed themselves quite largely of the privilege of utilizing non-Departmental publications. The last two volumes of the *Record*, corresponding to a year's work, contain titles of over five hundred such contributions.

The fact that these various channels of publication are now available is obviously of much advantage. It permits of a selection of the medium most suitable for a given purpose, and it relieves the congestion so rapidly replacing the scarcity of material complained of in the earlier days. It is, therefore, a matter of congratulation that the topical journals of agricultural science, which are rendering so useful a service, should have apparently passed the experimental stage and have established themselves among the recognized agencies for the dissemination of results of agricultural research.

RECENT WORK IN AGRICUTURAL SCIENCE.

AGRICULTURAL CHEMISTRY—AGROTECHNY.

Annual reports on the progress of chemistry for 1916, edited by J. C. CAIN, A. J. GREENAWAY, and C. SMITH (*Ann. Rpts. Prog. Chem.* [*London*], *13* (*1916*), *pp. VIII+284*).—This report corresponds to those of previous years (E. S. R., 35, p. 201).

Pervaporation, perstillation, and percrystallization, P. A. KOBER (*Jour. Amer. Chem. Soc., 39* (*1917*), *No. 5, pp. 944-948, figs. 5*).—Experiments are described in which collodion bags or containers are used for the procedures of evaporation, distillation, and crystallization. "Collodion and parchment membrane containers permit water to evaporate through the walls as though no membrane were present. This phenomenon is called pervaporation. Distillation by means of pervaporation is called perstillation, and can be conducted at ordinary atmospheric pressure with low temperatures as well as with vacuum. When a dialyzable constituent of a liquid within these containers reaches saturation, crystallization usually takes place on the outside. This phenomenon is called percrystallization."

The theory of the phenomena is briefly discussed.

On the quinone-phenolate theory of indicators: The electrical conductivity of solutions of phenolsulphonphthalein and of its bromo and nitro derivatives, E. C. WHITE and S. F. ACREE (*Jour. Amer. Chem. Soc., 39* (*1917*), *No. 4, pp. 648-652*).

Reducing matter extractable from filter paper, R. S. McBRIDE and J. A. SCHERRER (*Jour. Amer. Chem. Soc., 39* (*1917*), *No. 5, pp. 928-933*).—In the study reported the authors conclude that some substance is extracted from the filter papers ordinarily used which reduces permanganate. It is indicated as being furfural or a closely related substance produced by oxidation and hydrolysis of the cellulose. Washing the filter paper previous to use is indicated as a great aid in avoiding excessive consumption of permanganate. Titration, however, even in the presence of the paper is not considered objectionable.

The preparation of hydrochloroplatinic acid by means of hydrogen peroxid, P. RUDNICK and R. D. COOKE (*Jour. Amer. Chem. Soc., 39* (*1917*), *No. 4, pp. 633-635*).—The following procedure is described:

Ten gm. of dried (but not ignited) platinum black is covered with 50 cc. of concentrated hydrochloric acid warmed to about 50 or 60° C. and 3 per cent hydrogen peroxid slowly added. Just enough hydrogen peroxid is kept present to maintain a moderate evolution of chlorin, which originates entirely on the platinum. When the platinum has been entirely dissolved the solution is evaporated to a volume of 100 cc. and is then ready for use. The use of dilute peroxid may cause the volume to become too great, in which case it is necessary to evaporate to a smaller bulk before all the platinum has been dissolved. Hydrogen peroxid of from 20 to 30 per cent strength has been found satisfactory in keeping down the volume of the solution.

Earlier references to the use of hydrogen peroxid as an oxidizer and the mode of the reaction are noted and briefly discussed.

The arsenates of lead.—III, Basic arsenates, C. C. McDonnell and C. M. Smith (*Jour. Amer. Chem. Soc., 39 (1917), No. 5, pp. 937–943*).—Continuing previous work (E. S. R., 36, p. 501) the authors describe the preparation and properties of a number of basic arsenates of lead.

Indirect measurements of the rotatory powers of some alpha and beta forms of the sugars by means of solubility experiments, C. S. Hudson and E. Yanovsky (*Jour. Amer. Chem. Soc., 39 (1917), No. 5, pp. 1013–1038*).

The preparation of beta glucose, A. W. Mangam and S. F. Acree (*Jour. Amer. Chem. Soc., 39 (1917), No. 5, pp. 965–968*).

The preparation of xylose, C. S. Hudson and T. S. Harding (*Jour. Amer. Chem. Soc., 39 (1917), No. 5, pp. 1038–1040*).—A procedure for preparing xylose from cottonseed hulls is described. The yield obtained varies from 8 to 12 per cent, and the first lot of crystals obtained are almost colorless and pure.

On the cleavage in starch grains, A. Reuss (*Ztschr. Untersuch. Nahr. u. Genussmtl., 32 (1916), No. 6, pp. 269, 270, figs. 6*).—In the examination of a sample of bouillon cubes, starch grains were observed which exhibited peculiar cleavage. The cubes contained 50 per cent sodium chlorid. A preliminary study of the effect of various solutions on the cleavage of different kinds of starch grains was made, and the results are briefly noted.

The determination of gelatinization temperatures of starches by means of an electrically heated chamber on the microscope stage, A. W. Dox and G. W. Roark, jr. (*Jour. Amer. Chem. Soc., 39 (1917), No. 4, pp. 742–745*).—The authors, at the Iowa Experiment Station, describe an apparatus similar to that previously noted by Francis and Smith (E. S. R., 35, p. 108). In the modified apparatus the chamber containing the slide is electrically heated. The manipulation of the apparatus and the procedure for determining the gelatinization temperature are described in detail.

The gelatinization temperature of starches of 13 different varieties of corn are submitted in tabular form.

Inflammability of carbonaceous dusts in atmospheres of low oxygen content, H. H. Brown and J. K. Clement (*Jour. Indus. and Engin. Chem., 9 (1917), No. 4, pp. 347–349, fig. 1*).—Continuing previous work (E. S. R., 37, p. 109) it has been shown that an inert gas mixture containing 12 per cent or less of oxygen would prevent a dust explosion from starting or propagating.

Hydrolysis of the soluble protein of Swede turnips, G. Williams (*Jour. Agr. Sci. [England], 8 (1917), No. 2, pp. 182–215*).—The following percentage composition of the protein obtained from the juice of Swede turnips (rutabagas) by heating to 90° C. for one-half hour is reported: Glycin, 0.27; alanin, 3.58; valin, 9.95; leucin and isoleucin, 9.01; phenylalanin, 4.47; tyrosin, 2.92; cystin, present; prolin, 4.17; aspartic acid, 6.98; glutaminic acid, 3.18; tryptophan, present; arginin, 3.12; histidin, 3.04; lysin, 4.35; ammonia, 1.21; humin bodies, 4.74; total, 60.99. One preparation of the protein prepared contained 14.09 per cent of nitrogen, 1.81 per cent of water, and 8.6 per cent of ash.

The procedures of Kossel and Kutscher, the ester method, and methods for isolating individual amino acids were used. The procedures are described in detail and the analytical data obtained discussed.

Experimental investigations of the plum (Prunus domestica).—II, Composition of plum seed oil, D. Feruglio and G. B. Bernardis (*R. Lab. Chim. Agr. Udine Ric. Sper. e Attiv. Spiegata, 4 (1911–1914), pp. 111–118*).—Experimental data relative to the physical and chemical constants and color reactions of the oil obtained by ether extraction of the finely ground material and qualitative tests of the fatty acids of the oil are submitted.

The oil is deemed to consist largely of the glycerid of oleic acid, together with smaller amounts of the glycerids of linoleic and palmitic acids. A small amount of an unidentified phytosterol was also present in the oil.

Tobacco seed oil, N. H. COHEN (*Proefstat. Vorstenland. Tabak [Dutch East Indies], Meded. 14 (1915), pp. 57–65*).—Some data relative to the yield of oil from the seeds of various crops of tobacco and the fertilizing value of the press cake are submitted and discussed, together with notes on the possible economic importance of the industry.

A sample of seed yielded on analysis the following percentage composition: P_2O_5, 1.5; K_2O, 2.06; nitrogen, 4.21; and oil, 14.38

The oleoresin of Douglas fir, A. W. SCHORGER (*Jour. Amer. Chem. Soc., 39 (1917), No. 5, pp. 1040–1044*).—The oleoresin in the heartwood of Douglas fir (*Pseudotsuga taxifolia*) was found to contain a volatile oil consisting largely of *l*-α-pinene, with small amounts of *l*-limonene and *l*-terpineol. The oil from the oleoresin obtained from the sapwood contained *l*-α-pinene, *l*-β-pinene, and probably *l*-limonene. The "firpene" previously described as a new terpene is indicated as being highly active *l*-α-pinene.

The oxidase of Rhus diversiloba, J. B. McNAIR (*Jour. Infect. Diseases, 20 (1917), No. 5, pp. 485–498, figs. 4*).—The results of the investigation show that the darkening of the sap of *R. diversiloba* is due to oxidation and that the oxidation results in the total loss of the irritating poisonous properties of the sap. The oxidase found accelerated the transfer of molecular oxygen to phenols and aromatic amins. The oxidizing power is accelerated by dilute alkalis and retarded by dilute acids, and when boiled for a short time in aqueous solution is destroyed. The similarity of the oxidase to others previously isolated is noted.

In the study of the oxidase the author applied the Van Slyke apparatus (E. S. R., 31, p. 610).

Achroodextrinase, J. EFFRONT (*Compt. Rend. Acad. Sci. [Paris], 164 (1917), No. 10, pp. 415, 416*).—The preparation of a dextrinase which rapidly converts into achroodextrin, amylodextrin, and erythrodextrin from *Bacillus mesentericus* found in various seed press cakes, distillery malt, and similar amylaceous material is noted. The enzym is precipitated by alcohol and ammonium sulphate at an optimum temperature of 40° C. It acts best in a medium neutral to methyl orange but is also active in slightly alkaline solution. Its action is retarded, however, by even very low acid concentration.

The use of the bacterial diastase in the textile industry, in converting starch residues into dextrin sirup, etc., is indicated.

The chemical nature of the vitamins.—III, The structure of the curative modifications of the hydroxypyridins, R. R. WILLIAMS (*Jour. Biol. Chem., 29 (1917), No. 3, pp. 495–520, pl. 1*).—Continuing the study previously noted (E. S. R., 36, p. 314) it has been found that the two crystalline forms of α-hydroxypyridin are isomeric and mutually convertible. The needle form alone is curative for polyneuritis. The corresponding crystal form of β-hydroxypyridin and the anhydrous forms of methylpyridone, trigonellin, and betain produced similar curative effects on polyneuritic birds. The last three, however, yielded negative results when tested for protective properties.

It is concluded that "the curative form of α-hydroxypyridin is a pseudo betain, and that a feature conforming more or less closely in structure or energy conditions to the type of a betain ring is probably an essential characteristic of antineuritic vitamins." The theoretical possibility of the existence of such a structure in most of the simpler nitrogenous constituents of animal tissues, but especially in the nuclein bases, is pointed out.

Preliminary experiments are noted which indicate that "nicotinic acid may exist in a betain form and that the curative properties of Funk's vitamin fractions of yeast and rice polishings may have been due in part to this isomeric form of nicotinic acid or a polymer or simple derivative of it."

Titration of magnesium, F. W. BRUCKMILLER (*Jour. Amer. Chem. Soc.*, *39* (1917), *No. 4, pp. 610–615*).—From experimental results obtained in the titration of magnesium as applied to water analysis the author indicates that magnesium can be determined volumetrically, provided great care is exercised in the formation of the phosphate precipitate in the one procedure, and special precautions taken in the titration of the iodin liberated by the arsenate precipitate from potassium iodid or the arsenious acid remaining after all the iodin has been expelled in the other procedure.

The modified methods are described in detail. Experimental data submitted indicate the accuracy of the methods as compared to the gravimetric procedure.

A study of the volumetric or Pemberton method for determining phosphoric acid, with some experiments showing the influence of temperature and the sulphuric acid radical on results, P. McG. SHUEY (*Jour. Indus. and Engin. Chem.*, *9* (1917), *No. 4, pp. 367–370*).—The author discusses the method and points out certain precautions necessary in the use of the procedure. Some experimental data relative to. the temperature of titration are also submitted and discussed.

It is concluded in general that, "with a knowledge of the method and with strict attention to detail, very accurate and reliable results may be obtained. The fact that it is extremely delicate is a point in its favor."

The iodometric determination of ammonium sulphate, W. S. J. SCHOUTEN-ILCKEN and R. W. TUINZING (*Verslag. Landbouwk. Onderzoek. Rijkslandbouw-proefstat.* [*Netherlands*], *No. 20* (1917), *pp. 12–20*).—The authors briefly review the distillation and other procedures used for the determination of ammonia in ammonium sulphate and other fertilizers. A procedure which depends on the following reactions is described:

(1) $2NH_3 + 3NaOBr = 3NaBr + 3H_2O + N_2$

(2) $(NH_4)_2SO_4 + 3NaOBr + 2NaOH = Na_2SO_4 + 3NaBr + 5H_2O + N_2$

(3) $NaOBr + 2HI = NaBr + H_2O + I_2$

(4) $2Na_2S_2O_3 + I_2 = Na_2S_4O_6 + 2NaI$

The alkaline-bromin solution is prepared by adding, with constant stirring, 15.5 gm. of bromin to 5 liters of sodium hydroxid solution (containing 15.5 gm. of NaOH). This solution is allowed to stand for several days and its titer then determined with a standard thiosulphate solution. Since the titer does not remain constant it should be determined every few days.

The ammonia determination is made by treating 10 cc. of a solution of ammonium sulphate (0.5 gm. in 100 cc. water) or a solution of ammonium superphosphate (1 gm. in 100 cc. of water) in a 700-cc. flask with 75 cc. of the alkaline-bromin solution. After having been set aside for several minutes 5 cc. of a 10 per cent solution of potassium iodid, 20 cc. of a 10 per cent hydrochloric acid solution, 5 cc. of a saturated solution of sodium carbonate, drop by drop, and 200 cc. of water are added to the mixture, in the order named. The liberated iodin is titrated with standard thiosulphate solution, using methylene blue as an indicator. From the amount of alkaline-bromin solution used the amount of nitrogen and ammonium sulphate present in the sample is calculated.

Analytical data submitted indicate the accuracy of the procedure. The method is recommended as being more economical than the usual distillation procedure in point of time and materials.

The determination of nitrogen in the form of calcium cyanamid in lime nitrogen, A. D. BERKHOUT, R. D. HENDRIKSZ, and J. WIND (*Verslag. Landbouwk. Onderzoek. Rijkslandbouwproefstat.* [*Netherlands*], No. 20 (*1917*), pp. 43–52).— The following method has been found to yield most reliable results:

Two gm. of the finely pulverized sample is rubbed up with repeated small amounts of distilled water and transferred to a 1,000-cc. measuring flask by decantation, using about 900 cc. of water. The flask is then placed in the shaking machine and thoroughly shaken for about one hour. The solution, after being made up to volume, is thoroughly shaken, and treated by either of the following methods:

(1) Fifty or 100 cc. of the solution is neutralized in a flask with 10 per cent nitric acid and then treated with from 2.5 to 5 cc. of 2.5 per cent ammonia. Tenth-normal silver nitrate solution is immediately added in excess from a burette while the solution is being thoroughly shaken to precipitate the cyanamid as silver cyanamid. The material in the flask is made up to volume and after thorough agitation is filtered. After this precipitation the solution should be decidedly alkaline. From 50 to 100 cc. of the filtrate, after being acidified with from 5 to 10 cc. of 10 per cent nitric acid, is titrated with tenth-normal ammonium thiocyanate solution, using from 2.5 to 5 cc. of a cold saturated ferric ammonium alum solution as indicator. If chlorids are present they should be previously determined and the proper correction made.

(2) One hundred cc. of the solution is transferred to a 250-cc. beaker, neutralized with 10 per cent nitric acid, and after the addition of 2 cc. of 10 per cent ammonia a slight excess of tenth-normal silver nitrate is added with thorough agitation. The precipitated silver salt is quantitatively filtered, thoroughly washed, and the wet filter and contents subjected to a Kjeldahl nitro gen determination, using 10 cc. of 50 per cent sulphuric acid, 0.6 gm. of mer cury, and 20 cc. of a mixture of 1 liter of sulphuric acid (specific gravity 1.84) and 200 gm. phosphorus pentoxid.

On the Duclaux method for the estimation of the volatile fatty acids, F. W. UPSON, H. M. PLUM, and J. E. SCHOTT (*Jour. Amer. Chem. Soc., 39 (1917), No. 4, pp. 731–742*).—From the results of a critical study the authors conclude that small, unavoidable variations in the experimental results such as are within the limits of error of the method may cause such wide variation in the calculated results as to make them of no quantitative value. When more than two acids are present in a mixture practically identical series may be calcu· lated from mixtures of different acids in varying proportions. "Results which indicate the presence of one acid may just as well be calculated in terms of three or more acids. Small amounts of acids may be distributed just as well between the acids next higher and lower in the series."

The theory of the method is deemed to be unsound, and the procedure therefore not to be applicable for either quantitative or qualitative determinations of the composition of unknown mixtures of fatty acids.

The experimental data are submitted and discussed in detail.

A note on the Duclaux method for volatile fatty acids, A. R. LAMB (*Jour. Amer. Chem. Soc., 39 (1917), No. 4, pp. 746, 747*).—From a critical study of the method in connection with some investigations on the fermentation of corn silage the author, at the Iowa Experiment Station, considers it to be impracticable to attempt to determine more than two or three acids in the same fraction. "By proper fractional distillation the acids in the mixture may be quite well separated. This obviates the necessity of calculating as many as four acids from a single distillation, which is objected to by Upson et al." (as noted above).

The lack of agreement between different sets of Duclaux's constants is considered to be due to impurities in the acids used and to avoidable experimental variations, rather than to unavoidable experimental variations claimed above. The author considers that "it is possible under proper conditions to obtain much more accurate results with the method than have generally been obtained."

The Duclaux method, F. W. J. Boekhout and J. J. O. De Vries (*Verslag. Landbouwk. Onderzoek. Rijkslandbouwcproefstat. [Netherlands], No. 20 (1917). pp. 79–90*).—In a critical study of the Duclaux method the authors have determined constants practically the same as those obtained by the originator of the method. Results obtained from a mixture of more than two acids are considered not to be trustworthy.

The theory and use of the procedure are discussed in some detail, and analytical data submitted in tabular form.

The systematic extraction of aqueous solutions with ether, J. Pinnow (*Ztschr. Untersuch. Nahr. u. Genussmtl., 32 (1916), No. 6, pp. 257–268*).—Physical-chemical data relative to extraction with varying volumes of the solution, concentration of the solution, time, etc., of citric, succinic, and lactic acids, pyrogallol, and caffein are submitted and discussed.

The determination of added water in ground meats and sausages, C. Baumann and J. Grossfeld (*Ztschr. Untersuch. Nahr. u. Genussmtl., 32 (1916), No. 11, pp. 489–493*).—The use of the ratio total water : nitrogen is considered to be easier and more reliable than that of the others commonly used for the determination of added water. For fresh meats this ratio (average) has been found to be 18.3. The following formula is proposed for calculating results:

Added water = Total water − (nitrogen × 18.3).

Some analytical data are submitted.

The alkalinity of cocoa, Arpin (*Ann. Falsif., 10 (1917). No. 99–100, pp. 10–14*).—Analytical data of a number of samples of cocoas with especial reference to the alkalinity of the ash are submitted and discussed.

The determination of the alkalinity of cocoa, X. Rocques (*Ann. Falsif., 10 (1917), No. 99–100, pp. 14–17, fig. 1*).—Modified procedures of the official French method for the determination of total ash, water-soluble and insoluble ash, alkalinity of the soluble ash, and the phosphoric acid in the soluble ash are described and discussed.

Moisture determination in spices and similar products, A. Scholl and R. Strohecker (*Ztschr. Untersuch. Nahr. u. Genussmtl., 32 (1916), No. 11, pp. 493–499*).—This is a general discussion of the subject, together with some experimental data obtained in a study of methods commonly used for moisture determinations.

It is concluded that in general the distillation procedure for the determination of moisture is applicable to spices, and that comparatively accurate results are obtainable. The procedure is especially suited to samples which contain large amounts of volatile matter. It could not well be applied, however, to samples which contain inorganic salts with water of crystallization without some modification.

The determination of ammonia in wine and its significance, W. J. Baragiola and C. Godet (*Ztschr. Untersuch. Nahr. u. Genussmtl., 30 (1915), No. 5, pp. 169–216. fig. 1*).—The literature on the determination of ammonia in wine and other biochemical studies is reviewed and the results of an original investigation on the subject submitted.

The distillation with magnesium oxid in vacuo is deemed to be accurate and satisfactory for all practical and control determinations since the amount of amins or other bases is ordinarily only very small. For very exact work where it is desired to separate the ammonia from the amins and other bases the precipitation of ammonia as ammonium-magnesium phosphate is recommended.

The procedures which are applicable to fermented and unfermented fruit wines and juices, together with analytical data relative to the effect of other substances present on the determination of ammonia, are described in detail.

The amount of ammonia in wines was found to vary from nothing to 150 mg. per liter. The French limit of 20 mg. per liter for maximum content is considered to be unsatisfactory. Fruit wines appear to be very poor in ammonia.

The significance of the determination of ammonia for both practical and scientific purposes is indicated.

The determination of ammonia in wine, W. J. Baragiola and O. Schuppli (*Ztschr. Untersuch. Nahr. u. Genussmtl.*, *32* (*1916*), *No. 10, pp. 441–444*).—Supplementary to the study noted above the distillation with magnesium oxid is again strongly recommended. The use of the precipitation procedure is advised only in cases where it is desired to determine small amounts of volatile amins and other bases that might be present.

The precipitation of ammonia was found not to be complete except in an excess of sodium phosphate. The use of 12 gm. of sodium phosphate rather than 5 gm. as in the previous procedure is recommended.

A method for the examination of methyl salicylate, A. R. Albright (*Jour. Amer. Chem. Soc., 39* (*1917*), *No. 4, pp. 820–825*).—A method for examining a methyl salicylate oil and other phenolic substances or impurities present which depends on the conversion of the substances into the same crystalline derivative (the benzoate) and the microscopical examination of the resulting crystals is described and discussed.

A study of certain ferments with a view to determining a method for the differentiation of pasteurized milk from raw milk.—I, Reductases, R. E. Lee and M. G. Mellon (*Jour. Indus. and Engin. Chem., 9* (*1917*), *No. 4, pp. 360–367, figs. 7*).—From the study reported the authors conclude that methylene blue, as it occurs in Schardinger's F. M. reagent (5 cc. of a saturated alcoholic solution of methylene blue, 5 cc. of 40 per cent formaldehyde, and 190 cc. of water), is not decolorized by normal milk in less than 20 minutes. In cases of decolorization effected in 10 minutes or less the milk was found to contain 1,000,000 or more microorganisms per cubic centimeter. Milk pasteurized at 70° C. for 10 minutes, unless allowed to stand for 48 hours before testing (or until the bacterial content was largely increased), or old milk in which the preservative (formaldehyde) inhibited the growth of bacteria, also did not decolorize methylene blue. The reagent was ordinarily decolorized by normal milk which had stood under ordinary temperature conditions for from 24 to 48 hours. Pasteurization increased the time required for the decolorization of the reagent.

In general, no ratio was found to exist between the time required for decolorization and the number of bacteria in the milk. A general relation, however, appeared to exist between these two factors up to a given point of acidity. Because of a lack of parallelism between these two factors it is indicated that "reductase is of bacterial origin but that not all bacteria found in milk produce this enzym. . . . It seems probable that formaldehyde either gradually retards the action of the reductase or destroys it. This is a matter, however, for more careful investigation in the future."

The experimental data are submitted in tabular and graphical form.

Characteristic milk powder forms, C. Griebel (*Ztschr. Untersuch. Nahr. u. Genussmtl., 32* (*1916*), *No. 10, pp. 445–447, figs. 2*).—Some notes on the differences in the microscopic appearance of whole milk and skim milk powders are submitted.

A further contribution to the method for the determination of fat in cheese, N. A. BRODRICK-PITTARD (*Ztschr. Untersuch. Nahr. u. Genussmtl., 32 (1916), No. 8, pp. 354–358*).—Data submitted show that the presence of greater or lesser amounts of lactic acid in cheese does not exercise an influence on the results in the determination of fat by extraction with ether. The difference in the acid content of fat obtained by extraction with petroleum ether and that extracted with ether is considered to be chiefly due to the insolubility of the oxy-fatty acids in petroleum ether.

From results previously obtained, together with those submitted, the extraction with ether is considered to be the preferable procedure.

The microscopic examination of colza and rape seed cake, J. A. EZENDAM (*Verslag. Landbouwk. Onderzoek. Rijkslandbouwproefstat. [Netherlands]. No. 20 (1917), pp. 1–11, pls. 5*).—The preparation of samples for microscopic examination and the microscopic appearance of various species of Brassica are described. The value of microscopical examination in the control of feeding stuffs is indicated.

The chemical examination of rape seed press cake with reference to its deleterious effect as a feeding stuff, G. B. VAN KAMPEN (*Verslag. Landbouwk. Onderzoek. Rijkslandbouwproefstat. [Netherlands], No. 20 (1917), pp. 53–70, fig. 1*).—Previous work in regard to the determination of mustard oil in samples of rape seed cake is reviewed.

From the study reported it is concluded that when the odor test is used to determine whether or not the sample is harmful it should always be made with the addition of thymol or sodium fluorid. The determination of the amount of mustard oils and the nitrogen content of the thiosinamins is considered to be a more reliable procedure. The limiting figures for these substances reported by earlier workers are, however, not considered to be reliable.

The determination of the water-soluble carbohydrates is deemed to be very important in determining the freshness of the sample and thus indicating the probable harmfulness of the material as a feeding stuff.

Cider and the cider industry in England, G. WARCOLLIER ET AL. (*Bul. Mens. Off. Renseig. Agr. [Paris], 15 (1916), Jan.–July, pp. 167–199; Aug.–Sept., pp. 314–335*).—This is a detailed report of the findings of the French commission appointed by the minister of agriculture to investigate the industry in England.

Washing fruits and vegetables, A. W. BITTING (*Nat. Canners Assoc. Bul. 12 (1917), pp. 28, figs. 31*).—This is a brief general discussion of the subject, together with a description of the various forms of apparatus which have been proposed and used in the canning industry.

Beet molasses: Its composition and utilization, S. J. OSBORN (*Metallurg. and Chem. Engin., 16 (1917), No. 8, pp. 436–443, figs. 3*).—This is a general discussion of the subject under the topics of theories of molasses formation, commercial importance of molasses formation, melassigenic action of various nonsugars, composition of molasses, cane molasses, utilization of beet molasses, cattle feeding, alcohol production, molasses processes, recovery of potash, and miscellaneous processes.

Notes on the preparation, by the distillation and by the combustion of wood, of acid coagulants, and on their effect on the quality of rubber, B. J. EATON and G. S. WHITBY (*Agr. Bul. Fed. Malay States, 5 (1917), No. 4, pp. 124–134*).—Data relative to the use of crude pyroligneous acid, obtained from rubber wood and mangrove, and a "smoke solution" (obtained by passing smoke through water) as coagulants, together with vulcanization and strength tests, are reported.

Pyroligneous acid was found to retard the vulcanization somewhat, although the effect was not constant. The acid distilled from the mangrove had a more marked effect than that distilled from the rubber wood. The results are discussed in detail.

Notes on the rubber from Eucommia ulmoides, A. F. SIEVERS (*Jour. Amer. Chem. Soc.*, *39* (*1917*), No. *4*, pp. *725-731*, *fig. 1*).—Extraction data of the elastic constituent of the bark of *E. ulmoides*, solubility of the ether-extracted caoutchouc in various solvents, percentage of elastic constituent extracted from the bark by various solvents and in various time periods under constant agitation, comparative effect of various solvents on caoutchouc from Eucommia as compared with genuine specimens of crude rubber, and relative rapidity of solvent action of various organic solvents on a Siam, a Ceylon, and a Eucommia specimen of rubber are submitted and discussed.

The artificial drying of tobacco, O. DE VRIES (*Proefstat. Vorstenland. Tabak* [*Dutch East Indies*], *Meded. 10* [*1914*], pp. *1-13*, *figs. 3*).—Experiments on the artificial drying of tobacco are described and discussed. The value of the control of ventilation, temperature, and humidity in artificial drying is indicated.

METEOROLOGY.

A new system of weather prediction, R. PARESCE (*Sci. Amer. Sup.*, *83* (*1917*), No. *2165*, p. *403*, *figs. 4*).—This is a brief review of a report by F. Vercelli on periodic oscillations and prediction of atmospheric pressure. It is claimed that these furnish a basis for predicting weather conditions months in advance.

Normal anomalies of the mean annual temperature variation, H. ARCTOWSKI (*Phil. Mag. and Jour. Sci.*, *6. ser.*, *33* (*1917*), No. *198*, pp. *487-495*, *figs. 4*).—It is stated that if in case of long series of observations the averages for each day of the year are taken into consideration instead of monthly means, curves representing the annual variations of atmospheric temperature show most remarkable anomalies. From a study of certain typical examples of such curves, the author reaches the conclusion "that in a comparative study of the anomalies of the annual temperature variation Teisserenc de Bort's conception of the great centers of action of atmospheric circulation will find an extensive application; because, although at present it would be premature to try to explain why it is that some changes of phase may occur simultaneously in the Arctic and Antarctic regions, or in North America and Siberia, it seems impossible to conceive such correlations without supposing some relationship with the exchange of pressure between the seasonal and permanent centers of action."

Effect of short period variations of solar radiation on the earth's atmosphere, H. H. CLAYTON (*Smithsn. Misc. Collect.*, *68* (*1917*), No. *3*, pp. *18*, *pls. 8*, *figs. 3*).—Using the Pearson method in correlating the bolometric measurements of variations in solar radiation as recorded by Abbott and his associates at the Mount Wilson observatory with atmospheric changes as observed at Pilar in central Argentina, the author concludes "(1) that there is an intimate relation between solar changes and meteorological changes of short period, and that measurements of solar radiation like those made by Dr. Abbott and his associates have the greatest importance for meteorology; (2) that there is a class of meteorological changes which have their origin in equatorial regions, and by a transference of air, probably in the upper layers, are felt within a few days in higher latitudes. These changes are the complement of the complex meteorological drift which goes from west to east in temperate latitudes with a component of motion from pole to equator in both hemispheres."

The influence of intense and prolonged cannonading on rainfall, H. DES-
LANDRES (*Compt. Rend. Acad. Sci.* [Paris], *164 (1917), No. 17, pp. 613–615;
abs. in Rev. Sci.* [Paris], *55 (1917), No. 9, p. 284*).—It is stated that artillery
discharges electrify and ionize the atmosphere to an extent which apparently
influences rainfall, although to a much less extent than the great atmospheric
currents and depressions. To reach a positive conclusion on this point, however, one must carefully consider all of the elements which enter into the
phenomenon, particularly the degree of ionization of the air and the intensity
and character of the electric field.

Commenting on the above, G. Lemoine expresses the opinion that if frequent
and prolonged artillery discharges have any influence on rainfall it is only in
connection with light rains.

Does violent cannonading induce rainfall? SEBERT (*Compt. Rend. Acad.
Sci.* [Paris], *164 (1917), No. 18, pp. 663–669; abs. in Rev. Sci.* [Paris], *55
(1917), No. 10, p. 317*).—Referring to discussions of this subject by Deslandres
and Lemoine, noted above, a question is raised as to whether intense cannonading does not create atmospheric disturbances which may induce heavy and prolonged rainfall. The author is of the opinion that the subject is of sufficient
importance to warrant careful investigation in certain restricted areas by
meteorological bureaus and agricultural experiment stations.

Investigation of the influence of climatic conditions on the composition
of plant oils, G. V. PIGULEVSKI (*Zhur. Russ. Fiz. Khim. Obshch., 48 (1916), pp.
324–341; abs. in Jour. Chem. Soc.* [London], *112 (1917), No. 653, I, p. 189*).—
"Evidence is adduced showing that among plants belonging to one and the
same subfamily the iodin number of the essential oil increases as the geographical distribution of the plant extends farther toward the north."

The past winter, C. HARDING (*Nature* [London], *99 (1917), No. 2484, pp. 294,
295*).—The characteristic features of the five months December, 1916, to April,
1917, which was an abnormally cold and wintry period generally over the
British Islands, are briefly reviewed. Similar conditions prevailed over western
and northern Europe.

SOILS—FERTILIZERS.

Soil moisture and plant succession, G. D. FULLER (*Trans. Ill. Acad. Sci., 7
(1914), pp. 68–73*).—Data representing the range of soil moisture in the upper
subterranean strata of the vegetation of various associations are reported.

"The rate of evaporation in the cottonwood dune association, both by its
great amount and by its excessive variation, seems a quite sufficient cause for
the xerophytic character of the vegetation and for the absence of undergrowth,
in spite of the constant presence of growth water. The pine and oak dune
association resemble one another closely in their supply of growth water. The
former is slightly more xerophytic during the midsummer weeks. The amount
of growth water in the various associations varies directly with the order of
their occurrence in the succession, the pioneer being the most xerophytic.
The ratios between the evaporation and growth water in the beech-maple
forest, oak-hickory forest, oak dune, pine dune, and cottonwood dune associations have been shown to have comparative values of 100, 65, 20, 17, and 15,
respectively, and the differences thus indicated are sufficient to be efficient
factors in causing succession."

Eight references to literature bearing on the subject are appended.

Evaporation and soil moisture in forests and cultivated fields, J. F.
GROVES (*Trans. Ill. Acad. Sci., 7 (1914), pp. 59–67, figs. 5*).—Experiments on

a beech-maple forest soil and on the bordering cultivated fields of wheat and oats are reported.

It was found that "the evaporation rate at the surface of cultivated fields is somewhat parallel to that of the climax beech-maple forest and shows corresponding variations due to changes in weather conditions. After crops are harvested the evaporation rate is greatly increased, due to the increased exposure. In the beech-maple forest the soil moisture is much higher in the stratum, due largely to the great amount of humus. In this association the wilting coefficient was reached only once during the season. In the wheat field the upper stratum shows a marked response in soil moisture due to periodic rainfall. In this association the soil moisture falls decidedly below the wilting coefficient after the wheat is harvested. The upper stratum of the oat field also shows considerable variations which correspond more or less to those in the wheat field."

Three references to literature bearing on the subject are appended.

Tobacco soils and the tobaccos grown thereon, N. H. COHEN (*Proefstat. Vorstenland. Tabak [Dutch East Indies], Meded. 11 (1914), pp. 18, pls. 3*).—Analyses of 20 samples of tobacco soils from eight different localities in Java are reported and compared with analyses of the tobacco grown on these soils.

It was found that the solubility in citric acid of the phosphoric acid of the soils decreased as the soils were heavier and more weathered. The content of available lime of the different soils increased with the content of finest particles in the soil. The quotient of the content of lime soluble in 25 per cent hydrochloric acid and content of available lime decreased as the content of finest particles increased and approached unity. No relation was found between the content of potash in a soil and the tobacco grown thereon, and little relation was shown for phosphoric acid.

Heavy soils with a low content of citrate-soluble phosphoric acid bore tobacco with a lower phosphoric acid content than light soils. Parallel relations existed between the content of available lime in soil and the lime content of the corresponding tobacco. No relation was established between the chlorin and potash content of tobacco and its burning qualities. The whiteness of the ash of the tobacco increased with the lime content, but its relation with the magnesia content was doubtful.

Soil survey of Cowley County, Kansas, E. C. and R. H. HALL and B. W. TILLMAN (*U. S. Dept. Agr., Advance Sheets Field Operations Bur. Soils, 1915, pp. 46, pls. 2, fig. 1, map 1*).—This survey, made in cooperation with the Kansas Agricultural College and Experiment Station, deals with the soils of an area of 725,120 acres in southeastern Kansas, the surface of which is predominantly undulating or gently rolling. The county lies in the Great Plains region. The surface drainage is said to be generally good.

The upland soils of the county are of residual origin and the stream bottom lands of alluvial origin. Twenty-three soil types of nine series are mapped, of which the Summit silty clay loam, the Summit silt loam, Crawford silt loam, and Gerald silt loam cover 29.5, 13.2, 11, and 10.8 per cent of the area, respectively. Chemical analyses are included of some of these soils.

Report on Mecklenburg County soils, agriculture, and industries, C. B. WILLIAMS, W. E. HEARN, J. K. PLUMMER, and W. F. PATE (*Bul. N. C. Dept. Agr., 38 (1917), No. 4, pp. 47, pl. 1, figs. 12*).—This is No. 1 of the North Carolina soil reports. It supplements the survey made in cooperation with the Bureau of Soils of the U. S. Department of Agriculture (E. S. R., 29, p. 16), and includes average chemical analyses of the soil types of the county, together with recommendations as to fertility requirements based on field experiments with the prevailing types.

"Experiments which have been conducted in this county on the Cecil clay, in Iredell on Cecil clay loam, and in Gaston on Cecil sandy loam have shown for several years that nitrogen and phosphoric acid are the constituents chiefly needed. Potash has not been generally shown to be essential except for such crops as tobacco and potatoes."

Lime requirements of some acid soils, S. D. CONNER (*Jour. Assoc. Off. Agr. Chem.*, *3* (*1917*), *No. 1, pp. 139, 140*).—Studies at the Indiana Experiment Station of the lime requirements of very acid peat, peat, peaty sand, loam well supplied with organic matter, and silt loam soils, using the Hopkins potassium-nitrate method, the Veitch limewater method, the Hutchinson-MacLennan calcium-bicarbonate method, and the Jones calcium-acetate method, are reported.

It was found that the Hopkins method gave much lower results than the others, especially on soils containing much organic matter. "This method possibly gives too low an estimate as an average; but . . . in most cases it is just as near as any other method to the amounts of lime which have given profitable returns by actual tests on the crops. While the Veitch method doubtless more accurately determines the amount of lime that a soil has the capacity to absorb, . . . it is not profitable to add this much lime to soils high in organic matter. The results of these tests indicate that organic acidity is much less toxic in soils than inorganic acidity. The Jones calcium-acetate method gives higher results than the calcium-bicarbonate method. . . . None of the soil-acidity methods can be used as an exact estimate of the most profitable amount of lime to be added to the soil."

In this connection the opinion is expressed that "a soil-acidity estimation is probably the most important single test that can be made in the laboratory to determine the chemical requirements of the soil."

Study of soil containing residual limestone, H. A. NOYES (*Jour. Assoc. Off. Agr. Chem.*, *3* (*1917*), *No. 1, pp. 151–153*).—Studies at the Indiana Experiment Station of the acidity of a residual silty clay orchard soil containing about 60 per cent of fine silt and 20 per cent of clay and underlaid with limestone rock are reported. Samples were taken representing the following depths: Surface to 9 in., 9 to 18 in., 18 to 27 in., 27 to 36 in., and 36 to 45 in. Acidity was determined by the Hopkins potassium-nitrate method.

It was found that the acidity did not decrease with the depth and showed no regular decrease or increase dependent upon the distance from bed rock. The acidity results could not be correlated with either the percentage of nitrogen or the volatile matter in the samples. The presence of limestone fragments in this acid soil leads to the conclusion that coarse screenings would not correct the acidity and that for acid silt and clay soils finely ground limestone is necessary.

The character of certain soils in the area devastated by the eruptions of the Soufrière of St. Vincent in 1902–3, H. A. TEMPANY (*West Indian Bul.*, *16* (*1917*), *No. 2, pp. 126–137, fig. 1*).—Physical, chemical, and biological studies of samples from the ash deposits in the Carib country of St. Vincent which were laid down at the time of the eruption of the St. Vincent Soufrière in 1902 are reported. These deposits are said to range in thickness from 14 to 18 in.

"Physically the soils were found to consist of coarse sandy types; they showed shrinkages ranging between 1 and 2 per cent, thereby indicating the formation of a certain amount of colloidal material. Chemically the soils showed small contents of organic carbon and nitrogen; they were extremely deficient in calcium carbonate; [and] they showed the presence of moderate amounts of available phosphoric acid and potash. Characteristically the soils all possessed an appreciable degree of acidity, as evidenced by the lime requirement for neutralization.

"The biological activity of the soils was found to be as follows: The value for the figure for partial sterilization indicated the existence of a moderate activity of putrefactive bacteria. Nitrogen-fixing organisms of the Azotobacter type were found to be present, and the soils showed small, but appreciable, nitrogen-fixing power. The soils also possessed appreciable ammonifying power, but were completely deficient in nitrifying power.

"During the 14 years which have intervened between the eruption and the date on which the samples were taken, considerable progress has been made in the conversion of the sterile ash deposits then laid down into fertile soil."

The "gall patches" in Antigua soils, H. A. TEMPANY (*West Indian Bul. 16 (1917), No. 2, pp. 137–144, fig. 1*).—Chemical and biological studies of so-called gall patches in sugar cane soils, together with cultural experiments with cane and examinations of cane, are reported.

"The results indicate clearly that the effect in question is due to the presence of sodium carbonate in the soil. The origin of this sodium carbonate is attributed to interaction between the calcium carbonate and the sodium chlorid dissolved in soil water and brought up from saliniferous deposits at deeper levels."

Sterilization and fatigue of soil (*Sta. Agron. Finistère et Lab. Dept. Bul., 1914–15, pp. 24–36*).—Experiments on the treatment of soil-growing turnips with benzin and toluene in amounts equivalent to 100, 125, 150, 175, and 200 liters per hectare showed that the largest yield by weight was obtained with benzin added at the rate of 100 liters per hectare (about 10.7 gal. per acre). The benzin was also superior to toluene in amounts of 125 liters per hectare. The toluene gave better results in the higher concentrations, but a treatment of 100 liters per hectare of benzin gave as good result as 175 liters of toluene.

Influence of crop, season, and water on the bacterial activities of the soil, J. E. GREAVES, R. STEWART, and C. T. HIRST (*U. S. Dept. Agr., Jour. Agr. Research, 9 (1917), No. 9, pp. 293–341, fig. 1*).—The work of others bearing on the subject is briefly reviewed and investigations conducted at the Utah Experiment Station with a rich sedimentary soil are reported Twenty $\frac{1}{16}$-acre plats were divided into five equal sets of plats. The first set was left fallow, the second was planted to alfalfa, the third to corn, the fourth to potatoes, and the fifth to oats. One of these sets received a maximum, one a medium, and one a minimum application of water, and one set was unirrigated. The plats were sampled during the spring (about the middle of April), midsummer (about the last of July), and in the fall (the last of October or the first of November). The samples were analyzed for moisture, nitric nitrogen, number of bacteria developing on synthetic media, and the ammonifying and nitrifying powers.

It was found that "the quantity of nitric nitrogen in the surface 6 ft. of alfalfa soil is comparatively low throughout the season, but is higher in the fall than in the spring or summer. The quantity present decreases as the water applied increases; yet the quantity formed in the soil increases as the water applied increases, but is greatest per acre-inch of water when only 15 in. of water are applied. The quantity of nitric nitrogen in the surface 6 ft. of potato, oats, corn, and fallow soil decreases as the water applied increases; but the quantity formed for each of the cropped soils is greatest where the largest quantity of water was applied. The quantity formed per acre-inch of water applied is greatest where only 15 in. of water were applied.

"Large quantities of nitric nitrogen disappeared from the fallow soil during the summer months. This is attributed to the growth of bacteria, which transforms it into protein substances and not to denitrification.

"The larger applications of irrigation, 37.5 and 25 in. of water, carry much of the nitric nitrogen beyond the sphere of action of the plant, and this accounts for the decrease in crop yield, which is often noted when excessive quantities of irrigation waters are applied to a soil. The application of water to a soil depresses the number of organisms which will develop upon synthetic agar in alfalfa, oats, and potato soil, but increases them in fallow. The results obtained with the corn are irregular. The ammonifying powers of all the soils, except the alfalfa, were increased by the application of irrigation water. Water increased the nitrifying powers of all the soils except the oats soil.

"There was a difference of 2° F. in the temperature of the soil of irrigated and unirrigated in favor of the unirrigated. This difference in temperature was perceptible to a depth of 4 ft. The number of organisms was higher in the cropped than in the fallow plats, and this is probably due to the plant residues left upon the cropped soil."

The soils in the order of increasing ammonifying powers were alfalfa, oats, corn, potato, and fallow soils. "By naming them in the order of increasing nitrifying powers, they are fallow, corn. oats, alfalfa, and potato [soils]. The alfalfa not only feeds closer upon the nitric nitrogen of the soil than do other crops but it also increases the nitrifying powers of the soil. Hence, it would deplete the soil of its nitrogen more rapidly where the entire crop is removed than would other crops.

"The use of irrigation water increases the bacterial activities of the soil which render soluble the nitrogen, and where excessive quantities of water are used considerable of this is washed from the soil, thus unnecessarily depleting the soil of its nitrogen. This in turn gives diminished yields on the soil."

The behavior of legume bacteria in acid and alkaline media, R. C. SALTER (Proc. Iowa Acad. Sci., 23 (1916), pp. 309–313, figs. 2).—Experiments made to compare the effects of acid and alkali on legume bacteria are reported, in which it was found that "alfalfa bacteria are benefited by an alkaline reaction, while the clover bacteria do best in a neutral or slightly acid medium. The difference in behavior of alfalfa and red clover plants in acid soils is characterized by a corresponding difference in the behavior of their symbiotic bacteria."

Effect of decomposing organic matter on the solubility of certain inorganic constituents of the soil, C. A. JENSEN (U. S. Dept. Agr., Jour. Agr. Research, 9 (1917), No. 8, pp. 253–268).—This paper "deals with the solvent action on certain inorganic soil constituents of the water-soluble decomposition products of manures and other organic fertilizers. Soils were extracted (1) with soluble organic matter obtained from decomposing green manures and from stable manures; (2) with soluble organic matter obtained from thoroughly decomposed green manures; (3) with artificially prepared humus solutions obtained by hydrolyzing organic substances with acids; and (4) with osmosed organic solutions derived from the decomposition of organic matter. In addition, stable and green manures were added directly to the soil and the effect of this treatment was noted (1) on the amounts of certain soil minerals dissolved out with water, and (2) on the change produced in the specific electrical conductivity of the soil. . . . Two types of soil, a clay loam and a sandy loam, were used.

"In the four soil extractions these organic solvents removed from the soil from two to five times as much calcium as was added to the soil with the solvents. In most cases these solvents removed more magnesium from the soil in the four extractions than was added with the solvents, the increase varying from a small fraction to about 80 per cent. The amount of iron and phosphoric acid removed from the soil by these organic solvents in the four soil extractions did not equal the total amount added to the soil with the solvents. However, the amount of iron dissolved from the soil by the organic solvents exceeded the amount dissolved by distilled water from 1 to 5.5 times. The amount of phosphoric acid dissolved from the soil exceeded the amount dissolved by water from 1.7 to 5.4 times. These various organic solvents, whether derived from a leguminous or a nonleguminous crop, had about equal solvent action on the soil minerals.

"Organic solvents obtained from cow manure treated in a manner similar to the freshly decomposing green manures did not dissolve as much calcium from the soil as the solvents derived from the latter substance. They exerted about the same solvent action, however, on the other elements under investigation. The solvent action of these organic extracts on the soil minerals appeared to be due both to the inorganic salts present in the organic solvents and to the organic compounds. Green manures kept moist until thoroughly decomposed gave organic solvents which removed calcium from the soil in amounts several times that added with the organic solvents. These solvents also removed magnesium, phosphoric acid, and iron considerably in excess of the amount dissolved by water alone. The organic solvents showed no alkaline reaction with phenolphthalein nor acid reaction with methyl orange. Three per cent of green manures and stable manure mixed with soil and allowed to undergo partial decomposition increased the solubility of calcium and phosphoric acid in the soils from 30 to 100 per cent.

"Artificial humus solutions free from calcium, magnesium, iron, and phosphoric acid were prepared by hydrolyzing green manures and sugar with strong acid, washing them free from acid, and extracting with ammonia. These organic solvents, when freed from ammonia, increased the solubility of calcium in the soil, compared with its solubility in water, by amounts varying from a few parts to 240 parts per million of soil. They also increased the solubility of magnesium, phosphoric acid, and iron, but to a less extent.

"In brief, the solubility of calcium, magnesium, iron, and phosphoric acid in citrus soils of the Riverside [Cal.] district is measurably increased by the addition of green manure, stable manure, or their extracts. This increase in solubility is due in part to the action of the inorganic salts contained in the organic substances or their extracts and in part to the solvent action of the soluble organic compounds formed during organic decomposition. The fact that a deficiency in soluble iron is known to induce certain types of chlorosis suggests that the beneficial effects following the addition of organic matter to citrus soils may have been in part due to its solvent action on iron and other soil compounds."

Conversion of soluble phosphoric acid into insoluble phosphoric acid in the soil under the influence of physical, chemical, and biological factors, S. SKALKIJ (*Iuzh. Russ. Selsk. Khoz. Gaz., 17 (1915), Nos. 33, pp. 6, 7; 34, pp. 6, 7; 36, pp. 7, 8; 37, pp. 9–11; 38, pp. 6–8; abs. in Internat. Inst. Agr. [Rome], Internat. Rev. Sci. and Pract. Agr., 7 (1916), No. 8, pp. 1084–1086; Jour. Soc. Chem. Indus., 36 (1917), No. 2, p. 94; Chem. Abs., 11 (1917), No. 9, p. 1237).*—Field and laboratory experiments conducted at the Ploty Agricultural Experiment Station on the fixation of water-soluble phosphoric acid in April fallow soil, uncultivated land, kitchen garden soil, and forest soil are reported.

The soils were studied in two depths, 0 to 17.7 cm. (about 6.97 in.) and 17.7 to 35.5 cm. (about 13.98 in.). In the first series of experiments potassium nitrate at the rate of 3.605 gm. per kilogram was applied in addition to acid phosphate at the rate of 1.3312 gm. per kilogram. In the second series part of the soil was treated with chloroform at the rate of 50 cc. per kilogram. The results are given in the following table:

Fixation of phosphoric acid soluble in water in percentages of the quantity added to the soil (1.3312 gm. of P₂O₅ per kilogram).

Treatment.	Layer 0 to 17.7 cm.				Layer 17.7 to 35.5 cm.			
	April fallow.	Uncultivated land.	Kitchen garden soil.	Forest soil.	April fallow.	Uncultivated land.	Kitchen garden soil.	Forest soil.
First series:	Per ct.	Per ct.	Per ct.	Per ct.	Per ct.	Per ct.	Per ct.	Per ct.
Total fixation (with potassium nitrate)	89.89	87.93	....	....	92.56	89.87	....	....
Total fixation (without potassium nitrate)	87.14	84.04	....	....	91.64	86.92	....	....
Second series:								
Total fixation (in chloroformed soil)	87.14	84.04	84.06	75.28	91.64	86.92	84.11	83.87
Physico-chemical fixation (in chloroformed soil)	84.90	81.92	82.58	73.16	89.94	86.05	83.29	83.65
Biological fixation	2.24	2.12	1.48	2.12	1.70	.87	.82	.22

It is concluded that the process of fixation of water-soluble phosphoric acid in soil depends on physical, chemical, and biological factors, and that the intensity of the total fixation is in direct relation to the cultural conditions and increases with the addition of potassium nitrate to the soil. Fixation was greater in natural soils than in chloroformed soils. The total fixation and the physical and chemical fixation were less in the arable layer, 0 to 17.7 cm., than in that lying immediately beneath, from 17.7 to 35.5 cm.

Further experiments with the bacterial flora of each of the soil samples capable of multiplying in peptonized meat bouillon led to the deduction that the quantity of these bacteria increased with the improvement of the cultural conditions of the soil.

The gases of swamp rice soils.—IV, The source of the gaseous soil nitrogen, W. H. HARRISON and P. A. SUBRAMANIA AIYER (*Mem. Dept. Agr. India, Chem. Ser., 5 (1916), No. 1, pp. 1–31, pls. 6, fig. 1*).—Continuing previous experiments (E. S. R., 36, p. 116), " it has been demonstrated that a very considerable proportion of the gaseous nitrogen normally found in swamp paddy soils is produced through the decomposition of organic matter. . . . The nitrogen gas thus liberated is derived from two distinct sources, namely, (1) from the decomposable organic matter of the soil or of the green manure used, and (2) from a certain proportion of the roots of the crop which die and subsequently decompose. The production of gaseous nitrogen from soil organic matter and green manure persists throughout the growing season but is most prominent during the earlier period, whereas that derived from root decomposition is most prominent during the later stages of growth and persists after harvest time.

" There is no evidence forthcoming to show that the crop interferes with, or materially alters, the normal course of the fermentation of the soil organic matter and green manure; in fact the balance of evidence is distinctly against this theory. Under normal conditions in uncropped soils the nitrogen gas thus produced escapes from the soil into the air at a fairly uniform rate. On the other hand, that produced in cropped soils does not escape in any quantity until about the time when the plant is running up for flower. At this stage a very marked escape of gas occurs which continues up to and past harvest time. This irregularity in the escape of the soil gases from cropped paddy soils is a purely physical phenomenon, and is caused by the roots of the crop forming, in conjunction with fine soil, a surface layer which resists the passage of the gases. The gas is thus trapped and retained in the soil until the accumulation is sufficient to cause a passage to be forced, or until the decay of some of the roots opens out such a passage."

With reference to the change in the composition of the soil gases under the action of a paddy crop, it is shown that "the physical retention of the soil gases through the action of the roots of the crop, taken in conjunction with the oxidizing action of the film, offers a simple and complete explanation of the change in composition of the soil gases under the action of the crop."

With reference to the relations of green manures to the soil and crop, the conclusion is drawn "that the nitrogen of these manures has little actual manurial value, that the crop is mainly dependent upon soil nitrogen for its support, and that green manures owe their efficiency mainly to their indirect action on the soil and by increasing root aeration." It is tentatively concluded that the practice of bringing green manure into paddy soils from external sources is preferable to growing a green crop on the soil to be puddled in, owing to the loss of nitrogen incident to the latter method.

Maintaining the nitrogen supply of the soil, A. W. BLAIR (*New Jersey Stas. Bul. 305 (1917), pp. 5–16, figs. 8*).—A general discussion of the soil nitrogen supply and its maintenance is followed by the results of an eight-year experiment in which wheat and rye were grown continuously on one-twentieth-acre plats of sandy loam soil with and without a leguminous green manure crop of cowpeas and soy beans grown between the time of harvesting the grain crop and the fall seeding of the following crop. While the yields of wheat and rye were small on all plats, those on plats receiving green manure treatment were from 50 to 100 per cent greater than those without green manure treatment.

The average yields for the legume plats and also those without legumes for the last four years were smaller than the corresponding averages for the entire eight years. This is taken as an indication that the nitrogen supply of the soil is not being maintained even where the leguminous crop is grown. The average gain in nitrogen for the legume plats for the last four years, as indicated by the amount recovered in the crop, amounted to about 15 lbs. annually.

It is suggested that farmers endeavor to maintain the nitrogen supply of their soils by growing leguminous crops either as a part of the regular rotation or as green manure crops between the main crops of the rotation as often as possible, and that for the most crops they further supplement the nitrogen thus secured by the use of a few hundred pounds of a material supplying nitrogen in a readily available form.

Fertilizers and increased production, F. T. SHUTT (*Amer. Fert., 46 (1917), No. 10, pp. 44, 46, 48, 52*).—The author reviews Canadian experience with fertilizers, and concludes "that the exclusive use of fertilizers will neither keep up the fertility of the soil nor yield profitable returns; that it is on soils of medium rather than poor quality that a lucrative response from their employment is to be expected; that they can profitably be used to supplement the home source of fertility, farm manures; that the largest returns are not necessarily from the largest applications; and that it is on the money crop of the rotation, such as potatoes, that their application is most profitable."

Is the recovery of the nitrogen in sewage sludge practicable? W. R. COPELAND (*Jour. Indus. and Engin. Chem., 9 (1917), No. 4, pp. 374–376*).—Experiments conducted at the sewage testing station at Milwaukee, Wis., are reported in which it was found "that the dried sludge has a market value upon present figures of $9 to $15 per ton of material containing 10 per cent moisture. The total cost of getting this product and placing it on the market will probably run from $8 to $12 commercially per dry ton, depending upon local conditions. For large plants this cost may possibly be reduced as a result of further experience.

"The activated sludge containing 4 per cent or more of nitrogen is much nearer a commercial possibility than the sludges obtained by the older methods of treatment, such as chemical precipitation, septic tanks, or the Imhoff process, which . . . contain only 1.5 to 3 per cent of nitrogen." The data indicate "that the recovery of the nitrogen in sewage sludge has at last been brought within the range of a commercially practicable problem."

Report on humogen, E. J. Russell (Jour. Bd. Agr. [London], 24 (1917), No. 1, pp. 11–20).—Reviewing fully the experimental work which has been done on the subject, the author finds "no evidence that humogen possesses any special agricultural value. There is not the least indication that it is '50 times as effective as farmyard manure,' to quote an often repeated statement, and there is nothing to show that it is any better than any other organic manure with the same content of nitrogen. It is offered at present at £5 per ton in 2-ton lots; . . . [the Rothamsted] experiments give no reason for supposing that it is worth anything like so much."

The investigations have shown wide variations in the composition of the material, as well as in the results of tests of its fertilizing value. The author states that "there is no definite evidence that 'bacterization' really adds to the value of peat."

Further careful experimental work on the subject is recommended.

Grape cake as a fertilizer, L. Roos (Prog. Agr. et Vit. (Ed. l'Est-Centre), 37 (1916), No. 46, pp. 463–468).—It is stated that grape cake contains on the average 1 per cent of nitrogen, 0.5 per cent of potassium, 0.5 per cent of phosphoric acid, and 35 per cent of organic matter. Its fertilizing value is considered to be double that of barnyard manure.

Information on its use as a fertilizer is also given.

Comparison of four nitrogenous materials as sources of nitrogen, Z. Bonomi and G. Margbeth (R. Lab. Chim. Agr. Udine, Ric. Sper. e Attiv. Spiegata, 4 (1911–1914), pp. 29–34).—Comparative tests with grain, on a soil low in nitrogen and organic matter, of calcium nitrate, sodium nitrate, ammonium sulphate, and calcium cyanamid are reported. In the order named the fertilizers are applied at rates of 8.57, 6, 4.5, and 6 kg. per hectare (7.62, 5.34, 4, and 5.34 lbs. per acre).

In grain production, the best results were obtained with calcium nitrate, followed in order by sodium nitrate, ammonium sulphate, and calcium cyanamid. In straw production, calcium nitrate showed the best results, followed in order by ammonium sulphate, sodium nitrate, and calcium cyanamid. Considering the value of the results obtained with calcium nitrate as 100, sodium nitrate, ammonium sulphate, and calcium cyanamid stood, respectively, as 42, 37, and 31.

The action of superphosphate in tests in 1913, J. M. Geerts (Meded. Proefstat. Java-Suikerindus., 6 (1916), No. 19, pp. 543–651, figs. 7; Arch. Suikerindus. Nederland. Indië, 24 (1916), No. 52, pp. 2065–2173, figs. 7).—This is an extensive report of fertilizer experiments with double superphosphate on cane soils.

It was found that double superphosphate had a distinct action on cane soils poor in phosphoric acid, but in soils rich in phosphoric acid no effect was observed. When the supply of available phosphoric acid in the soil was low, and also when the total supply of phosphoric acid was low, an effect of double superphosphate could be expected. While the experiments on the lighter soils showed no action, those on the heavier soils showed a distinct action of double superphosphate.

It is concluded that for these soils there is a distinct limit for phosphate content. Whenever the total content was less than 0.026 per cent or the available content less than 0.009 per cent, an effect of fertilizing with super-phosphate could be expected, and in some cases also where only one, more particularly the available phosphorus, was less than these limits. It is further concluded that an analysis of soil is not sufficient to determine the need for fertilization with double superphosphate. Fertilization with double superphosphate did not hasten ripening.

The extraction of potash from silicate rocks, II, W. H. Ross (*Jour. Indus. and Engin. Chem., 9 (1917), No. 5, pp. 467–472, fig. 1; abs. in Amer. Jour. Sci., 4. ser., 43 (1917), No. 258, p. 485*).—A study of the various methods, now including over 100 patented processes, that have been proposed for the extraction of potash from feldspar is reported in continuation of work previously noted (E. S. R., 27, p. 628).

It is concluded that the economic success of any process depends upon the recovery at the same time of some other product of value in addition to potash, the most promising by-product being cement. In experiments in which feldspar was subjected to the action of water at high temperature and pressure, there was no decomposition. When, however, the powdered feldspar was digested with water containing 1.7 parts lime at a steam pressure of from 10 to 15 atmospheres, about 90 per cent of the potash went into solution in the form of hydroxid and the residue had the composition required for Portland cement clinker.

Potash from Canadian feldspar, D. J. BENHAM (*Canad. Chem. Jour., 1 (1917), No. 1, pp. 8–11*).—The author describes a process for the extraction of potash from Canadian feldspar which it is claimed yields muriate which is almost chemically pure and permits the collection of at least 87 per cent of all the potassium chlorid vapors released from a raw mixture containing from 9.5 to 12.5 per cent of potash. "The process . . . consists in heating to a high temperature in a blast furnace 110 tons of a mixture of feldspar, coal, calcium, chlorid, and limestone. The limestone is used to render the slag fluid, while the chlorin of the calcium chlorid combines with the potash, forming potassium chlorid which distills over at the temperature of the blast furnace into a condenser, where it meets a current of steam in which it dissolves. By a process of evaporation and crystallization of the solution thus obtained, the salt is obtained in a high state of purity."

Report on wood and plant ashes as a source of potash, R. A. BERRY (*West of Scot. Agr. Col. Bul. 73 (1916), pp. 141–149*).—Analyses showing the potash content of the ashes of bracken, spruce, forest hardwoods, flue dust, and miscellaneous organic substances are reported and discussed.

Bracken was found to contain 20.45 per cent of potash soluble in strong hydrochloric acid. Flue dust from blast furnaces was poor in potash, containing under 4 per cent. Spruce and forest hardwood ashes contained 11.94 and 11.79 per cent, respectively, of potash soluble in strong hydrochloric acid.

[Liming and manurial experiments] (*Ann. Rpt. Agr. Expt. Stas. Assam, 1916, pp. 26–38*).—This is a progress report of miscellaneous liming and manurial experiments. On an old alluvial soil it was found that annual dressings of wood ashes will replace the more expensive lime as a soil ameliorant.

The effect of fineness of division of pulverized limestone on the yield of crimson clover and lime requirement of soils, N. KOPELOFF (*Science, n. ser., 45 (1917), No. 1163, pp. 363–365*).—Pot experiments with crimson clover on Iowa, Ohio, and Tennessee silt loams, on Virginia and California sandy loams, and on New Jersey acid muck to determine the influence of calcium oxid and limestone of 20 to 40, 60 to 80, 100 to 200, and 200+ mesh fineness when added in quantities sufficient to satisfy the lime requirement of each soil, as determined by the Veitch method are reported.

In all the soils there was an increase in the crop as the fineness of the limestone was increased. The yields with the 200-mesh limestone were fully one-third larger than those with the 20-mesh limestone. There was little difference between the results obtained with 200-mesh limestone and the calcium oxid. An analysis of the crops showed that as the fineness of the limestone used increased the total nitrogen increased. "The California soil, being decidedly alkaline, responded unfavorably to the application of limestone. The yield of clover as well as the total nitrogen decreased with increasing fineness of division of pulverized limestone. With the acid muck soil, however, the results were similar to those obtained with the other typical soils, i. e., an increase in fineness of division was responsible for an increase in crop yield and total nitrogen."

Determinations of the lime requirement of the soils after harvesting the clover showed that the lime requirement tended to decrease as the limestone previously applied increased in fineness. The calcium oxid was not so effective in this respect as was the 200-mesh limestone.

Limestones of Michigan, R. A. SMITH (*Mich. Geol. and Biol. Survey Pub. 21, Geol. Ser. 17 (1916), pp. 103–311, pls. 10, figs. 13*).—This report embraces (1) a discussion of the character, origin, and classification of limestones; (2) an outline of the geology of the limestone formations of Michigan; (3) their uses; and (4) descriptions of the occurrence, character, development, and economic possibilities of the limestone beds of the different counties of the State.

Agricultural lime, M. F. MILLER and H. H. KRUSEKOPF (*Missouri Sta. Bul. 146 (1917), pp. 25, figs. 7*).—This is a popular review of experience in liming Missouri soils, with a description of the limestone resources of the State.

It is stated that approximately two-thirds of the samples of Missouri soils examined at the station have shown more or less need for lime. About one-fourth of these have shown a lime requirement of 2 tons or over per acre to a depth of 7 in. Ground limestone is considered to be as a rule the cheapest form to apply.

"Missouri has much limestone suitable for agricultural purposes. The most extensive region of high-grade, high calcium stone extends from southwest Missouri in a northeasterly direction to the Missouri River, spreading out and covering the eastern part of the State both north and South. The Ozark limestones contain much magnesium, and while these are not usually considered so desirable as the high calcium stones they are yet very satisfactory for agricultural purposes."

Tabulated analyses of agricultural lime (*Off. Bul. Bd. Agr. Ohio, 8 (1917), No. 1, pp. 62–64*).—This section of the report contains the results of actual and guaranteed analyses of 40 samples of limestone, calcium carbonate, quicklime, and hydrated lime collected for inspection in Ohio during 1916.

Inspection of commercial fertilizers, 1916, P. F. TROWBRIDGE (*Missouri Sta. Bul. 145 (1917), pp. 41, fig. 1*).—This bulletin contains the results of actual and guaranteed analysis of 331 samples of fertilizers and fertilizing materials collected for inspection in Missouri during 1916, together with the results of tests of the relative value of 163 samples of limestone for correcting soil acidity. A list of brands registered for sale in the State for 1917 is also given.

[Commercial fertilizer analyses] (*Off. Bul. Bd. Agr. Ohio, 8 (1917), No. 1, pp. 65–82*).—This section of the report contains the results of actual analyses of 76 samples of mixed fertilizers, 5 samples of bones, and 4 samples of unmixed fertilizing materials collected for inspection in Ohio during 1916, together with a list of brands of fertilizers licensed from January 1 to February 1, 1917.

Fertilizer registrations for 1917, C. S. CATHCART (*New Jersey Stas. Bul. 304 (1917), pp. 5–42*).—This bulletin contains the list of fertilizer registrations received in New Jersey for 1917 up to January 22.

AGRICULTURAL BOTANY.

Periodicity in transpiration, SOPHIE J. WILKIE (*Trans. and Proc. Bot. Soc. Edinb., 27 (1915–16), pt. 1, pp. 59–64, figs. 2*).—The author has employed the apparatus previously described (E. S. R., 34, p. 729) in tests with *Pinus sylvestris, Opuntia occidentalis,* and *Lilium rubrum* as herein detailed. She has found that under ordinary conditions there is a daily periodicity in transpiration by these plants, which show also individual differences in this respect, transpiration being active but erratic in darkness.

Comparison of the hourly evaporation rate of atmometers and free water surfaces with the transpiration rate of Medicago sativa, L. J. BRIGGS and H. L. SHANTZ (*U. S. Dept. Agr., Jour. Agr. Research, 9 (1917), No. 9, pp. 277–292, pls. 3, figs. 4*).—The authors report a study of the individuality of evaporating surfaces as related to the hourly transpiration rate, employing *M. sativa* and the four types of porous-cup atmometers designed and used by Livingston (E. S. R., 33, p. 320; 34, pp. 34, 521), evaporation tanks which are described, and a filter-paper evaporimeter of special design. The measurements were made at Akron, Colo., during a period of hot, dry weather in July, 1916.

The various atmometers, though differing widely in form, gave graphs which are similar in their characteristics. No very close correspondence was observed between the hourly transpiration rate of alfalfa and the hourly evaporation rate, as given, of any of the systems employed. The departure of the hourly evaporation rate of the porous-cup atmometer from the hourly transpiration rate of alfalfa is considered to be due largely to the increase in evaporation over transpiration during the night, to the sensitivity of the atmometers to changes of wind velocity (not accompanied by like changes in transpiration), and to deficient response by the atmometers to changes in solar radiation.

Lack of high correlation between evaporation and the hourly transpiration rate does not necessarily involve low correlation on a daily basis.

The plant may not respond freely to its environment, but that fact is not considered proved by a departure of relative transpiration rate from evaporation rate in an arbitrarily chosen physical system.

The relationship existing between the oxidase activity of plant juices and their hydrogen ion concentrations, with a note on the cause of oxidase activity in plant tissues, H. H. BUNZEL (*Jour. Biol. Chem., 28 (1916), No. 1, pp. 315–333, figs. 3*).—In continuation of a general body of work begun some years ago, reports on which have been noted as given by the author (E. S. R., 27, p. 9; 29, p. 48; 31, p. 748) or by True and Stockberger (E. S. R., 36, p. 127), the author undertook to study the oxidase activities of various plant tissues in different hydrogen ion concentrations, hoping that such study might throw some light on the nature of the acid effect and furnish further data on the comparative behavior of oxidases from different sources. An account is given of the methods employed. The results as tabulated are considered to corroborate in a quantitative way the findings of other experimenters cited on the inhibition of oxidase by acids, no experiments being made in alkaline solutions owing to the inadequacy of the technique at present available.

The experiments, while not sufficiently numerous to establish clearly the relationship between oxidase activity and hydrogen ion concentration, suggest the agency of two factors, the direct destructive effect of acidity on the active matter and the retardation of oxidation rate by the hydrogen ions. These factors may prove to be easily separable.

It appears that the hydrogen ion concentration for each type of plant material covers only a comparatively narrow range, a fact which may prove to be important. It would seem that the nature of the material related to oxidase activity is identical in closely related plants.

Just what particular agency is responsible for oxidase activity is not yet determined, although it is widely distributed in nature. Active and inactive modifications probably exist side by side, some characteristics noted strongly suggesting the agency of colloids.

Evidence of the action of oxidases within the growing plant, J. H. KASTLE and G. D. BUCKNER (*Jour. Amer. Chem. Soc., 39 (1917), No. 3, pp. 478-482*).— The authors have attempted to establish the presence of oxidases and available oxygen in growing plants. Sweet corn and okra were injected with phenolphthalein, then sectioned and tested with alkali, which showed the pink coloration of phenolphthalein mostly above the point of injection and in some instances extending nearly to the leaf tips. The reagents seem to have traveled along the vascular bundles, spreading in some cases into the neighboring cells. The facts observed are considered to show the occurrence of oxygen and oxidation in the living cells in both monocotyledons and dicotyledons.

The occurrence and physiological significance of flavone derivatives in plants, K. SHIBATA, I. NAGAI, and M. KISHIDA (*Jour. Biol. Chem., 28 (1916), No. 1, pp. 93-108, pl. 1*).—The authors, continuing the work previously noted (E. S. R., 36, p. 329) on flavone derivatives and their relations to other bodies. such as anthocyanin, have carried on a series of studies on the occurrence and the physiological and biological significance of such substances in plants.

It is claimed that a general occurrence of flavone derivatives in plants is now established, but that these, with a few exceptions noted. are limited almost exclusively to the epidermis and the peripheral parenchymatous layer of the aerial parts. It is assumed that flavone derivative solutes in cell sap are important as aiding absorption of ultraviolet waves and as thus protecting the protoplasm and its biochemical activities. This assumption is said to have been supported by observations on plants from alpine and tropical regions where the sun's rays are intense, the plants grown in strong insolation being always rich in flavones except in case of those protected by anatomical and morphological peculiarities. Green leaves of deciduous trees, destined to produce anthocyanin pigment in autumn, are said to contain considerable flavone, the production of autumnal anthocyanin color being due to the reduction of such flavones and initiated by physiological conditions at the end of the growing season.

The acidity of plant cells as shown by natural indicators, A. R. HAAS (*Jour. Biol. Chem., 27 (1916), No. 1, pp. 233-241*).—The author has endeavored to ascertain to what extent natural indicators in living cells can be utilized to determine their reaction (the actual acidity of the dissociated hydrogen ions as contrasted with the total acidity, which includes both dissociated and undissociated hydrogen ions). He has found that the reaction of the sap in some entirely normal cells may be decidedly acid and that a blue color in living cells does not necessarily indicate an alkaline reaction, also that in a dying cell a considerable alteration of reaction may occur.

Germination of seeds of Lepidium sativum in solutions of electrolytes, P. LESAGE (*Compt. Rend. Acad. Sci.* [Paris], *164 (1917), No. 2, pp. 119–121*).—Having observed in the work previously noted (E. S. R., 37, p. 26) that the osmotic pressure of the solution in which seeds of *L. sativum* were being soaked plays an important part in germination, and having entered upon a study of the part played by dissociation in that connection, the author here discusses some of the mathematical and practical phases of that work.

The influence of different media on the histology of roots, SOPHIE J. WILKIE (*Trans. and Proc. Bot. Soc. Edinb., 27 (1915–16), pt. 1, pp. 76–78, pl. 1*).—This is a short note on the differences found to exist in the anatomical structure of roots of *Monstera deliciosa* grown in air, soil, water, wet gravel, and damp soil.

It was found that the development of the absorptive layer varies inversely, and the mechanical tissue directly, with the humidity of the medium. There is no variation in the size of the intercellular spaces of the fundamental tissue, excepting the presence of lacunæ in the cortex of the water roots.

The permeability of living cells to acids and alkalies, A. R. HAAS (*Jour. Biol. Chem., 27 (1916), No. 1, pp. 225–232*).—In view of the fact that metabolism is strongly influenced by changing the chemical reaction of the protoplasm, the author has made a study of the penetration of the cell by reagents, employing as indicators petals of *Browallia speciosa* and Pelargonium, the perianth of the hyacinth, and the root of the red radish, which prove to be well adapted to this purpose. Differences noted in the relative rate of penetration by the hydrogen ion on employment of different methods are thought to be explainable by the dissociation of the acids concerned.

Salt antagonism in gelatin, W. O. FENN (*Proc. Nat. Acad. Sci., 2 (1916), No. 9, pp. 534–538, figs. 3*).—Discussing previous contributions with explanations regarding observed salt antagonisms, the author presents his own hypothesis, which is said to be supported by experimentation on gelatin. This is that anions antagonize cations in their effects upon organisms, the point of maximum antagonism being an isoelectric point at which the amount of alcohol needed for precipitation is at a minimum and the aggregation or amount of precipitation at a maximum.

Similarity in the behavior of protoplasm and gelatin, W. O. FENN (*Proc. Nat. Acad. Sci., 2 (1916), No. 9, pp. 539–543, figs. 2*).—Discussing the above and other investigations, the author concludes that if we assume that the effect of time in the Laminaria experiments of Osterhout (E. S. R., 32, p. 728) is to increase the concentration of the salts in the cells of the tissue, a close analogy to these experimental results is found in gelatin to which sodium hydroxid has been added.

Tolerance of fresh water by marine plants and its relation to adaptation, W. J. V. OSTERHOUT (*Bot. Gaz., 63 (1917), No. 2, pp. 146–149*).—The author has followed up studies previously noted (E. S. R., 30, p. 130) regarding the effects of distilled water on protoplasm. He has found that remarkable differences exist between plants, and even between different cells of the same plant, with respect to their tolerance of fresh water. These differences may prove to be of significance in connection with adaptation.

In case of Polysiphonia, many cells are killed by exposure to pure distilled or fresh water for less than one minute. Instances are discussed of remarkable tolerance by plants naturally, accidentally, or experimentally subjected to great and quick alterations of salinity in the water. It is supposed that some characters attributed to adaptation may have been present from the beginning and that they may have been due originally to entirely different causes. The fact that leaf cells, as compared with root cells of the same plant, withstand a much longer exposure to fresh water is considered significant. Suggestions are made that some protoplasm may part more readily than other with certain salts with which it may be chemically or mechanically united, and that the less tolerant protoplasm may consist more largely of such substances as globulins or other colloids, which undergo a change of state as soon as the concentration of the salts falls below a certain limit.

Copper in the flora of a copper-tailing region, W. G. BATEMAN and L. S. WELLS (*Jour. Amer. Chem. Soc.*, *39* (*1917*), *No. 4*, *pp. 811–819*).—Plants growing in a copper-tailing region were found to contain copper, arsenic, antimony and zinc, the amounts of copper ranging from 0.0046 to 0.621 per cent. Larger quantities were present in the dead than in the living tissue and in the bark than in the other parts of the plant.

It is noted that "many plants are unable to adapt themselves to this novel factor of environment, while others flourish in spite of it, thus showing a decided selective activity."

Models to illustrate segregation and combination of Mendelian characters, H. M. CHIBBER (*Agr. Jour. India, Indian Sci. Cong. No., 1916, pp. 80–85, figs. 2*).—This paper describes a scheme for demonstrating the behavior of hereditary characters that conform with the Mendelian principles. The dominant determiners are represented by colored beads, while the recessive determiners are represented by beads identical in size and shape but colorless. The method of demonstrating the composition of different zygotes and of their gametes is illustrated with reference to one, two, and three characters, respectively. The demonstration of the phenotypic composition is also illustrated.

The probable error of a Mendelian class frequency, R. PEARL (*Amer. Nat.*, *51* (*1917*), *No. 603, pp. 144–156*).—In view of the growing need for adequate and clearly understood tests for the statistical significance of differences between expectation and observed results in Mendelian experimentation, the author offers a method supplementary to those in use of calculating and expressing the errors, due to random sampling, of a Mendelian class frequency. The method consists essentially in expressing each expected frequency as the probable quartile limits, determined from the ordinates of a hypergeometrical series, for that class frequency in a supposed second sample of the same size as the observed sample drawn from the same population. Simplifications of method are suggested and illustrated.

Note on the inheritance of crossability, W. O. BACKHOUSE (*Jour. Genetics*, *6* (*1916*), *No. 2, pp. 91–94*).—The author found that in the progeny of a hybrid wheat crossed with rye there was a segregation of crossability. The data here obtained from this and other crossings described are considered to justify caution in ascribing importance to the production and fertility of hybrids as a guide to relationship. It is considered as very probable that the deciding factor as to whether two individuals will hybridize or not may depend upon one simple Mendelian factor.

The results of hybridization in Salix, S. IKENO (*Bot. Mag.* [*Tokyo*], *30* (*1916*), *No. 357, pp. 316–320*).—Experimentation, including artificial hybridization since 1910 between *S. purpurea multinervis* and *S. purpurea gracilistyla*, is said to have shown that the hybrids are not always constant. A certain amount of splitting was revealed, somewhat obscured by the failure of some of the plants to live, so that the question as to Mendelian behavior in this respect is not yet settled.

Evolution by means of hybridization, J. P. LOTSY (*The Hague: Martinus Nijhoff, 1916, pp. X+166, figs. 2*).—Discussing some evidences and views which have been offered regarding the problems and methods of organic evolution, the author claims that crossing is the cause of the origin of new types which are perpetuated by heredity, natural selection being the cause not of their origin but of their gradual extinction. It is considered correct, in a sense, to say that species are related to one another in the same way that human brothers or cousins are, being in each case simply separates resulting from a previous crossing.

The bearing of some general biological facts on bud variation, E. M. EAST (*Amer. Nat., 51 (1917), No. 603, pp. 129-143*).—The author, dealing with the possible relation to bud variation of such conditions as environment, mutilations, diseases, and changes in food supply, states that bud variations are comparable to seed variations in their nature and in the abundance of types produced thereby, but handicapped by the fact that recombinations of variant characters are possible only in case of sexual reproduction. It is held that environment must have been an immense factor during the long periods involved in organic evolution, but its effects are shown so infrequently that it may be neglected for the practical purposes of plant breeding. It would not, however, be safe to deny importance to bud variation as an adjunct to plant breeding.

Mendelian factor differences *v.* reaction system contrasts in heredity, I, II, T. H. GOODSPEED and R. E. CLAUSEN (*Amer. Nat., 51 (1917), Nos. 601, pp. 31-46; 602, pp. 92-101*).—In this work, which besides listing related contributions deals with a number of facts and conclusions drawn from contributions by Goodspeed, alone or with others (E. S. R., 34, p. 136; 37, p. 225), it is stated that *Nicotiana sylvestris*, when crossed with varieties of *N. tabacum*, gives an F_1 hybrid which is a replica, on a large scale, of the *tabacum* variety employed. Such hybrids produce a small number of functional ovules which represent the *sylvestris* and *tabacum* extremes of a recombination series, most members of which fail to function because of mutual incompatibility of the elements of the two systems. Back crosses with *sylvestris* give both *sylvestris* and aberrant forms, of which the former only are fertile and breed true. Back crosses with *tabacum* produce apparently only *tabacum* forms, some of which are fertile and breed true.

The authors reach the general conclusion that Mendelian factors may be considered as making up a reaction system, the elements of which exhibit more or less specific relations to one another. Strictly Mendelian results are to be expected only when the contrast is between factor differences within a common Mendelian system, as ordinarily in varietal hybrids. When distinct reaction systems are involved, as in species crosses, the phenomena are to be regarded as a contrast between systems rather than between specific factor differences. Sterility in such cases depends upon nonspecific incompatibility between elements of the systems involved, and its degree depends upon the degree of incompatibility rather than upon the number of factors. The consequences of the application of such a conception to the complex type of behavior in Œnothera are pointed out and the suggestion is made that the type of behavior exhibited by *Œ. lamarckiana* and its segregants in hybridization may be referred to such complex system interactions.

Œnothera mutants with diminutive chromosomes, ANNE M. LUTZ (*Amer. Jour. Bot., 3 (1916), No. 9, pp. 502-526, pl. 1, figs. 7*).—In this report, the first of a projected series of three on studies continuing for several years in Europe and America and dealing with somatic chromosome number in mutants of the *lamarckiana* group of Œnothera, the author considers the 14-chromosome mutants, the 14^{+1}-chromosome mutants and offspring of certain hybrids, the origin of the small chromosome and its fate in succeeding generations, chromosomal individuality as evidenced by the small chromosomes, and some observations on *Œ. rubrinervis*.

Root cuttings, chimeras, and sports, W. BATESON (*Jour. Genetics, 6 (1916), No. 2, pp. 75–80, pl. 1*).—The author states that some unsuspected plants are really periclinal chimeras, having an outer layer or cortex distinct in genetic composition from the inner core, and that whenever plants grown from root cuttings differ from those grown from corresponding stem cuttings, it may be inferred, at least provisionally, that the plant is a periclinal chimera. Some studies have been undertaken and are still in progress with Bouvardia, some doubles of which are said to give singles from their root cuttings, differences in color appearing also in several instances.

Fasciation in Pharbitis hederacea, Y. YAMAGUCHI (*Jour. Col. Sci., Imp. Univ. Tokyo, 39 (1916), Art. 2, pp. 56, pls. 2, figs. 5*).—The author, reporting a study of P. *hederacea*, states that Knop's solution in 1, 2, and particularly 5 per cent strength favored the production of fasciation. The higher concentrations hindered greatly the development of the fasciated plants, while the normal plants were but little retarded thereby. Darkness had little effect upon the development of fasciation and topping produced no fasciation in normal plants. Longitudinal splitting at the top of the stem resulted in slight fasciation, as did removal of the blooms, the same treatment giving uncertain results when applied to the leaves and tending to recovery of fasciated plants when applied to the roots.

The woody structure was looser and less developed in fasciated plants, with a relatively greater development of the vascular bundles and a diminution of size with increase in length of the cells. This phenomenon appears to be hereditary, showing from the earliest stages. The production of fasciation, so far as its mechanical phases are concerned, is due to the early coalescence of the leaf stalk with the plant stem in conjunction with leaf growth in the early stages of development.

Plant succession.—An analysis of the development of vegetation, F. E. CLEMENTS (*Carnegie Inst. Washington Pub. 242 (1916), pp. XIII+512, pls. 61, figs. 51; rev. in Jour. Ecology, 4 (1916), No. 3–4, pp. 198–204*).—This book constitutes the general part of a monograph on Rocky Mountain vegetation, a study of which has been in progress since 1899. The general principles herein set forth are an outgrowth of the treatment in the contributions previously noted (E. S. R., 15, p. 955; 19, p. 529), the original concepts in which have been confirmed and generalized by the studies since carried on.

It is thought that the earlier concept of the formation as a complex organism with a characteristic development and structure in harmony with a particular habitat is fully justified, representing really the only possible complete and adequate view of vegetation. This concept has been broadened and definitized by the recognition of the developmental unity of the habitat, so that formation and habitat are regarded as the two inseparable phases of a development which terminates in a climax controlled by climate. All vegetation has thus been developmentally related, every climax formation having its phylogeny as well as its ontogeny. Essentially the same processes or functions of vegetation have held throughout geologic time, so that it is possible to sketch the succession of plant populations throughout eras and periods, organizing in a tentative fashion the new field of paleoecology.

A bibliography is appended.

Polar bear cacti. O. F. COOK and ALICE C. COOK (*Jour. Heredity, 8 (1917), No. 3, pp. 113–120, figs. 6*).—Opuntia *floccosa*, found on exposed slopes of the bleak plateaus of the Andes of southern Peru, is described in connection with environmental relations as regards protection against direct sunshine and cold. It is suggested that there may be a real analogy between these cacti and the animal from which they are named as regards adaptation to extreme special conditions.

A quantitative, volumetric, and dynamic study of the vegetation of the Pinus tæda belt of Virginia and the Carolinas, R. M. HARPER (*Bul. Torrey Bot. Club, 44 (1917), No. 1, pp. 39-57, fig. 1*).—This is an account of a very rapid survey of the *P. tæda* belt of the Atlantic coastal plain as regards its boundaries, topography, hydrography, soils, climate, and vegetation, giving lists of plants observed with estimated percentages of the several species.

Meadow vegetation in the montane region of northern Colorado, E. L. REED (*Bul. Torrey Bot. Club, 44 (1917), No. 2, pp. 97-109, fig. 1*).—The results of studies made during two summer seasons are embodied chiefly in descriptions of seven plant societies of meadows of the Boulder Park region, at Tolland, in northern Colorado, with an altitude of 2,710 meters (8,891 ft.). Societies of the lower montane region are indicated and the different characteristics of the subalpine meadows are also briefly discussed. A list of the meadow plants of Boulder Park with their frequency and soil moisture index is also given.

Taxonomic botany and the Washington botanist, A. S. HITCHCOCK (*Jour. Wash. Acad. Sci., 7 (1917), No. 9, pp. 251-263*).—This is a plea for a better utilization of the opportunities in the vicinity of Washington, D. C., as regards observation and taxonomic study of local flora.

FIELD CROPS.

Forage and root crops, C. S. KNIGHT (*Nevada Sta. Bul. 86 (1917), pp. 3-20, figs. 13*).—Variety tests with alfalfa, corn (for silage), sorghum, and potatoes; irrigation tests with alfalfa and red clover; field tests of sweet clover, Sudan grass, and beets and mangels; and tests of forage crops for seed and hay production are reported.

Australia alfalfa No. 23753 was first of 66 varieties with a yield of 6,920 lbs. and North Dakota No. 27247 second with 6,875 lbs. of cured hay per acre. The proportion of leaves to the entire plant was 36.8 and 36.5 per cent, respectively. Nevada No. 6 was lowest with a yield of 2,100 lbs. The proportion of leaves to stems for all the varieties tested varied from 48.5 per cent in France No. 12694 to 30 per cent in Media No. 16400, although the yields of the two varieties named were identical, 3,004 lbs. of hay per acre.

Improved Learning corn gave the highest average yield of silage per acre, 11.3 tons, for the 4-year period 1913 to 1916. Wisconsin Yellow Dent, with a yield of 8.5 tons, was lowest. No variety has matured grain.

The sorghums did not mature seed and were considered inferior to corn for silage purposes. Broom corn produced a heavy brush, but did not mature seed.

The Great Divide and Burbank varieties of potatoes, with average yields of 12,161 and 10,204 lbs. per acre, respectively, have given the best results in potato variety tests for the 4-year period 1913 to 1916.

Irrigation tests with alfalfa and red clover included 6, 9, and 12 in. applications of water at three successive stages of wilt. With the advance in the wilting stage, the average variations in alfalfa for a 3-year period were from 64 to 21 in. in total irrigation, 83.9 to 76.4 per cent in total water content, 37.3 to 43.2 per cent in proportion of leaves to stem, 6.68 to 4.41 tons in yield per acre, and 1.29 to 2.05 tons in yield per acre-foot of water. The heaviest yield per acre, 7.32 tons, was secured with the heaviest total irrigation of 72 in., but the yield per acre-foot of water was only 1.23 tons. These results indicate that the most economical use of water favors 12-in. applications (with a total irrigation of about 36 in.) between the last two stages of wilting, this resulting in an average yield of 5.7 tons per acre and of 1.85 tons per acre-foot of water. In all three stages the 6-in. applications gave the lowest and the 12-in. the highest yields, with but little variation in yield per acre-foot of water. A gradual decrease in yield was noted with the same applications made as the wilting stage advanced. Alfalfa responded better than wheat and potatoes to heavy applications of water.

The highest clover yield, 6.97 tons per acre, was secured from a total of 57 in. of water in 12-in. applications (the first application being 9 in.), with a yield of 1.47 tons per acre-foot of water. The lowest yield, 2.71 tons, was secured with four 6-in. irrigations and gave 1.35 tons per acre-foot of water. The results indicate that clover can not be allowed to reach the wilting stages without a material decrease in the yield of hay. The nitrogen content varied inversely with the total yield of forage per acre.

Sudan grass yielded 3.8 tons of forage and 1,912 lbs. of seed per acre in the 1916 trials and is especially recommended for seed production for well-drained soils of Nevada.

Field trials with root crops gave average yields of 15.73 tons of roots for Our Ideal mangels and 12.06 tons for sugar beets, with an average sugar content of 4.5 and 19.5 per cent, respectively. In date-of-planting tests with sugar beets the yield varied from 20.79 and 20.35 tons for beets planted April 23 and 30, respectively, to 4.79 tons for beets planted July 2. Nevada-grown sugar beet seed yielded at the rate of 20.9 tons per acre, with 19.5 per cent sugar and 82.1 per cent purity of juice, while seed of Russian origin produced 20.8 tons per acre, with 17.5 per cent sugar and 75.3 per cent purity of juice.

Sudan grass, beans, and field peas were compared for seed production. The Kaiser field pea, with an average yield of 1.667 lbs. per acre, was highest and California Mexican Large bean lowest, with 505 lbs. Sudan grass gave an average yield of 1,506 lbs. A similar test with Sudan grass, millet, and field peas for hay production resulted in an average yield of 2.7 tons per acre with Siberian millet, while Bangalia field pea was lowest, with 1.27 tons. Sudan grass gave an average yield of 2.5 tons and Green Canada field pea an average yield of 2.1 tons per acre.

Field crops for late planting, C. S. Knight (*Nevada Sta. Bul. 88 (1917), pp. 15, figs. 5*).—The value of wheat and oats for hay, and of potatoes, sugar beets, Sudan grass, and millet for late planting, due to a late, cold spring, is discussed in a popular manner, including cultural directions.

[Field crops] (*Izv. Khartov. Oblast. Selsk. Khoz. Opytn. Sta., Otd. Polevod., No. 3 (1915), pp. XII+112, fig. 1*).—Field experiments conducted at the Kharkov Experiment Station in 1912, 1913, and 1914 are reported, and include fertilizer, manurial, variety, and cultural tests with rye, corn, sorghum, spring wheat, winter wheat, barley, oats, millet, and potatoes.

[Field crops], E. A. Nobbs (*Rhodesia Agr. Jour., 13 (1916), Nos. 4, pp. 474–488; 5, pp. 659–672, pl. 1*).—Field tests with varieties, fertilizers, and cultural methods on various crops at the Gwebi Experiment Farm for the season of 1915–16 are reported.

[Field experiments], A. W. K. De Jong and C. van Rossem (*Dept. Landb., Nijv. en Handel [Dutch East Indies], Meded. Agr. Chem. Lab., No. 12 (1916), pp. 150, pl. 1, figs. 41*).—This is a detailed report of field experiments in the testing of fertilizers, stable manure, and crop rotations for the year 1914–15.

[Field crops] (*Rpt. Nagpur Expt. Farm [India], 1915, pp. 21, 22*).—A glossary of the botanical, English, and vernacular names of a number of crops grown in India is given, together with several local agricultural terms and their meanings.

[Registration of varieties], E. G. Montgomery, C. G. Williams, and H. K. Hayes (*Jour. Amer. Soc. Agron.*, *8 (1916)*, *No. 6*, *pp. 391–394*).—This is the report of the committee on varietal nomenclature of the American Society of Agronomy previously noted (E. S. R., 36, p. 198). A suggested form of application for registration of varieties of winter wheat is included.

[Field crops] (*Proc. Amer. Seed Trade Assoc.*, *34 (1916)*, *pp. 125, pl. 1*).— The following papers relating to field crops were read at the thirty-fourth annual convention of the American Seed Trade Association: The Evolution of Corn Growing and Feeding in the Northwest, by A. K. Bush; Farmers' Associations, by W. D. Weedy, with special reference to the dissemination of pedigreed seed; Report of Committee on Experiment Stations, by L. L. Olds; Report of the Committee on Nomenclature, by H. G. Hastings; and The Vegetable Growers' Attitude Toward Nomenclature, by C. E. Durst.

[Field crops] (*Proc. Dry Farming Cong.*, *10 (1915)*, *pp. 69–126, 207–238, figs. 3*).—At the tenth annual session of the International Dry-farming Congress the following papers relating to field crops were presented: High Altitude Crops, by T. S. Parsons; Grasses in Relation to Dry Farming, by C. V. Piper; Dry Farming in Western Canada, by J. Bracken; Cultivation to Conserve Soil Moisture, by W. W. Burr; Effect of Soil Alkali on Dry-farm Crops, by F. S. Harris; Dry-land Agriculture Investigations in the Great Plains Area, by E. C. Chilcott; and Arizona Indian Agriculture, by A. M. McOmie.

Notes on dry farming in the following countries were given by their respective representatives: Colombia, Nicaragua, Australia, South Africa, China, Greece, Russia, Belgium, Sweden, Roumania, Guatemala, Iceland, and Argentina.

Dry farming in Colorado, A. Kezer (*Colorado Sta. Bul. 227 (1917)*, *pp. 3–40, figs. 12*).—General principles of dry-land farming applicable to Colorado conditions are discussed in detail, and crops deemed suitable for dry farming recommended and their production described.

Grasses under drought conditions at Hawkesbury Agricultural College, W. D. Keble (*Agr. Gaz. N. S. Wales*, *27 (1916)*, *No. 10*, *pp. 694–697, figs. 3*).— Brief notes are given on the behavior of certain grasses under extreme drought conditions during the year 1915 and part of 1916. The precipitation for the year ending December 31, 1915, was 16.725 in., the lowest in 51 years; and for the year ending May 31, 1916, only 13.195 in. The grasses noted are *Eragrostis curvula*, *Chloris gayana*, *Andropogon intermedius*, *E. leptostachya*, *Paspalum dilatatum*, *Anthistiria avenacea*, *Pollinia fulva*, and *Andropogon sorghum*.

Artificial reseeding of range lands, A. W. Sampson (*Nat. Wool Grower*, *6 (1916)*, *No. 11*, *pp. 23–25, figs. 5*).—This is a discussion of the results obtained in various tests undertaken by the U. S. Forest Service in reseeding range lands in restricted localities extending from Canada to Mexico.

Fall sowing is recommended and the trampling of the seed by sheep was found to be sufficient to work it into the soil. Successful seedings were obtained with timothy, smooth brome grass, perennial rye grass, Italian rye grass, redtop, and Kentucky blue grass, in the order named. Of the clovers, white clover gave the best returns. The moisture conditions of the land will determine to a large extent the plants to be seeded, and with that in view the following recommendations are made: Mixture for wet lands, redtop 5 lbs., timothy 3 lbs., Italian rye grass 3 lbs., and alsike clover 2 lbs. per acre; mixture for moist lands, timothy 3 lbs., orchard grass 5 lbs., Kentucky blue grass 5 lbs., and white clover 2 lbs.; and mixture for medium moist lands, smooth brome grass 6 lbs., timothy 4 lbs., slender wheat grass 5 lbs. Attempts at seeding the drier lands have not been successful.

Cereal experiments, A. C. Tonnelier (*Experiencias sobre Cereales. Buenos Aires: Min. Agr., 1914, pp. 239, figs. 38*).—Field tests with wheat, barley, rye, and oats from 1910 to 1913, inclusive, are reported, including general notes on variety tests with each cereal for 1910 and 1911 (pp. 5–75) ; notes on variety tests for 1911 and 1912 (pp. 79–133) ; notes on fertilizer and cultural experiments with wheat and barley for 1911 and 1912 (pp. 137–169) ; and notes on variety tests with wheat, barley, and rye for 1912 and 1913 (pp. 173 to 239).

Seed grain inspection and crop reports, 1915–16, J. J. Garland (*Ann. Rpt. Wis. Agr. Expt. Assoc., 14 (1916), pp. 11–16*).—The reports of members of the Wisconsin Agricultural Experiment Association on the yields of pedigree grains grown in 1915 show that pedigreed barley yielded 5.5 bu. per acre in excess of the United States average, pedigreed oats No. 1 9.3 bu. and pedigreed winter rye 4.4 bu. over other varieties, and pure-bred corn (Wis. No. 7) 23 bu., select winter wheat 10.4 bu., and spring wheat 10 bu. over the United States averages. Data are also presented from experiments conducted by members of the association on rates of seeding, drilling v. broadcasting, and spring v. fall plowing.

Some effects of legumes on associated nonlegumes, M. W. Evans (*Jour. Amer. Soc. Agron., 8 (1916), No. 6, pp. 348–357, pls. 2*).—This is a further study of some of the effects of legumes on nonlegumes growing in a mixture with them. The experiments described were performed during 1912, 1913, 1914, and 1915 at the timothy breeding station at New London, Ohio, which is conducted cooperatively by the U. S. Department of Agriculture and the Ohio Experiment Station. The leguminous plant used was clover (*Trifolium pratense* and *T. repens*), while timothy (*Phleum pratense*), redtop (*Agrostis alba*), and Kentucky blue grass (*Poa pratensis*) were grown alone and in mixture with the clover.

The following table shows the percentage of increase in the protein content and length of leaf in the grasses grown with clover over those grown alone:

Percentage of increase in the protein content and in the length of leaf growth in grasses grown with clover over grasses grown alone.

Kind of grass.	Protein (N×6.25).	Length o. leaf.
	Per cent.	*Per cent.*
Timothy grown in lawn plat	18.89	21.27
Timothy grown in field	7.68	19.41
Redtop	9.48	13.25
Kentucky blue grass	16.03	30.13
Average	13.02	21.01

Timothy plats receiving ammonium nitrate showed a somewhat greater increase in percentage of protein in the grass over those plats where the grass was grown in mixture with clover.

Clippings from plats where grass was grown in mixture with clover showed a larger proportion of green leaves and a correspondingly smaller proportion of dry brown leaves than clippings from plats where grass was grown alone.

Soy beans and cowpeas in Illinois, W. L. Burlison and O. M. Allyn (*Illinois Sta. Bul. 198 (1917), pp. 20*).—The adaptability and production of soy beans and cowpeas in central and southern Illinois are briefly discussed, with a report of extensive variety tests at Urbana (Champaign Co.) and Fairfield (Wayne Co.).

The soy bean appears to be much better suited to Illinois conditions than the cowpea, except on poor, unfertilized, sour soil in southern Illinois, where the latter may be more hardy.

A seeding rate of from 30 to 40 lbs. per acre for soy beans is recommended when the beans are planted in rows, with a rate of from 1 bu. to 6 pk. when sown broadcast.

The variety tests included a comparison of yields of seed, hay, and straw. Recommendations of soy bean varieties for central Illinois include Haberlandt, Hong Kong, Chestnut, Amherst, Ebony, Sherwood, Meyer, and Nuttall for seed production. Ebony is a consistent-yielding, medium late, standard variety, while Medium Yellow, although not a high-yielding variety, is early and is recommended for planting when winter wheat is to follow soy beans. The two last-named varieties are considered the best for southern Illinois conditions. The agronomic characteristics of 27 varieties of soy beans are listed in tabular form.   •

In variety tests with cowpeas for seed production Extra Early Black Eye for central Illinois and Michigan Favorite for southern Illinois gave the best results. Cowpea tests were abandoned at Urbana in 1909, due to the superiority of soy beans. At Fairfield the range of average yields of soy beans was from 6.5 to 16 bu. per acre, while the range of cowpeas was only from 3.4 to 7.2 bu. per acre.

A test of soy beans grown in rows 24 in. apart and cultivated, at Fairfield, gave a 3-year average yield of 14.4 bu., as compared with a yield of 15.5 bu. from beans sown in rows 8 in. apart and not cultivated. The highest average yields of beans were secured for two consecutive years from a row spacing of 24 in. as compared with spacings of 32 and 40 in.

The dry-matter content of field-cured and green forage, A. C. ARNY (*Jour. Amer. Soc. Agron., 8 (1916), No. 6, pp. 358–363, pl. 1*).—This is a comparison of the determination of the yields of alfalfa and other forage crops by weighing the field-cured hay with weighing the crop green. The data were obtained under field conditions from a large number of plats on the university farm, Minnesota College of Agriculture. The crops of 1915 were weighed and sampled as soon as cut and are compared with those of 1914, which were weighed and sampled when field-cured.

The coefficient of variation appears to be the most satisfactory basis for comparison and is given, together with the mean of the dry-matter percentages and the standard deviations. Data are given for three cuttings of alfalfa, two cuttings of timothy and clover mixed, and one cutting of sweet clover for each year.

The alfalfa and timothy and clover plats were less variable in dry-matter content in 1914 than when weighed as soon as cut in 1915. Sweet clover was more variable in dry-matter content when weighed and sampled in the field-cured condition than when weighed and sampled as soon as cut. A more accurate estimate of the weights of alfalfa and timothy and clover mixed was secured from the weights based on the field-cured hay than on the crop cut green. Sweet clover showed a higher moisture content than the other crops at the time of cutting, indicating that it could be less easily cured than alfalfa or timothy and clover mixed, and that less representative samples could be secured.

A variation of 5 per cent or more in the moisture content of the crops on different plats is deemed too great for accurate results; therefore, samples for making corrections of yields on the air-dry or water-free basis are necessary. When such samples are taken it has been found more desirable to weigh the product of each plat as soon as cut, especially if nitrogen determinations or complete analyses are to follow the determination of dry-matter content.

Alfalfa in Kansas, H. W. DOYLE ET AL. (*Quart. Rpt. Kans. Bd. Agr., 35 (1916), No. 138, pp. 11–338, 447–472, figs. 288*).—A detailed discussion of the production and marketing of alfalfa in Kansas.

12883°—17—No. 5——4

[Alfalfa], L. F. GRABER and A. C. JOHNSON (*Ann. Rpt. Wis. Agr. Expt. Assoc., 14 (1916), pp. 68–88, pls. 2*).—According to the secretary's report at the fourth annual meeting of the Alfalfa Order of the Wisconsin Agricultural Experiment Association, out of 487 reports received from 796 farmers to whom alfalfa seed was distributed in the spring of 1914, 81 per cent reported good or fair success. Of the 19 per cent which reported poor stands or failures, the reasons given included lack of lime, lack of inoculation, poorly drained flat land, nurse crop too thick, early spring freezing and thawing, land of poor fertility, weeds and poor preparation of seed bed, crowded out by blue grass, drought after nurse crop was harvested, lack of snow covering, loose seed bed due to late spring plowing, and late fall cutting or pasturing.

Field experiments indicated that a 20-lb. rate of seeding gives the best results. There was no appreciable difference in winterkilling between southwestern- and northern-grown seed.

General notes on alfalfa production in Wisconsin are given, as well as statistics by A. C. Johnson concerning alfalfa in South Dakota.

Bermuda grass, S. M. TRACY (*U. S. Dept. Agr., Farmers' Bul. 814 (1917), pp. 19, figs. 2*).—The characteristics, adaptations, and uses of Bermuda grass in the South are discussed, including cultural directions and analyses.

Bermuda grass is said to compare favorably with timothy in feeding value, although its market value is usually less. Notes are given on the eradication of Bermuda grass by freezing the "roots," or by growing a winter smother crop of oats or rye followed by a summer crop of cowpeas or velvet beans.

Irrigation and manuring studies.—II, The effect of varying quantities of irrigation water and manure on the growth and yield of corn, F. S. HARRIS and D. W. PITTMAN (*Utah Sta. Bul. 154 (1917), pp. 3–29, figs. 14*).—In continuation of work previously noted (E. S. R., 31, p. 428), the results of irrigation and manuring experiments with corn are reported for the six-year period of 1911 to 1916, inclusive. In addition to the material discussed in the previous report, data on the composition of corn as affected by the irrigation and manurial treatments are presented for the first time. Detailed tabulated data regarding the crop are given for each treatment during the six years of the experiment.

The highest average yield of grain, 84.8 bu. per acre, was obtained with 20 in. of water, and the highest average yield of stover, 3.943 tons, with 30 in. With 40 in. of water the average yields were 79.2 bu. of grain and 3.817 tons of stover per acre, a decided decrease resulting in a waste of water and loss of time. The value of an acre-inch of water for applications of 5, 10, 20, 30, and 40 in. was $1.90, $0.87, $0.69, $0.42, and $0.24, respectively, for each acre-inch.

Manure applied at the rate of 5 tons per acre showed an increased crop value of $3.57 for each ton of manure. When applied at the rate of 15 tons per acre, the increased crop value was $1.56 for each ton. These estimates do not take into account the cost of handling the increased crops produced by the different applications.

The influence of irrigation and manure on the yield of shelled grain, cobs, husks, stalks, leaves, and the percentage of each part is discussed in detail. The greatest yield of grain, cobs, and leaves was produced with 20 in. of water, while the yield of stalks was highest with 30 in., and of husks with 40 in. The yield of all parts was decidedly increased by manure, but not all in the same proportion. The amount of grain in proportion to the other plant parts was slightly decreased by manure, while the proportion of stalks was decidedly increased. Neither the size of the kernels nor the weight of a measured bushel of grain was greatly affected by the irrigation treatments. Manure, however, increased both the weight of the individual kernels and of a bushel of grain.

The height of the stalk of the plant increased with increased irrigation up to 30 in., but decreased with 40 in. of water. Unmanured corn was decidedly shorter than manured corn, but 5 tons of manure gave slightly higher stalks on the average than 15 tons. The longest ears were produced with no manure and with 30 in. of water. The length and width of the leaves increased with an increase of water up to 30 in., while manuring decidedly increased the leaf measurements.

Manuring greatly stimulated tillering, while the irrigation water was added too late to affect tillering. The number of leaves per stalk and the number of ears per plat increased with increased irrigation up to 20 in. and with manure. The average number of branches per tassel was affected by the same conditions that affected grain production.

The nitrogen content of the grain was reduced by the same irrigation treatments that increased crop yields, the percentage decreasing from 1.923 with no irrigation to 1.901 with 20 in. Manure, on the other hand, as a rule, increased the nitrogen percentage in the grain. In the total nitrogen per acre, however, the highest average production was secured with 20 in. of water, and amounted to 58.365 lbs.

The phosphorus content of the grain was affected irregularly by irrigation, but was increased by the manure. The calcium and magnesium content of the grain was not regularly influenced by the treatments.

From the results of the experiments, it was concluded that under similar conditions 20 acre-inches of water is the best amount for corn production, and that an annual application of 5 tons of manure per acre is sufficient for profitable corn production on Greenville soil.

Cotton production and distribution, 1915–16 (*Bur. of the Census* [*U. S.*], *Cotton Prod. U. S.*, *1916. pp. 99, figs. 14*).—Statistics are given on the supply and distribution of cotton in the United States, cotton production in the United States, consumption and stocks of cotton, imports and exports, the world's production of cotton, the world's consumption of cotton, cottonseed products, and cotton ginned by counties. Maps are given showing the cotton-producing area of the United States in 1915 and the center of production for the period of 1859 to 1914, the classification of States according to the quantity of cotton consumed in 1916, and the production of cotton in 1915 by counties for Alabama, Arkansas, Florida, Georgia, Louisiana, Mississippi, North Carolina, Oklahoma, South Carolina, Tennessee, and Texas.

Cotton in Brazil, W. W. COELHO DE SOUZA (*Lavoura: Bol. Soc. Nac. Agr.* [*Brazil*], *20 (1916), No. 1–6, pp. 9–19*).—A general discussion of the production of cotton in Brazil. A brief history of the crop in Brazil is given.

Cotton varieties in Brazil, E. C. GREEN (*Classificação Summaria das Diversas Especies de Algodoeiros Cultivadas no Brasil. Rio de Janeiro: de Rodrigues & Co., 1916, pp. 14*).—This is a brief summary and description of the cotton varieties grown in Brazil.

Third report on the improvement of indigo in Bihar, A. and GABRIELLE L. C. HOWARD (*Agr. Research Inst. Pusa Bul. 67 (1916), pp. 34, pl. 1; abs in Nature* [*London*], *98 (1916), No. 2461, p. 335*).—This is a supplementary report of work previously noted (E. S. R., 34, p. 36). The principles underlying the production of natural indigo are discussed, as well as seed production and improvement through selection and breeding.

The authors state that since the best color is obtained from those plants which secure their chief nitrogen supply from the root nodules good soil aeration is the most important phase of cultivation. Further notes are given on indigo wilt, together with recommendations for its prevention.

Peanut growing in the cotton belt, H. C. THOMPSON (*Nat. Provisioner, 55 (1916), No. 19, pp. 26, 27, 35*).—This is a popular article on the production of peanuts for oil in the cotton-producing sections of the South. The author states that with modern processes it is possible to obtain from 42 to 44 per cent of oil from shelled Spanish peanuts, 1 bu. of nuts weighing 30 lbs. yielding about 1 gal. of oil. The oil cake has about the same food value as cottonseed meal.

Home potato patches, C. S. KNIGHT (*Nevada Sta. Bul. 87 (1917), pp. 8, figs. 2*).—A brief, popular discussion of Irish potato production on small tracts in Nevada.

Potato growing in Wisconsin, J. G. MILWARD (*Wisconsin Sta. Bul. 280 (1917), pp. 26, figs. 14*).—Approved field practices and cultural methods employed in potato production in Wisconsin are discussed in detail and the standard varieties for the State briefly described.

Rice growing in New South Wales (*Agr. Gaz. N. S. Wales, 27 (1916), No. 11, pp. 799, 800*).—A brief report is made of the successful production of rice at the Yanco and Grafton experiment farms, New South Wales, in the season of 1915–16, with a variety known as Takasuka. At Yanco the crop was grown under irrigation. The results secured were deemed sufficient to justify further trials.

Soy beans, N. SCHMITZ (*Maryland Sta. Bul. 201 (1917), pp. 131–158, figs. 6*).—The adaptation of soy beans to Maryland conditions, their uses, and the field practices employed in their production both for seed and hay are discussed, extensive variety tests reported, and numerous varieties briefly described.

Thirty-six varieties have been tested for seed production for three years and more. Virginia has given the highest average yield, 20.06 bu., with Ebony second, with 19.84 bu. Cloud and Haberlandt have yielded 18.39 and 17.45 bu., respectively. The lowest average yield was secured from Mammoth, 10.12 bu. Of eight varieties tested for two or more years for hay production, the highest average yield was secured from Ebony, 4.29 tons, with an unnamed variety No. 3691 second, with 4.09 tons per acre. Virginia yielded 3.13 tons per acre. The lowest average yield, 2.58 tons, was secured from Edna.

Observations regarding inoculation indicate that on soils of low-to-medium fertility the best results can not be secured without inoculation, and even on those of high fertility inoculation is recommended. Soil inoculation is reported as much more satisfactory than the use of artificial cultures.

A 2-year test with 4 varieties for a comparison of the yield of seed when planted in 3.5-ft. rows and when drilled broadcast gave average yields of 13.38 and 16.41 bu. for the Edna and Virginia varieties, respectively, when planted in rows, as compared with yields of 19.1 and 16.9 bu., respectively, when drilled broadcast. Wilson and Ebony yielded 14.74 and 15.1 bu., respectively, when sown in rows, and 11.66 and 12.13 bu., respectively, when drilled broadcast.

Some recent investigations in sugar beet breeding, F. J. PRITCHARD (*Bot. Gaz., 62 (1916), No. 6, pp. 425–465, figs. 51*).—The studies reported in this paper have been briefly noted (E. S. R., 35, p. 442). The effect of environment on consecutive check and progeny rows is graphically illustrated in this paper, as it presents a number of phenomena having an important bearing on the final results of the investigations. The points studied included the relationships between a few commonly determined characters of the root and its yield of seed, the relationship between a root's yield of seed and the percentage of sugar in its progeny, the transmission of selected qualities of mother roots, selection of families, variability of progeny rows, effect of soil irregularities upon the variability of beet families, transmission of qualities exhibited by selected families, deterioration from lack of selection, and the relationships between percentage of sugar, yield of sugar, and average root weight of sugar beet rows.

The observations reported indicate that although sugar beet improvement has been accomplished, continuous selection is not necessarily the basis upon which it has been attained. That the best roots transmit no better qualities than do the mediocre roots is shown by the tables and graphs submitted. The differences are mere fluctuations and have no definite influence upon improvement, although continuous selection applied to real differences as a possibility of improvement is still an open question. The real differences between sugar beet families are usually very slight and are greatly exceeded by their fluctuations. Both the best and the poorest families transmit average qualities, so that continuous selection is not an efficient means of improvement.

The isolation of mutants offers promise for improvement, but the number of individuals entering into these investigations was too small and the period of time over which the experiments extended (two generations) was too brief to determine the fact or the frequency of their appearance. If the mutation method is to be used for improvement, it is deemed essential that more efficient experimental methods be devised to reduce the effects of soil differences and make it possible to distinguish real differences more clearly. This can be accomplished by the more frequent use of check rows and by replications of the progeny rows. Whether the original stock or the new variety should be used as a source of material from which to isolate more valuable mutants can be determined only when it is known in which the mutants occur with the greater frequency.

Fundamentals of sugar beet culture under California conditions, R. L. ADAMS (*California Sta. Circ. 165 (1917), pp. 22, figs. 4*).—The field practices and cultural methods employed in sugar beet production in California are described and economic factors in the sugar beet industry briefly discussed.

The cost, value, and profit per acre for 10, 15, and 20 ton crops are estimated, the profits per acre being estimated at $17.75, $44.75, and $67.25, respectively, indicating the advantage of good yields.

Russian sugar beet seed, T. G. PALMER (*Sugar [Chicago], 18 (1916), No. 3, pp. 122, 123*).—This is a general discussion of the sugar beet seed industry in Russia, with special reference to the extent of the industry in that country, the quality of Russian seed, and a comparison of the normal price of Russian seed with German and Austrian seed.

[Sugar cane varieties], J. JESWIET (*Arch. Suikerindus. Nederland. Indië, 24 (1916), Nos. 12, pp. 359–429; 17, pp. 625–636; 34, pp. 1321–1349, pls. 2, figs. 81; Meded. Proefstat. Java-Suikerindus., 6 (1916), Nos. 5, pp. 67–137; 8; 13, pp. 383–411, figs. 81*).—This is a detailed botanical description, profusely illustrated, of the more important sugar cane varieties of the Dutch East Indies. A discussion of the morphology of the sugar cane, dealing with each portion of the plant in detail, descriptions of the two most important seed-producing varieties, and descriptions of the six varieties next in importance are included.

Notes on fallowing in sugar cane cultivation, F. LEDEBOER (*Arch. Suikerindus. Nederland. Indië, 24 (1916), No. 30, pp. 1157–1165; Meded. Proefstat. Java-Suikerindus., 6 (1916), No. 11, pp. 323–331*).—This is a discussion of some rather limited experiments with fallowing in sugar cane cultivation extending over a three-year period. The results indicate that slightly higher yields were obtained from this practice, especially in dry seasons.

Lodging in sugar cane, and its prevention, H. F. K. DOUGLAS (*Arch. Suikerindus. Nederland. Indië, 24 (1916), Nos. 18, pp. 667–688, figs. 2; 21, pp.*

821–823).—The author indicated that the younger a plant at the time of lodging the greater is the loss. The loss also varied directly with the degree of brittleness of the stem. Poor drainage aggravated lodging, while the removal of the dead leaves served to decrease the loss through lodging. Other causes which contribute to lodging are a lack of silicic acid in the stem; too frequent cultivation; overfertilization; shallow planting, whereby the cane becomes top-heavy; and severe wind and rain storms.

The prevention of lodging is said to be by " direct " and " indirect " methods. Direct methods are described as those which act without exerting any disturbing influence on the growth of the plant itself as deep planting, planting at different distances, and planting in such a way that the individual plants afford each other support. The indirect methods include such practices as light fertilization, whereby the growth of the cane is less rapid and luxuriant; the application of phosphates to hasten maturity; the removal of dead leaves to permit of freer circulation of air and light; the strengthening of the stalk by the removal of some of the green leaves; and improved drainage, especially as the cane increases in height. Several authorities are quoted to some length in the course of the discussion.

Excerpts from correspondence between the author and other investigators on the value of potash fertilizers in regard to lodging are included. Opinion was found to be divided on this point.

Lodging in sugar cane, and its prevention, P. W. HOUTMAN (*Arch. Suikerindus. Nederland. Indië, 24 (1916), No. 17, pp. 637–665, figs. 6*).—The causes and effects of lodging in sugar cane are discussed, and suggestions made for its prevention.

The author outlines the causes of lodging as rank growth on fertile soil, too high nitrogen fertilization, the continuation of heavy rains through the vegetative period, wind and severe rain storms, and light, peaty soils affording insufficient support to the roots of the cane. Data and graphs are presented showing the degree and the effect on yield of lodging at different experimental centers and with different varieties.

While, as a rule, no attempt has been made to prevent lodging, there are certain definite measures that have proved beneficial. The author discusses these and presents data in support of his arguments. The methods noted are the tying up of the cane, less fertilization, earlier applications of the fertilizers used, wider plantings of the cane, and the use of varieties not addicted to lodging.

[Sugar cane] (*Hawaii. Sugar Planters' Assoc., Rpt. Com. Cult. and Fert. Unirrig. Plantations, 1916, pp. 39, pl. 1, figs. 2*).—The points taken up in this report include topping experiments, crop of 1916; stubble shaving; deterioration in the first mill juice; the handling of plant and ratoon fields and their green soiling; and fertilization by means of soil bacteria.

The relation of applied science to sugar production in Hawaii, H. P. AGEE ET AL. (*Hawaiian Sugar Planters' Assoc. Rpt. 1915, pp. 5–84, pl. 1, figs. 25*).— A report compiled by the director of the Hawaiian Sugar Planters' Station at the request of the U. S. Department of Commerce, and with the cooperation of the station staff. The report includes an introduction and chapters on the experiment station work, and publications dealing with the application of scientific knowledge and discoveries to the sugar industry.

Sweet clover: Utilization, H. S. COE (*U. S. Dept. Agr., Farmers' Bul. 820 (1917), pp. 32, figs. 13*).—The use of sweet clover for pasture, hay, silage, soiling, soil improvement, and as a honey plant is discussed in some detail.

Feeding tests noted from several sources indicate that this crop compares favorably with alfalfa and is an excellent feed for cattle and sheep. An acre of sweet clover will ordinarily support 20 to 30 shotes.

Instructions are given for the production of sweet clover hay and for the preservation of sweet clover as silage.

[Tobacco], D. ARGERIO (*Rev. Min. Indus. Uruguay, 4 (1916), No. 20, pp. 27-58, figs. 12*).—A general discussion of tobacco growing in Uruguay, with notes on the production of seedlings, transplanting, cultivation, harvesting, and yields.

Tobacco culture in Albania, A. BALDACCI (*Bol. Tec. Coltiv. Tabacchi [Scafati], 15 (1916), No. 1-2, pp. 3-23*).—A general discussion of tobacco culture in Albania and adjacent territory, especially as regards locally adapted varieties and general methods of cultivation.

Velvet beans: How to grow and use, C. B. WILLIAMS (*North Carolina Sta. Circ. 35 (1917), pp. 4, fig. 1*).—The production and use of velvet beans are briefly discussed, and varieties recommended for forage and seed production for different soil conditions.

Spring wheats, R. H. BIFFEN (*Jour. Roy. Agr. Soc. England, 76 (1915), pp. 37-48, figs. 5*).—The production of spring wheat in England and western Europe and the economic value of spring wheat as compared with the crops now in vogue are discussed, and a number of the more important spring wheat varieties available for use in these regions noted.

Red Fife, Burgoyne Fife, and Marquis are recommended as being superior to other varieties for early sowing. With Nursery and Red Marvel available for seeding late in February, Marquis and April Bearded can be safely sown as late as March.

A new hybrid yellow wheat, G. GAUDOT (*Jour. Agr. Prat., n. ser., 28 (1915), No. 58, p. 581, fig. 1; abs. in Internat. Inst. Agr. [Rome], Mo. Bul. Agr. Intel. and Plant Diseases, 6 (1915), No. 12, pp. 1621, 1622*).—A new wheat hybrid named Ceros, obtained by crossing Yellow Briquet with Autumn Victoria, is described. It has been grown ten years under varying conditions of soil and climate, and is reported to be perfectly hardy and remarkably rust-resistant.

On growing two white-straw crops in succession, E. J. RUSSELL (*Jour. Bd. Agr. [London], 22 (1915), No. 6, pp. 533-542, fig. 1; abs. in Internat. Inst. Agr. [Rome], Mo. Bul. Agr. Intel. and Plant Diseases, 6 (1915), No. 12, p. 1619*).— In an effort to determine to what extent fluctuations in yield are liable to occur in continuous wheat growing, the author compared the results obtained from the continuous wheat and barley plats of the Rothamsted Experimental Station.

It was found that the yields varied much more on the plats receiving artificial fertilizers than on those receiving farmyard manures. In a favorable season the yield increased to a greater extent by artificial fertilizers than by farmyard manure, but in unfavorable seasons the conditions were reversed. Wheat in rotation with clover gave higher yields and less variation than when grown continuously, so that continuous growing is deemed justifiable only where the cost of production is low or the prices high.

Two conditions essential to success are that the land be clean and that a suitable spring top-dressing be applied. The top-dressing will be determined by the needs of the second crop. Where the tilth is unsatisfactory soot or ammonium sulphate is recommended; otherwise, sodium nitrate.

Agriculture and the wheat supply, E. J. RUSSELL (*Nature [London], 98 (1916), No. 2458, pp. 269-271*).—This is a general discussion of the ways and means of increasing the production of home grown wheat in England.

The wheats of Baluchistan, Khorassan, and the Kurram Valley, GABRIELLE L. C. HOWARD (*Mem. Dept. Agr. India, Bot. Ser.*, 8 (1916), No. 1, pp. 88, pls. 2, fig. 1).—This is a botanical classification and detailed description of the wheats of Baluchistan, Khorassan, and the Kurram Valley, and a brief description of the barleys of Khorassan.

Third annual seed laboratory report, 1915–16, W. L. OSWALD (*Minnesota Sta. Bul. 165 (1917), pp. 12, figs. 4*).—During the year 9,564 voluntary samples and 104 official inspection samples were tested for germination or purity, or both, and the results reported in tabular form. A 3-year summary of the seed-testing work is included in this report.

Seed impurities, A. H. COCKAYNE (*Jour. Agr. [New Zeal.], 13 (1916), No. 3, pp. 208–212*).—This is a list of 225 extraneous seeds found in commercial samples of seed on the New Zealand market, together with a key showing the relative frequency of occurrence and harmfulness of each.

Weeds on arable land and their suppression, WINIFRED E. BRENCHLEY (*Jour. Roy. Agr. Soc. England*, 76 (1915), pp. 14–37, pl. 1, figs. 10).—This is a general discussion of weeds on cultivated land, including a glossary of 76 weeds mentioned in the paper.

Weed control with pulverized kainit, H. LINDEMAN (*Tijdschr. Plantenziekten*, 22 (1916), No. 5, pp. 107–121, pls. 10).—This is a general discussion of weed control with the application of finely ground kainit, including a comparison of kainit with ferrous sulphate in weed control.

HORTICULTURE.

The persistence of lawn and other grasses as influenced especially by the effect of manures on the degree of soil acidity, B. L. HARTWELL and S. C. DAMON (*Rhode Island Sta. Bul. 170 (1917), pp. 3–24, pls. 4*).—This bulletin briefly reviews earlier work of the station on the subject (E. S. R., 20, p. 144), and reports in detail further experiments that have been in progress for a number of years. The effect on different kinds of grasses of changes in the degree of so-called soil acidity has received special attention. Soil acidity was modified not only by liming but by applying fertilizer combinations having acid, neutral, and alkaline reactions. Observations are also given on the effect on mixed herbage of variations in the amount of different nutrients, on the relative effectiveness of different sources of nitrogen used as top-dressings, and on the nature of the turf from different individual grasses and mixtures which were seeded in 1905.

The study as a whole has shown that with other conditions equal variations in the supply of individual nutrients may be expected to cause changes in the proportion of different grasses in a mixture. The most potent factor leading to the replacement of one grass by another appears to be variation in the degree of so-called soil acidity. The most common example of variation in herbage caused by modifications in the degree of acidity is the gradual replacement of timothy by redtop when manurial substances which are physiologically acid are applied and vice versa when alkaline substances are added. That the differences are not due merely to the physical and nutrient effects of the fertilizer was indicated in experiments where these effects were eliminated by the maintenance of optimum physical and nutrient conditions.

Having added at the time of seeding sufficient lime to create a soil reaction thought to be suited to the kind of grass adopted, any changes in reaction which are subsequently desired may be made by modifications in the annual top-dressing. The authors point out, however, that even when the specific needs of a grass are known it is not always advisable to maintain these needs because the growth of certain undesirable plants may be promoted by the same conditions. For example, alkaline fertilizers suitable for promoting the best growth of blue grass are also favorable for the growth of dandelions and plantains. These weeds, as well as certain grasses like blue grass and also clover, are apparently checked by a degree of acidity which is not especially detrimental to the growth of bent and red fescue, which condition may be brought about by introducing sulphate of ammonia into the top-dressing in place of nitrate of soda.

The small vegetable garden (*U. S. Dept. Agr., Farmers' Bul. 818 (1917), pp. 44, figs. 22*).—A popular treatise on vegetable gardening, discussing essentials of gardening, planning the small garden, choosing crops, aids to earliness (hotbed, seed box, and cold frame), tools, preparing the soil, planting vegetables in the open, gardener's planting table, cultivation, irrigation, protecting plants from diseases and pests, cultural suggestions for the commoner vegetables, vegetables for winter use, and fruits in the small garden.

Small fruit culture in California, A. H. HENDRICKSON (*California Sta. Circ. 164 (1917), pp. 24, figs. 13*).—A popular treatise on the culture of bush fruits and strawberries, including a discussion of soils, methods of propagation, planting, cultivation, pruning, renewing the plantation, berries as intercrops, fertilizers, insects and diseases, harvesting, and varieties.

Spraying experiments in Nebraska, J. R. COOPER (*Nebraska Sta. Research Bul. 10 (1917), pp. 5–98, figs. 26*).—In continuation of previous work (E. S. R., 24, p. 758) this bulletin reports spraying experiments conducted on a large scale during the period 1913 to 1915 by the station in cooperation with the extension service of the university and growers in different parts of the State. The work was carried on to demonstrate known methods and evolve new methods of practice from a commercial as well as an experimental standpoint. The data secured each year in spraying for the codling moth, plum curculio, apple scab, and apple blotch are presented in detail and fully discussed. Tests of Bordeaux v. lime-sulphur and newer spray materials, together with data on the cost and efficiency of different methods of spraying, are also reported.

The results of the experiments as a whole show that the codling moth, plum curculio, apple scab, and apple blotch, together with incidental diseases such as rust and sooty blotch, may all be controlled by combining fungicides and insecticides and applying the first spray before the flowers open. The second spray should be given immediately after two-thirds to three-fourths of the petals have fallen, and the third spray immediately after the eggs from which the second brood of codling moth larvæ hatch are laid. A fourth spraying for the codling moth and apple scab may be necessary in certain seasons.

Practically no difference was found in the efficiency of Bordeaux and lime-sulphur in controlling fungus diseases, except in cases of apple blotch, where Bordeaux was more efficient but also more liable to injure the fruit when used early in the season. No way of eliminating Bordeaux injury has been found. The application of milk of lime following rains to trees which have been sprayed with Bordeaux does not lessen the injury to any appreciable extent. Bordeaux and lime-sulphur sprays may be interchanged in a schedule so as to form a maximum amount of control with a minimum amount of injury. Home-boiled lime-sulphur has been found as efficient a fungicide as the ordinary commercial product, but to avoid russeting the fruit care should be taken to screen out the coarse particles in the sludge, using only the clear liquid.

None of the new fungicides was found to be in any way superior to the two standard fungicides now in use. Bordeaux arsenate, Pyrox, and tuber tonic were effective in controlling fungi but more dangerous to fruit and foliage and more expensive than Bordeaux. Soluble sulphur and atomic sulphur proved effective in controlling apple scab but did too much damage to fruit and foliage to warrant their use in their present form.

Practically no difference was found in any of the standard brands of arsenate of lead. Two lbs. of arsenate of lead paste or 1.25 lbs. of arsenate of lead powder have been found to be as efficient as larger quantities.

Spray applied with hollow stream nozzles was found fully as effective as when applied with the solid stream type. More spray injury and waste of material accompanies the use of the latter.

The results of the work of the last three seasons indicate that while it is sometimes possible to omit either the fungicide or the insecticide in the first spray, or to omit the first spray altogether without suffering serious loss, it is never safe to do so and is more hazardous to omit the fungicide than the insecticide. Clean culture was found to be of paramount importance in controlling the plum curculio and apple scab. Power machines are the most satisfactory where the orchard is large enough to warrant their use, though not necessarily more efficient than a good type of hand outfit when the latter is properly used.

Five years' investigations in apple thinning, E. C. AUCHTER (*West Virginia Sta. Bul. 162 (1917), pp. 3–56, figs. 9*).—This bulletin reports thinning experiments carried on by the station for the 5-year period 1912 to 1916. During this period 187 trees of different ages, growing under different environmental conditions and consisting of the varieties Rome, Baldwin, York Imperial, Delicious, and Ben Davis, were under test. For the most part the experiments were not conducted continuously on the same trees owing to the failure of the trees to set fruit in certain years, hence the results for each season are presented in detail. Owing to the lack of an apple crop in 1913 a thinning experiment with peaches was conducted and is here noted.

The results from the thinning experiments as a whole indicate that it does not pay to thin in years of light crop production if the trees are vigorous and growing in fertile soil. Where apple trees are bearing from a medium to a heavy crop of fruit the removal of a part of this fruit by thinning is a very profitable practice. In all cases where the trees had a good crop thinning increased the size and improved the color of the fruit, thus enhancing its market value. The results of the experiments indicate that thinning does not influence subsequent crops nor cause trees naturally biennial in bearing habit to bear a crop each year.

Winter varieties of apples may be thinned just after the June drop, since much of the fruit removed by too early thinning will drop off naturally at the time of the June drop and the remaining apples on the thinned trees may then be thinned too much. In the case of summer or early autumn varieties it is suggested that it will probably pay to delay thinning until the fruit is large enough to use and then several thinnings should be made as the fruits size up. In most cases the best results were obtained when the fruits were thinned 6 to 7 in. apart. In the case of old trees bearing good crops 9 to 10 in. apart gave slightly better results.

One year in one lot of 12 trees the thinned trees returned twice as much net per tree as did the unthinned trees. Another year the thinned trees gave at least a 75 per cent greater net return per tree. In some cases the increases were not so striking. The cost of thinning ranged from 8½ cts. to 43½ cts. per tree, depending on size of crop and tree. The author concludes that only a small part, if any, of the cost of thinning should be charged against the thinned trees, partly because the fruit thinned off would have to be removed at picking time anyway and partly because it takes much longer and costs more in sorting to pick out the larger amount of unsalable culls from the unthinned trees.

The results of other investigators dealing with thinning apples are cited and a bibliography on the subject appended.

Inheritance of sex in Vitis rotundifolia, L. R. DETJEN (*North Carolina Sta. Tech. Bul. 12 (1917), pp. 5–43, figs. 37*).—This is the fourth report on the station's investigations of *V. rotundifolia* (E. S. R., 31, p. 636), and deals specifically with the problems of transmission of sex. The important results secured in the work are summarized as follows:

"Hope, the first discovered hermaphrodite grapevine of the species *V. rotundifolia*, which bears upright stamens, is self-fertile. The self-fertility of the Hope vine is variable, and seems to depend on its inner constitution.

"Floral types in *V. rotundifolia* are transmitted to the progeny in definite ratios. Substituting S for staminate flowers, R for hermaphrodite flowers with reflexed stamens, and U for hermaphrodite flowers with upright stamens, we find that

$$R \times S = 1 \ R : 1.06 \ S.$$
$$R \times U = 1.07 \ R : 1 \ U.$$
$$U \times U = S : R \text{ (ratios not determined)}.$$

"The Hope vine and some of its self-fertile progeny apparently will not cross with staminate vines. In *V. rotundifolia* the upright stamen in hermaphodite flowers is correlated with normal, viable pollen and self-ferility; the reflexed stamen in hermaphrodite flowers is always associated with defective pollen and self-fertility. The Hope vine and all of its seedlings, which bear upright stamens, appear and behave essentially like staminate vines except for the facts that the flowers usually contain well-developed pistils and that fruit is subsequently produced. The Hope vine probably is a staminate vine whose long suppressed pistils have suddenly been regenerated and have recovered the power to function. The prototype of our present-day rotundifolia vines probably was a true and functioning hermaphrodite."

Breeding southern grapes, L. R. DETJEN (*Jour. Heredity, 8 (1917), No. 6, pp. 252–258, figs. 4*).—A popular discussion of this subject based upon the above noted investigation.

The use of commercial fertilizers in growing roses, F. W. MUNCIE (*Illinois Sta. Bul. 196 (1917), pp. 511–564, figs. 37; abs. ed., pp. 4*).—This bulletin describes in detail experiments with dried blood, acid phosphate, and potassium sulphate used in growing Killarney, Bride, and Richmond roses in the greenhouse during the period 1910 to 1913. These fertilizers were used both alone and in various combinations. Supplementary experiments were conducted during the period 1913 to 1915 to determine the value of acid phosphate with and without lime as a rose fertilizer. The results secured are presented in tabular form, also illustrated by a series of curves, and fully discussed.

Summarizing the experiments as a whole it was found that for the soil used at the station, a brown silt loam, fertilization is necessary to produce a maximum crop of roses. The benefit from fertilizing was in number of flowers produced and to a slight extent in the average stem length, though not in percentage of long-stemmed flowers. No measurable change in length of petals followed fertilization with acid phosphate, but applications of phosphatic fertilizer gave the most pronounced increase in the production of roses. Twenty lbs. of acid phosphate per 100 sq. ft. of bench space gave a profit of $176 per 1,000 plants. Four times this quantity may be used without injury from overfeeding. The beneficial effect of acid phosphate was continuous throughout the year.

Dried blood in small amounts proved beneficial, but with amounts exceeding 8 lbs. per 100 sq. ft. of bench space there was a decrease in production with own-root and grafted Brides and grafted Killarneys. The effect of dried blood upon weekly production was found to be a decrease during the fall months, no difference during winter, and an increase in the spring.

No benefit was obtained from the use of potassium sulphate under the conditions of the experiment. Mixing ground limestone with the soil resulted in decreased production whether or not acid phosphate had been added. Hence ground limestone is not recommended for general use.

A definite relation was found to exist between the variation in hours of sunshine and the subsequent production of flowers. The experiment showed the desirability of planting grafted stock, since its larger production during the first year more than paid for the increase in initial cost.

Based on the experiments, the author recommends that the nitrogen content of rose soils be maintained by turning under green or farm manures before use. If lack of nitrogen is indicated by a lightening of the color of the foliage, applications of liquid manure, mulches of manure, or top-dressings of dried blood may be used, the last in applications not exceeding 5 lbs. per 100 sq. ft. of bench space, to be applied not oftener than six weeks apart. Nitrogenous fertilizers should be applied only during sunshiny weather and most generously during periods of heavy production. Generous quantities of acid phosphate should be added to the soil. It may be applied in the field at the rate of 4 to 8 tons per acre and in the bench soil at the rate of 40 to 80 lbs. per 100 cu. ft. of soil. Neither lime nor limestone should be mixed with the soil. If needed for sweetening the soil and for preventing the growth of algæ a top-dressing of finely-ground limestone at the rate of 10 lbs. per 100 sq. ft. of bench space may be applied.

FORESTRY.

Proceedings of the Southern Forestry Congress, held in Asheville, N. C., July 11 to 15, 1916 (*Proc. South. Forestry Cong., 1916, pp. 187*).—A report of numerous papers, addresses, and discussions at this meeting of the Southern Forestry Congress. Problems dealing with forest protection, organization, legislation, and management in their relation to the protection and development of southern forest industries received special consideration.

Tree growth and climate in the United States, K. W. WOODWARD (*Jour. Forestry, 15 (1917), No. 5, pp. 521–531*).—A summary of the available information with regard to forest yields in the United States and a discussion of the relation of these yields to climate and soil. Fifteen forest types are differentiated with special reference to climatic and soil characteristics.

Laws of tall-tree growth investigated mathematically, R. D. BOHANNAN (*Jour. Forestry, 15 (1917), No. 5, pp. 532–551*).—In this article the author undertakes to prove a number of formulas and laws relating to height growth in forest trees, presents age-height-diameter tables for various American trees, and gives notes on the measurements of the different species.

The problem of making volume tables for use on the National Forests, T. T. MUNGER (*Jour. Forestry, 15 (1917), No. 5, pp. 574–586*).—In this paper the author calls attention briefly to the part that the Branch of Research of the Forest Service of the U. S. Department of Agriculture should take in the preparation of volume tables, sketches some of the questions that arise in their preparation, and suggests some of the principles that should guide the work.

Site determination, classification, and application, R. WATSON (*Jour. Forestry, 15 (1917), No. 5, pp. 552–563, fig. 1*).—The purpose of this article is to indicate a possible standard method of site determination and of site classification. In order to test the validity of the methods advocated they are applied in a practical manner to a timber survey.

Volume of western yellow pine logs from an actual mill tally, S. BERRY (*Jour. Forestry, 15 (1917), No. 5, pp. 615–618*).—A mill tally of western yellow and Jeffrey pine is here described with special reference to the application of the data secured in estimating the quality of standing timber in a given area.

The Swiss method of regulating the cut in practice, C. H. GUISE (*Jour. Forestry, 15 (1917), No. 5, pp. 564–573*).—The author used the Swiss method of regulating timber cut in the preparation of working plans for two forest tracts. The data secured are here given and discussed. It is believed that the results secured warrant the further use of the Swiss method in regulating the cut in mixed selection forests.

Effect of depth of covering seed upon the germination and quality of stock, S. B. SHOW (*Jour. Forestry, 15 (1917), No. 5, pp. 619–623*).—The results are given of a series of experiments conducted at the Feather River Experiment Station of the Forest Service of the U. S. Department of Agriculture on the effect of depth of covering seed upon germination and quality of stock. The species included in the experiment were western yellow pine, Jeffrey pine, sugar pine, Douglas fir, white fir, and bigtree. With the exception of sugar pine, the conclusions regarding all the species are based on spring sowing only. The results secured for each species are presented in tabular form and discussed.

A study of reforested chestnut cut-over land, E. C. M. RICHARDS (*Jour. Forestry, 15 (1917), No. 5, pp. 609–614*).—Experiments on the reforestation of chestnut cut-over land with pine transplants, here described, lead the author to conclude that pine will establish itself readily on cut-over land, but that chestnut and other hardwood sprouts should be cleaned out not later than three years after planting the pine and this should be repeated every three to five years until the pine attains a height of 12 to 15 ft. and overtops neighboring hardwoods.

In these plantings, which were made in New Jersey and Connecticut, chestnut blight did not kill the sprouts soon enough to prevent injury to the pine.

Forest succession in the central Rocky Mountains, C. G. BATES (*Jour. Forestry, 15 (1917), No. 5, pp. 587–592*).—In this paper, which is based upon general observations over a number of years in the mountainous territory of Colorado and Wyoming, the author discusses different tree associations and successions with the view of indicating the practical importance to the forester of taking into account the systematic development of vegetation by definite stages.

The woodlot, C. A. SCOTT (*Kansas Sta. Circ. 58 (1917), pp. 37, figs. 24*).—A treatise on woodlot management with special reference to conditions in Kansas. A list is given of desirable trees for Kansas woodlots, including data on the uses of each kind of wood and estimated yield per acre in lumber and other products. A table is given showing an itemized account of the cost of growing a 20-acre catalpa plantation and the returns received from it. The total expense per acre for growing and harvesting the plantation, which was about 16 years old at the time of cutting, was $109.83. The net proceeds per acre was $152.17, equivalent to an annual net income of $9.31 per acre.

Some timely suggestions for the owners of woodlots in New England, F. H. MOSHER and G. E. CLEMENT (*U. S. Dept. Agr., Bur. Ent,. 1917, pp. 8*).—Based on observations conducted by the Bureau of Entomology over a number of years some 75 species of native and naturalized trees are here grouped into

the following classes: Species that are favored food of gipsy moth larvæ in all
their stages, species that are favored food for gipsy moth larvæ after the earlier
larva stages, species that are not particularly favored but upon which a small
proportion of the gipsy moth larvæ may develop, and species that are unfavored
food for gipsy moth larvæ. The suggestions herein given constitute, in a general
way, a guide for the thinning of the above classes of trees in New England
woodlots, with reference both to the utilization of the wood and the protection of the trees from gipsy moth attacks.

Tree planting needed in Texas, J. H. FOSTER and H. B. KRAUSE (*Bul. Agr.
and Mech. Col. Tex., 3. ser., 3 (1917), No. 1, pp. 32, figs. 12*).—A popular treatise
on tree planting for windbreaks, shelter belts, fence posts, and fuel, as well as
planting in streets, city parks, and school and home grounds.

Report of committee on forestry, L. A. THURSTON ET AL. (*Proc. Hawaii.
Sugar Planters' Assoc., 36 (1916), pp. 333–368*).—A report of tree planting and
other forest activities of the Hawaiian Sugar Planters' Association, including
a report by C. S. Judd upon the present status of forestry in Hawaii.

Douglas fir shipbuilding, H. B. OAKLEAF (*[Portland, Oreg.], 1916, pp. 9, figs.
2*).—A general account of the utilization of Douglas fir in shipbuilding.

Brazilian woods: Their utilization for the manufacture of wood pulp
(*Jour. Forestry, 15 (1917), No. 5, pp. 624–627*).—This is a reprint of an article
from the *London Times,* giving analyses of a number of woods suitable for wood
pulp, together with information relative to the volume and distribution of these
woods, conditions, and estimated cost of exploitation, etc.

The purchase of pulpwood.—Some suggestions, C. P. WINSLOW and R.
THELEN (*[Madison, Wis.], 1916, pp. 8, figs. 2*).—A paper read before the Tech-
nical Association of the Pulp and Paper Industry at a meeting held at Columbia
University, New York City, on September 28, 1916.

DISEASES OF PLANTS.

Fungus and bacterial diseases, W. NOWELL (*West Indian Bul., 16 (1916),
No. 1, pp. 17–25, 28, 29*).—This is a descriptive and tabular account of the distribution and severity, during 1915, of fungus and bacterial diseases, including
root disease (*Marasmius sacchari*), rind fungus (*Melanconium sacchari*), red
rot (*Colletotrichum falcatum*), pineapple disease (*Thielaviopsis paradoxa*),
and *Cephalosporium sacchari* of sugar cane; anthracnose (*Colletotrichum
gossypii*), West Indian leaf mildew, a bacterial boll disease, angular leaf spot,
black arm, and other diseases of cotton; root disease (*Rosellinia pepo*), canker
(*Phytophthora faberi*), black pod rot (P. *faberi*), brown pod rot (*Lasiodiplodia
theobromæ*), dieback and stem diseases (L. *theobromæ*), pink disease (*Corticium salmonicolor*), horse-hair blight (*Marasmius sarmentosus*) and other
diseases of cacao; black root disease (*Rosellinia* spp.), red root disease
(*Sphærostilbe* sp.), pink disease (C. *salmonicolor*), and an unidentified root
or collar disease of limes and citrus trees, and other diseases of limes; root
disease (M. *sacchari*) and white rust (*Albugo* (*Cystopus*) sp.) of sweet potatoes;
bud rot, root disease, and leaf diseases (*Pestalozzia palmarum*) of coconuts;
brown rust (*Puccinia maydis*), smut (*Ustilago zeæ*), and root disease of Indian
corn; rust (P. *purpurea*) and smut (*Sphacelotheca sorghi*) of sorghum and
Guinea corn; root disease (*Sclerotium* sp.), leaf rust (*Uredo arachidis*), and
leaf spot (*Cercospora personata*) of peanuts; bacterial rot and damping-off of
onions; and tuber and wilt diseases of yams.

The wet year, 1915, was highly favorable to fungi parasitic on scale insects.
Phanerogamic parasites noted include *Cuscuta americana, Cassytha filiformis,*

Dendropemon sp., and *Phorandendron* sp. Some other plant troubles having different causes are noted.

Annual report of the mycologist for the year 1913–14, W. J. Dowson (*Dept. Agr. Brit. East Africa Ann. Rpt. 1913–14, pp. 118–121*).—A disease of sisal is thought to be due to climatic conditions.

The coffee leaf disease due to *Hemileia vastatrix* was treated successfully with Bordeaux mixture. Formalin in weak solution was found protective but it retarded germination.

Diseases identified included the coffee leaf disease (*H. vastatrix*), rusts of wheat (*Puccinia graminis*, P. *glumarum*, and P. *triticina*), barley (P. *simplex*), maize (P. *sorghi*), peach (P. *pruni-spinosæ*), fig (*Uredo fici*), carnation (*Uromyces caryophyllinus*), bean (*U. appendiculatus*), mildew of rose (*Sphærotheca pannosa*), tobacco (*Erysiphe communis*), cucumber and marrow (*E. cichoracearum*), and grape anthracnose (*Glœosporium ampelophagum*). Diseases still unidentified include the bud rot of *Cocos nucifera*, a blackening of the stems of *Manihot glaziovii*, a root disease of young *Juniperus procera*, a heart rot of the same plant due to a Fomes, and a leaf disease attacking citrus trees, other than limes.

Annual report of the mycologist for the year ending March 31, 1915, W. J. Dowson (*Dept. Agr. Brit. East Africa Ann. Rpt. 1914–15, pp. 94–107*).— In this report, which is particularly concerned with administrative and other matters, it is stated that coffee is regularly attacked by *Hemileia vastatrix*, but that the disease is not very virulent and is not considered a dangerous pest if properly handled. The effects on this parasite of seasonal and weather conditions, and of various fungicides and combinations thereof, are detailed.

Withertip of citrus trees is under investigation, the only organism found in connection with the specimens examined being *Colletotrichum glœosporioides*. Dead leaves on the ground are thought to aid in spreading the disease..

Rose leaf mildew (*Sphærotheca pannosa*) is reported as again very prevalent on susceptible varieties. Copper sprays control the disease but scorch the foliage of certain varieties.

Bud rot disease of the coconut palm, or a root rot disease. or both together, caused mortality among the older trees. Drainage and manuring are considered the only practicable remedies. Of the several bacteria isolated from diseased material, one closely resembled *Bacillus coli communis*.

A list is given of parasitic fungi recorded during 1914–15, in connection with associated plant diseases.

Some problems connected with the treatment of fungus diseases by spraying, E. S. Salmon and J. V. Eyre (*Gard. Chron., 3. ser., 60 (1916), No. 1559, pp. 229, 230*).—In this paper the authors, discussing some of the results of experimentation and practice in the use of fungicides against plant diseases, state that to make this work thoroughly efficient its problems must receive detailed attention from three sides, relating to the fungus, the host plant, and the chemical substance of the fungicide. These phases are briefly discussed.

Control of root knot by calcium cyanamid and other means, J. R. Watson (*Florida Sta. Bul. 136 (1917), pp. 145–160, fig. 1*).—A description is given of plant and greenhouse experiments with calcium cyanamid for the control of root knot on various plants.

As a result of his investigations, the author recommends the use of calcium cyanamid thoroughly mixed with the soil, after which the beds are to be well irrigated. This treatment, it is said, will so greatly reduce the number of nematodes as to make the growing of susceptible crops profitable. The amount of cyanamid required will vary from one thousand to several thousand pounds per acre, according to the depth and nature of the infested soil. On account of the burning effect of the cyanamid, an interval of one to several weeks should intervene between the treatment of the soil and the planting of the seed. The cost of the treatment is such that its use is recommended only on seed beds and truck lands under intensive cultivation, but as cyanamid is an important source of nitrogen its use as a fertilizer should be considered in connection with nematode control.

Rosellinia root diseases in the Lesser Antilles, W. NOWELL (*West Indian Bul.*, 16 (1916), No. 1, pp. 31–71, pls. 7, figs. 2).—Rosellinia, several species of which cause root disease in numerous temperate and tropical countries, occurs in this relation in the Lesser Antilles, Guadeloupe, Dominica, Martinique, St. Lucia, St. Vincent, and Grenada, but not on the other islands of the group which have drier climates. Though the range of hosts as regards classification is also very wide, the plants most affected in this region are cacao, coffee, limes, and arrowroot. Cacao is attacked usually by *R. pepo* (possibly in certain localities by another species not yet identified), which spreads from roots of dead or dying shade trees. Limes and coffee plants are attacked by both *R. pepo* and *R. bunodes*.

Infested trees may be killed by the progressive investment of the roots (spreading from roots of other trees) or by the destruction of the bark around the collar. The fungus penetrates quickly both bark and wood, conidia being readily formed where the mycelium is exposed, and perithecia occurring later.

Preventive measures include periodical inspection, aeration, insulation, disinfection, liming, flaming, and removal of infected wood.

Observations on a new disease in cotton, M. L. PATEL (*Poona Agr. Col. Mag.*, 8 (1916), No. 1, pp. 45–48).—A disease, affecting most of the native varieties of cotton in certain districts, is described. The leaves on some branches turn pinkish yellow just before blooming, the number of blooms is reduced, and the young bolls produced remain small and dry up quickly.

The trouble, locally termed sterility, was more severe in 1915–16 than in 1914–15. It varies somewhat in severity with season, soil, and variety, but it does not appear to be due primarily to diminished water supply or to lack of nutrient material. An observed shortness of the taproot is thought to be a result, not a cause, of the disease. Belated attacks are less severe. Mites are observed to be more common on affected than on other portions of the plant. No disease organism has been isolated. The bolls open poorly on affected plants. The seeds are lighter in affected cotton, but the lint is proportionate.y still lighter, as shown by a lowered ginning percentage; also the lint is said to be more brittle in diseased cotton.

Removal of all affected branches appears to prevent the disease so far as the individual plant is concerned.

Studies on clubroot of cruciferous plants, C. CHUPP (*New York Cornell Sta. Bul.* 387 (1917), pp. 419–452, figs. 16).—The author has made a study of the clubroot of cruciferous plants due to *Plasmodiophora brassicæ* in an attempt to determine the part played by swarm spores in the dissemination of the fungus, spore germination, the manner in which the pathogene enters the host, the distribution of the organism throughout the tissues of the root, the formation and size of the spores, and the reputed relation of bacteria to the normal development of the myxomycete.

As a result of his investigations he has found that neither the motility of swarm spores nor the action of winds is an important factor in the dissemination of the parasite. Each spore is said to produce one swarm spore which, if not supplied with a host, develops no further. Penetration of the host takes place through the wall of the root hair while the organism is in a uninucleate stage. The root hair at once shows hypertrophy. The amœba increases in size as it passes rootward, and finally, by direct cell-wall penetration as well as by the division of the host cells, the pathogene is distributed throughout the cortical tissue. Aside from *P. brassicœ* there is said to be often present another organism which causes no hypertrophy and which is probably *Olpidium brassicœ*.

In the experiments to determine the relation of bacteria to *P. brassicœ*, as claimed by Pinoy (E. S. R., 14, p. 946), all the results obtained indicate that the bacteria do not enter the host as soon as the slime mold does, but follow only after there has been a rupture of the epidermis. Consequently the bacteria can be of no vital importance in the nutrition of the parasite.

Bitter pit investigation.—The experimental results in their relation to bitter pit and a general summary of the investigation, D. McAlpine (*Rpt. Bitter Pit Invest.* [*Aust.*], *4 (1914–15), pp. 178, pls. 41, figs. 2*).—This is the author's fourth report on this work (E. S. R., 33, p. 852), and sums up the results of the study carried on by him for four years under appropriations by the Commonwealth and State governments of Australia.

The causation and prevention of the disease by direct measures received the greater portion of attention, as breeding experiments were precluded by the time limitation imposed. Extended investigations failed to connect the disease with any parasitic organism. It is claimed to be due to a disturbance of the normal functions of the plant itself. In some apple varieties, the majority of the trees showed a tendency to the pitting habit, and some individual trees showed bitter pit to the extent of 60 or 80 per cent of their crop. Abundance of material was obtained from the six States included in the investigation.

It is held that success against bitter pit depends entirely upon the ability of orchardists to control the conditions in the individual trees, and the ability of shippers to control conditions, chiefly temperature, during transit. Apparently, the factors operative in the production of bitter pit include every phase in the life of the tree, from the nursery to the marketed fruit. The experimental work is reported in considerable detail and the practical applications of the results obtained are pointed out. It appears that apples apparently faultless can be shown, by means of the X-ray, to be affected, the honeycombed appearance of a pitted apple contrasting sharply with the solid flesh of a healthy fruit. Apparently the disease begins on the tree and continues to develop under certain unfavorable storage or shipping conditions.

Biochemical researches were conducted by Rothera, Jackson, and Kincaid. The absence of development of bitter pit in apples kept at 32° F. is thought to be simply the usual phenomenon of arrest due to slowing up of all vital activities at that temperature, as nothing indicates a permanent influence of such temperature on this disease. It appears that the pitting of apples is determined before they are picked and before their starch is converted into sugar, though laboratory experiments indicate some possible influence of treatment (as handling) after picking. Further work needs to be done in this connection.

Other studies were conducted in cooperation at various points by different persons, who are named. Susceptible and nonsusceptible varieties were compared as regards the composition of the fruit and the nature of the leaf, since it appeared evident that retardation in the leaves would result in increased transportation of water to the fruits. Yates, which is nearly immune, appears to be more nearly allied to the wild crab apple than is the susceptible variety,

12883°—17—No. 5——5

Cleopatra. It is stated that the tendency to bitter pit is more or less inherent in the constitution of the cultivated apple, no matter where it is grown.

Bitter pit is considered a functional disorder, the vascular system, or conducting tissue, being largely concerned. The cultivated apple has evidently lost, in large degree, the hardy nature of its wild ancestors, its vascular system having failed to keep pace with the requirements laid upon it during the development of such various desirable qualities as size. A softening of the fiber, a delicacy of constitution, and a feebleness in the power of rapid transportation of water, etc., have necessitated measures to counteract the inadequate conduction in the tissues.

Studies on the relation of laterals to bitter pit were inconclusive. Ringing and fracturing the branches was tried, and it was found that checking the flow of sap in September resulted in a diminution of pitting, and for the last two seasons there was none at all. The results from constricting the branches with wires were inconclusive, as were those from ringing pear trees. The fall of the leaves was not affected.

Observations described seem to indicate that apples should not be kept in an ordinary storeroom where the air is overdry. In case of apples on the tree, the temperature of the atmosphere and its humidity appear to modify the effects of the sun's rays. Slightly less pit developed in apples grown in sheltered situations, transpiration being reduced when the drying effects of wind are moderated.

A study of bitter pit in its relation to weather shows that it is not strong transpiration in dry air or weak transpiration on dry soil that induces bitter pit, but that it is the amount of transpiration relatively to the water supply that is the important factor. The general evidence indicates that the nature of the scion, and not that of the stock, is the deciding factor in varietal susceptibility. As regards situation, the least suitable is one having a southerly exposure, and the most favorable is one having a northeasterly aspect, well sheltered from west and south winds.

Of all orchard operations, pruning appears to have the most direct effect upon the development of bitter pit, which is least prevalent when there is a good average crop with fruit, generally of normal size, well distributed over the tree. The pruning operation should be carried on continuously from the time of planting through the bearing period. The objects to be aimed at are not only increased vigor and luxuriant growth, but also the distribution of the fruits on the tree so that each receives its due share of sun, shade, air, and nourishment.

While many facts and suggestions are variously presented in the body and conclusion of this report, it is thought that the ultimate solution of the problem must be obtained from breeding experiments looking to the production of otherwise desirable varieties which do not develop bitter pit.

A brief bibliography is appended.

Xylaria root rot of apple, F. A. WOLF and R. O. CROMWELL (*U. S. Dept. Agr., Jour. Agr. Research, 9 (1917), No. 8, pp. 269–276, pl. 1, figs. 3*).—In continuation of a preliminary report on the black root rot of apple (E. S. R., 36, p. 147), the authors give an account of further investigations carried on at the North Carolina Experiment Station on this disease. This trouble is found to be widely distributed in North Carolina, and it is believed to be the same disease which has been reported in Virginia and Pennsylvania.

There are said to be no above ground symptoms by which this disease may be distinguished from other apple root rots. The roots, however, are said to be characteristically covered with black fungus incrustations from whose margins radiate minute black rhizomorphs. Isolations have constantly yielded a form whose conidial fructifications and stromatic arms indicate its relationship to *Xylaria* spp., and from a study of the perithecial material, the fungus is considered morphologically quite like *X. hypoxylon*. The pathogenicity of the organism has been repeatedly established by inoculation with pure cultures into the roots of living apple trees. The ascigerous stage of a species of Xylaria has been found on diseased apple roots, but this has not yet been connected with the conidial stage developed in artificial cultures.

[**Brown rot of plum and apple**] (*Gard. Chron., 3. ser., 60 (1916), No. 1561, p. 251, figs. 2*).—Brown rot, due to *Sclerotinia (Monilia) fructigena*, is reported as having been severe early in the season of 1916 on apples, and later on plums. This disease is said to have been increasingly common during recent years, supposedly due to the exceptional prevalence of moisture in winter and spring.

The best plan for protection is considered to be that of drenching the trees with lime-sulphur of winter strength, or Bordeaux mixture, just before the buds begin to open and afterwards cutting off and burning all diseased material. Turning the ground during the winter is also recommended.

Further studies of the orange rusts of Rubus in the United States, L. O. KUNKEL (*Bul. Torrey Bot. Club, 43 (1916), No. 11, pp. 559–569, figs. 5*).—According to the author, there are two forms of the orange rust of blackberries in the United States. One is the cæoma stage of *Gymnoconia interstitialis* and the other a short-cycle rust with a life history similar to the Endophyllums. The two rusts are morphologically alike in their cæoma stage, though quite different in their life histories. The short-cycled *Cæoma nitens* seems to be more widely spread in the United States than is *G. interstitialis*, and to the first species is attributed most of the injury of orange rust on blackberries and raspberries.

Note on a Botrytis disease of fig trees, W. B. BRIERLEY (*Roy. Bot. Gard. Kew, Bul. Misc. Inform., No. 9 (1916), pp. 225–229, pls. 2*).—An account is given of the development of *B. cinerea* when tested in pure culture, and when inoculated into twigs, in which it causes a dieback, and into fruit, which becomes mummified, any leaves developing the following season being dwarfed and primitive in form.

The "band" disease of betel-nut palms in the Konkan, V. G. GOKHBLE, R. S. KASARGODE, and S. L. AJREKAB (*Poona Agr. Col. Mag., 8 (1916), No. 1, pp. 49–53*).—A disease of betel-nut palms, known locally as "band" and causing decline, barrenness, and finally death of the trees, has been known in portions of the Ratnagiri district for more than 30 years, reducing the yield materially. There is no indication that the trouble is communicable. Soil conditions, which are thought to be largely or wholly responsible for the development of the disease, include the presence of soil exhaustion, bad drainage, acidity, and toxic substances. Spacing and intergrowths may also be factors. Progress as regards remedial measures is at present hampered by lack of knowledge regarding the physiology of the betel palm.

An epidemic of rust on mint, A. H. CHIVERS (*Mycologia, 9 (1917), No. 1, pp. 41, 42*).—In gardens at Hanover, N. H., early in the summer of 1915, an epidemic of rust (*Puccinia menthæ*) on mint developed suddenly and increased rapidly after a period of heavy and continuous rainfall, this being the first outbreak of the rust in this locality so far as known. Though nothing was done in the way of control or prevention, the disease did not reappear in 1916. It is thought that this disease, which is capable of destroying the foliage of mint during a wet season, may become inactive on return of normal seasons.

[Lophodermium pinastri and Phacidium infestans on pine], T. LAGERBERG (*Statens Skogsförs. Anst.* [*Sweden*], *Flygbl. 5* (1915), pp. 10, figs. 6).—This is a brief discussion of *L. pinastri*, which causes a pine needle cast, and *P. infestans*, which is said to kill out young pines in the nursery.

The pine blister disease (*Amer. Forestry, 22* (1916), No. 276, pp. 748–750, figs. 2).—It is stated that the white pine blister, or canker, has made steady progress in the portions of New England from which it has been previously reported, and that what are thought to be the areas of new infection have been discovered recently, so that the situation is constantly becoming more serious.

Recent study of pod disease and canker in Hevea, A. A. L. RUTGERS (*Meded. Adv. Alg. Ver. Rubberplanters Oostkust Sumatra. No. 5* (1916), pp. 63–66).—The author, having carried on for some time a study of Hevea canker (E. S. R., 32, p. 242), which is claimed to be caused by *Phytophthora faberi*, states that slightly infected trees recovered in nearly every case, and trees severely infected in a number of cases. This form of the fungus is thought to be identical with that causing a disease of cacao and other plants. Infection experiments with Hevea fruits succeeded, causing a rot thereof in several instances.

A root disease of plantation rubber in Malaya due to Poria hypolaterita, W. N. C. BELGRAVE (*Agr. Bul. Fed. Malay States. 4* (1916). No. 11. pp. 347–350).—This is a preliminary report on investigations continued since 1915, and still in progress, on a wet foot rot of mature rubber trees in Malaya, which is described as due to *P. hypolaterita.*

The disease is spread by root contact, its progress being slow and insidious, the trees yielding latex until they are very far gone. The fungus is suspected to be too common in jungle lands to justify the use of isolation trenches except, possibly, to isolate the larger-infected areas. This may be done with deep drains, the trees being then tapped until they die, which may require at least five years.

Some suggestions on the control of mistletoe in the National forests of the Northwest, J. R. WEIR (*Forestry Quart., 14* (1916). No. 4. pp. 567–577).—This article, while relating mainly to forestry measures and methods, notes also the fact that mistletoe brooms, and eventually the uninfected parts of the tree, cease to produce seed, which may be a serious matter in view of the trying conditions related to reproduction and survival of forest growths. It is stated also that the false mistletoes (Razoumofskya) are of much greater importance in the western than in the eastern portions of the United States, practically every western conifer being attacked by at least one of these parasites, which may be inconspicuous but usually show a greater degree of parasitism than do the Phoradendrons.

The author reports briefly on a study of the more minute details of the anatomy of the sinkers and horizontal root system of the parasite, stating that the phloëm of the host is found to be, in some species, in direct union with the absorbing cells of the parasite. The weakening of heavily infested young trees, and other facts noted, are considered as proof of a heavy drain on the host by the parasite. The fact that if a seed of one of these species falls on a plant other than an accustomed host it will exhaust its energy in producing a long hypocotyl without penetrating the substratum is considered proof of a special adaptation of the parasite to particular types of cell structure or chemical constitution of the hosts. This fact may become important in connection with the planting of mixed forests. Mistletoe attacks hosts of all ages, and trees attacked when young are apt to be otherwise diseased.

ENTOMOLÒGY.

Recognition among insects, N. E. McINDOO (*Anat. Rec., 11 (1917), No. 6, pp. 517, 518*).—The experimental results here reported deal only with the odors emitted by honeybees.

Proceedings of the Entomological Society of British Columbia (*Proc. Ent. Soc. Brit. Columbia, Econ. Ser., No. 9 (1916), pp. 49–88, figs. 17*).—The more important papers of practical or popular interest to fruit growers and farmers presented at the fifteenth annual meeting of the society, held at Victoria, British Columbia, in 1916, are here given, namely, Notes on the Wood Tick (*Dermacentor venustus*), by J. W. Cockle (pp. 53–57) ; The Cottony Maple Scale (*Pulvinaria innumerabilis*), by T. Wilson (pp. 57–59) ; The Pea Weevil in British Columbia, by R. C. Treherne (pp. 59, 60) ; Entomology in the Public School, by J. A. Hamilton (pp. 60–62) ; The Forest-insect Problem in Stanley Park, by R. N. Chrystal (pp. 63–66) ; Some Orchard Insects of Economic Importance in British Columbia, by R. C. Treherne (pp. 66–83) ; Superheating as a Control Method for Insects Which Infest Stored Products, by A. Gibson (pp. 83, 84) ; and Control of Cabbage Aphis by Parasites in Western Canada, by E. H. Strickland (pp. 84–88).

Seventh annual report of the State entomologist, C. P. GILLETTE and G. M. LIST (*Off. State Ent. Colo. Circ. 19 (1916), pp. 43*).—This is the usual annual report, dealing particularly with the inspection work of the year.

[Parasite work in Maine], J. N. SUMMERS (*Agr. of Maine, 1915, pp. 116–127, pls. 4*).—The first of the two papers, here presented, reports (pp. 116–119) upon the work of 1915 at the Maine Parasite Laboratory. The second (pp. 120–127) consists of a discussion of the parasites of the gipsy and brown-tail moths in Maine, including a brief history of those thus far introduced into the State, namely, *Anastatus bifasciatus, Apanteles lacteicolor, Meteorus versicolor, Compsilura concinnata,* and *Monodontomerus æreus,* and the predator *Calosoma sycophanta.*

Report of the economic zoologist, H. A. SURFACE (*Ann. Rpt. Penn. Dept. Agr., 21 (1915), pp. 174–205, pls. 4*).—This report consists largely of details relating to the work of the year, particularly as relate to orchard, nursery, and apiary inspection, etc.

The results of studies of the life history and habits of the red leaf or cherry leaf beetle (*Galerucella cavicollis*), which was recently found in Pennsylvania, are briefly reported. This beetle is said to have been very destructive in several counties in the northern and central portions of the State, feeding upon the foliage of cherry, peach, apple, pear, and some other trees, shrubs, and plants.

A detailed account of this leaf beetle by Cushman and Isely has been noted (E. S. R., 35, p. 260).

[Insect pests], H. A. SURFACE (*Bi-Mo. Zool. Bul. Penn. Dept. Agr., 6 (1916), Nos. 1, pp. 58, pls. 5, figs. 19; 2, pp. 59–118, pls. 5, figs. 10; 3, pp. 119–149, figs. 6; 4, pp. 23*).—These papers deal, respectively, with (1) pests of truck and farm crops and live stock; (2) pests of trees; (3) pests of the household, etc.; and. (4) bee diseases in Pennsylvania.

[Report of the] division of entomology, E. E. SCHOLL (*Ann. Rpt. Comr. Agr. Tex., 9 (1916), pp. 10–27*).—This report deals with the occurrence of some of the more important insect pests of the year in Texas and measures for their control.

[Report of entomological work], H. P. AGEE (*Hawaii. Sugar Planters' Assoc., Rpt. Expt. Sta. Com., 1916, pp. 4–10*).—This reports upon the progress of work for the year ended September 30, 1916.

Several additional egg parasites of the leaf-hopper were introduced, one belonging to the genus Paranagrus and two to the genus Ootetrastichus. The Anomala beetle is slowly extending its damage into the cane fields at the outskirts of the infested district. Mention is made of several predators and parasites of this pest which are being introduced.

Insect pests [in the West Indies during 1915], H. A. BALLOU (*West Indian Bul. 16 (1916), No. 1, pp. 3–16, 26, 27*).—This is a record of the occurrence of the more important insect pests during 1915.

[Insect pests in St. Vincent] (*Imp. Dept. Agr. West Indies, Rpt. Agr. Dept. St. Vincent, 1915–16, pp. 7–9, 11–13, 15–17, 18, 19, 20–28, 31–34*).—This paper deals with the occurrence of the more important insect pests of cotton, cassava, corn, Lima beans, etc., and includes a report of a special study of the egg parasite *Trichogramma minuta*, a report of the work connected with insect and fungus pests and their control, and an account of the native food plants and feeding habits of the cotton stainer. Much of the data has been previously noted from other sources (E. S. R., 35, p. 355; 36, pp. 153, 253, 654).

[Insects of economic importance in South America] (*An. Zool. Aplicada, 1 (1914), No. 1, pp. 17–22, 25–27, 29, 30, 37–41, 44–79, figs. 28*).—The papers here presented, relating to insects in Chile, include the following: Simulidæ of Northern Chile, by F. Knab (E. S. R., 35, p. 258); A New Scolytid in Chile, *Phlœotribus porteri*, by C. Bruch; Description of a New Prionomitus in Chile, by J. Brèthes; Insecticide Formulas Recommended for the Destruction of Coccids and Other Insects, by E. Molina; Résumé of Work in Peru on *Phlebotomus verrucarum* and Its Agency in the Transmission of Verruga, by C. H. T. Townsend (E. S. R., 35, p. 258); and Contribution to the Economic Entomology of Chile, by C. E. Porter.

[Insects of economic importance in South America] (*An. Zool. Aplicada, 3 (1916) No. 1, pp. 6–29, 31–54. figs. 9*).—The papers here presented include the following: Discovery and Interpretation of the Stages in the Asexual Cycle of the Organism of Verruga Peruviana, by C. H. T. Townsend; Description of a New Genus and a New Species of Ortalidæ in Chile, namely, *Eupterocalla opazoi*, by J. Brèthes; Description of a New Chilean Dipteran (*Agromyza gayi*), by C. E. Porter; The Codling Moth, by A. Paillot; Description of Two Chilean Hymenoptera, namely, *Pteroptrix australis* n. sp., and *Heterobelyta chilensis* n. g. and n. sp., by J. Brèthes; *Phlebotomus papataci*, the Transmittor of Three Days' Fever, by R. Morales; Lepidoptera of Economic Importance in La Rioja, Argentina, by E. Giacomelli; Introduction of *Diaspis pentagona* and the Control of This Pest in Argentina, by A. Gallardo; and A Contribution to the Economic Entomology of Chile, by C. E. Porter.

[Insects and insect control in Germany] (*Mitt. K. Biol. Anst. Land u. Forstw., No. 16 (1916), pp. 15–58, figs. 5*).—Several papers relating to insects and their control are here presented, namely, Tests of Insecticides, by Schwartz (pp. 15, 16); Observations on Insect Pests (pp. 16–19) and On the Knowledge of Red Spider Mites (pp. 19–25), by Zacher; Contribution to the Knowledge of the Migratory Plant Lice in Germany, by Börner and Blunck (pp. 25–42); The Appearance of Winged Forms of Plant Lice (pp. 42, 43) and The Blood-dissolving Fluids in the Body of Plant Lice and Their Behavior Toward Plant Juices (pp. 43–49), by Börner; and Bee Diseases, by Maassen (pp. 51–58).

Annual report of the entomological laboratory for the year ended March 31, 1915, T. J. ANDERSON (*Dept. Agr. Brit. East Africa Ann. Rpt. 1914–15, pp. 38–54*).—This consists largely of a preliminary annotated list of 129 economic insects of British East Africa.

Some reasons for spraying citrus trees in Florida, W. W. YOTHERS (*Fla. Grower, 15 (1917), Nos. 10, pp. 5, 6; 11, pp. 7, 8; 12, pp. 9, 10*).—The advantages resulting from spraying for the control of insect pests and mites as a supplement to the benefits resulting from natural enemies are pointed out.

The cat-tail rush, Typha latifolia, as a summer host of injurious insects, W. M. DAVIDSON (*Mo. Bul. Com. Hort. Cal.*, *6 (1917), No. 2, pp. 64, 65, fig. 1*).— This rush, which serves as a summer host for a number of important pests, is abundant in California along water courses, in ponds and marshes, and in irrigation ditches. It frequently thrives in close proximity to orchards and remains green throughout the long, dry summers while the grasses and weeds in great part begin to die off in the late spring.

The plum aphis (*Hyalopterus arundinis*) is perhaps the chief insect pest which feeds upon it, spring migrants arriving from plums and apricots at the end of April and continuing to arrive until the end of July. The reddish-brown plum aphis (*Rhopalosiphum nympheæ*), which occurs on plums of both European and Asiatic origin, uses the cat-tail as summer host along with other water plants, including Alisma, Nymphea, Potamogeton, etc. Ordinarily predators control this aphid quite effectively, while the smaller colonies of the mealy aphis more frequently escape. The grain aphis colonizes *T. latifolia* during the summer and fall, winged forms arriving in May and June, and another such generation departing in the late autumn. *Aphis avenæ*, the oat aphis, is another grass species that may be found on it, often in large colonies, during the summer and fall. A small, black aphis, probably *A. gossypii*, also occurs in small numbers on this host plant during the summer and fall months, migrating forms appearing at the end of October. Red spider mites of the genus Tetranychus feed on it, sometimes in abundance, during the summer months.

Hackberry insects and their control, F. B. PADDOCK (*Proc. Texas Farmers' Cong.*, *18 (1915), pp. 103–106*).—This is a brief summary of the insect enemies of the hackberry and means for their control.

Contribution to a study of the toxins of spiders, R. LÉVY (*Ann. Sci. Nat. Zool.*, *10. ser., 1 (1916), No. 4–6, pp. 161–399, figs. 6*).—This work reviews the literature and reports upon investigations conducted.

The genera and species of Mallophaga, L. HARRISON (*Parasitology, 9 (1916), No. 1, pp. 156*).—This paper has been prepared primarily with the view of placing a complete list of the systematic nomenclature of the group in the hands of students of Mallophaga, no attempt having been made to bring the host list up to date. The subject matter is divided into eight parts under the headings of general introduction; list of species of Mallophaga included in the genera Pediculus, Ricinus, and Nirmus; list of generic and subgeneric names, valid and invalid, used for Mallophaga; scheme of classification; list of species and subspecies, valid and invalid, of Mallophaga; bibliography; list of new names introduced in this publication; and index to genera.

Field notes on Virginia Orthoptera, H. Fox (*Proc. U. S. Nat. Museum, 52 (1917), pp. 199–234*).

Fourth campaign against locusts (Schistocerca peregrina) in Algeria by means of Coccobacillus acridiorum, BÉGUET (*Bul. Soc. Path. Exot., 9 (1916), No. 9, pp. 679–682*).—A continuation of the work previously reported (E. S. R., 36, p. 356).

The distribution of virulent cultures of *C. acridiorum* on the food has always started an epidemic in the bands of *S. peregrina*. Such epizootics, however, have never brought about their complete disappearance.

The fungus on cacao thrips, W. NOWELL (*Agr. News [Barbados], 15 (1916), No. 383, p. 430*).—The fungus which occurs as a white mold on the body of *Heliothrips rubrocinctus* in St. Vincent has been identified by R. Thaxter as *Sporotrichum globuliferum*.

The cost of spraying in the control of the pear thrips in British Columbia, A. E. CAMERON, R. C. TREHERNE, and E. W. WHITE (*Agr. Gaz. Canada, 4 (1917), No. 1, pp. 13–16*).—These data are based upon spraying work in the spring of 1916 with hand and power outfits in which some 138 acres, comprising 11,569 bearing fruit trees of mixed varieties, were treated.

The green apple bug in Nova Scotia, W. H. BRITTAIN (*Nova Scotia Dept. Agr. Bul. 8 (1917), pp. 56, pls. 8, figs. 6*).—This bulletin relates to a form previously described by Knight as *Lygus communis novascotiensis* (E. S. R., 36, p. 550), one of the most serious pests of apples and pears in Nova Scotia. It contains much data based upon work during 1916 in addition to that for 1915 noted from another source (E. S. R., 36, p. 457).

"The young begin to emerge several days before the blossoms open, the maximum emergence coinciding with the period of full bloom of the Bartlett pear, or just as the Gravenstein blossoms begin to open. The nymphal stage is of about 32 days duration. The adults begin to die off within a couple of weeks after reaching maturity, but are found in diminishing numbers throughout the summer and early autumn. The winter is passed in the egg state, beneath the bark of the twigs.

"The young bugs or nymphs are very active and elusive in their habits, and as they increase in size, exhibit an increased tendency to drop to the ground. Leaves, stems, blossoms, and fruit are freely attacked, but blossoms and fruit are preferred. They are occasionally predacious in habit, and though apparently fragile, can exist for several days without food and are able to make their way over the ground for comparatively long distances. The adults are active insects and strong fliers, though under ordinary conditions they do not appear to wander far from the orchard in which they have developed. In feeding, the adults prefer a diet of fruit, and that of pears is most attractive to them when they first reach maturity."

The spiny citrus white fly.—A potential pest of citrus trees, J. C. HUTSON (*Agr. News [Barbados], 16 (1917), No. 384, pp. 10, 11*).—An account is here given of *Aleurocanthus woglumi*, a species recently described by Quaintance and Baker (E. S. R., 35, p. 552), which is already attracting considerable attention in Jamaica, the Bahama Islands, and Cuba.

The author reports observations of the past in the Guantanamo Valley, Cuba, where it was discovered in August, 1915, attacking a few citrus trees in a grove of about 8,000. During the course of an inspection made in the early months of 1916, it was found that this aleyrodid had spread so rapidly in the infested grove that practically all the trees were infested. It was prevalent in the neighboring town of Guantanamo, and an inspection of the main portion of the valley showed that practically all the citrus trees within a well-defined area of the valley and foothills were more or less infested by it. In addition to attacking oranges and grapefruit, it occurs on other species of citrus, mango, coffee, guava, sapodilla, star-apple, etc.

The spiny citrus white fly and means for its control in Cuba (*Sec. Agr. Com. y Trab., Com. Sanid. Veg. Cuba, Circ. 1 [1916], pp. 6*).—This gives a brief description of *Aleurocanthus woglumi* and methods of combating it.

On the supposed varieties of Chrysomphalus dictyospermi, E. MALENOTTI (*Redia, 12 (1916), No. 1, pp. 109–123, figs. 6; abs. in Rev. Appl. Ent., Ser. A, 4 (1916), No. 11, p. 468*).—The author takes the view that there are no true varieties of *C. dictyospermi*, a scale which infests at least 80 different species of plants belonging to about 25 quite dissimilar families in both tropical and temperate climates.

The codling moth and its control in the Western Province, F. W. Pettey (*Union So. Africa Dept. Agr., Sci. Bul. 9 (1916), pp. 48, figs. 7*).—A report of a detailed study of the codling moth commenced in the summer of 1915.

Statistics on the production of silk in France and elsewhere (*Statistique de la Production de la Soie en France et a l'Etranger. Lyon: Syndicat de l'Union des Marchands de Soie de Lyon, 1917, pp. 68*).—This, the usual annual summary (E. S. R., 36, p. 655), covers the year 1915.

The meadow foxtail midge, A. H. Cockayne (*Jour. Agr.* [*New Zeal.*], *13 (1916), No. 6, pp. 459–466, figs. 5*).—*Oligotropus alopecuri*, originally thought to be a variety of the wheat midge, is probably distributed wherever meadow foxtail is cultivated. During 1915 the crop was virtually ruined in the Manawatu district, one of the two principal seed-producing localities in New Zealand. In many cases 70 per cent of the seed was destroyed and the output rendered quite unsalable. In 1916 the infestation was even worse in this district and no seed was harvested.

Anopheline mosquitoes.—Their distribution and infection under field conditions, M. B. Mitzmain (*Pub. Health Rpts.* [*U. S.*], *32 (1917), No. 15, pp. 536–540*).—This is a report of investigations, conducted in continuation of those previously noted (E. S. R., 36, p. 757), that were undertaken primarily for the purpose of ascertaining the relative distribution of anophelines under field conditions and included also an effort to determine for a particular locality (Talladega Springs, Ala.) the seasonal period at which parasitism of mosquitoes could no longer be demonstrated.

In the above-mentioned region the maximum parasite index among 200 persons was found to be 18.6 per cent. With a view to determining whether conditions exist in nature in the presence of which this mosquito may be of epidemiological significance, a total of 1,377 specimens of two species of Anopheles (*A. quadrimaculatus* and *A. punctipennis*) were collected during the period from September 18 to November 15, 1916. "It is indicated that in the three sources of direct human influence, namely, inside dwellings, under dwellings, and in privies, the last produced the greatest number of specimens of *A. punctipennis*. This species comprised less than one-third (30 per cent) of the catch in houses, while under dwellings 62 per cent of the mosquitoes collected proved to be *A. punctipennis.*"

The preponderant numbers of *A. punctipennis* infesting houses were usually found in an engorged state resting under the flooring of dwellings. Although *A. punctipennis* rarely bites while inside a dwelling, it is found to attack persons seated on the porch or gallery of the house, after which these mosquitoes seek rest, presumably under the house in preference to the interior. In one instance infection was noted in a specimen of *A. quadrimaculatus* examined on November 15.

Is mosquito or man the winter carrier of malaria organisms? M. B. Mitzmain (*Pub. Health Serv. U. S. Bul. 84 (1916), pp. 32, pls. 8*).—This is a report of investigations made in a territory comprising 15 plantations in Bolivar and Washington Counties, Miss.

It is concluded after an examination of 2,122 dissected anophelines collected in this region that hibernating anophelines did not harbor parasites of malaria. In the investigation of man as the responsible winter carrier, 1,184 persons residing in the section above mentioned were examined for malarial parasites and 492 infections were identified microscopically, i. e., nearly one-fourth of the human carriers harbored gametocytes. Of these, 317 cases were of the subtertian type, 8 were mixed infections, and the remainder were of the simple tertian type, with the exception of one quartan case.

" The incrimination of man as the sole winter carrier is emphasized by the fact that three malaria-infected *Anopheles quadrimaculatus* were found in the homes of these gametocyte carriers during May 15 to May 26, previous to which time, 1,180 specimens of Anopheles from this source were found to be negative."

See also previous notes (E. S. R., 36, pp. 255, 757).

Experimental studies with muscicides and other fly-destroying agencies, E. B. PHELPS and A. F. STEVENSON (*Pub. Health Serv. U. S., Hyg. Lab. Bul. 108 (1917), pp. 57, figs. 2*).—A detailed report of experimental studies which have been substantially noted from another source (E. S. R., 37, p. 53).

The limitations of kerosene as a larvicide, with some observations on the cutaneous respiration of mosquito larvæ, J. W. S. MACFIE (*Bul. Ent. Research, 7 (1917), No. 3, pp. 277-295, fig. 1*).—It is pointed out that many localities are ill-suited for the application of kerosene, that many surfaces of water can not be efficiently oiled, and that by no means all the species of mosquitoes that bite man breed close to houses.

Experiments made to determine the action of kerosene as a larvicide, the survival of submerged larvæ, etc., are reported.

Observations on the distribution of warble flies in Ohio, D. C. MOTE (*Ohio Jour. Sci., 17 (1917), No. 5, pp. 169-176, figs. 2*).—This is a report of studies conducted in Ohio largely during 1914 and 1916, in which it is shown that *Hypoderma bovis* is the most abundant species, comprising nearly 83.5 per cent of 628 grubs and 15 adults collected in 32 counties. See also work noted in Ohio Station Bulletin 278 (E. S. R., 32, p. 796).

The poplar and willow borer (Cryptorhynchus lapathi), R. MATHESON (*New York Cornell Sta. Bul. 388 (1917), pp. 457-483, pl. 1, figs. 18*).—The poplar and willow borer is a European beetle, first discovered in this country in 1882, which has become so abundant in many eastern nurseries during the past 10 to 20 years that in many cases the nurserymen have almost abandoned the raising of Carolina and other species of poplars. It is also a serious enemy of practically all species of willows and where the beetle is abundant the damage done is extensive, this being especially true of all varieties of ornamental willows, while the production of basket willows is greatly reduced and in many cases stopped by its work. In addition to poplars and willows it has been recorded as attacking several species of alders and two species of birch. At the present time it is known to occur from Maine west to Ontario and North Dakota and south to the District of Columbia.

In New York State the adults begin to appear during the latter part of July, are abundant in August, and have been found present on poplar trees as late as October 7. Shortly after emerging from the pupal cells they begin to feed, selecting young, tender shoots. The bark is punctured by the beak, a round hole being formed down to the cambium layer, on which the beetles largely feed. They are such voracious feeders that when abundant the young 1-year-old shoots may be so completely, riddled that they shrivel and die. Punctures in old bark are for the deposition of eggs, and these always appear some weeks after the beetles have been feeding. While their wings are perfect and apparently suitable for flying the beetles have never been observed in flight or attempting to fly, and in the nursery it is not uncommon to find one block badly infested, whereas a block somewhat distant may be only slightly injured.

The eggs are placed in corky parts of the bark on branches or parts of the tree more than a year old, from 1 to 3 or 4 eggs being deposited in a cavity. Oviposition continues from early August until October, but the number of eggs deposited by a single female has not been determined; from 18 to 25 days are required for their incubation, the first of which out-of-doors were observed to hatch on October 2.

The young larva feeds on the tender tissues of the plant and soon reaches the soft cambium layer. Externally the beginning of feeding can be easily recognized by the blackish wet frass that fills the outer part of the egg cavity. Feeding continues until cold weather and commences the following spring as soon as the weather becomes sufficiently warm.

Pupation begins in the last few days of June and continues throughout July, the pupal period varying from 10 to 18 days, those formed early in July requiring only 10 days while those late in July require the full 18 days. Individuals maturing early in the season usually remain in the pupal cells for two or three weeks before emerging, a general emergence of adults occurring the latter part of July.

It is pointed out that the observations of European workers do not entirely agree with those made in New York State, thus indicating that the life history and habits of this insect are complex and vary greatly.

Extensive experiments were carried out on large blocks of trees in nurseries in which varying strengths of miscible oils, emulsions, etc., were applied both in the fall and in the spring. Such work carried on during 1913–14, 1914–15, and 1915–16 has shown that carbolineum avenarius, when applied to the trunk to a sufficient height, gives nearly absolute control. A high-grade creosote which has been tried in a limited way has also given a perfect control. Carbolineum is not injurious to the hands and can best be applied by dipping cotton waste into the material, then rubbing carefully up and down the trunk of the tree to a height of 4 or 5 ft. It is pointed out that great care should be exercised to see that the base of the tree is well treated and all parts of the trunk well covered.

Carbolineum gives the bark of the trees a deep-brown color but in no way affects their vigor. While this brownish coloration gradually becomes reduced during the summer, the treated trees can be recognized easily for at least three years after treatment. In the experimental plats treated in 1913–14 trees were not attacked during 1914 and 1915 and only a single larva was found in them during 1916, indicating that they are not readily selected by the females for oviposition, provided untreated trees are available.

In nurseries the carbolineum should be applied by hand during the latter part of March and the first week in April. This can be most advantageously done just after the trees are pruned. A careful account of the entire cost of treatment in one nursery showed it to average not more than 0.2 ct. per tree.

Studies of this beetle by Schoene have been noted (E. S. R., 18, p. 957). A 3-page bibliography is included.

Experimental evidence that bark borers are able to kill healthy fir trees, A. WELANDER (*Skogsvårdsför. Tidskr.*, *No. 6–7 (1916), pp. 520–526, figs. 3; abs. in Rev. Appl. Ent., Ser. A, 4 (1916), No. 12, pp. 507, 508*).—Experiments reported indicate that *Ips typographus* is able to kill perfectly healthy trees.

The bean beetle (Epilachna corrupta), D. E. MERRILL (*New Mexico Sta. Bul. 106 (1917), pp. 3–30, pls. 4, fig. 1*).—This is a report of studies of *E. corrupta*, a leaf-eating coccinellid or lady beetle which is the most injurious insect attacking the bean in New Mexico. Although its yearly damage is estimated in various localities at from 5 to 100 per cent, the author considers an average of 10 per cent to be a conservative estimate. The injury is caused by both the adult beetles and the larvæ eating outright or skeletonizing the leaves.

The larvæ feed on the under surface of the leaves in colonies when they are young, but scatter later. When at all numerous they eat off the lower epidermis and all the green substance of the central layers of the leaf, whereas the adults eat holes here and there entirely through the leaves, rarely destroying the whole leaf. The young pods may be attacked, holes being scraped in their sides, or an occasional flower eaten.

The species was first described from Mexico in 1851 and occurs in Arizona, Colorado, New Mexico, Texas, and Utah. There are two broods of the bean beetle each year in the southern part of New Mexico, where the life-history studies were conducted. The hibernated adults oviposit from June 15 to August 1. The first-brood larvæ were found from June 19 to August 23; the first-brood pupæ from July 5 to August 28; and first-brood adults from July 10 throughout the season, of which some may hibernate. The second-brood eggs are found from July 16 to the end of the season; second-brood larvæ from July 20 to the end of the season; second-brood pupæ from August 5 to the end of the season; and second-brood adults from August 10 on, in which stage they hibernate.

The eggs are deposited in clusters, as a rule not contiguously, on the underside of the leaves, 46 being the average number of eggs per cluster for 39 clusters counted. The maximum egg production among 8 females observed was 754 in 14 clusters, the minimum was 93 eggs in two clusters, and the average 291 eggs per female. The average period of incubation was 5.8 days, with 4 days as the minimum and 9 days the maximum. The larval period (4 instars) required an average of 16.8 days for the first brood, with a maximum of 21 and a minimum of 15 days; for the second brood an average of 15.7 days, with a maximum of 19 and a minimum of 15 days. The pupal period averaged 4.7 days for either brood, with 5 days as a maximum in each, while the minimum for the first brood was 3 days and for the second 4 days. The average total time from egg to adult was 25.9 days for the first brood and 25.4 days for the second brood; the shortest time was 22 and the longest 28 days.

It is pointed out that injury may be reduced to a minimum by cooperation in the use of preventive measures of control, including time of planting, rotation, clearing of fields, etc. Attention is called to the fact that a gain of from one to two weeks in planting is of considerable importance at the crucial point of the infestation. But few natural enemies have been observed. Preliminary experiments with arsenicals and blackleaf 40, briefly reported, indicate that lead arsenate may be of value.

The 1916 tests of sulphur-arsenical dusts against the strawberry weevil, T. J. HEADLEE (*New Jersey Stas. Circ. 65 (1917), pp. 3–7, fig. 1*).—The remarkably efficient results obtained from the use of mixtures of arsenate of lead and sulphur for the strawberry weevil during 1915 (E. S. R., 35, p. 364) led to more extensive tests in Atlantic, Cumberland, and Burlington Counties during 1916.

The results obtained on a representative farm in Atlantic County on which careful records were kept, presented in tabular form, show net returns at the rate of more than $100 per acre or a maximum increase of 200 per cent. The mixture of one part of lead arsenate to five parts of sulphur, while a little less effective than the 1:1 mixture, was much the better from the standpoint of net returns. It is shown that neither sulphur by itself nor arsenate of lead used alone is anywhere nearly so effective as the two combined. This is thought to be due to the fact that while neither substance alone flows freely through a powder gun a mixture of the two does so readily, and thus permits the application of a much more even and complete coating. Since careful examinations again failed to reveal any considerable number of dead beetles on treated plats, it is concluded that the mixtures act as repellents.

The year's experience with machinery for making applications is said to have been largely unsatisfactory. Mention is made of a satisfactory hand sifter which has been devised by T. Rizzotte, consisting of a common wire nose muzzle covered with one thickness of copper mosquito netting, 15 wires to the inch, the open edges of which are drawn up and tied to the rim. By using a 3-ft. hickory sapling bent as a bow and the ends fastened to the opposite sides of the rim a good coating can be applied to rows varying in width from 18 in. to 3 ft. by twirling the apparatus over the row as the operator walks along.

From 80 to 90 lbs. of the mixture are required per acre for each treatment. Ordinarily two applications are sufficient, the first when weevil-feeding on the bud begins and the second about one week later or as soon as the coating given by the first treatment has lost its completeness. Every bud should be kept dusty.

Further trial of sulphur-arsenate of lead dust against the strawberry weevil, T. J. HEADLEE (*Jour. Econ. Ent., 10 (1917), No. 2, pp. 287–290, fig. 1*).— Noted above.

Method of cockchafer control used in Germany, K. ESCHERICH (*Ztschr. Angew. Ent., 3 (1916), No. 1, pp. 134–156; abs. in Internat. Inst. Agr. [Rome], Internat. Rev. Sci. and Pract. Agr., 7 (1916), No. 6, pp. 910–912*).—Control experiments with the cockchafer (*Melolontha vulgaris* and *M. hippocastani*) in the Bienwald in the Upper Palatinate are reported.

Descriptions of various chalcidoid Hymenoptera with observations, [III], A. A. GIRAULT (*Entomologist, 50 (1917), No. 645, pp. 36–38*).—This third (not fourth) paper (E. S. R., 36, p. 555) with descriptions of three parasites new to science, includes *Podagrion mantidiphagum* reared from an egg mass of a mantid in the British West Indies, and *Paraleptomastrix notatus* reared from *Pseudococcus bakeri* on the grape at Fresno, Cal.

Notes on chalcid flies, chiefly from California, A. A. GIRAULT (*Jour. Ent. and Zool., 9 (1917), No. 1, pp. 8–12*).—Descriptions of seven new species are given.

Notes on coccid-infesting Chalcidoidea, II, J. WATERSTON (*Bul. Ent. Research, 7 (1917), No. 3, pp. 231–257, figs. 9*).—This second paper (E. S. R., 37, p. 162) presents descriptions of seven chalcidoid parasites of Coccidæ from the Gold Coast that are new to science.

Annual reports of the State bee inspector for the years 1915 and 1916, F. C. PELLETT (*Ann. Rpt. State Bee Insp. Iowa, 4 (1915), pp. 72, pls. 2, figs. 9; 5 (1916), pp. 103, figs. 11*).—These reports of the work for the years 1915 and 1916 include the proceedings of the fourth and fifth annual conventions of the Iowa State Beekeepers' Association.

The question of denatured sugar for the feeding of honeybees, E. ÍA. ZARIN (*Trudy Selsk. Khoz. Bakt. Lab., 5 (1915), pt. 3, pp. 371–390*).—This discussion includes a report upon the experimental feeding of bees with sugar denatured with various substances. In experiments with paprika and methyl violet, coal tar and animal oils, the latter was found the better, as a moderate addition of the animal oil can not influence harmfully the color or taste of the honey.

Beauveria peteloti n. sp., a polymorphous Isaria parasite of Hymenoptera in tropical America, F. VINCENS (*Bul. Soc. Bot. France, 62 (1915), No. 4–6, pp. 132–144, pls. 4*).—This fungus is parasitic on two wasps (*Polybia chrysothorax* and *Polystes canadensis*) and an undetermined bee.

FOODS—HUMAN NUTRITION.

The effect of high temperatures on the nutritive value of foods, A. G. HOGAN (*Jour. Biol. Chem., 30 (1917), No. 1, pp. 115–123, figs. 9*).—Earlier work by the author (E. S. R., 36, p. 158) indicated that young laboratory animals (rats) were unable to grow upon a diet which had been subjected to high temperatures. Accordingly, further experiments with rats were made on the nutritive properties of heated foods. In some instances the ration consisted of corn and in others of corn and egg white, a salt mixture being added to the diet to compensate for the mineral deficiencies of maize. The heating process was continued for six hours at 30 lbs. pressure.

It was found that heating the egg white had little or no effect, but in every case where corn was heated the diet was inadequate in some respect and the animals were unable to maintain body weight. It was suggested that some factor other than that of food accessories was altered, and to investigate this point a comparatively pure protein, egg white, was heated in an autoclave for six hours at 30 lbs. pressure. This was dried and combined with protein-free milk, butter, starch, and agar in such proportions that the protein formed about 9 per cent of the ration. "This diet did not permit maximum growth, and possibly these rats grew somewhat more slowly than other animals receiving a similar ration in which the protein had not been heated. Evidently, however, the nutritive value of the protein had not been seriously impaired."

Similar experiments with casein in the ration instead of egg white were carried out, the casein being heated for two hours, but at different pressures, namely, 15, 30, and 45 lbs., while unheated casein was given to one lot of control animals. In these rations protein formed approximately 12 per cent. "In all cases animals of the same sex grew at approximately the same rate, indicating that the nutritive value of the casein had not been materially lowered by the high temperature. . . .

"The heating process described in this paper does not materially lower the nutritional value of protein. It is suggested that one or more of the so-called food 'accessories' may be injured by high temperatures."

Bread making, MAY C. McDONALD (*N. Dak. Agr. Col. Ext. Bul. 7 (1917), pp. 16, figs. 4*).—This bulletin discusses the ingredients used in bread making and describes the processes of mixing, rising, and baking. Recipes are given for making different kinds of breads.

The proteins of the peanut, Arachis hypogæa, C. O. JOHNS and D. B. JONES (*Proc. Nat. Acad. Sci., 3 (1917), No. 5, pp. 365–369*).—Two globulins, arachin and conarachin, together with a trace of albumin, have been isolated by the authors from the peanut. The greatest difference between the two globulins is in the percentage of sulphur, conarachin containing nearly three times as much as arachin. Both equivalents are characterized by a high percentage of basic nitrogen.

The article also discusses briefly the nutritive value of the peanut and especially the question of supplementing wheat and corn with peanut meals.

[Bacteriological examination of milk, ice, oysters, ice cream, and catsup], W. R. STOKES (*Ann. Rpt. Bd. Health Md., 1913, pp. 166–170*).—The results are reported of the examination of several samples of these products.

[Report of the State Food and Drug Commissioner and the Bureau of Chemistry of the Maryland State Board of Health], C. CASPARI, JR., and W. B. D. PENNIMAN (*Ann. Rpt. Bd. Health Md., 1913, pp. 179–193*).—This report covers the work done in the inspection and examination of foods during the year ended December 31, 1913, data being given regarding a number of samples of miscellaneous food products and the inspection of a large number of establishments where food is prepared and sold.

[Pure food topics and drug inspection], E. F. LADD and ALMA K. JOHNSON (*North Dakota Sta. Spec. Bul., 4 (1917), No. 12, pp. 331–338, 341–346*).—This bulletin contains a brief article on The So-called "Vitamins" or "Food Accessories" and Their Importance in the Nutrition of Animals, by F. W. Christensen, and reports the results of the examination of a number of samples of drugs.

Food and efficiency, MARTHA TRACY (*N. Y. Med. Jour., 104 (1916), Nos. 16, pp. 748, 749; 18, pp. 851–853; 20, pp. 953, 954; 22, pp. 1054–1056; 24, pp. 1149–1151; 26, pp. 1245–1247; 105 (1917), No. 2, pp. 75–78*).—This is a summary and digest of recent experimental data on various topics of food and nutrition.

Food, fuel for the human engine, E. L. FISK (*New York: Life Extension Institute, Inc., 1917, pp. 32, fig. 1*).—A popular bulletin on the selection and use of food. Much of the material given is based on a three-weeks' dietary test with 12 young men, in which the cost of food was kept within the limit of 25 cts. per day. The menus and recipes used in this test are given and a modification is suggested of the menus for a family including young children.

Practical suggestions regarding food values and the proper selection of a nutritious and economical diet, A. M. G. SOULE (*Bul. [Maine] Dept. Agr., 16 (1917), No. 1, pp. 36, figs. 2*).—This publication contains data regarding the classification of foods and the composition of different food materials and suggestions for the economical selection of the different foods.

Diet lists, compiled by H. S. CARTER (*Philadelphia: W. B. Saunders Co., 1913, pp. VII+129*).—This is a compilation of different lists prepared primarily for use in the Presbyterian Hospital, New York City. Among the lists included are the regular house diet for each day of the week, which includes the convalescent and soft diets, and typhoid, salt-poor, purin-free, gastric, diabetic, and other special diets. In the publication are also included a number of special recipes and miscellaneous tables.

Reports of the [Massachusetts] Commission on Cost of Living, R. LUCE ET AL. (*[Boston]: State, 1917, pp. 8+7+6+3+14*).—This publication contains reports on anthracite coal, bread, the relation of transportation to prices, and department stores, and a final report which summarizes basic causes of the recent increase in prices, and the effect of the war, short crops, abnormal buying, inflation of currency, waste, etc., upon the cost of living. The report contains some recommendations.

Government control of food supplies in France (*Mo. Rev., U. S. Bur. Labor Statis., 4 (1917), No. 4, pp. 525–533*).—Information is given regarding the fixing of maximum prices for wheat, flour, bread, and other commodities; municipal and cooperative meat markets; the limitation of the sale and service of food, etc.

The interrelation between diet and body condition and the energy production during mechanical work in the dog, R. J. ANDERSON and G. LUSK (*Proc. Nat. Acad. Sci., 3 (1917), No. 5, pp. 386–389*).—From the experimental data here reported, the following conclusions are drawn by the authors:

"The accomplishment of a given amount of mechanical work is always at the expense of a given amount of energy, and . . . the amount of energy required for mechanical work is independent of the physical condition of the subject and independent of the quantity of carbohydrate food present in the gastrointestinal tract. . . .

"Protein in the dietary is primarily for the repair of the tissues. It is not beneficial for the economical performance of work. In excess, it largely increases the heat production which a working organism is called on to eliminate.

"One may reduce the basal requirement for energy by starvation, and this process may economize food in the case of those who do no mechanical work.

"To accomplish a given amount of work a given amount of fuel energy is required, irrespective of the nutritive condition of the organism. This is of primary importance in the maintenance of armies or munition workers. Carbohydrate food fuel is utilized without loss."

The influence of the protein intake on the excretion of creatin in man, W. DENIS and ANNA S. MINOT (*Jour. Biol. Chem., 30 (1917), No. 1, pp. 47–51*).—Observations upon five individuals suffering from Graves's disease showed that the amount of creatin excreted depended on the intake of protein. It was increased by high protein feeding and decreased by low protein feeding.

Inhibition of digestion of proteins by adsorbed tin, B. C. Goss (Jour. Biol. Chem., 30 (1917), No. 1, pp. 53–60, fig. 1).—This paper reports experiments in which artificial gastric and tryptic digestions of proteins were carried out in the presence and absence of adsorbed tin. The main object was to determine whether or not the stable tin-protein complex, formed by the adsorption of tin by foods having a high protein content, would pass through the body without being broken up by digestion.

It was found that "tin is readily adsorbed from solutions by coagulated proteins in amounts varying with the concentration according to the adsorption law of Freundlich. This adsorption takes place rapidly at first and then continues to increase slowly for several days, presumably because of the time required for diffusion into the solid. The adsorption complex is extremely stable and does not lose tin to a dilute acid or alkaline aqueous phase containing no tin, although the percentage of tin in the solid may be as high as 50 per cent. The presence of this tin, even in small amounts, interfered markedly with the digestion of the protein by either peptic or tryptic digestion, as was indicated by the change in color of the biuret reaction and by the visible retardation of the solution of coagulated proteins."

It appeared that it was only part of the protein, directly joined to the tin, whose digestion was hindered. "The effect of this retardation on the food value of a protein containing tin can only be a matter of conjecture, but it is probably small, since the total tin in foods rarely exceeds 0.03 per cent."

It was found that even after two days, in the case of artificial peptic digestions of the tin albumin containing 32 per cent of tin, there was no tin in a dialyzable form and only a very small amount in a filterable form, the latter probably being present as a colloid suspension of particles of the tin protein complex, split away from the solid by solution of the connecting albumin. "In the tryptic digestions no dialyzable tin was found in the liquor and only traces of filterable tin. Moreover, during digestion the percentage of tin in the solid rapidly increased, indicating that the protein which was not directly bound to the tin was being dissolved away."

The insoluble complex formed when coagulated proteins are brought into contact with solution containing tin was not broken up to any extent by artificial gastric and tryptic digestions. The author states that "while it is impossible to predict what the action of bacteria in the stomach and intestine would be, it is to be questioned whether the tin-protein complex is broken up in the actual digestive processes in the body and whether the tin which is combined in this way can have any toxic action."

Effect of ingestion of coffee, tea, and caffein on the excretion of uric acid in man, L. B. MENDEL and EMMA L. WARDELL (Jour. Amer. Med. Assoc., 68 (1917), No. 24, pp. 1805–1807, fig. 1).—The authors review the literature of the physiological effect of caffein and report the results of a study undertaken to determine the effect of caffein ingestion upon the excretion of uric acid. The subject of the experiment received a purin-free diet and, after the endogenous level of uric acid excretion had been reached, a definite quantity of coffee infusion of known caffein content was added to the diet on each of five consecutive days. Experiments were also made with decaffeinated coffee, caffein, and tea.

The authors state that a modification of Benedict's method for determining uric acid made possible more accurate determinations than had hitherto been obtained.

The experiments showed that the addition of the strong coffee infusion to a purin-free diet caused a marked increase in the excretion of uric acid.

The addition of a commercial decaffeinated coffee to a purin-free diet did not cause any increase in the excretion of uric acid. If, however, caffein was added to this preparation the excretion of uric acid was increased decidedly, as was the case with coffee. The effect of adding tea to the purin-free diet was similar to that of adding coffee to the same diet. The increase in the quantity of uric acid excreted after the addition of coffee, tea, or caffein to the purin-free diet seemed to be proportional to the quantity of caffein ingested and was equal to the quantity of uric acid which would be obtained by the demethylation and subsequent oxidation of from 10 to 15 per cent of the ingested caffein.

The action of xanthin and methyl xanthins on the isolated intestine, W. SALANT and E. W. SCHWARTZE (Proc. Soc. Expt. Biol. and Med., 14 (1916), No. 1, p. 15).

The action of succinate, malate, tartrate, and citrate on the isolated intestine, W. SALANT, C. W. MITCHELL, and E. W. SCHWARTZE (Proc. Soc. Expt. Biol. and Med., 14 (1916), No. 1, pp. 16, 17).

ANIMAL PRODUCTION.

How feed inspection helps the farmer, W. H. STROWD (Wisconsin Sta. Bul. 281 (1917), pp. 56, fig. 1).—Information with reference to feeding stuffs is summarized and analyses are given of cottonseed meal, cottonseed feed, linseed meal, gluten feed, corn oil meal, distillers' grains, hominy feed, corn feed meal, wheat bran, wheat middlings, red dog flour, germ middlings, oat middlings, rye middlings, rye bran, rye shorts, barley shorts, brewers' grains, malt sprouts, vinegar grains, alfalfa meal, bone meal, meat meal, meat scrap, tankage, dried beet pulp, screenings, and mixed and proprietary feeding stuffs.

How to feed live stock successfully, C. A. WILLSON (Tennessee Sta. Bul. 116 (1916), pp. 49–106, figs. 8; Col. Agr. Univ. Tenn., Ext. Div. Pub. 24 (1917). pp. 58, figs. 8.)—This popular treatise upon live-stock feeding discusses the traits of a successful feeder, principles to be considered in the feeding of farm animals, limitations as to the amounts of feed that should be given under various conditions, general rules for comparative valuations of feeding stuffs, balanced and standard rations, how to balance a ration, and the feeding of various kinds of live stock and poultry. The appendix gives in tabular form from sources already noted the average composition, digestible nutrients, and fertilizing constituents of American feeding stuffs, modified Wolff-Lehmann feeding standards, manurial values of farm products, fertility removed per acre by various farm crops, weights and measures of feeding stuffs, and suggested rations for beef and dairy cattle, horses, and mules.

How live stock is handled in the blue-grass region of Kentucky, J. H. ARNOLD (U. S. Dept. Agr., Farmers' Bul. 312 (1917), pp. 14).—This discusses the importance of knowing the best practice, what the blue-grass region farmer may do to increase his profits through live stock, utilization of waste products by means of animals, and feeding practice and cost of feed for different kinds of animals common on blue-grass farms, and presents analyses of the business on six individual farms. These farmers made beef cattle their leading stock enterprise, keeping sheep and hogs principally to utilize materials that otherwise would be wasted.

A study of the rate and economy of gains of fattening steers, H. W. MUMFORD, H. S. GRINDLEY, A. D. EMMETT, and S. BULL (Illinois Sta. Bul. 197 (1917), *pp. 567–604; abs. ed., pp. 3*).—This bulletin reports results relating to the effect upon the rate and economy of gains of variations in the amount of feed consumed ranging from maintenance to full-feed rations, of variations in the proportions of roughage and concentrates in the ration, and of the substitution of a nitrogenous concentrate for a part of the grain in a ration of clover hay and ground corn in the ratio of 1:5.

The experiment reported lasted for 37 weeks and was divided into five test periods, the first of five weeks, the second, third, and fourth of six weeks, and the fifth four weeks in length. The animals used were 2-year-old choice feeder steers, four lots of four each. One lot was fed a ration slightly above maintenance; another, an amount of feed equal to the maintenance ration plus one-third of the difference between the maintenance and the full-feed rations; another an amount equal to the maintenance ration plus two-thirds of the difference between the maintenance and the full-feed rations; and another as much feed as the animals would eat readily. The rations of the first test period consisted of clover hay and ground corn in the ratio of 1:1; that of the second the same, in the ratio of 1:3; that of the third the same, in the ratio of 1:5; of the fourth and fifth, of clover hay, ground corn, and linseed meal in the ratio of 1:4:1.

The average daily gains per head for the entire experiment of 37 weeks were for the maintenance ration 0.7 lb., for the one-third additional ration 1.32 lbs., for the two-thirds additional ration 1.79 lbs., and for the full-feed ration 2.13 lbs. The variations for individual animals were for the respective lots 0.37–1.05, 1.23–1.39, 1.75–1.81, and 1.98–2.29 lbs. These averages include, however, data for two steers which were upon full feed from the thirty-first to the thirty-seventh week, inclusive.

Other data are shown in the following table:

Consumption of digestible dry substance and net energy per pound of gain.

Lot.	Dry substance.		Digestible dry substance.		Net energy.	
	Average.	Variations.	Average.	Variations.	Average.	Variations.
	Pounds.	*Pounds.*	*Pounds.*	*Pounds.*	*Therms.*	*Therms.*
One-third feed...............	[1] 9.51	[1] 9.17–10.04	[1] 6.96	[1] 6.73–7.29	[1] 7.22	[1] 6.97–7.55
Two-thirds feed...............	[1] 9.40	[1] 8.95– 9.64	[1] 6.67	[1] 6.48–6.86	[1] 6.90	[1] 6.67–7.10
Full feed.....................	9.63	8.41–10.47	6.60	5.95–7.23	6.73	6.10–7.48

[1] This average includes the data for two steers which were upon full feed from the thirty-first to the thirty-seventh week, inclusive.

It is concluded that "2-year-old steers may be maintained on 8 to 9 lbs. of dry substance, 0.39 to 0.44 lb. of digestible crude protein, and 6.5 to 6.8 therms of net energy per 1,000 lbs. live weight. Fattening 2-year-old steers may make satisfactory gains over a period of 37 weeks on 14.3 to 22.1 lbs. of dry substance, 0.72 to 1.44 lbs. of digestible crude protein, and 11.9 to 13 therms of net energy per 1,000 lbs. live weight. Fairly good gains may be made even on less amounts than these."

The rate of gains of 2-year-old steers is considered to depend upon the amount of feed consumed. "However, the amount of feed consumed between one-third feed and full feed apparently has no effect upon the economy of gains as measured by the consumption of feed, of total dry substance, of digestible dry substance, and of net energy per pound of gain."

When a ration consisting of clover hay and ground corn was changed to a similar ration in which the amounts of digestible dry substance and net energy remained practically unchanged but the amount of protein was reduced from 10 to 12 per cent the rate of economy of gains was considerably decreased. A decrease was also observed where there was a change to a ration in which the digestiblé dry substance, digestiblc protein, and energy were slightly reduced. The substitution of the linseed meal in the fifth feeding period materially increased the rate of gains and the economy of gains.

"Steers which have been kept on a low plane of nutrition (maintenance) for a considerable time make more economical gains when put upon a full-feed ration than steers which have been upon full feed for some time. However, steers receiving more than a maintenance but less than a full-feed ration make no more economical gains when put upon full feed than steers which have already been on full feed."   .

The investigation indicates that "steers may be maintained or fattened with the ordinary rations of the corn belt on less digestible dry matter, on less digestible protein, and on less net energy than the amounts prescribed by the generally accepted feeding standards."

Information for horse breeders, L. L. LEWIS and W. P. SHULER (*Oklahoma Sta. Circ. 43 (1917), pp. 11, fig. 1*).—This circular gives in concise form information for persons engaged in horse raising. The topics discussed include artificial insemination, some diseases of the reproductive organs of mares and stallions, and the general care of mares and foals.

Preserving eggs for the home, B. ALDER (*Utah Sta. Circ. 25 (1917), pp. 8*).— This circular briefly reviews recent experiments on the preservation of eggs and gives directions for the home preservation of eggs in limewater and water glass.

In tests at the station 12 doz. eggs were placed in a crock jar and covered with a 10·per cent solution of water glass on April 1, 1913. During the following winter some of these eggs were tested and found to be in very good condition. Some of them were kept in the solution until the latter part of June, 1914, when most of the eggs retained a fairly fresh appearance as far as ordinary observation could determine. There was no change in the size of the air cell.

In similar tests conducted more recently the quality of the eggs deteriorated rather rapidly after about eight or ten months of storage. During the last two years water glass and a patented preservative for coating eggs have been compared. Good results were obtained with each method, but after five or six months of storage the eggs preserved with the patented preservative deteriorated the more rapidly.

DAIRY FARMING—DAIRYING.

Selecting dairy bulls by performance, W. E. CARROLL (*Utah Sta. Bul. 153 (1917), pp. 3–19, figs. 3*).—The author discusses the selection of dairy sires by performance, which in the sense here used is meant the ability of the sire to transmit to his daughters the potentiality of high milk and fat production.

Results are given of a study of standards of measuring performance or comparative value of dairy bulls. The data reported consist of seven-day milk and fat production records taken from the Holstein-Friesian Yearbook. Only bulls having 50 or more A. R. O. daughters were considered. The 32 bulls whose progeny were studied have to their credit a total of 2,579 tested daughters and 1,052 proved sons, who in turn have 7,632 tested daughters, making a total of 10,211 individual milk-fat records, as every tested daughter of each bull was considered in the study. The records are classified by age groups, and they show that these cows exceeded the present association age requirements by averages of from 64.8 per cent in the junior three-year-old group to 48.3 per cent in the aged cow group. Revised Advanced Registry requirements are calculated from the actual average fat production of cows in the different age groups based on 12 lbs. for an aged cow—the present aged requirement. Except for the aged cows, the revised standard is higher for all age groups than the present standard.

The A. R. O. fat production record of every daughter of each sire is reduced to a percentage of the association requirements, and the averages of these percentages for the daughters of each bull are considered the comparative values of the bulls as revealed by the performance of their A. R. O. daughters. Of the 32 bulls compared on this basis King of the Pontiacs heads the list, having 149 A. R. O. daughters, with an average percentage value of 186.4; King Segis stands second, with a value of 181.2 per cent; and Lord Netherland De Kol stands lowest among the 32, with an average value of 133.9 per cent. When compared on the basis of the number of A. R. O. daughters Lord Netherland De Kol, who has 122 such daughters, is exceeded only by King of the Pontiacs. The 32 sires are also compared on the basis of percentage performance of their A. R. O. daughters based on the revised age requirements above mentioned. No very great differences occur in the relative standing of the sires when compared on the two bases.

An attempt was also made to obtain a measure of the performance of a bull by the performance of his sons. To this end the records of the 7,632 daughters of the sons of the bulls in question were calculated to a percentage basis, as outlined above, these records being taken as a measure of the son's performance. The correlation coefficient between the average value of bulls and the average value of sons of these same bulls as shown by the average percentage values of their daughters is 0.6326 ± 0.0715. This high correlation is not considered evidence that fat production is transmitted through the male line.

The method suggested by the author of testing out a new sire is to "breed him only to a few older cows of known breeding capacity, then hold him in reserve, using him only when absolutely necessary, till the results of this first trial are completed. If the majority of these first heifers prove to be satisfactory producers, the bull could then safely be used generally in the herd; if not. he should be discarded."

Cow-testing associations, E. M. CLARK (*Illinois Sta. Circ. 196 (1917), pp. 10, figs. 2*).—Brief information is given on the advantages of cooperative cow-testing associations. including hints on their formation and operation.

Feeding dairy cattle, A. C. McCANDLISH (*Iowa Sta. Circ. 34 (1917), pp. 32*).— This popular treatise deals with the subject under the headings of constituents of feeds, functions of nutrients. definitions and characteristics of feeds, requirements of a ration. and the feeding of dairy animals.

Studies in the cost of market milk production, A. C. ANDERSON and F. T. RIDDELL (*Michigan Sta. Bul. 277 (1916), pp. 38, figs. 9*).—Data are presented on the cost of producing milk for the city market on 29 farms in the territory of the Grand Rapids Milk Producers' Association. These data cover the years 1914 and 1915, 25 farms being studied each year, and one of the authors spending his entire time on the farms.

On all of the farms where the investigations were carried on the production of milk was only one of the enterprises of the farm. On a few of them it was practically the sole enterprise, and crops were grown simply to feed the herd. On other farms milk production was coupled with grain. vegetables. live stock. or. fruit production for the market. None of these other enterprises were considered in any manner.

The average number of cows per year on the 25 farms was 459.46 in 1914 and 428.57 in 1915. The average daily labor requirement per cow when all the cows are considered was 28.73 minutes in 1914 and 28.56 minutes in 1915. The average yearly feed cost per cow varied from $39.27 to $93.54 on the different farms, the general average for the two years being $65.24. Of this amount the average charge for pasture was $7.98 per year. The total expenses per cow in 1914 were $150.57, and in 1915, $150.29. Of these amounts 30 per cent was for labor, 45 per cent for feed, and 25 per cent for overhead charges. The total value of products per cow was $158.80 in 1914 and $156.60 in 1915. The average milk yield per cow was 6,928 lbs. in 1914 and 7,156.8 lbs. in 1915. The cost of production and delivery of milk per hundredweight was $1.916 in 1914 and $1.854 in 1915. The net profit on milk was 1 ct. per gallon in 1914 and 0.7 ct. in 1915.

According to the data obtained in this study, 72 per cent of the dairies were profitable and 28 per cent were operated at a loss. In discussing conditions under which these profits and losses were brought about, it is stated that "no one factor seems to determine a profit or loss. In some cases high producing herds have failed to be remunerative, while in others very low producing herds have made a profit. The cost of labor, feeds, and the investment, as well as the system of management of the business, are important factors. Losses due to tuberculosis played a very important part in raising the cost of milk, and since these losses are occasioned by and sustained wholly in compliance with city ordinance, it is eminently fair and equitable that the producer should receive sufficient compensation for his improved product to safeguard him against losses from this source. Buildings poorly arranged, hauling feed and milk in small quantities for long distances, and the maintaining of low-producing cows tend to raise the cost of production. Moderate investment in buildings and equipment, systematized labor, moderate-priced feeds, and high-producing cows are inducive to profits. On the other hand, the price received for the product determines a profit or loss when milk is produced under economical conditions. The price secured should be great enough to allow a fair margin of profit."

A summation of the receipts and expenditures of each of the dairies under investigation for each year and other data brought out in the investigations are presented in graphic charts and diagrams.

Clarification of milk, T. J. McINERNEY (*New York Cornell Sta. Bul. 389* (*1917*), *pp. 487–504, figs. 7*).—The author briefly reviews the history of clarification studies, and gives detailed results of experimental work the object of which was to determine the advantages and disadvantages of the clarifier in commercial work. The points studied were the effect of clarification on the germ content and chemical and physical qualities of milk. In the experiments samples of milk were examined immediately before and after clarifying. The germ content was determined by the plate method, the total solids by the chemical method, and the fat content by the Babcock method. The acidity was determined by titrating 18 gm. of the sample with a tenth-normal alkali solution. The amount of insoluble dirt was determined by filtering equal quantities of clarified and unclarified milk through absorbent cotton. The amount of cream rising was determined by filling graduated, straight-sided cylinders with the samples and allowing them to stand for 24 hours. The keeping quality was determined by holding samples of clarified and of unclarified milk at definite temperatures and noting the time required for the milk to curdle.

An average increase in the bacterial content of milk due to clarification in these experiments was noted of 87.15 per cent in the case of fresh milk and

114.77 per cent in the case of old milk. "Bacteria increase more rapidly in unclarified milk than in clarified milk. The fat content before and after clarification is practically the same. The percentage of total solids is slightly reduced by clarification. This is probably due to the slime removed. The development of acidity is slightly more rapid in clarified milk than in unclarified milk. The keeping quality of milk remains about the same after clarification as it was before. About 99 per cent of the insoluble dirt in milk is removed by clarification. The volume of cream that is separated by gravity is reduced from 2 to 3 per cent by clarification. This is probably due to the agitation of the milk in passing through the clarifier."

Average analyses of eight samples of clarifier slime show the following percentage composition: Water 71.33, total solids 28.67, nitrogen 0.33, casein 2.13, fat 4, and ash 3.15.

A bibliography of 18 titles is given.

Pasteurization of cream, C. LARSEN, J. M. FULLER, V. R. JONES, H. GREGORY, and M. TOLSTRUP (South Dakota Sta. Bul. 171 (1916), pp. 529–548, figs. 6).— The objects of the experiments reported in this bulletin were to determine the efficiency and practicability of the coil cream vat as a cream pasteurizer in the manufacture of butter, the effectiveness of different temperatures of cream pasteurization, and also the keeping properties of the butter made from the cream pasteurized at the different temperatures. The cream used in the experiments was obtained from the regular college creamery patrons and contained about 30 per cent of fat.

In one series of experiments 19 vats of cream averaging 761 lbs. each were pasteurized at 140° F. With a steam pressure of 73.9 lbs. it required an average of 16.8 minutes to raise the temperature from 56.5 to 140°. In pasteurizing cream at 160° 20 vats were used, averaging 765 lbs. each. With a steam pressure of 72.3 lbs. it required an average of 22.2 minutes to raise the temperature from 56.8 to 160°. In a third series 19 vats of cream averaging 758 lbs. each were pasteurized at 180°. With a steam pressure of 74 lbs. it required an average of 34.4 minutes to raise the temperature from 57.6 to 180°.

The cream pasteurized at 140° was cooled to the churning temperature at an average rate of 2.9° per minute, that pasteurized at 160° was cooled 3.4° per minute, and that pasteurized at 180° was cooled 3.9° per minute. In the cooling experiments the water at the intake averaged about 50° in temperature.

The authors conclude that "in pasteurization of cream at different temperatures, namely, 140° for 25 minutes, 160° for 10 minutes, and 180°, with immediate cooling, the temperature of 160° for 10 minutes was the most effective in destroying total microorganisms. Pasteurization of cream at 160 or 180° proved more efficient in killing molds and nonacid-forming organisms than pasteurization at 140°.

"The only noticeable change in composition of cream due to pasteurization was a slight decrease in percentage of water, and a consequent increase in percentage of total solids. There was a slight decrease in acidity of the cream after pasteurization at temperatures of 140 and 160°. Cream pasteurized at 180° showed on the average less decrease in percentage of acid. . . . The numerous microscopical examinations of fat globules in raw and pasteurized cream show that at the higher temperatures (160 and 180°) the fat globules tend to coalesce or unite. . . .

"In no instance was it noticed that the high pasteurization temperatures unfavorably affected the body of the butter. Butter made from cream pasteurized at 180° retained its keeping qualities the best. The different temperatures of pasteurization did not have any important effect on the chemical composition of the butter."

VETERINARY MEDICINE.

Eighth biennial report of the State veterinarian of California for the two years ending June 30, 1916, C. KEANE (*Bien. Rpt. State Vet. Cal.*, 8 (1915–16), pp. 24).—This report, dealing with the occurrence of and work with the more important contagious diseases of live stock in California, includes papers on Hemorrhagic Septicemia, by J. P. Iverson (pp. 8–10), and Studies to Diagnose a Fatal Disease of Cattle in the Mountainous Regions of California, by K. F. Meyer (pp. 10–17).

Report of the bureau of veterinary science, C. F. DAWSON ET AL. (*Ann. Rpt. Bd. Health Fla.*, 28 (1916), pp. 216–247, figs. 2).—This report of the work of the year, dealing especially with tick eradication, includes directions for the preparation of dips and the dipping of cattle, together with plans for the construction of a dipping vat. Some diseases hitherto not known to exist in Florida are also briefly considered, among which are a tapeworm (*Tænia marginata*) in the liver of swine, enzootic pneumonia in young pigs, takosis in goats, stomach roundworm in sheep, and demodectic mange in swine.

Fifth annual report of the commissioner of animal industry for the year ended November 30, 1916, L. H. HOWARD (*Ann. Rpt. Comr. Anim. Indus.* [*Mass.*], 5 (1916), pp. 53).—Reports are given on the occurrence of and control work with the more important infectious diseases of animals, particularly tuberculosis and hog cholera.

Live-stock sanitation, H. T. GRAVES ([*Bien.*] *Rpt. Dept. Agr. Wash.*, 2 (1915–16), pp. 63–89).—This report deals with the occurrence of and work with contagious diseases of animals in Washington State, including bovine tuberculosis, foot-and-mouth disease, glanders, hog cholera, etc. A discussion of the pure-bred accredited herd plan as related to tuberculosis is included.

Proceedings of the Wisconsin Veterinary Medical Association (*Proc. Wis. Vet. Med. Assoc.*, 2 (1917), pp. 176, figs. 4).—The proceedings of the second annual meeting, held at Madison in January, 1917, are reported in full.

Biennial report of the State veterinarian of the State of Wyoming for the years 1913 and 1914 ending September 30, 1914, B. F. DAVIS (*Bien. Rpt. State Vet. Wyo.*, 1913–14, pp. 120).—In reporting upon the work with diseases of live stock particular attention is given to tuberculosis and dourine eradication.

Biennial report of the State veterinarian, State of Wyoming, for the period September 30, 1914, to September 30, 1916, A. W. FRENCH (*Bien. Rpt. State Vet. Wyo.*, 1915–16, pp. 90, figs. 6).—A report similar to the above.

Progress in veterinary work [in India] (*Rpt. Prog. Agr. India*, 1915–16, pp. 95–100).—A progress report on veterinary work for the year ended June 30, 1916.

Chlor-antiseptics, H. S. EAKINS (*Jour. Amer. Vet. Med. Assoc.*, 51 (1917), No. 2, pp. 221–229).—Formulas for the preparation of Dakin's solution and its various modifications are submitted and discussed.

The treatment of wounds with the polyvalent serum of Leclainche and Vallée, A. GUILLAUME and G. BITTNER (*Rev. Gén. Med. Vét.*, 26 (1917), No. 302–303, pp. 67–79).—Observations of a number of cases of wound treatment in horses injured on the field with a polyvalent serum are noted in detail. The use of the serum has yielded excellent results and is considered to be an important adjuvant in wound therapy.

Mechanism of the serum reactions, H. R. DEAN (*Lancet* [*London*], 1917, I, No. 2, pp. 45–50, figs. 4).—This is a general review of the work on the subject, in which the author concludes that in all the serum reactions (precipitation, complement fixation, and agglutination) the immediate result is an aggregation of the globulin particles around the antigen. " The degree to which the aggregation or precipitation proceeds depends entirely on the experimental conditions, on the relative proportions of antigen and antibody in the mixture, on the nature of the antigen-containing substance, red corpuscle, bacillus, or normal serum, on the presence of some third factor, a normal serum containing complement or conglutinin."

The various serum reactions are thus considered to be the observation and measurement of a single reaction. It is indicated that the main phenomena of the reaction are most readily accounted for by the adsorption rather than by the side-chain theory.

The influence of serum upon the staining of bacteria in suspensions, M. S. FLEISHER (*Jour. Med. Research,* 36 (1917), No. 1, pp. 31–49).—Serum added to a mixture of bacteria and certain dilute basic stains (neutral red, methylene blue, gentian violet, methyl green, and Bismark brown), 1 part in 25, prevented the staining of the organisms. A similar although weaker action was produced by using egg albumin in the place of serum, and a very weak action was exerted by 3 per cent gelatin solutions.

The addition of acids or alkalis did not interfere with the inhibitory action of the other substances. The action of the serum diminished with its diminishing concentration. and an increasing concentration of the stain tended to overcome the inhibitory action of the serum. Heating the serum or the bacteria did not interfere with the inhibition of the staining.

It is deemed probable that this inhibitory phenomenon of the serum is due to a protective colloid action.

On the cause of negative tissue transplantation.—III, The cleavage of tissue protein of one animal species by the blood serum of an animal of another species, A. ALBANESE (*Atti R. Accad. Lincei, Rend. Cl. Sci. Fis., Mat. e Nat.,* 5. ser., 25 (1916), II, No. 12, pp. 501–505).—Tabulated data of the action of the blood serum of the rat on the protein of the mouse, rabbit, guinea pig. and dog; of the blood serum of the mouse on the protein of the rat; of the blood serum of the guinea pig on the protein of the rat, mouse, dog, and rabbit; and of the blood serum of the rabbit on the protein of the rat, mouse, and guinea pig are submitted. The Abderhalden procedure was used in the study. The results are briefly discussed.

The origin of the proteolytic ferments of the blood.—The question of the specific character of certain ferments, L. H. SLOAN (*Amer. Jour. Physiol.,* 39 (1915), No. 1, pp. 9–19).—Data relative to the action of blood serum from pregnant individuals on human placenta and on various tissues (pancreas, liver, and kidney) and of blood serum from normal individuals and blood serum from various pathological conditions on human placenta are reported.

From the results it is concluded that there is an increased proteolytic ferment action of the blood serum during pregnancy. This increased activity is considered probably due to an increase in the polyvalent ferments. Normal blood serum was found to have a weak nonspecific proteolytic action. Since many advanced pathological conditions gave a positive reaction, it is indicated that the Abderhalden method does not " provide a reliable test for the differential diagnosis between the strictly physiological state of pregnancy and certain pathological conditions." The test is considered to be quantitative and not qualitative.

The origin of the proteolytic ferments.—II, Concerning the character of certain ferments, L. H. SLOAN (*Amer. Jour. Physiol.,* 42 (1917), No. 4, pp. 558–571).—The author has studied in detail the action of blood serum of normal and pregnant dogs on human placenta, the action of blood serum of dogs injected with placental suspension, the action of serum of dogs injected with split products of pepsin-trypsin digestion of human placenta, the action of serum of pregnant dogs injected with placental suspension, and the effect of feeding on the amino-acid content and the ferment strength of the blood serum, using placenta as substrate.

It is concluded that normal blood serum contains a weak proteolytic ferment which carries digestion to the amino-acid stage. The concentration of this ferment is not constant. "There is an increased proteolytic ferment action of serum during pregnancy as shown by the dialysis method of Abderhalden. This can not be detected by the Van Slyke method [E. S. R., 34, p. 577]. The injection of placental suspension does not give rise to an increased production or mobilization of ferments when tested by the dialysis method or the Van Slyke method. The injection of the split products of pepsin-trypsin digestion of human placenta gives rise to an increase in the ferments. This increase can be shown by the dialysis method but not by means of the Van Slyke method. The theory underlying the Abderhalden reaction as advanced by Abderhalden does not explain the increase in ferments found during pregnancy. The basis of the theory would seem to be the entrance of split products of placental hydrolysis rather than of chorionic villi and cells. The Van Slyke method is not applicable to determinations of the above character in which a nonsoluble, moist, complex, protein substance is incubated with serum in a test tube but without dialysis."

Desiccated anthrax antigen for immunization purposes, N. S. FERRY (*Jour. Amer. Vet. Med. Assoc.*, 51 (1917), No. 2, pp. 200–203).—The preparation of a desiccated spore vaccine in a manner similar to the preparation of spore vaccine in suspension (E. S. R., 34, p. 579) is noted. The growth was scraped from the agar and incorporated with a sterile diluent and dried at room temperature.

No deterioration in the virulence of a preparation one year old and kept at room temperature was observed. It is indicated that the most satisfactory method of using the vaccine would be in the form of properly standardized pellets.

Special report of the State veterinarian on foot-and-mouth disease in Virginia, its cause, how spread among cattle, other ruminants, and swine, and its control and eradication, J. G. FERNEYHOUGH (*Richmond, Va.: State, 1916, pp. 38, pls. 4*).—This reports upon control and eradication work by the Virginia State Live Stock Sanitary Board during the outbreak of foot-and-mouth disease which occurred in the fall of 1914.

Johne's disease.—The reactions of animals to " Johnin," J. McFADYEAN, A. L. SHEATHER, and J. T. EDWARDS (*Jour. Compar. Path. and Ther.*, 29 (1916), Nos. 2, pp. 134–171; 3, pp. 201–243, figs. 25).—The substance " Johnin," used in the experiments reported, is analogous to tuberculin. The material was prepared from a strain of Johne's bacillus isolated from the intestine of a typical case of the disease, and the absence of tubercle bacilli from the strain was proved by animal experimentation. The strain, which had been cultivated for a number of years, would not grow on liquid or solid media unless extracts of some other acid-fast bacilli were present.

The first Johnin used was prepared from a surface growth on broth to which 4 per cent of an extract of human tubercle bacilli in 20 per cent glycerin had been added. The culture in the flask was heated for one hour and the organisms removed by passing the liquid through a Berkefeld filter. The clear filtrate thus obtained was used in some of the tests.

A preparation was also made by separating the bacilli from the liquid culture media by sedimentation, suspending in sterile distilled water, and then removing by centrifugalization. A second washing was carried out, and the bacilli remaining were extracted by heating for one hour with 5 per cent glycerin in distilled water, then removed by centrifugalization or passing the liquid through a Berkefeld filter.

These preparations were approximately of the same strength, 10 cc. of the liquid representing the extract from 1 gm. of the wet bacilli. A concentrated Johnin used in the conjunctival and intracutaneous tests was prepared by evaporating the ordinary Johnin to one-fifth of its original volume or by extracting washed bacilli with 5 per cent glycerin in water in the proportion of 2 cc. to 1 gm. of the wet bacilli.

Subcutaneous, intracutaneous, and conjunctival tests of animals experimentally infected with the disease and animals experimentally infected with human, avian, and bovine tubercle bacilli are reported in detail. The Johnin produced distinct temperature reactions in animals affected with Johne's disease. Positive results were obtained by the intracutaneous procedure, but the application of the Johnin to the conjunctiva appeared to be incapable of producing distinct reactions. Reactions with the Johnin were also obtained in young animals infected with human, avian, or bovine tubercle bacilli.

A new Italian method for antirabic treatment, C. FERMI (*Ann. Ig. Sper., n. ser., 26 (1916), Sup., pp. 164*).—This volume describes the results of an experimental investigation. Part 1 consists of a description of the new method and its evolution; part 2 gives a comparison of the efficacy of the new method with other methods of antirabic treatment; and part 3 shows the duration of the immunizing power of the vaccine and serum vaccine and of the immunizing and neutralizing power of the new antirabic serum.

In the procedure a vaccine consisting of a 5 per cent emulsion of the virus, an antirabic serum obtained from the horse, and a serum vaccine consisting of one part of the antiserum and two of the vaccine. together with 1 per cent phenol, are used. The method of treatment and detailed tabulated data are described and discussed.

Rinderpest.—Preparation of antiserum. A. W. SHILSTON (*Agr. Research Inst. Pusa Bul. 64 (1916), pp. 18*).—Experiments to determine the potency of sera taken 8, 12, and 16 days after the injection of virus, and to compare the results with those given by sera taken 15 and 17 days after injection, are reported.

The results indicate that the immune bodies are present in full amount in the serum 8 days after the injection of the virulent blood and citrate solution mixture. " By taking three bleedings at the rate of 6 cc. per pound body weight on the eighth, twelfth, and sixteenth days after injection a mixed serum was obtained of equal (hill bulls) or increased (buffaloes) potency to that obtained by taking two bleedings 15 and 17 days after injection at the rate of 6 cc. and 8 cc. per pound body weight, respectively. . . . The actual yield of serum after each injection was increased from 6.79 cc. per pound body weight by the two bleedings system to 9.6 cc. by the three bleedings system or an additional 2.81 cc. of serum per pound body weight; an increase of 41.4 per cent on the former output."

The saving of cost in the production of a large amount of serum by the new procedure is noted.

The piroplasmoses and means for their prevention and control, G. ALESSANDRINI (*Ann. Ig. [Rome], 27 (1917), No. 2, pp. 100–110; abs. in Rev. Appl. Ent., Ser. B, 5 (1917), No. 5, p. 71*).—A brief review of the present status of the knowledge of piroplasmoses and babesiases and their control, including an account of the ticks implicated in their transmission.

The pathogenic action of **Ixodidæ**, S. E. PARODI (*An. Soc. Rural Argentina, 51 (1917), No. 2, pp. 111–125, figs. 4*).—An account of the protozoan parasites transmitted by ticks in Argentina and their effect upon the host.

Application of the complement-fixation test to tuberculosis, N. B. BURNS, F. H. SLACK, P. CASTLEMAN, and K. BAILEY (*Jour. Amer. Med. Assoc., 68 (1917), No. 19, pp. 1386–1389*).—From the results of the investigation reported the authors indicate that the complement-fixation test appears specific for tuberculosis.

It is considered that the test will prove of great value as a diagnostic aid in cases showing suggestive physical signs, but in which it is impossible to demonstrate the presence of tubercle bacilli in the sputum. "In such cases positive complement-fixation reactions would be strong evidence of the disease. A single negative would be inconclusive, but several negatives would indicate that no active tuberculous process was present."

The value of determining whether a case of tuberculosis clinically apparently arrested still has an active focus, as indicated by positive reaction, is noted.

Complement fixation in tuberculosis with the "partial antigens" of Deyke and Much, A. C. WOODS, G. E. BUSHNELL, and C. MADDUX (*Jour. Immunol., 2 (1917), No. 3, pp. 301–325*).—One hundred and seventy-six normal and tuberculous sera were tested against partial antigens and against whole bacillus emulsion antigen. Ninety-one per cent of the sera from cases classed clinically as inactive tuberculosis reacted negatively to the antigens. Ninety per cent of the sera classed clinically as incipient tuberculosis, 87 per cent of those classed as active, and 92 per cent of those from advanced cases reacted positively to the partial antigens.

The results are discussed in some detail. A list of 26 references to the literature cited is included.

The influence of certain organic substances on the growth of the tubercle bacillus, P. A. LEWIS (*Jour. Expt. Med., 25 (1917), No. 3, pp. 441–459*).—The growth-restraining power of a large number of anilin dyes on *Bacillus tuberculosis* and *B. typhosus* has been determined.

Many dyes were found to possess a special restraining power for the tubercle bacillus. "This capacity to restrain growth in the case of the tubercle bacillus apparently bears no simple relation to true disinfectant action. Opinion as to whether the active substances exert a truly specific activity against the tubercle bacillus or whether the activity is determined by the peculiar conditions imposed by the growth of this bacterium as a surface membrane is left for future consideration."

The influence of typhoid vaccine on tuberculous guinea pigs, HELEN BALDWIN and ELISE S. L'ESPERANCE (*Jour. Immunol., 2 (1917), No. 3, pp. 283–299, pl. 1, figs. 11*).—Experiments are reported which show that a greater resistance to tubercle inoculation developed in animals immunized against typhoid than in the unimmunized animals, and that animals with active tuberculosis appeared to possess an increased resistance when given typhoid vaccine.

The presence of the tubercle bacillus in butter, A. C. MARCHISOTTI (*Rev. Facult. Agron. y Vet. La Plata, 2. ser., 12 (1917), No. 3, pp. 279–298*).—In a bacteriological study of 25 samples of commercial butters the author found that 24 per cent contained tubercle bacilli. Fifty-two and nine-tenths per cent of the samples contained acid-fast organisms, the greater number of these, however, being pseudo-acid-resistant. The hygienic aspects of the results of the study are noted.

The procedures used and the detailed inoculation data are submitted.

Tuberculosis in the goat, MOUSSU (*Compt. Rend. Acad. Agr. France, 3 (1917), No. 12, pp. 341–348*).—A general discussion with special reference to the hygienic importance of a proper diagnosis, especially where the milk is to be used. The difficulty often encountered in diagnosis is indicated.

Age determination of cattle **in** different countries (*Abs. in Agr. News [Barbados], 16 (1917), No. 392, p. 133*).—Attention is called to the fact that dentition formulas for the determination of age in cattle vary according to breed and environment.

Health herd book for breeders of pure-bred cattle **and** owners of high-grade dairy animals, V. A. MOORE (*Ithaca, N. Y.: Carpenter & Co., 1915, pp. [204], figs. 51*).—This loose-leaf book contains blanks for recording the name of the animal, date of birth, date of purchase, price, etc.; identification markings; progeny; health, including record of tuberculin tests and statement and date of any sickness, abortion, udder trouble, or injuries; milk production; and pedigree.

In a prefatory note the author calls attention to the importance of a carefully kept record of the health of every animal of a herd, not only to the owner in the management of his herd but also to the prospective purchaser.

A rational and successful method of preventing abortion in cattle, A. T. PETERS (*Jour. Amer. Vet. Med. Assoc., 51 (1917), No. 2, pp. 211-214*).—The author has obtained successful results in 106 herds through feeding a perfectly blended formula of mineral matter in sufficient quantity to replenish the lost mineral in the animal body. This was supplemented by a thorough disinfection of the stables and, where the cows showed indications of discharge, by injections of a saturated solution of bicarbonate of soda.

Abortion in dairy cattle, W. L. WILLIAMS (*Jour. Amer. Vet. Med. Assoc., 51 (1917), No. 3, pp. 348-363, figs. 3*).—A paper presented at the twentieth annual meeting of the U. S. Live Stock Sanitary Association, held at Chicago in December, 1916, which summarizes the present status of knowledge of the disease. See also a previous note (E. S. R., 34, p. 386).

A report upon an outbreak of stomatitis contagiosa, H. E. GIBBS (*Vet. Jour., 73 (1917), No. 503, pp. 147-155, figs. 4*).—A report of experiments conducted during a recent outbreak.

Investigation of a new variety of Nocardia bovis, Actinomyces lanfranchii, L. SANI (*Ann. Ig. [Rome], 26 (1916), Nos. 9, pp. 570-580, figs. 5; 10, pp. 646-658*).—Biological and morphological studies which have led to the identification of this new variety of the ray-fungus are reported.

Sheep poisoned by western goldenrod (Solidago spectabilis), S. LOCKETT (*Jour. Amer. Vet. Med. Assoc., 51 (1917), No. 2, pp. 214-221*).—The author reports upon losses among sheep in Nevada through feeding upon *S. spectabilis,* a plant which possesses definite nerve-poisoning properties, both in its natural green condition and when cured in hay.

"The symptoms produced may be acute (maniacal), subacute (producing slight cerebral stimulation and increased normal reflexes), or chronic (resulting finally in mental depression, ataxia, and palsy). These appear to depend upon the amount of the plant ingested in a given period of time. Five hundred gm. eaten in 8 hours produced within 23 hours a severe type of poisoning in a six to seven months lamb.

"Chloral hydrate in proper dosage would seem indicated as an antidote. The administration of 45 grains per rectum followed in 20 minutes by 90 grains per os was excessive in the case of the experimental lamb of six to seven months of age. This animal remained too long under the effect of the drug and the after stupor produced would in field practice militate against the chances of recovery under herd conditions."

The kidney worm of swine (Stephanurus dentatus), E. L. LUACES (*Estac. Expt. Agron. Cuba Circ. 52 (1916), pp. 13, figs. 3*).—A brief summary of information relative to this parasite, the disease which it causes, and remedial measures.

"**Piroplasmosis,**" " equine malaria," R. A. STOUTE (*Jour. Amer. Vet. Med. Assoc., 51 (1917), No. 2, p. 239*).—The author records the occurrence of this affection in Barbados in a 10-year-old mare imported from St. Croix.

Parasites of the dog in Michigan, M. C. HALL (*Jour. Amer. Vet. Med. Assoc., 51 (1917), No. 3, pp. 383–396*).—This is a summary of information based upon personal investigations and a review of the literature.

Trichina spiralis in the polar bear, H. FOX (*Ann. Rpt. Zool. Soc. Phila., 45 (1917), p. 38*).—The author records the discovery of encysted forms of trichina in almost unbelievable numbers, made at post-mortem examination of a polar bear which succumbed to disease at the Philadelphia Zoological Garden.

Mortality statistics of the fifth national egg-laying contest, Missouri, G. D. HORTON (*Jour. Amer. Assoc. Instr. and Invest. Poultry Husb., 3 (1917), No. 9, pp. 70, 71*).—It is concluded from the data here presented that at least 80 per cent of all sick or out-of-condition fowls, if treated in time, may be cured readily and at small cost.

A study of the fermenting properties of Bacterium pullorum and B. sanguinarium, S. A. GOLDBERG (*Jour. Amer. Vet. Med. Assoc., 51 (1917), No. 2, pp. 203–210*).—The author's investigations " show that the principal differences in the strains of *B. pullorum* and *B. sanguinarium* studied lie in the fact that *B. pullorum* produces gas in various carbohydrates while *B. sanguinarium* lacks this power in any of the carbohydrates used. This difference appears to be constant. Judging from the present classification of species of bacteria this difference in gas production as well as their different actions on milk, maltose, dulcite, dextrin, and isodulcite seem to indicate that these two organisms are two distinct species of bacteria."

Is Leucocytozoon anatis the cause of a new disease in ducks? A. B. WICKWARE (*Jour. Amer. Assoc. Instr. and Invest. Poultry Husb., 3 (1917), No. 9, pp. 67, 68*).—Noted from another source (E. S. R., 36, p. 275).

RURAL ENGINEERING.

Irrigation of rice in California, R. D. ROBERTSON (*California Sta. Bul. 279 (1917), pp. 253–270, figs. 7*).—This report, based on work done during 1913 to 1916 in cooperation with the Office of Public Roads and Rural Engineering and the Bureau of Plant Industry of the U. S. Department of Agriculture and the California State Department of Engineering and State Water Commission, describes the irrigation of rice in California, principally in the Sacramento Valley.

"Approximately 67,000 acres of rice were irrigated in California in 1916, the water supply being obtained principally from Sacramento and Feather Rivers. Only about 3,700 acres were irrigated by pumping from wells.

"Land is prepared for irrigation in contour checks, preparation consisting mainly in making ditches and levees and installing gates. The gates must be wide enough to admit the large heads of water used in the initial floodings. The irrigation season consists of two periods. Frequent light irrigations with relatively large heads of water are given to germinate the seed and to maintain growth until the plant is 4 to 6 in. high, and thereafter the land is continually submerged to a depth of 6 to 8 in. until the rice is matured.

"Measurements of the use of water in 1916 on 18 typical fields in Sacramento Valley showed a range of from 4.27 to 14.83 acre-feet per acre, an average depth applied of 8.23 ft., and an average of 47 acres served per cubic foot per second. The heads of water used per acre averaged 0.052 cu. ft. per second before submergence and 0.034 during submergence. The lowest used was on fields with heavy retentive soil, where the preparation was good and the water carefully handled. The average annual use over a three-year period on a field near Biggs was 4.6 acre-feet per acre. During the three irrigation seasons the average precipitation was 0.23 ft. and evaporation 3.19 ft. Irrigation practice and requirements in California differ from those in the Gulf States, due mainly to different climatic conditions.

"Adequate drainage is essential to successful rice production. Planting and harvesting are both delayed while the soil remains wet and the removal of alkali salts and the relief of water-logged lands are dependent upon drainage facilities.

"The results of experiments made in 1914 to 1916, inclusive, on black clay adobe soil near Biggs indicated that 30 days after emergence of the plant is the best time for commencing submergence and that 6 in. is probably the most advantageous depth of submergence. Very poor yields were secured where no water was held on the land. Fluctuating the depth of water had very little effect on plant growth. More uniform temperatures of the water were found with the greater depths of submergence."

Annual irrigation revenue report of the Government of Bengal for the year 1915–16 (*Ann. Irrig. Rev. Rpt. Bengal, 1915–16, pp. 73, pl. 1*).—This reports administration work, expenditures, engineering projects, and revenues for the year 1915–16.

River discharge, J. C. Hoyt and N. C. Grover (*New York: John Wiley & Sons, 1916, 4. ed. rev. and enl., pp. XII+210. pls. 11, figs. 39*).—This is the fourth revised and enlarged edition of this book (E. S. R., 33, p. 287). Chapter 5, on Discussion and Use of Data, has been largely rewritten, and chapter 6, formerly entitled Conditions Affecting Stream Flow, has been expanded in scope to cover the field of hydrology as related to stream flow and the title changed accordingly.

Geology and water resources of Big Smoky, Clayton, and Alkali Spring Valleys, Nevada, O. E. Meinzer (*U. S. Geol. Survey, Water-Supply Paper 423 (1917), pp. 167, pls. 15, figs. 11*).—The first part of this report deals with the geology and water resources of a desert area of 1,300 square miles extending from the center of Nevada to within 20 miles of the California line.

"Several tens of thousands of acre-feet of ground water is probably contributed each year to the underground reservoirs of Big Smoky Valley. A part of this supply could be recovered for irrigation. Most of this water is in the upper valley, but a part is in the vicinity of Millers, in the lower valley. The water is in general of satisfactory quality for irrigation. Nearly all the poor water is in the southwestern part of the lower valley, where prospects for irrigation are practically lacking.

"A small part of the ground-water supply can be recovered by flowing wells, but full use of the supply is possible only by pumping. Throughout the extensive areas in which the depth to the water table does not exceed 10 ft. the soil contains injurious amounts of alkali. In the areas in which the depth to the water table ranges between 10 and 50 ft. there is enough good soil to utilize all the available ground water. These areas, however, also contain considerable gravelly, sandy, and alkaline soil.

"There are some prospects of obtaining flowing wells wherever the water table is near the surface, but the prospects are best on the west side of the upper valley. The flowing-well areas will be found to lie chiefly within the areas of alkali soil, but they may extend into adjacent areas of good soil.

"Full utilization of the ground-water supply for irrigation will not be economically practicable until cheaper power or more valuable crops can be introduced than are now in sight. The Developments that may be practicable at present are (1) the sinking of flowing wells of moderate depths in the restricted areas where fairly copious flows can be obtained and the soil is not irreclaimably alkaline; (2) the sinking of nonflowing wells and the installation of pumping plants for raising high-priced crops or for raising ordinary crops in localities where the conditions are exceptionally favorable or where the well water can be used to supplement surface-water supplies. . . . Existing conditions do not warrent the influx of a large number of settlers, nor of any without means to sink wells and make other necessary improvements."

The second part of this report deals with the geology and water resources of Clayton Valley, an area of about 570 square miles in Esmeralda County, Nev.

"Most of the soil of Clayton Valley is too gravelly, sandy, or alkaline for cultivation, but there is a small area, lying chiefly between the 50-ft. line and the salt-grass boundary, that can apparently be classed as agricultural soil. . . . The information available indicates that although water underlies Clayton Valley in considerable quantities, it can not be successfully utilized for irrigation because of its saline character and other unfavorable conditions."

The third part of the report deals with the geology and water resources of Alkali Spring Valley, an area of about 310 square miles lying almost entirely in Esmeralda County, Nev. "The wells that have been sunk in Alkali Spring Valley prove the existence of ground water in the valley fill. . . . If 5 per cent of the precipitation in the basin finds its way to the underground reservoir the annual contributions amount to about 5,000 acre-ft. . . .

"The valley fill of Alkali Spring Valley contains a supply of water that is of fairly good quality for domestic and boiler use and for irrigation. Although the quantity of water is not large, it is adequate for ordinary domestic, stock, and industrial purposes, and would probably be adequate for a small amount of irrigation. The valley contains considerable good soil, but the depth to the water table is too great to make pumping for irrigation profitable under present conditions except possibly for intensive market gardening."

Ground water in San Simon Valley, Arizona and New Mexico, A. T. SCHWENNESEN (*U. S. Geol. Survey, Water-Supply Paper 425–A (1917), pp. 35, pls. 3, figs. 2*).—This report, prepared in cooperation with the Arizona Experiment Station, deals with the geology, physiography, water supply, and agriculture of an area 85 miles long and varying in width from 10 to 35 miles, which is located in southeastern Arizona and the adjacent part of New Mexico.

"Practically all the water in San Simon Valley is derived from the precipitation on the drainage basin; there is no considerable inflow of water from other basins. In the San Simon and Bowie areas there are two distinct ground-water horizons; an upper horizon in the younger stream deposits and a lower or artesian horizon in the deposits below the dense clay of the lake beds. In the San Simon area the ground water of the upper horizon is less than 100 ft. below the surface throughout a large tract extending along the axis of the valley. The supply has proved ample for watering stock, for domestic needs, and for the heavier demands of the railroad, and if it can be pumped economically it is probably large enough for considerable irrigation. It is doubtful whether it would be profitable at present to pump this supply for irrigation. In the Bowie region the supply at the upper ground-water horizon is very scanty and it is generally necessary to sink to the lower horizon, even for small supplies,

"In the lower ground-water horizon the water is under hydrostatic pressure, so that it rises in wells when the water-bearing beds are penetrated. In the San Simon flowing-well area the pressure is sufficient to cause this water to rise above the surface in wells. In the Bowie area the water is also under pressure and in some localities it rises close enough to the surface to be economically pumped for irrigation. Measurements show that the head and yield of wells has decreased considerably in the two-year period between 1913 and 1915. This increase is largely due to the filling of the uncased wells with sand and the caving of the walls of these wells, but it may in part be due to the increase in the number of wells and depletion of the artesian supply. It is of the utmost importance for the future welfare of the valley that all wells be properly cased to the bottom with heavy casing and be fitted with valves which will be closed when the water is not needed. . . .

"The flowing-well waters are mostly of the sodium carbonate type, but they generally contain only small amounts of dissolved solids and are of good quality for irrigation and domestic use. In the vicinity of Apache and Moore's Spur the ground-water supply is small and uncertain, but some water for stock and domestic purposes is obtained from shallow wells and springs. In the vicinity of Rodeo and in the central part of the valley north of Rodeo there is a considerable area in which the depth to the water table is less than 100 ft. In this area the supply is probably large, but on account of the lift that would be required it would probably not be profitable at present to pump it for irrigation. All the waters analyzed from the Rodeo area are good irrigating and domestic waters."

A section on general agriculture in the valley, by R. H. Forbes, is also included.

Report [of the California] State water problems conference (*Sacramento, Cal.: State, 1916, pp. 125*).—This report deals with the conservation and use of water, the flood problems of California, riparian rights, irrigation, underground water, reclamation, inland waterways, relation between navigation and irrigation, storage for flood control, interstate waters, water for mining, water for municipal purposes, expense and delay in water litigation and State aid in the interest of conservation.

Ditch flow found quickly and accurately with new portable weir, E. S. Fuller (*Engin. News-Rec., 78 (1917), No. 7, pp. 373, 374, fig. 1*).—A portable weir for use in quickly determining seepage losses along a canal is described and diagrammatically illustrated.

Determining daily discharge of canals affected by check control, H. W. Humphrey (*Reclam. Rec. [U. S.], 8 (1917), No. 6, pp. 288–290, fig. 1*).—The use of the Hall slope method in determining daily discharge of canals affected by variable slopes due to check control is demonstrated (E. S. R., 32, p. 382.).

The turbidity of water, A. A. Bado and R. A. Trelles (*An. Soc. Quím. Argentina, 4 (1916), No. 16, pp. 283–293, figs. 4*).—New methods and apparatus for determining turbidity in river waters, which are considered to be especially applicable to South American river waters, are described. All are based on the relative distances through which light or objects may be seen through the water.

Silt observations at Yuma gauging station, compiled by L. M. Lawson (*Reclam. Rec. [U. S.], 8 (1917), No. 5, pp. 240, 241, fig. 1*).—Silt determinations begun in 1909 on the Colorado River are summarized.

"The maximum percentage of silt during the rising stage is carried at a discharge of approximately 26,000 second-feet, which is also the stage at which the river at this point reaches its maximum velocity—6.2 ft. per second.

During the falling stage of the river, the maximum percentage of silt is carried
at a somewhat higher discharge. The maximum percentage of silt by weight
observed is 4.16 per cent. The mean silt content and percentage by weight,
1909 to 1916. of the Colorado River at Yuma, without the Gila flow, is 0.7 per
cent. At times of Gila discharge this percentage is 0.93. The weight of the
wet deposited silt per cubic foot when dried is 86 lbs. The weight of 1 cu. ft. of
solid dried silt is 159.3 lbs. The specific gravity of the silt is 2.6."

Sluicing silt to reduce canal leakage, F. J. BARNES (*Engin. News-Rec.*, 78
(*1917*), No. 7, pp. 337–339, figs. 3).—This article summarizes operating experience on an experimental plant installed on the U. S. Reclamation Service
Irrigation Project at Grand Valley, Colo.

Modern practice in wood-stave pipe design and suggestions for standard
specifications, J. F. PARTRIDGE (*Proc. Amer. Soc. Civ. Engin.*, 43 (*1917*), No. 4,
pp. 559–594).—"The object of this paper is to give engineers an idea of the
difference between the various grades of wood pipes; to set forth a standard
set of specifications for the assistance of engineers who have had no opportunity to become versed in their design; to safeguard those who contemplate
building such pipe; and to remove doubt from the minds of those who view
wood pipe as one of the vagaries of engineering practice and a medium to be
resorted to only in temporary and cheap work."

The elements causing success or failure in wood stave pipe are enumerated
as (1) kinds of wood used, (2) grade of lumber used. (3) method of curing
lumber, (4) method of treating lumber, (5) location of pipe when built, (6)
size and spacing of bands, and (7) methods used in erection, and quality of
workmanship. These are discussed as applied to continuous-stave pipe and
machine-banded pipe, and a plea is made for the adoption of uniform specifications, dividing each type into classes A, B, and C. The appendix contains the
specifications for the two types and three classes of pipes, which are proposed
as a basis for adoption by engineers.

The classification of continuous-stave pipe is as follows: "Class A—a pipe
having a maximum life, under all conditions, and this will be 25 years when
receiving no care whatsoever; a life greater than 25 years, if under continuous operation; and a probable life of 50 years, or more, if in continuous operation under at least a moderate head, if the bands are given attention and cor-
roded ones are renewed. This includes pipe made from clear, air-dried redwood. Class B—this class includes coated pine or fir, in such a situation as to
be open to continuous inspection, so that it may be given constant attention,
comprising repainting staves and renewing bands. This pipe will be placed
under class A, on theory only, as experience has not yet confirmed such an
assumption. Class C—this class will have a maximum life of 10 years and an
average life of 7 years. It will include uncoated fir, pine, or other suitable
wood."

The classification of machine-banded pipe is as follows: "Class A—this
class will have a life of from 15 to 25 years when receiving no attention; a
longer life under ideal conditions, as when laid in soils having the least possible corrosive effect on the galvanized wire, and when operating under pressure, so as to insure complete saturation of the wood. Pipes of this class will
be guaranteed to withstand severe conditions of overload, such as in hydroelectric work, general waterworks for city supply, and high-pressure pumping
lines; and will be guaranteed to withstand an overload of 100 per cent under
test. It will include pipes of clear, air-dried redwood, manufactured according to the specifications in the appendix. Class B—this class will have a life
of at least 10 years, and a probable life not exceeding 15 years. It will include

pipe made of redwood, or of coated fir or pine, etc., manufactured according to present-day standards, as indicated by the specifications covering this class. Class C—pipes of this class will be used for temporary work only and may be manufactured from redwood, fir, pine, or any other wood, with or without coating, as desired."

Analyses of Fargo city water supply, R. HULBERT (*North Dakota Sta. Spec. Bul., 4 (1917), No. 12, pp. 338–341*).—Chemical and bacteriological analyses of samples of water from the Red River and of the same after undergoing purification at the Fargo city filtration plant showed that the purification process removed better than 99 per cent of the organisms present in the raw river water.

Investigations on the filtration of drinking water.—I, The theory of slow sand filtration, K. KISSKALT (*Ztschr. Hyg. u. Infektionskrank., 80 (1915), No. 1, pp. 57–64. fig. 1*).—Experiments are reported on the slow filtration of water through sand in which it was found that the addition of potassium cyanid killed the protozoa in the filter but did not injure the bacteria and thus destroyed the purifying action of the filter almost completely for some time. It is concluded, therefore, that the greatest part of the purification process of slow-sand filtration is due to the protozoa.

A bibliography is appended.

A new process for the chemical sterilization of drinking water in the field, M. RHEIN (*Ztschr. Hyg. u. Infektionskrank., 78 (1914), No. 3, pp. 562–570. fig. 1*).—It was found that by the addition of 2.1 cc. of antiformin and 1.1 cc. of 25 per cent hydrochloric acid to 1 liter of contaminated water which had been filtered through wadding coli bacteria were killed in five minutes at the rate of 4,000,000 per cubic centimeter of water. The chlorin was removed from the treated water by means of a tablet containing 1.7 gm. of sodium bicarbonate and 0.45 gm. of sodium thiosulphate. The treated water had then a slightly alkaline taste, was clear and odorless, and was found safe to drink. Sodium sulphite was also found to be effective for the removal of the chlorin when bathing water was treated.

A bibliography is appended.

The manner of action of biological sewage purification media. T. MESSERSCHMIDT (*Ztschr. Hyg. u. Infektionskrank., 78 (1914), No. 3, pp. 475–488, figs. 2; 80 (1915), No. 3, pp. 447–456*).—From a comparison made in the laboratory of the so-called absorption and nitrification theories of the action of sewage purification media, it is concluded that the nitrification theory is not entirely correct and that the action of biological filters may be explained primarily on the grounds of absorption. Nitrification is considered merely a part of the total process.

Further experiments showed that in a perfectly purified sewage the albuminous substances are so completely destroyed that they have lost their antigen character. A third set of experiments in which a natural and highly infective sewage was put through the biological filter process in the laboratory showed that under optimum conditions a complete sterilization could not be obtained.

A bibliography is appended.

A new type of trickling filter, G. G. NASMITH (*Surveyor. 51 (1917), No. 1303, pp. 4, 5, fig. 1*).—Experiments on a trickling sewage filter made of wood lath are reported.

"The laths of the lowest layer were laid parallel to one another, the spaces between the laths being a little less than the width of the laths themselves. A second layer was laid on top of this and at right angles to it, with the same interspace. A third row was laid parallel to the bottom row. but in such a manner that the laths covered the spaces left between the laths of the lower series. In this way a filter 4 ft. in depth was constructed in which the sewage in order to reach the bottom had to flow over a very large surface of filter. Air could enter from all sides and the top through the regular channels provided. . . .

"Sedimented sewage was allowed to trickle over the surface of this lath filter. In less than a month the filter was mature, and the results obtained thereafter exceeded all expectations. Where the standard type of stone filter, operated side by side with it as a control, treated 2,000,000 gal. of sewage per acre per day, the lath filter treated 6,000.000 gal. and yielded a nonputrescible effluent. This lath filter has now been in continuous use for 3.5 years and has never failed to give satisfactory results."

Satisfactory results were also obtained with a brushwood filter which within two months was treating sewage at the rate of 6,000,000 gal. per acre per day.

Brushwood as a medium for sewage filters, G. PHELPS *(Canad. Engin., 32 (1917), No. 6, pp. 117–120, figs. 6; Surveyor, 51 (1917), No. 1312, pp. 254, 255).*— Experiments using brushwood and washed and graded steel slag as filter media are reported. The depth of medium in each case was 5.5 ft., both filters being 50 ft. in diameter.

"After two months' working, the brushwood had become thickly coated with gray slime and a very satisfactory effluent was obtained, and from that time on the flow to the filter has been periodically increased up to the present average rate of 7,250,000 gal. per acre per day. . . . Witch-hazel was found to be the best material for making up, but almost any kind of brush is suitable provided no dead wood is used. It requires to be cut in the fall or early spring when no leaves are on."

The slag filter "was started at a rate of 1,250,000 gal. per acre per day and worked up to 2,500,000 in six months. The rate was increased for a short time to 3,000,000, but this resulted in clogging and ponding on the surface and the rate had consequently to be reduced. The effluent from this filter has always been satisfactory, but its capacity is limited to about 2,000,000 gal. per acre per day, the rate at which the sewage will pass through without clogging.

"The effluent from both filters contains usually from 0.1 to 0.2 cc. of sediment per liter. This is a fine humus which is settled out by a half-hour retention in tanks. It is liable to increase with sudden rushes of storm water but is easily got rid of."

Analyses of samples of effluent from both filters "show that nitrates are not formed in the brushwood as readily as in the slag filter, which is no doubt due to the rapidity with which the sewage passes through the brushwood. . . . The open nature of the brush allows good aeration, and it is very efficient when working at a high rate of flow. The rotary distributor also seems well adapted for this type of filter. It gives a good distribution, does not require a great deal of attention, and requires only about a foot of head for its operation. . . .

"Brushwood shows itself to be particularly suitable as a medium for inducing the slimy growth characteristic of sewage filters. The thick coating of this slime over every particle of the brush is in marked contrast to anything that can be seen on a medium such as stone or slag. . . . To engineers constructing filters of this type, it is recommended that they be made at least 7 ft. deep if possible, and made up to this depth again when the bed has been in work for 12 or 18 months, in which time it will have shrunk down considerably."

Regulations respecting highways, 1916, F. G. MACDIARMID *(Ann. Rpt. Dept. Pub. Highways Ontario, 1916, App., pp. 11).*—The text of the regulations is given.

Intelligent use of road oil reduces maintenance, T. R. Agg (*Engin. News-Rec.*, 78 (1917), No. 8, pp. 412, 413, figs. 4).—It is pointed out that the use of road oil is of little actual value unless good drainage is provided. All soils are benefited. but under Iowa conditions the gumbos give the best results.

Colorimetric test for organic impurities in sands, D. A. Abrams and O. E. Harder (*Struct. Materials Research Lab.* [*Lewis Inst*], Circ. 1 (1917), pp. 7; abs. in *Engin. and Contract.*, 47 (1917), No. 12, pp. 273).—A detailed description of the field and laboratory methods for the colorimetric test for organic impurities in sand.

"A sample of sand is digested at ordinary temperature in a solution of sodium hydroxid (NaOH). If the sand contains certain organic materials, thought to be largely of a humus nature, the filtered solution resulting from this treatment will be found to be of a color ranging from light yellow up through the reds to that which appears almost black. The depth of color has been found to furnish a measure of the effect of the impurities on the strength of mortars made from such sands. The depth of color may be measured by comparison with proper color standards."

Effect of water on the strength of concrete, D. A. Abrams (*Concrete Highway Mag.*, 1 (1917), No. 4, pp. 5–7, fig. 1; abs. in *Engin. and Contract.*, 47 (1917), No. 18, pp. 422, 423, fig. 1; *Engin. News-Rec.*, 78 (1917), No. 4, p. 206, fig. 1).—The results of compression tests on 6 by 12 in. concrete cylinders made in mixes ranging from 1 part cement and 9 parts aggregate to 1 part cement and 2 parts aggregate by volume are summarized.

"These tests show that the effect of proportional changes in the mixing water is approximately the same for all mixes of concrete. . . The amount of water which gives the maximum strength in concrete produces a mix which is too stiff for most purposes." The following table. based on the experiments, is given to indicate the approximate quantities of water which should be used for mixes commonly employed in concrete road construction:

Concrete road mixtures.

Mix.		Approximate mix as usually expressed.			Water required per sack of cement.	
Cement.	Volume of aggregate after mixing.	Cement.	Aggregate.		Minimum.	Maximum.
			Fine.	Coarse.		
					Gallons.	Gallons.
1	5	1	2	4	6	6½
1	4½	1	2	3	5¾	6¼
1	4	1	1½	3	5¼	6
1	3	1	1¼	2½	5	5½

Bearings for agricultural machinery, V. W. Page (*Amer. Thresherman, 19* (1917), Nos. 9, pp. 44–46. figs. 3; 10. pp. 16–18, figs. 4).—This is a discussion of the design and purpose of bearings for agricultural machinery.

Review of mechanical cultivation, M. Ringelmann (*Bul. Soc. Encour. Indus. Nat.* [*Paris*], 127 (1917), No. 1, pp. 197–218, figs. 15).—This is a review of the status of mechanical cultivation in Europe, with special reference to wartime conditions. Typical tests of different outfits are discussed.

A press for the Georgia carrier, M. A. Blake and H. C. Haines (*New Jersey Stas. Circ. 64* (1917), pp. 8, figs. 4).—This circular describes and diagrammatically illustrates a press designed at the station for use in pulling down into place the covers of peach shipping crates for proper nailing.

The drying of potatoes, C. DANTIN (*Génie Civil, 70 (1917), No. 11, pp. 171–175, figs. 10*).—Apparatus for the drying of potatoes is described and illustrated.

Some details in the construction of wooden hoop silos, I. D. CHARLTON (*Washington Sta., West. Wash. Sta. Mo. Bul., 5 (1917), No. 2, pp. 20–23, figs. 4*).—Brief instructions, with illustrations, for the construction of wooden hoop silos are given, together with a bill of material and costs for a 14 by 32 ft. silo of 100 tons capacity.

Housing of chickens, J. DRYDEN (*Oreg. Agr. Col. Bul., Ext. Ser. 7, No. 2 (1916), pp. 18, figs. 16*).—This bulletin discusses the essentials of poultry-house construction, and gives plans, specifications, and bills of materials for both portable and stationary houses.

RURAL ECONOMICS.

A theory of rural attitudes, L. L. BERNARD (*Amer. Jour. Sociol., 22 (1917), No. 5, pp. 630–649*).—The author discusses certain traits of the farmer under the following topics: The lack of scientific methods in his farm operations, the lack of contact with cultural centers, the effect of geographical isolation, seasonal labor requirements, conservatism, emotionalism, and frugality. The author points out the causes for these various traits, as well as their effect upon the mind of the person living on a farm.

Farm organization, balance between crops and stock, crop rotation and labor distribution, K. C. LIVERMORE (*N. Y. Dept. Agr. Bul. 86 (1916), pp. 2432–2448, figs. 2*).—The author outlines methods that may be used to measure the efficiency of the various factors affecting the farm income and cites a number of typical examples.

Minor articles of farm equipment, H. N. HUMPHREY and A. P. YERKES (*U. S. Dept. Agr., Farmers' Bul. 816 (1917), pp. 15*).—This is a revision of circular 44 of the Bureau of Plant Industry, previously noted (E. S. R., 22, p. 492).

In the summary list of the inventories of minor equipment for 33 general farms in Ohio the articles are classified as " essential " (found on at least 20 per cent of the farms) or as " not essential but very desirable." It was found that the total value, under normal price conditions, of the essential articles amounted to $114.70 and the other articles to $121.15.

Food preparedness, H. R. SEAGER and R. E. CHADDOCK (*Columbia [Univ.] War Papers, 1. ser., No. 6 (1917), pp. 23*).—In this pamphlet, which is one of a series of war papers issued by the Division of Intelligence and Publicity of Columbia University, the authors have pointed out the decrease in the per capita production in the United States and in the exports of agricultural products, but call attention to the increase in meat products due to the slaughtering of animals already on hand. They advocate the mobilization of food supplies and an increase in production through the augmenting of farm labor, the introduction of home gardening, a guaranteed minimum price to producers, the use of war bread, and the elimination of waste.

A farm census of New York State (*N. Y. Dept. Agr. Bul. 89 (1916), pp. 32*).—This bulletin gives the results of a census taken by the school children in New York State during January, 1916. It describes the methods used and presents the details by counties of the results obtained.

Redistribution of farm land in France, P. DE CABAUSSEL (*Vie Agr. et Rurale, 7 (1917), No. 15, pp. 257–264*).—The author discusses the question of the redistribution of farm land in its effect upon the rural proprietor, the inconvenience that will be caused to the occupants by the breaking up of farms, and the insufficiency of legislation to accomplish this purpose. He calls attention to methods being used in other countries and the difficulties likely to be experienced in determining the boundaries of farms in the territories that have been devastated by the war.

The Torrens system, E. C. Massie (*Richmond, Va.: Everett Waddey Co,. 1916, pp. XVII+206, figs. 25*).—This volume is a manual of the Uniform Land Registration Act of Virginia and has appended the annotated act, proposed rules of court, and a complete system of forms. It also contains references to all decisions made in the United States relating to this system.

Agricultural labor, T. B. Ponsonby (*Better Business, 2 (1917), No. 3, pp. 240–264*).—The author discusses the methods that may be used in standardizing the activities of agricultural labor as a means of improving the conditions of rural employment in Ireland.

[Agricultural wages in Sweden, 1915] J. G. Richert (*Arbetartillgång, Arbetstid och Arbetslön. Stockholm: K. Socialstyrelsen, 1916, pp. 39*).—The author discusses wages received by various types of agricultural laborers in Sweden under the different kinds of working conditions found in that country.

The Federal Farm Loan Act and the farmer, F. B. Bomberger (*Md. Agr. Ext. Serv. Bul. 4 (1917), pp. 87*).—This bulletin explains the purpose and function of the Federal Farm Loan Act, and contains models of statements that may be used in making application for loans, organizing the associations, and transacting the business of local associations.

Oregon rural credits primer, H. Macpherson (*Oreg. Agr. Col. Ext. Serv. Bul. 201 (1917), pp. 15*).—The author has given answers to a large number of questions raised in his State regarding the subject of the Federal Farm Loan Act.

Organizing cooperative associations, J. E. Boyle (*North Dakota Sta. Circ. 16 (1917), pp. 24*).—The author explains the function of cooperative organizations, and methods of organizing, and gives a model form for the articles of incorporation and for the by-laws for a cooperative elevator, a cooperative creamery, cooperative egg association, cow-testing association, live-stock shipping association, and a potato warehouse company. There is also included text of the North Dakota law governing cooperative corporations.

[Bulk handling of wheat in the Inland Empire]. G. B. Hegardt (*Portland, Oreg.: Com. Pub. Docks, 1916, pp. 40, pls. 16; appendix, pp. 61*).—This is a report covering an investigation of the movement now under way to adopt the system of bulk handling of wheat to tidewater and conclusions regarding it, together with a statement of present and required terminal facilities for bulk handling and shipping. The report relates especially to conditions surrounding Portland, Oreg. It is accompanied by an appendix, bound in a separate volume, which contains evidence obtained in gathering data for the report.

Statistical information relating to stocks, cotton, grain. provisions, live stock, and seeds, 1916 (*Chicago: Howard, Bartels & Co., 1916, pp. 54*).—This report continues data previously noted (E. S. R., 35, p. 894), adding statistics for 1916.

[Livestock statistics of Sweden] (*Internat. Inst. Agr. Rome, Internat. Crop Rpt. and Agr. Statis., 8 (1917), No. 4, p. 322*).—This contains data showing for the different classes of live stock the number on June 1, 1916, December 31, 1914, and December 31, 1913.

Statistics of live stock and animal produce for the year 1916 [in Rhodesia], E. A. Nobbs and F. Eyles (*Rhodesia Agr. Jour., 14 (1917), No. 2, pp. 184–188*).—These pages continue the data previously noted (E. S. R., 35, p. 500).

[Agriculture in Japan] (*Statis. Rpt. Dept. Agr. and Com. Japan, 32 [1915], pp. 1–130*).—These pages continue the statistical data previously noted (E. S. R., 36, p. 594).

AGRICULTURAL EDUCATION.

Agricultural education, E. Tisserand (*Bul. Soc. Encour. Indus. Nat.* [*Paris*], *127* (*1917*), *No. 1, pp. 56–77*).—The author reviews the development and present status of agricultural education in France, and discusses its reorganization and improvement.

Among his recommendations are the reorganization of the entire agricultural education service, including all grades of institutions, and the establishment of a higher council of agricultural education, consisting of 24 members, to supervise the functions of all parts of the service. The council should comprise three sections, dealing respectively with (1) higher instruction, including the National Agricultural Institute, the national schools of agriculture, horticulture, agricultural industries, and dairying and cheese making, and agricultural instruction in the faculties of universities; (2) the practical and special schools of agriculture, farm schools, seasonal schools, winter schools, and agricultural orphanages; and (3) the departmental and district chairs of agriculture, and itinerant and home economics instruction.

The character of the higher scientific instruction of the agricultural institute should be strengthened and its equipment improved and extended. Its course of study should be so revised as to turn out graduates who will assure competent recruits for the national schools of streams and forests and of horse breeding, and to make the institute, together with the national schools of agriculture, a center for the training of professors and assistants, directors of stations and laboratories, and technical agents for the public agricultural service. The courses of study of the national schools of agriculture should also be revised.

Further recommendations include an increased number of practical schools of agriculture, conserving their character of peasant schools, the revision of their course of study and its limitation to two years, and the establishment in connection with them as well as the farm schools of wood and machine shops for the practical work of students; the development of the staff of departmental and special district professors of agriculture; the multiplication of chairs of agriculture in the lyceums, colleges, and higher primary schools, as well as of special winter schools and home economics instruction for girls in rural districts; the revision of the salaries of the scientific research and instruction staff, so that its members need not seek outside employment for a livelihood, but could give their entire time and effort to their profession; and finally the organization of correspondence courses in agriculture at the agricultural institute, the national schools, and the practical schools.

Report of the acting secretary for agriculture (education) for the year 1914–15, A. Holm (*Union So. Africa, Rpt. Sec. Agr. (Ed.), 1914–15, pp. 37*).—This is the third annual report of the section of the department of agriculture of the Union of South Africa which deals with agricultural education. Detailed information is given with reference to the staff, students, courses of studies, extension and experimental work, buildings and equipment, cost of education and maintenance, and finances, of each of the four agricultural schools now in operation, located respectively at Elsenburg and Middelburg in the Cape Province, Cedara in Natal, and Potchefstroom in the Transvaal. A fifth school, with accommodations for 40 students, and a farm of 4,000 acres, has been erected at Glen in the Orange Free State, but its opening has been postponed because of the financial stringency created by the war.

At the beginning of the school year 1914 there were 205 students in residence at the four schools, but a large number left during the year to join the military forces. At the beginning of the 1915 school year the attendance, which had dropped to 83, increased to 105, with an average age of from eighteen to nineteen years. The schools, which are located on large, well-stocked, and well-equipped farms, offer a 1-year certificate course, a 2-year diploma course, a 3-year advanced diploma course, a special course in dairying (at the Grootfontein school at Middelburg), followed by practical work in a factory dairy, a 2-week short winter course open also to women, and special short courses in the various subjects. At the request of the university council of the Cape of Good Hope, courses have been prepared and submitted for the third and fourth years at the agricultural schools for the degree of B. S. in agriculture.

Although the war and consequent disturbed conditions of the country interfered with the extension work, 190 lectures and demonstrations outside of the schools were held, attended by 7,000 people, as compared with 328 lectures and demonstrations in the previous year, attended by 20,000 people. Eleven agricultural education exhibits were made at shows, 440 farms and poultry yards were visited for the purpose of giving advice, etc.

[**Agricultural instruction in the Philippine Islands**], N. H. FOREMAN ET AL. (*Philippine Craftsman, 5 (1916), No. 4, pp. 235–311, figs. 25*).—This issue comprises the following articles: Agricultural Activities of the Bureau of Education, Results of Agricultural Education As Shown in Graduates of the Central Luzon Agricultural School, Demonstration Work in Rice Culture for Farm Schools, How Specialization in Gardening Pays, Suggestions for Primary and Intermediate Gardening Teachers, Correlation of Field and Class Work in Farming, Poultry Raising at the Santa Maria Farm School, Agricultural Instruction in the Primary Grades, Agricultural Training of Manobo Boys, Agricultural Extension in the Ilongot Settlement Farm Schools. Hog Raising at Lagangilang, Garden Days with Prizes, and Clean-up Week in Oriental Negros; an editorial on Two Kinds of Agricultural Instruction, viz, general and vocational; resolutions of the annual industrial conference held May 1–5, 1916; and notes on industrial work in the schools of the various Provinces.

Agriculture in the high school, H. N. GODDARD and J. A. JAMES (*Madison, Wis.: Dept. Pub. Instr., 1917, pp. 191, figs. 24*).—This bulletin has been prepared to furnish a guide to high schools giving instruction in agriculture, and especially to those that maintain four-year agricultural departments. It contains the texts of the laws relating to agricultural instruction in the schools of Wisconsin; outlines of courses of study; a discussion of general methods and lines of work, including field work, laboratory experiment and observation, class instruction, practical school and home projects, contests and exhibits, manual-training work, and community or extension work; equipment; general and topical outlines suggestive of work that should be done in farm plant life, animal husbandry, soils, farm mechanics, farm management, and manual training; and a list of agricultural literature. A list of national registry associations, standards for Wisconsin crops, and official Wisconsin score cards are appended.

[**Agricultural and home economics in the public schools of New Hampshire**], G. H. WHITCHER (*N. H. Dept. Pub. Instr., Div. Insts., 1915–16, Nos. 55, pp. 7; 56, pp. 16, figs. 10; 57, pp. 13, fig. 1; 1916–17, 66, pp. 5*).—These circulars for teachers deal with experiments in nature study, field projects, rational methods in teaching cooking, and domestic arts courses in a high-school of the usual four-year type.

Suggestive outlines of industrial courses for consolidated and rural schools (*Minn. Dept. Ed. Bul. 42, rev. ed. (1917), pp. 116, figs. 29*).—Part 1 of this bulletin deals with suggestive outlines for home training, which are arranged in two groups. The first group includes lessons for the entire school, comprising topics with which boys and girls alike should become familiar, such as the preservation of food, the handling of the school lunch, the use of small tools, social customs, labor-saving equipment for farm and home, public-health questions, shelter, family income, sanitation, civic responsibilities, etc. The lessons in the second group are arranged in three plans, designed respectively for schools having one 60-minute period a week in the sixth grade and two 80-minute periods a week in the seventh and eighth grades for industrial work; those having two 60-minute periods a week in the seventh and eighth grades; and those having one 80-minute period a week in the seventh and eighth grades. The work of the sixth grade involves the principles and processes of garment making carried out with simple garments; that of the seventh grade relates to the care of the house and its equipment, laundry work, the care of children, the planning and preparation of meals, garment making, and the care and repair of clothing; the eighth grade work deals with home management, including the responsibility of the home maker, the family income, an efficient home, shelter, house planning, labor-saving equipment, cooking, planning, preparation, and serving of meals, household accounts, the care of young children and of the sick, civic responsibilities, elementary dressmaking, the study of clothing, etc.

Part 2 consists of outlines for manual training.

The organization and administration of a collegiate department in poultry husbandry, H. R. LEWIS (*Jour. Amer. Assoc. Instr. and Invest. Poultry Husb.,* *3* (*1917*), *No. 7, pp. 49–52, 53, 54*).—In this discussion of the most essential factors of the successful organization and administration of a department of poultry husbandry, the author calls special attention to the importance of department individuality and unity of departmental responsibility, and of a definite, clean-cut organization. In his opinion responsibility for the policy, administration, and efficiency of all research, instruction, and extenson work should be centered in one individual, who should be professor of poultry husbandry in the college and poultry husbandman in the station. Next in line and responsible to him should be a number of scientifically trained men, viz., an instructor in the college, a research assistant in poultry husbandry, an extension specialist in poultry husbandry, and a research biologist. In order that their highly specialized activities may not result in a narrow viewpoint, it is desirable that each division head should be given some work in the other branches, that is, the instructor and research specialist should at some time during the year go around the State to do some extension teaching and thus get in contact personally with the problems of the commercial poultrymen, thereby becoming intimately associated with the questions which must be investigated and taught.

Weekly staff meetings of the department, at which the head of each division makes a written report as to the condition of the work for which he is responsible; special conference hours between the head of the department and members of the staff for the discussion of problems in detail; issuing regular departmental instructions in the forms of a single, loose-leaf note book, which can be added to from time to time; and planning and arranging all important departmental activities by means of conferences also are suggested as conducive to efficiency. Methods of keeping in touch with the results of research projects and extension activities are also suggested.

NOTES.

Alabama College and Station.—Dr. Wright A. Gardner, formerly associate professor of botany and plant physiologist at the Idaho University and Station, has been appointed plant physiologist and head of the department of botany.

California University and Station.—Dr. Robert H. Loughridge, widely known as a pioneer research worker in soil chemistry and emeritus professor of agricultural chemistry, died July 1 at Waco, Texas.

Dr. Loughridge was the son of the first missionary to go to the Creek Nation after these Indians moved from Florida, and was born at the Presbyterian mission station at Koweta, Indian Territory, on October 9, 1843. He was educated at the mission school established by his father and entered La Grange Synodical College in Tennessee in 1860. He left college in 1862 to serve in the Civil War, and at its close became a student in the University of Mississippi. Here he became acquainted with Dr. E. W. Hilgard, with whom he was subsequently so closely associated.

Dr. Loughridge was graduated from this institution in 1871 and in 1878 received the degree of Ph. D. From 1874 to 1878 he was adjunct professor of chemistry in the university and assistant State geologist of Mississippi. Subsequently he assisted Professor Hilgard in the preparation of his report on cotton production for the Tenth Census and served as assistant State geologist in turn of Georgia, Kentucky, and South Carolina. He was also professor of agricultural chemistry of the University of South Carolina from 1885–1890, and instituted considerable experimental work with field crops, fertilizers, etc., at that institution.

In 1891 he came to the University of California, teaching agricultural chemistry and participating in the classical researches of Professor Hilgard as to the chemistry, physics, and geology of the soils of California, methods for the reclamation of alkali lands, scientific problems of the relation of the irrigation and drainage to the qualities of California soils, and the problem of maintaining and increasing nitrogen in those soils. His retirement from active service in 1909 was noted editorially in the *Record* (E. S. R., 21, p. 4).

Dr. Loughridge was a fellow of the American Association for the Advancement of Science and the Geological Society of America and a member of the Society for the Promotion of Agricultural Science and many other organizations. He was also the author or joint author of numerous publications.

Connecticut College and Storrs Station.—According to a note in *Science*, Austin C. Dunham has offered the college his farm of 130 acres at Newington for use for school purposes. About $50,000 has been expended in improving the property, which is considered one of the best equipped in the State.

Arthur G. Gulley, for 23 years professor of horticulture, died August 16 at the age of 68 years. Professor Gulley was a graduate of the Michigan College in 1868 and received the master's degree from the same institution in 1873.

B. G. Southwick, assistant agronomist, has been appointed extension agronomist and station field agent, devoting one-quarter of his time to the station and the remainder to extension work.

496

·Hawaiian **Sugar Planters' Station.**—The station has recently been provided with a building of reinforced concrete construction, which will house the business offices, the offices of the agricultural department, the office and laboratory of the entomological department, and the library. The building offers increased floor space to accommodate the growth of the station, and also provides fireproof quarters for the station library and entomological collections, which were heretofore housed in a frame building.

Idaho University.—The department of forestry has been segregated from the college of arts and sciences, as an independent school. F. G. Miller, head of the department of forestry in the Washington College, has been appointed dean of the school and professor of forestry.

A modern horse barn 40 by 112 feet and a sheep barn 32 by 80 feet are being erected.

Purdue University and Station.—F. G. King, associate in animal husbandry, has received a commission as captain in the National Army.

Iowa Station.—Dr. A. W. Dox, chief of the section of chemistry, has been granted leave of absence to accept an appointment as captain in the food division of the Sanitary Corps of the National Army.

Kansas College and Station.—Among the members of the staff engaged in military service are the following: E. N. Wentworth, professor of animal breeding; H. B. Walker, associate professor of irrigation and drainage engineering; Robert Schmidt assistant in botany; Herschel Scott, fellow in soils; Ernest E. Dale, fellow in horticulture; and C. E. Aubel, fellow in animal husbandry.

Recent appointments include K. J. T. Ekblaw as professor of farm engineering, A. C. Hartenbower as superintendent of institutes and extension schools, John H. Parker as assistant professor of farm crops, L. H. Fairchild as assistant in dairy husbandry, H. F. Lienhardt as instructor in bacteriology, W. F. Pickett as assistant in plant propagation and foreman of the greenhouse, ·E. C. Thurber as hog herdsman, H. H. Amos as assistant in poultry husbandry, W. L. French as specialist in agriculture in the home study department, Miss Lena L. Price as research assistant to the director of the station, W. S. Stevens as associate in stock remedy analysis, and William E. Paterson as specialist in dairy husbandry in the division of extension.

Kentucky University.—Dr. Frank Le Rond McVey, president of the University of North Dakota since 1909, has been appointed president.

Maine University and Station.—Leave of absence has been granted for the duration of the war to Drs. Raymond Pearl and F. M. Surface, for service with the statistical department of the U. S. Food Administration. Dr. H. R. Willard, of the university, and John R. Miner, of the station, are also associated in this work.

Massachusetts College.—E. L. Quaife, assistant professor of animal husbandry, has resigned to accept a position in the extension work in animal husbandry in the Iowa College.

Minnesota University and Station.—Clyde H. Bailey, cereal technologist and assistant professor of agricultural chemistry, who has been on leave of absence as chemist for the State Board of Grain Appeals, has returned as associate professor of agricultural biochemistry. Simon Marcovitch, assistant entomologist, has resigned to become head of the department of biology at the National Farm School of Pennsylvania. ·

Mississippi College.—J. Wendell Bailey, assistant professor in the general science school, has accepted an appointment with the Bureau of Entomology of the U. S. Department of Agriculture and is engaged in studies of insects affecting cereal and forage crops at Tempe, Ariz.

Montana Station.—B. W. Whitlock, for the past four years superintendent of the State grain laboratory of the station, has resigned to accept a position as Federal grain supervisor with headquarters at Salt Lake City. E. W. Jahnke, assistant in the laboratory, has been appointed superintendent.

Nevada University and Station.—Dr. Walter E. Clark, head of the department of political science of the College of the City of New York, has been appointed president, to take effect January 1, 1918. James B. McNair has been appointed assistant chemist in the station.

A joint study of poisonous plants has been arranged. The department of range management will take up the study of methods of handling live stock on the range for the prevention of losses due to poisonous plants. The veterinarian will study the characteristic symptoms of poisoning by various plants and will make post-mortem examinations of poisoned animals to determine the character of the injury caused by plant poisons. The department of chemistry will attempt to isolate the poison and to determine the part of the plant in which poisonous matter is most abundant and the stage of plant growth at which injury is most certain to occur.

New Hampshire College.—A. W. Richardson, instructor in poultry industry at the University of Maine, has been appointed assistant professor in charge of the poultry department, vice R. V. Mitchell. J. R. Hepler, of the Wisconsin University and Station, has been appointed assistant professor of horticulture, and H. F. Depew assistant in dairying.

New Jersey College and Stations.—F. C. Minkler, professor of animal husbandry and animal husbandman, director of the short courses in agriculture, and live-stock commissioner for the State Department of Agriculture, has resigned to accept a position in charge of live stock on a private estate in the State.

Cornell University and Station.—*School and Society* states that on account of the financial uncertainty caused by the war, a temporary rule has been adopted making all terminable appointments in the instruction staff for next year effective for one year only. Heretofore, instructors and assistant professors have been appointed for terms of from one to five years.

A. R. Mann has been appointed dean of the College of Agriculture and director of the station.

Chas. H. Tuck, who has been absent on leave since January, 1916, to engage in agricultural explorations in Manchuria for an American syndicate, has resigned and has been succeeded by M. C. Burritt as professor of extension teaching and vice director of extension. Other promotions include J. R. Schramm as professor of botany, R. H. Wheeler as professor of extension teaching, and H. O. Buckman as professor of soil technology.

Ohio State University and Station.—Frank Beach, assistant in horticultural extension at Purdue University, has been appointed specialist in horticulture in the university beginning July 1.

In the station Horatio Markley has resigned from the board of control to take charge of fair exhibits, vice F. M. Lutts, who has been appointed a superintendent of experiment farms. James Devol, of Marietta, has been appointed to the board of control to succeed Mr. Markley. Other appointments include the following: William H. Alexander, section director of the U. S. Weather Bureau, as climatologist; Firman E. Bear, of the College of Agriculture, as associate in soil technology (nonresident); J. T. Parsons, assistant in soil technology; O. I. Snapp, assistant in soils; J. R. Stear, assistant entomologist; I. P. Lewis, field assistant in horticulture; and M. O. Bugby, S. C. Hartman, and W. J. Smith, superintendents of experiment farms.

Pennsylvania College and Station.—Among recent appointments are the following: Effective July 1, A. A. Farnham, instructor in landscape gardening; and Grace Armstrong and Mary R. Fisher, instructors in home economics extension; July 7, Clair W. McDonald, assistant in animal husbandry; August 1, M. F. Grimes, assistant professor of animal husbandry; H. C. Yerger, jr., instructor in dairy manufacture; and J. N. Else, assistant in agronomy; September 1, H. G. Parkinson, assistant professor of rural education; Fred Hultz, assistant in animal husbandry; and W. T. White, teaching fellow in agriculture; and September 24, C. A. Hunter, assistant professor of bacteriology. G. S. Bulkley has been transferred from the dairy husbandry department to extension work as assistant professor of dairy husbandry extension. J. M. Sherman, assistant professor of bacteriology; E. O. Anderson, instructor in farm management; and H. R. Kraybill, instructor in agricultural chemistry, have resigned.

Oregon College and Station.—An apple and pear packing school was conducted by the horticultural division September 4 to 15. A short course in pruning will be offered during December.

P. M. Brandt, assistant to the dean and director at the Missouri University and Station, has been appointed professor of dairy husbandry. L. W. Wing, assistant in dairying at the same institution, has been appointed instructor in dairying. Bernard F. Sheehan, in charge of alfalfa investigations at the Iowa College, has been appointed instructor in farm crops and will assist in plant breeding at the station.

South Carolina Station.—J. L. Seal, formerly with the Bureau of Plant Industry and the States Relations Service of the U. S. Department of Agriculture, has been appointed extension pathologist and will devote his entire time to extension work in plant disease control in the State. G. M. Armstrong has been appointed instructor in the college and assistant in botany in the station, his time being equally divided between teaching and research work with cotton. W. E. Hunter, W. C. Harron, J. G. Gee, and J. L. Cathcart have been appointed graduate assistants in the divisions of botany, chemistry, and veterinary science.

The horticultural division has given intensive training to a number of the 1917 graduates of the college who are managing cooperative canneries in different sections of the State. It is stated that this has proved to be a very successful step in the food conservation campaign.

Tennessee Station.—A plant house is being built for the department of botany to be used in the further study of tomato blight, especially in the inoculation of plants with cultures of fungi isolated from blighted plants secured in different sections of the State.

The corn disease, Physoderma, has been found to be prevalent in east and west Tennessee, and the station is engaged in a campaign, in cooperation with the Plant Disease Survey of this Department, to locate the disease.

A valuable addition to the equipment of the entomological laboratory is an electric incubator, provided with an extremely sensitive thermoregulator. It has ample space for a large amount of material, also for a recording thermograph and hygrograph and thermometers, and a hygrograph by which the recording instruments are kept adjusted.

Vermont University and Station.—Dr. H. B. Ellenberger has been appointed associate professor of animal and dairy husbandry and extension specialist in dairying. B. A. Chandler has resigned as acting professor of forestry and acting forester of the station to become assistant professor of forestry at Cornell University. W. G. Hastings has been appointed professor of forestry in the university and chief forester for the State.

Virginia Station.—Recent appointments include M. O. Wilson as superintendent of the Charlotte County substation, vice A. P. Moore, resigned to enter a reserve officers' training camp; W. G. Harris as associate chemist; S. A. Wingard, previously assistant in agronomy at the Alabama Station, as assistant plant pathologist; and S. C. Harmon as assistant agronomist.

Virginia Truck Station.—J. T. Rosa, jr., has resigned as assistant horticulturist to become instructor in horticulture at the University of Missouri.

States Relations Service.—Dr. E. R. Flint, professor of chemistry in the University of Florida, has been appointed scientific and administrative assistant, succeeding Dr. E. V. Wilcox, whose resignation has been previously noted. D. W. May, agronomist in charge of the Porto Rico Station, will be located in Washington, D. C., for several months, during which time he will continue his connection with the station and will also assist in the abstracting in animal production for *Experiment Station Record.* H. L. Lang, of the Office of Home Economics, for several years associated with the abstracting in foods and human nutrition, has accepted an appointment as assistant professor of biology and public health in the Carnegie Institute of Technology.

U. S. Plant Disease Survey.—On July 1 there was organized as an office of the Bureau of Plant Industry, the Plant Disease Survey, with G. R. Lyman in charge. The principal objects of the survey are to collect information on plant diseases in the United States, covering such topics as prevalence, geographic distribution, severity, etc., and to make this information immediately available to all persons interested, especially to those concerned with disease control. Collaborators have been appointed from every State, and in addition, special investigations will be carried on to collect data on diseases of particular importance. The Plant Disease Survey has begun the issuing of a bulletin, which will appear at frequent intervals during the crop season and will contain summaries of all the important information obtained.

New Journals.—The *Journal of Dairy Science* is being published bi-monthly as the official organ for the American Society of Dairy Science, formerly the Official Dairy Instructors Association. Abstracts of all papers read at the meetings of the association are to be published in the journal, and many of the more important papers and reports will be presented in full. Opportunity will also be afforded for the publication of other material. The initial number contains the address of President Pearson, of the Iowa College, at the dedication of the new dairy building at the University of Nebraska, A Preliminary Report on a Series of Cooperative Bacterial Analyses of Milk, by R. S. Breed and W. A. Stocking, a report of the committee on relations to breed associations. Specifications and Directions for Testing Milk and Cream for Butter Fat, by O. F. Hunziker, and a report of the committee on statistics of milk and cream regulations. A board of 21 editors is in charge of the journal, with J. H. Frandsen, of the Nebraska University and Station, as editor-in-chief.

Journal of the Massachusetts Poultry Society is being published bi-monthly, with J. C. Graham, of the Massachusetts College and Station, as editor. One of the primary objects is to afford a means of publishing the papers delivered at the annual poultry convention. The opening numbers also report some experimental work.

Following protests by numerous scientific organizations and others, it is announced that publication of the *Keio Bulletin*, which was suspended as a war economy measure a short time ago, is to be resumed, with some modifications as to subject matter.

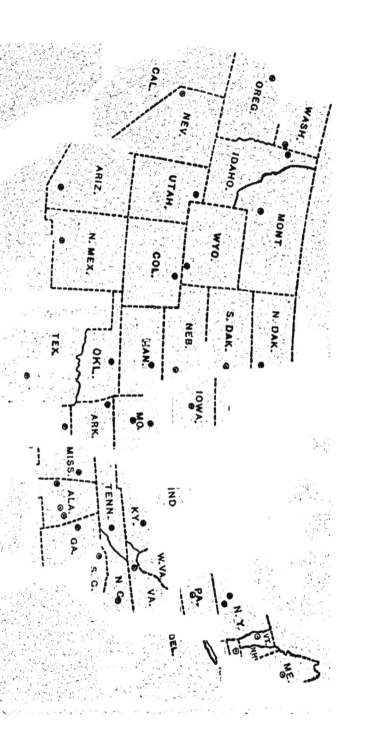

Issued November 20, 1917

U. S. DEPARTMENT OF AGRICULTURE
STATES RELATIONS SERVICE
A. C. TRUE, DIRECTOR

Vol. 37   ABSTRACT NUMBER   No. 6

EXPERIMENT STATION RECORD

WASHINGTON
GOVERNMENT PRINTING OFFICE
1917

EXPERIMENT STATION RECORD.

Editor: E. W. ALLEN, Ph. D., *Chief, Office of Experiment Stations.*
Assistant Editor: H. L. KNIGHT.

EDITORIAL DEPARTMENTS.

Agricultural Chemistry and Agrotechny—E. H. NOLLAU.
Meteorology, Soils, and Fertilizers{W. H. BEAL.
{R. W. TRULLINGER.
Agricultural Botany, Bacteriology, and Plant Pathology{W. H. EVANS, Ph. D.
{W. E. BOYD.
Field Crops{J. I. SCHULTE.
{J. D. LUCKETT.
Horticulture and Forestry—E J. GLASSON.
Economic Zoology and Entomology—W. A. HOOKER, D. V. M.
Foods and Human Nutrition{C. F. LANGWORTHY, Ph. D., D. Sc.
{H. L. LANG.
Zootechny, Dairying, and Dairy Farming{M. D. MOORE.
Veterinary Medicine{W. A. HOOKER.
{E. H. NOLLAU.
Rural Engineering—R. W. TRULLINGER.
Rural Economics—E. MERRITT.
Agricultural Education{C. H. LANE.
{M. T. SPETHMANN.
Indexes—M. D. MOORE.

CONTENTS OF VOL. 37, NO. 6.

	Page.
Recent work in agricultural science	501
Notes	600

SUBJECT LIST OF ABSTRACTS.

AGRICULTURAL CHEMISTRY—AGROTECHNY.

	Page
The essentials of chemical physiology, Halliburton	501
International catalogue of scientific literature. D—Chemistry	501
Annual chemical directory of the United States, 1917, edited by Lovelace	501
The physical properties of colloidal solutions, Burton	501
The proteins of the peanut, *Arachis hypogæa*, II, Johns and Jones	501
Levulose the preponderant sugar of apple juices, Eoff, jr	502
Sedoheptose, a new sugar from *Sedum spectabile*, I, La Forge and Hudson	502
Rotary powers of some new derivatives of gentiobiose, Hudson and Johnson	502
The inosit phosphoric acids of cottonseed meal, Rather	502
The chemistry of wood, Schorger	502
Chemical composition of higher fractions of maple wood creosote, Pieper et al.	502
Toxicity to a wood-destroying fungus of maplewood creosote, Pieper et al	502
Application of Chodat's paracresol-tyrosinase reaction, Breslauer	502
A course in food analysis, Winton	503
Device for evaporating solutions to a definite volume, Plaisance and Pervier	503
An evaporating bath of seasand heated by steam, Peterson	503
Handling laboratory solutions by suction, Beals	503

Page.

An automatic suction attachment for an ordinary pipette, Schroeder.......... 503
Device for the automatic and intermittent washing of precipitates, Lathrop... 503
An improved form of a fumeless digestion apparatus, McHargue............... 503
An apparatus for the purification of mercury, Patten and Mains............. 503
Recovery of molybdenum residues, Lenher and Schultz..................... 504
Determination of total nitrogen, Lagers................................. 504
Nitrate determinations in the presence of chlorids, Gericke.................. 504
Study of determination of potash chiefly the Lindo-Gladding method, Hibbard. 504
Action of solutions of ammonium sulphate on muscovite, Gardiner and Shorey.. 505
Influence of calcite on determination of organic carbon, Shorey and Fry...... 505
New method for silicic acid (zeolitic) in soils, Gedrolts...................... 505
A note on the phenolsulphonic acid method for nitrates in waters, Nichols.... 506
Note on the determination of strontium and lithium in water, Averitt........ 506
Improved chemical methods for differentiating bacteria, Clark and Lubs..... 506
The colorimetric determination of hydrogen in concentration, Clark and Lubs.. 506
Improvements in the copper method for estimating amino acids, Kober....... 506
A simplified inversion process for the determination of sucrose, Walker....... 506
A method for the estimation of levulose in presence of glucose, Loewe........ 507
The determination of fat in certain milk products, Francis and Morgan........ 507
Determination of water soluble fatty acids in butter and other fats, Kauffman.. 508
Correction required in applying Babcock formula to evaporated milk, Evenson. 508
The analysis of desiccated milk.—Determination of moisture and fat, Porcher.. 508
Index of refraction of olive oil in relation to acidity and rancidity, Cutolo.... 508
The identification of emodin-bearing drugs, Hubbard....................... 509
The biochemistry of tobacco, I, Paris................................... 509
The drying of fruits and vegetables, MacDonald.......................... 509
Influence of nitrogenous substances on wines, Müller-Thurgau and Osterwalder. 509
Chemical control in cane sugar factories, Prinsen Geerligs................... 509
[Report of the] bacteriological department, Owen........................ 509
Chemical changes caused by defecation of sorghum juice for sirup, Anderson.. 511
Sugar-beet sirup, Townsend and Gore................................... 511
American vegetable food oils, their sources and methods of production, Bailey.. 511
Brazilian oilseeds, Bolton and Hewer.................................... 511
The natural accelerator of Para rubber, Stevens........................... 512

METEOROLOGY.

Hail in the United States, Henry.. 512
Observations on possible influence of violent cannonading on rainfall, Sebert.. 512
Lightning and forest fires in California, Palmer............................ 512
Bacteriological study of the air of Buenos Aires, Riganti................... 513
Monthly Weather Review.. 513
Meteorological, magnetic, and seismic observations at Havana, 1916, Gangoiti.. 513
Meteorology, Trivett.. 513

SOILS—FERTILIZERS.

Edgar County soils, Hopkins, Mosier, Van Alstine, and Garrett............... 514
Soil survey of Clinton County, Iowa, Hawker and Howe..................... 514
The soil resources of Maryland, McCall.................................. 514
Soil survey of Schoharie County, N. Y., Maxon and Fuller.................. 514
Geology of southern Ohio, Stout... 514
Survey of Fairfax and Alexandria Counties, Va., Carter, jr., and Yingling, jr.. 514
Principal plantation soil types found on Island of Hawaii, Burgess........... 515
Method of botanical soil investigations, Chafanov and Mushchenko........... 515
Degradation of chernozems of western part of northern Caucasus, Iakovlev.... 516
Soil flora studies.—I, General characteristics. II, Methods, Conn............. 516
Soil flora studies.—III, Spore-forming bacteria in soil, Conn................. 516
Soil flora studies.—IV, Nonspore-forming bacteria in soil, Conn.............. 516
Soil flora studies.—V, Actinomycetes in soil, Conn......................... 517
Soil bacteria and streptothrices that develop on dextrose agar, Emerson....... 517
Some effects of auximones on soil organisms, Mockeridge.................... 517
The organic matter of the soil.—V, Nitrogen distribution, Morrow and Gortner. 517
The nitric nitrogen content of the country rock, Stewart and Peterson........ 518
The significance of nitrification as a factor in soil fertility, Gainey........... 519
Soil constituents which inhibit the action of plant toxins, Truog and Sykora.. 519

Page.
The extraction and saturation of soils with volatile antiseptics, du Buisson....   519
Farms, forests, and erosion, Dana...   520
Measuring the surface temperature of soil, Dobiasha (Dobiache)..............   520
Studies on soil colloids, II, Wolkoff..   520
Facilities for lysimeter and outdoor pot culture work at the station, Barker....   521
[Fertilizer experiments], Émanuèl..   521
The stable-manure business of big cities, Fletcher.............................   521
Effect of soil reaction on ammonium sulphate, Cook and Allison..............   521
The forms of phosphorus in granitic soils, Vincent............................   522
Report on availability of potash, Vanatta......................................   522
Importance of developing our natural resources of potash, Brown..............   522
Fertilizer experiments with lime on tobacco soils, 1912–13, Cohen.............   522
Fertilizer experiments with lime on tobacco soils, 1913–14, Sidenius..........   523
Ground limestone for use in New York State, Barker and Baer.................   523
The international trade in fertilizers, Van Hissenhoven.......................   523
Fertilizer analyses, Patten, Berger, Smoll, and De Windt....................   524

AGRICULTURAL BOTANY.

Department of botanical research, MacDougal....................................   524
Osmotic pressure in roots and leaves in relation to moisture, Iljin et al........ 525
Nitrogen compounds in mulberry leaves, Katayama...........................   525
The emergence of the aerial organs in woodland plants, Salisbury..............   525
Linkage in maize: Aleurone and chlorophyll factors, Lindstrom..............   526
The different meanings of the term "factor," Frost............................   526
Notes on the flora of Sitka, Alaska, Anderson..................................   526
The chief types of vegetation in South Africa, Bews.........................   526
Effects of constituents of solid smelter wastes on barley, Lipman and Gericke.   526
Some effects of salt-treated soils on absorption by seeds, Gericke.............   527
Certain effects under irrigation of copper compounds upon crops, Forbes......   527
Protection against pollution of waters and smoke and dust injury, Stoklasa....   528

FIELD CROPS.

Field experiments and compensating calculations, Leidner...................   528
[The experimental error in field tests], Batyrenko.........................   528
[Report of field crops work], Taggart, Kerr, Hester, and Quereau.............   529
Dry farming investigations at Moro, Oreg., Stephens and Hill.................   529
Progress report, Substation No. 4, Beaumont, Tex., 1909–1914, Laude..........   532
[Field crops], Zavitz..   533
Cultivated plants: Potatoes and sugar beets, Hitier...........................   533
Contribution to the study of Gramineæ, Girola...........................   533
Relation of winter temperature to winter and spring grains, Salmon...........   533
Effect of greenhouse temperatures on the small grains, Hutcheson and Quantz.   533
Experiments with spring wheat and oats, Fedorov (Fedoroff)..................   534
Thrashing injuries of wheat and rye, Walldén..............................   534
Fibers from the Belgian Congo...   534
The agave fibers of Tunis, Guillochon..   535
Alfalfa culture, Williams..   535
Cassava as a competitor of maize and potatoes in production of starch.........   535
Anatomical structure and peculiarities of varieties of clover, Zholtkevich.....   535
Corn culture, Hutcheson, Hodgson, and Wolfe...............................   535
Corn variety tests, 1915 and 1916, Osborn....................................   536
Hybrids of Zea ramosa and Z. tunicata, Collins..............................   536
A method for determining the percentage of self-pollination in maize, Waller..   537
Danthonia in New Zealand, Cockayne.......................................   537
The dasheen; its uses and culture, Young.....................................   537
Flax-growing experiments, 1914 and 1915......................................   537
Notes on the cultivation of flax by the ancient Egyptians, Munier.............   537
Influence of methods of sowing oats on crop yield, Archangelskij.............   537
Percentage of husk in varieties of oats, Pridham...........................   537
Standardization and classification of potato varieties for Michigan, Waid......   538
[Potatoes], Cadoret..   538
The production of potatoes by cuttings, Cadoret..............................   538
Potato growing and potato diseases from Maine to California, Morse...........   538
Spraying potatoes in 1916..   538
The transplanting of rice in Egypt, Mosséri..................................   538

Page.
Studies in rice, Rundles... 538
[Rice improvement], Marcarelli... 539
The nitrogen fertilization of rice, Novelli.................................... 539
A remarkable cultural variety of rye, Cerriana................................. 539
The composition of grain sorghum kernels, Le Clerc and Bailey.............. 539
The sugar beet during vegetation, Saillard.................................... 540
Present status of sugar-beet seed industry in United States, Townsend........ 540
Present status of sugar-beet seed industry in United States, Townsend........ 540
[Experimental work with sugar cane], Easterby................................. 540
Sweet clover: Growing the crop, Coe... 540
Timothy fertilization and culture, Schmitz.................................... 540
Tobacco culture in North Carolina, Matthewson and Moss........................ 541
Tobacco, Baldassarre.. 541
Composition of the ash and fertilizing of tobacco, Tijmstra................... 541
Agricultural seed inspected in 1915, Smith.................................... 541
Information concerning the origin of red clover and alfalfa seed, Lakon....... 541
The disinfection of seeds with bromin, Artsikhovskiĭ and Stom................. 542
Investigations in 1914 on the weeds occurring in Russia, Pachoskiĭ............ 542
Crowfoot (Ranunculus arvensis), Martin.. 542
The flea-seed, a new weed plant, Osborn....................................... 542
[Notes on species of Xanthium and their destruction].......................... 542

HORTICULTURE.

The plant introduction gardens of the Department of Agriculture, Dorsett.... 542
Development and localization of truck crops in the United States, Blair...... 543
Home vegetable gardening, Durst... 543
How to make the garden pay, Morrison and Brues................................ 543
Vegetable culture for all, Eva.. 543
The allotment book, Brett... 543
A book about potatoes and other vegetables, Wright............................ 543
Late cabbage, Reed.. 543
Adult characters in sunflower seedlings, Cockerell............................ 543
The effect of continued capillary watering, Daniel............................ 543
Color as an indication of picking maturity of fruits and vegetables, Corbett.... 543
Arkansas Plant Act of 1917 and rules and regulations pursuant thereto......... 544
Colorado's amended horticultural inspection law............................... 544
Horticultural laws of Idaho... 544
Suggestions for the control of injurious insects and plant diseases, Bentley.... 544
Why, when, and how to spray, Cooper... 544
The preparation and use of lime-sulphur in orchard spraying, Morse........... 544
Practical guide to the culture of fruit trees in Chile, Opazo................. 544
National fruit culture, Davidson.. 544
The pear in Ontario, Clement and Robb... 544
Bush fruits, Card... 544
Muscadine grape breeding, Dearing... 544
Vinifera grapes in New York, Anthony.. 544
European grapes succeed in New York, Hall..................................... 545
Olive growing and production in Spain, Priego................................. 545
Citrus stock experiments at Warm Baths, Transvaal, Simmonds................... 545
The origin and dispersal of Cocos nucifera, Beccari........................... 545
Note on the coffees and their culture at Lula, Mertens........................ 545
The coffee industry of French Indo-China, Briggs.............................. 545
Filbert growing in the Puget Sound country, Quarnberg......................... 545
Further notes on the germination of belladonna seed, Sievers.................. 545
Report on cooperative experiment [with Datura], Woodworth and Langenhan.. 546
Possibility of commercial production of lemon-grass oil in United States, Hood.. 546
The sweet pea (Lathyrus odoratus) in the flower garden, Ghosh................. 546
The culture and diseases of the sweet pea, Taubenhaus......................... 546
The ornamental trees of Hawaii, Rock.. 546
A bud variation of Pittosporum, Shamel.. 546
Hints on landscape gardening, von Pückler-Muskau, trans. by Sickert........ 546
The natural style in landscape gardening, Waugh............................... 547

FORESTRY.

Forest laws... 547
Annual report for 1916, Department of Conservation and Development........ 547

Page.

Opening up the National Forests by road building, Merrill.................. 547
The work of the forest department in India, edited by Troup................ 547
Silviculture, Marsden.. 547
Relation of storage of seeds of oaks and hickories to germination, Delavan...... 547
Evergreen trees for Iowa, MacDonald....................................... 548
The structure and identification of Queensland woods, Jolly.................. 548
Utilization of ash, Sterrett.. 548
Grass trees: An investigation of their economic products, Earl.............. 548
Note on Indian sumac (*Rhus cotinus*), Puran Singh........................ 548
Notes on *Funtumia elastica* and Funtumia hybrids, Miny.................... 548
Cicatrization of tapping wounds among rubber-yielding plants, Heim....... 548
Economic forest . products, Pearson.. 548
Marketing woodlot products in Tennessee, Sterrett........................ 548

DISEASES OF PLANTS.

A method for studying the humidity relations of fungi in culture, Stevens.... 549
Celluloid cylinders for inoculation chambers, Hubert....................... 549
Nematode technique, Magath.. 549
Presence of nitrites and ammonia in diseased plants, Boncquet.............. 549
Influence of *Æcidium clematidis* on the leaves of its host, Montemartini....... 549
Work connected with insect and fungus pests and their control.............. 550
Reports of laboratory for plant diseases, Linsbauer et al.................... 550
Some new or rare plant diseases, Montemartini........................... 550
Phytopathology, Stockdale.. 550
Report of the microbiologist, Nicholls..................................... 551
Notes as to Gymnosporangia on Myrica and Comptonia, Dodge and Adams.. 551
Studies in life histories of some Septoria occurring on Ribes, Stone........... 551
The Uredinales found upon the Onagraceæ, Bisby......................... 552
Endophyllum-like rusts of Porto Rico, Olive and Whetzel.................. 552
The barberry bush and black stem rust of small grains, Melhus and Durrell ... 552
Sclerotinia libertiana on snap beans, McClintock.......................... 552
The Peronospora disease of maize, Rutgers................................ 552
Flower-bud and boll shedding of cotton in Nigeria, Thornton................ 553
Onion mildew, Blin.. 553
Some potato problems, Cowan.. 553
Cryptogamic diseases of sugar cane, Averna Saccá........................ 553
Pathology and physiology of tobacco in the Crown lands, Jensen et al........ 553
Lanas disease of tobacco in the Crown lands, Jensen...................... 553
Gummosis in tobacco, Jensen.. 554
Leaf roll in tomatoes, Güssow.. 554
Watermelon diseases, Orton.. 554
The varietal relations of crown gall, Shaw................................ 554
Fire blight, Létourneau... 554
Dieback of apple trees, caused by *Cytospora leucostoma*, van der Bij (Byl). 554
The period of ascospore discharge of the apple scab fungus, Childs.......... 555
The black knot of plum and cherry, Hutchings............................. 555
Rougeot of grapevines, Faes.. 555
A Pythiacystis on avocado trees, Fawcett.................................. 555
Banana disease on the Salayer Islands, Rijks.............................. 556
Characteristics of citrus canker and of the casual organism, Jehle........... 556
Cooperative work for eradicating citrus canker, Kellerman.................. 556
Department of citrus canker eradication, Sterling.......................... 556
Citrus scab, Fawcett... 556
Report of the mycologist, Nowell... 556
Dieback disease of *Paulownia tomentosa* caused by new species of Valsa, Hemmi. 557
Diseases of woody plants in North Africa, Maire........................... 557
Influence of certain climatic factors on *Endothia parasitica*, Stevens.......... 557
Influence of temperature on the growth of *Endothia parasitica*, Stevens........ 557
Chestnut blight in West Virginia.. 558
Pycnia of *Cronartium pyriforme*, Boyce................................... 558
The white pine blister rust in Canada, McCubbin.......................... 558

ECONOMIC ZOOLOGY—ENTOMOLOGY.

The Wyoming ground squirrel in Colorado with suggestions for control, Burnett. 558
Destroying rodent pests on the farm, Lantz................................ 558
Bird life in Washington, Getty.. 558

Page.

Observations on polycystid gregarines from Arthropoda, Watson............... 558
On a trematode larva encysted in a crab, *Helice tridens*, Yoshida............... 558
The death-feigning instinct, DuPorte............... 559
Arsenic as an insecticide, Lovett and Robinson............... 559
Toxicity of various benzene derivatives to insects, Moore............... 559
Carbon disulphid as an insecticide, Hinds............... 559
Nicotin sulphate as a poison for insects, Lovett............... 559
The practical use of the insect enemies of injurious insects, Howard............ 559
Losses caused by imported tree and plant pests, Marlatt............... 559
Notes on a southern trip, Pierce............... 560
Second biennial report of the Montana State Board of Entomology, Cooley..... 560
Annual report of the Government entomologist, Gowdey............... 560
Cotton pests in the arid and semiarid Southwest, Morrill............... 560
Some problems in insect control about abattoirs and packing houses, Bishopp.. 560
Insects injurious to man and stock in Zanzibar, Aders............... 560
Guide to specimens and enlarged models of insects and ticks............... 560
Methods of controlling grasshoppers, Milliken............... 560
Grasshoppers and their control, Severin and Gilbertson............... 561
Destroy the grasshoppers. Urbahns............... 561
Report on the great invasion of locusts in Egypt in 1915, McKillop and Gough. 561
New Thysanoptera from Florida, Watson............... 561
An annotated list of the Thysanoptera of Plummer's Island, Md., Hood........ 561
Two new species of Dicyphus from Porto Rico, Gibson............... 561
The green bug (*Toxoptera graminum*) outbreak of 1916, Kelly............... 561
Plant lice injurious to apple orchards, II, Parrott, Hodgkiss, and Lathrop.... 561
The reddish-brown plum aphis (*Rhopalosiphum nymphex*), Davidson.......... 562
The migratory habits of *Myzus ribis*, Gillette and Bragg............... 562
Little-known western plant lice. II, Davidson............... 562
Methods for the study of mealy bugs, Ferris............... 563
Insect parasites and predators as adjuncts in control of mealy bugs, Smith.... 563
Some comparisons of *Coccus citricola* and *C. hesperidum*, Quayle............... 563
A scale insect new to California, Smith............... 563
The Mediterranean fig scale (*Lepidosaphes ficus*), Roullard............... 563
Two new species of lace bugs. Heidemann............... 563
Notes on *Leptobyrsa rhododendri*, Dickerson............... 563
Check list of the Lepidoptera of Boreal America. Barnes and McDunnough... 563
The Barnes and McDunnough "list," Dyar............... 563
Suppression of the gipsy and brown-tail moths and its value. Burgess......... 563
Solid-stream spraying against the gipsy and brown-tail moth. Worthley....... 563
Louisiana records of the bindweed prominent (*Schizura ipomex*), Tucker...... 564
Nepticulidæ of North America, Braun............... 564
The pink bollworm, *Pectinophora gossypiella*, Busck............... 564
[New Lepidoptera], Dyar............... 564
Effect of time of seeding and volunteer wheat on Hessian fly, Parks............ 564
The mosquitoes of the mountains of California, Dyar............... 564
Bromelicolous anopheles, Dyar and Knab............... 565
A State-wide malaria-mosquito survey of California, Herms............... 565
The rice fields as a factor in the control of malaria. Freeborn............... 565
A plea and a plan for the eradication of malaria. Hoffman............... 565
Notes on horse flies as a pest in southern Florida. Snyder............... 565
A synoptic revision of the Cuterebridæ, Townsend............... 565
The head and throat of American game animals, Townsend............... 565
Notes on "Pœcilanthrax," with descriptions of new species, Cole............... 565
The occurrence of *Eumerus strigatus* in Canada, Gibson............... 565
The Mediterranean fruit fly, Back............... 565
Mediterranean fruit fly (*Ceratitis capitata*) breeds in bananas, Severin......... 565
Dark currant fruit fly in California, *Rhagoletis ribicola*, Severin............... 566
The melon fly in Hawaii, Back and Pemberton............... 566
The root maggot pest, Stookey............... 566
Notes on some western Buprestidæ, Burke............... 566
A new species of Agrilus from California, Fisher............... 566
The locust borer (*Cyllene robiniæ*), Sanborn and Painter............... 566
A new species of Xylotrechus, Fisher............... 566
The horse-radish flea-beetle, Chittenden and Howard............... 566
The two-banded fungus beetle, Chittenden............... 567
A troublesome household pest (*Attagenus plebius*) of Hawaii, Illingworth...... 567

Page.
Studies on the life history of *Ligyrus gibbosus*, Hayes........................ 567
Notes on an introduced weevil (*Ceutorhynchus marginatus*), Hyslop............ 568
The strawberry root weevil in British Columbia, Treherne..................... 568
[The rice water weevil], Quereau... 568
A newly-introduced clover beetle (*Sitones hispidulus*), Van Dyke............. 568
The A B C and X Y Z of bee culture, Root................................... 568
Diprion simile in North America, Rohwer.................................. 568
The Argentine ant as an orchard pest, Smith................................ 568
Ants protecting acacia trees in Central America, Schwarz..................... 569
Notes on *Trichogramma minutum*, Harland.................................. 569
A nearctic species of Dolichurus, Rohwer.................................... 569
Life history and successful introduction of Sicilian mealy bug parasite, Smith.. 569
Some new Australian chalcid flies, mostly of the *Encyrtidæ*, Girault.......... 569
New Australian chalcid flies, Girault....................................... 569
A chalcid parasite of the pink bollworm, Girault............................. 569
Two bethylid parasites of the pink bollworm, Rohwer......................... 569
Occurrence of the genus Parachrysocharis in the United States, Girault....... 570
Two apple leaf mites of economic importance, Brittain....................... 570

FOODS—HUMAN NUTRITION.

Goat's milk as food for infants and very young children, Jordan and Smith.... 570
Milling properties of Ohio wheat, Corbould................................. 570
The value of sugar and honey as foods, Perucci............................. 570
Miscellaneous drug preparations, Woods................................... 570
[Food and drug inspection], Ladd and Johnson............................. 570
Preliminary report of the dairy and food commissioner for 1916, Foust......... 570
Food and drug laws of the State of Rhode Island............................ 570
What to eat in war time, Lusk... 571
Food economy in war time, Wood and Hopkins............................. 571
Food values and the rationing of a country, Smith.......................... 571
The restricted supply of food: Its relation to health and efficiency, Pembrey.. 571
The gaseous-exchange of subjects receiving a rice diet, Ramoino............. 571
The physiological behavior of raffinose, Kuriyama and Mendel.............. 571

ANIMAL PRODUCTION.

The function of live stock in agriculture, Rommel........................... 572
[Japanese cane for steers], Kerr... 572
Progress in handling the wool clip: Development in the West, Marshall....... 572
The production of pork in the four-year rotation, Kerr...................... 572
Stallion legislation and the horse-breeding industry, Glenn.................. 572
The poultryman's problems in 1917, Lewis................................. 573
The Thanksgiving turkey, Weiant.. 573
Fur farming as a side line, Dearborn....................................... 573
A critique of the theory of evolution, Morgan.............................. 573

DAIRY FARMING—DAIRYING.

An experiment in community dairying, Welch............................... 573
The cow makes farming more profitable, Holden and Carroll.................. 574
Beginning of the dual-purpose Shorthorn type, Graham..................... 574
Cooperative bull associations, Winkjer..................................... 574
[Dairy herd records].. 574
Pasturing cows *v.* stable feeding... 574
Cost of milk production... 575
Standard calf rearing chart.. 575
Goat's milk for infant feeding, Jordan and Smith........................... 575
Goat milk good for babies... 576
Dairying.. 576
Skim-milk cheese... 576

VETERINARY MEDICINE.

Meat inspection service of the Department of Agriculture, Ditewig........... 577
Report of State veterinarian for 1914 and 1915, Marshall.................... 577
Report of proceedings under the diseases of animals acts, 1915, Prentice...... 577
Further note on life history of *Gongylonema scutatum*, Ransom and Hall...... 577

Page.
Spirochæta icterohæmorrhagiæ in American wild rats, Noguchi... 577
Effects of radiation on development of *Trichinella spiralis*, Tyzzer and Honeij... 578
Oil of Chenopodium and chloroform as anthelmintics, Hall and Foster........ 578
Anaphylatoxin and anaphylaxis... 578
A study of five members of the septicemia hemorrhagica group, Besemer...... 583
Virulence of apparently sound muscle and glands in tuberculosis, Chaussé.... 583
Eupatorium ageratoïdes, the cause of trembles, Curtis and Wolf.............. 583
The control and prevention of infectious diseases of cattle, Schroeder........ 583
Bacteriotherapeutic treatment of ulcerous lymphangitis in the horse, Truche.. 583
Salvarsan in the treatment of canine distemper, Krocber..................... 584
Occurrence of a pseudoparasitic mite, Hirst................................. 584
Chicken pox in poultry.—Preventive suggestions, Upton..................... 584

RURAL ENGINEERING.

A textbook of practical hydraulics, Park...................................... 584
Report of the State water commission of California, 1917..................... 585
Report of the water conservation and irrigation commission for 1916.......... 585
Administration report, irrigation department, Punjab, 1915–16................ 585
Surface water supply of North Atlantic slope drainage basins, 1915 585
Surface water supply of Ohio River Basin, 1915.............................. 585
Centrifugal pumps and suction dredgers, Sargeant 585
Some costs of maintenance of motor-driven deep-well pumps, Enger.......... 585
Unlined earth reservoirs for pumping plants................................. 585
Pumping for irrigation on the farm, Fuller.................................. 585
Divisors (for the measurement of irrigation water), Cone..................... 586
The composition of irrigation waters in upper Italy, Menozzi and De Vecchi.. 586
Economical irrigation of alfalfa in Sacramento Valley, Beckett and Robertson. 586
Irrigation and drainage, Risler and Wery.................................... 587
Drainage of irrigated farms, Hart... 587
Standard specifications for drain tile....................................... 587
The quality of water and confirmatory tests for *Bacillus coli*, Wolman........ 587
Ultra-violet rays in the purification of drinking water, Spencer............... 588
Sterilization by liquid chlorin and hypochlorite of lime, Dutton.............. 588
The disposal of wastes from the dairy industry, Kimberly..................... 588
Sewage disposal on the farm, Warren....................................... 589
Modern road construction, Byrne... 590
Good roads yearbook, 1917.. 590
Report of the State highway commission of Minnesota, 1915–16.............. 590
Wisconsin highway commission, second biennial report...................... 590
The Highway Law [of New York].. 590
Automobile registration, licenses, and revenues in the United States, 1916.... 590
A treatise on concrete, plain and reinforced, Taylor and Thompson........... 590
Extracting alcohol from garbage would conserve grain and potatoes.......... 590
Agricultural practice, Lougher 591
The necessity of mechanical cultivation of soil, Héron...................... 591
Public tests of motor cultivation, Sourisseau............................... 591
Homemade silos, Hillman.. 591
How to build the wooden-hoop silo, Blasingame............................ 591
The Tenessee wood-hoop silo.—How to build it, Hutton..................... 591
A dairy farm plant, Charlton... 591
Cooling tanks and milk houses as factors in cream improvement, Frandsen.... 591
Why hot water pipes in the household burst more frequently, Brown and Noll. 592
Community sanitation.. 592

RURAL ECONOMICS.

Meeting the farmer halfway, Vrooman....................................... 592
The Nonpartisan League, Russell.. 592
Rural surveys, Thompson... 592
The results of some rural social surveys in Iowa, Von Tungeln................ 592
The mind of the farmer, Groves.. 592
The development of rural leadership, Fiske.................................. 563
The consolidated school as a community center, Cook....................... 593
Social control: Rural religion, Gill... 593
Countryside and Nation, Vincent... 593
Country versus city, Wilson.. 593

Page.

Folk depletion as a cause of rural decline, Ross.........................·.......... 593
Farm tenantry in the United States, Spillman and Goldenweiser............. 593
The land problem and rural welfare, Vogt................................... 593
Cooperation and community spirit, Wilson.................................. 594
Business essentials for cooperative fruit and vegetable canneries, Kerr........ 594
Cooperative cheese manufacturing and marketing, Macpherson and Kerr...... 594
Farmers' mutual fire insurance, Valgren.................................... 594
State hail insurance in North Dakota....................................... 594
Possibilities of a market-train service, White and Powell.................... 594
A system of accounts for cotton warehouses, Newton and Humphrey.......... 594
Essentials in larger food production, Hopkins.............................. 594
The high cost of low crop yields, Thorne................................... 595
The net output from agriculture and its distribution, Orwin................. 595
Agriculture on Government reclamation projects, Scofield and Farrell........ 595
British agriculture the nation's opportunity, Strutt et al...........·......... 595
[Progress of agriculture in India]... 595
A graphic summary of world agriculture, Finch et al....................... 595
Price Current Grain Reporter Yearbook, 1917, Osman...................... 595

AGRICULTURAL EDUCATION.

[Agriculture and home economics at National Education Association in 1916].. 596
State higher educational institutions of North Dakota....................... 596
A survey of educational institutions of the State of Washington.............. 597
Agricultural instruction.—The Central Development Farm, Weraroa, Pope.... 597
Report of the agricultural society of Malmöhus Province for 1916............. 597
What is the Federal vocational education law?.............................. 597
The chemistry of farm practice, Keitt...................................... 598
Nature study or stories in agriculture...................................... 598
The culture of the mulberry silkworm, Keleher............................. 598
Vocational mathematics for girls, Dooley................................... 598
Live-stock classifications at county fairs, Ray.............................. 598
Illustrated lecture on public-road improvement............................. 598
[School home gardening].. 598
Effect of home-demonstration work in the South, Knapp and Creswell........ 598

MISCELLANEOUS.

Yearbook of the Department of Agriculture, 1916............................ 599
Annual report on work done under the local experiment law in 1916, Duggar.. 599
Twenty-ninth Annual Report of Colorado Station, 1916...................... 599
Twenty-ninth Annual Report of Louisiana Stations, 1916, Dodson............ 599
Twenty-eighth Annual Report of Maryland Station, 1915.................... 599
Twenty-ninth Annual Report of Maryland Station, 1916..................... 599
Monthly Bulletin of the Ohio Experiment Station........................... 599
Monthly Bulletin of the Western Washington Substation..................... 599

LIST OF EXPERIMENT STATION AND DEPARTMENT PUBLICATIONS REVIEWED.

Stations in the United States.

Alabama College Station: Page.
    Circ. 35, Feb., 1917........... 599
Arkansas Station:
    Bul. 130, Mar., 1917.......... 536
    Bul. 131, Mar., 1917.......... 502
California Station:
    Bul. 280, May, 1917.......... 586
Colorado Station:
    Bul. 228, Apr., 1917.......... 586
    Twenty-ninth An. Rpt. 1916. 599
Hawaiian Sugar Planters' Station:
    Agr. and Chem. Bul. 45. 1917. 515
Illinois Station:
    Circ. 197, May, 1917.......... 594
    Circ. 198, May, 1917.......... 543
    Soil Rpt. 15, Mar., 1917....... 514
Iowa Station:
    Bul. 170, Mar., 1917.......... 548
    Circ. 35, Apr., 1917........... 552
Kansas Station:
    Bul. 215, Nov., 1916.......... 560
Louisiana Stations:
    Twenty-ninth An. Rpt. 1916. 509,
Maine Station: [529, 568. 572, 599
    Off. Insp. 82, Feb., 1917...... 570
    Doc. 522, Feb., 1916.......... 538
    Doc. 523, Mar., 1916.......... 544
    Doc. 531, Dec., 1916.......... 538
Maryland Station:
    Bul. 202, Feb., 1917.......... 540
    Bul. 203, Mar., 1917.......... 541
    Twenty-eighth An. Rpt. 1915. 599
    Twenty-ninth An. Rpt. 1916. 599
Michigan Station:
    Bul. 278, Dec., 1916.......... 524
Nebraska Station:
    Bul. 158, Feb. 15, 1917....... 543
    Circ. 3, May 5, 1917.......... 591
New Jersey Stations:
    Hints to Poultrymen, vol. 5.
      No. 9, June, 1917........... 573
New York State Station:
    Bul. 429, Feb., 1917.... 570, 575, 576
    Bul. 430, Mar., 1917.......... 523
    Bul. 431, Mar., 1917.......... 561
    Bul. 432, Apr., 1917........ 544, 545
    Tech. Bul. 57, Jan., 1917...... 516
    Tech. Bul. 58, Mar., 1917..... 516
    Tech. Bul. 59, Mar., 1917..... 516
    Tech. Bul. 60, Mar., 1917..... 517
    Tech. Bul. 61, Mar., 1917..... 521
North Carolina Station:
    Bul. 237, Apr., 1917.......... 541
North Dakota Station:
    Spec. Bul., vol. 4, No. 13.
      May, 1917.................. 570

Stations in the United States—Con.

Ohio Station: Page.
    Mo. Bul., vol. 2, No. 6, June,
      1917........ 535, 570, 575, 595, 599
Oklahoma Station:
    Bul. 113, Mar., 1917.......... 566
    Bul. 114, Apr., 1917.......... 507
Oregon Station:
    Bul. 143, May, 1917.......... 555
    Bul. 144, Apr., 1917.......... 529
South Dakota Station:
    Bul. 172, Feb., 1917.......... 561
Tennessee Station:
    Bul. 117, Mar., 1917.......... 544
Texas Station:
    Bul. 200, Dec., 1916.......... 532
Utah Station:
    Bul. 150, May, 1917.......... 518
Virginia Station:
    Bul. 214, Mar., 1917.......... 535
Washington Station:
    West. Wash. Sta. Mo. Bul.,
      vol. 5. No. 3. June. 1917..... 566.
                    591, 599

U. S. Department of Agriculture.

Jour. Agr. Research, vol. 9:
    No. 10, June 4, 1917.......... 564
    No. 11, June 11, 1917... 536. 559. 583
Bul. 480, Solid-stream Spraying
    against the Gipsy Moth and the
    Brown-tail Moth in New Eng-
    land, L. H. Worthley........... 563
Bul. 491, The Melon Fly in Ha-
    waii, E. A. Back and C. E. Pem-
    berton......................... 566
Bul. 520, A System of Accounts for
    Cotton Warehouses. R. L. New-
    ton and J. R. Humphrey........ 594
Bul. 523, Utilization of Ash, W. D.
    Sterrett........................ 598
Bul. 535, The Horse-radish Flea-
    beetle: Its Life History and Dis-
    tribution. F. H. Chittenden and
    N. F. Howard.................. 566
Farmers' Bul. 797, Sweet Clover:
    Growing the Crop, H. S. Coe.... 540
Farmers' Bul. 799, Carbon Disul-
    phid As an Insecticide, W. E.
    Hinds......................... 559
Farmers' Bul. 805, The Drainage of
    Irrigated Farms, R. A. Hart.... 587
Farmers' Bul. 821, Watermelon
    Diseases, W. A. Orton.......... 554
Farmers' Bul. 822, Live-stock
    Classifications at County Fairs,
    S. H. Ray..................... 598

U. S. Department of Agriculture—Con.

Farmers' Bul. 823, Sugar-beet Page.
Sirup, C. O. Townsend and H.
C. Gore...................... 511
Yearbook, 1916........ 511, 520, 521, 522
537, 540, 542, 543, 547, 556, 558,
559, 563, 572, 573, 574, 577, 585,
589, 592, 593, 594, 595, 598, 599
Office of the Secretary:
Circ. 73, Autombile Registra-
tions, Licenses, and Reve-
nues in the United States,
1916...................... 590
Bureau of Soils:
Field Operations, 1915—
Soil Survey of Clinton
County, Iowa, H. W.
Hawker and F. B. Howe. 514
Soil Survey of Schoharie
County, New York, E.
T. Maxon and G. L.
Fuller................ 514
Soil Survey of Fairfax and
Alexandria Counties,
Virginia, W. T. Carter,
jr., and C. K. Yingling, jr. 514
States Relations Service:
Syllabus 29, Illustrated Lec-
ture on Public-road Im-
provement................ 598
Weather Bureau:
Mo. Weather Rev., vol. 45,
Nos. 3–4, Mar.–Apr., 1917.. 512, 513
Scientific Contributions:[1]
The Proteins of the Peanut,
Arachis hypogæa.—II, The
Distribution of the Basic
Nitrogen in the Globulins
Arachin and Conarachin, C.
O. Johns and D. B. Jones... 501
Sedoheptose, a New Sugar
from *Sedum spectabile,* I, F.
B. La Forge and C. S. Hudson 502
The Rotatory Powers of Some
New Derivatives of Genti-
obiose, C. S. Hudson and J.
M. Johnson................ 502
The Chemistry of Wood, A. W.
Schorger................... 502
The Chemical Composition of
the Higher Fractions of
Maple Wood Creosote, E. J.
Pieper, S. F. Acree, and C.
J. Humphrey............... 502
On the Toxicity to a Wood-
destroying Fungus of Maple
Wood Creosote and of Some
of Its Constituents and De-
rivatives, together with a
Comparison with Beech-
wood Creosote, E. J. Pieper,
S. F. Acree, and C. J. Hum-
phrey..................... 502
A Note on an Automatic Suc-
tion Attachment for an Ordi-
nary Pipette, J. P. Schroeder 503

U. S. Department oj Agriculture—Con.

Scientific Contributions—Contd. Page.
A Simple Device for the Auto-
matic and Intermittent
Washing of Precipitates, E.
C. Lathrop................. 503
An Apparatus for the Purifica-
tion of Mercury, H. E. Pat-
ten and G. H. Mains....... 503
The Action of Solutions of
Ammonium Sulphate on
Muscovite, R. F. Gardiner
and E. C. Shorey.......... 505
The Influence of Calcite In-
clusions on the Determina-
tion of Organic Carbon in
Soils, E. C. Shorey and W.
H. Fry.................... 505
Improved Chemical Methods
for Differentiating Bacteria
of the Coli-ærogenes Family,
W. M. Clark and H. A. Lubs. 506
The Colorimetric Determina-
tion of Hydrogen Ion Con-
centration and Its Applica-
tions in Bacteriology, W. M.
Clark and H. A. Lubs...... 506
The Correction Required in
Applying the Babcock
Formula to the Estimation
of Total Solids in Evapo-
rated Milk, O. L. Evenson.. 508
The Identification of Emodin-
bearing Drugs, W. S. Hub-
bard...................... 509
The Composition of Grain Sor-
ghum Kernels, J. A. Le
Clerc and L. H. Bailey.... 539
The Present Status of the
Sugar-beet Seed Industry in
the United States, C. O.
Townsend................. 540
Tobacco Culture in North
Carolina, E. H. Matthewson
and E. G. Moss............ 541
Muscadine Grape Breeding,
C. Dearing................ 544
Further Notes on the Germina-
tion of Belladonna Seed,
A. F. Sievers............. 545
Possibility of the Commercial
Production of Lemon-grass
Oil in the United States,
S. C. Hood................ 546
A Bud Variation of Pitto-
sporum, A. D. Shamel...... 546
Marketing Woodlot Products
in Tennessee, W. D. Ster-
rett...................... 548
A Method for Studying the
Humidity Relations of Fun-
gi in Culture, N. E. Stevens. 549
The Influence of Certain Cli-
matic Factors on the Devel-
opment of *Endothia para-
sitica,* N. E. Stevens....... 557

[1] Printed in scientific and technical publications outside the Department.

U. S. Department of Agriculture—Con.

Scientific Contributions—Contd.   **Page.**
The Influence of Temperature on the Growth of *Endothia parasitica*, N. E. Stevens... 557
Losses Caused by Imported Tree and Plant Pests, C. L. Marlatt...................... 559
Notes on a Southern Trip, W. D. Pierce............... 560
Some Problems in Insect Control about Abattoirs and Packing Houses, F. C. Bishopp.................... 560
Destroy the Grasshoppers, T. D. Urbahns................ 561
An Annotated List of the Thysanoptera of Plummer's Island, Md., J. D. Hood... 561
Two New Species of Dicyphus from Porto Rico, E. H. Gibson.......................... 561
The Green Bug (*Toxoptera graminum*) Outbreak of 1916, E. O. G. Kelly............. 561
The Reddish-brown Plum Aphis (*Rhopalosiphum nymphex*), W. M. Davidson. 562
Little-known Western Plant Lice, II, W. M. Davidson.. 562
Two New Species of Lace Bugs, O. Heidemann....... 563
The Barnes and McDunnough "List," H. G. Dyar........ 563
A Note on Cisthene, H. G. Dyar...................... 564
Three New North American Phycitinæ, H. G. Dyar.... 564
A New Phycitid from the Bahamas, H. G. Dyar...... 564
A New Noctuid from Brazil, H. G. Dyar................ 564
Miscellaneous New American Lepidoptera, H. G. Dyar... 564
Notes on North American Pyraustinæ, H. G. Dyar... 564
Notes on North American Nymphulinæ, H. G. Dyar.. 564
Notes on North American Schœnobiinæ, H. G. Dyar.. 564
Seven New Crambids from the United States, H. G. Dyar.. 564
Seven New Pyralids from British Guiana, H. G. Dyar. 564
The Mosquitoes of the Mountains of California, H. G. Dyar...................... 564
Bromelicolous anopheles, H. G. Dyar and F. Knab......... 565
Notes on Horse Flies as a Pest in Southern Florida, T. E. Snyder.................... 565
A Synoptic Revision of the Cuterebridæ, with Synonymic Notes and the Description of One New Species, C. H. T. Townsend... 565

U. S. Department of Agriculture—Con.

Scientific Contributions—Contd.   **Page.**
The Head and Throat Bots of American Game Animals, C. H. T. Townsend........ 565
Notes on Osten Sacken's Group "Pœcilanthrax," with Descriptions of New Species, F. R. Cole................. 565
The Mediterranean Fruit Fly, E. A. Back................. 565
Notes on Some Western Buprestidæ, H. E. Burke......... 566
A New Species of Agrilus from California, W. S. Fisher..... 566
A New Species of Xylotrechus, W. S. Fisher............. 566
The Two-banded Fungus Beetle, F. H. Chittenden...... 567
Notes on an Introduced Weevil (*Cautorhynchus marginatus*), J. A. Hyslop............... 568
Diprion simile in North America, S. A. Rohwer.......... 568
Ants Protecting Acacia Trees in Central America, F. A. Schwarz.................. 568
A Nearctic Species of Dolichurus, S. A. Rohwer...... 569
Some New Australian Chalcid Flies, Mostly of the Family Encyrtidæ, A. A. Girault.. 569
New Australian Chalcid Flies, A. A. Girault............. 569
A Chalcid Parasite of the Pink Bollworm, A. A. Girault... 569
Two Bethylid Parasites of the Pink Bollworm, S. A. Rohwer....................... 569
The Occurrence of the Genus Parachrysocharis in the United States, A. A. Girault. 570
A Further Note on the Life History of *Gongylonema scutatum*, B. H. Ransom and M. C. Hall................. 577
Oil of Chenopodium and Chloroform As Anthelmintics.— Preliminary Note, M. C. Hall and W. D. Foster..... 578
The Control and Prevention of Infectious Diseases of Cattle, E. C. Schroeder.......... 583
Divisors (for the Measurement of Irrigation Water), V. M. Cone...................... 586
The Economical Irrigation of Alfalfa in Sacramento Valley, S. H. Beckett and R. D. Robertson. 586
Rural Surveys, C. W. Thompson....................... 592
Mass Instruction through Group Training, O. B. Martin........................ 596

EXPERIMENT STATION RECORD.

VOL. 37.   ABSTRACT NUMBER.   No. 6.

RECENT WORK IN AGRICULTURAL SCIENCE.

AGRICULTURAL CHEMISTRY—AGROTECHNY.

The essentials of chemical physiology, W. D. HALLIBURTON (*London and New York: Longmans, Green & Co., 1916, 9. ed., pp. XI+324, pl. 1, figs. 71*).— This is the ninth edition of this well-known work. Some additions have been made, and the revision has been thorough so as to bring the volume up to date. The work contains an introduction, elementary course, advanced course, and appendix. The subject matter is treated both from a descriptive and experimental standpoint.

International catalogue of scientific literature. **D**—Chemistry (*Internat. Cat. Sci. Lit., 13 (1916), pp. VIII+836*).—The thirteenth annual issue of this catalogue (E. S. R., 34, p. 407). The material catalogued was received between September, 1913, and September, 1914.

Annual chemical directory of the United States, 1917, edited by B. F. LOVELACE (*Ann. Chem. Dir. U. S., 1917, pp. 305*).—This volume contains alphabetically arranged lists of American manufacturers of chemicals and dealers in chemicals; American manufacturers of and dealers in apparatus and equipment, machinery and mechanical supplies for scientific and technical laboratories, industrial plants and organizations; professional chemical firms; Federal, State, municipal, industrial, and professional laboratories; American and foreign colleges offering courses in chemistry; experiment stations of the United States and the principal foreign stations; Federal and State officials of dairying, foods, drugs, health, and feeding stuffs; American and foreign technical and scientific societies; American and foreign chemical publications; a chemical survey of 1916; and new devices, methods, and appliances for handling industrial chemical problems.

The physical properties of colloidal solutions, E. F. BURTON (*London and New York: Longmans, Green & Co., 1916, pp. VII+200, figs. 18*).—This monograph considers the subject under the topics of preparation and classification of colloidal solutions, the ultramicroscope, the Brownian movement, the optical properties of colloidal solutions, measurement of the sizes of ultramicroscopic particles, motion of colloidal particles in an electric field, cataphoresis, the coagulation of colloids, theory of the stability of colloids, and practical applications of the study of colloidal solutions. A list of references is appended to each chapter.

The proteins of the peanut, Arachis hypogæa.—II, The distribution of the basic nitrogen in the globulins arachin and conarachin, C. O. JOHNS and D. B. JONES (*Jour. Biol. Chem., 30 (1917), No. 1, pp. 33-38*).—The globulins arachin and conarachin previously isolated from the peanut (E. S. R., 37, p. 8) were analyzed by the Van Slyke method (E. S. R., 26, p. 22) with the following average percentage results as to nitrogen, respectively: Amid, 11.81 and 11.08; humin adsorbed by lime, 0.57 and 0.65; humin in amyl alcohol extract, 0.43 and 0.13; cystin, 0.74 and 0.75; arginin, 23.77 and 25.78; histidin, 2.78 and 2.72; lysin, 5.22 and 6.35; amino of filtrate, 53.3 and 50.23; nonamino of filtrate, 1.65 and 1.94; total, 100.27 and 99.63.

It is indicated that the relatively high percentage of lysin in the peanut proteins might make its use advantageous in supplementing diets deficient in lysin.

Levulose the preponderant sugar of apple juices, J. R. Eoff, jr. (*Jour. Indus. and Engin. Chem.*, 9 (1917), No. 6, pp. 587, 588).—Tabular analytical data relative to the acidity, gravity (Brix), sucrose, levulose, and dextrose of the juices of 20 varieties of apples are reported. The data show that in all cases the amount of combined levulose exceeds the amounts of the other sugars present.

See also a previous note by Thompson and Whittier (E. S. R., 29, p. 711).

Sedoheptose, a new sugar from Sedum spectabile, I, F. B. La Forge and C. S. Hudson (*Jour. Biol. Chem.*, 30 (1917), No. 1, pp. 61–77).

The rotatory powers of some new derivatives of gentiobiose, C. S. Hudson and J. M. Johnson (*Jour. Amer. Chem. Soc.*, 39 (1917), No. 6, pp. 1272–1277).

The inosit phosphoric acids of cottonseed meal, J. B. Rather (*Arkansas Sta. Bul. 131 (1917), pp. 3–20).*—The author has isolated from cottonseed meal as the crystalline strychnin salt an inosit phosphoric acid which corresponds to inosit triphosphoric acid, $C_6H_6(OH)_3(H_2PO_4)_3$. The acid was found, however, not to be of constant occurrence in cottonseed meal. From other samples of cottonseed meal an acid was isolated which agrees with the formula $C_{12}H_9O_{42}P_5$ of the inosit phosphoric acid previously isolated from cottonseed meal and other feeding stuffs (E. S. R., 29, p. 804). "The composition corresponds equally as well to that of salts of inosit pentaphosphoric acid, $C_6H_6(OH)(H_2PO_4)_5$, and in view of the similarity of the formulas and the theoretical possibility of the existence of inosit pentaphosphoric acid it appears best to ascribe the latter formula to the acid."

Products prepared according to the method of Anderson (E. S. R., 31, p. 707) did not yield strychnin and silver salts which were similar to the salts of inosit hexaphosphoric acid claimed to have been isolated. "The composition of these materials agreed with that calculated for salts of inosit pentaphosphoric acid." Experimental data are submitted in detail and discussed.

The chemistry of wood, A. W. Schorger (*Jour. Indus. and Engin. Chem.*, 9 (1917), No. 6, pp. 556–566, figs. 3).—Two studies are reported. The first takes up methods and results of analysis of some American species. Tabulated analytical data of longleaf pine, Douglas fir, western larch, white spruce, basswood, yellow birch, and sugar maple are reported, together with a description of the methods of analysis used. In the second paper a general discussion is given of the methods used and the analytical results obtained.

The chemical composition of the higher fractions of maple wood creosote, E. J. Pieper, S. F. Acree, and C. J. Humphrey (*Jour. Indus. and Engin. Chem.*, 9 (1917), No. 5, pp. 462–465, fig. 1).

On the toxicity to a wood-destroying fungus of maple wood creosote and of some of its constituents and derivatives, together with a comparison with beechwood creosote, E. J. Pieper, S. F. Acree, and C. J. Humphrey (*Jour. Indus. and Engin. Chem.*, 9 (1917), No. 6, pp. 566–569, figs. 2).

The application of Chodat's paracresol-tyrosinase reaction to a study of the proteolysis by microorganisms, Alice Breslauer (*Bul. Soc. Bot. Genève,*

2. ser., 8 (1916), No. 7–9, pp. 319–352).—From the results of the study it is concluded that the different species of microorganisms can be differentiated colorimetrically by means of the paracresol-tyrosinase reaction. Most of the amino acids give with equimolecular proportions of paracresol and tyrosinase a red color, which, in the presence of an excess of the amino acid, more or less rapidly turns blue. Glycyltyrosin and a great number of other polypeptids react with less intensity. The rapidity and intensity of the reaction depends upon the quantity of the culture present and also upon the age of the culture. These functions vary with the different species. The nature of the culture medium was also found to influence the reaction. A parallelism between the color and the amount of gelatin liquefied was noted. Light did not affect the reaction. Low temperatures, however, greatly retarded the development of the color. The reaction was found to be valuable in detecting indol, especially when present only in very small amounts with skatol.

The relation of microorganisms to the ripening of cheese is noted.

The data are submitted in detail and discussed.

A course in food analysis, A. L. WINTON (*New York: John Wiley & Sons, Inc., 1917, pp. IX+252, figs. 107*).—This volume considers dairy products, meat and fish, natural vegetable foods and mill products, microscopic examination of vegetable foods, saccharine products, fats and oils, fruits, fruit products, liquors and vinegars, flavoring extracts, coffee, tea, and cocoa. Calculation tables and a list of apparatus, reagents, and practice material are appended.

The book is intended to give an introductory course in the subject prior to the use of more extensive works or to meet the needs of the general student.

A simple device for evaporating solutions to a definite volume, G. P. PLAISANCE and N. C. PERVIER (*Jour. Amer. Chem. Soc., 39 (1917), No. 6, pp. 1238–1240, figs. 3*).—An easily assembled apparatus and its manipulation are described in detail.

An evaporating bath of sea sand heated by steam, P. P. PETERSON (*Jour. Indus. and Engin. Chem., 9 (1917), No. 7, p. 686, figs. 2*).—An apparatus in which the sand bath is heated by coils of pipe through which superheated steam is passed and controlled by a suitable steam trap is described.

Handling laboratory solutions by suction, C. L. BEALS (*Jour. Indus. and Engin. Chem., 9 (1917), No. 6, p. 603, fig. 1*).—The author, at the Massachusetts Experiment Station, describes an apparatus and its construction for obtaining solutions from large containers. The apparatus was successfully applied to measuring dilute acid and alkali solutions used in fiber determinations.

A note on an automatic suction attachment for an ordinary pipette, J. P. SCHROEDER (*Jour. Indus. and Engin. Chem., 9 (1917), No. 7, pp. 687, 688, figs. 3*).—An apparatus which consists essentially of the attachment of a stopcock to an ordinary pipette, or for automatic measurement a Gooch crucible filter tube and a stopcock, is described.

A simple device for the automatic and intermittent washing of precipitates, E. C. LATHROP (*Jour. Indus. and Engin. Chem., 9 (1917), No. 5, pp. 527, 528, fig. 1*).—An apparatus which has yielded excellent results and its manipulation are described in detail.

An improved form of a fumeless digestion apparatus, J. S. McHARGUE (*Jour. Indus. and Engin. Chem., 9 (1917), No. 7, pp. 686, 687, fig. 1*).—The author, at the Kentucky Experiment Station, describes an enlarged and modified Sy fumeless nitrogen digestion apparatus (E. S. R., 28, p. 311). The apparatus is indicated as yielding excellent results.

An apparatus for the purification of mercury, H. E. PATTEN and G. H. MAINS (*Jour. Indus. and Engin. Chem., 9 (1917), No. 6, pp. 600–603, figs. 3*).—

An apparatus, which has yielded satisfactory results, and its manipulation are described in detail.

Recovery of molybdenum residues, V. Lenher and M. P. Schultz (*Jour. Indus. and Engin. Chem.*, 9 (*1917*), No. 7, pp. 684, 685).—The authors present a method for recovering molybdenum residues which consists of the precipitation of molybdenum sulphid by hydrogen sulphid from a solution slightly acid with nitric acid or the formation of a sulpho-molybdate solution by adding hydrogen sulphid to the alkaline solution of the "yellow precipitate" and subsequent precipitation of molybdenum sulphid with hydrochloric acid. The molybdenum sulphid when ignited yields MoO₃, which is in a condition to be readily used.

When an acid solution is used the acidity should be kept between 0.1 and 0.4 per cent. In case much iron is present the sulphid should be washed with water containing hydrochloric acid. When the "yellow precipitate" is dissolved in alkali any iron, if present, will be precipitated as the hydroxid and can be easily removed by filtration.

Determination of total nitrogen, G. H. G. Lagers (*Chem. Weekbl.*, 14 (*1917*), No. 21, pp. 492–499).—Experimental data on the determination of nitrogen in various fertilizers containing both organic and inorganic (nitrate) nitrogen by the method of Jodlbaur, the Kjeldahl method, the Kjeldahl method plus zinc, the Kjeldahl method plus ferrous sulphate, and a procedure involving the Kjeldahl and Schlösing methods are reported in tabular form.

The Jodlbaur method yielded low results in samples which contained ammonia or nitrates. Exact results were obtained, however, by a combination of the Schlösing and Kjeldahl methods in which the sample was first treated with ferrous chlorid and hydrochloric acid and then according to the regular Kjeldahl procedure.

The methods used are described in detail and the results discussed.

Nitrate determinations in the presence of chlorids, W. F. Gericke (*Jour. Indus. and Engin. Chem.*, 9 (*1917*), No. 6, pp. 585, 586).—The author, at the California Experiment Station, proposes a modification of the phenoldisulphonic acid method in which the evaporation of the solution to dryness is obviated by the use of concentrated sulphuric acid, which is added to the aqueous extract. The addition of the sulphuric acid and phenoldisulphonic acid to the aqueous solution prevents the loss of nitrates, which in the old procedure was occasioned by the addition of acid to the dry salts after evaporation. It is noted that the temperature of the final evaporation and concentration of the aqueous solution should not exceed 70° C.

Some analytical data are submitted.

A study of the determination of potash chiefly concerned with the Lindo-Gladding method, P. L. Hibbard (*Jour. Indus. and Engin. Chem.*, 9 (*1917*), No. 5, pp. 504–513).—From a critical study of the method, the author has found that in preparing a solution for the determination of potash considerable variation in the volume of water used, amount and time of boiling, excess of ammonia, and time of standing after boiling but before filtering have but little effect on the results.

Higher results and fewer impurities in the solution are obtained by extraction of the material with hot water on a filter. For this extraction a tube filter was found to be much more efficient than the ordinary paper filter in a funnel.

For correct results the ignition of the ash must be so gradual that spattering does not occur. The addition of 10 mg. of sugar during the evaporation was found to be a material aid. "The final temperature need not be above a moderate red heat for a few minutes. Long heating near the fusion point of the salts causes loss of potash. A little SO₄ remaining as bisulphate does no harm. In case the residue is not easily burnt white, it is best to dissolve in water and a little hydrochloric acid and filter out insoluble matter. In many cases organic matter and ammonium salts may be conveniently removed by evaporation of the solution with aqua regia." After ignition the residual salts are best dissolved by adding a few drops of hydrochloric acid and heating before adding much water.

"Separation of K_2PtCl_6 requires certain conditions for an accurate result. Concentration of potassium at time of adding platinum must be low enough so that no K_2PtCl_6 is precipitated at once. Free sulphuric acid, nitric acid, or organic matter must not be present. The amount of platinum used should be only slightly in excess of that necessary to combine with all the potassium. Excess of hydrochloric acid is unimportant. Evaporation should cease while some free hydrochloric acid still remains; if evaporation is carried too far dilute hydrochloric acid should be added and the evaporation repeated."

Five or six successive washings with 10 cc. of the wash fluids were found to be sufficient. In the presence of large amounts of sodium, potassium is better separated as cobaltinitrite than as platinichlorid. An ordinary Gooch crucible with asbestos felt was found to be most suitable and reliable for accurate work in collecting and purifying the precipitate. Drying can be accomplished at any temperature between 100 and 140° C., and is usually complete in an hour at 120°. The final weighing should not be made in less than half an hour after the removal from the oven.

The perchlorate procedure for the determination of potassium was found to be less reliable than the platinum method, and to be longer, more difficult, and more expensive in regard to the reagents.

A list of 30 references to the literature is cited.

The action of solutions of ammonium sulphate on muscovite, R. F. GARDINER and E. C. SHOREY (*Jour. Indus. and Engin. Chem., 9 (1917), No. 6, pp. 589, 590*).—Analytical data relative to the extraction of potassium from muscovite by ammonium sulphate are submitted and briefly discussed.

The influence of calcite inclusions on the determination of organic carbon in soils, E. C. SHOREY and W. H. FRY (*Jour. Indus. and Engin. Chem., 9 (1917), No. 6, pp. 588, 589*).—The authors report the presence of calcite inclusions in quartz of soils derived from limestones, as previously noted by McCaughey and Fry (E. S. R., 28, p. 812) and by Robinson (E. S. R., 31, p. 719). The effect of these inclusions on the determinations of the total carbon in such soils by the cupric oxid combustion method is indicated by the analytical data submitted. The inclusions were found to introduce no error when the carbon was determined by the wet oxidation method.

The subject is briefly discussed.

A new method for the determination of silicic acid (zeolitic) in soils, K. K. GEDROÏTS (C. GUÉDROÏTZ) (*Zhur. Opytn. Agron. (Jour. Agr. Expt.), 17 (1916), No. 5, pp. 400–407*).—The value of silicic acid determinations in studying the transformations and origin of soils is indicated, and the disadvantages of the procedures commonly used are noted. The following procedure is described and deemed to yield excellent results:

Five gm. of the sample is treated with 10 per cent hydrochloric acid and heated in a small platinum crucible over a spread burner to a temperature not higher than 625° C. After cooling, the mass is transferred with a little water to a beaker, and 100 cc. of 5 per cent potassium hydroxid added. The material is heated on the water bath for one-half hour, filtered, and washed with 1 per cent potassium hydroxid. The filtrate is acidulated with hydrochloric acid, evaporated, and heated on a sand bath for from one to one and one-half hours. The silicic acid becomes completely insoluble, and after the addition of water is separated by a filtration, washed free from chlorids, dried, and weighed in the usual manner.

A note on the phenolsulphonic acid method for nitrates in waters high in magnesium salts, M. S. NICHOLS (*Jour. Indus. and Engin. Chem., 9 (1917), No. 6, pp. 586, 587*).—To obviate the precipitation of magnesium and iron hydroxids after neutralization of the excess phenolsulphonic acid, the addition of saturated ammonium chlorid solution was found to be satisfactory. This modification is deemed preferable to filtering the solution, as by the latter procedure a small quantity of the color always remains in the filter.

Note on the determination of strontium and lithium in water, S. D. AVERITT (*Jour. Indus. and Engin. Chem., 9 (1917), No. 6, pp. 584, 585*).—The author, at the Kentucky Experiment Station, submits the following indirect methods.

For the determination of strontium, the weighed calcium and strontium oxids are dissolved in hydrochloric acid, reprecipitated as oxalates, and then titrated with standard potassium permanganate. For calculating the amount of strontium oxid, the following formula is submitted:

(W—CaO equivalent of KMnO, titration) 2.179=strontium oxid.

W=weight of CaO and SrO. The derivation of the formula is explained.

For the determination of lithium, the aqueous solution of the combined chlorids of sodium, potassium, and lithium is made up to a suitable volume, from which an aliquot is taken for the determination of potassium. From this determination the potassium and the potassium chlorid in the solution are calculated. The total chlorin is determined in another aliquot by titration with standard silver nitrate. The lithium chlorid is then calculated by the following formula:

NaCl equivalent of C—Cl in KCl—(W—KCl)×2.64=lithium chlorid.

C=weight of total chlorin and W=weight of NaCl+KCl+LiCl.

Experimental data submitted indicate the accuracy of the procedures.

Improved chemical methods for differentiating bacteria of the coli-aerogenes family, W. M. CLARK and H. A. LUBS (*Jour. Biol. Chem., 30 (1917), No. 2, pp. 209–234, fig. 1*).—A new medium for differentiating bacteria of the coli-aerogenes family by accurate determination of the carbon dioxid and hydrogen ratios and its use are described. The differences in the intensities of the acid fermentations are determined by the use of the indicator method of hydrogen ion concentration.

The colorimetric determination of hydrogen ion concentration and its applications in bacteriology, W. M. CLARK and H. A. LUBS (*Jour. Bact., 2 (1917), Nos. 1, pp. 1–34; 2, pp. 109–136; 3, pp. 191–236, pl. 1, figs. 8*).—A monographic review, including the original work on the subject by the authors.

It is concluded in general that with the improvements presented the colorimetric method for the determination of hydrogen ion concentration is applicable to routine as well as research purposes in bacteriology.

Improvements in the copper method for estimating amino acids, P. A. KOBER (*Jour. Indus. and Engin. Chem., 9 (1917), No. 5, pp. 501–504, figs. 2*).— Simple methods for dehydrating and weighing copper sulphate for use in making standard solutions, keeping a saturated solution of potassium iodid containing starch and acetic acid, and making a permanent suspension of cupric hydroxid are described in detail. A concise description of the procedure for amino acid determination by the copper method is included.

A simplified inversion process for the determination of sucrose by double polarization, H. S. WALKER (*Jour. Indus. and Engin. Chem., 9 (1917), No. 5.*

pp. 490–492).—From some preliminary experimental data the following procedure was devised:

From 50 to 75 cc. of the sample used for direct polarization is placed in a 100-cc. flask and heated in the water bath to 65° C. In case a 50-cc. sample is used 25 cc. of water should be added. After removal from the bath 10 cc. of a mixture of equal volumes of hydrochloric acid (specific gravity 1.188) and water is added, the mixture allowed to cool spontaneously in the air for 15 minutes, and then in water to room temperature. It is made up to 100 cc. and polarized as usual.

A method for the estimation of levulose in presence of glucose, L. LOEWE (*Proc. Soc. Expt. Biol. and Med., 13* (*1916*), *No. 4, pp. 71–73*).—The following qualitative test is described:

To 1 cc. of the sample, from 6 to 8 drops of orcein solution (0.2 per cent aqueous solution) and 1 cc. of 85 per cent phosphoric acid are added. The test tube is heated to boiling over a free flame and placed in a boiling water bath for ten minutes. In the presence of levulose a yellow color appears, the depth of which is proportionate to the concentration of the sugar. On cooling, a yellow precipitate settles out. Upon the addition of sodium or potassium hydroxid sufficient to neutralize the acid the yellow color changes to a distinct orange.

The development of this characteristic orange color was made the basis for a quantitative determination of levulose, using suitable standards. In the qualitative test levulose was detected in 1 cc. of a 0.005 per cent solution. Maltose, lactose, galactose, and arabinose in solutions of various strengths did not interfere with the tests. Cane sugar yielded a positive test, due to the presence of levulose, from the cleavage of the sugar in the presence of the phosphoric acid.

The determination of fat in certain milk products, C. K. FRANCIS and D. G. MORGAN (*Oklahoma Sta. Bul. 114* (*1917*), *pp. 3, fig. 1*).—The following modified Babcock procedure for the determination of fat in ice cream and evaporated milk is described:

To 9 gm. of a uniform sample weighed in a 30 per cent cream test bottle from 4 to 5 cc. of a mixture of equal parts of glacial acetic and sulphuric acids is added with thorough mixing after each addition until a dark brown color develops. Two or three additions of one or two drops of concentrated nitric acid are now made and the mixture thoroughly agitated after each addition. The amount of nitric acid added may be increased, but precautions should be observed so that there is no loss through excessive foaming. When a light yellow color results the bottle is immersed in boiling water for from 3 to 4 minutes until the dark brown color returns. The mixture is then centrifugalized for 5 minutes, the bottle filled nearly to the neck with hot water, and again centrifugalized for 10 minutes. The fat column is brought into the scale of the neck with more hot water and again centrifugalized for another minute. The meniscus is reduced with glymol and the reading multiplied by two for a 9-gm. sample.

For malted milk, from 1 to 1.5 cc. at a time of a mixture of sulphuric and nitric acids (20 cc. H_2SO_4 to 1 cc. HNO_3) is added to a 4.5-gm. sample in a 30 per cent cream test bottle until a light yellow color is obtained. About 15 or 20 cc. of the acid mixture is usually required. The bottle is then immersed in boiling water until a dark brown color develops. A mixture of sulphuric and nitric acids (10 cc. H_2SO_4 to 2.5 cc. HNO_3) is added, 1 cc. at a time, with thorough shaking after each addition, until a light red color is developed. It is again immersed in boiling water until the dark brown color returns, centrifugalized for 5 minutes, hot water added, and again centrifugalized for 2 minutes. The fat column is then measured as usual and the reading multiplied by four.

For dried milk from 5 to 6 cc. portions of concentrated sulphuric acid are added to a 4.5-gm. sample until a dark brown color develops. The sulphuric-nitric acid mixture used for malted milk is then added, 0.5 cc. at a time, with thorough agitation, until a light red color results. The material is then immersed in boiling water until the dark brown color returns, more of the acid mixture added until the light color is produced, and again immersed in boiling water until the dark brown color reappears. The procedure is then carried out the same as for malted milk.

Experimental data submitted indicate uniformly higher results with the proposed procedure than with the Röse-Gottlieb method. Directions for the preparation of the samples of the various products, together with a graphical chart showing the variation in the fat content of 75 samples of ice cream, are included.

The determination of water soluble fatty acids in butter and other fats, M. KAUFFMAN (*Chem. Weekbl., 14 (1917), No. 16, pp. 364–367*).—The following procedure, which is deemed to yield accurate results and to be much simpler than the usual procedure, is described:

One gm. of the sample is treated in a 200-cc. flask with 50 cc. of 13/100-normal alcoholic potash solution. After saponification under a reflux condenser, a small amount of water at about 90° C. and 50 cc. of 15/100-normal sulphuric acid are added. After cooling, the volume is made up to 200 cc., the liquid filtered, and 100 cc. of the filtrate titrated with tenth-normal alkali, using phenol-phthalein as indicator. An excess of acid should be present to insure complete liberation of all the fatty acids and a proper correction for the amount added made.

Analytical data submitted indicate the accuracy of the procedure.

The correction required in applying the Babcock formula to the estimation of total solids in evaporated milk, O. L. EVENSON (*Jour. Indus. and Engin. Chem., 9 (1917), No. 5, pp. 499–501*).—Experimental data submitted show that the Babcock formula (E. S. R., 8, p. 721) can not be applied directly to the determination of total solids in evaporated milk at either 5° C. or at 37 to 40° when exact results are desired. The formula

$$T = \frac{L-1.8}{4} + 1.2 \times \text{percentage of fat}$$

is submitted for obtaining results which are comparable with those obtained with the Babcock formula on whole milk cooled to its maximum specific gravity, and the formula

$$T = \frac{L-0.5}{4} + 1.2 \times \text{percentage of fat}$$

for milk kept at 37 to 40° for 1.5 hours, or until there is no further change in the specific gravity.

The analysis of desiccated milk.—Determination of moisture and fat, C. PORCHER (*Ann. Falsif., 9 (1916), No. 97–98, pp. 450–456*).—The best procedure for the determination of moisture was found to be desiccation over phosphorus pentoxid for 48 hours, or 72 hours if necessary. Drying over sulphuric acid was found not to be satisfactory, and drying over calcium chlorid to be very slow. Ordinary drying in a steam oven caused a brown coloration in the material and an apparent change in some of its constituents.

The Röse-Gottlieb procedure was found to be entirely satisfactory for the determination of fat. Direct extraction with ether, however, consistently yielded low results.

The index of refraction of olive oil in relation to acidity and rancidity, A. CUTOLO (*Staz. Sper. Agr. Ital., 49 (1916), No. 7–8, pp. 377–387*).—Data relative to the acidity and index of refraction of 15 samples of oil from different Italian Provinces are submitted in tabular form.

The results show in general that where the acidity is less than 2 per cent the index of refraction is nearly always 63. With increasing acidity there is a decrease in the index of refraction. The index of refraction was also found to increase with the rancidity.

The identification of emodin-bearing drugs, W. S. HUBBARD (*Jour. Indus. and Engin. Chem., 9 (1917), No. 5, pp. 518–521*).

The biochemistry of tobacco.—I, Critical examination of methods for determining nitrogenous substances in tobacco leaves, G. PARIS (*Staz. Sper. Agr. Ital., 49 (1916), No. 7–8, pp. 405–424*).—The author examined the various methods for determining ammonia, amid, and nicotin nitrogen in tobacco, and submits the methods which he has adopted for the continued study of the subject.

The drying of fruits and vegetables, PEARL MACDONALD (*Penn. State Col. Ext. Circ. 61 (1917), pp. 12, figs. 10*).—This circular gives brief directions for drying cherries, currants, huckleberries, apples, pears, quinces, peaches, shelled peas and beans, green string beans, corn, and pumpkins, together with methods of preparing dried fruits and vegetables.

The influence of nitrogenous substances on the fermentation of fruit wines, H. MÜLLER-THURGAU and A. OSTERWALDER (*Landw. Jahrb. Schweiz, 31 (1917), No. 1, pp. 44–98, figs. 4*).—In the study reported it was found that, in cases where the fruit juices were fermented only by the organisms that were present on the fruit and without the addition of nitrogenous substances, there was great variation in the fermentation, not only in the time of beginning, but also in intensity. Even though the fermentation was slow where no pure yeast or nitrogenous material was added, all the juices proceeded to complete fermentation. Retardation of the fermentation in most of the juices is attributed to the small amount of assimilable nitrogen present, as was indicated by the addition of various materials.

The addition of ammonium chlorid stimulated the fermentation in juices to which no pure yeast had been added. The stimulation varied in the different juices, and also with the amount of ammonium chlorid added, and it was evident only after the yeast cells had multiplied and required more nitrogen. The addition of ammonia either exercised no influence or had an inhibitory action on the fermentation. The influence of ammonium phosphate showed no appreciable difference from that of ammonium chlorid.

The use of pure yeast always stimulated the fermentation. The results of the use of nitrogenous adjuvants with the pure yeast were similar to those obtained in the autofermentation experiments, the effect, however, being somewhat greater.

The addition of the nitrogenous substances to grape fermentations exercised no stimulating action. A greater number of yeast cells and a marked improvement in their general condition was observed in the cases where nitrogenous substances were used.

Chemical data relative to acid formation and other fermentation data are submitted in tabular and graphical form and discussed.

Chemical control in cane sugar factories, H. C. PRINSEN GEERLIGS (*London: Norman Rodger, 1917, rev. and enl. ed., pp. XII+140, fig. 1*).—This volume considers analytical methods, determination of quantities, stock taking, various calculations, factory and laboratory instruments, tables, and models of books.

[Report of the] bacteriological department, W. L. OWEN (*Louisiana Stas. Rpt. 1916, pp. 11–15*).—Continuing work on the deterioration of sugars and the principal factors affecting it (E. S. R., 35, p. 316), a number of samples were inoculated in duplicate and a triplicate portion retained as a control. Only 10 per cent of the inoculated samples showed a greater deterioration than the controls. The results indicate that "the original infection of the majority of these samples was sufficient to cause their deterioration when suitable conditions for this action obtained."

Experiments conducted to determine the relative rate of deterioration of sugar with varying amounts of absorbed moisture showed that deterioration occurred only in samples having a factor higher than 0.25.

In a study to determine the relations between the rate of deterioration and the density of the films of molasses surrounding the sugar crystals a series of sugars was used which had factors of safety varying from 0.136 to 0.677, with molasses films varying in density from 69 to 79° Brix. The samples were stored for three months and a percentage deterioration was noted of 0.7 on a sugar with a factor of 0.677, 0.6 on a sugar with a factor of 0.369, and 1.42 with a sample having a factor of 0.472. The small deterioration on the sugar with the factor 0.677, which would ordinarily be considered very unsafe, is indicated as being probably due to the lack of certain impurities usually present in plantation granulated sugar.

Experiments on the influence of cold storage on the keeping of sugars suggested the possible cold-storage warehousing of white sugar. In a further study of the species of microorganisms causing the deterioration of sugar, the 18 bacterial cultures previously isolated showed a great variation in deteriorative power, some cultures having as much as four times the deteriorative power of others. Only two of the 20 yeast cultures isolated showed any inverting power, and this was very slight when compared to the action of the bacterial species. "Mixed inoculations of torula and bacteria invariably resuited in a deterioration greater than that produced by the torula, and much less than where pure cultures of bacteria were introduced alone. No symbiotic relationship between the two is therefore indicated in the results of these experiments.

"The maximum limit of density of the bacterial cultures was found to be between 60 and 72° Brix, while no limit has yet been found for the activity of the torula in fermenting invert sugar. Above 65° Brix the action of the torula upon sugar solutions containing both sucrose and invert sugar is exclusively confined to the latter, thus explaining the decrease in invert sugar during the storage of sugars with low factors of safety. The bacterial species associated with the deterioration of sugars have a very low minimum nutrient requirement. Standard granulated sugar and distilled water in a 35 per cent solution showed a loss of sucrose 2.69 per cent when inoculated with cultures of deteriorative bacteria. Plantation granulated sugar showed a loss of 2.9 per cent under the same condition. The addition of 1 cc. of a 1 : 1,000 molasses solution to 100 cc. of the standard granulated sugar solution gave a deterioration of 2.8 per cent, while the same addition to the plantation granulated resulted in a deterioration of 4.9 per cent. The addition of 1 cc. of a 1 : 1,000 dirt suspension caused a deterioration of plantation granulated of 8.3 per cent. These experiments emphasize the importance of cleanliness in the manufacture of white sugar of keeping qualities."

Experiments to determine acquisition of deteriorative power by the same species of bacteria as those found in sugar, but isolated from other products, showed in one case an increase in deteriorative power of about 1,100 per cent when grown for successive generations in sugar solution. "This would indicate that the most active infection of sugar comes from old sources of contamination in the house, rather than from the dirt immediately introduced into the juice from the soil adhering to the cane."

In experiments made on the retention of microorganisms contained in their respective massecuites by unwashed sugars, the results showed that on an average 13 per cent of the microorganisms of the massecuite were retained by the sugar crystals. They were reduced approximately one-half by washing.

The chemical changes which are caused by defecation of sorghum juice for sirup manufacture, A. K. ANDERSON (*Jour. Indus. and Engin. Chem., 9* (*1917*), *No. 5, pp. 492–499*).—The results of a study by the author at the Minnesota Experiment Station which included both factory and laboratory trials show that the acidity of the juice of sorghum cane decreases during defecation and increases during evaporation with the lime and phosphate methods. The acidity was found to vary inversely with the amount of lime used. The volume of the lead subacetate precipitate is not considered a good indication of the efficiency of defecation. In cases of high acidity there is a large precipitate. The ash content was found to increase after lime had been added. In the phosphate method a decrease in the amount of ash was noted. Calcium oxid increased during defecation and decreased during evaporation. An apparent increase in sucrose and decrease in reducing sugar was observed during defecation.

"The nitrogen content decreases during defecation. In cane which has stood after being cut the nitrogen is changed to a nonprecipitable form which is not removed by defecation. Solids-not-sugar decrease during defecation and evaporation, the larger decrease being during the latter process. The color of the juice is not darkened materially until more than the theoretical amount of lime has been added. The amount of lime to produce alkalinity is 2.2 times the theoretical amount.

"Acidity in sirups varies inversely with the amount of lime used. In sirups the total ash, insoluble ash, and calcium oxid increase with the amount of lime added. Sucrose increases and dextrose decreases with the amount of lime used. Crystallization is due to a high percentage of dry matter, a relatively high sucrose content, and a juice relatively free from 'gummy materials.' It occurs most frequently in samples where lime was used in defecation. The darkness of color of a sirup varies directly with the amount of lime used in defecation and with the time required for evaporation.

"The phosphate and lime methods give the best tasting sirups. For economic reasons the lime method is considered the better to use. The theoretical amount of lime gives proper defecation with the minimum darkening of the juice. The titration of the juice is an efficient method of factory control."

The data are submitted in tabular form.

Sugar-beet sirup, C. O. TOWNSEND and H. C. GORE (*U. S. Dept. Agr., Farmers' Bul. 823* (*1917*), *pp. 13, figs. 9*).—Detailed directions for growing sugar beets for sirup and for making a sirup from the beets are given. The preparation of the sirup consists in extracting the sliced beets with water at from 70 to 80° C. (158 to 176° F.), and evaporating the extract to the desired consistency. The sirup, although dark in color, is indicated as being very palatable and nutritious and to be easily prepared.

Some American vegetable food oils, their sources and methods of production, H. S. BAILEY (*U. S. Dept. Agr. Yearbook 1916, pp. 159–176, pls. 4*).—This article describes the commercial methods for producing olive, cottonseed, peanut, and corn oils, and their uses.

Brazilian oilseeds, E. R. BOLTON and DOROTHY G. HEWER (*Analyst, 42* (*1917*), *No. 491, pp. 35–45, pl. 1*).—Tabulated data of the physical and chemical constants of the oils of the seeds of 10 palms and the oils of 10 other oilseeds found in Brazil are submitted. Brief botanical notes on the seeds, together with notes on the properties of the oils, are also given.

The natural accelerator of Para rubber, H. P. Stevens (*Jour. Soc. Chem. Indus., 36 (1917), No. 7, pp. 365–370*).—Experimental data are submitted which show "that the rapid curing property of matured coagulum is due to organic nitrogenous bases formed during putrefaction, as small quantities of these bases can be extracted from the rapidly curing rubber which has undergone putrefaction while only a trace can be extracted from the ordinary pale crêpe." Similar bases were extracted from the residual liquors. Very small amounts of these bases were found to exert a marked effect in promoting vulcanization.

METEOROLOGY.

Hail in the United States, A. J. Henry (*U. S. Mo. Weather Rev., 45 (1917), No. 3, pp. 94–99, pls. 5*).—This article reviews geographic, seasonal, and general distribution of hail in the United States and discusses theories of hail. It is based upon 167 records covering an area of 3,026,789 square miles.

"The region of most frequent occurrence, four or more storms per year, is in southeastern Wyoming and eastward therefrom, including the western portions of Kansas, Nebraska, and Oklahoma. Adjoining this region of maximum frequency, especially to the eastward, the average number of storms per annum decreases to three. . . .

"Hail in the United States is, in general, a phenomenon of the warm season, the only notable exception being along the immediate Pacific coast from San Francisco northward. On that strip of coast hail occurs chiefly from November to March, a season that is substantially the same as that of the rains in that part of the United States. . . . Practically no damage to agricultural crops by hail is possible in the Pacific Coast States and only small damage is possible in the Gulf States both by reason of the infrequency of the phenomenon and the absence of crops at the time of greatest frequency. In Kansas, Nebraska, South Dakota, western Iowa, and northwestern Missouri hail falls at a time when destruction of crops is possible."

Reviewing the data for hail distribution in Europe, as well as in the United States, the conclusion is reached that "hailstorms over both land and water occur most frequently in temperate latitudes, the belt of greatest frequency being between the thirty-fifth and the sixtieth parallels in both hemispheres. They are infrequent in the Tropics, especially over the lowlands. In Arctic and Antarctic regions, while hail occurs more frequently than was once supposed, lack of precise observations make it somewhat conjectural whether the hail reported is graupel or true hail."

It is stated that in the United States the region of greatest thunderstorm frequency does not coincide with the region of greatest hail activity, and although hail is generally associated with tornadoes the author doubts whether the fundamental conditions for the formation of a tornado are always present in a hailstorm.

Observations on the possible influence of violent cannonading on rainfall, Sebert (*Compt. Rend. Acad. Sci. [Paris], 164 (1917), No. 19, pp. 703, 704*).—Supplementing a previous note (E. S. R., 37, p. 418) the author calls attention to a series of observations which have been made at the Central Meteorological Bureau at Paris which may be useful in the study of this subject.

Lightning and forest fires in California, A. H. Palmer (*U. S. Mo. Weather Rev., 45 (1917), No. 3, pp. 99–102, pls. 3, fig. 1*).—It is shown in this article that lightning is an important cause of forest fires, and the development of the fire-weather warning service, as well as the making available of facilities to subdue forest fires, is urged.

Bacteriological study of the air of Buenos Aires, H. RIGANTI (*1. Conf. Soc. Sud Amer. Hig., Microbiol. y Patol., 1916, pp. 873–885, fig. 1*).—Results of examinations of samples of air taken under various conditions in different parts of the city show wide variation in the germ content, depending upon conditions of temperature, illumination, ventilation, and character of the street surfaces. Samples taken from the more densely populated parts of the city, where traffic is greatest and the streets narrow and unpaved, showed a high germ content. Under similar conditions with stone pavement the germ content was slightly smaller, and it was decidedly less where the streets were paved with asphalt. The width of the streets, the height of the buildings, and the density of the population influenced the germ content to a marked extent.

Monthly Weather Review (*U. S. Mo. Weather Rev., 45 (1917), Nos. 3, pp. 91–148, pls. 17, figs. 8; 4, pp. 149–201, pls. 10, figs. 25*).—In addition to weather forecasts, river and flood observations, and seismological reports for March and April, 1917; lists of additions to the Weather Bureau Library and of recent papers on meteorology and seismology; notes on the weather of the months; solar and sky radiation measurements at Washington, D. C., during March and April, 1917; condensed climatological summaries; and the usual climatological tables and charts, these numbers contain the following articles:

No. 3.—Hail in the United States (illus.), by A. J. Henry (see p. 512); Lightning and Forest Fires in California (illus.), by A. H. Palmer (see p. 512); The Density of Snow, with a Note on the Disappearance and Settling of Snow in 1915–16 near Reno, Nev. (illus.), by A. J. Henry and H. F. Alciatore; A Modern Chinese Meteorological Monthly; Meteorological Observations on United States Lightships, by H. E. Williams; Avalanche Wind at Juneau, January 26, 1917, by M. B. Summers; Tornado at Cincinnati, Ohio, March 11, 1917 (illus.), by W. C. Devereaux; Tornadoes of March 11, 1917, in Montgomery County, Ohio (illus.), by R. F. Young; Unusual Hailstorm at Ballinger, Tex.; Severe Local Storm at San Diego, Cal., February, 1917; Winter of 1916–17 at Greenwich, England (reprinted); Cold Waves and Freezing Temperatures at Tampa, Fla., by W. J. Bennett; and A Skew Frequency Curve Applied to Stream Gauge Data (illus.), by W. G. Reed.

No. 4.—Equation of Horizontal Rainbows (illus.) (reprinted), by K. Otobe; Improved Kite Hygrometer and Its Records (illus.), by W. R. Gregg; Anemometer Records on a Buffalo Office Building Compared with Those Secured Near the Surface of Lake Erie (illus.), by B. C. Kadel; Some New Instruments for Oceanographical Research (illus.), by H. Pettersson; On Working Up Precipitation Observations (trans.), by H. Meyer; Tornado of April 5, 1917, at Tampa, Fla. (illus.), by W. J. Bennett; Tornado of March 23, 1917, at New Albany, Ind. (illus.), by F. J. Walz; Fish Killed by the Cold Wave of February 2–4, 1917, in Florida, by R. H. Finch; Relation between Rainfall and Run-off in Hillebrand Glen, Nuuanu Valley, Oahu, Hawaii (illus.), by R. C. Rice; and The Missouri Earthquake of April 9, 1917 (illus.), by R. H. Finch.

Meteorological, magnetic, and seismic observations of the College of Belen, Havana, 1916, L. GANGOITI (*Observatorio Meteorologico, Magnetico y Seismico del Colegio de Belen de la Compañia de Jesus en la Habana, año de 1916. Habana, 1917, pp. 94*).—Detailed daily and monthly summaries are given and the characteristic features of each month are described in notes.

Meteorology, J. B. TRIVETT (*N. S. Wales Statis. Reg., 1915–16, pt. 6, pp. 345–414*).—Detailed tabular summaries of observations at Sydney and other places in New South Wales during 1915 on temperature, pressure, precipitation, and wind are given.

SOILS—FERTILIZERS.

Edgar County soils, C. G. HOPKINS, J. G. MOSIER, E. VAN ALSTINE, and F. W. GARRETT (*Illinois Sta. Soil Rpt. 15 (1917), pp. 56, pls. 2, figs. 8*).—Edgar County is located in the central eastern border of Illinois and lies principally in the early Wisconsin glaciation, with the southern part in the lower Illinoisan glaciation. The topography varies from flat to slightly rolling. The southeastern part is quite hilly.

The soils of the county are classed as upland prairie soils rich in organic matter, upland timber soils, terrace soils, and swamp and bottom lands. The brown silt loam upland prairie soil covers 52.37 per cent of the area, and the yellow-gray silt loam upland timber soils, 19.17 per cent.

Soil survey of Clinton County, Iowa, H. W. HAWKER and F. B. HOWE (*U. S. Dept. Agr., Adv. Sheets Field Oper., Bur Soils, 1915, pp. 64, pls 3, fig. 1, map 1*).— This survey, made in cooperation with the Iowa Experiment Station, deals with the soils of an area of 442,240 acres on the central eastern border of Iowa. "The county comprises three physiographic divisions. a plain of Kansan drift covered by Mississippi loess in the northern and western parts of the county, a plain of modified Iowan drift in the southern part, and an alluvial plain adjoining the Mississippi River and its tributaries in the county. . . .

"The soils of the county are derived mainly from loess. glacial drift, and alluval deposits." Including river wash and muck. 24 soil types of 13 series are mapped, of which the Memphis, Muscatine, and Carrington silt loams cover 29.2, 22.2, and 17.1 per cent of the area, respectively.

The soil resources of Maryland, A. G. MCCALL (*Rpt. Md. Agr. Soc., 1 (1916), pp. 211–224*).—This is an address delivered to the Maryland Agricultural Society in which some of the problems concerning the maintenance of the fertility of Maryland soils were discussed on the basis of experience at the Maryland Experiment Station.

Soil survey of Schoharie County, N. Y., E. T. MAXON and G. L. FULLER (*U. S. Dept. Agr., Adv. Sheets Field Oper., Bur. Soils, 1915, pp. 34, pls. 4, fig. 1, map 1*).—This survey, made in cooperation with the New York State College of Agriculture, deals with the soils of an area of 396,800 acres in eastern New York. "The topographic features are the rolling uplands in the northern part of the county and the rugged mountainous section in the southern part." . . . "Practically the entire county, with the exception of the extreme northeastern part, is adequately drained."

The soils are grouped as ice laid, stream terrace. lake laid, and alluvial soils. Including muck, rough stony land, rock outcrop. and meadow, 22 soil types of 14 series are mapped, of which the Lordstown stony silt loam and the Volusia silt loam cover 46.4 and 10 per cent of the area, respectively.

Geology of southern Ohio, W. STOUT (*Geol. Survey Ohio, 4. ser., Bul. 20 (1916), pp. 723, pls. 35*).—This report, including Jackson and Lawrence Counties and parts of Pike, Scioto, and Gallia. contains information which should be of value in a study of the soils of Ohio.

Soil survey of Fairfax and Alexandria Counties, Va., W. T. CARTER, JR., and C. K. YINGLING, JR. (*U. S. Dept. Agr., Adv. Sheets Field Oper., Bur. Soils, 1915, pp. 43, pls. 4, fig. 1, map 1*).—This survey deals with the soils of an area of 287,360 acres in extreme northeastern Virginia. the topography of which ranges from gently undulating to very rolling and hilly, being predominantly gently rolling. Drainage is said to be good throughout. The western two-thirds of the area lies within the Piedmont plateau province and the eastern third within the Coastal Plain province.

The soils are of residual, sedimentary, and alluvial origin. Including clay pits and tidal marsh, 26 soil types of 19 series are mapped, of which the Chester and Manor loams cover 23.9 and 22.8 per cent of the area, respectively.

A study of the principal plantation soil types as found on the Island of Hawaii, P. S. BURGESS (*Hawaii. Sugar Planters' Sta., Agr. and Chem. Bul. 45 (1917), pp. 100, pl. 1, figs. 3*).—This bulletin discusses the mineralogy, chemistry, physics, and biology of soils in general and deals with those of the Island of Hawaii in particular. The soils of the island are classed physically as high humus clay and silty clay loams. Colloidal aluminum and iron hydroxids are said to give the soils their apparent clayey character.

"The hygroscopic coefficients vary from 9 to over 26 per cent when determined by Hilgard's standard method, while the optimum moisture capacity averages about 45 per cent of the dry weight of the soils. The 'free water' varies from 15 to 38 per cent, while the maximum moisture-holding capacity is in all cases well above that for average mainland soils. These soils do not usually cake badly unless thoroughly puddled. When worked under optimum conditions they are fluffy and show good tilth. . . .

"The soils, with but few exceptions, are high in total nitrogen, but its availability is universally low. The same is more or less true of phosphoric acid. Potash, both total and available, is high in all of the soils examined except in those of the Hilo district. . . . The amounts of total and available soil potash follow with surprising regularity the amounts of total potash as determined in the final molasses and in the molasses ashes from the mills of the several plantations. The total lime figures vary from over 5 per cent in the alkaline Kau soils to less than 0.2 per cent in acid Hamakua. . . .

"The lime requirements for the surface soils vary from 1 ton of calcium carbonate to 11 tons, depending on location. . . . The amounts of alkali salts (the chlorids, carbonates, and sulphates of sodium) are in all cases negligible. All of the surface soils are fair ammonifiers."

Six series of nitrification experiments are also reported. "In the first, the soils received no additions of nitrogen but were incubated under standard conditions of moisture and temperature to ascertain the nitrifiability of their own organic nitrogen. In the second, ammonium sulphate was added; in the third, dried blood; in the fourth, dried blood plus sufficient calcium carbonate to exactly neutralize acidity; in the fifth, dried blood plus gypsum; and in the sixth, dried blood plus reverted phosphate."

It was found that "considering the large quantities of total nitrogen which these soils contain, the absolute amounts and the percentages of it nitrified are very low. Ammonium sulphate nitrogen is nitrified approximately twice as fast as dried blood nitrogen. As an average for the soils of the entire island, the addition of lime doubles the nitrification of dried blood. In some instances it multiplies it by three and four. Gypsum has practically no effect upon nitrification in these soils. In some instances a loss is recorded. Reverted phosphate increases nitrification by aproximately 35 per cent.

"Nitrogen fixation as determined both by solution and by soil culture methods is fair in Hawaii soils. Azotobacter forms are well distributed. Three different species (*A. chroococcum, A. vinelandii,* and *A. vinelandii,* n. sp. ?) were isolated in pure cultures and tested for nitrogen fixation in both solutions and soils."

A discussion of the analytical methods used in this work is appended.

Method of botanical soil investigations on the Voronezh Zemstvo Experimental Field, S. K. CHAĬNOV and S. S. MUSHCHENKO (*Mctodika Pochvenno-Botanicheskikh Izslědovanii na Voronezhskom Opytnom Polĕ Gubernskago Zemstva. [Voronezh]: Voronezh Prov., 1915, pp. V+17*).—The method used consists primarily of determining the relation of relief to soil characteristics on every section of a field. The soil characteristics are determined by the morphology; botanical growths; the relation of climate to soil temperature and moisture; and physical, mechanical, and chemical composition.

The degradation of the chernozems of the western part of the Northern Caucasus, S. A. IAKOVLEV (*Pochvověděnïe* (*Pédologie*), *16* (*1914*), *No. 4, pp. 1–20; 17* (*1915*), *No. 1, pp. 1–35*).—The chernozem soils of the region are discussed with reference to mechanical and chemical composition.

Soil flora studies.—I, The general characteristics of the microscopic flora of soil: II, Methods best adapted to the study of the soil flora, H. J. CONN (*New York State Sta. Tech. Bul. 57* (*1917*), *pp. 3–42*).—This is the first and second of a series of five reports on a study conducted for eight years on the microscopic flora of various New York State soils, in which determinations of the total number of bacteria have been made by the plate method. About 1,000 pure cultures of different organisms were isolated and their general characteristics studied.

Nonspore-forming bacteria (mostly immotile rods) were found to be the most abundant of all soil microorganisms. Next to them in abundance were the various types of Actinomyces. Certain spore-forming bacteria were also found, but not in great numbers and apparently they are not of great importance in normal soil. It is thought that soil bacteria are quite different from those found in milk, cheese, or water and that soil has its own characteristic bacterial flora.

A discussion of the methods used in these studies, the reasons for using them, and their possible development is also included.

Soil flora studies.—III, Spore-forming bacteria in soil, H. J. CONN (*New York State Sta. Tech. Bul. 58* (*1917*), *pp. 3–16, figs. 4*).—This is the third of the reports of studies on the flora of New York soils and deals with the spore-forming bacteria of soil.

"Certain spore-forming bacteria are always found in soil, but in comparatively small numbers. The three most abundant spore formers found in the soils investigated are *Bacillus megatherium*, *B. mycoides*, and *B. cereus*. *B. simplex* occurs in somewhat smaller numbers. Occasionally other spore-forming bacteria have been encountered, but not in large enough numbers to be considered important.

"In the past, the spore-forming bacteria have been considered important soil bacteria. The technic used in this work, however, shows that they comprise but a small part of the flora and apparently occur in normal soil only in the form of spores. This indicates that they are ordinarily inactive in soil."

Soil flora studies.—IV, Nonspore-forming bacteria in soil, H. J. CONN (*New York State Sta. Tech. Bul. 59* (*1917*), *pp. 3–18*).—This is the fourth of the reports of studies on the soil flora of New York soils and deals with the nonspore-forming bacteria in soil.

"The majority of colonies on culture plates made from soil are those of nonspore-forming bacteria. The only nonspore former that has been successfully identified with previously described species is *Pseudomonas fluorescens*. This organism is most abundant in freshly aerated soil or in soil to which organic matter has been recently added. It is known to cause ammonification in pure culture, and is therefore thought to take part in the decomposition of organic matter in soil. There are other liquefying nonspore formers in soil that seem to be closely related to P. *fluorescens*. They increase in numbers under much the same conditions and are thought to have similar functions.

"The great majority of the asporogenous bacteria of soil grow so poorly in ordinary laboratory media and produce such small noncharacteristic colonies on culture plates that little is known about them. One of the greatest present needs for a soil flora study is the development of methods by which the different species in this group may be identified.

" The numbers of the nonspore-forming bacteria in soil show greater fluctuations than do those of spore-forming bacteria or of Actinomycetes (the two other large groups of soil bacteria). High numbers of nonspore formers have been especially noticed in freshly aerated and in freshly manured soil. This indicates that they are among the most active soil microorganisms."

Soil flora studies.—V, Actinomycetes in soil, H. J. Conn (*New York State Sta. Tech. Bul. 60 (1917), pp. 3–25*).—This bulletin completes the series of five soil flora studies and deals with Actinomycetes or the higher bacteria.

It was found that " ordinarily from 12 to 50 per cent of the colonies on plate cultures made from soil are those of Actinomycetes. Description of species of Actinomycetes is at present very difficult. The literature abounds with descriptions that have become invalidated as better methods of study have been developed. About 70 different types have been found in the soils studied. Three of them are of fairly common occurrence. One of these three, *A. pheochromogenus* n. sp., is considered distinct enough to be given a specific name. One of the other two types agrees in cultural characteristics with the potato-scab organism, but its pathogenicity has not yet been tested. The other common type probably is not a distinct species. . . . The significance of these organisms in soil needs further investigation. There are good indications that they are active as well as numerically important."

Are all the soil bacteria and streptothrices that develop on dextrose agar azofiers? P. Emerson (*Soil Sci., 3 (1917), No. 5, pp. 417–421*).—Experiments conducted at the Iowa State College are reported in which it was found that 97 per cent of the soil organisms developing on dextrose agar plates were azofying bacteria. " No Azotobacter were present, showing clearly that there are a large number of organisms in the soil other than Azotobacter and Radicicola which have the power of fixing atmospheric nitrogen."

Some effects of organic growth-promoting substances (auximones) on the soil organisms concerned in the nitrogen cycle, F. A. Mockeridge (*Proc. Roy. Soc. [London], Ser. B, 89 (1917), No. B 621, pp. 508–533; abs. in Jour. Soc. Chem. Indus., 36 (1917), No. 13, p. 729*).—Experiments on the influence of so-called organic growth-promoting substances (auximones) extracted with water from bacterized peat on the nitrogen-fixing, nitrifying, denitrifying, and ammonifying bacteria of soil are reported.

It was found " that soluble humus, and especially that produced by bacterial decomposition, is a very important factor from the point of view of the activities of soil bacteria. Its effect upon the organisms appears to be largely independent of any inorganic matter which it may contain or any physical action brought about by its colloidal nature, and is shown to be due to the presence in the humus of growth-promoting substances or auximones. The influence of these auximones upon the organisms concerned in the nitrogen cycle may be briefly summed up in the general statement that they increase the rate of nitrogen fixation and nitrification, depress the rate of denitrification, and do not appreciably affect the rate of ammonification."

The organic matter of the soil.—V, A study of the nitrogen distribution in different soil types, C. A. Morrow and R. A. Gortner (*Soil Sci., 3 (1917), No. 4, pp. 297–331*).—Continuing previous work (E. S. R., 37, p. 121), studies conducted at the Minnesota Experiment Station are reported on the nitrogen distribution in fibrin, hydrolyzed in the presence of an ignited mineral subsoil; calcareous black peat; an acid sphagnum covered peat, hydrolyzed alone, in the presence of a mineral subsoil, and in the presence of stannous chlorid; an acid muck soil; samples of mineral surface soil representative of Fargo clay loam,

Fargo silt loam, Carrington silt loam, Hempstead silt loam, prairie covered loess, and forest covered loess; and extracts of a sphagnum covered peat soluble in (1) 1 per cent hydrochloric acid, (2) 4 per cent sodium hydroxid but precipitated by acid, and (3) 4 per cent sodium hydroxid and not precipitated by hydrochloric acid. The following conclusions are drawn:

"The figures for the ammonia nitrogen in a protein analysis are not appreciably changed when the hydrolysis is carried out in the presence of an ignited mineral soil equal to 20 times the weight of the protein material. The 'humin' nitrogen was greatly increased by hydrolysis in the presence of ignited mineral soil. The histidin fraction entirely disappeared. . . . The analysis of a pure protein in the presence of an ignited mineral soil does not give reliable results for the different fractions. Therefore, the figures obtained for the nitrogen distribution in soils are of value only when used for purposes of comparison. Such data should not be compared with analyses of pure proteins.

"Since practically all mineral soils give furfural on treatment with acid, it is very likely that a very considerable amount of the total humin nitrogen found is due to the presence of carbohydrates in the soil, which give rise to furfural during hydrolysis. This may combine with certain of the nitrogenous compounds and cause an increase in the humin nitrogen, as well as adsorb or occlude nitrogenous compounds in the 'humin' formed from furfural by polymerization.

"This investigation of the distribution of organic nitrogen in the soil has indicated a new fraction which should be recorded separately. This is the fraction of nitrogen removed from a colorless solution by calcium, iron, and aluminum hydroxids on the addition of calcium hydroxid. The nitrogen retained in this fraction must consist almost entirely of material of nonprotein origin, since the organic substances in this precipitate have been shown to be colorless organic compounds adsorbed by or combined with the metallic hydroxids. This fraction has been reported as nitrogen precipitated by calcium hydroxid.

"The true humin nitrogen remains in the residual soil after hydrolysis, but in addition nonhumin nitrogenous compounds are also retained in this fraction. The strength and volume of the hydrochloric acid used in hydrolysis has little effect on the nitrogen distribution of the hydrolysate, provided acid as strong as constant boiling acid is used, in the proportion of at least two parts of acid to one of soil. Results gained from a study of different soils indicate that the organic nitrogen dissolves during hydrolysis to almost the same extent regardless of the origin and nature of the soil. . . .

"In the comparison of the different extracts from sphagnum-covered peat the portion soluble in sodium hydroxid and not precipitated by hydrochloric acid gives a nitrogen distribution approximating very closely that of a normal plant protein. The nitrogen dissolving in the preliminary hydrochloric acid leaching shows a nitrogen distribution which is certainly not due exclusively to protein materials, e. g., an ammonia nitrogen percentage of 65.4 and amino nitrogen in the filtrate from bases of 17.11 per cent.

"The most significant fact brought out by this study is that the organic nitrogen distribution in different soil types is very uniform. This is to be expected, since it has been pointed out that the nitrogen distribution in soils is an average distribution of all the plant and animal nitrogenous products that find their way into the soil."

Further studies of the nitric nitrogen content of the country rock, R. STEW-ART and W. PETERSON (*Utah Sta. Bul. 150 (1917), pp. 5–20, fig. 1*).—The substance of this bulletin has been previously noted from another source (E. S. R., 36, p. 423).

The significance of nitrification as a factor in soil fertility, P. L. GAINEY (*Soil Sci., 3 (1917), No. 5, pp. 399–416*).—The author reviews the work of others bearing on the subject and work by himself at the Kansas Experiment Station in an effort to show that productivity in nonproductive soils, in so far as nitrogen is the limiting factor, is not limited by the processes of nitrification.

Soil constituents which inhibit the action of plant toxins, E. TRUOG and J. SYKORA (*Soil Sci., 3 (1917), No. 4, pp. 333–351, pls. 5*).—Studies conducted at the Wisconsin Experiment Station on the constituents of soils which inhibit the action of plant toxins are reported. The soils used were acid Plainfield sand and acid Wabash silt loam.

"The experiments indicate that chemical reactions are probably very important factors in lessening the harmful effects of plant toxins in soils. Calcium carbonate, a very common soil constituent, inhibited to a remarkable degree the toxicity, to wheat seedlings, of copper sulphate and copper nitrate. . . . The toxic effects of the strong base guanidin were markedly inhibited by the presence of either kaolin or an acid clay soil. . . . The results of pot experiments with natural soils indicate . . . that vanillin can, at most, be but a very slight factor in soil fertility if the soil has an adequate supply of the fertility elements and is not acid in reaction. Here, again, calcium carbonate seems to inhibit or prevent the harmful effects of the toxic agent. . . . It is believed that the data presented show that, in the amelioration of toxicity in soils, chemical reactions probably play fully as important a rôle as physical phenomena such as adsorption, and possibly the former have the greater effect."

The extraction and saturation of soils with volatile antiseptics, J. P. DU BUISSON (*Soil Sci., 3 (1917), No. 4, pp. 353–391, pls. 2*).—Experiments conducted at Cornell University with Dunkirk clay loam and Volusia silt loam soils to determine the influence of treatment with the volatile antiseptics alcohol, benzene, ether, commercial gasoline, and toluene are reported. The treatment in general consisted in extracting and saturating each type of soil with the individual solvents.

It was found that "the application of volatile antiseptics to the soils used in this investigation gave beneficial results on the crops subsequently grown thereon." A beneficial, residual effect was observed for the second crop after the application of the antiseptics, but this was in all cases less marked than with the first cropping. Both types of soils responded to treatment, but somewhat differently.

The volatile antiseptics had a definite effect upon the ammonification and nitrification of the soil, enhancing the former and inhibiting the latter. There was a tendency to increase the water-soluble salts of the soil. The effect of the antiseptics upon the ammonifying and nitrifying processes of the soils after two crops were grown seemed to disappear. No marked differences were observed as to plant growth and biological activity between the saturation and extraction methods of applying the antiseptics to the soil. In these experiments the physical condition of the soil as indicated by its ammonification and nitrification did not seem to be the cause of the influences noted upon plant growth and bacterial action. By the extraction of soil with alcohol, a substance was removed which was toxic in water cultures but not at all toxic when in the soil itself. The development of acids in the soil as a result of some action or change of the alcohol was found to be too slight to account for the marked effects of volatile antiseptics upon plant growth and bacterial action.

It is finally concluded that "the beneficial influences obtained by treating the soil with volatile antiseptics can not be ascribed to a change in physical condition, to a suppression of some toxic material, or to a development of acids from the action of the antiseptics. The method of applying the antiseptics seems to have no marked influence upon the results obtained. The closely coordinated stimulation of plant and bacterial activity due to the treatment of the soil with volatile antiseptics points strongly toward a biological interpretation, with due regard for the chemical considerations, of the effects therefrom."

Farms, forests, and erosion, S. T. Dana (*U. S. Dept. Agr. Yearbook 1916, pp. 107–134, pls. 10*).—This article gives data on the injury to farm lands and agricultural and other industries of the United States resulting from erosion, floods, and washing. A direct relation between these and deforestation of the higher areas is shown.

It is concluded that " the problem of erosion and its control forms an integral part of any comprehensive plan for the development of our natural resources. If all land were put to its best use and so handled as to maintain its productivity the problem would be solved. This result can be attained, however, only by marked change in our present practice. A stop must be put to reckless destruction of the forest, to uncontrolled fires, to overgrazing, and to careless farming. For the sake of the farmer in particular and the public in general, steps should be taken to retain and restore the forest cover in the mountains under public ownership or supervision. There should be brought home to the people as a whole the extent and seriousness of erosion and the necessity for its control by the community."

Measuring the surface temperature of soil, A. A. Dobiasha (Dobiache) (*Zap. Selsk. Khoz. Inst. Imp. Petra I* (*Mem. Inst. Agron. Emp. Pierre I*), *1 (1916), pp. 101, 102, pl. 1*).—Methods of surface soil temperature measurements used in 30 years' experiments in Russia are described and compared. The methods of slightly pushing the thermometer into the surface soil or of placing it on the surface and covering it with soil were found to give inaccurate results.

In a third method three thermoelements on ebonite supports and made of thin wire were placed one below the other at equal distances of 1.5 mm. and covered with soil so that the upper one remained visible. Three mercury thermometers covered with soil and three open thermometers were placed parallel to the thermoelements. The day of test was hot and sunny and the temperature of the surface layer reached 60° C.

It was found that the mercury thermometers covered with soil showed a mean temperature some 2.4° higher than the uncovered ones. The thermoelements acted differently, the upper one showing the highest temperature and the difference reaching in some cases 5°. The temperature of the upper element reacted promptly to changes in temperature due to the passing of clouds before the sun. Only at depths of from 1.5 to 2 mm. were the temperatures recorded equal to that of the covered thermometer. It is concluded that the latter gives more accurate results. but that during strong radiation none gives trustworthy results.

Studies on soil colloids.—II, Influence of colloids on electrical conductivity of salts, M. I. Wolkoff (*Soil Sci., 3 (1917), No. 5, pp. 423–430, figs. 2*).—Experiments conducted at Rutgers College are reported in which fifth-normal solutions of aluminum potassium sulphate, ferric sulphate, lead nitrate. and hydrochloric acid and a saturated solution of calcium hydroxid were added to a colloidal solution obtained from a fresh clay soil.

It was found that " the inorganic colloid particles, as found in clay, especially the colloidal gels, hinder the electrical conductivity of salt solutions. The causes for such an interference lie possibly in (1) the fact that colloidal particles moving comparatively slowly are in the pathway of the free ions, and (2) that the change of the structure of the gel at the point of coagulation results in an increase in the adsorptive capacity of colloids. The adsorption of electrolytes by the gel increases with the increase of the electrolyte present for coagulation. The coagulation of the colloidal solutions by means of certain electrolytes can be employed for separation of colloids from crystalloids, provided that only a minimum amount of electrolyte be used for a complete coagulation in order to reduce to the minimum the error due to adsorption."

Facilities for lysimeter and outdoor pot culture work at the station, J. F. BARKER (*New York State Sta. Tech. Bul. 61 (1917), pp. 3-10, pls. 2, figs. 3*).—The equipment is described and illustrated.

[Fertilizer experiments], B. S. ÉMANUÉL (*Svodnyĭ Otchet Stĕti Kollektivnykh Opytov za Trekhafĕtïe 1910-1913 g. Stavropol, Russia: Stavropol-Kavkaz. Selsk. Khoz. Opytn. Sta., 1914, pp. 39*).—Fertilizer experiments on clay soil intermixed with dark loam at the Stavropol Caucasian experiment station for the years 1910 to 1913, inclusive, are reported.

It was found that phosphates generally increased the yield of all crops. Superphosphate was more effective on spring cereals than Thomas phosphate, and gave about equal results with potatoes. Sodium nitrate when used alone increased crop yields very little and when added with phosphates seemed to decrease the influence of the latter on crop yields. Potash frequently increased the yield of potatoes but when used with phosphates it decreased their effect. Phosphates increased the size of potato tubers but did not seem to affect their starch content. Broadcasting of fertilizers followed by deep plowing was apparently as effective as row fertilizing.

The stable-manure business of big cities, C. C. FLETCHER (*U. S. Dept. Agr. Yearbook 1916, pp. 375-379, pl. 1*).—This is a brief description of the process of collection, shipment, grading, storage, and treatment of stable manure from cities in the United States.

The effect of soil reaction on the availability of ammonium sulphate, R. C. COOK and F. E. ALLISON (*Soil Sci., 3 (1917), No. 5, pp. 487-498, figs. 2*).—Experiments conducted at Rutgers College are reported in which sand, silt loam, and sandy loam soils, with respective lime requirements per acre of 3,000, 3,000, and 4,000 lbs., were planted to buckwheat and treated with an excess of potassium and phosphorus and varying amounts of calcium oxid and ammonium sulphate.

From the standpoint of the utilization of the nitrogen applied it was found that the heavier the soil the less effect calcium oxid has in increasing the availability of ammonium sulphate. Buckwheat seemed to use ammonium sulphate almost as well in the heavier soils in the absence of lime as in its presence.

It was further found that "small applications of calcium oxid produced practically as large yields of buckwheat as where enough lime was added to neutralize all of the acidity or make the soil distinctly alkaline. Buckwheat grown on the more acid soils usually showed a higher percentage of nitrogen but the total yield of the crop was smaller. For this reason the recovery of the nitrogen from the more acid soils in many cases was as great as, or even greater than, that from the alkaline soils.

"The beneficial effects of calcium oxid on acid soils were much more noticeable on the sandy soils than on the silt loam. The addition of calcium oxid to acid soils allows the soil nitrogen to be made available to such an extent as to supply the needs of the crop. Hence, the use of ammonium sulphate on alkaline soils may produce a smaller increase in yield over checks than where the same amount of the fertilizer is added to an acid soil.

" Buckwheat is able to utilize the nitrogen from ammonium sulphate at an acidity of from 3,000 to 4,000 lbs. of calcium oxid per acre. The nitrogen is either taken up as ammonia or else nitrification proceeds to a considerable extent in the presence of the acid."

The forms of phosphorus in granitic soils, C. VINCENT (*Compt. Rend. Acad. Sci.* [*Paris*], *164* (1917), *No. 10, pp. 409–411; abs. in Jour. Soc. Chem. Indus.. 36 (1917), No. 8, pp. 465, 466*).—It is pointed out that while granitic soils are generally supposed to be poor in phosphoric acid since they respond to phosphatic applications, the application of lime or chalk has a similar effect. This is attributed to the existence of the phosphoric acid in unavailable organic combinations with humus which must be neutralized before the phosphoric acid becomes available.

" If these soils be digested near the boiling point with concentrated nitric acid for four hours, only a portion of the total phosphoric acid is found on analysis, but if the soil be first neutralized with lime, or dried and calcined. before digestion. the whole of the phosphoric acid is obtained; the difference may be very considerable. Under these conditions the granitic soils are found to be moderately rich in phosphoric acid and some of them very rich. In the majority of cases the application of a light dressing of lime, calculated for four to five years, combined if necessary with potash and farmyard manures, will suffice to make the phosphoric acid and a portion of the nitrogen readily available."

Report on availability of potash, E. E. VANATTA (*Jour. Assoc. Off. Agr. Chem., 3 (1917), No. 1, pp. 105–107*).—Pot experiments with sweet corn conducted at the Missouri Experiment Station are reported in which a mixture of washed quartz sand with sufficient fine ground feldspar to supply 0.06 per cent total potash was used. Sufficient other fertilizer for maximum plant growth was also added. Other individual treatments included the addition of blue grass at the rate of 30.000 lbs. per acre, heating the feldspar to 100° C.. and the addition of calcium carbonate at the rate of 4.500 lbs. per acre, of calcium oxid at the rate of 3,000 lbs. per acre. and of starch at the rate of 10,000 lbs. per acre.

It was found that " the addition of a large amount of organic matter in the form of blue grass . . . had a beneficial effect on plant growth, either by furnishing available potash on its decay or by liberating potash from the feldspar. The addition of organic matter in the form of starch . . . retarded plant growth. Calcium carbonate apparently . . . had slight effect on plant growth, while calcium oxid apparently . . . retarded plant growth. The results of this work indicate that the potash compounds in feldspathic rock are of little value in furnishing readily available plant food."

Importance of developing our natural resources of potash, F. W. BROWN (*U. S. Dept. Agr. Yearbook 1916, pp. 301–310, pl. 1*).—This article deals with the natural and artificial potash resources of the United States. including by-products of cement manufacture, blast-furnace gas, wool and wood wastes, natural lake brines, alunite, and kelp. Processes of extracting potash from these are briefly described.

"At present the Pacific kelps appear to be one of the most hopeful sources of an adequate supply of potash for the country's needs."

Fertilizer experiments with lime on tobacco soils, 1912–13, N. H. COHEN (*Proefstat. Vorstenland. Tabak* [*Dutch East Indies*], *Meded. 17 (1915), pp. 5–15*).—Fertilizer experiments to determine the influence of liming on the quality, color, and burning qualities of tobacco showed that liming did not increase the tobacco yield but improved its quality and color and the color of the ash. Its burning qualities were injured, however.

Fertilizer experiments with lime on tobacco soils, 1913–14, E. SIDENIUS (*Proefstat. Vorstenland. Tabak* [*Dutch East Indies*], *Meded. 17 (1915), pp. 19–40*).—Experiments on the influence of liming on tobacco soils are reported.

It was found that in some cases the quality of the tobacco was improved and in some cases injured. In the majority of cases the lime was especially active. Liming reduced the percentage of light-colored leaves, but in no case the burning qualities of the tobacco. The color of the ash was improved by liming in some cases, but in most cases no difference was observed between limed and unlimed plats. The results as a whole are taken to indicate that no great profit resulted from the liming of tobacco soils.

Ground limestone for use in New York State, J. F. BARKER and W. W. BAER (*New York State Sta. Bul. 430 (1917), pp. 21–32, pls. 4, fig. 1*).—This gives data on the distribution of limestone production in New York, reports analyses of 69 samples of ground limestone produced by New York plants and by companies in near-by States shipping limestone into New York, and gives general information on the comparative values of ground limestones and on their use in agriculture.

The international trade in fertilizers and chemical products useful to agriculture, P. VAN HISSENHOVEN (*Internat. Inst. Agr. Rome, Internat. Crop Rpt. and Agr. Statis., 8 (1917), No. 3, pp. 239–308*).—This, the sixth of these semiannual reviews, is dated March, 1917, and gives comparatively complete statistics for 1913 and 1914 and incomplete data for 1915 and 1916. The data are taken from both official and private sources. Generally speaking, the more recent information is largely from private sources, while the official data are, as a rule, not later than 1913 and 1914.

It is stated that the phosphate mined in the United States fell to 1,865,123 metric tons in 1915. The shipment of Florida hard rock was almost insignificant in 1916, namely, 33,000 tons, of which 4,600 tons was for domestic use. The decline in shipment of land pebble was not so great. "In 1916 and in 1915 shipments to countries other than the United States were practically identical in quantity, but they both show a deficiency of nearly 700,000 tons as compared with the shipments of this description of phosphates effected prior to the war." Shortage of labor and of sulphuric acid are named as causes of this decline. The exports of Tunisian phosphate increased in 1916 to 352,000 tons as compared with 226,000 tons in 1915 and 355,000 tons in 1914. There was increased activity in 1916 in exploitation of the Pacific islands phosphates. The exports of Egyptian phosphates declined something over one-third in 1916.

The estimated total production of potash salts in Germany in 1916 is reported to have been 900,000 tons. Of the 24,638 tons of saltpeter produced in India in 1916, 21,749 tons went to Great Britain and Ireland. The average prices per metric ton of the principal potash salts in the United States (New York) during 1916 were as follows: Kainit, $45.26; sulphate of potash, $315; and muriate of potash, $400. The prices for these salts remained fairly constant during the year, being slightly lower on the whole at the end than at the beginning of the year.

The production of nitrate of soda was slightly less during the second half of 1916 than during the first. The stocks on hand on the Chilean coast were not more than 718,315 tons at the close of 1916. The total production for the year was 2,914,542 tons, and the export, 2,991,786. The exports to Europe and Egypt amounted to 957,772 tons during the last half of 1916, as compared with 673,348 tons during the corresponding period of 1915. The exports to the United States during the second half of 1916 amounted to 592,901 tons, as against 452,582 tons in 1915. Of the amount exported to the United States, 526,261 tons went to the Atlantic States and 51,683 tons to the Pacific States. The average price in New York during 1916 was $72.35 per metric ton.

The statistics for production of sulphate of ammonia during 1916 are very incomplete. The production in Great Britain and Ireland from all sources in that year was 445,029 tons, of which 263,473 tons was exported. The production in the United States was 294,835 tons, as compared with 199,571 tons in 1915. Of this amount, 246,754 tons was obtained from coke ovens and 48,081 tons from gas and carbonizing works. The United States imported 13,170 tons of sulphate of ammonia during the year. The average price of sulphate of ammonia in New York for 1916 was $83.86 per metric ton. Incomplete statistics show that synthetic nitrogen compounds were exported during the year by Norway to the extent of 82,276 tons.

As regards fertilizers in general, the statistics since the beginning of the war are very incomplete. In general, an increasing demand prior to the war was evident in Russia, Japan, South Africa, Australia, and Hawaii, with an inadequate supply since that date. Among other products useful to agriculture for which statistics are given are sulphur and copper sulphate.

An extensive bibliography of recent literature on fertilizers and chemical products useful for agriculture is given as usual.

Fertilizer analyses, A. J. PATTEN, E. F. BERGER, A. E. SMOLL, and E. A. DEWINDT (*Michigan Sta. Bul. 278 (1916), pp. 3–31*).—This bulletin contains the results of actual and guaranteed analyses of 549 samples of fertilizers and fertilizing materials collected for inspection in Michigan during 1916. It was found that of the 549 samples "30 (5.5 per cent) are below guarantee in nitrogen, 38 (6.9 per cent) are below in available phosphoric acid, 6 (1 per cent) in total phosphoric acid, and 23 (4.2 per cent) in potash."

AGRICULTURAL BOTANY.

Department of botanical research, D. T. MACDOUGAL (*Carnegie Inst. Washington Year Book, 15 (1916), pp. 51–95*).—A summary is given of the more important results as condensed from the reports by the several investigators taking part in the various phases of botanical work. The groupings under which the work is reported include photosynthesis, imbibition, and growth; ecology and phytogeography; genetics and taxonomy; eremography; equipment; and field work.

It is stated that the study of the available facts and accepted conclusions regarding photosynthesis eliminates the theory of Baeyer from the possible explanations. The initial stage is probably much more complex than a simple condensation of formaldehyde to sugar. A study of the cacti regarding the carbohydrate economy of plants yields no evidence of special formative substances. Sugar starvation may occur as a result of desiccation or of enzym-inhibiting temperatures even when plenty of starch is present.

The lower temperature limit of growth in a single plant may range from 10 to 25° C. and the upper from 26 to 43°, with a maximum of 49° for growth and as high as 53° for endurance. Temperature coefficients of 2 or more for every rise of 10° were found between 10 and 30 or 35°. All temperatures were those of the plant body itself, which may be as much as 8 to 9° above that of the surrounding air.

The precision auxograph now in use indicates reliably an increase or decrease in length or thickness to within 0.0004 in. No inhibiting effect of light on growth of *Eriogonum nudum* was shown, the maximum occurring in daylight and the rate depending largely upon the balance between absorption and water loss. Imbibition, defined as distensive force in the earlier growth of the cell, plays an important but diminishing part as vacuoles form and the protoplast enlarges, osmosis meanwhile increasing in importance. Acidity checks growth, most plants having a greater capacity for water when slightly alkaline. Water capacity of cacti increases with the dry weight up to the age of one year or more (maturity), then decreases. Gelatin with a little agar makes a mixture displaying imbibition comparable to that of plants. Imbibition capacity (which is less at night than in the daytime) influences transpiration and movements. Studies were made on the relative influences of imbibition and turgor in the growth of pollen tubes in cane sugar, acids, and alkalies. The contained colloids swell more in acid than in alkali of low concentrations.

The ratio of precipitation to evaporation is the factor which limits the areas of forest, grassland, and desert. A new subdivision of vegetational areas has been worked out, as well as a new method of determination of the domination of different growth forms.

Flattened plant bodies meridionally placed receive more heat than those set at right angles to this position, attaining temperatures of 53° C. (127.4° F.) or more and transpiration and dry weight corresponding to the exposure. Roots of different plants show varied relations to oxygen, which is correlated with soil penetration and habit, and similar differences appear as regards the temperature conditioning growth. The forms taken by root systems are greatly affected by environment. Roots of Salix will grow for some time without oxygen.

Extensive study has been made of the concentrations of the sap of plants in mountain and desert habitats. Sap of parasites is usually, but not always or necessarily, of higher concentration than that of their hosts.

Wide divergences appear in the progenies of single species of Œnothera from widely separated localities, and striking aberrants or mutants were noted. The revegetation of an island has been followed since 1908, when there were two individuals present, to 1916, when there were 470 individuals, representing 10 species.

Variations in climate as related to vegetation in earlier geological periods are attributed chiefly to the frequency and distribution of cyclonic storms. The study of the Mohave River yields evidence which is of value in making out the evolutionary history of the vegetation in this ancient desert. The underflow being of great importance to vegetation, it has been found that artesian conditions would not necessarily require a bowl-shaped basin, and some generalizations of practical value have been obtained.

Osmotic pressure in roots and in leaves in relation to habitat moisture, V. ILJIN, P. NAZAROVA, and M. OSTROVSKAJA (Jour. Ecology, 4 (1916), No. 3–4, pp. 160–173).—The authors have made a study of the vegetation (represented by various genera and species) of three types, swamp, meadow, and grass steppe, in the Valuyki district, in the Government of Voronezh. It is stated that the influence of differences in water supply can be noted in leaf and root. The osmotic pressure shows variations due to external influences as well as to internal structure. A close relation is always observable between intensity of osmotic pressure and the amount of water at the disposal of the plant cell.

Nitrogen compounds in mulberry leaves, E. KATAYAMA (Bul. Imp. Sericult. Expt. Sta. Japan, 1 (1916), No. 1, pp. 1–30).—The author reports on a study of the various nitrogen compounds and their percentages present in mulberry leaves, with some reference to their utilization by silkworms in their nutritive processes and in the manufacture of their products.

The emergence of the aerial organs in woodland plants, E. J. SALISBURY (Jour. Ecology, 4 (1916), No. 3–4, pp. 121–128, figs. 7).—A study has been made of the three principal types of adaptation to overcome the resistances to emergence from the soil by various plants on germination.

It is considered as an important feature of both spear leaves and spear shoots (in which the leaves are rolled parallel to the midrib) that the unfolding begins at the apex and travels downward, the tip of the leaf or shoot thus developing an increased periphery on reaching the light, while the part below remains small, thus greatly reducing resistance to the emergence of the remaining part of the shoot or leaf. The third (and in some respects more elaborate) type, in which the stem or petiole emerges in a bent condition, is dealt with in some detail. It is stated that the straightening of the bent organs is a growth phenomenon which normally takes place under the stimulus of light at a rate corresponding somewhat to its intensity, but sometimes occurring eventually in darkness.

Linkage in maize: Aleurone and chlorophyll factors, E. W. LINDSTROM (Amer. Nat., 51 (1917), No. 604, pp 225–237).—The author states that linkage between R, one of the aleurone factors (of which there are said to be 5 pairs), and G, one of the chlorophyll factors (of which the author has found that there are at least 7 pairs), shows approximately 20 per cent crossovers, the crossing over occurring in both male and female gametogenesis of the monœcious maize plant. Preliminary tests indicate that G is also linked with L, a seedling chlorophyll factor, the factor pairs Rr, Gg, and Ll constituting one factorial group in maize.

The different meanings of the term "factor" as affecting clearness in genetic discussion, H. B. FROST (Amer. Nat., 51 (1917), No. 604, pp. 244–250).— The author proposes to employ in genetic discussion the two distinct meanings now in use for the term factor, so that a genetic (Mendelian) factor will mean, in one sense, a property or characteristic of the germ plasm, more or less conveniently delimited for the analysis of segregating heredity; in the other, an actual material unit of genetic segregation, of unknown nature, but probably a genetically indivisible portion of a chromosome in a particular state. The presence-and-absence scheme employs properly the first only of these meanings; the Morgan-Castle scheme may use either.

Notes on the flora of Sitka, Alaska, J. P. ANDERSON (Proc. Iowa Acad. Sci., 23 (1916), pp. 427–482, figs. 16).—The author, presenting the results of collections, observations, and research of two years near Sitka, states that in the area in question the Canadian, Hudsonian, and Arctic-Alpine zones are represented. The plants segregate into five or six typical habitats, which are systematically discussed, as are economic plants including forest, fruit bearing, and other species. A number of fungi are listed with their hosts. The collections made are to be added to those at the Alaska Sitka Experiment Station.

An account of the chief types of vegetation in South Africa, with notes on the plant succession, J. W. BEWS (Jour. Ecology, 4 (1916), No. 3–4, pp. 129–159, fig. 1).—Giving a somewhat extended, though confessedly incomplete, account of the vegetation prevalent in portions of South Africa as related to various factors, the author states that the types of vegetation found there are very varied, showing many stages and tendencies as regards order of succession. One striking feature is the rarity of formations or associations dominated by a single species. In some cases, but not all, this may be considered to indicate a lack of stability in the environmental conditions.

Experiments on the effects of constituents of solid smelter wastes on barley growth in pot cultures, C. B. LIPMAN and W. F. GERICKE (Univ. Cal. Pubs. Agr. Sci., 1 (1917), No. 13, pp. 495–587).—Following some preliminary investigations by Lipman and Wilson previously noted (E. S. R., 30, p. 130), the present authors instituted in 1912 new and more complete experiments to ascertain whether sulphates of such metals as copper, zinc, lead, iron, and manganese in soil are toxic to barley; whether these substances are toxic in the proportions in which they may be present around smelters; whether they may be carried down to crops by water; whether they may prove to be permanently or temporarily stimulating to plants; and whether potassium aluminum sulphate can possess any value as a stimulant or as a source of potash. This work is herein described and its results are discussed in some detail, and some comparisons are shown with findings of other investigators.

The effect of various concentrations of the several compounds employed in connection with the different soils are indicated in connection with the growth attained by grain, straw, or roots. Stimulation usually attended the use of low and, in some cases, rather high concentrations.

Results are given regarding the effects of the salts on the nitrogen content of the grain, the nitrifying powers of the soil, and the amounts of copper and zinc taken up. Correlations are noted between some of these factors and the yields of dry matter. Some theoretical and practical phases of the smelter question are discussed, and evidence is cited to show that the solids of smelter waste are not a menace to agriculture.

Some effects of salt-treated soils on absorption by seeds, W. F. GERICKE (*Soil Sci.,* *3* (*1917*), *No. 3, pp. 271–278*).—The work above noted having raised the question whether, owing to absorption, an increase would occur in the weight of good viable seeds planted in soils containing solutions of certain toxic salts, the author has carefully studied the behavior in this respect of the seeds of several common economic plants.

It was found that smaller applications of copper sulphate to soil increased, and larger additions decreased, the absorption of water by bean and barley seeds. Small applications of sodium carbonate to soils increased the weight of bean, barley, and maize through increased absorption. Small applications of sodium chlorid decreased water absorption by all of these seeds.

Certain effects under irrigation of copper compounds upon crops, R. H. FORBES (*Univ. Cal. Pubs. Agr. Sci., 1* (*1917*), *No. 12, pp. 395–494, pls. 4, figs. 16*).—Investigations are reported which show that as a direct effect of the Clifton-Morenci mining operations in Arizona, copper is distributed throughout the water supplies, soils, and the vegetable and animal life of an underlying irrigated district.

"Smaller amounts of copper are found elsewhere in the State where the drainage basin includes mining operations or ore-bearing areas. Individual plants grown in water cultures or in soil containing copper show a comparatively small, and probably not injurious accumulation of copper in the aerial portions of the plants, but the root systems, carefully cleansed of externally adhering copper, contain relatively great amounts. Copper in root systems, as shown by the biuret test, is largely in combination with plant proteids, especially at the growing points of root systems and near vicinity. . . . Conditions favoring toxicity of copper compounds are the presence of carbon dioxid and certain soluble salts which assist in forming copper solutions that come into contact with plant roots; coarse, sandy soils favoring free access of copper solutions to plant roots and minimizing the withdrawal of copper from solution by adsorption; and the presence of copper in the form of the more soluble precipitated carbonate. . . .

"Conditions opposing toxicity of copper compounds are the presence of copper in the form of chrysocolla and chalcocite; adsorption through contact with finely divided soil particles; reactions with carbonates, silicates, and organic matter tending to precipitate copper from its solutions; the presence of certain soluble salts in the soil that overcome toxic action; and increased resistance of old plant roots. The stimulation by copper of vegetative growth in pot and water cultures has been observed. Stimulated growth of crops under field conditions is a possibility.

"Pot cultures may be used for comparative determinations of toxic effects upon plants of copper in soils, if conducted under rigidly uniform conditions. The copper content and the physiological response to copper of such material will be much greater than for similar cultures grown under plat or field conditions. Copper injury in field soils containing doubtfully toxic amounts of copper may be diagnosed by a combination of symptoms. Facts which indicate such injury in a soil containing 0.1 per cent of copper (more or less) are yellow tops (for winter grains) in absence of other conditions that cause yellow tops, crinkly root systems (in absence of excessive amounts of alkali salts), and a high copper content in dry matter of root systems. Combined evidence of this character, which may be observed in the district studied, indicates toxic copper effects.

"Field observations before and following the exclusion of tailings from the irrigating water supply indicate that conditions in the district studied are gradually improving, due to the cultivation of alfalfa and to the incorporation of river sediments with accumulations of tailings. Noticeable toxic effects in the field exist only where the roots of young, growing crops are exposed to surface soils containing maximum amounts of copper. The general tendency in the district is probably toward decreasing rather than increasing percentages of copper in irrigated soils."

Methods of experimental procedure are described.

Fifty-seven references to literature bearing on the subject are appended.

Protection against pollution of waters and smoke and dust injury to agriculture and forestry in Austria, J. STOKLASA (*Mitt. Verhandl. Landw. Rats* [*Austria*], *17* (*1913*), *pp. 141–163*).—Besides discussing reports on emanations from such sources as furnaces and chemical works in different countries during some years past, the author deals more specifically with several phases of water pollution and with such emanations as smoke, dust, and gases, and the injury done thereby to plants.

One of the most important of the injurious factors is sulphuric acid, which is discussed as regards its effects, both direct and indirect. The action on the leaves is far-reaching as regards results, though not necessarily apparent in the early stages of the processes. The effects of some other components are somewhat systematically discussed.

FIELD CROPS.

Field experiments and compensating calculations, R. LEIDNER (*Landw. Jahrb.*, *49* (*1916*), *No. 1*, *pp. 105–135*, *figs. 3*).—The author reviews experimental work by Rümker, Rodewald, Hummel, Remy, Ehrenberg, Pfeiffer, Mitscherlich, and others in an attempt to ascertain those methods that secure the greatest accuracy in field experiments. Considerable data are given and discussed.

The general conclusion is drawn that the most suitable means for conducting field experiments has not yet been found, although the transition from the early two-plat system to the newer method of using many small control plats and the detailed statement of the technical and mathematical phases of the subject studied are advances in the right direction. A more careful selection of experimental field plats and increased attention to all the details of experimental work are natural consequences following such a practice.

[The experimental error in field tests], V. G. BATYRENKO (*Zhur. Opytn. Agron.* (*Jour. Agr. Expt.*), *17* (*1916*), *No. 2*, *pp. 99–121*).—The author discusses the factors involved in experimental errors in field tests, with special reference to the influence they may have when the results obtained from plat tests are applied to open field practices. Two types of plat experiments are considered, those for testing methods and those for testing yields.

[Report of field crops work], W. G. TAGGART, A. P. KERR, C. E. HESTER, and F. C. QUEREAU (*Louisiana Stas. Rpt. 1916, pp. 7–9, 24, 25, 26–29*).—This continues work previously noted (E. S. R., 35, p. 336).

Fertilizer experiments with sugar cane at the Sugar Experiment Station showed an average increase of 3.03 tons of cane from sulphate of potash applied to first-year stubble, thus confirming results obtained the year before with plant cane but contradicting many experiments of previous years. An application of 500 lbs. each of acid phosphate and tankage on second-year stubble showed an increased production over an application of 250 lbs. of acid phosphate and 500 lbs. of tankage which a little more than paid for the extra amount of fertilizer. The failure of this experiment to yield tonnage equal to that obtained the past four years is attributed to a disturbance of the nitrogen balance by continuous cropping to sugar cane.

Four foreign varieties of sugar cane were tested. Louisiana seedlings L511 and L231 continued to maintain their high standard.

Attempts to develop a white flint corn were continued and a yield of 63 bu. per acre obtained in spite of injury by heavy winds. So-called prolific varieties of corn recommended by other southern experiment stations in the same latitude were obtained and grown in comparison with native Yellow Creole, but none gave superior yields.

In an attempt to increase the value of hay grown on Johnson grass infested land, two cuttings of clean red clover were secured before the Johnson grass got any headway. The early growing period of the clover, however, prevented the cutting of a mixed Johnson grass and clover hay. Further observations on the eradication of Johnson grass by kudzu were made and indicated that this plant will completely choke out the grass in a very few years.

In fertilizer experiments with rice at the Rice Experiment Station conducted since 1910 five profitable crops of rice have been grown on all plats receiving available phosphorus, the highest yield being 28 bbls. per acre. The last two crops, however, yielded less than the checks, due to the heavy growth of water crab grass and barnyard millet. Potash showed profitable yields the first year, but subsequently the yield has been little more than on the check. Cottonseed meal or manure appears to be profitable when applied to Honduras rice, but the increase was not so marked with Shinriki or Blue Rose rice.

Field tests are briefly noted with green mungo beans, the Biloxy soy bean, velvet beans, garlic, clovers, Japanese cane, teosinte, sorghum, and peas for silage, Sudan grass, corn, and oats.

Dry farming investigations at the Sherman County branch experiment station, Moro, Oreg., D. E. STEPHENS and C. E. HILL (*Oregon Sta. Bul. 144 (1917), pp. 3–47, figs. 13*).—Variety, crop improvement, and rotation tests and tillage experiments to determine the best cultural methods for wheat production under the summer-fallow system are reported. The tests were made at the Moro substation in eastern Oregon and were conducted in cooperation with the Office of Forage Crop Investigations of the U. S. Department of Agriculture. The history of the branch station, meteorological data, and a report of variety tests of spring cereals have been previously noted (E. S. R., 36, p. 830).

Four-year average yields of 17 winter wheat varieties show the Argentine (1569) to be first, with 32 bu. per acre, while Ghirka (1438) was last with 24.6 bu. The local Turkey variety commonly grown in the vicinity of Moro and taken as a standard, yielded 27 bu. per acre. The first 9 varieties—all wheats of the Turkey type, exceeded the local Turkey strain by from 6 to 18 per cent. The highest yielding Turkey variety exceeded Fortyfold, a popular variety in eastern Oregon, by 6.6 bu. per acre. Hybrid No. 123 yielded 43.8 bu. for a 2-year average.

Rate- and date-of-seeding tests with winter wheat indicate that from 45 to 55 lbs. of seed per acre, sown between October 10 and 25, will give best results.

A comparison of Turkey wheat grown from seed produced at Moro and Moccasin, Mont., and Nephi, Utah, gave 5-year average yields of 30.1, 30, and 28.1 bu. per acre, respectively.

In variety tests with spring wheats, using Bluestem as a standard, Koola, a pure-line selection, gave the highest average yield, 32 bu., for the 4 years 1913–1916, while Kubanka gave the lowest average yield, 21.2 bu. Bluestem yielded 25.4 bu.

Rate- and date-of-seeding tests with spring wheat gave a 5-year average yield of 17.7 bu. per acre for all rates sown early (March 28), while the late sowings (April 23) averaged 12.2 bu. per acre. The 8-pk. rate of seeding gave the highest average yield, 20.3 bu., for the early sowings, while the 3-pk. rate gave the highest yield, 13.6 bu., for late sowing.

Texas Winter barley gave the highest average yield of the 5 varieties tested, 49 bu., and Utah Winter the lowest, 36.8 bu. per acre. None of the beardless varieties tested have been winter hardy.

Of the 24 spring barleys tested for 4 years, Mariout has given the highest average yield of 51.6 bu., with White Smyrna second, with 50.1 bu. per acre. Manchuria gave the lowest average yield of 31.7 bu.

The highest 4-year average yield of spring oats was secured from Siberian and amounted to 62.1 bu., while Canadian was lowest with 52.3 bu. per acre. In seasons of normal or less than normal rainfall early-maturing varieties such as Sixty Day and Kherson gave the highest yields, while in cool seasons of high rainfall the late-maturing varieties gave considerably higher yields. The earlier varieties are recommended, however. Winter oats have not proved hardy.

The leading varieties of the cereals named above are briefly described.

In a comparison of emmer and spelt varieties tested for the 3-year period of 1914–1916, Red Winter spelt gave an average yield of 57.4 bu. as compared with a yield of 29.4 bu. from Black Winter emmer No. 2337, the highest-yielding emmer variety.

Abruzzes and Giant Winter ryes have given the highest yields of the winter types tested, while a spring rye, No. 26101, has proved exceptionally valuable.

Tabulated data are presented showing the acre value of the grain crops based on the highest-yielding varieties of winter and spring wheat and barley, spring oats, and winter spelt, and on 10-year average prices. Mariout spring barley, with an average yield of 2,477 lbs. per acre, gave the highest acre value, $33.06, and Red Winter spelt, with a yield of 1,837 lbs., the lowest, $24.52.

Field peas have proved to be the most profitable of all leguminous crops tested. The Lima variety gave the highest average yield in variety tests extending over the 4-year period of 1913–1916, yielding 22.8 bu. per acre, while White Scimitar was lowest with 14.9 bu. A few of the leading varieties are briefly described.

An average yield of 18.8 bu. per acre was obtained from field peas grown continuously on the same land without summer fallow from 1912 to 1916, inclusive. Field peas substituted for one summer fallow in a 4-course rotation of fallow, spring wheat, field peas, and spring wheat yielded 15.7 bu. per acre. Wheat after peas yielded 22.3 bu. and after fallow 23.5 bu. New field-pea and wheat rotations begun in 1916 on land sown to field peas continuously since 1912 gave average yields of 40.2 bu. of spring wheat after field peas, 27.4 bu. of field peas after field peas, and 38.5 bu. of wheat after summer fallow.

An attempt was made to determine the relative amounts of soil moisture used by field peas, wheat, and corn, as compared with the amount conserved by summer fallowing. The following average results were secured from two determinations: After spring wheat yielding 39.4 bu., 7.5 per cent moisture; after corn yielding 27.1 bu., 8 per cent; after field peas yielding 27.7 bu., 9 per cent; and after fallow, 13.4 per cent.

Numerous alfalfa varieties have been tested and produced excellent yields of forage but, with the exception of Baltic and Grimm, have failed to produce seed. Results obtained with sweet clover indicate that it may be equal to or even superior to alfalfa as a hay crop. Several varieties of vetch have been tested, with the best results being secured from fall-sown hairy vetch.

In variety tests with corn Northwestern Dent, with a 4-year average yield of 23.2 bu. per acre, was highest and Minnesota No. 23 lowest with 14.4 bu. Walla Walla White Dent and Minnesota No. 13, with average yields of 22.5 and 19 bu., respectively, are especially recommended for silage purposes.

Green Mountain, with a 4-year average yield of 184 bu. per acre, was first in potato variety tests, with Early Ohio lowest with 100.2 bu. Early Rose, Burbank, and Irish Cobbler gave average yields of 155.5, 150.3, and 141.8 bu., respectively.

In the tillage experiments, tests of methods for disposing of the wheat stubble resulted as follows:

Effects of various treatments of the stubble on the yield of winter wheat grown after fallow, 1913–1916, inclusive.

Date of plowing.	Disked in fall and spring.	Disked in spring only.	Not disked.
	Bushels.	Bushels.	Bushels.
April 1	26.6	29.9	33.5
May 1	27.2	29.0	27.2
June 1	27.2	25.9	21.0

Tests of the time and manner of plowing for winter and spring wheat showed an average yield of 28 bu. per acre for early fall plowing, as compared with 25 bu. for late fall plowing and 29.9 bu. for early spring plowing (April 1). Disk plowing gave an average yield of 25.7 bu., while moldboard plowing averaged 27.2 bu. In early fall plowing with a disk plow the average yield amounted to 26.5 bu. and with the moldboard plow to 29.2 bu., while in late fall plowing the difference was negligible. The 4-year average yield of winter wheat on plats plowed April 1 amounted to 7.8 bu. per acre more than the average yields of plats plowed June 1, although these variations are said to be largely dependent upon seasonal conditions. Spring wheat sown on plats plowed deep yielded 19.1 bu. and on plats plowed shallow 18.7 bu. per acre.

Analyses of samples of wheat grown on land plowed April 1 and June 1 showed a marked increase in yellow-berry on the late-plowed land, amounting to almost 84 per cent in 1915. The protein content of the kernel on the early and late plowed lands amounted to 13.35 and 8.49 per cent, respectively. The moist gluten content with early plowing amounted to 30.4 per cent and after late plowing to 18.7 per cent.

Winter wheat grown after a fallow and on land packed with a subsurface packer gave a 4-year average yield of 26.2 bu., as compared with 26.8 bu. from land not packed. The average yield from land packed by the surface packer was 26.4 bu. Spring wheat after a fallow yielded an average of 20.1 bu. when packed with the subsurface packer and 20 bu. per acre when not packed.

In a comparison of no harrowing, light harrowing, and heavy harrowing and weeding of the summer fallow for winter wheat, 4-year average yields for three plowing dates April 1, May 1, and June 1 amounted to 24.2, 26.6, and 27.2 bu., respectively. There was little difference between the treatments for any but the earliest plowing date (April 1), when average yields of 25.6, 30.2, and 33.5 bu., respectively, were secured.

The average yield of winter wheat on plats harrowed in the spring amounted to 26.4 bu., as compared with 27.4 bu. from plats not harrowed, thus indicating that except for weed eradication spring harrowing of winter wheat is not necessary or desirable.

Considerable tabulated data are presented and discussed, summarizing the results obtained in rotation experiments with spring and winter wheat, spring barley, spring oats, corn, field peas, and potatoes for the period of 1913–1916. The results, however, are not considered conclusive.

Progress report, Substation No. 4, Beaumont, Tex., 1909–1914, H. H. LAUDE (*Texas Sta. Bul. 200 (1916), pp. 3–18, figs. 4*).—The history and development of this substation are briefly outlined and the work and results obtained from its establishment through the crop season of 1914 are discussed. The substation is located on a so-called "old rice field" at an elevation of from 26.5 to 29.8 ft. above sea level, near the southeastern corner of the State. Red rice, weeds, and grass common to old rice fields were present, and the whole farm was characterized by the poor drainage facilities which predominate on most of the rice farms of the region. The rainfall is well distributed throughout the year and totals approximately 45.09 in.

Experimental work has dealt largely with rice and a study of the practices related to rice farming, including cultural methods and variety and rotation tests. In date-of-seeding trials the average yields for 1913 and 1914 varied from 270 lbs. per acre for seedings made March 24 to 1,660 lbs. for seedings made June 3. Rate-of-seeding tests conducted during 1913 and 1914, employing 60-, 80-, and 100-lb. rates per acre, resulted in average yields of 1,270, 1,260, and 1,525 lbs. per acre, respectively. A comparison of broadcasting with drilling in rice on dry land in 1913 resulted in yields of 927 lbs. per acre with the former method and 1,930 lbs. with the latter.

The yields of rice obtained in 1914 on plats sown to various other crops in 1913 are reported in tabular form. The highest yield of rice, amounting to 1,911 lbs. per acre, was secured after cotton, while the lowest yield, 1,068 lbs., was obtained after rice. The legumes (cowpeas, peanuts, sweet clover, and soy beans) also proved beneficial to the succeeding rice crop, giving yields ranging from 1,721 lbs. after soy beans to 1,774 lbs. after cowpeas. Rice after fallow yielded 1,412 lbs.

Rod-row tests have been conducted with 122 varieties of rice and 3-year average yields of 18 of these varieties are reported in tabular form. The average yields reported varied from 3.23 lbs. per nursery row for the Chien-Yu variety to 1,603 lbs. for the Honduras variety.

Methods for the control of red rice, grass, and weeds are suggested.

Hay crops have not proved very satisfactory, due to the high humidity prevailing at harvest time. Sudan grass yielded 2.48 tons of cured hay per acre from a 15-lb. rate of seeding in 1914, but suffered a large percentage of loss. Japanese sugar cane (E. S. R., 37, p. 140) is considered the best forage crop grown at the station, producing as high as 24 tons of green forage per acre. A rate-of-seeding test with Japanese sugar cane in 1914, using rates of approximately 800, 2,000, and 4,000 lbs. of cane, gave yields estimated at 19,226, 27,687, and 36,524 lbs. per acre, respectively.

An experimental planting of Bermuda grass, burr clover, and Lespedeza is reported to have given good results in a test of pasture mixtures begun in 1911 and 1912.

[Field crops], C. A. ZAVITZ (*Ann. Rpt. Ontario Agr. and Expt. Union, 37 (1915), pp. 12–38*).—This is a report of cooperative field experiments in Ontario with different varieties of grain crops, roots, forage and silage crops, and fertilizer tests with potatoes, mangels, and rape for the year 1915.

Cultivated plants. Potatoes and sugar beets, H. HITIER (*Plantes Sarclées. Pomme de Terre et Betterave. Paris: J. B. Baillière & Sons, 1916, pp. 498, figs. 26*).—This work is presented in two sections, one dealing with potatoes and the other with sugar beets, each crop being discussed in considerable detail.

Contribution to the study of Gramineæ, C. D. GIROLA (*Bol. Min. Agr. [Argentina], 19 (1915), No. 10–12, pp. 867–874, fig. 1*).—Some notes are given on *Sporobolus phleoides,* including chemical and physical analyses.

The relation of winter temperature to the distribution of winter and spring grains in the United States, S. C. SALMON (*Jour. Amer. Soc. Agron., 9 (1917), No. 1, pp. 21–24, figs. 2*).—This paper discusses some studies begun during the winter of 1913–14, at the Kansas Experiment Station, to determine the relation between winter temperatures and the distribution of winter and spring grain in the United States. The data have been collected from the Census reports and Weather Bureau records of the United States and Canada. Two outline maps of the United States and Canada, upon which isotherms have been plotted, illustrate the distribution of winter and spring wheat. The isotherms connect points of equal daily minimum temperature for January and February.

The isotherm of 10° F. coincides with the line which divides the winter from the spring wheat belt. Practically the only exception is where spring wheat is grown south of the isotherm, rather than where winter wheat is produced north of it.

The isotherms of 20 and 30° coincide very closely with the northern limits for winter barley and winter oats, respectively, agreeing with the statements of Derr (E. S. R., 28, p. 432), Stephens (E. S. R., 32, p. 730), and Warburton (E. S. R., 25, p. 133).

The absence of any correlation between the northern limit of winter cereal culture and snowfall is noted, and may be due to the fact that heavy spring snows, increasing the moisture content of the soil, increase the danger from heaving, thus offsetting the protection afforded by earlier snows.

The effect of greenhouse temperatures on the growth of small grains, T. B. HUTCHESON and K. E. QUANTZ (*Jour. Amer. Soc. Agron., 9 (1917), No. 1, pp. 17–21, pls. 2, figs. 1*).—This paper reports the results of an experiment conducted by the authors during the winter of 1915, at the Virginia Agricultural Experiment Station, to test the effect of temperature upon winter wheat, oats, barley, and rye grown in greenhouses. The greenhouses were kept as near the following temperatures as outside influences would permit: House No. 1, 75° F.; house No. 2, 65°; house No. 3, 62°; and house No. 4, 58°. The seeds were sown in 4-in. earthen pots on December 21, 1915, and the experiment discontinued May 27, 1916. The results of the experiments showed the effects of temperature to be as follows:

Except in the case of oats, the cool temperature produced earlier maturity, while high temperatures stimulated rank growth of tillers and thus wasted energy needed for the formation of heads. Barley was affected by heat. while wheat and rye suffered, though not as much as barley. Oats showed very little ill effect from high temperatures, indicating that they are better suited for soil work in greenhouses where temperatures can not be accurately controlled. The setting of seed was best in the cooler houses, although with oats there was apparently no difference in this respect. Tillering was greatest in the warmer temperatures and least in the cooler houses, but the difference in the number of heads was overcome by the large percentage of seed produced per head, except with oats. A temperature ranging from 55 to 70° is deemed most desirable for growing grain in the greenhouse.

Experiments with spring wheat and oats, P. R. FEDOROV (FEDOROFF) (*Bezenchuk. Selsk. Khoz. Opytn. Sta., No. 71 (1916). pp. 14*).—Field experiments are reported with spring wheat and oats for 1915. The plan of the experiments included a study of the influence of the preceding crop. plowing at different depths and at different times, fertilizers, various methods of sowing, and seed selection tests. The crops were grown after wheat, peas, corn, sunflowers, millet, potatoes, and carrots.

The best results were obtained from the crops following carrots and potatoes. Late, shallow plowing for wheat appeared to increase yields slightly, but no very definite results were obtained with oats. Mineral fertilizers, consisting of acid phosphates and Thomas slag, showed no increased yields with wheat, but a slight increase with oats. Manure showed good results for both crops.

Broadcasting the seed gave better results than any of the other methods tested.

Thrashing injuries of wheat and rye and their influence on the germination and keeping qualities of the grain, J. N. WALLDÉN (*Sveriges Utsädesför. Tidskr., 26 (1916), No. 1, pp. 24–47, pl. 1, fig. 1*).—This article deals with experiments by the author to determine the extent of injuries to wheat and rye during thrashing and the resultant effect of subsequent copper sulphate treatment on the germination of the seed. A study is also made of the effect of such injuries on the keeping qualities of the grain.

A 0.4 per cent aqueous solution of eosin was used to determine the location and extent of the injury, the seeds being dipped in the solution for one minute, removed and washed with water. The injured portions stained red. while the remaining surface was practically uncolored. The author considered any injury unimportant except such as occurred directly over the embryo. The following gradations are suggested as an indication of the probable degree of injury to the embryo: (1) No color, or only a perceptible tinge, (2) only the apex above the embryo strongly colored, (3) at least one-half (usually the lower half) of the embryo surface strongly colored, and (4) the entire embryo surface strongly colored. It is claimed that this method will enable one to control the thrashing of wheat and rye when there is risk of injury to the seed.

The keeping qualities of both wheat and rye, but especially the latter, were reduced by injury to the seed coat. Rye showed a marked reduction in its germinability after two weeks, corresponding to the degree of injury sustained.

Further tests showed that in the case of seed with uninjured integument copper sulphate solutions of the highest concentration could be used without subsequent damage to the germinability of the seed, but that a 0.2 to 0.3 per cent formaldehyde solution materially reduced the germinability of such seed. The use of 0.1 to 0.2 per cent formalin, however, had no injurious effect.

The data are presented in tabular form.

Fibres from the Belgian Congo (*Bul. Imp. Inst. [So. Kensington], 14 (1916), No. 3, pp. 385–388*).—Brief notes are given on fibers received for analysis from the Belgian Congo. The materials comprised baobab bark (*Adansonia digitata*), punga bark (*Cephalonema polyandrum*), and several Agave and Furcræa fibers. Both the baobab and punga barks are reported as being suitable for paper making.

The agave fibers of Tunis, L. GUILLOCHON (*Vie Agr. et Rurale, 6 (1916), No. 52, pp. 458–461, figs. 4*).—This is a general discussion of the production of agave fiber in Tunis, with special reference to sisal.

Alfalfa culture, C. G. WILLIAMS (*Mo. Bul. Ohio Sta., 2 (1917), No. 6, pp. 173–177, figs. 2*).—The essentials in growing alfalfa the first year are enumerated and briefly discussed.

An increased yield of more than 1,200 lbs. of hay per acre for the first year is reported from a 320-lb. application of acid phosphate at Wooster.

Comparative tests with different amounts of seed sown broadcast for three years gave the highest average yield, 9,148 lbs. per acre, with a 10-lb. rate. Further tests using the same rates but comparing broadcasting with drilling in the seed are reported for 1913 and 1914. The highest average yield, 9,569 lbs., was obtained from the 5-lb. rate drilled in, with a 10-lb. rate broadcasted second, with a yield of 9,216 lbs. Counts of the original plants showed 75 per cent remaining after two years from the 10-lb. rate, but only 23 per cent from the 25-lb. rate.

Tests with clipping alfalfa in 1907 indicated that a growth of from 12 to 18 in. might remain without cutting in the fall with no harmful effect to new seedings. Clippings made in September and October of that year were estimated to have reduced the yield from 500 to 1,300 lbs. per acre the following year, and to have increased the percentage of weeds. Clipping in August may be admissible if weeds are serious.

Cassava as a competitor of maize and potatoes in the production of starch and allied products (*Queensland Agr. Jour., n. ser., 6 (1916), No. 5, pp. 313–317, figs. 3*).—This is a general discussion of cassava growing and its substitution for corn and potatoes as a source of starch.

The relation between the anatomical structure and some peculiarities of the different varieties of clover, V. ZHOLTKEVICH (W. JOLTKEWITCH) (*Zhur. Opytn. Agron. (Jour. Agr. Expt.), 17 (1916), No. 3, pp. 239–250, figs. 3*).—The author presents data obtained from two years' observations on the flowering habits and certain anatomical measurements of several varieties of clover. A definite relationship was found to exist between the flowering habits and the length of the cells of the stomata, the diameter of the palisade cells, the internodal length of the stems, and the length of the corolla tube of the different varieties.

Corn culture, T. B. HUTCHESON, E. R. HODGSON, and T. K. WOLFE (*Virginia Sta. Bul. 214 (1917), pp. 3–12, figs. 2*).—A brief review of experimental work conducted in various sections of the country, relative to the value of cultivation for corn, is given, and results obtained at the Virginia Station in similar experiments are reported for 1913–1916, with averages as follows:

Average results of corn-cultivation tests, 1913–1916.

| Year. | No cultivation. | | | | Three cultivations. | | Five cultivations. | |
| | Weeds allowed to grow. | | Weeds cut with hoe. | | | | | |
	Grain.	Fodder.	Grain.	Fodder.	Grain.	Fodder.	Grain.	Fodder.
	Bushels.	*Tons.*	*Bushels.*	*Tons.*	*Bushels.*	*Tons.*	*Bushels.*	*Tons.*
1913	7.49	0.65	27.81	0.88	34.99	1.14	40.56	1.29
1914	No test.		64.50	1.74	75.70	1.77	73.10	1.92
1915	2.84	0.45	38.26	1.20	51.51	1.40	53.56	1.26
1916	14.18	1.02	65.59	1.83	75.53	2.07	67.50	1.76
Average	8.17	0.71	49.04	1.41	59.43	1.59	58.68	1.56

An average increase of 40.87 bu. per acre was thus obtained by removing the weeds without any cultivation. Valuing corn at 50 cts. a bushel, the estimated damage sustained by an acre of corn from weeds alone amounted to $20.44.

Data showing the rainfall during the growing season for each year of the test failed to establish any significant relationship between rainfall and the amount of cultivation necessary.

Recommendations regarding cultivation, the choice of varieties, and the fertilization of the corn crop are discussed in a general manner.

Corn variety tests, 1915 and 1916, L. W. OSBORN (*Arkansas Sta. Bul. 130* (*1917*), *pp. 3–31*).—Corn variety tests at Fayetteville and at the Mena and Marianna substations, and numerous cooperative tests in different parts of the State during 1915 and 1916 are reported, preliminary to a more complete report of all corn experiments since 1903. The results of the tests of each year at each experimental center are tabulated and briefly discussed.

The moisture supply appears to be the limiting factor in corn production, the relative standing of the varieties being closely related to their time of maturity. Early and medium maturing varieties have led in practically all tests, unless seasonal and soil conditions were exceptionally favorable.

A study of the data relative to barren stalks indicates a close correlation between moisture supply, as determined by the character of the soil and season, and the percentage of such stalks produced. Early and medium varieties, as well as the more prolific sorts, showed the lowest number of barren stalks. Surcropper, Hickory King, Biggs Seven-ear, Southern Beauty, Neal Paymaster, Pool Prolific, White Wonder, Leaming, Reid Yellow Dent, and Diamond Joe have contained a minimum of barren stalks in three or more tests.

Hybrids of Zea ramosa and Z. tunicata, G. N. COLLINS (*U. S. Dept. Agr., Jour. Agr. Research, 9 (1917), No. 11, pp. 383–396, pls. 9*).—*Z. tunicata* and *Z. ramosa* are described, the nature of their variations from normal maize outlined, and a hybrid strain secured from a cross of the two made at Lanham, Md., in 1914 discussed in detail. The female parent was a plant of *Z. ramosa*, while the male was a tunicate strain designated as half tunicate.

Nine F_1 plants of this cross were grown at Chula Vista, Cal., in 1915, of which 4 were tunicate and 5 normal, indicating the heterozygous nature of the half tunicate parent. The tunicate plants were all half tunicate and no trace of *ramosa* characters were discernible.

F_2 plants were grown at Lanham in 1916 from 3 tunicate and 2 normal ears. The 3 tunicate ears produced 326 mature plants and the 2 normal ears 82 plants. The F_2 progeny of the nontunicate or normal F_1 plants showed segregation into normal and *Z. ramosa* types in the ratio of 3:1, the numbers being 65 normal and 17 *ramosa*. No evidence of tunicate characters was observed.

The progeny of the tunicate plants, however, presented many intermediates which have been divided into groups and discussed in detail.

The author concludes that *Z. ramosa* and *Z. tunicata* should be regarded as mutative reversions, the one recessive and the other dominant, as compared with normal maize. The hybrid demonstrated that both behave as independent Mendelian units. The F_1 progeny was composed of normal maize, showing none of the characters of either mutation, the recurrence of both parental types in an apparently pure form, and individuals combining the characters of both mutants. In the last group normal expression was inhibited, resulting frequently in the appearance of a totally different type of inflorescence, which was sterile and abnormal to the extent that the tissue remained in an embryonic state, appearing as a much-branched, white, succulent mass, similar to that described by

Blaringhem (E. S. R., 19, p. 1128) and termed by him "cauliflower" inflorescence.

A method for determining the percentage of self-pollination in maize, A. E. WALLER (*Jour. Amer. Soc. Agron., 9 (1917), No. 1, pp. 35–37*).—This paper reports an attempt to determine the percentage of selfing in corn. The test was conducted by the author at the Ohio State University, using Reid Yellow Dent and Wing Hundred-Day White. The hills containing the white corn were spaced a distance of 38½ ft. from hill to hill east and west, and 35 ft. from hill to hill north and south. At the time of tasseling two of the three plants in each hill of white corn were detasseled.

Only one pair of endosperm characters were contrasted, the white and yellow. In endosperm formation in maize, the second nucleus from the pollen fuses with the two polar nuclei in triple fusion. If the male nucleus is the bearer of determiners for a dominant character expressing itself in the endosperm, the phenomenon called xenia then results. The author presents the analysis of 38 ears of white corn, showing the number of yellow (cross-pollinated) and of white (selfed) kernels, with the percentage of selfed kernels.

The average amount of self-pollination obtained was 5.13 per cent, although under field conditions such factors as humidity and wind determine the zone of infection between hills. The author believes that the effect of xenia can be better illustrated by contrasting more than one pair of characters.

Danthonia in New Zealand, A. H. COCKAYNE (*Jour. Agr. [New Zeal.], 13 (1916), No. 5, pp. 352–355, figs. 2*).—The two "composite" species of Danthonia used in New Zealand pasture formation, *D. semiannularis* and *D. pilosa*, are described and compared. Brief cultural notes are given.

The dasheen; its uses and culture, R. A. YOUNG (*U. S. Dept. Agr. Yearbook 1916, pp. 199–208, pls. 6*).—The production and uses of the dasheen, with special reference to its place in the agriculture of the Southern States, are discussed, and the origin and the introduction of the crop into the United States briefly outlined.

Flax growing experiments, 1914 and 1915 (*Dept. Agr. and Tech. Instr. Ireland Jour., 17 (1916), No. 1, pp. 3–19*).—This is a continuation of work previously noted (E. S. R., 32, p. 136), reporting results for 1914 and 1915, which are, in a large part, confirmatory of previous results.

Notes on the cultivation of flax by the ancient Egyptians, H. MUNIER (*Bul. Union Agr. Égypte, 14 (1916), No. 114, pp. 22–26*).—This is a brief historical note on the cultivation of flax in ancient Egypt.

Influence of methods of sowing oats on crop yield, M. ARCHANGELSKIJ (*Zeml. Ghaz., No. 12 (1916), pp. 313–318; abs. in Internat. Inst. Agr. [Rome], Internat. Rev. Sci. and Pract. Agr., 7 (1916), No. 6, p. 826*).—This reports the results of field experiments with oats conducted at Tambov in 1914, comparing broadcasting, sowing in rows in the ordinary way, and sowing in sets of rows alternating with bare strips varying in width up to about 12 in. The quantity of seed sown ranged from 0.6 to 1.41 cwt. per acre (2 to 4 bu.). Moisture determinations were made during the summer to a depth of 3 ft., in order to ascertain how the various methods influenced the moisture content of the soil.

With equal quantities of seed, the ordinary method of sowing in rows gave the largest yield and broadcasting the smallest. Increases in the quantity of seed sown influenced the yield, the maximum being attained with 1.41 cwt. sown in ordinary rows. Periodic, superficial plowing of the bare strips showed the greatest conservation of soil moisture and increased the yield.

Percentage of husk in varieties of oats, J. T. PRIDHAM (*Agr. Gaz. N. S. Wales, 27 (1916), No. 9, pp. 625, 626*).—A number of standard oat varieties and

16179°—17—No. 6——4

hybrids were grown at the Glen Innes Experiment Farm for the years 1912, 1913, 1914, and 1915, and 100 uniform grains of each variety selected each year, carefully husked, the kernels and husks weighed, and the percentage of husks determined. Tartar King with 39.94 per cent and Sunrise with 26.31 per cent husks represented the extreme limits in the results obtained.

Standardization and group classification of potato varieties for Michigan, C. W. WAID (*Mich. Agr. Col., Ext. Div. Bul. 5 (1916), pp. 15, figs. 8*).—A group classification and description of potato varieties best suited to Michigan conditions, based on the classification given by Stuart (E. S. R., 32, p. 830).

[Potatoes], A. CADORET (*Prog. Agr. et Vit. (Ed. l'Est-Centre), 37 (1916), No. 15, pp. 355, 356; abs. in Internat. Inst. Agr. [Rome], Internat. Rev. Sci. and Pract. Agr., 7 (1916), No. 6, p. 828*).—After a brief review of various methods for a more economical use of seed potatoes, the author describes his own method, which has given good results for several years. The tubers are placed in a dry cellar at a temperature above 17° C. (62.6° F.), and before they wrinkle rooting sprouts are obtained. These sprouts are planted at distances of 8 by 20 in. at a depth of from 2¾ to 3½ in., according to the soil. The author states that a crop of 8½ tons (approximately 280 bu.) per acre of marketable potatoes may be obtained. The method is applicable to all loose, light, and relatively dry soils.

The production of potatoes by cuttings, A. CADORET (*Prog. Agr. et Vit. (Ed. l'Est-Centre), 38 (1917), No. 14, pp. 325–327*).—An economic discussion of the above, emphasizing the saving in seed made possible by this scheme. It is estimated that from 595 to 800 kg. of seed per hectare (8.8 to 11.8 bu. per acre) would suffice as compared with 3,333 kg. of seed required by the Girard method (E. S. R., 5, p. 117).

Potato growing and potato diseases from Maine to California, W. J. MORSE (*Maine Sta. Doc. 531 (1916), pp. 20*).—This is a partial report of the author's observations on a tour of inspection through the leading potato-growing sections of the Northern and Western States in 1914, in company with Appel et al., in order to secure first-hand information on the growing of potatoes and on potato diseases under a variety of conditions. It was presented at the annual meeting of the Maine Seed Improvement Association at Lewiston in December, 1915.

Spraying potatoes in 1916 (*Maine Sta. Doc. 522 (1916), pp. 12, fig. 1*).—A popular discussion of potato spraying for the control of disease and insect enemies under the market conditions of spray materials then existing.

The transplanting of rice in Egypt, V. MOSSÉRI (*Bul. Union Agr. Égypte, 14 (1916), No. 114, pp. 5–13*).—This is a preliminary note on two experiments to determine the comparative value of seeding rice in the field and transplanting it from a seed bed. A comparison was also made of early and late seeding and early and late transplanting.

It was found that the cost of production was slightly greater when the rice was transplanted, and the yield considerably less than where the seed was sown in the field, resulting in a net return decidedly in favor of the latter system of cultivation. Early seeding and early transplanting gave larger net returns than late seeding and late transplanting.

Studies in rice, J. C. RUNDLES (*Philippine Jour. Sci., Sect. C, 10 (1915), No. 6, pp. 351–378, pls. 5*).—Rice seed selection is discussed in detail, with emphasis on the methods of selection and the factors which should govern the selection of standard varieties, such as production, market demand, maturity, character of the plants, and character of the paddy. Rice growing is discussed in some detail with special reference to the preparation, seeding, and care of the nursery seed bed.

The growing of cultivated leguminous catch crops on the paddy fields during the dry season is recommended, such crops as the peanut, mungo bean, cowpea, and sitao being deemed most suitable for this purpose.

The production of upland rice is briefly discussed.

[Rice improvement], B. MARCARELLI (*Gior. Risicolt.*, 6 (1916), No. 16, pp. 253–257).—This is a general discussion of rice improvement through seed selection.

The nitrogen fertilization of rice, N. NOVELLI (*Gior. Risicolt.*, 6 (1916), No. 10, pp. 161–164).—This is a brief general discussion of the fertilization of rice with ammonium sulphate, sodium nitrate, and calcium cyanamid.

A remarkable cultural variety of rye in the upper valley of Dora Riparia, Italy, C. F. CERRIANA (*Coltivatore*, 62 (1916), No. 12, pp. 358–362, figs. 2; abs. in *Internat. Inst. Agr.* [Rome], *Internat. Rev. Sci. and Pract. Agr.*, 7 (1916), No. 6, pp. 825, 826).—This describes a variety of rye grown in certain mountain regions of Italy, and partially adapted to growing in the lower plains region.

The variety is described as differing from common rye in that the culms are shorter, leaves darker and wider, ears denser, grains larger and greenish in color even when fully ripe, yields of grain higher (approximately 27 bu. per acre), and flour whiter, yielding a whiter loaf. This rye tillers freely and, owing to the climatic conditions of the region, is often on the ground from 12 to 13 months. It is especially suited to poor, dry, and wind-exposed soils, and, in combination with common rye, is suitable for fertile soils, provided they are not exposed to excessive humidity or fog. The characteristic qualities of this variety disappear after the second reproduction outside of its natural environment, necessitating a renewal of the seed every three years.

The composition of grain sorghum kernels, J. A. LE CLERC and L. H. BAILEY (*Jour. Amer. Soc. Agron.*, 9 (1917), No. 1, pp. 1–16).—This paper gives the minimum and maximum results obtained, and the average composition found, in analyses of several hundred samples of grain sorghums grown at Amarillo, Tex., from 1908 to 1912, inclusive. The results are presented in tabular form and discussed so as to bring out the correlations between the percentage of protein and the weight per 1,000 kernels, and also to show how the composition of grain varies with a high and low protein content, a high and low weight per 1,000 kernels, and a high and low ash content. Data are given on the rainfall at various periods during the growth of different grain sorghums at Amarillo, annually from 1908 to 1912, in an effort to correlate protein content and yield with rainfall.

The competition of the grain sorghums is compared in tabular form with that of many of the other grains and seeds to ascertain their comparative food value.

Analyses are also given of shallu and broom corn, and of bread made in part from grain sorghum meal. This meal is reported as producing a pleasing loaf.

The authors conclude that in the grain sorghums low protein is correlated with high weight per bushel, low fiber, low ash, and low pentosans, and, except in the case of milos, with low weight per 1,000 kernels, although this last is not a definite relationship. From the data on rainfall it is evident that the amount of precipitation between the periods of emergence and ripening has less influence upon the composition and yield of the crop than has either the amount of rainfall before the period of emergence or the total yearly rainfall.

The sugar beet during vegetation, E. SAILLARD (*Monit. Sci.*, 5. ser., 6 (1916), I, No. 894, pp. 121–125).—This is a brief discussion of the effects of meteorological conditions on the sugar beet during the growing season. Averages are given for the 10-year period 1904 to 1913 for each week of August and September showing the rainfall, hours of sunshine, and mean temperature, and the yield of beets per hectare, the weight of the entire plant, the weight of the roots, the yield of sucrose, the amount of sugar produced per week per hectare, and the amount of sugar produced per root per week. Some notes are also given on the reducing sugars present in sugar beets.

The present status of the sugar-beet seed industry in the United States, C. O. Townsend (*U. S. Dept. Agr. Yearbook 1916, pp. 399–410, pls. 5*).—The importance and possibilities of developing an American beet-seed industry capable of meeting the requirements of American sugar-beet growers are outlined and discussed, and cultural methods are described. The necessity for establishing uniform and fixed types is emphasized.

The present status of the sugar-beet seed industry in the United States, C. O. Townsend (*Sugar [Chicago], 19 (1917), No. 5, pp. 176–180, figs. 6*).—This is a reprint of the above.

[Experimental work with sugar cane], H. T. Easterby (*Ann. Rpt. Bur. Sugar Expt. Stas. [Queensland], 16 (1916), pp. 34*).—Work with sugar cane at numerous experimental centers in Queensland, in continuation of that previously noted (E. S. R., 35, p. 230) is reported.

Sweet clover: Growing the crop, H. S. Coe (*U. S. Dept. Agr., Farmers' Bul. 797 (1917), pp. 34, figs. 11*).—The field practices and cultural methods employed in the production of sweet clover are discussed in some detail.

Tests of 237 samples of hulled seed gave an average of 53.25 per cent germination, with 18.7 per cent of hard seed, as compared with an average of 11.8 per cent germination and 70.9 per cent hard seed for 45 unhulled samples. A further comparison of 22 samples each of southern and northern grown seed and of 28 samples of imported seed gave an average germination of 14, 37, and 56 per cent, respectively, with 60, 43, and 12 per cent of hard seed.

Means for the eradication of sweet clover are briefly outlined.

Timothy fertilization and culture, N. Schmitz (*Maryland Sta. Bul. 202 (1917), pp. 159–178, figs. 3*).—Fertilizing experiments with timothy begun in 1911, employing different commercial fertilizers as top-dressings, are reported and discussed, and field practices and cultural methods in timothy production deemed best for Maryland conditions outlined.

The fertilizer tests included a comparison of the effects of different fertilizers used alone and in various combinations; of different nitrogen carriers; of nitrate of soda, acid phosphate, and basic slag; of different rates and numbers of applications; and of spring versus fall applications.

The highest average yield of the 1912, 1913, and 1914 crops was secured from an application of 250 lbs. each of nitrate of soda and acid phosphate and 100 lbs. of muriate of potash, and amounted to 2.86 tons of hay per acre, an increase of 1.66 tons over the untreated checks. The lowest increases in yield, considered to be within the limits of experimental error, were secured from applications of basic slag and acid phosphate used alone.

An average yield of 2.34 tons was secured from a 300-lb. application of ammonium sulphate during 1913 and 1914 as compared with a yield of 1.49 tons from a similar application of dried blood. The gain over the untreated checks amounted to 0.98 and 0.13 ton, respectively. Nitrate of soda and nitrate of potash showed average yields of 2.21 tons each, a gain of 0.85 ton per acre. In a comparison of nitrate of soda, calcium cyanamid, and alpha tankage, the average yields for 1912 and 1913 were 2.71, 2.13, and 1.73 tons, respectively, which represented gains of 1.2, 0.62, and 0.22 tons per acre.

A summary of the data relative to the yields and net profits of nitrate of soda used alone, acid phosphate and nitrate of soda, and basic slag and nitrate of soda show that the average increase in yield amounted to 1.2, 1.35, and

1.08 tons per acre, respectively, with average net profits per acre of $12.41, $14.66, and $9.57.

The average results of all applications of nitrate of soda used alone indicate that the 250-lb. rate gave the highest percentage increase, 61 per cent, while the 200-lb. rate gave the highest net profit, 152 per cent. The highest net profit from a single application of nitrate of soda, 359 per cent, was also obtained from a 200-lb. application.

The use of 150 lbs. of nitrate of soda and 250 lbs. of acid phosphate gave the highest single net profit, 341 per cent, of the different combinations tested, also giving the highest average net profit, 239 per cent. The average percentage of increase varied directly with the amounts of fertilizer applied, being highest, 69 per cent, with the heaviest application, 250 lbs. each of nitrate of soda and acid phosphate.

Applying half the fertilizer the first week in April and half the second week in May as compared with a single application of the whole amount the first week in April did not give as good results on the whole as the latter method. Any increase in yield secured from the two applications was deemed insufficient to pay for the extra labor involved.

The average net profit per acre of all fall applications of fertilizers was estimated to be $5.88, while that of all spring applications was estimated at $8.10.

Tobacco culture in North Carolina, E. H. MATTHEWSON and E. G. Moss (*North Carolina Sta. Bul. 237 (1917), pp. 40, figs. 13*).—This is a detailed account of the production of flue-cured tobacco in North Carolina, including cultural and curing directions. A brief historical sketch of the introduction and development of the crop in the State and tabulated statistics on production by counties in 1909 and on sales in the old and new tobacco belts for 1910–11 and 1914–15 are also given.

Tobacco, J. F. BALDASSARRE (*Bol. Min. Agr. [Argentina], 19 (1915), No. 10–12, pp. 752–826, pls. 2, figs. 32*).—This is a detailed discussion of the economic and cultural conditions pertaining to tobacco in Argentina, including statistics on tobacco production in Argentina and other countries and importations and general notes on tobacco production in Cuba, Paraguay, and Brazil.

Notes on the composition of the ash in relation to the fertilizing of tobacco, S. TIJMSTRA (*Meded. Deli-Proefstat. Medan, 10 (1916), No. 1, pp. 12–15*).— This is a brief note on the effect of various fertilizer treatments on tobacco ash. The results agree with those obtained by Bylert and Hissink in similar experiments.

Agricultural seed inspected in 1915, C. P. SMITH (*Maryland Sta. Bul. 203 (1917), pp. 179–230*).—The results of purity and germination tests of about 1,200 official samples collected during 1915 are reported in tabular form and include red, mammoth, crimson, and alsike clovers, alfalfa, soy beans, cowpeas, timothy, orchard grass, millets, redtop, and Dwarf Express rape.

The "tolerance" table for purity tests previously noted (E. S. R., 36, p. 442) was applied to the above tests, and a similar table devised and illustrated to determine the tolerance for variations in germination tests.

The percentage of hard seeds in the samples of legume seeds tested is also reported.

Some information concerning the recognition of the Italian origin of red clover and alfalfa seed, G. LAKON (*Landw. Jahrb., 49 (1916), No. 1, pp. 137–145, figs. 2*).—Numerous tests are noted for the determination of the origin of the red clover and alfalfa seed on the German market. It is demonstrated that with a knowledge of the weed flora of a region commercial seed from that region can be definitely identified.

Certain weed seeds have been designated as the "character" seeds in samples of red clover and alfalfa. Red clover samples from Italy were identified by the presence of *Hedysarum coronarium* and *Phalaris paradoxa*. Turkestan alfalfa was distinguished from alfalfa from other sources by the presence of *Acroptilon picris*. Out of 77 tests with alfalfa of supposedly Italian origin, 75 contained the following distinguishing weed seeds: *Helminthia echioides*, *Trifolium supinum*, *Arthrolobium scorpioides*, *Hedysarum coronarium*, *Phalaris paradoxa*, and *Andropogon halepensis*. The author states that while no one of these seeds can be regarded as characteristic as in the case of red clover, yet the weed flora as a whole is characteristic.

The origin of well-cleaned seed and mixed seed was obviously difficult to determine.

The disinfection of seeds with bromin, V. ARTSIKHOVSKIĬ (ARCICHOVSKIJ) and V. STOM (*Zap. Sta. Isp. Siem. Imp. Bot. Sad.* (*Ann. Inst. Essais Semences Jard. Imp. Bot. Pierre Grand*), *3* (*1915*), No. *2*, pp. *15*, figs. *6*).—The authors present data regarding the treatment of the seed of pumpkins, beans, peas, corn, flax, and wheat with 1 per cent bromin water for varying lengths of time. Their conclusion is that a 1 per cent bromin solution applied to the seed for half an hour will prove sufficient. See also a previous note (E. S. R., 35, p. 444).

Investigations in 1914 on the weeds occurring in the Government of Kherson, Russia, I. PACHOSKIĬ (PACZOSKY) (*Trudy Búro Prikl. Bot.* (*Bul. Appl. Bot.*), *8* (*1915*), No. *6*, pp. *816–820; abs. in Internat. Inst. Agr.* [*Rome*], *Internat. Rev. Sci. and Pract. Agr.*, *7* (*1916*), No. *6*, pp. *903, 904*).—The object of these investigations was to devise a method for the study of field weeds and to study the root system of the weeds peculiar to the region.

The author holds that the only practical method for determining the degree to which a field is infested with weeds is to confine the observations to one or a few selected plats, after a careful examination of the actual field conditions.

The roots of *Cirsium arvense* were found to reach a depth of 20 ft.; those of *Euphorbia virgata*, 9.84 ft.; of *E. glariosa*, 8.53; of *Centaurea scabiosa* and *Salvia nemorosa*, 7.22 ft.; of *Reseda lutea*, 9.18 ft.; and of *Melandrium album*, 6.9 ft.

Crowfoot (Ranunculus arvensis), J. B. MARTIN (*Compt. Rend. Acad. Agr. France*, *2* (*1916*), No. *13*, pp. *420–424*).—A brief note on the occurrence and habit of growth of crowfoot. Suggestions are made for its control, and the value of copper sulphate, copper sulphate and sodium nitrate, and ferrous sulphate in combating the weed is discussed. Ferrous sulphate is reported as giving the best results.

The flea-seed, a new weed plant, T. G. B. OSBORN (*Jour. Dept. Agr. So. Aust.*, *20* (*1916*), No. *5*, pp. *360–362*, fig. *1*).—This is a brief note on the appearance of flea-seed (*Plantago psyllium*) in South Australia.

[**Notes on species of Xanthium and their destruction**] (*Instrucciones sobre el "Abrojo Grande" y su destrucción. Buenos Aires: Min. Agr.*, *1915*, pp. *12*, figs. *7*).—Brief descriptive notes are given on a composite of *X. macrocarpum*, *X. italicum*, and *X. strumarium*, with suggestions for its eradication.

HORTICULTURE.

The plant introduction gardens of the Department of Agriculture, P. H. DORSETT (*U. S. Dept. Agr. Yearbook 1916*, pp. *135–144*, pls. *10*).—A descriptive account of the plant introduction field stations or gardens situated at Miami and Brooksville, Fla., Chico, Cal., Yarrow, near Rockville, Md., and Bellingham, Wash., including information relative to methods of preventing the introduction of injurious insects and diseases and recent introductions now being tested at the gardens.

Development and localization of truck crops in the United States, F. J. BLAIR (*U. S. Dept. Agr. Yearbook 1916, pp. 435–466, figs. 13*).—A statistical account of the development and localization of the truck crop industry in various parts of the United States.

Home vegetable gardening, C. E. DURST (*Illinois Sta. Circ. 198 (1917), pp. 3–56, figs. 29*).—A practical treatise on home vegetable gardening.

How to make the garden pay, E. MORRISON and C. T. BRUES (*Boston: Houghton Mifflin Co., 1917, pp. VII+176*).—A small popular manual for the intensive cultivation of home vegetable gardens.

Vegetable culture for all, EVA (*London: Herbert Jenkins, Ltd., 1917, pp. XI+144, figs. 21*).—A popular treatise with special reference to conditions in England.

The allotment book, W. BRETT (*London: C. Arthur Pearson, Ltd., 1917, pp. 92, figs. 27*).—A popular treatise on amateur vegetable gardening, with special reference to conditions in England.

A book about potatoes and other vegetables, W. P. WRIGHT (*London: Headley Bros., 1917, pp. 164, pls. 20, figs. 12*).—A small practical treatise on vegetable gardening, in which special consideration is given to the potato.

Late cabbage, E. N. REED (*New York: John Wiley & Sons, Inc., 1917, pp. XIII+131, figs. 38*).—A practical treatise on cabbage culture based upon the author's experience and upon the results of investigations conducted by the experiment stations in the cabbage belt.

Adult characters in sunflower seedlings, T. D. A. COCKERELL (*Jour. Heredity, 8 (1917), No. 8, pp. 361, 362, fig. 1*).—In continuation of previous studies of the sunflower (E. S. R., 34, p. 237), the author calls attention to a number of variations in sunflower seedlings. These, it is concluded, are evidently inherited like other characters and may be obviously correlated with adult characters, whereas the manifestation of their effects may be limited to the seedling stage.

The effect of continued capillary watering, L. DANIEL (*Compt. Rend. Acad. Sci. [Paris], 163 (1916). No. 19, pp. 525–527; abs. in Internat. Inst. Agr. [Rome], Internat. Rev. Sci. and Pract. Agr., 8 (1917), No. 1, pp. 84, 85*).—Experiments conducted by the author with lettuce, chicory, cabbage, and radishes indicate that the continuous capillary watering of plants is much more beneficial than the usual intermittent watering employed in market gardening. Continued capillary watering gave seedling plants much in advance of those given the usual intermittent watering and also resulted in the development of more uniform and healthy subsequent growth.

Color as an indication of the picking maturity of fruits and vegetables, L. C. CORBETT (*U. S. Dept. Agr. Yearbook 1916, pp. 99–106, pls. 6*).—The work of the Department has shown that immature apples when placed in storage develop various degrees of scald, depending upon the pigmentation or color development attained by the fruit up to the time of storage. As the apple matures and assumes its normal pigmentation, danger from scald becomes reduced. For best storage conditions, however, the normal pigmentation should not be too strongly developed, as overripe fruit suffers in storage as well as green fruit.

In the case of tomatoes, half-ripened red tomatoes will not produce a canned product or a catsup of bright red color, since the pigment in such fruits is not stable and fades slightly when the pulp is subjected to the temperatures required for sterilization or concentration. In fully ripe tomatoes the red pigment is fixed.

It is pointed out, in substance, that degree of color may be a measure of physiological activities in other fruits and vegetables as well as apples and tomatoes.

Arkansas Plant Act of 1917 and rules and regulations pursuant thereto (*State Plant Bd. Ark. Circ. 1 (1917), pp. 16*).—The law here presented is entitled " an act to prevent the introduction into and the dissemination within this State of insect pests and diseases injurious to plants and plant products of this State, to create a State plant board, and to prescribe its powers and duties."

Colorado's amended horticultural inspection law (*Off. State Ent. Colo. Circ. 22 (1917), pp. 8*).—This comprises the text of the law as amended in 1917.

Horticultural laws of Idaho (*Jerome, Idaho: Lincoln County Times, 1917, pp. 16*).—This pamphlet contains the text of the horticultural inspection, insecticide, and fungicide laws of Idaho.

Suggestions for the control of injurious insects and plant diseases. G. M. BENTLEY (*Tennessee Sta. Bul. 117 (1917), pp. 111–123, figs. 2*).—A revised edition of Bulletin 106 (E. S. R., 31, p. 635).

Why, when, and how to spray, J. R. COOPER (*Nebraska Sta. Bul. 158 (1917), pp. 3–20, figs. 13*).—A brief review of Research Bulletin 10 (E. S. R., 37, p. 447).

The preparation and use of lime-sulphur in orchard spraying, W. J. MORSE (*Maine Sta. Doc. 523 (1916), pp. 11, figs. 2*).—Directions are given for making home cooked lime-sulphur concentrate, together with dilution tables and brief suggestions on the use of lime-sulphur.

Practical guide to the culture of fruit trees in Chile, especially in the northern zone, A. OPAZO G. (*Cartilla Practica sobre Arboles Frutales que Debemos Propagar en Chile i Especialmente en la Zona Norte. Santiago de Chile: Serv. Agron. Rejion. i Enseñanza Agr. Ambulante, 1916, pp. 116, figs. 55*).—Directions are given for the propagation, cultivation, care, and management of fruit trees adapted for culture in Chile, especially in northern Chile.

Rational fruit culture, H. C. DAVIDSON (*London: Garden Life Press [1917], pp. [6]+127, figs. 48*).—A practical treatise, with special reference to conditions in England.

The pear in Ontario, F. M. CLEMENT and O. J. ROBB (*Ontario Dept. Agr. Bul. 249 (1917), pp. 28, figs. 24*).—In this bulletin the authors give a summarized account of the pear industry in Ontario, together with suggestions relative to varieties, culture, harvesting, and marketing of pears.

Bush fruits, F. W. CARD (*New York: The Macmillan Co., 1917, rev. ed., pp. XIII+409, pls. 16, figs. 58*).—The present edition of this work (E. S. R., 10, p. 756) has been revised to include recent information on the subject.

Muscadine grape breeding, C. DEARING (*Jour. Heredity, 8 (1917), No. 9, pp. 409–424, figs. 9*).—A short general account of the work being conducted by the U. S. Department of Agriculture with muscadine grapes in the South, including a review of some of the results secured from intercrossing and hybridizing these grapes with other species.

Vinifera grapes in New York, R. D. ANTHONY (*New York State Sta. Bul. 432 (1917), pp. 81–105, pls. 6*).—This bulletin gives the results of experiments conducted at the station for several years in an attempt to cultivate the European grape (*Vitis vinifera*).

Since 1911 the station has had under trial more than 70 varieties of *V. vinifera* which were grafted on a miscellaneous collection of station seedlings ranging from 6 to 10 years old. Most of the plants fruited in 1913. By giving the vines winter protection and the usual grape sprays they have been kept in a healthy condition. Most of the Vinifera varieties have originated in regions with a longer season and a much warmer climate than that of New

York; hence, many of the kinds tested have been discarded. It is believed that the chief value of the Vinifera grape at present in the State is as a home-garden grape, for the commercial growers supplying local markets demanding high quality, and for the plant breeder. The varieties are discussed under the following general groups: (1) Desirable varieties for the grape regions of the State for the table and wine; (2) sorts worthy of testing in the more favorable parts of the State for table and wine; (3) kinds still on probation; and (4) varieties of little or no value in the State.

Relative to the culture of these grapes it is recommended that the eastern grower graft cuttings on phylloxera-resistant roots, such as *V. riparia*. The vines may be grown on the regular 2-wire trellis and protected through the winter by bending the trunk to the ground and covering with a few inches of earth. A replacing spur should be left at the base of the trunk to use in forming a new trunk when the old one becomes too stiff.

European grapes succeed in New York, F. H. HALL (*New York State Sta. Bul. 432, popular ed. (1917), pp. 3–7*).—A popular edition of the above.

Olive growing and production in Spain, J. M. PRIEGO (*Internat. Inst. Agr. [Rome], Internat. Rev. Sci. and Pract. Agr., 7 (1916), No. 12, pp. 1727–1733*).— A general account of the olive industry in Spain, including information relative to the varieties grown, method of cultivation, development, and present condition of olive production.

Citrus stock experiments at Warm Baths, Transvaal, experimental orchard, C. A. SIMMONDS (*Agr. Jour. So. Africa, 2 (1915), No. 11, pp. 196–205*).— Brief notes are given on the condition and behavior of numerous citrus varieties, including oranges, tangerines, lemons, citrange, and grapefruit grafted on various stocks. The stocks used in the test, which has been carried on for a number of years, include rough lemon, Mazoe lemon, sweet orange, mandarin, sweet lime, *Citrus trifoliata*, shaddock, pomelo, Florida sour, and bitter Seville.

The origin and dispersal of Cocos nucifera, O. BECCARI (*Philippine Jour. Sci., Sect. C, 12 (1917), No. 1, pp. 27–43*).—In the present discussion the author reaches the conclusion that an Asiatic or Polynesian origin of the coconut palm is more probable than an American one, as suggested by Cook (E. S. R., 13, p. 714).

Note on the coffees and their culture at Lula, MERTENS (*Bul. Agr. Congo Belge, 7 (1916), No. 3–4, pp. 285–301, fig. 1*).—Notes are given on the various coffees being tested at the Lula Agricultural Station, Stanleyville, Belgian Kongo, including observations on the diseases and other enemies of coffee at the station during the years 1914 and 1915.

The coffee industry of French Indo-China, L. P. BRIGGS (*U. S. Dept. Com., Com. Rpts., No. 186 (1917), pp. 534–542*).—In this account the author discusses the range of the coffee industry in French Indo-China, the climatic and soil conditions, varieties, plants resistant to insect attacks, cultural operations, harvesting and preparation for the market, enemies of the coffee tree, production and exportation, and the future of the coffee industry.

Filbert growing in the Puget Sound country, A. A. QUARNBERG (*Seattle, Wash.: Puget Mill Co. [1917], pp. 36, figs. 19*).—This booklet contains practical information on the culture of the European filbert (*Corylus avellana*) as at present practiced in the Pacific Northwest.

Further notes on the germination of belladonna seed, A. F. SIEVERS (*Amer. Jour. Pharm., 89 (1917), No. 5, pp. 203–213, figs. 5*).—The author briefly summarizes previous work along this line (E. S. R., 32, p. 626) and gives the results secured from three different methods of gathering belladonna seed with reference to their influence on germination. In the first method, the berries were picked when ripe and succulent, the seed being at once removed from the pulp and dried. In the second, the berries were picked in a similar manner but allowed to dry spontaneously, which resulted in much molding and partial decomposition. In the third, the berries were allowed to remain on the plants until they were dry.

The first method produced the heaviest and the third method the lightest seed. The latter method is likely to result in the admixture of some immature seed. The first method produced seed of the best uniform color, while the second method resulted in seed of very poor color. The germination percentage was highest in the first and lowest in the third method. Seed from different individual plants was found to vary considerably in vitality.

Preliminary report on cooperative experiment [with Datura], C. M. WOODWORTH and H. A. LANGENHAN (*Bul. Univ. Wis., No. 829 (1916), pp. 51, 52*).—A brief statement of progress made in breeding experiments with Datura species, with special reference to a determination of the inheritance of alkaloidal content. Analyses made in 1915 showed that the alkaloidal content of leaves varied much, both in the same plant and in different plants of the same species. The alkaloidal content of leaves in 1916 appeared to be more uniform.

Possibility of the commercial production of lemon-grass oil in the United States, S. C. HOOD (*Amer. Jour. Pharm., 89 (1917), No. 4, pp. 180–191*).—This article is reprinted from the bulletin previously noted (E. S. R., 36, p. 538).

The sweet pea (Lathyrus odoratus) in the flower garden, A. C. GHOSH (*Agr. Jour. Bihar and Orissa [India], 4 (1916), Double No., pp. 53–63, pls. 2*).—In addition to cultural directions the varieties of sweet peas tested under the direction of the Botanic Garden at Sabour, India, are here described.

The culture and diseases of the sweet pea, J. J. TAUBENHAUS (*New York: E. P. Dutton & Co., 1917, pp. XXIV+232, pls. 22, figs. 16*).—A practical treatise on the subject, the successive chapters of which discuss the history, evolution, classification, and culture; culture of the sweet pea for seeds; culture of sweet peas under glass; diseases of greenhouse sweet peas; field diseases of sweet peas; diseases not yet known in America; insect pests; diseased seeds; physiological diseases; methods of control; and spraying.

The ornamental trees of Hawaii, J. F. ROCK (*Honolulu, Hawaii: Author, 1917, pp. V+210, pls. 2, figs. 79*).—Descriptive accounts are given of the ornamental trees and shrubs of Hawaii, including references to fruit trees and ornamental vines. The plants treated or mentioned in the volume have been identified and are represented by specimens in the College of Hawaii herbarium. The author points out that it is possible that a few introduced and indigenous species as yet not identified or unheard of may not be included in the present work.

A bud variation of Pittosporum, A. D. SHAMEL (*Jour. Heredity, 8 (1917), No. 8, pp. 357, 358, fig. 1*).—The author illustrates and describes bud sports occurring in the ornamental hedge plant *Pittosporum tobira variegatum* for the purpose of calling attention to the possibility of studying and utilizing bud variations for the propagation of valuable commercial varieties of ornamental plants.

Hints on landscape gardening, PRINCE VON PÜCKLER-MUSKAU, trans. by B. SICKERT, edited by S. PARSONS (*Boston: Houghton Mifflin Co., 1917, pp. XLV+196, pls. 33*).—The present work comprises the second of a series of books (E. S. R., 19, p. 1042) undertaken at the suggestion of and with the cooperation of the American Society of Landscape Architects.

In part one of the present work the author presents hints on landscape gardening based upon the results secured in developing his private park at Muskau,

Silesia. Frequent reference is also given to observations made on various types of English landscape gardening. Consideration is given to the laying-out of a park; size and extent; inclosure; grouping in general, and buildings; parks and gardens; concerning the laying-out of the lawns of parks, meadows, and gardens; trees and shrubs and their grouping, and plantations in general; roads and paths; water; islands; rocks; earthworks and esplanades; and maintenance.

`Part two contains a detailed description of the park in Muskau and its origin.

The natural style in landscape gardening, F. A. WAUGH (*Boston: Richard G. Badger, 1917, pp. 151, pls. 16, fig. 1*).—A general work on landscape gardening, in which the author places special emphasis on the development of natural landscapes. As defined by the author the natural style of landscape gardening endeavors to present its pictures in forms typical of the natural landscape and made vital by the landscape spirit. The subject matter is presented under the general headings of what is meant, the native landscape, form and spirit, the landscape motive, principles of structural composition, the art of grouping, features and furnishings, and the open field.

FORESTRY.

Forest laws (*N. H. Forestry Com. Circ. 7, rev. (1917), pp. 44*).—This pamphlet gives the State laws relating to forestry in general and particularly to the protection of forests from fire, the control of the white pine blister rust, the purchase and development of State forests, and the possibilities for woodlot owners to secure help in reforesting waste lands and improving woodlots.

·Annual report for the year ended October 31, 1916, Department of Conservation and Development (*Rpts. Dept. Conserv. and Develop., N. J., 1916, pp. 84, pls. 13, figs. 2*).—In addition to the report of the department as a whole, the reports of the State geologist, State forester, and State firewarden are given.

Opening up the National Forests by road building, O. C. MERRILL (*U. S. Dept. Agr. Yearbook 1916, pp. 521-529, pls. 3*).—A review of legislation dealing with road building in the National Forests, including an account of the work accomplished along this line.

The work of the forest department in India, edited by R. S. TROUP (*Calcutta: Govt., 1917, pp. [6]+65, pls. 13*).—This publication presents the main facts connected with the work of the forest department in India and sketches the outlook for future expansion. The subject matter is presented under the general headings of history of the forest department; area, classes, and types of forests; forest policy and legal control; administration and staff; research; forest organization and exploitation; forest products; forest industries; financial results; and future prospects and requirements.

Silviculture, E. MARSDEN (*Ann. Rpt. Bd. Sci. Advice India, 1915-16, pp. 123-129*).—A brief review of silvicultural operations conducted by the forest service of India, including a list of publications for the year 1915-16.

The relation of the storage of the seeds of some of the oaks and hickories to their germination, C. C. DELAVAN (*Rpt. Mich. Acad. Sci., 17 (1915), pp. 161-163*).—Different methods of storing oak and hickory seeds were compared at the University of Michigan to determine the influence of storage on the germination of the seeds. Three species of hickory, three species of the white-oak group, and two species of the black-oak group were included in the test.

The work showed in brief that a cold, even temperature, even if the atmosphere is very moist, is better than a warm, drier condition of storage. The best results from the standpoint of germination were secured by storing the seeds in closed but unsealed fruit jars placed in an ice box.

Evergreen trees for Iowa, G. B. MacDonald (*Iowa Sta. Bul. 170 (1917), pp. 31–59, figs. 31; abridged ed., pp. 16, figs. 7*).—This bulletin lists the most desirable evergreens to be used in Iowa for shelter belts, windbreaks, and ornamental planting, and gives brief descriptions of their characteristics and value for various purposes, as well as methods of planting and growing.

The structure and identification of Queensland woods, N. W. Jolly (*Dept. Pub. Lands, Queensland, Forestry Bul. 1 (1917), pp. 14, pls. 5*).—A descriptive account of the wood structure, with illustrations, of some 45 species of the more common trees of Queensland.

Utilization of ash, W. D. Sterrett (*U. S. Dept. Agr. Bul. 523 (1917), pp. 52, pls. 10, figs. 3*).—This bulletin discusses the value of ash for different uses, gives the amount of the different species of ash used in various industries, and indicates methods by which owners may utilize their ash timber profitably. An account is also given of the properties of ash wood, including results of tests conducted by J. A. Newlin with different species.

Grass trees: An investigation of their economic products, J. C. Earl (*So Aust. Dept. Chem. Bul. 6 (1917), pp. 19, pls. 5*).—A study of the grass trees, blackboys, or yackas (*Xanthorrhœa* spp.) of South Australia, with special reference to their botany, distribution, and exploitation for resin. A short chemical study of the resin extracted is included.

Note on Indian sumac (Rhus cotinus), Puran Singh ([*Indian] Forest Bul. 31 (1916), pp. 12*).—The author calls attention to the possibility of using the Indian sumac (*R. cotinus*) as a source of tannin, and gives an account of the cultivation, preparation, and quality of European sumacs (*Rhus* spp.) for this purpose.

Notes on Funtumia elastica and Funtumia hybrids, Miny (*Bul. Agr. Congo Belge, 7 (1916), No. 3–4, pp. 246–267, figs. 14*).—This comprises notes and observations on the growth and rubber-yielding value of *F. elastica* and other Funtumia hybrids as observed in plantations in the oriental Province of Belgian Kongo.

Investigations on the mechanism of the cicatrization of tapping wounds among rubber-yielding plants, F. Heim (*Bul. Off. Colon. [France], 10 (1917), No. 110–111, pp. 95–102, pl. 1*).—The author here summarizes the results of studies conducted by J. Maheu relative to the healing of wounds and development of new latex-yielding ducts among African rubber plants. The text is accompanied by a number of figures showing the process of cicatrization. The results show, in brief, that the tapping operation should consist in making numerous small wounds rather than large wide wounds inasmuch as abnormal growths are apt to occur on the latter wounds, thereby interfering with the reestablishment of the latex ducts.

Economic forest products, R. S. Pearson (*Ann. Rpt. Bd. Sci. Advice India, 1915–16, pp. 130–137*).—A report of investigations conducted by the forest service of India with economic forest products, including a list of publications relating thereto published during 1915–16.

Marketing woodlot products in Tennessee, W. D. Sterrett (*Resources Tenn., 7 (1917), No. 3, pp. 111–195, figs. 19*).—Information is given relative to the woodlot regions of the State; native tree species and their uses; available markets, classed both by products and by species; lumber and log values; best methods of estimating and marketing various woodlot products; and the care of cut woodlot products. A directory of wood-using firms is included.

DISEASES OF PLANTS.

A method for studying the humidity relations of fungi in culture, N. E. STEVENS (*Phytopathology, 6 (1916), No. 6, pp. 428–432*).—A description is given of a method used by the author in maintaining known humidities in small chambers which is applicable to the study of fungi in culture or growing on small fruits. It consists in keeping the cultures of fungi or the affected fruits in an atmosphere which is maintained at a constant humidity by exposure to an aqueous solution of sulphuric acid of known specific gravity.

Celluloid cylinders for inoculation chambers, E. E. HUBERT (*Phytopathology, 6 (1916), No. 6, pp. 447–450, fig. 1*).—The author describes a cylinder made of sheet celluloid which has proved adapted to use in inoculation experiments on tree seedlings and similar hosts.

Nematode technique, T. B. MAGATH (*Trans. Amer. Micros. Soc., 35 (1916), No. 4, pp. 245–256, figs. 6*).—The methods here presented are intended to serve as a guide for future work. While applicable for free-living nematodes, the methods have been worked out particularly for the parasitic forms.

Presence of nitrites and ammonia in diseased plants. Its significance with regard to crop rotation and soil depletion, P. A. BONCQUET (*Jour. Amer. Chem. Soc., 38 (1916), No. 11, pp. 2572–2576*).—The author, having continued some phases of the work previously participated in by him (E. S. R., 34, p. 645), states that in beets *Bacillus morulans* is able to reduce nitrates not only to nitrites but also partly or wholly to ammonia, these substances never being found in these tests apart from pathological indications.

Mosaic disease of tobacco was associated with a filterable organism which showed considerable reducing power and which was absent from normal leaves. An organism provisionally named *Streptococcus solani* n. sp. was present uniformly in certain potato vines and leaves. This proved to be an active nitrate reducer. Traces of ammonia were also detected. This organism may prove to be connected with brown streak and blossom abortion of potato. Some other plants which looked sickly gave a decided nitrite reaction, the intensity thereof corresponding to the severity of the sickly appearance shown by the plants.

Nitrites have not been detected in any plant tissue which can, in strictness, be called normal. The disturbance is ascribed to a partial and local nitrogen starvation of the tissues, as well as to mechanical laceration due to ulcer formation by the bacteria.

It is thought that soil depletion has a fundamental relation to nitrate reduction, a lack of rotation favoring the accumulation of nitrate-reducing organisms.

The influence of Æcidium clematidis on the leaves of its host, L. MONTE-MARTINI (*Riv. Patol. Veg., 8 (1916), No. 8–9, pp. 165–176*).—Having shown previously (E. S. R., 17, p. 981) that vegetable parasites produce in their hosts at first a stimulating, but later a depressing effect, the author has made a study of leaves of *Clematis vitalba* attacked by *Æ. clematidis*, from which it is concluded that the acceleration observed is a consequence of the increase of chlorophyll in the infested leaves. While the ash weight per unit of area was increased by the fungus attack, the ash weight per unit of dry matter was lessened thereby. Assimilation and transpiration appeared to be more energetic in diseased leaves than in sound ones, as shown by the total ash content. The calcium, however, was somewhat less in case of the diseased leaves, which showed a considerable increase in silica. These findings are compared with some reported by Pavarino (E. S. R., 18, p. 347).

Work connected with insect and fungus pests and their control (*Imp. Dept. Agr. West Indies, Rpt. Agr. Dept. Montserrat, 1915–16, pp. 23–26*).—Besides notes on cotton stainers, an account is given of attempts to control peanut leaf rust (*Uredo* sp.), which was accomplished with Bordeaux mixture; of a serious and spreading wilt of pineapple, involving root decay; and of two diseases of papaya, one of which appeared on the leaves in association with *Asperisporium caricæ* in an unsuitable situation, the other and more important one attacking stems and fruit and resembling considerably a disease reported from Barbados as produced on stems, leaves, leaf stalks, and fruits by a species of Colletotrichum.

Reports of the botanical laboratory and laboratory for plant diseases, L LINSBAUER, F. ZWEIGELT, and H. ZUDERELL (*Programm u. Jahresber, K. K. Höh. Lehranst. Wein u. Obstbau Klosterneuburg, 1914–15, pp. 91–101; 1915–16. pp. 117–130*).—Continuing previous work (E. S. R., 33, p. 444), the first of these two reports, along with insect enemies and other matters, deals with Fusicladium, Penicillium, *Gymnosporangium sabinæ, Mycosphærella scutina, Puccinia pruni-spinosæ*, and leaf curl as related to orchard plants; *Sphærotheca mors-uvæ* on gooseberry; *Plasmopara viticola* on grape; *Plasmodiophora brassicæ, Sclerotinia libertiana, Colletotrichum lindemuthianum, Bremia lactucæ*, and *Peronospora effusa* on vegetables; *Asteroma rosæ* and *Oidium cuonymi japonici* on ornamental plants; *Erysiphe tortilis, Cæoma euonymi, Lophodermium macrosporum, L. pinastri, P. effusa, Ustilago tragopogonis*, and *Ramularia violæ* on wild-growing plants.

The second report also gives data regarding *Septoria piricola, Cephalothecium roseum, Phytophthora cactorum, Exoascus bullatus*, and *E. deformans* on fruit trees; Boytrytis and Oidium on grape; *Pseudomonas phaseoli, P. campestris, Puccinia chondrillæ*, and *P. glumarum* on field or garden plants; *Gymnosporangium clavariæforme, Glœosporium tiliæ, G. nervisequum*, and *Phragmidium subcorticium* on various ornamentals.

Some new or rare plant diseases, L. MONTEMARTINI (*Riv. Patol. Veg.*, 7 (*1915*), No. 8–9, pp. 225–237; 8 (*1916*), No. 8–9, pp. 177–185).—In the first of these reports, continuing previous work (E. S. R., 30, p. 349), the author notes a leaf scorch of *Syringa vulgaris* associated with *Cladosporium syringæ* n. sp.; one of Anthurium with *Chætodiplodia anthurii* n. sp., *Glomerella anthurii* n. sp., and *Colletotrichum anthurii*; a leaf spot of *Corylus avellana* with *Cercospora coryli* n. sp.; of *Quercus sessiliflora* with *Septoria* sp. and *Phyllosticta italica* n. sp.; of *Camellia japonica* with *Alternaria camelliæ*; of Cratægus with *Hadrotrichum populi*; a leaf dieback of yucca with *Cylindrosporium yuccæ* n. sp.; a leaf perforation of peony with *Coniothyrium pæoniæ* n. sp.; and a Cicinnobolus, very similar to *C. cesatii evonymi* noted in France by Vuillemin (E. S. R., 24, p. 352), attacking Oidium on oaks.

In the second report, the author notes a bacteriosis of chestnut leaves; a leaf spot of Tilia ascribed to a fungus which is considered a new variety, *Phyllosticta bacteroides minima;* a fruit disease of pomegranate due to *Ceuthospora punicæ;* a leaf shot-hole and laceration of Acanthus connected with a fungus described as a new variety, *Septoria acanthi romana;* a leaf curl of cherry associated with *Exoascus cerasi;* a leaf spot of *Cratægus oxyacantha* associated with *P. bacillaris* n. sp., supposedly the pycnidial stage of *Venturia cratægi;* and a cucurbit leaf spot associated with several fungi named as probably saprophytic, with *Cercospora cucurbitæ, P. cucurbitacearum, Ascochyta* sp., and the new species *S. cucurbitæ* and *Leptosphæria cucurbitæ*, also supposed to be parasitic.

Phytopathology, F. A. STOCKDALE (*Ann. Rpt. Dept. Agr. Mauritius, 1915, pp. 14–16*).—The general conditions throughout 1915 are said to have been somewhat unfavorable to the spread of fungus diseases in this region. The extreme dryness favored the spread of a root disease of sugar cane due to a weakly parasitic Marasmius. Pithy deterioration of White Tanna cane, apparently due to a bacterium, was prevalent in certain districts, and some other varieties were affected. The gumming disease of sugar cane noted during the early part of the year (E. S. R., 34, p. 843) did not spread after May. Red rot (*Colletotrichum falcatum*) occurred in September and October on one estate, following an attack by borers (*Diatræa striatalis*). Smut (*Ustilago sacchari*) came under observation here this year for the first time.

The leaf disease of Arabian coffee due to *Hemileia vastatrix* was less common this year than usual. It was controlled by Bordeaux mixture in one instance.

The manioc leaf and stem disease (*Glœosporium manihotis*) was again common in some localities, causing defoliation in September. Some recently introduced varieties appear to be somewhat resistant to this disease.

A leaf spot of pistachio, due to *Uredo arachidis*, was again observed. The most serious leaf spotting of pistachio was due to *Cercospora personata*, which caused much damage to introduced varieties.

Leaf disease (*Phytophthora infestans*) of potato was common during July to September, inclusive. Cooperative spraying gave encouraging results. Spraying should begin early, and should continue at intervals of 8 to 10 days, owing to heavy dews in July and August.

Tomatoes raised from imported seeds suffer with leaf disease, but the local pomme d'amour is measurably resistant. Sleeping disease (*Fusarium lycopersici*) and a collar rot are common and injurious. Egg fruits (*Solanum melongena*) were badly affected with stem blight during March and April. A root disease of she oak (*Casuarina equisetifolia*) is under investigation. Turkish tobacco at Pamplemousses failed on account of attacks by an Erysiphe.

Lists are given of garden plants examined during the year, diseases noted, and causative organisms.

Report of the microbiologist, H. M. NICHOLLS (*Tasmania Agr. and Stock Dept. Rpt. 1913–14, pp. 28, 29*).—In a brief report which also deals with insect pests, the author notes the first appearance in Tasmania of cruciferous clubroot (*Plasmodiophora brassicæ*) and of cabbage leaf spot (*Glœosporium concentricum*). Considerable injury is done by a rust causing dieback in orchards.

The principal potato diseases noted were dry rot (*Fusarium solani*) and scab (*Oospora scabies*). The dry rot due to *Spondylocladium atrovirens* was noted here for the first time.

Notes relating to the Gymnosporangia on Myrica and Comptonia, B. O. DODGE and J. F. ADAMS (*Mycologia, 9 (1917), No. 1, pp. 23–29, pls. 2, fig. 1*).— A study has been made, with inconclusive results, regarding the relationships of a fungus found in 1916 to cause certain changes, which are described, in Comptonia. It is thought that the fungus may prove to be a relative or member of the genus Gymnosporangium, possibly identical with *G. myricatum* or *Æcidium myricatum* on Myrica.

Studies in the life histories of some species of Septoria occurring on Ribes, R. E. STONE (*Phytopathology, 6 (1916), No. 6, pp. 419–427, figs. 2*).—Additional investigations have confirmed the conclusion of the author that *S. ribis* has for its perfect stage *Mycosphærella grossulariæ* (E. S. R., 36, p. 246). The perfect stage has been reported on *R. grossularia* and *R. nigrum* in Europe and possibly on *R. rubrum*, but in North America it has been collected only on *R. nigrum*. *M. aurea* n. sp. is described as the perfect stage of *S. aurea*. This fungus is said to be more limited in its range, being known only in North America on *R. aureum*.

The Uredinales found upon the **Onagraceæ**, G. R. Bisby (*Amer. Jour. Bot.,* *3 (1916), No. 10, pp. 527–561*).—This is a study of the characters and correlations of Uredinales on Onagraceæ.

It is conceded that a perfectly consistent treatment of all the evening primrose rusts is impossible at this time, this study attempting rather to draw attention to some of the more insistent questions which arise. These rusts appear to fall into three somewhat definite groups, those with teliospores adherent in layers, those with teliospores free and short-ellipsoid, and those with teliospores free and long-ellipsoid, with a fourth group, the members of which may really belong to the second and third.

The main points brought out are the grouping of the long-cycled, autœcious forms of Puccinia upon the Onagraceæ into one species and the considerations involved; some notes upon heterœcious forms, which include the Onagraceæ in their life cycle; some correlations between species and races; and keys based respectively upon the life history, upon the spore forms independently, and upon the host (indicating also the geographic distribution). The hosts and rusts, an index to which is also given, present many parallelisms in their evolution.

Endophyllum-like rusts of Porto Rico, E. W. Olive and H. H. Whetzel (*Amer. Jour. Bot., 4 (1917), No. 1, pp. 44–52, pls. 3*).—A list given by the authors, with discussion of some rusts collected in Porto Rico early in 1916, includes, as new genera, Botryorhiza, represented by *B. hippocrateæ,* and Endophylloides, represented by *E. portoricensis;* also as new combinations, *Endophyllum circumscriptum, E. wedeliæ, E. decoloratum,* and *E. stachytarphetæ.*

The barberry bush and black stem rust of small grains, I. E. Melhus and L. W. Durrell (*Iowa Sta. Circ. 35 (1917), pp. 4, figs. 6*).—Attention is called to the relation of the common European barberry (*Berberis vulgaris*) to the black stem rust of cereals, for which this barberry acts as alternate host. The author recommends the eradication of all of the common European barberries. If such plants are desired, the Japanese species (*B. thunbergii*) may be substituted, as this is considered immune to rust attack.

Sclerotinia libertiana on snap beans, J. A. McClintock (*Phytopathology, 6 (1916), No. 6, pp. 436–441, figs. 2*).—A detailed account is given of a serious disease of a fall crop of snap beans which was investigated at the Virginia Truck Experiment Station, a popular account of the disease having already been noted (E. S. R., 36, p. 647).

The investigations have shown that the trouble is due to *S. libertiana,* and some evidence is said to have been obtained indicating varietal resistance toward the organism. In culture the fungus isolated from beans produced sclerotia, which differed in size and shape from those produced by the lettuce drop organism, thus suggesting that the former organism is a special strain of *S. libertiana.*

The Peronospora disease of maize, A. A. L. Rutgers (*Dept. Landb., Nijv. en Handel [Dutch East Indies], Meded. Lab. Plantenziekten, No. 22 (1916), pp. 30, pls. 7*).—This is a study of the lijer disease, said to be the most serious affecting Indian corn in Java, where it has been present for at least 25 years, occurring all over that island and Madura, and also in Achin, but never at an altitude of more than 4,000 feet.

The symptoms are described as differing according to the age of the plant. The disease is caused by *P. maydis,* which is provided with conidia, chlamydospores, and oospores, both the latter being found in decaying portions of young plants, especially in the leaf sheaths. Young plants are known to be susceptible to infection by conidia, but this is not known to occur normally in the field. Infected soil gave negative results. Seed which had been placed in water at 60° C. showed twice as high a degree of infection as did the control seed, owing supposedly to the weakening effect of the hot water upon the seed.

Flower-bud and boll shedding of cotton in the Ilorin Province, Nigeria, T. THORNTON (*Trans. 3. Internat. Cong. Trop. Agr. 1914, vol. 1, pp. 379–384*).— In this account, previously noted from another source (E. S. R., 34, p. 844), it is stated that native and imported cottons behaved alike as regards shedding. The nature of the influence of sunshine and humidity was not determined. Seed were preserved from a plant which retained all its blooms and ripened all its bolls, with a view to breeding a variety resistant to the extreme conditions and quick changes prevalent in this region.

Onion mildew, H. BLIN (*Rev. Hort. [Paris], 88 (1916), No. 9, pp. 141, 142*).— A mildew disease of onions, studied since 1913, is said to have been due to *Peronospora schleideni*, though *Macrosporium parasiticum sarcinula* was often present, and apparently took a certain part in the alteration observed. For the protection of plants from attack, the author suggests the use of Bordeaux mixture made up of 3 per cent copper sulphate and 2 per cent lime.

Some potato problems, P. R. COWAN (*Ann. Rpt. Quebec Soc. Protec. Plants [etc.], 8 (1915–16), pp. 59–63*).—Noting the growing importance of disease as affecting returns from potato culture in Canada, the author discusses varietal susceptibility and the symptoms of the various potato diseases. The several means of control considered effective are outlined.

Cryptogamic diseases of sugar cane, R. AVERNA SACCÁ (*Bol. Agr. [Sao Paulo], 17. ser., No. 8 (1916), pp. 610–641, figs. 27*).—This is a condensed account of information collected during several years regarding sugar cane diseases as related to *Schizophyllum commune* (*S. alneum*), *Valsaria subtropica*, *Linospora sacchari*, *Leptosphæria sacchari*, *Euryachora sacchari*, *Cytospora sacchari*, *Nectria* sp., *Otthia* sp., *Fusarium* sp., *Vermicularia sacchari*, *Colletotrichum falcatum*, *Lasiodiplodia theobromæ*, *Coniothyrium sacchari*, *Phyllosticta* sp., *Dendrophoma saccharicola*, *Sphæropsis pseudodiplodia*, and *Cladosporium graminum*.

Pathology and physiology of tobacco in the Crown lands, H. JENSEN ET AL. (*Proefstat. Vorstenland. Tabak [Dutch East Indies], Meded. 5 (1913), pp. 7–78, 122–130, 137, 197, 198, pls. 8*).—These selections include the botanical and phytopathological portions of a somewhat extended report embodying materials taken by the author from his own work and from that of M. Raciborski, O. de Vries, and M. Treub.

Tobacco diseases, or causes thereof as dealt with, include *Phytophthora nicotianæ* (here considered as possibly identical with P. *infestans*), gummosis (bacterial), leaf mosaic, tjakar, various fungi, nematodes and other animals, and diseases of undetermined causation. The abnormality of the flowers, characterized by their turning or remaining green, mutants with double blooms, three-parted seedlings, the influence of light on germination, and the influence of colored light on desiccation are also discussed.

Lanas disease of tobacco in the Crown lands, H. JENSEN (*Proefstat. Vorstenland. Tabak [Dutch East Indies], Meded. 1 (1913), pp. 35, pls. 5*).—Having made a study of a disease supposedly identical with that reported by J. Van Breda de Haan (E. S. R., 8, p. 237) as due to a fungus which that author described as a new species under the name *Phytophthora nicotianæ*, the present author distinguishes between this disease and one characterized by a gummosis (but showing a somewhat similar leaf wilt) by employing rather arbitrarily for these two diseases the Javanese terms lanas and lier, respectively.

16179°—17—No. 6——5

Lanas may attack in any one of four forms, namely, entire young plantlets on the seed bed, the crown at any age, the upper part of the stalk of grown plants, or the leaves thereof. Comparisons are made with tobacco diseases elsewhere.

Spraying affected plants and soil with fungicides and removal of affected plants are recommended.

Gummosis in tobacco, H. JENSEN (*Proefstat. Vorstenland. Tabak* [*Dutch East Indies*], *Meded. 6 (1914), pp. 3–10, fig. 1*).—The author gives the results of studies on the relation between lanas in the Crown lands and gummosis at the Deli station. These diseases may prove to differ but little, except in the greater severity noted in the former case.

Experiments carried on simultaneously by the author in the Crown lands and by J. A. Honing at Deli seemed to indicate that a strain of Kanari tobacco is somewhat resistant to diseases of this type, attaining more vigorous growth than either of the other two strains tested.

Leaf roll in tomatoes, H. T. GÜSSOW (*Phytopathology, 6 (1916), No. 6, p. 447*).—The author reports a disease of tomatoes at Lethbridge, Alberta, which shows phenomena closely resembling the leaf roll in potatoes, and he suggests that the disease is similar to one previously described from Austria by G. Köck, in which no parasitic organism was found. The Canadian specimens are said to have appeared sound with the exception of the rolling of the leaves.

Watermelon diseases, W. A. ORTON (*U. S. Dept. Agr., Farmers' Bul. 821 (1917), pp. 18, figs. 11*).—Popular descriptions are given of a number of diseases to which the watermelon is subject, together with suggestions for their control. Among the more common and destructive diseases are watermelon wilt, root knot, anthracnose, and stem-end rot. Descriptions are also given of several minor diseases.

The varietal relations of crown gall, J. K. SHAW (*Science, n. ser., 45 (1917), No. 1167, pp. 461, 462*).—Attention is called to the various forms of crown gall occurring on apple trees, and the author raises the question as to whether the different forms may not be due to varietal differences in the host plants. During the past few years several thousand apple trees of many varieties have been propagated on their own roots by means of the common whip graft, the seedling nurse root being cut off at the end of about two seasons' growth, thus leaving the scion growing on its own roots. It has been observed that where crown gall is present on such trees there is a tendency for a given variety to have only a single form of the disease. The Jewett shows usually the hard form of the gall, the Red Astrachan the simple form of the hairy root, and the Oldenburg the woolly knot form with many soft fleshy root growths. Some varieties on their own roots seem to be largely if not entirely immune to this disease, and it is suggested that this fact may offer a solution of the problem of the prevention of crown gall.

Fire blight, F. LÉTOURNEAU (*Ann. Rpt. Quebec Soc. Protec. Plants* [*etc.*], *8 (1915–16), pp. 42–45*).—Fire blight is said to be the worst disease of fruit trees in the Province of Ontario, attacking chiefly pear, but also apple, quince, and even plum, hawthorn, and mountain ash. The disease is said to be peculiar to North America, occurring all over the United States and in Ontario, Quebec, and British Columbia. The various forms and effects of attack are discussed, as are also the life cycle and means of control.

Dieback of apple trees, caused by Cytospora leucostoma, P. A. VAN DER BIJL (BYL) (*So. African Jour. Sci., 12 (1916), No. 12, pp. 545–557, pls. 6, figs. 4*).— The author describes a serious dieback of apple attributed to *C. leucostoma*, which is said to appear also in the same, or a closely related form, on peach, plum, and apricot trees. The fungus grows well in the laboratory on a number of media, developing pycnidia. The ascus stage has not been observed. The fungus appears to flourish through a rather wide range of temperature, growth being vigorous between 25 and 30° C. (77 and 86° F.). The mycelium is septate and branched.

Control measures suggested include destruction of diseased parts and cleansing sprays in winter.

New facts regarding the period of ascospore discharge of the apple-scab fungus, L. CHILDS (*Oregon Sta. Bul. 143 (1917), pp. 3–11, figs. 2*).—A report is given of a study of the activity of the apple-scab fungus made in Oregon during 1916 in order to determine the time at which primary infection could be expected and the bearing that it would have on the first application of a fungicide. The investigation has shown that there is a correlation between spore ejection and the prevailing weather conditions, the number of periods of ascospore discharge, and the length of ascospore activity during the season.

Mature ascospores were first ejected at Hood River on March 20, 1916, and the last ejection observed was on June 27. At Corvallis this activity was first noted on February 25, and the discharge was abundant as late as May 20, after which no observations were made. It was observed that, as a rule, the heaviest spore ejection occurred during the first two or three days of a rainy period, gradually becoming less toward the end of the wet weather.

This study is considered to have demonstrated that the delayed dormant application of fungicides given while the leaves are small and undeveloped can not be safely dispensed with in the Hood River and Willamette Valleys, as the ejection of ascospores begins before the foliage is even started. Owing to the great length of ascospore activity, it is stated that orchardists are not safe in omitting any of the later spring sprayings, even though conidial infections are not present.

The black knot of plum and cherry, C. B. HUTCHINGS (*Ann. Rpt. Quebec Soc. Protec. Plants [etc.], 8 (1915–16), pp. 85–88, fig. 1*).—Black knot, prevalent in Great Britain, the United States, and Canada wherever wild or cultivated plums and cherries grow, is said to be particularly severe in the Maritime Provinces, Quebec, parts of Ontario, and New York State. Notable exceptions occur in case of the plum and cherry orchards of the Niagara peninsula, owing to the thoroughness of the control measures there employed. Early removal and complete destruction of all knots before maturing is considered to be the simplest and most effective of all treatments for black knot.

Rougeot of grapevines, H. FAES (*Prog. Agr. et Vit. (Ed. l'Est-Centre), 37 (1916), No. 45, pp. 444–448, fig. 1*).—This is chiefly a discussion of the views of several investigators on the grapevine disease known for some years in Switzerland and elsewhere in Europe and designated by such descriptive names as rougeot, red scald, etc. The evidence is considered to favor the view of Müller-Thurgau (E. S. R., 30, p. 452) that the disease is associated with the blocking of the vessels by *Pseudopeziza tracheiphila.*

A Pythiacystis on avocado trees, H. S. FAWCETT (*Phytopathology, 6 (1916), No. 6, pp. 433–435; Rpt. Cal. Avocado Assoc., 1916, pp. 152–154*).—The author reports a disease of avocado trees in California in which the bark is killed and slightly sunken areas produced. It is accompanied by the exudation of gum. The disease is said to occur most frequently on trunks not far from the surface of the soil, and it is found not only on the trunks of larger trees but on small seedlings, especially if the latter have been overwatered.

Studies of the disease showed the presence of a Pythiacystis similar to P. citrophthora, and it is thought that under certain conditions this fungus may become at least a wound parasite of avocado trees. The fungus was isolated from two different specimens of avocado trees, was introduced into trunks of avocado trees in two different seasons, and produced effects similar to those on the trees from which it was isolated.

Banana disease on the Salayer Islands, A. B. RIJKS (*Dept. Landb., Nijv. en Handel [Dutch East Indies], Meded. Lab. Plantenziekten, No. 21 (1916), pp. 16, pls. 4*).—Observations made since November, 1915, are reported on the disease which is the cause of increasing loss to banana culture in several islands of the Salayer group. The author gives an account of some conditions apparently related to the prevalence of the disease, such as location, climate, soil, culture, light intensity, and varieties differing in resistance to the disease. The trouble appears in the young roots, later attacking the older ones and almost completely suppressing the root system of the plant.

Characteristics of citrus canker and of the causal organism, R. A. JEHLE (*Quart. Bul. Plant Bd. Fla., 1 (1917), No. 2, pp. 24–47, figs. 20*).—This paper aims to give such information, additional to that previously noted (E. S. R., 36, p. 352), as may enable citrus growers to obtain an adequate knowledge of citrus canker.

Apparently the disease is distributed by such mechanical carriers as rain, dew, insects, and in particular, men and domestic animals. Experiments on young plants kept in screened cages, which are described, indicated the causal agency of *Bacterium (Pseudomonas) citri*. Probably ripe fruits are not attacked, but they may serve as mechanical carriers.

The symptoms are described as being very similar on all the parts attacked. On twigs the cankers do not penetrate the wood. The period within which infection becomes obvious, after inoculation, may vary greatly, being influenced by weather or seasonal conditions and the vigor of the host, as are also the prevalence and severity of the canker.

Cooperative work for eradicating citrus canker, K. F. KELLERMAN (*U. S. Dept. Agr. Yearbook 1916, pp. 267–272, pls. 4*).—A popular description is given of the citrus canker due to *Pseudomonas citri*, together with an account of the cooperative work for the eradication of this disease carried on by the Department of Agriculture and various Gulf States as outlined.

Department of citrus canker eradication, F. STIRLING (*Quart. Bul. Plant Bd. Fla., 1 (1917), No. 2, pp. 50, 51*).—Giving data for 1914 to 1916 which he has compiled on the canker eradication work conducted in cooperation with the U. S. Department of Agriculture, the author states that citrus canker has been found on 441 properties in 22 Florida counties, there were still being classed as infected in 1916, 150 properties, 12 properties in 3 counties showing active infection at that time, of which 4 cases were regarded as new. The number of infected trees showed high maxima in August, of 1914, May and August, of 1915, and a much lower maximum in June, 1916, the range during that year being much lower than that for the other two years.

Citrus scab, H. S. FAWCETT (*Phytopathology, 6 (1916), No. 6, pp. 442–445*).— The author reviews and criticizes the conclusions of Grossenbacher regarding the cause of citrus scab (E. S. R., 36, p. 352). He also reviews some of his own investigations carried on at the Florida Experiment Station (E. S. R., 27, p. 653), which are considered to indicate definitely that *Cladosporium citri* is the cause of citrus scab.

Report of the mycologist, W. NOWELL (*Imp. Dept. Agr. West Indies, Rpt. Agr. Dept. Montserrat, 1915–16, pp. 9–12*).—Limes in the district near Plymouth exhibited a progressive dieback of the branches, and another, supposedly distinct therefrom, of the roots. The symptoms, which are discussed for each case, suggest that both troubles result from conditions unfavorable to vigorous growth in this locality. The conditions considered as significant are the amount of available water, degree of exposure to wind, and possibly some factor affecting nutrition.

On the dieback disease of Paulownia tomentosa caused by a new species of Valsa, T. HEMMI (*Bot. Mag.* [*Tokyo*], *30 (1916), No. 357, pp. 304–315, figs. 4; abs. in Mycologia, 9 (1917), No. 1, p. 40*).—Since 1914 the author has studied a dieback of P. *tomentosa*, due to a fungus described as a new species, *V. paulowniæ*, and said to be an almost omnivorous saprophyte. It attacks all parts of these trees of any age, but only at points where they have been injured, producing a layer of dead cells. Winter injury constitutes an important contributing factor in the vicinity of Sapporo, Japan.

Diseases of woody plants in North Africa, R. MAIRE (*Bul. Sta. Forest. Nord Afrique, 1 (1916), No. 4, pp. 121–130, pl. 1, figs. 4*).—*Arbutus unedo* in Algerian forests is subject to a disease producing a crowding together of the leaves, which persist after they become dead and dry, giving the appearance of a small witches' broom. The trouble is said to be due to a fungus described as *Exobasidium unedonis* n. sp., which is further discussed. The same branches as bear the above fungus show another fungus described as *Glœosporium conviva* n. sp., and a third designated as *Phoma arbuti* n. sp. *Rosa sempervirens* near Algiers is frequently attacked by a fungus thought to be new, and described as *Phragmidium rosæ-sempervirentis*.

The influence of certain climatic factors on the development of Endothia parasitica, N. E. STEVENS (*Amer. Jour. Bot., 4 (1917), No. 1, pp. 1–32, figs. 3*).—The author made a study during 1914 and 1915 of the behavior of chestnut blight on trees inoculated with *E. parasitica*. The experimental tracts ranged from Concord, N. H., to Charlottesville, Va., this stretch of country including a transition region for several important plant diseases which are named.

The average annual growth laterally of the chestnut cankers was found to increase at 11 stations trending from the north to south, but to decrease with elevation at stations in the Catskills. Rainfall seems to bear no relation to canker development. The fungus can resume growth at once on return of atmospheric warmth. No relation of climatic factors to pycnospore development could be traced. Ascospores were not developed in some cases within 18 months after inoculation. No mature perithecia developed during 1914, but both perithecia and ascospores appeared abundantly at many stations in the (late) winter, spring, and summer of 1915, atmospheric moisture appearing to have considerable connection, temperature much less, with ascospore development. Perithecia were first observed in the spring during a period of high humidity in 1915. Dry weather apparently tends to reduce the spread of the chestnut blight by lessening spore production.

The results of the present investigation are said to agree with those reported by Rankin for Ulster County, N. Y. (E. S. R., 32, p. 54). The data here presented are thought to indicate a probability that chestnut canker will spread more rapidly in the Southern than in the Northern States.

The influence of temperature on the growth of Endothia parasitica, N. E. STEVENS (*Amer. Jour. Bot., 4 (1917), No. 2, pp. 112–118, fig. 1*).—The observations above noted have been continued, though abandoned at all but six stations on account of the increased prevalence of the disease, and the results are here tabulated and discussed.

The lateral growth of the cankers of *E. parasitica* on *Castanea dentata*, as noted at these stations for the year ending with May, 1916, as for the previous year, was apparently not influenced by the amount or frequency of rainfall. The rate of growth of the fungus agrees closely with the temperature for the period, as computed by the system of remainder summation indices, or that of exponential summation indices, and less closely but still in a general way with that by physiological indices. It thus appears that temperatures is the chief climatic influence in determining the rate of growth of the chestnut-blight fungus.

Chestnut blight in West Virginia (*W. Va. Dept. Agr. Bul. 18 (1916), pp. 110–112*).—This is chiefly a discussion of information reported by Brooks as noted previously (E. S. R., 36, p. 150) and as supplemented by a later report. It is stated that late in May, 1916, the blight was found to be still spreading at the former rapid rate in the infected portions of West Virginia, but that by prompt and vigorous measures much could probably be done to check the disease in regions where infection is only sporadic and to keep it out of territory not yet infected.

Pycnia of Cronartium pyriforme, J. S. BOYCE (*Phytopathology, 6 (1916), No. 6, pp. 446, 447*).—The author reports having observed on seedlings and small saplings of the western yellow pine (*Pinus ponderosa*) typical spindle-shaped or fusiform swellings on the main stem which contained innumerable pycnospores. It is believed that the pines are probably infected in the summer or fall of one season, the pycnia not appearing until the summer of the next season at the earliest, while mature æcia are produced in the late spring or early summer of the third season.

The white pine blister rust in Canada, W. A. McCUBBIN (*Ann. Rpt. Quebec Soc. Protec. Plants [etc.], 8 (1915–16), pp. 64–72, figs. 3*).—While in both the United States and Canada numerous cases of white pine blister rust (*Peridermium strobi*) have appeared on pines imported from Europe, only one region in Ontario is known where the disease has attacked native white pines of considerable size. The degree of infection on that small area, however, suggests that this fungus might prove to be a very dangerous pest if it once obtains a foothold. Only five-leaved pines are known to be attacked. The main area affected (with the alternate stage on practically all species of Ribes but particularly on black currant) lies north of Lake Ontario, between Niagara Falls and Hamilton, with isolated areas in other localities which are named.

Experiments seem to show that the spread of the blister-rust fungus can be reduced by spraying currant bushes, but not entirely prevented by this indirect means.

ECONOMIC ZOOLOGY—ENTOMOLOGY.

The Wyoming ground squirrel in Colorado with suggestions for control, W. L. BURNETT (*Off. State Ent. Colo. Circ. 20 (1916), pp. 11, pl. 1, figs. 2*).—This account of the Wyoming ground squirrel (*Citellus elegans*) deals particularly with its distribution by counties and methods of control. The author states that from an agricultural standpoint it is the worst mammalian pest that has to be contended with in Colorado.

Destroying rodent pests on the farm, D. E. LANTZ (*U. S. Dept. Agr. Yearbook 1916, pp. 381–398, pls. 5, fig. 1*).—Means for destroying rodent pests are described.

Bird life in Washington, JENNIE V. GETTY (*Seattle, Wash.: Lowman & Hanford Co., 1916, pp. 8+134, pl. 1, figs. 61*).—A popular work dealing with the birds of Washington State, their songs, and nesting habits.

Observations on polycystid gregarines from Arthropoda, MINNIE E. WATSON (*Jour. Parasitology, 3 (1916), No. 2, pp. 65–75, pl. 1*).—A new genus, Bulbocephalus, with two new species, are described for the family Stylocephalidæ. New species are described for Pyxinia and Gregarina, and new data are given for gregarines already known.

On a trematode larva encysted in a crab, Helice tridens, S. YOSHIDA (*Jour. Parasitology, 3 (1916), No. 2, pp. 76–81, figs. 2*).—This paper relates to a trematode the larva of which was found to infest a crab (*H. tridens*) in Japan. Of some 250 specimens of crabs examined 90 per cent were found to be infested with cysts of this parasite. Though this crab is not used as food in Japan proper, it is said to be eaten in some parts of Korea and Formosa.

The death-feigning instinct, E. M. DuPorte (*Canad. Ent., 49 (1917), No. 7, pp. 221-225*).—The author concludes that there is no consciousness involved in the death feint and that the instinct is merely a physicochemical reaction to external stimulus. " The most probable theory is that in the death feint we have an example of negative thigmotaxis, that shrinking from contact characteristic of so large a proportion of all classes of animals."

Arsenic as an insecticide, A. L. Lovett and R. H. Robinson (*Jour. Econ. Ent., 10 (1917), No. 3, pp. 345-349*).—A brief report of experiments conducted in which lampblack and fullers' earth were used as adsorbents of arsenic from a water solution of arsenic acid.

It was found that under field conditions lampblack is not practical as the black color probably absorbs heat and increases the burn. Fullers' earth used as an adsorbent gave comparatively little burn. The results, based on a single season's observations, both as to toxicity for insects and as to amount of burn on apple foliage, indicate that there are possibilities in the use of adsorbents with arsenic.

Toxicity of various benzene derivatives to insects, W. Moore (*U. S. Dept. Agr., Jour. Agr. Research, 9 (1917), No. 11, pp. 371-381, pls. 2, figs. 2*).—In continuation of fumigation work for the destruction of external parasites, previously reported (E. S. R., 35, p. 656), the author reports upon a series of 28 benzene derivatives. The results obtained, at the University of Minnesota, are summarized as follows:

" All the benzene derivatives tested proved to be more toxic to insects, molecule for molecule, than carbon bisulphid. Physical characters, such as boiling point and vapor pressure, have more influence on the toxicity than chemical composition. Up to 250° C. the higher the boiling point the more toxic the compound to insects. Beyond 250° the compound is usually so slightly volatile that not enough of the chemical will evaporate to be effective. Lipoids are very soluble in compounds with low boiling points and but slightly soluble in compounds with high boiling points. Compounds with low boiling points, although less toxic, owing to their great volatility may give better results than compounds with high boiling points, particularly in the fumigation of grain."

Carbon disulphid as an insecticide, W. E. Hinds (*U. S. Dept. Agr., Farmers' Bul. 799 (1917), pp. 21*).—This is a revision of Farmers' Bulletin 145, previously noted (E. S. R., 13, p. 971).

Nicotin sulphate as a poison for insects, A. L. Lovett (*Jour. Econ. Ent., 10 (1917), No. 3, pp. 333-337*).—The author's experiments with *Malacosoma pluvialis* indicate that nicotin sulphate is a very powerful repellent for caterpillars. Where feeding does take place, the action of the nicotin is apparently rapid and sure, even small bits of foliage sprayed with comparatively weak solutions killing, when devoured, after a short time.

Tests of nicotin sulphate in the control of the codling moth made under unfavorable conditions are briefly considered.

The practical use of the insect enemies of injurious insects, L. O. Howard (*U. S. Dept. Agr. Yearbook 1916, pp. 273-288, figs. 8*).—A brief popular account in which attention is called to the benefits obtained from the use of insect parasites and predators. A technical account of some of the work has been previously noted (E. S. R., 25, p. 662).

Losses caused by imported tree and plant pests, C. L. Marlatt (*Amer. Forestry, 23 (1917), No. 278, pp. 75-80, figs. 12*).—A discussion of the losses resulting from imported insect pests, presented at the International Forestry Conference of the American Forestry Association at Washington, D. C., in January, 1917. See also a previous note (E. S. R., 17, p. 159).

Notes on a southern trip, W. D. PIERCE (*Proc. Ent. Soc. Wash., 18 (1916), No. 4, pp. 206, 207*).—The author records observations of the collection of Lachnosterna, etc., by insect-catching plants (*Sarracenia* spp.) in southern Georgia; the mining of leaves of the bay (*Magnolia virginiana*) by *Prionomerus calceatus*; the feeding of the cowpea weevil on the terminal buds of cotton; and the infestation of the flat galls of *Phylloxera caryæ-avellana* by larvæ of *Anthonomus hicoriæ*.

Second biennial report of the Montana State Board of Entomology, R. A. COOLEY (*Bien. Rpt. Mont. Bd. Ent., 2 (1915–16), pp. 66, figs. 8*).—Following a brief statement of the work of the year the following papers are presented: Report on the Investigation and Control of the Rocky Mountain Spotted Fever Tick in Montana during 1915–16, by W. V. King (pp. 13–23); Review of Rocky Mountain Spotted Fever Eradicative Work Conducted by the United States Public Health Service in the Bitter Root Valley, Mont., 1915–16, by L. D. Fricks (pp. 24–27); Rocky Mountain Spotted Fever.—A Report of Laboratory Investigations of the Virus, by L. D. Fricks (pp. 28–34), previously noted (E. S. R., 36, p. 158); The Etiology of Rocky Mountain Spotted Fever, by S. B. Wolbach (pp. 35–44); Some Facts of Importance Concerning the Rocky Mountain Spotted Fever Tick (*Dermacentor venustus*) in Eastern Montana, by R. R. Parker and R. W. Wells (pp. 45–56); and The House Fly and the Control of Flies, by R. R. Parker (pp. 57–66).

Annual report of the Government entomologist, C. C. GOWDEY (*Ann. Rpt. Dept. Agr. Uganda, 1916, pp. 48–53*).—This report deals with the more important insect enemies of coffee, cacao, cotton, etc., for the year ended March 31, 1916.

Cotton pests in the arid and semiarid Southwest, A. W. MORRILL (*Jour. Econ. Ent., 10 (1917), No. 3, pp. 307–317*).—This is a summary of information on the cotton pests of the Southwest, including an annotated list of 23 references to the literature.

Some problems in insect control about abattoirs and packing houses, F. C. BISHOPP (*Jour. Econ. Ent., 10 (1917), No. 2, pp. 269–277, pl. 1*).—This report of studies made by the Bureau of Entomology in cooperation with the Bureau of Animal Industry of the U. S. Department of Agriculture discusses some of the special problems involved and the species of insects concerned.

Insects injurious to man and stock in Zanzibar, W. M. ADERS (*Bul. Ent. Research, 7 (1917), No. 4, pp. 391–401*).—This consists largely of an annotated list of the more important insect and acarid pests of animals.

Guide to the specimens and enlarged models of insects and ticks exhibited in the central hall illustrating their importance in the spread of disease (*Brit. Mus. (Nat. Hist.) Spec. Guide No. 7 (1916), pp. 45, figs. 14*).—This is a special guide.

Methods of controlling grasshoppers, F. B. MILLIKEN (*Kansas Sta. Bul. 215 (1916), pp. 5–30, figs. 19*).—This is a report of control work with grasshoppers conducted during July, August, and September, 1911, with headquarters at Dodge City, and during July and August, 1912, at Garden City, Kans.

It is concluded that most of the damage can be prevented if proper control measures are introduced into the regular farm practice. These control measures consist of the destruction of the eggs by plowing and disking, and of the destruction of the young and adults by the use of poultry and hogs, the hopperdozer, the poisoned bran mash, or by burning where there is sufficient vegetation to carry fire.

Grasshoppers and their control, H. C. SEVERIN and G. I. GILBERTSON (*South Dakota Sta. Bul. 172 (1917), pp. 552–588, figs. 15*).—This is a popular account of grasshoppers, which were unusually abundant in alfalfa fields in the greater part of South Dakota in 1916 (though the most severe attacks occurred in the western two-thirds of the State), and means for their control.

Destroy the grasshoppers, T. D. URBAHNS (*Mo. Bul. Com. Hort. Cal., 6 (1917), No. 7, pp. 249–253, figs. 4*).—A popular account.

Report on the great invasion of locusts in Egypt in 1915 and the measures adopted to deal with it, A. T. McKILLOP and L. H. GOUGH (*Cairo: Min. Agr., 1916, pp. X+72, pls. 14, figs. 2*).—It is stated that in 1915 locusts appeared in the Nile Valley both from the west and from the east, as they apparently did the previous year. Driving the locusts into small trenches and burying them was found to be the best method of destruction under Egyptian conditions. Contact insecticides are useful but not to the same extent. Stomach poisons and *Coccobacillus acridiorum* were tested and found unsuitable for use in Egypt.

The several appendixes to this paper include Notes on the Migratory Locust (1904) (*Acridium peregrinum*), by W. Cartwright (E. S. R., 16, p. 485); a brief report on the cost of the locust campaign; etc.

New Thysanoptera from Florida, J. R. WATSON (*Ent. News, 26 (1915), No. 2, pp. 49–52, pl. 1; 27 (1916), No. 3, pp. 126–133, pls. 2*).—The second paper, continuing previous work (E. S. R., 29, p. 354), includes descriptions of two species and one variety new to science. The third paper presents descriptions of three species and one subspecies new to science, and includes a key to the North American species of Aeolothrips, Anthrothrips, and Liothrips. None of the new forms is said to be of economic importance, although *Aeolothrips floridensis* n. sp. was taken from oats and *Anthrothrips floridensis* n. sp. from Indian corn, and *Euthrips tritici projectus* n. var. is a very common type in Florida in blossoms of orange, tomato, roses, begonia, etc.

An annotated list of the Thysanoptera of Plummer's Island, Md., J. D. HOOD (*Insecutor Inscitiæ Menstruus, 5 (1917), No. 4–6, pp. 53–65*).—The author records the collection of 57 species representing 18 genera in addition to several unidentified uniques from Plummer's Island, Md., in the Potomac River near the District of Columbia, and 17 additional species taken within a few miles of the island.

Two new species of Dicyphus from Porto Rico, E. H. GIBSON (*Canad. Ent., 49 (1917), No. 6, pp. 218, 219*).—Two hemipterans *Dicyphus prasinus* and *D. luridus*, collected at Rio Piedras, P. R., where they are a source of injury to tobacco plants, are described as new.

The green bug (Toxoptera graminum) outbreak of 1916, E. O. G. KELLY (*Jour. Econ. Ent., 10 (1917), No. 2, pp. 233–248*).—This is a report of studies made of the outbreak of this pest in Kansas in the spring of 1916.

Plant lice injurious to apple orchards.—II, Studies on control of newly-hatched aphids, II, P. J. PARROTT, H. E. HODGKISS, and F. H. LATHROP (*New York State Sta. Bul. 431 (1917), pp. 33–79, pl. 1, figs. 4*).—This report of life history studies and experiments with apple plant lice (*Aphis sorbi*, [*A.*] *Sphocoryne avenæ*, and *A. pomi*), conducted with a view to the establishment of efficient spraying practices for the protection of bearing apple orchards, is in continuation of that previously noted (E. S. R., 35, p. 757).

The more important results and applications from these efforts are dealt with under the headings of classification of newly-hatched larvæ and stem mothers of the first brood, seasonal behavior of aphids, influence of aphids on fruits, tests with lime-sulphur and nicotin solution, auxiliary experiments during 1916, the delayed dormant application in the spraying schedule, and a plan for a spraying test. It is stated that, in general, infestation of orchards in western New York during 1916 was not severe. The oat aphis at the outset outnumbered the rosy aphis and the apple aphis in most orchards, although their comparative numbers varied locally. In relative abundance the three species exhibit a seasonal succession or cycle, which, while probably varying somewhat from year to year, appears to be fundamentally constant.

"At Geneva activities began with the hatching of goodly numbers of the oat aphis on April 22. A few rosy aphids were detected on the buds at the same date, but this species did not reach maximum numbers until four days later. The green aphis was the last species to hatch and began to emerge on April 26. As during the preceding year, dwarfing of apples was chiefly the work of the rosy aphis, although losses in fruit yields in this respect were rarely of serious extent.

" In experiments with the aphids all species attacked succulent tissues, as blossom and fruit stems, tender leaves, and young apples. As a result of their activities various distortions of apples developed. Severe infestation by *A. sorbi* and *A. pomi* was attended in a number of instances by destruction of entire clusters of apples.

" In an experiment on Rome apples an application on May 1 of lime-sulphur and nicotin sulphate at recommended strengths afforded efficient protection from the oat aphis and the rosy aphis. The trees receiving the treatment were also free from the green aphis until June, when there was a reinfestation of the plat due to invasion by winged migrants. Of 12 auxiliary experiments, 9 gave appreciable benefits from spraying. The remainder were inconclusive because of slight infestation by the insects or excessive defoliation by apple scab assisted in part by aphids."

The reddish-brown plum aphis (Rhopalosiphum nympheæ), W. M. DAVIDSON (*Jour. Econ. Ent., 10 (1917), No. 3, pp. 350–353, fig. 1*).—A report of observations made in California, where *R. nympheæ* is distributed in many of the plum and prune districts. It is generally confined to a few trees in an orchard and occasionally infests apricots and almonds; in the East it occasionally attacks peaches. Though apparently of European origin and recorded from many parts of Europe, it is known to occur from Maine to Virginia and in the Central States and Colorado, as well as Ontario and Japan.

Brief notes are given on its biology and habits and recognition characters, including comparative measurements. It is of especial interest in that it is double-hosted, spending the winter and spring on fruit trees and the summer and early fall on a large variety of water plants.

A paper on this pest by Patch has been noted (E. S. R., 34, p. 550).

The migratory habits of Myzus ribis, C. P. GILLETTE and L. C. BRAGG (*Jour. Econ. Ent., 10 (1917), No. 3, pp. 338–340, fig. 1*).—It is pointed out that while this aphid has long been known to leave the currant bushes during the middle of the summer no one has definitely determined the alternate hosts. The authors have repeatedly transferred the migrants from Ribes to Stachys and Leonurus and the fall migrants from these plants to the currant and had them take well, and thus feel safe in announcing these two genera, at least, as summer hosts of *M. ribis*.

Little-known western plant lice, II, W. M. DAVIDSON (*Jour. Econ. Ent., 10 (1917), No. 2, pp. 290–297. fig. 1*).—These notes relate to *Vacuna dryophila*, which occurs on valley oak (*Quercus lobata*) at Walnut Creek, Cal.; *Callipterinella annulata*, which infests the foliage and shoots of imported birch (*Betula alba*) in California and has been reported from other States; *Aphis neo-mexicana pacifica* n. var., which curls the terminal leaves of red currant at Walnut Creek, Cal.; and *Myzus ribifolii* n. sp., which curls and blisters the foliage of the wild flowering currant (*Ribes glutinosum*) near Walnut Creek, Cal.

Methods for the study of mealy bugs, G. F. Ferris (*Jour. Econ. Ent.*, 10 (1917), No. 3, pp. 321-325).—The author recommends the staining of specimens with magenta red in order to accentuate the characters that are of especial importance in the identification of mealy bugs. He asserts that for satisfactory study of mealy bugs and their allies the use of properly stained preparations is not only desirable but is in fact necessary. The method has also proved eminently satisfactory for use with other coccids, especially diaspine scales, as reported by Stafford,[1] certain aphids, particularly chermes and phylloxera, and with cecidomyiid larvæ.

Insect parasites and predators as adjuncts in the control of mealy bugs, H. S. Smith (*Mo. Bul. Com. Hort. Cal.*, 6 (1917), No. 3-4, pp. 108-114, figs. 10).—This paper gives brief accounts of the more important predacious and parasitic insect enemies of mealy bugs in California.

Some comparisons of Coccus citricola and C. hesperidum, H. J. Quayle (*Jour. Econ. Ent.*, 10 (1917), No. 3, pp. 373-376).—The author here points out some of the differences and also some of the similarities of these two scales, which are quite distinct.

A scale insect new to California, H. S. Smith (*Mo. Bul. Com. Hort. Cal.*, 6 (1917), No. 7, p. 249).—The author records the infestation of a palmetto near Riverside by the palmetto scale (*Comstockiella sabilis*).

The Mediterranean fig scale (Lepidosaphes ficus), F. P. Roullard (*Mo. Bul. Com. Hort. Cal.*, 6 (1917), No. 7, pp. 246-248, figs. 4).—A brief account of *L. ficus*, a European scale pest which has been discovered in Fresno County, where investigations are being made with a view to eradicating it.

Two new species of lace bugs, O. Heidemann (*Proc. Ent. Soc. Wash.*, 18 (1916), No. 4, pp. 217-219).—*Leptophya distinguenda*, which abounds on witch-hazel from early spring until late fall in the vicinity of Washington, D. C., and *Acalypta grisea* from Massachusetts, North Carolina, and Maryland are described as new.

Notes on Leptobyrsa rhododendri, E. L. Dickerson (*Jour. N. Y. Ent. Soc.*, 25 (1917), No. 2, pp. 105-112, pl. 1).—These notes relate to the biology of a lace bug, previously described under the name *L. explanata* (E. S. R., 21, p. 451), which has since been shown to be the same as the Old World form *L. rhododendri* (E. S. R., 36, p. 656).

Check list of the Lepidoptera of Boreal America, W. Barnes and J. McDunnough (*Decatur, Ill.: Herald Press, 1917, pp. IX+392*).—This comprises a list of 8,495 species of Lepidoptera from North America, a list of species omitted as European or foreign, and a complete index (pp. 201-392).

The Barnes and McDunnough "list," H. G. Dyar (*Insecutor Inscitiæ Menstruus, 5 (1917), No. 1-3, pp. 41-44*).—This is a critical review of the above list.

Suppression of the gipsy and brown-tail moths and its value to States not infested, A. F. Burgess (*U. S. Dept. Agr. Yearbook 1916, pp. 217-226, pls. 7*).—A popular discussion of suppression work in which attention is called to the benefits resulting.

Solid stream spraying against the gipsy moth and the brown-tail moth in New England, L. H. Worthley (*U. S. Dept. Agr. Bul. 480 (1917), pp. 15, pls. 16*).—The methods of spraying and the apparatus developed during the course of work with the gipsy and brown-tail moths in New England are described and illustrated.

[1] Ann. Ent. Soc. Amer., 8 (1915), No. 1, pp. 65-73.

Louisiana records of the bindweed prominent (Schizura ipomeæ), E. S. TUCKER (*Canad. Ent., 49 (1917), No. 8, pp. 280, 281*).—Observations of the occurrence and food habits of this lepidopteran in Louisiana are recorded.

Nepticulidæ of North America, ANNETTE F. BRAUN (*Trans. Amer. Ent. Soc., 43 (1917), No. 2, pp. 155–209, pls. 4*).—In this synopsis of the family which includes the smallest species of Lepidoptera, the author recognizes 4 genera and 61 species (8 new), of which 54 belong to the genus Nepticula, 5 to Ectoedemia, 1 to Obrussa, and 1 to Glaucolepis n. g. With the exception of several gall-making species of Ectoedemia, the larvæ of all species of which the life histories are known are miners within the tissues of leaves or in bark, but rarely in fruit. They show a preference for trees and shrubs, but not a few mine leaves of herbaceous plants, when full grown, the larva, with a few exceptions, leaves of herbaceous plants. When full grown, the larva, with a few exceptions, amongst the rubbish or in the loose surface soil. The species of Ectoedemia are gall producers or bark miners in forest trees. A list of their food plants and descriptions of mines occurring on them, compiled as an aid in identification, is included.

The pink bollworm, Pectinophora gossypiella, A. BUSCK (*U. S. Dept. Agr., Jour. Agr. Research, 9 (1917), No. 10, pp. 343–370, pls. 6, figs. 7*).—This is a summary of the present status of knowledge of the pink bollworm, (*Gelechia*) *Pectinophora gossypiella*. This is based upon a review of the literature and investigations conducted by the author, the biological part of which was made in the Hawaiian Islands, where the cultivation of cotton has been abandoned on account of its injury.

The new genus Pectinophora is erected by the author for this species. It is pointed out that even a fraction of the insect in any of its stages can be recognized under the microscope by the characters given in this paper.

The paper includes (pp. 362–366) a similar detailed descriptive and anatomical account of another lepidopterous insect (*Pyroderces rileyi*), known as the "scavenger bollworm," since it frequently occurs in decayed or dried bolls injured by other insects. This frequently has been and may be mistaken for the pink bollworm, but the anatomical details given in this paper make it possible for the inspector to distinguish readily these two insects.

A bibliography of 48 titles is included.

[New Lepidoptera], H. G. DYAR (*Insecutor Inscitiæ Menstruus, 5 (1917), Nos. 1–3, pp. 8–10, 45–47, 50, 51; 4–6, pp. 65–92*).—Several papers are here presented, all of which include descriptions of species new to science, namely, A Note on Cisthene (pp. 8–10) ; Three New North American Phycitinæ (pp. 45–47) ; A New Phycitid from the Bahamas (p. 50; A New Noctuid from Brazil (p. 51) ; Miscellaneous New American Lepidoptera (pp. 65–69) ; Notes on North American Pyraustinæ (pp. 69–75) ; Notes on North American Nymphulinæ (pp. 75–79) ; Notes on North American Schœnobiinæ (pp. 79–84) ; Seven New Crambids from the United States (pp. 84–87) ; and Seven New Pyralids from British Guiana (pp. 88–92).

A county-wide survey to determine the effect of time of seeding and presence of volunteer wheat upon the extent of damage by the Hessian fly, T. H. PARKS (*Jour. Econ. Ent., 10 (1917), No. 2, pp. 249–253*).—A report of investigations during the season of 1916, based upon a questionnaire and examinations of 306 fields in McPherson County, Kans.

The mosquitoes of the mountains of California, H. G. DYAR (*Insecutor Inscitiæ Menstruus, 5 (1917), No. 1–3, pp. 11–21*).—The author presents notes on all the mosquitoes found in the northern half of the Sierra Nevada Mountains of California, of which six species are described as new.

Bromelicolous anopheles, H. G. DYAR and F. KNAB (*Insecutor Inscitiæ Menstruus*, 5 (1917), No. 1–3, pp. 38–40).—These notes relate to four species of Anopheles, of which one, *A. hylephilus*, is described as new to science.

A State-wide malaria-mosquito survey of California, W. B. HERMS (*Jour. Econ. Ent.*, 10 (1917), No. 3, pp. 359–370).—The author reports upon a systematic anopheline survey in California and discusses the object and method of the survey and the results obtained.

The rice fields as a factor in the control of malaria, S. B. FREEBORN (*Jour. Econ. Ent.*, 10 (1917), No. 3, pp. 354–359).—A discussion of the relation of rice fields to the occurrence of Anopheles in the Sacramento and San Joaquin Valleys of California, where rice has been introduced and is being grown commercially and malaria is already endemic.

A plea and a plan for the eradication of malaria throughout the Western Hemisphere, F. L. HOFFMAN (*Newark, N. J.: Prudential Press, 1917, pp. 65, figs. 4*).—The several parts of this work on the eradication of malaria, particularly through the control of mosquitoes, consist of a plea for organized action, a plan for organized prevention and control, and some essential statistical considerations.

Notes on horse flies as a pest in southern Florida, T. E. SNYDER (*Proc. Ent. Soc. Wash.*, 18 (1916), No. 4, pp. 208–210).—These notes relate particularly to species of Tabanus.

A synoptic revision of the Cuterebridæ, with synonymic notes and the description of one new species, C. H. T. TOWNSEND (*Insecutor Inscitiæ Menstruus*, 5 (1917), No. 1–3, pp. 23–28).—This paper includes a description of *Bogeria scudderi* n. sp., the larva of which is a parasite in the larynx of the hog in Virginia and Tennessee.

The head and throat bots of American game animals, C. H. T. TOWNSEND (*Jour. N. Y. Ent. Soc.*, 25 (1917), No. 2, pp. 98–105).—A review of the present status of information on the biology of œstrids of the genus Cephenemyia.

"The flies of this genus larviposit at the entrance of the nostrils or on or about the nose or mouth of various members of the Cervidæ, and probably at times of certain allied families of ruminants. The newly deposited larvæ gain entrance to the host normally through the nostrils, but no doubt also at times through the mouth. They cling by their spines and mouth hooks to the mucous membranes near the point of entrance, and feed upon the mucous exudation which their irritation causes the membranes to secrete. On reaching the second stage they penetrate farther within."

Notes on Osten Sacken's group "Pœcilanthrax," with descriptions of new species, F. R. COLE (*Jour. N. Y. Ent. Soc.*, 25 (1917), No. 1, pp. 67–80, pls. 5).—Four species of Anthrax and one variety are described as new.

The occurrence of Eumerus strigatus in Canada, A. GIBSON (*Canad. Ent.*, 49 (1917), No. 6, pp. 190, 191).—This relates briefly to the occurrence and distribution of this European dipteran in North America.

The Mediterranean fruit fly, E. A. BACK (*Mo. Bul. Com. Hort. Cal.*, 6 (1917), No. 3–4, pp. 69–80, pls. 2, figs. 5).—A summary of information relating to *Ceratitis capitata*, including colored plates which illustrate its infestation of peaches and citrus fruits. Reports of studies of this pest by the author and Pemberton have been prevously noted (E. S. R., 35, pp. 362, 760).

Mediterranean fruit fly (Ceratitis capitata) breeds in bananas, H. H. P. SEVERIN (*Jour. Econ. Ent.*, 10 (1917), No. 3, pp. 318–321).—In referring to the paper by Back and Pemberton, previously noted (E. S. R., 34, p. 655), the author presents evidence in addition to that given in the previous paper (E. S. R., 29, p. 54), which supports the view that *C. capitata* may breed in bananas.

Dark currant fruit fly in California, Rhagoletis ribicola, H. H. P. Severin (*Mo. Bul. Com. Hort. Cal.*, *6* (*1917*), *No. 7, pp. 258–260. fig. 1*).—The collection in California of a specimen of the dark currant fly (*R. ribicola*), which has been reported by Piper and Doane (E. S. R., 10, p. 869) to be of considerable economic importance in the State of Washington, is recorded.

The melon fly in Hawaii, E. A. Back and C. E. Pemberton (*U. S. Dept. Agr. Bul. 491* (*1917*), *pp. 64, pls. 24, figs. 10*).—This is a summary of the present status of the knowledge of (*Dacus*) *Bactrocera cucurbitæ*, based upon a review of the literature and the authors' investigations conducted during a period of several years, and including the studies previously noted (E. S. R., 32, p. 452).

An annotated bibliography of 51 titles is appended.

The root maggot pest, E. B. Stookey (*Washington Sta., West. Wash. Sta. Mo. Bul.*, *5* (*1917*), *No. 3, pp. 32–34, figs. 4*).—The root maggot is said to be very common throughout western Washington and to do considerable damage each year to various cruciferous plants and also to onions. The work of the year was largely in connection with the kale crop. Previous experiments indicate "that to use fall-seeded kale for early transplanting in the spring is a good practice, both from the standpoint of size and freedom from root maggot; that transplanted plants should be protected by tarred felt pads; and that the later seedings and transplantings are usually less damaged by root maggot than those from early spring seeding.

"The average loss the past year on transplanted kale protected by tarred felt pads varied from 8.65 to 12.1 per cent, as against averages of 28.36 to 45.9 per cent loss where no pads were used. The average loss from transplanted fall-seeded plants was 28.36 per cent, as against an average loss of 33.7 per cent for transplants from spring seeding. The average loss from kale seeded in the field May 8 and thinned June 20 amounted to 11.2 per cent, as against 21.5 per cent from spring-seeded plants transplanted at the same time."

Notes on some western Buprestidæ, H. E. Burke (*Jour. Econ. Ent.*, 10 (*1917*), *No. 3, pp. 325–332*).—The author notes the occurrence of, habits, and injury caused by 44 species of the flat-headed borers. A table for the separation of the various genera of borers and other data are given in a bulletin previously noted (E. S. R., 36, p. 554).

A new species of Agrilus from California, W. S. Fisher (*Canad. Ent.*, 49 (*1917*), *No. 8, pp. 287–289*).—Under the name *Agrilus burkei* the author describes a new buprestid, the larvæ of which mine in the inner bark and wood of normal, injured, and dying white alder (*Alnus rhombifolia*) and paper-leaf alder (*A. tenuifolia*) at Placerville, Cal.

The locust borer (Cyllene robiniæ), C. E. Sanborn and H. R. Painter (*Oklahoma Sta. Bul. 113* (*1917*), *pp. 3–8, figs. 4*).—A brief summary of information on this beetle, which is one of the most injurious pests of the locust tree in Oklahoma, where many of these trees are grown for posts as well as for shade. A bibliography of 24 titles is included.

Studies of this pest by Garman in Kentucky have previously been noted (E. S. R., 35, p. 552).

A new species of Xylotrechus, W. S. Fisher (*Proc. Ent. Soc. Wash.*, 18 (*1916*), *No. 4, pp. 214–216*).—*Xylotrechus aceris,* a new cerambycid which makes galls on maple trees, is described from Washington, D. C. It also occurs in Pennsylvania, Delaware, and Kentucky.

The horse-radish flea-beetle: Its life history and distribution, F. H. Chittenden and N. F. Howard (*U. S. Dept. Agr. Bul. 535* (*1917*), *pp. 16, figs. 6*).—(*Haltica*) *Phyllotreta armoraciæ*, a European pest thought to have been introduced in horse-radish, having first been collected at Chicago in 1893, now occurs from New York and New Jersey to Quebec, Canada, and westward to

Nebraska. The injury is caused by the larvæ, which bore into the petioles or midribs of horse-radish ([*Nasturtium*] *Radicula armoracia*), and by the adults, which feed on the leaves, causing the characteristic flea-beetle injury—withering and dying—or gouge deep pits in the petioles or midribs. In 1914 it became of economic importance in the growing of horse-radish on a commercial scale in Brown County, Wis., and in the two years following reappeared in large numbers. It is also a source of injury at Shermerville, Ill., to the extent of thousands of dollars every year. This beetle is partial to horse-radish and marsh cress but has once been taken on young cabbage in hotbeds in early spring.

The species hibernates as an adult, appearing in its northern range in April and May. The eggs are deposited from the latter part of April or early May until early August, the crevices of the tender petioles of young leaves where they leave the root usually being the preferred location. A total of 418 eggs deposited at intervals in numbers of about 22 were recorded from a single female. The incubation period of the egg required from 7 to 14 days.

On hatching, the larvæ crawl about the leaf for some time, examination of a small tender petiole showing that they enter at different places along the inner side. The larvæ grow and feed in the tissues of the petioles and midribs of the leaves, and when very numerous the petioles are tunneled to the extent that they shrink considerably, causing the leaf to wither and die at the tip and about the margins.

When the larvæ are ready for pupation, they leave the petioles and enter the ground. That the larvæ may also live in the root of the plant is said to have been clearly demonstrated. After leaving the plant the larva enters the soil to a depth of from ⅛ to ¼ in., or even 3 in., where it remains for 4 or 5 days, pupating in from 2 to 6 days. Forty-eight days was the total larval period of an individual which was deposited as an egg on May 1; others required periods of from 52 to 66 days and 10 to 13 days for pupal development.

The length of the oviposition period was found to be about 75 days, from the middle of May to the first of August. The total period of time from egg laying to adult ranges from 77 days to about 90 days in the cases where complete records were obtained. The adult appears to live about a year, there being but one generation annually in Wisconsin.

Bordeaux applied on the first appearance of the beetle is recommended as a preventive to be followed by arsenate of lead where necessary.

A bibliography of 10 titles is appended.

The two-banded fungus beetle, F. H. CHITTENDEN (*Jour. Econ. Ent., 10* (*1917*), *No. 2, pp. 282–287. fig. 1*).—*Alphitophagus bifasciatus*, a cosmopolitan fungus beetle, is a scavenger usually found in refuse, such as decaying vegetable matter, in flour and feed stores, in mills, and in grain warehouses, and is not uncommon in the open as well as indoors. The present paper gives a brief summarized account of observations of the pest.

A troublesome household pest (Attagenus plebius) of Hawaii, J. F. ILLINGWORTH (*Jour. Econ. Ent., 10* (*1917*), *No. 3, pp. 340–344, fig. 1*).—This dermestid, which has habits somewhat similar to the black carpet beetle (*A. piceus*) of the United States, is said to be an important household pest in the Hawaiian Islands, though apparently not found elsewhere. A note is given on its life history, together with technical descriptions of its several stages, and brief mention is made of control measures. A second fumigation with carbon bisulphid is necessary, as the eggs are not thus destroyed.

Studies on the life history of Ligyrus gibbosus, W. P. HAYES (*Jour. Econ. Ent., 10* (*1917*), *No. 2, pp. 253–261, pl. 1*).—*L. gibbosus*, which first came into prominence as an enemy of the wild sunflower, is growing in importance as a pest of staple crops, among which are carrots, sugar beets, sugar cane, corn, cotton, celery, etc. In the present paper the author first gives a brief review of the present status of knowledge of the species, with references to the literature, and then reports upon studies made at the Kansas Experiment Station.

The adults are present in the soil throughout the winter and early spring. During the latter part of April, or the first few days of May, and continuing throughout the summer, they emerge at night and fly to lights, returning to the soil before daybreak. During the summer of 1916, eggs were plentiful at Manhattan from the last of May to late in July. Larvæ were present from June throughout the remainder of the summer and early fall, and pupæ from the last of July to the last of October. Thus far no satisfactory method of control has been worked out. No special time can be set for the destruction of the pupæ by plowing due to the fact that pupation extends over a long period.

Notes on an introduced weevil (Ceutorhynchus marginatus), J. A. HYSLOP (Jour. Econ. Ent., 10 (1917), No. 2, pp. 278-282, fig. 1).—This European weevil (C. marginatus) was found by the author to infest nearly every seed head of the dandelion at Bridgeport, N. Y., in 1916.

The strawberry root weevil in British Columbia, R. C. TREHERNE (Canad. Ent., 49 (1917), No. 8, pp. 257-260).—The data here presented supplement those given in a bulletin previously noted (E. S. R., 32, p. 556).

[The rice water weevil], F. C. QUEREAU (Louisiana Stas. Rpt. 1916, pp. 25, 26).—Oil experiments with Lissorhoptrus simplex indicate that the application of 15 gal. per acre will result in a 25 to 40 per cent increase in yield. It is stated that 40 gal. of crude oil has been used to a single acre without injury to rice when the leaves were not resting on the surface of the water. By draining the land and allowing it to become dry 15 days after the initial irrigation the damage from the " maggot " is largely prevented.

A newly-introduced clover beetle (Sitones hispidulus), E. C. VAN DYKE (Mo. Bul. Com. Hort. Cal., 6 (1917), No. 7, pp. 248, 249).—The author records the occurrence of this European clover beetle in California for the first time.

The A B C and X Y Z of bee culture, A. I. and E. R. ROOT (Medina, Ohio: The A. I. Root Co., 1917, rev. and enl. ed., pp. 8+830, pl. 1, figs. 732).—A new revised and enlarged edition of the work previously noted (E. S. R., 19, p. 1058).

Diprion simile in North America, S. A. ROHWER (Proc. Ent. Soc. Wash., 18 (1916), No. 4, pp. 213, 214).—The European pine sawfly D. simile, previously reported by Britton as occurring in several localities in Connecticut (E. S. R., 35, p. 53), is said to have been received from inspectors in Massachusetts, Pennsylvania, and New Jersey, though it is not known to have become established in any of these three States. It has, however, been received from one nursery in New York under conditions which indicate that it has become established.

The Argentine ant as an orchard pest, H. S. SMITH (Mo. Bul. Com. Hort. Cal., 6 (1917), No. 7, pp. 254-258, figs. 3).—This ant has become an important orchard pest in California through its protection of mealy bugs and scale insects from their natural enemies. In investigations thus far poisoned sirup, placed in paraffin paper bags attached to trees, has given more promising results than banding.

Ants protecting acacia trees in Central America, E. A. SCHWARZ (Proc. Ent. Soc. Wash., 18 (1916), No. 4, pp. 211, 212).—Observations by the author in the Canal Zone of Panama and at Tampico, Mex., fully corroborate the original observations of T. Belt[1] to the effect that the ants effectually defend the acacia

---

[1] The Naturalist in Nicaragua. London: Edward Bumpus, 1888, 2. ed., rev., pp. XXXII + 403.

trees against the attacks of man, cattle, and insects. No leaf-eating caterpillars, no aphids, and no coccids were seen on the trees, and no leaf-cutting ants ever defoliate them.

Notes on Trichogramma minutum, S. C. HARLAND (*West Indian Bul., 15* (*1915*), *No. 3, pp. 168–175*).—The author's experiments with this important parasite indicate that it parasitizes the eggs of the sugar-cane borer, the bollworm, the fall army worm, *Utetheisa ornatrix, Calpodes ethlius*, and an unidentified cutworm. It is pointed out that other egg parasites confine themselves to one particular host. Experiments show that *T. minutum* will not parasitize the eggs of a nonlepidopterous insect nor of a spider. In every case *T. minutum* was a subsidiary parasite, as the number obtained in the field was always less than that of the other egg parasites of the same host. Work is being carried on with *U. ornatrix*, with a view to making use of it in the control of the sugar-cane borer through serving as a host for *T. minutum*.

A nearctic species of Dolichurus, S. A. ROHWER (*Proc. Ent. Soc. Wash., 18* (*1916*), *No. 4, pp. 212, 213*).—*Dolichurus greenei* n. sp. is described from Falls Church, Va.

On the life history and successful introduction into the United States of the Sicilian mealy bug parasite, H. S. SMITH (*Jour. Econ. Ent., 10* (*1917*), *No. 2, pp. 262–268, pls. 2, figs. 5*).—This paper relates to the Italian encyrtid parasite of mealy bugs, described by Girault as *Paraleptomastix abnormis* (E. S. R., 34, p. 456), accounts of which have previously been noted (E. S. R., 34, p. 451).

Reproduction took place so rapidly that before many months large colonies were placed in the orchards of southern California. The parasite is now quite thoroughly distributed throughout the mealy-bug infested sections of the State and has become established in practically every colony. In many of the orchards under investigation it has successfully passed through two fumigations, probably as larvæ and pupæ within the young mealy bugs. Spraying does not destroy it, except where it is successful in killing the mealy bugs. While it will occasionally deposit eggs in *Pseudococcus bakeri*, the author has never succeeded in rearing it from this host. In work in Hawaii Swezey has succeeded in getting it to breed upon P. *sacchari*, though it does not thrive greatly on that species.

Some new Australian chalcid flies, mostly of the family Encyrtidæ, A. A. GIRAULT (*Insecutor Inscitiæ Menstruus, 5* (*1917*), *No. 1–3 pp. 29–37*).

New Australian chalcid flies, A. A. GIRAULT (*Insecutor Inscitiæ Menstruus, 5* (*1917*), *No. 4–6, pp. 92–96*).—The author erects a new genus (Paramyiocnema) and describes six species as new to science.

A chalcid parasite of the pink bollworm, A. A. GIRAULT (*Insecutor Inscitiæ Menstruus, 5* (*1917*), *No. 1–3, pp. 5, 6*).—Under the name *Stomatoceras pertorvus*, the author describes a parasite reared from pupæ of (*Gelechia*) *Pectinophora gossypiella* at Honolulu, Hawaii, which has previously been referred to as *Hockeria* sp.

Two bethylid parasites of the pink bollworm, S. A. ROHWER (*Insecutor Inscitiæ Menstruus, 5* (*1917*), *No. 1–3, pp. 1–3*).—*Perisierola nigrifemur* Ashm. is recorded as parasitic on the larvæ of the pink bollworm (*Gelechia*) *Pectinophora gossypiella* in Brazil. P. *emigrata*, which has been reared in great numbers from the larva of the pink bollworm in Honolulu, Hawaii, is here described as new. Specimens from Texas referred to under the name P. *distinguenda* and recorded as parasites of *Bruchus prosopidis* and *Bruchus* sp. are considered to be P. *emigrata*.

The occurrence of the genus **Parachrysocharis** in the United States, A. A. GIRAULT (*Canad. Ent., 49 (1917), No. 4, p. 129*).—A new species, based on specimens collected at Austin, Tex., is here described as *Parachrysocharis semiflava.*

Two apple leaf mites of economic importance, W. H. BRITTAIN (*Canad. Ent., 49 (1917), No. 6, pp. 185–189, pl. 1*).—This article deals with the silver-leaf or rusty leaf mite (*Phyllocoptes schlechtendali*), which is extraordinarily abundant in the Okanogan Valley and other parts of the dry belt of British Columbia, and the apple leaf mite (*Eriophyes malifoliæ*), which, though it has not appeared in destructive outbreaks, may yet prove of greater economic importance than is commonly supposed, at least under conditions that exist in the Okanogan.

FOODS—HUMAN NUTRITION.

Goat's milk as food for infants and very young children, W. H. JORDAN and G. A. SMITH (*New York State Sta. Bul. 429 (1917), pp. 12–20*).—This is a reprint of a report of a practical study of goat's milk in infant feeding when compared to cow's milk, by D. H. Sherman and H. R. Lohnes (E. S. R., 32, p. 66), together with reports of results obtained with 16 children as reported by parents or physicians.

Milling properties of Ohio wheat.—Differences in physical characteristics and milling qualities, MABEL K. CORBOULD (*Mo. Bul. Ohio Sta., 2 (1917), No. 6, pp. 188–192, fig. 1*).—This reports the methods used in determining the physical and milling characteristics of wheat and gives the score card and milling record of several samples of Ohio wheats. The experiments showed the following results:

"The Poole and Fultz wheats and their pure line selections (Ohio 9,920, Portage and Trumbull) have good milling qualities and make good flour. The Mediterranean, a good milling wheat, and its selection (Ohio 9,700) give a creamy flour. Early Ripe flour is a dirty gray, a very objectionable characteristic. The Gypsy mills well and makes a satisfactory flour. Gladden flour excels Gypsy, from which it was originally selected, in baking qualities. Dawson Golden Chaff gives a large percentage of bran, and a·very white, starchy flour. Mealy produces a very deep cream flour, granular to the touch, due to poor milling qualities."

The value of sugar and honey as foods, E. PERUCCI (*Agr. Mod. [Milan], 23 (1917), No. 4, pp. 41–43*).—The food values of honey and sugar are compared and analyses of nectar and honey are given. The author claims that honey contains radium in addition to other salts.

Miscellaneous drug preparations, C. D. WOODS (*Maine Sta. Off. Insp. 82 (1917), pp. 29–36*).—Results of analyses of samples of nitrous ether, spirit of peppermint, tincture of iodin, and spirit of camphor are reported.

[Food and drug inspection], E. F. LADD and ALMA K. JOHNSON (*North Dakota Sta. Spec. Bul., 4 (1917), No. 13, pp. 347–362*).—This contains the results of analyses of several samples of beer and general information regarding a number of drugs and patent medicines, together with miscellaneous information on food and drug topics.

Preliminary report of the dairy and food commissioner for the year 1916, J. FOUST (*Penn. Dept. Agr. Bul. 292 (1917), pp. 53*).—This is a preliminary report which reviews the work of the food inspection department during the year ended December 31, 1916.

Food and drug laws of the State of Rhode Island (*Providence: E. L. Freeman Co., 1917, pp. 32*).—The texts of the laws and the rules and regulations for their enforcement are given.

What to eat in war time, G. LUSK (*World's Work*, *34* (*1917*), *No. 4, pp. 446-452*).—A more or less popular statement of the food needs of the body, together with information regarding food costs and some plans adopted to meet the shortage of food in Europe.

Food economy in war time, T. B. WOOD and F. G. HOPKINS (*London: Cambridge University Press, 1916. pp. 35*).—This bulletin deals with the uses of food, food values, and food costs.

Food values and the rationing of a country, R. SMITH (*London: Author,* [*1917*], *2. ed., rev., pp. 19*).—This publication considers the question of food supply and food regulation in the light of war conditions. Tables are included which show the composition of different foods and various so-called standard diets.

The restricted supply of food: Its relation to health and efficiency, M. S. PEMBREY (*Brit. Med. Jour., No. 2941, Epit.* (*1917*), *pp. 605-607*).—A summary and digest of data relative to the food requirements and standard diets, together with suggestions regarding the regulation of the food supply.

Contribution to the study of incomplete diets.—Researches on the gaseous exchange of subjects receiving a rice diet, P. RAMOINO (*Arch. Ital. Biol., 65* (*1916*), *No. 1, pp. 1-16*).—Present-day theories regarding the etiology of polyneuritis are given and accounts of experiments made by the author are reported in detail. Four pigeons were fed upon a rice diet, and observations were made of the daily weight, the hourly consumption of oxygen per 100 gm., and the hourly production of carbon dioxid per 100 gm., as well as the respiratory quotient.

In general, it was found that pigeons maintained on the diet of polished rice died; this being in agreement with the results of other workers. The administration of the polishings or the extracts of rice bran served to retard or. even to prevent the appearance of the symptoms, and this substance was active even in extremely small quantities. Discontinuing this administration caused a reduction of weight and the appearance, after a short interval, of the symptoms.

The study of the respiratory exchange showed in a like manner a progressive and rapid lowering of the respiratory quotient in passing from a diet rich in vitamins to a diet deprived of them. This lowering was due to the fact that the quantity of oxygen consumed did not follow a descending curve parallel to that of the carbon dioxid emitted.

The value of the respiratory quotient increased promptly to normal when the polishings were administered. After the administration of the polishings was discontinued the quotient again fell to an extremely low point.

The physiological behavior of raffinose, S. KURIYAMA and L. B. MENDEL (*Jour. Biol. Chem., 31* (*1917*), *No. 1, pp. 125-147, fig. 1*).—From experiments with laboratory animals (rabbits and dogs) which are reported, the following conclusions in part were drawn:

Human saliva and the bile, pancreas, liver, and intestinal mucous membranes of laboratory animals did not contain raffinase. Under suitable conditions the gastric juice may invert raffinose. When raffinase and raffinose were injected successively into the circulation, the sugar was no better utilized than when it was injected alone.

"No noteworthy glycogen formation in the liver was found after feeding raffinose to fasting white rats. The sugar was scarcely inverted in the stomach and small intestine. It was, however, changed in the large intestine.

"When raffinose was administered directly into loops of the small intestine of [fasting] dogs, most of it was recovered after two hours without evidence of its inversion. In a loop of the large intestine, however, raffinose was easily inverted. This was probably due to bacteria. Part of the raffinose can pass unchanged through the intestinal wall and reappear in the urine. . . .

"The sterilized feces of dogs and rabbits seems to contain a small amount of raffinase, probably of bacterial origin.

"Raffinose is devoid of food value until after its inversion. It may be that raffinose-digesting bacteria occur more frequently in the large intestine of species which consume foods containing raffinose and thus render the physiological utilization more probable for them."

A bibliography is appended.

ANIMAL PRODUCTION.

The function of live stock in agriculture, G. M. ROMMEL (*U. S. Dept. Agr. Yearbook 1916, pp. 467–475*).—This paper which was read at a meeting of the Second Pan American Scientific Congress, Washington, D. C., has already been noted (E. S. R., 34, p. 305).

[Japanese cane for steers], A. P. KERR (*Louisiana Stas. Rpt. 1916, pp. 16, 17*).—To determine the value of Japanese cane as a grazing crop 20 steers were grazed for 60 days during the fall and winter of 1915–16. The steers were practically maintained on this crop although the season was very cold and wet.

Progress in handling the wool clip: Development in the West, F. R. MARSHALL (*U. S. Dept. Agr. Yearbook 1916, pp. 227–236, pls. 4, fig. 1*).—An account is given of the more businesslike methods of handling the wool clip in the Western States during the past two seasons. In 1915 the wool growers began to grade their wools before shipment, and in 1916 about 7,000,000 lbs., including 81 clips and representing about 870,000 sheep in three far Western States, was graded and baled at the time of shearing. This wool when shipped was ready for final sale without the usual further handling undergone by most clips in the dealers' warehouses before sale to manufacturers.

Descriptions, with an illustration of floor plan, are given of shearing sheds which have been erected or remodeled to include the main features of the Australian plan. The author describes the principal methods used in preparing the clips in 1915–16 and discusses the advantages of grading at the ranch and the methods of selling ranch-graded wool. The new plan makes it possible for the flockmaster who studies his wool to appraise his clip closely when considering offers, but the full financial value of the system is not expected to be obtained until the growers have made a more general use of the system, thus securing wider competition for the purchase of their wools.

The adaptability of the plan to other States is pointed out, and examples of cooperative selling of wool in New York State and Louisiana are noted.

The production of pork in the four-year rotation, A. P. KERR (*Louisiana Stas. Rpt. 1916, p. 17*).—In a four-year rotation of corn and cowpeas, soy beans, sweet potatoes, and mangels from 12 to 16 lbs. of pork were produced per bushel of corn, the amount depending a great deal on the crop of cowpeas in the corn. In this test from 2.5 to 3 bu. of sweet potatoes were equal in feeding value to 1 bu. of corn. The yields of soy beans have been very variable but the crop has proved a valuable one in the rotation as it is ready to graze between the corn and cowpeas and the sweet potatoes.

Stallion legislation and the horse-breeding industry, C. C. GLENN (*U. S. Dept. Agr. Yearbook 1916, pp. 289–299, pls. 4, fig. 1*).—The author notes that progress in horse breeding has not kept pace with that of many other agricultural lines. He attributes this condition largely to the too general use of stallions lacking in quality of breeding and to the failure on the part of owners of mares to appreciate fully the value of sound pure-bred sires of desirable conformation. A brief review is made of the requirements and effects of laws regulating the public service of stallions and jacks in the various States. The first of these laws was that of Wisconsin which became effective on January 1, 1906, since when 20 additional States have enacted legislation of similar character.

Latest available statistics from 18 of these States are tabulated. Of the 55,553 stallions licensed for public service in these States 59 per cent are pure-bred, 33 grade, and 8 cross-bred and mongrel. It is noted that since the beginning of stallion legislation in these States there has been a general increase in pure-bred stallions and a decrease of grades and mongrels.

A list is given of the various State stallion registration boards or commissions.

The poultryman's problems in 1917, H. R. LEWIS (*New Jersey Stas. Hints to Poultrymen, 5 (1917), No. 9, pp. 4*).—The importance of the production of infertile eggs for market is emphasized and suggestions are given for the systematic culling of layers, compounding war-time rations, and caponizing.

The Thanksgiving turkey, A. S. WEIANT (*U. S. Dept. Agr. Yearbook 1916, pp. 411-419, pls. 3*).—This is a brief review of the market turkey industry in this country, including methods of raising, marketing, killing and dressing, and shipping.

Fur farming as a side line, N. DEARBORN (*U. S. Dept. Agr. Yearbook 1916, pp. 489-506, pls. 2*).—It is stated that the solution of the problem of obtaining from a waning source the necessary stock for the permanent development of the fur industry is to " domesticate the fur bearers and farm them, as has been done over and over with other animals. The killing pressure on those remaining in the wild state will then be reduced, the fur trade supported, and a new farm product developed." Of about a dozen kinds of fur-bearing animals native to North America which are considered to be suitable for domestication, the skunk, mink, and silver fox have already been bred successfully in captivity in widely scattered localities, and the marten, fisher, otter, blue fox, raccoon, and beaver have been partially tested under domesticated conditions.

The habits and climatic conditions suitable for the raising of fur-bearing anicals are noted, and directions are given for the choice of species, construction of inclosures, feeding, breeding, treatment of diseases, care of skins, and the dressing of furs. The cooperation of breeders of fur-bearing animals is strongly urged.

A critique of the theory of evolution, T. H. MORGAN (*Princeton: Princeton University Press, 1916, pp. X+197, figs. 95*).—This is a series of lectures delivered at Princeton University, in which the author (1) attempts to put a new valuation on the traditional evidence for evolution, (2) deals with the most recent work on heredity, (3) examines in the light of new observations the physical basis of heredity and the composition of the germ plasm stream, and (4) develops the thesis that chance variation, combined with a property of living things to manifold themselves is the keynote of modern evolutionary thought.

DAIRY FARMING—DAIRYING.

An experiment in community dairying, R. R. WELCH (*U. S. Dept. Agr. Yearbook 1916, pp. 209-216, pl. 1, fig. 1*).—An account is given of an experiment conducted by the Dairy Division in developing community dairying at Algona, Iowa, in a region where most of the farmers were engaged in grain farming and stock raising, dairying being only a side line. During the five years of the experiment the project was constantly in charge of a field man who worked among the farmers and was assisted by the butter maker at the Algona creamery.

For the five years it is estimated that, as a result of the experiment, the net profits to the creamery patrons from larger and more economical production of milk fat and better quality of butter manufactured were increased by $20,973. The effects of the work were also shown in the organization of a county butter makers' association, a cow-testing association, a Holstein breeders' association, and various other activities looking to the betterment of dairying in the region.

The author believes that community development in dairying can be carried on with advantage in close cooperation with, and perhaps under the direction of, county agricultural agents.

The cow makes farming more profitable, compiled and edited by P. G. HOLDEN and C. M. CARROLL (*Chicago: International Harvester Company of New Jersey, 1917, pp. 122, figs. 84*).—This manual is a compilation of brief articles on the care and management of dairy cattle and the production and sale of milk and butter.

Beginnings of the dual-purpose Shorthorn type, W. GRAHAM (*Breeder's Gaz., 71 (1917), No. 25, pp. 1235, 1236, fig. 1*).—In this article the author reviews the rise of Shorthorn cattle-breeding interests in Cumberland and Westmoreland Counties, England. The data are taken for the most part from original catalogues of sales.

Cooperative bull associations, J. G. WINKJER (*U. S. Dept. Agr. Yearbook 1916, pp. 311-319, pls. 3, fig. 1*).—A brief review is given of the activities of this Department and the State agricultural colleges in the formation of cooperative bull associations and of the advantages arising from such associations.

The first of these associations in the United States was formed in Michigan in 1908. In 1916 there were 32 active associations in this country, with a membership of 650, owning about 120 pure-bred bulls.

Cooperative bull associations which are formed by farmers for the joint ownership, use, and exchange of high-class pure-bred bulls have been found especially adapted to small herds where a valuable bull for each herd is too large an investment. Among the advantages noted are better and fewer bulls, low cost per member, quick returns on investment, opportunity for more intelligent breeding, elimination of the scrub, encouragement of community breeding, and improvement of herd production due to the use of good sires.

[Dairy herd records] (*Ann. Rpt. Ontario Agr. Col. and Expt. Farm, 42 (1916), pp. 24-26*).—Tabular data show in detail for each of 34 pure-bred cows of the Macdonald College herd the amount and cost of feed consumed, cost of pasturage, amount and value of milk and fat produced, profit, and cost of production of milk and fat.

The highest record of the year was made by the 5-year-old Holstein cow, Young Springwood. This cow produced 20,110 lbs. of milk containing 821 lbs. of fat in one year, and returned a profit above cost of feed of $188.57.

Pasturing cows v. stable feeding (*Ann. Rpt. Ontario Agr. Col. and Expt. Farm, 42 (1916), pp. 26, 27*).—A comparison was made of the performance of nine cows fed during the year exclusively in the stable but allowed outdoor exercise in a moderate sized yard, and of nine other cows from the college herd pastured during the summer.

The cows fed in the stable showed an average annual record of 14,048 lbs. of milk and 528 lbs. of fat, and produced a profit of $89.35 from $119.04 worth of feed. Those pastured showed an average annual record of 12,361 lbs. of milk and 468 lbs. of fat, and produced a profit of $95.38 from $86.26 worth of feed and pasture.

Cost of milk production (*Mo. Bul. Ohio Sta., 2 (1917), No. 6, pp. 193–197).*— A brief review is given of the work done by the station since 1907 in assisting dairy farmers of the State in keeping production records of their cows and in computing profits and losses. Complete and dependable cost data giving yearly records of from one to five years for a number of herds are briefly summarized. These indicate that for the period covered there was an average loss of $1.95 per head for veal calves sold on the 26 farms on which one or more veal calves were sold annually. In 30 herds the average loss in raising heifer calves to one year of age was $6.90 per calf, and the calves were raised at a profit in only 5 of these herds. The average total cost of raising calves was $32.32 to one year of age and $67.22 to two years of age. In 22 of the herds there was a loss of $10.94 per head on heifers grown from one or two years of age and in eight herds there was a gain of $1 per head.

Data extending from 1910 to 1916, inclusive, and covering 76 yearly herd records from 31 herds indicate that the labor cost per cow annually, at 15 cts. per hour for man labor and 8.2 cts. per hour for horse labor, was $26.55. The feed cost per cow annually ranged from $35.33 to $85.12, with an average of $52.86. The total cost per cow ranged from $73 to $147 per year, with an average of $102 per year. The herd average of annual milk production ranged from 4,329 to 9.400 lbs. per cow, with an average of 5,868 lbs. The cost per 100 lbs. of milk, including loss on young stock, ranged in the various herds from about $1.50 to more than $3, and the average was approximately $1.90. The average cost per 100 lbs. of milk, less the loss on young stock, was about $1.56.

Standard calf rearing chart (*Irish Homestead, 24 (1917), No. 31, pp. 590, 591).*—This chart shows the average weights, condition of teeth, and methods of feeding normal dairy calves by weeks to the age of 24 weeks. Brief directions are given for the use of the chart.

Goat's milk for infant feeding, W. H. JORDAN and G. A. SMITH (*New York State Sta. Bul. 429 (1917), pp. 3–12, pls. 2).*—Data are given on the amount of feed consumed and the quantity and composition of milk produced during the years 1910 to 1912, inclusive, by a herd of milch goats at the station. The flock consisted of some very good animals, including one pure-bred Saanen and several pure-bred Toggenbergs. The number of animals of which complete records were kept varied from 10 to 26. During 1912, 31 adults and 9 partially grown animals consumed $441.95 worth of feed. The average cost per month per goat varied from 79.1 cts. to $1, and per goat per year was $11.05. The yearly production of milk, including some animals in the first period of lactation, varied from 301.7 to 1,845.2 lbs. The average yearly yield for 10 animals of which records were kept during three years, including 28 lactation periods, was 800.4 lbs. The feed cost of the milk per goat for all the goats during the year 1912 was 4 cts. per quart and for the three years during which the record was kept, 3.4 cts. The lowest cost was with the Saanen goat for the year 1911, which was estimated to be 1.27 cts. per quart.

The range of composition of the mixed milk of the whole flock as determined during May and June of the year 1912 was as follows: Solids, from 11.4 to 11.9 per cent; solids-not-fat, from 7.72 to 8.61 per cent; fat, from 3.5 to 3.8 per cent. The composition of milk from individual goats was found to vary in total solids from 9.22 to 18.55 per cent; in protein, from 2.24 to 4.96 per cent; in casein, from 1.56 to 4.6 per cent; in fat, from 1.08 to 8.4 per cent; and in ash, from 0.43 to 0.8 per cent.

A chemical study of the milk has already been noted (E. S. R., 34, p. 708).

Goat milk good for babies (*New York State Sta. Bul. 429, popular ed. (1917), pp. 3–7, fig. 1*).—A popular edition of the bulletin noted above and on page 570.

Dairying (*Ann. Rpt. Ontario Agr. Col. and Expt. Farm, 42 (1916), pp. 18–21*).—A brief report is made of dairy investigations conducted during the year at Macdonald Agricultural College.

It was found practicable to make rennet at home or at the cheese factory where a supply of calves' stomachs is available. Pepsin in various forms was found to be a good substitute for rennet, but a mixture of pepsin and rennet is deemed preferable to the use of pepsin alone. It was not found economical to use less than the standard quantity of rennet (3 oz. to 1,000 lbs. of milk) in cheese manufacture even with rennet at the present high price. An increase of 5.6 lbs. of cheese per 1,000 lbs. of milk was obtained as a result of pasteurizing the milk. The use of 5 per cent lactic culture in pasteurized milk was found more satisfactory than the use of hydrochloric acid.

In experiments in operating hand cream separators, it was found that a reduction of 8 revolutions per minute below normal caused a decrease of about 3 per cent in the fat content of the cream, while an increase of 8 revolutions above normal caused an increase of about 3 per cent in the fat content of the cream. An increase in the temperature of the milk at the time of separating from 80 to 90° F. and from 90 to 100° had very little effect on results, except that the fat in the cream averaged about 1 per cent lower when separating at 100° as compared with separating at temperatures of from 80 to 90°. Variations of different depths of milk in the supply-tank of the separator from full to one-half and one-quarter full, had very little effect on results, except that less than a full supply of milk in the supply can tended to reduce the capacity of the machine about 20 lbs. per hour. A variation from 3 to 4.1 in the percentage of fat in the milk separated had little effect, except that the milk containing the higher percentages of fat, averaging 3.8, produced cream testing an average of 31.3 per cent fat, while milk averaging 3.1 per cent fat, separated under similar conditions with 8 different types of machines, averaged 26.3 per cent fat in the cream. Rich, or high-testing milk, produces higher testing cream than low-testing milk.

Pasteurized sour cream showed a higher loss of fat in the buttermilk and a lessened yield of butter as compared with raw sour cream. These results emphasize the need of sweet cream for pasteurization for butter making.

Salt added to the drained butter in the churn at the rates of 4, 5, 7, and 8 oz. per 100 lbs. of butter produced finished butter containing 2, 2, 2.6, and 3.95 per cent of salt, respectively. This butter, made in June, was held in cold storage until September 28, when it was scored. The lot to which 8 per cent salt had been added was found to be "gritty," scored 42 out of 50 points for flavor, and a total of 87.5 points out of 100. The other lots were scored full for salt, and 44.5, 45, and 44, respectively, in flavor for the lots having 4, 5, and 7 per cent salt added, with total scores of 92.5, 92.5, and 92. The heavier salted lots were poorer in flavor after being held over three months in cold storage.

Skim milk cheese (*Jour. Bd. Agr. [London], 24 (1917), No. 2, pp. 175–179*).—A description is given of a method worked out by A. Todd, of the British Dairy Institute at Reading, for the manufacture of skim milk cheese from milk from which the cream is removed by hand-skimming or from separator skim milk to which enough whole milk is added to raise the fat content to about 1.5 per cent. Some of the essentials of the method are as follows:

The skim milk is raised to a temperature of 82° F., and when the acidity reaches about 0.19 per cent enough rennet is added to coagulate the milk in 35 minutes. When the curd has reached the proper consistency it is cut into ⅓-in. cubes, gently stirred by hand, and allowed to settle for 15 minutes.

The curd is then brought to 86°, with constant stirring, and allowed to settle for 30 minutes. It should then be firm and spongy and should readily sink to the bottom of the vat. When these conditions are obtained the whey should be poured off and the curd tied in cheesecloth and drained on a rack for about 1½ hours, the curd mass being cut into 4-in. cubes three or four times to facilitate drainage.

The curd is next broken up by hand and salt added at the rate of 1 oz. to 3 lbs. of curd. After a thorough stirring the curd is again inclosed in cheesecloth and weighted in molds. After being pressed overnight the cheese is trimmed, bandaged in clean calico, again pressed for 2 hours, removed from the mold, placed in the making room, and turned daily for 2 or 3 days. It is then removed to a shelf in a cooling room and turned daily. The cheese is ready for use in from 3 to 5 weeks, and should keep in good condition for from 8 to 10 weeks. The yield is said to be about 3 lbs. of cheese for each 4 gal. of skim milk.

VETERINARY MEDICINE.

The meat inspection service of the United States Department of Agriculture, G. DITEWIG (*U. S. Dept. Agr. Yearbook 1916, pp. 77–97, pls. 11, figs. 5*).— This is a description of the manner in which the Federal meat inspection is carried out under the regulations previously noted (E. S. R., 32, p. 777).

Report of State veterinarian and State live stock sanitary board for 1914 and 1915, C. J. MARSHALL (*Ann. Rpt. Penn. Dept. Agr., 21 (1915), pp. 89–173*).—This report deals with the occurrence of and work with transmissible diseases of live stock in Pennsylvania, and includes an account of control work with foot-and-mouth disease, hog cholera, rabies, tuberculosis, etc.

Report of proceedings under the diseases of animals acts, with returns of the exports and imports of animals, for the year 1915, D. S. PRENTICE (*Dept. Agr. and Tech. Instr. Ireland, Rpt. Diseases Anim., 1915, pp. 34*).—This is the usual report (E. S. R., 35, p. 279) dealing with the occurrence of infectious diseases of animals, and including statistical data.

A further note on the life history of Gongylonema scutatum, B. H. RANSOM and M. C. HALL (*Jour. Parasitology, 3 (1917), No. 4, pp. 177–181*).—The questioning by Seurat, as previously noted (E. S. R., 37, p. 361) and elsewhere,[1] of the identity of the species studied by the authors (E. S. R., 34, p. 783) has led to the further work here reported.

The authors have definitely proved that dung beetles and croton bugs fed upon the eggs of *G. scutatum* become infested with an encysted larval stage of the parasite. The evidence is also very strong, if not quite conclusive, that sheep, cattle, and other suitable mammalian hosts become infested as a result of swallowing infested insects which usually under natural conditions are various species of dung beetles.

"The nematodes found in several species of Blaps in Algeria and identified by Seurat as the larvæ of *G. scutatum* belong to some other species. It is not improbable that the nematodes found in Algerian beetles, which Seurat has considered to be the larvæ of *G. mucronatum* in reality belong to *G. scutatum*."

Spirochæta icterohæmorrhagiæ in American wild rats and its relation to the Japanese and European strains, H. NOGUCHI (*Jour. Expt. Med., 25 (1917), No. 5, pp. 755–763*).—"Wild rats captured in this country carry in their kidneys a spirochete which possesses the morphological and pathogenic properties characteristic of *S. icterohæmorrhagiæ* discovered by Inada in the Japanese

---

[1] Compt. Rend. Soc. Biol. [Paris], 79 (1916), No. 14, pp. 717–742, figs. 5.

form of infectious jaundice. Cultures of the American, Belgian, and Japanese strains of the spirochete were obtained by special technique described, the first two strains having been cultivated artificially for the first time. Animals actively immunized against the Japanese strain resist inoculation, not only of the same strain, but also of the Belgian and American strains. The Belgian strain produces immunity equally effective against all three strains. Experiments to ascertain whether the immunity afforded by the American strain also protects against the Japanese and Belgian strains are in progress. These findings warrant the conclusion that the spirochetes designated here as the Japanese, Belgian, and American strains are probably identical.

"On account of its distinctive features a new genus, Leptospira, has been suggested as the designation of this organism."

The effects of radiation on the development of Trichinella spiralis, with respect to its application to the treatment of other parasitic diseases, E. E. TYZZER and J. A. HONEIJ (Jour. Parasitology, 3 (1916), No. 2, pp. 43–56, pl. 1).— "By radium radiation from the surface of the abdomen of the rat the injury of fully developed T. spiralis has not been accomplished. These worms appeared well developed and persisted longer than in controls. Similar treatment from the second day after the ingestion of cysts has apparently resulted in a retardation of development, 30 per cent of the females being immature. In a rat radiated in this manner from the time it was fed trichinous meat, only two immature worms were found seven days later, indicating that radiation of the larvæ before they have entered upon their period of development free in the intestine is fatal to them. . . .

"Observations on the life history of T. spiralis made in the course of these experiments indicate that certain points emphasized in books of reference do not apply to the development of this parasite in rats and mice. T. spiralis is found only in small numbers in the duodenum and jejunum of rats and mice which show great numbers in the lower portion of the small intestine. It is also occasionally found in the cecum and large intestine. The life of this parasite is comparatively short in the rat, and it is found to have disappeared or is present only in small numbers 18 days after infection. No evidence has been obtained that the males disappear early in the infection. A sex ratio of one male to two females observed six and seven days after infection has shown no marked change for the ten days following. A male Trichinella has been found in a rat from which all females had disappeared."

Oil of Chenopodium and chloroform as anthelmintics.—Preliminary note, M. C. HALL and W. D. FOSTER (Jour. Amer. Med. Assoc., 68 (1917), No. 26, pp. 1961–1963).—The authors' experimental findings indicate that oil of Chenopodium should be accompanied by large doses of castor oil, and that when so given it is an uncommonly effective and quite safe anthelmintic for use against ascarids. Chloroform in castor oil, in therapeutic doses, is the most effective anthelmintic that they have found for use against hookworms, and they consider it as safe as thymol or any other effective drug for use against hookworm disease.

Anaphylatoxin and anaphylaxis (Jour. Infect. Diseases, 20 (1917), Nos. 5, pp. 499–656; 6, pp. 657–854, figs. 19).—Ten studies are here reported.

I. Trypanosome anaphylatoxin, F. G. Novy, P. H. DeKruif, and R. L. Novy (pp. 499–535).—In the course of a study on immunity against the trypanosomes of surra and nagana it was found that severe toxic effects with marked hypothermia often followed the injection of autolyzed suspensions of the organisms. Reinjection usually resulted fatally.

This phenomenon was further studied and anaphylatoxin found to be produced by the trypanosomes of surra (Trypanosoma evansi), caderas (T.

equinum), dourine (*T. equiperdum*), nagana (*T. brucei*), and the nonpathogenic trypanosome, *T. lewisi.* The anaphylatoxin was made not only by the living cells but also by those dead and more or less autolyzed, and even by those heated to 60° C. The same mass of trypanosomes could be used repeatedly to toxify different lots of serum. Rat serum was found preferable to guinea pig serum since it yielded a poison 12 or more times as active as that obtained with the latter, the lethal doses being 0.25 cc. and 3 cc., respectively.

"The speed of poison production under favorable conditions is very rapid and quickly reaches a maximum, the poison then persisting for a long time. Thus, infected, defibrinated rat blood or serum, when incubated for one or two minutes, may become fatally toxic. With an incubation of about 15 minutes it is possible to produce a toxic serum such that 0.25 cc. will cause acute anaphylactic death." The anaphylatoxin was found to persist at 37° for more than four hours and at about 0° for an indefinite time.

"Toxic sera can induce toxicity in normal sera, the mixtures representing a high dilution of the former. This result is not due to the action of a ferment, but to minute amounts of trypanosomes still present in the inciting serum; or, in the case of very prolonged incubation, to the production of autoanaphylatoxin. . . .

"Transfusion experiments indicate the possible presence of anaphylatoxin in heavily infected rats. The formation of this poison in corpore may lead to sudden deaths or to chronic intoxication or cachexia. . . .

"The injection of large amounts of washed trypanosomes into guinea pigs may result in the production of anaphylatoxin in corpore. The effects are not due directly to the organisms but to the disturbance in the colloidal state of plasma constituents caused by the alien material. The 'trypanotoxins' are therefore disturbers of equilibrium; the result is a poison production in vivo as well as in vitro. The mode of action of endotoxins in general will be found to be of the same nature.

"The participation of a ferment in this reaction is contraindicated by the speed of production, the rapid attainment of maximal level, the behavior of inactivated sera, and by the results of centrifugation.

"The syndrome of symptoms and autopsy findings consequent on the injection of the trypanosome anaphylatoxin are those of the intoxication of true anaphylaxis. The two poisonings are to be considered as identical."

II. *Agar anaphylatoxin: Guinea pig serum,* F. G. Novy and P. H. DeKruif (pp. 536–565).—Anaphylatoxin was produced in guinea pig serum by using agar in place of the trypanosomes. Incubation from 8 to 10 minutes at 37° was found to render the serum fatal in a dose of 3 cc. The lethal dose can be reduced to 1 cc. "The toxicity of such serum, when tested at regular intervals, appears to show more or less oscillation, as in the case of the trypanosome anaphylatoxin. Such variations are not due to a change in the amount of the poison, but to a varying resistance of the test animals. The physical state of the agar is an important factor in the production of the poison."

Incubation at 37° is necessary, and serum contact does not result in poison production, which contraindicates absorption as a factor in the reaction. Individual variation in the ease with which sera can be toxified was noted.

III. *Agar anaphylatoxin: Rabbit serum,* F. G. Novy and P. H. DeKruif (pp. 566–588).—The production of anaphylatoxin in normal rabbit serum was found not to be as easy as in the case of guinea pig or rat serum. Individual variation in the ease with which the serum yielded the poison was again observed. The presence of lipoidal matter was not found to be inhibitive. After a short fast the sera appeared to be more reactive, and a varied diet was favorable to the reaction. The results were similar to those noted in the case of the guinea pig serum.

IV. *Agar anaphylatoxin: Rat serum*, F. G. Novy and P. H. DeKruif (pp. 589–617).—"Rat serum can be toxified with agar in 7.5 minutes so that 0.25 cc. will cause acute fatal shock; after incubation for only 2.5 minutes 1 cc. may be fatal. The reaction concerned in the production of anaphylatoxin is one of great speed. Agar and trypanosomes can work at the same speed since they can toxify 1 cc. in 2.5 minutes.

"The individual sera show some variation in the ease with which they can be toxified. This is not due to the age of the serum or to the presence of lipoids. Normal rat serum, without any addition, on long incubation may become toxic so that 1 cc. will be fatal.

"The physical state of the agar is an important factor in the production of the poison. Its inducing power is not affected by sterilization at 140°."

The poison is not destroyed when kept at 56° for 24 hours, but is partially destroyed in half an hour at 70°, and apparently completely in 5 minutes at 100°.

V. *Effect of multiple doses of anaphylatoxin*, F. G. Novy and P. H. DeKruif (pp. 618–628).—Rat anaphylatoxin, in amounts representing from 1 to 40 lethal doses, invariably produced death in guinea pigs in essentially the same time. "The larger doses gave an intense quiet shock; the autopsy findings in all cases were typical, but with larger doses the petechiæ in the lungs were most pronounced; the blood was always free from clot. The blood when transferred to a test tube showed delay in coagulation. Slow injection of very large doses gave an almost incoagulable blood. The in vitro mixtures of rat anaphylatoxin and normal blood likewise showed retarded coagulation. The white rat possesses a remarkable immunity against anaphylatoxin; weight for weight it can tolerate more than 100 times as much as the guinea pig. The dosage with serum reached 10 per cent of the body weight. . . .

"The rabbit like the rat is not affected by large doses of anaphylatoxin and this fact parallels the behavior of rabbits on injection of large doses of the toxic antisheep immune rabbit serum. It is this tolerance of the rabbit for the poison that permits the formation of large amounts of anaphylatoxin during life. Antisheep guinea pig serum is not toxic since the formation of anaphylatoxin to the extent of a single lethal dose would mean the death of the animal. This tolerance likewise accounts for the known resistance of the rabbit to specific anaphylaxis."

A transfusion experiment indicated the rapid disappearance of the anaphylatoxin from the blood.

VI. *Effect of intravenous injections of agar*, F. G. Novy and P. H. DeKruif (pp. 629–656).—Agar injected into guinea pigs may produce a typical anaphylactic shock and death with characteristic autopsy findings. The rabbit appears to be somewhat less susceptible than the guinea pig to the agar injections and the rat still less inactive. "With a transfer time of 1 minute, the transfusion of 4 cc. of normal rat blood resulted in typical fatal anaphylactic shock, due to the anaphylatoxin formed as the result of the precoagulation disturbance.

"The transfusion method has shown that the blood of normal untreated rabbits may be toxic in dose of 2 cc., and that the serum from such animals may be fatal in dose of 1 cc. The apparently healthy rabbit may carry 50 guinea pig lethal doses per kilogram.

"This inherent or acquired toxicity is to be correlated with that developed by immunizing injections, also with the precoagulation toxicity, and with that of normal serum, as well as with that induced in normal serum by alien substances."

It is concluded that the so-called "endotoxin" of various pathogenic organisms is similar to the toxicity of agar, and that the common conception· of endotoxin is fundamentally wrong. "The disturbance in the plasma caused by the introduction of alien substances results in the formation of anaphylatoxin, the poisonous effects of which have been erroneously attributed to a liberation of the so-called endotoxin."

VII. *Peptone anaphylatoxin*, F. G. Novy, P. H. DeKruif, and F. O. Novy (pp. 657–716).—The symptoms and findings in guinea pigs injected with peptone were the same as those produced by anaphylatoxin, agar, or by specific anaphylactic shock. A marked exophthalmos was observed and was especially marked in rabbits. Guinea pigs showed the same individual variation to peptone as has been demonstrated for anaphylatoxin and agar. In white rats the injection of peptone resulted in symptoms and findings identical with those caused by anaphylatoxin and agar. The coagulation time of the blood was retarded for an appreciable period.

It was found necessary to employ very large doses of peptone in rabbits to obtain typical anaphylactic shock and findings. Considerable variation in resistance was observed in rabbits, as in rats and guinea pigs. An immunity or tolerance was shown by the rabbit to repeated injections of peptone similar to that exhibited by the dog or guinea pig.

"Rat serum on treatment with peptone rapidly yields anaphylatoxin. A peptone suspension is more active than a perfectly clear solution. The fully dissolved peptone does not toxify rat serum as easily, nor does it yield as high a degree of toxicity as do the agar and trypanosome suspensoids. Extreme dispersion is, therefore, unfavorable for the reagent." Anaphylatoxin was also produced when guinea pig serum was treated with peptone.

"A comparison of the effective agar-serum ratio with that of peptone-serum shows that, with regard to rat serum, agar is 500 times more active than peptone; with regard to guinea pig serum, it is from 200 to 1,000 times as active. . . . Peptone itself is not toxic, but when brought into contact with a reactive serum or plasma it induces the change which results in anaphylatoxin production."

VIII. *The primary toxicity of normal serum*, P. H. DeKruif (pp. 717–775).— "Very rapid transfusion of the blood of normal rabbit to the guinea pig or white rat shows that the toxicity of such blood is subject to great variation. It is often possible to transfuse 10 cc. of heart blood without much effect. Exceptionally, however, the blood from apparently normal rabbits is inherently toxic in dose of 2 or even 1 cc., and the plasma and serum from such blood may be correspondingly toxic. The natural resistance of the rabbit enables it to act as a carrier of the poison which may be generated in the normal animal as a result of changed conditions, notably diet. The toxicity of the blood of an apparently normal rabbit may correspond to 100 guinea pig lethal doses per kilogram. A blood which is initially nontoxic becomes poisonous in 3 cc. dose, just prior to the appearance of coagulation. The speed of poison production corresponds to that of anaphylatoxin by agar, inulin, trypanosomes, etc."

The symptoms and autopsy findings in guinea pigs after injection of toxic blood or serum were essentially those produced by anaphylatoxin and in anaphylactic shock. When rat or guinea pig blood or serum was used instead of that of the rabbit identical results were obtained. Homologous blood was found to be distinctly less toxic than heterologous. Large doses of normal rabbit serum which killed guinea pigs rapidly caused death with thrombi in the heart and enlarged vessels.

IX. *Specific anaphylactic Shock*, F. G. Novy and P. H. DeKruif (pp. 776–832).—It is noted that the rat is an invaluable agent in the study of anaphylaxis. Nonspecific anaphylactic shock was induced in sensitized rats by the injection of distilled water in amounts which had no effect on the normal rat. Salt solution in like doses was tolerated with practically no effect. The specifically sensitized guinea pig was found not to be more susceptible to distilled water than the normal animal.

"The relative behavior of the rat and guinea pig to distilled water is paralleled in the relative ease with which the serum of the former, as compared with that of the latter, is toxified by agar. Normal guinea pigs on rapid injection of very large doses of saline, and especially of distilled water, respond with shock effects. . . . A mixture of distilled water and sensitized rat serum is rapidly toxified at 37° C., the speed increasing with the dilution. The dose containing 1 cc. serum equivalent, incubated for 5 minutes, is fatally toxic." A mixture of distilled water and serum of the rat sensitized to horse serum was likewise rapidly toxified at 37°.

"The speed of poison production in normal serum or in sensitized serum is the same as that which has been demonstrated for agar, trypanosomes, peptone, etc. The in vivo production of anaphylatoxin in specific shock, and its production, in vitro, in mixtures of sensitized sera and antigen or distilled water, is therefore an accomplished fact. The results contraindicate the theories of adsorption and of proteolysis. The specific anaphylactic shock is the result of anaphylatoxin production, in corpore, consequent upon the inducing action of a body which is formed by the union, or otherwise, of antigen and its specific antibody. It is not necessary for this inducing body to exist as a visible precipitate, since substances in solution are capable of giving rise to anaphylatoxin. The specificity of the reaction concerns the production of this inducing substance, and not that of the poison; and further, the antigen is in no wise the source of the anaphylatoxin which is brought into being in shock."

X. *Anaphylatoxin and amino nitrogen*, P. H. DeKruif and W. M. German (pp. 833–854).—No relationship between serum autolysis and anaphylatoxin production was observed when the method of Van Slyke for the determination of aliphatic amino nitrogen was used.

"Rat and guinea pig sera, toxified rapidly by the addition of 5 per cent agar-hydrogel, show a marked decrease in amino nitrogen as compared with controls from the same pool of serum. This decrease takes place at once upon addition of agar to serum. After this preliminary drop in amino nitrogen a very gradual rise to a value not exceeding that of the control may take place. Maximal toxicity appears before this increase begins to be noticeable. The cause of this drop in amino nitrogen in serum treated with agar is not known, but is probably to be referred to adsorption of amino acid by the agar. Attempts to recover this supposedly adsorbed amino acid have failed.

"A similar drop in amino nitrogen along with a marked increase in toxicity is to be observed in the case of rat serum incubated with inulin. Guinea pig serum treated in a like manner shows a slight increase in amino acids, which, however, does not keep pace with the increase in toxicity. Rat serum behaves peculiarly when diluted with distilled water. Sensitive rat serum shows an increase, normal rat serum a decrease in amino nitrogen when incubated with six volumes of distilled water. Despite this difference, both become toxic."

The most potent anaphylatoxin was produced by mixing inulin in the proportion of 1 to 10 with normal rat serum.

A study of five members (or so-called species) of the septicemia hemorrhagica (Pasteurella) group of organisms with special reference to their action on the various carbohydrates, A. M. Besemer (*Jour. Bact.*, *2* (*1917*), No. *2*, pp. *177–184*).—"The members of the septicemia hemorrhagica group studied were practically uniform in their biochemical actions. The passing of an organism through a rabbit did not change its biochemical characters, except to a very slight degree."

The virulence of apparently sound muscle and lymph glands in general bovine and porcine tuberculosis, P. Chaussé (*Ann. Inst. Pasteur*, *31* (*1917*), No. *1*, pp. *1–18*).—The literature on the subject is reviewed and data submitted in tabular form.

In the original study reported material from 18 tubercular hogs and 40 tubercular cattle was used. Extracts were made of the muscular and lymphatic tissue and injected into guinea pigs. Of the animals injected with the material obtained from the muscle tissue none exhibited tubercular symptoms or lesions on autopsy. These results indicate the freedom from virulent material of the muscles of animals which have died from the disease. Of 53 samples of lymphatic material 13 were found to be virulent. The relative frequency of the virulence of this material is considered to be strong proof of the rôle of filtration of the lymphatic system as a defensive agency.

The results of the investigation are discussed and their hygienic importance emphasized.

Eupatorium ageratoides, the cause of trembles, R. S. Curtis and F. A. Wolf (*U. S. Dept. Agr., Jour. Agr. Research*, *9* (*1917*), No. *11*, pp. *397–404*. pls. *3*).—This is a progress report of investigations conducted at the North Carolina Experiment Station, in the mountainous sections of which State considerable losses of domestic animals result from a malady known as trembles. The disease is thought to be transmissible to man through milk products or flesh of animals affected with the disease, and is known by physicians as milk sickness.

The report is summarized as follows: "*E. ageratoides*, commonly known as white snakeroot and locally known in North Carolina as richweed, had previously been claimed by Moseley [E. S. R., 21, p. 383] to cause trembles in animals. This claim has been substantiated by experiments with sheep in which green plants of *E. ageratoides* were fed during the months of June, July, August, September, and October, 1916. Fifteen cases of trembles in sheep have been developed from feeding *E. ageratoides*. Fourteen of these resulted fatally and one of them recovered. Death of one of these sheep was probably due in part to an infestation of stomach worms. Death resulted in from 5 to 27 days following the beginning of feeding of *E. ageratoides*. Considerable variation existed in the several ewes, also, with reference to the quantity of weed ingested before trembles appeared.

"Indirect evidence against the infectious nature of the disease was secured by failure to communicate trembles from sheep characteristically affected to healthy sheep when they were confined and fed together in a small lot.

"Salt and soda in the amounts given along with a ration of grain and *E. ageratoides* were without apparent antidotal effect. No harmful effect followed the feeding for 69 days of aluminum phosphate mixed with grain and supplemented with alfalfa hay."

The control and prevention of infectious diseases of cattle, E. C. Schroeder (*Ann. Rpt. Internat. Assoc. Dairy and Milk Insp.*, *5* (*1916*), pp. *167–180*).

The bacteriotherapeutic treatment of ulcerous lymphangitis in the horse, C. Truche (*Compt. Rend. Acad. Sci.* [Paris], *164* (*1917*), No. *12*, pp. *497–499*).—

The successful treatment of the disease with a vaccine made from the Preisz-Nocard bacillus is noted.

The vaccine was prepared by heating a suspension of the organism in physiological salt solution for 24 hours at 37° C., separating the organisms by centrifugalization, treating with alcohol-ether mixture, and finally drying over sulphuric acid. It produced no general reaction, the thermic reaction being only from 0.5 to 1° and the appetite and general condition remaining normal. The number of injections found necessary varied with the degree and duration of the disease, two or three generally being sufficient. The value of local treatment with tincture of iodin and other antiseptics is noted.

Salvarsan in the treatment of canine distemper, C. KROCHER (*Abs. in Jour. Amer. Vet. Med. Assoc., 51 (1917), No. 4, pp. 565, 566*).—It appears that salvarsan does not exert either a curative or an otherwise favorable action on the course of canine distemper.

On the occurrence of a pseudoparasitic mite (Cheletiella parasitivorax) on the domestic cat, S. HIRST (*Ann. and Mag. Nat. Hist., 8. ser., 20 (1917), No. 115, pp. 132, 133, fig. 1*).—This records the finding, on post-mortem examination of a cat affected with mange, of numerous specimens of *C. parasitivorax* on various parts of the body and a few isolated eggs, each fixed to a hair. Presumably this mite fed on the acarid *Notœdrus cati.*

Chicken pox in poultry.—Preventive suggestions based on practical experiments, H. E. UPTON (*Brit. Columbia Dept. Agr., Circ. Bul. 20 (1917), pp. 5, figs. 5*).—The author has vaccinated approximately 3.000 birds ranging from 5 weeks to 3 years in age without observing any bad effects aside from 3 deaths, due mainly to emaciation before vaccination. Control birds were left in each flock, and 40 per cent died. Egg production was not affected by vaccination in any way other than the handling of the birds would cause.

"Some flocks were vaccinated with vaccine made from scabs only. Others were vaccinated from vaccine made from scabs and cheesy exudate. Some were vaccinated with vaccine made up of scabs and exudate mixed together before attenuated. Others were vaccinated with vaccine made by attenuating scabs and exudate separately and mixing the two vaccines together before injection. The best results were obtained amongst the 7 flocks by the use of the vaccine made up of the scabs and exudate ground together before being attenuated.

"Data were not obtainable from any source relating to the vaccination of young chicks. Our experiments show that good results are obtainable by vaccinating 5- to 8-week-old chicks (majority showing signs of disease after severe chilling) twice with 0.5 cc. of vaccine at intervals of 3 to 4 days. Two cc. was injected in 3 or 4 very bad cases expected to die in a few hours. Cases recovered and can not be noticed other than by band number in flocks after expiration of 7 months.

"Strong tincture of iodin is recommended as the best disinfectant for use with this disease. The scabs and exudate should be removed with a sterile pair of forceps and tincture of iodin applied to the exposed surface."

RURAL ENGINEERING.

A textbook of practical hydraulics, J. PARK (*Philadelphia: J. B. Lippincott Co., 1916, pp. XVI+284, pls. 47, figs. 115*).—This is a handbook for the practical use of irrigation, hydraulic, and power development engineers. It comprises chapters on some first principles: definition of terms; flow of water through orifices; friction in pipes and channels; the discharge of pipes; flow of water in open channels, over weirs and notches, and in rivers; construction of pipes, flumes, ditches, masonry and concrete dams, and earthen dams; and water power and water prime motors.

Report of the State water commission of California, 1917 (*Rpt. State Water Com. Cal., 1915-16, pp. 183, pls. 10, figs. 5*).—This report contains data on water rights and water supply in California, duty of water, ground water and its relation to surface water, water spreading, check dams, interstate water rights, rice culture, the irrigation districts of California, and the principal private irrigation enterprises. A list, by counties, of all applications for the appropriation of water, together with a statement of their status, is included.

Report of the water conservation and irrigation commission [of New South Wales] for the year ended June 30, 1916 (*N. S. Wales Rpt. Water Conserv. and Irrig. Com., 1916, pp. 128, pls. 10*).—This report for 1916 contains data on irrigation areas in New South Wales established and controlled by the State, irrigation schemes under consideration for State control, water conservation works constructed by the State but administered by local trusts, national works maintained by the commission, artesian and shallow boring, and water conservation and irrigation works constructed by private persons. Eleven appendixes of financial and statistical data are included.

Administration report, irrigation department, Punjab, 1915–16 (*Punjab Irrig. Branch Admin. Rpt. 1915-16, pp. 178, pls. 13*).—This is an administrative report, including statistical data on expenditures and revenues for irrigation in the Punjab.

Surface water supply of North Atlantic slope drainage basins, 1915 (*U. S. Geol. Survey, Water-Supply Paper 401 (1917), pp. 155+XXXVI, pls. 2*).—This report contains the results of measurements of flow made on the drainage basins of streams in the North Atlantic slope during 1915, together with the usual list of gauging stations and publications.

Surface water supply of Ohio River Basin, 1915 (*U. S. Geol. Survey, Water-Supply Paper 403 (1917), pp. 175+XXXIV, pls. 2*),—This report presents the results of measurements of flow made on streams in the Ohio River Basin during 1915, together with the usual list of stream-gauging stations and publications.

Centrifugal pumps and suction dredgers, E. W. SARGEANT (*Philadelphia: J. B. Lippincott Co., 1916, pp. VIII+188, pls. 16, figs. 131*).—This book is essentially a manual of centrifugal pumping machinery for the use of engineers and designers and those responsible for the installation and supervision of centrifugal pumping plants. It contains chapters on the design and construction of centrifugal pumps of different types; pumps in series and parallel; high capacity, low-head pumps; charging apparatus; testing of centrifugal pumps; centrifugal pumping machinery for drainage, irrigation, and sewage; and pumps for dredging and conveying solids.

Some costs of maintenance of motor-driven deep-well pumps, M. L. ENGER (*Jour. Amer. Water Works Assoc., 4 (1917), No. 2, pp. 190, 191*).—Records made at the University of Illinois are reported.

Unlined earth reservoirs for pumping plants, (*Jour. Electricity, 38 (1917), No. 10, pp. 395–397, figs. 2*).—Cost data per acre-foot for different capacities of unlined reservoirs for irrigation are graphically given, together with tabular and other data on the details in the construction of typical unlined earth reservoirs.

Pumping for irrigation on the farm, P. E. FULLER (*U. S. Dept. Agr. Yearbook 1916, pp. 507–520, pl. 1, fig. 1*).—This article deals with types of pumps and their special adaptations, and with the general features of proper installation of an irrigation pumping plant, including well construction.

16179°—17—No. 6——7

With regard to cost, it is stated that " a first-class pumping plant, including well, may be installed, under average conditions of head and capacity, at a cost of from $5,000 to $7,000, with ample capacity to irrigate 160 acres of average forage crops. A smaller plant with a capacity of several hundred gallons a minute may be installed complete, including the well, for $2,000 or less if water-supply conditions are favorable. The cost of a reservoir may be $500 or even $1,000 if it be concrete lined. The operation of a pumping plant should extend over as great a period of time during an irrigation season as possible, so as to reduce the unit overhead cost."

Divisors (for the measurement of irrigation water), V. M. Cone (*Colorado Sta. Bul. 228 (1917), pp. 3–52, figs. 8*).—This bulletin, based on work done under a cooperative agreement between the Colorado Station and the Office of Public Roads and Rural Engineering, U. S. Department of Agriculture, reports the results of 341 tests of divisors for the measurement of irrigation water and 196 tests on dividing the flow over rectangular and Cipolletti weirs. Eight different divisors were tested, each under four different sets of conditions.

In the weir tests " crest lengths of 2 and 4 ft. were used for both types. A thin metal plate was placed on the downstream side of the weir so that its edge touched the crest of the weir and extended vertically above the weir crest into the weir notch. This plate was set for different experiments at intervals of 2 in. across the entire width of the weir, and separate channels caught the flow over the weir on the two sides of the plate. These channels were placed far enough below the crest of the weir to allow a free passage of air under the overpouring sheet of water.

" Under these conditions both types of weirs give reasonably accurate divisions, the greatest error being with the rectangular weir set to divide the flow between two parties on a basis of one-fourth and three-fourths, when the actual deliveries will be 24 and 76 per cent for a head of 0.2 ft., and 22.5 and 77.5 per cent for a head of 0.8 ft. The errors with Cipolletti weirs used as divisors were in the opposite direction and about one-half as great. When either weir would be used to divide the water equally between three parties the error would be quite negligible.

" If the divisor plate is placed out some distance from the weir, or the edge is placed in a horizontal position below the weir crest, the discharge for the end division would be considerably short, and the flow for the middle division would be accordingly greater than the desired amount."

The composition of irrigation waters in upper Italy, A. Menozzi and A. De Vecchi (*Rend. R. Ist. Lombardo Sci e Let., 2. ser., 49 (1916), No. 7–8, pp. 291–297*).—Analyses of representative samples of irrigation waters from irrigation canals of Lombardy are reported and discussed.

The economical irrigation of alfalfa in Sacramento Valley, S. H. Beckett and R. D. Robertson (*California Sta. Bul. 280 (1917), pp. 273–294, figs. 2*).—This bulletin reports the results of work done under cooperative agreement between the Office of Public Roads and Rural Engineering, U. S. Department of Agriculture, and the State Engineering Department of California, and between the Office of Public Roads and Rural Engineering and the California Experiment Station. The practices found most desirable are summarized in the table following.

Results of studies of alfalfa irrigation practices.

Soil type.	Number of irrigations.	Depth of each irrigation.	Total depth of irrigation.	Desirable dimensions of checks.		Desirable grade of checks. per 100 feet.	Desirable irrigation heads per second per check.
				Width.	Length.		
		Inches.	*Inches.*	*Feet.*	*Feet.*	*Inches.*	*Cu.ft.*
Medium loam............	3 to 5...........	6 to 9	30 to 36	50	300 to 600	3 to 6	2 to 10
Gravelly or sandy soil..	2 to 3 per cutting.	3 to 4	48 to 60	100	100	....	5 to 6
Heavy soil..............	2 to 3 per cutting.	2 to 4	30 to 36	30 to 50	300 to 600	1 to 3	1 to 4

The general conclusion drawn is that "from 2.5 to 3 acre-feet of irrigation water per acre per year is sufficient for the growth of maximum economic yields of alfalfa on the medium loam soils of Sacramento Valley."

Irrigation and drainage, E. RISLER and G. WERY (*Irrigations et Drainages. Paris: J. B. Baillière & Sons, 1916, 3. ed., rev. and enl., pp. 566, figs. 186*).— This is the third revised and enlarged edition (E. S. R., 15, p. 934) of one of the volumes of the Encyclopédie Agricole.

Part 1, on water plants and the soil, contains chapters on the physical and chemical relations between water, soil, and plants; the régime of water in geological formations; and fertilizing substances. Part 2, on irrigation, contains chapters on effects of irrigation; quality, methods of obtaining, and distribution of irrigation water; cost, technique, assessments, practice, and economics of irrigation; irrigation ditches and canals; duty of water; drainage of irrigated lands; irrigation in mountain regions; silting; maintenance of prairie irrigation systems and prairie irrigation practice. Part 3, on drainage, contains chapters on the origin, indications, and bad results of excess of water in soil; reclamation and drainage and methods therefor; definition and history of drainage; theory, execution, and results of drainage; obstructions of drains and methods of prevention; drainage economics; and types of drains and their proper use.

Drainage of irrigated farms, R. A. HART (*U. S. Dept. Agr., Farmers' Bul. 805 (1917), pp. 31, figs. 19*).—This describes methods of draining irrigated farms. See also a technical report by the author (E. S. R., 33, p. 88).

Standard specifications for drain tile (*Amer. Soc. Testing Materials, A. S. T. M. Standards, 1916, pp. 452–468, pl. 1, figs. 4*).—Specifications for farm, standard, and extra quality drain tile are given each for 1916.

The quality of water and confirmatory tests for Bacillus coli, A. WOLMAN (*Jour. Amer. Water Works'Assoc., 4 (1917), No. 2, pp. 200–205, fig. 1*).—Experimental data are reported from which it is concluded that "a water showing the highest degree of actual pollution, as determined by the highest percentage of samples giving a positive isolation test for colon, in general gives the highest percentage of presumptive tests confirmed. A water showing the lowest degree of actual pollution in general gives the lowest percentage of presumptive tests confirmed. . . .

"A rough quantitative test for pollution, in a general study of a water, might with safety consist only of a determination of the presumptive tests confirmed, rather than of a detailed estimate of the percentage of samples showing isolation tests in varying dilutions. In such a procedure one might establish as bases for comparison a maximum and minimum percentage of tubes confirmed, using for this purpose waters grossly polluted in the first case, and unquestionably pure in the second. With these maximum and minimum values as standards, the relative position of the water under consideration could be determined with ease by the use of the ʻpercentage of tubesʼ scoring method."

Ultra-violet rays, their advantages and disadvantages in the purification of drinking water, R. R. SPENCER (*Jour. Amer. Water Works Assoc., 4 (1917), No. 2, pp. 172–182, figs. 2*).—The author expresses the opinion that the use of ultra-violet rays in the purification of drinking water is capable of further development, with a corresponding increase in efficiency.

"The method is especially recommended for treating water in circulating systems, in which the water may be exposed many times to the ultra-violet rays. . . . The chief advantages of this method of treatment over chemical methods lie in the fact that objectionable overdosage is impossible. Again, from the standpoint of potability, the water is absolutely unchanged, and, hence, in this respect, is superior even to boiled water. . . .

"The present forms of apparatus need considerable attention when in operation. Care should be taken to prevent an accumulation of grease or dirt of any kind on the quartz tube. Experience has shown that a very small amount of grease will obstruct the light sufficiently to allow many organisms to pass. Furthermore, the light chamber should be emptied if the machine remains idle for any length of time. This will prevent the growth of algæ and other organisms which will obstruct the light when the machine is again operated. . . .

"In the tests [described], since the gravity type gave a higher efficiency than the pressure type, and inasmuch as any lamp operating at a higher voltage is known to emit a larger amount of ultra-violet radiation, the use of lamps at a higher voltage, combined with the gravity system. suggests itself as a reasonable line of development. In regard to cost, the method is not expensive when treating relatively small quantities of water."

Sterilization by liquid chlorin and hypochlorite of lime, M. S. DUTTON (*Jour. Amer. Water Works Assoc., 4 (1917), No. 2, pp. 228–230*).—A comparison of calcium hypochlorite and liquid chlorin for water sterilization showed that, "the cost of hypochlorite being considered as 7 cts. per pound and the cost of liquid chlorin as 20 cts. per pound, the average cost of sterilization by means of hypochlorite was $1.07 per million gallons of water treated and 28 cts. per million gallons when using liquid chlorin. The saving, then, in chemicals alone amounted to 79 cts. per million gallons of water treated.

"In summarizing the results of sterilization, the average reduction in bacteria count of daily plates made on nutrient agar incubated at 37° C. for 24 hours was as follows: In January, when hypochlorite was used, the average raw water count was 6,300 and the filtered water count was 15. In June, when liquid chlorin was used, the average raw water count was 7,980 and the filtered water count was 11. In *Bacillus coli* tests, the raw water shows 100 per cent + for both months, while the filtered water shows 1.6 per cent + in January and 0 per cent + in June. These results were obtained by means of 1 cc. samples in all cases. While hypochlorite was used 0.46 parts per million of chlorin was applied and while using liquid chlorin 0.22 parts per million of chlorin was applied."

The disposal of wastes from the dairy industry, A. E. KIMBERLY (*Ohio Pub. Health Jour., 7 (1916), No. 7, pp. 250–285, pl. 1; abs. in Chem. Abs. 10 (1916), No. 21, p. 2779*).—This paper reviews existing information on the dairy wastes disposal problem, covering American and foreign experience, and suggests practical solutions of given problems, including plant design and estimates of cost. It is based especially on experience by the Ohio State Board of Health. The following conclusions are drawn:

"Not only do the actual wash waters cause nuisances, but in a practical way also whey, buttermilk, and skimmed milk remaining at the end of the day's operation, all three of which require extended dilution to admit of their satisfactory disposal in running streams. . . . No practical process appears available for whey treatment unless the small plant ships the waste to a central station for evaporation. Whey-butter making would, of course, remove but little of the organic matters of the whey. Whey contains so much albuminous matter as to render ineffective the bacterial processes availed of in the treatment of the other wastes of the dairy industry and its removal by cartage appears the most practical method of disposal at present available. . . . Dependable whey disposal in a practical way means definite provision for its systematic removal through such part of the year as dilution disposal in the local stream can not be employed.

"Tank treatment by septic tanks requires land or artificial filters in the absence of 30-fold dilution. With proper construction . . . tanks of 48 or 72 hours' retention, according to the character of the processes carried out at the plant, and filters of sand on a basis of 25,000 gal. per acre per day, can be depended upon to prevent nuisances. The rectangular tank has at best certain disadvantages, particularly as regards the intermittent discharge of sludge with the effluent. Data are too few to indicate the applicability of two-story tanks, but it would seem that such tanks can be advantageously used for wastes of the dairy industry, subject to proper construction details, especially as to detention period. Combined septic and two-story tanks may solve this problem to good advantage. . . .

"Tanks remove suspended matter, increase acidity by encouraging the lactic fermentation, and to a certain extent modify the chemical character of these wastes. Filters, subsurface tile systems, or running streams supply the oxygen essential to render the organic matters of these wastes no longer amenable to putrefactive decomposition. Each has its own function to perform. These processes cover the field at present available for waste treatment. All methods applicable to the treatment of domestic sewage have been applied in the past with varying degrees of success to dairy wastes, and it is possible that the activated sludge process may find in these wastes a fruitful field. Unless activated sludge methods will result in by-product recovery, bringing financial gain to the plant, it is the author's viewpoint that the process would be of limited utility because the operation of such plant would involve a daily expense and because dairy waste disposal to be successful under practical conditions must be cheap and simple in operation and require but little daily attention."

Forty-two references to literature bearing on the subject are appended.

Sewage disposal on the farm, G. M. WARREN (*U. S. Dept. Agr. Yearbook 1916, pp. 347–373, figs. 10*).—This article deals with sewage as a menace to health and with sewage purification by natural agencies, and describes and diagrammatically illustrates pit, dry earth, and wet closet privies, chemical closets, cesspools, and septic tanks.

An especially important point brought out regarding septic-tank systems is that "the septic tank is not a complete method of sewage treatment. With the general run of small septic tanks it is close to the facts to say that of all the solid matter in the crude sewage one-third is reduced to liquids and gas, one-third remains in the tank, and one-third escapes with the effluent. Every septic-tank installation is a problem by itself. As a suit is fashioned to the size and needs of an individual, so should the design of a septic tank and the after disposition of the effluent be decided upon, with full consideration for the size of the family, the amount of water used, the location of property lines, buildings, wells, and drainage outlets, the slope of the land, and the character of the soil and subsoil."

Modern road construction, A. T. BYRNE (*Chicago: Amer. Tech. Soc., 1917, pp. [VIII]+187, pl. 1, figs. 113*).—This is a treatise on the engineering problems of road building, with a compilation of highway specifications. It is the purpose to cover the field of road building for both rural and urban conditions. The following chapters are included: Country roads and boulevards—resistance to movement of vehicles, location of roads, preliminary road construction methods, culverts, earthwork, and maintenance and improvement of roads; city streets and highways—foundations, stone-block pavements, brick pavements, wood-block pavements, asphalt pavements, miscellaneous pavements, miscellaneous street work, curbstones and gutters, street cleaning, and selecting the pavement.

Good roads yearbook, 1917 (*Good Roads Year Book, Amer. Highway Assoc., 1917, pp. VII+556, figs. 36*).—This is the sixth annual edition of this book (E. S. R., 35, p. 583). It gives information regarding road improvements under Federal, State, Territorial, and local control and on the construction and maintenance of rural roads and miscellaneous information and tables.

Report of the State highway commission of Minnesota, 1915–16 (*Rpt. Highway Com. Minn., 1915–16, pp. 40, pls. 3, figs. 16*).—This is a report on the work and expenditures on road and bridge design, construction, and maintenance in Minnesota during the years 1915–16, including data on reinforced concrete bridge and culvert tests.

Wisconsin highway commission, second biennial report (*Wis. Highway Com. Bien. Rpt., 2 (1913–14), pp. IX+260, pls. 5, figs. 85*).—This is a statement of work and expenditures on highway construction, maintenance, and repair in Wisconsin for the two calendar years ended December 31, 1914, together with the cost of construction for the year 1912.

The highway law [of New York] (*Albany, N. Y.: State, 1916, pp. 344*).— The text of the law is given.

Automobile registrations, licenses, and revenues in the United States, 1916 (*U. S. Dept. Agr., Office Sec. Circ. 73 (1917), pp. 15, fig. 1*).—This circular was prepared in the Office of Public Roads and Rural Engineering.

"In 1916 a total of 3,512,996 motor cars—including commercial vehicles—and 250,820 motorcycles, were registered in the several States on account of which the States collected in registration and license fees, including those of chauffeurs and operators, a total gross revenue of $25,865,369.75. As compared with 1915, this was an increase of 1,067,332 cars, or 43 per cent in number, and $7,619,659, or 42 per cent in revenue. This corresponds very closely to the annual percentage increase of the three preceding years, which was about 40 per cent for motor cars and 50 per cent for revenues."

Data are also reported showing motor vehicle registrations and license fees in force January 1, 1917, and administrative provisions in force January 1, 1917, affecting motor vehicle registrations, licenses, and revenues.

A treatise on concrete, plain and reinforced, F. W. TAYLOR and S. E. THOMPSON (*New York: John Wiley & Sons, Inc.; London: Chapman & Hall, Ltd., 1916, 3. ed., rev. and enl., pp. XX+885, pl. 1, figs. 268*).—This is the third revised and enlarged edition of this book (E. S. R., 28, p. 186). The most important changes are in the portions treating of reinforced concrete. Prominent among the additions in the first part of the book are specifications for reinforced concrete and new cement specifications.

Extracting alcohol from garbage would conserve vast quantities of grain and potatoes (*Engin. News-Rec., 78 (1917), No. 11, pp. 534, 535, fig. 1*).—Experiments at the Columbus, Ohio, garbage reduction works showed "that 1 ton of Columbus green garbage will yield 4.8 gal. of 95 per cent alcohol of satisfactory quality. Estimates indicate that a $36,000 plant would produce from the 20,000 tons of garbage treated annually at the reduction works a total of 96,000 gal. of alcohol, giving a profit of 42 cts. per gallon at war-time prices or 30.5 cts. under normal conditions. A year's garbage, the tests indicate, would yield as much alcohol as could be produced from 33,600 bu. of shelled corn, 39,529 bu. of wheat, or 110,344 bu. of potatoes. . . .

"The process consists of extracting grease from garbage by cooking with sulphuric acid and steam, thereby converting the starch and allied products to dextrose, separating the grease from the tank liquor, neutralizing the acid sufficiently to allow fermentation, fermenting the liquor with yeast, thereby converting the dextrose to alcohol, and then recovering the alcohol by distillation."

Agricultural practice, T. H. Lougher (*Estac. Expt. Agron. Cuba Bol. 31* (*1916*), *pp. 35, pls. 30*).—This bulletin deals mainly with the types of machinery best adapted to Cuban agriculture and discusses soils and crops in general.

The necessity of mechanical cultivation of soil, G. Héron (*Prog. Agr. et Vit. (Ed. l'Est-Centre), 37 (1916), No. 29, pp. 61–69*).—This is a brief comparison of animal with motor power, made on the basis of net expense of cultivating a hectare of soil for one year.

Public tests of motor cultivation, J. H. Sourisseau (*Prog. Agr. et Vit. (Ed. l'Est-Centre), 37 (1916), Nos. 30, pp. 82–93; 32, pp. 133–138; 33, pp. 160–166; 34, pp. 178–180; 35, pp. 205–212, figs. 12*).—Tests of a number of motor plowing and cultivating outfits are reported and discussed. The purpose was to determine some of the factors in the selection of motor-drawn tillage machines and the cost of different motor tillage operations under French conditions.

Homemade silos, F. M. Hillman (*Mont. Col. Agr. Ext. Serv.* [Pub.] *21 (1917), pp. 31, figs. 23*).—This circular describes the construction of different types of silos under Montana conditions, special attention being given to the less expensive types such as the pit silo.

How to build the wooden-hoop silo, R. U. Blasingame (*Ala. Polytech. Inst. Ext. Serv. Circ. 9 (1917), pp. 6–12, pls. 4, figs. 2*).—This circular describes the construction and gives bills of materials and costs for several sizes of wooden-hoop silo.

The Tennessee wood-hoop silo.—How to build it, C. A. Hutton (*Col. Agr. Univ. Tenn., Ext. Div. Pub. 26 (1917), pp. 19, figs. 15*).—This circular describes the construction of wooden-hoop silos under Tennessee conditions.

A dairy farm plant, I. D. Charlton (*Washington Sta., West. Wash. Sta. Mo. Bul., 5 (1917), No. 3, pp. 35–39, figs. 4*).—This plant is described and diagrammatically illustrated.

Cooling tanks and milk houses as factors in cream improvement, J. H. Frandsen (*Nebraska Sta. Circ. 3 (1917), pp. 19, figs. 13*).—This describes and illustrates cream cooling tanks and milk houses, and gives the results of winter and summer tests of a square tank built of 2-in. cypress, a square tank insulated with 1 in. of ground cork or mineral wool, and a round tank built of 2-in. Washington fir.

In the summer tests it was found that the difference in the results obtained with these three tanks was so slight that one would scarcely be jusified in going to the expense of providing insulation other than that furnished by the wood itself. The water within the tank responded slowly to a change in atmospheric temperature.

"In the winter experiments the tanks were exposed out-of-doors. The only protection given consisted of a double layer of 10-oz. canvas thrown over the top of the tank. In these experiments the water was adjusted at 6 p. m. daily to a temperature at or as near as possible 50° [F.] (the temperature of the well water). Twice daily record was made of the temperature of the cream in each tank. . . . Although the temperature dropped below zero on several occasions the temperature of the cream remained well above the freezing point. On the coldest nights a very small amount of ice was in evidence on the surface of the cream, but this condition did not exist below the surface, showing that the volume of water in one of these tanks is sufficient protection, even in rather cold weather."

Brief sections on ice for cream cooling and on cream grading and improvement are also included.

Why hot water pipes in household plumbing burst more frequently than cold water pipes, F. C. BROWN and W. NOLL (*Proc. Iowa Acad. Sci., 23 (1916), pp. 237–240*).—Experiments are reported on the difference in the time required to burst hot and cold water plumbing pipes and the reasons therefor.

"In summing up the results of the experiments it was concluded that the occluded air affects the difference in bursting. It does this, first, by acting as a nucleus for crystallization, so that ordinary water freezes less solidly than boiled water; second, by causing the ice to freeze less solidly especially at the center, until a very low temperature is reached the pressure along the center is relieved by the water and slush flowing away. Third, the air acts as a compressible medium, which relieves the pressure by an unknown amount."

Community sanitation (*Winthrop Normal and Indus. Col. S. C., Home Demonstr. Course for Women, 2. ser., No. 4 [1917], pp. 12*).—This is an outline of proposed activities in rural sanitation, including water supply, sewage disposal, fly and mosquito control, etc.

RURAL ECONOMICS.

Meeting the farmer halfway, C. VROOMAN (*U. S. Dept. Agr. Yearbook 1916, pp. 63–75*).—The development of the Federal Department of Agriculture, in response to a demand on the part of the farmers of the country, is briefly traced, and some of the results obtained enumerated. Special notice is made of the increased attention given to the dissemination of information under the Extension Act and otherwise, and to the organization of the Office of Markets and Rural Organization to assist the farmer in solving problems of distribution. Other recent legislation under the Federal Farm Loan Act, Grain-Standards Act, Warehouse Act, Federal-Aid Road Act, and Cotton-Futures Act is also reviewed.

The Nonpartisan League, C. E. RUSSELL (*Pubs. Amer. Sociol. Soc., 11 (1916), pp. 31–36*).—An account is given of this league, organized recently by the farmers of North Dakota. Its principles are said to introduce the State into business in the owning and operating of elevators, flour mills, and packing plants at terminal points. It also advocates State insurance against hail, State loans to farmers, and aid in general to make farming more practical and profitable.

Rural surveys, C. W. THOMPSON (*Pubs. Amer. Sociol. Soc., 11 (1916), pp. 129–133*).—This paper enumerates the purposes for which surveys are made, kinds of surveys made, sources of information, and methods used.

The results of some rural social surveys in Iowa, G. H. VON TUNGELN (*Pubs. Amer. Sociol. Soc., 11 (1916), pp. 134–162*).—The author defines the purposes of rural surveys and the argument for making them. The results of detailed surveys of two Iowa townships are given under (1) population and conjugal conditions, (2) economic conditions, (3) organizations, (4) church and Sunday school membership, and (5) social conditions and the social mind.

The mind of the farmer, E. R. GROVES (*Pubs. Amer. Sociol. Soc., 11 (1916), pp. 47–53*).—Influences that tend to shape the mind of the farmer are the occupation of farming itself, his isolation, and suggestions from various sources. The author concludes, however, that owing to the differences between rural communities and close relationship of rural and urban people, no distinctive American farmer's mind is conceivable.

The development of rural leadership, G. W. FISKE (*Pubs. Sociol. Soc.*, 11 (1916), pp. 54–70).—The author considers influences in the rural community itself, such as rural individualism, lack of socialization, and natural difficulties of development, that hinder the development of rural leadership. He concludes that the rural community will organize and develop its leadership from within its own ranks.

The consolidated school as a community center, J. H. COOK (*Pubs. Amer. Sociol. Soc.*, 11 (1916), pp. 97–105).—The author contrasts the advantages of the consolidated school with the one-room school. His conclusion is that " every improvement in rural life and education depends either partially or entirely upon the centralization of schools for its permanent success."

Social control: Rural religion, C. O. GILL (*Pubs. Amer. Sociol. Soc.*, 11 (1916), pp. 106–112).—Resident ministers and interdenominational cooperation is deemed necessary to organize the rural church more effectively. The author considers this action basic for cooperation in rural business as well as for the conservation of rural life itself.

Countryside and Nation, G. E. VINCENT (*Pubs. Amer. Sociol. Soc.*, 11 (1916), pp. 1–11).—This article is a review in its broader aspects of American agriculture to-day. The problem of tenancy and the possibility of land ownership by large corporations are contrasted with the more auspicious tendency to individual ownership.

Country versus city, W. H. WILSON (*Pubs. Amer. Sociol. Soc.*, 11 (1916), pp. 12–20).—The relations between country and city are discussed. The author concludes that the country and city are dynamically one.

Folk depletion as a cause of rural decline, E. A. ROSS (*Pubs. Amer. Sociol. Soc.*, 11 (1916), pp. 21–30).—From a personal survey of several rural counties in New England, as well as other districts in various parts of the country, the author concludes that the evident rural decline is due to migration of the natural leaders and not to rural degeneracy. Several remedies for folk depletion are suggested.

Farm tenantry in the United States, W. J. SPILLMAN and E. A. GOLDEN-WEISER (*U. S. Dept. Agr. Yearbook 1916*, pp. 321–346, figs. 9).—The authors discuss the conditions with reference to tenantry in different parts of the United States.

They conclude that where land is increasing rapidly in value, unless other factors have a preponderating influence, there is a tendency for the percentage of tenantry to increase, while where land is increasing slowly in value the percentage of tenantry does not tend to increase. Among the factors that reduce the normal percentage of tenantry are the availability of public lands, smallness of farms, and low productivity of land. Factors that tend to increase the percentage of tenantry include large size of farms, high productiveness of land, and the capitalization of the advantages of land ownership. The authors also point out that tenantry is encouraged by the higher rate of income on working capital than on fixed capital.

The principal defect of the American system of tenant farming is considered to be the lack of suitable provision for maintaining the fertility of the soil.

The land problem and rural welfare, P. L. VOGT (*Pubs. Amer. Sociol. Soc.*, 11 (1916), pp. 82–94).—The author finds the essence of the problem in the centralization of land ownership and the resulting increase in tenantry. Development of a more successful agriculture and better rural life occurs only through effective organization depending on intelligence, homogeneity of population, stability, intimate acquaintance, and community of social interests. Increase in tenantry destroys each one of these as a basis of successful organization.

The solution of the problem is thought to be in State action as well as through individual education.

Cooperation and community spirit, A. D. WILSON (*Pubs. Amer. Sociol. Soc., 11 (1916), pp. 113–125*).—Farmers' clubs with their social, educational, and business activities, and live-stock shipping associations, are cited by the author as examples of successful rural cooperation, while the cooperative store, however, is regarded as one form of cooperation likely to fail. The attitude of Minnesota business men and farmers and that of the U. S. Department of Agriculture and the University of Minnesota toward rural cooperation is explained.

Business essentials for cooperative fruit and vegetable canneries, W. H. KERR (*U. S. Dept. Agr. Yearbook 1916, pp. 237–249*).—The author believes that although cooperative canneries sold only $3,500,000 worth of the approximately $158,000,000 worth of canned fruits and vegetables marketed in 1914, they have a legitimate place in the marketing of perishable products. A close examination of the many failures as well as the successes indicates that the business of canning is not a by-product business, that a suitable location is vital, that ample capital must back the enterprise, that an experienced manager salesman must be secured, that contracts with growers are necessary, that a liberal and inclusive budget be followed, that cost accounting methods be adopted, and that goods be packed to meet market demands.

A federated cooperative cheese manufacturing and marketing association, H. MACPHERSON and W. H. KERR (*U. S. Dept. Agr. Yearbook 1916, pp. 145–157*).—A survey is given of the cheese industry of Tillamook County, Oreg., where much success is reported to have followed the formation of a cooperative county creamery association in 1909. The plan of operation, benefits of centralized market control, and quality standardization, and the business practice followed are described.

Farmers' mutual fire insurance, V. N. VALGREN (*U. S. Dept. Agr. Yearbook 1916, pp. 421–433, figs. 4*).—The author traces the origin and growth of this form of insurance and discusses its practical workings and possibilities. See also a previous note (E. S. R., 37, p. 391).

State hail insurance in North Dakota (*Internat. Inst. Agr. [Rome], Internat. Rev. Agr. Econ., 8 (1917), No. 2, pp. 41–49*).—The working features of the State hail insurance act of North Dakota, providing State insurance for "growing grain crops in any county in the State against loss or damage by hail," are described. Balance sheets showing financial conditions are appended.

Possibilities of a market-train service, G. C. WHITE and T. F. POWELL (*U. S. Dept. Agr. Yearbook 1916, pp. 477–487*).—In this article several market trains in operation are described. The authors take the position that this form of service, where practicable, affords an excellent method of restoring the custom of direct dealing between producer and consumer. "Such a service, to be successful, depends on the organized effort of the producing community, intelligently directed in sympathetic cooperation with the carrier."

A system of accounts for cotton warehouses, R. L. NEWTON and J. R. HUMPHREY (*U. S. Dept. Agr. Bul. 520 (1917), pp. 31*).—The system outlined requires twelve forms, which are described and illustrated.

Essentials in larger food production, C. G. HOPKINS (*Illinois Sta. Circ. 197 (1917), pp. 4*).—This is an address given before a conference of Illinois mayors April 27, 1917.

The author believes that the two factors of primary importance are sufficient labor to perform the necessary farm work and sufficient soil fertility to make the larger crop yields possible. He advocates the erection in every town of a storehouse for ground limestone and phosphate rock, to be kept on hand ready for farmers to haul and apply whenever the conditions of the roads and fields and farm labor permit.

The high cost of low crop yields.—Intensive cultivation most profitable on average farms, C. E. THORNE (*Mo. Bul. Ohio Sta., 2 (1917), No. 6, pp. 181–187*).—Experiments using a 10-acre tract, fertilized, limed, and treated with acid phosphate were compared with larger unfertilized tracts of a size to produce about the same yield. A regular rotation of corn, oats, wheat, and clover was followed at Wooster, and one of corn, wheat, and clover at Germantown.

The relative costs of producing the entire rotation were $613 and $1,095 for the high and low-yielding tracts at Wooster, and of $271 and $396.10 for those at Germantown. It is concluded that "the intelligent use of fertilizer and manure not only increases the yield of the land but also reduces both the labor cost per unit of crop production and the cost of seed and rental."

The net output from agriculture and its distribution, C. S. ORWIN (*Jour. Bd. Agr. [London], 24 (1917), No. 2, pp. 158–161*).—Tabulated results of surveys of several farms indicate that the net output, the difference between cost of production and value on the farm, is distributed to the farmer, laborer, and landlord on the basis of 47.9, 29.9, and 22.2 per cent, respectively. Net returns, however, after the farmer and landlord have deducted ordinary expenses, are found to be distributed on the basis of 40.7, 39.5, and 19.8 per cent, respectively.

Agriculture on Government reclamation projects, C. S. SCOFIELD and F. D. FARRELL (*U. S. Dept. Agr. Yearbook 1916, pp. 177–198, pls. 3*).—The purpose of this paper is "to discuss briefly a number of the industries that have been or may become important on reclamation projects."

The authors find that crop production on reclaimed land follows a "regular sequence of development, beginning with the production of alfalfa and small grains and gradually reaching a great diversity of crops and industries. Finally, out of this diversity a few major industries became permanent."

Crop disposal is said to constitute a more serious problem than that of production.

The sugar-beet industry, potato production, seed production, cotton production, fruit production, pork production, dairying, the sheep industry, and beef production are among the phases discussed.

British agriculture the nation's opportunity, E. G. STRUTT, L. SCOTT, and G. H. ROBERTS (*London: John Murray, 1917, pp. XI+168*).—This book, after a review of English agricultural policy and problems of land settlement before the war, consists of a discussion of the findings and recommendations of the minority report of the departmental committee on the employment of sailors and soldiers on the land referred to in a previous note (E. S. R., 35, p. 296).

[Progress of agriculture in India] (*Rpt. Prog. Agr. India, 1915–16, pp. 84–89*).—Such forms of agricultural cooperation as societies for the sale of manure, cooperative dairies, cattle breeding societies, registered seed unions, and cattle insurance societies are briefly mentioned. Various recommendations and tendencies are discussed.

A graphic summary of world agriculture, V. C. FINCH, O. E. BAKER, and R. G. HAINSWORTH (*U. S. Dept. Agr. Yearbook 1916, pp. 531–553, figs. 19*).—Production and acreage of important crops are compared for the important countries of the world. Several page maps indicate graphically crop and acreage comparisons.

Price Current Grain Reporter Yearbook, 1917, E. G. OSMAN (*Price Current Grain Rptr. Yearbook 1917, pp. 96*).—This issue continues data previously noted (E. S. R., 35, p. 893), giving statistics for a later year.

AGRICULTURAL EDUCATION.

[Agricultural and home economics instruction at the National Education Association in 1916] (*Addresses and Proc. Nat. Ed. Assoc., 54 (1916), pp. XII+1112, figs. 10*).—This report contains the papers presented at the 1916 meeting previously noted (E. S. R., 35, p. 197), and in addition the following papers relating to agriculture and home economics: First Aid to the Country Teacher—A Suggestion as to Vitalizing the Country Schools through Our Present Teachers [by means of instruction in gardening, poultry raising, and domestic science for girls], by J. D. Eggleston (pp. 58–63) ; Mass Instruction through Group Training [illustrated by the home-demonstration work in the Southern States], by O. B. Martin (pp. 97–101) ; Preparing Teachers for Leadership in All Special Education, J. W. Crabtree (pp. 122–127) ; Thrift in Its Relation to Country Life, by R. H. Wilson (pp. 201–205) ; The Conservation of Natural Resources through Education, by L. W. Goldrich (pp. 722–726) ; The Teaching of Home Nursing and the Care of Children to Elementary and High-school Pupils, by Isabel M. Stewart (pp. 767–771) ; and Vacation-club Work, by J. H. Beveridge (pp. 1060–1063).

State higher educational institutions of North Dakota (*U. S. Bur. Ed. Bul. 27 (1916), pp. 204, figs. 26*).—This is a report to the North Dakota State Board of Regents of a survey made under the direction of the U. S. Commissioner of Education. A very detailed report is given on the legal provisions for the establishment of the North Dakota Agricultural College, its organization, functions, finances, etc. Among the recommendations of the survey committee are the following:

The agricultural college should devote its energies and means to instruction in agriculture and its immediate allied subjects, offer courses in liberal arts and sciences only as service courses, and give no degrees therein. Agricultural, industrial, and chemical engineering courses should be given only at the agricultural college, and degree courses in other forms of engineering only at the university.

While the university should prepare high school teachers, school superintendents, supervisors for both elementary and high schools, and expert special teachers, the agricultural college only should prepare special teachers of agriculture, home economics, and industrial subjects. The latter should offer both major and normal courses in home economics, while the university should give sufficient instruction in this subject and in methods of teaching it to fit young women for the duties of intelligent home making, and to enable them to combine the teaching of home economics with other subjects in the high school.

The agricultural high school at the agricultural college should be discontinued as a preparatory school, and the 22-week courses strengthened and organized into a school of agriculture, elementary mechanic arts and home economics, with 3-year winter sessions of five and one-half or six months each, for young men and women who do not expect to attend cllege or to become teachers. The short winter courses in extension work for farmers and farmers' wives are to be commended, but those attending these courses should not be taught in the regular classes of the college, the agricultural high school, or the 22-week courses.

In view of the liberal Federal and State provision for extension work in agriculture and home economics under the direction of the agricultural college, no other institution in the State should undertake extension work in these subjects. Any extension work done by instructors in agricultural schools in the State should be under the direction of the college.

Graduate work at the university and the agricultural college should for the present continue to be limited to the requirements for the master's degree, and each institution should give graduate instruction only in its major subjects. Graduate courses in education may be given at each institution.

The president of the agricultural college should have general control of the experiment station and of its branches and of the extension department, and be held responsible to the board of regents for their management. Men and women engaged in research work at the experiment station at Fargo should, except in case of those whose duties are such as to make it inexpedient, be expected to teach some classes in the college, and the experiment station and its farms and laboratories, as well as the laboratories of the regulatory services, should be used under necessary restrictions as teaching agencies for undergraduate college students and as research agencies for graduate students. It is recommended that a careful study be made of the operations of the substations and demonstration farms, with a view to determining whether or not much of the experimental work now under way might be carried on by farmers on their own premises without other expense to the State than that of necessary supervision.

The forestry and nursery work required of the school of forestry at Bottineau should be put under the direction of the agricultural college and all necessary instruction of college grade in forestry given at Fargo.

A survey of educational institutions of the State of Washington (U. S. Bur. Ed. Bul. 26 (1916), pp. 228, figs. 46).—This is a report of a survey made under the direction of the U. S. Commissioner of Education, at the request of the commission of educational survey created by the State legislature, of the State institutions of higher education, and such a study of the elementary and secondary schools and of the preparation of teachers in these schools as was deemed necessary to an intelligent consideration of the functions and standards of the higher schools. A report of the findings and recommendations of the commission of educational survey, as submitted to the governor, is included. Subsequent action of the legislature has been previously noted (E. S. R., 36, p. 296).

Agricultural instruction.—The Central Development Farm, Weraroa, F. S. POPE (Jour. Agr. [New Zeal.], 14 (1917), No. 2, pp. 83–88).—The author briefly discusses the defects in existing schemes of agricultural education and development in New Zealand, and the objects of the Central Development Farm (operated until recently as the Weraroa Experimental Farm), which is intended as the main factor in a system to overcome these difficulties.

Report of the agricultural society of Malmöhus Province for 1916 (Malmö. Läns. Hushåll. Sällsk. Kvrtlsskr., 1916, No. 4, pp. VIII+505–928, figs. 2).—The activities of the society reported on include the work of the farm schools at Vilan, Fridhem, and Skurup, the dairy school at Näsbygård, the agricultural school at Dala, the home economics schools at Fridhem and Östra Grefrie, the dairy school at Alnarp, the fruit culture school at Apelryd, special courses in agriculture and home economics for adults and teachers, the seed-control station at Lund, the chemical station at Alnarp, the swine breeding stations, etc.

What is the Smith-Hughes bill providing Federal grants to vocational education? And what must a State do to take advantage of the Federal vocational education law? (Nat. Soc. Prom. Indus. Ed. Bul. 25 (1917), pp. 1–42).—This bulletin contains information as to the essential points of the Federal Aid Vocational Education Act (E. S. R., 36, p. 701) and of the steps the States should take to secure the benefits of the act; the text of the act; tables showing the Federal funds available for each State; principles and policies of vocational education as a means for the educational conservation of children; principles and policies that should underlie State legislation; and a form of bill, for enactment by a State accepting the act, framed and distributed by the Federal Board for Vocational Education.

The chemistry of farm practice, T. E. Keitt (*New York: John Wiley & Sons, Inc., 1917, pp. XII+253, figs. 81*).—This text, which has been prepared for high schools in farming communities, vocational and industrial schools, and short-course students in agricultural colleges, deals with the fundamental principles of chemistry and their application to the problems which arise in the life on a farm, including the study of soils, fertilizers, and manures, feeds and the calculation of rations, animal nutrition, milk and its products, sanitary water, boiler water, insecticides, fungicides and disinfectants, paints and whitewashes, materials producing heat and light, and concrete.

Nature study or stories in agriculture (*Ontario Dept. Agr. Bul. 243 (1916), pp. 70, figs. 46*).—This is a revised edition of the bulletin previously noted (E. S. R., 14, p. 822).

The culture of the mulberry silkworm, T. A. Keleher (*Washington: Author, 1917, pp. 13, figs. 3*).—This brief manual, adapted for practical use or for study in the classroom, gives instruction regarding the life history and rearing of silkworms as adapted to commercial puprsuits.

Vocational mathematics for girls, W. H. Dooley (*Boston, New York, and Chicago: D. C. Heath & Co., 1917, pp. VI+369, figs. 79*).—This text is offered as an introduction to the regular secondary school course in mathematics. It consists of six parts dealing respectively with a review of arithmetic; problems in home making, including the distribution of income, food, construction of a house, cost of furnishing a house, and thrift and investment; problems in dress-making and millinery; office and store problems; arithmetic for nurses; and problems on the farm. An exposition of the metric system, graphs, formulas, and useful mechanical information are appended.

Live-stock classifications at county fairs, S. H. Ray (*U. S. Dept. Agr., Farmers' Bul. 822 (1917), pp. 12, fig. 1*).—This discusses, in a general way and with reference to increasing the educational value of the county live-stock exhibit, cooperation with live-stock organizations; uniformity of classification; special features, such as futurity and judging contests; selection of superintendents, judges, etc.; arrangement of exhibits; announcement of judges, prize winners, etc.; exhibition of prize winners; rules governing an exhibition; premiums; and a suggested scheme of classifications.

Illustrated lecture on public-road improvement (*U. S. Dept. Agr., States Relat. Serv. Syllabus 29 (1917), pp. 12*).—This syllabus has been prepared in the Office of Public Roads and Rural Engineering. It considers only the general features of public-road improvement, including the three distinct phases of public sentiment, finance, and engineering entering into most road problems. Points to be studied in the location and design of roads to balance the convenience of travelers against the question of economy, types of surface, and maintenance are discussed. A list of 56 lantern slides to illustrate the syllabus is appended.

[School home gardening] (*U. S. Dept. Int., Bur. Ed., School Home-Gard. Circs., 1917, No. 12, pp. 13; 1916, No. 13, pp. 5; 1917, Nos. 14, pp. 4; 15, pp. 4; 16, pp. 3*).—The following subjects are dealt with in these circulars: School home garden results of 1916, mainly in those cities that are cooperating with the U. S. Bureau of Education in working out the plan for school-directed home gardening; garden projects in seed planting; flower growing for school children in elementary grades; the part played by the root in the production of a crop; and home gardening for town children.

The effect of home-demonstration work on the community and the county in the South, B. Knapp and Mary E. Creswell (*U. S. Dept. Agr. Yearbook 1916, pp. 251–266, pls. 3*).—The authors describe the home-demonstration work for women and girls in eight counties of the South and some of the benefits resulting. "This work began in 1910 with the girls' canning clubs, and led by gradual and logical steps into the present very broad and comprehensive work with both individuals and groups. In the fall of 1916 home-demonstration work was in progress in 420 counties in the southern States."

MISCELLANEOUS.

Yearbook of the Department of Agriculture, 1916 (*U. S. Dept. Agr. Yearbook, 1916, pp. 783, pls. 97, figs. 74*).—This contains the report of the Secretary of Agriculture, previously noted (E. S. R., 37, p. 297); 33 special articles abstracted elsewhere in this issue; and an appendix containing a directory of the agricultural colleges and experiment stations and the State officials in charge of agricultural and extension work, and statistics of the principal crops, farm animals and their products, the Federal meat inspection, estimated value of farm products, tonnage carried on railways, 1913–1915, imports and exports of agricultural products, rural and agricultural populations, number of persons engaged in agriculture and area of agricultural land in various countries, and the utilization of the National Forests.

Annual report of the director of the experiment station on work done under the local experiment law in 1916, J. F. Duggar (*Alabama Col. Sta. Circ. 35 (1917), pp. 35*).—This includes a report by the director on the progress of the work under this law (E. S. R., 24, p. 400), a financial statement for the year, and reports from heads of departments, including detailed reports of boys' and girls' club work and other extension activities.

Twenty-ninth Annual Report of Colorado Station, 1916 (*Colorado Sta. Rpt. 1916, pp. 39, fig. 1*).—This contains the organization list, a financial statement for the fiscal year ended June 30, 1916, a report of the director on the work and publications of the station, and departmental reports.

Twenty-ninth Annual Report of Louisiana Stations, 1916, W. R. Dodson (*Louisiana Stas. Rpt. 1916, pp. 29*).—This contains the organization list, a report by the director including brief departmental reports, and a financial statement as to the Federal funds for the fiscal year ended June 30, 1916, and as to the State funds for the fiscal year ended November 30, 1916. The experimental work reported is for the most part abstracted elsewhere in this issue.

Twenty-eighth Annual Report of Maryland Station, 1915 (*Maryland Sta. Rpt. 1915, pp. XXX+214, pls. 9, figs. 50*).—This contains the organization list; a report by the director on the organization, work, and publications of the station; a financial statement for the fiscal year ended June 30, 1915; and reprints of Bulletins 185–190, previously noted.

Twenty-ninth Annual Report of Maryland Station, 1916 (*Maryland Sta. Rpt. 1916, pp. XII+95, figs. 16*).—Data corresponding to the above are given for the fiscal year ended June 30, 1916, including reprints of Bulletins 191–196, previously noted.

Monthly Bulletin of the Ohio Experiment Station (*Mo. Bul. Ohio Sta., 2 (1917), No. 6, pp. 171–209, figs. 8*).—This contains several articles abstracted elsewhere in this issue, together with the following: Handling Alfalfa Hay, by J. W. Ames and G. E. Boltz, an extract from Bulletin 247 (E. S. R., 29, p. 32); The Currant Worm, by W. H. Goodwin; The Colorado Potato Beetle, by H. A. Gossard; and notes.

Monthly bulletin of the Western Washington Substation (*Washington Sta., West. Wash. Sta. Mo. Bul., 5 (1917), No. 3, pp. 29–44, figs. 8*).—This number contains brief articles on the following subjects: Second Crops for Milk and Meat, by H. L. Blanchard; The Root Maggot Pest, by E. B. Stookey (see p. 566); A Dairy Farm Plant, by I. D. Charlton (see p. 591); Weeding Out the Poor Producers, by Mr. and Mrs. G. R. Shoup; and Home Canning, by T. J. Newbill.

NOTES.

California University.—Dr. C. H. Shattuck, whose resignation as head of the department of forestry at the University of Idaho has been previously noted, has accepted an appointment as professor of forestry.

Delaware College and Station.—Recent appointments include R. V. Mitchell, of the New Hampshire College, as professor of poultry husbandry, vice H. V. Cory resigned to become captain in the National Army; R. W. Goss as associate plant pathologist; and H. T. King as assistant chemist in the station, vice L. W. Tarr.

Iowa College.—A special short course has been arranged to begin November 12 and continue until about April 1, 1918. This course will include instruction in agriculture, home economics, engineering, and industrial science, and will be open to young people who have not yet completed high-school work, as well as to those prepared for full collegiate instruction.

Minnesota Station.—Andrew Boss has been appointed vice director in addition to his present duties. R. P. Ingram resigned as seed inspector in the division of plant pathology and botany July 31. Miss Mildreth J. Haggard has been appointed chemist in animal nutrition beginning September 1, and Miss Anna Wuentz, graduate assistant in entomology, beginning January 1, 1918. J. J. Willaman has been promoted from assistant chemist to plant chemist.

Mississippi Station.—The large breeding barn was struck by lightning July 26, and was completely destroyed together with two other barns located near by and some farm machinery and other equipment. The total loss was between $15,000 and $18,000.

Nebraska University.—Dr. A. R. Davis, assistant professor of agricultural botany, has been commissioned captain in the Coast Artillery.

Cornell University and Station.—The trustees have voted to pay members of the staff who enter war service the difference in salary between the army wage and that previously received.

South Carolina Station.—A class of 15 scouts received training in the botanical laboratories during the first two weeks in September, preliminary to taking up survey work in the South for the Plant Disease Survey of the U. S. Department of Agriculture. Leon H. Leonian has been appointed research assistant in horticulture.

Tennessee University and Station.—The bond issue of $1,000,000 voted by the last legislature for the university has been sold and it is expected that the money will be immediately available. Among the first expenditures was an allotment for barns and laborers' cottages on the new Cherokee Farm donated to the university for station purposes.

Texas Station.—P. V. Ewing, of the Georgia Station, has been appointed animal husbandman in swine investigations and has entered upon his duties. Wellington T. Brink, a 1916 graduate of the Kansas College and engaged in newspaper work, has been appointed technical assistant to the director, in charge of the station library, and editor of publications.

Utah Station.—H. P. Anderson, assistant chemist and bacteriologist, has resigned to become instructor in agriculture in the Price High School and local leader of boys' club work. O. P. Madsen has resigned as assistant poultryman to become county agent in Emery County. Yeppa Lund and Harold Goldthorpe have been appointed assistants in the department of chemistry and bacteriology.

THE AGRICULTURAL EXPERIMENT STATIONS OF THE UNITED STATES.

U. S. DEPARTMENT OF AGRICULTURE
STATES RELATIONS SERVICE
A. C. TRUE, DIRECTOR

ol. 37   NOVEMBER, 1917   No. 7

EXPERIMENT STATION RECORD

WASHINGTON
GOVERNMENT PRINTING OFFICE
1917

U. S. DEPARTMENT OF AGRICULTURE.

Scientific Bureaus.

WEATHER BUREAU—C. F. Marvin, *Chief.*
BUREAU OF ANIMAL INDUSTRY—J. D. Mohler, *Chief.*
BUREAU OF PLANT INDUSTRY—W. A. Taylor, *Chief.*
FOREST SERVICE—H. S. Graves, *Forester.*
BUREAU OF SOILS—Milton Whitney, *Chief.*
BUREAU OF CHEMISTRY—C. L. Alsberg, *Chief.*
BUREAU OF CROP ESTIMATES—L. M. Estabrook, *Statistician.*
BUREAU OF ENTOMOLOGY—L. O. Howard, *Entomologist.*
BUREAU OF BIOLOGICAL SURVEY—E. W. Nelson, *Chief.*
OFFICE OF PUBLIC ROADS AND RURAL ENGINEERING—L. W. Page, *Director.*
BUREAU OF MARKETS—C. J. Brand, *Chief.*

STATES RELATIONS SERVICE—A. C. True, *Director.*
OFFICE OF EXPERIMENT STATIONS—E. W. Allen, *Chief.*

THE AGRICULTURAL EXPERIMENT STATIONS.

ALABAMA—
　College Station: *Auburn;* J. F. Duggar.[1]
　Canebrake Station: *Uniontown;* J. M. Burgess.[1]
　Tuskegee Station: *Tuskegee Institute;* G. W. Carver.[1]
ALASKA—*Sitka:* C. C. Georgeson.[1]
ARIZONA—*Tucson:* R. H. Forbes.[1]
ARKANSAS—*Fayetteville:* M. Nelson.[1]
CALIFORNIA—*Berkeley:* T. F. Hunt.[1]
COLORADO—*Fort Collins:* C. P. Gillette.[1]
CONNECTICUT—
　State Station: *New Haven;* ⎰
　Storrs Station: *Storrs;* ⎱E. H. Jenkins.[1]
DELAWARE—*Newark:* H. Hayward.[1]
FLORIDA—*Gainesville;* P. H. Rolfs.[1]
GEORGIA—*Experiment:* J. D. Price.[1]
GUAM—*Island of Guam:* C. W. Edwards.[2]
HAWAII—
　Federal Station: *Honolulu;* J. M. Westgate.[3]
　Sugar Planters' Station: *Honolulu;* H. P. Agee.[1]
IDAHO—*Moscow:* J. S. Jones.[1]
ILLINOIS—*Urbana:* E. Davenport.[1]
INDIANA—*Lafayette:* C. G. Woodbury.[1]
IOWA—*Ames:* C. F. Curtiss.[1]
KANSAS—*Manhattan:* W. M. Jardine.[1]
KENTUCKY—*Lexington:* A. M. Peter.[4]
LOUISIANA—
　State Station: *Baton Rouge;* ⎫
　Sugar Station: *Audubon Park,* ⎬W. R. Dodson.[1]
　　New Orleans; ⎪
　North La. Station: *Calhoun;* ⎭
MAINE—*Orono:* C. D. Woods.[1]
MARYLAND—*College Park:* H. J. Patterson.[1]
MASSACHUSETTS—*Amherst:* W. P. Brooks.[1]
MICHIGAN—*East Lansing:* R. S. Shaw.[1]
MINNESOTA—*University Farm, St. Paul:* R. W. Thatcher.[1]
MISSISSIPPI—*Agricultural College:* E. R. Lloyd.[1]

MISSOURI—
　College Station: *Columbia:* F. D. Mumford.[1]
　Fruit Station: *Mountain Grove:* Paul Evans.[1]
MONTANA—*Bozeman:* F. B. Linfield.[1]
NEBRASKA—*Lincoln:* E. A. Burnett.[1]
NEVADA—*Reno:* S. B. Doten.[1]
NEW HAMPSHIRE—*Durham:* J. C. Kendall.[1]
NEW JERSEY—*New Brunswick:* J. G. Lipman.[1]
NEW MEXICO—*State College:* Fabian Garcia.[1]
NEW YORK—
　State Station: *Geneva:* W. H. Jordan.[1]
　Cornell Station: *Ithaca:* A. R. Mann.[1]
NORTH CAROLINA—
　College Station: *West Raleigh;* ⎰
　State Station: *Raleigh;* ⎱B. W. Kilgore.[1]
NORTH DAKOTA—*Agricultural College:* T. P. Cooper.[1]
OHIO—*Wooster:* C. E. Thorne.[1]
OKLAHOMA—*Stillwater:* J. W. Cantwell.[4]
OREGON—*Corvallis:* A. B. Cordley.[1]
PENNSYLVANIA—
　State College: R. L. Watts.[1]
　State College: Institute of Animal Nutrition H. P. Armsby.[1]
PORTO RICO—*Mayaguez;* D. W. May.[2]
RHODE ISLAND—*Kingston:* B. L. Hartwell.[1]
SOUTH CAROLINA—*Clemson College:* H. W. Barre.[1]
SOUTH DAKOTA—*Brookings:* J. W. Wilson.[1]
TENNESSEE—*Knoxville:* H. A. Morgan.[1]
TEXAS—*College Station:* B. Youngblood.[1]
UTAH—*Logan:* F. S. Harris.[1]
VERMONT—*Burlington:* J. L. Hills.[1]
VIRGINIA—
　Blacksburg: A. W. Drinkard, jr.[1]
　Norfolk: Truck Station: T. C. Johnson.[1]
WASHINGTON—*Pullman:* Geo. Severance.[4]
WEST VIRGINIA—*Morgantown:* J. L. Coulter.[1]
WISCONSIN—*Madison:* H. L. Russell.[1]
WYOMING—*Laramie:* H. G. Knight.[1]

[1] Director. 　[2] Agronomist in charge. 　[3] Animal husbandman in charge. 　[4] Acting director.

EXPERIMENT STATION RECORD.

Editor: E. W. ALLEN, Ph. D., *Chief, Office of Experiment Stations.*
Assistant Editor: H. L. KNIGHT.

EDITORIAL DEPARTMENTS.

Agricultural Chemistry and Agrotechny—E. H. NOLLAU.
Meteorology, Soils, and Fertilizers{W. H. BEAL.
R. W. TRULLINGER.
Agricultural Botany, Bacteriology, and Plant Pathology{W. H. EVANS, Ph. D.
W. E. BOYD.
Field Crops{J. I. SCHULTE.
J. D. LUCKETT.
Horticulture and Forestry—E. J. GLASSON.
Economic Zoology and Entomology—W. A. HOOKER, D. V. M.
Foods and Human Nutrition{C. F. LANGWORTHY, Ph. D., D. Sc.
H. L. LANG.
Zootechny, Dairying, and Dairy Farming{M. D. MOORE.
Veterinary Medicine{W. A. HOOKER.
E. H. NOLLAU.
Rural Engineering—R. W. TRULLINGER.
Rural Economics—E. MERRITT.
Agricultural Education{C. H. LANE.
M. T. SPETHMANN.
Indexes—M. D. MOORE.

CONTENTS OF VOL. 37, NO. 7.

Editorial notes: Page.
The Thirty-first Annual Convention of the Association of American Agricultural Colleges and Experiment Stations........................... 601
Recent work in agricultural science... 612
Notes... 700

SUBJECT LIST OF ABSTRACTS.

AGRICULTURAL CHEMISTRY—AGROTECHNY.

Isolation of cyanuric acid from soil, Wise and Walters......................... 612
Analysis of ragweed pollen, Heyl.. 612
The pungent principles of ginger.—I, A new ketone, zingiberone, Nomura.... 612
Gingerol and paradol, Nelson... 612
Microorganisms and heat production in silage fermentation, Hunter.......... 613
The citric acid fermentation of *Aspergillus niger*, Currie................... 613
Influence of certain electrolytes on hydrolysis of starch, Sherman and Walker. 614
A noteworthy effect of bromids upon the action of malt amylase, Thomas..... 614
A handbook of organic analysis, Clarke.. 614
A titration flask, Bezzenberger.. 614
The estimation of sulphur in plant material and soil, Olson.................. 614
Influence of calcium carbonate on Dyer's method, Jatindra Nath Sen....... 615
Phosphoric acid determination in phosphate rock, Semple.................... 615
Determination of carbonates in limestone and other materials, Barker........ 616

Page.
Determination of water-soluble arsenic in lead arsenate, Scholz and Waldstein.   616
Inadequacy of ferric basic acetate test for acetates, Curtman and Harris.......   617
Gluten, Arpin...   617
Determination of pentoses and glutose by Fehling's solution, Pellet...........   617
The quantitative estimation of dextrose in muscular tissue, Hoagland.........   617
Determination of sugar in hay and turnips, Kristensen......................   618
Determination of alkalinity and phosphoric acid content of foodstuffs, Kolthoff.   618
Specifications for testing milk and cream for butter fat, Hunziker............   618
Shrewsbury and Knapp process for coconut oil, Elsdon and Bagshawe....   618
Observations and experiments on the preparation of tea, Deuss...............   619

METEOROLOGY.

Forecasting the seasons, McAdie..   619
Climatological data for the United States by sections.........................   619
Meteorological observations at Massachusetts Station, Ostrander and Saunders..   619
The meteorology of Brazil, Delgado de Carvalho...............................   619
The rainfall régime of Indo China, Le Cadet..................................   620
Dissolved oxygen in rain water, Richards.....................................   620
The coefficient of correlation, Reed...   621

SOILS—FERTILIZERS.

Soil survey of Barbour County, Ala., Smith, Bell, and Stroud................   621
Soil survey of Chickasaw County, Miss., Jones et al..........................   621
Soil survey of Anson County, N. C., Vanatta and McDowell...................   621
Analyses of soils of Belgian Kongo by the physiological method, Smeyers.....   622
The wheat soils of Alexandria division, Cape Province, Juritz...............   622
Some soils of New Zealand, with special reference to lime requirements, Wild..   622
Causes of acidity of soils which are acid through exchange of ions, Kappen....   623
Movement and distribution of moisture in the soil, Harris and Turpin........   623
Adsorption by soils, Harris...   624
Results of soil fertility studies, Williams...................................   625
Thirty-five years' results with fertilizers, Gardner, Noll, and Baker..........   626
Injurious effect of manure on balance of nitrogen in the soil, Sabashnikov.....   627
[Manure conservation experiments], Woods...................................   628
Effect of phosphoric acid on decomposition of sugar in the soil, Herke.........   628
The potash question and general farm crops, Blair...........................   629
Potash in New Zealand and other countries, Morgan.........................   629
A discussion concerning the rational use of lime on the farm.................   629
Notes on humus, humogen, and its accessory plant food substances, Stead.....   629
The plant food materials in the leaves of forest trees, Serex, jr..............   629
Fertilizers and industrial wastes, Brown....................................   630
Analyses of fertilizers..   630
Fertilizer analyses...   630

AGRICULTURAL BOTANY.

International catalogue of scientific literature. M—Botany...................   630
[Some investigations in the department of experimental evolution]...........   630
Wild flowers worth knowing, Blanchan, adapted by Dickinson.................   630
Fungi from Val d'Aosta, Saccardo...   630
Fungi causing discolorations in paper, Sée..................................   630
On *Stigeosporium marattiacearum* and the mycorrhiza of the Marattiaceæ, West.   630
Chemical conditions for development of reproductive organs in yeasts, Saito...   631
Microchemical studies in progressive development of wheat plant, Eckerson....   631
The physiological rôle of calcium in vegetable life, Robert...................   631
The influence of some organic substances on plants, I, Ciamician and Ravenna.   632
Experiments demonstrating mechanism of inhibition of growth, Loeb.......   632
Studies in permeability, IV, Stiles and Jörgensen...........................   632
Osmotic concentration of sap of leaves of mangrove trees, Harris and Lawrence.   632
Origin of chromoplasts and mode of formation of pigments, Guilliermond.....   632
The anthocyanin pigments of plants, Wheldale..............................   633
Environmental influences on nectar secretion, Kenoyer......................   633
The consequences of precocity in spring vegetation, 1916, Opoix.............   633
Fruit injury during the fumigation of citrus trees, Woglum..................   634
The history and legal phases of the smoke problem, Johnson..................   634

FIELD CROPS.

Page.

The experimental error in field trials and the effect on sampling, Miyake..... 634
[Report of field crop work], Scott.. 635
[Experiments with field crops in Maine], Woods................................ 635
Results of breeding experiments, Williams...................................... 636
Daily variation of water and dry matter in corn and sorghums, Miller et al.... 637
Experiments with legume crops under irrigation, Welch....................... 639
The management of irrigated grass pastures, Welch............................ 640
Experiments with small grains under irrigation, Welch........................ 640
Yields of winter grains in Illinois, Burlison and Allyn........................ 641
Bean culture, Bryant... 641
Dried bean production in Illinois, Durst....................................... 642
Field bean production, De Baun.. 642
Studies of correlation of weight and sugar content of beets, Oetken........... 642
Corn, App... 642
Varieties of cotton, 1916, Ayres... 642
The recurving of milo and some factors influencing it, Conner and Karper..... 642
The culture of early potatoes under glass...................................... 643
The morphology and development of transplanted rice, Marcarelli............. 643
Studies of the volume weight of hulled rice grains, Kondo.................... 643
Rhodes grass, Rolfs... 644
Sugar beet culture, Stewart.. 644
The tillering of winter wheat, Grantham....................................... 644
Labeling, inspection, and analysis of seeds in New Jersey, Helyar............ 645
The seed situation, Helyar... 645

HORTICULTURE.

Gardening.—A complete guide, Thomas... 645
The beginner's gardening book, Thomas....................................... 645
The manuring of market garden crops, Shutt and Emslie...................... 645
Possibilities of the fall vegetable garden, Durst............................... 645
Variety tests of potatoes, tomatoes, cabbage, and other vegetables, White...... 645
Potatoes and root crops, Thomas.. 645
Tomatoes and salads, Thomas and Castle...................................... 645
Harvesting and storing vegetables for home use, Gardner..................... 646
Commercial onion culture in Idaho, Vincent................................... 646
Studies on dying out of pepper vines in Dutch East Indies, III, Rutgers..... 646
Report on the Government Horticultural Gardens, Lucknow, for 1917, Davies. 646
Fifteenth annual report of the State nursery inspector, Fernald............... 646
Factors governing fruit bud formation, Barker and Lees...................... 646
Miscellaneous notes on experiments in fruit culture, Barker et al............. 646
Methods of handling basket fruits, Smith and Creelman...................... 647
A systematic study of Iowa apples, Hartill..................................... 647
Fertilizer experiments on apple trees at Highmoor Farm, Woods.............. 647
Winter v. summer pruning of apple trees, Vincent............................ 647
Field experiments in spraying apple orchards, Pickett et al................... 647
Modern methods of packing apples, Flack and Carey......................... 648
Report on apple-packing houses in the Northwest, Scott and Alwood....... 648
Plum growing in Maryland, Holmes... 648
Profitable small fruits, Thomas.. 648
The strawberry in North America, Fletcher.................................... 648
Soil influence on the composition of strawberries, Gimingham................ 648
New or noteworthy tropical fruits in the Philippines, Wester.................. 648
Report on manurial experiments... 648
Citrus experimental grove, Collison.. 649
Do fertilizers influence the composition of oranges? Webber.................. 649
Standards of maturity for the Washington navel orange, Chace............... 649
Some notes on frost protection in orange groves, Vaile........................ 649
Preventing frost damage in transit, McKay.................................... 649
Effect of different methods of transplanting coffee, McClelland............... 649
A preliminary report on some breeding experiments with foxgloves, Warren... 649

FORESTRY.

Second biennial report Nebraska Forestation Commission, Rohde et al......... 649
Report of the State forester and firewarden, Wilber........................... 650

                                                                        Page.
Report of the chief forest firewarden for the year 1916, Wirt 650
Report of the forest branch of the department of lands for 1916................. 650
French forests and forestry.—Tunis, Algeria, Corsica, Woolsey, jr............. 650
Report on forest operations in Switzerland................................. 650
Report of forest administration in United Provinces for 1915–16, Billson....... 650
Report of forest administration in Jammu and Kashmir for 1915–16, Coventry. 650
Progress report of forest administration in Coorg for 1915–16, Tireman......... 650
Report of forest circles in Bombay Presidency, for 1915–16.................. 650
Notes on the principal timbers of Queensland.............................. 650
Georgia forest trees.. 650
Reproduction in the coniferous forests of northern New England, Moore...... 651
Growth study of planted trees, Door, jr., and Boag......................... 651
Frustum form factor volume tables for sugar maple, Hamlin.................. 651
A study of breakage, defect, and waste in Douglas fir, Hanzlik et al.......... 651
Influence of the age of the trees in the quality of the rubber, de Vries......... 651
The preservative treatment of poles, Grondal............................... 651
Mapping methods, Cade.. 651

                          · DISEASES OF PLANTS.

Report of the associate plant pathologist, Sherbakoff......................... 651
Report of the laboratory assistant in plant pathology, Matz.................. 652
[Plant diseases in New Jersey, 1915], Cook.............................. 652
[Fungus pests and their control]... 652
Some parasitic fungi of Japan, Hemmi...................................... 652
Combating nematodes by the use of calcium cyanamid, Watson............... 652
A new disease of wheat, Smith... 653
Observations on stalk disease of wheat, Capus............................. 653
Common diseases of cucumbers and melons, Martin......................... 653
A form of potato disease produced by Rhizoctonia, Ramsey.................. 653
A new strain of Rhizoctonia solani on the potato, Rosenbaum and Shapovalov.. 654
An investigation of the potato rot occurring in Ontario during 1915, Jones..... 654
Diseases of tomatoes, Cook and Martin.................................... 654
Apple blotch and its control, Roberts...................................... 654
Apple scab control in British Columbia, Winslow........................... 655
The biology of Exoascus deformans, Manaresi............................... 655
Comparative resistance of Prunus to crown gall, Smith...................... 655
Winter injury of grapes, Gladwin.. 655
Why and when winter kills grapes, Hall.................................... 655
A fatal disease of mulberry, Montemartini.................................. 655
Anthracnose of Japanese persimmon, Maffei................................ 656
Report of the plant physiologist, Floyd.................................... 656
Injury to citrus trees apparently induced by ground limestone, Floyd......... 656
Report of the plant pathologist, Stevens.................................... 656
The origin and cause of citrus canker in South Africa, Doidge............... 657
Anaberoga, Venkata Rao... 657
Diseases and pests of the mango, Kunhikannan and Norouha................. 657
Powdery mildew of dwarf magnolias, Turconi............................... 657
Black canker of chestnut, Peyronel.. 657
Black canker of chestnut, Petri... 657
The primary infection in black canker of chestnut, Petri.................... 658
Leaf cast in horse chestnut, Montemartini................................. 658
A needle blight of Douglas fir, Weir....................................... 658
[White pine blister rust in Canada], Güssow............................... 658
White pine blister rust on currants, McCubbin............................ 658

                       ECONOMIC ZOOLOGY—ENTOMOLOGY.

A check list of mammals of North America, Elliot........................... 658
Report of the entomologist, Watson.. 659
Undesirable insect immigration into New Jersey, Weiss...................... 660
Fumigation of greenhouses, Cory.. 660
A neglected factor in the use of nicotin sulphate as a spray, Moore and Graham. 660
Grasshopper control, Jones.. 661
A further contribution to the study of Eriosoma pyricola, Baker and Davidson. 661
The aphid of tea, coffee, and cacao (Toxoptera coffeæ), Theobald 662
Observations on Lecanium corni and Physokermes piceæ, Fenton.............. 662

Page.

Pupæ of some Maine species of Notodontoidea, Mosher...................... 663
Life history of *Plutella maculipennis*, the diamond-back moth, Marsh......... 663
The tobacco bud worm and its control, Morgan and McDonough.............. 663
Some recent advances in knowledge of mosquitoes, Headlee................. 664
The domestic flies of New Jersey, Richardson.............................. 665
Some fly poisons for outdoor and hospital use, Jackson and Lefroy........... 665
The apple maggot in British Columbia, Treherne.......................... 665
The dipterous families Sepsidæ and Piophilidæ, Melander and Spuler........ 665
Notes on some Buprestidæ of northern California, Chamberlain.............. 666
Biological investigation of *Sphenophorus callosus*, Metcalf............... 666
An annotated list of the scolytid beetles of Oregon, Chamberlin.............. 666
Destruction of wheat by wasps, Frohawk................................. 667
The host of *Ablerus clisiocampæ*, Porter................................ 667
A new West Indian chalcid fly, Girault.................................. 667
Notes on *Perisierola emigrata*, a parasite of the pink bollworm, Busck......... 667
Notes on coccid-infesting Chalcidoidea, III, Waterston..................... 667
Two new species of Macrophya, Rohwer................................. 667
The occurrence of the genus Monobæus in North America, Girault........... 667
Notes on some parasites of sugar cane insects in Java, Girault................ 667
The hothouse milliped, Cory and O'Neill................................. 667

FOODS—HUMAN NUTRITION.

How to select foods.—II. Cereal foods, Hunt and Atwater.................... 668
Eggs in a thousand ways, Meyer... 668
Milk as a food... 669
How to use skim milk to advantage in cookery............................ 669
Buttermilk a food drink.. 669
The food value of American cheese...................................... 669
Ways to use cottage cheese... 669
The nutritive value of edible fungi...................................... 669
Cider fruit for table use, Barker.. 669
Botulism from vegetables canned by the cold-pack method, Dickson......... 669
Canned food safe.. 670
Food supplies in war time, Rew... 670
Utilization of food... 670
High cost of living.. 670
Report on the increased cost of living in New York City.................... 670
Evidence regarding food allowances for healthy children, Gillett............. 671
The influence of diet on the heat production during mechanical work, Lusk.. 671

ANIMAL PRODUCTION.

Alfalfa silage, Reed and Fitch.. 671
Sudan grass silage, Francis and Friedemann.............................. 672
A study of methods of estimation of metabolic nitrogen, Forbes et al......... 672
Rate of passage of feed residues and its influence, Ewing and Smith......... 673
[Feeding experiments with beef cattle], Gray.............................. 674
Sheep, Gray....:.. 676
The management of farm flocks in Idaho, Iddings......................... 676
Are sheep profitable in winter? Woods................................... 676
Family performance as a basis for selection in sheep, Ritzman and Davenport. 676
Digestion experiments with pigs, Grindley et al........................... 677
The digestibility of some Arkansas feeds for hogs, Rather.................. 678
Pork production on irrigated land in western Nebraska, Holden............... 678
[Feeding experiments with pigs], Gray................................... 679
Are swine profitable in winter? Woods................................... 680
Orokinase and salivary digestion studies in the horse, Palmer et al........... 681
[Cottonseed meal for work horses and mules], Gray....................... 681
Licensed stallions in Utah during the season of 1916, Carroll................ 681
[Poultry investigations], Gray.. 681
Preparing poultry produce for market, Elford............................. 682
Preserving eggs for home use, Templeton................................. 682

DAIRY FARMING—DAIRYING.

Dairy investigational work, Gray.. 682
[Feeding experiments with dairy cattle], Scott............................ 683

Page.

Feed and care of the dairy calf, Hulce and Nevens............................ 683
Selecting rations for dairy cows, White and Musser.......................... 684
Dairy feeding and the calculation of rations, Riford........................ 684
Dairy herd [record], Scott... 684
Germ content of milk.—I. As influenced at the barn, Prucha and Weeter.... 684
Fishiness in evaporated milk, Hammer....................................... 686
The manufacture of cottage cheese in creameries and milk plants........... 686
Simple directions for making cottage cheese on the farm................... 686
A substitute for litmus for use in milk cultures, Clark and Lubs.......... 686

VETERINARY MEDICINE.

Annual reports of the State veterinarian of Alabama, 1914 and 1915, Cary.... 687
Report of the Montana Live Stock Sanitary Board for 1915–16................. 687
Diseases of domestic animals.. 687
Reports of the chief veterinary officer for 1914 and 1915, Stockman........ 687
Immunity in its relation to the stock diseases of southern Rhodesia, Bevan... 688
Anaphylatoxin and anaphylaxis, Novy and DeKruif........................... 688
Effect of temperature on complement fixation, Bronfenbrenner and Schlesinger. 688
The specific serum treatment of wounds, Leclainche and Vallée.............. 688
Plants poisonous to live stock, Long...................................... 688
Potassium permanganate as an antidote for poisonous plants, Marsh......... 688
Studies in forage poisoning, IV, Graham and Himmelberger.................. 689
Cottonseed meal work, Withers... 689
Blackleg filtrate, Eichhorn... 689
Virulence of blood of animals with foot-and-mouth disease, Cosco and Aguzzi.. 689
Allergic reaction of mallein for the diagnosis of glanders, Fava.......... 689
Milk sickness, Gray... 690
Studies on the paratyphoid-enteritidis group, III, Krumwiede, jr. et al... 690
Studies on the paratyphoid-enteritidis group, IV, Krumwiede, jr. and Kohn.... 690
Effect of injection of nonspecific foreign substances on rabies, Burmeister... 690
Tuberculosis in camels, Mason... 690
Brisket disease, Glover and Newsom.. 690
Report of the division of veterinary science, Roberts..................... 690
Keratitis infectiosa in cattle, Poels, trans. by Kappeyney and Ward....... 691
The life history of Hypoderma bovis and H. lineatum, Hadwen............... 691
Feeding lambs in the summer to prevent stomach worms, Gray................ 691
Hog cholera transmission through infected pork, Birch..................... 691
Transmission of piroplasmosis to three pigs by ingestion, Sparapani....... 691
A note on dourine in the horse, Pease..................................... 692
Abortive treatment of equine filariasis by hypodermic injection, Monbet.... 692
[Epizootic lymphangitis in France].. 692
Epizootic lymphangitis in France: Its diagnosis and treatment, Bridré..... 692
"Stomatitis contagiosa" in horses, Burton................................. 692
Note on an outbreak of contagious pneumonia in donkeys, Branford.......... 692
Another cestode from the young cat, Ackert and Grant...................... 693
Some of the infectious diseases of poultry, Pickens....................... 693

RURAL ENGINEERING.

Flow through sharp-edged V-notches or weirs, Doebler and Rayfield......... 693
Spray irrigation, Tolley.. 693
Irrigation laws of the State of Washington, compiled by Howell............ 693
Irrigation revenue report of the Bombay Presidency, excluding Sind, 1914–15. 693
Annual report, Ministry of Public Works, Egypt, 1915–16, MacDonald........ 693
[Water analyses].. 693
Reaeration as a factor in the self-purification of streams, Phelps........ 693
The javellization of water in the field, Arbinet......................... 694
Comparison of activated sludge and Imhoff processes of sewage treatment, Eddy. 694
Marked advance in treating sewage from packing houses, Zimmele........... 694
The relation of sewage disposal to the spread of pellagra, Siler et al.... 694
Rational and economic sanitary treatment of human wastes, Garrigou....... 694
Rural sanitation 695
Report of highway commissioner of Milwaukee County, Wis., 1916, Kuelling.. 695
Road problems in the Ozarks, Harris....................................... 695
Report of the fourth annual road drag competition, Kuehne and Hettle...... 695
Determining road making qualities of deposits of stone and gravel, Reinecke.... 695

Page.

The arrangement of rectangular dairy barns, Hulce and Nevens.............. 696
Wooden silos used in Nebraska, Chase and Wood............................ 696
The principles of poultry house construction, Elford........................ 696
Better conveniences for rural schools, Scott................................. 696

RURAL ECONOMICS.

The marketing of Kansas butter, Macklin..................................... 696
The wheat question, Perchot... 697
Observations on the recent agricultural inquiry in California, Hunt........... 697
The great war: Its lessons and its warnings, Collings......................... 697
The land and the Empire, Turnor... 697
The English land system, Marriott... 697
Land improvement in the Province of the Rhine, Heimerle.................. 697
Madras agriculture.—A brief survey... 697
Monthly crop report... 697

AGRICULTURAL EDUCATION.

Proceedings of Association of Agricultural Colleges and Stations, ed. by Hills.. 698
Short courses in agriculture and home economics, Reid et al................... 699
Household science in normal schools, Bridges, et al.......................... 699
[Agricultural and home economics, New Hampshire], Whitcher and Damon. ... 699
Some exercises in farm handicraft for rural schools, Sampson................. 699
Working drawings and photographs showing the construction of farm buildings. 699

MISCELLANEOUS.

Annual Report of Florida Station, 1916...................................... 699
Thirty-ninth Annual Report of North Carolina Station, 1916.................. 699
Barn and field experiments in 1916, Woods................................... 699
Monthly Bulletin of the Western Washington Substation..................... 699

LIST OF EXPERIMENT STATION AND DEPARTMENT PUBLICATIONS REVIEWED.

Stations in the United States.

Page.

Alabama College Station:
Circ. 36, Apr., 1917........... 682
Arkansas Station:
Bul. 129, June, 1917 642
Bul. 133, Apr., 1917........... 678
California Station:
Bean Culture.................. 641
Observations on the Recent
Agricultural Inquiry in Cali-
fornia...................... 697
Colorado Station:
Bul. 229, May, 1917........... 690
Bul. 232, June, 1917........... 646
Bul. 233, June, 1917........... 661
Connecticut Storrs Station:
Bul. 90, Feb., 1917 684
Delaware Station:
Bul. 117, Mar., 1917........... 644
Florida Station:
Bul. 137, June, 1917........... 656
Bul. 138, June, 1917........... 644
An. Rpt. 1916 635,
649, 651, 652, 656, 659, 683, 684, 699
Idaho Station:
Bul. 93, Jan., 1917............. 640
Bul. 94, Jan., 1917............. 639
Bul. 95, Jan., 1917............. 640
Bul. 96, Jan., 1917............. 676
Bul. 97, Feb., 1917............ 646
Bul. 98, Feb., 1917 647
Illinois Station:
Bul. 199, May, 1917........... 684
Bul. 200, May, 1917......... 645, 677
Bul. 201, June, 1917........... 641
Circ. 199, June, 1917........... 696
Circ. 200, June, 1917.......... 645
Circ. 201, June, 1917.......... 642
Circ. 202, June, 1917.......... 683
Iowa Station:
Research Bul. 37, Nov., 1916.. 633
Research Bul. 38, Jan., 1917.. 686
Kansas Station:
Bul. 216, Apr., 1917........... 696
Bul. 217, May, 1917........... 671
Maine Station:
Bul. 259, Feb., 1917........... 663
Bul. 260, Mar., 1917........... 628,
635, 647, 676, 680, 699
Maryland Station:
Bul. 204, Mar., 1917........... 645
Bul. 205, Apr., 1917 660
Bul. 206, Apr., 1917 667
Bul. 207, May, 1917 648
Massachusetts Station:
Met. Buls. 341–342, May–June,
1917 619

Stations in the United States—Continued.

Page.

Nebraska Station:
Bul. 159, Apr. 10, 1917........ 678
New Jersey Stations:
Bul. 306, Oct. 17, 1916........ 664
Bul. 307, Feb. 7, 1917......... 665
Circ. 66, Mar. 25, 1917........ 645
Circ. 67, Mar. 15, 1917........ 629
Circ. 68, Apr. 4, 1917......... 653
Circ. 69, Apr. 18, 1917........ 642
Circ. 70, Apr. 18, 1917........ 642
Circ. 71, Apr. 25, 1917........ 654
Circ. 72, Apr. 25, 1917........ 645
Circ. 73, May 1, 1917.......... 684
New Mexico Station:
Bul. 107, May, 1917........... 644
New York State Station:
Bul. 433, Apr., 1917 655
Tech. Bul. 62, May, 1917...... 616
North Carolina Station:
Tech. Bul. 13, Jan., 1917...... 666
Thirty-ninth An. Rpt. 1916... 625,
636, 674, 676, 679, 681,
682, 689, 690, 691, 699
Oklahoma Station:
Bul. 115, Apr., 1917 672
Pennsylvania Station:
Bul. 14, May, 1917........... 626
Porto Rico:[6,]
Bul. 22, June 29, 1917......... 649
Texas Station:
Bul. 204, Feb., 1917........... 642
Utah Station:
Circ. 24, Mar., 1917........... 681
Washington Station:
Bul. 139, Mar., 1917 631
Bul. 143, Apr., 1917 665
Bul. 145, Apr., 1917 614
West. Wash. Sta. Mo. Bul.,
vol. 5, No. 4, July, 1917...... 699

U. S. Department of Agriculture.

Jour. Agr. Research:
Vol. 9, No. 12, June 18, 1917. 653,
654, 672
Vol. 10, No. 1, July 2, 1917... 637,
653, 660, 663
Vol. 10, No. 2, July 9, 1917... 612,
658, 660, 673, 676
Vol. 10, No. 3, July 16, 1917. 626. 686
Bul. 527, Some Exercises in Farm
Handicraft for Rural Schools,
H. O. Sampson................ 699

*U. S. Department of Agriculture—*Contd.

Page.

Bul. 534, Apple Blotch and Its
Control, J. W. Roberts......... 654
Farmers' Bul. 817, How to Select
Foods: II, Cereal Foods, Caro-
line L. Hunt and Helen W.
Atwater......................... 668
Farmers' Bul. 819, The Tobacco
Budworm and Its Control in the
Southern Tobacco Districts,
A. C. Morgan and F. L. Mc-
Donough........................ 663
Weekly News Letter, 5 (1917), No.
16, Nov. 21, 1917.............. 670
Bureau of Crop Estimates:
Mo. Crop Rpt., vol. 3—
No. 6, June, 1917.......... 697
No. 7, July, 1917......... 697
Bureau of Markets:
Doc. 4, June 8, 1917.......... 648
Bureau of Animal Industry:
How to Use Skim Milk........ 669
Milk as a Food.............. 669
Simple Directions for Making
Cottage Cheese on the Farm. 686
Ways to Use Cottage Cheese... 669
The Manufacture of Cottage
Cheese in Creameries and
Milk Plants.'................. 686
The Food Value of American
Cheese........................ 669
Buttermilk a Food Drink..... 669
Bureau of Soils:
Field Operations, 1914—
Soil Survey of Barbour
County, Ala., H. C.
Smith, N. E. Bell, and
J. F. Stroud............. 621
Field Operations, 1915—
Soil Survey of Chickasaw
County, Miss., E. M.
Jones and C. S. Waldrop. 621
Soil Survey of Anson
County, N. C., E. S.
Vanatta and F. N. Mc-
Dowell................. 621
Weather Bureau:
Climat. Data, vol. 4, Nos. 3–4,
Mar.–Apr., 1917........... 619

*U. S. Department of Agriculture—*Contd.

Page.

Scientific Contributions: [1]
Gingerol and Paradol, E. K.
Nelson...................... 612
The Citric Acid Fermentation
of *Aspergillus niger*, J. N.
Currie...................... 613
The Quantitative Estimation
of Dextrose in Muscular
Tissue, R. Hoagland........ 617
The Coefficient of Correlation,
W. G. Reed................. 621
Fertilizers and Industrial
Wastes, F. W. Brown....... 630
Fruit Injury during the Fumi-
gation of Citrus Trees, R. S.
Woglum.................... 634
Standards of Maturity for the
Washington Navel Orange,
E. M. Chace................ 649
Preventing Frost Damage in
Transit, A. W. McKay..... 649
A Study of Breakage, Defect,
and Waste in Douglas Fir,
E. J. Hanzlik, F. S. Fuller,
and E. C. Erickson......... 651
A New West Indian Chalcid
Fly, A. A. Girault.......... 667
Notes on *Perisierola emigrata*,
a Parasite of the Pink Boll-
worm, A. Busck............ 667
Two New Species of Ma-
crophya, S. A. Rohwer..... 667
The Occurrence of the Genus
Monobæus in North Ameri-
ca, A. A. Girault.......... 667
Notes on Some Parasites of
Sugar Cane Insects in Java,
with Descriptions of New
Hymenoptera Chalcidoidea,
A. A. Girault.............. 667
Potassium Permanganate as an
Antidote for the Effects of
Poisonous Plants, C. D.
Marsh...................... 688
Economic Factors to Be Con-
sidered in Connection with
the Project for Extension
Work Among Farm Women,
E. Merritt................. 699

[1] Printed in scientific and technical publications outside the Department.

EXPERIMENT STATION RECORD.

VOL. 37. NOVEMBER, 1917. No. 7.

The thirty-first annual convention of the Association of American Agricultural Colleges and Experiment Stations, held in Washington, D. C., November 14–16, seems likely to be long remembered as one of the most interesting and inspiring in the history of the organization. As was pointed out by Secretary Houston in his address of greeting, according to the calendar barely a year had gone by since the previous meeting, but "judged by the experiences through which we have passed, it has seemed more like a generation." The profound changes during this period which the entrance of the Nation into the war has brought to every institution represented were reflected in the program, the point of view, and the predominating spirit of the convention.

Official delegates were in attendance from every State in the Union, as well as Porto Rico, and a delegation was also present from Canada which was given the privileges of the floor. From many institutions there were representatives for each of the five divisions of college, station, extension, engineering, and home economics work. The total registration of delegates and visitors aggregated three hundred and seventy, surpassing all previous records.

The large attendance was the more noteworthy since the number of other organizations meeting with the association was somewhat smaller than in 1916. Prior to the opening of the convention itself, a four-day conference was held of State leaders of home demonstration agents and the States Relations Service. The Society for the Promotion of Agricultural Science, the American Society of Agronomy, the National Potato Association, the American Association for the Advancement of Agricultural Teaching, the American Association of Farmers' Institute Workers, and the Association of Official Agricultural Chemists also held sessions before or after the convention. The attendance at many of these meetings was likewise unusually large, and while many of their papers followed the usual scientific and technical lines a distinctly war-time flavor permeated their programs and proceedings.

The program of the Association of American Agricultural Colleges and Experiment Stations naturally gave primary consideration to questions associated with the war and its relations to the land-grant institutions. The presidential address, for example, was entitled The Morrill Act Institutions and the New Epoch. It considered some of the far-reaching changes which the war is bringing to the Nation, and the responsibilities and opportunities of these institutions not only during the conflict itself but in the era to follow.

In this address President Butterfield outlined some of the ideals of the democracy for which the Nation is contending, such as real equality of opportunity, the exaltation of manhood and of the religious motive, and the substitution of cooperation for coercion. He indicated that the Nation would look to the agricultural colleges for their full share of leadership in bringing these ideals to realization. As he brought out, this will mean far more than the training of experts to increase production, important as this will continue to be. Its aim will be to develop leaders, men and women broadly educated and with vision and sympathetic understanding of what the new democracy will represent in rural life. As a preliminary step to meet the changing conditions, President Butterfield suggested the appointment of a national agricultural committee to consider the whole rural situation as affected by the war.

Practically an entire afternoon was devoted to a discussion of food and food administration, with addresses by Hon. Herbert C. Hoover, director of the Federal Food Administration; Prof. Isabel Bevier, of Illinois; Dean Catharine J. MacKay, of Iowa; and President C. R. Van Hise, of Wisconsin. The address of Secretary Houston, already referred to, discussed the season's work in food production and similar needs of the future. The experiment station section devoted its entire attention to this topic, with papers by Dr. Graham Lusk, entitled Calories in Common Life, this being mainly a discussion of the economic use of foods on the basis of their energy values, and a symposium on what the stations can most profitably do to increase the efficiency of food production and conservation in the present national emergency, participated in by Dr. Raymond Pearl, of Maine; Dr. E. W. Allen, of the Office of Experiment Stations; and others. From a somewhat different point of view the home-economics division took up the food-conservation program in a joint session with the conference of home-demonstration agents, Dr. A. E. Taylor, of the Food Administration, discussing the necessity and purpose of food conservation, and others, representing the Food Administration and the States Relations Service, describing the past summer's work and projected plans for the future.

An economic study of the farmer's income as affected by war conditions was presented at one of the general sessions by Prof. T. N. Carver, of Harvard University, in which he considered in detail various items of income and outgo during the past season. Wide variations were found in the net profits accruing from different types of farming, ranging from losses on many dairy farms in the Northeastern States, where much grain is purchased, to profits somewhat larger than the average in sections where little or no fertilizer is required and the primary staple crops are marketed. The duty to the Nation at this time of conserving profits, however reasonable or legitimately acquired, was strongly emphasized.

Special mention should also be made of the stirring speech of President G. C. Creelman, of the Ontario Agricultural College, on Canada's part in the war. Some of the remarkable accomplishments of Canada, particularly that of materially increasing wheat production despite the wholesale withdrawal of labor to make up an army as large in proportion to population as would be one of 5,000,000 men from the United States, were impressively narrated, and tribute paid to the substantial aid being rendered by the Canadian agricultural colleges and experiment stations.

The important service of the land-grant institutions in this country was attested by several speakers. Thus Secretary Houston declared that while at the time the country entered the war the Nation was not fully prepared for war in any respect " it was fortunately circumstanced in the character of its agricultural organization and the number and efficiency of its expert agencies. In fact, in efficient machinery for directing agricultural activity as represented by the land-grant colleges, the Federal Department of Agriculture, farmers' organizations, and its alert and patriotic rural population, it excelled any other two or three nations in the world combined."

" The Nation may well pride itself," he said, " on the fact that it had had the foresight generations ago to lay deep its agricultural foundations." He congratulated the representatives of the land-grant colleges on the fine opportunity for service presented to them and on the splendid way in which they had seized it. " The Department of Agriculture has had great comfort in the thought that these institutions, ably planned and wisely directed, existed in every part of the Nation and stood ready not only to place themselves at the service of the National Government but also to take the initiative in a vast number of directions."

Similarly, President E. C. Perisho, of South Dakota, in a paper before the college section on The Best Things Done by the Land-grant Colleges to Meet the War Emergencies of the Nation, maintained that "no portion of our people responded more quickly or more intelligently than did the men and women of the land-grant colleges. From every one of these institutions there was sent at once to State and Federal authorities not only assurance of loyalty but the free offer of men, military departments, laboratories, machine shops, experiment plats, engineering plants, agricultural workers, and the entire staff of our extension divisions." This service took the form of cooperation with State and Federal governments, assistance in the production and conservation of food materials, the work of the extension divisions and experiment stations, aid rendered along military lines, the offering of special emergency courses, and many forms of individual aid by students, faculty, and alumni.

Appreciation of the part played by the land-grant institutions along military lines was voiced by Major Clark, representing the Adjutant-General's Office of the War Department, who specially commended the work of the men entering the officers' training camps; and by President James of the University of Illinois, who drew attention to some of the potentialities of these institutions as military assets. Maj. David S. White, of the Veterinary Corps of the U. S. Army, in a discussion of the organization and workings of this branch of the service, indicated the substantial aid rendered by many institutions in supplying competent veterinarians.

Interest in past achievements of the colleges and stations, however, was far overshadowed by the evidence of their desire to serve the Nation in the most effective way possible in its present and future needs. The program was, therefore, constructive rather than reminiscent, and dealt quite largely with ways and means for immediate application. For example, in addition to papers already referred to, President Soule, of Georgia, took up in the college section the question of how the land-grant colleges may be organized to serve the Government in the war emergency, and the engineering and home economics divisions considered modifications in their respective curricula to meet the emergency conditions.

As would be expected, special interest centered in the developments along the line of extension work. The Federal program for extension work during the war period was outlined by Dr. A. C. True. The program suggested for the agricultural colleges and the Department of Agriculture included as its principal items the full maintenance of the food supply and its conservation, the preservation of a permanent and safe sytsem of agriculture, the rendering of assistance in the solution of such problems as farm labor and the handling and marketing of farm products, and assisting the Federal Government in spe-

cial work from time to time. Some of these phases were discussed
by others in considerable detail.

For instance, President Pearson, of Iowa, took up the cooperation
of the extension service with State councils of defense and other
public and private organizations. Vice-director M. C. Burritt, of
New York, and Director John T. Caine, of Utah, discussed forms
of organization required in the county before funds are available for
the employment of emergency food agents; and Director C. A. Keffer,
of Tennessee, and Miss Florence E. Ward, of the States Relations
Service, described the correlation of men and women agents. Under
the general subject of Methods of Meeting the Farm Labor Shortage,
Director C. W. Pugsley, of Nebraska, discussed the Organization of
Farm Labor Bureaus, and Director William D. Hurd, of Massachusetts, the Utilization of Nonproductive or Partially Nonproductive
Labor, such as the boys' working reserve and similar agencies.

An important problem as regards extension publications was referred to in the report of the bibliographer, which dealt with agricultural literature and the war. The vitally significant change in
the character of this literature during the year has been, as Dr.
True stated, the tremendous output of popular emergency material
of a new sort, "exhortation and precept cast into pictorial, mimeographed, or printed form, bulletins, posters, circular letters, and
what not." This material has been distinguished alike "by its
endless variety in form of presentation and its endless repetition
of subject matter."

Much of the duplication has been of course unavoidable under
the circumstances, but as Dr. True maintained, "the situation no
longer justifies the same degree of duplication of effort or breath-
less haste of issue and distribution. It is now possible to foresee,
for a sufficiently extended period, the subjects which will claim attention, and it will, therefore, be possible carefully and thoughtfully
to plan for the advantageous use of existing and available material, as well as for the preparation of such new matter as may be
needed. The variety in form and subject of what has been issued
gives ample opportunity for matured, well-considered selection of
suitable forms of presentation, and will be valuable as a guide to
the formulation of more definite principles by which future activities may be guided."

The discussion of the part which the experiment stations should
play in the war program has already been referred to. Interest
in this topic was decidedly keen, and the strong desire of station
workers to bring their work into close relations with the emergency
conditions was much in evidence. It was recognized that the fundamental character of the stations as research institutions must be

preserved, but there was general concurrence in the view expressed that "the emergency presents special reason for some degree of temporary adaptation and less rigid adherence to strict limitations and the pursuit of established projects than under normal conditions."

Numerous specific suggestions were made as to how this redirection of effort could be accomplished. The situation may be summarized by the following quotation from one of the addresses: "The experiment stations can be of the greatest service at this time by continuing to serve in the capacity of experts in agricultural science and its interpretation, by supplying tested and reliable information and making this available and applicable, by expert study of the general situation in its relation to agricultural production, by supplying counsel and formulating broad plans and policies, by being alert to detect and act upon the present necessities, and by exercising foresight in preparing for post-bellum conditions. They can do this—

"(1) By letting their work be known—by seeing to it that it is written up and published promptly.

"(2) By maintaining unusually close relations with the publicity and teaching agencies, seconding the efforts of the extension and other agencies in helping and protecting the producer.

"(3) By a revision of their project programs, selecting for special attention those having an emergency or present importance, and by adapting others so as to take account of the changed conditions resulting from the war.

"(4) By working close to the ground, reaching out into the State and maintaining an unusually close contact with the actual conditions of production.

"(5) By inaugurating, to a limited extent naturally, new investigations having war-time and post-bellum significance.

"(6) By working close together, either in cooperation or with mutual understanding, and at least with full recognition of other similar work, in order that greater accuracy may be attained and time economized."

Aside from war questions the convention had before it a number of other important matters. A development of the year which received special consideration was the enactment of the Federal Vocational Education Aid Act. Although this measure, as is well known, deals with instruction of subcollegiate grade and makes no direct reference to the land-grant institutions in its scheme of administration, its workings are none the less of great interest to them. One of the general sessions was largely devoted to this subject, and in addition a round-table conference was held by the home economics division on the training of teachers in that subject. The topic likewise assumed great prominence in the meetings of the Association for the Advancement of Agricultural Teaching, with addresses by a member of the Federal Board for Vocational Education and several others of the staff.

At the general session of the association, some of the policies and plans of the Federal Board were outlined by Mr. Charles A. Prosser, director of vocational education, while some requisites in the training of teachers under the act were discussed for agriculture, the trades and industries, and home economics by the assistant directors for each of these subjects. Dean Alfred Vivian, chairman of the State Board of Education of Ohio, closed the discussion as spokesman from the points of view of the association and the State boards.

The address of Mr. Prosser drew attention to the large measure of authority given under the act to the State boards of vocational education in correlating the new system with the work of existing institutions, but he expressed the opinion that the land-grant colleges would render very useful service. The greatest needs in developing vocational education he considered to be intelligent supervision and a competent teaching force, and he maintained that the colleges, with their unique advantages as sources of subject matter, possess a special opportunity for developing strong courses to meet these needs.

A similar view as to the opportunity and duty of the agricultural colleges in teacher training was taken by the standing committee on instruction in agriculture in its report on college teaching in agriculture, with particular reference to the improvement of methods. In this report the committee expressed the view that "strong departments of agricultural education will be needed under the administration of the Smith-Hughes Act in order to give the colleges of agriculture the positions they should occupy in the training of teachers of agriculture. Unless these colleges take up the teacher training work actively at the present time, the funds provided for this work under the Smith-Hughes Act are likely in many States to be divided among a number of institutions, including some of relatively low grade and poor equipment, with the result that our whole system for training teachers of agriculture will be fundamentally weak. The agricultural colleges ought to have a clear leadership in this field, and they can not have this unless they adequately equip their departments of agricultural education."

The committee also urged the development of such departments as a means of improvement of college teaching in general. It was recognized that in the past a large proportion of college graduates without special pedagogical training have done well as teachers, but, "they have succeeded in spite of the lack of professional training, and the percentage and degree of successes might have been much larger if the professional training had been provided. No matter how well manned and equipped the subject matter departments of the colleges of agriculture may be, they need the help of strong departments of agricultural education, not only in the training of undergraduates for teaching positions but also in improving the quality of teaching within the subject matter departments."

Two other papers of direct interest to educators were presented. One of these was a study of the prevailing requirements for graduation in agriculture in the land-grant colleges, presented before the college section by Dr. C. D. Jarvis of the U. S. Bureau of Education. The second was a discussion of the status of agricultural engineering instruction in the land-grant colleges, by Dean Stout of Nebraska.

In Dr. Jarvis' study, a decided increase was noted in the entrance requirements for college work in agriculture within recent years, coupled with greater uniformity among institutions and considerable optional substitution of vocational for academic subjects. Much difficulty was found, however, in comparing the requirements for graduation, mainly because of the diversity of practice as to units of credit. Wide variations were also encountered in subject matter, its distribution by courses, proportion and kind of prescribed and elective work, and similar matters. The study made it apparent that there is still much difference of opinion as to the optimum college course in agriculture, although the discussion following its presentation indicated general agreement on the part of those present that as much uniformity should be obtained as would be feasible under varying conditions.

The report of the committee on college organization and policy was in two sections. The first section dealt with administrative organization, presenting fourteen recommendations for consideration. Under the plan proposed, the individual specialist capable of working independently is regarded as the unit of organization. A subject matter department would consist of the group of working specialists on that subject, regardless of the kind of service, and authority for subject matter would be confined to this group of specialists, administrative control being limited to the amount and method of work. Administrative authority would be on the basis of kind of service, with the various kinds coordinated under a chief executive.

The remaining section of the committee's report, and likewise the report of the committee on extension organization and policy, dealt largely with the relations of the colleges to other agencies, such as the Federal Board of Vocational Education, the Food Administration, and the emergency and other work of this Department. The executive committee of the association was instructed to represent the interests of the association in these matters. A request from the college committee that the executive committee report on the feasibility of the preparation of a history of the Morrill Acts and supplementary legislation was also adopted.

The committee on graduate study discussed the status of the Graduate School of Agriculture under the emergency conditions. In view of the altered situation it advised the postponement for another year of a decision as to continuing the school. This recommendation was accepted by the association.

The familiar question of the form and content of station publications was discussed from various points of view. A comprehensive report was submitted by the committee on experiment station organization and policy, which drew attention to the prevailing diversity in practice. More than a score of existing series of publications were enumerated, and it was stated that many of the individual series may "mean one thing at one station or at one time, but another thing at a different place and time."

To relieve some of the existing confusion, the committee suggested five series of publications as covering the usual needs. These include, besides technical papers published in scientific journals, regular bulletins designated as bulletins, research bulletins, regulatory bulletins, circulars, and the annual report. Of these the bulletins are for the general reader, and devoted primarily to the publication of such "results of the station's own work as appear to be important or directly useful or interesting to the serious student of practical agriculture, especially the farmer." Technical material should be given special distribution, either by publication in scientific journals or in regular or research bulletins, issued in limited editions. Circulars when deemed necessary would include, not the popular information now largely disseminated through extension series, but popular accounts of small pieces of work, matter too ephemeral in nature to appear in the bulletin series, preliminary announcements, popular editions of bulletins, and similar material. The annual report is regarded as an administrative document, and designed to be an epitome and permanent record of the station's progress during the year.

As to subject matter, the thesis was laid down that, "the publications of an experiment station properly consist of accounts and records of its experiments and investigations and of their applications, leaving to other agencies the dissemination of general information and experience, propaganda, descriptions of farm devices,

methods in farming, etc." The committee also pointed out that any
scheme for publishing will require some supervision, and suggested
the desirability for providing in connection with the director's office
some machinery for assuring systematic attention to manuscript and
matter in course of publication.

A report on publications from a committee of the Agricultural
Libraries section of the American Library Association was also received, and is to be included in the proceedings of the association.
This report dealt more specifically with the details of distribution of
the publications among libraries, and their most effective utilization.

Still another phase of the subject was touched upon in the report
of the association's committee on the publication of research, which
again indicated very clearly some of the advantages accruing from
the use of the *Journal of Agricultural Research* as a medium of publication. It was stated that of the one hundred and eleven papers
appearing in the journal during the past year, fifty-seven were from
station workers, representing twenty-four institutions.

The proposed initiation of Federal aid to research in engineering
was again considered by the engineering section, and a compromise
measure submitted by a committee of that section was subsequently
approved by the association itself. This measure would provide
$15,000 per annum of Federal funds to each State and Territory for
engineering experimentation at the land-grant college, but would
involve an equal appropriation by the States for similar work to be
conducted either at the same institution or elsewhere as determined
by the legislature. The executive committee was instructed to urge
the consideration of legislation along these lines as a war measure.

The election of officers resulted in the selection of Dean Eugene
Davenport of Illinois as president; President C. A. Lory of Colorado, President A. M. Soule of Georgia, Director J. G. Lipman of
New Jersey, President A. F. Woods of Maryland, and Dean R. W.
Thatcher of Minnesota, vice presidents; and the reelection of the previous secretary-treasurer and bibliographer. The membership of the
various committees underwent few changes. The vacancies caused
by the retirement from land-grant college work of Presidents Waters
of Kansas and Duniway of Wyoming were filled respectively by the
appointment of Prof. G. A. Works of Cornell University to the
committee on instruction in agriculture and President C. A. Lory
of Colorado to the committee on college organization and policy.
President W. M. Riggs of South Carolina succeeded President
Waters on the executive committee, the personnel of which was otherwise continued unchanged. An amendment to the constitution pro-
posing the enlargement of the executive committee to six members,

the additional member to be selected by the extension section, was offered for consideration at the next annual meeting.

The section officers included for college work and administration, President E. C. Perisho, of South Dakota, chairman, and President R. D. Hetzel, of New Hampshire, secretary; in the station section, Dean W. M. Jardine, of Kansas, chairman, Director W. P. Brooks, of Massachusetts, secretary, and Mr. W. H. Beal, of the States Relations Service, recording secretary; and in the extension section, Director C. R. Titlow, of West Virginia, chairman, Dean E. C. Johnson, of Kansas, secretary, and Mr. Bradford Knapp, of the States Relations Service, recording secretary. The engineering division elected President W. M. Riggs, of South Carolina, chairman, and Dean A. A. Potter, of Kansas, secretary; and the home economics section, Miss Isabel Bevier, of Illinois, chairman, and Miss Mary Sweeny, of Kentucky, secretary.

The 1917 convention was thus an unusually interesting gathering, quite different in many respects from any which had preceded it. It revealed how closely the war has been brought home to the land-grant institutions, depleting the faculty and student body, interrupting many well established projects, and compelling a redirecting of their entire program and point of view. More strongly, however, did it indicate how largely the Nation is relying on these institutions in the present emergency, and how important are the functions which are theirs to fulfill. It put this great body of public service institutions, already conspicuous for a season's successful endeavor, formally on record as enlisted for the war, and with their full resources mobilized in the national service.

RECENT WORK IN AGRICULTURAL SCIENCE.

AGRICULTURAL CHEMISTRY—AGROTECHNY.

Isolation of cyanuric acid from soil, L. E. WISE and E. H. WALTERS (*U. S. Dept. Agr., Jour. Agr. Research, 10 (1917), No. 2, pp. 85–92, pl. 1*).—The authors note the isolation of a nitrogenous compound from an Indiana soil whose identity with cyanuric acid prepared by heating urea with zinc chlorid was established. The largest amount of the acid isolated from any of several lots of 23 kg. of the Indiana soil was about 0.15 gm. Cyanuric acid was also isolated from a Maine soil, 46 kg. of soil yielding about 0.165 gm. of acid; a Florida soil, yielding approximately 0.04 gm. of acid from 23 kg. of soil; and a Texas soil, which yielded about 0.04 gm. from 46 kg. of soil.

The procedure used in the isolation of the acid from the soil samples and the identification tests are described in detail. The possibility of the formation of cyanuric acid in the soil by the decomposition of nucleoprotein or purin bases, some of which have been previously isolated, and its possible derivation from urea are suggested.

Analysis of ragweed pollen, F. W. HEYL (*Jour. Amer. Chem. Soc., 39 (1917), No. 7, pp. 1470–1476*).—The following percentage composition is reported for the pollen of the ragweed (*Ambrosia artemisifolia*): Alcohol-soluble material, 42.9; moisture, 5.3; crude fiber, 12.2; pentosans, 7.3; ash, 5.4; dextrin, 2.1; and protein, 24.4. Of the protein about 7.5 per cent could not be extracted, while 6.75 per cent was extracted with dilute alkali and only about 5 per cent with 10 per cent salt solution. The albumin and globulin fractions thus appear to be small. The presence of proteoses is indicated. The alcoholic extract was found to have the following percentage composition: Fat, 10.8; lecithin, 0.75; ether-soluble (but not soluble in ligroin), 1.75; sucrose, 0.4; glucose, 1.6; resin, 17.4; and a nitrogenous base.

Some ophthalmic tests obtained in the case of two hay-fever subjects are noted.

The pungent principles of ginger.—I, A new ketone, zingiberone, occurring in ginger, H. NOMURA (*Sci. Rpts. Tohoku Imp. Univ., ser. 1, 6 (1917), No. 1, pp. 41–52*).—The author notes the isolation from ginger of a ketone, zingiberone, having the composition $C_{11}H_{14}O_3$. The experimental procedures used in this isolation and the determination of its chemical constitution are described in detail.

Gingerol and paradol, E. K. NELSON (*Jour. Amer. Chem. Soc., 39 (1917), No. 7, pp. 1466–1469*).

Microorganisms and heat production in silage fermentation, O. W. HUNTER (*U. S. Dept. Agr., Jour. Agr. Research, 10 (1917), No. 2, pp. 75–83, figs. 10*).—In the study reported by the author at the Kansas Experiment Station an endeavor was made to determine the exact cause of heat production in silage fermentation. Alfalfa, corn, cane, and Kafir corn forage, siloed under laboratory conditions, were used for silage production. Heat production was observed in normal fermenting forage, forage treated with a weak antiseptic, forage treated with heat, heated forage inoculated with bacteria, and cured or dried forage. Normal check fermentations were provided by siloing untreated forage.

The untreated and inoculated forage all showed a marked increase in acid production, while the chloroformed and heated samples exhibited no increase. "Good clean-flavored silage resulted in every instance from the fermentation of the untreated, green, cured, and inoculated forage. The treated forage, that saturated with chloroform and that heated, exhibited no characteristics of silage." Heat production was observed only in the untreated and inoculated forage, with no indication of heating in any of the treated samples. The heat production of the different kinds of silage is represented in graphical charts.

From the investigation it is concluded that "heat production in forage fermentation results from microbial activity and not from intramolecular respiration of the tissue cells."

The citric acid fermentation of Aspergillus niger, J. N. Currie (Jour. Biol. Chem., 31 (1917), No. 1, pp. 15–37, pls. 2, figs. 2).—The author has studied the inorganic salt requirements, the general equation of metabolism, and the reaction of the medium of the citric acid fermentation of A. niger. From observations of a large number of cultures, iron is not considered necessary for the development of spores. It is suggested, however, that some definite chemical reaction involved in the utilization of nitrates is accelerated in the presence of iron.

The fermentation of a sugar by A. niger is considered an oxidation proceeding in three stages and producing citric acid, oxalic acid, and carbon dioxid. The proportion in which the products of the metabolism appear can be varied at will. Quite different results are given by cultures, even under the same conditions, which can not be distinguished morphologically. By proper selection of cultures and conditions the yield of citric acid can be varied from none at all to over 50 per cent of the sugar consumed. Low nitrogen supply, high concentration of sugar, and nitrogen supplied as ammonium salts rather than as nitrates are conditions especially favorable to the fermentation. Where the nitrogen was supplied as ammonium salts or as asparagin, iron was not found to stimulate the metabolic processes in any way. In the case of nitrates the stimulating effect of iron, however, was especially noticeable in the increased production of carbon dioxid and weight of mycelium.

From the general consideration of the data obtained the following medium is considered the most suitable for conducting the citric acid fermentation with A. niger: Per 1,000 cc. of solution, saccharose 125 to 150 gm., NH_4NO_3 2 to 2.5 gm., KH_2PO_4 0.75 to 1 gm., $MgSO_4.7H_2O$ 0.2 to 0.25 gm., HCl to P_H 3.4–3.5 (5–4 cc. fifth-normal).

Influence of certain electrolytes upon the course of the hydrolysis of starch by malt amylase, H. C. Sherman and Jennie A. Walker (Jour. Amer. Chem. Soc., 39 (1917), No. 7, pp. 1476–1493, figs. 7).—The rate of formation of reducing sugar by the action of purified malt amylase on soluble starch, both in neutral solution and in solution with the addition of regulated amounts of hydrochloric or phosphoric acids or primary potassium phosphate, was investigated.

"When the activating electrolyte was added in such amount as to give optimum or nearly optimum concentration of hydrogen ion, the action of the enzym was increased not only in the earlier stages but throughout the entire range investigated. The greater the concentration of enzym the less the effect of the added electrolyte. . . . Throughout the first half of the hydrolysis, or up to a yield of half the theoretical amount of maltose, the rate of maltose formation from soluble starch was found to be proportional to the concentration of substrate, at least in solutions containing favorable amounts of acid or acid phosphate. When, in similar experiments, enzym concentration is varied within limits suitable for such quantitative study, the rate of maltose formation is found to be directly proportional to the enzym concentration up to a yield of about half the theoretical amount of maltose. This broadens the range within which diastatic activities may be compared quantitatively."

No "region of linear relationship" in which the yield of reducing sugar is directly proportional to the time was found. No cessation of hydrolysis nor true equilibrium at 80 per cent was shown in experiments with widely varied enzym concentration, as was claimed by some previous investigators.

A noteworthy effect of bromids upon the action of malt amylase, A. W. Thomas (Jour. Amer. Chem. Soc., 39 (1917), No. 7, pp. 1501–1503, fig. 1).—In an investigation on the activation of malt amylase by acids and salts it was observed that bromids when present in small amounts exercised an inhibitory effect on the action, but an activating action was observed when the concentration of the salt was increased. As previously shown, the chlorid, nitrate, sulphate, and phosphate of sodium and potassium activated malt amylase proportionately to the concentration of the salt present. The experiments were repeated with sodium and potassium bromid which had been recrystallized several times, positive results being obtained.

Experimental data are submitted in tabular and graphical form.

A handbook of organic analysis, H. T. Clarke (London: Edward Arnold, 1916, 2. ed., pp. VIII+263, figs. 23).—The subject is treated under the topics of preliminary investigation, examination for radicles, separation of organic compounds, quantitative determination of constituent elements, quantitative determination of radicles, and determination of some physical properties.

Classified tables which give the melting or boiling points and common reactions of the more common organic compounds are included. A detailed index of the tables is appended.

A titration flask, F. K. Bezzenberger (Jour. Amer. Chem. Soc., 39 (1917), No. 7, p. 1321, fig. 1).—A titrating flask, to be used in place of the weighing burette, which has been found to possess some advantages in volumetric analyses is described.

The estimation of sulphur in plant material and soil, G. A. Olson (Washington Sta. Bul. 145 (1917), pp. 3–12, figs. 2).—Tabular analytical data relative to the sulphur content of linseed meal, corn, peas, beans, wheat, casein, and gluten obtained by the Parr bomb calorimeter method and compared with the official and Osborne methods show that with certain precautions the bomb method can be successfully used without sacrificing any degree of accuracy for speed. The material should be very finely ground, the silica removed, and the precipitate of barium sulphate well washed.

For the determination of sulphur in plant materials a charge of 0.687 gm. was found to be the most satisfactory. The fusion mixture used was the same as that recommended by Parr, except that sodium nitrate was substituted for potassium nitrate because of the tendency of potassium salts to form double salts with barium. The mixture consisted of boric acid 5, sodium nitrate 3, and magnesium metal 1 parts by weight. The exact amount of sodium peroxid necessary was found to vary with the nature of the material, approximately 16 gm. being necessary for gluten and similar nitrogenous substances, while for starchy substances, such as flour, etc., from 12 to 14 gm. was found sufficient. Shortening of the electrodes about ⅜ in. in the Parr bomb apparatus was found to be more satisfactory with the quantity of material used in the charges. A bomb having a bottom cast in one piece with the shell is considered preferable to one with a removable bottom.

For the determination of sulphur in soil a 2-gm. charge with 1 gm. of fusion mixture was used. In addition 0.5 gm. of sugar was added and from 10 to 12 gm. of sodium peroxid. Some slight precautions were found necessary in the application of the method to sulphur determination in soil. The method as adopted is described in detail.

The successful use of the bomb method for the determination of phosphoric acid is noted, but because of the easier manipulation of other procedures it is not considered desirable.

The influence of the presence of calcium carbonate on the determination of available phosphoric acid in soils by Dyer's method, JATINDRA NATH SEN (*Agr. Jour. India, 12 (1917), No. 2, pp. 258–265*).—Some experimental data on the effect of large amounts of calcium carbonate in soils on the amount of phosphoric acid extracted by treatment with 1 per cent citric acid are submitted and discussed. Other factors which might affect the rate of solution, such as fineness of soil, composition, etc., are also discussed.

The retarding influence of calcium carbonate was considered not to be solely due to neutralization of citric acid, since the fall in the amount of phosphoric acid extracted was maintained up to a calcium carbonate content of 20 per cent when only 7.1 gm. of calcium carbonate was required to neutralize the citric acid used in the extraction. It thus appears that the phosphoric acid is actually absorbed or "fixed" from the solution by the calcium carbonate.

Phosphoric acid determination in phosphate rock, O. C. SEMPLE (*Engin. and Min. Jour., 103 (1917), No. 26, pp. 1140, 1141*).—On account of the difficulty of obtaining molybdic acid the following procedure was devised for the determination of phosphoric acid in phosphate rock:

A 0.5-gm. sample of material containing 20 per cent or more phosphoric acid (or a proportionate sample of material containing less) is treated in a 75-cc. casserole with 10 cc. concentrated nitric acid and stirred until all the material is moistened and effervescence ceases. Twenty cc. of concentrated hydrochloric acid is then added and the material gently boiled on the hot plate. If soluble silicates are present they should be dehydrated by evaporating the material to dryness several times with concentrated hydrochloric acid.

The material is finally taken up with 10 cc. concentrated hydrochloric acid and boiled for a few minutes to dissolve all soluble salts. Boiling water is then added and the material allowed to set until the residue settles, after which the bulk of the solution is decanted on a filter and the filtrate received in a 300-cc. beaker. The residue in the casserole is again treated with concentrated hydrochloric acid and hot water, and finally transferred to the filter and washed with boiling water until the bulk of the filtrate is about 175 to 200 cc.

Ammonium hydroxid, a little at a time, is then added to the filtrate until the gelatinous precipitate of calcium, iron, and aluminum phosphates begins to form, after which 30 cc. of ammonium hydroxid (specific gravity 0.9) is added and the liquid well stirred. Ten cc. of a saturated solution of citric acid is added and the solution stirred for two minutes. Enough citric acid should be added to insure complete solution of all the precipitated phosphates.

Thirty cc. of magnesium mixture is added and the beaker set aside to allow precipitation. It is indicated that, although complete precipitation has been obtained in 1.5 hours, it is advisable to allow at least 3 hours and to keep the filtrate for 24 hours to be certain that complete precipitation has taken place. After complete precipitation the liquid is decanted, the precipitate finally collected on a filter, and washed with the usual wash solution, consisting of ammonium hydroxid and ammonium nitrate. The filter and precipitate are then placed in a crucible, dried, ignited, and weighed as magnesium pyrophosphate.

Comparative analytical data with the molybdate method indicate the accuracy of the procedure.

Approximate results may be obtained at the time of adding the citric acid, since the amount of acid required is proportionate to the amount of phosphate present. A solution of citric acid standardized against a known sample is added to the solution containing the precipitates until it just clears. Results within from 0.5 to 1 per cent of those obtained by the regular procedure are secured.

For the determination of lime in a complete analysis of phosphate rock the following procedure is proposed: A 0.5-gm. sample is treated in the same manner as in the phosphoric acid determination. The acid is entirely boiled off and the residue dehydrated. Hydrochloric acid is again added and the material heated to dryness. Fifteen cc. of concentrated hydrochloric acid is finally added and the material boiled, after which 50 cc. of boiling water is added and the material filtered and washed.

Since iron can not be separated from the filtrate by the addition of ammonia, because of the precipitation of calcium phosphate, ammonia is added until the precipitate begins to appear, and then hydrochloric acid, drop by drop, until the filtrate is clear again. Two cc. of hydrochloric acid is added in excess, the liquid heated to boiling, and 5 gm. of crystallized oxalic acid added, and, after solution, 40 cc. of boiling saturated solution of ammonium oxalate. After boiling for 30 minutes the precipitate is filtered, washed, ignited, and weighed as CaO, or dissolved in sulphuric acid and titrated with standard permanganate. The presence of the free oxalic acid keeps the iron in solution.

The use of fused quartz and alundum crucibles in place of platinum crucibles in phosphate work was found satisfactory.

Directions for preparing magnesium mixture and the wash solution are included.

Determination of carbonates in limestone and other materials, J. F. BARKER (*New York State Sta. Tech. Bul. 62 (1917), pp. 3–7, fig. 1*).—An apparatus which depends on the principle of the hydrometer and its manipulation are described.

In the apparatus the carbon dioxid is liberated from the material by dilute hydrochloric acid and the weight of the hydrometer decreased by the escaping gas. The rise of the graduated tube above the water thus records the percentage of carbonates from which the carbon dioxid was liberated. The method requires no weighing or computation of results, since the latter are given by direct reading of the graduated scale.

Comparative analytical data with the standard method indicate the accuracy of the proposed procedure. Some notes on details of manipulation, composition of limestone, and application of the method are included.

A rapid method for the determination of water-soluble arsenic in lead arsenate, H. A. SCHOLZ and P. J. WALDSTEIN (*Jour. Indus. and Engin. Chem., 9 (1917), No. 7, pp. 682, 683*).—A procedure similar to that noted by Gray and Christie (E. S. R., 36, p. 715) is described, as follows:

Five-tenths gm. of the dried and pulverized sample or 1 gm. of paste is weighed into a 250-cc. volumetric flask. Two hundred cc. of recently boiled distilled water is added and the mixture vigorously boiled for 3 to 5 minutes, allowed to stand 10 or 15 minutes, cooled, made to volume, and filtered through a dry paper. Two hundred cc. of the clear filtrate is measured into a 500-cc. Erlenmeyer flask, a few crystals of potassium iodid and 7 cc. of concentrated sulphuric acid added, and the liquid then boiled down to about 50 cc. It is then diluted with cold water, made alkaline to methyl orange with sodium hydroxid, acidified with dilute sulphuric acid, and an excess of sodium bicarbonate added. It is then titrated with twentieth-normal iodin solution.

Experimental data submitted indicate closely agreeing or somewhat higher results by the proposed procedure when checked against official methods.

The inadequacy of the ferric basic acetate test for acetates, L. J. Curtman and B. R. Harris (*Jour. Amer. Chem. Soc., 39 (1917), No. 7, pp. 1315–1317*).— Data are reported which show that the ferric basic acetate test is not suf- ficiently sensitive and that it does not furnish a means of roughly estimating the amount of acetate present in a solution.

Gluten, M. Arpin (*Liverpool: Offices of "Milling," 1917, pp. 23, figs. 5*).— This is a translation, together with some notes, by W. Jago of the official French method for the estimation of gluten. Some notes on the interpretation of the results of the analysis of flours are also included.

The determination of pentoses and of glucose by means of Fehling's solu- tion, H. Pellet (*Internat. Sugar Jour., 19 (1917), No. 222, pp. 275, 276*).— The reduction of Fehling's solution by pentoses (arabinose and xylose) and by glutose is discussed.

The importance of treating the sample with Fehling's solution at from 63 to 65° C. and maintaining it at such a temperature for 10 minutes in the de- termination of reducing sugars in impure samples which may not contain either pentoses or glutose is emphasized. In products supposed to contain either pentoses or glutose the heating should be continued for 30 minutes, or else at boiling temperature for 3 or 4 minutes.

It is indicated that "the organic matter of beet molasses behaves much less actively toward Fehling's solution than that contained in cane molasses."

The quantitative estimation of dextrose in muscular tissue, R. Hoagland (*Jour. Biol. Chem., 31 (1917), No. 1, pp. 67–77*).—On account of the reducing action on Fehling's solution, creatinin was found to be an important source of error in the determination of dextrose in muscular tissue. For the removal of creatinin and also as an efficient precipitant for other nitrogenous con- stituents of muscular tissue, an excess of phosphotungstic acid was found to yield excellent results. After considerable preliminary work the following method, which has yielded accurate results, was devised:

One hundred gm. of finely ground muscular tissue previously freed from visible fat and connective tissue is treated in a 600-cc. beaker with 200 cc. of distilled water, gradually heated to boiling, and boiled for a few minutes. During the extractions the contents of the beaker must be frequently stirred. After boiling, the insoluble material is allowed to settle and the clear liquid decanted on to the previously prepared asbestos filter in a 4-in. funnel. Fil- tration is carried on by the aid of suction. The residue is again extracted with 150 cc. of hot distilled water as above. The operation is repeated and the residue finally transferred to the filter, washed with hot water, and filtered as dry as possible.

The contents of the filter flask are transferred to an 800-cc. beaker and con- centrated on the steam bath to a volume of about 25 to 30 cc. The concen- trated liquid is then transferred to a 100-cc. volumetric flask, but the volume should not be allowed to exceed 60 to 70 cc. It is cooled to room temperature, from 25 to 30 gm. of phosphotungstic acid dissolved in about 25 cc. of water added, shaken thoroughly, and let stand for a short time. The solution is then made to volume, shaken, and either filtered or centrifugalized to remove the solid matter. The use of the centrifuge is preferable. A portion of the fil- trate is tested for complete precipitation by the addition of dried phospho- tungstic acid. If an appreciable precipitate forms, an aliquot portion of the filtrate should be taken, treated with an excess of dry phosphotungstic acid, made to volume, filtered, and the filtrate tested for complete precipitation.

When the precipitation is complete sufficient dry potassium chlorid is added to precipitate the excess of phosphotungstic acid. The potassium phosphotungstate is filtered off and the filtrate tested for the presence of creatinin. When an appreciable excess of phosphotungstic acid has been used for clarification not more than a trace of creatinin should be found. The sugar is then determined in aliquot portions of 25 cc. of the filtrate by Allihn's method and the reduced copper by Low's iodid method.

In view of the reported increased formation of dextrose in muscular tissue during grinding for analysis, it is suggested that when the dextrose content of the sample is to be determined immediately after the death of the animal the weighed sample be cut into several pieces, plunged into boiling water, and the boiling continued for from five to ten minutes. The clear liquid should then be decanted, the residue ground in a meat grinder, and the extraction carried out as usual.

Determination of sugar in hay and turnips, R. K. KRISTENSEN (*Tidsskr. Planteavl, 23 (1916), No. 5, pp. 757–777*).—Continuing previous work (E. S. R., 36, p. 807), it has been found that either water or alcohol can be satisfactorily used for extraction of the sugar in the materials. For cruciferous plants alcohol extracts have been found to yield the most reliable results. Basic lead acetate could not be used for clarifying the solutions, but mercuric nitrate was entirely satisfactory, and its use is recommended. The reduction of the precipitated cuprous oxid to metallic copper is considered not to be necessary unless the solution has not been clarified by some defecating agent.

Determination of the alkalinity and phosphoric acid content of foodstuffs, I. M. KOLTHOFF (*Chem. Weekbl., 14 (1917), No. 24, pp. 547–558*).—This is a discussion of the comparative merits of the author's method (E. S. R., 36, p. 204) and the method of Pfyl,[1] which depends on precipitating the phosphates as tricalcium phosphate with calcium chlorid and titrating the liberated hydrochloric acid with standard alkali, using phenolphthalein as an indicator, after converting the phosphates into primary phosphates. Some comparative analytical data obtained in the examination of pure solutions and the ash of bread, pepper, and milk powder by the above methods and the procedure of Lorenz (E. S. R., 13, p. 14) are submitted.

It is concluded in general that the method of Pfyl does not possess any advantages over the method previously proposed by the author.

Specifications and directions for testing milk and cream for butter fat, O. F. HUNZIKER (*Jour. Dairy Sci., 1 (1917), No. 1, pp. 38–44*).—This is a report of the data on official methods of testing milk and cream for milk fat submitted at the Official Dairy Instructors' Association meeting held at Springfield, Mass., October 16 and 17, 1916 (E. S. R., 35, p. 799).

The Shrewsbury and Knapp process for the estimation of coconut oil, G. D. ELSDON and C. R. BAGSHAWE (*Analyst, 42 (1917), No. 492, pp. 72–83, figs. 2*).—The authors have studied the method previously noted (E. S. R., 24, p. 515) and have found that the most suitable strength of alcohol to use is of specific gravity 0.92 at 15.5° C. With alcohol of this strength concordant results could be obtained with mixtures of coconut oil and butter and coconut oil and margarin containing up to about 60 to 65 per cent coconut oil. With mixtures containing greater percentages of coconut oil the results obtained were not so satisfactory. Where the samples contained 70 per cent or more of coconut oil, alcohol of specific gravity 0.91 was found to yield satisfactory results.

---

[1] Arb. K. Gsndhtsamt., 47 (1914), No. 1, pp. 1–44.

Washing the fatty acids once with 50 cc. of cold water was found to be sufficient.

It is indicated that the filtration should be carried out as nearly as possible at 15.5°. Cooling the alcoholic solution to about 14° and violently shaking before bringing to the final temperature of 15.5° has been found to yield more concordant results.

The modified procedure is described in detail and experimental data obtained in the examination of mixtures containing coconut oil submitted.

Observations and experiments on the preparation of tea, J. J. B. Deuss (*Dept. Landb., Nijv. en Handel* [*Dutch East Indies*], *Meded. Proefstat. Thee, No. 52 (1917), pp. 34, pl. 1*).—This pamphlet discusses the withering and fermentation of tea and gives results of some experiments on artificial and natural drying of tea. The data are submitted in tabular and graphical form.

METEOROLOGY.

Forecasting the seasons, A. McAdie (*Sci. Amer. Sup., 84 (1917), No. 2169, pp. 50, 51, figs. 2*).—This article briefly discusses the so-called Réseau Mondial, or world net, in its relation to the forecasting of seasonal conditions on the basis of the position of infrabars and hyperbars. It is shown that the survey thus provided makes possible certain important deductions regarding the control of seasonal conditions by the large pressure areas. The article also deals with the relation of sun spots, volcanic eruptions, and heavy cannonading to weather changes.

It is stated that " we may dismiss the question of the effect of war in making unseasonable weather; but we can not disregard the rather more important question—the effect of an abnormal season upon the operations of man, including war. An unseasonable continuance of south and east winds over central Europe due to a temporary displacement of the continental infrabar may cause deficient rainfall if not drought during the growing period and so affect the harvests."

Climatological data for the United States by sections (*U. S. Dept. Agr., Weather Bur. Climat. Data, 4 (1917), Nos. 3, pp. 250, pls. 3, figs. 8; 4, pp. 217, pls. 3, figs. 3*).—These numbers contain brief summaries and detailed tabular statements of climatological data for each State for March and April, 1917, respectively.

Meteorological observations at the Massachusetts Agricultural Experiment Station, J. E. Ostrander and W. P. Saunders (*Massachusetts Sta. Met. Buls. 341–342 (1917), pp. 4 each*).—Summaries of observations at Amherst, Mass., on pressure, temperature, humidity, precipitation, wind, sunshine, cloudiness, and casual phenomena during May and June, 1917, are presented. The data are briefly discussed in general notes on the weather of each month.

The meteorology of Brazil, C. M. Delgado de Carvalho (*Météorologie du Brésil. London: John Bale, Sons, & Danielsson, Ltd., 1917, pp. XIX+528, pls. 12, figs. 34; rev. in Scot. Geogr. Mag., 33 (1917), No. 7, pp. 315–325*).—This is in the main a compilation of the principal things that have been published about the climates of Brazil, with numerous references to sources of information. It includes sections of special interest from the standpoint of agricultural meteorology, as, for example, droughts and measures taken to mitigate them; frost; and the weather conditions prevailing in the regions especially adapted to coffee, cacao, and sugar cane.

Three groups of climates are recognized, "(1) equatorial and subequatorial climates, which include those of the region extending to the latitude of the lower São Francisco, about 11° S.; (2) tropical and subtropical climates, embracing the greater part of the remaining area within the Tropic of Capricorn; and (3) temperate climates—that is, practically those of the four southern States of Brazil, beginning on the coast with Santos, just outside of the Tropic, but extending in the higher interior 2 or 3 degrees north of that line. These groups are then subdivided into regions in accordance with the rainfall and humidity, altitude, and situation with respect to the ocean, and under each of these the climates of minor regions are studied with reference to selected typical stations. The first group is divided into the superhumid or Amazonian type, and the semiarid or northeast Brazilian type; the second, into the semihumid type of the middle latitudes, and the semihumid altitude type."

It is stated that droughts are more often due to irregular and badly distributed rainfall than to actual deficiency. One of the peculiarities of farming in the drier areas of northeastern Brazil is the use of artificial reservoirs (açudes) "dotted over the surface, not for the supply of irrigation water to be led to adjacent fields, but merely to allow of the marginal tracts of silt exposed after floods being cultivated during the dry season. The topography of large parts of this region is such that the lowering of the water surface in one of these reservoirs by the evaporation of 5 ft. in depth of water is enough to expose immense tracts of cultivable ooze."

The weather conditions, especially distribution of the rainfall, of the plateau of São Paulo are peculiarly suited to the growth of coffee. The fact that Brazilian coffee has suffered so little comparatively from diseases is attributable to the favorable weather conditions.

As regards cacao, humidity is a more important climatic requirement than temperature, since this plant is especially susceptible to injury from drought.

It is noted that among the essential climatic requirements for sugar cane is an abundance of rain. In the Campos region, where sugar cane is principally grown, there is sufficient rainfall during two or three months to make conditions exceptionally favorable for the growth of this crop. There are, however, occasional dry years, which are seriously injurious unless irrigation is freely practiced. The irregularity of the precipitation in this region is shown by the fact that during the 20 years, 1888 to 1907, the total annual rainfall varied from 8 to 95 in.

Frosts are very irregular in occurrence and distribution and do not form a constant phenomenon at any given place.

A classified bibliography is given.

The rainfall régime of Indo China, G. LE CADET (*Bul. Écon. Indochine, n. ser., 20 (1917), No. 123, pp. 1–50, pls. 4*).—Tables and charts are given which show the mean rainfall and number of rain days per month and per year, as well as the extremes of such data, at stations well distributed throughout the country, for periods varying from five to ten years. The characteristic features of the rainfall of the region as shown by the data are discussed, as well as certain features of the relation of the amount and distribution of rainfall to plant growth.

The average annual rainfall shown by the data reported appears to be about 1,800 mm., varying widely, however, in different years and localities. The number of rain days averages over 100. Attention is called especially to the greater plant response to freshly fallen rain due to its higher radioactivity.

Dissolved oxygen in rain water, E. H. RICHARDS (*Jour. Agr. Sci. [England], 8 (1917), No. 3, pp. 331–337, figs. 2*).—Reference is made to the importance of dissolved oxygen in rain water as one of the chief factors controlling bacterial activity in soil, particularly in relation to the decomposition of organic matter. Previous investigations on the subject are briefly reviewed, and the results of a year's observations at Rothamsted on the dissolved oxygen content of rainfall are reported and discussed, with descriptions of the apparatus and methods used.

The results show that rain water is very nearly saturated with oxygen when the temperature of collection is below 15° C., but is always below saturation, occasionally as much as 25 per cent, when the temperature is above 15°.

The coefficient of correlation, W. G. Reed (*Quart. Pubs. Amer. Statis. Assoc., n. ser., 15 (1917), No. 118, pp. 670–684, figs. 4*).—The limitations and applicability of the coefficient of correlation as a measure of relationships, as, for example, between July rainfall and yield of corn in Ohio, are discussed.

"The coefficient of correlation is obtained by applying the least square adjustment to all the material and is, therefore, the straight line of closest fit. If the relationship is not that of a straight line, it is obvious that the straight line of closest fit is not a good measure of the relationhip and that some other measure (e. g., the correlation ratio) must be used. Therefore, the coefficient of correlation should never be used to show relationship until after the phenomena have been investigated, at least far enough to show whether a straight line satisfies the relationship as well as any other curve."

The method of procedure to be followed in applying the method is explained in some detail, and a bibliography of the subject is given.

SOILS—FERTILIZERS.

Soil survey of Barbour County, Ala., H. C. Smith, N. E. Bell, and J. F. Stroud (*U. S. Dept. Agr., Adv. Sheets Field Oper. Bur. Soils, 1914, pp. 50, fig. 1, map 1*).—This survey, made in cooperation with the State of Alabama, deals with the soils of an area of 579,840 acres in southeastern Alabama, the topography of which ranges from hilly and broken to nearly level. The drainage is well developed.

The area is included in the coastal plain province, and the soils are classed as upland, stream terrace, and bottom-land soils. Including meadow, 23 soil types of 13 series are mapped, of which the Ruston sandy loam, Norfolk sand, and Ruston gravelly sandy loam cover 21.3, 14.3, and 10 per cent of the area, respectively.

Soil survey of Chickasaw County, Miss., E. M. Jones, C. S. Waldrop, and H. H. Bennett (*U. S. Dept. Agr., Adv. Sheets Field Oper. Bur. Soils, 1915, pp. 53, fig. 1, map 1*).—This survey, made in cooperation with the State of Mississippi, deals with the soils of an area of 320,640 acres in northeastern Mississippi, the topography of which ranges from level or undulating to rolling or hilly. Except in the Flatwoods section the drainage system of the county is well developed.

The upland soils derived from coastal plain deposits cover over three-fourths of the area. The alluvial soils of the overflowed stream bottoms consist mainly of silt and clay. Including chalk and rough gullied land, 24 soil types of 14 series are mapped, of which the Lufkin silt loam, Oktibbeha clay, Ruston fine sandy loam, and Lufkin clay cover 9.6, 9, 8.6, and 8.1 per cent of the area, respectively.

Soil survey of Anson County, N. C., E. S. Vanatta and F. N. McDowell (*U. S. Dept. Agr., Adv. Sheets Field Oper. Bur. Soils, 1915, pp. 65, pls. 7, figs. 2, map 1*).—This survey, made in cooperation with the North Carolina Department of Agriculture, deals with the soils of an area of 344,960 acres in central southern North Carolina, which lies on the boundary between the Coastal Plain and the Piedmont Plateau provinces. The topography is undulating to hilly.

"The county is thoroughly dissected by streams, and there are no large upland areas without natural drainage outlets. While there are many flat areas and depressions, in both the uplands and bottoms, which are naturally poorly drained, there is a much larger area from which the water flows off so rapidly as to cause severe erosion."

The soils of the county are of residual, sedimentary, and alluvial origin. Twenty-eight soil types of 13 series are mapped, of which the Georgeville silt loam and the Cecil gravelly loam cover 11.2 and 10.5 per cent of the area, respectively.

Analyses of soils of the Belgian Kongo by the physiological method, F. Smeyers (*Bul. Agr. Congo Belge, 7 (1916), No. 3–4, pp. 268–284, figs. 13*).—Pot experiments are reported with oats, white mustard, and barley to determine the fertility requirements of seven typical soils of the lower Belgian Kongo, including black, dry, and tenacious lowland soil, fine-grained sandy soil, calcareous prairie soil, alluvial clay soil, brown clay forest soil, upland soil with lateritic subsoil, and upland sandy soil. The surface soils were tested to a depth of about 30 cm. (11.81 in.). Fertilizer treatment consisted of complete fertilization and of complete fertilization without nitrogen, phosphoric acid, potash, and lime, respectively.

The results indicate that the soils of the lower Kongo are generally deficient in nitrogen, this being the limiting factor. The addition of the other fertilizing elements without nitrogen had no appreciable effect on the vegetation. The fine-grained sandy soil and the upland sandy soil were the only soils tested showing a notable deficiency in phosphoric acid. while the upland sandy and brown clay forest soils were the only soils not somewhat deficient in potash. The fine-grained sandy soil was the only soil seriously deficient in lime.

The wheat soils of Alexandria division, Cape Province, C. F. Juritz (*So. African Jour. Sci., 13 (1917), No. 6, pp. 211–237*).—Mechanical and chemical analyses of 10 cultivated and 10 virgin soils are reported and compared with similar analyses of wheat soils in the United States and England. Deterioration was observed for some years in the crops from these soils, especially wheat.

"Mechanical analysis showed the soils to range in physical character from medium sands to fine sandy loams, the proportions of very fine sand, silt, and clay together varying between 16 and 63 per cent, while pebbles, gravel, and coarse sand were practically absent. . . . The causes of inadequate production, therefore, seem to be (1) the rather sandy character of some of the soils, conjoined with their inherent poverty in plant-food constituents; (2) the removal of some of those constituents by continuous cropping without manure; and (3) the further losses caused by the surface soil suffering depletion in respect of silt and clay. The moisture conditions of the soil have not been investigated. Out of the 10 localities investigated only one is not in immediate need of manuring of any kind, in order to fit it for wheat production. Eight require manuring with nitrogen, five need potash fertilizers, and six need fertilizing with phosphates."

Some soils of the southern island of New Zealand with special reference to their lime requirements, L. J. Wild (*Jour. Agr. Sci. [England], 8 (1917), No. 2, pp. 154–177, figs. 2*).—Studies of the lime requirements of certain New Zealand soils, including so-called shingly inland soils, deep loams underlain by deep clay, and alluvial soils resting on gravel and in river beds, using the Hutchinson-MacLennan method (E. S. R., 33, p. 622), are reported.

It was found that "the Hutchinson-MacLennan method for determining the lime requirements of soils, when practiced under suitable standard conditions. gives more reliable indications than are obtainable by the ordinary methods of chemical analysis. The method gives indications which appear to be uniformly in excess of the actual requirement of the soil for lime as judged by economic standards; hence a correcting value seems advisable. The correcting value for the soils of Canterbury Plains is about 0.1 per cent. The greater acidity and higher lime requirement of soils of the Southland Plains appears to be due to a combination of lack of natural underdrainage and high rainfall, which prevents aeration and oxidation of organic matter, so that 'sour' humus accumulates in the soil."

Causes of acidity of soils which are acid through exchange of ions, H. KAPPEN (*Landw. Vers. Stat., 89 (1916), pp. 39–80; abs. in Jour. Chem. Soc. [London], 110 (1916), No. 650, I, p. 876; Chem. Abs., 11 (1917), No. 8, p. 1008).—* Experiments with two pine-forest soils and a soil on which the vegetation consisted of a few bilberry bushes are reported.

The forest soils, which were covered with a layer of humus from 2 to 3 cm. (0.79 to 1.18 in.) deep, showed considerable activity when treated with a normal solution of potassium chlorid, while the third soil failed to react. The latent activity of the forest soils is attributed to the action of humic acids on the mineral soil and the production of aluminum and iron salts. It is shown that the true acidity of humus extracts is approximately the same as that of acetic acid of the same strength, and that latent acidity can be produced by treating mineral soils with raw humus. The same result was obtained with only partially humified vegetable substances. It is also thought possible that latent acidity can arise from the production of soluble aluminum and iron compounds in the humus itself and the penetration of the soluble salts into the mineral soil below the humus.

Movement and distribution of moisture in the soil, F. S. HARRIS and H. W. TURPIN (*U. S. Dept. Agr., Jour. Agr. Research, 10 (1917), No. 3, pp. 113–155, figs. 31*).—Field and laboratory soil moisture experiments conducted at the Utah Experiment Station under irrigation and dry-farming conditions, and representing several thousand moisture determinations, are reported. The field studies included the effect of fallow, kind of crop, manure, irrigation water, surface mulches, cultural methods, and seasonal conditions on the movement and distribution of soil moisture. The laboratory studies included the effect of the initial percentage of moisture, gravity, soil type, source of supply, etc.

In field soils the moisture content of the fallow soils averaged greater than that of the cropped soils. Unmanured irrigated land showed less difference in moisture between cropped and fallow than did the manured. Irrigation influenced the top feet of the cropped plats proportionately more than the fallow, but water did not appear to penetrate the fallow plats below 7 ft. as readily as it did the cropped ones.

Under dry-farming conditions the difference in moisture between cropped and fallow plats was not noticeable until after June 16. Cropped plats showed more fluctuation than fallow ones. Wheat, corn, potatoes, and peas drew most of their moisture from the first 4 ft. in depth. The wheat land contained less moisture in the fall than the other cropped soils, with corn following.

The increase in moisture due to applications of from 5 to 7.5 in. of irrigation water was felt to depths of 10 ft. in 24 hours, although most of the increase was in the first 4 ft.

The effect of mulches in preventing moisture loss under both irrigation and dry farming was noticeable several feet below the surface of the ground, but the surface foot showed the greatest benefit from mulches. A straw mulch proved considerably better than a 2-in. soil mulch. Mulches on irrigated plats appeared to influence the moisture content of the soil to greater depths than did those under dry-land conditions. A dry-farm plat kept free from weeds in

1916 but not mulched lost very little more water than one mulched 2 in. deep. A 6-in. cultivation on spring-plowed and a 2-in. cultivation on fall-plowed dry-farm land seemed to conserve the moisture best.

Subsoiling 15 in. deep had little influence on the moisture; spring disking was a rather distinct benefit. Spring plowing under dry-farming conditions at Nephi conserved moisture better than fall plowing, this difference in favor of spring plowing being shown more below the first foot than in the first foot, and more in the summer and fall than in the spring.

A precipitation as small as 0.1 in. under dry-farming conditions could not be detected in moisture determinations soon after, but when as much as 0.5 in. fell within a short time an increase in moisture was noticed to a depth of 6 ft.

"When freely supplied with water, a soil with a high initial percentage of moisture will come to a moisture equilibrium sooner than a drier one, but if given time the drier soil will absorb a greater quantity through a long distance either upward or downward than will the wet one. The rate of moisture penetration in the first 10 days was nearly twice as great with initial percentages above 15 as with 5 or below, and nearly twice as rapid after a 15-in. irrigation as after a 5-in. one. Under the most favorable conditions 7 ft. was influenced in 10 days. Moisture movement from soils of optimum moisture content into soils of differing initial percentages varied to an extent inversely as the initial content of the dry soil. At the end of six weeks, however, the amount of water actually in the soils still varied directly as the initial percentage. The higher the percentage of moisture in the soil supplying the water to a dry soil, the more rapidly and farther from the source of water did the moisture move. Even when the source of water was an unsaturated soil, greater and faster movement took place when the water was moving downward than upward. When the quantity of soil yielding the water was so small as to make the total moisture content of both moist and dry soils very low if equally distributed, the effect of gravity was not great.

"Moisture from a nearly saturated soil moved a greater distance into loam than into sand in 139 days and into sand farther than into clay. The clay, however, contained more moisture in the layer of soil next the water supply than the others, and sand contained by far the least. Sand, with 7.77 per cent of moisture, gave up its moisture to loam much more readily than did loam with 31.09 or clay with 24.62 per cent of moisture. The rate of rise of moisture from soils of varying fineness when used either as water sources or water absorbers varied inversely with the fineness. Water rose to a height of over 30 in. in a loam soil from a moist sand in 94 days, while from a moist clay it rose little more than 6 in. in this length of time. In all soils the most rapid rise of the water was during the period soon after being placed in contact with the water. Although the rise of the moisture was more rapid in the sand and loam than in the clay, the rise continued steady longer in the clay than in the others."

Adsorption by soils, J. E. Harris (Jour. Phys. Chem., 21 (1917), No. 6, pp. 454–473).—Further experiments at the Michigan Experiment Station on the subject (E. S. R., 31, p. 814), using uniform samples of sandy loam soil, are reported. The purpose was to secure additional evidence that the cause of soil acidity is due to colloidal adsorption or to the presence of true acids, and to secure data on the action of fertilizer salts.

It was found that "when a soil or kaolin is treated with salt solutions of varying concentrations the quantities of the cation adsorbed follow very closely the adsorption isotherm represented by the equation $x/m = ac^{1/n}$, indicating that the action is one of adsorption and not of double decomposition.

"When the soil was treated with different salt solutions it was found that the number of equivalents of the different cations adsorbed was not the same. The cations with reference to their tendency for being adsorbed occurred in the order: Al, K, Ca, Mn, Mg, and Na. The numbers for the ions Ca, Mn, and Mg were very nearly the same. . . . The metals, with the exception of the potassium occur in the order of their valence and . . . metals of the same valence give practically the same values.

"It was found that a soil that had adsorbed large quantities of potassium would give part of this up when treated with various salt solutions. In the case of the solutions tried it was found that, with reference to their ability to set free adsorbed potassium, the salts occurred in the following order: $AlCl_3$, NH_4Cl, $MnCl_2$, $CaCl_2$, $CaSO_4$, $MgCl_2$, NaCl, $CaCO_3$.

"When the soil was treated with a mixture of salts it was found that the amount of each ion adsorbed was cut down by the presence of the other. The total number of equivalents adsorbed from the mixture was greater, however, than from either of the salts alone."

Results of soil fertility studies, C. B. WILLIAMS (*North Carolina Sta. Rpt. 1916, pp. 14–16*).—Chemical and petrographic studies of the soils of North Carolina have shown that "wide variations in the total amount of the elements of plant food ... . exist between the soils of the Appalachian Mountains, Piedmont plateau, and Atlantic coastal plain. The soils of the first physiographic province are better supplied with phosphoric acid, potash, and lime than are those of the other two provinces. . . . Those of the Piedmont plateau are, as a rule, amply supplied with potash and lime and with phosphoric acid in rather large amounts in some cases. On the other hand, the soils of the coastal plain south of Albemarle Sound are markedly deficient in all essential elements of plant growth. Nitrogen is usually low in a majority of the soils of all three sections of the State."

Petrographic studies of these soils correlate markedly with the chemical studies. Topography plays an important part in their chemical composition. Soils of the mountains are formed from the same or similar rock as are those of the Piedmont section, but in the mountains the soil mantle is not so well defined, consequently there are more of the minerals found in the parent rock when the superficial covering has been removed. The coastal plain soils are markedly deficient in minerals except quartz.

In coordinating these studies with the field tests, using various crops as indicators for measuring the relative densities of the soil solution, close relationships appear to exist between the chemical and mineral composition of the soils of each province and their requirements for plant nutrients. Nitrogen is either the first or second element required by all the soils under experiment.

Field tests with four distinct types of soil in the mountain sections, namely, Porter's clay, Porter's loam, Toxaway silty loam, and Toxaway loam, show that with all four types "phosphoric acid is needed first, and potash shows no gain with different crops, except where complete fertilizer is used and large crops produced. Lime alone shows gains on leguminous crops, and when used with complete fertilizer a gain is made. On Porter's clay and Porter's loam nitrogen is second in importance to phosphoric acid, and has to be supplied to produce good crops. Toxaway loam and Toxaway silty loam need nitrogen for best results, but not so much as the upland mountain soils to produce remunerative crops."

Field tests of Piedmont soils, Cecil clay near Charlotte, Cecil clay loam near Statesville, and Cecil sandy loam near Gastonia, all show phosphoric acid to be the limiting constituent of plant food, with nitrogen second. Very little benefit is derived from potash, except where used in a complete fertilizer. The tests on the Iredell loam near Charlotte show that nitrogen is the first element of plant food needed, with potash and lime next. Although a complete fertilizer with lime gives best returns where phosphoric acid alone is used, no increase is secured. Alamance silt loam near Monroe, Durham sandy loam near Oxford, and Norfolk coarse sand near Hoffman all show nitrogen to be the most needed element of plant food, with phosphoric acid and potash, giving good yields when used with phosphoric acid and nitrogen. For large crops a good supply of all of the plant food constituents with lime is needed, as well as an increased supply of vegetable matter. On the Cecil clay soils potash either gives no gain or depresses the yields. On other phases of the Cecil series of soils experiments show that nitrogen is the chief limiting element of plant food for large yields of crops, with additions of phosphoric acid needed for best crops. Potash is of least importance.

Field tests with coastal plain soils show that "with the exception of muck, nitrogen is the limiting element of plant food, . . . with potash and phosphoric acid needed to produce good gains in crop yields. The results on Norfolk sandy loam at Elizabeth City have shown that phosphoric acid comes before potash in importance. . . . On the muck soil, lime seems to be of first importance, [followed in order by] . . . phosphoric acid, potash, and nitrogen. . . . Nitrogen, potash, and phosphoric acid give best returns when used in connection with lime. Norfolk sand at Greenville gives evidence of needing humus-forming material before any fertilizer can be used with profit. With peaty soils, the addition of potash and phosphoric acid seems to have a depressing effect so far when used alone or in combinations without lime."

Thirty-five years' results with fertilizers, F. D. GARDNER, C. F. NOLL, and P. S. BAKER (*Pennsylvania Sta. Bul. 146 (1917), pp. 3-29, figs. 11*).—This is a summary of the results of experiments begun in 1881 and previously noted (E. S. R., 34, p. 128) on the use of commercial fertilizers, barnyard manure, lime and land plaster in a rotation of corn, oats, wheat, and mixed clover and timothy grown on residual limestone soil varying from clay to silt loam in character.

It was found that in the absence of manure or fertilizers of any kind the fertility of this soil showed a marked decline. The average yield of all crops in the rotation for all of the untreated plats during the last five years was only 61 per cent as much as the yield for the same plats and crops during the first five years. The reduction in yield was most pronounced in case of hay and corn. Wheat started with a comparatively low yield and showed the smallest decline in yield. The average yield of both wheat and wheat straw during the last five years equaled 94 per cent of the yield during the first five years.

"Phosphoric acid is the limiting factor in crop production on this soil. The average yield on the plats treated with phosphoric acid alone is 18 per cent more than the average of the check plats and 41 per cent more than the average of check plats which are nearest to the phosphoric acid treated plat. Ground bone as a source of phosphoric acid appears to be slightly more efficient than dissolved bone black."

Potash alone had no appreciable effect on the yield of crops, but potash applied with phosphoric acid gave a very marked increase in yield over phosphoric acid alone, and very materially increased the profits on the fertilizer applied. The use of 100 lbs. of muriate of potash per acre in alternate years is believed to be sufficient to meet the needs for the crops grown on this soil. Potash and phosphoric acid in combination proved to be the most profitable mixture used. This combination in this rotation, in which clover occurs once every four years, practically maintained the fertility of the soil for a period of 35 years.

Nitrogen alone and a combination of nitrogen and potash had no appreciable effect on these crops. Nitrogen in addition to phosphoric acid and potash produced a considerable increase in yield of crops. Of the three forms of nitrogen, sodium nitrate gave a larger average increase in crops than either dried blood or ammonium sulphate. During the first ten years of the experiment, ammonium sulphate was superior to either sodium nitrate or dried blood, but later the yields declined and crops began to fail on the ammonium sulphate plats.

None of the plats used in this comparison of sources of nitrogen have been limed since the experiment was begun. " On the plats where the heaviest applications of sulphate of ammonia have been made there are large areas where all crops fail. This we believe is due to the acidity of the soil, especially since in pot cultures, when soil from these most acid plats was limed, the yields of clover were excellent. . . . The nitrate of soda plats are least acid, and the crop yields are probably not reduced by a lack of lime. On some of the dried blood plats the acidity has become too great for a good growth of clover though other crops do not show signs of injury."

Complete commercial fertilizers, except where ammonium sulphate was used, and barnyard manure were about equally efficient in maintaining the fertility of the soil. The heavier applications of each caused the yields during the last five or ten year periods to exceed those of the first five or ten year periods of the experiment.

Manure applied in different amounts showed that there is economy in light applications when used for general farm crops. The money return per ton of manure, when applied at the rate of 6 tons per acre twice in a rotation, was $3.29 as compared with $2.29 per ton when applied at the rate of 10 tons per acre twice in the rotation.

Lime either as slaked lime or as carbonate of lime applied alone in large amounts frequently gave a small increase in yields of crops. Burnt lime alone during a period of 35 years gave an average increase of 701 lbs. of total products per acre in a rotation, as compared with the untreated plats immediately adjacent. Pulverized raw limestone under the same conditions gave an average increase of 1,334 lbs. of total products in a rotation, as compared with untreated plats nearest to the pulverized limestone plats. The larger return from burnt lime was where it was used in conjunction with barnyard manure. In this case there was an increase of 1,001 lbs. of produce per acre in a rotation valued at $6.38. Land plaster or gypsum had no measurable effect on the crops grown and did not prevent the soil from becoming acid.

"For the limestone soils of Pennsylvania it is recommended that manure be applied at the rate of about 6 tons per acre for corn, and supplemented with 200 lbs. per acre of acid phosphate. For oats which follow the corn, no fertilizer will be required. For the wheat which follows oats, 350 lbs. per acre of acid phosphate, 100 lbs. of muriate of potash, and not more than 10 lbs. of nitrogen, preferably in an organic form, is recommended. For the clover following wheat, no fertilizer will be required. On timothy occurring the fifth year in a rotation, a top-dressing of 150 lbs. of acid phosphate, 150 lbs. of nitrate of soda, and 50 lbs. of muriate of potash will give good results."

Injurious effect of farmyard manure on the balance of nitrogen in the soil, A. SABASHNIKOV (SABACHNIKOV) (*Selsk. Khoz. i Læsov.*, *250 (1916)*, *Jan.*, *pp. 5–19; abs. in Internat. Inst. Agr. [Rome], Internat. Rev. Sci. and Pract. Agr.,* *7 (1916), No. 6, pp. 802, 803; Chem. Abs., 11 (1917), No. 9, p. 1242*).—The chief influence of barnyard manure on the balance of nitrogen in the soil is attributed to the organic matter it contains and not to microorganisms, which are considered of secondary importance. The organic matter in the manure (especially undecomposed straw), being a good source of carbon for the soil microorganisms, contributes (1) in an aerobic environment to the assimilation of nitrates, ammonia, amids, and gaseous nitrogen, and their deposition in protein form; and (2) in an anaerobic environment in the presence of nitrate to the assimilation of the latter, and also on the other hand to its denitrification.

The nitrogen in barnyard manure is considered to be chiefly in an organic form and its loss in the gaseous state is thought to be possible without its passing into the nitric state, both in the aerobic and anaerobic environment. The organic matter, contributing to the conversion of the protein nitrogen, indirectly promotes the loss of nitrogen in further decomposition. A local retardation in furrows, etc., of the nitrifying processes is also possible owing to the organic matter, to the presence of which the nitrifying organisms are known to be very sensitive.

As to the question whether barnyard manure supplied to the soil in quantities up to 28 tons per acre reduces nitrification or not, it is thought that a negative conclusion can not be drawn. It is considered possible that the presence of vegetable residues in the soil and the continuous conversion of nitrogen from the soluble form into the organic form or vice versa may cause such heavy losses of nitrogen (although compensated by its assimilation from the air) that the effect of the additional organic matter in the form of barnyard manure is relatively unimportant.

[Manure conservation experiments], C. D. Woons (*Maine Sta. Bul. 260* (*1917*), *pp. 94–99*).—An experiment on the storage of cow, horse, hog, and sheep manure during the winter is reported, in which an account was kept of all feed eaten and the manure was stored in a water-tight platform (which is described) and kept worked by swine to prevent fire fanging. The composition of the mixture of cow, horse, and hog manure as removed from the pit was nitrogen 0.457 per cent, phosphoric acid 0.19, and potash 0.5. The sheep manure contained nitrogen 0.74 per cent, phosphoric acid 0.29, and potash 1.04. "Seventy-nine per cent of the nitrogen, 87 per cent of the phosphoric acid, and 87 per cent of the potash in the feeding stuffs used were found in the sheep manure, and 61 per cent of the nitrogen, 56 per cent of the phosphoric acid, and 67 per cent of the potash in the feed and bedding given the cows and horses were found in the mixed manure."

It is estimated that the sheep and swine manure was worth about $6 and the mixed manure about $3 per cord at the manure pit.

The effect of phosphoric acid upon the decomposition of sugar in the soil, S. Herke (*Kisérlet. Közlem.*, *18* (*1915*), *No. 5–6, pp. 857–886; abs. in Internat. Inst. Agr. [Rome], Internat. Rev. Sci. and Pract. Agr., 7 (1916), No. 5, pp. 645, 646; Jour. Soc. Chem. Indus., 35 (1916), No. 21, p. 1125; Chem. Abs., 11 (1917), No. 10, p. 1511*).—Experiments are reported which showed that the decomposition of sugar in a soil, as indicated by the liberation of carbon dioxid, is influenced by the chemical composition of the soil and by the presence of certain nutritive salts. In a soil to which phosphoric acid was added the sugar decomposed more quickly than in the same soil without the addition of phosphoric acid. The difference between the amounts of carbon dioxid liberated from the treated and untreated soils increased for a certain time and then decreased.

A certain correlation was observed between the effect of the phosphoric acid on the decomposition of the sugar and the increased yield produced by it in fertilizer experiments. Thus, in a soil where the addition of 0.06 gm. of phosphoric acid per kilogram of soil increased the yield of oats and mustard, the same amount of phosphoric acid increased the amount of carbon dioxid liberated in the presence of 2 per cent of dextrose or saccharose. Increasing amounts of phosphoric acid also gradually increased the liberation of the carbon dioxid liberated.

The presence of calcium carbonate and of ammonium sulphate at the rate of 0.05 gm. of nitrogen per kilogram of soil promoted the decomposition of sugar. Small amounts of nitric nitrogen (0.05 gm. of nitrogen, in the form of sodium nitrate, per kilogram) also increased the liberation of carbon dioxid except in a nutritive solution in which 0.1 per cent sodium nitrate exercised an inhibiting effect. Potassium sulphate increased the liberation of carbon dioxid in some soils and decreased it in others.

. These results are taken to indicate that the effect of phosphoric acid is differently influenced by the addition of nitrogenous and potassic compounds according to the nature of the soil, any quantitative variation in one as a rule modifying the action of the other.

The potash question and general farm crops, A. W. BLAIR (*New Jersey Stas. Circ. 67 (1917), pp. 3–7*).—It is stated in this circular that with the exception of the very sandy sections of the State, New Jersey soils contain a fair supply of potash which has been derived from the original rocks and glaciated materials. The greater part of this potash is unavailable and, on the basis of work at the station, the incorporation of organic matter, deep plowing, thorough cultivation, and liming are recommended for setting some of it free.

Potash in New Zealand and other countries, P. G. MORGAN (*Jour. Agr. [New Zeal.], 14 (1917), No. 4, pp. 257–273*).—This article gives general information concerning the present potash situation, possible sources of potash, and methods for rendering potash available to the farmer, with special reference to New Zealand conditions. Some of the natural sources of potash recommended for use by farmers in New Zealand are calcareous clay stones, glauconitic rocks, and calcareous green sandstone.

A discussion concerning the rational use of lime on the farm (*Bul. N. C. Dept. Agr., 38 (1917), No. 1, pp. 22*).—This circular gives information on the selection, purchase, and use of lime for agricultural purposes.

Notes on humus, humogen, and its accessory plant food substances, A. STEAD (*So. African Jour. Sci., 13 (1917), No. 6, pp. 239–250*).—This is a review of the work of others on the soil humus question, special attention being given to the Bottomley bacterized peat process.

The plant food materials in the leaves of forest trees, P. SEREX, JR. (*Jour. Amer. Chem. Soc., 39 (1917), No. 6, pp. 1286–1296*).—Experiments conducted to determine the plant food constituents of the leaves of the chestnut, sugar maple, and white oak at the beginning of their activity in spring and at the end of their growth in the fall are reported.

It was found that " the leaves collected in the spring show a higher content of nitrogen and potash than those collected in the fall from the same trees. The phosphoric acid content varies with the species of tree and also with the section of the tree from which the leaves were obtained. The lowest amount of nitrogen and phosphoric acid occurred in those leaves collected from trees grown upon a clay soil. The highest content of nitrogen, phosphoric acid, and potash occurred in those leaves collected from trees grown upon the Holyoke stony loam and Wethersfield loam. The leaves from the upper branches of the maple and oak have a higher content of nitrogen, phosphoric acid, and potash in the majority of cases than those taken from the lower branches. In the case of the chestnut the reverse appears to be true, the leaves from the lower branches having the larger amount of nitrogen, phosphoric acid, and potash, with some exceptions, than those removed from the upper branches. The estimated theoretical cash value of a ton of leaves calculated upon a 20 per cent moisture basis varies from $3 to $6.50, depending upon the kind of leaves and upon what portion of the tree they were grown. The cost of collecting and handling would probably be greater than the value of the leaves, thus making it inadvisable in most cases for farmers to spend their time in this way."

Fertilizers and industrial wastes, F. W. Brown (*Saturday Even. Post, 189* (1917), No. 48, pp. 121, 122; *Amer. Fert.*, 47 (1917), No. 1, pp. 58, 62, 64, 68).—Attention is called to the loss of nitrogen, potassium, and phosphoric acid compounds in industrial wastes, especially of potash in cement mills and blast-furnace gases.

Analyses of fertilizers (*Bul. N. C. Dept. Agr., Sup., 38* (1917), No. 2, pp. 4).—This bulletin contains the results of actual and guaranteed analysis of 54 samples of fertilizers and fertilizing materials collected for inspection in North Carolina in February, 1917.

Fertilizer analyses (*Bul. N. C. Dept. Agr., 38* (1917), No. 3, pp. 14).—This bulletin contains the results of actual and guaranteed analyses of 268 samples of fertilizers and fertilizing materials collected for inspection in North Carolina during the spring of 1917.

AGRICULTURAL BOTANY.

International catalogue of scientific literature. M—Botany (*Internat. Cat. Sci. Lit.*, 13 (1916), pp. VIII+812).—This volume (E. S. R., 35, p. 29), though listing mainly the literature of 1913, includes some of previous years, going back as far as 1901.

[Some investigations in the department of experimental evolution] (*Carnegie Inst. Washington Year Book*, 15 (1916), pp. 133, 134).—This section of the report of this department includes condensed information on the results of work by J. A. Harris on the correlation between characters of leaves in normal and abnormal bean seedlings, the correlation between homologous parts of a plant, and a table of osmotic pressures based on depression of freezing point; by him with Lawrence on plant sap in relation to environment on the Arizona deserts; and by these with Gortner on expressed vegetable saps as affected in their concentration by continued pressure.

Wild flowers worth knowing, N. Blanchan, adapted by A. D. Dickinson (*Garden City, N. Y.: Doubleday, Page & Co., 1917, pp. XVIII+270, pls. 48, figs. 39*).—This book, adapted from Nature's Garden, a previous work by the author, deals with a number of well-known families of plants. The nomenclature and classification of Gray's New Manual of Botany, seventh edition, are followed throughout.

Fungi from Val d'Aosta, P. A. Saccardo (*Nuovo Giov. Bol. Ital., n. ser., 24* (1917), No. 1, pp. 31-43).—Among a number of fungi collected at various altitudes in Val d'Aosta in 1916 and submitted for examination to the author, he has designated as new species *Clitocybe thuilensis, Exobasidium æquale, Sphæronema oreophilum, Næmosphæra chanousiana, Rhabdospora bernardiana, Cylindrosporium vaccarianum, Sporodesmium fumagineum,* and *Nothodiscus antoniæ,* the last named being considered also as representing a new genus.

Fungi causing discolorations in paper, P. Sée (*Compt. Rend. Acad. Sci. [Paris], 164* (1917), No. 5, pp. 230-232).—Brief descriptions are given of discolorations caused in paper by the development of spores of certain fungi, also an account of culture studies therewith.

On Stigeosporium marattiacearum and the mycorrhiza of the Marattiaceæ, C. West (*Ann. Bot. [London], 31* (1917), No. 121, pp. 77-99, pl. 1, figs. 9).—The author describes a fungus, supposedly a new species and here named *S. marattiacearum,* which forms an endotrophic mycorrhiza with roots of certain genera (Angiopteris, Archangiopteris, Kaulfussia, and Marattia) of Marattiaceæ, giving a discussion of its biology, systematic position, and probable life history. A brief description is also given of a mycorrhizal fungus said to enter into association with roots of Danæa.

The chemical conditions for the development of reproductive organs in yeasts, K. SAITO (*Jour. Col. Sci. Imp. Univ. Tokyo, 39 (1916), Art. 3, pp. 73*).— The author has made a study of the influences bearing upon the production of the organs of reproduction in *Zygosaccharomyces mandshuricus*, *Schizosaccharomyces octosporus*, and *Saccharomyces mandshuricus*. He states that though these resemble other fungi in that reproduction stands in close relation to the quantity and quality of the chemical substances available, reproduction depends also, in case of certain organisms, upon the presence of specific chemical substances. Several such requirements are indicated. Among the significant physical considerations, osmotic activity plays an important rôle in determining concentrations and consequent development of reproductive parts. The factors, both internal and external, are thought to be very numerous, and together to constitute a very complex mechanism.

Microchemical studies in the progressive development of the wheat plant, SOPHIA H. ECKERSON (*Washington Sta. Bul. 139 (1917), pp. 3-21, figs. 13*).— The author states that the progressive chemical changes during the development of the wheat grain are correlated with morphological changes, each definite period of the morphological development being characterized by some chemical difference. The progression of these chemical changes was found to be alike in all varieties tested of both winter and spring wheat.

Summarizing her results, the details of which are given, the author reports that inorganic materials are high in the young plant. The largest amount of potassium nitrate was found, chiefly in the root and stem, just before the formation of the spike, after which it decreased gradually. Free magnesium quickly fell to a minimum during the formation of the aleurone, while free phosphate rose to a maximum during development of the sporogenous tissue, falling to a minimum after the development of the sex cells.

Asparagin is thought to be a very important nutritive substance, and it was found together with fructose in all young growing parts. The occurrence of pectic substances on the stigma is considered especially important in reducing the rate of water absorption by pollen grains. During the period from the fertilization of the egg to the mature grain, there is said to be a stream of nutrient materials for the growing embryo coming to the endosperm from the leaves and glumes. Any excess of sugar was found to condense immediately into starch. Excess of asparagin and amino acids remained as such in the endosperm cells until desiccation of the grain. The nitrogenous compounds in the endosperm just before ripening of the grain, aside from aleurone and protoplasm, are asparagin, arginin, histidin, and some leucin. No glutamin was found.

Protein, which has the physical characteristics of gluten, is said to appear in the storage cells on desiccation of the grain, the amino acids and most of the asparagin disappearing. The formation of the storage protein in wheat is believed to be a condensation process.

The physiological rôle of calcium in vegetable life, THÉRÈSE ROBERT (*Rev. Gén. Sci., 28 (1917), No. 4, pp. 101-108*).—The author discusses the ability of plants to utilize calcium in their economy, as deduced from the examination of a very large number of investigations by various authors, taking up more particularly the relation of calcium to phanerogams, including the distribution of calcium in its various forms in the plant body; its necessity, or at least utility, in relation thereto; its mode of action or rôle as plastic, catalytic, toxic, or antitoxic; and its replacement or substitution by other elements.

The influence of some organic substances on plants, I, G. CIAMICIAN and C. RAVENNA (*Atti R. Accad. Lincei, Rend. Cl. Sci. Fis., Mat. e Nat., 5. ser., 26 (1917), I, No. 1, pp. 3–7*).—This article, which is related to previous work (E. S. R., 36, pp. 329, 432) and is regarded as suggestive of further studies on a larger scale, discusses briefly the effects on plant growth of several organic substances, including mandelic nitrile, nicotin, strychnin, caffein, and morphin.

Quantitative experiments demonstrating the mechanism of the inhibition of growth, J. LOEB (*Proc. Soc. Expt. Biol. and Med., 14 (1917), No. 7, pp. 131, 132*).—The author has studied by a quantitative method the laws of inhibition, several reports regarding which have been noted previously (E. S. R., 34, p. 730; 35, p. 820; 37, pp. 324, 325). Proceeding upon the hypothesis of inhibition of growth by one organ in relation to another by the removal of material necessary for growth, and upon the expectation that if such were the case the total mass of shoots produced by a leaf in a certain time would be approximately the same regardless of their number, he claims to have found that this is true to a surprising degree of exactness. The quantitative data so obtained, as briefly indicated in the statement, are relied upon to furnish the basis of a chemical theory of regeneration.

Studies in permeability.—IV, The action of various organic substances on the permeability of the plant cell, and its bearing on Czapek's theory of the plasma membrane, W. STILES and I. JÖRGENSEN (*Ann. Bot. [London], 31 (1917), No. 121, pp. 47–76, figs. 15*).—The authors have carried forward the series of studies the last noted of which was contributed by Mildred Hind (E. S. R., 36, p. 433). The present contribution relates partly to tests made by the author as bearing upon Czapek's theory of a plasma membrane, earlier (E. S. R., 24, p. 137) and later reports on which are discussed, with a statement of alleged reasons for the rejection of some views held by that author.

The method employed is here described in more detail than in the article previously noted (E. S. R., 35, p. 224), with an account of its supposed advantages over the methods formerly used, such as greater exactness and more general applicability.

It is stated that with each organic substance a higher rate of exosmosis corresponded to a higher concentration of the substance employed. Equimolecular solutions of different substances do not bring about the same exosmosis. The rate of exosmosis produced by a solution is not a function of its surface tension alone. A concentration below which exosmosis of electrolytes could not take place was not found. In the attempt to deduce a mathematical time-rate expression for exosmosis, it was found that the equation expressing the results of actual experiments exactly resembled that expressing theoretical considerations.

The osmotic concentration of the sap of the leaves of mangrove trees, J. A. HARRIS and J. V. LAWRENCE (*Biol. Bul. Mar. Biol. Lab. Woods Hole, 32 (1917), No. 3, pp. 202–211*).—Presenting the results of a series of determinations of the leaf tissue fluids of *Avicennia nitida, Rhizophora mangle,* and *Laguncularia racemosa* on the southern shore of Jamaica and in southern Florida, the authors state that the concentration of these fluids is relatively high throughout, the range as noted lying between the limits of 20 and 50 atmospheres. Avicennia apparently developed a much higher concentration than the other species in the same environment.

The origin of chromoplasts and the mode of formation of xanthophyll and carotin pigments, A. GUILLIERMOND (*Compt. Rend. Acad. Sci. [Paris], 164 (1917), No. 5, pp. 232–235*).—Giving a résumé of related studies to date, the author states that the various forms in which pigments may appear can be arranged under three general heads. These are according as to whether the pigment in question occurs in a diffused or finely granulated state in the mitochondria or the chloroplasts derived from them, as a result of a process of crystallization subsequent to such origin, or in diffused granular or crystalline form in the large chromoplasts resulting from the metamorphosis of the chloroplasts previously formed out of the mitochondria, such mitochondrial origin explaining the elongated early form of the chloroplasts. The formation of vegetable pigments is effected by a process very similar to that which has been recently shown to occur in the cells of animals.

The anthocyanin pigments of plants, MURIEL WHELDALE (*Cambridge: University Press, 1916, pp. X+318).*—The object of this book is to provide a somewhat complete account of the various reports which have been made regarding the anthocyanin pigments as studied along botanical, chemical, and genetical lines. While not claiming that anthocyanins will ever possess great botanical significance, when compared with that of chlorophyll, for example, the author thinks they may develop a wide field for research in connection with problems of inheritance. Owing to the increasing availability of satisfactory methods for the isolation, analysis, and determination of the constitutional formulæ of these pigments on the one hand and Mendelian methods for determining inheritance on the other, the two methods combined furnish a reasonable hope that inheritance phenomena may eventually be expressed in terms of chemical composition and structure.

The eight chapters of the first part deal with the anthocyanins as regards their morphological and histological distribution, their properties and reactions, isolation and constitution, physiological conditions, factors, reactions, and significance. The second part considers the anthocyanins in relation to genetics.

An extensive bibliography is given.

Environmental influences on nectar secretion, L. A. KENOYER (*Iowa Sta. Research Bul. 37 (1916), pp. 219–232, fig. 1).*—The results are given of studies of a number of species of flowers, among them varieties of clovers, alfalfas, dandelions, and lilies, to determine the factors which stimulate or retard the secretion of nectar.

It was found that by increasing humidity, the secretion by the nectaries of water, but not of sugar, was increased. Excessive water supply lessens the sugar surplus, and dilution and washing by rain causes much of the sugar of the nectaries to be lost. The rate of secretion for both sugar and water increases with the temperature up to a certain optimum. Accumulation of sugar in the flower varies inversely as the temperature. The optimum condition for sugar secretion was found to be an alternation of low and high temperatures. Variation of atmospheric pressure has no marked influence on secretion. Sugar excretion is markedly diminished in darkness on account of the limitation of the food reserves of the plant. Water excretion may or may not be limited in this manner, depending on the species. The greatest amount of sugar was found to be secreted under the most favorable conditions for growth and vigor for the plant. Other things being equal, nectar is most abundant early in the blooming season, and the accumulation and secretion of sugar is most pronounced near the time of the opening of the flower.

Environmental influences on nectar secretion, L. A. KENOYER (*Bot. Gaz., 63 (1917), No. 4, pp. 249–265, fig. 1).*—This is essentially the same as the article noted above.

The consequences of precocity in spring vegetation, 1916, O. OPOIX (*Compt. Rend. Acad. Agr. France, 3 (1917), No. 1, pp. 49–52).*—Warm weather during nearly all of the winter and spring of 1915–16 resulted in the production of three periods of blooming in apricot trees, occurring about the middle of the months of January, March, and April. A heavy snow February 25 and continned cold completely arrested growth for the time being, and resulted in a very great reduction of the fruit crop.

Fruit injury during the fumigation of citrus trees, R. S. WOGLUM (*Fruit World Austral.*, *17 (1916), No. 3, pp. 70–72).*—Giving the results of observations on the degrees and phases of fruit pitting after the use of cyanid gas to kill insects on citrus trees, the author holds that the cyanid gas itself is the basic cause of general fruit pitting, other factors being the strength of the gas used, length of exposure, condition of plants treated, and moisture, along with minor or contributing factors.

Mechanical injury, favoring the gas injury, is caused by drawing the tents over the trees, especially when they are wet or when the tent poles are low. Pressures on the growing fruit appear to weaken resistance near such points, as in cases where fruits are pressed together. Trees which have been sprayed with Bordeaux mixture should not be fumigated for about a year after spraying, as leaves and fruit may be dropped as a result of such treatment.

The history and legal phases of the smoke problem, L. JOHNSON (*Metallurg. and Chem. Engin.*, *16 (1917), No. 4, pp. 199–204).*—Dealing very briefly with the history and bearings of smoke-injury problems, the author reviews some phases of the investigation carried out by, or in connection with, the Selby Smelter Commission selected to investigate the questions arising in the Selby smelter smoke zone (E. S. R., 34, p. 716; 35, pp. 133, 243, 244).

It is said to have been found that dust and acid vapors were practically negligible factors in the fume problem so far as vegetation is concerned, any damage actually done being traceable almost wholly to sulphur dioxid. Vegetation can stand on the average, it is said, 50 times the strength of sulphuric acid that it can bear of sulphur in the form of sulphur dioxid, the latter, however, producing little or no injury when the plants are not in leaf. Both crude sulphur and sulphuric acid increased crop yields in most instances, and practically without exception in alkaline soils. When leaf stomata were closed, as in darkness, the plants were very resistant to sulphur dioxid.

Four prominent factors in this connection were light, humidity, temperature, and direction of the wind (where the latter is constant, puffs of wind having but little influence in this connection). Much of the injury previously ascribed to smoke is said to have been due to such factors as fungus diseases.

FIELD CROPS.

The experimental error in field trials and the effect on this error of various methods of sampling, C. MIYAKE (*Ber. Ōhara Inst. Landw. Forsch.*, *1 (1916), No. 1, pp. 111–121, figs. 2).*—The experimental error of field tests with barley and rice on single unit plats, successive unit plats, and scattered unit plats is discussed, and data giving the standard deviation on the plats and the estimated standard deviation are presented in tabular form. The conclusions reached from these data are that the standard deviation decreases with the size of the plat, that it is smaller with the scattered unit plats than with the successive unit plats, and that the scattered unit plat method is superior to the successive unit plat method in point of sampling.

The author found the probable error on a $\frac{1}{40}$-acre plat of barley to be about ±3.3 per cent, and of rice about ±1.8 per cent. He concludes that the probable error in plats of this size is about ±2 per cent as contrasted with the results obtained by Hall and Wood (E. S. R., 26, p. 732), from which they calculated the probable error in field experiments to be approximately ±5 per cent. He attributes this difference to the more intensive cultural methods employed in Japan.

Five methods for sampling a rice crop in the field to estimate the total yield are described and were tested, and the results presented in tabular form. In order to place the results on some basis for comparison, the estimated standard error has been calculated in each case according to the following formula:

$$\omega = \sigma \sqrt{\frac{n}{300}},$$

when n is the total number of plants sampled, σ the real standard error, and 300 a constant. From these results the author concludes that either the "diagonal" or "scattered" method of sampling is superior to the other methods tested.

[Report of field crop work], J. M. SCOTT (*Florida Sta. Rpt. 1916, pp. 23–29*).—Fertilizer tests with Japanese cane, velvet beans, and sweet potatoes, variety tests with cowpeas and velvet beans, and field tests with cotton and sorghum are briefly noted.

The 1915 yield of Japanese cane showed a decrease, as compared with that of 1914, of more than 50 per cent on some plats, while on others the decrease varied from 10 to 20 per cent. In the spring of 1915 land grown continuously with Japanese cane under varying fertilizer treatments since 1908 was plowed and replanted to cane, using the same fertilizers. The results are interpreted as strongly indicating the advisability of replanting Japanese cane every three or four years. The highest yield, 31.9 tons of green forage per acre, was secured from the plats receiving 84 lbs. of muriate of potash and 224 lbs. of acid phosphate. The lowest yield, 18 tons per acre, was obtained from the plat receiving 112 lbs. of dried blood and 224 lbs. of acid phosphate. Applications of ground limestone failed to show any substantial benefit after the first application in 1909.

Fertilizer tests with velvet beans gave the highest average yield, 658.4 lbs. of pods per acre, with an application of 360 lbs. of Thomas slag, while the lowest yield, 583.9 lbs., was secured from a 400-lb. application of acid phosphate. The untreated checks yielded 616 and 642.8 lbs. per acre, respectively.

An application of 112 lbs. of dried blood, 224 lbs. of acid phosphate, 84 lbs. of sulphate of potash, and 2,000 lbs. of ground limestone showed the highest average yield of sweet potatoes, estimated at 269.6 bu. per acre. The lowest yield, estimated at 99.6 bu., was obtained from a plat receiving 112 lbs. of dried blood and 224 lbs. of acid phosphate.

Of the four varieties of cowpeas tested for forage production, Monette S. P. I. No. 1541 was highest with a yield of 1,705.1 lbs. per acre and Brabham second with a yield of 1,577.9 lbs. In seed production Monette S. P. I. No. 1541 yielded 531.7, Brabham 517.3, and S. P. I. No. 27863 258.2 lbs. of seed pods per acre.

Tests with velvet beans included the Yokohama, Osceola, Florida, Chinese, and Wakulla varieties, which yielded 1,893, 1,394.6, 1,320, 1,229.5, and 856 lbs. of pods per acre, respectively.

The average acre yield of seed cotton amounted to 349.5 lbs. per acre. Selection work with cotton is being continued.

The seed heads of Sumac sorghum grown on the station farm amounted to 1,236.25 lbs. per acre green weight and 1,129 lbs. dry weight. The average yields in green and dry forage amounted to 9,512 and 3,037 lbs. per acre, respectively, based on a 2-acre yield.

[Experiments with field crops in Maine], C. D. WOODS (*Maine Sta. Bul. 260 (1917), pp. 102–120*).—Variety and rate-of-seeding tests with oats were continued as previously noted (E. S. R., 35, p. 33), and fertilizer experiments with oats and potatoes reported.

Sixteen varieties of oats were tested at Aroostook farm in 1916, giving an average yield of 61.4 bu. of grain and 3,412 lbs. of straw per acre. Maine 340 was highest, with a yield of 75.6 bu. It also matured from three to six days earlier than Early Pearl and Siberian, which yielded 66.6 and 66 bu. per acre, respectively. The early varieties Kherson and Daubeney, maturing from a week to ten days earlier than the other varieties, yielded only 61.3 and 57.2 bu., respectively.

Eight commercial varieties of oats and ten pure-line selections were tested during 1916 at Highmoor farm. The season is reported as having been very unfavorable for the oat crop. Early Pearl, with a yield of 56.7 bu., was the leading commercial variety tested, while Maine 340, with a yield of 52.7 bu. per acre, was first of the pure-line selections.

In the rate-of-seeding tests with oats the 14-pk. rate again gave the highest yield, 71.8 bu. per acre. The 16- and 20-pk. rates yielded 70.2 and 69.5 bu., respectively, but showed a distinct tendency to lodge.

Fertilizer experiments with oats on the Aroostook farm included a series of plats receiving an application of 500 lbs. of commercial fertilizers each per acre, having 4 per cent nitrogen, 8 per cent available phosphoric acid, and from 0 to 8 per cent potash. Oats were also grown on land seeded to potatoes in 1915 with and without potash. The results indicate that potash is not a limiting factor in oat production in these soils, and that the application of potash the previous year does not affect the oat crop following.

Experiments on the effect of omitting potash fertilization upon the potato crop were continued. with more pronounced effects in favor of potash fertilization than previously observed (E. S. R., 35, p. 34). The average yield for the two years from the plats receiving no potash was estimated to be 111 barrels. and from those plats receiving 8 per cent potash 134 barrels. It is concluded that as little as 45 lbs. of potash per acre will give a profitable increase in the yield of potatoes. at least when grown on sod land, while a profitable yield can be obtained without the use of potash for at least one year.

The comparison of sulphate of ammonia with nitrate of soda as a source of nitrogen for potato fertilization was continued. From the results of three years of experimental work it is concluded that at least two-thirds of the total nitrogen can be supplied in the form of sulphate of ammonia without decreasing the yield. These experiments are to be continued in order to determine the effect of these different substances under different seasonal conditions.

In comparing methods of application of fertilizers to the potato crop it has been concluded that fully as good, if not better. results can be obtained by applying all the fertilizer in the planter. It appeared that up to 1.500 lbs. per acre nothing was gained either by broadcasting before planting or by applying a part at the first cultivation.

Field tests are briefly noted on the use of common salt in fertilizing oats. potatoes, grass, and turnips to liberate the unavailable potash in the soil. Increased yields of turnips were noted. but no benefit was found with the other crops. No appreciable effect of the salt on the soil potash was observed.

Results of breeding experiments, C. B. WILLIAMS (*North Carolina Sta. Rpt. 1916, pp. 16–18*).—Selection and variety tests with cotton, corn, soy beans. and velvet beans are briefly reported.

Cotton Selection No. 29 is deemed the best yielder thus far secured, producing 252 lbs. of seed cotton per acre more in 1915 than the unselected seed and leading in the variety tests at the station farm by 94 lbs. of seed cotton per acre. A uniform strain of cotton was secured at Aberdeen in 1915, which gave a staple 1$\frac{7}{8}$ in. in length and compared favorably in yield with the local short-staple cottons. A strain introduced into Edgecombe County in 1915 produced 158 lbs. of lint per acre more than the prevailing local variety.

Cooperative ear-to-row corn tests resulted in yields estimated to range between 23.1 and 58.7 bu. of shelled corn per acre from selections made the previous fall. The 10 best selections averaged 54.2 bu. while the average yield of all selected seed was 42 bu. per acre.

Mammoth Yellow and Tokyo soy beans are recommended for seed production for the eastern and lower Piedmont sections of the State, while Haberlandt and Wilson are recommended for the upper Piedmont and mountains. Virginia is deemed superior to all varieties tested for hay production in all sections of the State.

Velvet beans have not proved successful in the western portion of the State, while from Wake County eastward the varieties are classed as follows: For hay production, Florida Velvet, One Hundred Day Speckle, Chinese, Wakula, and Yokohama; and for seed production, One Hundred Day Speckle, Wakula, Yokohama, Chinese, and Florida Velvet. One Hundred Day Speckle is deemed best for North Carolina conditions generally.

Daily variation of water and dry matter in the leaves of corn and the sorghums, E. C. MILLER ET AL. (*U. S. Dept. Agr., Jour. Agr. Research, 10 (1917), No. 1, pp. 11–46, pl. 1, figs. 10*).—In connection with studies previously noted (E. S. R., 35, pp. 437, 529), the author has determined the daily variation of the water and dry matter content of the leaves of Pride of Saline corn, Dwarf milo maize, and Blackhull Kafir corn. A knowledge of the variations of the amount of water in the leaves was expected to throw light on the relative ability of these plants to absorb water from the soil and transport it to regions of loss through transpiration, while a study of the variations of dry matter in the leaves was expected to show the relative power of the plants to manufacture food under different climatic conditions. The experiments were conducted during the summers of 1914, 1915, and 1916 at the Garden City substation of the Kansas Experiment Station.

Soil samples for moisture determinations were taken for each foot to a depth of 6 ft. either a few days before or after the experimental work with the leaves. The results of the determinations, together with the wilting coefficient and moisture equivalent for each of the several plats, are reported in tabular form.

Livingston's porous-cup atmometers with a coefficient of 74 were employed to determine hourly evaporation. The atmometers were placed 2 ft. from the ground, connected with burettes so that readings could be made to 0.1 cc., and evaporation in cubic centimeters reported in tabular form for the different periods of leaf sampling for each year of the experiment.

Leaf samples, each with an area of 1 sq. cm., were taken every two hours during an experiment from 30 representative plants of each variety. One leaf was chosen on each plant to furnish all the samples desired for a given experiment. The samples were taken by means of a Ganong leaf punch.

Nine experiments were conducted in 1914, two in 1915, and four in 1916. Four of the 1914 experiments extended through the daylight hours only, all others ranging from 24 to 40 hours in length. The amount of water and dry matter for each square meter of leaf were determined every two hours for a total of 22 days and 10 nights, and the percentage of water calculated on both a wet and dry basis. The data obtained are presented in tabular form, expressed graphically, and the results discussed in some detail.

The following summarized statement shows the variation of the water content of the leaves of the plants studied during the three years 1914–1916:

Variation of the water content of the leaves of corn, Kafir corn, and milo maize, 1914–1916, at Garden City, Kans.

Time of day.	Kind of plant.	Loss.			Gain.			Net gain (+) or loss (−).	
		Number of cases.	Average loss of leaf water per square meter of leaf.	Average percentage of loss based on leaf water at beginning of period.	Number of cases.	Average gain of leaf water per square meter of leaf.	Average percentage of loss based on leaf water at beginning of period.	Per square meter of leaf.	Percentage based on leaf water at beginning of period.
			Gm.	*Per cent.*		*Gm.*	*Per cent.*	*Gm.*	*Per cent.*
7–9 a. m.	Corn	21	4.1	3.5	0	0	0	−4.1	−3.5
	Kafir corn	15	3.3	2.8	1	3.8	3.2	−3.0	−2.5
	Milo maize	18	4.2	4.0	3	1.3	1.3	−3.6	−3.4
9–11 a. m.	Corn	19	4.8	4.2	2	2.5	2.2	−4.1	−3.8
	Kafir corn	16	3.9	3.4	1	1.3	1.0	−3.7	−3.4
	Milo maize	20	2.2	2.1	1	5.2	5.6	−1.9	−1.8
11 a. m.–1 p. m.	Corn	15	3.7	3.4	6	2.9	2.4	−2.5	−2.2
	Kafir corn	14	3.1	2.8	3	4.2	3.6	−2.5	−2.2
	Milo maize	13	1.9	1.9	7	1.7	1.6	−1.1	−1.1
1–3 p. m.	Corn	10	3.1	2.8	10	2.5	2.2	−1.8	−1.6
	Kafir corn	4	2.5	2.1	13	3.1	2.7	+2.0	+1.7
	Milo maize	11	3.3	3.3	10	2.6	2.5	−1.7	−1.6
3–5 p. m.	Corn	4	2.7	2.3	17	5.7	4.9	+4.6	+4.0
	Kafir corn	0	0	0	17	4.3	3.6	+4.3	+3.6
	Milo maize	4	4.1	4.2	17	3.9	3.7	+3.2	+3.0

The average rate of increase of dry matter for each square meter of leaf for corn, Kafir corn, and milo maize during each two-hour period of the day has been estimated as follows:

Average rate of increase of dry matter per square meter of leaf.

Kind of plant.	7–9 a. m.	9–11 a. m.	11 a. m.–1 p. m.	1–3 p. m.	3–5 p. m.
	Gm.	*Gm.*	*Gm.*	*Gm.*	*Gm.*
Corn	2.2	1.1	0.8	0.7	0.8
Kafir corn	1.7	1.2	.7	1.2	.7
Milo maize	1.3	1.5	2.2	2.0	.8

The author summarizes his observations and conclusions as follows:

The amount of water in the leaves of milo maize was found to be lower at all times of the day and night than that of corn or Kafir corn leaves at a similar stage of development, while the average water content of these two was practically the same. The water content of the leaves of corn, Kafir corn, and milo maize averaged 118.5, 120, and 107 gm., respectively, for each square meter of leaf during the day (7 a. m. to 7 p. m., inclusive) and 127.9, 132.7, and 115.5 gm., respectively, for the night periods (7 p. m. to 7 a. m., inclusive). The average variation between the maximum and minimum water contents of the leaves from 7 a. m. to 7 p. m. was 13.8, 8.4, and 7.8 gm. for each square meter of leaf of corn, Kafir corn, and milo maize, respectively, and the average range between the maximum water content of the leaves during the night and the minimum amount during the day, 23.8, 25.9, and 21.7 gm., respectively.

Evaporation during the 22 days reached a maximum 18 times between 2 and 3 p. m. and 4 times between 3 and 5 p. m. Two-thirds of the observations for corn and milo maize and nine-tenths of those for Kafir corn showed a minimum water content of the leaves from two to four hours before maximum evaporation was reached, while in the remaining tests the minimum amount of leaf water occurred at the time of maximum evaporation.

On a wet basis the maximum and minimum percentages of water in the leaves showed an average variation during the day of 3.5 for corn, 3.2 for Kafir corn, and 4.5 for milo maize. The average variation between the minimum percentage of water during the day and the maximum during the night was 5.4, 5.9, and 6, respectively. On a dry basis the average difference between the minimum and maximum percentages of water during the day was 39.5 for corn, 31.1 for Kafir corn, and 35.9 for milo maize. The average range between maximum and minimum water content during the night was 37.5, 47.5, and 40 per cent, respectively, while the average range between the minimum percentage of water during the day and the maximum percentage during the night was 67.8, 67.2, and 51.2, respectively.

The average dry weight of a square meter of leaf for all observations was 48.2 gm. for corn, 52.5 for Kafir corn, and 56.2 for milo maize. The average difference between the minimum and maximum amounts of dry matter in the leaves for each square meter during the day was 4, 4.8, and 8 gm. for corn, Kafir corn, and milo maize, respectively. The increase in dry matter began at daybreak and usually reached a maximum between 2 and 5 p. m., the rate of increase during that portion of the day when the climatic conditions were severe being higher for milo maize than for either corn or Kafir corn.

The results are held to indicate that the sorghums, more particularly milo maize, can absorb water from the soil and transport it to leaves more rapidly in proportion to the loss of water from the plant than can corn. As a result of this the sorghums are enabled to produce more dry matter per unit of leaf area under severe climatic conditions than can the corn plant.

Experiments with legume crops under irrigation, J. S. WELCH (*Idaho Sta. Bul. 94 (1917), pp. 14, figs. 5*).—Field tests and observations with various legumes under irrigation at the Gooding substation in southern Idaho are noted and briefly discussed.

Rate-of-seeding tests with alfalfa during the period of 1910–1912, inclusive, gave average yields of 4.021, 3.726, 4.364, 3.855, and 3.702 tons per acre, with 20-, 16-, 12-, 8-, and 4-lb. rates, respectively.

A comparison of the corrugation method with the flooding method for irrigating alfalfa showed the former to be far superior for the first season of growth, after which it failed to show any advantage over the latter method. A comparison of different sized streams for the application of irrigation water during 1915–16 gave average yields of cured hay of 4.246, 2.842, and 2.291 tons per acre for streams of 0.3, 0.65, and 1.2 cu. ft. per second, respectively. Tests on the duty of water for alfalfa hay during 1911–1914, inclusive, indicated that for three crops of hay an application of about 2.75 acre-feet per acre gave best results.

For alfalfa-seed production light, frequent applications of water sufficient to maintain a uniform but not excessive soil moisture content were deemed best.

Field tests with red clover indicate that the common is the most important strain, and that grown for hay it requires practically the same treatment as alfalfa. The heaviest yields of seed were obtained from plats clipped late in May. Increased yields of barley, wheat, and oats estimated at 17.57, 10.74, and 9.47 bu. per acre, respectively, were attributed to the plowing under of a red clover crop as a green manure.

Alsike and white clovers are deemed valuable as pasture mixtures, while crimson clover has not proved to be sufficiently hardy for Idaho conditions.

In variety tests with field peas the Amraoti was first, with an average yield of 39.01 bu. per acre for 1912–1915, inclusive. Other varieties have given satisfactory yields. Field peas sown in rows 21 in. apart and cultivated gave an average yield of 32.49 bu. per acre as compared with an average of 38.98 bu. for peas drilled in. The best results with field peas were secured with one irrigation just before blooming, followed by a second application when the peas were forming.

In rate-of-seeding tests with different mixtures of field peas and oats the highest average yield, 3.223 tons of cured hay per acre, was secured from a rate of 70 lbs. of peas and 50 lbs. of oats. An estimated net return of $39.68 per acre was secured from " hogging off " field peas alone in 1916, while a mixture of three-fourths field peas and one-fourth wheat sown at the rate of 90 lbs. per acre was estimated to give a net return of $45.20.

Vicia villosa, the White Navy field bean, and the horse bean have proved valuable as forage crops. Soy beans and cowpeas have not proved hardy.

The management of irrigated grass pastures, J. S. WELCH (*Idaho Sta. Bul. 95 (1917), pp. 17, figs. 4*).—Results at the Gooding substation previously noted (E. S. R., 32, p. 628) are reviewed, together with additional data secured from grazing tests and observations during 1915–16. Certain important phases of pasture management under irrigation conditions are emphasized.

Experiments with small grains under irrigation, J. S. WELCH (*Idaho Sta. Bul. 93 (1917), pp. 24, figs. 5*).—The results of variety and irrigation experiments with spring and winter wheat and barley and spring oats at the Gooding substation, conducted in cooperation with the Irrigation Investigations of the U. S. Department of Agriculture, are reported for the period of 1909–1916, inclusive.

The soft, white, spring wheats are considered best adapted for growth under irrigation. The Dicklow, with a 6-year average yield of 46.1 bu. per acre, was deemed the best spring wheat variety, and Jones Fife and Turkey Red, with 2-year average yields of 53.6 and 52.4 bu., respectively, the best winter varieties. Although drought-resistant, the durum wheats are not recommended for average irrigation conditions.

The irrigation experiments with spring wheat indicated that the highest yields were secured from one irrigation in each of three successive stages of growth and amounted to an average of 43.9 bu. per acre for the period of 1911–1916, inclusive. One irrigation in the first and second stages each gave an average yield of 43.5 bu., and one irrigation in the first stage only, an average of 33.6 bu. per acre. When irrigation was withheld until the third stage the average yield was 22.7 bu., and it was considered as of no value to the crop. It is recommended that if but one irrigation can be made it be applied just before the first jointing stage of growth.

Duty-of-water experiments with spring wheat from 1910–1916, inclusive, indicated that a total application of not more than 1.25 acre-feet of water per acre gave the best results. For winter wheat production one irrigation of slightly less than 0.75 acre-foot of water per acre applied just before heading was deemed sufficient from results secured in tests conducted in the years 1910, 1911, and 1912.

In variety tests with spring barleys Trebi, with 95.5 bu., Beldi No. 1209, with 87.3 bu., and Sandrel, with 82.9 bu. per acre gave the highest yields for the 6-rowed types; Bohemian, with 84.21 bu., and Horn, with 81.65 bu. for the 2-rowed types; and Eureka, with 63.4 bu. for the hull-less type.

In irrigation tests with spring barley a study was made of the influence of different sized streams, employing 1.2, 0.65, and 0.3 cu. ft. per second. The tests were conducted during 1915–16, and the average yields were 54.7, 55.9, and 49.2 bu. per acre, respectively. Duty-of-water experiments with spring barley extending over the period of 1910–1914, inclusive, indicated the use of approximately 1.5 acre-feet of water per acre as sufficient.

The Utah and Tennessee winter barleys yielded 69.7 and 60.8 bu. per acre, respectively, for a 2-year average. Duty-of-water experiments with winter barley extending over the 3-year period of 1913–1915 gave the best results with one irrigation of about 0.43 acre-foot of water per acre applied just before heading.

The leading varieties of oats included Swedish Select, Wisconsin Pedigree No. 1, and Silver Mine, with average yields of 96.6, 96.5, and 96 bu. per acre, respectively.

Duty-of-water experiments with oats indicate that the oat crop requires approximately 1.75 acre-feet of water per acre.

Yields of winter grains in Illinois, W. L. BURLISON and O. M. ALLYN (*Illinois Sta. Bul. 201 (1917), pp. 96–110, figs. 3*).—Field tests with winter varieties of wheat, rye, and barley conducted at DeKalb (DeKalb Co.), Urbana (Champaign Co.), and Fairfield (Wayne Co.) are reported and briefly discussed. The results of the wheat variety tests conducted at Cutler (Perry Co.) and previously noted (E. S. R., 19, p. 1035) are summarized, and tests with rye, barley, emmer, and oats reported for the winter of 1915–16. The data are presented in tabular form.

The winter wheat variety tests at DeKalb were begun in 1907 and Dawson Golden Chaff employed as a standard of comparison. Turkey Red is deemed the principal high-yielding variety for northern Illinois, while other high-yielding varieties grown for a minimum of three years include Turkey 9–233, Malakoff 5–458, Minnesota Reliable, Wheedling 5–464, Kharkof, and Malakoff, with average yields of 37.2, 36.7, 36.1, 35.2, 32.6, and 31.4 bushels, respectively. Turkey Red has given a 7-year average yield of 35.4 bu. per acre.

Winter barley all winterkilled. Average yields of 55.5 and 47 bu. per acre, respectively, were secured from four tests each of Petkus winter rye and Wisconsin Pedigree rye.

Variety tests with winter wheat at Urbana were begun in 1904, using Turkey Red as a standard variety. The average yields of the leading varieties tested five years or more were as follows: Turkey Red 42.4 (12 years), Malakoff 42, Fultz, 42.1, Hungarian 39.7, Pesterboden 41.8, Beloglina 40.4, Kharkof 42.6, and Dawson Golden Chaff 39.5 bu. per acre. Other promising strains for central Illinois are Turkey Hybrid 509 and Dawson Golden Chaff 9–225.

Tests with winter wheat at Fairfield were begun in 1906, using Fulcaster as a standard variety. The following varieties have given the highest average yields on a percentage basis for a minimum of three years: Fulcaster, Economy, Missouri Pride, Indiana Swamp, Wheedling, Harvest King, Rudy, and Poole, with 15.9 (10 years), 16.9, 15.8, 14.9, 14.5, 14.3, 12.3, and 12 bu. per acre, respectively. Fulcaster was outyielded several years by Economy, Wheedling, Missouri Pride, and Harvest King. The hard wheats such as Turkey Red and Kharkof did not prove to be adapted to southern Illinois conditions.

The following results were secured with winter grain at Cutler in 1916: Wisconsin Pedigree rye 43.4 bu., Wing Black rye 46.8 bu., Salzer winter barley 22.7 bu., Michigan winter barley 17.5 bu., and Winter emmer 52 bu. Winter oats did not prove hardy.

The characteristics of the winter wheat varieties tested at DeKalb, Urbana, and Fairfield are noted in tabular form.

Bean culture, V. C. BRYANT (*California Sta. [Pub., 1917], pp. 2*).—A brief popular outline of the cultural practices deemed best for bean production in California.

Dried bean production in Illinois, C. E. DUBST (*Illinois Sta. Circ. 201 (1917), pp. 8*).—A general discussion of the production and harvesting of beans for drying as human food, together with a brief note on insects and diseases.

Field bean production, R. W. DE BAUN (*New Jersey Stas. Circ. 70 (1917), pp. 4*).—The methods for production of field beans in New Jersey are briefly discussed.

Studies of variation and correlation of weight and sugar content of beets, especially sugar beets, W. OETKEN (*Landw. Jahrb., 49 (1916), No. 1, pp. 1–103, figs. 4*).—The author outlines the object of his investigations and describes the material used and the methods employed in connection with a series of experiments previously noted (E. S. R., 35, p. 640). A number of formulas are presented and explained for determining the mean, the standard of deviation, the coefficient of variation, regression, the correlation coefficient, the excess, etc.

The variability in weight and sugar content was studied in respect to the individual and to a series of individuals. Considerable data are presented in tabular form and discussed in detail.

A list of 75 articles comprising the literature cited is appended.

Corn, F. APP (*New Jersey Stas. Circ. 69 (1917), pp. 7*).—The advantages of an increased corn acreage under present food conditions are briefly discussed and the field practices employed in corn production in New Jersey outlined.

Varieties of cotton, 1916, W. E. AYRES (*Arkansas Sta. Bul. 129 (1917), pp. 3–32, fig. 1*).—Extensive variety tests with cotton at Scotts, Mena, and Fayetteville and cooperative tests throughout the State are reported, with considerable tabulated data.

The highest-yielding varieties at Scotts were Cleveland, with 946.2 lbs. of lint per acre, and Cook No. 920, with 813.8 lbs. per acre. At Mena Half and Half was first, with 265.4 lbs. of lint, and Arkansas Trice second, with 225.4 lbs. per acre. Brief descriptive data are submitted for the varieties tested at Fayetteville.

The recurving of milo and some factors influencing it, A. B. CONNER and R. E. KARPER (*Texas Sta. Bul. 204 (1917), pp. 3–30, figs. 13*).—Experiments were conducted by the authors during 1916 at Lubbock, Tex., pertaining to the recurving, or "goosenecking," of milo maize, which is deemed undesirable on account of the difficulty of harvesting the crop with machinery and the reduction in yield through loss of heads during the early stages of growth. Some conclusive data are presented on the anatomy of the milo maize plant and variation in anatomy of both milo maize and Katir corn plants under different environmental conditions. No definite conclusions are drawn as to the fundamental causes of recurving, although a number of the factors which heretofore were considered responsible for the phenomenon have been eliminated and evidence advanced to indicate that recurving is due to the structure and development of the upper leaf sheath.

Considerable tabulated data are presented and discussed in detail. The studies are to be continued in the hope of obtaining a proper basis for the selection of strains having erect heads. The observations for the season of 1916 may be summarized as follows:

Tallness or dwarfness in the same strain was a result of the lengthening or shortening of the internode. No apparent difference was observed in the tenderness of the peduncle of different grain sorghums at similar stages of growth. Dwarfness was associated with a high percentage of erect heads, while tallness was attended by a high percentage of pendant heads. Rapid growth was conducive to tallness and slow growth to dwarfness.

The removal of a vertical section of the back of the upper leaf sheath always resulted in a complete recurving of the peduncle in the direction of the opening. The upper leaf is attached to its sheath at an angle of approximately 45°, and the long side of the sheath first begins inrolling. Tall plants showed a long inroll of the upper sheath as compared with dwarf plants, that character being also associated with a large number of pendant heads.

Root pruning and a consequent limitation of the food supply increased the number of erect heads and decreased the number of pendant heads. Furthermore, a limitation of the moisture and food supply of the individual plants by reducing the feeding area per plant resulted in an increased number of erect heads and a decreased number of pendant heads.

Measurements of internode and sheath lengths in both milo maize and Kafir corn showed that while the internode lengths varied widely under different environmental conditions, the sheath length remained quite stable. A variation of the internode length without a corresponding change in the sheath length resulted in an overlapping of the internode in varying degrees when the same plant was grown under different conditions. Long overlapping of the sheath probably furnished support to the stem and the peduncle, while a short overlapping supplied correspondingly little support. The removal of the inrolled sheath tip before any part of the head appeared resulted in an increased percentage of erect heads. It appeared that in milo maize the tightly inrolled upper leaf sheath tip influenced the position of the head.

The culture of early potatoes under glass (*Jour. Bd. Agr. [London]*, *23* (*1917*), *No. 10, pp. 976–978*).—This is a brief general discussion of the production of early potatoes under glass. Several early and second early varieties are recommended for use, and directions are given for the preparation of the soil, planting, and the care of the house during the growing season.

The morphology and development of transplanted rice, B. MARCARELLI (*Gior. Risicolt., 6 (1916), Nos. 13–14, pp. 211–222; 22, pp. 341–347; 23, pp. 357–364; 24, pp. 372–378, figs. 21*).—The morphology and development of transplanted rice is compared with that of rice seeded in the field. The author discusses in particular the morphological effects of transplanting on the root system, the aerial portions of the plant, stem development, and development of the rachis.

The increased development following transplanting is illustrated.

Studies of the volume weight of hulled rice grains, M. KONDO (*Ber. Ohara Inst. Landw. Forsch., 1 (1916), No. 1, pp. 1–26, pls. 2*).—This reports studies with rice to determine the correlation between volume weight and such grain characteristics as size and form of kernel, water content, mixture of whole and broken kernels, impurities, etc., since volume weight is a recognized factor in determining the value of rice on the Japanese market.

Similar studies with barley, wheat, rye, and oats are noted.

Considerable data are presented in tabular form and graphs drawn to illustrate the correlations studied.

In studying the relationship between the water content of hulled rice and its volume weight, the experiments included drying by the heat of the sun, drying in a desiccator with sulphuric acid or calcium chlorid, and drying in an oven. A fourth experiment was planned to study this relationship in hulled rice kernels which had been dried by the sun's heat before hulling.

The volume weight of hulled rice kernels is influenced by different factors, the relationship between volume weight and these factors being as follows: Factors causing an increase in volume weight were smooth seed coat; thick, round, short-elliptical kernels; the addition of small kernels; the mixing. of large and small kernels of the same kind; and sun or oven drying of the seed before hulling. Factors which caused a decrease in volume weight were a rough seed coat; long, thin kernels; broken shrunken kernels, straw, chaff, etc.; drying by the sun's heat or by means of chemicals; and the absorption of water. The one factor which exerted no definite influence was size of kernel.

The author concludes that in view of the complex nature of these correlations it is practically useless to attempt a determination of the quality or moisture content of rice by means of volume weight.

Rhodes grass, P. H. ROLFS (*Florida Sta. Bul. 138 (1917), pp. 182–190, fig. 1*).— The value of Rhodes grass for hay and pasture in central and southern Florida has been demonstrated by field tests at the station since 1909, and its use is recommended on well-tilled, moist lands in regions where the winter temperatures do not go below 23° or 22° F.

Sugar beet culture, R. L. STEWART (*New Mexico Sta. Bul. 107 (1917), pp. 30, figs. 7*).—The production of sugar beets in New Mexico is discussed in detail. The results of rather extensive experiments begun in 1916 are reported as planned to study the best cultural methods and the effect of low humidity and high temperature upon the yield and sugar content of the beets and the purity of the juice.

The experimental work was conducted on light sandy, silt loam, and moderately heavy adobe soils. Plantings were made on all sandy and adobe soils in December, January, and February, and on the silt loam beginning with March 15 and at 15-day intervals for the remainder of the season. Irrigation consisted of flooding after planting, furrowing after planting, or planting in a moist seed bed. The best stands were secured from plantings made May 1, while little difference was noted in the stands under different methods of irrigation.

Analyses of samples from the different plats gave an average of 13.1 per cent sugar and 79.1 per cent purity. The maximum sugar content was 20.3 per cent and the maximum purity 94.2 per cent.

The results of the first year's test indicate that beets grown on heavy soil are lower in sugar content and in purity than those grown on light soils.

The tillering of winter wheat, A. E. GRANTHAM (*Delaware Sta. Bul. 117 (1917), pp. 3–119, figs. 18*).—An extensive study of tillering of winter wheat is reported in an effort to determine to what extent certain factors affected the rate of tillering and, through tillering, the yield of grain. The studies included an investigation of (1) the effects of environmental factors on tillering, such as time, rate, and depth of seeding and fertilization, (2) of the relation of heredity to tillering, including the relation of variety to tillering, and the inheritance of tillering, and (3) a study of the number of tillers in relation to length of culm, length of spike, yield per plant, yield per spike, and quality of grain. Considerable tabulated data are presented, discussed in detail, and may be briefly summarized as follows:

The time of seeding directly influenced tillering, early seeding being accompanied by a higher rate of tillering than late seeding. The yield per spike of high-tillering plants usually exceeded that of low-tillering plants.

Rate of seeding influenced tillering in that the thicker the seeding the fewer the tillers per plant. Close seeding resulted in earlier maturity and shorter spikes. A high seeding rate lessened the number of tillers, the length of culm and spike, and the yield of grain in smooth wheats to a greater extent than in bearded wheats.

Nitrogen and phosphoric acid appeared to stimulate tillering, while potash had little or no effect. Wheat was observed to tiller equally as well when sown late on fertile soil as when sown earlier on thin soil.

The capacity for tillering appeared to be a variental characteristic, varieties differing considerably in this respect. Bearded wheats as a class tillered more freely than smooth wheats, the environmental factors appearing to influence the rate of tillering in the former to a less extent. A tendency was noted for high tillering mother plants to produce a larger proportion of plants with a larger number of tillers than the average, but the inheritance of tillering as indicated by the performance of individual plants was not marked.

Increased yields per spike accompanied an increase in the number of tillers per plant up to 4 or 5 tillers, beyond which the yield was more or less uniform. Low tillering plants of a variety produced smaller yields per spike and grain of poor quality. Within a variety under similar conditions of planting the quality of grain was correlated to some extent with the number of tillers per plant. Varieties with coarse, stiff straw did not tiller so freely as those with finer, more pliable straw. Depth of planting did not appear to affect materially the number of tillers per plant. The improved quality of grain used for seed, as indicated by size, plumpness, and weight, favored a higher rate of tillering.

Regulations and instructions relating to the labelling, inspection, and analysis of seeds in New Jersey, J. P. HELYAR (*New Jersey Stas. Circ. 66 (1917), pp. 3–10*).—This outlines the rules and regulations promulgated by the station for the enforcement of the New Jersey seed law of 1916.

The seed situation, J. P. HELYAR (*New Jersey Stas. Circ. 72 (1917), pp. 3–7*).—This is a brief consideration of the most feasible means for meeting the situation in respect to agricultural seeds for the 1918 planting.

HORTICULTURE.

Gardening.—A complete guide, H. H. THOMAS (*London and New York: Cassell & Co., Ltd., 1917, pp. [8]+152, figs. 78*).—A guide to the culture of ornamentals, fruits, and vegetables, both in the open and under glass.

The beginner's gardening book, H. H. THOMAS (*London and New York: Cassell & Co., Ltd., 1917, pp. 80, figs. 18*).—A small popular treatise on ornamental and kitchen gardening.

The manuring of market garden crops, with special reference to the use of fertilizers, F. T. SHUTT and B. L. EMSLIE (*Canada Expt. Farms Bul. 32, 2. ser. (1917), pp. 36*).—This bulletin deals briefly with some of the important features of market gardening in Canada, with special reference to the selection and use of fertilizers and fertilizing materials. Data on fertilizer experiments with vegetables conducted in 1915 are appended. The results as a whole indicate the economic advantage of a medium application of manure with suitable commercial fertilizers as compared with the use of a large quantity of manure alone.

Possibilities of the fall vegetable garden, C. E. DURST (*Illinois Sta. Circ. 200 (1917), pp. 8, fig. 1*).—This circular deals with vegetables which can be made available for fall use. Consideration is given to vegetables planted in early spring and which are capable of surviving hot dry weather, vegetables planted in late spring and early summer, and quick maturing vegetables planted in late summer or early fall especially for fall use.

Variety tests of potatoes, tomatoes, cabbage, and other vegetables, T. H. WHITE (*Maryland Sta. Bul. 204 (1917), pp. 231–262, figs. 5*).—This bulletin contains the hitherto unpublished notes and records of vegetables that have been tested at the station during the past ten years.

Potatoes and root crops, H. H. THOMAS (*London and New York: Cassell & Co., Ltd., 1917, pp. 80, figs. 23*).—A small popular treatise on the culture of potatoes and other garden root crops.

Tomatoes and salads, H. H. THOMAS and F. R. CASTLE (*London and New York: Cassell & Co., Ltd., 1917, pp. 79, figs. 27*).—A small popular treatise on the culture of tomatoes and various salad plants.

Harvesting and storing vegetables for home use, J. J. GARDNER (*Colorado Sta. Bul. 232 (1917), pp. 3–7, figs. 3*).—Suggestions are given relative to time of planting and harvesting with reference to storing vegetables, together with directions for storing home supplies of the more common vegetables.

Commercial onion culture in Idaho, C. C. VINCENT (*Idaho Sta. Bul. 97 (1917), pp. 3–16, figs. 9*).—This bulletin embodies the results of variety and cultural tests conducted at the station during the last three years, together with the cultural methods followed by the largest and most successful onion growers in the State.

Studies on the dying out of pepper vines in the Dutch East Indies.—III, Pepper cultivation in the Lampong district, A. A. L. RUTGERS (*Dept. Landb., Nijv. en Handel [Dutch East Indies], Meded. Lab. Plantenziekten, No. 27 (1916), pp. 65, pls. 14*).—This is the third report (E. S. R., 35, p. 835) on a study of the causes leading to the dying out of pepper vines in the Dutch East Indies.

The author concludes in substance that the dying out prematurely can not be explained by the action of insect and fungus troubles but is rather to be attributed to the general state of cultivation. The indications are that with proper methods of tillage, manuring. and other cultural measures peppers may be successfully grown on soils where they have been regularly dying out prematurely.

Report on the Government Horticultural Gardens, Lucknow, for the year ended March 31, 1917, H. J. DAVIES (*Rpt. Govt. Hort. Gardens Lucknow, 1917, pp. [6]+10*).—A brief statement relative to the condition of various fruits and other economic plants grown at the gardens, including a financial statement for the year.

Fifteenth annual report of the State nursery inspector, H. T. FERNALD (*Agr. of Mass., 64 (1916), pt. 1, pp. 69–97, pls. 4*).—A report of activities during 1916, with special reference to the inspection of nursery stock for the detection and control of the gipsy and brown-tail moths and white pine blister rust.

Factors governing fruit bud formation, B. T. P. BARKER and A. H. LEES (*Univ. Bristol, Ann. Rpt. Agr. and Hort. Research Sta., 1916, pp. 46–64, figs. 4; Jour. Bath and West and South. Counties Soc., 5. ser., 11 (1916–17), pp. 171–191, figs. 4*).—A discussion of various factors affecting fruit bud formation, including a summarized report on long-continued pruning investigations with several varieties of apples conducted at the Agricultural and Horticultural Research Station of the National Fruit and Cider Institute, Long Ashton, Bristol.

Thus far no definite conclusions are reached relative to the direct effect of pruning on fruit bud formation. The evidence secured indicates that both heavy and light winter pruning have given practically the same number of laterals and fruit buds, although these were distributed differently on the trees, the light pruned trees showing a greater amount of growth but much more bare wood.

A study of meteorological conditions prevailing at Long Ashton led the authors to conclude that any results secured from pruning are of only a local value and that the question of fruit bud formation should be investigated with the idea of determining the ultimate cause. Among the factors to be studied in continuing the work are excess of water in the soil, deficiency of water in the soil, the effect of artificial manures, light, and shade.

Miscellaneous notes on experiments in fruit culture, B. T. P. BARKER. A. H. LEES, and G. T. SPINKS (*Univ. Bristol, Ann. Rpt. Agr. and Hort. Research Sta., 1916, pp. 71–73; Jour. Bath and West and South. Counties Soc., 5. ser., 11*

(1916–17), pp. 196–198).—The notes here given deal with the progress being made in fruit-breeding investigations at Long Ashton, Bristol, experiments in planting different aged plum trees and the influence of stock on fruit trees. Thus far no definite conclusions have been drawn.

Methods of handling basket fruits, E. SMITH and J. M. CREELMAN *(Canada Dept. Agr., Dairy and Cold Storage Branch Bul. 52 (1917), pp. 13, figs. 10).*— The methods here described are based primarily on data obtained in the operation of the Dominion precooling and experimental fruit-storage warehouse at Grimsby, Ont.

A systematic study of Iowa apples, L. R. HARTILL *(Trans. Iowa Hort. Soc., 51 (1916), pp. 162–248).*—A paper on this subject prepared for the Iowa State College and State Horticultural Society, and comprising a descriptive list of the more important varieties of apples grown in Iowa. A list of cited literature is included.

Fertilizer experiments on apple trees at Highmoor Farm, C. D. WOODS *(Maine Sta. Bul. 260 (1917), pp. 99–102).*—A brief statement of progress made on long-continued experiments being conducted by the station.

Experiments to determine the value of highly nitrogenous fertilizers as a means of forcing trees into bearing have thus far shown no differences that could be attributed to the additional nitrogen in the fertilizer. Experiments conducted since 1912 appear to confirm partially the results secured at the New York State Station in which the use of fertilizers did not materially affect the yield and growth of apple trees (E. S. R., 25, p. 643). In the present investigation no differences could be observed between the trees fully fertilized, those partially fertilized, and those not fertilized at all during the past three years. On the other hand, the limited data available relative to yield of these trees indicate larger yields on the fertilized plats and a consistent increase with the amount of fertilizer applied. The experiment is to be continued for a number of years.

Winter v. summer pruning of apple trees, C. C. VINCENT *(Idaho Sta. Bul. 98 (1917), pp. 28, pls. 2, figs. 23).*—This bulletin gives the results secured for a period of 11 years in a comparative test of winter and summer pruning. The four varieties included in the test were Jonathan, Rome, Grimes, and Wagener. The winter-pruned trees received a moderate annual pruning during the dormant season from the time the trees were planted in 1905 until the present time. Similar pruning in the summer-pruned plat took place after the terminal growth had stopped for the year. A complete record of the yields of each individual tree in both plats is given from the time the trees commenced bearing until the present time. Observations were also made on color and growth performance.

On the basis of the total production for the first seven crops summer pruning has produced the greatest yield in all varieties. Color in the three red varieties was intensified by summer pruning. As determined by both color and yield, the crop value per acre under summer pruning as compared with winter pruning shows an average gain of $52.33 for Jonathan, $53.64 for Rome, and $30.69 for Wagener. In some cases summer pruning has hastened the bearing of the young trees. Summer pruning increased the average terminal growth somewhat but tended to check the total wood growth slightly. The average diameter of the tree trunks in the winter-pruned plat was somewhat larger. The experiment as a whole shows that thinning has a direct relation to pruning and crop production.

Field experiments in spraying apple orchards, B. S. PICKETT ET AL. *(Illinois Sta. Bul. 185, abs. (1916), pp. 12, figs. 4).*—A popular edition of Bulletin 185, previously noted (E. S. R., 35, p. 39).

Modern methods of packing apples, A. H. FLACK and P. J. CAREY (*Canada Dept. Agr., Fruit Branch, Fruit Comr. Ser. Bul. 2 (1917), pp. 62, figs. 57*).—This bulletin gives instructions for packing apples in boxes and barrels, the subject matter being largely a revision of previous information on the subject (E. S. R., 19, p. 741).

Preliminary report on apple-packing houses in the Northwest, W. M. SCOTT and W. B. ALWOOD (*U. S. Dept. Agr., Off. Markets and Rural Organ. Doc. 4 (1917), pp. 31, figs. 9*).—This comprises a preliminary report on an investigation conducted in the States of Washington and Oregon during the apple packing season of 1916, with reference to the handling of apples from the orchard to and through the packing house and into the cars ready for shipment to market.

The subject matter is presented under the general headings of community packing houses, community packing-house equipment, packing-house organization and personnel, a suggested floor unit, some of the details of operation, and the operations in two typical houses.

Plum growing in Maryland, F. S. HOLMES (*Maryland Sta. Bul. 207 (1917), pp. 295-326*).—This bulletin presents information relative to the status of the plum growing industry in Maryland and gives the results with varieties tested at the station, together with brief suggestions on orchard management, picking, packing, and marketing.

Profitable small fruits, H. H. THOMAS (*London and New York: Cassell & Co., Ltd., 1917, pp. 80, figs. 25*).—A popular treatise on the culture of strawberries and bush fruits.

The strawberry in North America, S. W. FLETCHER (*New York: The Macmillan Co., 1917, pp. XIV+234, figs. 26*).—A companion work to the author's treatise on strawberry growing (E. S. R., 37, p. 42), and dealing mainly with the origin and history of the North American type of strawberries, including information relative to the improvement of strawberries by breeding and the development of commercial strawberry growing. A list of breeders since 1854 is given.

Soil influence on the composition of strawberries, C. T. GIMINGHAM (*Univ. Bristol, Ann. Rpt. Agr. and Hort. Research Sta., 1916, pp. 65-70; Jour. Bath and West and South. Counties Soc., 5. ser., 11 (1916-17), pp. 191-196*).—The results secured with two varieties of strawberries as grown on several different types of soil in the three years, 1914 to 1916, at Long Ashton, Bristol, are here presented.

Among the general conclusions thus far deduced it was found that the two varieties tested show a marked variety distinction in respect to degree of acidity. As to sugar content seasonal influence appears to outclass other factors. With one or two exceptions no soil effect was sufficiently pronounced in the trials to show itself in the presence of the other factors concerned.

The study is to be continued.

New or noteworthy tropical fruits in the Philippines, P. J. WESTER (*Philippine Agr. Rev. [English Ed.], 10 (1917), No. 1, pp. 8-23, pls. 9*).—In continuation of previous papers (E. S. R., 34, p. 639) the author describes and gives notes on a number of tropical fruits which have been tested at the Lamao Experiment Station.

Report on manurial experiments (*Imp. Dept. Agr. West Indies, Rpt. Agr. Dept. Dominica, 1916-17, pp. 45-58, pl. 1*).—This is the customary progress report on manurial experiments with cacao and limes in Dominica (E. S. R., 36, p. 141). The data secured on the various plats are presented in tabular form and discussed. Work on the lime plats was interfered with by hurricanes in 1916 and the experiments have been reorganized. The results to date are similar to those previously noted.

Citrus experimental grove, S. E. COLLISON (*Florida Sta. Rpt. 1916, pp. 113-118*).—In continuation of previous reports (E. S. R., 35, p. 839) measurements are given showing the average gain in diameter of trees from June, 1909, to June, 1916, growing on the various fertilizer plats in the citrus experimental grove. The lime requirements as studied for each plat are also presented in tabular form.

The data secured show that the acidity of the plats varies from season to season, being greatest in summer and least in winter. The greater increase in acidity during the summer is attributed to the increased decay of vegetable matter. Plats receiving strongly alkaline materials, such as lime, limestone, and hardwood ashes were alkaline in reaction, and those receiving mildly alkaline materials such as Thomas slag and nitrate of soda showed a decrease in acidity. The use of phosphoric acid from floats has not served to decrease the acidity of the soil.

Do fertilizers influence the composition of oranges? H. J. WEBBER (*Cal. Citrogr., 2 (1917), No. 6, pp. 17-19*).—A brief analysis of experiments previously reported by H. D. Young (E. S. R., 36, p. 642).

Standards of maturity for the Washington navel orange, E. M. CHACE (*Mo. Bul. Com. Hort. Cal., 6 (1917), No. 8, pp. 325-330*).—The substance of this article has been noted from another source (E. S. R., 37, p. 345).

Some notes on frost protection in orange groves, R. S. VAILE (*Cal. Citrogr., 2 (1917), No. 6, pp. 10, 11, 16*).—A paper on this subject read at the Orange Show Convention, in which the author reviews the work of various citrus associations and individual growers in protecting groves from frost and makes some deductions relative to the value of frost-protective methods.

It is concluded in brief that although it is entirely possible to protect orange groves against frost it may or may not be profitable, depending upon the size of the crop, amount of actual risk, and amount of protection necessary for any particular grove. It is believed that more attention should be given to the adding of heat units than to the prevention of radiation by the formation of a cloud of smoke.

Preventing frost damage in transit, A. W. McKAY (*Col. Citrogr., 2 (1917), No. 6, pp. 4, 5, 17, figs. 4*).—The results of experiments conducted by the U. S. Department of Agriculture during two seasons to determine means of preventing frost injury to citrus fruits in transit are here reported.

Effect of different methods of transplanting coffee, T. B. McCLELLAND (*Porto Rico Sta. Bul. 22 (1917), pp. 11, pl. 1*).—This bulletin reports the result of a trial test of different methods of transplanting coffee, shows the advantages and disadvantages of each method, and gives suggestions relative to the correction of bad practices.

Briefly stated, the test shows that the transplanting of moderately large coffee seedlings, either from or into a heavy clay soil, should unquestionably be done with the roots still incased in the soil in which they grew.

A preliminary report on some breeding experiments with foxgloves, E. WARREN (*Biometrika, 11 (1917), No. 4, pp. 303-327*).—A discussion of the results secured in a number of first generation crosses.

FORESTRY.

Second biennial report Nebraska Forestation Commission, C. ROHDE, A. H. METZGER, and W. BALL (*Bien. Rpt. Nebr. Forestation Com., 2 (1916), pp. 19*).—This report contains recommendations and outlines of proposed legislation dealing with forestry in Nebraska.

Report of the State forester and firewarden, C. P. WILBER (*Rpts. Dept. Conserv. and Develop., N. J., 1916, pp. 49–84, pls. 9, figs. 2*).—A brief statement of activities during the year, including a description of the forests of the State forest reserves and detailed information relative to fire protective work.

Report of the chief forest firewarden for the year 1916, G. H. WIRT (*Penn. Dept. Forestry Bul. 16 (1917), pp. 123, pls. 3, figs. 3*).—A report on forest protective measures in Pennsylvania during 1916, including data on forest fires for the year.

Report of the forest branch of the department of lands for the year ended December 31, 1916 (*Rpt. Forest Branch Dept. Lands, B. C., 1916, pp. 35, figs. 2*).—This report deals with the development of markets for British Columbia lumber, together with statistics on sawmill operations, lumber cut, timber sales, fire protection, and miscellaneous work conducted during 1916.

French forests and forestry.—Tunis, Algeria, Corsica, T. S. WOOLSEY, JR. (*New York: John Wiley & Sons, Inc., 1917, pp. XV+238, figs. 20*).—The author here presents the results of a study of the more important phases of forest practice in Corsica, Algeria, and Tunis and a translation of the Algerian forest code of 1903. A subsequent work will be descriptive of methods employed in the forests in France proper. In presenting the subject matter as a whole the aim has been to set forth the essentials of method which may be applied directly in the United States or which may be indirectly of value to English-speaking foresters.

Report on forest operations in Switzerland (*Rap. Dépt. Suisse Int., 1916, pp. 1–12*).—The usual report (E. S. R., 35, p. 543) relative to the administration and management of State, communal, and private forests in Switzerland, including data on forest products, revenues, expenditures, etc., in 1916.

Annual progress report of forest administration in the United Provinces for the forest year 1915–16, H. G. BILLSON (*Ann. Rpt. Forest Admin. United Prov., 1915–16, pp. 27+LXX+[7]*).—The usual report relative to the administration and management of the State forests in the United Provinces. All important data relative to alterations in forest areas, forest surveys, working plans, miscellaneous work, yields in major and minor forest products, revenues and expenditures, etc., are appended in tabular form.

Progress report of forest administration in the Jammu and Kashmir State for the year 1915–16. B. O. COVENTRY (*Rpt. Forest Admin. Jammu and Kashmir [India], 1915–16, pp. II+26+LV*).—A report similar to the above on the administration and management of the State forests in Jammu and Kashmir State.

Progress report of forest administration in Coorg for 1915–16, H. TIREMAN (*Rpt. Forest Admin. Coorg. 1915–16, pp. [4]+11+13*).—A report similar to the above, relative to the administration and management of the State forests of Coorg for the year 1915–16.

Administration report of the forest circles in the Bombay Presidency, including Sind, for the year 1915–16 (*Admin. Rpt. Forest Circles Bombay, 1915–16, pp. II+172+6*).—A report similar to the above relative to the administration and management of the State forests of the Northern, Central, Southern, and Sind Circles in the Bombay Presidency for the year 1915–16.

Notes on the principal timbers of Queensland (*Dept. Pub. Lands, Queensland, Forestry Bul. 2 (1917), pp. 20*).—Notes are presented on the more important timbers of Queensland with reference to their distribution, general characteristics, uses, strength, and durability.

Georgia forest trees (*Forest Club Ann., Ga. State Forest School, 1917, pp. 69, figs. 70*).—A handbook describing the coniferous and hardwood trees of Georgia. A key to the hardwoods is included.

Reproduction in the coniferous forests of northern New England, B. MOORE (*Bot. Gaz., 64 (1917), No. 2, pp. 149–158*).—A paper on this subject delivered at the meeting of the Ecological Society of America in New York City in December, 1916, in which the author gives the results of an investigation undertaken to determine the factors governing the reproduction of the more important coniferous trees in the forests of northern New England. A bibliography of literature cited is included.

Growth study of planted trees, H. DORR, JR., and W. A. BOAG (*Forestry Ann.* [*Mich. Agr. Col.*], *2 (1917), pp. 37, 38*).—A table is given showing the growth performance of various hardwood species planted in 1909 in the forest nursery of the Michigan Agricultural College.

Frustum form factor volume tables for sugar maple, E. G. HAMLIN (*Forestry Ann.* [*Mich. Agr. Col.*], *2 (1917), pp. 14–18, fig. 1*).—The tables here presented were prepared with a view to determining the feasibility and accuracy of the frustum form factor method in preparing volume tables. The data were secured in Wexford County, Mich., during 1915 and 1916.

A study of breakage, defect, and waste in Douglas fir, E. J. HANZLIK, F. S. FULLER, and E. C. ERICKSON (*Univ. Wash. Forest Club. Ann., 5 (1917), pp. 32–40, fig. 1*).—A short study was made in the spring of 1916 to secure data upon breakage, defect, and waste in logging Douglas fir timber. The results are here presented in tabular form and are supplemented by a report on breakage in Douglas fir timber as observed in three typical logging camps during 1915.

On the influence of the age of the trees on the quality of the rubber, O. DE VRIES (*Arch. Rubbercult. Nederland. Indië, 1 (1917), No. 3, pp. 169–177*).—A number of special experiments were conducted to determine the influence of the age of rubber trees on the quality of the rubber.

The results in general show that the tensile strength of rubber from older trees is not appreciably better than from young trees. The slope or type of the stress strain curve is generally the same, although sometimes somewhat better for old trees. The rate of cure diminishes in an appreciable degree with the age of the tree and the viscosity for old trees is nearly always better.

The preservative treatment of poles, B. L. GRONDAL (*Univ. Wash. Forest Club Ann., 5 (1917), pp. 8–11, fig. 1*).—In this paper the author discusses modern methods of treating poles, including the recently developed perforation process in which the poles are pierced in a number of places to insure greater penetration of creosote just above and just below the ground line where fungi are most active.

Mapping methods, C. M. CADE (*Forestry Ann.* [*Mich. Agr. Col.*], *2 (1917), pp. 19–24, fig. 1*).—A discussion of present practice in mapping land areas, including forest tracts.

DISEASES OF PLANTS.

Report of the associate plant pathologist, C. D. SHERBAKOFF (*Florida Sta. Rpt. 1916, pp. 80–98, figs. 5*).—The line of investigations reported upon is similar to that previously noted (E. S. R., 35, p. 844), including studies of diseases of vegetables and a disease of pineapples.

Chief attention has been paid to damping-off of seedlings, *Rhizoctonia* sp. being the most troublesome fungus in Florida in this respect. Experiments in the control of damping-off have been carried on, and the application of 0.5 per cent copper sulphate solution has given good results with lettuce, the seeds germinating normally and no damping-off following. For seed disinfection, formalin and corrosive sublimate have been compared, the author having found in the use of corrosive sublimate with a number of kinds of seeds, particularly celery, that the temperature of the solution bears an important relation to the amount of injury produced.

A brief description is given of a rot of tomato fruit due to an undetermined species of Phytophthora. This disease, which is called buckeye rot, is to be the subject of a special publication. Brief notes are given on bacterial diseases of celery, lettuce, peppers, tomato, and potato, and on fungus diseases of a number of other vegetables.

In connection with the pineapple wilt studied by the author, in which study field observations and laboratory experiments were carried on, nematodes were found in almost every instance to be the cause of some of the injury. In addition to nematodes, *Thielaviopsis paradoxa* was found to attack the roots and stems of pineapples, causing considerable loss.

Report of the laboratory assistant in plant pathology, J. MATZ (*Florida Sta. Rpt. 1916, pp. 99–112, figs. 7*).—The author reports upon his investigations on pecan dieback and the leaf blight of the fig.

The investigations of the dieback are in continuation of those previously described (E. S. R., 35, p. 849). Experiments in controlling the organism, *Botryosphæria berengeriana*, have been continued, and pruning dead wood from the trees has been found satisfactory in keeping down the disease. Spraying with lime-sulphur solution did not seem to have any effect.

The leaf blight of fig is described as characterized by a yellowish, water-soaked appearance on both surfaces of the leaves. The twigs and fruit may be infected by the spreading mycelium, although the blight is primarily one of the leaves. An organism has been isolated which experiments have shown to be the cause of the trouble and which has been determined as *Rhizoctonia microsclerotia* n. sp.

[Plant diseases in New Jersey, 1915], M. T. COOK (*Ann. Rpt. N. J. Bd. Agr., 43 (1916), pp. 48–54*).—Besides notes on plant diseases, 214 of which were observed during 1915, and mention of the four epidemics of economic diseases occurring in New Jersey during the year, namely, fire blight of pear and apple, anthracnose of bean, mosaic of tomato, and Rhizoctonia of potato, the author reports more specifically on potato diseases, including scab, leaf roll, blackleg, discolorations (*Fusarium oxysporum* and *F. radicicola*), and powdery scab (*Spongospora subterranea*), also on some preliminary experiments regarding the control of the diseases, the results of which varied considerably. The administrative report for 1915 of the State plant pathologist is included.

[Fungus pests and their control] (*Imp. Dept. Agr. West Indies, Rpt. Agr. Dept. St. Vincent, 1915–16, pp. 24–30*).—The information here given relates to both insect enemies (particularly thrips on cacao) and fungus diseases of plants, with a discussion of conditions and remedial measures. Specimens were examined of arrowroot rhizomes affected with the so-called burning disease, which appears to be due to *Rosellinia bunodes*. Internal boll disease of cotton is thought to be related to the presence of cotton stainers.

Some parasitic fungi of Japan, T. HEMMI (*Bot. Mag. [Tokyo], 30 (1916), No. 353, pp. 334–344, figs. 5*).—A discussion is given of *Clasterosporium degenerans* on *Prunus mume, Septoria perilæ* on *Perilla ocimoides*, and *Armatella litseæ* on *Litsea glauca*, and a discussion with technical descriptions of the new species *Septoglœum niisimæ* on *Quercus dentata* and *Septoria petasitidis* on *Petasites japonica*.

Combating nematodes by the use of calcium cyanamid, J. R. WATSON (*Florida Sta. Rpt. 1916, pp. 55–63*).—In addition to a previous account (E. S. R., 37, p. 453), the author describes experiments in the use of calcium cyanamid for the control of nematodes, particularly with tomatoes, peach trees, and pineapples.

Tomato plants were so badly burned as to be practically worthless when placed in the soil nine days after the application of the cyanamid. A second crop planted after an interval of about four months gave a fair crop of tomatoes, while plants in check plats yielded nothing. Nematodes were found in all the plats. Experiments in which cyanamid was applied at the rate of 1,500 lbs. per acre on light soil, and in which tomato plants were set out at once, showed that while the plants were severely burned, they recovered, made good growth, and were nearly free from nematodes. These experiments seem to indicate a correlation between the character of the soil and the amount of cyanamid used.

Where cyanamid was applied to peach trees at the rate of 1 to 6 lbs. per tree, it was found to reduce the number of nematodes present, although not penetrating the soil readily.

With pineapples, it was found that cyanamid could be applied at the rate of 1,500 lbs. per acre without injuring the plants, the nematodes being fewer than on untreated plants and the pineapples having a better color, probably due to the nitrogen of the fertilizer.

A new disease of wheat, E. F. SMITH (*U. S. Dept. Agr., Jour. Agr. Research, 10 (1917), No. 1, pp. 51-54, pls. 5*).—The author reports the occurrence of a disease of wheat that has appeared in Indiana, Arkansas, Kansas, Missouri, Oklahoma, and Texas, and is believed to be present in other States. Numerous bacteria have been found associated with this disease, and while not definitely claiming that it is a bacterial disease, the author believes it to be of bacterial origin. A description is given of infected parts of plants, and attention is called to the disease in the hope that material may be forwarded to the author for further study.

Observations on stalk disease of wheat, J. CAPUS (*Bul. Soc. Path. Vég. France, 2 (1915), No. 2, pp. 94-104*).—Giving the results of observation and experimentation on *Leptosphæria herpotrichoides*, as causally connected with the appearance of foot or stalk disease in wheat, the author states that the trouble is favored by the susceptibility of some varieties, by soil and atmospheric humidity and warmth (during winter and early spring), by close seeding, by the presence of weeds, and probably by continued seeding of the same land to wheat.

Sulphuric acid in dilute solution, when used in early spring, kills the lower leaves and sheaths, admitting air and sunshine, both of which are unfavorable to the development of the foot or stalk disease fungi. This treatment is helpful if used during latency or imminence of the disease, but not markedly so after the attacks are well developed.

Common diseases of cucumbers and melons, W. H. MARTIN (*New Jersey Stas. Circ. 68 (1917), pp. 11, figs. 5*).—Popular descriptions are given of a number of the more common fungus and bacterial diseases to which cucurbitaceous plants are subject, together with suggestions for their control so far as definite means are known.

A form of potato disease produced by Rhizoctonia, G. B. RAMSEY (*U. S. Dept. Agr., Jour. Agr. Research, 9 (1917), No. 12, pp. 421-426, pls. 4*).—In this contribution from the Maine Experiment Station the author gives a description of a type of potato tuber disease observed for the first time in southern Maine a few years ago. No positive evidence has been found of the trouble in northern Maine nor any reference to this form of injury elsewhere in the country.

Two phases of injury are produced by the fungus, one whose external appearance somewhat resembles scab and which extends as a dry core into the tuber, another in which the shrinkage of tissues has formed a pit or canal in the center of the infected area, frequently suggesting wireworm injury. Histological studies in all stages of the progress of the disease show the presence of Rhizoctonia, and pure cultures of the fungus have been repeatedly obtained from the interior of the diseased areas. Evidence is presented that indicates that the host cells die and lose their contents and the walls suberize and are more or less broken down in advance of the fungus filaments. This, the author states, might lead to the supposition that part of the action is due to a toxin secreted by the fungus. Cell wall penetration by the hyphæ is thought to occur, but this is believed to be the exception rather than the rule.

A new strain of Rhizoctonia solani on the potato, J. ROSENBAUM and M. SHAPOVALOV (*U. S. Dept. Agr., Jour. Agr. Research, 9 (1917), No. 12, pp. 413–420, pls. 2, figs. 3*).—A description is given of a strain of *R. solani* which was isolated from the stems of potatoes in Maine during the summer of 1916. This strain is distinguished from the more common form of *R. solani* by the more pronounced lesions produced when inoculated on injured stems or tubers; by the reaction, growth, and character of sclerotia on definite media; and, morphologically, by measurements of the mycelium, also of the short sclerotial cells, and by the measurement of the diameter of germ tubes when the short, or barrel-shaped, cells enveloping the sclerotia are placed in drops of water to germinate.

An investigation of the potato rot occurring in Ontario during 1915, D. H. JONES (*Abs. Bact., 1 (1917), No. 1, pp. 37, 38*).—Reporting briefly the result of studies made during 1915 and 1916, the author states that potato diseases are greatly favored by such continued wet weather as prevailed during 1915. Rhizoctonia was the principal and soft rot bacillus the secondary cause of the black basal stem rot and collapse which occurred in many places during 1915, the organism producing only a slightly shrunken, brown canker where the cortical tissue alone was punctured. The soft rot bacillus could not penetrate healthy, unbroken epidermal tissue, but when introduced beneath the punctured epidermis of a young potato stem or tuber, or of carrot, turnip, or cauliflower, it produced a characteristic soft rot. Seed tubers showing sclerotia of Rhizoctonia (black scab) are most likely to give a diseased crop unless disinfected. which may be done by soaking them in water for two or three hours and then in 0.1 per cent corrosive sublimate for five or six hours.

Fusarium sp. caused much of the tuber rot observed at harvesting time and in storage. The disease may be carried over in débris of the potato crop left in the soil, high humidity favoring its development.

Diseases of tomatoes, M. T. COOK and W. H. MARTIN (*New Jersey Stas. Circ. 71 (1917). pp. 8, figs. 6*).—The authors briefly describe the more prevalent fungus, bacterial, and other diseases of tomatoes, and offer suggestions for their control.

Apple blotch and its control, J. W. ROBERTS (*U. S. Dept. Agr. Bul. 534 (1917), pp. 11, pls. 2, figs. 3*).—The author describes the blotch of fruit, foliage, and twigs of the apple due to the fungus *Phyllosticta solitaria*, and gives the results of his investigations on the disease and on methods of control. His cross-inoculation experiments are said to confirm the inoculation work of Scott and Rorer (E. S. R., 20, p. 1044).

As an explanation for the few infections which occur late in the season, the author suggests an increased resistance of the host as well as a gradual decrease in the number of spores produced by the fungus. A large number of mummied fruits were examined throughout the spring but no spores were found, and hence the author concludes that mummies are not an important source of infection.

It is claimed that apple blotch may be controlled by three sprayings with 3:4:50 Bordeaux mixture applied at intervals of three weeks, the first spray being applied about three weeks after the petals have fallen. Summer-strength lime-sulphur solution may be substituted for Bordeaux mixture where the disease is not severe, thus lessening the risk of injury.

Apple scab control in British Columbia, R. M. WINSLOW (*Canad. Hort.*, *40 (1917), No. 2, pp. 32, 56–58, fig. 1*).—The rapid spread of apple scab in British Columbia during the last three years is said to have caused much alarm, discouraging some very careful growers. In view of the losses of 1915, an extensive series of tests was carried out in 1916 with lime-sulphur, which was applied when the leaves were from $\frac{1}{4}$ to $\frac{1}{2}$ in. in length, when the blooms were just about to open, when the blooms were falling, and again 14 days later, the last three of these sprays proving to be of the greatest general utility. A wet July makes a summer spray advisable, in addition to those above mentioned. An abnormally bad year for scab may be followed by one almost free therefrom. The sprays increased the percentages of absolutely clean and marketable fruit, the average weight of the fruit, the total yield, the set of fruit, and the vigor of the foliage. Tests with Bordeaux mixture and with atomic sulphur gave less favorable results than those with lime-sulphur, which gave fair control of scab even when unsprayed trees showed from 98 to 100 per cent infection.

The biology of Exoascus deformans, A. MANARESI (*Riv. Patol. Veg.*, *7 (1915), No. 7, pp. 193–201*).—The author during 1912 to 1915 made a study of several varieties of peach in the Province of Bologna as affected by *E. deformans*, the cause of leaf curl, in connection with the weather during that period and the treatments employed. The results are tabulated and discussed. Strong Burgundy mixture applied about the middle of March gave good results, later applications being ineffective.

Comparative resistance of Prunus to crown gall, C. O. SMITH (*Amer. Nat.*, *51 (1917), No. 601, pp. 47–60, figs. 6*).—This is a more detailed account of the work already noted (E. S. R., 36, p. 352).

Winter injury of grapes, F. E. GLADWIN (*New York State Sta. Bul. 433 (1917), pp. 107–139, pls. 8*).—As a result of a study of light crops of grapes during the years 1909 to 1916, the author was led to the conclusion that such crops are due to injury to immature shoots by low temperatures. Embryo flower clusters were found to be injured by low temperatures if they entered the dormant period immature, yet the foliage of the bud might expand normally. The effect of low temperatures following various periods when temperatures rose high enough and continued for sufficient time to start activity is discussed.

Experiments testing the effect of various fertilizer elements on maturity indicate that neither nitrogen, phosphoric acid, nor potash influenced maturity, and hence their effect was not apparent as influencing the degree of killing. The extent of injury was observed to be closely correlated with poor drainage of soils, although some killing occurred where drainage was reported as satisfactory. Severe pruning after late frost injury in the spring is believed to favor bud killing indirectly through inducing rank wood growth. Maturity of bud and wood is probably correlated with the ripeness of the fruit, as determined from sugar analyses of the fresh juice.

Resistance to low temperature is considered a species character and is possibly correlated with hardness of wood.

Why and when winter kills grapes, F. H. HALL (*New York State Sta. Bul. 433, popular ed. (1917), pp. 3–8, figs. 4*).—A popular edition of the above.

A fatal disease of mulberry, L. MONTEMARTINI (*Riv. Patol. Veg.*, *7 (1915), No. 8–9, pp. 238–242*).—The results to date of the inquiry regarding a disease of mulberry (E. S. R., 33, p. 448) in seven Provinces have already shown it to be widely diffused and of considerable importance, but not so severe on clayey and limy soils as on some others indicated.

Anthracnose of Japanese persimmon, L. MAFFEI (*Riv. Patol. Veg., 7 (1915), No. 6, pp. 161–163*).—A brief description is given of a disease of fruits of Japanese persimmon in the botanical garden at Pavia, caused by *Glœosporium kaki.*

Report of the plant physiologist, B. F. FLOYD (*Florida Sta. Rpt. 1916, pp. 30–50, figs. 6*).—This report gives the results of a study of the toxic effect of certain organic chemicals on citrus and of injury to citrus trees by ground limestone.

Previous investigations (E. S. R., 29, p. 248) having shown that dieback of citrus trees could be induced by organic nitrogenous fertilizers, the author reports on experiments to test the action of vanillin on both citrus seedlings and citrus cuttings. This organic compound was added to nutrient solutions used at various rates in the growth of seedlings, and, while marked injury to the roots was produced, no gum, which is characteristic of the disease dieback, was formed in grapefruit seedlings. With citrus cuttings vanillin produced no gum, but, as no gum was formed in a series of experiments in which copper sulphate was used, it is believed that the lack of gum formation in cuttings may have been due to the absence of growth.

The attention of the station having been called to apparent injury in a number of groves where ground limestone had been applied, an investigation was made. Pot experiments indicated that ground limestone can, under limited conditions, induce injury to citrus trees, and that this injury shows itself by a frenching, or chlorosis, of the foliage of the trees.

Some cases of injury to citrus trees apparently induced by ground limestone, B. F. FLOYD (*Florida Sta. Bul. 137 (1917), pp. 161–179, figs. 6*).—This bulletin is essentially a reprint from the article noted above, with suggestions for the control of the injury.

Report of the plant pathologist, H. E. STEVENS (*Florida Sta. Rpt. 1916, pp. 66–79, figs. 2*).—The investigations reported by the author have been continued along about the same lines as previously.

A number of citrus trees which had been treated for gummosis have been kept under observation for three years (E. S. R., 33, p. 55), and many of the active areas have healed following the treatment. A study is being made of the fungus and bacterial flora associated with gummosis and several organisms are under observation, among them *Phomopsis citri* and *Diplodia natalensis,* to determine whether these fungi are active agents in producing the disease.

Pruning experiments for the control of melanose have been continued with some success, summer pruning giving very good results in reducing the amount of injury.

The author is continuing his investigations on citrus canker, paying particular attention to laboratory studies of the organism, especially in relation to soils. *Pseudomonas citri* has been cultured in sterilized soil for more than a year, and experiments have demonstrated that it grows readily on sterilized soil under moist conditions. Soil cultures made in the spring of 1915 have been kept under observation and in nearly every instance the organism has been found present. The infected soil has been applied to healthy citrus foliage and in all cases canker infections have resulted. Tests have been made of field soil collected under infected trees, and while in a majority of the tests there were negative results, in a few instances the presence of the organism was established by inoculation experiments.

Brief descriptions are given of lightning injury to citrus trees, the lemon brown rot fungus, citrus scab, withertip, and stem end rot. In connection with the investigation of the lemon brown rot fungus, the author reports having isolated from gumming citrus trees an organism which, when inoculated upon healthy lemons, developed a brown rot similar to that produced by *Pythiacystis citrophthora.*

The origin and cause of citrus canker in South Africa, ETHEL M. DOIDGE (*Union So. Africa Dept. Agr., Sci. Bul. 8 (1916), pp. 20, pls. 10, figs. 3; ditto, Div. Bot. [Pub.] 20 (1916), pp. 8, pls. 6*).—Citrus canker, claimed by Hasse (E. S. R., 33, p. 149) to be caused by an organism described by her as *Pseudomonas citri,* but designated by the present author as *Bacterium citri,* is said to have been imported on grapefruit trees from Florida. A brief history of the disease in Africa and elsewhere is given, with an account of study by the author.

At first the trouble was taken to be a severe outbreak of scab (*Cladosporium citri*). Serious effects may be produced even in the nursery. The organism works in buds, leaves, fruits, and branches. Orange, lime, and related plants are attacked. It is claimed that under the dry conditions of the Transvaal the disease has been effectively controlled with a 4:4:50 Bordeaux spray. This should be used two or three times the first year with a single spraying every year or two thereafter. Badly infected stock should be burnt and old cankers should be searched for, as infection may occur after four years of apparent freedom from canker.

Anaberoga, M. K. VENKATA RAO (*Mysore Agr. Calendar, 1917, pp. 26, 27, 30, fig. 1*).—Anaberoga of the areca palm in parts of Mysore is described in connection with the fungus locally known as "anabe," which attacks trees, usually over 10 years of age, at the roots and collar and apparently spreads through the soil and by air-borne spores. Other plants of different genera, and even different orders, are also attacked by the fungus, which causes the same general symptoms, ending in the death of the tree. No remedial measures are effective after the tree is attacked.

Diseases and pests of the mango, K. KUNHIKANNAN and C. NORONHA (*Mysore Agr. Calendar, 1917, pp. 7, 10, 11, figs. 3*).—Failure of mango trees in Mysore to set fruits has been shown by recent observations to be due to a fungus which attacks young leaves and flower spikes. It develops most rapidly under moist conditions, the drying up of the flowers following a succession of misty or damp nights. This fungus is distinguished from other local mildews which attack tobacco and roses. Bordeaux mixture applied to the young leaves and flower spikes just before the blooms open controls the disease. A combined treatment is being sought for both fungi and troublesome insects, some of which are mentioned in this article.

Powdery mildew of dwarf magnolias, M. TURCONI (*Riv. Patol. Veg., 7 (1915), No. 6, pp. 164–167*).—The disease produced by species of Erysiphe on several plants is said to be associated in the case of *Magnolia pumila* with a fungus, the characters of which, as described, are considered to agree with those of *E. polygoni.*

Black canker of chestnut, B. PEYRONEL (*Atti R. Accad. Lincei, Rend. Cl. Sci. Fis., Mat. e Nat., 5. ser., 25 (1916), II, No. 11, pp. 459–461*).—This is a preliminary discussion of a study of black canker of chestnut, now becoming important in Italy, its manifestations, the causal or contributing agents (such as atmospheric conditions), and various related problems, such as the mode of penetration by the fungi, no trace of which appears outwardly in the early stages of the disease.

Black canker of chestnut, L. PETRI (*Atti R. Accad. Lincei, Rend. Cl. Sci. Fis., Mat. e Nat., 5. ser., 25 (1916), II, No. 5, pp. 172–176, figs. 2*).—Previous reports on black canker of chestnut (E. S. R., 33, p. 854; 35, p. 250) are continued.

The author states that whether near the basal portions of the larger roots or at the collar and above that region, necrosis of the cortical tissue is a phenomenon secondary to the death of the cambium. The former portion showed at first no microorganisms, but these could be demonstrated by means of the microscope and sometimes by means of culture methods in the cambium, sapwood, and heartwood. It appears that the rapidly progressing primary infection is independent of the deeper fungi, which are probably secondary. The infection, which proceeds up the trunk, appears to have its origin at the collar.

The primary infection in black canker of chestnut, L. Petri (*Atti R. Accad. Lincei, Rend. Cl. Sci. Fis., Mat. e Nat., 5. ser., 25* (1916), II, No. 12, pp. 499–501, figs. 2).—More recent study by improved methods confirms the observations above noted regarding the phases or stages of black canker of chestnut. The attack originates near the junction of the roots and trunk. The identity of the primarily causal fungus remains unknown.

Leaf cast in horse chestnut, L. Montemartini (*Riv. Patol. Veg., 7* (1915), No. 8–9, pp. 243–248).—This is a discussion of the factors involved in the early shedding of leaves by horse chestnut, including foliar surface and branching as related to transpiration surface and conduction. The author states that the number of conducting elements is the same as that of actively transpiring elements, both increasing in number with the amount of branching.

A needle blight of Douglas fir, J. R. Weir (*U. S. Dept. Agr., Jour. Agr. Research, 10* (1917), No. 2, pp. 99–104, pl. 1, figs. 3).—A description is given of a serious disease of Douglas fir which is causing damage to young trees and seedlings in the Northwest both in the nursery and the forest. A study of the disease indicates that it is due to a fungus, the systematic position of which has not been definitely determined.

Some preliminary experiments in spraying with a solution of soap and Bordeaux mixture give indications that this will prove a successful means of controlling the fungus.

[White pine blister rust in Canada], H. T. Güssow (*Canad. Forestry Jour., 13* (1917), No. 1, pp. 900–906, figs. 6).—In this article, which has been issued also in pamphlet form, a brief popular account is given of the importation of the American 5-leaved pine (*Pinus strobus*) into Europe, its attack there by the blister rust fungus, the importation of the latter into America on seedlings, and the spread of the disease to such an extent that this pine and all the interests connected with it are seriously threatened. A plea is made for concerted action looking to the control of this disease. Eradication of all currant and gooseberry plants in the neighborhood of the pines is the remedy which is offered with most confidence.

White pine blister rust on currants, W. A. McCubbin (*Canad. Hort., 40* (1917), No. 2, p. 34, fig. 1).—Certain features observed in the Ontario outbreak of white pine blister rust suggest that the fungus may overwinter on currant bushes. Besides the large area on the Niagara Peninsula previously known to be infected, the disease occurred, so far as known, only in small isolated patches in Ontario in localities which are named. The disease has also been reported from Quebec. The appearance and behavior of the disease on both white pine and currant are briefly described.

ECONOMIC ZOOLOGY—ENTOMOLOGY.

A check list of mammals of the North American continent, the West Indies, and the neighboring seas, D. G. Elliot (*Pubs. Field Columb. Mus. [Chicago], Zool. Ser., 6* (1905), pp. V+761, pl. 1; Sup., New York: Amer. Mus. Nat. Hist., 1917, pp. IV+192).—The check list proper is supposed to include all the species and races of mammals, described up to the date of publication, which inhabit the North American continent from the Arctic Ocean to the Province of Cauca in Colombia, South America, together with those of the West Indies Islands and the adjoining seas. They are arranged systematically according to the author's views, and descriptions are given of those forms that have received names since his two previous works were published[1] (E. S. R., 16, p. 233). The species enumerated in the list number 1,309 and 676 races of species found within the geographical limits embraced, together with 22 races of exotic species originating in South America. The type locality and geographical distribution, where known, are given in every instance.

The supplement, which is edited by J. A. Allen, lists the species and subspecies that have for the most part been described since the publication of the earlier works on which the check list was based, down to the end of the year 1914. In addition to being a supplement to the check list, it is also a continuation of the preceding two manuals on the subject, since it gives descriptions of forms added as well as the usual check list matter. It contains many changes in generic nomenclature from that of the check list proper, many groups treated in the latter as subgenera being given the rank of genera, while the changes in generic names shown to be necessary since the publication of the check list are duly recorded.

Report of the entomologist, J. R. WATSON (*Florida Sta. Rpt. 1916, pp. 51–65*).—Attempts to establish *Calosoma sycophanta* were not successful and it appears that this beetle is not adapted to the climatic conditions of Florida.

In further observations (E. S. R., 35, p. 852) of the Florida flower thrips ([*Euthrips*] *Frankliniella tritici projectus*) kept in test tubes constantly supplied with fresh rose petals, many lived for several weeks, and one individual lived for 59 days. The observations establish the fact that they spend the winter as adults, though there may be some breeding during the warm periods in any month of the year, but there are no indications that they ever enter the ground or seek other shelter than the depths of the flowers. The author's observations show that prolonged and dashing rain is the chief natural factor in reducing the numbers of thrips. Spraying work in the control of thrips on citrus indicates that it will pay well for one spraying even when the bloom is unusually irregular and scattering.

Studies made of an outbreak of thrips on strawberries at Waldo showed the infestation to be heavy, as many as 50 adults and larvæ being found in a single bloom. When thus heavily infested the bloom failed to set fruit. Successful control of the pest was obtained through the application of a home-made tobacco decoction of tobacco stems soaked overnight in enough water to cover them, applied at the rate of 3 gal., and a pound of soap to each 15 gal. of water.

In April, 1916, the Florida flower thrips was found to injure camphor trees, the damage to the unfolding buds of camphor being very similar to that caused by the camphor thrips, previously noted (E. S. R., 31, p. 751).

Work on combating nematodes by the use of calcium cyanamid is noted on page 652.

The report concludes with brief notes on the insects of the year, including accounts of an unusual outbreak of the striped cucumber beetle in south Florida, where they killed bearing okra plants and watermelons and even attacked Irish potatoes, and destroyed the young growth of citrus, it being the first record of injuries to citrus in Florida by this pest. The woolly white fly (*Aleurothrixus howardi*) continued to extend slowly into the regions adjacent to its previous range. The cowpea pod weevil (*Chalcodermus aeneus*) is said to have

---

[1] Synopsis of North American Mammals. (Field Columbian Mus., Zool. Ser., 2 (1901).

been more abundant than usual during the spring of 1916, it being especially so on the California black-eyed variety of cowpeas. A June bug (*Anomala marginata*) was especially abundant in June. The twig girdler (*Oncideres cingulatus*) was the cause of several complaints from the lower east coast where it attacked "Australian pines."

Undesirable insect immigration into New Jersey, H. B. WEISS (*Canad. Ent., 49 (1917), No. 9, pp. 293–298, pl. 1*).—The author calls attention to the fact that fully one-half of the principal injurious hexapods in the United States have been introduced from foreign countries and that the injuries inflicted by them have been enormous. Mention is made of the introduction into New Jersey of the mole cricket *Gryllotalpa gryllotalpa* from Holland (E. S. R., 34, p. 653), the large cockroach *Blaberus discoidalis* from South America (E. S. R., 37, p. 255), *Stephanitis pyrioides* from Japan, and *Cholus forbesii* from Colombia.

Fumigation of greenhouses, E. N. CORY (*Maryland Sta. Bul. 205 (1917), pp. 263–284*).—This bulletin is based upon fumigation experiments conducted with the view of ascertaining the effect of certain doses of hydrocyanic-acid gas on insects and plants when certain factors are known, including moisture and temperature, meteorological conditions, time (day or night), and length of exposure. The investigations were largely limited to the determination of effective dosage for certain insects under normal conditions, but little work having been done with one factor constant and others variable in order to ascertain the effect of the variables, which, it is pointed out, is a very important phase of fumigation.

The conclusions drawn from the work carried on are as follows: " Fumigation in the presence of daylight is likely to result in injury to the plants if a sufficient dose is used to control the ordinary insects. . . . Overnight fumigation is recommended because (1) fumigation in late afternoon for a short period is impractical in winter, since ventilation after nightfall is likely to result in chilled or frozen plants; (2) long exposure at night does not give as much injury as a short exposure during the day.

" Definite doses under optimum conditions of moisture and temperature for different horticultural varieties of plants can be recommended. Definite doses, under the normal greenhouse conditions, that will kill certain species of insects are recommended. Slight reductions in the doses may be effected by increasing the temperature up to a maximum of 70° F. without danger of injury to the plants if the moisture is kept at or below 50 per cent saturation. High moisture is decidedly an important factor as far as injury to the plant is concerned. High moisture will increase the mortality if the dose is below the optimum for the insect involved.

" High temperature will increase the mortality if the dose is below the optimum for the insect involved. Plants that are normally grown under warm conditions, such as ' stove plants,' will not be injured by fumigations in a temperature that would injure bedding plants and plants grown for cut flowers. Plants other than ' stove plants ' should be fumigated if possible with the optimum dose for the insect involved, at a night temperature at or below 50° and with the atmosphere about half saturated."

In an appended table the author gives the maximum safe dose for various plants under normal greenhouse conditions.

A neglected factor in the use of nicotin sulphate as a spray, W. MOORE and S. A. GRAHAM (*U. S. Dept. Agr., Jour. Agr. Research, 10 (1917), No. 1, pp. 47–50*).—Illness caused by the consumption of greenhouse lettuce that had been sprayed with nicotin sulphate led to the studies at the Minnesota Experiment Station here reported.

The results show that nicotin sulphate is nonvolatile, but that alkalies contained in hard water and soap set free the nicotin contained in nicotin sulphate sprays. Thus, in order to obtain the maximum efficiency of tobacco extracts containing nicotin sulphates, they should be rendered alkaline before using. This is thought to explain the different results obtained in the use of tobacco extracts, and also why soap greatly increases the efficiency of sprays containing nicotin sulphate. The fact that nicotin sulphate is nonvolatile also explains the cases of poisoning from eating lettuce sprayed with tobacco extracts containing this material.

"Commercial tobacco extracts containing nicotin sulphate should not be used in the greenhouse, at least not on plants which are later to be used for food. Tobacco extracts or tobacco papers containing free nicotin may safely be used in the greenhouse on plants such as lettuce without endangering the lives of the consumers. Food plants such as lettuce sprayed with tobacco extracts containing free nicotin should not be cut for the market until the day after spraying. If the temperature of the house is low, a longer period should be given the nicotin to evaporate from the leaves."

Grasshopper control, C. R. JONES (*Colorado Sta. Bul. 233 (1917), pp. 3–29, figs. 17*).—A summary of information on the general life history, habits, and practical methods of control of grasshoppers, based upon work in Colorado during the outbreaks of 1916. The subject is taken up under the headings of life history; food habits—the plants affected; natural and artificial control; apparatus for capturing grasshoppers, including the hopperdozer, balloon catcher, and the live hopper machine; insecticides; diseases; etc. The bulletin concludes with a discussion of the work during 1916.

A further contribution to the study of Eriosoma pyricola, the woolly pear aphis, A. C. BAKER and W. M. DAVIDSON (*U. S. Dept. Agr., Jour. Agr. Research, 10 (1917), No. 2, pp. 65–74, pls. 2, fig. 1*).—In the present paper, which gives the complete life of cycle of *E. pyricola*, the authors first discuss the history of the different species of plant lice recorded on pear roots (*Pyrus communis*) at some length. The species *Prociphilus pyri* (Fitch) has been found to be a homonym and the name P. *fitchii* is proposed for it. It is shown to be definitely established that the European pear-root aphis (*E. pyri* Goethe), described in 1884, is the alternate form of the elm species *E. lanuginosa* (Hartig) of 1841.

In a paper previously noted (E. S. R., 35, p. 463) the authors described the American woolly pear aphis, previously thought to be the woolly apple aphis, under the name *E. pyricola* and called attention to its close resemblance in general structure to European specimens of *E. lanuginosa*. Studies since conducted have shown that the marked difference in the wax pores and minor differences in the sensoria then considered as representing a very distinct species are not the same in the spring forms living on elms as in the summer and fall forms living on pear roots, those in the spring forms being very similar to those of *E. lanuginosa*. The very great similarity between the spring forms of *E. pyricola* and *E. lanuginosa* has led the authors to believe that the same variation will be found between the spring and fall forms of *E. lanuginosa*, which if it proves true—and it is regarded as all but proved—will result in *E. pyricola* becoming a synonym of *E. lanuginosa*.

Thus it would appear that "the destructive woolly pear aphis of this country is a European insect imported into the Western States on pear stock. It has spread rapidly in the West in the last 25 years and now occurs from Washington to California, although as yet it is most destructively abundant in California. The isolated infestations in the Middle West and in the East are due to separate infested importations. While the alternate winter forms thrive best on European elms, the species is able to live successfully upon the common American elm and at no very distant date may become entirely adapted to this native tree. The species is liable through importations to gain a foothold in any pear-growing region, for, as recently as 1916, skins have been collected on seedling nursery stock. . . .

"The fall sexuparous migrants leave the pear roots upon which they have developed and fly to elm trees to deposit the sexes on the trunks and limbs. These migrants settle on *Ulmus americana* and *U. campestris*. The latter tree is distinctly preferred; in fact, no perfect galls have been produced on the former. The sexed female after mating deposits a single egg in a crack in the bark or underneath a bud scale. . . . From this egg hatches the young stem mother which ascends a trunk or limb and seeks an expanding leaf. In 1916 hatching commenced March 23 and extended until April 18, the majority hatching during the first two weeks of April."

The newly-hatched stem mother settles on the underside of the elm leaf near the midrib, generally not far from the base. "After the young aphid has fed for a very few days, the leaf begins to curl around it, and the curling and twisting become more pronounced as the insect grows, so that by the time it has reached the third instar the leaf in the form of a gall has completely closed around it." Following upon the maturing of the stem mother the galls grow very rapidly and change their shape. "The possibility of the second generation's wingless forms leaving the parent gall and founding new galls should not be overlooked; yet the observations made indicate either that no such movement exists or that it is uncommon."

In 1916 nearly every gall examined contained winged forms by the fourth week in June, large numbers of the earlier galls had been vacated by July 10, and by the end of July hardly a gall with living inmates could be found. Spring migrants were observed resting on pear foliage and actively crawling up and down the lower part of the pear trunks, young deposited by them were taken in spider webs at the base of pear trees, and it appears that the young are normally deposited on pear trunks at or near to the soil surface. Spring migrants when placed in Petri dishes with pieces of pear roots on wet sand deposited young which readily settled and fed upon the roots and which precisely resembled in structure the newly-born larvæ of the pear-root aphis. The young deposited by the spring migrants readily fed on pear stocks of Kieffer, French, and Japanese varieties, but like the root-dwelling larvæ absolutely refused to feed upon apple roots and fed only in very rare instances upon roots of the quince.

The life history account is accompanied by a diagram of the complete life cycle of the species. A list of ten titles cited is appended.

The aphid of tea, coffee, and cacao (Toxoptera coffeæ), F. V. THEOBALD (*Bul. Ent. Research, 7 (1917), No. 4, pp. 337–342, figs. 3*).—A summarized account of *T. coffeæ*.

Observations on Lecanium corni Bouche and Physokermes piceæ Schr., F. A. FENTON (*Canad. Ent., 49 (1917), No. 9, pp. 309–320, pl. 1, figs. 13*).—A report of biological studies of the European fruit lecanium (*L. corni*) and the spruce scale (*P. piceæ*) at Madison, Wis.

L. corni, observations of which in New York by Slingerland (E. S. R., 6, p. 1004) and by Lowe (E. S. R., 9, p. 71) have been noted, now occurs throughout most of the United States. It has a wide variety of host plants, a list here given including 36 genera, representing 21 families. In spite of the wide range of its host plants and its general distribution this insect seldom becomes of economic importance, although serious outbreaks of it have been recorded, it having occurred in New York in destructive abundance on the plum and in

California on apricots and prunes. Successful transference to different host plants is recorded.

Several parasites have been reared in Michigan from *L. corni*, which on some trees was so badly parasitized as to be almost exterminated. In the vicinity of Madison, Wis., *Coccophagus lecanii* was by far the most numerous and effective, though in California *Comys fusca* appears to be the chief check. Several insect predators are mentioned and the adult females are said to be susceptible to several fungus diseases, of which that caused by *Cordyceps clavulatum* is the most important.

The spruce scale, a European pest first discovered in this country at Hartford, Conn., in 1906, and since found in various northern localities as far west as Wisconsin has become a serious pest. It appears to be dependent upon spruce and pine for host plants, preferring the Norway spruce (*Picea abies*). A parasite representing a new species, described by Girault as *Holcencyrtus physokermis* (E. S. R., 36, p. 555), which appears to have been introduced with *P. piceæ* from Europe, is effective in checking its spread. *Cheiloneurus albicornis* and several encyrtids were also reared from this scale.

Pupæ of some Maine species of Notodontoidea, EDNA MOSHER (*Maine Sta. Bul. 259 (1917), pp. 29–84, figs. 5*).—The importance of being able to recognize insect pests in any stage of their life cycle led to studies of the pupæ of some of the more common forms of notodontid moths found in Maine, a report of which is here presented. Twenty-eight species representing 21 genera are thus dealt with.

Life history of Plutella maculipennis, the diamond-back moth, H. O. MARSH (*U. S. Dept. Agr., Jour. Agr. Research, 10 (1917), No. 1, pp. 1–10, pls. 2*).—This report, based largely upon studies made since 1908 at Rocky Ford, Colo., includes observations at Phoenix, Ariz.

P. maculipennis is a cosmopolitan species which in the United States apparently occurs wherever cabbage is grown. It feeds exclusively on cruciferous plants, having been observed by the author to feed upon cabbage, cauliflower, turnip, radish, rape, kale, mustard, Chinese mustard, kohl-rabi, water cress, horse-radish, sweet alyssum, and candytuft, and also on two weeds, wild water-cress (*Roripa sinuata*) and hedge mustard (*Sisymbrium* sp.). While cabbage is decidedly the favorite, rape, cauliflower, turnip, and mustard are readily eaten.

Seven generations occur annually at Rocky Ford, where the winter is passed as an adult. The egg stage covered from 3 to 6 days, the larva stage from 9 to 28 days, and the pupa stage from 5 to 13 days. In the South the diamond-back moth is active throughout the year, and the larvæ are to be found at all seasons. The larvæ reared at Rocky Ford during May lived as leaf miners for the first two or three days of their existence, whereas those reared at Phoenix during February lived in mines for four days.

While potentially a serious pest, it is normally held in suppression by parasites, of which the most effective is an ichneumonid, *Angitia plutellæ*, which in turn is occasionally parasitized by *Spilochalcis delira*. From 50 to 70 per cent of the larvæ of later generations of the diamond-back moth are commonly found parasitized by *A. plutellæ*. Other parasites reared by the author proved to be *Meteorus* sp., *Mesochorus* sp., and a new species of Microplitis. No parasites of the eggs or pupæ and no predacious or fungus enemies have been observed. It is readily controlled by the use of arsenicals, of which Paris green 2 lbs. and soap 6 lbs. to 100 gals. of water is the most effective. Powdered arsenate of lead at the rate of 4 lbs. in 100 gal. of water is also effective.

The tobacco budworm and its control in the southern tobacco districts, A. C. MORGAN and F. L. McDONOUGH (*U. S. Dept. Agr., Farmers' Bul. 819*

(1917), pp. 11, figs. 2).—This lepidopteran (*Chloridea virescens*) is a very serious pest in the tobacco-growing sections of Florida, Georgia, Alabama, and Louisiana. Although common in North Carolina, South Carolina, and Virginia, it is much less injurious there than in the more southern part of its range and is rarely injurious in Kentucky and Tennessee. In addition to tobacco, the species has been recorded in the United States as attacking deer grass (*Rhexia virginica*), geranium, and ageratum, and has been reported to feed upon wild solanaceous plants, including ground cherry (*Physalis viscosa*) and other species of the same genus, and *Solanum seiglinge.*

Eggs are deposited singly on the leaves and in Florida during the growing season of tobacco hatch in from 3 to 5 days. The young larvæ migrate to and reach the buds in about 24 hours. Studies have shown the larval period to cover from 18 to 31 days during May and June, the pupal stage varying during the summer from 13 to 21 days. The emergence of adults from the ground is affected materially by moisture conditions, it having been observed that a great many moths often appear at the expiration of a dry period. In captivity moths laid an average of 334 eggs. The average duration of the life cycle during May and June, 1916, was determined to be 37.5 days.

A larval parasite (*Toxoneuron* sp.) is said to be its most important enemy. In control work 30 different insecticide formulas were tested during the seasons from 1913 to 1916. Of all the poisons used Paris green, arsenate of lead, and golden antimony sulphid applied directly to the bud with corn meal as a carrier gave the most promising results, there being, however, a great variation in the efficiency and cost in their application. A mixture of 1 lb. of arsenate of lead and 75 lbs. of corn meal has proved to be the most efficient combination, the loss from burning which follows the use of Paris green thus being eliminated. For the best results the buds must be treated twice a week until topping has been completed. Other supplementary control measures recommended include the removal from the field and destruction of suckers, 55 per cent of those removed having been found to be infested; the removal at the end of the season of the tobacco plants that remain standing in the fields; patching of holes in the cheesecloth and gates kept closed where tobacco is grown under cloth; destruction of plants left growing within and around old seed beds; and the covering and walling in of seed beds with cloth so as to prevent the entrance of moths.

Some recent advances in knowledge of the natural history and the control of mosquitoes, T. J. HEADLEE (*New Jersey Stas. Bul. 306 (1916), pp. 5–26, figs. 10*).—Reference is first made to the influence of salinity on the development of certain species of mosquito larvæ, an account of studies of which by Chidester has been noted (E. S. R., 37, p. 259). Studies in the laboratory and salt marsh have shown "that highly saline water (10 to 15 per cent) is favorable to the growth of the wrigglers of the white-banded salt-marsh mosquito (*Aedes sollicitans*) and injurious (deadly if sufficiently high) to the wrigglers of the brown salt-marsh mosquito (*A. cantator*), while only slightly salt water (6 to 8 per cent) is favorable to the latter and injurious to the former. The younger the larvæ the more acutely are they affected by the degree of salinity."

A method of rapidly tracing the migrating mosquitoes to their origin by use of an automobile, starting in uninfested territory close to the infested area and collecting at regular distances, 0.5 to 2 miles, until the mosquito zone had been traversed and uninfested country found on the other side, resulted in the discovery of the breeding places of many broods. This method is illustrated by a diagram. It was clearly shown in one case by collections between 8 and 9.30 p. m. that *Culex pipiens* migrated a distance of 2.5 miles from its place of breeding, though as a matter of fact much study of this species on the wing indicates that except when bred in enormous numbers over many acres of sewage-charged water, the areas of great density are small and isolated from each other, showing clearly that slight, if any, migration, has taken place.

Drainage and the elimination of mosquito breeding areas are considered at some length under the headings of upland drainage, salt-marsh drainage, diking and tide-gating, and pumping.

The work with larvicides has seemed to indicate that fuel oil is the best for general use. Tests of sulphuric acid indicate that it can not have any great importance as a larvicide, while work with chlorin (bleaching powder) seems to show that it can not have more than a limited use. Electrolytic tests made of a machine consisting of a gasoline-engine-driven dynamo, connecting wires, and electrodes, in a meadow near Grasselli gave no evidence of their destruction of mosquito larvæ. In a test of niter cake it was found that the pupæ survived in a saturated solution.

The domestic flies of New Jersey, C. H. RICHARDSON (*New Jersey Stas. Bul. 307 (1917), pp. 5–28, figs. 18*).—A summary of information on the more important domestic flies, based upon studies conducted for the past three years at the station, the results of which have been previously noted (E. S. R., 32, pp. 60, 550; 34, p. 160; 36, p. 156).

The species concerned are the house fly, flesh flies, blow flies and allied species, the stable fly (*Muscina stabulans*), the little house fly (*Fannia canicularis*), the cluster fly (*Pollenia rudis*), etc. A summary of information on the breeding places of domestic flies, their eradication, a key to the common domestic flies of New Jersey, and a bibliography of 20 titles are included.

Some fly poisons for outdoor and hospital use, A. C. JACKSON and H. M. LEFROY (*Bul. Ent. Research, 7 (1917), No. 4, pp. 327–335*).—"The fluorids, iodates, and salicylates are all excellent for indoor purposes and used at 1 per cent in sugar solution are not in any way dangerous or offensive. Formaldehyde is so uncertain that its use is not indicated when any other safe liquid can be employed; the reasons for the variability of its action are now under investigation. For hospital use, particularly, the very small quantity needed makes even the salicylates possible as useful fly poisons; an ounce of salicylate to 5 pints of water would poison flies for some time throughout quite a large hospital, and this amount could probably be spared. The fluorids are in use as indoor fly poisons in the Imperial College, where they successfully destroy flies that escape to the laboratories from the fly rooms."

The apple maggot in British Columbia, R. C. TREHERNE (*Canad. Ent., 49 (1917), No. 10, pp. 329, 330*).—The author records the collection at Penticton, B. C., on July 26, 1916, of two adult flies of the apple maggot. This is said to be the first record of its collection in the Province of British Columbia and is practically an original record for the Pacific coast of North America.

The dipterous families Sepsidæ and Piophilidæ, A. L. MELANDER and A. SPULER (*Washington Sta. Bul. 143 (1917), pp. 3–103, figs. 28*).—In the present bulletin the authors deal with the flies commonly combined as the family Sepsidæ. These are of economic importance as they are principally scavengers, feeding and breeding in filth, sewage, excrement, carrion, and other decomposing vegetable or animal matter. A synopsis of the Sepsidæ is first presented (pp. 6–53), followed by a synopsis of the Piophilidæ. The authors recognize 51 species belonging to 18 genera, of which 19 are described as new.

A catalogue of described species is included.

Notes on some Buprestidæ of northern California, W. J. CHAMBERLIN (*Ent. News, 28 (1917), Nos. 3, pp. 129–139, figs. 10; 4, pp. 166–169*).—These notes, which relate to 61 species, include data on their occurrence and hosts. .

Biological investigation of Sphenophorus callosus, Z. P. METCALF (*North Carolina Sta. Tech. Bul. 13 (1917), pp. 5–123, pl. 1, figs. 68*).—Investigations of the southern corn bill bug commenced by the author in the spring of 1912 and carried on until the fall of 1915 are reported in connection with the earlier work by Smith, as previously noted (E. S. R., 29, p. 56). The biologic and economic aspects of the investigation are dealt with, other phases of the problem being left for a later report. Much of the data is presented in tabular form.

Observations of its biology made in the southwestern part of the State, thought to apply throughout the area of its greatest abundance in North Carolina, have been summarized as follows: "The adults hibernate over winter, going into hibernation in late October (October 17 being the latest recorded date). They emerge from hibernation in mid-April (April 10 being the earliest date recorded). Their numbers seem to increase rather rapidly until late May, and after that rather slowly until mid-August. . . . After mid-August the numbers of adults diminish rapidly, so that in early corn practically all the adults have disappeared by the end of August. A few adults remain active to late October.

"The adults commence to lay eggs by early May (May 5 being the earliest recorded date). The number of eggs found in the field increases rather rapidly until mid-June and then less rapidly until mid-July, the number of eggs falling off slightly toward mid-August. After this the number decreases rather rapidly. The latest date recorded for finding eggs in the field is September 23, but as they were still rather common at that time, it seems safe to conclude that egg laying continues until early October, especially as the adults are active in the fields till late October.

"The distribution of the larvæ throughout the year seems to coincide rather closely with the distribution of the eggs. The earliest larvæ have been found in the field in mid-May, but the time of greatest abundance seems to be from late July to mid-August. After this time their numbers fall off rapidly, the latest larvæ being found in late October (larvæ in what appeared to be the fourth molt being found on October 27).

"The earliest pupæ have been found in late June. The number increases rather rapidly till late July and seems to remain nearly constant till late September, the latest pupa being found on November 9. These late-maturing pupæ seem to all change to adults before winter, and these adults seem to remain in the pupal cells over winter, not becoming active until the following spring. There is some evidence to show that the early maturing adults lay eggs the same summer that they reach maturity, these eggs hatching and reaching maturity late in the season."

The following are thought to be the most important factors involved in any system for the control of this pest, both from the standpoint of ease and cheapness of application: (1) Time of planting, (2) rotation of crops, (3) fertilization, (4) drainage, (5) ridging, (6) fall and winter plowing, (7) thorough cultivation, and (8) destruction of native food plants. These indirect measures are the only means of control, since the habits of the pest make it impossible to apply direct measures.

A bibliography of 17 titles is included.

An annotated list of the scolytid beetles of Oregon, W. J. CHAMBERLIN (*Canad. Ent., 49 (1917), Nos. 9, pp. 321–328; 10, pp. 353–356*).—This list includes descriptions of seven new species.

Destruction of wheat by wasps, F. W. FROHAWK (*Entomologist, 50 (1917), No. 649, pp. 132, 133, fig. 1*).—*Vespa vulgaris*, a common wasp in England, is said to feed upon and damage the heads of wheat in that country.

The host of Ablerus clisiocampæ, B. A. PORTER (*Ent. News, 28 (1917), No. 4, p. 186*).—The author records the rearing of *A. clisiocampæ* in some numbers from the egg masses of the tent caterpillar, together with *Telenomus coloradensis, Tetrastichus malacosomæ*, and *Ooencyrtus* sp., of which *T. malacosomæ* was by far the most abundant.

A new West Indian chalcid fly, A. A. GIRAULT (*Canad. Ent., 49 (1917), No. 10, pp. 356, 357*).—*Achrysocharella albitibiæ* n. sp. is described from a single female collected in St. Vincent.

Notes on Perisierola emigrata, a parasite of the pink bollworm, A. BUSCK (*Insecutor Inscitiæ Menstruus, 5 (1917), No. 1-3, pp. 3-5*).—These notes relate to observations in Hawaii of the species described as new and previously referred to as *Goniozus cellularis*, the larva of which is an external parasite of the full-grown pink bollworm. It was found to occur commonly in all the cotton fields on the island of Oahu and in the Kona cotton district of Hawaii, and is at present the only parasite of the pink bollworm of any importance. It is, however, by no means an effective check, and destroys only a small percentage of the cotton pest.

Notes on coccid-infesting Chalcidoidea, III, J. WATERSTON (*Bul. Ent. Research, 7 (1917), No. 4, pp. 311-325, figs. 7*).—This continuation of the article previously noted (E. S. R., 37, p. 467) includes descriptions of three new species and one new variety from the West Coast of Africa.

Two new species of Macrophya, S. A. ROHWER (*Ent. News, 28 (1917), No. 6, pp. 264-266*).

The occurrence of the genus Monobæus in North America, A. A. GIRAULT (*Ent. News, 28 (1917), No. 3, p. 106*).—A new species, *Monobæus hegeli*, is described from a female specimen from Michigan.

Notes on some parasites of sugar cane insects in Java, with descriptions of new Hymenoptera Chalcidoidea, A. A. GIRAULT (*Entomologist, 50 (1917), No. 649, pp. 134-136*).—Three parasites, probably of economic importance, are here described as new, namely, *Gonatocerus bifasciativentris* reared from eggs of a leafhopper embedded in the leaves of sugar cane; *Parachrysocharis javensis*, n. g. and n. sp., from *Flata affinis;* and *Cyrtogaster javensis*, from lepidopterous eggs.

The hothouse milliped, E. N. CORY and F. H. O'NEILL (*Maryland Sta. Bul. 206 (1917), pp. 283-294, figs. 3*).—Reports received at various times attributing injuries to the hothouse milliped (*Oxidus gracilis*) and requests by florists and gardeners for information regarding its economic status led to the hothouse studies here reported.

This myriapod, a species of tropical origin widely distributed in temperate climates, is thought to have been introduced into the United States from Europe. Its distribution in this country seems to include the States along the Atlantic coast and as far west as the Mississippi Valley.

It is rarely seen during the day, being nocturnal in its habits. There appears to be but one generation a year, although the date of the oviposition period varies so much with individuals that specimens of all sizes may be found at almost any time.

The eggs are usually laid in the spring in masses, those counted containing from 9 to 327 eggs, and the average cluster containing from 175 to 250 eggs. The first eggs were observed on February 9, although the greatest number were found during April and May. The depth to which they are placed in the soil varies with its nature and not in any special cavities in the soil or apparently with any relation to the proximity of food. In packed clay soil the depth to which the eggs were deposited varied from 0.5 to 1 in. below the surface, and in light sandy soil the average depth was from 1.5 to 2 in., although some few clusters were found as deep as 3 or even 4 in. below the surface. The eggs hatched in 20 days at a greenhouse temperature ranging from 58 to 76° F.

Five larval stages are described. The first stage has 5 pairs of legs and the succeeding larval stages 10, 29, 31, and 35 pairs, respectively. Roomy cells are formed in the earth in which they pass the molts.

Observations show that manure or decaying vegetable matter is the principal food of these millipeds. Experimental feedings indicate that they will not burrow in sand after the raw ends of cuttings or the newly formed roots, that they will not attack the stems of plants even under the stress of hunger, and that they can subsist for some time on the humus in the soil. The millipeds occasionally attack sprouting seeds, and it is believed that they can be starved into attacking the roots of some plants and under certain conditions may damage them to a limited extent.

The green alga that grows on moist flower pots appears to be an important source of food for this species. Observations indicate that it has predacious habits also, a half-grown milliped having been observed to attack and destroy a dipterous larva that was about 3 mm. long, and it was also observed to feed upon the remains of an earthworm, a green aphid, etc.

No parasites have been reared up to the present time but a small centiped is thought to attack it. In control work the authors' experiments with poison baits gave negative results, although they have been recommended as being efficient in some localities. Tests of tobacco products show that they are probably the best material for the control of the hothouse milliped. Tobacco dust sprinkled on the beds at the rate of 300 lbs. to the acre (1 oz. to 9 sq. ft.) has proved fairly effective, about 85 per cent of the millipeds on the beds being found dead the following day, although some apparently normal individuals were moving around through the dust, and only about 5 per cent of the millipeds below the surface were dead. Forty per cent nicotin sulphate was applied with good results at strengths varying from 1 part to 750 parts of water to 1 part to 1,000 parts of water. When applied at the weaker strength with a watering can until the soil of the beds was thoroughly drenched about 90 per cent were killed by the treatment, including nearly every milliped within 3 in. of the surface.

FOODS—HUMAN NUTRITION.

How to select foods.—II, Cereal foods, CAROLINE L. HUNT and HELEN W. ATWATER (*U. S. Dept. Agr., Farmers' Bul. 817 (1917), pp. 23, figs. 5*).—Continuing previous work (E. S. R., 37, p. 364), this publication deals with foods rich in starch and especially with the cereals and foods made from them.

Cereals, it is pointed out, are mild-flavored and comparatively inexpensive foods, which are very largely depended upon to yield energy to the body. In addition to this, they also yield varying but important amounts of tissue-building and body-regulating substances. Rightly combined with well-chosen food materials from other food groups, cereals can be safely used as the main part of the ration. Wisely planned, a diet in which cereals are so used can be made adequate, attractive, and at the same time economical.

Eggs in a thousand ways, A. MEYER (*Chicago: The Hotel Monthly Press, 1917, pp. 140*).—A compilation of recipes for the preparation of eggs for the table.

Milk as a food (*U. S. Dept. Agr., Bur. Anim. Indus.* [*Pub.*, *1917*], *p. 1*).—A summary of data comparing milk and other foods.

How to use skim milk.—Ways in which this nutritious food material may be used to advantage in cookery (*U. S. Dept. Agr., Bur. Anim. Indus.* [*Pub.*, *1917*], *p. 1*).—A summary of popular information with recipes.

Buttermilk a food drink (*U. S. Dept. Agr., Bur. Anim. Indus.* [*Pub.*], (*1917*), *pp. 2*).—A summary of data, with recipes.

The food value of American cheese (*U. S. Dept. Agr., Bur. Anim. Indus.* [*Pub.*], (*1917*), *pp. 2*).—A popular comparison of cheese with other foods.

Ways to use cottage cheese (*U. S. Dept. Agr., Bur. Anim. Indus.* [*Pub.*], (*1917*), *pp. 2*).—Popular information and recipes.

The nutritive value of edible fungi (*Jour. Bd. Agr.* [*London*], 24 (*1917*), *No. 4, pp. 416–419*).—A discussion of data in which the general conclusion is drawn that, while fungi can not be compared with meat or ranked with the essential foods, they should not be looked upon as absolutely worthless. They may be made to serve useful purposes as food accessories because of their agreeable flavor.

Cider fruit for table use, B. T. P. BARKER (*Jour. Bd. Agr.* [*London*], 24 (*1917*), *No. 4, pp. 394–402*).—The author concludes that, under present conditions, apples commonly used for cider should be used for cookery and the culls for jam making.

Botulism.—The danger of poisoning from vegetables canned by the cold-pack method, E. C. DICKSON (*Jour. Amer. Med. Assoc., 69* (*1917*), *No. 12, pp. 966–968*).—The occurrence of a number of cases of botulism in the Pacific coast region led to a study of the possibility of conveying this disease by canned goods, especially those prepared by the cold-pack method. In experimental tests quart jars of peas, beans, and corn were inoculated with an emulsion containing spores of *Bacillus botulinus*, the jars of peas and beans being left in boiling water in a wash boiler for 120 minutes, and the jars of corn for 180 minutes. They were sealed immediately after removal from the boiler, inverted, and placed in a dark closet.

Within three weeks fermentation with the formation of gas was noted in all the jars. Some of the jars were leaking. On opening the jars a strong odor, resembling butyric acid, was noticed and cultures from all the jars showed a mixture of *B. botulinus* and *B. subtilis*.

Portions of the juice from all the jars were injected into guinea pigs and some of the canned peas were fed to a chicken. "All the guinea pigs died within 20 hours, and the chicken developed symptoms of limber-neck and died within 30 hours. A portion of the juice from the corn was passed through a diatomaceous filter and injected into a guinea pig, and the animal died within 24 hours. The symptoms of all the guinea pigs and of the chicken were identical with those produced by the toxin of the *B. botulinus* which is formed in meat broth."

The author believes that the experimental data reported prove that "the cold-pack method of canning vegetables is not efficient if the raw material happens to be contaminated with spores of the *B. botulinus*. The fact that both *B. subtilis* and *B. botulinus* were recovered in cultures from the contents of the jars proves that a single sterilization for the time recommended in the published directions is not sufficient to cause the destruction of spores. Fortunately, the number of spore-bearing bacteria which are responsible for producing poisonous changes in food is small, but the *B. botulinus* belongs to this small group, and since it is also an obligative anaerobe, the conditions which exist in the sealed jar or can are ideal for its growth and toxin formation."

In discussing the results it is also pointed out that the percentage of canned goods which would be normally infected with spores of *B. botulinus* would probably be small.

The practical conclusion drawn by the author is that "the botulinus toxin is easily destroyed by heating, and all danger of botulism will be removed from home-canned products if the food is always boiled before it is eaten or even tasted. Under no circumstances should home-canned vegetables which have been prepared by the cold-pack method be served as salad unless they have been cooked after their removal from the container, and, until it is established what fruits are suitable for the formation of the toxin, it will be safer to reheat all fruits which have been prepared by this method, even though there may be no apparent evidence that the food has spoiled."

Canned food safe (*U. S. Dept. Agr., Weekly News Letter, 5 (1917), No. 16, p. 6*).—The following statement prepared by bacteriologists of the Bureau of Chemistry and the States Relations Service has been issued:

"There is no danger that the type of food poisoning known as 'botulism' will result from eating fruits or vegetables which have been canned by any of the methods recommended by the U. S. Department of Agriculture, provided such directions have been followed carefully. It is possible that in a number of instances the directions were not strictly followed and that spoilage has occurred. Of course, extreme care should be taken to ascertain before eating canned goods of any kind whether they are in good condition, and if they have spoiled they should not be consumed.

"In case of any doubt as to whether the contents of a particular can have spoiled, the safest plan is to throw it away, although all danger of botulism may be avoided by boiling the contents of the can for a few minutes, since the *Bacillus botulinus* and the toxin or poison which it produces are killed by such treatment. No canned food of any kind which shows any signs of spoilage should ever be eaten. In the cold-pack method of canning given out by the Department of Agriculture, only fresh vegetables are recommended for canning, and sterilization is accomplished by the following processes: Cleansing, blanching, cold dipping, packing in clean hot jars, adding boiling water, sealing immediately, and then sterilizing the sealed jars at a minimum temperature of 212° F. for one to four hours, according to the character of the material. Since the spores of *B. botulinus* are killed by heating for one hour at 175° F. (according to Jordan's Bacteriology and other recognized textbooks) there is no reason to believe that the botulinus organism will survive such treatment."

Food supplies in war time, R. H. REW (*London: Oxford University Press, 1914, pp. 19*).—A digest of data regarding the quantities of food available.

Utilization of food (*[Columbus], Ohio: Agr. Div. Ohio Branch Council Nat. Defense, [1917], pp. 44*).—This publication is prepared by the home economics department of the Ohio State University. Suggestions and recipes are given for the preparation of fresh and dried fruits, vegetables, salt fish, and cereals.

High cost of living (*Washington: Govt., 1917, pp. 119*).—This is a report of the minutes of a conference of the Federal Trade Commission with delegates appointed by the governors of the several States to confer regarding food and fuel supplies and prices.

Report on the increased cost of living for an unskilled laborer's family in New York City (*New York: City, 1917, pp. 32*).—This publication reports the results of comparative studies made in February, 1915, and February, 1917, by the Bureau of Personal Service of the Board of Estimate and Apportionment, as to the cost of living for the family of an unskilled laborer, which consisted of two adults and three children aged 6, 10, and 13 years.

A survey of evidence regarding food allowances for healthy children, LUCY H. GILLETT (*N. Y. Assoc. Imp. Condition Poor Pub. 115 (1917), pp. 24*).— This publication summarizes, under three headings, the evidence regarding the energy and protein requirements of children, consisting of (1) dietary studies, in which the weight of food eaten has been recorded for a given period of time and food values determined by analysis or calculated from average composition; (2) metabolism experiments, in which measurements have been made of the amount and composition of the food eaten and of the excretory products; and (3) respiration experiments in which the body heat has been estimated from the respiratory quotient.

A bibliography is appended.

The influence of diet on the heat production during mechanical work in the dog, G. LUSK (*Proc. Soc. Expt. Biol. and Med., 14 (1917), No. 5, pp. 92, 93*).—The data here reported show that "when a dog runs at the rate of about 2½ miles an hour the heat production is almost exactly the same whether the dog has had no food or whether 70 gm. of glucose has been administered. In the resting dog 70 gm. of glucose would have increased the heat production 6 calories. The experiment proves the economical use of carbohydrate during periods of work. On the contrary, when 700 gm. of meat were given and the dog was compelled to run, the heat production was increased by that quota which would have been added from the specific dynamic action of the protein metabolized."

ANIMAL PRODUCTION.

Alfalfa silage, O. E. REED and J. B. FITCH (*Kansas Sta. Bul. 217 (1917), pp. 3–19, figs. 2*).—Experiments conducted in 1914 and 1915 on the preservation of alfalfa in silos are reported. The silos were 7 ft. in diameter and 16 ft. in height and held about 10 tons of silage each. One of the silos was filled each year with alfalfa alone, another with rye alone, and the others with alfalfa in combination with corn chop, blackstrap molasses, straw, sweet sorghum stover, or green rye. A palatability test was made each year to see how cattle would relish the various combinations. Chemical analyses were made each year of the silages and of the mixtures from which they were made.

The silos were filled in May, 1914, the alfalfa used being the first cutting, cut when about one-tenth in bloom, and they were opened in January, 1915. The results were not entirely satisfactory, due in part to the fact that there was not sufficient weight in the silos to cause thorough filling and packing and also to the fact that the silos were not entirely air-tight. In the palatability test silage from each of the silos was placed in a separate feed bunk in a feed lot to which 40 beef cattle had access. The cattle showed their preference for the mixtures in the following order: Alfalfa and molasses (17:1), alfalfa and corn chop (13:1), alfalfa alone, alfalfa and rye (1.5:1), alfalfa and molasses feed (11:1), alfalfa and straw (4:1), and rye alone. Analyses of the silage used in this test showed that the moisture content of all the silages was low with the exception of alfalfa and rye.

Before filling the silos the second year they were painted on the outside and inside, thick asphalt paint being used on the inside. In order to pack the silage more firmly and prevent such a large amount of silage from being spoiled, additional weight was obtained by placing bags of sand on top of the silage after the silos were filled. They were filled in the spring of 1916 and opened in December, after standing 6.5 months. There was only about 8 in. of spoiled silage on the surface of each silo, and the silage was in much better condition than in the previous test. In a palatability test conducted for 12 days on the plan of the previous year the silage mixtures were preferred by the animals in the following order: Alfalfa-molasses (20:1), alfalfa-molasses (10:1), alfalfa and corn chop (10:1), alalfa and rye (2:1), alfalfa and sweet-sorghum stover (6:1), and alfalfa alone. Very little difference was shown between the first five mixtures. In a few cases the alfalfa and sorghum stover seemed to be preferred to the alfalfa and corn chop and alfalfa and rye silage. The poor quality of the sorghum stover accounts for the fact that the alfalfa and sorghum stover silage was not relished at times. The cattle ate very little of the alfalfa silage alone.

No attempt was made either year to determine the feeding value of the different mixtures used. A study of the chemical composition of the silages shows that both years those containing the highest percentage of acid were most palatable to the cattle, with the exception of rye alone.

Sudan grass silage, C. K. FRANCIS and W. G. FRIEDEMANN (*Oklahoma Sta. Bul. 115 (1917), pp. 8, figs. 2*).—This bulletin gives results of experiments on the preservation of Sudan grass silage in a steel silo. The Sudan grass was cut when about one-sixth of the plants had reached the milk stage. The composition is given of Sudan grass hay as compared with other hays and of Sudan grass silage and corn silage. It is noted that the composition of Sudan grass silage is very similar to that of corn silage, except that the former averages about 33 per cent in fiber and the latter about 23 per cent.

Temperature records taken at several depths in the silo show that the maximum temperature was reached in about 21 to 30 days and that no great increases occurred thereafter. It is stated that the Sudan grass silage was fed to the college sheep and, "while proving a good feed, it did not appear to be relished by the animals so well as the corn silage, but quite as well as that made from other grain sorghums, and was relished much more in this form than as cured hay."

A study of methods of estimation of metabolic nitrogen, E. B. FORBES, C. E. MANGELS, and L. E. MORGAN (*U. S. Dept. Agr., Jour. Agr. Research, 9 (1917), No. 12, pp. 405–411*).—In the work reported, carried on at the Ohio Experiment Station, a basal ration of corn alone was fed to each of five pigs during the first period and nitrogenous supplements added to this corn ration in subsequent periods. In selecting the supplements an endeavor was made to choose foods the protein of which would probably be entirely digestible. Milk, blood albumin, and commercial dried egg albumin were used.

The analytical methods compared were the acid-pepsin method, the acid-pepsin and alkaline-pancreatin method, and the alcohol, ether, hot-water, and cold-lime water method suggested by Jordan.[1] In the first two methods it is assumed that by the use of digestive enzyms the nitrogen which has been digested, absorbed, and returned to the feces may be separated from the indigestible nitrogen, and that there is no further digestion during the course of the estimation of that part of the protein which escaped digestion in the alimentary tract of the experimental animal. It is noted that there is no means of proving the truth of this assumption. The experimental methods are described.

The results show that the apparent digestibility of corn, based on the total nitrogen of the feces, is about 75 per cent. The results of the acid-pepsin method make it appear that the real digestibility is about 92 per cent, and the pepsin-pancreatin method, about 96 per cent. Jordan's method yielded appreciably lower figures, averaging 86 per cent. The results of the acid-pepsin

---

[1] Maine Sta. Rpt. 1888, pp. 196, 197 ; abs. in U. S. Dept. Agr., Office Expt. Stas. Bul. 2 (1891), pt. 2, p. 60.

method indicate that 70 per cent of the nitrogen of the feces from corn is of metabolic origin, while those of the pepsin-pancreatin method and Jordan's method indicated 84 per cent and 46 per cent, respectively.

"All of the methods make the nitrogen of blood albumin appear more than completely digestible, even the apparent digestibility being over 100 per cent; thus, the feeding of blood albumin with corn seems to increase the digestibility of the corn protein to an extent more than sufficient to offset the incompleteness of digestibility of the protein of this supplement."

The apparent digestibility of skim milk varied from 95.97 to 104.44 per cent, the average being 99.15. The proteins of skim milk appear to be more nearly completely digestible by the acid-pepsin method than by the other methods.

It is indicated that "important inaccuracy seems to be inevitable in any determination of digestibility of supplementary foods in the usual way, by difference; and no other method seems more satisfactory. This applies equally to computations of real digestibility and of apparent digestibility (based on total nitrogen of the feces). The digestion coefficients for protein involved in the feeding standards of our reference works on animal production assume that the nitrogen of the feces is entirely an indigestible food residue. The rough measures afforded by the results of this study indicate that, as applying to the digestive capacities of swine, this assumption underestimates the digestibility of protein by about 20 per cent."

No significant differences were observed in the study of the effects on metabolic nitrogen of storage of the feces in a frozen condition for 20 days, with or without the addition of thymol, or air-drying the fresh material with or without thymol.

The acid-pepsin and the pepsin-pancreatin methods are considered to give results which are more nearly true than does Jordan's method. The latter does not digest the bacteria which may contain large proportions of the nitrogen of the feces and which presumably are more largely the product of digestible. than of indigestible protein. The lack of an accurate scientific basis for the determination of the digestibility of protein is noted.

A study of the rate of passage of feed residues through the steer and its influence on digestion coefficients, P. V. Ewing and F. H. Smith (*U. S. Dept. Agr., Jour. Agr. Research, 10 (1917), No. 2, pp. 55–63*).—In the investigations here reported, which were made at the Georgia Experiment Station, the attempt was made (1) to determine by means of digestion experiments the relationship between the moisture content of the feces and the digestion coefficients in order to see if there is a correlation between the time required for the passage of the food through the animal and the moisture content of the feces, (2) to follow more closely and directly by means of rubber markers the time required for passage of the feed residues through the steers, and (3) to determine the rate of passage by means of calculations based upon the intake of food and outgo of feces and the alimentary tract contents as ascertained on slaughtering.

In studying the problem by the first method essentially the digestion experiments already noted (E. S. R., 34, p. 169) were repeated. To avoid the complications in the calculations and results which would arise if comparisons were made of the data obtained while on different rations, studies were made on the correlations between the high and low moisture contents of the feces and the corresponding digestion coefficients where the same rations were employed. The correlations, as obtained from the results of the two series of digestion experiments each made in duplicate, indicate that with a higher moisture content of the feces there is a more complete digestion of all nutrients except nitrogen and fat. Commenting on the weakness of this method the authors state that "it still remains to be proved definitely that the rate of passage of feed residue through the steer can be measured by the moisture content of the feces. Our work has shown that if a high moisture content of the feces is indicative of rapid passage then the apparent digestion is more complete probably for all the nutrients with the more rapid passage and less complete with the slower movement. Unfortunately, the method of study shows only the relationship and not the extent of the variation in digestion associated with a high moisture content."

In studying the problem by the second method soft rubber discs cut from heavy rubber tubing were fed at the beginning of a ten-day digestion trial and a count was made of them as they appeared in the feces. Some of the indicators appeared within 12 hours, while others were recovered as late as 60 days following, and still others never came out until the steers were slaughtered. While this method proved impractical, the slaughter tests showed that hard particles of feed and foreign substances were especially prone to become delayed in transit either in the reticulum, in the fourth, or true, stomach, or in the first few ventral folds of the duodenum. The coarse feeds and roughages retard the rate of passage of feed residues, a point proved conclusively by the slaughter tests. In connection with this method the use of 60 or 120 gm. per steer daily of calcium carbonate or magnesium sulphate exerted no appreciable effect upon the rate of passage of feed residue or upon the digestion coefficients.

Studying the problem by the third method, an accurate measure of the time required for the passage of the residue of feed was obtained by use of a formula. The inaccuracies of the method arising from certain metabolic processes are recognized, but it is stated that their influence would be no greater on these results than on the digestion coefficients, if as much.

The data obtained by this method indicate that with the rations used and the quantities fed the time required for the passage of the feed residues through the animals varied from 2.9 to 5.2 days. "The two most important factors determining the rate of passage are the nature of the ration and the amount fed. Coarse roughages seem to require a considerably greater time than the more finely ground concentrated feeds. . . . As to the influence of quantity, it appears that, when the coarse feeds were fed, a smaller quantity required a greater time for passage of the residues, but when the feed was a concentrate in pulverized form the variation was not so pronounced. . . . In dealing with the influence which the rate of passage of the feed residue may have had on the digestion coefficients we are unable definitely to attribute changes to the rate of passage, and at best it can only be said that associated with the more rapid passage there occurred an apparent gain in the digestibility of the ash, negligible results in the case of nitrogen, a decided loss in the digestibility of the crude fiber, a gain in the case of the nitrogen-free extract, and negligible results in the case of fat."

[Feeding experiments with beef cattle], D. T. GRAY (*North Carolina Sta. Rpt. 1916, pp. 31–34*).—To ascertain the best feed for wintering stock cattle, 67 grade steers were fed varying amounts of cottonseed meal and corn silage for 148 days at the station farm during the winter of 1915–16. The steers in lot 1 were fed an average daily ration of 20 lbs. of corn silage and 1 lb. of cottonseed meal, those in lot 2 an average ration of 23 lbs. of corn silage, those in lot 3 an average ration of 20 lbs. of corn silage, and those in lot 4 an average ration of 20 lbs. of corn silage and 0.5 lb. of cottonseed meal. During the last 44 days of the experiment all the lots also received 5 lbs. of corn stover per head daily. The steers in the first lot lost 16.2 lbs. during the entire period, those in the second lot 52.9 lbs., those in the third lot 72.2 lbs., and those in the fourth lot 69.4 lbs.

In a similar experiment at the Iredell substation one lot of steers wintered on a daily ration of 20 lbs. of corn silage and 1 lb. of cottonseed meal gained 24 lbs. per head in 160 days. Another lot on a daily ration of 20 lbs. of corn silage alone lost 55 lbs. per head during the same period.

Work was carried on at the Edgecombe substation during the past winter to determine the best feeds for wintering beef calves, especially to see if cottonseed meal could be fed profitably. One lot of calves averaging 340 lbs. each in weight gained 19 lbs. per head in 98 days on an average daily ration of 15 lbs. of corn silage and 1 lb. of cottonseed meal. Another lot averaging 321 lbs. each in weight lost 16 lbs. per head during the same period on an average daily ration of 15 lbs. of corn silage alone. With silage at $4 and cottonseed meal at $40 per ton, the respective feed costs per calf were $4.90 and $2.94. The cottonseed meal did not injure the calves in any way.

At the station farm the attempt is being made to determine the amounts of cottonseed meal that can be safely fed to growing calves, with special reference to the kinds of roughage and antidotes. During the past winter 20 grade Jersey calves weighing from 150 to 450 lbs. each were divided into four lots and fed the following daily rations: Lot 1, cottonseed hulls and 1 lb. of cottonseed meal per 100 lbs. live weight; lot 2, cottonseed hulls and 1 lb. per 100 lbs. live weight of a mixture of cracked corn and cottonseed meal (1:1); lot 3, a mixture of beet pulp and cottonseed hulls and 1 lb. of cottonseed meal per 100 lbs. live weight; and lot 4, the same as lot 1 plus 1 qt. of iron sulphate solution per pound of cottonseed meal. This experiment was closed May 1, as one of the calves in the third lot died on April 12 as a result of cottonseed-meal poisoning and several of the other calves were losing their sight. The calves in lots 2, 3, and 4 were then turned on pasture and weighed again on October 31. All of them showed subsequent gains for the summer, and their eyes had apparently entirely recovered from the trouble. A repetition of the above experiment ended with practically the same results.

In a cooperative experiment in Haywood County the attempt is being made to solve the problem of maintaining beef cattle through the winter with a view to finishing on pasture the subsequent summer. During the past winter 114 stockers were divided into five lots and wintered for 119 days as follows: Lot 1 was fed a daily ration of 3.15 lbs. of ear corn and 11.4 lbs. of a mixture of corn stover, hay, and straw; lots 2 and 3, a daily ration of 18 lbs. of corn silage and 6 lbs. of the hay mixture; lot 4, pasture alone; and lot 5, which consisted of calves averaging 270 lbs. each in weight, a ration of 0.5 lb. of shelled corn and 0.5 lb. of cottonseed cake. The stockers in lots 1, 2, 3, and 4 averaged from 762 to 813 lbs. each in weight. During the winter the cattle in the first three lots lost in weight 34, 41, and 40 lbs., respectively, per head, while those on pasture alone gained 26 lbs. each. The calves gained 9 lbs. each. Counting pasture at $1 a month per animal and the other feeds at local prices, it cost $12.14 to winter each steer in the first lot, $7 in lots 2 and 3, $5.30 in the winter pasture lot, and $4.18 to feed each one of the calves.

The cattle were placed on summer pasture from April 13 until August 31, lot 1 also receiving 4 lbs. of cottonseed cake per head daily. All the steers made good gains, but those fed cottonseed cake did not make much more rapid gains than those on pasture alone and it did not pay to feed it. The steers in lots 2, 3, and 4 yielded a net profit of $21.63, $20.94, and $24.02 per head, respectively, while the steers in lot 1 yielded a net profit of only $13.01 each.

Sheep, D. T. Gray (*North Carolina Sta. Rpt. 1916, pp. 34, 35, 36*).—Two years' work on the effect of cottonseed meal upon the health and reproductive organs of breeding ewes showed no detrimental results from a ration of cottonseed meal and cracked corn (2:1). In the work of crossing Barbado sheep with those of the Shropshire and Merino blood, wool from the cross-bred animals was sold the past season for the same price as the wool from the Shropshire and Merino ewes. The Barbado sheep have not proved immune to the ravages of the stomach worm.

At the Iredell substation a lot of breeding ewes kept in shed or corral during the winter of 1915–16 and fed corn silage and a mixture of cracked corn, cottonseed meal, and wheat bran (2:1:1) gained about 5 lbs. per head. Another lot pastured during the winter on a meadow from which hay had been cut gained 20 lbs. each. The cost of wintering the barn-fed ewes was about twice that of the lot on pasture. In the spring the ewes were all sheared, the wool selling at 36 cts. per pound, or $2.99 per ewe, which was about the cost of wintering ewes on good pasture.

The management of farm flocks in Idaho, E. J. Iddings (*Idaho Bul. 96 (1917), pp. 20, figs. 9*).—This bulletin gives general information and suggestions for the management of farm flocks of sheep under Idaho conditions.

Are sheep profitable in winter? C. D. Woods (*Maine Sta. Bul. 260 (1917), pp. 86–92*).—A two years' progress report is given of the experiment with grade Hampshire sheep at Highmoor farm, already noted (E. S. R., 33, p. 73).

On the flock of 73 ewes, 3 rams, and 22 ewe lambs there was a loss of $375.55 during the year ended October 31, 1915, the estimated value of manure being credited. During the year ended October 31, 1916, the flock was kept at a loss of $207.56, no account being taken of manure, or allowing full value for manure and omitting overhead charges, a credit balance of about $100 on the flock for 1915–16.

Family performance as a basis for selection in sheep, E. C. Ritzman and C. B. Davenport (*U. S. Dept. Agr., Jour. Agr. Research. 10 (1917), No. 2, pp. 93–97*).—An outline is given of a system of selection on the basis of family performance being used in sheep-breeding work at the New Hampshire Experiment Station.

By "family" is meant the brothers and sisters and the two parents of the individual being studied. The aim of these breeding experiments being to produce a race of sheep that will combine good qualities of conformation, size, and wool, weights are assigned to various quantities which are thought to be correlated with the traits that are desired. The families from which individuals are to be selected are rated according to the average weights obtained in grading. In the selection of breeding rams, if the individual belonging to the "best" family is sickly or has any physiological quality that would interfere with its success as a breeder, the male from the next higher family may be preferred— that is, selection is made primarily on the basis of family performance, but the somatic insufficiency of the individual is permitted to veto the choice based on family alone. It has been found, however, that the best individuals usually come from the families that stand high in the scale.

The use of the method is illustrated in a particular case. The experiment has not yet proceeded far enough to show definite results, but the authors state that "the uniformity of the progeny and the high quality already shown by the earlier generations give us every reason for confidence that this method of selecting by family performance in place of individual traits is well worth the extra trouble it entails, if, indeed, it is not indispensable."

Digestion experiments with pigs, with special reference to the influence of one feed upon another, and to the individuality of pigs, H. S. GRINDLEY, W. J. CARMICHAEL, and C. I. NEWLIN (*Illinois Sta. Bul. 200 (1917), pp. 55–94, figs. 4*).—The objects of the experiments reported in this bulletin were (1) to determine the influence of one feed upon the digestibility of the nutrients of another feed, (2) to study the individuality of pigs as to the thoroughness with which they digest their feed, and (3) to determine the coefficients of digestibility of the nutrients of the following rations: Wheat middlings, ground corn, ground barley, wheat middlings and ground corn (1:1), ground barley and ground corn (1:1), and tankage and ground corn (1:7.5). The feeding stalls used in these experiments were large enough to allow the pigs to turn around freely and were raised some 3 ft. from the floor to enable an easy collection of the urine. The feces were collected in rubber-lined canvas bags held in place by specially constructed harness. Illustrations are given of the digestion harness and of the feeding stalls.

Each of the rations was fed for two 10-day periods. Each test period was preceded by a preliminary period of from 25 to 32 days during which the pigs were accustomed to the test rations and to the stalls and harness. Four 7-months-old pigs were used in each of the series, those in 1913–14 being cross-bred Berkshire-Chester Whites, all from the same litter, and those in 1914–15 cross-bred Duroc Jersey-Poland Chinas, all from the same litter. Analyses are given of the feeds and feces.

The following table gives the average coefficients of digestibility of the rations fed in these experiments:

Digestion coefficients of rations when fed to swine.

Ration.	Number of experiments.	Dry substance.	Protein.	Ether extract.	Nitrogen-free extract.	Crude fiber.
		Per cent.	*Per cent.*	*Per cent.*	*Per cent.*	*Per cent.*
Wheat middlings........................	16	74.4	80.0	85.4	81.2	21.0
Ground corn............................	16	87.1	74.5	68.3	92.1	34.8
Ground barley.........................	8	70.8	54.0	33.0	81.2	14.1
Wheat middlings and ground corn (1:1)..	8	79.1	77.3	83.4	85.9	12.1
Ground barley and ground corn (1:1).....	8	80.9	66.5	67.8	88.9	15.0
Tankage and ground corn (1:7.5).........	16	86.0	74.8	80.8	92.2	51.2

Discussing the influence of one feed upon the digestibility of another feed as indicated by results obtained in these experiments, the authors conclude, "first, that the coefficients of digestibility of feeds calculated indirectly by subtracting the weights of the digestible nutrients of one feed as directly determined in other periods from the corresponding values for two feeds combined may be, and probably often are, decidedly inaccurate, and, second, that the weights of the digestible nutrients of a mixed ration calculated by the use of the coefficients of digestibility of the nutrients obtained directly for the individual feeds when fed alone may be decidedly inaccurate. It, therefore, seems evident from these considerations that, in order to obtain accurate results for the cofficients of digestibility of mixed rations, digestion experiments should be made directly upon the mixed rations as fed. In other words, in the future, coefficients of digestibility of the nutrients for mixed rations should be obtained and reported, rather than merely those for the individual feeds composing the rations."

The following table is a summary of the average results, which show the influence of one feed upon the digestibility of another feed:

Coefficients of digestibility of feeds, directly and indirectly determined.

Ration.	Number of experiments.	Dry substance.	Protein.	Ether extract.	Nitrogenfree extract.	Crude fiber.
		Per cent.	*Per cent.*	*Per cent.*	*Per cent.*	*Per cent.*
Middlings—direct..........................	8	74.7	79.3	82.3	82.2	22.8
Middlings—indirect........................	8	70.7	78.3	89.3	77.2	6.1
Corn—direct..............................	8	87.8	75.1	71.7	92.7	30.8
Corn—indirect............................	8	83.7	73.0	81.3	88.9	-2.2
Barley—direct............................	8	70.8	54.0	33.0	81.2	14.1
Barley—indirect..........................	8	76.1	60.2	68.9	86.2	3.7
Corn—direct..............................	8	86.2	74.0	64.9	91.5	38.8
Corn—indirect............................	8	91.8	81.4	68.7	96.6	15.6
Middlings and corn—direct................	8	79.1	77.3	83.5	86.0	12.1
Middlings and corn—indirect [1]..........	8	81.1	78.0	78.8	88.1	24.8
Middlings and corn—indirect [2]..........	8	77.1	76.6	88.1	83.8	-0.7
Barley and corn—direct...................	8	80.9	66.5	67.8	88.9	15.0
Barley and corn—indirect [1].............	8	78.3	63.2	54.0	86.3	20.4
Barley and corn—indirect [2].............	8	83.7	69.9	50.7	91.3	6.6

[1] Calculated from direct determinations of coefficients of individual feeds.
[2] Calculated from indirect determinations of coefficients of individual feeds.

Data are also tabulated showing the thoroughness with which each pig digested its feeds, from which it is concluded that "under conditions that are practically identical throughout the same experiment, the coefficients of digestibility of the nutrients of a number of different rations show significantly higher values for some pigs than for others. However, the differences in the coefficients of digestibility of the nutrients of the same feeds by the different pigs are probably too small to be considered of much, if any, practical or economic importance."

The digestibility of some Arkansas feeds for hogs, J. B. Rather (*Arkansas Sta. Bul. 133 (1917), pp. 16, fig. 1*).—The results of digestion experiments on hogs are reported, including analyses of the feeds and a description of the digestion crate used in the experiments. The following table gives the coefficients of digestibility as determined:

Coefficients of digestibility of various feeding stuffs.

Number of trials.	Kind of feed.	Protein.	Ether extract.	Crude fiber.	Nitrogenfree extract.
		Per cent.	*Per cent.*	*Per cent.*	*Per cent.*
4	Corn chop..........................	82.37	70.75	42.38	93.58
4	Cottonseed meal....................	79.53	85.04	39.56	63.34
2	Kafir corn.........................	77.14	62.14	67.31	96.22
2	Oats...............................	78.37	86.29	21.85	78.31
1	Wheat bran.........................	76.26	80.20	19.23	68.33
2	Wheat shorts.......................	85.83	79.93	34.86	85.73
2	Rice bran..........................	75.69	86.49	20.52	80.63
2	Rice polish........................	87.49	87.07	55.21	95.55

Pork production on irrigated lands in western Nebraska, J. A. Holden (*Nebraska Sta. Bul. 159 (1917), pp. 4–31, figs. 3*).—Results of grazing experiments with hogs at the Scottsbluff experiment farm from 1912 to 1916, inclusive, are reported. Results secured from 1912 to 1915, inclusive, have been noted from another source (E. S. R., 36, p. 767).

In 1916 corn and ground barley were compared as supplements for alfalfa pasture. Although the one acre of pasture on which these tests were made was severely damaged by wind and hail storms, the results were fairly satisfactory and added strength to the previous years' data which showed that ground barley is equal to shelled corn as a hog feed. For the entire season the gain from the corn lot was 3,142 lbs., and from the barley lot 2,701 lbs. The corn lot consumed 2.74 lbs. of corn and the barley lot 2.92 lbs. of ground barley for each pound of gain made. When the gains made are figured at 7 cts. per pound and the lots charged $1.07 per hundredweight for corn and $1 for ground barley, the net returns for the one-acre alfalfa pastures were $127.84 where corn was fed and $110.11 where barley was fed. The pasture of the barley lot, however, was more severely damaged by the windstorms and one of the shoats in this lot became sick 28 days after the experiment began and was removed.

Sows and their litters grazed on alfalfa pasture with 2 lbs. of corn per 100 lbs. of live weight made a gain of 1,285 lbs. and a net return of $57.20 per acre in 1916. The average for the five years in these tests, in one of which barley was used instead of corn, was 1,516 lbs. of gain and a net profit of $63.11 per acre.

In an experiment which lasted two months in 1916 where corn and alfalfa pasture were compared with corn alone in a dry lot for finishing shoats for market, 1¾ acres of pasture supplemented with 9,677 lbs. of corn produced 2,497 lbs. of pork, and 11,300 lbs. of corn on dry lot produced 2,202 lbs. of pork, or a gain of 25.8 lbs. on pasture and 19.5 lbs. on dry lot per 100 lbs. of corn.

Results in 1916 in hogging corn without supplementary feed showed a gain of 840 lbs. of pork worth $58.80 per acre, or $1.56 per hundredweight for the estimated yield of corn. The average gain per acre in four years of these tests was 882 lbs. of pork worth $61.74 per acre, or $1.52 per hundredweight of the estimated yield of corn.

[Feeding experiments with pigs], D. T. GRAY (*North Carolina Sta. Rpt. 1916, pp. 23–31*).—At the Edgecombe substation 18 pigs weighing 87 lbs. each were pastured on 5 acres of soy beans for 60 days. In addition to the pasture they received a small amount of corn and tankage (9:1). As a check 3 pigs were fed a full ration of corn and tankage (9:1) on dry lot. The pigs on soy-bean pasture gained 1.38 lbs. per head daily at a cost of 4.96 cts. per pound of gain and returned a value of $19.25 per acre for the soy beans, the yield of which was below normal. The pigs on dry lot gained 1.28 lbs. each daily at a cost of 5.6 cts. per pound of gain.

To determine the relative value of peanuts and soy beans as grazing crops for pigs, 1.65 acres of soy beans and 1.72 acres of peanuts were planted in the spring of 1915 at the Pender substation. Nine pigs averaging 112 lbs. each were turned into each field September 16 and given a half ration of corn. The soy beans afforded feed for the 9 pigs for 61 days, but an equivalent area of peanuts afforded grazing only 36 days. The soy bean-fed pigs gained an average of 0.98 lb. per head daily at a cost of 5.2 cts. per pound of gain. The peanut-fed pigs gained 1.36 lbs. per head daily at a cost of 5.41 cts. per pound of gain. Deducting the cost of grain the soy beans produced $18.80 and the peanuts $16.61 worth of pork per acre.

In an experiment to test the relative value of peanuts damaged in the shock and peanut meal for pigs at Edgecombe, 30 pigs averaging 98 lbs. each were divided into three lots and fed for 149 days, beginning January 25, 1916. The pigs in the first lot were fed a ration of corn and shorts (2:1), those in the second lot corn and damaged peanuts (2:1), and those in the third lot a ration of corn and peanut meal (2:1). Those in the first lot gained 0.69 lb. per head daily at a cost of 10.35 cts. per pound of gain, those in the second lot 0.71 lb. at a cost of 9.83 cts., and those in the third lot 0.81 lb. at a cost of 8.81 cts.

The waste peanuts were marketed by means of these hogs at more than 75 cts. per bushel.

In a preliminary experiment at the main station as to the relative value of wheat shorts, soy-bean meal, and peanut meal as supplements for corn, pigs averaging about 43 lbs. each were fed for 140 days in very small cement-floored lots. The pigs fed corn and shorts (2:1) gained an average of 0.29 lb. per head per day at a cost of 19.8 cts. per pound of gain, those fed corn and soy-bean meal (2:1) gained 0.44 lb. at a cost of 11.79 cts., and those fed corn and peanut meal (2:1) gained 0.37 lb. at a cost of 14.56 cts. In this test corn was valued at $1 a bushel, soy-bean meal at $40 a ton, and peanut meal at $30 a ton.

Continuing the work on the use of iron sulphate and citrate of iron and ammonia to neutralize the effects of cottonseed meal upon hogs (E. S. R., 34, p. 79), it was found that while these chemicals did not completely overcome the toxic effects of cottonseed meal, gains were more satisfactory where they were used.

Tests were made on the feed and labor cost of raising pigs to weaning time at eight weeks of age. At Edgecombe with sows that raised an average of $5\frac{7}{11}$ pigs the cost was $1.94 per pig and the weight at weaning time averaged 24.3 lbs. At Pender the sows raised an average of $6\frac{1}{4}$ pigs each, averaging 28.8 lbs. each in weight and $3.34 in cost at weaning time. At the Iredell substation the sows raised an average of $6\frac{1}{4}$ pigs each, averaging 31.8 lbs. in weight and cost $2.24 each.

Extensive experiments are being made by the station on the softening effects of peanuts, soy beans, and mast upon the fat of hogs. In this work corn-fed hogs are used as a standard, it having been found that the melting point of the lard from the kidney fat of hogs fattened on corn alone is approximately 43° C. In a cooperative experiment hogs were grazed on waste peanuts for 82 days, at the end of which time their bodies were very soft. During the finishing or hardening period of 26 days the hogs were fed on corn alone and corn in combination with various amounts of cottonseed meal, but in none of the lots was the average melting point of the leaf lard of these hogs as high as 40° after the hardening period. At Pender a lot of pigs was grazed on soy-bean pasture supplemented with a partial ration of corn for 61 days, when the melting point of the leaf lard of two of the pigs averaged 37°. The remaining pigs were finished for 41 days on corn alone, and the average melting point of the leaf lard of these pigs was 39.8°. With another lot not pastured on peanuts and fed some corn in addition for 36 days the average melting point was 33.4°, while the remaining pigs of this lot, after being finished for 66 days on corn alone, showed a melting point of 37.2°. At Edgecombe the leaf fat of pigs fed in dry lot on corn and tankage (9:1) for 60 days had a melting point of 43.3°, while in other pigs fed this ration supplemented with soy-bean pasture for 60 days it was 33.3°. The remaining pigs in the soy-bean lot were finished in dry lots for 21 days, when the lards taken from those finished on corn and tankage had a melting point of 35.6°, and from those finished on corn and cottonseed meal 38.5°. The results of more recent work indicate that soft-bodied hogs can be brought back to normal in from 32 to 49 days when corn is fed in conjunction with cottonseed meal.

Are swine profitable in winter? C. D. Woods (*Maine Sta. Bul. 260 (1917), pp. 92–94*).—In an experiment on the care of manure noted on page 628, it was necessary to keep the manure well worked over and compacted to prevent losses from heating. The experiment here reported was undertaken to determine whether swine would perform this work.

A brood sow and 14 2-months-old pigs were placed on the manure December 1, 1915, and were kept there until June 7, 1916. They were fed cooked turnips and ground feed, and some whole corn was scattered over the manure at times to keep the swine at work stirring the manure. Reckoning the turnips at 15 cts. per bushel, corn at $30 per ton, corn meal at $31 per ton, middlings at $27 per ton, and labor at 15 cts. per hour, and crediting the sow and shoats at the end of the experiment at 8 cts. per pound, live weight, increased by a litter of 8 pigs at $2 each, and $27 for manure, there was a profit of $23.68, or a return of 15 per cent on the whole investment. Moreover, the manure in the pit was thoroughly worked and in excellent shape for application to the land.

Orokinase and salivary digestion studies in the horse, C. C. PALMER, A. L. ANDERSON, W. E. PETERSON, and A. W. MALCOMSON (*Amer. Jour. Physiol.*, *43* (*1917*), *No. 3, pp. 457–474*).—The name orokinase is proposed by the senior author, at the Minnesota Experiment Station, for the enzym produced in the mouth and found in the saliva which activates the saliva of the horse. Saliva obtained from the parotid ducts or extracts of the salivary gland was found not to digest starch, while mixed mouth secretions obtained from an esophageal fistula were found to have a very powerful amylolytic action. The amylolytic action of mixed horse saliva was equal to that of human saliva on cooked starches and greater on raw starches. The saliva collected from the mouth was hardly ever as powerful as that obtained from an esophageal fistula.

Attempts were made to activate artificially fistula saliva or gland extracts, but these were unsuccessful. The gland extracts, however, became self-active with age. Considerable reducing sugar in food caught from an esophageal fistula a few minutes after feeding a diet of raw corn and oats was demonstrated. It is noted that "salivary digestion started in the mouth is very likely continued in the stomach, and this digestion is more important in the horse than most investigators have been lead to believe."

The amylolytic action of parotid fistula saliva was studied by methods previously noted by Palmer (E. S. R., 36, p. 82).

[Cottonseed meal for work horses and mules], D. T. GRAY (*North Carolina Sta. Rpt. 1916, pp. 46, 47*).—At the Iredell, Pender, and Edgecombe substations the work horses and mules have been divided into two lots, one lot receiving no cottonseed meal and the other lot the same kind of ration, except that cottonseed meal makes up a part.

It has been found that "while cottonseed meal can be used in very limited amounts, we can not, as a rule, induce a horse or mule to use more than 1 lb. a day for any length of time. This 1 lb., however, has proved to be an economical addition to the ration, and has also had much to do with maintaining the horses and mules in better condition. The saving in money, however, is not the chief advantage in using cottonseed meal, or at least it does not appear so at the present time. It seems that the chief advantage will be that the horses which eat cottonseed meal stay in better condition. This is indicated plainly during the spring months, as the animals which eat cottonseed meal shed off earlier and smoother than those which do not eat it."

Licensed stallions in Utah during the season of 1916, W. E. CARROLL (*Utah Sta. Circ. 24 (1917), pp. 3–25, fig. 1*).—Tables are given showing the distribution of licensed stallions and jacks in the State, the number of licensed animals in each county and the percentage which are pure bred, and the distribution among the various breeds.

[Poultry investigations], D. T. GRAY (*North Carolina Sta. Rpt. 1916, pp. 43–45*).—In tests on the cost of raising chicks to eight weeks of age it was found that to produce 1 lb. of gain with the Mediterranean and Continental breeds it required 2 lbs. of feed, and with the English and American breeds 2.1 lbs. of feed. At the end of eight weeks chicks of the former classes averaged 1.2 lbs. in weight, while those from the latter classes averaged 1.6 lbs. It cost slightly over 8 cts. per pound to produce gains in all the breeds.

In fertility experiments it was found that ordinarily from 80 to 90 per cent of the eggs are fertile when cocks are continually with the hens, and from 80 to 90 per cent of these eggs hatch. When cocks were removed from the hens the fertility of the eggs declined rapidly, no fertile eggs being found after from 15 to 18 days. When cocks were placed with laying hens fertile eggs began to appear after the fifth or sixth day.

An experiment was begun November 1, 1915, with three lots of hens to determine the effects of continued feeding of cottonseed meal upon the health, vigor, and egg production. Rations were fed made up of 30 per cent, 5 per cent, and no cottonseed meal, respectively. During the first year 26, 12, and 10 per cent of the respective flocks died. There has not been so far a marked difference in the amount of eggs produced.

Eight different breeds and some mixed lots were compared as to the amount of feeds eaten, the cost of feeds, and the amount of manure produced. Of the breeds tested, the Silver Campines consumed the least amount of feeds. In cost of eggs produced, the Buff Plymouth Rock was the most expensive breed. In this test the hens produced an average of 22 lbs. of manure per head per year.

In experiments in marketing eggs by parcel post and express it was found that such materials as sawdust, bran, and cottonseed hulls pack so closely that there is not sufficient spring to the material about the eggs, and about 10 per cent of the eggs are broken in transit. These materials were particularly unsatisfactory when breeding eggs were shipped. When the eggs were wrapped in soft paper, felt, moss, or prairie hay very few were broken.

At the Pender substation soy-bean meal practically took the place of rolled oats for chicks and was much cheaper. At the Edgecombe substation peanut meal proved a valuable feed for young chicks up to eight weeks of age. Chicks fed a ration of peanut meal, corn meal, and ground oats (1:1:1) and buttermilk weighed an average of a little over 1 lb. each at eight weeks of age, while those fed a similar ration with peanut meal omitted weighed only 0.7 lb. each.

Preparing poultry produce for market, F. G. ELFORD (*Canada Expt. Farms Bul. 88 (1916), pp. 31, pl. 1, figs. 19*).—In addition to notes on the need and value of preparing poultry for market and systems of marketing, this bulletin contains general directions for packing and shipping market eggs, for crate feeding, killing, plucking, packing, and marketing poultry, and for crating and shipping breeding stock and eggs for hatching.

Preserving eggs for home use, G. S. TEMPLETON (*Alabama Sta. Circ. 36 (1917), pp. 39–42, fig. 1*).—Brief directions are given for preserving eggs in water glass or sodium silicate.

DAIRY FARMING—DAIRYING.

Dairy investigational work, D. T. GRAY (*North Carolina Sta. Rpt. 1916, pp. 36–40*).—Work has been carried on at the Pender substation for three years to determine the value of corn silage for milch cows. During the three winters the cows fed silage have produced 3,878 lbs. of milk more than those fed cottonseed hulls and corn stover. This was produced at a saving of $11.42 in cost of feed.

A progress report is made of four years' work at Pender substation and near Greensboro in cooperation with farmers to test the value of a limited ration of cottonseed meal for wintering growing dairy calves. Each year one lot of calves was fed a grain ration of cottonseed meal alone and another lot a grain ration of cottonseed meal and bran (1:1). The roughage was the same for both lots. Summarizing the four years' work, during which the calves were upon experimental feeds for 553 days, it was found that the respective feed costs were $99.33 and $98.88, while the calves fed no bran gained an average of 54.8 lbs. more per head. At Pender the same feeds were also compared as supplements for scant pasture for dairy heifers during the spring and summer. During the three summers this experiment has been running the calves fed cottonseed meal have made the better gains, but this ration was somewhat the more expensive.

Data on the cost of raising 22 calves at Pender show that when these calves were 6, 12, and 18 months old they averaged per head 264, 373, and 478 lbs. in weight, respectively, at total costs of $13.57, $26.12, and $34.30. Four of the calves which attained the age of 30 months averaged 646 lbs. in weight at a total cost of $52.06. These figures include market prices for feeds and $1 per month each for pasture, no credit being made for manure. Cooperative experiments with farmers in Guilford and Forsyth Counties show a cost of $31.58 to raise a dairy calf to the age of 12 months.

A study is being made at Pender relative to the feasibility of overcoming onion flavors in milk. In one case a strong onion flavor was found in the milk of a cow milked 19 hours after the onions had been eaten. It has been found that molasses fed in conjunction with other feeds materially weakens the onion flavor, but does not remove it completely. Other remedies being tried are charcoal, soda, mixtures of charcoal, soda and molasses, and patent preparations. These have been without effect, except that one of the patent preparations has caused some weakening of the onion flavor.

[Feeding experiments with dairy cattle], J. M. Scott (*Florida Sta. Rpt. 1916, pp. 18–23*).—In a comparison of sorghum silage and Japanese cane silage as supplements for wheat bran and cottonseed meal for dairy cows, ten cows were fed during four periods of 16 days each with four days between experimental periods for changing feeds. The cows were fed in lots of five by the reversal system. Those on sorghum silage produced 539.72 gal. of milk at a feed cost of 12.1 cts. per gallon and those on Japanese cane silage 509.74 gal. of milk at a feed cost of 12.8 cts. per gallon. In this experiment the silage was valued at $4 per ton. All the cows gained slightly in weight during the test, there being no difference between the two rations in maintaining the animal's initial weight.

A comparison was also made of sorghum silage and sweet-potato silage as supplements for wheat bran and cottonseed meal. In this test ten cows were fed by the reversal system during two periods of 20 days each with three days for change of feeds. The five cows on sorghum silage produced 280.9 gal. of milk at a feed cost of 14.8 cts. per gallon. The five cows fed sweet potato silage produced 307.1 gal. of milk at a feed cost of 15.4 cts. per gallon. In this experiment sorghum silage was valued at $4 and sweet-potato silage at $13 per ton. Each of the cows gained in weight during the test. This work has shown that it is practicable to preserve sweet potatoes in the silo for cattle feeding and hog feeding purposes.

During the winter of 1915–16 sorghum silage and Japanese cane silage were compared for feeding young cattle. Grade Jersey heifers from 15 to 20 months old were fed for 60 days all the silage they would eat and 1 lb. of cottonseed meal each daily. The animals fed sorghum silage gained an average of 8.25 lbs. each during the 60 days, and those fed Japanese cane silage barely maintained their weights.

Feed and care of the dairy calf, R. S. Hulce and W. B. Nevens (*Illinois Sta. Circ. 202 (1917), pp. 13, figs. 6*).—Methods of feeding and care are given which have been found by experience to give good results in the rearing of calves.

The average weights at one day of age of calves born in the university herd are classified according to breed and sex as follows, the first figure under each breed being for females and the second for males: Jersey 59.7 and 62.4, Guernsey 68.8 and 70, Ayrshire 71.4 and 77.7, and Holstein 88 and 90 lbs. At the station a group of 20 Holstein heifers from birth to one year of age consumed 244 lbs. of whole milk, 860 lbs. of skim milk, 1,107 lbs. of grain, 1,067 lbs. of hay, and 1,669 lbs. of silage per head. These heifers averaged 92 lbs. at birth and 532 lbs. at one year and made an average daily gain of 1.2 lbs.

Selecting rations for dairy cows, G. C. WHITE and K. B. MUSSER (*Connecticut Storrs Sta. Bul. 90 (1917), pp. 3–38*).—The requirements to be considered in formulating dairy rations are discussed and tables are given showing the characteristics of some common feeds; the nutrients required by dairy cows for maintenance and milk production; the digestible nutrients, fertilizing constituents, and value of feeding stuffs; the average wholesale prices for 13 years of feeding stuffs in carload lots at Boston points; high and low prices of some common feeds by months for five years; cost per hundredweight of digestible nutrients at different prices for feeds, etc. Full directions are given for selecting and compounding rations, and suggestions are offered for analyzing the feed market.

Dairy feeding and the calculation of rations, L. S. RIFORD (*New Jersey Stas. Circ. 73 (1917), pp. 15*).—This circular explains briefly some common feeding terms, gives directions for the use of the feeding standard, and offers suggestions for the purchase of concentrates and the use of home-grown feeds.

Dairy herd [record], J. M. SCOTT (*Florida Sta. Rpt. 1916, pp. 14–17, figs. 3*).— Tables show the calving record, age and breed of cows, time in milk, milk and fat production records, and cost data of the station dairy herd during the fiscal year. Of 19 pure-bred and grade Jerseys being milked during the year, the highest yield was 5,907.7 lbs. of milk and 360.75 lbs. of fat. The cost of feed for this cow was $94.86. Valuing butter at 40 cts. per pound and milk at 32 cts. per gallon, she returned a profit of $124.95 over cost of feed.

Germ content of milk.—I, As influenced by the factors at the barn, M. J. PRUCHA and H. M. WEETER (*Illinois Sta. Bul. 199 (1917), pp. 25–51, figs. 3*).— The investigation here reported is a part of that begun by Harding et al. (E. S. R., 29, p. 878). Its purpose was to measure the collective influence of all the barn conditions and operations upon the germ content of the milk produced therein. The data were obtained in three dairy barns during the years 1914 and 1915. A description is given together with an illustration of the interior of each of the barns. The three barns "in a general way represent three classes of dairy barns, barn 1 being in excellent condition, barn 2 being good, and barn 3 poor. The difference between barns 1 and 2 as to cleanliness, however, was not very great. On the other hand, barn 3 would be classed as a dirty barn."

The utensils used were thoroughly steamed before each milking. In 1914 the udders of all the cows were wiped with a damp cloth previous to each milking, but in 1915 this practice was discontinued. All samples were taken from the milk of the individual cows when the milker brought it in pails from the barn into the adjacent milk room. The bacteriological examination of the milk was made by the plate method. In order to ascertain the extent of variation in bacterial count due to the laboratory methods employed, ten experiments were undertaken in each of which 100 plates were seeded with the same milk. None of the individual counts varied much more than 25 per cent from the average.

A total of 1,665 samples were taken from 138 cows. Data from the analyses of these samples are tabulated. Among the samples from barn 1 the lowest germ content was 17 and the highest was 218,250 bacteria per cubic centimeter of milk; in barn 2 the lowest was 3 and the highest was 33,000; and in barn 3 the lowest was 307 and the highest was 63,835. "These are wide limits of variation in the germ content of milk produced under uniform barn conditions."

The following table shows the grouping of all milk samples according to germ content and the average germ content of the milk from the three barns:

Arrangement of milk samples according to germ content and average number of bacteria per cubic centimeter.

Barn.	Below 1,000 per cubic centimeter.	Between 1,000 and 5,000 per cubic centimeter.	Between 5,000 and 10,000 per cubic centimeter.	Between 10,000 and 50,000 per cubic centimeter.	Over 50,000 per cubic centimeter.	Average germ content per cubic centimeter of milk.	
						1914.	1915.
I	472	297	56	29	6	2,140	3,260
II	405	153	4	5	0	973	830
III	19	127	57	34	1	6,189	5,050
Total	896	577	117	68	7	2,133 (Av.)	2,552 (Av.)

Most of the samples of high germ content in barn 1 came from a few animals. One of these animals persistently gave milk with high germ content and subsequent studies showed that her udder was the source of these large numbers of bacteria in her milk. Data are tabulated showing the average content of the milk of each animal for each of the two years. Of the 72 averages in barn 1, 30 were below 1,000 bacteria per cubic centimeter of milk, 35 were between 1,000 and 5,000, only 7 were over 5,000, and of these 7 only 2 were over 10,000. In barn 2, 30 of the 47 averages were below 1,000, and the highest average was only 3,599. In barn 3 all the averages were above 1,000 bacteria per cubic centimeter of milk, 11 were below 5,000, 6 were between 5,000 and 10,000 and 2 were over 10,000.

It is thus seen that in the production of milk of low germ content the udder of some cows may become the principal source of contamination. It is stated that "no conclusion can be drawn from the data concerning the relative importance of the practice of wiping the udders, as compared with the other sources of contamination in these barns. The data, however, do point to the conclusion that the wiping of the udders under the conditions obtaining in these barns did not affect the germ content of the milk to any appreciable extent."

Commenting on the results of this investigation, the authors state that it might be argued from the results obtained in barns 1 and 2 "that a dirty barn does not contribute more bacteria to the milk than a clean barn. Such conclusion, however, would be against a well-established fact. This apparent discrepancy is only a side issue to the general problem, and it would be a mere conjecture to attempt to explain it. The real significance of the results from these two barns lies in the fact that the number of bacteria in the milk from both barns was remarkably small, and that the difference in the conditions and the operations in the two barns exerted practically negligible influence upon the germ content of the milk.

"Even more significant are the results from barn 3. The average contamination here was 5,777 bacteria per cubic centimeter. This milk, so far as the germ content was concerned, would meet the requirements for certified milk, and yet the conditions of the barn as to cleanliness were such that it is doubtful whether the milk produced here would have been admitted to the milk supply of some cities. These results must not be construed as a defense of dirty barns. They simply point to the fact that the large numbers of bacteria commonly found in milk do not have their origin in the barn."

Fishiness in evaporated milk, B. W. HAMMER (*Iowa Sta. Research Bul. 38* (1917), pp. 235-246, fig. 1).—The author briefly reviews recent literature pertaining to fishy flavor in milk and butter and reports results of a study of the cause of the very fishy odor and flavor that had developed in one can of evaporated milk. From this can an organism was isolated that was capable of producing fishiness in milk, cream, or evaporated milk into which it was inoculated. In inoculated milk there was, in addition to the development of a fishy odor, a coagulation and a rapid digestion. The isolated organism when inoculated into butter, either directly or into sweet or sour cream either pasteurized or sterilized before churning, failed to produce fishiness. In some lots of butter, salt was used while other lots were unsalted. The counts made showed that the numbers of bacteria per gram deceased throughout the holding period with butter made from sour cream and with salted butter made from sweet cream, while with unsalted butter made from sweet cream there was an increase which was followed by a decrease.

A description is given of the organism under the name *Bacillus ichthyosmius*, apparently a new species closely related to the Proteus group. It is suggested that the organism, which fails to resist heat, may have gained entrance to this can after heating, probably through some hole in the metal which was sealed shortly after sterilization.

The manufacture of cottage cheese in creameries and milk plants (*U. S. Dept. Agr., Bur. Anim. Indus.* [Pub.], (1917), pp. 4).—This circular points out the advantages of pasteurizing skim milk for the purpose of controlling the flavor of cottage cheese, describes in brief the methods of manufacture, packing, and marketing, and gives an estimate of the yield of cottage cheese to be expected from skim milk.

Simple directions for making cottage cheese on the farm (*U. S. Dept. Agr., Bur. Anim. Indus.* [Pub.], (1917), pp. 3).—Brief directions are given for the utilization of skim milk for making cottage cheese on farms.

A substitute for litmus for use in milk cultures, W. M. CLARK and H. A. LUBS (*U. S. Dept. Agr., Jour. Agr. Research, 10* (1917), No. 3, pp. 105-111).— "The color changes which occur in litmus-milk cultures may be due to changes in the hydrogen-ion concentration of the medium, or to reduction, or even destruction of the dye. If it is the degree of acid or alkali fermentation which is sought, it is advisable to use an indicator which will not be affected except by a change in the hydrogen-ion concentration." Dibromoorthocresolsulfonphthalein, for which the short name bromcresol purple is suggested, is said to fulfill this condition. The authors have described the preparation of this compound (E. S. R., 36, p. 111) and have suggested its use in the determination of hydrogen-ion concentration (E. S. R., 37, p. 506.) For ordinary indicator purposes a 0.04 per cent aqueous solution of the monosodium salt is recommended, but as a stock solution for the present purpose a solution of the salt containing 0.5 per cent of the acid is suggested. A method is given for the preparation of this solution.

In comparing litmus and bromcresol purple as indicators in milk cultures it is stated that "litmus undergoes a temporary reduction during sterilization in the presence of milk. Bromcresol purple does not. The coloring power of litmus is relatively weak; bromcresol purple in very high dilution is useful. Litmus and azolitmin are indicators of uncertain composition; bromcresol purple is a definite individual compound obtainable in crystalline form and therefore reproducible. Its cost is not excessive.

"The impurities of litmus preparations vary in their effect upon the P_H of milk and often necessitate elaborate adjustment either of the litmus solution, of the milk, or of the mixture if reproducible color is to be obtained. Bromcresol purple, on the other hand, may be used with the assurance that, if other conditions are constant, it will always produce the same coloration. Some of the difficulty experienced in reproducing a particular initial color with either indicator is shown to be due to the changes in P_H which occur when milk is sterilized by heat.

"The comparative value of litmus and bromcresol purple in milk cultures was tested with a variety of organisms. It was found that no change in reaction could be observed with litmus which could not be followed equally well with bromcresol purple. In many instances litmus was rendered useless by reduction or destruction while bromcresol purple continued to act as a true indicator of the hydrogen-ion concentration."

VETERINARY MEDICINE.

Annual reports of the State veterinarian of Alabama, 1914 and 1915, C. A. CARY (*Ann. Rpt. State Vet. Ala.*, 8 (*1914*), pp. 28; 9 (*1915*), pp. 48).—These reports, dealing with the work of the years 1914 and 1915, respectively, include accounts of the occurrence of and control work with diseases of live stock, including tick eradication.

Report of the Montana Live Stock Sanitary Board and State veterinary surgeon for years 1915–16 ([*Bien.*] *Rpt. Mont. Live Stock Sanit. Bd.*, *1915–16*, pp. 50, pl. 1).—This report, dealing with the work of the year with infectious and other diseases of live stock, includes a discussion of tuberculosis free accredited herds, contagious abortion, etc., and gives a list of official dips and disinfectants, live stock sanitary board orders, regulations governing importation of live stock into Montana, etc. A short popular article on cattle lice in Montana, by R. A. Cooley and R. R. Parker, is included.

Diseases of domestic animals (*Rpt. Dept. Agr.* [*N. H.*], *54* (*1915–16*), pp. 85–99).—This reports upon the occurrence of and control work with infectious diseases of live stock in New Hampshire.

Annual reports of the chief veterinary officer for the years 1914 and 1915, S. STOCKMAN (*Bd. Agr. and Fisheries* [*London*], *Ann. Rpt. Chief Vet. Off.*, *1914*, pp. 62; *1915*, pp. 12).—These report briefly upon the occurrence of and work with the more important diseases of animals during 1914 and 1915.

In the report for 1914 some cross-immunization tests with *Piroplasma bigeminum* and *P. divergens* are noted which indicate that animals immunized against *P. bigeminum* are not protected against infection by *P. divergens*, or vice versa.

For obtaining massive cultures of *Bacillus abortus* a medium prepared as follows was used: Five hundred gm. of raw potato in small pieces is macerated in 2,000 cc. of water, placed in an incubator for 12 hours at 60° C. and then strained through a flannel bag. To the filtrate, 10 gm. of meat extract, 10 gm. of salt, and 20 gm. of Witte's peptone are added. The mixture is steamed for 1 hour, strained through a flannel bag, rendered slightly alkaline, and again steamed for 1.5 hours. A slight precipitate results which is removed by filtration through paper. The filtrate is finally sterilized in the autoclave and kept as a stock solution. With the addition of 1 per cent of sugar and 1 per cent of glycerin the material constitutes an excellent liquid medium for cultivating the organism.

For making a solid medium, 60 gm. of agar is added to 2,000 cc. of the stock solution and melted in the usual way. After clarifying by the usual method, the medium is again neutralized, if necessary, and grape sugar and glycerin added as for the liquid medium. The material is then sterilized in the autoclave, either in bulk or in culture flasks.

Immunity in its relation to the stock diseases of Southern Rhodesia, L. E. W. BEVAN (*Rhodesia Agr. Jour.,* 13 (1916), Nos. 5, pp. 640–651; 6, pp. 800–812, pls. 2; 14 (1917), No. 2, pp. 213–234, pls. 2).—This is a general review of the subject with special reference to the stock diseases of Southern Rhodesia.

Anaphylatoxin and anaphylaxis, F. G. NOVY and P. H. DEKRUIF (*Jour. Amer. Med. Assoc.,* 68 (1917), No. 21, pp. 1524–1528).—This is a general summary of the studies previously noted (E. S. R., 37, p. 578).

The effect of temperature on the rate of complement fixation, J. BRONFENBRENNER and M. J. SCHLESINGER (*Proc. Soc. Expt. Biol. and Med.,* 14 (1917), No. 7, pp. 139, 140).—The authors have studied the relation between the temperature and the rate of fixation and have found that "if sufficient antibody is present in the serum (three to five units or more) fixation of two units of complement takes place within the first five minutes, provided the amount of antigen used contains several antigenic units. We find it possible to use this procedure for presumptive elimination of strongly positive sera from a large series of cases. One places in a tube 0.05 cc. of the patient's serum· adds the proper amount of antigen and salt solution and incubates at 87° C. in the water bath for five minutes, and then adds sensitized cells to test for free complement." Where a rapid fixation of complement is desired a temperature of 37° is indicated as being the best. One-half hour of incubation at this temperature is considered to be the most efficient for diagnosis.

Where the time element is of little importance, but complete fixation is desired, incubation in the ice box for from eight to ten hours is found to be the best. "These fixations on ice, however, may not be specific, for the reaction of fixation is so complete under these conditions that even traces of secondary circulating antigens and their corresponding antibodies may cause fixation of complement. The ice-box fixation can, therefore, be used only as a presumptive test to eliminate the negative cases."

For the fixation of complement at temperatures below the freezing point such a procedure was found to produce undesirable changes in the reagents. especially in the antigen, and was therefore unsuitable for the test.

The specific serum treatment of wounds, E. LECLAINCHE and H. VALLÉE (*Jour. Compar. Path. and Ther.,* 29 (1916), No. 4, pp. 283–290).—This is an English translation of the material previously noted (E. S. R., 35, p. 882).

Plants poisonous to live stock, H. C. LONG (*Cambridge: University Press, 1917, pp. VII+119, pl. 1*).—A brief summary of the present knowledge of plants poisonous to live stock in Great Britain, with symptoms, toxic principles, and a list of the more important references to the bibliography in relation to each plant. The poisonous plants are dealt with under their respective orders, and accounts are given of plants suspected of being poisonous, the effects of plants on milk, plants which cause mechanical injury, and the classification of poisons. A bibliography of 267 titles is appended and a subject index included.

Potassium permanganate as an antidote for the effects of poisonous plants, C. D. MARSH (*Jour. Amer. Vet. Med. Assoc.,* 51 (1917), No. 3, pp. 419, 420).—The author calls attention to the fact that for practical purposes the use of a drench of potassium permanganate in the case of ruminants poisoned by plants is without value, as previously shown (E. S. R., 35, p. 779). While potassium permanganate, tannic acid, or sodium bicarbonate would be logical antidotes for alkaloidal poisonings, they are effective only as they come into actual contact with the poisonous substances. It has been found experimentally that if the antidote is given repeatedly at intervals of 30 minutes or less

It is effective, for it then attacks the poisonous substance as it passes through the abomasum.

Studies in forage poisoning, IV, R. GRAHAM and L. R. HIMMELBERGER (*Jour. Amer. Vet. Med. Assoc.*, *51* (*1917*), *No. 2, pp. 164–187, figs. 6*).—This report is based upon investigations conducted at the Kentucky Experiment Station and previously noted (E. S. R., 36, p. 581).

During the course of investigations in connection with a definite outbreak of forage poisoning various types of microorganisms that proved to be quite uniformly poisonous to horses and mules were isolated from oat hay. Among these was a spore-forming, Gram negative, aerobic bacillus which was pathogenic for horses and mules and less so for cattle, sheep, and goats, but to which guinea pigs, rabbits, and white mice were apparently immune. Sterile filtrates of this bacillus subsequent to daily intravenous injections in some experimental horses proved pathogenic and capable of exciting clinical manifestations somewhat analogous to affected animals in the original outbreak as the result of feeding on oat hay.

The bacillus previously noted (E. S. R., 36, p. 581) was isolated from silage in a remote outbreak of forage poisoning among cattle.

Cottonseed meal work, W. A. WITHERS (*North Carolina Sta. Rpt. 1916, pp. 19, 20*).—This is a brief review of investigations during the year of the toxicity of cottonseed meal which have confirmed the views previously presented (E. S. R., 34, p. 381) that gossypol is the toxic substance of cottonseed.

Blackleg filtrate, A. EICHHORN (*Jour. Amer. Vet. Med. Assoc.*, *51* (*1917*), *No. 3, pp. 406–413; Amer. Jour. Vet. Med.*, *12* (*1917*), *No. 6, pp. 375–378*).—The biological products proposed and used in blackleg are briefly reviewed. Preparation of a filtrate from media containing meat upon which the organism was grown until no more gas was produced, together with a procedure for its standardization, is noted.

The filtrate is considered to be an effective immunizing agent, conferring an active immunity which protects cattle against blackleg for as long a time as the germ-free extracts prepared from the juices of the tissues of affected animals. The losses incidental to vaccination with the powder or pellets are entirely avoided, since the preparation does not contain the blackleg germ.

The material in a concentrated form was found to retain its potency for almost an indefinite time. The necessity of the usual sterility tests of the filtrate, in order to guard against possible contamination, is indicated.

The virulence of the blood of animals affected with foot-and-mouth disease and immunity tests, G. Cosco and A. AGUZZI (*Gior. Med. Vet.*, *66* (*1917*), *No. 14, pp. 313–320*).—This is a brief report of the investigation ordered by the Italian minister of the interior in 1916. The topics treated are incubation, fever, time of maximum virulence of blood, virulence of red blood corpuscles, minimum dose of blood, increase of virulence of red blood corpuscles, temporary infection through the mouth, intravenous injection, and immunity tests.

Allergic reaction of mallein for the diagnosis of glanders, E. FAVA (*Arch. Sci. Med. Vet.* [*Turin*], *14* (*1916*), *No. 1–12, pp. 1–131, figs. 27*).—The author describes and submits experimental data obtained through the application of the subcutaneous, ophthalmic, and intrapalpebral mallein tests, and discusses the specificity of the intrapalpebral reaction and its advantages over the other methods of malleinization, the intrapalpebral test for the prophylaxis of glanders, and its application.

It is concluded in general that the intrapalpebral test posseses advantages over the other procedures for the diagnosis of glanders, the advantages being those essentially noted by other investigators.

Milk sickness, D. T. GRAY (*North Carolina Sta. Rpt. 1916, p. 56*).—A brief statement of work by Curtis and Wolf (E. S. R., 37, p. 583).

Studies on the paratyphoid-enteritidis group.—III, Some cultural characteristics and their relation to host origin, C. KRUMWIEDE, JR., JOSEPHINE S. PRATT, and L. A. KOHN (*Jour. Med. Research. 35 (1917), No. 3, pp. 357–366*).—"The quantitative differences in the reduction of fuchsin, added to the fermentative results, especially of dulcit and arabinose, give fairly defined groups. This grouping is only suggestive in that it correlates to some extent with host origin, a correlation hitherto not observed. It also correlates with the primary or secondary invasive properties of the various types. As would be expected, the latter are much more heterogeneous.

"Some of the results do not correlate with agglutinative results and suggest the necessity of further study in relation to such correlation."

Studies on the paratyphoid-enteritidis group.—IV, The differentiation of the members of the paratyphoid-enteritidis group from B. typhosus with special reference to anaerogenic strains and observations on the fermentative characteristics of the avian types, C. KRUMWIEDE, JR., and L. A. KOHN (*Jour. Med. Research, 36 (1917), No. 3. pp. 509–518*).—"The ability to produce acid from rhamnose is the essential characteristic of the paratyphoid-enteritidis group, differentiating both the aerogenic and anaerogenic members from *B. typhosus*. Additional cultural differences between *B. typhosus*, *B. sanguinarium*, and *B. pullorum* are presented. The agglutinative relationship of the strains studied is recorded. Observations are added on the low or latent avidity for carbohydrates in relation to variability and practical differentiation. Without due regard to these factors, erroneous differential significance might easily be given to variation even among members of the fixed groups."

Effect of the injection of nonspecific foreign substances on the course of experimental rabies, W. H. BURMEISTER (*Jour. Infect. Diseases, 21 (1917), No. 1, pp. 95–107*).—"The injection of certain nonspecific substances (horse serum, serum globulin, egg white, egg yolk. broth, typhoid vaccine, or tuberculin) does not inhibit the course of experimental rabies in rabbits produced by nonattenuated virus. The seemingly beneficial effect of tuberculin in the early series of the experiments must be disregarded because of the survival of some control animals inoculated at a later date with the same virus. . . . Rabbits surviving an intracerebral inoculation of attenuated rabies virus (fixed or street virus) may become hypersensitive to a reinoculation of the same virus made in the same way."

Tuberculosis in camels, F. E. MASON (*Jour. Compar. Path. and Ther., 30 (1917), No. 1, pp. 80–84*).—The literature on the occurrence of tuberculosis in camels is briefly reviewed. Continuing the work previously noted (E. S. R., 29, p. 676), the author has examined and made bacteriological studies of a large number of camels slaughtered in the Cairo abattoir. The disease appears to occur chiefly in Egyptian camels and the causative organism to be of the bovine type.

The source, method of infection, course, distribution of lesions, and histology of lesions of tuberculosis in the camel are briefly discussed.

The subcutaneous tuberculin test with ordinary tuberculin was successfully employed on infected animals. Data relative to the variations in the normal temperature of camels are submitted.

Brisket disease, G. H. GLOVER and I. E. NEWSOM (*Colorado Sta. Bul. 229 (1917), pp. 3–8, figs. 3*).—This is a revised and abbreviated edition of Bulletin 204, previously noted (E. S. R., 32, p. 781).

Report of the division of veterinary science, G. A. ROBERTS (*North Carolina Sta. Rpt. 1916, pp. 55–57*).—The principal work of the year was with contagions abortion, some 2,500 cows and heifers in 70 herds at 35 different points in the State being examined. In agglutination and complement fixation tests of 203 samples of blood from cattle in various sections of the State 65 per cent gave positive reactions with one test or the other, 17 per cent negative reactions to both tests, and 18 per cent suspicious reactions.

Keratitis infectiosa in cattle (keratitis pyobacillosa), J. POELS, trans. by J. KAPPEYNEY and A. R. WARD (*Jour. Amer. Vet. Med. Assoc., 51 (1917), No. 4, pp. 526–531*).—The author's investigations have led to the conclusion that *Bacillus pyogenes* is the specific cause of the infectious eye disease of cattle now existing in Holland, and that the two species of micrococci found present are secondary invaders. The author has used pyogenes serum as a prophylactic and as a curative agent with favorable results.

The life history of Hypoderma bovis and H. lineatum, S. HADWEN (*Jour. Amer. Vet. Med. Assoc., 51 (1917), No. 4, pp. 541–544*).—The observations here reported are based upon work at Agassiz, B. C. The principal differences between the two warble flies, both anatomically and biologically, are pointed out. It is thought that with *H. lineatum* several larvæ enter through the same opening in the skin.

Feeding lambs in the summer to prevent stomach worms, D. T. GRAY (*North Carolina Sta. Rpt. 1916, p. 35*).—A first year's feeding experiment which was carried on to determine whether a heavy grain ration had any effect in overcoming the ravages of the stomach worm, in which 30 lambs were used, indicates "strongly that there is a very definite relationship between deaths by stomach worms and grain fed through the pasture season."

Hog cholera transmission through infected pork, R. R. BIRCH (*Jour. Amer. Vet. Med. Assoc., 51 (1917), No. 3, pp. 303–330, figs. 3*).—Detailed experimental data of a study on the effects of feeding susceptible pigs bits of pork such as might be found in garbage are reported in tabular and graphical form and discussed.

It was found that the meat and bone taken from carcasses of hogs killed before any manifestation of hog cholera other than elevation of temperature, at a time when they will pass inspection, will usually produce the disease when fed in small quantities to susceptible pigs. In hog-cholera infected carcasses that passed inspection the virus was not often killed in parts sold as fresh or refrigerated products. In sugar-cured hams the virus was killed in 12 out of 21 experimental cases.

"Measures to prevent hog-cholera infections due to feeding trimmings from market pork should include efforts to prevent marketing infected herds, efforts to prevent the sale of carcasses in products in which the virus is not killed, and efforts to acquaint swine breeders with the danger incident to feeding kitchen refuse. Farmers can avoid the danger mentioned by discontinuing the feeding of kitchen refuse, by placing all pork trimmings elsewhere than in the garbage pail, by thoroughly cooking all garbage before it is fed, or by immunizing their hogs. Men who collect and feed city garbage can avoid the danger by cooking all the material they feed or by immunizing their hogs."

The importance of severe interpretation of temperatures, symptoms, and lesions observed during inspection to indicate the proper treatment of any animals that might be infected without condemnation of appreciable numbers is indicated.

Transmission of piroplasmosis to three pigs by ingestion, SPARAPANI (*Pathologica, 9 (1917), No. 196, pp. 21, 22; abs. in Trop. Vet. Bul., 5 (1917), No. 2, p. 90*).—The author reports upon infection in pigs apparently brought about by ingestion of the flesh of infected sheep.

A note on dourine in the horse, H. T. Pease (*Agr. Jour. India, 12* (*1917*), *No. 2, pp. 230–251, pls. 5, fig. 1*).—A discussion of the disease and its treatment.

Abortive treatment of equine filariasis by the hypodermic injection of a permanganate of potassium solution, Monbet (*Rev. Gén. Méd. Vét., 22* (*1913*), *No. 262, pp. 534–537; abs. in Vet. Rec., 27* (*1915*), *No. 1394, p. 498*).—The subcutaneous injection of 10 cc. of a 1 per cent solution of permanganate of potassium at six points in the pericicatricial zone has resulted in the cure of summer sores. The author is of the opinion that this treatment will give good results and that it may also be employed in filariasis of the tendons.

[Epizootic lymphangitis in France] (*Bul. Soc. Cent. Méd. Vét., 92* (*1916*), *Nos. 8, pp. 136–142, pl. 1; 11–12, pp. 144–155, pls. 4; 22, pp. 334–346; 24, pp. 385–388, 402–404; 93* (*1917*), *Nos. 3–4, pp. 64–68; 6, pp. 99–109; 9–10, pp. 191–204; Rec. Méd. Vét., 92* (*1916*), *No. 21, pp. 614–618; 93* (*1917*), *No. 7–8, pp. 179–196, figs. 5*).—Epizootic lymphangitis, a disease rarely seen in France before the war, has since been introduced with horses imported from northern Africa and is of quite frequent occurrence.

Several papers relating to the disease are presented as follows: Epizootic Lymphangitis in France: Diagnosis and Treatment, by J. Bridré; Treatment of Epizootic Lymphangitis—Trials with Galyl (Tetraoxydiphosphaminodiarsenobenzene), by Douville; Treatment of Epizootic Lymphangitis by Novarsenobenzol, by Velu; Note on the Treatment of Epizootic Lymphangitis by Potassium Iodid, by J. Cartier (E. S. R., 37, p. 377); Epizootic Lymphangitis in France—Its Treatment by the Chatelain Method and Its Prophylaxis, by E. Nicolas; Epizootic Lymphangitis in the Region of Mekinez, by Aubry; Epizootic Lymphangitis, by Velu; Observations Relative to the Incubation of Epzootic Lymphangitis, by H. Chapron; Contribution to the Study of Epizootic Lymphangitis, by Truche and Guignard; Epizootic Lymphangitis—Symptomatology, by Velu; Apropos of Epizootic Lymphangitis and Its Treatment, by Fayet; Epizootic Lymphangitis, by Charmoy; Notes on the Determination of the Incubation Period of Epizootic Lymphangitis in France, by Perrin; and The Curative Treatment of Epizootic Lymphangitis by Vaccine Therapy, by Velu.

Epizootic lymphangitis in France: Its diagnosis and treatment, J. Bridré (*Vet. Jour., 73* (*1917*), *No. 503, pp. 173–175*).—This is a review of the article by Bridré above noted.

The author, together with Negri and Trouette, has obtained excellent results from the intravenous injection of arsenobenzol, but novarsenobenzol is deemed much more convenient to use and quite as effective. He recommends a dose of from 2 to 3 gm. in 20 cc. of distilled water, the injection to be made in the jugular vein.

"Stomatitis contagiosa" in horses, A. C. Burton (*Vet. Jour., 73* (*1917*), *No. 505, pp. 234–242, figs. 4*).—The author has found that this disease of the horse is transmissible to man, both he and two assistants having contracted it. The disease in man was of short duration and mild, but very painful. The incubation period appeared to be from one to three days. Any immunity conferred by an attack appears to be short, reinfection having apparently taken place in less than two months.

The author has found frequent irrigation and cleansing of the mouth with potassium permanganate (0.5 oz. to 5 gal. of water) by means of a Vermorel sprayer carried on the back, the nozzle covered with a piece of rubber hose pipe, to be a very satisfactory means of treatment for army horses.

Note on an outbreak of contagious pneumonia in donkeys, R. Branford (*Agr. Jour. India, 12* (*1917*), *No. 2, pp. 268–273, pls. 2*).—This reports upon an outbreak of this disease among the young stock donkey jacks at the Government Cattle Farm, Hissar, on July 20, 1916.

Another cestode from the young cat, J. E. ACKERT and A. A. GRANT (*Trans. Amer. Micros. Soc., 36 (1917), No. 2, pp. 93–96*).—The authors find that the dog tapeworm (*Tænia pisiformis*) may develop in the young cat (*Felis domestica*) and that evagination of *Cysticercus pisiformis* occurs in the duodenum of the domestic kitten.

Some of the infectious diseases of poultry, E. M. PICKENS (*Cornell Vet., 7 (1917), No. 3, pp. 151–184*).—A systematic summary of information on the more important infectious diseases of poultry.

RURAL ENGINEERING.

Flow through sharp-edged V-notches or weirs, E. W. DOEBLER and F. H. RAYFIELD (*Cornell Civ. Engin., 25 (1917), No. 8, pp. 389–397, figs. 7*).—Experiments are reported on the flow of water through V-notch weirs to determine the experimental coefficient μ in the formula

$$Q = \mu 8/15 \tan 1/2\alpha 2 \, gh \, {}^{u_2}$$

for heads higher than those used in previous experiments by others. Four notches were studied. The smallest had the Cippoletti side slopes of one horizontal to four vertical, an angle of approximately 28°. The other three angles were 60, 90, and 120°. Heads were used up to 3 ft.

It was found that "the 60° notch has the lowest average coefficient, about 0.578, with the value for the 90° a very little higher, about 0.58. The average values of μ for the 28 and 120° notches are respectively about 0.59 and 0.591, or about 2 per cent higher than the values for the intermediate notches. These averages are for the medium heads. . . . For all of the notches there is a rapid increase in the value of the coefficient at the high heads. This increase is, no doubt, partly due to the velocity in the channel of approach. . . .

"For those runs for which the velocity measurements were made, the mean heads were increased by their respective velocity heads and another coefficient computed. Considering these coefficients, there is still a marked increase in the value of the coefficients which tends to show that it is not entirely due to velocity. The nearness of the edges of a notch to the sides of the channel has an effect upon the coefficient."

Spray irrigation, G. H. TOLLEY (*Water Conserv. and Irrig. Com., N. S. Wales, Bul. 1 (1917), pp. 32, figs. 36*).—This pamphlet discusses the general principles of spray irrigation, and describes service tests of several different systems of spray irrigation.

Irrigation laws of the State of Washington, compiled by I. M. HOWELL (*Olympia, Wash.: State, 1916, 2. ed., pp. 173*).—The text of the laws is given.

Irrigation revenue report of the Bombay Presidency, excluding Sind, 1914–15 (*Irrig. Rev. Rpt. Bombay Pres., 1914–15, pp. 49*).—Data on expenditures and revenues for irrigation works in Bombay for the year 1914–15 are reported.

Annual report, Ministry of Public Works, Egypt, 1915–16, M. MACDONALD (*Ann. Rpt. Min. Pub. Works Egypt, 1915–16, pp. 87, pls. 9*).—A large part of this report is devoted to drainage and irrigation projects in Egypt, especially as they are affected by the European war.

[Water analyses] (*An. Min. Agr. Argentina, Secc. Geol., Mineral. y Min., 11 (1916), No. 4, pp. 53–63*).—Analyses of 13 samples of 8 water supplies from 5 Provinces in Argentina showed 7 of the supplies to be potable. Analyses of 102 samples of 35 water supplies of 12 Provinces showed 19 samples potable.

Reaeration as a factor in the self-purification of streams, E. B. PHELPS (*Jour. Indus. and Engin. Chem., 9 (1917), No. 4, pp. 403–405*).—It is. pointed out, on the basis of work by the U. S. Public Health Service, that "in the development of the maximum economic use of a stream, its capacity to dispose of sewage and waste within any specified degree of depreciation or nuisance is a factor of first importance. This capacity is limited by stream conditions and is a function of the capacity for reaeration. For this reason the dilution unit is an improper one for a discussion of nuisance and self-purification, and results obtained upon one stream, expressed in such units, are not applicable to another. Reaeration is capable of experimental determination not only in single instances but in terms of general applicability. Its determination in such general terms involves laborious work of a hydraulic and analytical nature."

The javellization of water in the field, E. ARBINET (Rev. Hyg. et Pol. Sanit., 39 (1917), No. 2, pp. 98–104, figs. 3).—This process is described.

A comparison of the activated sludge and the Imhoff tank trickling filter processes of sewage treatment, H. P. EDDY (Jour. West. Soc. Engin., 21 (1916), No. 10, pp. 816–852, figs. 11; Surveyor, 51 (1917), No. 1317, pp. 370–372, figs. 2).— From a comparison of the two processes of sewage treatment it is concluded that at the present time " the Imhoff tank trickling filter process is a less expensive means of oxidizing the organic matter of sewage wastes than the activated sludge process, where oxidation alone is considered. If the areas of land required for isolation, the loss of head in the plant, the danger of objectionable odors and of the fly annoyance, and other disadvantages of the trickling filter process are of marked importance in any specific case, the balance may be decidedly in favor of the activated sludge process, even in its present state of development. . . . Further attention should be given to improvement in the design and operation of the oldest processes of sewage treatment."

Marked advance in treating sewage from packing houses, G. B. ZIMMELE (Engin. News-Rec., 78 (1917), No. 9, pp. 436, 437, fig. 1).—Experiments conducted at Forth Worth, Tex., on the treatment of packing-house waste by means of a small activated sludge plant showed that this sewage can be successfully handled by the activated sludge treatment. With reference to the fertilizing value of the sludge it was found that " the addition of the acid holds the ammonia—contrary to the effect of adding lime. Second, the availability of the nitrogen is increased. By the neutral permanganate method, blood contains about 90 per cent available nitrogen, but this treated sludge contains about 93.5 per cent available nitrogen."

An experimental test of the relation of sewage disposal to the spread of pellagra, J. F. SILER, P. E. GARRISON, and W. J. MACNEAL (Arch. Int. Med., 19 (1917), No. 5, pt. 1, pp. 683–694, figs. 2).—An account is given of an experiment conducted in a small milling community in South Carolina which had long been a conspicuous endemic center of pellagra. In the fall of 1913 the installation of a water carriage sewerage system was begun and a few houses were equipped with water and fly tight pail closets. As far as possible all privies in the community were made fly and water tight regardless of their character.

"The diminution in new cases of pellagra in this community from 30 in 1913 to 18 in 1914, eight in 1915, and two in 1916 has been very remarkable, and the obvious cause of this improvement would appear to be the intentional experimental factor, namely, the installation of the sewerage system. . . . The installation of sanitary systems of sewage disposal is recommended as a measure for the restriction of the spread of pellagra in the general population."

Rational and economic sanitary treatment of human wastes, F. GARRIGOU (Compt. Rend. Acad. Sci. [Paris], 162 (1916), No. 17. pp. 649–651; abs. in Chem. Abs., 10 (1916), No. 19, p. 2490; Internat. Inst. Agr. [Rome], Internat. Rev. Sci. and Pract. Agr., 7 (1916), No. 7, pp. 947, 948).—A method of sewage treatment considered as an economic war measure in France is described.

The liquid and solid constituents are separated by sedimentation and decantation. The treatment of the liquid portion is based on the double decomposition of calcium sulphate in the presence of ammonium carbonate, giving calcium carbonate and amonium sulphate. The calcium carbonate settles out and the liquid containing ammonium sulphate is concentrated until the crystals separate. The precipitated calcium carbonate contains much organic matter rich in nitrogen. The solid matter from the decantation process is filter pressed and then autoclaved for 15 minutes at 140 to 150° C. The vapors from the autoclave are condensed to recover the ammonia salts in them, and the solids remaining in the autoclave are dried for fertilizer. This process, it is stated, requires only a simple apparatus and cheap chemicals and is considered to be adapted for use on farms and in rural communities of France, as well as in larger towns, for the production of fertilizer from sewage.

Rural sanitation (*Cal. Bd. Health Mo. Bul., 12 (1916), No. 2, pp. 74–81; abs. in Chem. Abs., 10 (1916), No. 21, p. 2780*).—This article outlines the public health methods of the California State Board of Health and describes common unhealthful conditions, including sewage entering streams, contaminated wells and water supplies, carelessness in producing and handling milk, manure piles, fly and mosquito breeding places, and insanitary privies. A form of notice to abate nuisances issued by the board is included.

Fifth annual report of the county highway commissioner of Milwaukee County, Wis., 1916, H. J. KUELLING (*Ann. Rpt. Co. Highway Comr., Milwaukee Co., Wis., 5 (1916), pp. 93, figs. 28*).—This is a statement of the work and expenditures of the office of the highway commissioner of Milwaukee County, Wis., on highway construction, maintenance, and repair for 1916.

Road problems in the Ozarks, E. G. HARRIS (*Bul. School Mines and Metallurg., Univ. Missouri, 9 (1917), No. 1, pp. 23, figs. 6*).—This bulletin is a discussion of the road problems encountered in the average sparsely settled, rugged portion of the Ozark uplift, embracing about one-fourth of the area of Missouri. It is stated that in this region the present bad location of many of the roads constitutes the chief reason why improvement is impossible or possible only at great and continuous expense.

A list of references, compiled by H. L. Wheeler, on the construction and maintenance of rural roads is included.

Report of the fourth annual road drag competition, J. KUEHNE and H. W. HETTLE (*Saskatchewan Highway Comrs., Rpt. Road Drag Compet., 4 (1916), pp. 22, figs. 8*).—An outline is given of the procedure and results of a road dragging competition in the Province of Saskatchewan lasting through the summer of 1916.

Methods of determining the road making qualities of deposits of stone and gravel, L. REINECKE (*Good Roads, 51 (1917), No. 20, pp. 293–297, figs. 9*).—This is an outline of the methods used by the department of mines of Canada in arriving at the relative values of deposits of stone and gravel available for road construction.

" In order to determine the road making values of the rocks in a certain district, they are first divided into formations and then into rock types. Their average values and the variation in strength and cementing value of each type are obtained by laboratory tests on a number of samples, and the results thus obtained are compared with actual service tests in the roads wherever possible. Laboratory studies with the microscope and by chemical analyses are then undertaken to discover the cause of such variations in order to furnish data which will enable the field man to distinguish a good stone from a poor one in the outcrop.

" With a working knowledge of the strength of the bedrock in a district, an attempt is made to devise a classification of the kinds of bowlders in the field stone deposits in such a way that their composition expressed in percentages of durable, intermediate, and soft bowlders will bear a direct relation to their percentage of wear as determined in the laboratory and to their durability under traffic conditions. The pebbles in the gravels of the district are classified in a manner that will bring about the same result. The impurities present and the texture or grading of the gravels are studied in order to furnish advance data as to their probable value in concrete and sheet-asphalt work."

The arrangement of rectangular dairy barns, R. S. HULCE and W. B. NEVENS (*Illinois Sta. Circ. 199 (1917), pp. 3–30, figs. 23*).—This circular enumerates the factors to be considered in the location, lighting, ventilation, and general arrangement of rectangular dairy barns and gives information regarding principles of construction.

Wooden silos used in Nebraska, L. W. CHASE and I. D. WOOD (*Univ. Nebr., Col. Agr. Ext. Bul. 40 (1917), pp. 16, figs. 11*).—This bulletin relates especially to the construction of wooden silos under Nebraska conditions and includes diagrammatic illustrations and bills of materials.

The principles of poultry house construction with general and detailed plans, F. C. ELFORD (*Canada Expt. Farms Bul. 87 (1916), pp. 55, figs. 55*).—This bulletin enumerates the principles of construction and gives general and detailed plans and specifications for farm and commercial poultry houses, including their interior arrangement and equipment.

Better conveniences for rural schools, L. E. SCOTT (*Wis. Farmers' Insts. Bul. 30 (1916), pp. 48–55, figs. 7*).—Sanitary conditions and conveniences for rural schools, especially with reference to lighting, heating, ventilation, water supply, and sewage disposal, are discussed.

RURAL ECONOMICS.

The marketing of Kansas butter, T. MACKLIN (*Kansas Sta. Bul. 216 (1917), pp. 3–79, figs. 42*).—This investigation was made for the purpose of determining the methods, processes, and costs of marketing butter made both on farms and in creameries of the State.

It is concluded that " dairy farming in Kansas has been and continues to be a side line on the average farm. Experience with whole-milk creameries, local private creameries, and skimming-station centralizers proved that they were not adapted to Kansas conditions, and led to the establishment of cream-station direct-shipper centralizers, which are well adapted to the conditions of Kansas dairy farming. Farm butter making has rapidly declined in Kansas owing to the rapid increase in the efficiency of creameries. . . . The average farmer does not live close enough to favorable markets to make and market butter profitably, except in so far as the stores follow the practice of paying the same price for both good and poor butter. . . .

" Kansas has 78 creameries. Forty-one are centralizers, which make more than 95 per cent of the creamery butter of the State. . . . Centralizers are necessary because there is only one creamery for each 1,053 square miles, and the average farmer lives 19 miles from a creamery. . . .

" The prices paid for delivered butter fat by centralizers averaged above Elgin prices, and according to prevailing economic conditions, appear to be fair. The fact that butter-fat prices in Kansas are somewhat lower than in some other States is because farmers choose to sell four-fifths of their butter fat through cream stations rather than to deliver the cream at their own expense.

" More and better dairy cows would have the effect of reducing the cost of getting butter fat to the creameries, of lowering the cost of making and marketing butter by the creameries, and would result in higher net prices and greater profits to the farmer."

The wheat question, M. PERCHOT (*Vie Agr. et Rurale, 7 (1917), No. 25, pp. 433–440*).—This report discusses the stock of wheat on hand, the consumption requirements, the influence of fixing of the price on production, and methods of restricting consumption.

Observations on the recent agricultural inquiry in California, T. F. HUNT (*California Sta. [Pub., 1917], pp. 20*).—The author discusses the findings of the committee on resources and food supply of the State council of defense. He recommends that the council devise means to bring city labor resources in touch with country needs, to organize tractor garages, to urge city capital and people to engage in the production of food, to promote plans of meeting the livestock situation, to urge conservation of food and elimination of waste through organizations of women, and to assure the producer of high prices.

The great war: Its lessons and its warnings, J. COLLINGS (*London: The Rural World Publishing Co. [1917], pp. 113, pls. 2*).—The author deals in a general way with the deficiencies of English agriculture in meeting national demands in time of war. A material reduction of the acreage in grass, more intensive cultivation and division of agricultural lands, reclamation of waste lands, and state aid to bring about reform are lessons emphasized.

A comparison of the systems of agriculture on the Continent, where intensified farming predominates, with that in England, is carried through the book.

The land and the Empire, C. H. TURNOR (*London: John Murray, 1917, pp. 144, figs. 28*).—The author treats of errors in the policy of English agriculture in the past, which permitted a decrease in rural population as well as agricultural production. Occupying ownership, more practical education, betterment of labor conditions, and a more efficiently organized agricultural industry are urged as essentials in the solution of the problem.

The English land system, J. A. R. MARRIOTT (*London: John Murray, 1914, pp. X+168*).—The author traces the development of the English land system from the viewpoint of social and economic history. Its origin in the manorial system, the effect of the Black Death and peasant revolts, the agrarian revolutions of the sixteenth and eighteenth centuries, resulting in large estates and decay of yeomanry, and the causes and outcome of the periods of plenty, as well as depression, of the nineteenth centry agriculture are noted with some detail.

The concluding chapter deals with the land problem to-day, reviewing such suggested solutions as land nationalization, a land commission to settle on such questions as "fair rent" and "security of tenure," and the increase in small holdings through a system of land purchase involving State assistance.

Land improvement in the Province of the Rhine, HEIMERLE (*Landw. Jahrb., 48 (1915), No. 2, pp. 171–277, pl. 1*).—This is a survey of improvements made in Rhenish irrigation and drainage conditions during the past century. Technical, legal, and economic phases are studied, including soil and climatic conditions, drainage and drainage regulations, financial aid, economy of improvement and production increase, and general effect on commerce and population.

Madras agriculture.—A brief survey (*Madras: Dir. Agr. [1916], pp. 87*).— The introduction briefly reviews conditions pertaining to general land economics. Following data of a general nature concerning the variety of crops produced, with the acreage distribution, each crop is considered separately in reference to its locality, manner of cultivation, improvement, and comparative quality. Statistical tables are presented for the principal commercial crops showing the quantity, value, months when available for export, and distribution of foreign trade.

Monthly crop report (*U. S. Dept. Agr., Mo. Crop Rpt., 3 (1917), Nos. 6, pp. 45–56, figs. 2; 7, pp. 57–68, fig. 1*).—These two numbers contain the usual data regarding the estimated crop conditions of the more important crops, the estimated farm value of important products, and range of prices of these products at important markets.

In the first number special data are also given regarding the United States summary of farm prices, the monthly composite crop-condition estimates, index figures of crop prices, ten-year averages of conditions of crops, the estimated production in 1916 of the different varieties of wheat in the three spring-wheat States, special reports regarding Florida and California crops, the commercial production of strawberries, Bermuda onions, and early Irish potatoes, the date of harvesting watermelons, fertilizer used on cotton in 1917, the peanut acreage, the world's production of cereals by five-year periods, and the estimated acreage of hay. The number also includeds a reprint of a special article on the uses made of the corn crop (E. S. R., 28, p. 595), the length of cotton lint for the crops of 1916 and 1915, the international exports of wheat, and the monthly world export of wheat and flour for the five years 1910 to 1914, inclusive.

The second number contains special reports relating to honey yields and prospects, the commercial cherry crop, area planted to sugar beets, prices to producers of cotton and cotton seed, the production and acreage of grain sorghums, a special bean report, potato forecasts by harvest periods, data relating to prices indicating the increase in average of prices, and index figures of crop prices, commercial acreage and production of cantaloups, and acreage and conditions of tobacco by types and districts, together with data relating to the acreage devoted to onions, etc.

AGRICULTURAL EDUCATION.

Proceedings of the thirtieth annual convention of the Association of American Agricultural Colleges and Experiment Stations, edited by J. L. HILLS (*Proc. Assoc. Amer. Agr. Cols. and Expt. Stas., 30 (1916), pp. 363, figs. 3*).—This is a detailed report on the proceedings, including the papers submitted and discussions thereof, of the meeting of the association held at Washington, D. C., November 15–17, 1916.

In addition to the papers and reports previously noted (E. S. R., 35, p. 700), the proceedings also contain the following: Proposed Legislation to Establish Engineering Experiment Stations, by A. Marston (pp. 26–33) ; Scientific Management as Applied to the Farm, Home, and Manufacturing Plants, by C. R. Jones (pp. 108–115) ; Report of Joint Standing Committee on Projects and Correlation of Research (p. 133) ; Report of the Executive Committee (pp. 140–142) ; The Reserve Officers' Training Corps, Historical Statement, by W. O. Thompson (pp. 142–144) ; Problems and Opportunities Presented by the New Federal Army Reserve Law, by G. P. Benton (pp. 145–150) ; The Reserve Officers' Training Corps, by W. M. Riggs (pp. 150–152) ; Report of the Secretary, A. A. Potter, of the Engineering Division of the Section on College Work and Administration, setting forth in brief the history of the campaign in connection with the engineering experiment station bill (pp. 198,199) ; The Appropriate Field in Engineering Extension for the Separate Land-grant College and the State University, by D. W. Spence (pp. 200–202) ; and by C. H. Benjamin (p. 207) ; Mechanic Arts of Sub-collegiate Grade in Land-grant Colleges, by C. E. Hewitt (pp. 212–215) ; and by W. N. Gladson (pp. 215–218) ; The Field of Engineering Experimentation, by R. L. Sackett (pp. 224–229), followed by a review by A. P. Davis of some of the possibilities or facilities of the U. S. Reclamation Service along these lines ; Control of Engineering Experimentation in the Land-grant Colleges, by H. S. Boardman (pp. 232–234) ; The Cooperation of Teachers of Agriculture and Engineering in the Agricultural and Engineering Curriculum, by R. J. Aley (pp. 241–245) ; The Status of the Land-grant College as Outlined in Reports of Surveys Recently Made by the U. S. Bureau of

Education, by S. P. Capen (pp. 246–252); and Economic Factors to Be Considered in Connection with the Project for Extension Work among Farm Women, by E. Merritt (pp. 339–346).

Short courses in agriculture and home economics, W. J. REID ET AL. (*Agr. Gaz. Canada, 4 (1917), No. 5, pp. 363–386, figs. 6*).—This is a symposium on short courses in argiculture and home economics held in the past winter in the various Provinces of Canada. Approximately 500 short courses were held, with an aggregate attendance of 175,000 persons. Upwards of $160,000 was appropriated for 1916–17 for instruction and demonstration and women's work.

Household science in normal schools, H. V. B. BRIDGES ET AL. (*Agr. Gaz. Canada, 4 (1917), No. 5, pp. 400–407, figs. 2*).—This is an account of the instruction in household science given in the normal schools of Ontario, Saskatchewan, and Alberta.

[Agricultural and home economics instruction in the public schools of New Hampshire], G. H. WHITCHER and F. H. DAMON (*N. H. Dept. Pub. Instr., Inst. Circ., 1915–16, Nos. 58, pp. 11; 59, pp. 22; 1916–17, No. 72, pp. 11, figs. 6*).—These circulars deal respectively with methods of cooking meat and diets for invalids, including suggestions as to methods of teaching these subjects, and a description of a poultry plant made by the boys of the Dover (N. H.) high school.

Some exercises in farm handicraft for rural schools, H. O. SAMPSON (*U. S. Dept. Agr. Bul. 527 (1917), pp. 38, figs. 41*).—This bulletin is intended primarily for rural school teachers and for pupils of the seventh and eighth grades. It contains outlines of 25 exercises in the making of useful articles for the school, farm, and home. The exercises have practical application in the agricultural work of the school and also to the various club projects in agriculture.

Working drawings and photographs showing the construction of farm buildings for use in manual training schools (*Nat. Lumber Manfrs. Assoc., Trade Ext. Dept., Ed. Ser. [Pub.] 3 (1917), pp. 15, figs. 16*).—This includes a corn crib, implement shed, granary, dairy house, poultry house, garage, and general-purpose barn.

MISCELLANEOUS.

Annual Report of Florida Station, 1916 (*Florida Sta. Rpt. 1916, pp. 118+ IV, figs. 22*).—This contains the organization list, a financial statement for the fiscal year ended June 30, 1916, a list of the publications of the year, a general review of the work of the station during the year, and departmental reports, the experimental features of which are for the most part abstracted elsewhere in this issue.

Thirty-ninth Annual Report of North Carolina Station, 1916 (*North Carolina Sta. Rpt. 1916, pp. 207, pl. 1, figs. 56*).—This contains the organization list, a report of the director and heads of departments, a financial statement for the fiscal year ended June 30, 1916, and reprints of Bulletins 232–236. The experimental work reported is for the most part abstracted elsewhere in this issue.

Barn and field experiments in 1916, C. D. WOODS (*Maine Sta. Bul. 260 (1917), pp. 85–120*).—These experiments are presented in 13 articles abstracted elsewhere in this issue.

Monthly Bulletin of the Western Washington Substation (*Washington Sta., West. Wash. Sta. Mo. Bul., 5 (1917), No. 4, pp. 45–60, figs. 7*).—This number contains brief articles on the following subjects: Hay Caps, by H. L. Blanchard; Blanching, Harvesting, and Marketing of Celery, by J. L. Stahl; Summer Spraying for Garden Pests, by A. Frank; Summer Feeding, by G. R. Shoup; Poultry Accounts, by Mrs. G. R. Shoup; and Concerning Moles, by T. H. Scheffer.

NOTES.

Alabama College and Station.—R. U. Blasingame, professor of agricultural engineering and agricultural engineer, resigned November 1 to become associate professor of farm mechanics in the Pennsylvania College.

Arizona University and Station.—Recent appointments to the board of regents include Dr. William V. Whitmore, of Tucson, formerly treasurer of the board, as president and chancellor; John P. Orme, of Phoenix; E. Titcomb, of Nogales; Dr. John W. Flinn, of Prescott; and Captain J. P. Hodgson, of Bisbee. State appropriations for the college and station have been made of $72,569.59 for 1917–18, and $75,164.15 for 1918–19.

California University.—The dedication of Hilgard Hall took place October 13. The new building is an elaborate 4-story structure, of reinforced concrete, 60 by 300 ft., costing with equipment about $370,000 and constituting the second of the three buildings which will complete the agricultural quadrangle. It will serve as the headquarters of the college of agriculture, housing the departments of agronomy, citriculture, forestry, genetics, pomology, soil technology, and viticulture. A feature of the dedication exercises was a series of popular conferences on subjects connected with the work of each of these departments. A number of addresses commemorating the life and activities of Dr. Hilgard were also given, including one by Dean Hunt entitled Carrying Hilgard's Work Forward.

Connecticut State Station.—W. C. Pelton, county agent for Sussex County, Del., has succeeded Howard F. Huber as vegetable expert.

Illinois University and Station.—Warren R. Schoonover, instructor in soil biology in the department of agronomy and assistant biologist in the station, has enlisted in the gas defense service of the Sanitary Corps, U. S. Army.

Purdue University and Station.—W. J. Jones, Jr., professor of agricultural chemistry and State chemist for the past 10 years, died August 31, aged 46 years. He was a graduate of the university in 1891, and received the degree of M. S. in 1892 and that of agricultural chemist in 1899. His entire career was spent at the university and dealt especially with control work. He had long been a prominent figure in the Association of Official Agricultural Chemists and was widely known among fertilizer and feeding stuff control officials throughout the country.

Laurenz Green, chief in pomology in the Iowa Station, has been appointed head of the horticultural department. Harry M. Weeter has been appointed associate professor of dairy bacteriology and associate dairy bacteriologist, vice H. B. Switzer, who has accepted a position with the U. S. Department of Agriculture under the Food and Drugs Act with headquarters at Chicago.

Kansas College.—President Henry J. Waters has resigned to become managing editor of the weekly *Kansas City Star*.

Louisiana Stations.—Nicholas Kozeloff, Ph. D. (Rutgers, 1917), has been appointed bacteriologist of the Sugar Station, vice W. L. Owen, whose resignation has been previously noted.

Vermont University.—President G. P. Benton has been given a year's leave of absence for service with the National War Council in France. Dean G. H. Perkins, of the College of Arts and Sciences, has been designated acting president.

700

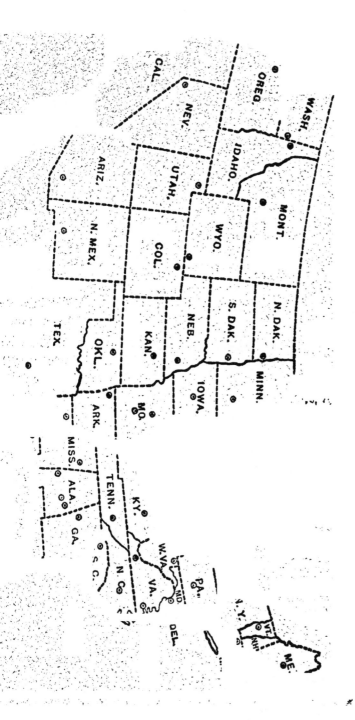

U. S. DEPARTMENT OF AGRICULTURE
STATES RELATIONS SERVICE
A. C. TRUE, DIRECTOR

Vol. 37   DECEMBER, 1917   No. 8

EXPERIMENT STATION RECORD

WASHINGTON
GOVERNMENT PRINTING OFFICE
1918

U. S. DEPARTMENT OF AGRICULTURE

Scientific Bureaus.

WEATHER BUREAU—C. F. Marvin, *Chief.*
BUREAU OF ANIMAL INDUSTRY—J. R. Mohler, *Chief.*
BUREAU OF PLANT INDUSTRY—W. A. Taylor, *Chief.*
FOREST SERVICE—H. S. Graves, *Forester.*
BUREAU OF SOILS—Milton Whitney, *Chief.*
BUREAU OF CHEMISTRY—C. L. Alsberg, *Chief.*
BUREAU OF CROP ESTIMATES—L. M. Estabrook, *Statistician.*
BUREAU OF ENTOMOLOGY—L. O. Howard, *Entomologist.*
BUREAU OF BIOLOGICAL SURVEY—E. W. Nelson, *Chief.*
OFFICE OF PUBLIC ROADS AND RURAL ENGINEERING—L. W. Page, *Director.*
BUREAU OF MARKETS—C. J. Brand, *Chief.*

STATES RELATIONS SERVICE—A. C. True, *Director.*
OFFICE OF EXPERIMENT STATIONS—E. W. Allen, *Chief.*

THE AGRICULTURAL EXPERIMENT STATIONS.

ALABAMA—
  College Station: *Auburn;* J. F. Duggar.[1]
  Canebrake Station: *Uniontown;* J. M. Burgess.[1]
  Tuskegee Station: *Tuskegee Institute;* G. W. Carver.[1]
ALASKA—*Sitka:* C. C. Georgeson.[3]
ARIZONA—*Tucson:* R. H. Forbes.[1]
ARKANSAS—*Fayetteville:* M. Nelson.[1]
CALIFORNIA—*Berkeley:* T. F. Hunt.[1]
COLORADO—*Fort Collins:* C. P. Gillette.[1]
CONNECTICUT—
  State Station: *New Haven;* } E. H. Jenkins.[1]
  Storrs Station: *Storrs;*
DELAWARE—*Newark:* H. Hayward.[1]
FLORIDA—*Gainesville:* P. H. Rolfs.[1]
GEORGIA—*Experiment:* J. D. Price.[1]
GUAM—*Island of Guam:* C. W. Edwards.[3]
HAWAII—
  Federal Station: *Honolulu;* J. M. Westgate.[3]
  Sugar Planters' Station: *Honolulu;* H. P. Agee.[1]
IDAHO—*Moscow:* J. S. Jones.[1]
ILLINOIS—*Urbana:* E. Davenport.[1]
INDIANA—*Lafayette:* C. G. Woodbury.[1]
IOWA—*Ames:* C. F. Curtiss.[1]
KANSAS—*Manhattan:* W. M. Jardine.[1]
KENTUCKY—*Lexington:* A. M. Peter.[4]
LOUISIANA—
  State Station: *Baton Rouge;*
  Sugar Station: *Audubon Park,* } W. R. Dodson.[1]
    New Orleans;
  North La. Station: *Calhoun;*
MAINE—*Orono:* C. D. Woods.[1]
MARYLAND—*College Park:* H. J. Patterson.[1]
MASSACHUSETTS—*Amherst:* W. P. Brooks.[1]
MICHIGAN—*East Lansing:* R. S. Shaw.[1]
MINNESOTA—*University Farm, St. Paul:* R. W. Thatcher.[1]
MISSISSIPPI—*Agricultural College:* E. R. Lloyd.[1]

MISSOURI—
  College Station: *Columbia;* F. B. Mumford.[1]
  Fruit Station: *Mountain Grove;* Paul Evans.
MONTANA—*Bozeman:* F. B. Linfield.[1]
NEBRASKA—*Lincoln:* E. A. Burnett.[1]
NEVADA—*Reno:* S. B. Doten.[1]
NEW HAMPSHIRE—*Durham:* J. C. Kendall.[1]
NEW JERSEY—*New Brunswick:* J. G. Lipman.[1]
NEW MEXICO—*State College:* Fabian Garcia.[1]
NEW YORK—
  State Station: *Geneva;* W. H. Jordan.[1]
  Cornell Station: *Ithaca;* A. R. Mann.[1]
NORTH CAROLINA—
  College Station: *West Raleigh;* } B. W. Kilgore.[1]
  State Station: *Raleigh;*
NORTH DAKOTA—*Agricultural College:* T. P. Cooper.[1]
OHIO—*Wooster:* C. E. Thorne.[1]
OKLAHOMA—*Stillwater:* J. W. Cantwell.[1]
OREGON—*Corvallis:* A. B. Cordley.[1]
PENNSYLVANIA—
  State College: R. L. Watts.[1]
  State College: Institute of Animal Nutrition H. P. Armsby.[1]
PORTO RICO—Federal Station: *Mayaguez;* D. W. May.[3]
RHODE ISLAND—*Kingston:* B. L. Hartwell.[1]
SOUTH CAROLINA—*Clemson College:* H. W. Barre.[1]
SOUTH DAKOTA—*Brookings:* J. W. Wilson.[1]
TENNESSEE—*Knoxville:* H. A. Morgan.[1]
TEXAS—*College Station:* B. Youngblood.[1]
UTAH—*Logan:* F. S. Harris.[1]
VERMONT—*Burlington:* J. L. Hills.[1]
VIRGINIA—
  Blacksburg: A. W. Drinkard, Jr.[1]
  Norfolk: Truck Station; T. C. Johnson.[1]
WASHINGTON—*Pullman:* Geo. Severance.[4]
WEST VIRGINIA—*Morgantown:* J. L. Coulter.[1]
WISCONSIN—*Madison:* H. L. Russell.[1]
WYOMING—*Laramie:* H. G. Knight.[1]

[1] Director.   [3] Agronomist in charge.   [2] Animal husbandman in charge.   [4] Acting director.

EXPERIMENT STATION RECORD.

Editor: E. W. ALLEN, PH. D., *Chief, Office of Experiment Stations.*
Assistant Editor: H. L. KNIGHT.

EDITORIAL DEPARTMENTS.

Agricultural Chemistry and Agrotechny—E. H. NOLLAU.
Meteorology, Soils, and Fertilizers {W. H. BEAL.
                                     {R. W. TRULLINGER.
Agricultural Botany, Bacteriology, and Plant Pathology {W. H. EVANS, Ph. D.
                                                       {W. E. BOYD.
Field Crops {J. I. SCHULTE.
            {J. D. LUCKETT.
Horticulture and Forestry—E. J. GLASSON.
Economic Zoology and Entomology—W. A. HOOKER, D. V. M.
Foods and Human Nutrition—C. F. LANGWORTHY, Ph. D., D. Sc.
Zootechny, Dairying, and Dairy Farming {D. W. MAY.
                                       {M. D. MOORE.
Veterinary Medicine {W. A. HOOKER.
                    {E. H. NOLLAU.
Rural Engineering—R. W. TRULLINGER.
Rural Economics—E. MERRITT.
Agricultural Education {C. H. LANE.
                       {M. T. SPETHMANN.
Indexes—M. D. MOORE.

CONTENTS OF VOL. 37, NO. 8.

	Page.
Editorial notes:	
Attendance at the agricultural colleges as affected by the war	701
Recent work in agricultural science	709
Notes	797

SUBJECT LIST OF ABSTRACTS.

AGRICULTURAL CHEMISTRY—AGROTECHNY.

Chemical studies in making alfalfa silage, Swanson and Tague	709
The isolation of parahydroxybenzoic acid from soil, Walters	709
Studies on the seed of *Spartium junceum*, Raffo	710
Occurrence of raffinose in the seed of the jute plant, Annett	710
The chemistry of wood.—III, Mannan content of the gymnosperms, Schorger	710
The effects of exposure on some fluid bitumens, Reeve and Lewis	711
Importance of uniform culture media in examination of disinfectants, Wright	711
A simple ultramicroscope, Kiplinger	711
Sampling tubes for manure, alfalfa, or other organic materials, Shamel	711
A sampling press, Clark	711
A new filter flask, Shaw	711
Simple apparatus for hydrogen sulphid precipitation under pressure, Fuller	712
Ashing organic materials for determination of potassium, Blumenthal et al	712
A revision of the cobalti-nitrite method for potash, Haff and Schwartz	712
The solubility of calcium phosphates in citric acid, Ramsay	713
A method for the destruction of organic matter, Gautier and Clausmann	713
Iodometric determination of chlorin in chlorids, Torossian	714
A new test for chlorin in drinking water, Wallis	714
The chemical examination of potable waters.—I, Organic matter, Kolthoff	714

Page.

A new method for the determination of aldehyde sugars, Bougault........... 714
The acid content of fruits, Bigelow and Dunbar.............................. 714
Sources and composition of commercial invert sugar sirups, Jordan and Chesley 715
Relative value of different weights of tin coating on canned food containers... 715
War food, Handy.. 715
The evaporation of fruits and vegetables, Caldwell.......................... 715
A new method for the preparation of pectin, Caldwell........................ 715
Carbonation studies.—I, Mechanical stirrer for carbonation, Patten and Mains. 716
Vinegar investigation.—Changes that cider undergoes, Hartman and Tolman. 716
Preserving fish for domestic use, Moore.................................... 716
A practical small smokehouse for fish...................................... 716

METEOROLOGY.

New methods of weather prediction, Voss................................... 716
Factors influencing condensation of aqueous vapor in the atmosphere, Masini.. 716
Relation between forests and atmospheric and soil moisture in India, Hill.... 716
Rainfall and gunfire, Angot... 717
Correlation between atmospheric phenomena and the yield of crops.......... 717
Phenological observations in the British Islands, Clark and Adames.......... 717
Climatological studies.—German East Africa, Lyons......................... 717

SOILS—FERTILIZERS.

The soil solution obtained by the oil pressure method, Morgan............... 717
Is the humus content of the soil a guide to fertility? Carr.................. 718
Effect of addition of organic matter on development of soil acidity, Miller.... 718
Is there any fungus flora of the soil? Waksman............................. 718
Biological variations in soil plats, Allison and Coleman..................... 719
The effect of sterilization of soils by heat and antiseptics, Koch............. 719
Some effects of auximones on the growth of Lemna minor, Bottomley......... 719
Du Page County Soils, Hopkins, Mosier, Van Alstine, and Garrett............ 720
Soil survey of Dickey County, N. Dak., Bushnell et al...................... 720
Sand devastation, Collins... 720
The improvement of the poor soils and run-down soils of New Jersey, Dickey.. 720
Manure and fertilizers for peat soil poor in nitrogen, von Feilitzen........... 720
American sources of nitrogen, Norton..................................... 721
The production of sulphate of ammonia for 1915-16......................... 721
Adsorption of ammonium sulphate by soils and quartz sand, Wolkoff......... 721
Saltpeter: Its origin and extraction in India, Hutchinson.................... 722
Potash from incinerator ash of the Northwest, Thing....................... 722
Tetraphosphate, Vinassa.. 722
Basic slag as affecting agricultural development, Gilchrist and Louis.......... 723
The liming of limy lands, Rosenfeld....................................... 723
Rules and regulations for the enforcement of the lime-barrel act, Stratton..... 723
The fertilizer value of city wastes.—II, Garbage tankage, Schroeder.......... 723
Turf bedding and compost, Vikhlíaev...................................... 723
Artificial fertilizers, their present use and future prospects, Russell........... 724
The American fertilizer handbook.. 724
Commercial fertilizers, Jones, jr., et al.................................... 724
Results of fertilizer inspection, spring season 1917, Patten.................. 724

AGRICULTURAL BOTANY.

Metroclinic inheritance in Œnothera reynoldsii, La Rue and Bartlett.......... 724
A new type of non-Mendelian variation in plants, Ikeno.................... 725
The relation between evaporation and plant succession in a given area, Gates.. 725
Adaptations of vegetation to climate, Massart............................. 725
Temperature and life duration of seeds, Groves............................ 725
Duration of leaves in evergreens, Pease................................... 726
The reaction of plant protoplasm, Haas................................... 726
The mode of action of plant peroxidases, Reed............................ 726
Action of potassium permanganate with peroxidases, Bunzel and Hasselbring.. 726
The response of plants to illuminating gas, Doubt......................... 726
Damage to greenhouse crops and soil from escaping illuminating gas, Stone.... 727
Leaf nectaries of Gossypium, Reed.. 727
On the formation of nodules in the cortex of Hevea brasiliensis, Bryce......... 727

Page.
Preliminary observations on distribution of certain hymenomycetes, Peyronel..   727
Studies in the physiology of the fungi, III, Zeller..............................   727
Studies in the physiology of the fungi, IV, Duggar, Severy, and Schmitz......   728
Microorganisms in silage, Reed and Barber....................................   728

FIELD CROPS.

General agriculture, Diffloth...   728
Agronomical investigatoins [at Guam Experiment Station, 1916], Hartenbower.   728
[Report on field crops work at the Missouri Experiment Station]...............   730
[Field crops], Watts...   732
The twenty-sixth year of crop experiments, Larsen et al......................   732
Report on cultural experiments, 1914–15, Hasund and Borgedal...............   733
[Experiments with field crops], Sjöström....................................   733
[Field crops], Burt..   734
[Field crops], MacDonald..   734
Experiments in Denmark with different mixtures of forage plants, Lindhard..   734
Pollination and fertilization studies with grasses and legumes, Frandsen......   734
Experiments with bird-foot clover and alfalfa in grass mixtures, Lindhard.....   735
Germinability of rice and corn as regards temperature and humidity, Da Fano..   736
Wheat and rye production in Iowa, Hechler...................................   736
Plants growing on moor soils as a source of fiber, von Feilitzen...............   736
Origin and cultural history of Danish strains of Barres field beet, Helweg......   736
Genetical studies of variegated pericarp in maize, Emerson...................   737
Contribution to the study of cotton production and its future, Natta Maglione..   738
Studies on oat breeding, V, Zinn and Surface...............................   738
[Potato culture], Weber and Kleberger......................................   739
The irrigation of potatoes, Harris...   740
Shallu, or "Egyptian wheat," a late-maturing variety of sorghum, Rothgeb...   740
The irrigation of sugar beets, Harris..   741
The weeding of wheat, Rey..   742
Effect of heating seeds upon development of wheat, Worobiew...............   742
Root-crop seeds.—Harvest and trade of 1915–16, Helweg.....................   742
Yellow rocket, a dangerous weed, Bessey....................................   742

HORTICULTURE.

One thousand hints on vegetable gardening, Croy............................   742
[Report of horticultural investigations], Hartenbower.........................   742
[Progress report on horticultural investigations]..............................   743
Protection of fruit against late spring frosts, Beeler.........................   744
[Spray calendars]...   744
Blooming period of the apple in northwest Arkansas, Wicks...................   744
The apple grading and packing law enacted by the Delaware Legislature, 1917..   745
Experimental work in cherry orchards in Kent during 1915–16, Berry.........   745
A census of the peach crop of 1917 in West Virginia, compiled by Somers......   745
Report on fertilizer experiments with cranberries, Schlatter..................   745
Spoilage of cranberries after picking, Shear.................................   745
First report on cacao selection in Assinan, Homburg and van Hall.............   745
Additional observations on the citrus fruits in the Philippines, Wester........   745
A contribution to the history of the mango in Florida, Wester.................   746
The pistachio, Falci...   746
Trees suitable for the farm and for ornamental purposes, Dowsett.............   746
Plant materials of decorative gardening: The woody plants, Trelease..........   746
Annuals and biennials, Jekyll...   746
Garden flowers of spring, Shaw...   746
Garden flowers of summer, Shaw..   746
Garden flowers of autumn, Shaw..   746
Flowers of winter, indoors and out, Free....................................   746
The livable house.—Its garden, Dean.......................................   746
How to make concrete garden furniture and accessories, edited by Fallon.....   746

FORESTRY.

General survey of Texas woodlands, including a study of mesquite, Foster et al..   747
Forest resources of eastern Texas, Foster et al...............................   747
The Patagonian forests, Rothkugel..   747

Page.
Timber-estimating methods used in eastern North Carolina, Krinbill.......... 747
Report of the State forester for 1916, Elliott................................... 747
Forestry, Viquesney.. 747
Law of the woods and yerbales... 747
Amendments to the Central Provinces Forest Manual (third edition).......... 747
On the sun and shade leaves of some trees, Doi............................... 747
The carob and its rational culture, Amico..................................... 747
The black wattle industry.—*Acacia mollissima, A. decurrens* var. *mollis*, Sim... 748
Catalogue of wood specimens exhibited in the economic section, Narasinga Rao. 748
The grouping of ties for treatment, Winslow.................................. 748
Paper and wood pulp industry, Ruff... 748
Forest products of Canada, 1916.—Pulpwood.................................. 748

DISEASES OF PLANTS.

New or interesting species of fungi, House.................................... 748
Texas parasitic fungi.—New species and amended descriptions, Tharp........ 748
Uredinales of Porto Rico based on collections by Whetzel and Olive, Arthur.. 749
A short-cycled Uromyces of North America, Bisby............................ 749
A systematic and physiological study of rusts, Reed, Hursh, and Brentzel.... 749
The physiological relation of the powdery mildews to their hosts, Reed....... 749
Control of *Phytophthora infestans* in Xochimilco, Madariaga and Villarreal..... 749
Economic hosts of *Sclerotinia libertiana* in tidewater Virginia, McClintock..... 749
A new strain of *Puccinia graminis*, Stakman and Piemeisel.................... 749
Grain-smut investigation and control, Reed.................................. 750
Ecological observations on *Ustilago zeæ*, Potter and Melchers............... 750
The formalin treatment for controlling oat smut, Krall....................... 750
Some new facts concerning wheat smut, Heald............................... 750
The prevention of wheat smut, Woolman..................................... 751
Puccinia graminis on wheat kernels, Hungerford............................ 751
The Pseudopeziza leaf spot diseases of alfalfa and red clover, Jones.......... 751
Bean mosaic, Stewart and Reddick... 751
Lima bean mosaic, McClintock... 751
The celery-rot bacillus, Wormald... 751
Development of the æcial stage of Nigredo on red clover, Melhus and Diehl.... 752
The æcial stage of the red clover rust, Davis and Johnson.................... 752
Two transmissible mosaic diseases of cucumbers, Jagger...................... 752
A Gnomonia on eggplant, Edgerton... 752
A malnutrition disease of Irish potato and its control, Edson and Schreiner.. . 752
The economic importance of mosaic of potato, Murphy....................... 752
Strains of Rhizoctonia, Rosenbaum and Shapavalov.......................... 753
Will *Spongospora subterranea* prove serious in Virginia? McClintock.......... 753
Host plants of *Synchytrium endobioticum*, Cotton............................ 753
Bordeaux spray for tip burn and early blight of potatoes, Erwin.............. 753
Seed potato certification in Nova Scotia, Murphy............................. 753
Root disease of sugar cane, Johnson... 753
Tobacco diseases and their control, Johnson................................. 753
A Colletotrichum leaf spot of turnips, Higgins............................... 753
Temperature relations of apple rot fungi, Brooks and Cooley.................. 754
Black root rot of the apple, Fromme and Thomas............................. 754
Treatment of apple canker diseases, Whitten................................ 754
Jonathan spot, Brooks and Cooley.. 754
Control of apple scab by bleaching powder, Brock and Ruth.................. 755
Observations on pear blight in Illinois, Stevens et al......................... 755
Studies on peach yellows and little peach, Blake, Cook, and Schwarze........ 755
Second progress report on leaf spot of cherries and plums in Wisconsin, Keitt.... 755
A new disease of cacao, Turconi.. 755
Diseases of chayote, Ramírez... 755
Mango disease in Yucatan, Ramírez.. 755
Additional suggestions on treatment of hazel blight, Waite................... 755
Winterkilling, sun scald, or sour sap of pecans, McMurran................... 755
Notes on pecan diseases, McMurran.. 756
Blight and melaxuma of walnut, Beers....................................... 756
An investigation of forest tree diseases, Reed et al........................... 756
Boleti and mycorrhiza upon forest trees, Pennington......................... 756
Blight-resistant chestnuts from China, Corsan............................... 756
Breeding chestnuts for disease control.. 756

Page.

Violent outbreak of Oïdium on oak in France, Noffray........................ 756
Oïdium on oak, Convert.. 756
American oaks resistant to Oïdium in Sologne, Noffray....................... 756
A species of Chrysomyxa new to North America, Jackson...................... 757 ·
Mycelium of the white pine blister rust, Colley............................. 757
Pycnial scars, an important diagnostic character for blister rust, Colley....... 757
"Black thread" disease of Hevea in Burma, Dastur.......................... 757
Phytophthora sp. on *Hevea brasiliensis*, Dastur............................. 757

ECONOMIC ZOOLOGY—ENTOMOLOGY.

New mammals from North and Middle America, Goldman.................... 757
The conservation of our northern mammals, Hewitt.......................... 757
Control of the pocket gopher in California.................................. 757
Varying hares of the prairie Provinces, Criddle............................. 758
On the ecology of the vegetation of Breckland, Farrow...................... 758
Description of a new race of Say's ground squirrel from Wyoming, Howell..... 758
Two new pocket mice from Wyoming, Goldman............................. 758
Mutanda ornithologica, I, II, Oberholser.................................. 758
The birds of South America, Brabourne and Chubb......................... 758
Illustrations to the birds of South America, Grönvold...................... 758
A new honey eater from the Marianne Islands, Wetmore..................... 758
A new shrew from Nova Scotia, Jackson................................... 758
Description of a new genus of Anatidæ, Oberholser......................... 758
Rearing insects for experimental purposes and life history work, Wilcox...... 758
The growth of insect blood cells in vitro, Glaser........................... 759
Toxic values and killing efficiency of the arsenates, Lovett and Robinson..... 759
Winter cover washes, Lees.. 759
Accessory wetting substances, especially paraffin emulsions, Lees........... 759
[Progress report of investigational work in entomology].................... 760
Report on injurious insects and fungi of trees in 1914, Schöyen............. 760
Preliminary account of entomological work in 1914, Zolotarevskiï........... 760
Some East African insects of economic importance, Deakin................. 760
Insect enemies of man and the household and the diseases they convey, Berlese. 760
Household and camp insects, Felt.. 760
Coccobacillus acridiorum and intestinal organisms, DuPorte and Vanderleck.... 760
The azalea lace bug, *Stephanitis pyrioides*, Dickerson and Weiss............. 761
The Cicadellidæ of Wisconsin, with new species, Sanders and DeLong........ 761
Spraying for apple sucker (*Psylla mali*), Petherbridge...................... 761
Some observation on the egg of *Psylla mali*, Lees.......................... 761
Plant lice on potatoes, Brown... 761
The louse and its relation to disease, Cummings............................ 762
Rate of increase of pink bollworm in bolls, July to November, 1916, Gough... 762
Rate of increase of *Gelechia gossypiella* in green bolls during 1916, Gough...... 762
The pink bollworm, Buchanan... 762
What effect has flooding on the pink bollworm?............................ 762
Sciara tritici, a fly injurious to seedlings, Edwards and Williams.............. 762
The mosquitoes of North and Central America and the West Indies, Howard et al 762
Relation between hatching of the eggs, development of larvæ of *Stegomyia*   763
    fasciata (*Aedes calopus*), and presence of bacteria and yeasts, Atkin and Bacot. 763
On the biology and economic significance of *Tipula paludosa*, Rennie.......... 763
Notes on New England Tachinidæ, Smith................................... 763
Seasonal abundance of flies in Montana, Parker............................ 764
Empusa muscæ versus *Musca domestica*, Güssow........................... 764
Report on a trial of tarred felt disks for cabbage root fly, Wadsworth......... 764
Two new cambium miners, Greene... 764
Investigations of the Anthomyidæ, the larvæ of which are carnivorous, Keilin. 764
New genera and species of American muscoid Diptera, Townsend............. 764
The viability of *Melophagus ovinus*, Sweet and Seddon...................... 764
Fleas as a menace to man and domestic animals, Waterston.................. 764
Observations on the larval and pupal stages of *Agriotes obscurus*, Ford........ 765
Note on attacks of *Phyllotreta vittula* on spring corn, Petherbridge........... 765
A fleabeetle which attacks potato plantations on the plateaus, Dawe.......... 765
The bark borer (*Dendroctonus micans*), Trägårdh.......................... 765
On new neotropical Curculionidæ, Marshall............................... 765
Fauna of British India.—Coleoptera. Rhynchophora: Curculionidæ, Marshall. 765

                                                                      Page.
The fauna of British India.—Hymenoptera: Ichneumonidæ, I, Morley.......   765
Guide to the insects of Connecticut.—III, The Hymenoptera, Viereck et al...   765
Observations on the occurrence of the Argentine ant in Silesia, Pax..........   766
On some North American species of Microdon, Knab.........................   766
On some North American species of Microdon, Knab.........................   766
New chalcid flies from Maryland, II, Girault..............................   766
A new aphis-feeding Aphelinus, Howard....................................   766
The cyclamen mite, Ross..   766

ANIMAL PRODUCTION.

Physiological effect of rations balanced from restricted sources, Hart et al.....   766
Some nutritional characteristics of corn, Willard............................   767
Feeds and feeding abridged, Henry and Morrison............................   767
Cost of digestible nutrients in principal cattle feeds, Winters.................   767
Commercial feeding stuffs, Wessels et al...................................   767
Digest and copy of revised feeding-stuffs law...............................   767
[Live-stock investigations], Hartenbower, Barbour, and Barber...............   767
[Animal husbandry studies at the Missouri Experiment Station]...............   768
Live stock of the farm.—V, Pigs and poultry, edited by Jones................   769
Live stock of the farm.—VI, edited by Jones................................   769
[Swiss live-stock industry], Borgeaud, Frey, and Bouret.....................   769
Statistics of Swiss live-stock industry.....................................   769
Nineteenth and twentieth conventions of American Live Stock Association....   769
Inbreeding, Bruce..   769
Report on cattle feeding experiments at Cedara, Natal, and Potchefstroom....   769
Experiment with palm kernel meal and earthnut cake, Hendrick and Profeit.   769
Ageing Egyptian cattle, Mohammed Askar...................................   770
Live stock of the farm.—IV, Sheep, edited by Jones.........................   770
Sheep production, García..   770
Sheep and wool for farmers. Crossbreeding experiments, Mathews...........   770
Horses, Pocock...   770
Horse breeding and horse racing, Ewart....................................   771
A history of the Percheron horse, compiled by Sanders and Dinsmore........   771
The diastatic action of saliva in the horse, Seymour........................   771
Sex-linked inheritance of spangling in poultry, Lefevre.....................   771
Mendelian inheritance in poultry, Lefevre..................................   772
The structure of the fowl, Bradley...   772
Studies on the physiology of reproduction in birds, I–VII, Riddle et al........   772
A study of the incubation periods of birds, Bergtold.........................   774
The molting of fowls, Irvin..   774
Protein feeds for laying hens, Kempster....................................   774
The poultry keeper's manual, Allman.......................................   775
Commercial egg farming, Hanson...   775
Poultry standards in their relation to utility, Hadlington....................   775
American squab culture, Eggleston..   775
Squab culture, Wood..   775
The raising and care of guinea pigs, Smith..................................   775
The rabbit: How to select, breed, and manage, Richardson..................   775

DAIRY FARMING—DAIRYING.

Cattle breeding problems and their solution, Pearl...........................   775
The Kerry: Its advantages under present conditions, Cheviot.................   776
Studies from the survey on the cost of market milk production, Musser et al....   776
The milk supply—a suggestion, Williams and Cornish......................   777
Manual of milk products, Stocking...   777
Modern pasteurization at low temperature, Vanderleck......................   777
Cause and prevention of mold on butter, Hastings...........................   777
Minnesota creameries; cheese, ice cream, and canning factories..............   777
Siberian butter and cheese...   778
Cheese making on an Irish farm, O Brien....................................   778
Experiments on the preparation of homemade rennet, Todd and Cornish.......   778
Experiments with pepsin to replace rennet, Steuart.........................   778

VETERINARY MEDICINE.

Page.

[Veterinary handbooks]... 778
[Diseases and parasites of live stock], Barber.................................. 778
[Report of the veterinary department], Connaway and Durant................. 779
Proceedings under the diseases of animals acts, etc., for 1916, Anstruther..... 779
Report on the veterinary sanitary service of Paris during 1915, Martel........ 780
Report of Bengal Veterinary College and Civil Department, 1915–16, Smith.. 780
Animal diseases regulations with notes on diagnoses, Lionnet.................... 780
Manure disposal as a factor in control of parasitic diseases of stock, Hall 780
Poisonous properties of the two-grooved milk vetch (*Astragalus bisulcatus*).... 780
Immunization with sensitized and nonsensitized bacteria, Swift and Kinsella.. 780
Toxin and antitoxin of inoculation against *Bacillus welchii*, Bull and Pritchett.. 781
Glanders in Australia from 1911 to 1913, Schnürer............................. 781
Neosalvarsan in the treatment of epizootic lymphangitis, Houdemeyer.......... 781
Studies on the paratyphoid-enteritidis group, I, II, Krumwiede, jr., et al..... 781
Antitetanic serum in articular rheumatism, Dalrymple 782
The vitality of the tubercle bacillus outside the body, Soparkar............... 782
Incidence of bovine infection of tuberculosis in children, Ching Yik Wang.... 782
The etiology of hog cholera.—Second report, Proescher and Seil.............. 782
The virulence of hog-cholera blood at different periods, Whiting............... 784
Observations on 1,470 hogs hyperimmune to hog cholera, Kernkamp 784
Serum therapy for trichinosis, Schwartz..................................... 784
Special equine therapy, Steffen.. 784
Trichomonasis of chicks: A new and highly fatal disease, Weinzirl............. 784

RURAL ENGINEERING.

Evaporation from the surfaces of water and river-bed materials, Sleight........ 785
Use of power and rates for irrigation pumping, Kenny 786
The use of cement on national irrigation works, Davis........................ 787
Improvements proposed in javellization of water for field service, Comte.... 787
Experiments upon the purification of sewage and water...................... 787
Annual report of the Baltimore County [Md.] roads engineer for 1916, Sucro.. 787
Influence of grading on fine aggregate used in road construction, Jackson, jr.... 787
The effect of alkali on Portland cement, Steik 788
Spontaneous combustion as a cause of fires, Lamb........................... 788
Report of tractor ratings committee, Olney et al............................. 788
Farm buildings, with plans and descriptions, Shearer........................ 789
Silo building, Nicholls.. 789
Pit silos, Metcalfe and Scott.. 789
Reinforced concrete silos and small grain bins, Fowler....................... 789

RURAL ECONOMICS.

Farm management [in Missouri], Johnson and Green........................... 789
[Farm cost accounts at the Ontario agricultural experimental farm]........... 790
Plan for handling the farm-labor problem.................................... 790
Agricultural labor question in Switzerland, IV............................... 790
[Agricultural societies in Finland]... 790
California resources and possibilities.. 790
New Hampshire farms.—Your opportunity.................................. 790
[Agricultural resources of the State of New York], Wilson et al................ 790
New York State rural market conditions and farm trade...................... 790
Corn is king in South Dakota... 790
Statistics and resources of Utah, Haines..................................... 790
Conditions in the Cagayan Valley in relation to tobacco, Hoskins et al........ 791
British industries after the war.—I, The land industry, Earnshaw-Cooper..... 791
A national agricultural policy, Johnston..................................... 791
Allotments and small holdings in Oxfordshire, Ashby........................ 791
The economic resources of Russia, Heyking.................................. 791
Agricultural colonization of Tripoli.. 791
[La d tenure and settlement; agriculture and live stock in New Zealand]..... 791
Prices and wages in India... 792
[Agricultural statistics of Japan].. 792

AGRICULTURAL EDUCATION.

                                                                    Page.
Secondary agricultural schools in Russia, Jesien............................... 792
Twenty-third annual report of the inspector of State high schools, Phillips.... 793
Introduction of agriculture into public schools............................... 793
The education of the farmers by the regional agronomes, Marotta.............. 793
Report of the work of the school garden association in 1915 and 1916......... 793
Chronicle of the woman movement in German Switzerland in 1915–16, Strub.. 793
Report of the committee on teaching.. 794
Farm management summer practice courses, Adams......................... 794
The scope and methods of instruction in rural sociology, Gillette.............. 794
The teaching of rural sociology, Sanderson................................... 794
Preparation for editorial work on farm papers, Crawford..................... 794
Report of committee on suggestive course in agriculture for use in land-grant
    colleges of the South which give teacher-training courses in agriculture..... 794
Practical agriculture through school, home, and community, Blackwell....... 794
Practical education: A home library, Holden et al........................... 795
School and home gardens, Mairs.. 795
Home project at an agricultural school, Lane............................... 795
Productive plant husbandry, Davis... 795
Agricultural botany, Whitney... 795
Feed manual and note book, Woll.. 795
Proceedings of Association of Farmers' Institute Workers, edited by Taft.... 796

MISCELLANEOUS.

Report of the Guam Agricultural Experiment Station, 1916.................. 796
Work and progress of the agricultural experiment station for 1916............. 796

LIST OF EXPERIMENT STATION AND DEPARTMENT PUBLICATIONS REVIEWED.

Stations in the United States.

Page.

Arkansas Station:
Bul. 134, May, 1917.......... 744
California Station:
Bul. 281, July, 1917........... 757
Guam Station:
Rpt. 1916..... 728, 742, 767, 778, 796
Illinois Station:
Soil Rpt. 16, May, 1917....... 720
Indiana Station:
Bul. 199, Apr., 1917.......... 724
Iowa Station:
Bul. 171, July, 1917......... 753
Circ. 36, July, 1917 788
Circ. 37, July, 1917........... 736
Michigan Station:
Spec. Bul. 80, May, 1917..... 742
Circ. 33, July, 1917........... 724
Missouri Station:
Bul. 147 (An. Rpt., 1916),
June, 1917.............. 718, 728,
730, 743, 749, 754, 756,
760, 768, 779, 789, 796
Circ. 82, June, 1917.......... 774
New Jersey Stations:
Circ. 74, May 10, 1917........ 767
Circs. 75–79, May 10, 1917.... 744
Hints to Poultrymen, vol. 5,
No. 10, July, 1917......... 774
North Dakota Station:
Bul. 121, Jan., 1917........... 720
Rhode Island Station:
Insp. Bul., May, 1917......... 767
Utah Station:
Bul. 156, June, 1917.......... 741
Bul. 157, June, 1917.......... 740
Washington Station:
Bul. 147, Apr., 1917.......... 715
Bul. 148, June, 1917.......... 715
Wyoming Station:
Bul. 112, Jan., 1917........... 780
Bul. 113, Mar., 1917.......... 788

U. S. Department of Agriculture.

Jour. Agr. Research, vol. 10:
No. 4, July 23, 1917. 753, 754, 759, 766
No. 5, July 30, 1917........ 785, 787
No. 6, Aug. 6, 1917.... 709, 738, 764
Farmers' Bul. 825, Pit Silos, T. P.
Metcalfe and G. A. Scott....... 789
Farmers' Bul. 827, Shallu, or
"Egyptian Wheat," B. E. Roth-
geb............................. 740

U. S. Department of Agriculture—Cont'd.

Page.

Office of the Secretary:
Office of Farm Management—
Circ. 2, June 5, 1917...... 790
Scientific Contributions:[1]
The Isolation of Parahydroxy-
benzoic Acid from Soil,
E. H. Walters............. 709
The Chemistry of Wood.—III,
Mannan Content of the Gym-
nosperms, A. W. Schorger... 710
The Effects of Exposure on
Some Fluid Bitumens, C. S.
Reeve and R. H. Lewis..... 711
Sampling Tubes for Manure,
Alfalfa, or Other Organic
Materials, A. D. Shamel.... 711
A Sampling Press, W. B.
Clarke.................... 711
A Simple Improvised Appara-
tus for Hydrogen Sulphid
Precipitation under Pres-
sure, A. V. Fuller.......... 712
The Acid Content of Fruits,
W. D. Bigelow and P. B.
Dunbar.................... 714
Carbonation Studies.—I, A
Mechanical Stirrer for Car-
bonation Direct in the Bot-
tle, H. E. Patten and G. H.
Mains..................... 716
Vinegar Investigation. — A
Study of the Changes That
Cider Undergoes during Fer-
mentation and Prolonged
Storage and Its Subsequent
Conversion into Vinegar in
Rotating Generators, B. G.
Hartman and L. M. Tolman. 716
Soil Survey of Dickey County,
N. Dak., T. M. Bushnell,
E. H. Smies, W. I. Watkins,
A. C. Anderson, M. Thomas,
M. E. Stebbins, R. C. Don-
eghue, and J. W. Ince...... 720
The Fertilizer Value of City
Wastes.—II, Garbage Tank-
age.—Its Composition, the
Availability of Its Nitrogen,
and Its Use as a Fertilizer,
P. J. Schroeder............. 723

[1] Printed in scientific and technical publications outside the Department.

U. S. Department of Agriculture—Contd.
Scientific Contributions—Contd.   Page.

Matroclinic Inheritance in Mutation Crosses of *Œnothera reynoldsii*, C. D. La Rue and H. H. Bartlett.............. 724

The Supposed Action of Potassium Permanganate with Plant Peroxidases, H. H. Bunzel and H. Hasselbring. 726

Spoilage of Cranberries After Picking, C. L. Shear........ 745

The Grouping of Ties for Treatment, C. P. Winslow....... 748

Additional Suggestions on Treatment of Hazel Blight, M. B. Waite.............. 755

Winterkilling, Sun Scald, or Sour Sap of Pecans, S. M. McMurran................ 755

Notes on Pecan Diseases, S. M. McMurran................ 756

New Mammals from North and Middle America, E. A. Goldman...................... 757

Description of a New Race of Say's Ground Squirrel from Wyoming, A. H. Howell.... 758

Two New Pocket Mice from Wyoming, E. A. Goldman.. 758

Mutanda ornithologica, I, II, H. C. Oberholser.......... 758

A New Honey Eater from the Marianne Islands, A. Wetmore.................... 758

A New Shrew from Nova Scotia, H. H. T. Jackson.... 758

Description of a New Genus of Anatidæ, H. C. Oberholser.. 758

Notes on Rearing Insects for Experimental Purposes and Life History Work, A. M. Wilcox.................. 758

U. S. Department of Agriculture—Contd.
Scientific Contributions—Contd.   Page.

The Growth of Insect Blood Cells in Vitro, R. W. Glaser. 758

The Mosquitoes of North and Central America and the West Indies, L. O. Howard, H. G. Dyar, and F. Knab.. 762

Notes on New England Tachinidæ, with the Description of One New Genus and Two New Species, H. E. Smith.. 763

New Genera and Species of American Muscoid Diptera, C. H. T. Townsend........ 764

On Some North American Species of Microdon, F. Knab.. 766

New Chalcid Flies from Maryland, II, A. A. Girault...... 766

A New Aphis-feeding Aphelinus, L. O. Howard........ 766

Serum Therapy for Trichinosis, B. Schwartz............ 784

Home Project at an Agricultural School, C. H. Lane.... 795

The Work of the U. S. Department of Agriculture, C. Vrooman 796

The Extent and Possibilities of Cooperative Marketing, C. E. Bassett.............. 796

The Relation of the Smith-Lever Funds to Farmers' Institutes, A. C. True...... 796

The Present Relation of Farmers' Institutes and Extension Schools, D. J. Crosby.. 796

Statistics of Farmers' Institutes in the United States, 1915–16, J. M. Stedman.... 796

EXPERIMENT STATION RECORD.

Vol. 37.   December, 1917.   No. 8.

The beginning of the new academic year this fall was awaited by most institutions devoted to higher education with unusual uncertainty and apprehension. The declaration of a state of war in April had profoundly affected these institutions almost immediately. Attendance, which in most colleges and universities had been steadily rising from year to year, was suddenly depleted as the call came for one form or another of National service, in some places the campus emptying almost over night. Some institutions closed their doors early in May, and in others work went on under greatly altered conditions. Commencements were quite generally omitted or curtailed, and July 1 found the undergraduates nearly as widely scattered as the alumni, with every indication that a considerable percentage would never return and that entering classes might also be much smaller than for many years.

The seriousness of such an outcome, not merely to the institutions but to the ultimate welfare of the Nation, was quite generally foreseen, but there was also more or less uncertainty as to the duty of the institutions and the individual students under the emergency conditions. It was apparent that the Nation had immediate need of thousands of its young men, many for military service and many along other lines; that the shortage of labor on the farms, in the factories, and elsewhere was enormous; and it was inevitable that such factors would influence many a boy against beginning or continuing a college course which would even temporarily keep him from active participation in the strenuous work of the conflict itself. On the other hand it was also seen that the war had vastly increased the need for trained men and that the supply of these men could not safely be allowed to fail.

In response to an inquiry from the Secretary of the Interior as to the duty of the colleges and technical schools during the war, the situation was admirably stated by President Wilson in a letter of July 20, 1917, as follows: "The question which you have brought to my attention is of the very greatest moment. It would, as you suggest, seriously impair America's prospects of success in this war if the supply of highly trained men were unnecessarily diminished.

701

There will be need for a larger number of persons expert in the various fields of applied science than ever before. Such persons will be needed both during the war and after its close. I therefore have no hesitation in urging colleges and technical schools to endeavor to maintain their courses as far as possible on the usual basis. There will be many young men from these institutions who will serve in the armed forces of the country. Those who fall below the age of selective conscription and who do not enlist may feel that by pursuing their courses with earnestness and diligence they also are preparing themselves for valuable service to the Nation. I would particularly urge upon the young people who are leaving our high schools that as many of them as can do so avail themselves this year of the opportunities offered by the colleges and technical schools, to the end that the country may not lack an adequate supply of trained men and women."

Subsequently, under date of November 23, 1917, a letter of much the same tenor from the Secretary of War to the chairman of the special committee on universities and colleges of the Council of National Defense was made public, which reads as follows: " The successful outcome of the war is so dependent upon the applications of science that the United States can ill afford at this time to risk any diminution of this supply of technically trained men. Such diminution we must in part suffer by reason of the fact that class exemptions in the execution of the selective service law are prejudicial to its general success, but I have constantly in mind the fact that the Government service will demand more and more scientifically trained men, and so I hope those who are in charge of scientific institutions will impress upon the young men the importance and desirability of their continuing their studies except to the extent that they are necessarily interrupted by a mandatory call under the provisions of the selective conscription law."

It will be noted that in both these statements particular stress is laid upon the need for men trained in applied science. In this group would be included, of course, the graduates of the agricultural colleges. In view of the important and unique functions which these institutions have to fulfill, and the realization that in some ways the conditions regarding their prospective attendance differed from those in other institutions, it was deemed of general interest to attempt to ascertain, after their reopening, how they had fared as regards enrollment. Information was, therefore, sought by the States Relations Service as to the initial registration of college students in agriculture this fall as compared with the previous year, and also as to how any changes in the enrollment in agriculture compared with other kinds of education. A general survey of the existing situation, rather than a collection of statistical data, was intended, although numerical data were gathered so far as readily available. Opinions were also sought as to any obvious changes in the character of the enrollment, as in age of students, relative proportion from farms and cities, proportion of men and women, purpose in coming to college, selection of courses of study, and similar matters, and especially as to the apparent underlying causes for such changes as were noted.

Information was supplied on some of these points by 48 institutions, located in 42 States and Hawaii. The reports covered nearly all sections of the country, and it is believed are representative of the situation as a whole. Although the inquiry necessarily reached the presidents, deans, and registrars at an exceptionally busy period, in most cases very complete data were furnished by these officials, through whose courteous response the preparation of this summary is made possible.

The data available indicate very clearly that a considerable shrinkage in total student enrollment in higher education occurred quite generally throughout the country. For the land-grant institutions this apparently averaged slightly over 20 per cent. In no institution reporting was there any considerable gain, although in such widely separated States as North Dakota, Oregon, South Carolina, Texas, and Virginia, substantially the registration of the previous year was maintained. On the other hand, decreases of nearly 50 per cent were encountered in a large university of the Middle West and a small southwestern college. The average percentage of falling off for the group, however, was probably less than for many of the oldest and best known universities of the country, press reports announcing, for instance, decreases of about 40 per cent for Harvard, Yale, and Princeton.

As regards students in agriculture, the showing is considerably less favorable than for total enrollment. The average decrease for the institutions reporting was slightly over 30 per cent and in numerous cases exceeded 50 per cent. Some sectional variation was noticeable, several southeastern colleges maintaining their previous registration and others falling only slightly below it, while losses were exceptionally heavy in the Southwest and in the Middle West.

On the other hand, the average decrease in the mechanic arts was approximately only 15 per cent and did not exceed 36 per cent for any institution. Four colleges reported gains of from 11 to 14 per cent, and in eight others the loss was under 10 per cent. These comparatively small losses were apparently typical of the technical schools in general, the Massachusetts Institute of Technology, for instance, reporting a loss of 18 per cent and the Carnegie Institute of Technology one of 16 per cent.

It seems probable that the explanation for the great difference noted between agriculture and the mechanic arts needs be sought in several directions. The unprecedented shortage of farm labor and the emphasis placed on an adequate food supply as a war measure doubtless kept many a boy on the farm, where his services could ill be spared, and the fact that his college training was unfinished, or even not begun, seemed much less important than his immediate availability as a dependable labor unit. More of the mechanic arts students, however, are recruited from the towns and cities, and while the labor shortage afforded them unusual opportunities for lucrative employment along industrial lines, they were often freer to follow their inclinations and the temptation to drop out of college was less keen because the opportunities were less closely associated with their chosen professional work. The enormous demand for trained engineers, chemists, and similar technically educated men was a strong inducement to boys graduating from high school to go to college and prepare themselves along these lines, while the limited field for half-trained workers discouraged the abandonment of the courses already begun. In short the feeling, formerly well-nigh universal and never entirely overcome, that thorough training is a necessity in the mechanic arts but less essential in agriculture, very likely explains some of the differences in relative enrollment.

In general the remaining courses offered by the land-grant institutions showed losses greater than for the mechanic arts and smaller than for agriculture, but there were many local variations. Even the enrollment of women, whether in home economics courses or in colleges of liberal arts, showed a considerable decrease in many cases, though this as a rule was less than the diminution of men and in some cases there were slight gains. The number of women students in agriculture continued to be too small for safe generalizations, but gives little indication of any increasing trend in this direction.

Analysis of the registration by classes revealed heavy losses at every stage. As would be expected, the senior class was largely effected, decreases of from 40 to 60 per cent being not uncommon. Obviously this class contains more men of draft age than those below it, and in many institutions men with longer military training, hence the call to the colors has been specially strong. Senior students also possess the maximum of specialized agricultural training and their services are in great demand along these lines. While it is desirable that the seniors should return and complete their work, particularly since these students include some of the most mature and otherwise promising material for development as teachers, investigators, and extension workers, withdrawals seem in many instances inevitable under the existing conditions.

The depletion of the junior and sophomore ranks was found to be somewhat smaller in most institutions. The reasons actuating withdrawals were substantially the same as with seniors, but applied with decreasing force, so that it seems probable that losses will be relatively somewhat less numerous and less detrimental.

The entering classes, however, present a special problem for consideration. Before the war steadily increasing numbers of freshmen, in many cases taxing the capacity of the college, had been the rule, but this fall thirty-six institutions reported losses ranging from 8 to 60 per cent. The Texas College, to be sure, reported an increase of over 12 per cent, resulting in the largest class in its history, and four others showed smaller gains, but the average for the entire group is a loss of about 25 per cent.

This percentage is, of course, smaller than for the entire enrollment in the colleges of agriculture, but it is none the less disquieting. In eighteen institutions it ranged from 30 to 40 per cent, whereas in mechanic arts courses only one institution showed an entering class more than 25 per cent below that for the previous year, while in fourteen others the losses were under 10 per cent and six showed gains of from 78 to 165 per cent. The percentage loss in freshman agricultural students was also considerably greater in the majority of institutions than for most other courses, although in some cases the falling off among male students in liberal arts was also large.

Expressed not in percentages, but in actual numbers, the data are even more striking. For the institutions available the freshmen aggregated in 1916, 4,630, and in 1917, only 3,463. This means a decrease of 1,167 freshmen students in agriculture in the 41 States reporting this item.

So heavy a decrease in this group, especially if it portends similar small entering classes for several years to come, must be regarded as unfortunate. It is unlikely that many of the boys who are thus foregoing a college course are of draft age or that any considerable proportion is engaged in military service. It seems probable that most of them have stayed on the farm, where they have indeed rendered sorely needed assistance, but it may be at a cost of an ultimate serious loss of hundreds of trained men to the Nation. The fact that the full extent of this loss will not be evident for several years only emphasizes how difficult it will be to remedy it when it becomes apparent. It would seem that special efforts should be made by the colleges to enlighten prospective students as to the unusual opportunities for trained agricultural workers within the next few years. Some institutions have already begun work along this line.

The group of students most seriously affected of all is, as would be expected, that of graduate students. The data reported as to these students are somewhat less complete than for undergraduates, since in the larger universities they are quite often enrolled in general graduate schools instead of in the colleges of agriculture. For eighteen institutions reporting graduate students in agriculture in 1916, the aggregate enrollment has dropped from 410 to 202, or over 50 per cent. This condition will doubtless continue or perhaps be aggravated, since most of these students are of draft age and openings for active employment were never more numerous.

Another phase of the matter which needs consideration is the subsequent dropping out of the students who have returned to college. Hardly an issue of a college paper has appeared this fall without items announcing such withdrawals. Many of these are for military service, but others are often for less vital reasons and should be kept at a minimum. As the committee on instruction in agriculture pointed out in its recent report to the Association of American Agricultural Colleges and Experiment Stations, "in this country and abroad, agriculture is now recognized to be of importance second only to the military service, even under war conditions. On this account there is a heavier burden of responsibility upon the young men of our agricultural colleges—students and graduates alike—who have not been called to military service. The burden is greater not only because of the demand for greater production, but also because of the smaller number of young men available for positions as teachers, as specialists, and as organizers in field demonstration work. It is, therefore, highly important that the agricultural college students who are not yet subject to the draft, as well as those who have been excused from military service, remain in college and make the best of every opportunity to prepare themselves for these heavier burdens, and it is incumbent upon the colleges of agriculture not only to urge this point of view, but to provide for these young men the best teaching and the most thorough training to be had."

Something can doubtless be done in many colleges to provide special courses to meet the emergency needs. Thus, as regards the training of teachers, the same committee states that whereas at the outbreak of the war there were upwards of a thousand college-trained young men teaching agriculture in schools below college grade, the number has now been seriously depleted, while the development of work under the Federal Vocational Education Aid Act alone will create a demand for several hundred additional instructors with such training. It is suggested that the colleges can do much to "prevent the serious lowering of standards by increasing their facilities for training undergraduates for the teaching profession, by conducting emergency courses for teachers now in service, and by the intensive training along agricultural lines of college graduates in arts and science courses."

In some States the pressure upon students to return to the farms has been lessened and considerable assistance rendered in alleviating the labor problem by shortening the college year and providing a more intensive training. Many institutions deferred the opening of their doors until October, and others made special provisions for students whose return was retarded because of farm needs. The University of Nebraska has already announced its intention of closing its school of agriculture early in March next year and the college of agriculture early in April.

Recognition of the work of students leaving before graduation to engage in war service by some form of war certificate has been suggested by the executive committee of the Association of American Agricultural Colleges and Experiment Stations. It was pointed out that such a certificate would not only be much appreciated by many former students and their relatives, but would also serve to strengthen the bond between the student and the institution, and perhaps facilitate and render more probable his eventual return for the completion of his work.

Emergency short courses in agriculture have already been offered by a number of institutions and their further development seems logical. One interesting innovation along this line is being undertaken at the University of California, which is offering to a limited number of inexperienced men practical training as milkers, teamsters, and other branches of farm labor. Such courses, if successful, would help relieve the dearth of labor and it is possible that modifications of the idea might be worked out to attract greater numbers of town and city-bred boys to regular college work. One large college of agriculture in the Middle West reported that an increasing realization of the need for practical farm experience had in a measure decreased the registration from the cities in recent years, and the present inquiry indicated that the war had thus far not materially affected the proportion of country and city-bred students. It is well understood that the city-bred boy in the agricultural college has in the past been more or less of a problem, but his presence there in increasing numbers would at least possess the advantage of not diminishing appreciably the supply of available farm labor, while under the present conditions provision for the necessary farm experience before graduation would probably be found somewhat less difficult than formerly.

Serious as the shrinkage of students appears, it need not prove an absolute calamity. The efficiency of educational institutions is not measured by the enrollment, and this is specially true of the agricultural colleges, the tuition fees in which constitute under normal conditions little over 10 per cent of their income. To quote

24656°—18—No. 8——2

again from the committee on instruction in agriculture, " during the past fifteen or twenty years nearly every agricultural college in the country has been working at high pressure. Nearly all of them have been growing more rapidly in enrollment than in teaching staff and equipment. The result has been crowded class rooms, large laboratory sections, many hours in class and laboratory for teachers with correspondingly few hours for preparation, and too much of a tendency to get things done somehow, whether well done or not.

" Just now there seems to be a breathing spell so far as the resident teaching work is concerned. There are fewer students, probably 30 per cent less. The class rooms are less crowded. The sections are smaller, and the number of students each instructor is required to teach has in many cases decreased. The present time seems, therefore, to be opportune to consider how we have been doing things and how we may do better."

The committee was of the opinion that for these reasons not within a decade " has there been a time so favorable for giving serious attention to measures for improving the quality of teaching in the colleges themselves as the present war emergency affords." It is to be hoped that this optimistic view will prove justified though there should not be overlooked the serious depletion of faculties or the possibility that in some States the reduction in enrollment may afford a pretext for a curtailment of financial support.

The decreased burden of teaching may also open up opportunities in many cases for greater attention to research and extension work. It may thus permit, for example, considerable additional investigation and experimentation which has a definite and direct bearing on present agricultural problems and so render a most timely and valuable service.

If the reduction in enrollment of agricultural students by nearly one-third seems discouraging, it is well to reflect that in England wholesale losses of faculties and students have occurred, that several institutions have closed their doors, and that others have been very seriously restricted in their operations. Likewise the Ontario Agricultural College reports a smaller registration in the entire institution than in its freshman class prior to the war. In our own country no such developments are expected and often the enrollment is far in excess of that of a few years ago. Some of this difference is probably due to the fact that in this country the principle of selective service was adopted as the basis of raising the National Army. When the importance of trained agricultural leadership becomes thoroughly realized, particularly in its relations to the existing emergency, there need be little doubt that the agricultural colleges, as the training ground for such leadership, will receive and retain the full support in every direction which they will need for this vital service.

RECENT WORK IN AGRICULTURAL SCIENCE.

AGRICULTURAL CHEMISTRY—AGROTECHNY.

Chemical studies in making alfalfa silage, C. O. SWANSON and E. L. TAGUE (*U. S. Dept. Agr., Jour. Agr. Research, 10 (1917), No. 6, pp. 275-292*).—This is a preliminary report of two series of experiments on chemical studies in the making of alfalfa silage, carried out at the Kansas Experiment Station. The first series of experiments, started in 1912 and continued for four years, was carried out in quart milk bottles; the second series, started in 1914 and continued in 1915, in 10-ton experimental silos. A portion of the work has been referred to (E. S. R., 37, p. 671), and a complete report will be published later. The conclusions drawn by the authors are based on the results obtained from both series of experiments.

It was found that silage could be made from alfalfa alone if absolute exclusion of air and retention of carbon dioxid could be secured. These conditions are, however, indicated as not practical of realization. The addition of supplements was found to insure a more rapid and plentiful production of acids, which makes conditions for putrefactive organisms unfavorable. Wilted alfalfa was more suitable for silage than unwilted. The addition of water to unwilted alfalfa was harmful, while no decisive results were obtained by the addition of water to wilted alfalfa.

Molasses was found to be the most effective supplement tried. Germinated corn was more effective as a supplement to alfalfa than sound corn, the results produced being similar to those produced by molasses. It is indicated that rye would be a suitable supplement but for the strong odor which it imparts to the silage.

The value of tightness of packing lies only in the fact that it makes the exclusion of air more certain.

In good alfalfa silage about one-third of the nitrogen was found to be in the amino form, while in bad silage the amount was sometimes one-half that of the total nitrogen.

"Most of the acids present in alfalfa silage are produced in the first two weeks. The percentage of acidity may increase after that, but the increase is comparatively slight. The alfalfa, as it is put into the silo, contains only a small amount of nitrogen in amino form. Most of the change of nitrogen into amino form takes place in the first 10 days. Silage from wilted alfalfa contains more nitrogen in this form than that made from fresh alfalfa. Sugar present in the materials used in making silage disappears very rapidly. Completely matured silage contains no sugar."

The isolation of parahydroxybenzoic acid from soil, E. H. WALTERS (*Jour. Amer. Chem. Soc., 39 (1917), No. 8, pp. 1778-1784*).—An aromatic acid whose identity with parahydroxybenzoic acid was established was isolated from a sandy soil from Florida. Benzoic acid was also isolated from this soil, but in a much smaller quantity.

Parahydroxybenzoic acid was isolated by the extraction of 23 kg. of soil with about 75 liters of an aqueous 2 per cent solution of sodium hydroxid at room temperature for 24 hours. The extract was acidified slightly with sulphuric acid and filtered. The acid filtrate was extracted with ether, the ether extract concentrated to a volume of about 200 cc., and then treated with a concentrated solution of sodium bisulphite to remove aldehydes, etc. The bisulphite solution was drawn off and extracted several times with fresh ether, and the ether extracts combined and slowly evaporated on the surface of a small volume of warm water. The water solution was heated to boiling and filtered while hot to remove any insoluble oily residue. A crystalline compound separated from the cold concentrated aqueous solution. This was purified by re peated crystallizations from water, but the product thus obtained persistently retained a slight tinge of color which was removed only after many crystallizations and boiling with a small quantity of purified bone black. Much of the material was lost in this procedure. The aqueous solution was finally subjected to steam distillation to remove benzoic acid and other volatile substances which might be present. The solution in the distilling flask was evaporated to dryness and the residue extracted with chloroform to remove final traces of ‚benzoic acid. The substance was finally recrystallized from water.

The confirmatory tests of the acids are described and the significance of their presence in the soil discussed.

Studies on the seed of Spartium junceum, M. RAFFO (*Ann. Chim. Appl.* [*Rome*], 7 (*1917*), *No. 5–8, pp. 157–164*).—The seed examined was found to contain a lipolytic enzym having but slight action in an acid medium, but a marked action in the presence of sodium carbonate.

A yield of about 10 per cent of a green-colored oil with an aromatic odor was obtained from the seeds. The following constants were determined for the oil: Specific gravity at 15° C., 0.9403; refractive index at 25°, 73.5; acid value, 9.1; saponification value, 198.6; iodin value, 134; Hehner value, 89.85; and Reichert-Meissl value, 0.44. The fatty acids obtained from the oil yielded the following constants: Specific gravity at 17°, 0.9208; melting point, 26.6–27°; solidifying point, 21.3°. The oil is classed with the group of semidrying oils.

Occurrence of raffinose in the seed of the jute plant (Corchorus capsularis), H. E. ANNETT (*Biochem. Jour.*, *11* (*1917*), *No. 1, pp. 1–6*).—The author reports the isolation of raffinose from the seed of the jute plant. The seed examined contained about 2.25 per cent of the sugar. The crude raffinose was obtained by precipitating an alcoholic extract of the seed (after previous extraction with ether and petrol) with ether. The impure material so obtained was recrystallized from 80 per cent alcohol, rosettes of white needles depositing in several days.

The confirmation tests are described in detail.

The chemistry of wood.—III, Mannan content of the gymnosperms, A. W. SCHORGER (*Jour. Indus. and Engin. Chem.*, 9 (*1917*), *No. 8, pp. 748–750, fig. 1*; *Jour. Forestry, 15 (1917), No. 2, pp. 197–202, fig. 1*).—Continuing the study previously noted (E. S. R., 37, p. 502), the author examined 22 different species of gymnosperms and 6 of angiosperms for mannan and found it present in appreciable quantities in all of the conifers, but absent in the hardwoods. The sapwood was generally found to contain larger amounts of mannan than the heartwood. The content was found to decrease from the base upward but was uniform throughout the heartwood in a radial direction.

The industrial importance of mannan in the production of ethyl alcohol from sulphite liquor and by the hydrolysis of sawdust with catalyzers is pointed out.

The mannan was determined by precipitation of the mannose formed on hydrolysis as mannose hydrazone.

The effects of exposure on some fluid bitumens, C. S. REEVE and R. H. LEWIS (*Jour. Indus. and Engin. Chem.*, *9 (1917), No. 8, pp. 743–746, fig. 1*).

The importance of uniform culture media in the bacteriological examination of disinfectants, J. H. WRIGHT (*Jour. Bact.*, *2 (1917), No. 4, pp. 315–346, figs. 4*).—The results of the study reported show that variations in culture media are the cause of the majority of the discrepancies obtained in the bacteriological examination of disinfectants. The hydrogen ion concentration of the culture medium was found to exert important influences on its composition and on its suitability for the growth of the typhoid organism. A marked relationship between the hydrogen ion concentration of the culture medium and the resistance of the test organism to the action of disinfectants was observed.

"The most satisfactory and uniform results have been obtained with a culture medium in which the P_H value falls between 6 and 7. This condition is easily obtained with a medium containing 10 gm. of Witte's peptone, 3 gm. of Liebig's meat extract, and 5 gm. of salt, boiled 15 minutes, filtered, tubed, and sterilized, with no attempt to adjust the acidity."

The experimental data are submitted in tabular and graphical form.

A simple ultramicroscope, C. C. KIPLINGER (*Jour. Amer. Chem. Soc.*, *39 (1917), No. 8, p. 1616, figs. 2*).—A simple apparatus, which has yielded good results in practice, and its manipulation are described.

Sampling tubes for manure, alfalfa, or other organic materials, A. D. SHAMEL (*Mo. Bul. Com. Hort. Cal.*, *6 (1917), No. 7, pp. 225–228, figs. 4*).—A device for sampling organic materials is described and illustrated.

"The apparatus . . . consists of a tube somewhat similar in arrangement and appearance to the King soil tube. Two different sizes of sampling tubes have been made, one for use in sampling car load or other large lots of manure, and the other for sampling bales of alfalfa, bean straw, cornstalks, or other similar materials. The manure sampling tube is about 6 ft. in length and about 2 in. in diameter. One end is made with a sharp sawtooth-like cutting edge so arranged as to cut down through the manure somewhat on the principle of the knives commonly used for cutting hay in the stack. At the other end of the tube an extra ring of metal is welded onto the tube in order to give it added support. A hole is cut through this ring and the tube so that a handle can be pushed through it for use in twisting the tube when the sample is being taken."

A sampling press, W. B. CLARK (*Jour. Indus. and Engin. Chem.*, *9 (1917), No. 8, pp. 788–790, figs. 4*).—An apparatus for the sampling of roots, tubers, melons, and such fruits as are easily separated from the seeds and skins, which consists essentially of a plunger and a cylinder, the latter having a stout sieve bottom, and its manipulation are described.

The apparatus has also been found to be well adapted for obtaining raw cultures of finely divided substance which is sterile except for such inoculations as may already exist in the interior of the material. It is indicated that, while this work has not been fully developed as yet, very satisfactory results have been obtained with ordinary precautions.

A new filter flask, J. A. SHAW (*Jour. Indus. and Engin. Chem.*, *9 (1917), No. 8, p. 793, fig. 1*).—An apparatus which is considered equal to the ordinary filter flasks and superior to the use of a bell jar for suction filtration and its manipulation are described. The flask is pear-shaped, with a wide-mouthed stopcock at the bottom and a heavy glass tubing leading off to the suction pump from near the flask mouth, which is of a size suitable to take the filtering funnel.

Advantages claimed for the flask are better air seals than those obtained with the bell-jar type of filter, and easy removal of the filtrate and washing of the flask, thus practically eliminating the danger of contamination.

A simple improvised apparatus for hydrogen sulphid precipitation under pressure, A. V. FULLER (Jour. Indus. and Engin. Chem., 9 (1917), No. 8, pp. 792, 793, fig. 1).—The apparatus described consists of an ordinary 500-cc. Kipp generator provided with a two-holed rubber stopper which carries a one-way stopcock and a small-bore glass tube about 3 ft. long which terminates at its upper end in a reservoir bulb of about 100 cc. capacity. The lower end of this tube extends several inches below the acid level. The gas outlet is fitted with a rubber stopper carrying a two-way stopcock. The manipulation of the apparatus is described.

It is noted that the precipitates obtained appear very granular and settle readily. The point of saturation is easily determined by rotating the flask and noting the absence of gas bubbles.

A method of ashing organic materials for the determination of potassium, P. L. BLUMENTHAL, A. M. PETER, D. J. HEALY, and E. J. GOTT (Jour. Indus. and Engin. Chem., 9 (1917), No. 8, pp. 753-756).—To reduce materially losses by spattering and volatilization in ashing organic material, the authors, at the Kentucky Experiment Station, have found that direct evaporation of the sample with nitric and sulphuric acids preliminary to burning off organic matter has proved the best method for securing uniform results. Simple moistening of the sample with sulphuric acid was found not to be sufficient, and enough acid must be added to oxidize the carbon and to convert all inorganic elements present to sulphates. This conversion of the potassium salt present in the material to the sulphate reduces the volatilization losses to a minimum.

Burning off the carbon in a muffle furnace yielded more uniform results than direct heating over a free flame.

The data are submitted in tabular form and discussed.

A practical revision of the cobalti-nitrite method for the determination of potash, R. C. HAFF and E. H. SCHWARTZ (Jour. Indus. and Engin. Chem., 9 (1917), No. 8, pp. 785, 786).—The following revision of the procedure previously described by Bowser (E. S. R., 22, p. 510) is submitted:

To a 2-gm. sample of raw material 0.5 gm. of ammonium chlorid is added and thoroughly mixed in a mortar. Four gm. calcium carbonate is then added and the contents of the mortar further mixed and ground. The mixture is transferred to a 20-cc. platinum crucible, the bottom of which has been covered with a generous layer of calcium carbonate, usually about 2 gm., the contents of the crucible are covered with about 2 gm. of calcium carbonate, and the heating and sintering carried out as in the J. Lawrence Smith method. After the mass has been slaked in a small casserole it is placed on a hot-water plate and heated to boiling, filtered into a flat-bottomed porcelain dish, and the precipitate washed three or four times with very hot water. An excess of acetic acid (5 to 10 cc.) is added to the filtrate and the solution then evaporated on a steam bath until no odor of acetic acid remains.

The residue is taken up with a little hot water and the sides of the dish thoroughly washed. From 10 to 15 cc. of the cobalt reagent is added and the liquid evaporated on a steam bath to a pasty consistency. It is removed from the bath, cooled, and about 30 cc. of cold water added, breaking up the precipitate thoroughly. The precipitate is then filtered through an asbestos padded Gooch crucible, washed once with cold water, the contents of the crucible transferred to a 400-cc. beaker containing an excess of standard fifth-normal potassium permanganate, and diluted to 250 cc. The beaker is then placed on a steam bath for about 15 minutes and acidulated with 10 cc. of 1:1 sulphuric acid, the excess permanganate is removed with standard fifth-normal oxalic acid, and the clear solution retitrated with standard potassium permanganate solution.

For determining "water-soluble" potash 10 gm. of the material is weighed into a 600-cc. beaker and boiled with 250 cc. of water for 30 minutes. It is then transferred to a 500-cc. flask, cooled to room temperature, and made to the mark. After shaking well, a portion of the solution is filtered through a dry paper and 50 cc. of the filtrate placed in a platinum or porcelain dish. The procedure is then carried out as given above.

Directions for preparing the cobalt-nitrite solution and calculation of the potassium oxid factor are given.

The method has been used for some time and has yielded most satisfactory results on total potash when checked against the J. Lawrence Smith method, and on water-soluble potash when checked against the official method.

The solubility of calcium phosphates in citric acid, A. A. RAMSAY (*Jour. Agr. Sci.* [*England*], 8 (*1917*), No. 3, pp. 277–298).—The results of the study reported show that the materials sold as "phosphate of lime" and "Calcii Phosphas B. P." are not tricalcium phosphate, but mixtures of di- and tricalcium phosphates. By adding disodium phosphate to ammoniacal calcium chlorid a mixture of di- and tricalcium phosphate and calcium hydrate is obtained. Bone ash dissolved in hydrochloric acid and precipitated with ammonia (as in the directions for preparing tricalcium phosphate according to the British Pharmacopœia) also yields a mixture of di- and tricalcium phosphate and calcium hydrate. When three equivalents of calcium oxid act on one equivalent of phosphoric acid and the resulting precipitate is immediately removed pure tricalcium phosphate is obtained. When two equivalents of calcium oxid react on one equivalent of phosphoric acid the product obtained is not dicalcium phosphate, but a mixture of di- and tricalcium phosphate.

Of the total phosphoric acid of pure tricalcium phosphate 91 per cent is soluble in 2 per cent citric acid solution in 30 minutes, as determined by the method adopted for the determination of "citrate-soluble" phosphoric acid. By addition of calcium carbonate to a pure tricalcium phosphate the "citrate solubility" of the phosphoric acid is reduced from 91 to 84 per cent. It is noted that the 2 per cent citric acid solution is rather a solvent for lime than for phosphoric acid.

"Since tricalcic phosphate and dicalcic phosphate are both soluble in the prescribed 2 per cent citric acid solution the statement that dicalcic phosphate can be differentiated from tricalcic phosphate by means of the selective action of this solvent is untenable. It follows that the manurial value of phosphates can not be determined by a 2 per cent citric acid solvent in the method prescribed, and it therefore is a matter for consideration whether or not the further use of this method should be continued."

See also previous notes of Hopkins (E. S. R., 37, p. 214) and Jatindra Nath Sen (E. S. R., 37, p. 615).

A method for the destruction of organic matter in animal and vegetable materials for the determination of arsenic and the examination of the ash, A GAUTIER and P. CLAUSMANN (*Compt. Rend. Acad. Sci.* [*Paris*], 165 (*1917*), No. 1, pp. 11–16).—The procedure, which consists essentially of heating the dry, finely pulverized material with calcium oxid, is described in detail. The method can also be used for preparing material for the determination of boric, phosphoric, and silicic acids, fluorin, nickel, silver, and copper. The procedure recommended eliminates the use of large amounts of acid ordinarily used for oxidation.

Iodometric determination of chlorin in chlorids, G. TOROSSIAN (*Jour. Indus. and Engin. Chem., 9 (1917), No. 8, pp. 751, 752, fig. 1*).—In the proposed method the sample is mixed with finely powdered manganese dioxid and treated with sulphuric acid (1:1 by volume) in a distilling flask. The chlorin produced by the interaction of the MnO_2 and liberated hydrochloric acid is distilled into potassium iodid solution and the liberated iodin titrated as usual with tenth-normal sodium thiosulphate.

Comparative analytical data with the standard silver nitrate procedure indicate the accuracy of the proposed method.

A new test for chlorin in drinking water and its application for the estimation of the chlorin present, R. L. M. WALLIS (*Indian Jour. Med. Research, 4 (1917), No. 4, pp. 797-799*).—A colorimetric procedure which depends on the production of a yellow color in a solution of benzidine or tolidin by chlorin is described as follows:

To 100 cc. of the sample to be tested in a Nessler tube 1 cc. of a 0.1 per cent solution of benzidine in 10 per cent hydrochloric acid is added. The solution first becomes blue, but on stirring the blue color rapidly changes to a bright yellow. The mixture is allowed to stand for exactly five minutes and then compared with standards prepared under similar conditions.

The production of the color is not affected by the salts present in drinking water or other chemical reagents added for purposes of sterilization. The delicacy of the test is indicated by its being able to detect 0.005 parts per million of chlorin in drinking water.

For effective chemical sterilization of water 1 part of chlorin in 500,000 parts of water is considered necessary.

The chemical examination of potable waters.—I. Determination of organic matter, I. M. KOLTHOFF (*Pharm. Weekbl., 54 (1917), No. 22, pp. 547-553*).—The addition of 5 cc. of four-normal sulphuric acid and 25 cc. of $\frac{1}{10}$-normal potassium permanganate to 100 cc. of the water sample and the determination of the excess potassium permanganate iodometrically after 24 hours is considered to be the best procedure for the determination of organic matter in potable waters and to yield satisfactory results.

A new method for the determination of aldehyde sugars, J. BOUGAULT (*Compt. Rend. Acad. Sci. [Paris], 164 (1917), No. 26, pp. 1008-1011*).—A new method for the determination of aldehyde sugars which depends on the oxidation of the aldehyde to the corresponding monobasic acid with iodin in the presence of sodium carbonate is noted. The presence of ketonic sugars does not affect the result. In mixtures containing sucrose and other nonreducing sugars the accuracy of the procedure depends on the relative proportion of the sugars present. With increasing amounts of nonreducing sugars the necessary correction increases, and so slightly diminishes the accuracy of the results. The principal disadvantage of the method indicated is the interfering action of other organic substances that are likely to be present with the aldehyde sugars.

The details of the reaction and of the method are reserved for a future communication.

The acid content of fruits, W. D. BIGELOW and P. B. DUNBAR (*Jour. Indus. and Engin. Chem., 9 (1917), No. 8, pp. 762-767*).—The following results obtained in an examination of the acids found in various fruits are reported: Apple, cherry, and plum, malic only; banana, peach, persimmon, probably malic only; cantaloup, malic none, probably all citric; cranberry, citric probably predominates, malic also present; currant, citric probably predominates, malic sometimes present; gooseberry, malic and citric; pear, malic only in some varieties—citric probably predominates in others with small amounts of malic; pomegranate, probably all citric, no malic nor tartaric; quince and watermelon, malic, no citric; and raspberry (red), probably citric only—malic, if present, in traces only. Apricots, blackberries, and huckleberries were also examined, but no definite results on their acid content were obtained.

The danger of drawing general conclusions as to the acid content of fruits from analysis of a limited number of varieties, or even samples, is indicated as being emphasized by the varying results obtained with pears.

A table giving results and references thereto as to the acids in various fruits reported by previous investigators is included.

Sources and composition of some commercial invert sugar sirups with notes on sorghum sirups, S. JORDAN and A. L. CHESLEY (*Jour. Indus. and Engin. Chem., 9 (1917), No. 8, pp. 756-758*).—This is a general discussion of the topics of methods of analysis, moisture-holding properties, specifications, and sorghum sirup. Analytical data, including invert sugar, sucrose, and ash of a number of sirups collected from various sources, are submitted.

Relative value of different weights of tin coating on canned food containers (*Washington, D. C.: Nat. Canners Assoc., 1917, pp. 51+666, figs. 9*).— This is the report of an investigation by a technical committee representing the National Canners' Association, the American Sheet and Tin Plate Company, and the American Can Company. Products from various parts of the country typical of those usually canned in tin were used. In general, no great differences in the products were observed by using tins with varying weights of coating.

Data relative to the discoloration of cans and average tin content of various products are submitted in graphical form. Other experimental and analytical data of the investigation are reported in detail in 10 appendixes.

War food, AMY L. HANDY (*Boston: Houghton Mifflin Co., 1917, pp. IX+76, figs. 2*).—This small volume gives directions for drying fruits and vegetables; preserving meat; canning with and without sugar; preparing jellies; salting; pickling; and making cider, potato, and corn vinegar.

The evaporation of fruits and vegetables, J. S. CALDWELL (*Washington Sta. Bul. 148 (1917), pp. 7-111, figs. 26*).—This is in part a revision of the bulletin previously noted (E. S. R., 35, p. 418), with new sections discussing in detail the drying of cherries, berries, peaches, apricots, prunes, and various vegetables, together with directions for preparing the materials for drying and for storing and packing the dry products.

A new method for the preparation of pectin, J. S. CALDWELL (*Washington Sta. Bul. 147 (1917), pp. 3-14*).—A method of preparing pectin from cull apples or other fruits rich in the substance for future use in jelly making from fruit juices poor in pectin is described. The method consists essentially of the separation of a portion of the water of the juice by freezing, removal of the concentrated liquid from the ice by centrifugalization (or draining through muslin), and repetition of the process until the desired concentration has been obtained. The concentration is finally completed by evaporating the residue at a low temperature. The method has been simplified and adapted so that it may be easily carried out with very little equipment.

The concentrated extracts were found to retain their gelatination properties perfectly after long periods if the acid was removed from the juice by calcium carbonate. A tasteless and odorless dry product may be secured by precipitating the pectin from the concentrated extract by alcohol and subsequently drying at a low temperature.

Some general notes on the occurrence, distribution, and use of pectin are included.

Carbonation studies.—I, A mechanical stirrer for carbonation direct in the bottle, H. E. PATTEN and G. H. MAINS (*Jour. Indus. and Engin. Chem., 9 (1917), No. 8, pp. 787, 788, figs. 2*).—An apparatus and its manipulation are described in detail.

Vinegar investigation.—A study of the changes that cider undergoes during fermentation and prolonged storage and its subsequent conversion into vinegar in rotating generators, B. G. HARTMAN and L. M. TOLMAN (*Jour. Indus. and Engin. Chem., 9 (1917), No. 8, pp. 759–762*).—The results of the investigation, which extended over a period of two years, show that during fermentation a large part of the malic acid of the apple juice is destroyed to form lactic acid. During acetification the remaining malic acid is almost entirely oxidized. The fixed acid in the vinegar is chiefly lactic acid. The presence of acetates in the vinegar and indications of minute amounts of formic acid were demonstrated. Analysis of the ash showed it to contain 75 per cent of potassium carbonate.

Complete analytical data are submitted.

Preserving fish for domestic use, H. F. MOORE (*U. S. Dept. Com., Bur. Fisheries Econ. Circ. 28 (1917), folio*).—This circular gives detailed general directions for canning and salting fish for home consumption.

A practical small smokehouse for fish (*U. S. Dept. Com., Bur. Fisheries Econ. Circ. 27 (1917), pp. 7, figs. 3*).—This gives directions for constructing the smokehouse and cleaning, salting, and smoking the fish, and discusses the fuel used in smoking and protection from mold.

METEOROLOGY.

New methods of weather prediction, A. VOSS (*Mitt. Deut. Dendrol. Gesell., 24 (1915), pp. 133–149, figs. 2*).—The author points out certain alleged deficiencies in ordinary methods of weather forecasting, particularly from the standpoint of the farmer and gardener, and explains methods devised by himself which he thinks overcome these deficiencies.

Factors influencing the condensation of aqueous vapor in the atmosphere, A. MASINI (*Nuovo Cimento, 6. ser., 12 (1916), II, No. 9, pp. 110–129, fig. 1; abs. in Sci. Abs., Sect. A.—Phys., 20 (1917), No. 235, pp. 261, 262; Sci. Amer. Sup., 84 (1917), No. 2180, p. 238*).—Experiments bearing upon the action of ozone, nitrogen peroxid, and, indirectly, ammonia, as well as of dust, in forming condensation nuclei in the atmosphere are reviewed. The effect of electrical discharges, flames, and glowing bodies in favoring condensation is also referred to.

Ultraviolet light is not considered necessary for the formation of nuclei and functions only as a source of ozone. Gaseous ions exhibit no power to constitute condensation nuclei. "Trees, especially tall ones and those rich in resins, give rise to ozone, and should therefore favor production of rain. Opinions on the actual influence exerted by trees are, however, very variable."

The relation between forests and atmospheric and soil moisture in India, M. HILL [*Indian*] *Forest Bul. 35 (1916), pp. 41, pls. 2; abs. in Internat. Inst. Agr. [Rome], Internat. Rev. Sci. and Pract. Agr., 8 (1917), No. 4, pp. 554–556; Nature [London], 99 (1917), No. 2492, pp. 445, 446*).—This is a report based upon replies to a letter of inquiry sent out by the Government of British India, asking information regarding (1) rainfall, (2) differences in level of the underground water table, and (3) flow of rivers and streams in different parts of India.

The data obtained indicate that during the last 50 years there have been no permanent changes in the rainfall which can be directly connected with the monsoons. It appears, however, that forests may increase rainfall to a certain limited extent (not exceeding 5 per cent) by promoting the condensation of aqueous vapor. There appears to have been no change in the level of the underground water during the last 50 years, except such as depends upon the rainfall. Apparently in most Provinces there has been no serious damage to the flow of rivers and no great injury to cultivation as a result of floods due to forest denudation. There are, however, local exceptions, and much flood damage has been done in the Punjab, in Bengal, and in Assam.

Rainfall and gunfire, A. ANGOT (*Compt. Rend. Acad. Agr. France, 3 (1917), No. 18, pp. 501–508; rev. in Nature [London], 99 (1917), No. 2493, pp. 467, 468; Sci. Amer. Sup., 84 (1917), No. 2180, p. 227*).—This paper deals with the historical aspects of the subject, reviews the various theories advanced, and adduces evidence to show that there is no causal relation between gunfire and rainfall.

Correlation between atmospheric phenomena and the yield of crops (*Rev. Sci. [Paris], 55 (1917), No. 14, p. 436*).—This is a brief note on studies by Marenghi on the influence of precipitation on the yield of alfalfa, in which a record was kept during 10 years of the spring rainfall and of the yield of the crop. The coefficient of correlation was found to be 0.49 for the particular period and place in which the studies were made.

Phenological observations in the British Islands, J. E. CLARK and H. B. ADAMES (*Quart. Jour. Roy. Met. Soc. [London], 43 (1917), No. 183, pp. 285–316, figs. 2*).—Observations from December, 1915, to November, 1916, at 117 stations on wild plants, birds, and insects are summarized. Tentative isophenal lines or zones similar to those of Ihne for Continental Europe are shown for several flowering plants for periods of 120 (April 29), 130 (May 9), and 140 days (May 19) for the British Isles. The usual data for farm crops are not included, although the status of farm work and crops at different dates is noted.

Climatological studies.—German East Africa, H. G. LYONS (*Quart. Jour. Roy. Met. Soc. [London], 43 (1917), No. 182, pp. 175–195, pls. 8, figs. 5*).—This article is based upon observations covering the 20 years from 1892 to 1911.

"On account of its position close to the equator most of the colony receives heavy tropical rains in the wet season, while the drier northeasterly and southeasterly air currents of northern and southern Africa, respectively, sweep over it and give rise to dry seasons which are in some parts of several months' duration and of considerable aridity." Seasons, as understood in the Temperate Zone, do not exist, but instead there is an alternation of the dry season and the rainy season which divides the year and determines the cycle of agricultural operations. The coastal region, as a result of air currents from the Indian Ocean, has a heavier rainfall than many parts of the interior.

Such climatic variations as occur are largely those due to the physical character of the country. The climatic conditions of each district are discussed in some detail with reference to vegetation.

SOILS—FERTILIZERS.

The soil solution obtained by the oil pressure method, J. F. MORGAN (*Soil Sci., 3 (1917), No. 6, pp. 531–545*).—Experiments at the Michigan Experiment Station with the paraffin oil displacement-pressure method are reported. In this method the solution is displaced by forcing paraffin oil by pressure through the soil.

It was found that "the paraffin oil pressure method furnishes in most cases plenty of solution for the necessary analytical work. In sandy soils as high as 74 per cent of the moisture present in the soils was obtained. A large amount of solution may be obtained without its coming in contact with the oil. If it does it can be easily separated by cooling and by the separatory funnel.

"The concentration of the soil solution from different samples of the same type of soil varies according to the moisture content of the samples from which it is derived. Successive portions of the same extraction vary only slightly in their physical properties, but to a considerable extent in the various forms of nitrogen. The forms of nitrogen vary in the different solutions. . . . Calcium and magnesium also vary according to the treatment and reaction of the soil. The phosphoric acid is fairly constant. Potash varies somewhat. A small percentage of the bacteria are removed from the soil, since the soil acts as a filter. Anaerobic changes take place in the cylinder if it is allowed to stand for a long time.

"The paraffin oil displacement-pressure method furnishes . . . a fair representative of the solution as it exists in the soil. The method permits the use of a large amount of soil, thus a better representative sample. Work now in progress indicates that it furnishes a valuable index of the microbial changes in the soil."

Is the humus content of the soil a guide to fertility? R. H. CARR (Soil Sci., 3 (1917), No. 6, pp. 515–524, figs. 3).—Experiments conducted at Purdue University using a surface clay soil very deficient in organic matter and different organic manures are reported.

"The results of the vegetation and humification tests seem to show that whenever there is rapid humification of manure the growth of the plant is greatly stimulated, indicating that 'the decay of organic matter is desirable in plant growth and not just its mere presence.' This was especially noticeable when green manures were rolled under and limed as compared with disking or mixing the manures uniformly with the soil.

"Certain of the manures seem to be as soluble in a 4 per cent ammonia when just mixed with the soil as after humification. This was found to be true with alfalfa and steer and somewhat with cow manures. Horse manure seemed to humify slowly and its plant food was largely unavailable to corn during the first year, but the humification and vegetation tests show it becomes more available in the second year. It was possible to increase the rate of humification of horse manure in the first year by adding dolomitic limestone, which resulted in a greater yield of corn than where humification had not taken place.

"The organic residues left in the soil from manure treatment were not very effective during the second year in producing a growth of corn, probably because the most available or valuable complexes had disappeared in the first year. There is no apparent relationship between the percentage of ash in humus and the growth of corn. The humification and vegetation tests seem to indicate a rather close relationship between the amount of humus and the growth of corn."

Effect of the addition of organic matter to the soil upon the development of soil acidity, M. F. MILLER (Missouri Sta. Bul. 147 (1917), pp. 50, 51).—The results reported in general indicate "that the ordinary green manures turned under either dry or fresh do not increase soil acidity, although a crop containing much sugar, as in the case of sorghum, does appreciably increase soil acidity for a few weeks. This acidity later decreases."

Is there any fungus flora of the soil? S. A. WAKSMAN (Soil Sci., 3 (1917), No. 6, pp. 565–589).—Studies at the New Jersey Experiment Stations of the fungus content of 25 soils collected under sterile conditions from different parts of North America and the Hawaiian Islands are reported.

Over 200 species of fungi were isolated. It was found that the more fertile soils contained more fungi, both in number and species, than the less fertile soils. The soils of the cooler climate seemed to contain a greater number of Mucorales and Penicillium, while those of the warmer climate were more abundant in Aspergillus. The acid and water-logged soils were richer in numbers and species of Trichoderma than normal agricultural soils.

Biological variations in soil plats as shown by different methods of sampling, F. E. ALLISON and D. A. COLEMAN (*Soil Sci.*, *3* (*1917*), No. 6, pp. *499–505, figs. 2*).—Experiments conducted at Rutgers College to determine the influence of method of sampling soils on biological variations are reported. Two one-twentieth acre plats, one of heavy clay growing timothy sod and the other of sandy loam growing corn, were used. Samples were taken by the Brown method (E. S. R., 28, p. 120) and by the Lipman sampling tube (E. S. R., 14, p. 556).

The data obtained led to the belief that "where plats are uniform in character the biological variations of the soil at different points in the plat are not great, or else we are not able to detect these differences by the present methods. The tube method is superior to Brown's method both for ease of taking the sample and from the standpoint of destruction of the plat, especially in an uncultivated area."

The effect of sterilization of soils by heat and antiseptics upon the concentration of the soil solution, G. P. KOCH (*Soil Sci.*, *3* (*1917*), No. 6, pp. *525–530*).—Experiments conducted at Rutgers College to determine the influence on the concentration of the soil solution of commercial sterilization as practiced in greenhouses, sterilization as used in biological laboratories, and of the presence of organic matter during the process of sterilization are reported. The following conclusions were drawn:

"The lowering of the freezing-point method is a satisfactory means of determining soil solution concentration as influenced by sterilization. In commerical as well as laboratory methods of steaming soils, the heavier soils are more influenced by sterilization than lighter soils. Steaming alone was more effective in increasing the concentration than . . . the formalin treatments.

"Applying formalin (1:50) and then steaming at 10 lbs. pressure increased the concentration more than any other method tried. By this method the concentration was increased to three times the original concentration of the soil solution. A considerable amount of soluble material is leached out of the soil, and thus the concentration is lowered if the quantity of antiseptic solution applied is so great that the soil can not hold it against the force of gravity. . . .

"Sassafras loam and . . . Penn loam soils were affected in the laboratory sterilization method so that the concentration was increased 0.24 and 0.3 atmosphere, respectively. The concentration of . . . Norfolk sand containing a very small amount of organic matter was not affected so that it could be detected by the method employed. One per cent of dried blood increased the concentration of the soil solution of . . . Norfolk sand 0.09 atmosphere, while 2 per cent cottonseed meal increased the concentration three times this amount."

Some effects of organic growth-promoting substances (auximones) on the growth of Lemna minor in mineral culture solutions, W. B. BOTTOMLEY (*Proc. Roy. Soc. [London], Ser. B, 89* (*1917*), No. B 621, pp. *481–507, pls. 2, figs. 7*).—Experiments on the influence of extracts of bacterized peat on the growth of *L. minor* plants in mineral culture solutions showed that "the addition to the mineral culture solution of 368 parts per million of organic matter from the water extract of bacterized peat resulted, after six weeks, in a multiplication of the number to 20 times, and an increase in weight to 62 times, that of the control plants. The water extract free from humic acid, representing an addition of 97 parts of organic matter per million, gave $9\frac{1}{2}$ times the number and 29 times the weight; 32 parts per million from the alcoholic extract gave 3½ times the number and 7½ times the weight; 13 parts per million from the phosphotungstic fraction gave 1½ times the number and 2½ times the weight.

"The effect of the reduction in amount of auximones with successive fractionation of the bacterized peat was also manifest from the general appearance of the plants. Those in mineral nutrients only decreased in size week by week, and became very unhealthy in appearance, while there was a progressive improvement in the appearance of the plants supplied with increasing amounts of auximones. Those receiving the larger amounts retained their normal healthy appearance throughout the experiment and increased in size.

"The beneficial effect of the auximones was not due to a neutralization of the toxic substances present in the ordinary distilled water, since comparable results were obtained with conductivity water. An interchange of culture solutions, with and without auximones, showed that the plants are very sensitive to the presence or absence of these substances. It is suggested that some of these growth-promoting substances may act directly as organic nutrients, and others may be of the nature of accessory food substances."

Du Page County soils, C. G. HOPKINS, J. G. MOSIER, E. VAN ALSTINE, and F. W. GARRETT (*Illinois Sta. Soil Rpt. 16 (1917), pp. 56, pl. 1, figs. 8*).—Du Page County is located in northeastern Illinois within the late Wisconsin glaciation. The topography varies from rolling to slightly undulating. The natural drainage is said to be poorly developed.

The soils of the county are divided into upland prairie soils, rich in organic matter, upland timber soils, terrace soils, late swamp and bottom-land soils, and miscellaneous types. Of these the brown silt loam upland prairie soil covers 59.95 per cent, the yellow-gray silt loam upland timber soil, 20.65 per cent, and the black mixed loam bottom-land soil, 12.01 per cent of the area.

It is pointed out that the soils of the county vary widely in content of fertility constituents. "The deep peat contains in the plowed soil of an acre 18 times as much nitrogen as yellow silt loam, and about 5 times as much nitrogen, but only one-eighth as much potassium as brown silt loam. The total supply of phosphorus in the surface soil varies from 760 lbs. per acre in the yellow silt loam to 2,360 lbs. in the black clay loam. The amounts of magnesium and calcium vary from about 4,000 to 5,000 lbs. in some types to more than 20,000 lbs. in others. Some types contain an abundance of limestone; others are practically neutral or slightly acid; and still others, such as the yellow-gray silt loam and the brown sandy loam, are acid in the surface and more strongly acid in the subsurface, but sometimes contain an abundance of limestone in the subsoil. More than 90 per cent of the soils of the county contain no limestone in the surface or subsurface to a depth of 20 in."

Soil survey of Dickey County, N. Dak., T. M. BUSHNELL, E. H. SMIES, W. I. WATKINS, A. C. ANDERSON, M. THOMAS, M. E. STEBBINS, R. C. DONEGHUE, and J. W. INCE (*North Dakota Sta. Bul. 121 (1917), pp. 5–56, pls. 2, fig. 1, map 1*).—This survey has been previously noted (E. S. R., 36, p. 421).

Sand devastation, P. COLLINS (*Sci. Amer. Sup., 83 (1917), No. 2157, pp. 280–282, figs. 12*).—Information on how sand dunes advance and how their movement is checked is given.

The improvement of the poor soils and run-down soils of New Jersey. J. B. R. DICKEY (*N. J. Agr. Col. Ext. Bul., 1 (1917), No. 11, pp. 31, figs. 2*).—This is a brief general statement of methods of improving and maintaining soil fertility, with special reference to the poor and run-down soils of New Jersey.

Manure and artificial fertilizers for peat soil poor in nitrogen, H. VON FEILITZEN (*Svenska Mosskulturför. Tidskr., 30 (1916), No. 5–6, pp. 409–436, figs. 7*).—Eleven years' experiments with manure and artificial fertilizers on

Swedish peat soil deficient in nitrogen showed that manure alone did not give good results but that excellent results were obtained with artificial fertilizers. It is concluded that manure should be used on such soils only in moderate amounts to stimulate bacterial action. while plant nutrients should be supplied by the use of artificial fertilizers. Manure also gave poor results on white moss soil previously treated with phosphates and potash.

American sources of nitrogen. T. H. NORTON (*Sci. Amer.* 116 (1917). No. 16. pp. 394. 410. 411. figs. 4).—This is a review of the present situation with reference to the economic production in the United States of combined nitrogen for military, agricultural. and industrial needs.

The production of sulphate of ammonia for 1915–16 (*New York: The Barrett Co.. pp. 16. pl. 1. fig. 1*).—This pamphlet summarizes data on the production of ammonium sulphate in the world during 1916. but states that no figures have been available from Germany since 1913. The production in the United States for 1916 is estimated at 325.000 tons. an increase of 50 per cent over the figures for 1915. Of this production 272.000 tons are credited to coke ovens and 53.000 tons to gas works and bone carbonizing plants. The consumption of all forms of ammonia in the United States totaled 315.424 tons in 1915 and 347,708 tons in 1916.

Adsorption of ammonium sulphate by soils and quartz sand.—Preliminary communication. M. I. WOLKOFF (*Soil Sci.* 3 (1917). No. 6. pp. 561–564).—A summary of the results of experiments at Rutgers College is reported on the adsorption of ammonium sulphate solutions of 1/2. 1/4. 1/8. 1/16. 1/32. 1/64. 1/128, and 1/256 normal concentrations by medium sandy loam. medium loam. medium silt loam. heavy silt loam. shaley loam. muck. and quartz sand passing the 24. 60. and 124 mesh and 5'0 and 7'0 bolting cloth.

The results in general showed that with the increase in concentration of the ammonium sulphate solution the percentage of adsorption decreased. while the total amount of salt that went out of solution increased. The quartz sand did not wholly follow the general rule. as did the agricultural soils, for instead of the decrease of the concentration of the salt solution on its addition to the soil. its concentration became greater. This phenomenon was most pronounced in the coarse quartz sand and diminished with the increase in the fineness of the material. Also the effect was more noticeable in the more concentrated solutions than in those less concentrated. In the finer grades of the quartz treated with the comparatively dilute solutions the point was reached after which the concentration of the resultant solution in the mixture with sand was less than that of the original solution. After a certain point. which evidently is specific for a given quartz sand. the quartz sand followed the same general rule that soils follow. In the case of the coarse sand which is designated as 24-mesh the depression of the salt solution after application was greater in every instance than the depression of the freezing point of the solution before application. The percentage of the increase in depression. however. gradually decreased with the dilution of the applied solution. With the finer grade of the quartz sand (60-mesh) in the first three concentrations there was a striking similarity to the results obtained with the coarsest material. But beginning with the concentration 1/32-normal, there was an adsorption of the salt by the quartz sand. the percentage of this adsorption increasing with the dilution of the solution.

"The results tend to show that the heavier the soil the greater is the amount of the salt adsorbed. The time in which the soil is allowed to be acted upon by the salt solution influences the percentage of the salt adsorbed. In the light sandy soil the maximum adsorption was reached in about 24 hours, while in the heavier type this point occurs after as many as 72 hours. The temperature from 0 to 31° C. at which the reaction is allowed to proceed effects the degree of adsorption, this being greater at the higher temperature in a given time than at the lower one. The presence of the organic matter in the form of dried blood, cottonseed meal, alfalfa, barley straw, or wheat straw affects the adsorption of ammonium sulphate in the soil. Moreover, the application of these materials alone increases the concentration of the soil solution."

Saltpeter: Its origin and extraction in India, C. M. HUTCHINSON (*Agr. Research Inst. Pusa Bul. 68 (1916), pp. 24, pls. 4*).—The methods in use by the natives of India for the extraction of nitrate salts from soils and organic matter are described. It is pointed out that the present sources of saltpeter are not fully utilized on account of the native methods used and the low price of saltpeter. The native methods do not allow of recovery of all the nitrate present in the soil used. It is thought probable that owing to the favorable soil and climatic conditions in Bihar, artificial niter beds would form a useful additional source of nitrate.

Potash from incinerator ash of the Northwest, C. W. THING (*Jour. Indus. and Engin. Chem., 9 (1917), No. 5, pp. 472–474*).—Experiments conducted at the University of Washington on the extraction of potash from the ash of the burned waste from the lumber industry are reported. The following conclusions are drawn:

" Potash production from incinerator ash can not be put on a paying commercial basis . . . because of (1) low potash content, (2) higher cost of production, (3) insufficient supply of raw material. Unless a new method for the disposal of waste is suggested, the prevailing method of disposal of incinerator ash is as economical as can be found. Analyses show it to be of little value for fertilizer. If any plan were to be suggested for the successful production of potash from wood ashes, it must fulfill the following conditions: (1) Dispose of the waste as fast as it is produced; (2) operate at low temperatures and with slight draughts; (3) successfully meet foreign and domestic competition."

Tetraphosphate, G. VINASSA (*Staz. Sper. Agr. Ital., 49 (1916), No. 7–8, pp. 357–365; abs. in Internat. Inst. Agr. [Rome], Internat. Rev. Sci. and Pract. Agr., 7 (1916), No. 10, pp. 1419, 1420*).—A new phosphatic fertilizer called tetraphosphate is described, which has been recently put on the market as a substitute for basic slag. It is prepared by mixing powdered phosphorite with carbonates of the alkaline earths, at the rate of 6 per cent by weight of the carbonates, and heating the mixture to 400° C. in special ovens. The mass is then moistened and inert bodies are added until a substance containing 20 per cent total phosphoric acid is obtained. The finished product is a dry grayish-white powder almost insoluble in water, with which it gives an alkaline reaction, and partly soluble in acids which cause an evolution of carbon dioxid.

Tetraphosphate was treated with a number of solutions, including water; water saturated with carbon dioxid; sodium chlorid and nitrate; ammonium chlorid and sulphate; 18 per cent ammonium acetate; 40 per cent ammonium malate; 20 per cent ammonium tartrate; 40 per cent ammonium citrate; 0.5, 2, and 10 per cent citric acid; and a mixture of 4 per cent citric acid, 6 per cent formic acid, and 10 per cent sodium chlorid. Similar tests were conducted with Sfax phosphorite. The solution of citric and formic acids and sodium chlorid was proposed as a suitable reagent for tetraphosphate, but indicated a larger percentage of soluble phosphoric acid in phosphorite than in tetraphosphate. The same result was obtained with all the other solvent solutions.

" These results would indicate that no valuable changes take place when the phosphorite is heated with the carbonates of the alkaline earths, and that the process, which is complicated and costly, is also useless. The name tetraphosphate is very inappropriate, as its insolubility clearly proves it to contain neither tetraphosphate nor calcium silicophosphate, both of which products have been isolated from basic slag. From the purely chemical point of view, there is no analogy between basic slag and tetraphosphate, which may be simply considered a ground phosphate mixed with inert compounds."

Basic slag as affecting agricultural development, D. A. GILCHRIST and H. LOUIS (*Jour. Soc. Chem. Indus.*, *36* (*1917*), No. *5*, pp. *261–264*).—This is a review of experience in Europe and the United States on the use of basic slag and rock phosphate for fertilizer, special attention being given to the difference between the citrate solubilities of the basic slag derived from the Bessemer steel process and of that derived from the English basic open hearth process.

The conclusion is drawn that "citric solubility is certainly not the only criterion, and is apparently not even a reliable criterion, of the value of phosphatic material as a manurial agent. It is therefore submitted that total phosphoric acid content is a far more reliable test of manurial value, and possesses the further advantage that it depends on the definite analytical determination of a substance, instead of being an empirical test liable to be affected by the conditions and methods of its application, and that it should therefore be authoritatively substituted for the citric solubility test throughout the country. This change would not only render available for the use of British agriculturists an annual amount which may reach up to 100,000 tons of phosphoric acid, most of which is now merely a troublesome waste product, but would at the same time render valuable assistance to the steel trade of the country."

The liming of limy lands, A. H. ROSENFELD (*Internat. Sugar Jour.*, *19* (*1917*), No. *221*, pp. *209–213*).—Experiments conducted at the Tucumán Experiment Station in Argentina with lime on typical sugar cane soils which were high in lime, but low in carbon dioxid are reported. Unslaked lime was applied at the rate of 1,600 kg. per hectare (1,424 lbs. per acre). It was found that the cane crops on the limed plats were 5 tons per acre greater than on the unlimed, the cane sprouted better, and the average weight of the stalks for five years was almost 10 per cent better.

Rules and regulations for the enforcement of the lime-barrel act, S. W. STRATTON (*U. S. Dept. Com., Bur. Standards Circ. 64* (*1917*), pp. *6*).—The text of these regulations, which should be of interest to users of agricultural lime, is given.

The fertilizer value of city wastes.—II, Garbage tankage.—Its composition, the availability of its nitrogen, and its use as a fertilizer, P. J. SCHROEDER (*Jour. Indus. and Engin. Chem.*, *9* (*1917*), No. *5*, pp. *513–518*).—In a second contribution to the subject (E. S. R., 36, p. 728) studies on the composition of garbage tankage, the availability of its nitrogen, and its fertilizer value are reported.

The examination of various garbage tankages "revealed no important fact that shows that they are unsuited for fertilizer material. The position is not taken that it is possible to determine the value of a fertilizer material definitely by present methods of chemical analysis, but from the examination the expectation would seem entirely justified that the proper use of garbage tankage should give the usual results obtainable from medium or low-grade fertilizers."

Turf bedding and compost, I. I. VIKHLIĂEV (*Torfíanaíā Podstílka i Kompost. Petrograd: Glav. Uprav. Zeml. i Zeml., Otd. Zemel. Uluch., Torfmeistersk. Chast., 1915, pp. 50, pls. 2, figs. 19*).—A review is given of experience with turf and moss as a bedding for cattle and horses and as a manure.

The best material was young, not greatly decomposed, mossy turf. Sphagnum was also good for this purpose. Air-dried moss, frozen while damp, made excellent bedding with very little dust. It was found to be very absorbent both of water and gases, destroyed disagreeable stable odors, and made an excellent small-grained manure which was easily and uniformly spread under the plow. Compressed turf was also found to be cheaper, occupy less storage space, and to be less dangerous as regards fire than straw. The resulting manure was found to contain from 0.5 to 1 per cent of nitrogen, 0.2 per cent of phosphoric acid, 1.3 per cent of sulphuric acid, 0.2 per cent of potassium, 1.2 per cent of calcium, and 2.1 per cent of magnesium.

Artificial fertilizers, their present use and future prospects, E. J. RUSSELL (*Jour. Soc. Chem. Indus., 36* (1917), No. 5, pp. 250–261, fig. 1).—The author reviews the commercial fertilizer situation, dealing especially with the general production and use, manner of use, and results obtained therefrom in Europe under war-time conditions.

The American fertilizer handbook (*Philadelphia: Ware Bros. Co., 1917, 10. ed., pp.* [434], *figs. 10*).—This handbook contains the usual data and information relating to the fertilizer industry (E. S. R., 36, p. 124). Among the more important special articles included are the following: Dictionary of Fertilizer Materials, by T. C. Pinkerton; The Sulphuric Acid Industry, by A. M. Fairlie; Sulphate of Ammonia Statistics; Fertilizers and Farm Efficiency, by J. W. Henceroth; Use Fertilizers to Keep More Stock, by S. B. Haskell; Sulphur, by P. S. Smith; Potash Salts; 1915, by W. C. Phalen; and Potash, 1916, by H. S. Gale.

Commercial fertilizers, W. J. JONES, JR., E. G. PROULX, R. B. DEEMER, R. O. BITLER, and H. C. MUGG (*Indiana Sta. Bul. 199* (1917), pp. 3–114, figs. 2).—This is the report of official fertilizer inspection and analyses in Indiana for 1916, including information on the selection, purchase, use, and home mixing of fertilizers.

Results of fertilizer inspection, spring season 1917, A. J. PATTEN (*Michigan Sta. Circ. 33* (1917), pp. 3).—This is the report of fertilizer inspection and analyses in Michigan for the spring season of 1917. "Of the 518 samples analyzed, 135 (26 per cent) were found to be below guaranty in one or more constituents and 92 (17.8 per cent) were below guaranty in potash."

AGRICULTURAL BOTANY.

Matroclinic inheritance in mutation crosses of Œnothera reynoldsii, C. D. LA RUE and H. H. BARTLETT (*Amer. Jour. Bot., 4* (1917), No. 3, pp. 119–144, figs. 4).—This paper is concerned primarily with the type of inheritance previously discussed (E. S. R., 35, p. 128) as mass mutation.

It has been found that the mutations characteristic of mass mutation in *Œ. reynoldsii*, when crossed either way among themselves or with the parent form, give progeny conforming exactly to the type of the pistillate parent. The author states that in *Œ. reynoldsii* mass mutation consists in the production of inordinate numbers of mutations of several characteristic types by certain individuals, which may be looked upon as having undergone a premutative modification. Their production of a large number of abortive seeds is regarded as one manifestation of mutability. The characteristic mutations form a series, each member of which may give rise to a succeeding member, such a series being that formed by the mutants *semialta, debilis,* and *bilonga*.

The observed facts of inheritance are supposed to be best explained by the hypothesis that two types of nonequivalent gametes, designated as a and β, are normally produced, the a gametes being usually eggs and the β gametes sperms, the mutant *bilonga*, however, producing both a and β sperms. Mutation in *Œ. reynoldsii* consists in the modification in a gametes of factors that have no counterpart in the β gametes. Sperms of the form *typica* being β gametes, mutations appear whenever a mutated a gamete is fertilized. They do not appear as a result of segregation.

A new type of non-Mendelian variation in plants, S. IKENO (*Bot. Mag.* [*Tokyo*], *29* (1915), *No. 3/6, pp. 216–221, fig. 1; abs. in Ann. Bot.* [*Rome*], *14* (1916), *No. 2, p. 109*).—The author reports having found in heredity tests with *Capsicum annuum* that variegation was transmitted from either parent or both. The numbers produced, however, were smaller when variegated plants were crossed with green than with variegated ones, the Mendelian formula not applying in these results.

The relation between evaporation and plant succession in a given area, F. C. GATES (*Amer. Jour. Bot., 4* (1917), *No. 3, pp. 161–178, figs. 9*).—Experimentation was carried on during the summers of 1915 and 1916 with 42 standard atmometers, employing the usual methods. Owing to the smallness of the area covered the influence of edaphic factors was not obscured by the operation of broad climatic factors.

Invasion, the initial stage of succession, must take place, it is claimed, under the conditions already existing. A change of conditions coincident with mesophytic succession may result in a decrease in the rate of evaporation in the ground or chamæphytic layer. Evaporation differences are due to the size and density of the surrounding vegetation. While a decrease in the evaporation is not a prerequisite to succession, a change in the dominant species of an area is fundamental thereto. The change in evaporation is a result and not a cause of succession. While certain species develop under existing conditions to bring about succession, species of narrower physiological limitations can not develop until the conditions come within their range. These are secondary species, unable to cause succession, the occurrence of which requires the arrival and development of the dominant species of a higher genetic association.

Adaptations of vegetation to climate, J. MASSART (*Ann. Géogr., 26* (1917), *No. 140, pp. 94–105, pl. 1*).—This is an account of the conditions and behavior observed in a study of vegetation in portions of France which are subject to somewhat exceptional climatic and seasonal influences and changes. It is stated that each function in the economy of the plant, as germination, growth, rosette production, etc., has its optimum temperatures lying within limits which are more or less narrow according to species, and that in order to understand the adaptation of a plant to heat (as an example of influential climatic elements) it is necessary to study the plant in all the successive phases of its life and in relation to the various exigencies to which it is normally subjected.

Temperature and life duration of seeds, J. F. GROVES (*Bot. Gaz., 63* (1917), *No. 3, pp. 169–189, figs. 5*).—Employing Turkey red wheat, the author has sought to determine to what extent a study of the life duration of seeds at high temperatures (50 to 100° C.) will explain the process of degeneration of air-dried seeds at ordinary storage temperatures. The life durations of wheat with 9, 12, and 17.5 per cent moisture are given for various temperatures, and the degree of application at high temperatures of the Lepeschkin formula (E. S. R., 29, p. 27) is indicated.

No definite trend appears in the value of the temperature coefficient Q_{10} (symbolizing the Van't Hoff law), and its range is confined to rather narrow limits. It is held that there is no justification for placing much emphasis on predicted longevities at low temperatures.

This work indicates some of the possibilities of throwing light on the nature of the processes of the loss of viability in seeds in storage conditions, and it makes possible a quantitative statement of the significance of storage conditions, especially moisture content and temperature as regards the longevity of seeds.

Duration of leaves in evergreens, VINNIE A. PEASE (*Amer. Jour. Bot.*, *4* (*1917*), *No. 3, pp. 145–160, figs. 13*).—Observations by the author in the western part of the State of Washington show that leaf persistence varies among evergreens from about 2 to 23 years. It is influenced by age and habitat, being shortened in saplings, by sunshine, on windward coasts, and in moist climates. Peat bogs show an influence similar to that of dry climate in the retention of leaves. Increased duration of leaves corresponds to such factors as favor slowness of growth, also decrease of leaf surface and of photosynthetic and transpiring activity. It is considered as possible that variations in leaf duration in a given species may be due to differences in transpiration or photosynthetic activity caused by a difference in age or habitat.

The reaction of plant protoplasm, A. R. HAAS (*Bot. Gaz.*, *63* (*1917*), *No. 3, pp. 232–235*).—Determinations of the actual and total acidity of a number of plant tissues are said to have shown that there is no constant relation between the two. Great variations occur in different portions of the same plant, one case (that of cranberry fruits) showing an actual acidity of $4/1,000$ normal in the living cells.

The mode of action of plant peroxidases, G. B. REED (*Bot. Gaz.*, *63* (*1916*), *No. 3, pp. 233–238, figs. 2*).—Having followed up the work previously noted (E. S. R., 35, p. 713), the author reports on a study of the very active ferment of horse-radish obtained after soaking the finely chopped tissue in water for 24 hours.

The results, as detailed and shown in graphical form, are considered to indicate that just as colloidal platinum is recharged with oxygen by hydrogen peroxid as soon as some of the oxygen has been removed by a reducing agent, so the horse-radish peroxidase is recharged by hydrogen peroxid under similar conditions. A study of potato peroxidase gave similar results. It is thought that in such oxidation processes the peroxidase combines with oxygen to form an intermediate compound which is a more energetic oxidizing agent than the original source of the oxygen, the final stage in the oxidation being thus affected by this intermediate compound. It is thought that this throws an important light on the difficult question of the mechanism of oxidation in living tissues.

The supposed action of potassium permanganate with plant peroxidases, H. H. BUNZEL and H. HASSELBRING (*Bot. Gaz.*, *63* (*1917*), *No. 3, pp. 225–228*).— The authors describe experimentation and other data which are considered to indicate that the conclusions drawn by Reed, as above noted, are too sweeping for the experimental grounds upon which they are based. The oxidation phenomena observed by that author are thought to have been brought about by the action of manganese peroxid and not by activated plant peroxidases.

The response of plants to illuminating gas, SARAH L. DOUBT (*Bot. Gaz.*, *63* (*1917*), *No. 3, pp. 209–224, figs. 6*).—The author, studying the effects of illuminating gas on flowers, potted plants, and root systems of a number of plants, found that certain ones named were injuriously affected by proportions of gas far below the limits of perceptible odor. An ethylene content corresponding to that of ordinary illuminating gas gave unfavorable results with several species. Some were not materially injured unless the odor was noticeable, and two were very resistant to gas. Lists are given of plants injured by gases in the soil, with forms of injury suffered by them.

Young trees at least may be injured by leakage of gas imperceptible to the senses, the foliage showing no indication of injury above ground. The killing of trees by gas is thought to be a slow process, sometimes requiring months or years. It appears that a perceptible odor of gas near trees is a certain indication that they are being injured.

Damage resulting to greenhouse crops and soil from escaping illuminating gas, G. E. STONE (*Florists' Ex. 42 (1916), No. 2, pp. 61, 85, fig. 1*).—Cases are cited in which illuminating gas was known to travel for considerable distances under frozen soil or more or less impervious strata, or to escape otherwise and injure vegetation in ways which are described, even when the concentrations were hardly, if at all, noticeable to the sense of smell. Roses are extremely sensitive to gas poisoning, and Easter lilies are greatly stunted thereby. Gas in the soil may be taken up by water and carried to plants some distance away. Sewer gas may be injurious if abundant, and certain paints give off gases which are injurious. On the other hand, certain gases in low concentrations are stimulating to growth.

A plan is presented for the protection of plants near a leaking pipe, consisting of a covering like an inverted trough for the gas main and connecting pipes to carry the gases to the open air, where they do comparatively little damage.

Leaf nectaries of Gossypium, E. L. REED (*Bot. Gaz., 63 (1917), No. 3, pp. 229–231, pls. 2, fig. 1*).—The author describes certain nectar glands found on the midrib and other principal veins of leaves of *C. hirsutum*.

On the formation of nodules in the cortex of Hevea brasiliensis, G. BRYCE (*Dept. Agr. Ceylon Bul. 23 (1916), pp. 23*).—Giving a somewhat detailed account of nodular and related structures in *H. brasiliensis*, the author states that such nodules are produced as the result of an alteration in the content of the latex vessels. This has not been referred to any parasitic organism and is thought to be due to physiological changes in the latex, certain trees showing a predisposition to develop this condition on tapping. Four types of nodule are described.

Globular shoots are to be distinguished from nodules, being formed by the growth of latent buds and never forming a core or the large masses of woody tissue sometimes resulting from nodule growth.

Nodules formed around altered latex vessels do not appear on trees that have not been tapped. These structures are formed on Hevea both in its native habitat and in plantations. The condition is not infectious.

Preliminary observations on the distribution of certain hymenomycetes and on their probable relation to the ectotrophic mycorrhiza of phanerogams, B. PEYRONEL (*Atti R. Accad. Lincei, Rend. Cl. Sci. Fis., Mat. e Nat., 5. ser., 26 (1917), I, No. 5, pp. 326–332*).—Some details are given of associations, so far as observed, between hymenomycetous fungi and woody forest plants of various groups having ectotrophic but not endotrophic mycorrhiza.

Studies in the physiology of the fungi.—III, Physical properties of wood in relation to decay induced by Lenzites sæpiaria, S. M. ZELLER (*Ann. Missouri Bot. Gard., 4 (1917), No. 2, pp. 93–164, pls. 16, fig. 1*).—The author follows up the previous report (E. S. R., 37, p. 129) with an account of preliminary experiments regarding the effects of *L. sæpiaria* on wood of *Pinus palustris*, P. *echinata*, and P. *tœda*, including a review of observation and opinion by others.

He concludes that resin is no safe or practical index of the durability of the three species of yellow pine investigated, except as its presence tends to exclude moisture, which is favorable to the fungi. High specific gravity of the heartwood, on the other hand, materially increases resistance to these fungi on all these pines. Specific gravity can be somewhat reliably estimated from the proportion of the summer wood to the spring wood. The width of the growth rings furnishes a further index of durability, which is greater in case of the narrower rings. Age, or distance from the central pith, shows no relation to durability up to 8 in. in radius. Sapwood decays irrespective of resin content, specific gravity, width of annual rings, or species.

The practical conclusion drawn is that specifications for great durability should be based on a judicious combination of high specific gravity, large number of rings per inch, and small percentage of sapwood present. The more durable timber is that showing broad bands of summer wood and narrow bands of spring wood as seen in the cross section.

Studies in the physiology of the fungi.—IV, The growth of certain fungi in plant decoctions, preliminary account, B. M. DUGGAR, J. W. SEVERY, and H. SCHMITZ (*Ann. Missouri Bot. Gard., 4 (1917), No. 2, pp. 165–173, figs. 4*).— Employing standardized decoctions, with or without additions as given, the authors have made a study of fungi with somewhat different habits of growth, employing for this purpose *Macrosporium commune, Aspergillus niger, Glomerella (Glœosporium) gossypii,* and *Penicillium expansum.* The results from each fungus are plotted and discussed.

The addition of sugar, nitrate, and phosphate gave in every case, except with Glomerella on bean decoction, an increase in growth over the addition of sugar alone. The next highest growth was obtained in most cases when sugar and nitrate were added. The changes produced in the hydrogen ion concentrations due to the growth of the fungi are also indicated.

Microorganisms in silage, G. M. REED and LENA BARBER (*Missouri Sta. Bul. 147 (1917), p. 29*).—Twenty-two different species of fungi are reported to have been identified from 15 samples of moldy silage. *Penicillium italicum* was the species most commonly found, while *P. roquefortii, Mucor circinelloides, Rhizopus nigricans,* and *Oïdium lactis* were found in the order named. All of these fungi were isolated from silage that had been reported as injurious to stock as well as from silage that was entirely harmless. No evidence was obtained indicating clearly the connection of *Aspergillus fumigatus* with stock poisoning from moldy silage.

FIELD CROPS.

General agriculture, P. DIFFLOTH (*Agriculture Générale. Paris: J. B. Baillière & Sons, 1917, vol. 2, 4. ed. rev. and enl., pp. 552, figs. 276*).—A revised and enlarged edition of the work by the same author, previously noted (E. S. R., 14, p. 1032).

Agronomical investigations [at the Guam Experiment Station, 1916], A. C. HARTENBOWER (*Guam Sta. Rpt. 1916, pp. 6–25, pls. 4*).—This reports the continuation of work previously noted (E. S. R., 35, p. 829), including improvement work with corn and field tests with cotton, rice, tobacco, leguminous forage crops, Kafir corn, feterita, milo maize, and grasses.

Seedings of the Yellow Dent and Chisholm varieties of corn from Texas failed to set ears, while a white variety from Hawaii produced a few small inferior ears.

In 1915 Gila, an Egyptian cotton, and Columbia and Covington-Toole, Upland types, were heavily pruned and left in the plats to study the ratoon crops produced. Yields of seed cotton were secured which amounted to 301, 1,137, and 1,012 lbs. per acre, respectively. The highest yielding variety for both the first and second 1916 crops was Hartsville, with 1,820 and 1,754 lbs. of seed cotton per acre. Sea Island and Caravonica have proved unsatisfactory in all tests to date. Cotton growing throughout the island is briefly noted, and the following general conclusions drawn from accumulated data of cotton experiments: Cotton planting about May 1 is deemed unprofitable, as the ground is so occupied that the production of any other crop that year is prohibited, and because the crop does not mature sufficiently early the next dry season to produce a ratoon crop that season. Cotton planted June 22 was completely harvested only 3.5 weeks before that planted December 7 following, the later crop maturing more uniformly and producing a higher quality ratoon crop. Cultivation during the rainy season proved impossible and weed control through the use of an arsenical spray difficult because of almost daily rains. The June planting required eight pickings, extending over 3.5 months, while the later planting required only three pickings, extending over but 3.5 weeks. Plantings made at the end of the dry season were of low grade and weak fiber as compared with the December plantings. The ratoon crop referred to required two seasons for its production.

Results obtained with Egyptian cotton in 1916 did not compare favorably with those secured in 1915, the difference being attributed to the date of planting and the source of the seed, the 1915 crop having been grown from Hawaii seed planted December 19, while the 1916 crop was grown from Arizona seed planted December 27—too late for seed from this source.

The native methods of rice growing are briefly described and fertilizer experiments with rice reported. The highest yield, 1,087 lbs. of rough rice per acre, was secured from an application of 95 lbs. of sulphate of potash. The untreated check yielded 259 lbs. With acid phosphate and nitrate of soda used alone the yield was 674 and 652 lbs. of rough rice per acre, respectively, while with a complete fertilizer it was 783 lbs. In variety tests, Hawaiian Gold Seed yielded 122 lbs., See Miu 704 lbs., and Porto Rico 105 lbs. The two native rice plats yielded 364 and 324 lbs., respectively. The imported varieties headed out about three weeks earlier than did the native rice. The native rice and Hawaiian Gold Seed lodged badly, while the other two varieties showed very little lodging.

Limited tests with alfalfa indicated that it is adapted to Guam conditions, although the results of an entire rainy season are deemed necessary for determination of its real value. Peruvian alfalfa has given the best results to date.

Tobacco investigations included variety and fertilizer tests and studies on the effects of shading and of lead arsenate treatment for the control of *Heliothis obsoleta.* The highest yield per plant from the unshaded plats was 11.14 oz. from White Burley with fertilization, and the lowest yield 3.5 oz. from Connecticut Broadleaf without fertilization. The average yield per plant for fertilized and unfertilized plats was: Oronoco 7.2 oz., White Burley 9.7 oz., Connecticut Broadleaf 5.8 oz., and Connecticut-Havana 5.2 oz. Shaded plants of White Burley and Oronoco gave an average yield of 48.6 per cent less tobacco per plant than unshaded plants on the same plats. An increased yield of 7.4 per cent was obtained with lead arsenate treatment. The unshaded plants gave an average increased yield of 21.88 per cent with fertilizers and the shaded plants an average increase of 10.1 per cent.

Soil inoculation tests with cowpeas gave yields of 885 and 808 lbs. of grain per acre, respectively, for inoculated and uninoculated fields, and 15,125 and 9,790 lbs., respectively, of green forage. Plantings of cowpeas on a lowland field yielded at the rate of 4.01 bu. of grain and 4,099 lbs. of green vines per acre. Other leguminous forage crops tested included soy beans, pigeon peas, jack beans, and velvet beans, the latter being deemed an especially valuable grain and cover crop for Guam. In variety tests with velvet beans, the Florida variety appeared to be best for grain production, yielding at the rate of 14.3 bu. of grain and 7.3 tons of green forage per acre in 1916 from plantings made in June, 1915. Guam-grown Florida velvet beans yielded 11.4 bu. per acre as compared with a yield of 9.5 bu. from imported Florida seed.

Field tests with Kafir corn, feterita, and milo maize are reported, and the value of the first two as soiling or grain crops indicated. Yields of forage amounting to 22,700 lbs. of feterita and 12,501 lbs. of Kafir corn per acre were secured on lowland in 1915. Successive cuttings of feterita stubble yielded 19,199, 4,612, and 11,416 lbs. of stover or fodder for the second, third, and fourth cuttings, respectively, with grain yields of 10.8 and 9.8 bu. per acre for the third and fourth cuttings. Plantings of feterita, milo maize, and Kafir corn on relatively high but fairly fertile land on November 20 gave average yields of 11.4, 9.3, and 13.2 bu. per acre, respectively, while plantings made in the same field on December 10 gave average yields of 7.8, 6.8, and 9.1 bu. per acre, respectively. Seedings made January 10 on heavy lowland soil yielded 23.56 bu. with black-hulled Kafir corn, 18.18 bu. with feterita, and 15.7 bu. with dwarf milo maize, the yields of green stover amounting to 7,995, 8,038, and 5,628 lbs. per acre, respectively. Counts of suckers and side branches showed an average of 3 suckers and 2 side branches per plant for feterita, 1 sucker and 1 side branch for milo maize, and only occasional side branches or suckers for Kafir corn. Approximately 25 per cent of the feterita heads were in the flowering stage when harvested, while Kafir corn and milo maize were quite uniform in maturity and in height of plant.

In the renovation of Para grass fields the best results were secured from the use of barnyard manure, when six cuttings were obtained yielding 65,604 lbs. of green forage per acre. A mowing of Para grass was scattered in furrows about 3 ft. apart and covered with soil for comparison with the usual propagation method of setting out roots. The estimated cost of the planting, exclusive of plowing, was $3.60 per acre as compared with $10 per acre for the old method. The grass attained an average height of 3 ft. at the end of six weeks, while approximately four months was required by the former system to attain sufficient growth for pasture. The new method is deemed especially desirable because it permits planting before the regular rains start, thereby providing pasture and a soiling crop during the rainy season.

The data from numerous tests with *Paspalum dilatatum* has led to the following general conclusions regarding the adaptability and planting of this grass: P. *dilatatum* on relatively high land has a value of fully one-half of that planted on low land during the rainy season. Large divisions of roots in plantings set not more than 2 ft. apart each way were found to be advisable even on low land for a thick turf and a quick pasture. Deep preparation of the soil before planting and careful weeding after planting are deemed essential for the best results. Live stock should not be pastured on the grass until four months after planting under ideal conditions, whereas on the higher lands fully six months should be allowed for the grass to become established.

Field tests with Guinea grass (*Panicum maximum*), millet, *Elephantorrhiza elephantina*, and Russian sunflower are briefly noted, the last-named crop alone being deemed sufficiently suited to Guam conditions for extended use.

[Report on field crops work at the Missouri Experiment Station] (*Missouri Sta. Bul. 147* (1917), pp. 35–37, 49, 50, 51, 52–54, figs. 4).—This reports the continuation of work previously noted (E. S. R., 35, p. 825).

Corn investigations conducted by C. B. Hutchison, E. M. McDonald, and A. R. Evans included a continuation of variety tests at Columbia and on various fields throughout the State, the leading varieties remaining as previously reported (E. S. R., 36, p. 135), and cultural tests on the Maryville and Warrensburg fields. The highest corn yields at Maryville were secured for the first time from plantings made with a furrow opener, while single listing gave the next best yields, and surface planting the lowest yield. On the Warrensburg field little difference in yield was noted with corn planted on stalk land plowed both deep and shallow in the spring and that which had been plowed both deep and shallow in the fall. Fall-plowed sod land gave slightly increased yields, while shallow fall plowing gave higher yields than deep fall plowing, both giving higher yields than spring plowing. Deep spring plowing gave much higher yields than shallow spring plowing.

Rate-of-planting tests and variety and breeding tests with wheat are reported. On the Shelbina field a seeding rate of 8 pk. per acre gave the highest yield, with the 7-pk. rate second, slightly decreased yields being recorded for the plats seeded at 5- and 6-pk. rates. The 10 leading wheat varieties at Columbia for the season of 1915 were Rudy, Lebanon, Harvest Queen, Fulcaster, Deitz, Pride of Genessee, Michigan Amber, Nigger, Pride of Indiana, and Gold Coin. In selection work the two best lines yielded 48.25 and 50.14 bu. per acre, respectively, while the original strains from which they were chosen yielded 31.45 bu. per acre.

Tests with winter oats were continued, some of the hardier strains giving promise for the future. An increased yield of 7.5 bu. per acre was obtained with oats sown on spring-plowed land as compared with the seedings on land disked and harrowed. Drilling in a seed bed prepared by disking and harrowing increased the yield over plats broadcasted and disked in by 8 bu. per acre. A seeding rate of 12 pk. per acre gave the best results. Variety tests with oats at Columbia gave an average yield of 44.3 bu. per acre for 24 varieties.

The improvement of winter barley varieties is reported as progressing favorably, while spring barley is deemed unsatisfactory at Columbia, due to the short growing season.

Cotton experiments, conducted by A. R. Evans, included variety and fertilizer tests. The five highest-yielding varieties are reported as Christopher Improved, Buck Long Staple, Hamilton Ounce Boll, Simpkin Prolific, and Ozier. The fertilizer tests included a comparison of applications of 200 lbs. of cottonseed meal, 200 lbs. of acid phosphate, and 3 tons of manure, resulting in increased yields of seed cotton of 470, 340, and 129 lbs. per acre, respectively, increases in no case deemed sufficient to pay the cost of the treatments.

E. M. McDonald conducted experiments on the influence of the spacing of rows of wheat and oats upon the yield and quality of grain. The 1915 oat crop was sown in rows, 3, 6, 8, and 12 in. apart, the 12-in. planting giving the highest yield, amounting to about 10 per cent more than the yield from the 6-in. planting. The 8- and 12-in. plantings of wheat were expected to yield from 10 to 25 per cent more than the 3- and 6-in. plantings in 1916.

This year completed the twenty-seventh year's work on crop rotation experiments conducted by M. F. Miller and R. R. Hudelson. The unmanured corn plat yielded 38 bu. per acre as compared with a yield of 45.7 bu. for the manured plat. The average yield for the untreated plat for the last six years was 11.14 bu. and for the treated plat 28.52 bu. per acre. The relatively high yield of the last year is attributed to the effect of sufficient rainfall. A complete fertilizer of 3 per cent nitrogen, 10 per cent phosphorus, and 4 per cent potash gave the highest yield of wheat for all treatments.

Experiments on the associated growth of corn and cowpeas resulted in higher yields of corn grown without cowpeas than when grown with them in the row or between the rows. A slight decrease in the nitrogen content of the corn and stover was noted where cowpeas were grown in the row. Determinations of the nitrates in the soil showed that cowpeas grown alone exhausted the supply of available nitrates as much as corn, indicating that the corn secured no nitrogen from the cowpeas. A pronounced physiological effect of the association of these two crops was observed in the green appearance of the corn foliage late in the season where cowpeas were grown either in the row or between the rows, but has not yet been explained.

Experiments to determine the effect of handling cowpea land in various ways on the wheat crop following indicated that land into which the cowpeas have been worked gave better wheat yields than land receiving no cowpeas or land from which cowpeas have been cut. Little evidence has been secured to show any deleterious effect of cowpeas on the following wheat crop.

A study of the factors influencing the development of the maize plant, by M. F. Miller and F. L. Duley, again demonstrated that the middle third of the growing period (from time of laying-by to time of silking) was the most critical from the standpoint of both moisture and nutrient supplies. The water requirement of the plant was found not to be greatly influenced by the variations in the supply during the growing period, but to vary greatly with different seasons. The optimum water supply during 1915 gave a weight of ears equal to 36.9 per cent of the total weight of the plant, while the minimum moisture supply gave an ear weight of 17.9 per cent of the total. An optimum supply of plant food gave grain representing 35.8 per cent of the total, while a minimum supply gave a grain weight of only 1.9 per cent of the total.

[Field crops], F. WATTS (*Imp. Dept. Agr. West Indies, Rpt. Agr. Dept. St. Vincent, 1915–16, pp. 5–7, 8–11, 13–15*).—Brief notes are given on the results of cotton selections based on the mean maximum length of fiber, percentage of available fiber, average weight of seed, and percentage of lint to seed. Further cotton investigations included studies with crinkled dwarf rogues, inheritance of the number of teeth in the bracts of cotton, resistance to leaf-blister mite (*Eriophyes gossypii*) in budded cottons and in cotton hybrids, Brazilian cotton, and fertilizer tests with Sea Island cotton.

Attempts to improve the native corn varieties through selection are reported along two lines, first, to produce uniform yellow corn, and second, to increase the size of grain and amount of grain per ear.

The twenty-sixth year of crop experiments, B. R. LARSEN, A. HEBSTADS, H. Foss, and K. VIK (*Aarsber. Norges Landbr. Höiskoles Akervekstforsök, 26 (1914–15), pp. 3–65, figs. 5*).—The extension of cooperative field crop tests in 1914 is discussed, and the results of several experiments are reported.

In experiments conducted for five years, potatoes planted about May 15 gave on the average a higher yield of tubers and a greater percentage of total production of dry matter than potatoes planted earlier or later. Plantings made about May 7, however, produced the largest tubers. Variations in yearly results were brought about by weather conditions. The late and medium late varieties proved better adapted to early planting than early or medium early sorts. It was found that under the prevailing conditions there was no advantage in planting potatoes, especially medium early varieties, before the soil at 25 cm. (10 in.) under the surface had reached a temperature of from 7 to 8° C. (44.6 to 46.4° F.). The date of planting seemed to have had no influence on the prevalence of dry rot.

Experiments on the influence of subsoiling to the depth of about 16 in. on soil consisting of a mixture of clay, sand, and gravel, and of a good moisture-holding capacity, with a subsoil of a clayey character but not very hard, were conducted for six years. The crops grown were turnips, potatoes, peas, spring wheat, and oats. The average results with all these crops showed an increase in yield from subsoiling, the largest increase in value being obtained with peas. The average results further indicated that the work had been done at a profit.

The results secured in an eight-year test of level and ridge culture of root crops indicated that the germination of the seed and the early growth of the

plants, especially during dry weather, is best with level culture, and that on
good soil well worked and under favorable moisture conditions the differences
in yield under these methods of culture are comparatively small.

Experiments with leguminous green forage crops on poor soils showed the
value of adding field peas, vetches, and other leguminous plants to mixtures of
forage crops for the purpose of increasing the yield of green forage and of
grain and of improving their quality.

Report on culture experiments at the Norwegian Agricultural High School,
1914–15, S. HASUND and P. BORGEDAL (*Ber. Norges. Landbr. Höiskoles Jordkltr.
Forsök, 1914–15, pp. 1–22, 31–54*).—The extension of cooperative field crop experiments in 1915 is pointed out, and the results of a number of these experiments are reported.

The average results of 81 cooperative fertilizer tests with nitrate of soda
and sulphate of ammonia showed that the unit of nitrogen in sulphate of
ammonia represented from 80 to 90 per cent of the value of the unit in nitrate
of soda. In other cooperative tests the action of lime was found quite marked
the first year on soil either unfertilized or fertilized with barnyard manure,
while on soil receiving commercial fertilizers the effect of lime was unimportant the first year but much more striking the second and third years.
In a cooperative series of 67 tests with lime, potatoes were not found benefited by its use, while meadows, as shown by 4-year experiments, gave an increase of 5.6 per cent in the yield of hay and barley fields of 4.4 per cent in the
yield of grain as apparently due to lime treatment. A larger increase from
liming was secured with unfertilized than with fertilized crops of barley.

Cooperative subsoiling tests in connection with the culture of different crops
gave varied results and did not allow drawing general conclusions.

[**Experiments with field crops**], A. SJÖSTRÖM (*Red. Ultuna Landtbr. Inst.
[Sweden], 1915, pp. 41–52*).—The results of cultural and variety tests with
cereals and root crops are briefly reported. Petkus rye sown at three different rates gave practically the same yields of grain and straw from the three different seedings. The differences in yield resulting from sowing Hannchen barley
on the first, fifth, and twentieth of May, as well as from pulverizing the soil
to depths of 3, 5, and 7 cm. (1.2, 2, and 2.8 in.), were also insignificant.

In a test of soiling crop mixtures the best yield in the green forage cut July
22 of dry matter and nitrogen, 4.6 tons and 83 kg. per hectare (4.1 tons and
73.8 lbs. per acre) respectively, was secured from a seed mixture consisting of
120 kg. of oats, 175 kg. of field peas, and 40 kg. of vetch per hectare. Analyses
made of a part of the crop allowed to ripen and harvested September 8 showed
that the dry-matter content had almost doubled since July 22.

In another experiment Petkus rye harvested and analyzed at weekly intervals
from June 1 to July 7 continued to increase in the yield of green forage until
June 22. The dry-matter production continued to increase and at the close of
the test was found to be four times as great as at the beginning, the average
weekly increase being 940 kg. per hectare. The ash and nitrogen content continued to increase up to June 22.

Crops of a seed mixture consisting of 110 kg. of oats and 160 kg. of vetch
per hectare and harvested weekly from July 7 to August 17 showed a continued
increase in dry-matter during the period, with the exception of the last two
weeks, when this factor remained constant. The percentage of vetch in the
yield of the crop mixture increased from 23 to 50.1 per cent during the experiment.

Turnips, swedes, and field beets grown in comparison produced 85.8, 70.3,
and 62.2 tons of roots per hectare, respectively. The average weight per root
was 1.17 kg. for the turnips, 1 kg. for the swedes, and 0.69 kg. for the field

beets. The percentage of dry matter was highest in the field beets and lowest in the turnips. On October 13 the yields of dry matter per hectare were 8.58, 7.60, and 8.24 tons, and on November 10, 7.93, 8.28, and 8.18 tons for the turnips, swedes, and field beets, respectively. During the period of maximum growth, or from the middle of August to the middle of September, the crops produced over a ton of dry matter per hectare per week. Immediately after this period the production of dry matter fell to 0.5 ton, and a little later to 0.3 ton per hectare per week, while after October 13 no further production of dry matter was perceptible. Analyses of the forage made at various intervals from August 4 to October 13 indicated that the more rapid formation of dry matter took place in the first half of September, while the greater percentage of water was found prior to September 1.

The results of planting these root crops at different distances were in favor of planting in rows 60 cm. apart with the plants 25 cm. apart in the row, or 1,500 sq. cm. (132 sq. in.) of space per plant. These results were influenced to a certain extent by a poorer stand on the closer planted plats.

In a variety test Ostersundom turnip outyielded Bortfeld and Yellow Tankard, and Red Eckendorf field beets produced a higher yield than Barres Halflong. Satisfactory yields of a variety of swedes and of sugar beets are reported.

[Field crops], B. C. Burt (*Rpt. Cawnpore [India] Agr. Sta., 1916, pp. 2–30*).— This reports work at the Cawnpore experiment station (E. S. R., 31, p. 732) for the year ended June 30, 1916.

Notes are given on fertilizer experiments with wheat, and green manure tests and cultural experiments with wheat, cotton, gram, sugar cane, millet, pigeon peas, tobacco, barley, flax, and peanuts. Other experiments reported included deep *v.* shallow sowing for maize, maize and peanuts as a mixed crop, tests of different spacings with American cotton, rotation tests, and fodder crop experiments.

[Field crops], A. C. MacDonald (*Dept. Agr. Brit. East Africa Ann. Rpt. 1913–14, pp. 191, pl. 1; 1914–15, pp. 145*).—These reports continue work previously noted (E. S. R., 26, p. 793). Brief notes are given on the production of sisal, cotton, flax, corn, wheat, tobacco, and certain tropical plants in British East Africa, with supplementary reports from the government experimental farms at Kibos, Nairobi, and Kabete.

The advancement of the agricultural industries and of stock breeding in the Protectorate is summarized for the past seven years.

Cultural experiments conducted in Denmark with different mixtures of the seeds of forage plants. E. Lindhard (*Tidsskr. Plantcavl, 22 (1915), No. 4. pp. 553–713, figs. 2; abs. in Internat. Inst. Agr. [Rome]. Internat. Rev. Sci. and Pract. Agr., 7 (1916), No. 2, pp. 224, 225*).—The author discusses the results obtained in a series of experiments with mixtures of seed of forage plants covering a period of twelve years, 1900 to 1912. The data are presented in tabular form. A mixture recommended by Nielsen and composed of the following ingredients per acre was used as a basis for comparison: Early red clover 6.4 lbs., *Trifolium hybridum* 1.8 lbs., *T. repens* 0.3 lb., *Agropyron repens* 3.2 lbs., *Avena fatua* 3.2 lbs., *Phleum pratense* 1.8 lbs., *Festuca pratensis* 1.1 lbs., *Lolium perenne* 1.8 lbs., and *L. italicum* 1.6 lbs.

A summary is given of the results obtained with ten other Gramineæ-Leguminosæ combinations. These together corresponded to the most varied cultural conditions, and, when used according to their individual adaptations, gave much better results than the Nielsen mixture.

Pollination and fertilization studies with grasses and legumes at the Tystofte Experiment Station, H. N. Frandsen (*Tidsskr. Planteavl, 23 (1916), No. 3, pp. 442–486, figs. 6*).—The studies described were conducted with orchard grass, tall oat grass, meadow fescue, English rye grass, Italian rye grass, timothy, meadow foxtail, *Poa fertilis*, field brome grass (*Bromus arvensis*), red clover, bird-foot clover, alfalfa, and yellow trefoil. In addition to the data secured the results obtained by other investigators are briefly reported.

Pollination experiments conducted with orchard grass for several years indicated that the species, while generally cross-pollinated, produced seed to some extent under self-fertilization. It was found that individual plants show considerable variation with reference to self-fertility. Similar experiments, but on a smaller scale, showed that tall oat grass under ordinary conditions is predominantly cross-pollinated. Pollination experiments with meadow fescue gave results very much the same as those secured with orchard grass. The two species of rye grass proved chasmogamous. In a series of pollination studies with timothy the plants behaved much like those of the foregoing species, but the results also indicated that types comparatively high in fertility when close-pollinated may be isolated.

Meadow foxtail proved to be generally cross-pollinated and did not seem to be lower in fertility when isolated than the species above mentioned. P. *fertilis* under ordinary conditions was found to be cross-pollinated, but when isolated close-pollination resulted in complete fertilization, and under unfavorable weather conditions during blossoming self-fertilization also took place. While field brome grass gave complete fertilization with pollen from the same plant, cross-pollination predominated when the weather conditions were favorable.

The results with red clover indicated the practically complete self-sterility of the plant. With reference to bird-foot clover it was concluded that cross-pollination is necessary for seed production and that pollination is dependent upon the action of insects.

In the case of alfalfa natural self-pollination produced some seed but artificial self-fertilization was much more effective in this regard, while artificial cross-pollination resulted in twice the number of seeds secured from artificially self-pollinated plants. The author discusses the possible relation of climate as a factor in this connection in addition to insects as pollinating agents.

Yellow trefoil showed a certain degree of self-fertility. In all the experiments conducted with this plant the blossoms of isolated individuals opened automatically.

Experiments with bird-foot clover and alfalfa in grass mixtures, E. LIND-HARD (*Tidsskr. Planteavl, 23 (1916), No. 4, pp. 605–622, figs. 2*).—The experiments described were conducted at Tystofte from 1910 to 1913. The mixtures used per töndeland (1.36 acres) in one series consisted of 8, 12, or 16 lbs. of bird-foot clover and varying quantities of orchard grass, tall oat grass, timothy, and *Poa fertilis*, the smaller quantities of grass seed being used with the larger quantities of bird-foot clover seed and vice versa. Where bird-foot clover was sown alone it was used at the rate of 20 lbs. per töndeland. The average yields of hay per töndeland for the three different quantities of seed for each mixture were as follows: Orchard grass 110, tall oat grass 140, timothy 120. P. *fertilis* 121, and bird-foot clover alone 125 cwt. The quantity of bird-foot clover in the hay of the different mixtures and the pure seeding was 36, 30, 43, 58, and 78 per cent, respectively.

In a second series of experiments 12 or 20 lbs. of alfalfa seed per töndeland was sown in a mixture of the different quantities of the grasses mentioned above. For the pure seeding of alfalfa 30 lbs. of seed per töndeland was used. The average yields of hay for the unit area for the two different quantities of seed for each mixture were as follows: Orchard grass 156, tall oat grass 178. timothy 171, P. *fertilis* 161, and the pure seeding of alfalfa 159 cwt. The proportion of alfalfa in the hay from these different seedings was 50, 47, 57, 74, and 89 per cent, respectively. The detailed results of the experiments are given in tables.

On the germinability of rice (Oryza sativa) and corn (Zea mays) in relation to temperature and humidity, ANNA DA FANO (*Atti Ist. Bot. R. Univ. Pavia, 2. ser., 16 (1916), pp. 17–39*).—This paper reports experiments with five varieties of rice and three varieties of corn in a study of the effect upon germination of varying the temperature, the loss of moisture in the seed during exposure to the various temperatures, and the percentage of moisture in the seed during germination. The plan of the experiment included the exposure of the seed of the different varieties for from one to three hours, at temperatures of 30, 40, 50, 60, 70, and 80° C., and for one hour at a temperature of 90°. The seeds were also germinated at the temperature of the surrounding air, approximately 23°. The data are presented in tabular form and discussed at some length.

The author concludes that in *O. sativa* the maximum germination was obtained after exposure of the seed for three hours at 30°, except with the Ranghino variety, which attained its maximum germination after two hours exposure at 40°, and the germination of the different varieties varying between 84 and 88 per cent. The minimum germination observed occurred with exposure for three hours at 80°, and varied between 18 and 24 per cent. while exposure for one hour at 90° entirely destroyed the power of germination. The maximum moisture content of the seed for successful germination did not correspond in any way to the maximum moisture content of the seed. The quantity of moisture best suited for germination in *O. sativa* apparently lies between the limits of 9.5 and 12.5 per cent. figures which correspond to the moisture content present at the maximum and minimum germination of the seed.

The results obtained with *Z. mays* were analogous to those noted above. Maximum germination was observed after exposure of the seed for two hours at 40°, varying between 93 and 95 per cent. The minimum germination occurred after exposure for three hours at 70°, while exposure for one hour or longer at 80° resulted in loss of germinability. As in *O. sativa*, maximum and minimum germination did not correspond to maximum and minimum moisture content of the seed, but to an intermediate value.

Wheat and rye production in Iowa, W. R. HECHLER (*Iowa Sta. Circ. 37 (1917), pp. 8, figs. 3*).—Recommendations are made for increased production of winter and spring wheat and winter rye in Iowa.

Plants growing on moor soils as a source of fiber, and the use of sphagnum in making bandages, H. VON FEILITZEN (*Svenska Mosskkulturför. Tidskr., 31 (1917), No. 1, pp. 96–109, pls. 2, figs. 4*).—This article discusses the value of *Eriophorum vaginatum* as a source of fiber for use in the textile industries and reviews briefly experimental and commercial work in this direction. The results of an experiment on the capacity for water absorption of air-dry fiber samples of *E. vaginatum*, flax, jute, cotton, and wool are reported. Brief notes are also given on the use of sphagnum moss in the preparation of bandages.

The origin and cultural history of the Danish strains of Barres field beet, L. HELWEG (*Tidsskr. Plantearl., 23 (1916), No. 2, pp. 289–339, figs. 20*).—An article discussing briefly the origin of the field beet and its development from the wild species *Beta maritima*. The early cultivated forms are briefly noted and the more important varieties grown in Denmark at the present time are described.

In reviewing the history of the Barres field beet in Denmark it is pointed out that this variety constituted 21.2 per cent of the field beets grown in 1884 as compared with 88.4 per cent in 1915. The area devoted to the variety in 1915 was approximately 270,000 acres. The history of different strains of

Barres field beet now recognized in Denmark is briefly traced, and five strains, known as Næsgaard, Sludstrup, Rosted, Ferritslev, and Lille Taarøje, are described in detail with reference to form, color, top, ease of lifting, yield, dry matter content, and uniformity.

Genetical studies of variegated pericarp in maize, R. A. EMERSON (*Genetics, 2 (1917), No. 1, pp. 1–35, figs. 4*).—This paper continues the study (E. S. R., 29, p. 333; 31, p. 135) of the inheritance of self-pattern in the pericarp of maize seeds, occurring as a sporophytic variation in variegated ears.

The later studies are in entire accord with those previously reported. The author formerly termed these changes somatic variations because they were first manifested in somatic cells. It was apparent from the beginning, however, that the factorial modification responsible for the visible change must often occur in meristematic cells from which later arise the germ cells as well as the somatic tissues of the pericarp, or even of the whole ear, and since such meristematic cells are germinal rather than somatic the variation is deemed to be better termed sporophytic.

Distinct variations in variegated ears of maize are described and new phases of the problem reported on. Most of the data presented were obtained in connection with heredity studies conducted at the Nebraska Experiment Station. The points studied were inheritance of sporophytic mutations from variegation to self-color, changes in type of variegation, reverse mutation—self-color to variegation, suggested explanation of the inheritance of certain sporophytic variations and the noninheritance of others, and the relation of variegation to unit-factor constancy.

"The seed ears used in the later studies have all been pollinated by colorless strains to avoid difficulties arising from the uncertainty of the purity of the pollen of variegated races. Self-colored, partly self-colored, variously variegated, and colorless seeds from variegated parent ears, thus pollinated, have given progenies containing a percentage of self-colored ears roughly proportional to the amount of self-color in the seeds planted, the maximum being approximately 50 per cent from self-colored and near-self seeds and the minimum none from colorless seeds. This has been equally true whether the parent ears have been homozygous or heterozygous for pericarp color. In the latter case, the self-colored ears have always occurred at the expense of variegated ears, never at the expense of colorless ones. Medium variegation has been found to be a simple Mendelian dominant to very light variegation. Self-colored ears appearing in the progeny of F_1 ears of this cross have occurred at the expense of medium variegated ears rather than in the place of very light variegated ones. These facts are held to indicate that a genetical factor for variegation mutates to a factor for self-color, that only one of the duplex factors ordinarily so mutates, and that the factor for medium variegation mutates much more frequently than that for very light variegation."

The results obtained indicate that there is an inheritance of a light type of variegation arising as a sporophytic variation on medium variegated ears, although this has not been fully investigated. A sporophytic change in the type of variegation resulting in seeds with strongly colored crown spots associated with self-colored cob glumes is not inherited as regards either pericarp or glume color.

From one to five wholly or partly variegated seeds per ear have occurred on about two-thirds of the self-colored ears descended from two presumably unrelated variegated ears. Other related and unrelated cultures have not exhibited such exceptional seeds, and no variegated seeds, as far as known, ever occurred on a homozygous self-colored ear. One test indicates the inheritance of these presumably reverse mutations from self-color to variegation.

Histological examinations of the developing ovary and glumes and of the mature seed suggest a possible explanation for the color peculiarities of distinct somatic variations and for the inheritance of some and the noninheritance of others. The change from variegated to near-self seeds associated with little change in the color of the glumes is thought to occur only in subepidermal cells and consequently may be inherited, while the change from variegated to darkcrown variegated seeds accompanied by self-colored glumes is thought to be limited to the epidermal layers and hence incapable of inheritance. ·

These results are thought to favor the idea that single allelomorphic factors, rather than two or more closely linked factors, are responsible for the color pattern of both glumes and pericarp.

"The phenomena studied are held to have an important bearing on the question of unit-factor constancy. The existence of the series of at least nine or ten multiple allelomorphs to which variegation belongs indicates that a factor for pericarp color has mutated several times. Some of the factors of this series have not been observed to mutate, while others have mutated rarely, and still others many times. In fact, the principal difference between certain of the factors is thought to lie in their relative frequencies of mutation. It is suggested that data such as is here presented may help to explain the somewhat diverse results of selection experiments within pure lines, clonal lines, and the like."

Contribution to the study of cotton production and its future, J. V. NATTA MAGLIONE (*Bol. Min. Agr.* [*Argentina*], 20 (1916), No. 7–8, pp. 631–646, figs. 8).— This is a general discussion of cotton production in Argentina. The cost of production is estimated and presented in tabular form.

Studies on oat breeding.—V, The F_1 and F_2 generations on a cross between a naked and a hulled oat, J. ZINN and F. M. SURFACE (*U. S. Dept. Agr., Jour. Agr. Research,* 10 (1917), No. 6. pp. 293–312. pls. 9).—In continuing work at the Maine Experiment Station previously noted (E. S. R.. 35, p. 831; 36, p. 834), the authors describe in detail a white naked oat, *Avena sativa nuda* var. *inermis,* and a black-hulled oat, *A. sativa patula* var. Victor, and the F_1 and F_2 generations of a cross between the two. The Victor oat was the female parent. and the naked oat the male parent, the F_1 progeny consisting of 11 hybrid grains. only 4 of which germinated when planted in 1915. The F_2 generation comprised 854 plants, all of which, together with the F_1 generation, were examined for hull character. grain color, pubescence at the base of the grain, and inheritance of awns.

The hulled parent was characterized by the presence of firm flowering glumes which adhered closely to the caryopsis, biflorous spikelets, black color of glumes, strong awns, and a long but rather sparse pubescence at the sides of the base of the lower grain. The naked parent was characterized by loose. membranous flowering glumes which did not adhere to the caryopsis, multiflorous spikelets. white or light yellow glume color, almost total absence of awns, and the absence of pubescence. It is suggested that the absence of awns and of pubesence may be due to the inability of these characters to express themselves on the thin membranous glumes.

The F_1 generation is described as distinctly intermediate in most characters. In regard to the glumes, both naked and firmly-hulled grain and intermediate forms were found on the same panicle and even in the same spikelet. The spikelets near the top of the panicle were entirely naked, or nearly so, while those near the base of the panicle tended to be firmly hulled. A similar but less marked relation was observed between the spikelets near the tip and base of each whorl.

A large number of intermediate forms appeared in the F_2 generation in addition to the two parental hulled types, four definite groups being distinguished. These intermediates contained all gradations from plants with perfectly hulled grain to the perfectly naked forms. The inheritance of the hulled characters presented a simple Mendelian ratio, giving 1 hulled, 2 intermediate, 1 naked. In grain color also there were three black plants to one white. It is shown that the genes for these two characters segregate independently of each other.

Multiflorous spikelets occurred only in connection with naked grain, plants with completely hulled grain bearing only biflorous spikelets.

The inheritance of pubescence at the base of the lower grain presented some difficulties, since it could not be manifested on plants with naked grain. By the use of a selected group of plants having hulled and intermediate grain, however, it was found that pubescence behaves as a bifactorial character, giving 15 pubescent plants to 1 without pubescence. Neither of these genes were linked with those for color. Available evidence indicates that one of these pubescent genes may come from the naked parent. Long and short pubescence at the base of the grain behaved as a monohybrid character and segregated independently of the other genes considered.

A remarkable feature of this cross was observed in the presence of pubescence at the base of the upper or second grain, no cultivated varieties of oats possessing this character. In this cross these forms occurred only on spikelets where the lower grain was naked or seminaked, and it is deemed probable that the presence of this pubescence was due to physiological disturbances caused by the presence of the naked lower grain.

The presence of awns was also affected by the nature of the glumes, a naked grain bearing only thin, weak awns. Considering only the hulled and intermediate types of grain, there appeared to be a simple 3:1 ratio between plants with medium strong to strong awns and those with weak awns.

[Potato culture], P. WEBER and KLEBERGER (*Jour. Landw.*, *64* (*1916*), *No. 3*, *pp. 181–199*).—The authors report experiments conducted on sandy, loamy, and clayey soils to test the effect of complete mineral fertilization, with especial reference to the nitrogen carrier, on the yield of potatoes and starch for each soil type. The nitrogenous fertilizers consisted of ammonium sulphate, calcium nitrate, ammonium nitrate, and liquid manure. The treatment of the plats was identical, and consisted of 352 lbs. of Thomas slag, 176 lbs. of 40 per cent potash salt, and either 176 lbs. of ammonium sulphate, 176 lbs. of calcium nitrate, 88 lbs. of ammonium nitrate, or 1,280 liters of liquid manure per acre. The soil type for each series of plats is described and the fertilizer treatment for each plat, together with the results obtained, are given in tabular form.

The results of the experiments indicate that nitrogen fertilization affects the yield of potatoes on the better loam and clay soils, while upon the sandy soils the potash and phosphorus fertilizers appeared to have the most pronounced effects. Satisfactory yields were not obtained on the heavier soils, however, with nitrogen alone. Of the nitrogen carriers tested, ammonium sulphate gave the best results on all soil types, although liquid manure gave very good results and is to be especially recommended at the present time.

The highest starch yields were obtained from the use of potash and phosphorus alone, liquid manure producing a slight and the remaining nitrogenous materials a decided reduction in the starch content.

The utilization of the nitrogen in the fertilizers did not always parallel the yields obtained. This was noticeable in the case of ammonium sulphate on clay soil, where only 90 per cent of the nitrogen was used, indicating that the nitrogen from the ammonium nitrate must have been used for the formation of vegetative parts, such as the stem and leaves. The utilization of the potash and phosphorous fertilizers was materially influenced by the nature of the nitrogen carrier, the most complete utilization being obtained in connection with ammonium sulphate. The effect of liquid manure in this respect is favorable on loam soils.

The irrigation of potatoes, F. S. HARRIS (*Utah Sta. Bul. 157 (1917), pp. 3-20, figs. 9*).—Rather extensive irrigation experiments with potatoes conducted on the Greenville Experiment Farm are reported for the 5-year period of 1912 to 1916, inclusive. The life of the potato plant was divided into four stages, (1) when the vines were 4 in. high, (2) when the tubers began to form, (3) when the potatoes were in full bloom, and (4) when the potatoes were nearly ripe. One, 2½, 5, and 7½ in. applications of irrigation water were made weekly, and 5-in. applications at the different stages of growth. Important literature on the subject is reviewed and detailed tabular data presented.

A comparison of the yields of tubers and vines on plats receiving different quantities of irrigation water weekly showed the highest average yield of tubers for the 5 years, 337.1 bu., to have been obtained from a total of 12.8 in. applied 1 in. per week during the growing season. The maximum application of 96 in., or 7½ in. weekly, resulted in a lower average yield of tubers, 140.5 bu., than where no irrigation water was given, 153.3 bu., although the weight of air-dry vines was nearly doubled.

In a comparison of single applications at different stages of growth the lowest yield of tubers, 139 bu. per acre, resulted from an application made after planting and before the vines were up. The best results were secured from applications made when the plants were in full bloom and averaged 229 bu. per acre. Neither 10, 15, nor 20 in. applied in two, three, or four irrigations of 5 in. each gave results equal to regular weekly applications of 1 in. each. Late applications, as well as large quantities, of water increased the relative growth of the vines.

The average size of the tubers was larger where the water was applied weekly with 1-in. applications, both 5 and 7½ in. weekly applications producing smaller tubers than where no irrigation water was used. The tubers on plats receiving water at the third and fourth stage and those receiving it at all four stages averaged the same size and were larger than for any other treatment.

The average number of tubers per hill was largest with a 2½-in. application per week, while early applications appeared to be conducive to a large production of tubers per hill.

The average weight of the hills, determined by weighing 100 average hills from each plat, was highest with 1 in. and 2½ in. weekly irrigations, while a rapid decrease in weight per hill was noted with an increase in the amount of water applied. Applications made in the third stage proved most effective in increasing the weight per hill.

All irrigation treatments produced vines that were higher than those produced with no irrigation, but a comparison of the vine growth is deemed insufficient as an indication of the relative value of the different irrigation treatments. A wide variation in the color of the vines was noted for the different methods of irrigation and was considered a reliable means of determining the moisture requirements of potato plants.

The experiments are held to indicate the importance of an even supply of moisture during the middle portion of the life of the potato, after the tubers begin to form and before they begin to ripen.

Shallu, or "Egyptian wheat," a late-maturing variety of sorghum, B. E. ROTHGEB (*U. S. Dept. Agr., Farmers' Bul. 827 (1917), pp. 8, figs. 3*).—Shallu is described as a late-maturing variety of sorghum exploited as Egyptian wheat, Mexican Desert wheat corn, and under many other local names.

The results obtained with shallu when grown under the dry-land conditions of the southern Great Plains are cited and compared with those secured from other grain sorghum varieties such as Dwarf milo maize, Dwarf Kafir corn. and feterita in variety, tests in Texas, Oklahoma, Kansas, and New Mexico.

Owing to its late maturity (125 to 140 days) shallu is subject to injury by drought and even under the most favorable dry-land conditions the yields are lower than those of Kafir corn and milo maize, while in unfavorable seasons it frequently fails entirely. Shallu often lodges badly and is not to be recommended where milo maize or Kafir corn can be grown successfully.

The irrigation of sugar beets, F. S. Harris (*Utah Sta. Bul. 156 (1917), pp. 3–24, figs. 14*).—Experiments with sugar beets are reported, showing the effect of different weekly irrigations and of standard 5-in. irrigations applied at certain periods in the growth of the plant on the yield of roots, yield of sugar, percentage of sugar and purity, and size and shape of beets. The life of the sugar-beet plant was divided into the following stages: (1) Just before thinning, (2) four weeks after thinning, (3) when the beets averaged 2 in. in diameter, and (4) when the beets were nearly ripe. The weekly irrigations consisted of applications of 1, 2.5, 5, and 7.5 in. of water, made during the regular irrigation season. Tabulated data are presented for the 5-year period of 1912–1916, inclusive, and the results compared graphically.

The highest average yield of beets on plats receiving weekly irrigations was secured from 1-in. applications, and amounted to 21.92 tons per acre, as compared with a yield of 12.98 tons without irrigation. When but one irrigation was given, that applied at the third stage of growth gave the highest average yield, 18.92 tons per acre. Where more than one application was made the highest average yield, 23.39 tons per acre, was secured from irrigations made at the first, third, and fourth stages of growth. Irrigation after planting but before the plants were up gave a yield of only 11.22 tons per acre. After the plants were up the least desirable time for irrigation was during the fourth stage of growth, when an average yield of but 15.09 tons was secured. Proportionately more tops were produced by the high and late irrigations than by opposite conditions.

Except where the water was applied quite late, the percentage of sugar and of purity was higher in the irrigated beets than in the nonirrigated. The highest average percentage of sugar was secured from a weekly application of 2.5 in. of water and amounted to 16.32 per cent. When one irrigation was given, the highest average percentage, 15.73 per cent, was obtained from an application made in the third stage of growth, while an average of 14.5 per cent was obtained from plats receiving no irrigation. The highest average purity was secured from weekly applications of 5 in. of water and amounted to 83.9 per cent, as compared with 78.4 per cent from nonirrigated plats and 83.2 per cent with 2.5 in. of water weekly.

The length of beets was not increased by delaying the time of application of the first irrigation, early irrigation apparently facilitating penetration of the roots into the soil. The average length of root from the nonirrigated plats was 10.6 in., while the longest roots were secured from the plats receiving applications of water during the first three stages of growth, and averaged 11.7 in. Weekly applications of 1 in. of water gave roots with an average length of 11.5 in.

Irrigation affected the size of the beets in about the same manner that it affected total yield. The highest average weight, 2 lbs., was secured from plats receiving 1 in. of water weekly, as compared with an average weight of 1.09 lbs.

from the nonirrigated plats. The percentage of forked beets bore no apparent relation to the amount of water used.

The author concludes that sugar beets do not require large quantities of irrigation water, provided it is properly applied, but that they are sensitive to the time of application.

The weeding of wheat, E. REY (*Jour. Agr. Prat., n. ser., 29 (1916), Nos. 19, pp. 324–326; 20, pp. 346–348; 23, pp. 392–394; 25, pp. 429, 430*).—This is a general discussion of the beneficial effects obtained from weeding wheat. The author cites a number of authorities in support of his arguments, giving the results of several experiments and emphasizing the economic phases.

The effect of heating seeds upon the development of the plant; experiments made in Russia with wheat, S. J. WOROBIEW (*Khoziaistvo, 10 (1915), No. 47–48, pp. 1075–1083; abs. in Internat. Inst. Agr. [Rome], Internat. Rcv. Sci. and Pract. Agr., 7 (1916), No. 4, pp. 527–530*).—The author reports experiments with "Arnaoutka" (a mixture of different varieties) and Kubanka wheats, strains of *Triticum durum*, to determine the effect of relatively high temperatures upon the plant embryo. The seeds were planted in pots after exposure for 20 minutes to a temperature of 80° C. (176° F.). The pots received 60, 40, and 20 per cent of the amount of water required to saturate the soil. The results obtained are summarized in an appended table.

The author concludes that heating has a stimulating effect upon the embryo and promotes a tendency to xerophytic structure, shown in the reduced height of the plant, the decreased relative weight of the leaves, and the dimensions of the cells. Since xerophilous plants best withstand a lack of water, it can be assumed that where moisture is abundant, heating the seed produces no modification in the structure of the plant, but where it is limited, heated seeds produce plants so modified as to withstand drought.

Root-crop seeds.—Harvest and trade of 1915–16, L. HELWEG (*Tidsskr. Planteavl, 23 (1916), No. 3, pp. 487–518, fig. 2*).—An article discussing at some length the yield and quality of turnip, field beet, rutabaga, and carrot seed secured in Denmark in 1915, including a review of a number of court decisions in settlement of cases arising in the root-crop seed trade.

Yellow rocket, a dangerous weed, E. A. BESSEY (*Michigan Sta. Spec. Bul. 80 (1917). pp. 3, 4*).—Yellow rocket, winter cress, or herb barbara (*Barbarea barbarea*), said to have been introduced as an impurity in clover and grass seeds, is briefly described and methods of eradication recommended.

HORTICULTURE.

One thousand hints on vegetable gardening, MAE S. CROY (*New York and London: G. P. Putnam's Sons, 1917, pp. VII+275*).—This work comprises practical hints arranged in short paragraphs on the culture of the common vegetables, fruits, and nuts, together with miscellaneous suggestions relating to gardening and garden equipment, planting tables, etc.

[Report of horticultural investigations], A. C. HARTENBOWER (*Guam Sta. Rpt. 1916. pp. 26–38, pls. 2*).—Notes are given on the acquisition and distribution of seeds and plants during the year, together with data on general fertilizer and cultural tests of beans, peppers, eggplants, radishes, carrots, muskmelons, cucumbers, watermelons, squash, okra, pumpkins, sweet corn, onions, and udo.

A test was started on August 1, 1915, to determine the longevity of vegetable seeds when stored in ground-glass top exhibition jars and when stored in cloth sacks in insect-proof wooden cabinet drawers. Germination tests were made at semimonthly intervals until the following June 15. The data as here presented in tabular form show a marked advantage in using closed jars as the time of storage increases.

Brief notes are given on the condition of fruit trees introduced at the station previous to July 1, 1914, and during 1915 and 1916. Tests of the inarching method of propagating mangoes resulted in a loss of 18 per cent of the plants. The size of fruit in the station lowland pineapple field was materially increased by providing good drainage. The station is to undertake work looking to the improvement of the coconut crop on the island.

[Progress report on horticultural investigations] (*Missouri Sta. Bul. 147 (1917), pp. 40–43, 44–47*).—In continuation of previous reports (E. S. R., 35, p. 837) concise statements are given of progress made along various lines of horticultural work during the year ended June 30, 1916.

Fruit nutrition studies in charge of J. C. Whitten and C. C. Wiggans were conducted with strawberries, peaches, and apples during the year. The work with strawberries was confined to the use of fertilizers containing phosphorus, since previous results from the use of potassium and nitrogen were negative. Acid phosphate applied directly to the row, either the current year or the previous year, caused a marked increase in yield, while bone meal even at the end of the second year caused no increase. The question has been raised as to whether or not the effect of the acid phosphate may not be wholly or in part due to the acid condition possibly resulting from its application rather than to the phosphorus it contains. Studies are to be conducted along this line.

In the nutrition experiments with peaches the trees receiving nitrogen over a period of years are markedly larger, more vigorous, and carry a greener foliage than those receiving no nitrogen. Also by far the greater effect in increasing yield has been shown on the nitrogen plants. During the last year the fruits on the trees fertilized with nitrogen were noticeably smaller in size, but not sufficiently so to injure the market quality, the larger number of peaches more than offsetting the reduction in size. The peaches seemed firmer and in better condition for long shipment.

The work with apples continued to show the superiority of nitrogen fertilizers on young trees, although the trees fertilized with nitrogen were more subject to blight. Blight was also found to be twice as prevalent on trees where cowpeas were grown and turned under the previous year as on plats where the trees were in timothy or alfalfa sod. Hence, it is concluded that where blight is destructive growers should use discretion in applying nitrogen fertilizer or in turning under leguminous crops. The results secured with fertilizers on older apple trees indicate in brief that the addition of fertilizer may or may not be profitable, depending on conditions in the individual orchard.

Among other investigations with fruits being conducted by J. C. Whitten work in breeding apples for late blooming habit was started. Planting tests of hardy fruit trees, such as the apple and pear, continued to show that fall planting causes uniformly much stronger growth than spring planting. During the last year late fall planting gave better results than early fall planting and late spring planting gave better results than early spring planting. The sour cherry profits more by fall planting, as compared with spring planting, than any other species that has been tested. The past year's results showed that approximately two-thirds of the spring-planted cherry trees died, while there was no loss among those planted in the fall. The surviving spring-planted trees made 25 per cent as much growth as the fall-planted trees.

Based on the yields secured from four crops, Ben Davis apple trees grown from fruit buds selected from a productive parent have shown no superiority over those selected from an unproductive parent. A similar experiment in straw berry selection (E. S. R., 33, p. 236) covering a period of 10 years and now completed also gave negative results.

Self-fertility studies of fruits by J. C. Whitten and C. C. Wiggans confirm the previous assumption that certain commercial varieties of apples have a tendency to self-fertility. Varieties such as Delicious, Ingram, Ben Davis, Gano, and York appear to be capable of fertilizing their own flowers when planted in large blocks.

Observations made on fruit trees in connection with tillage studies by J. C. Whitten and C. C. Wiggans indicate that the formation of fruit buds is induced by highly concentrated sap and wood growth, and lack of fruitfulness is indicated by less concentrated sap. In the tillage studies the tree sap was found to be more concentrated in orchards where cultivation is not extensive and where apparently greater competition with sod crops exists. Sap studies are to be conducted for a number of years with the view of determining a possible correlation between sap concentration and tillage methods.

The studies of fruit-bud development of trees as influenced by treatments and previous crops, conducted by C. C. Wiggans, confirm the conclusion previously drawn that only a small percentage of the spurs blossoms two years in succession and even a smaller percentage matures fruit two years in succession. It was found in every case where tests were made that the concentration of cortex sap from bearing spurs was greater than that from nonbearing spurs, if the determination was made during or soon after the fruiting season. Leaf sap from nonbearing spurs shows a higher concentration than leaf sap from bearing spurs. The high concentration of cortex sap from bearing spurs appears to exist only while the spur has fruit on it. Later the bearing spur comes back to normal concentration. So far as observed, there is no correlation between the number of leaves on a spur and its fruit development. Spurs bearing two or more fruits show little or no difference in sap concentration from those bearing only one fruit.

Examination of buds in winter for forecasting probable bloom, as made by C. C. Wiggans, indicates that it is possible to forecast the probable bloom of apple trees. Further observations are being made with the view of developing methods of forecasting that may be used by the average grower.

Protection of fruit against late spring frosts, A. D. Beeler (U. S. Dept. Com., Com. Rpts., No. 221 (1917), p. 1101).—A consular note on a new product, "agélarine" (antifrost), said to be a vegetable derivative compounded from the juices of certain plants. This material, it is claimed, has been successfully used for coating fruit trees, thereby retarding their blooming period without injuring the trees.

[Spray calendars] (New Jersey Stas. Circs. 75–79 (1917), pp. 2 each).—A series of circulars consisting of spray calendars for apples and quinces, pears, sweet cherries, plums, and peaches, as above numbered, respectively.

Blooming period of the apple in northwest Arkansas, W. H. Wicks (Arkansas Sta. Bul. 134 (1917), pp. 3–12, figs. 3).—This bulletin contains data collected in 1914, 1916, and 1917 to ascertain the blooming period of different varieties of apples. The work was limited to Washington and Benton Counties in northwest Arkansas. Records were kept by over 300 growers each year, in addition to records kept by the author.

A study of the data as a whole shows that the relative blooming period of varieties is not constant, that weather conditions preceding and during the blooming period exert an important influence on the earliness and length of the blooming period, and that varieties possess different degrees of susceptibility to climatic conditions. On certain slopes, elevations, and soils, and under certain methods of culture the same varieties will begin to bloom a few days earlier or later.

The varieties observed are classified according to time of blooming. A study of the data collected shows that the leading commercial varieties of the section, namely, Ben Davis, Jonathan, Winesap, Grimes, and Mammoth Black Twig, all blossom at about the same period, thus making it possible to secure the greatest benefit of cross-pollination, provided there is mutual affinity between them. Other varieties of less commercial importance also bloom during the same period with the leading varieties, and where bees are kept in or near the orchard the greatest benefit from cross-pollination is assured.

The apple grading and packing law enacted by the Delaware legislature, 1917 (*Bul. Bd. Agr. Del., 6 (1917), No. 4, pp. 11-15*).—The text of this law, which became effective on June 1, 1917, is here given in full.

Investigations and experimental work carried on in cherry orchards in Kent during the months of April and May, 1915-16, G. P. BERRY (*Jour. Bd. Agr. [London], 24 (1917), No. 3, pp. 288-298*).—Notes are given on varieties of cherries growing in Kent orchards, including information relative to their blooming period and relative sterility or fertility when grown alone and in admixture with other varieties. Some good pollenizers for the Early Rivers variety were determined by actual experiment.

A census of the peach crop of 1917 in West Virginia, compiled by W. H. SOMERS (*W. Va. Dept. Agr. Bul. 26 (1917), pp. 24*).—This comprises estimates for the 1917 season of the number of baskets of peaches in the various orchards in West Virginia.

Report on fertilizer experiments with cranberries, F. P. SCHLATTER (*Proc. Amer. Cranberry Growers' Assoc., 48 (1917), pp. 9-12*).—A progress report on cooperative experiments being conducted under the direction of the New Jersey Experiment Stations (E. S. R., 36, p. 641).

As a result of the work conducted during the past five years the author recommends the use of acid phosphate, rock phosphate, and bone meal for mud bottoms and iron ore bottoms. For sandy or savanna bottoms and possibly for mud bottoms having a heavy coat of sand on top, nitrate of soda, dried blood, cottonseed meal, acid phosphate, basic slag, bone meal, and rock phosphate, either singly or in proper and judicious mixtures, may prove of value. Potash has apparently no value. The use of sulphate of ammonia as a source of nitrogen is not recommended.

Spoilage of cranberries after picking, C. L. SHEAR (*Proc. Amer. Cranberry Growers' Assoc., 48 (1917), pp. 6-9*).—A paper on this subject outlining the cooperative investigations conducted by the U. S. Department of Agriculture in Massachusetts and New Jersey. The author briefly discusses spoilage due to fungus rots and premature death of the fruit caused by rapid ripening or suffocation.

First report on cacao selection in Assinan, G. HOMBURG and C. J. J. VAN HALL (*Meded. Proefstat. Midden-Java, No. 27 (1917), pp. 7*).—A record is given of the yield of parent trees included in the selection study, together with notes on the condition of stock budded from these trees.

Additional observations on the citrus fruits in the Philippines, P. J. WESTER (*Philippine Agr. Rev. [English Ed.], 10 (1917), No. 2, pp. 104-115, pls. 7*).—In continuation of a previous bulletin on citriculture in the Philippines (E. S. R., 30, p. 644), observations are given on a number of species that have fruited recently at the Lamao Experiment Station, including tabular data showing the degree of citrus canker affection in the station collection.

A contribution to the history of the mango in Florida, P. J. WESTER (*Philippine Agr. Rev. [English Ed.], 10 (1917), No. 2, pp. 146-149, ;ls. 2*).—This

EXPERIMENT STATION RECORD. [Vol. 37

contribution is based on the literature of the subject and on the data assembled by the author when connected with the subtropical garden in Miami, Fla.

The pistachio, R. FALCI (*Bol. R. Giard. Colon. Palermo, 3 (1916), No. 3–4, pp. 128–184, pls. 6, figs. 3*).—This comprises the results of a study relative to the biology, varieties, and culture of the pistachio in Sicily. A number of plates are appended showing the nature of the foliage and nuts of different species, hybrids, and varieties.

Trees suitable for the farm and for ornamental purposes, W. E. DOWSETT (*Rhodesia Agr. Jour., 14 (1917), No. 4, pp. 487–490, pls. 3*).—A descriptive list is given of trees suitable for the farm and homestead in Rhodesia.

Plant materials of decorative gardening: The woody plants, W. TRELEASE (*Urbana, Ill.: Author, 1917, pp. 204*).—A pocket guide to the generic and usually the specific name of the hardy trees, shrubs, and woody climbers found cultivated in the eastern United States (except in the extreme South) or in northern Europe, exclusive of nurseries, botanical establishments, and pretentious estates. In the generic descriptions more attention is given to wood, bud, leaf-scar, foliage, and inflorescence than to the more transient details of flower and fruit on which botanical classification largely rests. The nomenclature is in accord with that used in the Standard Cyclopedia of Horticulture. Other commonly used names are added as synonyms.

Annuals and biennials, GERTRUDE JEKYLL (*New York: Charles Scribner's Sons, [1916], pp. XIV+174, pls. 44*).—Part 1 of this volume discusses some ways of using annuals and biennials, raising annuals in greenhouse or frame, annuals and biennials for autumn sowing, annuals as edgings, color schemes with annuals, hedge-forming and climbing annuals, annuals in the rock garden, sweet scented annuals, and annuals and biennials for use as cut flowers. Part 2 comprises an alphabetical list, with description and culture, of the best annuals and biennials. In part 3 a chart of color and height together with selections for various purposes and aspects are given.

Garden flowers of spring, ELLEN E. SHAW (*Garden City, N. Y.: Doubleday, Page & Co., 1917, vol. 1, pp. 230, figs. 217*).—This is the first of a series of four volumes constituting the Pocket Garden Library, edited by L. Barron. The present volume contains descriptions with illustrations in color of garden flowers of spring.

Garden flowers of summer, ELLEN E. SHAW (*Garden City, N. Y.: Doubleday, Page & Co., 1917, vol. 2, pp. 251, figs. 238*).—A volume similar to the above describing garden flowers of summer.

Garden flowers of autumn, ELLEN E. SHAW (*Garden City, N. Y.: Doubleday, Page & Co., 1917, vol. 3, pp. 195, figs. 185*).—A volume similar to the above describing garden flowers of autumn.

Flowers of winter, indoors and out, M. FREE (*Garden City, N. Y.: Doubleday, Page & Co., 1917, vol. 4, pp. 206, figs. 196*).—A volume similar to the above describing flowers of winter, indoors and out.

The livable house.—Its garden, RUTH DEAN (*New York: Moffat Yard & Co., 1917, vol. 2, pp. XXI+174, figs. 107*).—This is one of a series of volumes dealing with the home and its surroundings. The successive chapters discuss the grounds as a whole; general planting; the flower garden; spring planting, trees, shrubs, flowers, bulbs, tall planting, and pruning; and garden architecture.

How to make concrete garden furniture and accessories, edited by J. T. FALLON (*New York: Robert M. McBride & Co., 1917, pp. XVIII+105, pls. 15, figs. 33*).—A treatise on the use of concrete in the garden. It discusses the selection and testing of material; how to proportion and mix the materials; making forms and placing the concrete; how to make garden walls, steps, and other simple utilities; how to make sundials, benches, swimming pools, bird baths, lanterns, pottery, and water gardens; and making concrete garden frames and garden rollers.

FORESTRY.

General survey of Texas woodlands, including a study of the commercial possibilities of mesquite, J. H. FOSTER, H. B. KRAUSZ, and A. H. LEIDIGH (*Bul. Agr. and Mech. Col. Tex., 3. ser., 3 (1917), No. 9, pp. 47, figs. 20*).—This comprises a general survey of forest and woodland conditions in Texas, including also a discussion of the geography, soil, and climate of the State. Data on a study of the commercial possibilities of mesquite, made by H. B. Krausz, are also given.

Forest resources of eastern Texas, J. H. FOSTER, H. B. KRAUSZ, and G. W. JOHNSON (*Bul. Agr. and Mech. Col. Tex., 3. ser., 3 (1917), No. 10, pp. 57, figs. 12*).—Data are given on the forest resources, industries, and outputs by counties of the east Texas timber belt.

The Patagonian forests, M. ROTHKUGEL (*Los Bosques Patagónicos. Buenos Aires: Min. Agr., 1916, pp. 207, pls. 23, figs. 99*).—This embraces the results of a reconnoissance of the forest regions of Patagonia. Information is given relative to the general distribution of the forests, distribution by species, data on density and yield from different stands, lumbering conditions and activities, and probable future distribution of commercial species. The more important species are considered in detail, and a number of maps are appended showing their distribution.

Timber estimating methods used in eastern North Carolina, H. R. KRINBILL (*Biltmorean, 4 (1917), No. 2, pp. 13–21*).—A descriptive account illustrating the application of these methods on various timber tracts.

Sixth annual report of the State forester to the governor for the year ended December 31, 1916, F. A. ELLIOTT (*Ann. Rpt. State Forester Oreg., 6 (1916), pp. 20, fig. 1*).—A report on forest fire protection work during the year ended December 31, 1916.

Forestry, J. A. VIQUESNEY (*Bien. Rpt. Forest, Game and Fish Warden W. Va., 1915–16, pp. 39–89, pls. 4, figs. 26*).—A report of forest activities in West Virginia for the biennial period ended July 1, 1916, including a discussion of State and Federal fire protection, the character of the fire season, and the assistance rendered by private landowners, railroads, and rural mail carriers. A plan prepared by E. S. Bryant for fire protection by the State of West Virginia in cooperation with the southern West Virginia fire protective association is here included.

Law of the woods and yerbales (*Ley de Bosques y Yerbales. Buenos Aires: Min. Agr. Nac., 1915, pp. 91, pls. 3*).—This comprises the text of a proposed forest law for Argentina as presented to the National Congress, Buenos Aires, on September 30, 1915.

Amendments to the Central Provinces Forest Manual (third edition) (*Nagpur, India: Govt., 1915–1917, pp. [67]*).—This comprises various additions, substitutions, and corrections to the manual previously noted (E. S. R., 36, p. 843).

On the sun and shade leaves of some trees, T. DOI (*Jour. Col. Sci. Imp. Univ. Tokyo, 40 (1917), Art. 1, pp. 37, pl. 1, figs. 4*).—A contribution to the knowledge of leaf structure as influenced by light and shade, based on investigations of plants and trees growing in the botanic garden of the Imperial University of Tokyo.

The carob and its rational culture, G. AMICO (*Il Carrubo Coltivato Razionalmente. Catania: F. Battiato, 1916, pp. 103, fig. 1*).—An account of the carob

(*Ceratonia siliqua*) with reference to its distribution ; botany ; varieties ; propagation ; flowering, pollination, and fruiting ; culture ; commercial importance ; and economic uses. The work has been written with special reference to the extension of carob culture in Italy.

The black wattle industry.—Acacia mollissima, A. decurrens var. mollis, T. R. SIM (*So. African Jour. Sci., 13 (1917), No. 7, pp. 279–301*).—A general and statistical account of the black wattle tanbark industry in Natal.

Catalogue of the wood specimens exhibited in the economic section, T. V. NARASINGA RAO (*Madras: Govt. Museum, 1916, pp. VI+114*).—A catalogue of the wood specimens exhibited in the Madras Government Museum, giving the common names of the wood, distribution, characteristics, and uses.

The grouping of ties for treatment, C. P. WINSLOW (*Proc. Amer. Wood Preservers' Assoc., 13 (1917), pp. 386–413, figs. 3*).—A paper presented at the annual meeting of the American Wood Preservers' Association in New York City in January, 1917, and discussing the proper grouping for preservative treatment of woods used as railroad ties.

Paper and wood pulp industry, W. A. RUFF (*Bur. of the Census [U. S.] Census of Manfr. 1914, Paper and Wood Pulp, pp. 19*).—This comprises a summary of the principal statistics for the paper and wood pulp industry as a whole for 1914 and 1909, together with special statistics relating to materials, products, equipment, imports, and exports.

Forest products of Canada, 1916.—Pulpwood (*Dept. Int. Canada, Forestry Branch Bul. 62B (1917), pp. 13, figs. 7*).—A statistical account of the pulpwood consumption in Canada in 1916. The Canadian mills consumed 1,764,912 cords valued at $13,104,458, while 1,068,207 cords valued at $6,866,669 were exported.

DISEASES OF PLANTS.

New or interesting species of fungi, H. D. HOUSE (*N. Y. State Mus. Bul. 188 (1916), pp. 29–58, pls. 4*).—Among other fungi this list includes, as more or less parasitic on economic plants, the new species Cercospora caricis on Carex folliculata, Cercospora lathyri on Lathyrus maritimus, Glœosporium alnicola on Alnus rugosa, G. falcatum on Benzoin œstivale, G. hydrophylli on Hydrophyllum canadense, Phoma pectinata on Abies pectinata. Phyllosticta steironematis on Steironema ciliatum, Ramularia cichorii on Cichorium intybus, Scolescosporium coryli on Corylus americana, Septoria mollisia on Antennaria neodioica and A. canadensis, S. tenuis on Carex tenuis, Stagonospora convolvuli on Convolvulus sepium, and Dothidella vacciniicola on Vaccinium atrococcum ; the newly named form Phoma bumeliœ (P. (Sphœropsis) maculans) on Bumelia ; and the newly formed combination Septoglœum ochroleucum (Septoria ochroleuca) on Castanea dentata.

Texas parasitic fungi.—New species and amended descriptions, B. C. THARP (*Mycologia, 9 (1917), No. 2, pp. 105–124*).—The pathogenic fungi described in this article, collected in 1914 to 1916 near Austin and in several points in east and northeast Texas, include, besides some previously known, the new species Ascochyta boerhaaviœ, Cercospora acalypharum, C. ammanniœ, C. apiifoliœ, C. arboriœ, C. bidentis, C. bliti, C. capitati, C. carolinensis, C. erythrinicola, C. ficina, C. helenii, C. hydrangeana, C. marrubii, C. mirabilis, C. modiolœ, C. nelumbonis, C. nigri, C. nyssœ, C. piaropi, C. populicola, C. pulcherrimœ, C. regalis, C. rosigena, C. salviicola, C. texensis, C. torœ, Colletotrichum cinnamoni, Coniothyrium rhois, C. ulmi, Exosporium liquidambaris, E. platanorum, E. phoradendri, Napicladium prosopodium, Phleospora pteleœ, Phyllachora texana, Phyllosticta cephalanthi. P. euonymi, P. verbenicola. Ramularia acalyphœ, R. salviicola,

Septoria angularis, S. antirrhinorum, S. argemones, S. asterina, S. hicoriæ, S. urticaria, and *S. wistariæ;* and the new varieties *Cercospora euphorbiæcola tragiæ,* and *C. pulcherrimæ minima.*

Uredinales of Porto Rico based on collections by H. H. Whetzel and E. W. Olive, J. C. ARTHUR (*Mycologia, 9 (1917), No. 2, pp. 55–104*).—Following the collection of fungus material during the spring of 1916 by Whetzel and Olive and its systematic study by the author, 122 species of the Uredinales are listed. A number of these are regarded as new species or treated as new combinations, some being of more or less importance in connection with ornamental or useful plants. A list is given of species previously reported from Porto Rico.

A short-cycled Uromyces of North America, G. R. BISBY (*Abs. in Phytopathology, 7 (1917), No. 1, p. 74*).—It is claimed that there are only 11 species of short-cycled Uromyces found in North America and that these are parasitic upon six families of monocotyledons and dicotyledons.

A systematic and physiological study of rusts, G. M. REED, C. R. HURSH, and W. E. BRENTZEL (*Missouri Sta. Bul. 147 (1917), p. 28*).—A report is given of tests under greenhouse conditions of 46 varieties of oats belonging to 9 species of Avena to determine their susceptibility to the crown rust of oats (*Puccinia coronifera*). Only one variety showed any degree of resistance and on this the rust developed to maturity. Additional tests were made with a number of species of grasses, and although the different grasses are known to be hosts of the rust P. *coronifera*, no infection was obtained by using uredospores from oats, this result indicating the existence of physiological races in this rust.

Notes are briefly reported on rust infection on varieties of wheat. With few exceptions, the varieties tested were all found badly infected with orange leaf rust (P. *triticina*).

A fundamental study of the physiological relation of the powdery mildews to their hosts, G. M. REED (*Missouri Sta. Bul. 147 (1917), p. 27*).—The author summarizes the results of previous investigations (E. S. R., 35, p. 651) in which he described the relation of powdery mildew to varieties of Triticum and Avena. In addition to the data previously reported, it is stated that a large number of experiments have been conducted with varieties of barley in relation to barley mildew, most of the varieties tested proving quite susceptible.

Control of Phytophthora infestans in the floating gardens of Xochimilco, A. MADARIAGA and R. VILLARREAL (*Bol. Dir. Agr. [Mex.], 2 (1916), No. 2, pp. 55–57*).—This is a discussion of local conditions affecting the success of cultivated plants in the floating gardens, more particularly the tomato, as affected by P. *infestans,* with suggestions for protection against that fungus.

Economic hosts of Sclerotinia libertiana in tidewater Virginia, J. A. Mc-CLINTOCK (*Abs. in Phytopathology, 7 (1917), No. 1, p. 60*).—In the warm, humid climate of tidewater Virginia, *S. libertiana* is said to be a serious parasite of lettuce, snap beans, tomatoes, winter-grown parsley, cauliflower, and eggplants.

A new strain of Puccinia graminis, E. C. STAKMAN and F. J. PIEMEISEL (*Abs. in Phytopathology, 7 (1917), No. 1, p. 73*).—The authors report a rust which behaves differently from any of the common biologic forms of P. *graminis.* This has recently been found on club wheat and a number of wild grasses, and is said to occur only west of the Rocky Mountains in Idaho and Washington, where it seems to take the place of ordinary P. *graminis tritici.*

Grain-smut investigation and control, G. M. REED (*Missouri Sta. Bul. 147 (1917), pp. 27, 28*).—Inoculations with spores of *Sphacelotheca sorghi* were made on 22 varieties of sorghum, including broom corn, kaoliang, and Kafir corn, four of which, feterita, Jerusalem corn, dwarf milo maize, and milo maize, remained free from infection, while all the others gave percentages of infection ranging from less than 1 to 31.

Inoculation experiments with bunt (*Tilletia foetens*) on 15 common varieties of wheat gave infection in all cases, the amount ranging from 8.3 to 62.8 per cent. The effect of date of planting on amount of infection was also tested, planting being made from October 2 to October 30, and it was found that seed planted latest in the year gave the highest degree of infection.

Other infection experiments are reported with oat smuts (*Ustilago avenæ* and *U. levis*), 38 varieties belonging to 10 species of Avena being inoculated with spores of both smuts. Most of the hosts became infected, the percentage of infection varying from less than 2 to more than 88. *A. barbata*, *A. brevis*, and *A. strigosa* remained entirely free from the smuts. Of the common varieties of oats, a few, notably Burt and Early Ripe, remained practically free from infection.

Ecological observations on Ustilago zeæ, A. A. Potter and L. E. Melchers (*Abs. in Phytopathology, 7 (1917), No. 1, pp. 73, 74*).—It having been reported that the nodal buds of maize were particularly subject to smut, the authors made an investigation of the matter. They report that conidia probably do not infect the corn plant directly, but that the result is rather the development of a virulent culture of the fungus in the leaf axil. A plant thus infected may become a center for aerial distribution, or, when rain occurs, the conidia may be washed down or splashed on other leaves.

The formalin treatment for controlling oat smut, J. A. Krall (*Proc. Iowa Acad. Sci., 23 (1916), pp. 593–620*).—Describing the loss annually caused by oat smut in Iowa and reviewing briefly the history and literature of oat-smut control measures, the author reports on his own experiments with treatments. Various fungicidal preparations were employed unsuccessfully as contrasted with formalin, 1 pt. of which to 20 gal. of water controlled the smut without materially decreasing the vitality of the seed. A bibliography is appended.

Some new facts concerning wheat smut, F. D. Heald (*Proc. Wash. State Grain Growers, Shippers and Millers Assoc., 10 (1916), pp. 38–45, figs. 2*).— Stinking smut, one of three types of smut that attack wheat, is the only one now serious in Washington. Recent studies have been noted in part (E. S. R., 34, p. 644). Two new features which stand out with special prominence are the occurrence of partially smutted grains and a general and extensive wind dissemination of the spores. These are discussed in connection with some of the better-known facts.

All or part of the heads of a stool may be smutted, and in a given head the smutting may be total or partial, showing wide variation. There is also great variation in the position and size of the smut mass in partially smutted grains. These grains in seed wheat would rarely be removed in cleaning, nor would the spores be killed by ordinary fungicidal treatment, and it is thought that a certain number will grow, vitiating the results from seed treatment. Fields may become infected by wind-blown spores. The spores of unbroken smut balls are not reached by fungicides, and will retain vitality in the soil for a year or more, though after liberation few remain alive for more than three months in moist soil and none of these are able to survive the winter. The records of spore traps show that during the thrashing period and the few weeks that follow there are probably many smut showers, the summer-fallowed fields becoming thickly strewn with spores borne by the wind.

The prevention of wheat smut, H. M. Woolman (*Proc. Wash. State Grain Growers, Shippers, and Millers Assoc., 10 (1916), pp. 45–49*).—In continuation of the above discussion, the author states that although it is practically impossible by any one process to clean a very smutty lot of seed perfectly, the wind or fanning-mill process, together with the open tank employing copper sulphate and salt or formaldehyde, will probably prove to be the best available means of control through seed treatment. However, this is admittedly inadequate to guard against the presence of partially smutted kernels.

Crop rotation is the best remedy for smut left in the field from former wheat crops, the rotation of oats, barley, or spring wheat with summer fallow being considered as fairly safe. Continuous alteration of wheat and summer fallow should be avoided. Deep plowing seems to help also, as will any operation on the stubble tending to crush the smut balls. Burning is advised in case of heavy stubble. Wind dissemination may occasionally be the sole cause of a smutty crop. Details of experiments regarding the viability of spores in the soil under varying conditions are considered to indicate that very early or very late sowing and replowing the summer fallow have considerable advantages. Another method suggested is tillage of the fallow after rains. Seed should be planted when the temperature is high.

Puccinia graminis on wheat kernels and its relation to subsequent infection, C. W. HUNGERFORD (*Abs. in Phytopathology, 7 (1917), No. 1, p. 73*).—The author briefly reports experiments carried on at Madison, Wis., to determine whether *P. graminis* is able to infect wheat through the seed. Although the work has not been fully completed, the results so far obtained are considered to show that seed wheat infected with *P. graminis* does not cause infection of the wheat plant. Similar experiments have been started in cooperation with the Oregon Experiment Station with wheat infected with *P. glumarum.*

The Pseudopeziza leaf-spot diseases of alfalfa and red clover, F. R. JONES (*Abs. in Phytopathology, 7 (1917), No. 1, p. 70*).—Studies have been made of the Pseudopeziza leaf spots of alfalfa and red clover to determine possible relationships of the parasites as well as other facts regarding their life history.

The author reports having found that both fungi may be obtained in pure culture, slight morphological and distinct physiological differences having been observed. Only ascospores have been found to be produced in nature, while conidialike structures occurred in cultures. The germinating ascospores are said to penetrate the epidermal cells directly, the mycelium developing within the host cells and penetrating the cell walls. The fungus is considered to overwinter on dead leaves which escape decay, and ascospores developed either in old or new apothecia are a source of spring infection.

Experiments in the disinfection of alfalfa seed have shown that this treatment can not be depended upon for the prevention of leaf spot.

Bean mosaic, V. B. STEWART and D. REDDICK (*Abs. in Phytopathology, 7 (1917), No. 1, p. 61*).—The authors report the extensive occurrence in New York in 1916 of a mosaic disease of beans, in some instances practically every plant being affected and the plants rarely setting pods. The disease was most frequently observed on pea beans, but other varieties of both· dry and snap beans showed some infection. Evidence has been obtained which indicates that the disease is seed borne and may be readily transferred by inoculation.

Lima bean mosaic, J. A. McCLINTOCK (*Abs. in Phytopathology, 7 (1917), No. 1, pp. 60, 61*).—The author reports having observed over 25 per cent of several hundred plants of certain varieties of lima beans which were stunted and bore the dwarfed, mottled, wavy leaves characteristic of mosaic. The disease is serious, because the yield on infected plants is greatly decreased and the pods are smaller and malformed.

The celery-rot bacillus, H. WORMALD (*Jour. Agr. Sci. [England], 8 (1917), No. 2, pp. 216–245, pls. 2*).—The author, in pursuance of an account previously given of a celery rot (E. S. R., 34, p. 244), states that the cause of this rot is a bacillus which is described as differing only in minor respects from *Bacillus carotovorus*. Other common vegetables are also susceptible to attack by the organism, which is itself very sensitive to antiseptic and germicidal reagents, also to desiccation.

The development of the æcial stage of Nigredo on red clover, I. E. MELHUS and W. DIEHL (*Abs. in Phytopathology*, 7 (1917), No. 1. p. 70).—Experiments have shown that the uredospore stage of *N. fallens* developed readily on red clover grown in greenhouses when the plants were about 6 in. tall. Subsequently, æcia were observed, and during a period of about two weeks the æcial stage became abundant and continued to develop for about a month when the temperature of the house was raised by increased sunshine.

White clover, alsike, and crimson clover in close proximity to the infected red-clover plants remained free from infection. Repeated attempts to transfer the rust to these hosts were without result, and it is believed that *N. fallens* is autœcious and not heterœcious as heretofore reported.

The æcial stage of the red-clover rust, W. H. DAVIS and A. G. JOHNSON (*Abs. in Phytopathology*, 7 (1917), No. 1. p. 75).—The observations and experiments of the authors are considered to have shown that the red-clover rust (*Uromyces fallens*) is a long-cycled, autœcious species, with pycnia, æcia, uredinia, and telia on the same host.

Two transmissible mosaic diseases of cucumbers, I. C. JAGGER (*Abs. in Phytopathology*, 7 (1917), No. 1, p. 61).—The author states that in addition to the mosaic disease known as white pickle, which has been previously described (E. S. R., 36, p. 350), a second distinct mosaic disease was observed in the vicinity of Rochester, N. Y. This disease is characterized by a mottling of the leaves, but shows no effect on the fruit. It has been repeatedly transmitted to healthy plants by rubbing them with crushed diseased leaves, and has also been transmitted to muskmelons and to summer crookneck squashes.

A Gnomonia on eggplant, C. W. EDGERTON (*Abs. in Phytopathology*, 7 (1917), No. 1, p. 78).—The author reports having observed a species of Gnomonia on old eggplant stems during the winter season at Baton Rouge, La. The fungus has been repeatedly cultured and found similar to, if not identical with, the fungus causing eggplant blight (*Phyllosticta hortorum*). Inoculation experiments, however, have always given negative results. While it is possible that there may be no connection between the two, it is very probable that they are closely related species.

A malnutrition disease of the Irish potato and its control, H. A. EDSON and O. SCHREINER (*Abs. in Phytopathology*, 7 (1917), No. 1, pp. 70, 71).—The authors report the occurrence, in potato fields from Maine to Virginia during the summer of 1916, of a disease of potatoes characterized by a downward curling of the leaf margins accompanied by a bronzing and later a browning but not a yellowing of the foliage. Death of the leaves and sudden collapse of the stems at the ground level followed. Fungi appeared at and above the point of collapse, but investigations indicate that they are only weak parasites acting as contributing factors and that the primary cause of the trouble is malnutrition resulting from insufficient potash or perhaps an excess of nitrates in the presence of a minimum potash supply. In Maine the disease appears to be correlated with certain soil types and certain varieties, though not entirely so. The use of stable manure was found to be an excellent corrective.

The economic importance of mosaic of potato, P. A. MURPHY (*Abs. in Phytopathology*, 7 (1917), No. 1, pp. 72, 73).—As a result of his investigations, the author concludes that in an average crop of 300 bu. per acre there is a loss of 1½ bu. per acre for every 1 per cent of mosaic present. The eating qualities of potatoes produced by mosaic plants are said to be unimpaired.

Strains of Rhizoctonia, J. ROSENBAUM and M. SHAPAVALOV (*Abs. in Phytopathology, 7 (1917), No. 1, pp. 74, 75*).—The authors report having isolated from potato stems a strain of Rhizoctonia which had produced a girdling and hollowing of the stems at or near the surface of the ground. Inoculation and culture experiments with this organism revealed certain characteristics, and it is considered possible that different strains of Rhizoctonia may offer an explanation for the conflicting reports regarding artificial infection.

Will Spongospora subterranea prove serious in Virginia? J. A. McCLINTOCK (*Abs. in Phytopathology, 7 (1917), No. 1, p. 72*).—As a result of planting in Virginia potatoes affected with powdery scab, the author concludes that powdery scab will not be prevalent either on the spring or on the fall planted potatoes even though the seed tubers are infected with the organism.

Host plants of Synchytrium endobioticum, A. D. COTTON (*Roy. Bot. Gard. Kew, Bul. Misc. Inform., No. 10 (1916), pp. 272–275*).—It is said to have been proved beyond doubt that certain potato varieties are absolutely immune to the wart disease organism, *S. endobioticum.* No varieties which appeared resistant after thorough tests have broken down in this respect.

Other plant hosts, however, have been discovered. A few minute sporangia of the wart disease have been known to form on *Solanum dulcamara* and on *S. nigrum.* It is thought that the latter constitutes a greater danger than the former. It is considered as possible that the organism may have spread from wild Solanums to potato in Hungary, where the disease is said to have been first described.

Bordeaux spray for tip burn and early blight of potatoes, A. T. ERWIN (*Iowa Sta. Bul. 171 (1917), pp. 62–75, pls. 2, figs. 6*).—Results are given of five years' experiments with tip burn and early blight of potatoes to determine whether, under corn-belt conditions, these diseases can be dealt with profitably by spraying with Bordeaux mixture.

The author has found that three applications of Bordeaux mixture gave an average annual increase of 10 bu. per acre, five applications 20 bu. per acre, and seven applications 22 bu. per acre. Basing his conclusions on these results, he recommends five sprayings with Bordeaux mixture, the first early in July, the applications to be repeated at approximately 10-day intervals.

A discussion is given of early blight and tip burn, their causes, temperature relations, etc.

Seed potato certification in Nova Scotia, P. A. MURPHY (*Abs. in Phytopathology, 7 (1917), No. 1, p. 72*).—A brief account is given of the method adopted in Nova Scotia for producing seed potatoes for the Bermuda seed trade.

Root disease of sugar cane, J. R. JOHNSON (*Hacienda, 12 (1917), Nos. 4, pp. 117, 118, figs. 2; 5, pp. 146, 147, fig. 1*).—This is a discussion of the destructive root disease of sugar cane, supposed to be caused primarily by *Marasmius sacchari* (though other fungi may be present), with suggestions for lessening injury therefrom, including such measures as insect control, soil selection and management, drainage, rotation, and resistance.

Tobacco diseases and their control, J. R. JOHNSON (*Hacienda, 11 (1916), No. 12, pp. 372–374, figs. 3; 12 (1916), Nos. 1, pp. 26–28, figs. 3; 2, pp. 63, 64, figs. 3; 3, pp. 91–93, figs. 2; 12 (1917), No. 4, pp. 124–126, figs. 2*).—Descriptions are given of several diseases, rots, or other sources of loss affecting the tobacco plant during its life or preparation for storage or market.

A Colletotrichum leaf spot of turnips, B. B. HIGGINS (*U. S. Dept. Agr., Jour. Agr. Research, 10 (1917), No. 4, pp. 157–162, pls. 2*).—The attention of the author, at the Georgia Experiment Station, was called in 1914 to a leaf-spot disease of young turnip plants near Macon, Ga. The spots are said to be ¼ in. or less in diameter, circular in outline, and of a pale green or straw color. The disease also attacks the stems and seed pods, but experiments indicate that the fungus is not carried over in the living seed.

The organism causing the disease has been isolated and inoculation experiments have proved its pathogenicity. The organism is described by P. A. Saccardo as *C. higginscanum* n. sp. The author believes that the disease occurs in various portions of Georgia.

Temperature relations of apple rot fungi, C. Brooks and J. S. Cooley (*Abs. in Phytopathology, 7 (1917), No. 1, p. 76*).—It is stated that most apple rot fungi will grow at a lower temperature on corn-meal agar than on fruit and at a lower temperature on ripe fruit than on green fruit. With several, if not all, of the storage-rot fungi the initial stages of rotting are found to be more inhibited at low temperatures than is the germination of the spores. Various rots may finally make a fairly rapid development at temperatures at which the fungus is at first barely able to make a start. Even at favorable temperatures most of the fungi pass through a period of incubation on apples that is not evident on culture media.

Black root rot of the apple, F. D. Fromme and H. E. Thomas (*U. S. Dept. Agr., Jour. Agr. Research, 10 (1917), No. 4, pp. 163–174, pls. 3, fig. 1; abs. in Phytopathology, 7 (1917), No. 1, p. 77*).—The authors give a detailed account, in continuation of a previous note (E. S. R., 36, p. 649), of their investigation at the Virginia Experiment Station on the black root rot of the apple, which is said to be an infectious disease of considerable economic importance in the orchard sections of Virginia.

No prominent leaf characters have been observed for the disease, but the black encrustations on the surface of affected roots and the accompanying dark zonations in the bark and wood are considered reliable diagnostic characters. Field observations show that the root rot is infectious but that its progress is comparatively slow. Apple trees planted on newly cleared land are said to be more liable to attack than those on land cleared and cultivated for some time prior to planting.

Three species of Xylaria have been obtained in pure cultures from the apple roots, *X. hypoxylon*, which proved to be an active wound parasite, *X. polymorpha*, which seems to be only slightly pathogenic, and an undetermined species. *X. hypoxylon* is considered the chief cause of the root rot in Virginia.

Exclusion of the fungus, proper attention to cultivation, and elimination of contact with stumps of forest land are recommended as control measures.

Treatment of apple canker diseases, J. C. Whitten (*Missouri Sta. Bul. 147 (1917), pp. 43, 44*).—In a previous publication (E. S. R., 35, p. 848), the author reported the checking of about 90 per cent of apple tree cankers by the use of copper sulphate or corrosive sublimate. Observations have been continued during the past year to determine whether the cankers would break out again, but no further progress has been noticed in wounds which were apparently healed during 1913 and 1914.

In connection with this treatment, the author reports that mixing corrosive sublimate with paint has proved as effective in controlling canker as treating the scraped parts with the disinfectant and later painting for protection. In this treatment, the corrosive sublimate is dissolved in turpentine and mixed in proper proportion into the paint.

Jonathan spot, C. Brooks and J. S. Cooley (*Abs. in Phytopathology, 7 (1917), No. 1, p. 76*).—The authors claim that Jonathan spot increases up to a temperature of 20° C. (68° F.), but it is entirely inhibited at 30°. The disease, it is said, can be readily produced in saturated air in closed moist chambers, but seldom develops in a stirred air of 70 to 95 per cent relative humidity.

Control of apple scab by bleaching powder, W. S. Brock and W. A. Ruth (*Abs. in Phytopathology, 7 (1917), No. 1, p. 76*).—The authors claim that the application of bleaching powder (calcium hypochlorite) to apple trees in 1916 reduced apple scab from 50 to 11.2 per cent without any injury to fruit or foliage.

Observations on pear blight in Illinois, F. L. Stevens, W. A. Ruth, G. L. Peltier, and J. R. Malloch (*Abs. in Phytopathology, 7 (1917), No. 1, p. 75*).—Experiments made by applying *Bacillus amylovorus* in suspension in water to pear buds in 1915 are believed to have indicated in 1916 that the bacilli did not hibernate in the buds. Infection of the spurs from hold-over trunk cankers was observed in 1916, but the organism appeared to be dead in all twig cankers. Leaves are said to be at no time naturally infected from the exterior, and on June 1 blades and pedicles could not be inoculated through the fruit while pedicles were still susceptible. The application of Bordeaux mixture is said to have controlled the floral infection without reducing the set of fruit.

Studies on peach yellows and little peach, M. A. Blake, M. T. Cook, and C. A. Schwarze (*Abs. in Phytopathology, 7 (1917), No. 1, pp. 76, 77*).—The results of investigations on these diseases are briefly described, and it is claimed that pits from diseased trees failed to germinate. Budding experiments with diseased buds indicate that the appearance of the disease in young trees varies with the source of bud wood.

Second progress report on investigations of leaf spot of cherries and plums in Wisconsin, G. W. Keitt (*Abs. in Phytopathology, 7 (1917), No. 1, pp. 75, 76*).—In continuation of investigations on the leaf spot due to *Coccomyces hiemalis* (E. S. R., 36, p. 149), the author reports having found that the trouble is satisfactorily controlled by the use of Bordeaux mixture of various strengths and lime-sulphur. Atomic sulphur, barium-sulphur, and self-boiled lime-sulphur in parallel applications did not control the disease satisfactorily.

A new disease of cacao, M. Turconi (*Atti R. Accad. Lincei, Rend. Cl. Sci. Fis., Mat. e Nat., 5. ser., 26 (1917), I, No. 1, pp. 75-78*).—In a preliminary note the author records the occurrence on *Theobroma cacao*, in the botanical garden at Pavia, of a leaf spot fungus described as a new species under the name *Physalospora theobromæ*, and of two associated fungi also described as new, which are given the respective names, *Stachylidium theobromæ* and *Helminthosporium theobromæ*.

Diseases of chayote, R. Ramírez (*Bol. Dir. Agr. [Mex.], 2 (1916), No. 2, p. 58, pl. 1*).—The chayote is subject to injury by Cuscuta, *Helix humboldtiana*, and a disease affecting leaves and fruits associated with a Sphærella presumably as a primary agent and with several fungi named as secondary.

Mango disease in Yucatan, R. Ramírez (*Bol. Dir. Agr. [Mex.], 2 (1916), No. 2, pp. 59, 60, pls. 2*).—A disease attacking branchlets, flowers, and fruits of mango, also other plants, is described as due to *Glæosporium mangiferæ*.

Additional suggestions on treatment of hazel blight, M. B. Waite (*Amer. Nut Jour., 3 (1915), No. 6, p. 97*).—The same treatment is recommended for hazel blight that has been found successful with black knot of plum and cherry, which yields to cutting out the blighted portions in February or early March before the spores have matured, and applying a dormant spray of Bordeaux mixture. Eradication of wild hazel is also considered important.

Winterkilling, sun scald, or sour sap of pecans, S. M. McMurran (*Amer. Nut Jour., 3 (1915), No. 5, p. 82*).—This is a descriptive account of the influence of cold weather succeeding warm days in November as causing injury or death to pecan trees which had renewed growth in the fall after a serious check due to summer drought. Wrapping the trees with sacking for about 4 ft. above the ground practically prevented the trouble.

Notes on pecan diseases, S. M. McMurran (*Amer. Nut Jour.*, *4* (*1916*), *No. 6*, *pp. 81, 86, figs. 3*).—In a block of pecan trees sprayed for scab with Bordeaux mixture five times about two weeks apart, from May 29 to August 8, 1914, the brown leaf spot disease (*Cercospora fusca*) was effectively controlled, while the unsprayed trees were almost entirely defoliated by September. Nursery leaf blight (*Phyllosticta caryæ*) was controlled with from three to five sprayings. A defoliation of pecan occurring in southern Louisiana in late summer appeared to be associated with water supply. A dieback observed at a point in Louisiana and one in Georgia were apparently due to soil and seasonal conditions. Black pit, a nut disease said not to have been described previously, is thought to be nonparasitic in character.

Blight and melaxuma of walnut, C. W. Beers (*Amer. Nut Jour.*, *4* (*1916*), *No. 2, pp. 18, 19, 21, figs. 3*).—Both blight and melaxuma of walnut are reported to have been brought under study and control.

An investigation of forest tree diseases, G. M. Reed, Lucile Keene, Jessie Cline, and Emily Hardesty (*Missouri Sta. Bul. 147* (*1917*), *pp. 28, 29*).—The authors report having collected a number of polyporous fungi on living trees during the year, among them *Fomes fraxinophilus* on ash, *F. robiniæ* on black locust, and *F. everhartii* on oak. Studies on fungi connected with the decay of fence posts are said to be in progress.

Boleti and mycorrhiza upon forest trees and an unusual mycorrhiza upon white oak, L. H. Pennington (*Abs. in Phytopathology, 7* (*1917*), *No. 1, p. 74*).—Six species of Boletus are reported as connected with mycorrhiza of forest trees, usually oaks. A peculiar form of mycorrhiza found upon white-oak roots is briefly described. Attempts to inoculate the roots of other trees with this fungus have thus far failed.

Blight-resistant chestnuts from China, G. H. Corsan (*Amer. Nut Jour.*, *2* (*1915*), *No. 4, p. 54, figs. 2*).—The author notes the observations made by Meyer in the course of studies carried out by him in northern China (E. S. R., 35, pp. 29, 140) regarding the high resistance of a Chinese chestnut (*Castanea mollissima*) to chestnut blight, the wounds caused by the attack on this species healing spontaneously.

Breeding chestnuts for disease control (*Amer. Nut Jour.*, *4* (*1916*), *No. 4, pp. 56, 57, figs. 4*).—Brief mention is made of work in progress in the testing of hybrids between the American native chinquapin and Japanese chestnut. The F₁ and F₂ hybrids are highly resistant to the chestnut bark disease and show other desirable characters, as do also four generations of hybrids between Japanese and Chinese chestnuts.

Violent outbreak of Oïdium on oak in France, E. Noffray (*Jour. Agr. Prat.*, *n. ser.*, *29* (*1916*), *No. 19, p. 326*).—A brief description is given of the mode of attack by Oïdium on oak, which, it is said, has not ceased since the time of its introduction to cause damage and which is becoming serious in Sologne.

Oïdium on oak, F. Convert (*Jour. Agr. Prat.*, *n. ser.*, *29* (*1916*), *No. 20, pp. 343, 344*).—The author, replying to the article noted above, states that an American oak which does well in France is resistant to Oïdium.

American oaks resistant to Oïdium in Sologne, E. Noffray (*Jour. Agr. Prat.*, *n. ser.*, *30* (*1917*), *No. 3, pp. 54, 55*).—Following up the information noted above, the author made examination of a number of oaks of the American species *Quercus palustris* in Sologne, finding them practically free from attack by Oïdium.

A species of Chrysomyxa new to North America, H. S. JACKSON (*Abs. in Phytopathology, 7 (1917), No. 1, p. 78*).—The author reports a short-cycled form referable to the genus Chrysomyxa occurring on leaves of *Picea engelmannii.*

Mycelium of the white pine blister rust, R. H. COLLEY (*Abs. in Phytopathology, 7 (1917), No. 1, p. 77*).—The author describes some of the morphological characters of the mycelium of *Cronartium ribicola* as it occurs on the white pine.

Pycnial scars, an important diagnostic character for the white pine blister rust, R. H. COLLEY (*Abs. in Phytopathology, 7 (1917), No. 1, p. 77*).—The occurrence of scars due to pycnia is said to offer a valuable diagnostic character for the identification of the white-pine blister rust.

"Black thread" disease of Hevea in Burma, J. F. DASTUR (*Dept. Agr. Burma Bul. 14 (1916), pp. 4, pl. 1*).—A brief account is given of the development and spread of the black thread disease of Hevea in Burma due to *Phytopthora* sp. The fungus remains dormant in the tissues during the monsoon after tapping is stopped, and resumes activity when tapping is resumed. The principal measures recommended as preventive are thinning out thickly planted areas, removal of diseased fruits, and suspension of tapping on trees showing black thread.

Phytophthora sp. on Hevea brasiliensis, J. F. DASTUR (*Mem. Dept. Agr. India, Bot. Ser., 8 (1916), No. 5, pp. 217-232, figs. 10*).—This is a more detailed account than that above noted of the Phytophthora disease of *H. brasiliensis,* which is thought to have been present in Burma since 1903, at least on Hevea fruits.

The effects of the fungus attack on the tapping areas and in the epidermal cells of the fruit are described, as are also studies in the morphology and biology of the fungus. These are claimed to show that there may be two stem diseases present in *H. brasiliensis* due to different species of Phytophthora, one of these being *P. faberi*. In those parts of Burma where the rainfall is not excessive, the author found that suspension of tapping during the rainy season checked the disease.

ECONOMIC ZOOLOGY—ENTOMOLOGY.

New mammals from North and Middle America, E. A. GOLDMAN (*Proc. Biol. Soc. Wash.; 30 (1917), pp. 107-116*).—The San Miguel Island opossum (*Didelphis marsupialis particeps*) from San Miguel Island, Panama; savanna marmosa (*Marmosa mexicana savannarum*) from Panama; Bangs collared peccary (*Pecari angulatus bangsi*) from Panama; Pinacate desert mouse (*Peromyscus eremicus papagensis*) from Sonora, Mex.; Nevada bushy tailed wood rat (*Neotoma cinerea lucida*) from Nevada; Wyoming kangaroo rat (*Perodipus ordii luteolus*) from Wyoming; black naped agouti (*Dasyprocta punctata nuchalis*) from Panama; Richmond's agouti (*D. punctata richmondi*) from Nicaragua; Nelson's false vampire (*Vampyrus spectrum nelsoni*) from Vera Cruz, Mex.; and the northern yellow-shouldered bat (*Sturnira lilium parvidens*) from Papayo, Guerrero, Mexico, are described as new.

The conservation of our northern mammals, C. G. HEWITT (*Com. Conserv. Canada Rpt., 7 (1916), pp. 32-40, pls. 2*).—This paper deals particularly with the caribou, musk ox, etc., and means for their protection. Colored maps show the approximate distribution of the barren ground caribou (*Rangifer arcticus*) and musk ox (*Ovibos moschatus*) and related forms in Canada.

Control of the pocket gopher in California (*California Sta. Bul. 281 (1917), pp. 15, figs. 4*).—The first of the two parts of this bulletin (pp. 3-13), by J. Dixon, deals with the natural history of the pocket gopher and various methods of control; the second part (pp. 14, 15), by E. R. de Ong, with a method of poisoning pocket gophers, which consists in the use of sweet potatoes, parsnips, or carrots, 8 qt.; flour paste, 0.5 pint; strychnin alkaloid, powdered, 0.25 oz.; and saccharin, 0.0625 oz.

Varying hares of the prairie Provinces, N. Criddle (*Agr. Gaz. Canada,* *4 (1917), No. 4, pp. 260-263*).—*Lepus americanus* and its various geographic races, with a range in western Canada almost as extensive as the woodlands, is a source of great injury to young trees through gnawing and eating the bark. The destruction of acres of aspen poplars in this way after a severe winter is said to be not an uncommon sight. Larches are also denuded of their bark, while spruce and pine are generally stripped of their branches. The greatest injury thus far recorded is said to have occurred during the winter of 1915-16. Enormous numbers of aspen poplars were destroyed in southern Manitoba and Saskatchewan and the infestation appears to have extended far northward. Practically all kinds of trees and shrubs were attacked, plum, cherry, and apple trees frequently being cut to the ground and in some instances quite old orchards were badly injured.

Their natural enemies are briefly considered, as are methods of protection by means of poultry netting, poisoning, and shooting.

On the ecology of the vegetation of Breckland, E. P. Farrow (*Jour. Ecology,* *5 (1917), No. 1, pp. 1-18, pls. 6, fig. 1*).—This deals with the general effects of rabbits on the vegetation.

Description of a new race of Say's ground squirrel from Wyoming, A. H. Howell (*Proc. Biol. Soc. Wash., 30 (1917), pp. 105, 106*).—*Callospermophilus lateralis caryi* n. subsp. is described from Wyoming.

Two new pocket mice from Wyoming, E. A. Goldman (*Proc. Biol. Soc. Wash., 30 (1917), pp. 147, 148*).

Mutanda ornithologica. I, II, H. C. Oberholser (*Proc. Biol. Soc. Wash., 30 (1917), pp. 75, 76, 125, 126*).

The birds of South America, Lord Brabourne and C. Chubb (*London: R. H. Porter, 1912, vol. 1, pp. XIX+504, pl. 1*).—This first volume, which consists of a list of South American birds, terminates a proposed 16-volume work, owing to the death of Lord Brabourne at the front in 1915. It contains a systematic index, a classified and systematic list of 4.561 forms representing 874 genera, and an alphabetical index.

Illustrations to the birds of South America, H. Grönvold (*London: John Wheldon & Co., vol. 2, 1915, pt. 1, pls. 19; 1916, pts. 2, pls. 4; 3, pls. 4; 4, pls. 4; 5, pls. 4; 1917, pt. 6, pp. 11, pls. 3*).—These six parts consist of colored plates of the game birds and waterfowl of South America, originally intended to form part of 400 hand colored plates illustrating the above-mentioned work. Short descriptive notes by H. K. Swann on most of the species illustrated preface the same.

A new honey eater from the Marianne Islands, A. Wetmore (*Proc. Biol. Soc. Wash., 30 (1917), pp. 117, 118*).—*Myzomela rubratra saffordi* n. subsp. is described from the islands of Guam and Saipan.

A new shrew from Nova Scotia, H. H. T. Jackson (*Proc. Biol. Soc. Wash., 30 (1917), pp. 149, 150*).—A new shrew is described under the name *Sorex fumeus umbrosus.*

Description of a new genus of Anatidæ, H. C. Oberholser (*Proc. Biol. Soc. Wash., 30 (1917), pp. 119, 120*).—The genus Horizonetta is erected for the Laysan teal (*Anas laysanensis*).

Notes on rearing insects for experimental purposes and life history work, A. M. Wilcox (*Psyche, 24 (1917), No. 1, pp. 7-12, pls. 2*).

The growth of insect blood cells in vitro, R. W. Glaser (*Psyche, 24 (1917),
No. 1, pp. 1-7, pl. 1*).—This is a report of observations on the morphology and
behavior of growing insect blood cells, made during the course of a study of the
pathological changes which take place in insect tissue, in which the tissue was
cultivated in vitro.

Toxic values and killing efficiency of the arsenates, A. L. Lovett and R. H.
Robinson (*U. S. Dept. Agr., Jour. Agr. Research, 10 (1917), No. 4, pp. 199-
207*).—This is a report of work carried on at the Oregon Experiment Station
in continuation of that of Tartar and Wilson previously noted (E. S. R., 34, p.
548). The results afford further verification of the earlier work and give material data on (1) the comparative time and (2) the approximate amount of lead
hydrogen arsenate and basic lead arsenate required to kill small caterpillars and
nearly mature caterpillars; and (3) the proportion of these arsenates devoured
by the small and mature caterpillars that passes through the alimentary canal
of the larvæ. The work has been summarized by the author as follows:

" Lead hydrogen arsenate has a higher killing efficiency at a given dilution
than either calcium or basic lead arsenate. It requires a longer period of time
to kill the nearly mature caterpillars than the small forms. All of the arsenic
devoured by the insects in feeding upon sprayed foliage is not assimilated, but a
portion passes through the intestinal tract in the excrement. The percentage
amount of the arsenic assimilated depends upon the arsenate used; lead hydrogen arsenate was assimilated readily and most of the arsenic was retained in the
tissue, while much of the basic lead arsenate was found in the excrement. It
requires approximately 0.1595 mg. of arsenic pentoxid to kill 1,000 small tent
caterpillars and approximately 1.84 mg. of arsenic pentoxid to kill 1,000 nearly
mature tent caterpillars, irrespective of the particular arsenate used as a spray.

" Preliminary experiments on the burning effects of calcium arsenate indicate
too severe injury to warrant the practical use of this spray."

Winter cover washes, A. H. Lees (*Ann. Appl. Biol., 2 (1916), No. 4, pp. 245-
250*).—In continuation of work previously noted (E. S. R., 34, p. 253), it was
found that the best cover wash consists of lime 30 lbs., glue 2 lbs., potassium
dichromate ¼ oz., and water 10 gal. "This lime-glue-dichromate mixture has
been tried against ordinary lime wash at Long Ashton and has given decidedly
superior results. An application to an apple tree stopped aphis hatching to
such an extent that hardly an aphis was to be seen on it throughout the season
though control trees were very badly attacked. The tree stood out all the
season from its fellows by the healthy green uncurled leaves and at the end of
the season by its very numerous well-developed fruit buds."

Accessory wetting substances with special reference to paraffin emulsions,
A. H. Lees (*Ann. Appl. Biol., 3 (1917), No. 4, pp. 141-149, fig. 1*).—This discussion is accompanied by a table which gives the results of tests of the wetting
power of paraffin emulsions and of other auxiliary wetting agents on certain
natural surfaces.

The author concludes that there is no object in introducing greater quantities of paraffin or soap since a 2 per cent soap-paraffin emulsion (20 lbs. soap
and 2 gal. of paraffin to 100 gal. water) gives perfect wetting. The work has
shown that it is not possible to reduce the quantity of either the paraffin or
soap without destroying the desirable qualities of the mixture, and that the
above mentioned mixture is the cheapest that can be used which at the same
time has the highest wetting power.

"The value of this 2 per cent emulsion lies not so much in its own killing
power as in the fact that it can act as a carrier, so to speak, for other fungicidal
or insecticidal bodies which, used alone, would prove themselves insufficient to

kill. Thus, liver of sulphur, used alone, has no great controlling effect on American gooseberry mildew but, combined with paraffin emulsion, has given promising results in a commercial scale experiment undertaken by Barker and myself. In the direction of insect control it also shows promise. While dilute solutions of nicotin are without decided action on adult caterpillars or difficultly killed beetles, such as *Byturus tomentosus*, the raspberry beetle, it has been found possible, at any rate on the small scale, to kill these by uniting the same nicotin solution with 2 per cent paraffin emulsion."

[Progress report of investigational work in entomology] (*Missouri Sta. Bul. 147 (1917), pp. 32–34*).—In dusting and spraying experiments on field corn for the control of the corn ear worm, by L. Haseman, six different treatments were applied on an area of 2 acres on creek bottom land, but the worms were so scarce that the results did not justify the expense of application. One plat dusted with 3 parts of arsenate of lead powder and 1 part of powdered sulphur showed a reduction in the infestation of 50 per cent, while another plat sprayed with a solution containing 1 tablespoonful of arsenate of lead powder to 1 gal. of water showed a reduction of 75 per cent, but on a plat of upland corn numerous treatments did not appear to check the pest in any degree.

Other work briefly reported upon includes investigations of the Hessian fly-resistant qualities of different varieties of wheat, by L. Haseman and C. G. Vinson, an account of which by Haseman has been previously noted (E. S. R., 35, p. 759); of insect pests of melon and related crops, by L. Haseman; of insects injurious to nursery stock, by L. Haseman, K. C. Sullivan, and A. H. Hollinger; and of the scale insects of Missouri, by A. H. Hollinger.

Report of the State entomologist on injurious insects and fungi of trees in 1914, T. H. Schöyen (*Indber. Norske Skogv., 1914, pp. 150–155, pl. 1*).—This report on the occurrence of important insect enemies and fungus diseases includes an account of the damage caused to trees by mice.

Preliminary account of entomological work in 1914, B. N. Zolotarevskiĭ (*Predvaritel'nyi Otchet o Rabotakh po Entomologii v 1914. Stavropol: Selsk. Khoz. Opytn. Sta., 1915, pp. 12*).—This report deals with the occurrence of the more important insects of the year, particularly those attacking cereal crops.

Some East African insects of economic importance, R. H. Deakin (*Ann. Appl. Biol., 2 (1916), No. 4, pp. 241–244*).—Brief notes based upon observations during a period of 18 months.

Insect enemies of man and the household and the diseases they convey, A. Berlese (*Insetti delle Case e dell' Uomo e Malattie che Diffondono. Milan: Ulrico Hoepli, 1917, pp. XII+293, figs. 100*).—A small handbook.

Household and camp insects, E. P. Felt (*N. Y. State Mus. Bul. 194 (1917), pp. 84, figs. 41*).—This is a summary of information on insects of the household and camp, particular attention being given to control measures.

Studies on Coccobacillus acridiorum and on certain intestinal organisms of locusts, E. M. DuPorte and J. Vanderleck (*Ann. Ent. Soc. Amer., 10 (1917), No. 1, pp. 47–62*).—Part 1 of this report of studies, made at McGill University, consists of experiments on the control of locusts by the use of *C. acridiorum*, and part 2 of descriptive studies on *C. acridiorum* and 16 related native organisms. The results indicate that the biological method for the control of the locust can not take the place of the measures now in use under the conditions which obtain in eastern Canada.

The pathogenicity of *C. acridiorum* was tested for all species of locusts and grasshoppers, seven in number, commonly occurring in large numbers in the region. *Gryllus pennsylvanicus*, one of the common field crickets, was also found to be susceptible to the disease. The yellow bear caterpillar [(*Spilosoma*) *Diacrisia virginica*] and the Colorado potato beetle, larvæ and adults, were also tested, and all individuals of the former were dead in less than 48 hours, but the latter was not susceptible to the disease.

The azalea lace bug, Stephanitis pyrioides, E. L. Dickerson and H. B. Weiss (*Ent. News, 28 (1917), No. 3, pp. 101–105, pl. 1*).—A report of studies of the morphology and biology of this tingitid which has recently become abundant and widespread enough in New Jersey to do considerable damage to azaleas.

This species, which was originally described by Scott from Japan in 1874, is said to have been introduced into New Jersey in the egg stage on evergreen azaleas from that country. It is also known to occur at Bala, Pa., and Washington, D. C., and in Holland. The nymphs and adults feed on the undersurface of the leaves, abstracting the sap and causing a discoloration of the foliage on the upper surface. In severe infestations the leaves become almost white, many of them drying completely and dropping off. The underside of the leaves is disfigured by the insect's excrement.

In central and southern New Jersey, the egg. in which stage the winter is passed, hatches the latter part of May. The length of each of the five nymphal stages varies from three to six days. The appearance of the adults the latter part of June is closely followed by oviposition which lasts for a period of two weeks. These eggs require on an average two weeks for hatching. Growth is completed by the last week in July and the first week in August and many new adults are present. During the first two weeks of August eggs are again laid and by the middle of and last week in September many adults of this brood are present, the overwintering eggs being deposited at this time and during the first part of October. Thus there are three broods in southern New Jersey, the average length of each being about one month. In the central and northern parts of the State, however, there are only two and a partial third.

The lace bug on azaleas may be controlled by spraying with whale-oil soap at the rate of 5 or 6 lbs. to 50 gal. of water, preferably shortly after the overwintering eggs have hatched.

The Cicadellidæ of Wisconsin, with description of new species, J. G. Sanders and D. M. DeLong (*Ann. Ent. Soc. Amer., 10 (1917), No. 1, pp. 79–97, figs. 49*).—The authors list 206 species and varieties representing 38 genera, of which 13 species are described as new.

Spraying for apple sucker (Psylla mali), F. R. Petherbridge (*Ann. Appl. Biol., 2 (1916), No. 4, pp. 230–234*).—"These experiments indicate that lime and salt [lime 150 lbs., salt 30 lbs., and water 100 gal.] may be effective in preventing a large proportion of apple sucker eggs from hatching. Lime wash was also fairly effective. Soft soap and nicotin, or treacle and nicotin, were the most effective after the suckers had hatched. Spraying to prevent the eggs from hatching is not sufficient to keep this pest under control, but should be followed by an application of nicotin and soft soap, or treacle and nicotin, to kill those which have hatched."

Some observations on the egg of Psylla mali, A. H. Lees (*Ann. Appl. Biol., 2 (1916), No. 4, pp. 251–257, figs. 9*).—A brief report of a morphological and embryological study.

Plant lice on. potatoes, W. R. Brown (*Rural New Yorker, 76 (1917), No. 4446, p. 1053, fig. 1*).—This records serious injury to the potato in Hampshire County, Mass., by the potato aphis during the summer of 1917.

An instance is cited of a promising 8-acre field which was killed by the plant lice before the tops were half grown. The first application of blackleaf 40 was inefficient due to too great a dilution. The second application killed the aphids, but the plants had been so weakened by the lice and the turning of the potato tops with a hand rake in order that the spray might hit the underside of the leaves that they died in a short time.

J. S. Regan, of the Massachusetts Agricultural College, who has conducted experiments, recommends the use of blackleaf 40, 1.25 teaspoonfuls, and 1 oz. of soap to a gallon of water, applied with an angle disk nozzle carried close to the ground so that it will direct the spray upwards and hit the underside of the leaves. Whale or fish-oil soap used at the rate of 1 lb. to 6 gal. of water is said to be nearly if not quite as good. Either of these insecticides properly applied was found to be from 98 to 99 per cent effective.

The louse and its relation to disease.—Its life history and habits and how to deal with it, B. F. Cummings (*Brit. Museum (Nat. Hist.), Econ. Ser., No. 2 (1915), pp. 16, pl. 1, figs. 2*).—This is a popular account.

The rate of increase of the pink bollworm in green bolls in the period July to November, 1916, L. H. Gough (*Min. Agr. Egypt, Tech. and Sci. Serv. Bul. 13 (1917), pp. 20, pl. 1*).—The data here given are based upon 106,400 bolls examined.

While the highest percentage of bolls attacked was found the second week of October, the largest number of bolls attacked must have existed during the third week in September. " If the figures on which our calculations have been based are accepted as sufficiently accurate, it can be estimated that when at its maximum the Gelechia population reached at least 4.500 individuals per thousand cotton plants (500 holes). Supposing 26.000 plants to the feddan [1.04 acres], this gives the alarming total of about 120.000 worms to the feddan. . .

" Considering that Gelechia is an imported pest, which has been in Egypt less than ten years, its increase has been enormous. It now occurs, everywhere where cotton is grown in Egypt ; in the last week of October, 87 per cent of the green bolls in Lower, 78 per cent in Middle, and 60 per cent in Upper Egypt were attacked by it ; and we have received specimens of the adult from the desert at Romani."

On the rate of increase of Gelechia gossypiella larvæ in green bolls during 1916, L. [H.] Gough (*Bul. Soc. Ent. Egypte, 9 (1916), No. 4, pp. 113–115*).—Substantially noted above.

The pink bollworm, J. P. Buchanan (*Cong. Rec., 55 (1917), No. 126, pp. 7140–7143*).—An address in which attention is called to the danger of this important cotton pest becoming established in the United States.

What effect has flooding of a cotton field by infiltration from high Nile on the numbers of the pink bollworm in that field? (*Bul. Soc. Ent. Egypte, 9 (1916), No. 4, pp. 105–108*).—It is pointed out that since (*Gelechia*) *Pectinophora gossypiella* pupates to a very large extent on the ground amongst fallen leaves, etc., it is very probable that a heavy flooding lasting for weeks will cause the death of the pupæ and pupating larvæ. Since *Earias insulana* larvæ pupate to a much greater extent on the plants they are much less likely to be destroyed by flooding.

Sciara tritici, a fly injurious to seedlings, F. W. Edwards and C. B. Williams (*Ann. Appl. Biol., 2 (1916), No. 4, pp. 253–262*).—This dipteran is reported to be the source of injury to Primula seedlings.

The mosquitoes of North and Central America and the West Indies, L. O. Howard, H. G. Dyar, and F. Knab (*Carnegie Inst. Washington Pub. 159, vol. 4 (1917), pp. 525–1064*).—This second part of the systematic description, the first part of which comprises volume 3 previously noted (E. S. R., 34, p. 453), completes the work. In these two volumes the authors recognize 380 species (besides two which are synonyms, as pointed out in the appendix) included in 25 genera occurring within the North American Continent from the southern edge of Canada to the Isthmus of Panama, including the Antilles and Trinidad. Adding to these the species previously mentioned as not included and the ones described since the appearance of volume 3, there is a total of 398 described species from the region included in this work.

In the tribe Sabethini (pp. 19–187 of vol. 3) 8 genera and 85 species are recognized, including Sabethes, represented by 3 species; Sabethinus, 2 species; Sabethoides, 1 species; Limatus, 3 species; Wyeomyia, 65 species (4 new to science) ; Prosopolepis, 1 species; Lesticocampa, 5 species (2 new) ; and Joblotia, 3 species. In the tribe Culicini (pp. 189–523 of vol. 3 and pp. 525–1038 of vol. 4) 17 genera and 297 species are treated, including Dinomimetes, represented by 1 species; Deinocerites, 5 species; Dinanamesus, 1 species; Culex, 104 species (6 new) ; Carrollia, 2 species; Lutzia, 2 species (1 new) ; Culiseta, 6 species; Mansonia, 7 species; Psorophora, 29 species; Aedes, 83 species (5 new) ; Hæmagogus, 4 species; Orthopodomyia, 5 species; Aedeomyia, 1 species; Uranotænia, 11 species (1 new) ; Megarhinus, 11 species; Anopheles, 21 species (1 new) ; and Cœlodiazesis, 1 species.

Under each species are given the synonymy with references to the literature; copies of the original description and the original descriptions of the synonyms; detailed descriptions of the male, female, and larva, when known; distribution, including a full citation of localities, date, and collector; and what is known of the life history and habits.

It is pointed out that only a few parts of the region have been at all adequately explored, many large areas not at all, so that many more species doubtless wait discovery. A large proportion of the material studied consists of bred specimens with larvæ associated. Sixteen pages are devoted to the yellow-fever mosquito, for which the name *Aedes calopus* is used, though, as shown in a foot-note, the strict application of the rule of priority will necessitate the use of the name *A. argenteus* (Poiret).

Errors noted in the preceding volumes are corrected in an appendix (pp. 1039–1042) to which are added a few supplementary notes.

The relation between the hatching of the eggs and the development of the larvæ of Stegomyia fasciata (Aedes calopus) and the presence of bacteria and yeasts, E. E. ATKIN and A. BACOT (*Parasitology, 9 (1917), No. 4, pp. 482–536*).—The authors find that the larvæ of *S. fasciata* greedily consume both bacteria and yeasts, on which they can thrive in the absence of any other food, whereas in very many instances they fail entirely to develop on a variety of nutritive fluids and particles, including dead bacteria, under sterile conditions. The rearing of adults under sterile conditions is so exceptional that they feel justified in concluding that the presence of bacteria or yeast is a practical necessity for the maintaining of the species.

On the biology and economic significance of Tipula paludosa, J. RENNIE (*Ann. Appl. Biol., 2 (1916), No. 4, pp. 235–240, pl. 1; 3 (1917), No. 2–3, pp. 116–137, pls. 3, figs. 3*).—The first part of this paper consists of a preliminary report of observations; the second part deals with hatching, growth, and habits of the larva.

Notes on New England Tachinidæ, with the description of one new genus and two new species, H. E. SMITH (*Psyche, 24 (1917), No. 2, pp. 54–58*).— *Pseudotachinomyia webberi* n. g. and n. sp. and *Sciasma frontalis* n. sp. from Massachusetts are described.

The larvæ of *Pelatachina pellucida*, which emerged from the larvæ of *Euvanessa antiopa* during August, hibernated in the puparia. From 344 of the lepidopterous larvæ 214 puparia were obtained, but since superparasitism existed to a great extent in the host larvæ, the figures do not indicate the exact percentage of parasitism. This is thought to be the first record of a species of the genus having been reared in North America, although the rearing of the genotype, P. *tibialis* from *Vanessa urticæ* in Europe has been recorded.

Compsilura concinnata, a European species introduced into and established in this country as one of the foremost primary parasites of the gipsy and brown-tail moths, is known to have been reared from more than 20 species of native North American Lepidoptera. It is said to be particularly prolific as a parasite of *E. antiopa*, in certain instances the percentage of parasitism of this host in the New England States being well over 50. The data at hand appear to establish the fact that it hibernates through the winter in New England in the pupa of *E. antiopa*.

The collection of *Exoristoides slossonœ* at Bennington, Vt., is recorded and *Exorista spinipennis* is said to be a synonym of *E. slossonœ*.

Seasonal abundance of flies in Montana, R. R. PARKER (*Ent. News, 28 (1917), No. 6, pp. 278-282, pl. 1*).—This is a report of the seasonal abundance of flies, especially the house fly, based upon work done at Laurel, Mont., during July and August, 1914.

Empusa muscæ versus Musca domestica, H. T. GÜSSOW (*Ann. Appl. Biol., 3 (1917), No. 4, pp. 150-158, pl. 1*).—In discussing the subject the author reviews the work of Hesse, previously referred to (E. S. R., 34, p. 254), and records cultural experiments and other observations on *E. muscæ*.

Report on a trial of tarred felt disks for protecting cabbages and cauliflowers from attacks of the cabbage root fly, J. T. WADSWORTH (*Ann. Appl. Biol., 3 (1917), No. 2-3, pp. 82-92, pl. 1*).—A detailed report of experiments with cabbage and cauliflower, conducted at Manchester University, which show tarred felt disks to be a very effective means of protection. A list of 15 references to literature on the subject is appended.

Two new cambium miners, C. T. GREENE (*U. S. Dept. Agr., Jour. Agr. Research, 10 (1917), No. 6, pp. 313-318, pl. 1*).—The author describes two new species of Agromyza, the larvæ of which mine in the cambium of the living tree, causing a scar which is known as "pith-ray fleck." The mines somewhat resemble those of the cambium miner (*Agromyza pruinosa*) in river birch (*Betula nigra*), an account of which has previously been noted (E. S. R., 30, p. 855).

The species first described is *Agromyza aceris*, which mines down the cambium in the trunk and roots of the red maple (*Acer rubrum*), occurring quite commonly at Falls Church, Va., and French Creek, W. Va. The second species, described as *A. amelanchieris*, was taken from the trunk near the ground and from the roots of the service berry or shadbush (*Amelanchier canadensis*) at French Creek, W. Va.

Investigations of the Anthomyidæ, the larvæ of which are carnivorous, D. KEILIN (*Parasitology, 9 (1917), No. 3, pp. 325-450, pls. 11, figs. 41*).—The species considered include *Melanochelia riparia, Graphomyia maculata, Allognota agromyzina, Phaonia* spp., *Myospila meditabunda, Mydæa* spp., *Hydrotœa* spp., *Muscina* spp., etc.

New genera and species of American muscoid Diptera, C. H. T. TOWNSEND (*Proc. Biol. Soc. Wash., 30 (1917), pp. 43-50*).—Thirteen genera and four species are here described as new.

The viability of Melophagus ovinus, the sheep louse fly, sheep ked, or sheep "tick," GEORGINA SWEET and H. R. SEDDON (*Vet. Jour., 73 (1917), No. 502, pp. 6-14*).—The authors' experiments show that the life of the sheep tick in shed wool is short under uniform temperature, whether cool or moderate. The state of nutrition does not seem to influence the viability of these ticks.

Fleas as a menace to man and domestic animals.—Their life history, habits, and control, J. WATERSTON (*Brit. Museum (Nat. Hist.), Econ. Ser., No. 3 (1916), pp. 21, pl. 1, figs. 6*).—A popular account.

Observations on the larval and pupal stages of **Agriotes obscurus**, G. H. FORD (*Ann. Appl. Biol., 3 (1917), No. 2-3, pp. 97-115, pls. 2, fig. 1*).—This is a report of studies of the immature stages of the common wireworm in Cheshire, North Staffordshire, and South Lancashire.

The life of the larva has been found to be probably four rather than five years. "The larva pupates in an earthen cell in the ground, down to 1 ft. deep; the pupal period is about three weeks; the imago remains resting motionless in the pupal cell for roughly two months, after which it comes to the surface, and hibernates under stones, clods, etc., until the next season."

A bibliography of 20 titles is appended.

Note on attacks of **Phyllotreta vittula** on spring corn, F. R. PETHERBRIDGE (*Ann. Appl. Biol., 3 (1917), No. 2-3, pp. 138, 139*).—The author records the injury caused by this beetle to young barley plants at Warminster and Rothamsted, England.

A flea-beetle which attacks potato plantations on the plateaus, M. T. DAWE (*Rev. Agr. [Colombia], 2 (1916), No. 8, pp. 458-461; abs. in Rev. Appl. Ent., Ser. A, 5 (1917), No. 3, pp. 133, 134*).—*Epitrix nigroœnea*, which closely resembles *E. cucumeris*, is said to attack the young, tender leaves of potatoes as soon as they appear and sometimes ruins an entire plantation in Colombia.

The bark borer (Dendroctonus micans), I. TRÄGÅRDH (*Skogsvårdsför. Tidskr., 14 (1916), No. 5, pp. 484-486, figs. 3*).—This borer, the largest of the European species, destroys an enormous number of both pine and fir trees each year, particularly those which have attained a growth of 25 to 50 years. The paper includes notes on its life history and habits, but no mention is made of control measures.

On new neotropical Curculionidæ, G. A. K. MARSHALL (*Ann. and Mag. Nat. Hist., 8. ser., 18 (1916), No. 108, pp. 449-469; abs. in Rev. Appl. Ent., Ser. A, 5 (1917), No. 3, p. 124*).—One genus, 17 species, and one subspecies, largely from the West Indies and South America, are described as new. The paper includes descriptions of one species and one subspecies of Diaprepes new to science and a review of the paper by Pierce on the genus Diaprepes previously noted (E. S. R., 33, p. 360).

The fauna of British India, including Ceylon and Burma.—Coleoptera. Rhynchophora: Curculionidæ, G. A. K. MARSHALL (*London: Taylor & Francis, 1916, pt. 1, pp. XV+367, figs. 108; rev. in Rev. Appl. Ent., Ser. A, 5 (1917), No. 3, p. 123*).—This volume contains an introductory account of the Curculionidæ in its wide sense, Lacordaire's system of classification being adopted. Two subfamilies, the Brachyderinæ and Otiorrhynchinæ, comprising 342 species, are dealt with in detail. Fifteen genera are erected and 179 species are described as new.

The fauna of British India, including Ceylon and Burma.—Hymenoptera: Ichneumonidæ, I, C. MORLEY (*London: Taylor & Francis, 1913, vol. 3, pp. XXXVI+531, pl. 1, figs. 152*).—This first part of volume 3 of the work previously noted (E. S. R., 15, p. 280), dealing with the subfamily Ichneumones deltoidei, first gives a bibliography of the literature consulted. This is followed by a summary of the known Indian forms, consisting of 406 species representing 140 genera; an index to the Indian hosts; a glossary of terms employed in the work; and a systematic index. In the introduction to the main part which follows, the author discusses the history of the group, metamorphoses, internal and external structure, and classification.

Twelve genera, 99 species, and 3 varieties are described as new.

Guide to the insects of Connecticut.—III, The Hymenoptera, or wasp-like insects of Connecticut, H. L. VIERECK ET AL. (*Conn. State Geol. and Nat. Hist. Survey Bul. 22 (1916), pp. 824, pls. 10, figs. 15*).—This third part of the work previously noted (E. S. R., 26, p. 147) deals with the Hymenoptera, and gives tables for the separation of the families, genera, and species of forms known to occur in Connecticut, together with brief descriptions and records of the distribution of such forms in the State. In collaboration with the author, A. D. McGillivray has prepared the part relating to the superfamily Tenthredinoidea; W. M. Wheeler that relating to the superfamily Formicoidea; C. T. Brues, the superfamily Serphoidea or Proctotrypoidea, and families Cosilidæ and Bethylidæ of the superfamily Vespoidea; and S. A. Rohwer, the superfamilies Sphecoidea and Vespoidea, with the exception of certain groups. The work records 86 families represented by 634 genera and 1,102 species from Connecticut, of which 366 species were originally described from the State. Complete indexes to the plant hosts, insect hosts, and Hymenoptera are included.

Observations on the occurrence of the Argentine ant (Iridomyrmex humilis) in Silesia, F. PAX (Illus. Schles. Monatschr. Obst, Gemüse u. Gartenbau, 4 (1915), No. 3, p. 33; abs. in Rev. Appl. Ent., Ser. A. 5 (1917), No. 3, pp. 97, 98).—The Argentine ant, which is known to occur in the open in Portugal, Bosnia, and Belgium, is reported to have been found in the greenhouse of the Botanic Gardens at Breslau.

On some North American species of Microdon, F. KNAB (Proc. Biol. Soc. Wash., 30 (1917), pp. 133-144).—Five new syrphid species are here described.

New chalcid flies from Maryland, II, A. A. GIRAULT (Ent. News, 28 (1917), No. 6, pp. 255-258).—In continuation of the paper previously noted (E. S. R., 36, p. 556) four species and one genus, Blattotetrastichus, are described as new.

A new aphis-feeding Aphelinus, L. O. HOWARD (Proc. Biol. Soc. Wash., 30 (1917), pp. 77, 78).—Aphelinus lapisligni reared from Aphis bakeri at Forest Grove, Oreg., is here described as new.

The cyclamen mite, W. A. Ross (Agr. Gaz. Canada, 4 (1917), No. 3, pp. 174, 175, fig. 1).—An undescribed species of Tarsonemus was reported by florists in Hamilton, Brantford, and Niagara Falls in the fall of 1916 as destroying the flowers and flower buds of cyclamen and causing the foliage to curl, resulting in the affected plants being rendered absolutely worthless.

ANIMAL PRODUCTION.

Physiological effect on growth and reproduction of rations balanced from restricted sources, E. B. HART, E. V. McCOLLUM, H. STEENBOCK, and G. C. HUMPHREY (U. S. Dept. Agr., Jour. Agr. Research, 10 (1917), No. 4, pp. 175-198, pls. 15).—In this contribution from the Wisconsin Experiment Station, work previously noted (E. S. R., 26, p. 467) is continued.

The experiment was carried out with grade Holstein heifers weighing from 200 to 400 lbs. The feeding period began in 1910 and continued for two years. It was proposed that one group should receive its nutrients wholly from the corn plant, another from the wheat plant, a third from corn grain and wheat straw, a fourth from wheat grain and corn stover, and a fifth from corn grain and the roughage equally divided between alfalfa hay and wheat straw. In carrying out the work other factors, as the baking of the wheat, the addition of certain mineral elements, etc., were introduced in an attempt to obviate the difficulties encountered.

A physiologically complete ration of corn-grain and corn-stover was not disturbed by altering the calcium-magnesium ratio through the addition of magnesium salts nor by the addition of mineral acids in excess.

A ration from the wheat plant alone did not sustain growth and the animals could not be bred. Blindness ensued, with feeble and emaciated condition and excitability, followed by collapse. The addition of salt did not improve the ration nor did the baking of the wheat. Additions of butter fat did not uniformly improve the ration. The causes are ascribed to an inherent toxicity of the wheat grains especially resident in the embryo. The addition of a large amount of wheat embryo was found likely to produce an early abortion. From a histological examination of the organs of the animals fed wheat products alone, attention is called to the similarity with conditions in beriberi in man. These animals also showed a low resistance to other diseases, notably anthrax.

Corn grain with wheat straw sustained growth at a slow rate. The offspring, however, were born weak or dead. The addition of salt to this ration made it normal, indicating that it was the needed factor lacking.

With wheat grain and corn stover growth was made but reproduction was only partially sustained, depending apparently on individuality. Where reproduction was successful in the first period, it failed in the second, due to the cumulative effects of the toxins of the wheat.

In the case of corn grain and a roughage made up of one-half each of wheat straw and alfalfa hay excellent growth was maintained and normal reproduction in the first period. In the second gestation period, however, weakness appeared. While this mixture made an improved ration, it was not perfect and might fail through accumulated toxicity.

The experiments indicate that modifications must be made of our present ideas of "balanced" rations and that we must take into consideration other factors as toxicity, a proper balance of salts, and certain growth-promoting compounds of unknown nature.

Some nutritional characteristics of corn, J. T. WILLARD (*Kans. Acad. Sci. Bul. 1 (1916), pp. 16*).—A paper read at the annual meeting, in which a number of tables of analyses from various sources are shown and data compiled. A popular discussion is given of the corn plant as a factor in nutrition, and various experiments, including recent ones at the Kansas Experiment Station, are quoted.

Feeds and feeding abridged, W. A. HENRY and F. B. MORRISON (*Madison, Wis.: Henry-Morrison Co., 1917, pp. VIII+440, figs. 116*).—A condensed edition of the sixteenth edition of Feeds and Feeding (E. S. R., 34, p. 261), to which have been added chapters on the feeding and care of poultry. An appendix contains tables showing the composition, digestible nutrients, and fertilizing constituents of the more important feeds. Each chapter closes with questions covering the subjects noted, and it is sought throughout to adapt the book to the needs of agricultural courses in secondary schools and short courses in agricultural colleges.

Cost of digestible nutrients in principal cattle feeds, H. B. WINTERS (*N. Y. Dept. Agr. Bul. 84 (1916), pp. 2147-2164*).—The value of available cattle feeds from June 1, 1915, to May 1, 1916, based upon the digestible nutrients, has been computed.

Commercial feeding stuffs, P. H. WESSELS ET AL. (*Rhode Island Sta. Insp. Bul., 1917, May, pp. 3-16*).—Analyses are reported of various brands of commercial feeding stuffs found for sale in Rhode Island in 1916, including meat scrap, fish scrap, tankage, cottonseed meal, linseed meal, gluten meal, gluten feed, distillers' dried grains, brewers' dried grains, wheat middlings, wheat bran, hominy feed, mixed and proprietary live stock and poultry feeds, ground oats, alfalfa meal, dried beet pulp, flax shives, and alfalfa.

Digest and copy of revised feeding-stuffs law (*New Jersey Stas. Circ. 74 (1917), pp. 2-8*).—A revision of Circular 10 (E. S. R., 28, p. 364), including the text of the law as amended March 16, 1916.

[Live-stock investigations], A. C. HARTENBOWER, J. BARBOUR, and L. B. BARBER (*Guam Sta. Rpt. 1916, pp. 39-44, 50-53, 54-57, pls. 4, figs. 5*).—An effort was made during the year to improve the live stock of the island by the further importation of pure-bred sires. New methods of feeding were also taken up, and all animals of the station were put upon definite rations.

The work with horses sought to improve the native stock by crossing with Morgan sires. The average weight of native horses is 460 lbs. They are hardier under local conditions, however, than imported animals. By crossing the size has been increased, and the crosses developed appear hardy on native pastures without extra feed. Native pasturage alone will not support Morgan horses. In a feeding experiment with two Morgan horses comparing alfalfa hay with Para grass, the former possessed a superior feeding value, although it can not be fed in Guam in the quantity and as successfully as in colder climates. For the station horses 5 lbs. of alfalfa hay and 40 lbs. of Para grass per day gave good results.

Native bulls average 690 lbs. and cows 512 lbs. The crossbred cattle compare favorably in hardiness with the native cattle, and the improvement by crossbreeding is most satisfactory.

During the year two Berkshire boars were imported. The stock in hand had deteriorated through inbreeding and parasitic infestation. A feeding experiment was carried out with two lots of four pigs each, comparing a ration of breadfruit and coconuts with corn and shorts. The animals were fed for 140 days. The pigs on the breadfruit-coconut ration made an average daily gain per head of 0.388 lb. at a cost of 11.58 cts. per pound. Those on the corn and shorts ration made an average daily gain of 0.45 lb. at a cost per pound of gain of 11.09 cts. Attention is called to the high cost of gain and the necessity of forage crops to lessen the cost. For pasturage Para grass was found to be very satisfactory for hogs, and with a light supplementary ration of breadfruit and coconuts the animals remained in excellent condition.

The work with goats during the year was much hampered by parasites.

The crossbreeding of poultry is showing good results. The best record of six native hens was 42 eggs per year, while that of six hens of the Brown Leghorn-native cross was 127 eggs. In feeding rice hulls to young chicks, death from crop impaction resulted in some cases, and it was found advantageous to use unhulled light rice instead. In a comparative test of brooders, it was demonstrated that for the first six weeks after hatching the chicks should be kept off the ground. An experiment was made comparing an imported grain ration made up of wheat, corn, and oats (2 : 1 : 1) with a Guam-grown ration made up of rough rice, a dry mash being used in each case. Two lots of 12 each of Brown Leghorns and two lots of crossbred fowls were employed. The experiment ran from September 1 to June 30. The Brown Leghorns on imported feeds laid 719 eggs, on native feeds 842. The crossbred fowls on imported feed laid 714 eggs and on native feed 915 eggs. In feeding grated coconut to chicks under 6 weeks old, the inclusion of more than 5 per cent in the ration invariably produced diarrhea, while 15 per cent or more caused a total loss of all chicks.

[Animal husbandry studies at the Missouri Experiment Station] (*Missouri Sta. Bul. 147 (1917), pp. 21–27, 48*).—This progress report includes, among others, the following studies:

The use of nitrogenous concentrates and heavy and light rations of silage for fattening two-year-old steers, by H. O. Allison.—The test indicates that the cost of fattening cattle can be greatly reduced by the extensive use of corn silage with nitrogenous concentrates.

The value of sour milk and beef scrap in rations for growing chicks, and the cost of growing chicks, by H. L. Kempster.—At the end of the first three weeks 100 chicks with skim milk in the ration weighed 21.4 lbs. at a cost of 2.76 lbs. of feed per pound of gain, the beef scrap chicks weighed 15.1 lbs. at a cost of

5.54 lbs. of feed per pound of gain, and the no-milk-or-meat chicks weighed 9.86 lbs. at a cost of 15.1 lbs. of feed per pound of gain. The mortality in the three lots was 13.4, 22, and 34 per cent, respectively.

Live stock of the farm.—V, Pigs and poultry, edited by C. B. JONES (*London: The Gresham Publishing Co., 1916, vol. 5, pp. XI+269, pls. 41, figs. 17*).—This treats of pigs and poultry, as to breeds, feeds, management, marketing, and diseases.

Live stock of the farm.—VI, Bees, goats, dogs, ferrets, asses, and mules, edited by C. B. JONES (*London: The Gresham Publishing Co., 1916, vol. 6, pp. VIII+199, pls. 19, figs. 13*).—The treatment is similar to the part noted above.

[Swiss live stock industry], A. BORGEAUD, J. FREY, and D. BOURET (*Vie Agr. et Rurale, 6 (1916), No. 36, pp. 164–180, figs. 12*).—In this special number, devoted to Swiss agriculture, pages 164–175 treat of the cattle industry, breeds of cattle, and cooperation among cattle raisers; pages 176–180, of goats (breeds and breeding).

Statistics of Swiss live stock industry (*Ergeb. Schweiz. Viehzähl, Kanton Zurich, 1916, pp. 31, figs. 2*).—Data covering several years are presented as to the number and kinds of animals owned in the various cantons. From 1911 to 1916 there was practically no change in the number of horses. Cattle increased 1 per cent, and smaller animals over 9 per cent.

Proceedings of the nineteenth and twentieth annual conventions of the American National Live Stock Association (*Proc. Amer. Nat. Live Stock Assoc., 19 (1916), pp. 171, pls. 14; 20 (1917), pp. 202, pls. 14*).—The proceedings and addresses are reported of these conventions, held respectively, at El Paso, Tex., in January, 1916, and Cheyenne, Wyo., in January, 1917.

Inbreeding, A. B. BRUCE (*Jour. Genetics, 6 (1917), No. 3, pp. 195–200*).—On the assumption that inbreeding is essentially "self-fertilization" in a greater or lesser degree, and that, in each generation, selfing and mating at random take place in a fixed ratio, the author proposes general formulas to express not only the array but also the genetic constitution of the individuals of which the family under investigation is composed.

Report on cattle feeding experiments conducted at the schools of agriculture and experiment stations at Cedara, Natal, and Potchefstroom, Transvaal (*Union So. Africa Dept. Agr. [Pub.] 15 (1916), pp. 40, figs. 22*).—The experiments reported were made on from 10 to 16 head of three types of cattle to determine whether a profit could be obtained by using feeds produced on the farm. The feeds covered a wide range of roughage, maize meal, and peanut cake.

With 6-year-old cattle, profits were made by grass fattening, but the addition of maize meal resulted only in a reduction in profits.

The results with 3-year-old cattle indicated that their raising and fattening with local feeds appears to be a remunerative business. It is believed that the future of the beef cattle industry in South Africa will be the fattening of younger cattle of this class.

In experiments with superannuated work oxen with feeds easily produced on South African farms, profits were returned at present prices. Because of the scarcity at present in the London market there was a profit in such cattle where extra feeding had produced a covering of fat. In fattening the old oxen better gains were obtained with animals possessing a dash of improved blood.

Feeding experiment with oil-extracted palm kernel meal and undecorticated earthnut cake, J. HENDRICK and W. J. PROFEIT (*North of Scot. Col. Agr. Bul. 21 (1916), pp. 10*).—In continuation of work previously reported (E. S. R., 34, p. 566), an experiment was carried out to compare the value of oil-extracted palm kernel meal and undecorticated peanut cake with linseed cake, and also to determine whether a home-grown product, crushed oats, could be profitably substituted for these imported feeds. The meal used was extracted with chemical solvents and contained less oil than the cake which was extracted under pressure.

Thirty-two crossbred bullocks in lots of 8 each were fed for 84 days, divided into periods of 28 days each. Turnips and straw were used as roughage. In addition, lot 1 received linseed cake and crushed oats; lot 2 peanut cake and crushed oats; lot 3 palm kernel meal, crushed oats, and a small portion of locust bean meal to induce the animals to eat the ration; and lot 4 crushed oats. The manurial value was deducted from the cost of the feed in each lot. On linseed cake bullocks made an average gain of 2.31 lbs. daily, on peanut cake 1.99 lbs., on palm kernel meal 2.15 lbs., and on oats alone 1.98 lbs. The net cost of gain per hundredweight was for lot 1, 48s. ($11.66) ; lot 2, 46s. 3d.; lot 3, 51s.; and lot 4, 50s.

Peanut cake gave the best monetary returns and was eaten readily. Crushed oats alone, while costing more than the other feeds, was considered a satisfactory concentrate with turnips and straw.

Ageing Egyptian cattle, MOHAMMED ASKAR *(Agr. Jour. Egypt, 6 (1916), pp. 73-78, pls. 12).*—A discussion of methods of determining the age, with 17 drawings of the teeth and mouth, of Egyptian cattle.

Live stock of the farm.—IV, Sheep, edited by C. B. JONES *(London: The Gresham Publishing Co., 1915, vol. 4, pp. X+252, pls. 38, figs. 18).*—Chapter 1 deals with sheep farming in the British Isles, the development and distribution of breeds, and statistics. Chapter 2, prepared by various authors, gives a description of the different breeds. Chapters 3, 4, and 5 are devoted respectively to profitable sheep farming, general management and feeding, and diseases.

Sheep production, P. V. GARCÍA *(Bol. Min. Agr. [Argentina], 20 (1916), No. 5-6, pp. 391-462, figs. 32).*—A statistical discussion of the production and exportation of sheep from Argentina from 1895 to 1915.

The number of sheep in the country has greatly decreased in this period, especially among the lower grades. The quality of the animals has improved, however, both as to wool and meat. The average weight of carcasses exported from 1896 to 1915 shows a gradual increase from about 23 to above 27 kg. (50.6 to 59.4 lbs.).

Sheep and wool for farmers. Crossbreeding experiments, J. W. MATHEWS *(Agr. Gaz. N. S. Wales, 27 (1916), Nos. 5, pp. 325-334, figs. 6; 6, pp. 397-407, fig. 1).*—This experiment, which is being continued, compares the crossing of wool and mutton type sheep. The work reported, covering five years, gives the results in crossing Lincoln, Leicester, and Border-Leicester rams with Merino ewes. The number of ewes employed was 218.

Exclusive of lambs, the average body weights of the three crosses for all ages were as follows: Lincoln-Merino 107 lbs. 11½ oz., Leicester-Merino 106 lbs. 6½ oz., Border Leicester-Merino 117 lbs. 2 oz. In wool weight, the Lincoln cross wethers average 1 lb. 4 oz. over the Leicester cross and practically 1 lb. over the Border-Leicester cross. With the ewes the differences were 1 lb. 1 oz. and 10 oz., respectively, in favor of the Lincoln.

The wool averaged in price for the whole period as follows: Lincoln-Merino 13.19d. (26.2 cts.) per pound, Leicester-Merino 13.71d., and Border Leicester-Merino 13.89d.

Horses, R. POCOCK *(London: John Murray, 1917, pp. X+252).*—The origin, history, and future of the horse are treated by a practical man who has gleaned his knowledge from the western plains and in war.

Horse breeding and horse racing, J. C. EWART (*Nature* [*London*], *99* (*1917*), *No. 2487, pp. 346, 347*).—The author points out the necessity for the preservation of the Thoroughbred horse and for the improvement of the breed for military and other purposes. As race horse breeding implies racing, the plea is made for the continuance of such racing as may be required to test the value of the stallions and mares now at stud in the United Kingdom.

A history of the Percheron horse, compiled by A. H. SANDERS and W. DINS-MORE (*Chicago: Sanders Publishing Co., 1917, pp. 602, pls. 131, figs. 10*).—In this history of the origin, evolution, development, and distribution of the modern heavy draft type of Percheron horses the effort has been made to throw new light upon the foundation history of the type in the district of the Perche in France. Data for this part of the work were obtained from books, records, and documents in the Government archives at Paris, including the official registration and inspection entries of stallions bought for the French Government stud at Le Pin, and lists of stallions approved and subsidized by the Government prior to the Stud Book in the Perche. The evidence thus obtained tends to show that the Percheron horse has existed as a distinct type from very ancient times, and that Arabian blood has played very little part in the production of the latter-day type of the breed.

A detailed account is given of the introduction and dissemination of the breed throughout the United States, to which is appended a symposium reflecting the views of contemporary importers and breeders on the selection, feeding, and general management of stallions, brood mares, and foals.

The diastatic action of saliva in the horse, R. J. SEYMOUR (*Amer. Jour. Physiol., 43* (*1917*), *No. 4, pp. 577–585*).—Both the mixed and the isolated secretions of the parotid and submaxillary glands of the horse were found to contain a diastase capable of converting starch into sugar. The diastase is indicated as being extremely feeble, requiring at least five hours for the conversion of boiled starch. The action of the diastase (pytalin?) was not increased by aeration, by acidifying, or by exposing to the action of weak alkalies.

The saliva of the horse was found to be inactive on cellulose and on sucrose. No evidence of the secretion of a zymogen with a subsequent conversion into active ptyalin was observed. "Salivary secretion may occur in the horse without mastication by stimulation with chemical substances, with an apparent augmentation through the psychic effect of the sight of food; the greatest flow occurs when the horse is permitted to masticate food material." Potassium sulphocyanid was not found in the saliva.

See also previous notes by Palmer (E. S. R., 36, p. 82) and by Palmer and others (E. S. R., 37, p. 681).

Sex-linked inheritance of spangling in poultry, G. LEFEVRE (*Abs. in Anat. Rec., 11* (*1917*), *No. 6, pp. 499, 500*).—A series of experiments has been carried out at the Missouri Station for the purpose of determining the mode of inheritance of spangling in poultry (E. S. R., 35, p. 867).

The initial crosses were made reciprocally between Silver Spangled Hamburgs and Brown Leghorns, and the material used for the analysis has been obtained from twelve different matings. The conclusion has been reached that spangling is determined in inheritance by a distinct factor which behaves in a typically sex-linked fashion, the cocks being homozygous and the hens heterozygous for it in Silver Spangled Hamburgs. When spangling is introduced through the male, both sexes in the F_1 generation show spangles, while the reciprocal cross gives only spangled males, the females being nonspangled and incapable of transmitting the pattern.

24656°—18—No. 8——6

It has been further shown that the expression of spangling may be greatly modified, or even entirely obscured, by the action of other factors, especially factors for black pigmentation, which, however, segregate independently of the factor for spangling. The independence of the spangling factor is indicated by the fact that, after segregation and recombination of the several factors concerned, some individuals are extracted in which all disturbing factors are absent and the spangled pattern is exhibited in its original purity. A number of such birds have been obtained from different matings, and these now breed as true to spangling as do the Silver Spangled Hamburgs themselves.

Mendelian inheritance in poultry, G. LEFEVRE (*Abs. in Missouri Sta. Bul. 147 (1917), pp. 47, 48*).—This is another abstract of the data reported above.

The structure of the fowl, O. C. BRADLEY (*London: A. & C. Black, Ltd., 1915, pp. XII+153, pls. 17, figs. 28*).—A concise descriptive anatomy of the fowl, with a chapter on the embryology of the chick.

Studies on the physiology of reproduction in birds, I–VII, O. RIDDLE ET AL. (*Amer. Jour. Physiol., 41 (1916), No. 3, pp. 387–437; 42 (1916), No. 1, pp. 151–162*).—In this series of articles, the first seven of which are here noted, results are given of studies of the physiology of avian reproduction in relation to the problem of heredity and sex.

I. *The occurrence and measurement of a sudden change in the rate of growth of avian ova,* O. Riddle.—Continuing studies already noted (E. S. R., 26, p. 164), it has been shown that when the oöcyte of the fowl reaches a diameter of about 6 mm. it increases its previous rate of growth to a rate nearly 25.8 times higher. The transition from the one rate to the other is made in a single day and sharply marks off the type of substance accumulated in the ovum. Under the slower rate this is white yolk. Under the greatly increased rate the yellow yolk is produced. The increased rate of deposition of yolk materials is accompanied by a pronounced alteration in the growth and activity of the membrane (follicular) which surrounds the ovum. A comparable change in growth rate occurs generally in other avian and sauropsidan eggs.

II. *On the chemical composition of white and yellow egg yolk of the fowl and pigeon,* Adelaide A. Spohn and O. Riddle.—By taking advantage of the fact that the ova of the fowl consist wholly of white yolk until they begin their final period of rapid development (see above) the authors were able to prepare samples of the two kinds of yolks for analysis. The results of the analyses of two samples of white yolk and of six samples of yellow yolk of the common fowl demonstrate that the two forms of yolk are strikingly different substances, and that the white yolk much the more nearly approximates the composition of small holoblastic eggs, and of living undifferentiated tissue generally. The ovarian egg (yellow yolk) of the fowl contains little more than 45 per cent of water. The solids of the fowl's egg contain 20.6 per cent of phosphatids, 49.5 per cent neutral fat, and 28.4 per cent protein.

Analyses were also made of two samples of yellow yolk of the jungle fowl and five samples of yellow yolk of the common pigeon. The results indicate that the yellow yolk of the jungle fowl has probably a lower lipoid and a higher protein content than the yolk of domestic fowls. The yellow yolk of the pigeon differs most from that of the fowl in its much higher moisture value, but probably differences in the amount of alcohol-soluble and protein materials also exist. The yellow yolk derived from different orders, genera, and species of birds probably varies more in the amount of water than in other fractions, but the yellow yolk from birds of different orders is relatively much alike as compared with yellow and white yolk from the same individual bird.

III. *On the metabolism of the egg yolk of the fowl during incubation,* O. Riddle.—In this study on the changes in the egg yolk during incubation the attempt was made to determine, by isolation and chemical analysis of the yolks of eggs subjected to various periods of incubation, the relative rates at which the various constituents of yolk are removed and utilized by the embryo.

A differential utilization of the elements of yolk prior to the twelfth day of incubation has not been shown to occur. A study of the unmetabolized yolk of 12, 18, and 20 day stages shows that after the twelfth day the phosphatids are utilized more rapidly than the neutral fats, and the neutral fats are utilized faster than the proteins. This order of utilization of these substances persists during the 18 to 20 day period when the embryo's sole source of protein is the protein of the yolk. The moisture value of the yolk undergoes very considerable fluctuations during incubation. At the twelfth day it is about 9 per cent higher than in fresh undiluted yolk. At the eighteenth day it has fallen to near the value for fresh yolk. At the very end of incubation this value probably rises considerably. Two forms of semisolid yolk bodies which are occasionally present in final stages of incubation were found to be wholly unlike in their chemical composition. Yolk resorbed by the follicle which secreted it shows a more rapid utilization of the phosphatids (lecithin), the neutral fats are utilized at a somewhat slower rate, while the proteins are metabolized more slowly than either the phosphatids or neutral fats.

IV. *When a gland functions for the first time is its secretion the equivalent of subsequent secretions?* O. Riddle and Adelaide A. Spohn.—A comparison was made of the composition of the albumin secreted by the pigeon's oviducal glands in their initial functionings with that of albumin secreted later by these glands.

Albumin produced in initial efforts contains a smaller percentage of water and a higher percentage of alcohol-ether-insoluble substance. During a few of the earlier functionings of the oviducal glands, there probably occurs a gradual change from the initial lower percentage of water to the later higher percentage of water. Partial analyses of the albumin of the pigeon's egg are recorded and one source of variation in the moisture value of this albumin has been identified. The amounts of alcohol-ether-soluble substance, and of inorganic matter probably do not vary widely nor consistently. The amount of water in the egg albumin of the pigeons studied shows no consistent variation in respect to summer and winter. The earliest secretion of the albumin-secreting gland of the pigeon's oviduct is, in several respects, a rather close approximation to the later products of the gland.

V. *The effect of alcohol on the size of the yolk of pigeon's egg,* O. Riddle and G. C. Basset.—In the studies here reported two common pigeons, two blond Ring doves, and three hybrids were used. Four of the birds were given alcohol by inhalation daily, with certain exceptions, for four months, and three for only two months. It was found that the yolks produced during the alcoholization period by these birds become smaller than during the prealcoholization period. This decrease occurs even during the season when the yolks of untreated birds normally grow larger than in the earlier period. Yolks produced during a few weeks or months after the alcoholization period are smaller than normal.

VI. *Sexual differences in the fat and phosphorous content of the blood of fowls,* J. V. Lawrence and O. Riddle.—Results are given of a study of the amount of fat and phosphorus in the blood, in relation to sex and sexual activity, in the common fowl.

The blood plasma of female fowls is found to be richer in alcohol-soluble substance and phosphorus than is the plasma of the male. The blood plasma of the sexually functioning female fowl contains more alcohol-soluble substance and more phosphorus than does the plasma of fowls with temporarily inactive ovary. The male, the nonlaying female, and the actively laying female fowl are three natural groups of fowls when these are considered from the standpoint of the fat and phosphorus content of the blood-plasma. The relative distribution of phosphorus in the alcohol-soluble and alcohol-insoluble fractions of the blood plasma is also different for these three groups of fowls. The differences here observed and measured are quantitative.

VII. *Variations in the chemical composition of reproductive tissues in relation to variations in functional activity*, O. Riddle and J. V. Lawrence.— The membranes which immediately surround different sizes of growing oöcytes of the fowl were analyzed. The phosphatids of all the membranes analyzed were found to exist in amounts relatively large in proportion to the neutral fats. The greatest disproportion of phosphatids to neutral fats, and the largest amounts of phosphatids, apparently were found in the membranes surrounding oöcytes from 5 to 6.5 mm. in diameter.

Analyses were also made of active and relatively inactive shell glands and albumin-secreting glands. In the shell glands the total alcohol-ether soluble substance is greatest when the gland is inactive and the moisture is greatest when the gland is active. While the alcohol-ether soluble phosphorus does not differ consistently in the active and inactive shell glands, it is perhaps higher in the active glands. In the albumin-secreting glands the alcohol-ether soluble phosphorus is much increased under inactivity. The percentage of water is somewhat larger in the active than in the inactive albumin-secreting glands.

The results are thought to indicate that an increase in the physiological activity of a tissue is accompanied by an increase in its phosphatid content.

A study of the incubation periods of birds, W. H. Bergtold (*Denver: The Kendrick-Bellamy Co., 1917, pp. 109*).—The author reviews the reasons assigned for the variations in the incubation periods of birds which are based on passive conditions, such as an anatomical character (size of body), a histologic character (size of egg), and effects which merely retard or suspend embryonic development.

Attention is also called to a factor that has received little attention, namely, bird temperatures. The importance of a study of bird temperatures is urged because it has been demonstrated that there is an optimum incubation temperature, which perhaps varies with different species. He puts forth the tentative conclusion that "a bird's temperature determines or fixes the time length of its incubation period, and that only an abiding change in the bird's temperature can permanently alter the time length of its incubation period."

The molting of fowls, R. F. Irvin (*New Jersey Stas. Hints to Poultrymen, 5 (1917), No. 10, pp. 4*).—A discussion of the molting of fowls from which the conclusion is drawn that it is better to feed the birds liberally during the period, and that no gain is made in forcing the molt by starving.

Protein feeds for laying hens, H. L. Kempster (*Missouri Sta. Circ. 82 (1917), pp. 11, figs. 4*).—In continuation of work already noted (E. S. R., 35, p. 773) three 10-bird pens of White Leghorn hens were fed from November 1, 1915, to October 31, 1916, to test the effect of sour milk on egg production. The rations of the different pens were identical with those of the previous year. The average number of eggs per hen laid by the no-meat-or-milk pen during the year was 59.7, by the beef-scrap fed pens 133.6, and by the sour milk fed hens 126.9. On the price basis of the previous year there was a loss of 5 cts. per hen on the no-meat ration, a profit of $1.04 per hen on the beef-scrap ration, and a profit of 92.4 cts. per hen on the sour-milk ratio.

In another test covering the same period linseed meal, gluten meal, and cottonseed meal were compared as sources of protein for laying hens. In this test, which involved three pens of 10 White Leghorn hens each, the birds were fed a mash composed of equal parts by weight of bran, shorts, corn meal, and one of the above protein feeds. During the year the linseed meal pen laid an average of 64.9 eggs per hen, the gluten meal fed hens an average of 63.8 eggs each, and the cottonseed meal fed hens an average of 66 eggs each. The hens did not relish the linseed meal mash as much as they did the other mashes. "So far as could be observed the hens in all pens were in perfect health throughout the entire experiment with vegetable proteins. No deleterious effects were observed in the use of the cottonseed meal.

"Beef scrap and sour milk are the most economical methods of supplying protein to laying hens. Protein concentrates of vegetable origin alone did not materially increase egg production It is poor economy not to furnish the laying hen a protein concentrate of animal origin."

The poultry keeper's manual, G. ALLMAN (*West. Aust. Dept. Agr. Bul. 47 (1916), pp. 96, pl. 1, figs. 25*).—A practical treatise on the growing of poultry and their diseases and remedies therefor.

Commercial egg farming, S. G. HANSON (*London: Constable & Co., [1916], pp. 62, pls. 8*).—Practical methods applying to English conditions are set forth.

Poultry standards in their relation to utility, J. HADLINGTON (*Agr. Gaz. N. S. Wales, 28 (1917), No. 3, pp. 208–216, figs. 6*).—Standards are given for the White Leghorn, Black Orpington, and Rhode Island Red breeds of fowls, together with photographs which represent the author's interpretation of the utility character of these breeds. A plea is made for a revision of the scale of points for these breeds set out in the English standards.

American squab culture, E. H. EGGLESTON (*Chicago: Author, 1916, pp. 191, figs. 37*).—A practical treatise for those in the business of raising squabs for market. The subjects treated are breeds, breeding, marketing, pests and ailments, houses, and equipment. Considerable miscellaneous information is also given on various problems likely to arise in the prosecution of the industry

Squab culture, D. R. WOOD (*Terre Haute, Ind.: The Indiana Squab Co., 1916, pp. 71, figs. 17*).—Practical instructions in raising and marketing squabs.

The raising and care of guinea pigs, A. C. SMITH (*Kansas City, Mo.: Author, 1915, pp. 35, figs. 5*).—This treats of the rearing, marketing, and uses.

The rabbit: How to select, breed, and manage the rabbit for pleasure or profit, W. N. RICHARDSON (*Syracuse, N. Y.: Clarence C. DePuy, 1916, 7. ed., pp. 64, figs. 14*).

DAIRY FARMING—DAIRYING.

Cattle breeding problems and their solution, R. PEARL (*Ann. Rpt. Comr. Agr. Maine, 14 (1915), pp. 215–242, figs. 4*).—Progress reports are presented on the following lines of work being conducted at the Maine Station:

The study and analysis of milk records.—In a study of the relation of milk flow to age in dairy cattle (E. S. R., 32, p. 575), a comparison was made of American and Scotch Ayrshires in respect to milk production. Comparing the mean weekly yields of American Advanced Registry and Scottish Milk Records Society Ayrshire cows, it was found that the American cows outyielded their Scottish sisters by 1.23 gal. per week in the 2-year-old class, 2.92 gal. in the 3-year-old class, 2.24 gal. in the 4-year-old class, and 1.76 gal. in the "mature" class. The mature American cows produced about 9 per cent more milk than the mature Scotch cows. The question is raised whether the American standard is high enough to get the best results in the direction of breed improvement.

For the purpose of comparing herds made up of cows of various ages and stages of lactation the author has constructed a dairy efficiency table in which it is assumed that cows from five to seven years of age and during the first month of lactation are 100 per cent efficient, and that cows of any other age or stage of lactation are less than 100 per cent efficient. The manner in which the table is to be used is shown by examples.

The study of inbreeding in dairy cattle.—A preliminary report is made of a study of inbreeding in American Jersey cattle. Tabulated data and diagrams are presented showing the coefficients of inbreeding for random samples of the general population of both Jersey bulls and cows and of samples of the animals in the Register of Merit. From these it is concluded that American Jersey cattle at the present time may be said, in general and on the average, to be about one-half as intensely inbred, when account is taken of the eighth ancestral generation, as would be the case if continued brother × sister breeding had been followed. That, in general and on the average, Register of Merit animals are less intensely inbred than the general population of Jersey cattle.

Physiology of cattle breeding.—In a study of the normal duration of oestrum in cattle it was found that of 834 successful services which are tabulated over 79 per cent occurred within 10 hours after the discovery of heat. No significant differences appeared between the distributions for the different breeds.

A study of 712 cows from the herds of about 150 leading dairymen of Maine shows that on the average these cows were dry about 4 days short of 2 months prior to calving. About 14 per cent of them were dry more than 79 days and about 29 per cent were dry less than 40 days.

In a study of the age of cattle used as breeders by dairymen in the State, it was found that of 967 calves included in the statistics 58.9 per cent were sired by bulls less than 3 years of age at time of service. Less than 15 per cent of the calves were sired by bulls 5 or more years old. The bearing of these facts on the progress in dairy cattle breeding is evident, since it is impossible to test the milk producing capacity of a bull's daughters before he is 3 years old. The average age of breeding cows in the study was approximately 5.5 years. Out of 878 calves 166 were the first calves of heifers. The average age of these heifers when successfully served for these first calves was approximately 1 year and 7 months. Three-quarters of the heifers were successfully served for their first calves before they were 2.1 years old.

The Kerry: Its advantages under present conditions, CHEVIOT (*Mark Lane Express, 118 (1917), No. 4483, pp. 206, 207, figs. 2*).—The advantages of the Kerry cattle as compared with the dairy type of Shorthorns and other dairy breeds under present war conditions are pointed out, and notes are given on the origin of the Kerry breed and of the type of the breed known as Dexter Kerry.

Studies from the survey on the cost of market milk production, K. B. MUSSER, G. C. WHITE, B. A. McDONALD, and H. F. JUDKINS (*Conn. Agr. Col. Ext. Serv. Bul. 7 (1917), pp. 27*).—Results are given of a survey of 193 representative dairy farms in Connecticut made for the purpose of determining the cost of producing milk for the year ended April 30, 1917, and for the month of April, 1917.

It was found that the cost of producing milk on 178 of these farms for the year ended April 30, 1917, was 5.53 cts. per quart. There was an average loss for the year per cow for the 178 farms of $18.42. The cost of producing milk on 179 farms for the month of April, 1917, was 6.29 cts. per quart, with labor at the yearly rates.

The 28 highest-producing herds produced milk on the average for 2.06 cts. per quart below the 25 lowest-producing herds. The greatest percentage of pure-bred bulls and milk records were in the 28 herds with the highest-producing cows, while the smallest percentage was in the 25 lowest-producing herds. The 28 highest-producing herds showed a profit above the net cost of production of $10.86 per cow per year, while the lowest-producing herds showed a loss of $33.75. The average milk production of the 3,258 cows on these 178 farms was

6,009 lbs. per year, whereas the general average for the State is estimated at 5,500 lbs.

Tabulated data show detailed cost data for each farm, and averages for each county in the State.

The milk supply—a suggestion, R S. WILLIAMS and ELFRIDA C. V. CORNISH (Cambridge, England: University Press, 1917, pp. 10, figs. 3).—The authors call attention to the present unsatisfactory method of handling the milk supply of cities, and suggest a scheme of handling raw milk. The essentials of this plan are that the milk be taken from healthy cows under cleanly conditions, cooled within three hours after milking, either at the farm or at factories within reach of a group of farms, put into sterile hermetically sealed cans, shipped in refrigerator cars to the destination, and kept cool until delivered to the consumer.

Manual of milk products, W. A. STOCKING (New York: The Macmillan Co., 1917, pp. XXVII+578, pls. 16, figs. 90).—In this manual the author has brought together the more important findings in regard to the handling of dairy products. The subject is treated under the headings of milk secretion, the chemical composition of milk, factors that affect the composition of milk, physical properties of milk, the testing of milk and cream, market milk, certified milk, butter making, cheddar cheese, fancy cheeses, farm dairying, condensed and powdered milk, fermented milk, ice-cream making, and the relation of bacteria to dairy products.

Modern pasteurization at low temperature, J. VANDERLECK (Agr. Gaz. Canada, 4 (1917), No. 7, pp. 614–619).—Results are given of experiments conducted by the department of bacteriology of Macdonald College in which milk was pasteurized at different temperatures in a small pasteurizer on a dairy farm. Data bearing on the subject obtained in the course of an investigation of the milk supply by municipal authorities in the district of Montreal are also tabulated.

The author concludes that " raw milk produced under sanitary conditions and pasteurized at 145° F. for 20 minutes contained virulent coli bacteria, causing enteritis in infants. Pasteurized milk of reliable concerns contained during the summer so many coli bacteria that it was bound to have a harmful effect. Milk pasteurized at 145° for 30 minutes by numerous small concerns contained so many coli bacteria (virulent gas producers) that the milk was unfit for consumption. In milk pasteurized at 152° the coli bacteria had lost their virulence and most of them were killed. In milk pasteurized at 152° in the proper way, the food value is unimpaired, and as the cream will not rise to the top it will be impossible to reduce its value as a beverage by skimming the cream off."

Cause and prevention of mold on butter, E. G. HASTINGS (Proc. Wis. Buttermakers' Assoc., 16 (1916), pp. 145–152, fig. 1).—In this popular summary of the cause and prevention of mold on stored butter, the author gives results of tests of bleaching powder and hot water on mold spores.

In a 1:3,330 solution of bleaching powder or chlorid of lime, mold spores were killed after an exposure of 10 minutes, and in solutions of 1:16,550 to 1:33,330 after an exposure of 20 minutes. Trials of the same mixture of spores resulted in the death of all spores in water heated to 131 and 140° F. An exposure of 15 minutes in water with a temperature of 122° failed to kill the mold spores. The author states that butter tubs and liners should be placed for a few minutes in water heated to 150° and as a further precaution the cream should also be pasteurized. If only mold spores are present salt is likely to prevent their germination.

Minnesota creameries; cheese, ice cream, and canning factories (St. Paul, Minn.: Minnesota Dairy and Food Dept., 1916, pp. [4]+69, figs. 15).—Dairy statistics for the State are tabulated and lists are given of Minnesota creameries and cheese, ice cream, and canning factories.

Siberian butter and cheese (*N. Y. Produce Rev. and Amer. Cream., 44 (1917), No. 14, pp. 550, 552, 554*).—In this article, which is taken from the *Weekly Bulletin* of the Canadian Department of Trade and Commerce, it is stated that the butter industry of Siberia began with the introduction of railway transportation in 1894. The growth of the industry is one of the chief features of the economic development of the country. In 1913, 72,500 tons of butter was exported from Siberia to Western Europe.

Attempts are also being made in an experimental way to develop the Cheddar cheese making industry. These are meeting with success, and on account of the natural advantages of the country for cheese making it is thought this industry will rapidly grow in importance.

Notes are given on the growth of cooperative enterprises and on the effect of the European war on the butter and cheese industry of Siberia.

Cheese making on an Irish farm, MABEL O BRIEN (*Better Business, 2 (1917), No. 3, pp. 214–225*).—This is an account of how an Irishwoman found cheese making both pleasant and profitable on a dairy farm located too far from market for the sale of whole milk.

Experiments on the preparation of homemade rennet, A. TODD and ELFRIDA C. V. CORNISH (*Jour. Bd. Agr. [London], 24 (1917), No. 3, pp. 307–312*).—Results are given of experiments on the home preparation of rennet from calves' stomachs, the method used being a modification of that already noted (E. S. R., 36, p. 378).

By the method described rennet extracts approximating in strength commercial rennet were often obtained. These extracts retained their coagulating properties for a period of several months, and often increased in strength during storage. The number of lactose-fermenting organisms in the extracts decreased with time. Several kinds of cheeses made by the use of rennet so prepared ripened normally and were of good quality.

Experiments with pepsin to replace rennet, D. W. STEUART (*Jour. Bd. Agr. [London], 24 (1917), No. 3, pp. 313–315*).—An attempt was made to prepare a pepsin solution which would keep fairly well and give results similar to those obtained with standard rennet extract. The pepsin solution was prepared by mixing $4\frac{1}{2}$ parts by weight of a 1:3,000 solution of pepsin, 1 part of boric acid, and 10 parts of salt to 50 parts of water. In cheese-making experiments this pepsin solution compared favorably with rennet extract when well-ripened milk was used, but when the milk was ripened to a less extent the time of coagulation was much longer with the pepsin than with the rennet.

The results of another test indicate that 1 oz. of soluble pepsin powder will curdle only 75 gal. of sweet milk.

VETERINARY MEDICINE.

[Veterinary handbooks] (*[Portland, Oreg.]: Vet. Sci. Assoc. Amer., 1917, pp. 171; pp. 75, pl. 1; pp. 91, pl. 1; pp. 87, pls. 7; pp. 123, figs. 4*).—The first of these handbooks, dealing with Veterinary Medicines, Their Actions, Uses, and Dose, is by G. F. Korinek. The other four, consisting of (2) Notes on Diseases of Cattle, Cause, Symptoms, and Treatment; (3) Notes on Diseases of the Horse, Cause, Symptoms, and Treatment; (4) Notes on Veterinary Anatomy; and (5) Notes on Diseases of Swine, Sheep, Poultry, and the Dog, are by C. J. Korinek.

[Diseases and parasites of live stock], L. B. BARBER (*Guam Sta. Rpt. 1916, pp. 44–49, 53, 57, 58, pl. 1, figs. 4*).—*Acacia farnesiana* known as aroma and

Andropogon aciculatus known as "enefuk" are troublesome to horses allowed to run in pastures. The thorns of the former plant cause local inflammation that results in the falling out of the hair, leaving raw sores, or the skin drying and peeling off, leaving a disfigured appearance, while the adherent awn of the latter plant causes conjunctivitis.

Use of the arsenical dip kept the cattle free from ticks, which was found impossible through picking and. the oil and kerosene treatment. The importance of keeping the stock free from ticks is emphasized by the work of the year. Charts of the temperatures of four animals suffering from tick infestation are included.

Brief mention is made of the kidney worm (*Stephanurus dentatus*), a lungworm (*Metastrongylus apri*), and a cecum worm (*Trichuris crenata*) in swine, the first two of which were described in detail in a previous report of the station (E. S. R., 35, p. 877). Infestation by the cecum worm results in emaciation and a rough, scaly skin, and diarrhea is present in the early stages. Post-mortem examination shows the mucus surface of the large intestines, especially that of the cecum, to be covered with a thick yellowish crust, the removal of which exposed many pitted ulcers, particularly in chronic cases. The parasites in many instances show through the serous coat of the intestines, and a marked cirrhosis of the liver is generally present.

The nodular worm (*Œsophagostomum columbianum*) and the fourth stomach worm (*Hæmonchus contortus*) appeared in the station herd of goats and caused the death of several kids. But few of the chicks in the station flock were lost during the year from diseases or intestinal parasites. A list of 7 external and 15 internal parasites collected, based upon identifications by the Bureau of Animal Industry of the U. S. Department of Agriculture, is included.

[Report of the veterinary department], J. W. CONNAWAY and A. J. DURANT (*Missouri Sta. Bul. 147 (1917), pp. 54–57*).—Continuing the study of hog cholera and the factors concerned in immunity against the disease (E. S. R., 35, p. 878), a preliminary investigation indicated that "no relation exists between the complement-fixation reaction and the potency of the antihog-cholera serum, and that the reaction observed was due to other immune bodies than the specific immune bodies of hog cholera." It is indicated, however, that these conclusions should not be accepted as final until proved by further work.

The contagious abortion. investigations were continued in cooperation with the dairy husbandry department and a number of cattle breeders in various parts of the State. Of 42 herds tested during the year for contagious abortion by the complement-fixation test, 31 proved to be infected. Of 638 animals tested, 212 yielded a positive reaction. Data on the question of the transmission of contagious abortion infection from immune positive-reacting dams to their apparently healthy offspring in utero or subsequent to birth through infected milk and the permanency of this infection in the offspring are submitted. While it is considered that more complete data will be necessary for final conclusions, from the data at hand it is provisionally concluded that "the probability of the abortion infection passing from an immune positive-reacting dam to the calf in utero is not great; or, if such apparently normal calf is infected at birth, the abortion infection is probably not conserved in its tissues until the first breeding period. Moreover, the danger of the permanent transmission of abortion infection to the calf through raw milk is small."

Annual report of proceedings under the diseases of animals acts, the markets and fairs (weighing of cattle) acts, etc., for the year 1916, A. W. AN-STRUTHER (*Bd. Agr. and Fisheries [London], [Vet. Dept.], Ann. Rpts. Proc. 1916, pp. 28*).—This reports upon the occurrence of and control work with foot-and-mouth disease, of which there was one outbreak, and hog cholera during the year. In hog-cholera work the serum treatment was resorted to from June 25, after which date slaughter in suspected outbreaks was limited to animals needed for diagnostic purposes.

Report on operations of the veterinary sanitary service of Paris and the Department of the Seine during the year 1915, H. MARTEL (*Rap. Opér. Serv. Vét. Sanit. Paris et Dépt. Seine, 1915, pp. 161, figs. 17*).—This is the usual report (E. S. R., 35, p. 279) giving a detailed account of the work of the year.

Annual report of the Bengal Veterinary College and of the Civil Veterinary Department, Bengal, for the year 1915–16, A. SMITH (*Ann. Rpt. Bengal Vet. Col. and Civ. Vet. Dept., 1915–16, pp. 4+II+5+VIII+3*).—This is the usual annual report (E. S. R., 35, p. 483).

Animal diseases regulations with notes on diagnoses, F. E. LIONNET (*Dept. Agr. Mauritius, Gen. Ser., Bul. 7 (1916), pp. 26*).—The regulations in force in Mauritius against animal diseases, which were completely remodeled in 1915, have been brought together in this report. Short notes on the diagnoses of the various infectious diseases specified in the regulations are included.

Manure disposal as a factor in the control of parasitic diseases of live stock, M. C. HALL (*Jour. Amer. Vet. Med. Assoc., 51 (1917), No. 5, pp. 675–678*).—The author calls attention to the fact that the proper disposal of manure is the first step to be taken in the control of parasitic infestation of live stock.

The poisonous properties of the two-grooved milk vetch (Astragalus bisulcatus) (*Wyoming Sta. Bul. 112 (1917), pp. 59–67, fig. 1*).—This brief preliminary report upon the two-grooved milk vetch, presented at this time in order to warn stockmen of the poisonous nature of the plant, consists of two parts, the first (pp. 59–65), by O. A. Beath, dealing with the chemical properties of the plant; and the second (pp. 66, 67), by E. H. Lehnert, with its physiological effect, etc.

Milk vetch, which grows on the plains and in the valleys throughout the Rocky Mountain region, appears during the month of May and goes to seed the latter part of July. A description and an analysis of the plant by Knight, Hepner, and Nelson have been previously noted (E. S. R., 20, p. 135). The plant has proved to be poisonous to cattle, from 80 to 90 per cent of the affected animals dying, and suspicion is held regarding its effect upon sheep. It was found that water easily removes the active poison from green or air-dried material, and that all parts of the plant contain poison with a slight excess in the leaves. The poison is neither precipitated by basic acetate of lead nor decomposed at the boiling point of water. It is nonalkaloidal, and the fact that it can be deprived of its toxicity by boiling with dilute acids indicates its probable glucosidic character. A definite crystalline substance has been isolated, giving chemical reactions common to glucosids. Thus far no chemical antidote has been obtained, but, as indicated by the physiological action of the poison, drugs that stimulate the heart and nervous system should prove beneficial in the case of vetch poisoning.

Active immunization with sensitized and nonsensitized bacteria, H. F. SWIFT and R. A. KINSELLA (*Proc. Soc. Expt. Biol. and Med., 14 (1917), No. 6, pp. 120–122*).—In the experiment noted four types of vaccine were studied, plain stock vaccine killed at 56° C., sensitized stock vaccine killed at 56°, freshly prepared sensitized vaccine killed at 56°, and an alcohol precipitate of sensitized vaccine. Type I pneumococcus was used in all the vaccines. Mice, guinea pigs, and rats were used as experimental animals, the rats being found the most satisfactory for comparative studies.

The results showed that in from 6 to 10 days after the last immunizing dose there was a higher degree of immunity in the plain vaccine series, but this fell off rapidly. In the series immunized with freshly sensitized vaccine the immunity, though present, was less marked early, but increased after from 12 to 16 days. No parallelism was observed between the degree of active immunity and the amount of agglutinin and bacteriotropin in the serum of the immune rats. Agglutinin was demonstrated only in the serum where plain stock vaccine killed at 56° was used. Bacteriotropins were much stronger in the serum of animals treated with this vaccine than in the serum of animals treated with freshly prepared sensitized vaccine killed at 56°. This indicates that "animals may possess a high degree of active immunity and still show practically no antibodies in their serum." It is suggested "that the immunity is due in part to a tissue immunity and not due entirely to antibodies circulating in the blood serum."

Toxin and antitoxin of and protective inoculation against Bacillus welchii, C. G. BULL and IDA W. PRITCHETT (*Jour. Expt. Med., 26 (1917), No. 1, pp. 119-138*).—"Antitoxic serum prepared from a given culture of *B. welchii* is neutralizing for the toxins yielded by the other four cultures of that microorganism. The antitoxin is protective and curative against infection with the spore and the vegetative stages of *B. welchii* in pigeons. The limits of the protective and curative action are now under investigation."

Glanders in Austria from 1911 to 1913, J. SCHNÜRER (*Wiener Tierärztl. Wchnschr., 1 (1914), No. 2, pp. 83–93; abs. in Vet. Rec., 28 (1916), No. 1438, pp. 339, 341*).—An account of glanders control work in Austria during 1911, 1912, and 1913.

Neosalvarsan in the treatment of epizootic lymphangitis, E. HOUDEMEYER (*Abs. in Vet. Rec., 29 (1917), No. 1496, pp. 372, 373*).—Of the various methods of administering neosalvarson the author prefers intravenous injection since intramuscular injection is painful and subcutaneous injection should be discarded altogether on account of the persistent edemas which it produces. A dose of 1.5 gm. which is injected corresponds to 1 gm. of salvarsan. Of seven horses affected with epizootic lymphangitis that were treated with neosalvarsan six recovered after the first injection and the seventh after the second. "It is always advisable to combine surgical intervention with the administration of neosalvarsan by puncturing the abscesses and treating the wounds with antiseptics, as in this manner the progress of recovery is hastened." Attention is called to the importance of commencing treatment before the disease has become generalized.

Studies on the paratyphoid-enteritidis group.—I, II, C. KRUMWIEDE, JR., JOSEPHINE S. PRATT, and L. A. KOHN (*Jour. Med. Research, 34 (1916), No. 3, pp. 355–358; 35 (1916), No. 1, pp. 55–62*).—Two papers are given.

Xylose fermentation for the differentiation of B. paratyphosus "A" from other members of the paratyphoid-enteritidis group.—"In a series of cultures representing nearly all the pathogenic types of the paratyphoid-enteritidis group, a group of cultures, including all the types agglutinatively *B. paratyphosus* 'A', failed to ferment xylose. We suggest, if the study of further strains shows that this is a constant characteristic, that the xylose-negative types from man be considered the paratyphoid A group on cultural grounds. Within this cultural group are encountered strains, presumably pathogenic, which differ agglatinatively from the normal 'A' type."

Observations on the reaction in litmus milk as a method of biological differentiation.—"With the strains we have studied, the reaction in litmus milk of the different members of the paratyphoid-enteritidis group is a gradient one. Although most of the paratyphoid 'A' types produce alkali more slowly than the other members of the group, this difference is quantitative only, and intermediate degrees of reaction, both temporal and quantitative, largely destroy the differential value of the medium. The usually described qualitative reaction, therefore, has not been verified by our results. With milk containing Andrade indicator somewhat sharper differences are obtained with most of the strains, although the general quantitative character of the reaction is preserved. This is probably due to the greater delicacy of this indicator and coincident reduction of the color. Some strains, however, react irregularly on this medium, as on litmus milk, and show its lack of value as a qualitative method of differentiation."

Antitetanic serum in articular rheumatism, W. H. DALRYMPLE (*Amer. Jour. Vet. Med., 12 (1917), No. 8, pp. 552, 553; Jour. Amer. Vet. Med. Assoc., 51 (1917), No. 5, pp. 692–694*).—The author, at the Louisiana Experiment Stations, reports the successful use of antitetanic serum in a case of articular rheumatism in a jack. Three doses of 500 units each were injected with apparent complete cure.

The vitality of the tubercle bacillus outside the body, M. B. SOPARKAR (*Indian Jour. Med. Research, 4 (1917), No. 4. pp. 627–650*).—The vitality of the tubercle bacillus was studied under varying external conditions.

The bacilli in the sputum when exposed to direct sunlight remained alive for six hours, but were killed after eight hours' exposure. On exposure to diffused daylight the organisms remained alive for six days, but were dead after exposure for eight days. Tubercle bacilli were kept alive and virulent for 309 days in sputum which was kept in darkness, even when it was completely desiccated. Living tubercle bacilli were isolated from decomposing sputum after 20 days, but not after 26 days. The bovine type was found to be more resistant to sunlight and diffused daylight than the human type. When exposed to electric light the bovine bacilli were found alive after 74 days, but were dead after 100 days. From three to four hours' exposure in direct sunlight and from three to four days in diffused daylight were found necessary for sputum to become sufficiently dried to be capable of being reduced to dust.

Incidence of bovine infection of tuberculosis in children, CHING YIK WANG (*Edinb. Med. Jour., 18 (1917), pp. 178–196; abs. in Abs. Bact., 1 (1917), No. 3, pp. 266. 267*).—Of 281 cases of tuberculosis examined in Edinburgh the bovine type of tubercle bacillus was isolated from 78.4 per cent of cases under 5 years of age, from 70.3 per cent of cases between the ages of 5 and 16 years, and from only 7.8 per cent of patients over 16 years. The bovine bacillus was found in 6 of 9 children who died of tuberculous meningitis and abdominal tuberculosis. The tuberculin test yielded positive results in 37.5 per cent of children fed on raw milk and in only 15.4 per cent of children fed on boiled milk.

The etiology of hog cholera.—Second report, F. PROESCHER and H. A. SEIL (*Jour. Amer. Vet. Med. Assoc., 51 (1917), No. 5, pp. 609–624. figs. 13*).—Continuing the study previously noted (E. S. R., 37, p. 382), data are reported which deal mainly with the blood changes, continued studies on the staining properties of the virus, microscopical changes in the organs, and the cultivation of the organism.

The blood changes in hog cholera were investigated with 12 pigs. Tabular data showing the absolute leucocyte count and the differential count, before and after incubation, are submitted. It is noted that the blood counts can not be regarded as conclusive on account of their incompleteness. The data obtained, however, show that in hog cholera there is at first a decrease in the absolute leucocyte count. In some of the animals a leucopenia was observed.

Shortly before death there may be a considerable increase in leucocytes. "In the majority of the cases the differential count showed a decided increase in the polynuclear neutrophils, with a decrease in the lymphocytes. The polynuclear eosinophils and basophils are greatly diminished in number or disappear entirely. Neutrophil myelocytes and plasma cells may appear shortly before death. If the increase in leucocytes just before death is occasioned primarily by the hog-cholera virus or is due to a secondary infection with *Bacterium suipestifer* or *suisepticus* can not be determined." Two pigs showing a high ante-mortem leucocyte count were secondarily infected with *B. suipestifer*.

The staining method used for blood smears is briefly as follows: The air-dried smears were stained in a methyl alcohol solution of eosin, methylene blue, and toluidin blue for three or four minutes, immersed for a few minutes in 96 per cent alcohol, washed in water, superficially dried, and then floated for 16 hours on a diluted Giemsa solution (1:10) alkalized with two drops of 1 per cent sodium carbonate or borax solution to 10 cc. The smears were then thoroughly washed in running water, air-dried, and mounted in cedar oil or in paraffin oil. This method is considered to be superior to that previously described.

Some observed histological changes in hog cholera which will be reported later in detail, together with the macroscopic changes, are noted.

For the cultivation of the virus both the blood and organs of pigs which succumbed to hog cholera were used. The blood was collected aseptically, defibrinated, centrifugalized, and the serum passed through a Berkefeld filter. The filtrate was tested aerobically and anaerobically for common bacterial contamination.

Only perfectly sterile serum was used for culture purposes. Unfiltered sterile carcinomatous ascites and sterile unfiltered horse serum were used as culture media. Either was placed in sterile test tubes to which a piece of fresh kidney or liver tissue from a guinea pig or rabbit was added, and covered with sterile paraffin oil. The tubes were then incubated for a week at 37° C. Tests were made to insure complete sterility.

To the sterile culture tubes filtered hog-cholera serum equal in amount to the culture medium was added by means of a sterile pipette. In one case blood taken directly from the heart which proved to be sterile was added directly to the culture medium. Cultures were made from the organs by taking pieces aseptically removed from the dead animal and immersing them in unfiltered sterile carcinomatous ascites or unfiltered sterile horse serum and then covering with sterile paraffin oil. The tubes which showed a high secondary infection were discarded. Those which were but slightly contaminated after incubation for a week were filtered through filter paper and then through a Berkefeld filter. The filtrates so obtained were used for subcultures, as previously described.

After two or three weeks the culture medium showed a slight opalescence which gradually disseminated through the liquid. In cultures made from filtered virus with the addition of a piece of fresh tissue a growth was observed in four weeks. In others, however, where the presence of the cocci was demonstrated microscopically, hardly any change in the culture medium could be noted. Several hundred cultures so prepared were examined microscopically. The data reported confirm the previous microscopic findings.

With the staining method described it was possible to demonstrate large masses of microorganisms attached to the red cells. These findings corroborate those of Meyer (E. S. R., 32, p. 475), who showed that hog-cholera virus adhered tenaciously to the red blood cells and that it was impossible to remove the virus by repeated washings with normal saline solution followed by centrifugalization.

It is indicated that "as soon as sufficiently distant subcultures are obtained, such that the transmission of the original virus is absolutely excluded, animal experiments will be made to furnish conclusive proof that this organism is the causative agent of hog cholera."

The virulence of hog-cholera blood at different periods during the disease, R. A. WHITING (*Jour. Amer. Vet. Med. Assoc.*, 51 (1917), No. 4, pp. 477-493).— The results of a study at the Indiana Experiment Station covering a period of several years show that there is a gradual increase in the virulence of hog-cholera blood as the disease progresses from four to eight days following inoculation. Eight-day blood was found to be the most virulent.

It is noted that in the production of virus for serum production hogs may be killed at six days following inoculation, providing there is a corresponding high temperature and a manifestation of symptoms, especially weakness. Blood obtained on slaughter seven or eight days following inoculation was found to be more virulent than any of the blood obtained by tail bleedings.

See also a previous note by Craig (E. S. R., 34. p. 783).

Summary of observations on 1,470 hogs hyperimmune to hog cholera, H. C. H. KERNKAMP (*Jour. Amer. Vet. Med. Assoc.*, 51 (1917), No. 4, pp. 537-540).—Observations on 1.470 hogs used in the production of antihog-cholera serum at the Minnesota State serum plant, covering a period of approximately 37 months, are reported.

During the first half of the period of observation two methods of hyperimmunization were used. designated as "slow intravenous" and "intravenous." In the slow intravenous method an interval of from four to eight days between the first and the second injection of the necessary dose of virus to effect a condition of hyperimmunity was allowed. In the intravenous method the injection was done at one operation, the virus being injected into the posterior auricular vein under a pressure of from 3 to 6 lbs. per square inch. A smaller amount of virus is necessary in this method, and it is considered much more satisfactory than the slow intravenous method.

Serum therapy for trichinosis, B. SCHWARTZ (*Jour. Amer. Med. Assoc.*, 69 (1917), No. 11, pp. 884-886).—The report by Salzer [1] that animals fed with infested meat later than 24 hours after the administration of serum from a convalescent animal prove to be immune. that infested meat mixed with immune serum does not produce trichinosis in animals to which it is fed, and that immune serum injected into animals suffering with the disease produces a curative effect led to the investigation here reported, which is summarized by the author as follows:

"Serum from animals convalescent from trichinosis when injected into other animals did not produce immunity to trichinosis in the latter. Trichinous meat mixed with serum from animals during the active or convalescent stage of the disease proved to be still capable of producing the disease. Animals once infected and harboring trichinæ in their muscles were not immune to further infection when fed trichinous meat. Serum from a trichinous animal had no observable ill effects on the larvæ freed from their cysts by artificial digestion. None of the results of the experiments appear to be in harmony with the assertions made by Salzer concerning the value of serum from convalescent animals as a prophylactic or curative agent in trichinosis."

Special equine therapy, M. R. STEFFEN (*Chicago: Amer. Vet. Pub. Co., 1917, pp. 212*).—This work gives special attention to diseases and conditions which are unnamed, atypical, or of infrequent occurrence, the discussions being entirely from the viewpoint of the general practitioner.

Trichomonasis of chicks: A new and highly fatal disease, J. WEINZIRL (*Jour. Bact.*, 2 (1917), No. 4, pp. 441-445, figs. 2).—Large losses of chicks on ranches in the Puget Sound region of Washington from disease led to the investigation here reported. It is concluded that a protozoan of the genus Tricho-

[1] Med. Rec. [N. Y.], 91 (1917), No. 6, p. 261.

monas, to which the name *Trichomonas pullorum* is given, is the cause. The disease appears the second week after hatching, commonly about the tenth day, young chicks only being affected. Stock that is a month old proves resistant, and chronic cases that reach this age usually recover. Diarrhea is absent in the early stages but is present in the chronic stage. In the acute stage the chick may succumb in a day or two, and only the more vigorous birds enter the chronic stage. On the ranch where the investigation was first made 800 of 900 chicks hatched at one time from a thrifty stock of White Leghorns died within 10 days after hatching.

"Examination showed that a single species was present, frequently in overwhelming numbers; that it was not present in healthy stock, or in newly hatched chicks; that healthy chicks kept in cages with sick chicks developed the disease and showed the protozoan in the ceca; and finally that control chicks did not develop the disease when kept under identical conditions. We concluded, therefore, that this protozoan is the cause of the disease."

RURAL ENGINEERING.

Evaporation from the surfaces of water and river-bed materials, R. B. Sleight (*U. S. Dept. Agr., Jour. Agr. Research, 10 (1917), No. 5, pp. 209–262, pls. 6, figs. 13*).—Part 1 of this report deals with evaporation from water surfaces.

Experiments on the evaporation from circular land tanks of different diameters showed that "over the range of areas 0.785 sq. ft. to 113.1 sq. ft., or diameters 1 to 12 ft., the range in evaporation for the year is 76.18 to 49.16 in., and in percentage 154.9 to 100 per cent."

In experiments on the relation between evaporation from circular tanks and square tanks set 3 ft. in the ground, of equal exposed water surface, circular tanks with diameters of 3.39 ft. and 2 ft., and square tanks of dimensions 3 by 3 ft. and 1.77 by 1.77 ft. were used. "Based upon the totals, the evaporation from the larger square tank is 102.7 per cent of that from the circular one of the same area. That from the other square one is 103.5 per cent of that from the circular one of the same exposed area. Based upon mean weekly averages, these figures are 104.7 and 104.9. In the case of the 9 sq. ft. area the ratio, perimeter divided by area, is 0.15 greater in the case of the square tank than for the circular one. This has apparently caused an increase in evaporation of 2.7 per cent. For the tanks of 3.14 sq. ft. area there is a corresponding increase of 0.26 in the ratio and an increase of 3.5 per cent in evaporation."

Experiments on the variation of evaporation with the depth of the tank set in the ground showed that "during the months when the cooling effects of the night were not so great, the shallow tanks show the greater evaporation, but later, when the day temperatures and the heat storage of the shallow tanks are more than offset by the low night temperatures, the shallow tanks indicate a lesser evaporation. This difference in evaporation is not great, but for general use a tank not less than 2 ft. deep is recommended, since its contents will not become heated or cooled as quickly as those of the shallower tank. The difference between the results from the 6 ft. tank and the 3 ft. one is so slight that under all ordinary conditions there is no necessity for using a tank deeper than 3 ft."

Experiments on evaporation from flowing water showed that "for the first set of tanks evaporation from the flowing water was 107 per cent of that from the still water under exactly the same conditions. For the other set, a tank 25 ft. long, the evaporation from the flowing water was 108 per cent of that from still water. . . . There seems to be no definite relation between evaporation and velocity within the limits of the experiment."

Experiments on effects of temperature on evaporation and on the extension of the evaporation depths from land pans to larger open water surfaces under the same conditions by use of a floating pan are also reported, together with the results of meteorological observations taken in connection with evaporation investigations in general.

Part 2 of the report deals with evaporation from river-bed materials. "The final figures indicate that for the period of the sand-tank work the evaporation from the surface of the sand from the smaller tank, approximately 2 ft. in diameter, was about 7.5 per cent greater than from the larger tank. This figure does not check that found for the water tanks, the corresponding difference there being 3.5 per cent."

Other data of these experiments are graphically reported.

Use of power and rates for irrigation pumping, G. R. Kenny (*Jour. Electricity, 38 (1917). No. 12, pp. 496, 497, fig. 1*).—Data on the character of electric pumping plants in their relation to power rates, compiled from the practice of a hydroelectric company in California, are reported. Some data from typical districts on acreage irrigated and cost of power per acre are given in the following table:

Data on irrigated districts served.

	Alfalfa territory.	Citrus fruit territory.	Entire territory.
Acreage irrigated	22, 893	9, 495	
Horsepower used	1,623. 84	1,470. 75	
Acres per horsepower	14. 10	6. 50	
Average acres per horsepower, all classes of crops			10. 50
Average costs per acre	$3 to $4	$6 to $7	About $4. 25

"Practically all of the pumps in use are of the direct-connected centrifugal type. For the deep well pumping, the turbine and plunger types of well pumps are installed. The pumping motors on the system vary in size from 3 to 75 horsepower, only a very few being in excess of 15 horsepower, while the average at the end of 1916 was 10.4 horsepower."

The rates used, based on the maximum demand, are given in the following table:

Rates based on maximum demand.

Months continuous service.	Contract flat rates, per horsepower.	Meter rates, meter charge of 0.5 ct. per kw.-hour added to following demand charges.
3	$17. 50	$10. 40
4	21. 55	12. 50
5	25. 15	14. 30
6	28. 50	15. 95
7	31. 65	17. 45
8	34. 55	18. 85
9	37. 35	20. 10
10	40. 00	21. 30
11	42. 55	22. 40
12	45. 00	23. 45

A survey of all gas engine pumping plants operating within one mile of the company's lines showed that "the gas engines were used where but little irrigation was required, when water was pumped from ditches, or where water was needed to supplement ditch irrigation after the ditches had gone dry. The engines are generally run for only a short period each year. About 1,200 engines were visited and the conclusion reached, after the information obtained was examined, was that in the majority of cases the plants now pumping by gas engines could not be taken over for electric service to the advantage of either the consumer or the company. There are certain classes of power irrigation for which the gas engine, due to its low annual cost, if operated but little, may be used with considerable economy as compared with electric power."

The use of cement on national irrigation works, A. P. DAVIS (*Proc. Nat. Assoc. Cement Users, 9 (1913), pp. 258–265, figs. 7*).—This is a statement of the use made by the U. S. Reclamation Service of cement in irrigation structures.

" Since its organization the Reclamation Service has used about 1,500,000 bbls. of Portland cement, representing about as many cubic yards of concrete. It has built about 7,000 miles of canals, 69 tunnels aggregating 111,000 ft., has built 18 storage dams and 25 diversion dams, about 2,000 concrete structures upon canals, and about 32,000 wooden structures. It has built altogether 2,908 bridges with an aggregate length of about 62,000 ft. It has built 436 offices and dwellings and about as many other buildings used for barns and store-houses."

Improvements proposed in the javellization of potable water for field service, COMTE (*Jour. Pharm. et Chim., 7. ser., 14 (1916), No. 9, pp. 261–263; abs. in Chem. Abs., 11 (1917), No. 6, p. 678*).—A summary of service experience leads to the recommendation that a solution of 20 gm. of powdered potassium permanganate in 1 liter of hot water and 20 gm. of concentrated sulphuric acid be used for cleaning and deodorizing containing vessels.

It has been found that a uniform method of javellization is not applicable, owing to the variation in the organic impurities in the water and variations in the Javelle solution. It is pointed out that a definite amount of a given Javelle solution corresponds to a given water. This ratio is determined rapidly by placing 100 cc. of the water to be examined into each of five vessels and adding, respectively, 1, 2, 3, 4, and 5 drops of a 1 : 100 strength Javelle solution. After stirring and a wait of 20 minutes about 1 cc. of a potassium iodid starch reagent is added and again stirred. Several samples will then be blue. The sample of lowest concentration giving a blue color indicates the number of drops of undiluted Javelle solution necessary for the treatment of 10 liters of the water with the same dropping instrument. The starch reagent contains 1 gm. each of starch, potassium iodid, and crystalline sodium carbonate.

Experiments upon the purification of sewage and water at the Lawrence Experiment Station during the year 1915 (*Ann. Rpt. Dept. Health Mass., 1 (1915), pp. 377–429, figs. 4*).—This section of the report gives in detail the results of the water and sewage purification experiments at the station for the year 1915.

Annual report of the Baltimore County [Md.] roads engineer for the year ending December 31, 1916, W. G. SUCRO (*Ann. Rpt. Roads Engin. Baltimore Co. [Md.], 1916, pp. 87, pl. 1, figs. 17*).—This is a report of work and expenditures on road construction, maintenance, and repair in Baltimore County, Md., for 1916.

Influence of grading on the value of fine aggregate used in Portland cement concrete road construction, F. H. JACKSON, JR. (*U. S. Dept. Agr., Jour. Agr. Research, 10 (1917), No. 5, pp. 263–274, figs. 10*).—Experiments showing in a general way the effects of variations in the grading of fine aggregate on the resistance to wear of road concrete are reported.

It was found " that but few naturally occurring concrete sands are as coarse as those making the strongest mortars, according to these tests. Neither has the fact been overlooked that the best mortar, when combined with stone or gravel without reference to its grading, will not necessarily produce the best concrete. A poorly graded, coarse aggregate will unquestionably require more mortar than will a well-graded one. Likewise, a coarse aggregate containing a large amount of small stone will allow the use of a somewhat finer sand than when the larger-sized stones predominate. . . . It might be considered practical to use a graded rather than a naturally occurring concrete sand in such important work as concrete road construction if, by so doing, the life of the pavement can be prolonged."

The effect of alkali on Portland cement, K. STEIK (*Wyoming Sta. Bul. 113* (*1917*), *pp. 71–122, figs. 19*).—Experiments are reported in which it was found that cement put into solutions of alkali salts set as well as in water. " In solutions of sodium sulphate $CaSO_4.2H_2O$ is formed. In solutions of magnesium sulphate $CaSO_4$, $2H_2O$, and $Mg(OH)_2$ are formed. In solutions of sodium chlorid a silicate is formed. The high percentage of sodium in this silicate is likely the reason for the increase of insoluble sodium in cement.

" Sodium chlorid in solution or its presence in solution with other alkali salts has its effect chiefly through a solvent action.

" Of the solutions tested, the 5 per cent sodium sulphate solution had the greatest disintegrating effects. Solutions containing chlorids, sulphates, and carbonates had the least effect. Mortars disintegrate faster than neat cement. The formation of compounds with molecular volumes larger than the molecular volume of calcium hydroxid is not the cause of disintegration of cement. The ultimate cause of the disintegration of cement by alkalies is due to the alkalies forming compounds with the elements of cement, which subsequently are removed from the cement by solution."

Spontaneous combustion as a cause of fires, A. R. LAMB (*Iowa Sta. Circ. 36* (*1917*), *pp. 4*).—This circular deals with the spontaneous combustion of coal, drying oils, and especially hay, and briefly outlines means of preventing it.

" The self-heating of hay generally reaches a dangerous point about a month or six weeks after being mowed or stacked. Means of prevention must . . . be employed before this time. The most effective means is proper curing of the hay before storing it. . . . The hay should be carefully cured until the stalks are so dry that no moisture can be squeezed out by twisting a bunch in the hands. It must also be free from outside moisture, as dew or rain, when put into the barn.

" If the hay has unavoidably been put into the barn when somewhat moist it should be watched for signs of heating. The first evidence is shown in the morning, a day or two later, when the mow is covered with moisture condensed from the water vapor driven off in the heating. If the heating continues, craters or openings may be found near the center of the mow. If gases or pungent odors are driven off, the heating is great enough to be dangerous, and the hay should be removed at once."

Report of tractor ratings committee, R. OLNEY ET AL. (*N. G. E. A. Bul., 2* (*1917*), *No. 12, pp. 7–9*).—The recommendations of the committee are " that the standard rating specifications for all tractors include belt horsepower, drawbar horsepower, drawbar pull in pounds, and engine and tractive speeds . . . but that for ordinary use in designating the different sizes or capacities of tractors, a standard rating be adopted such as is at present in general use. For example, tractors should be rated as 12–25, 10–20, 12–20, etc., in which the double number represents the drawbar and the belt horsepower, respectively.

" That the standard rating be on the following basis: (1) The drawbar horsepower rating must express the horsepower that the manufacturer will guarantee his tractor—when in good condition and properly operated at normal engine speed—to deliver at the drawbar continuously for two hours on a firm, dry, level, earth road, with the tractor traveling at its rated plowing speed; (2) that the belt horsepower rating must express the horsepower that the manufacturer will guarantee the engine of his tractor—when in good condition and properly operated at normal speed—to deliver at the belt pulley continuously for two hours."

Farm buildings, with plans and descriptions, H. A. SHEARER (*Chicago: Frederick J. Drake & Co., 1917, pp. 256, figs. 148*).—This book contains the following chapters: Economy of good farm buildings; two kinds of barn construction; horse and cow barn; enlarged dairy and horse barn; dairy barn for 28 cows; dairy barn for 30 cows; monitor roof dairy stable; new models for farm barns; miscellaneous farm buildings; hog houses for winter and summer; poultry, poultry houses, and poultry furniture; concrete on the farm; comfortable farm homes; and dictionary of building and architectural terms.

Considerable space is devoted to the chapter on comfortable farm homes, which includes plans and information regarding the construction of several types and sizes of farm dwelling. The section on the farm septic tank contains, among other matters, the following new information regarding sewage purification:

" A septic tank provides a scientific means of rendering sewage harmless. . . . Two kinds of bacteria work in a septic tank. Aerobic bacteria work in the first compartment and anaerobic bacteria work in the second compartment. . . . The size of the septic tank varies according to the amount of sewage to be disposed of. The capacity of the first box or compartment should be sufficient to hold two days' or three days' sewage before it runs over into the second compartment. The second compartment should be about the size of the first. . . . The final discharge from the septic tank is supposed to be inoffensive but it is generally recommended to discharge into 4-in. draintile so that the water can percolate away."

Silo building, W. D. NICHOLLS (*Univ. Ky. Col. Agr., Ext. Div. Circ. 48 (1917), pp. 7*).—This is a brief note on silo building in Kentucky.

Pit silos, T. P. METCALF and G. A. SCOTT (*U. S. Dept. Agr., Farmers' Bul. 825 (1917), pp. 14, figs. 6*).—This bulletin gives directions for constructing pit silos, indicating the proper size and best location, and describes the practices which have proved most satisfactory.

" Underground silos should be constructed only in soils that are firm and free from rocks, sand strata, and seeps, and where the water table is always below the bottom of the floor after they are dug. . . . The construction of pit silos is recommended only where a combination of soil and climatic conditions exists such as is found in the Great Plains region."

Reinforced concrete silos and small grain bins, E. S. FOWLER (*Proc. Nat. Assoc. Cement Users, 9 (1913), pp. 498–510, figs. 7*).—This article reviews statistical data on concrete silo construction and gives information regarding small concrete grain bins and tanks.

RURAL ECONOMICS.

Farm management [in Missouri], O. R. JOHNSON and R. M. GREEN (*Missouri Sta. Bul. 147 (1917), pp. 38-40*).—In these pages attention is called to the results of a survey to determine the cost of living in Missouri. It was found that the total cost of living on 191 farms in Saline County was $555.80, of which the farm furnished $239.80, while on 198 farms in Dade County the total cost was $406.80, of which the farm furnished $173.80. Data are also shown regarding animal units on Missouri farms, and the distribution of man and horse labor for various farm crops and live stock.

[Farm cost accounts at the Ontario agricultural experimental farm] (*Ann. Rpt. Ontario Agr. Col. and Expt. Farm, 42 (1916), pp. 21-29*).—These pages outline the method used to obtain the cost of producing crops, live stock, and livestock products on the farm of the Ontario Agricultural College, under the various systems employed in its management. The accounts indicate, for the crops, the various items of expense, the total yield, yield per acre, and cost per unit; for live stock, they indicate the quantity of the various feeds used, the value of the products, and the profit for the year and per unit.

Plan for handling the farm-labor problem (*U. S. Dept. Agr., Office Sec. Circ. 2 (1917), pp. 31*).—The plan as outlined in this circular contemplates a State organization and separate county organizations, and a local organization for the distribution of agricultural laborers, and also provides for ascertaining the needs of every farm, not only as to number of additional laborers but as to the time when they are wanted. In the plan presented, each unit acts as a clearing house for its territory, reporting to the units higher up only surpluses or deficits.

Forms for use in the work are appended.

Agricultural labor question in Switzerland, IV (*Pubs. Sec. Paysans Suisse, No. 54 (1917), pp. VII+194*).—To restrict the necessity for manual labor in agriculture in Switzerland, the author considers measures relative to the (1) general organization of the country, such as the influence of area, land improvements, and buildings, (2) specific organization for cultivation purposes in the substitution of motors and the use of proper implements and machines, and (3) management of the work.

[Agricultural societies in Finland] (*Landtbr. Styr. Meddel. [Finland], No. 114 (1914), pp. 91*).—In this volume are contained reports regarding the work of various agricultural societies, indicating the membership, type of organization, functions performed, and accomplishments during the year 1914.

California resources and possibilities (*Ann. Rpt. Cal. Develop. Bd., 27 (1916), pp. 64, pl. 1, figs. 5*).—This report continues data previously noted (E. S. R., 35, p. 795).

New Hampshire farms.—Your opportunity (*Concord, N. H.: Dept. Agr., 1916, 13. ed., pp. 42, pl. 1, figs. 30*).—In this issue many advantages which the State offers to farmers are suggested.

[Agricultural resources of the State of New York], C. S. Wilson et al. (*N. Y. State Food Sup. Com. Bul. 2 (1917), pp. 18*).—This is a preliminary report of the agricultural resources of the State, ascertained through cooperation with the extension agents and school children. It indicates the amount of crops and live stock wanted and for sale by farmers, the amount of live stock on hand, amount of pasture, and the use expected to be made of the farm land.

An auto trip in New York State and what three men found about rural market conditions and farm trade (*New York: Orange Judd Co., 1916, pp. 32, figs. 28*).—This report, based on interviews with farmers and country merchants, deals with rural market conditions and farm trade for the purpose of giving "advertisers first-hand, direct information regarding the attitude of rural merchants and farmers toward advertised goods, as well as a close view of the exact conditions, as reported by the dealers themselves, in the rural districts of New York State."

Corn is king in South Dakota (*Pierre, S. D.: State [1917], pp. 32, figs. 17*).—This bulletin is descriptive of the natural conditions, and the agricultural, mineral, and timber resources of the State, including opportunities for further development and settlement.

Statistics and resources of Utah.—Report of the State Bureau of Immigration, Labor, and Statistics, H. T. Haines (*Bien. Rpt. Bur. Immigr., Labor and

Statis. Utah, *3 (1915–1916)*, *pp. 492, pls. 11, figs. 190*).—This is a statistical and descriptive review of the various commercial, agricultural, mining, timber, and water-power resources of Utah, prepared to stimulate desirable immigration.

Joint report on the economic and agronomic conditions in the Cagayan Valley [Philippine Islands] in relation to tobacco, C. M. Hoskins et al. *(Manila, P. I.: Govt., 1916, pp. 36)*.—The authors find that general economic conditions in the Philippine Islands are unsatisfactory, due (1) to the scarcity and high cost of money, (2) to the inadequate transportation facilities, and (3) to the unsatisfactory marketing methods. They recommend an immediate cadastral survey for the Cagayan Valley, a government loan to a suggested rural agricultural cooperative association, and the construction of the necessary highways.

A survey of agronomic conditions as to tobacco culture indicated room for improvement in the cultivation of pure strains through seed selection, better and more modern methods of culture, control of insect pests, and construction of proper curing sheds.

British industries after the war.—I, The land industry, W. Earnshaw-Cooper *(London: Cent. Committee Nat. Patriotic Organs., [1917], pp. 52)*.— This report discusses the possible development of agriculture in England and Wales after the war. It recommends the increasing of the productiveness of the soil to its maximum capacity, enlarging the number of live stock, making land settlement in England and Wales as satisfactory as in other countries, and devising means whereby the country can grow a larger proportion of its own food.

A national agricultural policy, J. H. C. Johnston *(London: P. S. King & Son, Ltd., 1915, pp. 40, fig. 1)*.—The author presents a plan of land purchase for England, financially based on the principles of cooperative credit and occupying ownership, whereby the owner would receive part of the purchase price in cash and the balance in State guaranteed bonds, or the entire purchase price would be advanced to the farmer for a stipulated annuity.

Allotments and small holdings in Oxfordshire, A. W. Ashby *(Oxford, England: The Clarendon Press, 1916, pp. VII+198)*.—This survey, which supplements recently published information by Orr (E. S. R., 37, p. 291), considers the history of allotments and small holdings, present conditions in reference to the demand for allotments, conditions of tenancy, methods of cultivation and economic effects, distribution of holdings, small holding colonies, county council holdings, and conditions as to employment, crop, and stock. The view is taken that allotments are made to cover a deficient labor wage and that the system of small holdings, while conducive to better agriculture, shows need for general improvement.

The economic resources of Russia, with special reference to British opportunities, A. Heykine *(Jour. Roy. Statis. Soc., 80 (1917), No. 2, pp. 187–221)*.— With a discussion of the general economic resources, the author presents statistics concerning areas, production, and export of the wheat, rye, potato, oat, tobacco, and beet-sugar crops, and information is given showing the importance of live stock, bacon, and fruit. A discussion by members is appended.

Agricultural colonization of Tripoli *(Agr. Colon. [Italy], 11 (1917), No. 2, pp. 133–137)*.—This report recommends the appointment of a special commission to study methods of placing soldiers on the land and the ascertaining of the regions most favorable for agricultural development.

[Land tenure and settlement; agriculture and live stock in New Zealand] *(New Zeal. Off. Yearbook 1916, pp. 406–465, figs. 2)*.—These pages continue the data previously noted (E. S. R., 36, p. 690).

Prices and wages in India (*Dept. Statis. India, Prices and Wages India, 32 (1917), pp. [2]+IV+VIII+266, pls. 3*).—This volume continues data previously noted (E. S. R., 34, p. 195) by adding data for later years.

[Agricultural statistics of Japan] (*Résumé Statis. Empire Japon, 31 (1917), pp. 227, pls. 4*).—These pages give the area and production of the principal crops for 1915, with comparisons for earlier years, number of live stock for 1914, and area in forests and quantity of forest products harvested in 1915.

AGRICULTURAL EDUCATION.

Secondary agricultural schools in Russia, W. S. JESIEN (*U. S. Bur. Ed. Bul. 4 (1917), pp. 22*).—This bulletin deals with legislation for the maintenance of agricultural schools in Russia and the organization of secondary agricultural education, including admission requirements, statistics, sources of maintenance, courses of study, and the training of teachers. An account is also given of the organization and work of the Bessarabian School of Viticulture and Wine Making, at Kishenef.

The agricultural education act of 1904 places all private agricultural schools under the supervision of the ministry of agriculture and imperial domains, now known as the general office of land management and agriculture, and provides for the maintenance of schools controlled directly by this ministry and for a considerable part of the support of private schools. Government aid for agricultural schools controlled by the department of agriculture increased from $964,838 in 1907 to $2,000,440 in 1911.

The agricultural schools are divided into three classes—lower or primary, middle or secondary, and higher schools, the latter subject to regulations not included in this act. The secondary schools have for their object the furnishing to students of a practical agricultural education, based on scientific principles, in order to prepare them for agricultural work; the higher primary schools, preparation for practical farming; and the elementary schools, preparation mainly by practical instruction, of men informed and skilled in respect to farm work.

The secondary schools are stated to be admirably organized and managed and have a curriculum of wider scope than is necessary for purely practical instruction of peasant youths. Many of their graduates become managers of large estates, government officials, teachers, etc., while only a small part return to farming on a small scale. Almost all of the schools are boarding schools and nominal tuition fees are charged, but poorer children are aided by scholarships from government and private sources.

On January 1, 1910, there were 15 secondary agricultural schools, the oldest of which was founded in 1822 in Moscow. The number of instructors in these schools ranged from 7 to 26 per school, the number of students from 35 to 277, the annual expenditure from $17,609 to $54,550, and the value of school property from $49,834 to $598,400. The course of study extended over six years, the last year being devoted almost entirely to practical work. The general subjects taught have nearly the same scope as in the gymnasia. Horticulture is taught 2 hours weekly in the fourth year; agriculture 3 hours, zootechny 4 hours, farm economy 6 hours, survey of the farming industry 1 hour, agricultural technology 2 hours, agricultural machines and general mechanics 2 hours, and geodesy 2 hours weekly in the fifth and sixth years each; meteorology 1 hour weekly in the fifth year; and veterinary medicine and forestry 1 hour each a week in the sixth year. Courses for training teachers for primary agricultural schools have also been established at some of these schools.

Graduates of secondary agricultural schools may continue their education in higher agricultural schools where they are accepted without examination, while graduates of the viticultural school may continue their studies in the higher viticultural courses in Yalta, Crimea. The act of 1904 permits agricultural students to continue their studies after they have passed the age of conscription, which is 21 years, until the completion of the school program, but not after 24 years of age.

A bibliography of publications in the Russian language is included.

Twenty-third annual report of the inspector of State high schools, E. M. PHILLIPS (*Ann. Rpt. Insp. State High Schools Minn., 23 (1916), pp. 73, pls. 2*).—This is a report on the progress in the work of the Minnesota State high schools in 1915–16. It includes statistical data on the location of State-aided departments of agriculture, the number of pupils, agricultural subjects in each year of the course of each school, number of short courses, salary of instructors, etc. Similar information is given with reference to State-aided departments of home training.

A description is given of a community school building erected at Wheaton, Minn., believed to be the first building of its kind in this country. It houses among other departments those of agriculture and home training, the county agricultural agent, and the Traverse County farm bureau.

The report indicates that of a total of 230 State high schools, 152 maintained departments of agriculture and received a total of $142,992 State aid; 185 had departments of home training with a total of $108,855 State aid. The total enrollment in the grades in agriculture was 5,013 and in home training 7,438, as compared with 3,992 in agriculture and 6,708 in home training in the previous year. The total enrollment in the high schools in agriculture was 4,643 and in home training 9,813, as compared with 4,527 in agriculture and 5,853 in home training in 1914–15.

Introduction of agriculture into public schools (*Ann. Rpt. Dept. Agr. Prince Edward Island, 1916, pp. 46–51, fig. 1*).—A brief account is given of the progress in the work of the rural science department of the Prince of Wales College in training teachers to give instruction in nature study and agriculture in the rural schools.

The education of the farmers by the regional agronomes, F. P. MAROTTA (*Min. Agr. Nac. [Buenos Aires], Dir. Gen. Enseñanza e Invest. Agr. [Pub.] No. 62 (1916), pp. 5–19*).—The author describes various phases of the work of the 20 regional agronomes in Argentina, including itinerant chairs, consultations and information, temporary courses, cooperative experiment fields, competitions and expositions, and rural cooperation. This extension service was created in 1908.

Report of the work of the school garden association in 1915 and 1916 (*Ber. For. Skolehav. Virks. [Denmark], 1915–1916, pp. 47, figs. 22*).—A brief summary is given of the school garden work in 1915 and 1916, followed by reports on the work of individual gardens in Denmark. Reports are also included on the instruction in school gardening given by the training schools or seminars for teachers at Växjö, Lund, and Göteborg for men, and at Kalmar for women, and on the work of seven school gardens for children in Norway, including five in Christiania, and nine in Sweden.

Chronicle of the woman movement in German Switzerland in 1915–16, ELISA STRUB (*Jahrb. Schweizerfrauen, 2 (1916), pp. 9–39*).—The author reports on the progress in home economics, professional, social, and civic training of women, the activities of women's associations, and the professional and public life of women.

Report of the committee on teaching (*Amer. Farm Management Assoc. Rpt.*, *6 (1915), pp. 79–82*).—The committee confined its work to a study of graduate courses in farm management in different agricultural colleges. Answers to a questionnaire sent out indicate that graduate work is given in 13 institutions, 5 of which offer work leading to the doctor's degree. A list of problems for investigation and theses developed, leading to master's and doctor's degrees at different institutions, is included, as well as statistical data.

Farm management summer practice courses, R. L. ADAMS (*Amer. Farm Management Assoc. Rpt., 6 (1915), pp. 40–50*).—This is a description of the six-weeks' summer practice course, taken preferably between the sophomore and junior years, at the University of California, consisting of a tour of several of the distinctly agricultural sections of the State and detailed investigations in the various phases of agriculture. These trips have developed a decided farm-management aspect. Recommendations with reference to methods of carrying on the work are made, based on the results obtained from two years of these courses. The author states in conclusion that he feels so keenly the advantages which the students secure from this kind of work, that he is very reluctant for a man to substitute in any way whatever.

The scope and methods of instruction in rural sociology, J. M. GILLETTE (*Pubs. Amer. Sociol. Soc., 11 (1916), pp. 163–182*).—The author defines rural sociology and includes in its scope physical conditions, populations, economic production, communication, health, institutions and organizations, pathological social conditions, psychology of the rural social mind, problems of semirural communities, relation of country to city, and rural surveys. The methods of instruction are deemed identical with those used in other fields of social science.

The teaching of rural sociology, particularly in the land-grant colleges and universities, D. L. SANDERSON (*Pubs. Amer. Sociol. Soc., 11 (1916), pp. 181–208*).—This article summarizes replies to a questionnaire as to the teaching of rural sociology sent out to representative universities and colleges of the country. The points covered include courses offered; relation to elementary sociology, political economy, rural economics, and education; definition; prerequisites, etc.

Preparation for editorial work on farm papers, N. A. CRAWFORD (*Kans. State Agr. Col. Bul., 1 (1917), No. 5, pp. 35*).—A discussion based on replies by 146 managing editors of farm papers to a questionnaire as to the preparation desired of young men for agricultural journalism. In these replies, previous farm experience was given an average rating of 31.9, college training in agriculture 23.1, college training in journalism 13.2, experience on newspapers 17.1, and other qualifications 14.7 per cent.

Report of committee on suggestive course in agriculture for use in land-grant colleges of the South which give teacher training courses in agriculture, approved at New Orleans conference, April, 1916 (*High School Quart.* [Ga.], 5 (1917), No. 4, pp. 251–257*).—An outline is given of the course approved at this conference as previously noted (E. S. R., 34, p. 799).

Practical agriculture in Texas schools through school, home, and community, J. D. BLACKWELL (*Agr. and Mech. Col. Tex. Ext. Serv. Bul. 37 (1917), pp. 95, figs. 19*).—This bulletin is intended as a guide to teachers undertaking definite projects in agriculture, and incidentally as a supplement to the numerous textbooks on elementary and high-school agriculture. It contains an explanation of home projects, home work, and credit, suggested outlines for reports on home projects, and outlines of subject matter for plant culture, general animal husbandry, dairy husbandry, poultry husbandry, fruit production, elementary soil study, vegetable and landscape gardening, crop production, and farm engineering and farm management. The outlines are planned on the basis of a 1-unit course in general agriculture, which may, however, be enlarged upon and used in schools teaching two or more units. Each outline is followed by eight school exercises with directions for their performance, which may be given as a demonstration by the teacher or worked by groups or individuals, and which should be reported by the pupils in notebooks; also suggested field trips and home projects and home work, and lists of books and references. A monthly calendar for community projects is included.

Practical education: A home library of fourteen books in one, P. G. HOLDEN, E. J. McFADDEN, and O. T. BRIGHT (*Chicago: The W. E. Richardson Co., Inc., 1917, pp. 521, figs. 89*).—This text presents a plan for the cooperation of parent and teacher in organizing and conducting over 20 home school clubs. It includes directions for growing vegetables, fruit, and flowers in school-home gardens, raising poultry, pigs, and rabbits, keeping bees, cow testing and dairy work, stock judging, practical farm arithmetic and farm accounting, social center work, salesmanship and business efficiency, and outlines of work in sewing, cooking, canning, and home building, as well as suggestions to the teacher for correlating this work with other school subjects.

School and home gardens, T. I. MAIRS (*Penn. State Col., School Bul. 5 [1917], pp. 28, figs. 22*).—This bulletin contains a brief history of children's gardens and an enumeration of advantages that may be derived from children's gardens, an outline of a suggested classification of gardens based upon the purposes emphasized, suggestions with reference to gardens for schools in the country where probably for the most part the home garden should take the place of the school garden, selecting the site and crops, the size of the garden, and the preparation of the land, rules governing a garden contest for the high school, a home garden planting table, a form of records for a garden contest, plans of a model school garden prepared for the Panama-Pacific Exposition, and references to literature on gardening.

Home project at an agricultural school, C. H. LANE (*High School Quart. [Ga.], 5 (1917), No. 4, pp. 265–267*).—This is a brief statement of the home-project work required of students during the vacation between the second and third years of the 3-year courses in agriculture and horticulture for farm boys offered at the college of agriculture of the Ohio State University. These courses are complete in themselves and do not offer preparation for any of the four-year curricula, nor are they accredited toward a degree on any of these curricula.

Productive plant husbandry, K. C. DAVIS (*Philadelphia and London: J. B. Lippincott Co., 1917, pp. XVI+462, pl. 1, figs. 312*).—This textbook for high schools treats the subjects of plant propagation and breeding, soils, field crops, gardening, fruit growing, forestry, insects, plant diseases, and farm management. Field and laboratory exercises, including suggestions for home projects, and references to literature for supplementary reading are given at the close of each chapter. One school year is allowed for the completion of the studies and exercises, and a preliminary study of botany is not considered essential to the understanding of the lessons.

Agricultural botany, W. WHITNEY (*School Sci. and Math., 17 (1917), No. 6, pp. 488–494*).—The author considers briefly the principles which should underlie the construction of a course in botany, and outlines whole year and half-year suggestive courses in agricultural botany in which the order of topics is determined so far as practicable by the season.

Feed manual and notebook, F. W. WOLL (*Philadelphia and London: J. B. Lippincott Co., 1917, pp. 137*).—This manual, which has been prepared for students in agricultural schools and colleges, consists of exercises (1) relating to the value of the common feeding stuffs used in this country, their chemical composition and digestibility, methods of preparation, examination for purity, relative feeding values, etc.; and (2) illustrating calculations of rations for farm animals, the rights and wrong uses of the various feeds for feeding horses, cattle, sheep, swine, and poultry, and general problems connected with the feeding of farm stock. Digestion coefficients of common feeding stuffs, in percentages, and a brief list of suggested apparatus with prices are included.

Proceedings of the twenty-first annual meeting of the American Association of Farmers' Institute Workers, edited by L. R. TAFT (*Proc. Amer. Assoc. Farmers' Inst. Workers, 21 (1916), pp. 139, figs. 2*).—This is a detailed report of the proceedings of the meeting held at Washington, D. C., on November 13–15, 1916. It includes the reports of committees on institute organization, institute lecturers, cooperation of farmers' institutes with other educational agencies, movable schools of agriculture, young people's institutes, resolutions, etc., and the following papers: President's address, by F. S. Cooley; farmers' institute work in Wisconsin, Delaware, Michigan, Texas, Pennsylvania, and Iowa, by E. L. Luther, W. Webb, L. R. Taft, J. W. Neill, C. E. Carothers, and Catherine J. MacKay, respectively; extension work in Oregon, by Anna M. Turley; The Work of the U. S. Department of Agriculture, by C. Vrooman; The Extent and Possibilities of Cooperative Marketing, by C. E. Bassett; The Relation of the Smith-Lever Funds to Farmers' Institutes, by A. C. True; The Present Relation of Farmers' Institutes and Extension Schools, by D. J. Crosby; A Balanced Ration for a Community, by J. C. Ketcham; The Humus Content of the Soil, by H. J. Wheeler; Nebraska Junior Institutes in Agriculture and Home Economics; The School Lunch Basket and Its Preparation, by Mrs. D. H. Stockman; A Home Demonstration Project, by Anna M. Turley; Extension and Farmers' Institute Work in Home Economics, by Belle M. Hoover; Women's Institute Work in Ontario, by G. A. Putnam; Essentials in Home Economics Teaching, by Mrs. I. L. Harrington; Statistics of Farmers' Institutes in the United States, 1915–16, by J. M. Stedman; and special notes of the work in various States and notes on farmers' institute work in Canada.

MISCELLANEOUS.

Report of the Guam Agricultural Experiment Station, 1916 (*Guam Sta. Rpt. 1916, pp. 58, pls. 10, figs. 5*).—This contains reports of the agronomist in charge, the foreman of the Cotot stock farm, and the animal husbandman and veterinarian. The experimental work recorded is for the most part abstracted elsewhere in this issue.

Work and progress of the agricultural experiment station for the year ended June 30, 1916 (*Missouri Sta. Bul. 147 (1917), pp. 64, figs. 10*).—This contains the organization list, a report of the director on the work and publications of the station, and a financial statement for the Federal funds for the fiscal year ended June 30, 1916. The experimental work reported and not previously noted is for the most part abstracted elsewhere in this issue.

NOTES.

Alabama Canebrake Station.—J. M. Burgess, associate professor of dairying at Clemson College, has been appointed director beginning about December 1.

California University.—Several special short courses are being offered at Davis and Riverside on gas tractors, and at Davis to practical cheese makers on improved methods in cheese making.

New York State Station.—James E. Mensching, of the Pennsylvania Institute of Animal Nutrition, has been appointed associate agronomist to succeed R. C. Collison, promoted to agronomist and given leave of absence for postgraduate work at Columbia University for the year.

Ohio State University and Station.—Vernon H. Davis, professor of horticulture, has resigned to become director of the new State bureau of markets.

At the station Thomas L. Guyton and Jacob R. Stear have been appointed assistants in entomology. J. T. Parsons has been appointed assistant in soils.

Oklahoma College and Station.—W. L. Carlyle has resigned as dean and director to engage in business in Calgary, Alberta. President J. W. Cantwell has been designated acting director of the station.

Pennsylvania Institute of Animal Nutrition.—A frame building 25 by 45 feet is being erected for the use of the Institute. It will contain stalls and other appliances for the digestion and metabolism experiments carried on in connection with the investigations with the respiration calorimeter and will also afford storage for the feeding stuffs used.

Mark C. Lewis, a 1917 graduate of the college, has been appointed assistant in animal nutrition, vice William H. Matthews, resigned to enter the military service.

Tennessee Station.—The selection by the State commission of a site of 680 acres near Columbia in Maury County for the Middle Tennessee substation has been accepted by the county court of that county, which has appropriated approximately $100,000 for the purchase of the property. Another fund of $100,000 for buildings and a maintenance fund is available under the State legislation previously referred to (E. S. R., 37, p. 198).

Work has been begun on the new dairy barn on the Cherokee Farm of the main station. This is to cost $6,500, including two silos and accommodations for about 30 cows.

Utah Station.—The dairy barn has been renovated and additional equipment installed, including a new milk room. The poultry department has recently completed two semimonitor and two shed-roof poultry houses, which will accommodate about 400 birds and cost approximately $700. The department of meteorology has installed a complete set of meteorological instruments.

H. J. Maughan has resigned as assistant agronomist to engage in ranching in Wyoming, and A. O. Larson, as assistant entomologist, to accept a position in the high school at Manhattan, Mont.

Vermont University and Station.—H. E. Bartram, assistant plant pathologist in the station, resigned October 31 to begin demonstration work in plant pathology in connection with the extension service.

Washington College and Station.—F. J. Sievers, superintendent of the county school of agriculture at Wauwatosa, Wis., has been appointed professor of soils and soil physicist to succeed C. C. Thom. A. B. Nystrom, dairy husbandman, has resigned to accept an appointment as county agriculturist of Lewis County, effective October 1.

American Association for the Advancement of Agricultural Teaching.—The eighth annual meeting of this association was held in Washington, D. C., November 13, 1917. Special prominence was given to problems affecting secondary education, including developments under the Federal Vocational Education Aid Act.

W. H. French, of Michigan, president of the association, traced the development of secondary school agriculture in this country from 1888 to the present, calling attention to the prominence now given the subject through the passage of the Federal Vocational Aid Act. J. P. Monroe, of the Federal Board for Vocational Education, discussed the act in operation. He laid emphasis on the fact that this act provides for normal education for normal persons. It is not an inferior kind of education but aims to make broad and intelligent citizens. He also described the present Federal organization, and outlined some of its policies. L. S. Hawkins, assistant director of agricultural education for the board, under the subject What Constitutes Proper State Supervision of Home Projects, showed how the supervision should stimulate progress and encourage the teachers rather than merely standardize and contribute a check as to formal requirements.

F. B. Jenks, of the University of Vermont, showed how practical and valuable extension service might be the logical outgrowth of the high school work in agriculture and how this might cooperate with the work of the county agent within the territory of the school. Numerous examples of this service as rendered by high schools in Vermont were cited.

In a paper on Minimum Laboratory Equipment for Agriculture in Public Secondary Schools, by J. A. James, supervisor of secondary agriculture of Wisconsin, emphasis was laid on the necessity for useful apparatus which in many cases might be found and used at the home farms. The list of absolutely essential apparatus was very brief and for the most part comprised material useful in farm operations.

The relations of the association to the National Society for the Promotion of Industrial Education were discussed, and resolutions adopted declaring that the association should continue, but take steps looking toward the proper recognition and representation of agriculture in the society, and possibly to an amalgamation of these organizations. The incoming president, together with W. R. Hart of Massachusetts, and Z. M. Smith of Indiana, were appointed to represent the association in this matter.

The standing committee on the cooperative use of equipment and illustrative material presented a report by H. P. Barrows on Illustrative Material Through the States Relations Service. The committees on essential laboratory equipment for teaching agriculture in secondary schools and the relation of general science to agricultural instruction reported progress and were continued with the same personnel for another year, but a resolution was adopted substituting annual committees for standing committees.

The officers elected for the ensuing year were as follows: President, G. A. Works, Cornell University; vice president, W. G. Hummel, field agent of the Federal Board for Vocational Education; secretary-treasurer, F. E. Heald, States Relations Service; and additional members of the executive committee, L. S. Hawkins, Federal Board for Vocational Education; G. M. Wilson, Iowa State College; and Dean Alfred Vivian, Ohio State University.

American Society of Agronomy.—The tenth annual meeting of this society was held in Washington, D. C., November 12 and 13.

The presidential address was given by W. M. Jardine at a joint session held with the Society for the Promotion of Agricultural Science. Dean Jardine took for his subject The Agronomist of the Future, outlining the opportunities for service and the obligations imposed upon the trained agronomist with respect to the present emergency. He especially emphasized the necessity of gaining the confidence of the farmer by offering him ideas which are practical and workable as well as theoretically correct, and likened the agronomist to the " middleman " standing between the investigator in pure science and the farmer. Me maintained further that the primary duty of an agricultural college in granting the B. S. degree was to train agricultural teachers and farmers, not to turn out full-fledged scientific investigators. In concluding he urged that the agronomist be untiring in his study of the fundamentals and that the society encourage its members to pursue research studies.

Other papers presented before the society included the following: Mineral Food Requirements of the Wheat Plant at Different Stages in Its Development, by A. G. McCall; Effect of Sodium Nitrate Applied at Different Stages on the Yield, Composition, and Quality of Wheat, by J. Davidson and J. A. LeClerc; Some Facts Regarding the Soft or Flour Corns, by H. H. Biggar; Drainage Tanks for Soil Investigations—Some Preliminary Studies, by C. A. Mooers; Organizing Crop Production on the Basis of the Distribution of the Natural Vegetation, by A. E. Waller; Realtion of Weed Growth to Nitric Nitrogen Accumulation in the Soil, by L. E. Call and M. G. Sewell; Wheat Breeding Ideals, by H. Snyder; Red Rock Wheat and Rosen Rye, by F. A. Spragg; Calcium in Its Relation to Plant Nutrition, by R. H. True; The Triangle System for Fertilizer Experiments (with some remarks on the potash hunger of potatoes), by O. Schreiner and J. J. Skinner; Some Tests of an " All-Crops " Soil Inoculum, by P. Emerson; Corn and Wheat Soils in the United States, by C. F. Marbut; Methods Used in Cereal Investigations at the Cornell Station, by H. H. Love and W. T. Craig; The Significance of the Sulphur in Sulphate of Ammonia Applied to Certain Soils, by C. B. Lipman; and Aluminum as a Factor Influencing the Effect of Acid Soils on Different Crops, by B. L. Hartwell and F. R. Pember.

One entire session was devoted to varietal classification and nomenclature. A report of the committee upon varietal nomenclature embracing six years' work was read and discussed. This report is to be published in full in the Journal of the American Society of Agronomy. It included a " Code of Nomenclature," and a motion was adopted that the society appoint a committee to " act in cooperation with the American seed trade and any other agencies to secure uniformity in rules and practices of varietal nomenclature and registration." In connection with the presentation of the report, C. R. Ball discussed The Classification of Western Wheat Varieties, exhibiting mounted specimens to illustrate the scheme of classification employed, and gave a paper on Naming American Wheat Varieties, which outlined the use of the proposed Code of Nomenclature as applied to wheat. Mr. Ball emphasized the immediate necessity for a systematic naming of varieties, to be followed later by a scheme of classification.

Summarized reports were submitted by the committees on the standardization of field experiments and agronomic terminology. Brief reports were also submitted from local sections in Iowa, Kansas, Cornell, Ohio, South Dakota, New England, and Washington, D. C.

The following officers were elected for the ensuing year: President, T. L. Lyon; vice presidents, A. G. McCall and C. B. Lipman; and secretary-treasurer, P. V. Gardon.

Potato Association of America.—The fourth annual meeting of this association was held in Washington, D. C., November 9 and 10, 1917.

The program included addresses by Assistant Secretary Vrooman of the U. S. Department of Agriculture, Hon. H. C. Hoover, W. T. Macoun, C. A. Zavitz, and W. S. Blair, and papers on the following subjects: Feeding Value of Raw, Cooked, Silaged, and Pressed Dried Potatoes for Hogs, by F. G. Ashbrook; Feeding Value of Silaged and Pressed Dried Potatoes for Dairy Animals, by T. E. Woodward; The Farm Manufacture of Potato Starch, by H. C. Gore; The Preparation of Potato Silage, by L. A. Round; The Dehydration of Potatoes, by L. D. Sweet; Potato Utilization Work of the Bureau of Chemistry, by C. L. Alsberg; Fertilizer Studies on Potash Hunger of the Potato and Other Field Crops, by O. Schreiner; The Dietary Value of the Potato, by C. F. Langworthy; The Potato Situation and the Department's Work on Potatoes, by L. C. Corbett; Distribution of the Potato Crop, by E. P. Miller; Car Movement of Potatoes, by H. Elliott; Potato Growing and the Present Fertilizer Situation, by H. G. Bell; and The Production of High-Grade Seed Potatoes, by D. Dean.

Committee reports were also submitted upon seed improvement and certification, research, varietal nomenclature and testing, market standards and marketing, utilization of surplus stock and culls, transportation, potato contests and exhibitions, crop forecasting, publications, and education.

Officers were elected for the ensuing year, as follows: President, L. D. Sweet; vice president, W. T. Macoun; secretary-treasurer, W. Stuart; and members at large of the executive committee, H. G. Bell and H. E. Horton.

Miscellaneous.—The report of the committee of the Privy Council for Scientific and Industrial Research of Great Britain for 1916–17 states that substantial progress has been made for establishing a national research association for cotton. The committee has offered a grant of money to the Imperial Commissioner of Agriculture in the British West Indies, and it is hoped that in due course the new association may take over this work.

The food production department of Great Britain has established a seed-testing station in London. H. B. Renwich has been appointed director of feeding stuffs at the ministry of foods to organize the supply and distribution of feeding stuffs, particularly oil meal.

Plans are being devised in Great Britain for holding short training courses for soldiers who are available for agricultural work. Particular attention is to be given to the handling of farm machinery, especially tractors and plows.

A national institute is to be established in Italy to investigate the relations between malaria and agriculture, the cause of the unhealthfulness of malarial districts, and the organization of a campaign against these causes.

A chair of the pedagogy of agriculture has been established at the University of South Carolina. V. E. Rector, principal of the Antioch Industrial School, has been appointed to the position.

O

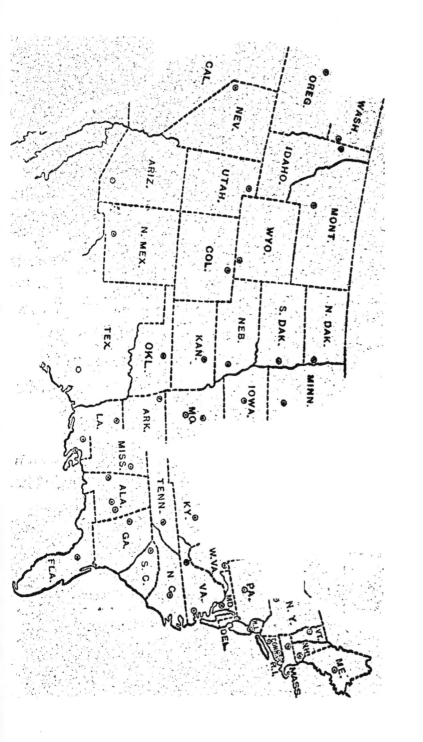

Issued February 28, 1918

DEPARTMENT OF AGRICULTURE
STATES RELATIONS SERVICE
A. C. TRUE, DIRECTOR

ABSTRACT NUMBER   No. 9

PERIMENT
TATION
RECORD

WASHINGTON
GOVERNMENT PRINTING OFFICE
1918

U. S. DEPARTMENT OF AGRICULTURE.

Scientific Bureaus.

WEATHER BUREAU—C. F. Marvin, *Chief.*
BUREAU OF ANIMAL INDUSTRY—J. R. Mohler, *Chief.*
BUREAU OF PLANT INDUSTRY—W. A. Taylor, *Chief.*
FOREST SERVICE—H. S. Graves, *Forester.*
BUREAU OF SOILS—Milton Whitney, *Chief.*
BUREAU OF CHEMISTRY—C. L. Alsberg, *Chief.*
BUREAU OF CROP ESTIMATES—L. M. Estabrook, *Statistician.*
BUREAU OF ENTOMOLOGY—L. O. Howard, *Entomologist.*
BUREAU OF BIOLOGICAL SURVEY—E. W. Nelson, *Chief.*
OFFICE OF PUBLIC ROADS AND RURAL ENGINEERING—L. W. Page, *Director.*
BUREAU OF MARKETS—C. J. Brand, *Chief.*

———

STATES RELATIONS SERVICE—A. C. True, *Director.*
OFFICE OF EXPERIMENT STATIONS—E. W. Allen, *Chief.*

———

THE AGRICULTURAL EXPERIMENT STATIONS.

ALABAMA—
College Station: *Auburn;* J. F. Dugger.[1]
Canebrake Station: *Uniontown;* J. M. Burgess.[1]
Tuskegee Station: *Tuskegee Institute;* G. W. Carver.[1]
ALASKA—*Sitka;* C. C. Georgeson.[3]
ARIZONA—*Tucson;* R. H. Forbes.[1]
ARKANSAS—*Fayetteville;* M. Nelson.[1]
CALIFORNIA—*Berkeley;* T. F. Hunt.[1]
COLORADO—*Fort Collins;* C. P. Gillette.[1]
CONNECTICUT—
State Station: *New Haven;* } E. H. Jenkins.[1]
Storrs Station: *Storrs;* }
DELAWARE—*Newark;* H. Hayward.[1]
FLORIDA—*Gainesville;* P. H. Rolfs.[1]
GEORGIA—*Experiment;* J. D. Price.[1]
GUAM—*Island of Guam;* C. W. Edwards.[3]
HAWAII—
Federal Station: *Honolulu;* J. M. Westgate.[3]
Sugar Planters' Station: *Honolulu;* H. P. Agee.[1]
IDAHO—*Moscow;* J. S. Jones.[1]
ILLINOIS—*Urbana;* E. Davenport.[1]
INDIANA—*Lafayette;* A. Goss.[1]
IOWA—*Ames;* C. F. Curtiss.[1]
KANSAS—*Manhattan;* W. M. Jardine.[1]
KENTUCKY—*Lexington;* T. P. Cooper.[1]
LOUISIANA—
State Station: *Baton Rouge;* }
Sugar Station: *Audubon Park,* } W. R. Dodson.[1]
New Orleans; }
North La. Station: *Calhoun;* }
MAINE—*Orono;* C. D. Woods.[1]
MARYLAND—*College Park;* H. J. Patterson.[1]
MASSACHUSETTS—*Amherst;* W. P. Brooks.[1]
MICHIGAN—*East Lansing;* R. S. Shaw.[1]
MINNESOTA—*University Farm, St. Paul;* R. W. Thatcher.[1]
MISSISSIPPI—*Agricultural College;* E. R. Lloyd.[1]

MISSOURI—
College Station: *Columbia;* F. B. Mumford.[1]
Fruit Station: *Mountain Grove;* Paul Evans.[1]
MONTANA—*Bozeman;* F. B. Linfield.[1]
NEBRASKA—*Lincoln;* E. A. Burnett.[1]
NEVADA—*Reno;* S. B. Doten.[1]
NEW HAMPSHIRE—*Durham;* J. C. Kendall.[1]
NEW JERSEY—*New Brunswick;* J. G. Lipman.[1]
NEW MEXICO—*State College;* Fabian Garcia.[1]
NEW YORK—
State Station: *Geneva;* W. H. Jordan.[1]
Cornell Station: *Ithaca;* A. R. Mann.[1]
NORTH CAROLINA—
College Station: *West Raleigh;* } B. W. Kilgore.[1]
State Station: *Raleigh;* }
NORTH DAKOTA—*Agricultural College;* L. Van Es.[4]
OHIO—*Wooster;* C. E. Thorne.[1]
OKLAHOMA—*Stillwater;* H. G. Knight.[1]
OREGON—*Corvallis;* A. B. Cordley.[1]
PENNSYLVANIA—
State College: R. L. Watts.[1]
State College: Institute of Animal Nutrition, H. P. Armsby.[1]
PORTO RICO—*Mayaguez;* D. W. May.[3]
RHODE ISLAND—*Kingston;* B. L. Hartwell.[1]
SOUTH CAROLINA—*Clemson College;* H. W. Barre.[1]
SOUTH DAKOTA—*Brookings;* J. W. Wilson.[1]
TENNESSEE—*Knoxville;* H. A. Morgan.[1]
TEXAS—*College Station;* B. Youngblood.[1]
UTAH—*Logan;* F. S. Harris.[1]
VERMONT—*Burlington;* J. L. Hills.[1]
VIRGINIA—
Blacksburg; A. W. Drinkard, Jr.[1]
Norfolk; Truck Station; T. C. Johnson.[1]
WASHINGTON—*Pullman;* Geo. Severance.[4]
WEST VIRGINIA—*Morgantown;* J. L. Coulter.
WISCONSIN—*Madison;* H. L. Russell.[1]
WYOMING—*Laramie;* A. D. Faville.[1]

[1] Director.   [2] Agronomist in charge.   [3] Animal husbandman in charge.   [4] Acting director.

EXPERIMENT STATION RECORD.

Editor: E. W. ALLEN, PH. D., *Chief, Office of Experiment Stations.*
Assistant Editor: H. L. KNIGHT.

EDITORIAL DEPARTMENTS.

Agricultural Chemistry and Agrotechny—E. H. NOLLAU.
Meteorology, Soils, and Fertilizers $\begin{cases} \text{W. H. BEAL.} \\ \text{R. W. TRULLINGER.} \end{cases}$
Agricultural Botany, Bacteriology, and Plant Pathology $\begin{cases} \text{W. H. EVANS, Ph. D.} \\ \text{W. E. BOYD.} \end{cases}$
Field Crops $\begin{cases} \text{J. I. SCHULTE.} \\ \text{J. D. LUCKETT.} \end{cases}$
Horticulture and Forestry—E. J. GLASSON.
Economic Zoology and Entomology—W. A. HOOKER, D. V. M.
Foods and Human Nutrition—C. F. LANGWORTHY, Ph. D., D. Sc.
Zootechny, Dairying, and Dairy Farming $\begin{cases} \text{D. W. MAY.} \\ \text{M. D. MOORE.} \end{cases}$
Veterinary Medicine $\begin{cases} \text{W. A. HOOKER.} \\ \text{E. H. NOLLAU.} \end{cases}$
Rural Engineering—R W. TRULLINGER.
Rural Economics—E. MERRITT.
Agricultural Education $\begin{cases} \text{C. H. LANE.} \\ \text{M. T. SPETHMANN.} \end{cases}$
Indexes—M. D. MOORE.

CONTENTS OF VOL. 37, NO. 9.

Page.

Recent work in agricultural science 801
Notes 896

SUBJECT LIST OF ABSTRACTS.

AGRICULTURAL CHEMISTRY—AGROTECHNY.

Principles of agricultural chemistry, Fraps 801
An introduction to the chemistry of plant products, Haas and Hill 801
Occurrence of mannite in silage and its use in explosives, Dox and Plaisance.. 801
Occurrence and significance of mannitol in silage, Dox and Plaisance 801
The occurrence of l-leucin in sweet clover silage, Plaisance 802
Action of acids on rotatory power of sucrose and invert sugar, Saillard 802
Glycolytic properties of muscular tissue, Hoagland and Mansfield 802
Function of muscular tissue in urea formation, Hoagland and Mansfield 802
Determination of carbonates in limestone and other materials, Barker 802
Insoluble phosphoric acid in organic base goods, Thomas 802
The decomposition of dilead arsenate by water, McDonnell and Graham 802
Allen's commercial organic analysis, edited by Davis 802
New apparatus for colorimetry, Moreau 803
Discontinuous extraction processes, Hawley 803
Simplified microcombustion method for carbon and hydrogen, Wise 803
Possibilities and limitations of the Duclaux method, Gillespie and Walters.... 803
Modification of the McLean-Van Slyke method for chlorids in blood, Foster... 804
Studies of acidosis, II, Van Slyke 804
Methods for the determination of saccharin in food products, Bonis 804

                                                                     Page.
Application of cryoscopic method for determining added water in milk, Keister.   804
The determination of fat in certain milk products, Francis and Morgan........   805
The estimation of unsaponifiable matter in oils, fats, and waxes, Wilkie.......   805
Thermal values of fats and oils.—II, Sulphuric acid number, Marden and Dover.   805
The pasteurization and biorization of fruit juices, Baragiola...................   805
Aldehydes in wine, Laborde...   806
Chemical composition of "separated musts," Baragiola and Kléber...........   806
Sauerkraut industry of the United States, Round and Coppersmith...........   806
Utilization of frozen and decayed potatoes, Schribaux........................   806
A moderate-sized evaporator for fruits and vegetables, Barss.................   806
The natural coagulation of the latex of *Hevea brasiliensis*, Denier and Vernet..   806
More about rice hull carbon, Zerban...   806
Local processes of coconut oil extraction in the Philippines, Gardiner........   806

METEOROLOGY.

Monthly Weather Review..   807
Free-air data at Drexel Aerological Station—April-June, 1916, Blair et al.....   807
Meteorological observations at Massachusetts Station, Ostrander et al.........   807
New England snowfall, Brooks..   807
Summer types of rainfall in upper Pecos Valley [N. Mex.], Hallenbeck.......   808
Showers of organic matter, McAtee..   808
The cold spring of 1917, Day..   808

SOILS—FERTILIZERS.

Relation of soil water movement to hygroscopicity, etc., Alway and McDole..   808
Origin of alkali, Stewart and Peterson...   809
A preliminary soil census of Alabama and west Florida, Harper...............   810
Soil survey of the Healdsburg area, Cal., Watson et al.........................   810
Soil survey of Cumberland County, Me., Van Duyne and Beck.................   810
Characteristics of Massachusetts peat lands and their uses, Dachnowski.......   810
The oxidizing power of some soils in Deli, Honing............................   811
Variation in the chemical composition of soils, Robinson et al.................   811
A soil sampler for bacteriological and chemical purposes, Neller..............   811
Influence of available carbohydrates on ammonia accumulation, Waksman....   812
Effect of paraffin on accumulation of ammonia and nitrates in soil, Gainey....   812
Nitrates and nitrification in relation to cultural practices, Noyes..............   813
A program of soil improvement for New York State, Fippin...................   813
Barnyard manure and products of decomposition, Murphy....................   813
Manure from the sea, Jenkins and Street.....................................   813
The value of coconut poonac as manure, Bamber............................   814
Experiments with humogen, Sutton..   814
The industrial chemist and the fertilizer crisis, Lint.........................   815
The effect of ammonium sulphate on soil acidity, Allison and Cook...........   815
The fixation of atmospheric nitrogen, Florentin..............................   815
Some conditions affecting value of calcium cyanamid as a manure, Mosscrop..   815
The value of Thomas slag phosphate for neutralizing soil, Hartwell et al.......   815
The rate of reversion of mixtures of superphosphate, Robertson..............   816
Phosphate rock in 1916, Stone...   816
Potash in agriculture.—III, Further researches, Aston........................   817
The recovery of potash from beet sugarhouse waste liquors, Zitkowski.........   817
Concentrated potash a by-product of cement mill..............................   817
The possibilities of developing an American potash industry, Meade...........   818
A key to the soil for better crops is soluble ground limestone..................   818
Lime report, 1916, Kellogg et al...   818
Fertilizer report, August 1 to December 31, 1916, Kellogg....................   818

AGRICULTURAL BOTANY.

The botany of crop plants, Robbins...   818
Important range plants: Their life history and forage value, Sampson..........   818
Inventory of seeds and plants imported from January 1 to March 31, 1914........   819
Inventory of seeds and plants imported from April 1 to June 30, 1914..........   819
Inventory of seeds and plants imported from July 1 to September 30, 1914......   819
New or noteworthy plants from Colombia and Central America, VI, Pittier....   819
The Middle American species of Lonchocarpus, Pittier........................   819

Page.

The families and genera of the bacteria, Winslow et al................ 819
Symbiosis between legume bacteria and nonlegumes, Burrill and Hansen 819
The behavior of self-sterile plants, East........................... 820
Twin hybrids from Œnothera lamarckiana and Œ. franciscana, Atkinson........ 820
Naming American hybrid oaks, Trelease............................ 820
The anatomy of woody plants, Jeffrey............................. 821
Ecology and physiology of the red mangrove, Bowman.................. 821
The chemical basis of regeneration and geotropism, Loeb.............. 821
The effects of acids and salts on biocolloids, MacDougal and Spoehr........... 821
Anesthesia and respiration, Haas................................. 831
The measurement of light in its physiological aspects, Macdougal and Spoehr.. 821

FIELD CROPS.

Effect of fall irrigation on yields at Belle Fourche, S. Dak., Farrell and Aune.. 822
Progress report, Substation No. 2, Troup, Tex., 1901–1914, Hotchkiss.......... 823
Report of the Bermuda Board of Agriculture, 1914–15, Wortley............... 823
[Field crops work in Argentina], Huergo.......................... 823
[Field crops], Symeonides...................................... 823
[Report of field crops work at the Bankipoor Station, 1915–16], Sherrard....... 823
[Report of work with field crops at the Benares Station], Sharma.............. 824
[Report of field crops work at the Cuttack Station, 1915–16], Sethi............ 824
[Report of field crops work at the Dumraon Station, 1915–16], Sherrard........ 825
[Report of work with field crops at the Orai Station], Burt................. 825
[Report of work with field crops at the Partabgarh Station], Sharma.......... 825
[Report of field crops work at the Ranchee Experiment Farm, 1915–16], Dobbs. 825
[Report of field crops work at Sabour Farm, 1915–16], Sil.................. 825
[Report of field crops work at Sepaya Experiment Farm, 1915–16], Mackenzie. 826
Fodder crops of Western India, Mann.............................. 826
Some wild fodder plants of the Bombay Presidency, Burns et al.............. 826
How to change the rotation system, Sotgia.......................... 826
Experiments in meadow culture on peat bogs, Fominykh.................. 826
Permanent pasture formation, Green.............................. 826
Grasses for pasture and hay in Texas, Garren....................... 827
The selection of cereals in Italy, Patanè.......................... 827
Influence of chemical fertilizers on the composition of the cereals............. 827
Statistics on the production of cereals and legumes, 1916................ 827
Growth of the root system of Medicago sativa, Shistovskij................. 827
The effect of phosphorus on alfalfa and alfalfa bacteria, Truesdell............. 828
A semiannual cropping system for bean lands, Hendry.................. 829
Determining the germinating capacity in beet seed, Vitek................ 829
Influence of low temperatures on germination of beet seeds, Urban and Vitek. 829
Boiling buffalo clover seed, McNair.............................. 829
An interesting seed corn experiment, Hughes....................... 830
Classification of American Upland cotton, Earle and Taylor.................. 830
Cotton production in the Belgian Kongo, Janssens..................... 830
The development of cotton culture in French West Africa, Barois............. 830
The opportunities for cotton production in the French colonies, Dybowski.... 830
Hemp culture in France, Blin................................... 830
The resources of Indo-China in oleaginous plants, Brenier................. 830
Growing potatoes under irrigation for profit, Stuart................... 830
Notes and observations on the culture of ramie, Hautefeuille.............. 830
Rice in Argentina, Girola...................................... 830
New rice varieties, Marcarelli................................... 831
Sweet clover (Melilotus), Fulmer................................ 831
Fertilizing the wheat crop, Thorne............................... 831
Acid phosphate versus raw phosphate rock for wheat, Williams............... 831
Adzuki beans and jimson weeds and Mendel's law, Blakeslee and Avery...... 831
The Canadian Seed Growers' Association and its work.................. 831
Determining impurity of cereals caused by Agrostemma githago, Âïnata........ 831

HORTICULTURE.

[Horticultural investigations at the Troup substation], Hotchkiss.............. 832
Report of horticultural experiment station, Vineland, Ont., 1906–1915........ 832
Plant breeding at the horticultural experiment station, Vineland, Palmer..... 832
[Vegetables at Wisley, 1915–16]................................. 832

Page.
Rules and regulations promulgated under the Federal Standard-Barrel Law ...   832
[Directions for the control of insect pests and diseases]   832
Dusting for tender fruits and apples, Caesar   832
Dusting as a substitute for spraying.—History and progress, Whetzel   832
New creations in fruits, Hansen   833
A list of the most desirable varieties of most kinds of fruits   833
Grass mulch.—A practical system of orchard management, Gourley   833
Orchard cover crops for the Moutere Hills, Hyde   833
Important factors in the successful cold storage of apples, Bird   833
The history and development of the red currant, Bunyard   833
Viticulture, Pacottet   834
Citrus culture in Japan, China, and Formosa, Clausen   834
Some abnormal water relations in citrus trees of the arid Southwest, Hodgson ..   834
Optimum moisture conditions for young lemon trees, Fowler and Lipman   834
Orange culture, de Mazières   835
The fig in Texas, Potts   835
The guavas of the Hawaiian Islands, MacCaughey   835
The pollination of the mango, Popenoe   835
Some results with oil palm (*Elæis guineensis*), van Helten   835
Coffee in Abyssinia, Spalletta   835
A review of coffee plantings in Buitenzorg garden, van Hall and van Helten ..   835
The germination and selection of tea seed, Bernard   835
[Flowers at Wisley, 1916]   836
Daffodil developments, Jacob   836
Practical book of outdoor rose growing for the home garden, Thomas, jr   836
Observations on tulips, Stout   836
Report of the tulip nomenclature committee, 1914–15, Bowles et al   836

FORESTRY.

The development of forest law in America, Kinney   836
Recent forestry propaganda in the Philippines, Sherfesee   836
Practical reforestation, Graves   836
How Louisiana is solving the reforestation problem, Alexander   836
An improved transplanting lath, Lyford-Pike   836
The preservation of leafy twigs of the beech, Boodle   837
The importance of plantation margins, Murray   837
Trees for nonirrigated regions in eastern Colorado, Morrill   837
Forest succession and rate of growth in sphagnum bogs, Rigg   837
Aspen as a permanent forest type, Fetherolf   837
The pitch pine, Piccioli   837
Notes on white pine 4-year transplants, Spring   837
Density of stand and rate of growth of Arizona yellow pine, Shreve   837
Probable error in field experimentation with Hevea, Bishop et al   837
Seed selection in the cultivation of *Hevea brasiliensis*, Petch   837
Effects of tapping and wintering on storage of plant food in Hevea, Rutgers ...   838
Rubber soils in Fiji, Wright   838
Report on forest administration in Bengal for 1915–16, Farrington   838
Forest Service stumpage appraisals, Girard   838
Marketing farm woodlot products in Maine, Lamb   838
Crossties purchased and treated in 1915, McCreight   838

DISEASES OF PLANTS.

Common and scientific names of plant diseases, Waite   838
[Plant diseases in British Guiana], Bancroft   838
Scolecotrichum graminis, Johnson and Hungerford   839
Bacteria of barley blight seed-borne, Jones et al   839
Corn disease caused by *Phyllachora graminis*, Dalbey   839
Smut diseases of wheat, Mercer   839
Tylenchus tritici on wheat, Byars   840
Bean diseases in New York State in 1916, Burkholder   840
Bacterial diseases of celery, Krout   840
Wintering of *Septoria petroselina apii*, Krout   840
Dissemination of the organism of cucumber anthracnose, Gardner   840
Do bacteria of angular leaf spot of cucumber overwinter on the seed? Carsner ..   840
Preliminary notes on a new leaf spot of cucumbers, Osner   840

Page.
Virulence of different strains of *Cladosporium cucumerinum*, Gilbert.......... 840
A nematode disease of the dasheen and its control by hot water, Byars........ 841
A bacterial stem and leaf disease of lettuce, Brown........................... 841
Studies upon the anthracnose of the onion, Walker............................ 841
Pink root, a new root disease of onions in Texas, Taubenhaus and Johnson.... 841
Black spot of pepper, Melchers and Dale...................................... 841
Notes on curly dwarf symptoms on Irish potatoes, Durrell..................... 841
Notes on mosaic symptoms of Irish potatoes, Melhus.......................... 842
Frost necrosis of potato tubers, Jones and Bailey............................. 842
A bacterial blight of soy bean, Johnson and Coerper.......................... 842
Further note on a parasitic saccharomycete of the tomato, Schneider.......... 842
Host limitations of *Septoria lycopersici*, Norton.............................. 842
Note on Coniothecium, especially *C. chomatosporum*, van der Bijl 842
Control of peach bacterial spot in southern orchards, Roberts................. 842
Black currant eelworm, Taylor... 843
Sulphuring Concord grapes to prevent mildew, Gladwin and Reddick...... 843
The generation of aldehydes by *Fusarium cubense*, Lathrop.................... 843
Citrus canker investigations at the Florida Tropical Laboratory, Jehle........ 843
Sour rot of lemon in California, Smith.. 843
Two new camphor diseases in Texas, Taubenhaus............................. 843
Diseases of cinchona, Rant.. 844
A disease of pecan catkins, Higgins... 844
Phytophthora on *Vinca rosea*, Dastur... 844
Notes on some species of Coleosporium, Hedgcock and Hunt.................. 844
The æcial stage of *Coleosporium elephantopodis*, Hedgcock and Long.......... 844
An alternate form for *Coleosporium helianthi*, Hedgcock and Hunt............. 844
Some new hosts for *Coleosporium inconspicuum*, Hedgcock and Hunt.......... 844
The Peridermium belonging to *Coleosporium ipomœæ*, Hedgcock and Hunt... 845
Some new hosts for *Coleosporium solidaginis*, Hedgcock and Hunt........... 845
A Peridermium belonging to *Coleosporium terebinthinaceæ*, Hedgcock and Hunt. 845
Notes on *Cronartium comptoniæ*, III, Spaulding............................. 845
Does *Cronartium ribicola* winter on the currant? McCubbin.................. 845
Evidence of the overwintering of *Cronartium ribicola*, Spaulding.............. 846
The pine blister, Paul... 846
The control of white-pine blister rust in small areas, Rankin.................. 846
Some new or little known hosts for wood-destroying fungi, Rhoads........... 846

ECONOMIC ZOOLOGY—ENTOMOLOGY.

A new subspecies of meadow mouse from Wyoming, Bailey.................... 846
Diagnosis of a new laniine family of Passeriformes, Oberholser................ 846
Description of a new Sialia from Mexico, Oberholser.......................... 846
Friends of our forests, Henshaw.. 846
Report of the entomologist of Arizona for 1916, Morrill....................... 846
Annual report of the State entomologist for 1915, Worsham................... 847
Report of the division of entomology, 1916, Ehrhorn.......................... 847
Report of the economic biologist, Bodkin...................................... 847
Observations on some insects attacking rice, Supino.......................... 847
Wild vegetation as a source of curley-top infection, Boncquet and Stahl....... 847
Meadow and pasture insects.—Practical methods of control, Osborn........... 847
Insects that factor in the grading of apples, Parrott.......................... 847
Spraying for insects affecting orchards in Nova Scotia, Sanders and Brittain... 848
Insects injuring stored food products in Connecticut, Britton.................. 848
The carriage of disease by insects, Howard.................................... 848
Key for identification of parasites in human feces, Martin and McKittrick.... 848
Volatility of organic compounds as an index of toxicity to insects, Moore...... 848
Lead arsenates, stone fruits, and the weather, Gray........................... 848
Locust control in various countries, Trinchieri................................ 848
Report on control work with the locust in Uruguay, Sundberg et al........... 849
Experiments in locust control in Argentina, Kraus............................ 849
Summary of locust work for the third quarter, 1916, South.................... 849
A new Sericothrips from Africa, Hood... 849
A new species of Corythuca from the Northwest, Gibson 849
The tomato and laurel psyllids, Essig... 849
The pink and green potato plant louse.—A new pest for Ohio, Houser.......... 849
Some sensory structures in the Aphididæ, Baker.............................. 850
Eastern aphids, new or little known, I, Patch................................. 850

Page.
Eastern aphids, new or little known, II, Baker............................ 850
The Aphididæ of Java, van der Goot...................................... 850
[Studies of pediculi]... 850
The louse problem, Bacot... 850
Isolation of *Bacillus typhi-exanthematici* from body louse, Olitsky et al........ 850
The lesser cornstalk borer, Luginbill and Ainslie.......................... 851
Control of the grape-berry moth in the Erie-Chautaqua grape belt, Isely....... 852
Pathogenicity of so-called Sotto bacillus of silkworms, Aoki and Chigasaki.... 853
The atoxogen type of *Bacillus sotto*, Aoki and Chigasaki.................... 853
Distance of flight of *Anopheles quadrimaculatus*, Le Prince and Griffitts........ 853
Notes on the early stages of Chrysops, Marchand.......................... 853
Sarcophage hæmorrhoidalis larvæ as parasites of human intestine, Haseman..... 853
Fly investigation reports, I–III, Saunders................................. 853
Flies and typhoid, Nicoll... 854
Relation of *Pegomyia fusciceps* to certain crops in Louisiana, Tucker.......... 854
A buprestid household insect (*Chrysophana placida*), Burke................. 854
The life history of *Diapus furtivus*, Beeson............................... 854
The weather and honey production, Kenoyer............................... 854
Seventh report of State inspector of apiaries, 1916, Gates.................... 855
The domestication of the Indian honeybee, Newton........................: 855
Life history and habits of *Polistes metricus*, Pellett....................... 855
Habits of western wheat stem sawfly in Manitoba and Saskatchewan, Criddle.. 855
An American species of the hymenopterous genus Wesmælia of Foerster, Myers.. 855
Report on a collection of Hymenoptera made by W. M. Giffard, Rohwer...... 855
Australian Hymenoptera Chalcidoidea, Girault............................ 855
Parasitism of Mediterranean fruit fly during 1916, Pemberton and Willard.... 856
Notes on the construction of the cocoon of Praon, Ainslie................... 856
An egg parasite of the sumac flea-beetle, Crosby and Leonard............... 856
An aphis parasite feeding at puncture holes made by the ovipositor, Rockwood. 856
Megastigmus aculeatus introduced into New Jersey from Japan, Weiss......... 856
The embryonic development of *Trichogramma evanescens*, Gatenby........... 856
Life history and habits of the spinose ear tick, *Ornithodoros megnini*, Herms... 856
Tarsonemus pallidus, a pest of geraniums, Garman......................... 856
The cyclamen mite, Moznette... 857
A synopsis of the genera of beetle mites, Ewing............................ 858
On the nymph and prosopon of *Leptotrombidium akamushi* n. sp., Nagayo et al. 858
Is *Trombidium holosericeum* the parent of *Leptus autumnalis?* Nagayo et al.... 859
Notes on the parasitic acari, Hirst....................................... 859
The chicken mite: Its life history and habits, Wood....................... 859
New mites, mostly economic, Banks...................................... 860

FOODS—HUMAN NUTRITION.

A comparison of several classes of American wheats, Thomas................. 860
Wheat and flour investigations, V, Olson.................................. 861
The milling and baking data for the 1915 crop of wheat, Sanderson........... 863
Shrimp: Handling, transportation, and uses, Clark et al.................... 863
Food products and drugs, Street.. 863
[Food and drug inspection], Ladd and Johnson............................. 863
How to select foods.—III, Foods rich in protein, Hunt and Atwater.......... 864

ANIMAL PRODUCTION.

A comparison of casein, lactalbumin, and edestin, Osborne, Mendel, et al.... 864
Effect of amino acid content of diet on growth of chickens, Osborne.......... 865
The productive value of some Texas feeding stuffs, Fraps.................... 865
Live stock feeding experiments... 866
Color inheritance in mammals, Wright.................................... 866
The value of good sires, Wright.. 866
The heredity of dual-purpose cattle, Euren................................ 866
Sheep breeding and feeding, Jones.. 866
Oestrus and ovulation in swine, Corner and Amsbaugh...................... 867
Cost of keeping farm horses and cost of horse labor, Cooper................. 867
Some important essentials in profitable horse production, McCampbell........ 868
Theory of sex as stated in terms of results of studies on the pigeon, Riddle.... 868
Factors influencing the sex ratio in the domestic fowl, Pearl................. 868
Crossing over in the sex chromosome of the male fowl, Goodale.............. 868

                                                                    Page.
Relation between gonads and soma of some domestic birds, Goodale..........   868
Determinate and indeterminate laying cycles in birds, Cole................   869
A study of broodiness in the Rhode Island Red breed, Goodale..............   869
Breeding for egg production.—II, Seasonal distribution, Ball and Alder.......   869
Selection: The basis of improving the poultry flock, Lewis.................   871
Feed cost of egg production at the Government poultry farm, Lamon and Lee.   871
Poultry feeds and feeding results, Harvey.................................   871
Poultry farm management, Jones, Davis, and McDonald......................   872
Finishing market poultry, Thompson.......................................   872

DAIRY FARMING—DAIRYING.

Dairy laboratory manual and notebook, compiled by Anthony................   872
Dairy cattle, Leitch, King, and Sackville................................   872
Palm kernel nut cake as a food for dairy cows, Lauder and Fagan..........   872
Calf feeding experiments...   873
The business of 10 dairy farms in the blue grass region of Kentucky, Arnold..   873
Effect of ingestion of desiccated placenta on milk, Hammett and McNeile..   873
The modern milk problem in sanitation, economics, and agriculture, MacNutt..   874
Rate of gas production by certain bacteria in raw and pastuerized milk, Allen..   874
The significance of colon bacilli in milk, Ayers et al...................   874
Influence of gargety and high count cows on bacteria in milk, Colwell..........   874
Dairy laws of Wisconsin..   875
Testing milk for butter fat by the Babcock test, compiled by Evans...........   875
Accounting records for country creameries, Humphrey and Nahstoll...........   875
Experiments with pepsin to replace rennet, Steuart......................   875
Loss of fat in the whey when using pepsin, Barr.........................   875
On the formation of "eyes" in Emmental cheese, Clark....................   876

VETERINARY MEDICINE.

[Live stock diseases]...   876
New and nonofficial remedies, 1916.......................................   876
Sugar in the treatment of wounds, Koheya................................   876
The use of chloramin-T paste for the sterilization of wounds, Daufresne.......   876
Sterilization of wounds with chloramin-T, Carrel and Hartmann.............   876
Dichloramin-T in the treatment of the wounds of war, Sweet................   876
The thromboplastic action of cephalin and its degree of unsaturation, McLean.   877
The reaction of sera as a factor in successful concentration, Homer.............   877
Equilibria in precipitin reactions, Bayne-Jones.........................   877
Notes on outbreak of foot-and-mouth disease at Butleigh, Somerset, Grenville..   878
Value of ophthalmic and conglutination tests in diagnosis of glanders, Gräub..   878
The temperature required for the "inactivation" of mule blood, Buxton......   878
Transmission of pulmonary and septicemic plague, Wu Lien-Teh and Eberson.   878
Note on transmission of animal trypanosomiasis in northern Rhodesia, Chambers   879
Tuberculosis and animal breeding, Duerst................................   879
Presence of tubercle bacilli in feces of cattle in dairy herds, Williams et al....   879
The incidence of bovine infection of tuberculosis in man, Chung Yik Wang....   879
Tuberculosis in carnivorous animals, Blair...............................   880
Tuberculosis in the horse, Chambers.....................................   880
Antituberculosis vaccination, Rappin.....................................   880
Effect of tethelin on experimental tuberculosis, Corper.................   880
Presence of Bacillus abortus bovinus in certified milk, Fleischner and Meyer..   881
Tick eradication laws and regulations of the State of Arkansas, Gow...........   881
A note on the immunity of suckling pigs to hog cholera, Birch.............   881
A serum test influenced by Ascaris infestation, Birch...................   881
Experiments in filtration of antihog-cholera serum, Edgington et al...........   881
Hog cholera control, Craig and Kigin....................................   882
Sanitary measures to prevent hog cholera, Graham.......................   882
Crude oil for hogs, Evvard...   882

RURAL ENGINEERING.

Construction and use of farm weirs, Cone.................................   882
A new evaporation formula developed, Horton.............................   882
Irrigation in the Novouzensk district, Frolov...........................   882
Irrigation experiments in rice culture, van der Elst.....................   883
Irrigation experiments in rice culture, van der Elst.....................   883

Page.
Organization, financing, and administration of drainage districts, Yohe........ 883
Report of the water laboratory, Barnard..................................... 883
Sterilization of water in the field, Penau................................... 884
Sewage disposal for school buildings in Ohio, Durroll and Adams.............. 884
The operation of sewage treatment plants for public buildings, Adams......... 884
Expansion and contraction of concrete roads, Goldbeck and Jackson, jr........ 884
Toughness of bituminous aggregates, Reeve and Lewis......................... 885
Concrete culverts.. 885
Mechanical properties of woods grown in the United States, Newlin and Wilson. 885
The seasoning of wood, Betts... 886
Creosoting for estate purposes, Greenfield................................. 886
[Farm machinery directory]... 886
Public tests of motor cultivation at Avignon, Zacharewicz................... 886
Tractor specifications, 1917... 886
Note on fencing construction, Gilbert...................................... 886
Dairy and general-purpose barns, White..................................... 886
Barns for work animals, Youngblood... 887
Measuring silage and capacity of silos, Chase.............................. 887
Poultry houses and poultry equipment for Texas, Harvey et al............... 887

RURAL ECONOMICS.

The farmers' handbook, compiled by Gilder.................................. 888
The Federal Office of Markets and Rural Organization, Gilbert.............. 888
Functions of a State bureau of markets, Cance.............................. 888
Cooperative purchasing and marketing organizations, Jesness and Kerr....... 888
The county farm bureau, Crocheron... 888
List of county and local agricultural societies, Wible.................... 888
Cooperative credit for the United States, Wolfe........................... 888
A survey of insurance of damage by fire to crops and forests, Vidière...... 888
The Torrens system of land title registration, Bomberger.................. 888
[Italian rules governing agriculture], Wilber............................. 888
Rural index, Hollister.. 889
Pounds to bushels tables, Davis... 889
Marketing grain at country points, Livingston and Seeds................... 889
Farm labor [conditions in Canada]... 889
Labor conditions among the forest workers in Sweden, Huss................. 890
Notes on methods and costs, California crop production, Adams.............. 890
Meeting the food crisis, Soule.. 890
The food supply in New England, McSweeney................................. 890
The food supply of the United Kingdom..................................... 890
Production of food in Scotland, Wason et al............................... 890
[Increasing agricultural production in France], Hitier.................... 890
The wheat question, Perchot... 890
Food crisis in Portugal... 890
[Agricultural development in Navarra], Nagore y Nagore.................... 891
Agricultural work in Egypt, Britain, America, and Japan, Roberts.......... 891
Monthly crop report... 891
[Agricultural statistics of Indiana]...................................... 891
Agricultural statistics for Wisconsin, 1915 and 1916...................... 891
Annual statistical report of the New York Produce Exchange for 1916....... 891
[Agriculture in Norway]... 891
Returns of produce of crops in Scotland................................... 891
[Agricultural statistics of British India for the year 1915–16], Shirras.. 891
Live stock statistics... 891

AGRICULTURAL EDUCATION.

Agricultural education and research....................................... 892
Report of elementary agricultural education division, New Brunswick, Steeves 892
[Agricultural instruction in Ontario, 1916], Hearst...................... 892
Uituna agricultural institute and farm, 1916.............................. 892
Agricultural education in Bulgaria, Murphy................................ 892
[Rural education].. 892
The school inspector and rural science, Robinson et al.................... 892
The agricultural subjects, Broyles.. 893
"Snap courses" in college: Agriculture v. engineering, Blodgett.......... 893
Experiments in agriculture for public schools of Louisiana, Guilbeau and Harris. 893

Page.

Dairy education, Pearson.. 893
Present position and future of dairy education.—Science, Mackintosh........ 893
Present position and future of dairy education.—Practice, McConnell........ 893
The part which women might play, Shanks.................................... 893
Productive dairying, Washburn... 894
First year course in home economics for southern agricultural schools, Stanley. 894
The story of foods, Crissey.. 894
Elements of the theory and practice of cookery, Williams and Fisher........ 894
Wool, Hart, edited by France.. 894
[Conference of the Alabama Home Economics Association].................... 895
Report of the supervisor of women's institutes, Winter.................... 895

MISCELLANEOUS.

Monthly Bulletin of the Ohio Agricultural Experiment Station.............. 895
Monthly bulletin of the Western Washington Substation.................... 895

LIST OF EXPERIMENT STATION AND DEPARTMENT PUBLICATIONS REVIEWED.

Stations in the United States.

Arkansas Station: **Page.**
    Bul. 132, 1917................. 881
California Station:
    Circ. 166, Aug., 1917........... 888
Connecticut State Station:
    Bul. 194, July, 1917........... 813
    Bul. 195, July, 1917........... 848
    An. Rpt. 1916, pt. 4........... 863
Illinois Station:
    Bul. 202, July, 1917........... 819
    Circ. 203, Aug., 1917........... 882
Indiana Station:
    Circ. 62, July, 1917........... 882
Iowa Station:
    Bul. 169, Mar., 1917.......... 854
Kansas Station:
    Insp. Circ. 2, Dec., 1916...... 868
Maryland Station:
    Bul. 208, June, 1917.......... 856
Massachusetts Station:
    Met. Buls. 343–344, July–Aug.,
    1917...................... 807
Nebraska Station:
    Circ.1, June 30, 1917........... 887
New Jersey Stations:
    Hints to Poultrymen, vol. 5—
      No. 11, Aug., 1917........ 872
      No. 12, Sept., 1917........ 871
North Dakota Station:
    Bul. 122, June, 1917.......... 863
    Spec. Bul., vol. 4, No. 14,
    June–July, 1917............ 863
Ohio Station:
    Mo. Bul., vol. 2—
      No. 7, July, 1917........ 831, 895
      No. 8, Aug., 1917. 831,847,849,895
Rhode Island Station:
    Bul. 171, June, 1917.......... 815
Texas Station:
    Bul. 203, Dec., 1916........... 865
    Bul. 205, Jan., 1917........... 866
    Bul. 206, Jan., 1917........... 871
    Bul. 207, Jan., 1917........... 887
    Bul. 208, Jan., 1917........... 835
    Bul. 209, Jan., 1917....... 823, 832
    Bul. 210, Jan., 1917........... 887
Utah Station:
    Bul. 149, Jan., 1917........... 869
Washington Station:
    Bul. 144, Mar., 1917.......... 861
    West. Wash. Sta., Mo. Bul.,
    vol. 5, No. 5, Aug., 1917.... 895

U. S. Department of Agriculture.

Jour. Agr. Research, vol. 10:   **Page.**
    No. 7, Aug. 13, 1917. 809,812,848,885
    No. 8, Aug. 20, 1917......... 808, 857
Bul. 532, The Expansion and Con-
    traction of Concrete and Con-
    crete Roads, A. T. Goldbeck and
    F. H. Jackson, jr................ 884
Bul. 538, Shrimp: Handling, Trans-
    portation, and Uses, E. D. Clark
    and L. MacNaughton............ 863
Bul. 539, The Lesser Corn Stalk-
    borer, P. Luginbill and G. G.
    Ainslie....................... 851
Bul. 540, A First Year Course in
    Home Economics for Southern
    Agricultural Schools, Louise
    Stanley....................... 894
Bul. 542, The Pollination of the
    Mango, W. Popenoe............. 835
Bul. 543, Control of Peach Bacte-
    rial Spot in Southern Orchards,
    J. W. Roberts................. 842
Bul. 545, Important Range Plants:
    Their Life History and Forage
    Value, A. W. Sampson.......... 818
Bul. 546, Effect of Fall Irrigation
    on Crop Yields at Belle Fourche,
    S. Dak., F. D. Farrell and B.
    Aune......................... 822
Bul. 547, Cooperative Purchasing
    and Marketing Organizations
    among Farmers in the United
    States, O. B. Jesness and W. H.
    Kerr......................... 888
Bul. 548, The Business of Ten
    Dairy Farms in the Bluegrass
    Region of Kentucky, J. H.
    Arnold........................ 873
Bul. 549, Crossties Purchased and
    Treated in 1915, A. M. Mc-
    Creight....................... 838
Bul. 550, Control of the Grape-
    berry Moth in the Erie-Chautau-
    qua Grape Belt, D. Isely........ 852
Bul. 551, Variation in the Chemi-
    cal Composition of Soils, W. O.
    Robinson, L. A. Steinkoenig,
    and W. H. Fry................. 811
Bul. 552, The Seasoning of Wood,
    H. S. Betts................... 886
Bul. 553, The Chicken Mite: Its
    Life History and Habits, H. P.
    Wood......................... 859

U. S. Department of Agriculture—Con.

Bul. 556, Mechanical Properties of Page.
Woods Grown in the United
States, J. A. Newlin and T. R.
C. Wilson........................... 885
Bul. 557, A Comparison of Several
Classes of American Wheats and
a Consideration of Some Factors
Influencing Quality, L. M.
Thomas............................ 860
Bul. 558, Marketing Grain at
Country Points, G. Livingston
and K. B. Seeds................. 889
Bul. 559, Accounting Records for
Country Creameries, J. R.
Humphrey and G. A. Nahstoll.. 875
Bul. 560, Cost of Keeping Farm
Horses and Cost of Horse Labor,
M. R. Cooper.................... 867
Bul. 561, Feed Cost of Egg Produc-
tion.—Results of Three Years'
Experiments at the Government
Poultry Farm, H. M. Lamon and
A. R. Lee....................... 871
Farmers'.Bul. 802, Classification of
American Upland Cotton, D. E.
Earle and F. Taylor............ 830
Farmers' Bul. 813, Construction
and Use of Farm Weirs, V. M.
Cone.....*...................... 882
Farmers' Bul. 815, Organization,
Financing, and Administration
of Drainage Districts, H. S. Yohe 883
Farmers' Bul. 824, How to Select
Foods.—III, Foods Rich in Pro-
tein, Caroline L. Hunt and Helen
W. Atwater..................... 864
Bureau of Crop Estimates:
  Mo. Crop Rpt., vol. 3, No. 8,
  Aug., 1917.................... 891
Bureau of Plant Industry:
  Inventory of Seeds and Plants
  Imported by the Office of
  of Foreign Seed and Plant
  Introduction during the
  Period from January 1 to
  March 31, 1914............... 819
  Inventory of Seeds and Plants
  Imported by the Office of
  Foreign Seed and Plant In-
  troduction during the Period
  from April 1 to June 30,
  1914......................... 819
  Inventory of Seeds and Plants
  Imported by the Office
  of Foreign Seed and Plant
  Introduction during the
  Period from July 1 to Sep-
  tember 30, 1914.............. 819
Bureau of Soils:
  Field Operations, 1915—
    Soil Survey of the Healds-
    burg Area, California,
    E. B. Watson et al...... 810

U. S. Department of Agriculture—Con.

Bureau of Soils—Continued. Page.
  Field Operations, 1915—Con.
    Soil Survey of Cumber-
    land County, Maine, C.
    Van Duyne and M. W.
    Beck.................... 810
Weather Bureau:
  Mo. Weather Rev., vol. 45,
  Nos. 5–6, May–June, 1917. 807, 808
  Mo. Weather Rev., Sup. 7.. 807, 808
Scientific Contributions:[1]
  Glycolytic Properties of Mus-
  cular Tissue, R. Hoagland
  and C. M. Mansfield....... 802
  The Function of Muscular Tis-
  sue in Urea Formation, R.
  Hoagland and C. M. Mans-
  field..................... 802
  The Decomposition of Dilead
  Arsenate by Water, C. C.
  McDonnell and J. J. T.
  Graham................... 802
  Discontinuous Extraction Pro-
  cesses, L. F. Hawley....... 803
  A Simplified Microcombustion
  Method for the Determina-
  tion of Carbon and Hydro-
  gen, L. E. Wise........... 803
  The Possibilities and Limita-
  tions of the Duclaux Method
  for the Estimation of Vola-
  tile Acids, L. J. Gillespie
  and E. H. Walters......... 803
  Application of the Cryoscopic
  Method for Determining
  Added Water in Milk, J. T.
  Keister................... 804
  Sauerkraut Industry of the
  United States, L. A. Round
  and S. C. Coppersmith...... 806
  The Formation and Character-
  istics of Massachusetts Peat
  Lands and Some of Their
  Uses, A. P. Dachnowski.... 810
  New or Noteworthy Plants
  from Colombia and Central
  America, VI, H. Pittier.... 819
  The Middle American Species
  of Lonchocarpus, H. Pittier. 819
  Growing Potatoes under Irri-
  gation for Profit, W. Stuart.
  Important Factors in the Suc-
  cessful Cold Storage of Ap-
  ples, H. S. Bird...........
  Practical Reforestation, H. S.
  Graves.................... 836
  Aspen as a Permanent Forest
  Type, J. M. Fetherolf...... 837
  Forest Service Stumpage Ap-
  praisals, J. W. Girard...... 838
  Marketing Farm Woodlot Prod-
  ucts in Maine, G. N. Lamb. 838

[1] Printed in scientific and technical publications outside the Department.

U. S. Department of Agriculture—Con.

Scientific Contributions—Con. **Page.**

The Generation of Aldehydes by *Fusarium cubense*, E. C. Lathrop.................... 843

Notes on *Cronartium comptoniæ*, III, P. Spaulding..... 845

A New Subspecies of Meadow Mouse from Wyoming, V. Bailey..................... 846

Diagnosis of a New Laniine Family of Passeriformes, H. C. Oberholser.............. 846

Description of a New Sialia from Mexico, H. C. Oberholser..................... 846

Friends of Our Forests, H. W. Henshaw................... 846

Wild Vegetation as a Source of Curly-top Infection of Sugar Beets, P. A. Boncquet and C. F. Stahl.................. 847

The Carriage of Disease by Insects, L. O. Howard...... 848

A New Sericothrips from Africa, J. D. Hood......... 849

A New Species of Corythuca from the Northwest, E. H. Gibson................... 849

Some Sensory Structures in the Aphididæ, A. C. Baker. 850

Eastern Aphids, New or Little Known, II, A. C. Baker.... 850

A Buprestid Household Insect (*Chrysophana placida*), H. E. Burke.................... 854

U. S. Department of Agriculture—Con.

Scientific Contributions—Con. **Page.**

An American Species of the Hymenopterous Genus Wesmaelia of Foerster, P. R. Myers...................... 855

A Report on a Collection of Hymenoptera (Mostly from California) Made by W. M. Giffard, S. A. Rohwer...... 855

Australian Hymenoptera Chalcidoidea, A. A. Girault..... 855

Parasitism of the Larvæ of the Mediterranean Fruit Fly in Hawaii during 1916, C. E. Pemberton and H. F. Willard.................... 856

Notes on the Construction of the Cocoon of Praon, C. N. Ainslie.................... 856

An Aphis Parasite Feeding at Puncture Holes Made by the Ovipositor, L. P. Rockwood. 856

New Mites, Mostly Economic, N. Banks.................. 860

Color Inheritance in Mammals, S. Wright.................. 866

The Significance of Colon Bacilli in Milk, S. H. Ayers et al..................... 874

On the Formation of "eyes" in Emmental Cheese, W. M. Clark..................... 876

The Federal Office of Markets and Rural Organization, J. C. Gilbert.................. 888

Functions of a State Bureau of Markets, A. E. Cance...... 888

ADDITIONAL COPIES
OF THIS PUBLICATION MAY BE PROCURED FROM
THE SUPERINTENDENT OF DOCUMENTS
GOVERNMENT PRINTING OFFICE
WASHINGTON, D. C.
AT
15 CENTS PER COPY
SUBSCRIPTION PRICE, PER VOLUME
OF NINE NUMBERS
AND INDEX, $1

▽

RECENT WORK IN AGRICULTURAL SCIENCE.

AGRICULTURAL CHEMISTRY—AGROTECHNY.

Principles of agricultural chemistry, G. S. FRAPS (*Easton, Pa.: The Chemical Publishing Co., 1917, 2. ed., pp. 501, figs. 94*).—This is the second edition of the work previously noted (E. S. R., 30, p. 10). A number of additions and changes have been made which include some of the recent advances in the subject, especially with reference to soil organisms, nutritive value of protein, and productive value of feeds.

An introduction to the chemistry of plant products, P. HAAS and T. G. HILL (*London and New York: Longmans, Green & Co., 1917, 2. ed., pp. XII+411, figs 5*).—This is the second edition of the work previously noted (E. S. R., 31, p. 803).

Due to the great advances made in the chemistry of plant pigments since the issue of the first edition, this section has been entirely rewritten. A few other minor additions and changes have been made and further references to the literature added.

The occurrence of mannite in silage and its possible utilization in the manufacture of explosives, A. W. DOX and G. P. PLAISANCE (*Science, n. ser., 46 (1917), No. 1182, pp. 192, 193*).—Analytical data obtained by the authors at the Iowa Experiment Station in the course of investigations on the fermentation processes that occur immediately after the ensiling of corn and the chemical products resulting therefrom show the presence of considerable amounts of mannite in various kinds of silage. The highest percentages of mannite were found in sunflower silage, cane silage, and an experimental corn silage to which sucrose had been added. It is indicated that the mother substance of the mannite is apparently sucrose or, more specifically, its fructose moiety. The presence of the mannite was shown not to be a local phenomenon, since the samples of silage examined were obtained from several different States. Corn and cowpea silage, sweet clover silage, and ensiled corn stover plus glucose contained no mannite.

A method of preparing quantities of mannite without special regard to quantitative yields and the use of its nitration product in the manufacture of explosives are noted.

See also a previous note by Manns (E. S. R., 1, p. 200).

The occurrence and significance of mannitol in silage, A. W. DOX and G. P. PLAISANCE (*Jour. Amer. Chem. Soc., 39 (1917), No. 9, pp. 2078-2087*).—This is a more detailed account of the material noted above.

The occurrence of 1-leucin in sweet clover silage, G. P. PLAISANCE (*Jour. Amer. Chem. Soc., 39 (1917), No. 9, pp. 2087, 2088*).—In the examination of sweet clover silage for mannite by the author, at the Iowa Experiment Station, no evidence of the substance was found. Instead a white substance crystallized in little round masses, which after recrystallization from dilute alcohol was identified as 1-leucin. In the samples of sweet clover silage examined leucin was recovered in amounts ranging from 0.4 to 1 per cent of the dry material.

The action of acids on the rotatory power of sucrose and invert sugar in the presence of soluble salts, E. SAILLARD (*Compt. Rend. Acad. Sci. [Paris], 165 (1917), No. 3, pp. 116–118*).—Data obtained in connection with work on beet molasses show that sulphurous acid and acetic acid do not change the rotatory power of sucrose in the presence of sodium chlorid. These acids do, however, diminish the rotation of invert sugar in the presence of sodium chlorid, with or without the addition of hydrochloric acid. Hydrochloric acid increases the polarization of a solution of invert sugar in the presence of salt. The solutions of invert sugar containing salt and sulphurous acid yield an unstable polarization because of the easy loss of part of the dissolved gas. Carbon dioxid does not influence the rotation of solutions of sucrose or invert sugar, undoubtedly because of its slight solubility.

Glycolytic properties of muscular tissue, R. HOAGLAND and C. M. MANSFIELD (*Jour. Biol. Chem., 31 (1917), No. 3, pp. 501–517*).

The function of muscular tissue in urea formation, R. HOAGLAND and C. M. MANSFIELD (*Jour. Biol. Chem., 31 (1917), No. 3, pp. 487–499*).

Determination of carbonates in limestone and other materials, J. F. BARKER (*Jour. Indus. and Engin. Chem., 9 (1917), No. 8, pp. 786, 787, fig. 1*).—Essentially noted from another source (E. S. R., 37, p. 616.)

Insoluble phosphoric acid in organic base goods, E. O. THOMAS (*Jour. Indus. and Engin. Chem., 9 (1917), No. 9, p: 865*).—Analytical data are submitted from which it is concluded that in the determination of citrate-insoluble phosphoric acid the official method gives the true value of acid phosphate, but that in the analysis of materials of the character of acidulated garbage tankage some modification should be used.

The decomposition of dilead arsenate by water, C. C. McDONNELL and J. J. T. GRAHAM (*Jour. Amer. Chem. Soc., 39 (1917), No. 9, pp. 1912–1918, figs. 2*).— Experimental data obtained in the study show that dilead arsenate is decomposed by water. The reaction is represented by the the equation

$$5PbHAsO_4 + HOH \leftrightarrows Pb_4(PbOH)(AsO_4)_3 + 2H_3AsO_4.$$

The reaction proceeds with the liberation of arsenic acid and the solution of a very small quantity of lead. Equilibrium is reached while the concentration of arsenic acid is very low. If the water is constantly changed, however, the reaction proceeds until the residue is converted to a definite basic lead arsenate (hydroxy mimetite, $Pb_4(PbOH)(AsO_4)_3.H_2O$.

Allen's commercial organic analysis, edited by W. A. DAVIS (*Philadelphia: P. Blakiston's Son & Co, 1917, 4. ed., rev., vol. 9, pp. XVIII+836, figs. 18*).— This is a supplementary volume to the work previously noted (E. S. R., 30, p. 309) which brings the text, especially that of the earlier volumes, up to date. The chapters included are alcohols; malt and brewing materials; wines and spirits; yeast; neutral alcoholic derivatives; sugars; starch and its isomerids; paper and paper-making materials; aliphatic acids; fixed oils, fats, and waxes; special characters and modes of examining fats, oils, and waxes; butter fat; lard; linseed oil; soaps; glycerol; cholesterol; wool, grease, and cloth oils; hydrocarbons; bitumens; naphthalene and its derivatives; phenols; aromatic acids; resins; india rubber, rubber substitutes, and gutta-percha; essential oils; special characteristics of essential oils; tannins; analysis of leather; analysis of coloring materials; coloring matters of natural origin; coloring matters in foods; printing inks; inks; amins and ammonium bases; anilin and its allies; the naphtylamins and their allies; the vegetable alkaloids; volatile alkaloids; estimation of nicotin; aconite alkaloids; atropin and its allies; cocaïne; opium alkaloids; strychnos alkaloids; cinchona alkaloids; berberin and its associates; caffein, tea, and coffee; other vegetable alkaloids; glucosids; nonglucosidal bitter principles; animal bases; animal acids; lactic acid; cyanogen and its derivatives; enzyms; proteins; vegetable proteins—flour; proteins of milk; milk products; albuminoids; meat and meat products; fibroids; and an appendix.

A complete author and subject index of the entire work is included in the volume.

New apparatus for colorimetry, E. MOREAU (*Ann. Falsif., 10 (1917), No. 103–104, pp. 235–237, fig. 1*).—A simple apparatus for routine analysis and its manipulation are described. It consists essentially of two colorimetric tubes, to one of which is attached at its lower end a piece of rubber tubing which is connected to a leveling bulb. This tube is used for the standard color solution, and by this arrangement the volume can be readily changed until the color corresponds with that of the unknown sample.

The calculation of the results is described.

Discontinuous extraction processes, L. F. HAWLEY (*Jour. Indus. and Engin. Chem., 9 (1917), No. 9, pp. 866–871*).

A simplified microcombustion method for the determination of carbon and hydrogen, L. E. WISE (*Jour. Amer. Chem. Soc., 39 (1917), No. 9, pp. 2055–2068, figs. 4*).—A modification of the Pregl[1] microcombustion method for the determination of carbon and hydrogen, in which 11- to 22-mg. samples are used and which does not require the use of a microbalance, is described. A sensitive analytical balance has been found to yield satisfactory results. The drying train of the original method has been modified, and the technique used in weighing and in carrying out the combustion has also been modified and standardized.

Analytical data obtained in the combustion of pure substances containing carbon, hydrogen, and oxygen indicate that the accuracy of the micromethod is comparable to that of the ordinary macrocombustion. Preliminary data indicate that the procedure, without further modifications, may be applicable to the microanalysis of a variety of nitrogenous organic compounds. The limitations and possible applications of the method are briefly discussed.

The possibilities and limitations of the Duclaux method for the estimation of volatile acids, L. J. GILLESPIE and E. H. WALTERS (*Jour. Amer. Chem. Soc. 39 (1917), No. 9, pp. 2027–2055, figs. 3*).—The authors have studied the Duclaux method in detail and have stated and verified the laws which must be assumed to calculate the results of analyses. Algebraic and graphic methods for the computation of results for mixtures of two or three acids have been described and the algebraic calculation for four or more acids indicated. Application of the methods to known mixtures shows that mixtures of two or three acids may be quantitatively analyzed without too great error. The errors, however, are in general too large for mixtures of four acids.

Data obtained show that the errors of the method are not proportional to the quantities of acid present. Mixtures containing four or more acids in significant quantities must be fractionated before applying the method into mixtures containing only three acids. "In order to apply the Duclaux method

---

[1] [Abderhalden's] Handb. Biochem. Arbeitsmethod., **5** (1912), pt. 2, pp. 1307–1356.

to unknown mixtures it is necessary to establish that not more than three acids are present in significant quantities. This fact established, a distillation by the Duclaux method should suffice for both qualitative and quantitative analysis of the mixture. The methods of calculation do not depend on the form of the laws governing the rates of distillation of pure acids in aqueous solution, and therefore do not necessarily depend on the mode of distillation. The calculations may therefore be applied to distillations made in other ways, for instance, to steam distillations at constant volume. It is merely necessary to conduct all distillations both of pure acids and of mixtures in the same manner."

A modification of the McLean-Van Slyke method for the determination of chlorids in blood, G. L. FOSTER (*Jour. Biol. Chem., 31 (1917), No. 3, pp. 483–485*).—The method previously described (E. S. R., 34, p. 507) has been modified in that a freshly prepared 25 per cent solution of metaphosphoric acid is used for coagulating the proteins. The procedure is described as follows:

To 2 cc. of the sample in a 25-cc. volumetric flask, 20 cc. of water is added and then slowly, with stirring, 1 cc. of a freshly prepared solution of metaphosphoric acid. The flask is filled to the mark, well shaken, and allowed to stand for ten minutes with occasional agitation. The contents of the flask are then filtered and 10 cc. of the filtrate used for the determination, as described in the original method.

Studies of acidosis.—II, A method for the determination of carbon dioxid and carbonates in solution, D. D. VAN SLYKE (*Jour. Biol. Chem., 30 (1917), No. 2, pp. 347–368, figs. 4*).—A simple one-piece apparatus for the determination of carbon dioxid or carbonates in water solutions and its manipulation are described.

The principle of the method is that of vacuum extraction. The apparatus was designed especially for analysis of 1-cc. samples of blood plasma, but is indicated as being applicable to aqueous solutions in general, as well as for the determination of dissolved gases other than carbon dioxid. A microapparatus with which the carbon dioxid content of 0.2 cc. of plasma can be determined with an accuracy of one volume per cent, designed on the same principle, is also described. The entire analysis is performed at room temperature and requires only about three minutes.

The calculation of the results is described in detail.

Methods for the determination of saccharin in food products, A. BONIS (*Ann. Falsif., 10 (1917), No. 103–104, pp. 210–218*).—A general review of the procedures for extracting saccharin and purifying the residue, and of methods of identification and quantitative determination.

Application of the cryoscopic method for determining added water in milk, J. T. KEISTER (*Jour. Indus. and Engin. Chem., 9 (1917), No. 9, pp. 862–865*).—It is concluded from the study that "the freezing-point figure of milk is the most constant one yet obtained and the safest basis upon which to draw conclusions as to the presence or absence of added water." Water added to fresh milk in excess of 5 per cent was detected with certainty by the freezing-point method. The use of sufficient formaldehyde for preservation was found to lower the freezing point. The test should be applied to the milk before any marked increase in acidity has taken place, since increased acidity affects the final results.

The freezing-point figures of the milk of 16 individual cows are submitted in tabular form, and the apparatus for determining the freezing point and its manipulation are described.

The determination of fat in certain milk products, C. K. FRANCIS and D. G. MORGAN (*Jour. Indus. and Engin. Chem.*, 9 (1917), No. 9, pp. 861, 862).—Essentially noted from another source (E. S. R., 37, p. 507).

The estimation of unsaponifiable matter in oils, fats, and waxes, J. M. WILKIE (*Analyst*, 42 (1917), No. 495, pp. 200–202).—The following modification has been found more satisfactory than the procedure usually recommended for the determination of unsaponifiable matter.

A 5-gm. sample is saponified with 12.5 cc. twice-normal alcoholic potassium hydroxid for one-half to one hour, transferred to a separatory funnel with 50 cc. of water, and extracted with 40, 30, and 30 cc. portions of ether. The ether extracts are combined in a separatory funnel containing about 20 cc. of water. Without shaking, the wash water is run off, the ethereal solution then washed by shaking vigorously with 2, 5, and 30 cc. portions of water, evaporated to dryness, and the residue weighed.

For solid waxes, such as beeswax, a sample of 0.5 gm. is used, and in the saponification a few grams of castor oil is added. The procedure is then the same as described above, with the exception of the addition of 40 cc. of water at 30° C. instead of 50 cc. of cold water, and the extraction with 50, 40, 40, and 30 cc. portions of ether. A suitable correction for the known unsaponifiable content of the castor oil is made.

Data submitted indicate the accuracy of the modified procedure.

The thermal values of the fats and oils.—II, The sulphuric acid or Maumené number, J. W. MARDEN and M. V. DOVER (*Jour. Indus. and Engin. Chem.*, 9 (1917), No. 9, pp. 858–860, figs. 2).—Continuing previous studies (E. S. R., 34, p. 803), the authors propose a method for the calorimetric determination of the sulphuric acid number of fats and oils. The method is indicated as being simple, a single determination requiring only about one-half hour, and accurate to 0.5 per cent. The rise in temperature on addition of the acid, multiplied by the heat capacity of the system divided by the weight of the oil, gives the sulphuric acid number in calories per gram of sample. The concentration of the acid was found to affect the results, but a variation in the amount used had little effect so long as the concentration remained constant. The importance of the use of a standard concentration of acid in the test is indicated.

The construction of an inexpensive apparatus (calorimeter) and its standardization are described.

Tabulated data of the heats of reaction of 20 oils examined are submitted.

The pasteurization and biorization of fermented and unfermented grape and fruit juices, W. J. BARAGIOLA (*Schweiz. Apoth. Ztg.*, 55 (1917), No. 29, pp. 396–400).—The disadvantages of the pasteurization of grape and fruit juices are discussed, and some preliminary results of the sterilization of these juices with the biorizator (E. S. R., 31, p. 276; 35, p. 677) are submitted. The results obtained were entirely satisfactory, and no cooked flavor was imparted to the product as is the case when the juices are pasteurized. Some slight modifications of the biorizator were, however, found necessary.

It is intended to continue the study.

Aldehydes in wine, J. LABORDE (*Ann. Inst. Pasteur*, 31 (1917), No. 5, pp. 215–252).—From the results of the study reported it is concluded that the catalytic and physiological agents which are responsible for the formation of aldehydes in wine exercise their greatest influence in young wines during storage in casks. Under these conditions the wine is more or less in contact with the air. There are, however, certain factors which inhibit the production of aldehydes and which are favored by the exclusion of air. This condition is indicated as being the reason for the small quantity of aldehyde in normally stored red wine. Formation of aldehydes in red wine is not considered to exercise any perceptible influence on the precipitation of tannin substances.

It is indicated that the aldehydes exercise not only a transitory influence but one which is wholly unfavorable to the aroma of red wines stored in casks. It is equally injurious to white wines, especially those which are deficient in sulphurous acid. Only those special wines in which part of the quality depends · on an energetic oxidation are benefited by the formation of aldehydes, as it is favorable to the development of their characteristic aroma.

The data obtained in the study are submitted in tabular form and discussed.

Chemical composition of " separated musts," W. J. BARAGIOLA and J. B. KLÉBER (*Landw. Jahrb. Schweiz, 31 (1917), No. 3, pp. 303–314*).—Analytical data of so-called separated musts prepared from the juice of overripe fruits are submitted and discussed.

The juice of such fruits is deficient in tannic acid and consequently turbid, and proper fermentation does not take place in such musts. They may be clarified, however, by proper treatment and are then known as separated musts, the fermentation of which proceeds as satisfactorily as that of a normal must.

Sauerkraut industry of the United States, L. A. ROUND and S. C. COPPERSMITH (*Canner, 44 (1917), Nos. 16, pp. 48, 50; 17, pp. 48, 50; 18, pp. 52, 54; 19, p. 52; 20, pp. 48, 50*).—This is a general discussion of the conditions necessary for the successful fermentation of sauerkraut.

Utilization of frozen and decayed potatoes, SCHBIBAUX (*Compt. Rend. Acad. Agr. France, 3 (1917), No. 26, pp. 716–718*).—The use and value of frozen and decayed potatoes as a stock food and in some instances as human food is noted. A procedure which can be easily carried out on the farm, and which consists of washing, pulping, and drying the pulp, is briefly outlined.

A moderate-sized evaporator for fruits and vegetables, A. F. BARSS (*Oreg. Agr. Col., Ext. Bul. 213 (1917), pp. 4, figs. 4*).—This bulletin describes the construction of a simple and efficient evaporator for drying fruits and vegetables.

Bacteriological study of the natural coagulation of the latex of Hevea brasiliensis, DENIER and VERNET (*Compt. Rend. Acad. Sci. [Paris], 165 (1917), No. 3, pp. 123–126*).—The authors have isolated 26 species of facultative aerobes and anaerobic organisms from the natural congulation of the latex. The organisms are indicated as being present in great numbers. The cultural and morphological characters of the organisms isolated are described.

Certain precautions necessary for a perfect coagulation of the latex are briefly outlined.

More about rice hull carbon, F. ZERBAN (*La. Planter, 59 (1917), No. 6, pp. 93, 94*).—This article reports the results of sugarhouse tests in which the new rice hull carbon was used for clarification. The results are considered entirely satisfactory and, while only of a preliminary nature, are indicated as having established the value of the new product.

Laboratory experiments carried out at the Louisiana Sugar Experiment Station have shown the rice hull carbon, properly prepared and purified, to have a very high decolorizing and deodorizing power which exceeds many times that of ordinary bone black. Its use extends over a large range. The impurities taken up by the carbon can be easily removed and the original decolorizing power restored.

Local processes of coconut oil extraction in the Philippines, C. A. GARDINER (*Philippine Agr. Rev. [English Ed.], 10 (1917), No. 1, pp. 27–31, figs. 6*).—This is a brief description of the machines and methods employed in the extraction of coconut oil in small mills owned and operated by the individual farmer.

METEOROLOGY.

Monthly Weather Review (*U. S. Mo. Weather Rev., 45* (*1917*), *Nos. 5, pp. 203-266, pls. 12, figs. 14; 6, pp. 267-333, pls. 20, figs. 34*).—In addition to weather forecasts, river and flood observations, and seismological reports for May and June, 1917; lists of additions to the Weather Bureau Library and of recent papers on meteorology and seismology; notes on the weather of the months; solar and sky radiation measurements at Washington, D. C., during May and June, 1917; condensed climatological summaries; and the usual climatological tables and charts, these numbers contain the following articles:

No. 5.—City Smoke and Daylight Illumination Intensities (illus.), by H. H. Kimball and A. H. Thiessen; On Horizontal Halos (illus.), by Y. Tsuiji (reprinted); Solar Halo at Vicksburg, Miss., April 24, 1917, by W. E. Barron; Halo Phenomena April 8, 1917, at York, N. Y., by M. N. Stewart; Summer Types of Rainfall in Upper Pecos Valley (illus.), by C. Hallenbeck (see p. 808); Showers of Organic Matter, by W. L. McAtee (see p. 808); Records at the Abbe Meteorological Observatory Compared with Those at the Government Building, Cincinnati (illus.), by W. C. Devereaux; Winter Indoor Aridity in Topeka, Kans., by S. D. Flora; The Preparation of Precipitation Charts, by W. G. Reed and J. B. Kincer; Some New Instruments for Oceanographical Research.—Supplemental Note (illus.); Hail Squall of May 1, 1917, and Accompanying Weather, Baltimore, Md., by L. K. Hirshberg; Photographs of the Antler, N. Dak., Tornado of August 20, 1911 (illus.), by H. E. Simpson; and Some Researches in the Far Eastern Seasonal Correlations.—Second Note (illus.), by T. Okada (reprinted).

No. 6.—Peculiar Streak in Line with Kite Wire, by B. J. Sherry; The World's Air Routes and Their Regulation, by Lord Montagu, of Beaulieu (reprinted abs.); New England Snowfall (illus.), by C. F. Brooks (see p. 807); The Cold Spring of 1917 (illus.), by P. C. Day (see p. 808); Some Aspects of the Cold Period, December, 1916, to April, 1917, by R. C. Mossman (reprinted abs.); Accidental Pressure Variations in the United States, by A. J. Henry; The Tornadoes and Windstorms of May 25–June 6, 1917 (illus.), by H. C. Frankenfield; Meteorological Courses for Aeronautical Engineers.—[Syllabus of 10 Lectures by R. DeC. Ward]; Some Researches in The Far Eastern Seasonal Correlations.—Third Note, by T. Okada (abs.); Kristian Birkeland, 1867–1917, by C. Chree (reprinted); Use of the Divining Rod in the Search for Hidden Things, by O. E. Meinzer (reprinted); Desiccation of Africa, by R. L. Harger (reprinted abs.); and Effect of Humidification of a School Room on Intellectual Progress of the Pupils, E. L. Thorndike and P. J. Kruse (abs.).

Free-air data at Drexel Aerological Station.—April, May, and June, 1916, W. R. BLAIR ET AL. (*U. S. Mo. Weather Rev. Sup. 7* (*1917*), *pp. 51, pls. 3*).— Detailed tabulated data are given on temperature, pressure, humidity, wind, and potential obtained in 140 free-air observations during a period of 91 days in which the mean altitude attained was 2,339 meters (7,672 ft.) above sea level.

Meteorological observations at the Massachusetts Agricultural Experiment Station, J. E. OSTRANDER ET AL. (*Massachusetts Sta. Met. Buls. 343-344* (*1917*), *pp. 4 each*).—Summaries of observations at Amherst, Mass., on pressure, temperature, humidity, precipitation, wind, sunshine, cloudiness, and casual phenomena during July and August, 1917, are presented. The data are briefly discussed in general notes on the weather of each month.

New England snowfall, C. F. BROOKS (*U. S. Mo. Weather Rev., 45* (*1917*), *No. 6, pp. 271-285, pl. 1, figs. 29*).—This is an amplification of an article which has already been noted from another source (E. S. R., 37, p. 16).

Summer types of rainfall in upper Pecos Valley, [N. Mex.], C. HALLEN-BECK (*U. S. Mo. Weather Rev.*, *45* (*1917*), *No. 5*, *pp. 209–216*, *figs. 5*).—From a study of data showing the rainfall, May to September, inclusive, for 12 years, 1905–1916, the author concludes that, while the summer rains of this portion of the United States are essentially daytime rains, there is a preponderance of night rains over the limited area occupied by the upper half of the Pecos Valley, due wholly to the occurrence of a peculiar type of nonconvective rainfall which is described.

Showers of organic matter, W. L. McATEE (*U. S. Mo. Weather Rev.*, *45* (*1917*), *No. 5*, *pp. 217–224*).—This article describes in some detail the various kinds of animal and vegetable matter, alive and dead, which are transported and distributed through the atmosphere. It is stated that the more spectacular phenomena of this kind, such as the distribution of live animals of various kinds, are the least important from the standpoint of the distribution of life. "The rains of larger animals have attracted much attention and excited wonder, but in many cases the animals have been dead; in others they were doomed to die because of falling in an unsuitable environment. Not often are all the conditions propitious for the species to secure a new foothold.

"The unobtrusive, but steady and widespread movement of minute eggs and spores by the atmosphere, however, is of great importance in distribution because these organic bodies are adapted to survive such transport; their numbers are so great and their dispersal so wide that some of them will necessarily fall in favorable places. The chances are, in fact, that every suitable environment will be populated."

The cold spring of 1917, P. C. DAY (*U. S. Mo. Weather Rev.*, *45* (*1917*), *No. 6*, *pp. 285–289*, *figs. 4*).—The unseasonable cold weather which persisted to an unusual degree in nearly all portions of the country during a period of three weeks, beginning about April 24 and continuing to the middle of May, is described. Discussing the agricultural effects of the low temperature, the author states that "while low temperatures retarded the planting and germination of corn, cotton, and other spring crops, and delayed the growth of gardens and truck over the southern districts, the cool weather was not unfavorable to winter wheat and other hardy cereals which are reported to have greatly improved during the month. Likewise fruit buds which had largely remained dormant escaped damage from the prevailing cold, although severe frosts were not experienced as late in the month as in some previous years. However, the cool weather was unfavorable in that it caused crops generally to be backward, which at the end of May were estimated to be from one to three weeks late throughout the country. This increases the liability to damage by fall frost for such crops as have a long period of growth."

SOILS—FERTILIZERS.

Relation of movement of water in a soil to its hygroscopicity and initial moisture, F. J. ALWAY and G. R. McDOLE (*U. S. Dept. Agr., Jour. Agr. Research*, *10* (*1917*), *No. 8*, *pp. 391–428*, *figs. 2*).—In experiments conducted at the Nebraska Experiment Station "17 soils, ranging from a coarse sand with a hygroscopic coefficient of 0.6 to a silt loam with one of 13.3, were placed in cylinders in three different degrees of moistness, 0.5, 1, and 1.5 times the hygroscopic coefficient, 1 in. of water was applied to the surface, the rate of movement during five days observed, and finally the moisture distribution at the end of this period determined.

"When placed in the cylinders the finer-textured soils showed a lower apparent specific gravity than the coarser, but within groups of somewhat similar texture this value was found to show no direct dependence upon the hygroscopicity.

"The moisture content of the moistened layer, even at the end of the first hour, was only from one-half to two-thirds the maximum water capacity, which shows that the latter has little significance as a direct index of the moisture retentiveness of a soil. The moisture content of the moistened layer fell much more rapidly with the finer-textured soils, at the end of 24 hours it being only between two and three times the hygroscopic coefficient, while in the coarser soils it varied from three to ten times the coefficient. At the end of the five days equilibrium had been practically attained in the finer-textured soils, but in the coarser ones this was far from being the case. The coarser the soil the more slowly was equilibrium reached.

"The rate of penetration showed little dependence upon the hygroscopicity, but was definitely affected by the moistness, the higher the initial moisture content of any soil within the limits employed the more rapid being the downward movement of water. The distance of penetration during the five days following the application of water increased with the initial moistness of the soil, but was not closely related to the hygroscopicity, owing partly to the slowness with which equilibrium is attained in the coarser soils.

"With the finer-textured soils the water content of the moistened layer was not distinctly affected by the initial moistness, but with the coarser members the drier the soil the wetter was the moistened layer. Provided that a period of high evaporation is to precede the next rain, the character of the weather immediately following a rain will have a greater effect upon the loss of moisture by evaporation in the case of a coarse than of a fine-textured soil.

"Glass tubes were filled with the same soils in the same three degrees of moistness and the lower ends placed in contact with water kept at a constant level. The rate of rise during eight or ten days was observed and the moisture in the uppermost layer of the moistened portion of the soil column at the end of this period determined. At first the rise was most rapid in the soils of low hygroscopicity, but the difference gradually lessened until those of intermediate hygroscopicity were in the lead. There was no definite dependence of the rise upon the hygroscopicity. No definite dependence of the rate of rise upon the initial moistness was shown, it being, in the case of the three moisture conditions studied, generally most rapid in the moistest condition and slowest in the intermediate.

"All the finer-textured soils showed the highest percentage of moisture at the head of the advancing moist layer when used in the driest condition, but the coarser members showed no difference. The moisture content of this moist layer shows a rather constant relation to both the hygroscopic coefficient and the moisture equivalent, being similar to the moisture retentiveness of the same soils.

"The relative rates and distances of penetration in the different soils are not similar to the relative rates and heights of capillary rise."

Origin of alkali, R. STEWART and W. PETERSON (*U. S. Dept. Agr., Jour. Agr. Research, 10 (1917), No. 7, pp. 331–353*).—In connection with the authors' well-known studies at the Utah Experiment Station of the origin of niter spots in soils (E. S. R., 36, p. 423), analyses were made of some 400 representative samples of sandstone, shale, "alkali," clay, and an ash consisting of a mixture of dry dust with crystals of "alkali" found just under the clay crust on the most affected parts.

" These investigations show a marked amount of water-soluble salts or alkali in the undistributed country rock with local accumulation wherever the movement of the underground water has caused a local concentration by seepage through the rock and deposition by evaporation. There is a marked variation in the amount of salts occurring in the country rock in any given geological series, but uniformly high results have been obtained at widely separated sections of the country, such as those found at Grand Junction, Colo.; Emery and Vernal, Utah; and Lyman, Wyo. There is a marked concentration of nitrates and alkali in the ashlike and alkali deposits in the uncultivated areas."

A tabulated summary of the average alkali material found in the country rock " brings clearly to mind the fact that in a widely disseminated form there are in the shales and sandstones of the Cretaceous and Tertiary of Utah, Colorado, and Wyoming enormous deposits of soluble salts consisting of the sulphates, chlorids, nitrates, and bicarbonates of calcium, magnesium, and sodium. In certain local areas these salts become concentrated so as to produce native alkali, or ' niter spots,' by the movement of the underground water without the instrumentality of the irrigation ditch. Wherever the shale is highly impregnated with the salts the evaporation of the water deposits the alkali salts on the surface in the form of an ashlike powder."

A preliminary soil census of Alabama and west Florida, R. M. HARPER (*Soil Sci., 4 (1917), No. 2, pp. 91–107, fig. 1*).—This census is based on all the soil surveys of the Bureau of Soils of the U. S. Department of Agriculture for Alabama and west Florida published up to the end of 1916.

Soil survey of the Healdsburg area, Cal., E. B. WATSON, W. C. DEAN, C. J. ZINN, and R. L. PENDLETON (*U. S. Dept. Agr., Adv. Sheets Field Oper. Bur. Soils, 1915, pp. 59, pls. 5, fig. 1, map 1*).—This survey, made in cooperation with the California Experiment Station, deals with the soils of an area of 222,720 acres in the central and northern parts of Sonoma County, in western California. The area consists of relatively level valley lands and low hills surrounded by higher hills which are mainly nonarable.

" The soils of the Healdsburg area include those of residual origin, those derived through weathering from old unconsolidated valley-filling deposits, and those of recent alluvial origin." Including rough mountainous land and riverwash, 30 soil types of 15 series are mapped, of which rough mountainous land covers 31.8 per cent, Goldridge fine sandy loam 12.8 per cent, and Madera loam 6.6 per cent of the area.

Soil survey of Cumberland County, Me., C. VAN DUYNE and M. W. BECK (*U. S. Dept. Agr., Adv. Sheets Field Oper. Bur. Soils, 1915, pp. 92, figs. 2, map 1*).—This survey deals with the soils of an area of 545,920 acres in southern Maine, the physiographic features of which are those of an uneven country with little or no systematic arrangement of its hills, valleys, and plains. Only small local areas are poorly drained.

With reference to origin, the soils of the area are classed as " soils derived from glacial till, from terrace deposits, from estuarine and glacial-lake deposits, from alluvial flood-plain deposits, from accumulations of organic matter, and miscellaneous nonagricultural. In all, 10 series with 21 soil types, 4 phases, and 4 miscellaneous types have been mapped." Of these the Gloucester sandy loam, Orono silt loam, Gloucester stony sandy loam, and the Merrimac sandy loam cover 27.3, 15.6, 15.5, and 11.5 per cent of the area.

The formation and characteristics of Massachusetts peat lands and some of their uses, A. P. DACHNOWSKI (*Trans. Mass. Hort. Soc., 1917, pt. 1, pp. 29–*

45).—This is an address delivered January 27, 1917, which was illustrated by means of lantern slides and samples of peat material, and is apparently intended to give the results of a reconnoissance of the peat lands of Massachusetts. It is concluded that the inequality in the character of the peat lands encountered and in the strata of their materials renders a more detailed study advantageous in their agricultural utilization.

"Information concerning the seasonal variations in the water table, the nature of the salt constituents, and the circumstances in the field conditions which lead to the augmentation or diminution of soluble constituents is of prime importance, the effect of any accumulation of iron compounds especially requiring attention in certain cases. The relation of cropping system to the several kinds of peat lands if ignored would be to the disadvantage of the real agricultural value of certain peat lands. Field trials are the more correct means under the existing conditions on the peat lands to determine the choice of crop varieties, seeding mixtures, etc., and the cultural practices to be followed."

The oxidizing power of some soils in Deli, J. A. HONING (*Bul. Deli Proefstat. Medan, No. 8 (1917), pp. 8*).—Tests of the Gerretsen method of determining the oxidizing power of soils (E. S. R., 35, p. 624) on the dry soils of Deli proved it to be impracticable and to give contradictory results on these soils. Frequently the hydrogen iodid value was high for samples taken at 1 or 2 ft. depth and low for surface soils having a high percentage of humus. The failure of the method on the nonirrigated soils of Deli is attributed to the presence of large quantities of humus and the irregular distribution of the ferric iron.

Variation in the chemical composition of soils, W. O. ROBINSON, L. A. STEINKOENIG, and W. H. FRY (*U. S. Dept. Agr. Bul. 551 (1917), pp. 16*).—This bulletin presents complete analyses of 45 samples of soil, representing 18 distinct soil types distributed in four provinces. These, with the analyses of 24 samples previously noted (E. S. R., 31, p. 719), are discussed with reference to variation of all samples, variation in composition within a soil province, variation of the same type, and the bearing of the limit of error in analysis on the interpretation of analytical data.

"It is thought that the analyses discussed represent nearly the extremes in composition of soils in the regions in which the samples were taken. Marked resemblances in composition of soils from the same province are pointed out. It is shown that some samples of the same type differ considerably in chemical composition. It is also shown that some soils of different types may resemble each other in chemical composition as closely as different samples of the same type. It is pointed out that the unavoidable error in analytical operations is in many cases of such magnitude that when analyses are stated in pounds per acre differences of several hundred pounds of some constituents are not significant."

A soil sampler for bacteriological and chemical purposes, J. R. NELLER (*Soil Sci., 4 (1917), No. 2, pp. 109–113, figs. 3*).—A soil sampler, devised at the New Jersey Experiment Stations, is described and diagrammatically illustrated.

The sampling tube is 3½ ft. long and has an inside diameter of 1¼ in. It is divided into two parts, *a* and *b*. Piece *a* is 11 in. long and has a point made so that the core slides easily up through the tube. The inner shoulder above the cutting edge is about ⅛ in. wide. Piece *a* is attached to piece *b* by means of a bayonet, or groove and key joint, made so that it closes and tightens when the upper part of the tube is turned to the right. A slight twist to the left enables one to detach the lower piece and remove the core of soil. The shoulders of this joint taper slightly into each other so as to come together and take up any looseness resulting from wear. The cleaning tube has an outside diameter that permits it to slip easily but snugly through the surface shield.

The use of the sampler is also described.

The influence of available carbohydrates upon ammonia accumulation by microorganisms, S. A. WAKSMAN (*Jour. Amer. Chem. Soc.*, *39* (*1917*), *No. 7, pp. 1503–1512*).—Experiments conducted at the University of California on the influence of carbohydrates on ammonia and amino nitrogen accumulations by soil microorganisms are reported. The organisms studied were *Aspergillus niger* and *Citromyces glaber*, isolated from soil by the author.

It was found that "the effect of sugar on the accumulation of ammonia by *A. niger* is marked. Where the sugar was absent the organism made a rather slow growth, as shown by the weight of the mycelium, but the ammonia accumulated in large quantities from the third till the sixteenth day, the amount increasing rapidly, so that on the sixteenth day about a half of the total nitrogen of the medium was in the form of ammonia. Where the sugar was present the ammonia accumulated only in very small quantities, while the weight of the mycelium increased rapidly until the seventh day, when autolysis set in and the weight of the fungus body began to decrease. The amount of ammonia accumulated was small when the organism grew rapidly; but as the maximum of growth was reached, which was also accompanied by the utilization of all the sugar in the medium, the ammonia began to accumulate very rapidly."

The same results were obtained with *C. glaber*, the excess of sugar corresponding to a decrease in the amount of ammonia present in the medium. "In the production of amino nitrogen *C. glaber* behaves in an entirely different manner from *A. niger;* it was found that many organisms which are not able to reduce the proteins to ammonia, whether in the presence or absence of available carbohydrates, may split the proteins into amino acids which accumulate in the medium.

"This experiment shows again that, when available carbohydrates are present, the organism will utilize all the nitrogen split off from the protein for its own metabolism; while in the absence of available carbohydrates, or where these have been used up, the protein molecule will be attacked not only for its nitrogen content but also for its carbon content."

Effect of paraffin on the accumulation of ammonia and nitrates in the soil, P. L. GAINEY (*U. S. Dept. Agr., Jour. Agr. Research. 10* (*1917*), *No. 7, pp. 355–364*).—In experiments at the Kansas Experiment Station paraffin and Parowax in thin shavings and paraffin oil were added to a soil having a vigorous ammonia and nitrate-forming flora at the rate of 2 gm. per 100 gm. of soil. In certain cases also the insides of the 500-cc. bottles used in the incubation test were paraffined or parowaxed. In certain cases no additions were made of nitrogen or calcium carbonate. In other cases nitrogen was added in the form of cottonseed meal and ammonium sulphate at rates of 50 mg., and calcium carbonate at the rate of 0.5 gm. per 100 gm. of soil.

In the tests in which no nitrogen was added, and regardless of whether calcium carbonate was added, paraffin in the three forms used not only inhibited the accumulation of ammonia and nitrate nitrogen, but caused that which was present at the beginning of the experiments to disappear. This effect was maintained for 13 weeks and even longer, and regardless of whether the paraffin was intimately mixed with the soil or simply lined the inner wall of the container.

When nitrogen was added in the form of cottonseed meal, there was vigorous formation of ammonia and nitrate in the presence of paraffin, but these disappeared so rapidly that "it is impossible to say whether such formation was equally as rapid as in the absence of paraffin." In no case did the quantity of ammonia or nitrate nitrogen, where Parowax or paraffin had been added, approach the quantity in the controls at the end of two weeks. The inhibitory effect of the paraffin oil was more marked than that of other forms of paraffin during the early stages of incubation. The effect of the oil appears to be quite largely an inhibition of formation rather than a disappearance of ammonia and nitrate nitrogen.

"When ammonium sulphate was added to the soil either with or without calcium carbonate, all three forms of paraffin exerted a very marked effect upon the accumulation of nitrate nitrogen. The decreased accumulation of nitrate nitrogen was not so evident during the early stages of incubation except with paraffin oil. With the oil the effect again seems to be to retard nitrification, the quantity of active nitrogen $[NO_3+NH_3]$ approaching very closely that in the controls. Parowax and paraffin, however, not only decrease the accumulation of nitrate nitrogen but also bring about a large reduction in the quantity of active nitrogen. The reduction in active nitrogen occasioned by the various forms of paraffin is not nearly so rapid where ammonium sulphate was added as where nitrogen in the form of cottonseed meal was added."

Further experiments with larger amounts of soil in paraffined 2-gal. earthenware containers showed that "no ordinary sized container used for cultural purposes can be protected with a coating of paraffin, as in these experiments, without the available nitrogen content throughout the whole mass of soil being affected."

Nitrates and nitrification in relation to cultural practices and plant growth, H. A. Noyes (*Abs. Bact., 1 (1917), No. 1, pp. 38, 39*).—A summary is given of the first two years' results of soil bacteriological investigations which are being conducted in an experimental orchard where different cultural practices are under direct comparison. The objects of these investigations are first, to find out if the behavior of the trees can be directly correlated with the activities of the bacteria in the soil, and second, to determine the effect of the activities of the bacteria on the soil.

"The results are as follows: The nitrates in the field correlate with tree growth (circumference gains). The lower nitrate content under field conditions does not mean lower nitrate content after incubation. The field nitrates when compared with the nitrates after incubation give the nitrifying efficiency of the organisms under field conditions." It is concluded that "knowledge of the nitrate content of field soil may throw more light on the activities of nitrifying bacteria than the nitrification test itself."

A program of soil improvement for New York State, E. O. Fippin (*N. Y. State Col. Agr., Cornell Univ. Ext. Bul. 15 (1917), pp. 499–534, figs. 5*).—"The purpose of this bulletin is to point out the primary elements of a comprehensive system of soil improvement, and to propose a program of work that will coordinate and unify, so far as that is now practicable, the field study of soils."

Barnyard manure and products of decomposition, H. Murphy (*Okla. Agr., 5 (1917), No. 9, pp. 13–16, 18*).—This is a brief summary of experience at several of the State experiment stations and at certain foreign experiment stations.

Manure from the sea, E. H. Jenkins and J. P. Street (*Conn. State Sta. Bul. 194 (1917), pp. 3–13, figs. 7*).—This bulletin treats of the manurial value of seaweeds and marine mud. Analyses of samples of these materials from the New England coast, made at the Rhode Island, Massachusetts, and Connecticut experiment stations, are given in the following table:

Average composition of seaweeds, calculated to 75 per cent moisture.

Kind of material.	Number of analyses.	Organic matter.	Nitrogen.	Phosphoric acid.	Potash.	Lime.	Magnesia.
		Per ct.	Per ct.	Per ct.	Per ct.	Per ct.	Per ct.
Laminaria saccharina	8	[1](19.76)	0.39	0.13	0.51	0.83	0.35
L. digitata	7		.45	.12	.62	.09	.38
Ascophyllum nodosum	11	(19.47)	.39	(0.02)	.79	.49	.38
Fucus vesiculosus	12	(19.34)	.43	.12	.50	.47	.30
Chondrus crispus	9	(18.75)	.70	.13	1.15		
Zostera marina	13	(10.90)	.41	.15	.42	.91	.30
Rhodymenia palmata	1		.68	.17	1.98	.87	.16
Phyllophora membranifolia	3		.80	.11	.72	3.66	.50
Cladostephus verticellatus	1		.39	.19	1.23	.75	.31
Polyides rotundus	1		.82	.15	.36	.60	.18
Ahnfeldtia plicata	1		.42	.09	.88	.22	.28
"Fine branching seaweed"	1		.98	.24	1.74	.31	.24
Sea lettuce	1		.33	.06	.48		
Coarse sponge	1		1.04	.25	.29	.14	.25

[1] Most figures in parentheses are results of single analysis and not average.

A comparison of average analyses of seaweed, New York horse manure, and cow manure with litter shows "that the average seaweed contains less organic matter, nitrogen, and phosphoric acid than New York horse manure, and compared with cow manure it has about the same amount of nitrogen, much less phosphoric acid, and more potash. Seaweeds are relatively deficient in phosphoric acid. . . . Eelgrass is generally regarded as inferior to the rockweeds as manure, though the composition of the fresh material is not strikingly different."

Analyses of 9 samples of marine mud from various places on the Connecticut shore showed an average moisture content of about 48 per cent, organic matter 3.95, and nitrogen 0.15 per cent. In four of these samples further determinations average, as follows: Potash, 0.35 per cent; soda, 0.72; lime, 0.43; magnesia, 0.52; phosphoric acid, trace; chlorin, 0.93; and sulphuric acid, 0.53 per cent. It is stated that although the percentages of organic matter, nitrogen, and potash in marine mud are small, "applications of from 1,000 to 2,000 bu. per acre have given excellent results, due in part, no doubt, to the action of the mud as an amendment, making the soil more retentive of water, and perhaps in part also to the action of salt."

The value of coconut poonac as manure, M. K. BAMBER (*Dept. Agr. Ceylon Leaflet 1 (1917), folio*).—Analyses of ordinary coconut poonac showed a content of nitrogen 3.33 per cent, phosphoric acid 1.47, potash 1.29, lime 0.9, and soda 1.17 per cent.

Experiments with humogen, M. H. F. SUTTON (*Reading, England: Sutton & Sons [1917], pp. 12, figs. 14*).—Experiments with mustard, Italian rye grass, and dwarf French beans to test the fertilizing value of humogen and also to compare it with barnyard manure and complete fertilizers are reported.

No great success attended the use of commercially manufactured humogen, although results were obtained with humogen made in the laboratory which were second only to those obtained with a complete fertilizer. "So far as the results of these tests show, it would appear that, however satisfactory humogen may be when prepared in the laboratory, some difficulty as yet exists in manufacturing this fertilizer efficiently on a commercial scale. The question also arises whether, when standardized, it can be placed on the market in a sufficiently concentrated form and at a price low enough to bring it within the reach of large users of fertilizers."

The industrial chemist and the fertilizer crisis, H. C. LINT (*Chem. Engin. and Manfr.*, 25 (1917), No. 3, pp. 86–89).—The author discusses the fertilizer problem from the standpoint of the industrial chemist, and discusses peat and muck as sources of organic ammoniates.

The effect of ammonium sulphate on soil acidity, F. E. ALLISON and R. C. COOK (*Soil Sci.*, 3 (1917), No. 6, pp. 507–512, fig. 1).—Experiments conducted at Rutgers College are reported in which it was found that "the increases in acidity in five greenhouse soils and a quartz sand receiving no nitrogenous fertilizer were practically the same during the course of a year whether these soils were cropped or kept in fallow. The quartz sand showed the smallest increase in acidity and a loam soil the largest, but there was no relation between the acid accumulation and the soil texture. The increases in acidity in the presence of ammonium sulphate were markedly higher than in the check pots. The partial removal of the nitrogen added decreased the acidity to an appreciable extent in the quartz sand and in the heavy clay soil, increased it in the loam, and left it practically the same in the other three soils. The average increase in acidity in the soils used, exclusive of the quartz sand, was 4,140 lbs. of calcium oxid per 3,000,000 lbs. of soil where no crop was grown, and 4,240 lbs. where four crops of buckwheat were harvested. On the average, the increase in acidity produced by ammonium sulphate in greenhouse pots was about 80 lbs. of calcium oxid for 100 lbs. of ammonium sulphate applied."

The fixation of atmospheric nitrogen, D. FLORENTIN (*Génie Civil*, 70 (1917), Nos. 20, pp. 319–322; 21, pp. 333–337; 22, pp. 353–355; 23, pp. 369–372; 24, pp. 384–386, figs. 14).—This article reviews recent processes and discoveries relating to the industrial fixation of atmospheric nitrogen for agricultural and industrial use.

Some conditions affecting the value of calcium cyanamid as a manure, T. D. MOSSCROP (*Jour. Agr. Sci.* [England], 8 (1917), No. 2, pp. 178–181).—Bell-jar and pot experiments with lettuce, turnips, barley, and wheat to determine the cause of the injurious influence of calcium cyanamid led to the conclusion that "any injurious effect on germination when calcium cyanamid is used is due to the formation of free ammonia produced at first more rapidly than it can be absorbed by the soil." It was further found that the injurious action disappeared eight days after the manure had been applied to a moist soil. "Any danger to nonoily seeds or those with a thin testa can be avoided by applying the calcium cyanamid a week before sowing the seeds."

The value of Thomas slag phosphate for neutralizing soil as well as for supplying phosphorus, B. L. HARTWELL, F. R. PEMBER, and S. C. DAMON (*Rhode Island Sta. Bul.* 171 (1917), pp. 3–34, pl. 1).—Experiments are reported the main object of which was to help furnish a basis for the adoption of analytical methods suited to the inspection of the various grades of Thomas slag phosphate from the standpoint of their agricultural value.

In experiments with barley, beets, and lettuce to determine the value of Thomas slag phosphates from different sources for neutralizing acid soils, using chemically pure, precipitated calcium carbonate as a standard of comparison, it was found that the calcium carbonate did not give results markedly superior to those given by the slags with the first two crops. "With the lettuce, however, the conditions were such that, for about the same amount of calcium oxid applied, that in the slags was only about a third as effectual as in the other form. . . .

"Data concerning the relative availability of the .phosphorus in slags and other phosphates were secured by four pot experiments with dwarf Essex rape and one with Japanese millet. A field experiment with these two crops was also conducted for two years. The later experiments, both in the pots and field, were carried out according to directions furnished by the basic slag committee of the Association of Official Agricultural Chemists. The use in the pots of a preceding crop of crimson clover as a green manure did not increase the relative availability of the phosphorus in the insoluble phosphates, slag, and raw rock phosphate, or floats, in comparison with that in the soluble sources. In the pot experiments, although the slags compared very favorably with the soluble sources, the floats were decidedly inferior; even in large applications the latter material failed to supply the needs of the plants. From soil to which no phosphorus was added the millet absorbed per pot more than twice as much as the rape did. . . . Even when applied in the most available source more than four-fifths of the phosphorus became inaccessible to the first crop planted after its application.

"In the field experiments with both millet and rape results were obtained for the year in which the various sources of phosphorus were applied as well as the after-effects in the following year. The raw rock phosphate was much less available than the other sources of phosphorus. . . . Basic phosphate yielded somewhat less than the other slags, which compared favorably with the soluble phosphates.

"It would seem from the results of the experiments . . . that if water-soluble phosphate is considered entirely available, then a laboratory method for determining the availability of Thomas slag phosphate should include the use of some solvent which would dissolve nearly all of the phosphorus."

The rate of reversion of mixtures of superphosphate with basic slag and rock phosphates, G. S. ROBERTSON (*Jour. Soc. Chem. Indus.*, *36 (1917)*, *No. 12*, *pp. 626–628*).—Experiments with mixtures of equal parts of 26 per cent water-soluble superphosphate and 26 per cent citric-soluble basic slag led to the conclusion that "on the whole it can not be said that a superphosphate and basic slag mixture has anything particular in its favor. If the basis of the mixture is one-half 26 per cent superphosphate and one-half basic slag, it is clear that if the slag contains 2 per cent of caustic lime practically all the water-soluble phosphate in the mixture will revert in a few hours."

Experiments with equal parts of 26 per cent superphosphate and Gafsa rock phosphate showed that "the water-soluble phosphate in the mixture reverts to a much less extent than in the slag and superphosphate mixture. The reversion is, comparatively speaking, so small that there would be no serious objection to farmers making and applying such a mixture. . . . There seems to be no serious difficulty in the way of manufacturers making such a mixture (1 of superphosphate to 1 of rock phosphate) and selling it with a guaranty of water-soluble phosphate, total phosphate, and, if advisable, citric-soluble phosphate."

Phosphate rock in 1916, R. W. STONE (*U. S. Geol. Survey, Min. Resources, U. S., 1916, pt. 2, pp. 29–41*).—This report states that "the quantity of phosphate rock marketed in the United States in 1916 was 1,982,385 long tons, valued at $5,896,993, an increase of 146,718 tons in quantity and of $483,544 in value over the production of 1915. This increase was comparatively small but it indicates an improvement in the industry, and suggests that in spite of the curtailment in the exports the production of former years may in time be approached. . . .

"The quantity mined in 1916 was 2,169,149 tons. Compared with the quantity mined in 1915, which was 1,935,341 tons, this was an increase of 12 per cent, as against a decrease of about 27 per cent in 1915 from 1914. In Florida the increase was about 17 per cent, 24 companies operating in 1916 instead of 17, as in 1915. In South Carolina there was a decrease of 46 per cent and in Tennessee an increase of 5 per cent. In Kentucky 1 producer reported rock mined. The production in the Western States decreased 55 per cent. . . .

"The western phosphate field includes about 2,500,000 acres, in which there are about 5,750,000,000 tons of high-grade rock within minable depth (5,000 ft.) of the surface, and in addition several billion tons of rock carrying from 15 to 40 per cent of tricalcium phosphate. Throughout most of the western field there is a main bed from 3 to 6 ft. thick which runs over 65 per cent in tricalcium phosphate. The workable deposits occur chiefly in public lands of the United States. The character and mode of occurrence of the rock are such that for the most part it must be mined by underground methods rather than by open pits. The rock can be ground and treated with acid, however, without the preliminary washing and drying which increase the cost of production of eastern phosphates."

Data on foreign sources of phosphoric acid are also given.

Potash in agriculture.—III, Further researches, B. C. Aston (*Jour. Agr.* [*New Zeal.*], *14* (*1917*), *No. 6, pp. 440–447*).—In a further discussion of the potash situation in New Zealand (E. S. R., 37, p. 218), it is pointed out that flax waste, wood ashes from sawmills, hedge clippings, weeds, and liquid stock excreta are some of the more important sources of potash in New Zealand which are now disregarded or wasted. It is also thought that bracken as a source of potash is worthy of investigation, as studies have shown that New Zealand bracken in the young stages contains as much potash as Scottish bracken and gives a higher yield per acre.

The recovery of potash from beet sugarhouse waste liquors, H. E. Zitkowski (*Sugar* [*Chicago*], *19* (*1917*), *No. 7, pp. 256–258; Metallurg. and Chem. Engin., 17* (*1917*), *No. 1, pp. 17–19*).—It is pointed out in this article that technically the recovery of the potash from beet sugarhouse waste liquors is a comparatively simple and perfectly feasible problem. "It is simply one of evaporating the dilute liquors as economically as practical, charring the residue to produce the crude ash, and leaching and recrystallizing if this is desired. The quantities of water to be evaporated, however, are large, the necessary equipment costly, and commercially such a procedure has possibilities only during war prices."

Concentrated potash a by-product of cement mill (*Engin. News-Rec., 78* (*1917*), *No. 13, pp. 630–632, figs. 3*).—Experience at a cement plant at Riverside, Cal., indicates that the possibilities of recovery of potash as a by-product in Portland cement manufacture are that 90 per cent of the potash contained in the raw mix can be volatilized, 10 per cent remaining in the clinker and 80 per cent being caught by the dust collector. Including filter losses, it is considered conservative to expect the recovery in the form of concentrated salt of 66⅔ per cent of the potash originally contained in the raw cement mix. A 100-ft. rotary kiln, it is stated, may produce from 4 to 7 tons of dust daily, the average potash content of which may range between 4 and 10 per cent.

With reference to the mechanical features of the process, the dust is drawn from bins under the electrical treatment into tanks, where it is put into solution by agitation in water of not less than 85° C., at a concentration of not over 5 per cent K₂O. The temperature soon rises to the boiling point, due to the hydration of the lime, and the potash goes rapidly into solution, the whole operation of extracting the water-soluble potash from 7 tons of dust being accomplished in less than 50 minutes. Under filter-press treatment a cake is formed and removed, and the remaining solution evaporated and the salt collected for grinding and sacking. Six lbs. of potassium sulphate is now being recovered at the plant for every barrel of clinker burned, which at present prices is worth from 40 to 50 cts. per barrel of cement produced.

The possibilities of developing an American potash industry, R. K. MEADE (*Metallurg. and Chem. Engin.*, 17 (*1917*), *No. 2, pp. 78–87; abs. in Sci. Abs., Sect. B—Elect. Engin.*, 20 (*1917*), *No. 10, p. 367*).—This is a rather comprehensive survey of the present potash situation in the United States and a discussion of future possibilities along this line.

The author believes " that the largest future source of cheap potash available in this country is in the iron industry and the cement industry. Germany is reported to have $150 invested in her potash mines and equipment for every ton of potash produced annually. On this basis $37,000,000 would be needed to produce the 250,000 tons of potash imported into this county. . . . The expenditure of this amount of money in this country in these two industries alone would result in the recovery of potash now lost amounting to nearly 200.000 tons. The balance could easily be obtained from the evaporation of lakes and brines, from beet-sugar waste, and from some of the processes now proposed for the manufacture of potash direct from feldspar or glauconite."

A key to the soil for better crops is soluble ground limestone (*Indianapolis, Ind.: Indiana Agr. Ground Limestone Assoc.* [*1917*], *pp. 15*).—This pamphlet briefly describes the use of ground limestone on soils.

Lime report, 1916, J. W. KELLOGG ET AL. (*Penn. Dept. Agr. Bul. 294* (*1917*), *pp. 33*).—This is the report of the official inspection and analysis of agricultural lime in Pennsylvania for 1916.

Fertilizer report, August 1 to December 31, 1916, J. W. KELLOGG (*Penn. Dept. Agr. Bul. 288* (*1917*), *pp. 71*).—This is a report of the official inspection and analysis of fertilizers in Pennsylvania for the period named.

AGRICULTURAL BOTANY.

The botany of crop plants, W. W. ROBBINS (*Philadelphia: P. Blakiston's Son & Co.*, 1917. pp. XIX+681. figs. 262).—This book, intended for agricultural and nonagricultural students. is designed to give a knowledge of the common orchard, field, and garden crops. more than 100 being treated. After an introductory part in which the fundamentals of plant structure, function, activity. and classification are dealt with, the different crops are taken up in the order of their families, the habits of the plants. their distinctive characteristics, distribution, production, and uses being described. Keys are given of the principal economic types that will aid the student in recognizing and identifying forms with which he is unfamiliar.

Important range plants: Their life history and forage value, A. W. SAMPSON (*U. S. Dept. Agr. Bul. 545* (*1917*), *pp. 63, pls. 56*).—The results are given of a study of the habits. requirements. and life history of more than 50 species of forage plants in the Wallowa National Forest in northeastern Oregon. Preliminary information regarding the palatability of the plants was obtained by observing sheep while feeding. and afterwards the relative value of the individual species was determined by studying their abundance, distribution. time of flower-stalk production, aggressiveness, reproduction (both vegetative and by seed). their palatability and nutritiousness at various times during the grazing season. and their ability to withstand trampling.

The data obtained relative to the life history of the different forage species are said to have made possible the adoption of what is known as the deferred or rotation grazing system in this forest.

Tables are presented giving the soil moisture requirements, time of flower-stalk production, time of seed maturity, and seed viability of the different species investigated.

Inventory of seeds and plants imported by the Office of Foreign Seed and Plant Introduction during the period from January 1 to March 31, 1914 (*U. S. Dept. Agr., Bur. Plant Indus. Inventory No. 38 (1917), pp. 105, pls. 10*).— This inventory includes importations of about 700 lots of seeds and plants.

Inventory of seeds and plants imported by the Office of Foreign Seed and Plant Introduction during the period from April 1 to June 30, 1914 (*U. S. Dept. Agr., Bur. Plant Indus. Inventory No. 39 (1917), pp. 183, pls. 10*).—A list is given, together with economic notes, on about 1,000 importations of seeds and plants.

Inventory of seeds and plants imported by the Office of Foreign Seed and Plant Introduction during the period from July 1 to September 30, 1914 (*U. S. Dept. Agr., Bur. Plant Indus. Inventory No. 40 (1917), pp. 110, pls. 10*).— This gives accounts of about 640 introductions, most of the material having been received from China, India, and Brazil.

New or noteworthy plants from Colombia and Central America, VI, H. PITTIER (*U. S. Nat. Mus., Contrib. Nat. Herbarium, 18 (1917), pt. 6, pp. 225–259+X, pl. 1, figs. 7*).—This paper is a continuation of a series of studies by the author on the flora of Colombia and Central America (E. S. R., 34, p. 827).

The Middle American species of Lonchocarpus, H. PITTIER (*U. S. Nat. Mus., Contrib. Nat. Herbarium, 20 (1917), pt. 2, pp. 37–93+X, pls. 6, figs. 43*).—A description is given of the species of Lonchocarpus known to occur in Central America and Mexico.

The families and genera of the bacteria, C. E. A. WINSLOW, JEAN BROAD-HURST, R. E. BUCHANAN, C. KRUMWIEDE, JR., L. A. ROGERS, and G. H. SMITH (*Jour. Bact., 2 (1917), No. 5, pp. 505–566*).—A preliminary report is given of the committee of the Society of American Bacteriologists appointed to consider the characterization and classification of bacterial types. An outline of the families and genera of bacteria is presented. The committee proposes the recognition of four orders of Schizomycetes, the Eubacteriales embracing 8 families and 31 genera. The adoption is recommended of the principles of the so-called Vienna Code of Botanical Nomenclature, with the exception of the requirement of Latin descriptions. It is also recommended that the date of publication of the third edition of Zopf's Spaltpilze be taken as the date for the beginning of bacteriological nomenclature in determining priority, except for a list of genera conservanda to be adopted by the society at its 1918 meeting.

Is symbiosis possible between legume bacteria and nonlegume plants? T. J. BURRILL and R. HANSEN (*Illinois Sta. Bul. 202 (1917), pp. 113–181, pls. 10, figs. 8; abs., pp. 4, fig. 1*).—This bulletin gives an account of investigations on legume bacteria and an attempt to develop symbiosis between legume bacteria and nonlegume plants similar to that which exists between *Pseudomonas radicicola* and leguminous plants.

Studies preliminary to the attempt to develop strains of bacteria that would exist in symbiosis with nonlegume plants showed that the nodule bacteria taken from the roots of leguminous plants may be divided into 11 groups according to the host plants to which they have become specifically adapted. By means of cultures, the authors have been able to isolate P. *radicicola* from all of the subfamilies of Leguminosæ, and while the various nodule bacteria exhibit serological and cultural differences which are permanent, yet in other characteristics they are so alike that it is considered best to regard the adapted forms as varieties of a single species. The nodules occurring on Ceanothus, Cycas, Alnus, and Myrica are said not to be caused by P. *radicicola*, those on Ceanothus differing morphologically from those found on the Leguminosæ. The authors do not consider conclusive the evidence that the nodules on Elæagnus and Podocarpus are caused by legume bacteria, nor is the proof conclusive that any of these nonlegume plants are concerned in the fixation of atmospheric nitrogen.

Extensive experiments were conducted in an attempt to infect nonlegume plants with nodule bacteria, always with negative results, and it is claimed that no conclusion can be drawn as to the possibility or probability of developing or finding nodule bacteria that will grow on nonlegume plants.

An extensive bibliography of the subject is appended.

The abstract is by A. L. Whiting.

The behavior of self-sterile plants, E. M. EAST (*Abs. in Science, n. ser., 46* (1917), *No. 1183, pp. 221, 222*).—According to the author, there are two problems connected with the inheritance of self-sterility in plants. One is the relation between self-sterile and self-fertile plants, the other the behavior of self-sterile plants when crossed together. In Nicotiana self-fertility is completely dominant over self-sterility. Either of the self-sterile species *N. alata* or *N. forgetiana* may be crossed with the self-fertile species *N. langsdorffii*, resulting in each case in an F_1 generation which is completely self-fertile. The F_2 plants are said to show the usual monohybrid ratio of 3 self-fertile to 1 self-sterile.

Discussing the results obtained in his investigations, the author concludes that the behavior of self-sterile plants in intercrosses is regulated by several transmissible factors, all of which are distinct from the single basic factor for self-sterility and which presumably may be carried by self-sterile plants. A plant homozygous for self-sterility can neither be fertilized by its own gametes nor by the gametes of any other self-sterile plant of like constitution as regards these regulation factors, but any two plants differing in these regulatory factors are cross-fertile.

Twin hybrids from Œnothera lamarckiana and Œ. franciscana when crossed with Œ. pycnocarpa, G. F. ATKINSON (*Abs. in Science, n. ser., 46* (1917), *No. 1183, p. 222*).—According to the author, when *Œ. lamarckiana* is crossed with *Œ. pycnocarpa*, there is a splitting in the F_1 generation with the production of twin hybrids. One of the twins is characterized by the *pycnocarpa* type, while the other is designated as a *lamarckiana* type. These twin types are fixed in the first generation, and are repeated in the F_2 and probably in the following generations in accordance with the usual behavior of twin hybrids determined by De Vries.

When *Œ. franciscana* and *Œ. pycnocarpa* are crossed, there is said to be a splitting in the F_1 with the production of twin hybrids, and in the F_2 generation there is a one-sided splitting similar to that which occurs in the F_2 of twins from *Œ. hookeri* and *Œ. lamarckiana*, as described by De Vries. In this second grouping the *pycnocarpa* type twin is said to have a hybrid constitution, while the *franciscana* type of this generation is fixed in the F_1 and repeats itself in the F_2. The *franciscana* twin is believed to carry the *pycnocarpa* factors, but in a subordinate or permanently latent condition.

Naming American hybrid oaks, W. TRELEASE (*Abs. in Science, n. ser., 46* (1917), *No. 1184, p. 244*).—In a study of American oaks, the author has investigated 38 known or probable hybrids among the oaks of the United States. To the number of accepted hybrids already recorded two are added in this paper.

So far no cases of hybridity have been observed in which a species of the white oak group has intercrossed with a species of the red oak group.

The anatomy of woody plants, E. C. JEFFREY (*Chicago: The University of Chicago Press, 1917, pp. X+478, pl. 1, figs. 307*).—In this book the author treats of the anatomy of vascular plants, with special reference to its historical and experimental aspects. In former standard works upon this subject the anatomy of existing forms is treated, but the author of the present work supplies many paleobotanical and developmental data that are fundamentally important for an understanding of the evolution of plant organization. A chapter on anatomical technique is given that may be used as a guide to the preparation of material for study.

Ecology and physiology of the red mangrove, H. H. BOWMAN (*Abs. in Science, n. ser., 46 (1917), No. 1184, p. 245*).—A report is given of an examination of the microscopic structure of the various tissues of the red mangrove, the material having been collected in the Gulf of Mexico along the lower Florida Keys. Particular attention has been paid to the presence of intercellular stone cells and to the occurrence of tannin cells. The physiological relations of transpiration and absorption of these plants growing in sea water and all dilutions of it, as well as in fresh water, have been studied.

The author has deduced the law that the transpiration of these plants varies directly as the concentration of the medium. It was also found that there is a definite relation between the amounts of sugar and tannin in the hypocotyls at different stages of growth of the plants.

The chemical basis of regeneration and geotropism, J. LOEB (*Science, n. ser., 46 (1917), No. 1179, pp. 115–118*).—In continuation of the author's investigations on Bryophyllum (E. S. R., 37, pp. 324, 325), additional information is given by which it is shown that the rate of geotropic bending of horizontally placed stems of *B. calycinum*, if an apical leaf is attached to the stem, increases with the mass of the leaf. The author believes that the phenomena of geotropism are due to the chemical mass action, probably of the common nutritive materials circulating in the sap, and they are apparently of the same nature as the growth of dormant buds, which is also due to a mass action of the same substances.

The effects of acids and salts on biocolloids, D. T. MACDOUGAL and H. A. SPOEHR (*Science, n. ser., 46 (1917), No. 1185, pp. 269–272*).—In continuation of investigations on what the authors term biocolloids (E. S. R., 37, p. 325), a report is given of the effects of various acids, alkalies, salts, and their various combinations in stimulating growth.

Anesthesia and respiration, A. R. C. HAAS (*Science, n. ser., 46 (1917), No. 1193, pp. 462–464*).—A preliminary account is given of investigations on the effect of anesthetics upon respiration, from which the author concludes that when Laminaria is exposed to the action of anesthetics in sufficient concentration to produce any result there is an increase in respiration. This may be followed by a decrease if the reagent is sufficiently toxic, but no decrease was observed with low concentrations which were not toxic.

The measurement of light in some of its more important physiological aspects, D. T. MACDOUGAL and H. A. SPOEHR (*Science, n. ser., 45 (1917), No 1172, pp. 616–618*).—The results are given of a test of the photoelectric cell developed by Elster and Geitel, comparisons being made with the Smithsonian pyrheliometer.

The authors state that the sodium cell connected with a suitable portable galvanometer offers many advantages for the measurement of light intensities

32950°—18—No. 9——3

in natural habitats and that the action of the photoelectric cell in light is more nearly parallel to that of the organism than that of any other light-measuring instruments hitherto available.

FIELD CROPS.

Effect of fall irrigation on crop yields at Belle Fourche, S. Dak., F. D. FARRELL and B. AUNE (*U. S. Dept. Agr. Bul. 546 (1917), pp. 13, fig. 1*).—The favorable results secured at Scottsbluff, Nebr. (E. S. R., 32, p. 36), with fall irrigation for spring-planted crops led to a repetition of the experiments under different soil conditions at the Belle Fourche Experiment Farm. The experiments were begun in 1913, and involved the use of oats, sugar beets, flax, potatoes, barley, corn, and wheat grown on duplicate check plats receiving the usual summer irrigation and on duplicate plats receiving in addition a fall irrigation. The results secured in 1914, 1915, and 1916 are reported and discussed.

The soil upon which these experiments were conducted is described as an extremely heavy clay, popularly known as "gumbo" and classified by the Bureau of Soils as Pierre clay. Mathews (E. S. R., 36, p. 210) reported that this soil would carry approximately 30 per cent moisture, about half of which would be available to crops, and that the wilting coefficient of the soil approximates 17 per cent. During the nine years 1908–1916, inclusive, the annual rainfall varied from 6.64 in. in 1911 to 21.02 in. in 1915, the mean being 14.05 in. The mean precipitation for the fall period (August to October, inclusive) for the 9-year period was 3.75 in. and for the winter period (November to March, inclusive) 2.15 in.

The average crop yields secured on the fall-irrigated plats and on the check plats are reported in tabular form and the summarized statement below given to show the probable errors of the average yields.

Summary of crop yields showing the probable errors of the averages.

Crop.	Unit of yield.	Fall-irrigated plats.		Check plats.		Difference in favor of fall irrigation.
		Number of plats averaged.	Average yield per acre.	Number of plats averaged.	Average yield per acre.	
Wheat	Bushels	6	22.1± 2.2	6	20.1± 1.4	+2.0± 2.6
Oats	...do	6	61.9± 5.0	6	67.8± 6.0	−5.9± 7.8
Barley	...do	6	33.9± 1.5	6	36.1± 2.5	−2.2± 2.9
Flax	...do	6	13.7± 1.4	6	15.2± 0.9	−1.5± 1.7
Corn	...do	6	42.2± 3.3	6	43.9± 3.1	−1.7± 4.5
Beets	Tons	6	8.4± 1.1	6	9.2± 1.1	−0.8± 1.5
Potatoes	Bushels	6	167.0±23.0	6	172.0±19.0	−5.0±30.0

Since none of the differences in favor of fall irrigation was as great as the probable error, all were regarded as insignificant. The lower average yields of the fall-irrigated plats are attributed to the relatively low productivity of one of the two fall-irrigated series, the 3-year average yield of which was 16 per cent lower than that of the duplicate series, while the corresponding averages of the two check series were identical. This low production was thought to have been associated with a heavy infestation of gumbo weed, *Iva axillaris*, on the low-yielding series.

Soil moisture determinations made in the spring and early summer of each year are reported and the data tabulated for each year of the experiment. In 1914 the first two samplings showed more moisture in the first 3 ft. of the fall-irrigated plats than in the corresponding depth of the check plats. No effect was noted beyond the third foot, the differences in the upper 3 ft. occurring at a time when all plats contained abundant moisture and disappearing before the end of June. No significant differences were found in 1915 or 1916.

The failure of fall irrigation to increase crop yields in these experiments appears to be attributable to the character of the soil. Being a heavy clay, absorption occurred only when the soil was dry, and was followed rapidly by expansion, which so compacted the soil that it became impervious and hindered the storage of water in the lower depths for the use of the crops.

Progress report, Substation No. 2, Troup, Tex., 1901–1914, W. S. HOTCH-KISS (*Texas Sta. Bul. 209 (1917), pp. 1–13, 33 fig. 1*).—Variety tests with cotton and corn for 1912–1914, inclusive, and fertilizer tests with sweet potatoes for 1907, 1908, and 1911 are noted, supplementing a previous report (E. S. R., 21, p. 536).

The average yields of the ten highest-yielding cotton varieties tested two or more times varied from 690 lbs. of seed cotton per acre for Half and Half to 756 lbs. for Texas Oak. Mebane, second with an average yield of 732 lbs. of seed cotton, is deemed superior to the other varieties tested because of its high yield of lint, averaging 38 per cent, and because of other desirable qualities.

In the corn variety tests Munson with 22.9 bu., Red Indian Chief with 22.1 bu., Strawberry with 20.5 bu., Oklahoma White Wonder with 20.4 bu., and Texseed Giant White with 19.1 bu. gave the highest average yields for two years.

In fertilizer tests with sweet potatoes the best results were obtained with acid phosphate and cottonseed meal, both when used singly and in combination, a mixture of the two being deemed advisable. An average increase of 30.3 bu. per acre for the three years of the test was attributed to acid phosphate and an increase of 33.3 bu. per acre to cottonseed meal. Potash is regarded as unnecessary on the soils on which these tests were conducted, while nitrate of soda, although giving good results, must compete with cottonseed meal as a source of nitrogen.

Report of the Bermuda Board of Agriculture, 1914–15, E. J. WORTLEY (*Rpts. Bd. Agr. Bermuda, 1914–15, pp. 21–26, 27–32*).—A general administrative report including a brief discussion of seed-potato improvement.

[Field crops work in Argentina], J. M. HUERGO (*Min. Agr. Argentina, Mem. Cong. Nac., 1914–15, pp. 42–45, 46, 50–53, 55, 56*).—Brief reports are given of wheat improvement through selection, the importation and production of potatoes, alfalfa seed importations, the cotton industry, the production of rice, seed analyses, the classification of commercial seeds, the production of barley for brewing purposes, and tobacco production, for the year 1914–15.

[Field crops], P. SYMEONIDES (*Cyprus Agr. Jour., No. 44 (1917), pp. 974–978, pl. 1*).—Fertilizer, variety, and cultural tests with wheat, barley, oats, rye, and canary seed are reported for the season of 1916. Further notes are given on " Sitarokrithi " (E. S. R., 34, p. 339), the so-called wheat-barley hybrid.

[Report of field crops work at the Bankipoor Agricultural Station, 1915–16], G. SHERRARD (*Rpt. Dept. Agr. Bihar and Orissa, 1915–16, pp. 43–49*).—Fertilizer and cultural experiments with rice are reported for the year. An application of 4 tons of manure showed a net profit of $6.18 per acre as compared with $4.43 from an application of one-half that amount. Acid phosphate applied at the rate of 120 lbs. per acre showed a net profit of $10.06, but when supplemented by 160 lbs. of ammonium sulphate of $7.48.

Experiments are reported with gram (*Cicer arietinum*) sown broadcast in the standing rice and left to grow through the cold weather after the rice is removed.

Rate-of-seeding tests with rice indicated that seedings of 410 lbs. per acre of seed bed gave considerably higher yields than seedings of 615 lbs. Transplanting 8 seedlings per hole showed higher yields than 1, 2, or 4 seedlings per hole.

Variety and cultural tests with sugar cane are briefly noted. The yield of cane cultivated by the local method as compared with trenching was considerably higher for the former.

[Report of work with field crops at the Benares Agricultural Station], L. C. Sharma (*Rpt. Benares Agr. Sta., United Provs. Agra and Oudh, 1916, pp. 3–14*).—Reports are given on variety tests with sugar cane, corn, cotton, wheat, rice, barley, and gram, together with tests of sunn hemp and millet and a study of the effect of hot-weather cultivation on wheat yields.

The sugar-cane experiments included a comparison of thick and thin varieties, rate-of-seeding tests, fertilizer tests, and irrigation tests. Saretha, the highest yielding thin variety, gave 6,888 lbs. of gur (crude sugar) per acre, while Red Mauritius, the highest yielding thick cane, gave 8,448 lbs. per acre. The most satisfactory seeding rate was 20,000 cuttings per acre, with a yield of 52,808 lbs. of cane. Of various irrigations the highest yield of cane, 63,296 lbs. per acre, followed eight irrigations. The highest percentage of gur in the juice in the fertilizer tests was 19.1, obtained on the plat receiving 480 lbs. of ammonium sulphate per acre, while the highest yield of cane was obtained from the use of 180 lbs. of ammonium sulphate and 350 lbs. of acid phosphate, but this gave only 17.3 per cent of gur.

Irrigation experiments with wheat resulted in a yield of 2,044 lbs. of grain and 3,608 lbs. of straw per acre from three irrigations, as compared with 1,120 lbs. of grain and 1,640 lbs. of straw from one irrigation. Considerable gain was also realized from flushing the field before seeding. Hot-weather cultivation to preserve soil moisture was found to give increased yields of wheat over the ordinary methods, both with and without supplementary irrigations.

[Report of field crops work at the Cuttack Agricultural Station, 1915–16], D. R. Sethi (*Rpt. Dept. Agr. Bihar and Orissa, 1915–16, pp. 56–63*).—Manurial and variety tests with rice and cultural and seed selection tests are briefly reported as heretofore (E. S. R., 35, p. 31).

The results of fertilizer tests indicated that green manuring is the cheapest and most efficient system of fertilization, but owing to the fact that all the rice of this section is broadcasted the introduction of green manures is difficult. About 10 lbs. of daincha (*Sesbania aculeata*) were planted with the rice and the daincha plants plowed under through the unique system of "beushan" prevalent in this region. By this system the broadcasted fields are plowed and cross-plowed during July to thin the crop and as a means of cultivation. This plowing is immediately followed by a weeding which serves to cover up the uprooted daincha plants. The results of the first year of this experiment showed an increased yield of 146 lbs. of grain and 386 lbs. of straw per acre over the untreated field.

The transplanting of 2 or 3 seedlings 9 or 10 in. apart gave higher yields than the common practice of transplanting 10 or 12 seedlings 5 or 6 in. apart.

A comparison of transplanting rice with broadcasting showed an increased yield of 243 lbs. of grain and 420 lbs. of straw per acre for the former method. Cultivation of the paddy fields during the hot weather (April) showed an increased yield of 246 lbs. of grain and 169 lbs. of straw over monsoon (June) cultivation.

Variety tests with jute, peanuts, and peas are briefly reported.

[Report of field crops work at the Dumraon Agricultural Station, 1915–16], G. SHERRARD (*Rpt. Dept. Agr. Bihar and Orissa, 1915–16, pp. 52, 53*).— A continuation of fertilizer and variety tests with rice as previously noted (E. S. R., 35, p. 32) is reported. An application of about 2 tons of manure per acre was followed by a net return of $15.34 as compared with $12.45 from an application of about 4 tons.

[Report of work with field crops at the Orai Experiment Station], B. C. BURT (*Rpt. Agr. Sta. Orai, Jalaun [India], 1916, pp. 4–16*).—Variety tests are reported with wheat, gram, millet, cotton, and pigeon peas. The Soharia variety of wheat is recommended for unirrigated regions, while Pusa 4 is recommended for all irrigated soils.

An average of 55.5 lbs. of wheat and 18.5 lbs. of gram per 0.1-acre plat was secured from a mixed seeding. Wheat in rotation after gram, however, yielded 107 lbs. per 0.1-acre plat, and gram after wheat 96 lbs.

An application of potassium nitrate equivalent to 25 lbs. of nitrogen per acre was followed by an increased wheat yield of only 10 lbs. of grain per acre, and a decrease of 350 lbs. of straw, as compared with the untreated check. The gram crop following gave an increased yield of 115 lbs. per acre on the fertilized plat.

[Report of work with field crops at the Partabgarh Agricultural Station], L. C. SHARMA (*Rpt. Partabgarh Agr. Sta. United Prov. Agra and Oudh, 1916, pp. 3–19*).—Varietal, cultural, and fertilizer tests with rice, and varietal and cultural tests with sugar cane, peanuts, wheat, barley, gram, peas, and potatoes are noted.

An increased wheat yield of 633 lbs. of grain and 927 lbs. of straw per acre was obtained from plats cultivated in the ordinary way with three irrigations, as compared with the yields from hot-weather cultivation.

[Report of field crops work at the Ranchee Experiment Farm, 1915–16], A. C. DOBBS (*Rpt. Dept. Agr. Bihar and Orissa, 1915–16 pp. 68–73*).—This is the first annual report of experimental work at the Ranchee station and briefly outlines the projects being studied. Extensive fertilizer experiments with peanuts are in progress. The highest yield for the past year, 3,680 lbs. per acre, was obtained from an application of 160 lbs. of gypsum.

[Report of field crops work at Sabour Farm and Agricultural College, 1915–16], S. N. SIL (*Rpt. Dept. Agr. Bihar and Orissa, 1915–16, pp. 18–25, 34–37*).—This reports the continuation of experiments previously noted (E. S. R., 35, p. 31).

Cultivation of the fallow during hot weather and the application of approximately four tons of manure per acre showed increased yields of grain over all other treatments.

Experiments with rice gave practically the same results as those of the previous year, with the following exceptions: The vitality of the seedlings appeared to be unaffected by thick planting in the seed bed; the wet seed-bed seedlings were inferior, due to the water-logged condition of the plats; on the manured plat the total yield was relatively small, due to lodging; and the difference between the "single" and "bunch" transplanting of seedlings in spacings 6 in. apart was very slight. Early transplanting (July 10) gave the best results. The green manuring of paddy lands has given good returns, which have been augmented by applications of lime and bone meal. Transplanting rice gave much higher yields of both grain and straw than sowing broadcast or dibbling.

Seedings of rahar (*Cajanus indicus*) in July gave higher yields than seedings in either May or June. Variety tests with rahar, wheat, and rice are reported.

[Report of field crops work at Sepaya Experiment Farm, 1915–16], M. M. MACKENZIE (*Rpt. Dept. Agr. Bihar and Orissa, 1915–16, pp. 76–79, 82–87*).— Experimental work with sugar cane, forage crops, and fertilizers is briefly outlined. Results of analyses of sugar-cane varieties grown at Sepaya are reported in tabular form.

Fodder crops of Western India, H. H. MANN (*Dept. Agr. Bombay Bul. 77 (1916), pp. 142*).—This is a compilation of available information relative to the cultivated fodder crops of Western India, showing the adaptation of each, method of cultivation, yield, and value of the fodder produced. The area under cultivated fodder crops in the Bombay Presidency is estimated to be about 124,920 acres.

Some wild fodder plants of the Bombay Presidency, W. BURNS, R. K. BHIDE, L. B. KULKARNI, and N. M. HANMANTE (*Dept. Agr. Bombay Bul. 78 (1916), pp. 24, pls. 34*).—This bulletin is a compilation of available information relative to some of the wild grasses and leguminous plants used as forage in the Bombay Presidency, giving their vernacular names, habitat, life history, chemical composition, and feeding value. Thirty-four such plants are described and illustrated.

How to change the rotation system, G. SOTGIA (*Agr. Terra Lavoro, 6 (1917), No. 1, pp. 2–8*).—The author describes in detail and illustrates with diagrams changing from a biennial rotation to a quadrennial rotation, based on *Trifolium pratense*, or to a septennial or octennial rotation, based on *Medicago sativa*. A method is also described for changing from a quadrennial system to an octennial one.

Experiments in meadow culture on peat bogs, V. A. FOMINYKH (*Selsk. Khoz. i Lěsov., 251 (1916), June, pp. 145–160*).—This reports experiments in 1914 and 1915 in an effort to convert peat bogs into meadows. The different treatments resulted in the increased yields noted below: Harrowing alone, 56.8 per cent; harrowing combined with fertilizing, 300 per cent; seeding to grass after harrowing and fertilizing, 350 per cent—also procuring a change in the flora of the bog; plowing, fertilizing, and seeding to grass, 600 to 900 per cent.

Permanent pasture formation, A. W. GREEN (*Jour. Agr. [New Zeal.], 14 (1917), No. 1, pp. 28–31*).—This reports pasture-formation experiments in progress at Ruakura, New Zealand, to determine (1) the influence of temporary fillers on the permanent grasses and clovers which will ultimately constitute the permanent pasture, (2) the value of temporary fillers in reducing the weed content in permanent pastures, and (3) the comparative value of different fillers for early feed. The fillers included in the experiment were prairie grass, cape barley, Italian rye-grass, broad-leaved Essex rape, and thousand-headed kale.

The results to date indicate that rape is the most valuable plant of those tested, due to its habit of growth and resistance to cold. Sheep turned into pasture on the unfenced plats at first preferred the rye-grass, but soon left it for barley and rape. The kale plat was left until last. The highest total live-weight gain, 379 lbs., was obtained from a seeding of 2 lbs. of rape per acre, at the minimum cost for all fillers of 40 cts. The least gain in live weight, 175 lbs., was realized from a seeding of 25 lbs. of barley per acre, at a cost of 78 cts.

Grasses for pasture and hay in Texas, G. M. GARREN (*Texas Agr. Col. Ext. Serv. Bul. B–32 (1916), pp. 16, figs. 4*).—A popular discussion of suitable hay and pasture grasses for Texas, with general recommendations for the establishment of meadows and pastures.

The selection of cereals in Italy, G. PATANÈ (*Internat. Inst. Agr. [Rome], Internat. Rev. Sci. and Pract. Agr., 7 (1916), No. 6, pp. 777–787; abs. in Jour. Heredity, 8 (1917), No. 3, p. 105*).—Systematic plant breeding, principally with cereals, is being conducted at 10 centers in Italy, and the work, modeled after that of the Svalöf station, is reviewed in this article. Selection and hybridization form the principal features of the investigations, and include studies with wheat, rice, barley, oats, corn, rye, pulses, potatoes, pumpkins, tomatoes, alfalfa, and other crops.

A study of cleistogamy and parthenogenesis from the standpoint of genetics, especially with the Cruciferæ and Leguminosæ, is being made by U. Brizi at the Royal Agricultural College, at Milan. Cereals and Leguminosæ are also being bred on Mendelian lines.

The influence of chemical fertilizers upon the composition of the cereals (*Agr. Mod. [Milan], 22 (1916), No. 24, pp. 284, 285*).—This reports analyses of grain grown on different soil types in France and under varying fertilizer treatments to determine the effect of the fertilizer upon the composition of the grain. The fertilizers used were acid phosphate, sodium nitrate, muriate of potash, and manure.

In every case the weight of the grain was materially higher with the fertilizer treatment. A complete chemical fertilizer in each case resulted in a higher percentage of protein in the grain than on the untreated plat or the plats receiving only partial fertilization. Manure alone showed a slight increase in the protein content, except with corn, which showed a slight reduction. With manure supplemented by chemical fertilizers slightly increased percentages of protein were obtained. The percentage of phosphoric acid in the grain was increased under all fertilizer and manurial treatments. See also a previous note by Tretiakov (E. S. R., 34, p. 230).

Statistics on the production of cereals and legumes, 1916 (*Estadística de la Producción de Cereales y Leguminosas en el año 1916. Madrid: Govt., 1916, pp. 32*).—Statistics are given on the acreage and production of wheat, barley, rye, oats, corn, chick-peas, vetch, field peas, beans, and other less important cereals and legumes in Spain for 1916. Brief observations are reported on the influence of meteorological conditions upon the cultivation and harvesting of cereals and legumes in each of 13 regions.

Growth of the root system of Medicago sativa, SHISTOVSKIJ (*Iuzh. Russ. Selsk. Khoz. Gaz., 17 (1915), No. 30, pp. 6, 7; abs. in Internat. Inst. Agr. [Rome], Internat. Rev. Sci. and Pract. Agr., 7 (1916), No. 8, pp. 1088, 1089*).—Observations are reported on the development of the root system of *M. sativa* at different stages of growth.

The alfalfa was sown in Rotmistrov boxes in the open field and the roots examined by washing with water at the ages of 1, 2, 2.5, 3, 3.5, and 4 months. The results of these observations are reported in tabular form. The data include the length in centimeters of the aerial portion and roots and the horizontal extension of the roots, together with the root coefficient, which is the product of the length and the horizontal extension of the root.

The results indicate that the growth of the root system continues uninterruptedly from germination to fructification, but that growth is not uniform. At the age of 2.5 months the roots had attained a length of from 45 to 51 centimeters (17.7 to 20.1 in.), and in the following 2 weeks, which form the pre-flowering period and actual growing period itself, the root growth was very intense, attaining a length at the age of 3 months of from 103 to 110 centimeters. Such great fluctuations in root growth were not observed previous to or follow-ing this period, and the author believes this fact to be the essential point in his investigations.

These observations are said to confirm those of Rotmistrov, but better specify the process of root growth by establishing the period of most intense develop-ment.

The effect of phosphorus on alfalfa and alfalfa bacteria, H. W. TRUESDELL (*Soil Sci., 3 (1917), No. 1, pp. 77–98, pls. 2*).—Investigations are reported in an effort to discover the reason for the beneficial influence of phosphorus upon alfalfa and other legumes, as simple nutrition (shown by chemical analysis) is deemed insufficient to account for this phenomenon. The hypothesis is ad-vanced that phosphorus fertilization may cause greater growth and activity of the root bacteria, resulting in greater nitrogen fixation and more rapid growth of the leguminous host. This theory has been tested experimentally in these investigations. The experiments fall into two parts, (1) those which treat of the influence of phosphorus upon the growth of the alfalfa organism (*Bacillus radicicola*) as shown by numerical counts, and (2) those which treat of the influence of phosphorus upon alfalfa as regards nodule formation, rate of growth, dry weight of plants, and percentage and absolute content of nitro-gen. The secondary phosphates of potassium, sodium, and calcium were used in quantities sufficient to supply a phosphorus equivalent of 0.1, 0.02, and 0.002 per cent. The studies were made at the University of Wisconsin.

The treatment of pure cultures of *B. radicicola* from alfalfa with phosphates resulted in large increases in the number of organisms, varying with the charac-ter and solubility of the salt. The highest counts were obtained from treat-ments supplying a phosphorus equivalent of 0.02 per cent, and disodium phos-phate gave the highest increase after seven days' incubation, with dipotassium phosphate next.

Pot culture experiments were conducted under greenhouse conditions to study the effect of dicalcium phosphate upon alfalfa. Alfalfa grown on unsterilized soil was inoculated, treated with phosphates and phosphorus plus nitrogen, and the results in nodule formation, dry weight, and percentage and absolute nitro-gen content compared with all possible control combinations. Percentages of phosphorus of 0.005, 0.015, and 0.045, equivalent to field applications of 700, 2,100, and 6,300 lbs. per acre of rock phosphate, respectively, were employed, and urea equivalent to 0.014 per cent used as a nitrogenous fertilizer.

The results of phosphorus fertilization of alfalfa may be briefly summarized as follows: The seedlings made a much more rapid growth, and increased nodule formation, dry weight, and total nitrogen content was observed. The third cutting (much more representative of normal average conditions) showed not only an increase in total nitrogen, but also an increase in the percentage of nitrogen associated with the addition of phosphorus fertilizer.

The author concludes that the early increase noted in the growth of phos-phorus-treated seedlings may be a result of nutrition of the plant and the stimulation frequently associated with cell reproduction and to the quickening of bacterial processes in the soil. The ultimate increases in growth resulting from phosphorus treatments may be due to increased infection with alfalfa organisms, increased growth and proliferation of the organism within the nodule, and consequently increased nitrogen fixation.

A bibliography of 26 articles comprising the literature cited is given at the end of the paper.

A semiannual cropping system for bean lands, G. W. HENDRY (*Univ. Cal. Jour. Agr., 4 (1917), No. 6, pp. 181, 182, fig. 1*).—Recommendations are made concerning the utilization of bean land during the winter months for the production of certain hardy leguminous crops in California. Increases in the market prices for 1916 over those received before the war, amounting to from 21 per cent for horse beans to 150 per cent for Large White (Lady Washington) beans, has resulted in increased rentals and share leasings, necessitating more intensive cultural conditions.

A semiannual cropping system such as proposed presupposes a well-drained soil not subject to winter inundations but readily irrigable in October and May, as well as facilities for rapid handling of the crops in the field. The winter crop should be planted during October and harvested not later than May 15. The following crops are suggested and their market value briefly discussed: Horse beans, garbanzos, garden peas, field peas, and lentils.

Investigations on the mode of determining the germinating capacity in beet seed, E. VITEK (*Ztschr. Zuckerindus. Böhmen., 40 (1916), No. 8, pp. 363–381; abs. in Internat. Inst. Agr. [Rome], Internat. Rev. Sci. and Pract. Agr., 7 (1916), No. 8, p. 1106*).—Experiments are reported to determine whether blotting paper or sand give more accurate results in germination tests. In 1913, 26 samples of seed were compared, 77 per cent showing a higher germination on blotting paper than on sand, and 88 per cent giving a larger number of embryos on blotting paper than on sand. Analogous results were obtained in 1914.

Influence of very low temperatures on the germination capacity of beet seeds, J. URBAN and E. VITEK (*Ztschr. Zuckerindus. Böhmen., 40 (1916), No. 7, pp. 29–300; abs. in Internat. Inst. Agr. [Rome], Internat. Rev. Sci. and Pract. Agr., 7 (1916), No. 8, pp. 1105, 1106*).—The authors report experiments with sugar beet seed to determine the influence of low temperature on germination. Samples of beet seed were exposed for 30 minutes at a temperature of $-180°$ C., produced by the spontaneous evaporation of liquid air, and germinated with unexposed seed at a temperature varying from 20 to 30°. After 15 days 95 per cent of the unfrozen seed and 96 per cent of the frozen seed had germinated, indicating that the heaviest frosts do not impair the germinability of beet seeds having a normal water content.

To test the behavior of seed harvested in wet weather samples of seed containing approximately 20 per cent water were exposed to the same temperatures as above from 2 to 72 hours. The results indicated that the germinative capacity of the seed had been impaired by freezing, but that exposure for 72 hours had had no more effect than exposure for a shorter length of time.

Boiling buffalo clover seed, A. D. MCNAIR (*Science, n. ser., 45 (1917), No. 1157, pp. 220, 221*).—The author reports tests with the seed of buffalo clover (*Trifolium reflexum*) in attempts to increase their germinability. The process of boiling the seed one minute as practised in the case of spotted bur clover (*Medicago arabica*) increased germination from 4 to 30 per cent. Experiments with bur clover conducted by the Alabama Experiment Station (E. S. R., 32, p. 829), in which the seed were soaked before boiling, led to similar tests with buffalo clover, with the following results as to percentages of germination: No treatment, 0; boiled 5 seconds, 53; boiled 30 seconds, 60; boiled 60 seconds, 60; soaked in cold water 12 hours, 0; soaked in cold water 12 hours and boiled 5 seconds, 47; soaked in cold water 12 hours and boiled 30 seconds, 87; and soaked in cold water 12 hours and boiled 60 seconds, 93.

An interesting seed corn experiment, H. D. HUGHES (*Iowa Agr.*, 17 (1917), *No. 9, pp. 424, 425, 448, fig. 1*).—This is a preliminary report on a test with prize-winning seed corn to determine whether such corn gives the highest production when planted in the field. Five hundred ears of corn were taken from the field in 1915 without any selection whatever, numbered, and scored by 25 judges. Later a portion of each ear was shelled and planted in separate field plats.

The results for the first year indicate that the ears receiving the highest scores were also the best ears from the standpoint of field production. The 50 best ears, as selected by a majority of the judges, averaged 5 bu. per acre better than the bulk of the ears.

Classification of American Upland cotton, D. E. EARLE and F. TAYLOR (*U. S. Dept. Agr., Farmers' Bul.* 802 (1917), pp. 28, figs. 15).—This is a revision of Farmers' Bulletin 591 (E. S. R., 31, p. 433), based on the Official Cotton Standards as established and promulgated by the Secretary of Agriculture under the United States Cotton Futures Act (E. S. R., 35, p. 693).

Cotton production in the Belgian Kongo, P. JANSSENS (*Bul. Agr. Congo Belge,* 7 (1916), No. 1-2, pp. 131-157, figs. 14).—A detailed review of the introduction and subsequent development of the cotton industry in the Belgian Kongo.

The development of cotton culture in French West Africa, J. BABOIS (*Compt. Rend. Acad. Agr. France,* 3 (1917), No. 5, pp. 141-148).—A general discussion of the possibilities of cotton production in the regions of Senegal and Niger.

The opportunities for cotton production in the French colonies, J. DYBOWSKI (*Compt. Rend. Acad. Agr. France,* 3 (1917), No. 5, pp. 149-155).—This is a general discussion directly bearing on the subject noted above. The economic necessity and desirability of developing the cotton industry in the territories of Senegal and the Sudan are emphasized.

Hemp culture in France, H. BLIN (*Jour. Agr. Prat., n. ser., 30 (1917), No. 2, pp. 34-36, figs. 4*).—A general discussion of the present status and future possibilities of hemp production in France.

The resources of Indo-China in oleaginous plants, BRENIER (*Compt. Rend. Acad. Agr. France,* 3 (1917), No. 7, pp. 185-195).—A general discussion of the oil plants produced commercially in Indo-China, including brief specific notes on cotton, rubber, soy beans, castor oil, sesame, peanuts, coconuts, and other palms.

Growing potatoes under irrigation for profit, W. STUART (*Reclam. Rec.* [*U. S.*], 8 (1917), No. 3, pp. 140-142, figs. 2).—The factors essential to the profitable production of potatoes under irrigation are enumerated and discussed as follows: Selection of a suitable soil type, deep plowing and thorough seed bed preparation, plentiful supply of available plant food, liberal use of good seed, good cultivation, intelligent application of irrigation water, protection against insect and fungus pests, careful harvesting and storing, and proper grading and intelligent marketing of the crop.

Notes and observations on the culture of ramie, L. NAUTEFEUILLE (*Bul. Écon. Indochine, n. ser.,* 18 (1915), No. 115, pp. 649-718).—A comprehensive discussion of ramie and its production, compiled largely from available literature and augmented by some personal observations of the author. A brief history of the various agencies engaged in the exploitation of the industry is included.

Rice in Argentina, C. D. GIBOLA (*An. Soc. Rural Argentina,* 50 (1916), No 6, pp. 596-620, figs. 9).—Rice production and the extent of the industry in Argentina are discussed and brief descriptions given of the Kiuskú, Carolina, and Valencia varieties.

New rice varieties, B. MARCARELLI (*Gior. Risicolt.*, 7 (1917), No. 1-2, pp. 4-10, figs. 2).—Two rice selections designated as Originario P. 7 and O. P. 6, developed by F. Sancio in the Province of Santhià from seed of Chinese origin, are described in detail. These strains are recommended as being of superior market quality. Data are presented in tabular form comparing them with the original.

Sweet clover (Melilotus), H. L. FULMER (*Ontario Dept. Agr. Bul. 235 (1916)*, pp. 32, figs. 10).—The value of sweet clover (Melilotus) as a pasture, hay, and soil improvement crop is discussed at some length.

A number of original analyses are presented showing (1) the composition of sweet clover at different stages of growth, (2) the yield and composition of sweet clover hay as compared with alfalfa, red clover, alsike, and timothy, (3) the dry matter and fertilizing constituents found in the tops (stems and leaves) and roots (in first foot of soil) and in the total crop at two different stages of growth and on two types of soil, (4) the composition of sweet clover and digestibility of its protein from two different types of soil and at six different stages of maturity, and (5) the total weight of nutrients and the amount of digestible protein furnished by one acre of sweet clover at six different stages of maturity.

Fertilizing the wheat crop, C. E. THORNE (*Mo. Bul. Ohio Sta.*, 2 (1917), Nos. 7, pp. 215-218, fig. 1; 8, pp. 251-253).—The results of experiments previously reported with acid phosphate, steamed bonemeal, and raw rock phosphate used with fresh stable manure as fertilizers for wheat are briefly noted to illustrate the value of phosphatic materials in increasing wheat production, and the value of fresh manure reenforced with a phosphorus carrier as a substitute for high-priced commercial carriers of nitrogen and potash. The relative importance of the phosphorus was shown by an increase valued at only $11 per acre where phosphorus was omitted, the nitrogen and potassium carriers remaining unchanged, as compared with an increase amounting to $39 upon the addition of acid phosphate valued at $2.60.

Acid phosphate versus raw phosphate rock—relative prices will determine the choice for wheat this fall, C. G. WILLIAMS (*Mo. Bul. Ohio Sta.*, 2 (1917), No. 8, pp. 249, 250).—The relative value of raw rock phosphate and acid phosphate for wheat is briefly considered in the light of experiments previously noted (E. S. R., 31, p. 217). The more profitable return in these tests was obtained from the investment in acid phosphate.

Adzuki beans and jimson weeds.—Favorable class material for illustrating the ratio of Mendel's law, A. F. BLAKESLEE and B. T. AVERY (*Jour. Heredity*, 8 (1917), No. 3, pp. 125-131, figs. 4).—The authors discuss the adaptability of the adzuki bean (*Phaseolus mungo*) and the jimson weed (*Datura stramonium* and *D. tatula*) as material for illustrative purposes in classes in genetics.

The closeness of the ratios to expectations in the jimson weed is indicated in summarized data on pigmentation and capsule characters obtained in connection with other studies. A study of variability in jimson weed is being made by the senior author.

The Canadian Seed Growers' Association and its work (*Ottawa: Association*, pp. 8, figs. 2).—This is a brief outline of the organization, purpose, and methods of procedure of the Canadian Seed Growers' Association, together with brief descriptions of some of the more important varieties of wheat, oats, barley, and peas distributed.

A method for determining the impurity of cereals caused by the seed of Agrostemma githago, A. AINATA (JANATA) (*Iuzh. Russ. Selsk. Khoz. Gaz.*, 17 (1915), No. 47, pp. 6-8; abs. in *Internat. Inst. Agr.* [Rome], *Internat. Rev. Sci. and Pract. Agr.*, 7 (1916), No. 9, pp. 1272, 1273).—A total of 1,820 seeds of

A. githago, taken from samples of oats, barley, rye, and wheat collected in 11 districts of the Government of Kharkov, were weighed, and the average weight of one seed found to be 0.0101 gm. The weight of individual seeds fluctuated between 0.0128 gm. and 0.0056 gm.

HORTICULTURE.

[Report on horticultural investigations at the Troup substation], W. S. HOTCHKISS (*Texas Sta. Bul. 209 (1917), pp. 13–33, figs. 3*).—Data are given on fertilizer experiments conducted with watermelons in 1904 and 1906, and with strawberries in 1907, 1908, and 1909. As a result of these tests mixtures of acid phosphate and cottonseed meal are advised, both for watermelons and strawberries.

Sixty-eight varieties of peaches and 105 varieties of grapes tested at the substation are here described, and varieties recommended both for market and home use.

Report of the horticultural experiment station, Vineland station, Ontario, 1906–1915 (*Rpt. Hort. Expt. Sta., Vineland, Ont., 1906–1915, pp. 79, figs. 42*).— This report comprises as a whole a record of the work of the Vineland station, Ontario, from the time of its establishment in 1906 up to October 31, 1915.

Most of the experimental work has been started in different years since 1912 and consists of plant breeding, variety tests, and various cultural investigations with orchard and small fruits and vegetables. A record is given of all crosses made with fruits and vegetables, together with lists of varieties being tested and the results to date of the more important cultural experiments.

Plant breeding at the horticultural experiment station, Vineland, E. F. PALMER (*Canad. Hort., 40 (1917), No. 11, pp. 286, 287, figs. 3*).—A summarized record of breeding experiments with fruits at the Vineland station, Ontario, in 1916 and 1917.

[Vegetables at Wisley, 1915–16] (*Jour. Roy. Hort. Soc., 42 (1917), No. 2–3, pp. 400–411*).—Notes are given on a number of varieties of cabbage tested at Wisley in 1915 and 1916.

Rules and regulations promulgated under authority of the Federal Standard-Barrel Law (*U. S. Dept. Com., Bur. Standards Circ. 71 (1917), pp. 8*).— Rules and regulations are given under the act previously described (E. S. R., 32, p. 499).

[Directions for the control of insect pests and diseases] (*Utah State Hort. Com. Bul. 1, rev. (1916), pp. 64*).—This bulletin briefly describes the more important insect pests and diseases of fruits and vegetables, and gives directions for their control. The text of the horticultural laws of Utah, regulations of the State Horticultural Commission, and the law governing the marking of closed packages of fruit are also given.

Dusting for tender fruits and apples, L. CAESAR (*Ann. Rpt. Fruit Growers' Assoc. Ontario, 48 (1916), pp. 47–51*).—A comparative test of dust and liquid sprays was carried out in 1916 on apples, plums, sweet cherries, peaches, and grapes in various orchards in Ontario.

Although the results were somewhat in favor of the dust method in this experiment, less favorable results from dusting were reported by others in Ontario and in New York State. Hence it is recommended that growers do not purchase dusting machines until further comparative studies have been made.

Dusting as a substitute for spraying.—History and progress, H. H. WHETZEL (*Ann. Rpt. Fruit Growers' Assoc. Ontario, 48 (1916), pp. 37–41*).—This is largely a review of studies conducted at the New York Cornell Experiment Station (E. S. R., 34, p. 738), including a summary of results secured in cooperative demonstration tests in New York apple orchards in 1916. Although the results of dusting as compared with spraying were less favorable in these cooperative tests than in the experimental work, the author is of the opinion that the failure was due to inexperience in the dusting method, use of improperly prepared mixtures, and poor dusting machinery rather than to the practice of dusting itself.

New creations in fruits, N. E. HANSEN (*Minn. Hort., 45 (1917), No. 12, pp. 464–469, figs. 4*).—This paper comprises a brief statement of progress being made in the author's work of breeding hardy fruits (E. S. R., 37, p. 142).

A number of plums recently sent out for trial are described. Of a large number of cherries tested at the South Dakota Experiment Station one variety, selected from a number of imported seedlings and which has been named Moscow, has been found to be both productive and perfectly hardy and was distributed for testing in the spring of 1917.

A list of the most desirable varieties of most kinds of fruits (*London: Roy. Hort. Soc., 1916, pp. 190*).—The list herein given was prepared by the fruit committee of the Royal Horticultural Society of England as a result of inquiries sent out to growers throughout the United Kingdom. A series of subsidiary lists, prepared by a number of gardeners living in various parts of the United Kingdom, is given of varieties which they consider most suitable for their various geographical divisions.

Grass mulch.—A practical system of orchard management, J. H. GOURLEY (*Ann. Rpt. Vt. State Hort. Soc., 14 (1916), pp. 36–41*).—In connection with orchard management studies being conducted at the New Hampshire Experiment Station (E. S. R., 36, p. 724), a grass mulch experiment was recently established on a small orchard. Various fertilizers were applied to the different plats. Data are here given showing the results secured in 1916.

The average yield of apples from the check rows was 10.5 bbls., from the nitrogen rows 23.5 bbls., and the average from the rows fertilized with potash, basic slag, or phosphate, but not including nitrogen, about 11 bbls. Although the color of the apples was not so good on the nitrogen plat the increase in production far outweighed the color factor and all the apples were sold at the same price. The results in general indicate that nitrogen is the only fertilizer to yield a profit, and that in this orchard at least the mulch system would be far from efficient unless supplemented with nitrogen.

Orchard cover crops for the Moutere Hills, W. C. HYDE (*Jour. Agr. [New Zeal.], 13 (1916), No. 6, pp. 472–477, figs. 7*).—The author outlines cooperative experiments being conducted in the Moutere district of New Zealand to determine the leguminous crop best suited for green manuring purposes in the young orchards of that locality. The experiments also included trials of various fertilizer combinations.

The crops tested were crimson clover, common vetch, white lupine, yellow lupine, white mustard, serradella, and partridge peas. The best results were secured with white lupine and white mustard, together with an application of 1 cwt. per acre each of blood and bone, acid phosphate, and muriate of potash.

Important factors in the successful cold storage of apples, H. S. BIRD (*Rpt. Proc. Mont. State Hort. Soc., 19 (1916), pp. 34–36*).—A brief discussion of the factors essential to the successful cold storage of apples, including some experimental data illustrating the damage by scald and decay due to storing immature fruit, over-mature fruit, and to delay in storage after picking the fruit.

The history and development of the red currant, E. A. BUNYARD (*Jour. Roy. Hort. Soc., 42 (1917), No. 2–3, pp. 260–270, pls. 6*).—A paper on this subject read before the Royal Horticultural Society, London, on September 12, 1916.

A bibliography of cited literature is appended.

Viticulture, P. PACOTTET (*Viticulture. Paris: J. B. Baillière & Sons, 1917, 3. ed., rev. and enl., pp. 554, figs. 217*).—This is one of the volumes of the Encyclopédie Agricole, published under the direction of G. Wery.

The introductory chapter contains a brief survey of the genus Vitis. Succeeding chapters deal with the anatomy and physiology of the grape, factors influencing quality and production, the viticultural geography of France and foreign countries, the details of grape growing, ampelography and reconstitution of vineyards, and the maladies and enemies of the grape.

Citrus culture in Japan, China, and Formosa, C. P. CLAUSEN (*Mo. Bul. Com. Hort. Cal., 6 (1917), No. 10, pp. 379–383, figs. 3*).—A brief account of cultural methods employed in Japan, China, and Formosa.

Some abnormal water relations in citrus trees of the arid Southwest and their possible significance, R. W. HODGSON (*Univ. Cal. Pubs. Agr. Sci., 3 (1917), No. 3, pp. 37–54, pl. 1, figs. 2*).—This paper deals with one phase of the investigation of a so-called physiological disease, June drop of the Washington navel orange.

As a result of observations and experiments, here noted, it was found that an abnormal water relation obtains periodically in citrus foliage and in the young fruits during the hot growing season in the dry interior valleys of California and Arizona. A diurnal decrease in water content of the fruits occurs during the afternoon and is accompanied by a considerable increase in the water deficit of the leaves. "Negative pressures of considerable magnitude are found in the water columns of citrus trees under these climatic conditions. These attain their maximum during the afternoon. The dropping of the fruits appears to be most severe where the above-mentioned water relations are most abnormal. Inasmuch as in the case of certain other plants the abscission of young fruits has been shown to be due to abnormal water relations it is suggested that such may be the case here."

Optimum moisture conditions for young lemon trees on a loam soil, L. W. FOWLER and C. B. LIPMAN (*Univ. Cal. Pubs. Agr. Sci., 3 (1917), No. 2, pp. 25–36, pls. 3, fig. 1*).—In the experiment here described, which was conducted at the Limoneira Ranch, Santa Paula, Cal., studies were made of the optimum moisture content of a rather heavy loam soil for young Lisbon lemon trees grown in cylinders. The data obtained in the course of the first two years of the work are summarized as follows:

"A moisture percentage of 20 based on the dry weight of the soil has produced the tallest trees. Trees grown with 16 and 18 per cent of moisture, while not as tall as those grown with 20 per cent of soil moisture, show better color and more vigor. The differences are not very marked, however.

"The foregoing facts seem to show that the range of optimum or nearly optimum moisture percentages for the soil and plant in question is a relatively wide one. Much more visible damage results to the young lemon trees from moisture percentages in excess of the optimum than from those below the optimum. Every successive increment of moisture beyond the optimum is accompanied by a sharp depression in growth, color, and general vigor of the trees. Every successive decrement of moisture from the optimum shows only a relatively slight depression in growth.

"The theoretical wilting point and the moisture equivalent for the soil studied are in close accord, respectively, with the actual wilting point as determined in the soil of the orchard and the optimum moisture content as determined in the experiment discussed above."

Orange culture, A. DE MAZIÈRES (*La Culture des Orangers. Paris: J. B. Baillière & Sons, 1917, pp. 96, figs. 28*).—A small treatise on the planting, culture, harvesting, and marketing of oranges.

The fig in Texas, A. T. POTTS (*Texas Sta. Bul. 208 (1917), pp. 41, figs. 13*).—A treatise on fig growing, with special reference to the development of the industry in Texas. Information is given relative to the climatic requirements of the fig, propagation, varieties, soil and its preparation, planting, culture, pruning, fertilizers, insects and diseases, splitting and souring, harvesting and marketing fresh fruit, preserving and drying, and the Smyrna fig and caprification.

The subject matter is based upon observations made in Texas and upon the industry as developed in other sections of the United States.

The guavas of the Hawaiian Islands, V. MacCAUGHEY (*Bul. Torrey Bot. Club, 44 (1917), No. 11, pp. 513–524*).—A descriptive account of the species and forms of guavas established in the Hawaiian Islands.

The pollination of the mango, W. POPENOE (*U. S. Dept. Agr. Bul. 542 (1917), pp. 20, pls. 4, fig. 1*).—This bulletin reports pollination studies conducted at Miami, Fla., during 1915 and 1916 to throw some light on the failure of many of the best imported varieties of mangoes to fruit satisfactorily in Florida. The flower structure, pollen, process of pollination, production of fruit, and flowering habits of the mango are considered in detail.

The author's experimental work shows that the mango requires pollination for the production of fruit and is benefited by cross-pollination, though normally self-fertile. The exclusion of insects is detrimental to pollination, but even in the presence of insects a large proportion of the stigmas are unpollinated and comparatively few stigmas receive more than one or two grains of pollen. Hand pollination with an abundance of pollen failed to improve fruit production.

The failure to set fruit is not deemed to be due to any morphological defect in the pollen or to defects in the mechanism of pollination, hence it is concluded that the problem is a physiological one connected with nutritional conditions, as influenced by changes in soil moisture and food supply, principally the former. Experiments have been undertaken in cooperation with E. J. Kraus, of the Oregon Experiment Station, who is working with pomaceous fruits, to test the practicability of inducing the formation of flower buds through ringing, girdling, and banding the limbs with wire.

Some results with oil palm (Elæis guineensis), W. M. VAN HELTEN (*Dept. Landb., Nijv. en Handel [Dutch East Indies], Meded. Cultuurtuin, No. 8 (1917), pp. 22, pl. 1*).—Data are given showing the yields of nuts and oil secured in 1916 from oil palms growing in the Buitenzorg Gardens and vicinity. These yields are compared with yields secured in other countries. Notes are also given on methods of propagation and planting the oil palm, based upon tests conducted at Buitenzorg and elsewhere.

Coffee in Abyssinia, A. SPALLETTA (*Agr. Colon. [Italy], 11 (1917), Nos. 1, pp. 70–88; 2, pp. 111–132, pls. 2; 3, pp. 196–222, pl. 1; 4, pp. 284–297*).—An account of the coffee industry in Abyssinia, including a discussion of varieties, soil, and climate, cultural details, harvesting and preparation for market, commerce, transportation, and the future of the industry. A bibliography of related literature is appended.

A review of coffee plantings in the Buitenzorg experimental garden, C. J. J. VAN HALL and W. M. VAN HELTEN (*Dept. Landb., Nijv. en Handel [Dutch East Indies], Meded. Cultuurtuin, No. 7 (1917), pp. 50, pls. 8*).—Notes are given on the character and condition of plantings of various species, hybrids, and varieties of coffee under observation at Buitenzorg.

The germination and selection of tea seed, C. BERNARD (*Indian Tea Assoc., Sci. Dept. Quart. Jour., No. 1 (1917), pp. 1–12, pl. 1*).—A translation of an article dealing with the author's experiments on the germination and selection of tea seed (E. S. R., 30, p. 742; 35, p. 745).

[Flowers at Wisley, 1916] (*Jour. Roy. Hort. Soc., 42 (1917), No. 2–3, pp. 412–429*).—This comprises notes on variety tests of a number of different flowers conducted at Wisley in 1916.

Daffodil developments, J. JACOB (*Jour. Roy. Hort. Soc., 42 (1917), No. 2–3, pp. 229–235*).—A brief historical review of the work of improvement in daffodils.

The practical book of outdoor rose growing for the home garden, G. C. THOMAS, JR. (*Philadelphia and London: J. B. Lippincott Co., 1917, 4. ed., pp. 215, pls. 120*).—The present edition of this work (E. S. R., 32, p. 339) has been largely rewritten to include improved cultural practices and revised lists of the best varieties of dwarf and climbing roses based on recent tests.

Observations on tulips, A. B. STOUT (*Jour. Hort. Soc. N. Y., 2 (1917), No. 14, pp. 201–206, pls. 2*).—Experiments conducted at the New York Botanical Garden indicate that it is difficult to attribute "blindness" of tulips to any one cause. Cultural tests made with two varieties prove that blind tulips may bloom excellently in the following year. Hence, they are not necessarily "rundown" or "run-out" bulbs. Different varieties have performed differently with respect to blindness under quite identical conditions of treatment and climate.

Data are also given showing the performance of sister bulbs of different sizes, and especially those of the smaller size, with respect to blooming, blindness, and scaling. Further observations are to be made on the performance of small bulbs which produced flowers in the experiment.

Report of the tulip nomenclature committee, 1914–15, BOWLES ET AL. (*London: Roy. Hort. Soc., 1917, pp. 164, pls. 22*).—A report of the tulip nomenclature committee of the Royal Horticultural Society of England, in which is presented a scheme for the classification of garden tulips, descriptions of garden tulips as tested at Wisley, descriptions of new cottage tulips, list of synonyms, alphabetical list of tulip names, and a bibliography on tulips.

FORESTRY.

The development of forest law in America, J. P. KINNEY (*New York: John Wiley & Sons, Inc., 1917, pp. XVIII+254+XXI*).—A historical presentation of the successive enactments, by the legislatures of the 48 States of the American Union and by the Federal Congress, directed to the conservation and administration of forest resources.

Recent forestry propaganda in the Philippines, F. SHERFESEE (*Jour. Forestry, 15 (1917), No. 6, pp. 740–756*).—The author reviews the forest propaganda in the Philippines and sketches the present attitude of the Filipinos with respect to forest activities.

Practical reforestation, H. S. GRAVES (*Proc. Cut-Over Land Conf. South, 1917, pp. 15–23*).—In this paper the author briefly summarizes the present status of cut-over pine land areas in the South and urges cooperation between public and private agencies in developing methods for the systematic use of these lands for grazing, agriculture, and forestry.

How Louisiana is solving the reforestation problem, M. L. ALEXANDER (*Proc. Cut-Over Land Conf. South, 1917, pp. 169–172*).—A brief summary of reforesting operations being conducted under the direction of the Department of Conservation of Louisiana.

An improved transplanting lath, J. LYFORD-PIKE (*Trans. Roy. Scot. Arbor. Soc., 31 (1917), pt. 2, pp. 160, 161, pl. 1*).—A lath or board designed for transplanting a large number of tree seedlings or other plants in one operation is described and illustrated.

The preservation of leafy twigs of the beech, L. A. Boodle (*Roy. Bot. Gard. Kew, Bul. Misc. Inform., No. 6 (1917), pp. 220–231*).—Experiments reported by the author indicate that leafy twigs of the common beech may be preserved for several months with very little wilting by cutting the twigs when the leaves are still green and placing the stems in a solution of calcium chlorid for about a week. The best results were secured by using solutions with specific gravities of 1.4 and 1.2. The lower ends of the twigs were trimmed every day or two to present freshly cut surfaces to the liquid and the twigs were exposed to direct sun for several hours during the treatment.

The importance of plantation margins, A. Murray (*Trans. Roy. Scot. Arbor. Soc., 31 (1917), pt. 2, pp. 156–159*).—A short paper on the selection of species for and the subsequent management of forest plantation margins or shelter belts.

Trees for nonirrigated regions in eastern Colorado, W. J. Morrill (*Colo. Agr. Col. Ext. Serv. Bul., 1. ser., No. 123 (1917), pp. 20, figs. 6*).—A descriptive list of trees and shrubs, including notes on their general behavior in eastern Colorado, is given, together with suggestions on tree planting.

Forest succession and rate of growth in sphagnum bogs, G. B. Rigg (*Jour. Forestry, 15 (1917), No. 6, pp. 726–739, figs. 3*).—A discussion of forest succession and rate of growth in six bogs of the Puget Sound region and four in Alaska, based on field observations conducted for several years.

Aspen as a permanent forest type, J. M. Fetherolf (*Jour. Forestry, 15 (1917), No. 6, pp. 757–760*).—In this paper the author brings out the more permanent features of aspen as a type, based on its behavior in habitats like the semiarid intermountain region.

The pitch pine, L. Piccioli (*Ann. R. Ist. Sup. Forestale Naz. Firenze, 2 (1916–17), pp. 401–431, pls. 4, figs. 6*).—An account of the various species of pine commonly known as pitch pine with reference to their distribution, anatomical characters, technical properties, and culture in Europe. The account is prepared with special reference to the selection of species adapted to Italian silviculture.

Notes on white pine 4-year transplants, S. N. Spring (*Jour. Forestry, 15 (1917), No. 6, pp. 761, 762*).—A growth record is given of white pine seedlings grown from three seed beds which were sown broadcast with different quantities of seed.

The density of stand and rate of growth of Arizona yellow pine as influenced by climatic conditions, F. Shreve (*Jour. Forestry, 15 (1917), No. 6, pp. 695–707, figs. 6*).—A contribution to our knowledge relative to the influence of climate on tree growth, based on observations and measurements made in the Santa Catalina Mountains in southern Arizona. Data are given showing the differences in population of the Arizona yellow pine at different altitudes, the differences in the character of the populations, and the differences or similarities in the rate of growth at the several elevations.

Probable error in field experimentation with Hevea, O. F. Bishop, J. Grantham, and M. D. Knapp (*India-Rubber Jour., 54 (1917), No. 15, pp. 13–16, 19–22, fig. 1*).—A review of recent literature on the subject, including actual records of experiments in Sumatra showing variations that may occur among carefully chosen experimental plats and the need of applying probable error methods. An example is given of the application of the probable error method to a series of 26 tapping experiments which were carried on in triplicate.

Seed selection in the cultivation of Hevea brasiliensis, T. Petch (*Roy. Bot. Gard. Kew, Bul. Misc. Inform., No. 3 (1917), pp. 118–120*).—A brief ac-

32950°—18—No. 9——4

count is given of seed selection studies of Hevea conducted under the direction of the Ceylon Department of Agriculture.

The effects of tapping and wintering on the storage of plant food in Hevea, A. A. L. RUTGERS (*Arch. Rubbercult. Nederland. Indië, 1 (1917), No. 2; Meded. Alg. Proefstat. Alg. Ver. Rubberplanters Oostkust Sumatra, Rubber Ser., No. 1–2 (1917), pp. 1–8, pls. 3*).—A brief summary of investigations on this subject conducted by Campbell and Bateson (E. S. R., 33, p. 543; 34, pp. 47, 240, 346). These authors are of the opinion that tapping should be stopped from the moment the new leaves are coming out until a week after the crown is full-grown. The reviewer, on the other hand, concludes that wintering takes only one-sixth of the starch reserve at the most, and since tapping takes practically none from a physiological point of view there is no reason to stop tapping during the winter.

Rubber soils in Fiji, C. H. WRIGHT (*Dept. Agr. Fiji Pamphlet 26 (1917), pp. 2*).—This pamphlet contains directions for distinguishing soils adapted for rubber growing in Fiji.

Annual progress report on forest administration in the Presidency of Bengal for the year 1915–16, H. A. FARRINGTON (*Rpt. Forest Admin. Bengal, 1915–16, pp. II+51+5*).—This is the usual report relative to the administration and management of the State forests of the Presidency of Bengal, including a financial statement for the year 1915–16. All important data relative to alterations in areas, forest surveys, working plans, forest protection, miscellaneous work, yields, revenues, expenditures, etc., are appended in tabular form.

Forest Service stumpage appraisals, J. W. GIRARD (*Jour. Forestry, 15 (1917), No. 6, pp. 708–725*).—This article deals with the appraisal of saw-log material and the logging methods employed in Montana, Idaho, and northern Washington.

Marketing farm woodlot products in Maine, G. N. LAMB (*Univ. Maine Ext. Bul. 113 (1917), pp. 38, figs. 5*).—This bulletin, which is published in cooperation with the Forest Service of the U. S. Department of Agriculture, discusses the woodlot situation in Maine; the common woodlot trees, including their growth, uses, and properties; estimating standing timber and saw logs; methods of selling timber; and the preparation and marketing of woodlot products destined for various industries.

Crossties purchased and treated in 1915, A. M. McCREIGHT (*U. S. Dept. Agr. Bul. 549 (1917), pp. 8*).—A statistical review for the year 1915. The total number of crossties bought by all classes of producers was approximately 121,-402,611. Treating plants reported a total of 37,085,585 crossties treated in 1915.

DISEASES OF PLANTS.

Common and scientific names of plant diseases, M. B. WAITE (*Abs. in Phytopathology, 7 (1917), No. 1, p. 60*).—The author makes a plea for definite common names for plant diseases which can attain proper status in discussions, literature, dictionaries, quarantine regulations, laws, and legal proceedings.

[Plant diseases in British Guiana], C. K. BANCROFT (*Rpt. Dept. Sci. and Agr. Brit. Guiana, 1914–15, App. 2, pp. 7–10*).—Besides a summary of organisms causing diseases of cultivated crops in the colony during three years, brief details are given of the South American leaf disease of Hevea (*Fusicladium macrosporum*); the dry disease (*Marasmius sacchari*) and the ring spot (*Leptosphæria sacchari*) of sugar cane; the fruit disease of mango and breadfruit (*Glœosporium mangiferæ*); witches' broom of cacao; a disease of leaves and fruit of the coffee plant due to a Colletotrichum (*C. coffeæ ?*); the bacterial disease of plantains; blast of rice (*Piricularia oryzæ*); collar rot of lime;

citrus knot; bud rot of coconut palm; root disease (*Fomes semitostus*) of Hevea; rose mildew (*Sphærotheca pannosa*); black blight (*Dimerosporium mangiferum*) of Hibiscus, Ixora, Barbados cherry, and Bougainvillea, besides several other plants; and a bacterial disease of orchids.

Scolecotrichum graminis on timothy, orchard grass, and other grasses, A. G. JOHNSON and C. W. HUNGERFORD (*Abs. in Phytopathology, 7 (1917), No. 1, p. 69*).—The authors report having observed *S. graminis* on timothy and orchard grass at various points from Wisconsin to the Pacific coast. The fungus is said to cause a serious disease of these hosts, especially in Wisconsin. A number of other species of grass are reported as hosts of the fungus, and observations at Madison, Wis., are considered to show that it overwinters readily in tufts of orchard grass and timothy.

Bacteria of barley blight seed-borne, L. R. JONES, A. G. JOHNSON, and C. S. REDDY (*Abs. in Phytopathology, 7 (1917), No. 1, p. 69*).—In continuation of a previous study of a bacterial blight of barley (E. S. R., 35, p. 845), the authors have given special attention to the dissemination of the disease over long distances, and they conclude that the organism may be carried with the seed grain and remain viable after at least two years of dormancy. Preliminary experiments are said to indicate that the organism may be destroyed by seed disinfection.

Corn disease caused by Phyllachora graminis, NOBA E. DALBEY (*Phytopathology, 7 (1917), No. 1, pp. 55, 56, fig. 1*).—A brief account is given of observations on the fungus *P. graminis* on leaves of maize collected in Porto Rico. A detailed description of the disease and fungus is to be given in a subsequent publication.

Smut diseases of wheat, W. B. MERCER (*Jour. Bd. Agr. [London], 23 (1916), No. 7, pp. 633–643, figs. 2*).—Along with a brief discussion of several smuts of economic cereals, the author gives brief notes of studies, to be published elsewhere in greater detail, regarding the life history of *Ustilago tritici*, the cause of loose smut of wheat.

The fungus is said to be capable of entering the young grain, but not the seedling. The chlamydospores germinate inside the flower and the tube penetrates the immature grain, giving rise to a small amount of mycelium in the embryo and the starchy endosperm, the grain developing in spite of this fact. When the infected grains are sown, the fungus grows with the young plant in a way similar to that of the bunt fungus. When the head begins to form, the mycelium begins to grow more rapidly, branches profusely, and forms a large number of spores, which are at first held together by a gelatinous substance enclosed in a thin membrane which usually ruptures as the ear emerges. Unless these spores thus freed reach a flower they become harmless, probably in a few days.

The control measures tried up to the present time are outlined. The fungus can not be reached with chemical fungicides. The method of picking out the smutted heads from the standing crops, while fairly effective, is not practicable on a large scale. Selection of seed on the basis of size or weight is ineffective. Steam has given some fair results, but is not considered safe as a seed treatment. Forcing hot water through the seed grain is impracticable. Hot-air kilns do not heat the grain evenly. Rolling the grain in heated drums has met with a measure of success. The treatment found most effective is to soak the wheat in water at a temperature of 25 to 30° C. (77 to 86° F.) for four hours and then for 10 minutes at 52 to 54° C. (125.6 to 129.2° F.), this treatment destroying the fungus with a comparatively slight lowering of germinability.

Tylenchus tritici on wheat, L. P. BYARS (*Phytopathology*, 7 (*1917*), *No. 1, pp. 56, 57*).—The author reports having determined the presence of the nematode *T. tritici* in wheat heads transmitted through the Office of Cereal Investigations of this Department from Nanking, China. The data presented are offered in order that measures can be taken to prevent the introduction of this parasite with wheat importations from infested countries.

Bean diseases in New York State in 1916, W. H. BURKHOLDER (*Abs. in Phytopathology*, 7 (*1917*), *No. 1, p. 61*).—In continuation of a report on diseases of the field bean (E. S. R., 36, p. 248), the author states that the most serious disease is due to a species of Fusarium which is considered nearly identical with *F. martii*. This causes a dry root rot of the bean plant. The organism is said to winter over in manure where bean straw has been used as feed, and there is evidence that it may live for several years in the soil. All varieties of beans are about equally susceptible to the attack of this fungus, although certain undesirable types of the white marrow are very resistant, and a few individuals of these have been selected for breeding experiments.

A blight, caused by *Bacterium phaseoli*, and mosaic are said to have been rather conspicuous in the bean crop of 1916, while the anthracnose which was destructive in 1915 caused little damage in the following year. The author claims that there is some indication that *B. phaseoli* causes a stem girdling.

Bacterial diseases of celery, W. S. KROUT (*Abs. in Phytopathology*, 7 (*1917*), *No. 1, p. 64*).—The author gives a description of a crown rot of celery which appears to be caused by a bacterium working simultaneously with a species of Fusarium, a crown rot wilt, and a bacterial heart wilt.

Wintering of Septoria petroselina apii, W. S. KROUT (*Abs. in Phytopathology*, 7, (*1917*), *No. 1, p. 65*).—As a result of the author's studies, it is believed that the above fungus is not carried on celery seed but in manures containing diseased, decomposed plants and probably by other methods. Laboratory investigations have shown that heating celery seed at 50° C. (122° F.) for half an hour will eliminate all chances, if there are any, of the disease being disseminated through the seed and pedicles.

Dissemination of the organism of cucumber anthracnose, M. W. GARDNER (*Abs. in Phytopathology*, 7 (*1917*), *No. 1, pp. 62, 63*).—The author presents evidence indicating that this disease of cucumbers is introduced by the seed and that subsequent spread is largely due to surface drainage.

Do the bacteria of angular leaf spot of cucumber overwinter on the seed? E. CARSNER (*Abs. in Phytopathology*, 7 (*1917*), *No. 1, pp. 61, 62*).—The fact that angular leaf spot appeared only on seedlings in six fields planted with seed from the same source and not in other fields in the vicinity is considered by the author as a basis for the hypothesis that the causal organism is seed-borne.

Preliminary notes on a new leaf spot of cucumbers, G. A. OSNER (*Abs. in Phytopathology*, 7 (*1917*), *No. 1, p. 62*).—During the seasons of 1915 and 1916, the author's attention was called to a peculiar leaf spot on cucumbers which was causing more or less damage in a number of fields. The spots for the most part were small and limited by the veins of the leaf. The disease is claimed to be due to a fungus, the exact generic position of which has not yet been determined.

Virulence of different strains of Cladosporium cucumerinum, W. W. GILBERT (*Abs. in Phytopathology*, 7 (*1917*), *No. 1, p. 62*).—As a result of investigations the author has found that different strains of *C. cucumerinum* vary widely in their ability to infect cucumber plants, some virulent strains killing the plants in two to four days, while nonvirulent strains failed to produce infection. Similar results were obtained from the inoculation of young cucumbers in moist chambers.

A nematode disease of the dasheen and its control by hot-water treatment, L. P. BYARS (*Abs. in Phytopathology*, 7 (*1917*), *No. 1, p. 66*).—The dasheen (*Colocasia esculenta*) is reported as having been found attacked by a nematode (*Heterodera radicicola*). The disease, it is claimed, can be successfully controlled by planting on uninfected land selected cormels from disease-free areas or diseased cormels which have been treated with water at 50° C. (122° F.) for 40 minutes.

A bacterial stem and leaf disease of lettuce, NELLIE A. BROWN (*Abs. in Phytopathology*, 7 (*1917*), *No. 1, p. 63*).—A wilt disease of lettuce is briefly reported, the disease having been observed in Beaufort County, S. C., in 1916. The affected plants were wilted and rotting was often rapid. Bacteria were abundant, and the organism isolated, when inoculated into lettuce, produced the blue-green color throughout the vascular system and pith which characterizes the normal appearance of the disease. The organism in its morphological and cultural characters is said not to correspond to any recorded as pathogenic to lettuce.

Studies upon the anthracnose of the onion, J. C. WALKER (*Abs. in Phytopathology*, 7 (*1917*), *No. 1, p. 59*).—It is claimed that a morphological study of the organism *Colletotrichum circinans* confirms the findings of Voglino that the fungus belongs to the genus Colletotrichum and not Vermicularia. Inoculation of the fungus from onion into apple fruits is said to have resulted in a rot very similar to the Volutella rot, but further study is necessary before the two fungi can be considered identical.

The fungus is said to winter over in the soil and consequently the disease is most severe on old onion fields. Spraying the bulbs before harvest or in the crates after harvest has not proved beneficial. Yellow and red varieties of onion are claimed to be highly resistant, and this fact is believed to offer encouragement for the development of a resistant white strain.

Pink root, a new root disease of onions in Texas, J. J. TAUBENHAUS and A. D. JOHNSON (*Abs. in Phytopathology*, 7 (*1917*), *No. 1, p. 59*).—A new disease of onions locally known as pink root is said to occur in Webb County, Tex., but only where onions are grown for two or more years on the same land. The roots of the affected sets in the seed bed or of the plants in the field turn pink in color, shrivel, and die. As fast as new roots are formed they become infected and the normal development of the bulbs is affected. The undersized bulbs resulting are worthless so far as market is concerned. The cause of the disease has not yet been determined.

Black spot of pepper, L. E. MELCHERS and E. E. DALE (*Abs. in Phytopathology*, 7 (*1917*), *No. 1, p. 63*).—A disease of peppers is described with which a species of Alternaria has been constantly associated. Inoculation experiments have shown that the organism is only weakly pathogenic to normal tissue and that it becomes established largely through injuries to peppers in the field, the principal means being sun scald and frost injury.

Notes on curly dwarf symptoms on Irish potatoes, W. L. DURRELL (*Abs. in Phytopathology*, 7 (*1917*), *No. 1, p. 71*).—Curly dwarf symptoms are said to have been very prevalent in Iowa during 1916, particularly on the varieties Irish Cobbler, Rural New Yorker, and Early Ohio. The disease made its appearance on the early plantings about June 10 and developed throughout the season. In August, plants that had been normal up to that time showed typical signs of curly dwarf on the foliage, and the upper third of the plants had shortened internodes and crinkled and curled leaves, giving the plants a bushy appearance. These symptoms are said to have been induced in the field by the hot, dry weather in August, and similar ones were later artificially developed in the laboratory. The plants showing these symptoms put forth normal foliage again in September with the advent of cooler weather.

Histological studies showed that the crinkling of the leaves was due to necrosis of certain epidermal and cortical cells of the veins, followed by the growth of the parenchyma cells which induced buckling of the leaf surface. Transpiration experiments indicated that dwarfed plants transpire more rapidly than normal ones.

Notes on mosaic symptoms of Irish potatoes, I. E. MELHUS (*Abs. in Phytopathology, 7 (1917), No. 1, p. 71*).—The author gives a description of the mosaic disease of potatoes and its effect on the production of tubers.

Frost necrosis of potato tubers, L. R. JONES and E. BAILEY (*Abs. in Phytopathology, 7 (1917), No. 1, pp. 71, 72*).—A type of noninheritable net necrosis of potato tubers is described, of which frost injury is apparently the primary cause. Experiments under artificial conditions have shown that exposure to freezing temperature may produce either ring or net necrosis. The stem end of the tuber is reported to be always more sensitive to injury than the other.

A bacterial blight of soy beans, A. G. JOHNSON and FLORENCE M. COERPER (*Abs. in Phytopathology, 7 (1917), No. 1, p. 65*).—The authors report having had a bacterial blight of soy bean under investigation at Madison, Wis., for several years. The disease has become quite common, occurring especially on the leaves, on which the organism causes the production of small, angular spots which, in later stages, become dark in color. Repeated isolation cultures have yielded a characteristic organism which is referred to the genus Pseudomonas. Studies on the physiological characteristics of the organism and its pathogenicity are said to be in progress.

Further note on a parasitic saccharomycete of the tomato, A. SCHNEIDER (*Phytopathology, 7 (1917), No. 1, pp. 52, 53*).—In continuation of investigations of a disease of tomato previously reported (E. S. R., 36, p. 749), the author has concluded that the fungus is a new species, and it is technically described under the name *Nematospora lycopersici*.

Host limitations of Septoria lycopersici, J. B. S. NORTON (*Abs. in Phytopathology, 7 (1917), No. 1, p. 65*).—Inoculation experiments in humid inclosures on seedlings of a number of species of Solanaceæ and 80 varieties of tomato with Septoria from tomato are said to have resulted in infections on several species of Solanum, eggplant, *Datura tatula*, potato, currant tomato, and *S. carolinense*. With larger plants outdoors, infection rarely occurs except on Lycopersicum.

Note on the genus Coniothecium, with special reference to C. chomatosporum, P. A. VAN DER BIJL (*So. African Jour. Sci., 12 (1916), No. 13, pp. 649–657, pls. 6, figs. 2*).—In view of a statement made by Massee (E. S. R., 34, p. 543), the author here presents more fully the results of an investigation, previously noted (E. S. R., 32, p. 344), which has not yet been completed.

This paper notes certain cultural characters of *C. chomatosporum*, the cause of a branch blister disease on apple and pear. The fungus develops between the cells, invading the middle lamellæ and rupturing the skin to produce the black blisters and fruit russeting. Evidence obtained is said to show that this organism is only a stage in the life cycle of *Phoma mali*.

Control of peach bacterial spot in southern orchards, J. W. ROBERTS (*U. S. Dept. Agr. Bul. 543 (1917), pp. 7, pl. 1*).—A description is given of the bacterial spot of peaches caused by *Bacterium pruni*. The disease, which is also known as bacteriosis, is said to occur in practically all the peach-growing sections of the eastern half of the United States, its most serious injury being confined to the most southerly portion of this district. Twigs, fruit, and leaves are affected, but the greatest amount of injury is done to the leaves.

Experiments carried on by the author and others indicate that the disease may be kept in check in southern peach orchards by proper pruning, cultivation, and especially fertilization. Of the fertilizers used, nitrate of soda proved most efficient.

In addition to the peach, *B. pruni* is said also to cause a disease of the plum, affecting especially the Japanese varieties.

Black currant eelworm, Miss A. M. Taylor (*Jour. Agr. Sci. [England]*, 8 (*1917*), No. 2, pp. 246–275, pl. 1, fig. 1).—The author notes an attack of nematodes on black currant near Cambridge, England. The evidence indicates that this parasite has been established here for some time, probably having been more or less masked by its association with the black currant mite, the symptoms of the two as described being similar in some respects. Although a study which has been made of the nematode is given in some detail, its relationships have not yet been determined.

Sulphuring Concord grapes to prevent powdery mildew, F. E. Gladwin and D. Reddick (*Abs. in Phytopathology,* 7 (*1917*), No. 1, p. 66).—The authors report the dusting of Concord grapevines with sulphur-lime mixtures containing 25, 50, and 75 per cent sulphur flour, 95 per cent or more of which would pass through a 200-mesh sieve. Comparisons were made with plants treated with Bordeaux mixture and where powdery mildew (*Uncinula necator*) was abundant, the vines receiving the dust mixture showed much less mildew on the grape clusters, although there was considerable burning with the larger amounts of sulphur-lime.

The generation of aldehydes by Fusarium cubense, E. C. Lathrop (*Phytopathology,* 7 (*1917*), No. 1, pp. 14–16).—Investigations having shown that aldehydes of various chemical constitution are detrimental to plant growth, the author experimented with *F. cubense,* the cause of the Panama banana disease, and found that aldehydes were formed during the growth of the fungus on synthetic culture media. The generation of aldehydes by *F. cubense* is believed to account, in a measure at least, for the pathological action of the organism.

Citrus canker investigations at the Florida Tropical Laboratory, R. A. Jehle (*Abs. in Phytopathology,* 7 (*1917*), No. 1, pp. 58, 59).—A description is given of some cultural characteristics of the canker organism, *Pseudomonas citri,* as obtained in the laboratory. Positive results are reported to have been secured from inoculations on grapefruit, ponderosa lemon, key lime, *Citrus trifoliata,* sour orange, tangelo, sweet orange, tangerine, king orange, mandarin lime, and kumquat. The disease also occurs on navel orange, mandarin, satsuma, common lemon, rough lemon, and *Ægle glutinosa.*

Sour rot of lemon in California, C. O. Smith (*Phytopathology,* 7 (*1917*), No. 1, pp. 37–41, figs. 2).—A description is given of a sour rot of lemons and other citrus fruits occurring during storage. The infected tissues soften, become straw-colored, and collapse, changing into a more or less slimy, watery mass.

A fungus has been isolated from diseased fruits which is considered identical with *Oospora citri-aurantii,* originally described by Ferraris (E. S. R., 14, p. 161). Artificial inoculations of the fungus on citrus fruits in moist chambers gave positive results with lemons, oranges, grapefruit, and tangerines, the rot showing within 48 hours. Green fruit of lemons, as well as twigs of Eureka lemon, when inoculated, gave negative results.

From the author's experiments, it is concluded that infection of lemons with the sour rot fungus takes place only through some injury or from contact with infected fruit.

Two new camphor diseases in Texas, J. J. Taubenhaus (*Abs. in Phytopathology,* 7 (*1917*), No. 1, pp. 59, 60).—Anthracnose of camphor, due to a species of Glœosporium which is tentatively named *G. camphoræ* n. sp., and a limb canker of camphor are briefly described.

Diseases of cinchona, A. RANT (*Meded. Kina Proefstat. [Dutch East Indies],* *No. 2 (1914), pp. 47, pls. 11).*—The author has listed with brief discussion the known diseases of adult plants of cinchona, grouped according to the portions affected, namely, leaves, branches, stems, and roots, and also separately the diseases affecting more particularly the young plants.

A disease of pecan catkins, B. B. HIGGINS (*Phytopathology, 7 (1917), No. 1,* *pp. 42–45, figs. 2).*—The author's attention was called during the spring of 1916 to an abnormality of the staminate catkins of pecans on the Georgia Experiment Station plats. An examination of the catkins showed the presence of a fungus in the infected anthers, which, while not killing the tissues outright, caused many of the pollen grains to become empty and to collapse.

A study of the trouble showed it to be due to a species of Microstroma, and as a similar fungus was observed on the leaves of hickory trees, it was suspected that the one on pecan was identical with that on hickory. Cultures of both forms were obtained and some differences were noted. Diligent search indicated that the fungus on pecan catkins differs from that on hickory, and the organism is technically described under the name *M. juglandis robustum* n. var. As pollen is always produced in great abundance by pecan trees, the loss of a comparatively large amount is considered of little importance, but the author suggests that this disease may become serious in the future.

Phytophthora on Vinca rosea, J. F. DASTUR (*Mem. Dept. Agr. India, Bot.* *Ser., 8 (1916), No. 6, pp. 233–242, figs. 14).*—During the wet period occurring in May and June, 1913, *V. rosea* suffered much from a parasitic fungus which was diagnosed as a Phytophthora. The attack weakens or disappears in dry weather and sunshine. The organism, which appears to be a weak parasite, has been studied by the author and is considered to be a biological strain of *P. parasitica,* previously described by him as a new species attacking the castor oil plant (E. S. R., 29, p. 548).

Notes on some species of Coleosporium, G. G. HEDGCOCK and N. R. HUNT (*Abs. in Phytopathology, 7 (1917), No. 1, p. 68).*—*C. delicatulum* is reported for the first time on two species of Euthamia, and the Peridermium form on a number of species of Pinus. The occurrence of *C. laciniariæ* on six species of Laciniaria is also reported.

The æcial stage of Coleosporium elephantopodis, G. G. HEDGCOCK and W. H. LONG (*Abs. in Phytopathology, 7 (1917), No. 1, pp. 66, 67).*—Young trees of *Pinus heterophylla* in the greenhouse at Washington, D. C., inoculated with teliospores of *C. elephantopodis,* are said to have produced æcia of *Peridermium carneum.* Inoculations with æciospores on the leaves of *Elephantopus tomentosus* produced both uredinia and telia of *C. elephantopodis.* Parallel sets of inoculations of plants of Vernonia and Elephantopus gave results indicating the identity of the two species of Coleosporium previously reported on the two hosts. *Peridermium carneum* is reported for the first time on the needles of *Pinus caribæa, P. clausa, P. echinata, P. glabra, P. heterophylla, P. ponderosa, P. rigida, P. scopulorum,* and *P. serotina.*

An alternate form for Coleosporium helianthi, G. G. HEDGCOCK and N. R. HUNT (*Abs. in Phytopathology, 7 (1917), No. 1, pp. 67, 68).*—*Peridermium helianthi* is described on *Pinus virginiana.* Inoculations made with the æciospores of the Peridermium on *Helianthus decapetalus, H. divaricatus, H. giganteus, H. glaucus,* and *H. hirsutus* proved the Peridermium to be the æcial stage of *C. helianthi.*

Some new hosts for Coleosporium inconspicuum, G. G. HEDGCOCK and N. R. HUNT (*Abs. in Phytopathology, 7 (1917), No. 1, pp. 68, 69).*—The Peridermium form of this fungus is reported for the first time on *Pinus echinata*. This material was used in inoculating *Coreopsis major œmleri* and *C. verticillata*, resulting in the formation of uredinia and telia of *Coleosporium inconspicuum*.

The Peridermium belonging to Coleosporium ipomœæ, G. G. HEDGCOCK and N. R. HUNT (*Abs. in Phytopathology, 7 (1917), No. 1, p. 67*).—The authors describe P. *ipomœæ*, a new foliicolus species on *Pinus echinata, P. palustris, P. rigida*, and *P. tœda*. Plants of *Ipomœa lacunosa, I. pandurata, I. triloba, Pharbitis barbigera, P. hederacea*, and *Quamoclit coccinea* under controlled conditions were successfully inoculated with the æciospores of this Peridermium, producing on their foliage the typical uredinia and telia of *C. ipomœæ*.

Some new hosts for Coleospórium solidaginis, G. G. HEDGCOCK and N. R. HUNT (*Abs. in Phytopathology, 7 (1917), No. 1, p. 68*).—*Peridermium acicolum*, the æcial stage of *C. solidaginis*, is reported for the first time on species of Pinus, and positive results are said to have been obtained from inoculations with the æciospores of P. *acicolum* on plants of species of Aster and Solidago.

A Peridermium belonging to Coleosporium terebinthinaceæ, G. G. HEDGCOCK and N. R. HUNT (*Abs. in Phytopathology, 7 (1917), No. 1, p. 67*).—The authors describe a new foliicolus species, P. *terebinthinaceum*, occurring on *Pinus echinata, P. rigida*, and *P. tœda*, with a range from North Carolina to Georgia. Inoculations were made under controlled conditions with the æciospores of this Peridermium on plants of *Silphium asteriscus, S. integrifolium, S. trifoliatum*, and *Parthenium integrifolium*, and in about two weeks the uredinia and later the telia of *C. terebinthinaceæ* appeared on the leaves of all these species. *C. terebinthinaceæ* has been reported on the leaves of *S. angustum, S. compositum, S. dentatum, S. glabrum*, and *S. pinnatifidum*.

Notes on Cronartium comptoniæ, III, P. SPAULDING (*Phytopathology, 7 (1917), No. 1, pp. 49–51*).—In continuation of notes on this and related fungi (E. S. R., 33, p. 351), the author presents additional data.

The additional pine hosts, *Pinus densiflora, P. jeffreyi, P. laricio, P. mugho*, and *P. resinosa*, have been reported for *C. comptoniæ*. Uredinia have been produced on plants of *Comptonia asplenifolia* with æciospores from a number of species of Pinus. Uredinia on Comptonia were successfully used to produce uredinia on Comptonia and *Myrica gale*. Uredinia from *M. gale* produced uredinia on Comptonia.

Observations made by the author in a number of localities have shown that *Cronartium comptoniæ* fruits on pines principally in a period of seven or eight weeks, reaching its maximum about June 1, a date considerably earlier than that previously reported. The author believes that P. *rigida* is much less susceptible to the disease than are P. *ponderosa* and P. *contorta*, the loss among which has been total.

Does Cronartium ribicola winter on the currant? W. A. McCUBBIN (*Phytopathology, 7 (1917), No. 1, pp. 17–31, fig. 1*).—In continuation of a previous note (E. S. R., 36, p. 652), the author offers data to substantiate his hypothesis that *C. ribicola* hibernates as mycelium in infected buds of currant. This is believed to be in agreement with known habits of other rusts under like conditions and of similar nature and is supported by the general and irregular appearance of the currant stage of the fungus over large areas in which there is reason to believe that there are no pine infections. Special cases where rust has occurred on currants which are distant from any possible source of infection are reported, and in one instance the only case of rust in one large black currant plantation was on two of four plants which had been badly infected in the preceding year. A report is also given of the occurrence of currant rust on plants set out in a rust-free district in order to test overwintering.

Evidence of the overwintering of Cronartium ribicola, P. SPAULDING (*Abs. in Phytopathology, 7 (1917), No. 1, p. 58*).—The author reports that currants are frequently infected with *C. ribicola* one summer but not the next and, further, that cooperative experiments in which 500 heavily infected black currants were used resulted in no disease. The author states that he has had under observation for seven years in greenhouses in Washington, D. C., hundreds of Ribes plants used in inoculation experiments, and in no case has the disease ever appeared the next season until artificial inoculations have been made. It is claimed that infection of petioles is not so rare as has been supposed, that no evidence of bud infection by way of the petiole has been obtained, and that direct examination of buds of infected plants has failed to show the presence of the fungus.

The pine blister, B. H. PAUL (*N. Y. State Conserv. Com. Bul. 15 (1916), pp. 18, pl. 1, figs. 8*).—This is a résumé of the proceedings of a conference held by the committee for the suppression of pine blister in North America at Albany, N. Y., November 20 and 21, 1916. A general account is given of the characteristics and importance of the disease in the United States and Canada, also the result of preliminary work showing the distribution of the disease as known to date, with recommendations and other information looking toward its control.

The control of white pine blister rust in small areas, W. H. RANKIN (*Abs. in Phytopathology, 7 (1917), No. 1, p. 58*).—A brief account is given of experiments in control of white pine blister rust on 85 forest plantings in New York State. Diseased or suspicious trees and all species of Ribes were removed within 500 ft. of the plantings, and the results obtained seem to indicate that this treatment prevented the appearance of *Cronartium ribicola* in these areas.

Some new or little known hosts for wood-destroying fungi, A. S. RHOADS (*Phytopathology, 7 (1917), No. 1, pp. 46–48*).—A list is given of host species of 16 wood-destroying fungi, the species being believed to be new or at least little known hosts for these fungi, which have not been previously reported upon them.

ECONOMIC ZOOLOGY—ENTOMOLOGY.

A new subspecies of meadow mouse from Wyoming, V. BAILEY (*Proc. Biol. Soc. Wash., 30 (1917), pp. 29, 30*).

Diagnosis of a new laniine family of Passeriformes, H. C. OBERHOLSER (*Jour. Wash. Acad. Sci., 7 (1917), No. 7, pp. 180, 181*).—The family Tylidæ is erected.

Description of a new Sialia from Mexico, H. C. OBERHOLSER (*Proc. Biol. Soc. Wash., 30 (1917), pp. 27, 28*).

Friends of our forests, H. W. HENSHAW (*Nat. Geogr. Mag., 31 (1917), No. 4, pp. 297–321, figs. 33*).—Brief accounts illustrated by colored plates, prepared by L. A. Fuertes, are given of 36 species of North American warblers.

Report of the entomologist of the Arizona Commission of Agriculture and Horticulture for the year ended June 30, 1916, A. W. MORRILL (*Ariz. Com. Agr. and Hort. Ann. Rpt., 8 (1916), pp. 11–57, pls. 3, figs. 17*).—The first part of this report (pp. 11–30) deals with inspection work, the alfalfa weevil protective service, insect control and eradication, etc. Part 2 (pp. 31–49) consists of notes on the more important insects of the year, and part 3 (pp. 51–57) takes up three plant diseases in 1916, namely, citrus gummosis, citrus scaly bark, and pear blight.

The more important insects of the year are considered under the headings of pests of deciduous fruits, small fruits, and vines; citrus and olive pests; pests of field and forage crops; vegetable crop pests; and cotton pests. During the year four species of insects and one species of red spider, not previously recorded as of economic importance, became injurious to crops in Arizona. These consist of a nitidulid beetle (*Conotelus mexicanus*) destructive to fruit blossoms, a variety of false chinch bug (*Nysius minutus*) destructive to flaxseed, a cotton stainer (*Dysdercus albidiventris*) injurious to cotton bolls, and a red spider (*Tetranychus modestus*) injurious to corn. Aside from these, the most noteworthy insect records of the year consist of that of a cornstalk borer, thought to be the larger cornstalk borer (*Diatræa zeacolella*), and that of an apparently new moth borer of pear trees.

Annual report of the State entomologist for 1915, E. L. WORSHAM (*Ga. Bd. Ent. Bul. 45 (1916), pp. 31, pl. 1, figs. 3*).—This reports upon the occurrence of the more important insects of the year in Georgia, particularly the boll weevil, and includes an account by I. W. Williams of cotton breeding work, of truck crop pests and miscellaneous insects affecting shade trees and ornamental plants, a report by C. S. Spooner on pecan pests, etc. A map showing the area in Georgia infested by the boll weevil in 1915 and the quarantined area in 1916 is attached.

Report of the division of entomology for the biennial period ending December 31, 1916, E. M. EHRHORN ([Bien.] *Rpt. Bd. Comrs. Agr. and Forestry Hawaii, 1915–16, pp. 79–109, pl. 1*).—This, the usual biennial report on inspection and other work of the year (E. S. R., 34, p. 59), includes a classified list of the insects collected. A report by D. T. Fullaway on beneficial insects (pp. 105–109) deals briefly with the parasites of the melon fly, corn leafhopper, fruit fly, mealy bug, and horn fly, and gives a tabulated list showing the liberation of beneficial insects in 1915–16.

Report of the economic biologist, G. E. BODKIN (*Rpt. Dept. Sci. and Agr. Brit. Guiana, 1915, App. 3, pp. 10*).—The author reports upon the occurrence of and work with the more important insect pests of the year in British Guiana.

Observations on some insects attacking rice, F. SUPINO (*R. Ist. Lombardo Sci. e Let. Rend., 2. ser., 49 (1916), No. 2–3, pp. 108–114*).—Three aquatic insects that are of importance in rice fields near Milan are reported upon by the author, namely, *Stratiomys chamæleon*, *Triænodes bicolor*, and *Hydrocampa* (*Nymphula*) *nymphæata*.

Wild vegetation as a source of curly-top infection of sugar beets, P. A. BONCQUET and C. F. STAHL (*Jour. Econ. Ent., 10 (1917), No. 4, pp. 392–397, pls. 2*).—*Malva rotundifolia*, a common weed in sugar beet fields, has proved to be at least a symbiotic host of the virulent factor of curly-top of sugar beets. Beet leaf hoppers, which were known to be nonvirulent when placed on sickly-looking mallow plants in the field and subsequently on healthy beets, produced curly-top in four experiments. "Insects known to be virulent were placed on healthy seedlings of *M. rotundifolia*. After a certain lapse of time they were removed and replaced with nonvirulent insects which were later transferred to healthy beets. All transfers brought about the disorder."

Meadow and pasture insects.—Practical methods of control for the more common forms, H. OSBORN (*Mo. Bul. Ohio Sta., 2 (1917), No. 8, pp. 268–273*).— A brief discussion of meadow and pasture insects and means for their control. The difficulties to be met with in their control are pointed out and emphasis placed upon the importance of crop rotation. The control measures applicable for permanent pastures and meadows consist of burning, hopperdozers or hopper catchers, baiting, and trap lights. Brief reference is made to their natural enemies.

Insects that factor in the grading of apples, P. J. PARROTT (*West. N. Y. Hort. Soc. Proc., 62 (1917), pp. 72–81, figs. 2; Rochester, N. Y.: Davis and Jeens Printing Co., 1917, pp. 10, figs. 2*).—An address, delivered before the Western

New York Horticultural Society on January 24, 1917, in which it is shown that the codling moth was by far the most important of the insects responsible for apple deformation during 1916, having been responsible for $58\frac{1}{3}$ per cent. It is followed in importance by aphids, $12\frac{2}{3}$ per cent; red bugs, $9\frac{5}{8}$; curculio, $4\frac{5}{8}$; lesser apple worm, $4\frac{1}{3}$; leaf roller, $3\frac{5}{8}$; green fruit worm, $1\frac{5}{8}$; San José scale, 1; case bearers, $\frac{2}{3}$; bud moth, $\frac{1}{2}$; Palmer worm, $\frac{1}{2}$; apple maggot, $\frac{1}{3}$; and other insects, 1.

Spraying for insects affecting apple orchards in Nova Scotia, G. E. SANDERS and W. H. BRITTAIN (*Canada Dept. Agr., Ent. Branch Circ. 8 (1916), pp. 11, pl. 1*).—This circular contains the results of spraying experiments carried on in Nova Scotia during the last two years, together with notes on the control of certain insects affecting apples and pears that are prevalent at the present time. A spray calendar, revised to include the results of later work, is also included.

Insects injuring stored food products in Connecticut, W. E. BRITTON (*Connecticut State Sta. Bul. 195 (1917), pp. 3–21, figs. 18*).—A brief summary of information on stored food products insect pests, to which is added information on control measures.

The carriage of disease by insects, L. O. HOWARD (*Jour. Wash. Acad. Sci., 7 (1917), No. 8, pp. 217–222*).—This is an abridgment of the presidential address delivered before the Washington Academy of Sciences on February 1, 1917.

A key for the identification of animal parasites found in the human feces, H. G. MARTIN and L. S. MCKITTRICK (*Bul. Univ. Wis., No. 828 (1917), pp. 24, figs. 43*).—An illustrated key.

Volatility of organic compounds as an index of the toxicity of their vapors to insects, W. MOORE (*U. S. Dept. Agr., Jour. Agr. Research, 10 (1917), No. 7, pp. 365–371, figs. 7*).—This is a report of investigations carried on at the Minnesota Experiment Station in continuation of those previously noted (E. S. R., 37, p. 559). By applying the chemicals to a strip of filter paper suspended in a flask the actual amount necessary to kill the housefly in 400 minutes was determined for a large number of chemicals, the results of which are here recorded.

"In general the toxicity of a volatile organic compound is correlated closely with its volatility. A decreasing volatility is accompanied by an increased toxicity. The boiling point of the chemical is a general index of its volatility. Compounds with boiling points of 225 to 250° C. are usually so slightly volatile that they do not produce death except after very long exposures. The structure of the respiratory system of the insect is probably responsible for the remarkable influence of volatility on the toxicity of the vapor of volatile organic compounds."

Lead arsenates, stone fruits, and the weather, G. P. GRAY (*Jour. Econ. Ent., 10 (1917), No. 4, pp. 385–392, pl. 1*).—Investigations of injury to stone fruits in California during April, 1915, have shown that the acid type of lead arsenate, often labeled "standard," is unsafe to use on the foliage of these fruits except under favorable weather conditions. Pome fruits sprayed under the same conditions for the control of cankerworm showed no injury. The foliage injury in the orchards of the Santa Clara Valley in the spring of 1915 was due to the decomposition of acid lead arsenate by the weather. The basic type of lead arsenate usually labeled "triplumbic" or "neutral," which is a slower acting poison, is a safer arsenical to use on stone fruits.

Locust control in various countries, G. TRINCHIERI (*La Lutte Contre les Sauterelles dans les Divers Pays. Rome: Inst. Internat. Agr., 1916, pp. XVI+187; rev. in Rev. Appl. Ent., Ser. A, 5 (1917), No. 3, pp. 100, 101*).—In an introduction by Saulnier (pp. IV-XVI) the circumstances relating to the compilation of this report by the author from information collected by means of a questionnaire circularized throughout the world are described.

The report considers the history and geographical distribution of locusts; gives a list of 142 injurious species observed in different countries and the locality in which each occurs, together with their food plants; and discusses the biology and habits of locusts and control organization in each country. The methods of control are discussed under the headings of natural enemies and mechanical, physical, and chemical methods. The work concludes with a discussion of an international understanding on the question of control, the following countries being reported as approving the principles of such an agreement: Portugal, Spain, Italy, Austria-Hungary, Roumania, Greece, China, India, Morocco, Tunis, Kamerun, Canada, the United States, Mexico, and Trinidad.

A 24-page bibliography is included.

Report on control work with the locust in Uruguay, R. SUNDBERG ET AL. (*Defensa Agr.* [*Uruguay*] *Mem.*, *1916, pp. 444, pls. 51*).—This report presents the details relating to work in Uruguay during 1915–16 and includes numerous large-sized colored maps showing the dissemination of and control work with the locust.

Experiments in locust control by means of Coccobacillus acridiorum in Argentina, R. KRAUS (*Centbl. Bakt.* [*etc.*], *2. Abt., 45 (1916), No. 18–25, pp. 594–599; abs. in Internat. Inst. Agr.* [*Rome*], *Internat. Rev. Sci. and Pract. Agr., 7 (1916), No. 9, pp. 1383, 1384*).—This paper is based upon investigations conducted by the author, as a member of a commission appointed by the Minister of Agriculture of Argentina, with a view to repeating the experiments of d'Herelle.

Organisms, morphologically identical with *C. acridiorum*, were isolated from the intestines of healthy locusts. The author was able to increase the virulence of the coccobacillus of d'Herelle and also found that the same effect can be obtained equally well with the micro-organisms from the intestines of locusts, although only negative results followed the feeding of locusts upon such organisms. His conclusions are as follows:

"It is not possible to produce in the open field the epidemic infection and the death of young locusts by spraying with a culture of coccobacillus, the virulence of which has been increased by successive passages. It may thus be concluded that this coccobacillus is a normal inhabitant of the intestine of healthy locusts and that it only kills the latter when injected into the abdominal cavity. By administering this bacterium to young locusts with food, no infection is obtained."

Summary of locust work for the third quarter, 1916, F. W. SOUTH (*Agr. Bul. Fed. Malay States, 5 (1916), No. 3, pp. 64–72*).—This is a report of work carried on in the Federated Malay States.

A new Sericothrips from Africa, J. D. HOOD (*Bul. Brooklyn Ent. Soc., 12 (1917), No. 2, pp. 32–34*).

A new species of Corythuca from the Northwest, E. H. GIBSON (*Ent. News, 28 (1917), No. 6, p. 258*).—*Corythuca pura*, collected from the prairie sunflower (*Balsamorhiza sagittata*) in several localities in the northwestern United States, is described as new.

The tomato and laurel psyllids, E. O. ESSIG (*Jour. Econ. Ent., 10 (1917), No. 4, pp. 433–444, pl. 1, figs. 2*).—Studies of 2 of the 50 species described from California, namely, the tomato psyllid (*Paratrioza cockerelli*) and the laurel psyllid (*Trioza alacris*), have been made by the author and are here reported upon.

The pink and green potato plant louse.—A new pest for Ohio causing serious losses this year, J. S. HOUSER (*Mo. Bul. Ohio Sta., 2 (1917), No. 8, pp.*

261–267, figs. 6).—A summary of information on *Macrosiphum solanifolii*, the first destructive outbreak of which in Ohio took place during 1917 and similar outbreaks occurred in Illinois and Missouri. In the vicinity of Cincinnati the attack, which started about the first of June, was so severe that within a few weeks entire fields were brown and dead. It was first observed to attack early potatoes and later spread to include early tomatoes and a rather wide range of host plants. Where potatoes were badly infested the vines were completely killed, while lighter infestations resulted in curling and distortion of the tops which stunted the plants and materially decreased the yield of tubers. On tomatoes the leaves were affected, but the main injury was to the blossom stems where the plant lice collected in enormous numbers, causing the blossoms to fall so that no tomatoes set. In one tomato field an expected return of about $900 an acre was reduced to not more than $100 an acre.

In control work in the Cincinnati district the most satisfactory material was nicotin sulphate used at the rate of 1 to 2 teaspoonfuls to 1 gal. of water, or a half pint to 50 gal. of water, with enough soap added to form suds. When desired nicotin sulphate may be used in combination with lead arsenate or Bordeaux mixture, or in a mixture of both, but when combined with either or both soap should not be used. Several applications should be made, preferably every other day for perhaps four or five times, depending upon the weather, in order to insure the destruction of the plant lice. The importance of directing the spray upward to reach the plant lice on the underside of the leaves is emphasized.

Some sensory structures in the Aphididæ, A. C. BAKER *(Canad. Ent., 49 (1917), No. 11, pp. 378–384, figs. 48).*

Eastern aphids, new or little known, I, EDITH M. PATCH *(Jour. Econ. Ent., 10 (1917), No. 4, pp. 416–420, fig. 1).*—This paper, based largely on a collection of Connecticut plant lice, includes descriptions of *Aphis viburniphila* n. sp. from several species of Viburnum, *A. rumexicolens* n. sp., from *Rumex acetosella*, and *Prociphilus approximatus* n. sp., from white ash.

Eastern aphids, new or little known, II, A. C. BAKER *(Jour. Econ. Ent., 10 (1917), No. 4, pp. 420–433, fig. 1).*—This second paper includes keys to the American species of several genera, namely, Myzocallis, Monellia, Euceraphis, Chaitophorus, and Pterocomma. Five species are described as new to science.

The Aphididæ of Java, P. VAN DER GOOT *(Inst. Sci. Buitenzorg, Contrib. Faune Indes Néerland., 1 (1917), No. 3, pp. 1–301, figs. 52).*—This summary of the knowledge of plant lice in Java includes descriptions of 2 new tribes, 14 new genera, and 54 species new to science. An index to the species of plant lice thus far known to occur in Java, namely, 82 species representing 34 genera, and a host plant index of the same are included, as is a list of 21 references to literature.

[Studies of pediculi] *(Parasitology, 9 (1917), No. 2, pp. 228–265, 293–324, pls. 2, figs. 16).*—Several papers relating to pediculi, here presented, include A Contribution to the Bionomics of *Pediculus humanus (vestimenti)* and P. *capitis*, by A. Bacot (pp. 228–258), consisting of a detailed report of life history studies, given to a large extent in tabular form; Notes on the Biology of P. *humanus*, by E. Hindle (pp. 259–265); and Studies on Pediculus.—I, The Copulatory Apparatus and the Process of Copulation in P. *humanus*, by G. H. F. Nuttall (pp. 298–324).

The louse problem, A. W. BACOT *(Brit. Med. Jour., No. 2931 (1917), pp. 296, 297).*—The data here presented are based upon the studies above noted.

The isolation of the Bacillus typhi-exanthematici from the body louse, P. K. OLITSKY, B. S. DENZER, and C. E. HUSH *(Jour. Amer. Med. Assoc., 68 (1917), No. 16, pp. 1165–1168).*—"Since 1910 many observers in different parts of the world have reported the finding of an organism in typhus-infected lice. This organism they believe to have a causal relationship to typhus fever. Owing to the fact that improper methods have been used, culture of this organism was impossible. In Mexico we have been able to grow this bacterium and to show that morphologically, culturally, and serologically it is identical with *B. typhi-exanthematici*."

The lesser corn stalk borer, P. LUGINBILL and G. G. AINSLIE (*U. S. Dept. Agr. Bul. 539 (1917), pp. 27, pls. 3, figs. 6*).—This is a report of studies conducted by the senior author at Columbia, S. C., during the seasons 1913, 1914, and 1915, and by the junior author at Lakeland, Fla., during 1913 and 1914.

The phycitid moth *Elasmopalpus lignosellus*, which has heretofore occurred in injurious abundance only in sporadic outbreaks, has now become of considerable economic importance in the Southern States. While particularly important as an enemy of corn, cowpeas, sorghum, and beans, it also attacks chufa (*Cyperus esculentus*), crab grass (*Eleusine indica*), Japanese cane, Johnson grass, milo maize, peanuts, sugar cane, turnips, and wheat. Though the larvæ are omnivorous, the investigations show that they have a decided fondness for Gramineæ, and probably would confine themselves almost exclusively to plants of this family if they were always obtainable. Crops grown on sandy soils or soils lacking humus are usually the most seriously affected.

The injury is caused by the larvæ boring into the stems of growing plants and feeding therein, such injury being particularly characteristic in young corn and sorghum, where the larvæ tunnel into the stalks at or slightly below the surface of the ground, through and sometimes up the heart for a distance varying from 1 to 2 in. The bud leaves of the affected plants are severed from the main plant, injury to corn in this manner resembling closely the work of the southern corn root worm (*Diabrotica 12-punctata*), but *E. lignosellus* is an upland species, found only in the driest of soils, while the corn root worm breeds generally in the moist lowlands. While some of the injured plants may survive, they remain dwarfed or become deformed. In older corn, sorghum, and cowpeas the damage consists primarily in the girdling of the stems at or slightly below the surface of the ground, and the larvæ also tunnel into the stems, thereby weakening them to such an extent that very little pressure is required to break them off. Cowpea plants have been found almost completely cut in two at a point near or slightly below the surface of the ground by the larvæ girdling the stem, while in other cases the larvæ were found tunneling into the stems as in the case of corn and sorghum. The larvæ in all stages spin a silken thread wherever they go, and the younger ones readily suspend themselves by it.

Originally described by Zeller in 1848 from Brazil, Uruguay, Colombia, and "Carolina," U. S. A., this moth is now known to occur in the United States throughout all the Southern States, westward, including the southern parts of New Mexico, Arizona, and California, and northward, including Oklahoma, eastern Kansas, southeastern Nebraska, southern Iowa, Illinois, Indiana, and Ohio, southeastern Pennsylvania, New Jersey, and along the Atlantic coast into Massachusetts.

Technical descriptions are given of its several stages, which include six larval instars. Oviposition apparently does not take place when the temperature falls much below 80° F. The eggs, which are thought to be deposited on the stems of plants, in the axils of the leaves, or on the ground at or near the bases of the stalks, hatch in 3 days in summer, 5 days in early fall, and in from 6 to 8 days in late fall. The number deposited under laboratory conditions varied from 91 to 342, with an average of 190, as many as 73 eggs being deposited in a single day. The larvæ may reach maturity in 13.8 days, but generally in about 16.8+ days during the summer months and from 22+ to

41.6 days in the fall. The number of instars and their length is quite variable, the larvæ molting four or five times in summer and five or six times in the fall. The length of the pupal stage varies from 7 to 11 days in July, 7 to 10 days in August, 8 to 18 days in September and October, and from 9 to 21 days in October and November. The longevity of the adults in rearing cages averaged 12.7 days for the summer months.

There are thought to be four generations of this species at Columbia, S. C., three complete generations having been reared from the middle of June to the middle of October in 1913. In the latitude of Columbia the first part of the winter is apparently passed as a larva and the latter part as a pupa and possibly adult, the larvæ having been found in the field in their burrows in the stalks as late as the middle of November. In Arizona it is thought to pass the winter in the larval stage, since larvæ in all sizes were found at Tempe as late as November 3.

The species apparently suffers very little from natural enemies, a single parasite (*Neopristomerus* sp.) having been reared at Columbia, S. C., and *Orgilus læviventris* at Gainesville, Fla.

Much can be accomplished in the control of this pest through late fall and early winter plowing after the removal or destruction of all remnants and waste material in the field, harrowing of the borders and terraces to break up the winter quarters of pupæ, the use of fertilizer to stimulate plant growth and make the plants more resistant to attacks by the pest, and the early planting of corn, sorghum, and allied crops to give the plants in the infested soil a good start before the insect begins its depredations.

An annotated bibliography of 27 titles is included.

Control of the grape-berry moth in the Erie-Chautauqua grape belt, D. ISELY (*U. S. Dept. Agr. Bul. 550 (1917), pp. 42, pls. 6, figs. 9*).—This bulletin, which relates particularly to control measures, is prefaced by a brief account of the economic status and a summary of seasonal history and habits of *Polychrosis viteana*, based upon observations by the author and his associates at North East, Pa., during the seasons of 1914, 1915, and 1916, and the work of Johnson and Hammar, previously noted (E. S. R., 28, p. 453).

The work has shown that the pest can be controlled by spraying, and that while other methods will reduce berry-moth infestation and some of them can be employed profitably to increase the efficiency of spraying, none offers a dependable control in commercial vineyards. The spray mixture recommended consists of arsenate of lead paste 3 lbs. or powder 1.5 lbs. and resin fish-oil soap 1 lb. in Bordeaux mixture (3:3:50). In case of extremely heavy infestation the amount of arsenate of lead should be increased to 5 lbs. paste or 2.5 lbs. powder, at least in the last application. The spray should be applied with "trailers," the first application immediately after falling of the grape blossoms and the second application (about two weeks later) when the grape berries are just touching. The cost of spraying material and labor required to control the grape-berry moth, if applied to control the berry moth alone, is about $5 per acre, it being assumed that an average of 6 acres are sprayed per day and that 150 gal. of liquid are applied to the acre.

"The applications of spray materials required for the control of the grape-berry moth are so timed that they may be combined with applications to control the grape rootworm, grape leafhopper, and powdery mildew, and some of the applications for downy mildew and black rot also may be combined with them. Nothing need be added to the spray solution for rootworm control; nicotin sulphate (40 per cent) at the rate of 1:1,600 should be added to the second application for leafhopper control; and Bordeaux mixture should be used in both applications for fungus diseases."

The other control measures considered include destruction of leaves in the fall, bagging grape clusters, hand picking infested berries, early harvesting, burying hibernating pupæ, etc.

A report of studies of this pest in Ohio by Goodwin has been previously noted (E. S. R., 35, p. 358).

On the pathogenicity of the so-called Sotto bacillus of silkworms, K. Aoki and Y. Chigasaki (*Bul. Imp. Sericult. Expt. Sta. Japan, 1 (1916), No. 1, pp. 97–139*).—The investigations show that the fatal action of old agar cultures of *Bacillus sotto* is due to a toxin which occurs in the spores.

The atoxogen type of Bacillus sotto, A. Aoki and Y. Chigasaki (*Bul. Imp. Sericult. Expt. Sta. Japan, 1 (1916), No. 1, pp. 141–149*).—A strain of *B. sotto* discovered by the authors—the atoxogen type—did not produce a fatal toxin when grown in agar culture, but did, however, possess the power to produce a septicemia. It was found that the so-called atoxogen and toxogen strains can be distinguished neither culturally or through immunization.

Flight of mosquitoes.—Studies on the distance of flight of Anopheles quadrimaculatus, J. A. A. LePrince and T. H. D. Griffitts (*Pub. Health Rpts. [U. S.], 32 (1917), No. 18, pp. 656–659, figs. 3*).—"Observations on the flight of *A. quadrimaculatus* in nature showed the flight to extend to approximately a mile from a breeding place producing very profusely. Beyond this distance stained specimens were not found. The distance of flight from a place producing very freely but less profusely than the above was decidedly less, approximately a half mile. Stained specimens of *A. quadrimaculatus* were taken as follows: One at 5,565 ft. from the point of liberation, two at 3,245 ft., three at 3,090 ft., one at 2,800 ft. *A. quadrimaculatus*, in one test, flew across a river 800 ft. wide in returning to a plantation from which they were originally caught for the test. Approximately 900 or 1,000 mosquitoes were liberated."

Notes on the early stages of Chrysops, W. Marchand (*Jour. N. Y. Ent. Soc., 25 (1917), No. 3, pp. 149–163, pls. 3*).—A contribution from the department of animal pathology of the Rockefeller Institute for Medical Research, Princeton, N. J., consisting of notes on the egg-laying habits and the earlier stages of Tabanidæ or horseflies of the genus Chrysops. Twelve of the 34 species occurring in New Jersey were found at Princeton.

Sarcophaga hæmorrhoidalis larvæ as parasites of the human intestine, L. Haseman (*Ent. News, 28 (1917), No. 8, pp. 343–346*).—This reports cases of parasitism by *S. hæmorrhoidalis* in Missouri.

Fly investigation reports, I–III, Winifred H. Saunders (*Proc. Zool. Soc. London, No. 3 (1916), pp. 461–463, 465–468, 469–479; abs. in Rev. Appl. Ent., Ser. B, 4 (1916), No. 11, pp. 167, 168*).—The first part of this report relates to some observations on the life history of the blowfly and of the house fly, made from August to September, 1915; the second part to trials for catching, repelling, and exterminating flies in houses, made during the year 1915; and the third part to investigations with stable manure to check the breeding of house flies, made during the year 1915.

As reported in the third paper, the author has found two very successful methods of treating stable manure for the destruction of flies, the first consisting in a surface dressing of the manure with green tar oil or with neutral blast furnace oil and soil at the rate of 1 part of oil to 40 parts of soil, and the second, the application of tetrachlorethane in the miscible form at the rate of 2 oz. to 10 cu. ft. of manure. Both treatments killed the maggots successfully and are harmless to plants. Tar oil has a permanent effect in being resistant to rain while the effect of the tetrachlorethane lasts only while the liquid vaporizes.

Flies and typhoid, W. NICOLL (*Jour. Hyg. [Cambridge]*, 15 (1917), No. 4, pp. 505–526).—"The chain of evidence incriminating the house fly as a disseminator of typhoid fever is at present fairly complete, but many of the links are weak and not thoroughly strengthened by experimentation. The bulk of experimental work has hitherto been done under highly unnatural and artificial circumstances and the results so obtained can not be accepted unreservedly as giving a correct view of conditions in nature.

"The experiments described in the present paper show that flies can ingest typhoid bacilli from natural matter, i. e., human feces and urine, and carry them for a certain period of time. There is no evidence to show that the typhoid bacilli multiply in the house fly. On the contrary the evidence goes to show that they are not adapted for prolonged life on or in the fly. It thus follows that the house fly is a purely mechanical carrier of the typhoid bacillus and is not a natural 'host' in the strict sense of the term.

"Many bacilli closely resembling *Bacillus typhosus* in cultural characteristics appear to be natural or, at least, common inhabitants of the intestine of the house fly. These are extremely likely to be mistaken for *B. typhosus* unless the most stringent tests are employed. As might be expected there is evidence to show that a process of bacterial selection occurs in the fly's intestine. Some bacteria appear to flourish, but others are rapidly eliminated. Among the latter must be numbered *B. typhosus*."

Relation of the common root maggot (Pegomyia fusciceps) to certain crops in Louisiana, E. S. TUCKER (*Jour. Econ. Ent.*, 10 (1917), No. 4, pp. 397–406).—The author reports upon injury in Louisiana to young tomato plants, garden peas, seed potatoes, young corn, and onions, and infestation of cottonseed used for fertilizer, by this root maggot.

A buprestid household insect (Chrysophana placida), H. E. BURKE (*Jour. Econ. Ent.*, 10 (1917), No. 4, pp. 406, 407).—The author records the injury to window casings and door frames of sugar pine, (*Pinus lambertiana*) by this buprestid at Placerville, Cal.

The life history of Diapus furtivus, C. F. C. BEESON (*Indian Forest Rec.*, 6 (1917), No. 1, pp. 29, pls. 2).—This paper reports upon studies of the life history and economic importance of *D. furtivus*, a species of shot-hole borer which attained notoriety in connection with the death of sal trees in Bengal. This borer is able to kill off trees with diseased roots, but its attack is not fatal to trees weakened by defoliation, creepers, unsuitable local conditions, etc. It normally breeds in newly dead or felled trees and is particularly abundant in felling areas and depots, being active throughout the year.

Its chief economic importance lies in the damage to unbarked timber, which takes the form of shot holes and lines and stained wood defects. It may be controlled by early barking on felling areas and the removal of newly dead trees in other parts of the forest.

The weather and honey production, L. A. KENOYER (*Iowa Sta. Bul. 169* (1917), pp. 15–26, fig. 1).—The author here reports studies, based on daily records for 29 years, kept by a successful beekeeper, as to the weight of a hive of bees and the accompanying weather conditions. These show that changes in the weather exert a marked influence on the production of honey. The conclusions drawn are as follows:

"June yields 56 per cent of the annual hive increase and July about half of the remainder. A large June increase is indicative of a good honey year. There is an evident alternation between good and poor years. A good year has a rainfall slightly above the average, the honey season being preceded by an autumn, winter, and spring with more than the average precipitation. A rainy May scarcely fails to precede a good honey season. South wind seems favorable and east wind unfavorable.

"The yield shows a gradual depression preceding and a gradual increase until about the fourth day following a rainy day, after which it remains fairly constant until about the fourteenth day following the rain. Good honey months average slightly higher in temperature than poor, this being especially true of the spring and fall months. Clear days are favorable to production of honey. Yield is best on days having a maximum of 80 to 90° F. and a wide daily range of temperature is favorable for a good yield. A low barometer is also favorable for good yield. The fluctuations in yield for a producing period seem to be closely correlated with the temperature range and the barometric pressure, acting jointly. A cold winter has no detrimental effect on the yield of the succeeding season, but a cold March reduces it. A winter of heavy snowfall is in the great majority of cases followed by a larger honey yield."

Seventh annual report of the State inspector of apiaries for the year 1916, B. N. GATES (*Mass. Bd. Agr., Apiary Insp. Bul. 11 (1917), pp. 26*).—This, the usual annual report (E. S. R., 35, p. 662), is devoted particularly to a discussion of the occurrence of bee diseases in the State, the effect of repellent sprays, etc.

The domestication of the Indian honeybee, L. V. NEWTON (*Agr. Jour. India, 12 (1917), No. 1, pp. 44–57, pls. 5*).—This paper relates particularly to *Apis indica.*

Life history and habits of Polistes metricus, F. C. PELLETT (*Proc. Iowa Acad. Sci., 23 (1916), pp. 275–284, figs. 2*).—A report of observations made in Iowa.

Further observations upon the habits of the western wheat stem sawfly in Manitoba and Saskatchewan, N. CRIDDLE (*Agr. Gaz. Canada, 4 (1917), No. 3, pp. 176, 177*).—The data here presented which relate to *Cephus occidentalis* are supplementary to those given in the bulletin previously noted (E. S. R., 34, p. 250).

The author finds that this sawfly is dependent largely on wild grasses, particularly those of the genus Agropyron, including *A. richardsoni, A. smithii,* and *A. repens,* for its perpetuation. Various species of lyme grass (*Elymus* spp.), most of which show a marked preference for deserted fields, roadsides, etc., have proved to be of greater importance as hosts of the sawfly than was thought at first to be the case. Couch grass (*A. repens*), which grows freely among the various cultivated crops, is probably a greater menace as a host of the sawfly than any of the others. As regards remedial measures, it has been found that a trap strip of rye or wheat sown between the previous season's infestation and the new crop early in the spring and plowed down about the middle of July or cut with a mower at that time may be used to considerable advantage.

An American species of the hymenopterous genus Wesmaelia of Foerster, P. R. MYERS (*Proc. U. S. Nat. Mus., 53 (1917), pp. 293, 294*).

A report on a collection of Hymenoptera (mostly from California) made by W. M. Giffard, S. A. ROHWER (*Proc. U. S. Nat. Mus., 53 (1917), pp. 233–249*).—This contains descriptions of 15 species new to science.

Australian Hymenoptera Chalcidoidea, A. A. GIRAULT (*Mem. Queensland Mus., 5 (1916), pp. 205–230; abs. in Rev. Appl. Ent., Ser. A, 5 (1917), No. 3, p. 129*).—Among the parasites here described as new are *Pterygogramma acuminata* n. g. and n. sp., reared from eggs of a jassid embedded in twigs of Eucalyptus; *Alaptus immaturus* n. sp., reared from sugar-cane leaves containing leaf-hopper eggs, but not proved to be parasitic on them; *Paranagrus optabilis* n. g. and n. sp., reared from eggs of *Perkinsiella saccharicida;* P. *perforator* n. sp., reared from the eggs of delphacid leaf-hoppers; *Polynema reduvioli* n. sp., parasitic in eggs of *Reduviolus blackburni* in the Hawaiian Islands; *Anagrus frequens* n. sp., reared from eggs of delphacids; and *Paruriella viridis* n. sp., reared from the seeds of grass (*Panicum* sp.).

Parasitism of the larvæ of the Mediterranean fruit fly in Hawaii during 1916, C. E. PEMBERTON and H. F. WILLARD ([Bien.] *Rpt. Bd. Comrs. Agr. and Forestry Hawaii, 1915–16, pp. 111–118*).—This is a general summary of the fruit-fly parasite situation in 1916.

The four parasites *Opius humilis, Diachasma tryoni, D. fullawayi,* and *Tetrastichus giffardianus,* are said to have become established in many localities in the Territory. Summaries are given of the percentage of parasitism of fruit flies infesting various crops, etc., in different localities. The average parasitism as taken from over 26,000 larvæ secured from the kamani nut (*Terminalia catappa*) was about 41 per cent. It is much higher during some weeks and at other times much lower. The average parasitism in larvæ secured from most other fruits throughout the ripening season was somewhat less than 40 per cent, although coffee was an exception, as the larvæ therefrom were found to be as a rule highly parasitized. There seems to have been very considerable fluctuation in relative abundance of at least three of the established species of fruit fly parasites. Whereas O. *humilis* spread rapidly in a few months after liberation, it took D. *tryoni* two years to gain a foothold, but within the four months prior to the preparation of this paper it had almost entirely supplanted O. *humilis,* particularly in Kona and about Honolulu.

Notes on the construction of the cocoon of Praon, C. N. AINSLIE (*Ent. News, 28 (1917), No. 8, pp. 364–367*).

An egg parasite of the sumac flea-beetle, C. R. CROSBY and M. D. LEONARD (*Ent. News, 28 (1917), No. 8, p. 368. fig. 1*).—A chalcidid parasite reared from the eggs of the sumac flea-beetle (*Blepharida rhois*) at Norfolk, Va., by L. B. Smith, is described as new under the name *Tetrastichus ovipransus.*

An aphis parasite feeding at puncture holes made by the ovipositor, L. P. ROCKWOOD (*Jour. Econ. Ent., 10 (1917), No. 4, p. 415*).—Observations of the feeding of *Aphelinus lapisligni* n. sp., on the juices of its host (*Aphis bakeri*) are recorded.

Megastigmus aculeatus introduced into New Jersey from Japan, H. B. WEISS (*Jour. Econ. Ent., 10 (1917), No. 4. p. 448*).—M. *aculeatus.* a hymenopteran which destroys the entire interior of seed of *Rosa multiflora.* appears to have become established in New Jersey and has also been reported as occurring at Ithaca, N. Y.

The embryonic development of Trichogramma evanescens, monembryonic egg parasite of Donacia simplex, J. B. GATENBY (*Quart. Jour. Micros. Sci.* [London], n. ser., 62 (1917), No. 246, pp. 149–187, pls. 3).—This chalcidid oviposits on the egg mass of a beetle (D. *simplex*), a single parasite emerging from a host egg, and is also known to parasitize eggs of dragon flies.

Contribution to the life history and habits of the spinose ear tick, Ornithodoros megnini, W. B. HERMS (*Jour. Econ. Ent., 10 (1917), No. 4, pp. 407–411*).—A report of observations of the biology of O. *megnini* in California, data relating to which species have been previously noted (E. S. R., 27, p. 865).

Tarsonemus pallidus, a pest of geraniums, P. GARMAN (*Maryland Sta. Bul. 208 (1917), pp. 327–342, figs. 13*).—This is a report of studies of the biology of T. *pallidus* (=T. *approximatus*), made during the course of an investigation of the cause and method of transmission of the geranium leaf spot, and to which the author gives the name " pallid mite."

The species was first noticed in America in New York in 1898 and described by Banks the following year under the name *T. pallidus*. Previous to that time a similar and apparently identical mite was described from cultivated verbenas in Illinois by Garman, who attributed the spread of a "black rust" to it. In Maryland it is fairly common in greenhouses and a source of injury to cyclamens, chrysanthemums, snapdragons, fuchsias, and geraniums. The author records the discovery of a female of a species of Tarsonemus identical with *T. pallidus* at College Park, Md., on linden trees, indicating that it may not be confined to greenhouses.

The injury to geraniums is sometimes severe, causing the leaves to curl, spot, and drop prematurely. The injury to heavy-wooded varieties is less pronounced. The presence of the mite is often first recognized by the appearance of scorched spots on the underside of the leaves. Cyclamen flowers are also attacked frequently, the flowers withering and curling in much the same manner as the leaves. It is most severe when the plants are crowded, the leaves in contact, and the humidity high. If the plants are well spaced the injury is seldom serious, and the mites disappear or are greatly reduced in numbers in a short time.

The eggs, which are laid during the night on the underside of the leaf or in a protected spot between the leaf and the main stem, were found to require from 3 to 7 days for incubation at a temperature of from 68 to 77° F. The larval stage of the female is divided into two periods, the first consisting of an active period lasting 1.5 to 3 days and the second a quiescent or inactive period lasting from 1 to 3 days. At the end of the quiescent period the insect molts and the adult mite emerges, oviposition commencing in about 2 days. The life cycle of a single reared male required 5 days for the egg, 2 days for active larva, 3 days for quiescent larva, and 6 days for the adult, or a total of 16 days. The species was found to be parthenogenetic, continuous generations being obtained, starting with a single egg or larva confined in glass cells, which lived more than five months without the appearance of the male. Its capacity to reproduce parthenogenetically is continued for at least three generations and probably more. In regard to the rate of reproduction the author concludes that with a minimum oviposition of one egg per day during the egg-laying period and a maximum of 12 eggs per female the number of individuals should total 40 at the end of one month, provided no males appear. His method of rearing the mites consisted in the use of shallow concave cells provided with a small square of lens paper and a piece of geranium leaf. Farrant's medium proved to be the best for mounting specimens.

Tests of the effect of various insecticides on *T. pallidus* are reported in tabular form. Those tested and discarded because of injury to geranium foliage include lime-sulphur 1:40 and 1:50, turkey red oil 1:30, carbon disulphid emulsions 0.5 to 5 per cent (with liquid soap), sodium fluorid, sodium chlorid 10 per cent solution, kerosene emulsion, and Tak-a-nap soap 1 lb. to 20 gal. Injury from chromic and picric acids is slow in appearing, and it is possible that a thorough watering of the plants on the day following treatment will reduce injury to a negligible factor. Small tests with blackleaf 40 seem unfavorable on the whole, but it is thought probable that nicotin has some repellent action and should prove valuable as a preventive. A stream of water will dislodge this mite more readily than it will red spider, due to the absence of webs. With geraniums the use of a stream of water as a control is available because the leaves do not curl sufficiently to hide the mite as is the case with snapdragons.

The cyclamen mite, G. F. Moznette (*U. S. Dept. Agr., Jour. Agr. Research, 10 (1917), No. 8, pp. 373–390, pls. 2, figs. 6).*—This is a report of studies of the biology of *Tarsonemus pallidus*, made in a badly infested greenhouse at the Oregon Experiment Station.

This species is a very serious floral pest found as far east as Connecticut, and is thought to occur throughout the United States wherever cyclamen stock is grown. In greenhouses in Washington and Oregon in several cases growers lost their entire stock of cyclamen during 1916 and it has been reported to injure seriously chrysanthemums and snapdragons. The distortion of the leaves and the discoloration of the flowers are the most noticeable effects of its attacks. The work of the mite resembles a gall on the older leaves as well as on the young, developing leaves, but the older leaves are not generally attacked. The continued growth of the damaged parts results in distortion of the leaves, giving the plants a very dwarfed and shriveled appearance. Often the leaves become very much thickened at the points immediately surrounding the injured parts. When the infestation is severe, the plants appear ultimately so badly curled and distorted as to be unsalable and they do not bloom normally. This mite is supposed to be spread by the shipment of seedlings and specimen plants from one place to another.

Technical descriptions are given of its several stages. In life history studies no nymphal stage was found, the larva transforming to a quiescent stage from which the adult emerges. Oviposition took place over a long period, the eggs being found from early November until the last of March. The eggs are laid in masses in moist, dark places provided by the curling and distortion of the leaves of the cyclamen plant. The average length of the incubation period of ten eggs at a temperature of about 70° was about 11 days. The average larval period for 10 individuals for the active stage was about 7 days, the larvæ being found from November to the last of March. The length of the quiescent stage averaged 3.5 days for 10 specimens. The adults are present from November until late spring, and it is thought that they may be found in the greenhouse throughout the year. The rearing methods employed are briefly described.

In discussing remedial measures it is pointed out that owing to the mites having an extremely primitive respiratory system fumigation is an unsatisfactory measure and spraying must be resorted to. After the older plants become badly infested there is not much hope of saving them as the mites are usually concealed under the calyx and penetrate even to the inner flower parts of the buds so that it is quite impossible to reach them, and it is advisable to burn the plants and sterilize the soil. The stable nicotin extracts and the volatile nicotin extracts, as blackleaf 40, are practically identical so far as killing properties are concerned, and used at the rate of 1:1,000 appear to be the most satisfactory means of control. The application of the nicotin spray containing a small quantity of soap should be started when the plants are quite young and continued every 10 days until the flower buds are well developed and begin to show color.

A list of 12 references to the literature is appended.

A synopsis of the genera of beetle mites with special reference to the North American fauna, H. E. EWING (*Ann. Ent. Soc. Amer., 10 (1917), No. 2, pp. 117–132, figs. 6*).—In addition to keys to the families, subfamilies, and genera of Oribatoidea descriptions are given of 12 new genera.

On the nymph and prosopon of the tsutsugamushi, Leptotrombidium akamushi n. g. (Trombidium akamushi Brumpt), carrier of the tsutsugamushi disease, M. NAGAYO, Y. MIYAGAWA, T. MITAMURA, and A. IMAMURA (*Jour. Expt. Med., 25 (1917), No. 2, pp. 255–272, pls. 4*).—The mite here dealt with is the carrier of the tsutsugamushi or kedani disease, an acute exanthematous infectious disease which up to the present occurs only in the northern coast districts of Japan and in Formosa. The mortality from this disease, which closely resembles Rocky Mountain spotted fever, varies from 20 to 50 per cent. In this paper the authors deal at length with the morphology and biology of the mite, for which they suggest the generic name Leptotrombidium. A bibliography of 16 titles is included.

Is Trombidium holosericeum the parent of Leptus autumnalis? M. NAGAYO, Y. MIYAGAWA, T. MITAMURA, and A. IMAMURA (*Jour. Expt. Med., 25 (1917), No. 2, pp. 273-276, pl. 1).*—While the tsutsugamushi, *Leptotrombidium (Trombidium) akamushi,* is almost identical with the European *L. autumnalis,* the authors' observations and study of the literature failed to convince them that *T. holosericeum* is the parent of *L. autumnalis.* Regarding the host relations of *L. autumnalis* the authors state that "there is perhaps no mammal, which comes within their reach, unmolested by them; they have been found on hares, rabbits, various kinds of mice, badgers, hedgehogs, molebat, shrew, dogs, and cats. On birds, reptiles, insects, and spiders I could, however, not effect any infestation, though on insects and spiders near relations of *L. autumnalis* parasitize. Our tsutsugamushi attacks field mice, rabbits, guinea pigs, monkeys, and other mammals, but not insects."

Notes on parasitic acari, S. HIRST (*Jour. Zool. Research, 1 (1916), No. 2, pp. 59-81, figs. 14).*—These notes relate to some species of acari parasitic on mammals and birds in Great Britain and include descriptions of two new African mites of the family Gamasidæ. Keys are given to the species of the genera Haemogamasus, Dermanyssus, and Laelaps occurring in Great Britain.

The chicken mite: Its life history and habits, H. P. WOOD (*U. S. Dept. Agr. Bul. 553 (1917), pp. 14, pl. 1, figs. 2).*—This is a report of studies made at Dallas, Tex., of the main points in the life history and bionomics of *Dermanyssus gallinæ,* especially those of importance in the application of control measures.

The incubation period of the eggs during the latter part of August at an average mean temperature of 78.43° F. was about 48 hours. At an average mean temperature of 73.5° the larva molts in about 24.5 hours without ever having fed. At an average mean temperature of 82.9° the first stage nymphs molt in somewhat less than 24 hours. With the exception of one individual observed the second stage nymphs molted to adults in 3 days after feeding. Fertilization normally takes place off the host and usually before feeding, followed by oviposition within about 12 hours after feeding. Females deposit an average of 4 eggs each at the rate of 4 eggs in 24 hours and they will continue to feed and deposit at least eight times with one fertilization.

The details presented relating to the life cycle show 10 days to have been the actual time taken to pass through the life cycle under favorable conditions, but under natural conditions it is thought that the period would be reduced in August to at least 8.5 days. A certain amount of moisture and a moderate temperature were found to favor longevity, while extreme dryness and high temperatures are unfavorable factors. Under favorable conditions during July, August, September, and October, adults and second stage nymphs lived from 91 to 98 days. The longest period for adults which had never fed was 88 to 96 days during October, November, December, and January. The longevity of the first stage nymphs was found to be about the same as the other stages. During the months of September to January, inclusive, all stages on wood lived from 91 to 113 days, while stages in a glass chimney with a cracked egg lived more than 107 days during the same months. The conclusions drawn from these observations are that the mite can be starved out of a chicken house by keeping fowls and other animals away from the house for four months during the summer season and for 5 months during the cooler season in the latitude of Dallas, Tex.

It was found that normal feeding takes place during the hours of darkness and that the mites leave the fowl soon after feeding, all stages attaching to, feeding, and leaving a fowl in less than 2 hours. It is pointed out that dispersion of the mites may take place by infested fowls being transferred to clean localities, by the use of boxes and crates in which infested fowls have been kept, through being carried by man on his clothing, on sparrows, pigeons, horses, cattle, dogs, cats, and certain wild animals, such as foxes, skunks, and weasels, and by migration of the mites to buildings in contact or close proximity to infested premises. Since the mites prefer to hide on roosts or adjacent thereto, the roosts should not be attached to the walls.

For control measures the author refers to Farmers' Bulletin 801, previously noted (E. S. R., 37, p. 357). The natural enemies mentioned include a small black ant (*Monomorium minimum*), the fire ant (*Solenopsis geminata*), and spiders.

New mites, mostly economic, N. BANKS (*Ent. News, 28 (1917), No. 5, pp. 193-199, pls. 2*).

FOODS—HUMAN NUTRITION.

A comparison of several classes of American wheats and a consideration of some factors influencing quality, L. M. THOMAS (*U. S. Dept. Agr. Bul. 557 (1917), pp. 1-28, figs. 21*).—From milling and baking tests undertaken in co-operation with the North Dakota Experiment Station with a view to procuring data of value in establishing a scientific basis for the classification and grading of wheat, the following conclusions were drawn:

"Normal, plump, dry, and sound wheat of all classes yields approximately the same percentage of flour. Over 80 per cent of the samples of each of the three classes of the more common wheats, soft and hard red winter and hard red spring, yielded between 67 and 75 per cent of flour.

"There is a direct relation between milling yield and the moisture content of wheat, and in a general way the yield varies inversely with the moisture content. . . .

"The weight per 1,000 kernels or average weight of kernels has very little value in judging the potential flour yield.

"Although there are frequent exceptions when individual samples are considered, average results show a very striking relation between weight per bushel and flour yield, the latter varying directly as the former. The ratio between these two figures, however, is not quite the same for the different classes, nor is it the same for all varieties within each class.

"In color the bread from the flour of the various classes of common wheat shows about the same ranges and averages. The flour from durum wheat is considerably more creamy and thus averages several points lower than that of any other class. Bread from all normal durum samples has a tinting or coloration varying from slightly creamy to bright yellow, while of the hard red winter samples 77.6 per cent show a noticeable creamy tint; of the hard red spring samples, 69.5 per cent; and of the soft red winter samples, only 18.9 per cent.

"The general results indicate that test weight and soundness, considered together, are of far more value in appraising quality than any one of them considered by itself.

"Small amounts of inseparable material are generally accompanied by a decrease in flour yield, as would be expected, in that as a rule a large part of such material usually finds its way into the bran and shorts.

"Loaf volume and texture are the two factors which are considered as indicative of strength. While a great range of strength was found within each class of wheat, the averages for each class show considerable differences between the various classes when considered as a whole. Given in order from weakest to strongest, the classes are soft white, soft red winter, durum, hard red winter, and hard red spring wheat.

"The average loaf volume in cubic centimeters for each of these classes is soft white wheat, 1,909; soft red winter, 1,965; durum, 2,070; hard red winter, 2,219; and hard red spring, 2,421. In the matter of texture the several classes stand in the same order, except that soft red winter has a slight advantage over durum wheat.

"Of the four more important classes of wheat under consideration, durum is the highest in crude-protein content; hard red spring, second; hard red winter, third; and soft red winter, fourth. High crude-protein content as a rule is accompanied by high strength, but the relation between these two factors varies with the different classes of wheat and extremely high crude-protein content is sometimes accompanied by a decrease in baking strength.

"The average water absorption of the flour from durum and from hard red spring wheat is about the same, and that of hard red winter is only slightly lower. The water absorption of the soft wheats averages from 3 to 4 per cent lower than for the hard wheats. The range of water absorption of each class varies within wide limits. There is a direct relation between the water absorption of the flour and the bread yield of a unit quantity of the same. As a rule, the higher the absorption the greater the weight of the loaf."

Wheat and flour investigations, V, G. A. OLSON (*Washington Sta. Bul. 144* (*1917*), *pp. 12–86, figs. 14*).—Cintinuing previous work (E. S. R., 26, p. 738), two of the three studies reported had to do with the baking quality of flour and the third with the milling value of water-soaked wheat.

In the first study a comparison of the results of the chemical and baking tests of flours from 12 States included offer evidence for the belief that there is no relation between the quality of flour and the total nitrogen, alcohol-soluble protein components, gluten content, water-soluble solids, and acidity. "Neither were relations between the gluten content and the water-retaining qualities of flour observed."

"Although no conclusions could be drawn, the volumes of the loaves appeared to be inversely proportional to the gluten content. A loaf of bread having an apparent specific gravity 0.25 or less may be regarded as a satisfactorily baked loaf."

With respect to the influence upon the baking quality of the removal from flour of water-soluble, alcohol-soluble, and salt-free extracts, and of the addition to flour of electrolytes, the following conclusions from the data are reported:

"The irregularities noted in the nitrogen-free and ash-free extract content of flours giving the same and different volume capacities indicate that the nitrogen-free and ash-free extracts do not bear the relation to volume that would be expected according to theory.

"There is strong evidence supporting Wood's theory that the ratio of soluble ash to total nitrogen determines the shape of the loaf. Our experiments indicate that the nature of the electrolytes contained in the soluble ash may have something to do with the property of shape, and this may account for the irregularities noted.

"The baking quality of flour was not perceptibly affected by the addition of lactic acid at the rate of 0.54 gm. per 100 gm. of flour; the addition of the mentioned amount of acid, however, did affect the amount of gluten that could be separated from the flour. The significance of modifying the quality of the gluten and its unnoticeable effect upon baking quality should not be overlooked.

" The removal of the 70 per cent alcohol extractives from flour impaired the baking qualities of the flour to the extent that it was impossible to obtain a satisfactory fermentation of the dough.

" Flour in which a part of the soluble salts had been removed through the process of dialysis also gave unsatisfactory fermentation action when compared with the same flour untreated."

The second of the studies has to do with the influence of the various components of flour upon baking quality and is a progress report. Some of the results obtained are summarized as follows:

" The water-soluble extractives from flour were added to both wheat and corn starch with beneficial results in volume production. Flour from which the gluten was removed gave similar results.

" The addition of gluten to both wheat and corn starch resulted in forming compact, rubbery masses. Flour from which the water-soluble extractives were removed also resulted in forming compact masses.

" The addition of the water-soluble extractives to flour made up of either wheat starch and gluten, or cornstarch and gluten. resulted in increased volumes, but these were not equal to the volumes obtained by mixing the water-soluble extractives with both the wheat starch and cornstarch or flour from which the gluten had been removed.

" While it is true that the significance of the water-soluble and gluten component of flour to baking quality are shown to a certain extent in our experiments it is impossible at this writing to express the exact importance of each."

The results obtained in the study of the milling value of water-soaked wheat are summarized as follows:

" Wheat which has been allowed to sprout loses in weight as the length of time allowed for germination advances. The milling value of germinated wheat decreases as the length of the plumule increases. The length of time required for the conversion of starch decreases as the length of the plumule increases, to at least twice the length of the kernel.

" The amount of gluten which can be recovered from flour from germinated wheat is less than that from ungerminated wheat. The yield of gluten decreases rapidly as the plumule increases in length.

" Expressed in percentage of total nitrogen. the alcohol-soluble nitrogen has been affected by the germination of wheat. The most marked changes were observed in the glutenin and amid nitrogen. In the former there was a sudden decrease in amount from the period where the plumule was equal to the length of the kernel to that where the plumule was equal to twice the length of the kernel. The amid nitrogen increased rapidly from the time when the plumule was equal to the length of the kernel.

" When germinated wheat flour was baked only the quality of the crumb of the bread was impaired; this was particularly noticeable in flours made from germinated wheat in which the plumule was equal to or twice the length of the kernel. The volume of the loaf increased, being exceptionally large in the bread made from partially germinated wheat flour.

" Using small quantities of germinated wheat flour with other flour, it was found that the volume of the loaf could be increased without impairing the texture of the loaf. Each particular flour requires a different amount of germinated flour in order to produce the best results. Too large an amount of strongly diastatic flour is less beneficial than none.

"A water-soaked wheat is not necessarily spoiled and can be used for milling purposes, providing it has been thoroughly cleaned and dried."

The introduction to the bulletin summarizes historical data, which are supplemented by a bibliography.

The milling and baking data for the 1915 crop of wheat, T. SANDERSON (*North Dakota Sta. Bul. 122 (1917), pp. 61–94*).—This includes a critical discussion of wheat grading and its effect upon the economies of the wheat industry from an agricultural standpoint. It is based upon milling and baking tests reported for a large number of wheats.

" Summing up this whole matter as to the trouble resulting from the sale of wheat it may be safely charged to the system used in grading. . . . It is evident that the majority of men engaged in the grain trade are not aware of the true milling value of the different lots of wheat coming to them and that they are conscientious in their application of the system in vogue, while it is the strict application of this system that is working such a hardshp on our local miller, as well as the farmers. If the local millers were aware of the actual value of the so-called lower grades of wheat, they would use more of them in their mixture, thus reducing the cost of their raw material. At the same time they would reduce the amount of low-grade wheat going to the terminal market; thereby increasing the cost of the raw material to their competitors."

" There is some wheat in almost every crop year that should not be used for human consumption, but should be condemned and only allowed to be sold as animal food, and if not fit for that prupose, should not be allowed on the market at any price, the same as is done with meat and many other food products, but under the present system the majority of this low-grade wheat is bought by the elevator companies and mixed in small quantities and eventually finds its way into the flour of the consumer. In many instances the price paid is far below what it is actually worth for feed. Many of the complaints from the consumers coming to the miller are just and could be attributed to this cause."

Similar data for other years have been noted (E. S. R., 34, p. 759; 36, p. 464).

Shrimp: Handling, transportation, and uses, E. D. CLARK, L. MACNAUGHTON, and MARY E. PENNINGTON (*U. S. Dept. Agr. Bul. 538 (1917), pp. 1–8, pls. 2*).—Handling, preparing, and shipping cooked and raw shrimps, dried shrimps, and other specialties, the utilization of shrimp waste as fertilizer, and the food value of shrimp meat are discussed in this bulletin, the data including analyses of cooked, canned, and dried shrimps.

" Cleanliness, proper cooking, and care in handling shrimp, combined with a discontinuance of the practice of using preservatives, have resulted in the production of a finely flavored product which is gradually increasing in popularity. At the same time improvements in methods of packing and preparation have made shrimp accessible to many new markets at long distances from the producing sections. . . .

" The increased consumption of shrimp and the opening of new markets are stimulating the industry to increase its catches. If shrimp are taken at the wrong time of year or in excessive numbers their extermination is probable. Those interested in the shrimp industry, therefore, should give early attention to the question of conservation. It is also to the interest of those whose livelihood is dependent upon catching and packing shrimp to encourage investigations planned to determine the periods of spawning, the times of migration, and the feeding habits of shrimp, and to do their part in helping to make such investigations result in the adoption of protective measures."

Food products and drugs, J. P. STREET (*Connecticut State Sta. Rpt. 1916, pt. 4, pp. 185–304*).—The 1,369 products here reported on include, among many others " hygienic coffees," diabetic foods, condensed and powdered milks, spices, vegetable extracts, baking powder, spices, and a proprietary article akin to meat extract made from squab.

[Food and drug inspection], E. F. LADD and ALMA K. JOHNSON (*North Dakota Sta. Spec. Bul., 4 (1917), No. 14, pp. 363–378*).—In addition to data regarding sanitary inspection and the examination of foods and beverages, information is given on a proprietary drug preparation by C. P. Guthrie, and on Stealing Bread and Butter, by R. E. Remmington, is included, the latter having to do with "a very general sale of short-weight butter" which "inspectors of the food department have discovered."

How to select foods.—III, Foods rich in protein, CAROLINE L. HUNT and HELEN W. ATWATER (*U. S. Dept. Agr., Farmers' Bul. 824 (1917), pp. 2–19, figs. 2*).—In this, the third of the series (E. S. R., 37, p. 668), the proper selection of foods rich in protein is discussed in relation to the other four food groups into which foods may be conveniently divided for the discussion of dietary problems.

"Since the protein foods include many of the more expensive foods in common use, and since an adequate supply of protein is essential to the growth and upkeep of the body, it is especially important for the housekeeper to know how much her family needs and to be able to choose the materials which, in her particular circumstances, will best provide the proper kind and amount."

Among the generalizations made are the following: "The foods usually classed as rich in protein are: Milk and cheese; eggs; meat, poultry, and fish; dried legumes, such as peas, beans, cowpeas, soy beans, and peanuts; and almond and some other nuts. Wheat, oats, and some other cereals also furnish considerable amounts of protein. Milk is the best source of protein for children. There is about one-fourth ounce of protein in each of the following: One glass of milk, one egg, 1½ to 2 ounces of meat, 1 ounce of cheese, and 13 ounces of bread." "A man at moderate muscular work is believed to need about 3½ oz. of protein a day, and a family consisting of father, mother, and three small children about 12 oz. a day."

"It is possible to plan an attractive and wholesome diet in which one-half of the necessary protein is supplied by bread and other cereal foods which are relatively cheap. The more milk, eggs, and other protein-rich foods are combined with other foods in cooking, the less protein-rich foods are needed for use as separate dishes. Skim milk is not a substitute for whole milk as a food for little children, but it can be so used as a source of protein in the diet of adults. A quart in cooking or to drink will add as much wholesome protein to the general diet as a quart of whole milk. Providing they are clean and wholesome, sour skim milk and buttermilk may be used instead of sweet. Real economy in the use of protein foods lies not in leaving them out of the diet, but in choosing and combining kinds which will supply the total amount needed as cheaply as circumstances permit."

ANIMAL PRODUCTION.

A quantitative comparison of casein, lactalbumin, and edestin for growth or maintenance, T. B. OSBORNE, L. B. MENDEL, ET AL. (*Jour. Biol. Chem., 26 (1916), No. 1, pp. 1–23, figs. 4*).—To avoid criticisms made in the case of previous experiments when food was given ad libitum, in this case the animals were fed equal amounts of the isolated food materials. By keeping the food below the amount ordinarily consumed and varying the amount from day to day the animals were kept growing at nearly the same rate.

The results of the test show that with rats of similar initial weights and with the same amount of food in equal portions daily, the lactalbumin foods in every case gave the largest gains. These later experiments prove also what was formerly indicated, namely, that the comparative inferiority of casein may be corrected by the addition of the essential amino-acid cystin. The experiments further show that protein beyond a concentration of approximately 12.5 per cent of the total calories failed to give increase of body weight.

In a second experiment instead of giving each animal equal amounts of food daily it was increased to each individual in proportion to the gains made. Lactalbumin again was superior, it taking 50 per cent more of casein and nearly 90 per cent more edestin to produce the same gain. With a lactalbumin food containing 8 per cent it took 12 per cent of casein and 15 per cent of edestin to produce the same gain in weight. The replacement of cystin by alanin in the ration with casein failed to bring about a nutritive advantage. In mature animals where maintenance requirements and not growth are to be met, the results with the different proteins are not so marked.

Further experiments were made in which the three proteins were fed daily in such a way that no essential gain or loss in body weight occurred. The total energy intake was made sufficiently liberal, the protein only being kept at the minimum. The results corroborate the former conclusions as to the comparative superiority of lactalbumin when fed with the other two proteins in minimum amounts.

The effect of the amino acid content of the diet on the growth of chickens, T. B. Osborne, L. B. Mendel, et al. (*Jour. Biol. Chem.*, 26 (*1916*), *No. 2, pp. 293–300, pl. 1*).—Experiments by the authors with rats have shown the importance of certain amino acids for growth, notably tryptophane, lysin, and cystin. Similar work by Buckner, Nollau, and Kastle (E. S. R., 34, p. 871) with chickens is noted. Further work was carried on with chickens, using foods similar to those employed with rats.

The results with chickens were found in accord with those obtained in the experiment with rats. Lactalbumin, rich in both tryptophane and lysin, proved to be an efficient adjunct to the proteins of corn gluten.

The productive values of some Texas feeding stuffs, G. S. Fraps (*Texas Sta. Bul. 203* (*1916*), *pp. 5–42*).—These experiments were conducted in the same manner as those previously noted (E. S. R., 27, p. 668; 31, p. 862). The coefficients of digestibility and productive values as determined on sheep are shown in the following table:

Average coefficients of digestibility of feeding stuffs and productive values.

Feeding stuff.	Protein.	Ether extract.	Crude fiber.	Nitrogen-free extract.	Ash.	Productive value.
	Per ct.	Per ct.	Per ct.	Per ct.	Per ct.	Lbs.
Acuff sorghum forage	9.1	37.1	58.2	45.6	1.4	5.3
Corn chop, Argentine	86.3	91.3	92.4	97.9	99.4	22.4
Corn silage	59.2	69.4	74.7	76.3	43.8	3.8
Cotton seed	79.5	96.3	52.5	68.1	58.4	18.1
Dolichos lablab hay	72.3	52.0	54.7	64.6	26.5	8.3
Feterita seed	90.0	74.5	50.0	96.6	89.0	21.2
Feterita fodder	50.1	58.7	66.3	60.9	29.2	8.2
Jack bean, chopped	89.6	81.6	80.2	96.8	89.6	19.6
Kafir stover	18.2	47.6	48.6	46.3	0	5.4
Kafir fodder	62.4	55.4	68.8	69.8	37.2	10.3
Milo head chop, average	75.6	86.7	51.7	90.8	30.9	18.6
Milo stover	0	56.6	65.8	49.2	0	6.8
Milo fodder	38.1	70.9	72.0	78.2	51.6	13.6
Moth bean hay	67.1	10.8	52.3	64.9	6.3	8.3
Peanuts, whole, average	80.8	93.3	34.4	12.8	0	22.7
Peanut hulls	62.2	95.9	16.4	57.6	6.8	1.5
Peanut hay with nuts, average	75.8	92.0	47.9	68.3	37.1	15.6
Peanut hay without nuts, average	64.0	63.8	49.6	75.5	29.6	10.7
Peat	0	100.0	0	0	1.6	.4
Prairie hay, average	10.8	42.0	58.4	51.8	9.4	7.1
Rhodes grass hay	43.8	45.3	67.9	58.0	27.9	8.2
Rough rice, ground, average	75.6	76.1	10.4	90.6	7.7	15.9
Rice hay	37.8	56.0	51.3	47.6	....	5.4
Shallu stover	0	32.3	64.7	50.4	49.2	6.7
Sorghum silage, average	0	56.0	58.0	64.0	4.0	2.6
Sorghum fodder, average	38.0	65.0	61.0	63.0	4.0	9.4
Sorghum forage	9.1	37.1	58.2	45.6	1.4	5.3
Sorghum hay	38.2	62.0	62.2	63.0	28.4	8.9
Sudan hay, average	49.4	54.0	61.2	52.9	24.8	7.4
Sudan straw	45.9	34.5	60.0	47.7	6.8	6.8
Wheat shorts	92.1	86.7	50.0	98.5	35.5	21.9

Live stock feeding experiments (*Dept. Agr. and Tech. Instr. Ireland Jour., 16 (1916), No. 3, pp. 418–430*).—The report deals with experiments carried out during two years, 1913–1915, under the supervision of agricultural instructors in almost every county in Ireland. The following conclusions are drawn:

In pig feeding raw meal showed a saving in fuel and labor. Cooking failed to give returns either in amount of feed consumed, length of fattening period, . or quality of the pork.

In calf feeding maize meal with separated milk showed practically as good results as a calf meal made up of 1 part ground flaxseed, 2 parts maize meal, and 2 parts oatmeal.

With cattle the feeding of a mixture of 2 parts undecorticated cotton cake and 1 part maize meal on second-rate pasture did not give a profitable increase in live weight. Indirectly it might give a profit by earlier maturity or better appearance at marketing.

With stall-fed cattle the extent to which turnips should be used is deemed a question for each farmer to decide. In most cases it seemed sound economy to grow them extensively and feed liberally. Cattle can be fattened successfully with 3 stone (42 lbs.) of turnips per head daily.

Almost similar results were obtained with two rations, one with 84 lbs. of roots and a moderate amount of concentrated food, and one of 42 lbs. of roots and an extra allowance (3 lbs.) of concentrated food.

Color inheritance in mammals, S. WRIGHT (*Jour. Heredity, 8 (1917), No. 5, pp. 224–235, figs. 2*).—An attempt is here made to relate the biochemical findings in regard to melanin with color relations that have come to light in genetic work. A scheme is proposed for showing the interrelations of the different mammalian coat colors, and a classification of color factors is suggested.

The value of good sires, J. K. WRIGHT (*Missouri Bd. Agr. Mo. Bul., 14 (1916), No. 9, pp. 5–86, figs. 58*).—This bulletin reviews in a general way the principles of heredity, environment, and variation, and shows by citation of a few great herds and from experimental data from other sources the value of good sires in the improvement of horses, asses, cattle, sheep, and swine.

The heredity of dual-purpose cattle, H. F. EUREN (*Norwich, [England]: A. D. Euren, 1917, pp. 96*).—A brief history is given of the origin and development of the dual-purpose Red Polled breed of cattle, including an account of the work of John Reeve, of Wheycurd Hall Farm, Wighton, England, and others in the development of the breed.

For the study of the heredity of the Red Polled, as evidenced by its milk production and its beef production, the author has prepared from the British and American Herd Books the extended pedigree of 29 cows in the United Kingdom and of 11 in the United States. In each of the pedigrees has been worked out the percentage of blood of polled " home-bred " cattle of Norfolk, polled Suffolk, and the Reeve blood-red breed.

Details are given of the breeding of noteworthy bulls that have been used in developing the Red Polled dual purpose cattle, together with data on the cost of feeding for milk and beef. Transcripts are also given from the British and American Herd Books showing the butter production and beef-making qualities of some of the leading strains and families of Red Polled cattle.

Sheep breeding and feeding, J. M. JONES (*Texas Sta. Bul. 205 (1917), pp. 3–24, figs. 5*).—The object of this test was to determine which of the most common mutton breeds of rams when crossed with fine-wooled ewes would produce the most thrifty and desirable lambs grown and fattened under Texas conditions.

Good Rambouillet range ewes of uniform type and breeding were used, 148 ewes being divided into six lots and bred to rams as follows: Lot 1, Rambouillet; lot 2, Shropshire; lot 3, Hampshire; lot 4, Southdown; lot 5, Lincoln; and lot 6, half-blood Karakule-Lincoln. The resulting lambs numbered 120, all of which were hardy and thrifty from birth. The highest average birth weight was shown by the Hampshire-Rambouillet cross, and they also made the greatest total gain and seemed to finish in a shorter period. The cost of feed per pound of gain in the experiment was, from October 13 to January 5, 3.32 cts., and from January 6 to 17, 5.03 cts.

Six of the best lambs were taken from each lot and fed from January 6 to March 8 for the National Feeders' and Breeders' Show. The cost of feed per pound of gain during this period was 6.32 cts. Pens of these lambs in competition at the show were ranked as follows: Lincoln-Rambouillet, Hampshire-Rambouillet, Southdown-Rambouillet, Rambouillet, Karakule-Rambouillet, and Shropshire-Rambouillet.

A novel salt trough used during the experiment, and which seemed to be effective, was made to apply pine tar to the lambs to keep the gadfly away from the nasal cavities. The trough, 4 in. by 6 in. by 4 ft., had a board 3½ in. wide placed 3 in. from the bottom. A strip of sheepskin, with the wool side out, was tacked to the edge of this board and smeared with pine tar every evening just before bringing the sheep into the lot.

Oestrus and ovulation in swine, G. W. CORNER and A. E. AMSBAUGH (*Abs. in Anat. Rec., 11 (1917), No. 6, p. 345*).—The authors found that animals killed during the period of heat usually show ruptured Graafian follicles, and in such animals the ova were recovered by washing out the Fallopian tubes. Rupture of the follicle is spontaneous, occurring even in the absence of the boar. Sows killed on the third day of heat showed regularly that ovulation had taken place. The unfertilized ripe ovum of the sow, as found in the tube, measures from 155 to 165 μ in diameter. The zona pellucida is from 7 to 8 μ thick, inclosing a yolk heavily laden with fat globules, obscuring the nucleus. The polar bodies are often clearly seen in the fresh ovum. Study of a small series of ova which have been cut into serial sections seems to show no deviation from the stages reported in other mammals. The first polar body is formed within the follicle just before rupture, the second in the tube. Entrance of the spermatozoön and fusion of the pronuclei occur in the tube.

Cost of keeping farm horses and cost of horse labor, M. R. COOPER (*U. S. Dept. Agr. Bul. 560 (1917), pp. 22, figs. 5*).—Results are given of a study of cost accounting records for 154 horses on ten farms in Illinois, 72 horses on seven farms in Ohio, and 90 horses on ten farms in New York. The purpose of the bulletin is to show how the annual cost of keeping a farm work horse and the cost per hour worked may be determined, and to point out that the cost per hour worked is the true measure of the profitableness of a horse to its owner.

The several items of cost and credit which make up the annual average cost per horse are analyzed in detail and tabulated. It was found that the annual net cost for keeping a horse was $100.65 in Illinois, $120.87 in Ohio, and $145.02 in New York. A study of the relation of work performed to the total feed cost shows that on an average on the farms studied there was a fairly uniform difference between the average feed cost and the total cost per hour of horse labor, showing that the number of hours worked and the feed cost per horse are the controlling factors in the total cost per hour of horse labor. On the Illinois farms the horses worked an average of 1,053 hours per year at an average cost of 9.56 cts. per hour, on the Ohio farms an average of 866 hours per year at an average cost of 13.9 cts. per hour, and on the New York farms an average of 1,020 hours at an average cost of 14.22 cts. per hour.

It was found that the large farms permit of a more efficient use of horse labor than do the small farms. On the large farms in Illinois there were 22.2

acres in crops per horse, while on the small farms there were but 16.8 acres per horse. Similar results were found on both the Ohio and the New York farms, though in these States the difference between the two groups was not as great as in Illinois.

Some important essentials in profitable horse production, C. W. McCamp-bell (*Kansas Sta. Insp. Circ. 2 (1916), pp. 3*).—In addition to brief notes on profitable horse production, a list is given of stallions licensed in Allen County during the year ended October 1, 1916. Similar lists are published for all the other counties of the State, each list being issued as Inspection Circular 2.

The theory of sex as stated in terms of results of studies on the pigeon, O. Riddle (*Abs. in Anat. Rec., 11 (1917), No. 6, p. 510*).—Studies on sex control in pigeons have indicated the nature of the initial difference between germs of prospectively different sex-value. "This difference rests upon different levels of metabolism, and when the metabolic level of a given germ is shifted from the level characteristic of the germ of one sex sufficiently toward the level of the other sex, it develops into an organism of the sex which corresponds to the acquired, or later, level. The initial difference characteristic of the two kinds of (sex) germs, tends to persist and characterize the adults of the two sexes.

"Sex is based on a quantitative difference. Intermediates of the normal extremes have been experimentally produced, and the normal extremes have themselves been experimentally accentuated."

Factors influencing the sex ratio in the domestic fowl, R. Pearl (*Science, n. ser., 46 (1917), No. 1183, p. 220*).—In this paper on the sex production question in the common fowl, results are given of eight years' experimentation at the Maine Station in which over 22,000 individuals were involved.

This work indicates first that the determination of sex in poultry is primarily a matter of a definite, hereditary mechanism, just as it is in insects and other forms which have been studied. At the same time, it is demonstrated that under certain physiological circumstances the operation of this mechanism may be modified in such a way as to lead to the production of more females in proportion to the number of males. The chief factor in bringing about the modification in the direction of a larger production of females is the fecundity or laying ability of the hens used as breeders. The larger the number of eggs which a hen lays before being put into the breeding pen, the larger will be the proportion of females and the smaller the proportion of males produced by her eggs.

Crossing over in the sex chromosome of the male fowl, H. D. Goodale (*Science, n. ser., 46 (1917), No. 1183, p. 213*).—In studying sex linkage in fowls, crossing over in the sex chromosomes of the male was seen to have occurred. This preliminary report deals only with the factors themselves, without regard to the somatic appearances of the individuals. "Three dominant sex-linked characters, namely, B, I, and S, were employed. B and I were introduced on one side, S on the other. Hence the F_1 males were all BI, S; B and I being in paternal (or maternal) sex chromosome, S in the maternal (or paternal). These males have been tested by mating them back to females of the composition b Is, b is.

"If there were no crossing over, offspring of this back cross showing the combination of somatic characters found in the F_1 male would not occur. Actually, however, they do occur, thus demonstrating that crossing over has occurred, a chromosome having the composition B I S having been formed. Other cross over classes have appeared, but the one cited is the one at the present age of the chicks most easily recognized."

Further data on the relation between the gonads and the soma of some domestic birds, H. D. Goodale (*Abs. in Anat. Rec., 11 (1917), No. 6, pp. 512-514*).—Published data on the ablation of the testes and ovaries of domestic birds, together with unpublished data on the transplantation of the ovary into castrated males, tend to show that different parts of the soma react in different ways to the secretion of the gonads. Each character appears to be more or less independent of every other character, just as they are in heredity. The characters affected are (1) those including some of the secondary sexual characters that are independent of either ovary or testis, such as size in the female, voice and some phases of behavior, and mandible color in ducks; (2) those affected by the testis, such as comb and wattles, fat deposition, size in the male, and some instincts and summer plumage in ducks; and (3) those that are affected by the ovary, such as plumage form and color and some phases of behavior.

"If the entire series of altered individuals is examined, it is apparent that it may be looked upon as a series of sex intergrades. That is, characters that are normally found in one sex may be experimentally transferred to the opposite sex while individuals composed of mixtures of such characters may be obtained."

Determinate and indeterminate laying cycles in birds, L. J. COLE (*Abs. in Anat. Rec., 11 (1917), No. 6, pp. 504, 505*).—The author has noted two distinct types of laying cycles in birds, one in which the number of eggs which will be laid in the clutch is definitely determined when laying begins, and the other in which the number of eggs that will be laid depends upon stimuli received after laying has begun. In other words, the stimulus for cessation of laying and inception of brooding has already been received and the reaction predetermined in the first case, while in the second the stimulus is received later and is followed by cessation of liberation of ova from the ovary, though laying continues for a time afterwards until the ova already discharged have received albumin and shells and have been expelled. The most important stimulus for the onset of broodiness and the consequent cessation of laying in the second class of cases is probably a physiological reaction of the female to a number of eggs in the nest. As a consequence, if the eggs are removed as laid the stimulus does not occur and laying continues beyond the regular clutch to an indefinite number.

Among domesticated birds the pigeon may be taken as an example of the determinate type and the common fowl of the indeterminate. Among wild birds experiments have been carried on with the English sparrow and the house wren, which also appear to represent the two types respectively.

A study of broodiness in the Rhode Island Red breed of domestic fowl, H. D. GOODALE (*Abs. in Anat. Rec., 11 (1917), No. 6, pp. 533, 534*).—In addition to results already noted (E. S. R., 36, p. 173), the author points out that the length of the period before the first broody period appears in Rhode Island Red hens may vary from a month up to two or even more years, while a very small percentage have never exhibited signs of broodiness. Ninety-five per cent, however, of the birds go broody before July 1 of their pullet year. The number of broody periods depends in part on the date of the first broody period and in part on the time the bird stops laying in the fall, and may vary from one to eleven times during the first year. In the second year broody periods begin as soon as the bird lays a comparatively few eggs.

Breeding for egg production.—II, Seasonal distribution of egg production, E. D. BALL and B. ALDER (*Utah Sta. Bul. 149 (1917), pp. 3–71, figs. 29*).—In continuation of previous data (E. S. R., 37, p. 369), this is a discussion of the seasonal distribution of egg production during the first, second, third, and later years of egg laying of the same flocks of hens, and a comparison of the distribution of production of high-laying and low-laying flocks in the same season and different seasons, as well as of high-laying and low-laying individuals of the same flocks. These studies are based on six flocks of White Leghorn hens ranging from nine to three years old and all descendants of a common flock.

The authors conclude that " environmental factors influence the records of the pullet year more than that of later years and influence flocks making low records more than those making high ones. Flocks of Leghorns with approximately the same yearly laying records will show the same distribution throughout the season regardless of whether the records were made in the first, second, or third year of production. Where a flock makes a low record the curve of distribution will be lower throughout than that of a high-laying flock, and, except for environmental fluctuations, the two curves will be practically parallel.

" Where the high and low layers of the same flock are compared, the low layers tend to fall off in production a little faster in the later part of the first season so that the first-year curves gradually separate toward the end. This was less noticeable in second-year production. High layers and low layers of the first and second years showed almost perfect agreement in distribution, with the curve of the low layers uniformly lower than that of the high layers or the difference slightly widening toward the ends. The distribution of production does not seem to be at all affected by age up to three years at least, but total production affects distribution regardless of age. . . .

" Winter egg production of flocks is more variable than annual production. This variation seems to be closely correlated with environmental factors. Flocks that made low winter records their first season made high ones the second, and vice versa. The flocks that made low records the first winter made higher three-year records than the high first-year flocks." The correlation between the first-winter production and that of later years averaged about 0.25. This correlation is less for the high first-year flocks than for the low ones. The higher the production of an individual the greater the percentage of this production that will be made in the " winter " period regardless of age.

The correlation between winter production (November 1 to February 28) and total production of the same year, as shown by 18 flock records from 1907 to 1912, inclusive, averaged 0.5848. This correlation was found to decrease slightly with age, the averages for the six years being 0.6325 between the first winter and first year, 0.5862 between the second winter and second year, and 0.5351 between the third winter and third year.

" The winter period as used does not seem correctly to represent a biological entity, but is made up of the end of one period and the beginning of another. There does not appear to be any foundation for the assumption of a division of the laying period into units. It appears that there is a fairly definite ' productive rhythm ' that not only affects annual production, but even influences the seasons so that a high fall production will be followed by a low spring one, and vice versa.

" The date of hatching when kept within a two-month period within the months of March, April, and May did not appear to affect total production in three years. The time between hatching and laying, while varying considerably under different environmental conditions, affected the total production in three years. The latest maturing pullets were always poorer producers."

Egg-production data from other sources are tabulated and discussed, from which it is noted that " the distribution of production of Leghorns in other flocks, including egg-laying contests, was found to agree with the corresponding curves from the Utah flocks. The distribution of production in the general-purpose breeds was found to be quite different from that of the Leghorns. The curves of the general-purpose breeds reached their maximum early in the season and then rapidly fell off again to very moderate production, from which they gradually declined to the end of the season, while the Leghorns reached their maximum a month or more later, but continued to produce heavily for several months and then rapidly fell off at the end."

Selection: The basis of improving the poultry flock, H. R. LEWIS (*New Jersey Stas. Hints to Poultrymen, 5 (1917), No. 12, pp. 4*).—Brief directions are given for improving the egg production of flocks of hens by eliminating the poor producers, the basis of selection being the external appearance of the individual hens. It is stated that when culling a flock of yearling hens in the fall the following factors should be studied in the order named, and the final decision with regard to the possibilities of each bird made on the basis of a combined grouping of all the factors: Health, or freedom from disease; weight, or condition of flesh; vigor and stamina; condition of comb; pigmentation—amount of yellow in vent, ear lobes, beak, and shanks; condition of pelvic arch—size and pliability of lay bones, and distance between lay bones and from keel to pelvic bones; and condition of plumage—degree of molt, if any.

Feed cost of egg production. Results of three years' experiments at the Government poultry farm, H. M. LAMON and A. R. LEE (*U. S. Dept. Agr. Bul. 561 (1917), pp. 42, pls. 8, figs. 5*).—Owing to the lack of complete data on the feed cost of egg production on general farms, this experiment was undertaken at Beltsville, Md., in 1912 with 6 pens of 30 pullets, later increased to 16 pens. Only the feed costs are considered, as the fowls were mostly on free range. Some of the results of the work are as follows:

The average egg yield for the first-year pullets was 131, at a cost for feed of 10 cts. a dozen; the second year, 92.7, at a cost of 14 cts.; the third year, 78.2, at a cost of 19 cts. The average value of eggs over feed cost the first year was $2.56 per hen, second year $1.41, third year $0.79.

Oats were not found necessary in the ration, but added variety. With the young fowls, especially, great gains were made with beef scrap or other animal protein. Cottonseed meal apparently produced brown or greenish spots on the yolks, rendering many of the eggs unfit for market. Fish meal at $7 a ton less can replace beef scrap with no unfavorable effect on the quality of the eggs.

No advantage was found in allowing the fowls to select their own mash constituents over feeding the mixture.

In comparison of Leghorn and general-purpose fowls, it was noted that the Leghorns ate an average of 55 lbs. of feed annually at a cost of 87 cts., the general-purpose fowls 72 lbs. at a cost of $1.13. The Leghorns produced eggs about 3 cts. per dozen cheaper during their first year than the general-purpose fowls, 6.4 cts. cheaper the second year, and 9.8 cts. cheaper the third year. The annual decrease in production was much less with the Leghorns than with the general-purpose breeds. The average weight per dozen of the eggs from the Leghorns during the first year was 1.45 lbs., second and third years 1.49 lbs.; from the general-purpose fowls, first year 1.53 lbs., second year 1.6 lbs., and third year 1.63 lbs.

Eggs were produced at the lowest cost in the spring and at the highest cost in the fall.

Poultry feeds and feeding results, R. N. HARVEY (*Texas Sta. Bul. 206 (1917), pp. 3–16, figs. 4*).—Part one of this bulletin consists of a discussion of Texas-raised feeding stuffs suitable for poultry, and includes methods of feeding and some rations that have proved satisfactory.

Part two is a report of results of a feeding test carried on for five periods of four weeks each for the purpose of comparing meat scrap, cottonseed meal, meat scrap and cottonseed meal, and sour skim milk as supplements of milo maize, wheat bran, and wheat shorts for laying hens. The fowls receiving meat scrap produced well during the first three periods, and those receiving skim milk did well throughout the whole 20 weeks. The flocks receiving cottonseed meal and cottonseed meal with meat scrap gave very poor results, the former being very low twice, high once, but falling again. The latter was lowest one month, but was next to the lowest all other times. During the 20 weeks the hens fed cottonseed meal laid an average of 62.68 eggs and returned a profit of 77.98 cts. each over the cost of feed; those fed meat scrap laid an average of 67.86 eggs per hen, at a profit of 85.67 cts.; those fed meat scrap and cottonseed meal averaged 63.81 eggs each, at a profit of 72.8 cts.; and those fed sour skim milk an average of 71.29 eggs, at a profit of 87.54 cts. per hen.

Poultry farm management, R. E. JONES, I. G. DAVIS, and B. A. McDONALD (*Conn. Agr. Col. Ext. Serv. Bul. 8 (1917), pp. 16, figs. 4*).—A study of the poultry business in Connecticut, based on the operation of 42 farms during one year. Receipts, expenditures, and inventories are noted, while labor income is taken as the measure of profit.

The average net receipts were $1,312. Deducting interest on capital at 5 per cent, $560, this gave a unit labor income of $752.

The range of egg production was from 54 to 160, averaging 97 per hen for the year. Receipts from market eggs were 46 per cent of the total, and nearly four times as much as from any other single source. The necessity for increased average egg production is emphasized.

Forty-eight per cent of the expense on these farms was for feed. The home production of more feeds and the cooperative buying of others is suggested as means of lowering costs.

The greatest returns were made on the farms with the largest range. The importance of range and shade are noted.

The number of poultry units per man varied from 319 to 2,000. The highest efficiency lay between 800 and 1,500. With less than 500 a man can not make a profit, and with more than 1,500 he can not give them the necessary care for best results. The ratio of poultry units to laying hens was 100 : 68. The larger farms gave the higher percentages of profit, owing to greater efficiency of labor, machinery, and capital.

Finishing market poultry, W. C. THOMPSON (*New Jersey Stas. Hints to Poultrymen, 5 (1917), No. 11, pp. 4*).—Market requirements and the best means to market poultry at a profit when there is a tendency to become overstocked in certain classes are discussed.

DAIRY FARMING—DAIRYING.

Dairy laboratory manual and notebook, compiled by E. L. ANTHONY (*Philadelphia and London: J. B. Lippincott Co., 1917, 2. ed., rev., pp. 72, figs. 15*).—A revised edition of these laboratory exercises (E. S. R., 31, p. 494).

Dairy cattle, A. LEITCH, H. M. KING, and J. P. SACKVILLE (*Ontario Dept. Agr. Bul. 253 (1917), pp. 72, figs. 23*).—A general treatise on the economy of dairy farming, breeds of Ontario dairy cattle, principles of nutrition, use of feeds, general problems in dairying, care and management of dairy cattle, common diseases, and plans for the construction and equipment of dairy barns.

Experiments on the use of palm kernel nut cake as a food for dairy cows, A. LAUDER and T. W. FAGAN (*Edinb. and East of Scot. Col. Agr. [Pamphlet]. 1916, pp. 9*).—Two experiments are here reported in which palm kernel nut cake and Bombay cottonseed cake were compared as feeds for dairy cows.

In the first experiment, which was conducted during the winter of 1915–16, two lots of nine Shorthorn dairy cows each were fed for eight weeks a daily ration of 4 lbs. bran, 1 lb. locust bean meal, 75 lbs. turnips, and oat straw, supplemented by 4 lbs. palm nut cake for lot 1 and 4 lbs. cottonseed cake for lot 2. The weekly yield of milk before the experiment was 17.25 lbs. more for lot 2 than for lot 1. During the eight weeks of the experiment lot 1 produced 11,215.75 lbs. and lot 2, 10,962.75 lbs. of milk.

During the summer of 1916 two lots of eight cows each were fed for seven weeks on pasture supplemented with 4 lbs. cottonseed cake, 4 lbs. bran, and 1 lb. locust bean meal per day for lot 1, and 4 lbs. palm nut cake, 4 lbs. bran, and 1 lb. locust bean meal for lot 2. Previous to the experiment the milk yield of the two lots was practically equal. During the experiment the milk yield was 13,622.5 lbs. for lot 1 and 12,836.25 lbs for lot 2. The animals ate the palm kernel nut cake less readily than the cottonseed cake.

Analyses are given of the concentrates used in these experiments.

Calf feeding experiments (*Dept. Agr. and Tech. Instr. Ireland Jour., 17 (1917), No. 2, pp. 257–259*).—In a series of experiments at 30 centers in 17 counties crushed oats was compared with a standard calf meal composed of ground flaxseed, oat meal, and maize meal (1 : 2 : 2).

In the experiments, which lasted an average of 116 days, 202 calves were used. They averaged one-half week of age at the beginning of the test. The crushed oats ration was fed dry and the calf meal was steeped in hot water for 12 hours. An average daily gain of 1.41 lbs. per head was made on crushed oats and 1.44 lbs. on the calf meal. On the basis of prewar prices, the cost of production was 5s. 3d. per hundredweight (1.1 cts. per pound) less on crushed oats than on the calf meal.

The business of ten dairy farms in the blue grass region of Kentucky, J. H. ARNOLD (*U. S. Dept. Agr. Bul. 548 (1917), pp. 12*).—A brief analysis is given of 10 dairy farms found among the 187 farms previously noted (E. S. R., 36, p. 789).

The average labor income on these 10 dairy farms was $1,773 and on the 187 farms $750. The labor income on the seven successful farms of the ten varied from $6,408 to $1,121. The principal source of income on these farms was market milk, with cream next in importance, while very little butter was marketed. Receipts from the dairy represented 71 per cent of the total, the remainder consisting of tobacco (5.8 per cent), wheat, steers, poultry, and the sale of dairy cows, young stock, and calves. It is estimated that the cost of feed per cow on these farms varied from $40 to $50. The advantages of the bluegrass region for dairying are discussed.

A comparison of the seven more successful farms is made with the average of the whole group of ten. It is noted that "the average successful farm had the largest business, as shown by the size of farm, the number of dairy cows, and the working capital. On the average successful farm there were more receipts from crops and miscellaneous sources than were shown for the average of the ten farms. This indicates the greater degree of diversity on the successful farms. The most important comparison is that shown for the receipts per cow [$164 and $126, respectively]."

The effect of the ingestion of desiccated placenta on the variations in the composition of human milk during the first 11 days after parturition, F. S. HAMMETT and L. G. McNEILE (*Jour. Biol. Chem., 30 (1917), No. 1, pp. 145–153*).—The results of this study demonstrate that the ingestion of desiccated placenta has an effect upon the factors concerned in the regulation of the chemical composition of milk. There is a stimulation of the sugar- and protein-producing mechanism with an apparent depression of the function of the fat-secreting apparatus.

From the peculiar characteristics of milk protein and carbohydrate it is presumable that these constituents are largely elaborated by the gland itself. Milk fat is apparently the sum total of the secretory and excretory activities of the mammary gland, the former being concerned with the elaboration of the fat peculiar to milk and the latter concerned in the inclusion in the milk of a part of the ingested fat as such. The evidence for this is admittedly incomplete. From the fact that the ingestion of desiccated placenta tends to produce a milk of greater uniformity in the change of production direction of fat, it does not seem improbable that its action may be stimulative to the secretory activity of the gland in this respect also.

A bibliography is included.

The modern milk problem in sanitation, economics, and agriculture, J. S. MacNutt (*New York: The Macmillan Co., 1917, pp. XI+258, pls. 16, figs. 22*).— This book, which consists largely of a compilation of data from various sources, is a treatise on the practical, economic, and sanitary factors involved in supplying cities with pure milk.

Comparisons of the rate of gas production by certain bacteria in raw and in pasteurized milk, P. W. Allen (*Jour. Infect. Diseases, 21 (1917), No. 2, pp. 219–225, figs. 3*).—In this comparison of the physiologic activity of bacteria in milk all factors were the same with the exception that part of the milk was raw and part was pasteurized at 60° C. (140° F.) for 30 minutes. It was found that pasteurization caused milk to become more favorable to the attack of the gas-forming colon bacilli and *Bacillus ærogenes*. These results indicate that pure raw milk has a power of resisting changes which the same milk does not possess when pasteurized.

The significance of colon bacilli in milk, S. H. Ayers, L. B. Cook, and P. W. Clemmer (*Abs. Bact., 1 (1917), No. 1, pp. 52, 53*).—In some experimental work in which a large number of samples of fresh milk produced under various conditions were examined, it was found that colon bacilli were present in 0.01 cc. in only a small percentage of the samples. When these organisms were found, their numbers ranged from 100 to 400 per cubic centimeter. There was apparently no increase in the colon count in milk held for 24 hours at 10° C. (50° F.) but a very great increase at 15.5° C. (60° F.).

In order to determine how many colon bacilli could be introduced into fresh milk, an examination was made of 70 samples produced under extremely filthy conditions and handled in unsterilized utensils. These conditions were far worse than would probably be found on any farm, yet in only 32 of the 70 samples were colon bacilli found in 0.01 cc. of fresh milk. The number of these organisms found in the 32 samples ranged from 100 to 28,400 per cubic centimeter, but only one sample showed more than 2,000. Leaving out this sample, the average colon count of the 31 samples was 648 per cubic centimeter.

The influence of gargety and high count cows on the number of bacteria in milk, R. C. Colwell (*Abs. Bact., 1 (1917), No. 1, pp. 48, 49*).—The investigation of a sanitary dairy of 140 cows from which raw milk was retailed in the city of Providence, R. I., showed two factors to be responsible for the production of milk with more than 10,000 bacteria per cubic centimeter, (1) high count cows, cows whose freshly and aseptically drawn milk contains more than 10,000 bacteria per cubic centimeter, and (2) gargety cows, cows affected with incipient, acute, or chronic mammitis. The results of 243 tests of individual cows showed that 72 per cent of the cows were producing milk containing less than 10,000 bacteria per cubic centimeter, and 28 per cent were cows of the high count type.

A certain few of these high count cows were infected with mammitis in one quarter of the udder and a bacteriological examination of each teat of such cows was made. In every instance where by physical examination one quarter was known to be infected one or more of the apparently healthy quarters proved to be infested with similar organisms. The custom of discarding only the milk from the infected quarter and of adding the milk from the remaining quarters to the whole milk of the herd was therefore responsible for infecting the entire output with the gargety milk.

Dairy laws of Wisconsin (*Madison, Wis.: Dairy and Food Comr., 1917, pp. 40*).—The text is given of the dairy laws of Wisconsin and of rules and regulations effective July 1, 1917, governing the licensing of butter makers and cheese makers and operators of butter and cheese factories, adopted by the dairy and food commissioner under authority of law.

Testing milk for butter fat by the Babcock test, compiled by W. E. EVANS (*Neffsville, Pa.: Author, 1917, pp. 16, figs. 13*).—Brief directions are given for making the Babcock fat test on whole milk, together with notes on the causes of variation in the fat content of milk.

Accounting records for country creameries, J. R. HUMPHREY and G. A. NAHSTOLL (*U. S. Dept. Agr. Bul. 559 (1917), pp. 37*).—This bulletin contains copies of forms and a description of their uses for a system of accounts which is being recommended by the Bureau of Markets and by the Dairy Division of this Department as a uniform system of accounting for country creameries. It is stated that the system presented is the result of careful study and practical experience in creameries operating under widely varying conditions.

Experiments with pepsin to replace rennet, D. W. STEUART (*Jour. Bd. Agr. [London], 24 (1917), No. 1, pp. 57–59*).—The author made up a pepsin solution that compared favorably with standard rennet extract and kept well. Caerphilly, Smallholder, and soft cheeses made by the use of the pepsin solution compared favorably with rennet cheese. In making a gallon of the pepsin solution, he advises the use of $13\frac{1}{3}$ oz. of 1.60 soluble pepsin powder, 2 lbs. salt, 3 oz. boric acid, and 1 gal. water. The brine must be cooled to 104° F. after boiling, before dissolving the pepsin. The solution should be filtered after a day or two.

Loss of fat in the whey when using pepsin, G. H. BARR (*Agr. Gaz. Canada, 4 (1917), No. 8, pp. 660–662*).—Tabulated results are given of cheese making experiments at the Finch Dairy Station from February 23 to May 10, 1917.

In using pepsin, the best results were secured by setting at a temperature of 85° F. and using enough pepsin to coagulate the milk ready to cut in from 25 to 30 minutes. Setting the milk at temperatures over 86° increased the loss of fat in the whey in nearly every case. The loss of fat in the whey was lessened by increasing the quantity of pepsin per 1,000 lbs. of milk from 4 oz. to 5.5 and 6 oz. Developing the acidity in the milk so that the curds dipped in less than 2 hours and 15 minutes from time of setting increased the loss of fat in the whey to a marked extent. It was found advisable to allow the curd to get fairly firm but not too firm before cutting.

Varying conditions in the milk from day to day as found in cheese factory work apparently affect the loss of fat in the whey to a greater extent when pepsin is used than when rennet extract is used. Care must therefore be exercised in cutting and stirring the curd when making cheese with pepsin.

On the formation of "eyes" in Emmental cheese, W. M. CLARK (*Jour. Dairy Sci., 1 (1917), No. 2, pp. 91–113, figs. 2*).—A review of the literature reveals little or no evidence that the eyes of Emmental cheese are strictly localized at points of excessive bacterial growth. On the contrary the evidence of bacterial counts and direct microscopical examination, as well as the gas production of different regions of the cheese, indicate a more or less uniform distribution of the eye distending gas.

Certain theoretical considerations are presented which lead to the hypothesis that the gas separates in aggregates according to laws governing the separation of gas from supersaturated aqueous solutions. This hypothesis has been tested upon viscous media with results directly applicable to the "eye" and "Nissler" hole formations in cheese.

It is concluded that the gas produced in Emmental cheese separates in aggregates whose localities have no necessary relation to the points where the gas is produced, and that a rapid gas production must tend to the formation of numerous small holes while a slow gas production must admit the formation of larger holes. This conclusion is shown to agree with the fact that Nissler holes are produced by a rapid fermentation while eyes are formed slowly. This conclusion also suggests that the gas of Nissler holes must separate at numerous points near its point of origin without regard to any particular locality of the cheese, while the eyes must form at favorable points. This was experimentally verified by a study of stained cheeses.

An extensive bibliography is given.

VETERINARY MEDICINE.

[Live stock diseases] (In *Live Stock of the Farm, edited by C. B. Jones, London: The Gresham Publishing Co., 1915, vol. 4, pp. 159–252, figs. 18; 1916, vol. 5, pp. 101–134, 249–269*).—The diseases of sheep are dealt with by T. W. Cave in volume 4 (pp. 159–252); and the diseases of pigs (pp. 101–134) and of poultry (pp. 249–269) by H. Leeney in volume 5.

New and nonofficial remedies, 1916 (*Chicago: Amer. Med. Assoc., 1916, pp. 428+XXII*).—Descriptions are given of the articles which had been accepted by the council on pharmacy and chemistry of the American Medical Association prior to January 1, 1916.

Sugar in the treatment of wounds, S. KOHEYA (*Chosen Igaku Kai Zassi, No. 13 (1916), pp. 11–18; abs. in Japan. Med. Lit. [Korea], 2 (1917), No. 1, pp. 7, 8*).—The successful use in wound treatment of commercial granulated sugar is noted. The sugar was found to inhibit the growth of most of the bacteria liable to be found in wounds. It possessed no disinfecting power, but stimulated tissue granulation and the formation of epithelial cells, prevented putrefaction of the secretions, and reduced the odor.

The use of chloramin-T paste for the sterilization of wounds, M. DAUFRESNE (*Jour. Expt. Med., 26 (1917), No. 1, pp. 91–93*).—"Dakin's toluene sodium *p*-sulphochloramid, mixed with sodium stearate, forms a paste sufficiently active and stable to be used in the treatment of wounds."

Sterilization of wounds with chloramin-T, A. CARREL and ALICE HARTMANN (*Jour. Expt. Med., 26 (1917), No. 1, pp. 95–118, figs. 20*).—"Under the conditions of our experiments chloramin paste maintains the asepsis of a wound already sterile, and sterilizes an infected wound. Under the same conditions chloramin paste causes no apparent modification of the cicatrization curve of an aseptic wound."

Dichloramin-T in the treatment of the wounds of war, J. E. SWEET (*Jour. Amer. Med. Assoc., 69 (1917), No. 13, pp. 1076–1078; Brit. Med. Jour., No. 2956 (1917), pp. 249, 250*).—The author concludes that Dakin's dichloramin-T in solution in eucalyptol and paraffin oil is of great advantage in wound treatment, even when the final results in wound healing are no better, because it saves the pain of wound dressing, it effects an appreciable saving of dressing material, the amount of solution is of small bulk, the number of wounds which a surgeon can dress in a given time is far greater than by any other method.

and the elimination of the Carrel tube simplifies the dressing, the problem of transportation of the wounded, and the time taken for the periodic flushing.

The relation between the thromboplastic action of cephalin and its degree of unsaturation, J. McLEAN (*Amer. Jour. Physiol.*, *43* (*1917*), *No. 4, pp. 586–596*).—Experiments with various samples of cephalin have shown that its thromboplastic action bears a direct relation to its degree of unsaturation. The greater the degree of unsaturation the greater the thromboplastic activity. Cephalin saturated beyond a certain degree, either by reduction or oxidation, loses completely its thromboplastic activity. The material in solution which has become saturated or partly saturated yields an acid reaction and retards the coagulation of blood. With increasing saturation the material gradually loses its property of solution in ether and chloroform.

It is noted that cephalin is most effective in its coagulative power shortly after its isolation from the tissues.

The reaction of sera as a factor in the successful concentration of antitoxic sera by the methods at present in use, ANNIE HOMER (*Biochem. Jour.*, *11* (*1917*), *No. 1, pp. 21–39, figs. 2*).—The results of the study reported show that in the Banzhaf[1] method for concentration of antitoxic sera the uncertainties of filtration are due to no account having been taken of the reaction of the serum, and that, as the precipitating power of 30 per cent ammonium sulphate is not appreciably increased during the heating, a certain amount of euglobulin escapes precipitation with the first fraction precipitate and appears in colloidal suspension in the final product. "The uncertainties in the filtration of the hot serum-ammonium-sulphate mixtures in the above method can be obviated by an adjustment of the hydrogen ion concentration. The filtration can also be improved by the addition of sodium chlorid to the mixtures, but in this case the improvement is due to a specific action of salt on the globulins."

Euglobulin can be completely eliminated by adjustment of the hydrogen ion concentration of the serum mixtures to the point at which the desired increased precipitation is assured, by brine extraction of the second fraction precipitate containing the pseudoglobulin-antitoxin combination, subjecting the serum to a preliminary prolonged heating at from 57 to 58° C., and the addition of organic substances such as phenol and its homologues, ether, or chloroform. "The extent of the heat denaturation of the serum proteins during the heating of serum at 57° for several hours is also influenced by the hydrogen ion concentration of the serum and can be controlled by the adjustment of the latter. The denaturation induced by heat in alkaline sera apparently does not involve the same type of change as that induced in acid sera."

Equilibria in precipitin reactions.—The coexistence of a single free antigen and its antibody in the same serum, S. BAYNE-JONES (*Jour. Expt. Med.*, *25* (*1917*), *No. 6, pp. 837–853, fig. 1*).—In the study reported the purified proteins, edestin from hempseed and crystalline ovalbumin from fresh eggs, were used as antigens. Although the albumin isolated was considered as pure as is obtainable by chemical means, moderately severe anaphylactic reactions were produced by it in animals sensitized with ovoglobulin. It is noted that "anaphylactic tests of the individuality of a protein can not be any longer regarded as the criterion of the purity of the substance as an antigen. . . .

"With edestin and crystalline egg albumin as antigens, phases in the precipitin reaction were found in which these substances and their specific precipitins could be demonstrated to be coexistent but ununited in the same serum. When edestin or crystalline egg albumin is injected into a rabbit immunized thereto, the antigen may be found in the circulating blood during 48 hours after

---

[1] Collected Studies Research Lab. Dept. Health N. Y. City, 4 (1908–9), pp. 230–232.

its injection, while at the same time the animal maintains a high titer of free precipitin in its blood. When the pure protein antigen is mixed in proper proportions with the serum of a specifically immunized rabbit and the resulting precipitate removed by centrifugation, the supernatant fluid contains both antigen and antibody. The serum drawn from a rabbit during the period in which free antigen and antibody are coexistent in the circulation undergoes slow spontaneous precipitation when kept in sterile tubes in the ice box." The interaction appears to take place according to a definite law.

The protective action of a solution of egg albumin as a third colloid inhibiting precipitation in a reaction between human serum and its antibody was demonstrated.

Notes on the outbreak of foot-and-mouth disease at Butleigh, Somerset, R. N. GRENVILLE (*Jour. Bath and West and South. Counties Soc., 5. ser., 11 (1916–17), pp. 82–84*).—Evidence is presented which indicates that the infection was carried to cows at Butleigh by a cart, probably in the mud on its wheels.

The value of the ophthalmic and conglutination tests in the diagnosis of glanders, E. GRÄUB (*Schweiz. Arch. Tierheilk., 59 (1917), No. 3, pp. 129–154*).—In the examination of a large number of remounts the ophthalmic reaction was found to yield fairly satisfactory results, although some doubtful reactions were obtained. The conglutination test was the most reliable, no doubtful reactions having been observed in the examination of 3,000 sera.

The ophthalmic reaction and a simplified conglutination reaction are described in detail. In the simplified technique, horse serum is used instead of guinea-pig serum to furnish complement.

The temperature required for the "inactivation" of mule blood for the complement fixation test for glanders, J. B. BUXTON (*Vet. Jour., 73 (1917), No. 505, pp. 245–247*).—In the examination of blood samples from a large number of mules by the complement fixation method it was found that an unusually large number of animals gave a definite positive or an indefinite reaction. Postmortem examination of certain animals which had given a positive reaction to the complement fixation test failed to show the presence of glanders lesions. The indefinite reaction was found to be due to insufficient inactivation of the mule serum and a consequent destruction of anticomplementary bodies. Experimental data submitted show that heating of the serum to 62° C. for one-half hour is necessary for complete destruction of these anticomplementary bodies.

Transmission of pulmonary and septicemic plague among marmots, WU LIEN-TEH and F. EBERSON (*Jour. Hyg. [Cambridge], 16 (1917), No. 1, pp. 1–11*).—Of marmots placed in contact with marmots infected with plague by inhalation, "52.6 per cent developed pulmonary plague and died within four to six days. Marmots suffering from pneumonic plague are infective at an early stage of the disease and the animals which such marmots infect acquire plague after a short incubative period.

"Pulmonary plague can be readily transmitted to the small marmot (*Spermophilus citellus*), and these animals, when suffering from pulmonary plague, are in turn capable of transmitting the same type of plague through the respiratory passages. Septicemic plague can be developed in marmots very easily as a result of respiratory infection, and also by direct subcutaneous inoculation with small amounts of culture. The marmot can acquire plague by way of the alimentary tract and spread the disease by feeding on plague-infected carcasses. The histological appearances observed in the lesions of these cases are characteristic."

In an appended note G. H. F. Nuttall reports upon the identification of ectoparasites collected from marmots by the senior author. These included a flea determined by Rothschild as a slightly aberrant specimen of *Ceratophyllus famulus* and a number of ticks closely resembling *Hæmaphysalis koningsbergeri.*

Note on the transmission of animal trypanosomiasis in northern Rhodesia by bloodsucking flies other than Glossina, F. CHAMBERS (*Vet. Rev., 1 (1917), No. 3, pp. 222–227).*—" From the evidence obtained it would appear that the trypanosome can be and is spread in tsetse-free areas by the agency of biting flies. That Tabanidæ are the worst offenders is becoming realized. Pangonia and Stomoxys have also been shown to be transmitting agents, and it is possible that any bloodsucking fly can transmit trypanosomiasis mechanically."

Tuberculosis and animal breeding, U. DUERST (*Schweiz. Arch. Tierheilk., 59 (1917), Nos. 2, pp. 65–91, figs. 2; 3, pp. 154–173, fig. 1).*—This is a general discussion of the subject, together with some original experimental data.

The author shows that the statistical data in regard to the frequency of tuberculosis in man as well as in animals, reported by districts, or findings in abattoirs do not, in general, give a correct indication of the spread of the disease among animals. The classification by age should be taken into account. As has been earlier suggested, the frequency of tuberculosis increases with age, but only to a definite point. This establishes an average curve of the frequency of the disease, and by its use the frequency can be calculated in any locality if the age classification of the animals in the particular locality is known.

In regard to the spread of the disease, the dust in the stable plays an important part, as well as the general condition of the stable. The larger the stable and the more animals together, the greater is the percentage of infections. It is indicated that more attention should be paid to construction of buildings for the animals. Small compartments, rather than the housing of many animals in one large compartment, are recommended.

The degree of susceptibility is considered to depend on the general state of the constitution of the animal. Experimental data show that excessive inbreeding weakens the constitution. Acclimatization and too frequent pregnacies are also considered to weaken the constitution and to be predisposing factors to the disease.

A bibliography of 81 references to the literature cited is appended.

Presence of tubercle bacilli in the feces of cattle in dairy herds, R. S. WILLIAMS, W. M. SCOTT, T. ROBERTS, and W. A. HOY (*Vet. News, 14 (1917), Nos. 695, pp. 171–173; 696, pp. 180–184, figs. 2).*—Samples of feces from 179 cows were examined for tubercle bacilli. Eliminating the cases which did not react to the tuberculin test and the tests which failed, virulent tubercle bacilli were found in the feces of 3 of the remaining 158 animals.

The experimental technique used is described and the results of the investigation discussed.

The incidence of bovine infection of tuberculosis in man, CHUNG YIK WANG (*Jour. Path. and Bact., 21 (1917), No. 2, pp. 131–172).*—The author divides the cases of tuberculosis examined by him into the following groups: Cases which showed definite active lesions of tuberculosis in the body on microscopic examination; cases which, while showing no evidence of a definite active tuberculous infection in any part of the body, revealed certain lesions apparently of a tuberculous nature in the form of caseous glands or calcareous deposits in the glands or the lungs; cases in which either no change or only a simple increase in size or softening of one or more glands, unassociated with any evidence of tuberculosis, could be demonstrated; and cases in which the sputum alone was examined.

The cases coming under the third group have been previously reported,[1] as well as those under the fourth group (E. S. R., 37, p. 180).

The 123 strains of tuberculosis bacilli obtained from 88 cases under groups 1 and 2 were investigated bacteriologically and found to conform to either human or bovine types of the bacillus. No atypical strain was demonstrated. When two or more strains were isolated from a single case their cultural characteristics were identified. Out of 68 cases of adults, bovine tubercle bacilli were separated in 7 instances, 1 from 29 sputum cases, 2 from 4 cases of abdominal tuberculosis, 2 from 7 cases of generalized tuberculosis, and 2 from 28 cases in which the only signs of the disease were the calcareous or caseous lesions. Three of the bovine cases gave indication on post-mortem examination that the path of infection was by way of the intestine. In three others the evidence of primary infection was inconclusive, while in the remaining case (sputum case) no post-mortem was performed.

The bacteriological examination of 20 cases in children resulted in the isolation of the bovine type in 11 instances. In 9 of these cases the primary site of infection was found to be in the intestine. In the remaining 2 instances the evidence was inconclusive.

The protocols of the cases of groups 1 and 2 are submitted, together with the bacteriological data, in detailed tabular form.

A bibliography of 26 references to the literature is appended.

Tuberculosis in carnivorous animals, W. R. BLAIR (*Jour. Amer. Vet. Med. Assoc., 51 (1917), No. 6, pp. 750–767*).—This is a general discussion of the prevalence, symptoms, and lesions of the disease, together with a number of case reports of dogs, cats, and other carnivorous animals in captivity.

The author's experience in the use of tuberculin as a diagnostic agent in dogs has been unsatisfactory. Its use on cats is indicated as being uncertain, and dangerous for animals free from the disease.

Tuberculosis in the horse, F. CHAMBERS (*Vet. Jour., 73 (1917), No. 505, pp. 242, 243*).—The author reports four cases of tuberculosis in the horse, the diagnosis of which was made on post-mortem examination. Autopsical data are included.

During the life of the animals tuberculosis was not suspected in any of these cases. It is thus indicated that all cases of general debility which show no improvement in a few weeks should be tested for tuberculosis.

Antituberculosis vaccination, RAPPIN (*Compt. Rend. Acad. Sci. [Paris], 164 (1917), No. 10, pp. 421, 422*).—The preparation of a vaccine which yielded good results is described as follows:

Tubercle bacilli obtained from bouillon cultures of different ages and desiccated for 24 hours are treated with a 2 or 3 per cent solution of sodium fluorid for several days. By this treatment the organisms lose their infective powers but retain their toxic properties. The bacilli are washed with physiological salt solution and then submitted for a longer or shorter period to the action of an antituberculosis serum. This emulsion of the bacilli in the serum constitutes the vaccine.

Effect of tethelin on experimental tuberculosis, H. J. CORPER (*Jour. Infect. Diseases, 21 (1917), No. 3, pp. 269–278*).—The subcutaneous injection of 25-mg. doses of tethelin, isolated by Robertson (E. S. R., 35, p. 8), on alternate days for 18 days into guinea pigs infected with virulent human tubercle bacilli had no appreciable effect on the progress of the disease or the duration of life of

---

[1] Lancet [London], 1916, II, No. 10, pp. 417–419.

the experimental animals. The daily subcutaneous administration of 25-mg. doses of tethelin to guinea pigs sensitized by dead and living human tubercle bacilli had no appreciable effect on the development, recession, or rupture of intracutaneous tubercles produced by dead human tubercle bacilli nor on deep puncture wounds of the skin in the animals used.

Observations on the presence of the Bacillus abortus bovinus in certified milk, E. C. FLEISCHNER and K. F. MEYER (*Amer. Jour. Diseases Children, 14* (*1917*), *No. 3, pp. 157–173*).—This is a report of preliminary studies at San Francisco, Cal., accompanied by a list of references to the literature.

The authors conclude from the examination of a limited amount of material that "*B. abortus* is, for practical purposes, always present in the certified milk produced in the San Francisco Bay regions. Tubercle bacilli are not present in this same milk in sufficient number to give tuberculosis to guinea pigs, although this conclusion may prove incorrect on further experimentation. If the above conclusion is correct, there is no necessity for pasteurizing certified milk on account of any danger that it may possess as a disseminator of bovine tuberculosis to infants.

"It is not unlikely that, in many previous milk tests for tubercle bacilli, the anatomic lesions of bovine abortion disease in the guinea pig were mistaken for tuberculosis. If the *B. abortus* is present in certified milk to the extent evident from these experiments, it is difficult to consider it pathogenic for infants, without, so far as is known, ever having produced recognizable lesions on post-mortem examination. The result of this work, however, is one more definite indication that it is of greatest importance to study the abortus problem from every angle to be absolutely certain of its bearing on the health of infants."

Tick eradication laws and regulations of the State of Arkansas, R. M. Gow (*Arkansas Sta. Bul. 132* (*1917*), *pp. 8*).—The text of the State tick eradication laws and regulations is given, with notes.

A note on the immunity of suckling pigs to hog cholera, R. R. BIRCH (*Cornell Vet., 7* (*1917*), *No. 3, pp. 199, 200*).—The author notes an instance in which two pigs of a hyperimmune sow died from natural exposure to hog cholera at the ages of 31 and 37 days, respectively. Another pig from the same litter died at the age of 27 days, but there was some doubt as to the definite cause of death in this animal. The pigs were all nursed by a hyperimmune mother until they refused food on account of sickness.

It is indicated that "these observations add emphasis to the fact that, although pigs of immune sows are often immune while being sucked, it is not always safe to depend on this immunity."

A serum test influenced by Ascaris infestation, R. R. BIRCH (*Jour. Amer. Vet. Med. Assoc., 51* (*1917*), *No. 5, pp. 694–696*).—The author, who has frequently observed that when exposed to hog cholera pigs infested with ascarids die much more quickly than normal ones, especially if the parasites have entered the gall duct, has found that ascarids are responsible for the differences obtained from serum and virus. He thinks it quite probable that disastrous results would follow simultaneous treatment of pigs badly infested if light doses of serum were administered.

Experiments in filtration of antihog-cholera serum, B. H. EDGINGTON, A. BROERMAN, and E. W. PORTER (*Jour. Infect. Diseases, 21* (*1917*), *No. 3, pp. 258–264*).—In the study reported attempts were made to produce bacteria-free antihog-cholera serum by passage through Berkefeld and Chamberland F filters.

The results obtained indicate that the immune bodies of antihog-cholera serum are restrained by filtration through Chamberland F filters. The Berkefeld filter was found to restrain the immune bodies of the serum as well as the Chamberland filter. "When Berkefeld filtrate was in turn passed through a Chamberland F filter, the resulting residuum was not sufficiently potent in a dose of 20 cc. to protect the test animal against simultaneous inoculation with 2 cc. of hog-cholera virus."

A potent bacteria-free antihog-cholera serum could not be obtained by filtration through either Berkefeld or Chamberland F candles. It is indicated that absorption of the proteins in the blood serum always takes place in the filter pores, so that finally the filtration is actually through a colloid filter. With such a condition, the first portion of the filtrate passing through the candles may have contained immune bodies, while the latter portion may have been free of these products.

The possibility of the production of a potent bacteria-free antihog-cholera serum by filtration of serum obtained through normal clotting or by centrifugalizing defibrinated blood is noted. No experiments to determine this, however, were carried out.

Hog cholera control, R. A. Craig and L. C. Kigin (*Indiana Sta. Circ. 62* (*1917*), *pp. 8, figs. 9*).—A popular summary of information on hog cholera and measures for its control.

The statistics for Indiana show that the death rate in hogs in that State varies from 6.2 to 24.7 per cent per year. The average for a period of six years (1910–1915) was about 13 per cent.

Sanitary measures to prevent hog cholera, R. Graham (*Illinois Sta. Circ. 203* (*1917*), *pp. 3–8*).—A popular summary of information.

Crude oil for hogs, J. M. Evvard (*Iowa Agr., 18* (*1917*), *No. 5, pp. 207, 208*).— The author recommends the use of crude oil for the destruction of lice and nits on hogs, applied by sprinkling over them.

RURAL ENGINEERING.

Construction and use of farm weirs, V. M. Cone (*U. S. Dept. Agr., Farmers' Bul. 813* (*1917*), *pp. 18, figs. 5*).—This is based on work done under a cooperative agreement between the Office of Experiment Stations of the U. S. Department of Agriculture and the Colorado Experiment Station. Its purpose is to give practical directions for the construction and use of the smaller sizes of weirs, such as are suited to the measurement of water on irrigated farms. A technical report on the experimental data involved has been previously noted (E. S. R., 34, p. 881).

A new evaporation formula developed, R. E. Horton (*Engin. News-Rec., 78* (*1917*), *No. 4, pp. 196–199, fig. 1*).—An empirical statement based on physical laws is given which was found to agree with observed facts and is held to be an improvement over existing formulas. The working formula is $E=C$ [Ψ V–v] in which E=evaporation, C=a constant, V=vapor pressure corresponding to liquid surface temperature, and v=atmospheric vapor pressure. A diagram is given showing values of Ψ, the wind factor variation for different wind velocities.

Investigations along the central and lower Volga region.—I, Irrigation in the Novouzensk district.—Basin of the Greater Utzen, N. S. Frolov (*Trudy Organizatsii po Izyskaniiam i Rabotam v Srednem i Nizhnem Povolzh'ĕ. vol. 3, pt. 1, sect. 1, Oroshenie v Novouzenskom Uĕzdĕ. Saratov: Min. Zeml., 1915. pp. IV+230, pls. 16*).—This volume covers the history and economics of irrigation in the Novouzensk district and gives the program and extent of irrigation investigations, special attention being given to so-called silt irrigation.

Irrigation experiments in rice culture, P. van der Elst (*Dept. Landb., Nijv. en Handel [Dutch East Indies], Meded. Proefstat. Rijst., No. 2 (1916), pp. 52, pl. 1, figs. 6*).—This is a description of the methods and purpose of irrigation water measurement and distribution experiments and of drainage of irrigated land experiments with special reference to rice lands.

Irrigation experiments in rice culture, P. van der Elst (*Dept. Landb., Nijv. en Handel [Dutch East Indies], Meded. Proefstat. Rijst., No. 3 (1916), pp. 71, pls. 4*).—The details of irrigation and drainage experiments on rice soils in several districts of Java are described. These included especially work on the measurement and distribution of irrigation water.

Organization, financing, and administration of drainage districts, H. S. Yohe (*U. S. Dept. Agr., Farmers' Bul. 815 (1917), pp. 37*).—This publication is intended to aid landowners, district officials, and others interested in forming drainage districts for the purpose of reclaiming swamp and overflowed lands. "It presents methods of organizing the interested property owners and principles which should be considered in the administration and financing of drainage districts. It is particularly applicable to drainage districts in the humid regions of the United States."

"Before promoting a drainage district consideration should be given to the economic conditions prevailing in the section in question, the agricultural value of the soil, and the demand for more agricultural land on the part of resident landowners. The cost of draining the land as compared with the market prices of other lands possessing equal agricultural value and not needing drainage should be learned. The sentiment of the property owners toward drainage should be ascertained. The success of the project requires the cooperation of more than a bare majority. Unless funds sufficient to construct adequate improvements can be obtained, the undertaking of the project generally would not be warranted. . . .

"Since drainage districts come into being only through the law, it is highly essential that the law be complied with in every detail. The need of retaining a competent attorney is apparent at the very beginning.

"The three principal reasons for forming a drainage district of wet lands which it is desired to reclaim are (1) to provide a method of equitably distributing costs among the landowners and a means of collecting such taxes, (2) to issue bonds to finance the district, (3) to obtain authority to condemn whatever land may be needed for the general use of the district. Each of these factors is vitally important to the promotion of the project. . . .

"The drainage commissioners must insist on employing the best talent they can afford to design and construct the improvements. So-called cheap engineering and construction must be guarded against. Bids for construction which on their face appear a great deal less than others should be scrutinized closely. . . . The importance of employing reputable consulting engineers to pass upon the plans before their final approval and adoption should not be overlooked. In selecting officials to administer districts the landowners should be guided by the same principles that govern the selection of directors for successful commercial and industrial enterprises. . . . In appointing engineers, attorneys, and other assistants, in awarding contracts, and in selling bonds the commissioners should so govern themselves as to win the confidence of the landowners."

Report of the water laboratory, H. E. Barnard (*Ind. Bd. Health, Ann. Rpt. Chem. Div. Lab. Hyg., 10 (1915), pp. 87–94, figs. 4*).—Of 1,520 samples of water from private and public sources in Indiana analyzed during 1915, 63.5 per cent were classed as good, 30.8 per cent as bad, and 5.7 per cent as doubtful. Of the total number examined 1,295 were from private supplies, of which 570 came from deep wells, 555 from shallow wells, 37 from cisterns, and 63 from springs; 785 of the private supplies were potable, 437 were bad, and 73 doubtful.

Of the total number of 690 deep well supplies examined 552 were classed as good, 103 as bad, and 35 of doubtful quality. Of the 569 shallow well samples analyzed but 243 were good, 291 were bad, and 35 were of doubtful quality. Of the 84 springs analyzed 56 were found to be good, 21 bad, and 7 were of doubtful quality. Of the 37 cistern waters examined but 14 were good, 18 were listed as bad, and 5 were of doubtful quality. Nineteen of the 23 pond and lake supplies examined were good and 4 were bad.

Sterilization of water in the field, H. PENAU (*Jour. Pharm. et Chim., 7. ser., 13 (1916), No. 12, pp. 377–385; abs. in Chem. Abs., 10 (1916), No. 19, p. 2487*).— A process is described in which a solution of sodium hypochlorite containing 10 gm. of active chlorin per liter is prepared by double decomposition of calcium hypochlorite with sodium carbonate and potassium permanganate and is added at the rate of 0.5 liter per 1,000 liters of water. After 45 minutes 60 cc. of an aqueous 10 per cent solution of sodium thiosulphate is added. It is found that colon bacilli are destroyed while the odor and taste of the water are not impaired.

Sewage disposal for school buildings in Ohio, R. S. DURRELL and D. E. ADAMS (*Ohio Pub. Health Jour., 7 (1916), No. 8, pp. 326–338, pls. 6*).—"The purpose of this bulletin is to acquaint boards of education, and their architects and engineers, in the general methods of sewage disposal for school buildings not accessible to sanitary sewers, and in the design of the separate features involved. It is not intended to provide standard working drawings for the construction of sewage-treatment plants for these buildings. The accompanying plates illustrate not only the essential details but also the principal features to be observed in preparing plans for submission. These plans illustrate sewage-treatment plants which are applicable for schoolhouse locations under typical Ohio conditions."

The operation of sewage treatment plants for public buildings, D. E. ADAMS (*Ohio Pub. Health Jour., 8 (1917), No. 1, pp. 20–30, figs. 2*).—Instructions as to the proper operation and maintenance of sewage-treatment plants for public and private institutions and schools are given.

The expansion and contraction of concrete and concrete roads, A. T. GOLDBECK and F. H. JACKSON, JR. (*U. S. Dept. Agr. Bul. 532 (1917), pp. 31, pls. 3, figs. 16*).—Laboratory and field tests begun in 1910 on expansion and contraction movements by concrete pavements are reported. These included detailed attention to the spacing, design, and movement of expansion joints.

It was found that neat cement, when allowed to dry, first contracted rapidly, then more slowly. The amount of contraction seemed to vary with the cement, size of specimen, and condition of atmosphere in which drying took place. The amount at 28 days was about 0.1 per cent and at six months about 0.2 per cent.

Mortar contracted on hardening in air and expanded on hardening in water. The contraction in warm, dry air at 28 days was about 0.045 per cent for 1:2 and 1:3 mortar and at six months was 0.078 for 1:3 mortar and 0.085 for 1:2 mortar. The expansion in water was 0.01 per cent for 1:3 and 0.017 for 1:2 mortar at 28 days, and at six months 0.013 for 1:3 and 0.02 per cent for 1:2 mortar.

Both 1:2:4 and 1:3:6 concrete contracted on drying in warm, dry air from 0.02 to 0.04 per cent at 28 days and from 0.04 to 0.07 per cent at six months. When hardening in water an expansion of about 0.01 per cent took place at 28 days and at six months in 1:2:4 and 1:3:6 concrete. The richness of the mix of concrete seemed to exert a small influence on the contraction; the richer the mix the greater was the change in length.

Concrete alternately wetted and dried was made to expand and contract owing to these causes. The expansion due to wetting was more rapid than the contraction on drying. The thoroughly dried specimens of concrete did not recover their original wet length when immersed. Concrete stored in the outer air and exposed to the weather did not contract to the same extent as the above-described specimens, except under very dry conditions. A waterproof covering, such as coal tar, prevented the rapid change in moisture content and greatly retarded the expansion and contraction. Reinforcement decreased but did not prevent the shrinkage and expansion of concrete due to drying, and had no effect on temperature changes.

"Reinforcement can not therefore entirely prevent cracks, but seems to distribute them and keep them small. Concrete roads are affected by both temperature and moisture. When the drainage is good and the sub-base not wet, the temperature effects seem to be most important. A wet sub-base may add to the temperature expansion by about 0.01 to 0.02 per cent. The restraining effect of friction at the base seems to be almost negligible when figuring temperature and moisture expansion and contraction. In very dry climates shrinkage due to drying must be added to contraction due to fall in temperature. A shrinkage of 0.04 per cent (0.25 in. in 50 ft.) is a safe allowance due to drying.

"Temperature at time of construction of road should be considered in designing joints. Cold-weather construction requires a full allowance for temperature expansion, and on wet sub-bases for moisture expansion also. Hot-weather construction theoretically requires no joints at all, even in wet sub-bases, as the temperature contraction exceeds the moisture expansion. However, the difficulty of keeping the cracks clear probably renders joints imperative."

Toughness of bituminous aggregates, C. S. REEVE and R. H. LEWIS (*U. S. Dept. Agr., Jour. Agr. Research, 10 (1917), No. 7, pp. 319–330, pls. 2*).—Tests of the toughness of several representative samples of various types of rock when used as aggregates in bituminous mixtures are reported, it being concluded that the toughness of bituminous aggregates in which a given bituminous material is tested will not be the same for every type of rock.

"Tests of laboratory specimens can be directly correlated with results in service. The difference in behavior of the various rock types can not be directly attributed to any of the routine physical test values of the rock, but appears to be due largely to differences in the surface character of the rock particles. While relatively soft or fluid bitumens may yield satisfactory results in bituminous concrete with some types of rock, their use with other types will lead to failure of the road surface. The impact or toughness test of bituminous aggregates offers possibilities as a means of determining in advance the relative behavior in service of bituminous concretes. While the authors at this time have no definite recommendations to offer with regard to their last conclusion, it may be stated that further experiments will be made with that end in view."

Concrete culverts (*Cement and Engin. News, 29 (1917), No. 4, pp. 109, 110, figs. 4*).—Comparative cost data on cast-iron and reinforced concrete culvert pipe for road use are given, showing in general the economy of the latter type of construction.

Mechanical properties of woods grown in the United States, J. A. NEWLIN and T. R. C. WILSON (*U. S. Dept. Agr. Bul. 556 (1917), pp. 47, pls. 3*).—This bulletin reports the results of about 130,000 tests on the mechanical properties of woods, including data on both green and air-dry timber. A glossary of terms

32950°—18—No. 9——7

used and a list of formulas used in computing are also given, together with a
list of publications and papers dealing with the mechanical properties of timber.

The seasoning of wood, H. S. BETTS (*U. S. Dept. Agr. Bul. 552 (1917), pp.
28, pls. 8, figs. 18*).—This bulletin enumerates the injuries to wood in seasoning,
as checking, casehardening, honey-combing, warping, and collapse, and describes
the processes of air seasoning and kiln-drying. Tabular and graphic data are
given on the average weights and shrinkages of various species of wood and
the rate at which crossties, poles, and sawed timbers of several species lose
moisture when freely exposed to the atmosphere.

Creosoting for estate purposes, W. P. GREENFIELD (*Quart. Jour. Forestry, 11
(1917), No. 2, pp. 94–111*).—The use of creosote as a preservative for farm
and estate structural timber is discussed.

[Farm machinery directory] (*Farm Machinery, No. 1342 (1917), pp. 20–
24*).—This directory lists the specifications for 188 internal-combustion tractors,
129 plows for tractor use, 23 huskers and shredders, and 104 silo fillers.

Public tests of motor cultivation at Avignon, E. ZACHAREWICZ (*Prog. Agr.
et Vit. (Ed. l'Est-Centre), 37 (1916), No. 31. pp. 109–115*).—Tests of six tractors on breaking and deep plowing of loose alluvial soil are reported. The
soil was dry and rather tenacious. The following table gives the results on
breaking:

Tests on soil breaking.

Horsepower.	Depth of plowing.	Width of plowing.	Area plowed.	Duration of test.		Fuel consumption.
	Cm.	Meters.	Sq. meters.	Hr.	Min.	Liters.
12–20	11	1.00	9,630	2	54	26.00
12–24	10	1.15	9,422	2	49	21.50
8–16	10	.90	9,210	3	5	22.30
8–16	12	1.15	9,150	2	6	15.12
10–20	8	1.30	9,650	3	5	17.30
12–25	12	1.60	10,000	2	22	18.40

The following table gives the results on deep plowing:

Tests on deep plowing.

Horsepower.	Depth of plowing.	Width of plowing.	Area plowed.	Duration of test.		Fuel consumption.
	Cm.	Meters.	Sq. meters.	Hr.	Min.	Liters.
12–20	20	1.00	9,518	3	26	30.0
12–24	20	1.15	9,525	0	0	30.0
8–16	20	.90	9,240	4	3	35.0
8–16	20	.65	11,220	4	0	31.9
10–20	20	.70	9,600	4	12	26.4
12–25	21	1.15	10,400	3	47	30.5

Tractor specifications, 1917 (*N. G. E. A. Bul., 2 (1917), No. 10, pp. 24; abs.
in Gas Engine, 19 (1917), No. 6, p. 278*).—Detailed specifications for 95 different
tractors are given.

Note on fencing construction, T. GILBERT (*Dept. Agr. Bombay Bul. 81
(1916), pp. 3, pls. 8*).—This bulletin describes briefly a few practical points to
be observed when erecting wire fences with wooden posts, with special reference
to conditions in India.

Dairy and general-purpose barns, F. M. WHITE (*Nat. Lumber Manfrs. Assoc.,
Trade Ext. Dept. Farm Bul. 7 (1917), pp. 40, figs. 31*).—This bulletin deals with
site and location, general shapes, light, ventilation, stalls, floors, and feed alleys

of dairy and general-purpose barns and gives details of construction. Diagrammatic illustrations of six types of barns are included.

Barns for work animals, B. YOUNGBLOOD (*Texas Sta. Bul. 210 (1917), pp. 3-23, figs. 18*).—It is stated that "satisfactory barns, large enough only for the work stock and a year's supply of feeding stuff, can be constructed in Texas at a cost of from $25 to $50 per animal. If as much as from $100 to $300 per animal is put into the barn, a proportionate amount of extra storage space for additional hay, grain, seeds, and so forth, may be had at less additional cost than would be the case if a separate storage building were constructed."

Suggestive plans are given which demonstrate principles applicable to Texas conditions. These are to be modified to meet local conditions. "The plans given begin with the cheapest possible, and end with a moderate-priced structure. The chief difference is in the size, convenience in feeding, and the amount of extra storage space supplied. No general-purpose barn plans are given, for the reason that it is better under southern conditions to have special-purpose buildings, separate and apart."

Bills of material and lumber necessary for the construction of various sized barns for work animals are also included.

Measuring silage and capacity of silos, L. W. CHASE (*Nebraska Sta. Circ. 1 (1917), pp. 14, figs. 5*).—As the result of silage weighing experiments a new table of weights of silage is proposed for determining the capacities of silos, the rule for which assumes that silage settles 10 per cent after filling ceases. A comparison of the new weights with those established by King at the Wisconsin Station shows that the new weights are from 11.5 to 13 per cent less than the Wisconsin weights. The new table of weights was found to be very nearly correct on the basis of actual weighing, being if anything a fraction too large.

The proposed weights are given in the following table:

Weight of silage per cubic foot.

Depth of silage.	Weight per cubic foot.	Depth of silage.	Weight per cubic foot.	Depth of silage.	Weight per cubic foot.	Depth of silage.	Weight per cubic foot.
Feet.	*Lbs.*	*Feet.*	*Lbs.*	*Feet.*	*Lbs.*	*Feet.*	*Lbs.*
1	16.13	14	25.24	27	32.91	39	38.48
2	16.89	15	25.88	28	33.43	40	38.88
3	17.64	16	26.52	29	33.94	41	39.27
4	18.38	17	27.15	30	34.44	42	39.65
5	19.12	18	27.77	31	34.93	43	40.02
6	19.83	19	28.38	32	35.41	44	40.39
7	20.54	20	28.99	33	35.88	45	40.75
8	21.24	21	29.58	34	36.34	46	41.11
9	21.93	22	30.16	35	36.79	47	41.46
10	22.61	23	30.73	36	37.23	48	41.81
11	23.28	24	31.29	37	37.65	49	42.16
12	23.94	25	31.84	38	38.07	50	42.50
13	24.59	26	32.38				

Tables are also given showing the relative capacities of silos and estimated tonnage of silage by volume, together with information regarding the determination of silo capacities. The experimental results on which the tables are based are included.

Poultry houses and poultry equipment for Texas, R. N. HARVEY, J. C. OLSEN, F. W. KAZMEIER, and T. J. CONWAY (*Texas Sta. Bul. 207 (1917), pp. 23, figs. 17*).—Plans of poultry houses and equipment are given and discussed, which, it is stated, with modifications of structure to fulfill needs imposed by climatic conditions may be used satisfactorily in almost any locality.

RURAL ECONOMICS.

The farmers' handbook, compiled by P. G. GILDER (*Sydney, N. S. Wales: Dept. Agr., 1916, 2. ed., pp. VI+886, pls. 5, figs. 443*).—This handbook is written for the use of practical farmers as well as a textbook for agricultural colleges, and high schools in New South Wales, and covers the entire field of agriculture with the exception of live stock, which subject is to be treated in a separate volume. The text is profusely illustrated.

The Federal Office of Markets and Rural Organization, J. C. GILBERT (*Agr. of Mass., 1916, pp. 109–121*).—The author describes the various activities of the Office of Markets and Rural Organization of the U. S. Department of Agriculture, as well as the marketing activities carried on through State bureaus and colleges of agriculture.

Functions of a State bureau of markets, A. E. CANCE (*Agr. of Mass., 1916, pp. 122–134*).—The author discusses the field to be covered by the State bureau, as well as the State agricultural colleges, and calls attention to conditions in the various States.

Cooperative purchasing and marketing organizations among farmers in the United States, O. B. JESNESS and W. H. KERR (*U. S. Dept. Agr. Bul. 547 (1917), pp. 82, pls. 15*).—The authors discuss the early history and growth of cooperative organization, different types of organizations and their characteristics, cooperation in representative States, representative types of cooperative organizations, and agencies which assist farmers in organizing. Statistical data are given showing the number of farm organizations, volume of business, and membership. There is also a brief digest of State cooperative laws and the text of a portion of the Clayton Amendment to the United States antitrust laws. A selected list of publications on cooperative purchasing and marketing is appended.

The county farm bureau, B. H. CROCHEBON (*California Sta. Circ. 166 (1917), pp. 16, figs. 12*).—The author points out the functions of the farm bureau, general plans of organization, methods of handling demonstrations, etc. He also includes a model constitution and by-laws.

List of county and local agricultural societies, L. H. WIBLE (*Penn. Dept. Agr. Bul. 296 (1917), pp. 9*).—This bulletin contains a list of local agricultural and horticultural societies, with dates of fairs to be held in Pennsylvania in 1917, information regarding attendance in 1916, receipts, premiums, etc.

Cooperative credit for the United States, H. W. WOLFF (*New York: Sturgis & Walton Co., 1917, pp. V+349*).—The author has endeavored to describe the cooperative credit organizations existing in the various European countries, with reference to their adaptability to conditions in the United States.

A survey of insurance of damage by fire to crops and forests, E. VIDIÈRE (*Précis D'expertises Aprés Incendies des Récoltes et des Bois. Paris: Libr. Agr. Maison Rustique, [1916], pp. VII+484, pl. 5, figs. 18*).—This report discusses, for France, the extent of the damage and methods of measuring the loss or destruction by fire of various types of crops, live stock, and forests.

The Torrens system of land title registration, F. B. BOMBERGER (*Md. Agr. Col. Bul., 14 (1917), No. 2, pp. 8*).—This contains a brief review of the history of the Torrens system and of its principal provisions.

[Italian rules governing agriculture], D. F. WILBER (*U. S. Dept. Com., Com. Rpts., No. 181 (1917), pp. 460–463*).—These pages contain parts of the decrees relating to agrarian contracts, the general use of agricultural machines, and the selection of agricultural committees and arbitrating committees for judicial districts.

Rural index, H. L. Hollister (*Chicago: Author, 1917 ed., pp.* [*23*], *pl. 1, figs. 3*).—This volume outlines a system for numbering rural homes so that they may be located as readily as city homes are by their street number.

Pounds to bushels tables, E. D. Davis (*Minneapolis, Minn.: Author, 1916, pp. 40*).—Tables are given for reducing pounds to bushels for oats, barley, buckwheat, shelled corn, ear corn, rye, flax seed, wheat, peas, beans, clover seed, and potatoes. Instructions are also given for determining the value of a load of grain, measuring the contents of bins, etc., measuring ear corn in a crib, measuring coal in a shed, computing freight rates per bushel from freight rates per hundred, estimating the value of mixed feeds, and loading cars by measurement.

Marketing grain at country points, G. Livingston and K. B. Seeds (*U. S. Dept. Agr. Bul. 558 (1917), pp. 44, figs. 4*).—Among the conclusions brought out by the authors are the following:

" Price and other factors being equal, farmers should patronize houses remaining open throughout the entire year.

" The producer of high-quality grain often receives less than it is worth in order.that an equal price may be paid to a grower of grain of inferior quality. The farmer who delivers clean, dry, sound grain should receive a premium over the price paid to his more careless competitor. Farmers who deliver grain of inferior quality should be willing to submit to a discount. . . . It is likely that the standardization of grain produced in a community would not only result in a reputation for uniform quality which at times may command a premium over general market prices, but also reduce the cost of handling grain through the local elevator.

" While the ' scoop-shoveler ' is usually a disturbing element, often causing loss to farmers and others having business relations with him, it is undoubtedly true that he frequently acts as a restraining influence upon the country dealer.

" Contracts with farmers for future delivery of grain should be entered into only after the interests of both parties concerned are safeguarded by a written contract clearly and concisely setting forth all the details of agreement. . . .

" When many elevators serve a community bad practices are usually introduced into the business, which increase the cost of marketing the farmer's grain and depreciate the value of all houses in the town and surrounding territory. Cooperative associations, as well as independent dealers, who desire to enter the business should purchase existing plants if this is practicable rather than build new ones.

" Losses from shrinkage and overgrading are usually ignored by country elevators. Managers should maintain a system of bookkeeping which shows accurately these as well as all other expenses, and a study of the results obtained should enable them to conduct their business in an economic and profitable manner. . . .

" When the organization of a cooperative-elevator association is contemplated, careful consideration should be given to the needs of the community for additional marketing facilities. Usually it is unwise to place too much confidence in the statements made by outsiders regarding the profits to be derived and the cost of operating a country elevator. Farmers should investigate fully the business circumstances which are to surround the new enterprise before affiliating themselves with the proposed cooperative-elevator association."

Farm labor [conditions in Canada] (*Agr. Gaz. Canada, 4 (1917), No. 5, pp. 387–393*).—These pages contain a series of articles indicating the plans adopted in a number of Provinces for the purpose of securing farm help necessary at the various seasons of production.

Labor conditions among the forest workers in Sweden, G. Huss (*Sveriges Off. Statis., K. Soc. Styr., 1916, pp. 399, figs. 66*).—This is a review of the social and labor conditions, wages, and hours of lumbermen and others employed in the forests of the Värmland, Dalarna, and Norrland regions of Sweden.

Notes on methods and costs, California crop production, R. L. ADAMS (*Berkeley, Cal.: Univ. Cal., [1917], pp. [7]+140*).—This volume contains data showing the requirements and methods of growing and cost of production of the various crops in that State. The statements are based upon the present practice of commercial producers, and are not designed to indicate what should be done but rather what is being done by men specializing in these crops. It also contains data concerning work capacity of farm machines, rules for determining work of implements, a day's work per man, a day's work per crew, annual amount of work required to care for live stock, costs of building materials, costs of fencing, costs of farm implements, costs of miscellaneous equipment, and annual rate of depreciation of farm machinery.

Meeting the food crisis, A. M. SOULE (*Atlanta, Ga.: South. Bell Telephone & Telegraph Co., 1917, pp. 19*).—In this speech the author discusses the deficit in food crop in Georgia, and the increase necessary to enable the State to feed itself. He also points out methods that may be used to obtain the necessary increase.

The food supply in New England, E. F. MCSWEENEY (*Boston, Mass.: New England Federation for Rural Prog., 1917, pp. 14*).—The author discusses the changes in the system of farming in New England, its effect upon the food supply, and some methods that may be adopted to improve it.

The food supply of the United Kingdom (*London: Bd. Trade, 1917, pp. 35*).—This report, drawn up by a committee of the Royal Society of London, discusses the food supply in the period of 1909-1913, the proportion of home produce and imported products used, the quantities of various classes of food used during 1916, the ration for the civil and military population, and possible methods of economizing the available food supply. The suggestions given include a better recovery of flour in milling, increase of economy in meat production, increase in the protein available for human consumption by increasing the manufacture of cheese at the expense of butter making, use as food of materials at present employed in brewing and distilling, and the diverting of food now used as feed for stock to use for human food.

Production of food in Scotland, E. WASON ET AL. (*Scot. Dept. Com. on Food Prod. Rpt., 2 (1916), pp. 6*).—This report discusses the land available for increased food production, methods of increasing labor supply, manures, and implements.

[Increasing agricultural production in France], H. HITIER (*Bul. Soc. Encour. Indus. Nat. [Paris], 116 (1917), I, No. 3, pp. 582-594*).—This article outlines the extent of the agricultural production in France, compares it with conditions in other countries, suggests methods of making agriculture more intensive, and gives recommendations adopted by the National Association of Economic Expansion with reference to the expansion of production.

The wheat question, PERCHOT (*Vie Agr. et Rurale, 7 (1917), No. 25, pp. 433-440*).—The author points out the available home supply of wheat and the possibilities of increasing it, the influence of Government intervention through price fixing and the guaranteeing of price, and the influence of price on production.

Food crisis in Portugal (*Bol. Assoc. Cent. Agr. Portuguesa, 19 (1917), No. 7, pp. 217-224*).—These pages outline methods that may be used to increase the production of cereals, sugar, cotton and other fibers, oil seeds, horticultural products, and live stock.

[Agricultural development in Navarra], D. NAGORE Y NAGORE (*Servicio de Agricultura y Ganadería. Pamplona, Spain: Prov. Printer, 1917, pp. 43*).—In this report are discussed the various types of agricultural organizations found, types of agricultural machines used and difficulties encountered in introducing new machines, natural products in Navarra, agricultural practices in different communities, and kinds of live stock and extent of live stock production.

Some observation on agricultural work in Egypt, Britain, America, and Japan, W. ROBERTS (*Lahore, India: Govt., 1917, pp. 12+XVIII*).—This report deals with the methods of growing cotton in the countries named, and schools and educational methods used for teaching the best practices.

Monthly crop report (*U. S. Dept. Agr., Mo. Crop Rpt.. 3 (1917), No. 8, pp. 69-80, fig. 1*).—This number contains the usual data relating to crop conditions, estimated farm value, average prices received by producers, and range of prices of agricultural products at important markets. It also includes special reports on the monthly marketings of wheat by farmers, production of sugar in the Philippine Islands, the acreage of beans by varieties, acreage of corn, peas, tomatoes, and snap beans contracted for by canners, and crop conditions in Florida and California, as well as on silos in the United States, fertilizers used on cotton, index numbers of food supplies in various countries, manufacture of vegetable oils for edible purposes, percentage and index number of foodstuffs in the export and import trade of the United States, data showing when farmers sell their crops, etc.

[Agricultural statistics of Indiana] (*Bien. Rpt. Bur. Statis. Ind., 16 (1915–16), pp. 444-446, 543-547, and 564-662*).—These pages contain data relating to the rural population, the increase of farm land, the assessed value of farm land, climatology, crops, and live stock. These data are based upon reports obtained by the township assessors.

Agricultural statistics for Wisconsin, 1915 and 1916 (*Wis. Dept. Agr. Bul. 11 (1917), pp. 145-192*).—This report contains statistical data, showing for 1916, by counties, the acreage, production, yield per acre, and area of the principal crops; number and value of live stock; number of silos; and average farm prices of important farm products on December 1, 1916.

Annual statistical report of the New York Produce Exchange for the year 1916 (*Ann. Statis. Rpt. N. Y. Produce Ex., 1916, pp. 139*).—This volume contains data relating to the receipts and exports of agricultural products from New York City, together with daily prices, freight rates, and the production of crops of the United States and in foreign countries for 1916, with comparative data for earlier years.

[Agriculture in Norway] (*Statis. Aarbok Konger. Norge, 36 (1916), pp. 24-35*).—These pages supplement data previously noted (E. S. R., 37, p. 93), by additional statistics for the year 1916.

Returns of produce of crops in Scotland (*Agr. Statis. Scotland, 4 (1915), pt. 2, pp. 59-79*).—These pages continue data previously noted (E. S. R., 33, p. 894) by adding statistics for a later year.

[Agricultural statistics of British India for the year 1915-16], G. F. SHIRRAS (*Agr. Statis. Brit. India, 1915-16, pp. 11*).—This report contains data by Provinces, showing the area cultivated and uncultivated in 1916 with comparative data for earlier years, area under irrigation, area under different crops, number of live stock, plows and carts, number of transfers of property and area transferred, together with area assessed, and incidents of land revenue settlement.

Live stock statistics (*Internat. Inst. Agr. Rome, Internat. Crop Rpt. and Agr. Statis., 8 (1917), No. 5, pp. 390-392*).—Data are shown indicating the number of the various classes of live stock in France on December 31, 1916, July 1, 1916, November 1, 1915, and December 1, 1915, together with similar data for Cuba for the second half year of 1915 and of 1916.

AGRICULTURAL EDUCATION.

Agricultural education and research (*Rpt. Bd. Agr. Scot., 5 (1916), pp. XII–XVIII*).—An account is given of the progress made in 1916 in the agri-, cultural education and research work under the control of the Board of Agriculture of Scotland.

Annual report of the director of the elementary agricultural education division, New Brunswick, 1916, R. P. STEEVES (*Dept. Agr. New Brunswick, Ann. Rpt. Dir. Elem. Agr. Ed. Div., 1916, pp. 26, pls. 2, figs. 2*).—This is a re-report on the progress made during the year in instruction in nature study and elementary agriculture, and the training of teachers in these subjects, including some of the difficulties encountered in the work.

During the year, 78 schools received grants for instruction in nature study and elementary agriculture with school gardening, an increase of 23 over the previous year. The number of school children receiving regular instruction in these subjects increased over 1,000, and the number of home plats, varying from ¼ acre to a few square feet each, from 378 to 727. The publication of a rural education monthly for the schools was begun to call attention to rural problems, to deepen interest in country life, etc.

[Agricultural instruction in Ontario, 1916], W. H. HEARST (*Rpt. Min. Agr. Ontario, 1916, pp. 5–20, 28–34, 46–77, figs. 25*).—This report contains information for 1916 similar to that given for 1914 (E. S. R., 34, p. 597). The number of school fairs held increased from 234 in 1915 to 275 in 1916, the number of children taking part from 48,386 to 60,262, and the number of home plats from 51,243 to 55,947. Among new features introduced in this work are interschool live-stock judging competitions and weed naming and driving contests. Public speaking contests are now recognized as an important feature of a school fair.

Ultuna agricultural institute and farm, 1916 (*Upsala, Sweden: Ultuna Landtbr. Inst., 1916, pp. 32, pl. 1, figs. 12*).—A report on the history, development, and present organization of the instruction and experimental work of this institution.

Agricultural education in Bulgaria, D. I. MURPHY (*U. S. Dept. Com., Com. Rpts., No. 110 (1917), pp. 554, 555*).—A brief statement is given concerning the course of study, cost, and entrance requirements of the agricultural schools at Roustchouk, Sadovo, Pleven, and Orhanie, the latter for girls, and of eight agricultural schools of lower grade.

[Rural education] (*Education. 37 (1917), No. 9, pp. 541–589*).—The principal addresses given at the Fifth Annual Conference on Rural Education held at Worcester, Mass., in March, 1917, are presented as follows: The New Conception of the Rural School Problem, by William B. Aspinwall; A Rational Program for Rural Education, by Payson Smith; How the Curriculum May Better Meet Present Day Social Needs, by William D. Hurd; Vitalizing School Studies—the Situation in One Massachusetts Town, by Mrs. Ella M. Clark; Vitalizing a Rural School Course, by Allen S. Woodward; The Revitalized Course of Study, by J. C. Muerman; Vitalizing Rural School Work in Massachusetts, by Grace C. Smith; An Example of a "Vitalized" School, by M. Harriet Bishop; and First Aid to the Citizen Makers, by Joseph D. Eggleston.

The school inspector and rural science, E. ROBINSON ET AL. (*Agr. Gaz. Canada, 4 (1917), Nos. 6, pp. 499–507; 7, pp. 608–610*).—This is a series of brief articles by school inspectors in Nova Scotia, Ontario, and Saskatchewan on what the school inspector can do to promote rural science instruction in the schools.

The agricultural subjects, W. A. BROYLES (*Quart. Jour. Univ. N. Dak., 6* (*1916*), *No. 2, pp. 138–144*).—The author discusses the wide range of the field of agricultural subjects, their cultural value, and elements of live educative processes in and out of school.

"Snap courses" in college: Agriculture v. engineering, F. H. BLODGETT (*School and Soc., 6* (*1917*), *No. 135, pp. 91–96*).—The author presents an analysis of the two fields of agriculture and engineering in an effort to discover why the biological sciences are so often regarded as "snap courses" in the average college. In his opinion, "It seems probable that the disrespect so often felt by students, either for the courses in the biological sciences themselves, or for the students who select such courses, will be largely diminished if there can be developed a more definite goal toward which the whole body of teaching and experiment may converge, each step being coordinated with each other step, and each essential to the whole. It should be the aim of agricultural science (or of biological science, of which agriculture is the field of application), to discover the sequence of details which together are necessary to build a foundation for the growth of the subject for its development into a branch of knowledge coordinate with the older topics."

Outline of experiments for departments of agriculture in the public schools of Louisiana, P. L. GUILBEAU and T. H. HARRIS (*Baton Rouge, La.: Dept. Ed., pp. 43, fig. 1*).—The author outlines exercises and experiments in agriculture to be used in connection with the various texts studied in grades 8, 9, and 11 of the public schools of Louisiana.

Dairy education, R. A. PEARSON (*Lincoln, Nebr.: Univ. Nebr., 1917, pp. 12*).— In this address, delivered at the dedication of Dairy Industry Hall at the University of Nebraska on January 17, 1917, the author discusses the growth of the dairy industry, the development of dairy cattle, improvements in methods of dairying, the recognition by the American people of the importance of making ample provision for instruction in the fundamental and vital industries of this country, the dignity of agricultural education, and future problems in dairying.

The present position and future developments of dairy education.—Science, J. MACKINTOSH (*Jour. Brit. Dairy Farmers' Assoc., 31* (*1917*), *pp. 92–107, fig. 1*).—The author gives a concise account of the system of dairy education which has been developed in Great Britain. This comprises instruction (1) provided by counties in the form of itinerant instruction and instruction at a fixed institution, either a county farm school or an agricultural college, or both, and (2) at provincial institutions. The most necessary lines of future development are also indicated.

The present position and future developments of dairy education.—Practice, P. MCCONNELL (*Jour. Brit. Dairy Farmers' Assoc., 31* (*1917*), *pp. 85–91*).— This is a review of progress made in practical dairy instruction in Great Britain, with special reference to feeding, records, selection, sanitation, and inspection. In the author's opinion "the best equipped dairy farmer—apart from questions of capital—is one who has spent some time in his youth on a dairy farm, taking his share of the work . . . and who then, equipped with practical knowledge, attends the usual courses at a dairy school."

The part which women might play, MARGARET SHANKS (*Jour. Brit. Dairy Farmers' Assoc., 31* (*1917*), *pp. 108–118*).—This is a review of what women have done in dairy production in the past and the lines upon which they have been advancing in recent years, and a consideration of what additional or special help they could give in the effort to increase the dairy production of Britain. The latter, the author concludes, "is a question first of education: Grades of education to suit the different classes of women who engage in dairying and, above all, an education that will come right into the farmhouse and influence the minds of the wives and daughters there. . . . And, added to that, let them have equal and honorable place beside men in all associations that concern the welfare of the industry in which they both labor with head and hands."

Productive dairying, R. M. WASHBURN (*Philadelphia and London: J. B. Lippincott Co., 1917, pp. XII+432, pls. 2, figs. 129*).—The object of this book is to furnish a foundation and guide for good practice in dairying. It is written for use in high schools, schools and colleges of agriculture, general courses, rural consolidated schools, and farmers. Its seven parts deal respectively with the why of dairying, the dairy breeds, care and management of dairy cows, winter feeding, clean milk production, farm dairying, and market milk. Tables showing the composition of feeding stuffs and data as to fat estimation are appended.

A first-year course in home economics for southern agricultural schools, LOUISE STANLEY (*U. S. Dept. Agr. Bul. 540 (1917), pp. 58, figs. 2*).—This bulletin outlines a first-year course in home economics, consisting of 160 lessons in cooking and sewing with related hygiene and sanitation, for southern agricultural schools. It emphasizes the connection between such instruction and actual home experience, discusses methods of teaching, and offers suggestions for correlating the work with other school subjects. A list of publications of this Department of interest in connection with this bulletin is appended.

The story of foods, F. CRISSEY (*New York and Chicago: Rand McNally & Co., 1917, pp. 501, figs. 271*).—This book gives a comprehensive world view of foods and their geographical and industrial background. It deals especially with the human agencies concerned in the production, preparation, and distribution of foods, including the work of the wholesaler and retailer. The foods dealt with are the grains, fruits, vegetables, dairy products, honey, poultry, meat, fish, canned and condensed foods, dried fruits, coffee, tea, and other drinks, nuts, sugar, spices, salt, and table delicacies.

Elements of the theory and practice of cookery, MARY E. WILLIAMS and KATHARINE R. FISHER (*New York: The Macmillan Co., 1916. 2. ed., rev. and enl., pp. XIII+405, pls. 16, figs. 30*).—This is the second edition, revised and enlarged, of a text in domestic science which may be used for individual or group instruction, and the subject matter of which can be covered in four terms or two school years by pupils in the sixth and seventh, or seventh and eighth grades of school, one two-hour lesson being given each week. The book deals with the following topics, taken up in an order that experience has shown to be natural and convenient: Homes and home-making; some starchy plants; tissue-building foods; bread; food in its relation to life; meat, fish, and poultry; fuel foods; fruits and vegetables; sugar and sweets; the preservation of food; special diets; tea, coffee, cocoa; the serving of food; laundering; and digestion. Principles are taught in connection with their application, followed by a classification of foods, their chief constituents, economic and food values, etc. Bibliographies are added.

Wool: The raw materials of the woolen and worsted industries, S. H. HART, edited by E. W. FRANCE (*Philadelphia: The Philadelphia Textile School, 1917, pp. XX+228, pl. 1, figs. 91*).—This book has been prepared for use as a text in connection with the course in the raw materials of the wool industries at The Philadelphia Textile School. It makes an effort to follow the various raw materials of the woolen and worsted industry from their origin to the point where actual machine processing begins, and comprises the following chapters: Structure, properties, and characteristics of wool; classes of fleece wool, including brief descriptions of important long and medium-wool breeds of sheep; grading and sorting; shrinkage; shearing, preparing, and marketing wool; pulled wools; mohair and other textile hair fibers; wool substitutes and waste products; fabric requirements; and historical synopsis. Statistics of wool production and importation in the United States, distribution of sheep, score cards for sheep, and other useful data are appended.

[Conference of the Alabama Home Economics Association] (*Ala. Girls Tech. Inst. Bul., n. ser., No. 38 (1916), pp. 37*).—This bulletin contains the following addresses given at the second annual conference of the Alabama Home Economics Association held at the Alabama Girls' Technical Institute, Montevallo, January 27–29, 1916: Home Economics in the New and Socialized Curriculum, by Z. Judd; Vocational Phases of Household Arts Education, and Survey of Household Economics in the High School, by Mary S. Woolman; and Club Work for Women and Girls; and a round table discussion of What Has Been Done in Home Economics in Alabama during 1915, including an outline of a suggested four-year course in home economics in the high schools of Alabama.

Report of the supervisor of women's institutes, Hazel E. Winter (*Rpt. Agr. New Brunswick, 1916, pp. 51–55*).—This is a report on the growth, patriotic work, short courses, and the fourth annual convention of the women's institutes of the Province of New Brunswick.

MISCELLANEOUS.

Monthly Bulletin of the Ohio Agricultural Experiment Station (*Mo. Bul. Ohio Sta., 2 (1917), Nos. 7, pp. 211–247, figs. 21; 8, pp. 249–281, figs. 14*).—These numbers contain, in addition to several articles abstracted elsewhere in this issue and miscellaneous notes, the following:

No. 7.—Buckwheat Culture.—A Bread-making Grain Commanding Unusual Attention this Year, by C. G. Williams; Wheat-flour substitutes.—Rolled Oats, Corn Meal, and Buckwheat Flour Provide Cheaper Food, by Mabel K. Corbould; Diseases of Wheat.—Methods of Control Possible by Seed Treatment, by A. D. Selby; Grain-bin Sanitation.—Insect Injuries to Stored Cereals Prevented by Cleaning Bins, by W. H. Goodwin; Silage for Fattening Cattle.—Economy in Winter Feeding Results, Experiment Proves, by B. E. Carmichael; Thinning Fruit.—Greater Yields of High Quality Result from Removing Part of Crop, by W. J. Green; and Insect Pests of Vegetables.—Methods of Control Suggested for the More Troublesome Kinds, by J. S. Houser.

No. 8.—Harvesting Soy Beans.—Special Care Needed in Cutting and Curing the Crop, by C. G. Williams, an extract from Bulletin 312 (E. S. R., 37, p. 235); Late Blight of Potatoes.—Weather Conditions May Necessitate Continued, Thorough Spraying, by D. C. Babcock; and Fuel and the Woodlot.—Marketing Wood Provides Winter Labor and Improves Timber Areas, by E. Secrest.

Monthly bulletin of the Western Washington Substation (*Washington Sta., West Wash. Sta., Mo. Bul., 5 (1917), No. 5, pp. 62–76, figs. 4*).—This number contains brief articles on the following subjects: Use of Soiling Crops, by H. L. Blanchard; Eradication of Rootstock Weeds, by E. B. Stookey; A Commercial Poultry Plant, by G. R. Shoup; Agricultural Fair Exhibits; Mountain Beavers; and Farmers' Excursions.

NOTES.

Connecticut College and Stations.—The legislature has authorized the trustees of the college to establish at least two scholarships from each county, and appropriated $4,000 for the purpose for the period ending September 30, 1919. The legislature also provided for State aid to one corporation or association organized in each county for the purpose of providing instruction and practical demonstration in agriculture and home economics, promoting advanced business methods among farmers, or assisting in any manner in the development of agriculture and the improvement of country life. Each organization may obtain annually from the State an amount equal to the sum received by it otherwise than under the provisions of the Federal Agricultural Extension Act, but not less than $1,000.

The chemical laboratory, occupied by the college and Storrs Station, was totally destroyed by fire, November 26, 1917. The apparatus and chemical laboratory of the station were destroyed, together with a large part of the samples of experimental crops which were awaiting analysis. The chemical work of the station is for the present being carried on at the State Station at New Haven.

John P. Street, chemist in charge of the analytical laboratory at the State station, has been granted leave of absence to become captain in the Sanitary Corps of the National Army. His duties are expected to deal largely with problems regarding the food supply at the cantonments. Waldo L. Adams, chemist, resigned December 1 to accept a commercial position.

Purdue University and Station.—A tract of 385 acres of virgin forest land in Randolph County has been given the university by the late Mrs. Henry Davis. Under the terms of the will the property is to be maintained as the Henry Davis Forestry Farm. The forest must be preserved and no commercial cuttings made, the tract used as a refuge for song birds, and experiments undertaken for the acclimatization of useful plants.

H. J. Reed, associate horticulturist, has been appointed assistant to the director. George N. Hoffer, assistant professor of botany in the school of science, has been transferred to the station as associate in botany, his college work being assumed by Eben H. Toole of the Kansas College. R. B. Easson, assistant in the poultry extension department, has resigned to enter a reserve officers' training camp, and H. C. Mills, associate in dairy manufactures, has resigned to engage in commercial work.

Kentucky University and Station.—Thomas P. Cooper, director of station and extension work in North Dakota, has been appointed dean of the college of agriculture and director of the station beginning January 1, 1918. R. H. Wilkins and L. B. Mann, of the animal husbandry department, have resigned. Recent appointments include J. R. Humphrey of the U. S. Department of Agriculture as head of the department of markets, and J. H. Martin, T. G. Yaxis, and H. C. Rhodes as assistants in animal husbandry.

Minnesota University and Station.—Dr. E. Dana Durand has resigned as chief of the division of research in agricultural economics to devote his entire attention to work in the college of science, literature, and arts. George B.

896

Holm, research assistant in agricultural biochemistry, has been commissioned first lieutenant in the Sanitary Corps of the Army Medical Department, and is expected to be assigned to investigations in the Gas Defense Service. G. R. McDole, assistant in soils, has enlisted in the Sanitary Corps for duty in the Gas and Flame Service.

F. L. Washburn has been transferred from professor of entomology in the college of agriculture, entomologist in the station, and State entomologist, to become professor of economic vertebrate zoolgy beginning February 6. Dr. C. C. Palmer, professor of physiology in the division of veterinary medicine, has accepted an appointment as professor of bacteriology, physiology, and hygiene at the Delaware College. Shinjiro Sato, assistant in agricultural biochemistry, has resigned to return to Japan.

Recent appointments include G. E. Weaver as assistant professor of dairy husbandry and assistant dairy husbandman, H. R. Searles as instructor in dairy production, and Paul L. Miller as superintendent of the Morris school of agriculture and substation, vice E. C. Higbie resigned.

Missouri University and Station.—M. F. Miller has been appointed assistant dean and director beginning November 1, 1917. Other appointments include Dr. O. S. Crisler as superintendent of the serum production work in the department of veterinary science, W. L. Nelson as assistant in the agricultural extension service, Frank L. Wright as assistant in boys' and girls' club work, L. L. Alexander as instructor in farm crops, Dr. C. H. Hays as extension assistant professor of veterinary science in charge of hog cholera extension work, Bliss F. Dana, M. H. Fohrman, and Turner H. Hopper as assistants in horticulture, dairy husbandry, and agricultural chemistry, respectively, Clifton R. Thomson, S. R. Miles, and I. F. Nuckols as assistants in animal husbandry, and E. H. Hughes as assistant to the dean and director and superintendent of short courses. R. R. Hudelson, assistant professor of soils, has been commissioned first lieutenant in artillery, E. M. McDonald, assistant professor in farm crops, as second lieutenant in infantry, and O. R. Johnson, professor of farm management, and F. C. Fenton, extension assistant in agricultural engineering, as second lieutenants in artillery. V. F. Payne, instructor in agricultural chemistry, resigned October 5.

Nebraska University and Station.—The corner stone of the new agricultural engineering building has been laid and it is expected that the building will be ready for occupancy next fall. Reinforced concrete construction has been substituted for steel in the new plans. Plans are also being drawn for a veterinary building, which it is hoped to erect in the spring.

H. B. Pier, assistant professor in animal husbandry, has resigned. H. W. Thurston, jr., has been appointed associate professor of plant pathology, vice G. K. K. Link on leave of absence from November 1, 1917, to take up special work with the U. S. Department of Agriculture. F. E. Mussehl, of the Wisconsin University and Station, has been appointed professor of poultry husbandry, vice M. E. Dickson resigned, effective October 20. R. P. Crawford has succeeded Floyd Wambeam, resigned, as agricultural editor. William B. Nevens, assistant dairy husbandman of the Illinois Station, has been appointed assistant professor of dairy husbandry. Miss Alice Loomis and Mrs. Emma R. Davisson have been granted leave of absence for the academic year, the former to take up work with the U. S. Bureau of Education and the latter to engage in extension work for the States Relations Service.

Nevada Station.—James B. McNair has resigned as assistant chemist, effective January 1, 1918. J. B. Menardi, assistant agronomist, has enlisted in the U. S. Navy.

Cornell University.—The college of agriculture has been assigned by the State Vocational Education Board the task of training teachers of agriculture and directors and supervisors of agricultural subjects. The training of teachers of home economics is to be divided between the college, the State Teachers' College at Albany, and the State Normal School at Buffalo. It is expected that eventually about $75,000 of the Federal funds will be available to the college annually, and that considerable graduate work will be developed by the department of rural education.

D. B. Carrick has resigned as instructor in pomology to accept a position in the Bureau of Markets of the U. S. Department of Agriculture.

Oregon College and Station.—A pruning school was held at the college the second week in December, with lectures and demonstrations in the forenoons of each week and pruning work in the nearby orchards in the afternoons. Some work on spraying was also carried on.

A joint antismut campaign has been conducted by the departments of botany, plant pathology, and farm crops, in cooperation with the U. S. Department of Agriculture as part of the plan to increase food production.

Ava B. Milam, head of the domestic science department, has been appointed dean of the school of home economics. Ralph McBurney, instructor in bacteriology, has been commissioned first lieutenant in the Sanitary Corps of the Army Medical Department. Chas. S. Brewster, of the Purdue University and Station, has been appointed instructor in poultry husbandry, vice A. C. McCulloch, now engaged in extension work in New Brunswick.

Other appointments include V. D. Chappell, instructor of dairy manufactures at the Iowa College, as assistant in dairy manufactures; L. W. Wing, as instructor in dairying; D. K. Tressler, of the Bureau of Soils of the U. S. Department of Agriculture, and E. H. Dougherty as instructors in agricultural chemistry; Bernard F. Sheehan as instructor in farm crops; L. F. Lingle as assistant professor and assistant in horticultural products; H. C. Woodham as instructor in horticulture; and E. J. Fjeldsted as instructor and assistant in animal husbandry, vice G. R. Samson.

Pennsylvania College and Station.—Plans have been approved for a commercial truck garden of about 10 acres. The work is to be done by students and is intended to afford an insight into commercial truck operations.

R. A. Andree, assistant professor in agronomy in charge of farm economics, has resigned to become head of the department of agricultural engineering at the Texas College. C. M. Arthur has resigned as instructor in agricultural extension to take up work connected with problems of distribution and marketing of farm products carried on with the Pennsylvania Committee on Public Safety. Dr. H. L. Fulmer, assistant professor of bacteriology, is now in military service. L. P. McCann, instructor in animal husbandry, resigned January 1, 1918.

Dr. D. S. Fox, assistant in farm management at the Montana Station, has been appointed assistant professor of farm management. Other appointments include E. L. Nixon as extension plant pathologist, C. A. Hunter as assistant professor of bacteriology and assistant bacteriologist, M. W. Lisse as assistant professor of agricultural chemistry, E. J. Klepper as assistant in botany, Chas. Cummings as instructor in dairy husbandry, and E. J. Holben as assistant in experimental agronomy.

Texas College and Station.—At the special session of the legislature, the acts establishing a West Texas Agricultural College and a Northeast Texas Junior A. and M. College were repealed. The John Tarleton Agricultural College at Stephenville and the Grubbs Vocational College at Arlington, junior colleges under the board of directors of the Texas A. and M. College, opened September

20. E. E. Binford, superintendent of the Beeville substation, became professor of agriculture in the John Tarleton College and was succeeded by I. E. Cowart, previously assistant professor of horticulture.

F. D. Fuller, formerly chief deputy State chemist of Indiana and more recently in commercial work, has been appointed chief of the division of feed control service. W. E. Jackson became assistant entomologist of the station, October 1, 1917, for work in combating foul brood. Dr. H. Schmidt, veterinarian, and Carl Abell, scientific assistant and station illustrator, are now in military service, the latter being succeeded by Miss Edith H. Phillips.

Virginia Truck Station.—A 75-acre farm in Accomac County has been rented for the use of the station in conducting experiments on sweet potatoes, Irish potatoes, strawberries, and other truck crops grown in the county. The farm will be equipped with modern buildings and operated for experimental purposes.

Albert White, instructor in horticulture at the Pennsylvania College, has been appointed assistant horticulturist, assuming his duties November 15.

Wyoming University and Station.—Dr. H. G. Knight, dean of the college of agriculture and director of the station, has accepted the corresponding position at the Oklahoma College and Station, effective February 1, and has been succeeded by A. D. Faville. Dr. H. M. Martin, assistant in animal diseases, is now in military service.

Society for the Promotion of Agricultural Science.—The thirty-eighth meeting of this society was held at Washington, D. C., November 12 and 13, 1917. The sessions were unusually well attended. The program dealt particularly with war conditions, but covered a wide range of subject matter.

The presidential address was given by Dr. Herbert Osborn at a joint session held with the American Society of Agronomy. Dr. Osborn took for his subject The Outlook in Agricultural Science, discussing some of the notable developments in various lines and some effects of the war upon agricultural science. He pointed out that when the war emergency arose, it found a great body of trained workers already mobilized, in whom the public had confidence and whose recommendations were accordingly widely followed. The outlook for material support of agricultural institutions he characterized as unusually favorable. The prospective shortage of younger workers he suggested might be lessened to some extent by the retention in service of older men who would ordinarily seek retirement. Since the immediate duty of agricultural science, as of all other interests, is to win the war, all efforts should be energetically put forth in this specific direction.

At the same session Dr. L. H. Bailey delivered an address of wide general interest entitled Permanent Agriculture and Democracy. This address was suggested by his observations of the agricultural situation in China, where 85 per cent of the people are engaged in agriculture but under a scale of living which he characterized as reduced to the lowest possible terms. On the basis of his observations he discussed such fundamental questions as the farmer's place in the Nation as the "keeper of the earth," the need of broad vision as well as specialized knowledge on the part of those attempting to advise on rural problems, the fallacy of too small holdings and overintensive methods, and the wide difference between "permanent" and "stationary" agriculture.

The program of technical papers was as follows: The Function of Organic Matter in the Maintenance of Soil Fertility, by C. E. Thorne; How Farmers Acquire Their Farms, by W. J. Spillman; Vegetation Experiments on the Availability of Treated Phosphates, by J. G. Lipman; Wheat Production and Consumption during Peace and War Times, by H. Snyder; Shall We Recommend the Use of Magnesium Limestone? by A. G. McCall; A Revolution in the Methods and Theories of Soil Chemistry, by C. B. Lipman; Abortiveness As Related to Position in the Pod of the Ovules of the Legume, by B. D. Halsted; The Station's Part in Winning the War, by B. Youngblood; Have the Agricultural Colleges Met Their Obligations in the War Emergency? by W. D. Hurd; The Most Pressing Development Problem of American Agriculture, by C. V. Piper; Some Factors of Success and Failure in Dry Farming, by A. Kezer; Some Results Obtained in the Use of Sulphur As a Fertilizer, by A. B. Cordley; Promoting Practical Forestry Work, by F. W. Rane; Inosit Phosphoric Acid in Feeding Stuffs, by J. B. Rather; The Mineral Metabolism of the Milch Cow, by E. B. Forbes; Influence of Degree of Fatness on Utilization of Feed, by H. P. Armsby and J. A. Fries; and A Prospective New Forage Crop for the Irrigated Portion of the Northwest, by F. B. Linfield.

At the business session the secretary, Director C. P. Gillette, reported that a canvass of members as to the enrollment in the society of members of the American Society of Agronomy and the American Farm Management Association and the formulation of a joint program had resulted in an affirmative vote of 47 to 39. In accordance with the results of this canvass, the executive committee was instructed to work out details for such a plan of reorganization and report at the next annual meeting.

Dean R. W. Thatcher was chosen vice-president of the society, the remaining officers being reelected.

Miscellaneous.—The death is noted of Dr. Arthur T. Neale, director of the Delaware Station from its organization in 1888 until 1906 and in charge of agronomy and animal husbandry work until 1907. Dr. Neale was 65 years of age, a graduate of Wesleyan University and the University of Halle, and served as assistant chemist in the laboratories of both institutions. He was also chemist of the New Jersey State Station from 1880 to 1888.

Dr. C. H. Higgins, chief pathologist of animals branch of the Canadian Department of Agriculture since 1902, has resigned to engage in commercial work in New York City, and has been succeeded by Dr. S. Hadwen, previously in charge of the veterinary research laboratory of the department in British Columbia.

T. B. Wood, professor of agriculture in the University of Cambridge, has been appointed to the Development Commission of Great Britain, vice A. D. Hall, now secretary of the Board of Agriculture and Fisheries.

The senate of the University of London has decided to institute for nonresident students a B. S. degree for courses dealing with the administration and management of urban and rural lands and estates.

A. C. Monahan, specialist in agricultural education and rural school administration of the U. S. Bureau of Education, has been commissioned major in the Sanitary Corps of the National Army.

W. V. Tower has resigned as director of the Porto Rico Insular Experiment Station at Rio Piedras.

○

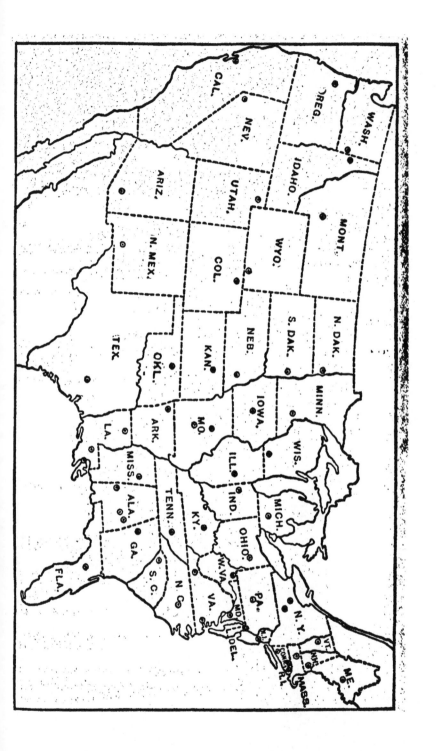

Issued May 15, 1918.

U. S. DEPARTMENT OF AGRICULTURE

STATES RELATIONS SERVICE
A. C. TRUE, DIRECTOR

Vol. 37   INDEX NUMBER

EXPERIMENT
STATION
RECORD

WASHINGTON
GOVERNMENT PRINTING OFFICE
1918.

U. S. DEPARTMENT OF AGRICULTURE.

Scientific Bureaus.

WEATHER BUREAU—C. F. Marvin, *Chief.*
BUREAU OF ANIMAL INDUSTRY—J. R. Mohler, *Chief.*
BUREAU OF PLANT INDUSTRY—W. A. Taylor, *Chief.*
FOREST SERVICE—H. S. Graves, *Forester.*
BUREAU OF SOILS—Milton Whitney, *Chief.*
BUREAU OF CHEMISTRY—C. L. Alsberg, *Chief.*
BUREAU OF CROP ESTIMATES—L. M. Estabrook, *Statistician.*
BUREAU OF ENTOMOLOGY—L. O. Howard, *Entomologist.*
BUREAU OF BIOLOGICAL SURVEY—E. W. Nelson, *Chief.*
OFFICE OF PUBLIC ROADS AND RURAL ENGINEERING—L. W. Page, *Director.*
BUREAU OF MARKETS—C. J. Brand, *Chief.*

STATES RELATIONS SERVICE—A. C. True, *Director.*
OFFICE OF EXPERIMENT STATIONS—E. W. Allen, *Chief.*

THE AGRICULTURAL EXPERIMENT STATIONS.

ALABAMA—
  College Station: *Auburn;* J. F. Duggar.[1]
  Canebrake Station: *Uniontown;* J. M. Burgess.[1]
  Tuskegee Station: *Tuskegee Institute;* G. W. Carver.[1]
ALASKA—*Sitka:* C. C. Georgeson.[2]
ARIZONA—*Tucson:* ———.
ARKANSAS—*Fayetteville:* M. Nelson.[1]
CALIFORNIA—*Berkeley:* T. F. Hunt.[1]
COLORADO—*Fort Collins:* C. P. Gillette.[1]
CONNECTICUT—
  State Station: *New Haven;*
  Storrs Station: *Storrs;* } E. H. Jenkins.[1]
DELAWARE—*Newark:* H. Hayward.[1]
FLORIDA—*Gainesville:* P. H. Rolfs.[1]
GEORGIA—*Experiment:* J. D. Price.[1]
GUAM—*Island of Guam:* C. W. Edwards.[4]
HAWAII—
  Federal Station: *Honolulu:* J. M. Westgate.[1]
  Sugar Planters' Station: *Honolulu;* H. P. Agee.[1]
IDAHO—*Moscow:* J. S. Jones.[1]
ILLINOIS—*Urbana:* E. Davenport.[1]
INDIANA—*La Fayette:* C. G. Woodbury.[1]
IOWA—*Ames:* C. F. Curtiss.[1]
KANSAS—*Manhattan:* W. M. Jardine.[1]
KENTUCKY—*Lexington:* T. P. Cooper.[1]
LOUISIANA—
  State Station: *University Station, Baton Rouge;*
  Sugar Station: *Audubon Park, New Orleans;* } W. R. Dodson.[1]
  North La. Station: *Calhoun;*
  Rice Station: *Crowley;*
MAINE—*Orono:* C. D. Woods.[1]
MARYLAND—*College Park:* H. J. Patterson.[1]
MASSACHUSETTS—*Amherst:* W. P. Brooks.[1]
MICHIGAN—*East Lansing:* R. S. Shaw.[1]
MINNESOTA—*University Farm, St. Paul:* R. W. Thatcher.[1]
MISSISSIPPI—*Agricultural College:* E. R. Lloyd.[1]

MISSOURI—
  College Station: *Columbia;* F. B. Mumford.[1]
  Fruit Station: *Mountain Grove;* Paul Evans.[1]
MONTANA—*Bozeman:* F. B. Linfield.[1]
NEBRASKA—*Lincoln:* E. A. Burnett.[1]
NEVADA—*Reno:* S. B. Doten.[1]
NEW HAMPSHIRE—*Durham:* J. C. Kendall.[1]
NEW JERSEY—*New Brunswick:* J. G. Lipman.[1]
NEW MEXICO—*State College:* Fabian Garcia.[1]
NEW YORK—
  State Station: *Geneva;* W. H. Jordan.[1]
  Cornell Station: *Ithaca;* A. R. Mann.[1]
NORTH CAROLINA—*Raleigh* and *West Raleigh:* B. W. Kilgore.[1]
NORTH DAKOTA—*Agricultural College:* L. Van Es.[4]
OHIO—*Wooster:* C. E. Thorne.[1]
OKLAHOMA—*Stillwater:* H. G. Knight.[1]
OREGON—*Corvallis:* A. B. Cordley.[1]
PENNSYLVANIA—
  State College: R. L. Watts.[1]
  State College: Institute of Animal Nutrition; H. P. Armsby.[1]
PORTO RICO—
  Federal Station: *Mayaguez:* D. W. May.[1]
  Insular Station: *Rio Piedras;* E. Colón.[1]
RHODE ISLAND—*Kingston:* B. L. Hartwell.[1]
SOUTH CAROLINA—*Clemson College:* H. W. Barre.[1]
SOUTH DAKOTA—*Brookings:* J. W. Wilson.[1]
TENNESSEE—*Knoxville:* H. A. Morgan.[1]
TEXAS—*College Station:* B. Youngblood.[1]
UTAH—*Logan:* F. S. Harris.[1]
VERMONT—*Burlington:* J. L. Hills.[1]
VIRGINIA—
  Blacksburg: A. W. Drinkard, jr.[1]
  Norfolk: Truck Station; T. C. Johnson.[1]
WASHINGTON—*Pullman:* Geo. Severance.[4]
WEST VIRGINIA—*Morgantown:* J. L. Coulter.[1]
WISCONSIN—*Madison:* H. L. Russell.[1]
WYOMING—*Laramie:* A. D. Faville.[1]

---

[1] Director.   [2] Agronomist in charge.   [3] Animal husbandman in charge.   [4] Acting director.

INDEX OF NAMES.

Abel, T. H., 198.
Abell, C., 899.
Abrams, D. A., 490.
Ackerman, E. B., 79.
Ackert, J. E., 693.
Ackroyd, H., 265.
Acree, S. F., 114, 201, 409, 410, 502.
Adames, H. B., 717.
Adams, B., 391.
Adams, C. S., 342.
Adams, D. E., 884.
Adams, F., 143, 190.
Adams, J., 15.
Adams, J. F., 551.
Adams, R. L., 190, 389, 443, 794, 890.
Adams, W. L., 893.
Aders, W. M., 560.
Agee, H. P., 339, 444, 459.
Agee, J. H., 21.
Agg, T. R., 490.
Aguzzi, A., 689.
Ahrens, B. A., 399.
Aicher, L. C., 30.
Aïnata, A., 831.
Ainslie, C. N., 358, 856.
Ainslie, G. G., 259, 851.
Aita, A., 322, 323.
Aiyer, A. K. Y. N., 175.
Aiyer, P. A. S., 424.
Ajrekar, S. L., 457.
Akemine, M., 141.
Albanese, A., 478.
Albaretto, E. C. d', 251.
Albrecht, W. A., 198, 300.
Albrechtsen, J., 379.
Albright, A. R., 415.
Alciatore, H. F., 513.
Alder, B., 389, 473, 869.
Alderman, W. H., 344.
Aldrich, J. M., 160.
Aleksiěev, A. I., 201.
Alessandrini, G., 480.
Alexander, L. L., 97, 897.
Alexander, M. L., 836.
Alexander, W. H., 498.
Aley, R. J., 698.
Allard, H. A., 224.
Allen, E. R., 212, 298.
Allen, E. W., 602.
Allen, F. W., 143.
Allen, J. A., 659.
Allen, P. W., 874.
Allen, R. W., 243.
Allen, W. J., 114.
Allison, F. E., 17, 120, 521, 719, 815.

Allison, H. O., 768.
Allison, L. W., 385.
Allison, W. F., 281.
Allman, G., 775.
Allyn, O. M., 438, 641.
Almy, L. H., 63, 311.
Alsberg, C. L., 800.
Alting, H. C., 91.
Altoff, A. T. d', 321.
Alvord, E. D., 237.
Alway, F. J., 20, 117, 808.
Alwood, W. B., 648.
Amadeo, T., 294.
Amalingan, D. B. P. y, 339.
Ames, J. W., 124, 195, 219, 599.
Amico, G., 747.
Amison, E. E., 280.
Amos, H. H., 497.
Amsbaugh, A. E., 867.
Anderson, A. C., 474, 720.
Anderson, A. K., 511.
Anderson, A. L., 681.
Anderson, C. R., 197.
Anderson, E., 218.
Anderson, E. O., 490.
Anderson, H. P., 600.
Anderson, J., 360.
Anderson, J. P., 526.
Anderson, P. A., 197.
Anderson, R. J., 469.
Anderson, T. J., 54, 460.
Andree, R. A., 898.
Andrews, J. B., 179.
Angot, P. A., 717.
Anken, I., 212.
Annett, H. E., 710.
Anstruther, A. W., 392, 779.
Anthony, E. L., 872.
Anthony, R. D., 240, 544.
Aoki, K., 853.
App, F., 642.
Appel, O., 247, 248, 249, 251.
Apperson, J. T., 197.
Arbinet, E., 694.
Arce, J., 377.
Archangelskij, M., 537.
Arcichovskij, V., 542.
Arctowski, H., 417.
Arden, J. A. P., 100.
Ardern, E., 286.
Arens, P., 347.
Argerio, D., 445.
Argyle, H., 99.
Armitage, E., 130.
Armsby, H. P., 900.
Armstrong, G., 499.

Armstrong, G. M., 300, 499.
Armstrong, W. B., 281.
Arnaud, G., 224, 248, 249, 250, 353.
Arnold, J. H., 471, 873.
Arny, A. C., 439.
Arny, L. W., 44.
Arpin, 414.
Arpin, M., 617.
Arthur, C. M., 898.
Arthur, J. C., 749.
Artsikhovskiǐ, V., 542.
Ashbrook, F. G., 800.
Ashby, A. W., 391, 791.
Ashe, W. W., 46.
Askar (Mohammed), 770.
Aspinwall, W. B., 892.
Aston, B. C., 218, 817.
Astruc, A., 130.
Athalye, M. G., 137.
Atkin, E. E., 763.
Atkins, W. R. G., 10.
Atkinson, A., 238.
Atkinson, G. F., 820.
Atwater, H. W., 364, 683, 864.
Aub, J. C., 266, 267.
Aubel, C. E., 497.
Aubry, 692.
Aubry, V. G., 71, 368.
Auchter, E. C., 344, 448.
Aune, B., 822.
Averitt, S. D., 506.
Averna Saccá, R., 553.
Avery, B. T., 831.
Awati, P. R., 358.
Ayers, S. H., 874.
Ayerza, A., 277.
Ayres, A. H., 225.
Ayres, W. E., 642.

Babcock, D. C., 895.
Babson, F. C., 189.
Bach, A., 309.
Back, E. A., 565, 566.
Backhouse, W. O., 432.
Bacot, A., 763, 850.
Bacot, A. W., 850.
Bado, A. A., 486.
Baer, W. W., 299, 523.
Bagshawe, C. R., 618.
Bahr, L., 162.
Bailey, C. H., 497.
Bailey, E., 842.
Bailey, H. S., 511.
Bailey, I. W., 46, 123.
Bailey, J. W., 497.
Bailey, K., 481.

901

Bailey, L. H., 41, 240, 539, 899.
Bailey, V., 846.
Bain, W., 167.
Baker, A. C., 157, 358, 661, 850.
Baker, C. F., 148, 200.
Baker, O. E., 595.
Baker, P. S., 98, 626.
Baker, W. H., 286.
Balangue y Rulloda, C., 338.
Balcom, R. W., 112.
Baldacci, A., 445.
Baldassarre, J. F., 541.
Baldwin, H., 481.
Ball, C. R., 799.
Ball, E. D., 257, 369, 869.
Ball, W., 649.
Balland, 164.
Ballou, H. A., 460.
Baltzer, A. C., 397.
Bamber, M. K., 144, 814.
Bancroft, C. K., 838.
Banks, N., 57, 860.
Bannwart, C., 346.
Banta, L., 394.
Banzhaf, 877.
Baragiola, W. J., 207, 310, 314, 414, 415, 805, 806.
Barbee, O. E., 99.
Barber, L., 728.
Barber, L. B., 767, 778.
Barber, T. U., 243.
Barbour, J., 767.
Barker, B. T. P., 646, 669.
Barker, F. D., 355, 361.
Barker, J. F., 299, 521, 523, 616, 802.
Barlow, J. T., 197.
Barnard, H. E., 63, 883.
Barnes, F. J., 487.
Barnes, J. H., 356.
Barnes, W., 563.
Barois, J., 830.
Barr, G. H., 274, 875.
Barr, W. A., 98.
Barron, L., 746.
Barron, W. E., 807.
Barrows, H. P., 395, 798.
Barss, A. F., 806.
Bartlett, H. H., 724.
Bartow, E., 87.
Bartram, H. E., 797.
Basset, G. C., 773.
Bassett, C. E., 796.
Bateman, W. G., 432.
Bates, C. G., 45, 46, 244, 451.
Bateson, W., 434.
Batyranko, V. G., 528.
Baumann, C., 414.
Baxter, G. P., 110.
Bayha, A. E., 398.
Bayliss, W. M., 166.
Bayne-Jones, S., 877.
Beach, F., 498.
Beach, J. R., 182.
Beacher, J. C., 190.
Beadle, C., 112.
Beal, A. C., 239, 346.
Beal, W. H., 611.

Beals, C. L., 503.
Bear, F. E., 498.
Beath, O. A., 780.
Beattie, J. H., 23.
Beccari, O., 545.
Bechdel, S. I., 197.
Bechtel, J. R., 197.
Beck, M. W., 810.
Becker, G. G., 158, 161.
Beckett, S. H., 586.
Beckwith, T. D., 86.
Bedard, A., 147.
Beegle, F. M., 169.
Beeler, A. D., 744.
Beers, C. W., 756.
Beeson, C. F. C., 854.
Béguet, 461.
Behring, E. von, 100.
Bekensky, P., 279.
Belgrave, W. N. C., 458.
Belin, M., 377.
Bell, H. G., 800.
Bell, N. E., 621.
Bell, R. D., 311.
Belov, S. A., 336.
Belt, T., 568.
Benham, D. J., 427.
Benjamin, C. H., 698.
Benjamin, E. W., 391.
Bennett, H. H., 621.
Bennett, R. L., 91.
Bennett, W. J., 513.
Benson, E. F., 281.
Benson, O. H., 290.
Bentley, G. M., 544.
Benton, G. P., 698, 700.
Berg, W. N., 77.
Berger, E. F., 524.
Berges, P., 271.
Bergman, A. M., 80.
Bergtold, W. H., 774.
Berkhout, A. D., 413.
Barlese, 360.
Beriese, A., 760.
Bernard, C., 835.
Bernard, L. L., 491.
Bernardis, G. B., 410.
Berry, G. P., 745.
Berry, J. T., 398.
Berry, O. C., 188.
Berry, R. A., 372, 373, 427.
Berry, S., 243, 451.
Berthault, P., 92.
Besemer, A. M., 583.
Besnard, J., 78.
Bessey, E. A., 742.
Besson, A. A., 207.
Best, T. R., 145.
Betts, G. H., 290.
Betts, H. S., 886.
Beulhne, F. R., 58.
Bevan, E. J., 112.
Bevan, L. E. W., 688.
Beveridge, J. H., 596.
Beverley, J., 136.
Bevier, I., 602, 611.
Bews, J. W., 526.

Bezzenberger, F. K., 614.
Bezzi, M., 160.
Bhide, R. K., 826.
Biazzo, R., 312.
Bibby, I. J., 98.
Biekart, H. M., 197.
Biffen, R. H., 445.
Bigelow, W. D., 714.
Biggar, H. H., 799.
Bijl, P. A. van der, 554, 842.
Billings, G. A., 390.
Billson, H. G., 650.
Bimbi, P., 82.
Binford, E. E., 899.
Bing, P. C., 197.
Birch, R. R., 691, 881.
Bird, H. S., 833.
Birkeland, K., 807.
Bisby, G. R., 552, 749.
Bishop, M. H., 892.
Bishop, O. F., 837.
Bishopp, F. C., 357, 560.
Bitler, R. O., 724.
Bittenbender, H. A., 299.
Bitting, A. W., 416.
Bittner, G., 477.
Blackman, V. H., 47.
Blackwell, J. D., 794.
Blair, A. W., 425, 629.
Blair, F. J., 543.
Blair, W. R., 115, 807, 880.
Blair, W. S., 242, 800.
Blake, A. F., 313.
Blake, M. A., 240, 490, 755.
Blakeslee, A. F., 831.
Blanchan, N., 630.
Blanchard, H. L., 96, 599, 699, 895.
Blaringhem, 137.
Blasingame, R. U., 591, 700.
Blatherwick, N. R., 308.
Blin, H., 553, 830.
Bliss, J., 198.
Bliss, J. W., 84.
Blodgett, F. H., 893.
Blumenthal, P. L., 712.
Blunck, 460.
Blunt, A. W., 146.
Boag, W. A., 651.
Boardman, H. S., 698.
Bock, J. C., 14, 206.
Bodkin, G. E., 155, 847.
Bookhout, F. W. J., 176, 414.
Boerner, F., jr., 179.
Bohannan, R. D., 398, 450.
Bolland, B. G. C., 233.
Bolton, E. R., 511.
Boltz, G. E., 599.
Bomberger, F. B., 492, 888.
Boncquet, P. A., 549, 847.
Bond, H. G., 80.
Bonis, A., 804.
Bonomi, Z., 426.
Bonsteel, J. A., 189.
Bontrager, W. E., 147.
Boodle, L. A., 837.
Boquet, A., 377.
Bordoli, J. B., 79.

Borgeaud, A., 769.
Borgedal, P., 733.
Borges, I., 81.
Börner, 460.
Borrino, A., 207.
Borthwick, A. W., 354.
Borzi, A., 333.
Boshart, C. F., 299.
Boss, A., 389, 600.
Bosscha, K. A. R., 44.
Bottomley, W. B., 719.
Bougault, J., 714.
Boulenger, C. L., 280.
Bouret, D., 769.
Boutwell, P. W., 108.
Bowles, 836.
Bowman, H. H., 821.
Boyce, J. S., 558.
Boyle, J. E., 492.
Boyles, F. M., 112.
Boynton, W. H., 79, 277.
Brabourne (Lord), 758.
Bracken, J., 437.
Brackett, E. E., 384.
Bradley, O. C., 772.
Bragg, L. C., 562.
Branch, G. V., 143.
Brandenburg, T. O., 379.
Brandt, P. M., 499.
Branford, R., 78, 692.
Branigan, E. J., 58.
Brannon, M. A., 397.
Braun, A. F., 564.
Braun, F., 814.
Breed, R. S., 500.
Bregger, J. T., 98.
Brehm, C. E., 300.
Breithaupt, L. R., 333.
Brenchley, 214.
Brenchley, W. E., 446.
Brenier, 830.
Brentzel, W. E., 749.
Breslauer, A., 502.
Brèthes, J., 460.
Brett, W., 543.
Brewster, C. S., 898.
Brewster, J. F., 8.
Brick, C., 148.
Bridges, H. V. B., 699.
Bridges, O. A., 388.
Bridgman, W. B., 281.
Bridré, J., 692.
Brien, M. O., 778.
Brierley, W. B., 457.
Briggs, L. J., 429.
Briggs, L. P., 545.
Brigham, R. O., 223.
Bright, O. T., 795.
Brindley, J. E., 89.
Bringard, 378.
Brink, W. T., 600.
Brinkley, L. L., 22.
Brittain, W. H., 157, 462, 570, 848.
Britton, W. E., 254, 255, 259, 848.
Broadhurst, J., 819.
Brock, W. S., 242, 755.
Brodrick-Pittard, N. A., 416.

Broerman, A., 881.
Bronfenbrenner, J., 688.
Brooks, C., 754.
Brooks, C. F., 15, 16, 807.
Brooks, E. C., 94.
Brooks, F. E., 58.
Brooks, S. C., 128, 326.
Brooks, W. P., 611.
Broughton, L. B., 218.
Brown, A. J., 25.
Brown, B. S., 41.
Brown, C. E., 289.
Brown, F., 314.
Brown, F. C., 592.
Brown, F. L. C. C., 146.
Brown, F. W., 522, 630.
Brown, G. G., 33, 41, 344.
Brown, H. H., 109, 410.
Brown, K. B., 53.
Brown, L. C., 345.
Brown, L. P., 113, 175.
Brown, N. A., 841.
Brown, P. E., 24, 119, 120, 126, 211.
Brown, W., 47, 245.
Brown, W. H., 79.
Brown, W. R., 761.
Browne, T. A., 190.
Broyles, W. A., 893.
Bruce, A. B., 769.
Bruce, E. A., 379.
Bruch, C., 460.
Bruckmiller, F. W., 412.
Brues, C. T., 356, 357, 543, 766.
Bruner, L., 157.
Bruner, S. C., 353.
Bryan, E. A., 281.
Bryant, E. S., 747.
Bryant, H. B., 146.
Bryant, H. C., 156.
Bryant, V. C., 641.
Bryce, G., 147, 727.
Brzesowsky, A., 44.
Bucci, P., 158.
Buchanan, J. P., 762.
Buchanan, R. E., 220, 819.
Buck, F. E., 143.
Buckley, J. S., 179.
Buckman, H. O., 498.
Buckner, G. D., 430.
Bueno, J. R. de la T., 357.
Bugby, M. O., 498.
Buisson, J. P. du, 519.
Bulkley, G. S., 499.
Bulkley, R. J., 91.
Bull, C. G., 781.
Bull, L. B., 279.
Bull, S., 471.
Bunnett, E. J., 55.
Bunting, B., 147.
Bunting, R. H., 349.
Bunyard, E. A., 833.
Bunzel, H. H., 9, 326, 429, 726.
Burge, W. E., 365.
Burgess, A. F., 258, 563.
Burgess, J. M., 797.
Burgess, P. S., 515.
Burk, L. B., 367.

Burke, H. E., 566, 854.
Burkholder, W. H., 840.
Burlison, W. L., 438, 641.
Burmeister, W. H., 690.
Burnett, W. L., 558.
Burns, J. C., 366.
Burns, N. B., 481.
Burns, W., 136, 826.
Burr, W. W., 437.
Burrill, T. J., 297, 819.
Burritt, M. C., 498, 605.
Burt, B. C., 734, 825.
Burton, A. C., 692.
Burton, E. F., 501.
Busck, A., 564, 667.
Bush, A. K., 437.
Bushnell, G. E., 481.
Bushnell, T. M., 21, 720.
Buss, W. J., 195.
Butler, M. D., 100.
Butterfield, K. L., 602.
Buxton, J. B., 878.
Byars, L. P., 840, 841.
Byl, P. A. van der, 554, 842.
Bylert, 541.
Byrne, A. T., 590.

Cabaussel, P. de, 491.
Cade, C. M., 651.
Cadet, G. le, 620.
Cadoret, A., 538.
Caesar, L., 832.
Cagurangan, A. B., 339.
Cain, J. C., 409.
Caine, J. T., 605.
Caldwell, F. W., 399.
Caldwell, J. S., 715.
Call, L. E., 212, 799.
Calland, J. W., 195.
Calvin, H. W., 393.
Cameron, A. E., 55, 462.
Camp, W. R., 36.
Campbell, L. E., 147.
Campus, A., 178.
Camuñas, M., 98.
Cance, A. E., 888.
Cannon, W. A., 213.
Cantwell, J. W., 797.
Capen, S. P., 699.
Capus, J., 152, 653.
Card, F. W., 544.
Card, L. E., 368.
Carey, P. J., 648.
Carles, P., 263.
Carlyle, W. L., 169, 797.
Carmichael, B. E., 195, 895.
Carmichael, W. J., 677.
Carothers, C. E., 796.
Carpenter, C. G., 97.
Carr, E. G., 263.
Carr, R. H., 718.
Carrel, A., 876.
Carrero, J. O., 222.
Carrick, D. B., 898.
Carris, L. H., 94.
Carroll, C. M., 574.
Carroll, W. E., 473, 681.

Carsner, E., 840.
Carson, W. J., 197.
Carter, H. S., 469.
Carter, L. M., 211.
Carter, W. T., jr., 514.
Cartier, J., 377, 692.
Carvalho, C. M. D. de, 619.
Carver, G. W., 364.
Carver, T. N., 603.
Cary, C. A., 687.
Case, L. N., 374.
Caspari, C., jr., 468.
Cassel, C. E., 299.
Casteel, C., 281.
Castle, F. R., 645.
Castle, M. A., 145.
Castleman, P., 481.
Cates, H. R., 36.
Cathcart, C. S., 219, 243, 429.
Cathcart, J. L., 499.
Cattaneo, E., 325.
Cattell, J. G., 274.
Cauda, A., 221.
Causse, P., 152.
Cauthen, E. F., 233, 234.
Cave, T. W., 876.
Center, O. D., 68, 399.
Cerriana, C. F., 539.
Chace, E. M., 345, 649.
Chaddock, R. E., 491.
Chafanov, S. K., 515.
Chamberlin, W. J., 666.
Chambers, F., 879, 880.
Chandler, B. A., 499.
Chandler, E. M., 281.
Chapais, J. C., 156.
Chapman, J. E., 398.
Chapman, J. W., 253.
Chappell, V. D., 898.
Chapron, H., 692.
Charles, V. K., 263.
Charlton, I. D., 96, 491, 591, 599.
Charmoy, 692.
Charron, A. T., 22.
Chase, L. W., 696, 887.
Chase, M., 281.
Chase, W. W., 42.
Chaussé, P., 82, 378, 583.
Chernoff, L. H., 9.
Chesley, A. L., 715.
Cheviot, 776.
Chibber, H. M., 432.
Chidester, F. E., 259, 260.
Chifflot, J., 250.
Chigasaki, Y., 853.
Chilcott, E. C., 437.
Childs, L., 51, 54, 56, 555.
Ching Yik Wang, 782.
Chirikov, F. V., 323.
Chittenden, F. H., 566, 567.
Chivers, A. H., 327, 457.
Chree, C., 807.
Christensen, F. W., 468.
Chrystal, R. N., 459.
Chubb, C., 758.
Chung Yik Wang, 180, 879.

Chupp, C., 454.
Ciamician, G., 632.
Cillis, E. de, 136.
Clapp, E. H., 44.
Clark, E. D., 63, 311, 863.
Clark, E. M., 474.
Clark, Ella M., 892.
Clark, J. E., 717.
Clark, W. B., 711.
Clark, W. E., 498.
Clark, W. M., 506, 686, 875.
Clarke, H. T., 614.
Clarkson, C. S., 197.
Clausen, C. P., 58, 834.
Clausen, R. E., 433.
Clausmann, P., 713.
Claypon, J. E. L., 174.
Clayton, R. H., 116, 417.
Clayton, J., 44.
Cleare, L. D., jr., 155.
Cleland, J. B., 181.
Clement, F. M., 212, 514.
Clement, G. E., 56, 451.
Clement, J. K., 410.
Clements, F. E., 434.
Clemmer, P. W., 874.
Cline, J., 756.
Clink, C. H., 378.
Cockayne, A. H., 142, 446, 463, 537.
Cockerell, T. D. A., 357, 543.
Cockle, J. W., 459.
Coe, H. S., 444, 540.
Coelho de Souza, W. W., 441.
Coen, V., 192.
Coerper, F. M., 842.
Cohen, N. H., 411, 419, 522.
Cohen, S. S., 274.
Cohn, A. E., 375.
Coit, J. E., 153, 154.
Cole, A. C., 351.
Cole, F. R., 565.
Cole, L. J., 869.
Cole, R. D., 328.
Coleman, D. A., 197, 213, 719.
Colley, R. H., 757.
Collings, J., 697.
Collins, C. W., 254.
Collins, G. N., 536.
Collins, P., 720.
Collison, R. C., 299, 797.
Collison, S. E., 649.
Colver, C. W., 39.
Colwell, R. C., 874.
Combs, W. B., 197, 399.
Commelin, J. W., 113.
Comte, 787.
Cone, V. M., 281, 282, 586, 882.
Conklin, R. S., 45.
Conklin, W. G., 45.
Conn, H. J., 516, 517.
Connaway, J. W., 779.
Connell, W. H., 188.
Conner, A. B., 642.
Conner, S. D., 420.
Connors, C. H., 239, 240.
Conolly, H. M., 297, 396.

Conradi, A. F., 395.
Converse, A., 152.
Convert, F., 756.
Conway, T. J., 887.
Cook, A. C., 434.
Cook, J. H., 593.
Cook, L. B., 874.
Cook, M. T., 652, 654, 755.
Cook, O. F., 335, 434.
Cook, R. C., 521, 815.
Cooke, J. V., 167.
Cooke, R. D., 409.
Cooley, A. M., 192.
Cooley, F. S., 796.
Cooley, J. S., 754.
Cooley, R. A., 255, 261, 560, 687.
Cooper, H. P., 123, 197.
Cooper, J. R., 447, 544.
Cooper, M. R., 867.
Cooper, T. P., 896.
Cooper, W. E., 791.
Copeland, W. R., 425.
Coppersmith, S. C., 806.
Corbett, L. C., 240, 543, 800.
Corbould, M. K., 570, 895.
Cordley, A. B., 299, 900.
Cordonnier, A., 153.
Corlett, D. S., 144.
Corner, G. W., 867.
Cornish, E. C. V., 777, 778.
Cornwall, J. W., 357.
Corper, H. J., 275, 890.
Corsan, G. H., 756.
Cory, E. N., 260, 660, 667.
Cory, H. V., 600.
Cory, V. L., 330.
Cosco, G., 689.
Cosens, A., 26.
Costa Lima, A. da, 59, 359, 360.
Costerus, J. C., 47.
Cotton, A. D., 753.
Cotton, R. T., 55, 256.
Cotton, W. E., 181.
Coventry, B. O., 244, 650.
Cowan, P. R., 553.
Cowart, I. E., 899.
Cowell, A. W., 197.
Cowgill, H. B., 236.
Cowley-Brown, F. L. C., 146.
Cox, F. E., 190.
Cox, J. B., 187.
Cove, W., 41.
Crabtree, J. W., 596.
Craig, C. F., 180.
Craig, R. A., 378, 882.
Craig, W. T., 799.
Crandall, C. S., 242.
Crawford, D. L., 196.
Crawford, N. A., 794.
Crawford, R. P., 322, 897.
Crawley, H., 53.
Creelman, G. C., 603.
Creelman, J. M., 647.
Creswell, M. E., 598.
Criddle, N., 355, 758, 855.
Crisler, O. S., 897.

Crissey, F., 894.
Crocheron, B. H., 888.
Cromwell, R. O., 50, 456.
Crosby, C. R., 856.
Crosby, D. J., 193, 796.
Cross, C. F., 112.
Cross, W. E., 139.
Crossman, S. S., 257.
Crowl, V. C., 398.
Crowther, C., 8, 130.
Croy, M. S., 346, 742.
Crumley, J. J., 298.
Cuesta, G. P. y de la, 339.
Cuevas, E., 217.
Culver, F. S.,-387.
Cummings, B. F., 762.
Cummings, C., 898.
Cunliffe, R. S., 345.
Cunningham, C. C., 136.
Cunningham, M. L., 385.
Currie, J. N., 613.
Currier, E. L., 290.
Curtis, F. R., 97.
Curtis, M. R., 371.
Curtis, R. S., 583.
Curtman, L. J., 617.
Cutler, G. H., 100.
Cutolo, A., 508.

Dabney, R. C., 398.
Dachnowski, A. P., 212, 810.
Da Costa Lima, A., 59, 359, 360.
Dadisman, A. J., 190.
Dadisman, S. H., 194.
Da Fano, A., 736.
D'Albaretto, E. C., 251.
Dalbey, N. E., 839.
Dale, E. E., 497, 841.
Dale, J. K., 109.
D'Alfonso, C., 173.
Dalmasso, G., 52.
Dalrymple, W. H., 179, 782.
D'Altoff, A. T., 321.
Dam, W. van, 175, 373.
Dammerman, K. W., 247.
Damon, F. H., 699.
Damon, S. C., 446, 815.
Dana, B. F., 897.
Dana, S. T., 520.
Dangeard, P. A., 250.
Daniel, L., 27, 325, 543.
Daniels, A. L., 166.
Dantin, C., 491.
Danysz, J., 76.
Darnell-Smith, G. P., 352.
Dastur, J. F., 154, 757, 844.
Daufresne, M., 876.
Davenport, C. B., 676.
Davenport, E., 290, 610.
Davidson, H. C., 544.
Davidson, J., 799.
Davidson, J. B., 90.
Davidson, W. C., 386.
Davidson, W. M., 461, 562, 661.
Davies, H. J., 646.
Davis, A. P., 84, 698, 787.

Davis, A. R., 129, 600.
Davis, B. F., 477.
Davis, C. E., 300.
Davis, C. W., 111.
Davis, E. D., 889.
Davis, (Mrs.) H., 896.
Davis, I. G., 872.
Davis, I. W., 259.
Davis, J. J., 261, 353.
Davis, K. C., 795.
Davis, L. V., 22.
Davis, V. H., 797.
Davis, W. A., 802.
Davis, W. H., 752.
Davison, C., 115.
Davisson, E. R., 897.
Dawe, M. T., 233, 357, 765.
Dawson, C. F., 477.
Day, P. C., 314, 807, 808.
Deakin, R. H., 760.
Dean, D., 800.
Dean, G. A., 260, 357.
Dean, H. R., 477.
Dean, R., 746.
Dean, W. C., 810.
Dearborn, N., 156, 573.
Deardorff, C. E., 122.
Dearing, C., 544.
De Baun, R. W., 642.
De Cabaussel, P., 491.
De Cillis, E., 136.
Deemer, R. B., 724.
De Favi, Remo, 314.
De Fazi, Romolo, 314.
De Jong, A. W. K., 345, 347, 436.
De Kruif, P. H., 578, 579, 580, 581, 582, 688.
De la Cuesta, G. P. y, 339.
De la Torre Bueno, J. R., 357.
Delavan, C. C., 547.
Delbridge, C. L., 137.
De Leon y German, J., 143.
Delépine, S., 378.
Delgado de Carvalho, C. M., 619.
DeLoach, R. J. H., 194.
DeLong, D. M., 761.
De Mazières, A., 835.
Denier, 806.
Denis, W., 469.
Dennis, J. S., 185.
Dennis, L. H., 192.
Denton, M. C., 166.
Denzer, B. S., 850.
De Ong, E. R., 758.
Depew, H. F., 498.
DePorte, E. M., 760.
Deslandres, H., 418.
De Sornay, P., 28.
De Souza, W. W. C., 441.
Detjen, L. R., 449.
Deuss, J. J. B., 619.
De Vecchi, A., 586.
Devereaux, W. C., 513, 807.
Devol, J., 498.
Devoto, F. E., 149.
DeVries, H., 131, 328.
De Vries, J. J. O., 176, 414.

De Vries, O., 347, 348, 417, 553, 651.
Dewell, H. D., 386.
Dewey, G. W., 37.
DeWindt, E. A., 524.
Dibble, B., 285.
Dick, J. H., 145.
Dick, M. V., 198.
Dickenson, C. G., 182.
Dickerson, E. L., 359, 563, 761.
Dickey, J. B. R., 720.
Dickinson, A. D., 630.
Dickson, E. C., 165, 669.
Dickson, M. E., 897.
Diehl, W., 752.
Dietrich, W., 270.
Diffloth, P., 728.
Dille, F. M., 355.
Dinsmore, W., 771.
Distant, W. L., 54.
Ditewig, G., 577.
Dixon, J., 757.
D'Lima, C., 233.
Dobbs, A. C., 334, 825.
Dobiache, A. A., 520.
Dobiasha, A. A., 520.
Dodd, S., 181.
Dodds, J. S., 89.
Dodge, B. O., 551.
Dodson, W. R., 599.
Döé, F., 253.
Doebler, E. W., 693.
Doi, T., 747.
Doidge, E. M., 657.
Doneghue, R. C., 720.
Dooley, W. H., 598.
Dorr, H., jr., 651.
Dorset, M., 81.
Dorsett, P. H., 542.
Dorsey, M. J., 240.
Doten, S. B., 97.
Doty, S. W., 390.
Doubt, S. L., 726.
Dougherty, E. H., 898.
Dougherty, J. E., 94.
Douglas, H. F. K., 443.
Douville, 692.
Dover, M. V., 805.
Downing, G. J., 57.
Dowsett, W. E., 746.
Dowson, W. J., 453.
Dox, A. W., 410, 497, 801.
Doyle, H. W., 439.
Draghetti, A., 219.
Dreyer, G., 14.
Drummond, J. C., 165.
Dryden, J., 491.
DuBois, C., 348.
DuBois, E. F., 266, 267.
Du Buisson, J. P., 519.
Ducceschi, V., 177.
Dudgeon, E. C., 336.
Dudgeon, G. C., 55, 138, 233.
Duerst, U., 879.
Duff, J. S., 155.
Duggan, M. L., 194.
Duggar, B. M., 129, 728.
Duggar, J. F., 97, 233, 234, 599.

Duggeli, M., 273.
Duley, F. L., 732.
Dunbar, P. B., 714.
Duncan, F., 346.
Dunham, A. C., 496.
Duniway, C. A., 198, 610.
Dunne, J. J., 172, 373.
Dunphy, G. W., 274.
DuPorte, E. M., 156, 559.
Durand, E. D., 896.
Durant, A. J., 779.
Durrell, L. W., 147, 552.
Durrell, R. S., 884.
Durrell, W. L., 841.
Durst, C. E., 437, 543, 642, 645.
Dutcher, R. A., 398.
DuToit, P. J., 389.
Dutt, H. L., 357.
Dutton, M. S., 588.
Dyar, H. G., 563, 564, 565, 762.
Dybowski, J., 830.
Dyer, D. C., 13.

Eakins, H. S., 477.
Earl, J. C., 548.
Earle, D. E., 830.
Earnshaw-Cooper, W., 791.
Easson, R. B., 896.
East, E. M., 433, 820.
Easterby, H. T., 540.
Eaton, B. J., 416.
Eberson, F., 180, 878.
Eckerson, S. H., 631.
Eckles, C. H., 71, 72, 94, 172.
Eddy, H. P., 694.
Eddy, W. H., 65.
Edelmann, R., 77.
Edgerton, C. W., 752.
Edgington, B. H., 881.
Edlefsen, N. E., 344.
Edmundson, W. C., 57.
Edson, H. A., 752.
Edwards, 163.
Edwards, A. L., 197.
Edwards, E. R., 193.
Edwards, F. W., 762.
Edwards, J. T., 479.
Edwards, R. W., 331.
Effront, J., 411.
Egbert, A. D., 369.
Eggleston, E. H., 775.
Eggleston, J. D., 596, 892.
Ehle, H. N., 100.
Ehrhorn, E. M., 847.
Eichhorn, A., 81, 689.
Ekblaw, K. J. T., 389, 407.
Ekholm, N., 116.
Eklof, C. M., 20.
Ekroth, C. V., 113, 175.
Elford, F. C., 682, 696.
Élladi, E. V., 203.
Ellenberger, H. B., 499.
Ellington, E. V., 75.
Elliot, D. G., 658.
Elliott, C. G., 186.
Elliott, F. A., 747.
Elliott, H., 800.
Elliott, J. A., 97, 353.

Elliott, L. S., 386.
Ellis, J. W., 149.
Ellis, W. E., 115.
Elsdon, G. D., 618.
Else, J. N., 499.
Elst, P. van der, 883.
Elvove, E., 111.
Émanuël, B. S., 521.
Embleton, H., 399.
Emelîanov, I. V., 355.
Emerson, P., 517, 799.
Emerson, R. A., 737.
Emmett, A. D., 471.
Emslie, B. L., 645.
Enger, M. L., 585.
Engle, C. C., 123.
Eoff, J. R., jr., 502.
Erickson, E. C., 651.
Erni, C. P., 21.
Erwin, A. T., 753.
Escherich, K., 467.
Escobar, R., 134.
Espino, R. B., 148.
Essig, E. O., 849.
Estes, C., 12.
Etchegoyen, F., 78.
Euren, H. F., 866.
Eva, 543.
Evans, A. C., 173.
Evans, A. H., 53.
Evans, A. R., 730, 731.
Evans, M. O., jr., 296.
Evans, M. W., 140, 438.
Evans, N. S., 98.
Evans, W. E., 875.
Evenson, O. L., 508.
Evvard, J. M., 90, 882.
Ewart, J. C., 771.
Ewing, H. E., 858.
Ewing, P. V., 65, 600, 673.
Eyles, F., 492.
Eyre, J. V., 47, 453.
Ezendam, J. A., 416.

Fabre, J. H., 358.
Faes, H., 555.
Fagan, F. N., 197.
Fagan, T. W., 872.
Fairchild, L. H., 497.
Fairlie, A. M., 724.
Falci, R., 746.
Fallon, J. T., 746.
Fano, A. da, 736.
Farmer, J., 78.
Farnham, A. A., 499.
Farnham, W. W., 198.
Farrell, F. D., 595, 822.
Farrell, J. J., 166.
Farrington, H. A., 838.
Farrow, E. P., 758.
Faulwetter, R. C., 49.
Fava, E., 689.
Favero, F., 82.
Faville, A. D., 899.
Fawcett, G. L., 139.
Fawcett, H. S., 555, 556.
Fuyet, 692.

Fazi, Remo de, 314.
Fazi, Romolo de, 314.
Fearnow, M. L., 218.
Fedoroff, P. R., 334, 534.
Fedorov, P. R., 334, 534.
Feilitzen, H. von, 134, 137, 720, 736.
Felder, E. A., 218.
Felt, E. P., 259, 760.
Fenger, F., 109.
Fenn, W. O., 431.
Fenton, F. A., 662.
Fenton, F. C., 897.
Ferguson, A. A., 14.
Ferguson, E. W., 181.
Ferguson, J. B., 205.
Fermi, C., 480.
Fernald, H. T., 646.
Fernandez, R. O., 110.
Ferneyhough, J. G., 479.
Fernow, B. E., 45.
Ferris, G. F., 563.
Ferry, N. S., 479.
Feruglio, D., 42, 410.
Fetherolf, J. M., 837.
Filaudeau, G., 12.
Finch, R. H., 513.
Finch, V. C., 595.
Finzi, G., 178.
Fippin, E. O., 215, 317, 813,
Fischer, W. 345.
Fish, E., 192.
Fisher, K. R., 894.
Fisher, M. L., 137.
Fisher, M. R., 499.
Fisher, W. S., 506.
Fisk, E. L., 469.
Fiske, G. W., 593.
Fiske, J. G., 197.
Fitch, C. P., 197.
Fitch, J. B., 671.
Fitts, F. O., 98.
Fitzpatrick, W. W., 300.
Fjeldsted, E. J., 898.
Flack, A. H., 648.
Flammarion, C., 16.
Flattely, F. W., 28.
Fleischmann, E. C., 831.
Fleisher, M. S., 478.
Fletcher, C. C., 521.
Fletcher, S. W., 42, 143, 648.
Fletcher, W. M., 266.
Flinn, J. W., 700.
Flint, E. R., 500.
Flora, S. D., 807.
Florentin, D., 815.
Floyd, B. F., 656.
Flume, A. J., 197.
Foex, E., 248, 240.
Foght, H. W., 393.
Fohrman, M. H., 897.
Folin, O., 311.
Folker, A. M., 398.
Folmer, C. J., 82.
Folpmers, T., 110.
Fominykh, V. A., 826.
Forbes, C. R., 384.
Forbes, E. B., 169, 195, 672, 900.

Forbes, R. H., 486, 527.
Ford, G. H., 765.
Foreman, N. H., 494.
Forteath, H. H., 348.
Fortier, S., 185, 281.
Foss, H., 732.
Fosseen, A. B., 281.
Foster, G. L., 804.
Foster, J. H., 348, 452, 747.
Foster, W. D., 361, 578.
Foust, J., 570.
Fowler, E. S., 789.
Fowler, L. W., 834.
Fowler, W. L., 169, 399.
Fox, D. S., 898.
Fox, H., 461, 483.
Fraenken, C., 77.
France, E. W., 894.
Francis, C. K., 399, 507, 672, 805.
Franco, E. E., 81.
Frandsen, H. N., 734.
Frandsen, J. H., 500, 591.
Frank, A., 96, 699.
Frankenfield, H. C., 807.
Franklin, H. J., 53.
Franklin, O. M., 376.
Fraps, G. S., 168, 363, 801, 865.
Frear, W., 406.
Freckmann, W., 333.
Fred, E. B., 133.
Free, E. E., 213.
Free, M., 746.
Freeborn, S. B., 179, 565.
Freeman, E. M., 398.
Frem, J. B., 281.
Frenais, H. M. la, 357.
French, A. W., 477.
French, J. A., 384.
French, W. H., 194, 793.
French, W. L., 497.
Frey, J., 769.
Frich, L., 192.
Fricke, F. H., 63.
Fricks, L. D., 560.
Friedemann, W. G., 672.
Fries, J. A., 900.
Froggatt, J. L., 160.
Froggatt, W. W., 55, 160.
Frohawk, F. W., 667.
Fröhner, E., 378.
Frolov, N. S., 882.
Fromme, F. D., 754.
Frost, H. B., 28, 526.
Frost, J. N., 277.
Frothingham, E. H., 45, 245.
Fry, W. H., 505, 811.
Fuertes, L. A., 846.
Fullaway, D. T., 162, 847.
Fuller, A. V., 712.
Fuller, E. S., 486.
Fuller, F. D., 899.
Fuller, F. S., 651.
Fuller, G. D., 418.
Fuller, G. L., 514.
Fuller, J. M., 476.

Fuller, P. E., 585.
Fulmer, H. L., 831, 898.
Futaki, K., 375.

Gabotto, L., 150.
Gahan, A. B., 359.
Gaines, E. F., 332, 334, 337.
Gainey, P. L., 519, 812.
Galang, F. G., 334.
Gale, H. S., 724.
Gallagher, B., 83.
Gallardo, A., 358, 460.
Galpin, C. J., 90.
Gangoiti, L., 513.
Garcia, F., 343.
Garcia, P. V., 770.
Gardiner, C. A., 806.
Gardiner, R. F., 505.
Gardner, A. D., 14.
Gardner, F. D., 626.
Gardner, J., 41.
Gardner, J. J., 646.
Gardner, J. S., 197.
Gardner, M. W., 840.
Gardner, V. R., 344.
Gardner, W. A., 496.
Gardon, P. V., 800.
Garland, J. J., 438.
Garman, H., 48.
Garman, P., 856.
Garren, G. M., 233, 827.
Garrett, F. W., 514, 720.
Garrigou, F., 694.
Garrison, P. E., 694.
Gastiaburu, J. C., 356.
Gatenby, J. B., 856.
Gates, B. N., 855.
Gates, F. C., 725.
Gaudot, G., 445.
Gautier, A., 713.
Gearhart, C. A., 232.
Gebhard, H., 91.
Gedrofts, K. K., 505.
Gee, J. G., 499.
Geerligs, H. C. P., 509.
Geerts, J. M., 123, 425.
George, F. A., 63.
Gephart, F. C., 267.
Gericke, W. F., 504, 526, 527.
Gerlach, 171.
Gerlaugh, P., 198, 365.
German, J. de L., y 143.
German, W. M., 582.
Gernert, 137.
Getty, J. V., 558.
Ghosh, A. C., 546.
Giacomelli, E., 460.
Gibbs, H. E., 482.
Gibson, A., 156, 459, 585.
Gibson, E. H., 157, 561, 849.
Gibson, J. W., 293.
Gibson, O. E., 96.
Giffard, W. M., 855.
Gilbert, A. W., 98.
Gilbert, C. G., 217.
Gilbert, J. C., 43, 888.

Gilbert, T., 886.
Gilbert, W. W., 840.
Gilbertson, G. I., 561.
Gilchrist, D. A., 723.
Gilder, P. G., 838.
Gile, P. L., 222.
Gill, A. H., 13.
Gill, C. O., 593.
Gillam, L. G., 251.
Gillespie, A., 182.
Gillespie, L. J., 803.
Gillett, L. H., 671.
Gillette, C. P., 459, 562, 900.
Gillette, J. M., 794.
Gilmore, J. W., 139.
Gimingham, C. T., 233, 648.
Girard, J. W., 838.
Girault, A. A., 59, 162, 360, 467, 569, 570, 667, 766, 855.
Girola, C. D., 533, 830.
Givens, M. H., 64.
Gladden, E. A., 44.
Gladson, W. N., 698.
Gladwin, F. E., 655, 843.
Glaser, R. W., 253, 759.
Glasgow, H., 359.
Glenn, C. C., 572.
Glover, G. H., 690.
Glover, G. J., 182.
Glover, H. M., 244.
Goddard, H. N., 494.
Goddard, L. H., 389.
Godet, C., 414.
Gokhble, V. G., 457.
Goldbeck, A. T., 88, 884.
Goldberg, S. A., 483.
Goldenweiser, E. A., 593.
Goldman, E. A., 757, 758.
Goldrich, L. W., 596.
Goldthorpe, H., 600.
Goodale, H. D., 868, 869.
Gooderham, C. B., 156.
Goodling, C. L., 197.
Goodman, A. L., 212.
Goodspeed, T. H., 225, 433.
Goodspeed, W. E., 99.
Goodwin, O. T., 171.
Goodwin, W. H., 262, 599, 895.
Goot, P. van der, 850.
Gore, H. C., 511, 800.
Gorria, H., 93.
Gortner, 630.
Gortner, R. A., 20, 121, 398, 517.
Goss, B. C., 12, 470.
Goss, L. W., 80.
Goss, O. P. M., 386.
Goss, R. W., 600.
Gossard, H. A., 53, 143, 195, 258, 261, 599.
Gott, E. J., 712.
Gough, L. H., 561, 762.
Gourley, J. H., 833.
Gow, R. M., 881.
Gowdey, C. C., 560.
Graber, L. F., 440.

Grady, R. I., 168.
Graf, J. L., 158.
Graham, J. C., 500.
Graham, J. J. T., 802.
Graham, P. A., 214.
Graham, R., 398, 689, 882.
Graham, S. A., 660.
Graham, W., 574.
Grant, A. A., 693.
Grant, J., 165.
Grantham, A. E., 644.
Grantham, J., 837.
Gräub, E., 878.
Graul, E. J., 133.
Graves, C. B., 281.
Graves, G. W., 21, 29.
Graves, H. S., 836.
Graves, H. T., 477.
Graves, R. R., 399.
Gray, D. T., 674, 676, 679, 681, 682, 690, 691.
Gray, G. P., 848.
Greathouse, C. A., 198.
Greaves, J. E., 120, 421.
Green, A. W., 139, 826.
Green, E. C., 441.
Green, L., 700.
Green, R. M., 789.
Green, S. N., 143, 150, 195, 338.
Green, W. J., 143, 241, 895.
Greenaway, A. J., 409.
Greene, C. T., 57, 764.
Greenfield, W. P., 886.
Greenway, J. O., 281.
Gregg, J., 182.
Gregg, W. R., 115, 513.
Gregory, G., 182.
Gregory, H., 476.
Grenville, R. N., 878.
Griebel, C., 415.
Griffin, E. L., 258.
Griffith, A. S., 181, 378.
Griffiths-Jones, E., 272.
Griffitts, T. H. D., 853.
Grimes, M. F., 499.
Grindley, H. S. 471, 677.
Grondal, B. L., 651.
Grönvold, H., 758.
Groom, P., 253.
Grossfeld, J., 414.
Grove, A. J., 356.
Grove, W. B., 149.
Grover, N. C., 484.
Groves, E. R., 592.
Groves, J. F., 418, 725.
Grulee, C. G., 174.
Grunsky, C. E., 183.
Gruse, W. A., 201.
Gruzit, O. M., 213.
Guédroitz, C., 506.
Gueylard, F., 356.
Guignard, 692.
Guilbeau, P. L., 893.
Guillaume, A., 477.
Guillebeau, A., 280.
Guilliermond, A., 632.
Guillochon, L., 535.

Guinier, M., 253.
Guinier, P., 53.
Guise, C. H., 451.
Gulley, A. G., 496.
Gunderson, A. J., 242.
Güssow, H. T., 554, 658, 764.
Guthrie, C. P., 864.
Guyer, M. F., 155.
Guyton, T. L., 797.

Haas, A. R., 222, 430, 431, 726.
Haas, A. R. C., 821.
Haas, P., 801.
Haberlandt, G., 222.
Hackedorn, H., 399.
Hadley, C. H., jr., 257.
Hadley, P. B., 183, 280.
Hadlington, J., 775.
Hadwen, S., 182, 379, 691, 900.
Haff, R. C., 712.
Hagan, H. R., 99.
Haggard, M. J., 197, 600.
Hahner, A. R., 397.
Haigh, F. L., 110.
Haines, H. C., 490.
Haines, H. H., 146.
Haines, H. T., 790.
Hainsworth, R. G., 595.
Hall, A. D., 900.
Hall, B. M., 84.
Hall, C. J. J. van, 745, 835.
Hall, E. C., 419.
Hall, F. H., 545, 655.
Hall, J. A., 139.
Hall, M. C., 82, 483, 577, 578, 780.
Hall, M. R., 84.
Hall, R. C., 46.
Hall, R. H., 419.
Hallenbeck, C., 807, 808.
Hallett, R. L., 110.
Halliburton, W. D., 165, 501.
Hallman, E. T., 274.
Halsted, B. D., 900.
Haltom, A. J., 285.
Hamilton, J. A., 459.
Hamilton, W. H., 98.
Hamlin, E. G., 651.
Hammer, B. W., 686.
Hammett, F. S., 273, 873.
Hammond, J., 272.
Hampson, C. B., 68.
Handy, A. L., 715.
Hanford, H. D., 281.
Hanmante, N. M., 826.
Hansen, A. A., 98.
Hansen, N. E., 142, 833.
Hansen, R., 819.
Hanson, S. G., 775.
Hanzlik, E. J., 651.
Hardenbergh, J. B., 179, 382.
Harder, O. E., 490.
Hardesty, E., 766.
Harding, C., 418.
Harding (Mrs.) E., 145.
Harding, T. S., 410.
Hardison, R. B., 22.
Harger, R. L., 807.

Harlot, P., 252, 253.
Harkins, M. J., 276.
Harland, S. C., 224, 569.
Harmon, S. C., 500.
Harper, J. D., 97.
Harper, R. M., 435, 810.
Harreveld-Lako, C. H. van, 23.
Harrington (Mrs.), I. L., 796.
Harrington, O. E., 221.
Harris, B. R., 617.
Harris, E. G., 695.
Harris, F. S., 340, 437, 440, 623, 740, 741.
Harris, J. A., 47, 630, 632.
Harris, J. E., 624.
Harris, N. L., 368.
Harris, T. H., 893.
Harris, W. G., 500.
Harrison, J. B., 144, 291.
Harrison, L., 461.
Harrison, W. H., 424.
Harron, W. C., 499.
Hart, E., 205.
Hart, E. B., 10, 766.
Hart, L. C., 188.
Hart, R. A., 587.
Hart, S. H., 894.
Hart, W. R., 798.
Hartenbower, A. C., 497, 728, 742, 767.
Hartill, L. R., 647.
Hartman, B. G., 716.
Hartman, S. C., 498.
Hartmann, A., 876.
Hartwell, B. L., 446, 799, 815.
Harvey, R. N., 871, 887.
Haseman, L., 760, 853.
Haskell, S. B., 724.
Haslam, T. P., 376.
Hasselbring, H., 726.
Hastings, E. G., 777.
Hastings, H. G., 437.
Hastings, R., 399.
Hastings, S. H., 90.
Hastings, W. G., 499.
Hasund, S., 733.
Haughs, D., 146.
Haverstick, H., 145.
Hawk, J. C., 272.
Hawker, H. W., 514.
Hawkes, E. W., 264.
Hawkins, L. S., 192, 293, 394, 798.
Hawley, L. F., 803.
Haydan, C. C., 195.
Hayes, H. K., 437.
Hayes, W. P., 567.
Haynes, D., 309.
Hays, C. H., 897.
Hays, E., 39.
Hays, F. A., 397.
Headden, W. P., 11, 38.
Headlee, T. J., 254, 466, 467, 664.
Heald, F. D., 150, 750.
Heald, F. E., 798.
Healy, D. J., 712.
Healy, W., 398.
Hearn, W. E., 419.

Hearst, W. H., 892.
Hechler, W. R., 736.
Hedgecock, G. G., 354, 844, 845.
Hedrick, U. P., 343.
Hegardt, G. B., 492.
Heidemann, O., 563.
Heim, F., 548.
Heimerle, 697.
Heinicke, A. J., 240.
Heinz, J. G., 281.
Heist, G. D., 274.
Hellmann, G., 115.
Helten, W. M. van, 835.
Helweg, L., 736, 742.
Helyar, J. P., 239, 645.
Hemmi, T., 251, 557, 652.
Hempl, H., 76.
Henceroth, J. W., 724.
Hendrick, H. B., 194.
Hendrick, J., 769.
Hendrickson, A. H., 447.
Hendriksz, R. D., 413.
Hendrixson, W. S., 205.
Hendry, G. W., 829.
Henika, G. W., 273.
Henley, R. R., 81.
Henning, E., 141.
Henry, A., 214.
Henry, A. J., 512, 513, 807.
Henry, W. A., 767.
Henshaw, H. W., 846.
Hepburn, J. S., 62.
Hepler, J. R., 498.
Herke, S., 628.
Hermann, H. A. van, 345.
Herms, W. B., 179, 565, 856.
Héron, G., 591.
Herron, W. H., 84.
Hershey, E., 198.
Herstads, A., 732.
Hervey, G. W., 97.
Hesler, L. R., 151.
Hess, A. F., 177.
Hess, C. L. V., 273.
Hess, G. L., 281.
Hester, C. E., 529.
Hettie, H. W., 695.
Hetzel, R. D., 197, 399, 611.
Hewer, D. G., 511.
Hewitt, C. E., 698.
Hewitt, C. G., 100, 156, 757.
Hewitt, J. L., 97.
Heyking, A., 791.
Heyl, F. W., 612.
Hibbard, P. L., 504.
Hibbard, R. P., 221.
Hickman, C. W., 66.
Hickok, (Mrs.) H. M., 192.
Higbie, E. C., 897.
Higgins, B. B., 48, 753, 844.
Higgins, C. H., 383, 900.
Higgins, J. E., 142.
Hilgard, E. W., 700.
Hill, C. E., 529.
Hill, M., 716.
Hill, S. B., 281.
Hill, T. G., 801.

Hillman, F. M., 591.
Hills, J. L., 698.
Hilson, G. R., 234.
Hiltner, L., 48.
Himmelberger, L. R., 689.
Hindle, E., 850.
Hinds, W. E., 262, 559.
Hine, G. S., 373.
Hines, C. W., 208.
Hirshberg, L. K., 807.
Hirst, C. T., 120, 421.
Hirst, S., 360, 584, 859.
Hissenhoven, P. van, 523.
Hissink, 541.
Hitchcock, A. S., 435.
Hitchner, E. R., 197.
Hite, B. H., 127.
Hitier, H., 189, 533, 890.
Hoagland, R., 617, 802.
Hoar, C. S., 131.
Hoare, E. W., 76.
Hobdy, J. B., 91.
Hodgkiss, H. E., 561.
Hodgson, E. R., 300, 535.
Hodgson, J. P., 700.
Hodgson, R. W., 153, 154, 834.
Hoek, P. van, 79.
Hoff, J. H., 216.
Hoffer, G. N., 896.
Hoffman, F. L, 565.
Hoffmann, M., 142.
Hogan, A. G., 164, 467.
Hogan, G., 272.
Holben, J., 898.
Holden, J. A., 678.
Holden, P. G., 574, 795.
Holder, A. E., 198.
Holder, C. H., 242.
Holding, W. A., 198.
Holland, W. J., 158.
Hollinger, A. H., 760.
Hollister, H. A., 93.
Hollister, H. L., 889.
Holm, A., 493.
Holm, G. E., 897.
Holman, R. M., 27.
Holmes, A. D., 364.
Holmes, E. M., 145.
Holmes, F. S., 648.
Holmes, O. W., 75.
Homburg, G., 745.
Homer, A., 376, 877.
Honeij, J. A., 578.
Honing, J. A., 554, 811.
Hood, J. D., 561, 849.
Hood, L. G., 197.
Hood, S. C., 346, 546.
Hoover, B. M., 796.
Hoover, H. C., 400, 602, 800.
Hopkins, A., 90.
Hopkins, C. G., 214, 514, 594, 720.
Hopkins, F. G., 166, 265, 266, 571.
Hopper, T. H., 897.
Horlacker, L. J., 196.
Horne, W. T., 51.
Horton, G. D., 280, 483.
Horton, H. E., 800.

Horton, J. R., 59.
Horton, R. E., 882.
Hoskins, C. M., 791.
Hotchkiss, W. S., 823, 832.
Hottes, A. C., 345.
Houdemeyer, E., 781.
House, H. D., 748.
Houser, J. S., 53, 849, 895.
Houston, D. F., 289, 601.
Houtman, P. W., 444.
Howard, A., 232, 238, 441.
Howard, C. W., 398.
Howard, G. L. C., 232, 238, 441, 446.
Howard, L. H., 477.
Howard, L. O., 559, 762, 766, 848.
Howard, N. F., 566.
Howard, W. L., 240.
Howe, F. B., 211, 514.
Howell, A. H., 758.
Howell, I. M., 693.
Hoy, W. A., 879.
Hoyt, J. C., 484.
Huard, V. A., 157.
Hubbard, P., 386.
Hubbard, W. S., 509.
Hubbell, C. D., 232, 234.
Huber, H. F., 197, 700.
Hubert, E. E., 549.
Huddleson, I. F., 79.
Hudelson, R. R., 731, 897.
Hudson, C. S., 109, 201, 410, 502.
Huergo, J. M., 823.
Hughes, E. H., 897.
Hughes, H. D., 830.
Hukam Chand, 146.
Hulbert, H. W., 397.
Hulbert, R., 488.
Hulce, R. S., 683, 696.
Hultz, F., 499.
Humbert, J. G., 150.
Hummel, W. G., 798.
Humphrey, C. J., 349, 502.
Humphrey, G. C., 766.
Humphrey, H. N., 491.
Humphrey, H. W., 486.
Humphrey, J. R., 594, 875, 896.
Hungerford, C. W., 751, 839.
Hunt, C. L., 364, 668, 864.
Hunt, N. R., 354, 844, 845.
Hunt, T. F., 289, 389, 697, 700.
Hunter, C. A., 499, 898.
Hunter, O. W., 612.
Hunter, S. J., 357.
Hunter, W. D., 358.
Hunter, W. E., 499.
Hunziker, O. F., 196, 500, 613.
Hurd, W. D., 605, 892, 900.
Hurd, W. E., 115.
Hursh, C. R., 749.
Hurwitz, S. H., 375.
Hush, C. E., 850.
Huss, G., 890.
Hutcheson, T. B., 533, 535.
Hutchings, C. B., 555.
Hutchins, D. E., 244.
Hutchinson, C. M., 19, 722.

Hutchinson, H. P., 337.
Hutchison, C. B., 730.
Hutson, J. C., 357, 462.
Hutton, C. A., 591.
Hyde, W. C., 833.
Hyslop, J. A., 568.

Iakovlev, S. A., 516.
ÍAkushkin, I. V., 321, 323.
Iddings, E. J., 66, 67, 676.
Ikeno, S., 432, 725.
Ilcken, W. S. J. S., 412.
Iljin, V. S., 129, 525.
Illick, J. S., 243.
Illingworth, J. F., 567.
Imamura, A., 858, 859.
Imes, M., 357.
Imms, A. D., 59.
Ince, J. W., 720.
Ingham, A. A., 99.
Ingram, R. P., 600.
Irvin, R. F., 71, 395, 774.
Isely, D., 852.
Ishiwara, K., 375.
Issoglio, G., 114.
Iverson, J. P., 477.
Ivy, R. H., 76.

Jack, R. W., 50.
Jackson, A. C., 665.
Jackson, F. H., jr., 386, 787, 884.
Jackson, H. H. T., 758.
Jackson, H. S., 757.
Jackson, W. E., 899.
Jacob, J., 836.
Jacobs, F. S., 100.
Jadin, F., 130.
Jager, F., 398.
Jagger, I. C., 752.
Jago, W., 617.
Jahnke, E. W., 238, 498.
Jakouchkine, I. V., 321, 323.
James, E. J., 604.
James, J. A., 494, 798.
Jamieson, R. A., 375.
Janata, A., 831.
Janensch, W., 317.
Jansen, B. C. P., 112.
Janssens, P., 830.
Jardine, W. M., 611, 799.
Jarnagin, M. P., 171.
Jarvis, C. D., 395, 608.
Jatrindra Nath Sen, 615.
Jayne, S. O., 281.
Jeffers, H. W., 389.
Jeffrey, E. C., 821.
Jeffrey, J. W., 352.
Jehle, R. A., 556, 843.
Jekyll, G., 746.
Jenkin, T. J., 230.
Jenkins, E. H., 231, 232, 234, 290, 813.
Jenks, F. B., 798.
Jensen, C. A., 352, 422.
Jensen, C. O., 380.
Jensen, H., 553, 554.
Jensen, L., 197.

Jepson, F. P., 359.
Jesien, W. S., 792.
Jesness, O. B., 888.
Jesseman, L. D., 197.
Jessup, L. T., 86.
Jeswiet, J., 443.
Jimenez, R. M., 78.
Johns, C. O., 8, 9, 468, 501.
Johns, H. A., 300.
Johnson, A. C., 440.
Johnson, A. D., 841.
Johnson, A. G., 752, 839, 842.
Johnson, A. K., 63, 468, 570, 863.
Johnson, E. C., 611.
Johnson, G. W., 747.
Johnson, H. W., 119.
Johnson, J., 37.
Johnson, J. M., 502.
Johnson, J. R., 252, 753.
Johnson, L., 634.
Johnson, M. O., 155, 165, 168.
Johnson, O. M., 190.
Johnson, O. R., 789, 897.
Johnson, T. C., 138.
Johnston, J. H. C., 791.
Jolly, N. W., 548.
Joltkewitch, W., 535.
Jones, C. B., 294, 760, 770.
Jones, C. R., 661, 693.
Jones, D. B., 8, 468, 501.
Jones, D. H., 149, 654.
Jones, E. G., 272.
Jones, E. M., 621.
Jones, F. R., 751.
Jones, G. C., 188.
Jones, J. G., 24.
Jones, J. M., 866.
Jones, J. S., 39.
Jones, L. R., 839, 842.
Jones, R. E., 383, 872.
Jones, R. S., 299.
Jones, S. B., 877.
Jones, S. C., 214.
Jones, T. H., 158.
Jones, V. R., 476.
Jones, W. J., jr., 700, 724.
Jong, A. W. K., de, 345, 347, 436.
Jongeward, M., 63.
Jordan, 672.
Jordan, E. O., 275.
Jordan, S., 715.
Jordan, W. H., 396, 570, 575.
Jörgensen, I., 26, 336, 632.
Joyeux, C., 163.
Judd, C. S., 146, 452.
Judd, R. C., 114.
Judd, Z., 895.
Judice, P. P. M., 151.
Judkins, H. F., 776.
Juritz, C. F., 622.

Kadel, B. C., 513.
Kaiser, W. G., 90.
Kalaida, F. K., 144, 145.
Kampen, G. B. van, 208, 416.
Kappen, H., 623.
Kappeyney, J., 691.

Karper, R. E., 642.
Kasargode, R. S., 457.
Kastle, J. H., 430.
Katayama, E., 525.
Kauffman, M., 508.
Kazmeier, F. W., 887.
Keane, C., 477.
Keefer, J. A., 398.
Keene, L., 756.
Keffer, C. A., 605.
Keil, J. B., 241.
Keilin, D., 764.
Keister, J. T., 804.
Keitt, G. W., 755.
Keitt, T. E., 598.
Keleher, T. A., 508.
Keller, E. R., 399.
Kellerman, K. F., 556.
Kellogg, J. W., 818.
Kelly, A., 39.
Kelly, E. O. G., 561.
Kelser, R. A., 220.
Kemner, N. A., 356.
Kempster, H. L., 763, 774.
Kempton, J. H., 136.
Kendall, E. C., 65.
Kendall, J. N., 225.
Kennedy, C., 24.
Kennedy, P. B., 236.
Kenney, R., 196.
Kenny, G. R., 786.
Kenoyer, L. A., 633, 854.
Kerle, W. D., 437.
Kernkamp, H. C. H., 784.
Kerr, A. F., 399.
Kerr, A. P., 529, 572.
Kerr, G. W., 346.
Kerr, W. H., 594, 888.
Ketcham, J. C., 796.
Keuchenius, P. E., 245.
Keyes, C. R., 115.
Kezer, A., 232, 437, 900.
Kidd, F., 26.
Kiesel, A., 201, 203, 204.
Kigin, L. C., 882.
Kilgore, B. W., 220.
Kimball, H. H., 115, 807.
Kimberly, A. E., 588.
Kincer, J. B., 114, 115, 807.
King, F. G., 270, 497.
King, H. M., 872.
King, H. T., 600.
King, J. L., 159, 396.
King, W. V., 560.
Kinman, C. F., 43.
Kinnaird, R. A., 97.
Kinney, J. P., 836.
Kinnison, F. I., 43.
Kinsella, R. A., 780.
Kiplinger, C. C., 711.
Kirkpatrick, M. W., 299.
Kirkpatrick, W. F., 368, 383.
Kishida, M., 430.
Kisskalt, K., 488.
Kizel, A., 201, 203, 204.
Kléber, J. B., 806.
Kleberger, 739.

Klepper, E. J., 898.
Knab, F., 357, 460, 565, 762, 766.
Knapp, B., 598, 611.
Knapp, M. D., 837.
Knight, C. S., 97, 435, 436, 442.
Knight, H. G., 99, 198, 899.
Knudson, L., 127.
Kobayashi, M., 110.
Kober, P. A., 205, 409, 505.
Koch, G. P., 719.
Köck, G., 554.
Koheya, S., 876.
Kohn, L. A., 690, 781.
Kokjer, T. E., 122.
Kolmer, J. A., 78, 274.
Kolthoff, I. M., 113, 613, 714.
Kondo, M., 643.
Kopeloff, N., 213, 428.
Korenblit, A. IA., 292.
Korinek, C. J., 778.
Korinek, G. F., 778.
Koser, S. A., 82.
Kozeloff, N., 700.
Kraemer, H., 220.
Krall, J. A., 750.
Kraus, E. J., 835.
Kraus, R., 849.
Krause, H. B., 452.
Krauss, F. G., 144.
Krausz, H. B., 747.
Kraybill, H. R., 499.
Krehan, 326.
Kreis, 207.
Kress, O., 109, 110.
Krinbill, H. R., 747.
Kristensen, R. K., 613.
Krocher, C., 584.
Krout, W. S., 840.
Krüger, 245, 248.
Krumwiede, C., jr., 690, 781, 819.
Kruse, P. J., 807.
Krusekopf, H. H., 428.
Kudo, R., 361.
Kuehne, J., 695.
Kuelling, H. J., 695.
Kulkarni, L. B., 826.
Kulp, W. L., 197.
Kunhikannan, K., 657.
Kunkel, L. O., 457.
Kunst, F. B., 127.
Kuriyama, S., 571.
Kusama, Y., 76.
Kuwana, S. I., 358.

Labitte, A., 355.
Laborde, J., 805.
La Cuesta, G. P. y de, 339.
Ladd, E. F., 63, 468, 570, 863.
Ladd, N. M., 53.
Laffer, H. E., 43.
La Forge, F. B., 9, 502.
La Frensis, H. M., 357.
Lagerberg, T., 458.
Lagers, G. H. G., 504.
Lako, C. H. van H., 23.
Lakon, G., 541.
Lamb, A. R., 413, 788.

Lamb, G. N., 838.
Lambert, R. A., 176.
Lambotte, 59.
Lamon, H. M., 871.
Lamson, G. H., jr., 258.
Lane, C. H., 193, 392, 795.
Lane-Claypon, J. E., 174.
Lang, H. L., 500.
Langenhan, H. A., 546.
Langston, W. W., 97.
Langworthy, C. F., 364, 800.
Lantz, D. E., 553.
Larmon, C. W., 390.
Larsen, B. R., 732.
Larsen, C., 476.
Larsen, H. C., 295.
Larson, A. H., 398.
Larson, A. O., 198, 797.
Larson, C. W., 172.
La Rue, C. D., 724.
Larue, P., 152.
Latham, H. A., 146.
Lathrop, E. C., 216, 503, 843.
Lathrop, F. H., 98, 561.
Latimer, W. J., 22.
Laubert, R., 248, 252.
Laude, H. H., 140, 532.
Lauder, A., 872.
Lawrence, 630.
Lawrence, J. V., 47, 632, 773, 774.
Lawson, L. M., 486.
Leather, J. W., 13.
Leavenworth, C. S., 8.
Leavitt, C., 45.
Le Cadet, G., 620.
Leclainche, T. P., 688.
Le Clerc, J. A., 539, 799.
Le Conte, J., 402.
Ledeboer, F., 443.
Lee, A. R., 871.
Lee, F. C., 281.
Lee, H. A., 154.
Lee, H. N., 245.
Lee, L. L., 123.
Lee, R. E., 415.
Leeney, H., 876.
Lees, A. H., 646, 759, 761.
Lefevre, G., 771, 772.
Lefroy, H. M., 665.
Lehmann, E. W., 90.
Lehnert, E. H., 780.
Leidigh, A. H., 140, 747.
Leidner, R., 528.
Leitch, A., 872.
Lemoine, G., 418.
Lende-Njaa, J., 135.
Lenher, V., 504.
Leon y German, J. de, 143.
Leonard, M. D., 856.
Leonian, L. H., 600.
Le Prince, J. A. A., 853.
Lesage, P., 26, 431.
L'Esperance, E. S., 481.
Létourneau, F., 554.
Levin, E., 197.
Levine, M., 220.
Lévy, R., 461.

Lewis, C. I., 41, 240.
Lewis, D. E., 151.
Lewis, H. R., 71, 495, 573, 871.
Lewis, I. P., 498.
Lewis, L. L., 169, 399, 473.
Lewis, M. C., 797.
Lewis, P. A., 379, 481.
Lewis, R. G., 245.
Lewis, R. H., 711, 885.
Liechti, P., 216, 219, 311.
Lienhardt, H. F., 497.
Lima, A. da C., 59, 359, 360.
Lima, C. d', 233.
Limaye, D. B., 147.
Limbocker, T. F., 41, 241.
Lindeman, H., 446.
Lindhard, E., 734, 735.
Lindley, E. H., 397.
Lindstrom, E. W., 526.
Linfield, F. B., 900.
Lingle, L. F., 898.
Link, G. A., sr., 158.
Link, G. K. K., 897.
Linsbauer, L., 550.
Lint, H. C., 815.
Lionnet, F. E., 780.
Lipman, C. B., 526, 799, 800, 834, 900.
Lipman, J. G., 610, 899.
Lippincott, J. A., 398.
Lippincott, W. A., 368.
Lisher, P. R., 196.
Lisse, M. W., 109, 898.
Lissone, S., 92.
List, G. M., 459.
Littlepage, T. P., 345.
Lûbimenko, V., 203.
Livermore, K. C., 491.
Livesay, E. A., 399.
Livingston, B. E., 26.
Livingston, C. D., 99.
Livingston, G., 889.
Lloyd, D. J., 178.
Lochhead, W., 156.
Lockett, S., 482.
Lodge, F. S., 9.
Loeb, J., 127, 324, 325, 632, 821.
Loewe, L., 707.
Long, C. W., 196.
Long, D. D., 211.
Long, H. C., 688.
Long, W. H., 354, 844.
Longley, A. T., 391.
Longmuir, J., 281.
Loomis, A., 897.
Lory, C. A., 610.
Lotsy, J. P., 432.
Lougher, T. H., 591.
Loughridge, R. H., 496.
Louis, H., 723.
Lounsbury, C., 21.
Lovchinovskaîa. E. I., 201, 202, 203.
Love, H. H., 799.
Lovelace, B. F., 501.
Lovett, A. L., 559, 759.
Lowry, M. W., 211.

Lowry, Q. S., 158, 254, 255.
Luaces, E. L., 482.
Lubs, H. A., 506, 686.
Luce, H. C., 397.
Luce, R., 469.
Ludlow, C. S., 57.
Luginbill, P., 851.
Luiggi, L., 183, 184.
Lund, H. H., 290.
Lund, Y., 600.
Lush, J. L., 196.
Lushington, P. M., 146.
Lusk, G., 267, 469, 571, 602, 671.
Lusk, W. F., 398.
Luther, E. L., 796.
Lutts, F. M., 140, 297, 498.
Lutz, A. M., 433.
Lyford, C. A., 393.
Lyford-Pike, J., 836.
Lyman, G. R., 500.
Lyman, H., 207.
Lyndon, L., 287.
Lyon, T. L., 800.
Lyons, H. G., 717.
Lythgoe, H. C., 165.
Lytle, W. H., 374.

Maassen, 460.
McAdie, A., 619.
McAlpine, D., 151, 455.
McAtee, W. L., 57, 355, 807, 808.
McBeth, I. G., 318, 353.
McBride, C. G., 98.
McBride, R. S., 409.
McBurney, R., 898.
McCall, A. G., 514, 799, 800, 900.
M'Call, M. A., 195.
McCall, T. M., 241.
McCampbell, C. W., 368, 868.
McCandlish, A. C., 474.
McCann, L. P., 197, 898.
McCartney, H. E., 169.
MacCaughey, V., 345, 835.
McClelland, C. K., 28, 35.
McClelland, T. B., 43, 649.
McClintock, J. A., 49, 249, 552, 749, 751, 753.
McColloch, J. W., 254, 260.
McCollum, E. V., 61, 99, 108, 163, 166, 264, 308, 766.
McConnell, O. J., 36.
McConnell, P., 893.
McCool, M. M., 116.
McCoy, E. J., 198.
McCray, A. H., 59.
McCreight, A. M., 838.
McCubbin, W. A., 558, 658, 845.
McCue, C. A., 42.
McCuistion, E. H., 91.
McCulloch, A. C., 898.
McDanell, L., 64.
McDermott, F. A., 313.
Macdiarmid, F. G., 489.
McDole, G. R., 20, 117, 808, 897.
MacDonald, A. C., 734.
McDonald, B. A., 776, 872.

McDonald, C. W., 499.
McDonald, E. M., 399, 730, 731, 897.
MacDonald, G. B., 548.
MacDonald, M., 693.
McDonald, M. C., 468.
MacDonald, P., 509.
McDonnell, C. C., 410, 802.
McDonnell, H. B., 24, 127.
McDonough, F. L., 663.
MacDougal, D. T., 325, 524, 821.
McDougall, W. B., 27.
McDowell, F. N., 621.
McDunnough, J., 563.
Mace, F. E., 243.
McFadden, E. J., 795.
McFadyean, J., 479.
McFarland, J., 76.
McFarland, J. H., 44, 145.
Macfarlane, W., 399.
McFeely, A., 398.
Macfie, J. W. S., 464.
McGill, A., 165.
McGillivray, A. D., 766.
McGinty, R. A., 241.
McGlennon, J. S., 243.
McGuire, F. X., 182.
McHargue, J. S., 503.
Machliss, J. A., 399.
McIndoo, N. E., 360, 459.
McInerney, T. J., 475.
McInnis, F. J., 197.
M'Intosh, C., 353.
McIntosh, R., 146.
Mack, W. B., 163.
McKay, A. A., 288.
McKay, A. W., 649.
MacKay, C. J., 602, 796.
Mackenzie, J. A. S., 375.
Mackenzie, M. M., 826.
McKillop, A. T., 561.
Mackintosh, J., 893.
McKittrick, L. S., 843.
Macklin, T., 696.
McLarty, J. E., 295.
McLaughlin, W. J., 175.
McLaughlin (Mrs.), W. J., 175.
McLean, J., 877.
McLean, W. A., 385.
McMurren, S. M., 755, 756.
McMurtis, E. (C.), 41.
McNair, A. D., 829.
McNair, J. B., 15, 411, 498, 897.
MacNaughton, E. B., 98.
McNaughton, G. C., 110.
Macnaughton, L., 863.
MacNeal, W. J., 76, 694.
McNeile, L. G., 873.
McNess, G. T., 140.
MacNutt, J. S., 874.
McOmie, A. M., 437.
Macoun, W. T., 240, 343, 800.
Macpherson, H., 492, 594.
McSweeney, E. F., 890.
McVey, F. L., 497.

McWhorter, V. O., 388.
Madariaga, A., 749.
Madden, I. A., 95.
Maddux, C., 481.
Madsen, O. P., 600.
Madson, B. A., 236, 338.
Maffei, L., 656.
Magath, T. B., 549.
Maglione, J. V. N., 738.
Magnan, J. C., 95.
Magness, J. R., 343.
Maheu, J., 548.
Mains, G. H., 503, 716.
Maire, R., 557.
Mairs, T. I., 795.
Malcomson, A. W., 681.
Malenotti, E., 360, 462.
Malloch, J. R., 755.
Malzew, A., 239.
Mameli, E., 325.
Manaresi, A., 655.
Manders, A. S., 347.
Mangam, A. W., 410.
Mangels, C. E., 672.
Mangin, L., 247, 250.
Mann, A. R., 498.
Mann, H. H., 215, 826.
Mann, L. B., 896.
Manning, D., 116.
Manning, W. H., 299.
Mansfield, A. B., 151.
Mansfield, C. M., 802.
Manter, J. A., 262.
Manwaring, W. H., 76.
Marbut, C. F., 799.
Marc, 244.
Marcarelli, B., 50, 539, 643, 831.
Marchand, W., 853.
Marchisotti, A. C., 481.
Marcovitch, S., 497.
Marcus, 163.
Marden, J. W., 805.
Marenghi, 717.
Marescalchi, A., 251.
Margreth, G., 420.
Markley, H., 498.
Marlatt, A., 192.
Marlatt, C. L., 559.
Marotta, F. P., 793.
Marre, F., 176.
Marriott, J. A. R., 697.
Marsden, E., 547.
Marsh, C., 399.

Marsh, C. D., 688.
Marsh, H. O., 663.
Marshall, C. E., 76.
Marshall, C. J., 577.
Marshall, F. M., 192.
Marshall, F. R., 572.
Marshall, G. A. K., 54, 161, 705.
Marshall, M. J., 309.
Marston, A., 698.
Martel, H., 780.
Martin, H. G., 843.
Martin, H. M., 899.

Martin, J. B., 542.
Martin, J. G., 37.
Martin, J. H., 896.
Martin, J. N., 30.
Martin, O. B., 596.
Martin, W. H., 653, 654.
Martinez, I. R., 141.
Martinotti, F., 152.
Masini, A., 716.
Mason, A. F., 197.
Mason, F. E., 690.
Mason, W. P., 187.
Masoni, G., 18.
Massart, J., 725.
Massey, L. M., 353.
Massie, E. C., 492.
Massonnat, 250.
Matheson, R., 156, 257, 464.
Mathews, J. W., 770.
Mattei, G. E., 336.
Matteson, E. B., 94.
Matthews, W. H., 797.
Matthewson, E. H., 541.
Mattos, A. T. de, 358.
Matz, J., 652.
Maufe, H. B., 212.
Maughan, H. J., 340, 797.
Maxon, E. T., 514.
Maxwell, F., 114.
May, D. W., 500.
Mazières, A. de, 835.
Mead, E., 184, 190.
Meade, R. K., 818.
Means, J. H., 266, 267.
Mebus, C. F., 385.
Meckstroth, G. A., 98.
Meigs, E. B., 308.
Meinzer, O. E., 484, 807.
Melander, A. L., 54, 143, 665.
Melchers, L. E., 750, 841.
Melhus, I. E., 552, 752, 842.
Mellon, M. G., 415.
Melvin, A. D., 77.
Menardi, J. B., 897.
Mendel, L. B., 60, 264, 470, 571, 864, 865.
Mendenhall, D. R., 166.
Mendiola, N., 148.
Menozzi, A., 586.
Mensching, J. E., 797.
Mentz, A., 135.
Mer, E., 147.
Mercer, W. B., 839.
Merrill, D. E., 465.
Merrill, J. H., 151, 157.
Merrill, M. C., 99.
Merrill, O. C., 547.
Merritt, E., 699.
Mertens, 545.
Messer, R., 287.
Messerschmidt, T., 488.
Metcalf, J. S., 91.
Metcalf, T. P., 789.
Metcalf, Z. P., 262, 666.
Metzger, A. H., 649.
Meyer, A., 668.
Meyer, A. H., 211.

Meyer, H., 513.
Meyer, K. F., 82, 477, 881.
Meyers, P. T., 198.
Michels, J., 172.
Mickelwaite, C. B., 21.
Miège, 319.
Miguel, L. A. san, 336.
Milam, A. B., 898.
Miles, S. R., 897.
Millar, C. E., 116.
Miller, A. H., 180.
Miller, D. G., 86.
Miller, E. C., 637.
Miller, E. P., 800.
Miller, F. G., 497.
Miller, M. F., 428, 718, 731, 732, 897.
Miller, M. R., 53.
Miller, P. L., 897.
Miller, R. W., 119.
Milligan, J. T., 398.
Milliken, F. B., 560.
Mills, H. C., 896.
Milo, C. J., 23.
Milward, J. G., 442.
Milward, R. C., 346.
Miner, J. R., 497.
Minges, G. A., 126.
Minkler, F. C., 498.
Minot, A. S., 469.
Miny, 548.
Mirande, M., 25.
Mitamura, T., 858, 859.
Mitchell, C. A., 112.
Mitchell, C. W., 206, 471.
Mitchell, R. V., 498, 600.
Mitra, J. M., 291.
Mitzmain, M. B., 180, 463.
Mix, A. J., 350.
Mixa, F. E., 368.
Mixter, W. G., 110.
Miyagawa, Y., 858, 859.
Miyake, C., 634.
Mockeridge, F. A., 517.
Moffitt, G. W., 110.
Mohammed Askar, 770.
Mohilevith, C., 376.
Mohler, J. R., 81, 182, 274.
Molina, E., 460.
Molisch, H., 220.
Molliard, M., 25, 223.
Monahan, A. C., 192, 294, 392, 900.
Monbet, 692.
Monnier, A., 111.
Monroe, J. P., 798.
Montagu (Lrod), 807.
Montemartini, L., 149, 327, 549, 550, 655, 658.
Montgomery, C. W., 195.
Montgomery, E., 380.
Montgomery, E. G., 437.
Montgomery, J. A., 91.
Mooers, C. A., 799.
Moore, A. P., 500.
Moore, B., 651.
Moore, H. F., 165, 716.
Moore, L. H., 97.
Moore, P., 70, 271.

Moore, V. A., 299, 482.
Moore, W., 559, 660, 848.
Morales, R., 460.
Moreau, E., 803.
Moreau, F., 129.
Morgan, A. C., 663.
Morgan, D. G., 507, 805.
Morgan, J. F., 717.
Morgan, L. E., 672.
Morgan, P. G., 629.
Morgan, T. H., 573.
Morison, A. E., 176.
Morison, C. G. T., 291.
Morley, C., 765.
Morley, L. W., 399.
Morrill, A. W., 560, 846.
Morrill, W. J., 837.
Morris, H., 179.
Morris, O. M., 139, 146.
Morrison, E., 543.
Morrison, F. B., 767.
Morrison, H., 360.
Morrison, T. M., 211.
Morrow, C. A., 398, 517.
Morse, F. W., 342.
Morse, W. J., 538, 544.
Mortlock, H. C., 22.
Mosher, E., 663.
Mosher, F. H., 451.
Mosier, J. G., 514, 720.
Moss, E. G., 541.
Mosscrop, T. D., 815.
Mosséri, V., 538.
Mossman, R. C., 807.
Mote, D. C., 464.
Moulton, C. R., 399.
Moussu, 481.
Moznette, G. F., 98, 857.
Muckleston, H. B., 185.
Muerman, J. C., 892.
Mugg, H. C., 724.
Mulford, F. L., 396.
Müller-Thurgau, H., 246, 509.
Mulraj, 45.
Mumford, H. W., 471.
Muncie, F. W., 449.
Mundell, J. E., 328.
Munerati, O., 28.
Munger, T. T., 450.
Munier, H., 537.
Munoz Jimenez, R., 78.
Munro, R. W., 345.
Munro, W., 56.
Munroe, J. P., 198.
Murdock, H. E., 283.
Murphy, D. I., 892.
Murphy, H., 813.
Murphy, J. B., 267.
Murphy, L. S., 45.
Murphy, P. A., 752, 753.
Murray, A., 837.
Murray, T. J., 221.
Mushchenko, S. S., 515.
Mussehl, F. E., 368, 897.
Musser, K. B., 684, 776.
Myers, C. E., 197.
Myers, P. R., 855.
Myrick, H., 389.

Nagai, I., 430.
Nagano, K., 57.
Nagayo, M., 858, 859.
Nagore y Nagore, D., 891.
Nahstoll, G. A., 875.
Nakamura, S., 115.
Narasinga Rao, T. V., 748.
Nasmith, G. G., 488.
Nath Sen, J., 615.
Natta Maglione, J. V., 733.
Nautefeuille, L., 830.
Nayudu, K. R., 342.
Nazarova, P., 525.
Neale, A. T., 900.
Négre, L., 377.
Negri, 692.
Neill, A. J., 365.
Neill, J. W., 796.
Neller, J. R., 811.
Nellis, J. C., 148.
Nelson, A., 399.
Nelson, B. E., 187.
Nelson, E. K., 612.
Nelson, S. B., 96.
Nelson, T. C., 197.
Nelson, W. L., 897.
Nestell, R. J., 218.
Nethersole, M., 184.
Neuwirth, I., 167.
Nevans, W. B., 683, 696, 897.
Newbill, T. J., 599.
Newbold, T., 299.
Newell, F. H., 184.
Newell, W., 162.
Newlands, E. M., 94.
Newlin, C. I., 677.
Newlin, J. A., 548, 885.
Newsom, I. E., 690.
Newton, L. V., 855.
Newton, R. L., 594.
Nicholls, H. M., 357, 551.
Nicholls, W. D., 789.
Nichols, B., 99.
Nichols, C. S., 286.
Nichols, M. L., 397.
Nichols, M. S., 506.
Nicolai, H. E., 281.
Nicolas, E., 692.
Nicoll, W., 854.
Nilsson-Ehle, H., 100.
Nipher, F. E., 115.
Nixon, E. L., 898.
Njaa, J. L., 135.
Nobbs, E. A., 436, 492.
Noble, E., 198.
Noble, G. B., 385.
Noble, T. A., 281.
Noffray, E., 756.
Noguchi, H., 577.
Noll, C. F., 197, 626.
Noll, W., 592.
Nomura, H., 612.
Nörgaard, V. A., 374.
Noronha, C., 657.
North, C. E., 175.
Northrup, Z., 76.
Norton, J. B. S., 842.

Norton, T. H., 721.
Nothnagel, M., 196.
Novelli, N., 539.
Novinskii, M., 339.
Novy, F. G., 578, 579, 580, 581, 582, 688.
Novy, F. O., 581.
Novy, R. L., 578.
Nowak, C. A., 208.
Nowell, W., 452, 454, 461, 556.
Noyes, H. A., 420, 813.
Nuckols, I. F., 897.
Nurenberg, L. I., 165.
Nuttall, G. H. F., 850, 879.
Nutting, P. G., 403.
Nystrom, A. B., 798.

Oakleaf, H. B., 452.
Oakley, R. A., 146.
Oberholser, H. C., 758, 846.
Oberlin, J. F., 91.
Obst, M. M., 183.
Oetken, W., 642.
Ohtawara, T., 375.
Okada, T., 807.
Olds, L. L., 437.
Olitsky, P. K., 850.
Olive, E. W., 552, 749.
Olney, R., 788.
Olsen, J. C., 887.
Olson, G. A., 341, 614, 861.
Olson, T. M., 399.
O'Neill, F. H., 667.
Onodera, I., 224.
Opazo, G. A., 544.
Opoix, O., 633.
Orme, J. P., 700.
Orr, J., 291.
Orton, C. R., 51, 52.
Orton, W. A., 554.
Orwin, C. S., 595.
Osborn, H., 847, 899.
Osborn, L. W., 536.
Osborn, S. J., 416.
Osborn, T. G. B., 542.
Osborne, T. B., 8, 60, 264, 864, 865.
Osman, E. G., 595.
Osner, G. A., 840.
Osterhout, W. J. V., 130, 431, 626.
Osterwalder, A., 509.
Ostrander, J. E., 116, 619, 907.
Ostrovskaja, M., 525.
Osugi, I. S., 118.
Osumi, S., 375.
Oswald, W. L., 398, 446.
Otoba, K., 115, 513.
Ousley, C., 306.
Overholts, L. O., 197.
Owen, W. L., 196, 509, 700.
Owens, J. S., 98.

Pachoskii, I., 542.
Pacottet, P., 834.
Paczosky, I., 542.
Paddock, F. B., 358, 461.
Padhye, G. R., 139.
Page, L. W., 89.
Page, V. W., 490.

Paguirigan y Amalingan, D. B., 339.
Paillot, A., 460.
Pailthorp, R. R., 397.
Painter, H. R., 566.
Palafox y de la Cuesta, G., 339.
Palladin, V. I., 201, 202, 203, 204.
Palladin, W., 201, 202, 203, 204.
Palmer, A. H., 512, 513.
Palmer, C. C., 276, 278, 380, 381, 681, 897.
Palmer, E. F., 832.
Palmer, F. E., 346.
Palmer, H. E., 206.
Palmer, L. S., 72, 172.
Palmer, T. G., 443.
Palmer, T. S., 355.
Pantel, J., 160.
Paranjpe, S. R., 215.
Paresce, R., 417.
Paris, G., 509.
Park, J., 584.
Park, J. B., 235.
Parker, H. N., 174.
Parker, J. H., 398, 497.
Parker, J. R., 255.
Parker, R. R., 560, 687, 764.
Parkinson, H. G., 499.
Parks, T. H., 564.
Parnell, R., 45.
Parodi, S. E., 481.
Parrott, P. J., 261, 359, 561, 847.
Parry, T. W., 285.
Parsons, J. T., 498, 797.
Parsons, S., 546.
Parsons, T. S., 198, 334, 437.
Partridge, J. F., 487.
Passerini, N., 113.
Patanè, G., 344, 827.
Patch, E. M., 850.
Pate, W. F., 419.
Patel, M. L., 454.
Paterson, W. E., 497.
Patrick, A. L., 123.
Pattan, A. J., 524, 724.
Patten, H. E., 503, 716.
Patterson, F. W., 263.
Paul, B. H., 846.
Pax, F., 766.
Payne, V. F., 897.
Peacock, E. A. W., 147.
Pearce, S. J., 299.
Pearl, R., 365, 370, 432, 497, 602, 775, 868.
Pearson, R. A., 605, 893.
Pearson, R. S., 245, 306, 500, 548.
Pease, H. T., 78, 692.
Pease, V. A., 726.
Péchon, R., 153.
Peck, F., 398.
Peck, F. W., 389.
Peelan, J. R. C., 345.
Peglion, V., 250.
Pellet, H., 13, 617.
Pellett, F. C., 262, 467, 855.
Peltier, G. L., 755.
Pelton, W. C., 700.

Pember, F. R., 34, 799, 815.
Pemberton, C. E., 566, 856.
Pembrey, M. S., 571.
Penau, H., 884.
Pendleton, R. L., 810.
Penniman, W. B. D., 468.
Pennington, L. H., 395, 756.
Pennington, M. E., 62, 863.
Perchot, 697, 890.
Perisho, E. C., 603, 611.
Perkins, A. E., 168.
Perkins, G. H., 700.
Perkins, G. W., 166.
Perold, A. I., 144.
Perrin, 692.
Perucci, E., 570.
Pervier, N. C., 503.
Petch, T., 253, 837.
Peter, A. M., 712.
Peters, 249.
Peters, A. T., 482.
Peters, F. H., 187.
Peterson, A., 159.
Peterson, P. P., 29, 503.
Peterson, W., 518, 809.
Peterson, W. E., 681.
Petherbridge, F. R., 351, 761, 765.
Pethybridge, G. H., 49, 350.
Petri, L., 657, 658.
Pettersson, H., 513.
Pettey, F. W., 463.
Pettibone, C. J. V., 24.
Pettit, S., 399.
Peyronel, B., 657, 727.
Pew, W. H., 379.
Pfyl, 618.
Phalen, W. C., 724.
Phelps, E. B., 53, 464, 693.
Phelps, G., 489.
Phelps, I. K., 206.
Phillips, E. F., 263, 360.
Phillips, E. H., 899.
Phillips, E. M., 793.
Phillips, S. W., 212.
Phillips, W. J., 263.
Piccioli, L., 837.
Piché, G. C., 148.
Pickell, J. R., 190.
Pickens, E. M., 693.
Pickett, B. S., 647.
Pickett, W. F., 497.
Piédallu, A., 220.
Piemeisel, F. J., 749.
Pieper, E. J., 502.
Pier, H. B., 897.
Pierce, W. D., 58, 560.
Piettre, 80.
Pigulevski, G. V., 418.
Pike, J. L., 536.
Pillai, N. K., 237.
Pinchot, G., 243.
Pinkerton, T. C., 724.
Pinnow, J., 414.
Pipal, F. J., 239.
Piper, C. V., 54, 146, 194, 437, 440, 900.

Pittard, N. A. B., 416.
Pittier, H., 819.
Pitz, W., 61, 99, 163, 264.
Plaisance, G. P., 206, 503, 801, 802.
Platishenskiĭ, P. G., 203.
Plotnitskiĭ, G. A., 144.
Plum, H. M., 413.
Plumb, C. S., 94, 172, 405.
Plummer, J. K., 419.
Pocock, R., 770.
Poels, J., 691.
Pollock, C., 399.
Ponsonby, T. B., 492.
Poole, R. F., 98.
Pope, F. S., 597.
Popenoe, F. O., 144.
Popenoe, W., 144, 835.
Porcher, C., 508.
Porter, A. E., 308.
Porter, B. A., 667.
Porter, C. E., 460.
Porter, E. W., 881.
Portier, P., 356.
Posey, G. B., 244.
Potebnia, A. A., 246.
Potter, A. A., 611, 698, 750.
Potter, G. M., 196.
Potts, A. B., 98.
Potts, A. T., 835.
Powell, T. F., 594.
Powers, W. L., 84.
Powley, J. O., 279.
Pratt, J. S., 690, 781.
Pratt, L. S., 110.
Pregl, 803.
Preissecker, K., 51.
Prentice, D. S., 577.
Preston, C. F., 98.
Price, L. I., 497.
Price, L. M., 99.
Price, W. A., 360.
Pridham, J. T., 537.
Priego, J. M., 545.
Priestley, H., 376.
Prinsen Geerligs, H. C., 509.
Pritchard, F. J., 28, 442.
Pritchett, I. W., 781.
Proescher, F., 382, 782.
Profeit, W. J., 769.
Prosser, C. A., 607.
Proulx, E. G., 724.
Prucha, M. J., 684.
Puckler-Muskau, (Prince) von, 546.
Pugsley, C. W., 605.
Punnett, R. C., 55.
Puran Singh, 548.
Putnam, G. A., 796.
Putnam, J. J., 20.
Putney, F. S., 172.

Quaife, E. L., 497.
Quaintance, A. L., 358.
Quantz, K. E., 533.
Quarnberg, A. A., 545.
Quayle, H. J., 563.
Quereau, F. C., 529, 568.

Raaij, C. J. van, 323.
Racíborski, M., 553.
Raffo, M., 710.
Raistrick, H., 8.
Ralston, G. S., 30).
Ramasastrulu Nayudu, K., 343.
Ramírez, R., 755.
Ramolno, P., 571.
Ramsay, A. A., 713.
Ramsay, J. M., 392.
Ramser, C. E., 87.
Ramsey, G. B., 653.
Ramsower, H. C., 388.
Ranc, A., 321.
Randall, J. L., 296.
Rane, F. W., 900.
Rankin, W. H., 327, 846.
Ransom, B. H., 277, 355, 577.
Rant, A., 352, 844.
Rapplin, 880.
Rasmussen, A. T., 156.
Rather, J. B., 502, 678, 900.
Ravaz, L., 43, 252.
Ravenna, C., 632.
Ray, F., 93.
Ray, G. S., 29.
Ray, S. H., 367, 598.
Rayfield, F. H., 693.
Rayner, M. C., 129.
Recknagel, A. B., 243.
Records, E., 183.
Rector, V. E., 100, 800.
Reddick, D., 751, 843.
Reddy, C. S., 839.
Reed, E. L., 435, 727.
Reed, E. N., 543.
Reed, G. B., 726.
Reed, G. M., 728, 749, 756.
Reed, H. J., 343, 896.
Reed, O. E., 671.
Reed, W. G., 11, 6, 513, 621, 807.
Reese, H .H., 368.
Reeve, C. S., 711, 885.
Reeve, J., 866.
Reeves, F. S., 242.
Reeves, G. I., 262.
Regan, J. S., 762.
Regan, W. M., 197.
Regnér, G., 80.
Reichel, J., 276.
Reid, H. W., 21.
Reid, W. J., 699.
Reinecke, L., 695.
Reitze, C. N., 281.
Remington, R. E., 63, 864.
Remy, T., 18.
Renacco, R., 349.
Rennie, J., 360, 763.
Renwich, H. B., 800.
Rettger, L. F., 82, 383.
Reuss, A., 410.
Rew, R. H., 670.
Rey, E., 742.
Reynolds, M. H., 197.
Rhein, M., 488.
Rhoads, A. S., 846.

Rhodes, H. C., 896.
Rice, R. C., 513.
Richard, J., 374.
Richards, D. E., 98.
Richards, E. C. M., 451.
Richards, E. H., 620.
Richardson, A. W., 498.
Richardson, C. H., 159, 665.
Richardson, W. N., 775.
Richert, J. G., 492.
Richez-Péchon, 153.
Ricker, P. L., 41, 220.
Riddell, F. T., 474.
Riddle, O., 772, 773, 774, 868.
Riehm, E., 247.
Ries, J. N., 382.
Riford, L. S., 197, 684.
Riganti, H., 513.
Rigg, G. B., 837.
Rigg, G. M., 27.
Riggs, W. M., 359, 610, 611, 698.
Rijks, A. B., 556.
Riley, W. A., 281.
Rindell, A., 18.
Ringelmann, M., 490.
Risler, E., 587.
Ritzman, E. G., 676.
Rizzotte, T., 466.
Roark, G. W., jr., 410.
Robb, O. J., 544.
Robbins, W. W., 209, 818.
Robert, T., 631.
Roberts, E. A., 128.
Roberts, G. A., 690.
Roberts, G. H., 595.
Roberts, J. W., 654, 842.
Roberts, T., 879.
Roberts, W., 891.
Robertson, G. S., 124, 816.
Robertson, R. D., 483, 586.
Robinett, P. M., 399.
Robinson, E., 892.
Robinson, J., 198.
Robinson, M. E., 399.
Robinson, R. H., 559, 759.
Robinson, W. O., 811.
Rock, J. F., 546.
Rockwood, E. W., 204.
Rockwood, H., 398.
Rockwood, L. P., 856.
Rocques, X., 414.
Rocton, 79.
Rodzianko, 160.
Roepke, W., 55.
Rogers, J. E., 346.
Rogers, L. A., 819.
Rogers, S. S., 143.
Rohde, C., 649.
Rohwer, S. A., 568, 569, 667, 766, 855.
Rolfs, P. H., 644.
Rommel, G. M., 572.
Roof, A., 192.
Roos, L., 426.
Root, A. I., 568.
Root, E. R., 568.
Rorer, J. B., 52.

Rosa, J. T., jr., 500.
Rose, R. E., 109.
Rosenbaum, J., 654, 753.
Rosenfeld, A. H., 139, 237, 723.
Rosenow, E. C., 273.
Ross, B. B., 219.
Ross, E. A., 593.
Ross, W. A., 766.
Ross, W. H., 427.
Rossem, C. van, 436.
Rost, C. O., 20.
Rothgeb, B. E., 740.
Rothkugel, M., 747.
Roullard, F. P., 563.
Round, L. A., 165, 208, 800, 806.
Rouse, I., 299.
Ruddick, J. A., 274.
Rudnick, P., 409.
Ruehe, H. A., 273.
Ruff, W. A., 748.
Rulloda, C. B. y, 338.
Rundles, J. C., 538.
Russell, C. E., 592.
Russell, J. J., 426, 445, 724.
Russell, H. L., 198.
Ruston, A. G., 130.
Rutgers, A. A. L., 247, 248, 458, 552, 646, 838.
Ruth, W. A., 755.
Rutherford, A., 158.
Ruttan, R. F., 309.

Sabachnikov, A., 627.
Sabashnikov, A., 627.
Sabinin, D. A., 202.
Saccá, R. A., 553.
Saccardo, P. A., 630, 754.
Saceghem, R. van, 377.
Sackett, R. L., 698.
Sackett, W. G., 248, 286.
Sackville, J. P., 872.
Sahr, C. A., 131.
Saillard, E., 539, 802.
St. John, E. Q., 62.
Saito, K., 631.
Salant, W., 266, 471.
Salisbury, E. J., 525.
Salmon, E. S., 47, 453.
Salmon, S. C., 533.
Salter, R. C., 422.
Salzer, 784.
Sampson, A. W., 437, 818.
Sampson, H. C., 343.
Sampson, H. O., 699.
Samson, G. R., 898.
Sanborn, C. E., 157, 566.
Sancio, F., 831.
Sanders, A. H., 771.
Sanders, G. E., 848.
Sanders, J. G., 761.
Sanderson, D., 93.
Sanderson, D. L., 794.
Sanderson, T., 863.
Sandsten, E. P., 37, 241.
Sani, L., 482.
San Miguel, L. A., 336.
Sarachaga, J. U., 318.

Sargeant, E. W., 585.
Sasscer, E. R., 257.
Sato, S., 897.
Sauder, P. M., 187.
Saunders, L. G., 157.
Saunders, W. H., 853.
Saunders, W. P., 116, 619.
Savastano, L., 155.
Savini, G., 312, 313.
Sawyer, H. L., 201.
Scammell, H. B., 56.
Schaaf, M., 348.
Schafer, E. G., 334, 337.
Schander, R., 150.
Scheffer, T. H., 355, 699.
Scherrer, J. A., 409.
Schimmel, E., 136.
Schlatter, F. P., 745.
Schlesinger, M. J., 688.
Schleussner, O. W., 43.
Schlick, W. J., 187.
Schlumberger, O., 138, 248, 249.
Schmidt, H., 899.
Schmidt, L. B., 189.
Schmidt, R., 497.
Schmitz, H., 250, 728.
Schmitz, N., 332, 340, 442, 540.
Schneider, A., 842.
Schnürer, J., 781.
Schoenfeld, W. A., 300.
Schoenleber, F. S., 376.
Schoevers, T. A. C., 155.
Scholl, A. 414.
Scholl, E. E., 459.
Schollenberger, C. J., 124, 195, 212, 219.
Scholz, H. A., 616.
Schoonover, W. R., 700.
Schorger, A. W., 411, 502, 710.
Schott, J. E., 413.
Schouten-Ilcken, W. S. J., 412.
Schöyen, T. H., 760.
Schramm, J. R., 498.
Schreiner, O., 752, 799, 800.
Schribaux, 263, 806.
Schroeder, E. C., 181, 379, 583.
Schroeder, J. P., 503.
Schroeder, P. J., 723.
Schryver, S. B., 309.
Schultz, M. P., 504.
Schuppli, O., 310, 415.
Schurmann, G., 358.
Schwartz, 460.
Schwartz, B., 784.
Schwartz, E. H., 712.
Schwartz, L., 98.
Schwartze, E. W., 471.
Schwarz, E. A., 568.
Schwarze, C. A., 755.
Schwannesen, A. T., 485.
Scofield, C. S., 595.
Scott, C. A., 46, 196, 451.
Scott, G. A., 789.
Scott, H., 497.
Scott, J. M., 635, 683, 684.
Scott, J. W., 374.
Scott, L., 595.

Scott, L. B., 345.
Scott, L. E., 696.
Scott, W. M., 648, 879.
Scot , W. W., 310.
Scoville, R. I., 98.
Seager, H. R., 491.
Seal, J. L., 499.
Seamans, H. L., 160.
Searles, H. R., 897.
Sebert, 418, 512.
Secrest, E., 895.
Seddon, H. R., 764.
Sée, P., 630.
Seeds, K. B., 889.
Séguin, P., 377.
Seil, H. A., 382, 782.
Selby, A. D., 143, 195, 895.
Sellards, A. W., 356.
Sellers, O. H., 233, 234.
Selvig, C. G., 192.
Semouchkine, V. V., 324.
Semple, C. C., 615.
Semushkin, V. V., 324.
Sen, J. N., 615.
Serbinov, I. L., 360.
Serex, P., jr., 629.
Sethi, D. R., 824.
Seurat, L. G., 361, 577.
Severance, G., 99, 281.
Severin, H. C., 561
Severin, H. H. P., 565, 566.
Severson, B. O., 365.
Severy, J. W., 728.
Sewall, T. R., 398.
Sewall, (Mrs.) T. R., 398.
Seward, W. B., 211.
Sewell, M. C., 212.
Sewell, M. G., 799.
Seymour, R. J., 771.
Shamel, A. D., 144, 145, 342, 345, 546, 711.
Shanks, M., 893.
Shannon, R. C., 57.
Shantz, H. L., 429.
Shapovalov, M., 654, 753.
Sharma, L. C., 824, 825.
Sharples, A., 52.
Shattuck, C. H., 87, 244, 397, 600.
Shaw, A. N., 16.
Shaw, C. F., 18.
Shaw, E. E., 746.
Shaw, J. A., 711.
Shaw, J. K., 554.
Shaw, S. B., 143, 342.
Shaw, W. M., 121.
Shaw-Mackenzie, J. A., 375.
Shear, C. L., 745.
Shearer, H. A., 789.
Sheather, A. L., 479.
Sheehan, B. F., 499, 898.
Sherbakoff, C. D., 651.
Sherfesee, F., 348, 836.
Sherman, H. C., 613.
Sherman, J. M., 499.
Sherrard, G., 823, 825.
Sherry, B. J., 807.
Sherwin, C. P., 308.

Sherwood, R. M., 368.
Shibata, K., 430.
Shields, R. L., 300.
Shilston, A. W., 480.
Shinji, G. O., 158, 163.
Shipley, A. E., 54, 156.
Shippen, L. P., 179.
Shirras, G. F., 891.
Shistovskij., 827.
Shorey, E. C., 505.
Shoup, G. R., 96, 599, 699, 895.
Shoup, Mrs. G. R., 96, 599, 699.
Show, S. B., 451.
Shreve, E. B., 26.
Shreve, F., 837.
Shuey, P. McG., 412.
Shuler, W. P., 473.
Shutt, F. T., 425, 645.
Shutts, G. C., 297.
Sibley, B. C., 100.
Sich, A., 57.
Sickert, B., 546.
Sidenius, E., 523.
Sievers, A. F., 417, 545.
Sievers, F. J., 798.
Sil, S. N., 825.
Siler, J. F., 694.
Silverstein, P., 109.
Sim, T. R., 748.
Simmonds, C. A., 545.
Simmonds, N., 61, 99, 163, 264, 308.
Simonot, J., 390.
Simpson, C. E., 79.
Simpson, H. E., 807.
Sinclair, T. A., 26.
Sivori, F., 277.
Sjogren, O. W., 384.
Sjöström, A., 733.
Skalkij, S., 423.
Skerrett, R. G., 359.
Skilling, W. T., 395.
Skinner, J. H., 270.
Skinner, J. J., 23, 799.
Slack, F. H., 481.
Sleight, R. B., 785.
Sloan, L. H., 478.
Slocum, R. R., 368.
Smales, C. B., 348.
Smeyers, F., 622.
Smies, E. H., 720.
Smillie, E. W., 384.
Smirnov, A. I., 322.
Smith, A., 780.
Smith, A. C., 775.
Smith, A. M., 196.
Smith, C., 409.
Smith, C. D., 281.
Smith, C. M., 410.
Smith, C. O., 655, 843.
Smith, C. P., 541.
Smith, E., 647.
Smith, E. F., 245, 653.
Smith, F .H., 65, 673.
Smith, G. A., 570, 575.
Smith, G. C., 892.
Smith, G. E., 278.
Smith, G. E. P., 185.

Smith, G. H., 819.
Smith, G. P. D., 352.
Smith, H. C., 621.
Smith, H. E., 763.
Smith, H. G., 328.
Smith, H. K., 114.
Smith, H. S., 58, 162, 563, 568, 569.
Smith, J. J., 47.
Smith, L. B., 856.
Smith, P., 892.
Smith, P. S., 724.
Smith, R., 571.
Smith, R. A., 428.
Smith, T., 383, 384.
Smith, W. J., 498.
Smith, W. S. A., 389.
Smith, Z. M., 296, 798.
Smits, M. B., 394.
Smoll, A. E., 524.
Snapp, O. I., 211, 498.
Snyder, E. R., 394.
Snyder, H., 165, 166, 799, 899.
Snyder, J. M., 122.
Snyder, T. E., 565.
Soderstrom, G. F., 266, 267.
Solis-Cohen, S., 274.
Somers, W. H., 745.
Somerville, 214.
Soparkar, M. B., 782.
Sornay, P. de, 28.
Sotgia, G., 826.
Souchon, 214.
Soule, A. M, 390, 604, 610, 800.
Soule, A. M. G., 469.
Sourisseau, J. H., 591.
South, F. W., 849.
Southwick, B. G., 496.
Souza, W. W. C. de, 441.
Spalletta, A., 835.
Sparapani, 691.
Spaulding, P., 845, 846.
Spence, D. W., 698.
Spencer, R. R., 588.
Spillman, W. J., 263, 389, 593, 899.
Spinks, G. T., 646.
Spoehr, H. A., 325, 821.
Spohn, A. A., 772, 773.
Sponsler, O. L., 346.
Spooner, C. S., 647.
Spragg, F. A., 799.
Sprague, C. B., 99, 143.
Spray, R. S., 197.
Sprecher, A., 150.
Spring, F. G., 147.
Spring, S. N., 837.
Spry, J. R., 385.
Spuler, A., 665.
Stacy, W. H., 196.
Stafford, 563.
Stahl, C. F., 847.
Stahl, J. L., 699.
Stakman, E. C., 749.
Standley, P. C., 244.
Stanley, L., 894.
Stapleton, R. G., 230.
Stead, A., 629.
Stear, J. R., 498, 797.

Stearns, T., 167.
Stebbins, M. E., 720.
Stebler, F. G., 47.
Stedman, J. M., 796.
Steenbock, H., 308, 309, 766.
Steeves, R. P., 892.
Steffen, M. R., 784.
Steik, K., 788.
Steinkoenig, L. A., 811.
Stephens, D. E., 529.
Sterrett, W. D., 548.
Steuart, D. W., 778, 875.
Stevens, F. L., 149, 755.
Stevens, H. E., 656.
Stevens, H. P., 512.
Stevens, J. C., 183.
Stevens, J. S., 314.
Stevens, N. E., 351, 549, 557.
Stevens, W. S., 497.
Stevenson, A. F., 53, 464.
Stevenson, C., 175.
Stevenson, J. A., 246.
Stevenson, W. H., 211.
Stewart, F. H., 374.
Stewart, G., 99.
Stewart, I. M., 596.
Stewart, J. S., 193.
Stewart, J. T., 197.
Stewart, M. N., 807.
Stewart, P. H., 211.
Stewart, R., 120, 421, 518, 800.
Stewart, R. L., 644.
Stewart, V. B., 751.
Stiles, W., 632.
Stinson, J. T., 399.
Stirling, F., 556.
Stober, J. P., 327.
Stockdale, F. A., 550.
Stockham, W. L., 362.
Stocking, W. A., 500, 777.
Stockman (Mrs.), D. H., 796.
Stockman, S., 277, 687.
Stockton, R. S., 185.
Stokes, W. R., 468.
Stoklasa, J., 528.
Stoik, D. van, 322.
Stoll, A., 222.
Stom, V., 542.
Stone, G. E., 727.
Stone, R. E., 551.
Stone, R. W., 217, 816.
Stookey, E. B., 96, 566, 799, 895.
Storey, G., 54.
Stout, A. B., 27, 836.
Stout, O. V. P., 608.
Stout, S. R., 97.
Stout, W., 514.
Stoute, R. A., 483.
Stoward, F., 149.
Stratton, S. W., 723.
Strausz, A. L., 136.
Street, J. P., 232, 234, 268, 813, 863, 896.
Strickland, E. H., 459.
Strohecker, R., 414.
Strong, R. P., 356.
Stroud, J. F., 621.

Strowd, W. H., 324, 471.
Strub, E., 793.
Strutt, E. G., 595.
Stuart, C. P. C., 43.
Stuart, W., 80C, 830.
Stuckey, H. P., 40, 44.
Subramania Aiyer, P. A., 424.
Sucro, W. G., 787.
Sudworth, G. B., 343.
Sullivan, K. C., 760.
Summers, J. N., 453.
Summers, M. B., 513.
Sundberg, R., 55, 849.
Supino, F., 847.
Sure, B., 10, 24.
Surface, F. M., 497, 733.
Surface, H. A., 459.
Sutto, S., 52.
Sutton, M. H. F., 814.
Swain, R. E., 64.
Swann, H. K., 758.
Swanson, C. O., 119, 206, 709.
Swart, N. L., 347, 343.
Sweany, L. C., 275.
Sweeny, M., 611.
Sweet, G., 764.
Sweet, J. E., 876.
Sweet, L. D., 800.
Swezey, O. H., 363.
Swift, H. F., 780.
Switzer, H. B., 700.
Sykora, J., 519.
Symeonides, P., 823.
Symons, T. B., 143.

Taft, L. R., 796.
Taggart, W. G., 529.
Tague, E. L., 206, 703.
Takaki, I., 375.
Takeoka, M., 275.
Tamura, K., 375.
Tanaka, Y., 158.
Taniguchi, T., 375.
Tarr, L. W., 600.
Tate, H. D., 300.
Taubenhaus, J. J., 155, 546, 841, 843.
Taylor, A., 344.
Taylor, A. E., 147, 166, 602.
Taylor, A. M., 843.
Taylor, E. P., 57.
Taylor, F., 830.
Taylor, F. W., 590.
Taylor, H. C., 290.
Taylor, R. B., 398.
Tchirikov, T. V., 323.
Teixeira de Mattos, A., 358.
Tempany, H. A., 420, 421.
Temple, J. C., 23.
Templeton, G. S., 682.
Tharp, B. C., 748.
Tharp, W. E., 21.
Thatcher, R. W., 398, 610, 900.
Thaxter, R., 461.
Thayer, P., 241.
Thelen, R., 452.
Theobald, F. V., 662.
Thiessen, A. H., 807.

Thing, C. W., 722.
Thom, C. C., 798.
Thomas, A. W., 614.
Thomas, B. A., 76.
Thomas, E. O., 802.
Thomas, G. C., jr., 836.
Thomas, H. E., 754.
Thomas, H. H., 41, 645, 648.
Thomas, L. M., 361, 860.
Thomas, M., 720.
Thomas, O., 357.
Thomas, W. A., 395.
Thompson, A. R., 320.
Thompson, C. A., 99.
Thompson, C. W., 291, 592.
Thompson, H. C., 297, 442.
Thompson, H. N., 100.
Thompson, I. F., 273.
Thompson, J. B., 132.
Thompson, S. E., 590.
Thompson, W. C., 82, 280, 872.
Thompson, W. O., 698.
Thomsen, O., 178.
Thomson, C. R., 897.
Thomson, E. H., 389.
Thomson, H. L., 399.
Thomson, W. W., 191.
Thorndike, E. L., 807.
Thorne, C. E., 132, 133, 195, 208, 337, 396, 595, 831, 999.
Thorne, J. F., 233.
Thornton, T., 553.
Thresh, J. C., 187.
Thrun, W. E., 393.
Thurber, E. C., 497.
Thurgau, H. M., 248, 509.
Thurston, H. W., jr., 897.
Thurston, L. A., 452.
Tijmstra, S., 541.
Tillman, B. W., 122, 412.
Tillotson, C. R., 348.
Tingle, A., 14.
Tinker, F., 25.
Tireman, H., 650.
Tisserand, E., 493.
Titcomb, E., 700.
Titlow, C. R., 611.
Tobiansky D'Altoff, A., 321.
Todd, A., 576, 778.
Todd, J. L., 76.
Tolley, G. H., 693.
Tolley, H. R., 269.
Tolman, L. M., 716.
Tolstrup, M., 476.
Tombave, W. H., 365.
Tompson, H. F., 94.
Tönjes, C. J., 90.
Tonnelier, A. C., 438.
Toole, E. H., 896.
Torossian, G., 714.
Torre Bueno, J. R. de la, 357.
Torrey, J., 347.
Tottenham, W. F. L., 146.
Tottingham, W. E., 24.
Toulaikoff, N. M., 128.
Tower, W. V., 900.
Townsend, C. H. T., 358, 359, 460, 565, 764.

Townsend, C. O., 511, 540.
Tracy, M., 469.
Tracy, S. M., 440.
Trafford, F., 348.
Trafton, G. H., 53.
Trägårdh, I., 163, 765.
Tregenna, C. J., 340.
Treherne, R. C., 55, 459, 462, 568, 665.
Trelease, W., 746, 820.
Trelles, R. A., 486.
Tressler, D. K., 98, 898.
Treub, M., 553.
Trinchieri, G., 848.
Trivett, J. B., 513.
Troop, J., 360.
Tropea, C., 339.
Trosper, E. J., 97.
Trotter, A., 250.
Trouchaud-Verdier, L., 152.
Trouette, 692.
Troup, R. S., 547.
Trowbridge, P. F., 428.
Troy, H. C., 175, 374.
Truche, 692.
Truche, C., 583.
True, A. C., 604, 605, 796.
True, R. H., 799.
Truelle, A., 15.
Truesdell, H. W., 828.
Trunninger, E., 219.
Truog, E., 519.
Tsuiji, Y., 807.
Tuck, C. H., 498.
Tucker, E. S., 564, 854.
Tuinzing, R. W., 412.
Tulaîkov, N. M., 128.
Tullgren, A., 158.
Tulloch, W. J., 176.
Tungeln, G. H. von, 592.
Tunstall, A. C., 52, 252.
Turconi, M., 155, 657, 755.
Turley, A. M., 796.
Turner, E. A., 95.
Turnor, C., 390.
Turnor, C. H., 697.
Turpin, G. M., 299.
Turpin, H. W., 623.
Tuttle, O. N., 398.
Tuttle, W. P., 196.
Tyzzer, E. E., 76, 356, 578.

Uchida, S., 109.
Uetsuki, T., 118.
Ultée, A. J., 348.
Underhill, F. P., 64.
Upson, F. W., 413.
Upton, H. E., 584.
Urbahns, T. D., 561.
Urban, J., 829.

Vaile, R. S., 144, 186, 649.
Valgren, V. N., 391, 594.
Vallée, H., 688.
Van Alstine, E., 514, 720.
Vanatta, E. E., 522.
Vanatta, E. S., 621.

Van Dam, W., 175, 373.
Van der Bijl, P. A., 554, 842.
Van der Byl, P. A., 554, 842.
Van der Elst, P., 883.
Van der Goot, P., 850.
Vanderleck, J., 760, 777.
Van Dine, D. L., 57.
Van Duyne, C., 810.
Van Dyke, E. C., 568.
Van Hall, C. J. J., 246, 247, 745, 835.
Van Harreveld-Lako, C. H., 23.
Van Helten, W. M., 835.
Van Hermann, H. A., 345.
Van Hise, C. R., 602.
Van Hissenhoven, P., 523.
Van Hoek, P., 79.
Van Kampen, G. B., 208, 416.
Van Pelt, W., 349.
Van Raaij, C. J., 323.
Van Rossem, C., 436.
Van Saceghem, R., 377.
Van Slyke, D. D., 804.
Van Stolk, D., 322.
Vasey, H. E., 51.
Vaughan, H. W., 194.
Veatch, J. O., 123.
Vecchi, A. de, 586.
Velu, 692.
Vendelmans, H., 136, 214, 215.
Venino, P., 141.
Venkato Rao, M. K., 657.
Vercelli, F., 417.
Verdier, L. T., 152.
Verge, G., 252.
Verkade, P. E., 108.
Vernet, 890.
Viala, P., 153.
Vidière, E., 888.
Viehoever, A., 9.
Viele, D., 190.
Vielle, 384.
Viereck, H. L., 765.
Vigdorcik, S., 312.
Vik, K., 732.
Vikhliâev, I. I., 723.
Villarreal, R., 749.
Vinall, H. N., 37.
Vinassa, G., 722.
Vincens, F., 252, 467.
Vincent, C., 522.
Vincent, C. C., 57, 646, 647.
Vincent, G. E., 593.
Vincent, H., 176.
Vinson, C. G., 763.
Viquesney, J. A., 747.
Vitek, E., 829.
Vivian, A., 607, 798.
Voegtlin, C., 308.
Voelcker, J. A., 215, 229.
Vogt, P. L., 290, 593.
Vosbury, E. D., 345.
Voss, A., 716.
Vries, H. de, 328.
Vries, J. J. O. de, 176, 414.
Vries, O. de, 347, 348, 417, 553, 651.
Vrooman, C., 592, 796, 800.

Waddell, J., 174.
Wadsworth, J. T., 764.
Wagner, P., 217.
Waid, C. W., 533.
Waite, M. B., 755, 833.
Waksman, S. A., 718, 812.
Walden, B. H., 156, 255.
Waldrop, C. S., 621.
Waldstein, P. J., 616.
Wale, J. H., 133.
Walker, H. B., 497.
Walker, H. S., 506.
Walker, J. A., 613.
Walker, J. C., 841.
Walker, S. S., 313.
Walldén, J. N., 534.
Waller, A. E., 537, 793.
Waller, O. L., 281.
Wallis, B. C., 15.
Wallis, R. L. M., 714.
Wallis, T. E., 205.
Walters, E. H., 612, 709, 801.
Walton, A. C., 163.
Walton, R. C., 195.
Walz, F. J., 513.
Wambeam, F., 897.
Warcollier, G., 416.
Ward, A. R., 276, 631.
Ward, F. E., 605.
Ward, R. DeC., 807.
Wardell, E. L., 470.
Warren, E., 649.
Warren, G. F., 94.
Warren, G. M., 583.
Washburn, F. L., 897.
Washburn, R. M., 894.
Wason, E., 890.
Waterman, H. I., 103.
Waters, H. J., 610, 703.
Waters, R., 150, 247.
Waterston, J., 162, 467, 667, 764.
Watkins, W. I., 720.
Watson, C. W., 211.
Watson, E. B., 810.
Watson, J. R., 355, 453, 561, 652, 659.
Watson, M., 86.
Watson, M. E., 53, 553.
Watson, R., 450.
Watt, W. M., 281.
Watts, F., 732.
Waugh, F. A., 189, 547.
Wauters, C., 183.
Weaver, G. E., 897.
Weaver, L. A., 69.
Webb, W., 793.
Webber, H. J., 144, 240, 649.
Weber, P., 739.
Webster, R. L., 262.
Weedy, W. D., 437.
Weeter, P. L., 684, 700.
Weiant, A. S., 573.
Weil, R., 275.
Weinberg, M., 377.
Weinzirl, J., 784.
Weir, J. R., 458, 653.
Weir, W. W., 297.

Weiss, H. B., 157, 255, 359, 660, 761, 856.
Welander, A., 465.
Welch, H., 278.
Welch, J. S., 68, 397, 639, 640.
Welch, R. R., 573.
Welles, W. S., 194.
Wellington, J. W., 240.
Wellington, R., 240.
Wellman, M. T., 396.
Wells, C. A., 65.
Wells, H. G., 77.
Wells, J. P., 315.
Wells, L. S., 432.
Wells, R. W., 560.
Welsford, E. J., 47.
Wentworth, E. N., 497.
Werth, E., 150, 249, 251, 253.
Wery, G., 587, 834.
Wessels, P. H., 767.
Wessling, H. L., 364.
West, C., 630.
West, F. L., 344.
Wester, P. J., 648, 745.
Westerdijk, J., 249.
Westover, E. L., 98.
Wetmore, A., 355, 758.
Wharton, L. D., 277.
Wheeler, H. J., 796.
Wheeler, H. L., 695.
Wheeler, R. H., 498.
Wheeler, W. M., 357, 766.
Wheelon, J. C., 281.
Wheldale, M., 633.
Whetzel, H. H., 151, 552, 749, 832.
Whipple, G. H., 167, 375.
Whipple, O. B., 241.
Whitby, G. S., 416.
Whitcher, G. H., 494, 699.
White, A., 899.
White, B., 233.
White, D. S., 176, 604.
White, E. A., 240.
White, E. C., 409.
White, E. W., 462.
White, F. M., 886.
White, G. C., 37, 594, 684, 776.
White, H. L., 399.
White, J. W., 197.
White, T. H., 320, 645.
White, W. T., 499.
Whiting, A. L., 820.
Whiting, R. A., 784.
Whitlock, B. W., 238, 498.
Whitmarsh, R. D., 258.
Whitmore, W. V., 700.
Whitney, W., 795.
Whitson, J., 342.
Whitten, J. C., 743, 744, 754.
Wiancko, A. T., 214.
Wible, L. H., 888.
Wichmann, H. J., 313.
Wicks, W. H., 744.
Wickware, A. B., 483.
Wiggans, C. C., 743, 744.
Wilber, C. P., 650.
Wilber, D. F., 888.

Wilcox, A. M., 758.
Wilcox, E. A., 387.
Wilcox, E. V., 500.
Wilcox, R. B., 351.
Wild, L. J., 622.
Wilde, E. I., 197.
Wiley, R. C., 324.
Wiley, W. E., 21.
Wilkerson, C. L., 192.
Wilkie, J. M., 805.
Wilkie, S. J., 429, 431.
Wilkins, R. H., 896.
Wilkins, S. D., 398.
Willaman, J. J., 109, 113, 600.
Willard, H. F., 856.
Willard, H. R., 497.
Willard, J. T., 324, 767.
Willcocks, F. C., 55.
Willett, G., 355.
Williams, C. B., 257, 358, 419, 445, 625, 636, 762.
Williams, C. G., 134, 235, 396, 437, 535, 831, 895.
Williams, G., 410.
Williams, G. I., 398.
Williams, H. E., 513.
Williams, H. S., 342.
Williams, I. W., 847.
Williams, M. E., 894.
Williams, P. C., 264.
Williams, P. F., 78.
Williams, R. J., 342.
Williams, R. R., 411.
Williams, R. S., 777, 879.
Williams, W. L., 379, 482.
Williamson, H., 98.
Williamson, J. T., 233, 234.
Willis, R. L., 243.
Willson, C. A., 471.
Willstätter, R., 222.
Wilson, A. D., 594.
Wilson, C. S., 790.
Wilson, E. G., 10.
Wilson, E. H., 145.
Wilson, G. M., 194, 798.
Wilson, M., 354.
Wilson, M. O., 500.
Wilson, R. H., 596.
Wilson, T., 100, 459.
Wilson, T. R. C., 885.
Wilson, W., 198, 301, 302, 701.
Wilson, W. H., 593.
Wimer, D. C., 197.
Wind, J., 413.
Windsor, W., 97.
Wing, L. W., 499, 898.
Wingard, S. A., 500.
Winkjer, J. G., 574.
Winslow, C. E. A., 819.
Winslow, C. P., 452, 748.
Winslow, R. M., 655.
Winter, H. E., 895.
Winterbottom, D. C., 322.
Winters, H. B., 767.
Winters, N. E., 329.
Winters, R. Y., 233.
Winton, A. L., 503.

Wirt, G. H., 650.
Wise, J. C., 192.
Wise, L. E., 612, 803.
Withers, W. A., 689.
Wittmer, J. H., 99.
Witwer, E., 62.
Woglum, R. S., 158, 634.
Wolbach, S. B., 560.
Wolcott, G. N., 255.
Wolf, E. L., 44.
Wolf, E. V., 144.
Wolf, F. A., 456, 583.
Wolfe, T. K., 300, 535.
Wolff, H. W., 588.
Wolkoff, M. I., 520, 721.
Woll, F. W., 94, 795.
Wolman, A., 587.
Wood, D. R., 775.
Wood, H. P., 357, 859.
Wood, I. D., 696.
Wood, T. B., 571, 900.
Woodbury, C. G., 97.
Woodham, H. C., 898.
Woodruffe-Peacock, E. A., 147.
Woods, A. C., 481.
Woods, A. F., 610.
Woods, C. D., 40, 218, 570, 628, 635, 647, 676, 680, 699.
Woodward, A. S., 892.
Woodward, E. G., 172.
Woodward, K. W., 450.
Woodward, T. E., 800.
Woodworth, C. M., 546.
Woolman, H. M., 750.
Woolman, M. S., 895.
Woolsey, T. S., jr., 650.
Work, P., 240.
Works, G. A., 192, 610, 798.
Wormald, H., 751.
Worobiew, S. J., 742.
Worsdell, W. C., 127.
Worsham, E. L., 847.
Worsham, W. A., jr., 211.
Worthley, L. H., 563.
Wortley, E. J., 823.
Wright, C. H., 838.
Wright, F. L., 897.
Wright, J. H., 711.
Wright, J. K., 866.
Wright, S., 866.
Wright, W. P., 543.
Wuentz, A., 600.
Wuerts, A. J., 398.
Wu Lien Teh, 180, 878.

Yakimoff, W. L., 360, 374.
Yamaguchi, Y., 434.
Yanovsky, E., 410.
Yarnell, D. L., 384.
Yaxis, T. G., 896.
Yeager, A. F., 197.
Yerger, H. C., jr., 499.
Yerkes, A. P., 491.
Yingling, C. K., jr., 514.
Yingling, H. C., 258.
Yohe, H. S., 883.
Yoshida, S., 558.

Yothers, M. A., 54, 157.
Yothers, W. W., 460.
Young, H. P., 123.
Young, R. A., 537.
Young, R. F., 513.
Youngblood, B., 887, 900.

Zacharewicz, E., 886.
Zacher, 460.
Zaporozhenko, A. P., 338.
Zapparoli, T. V., 28.

Zappe, M. P., 261.
Zarin, E. IA., 467.
Zavaritskii, V. N., 321.
Zavaritzki, V. N., 321.
Zavitz, C. A., 533, 800.
Zeller, S. M., 129, 727.
Zerban, F., 806.
Zholtkevich, V., 535.
Zimmele, G. B., 694.
Zimmerman, C. W., 89.

Zinn, C. J., 810.
Zinn, J., 738.
Zitkowski, H. E., 817.
Zlataroff, A. S., 273.
Zolotarevskii, B. N., 760.
Zon, R., 45.
Zuderell, H., 550.
Zunz, E., 376.
Zwart, S. G., 172.
Zweigelt, F., 550.

INDEX OF SUBJECTS.

NOTE.—The abbreviations "Ala.College," "Conn.State," "Mass.," etc., after entries refer to the publications of the respective State experiment stations; "Alaska," "Guam," "Hawaii," and "P.R.," to those of the experiment stations in Alaska, Guam, Hawaii, and Porto Rico; "Can.," to those of the experiment stations in Canada: and "U.S.D.A.," to those of this Department.

Abattoirs. (*See* Slaughterhouses.)

Ablerus clisiocampæ, parasitic on tent caterpillar.................................... 667

Abortion, contagious—
control in Michigan....................... 274
control in Oregon......................... 374
in cattle............................... 482, 687
in cattle, N.C........................... 691
in cattle, U.S.D.A....................... 181
in cattle, diagnosis...................... 276
in United States......................... 274
investigations, Mo....................... 779
transmission by milk..................... 78, 79

Aburachan seed, oil of..................... 109

Acacia farnesiana injurious to horses, Guam.. 778

Acalypta grisea n.sp., description........... 563

Acanthoscelides (Bruchus) obtectus, notes..... 262

Acari, parasitic on mammals and birds in Great Britain............................ 859

Acerbia maydis n.sp., notes.................. 148

Acetaldehyde in orchard fruits.............. 246

Acetates, determination..................... 617

Acetic acid, effect on—
inner qualities of rubber................. 347
rotatory power of sucrose and invert sugar 802

Achetoidea of South America................ 157

Achroodextrinase, bacterial, preparation... 411

Achrysocharella albitibiæ n.sp., description... 667

Acid phosphate. (*See* Superphosphate.)

Acids—
alkaline reaction in soils................. 18
amino. (*See* Amino acids.)
effect on plants.......................... 224
effect on rotatory power of sucrose and invert sugar........................... 802
effect on soil bacteria................... 213
excretion by roots....................... 222
fatty, determination in butter and other fats................................... 508
inhibition of oxidase activity by........ 9
of fruit wines........................... 310
reactions of ions and molecules.......... 201
volatile, determination.................. 803
volatile fatty, determination............ 13, 413

Acridians injurious in Nova Scotia.......... 156

Acridium peregrinum, notes.................. 561

Actinomyces—
lanfranchii, studies..................... 482
pheochromogenus n.sp., description, N.Y. State.................................. 517

Actinomycetes in soils, N.Y.State.......... 517

Adansonia digitata, fiber from............. 534

Adenin, isolation from cows' milk.......... 308

Adenitis, caseous, in swine................. 82

Adipocere, composition..................... 309

Adrenalin, effect on milk production...... 173, 272

Adzuki bean for classroom work in genetics.. 831

Æcidium clematidis, effect on leaves of host.. 549

Aedes calopus, development in relation to bacteria and yeasts........................ 763

Aeolothrips floridensis n.sp., description...... 561

Aeolothrips, North American species........ 561

Agar—
anaphylatoxin, studies................... 579
effect of intravenous injections.......... 580

Agave fibers of Tunis...................... 535

"Agélarine," notes......................... 744

Agglutination reaction, mechanism......... 576

Agglutinin—
disappearance from blood of anaphylactic and normal animals................. 76
from beans.............................. 81

Aggregates, bituminous, toughness, U.S.D.A. 885

Agoutis, new, from Panama and Nicaragua.. 757

Agricultural—
arithmetic, textbook.................. 95, 297
Chemical Institute at Bern-Liebefeld, report................................. 311
chemistry. (*See* Chemistry.)
colleges, attendance as affected by the war.................................. 701
colleges, response to war conditions...... 1, 603
(*See also* Alabama, Arizona, etc.)
colonization of Tripoli................... 791
conditions in Department of Corrèze, France................................ 92
cooperation, examples of................. 594
cooperation in Bengal.................... 291
cooperation in Saskatchewan............. 191
cooperation in Switzerland............... 392
cooperation in United States, U.S.D.A.. 888
cooperative associations, N.Dak......... 492
cooperative societies in Bombay Presidency................................. 91
courses, disrespect of students for........ 593
credit in California...................... 190
credit in Dutch East Indies.............. 91
credit in Texas.......................... 91
credit in United States................. 391, 888
development, factors in.................. 189

Agricultural—Continued. Page.
  education—
    at Panama-Pacific Exposition....... 393
    in Argentina........................ 793
    in Bulgaria......................... 892
    in France........................... 493
    in Iowa............................. 292
    in Netherlands...................... 193
    in North Dakota..................... 596
    in Saskatchewan.................... 394
    in Scotland......................... 892
    in Union of South Africa............ 493
    in Virginia......................... 192
    in Wales............................ 294
    in Washington...................... 597
    relation to National affairs........... 401
    secondary, in Russia................ 792
    vocational, in Pennsylvania......... 192
    (See also Agricultural instruction.)
  engineering, Federal aid.................. 610
  experiment stations. (See Experiment
    stations.)
  extension in Argentina.................. 793
  extension, response to war conditions.... 1,604
  fair exhibits, Wash....................... 895
  fairs, food training camps............... 400
  institutions and associations in Denmark 295
  instruction—
    class projects...................... 194
    home projects................. 194, 494, 795
    in Alaska........................... 393
    in Alberta.......................... 293
    in Argentina....................... 294
    in British Columbia................. 293
    in California........................ 394
    in Canada.......................... 699
    in elementary schools.............. 194, 295
    in high schools............. 93, 194, 494, 793
    in Ireland.......................... 294
    in Minnesota....................... 793
    in New Brunswick.................. 892
    in New Hampshire.................. 699
    in New York........................ 293
    in New Zealand..................... 597
    in North Dakota.................... 193
    in Norway.......................... 294
    in Ontario.......................... 892
    in Philippines....................... 494
    in Prince Edward Island............ 793
    in public schools.............. 192, 494, 893
    in secondary schools, U.S.D.A....... 395
    in Spain............................ 93
    in Texas............................ 794
    in United States................... 392, 798
    in Utah............................. 198
    in various countries................. 394
    lessons in.......................... 298
    papers on....................... 192, 596
    (See also Agricultural education.)
  insurance in France..................... 888
  journalism, instruction in.............. 794
  journals, new.......................... 200, 500
  journals, technical, development in
    America........................... 405
  labor in Canada........................ 889
  labor in Ireland........................ 492
  labor in North Carolina................. 190

Agricultural—Continued. Page.
  labor in Switzerland..................... 790
  labor, mobilization..................... 290
  labor problem, handling, U.S.D.A...... 790
  labor, seasonal distribution, U.S.D.A.... 390
  laborers in Finland..................... 91
  machinery, bearings for................. 490
  machinery, directory.................... 888
  machinery in Cuba...................... 591
  meteorology. (See Meteorology.)
  production in Great Britain............. 392
  production in Italy...................... 92
  production in United States............. 595
  products, bushel weights............... 889
  products, marketing.................. 89, 391
  products, marketing cooperatively, U.S.
    D.A............................... 888
  products, prices in India............... 792
  products, prices in Ireland............. 291
  products, receipts and exports at New
    York City......................... 891
  products, trade and commerce in Chicago 392
  research in Scotland.................... 892
  research, relation to National affairs..... 401
  resources of California.................. 790
  resources of New York.................. 790
  resources of Russia..................... 791
  resources of South Dakota.............. 790
  resources of Utah...................... 790
  rules in Italy........................... 888
  schools, district, in Georgia............. 193
  schools in New York.................... 394
  schools, laboratory equipment.......... 798
  small holdings in Oxfordshire.......... 791
  societies in Finland.................... 790
  societies in Pennsylvania.............. 888
  society of Malmöhus Province, report.... 597
  statistics—
    in British Guiana................... 291
    in Chile............................ 92
    in Denmark........................ 392
    in England and Wales.............. 392
    in Finland......................... 93, 291
    in India............................ 891
    in Indiana.......................... 891
    in Japan......................... 92, 792
    in Java and Madura................. 191
    in Norway.......................... 93
    in Ohio............................ 191
    in Scotland........................ 392
    in Spain........................ 191, 827
    in United Kingdom................. 191
    in Wisconsin....................... 891
  teachers, training courses............... 794
  tenancy in California................... 190
  tenancy in United States, U.S.D.A...... 593
  terms in India......................... 433
  wages in India......................... 792
  wages in Sweden....................... 492
Agriculture—
  and preparedness, treatise............. 389
  Department of. (See United States De-
    partment of Agriculture.)
  elementary, course in.................. 395
  elementary, textbook.................. 795
  graphic summary, U.S.D.A............. 595
  in America, economic history........... 189

Agriculture—Continued. Page.
 in Argentina............................. 190
 in British East Africa.................... 734
 in Cuba.................................. 591
 in England and Wales after the war..... 791
 in France................................ 890
 in Great Britain.................... 595, 697
 in India................................. 595
 in Madras................................ 697
 in Navarra............................... 891
 in New Zealand........................... 791
 in Norway................................ 891
 in Oxfordshire, treatise................. 291
 in Philippines........................... 791
 in San Simon Valley, Arizona and New
  Mexico................................. 486
 in Scotland.............................. 891
 in South Africa, improvement........... 389
 in Sweden............................. 93, 191
 Indian, in Arizona....................... 437
 net output from, in England............. 595
 on reclamation projects, U.S.D.A....... 595
 textbook.............................. 795, 888
 treatise................................. 728
Agrilus burkei n.sp., description............ 566
Agriotes obscurus, larval and pupal stages.... 765
Agromyza—
 gayi, n.sp., description................. 460
 n.spp., descriptions, U.S.D.A........... 764
Agrostemma githago, seed weight............. 831
Ahnfeldtia plicata, analyses, Conn.State.... 814
Air—
 of Buenos Aires, bacteriological study... 513
 routes and their regulation, U.S.D.A.... 807
 temperatures, reduction to true mean,
  U.S.D.A................................ 116
 (See also Atmosphere.)
Akebi seed, oil of........................... 109
Alabama—
 Canebrake Station, notes........... 97, 299, 797
 College, notes..................... 496, 700
 College Station, notes........... 97, 496, 700
 College Station, report.................. 599
Alanin, influence on action of alkali on glucose 109
Alaptus immaturus n.sp., description........ 855
Albugo (Cystopus) sp. on sweet potatoes..... 452
Alcohol—
 effect on egg yolk of pigeons............ 773
 effect on formation of carbon dioxid by
  dead yeast............................. 203
 effect on soils.......................... 519
 extracting from garbage.................. 590
Aldehydes, formation in wine................. 805
Aleurocanthus woglumi, notes................. 462
Aleurothrixus howardi, notes, Fla........... 659
Alfalfa—
 analyses, R.I............................ 767
 as a grazing crop for pigs, Nebr......... 679
 as a green manure........................ 320
 behavior in acid soils................... 422
 breeding experiments..................... 827
 cost of growing, Conn.State.............. 231
 culture experiments, Guam................ 729
 culture experiments, Idaho............... 30
 culture experiments, Minn........... 226, 227
 culture experiments, Ohio................ 535
 culture in Kansas........................ 439

Alfalfa—Continued. Page.
 culture in Wisconsin..................... 440
 culture in Wyoming, Wyo.................. 334
 effect on soil bacteria, U.S.D.A......... 421
 fertilizer experiments.............. 133, 215
 fertilizer experiments, Ohio............. 535
 fertilizer experiments, Oreg............. 33
 growth as affected by phosphates........ 828
 hay, digestibility, Tex.................. 168
 hay, effect on melting point of milk fat,
  Mo...................................... 73
 hay, handling, Ohio...................... 599
 in grass mixtures........................ 735
 irrigation experiments, Idaho............ 639
 irrigation experiments, N.Mex........... 32
 irrigation experiments, Nev.......... 30, 435
 irrigation experiments, Oreg............. 84
 irrigation in Sacramento Valley, Cal..... 586
 meal, analyses, Conn.State............... 268
 meal, analyses, R.I...................... 767
 meal, analyses, Wis...................... 471
 nectar secretion......................... 633
 nurse crop for, Minn..................... 226
 pollination experiments.................. 735
 pollination studies, Iowa................ 30
 Pseudopeziza leaf spots.................. 751
 root system.............................. 827
 sampling device for...................... 711
 seed, determination of origin............ 541
 seed, importations in Argentina......... 823
 seeding experiments, Ga.................. 29
 seeding experiments, Idaho............... 639
 seeding experiments, Ohio................ 535
 silage, chemical studies, U.S.D.A........ 709
 silage, preservation and use, Kans....... 671
 transpiration rate, U.S.D.A.............. 429
 varieties................................ 230
 varieties, Conn.State.................... 231
 varieties, Minn.......................... 229
 varieties, Nev........................... 435
 varieties, Oreg.......................... 531
 varieties, Tex........................... 331
 weevil, control in Arizona............... 846
 weevil, investigations................... 262
 weevil, notes, Mont...................... 255
 yield in relation to precipitation....... 717
 yields, determination.................... 439
Alkali—
 effect on cement, Wyo.................... 788
 effect on soil bacteria.................. 213
 origin, U.S.D.A.......................... 809
Alligator pears. (See Avocados.)
Allognota agromyzina, studies............... 764
Almonds, varieties, S.Dak................... 143
Alphitobius piceus, studies................. 356
Alphitophagus bifasciatus, notes............ 567
Alternaria—
 brassicæ, on collards, Ga................ 48
 camelliæ, notes.......................... 550
 dianthi, notes........................... 155
 solani, treatment........................ 50
 sonchi n.sp., description................ 353
Aluminum—
 as a factor in soil acidity.............. 799
 salts, effect on solubility of phosphates.. 323
Atypia octomaculata. (See Eight-spotted forester.)

Page.

American—
Association for the Advancement of Agricultural Teaching.................. 601,798
Association of Farmers' Institute Workers.................................. 601,796
Farm Management Association, report.. 389
National Live Stock Association........ 769
Society for Horticultural Science....... 239
Society of Agronomy.................. 601,799
Amino acids—
deficiency in diet......................... 265
determination............................. 506
determination in blood................... 207
determination in feeding stuffs.......... 10
effect on amylolytic enzyms............. 205
in diet, effect on growth................. 865
Ammonia—
determination in fertilizers.............. 412
determination in urine................... 311
determination in wine................. 414,415
fixation in soils, U.S.D.A................ 318
in dew, U.S.D.A........................... 116
in diseased plants........................ 549
Ammonification as affected by manganese salts, Iowa................................ 126
Ammonium—
nitrate, displacement of potash by....... 321
nitrate, effect on nodule formation....... 133
nitrate, effect on solubility of iron phosphate.................................... 324
nitrate, fertilizing value................. 739
sulphate, action on muscovite........... 505
sulphate, adsorption by soils and quartz sand.................................... 721
sulphate as a top-dressing for grains, Ga.. 29
sulphate, availability in relation to soil reaction.................................. 521
sulphate, effect on nodule formation..... 133
sulphate, effect on soil acidity........... 815
sulphate, fertilizing value.............. 123, 229,321,426,539,733,739,824
sulphate, fertilizing value, Me............ 636
sulphate, fertilizing value, Pa............ 627
sulphate, production in 1915-16........ 524,721
sulphate, use on peat soils............... 135
sulphid, fungicidal value................. 48
Amphrophora cicutæ n.sp., description....... 163
Amygdalus, new names in.................... 220
Amylases, nitrogenous stimulants........... 204
Anagrus frequens n.sp., description.......... 856
Anaphylactic—
and immune reactions, studies........... 76
shock, studies............................ 582
Anaphylatoxin—
and anaphylaxis, studies.............. 578,688
effect of multiple doses.................. 580
Anaphylaxis—
cause..................................... 76
hypodermal, in cattle and sheep......... 379
studies............................. 178,5í8,688
Anaplasmosis—
in Russian Turkestan.................... 374
review of literature...................... 178
Anas laysanensis. (See Horizonetta, new genus.)
Anastatus bifasciatus in Maine.............. 459

Page.

Andropogon aricuiatus injurious to horses, Guam.................................... 779
Anemia, infectious, in horses.............. 82,382
Anemometer records, comparison, U.S.D.A.. 513
Anesthetics—
effect on cyanogenetic compounds of sorghum.................................. 109
effect on plant respiration................ 821
(See also Ether and Chloroform.)
Aneurism, verminous. in the horse.......... 82
Anilin dyes, effect on tubercle bacilli........ 481
Animal—
diseases—
in Alabama.......................... 687
in Baluchistan....................... 274
in California.......................... 477
in Florida............................ 477
in Guam, Guam...................... 778
in Hawaii............................ 374
in India.......................... 274,477
in Ireland............................ 577
in Massachusetts..................... 477
in Mauritius......................... 780
in Michigan.......................... 274
in Montana........................... 687
in New Hampshire.................... 687
in Oregon............................ 374
in Paris and Department of the Seine. 780
in Pennsylvania...................... 577
in Russian Turkestan................. 274
in Southern Rhodesia................. 688
in United Kingdom................... 687
in United States...................... 274
in Washington........................ 477
in Wyoming.......................... 477
regulations among American countries.............................. 77
treatise.............................. 876
treatment............................ 876
(See also specific diseases.)
matter, showers of, U.S.D.A............. 808
micrology, handbook.................... 155
parasites found in human feces.......... 848
parasites in British Guiana.............. 155
Animals—
death-feigning instinct.....?............. 559
food, parasites transmissible to man..... 355
fur-bearing, domestication, U.S.D.A..... 573
hibernation............................. 156
Annona in Hawaii......................... 345
Anobium paniceum, notes.................. 156
Anomala marginata, notes, Fla............. 660
Anopheles—
hylephilus n.sp., description............. 565
quadrimaculatus, flight of............... 853
spp , infectibility....................... 463
spp., notes............................. 565
Anthocyanin—
formation in plants..................... 25
pigments of plants, treatise............. 633
Anthomyidæ, investigations................ 764
Anthonomus—
grandis. (See Cotton-boll weevil.)
hicoriæ, notes........................... 560
quadrigibbus. (See Apple curculio.)
signatus. (See Strawberry weevil.)

Page.

Anthostomella arecæ n.sp., notes.............. 148
Anthrax—
   affecting man............................ 179
   bacilli, resistance to sodium chlorid solu-
    tion.................................... 79
   control in Michigan....................... 274
   eradication.............................. 179
   immunization............................ 479
   investigations, Nev...................... 78
   outbreak among tannery workers........ 79
   symptomatic. (*See* Blackleg.)
Anthrax n.spp., descriptions................. 565
Anthrothrips floridensis n.sp., description.... 561
Anthrothrips, North American species...... 561
Antianaphylaxis, studies.................. 178
Antibodies, nature....................... 76
Antigen and antibody, coexistence in serum.. 877
Antigenic properties of β-nucleoproteins.... 77
Antineuritic substance from egg yolk........ 308
Antioxidase, notes........................ 203
Antiseptics—
   comparative study....................... 176
   effect on concentration of soil solution.... 719
   volatile, effect on soils................. 519
Antitoxic serum, concentration.............. 376
Ants—
   Argentine, as an orchard pest............ 568
   Argentine, in Silesia.................... 766
   protecting acacia trees in Central Amer-
    ica.................................... 568
   weather-proof bands for................. 59
   white. (*See* Termites.)
Apanteles lacteicolor in Maine............... 459
Aphelenchus ormerodis, notes................ 246
Aphelinus—
   lapisligni n.sp., description.............. 766
   lapisligni n.sp., feeding on juices of its
    host................................... 856
   mytilaspidis, studies.................... 59
Aphididæ—
   of Java................................. 850
   sensory structures...................... 850
Aphids—
   cat-tail as a summer host............... 461
   endoparasitism in, Wash................ 54
   new or little known, of eastern United
    States................................. 850
   notes................................... 258
   relation to fire blight.................. 151,157
   remedies................................ 256
   remedies, Conn.State.................... 254
   remedies, U.S.D.A...................... 358
Aphis—
   brassicæ. (*See* Cabbage aphis.)
   neo-mexicana pacifica n.var., description.. 562
   pseudobrassicæ, notes, Conn.State....... 254
Aphrophora paralleia, notes, Conn.State...... 255
Aphthous fever. (*See* Foot-and-mouth disease.)
Apiaries, inspection—
   in Connecticut, Conn.State.............. 254
   in Iowa................................. 467
   in Kansas............................... 357
   in Massachusetts........................ 855
   in Pennsylvania......................... 459
   in Wisconsin............................ 263

Page.

Apiculture. (*See* Beekeeping.)
Apis—
   indica, domestication................... 855
   mellifera. (*See* Bees.)
Apodemus sylvaticus, notes.................. 156
Aporphæria uiei, notes.................... 253
Appetite, studies.......................... 166
Apple—
   aphids, remedies........................ 156
   aphids, remedies, Oreg.................. 54
   aphids, studies, N.Y.State............... 561
   bitter pit, studies...................... 455
   bitter pit, treatment.................... 151
   black root rot, studies, U.S.D.A....... 456,754
   blister canker, notes.................... 151
   blister canker, treatment................ 51
   blotch, studies, U.S.D.A................ 154
   branch blister disease, notes............. 842
   brown rot, notes........................ 457
   bug, green, studies..................... 462
   canker, behavior in two grafts on same
    stock.................................. 250
   canker, treatment, Mo.................. 754
   cork, studies, N.Y.State................ 350
   crown gall, varietal relations........... 554
   curculio, remedies, Ill.................. 242
   dieback, studies........................ 551
   diseases, notes......................... 51
   diseases, treatment, Oreg............... 51
   drought spot, studies. N.Y.State........ 350
   flowers and fruits, abscission............ 240
   jelly, manufacture...................... 15
   juices, analyses........................ 502
   leaf-hopper, black, notes............... 157
   leaf mites, notes....................... 570
   leaf-roller, remedies, Oreg.............. 54
   maggot in British Columbia............. 665
   packing houses in Northwest, U.S.D.A.. 648
   rot, temperature relations.............. 754
   scab infection, relation to height of fruit,
    Oreg.................................. 51
   scab, studies, Oreg..................... 555
   scab, treatment.................. 242,655,755
   sucker, remedies........................ 761
   tree borer, round headed, remedies...... 161
Apples—
   acid content............................ 714
   blooming period, Ark................... 744
   breeding experiments.................... 242
   breeding for late blooming, Mo.......... 743
   bud selection experiments............... 240
   cambial activity........................ 128
   cider, use in cookery................... 669
   cold storage............................ 833
   crab. (*See* Crab apples.)
   culture in Mesa County Colo............ 241
   drying.............................. 114,503
   fall *v.* spring planting, Mo............. 743
   fertilizer experiments................ 344,833
   fertilizer experiments, Me.............. 647
   fertilizer experiments, Mo.............. 743
   fertilizer experiments, Oreg............ 41
   forecasting probable bloom, Mo.......... 741
   frost injury, Utah...................... 341
   grading and packing law in Delaware.... 745
   grading and packing law in Maryland... 143

Page.

Apples—Continued.
grafting on pear stocks. N.Mex.......... 40
insects affecting....................... 847, 848
Jonathan spot rot of.................... 754
keeping quality in relation to soil mois
ture, Wash........................... 41
marketing cooperatively................ 143
packing............................... 848
picking maturity, U.S.D.A............. 543
pruning............................... 344
pruning and training, W.Va............ 344
pruning experiments, Minn............. 240
pruning, winter v. summer, Idaho...... 647
selection experiments, Mo............. 743
self-fertility, Mo...................... 744
spraying, N.J.......................... 744
spraying, dust v. liquid............. 832, 833
spraying experiments, Ill.............. 242, 647
spraying experiments, Iowa............. 40
spraying experiments, Nebr............ 447
thinning experiments, W.Va........... 448
varieties, Minn........................ 240
varieties, Mont........................ 241
varieties, S.Dak...................... 143
varieties for Ohio, Ohio.............. 241
varieties of Iowa...................... 647
Apricot disease in Rhone valley.......... 250
Apricots—
acid content.......................... 715
blooming periods...................... 633
culture in Mesa County Colo........... 241
drying................................ 214
drying, Wash.......................... 715
varieties, Mont....................... 241
Aqueous solutions, extraction with ether.... 414
Arabinose, determination................ 617
Arachin—
basic nitrogen distribution in.......... 501
chemistry of.......................... 8
Archips argyrospila, remedies, Oreg........ 56
Areca palm anaberoga, description........ 657
Arginase—
in plants, studies.................... 204
preparation from fresh liver.......... 112
Arginin—
determination in proteins............. 112
rôle in purin metabolism.............. 265
Arithmetic, rural, textbook......... 95, 297, 598
Arizona University and Station, notes...... 700
Arkansas University and Station, notes..... 97
Armatella litseæ, notes................. 652
Army baking, manual.................... 62
Arsenates, toxicity, U.S.D.A............ 759
Arsenic—
determination in organic matter........ 713
insecticidal value.................... 559
occurrence and rôle in plants........ 130
water-soluble, determination in lead
arsenate............................. 616
Arthritis, infectious, in foals.......... 382
Artichokes—
culture experiments, Hawaii........... 132
variation in.......................... 342
Ascarids, remedies...................... 373
Ascaris—
canis and A. felis, comparison......... 163
lumbricoides and A. suilla, development
in rats and mice..................... 374

Page.

Ascaris infestation, effect on serum treatment
of hog cholera........................ 881
Aschersonia parænsis n.sp., notes.......... 143
Ascochyta—
bœrhaaviæ n.sp., description.......... 748
hortorum on artichoke................ 150
sp., notes........................... 550
Ascophyllum nodosum, analyses, Conn.State. 814
Asemantoideus dubius n. sp., description..... 59
Ash, utilization, U.S.D.A.............. 548
Ashes as a source of potash.............. 427
Asparagus, keeping after cutting, Mass...... 342
Aspen as a permanent forest type.......... 837
Aspergillus—
fumigatus, rôle in silage poisoning, Mo... 728
niger, citric acid fermentation.......... 613
niger, growth in plant decoctions........ 728
niger, nitrogen fixation by............. 129
niger, notes.......................... 51
niger on onions, Ohio................. 349
Asperisporium cariceæ, notes.............. 550
Aspidiotus perniciosus. (See San José scale.)
Asses—
improvement, value of good sires........ 866
treatise.............................. 769
Association of—
American Agricultural Colleges and Ex-
periment Stations.................. 601, 698
Official Agricultural Chemists.......... 601
Asterocystis radicis, notes............... 248
Asteroma rosæ, notes.................... 550
Astragalus bisulcatus, toxicity, Wyo........ 780
Astyage punctulata n.sp., notes.......... 359
Athyrosis, fetal, in pigs................ 273
Atmometers, relative merits, U.S.D.A....... 429
Atmosphere, condensation of aqueous vapor. 716
Atmospheric—
pressure. (See Barometric pressure.)
temperature. (See Temperature.)
water vapor, data on U.S.D.A.......... 314
Attagenus—
plebius, notes....................... 567
undulatus, studies................... 356
Aulacaspis major n.sp., description 158
Aurora of August 26, 1916, U.S.D.A........ 115
Automobile registrations, licenses, and revenues, U.S.D.A....................... 590
Auximones—
effect on plant growth................ 719
effect on soil bacteria................ 517
Auxoamylases, notes................... 204
Avian ova, change in rate of growth......... 772
Avocado root rot, notes................. 246
Avocados—
breeding experiments, Hawa 142
culture experiments.................. 144
culture in Florida and W st.ndies...... 144
varieties........................... 111, 243
varieties for California............... 345
varieties for Florida................. 345
Azalea lace bug, studies................ 761
Azotobacter—
development.......................... 221
nitrogen fixation by................. 129
Babcock test, use..................... 175, 875
Babesiasis, status and control......... 380

Page.

Bacillus—
abortus in certified milk.................. 881
abortus lipolyticus in milk................ 173
abortus, massive cultures of.............. 687
abortus, relation to abortion in women... 78
amylovorus, notes......................... 755
amylovorus, transmission by aphids.... 151, 157
botulinus, development in corn and apricots..................................... 165
botulinus, relation to forage poisoning.... 179
coli, determination in water............... 188
coli, significance in milk.................. 874
ichthyosmius, n.sp., description, Iowa.... 686
lathyri, investigations.................... 155
morulans, nitrate reduction by........... 549
œdematous, pathogenicity................. 377
pyogenes, relation to eye disease in cattle. 691
pyogenes, suppuration due to.............. 276
sotto, studies............................. 853
spp. on vegetables in Ontario............. 150
subtilis, rôle in utilization of organic compounds by plants...................... 223
typhi-exanthematici, isolation from body louse..................................... 850
welchii in pigeons, immunization......... 781

Bacteria—
classification......................... 220, 819
coli-aerogenes, differentiation........... 506
gas production by, in raw and pasteurized milk...................................... 874
in milk, soils, water, etc. (See Milk, Soil, Water, etc.)
legume, and nonlegume plants, symbiosis, Ill....................................... 819
legume, behavior in acid and alkali media 422
nodule, as affected by phosphorus....... 823
paratyphoid-enteritidis, studies.... 275, 690, 781
resistance to germicides.................. 176
sensitized and nonsensitized, immunization with............................... 780
spore-forming, of the apiary, U.S.D.A.... 59
staining, inhibitory action of serum..... 478

Bacterial—
emulsions, determination of turbidity... 14
infections, chemotherapy................. 274

Bactericidal tests in vitro.................... 274
Bacteriology, hydrogenion concentration in. 506

Bacterium—
citrarefaciens n.sp., description, U.S.D.A. 154
citri, notes........................... 556, 657
coli apium n.sp., description............. 360
lactis aerogenes in bottled milk.......... 273
phaseoli, notes........................... 840
pruni, treatment, U.S.D.A.............. 842
pullorum and B. sanguinarium, comparative studies......................... 82, 483
tumefaciens, notes.................. 245, 249, 252

Bakerophoma sacchari n.g. and n.sp., notes.. 148
Baking, army, manual....................... 63

Banana—
acid content.............................. 714
disease in Salayer Islands................ 555
fertilizer experiments.................... 215
Panama disease, studies.................. 843
weevil, notes............................. 161

Baobab bark, fiber from.................... 534

Page.

Barbarea barbarea, eradication, Mich........ 742
Barberry, relation to black stem rust of small grains, Iowa................................. 552
Barium, action on Spirogyra................. 130
Bark borers killing healthy fir trees.......... 465

Barley—
as a supplement for wheat in bread making..................................... 263
as affected by greenhouse temperature... 533
as affected by smelter wastes............. 526
bacterial blight, dissemination........... 839
breeding experiments..................... 827
breeding experiments, Wash............. 33
bushel weights............................ 889
correlation in............................. 141
culture, continuous....................... 445
culture experiments....... 436, 438, 734, 823, 825
culture in Argentina...................... 823
culture in Washington, Wash............ 334
culture under dry farming, N. Mex...... 329
embryo, morphology....................... 127
fertilizer experiments.......... 229, 436, 438, 823
fertilizer experiments, R.I................ 34
germination tests, Mont.................. 239
green manuring experiments.............. 734
ground, digestibility, Ill.................. 677
improvement, Mo......................... 731
improvement in Canada................... 831
inheritance in, Wash..................... 332
irrigation experiments, Idaho............ 640
irrigation experiments, U.S.D.A......... 822
liming experiments....................... 733
loose smut, treatment.................... 247
of Khorassan............................. 446
potassium and phosphorus requirements, R.I....................................... 34
rusts, notes............................... 453
seeding experiments...................... 733
seeding experiments, Minn.............. 226
seeds, selective permeability............. 25
selection experiments, Nev.............. 32
shorts, analyses, Wis.................... 471
varieties........... 135, 230, 436, 438, 823, 824, 825
varieties, Hawaii..'..................... 132
varieties, Idaho.................... 29, 30, 640
varieties, Ill............................. 641
varieties, Md............................. 332
varieties, Minn..................... 227, 228
varieties, Nev............................ 32
varieties, Oreg........................... 530
varieties, Tex............................ 330
varieties, Wash..................... 33, 334
volume weight and grain characteristics.. 643
winter, northern limits in United States.. 533
yields, determination..................... 634

Barns—
construction.............................. 886
construction, Tex......................... 887

Barnyard manure—
and products of decomposition........... 813
collection from cities, U.S.D.A........... 521
destruction of fly larvæ in............... 853
effect on nitrogen balance in soils........ 627
effect on peach trees, N.Mex............ 40
effect on soil acidity..................... 23
effect on soil bacteria, Ga............... 23

Barnyard manure—Continued.   **Page**
  effect on solubility of inorganic soil con-
    stituents, U.S.D.A...................... 422
  fertilizing value......................... 229
  fertilizing value, Md.................... 320
  fertilizing value, Pa.................... 626
  use on peat soils...................... 134, 135
  use with sodium nitrate............... 124
Barometric pressure variations in United
    States, U.S.D.A...................... 807
Barrel, standard, Federal law............. 832
Bartonella bacilliformis, notes............. 377
Bases, reactions of ions and molecules....... 201
Basic slag. (*See* Phosphatic slag.)
Bat, new, from Mexico.................... 757
Bay flea louse, notes.................... 157
Bean—
  anthracnose, notes.................... 652
  beetle, studies, N.Mex................ 465
  blight or bacteriosis, notes........... 750
  diseases, description and treatment, Colo. 848
  diseases in New York................ 840
  ands, semiannual cropping............ 829
  mosaic disease, notes................ 751
  rust, notes........................... 453
  seedlings correlation in.............. 630
  weevil, notes......................... 162
Beans—
  agglutinin from........................ 81
  analyses, Conn.State................ 568
  analyses, N.Mex....................... 343
  as a forage crop, Idaho.............. 640
  as a green manure, Hawaii............ 820
  bushel weights........................ 889
  culture, Cal........................... 641
  culture, Colo.......................... 832
  culture, N.J........................... 842
  culture, N.Mex........................ 843
  culture, Ohio.......................... 895
  culture, Wash......................... 136
  culture and harvesting for drying, Ill..... 642
  culture experiments, Guam........... 842
  culture for seed, Nev................ 436
  culture under dry farming, N.Mex...... 829
  dietary deficiencies.................. 161
  drying................................ 769
  fertilizer experiments, Guam........... 742
  Lima, insects affecting.............. 460
  mungo, culture experiments, La....... 829
  mungo, fertilizer experiments........... 336
  mungo, varieties...................... 536
  seed color variation in.............. 831
  selection experiments, Nev.......... 32
  varieties, N.Mex...................... 829
  varieties, Nev........................ 82
  velvet. (*See* Velvet beans.)
Beauveria peteloti n.sp., notes............. 467
Beavers, mountain, Wash................ 855
Bee diseases—
  in Germany........................... 460
  in Massachusetts.................... 855
  in Pennsylvania...................... 459
  notes.............................. 162, 360
  studies, U.S.D.A...................... 59
Beech—
  leafy twigs, preservation............. 837
  wood creosote, studies.............. 114
  wood creosote, toxicity to wood-destroying
    fungi................................ 802
Beef—   **Page.**
  baby, production, Tex................... 366
  baby, production, U.S.D.A.......... 269, 367
  scrap for growing chicks, Mo............ 768
Beekeeping—
  notes, Ind............................. 360
  treatise............................. 608, 769
Bees—
  as affected by weather, Iowa........... 854
  as carriers of fire blight.............. 53
  feeding.............................. 467
  from west coast of South America....... 357
  Indian, domestication................ 855
  infectious diarrhea of................ 360
  inspection.......................... 262
  Isle of Wight disease............... 360
  odors emitted by..................... 459
  sense organs on mouth parts......... 360
  wintering outdoors.................. 360
Beet—
  diseases in Switzerland.............. 47
  leaf-hoppers, host plants........... 847
  molasses, composition and use......... 416
  pulp, dried, analyses, Conn.State....... 268
  pulp, dried, analyses, R.I.......... 767
  pulp, dried, analyses, Wis......... 471
  seed, germination test.............. 829
  sugarhouse waste liquors as a source of
    potash.............................. 817
Beetle mites, synopsis.................. 858
Beets—
  anomalies in.......................... 28
  field or fodder. (*See* Mangels.)
  sugar. (*See* Sugar beets.)
Belladonna—
  breeding for atropin.................. 44
  seed, germination..................... 545
Belle Fourche reservoir as a bird reservation. 855
Bengal grass, culture.................... 136
Benzene—
  derivatives, insecticidal value, U.S.D.A.. 559
  effect on soils....................... 519
Benzoic acid, isolation from soil............ 710
Bermuda grass—
  as a pasture crop, Tex................ 533
  culture and use, U.S.D.A............. 440
  giant, notes, Ga...................... 29
  hay, digestibility, Tex............... 168
Berries, drying, Wash................... 715
Berseem, varieties....................... 233
Beschälseuche. (*See* Dourine.)
Besnoitia besnoiti n.g., studies............. 81
Betel-nut palm "band" disease............. 457
Bibliography of—
  agricultural education in Russia......... 793
  aneurism, verminous, in horses......... 82
  anthocyanin pigments of plants.......... 633
  apple bitter pit..................... 456
  apples, thinning experiments, W.Va..... 449
  bacteriology........................ 811
  botany.............................. 630
  cattle feeding....................... 172
  chemistry.......................... 411, 501
  Coccidæ of Porto Rico.............. 158
  coffee industry in Abyssinia.......... 835
  corn billbug, southern, N.C.......... 666
  cornstalk borer, lesser, U.S.D.A...... 852
  correlation as a measure of relationships. 621
  correlation in grains................ 141

Bibliography of—Continued	Page.
Coryneum spp. on trees and shrubs......	250
Cryptorhynchus lapathi, N.Y.Cornell.....	465
currant, red.............................	834
diet of children.........................	671
digitalis in pneumonia...................	375
Emmental cheese, eye formation........	876
fertilizers and chemical products........	524
flies of New Jersey, N.J.................	665
forests of northern New England........	651
grassland, herbage of...................	231
horse-radish flea-beetle, U.S.D.A........	567
Ichneumonidæ of British India..........	765
irrigation in Italy.......................	184
irrigation in United States..............	183
irrigation pumping, Nebr................	384
land-title registration...................	190
locust borer, Okla......................	566
locusts, control in various countries.....	849
Mallophaga............................	461
melon fly, U.S.D.A.....................	566
meteorology of Brazil...................	620
milk clarification, N.Y.Cornell..........	476
milk, human, composition...............	273
milk secretion..........................	874
nematodes, heteroxenous................	361
nitrates in soils........................	111
nitrogen of soils and fertilizers........	216
nodule bacteria, Ill....................	820
nodule formation in relation to nitrates..	134
peach borer, lesser, Ohio................	159
phosphorus, effect on legumes...........	829
pink bollworm, U.S.D.A.................	564
plant succession........................	434
plants poisonous to live stock...........	688
polyhedra in insects....................	254
raffinose, physiological behavior.........	572
rainfall, tropical.......................	17
roads, construction and maintenance....	695
roads in United States..................	188
sewage purification.....................	488
silkworm larval characters..............	158
silkworm pebrine.......................	361
soil sterilization.......................	213
specialization of parasitic fungi..........	149
strawberries, Va.......................	143
sugar beets, variation and correlation....	642
tea fermentation.......................	44
tsutsugamushi disease..................	859
tubercle bacilli, isolation...............	180
tuberculosis...........................	879,880
tulips.................................	836
variation in plants.....................	28,642
water purification......................	488
wheat, milling and baking qualities, Wash....	862
wireworm, common....................	765
Biliary fever. (*See* Piroplasmosis.)
Bindweed prominent in Louisiana........... | 564
Biocolloids, investigations................. | 325,821
Biographical sketch of Loughridge, R.H..... | 496
Biology, general and medical treatise....... | 78
Biotite as a source of potash............... | 321
Bird reservations on irrigation projects....... | 355
Birds—
egg-laying cycles....................... | 869
incubation periods..................... | 774
injurious to rice....................... | 247

Birds—Continued.	Page.
nomenclature.........................	753
of Culebra Island, Porto Rico...........	355
of Great Britain......................	53
of South America, treatise..............	753
of Washington, treatise................	553
reproduction in.......................	772
stomach examination...................	355
treatise.............................	53
Biscuit weevil, notes.....................	156
Bitumens, fluid, effect of exposure on........	711
Bituminous aggregates, toughness, U.S.D.A.	885
Blaberus discoidalis, notes.................	255,660
Black-head fireworm, remedies.............	56
Blackberries—
acid content......................... | 715
varieties, Oreg....................... | 243
Blackberry—
diseases, notes....................... | 52
orange rust, studies................... | 457
Blackboys of South Australia............ | 548
Blackhead in turkeys, studies........ | 280,383,384
Blackleg—
immunization......................... | 689
immunization, Kans................... | 376
Blast-furnace—
gases, loss of potash in............... | 630
slag, fertilizing value, Ohio........... | 126
Blattotetrastichus, new genus, description... | 766
Blood—
albumin, digestibility, U.S.D.A........ | 673
albumin-globulin ratio in experimental intoxications and infections............ | 375
coagulation.......................... | 177
culture media from.................... | 220
dried. (*See* Dried blood.)
of fowls, sexual differences.............. | 773
of pigs, morphology, U.S.D.A........ | 380,381
of various species, amino-acid nitrogen in | 206
proteins, studies..................... | 575
serum, action on protein of other animal species.............................. | 478
serum, coagulative and noncoagulative fractions............................ | 177
serum, primary toxicity................ | 581
sugar content in relation to diet.......... | 64
Blowflies—
life history and remedies................ | 853
studies, N. J........................ | 665
Blue grass as affected by companion crop of clover.............................. | 438
Boengkil, fertilizing value................ | 123
Bog water, toxicity...................... | 27
Bogeria scudderi n. sp., description........... | 865
Boletus spp. on tree roots................... | 756
Boll weevil. (*See* Cotton-boll weevil.)
Bollworm. (*See* Cotton bollworm.)
Bombyx mori. (*See* Silkworm.)
Bone—
analyses, Conn.State.................. | 268
black, dissolved, fertilizing value, Pa.... | 626
ground, analyses, N.J................. | 219
ground, fertilizing value, Pa............ | 626
meal, analyses, Wis................... | 71
meal, fertilizing value, Mo............. | 743
meal, use on peat soils................. | 135
residual effects....................... | 23

Books on—   Page.

agricultural credit...................... 391,888
agricultural insurance in France......... 888
agriculture........................ 728,795,888
agriculture and preparedness............ 389
agriculture in Great Britain....... 291,595,697
animal diseases.......................... 876
animal micrology......................... 155
anthocyanin pigments of plants.......... 633
arithmetic.......................... 95,297,598
beekeeping............................. 568,769
biology, general and medical............ 76
birds.............................. 53,358,758
botany............................... 220,818
bread making............................ 165
butter making on the farm............... 175
butterflies and moths.................... 358
cabbage................................. 543
cane-sugar factories, chemical control in.. 509
carob................................... 747
cattle feeding and management.......... 172
cellulose............................... 112
cheese, Camembert....................... 176
chemical analysis.............. 310,614,802
chemistry............................... 108
chemistry, agricultural............. 598,801
chrysanthemums.......................... 44
coconuts................................ 345
colloidal solutions..................... 501
concrete................................ 590
cookery............................. 94,894
cooking, Army........................ 63,166
corn.................................... 94
dairy cattle............................ 574
dairy laboratory exercises.............. 872
dairying.......................... 94,172,894
diet.................................... 469
drainage................................ 587
eggs, preparation....................... 668
electric heating........................ 387
evolution........................... 432,573
farm buildings....................... 10,789
farm equipment.......................... 388
farming................................. 290
fauna of British India.............. 54,765
feeding of farm animals............. 94,795
feeds and feeding....................... 767
fertilizers............................. 724
flowers......................... 145,630,746
food analysis........................... 503
foods.............................. 94,166,894
forest law in America................... 836
forestry................................ 243
forestry in Tunis, Algeria, and Corsica ... 650
fowls, anatomy.......................... 772
fruit culture....................... 41,544
fruit diseases.......................... 151
fruits, small....................... 544,648
garden furniture and accessories........ 746
gardening.............. 94,145,543,645,742
gardening, ornamental....... 145,346,746
green manures and manuring in the
    tropics............................. 28
guinea pigs............................. 775
home economics.......................... 696
home grounds........................ 44,346
horse diseases.......................... 784
horses.................................. 770

Books on—Continued.   Page.

horses Percheron........................ 771
house plants............................ 346
hydraulics.............................. 584
hydroelectric power..................... 287
immunology.............................. 76
incubation periods of birds............. 774
insects injurious....................... 395
insects injurious to man........... 156,761
irrigation................... 185,587,882
land reclamation........................ 214
land system of Great Britain............ 697
landscape gardening............... 546,547
Lepidoptera of North America............ 563
live stock judging...................... 94
live stock on the farm.................. 769
live stock remedies..................... 876
live stock types and market classes..... 194
locusts, control in various countries... 848
Luther Burbank.......................... 341
mammals of North America and adjacent
    seas................................ 658
manure.................................. 215
marketing and farm credits.............. 391
mathematics, vocational................. 598
meat inspection......................... 77
meteorology of Brazil................... 619
microbiology............................ 76
milk and its hygienic relations......... 174
milk products........................... 777
milk supply of cities.............. 174,874
milk supply of Massachusetts............ 372
mimicry in butterflies.................. 55
mosquitoes of North America and West
    indies.............................. 762
Orange culture.......................... 835
peonies................................. 145
physiology, chemical.................... 501
pigs.................................... 769
plant physiology........................ 220
plant propagation and breeding.......... 797
plant succession........................ 434
plants, ornamental...................... 746
plants poisonous to live stock in Great
    Britain............................. 688
potatoes................... 533,543,645
poultry............................. 769,775
pruning............................. 41,341
pumps and suction dredgers.............. 585
rabbits................................. 775
rabies.................................. 480
river discharge......................... 484
road construction....................... 590
root crops.............................. 645
roses.............................. 145,836
rubber industry......................... 347
rural sanitation in the Tropics......... 86
sheep farming in British Isles.......... 770
shrubs and trees, ornamental............ 44
squabs.................................. 775
strawberries........................ 42,648
sugar beets............................. 533
sugar manufacture....................... 114
sweet peas.......................... 346,546
tomatoes and salad plants............... 645
Torrens system of land registration..... 492
trees of United States.................. 343
trees, ornamental of Hawaii............. 546

Page.

Books on—Continued.
turf for golf courses...................... 146
veterinary medicine................. 76, 176, 778
vinegar.................................. 112
viticulture............................... 834
war food................................ 715
water supply............................ 187
wild flowers............................. 630
woody plants, anatomy.................. 821
wool.................................... 894
(*Boophilus*) *Margaropus annulatus*. (*See* Cattle tick.)
Bordeaux mixture—
analyses, N. J.......................... 243
fungicidal value, Nebr.................. 447
Borers, flat-headed, notes.................. 866
Boric acid, antiseptic and germicidal value.. 176
Botanical investigations at Carnegie Institution................................. 524, 630
Botany—
agricultural, course in.................. 795
international catalogue.................. 630
taxonomic, of Washington, D. C., and vicinity............................. 435
treatise............................. 220, 818
Botryodiplodia theobromæ, notes.......... 252, 253
Botryorhiza hippocrateæ n.g. and n.sp., notes.. 552
Botryosphæria—
berengeriana, treatment, Fla............ 652
minuscula n.sp., notes................. 148
Botrytis cinerea. (*See* Grape gray rot.)
Botrytis on flowers........................ 47
Bots, head and throat, of American game animals................................ 565
Botulism—
due to canned goods..................... 669
due to canned goods, U.S.D.A........... 670
notes.................................... 165
Bovine fetus, nutrients required to develop, Mo....:................................. 71
Box elder, poisoning of cows by............ 80
Boys, mobilizing for farm labor in Massachusetts.................................... 199
Bracken—
as a source of potash.................. 427, 817
poisoning in horses..................... 182
Bracon, nearctic species.................. 360
Bradsot or braxy etiology.................. 380
Bran, analyses............................ 873
(*See also* Wheat, Rye, *etc.*)
Bread—
crumbs, analyses, Conn.State............ 268
in the diet, U.S.D.A.................... 364
making, chemistry of.................... 165
making in the home, U.S.D.A............ 364
making, notes........................... 468
nutritive value and cost................ 165
staleness, N. Dak....................... 363
supply of French Army.................. 263
Breadfruit—
disease, notes.......................... 838
for pigs, Guam.......................... 768
Breakfast foods. (*See* Cereal foods.)
Bremia lactucæ, notes.................... 550
Brewers' grains—
analyses, Wis........................... 471
dried, analyses, Conn.State............. 268
dried, analyses, R.I.................... 767

Page.

Bridge stringers and ties, creosoting......... 386
Brisket disease in cattle, Colo.............. 190
Bromcresol purple, use in milk cultures, U.S.D.A............................... 686
Brome grass. pollination experiments........ 735
Bromids, effect on action of malt amylase.... 614
Bromin—
as a seed disinfectant................... 742
oxidation of carbohydrate mixtures by.. 10
Brooding, colony, N.J..................... 71
Broom—
corn, analyses.......................... 539
corn, culture under dry farming, N.Mex. 329
corn, varieties, N.Mex.................. 239
rape, notes............................. 239
Broomella zeæ n.sp., notes............... 148
Brown-tail moth—
control Conn.State...................... 254
control, U.S.D.A........................ 763
control in Massachusetts................ 646
in Connecticut......................... 259
parasites in Maine...................... 459
Bruchus—
chinensis. (*See* Cowpea-weevil.)
obtectus. (*See* Bean-weevil.)
pisorum. (*See* Pea-weevil.)
Bryophyllum calycinum, studies.... 127, 324, 325, 821
Buckthorn—
as a hedge plant, Minn................. 241
varieties, S.Dak........................ 143
Buckwheat—
as a supplement for wheat.............. 263
as a supplement for wheat Ohio......... 895
bushel weights......................... 889
cost of production, W.Va............... 191
culture, Ohio........................... 895
fertilizer experiments.................. 521
middlings, analyses, Conn.State........ 268
Bud—
development, studies.................... 324
variation, factors in.................... 433
Buffalo grass, digestibility, Tex........... 168
Bulbocephalus n.g. and n.spp., descriptions.. 558
Bull associations, cooperative, U.S.D.A...... 574
Bulls—
dairy, selection, Utah.................. 473
influence upon offspring................ 373
Bunostomum phlebotomum in Philippines.... 277
Buprestidæ—
notes.................................... 566
o. northern California.................. 666
Burbank, Luther, book................... 342
Bushes, pruning.......................... 242
Butter—
as affected by cottonseed products, Mo.. 72
fat. (*See* Fat and Milk fat.)
from pasteurized cream, keeping quality, S.Dak............................. 476
industry in Siberia..................... 778
making from pasteurized cream, Can.... 576
making on the farm, manual............. 175
marketing in Kansas, Kans.............. 696
mold, cause and prevention............. 777
renovation, use of lime in, U.S.D.A..... 313
substitutes, nutritive value............. 165
tubercle bacilli in...................... 481

Butterflies— Page.
   mimicry in............................... 55
   treatise................................... 358
Buttermilk as a food, U.S.D.A.............. 669
Butyric acid—
   effect on plants.......................... 224
   separation and determination in biologi-
    cal products........................... 206
Cabbage—
   aphis, control by parasites............... 459
   black rot or brown rot, notes............ 150
   clubroot, notes........................ 550,551
   clubroot, studies, N.Y.Cornell.......... 454
   clubroot, treatment.................... 150,248
   culture, Wash............................. 143
   culture, treatise...................... 543
   leaf spot, notes........................ 551
   root maggot, remedies................... 764
   varieties............................... 532
   varieties, Md........................... 645
   watering, continuous.................... 543
   yellows, control, Ohio.................. 150
Cacao—
   aphis, notes............................ 662
   culture experiments..................... 144
   diseases in Gold Coast.................. 349
   diseases in West Indies................. 452
   fertilizer experiments........... 144,345,648
   insects affecting....................... 560
   leaf spot, description.................. 755
   pink disease, studies................... 52
   pod disease in Philippines.............. 148
   root diseases in Lesser Antilles........ 454
   selection experiments................... 745
   thrips, notes................... 357,461,652
   witches' broom, notes................... 838
Cactus—
   physiological studies................... 524
   polar bear, description................. 434
Cæoma—
   euonymi, notes.......................... 550
   nitens, notes........................... 457
Caffein—
   determination in cocoa and chocolate.... 312
   effect on heat production............... 266
   effect on plant growth.................. 632
   effect on uric acid excretion........... 470
   extraction with ether................... 414
Cajanus indicus, seeding experiments........ 826
Calandra oryza. (See Rice-weevil.)
Calcium—
   arsenate as a spray, U.S.D.A............ 759
   carbonate, effect on solubility of iron
    phosphate............................. 524
   carbonate, effect on sulfofying power o.
    soils, Iowa........................... 120
   cyanamid, fertilizing value. 23,216,426,539,815
   cyanamid, fertilizing value, Md......... 543
   cyanamid for summer crops............... 217
   cyanamid, injurious action.............. 815
   cyanamid, use against nematodes, Fla. 453,652
   determination in blood and milk........ 207
   excretion in the dog, regulation........ 94
   hypochlorite, antiseptic and germicida
    value................................. 175
   hypochlorite, sterilization of water by.. 588
   hypochlorite, use against apple scab..... 755
   in blood of lactating cows.............. 308
   inorganic, in milk..................... 208

Calcium—Continued. Page.
   nitrate, effect on nodule formation....... 133
   nitrate, fertilizing value............. 426,739
   phosphates, citrate solubility.......... 713
   relation to plant nutrition........... 631,799
   sulphate. (See Gypsum.)
California—
   Station, notes.......................... 496
   University, notes....... 496,600,700,797
Callipterinella annulata, notes.............. 562
Callospermophilus lateralis caryi n.subsp., description............................... 758
Calophyllum inophyllum, oil of.............. 109
Calosoma sycophanta—
   in Florida, Fla......................... 659
   in Maine................................ 459
Calves—
   birth weights, Ill...................... 684
   cost of raising, N.C.................... 683
   dairy, feeding and care, Ill............ 683
   dairy, rearing chart.................... 575
   dairy, wintering experiments, N.C....... 682
   feeding and management, U.S.D.A........ 367
   feeding experiments.................... 866,873
   feeding experiments, N.C................ 675
   feeding experiments, Tex................ 366
   marketing in the South, U.S.D.A........ 391
   newborn, composition, Mo............... 72
   newborn, diseases of.................... 379
Cambium miners, new, U.S.D.A............. 764
Camels, variations in normal temperature... 690
Camphor— ·
   diseases, new, in Texas................. 843
   trees, growing in Florida............... 346
   trees of Mauritius...................... 310
Canadian—
   agricultural institutions, notes......... 100
   Seed Growers' Association............ 141,831
Canaigre, acclimatization in France......... 220
Canary seed, culture experiments........... 823
Canavalin, chemistry of.................... 8
Cancer, relation to crown gall.............. 245
Cane sugar—
   factories, chemical control in........... 509
   manufacture, clarifiers................. 208
Canine distemper. (See Dog distemper.)
Canna edulis—
   analyses, Hawaii........................ 165
   culture experiments, Hawaii............ 132
Canned foods—
   poisoning from.......................... 669
   poisoning from, U.S.D.A................. 670
   solution of tin by...................... 12
   tin coating on containers............... 715
Canning—
   factories, cooperative, U.S.D.A......... 594
   factories in Minnesota.................. 777
   factories, inspection in Indiana......... 63
   in the home, Wash...................... 590
   notes................................... 715
   sirups for.............................. 15
Cannonading, effect on rainfall.... 418,512,619,717
Cantaloups. (See Muskmelons.)
Caoutchouc. (See Rubber.)
Caponizing, directions, N.J.............. 308,573
Capons—
   care and management, N.J.............. 308
   cost of production, Iowa................ 70
Capsicum annuum, variation in.............. 725
Caramels, examination...................... 165

Carbohydrate—　　　　　　　　　　　　　　Page.
　metabolism, studies...................... 64
　mixtures, methods of analysis........... 10
Carbohydrates—
　as an index to quality of feeding stuffs... 208
　effect on ammonia accumulation by
　　micro-organisms........................ 812
Carbon—
　assimilation by plants.................... 26
　bisulphid, insecticidal value, U.S.D.A.... 559
　determination......................... 116,803
　dioxid, determination in carbonates..... 110
　dioxid, determination in solution........ 804
　dioxid, effect on rotatory power of sucrose
　　and invert sugar....................... 802
　organic, determination in soils........... 505
Carbonates—
　determination............................ 802
　determination, N. Y. State.............. 616
　determination in solution................ 804
Carbonation in bottles, stirrer for............ 716
Carbureter performance standards............ 188
Caribou, conservation....................... 757
Carnation—
　leaf spot in Italy......................... 155
　rust, notes............................... 453
Carob, treatise............................. 747
Carotin pigments, formation................. 632
Carpocapsa pomonella. (See Codling moth.)
Carrot seeds in Denmark..................... 742
Carrots—
　as a catch crop after wheat.............. 136
　culture experiments, Guam.............. 742
　fertilizer experiments, Guam............ 742
　varieties, Minn........................... 228
Carthamus tinctorius, culture for seed........ 230
Casein—
　hydrolysis as affected by carbohydrates.. 10
　value for growth or maintenance........ 864
Cassava—
　as a source of starch..................... 535
　culture................................... 535
　hydrocyanic acid in, Hawaii.............. 168
　insects affecting.......................... 460
　leaf and stem disease, notes............. 551
Cassia auriculata bark for tanning........... 147
Cassytha filiformis, notes.................... 452
Castor pomace, fertilizing value........ 144,321
Cat-tail rush as a summer host of insects.... 461
Catalpa, cost of growing, Kans............... 451
Catarrhal fever, malignant, in cattle........ 80
Caterpillar, yellow bear, control by parasites. 760
Cats, mange affecting....................... 584
Catsup, bacteriological examination......... 468
Cattle—
　anaphylactic shock due to ox-warble ex-
　　tract.................................. 379
　Ayrshire, milk production in relation to
　　Advanced Registry..................... 775
　breeding experiments, Iowa.............. 66
　breeding investigations................... 775
　dairy, care and management............. 872
　dairy, feeding, Iowa...................... 474
　dairy, manual............................ 574
　determination of age................. 482,770
　disease in mountainous regions of Cali-
　　fornia.................................. 477
　diseases, handbook....................... 778

Cattle—Continued.　　　　　　　　　　　Page.
　diseases, treatment....................... 583
　dual-purpose Red Polled, origin......... 866
　dual-purpose Shorthorn, origin.......... 574
　duration of œstrum in.................... 776
　feeding and management, textbook...... 172
　feeding experiments.................. 769,866
　feeding experiments, Idaho.............. 66
　feeding experiments, Minn.............. 269
　feeding experiments, Ohio.............. 895
　health herd book......................... 482
　improvement, Guam...................... 768
　improvement, value of good sires........ 866
　Jersey, inbreeding........................ 776
　judging................................... 94
　Kerry, origin and characteristics........ 776
　lice in Montana........................... 687
　marketing in the South, U.S.D.A....... 391
　plague. (See Rinderpest.)
　prices in Russia........................... 292
　tick, control in Argentina................ 277
　tick, eradication, Guam.................. 779
　tick, eradication in Alabama............. 687
　　(See also Ticks.)
　wintering experiments, Minn............ 268
　wintering experiments, N. C............ 674
Cauliflowers, culture, Wash................. 143
(Cecidomyia) Mayetiola destructor. (See Hes-
　sian fly.)
Celery—
　bacterial diseases, descriptions.......... 840
　bacterial diseases, notes, Fla............ 652
　blanching, harvesting, and marketing,
　　Wash.................................. 699
　culture, Wash............................ 143
　rot, cause................................ 751
Celluloid cylinders for inoculation chambers.. 549
Cellulose, treatise.......................... 112
Cement—
　as affected by alkali, Wyo............... 788
　dust as a source of potash........ 218,630,817
　specifications 386
　use in irrigation structures.............. 787
Centaurea scabiosa, root system............. 542
Cephaleuros virescens, notes................. 253
Cephalin, thromboplastic action............. 877
Cephalonema polyandrum, fiber from........ 535
Cephalosporium sacchari, notes.............. 452
Cephalothecium roseum, notes............... 550
Cephenemyia, biology....................... 565
Cephus occidentalis, habits.................. 855
Ceratitis capitata, notes.................... 565
Ceratonia siliqua, treatise.................. 748
Ceratophyllus femules, notes................ 879
Ceratostoma juniperinum in France.......... 253
Cercospora—
　beticola, notes........................... 249
　coryli n. sp., description.................. 550
　cucurbitæ, notes......................... 550
　fusca, treatment.......................... 756
　hevex n. sp., notes....................... 253
　n. spp., descriptions 748
　n. vars., descriptions..................... 749
　personata, notes.................. 349,452,551
Cercosporella herpotrichoides, notes.......... 248
Cereal—
　black stem rust, notes, Iowa............. 552
　diseases in Switzerland.................. 47

Page.

Cereal—Continued.
diseases, treatment...................... 247
foods, use in the diet, U. S. D. A......... 668
rusts, specialization.................... 149
Cereals—
culture, Wash........................... 96
culture experiments.................... 733
fertilizer experiments............. 323, 521, 827
improvement in Italy.................... 827
insects affecting...................... 156
mechanical winter covering............. 48
production in Spain..................... 827
recipes................................ 670
varieties.............................. 733
(See also Grain and specific kinds.)
Cerodonta femoralis—
investigations, U.S.D.A................. 160
notes, Mont............................ 255
Cerotoma ruficornis, studies.............. 256
Cestodes—
life history........................... 163
polyradiate, notes..................... 361
Ceuthospora punicæ, notes................. 550
Ceutorhynchus marginatus, notes........... 568
Chætodiplodia anthurii, n. sp., description.... 550
Chætosphæria eximia n. sp., notes.......... 148
Chaitophorus aceris, biology and anatomy.... 55
Chalcid flies—
new, of Australia...................... 569
new, of California.................. 360, 467
new, of Maryland....................... 766
of North America....................... 162
Chalcidoides, new, of West Coast of Africa... 667
Chalcodermus æneus, notes, Fla............. 659
Charbon. (See Anthrax.)
Charlock. (See Mustard, wild.)
Chayote diseases, notes................... 755
Cheese—
acidity................................ 373
Bulgarian and Kaschkawal, description. 273
Camembert, control in France........... 176
Cheddar, changes in, during ripening.... 373
curing. (See Cheese, ripening.)
Edam, cracking......................... 176
Edam, preparation...................... 373
Emmental, formation of eyes in......... 875
factories in Minnesota................. 777
food value, U.S.D.A.................... 669
industry in Siberia.................... 778
making from pasteurized milk, Can...... 576
making on the farm..................... 778
making, pepsin in.................. 175, 875
manufacturing and marketing association, cooperative, U.S.D.A.......... 594
ripening as affected by fat content.... 175
ripening, microorganisms in............ 503
skim milk, manufacture................. 576
Cheiloneuromyia javensis n. sp., description.. 59
Cheletiella parasitivorax on cats.......... 584
Chemical—
analysis, treatise.............. 310, 614, 802
directory of United States............. 501
Chemistry—
international catalogue................. 501
of plant products, treatise............ 801
progress in........................ 166, 409
textbook.................... 108, 598, 801

Page.

Chenopodium oil as an anthelmintic......... 578
Chermes coolcyi, notes, Conn. State........ 255
Cherries—
acid content........................... 714
blooming period and fertility.......... 745
breeding experiments................... 833
culture in Mesa County, Colo........... 241
drying................................. 509
drying, Wash........................... 715
fall v. spring planting, Mo............ 743
frost injury, Utah..................... 344
pruning and training, W. Va............ 344
spraying. N. J......................... 744
spraying, dust, v. liquid.............. 832
varieties, Mont........................ 241
varieties for Ohio, Ohio............... 241
Cherry—
black knot, notes...................... 555
leaf beetle, studies................... 459
leaf spot, studies..................... 755
witches' brooms, studies............... 250
Chestnut—
black canker, studies............. 657, 658
blight in West Virginia................ 558
blight, resistant species.............. 756
blight, studies........................ 557
leaf bacteriosis....................... 550
leaf injury in Paris................... 224
leaves, plant food constituents........ 629
Chicken—
diseases and intestinal parasites, Guam.. 779
flesh as affected by temperatures above
and below freezing.................. 62
lice, remedies......................... 258
mite, life history and habits, U.S.D.A... 859
pox, immunization...................... 584
Chickens—
American class, U.S.D.A................ 368
feeding experiments.................... 865
feeding experiments, Iowa.............. 70
Chicks—
artificial brooding, N. J.............. 71
care and management, Wash.............. 96
cost of raising, N. C.................. 681
diseases of. N. J...................... 280
feeding experiments. Guam.............. 768
feeding experiments, Mo................ 768
Chicory, watering, continuous.............. 543
Children, feeding................... 166, 671
Children's gardens. (See School gardens.)
Chilies. (See Pepper.)
Chinch bug, false, notes.................. 847
Chlor-antiseptics, formulas............... 477
Chloramin-T in treatment of wounds........ 576
(Chloridea) Heliothis obsoleta. (See Cotton
bollworm.)
Chloridea virescens, studies, U.S.D.A...... 664
Chlorids, determination in blood.......... 804
Chlorin—
determination in chlorids.............. 714
determination in drinking water........ 714
larvicidal value, N. J................. 665
liquid, sterilization of water by...... 588
Chloroform as an anthelmintic............. 578
Chlorophyll, photochemical reactions...... 26
Cholus forbesii, introduction into New Jersey. 660
Chondrus crispus, analyses, Conn. State.... 814

Page.

Chromoplasts, origin........................... 632
Chrysanthemum crown gall, notes........... 252
Chrysanthemums, culture.................... 44
Chrysomphalus dictyospermi, varieties........ 462
Chrysomyza sp., new to North America...... 757
Chrysopa, or golden-eyed fly, notes.......... 156
Chrysophana placida as a household pest..... 854
Chrysops, egg-laying habits and early stages. 853
Churches, rural—
 cooperation.............................. 593
 economic and social force, Wis........... 90
Cicada, periodical—
 in Ohio, Ohio........................... 258
 in western New York.................... 257
Cicadellidæ—
 of Missouri............................. 157
 of Wisconsin........................... 761
Cicer arietinum as a green manure for rice.... 824
Cicutin hydrobromid, use against tetanus.... 79
Cider—
 changes in during fermentation and stor-
 age.................................... 716
 industry in England.................... 416
Cigarette beetle, destruction by X-rays...... 359
Cimex rotundatus, relation to kala-azar....... 357
Cinchona—
 diseases, notes......................... 844
 gray root, notes........................ 352
Cinchonidin, methods of analysis............ 113
Cirsium arvense, root system................ 542
Cisthene, new, of North America............ 564
Citrate, action on isolated intestine......... 471
Citric acid, extraction with ether............ 414
Citrus—
 bacterial disease, new, in California...... 153
 bacterial disease, new studies, U.S.D.A. 154
 black spot and brown spot, treatment... 352
 blast, investigations.................... 153
 canker, control in Florida............... 556
 canker, eradication, U.S.D.A........... 556
 canker in Philippines................... 745
 canker in South Africa................. 657
 canker, notes........................... 556
 canker, studies......................... 843
 canker, studies, Fla.................... 656
 diseases in Porto Rico.................. 246
 diseases in West Indies................. 452
 diseases, notes, Fla.................... 656
 gummosis, notes........................ 846
 gummosis, studies, Fla................. 656
 knot, notes............................. 839
 leaf disease, notes..................... 453
 mealy bug, remedies.................... 158
 melanose, treatment, Fla.............. 656
 mottle leaf, studies, U.S.D.A.......... 352,353
 scab, cause............................. 556
 scaly bark, notes...................... 846
 sour rot, notes......................... 843
 withertip, notes........................ 453
Citrus fruits—
 abnormal water relations................ 834
 action of vanillin and limestone on, Fla. 656
 cost of production...................... 144
 cull, utilization, Fla................... 313
 culture................................. 345
 culture in Japan, China, and Formosa... 834

Page.

Citrus fruits—Continued.
 culture in Philippines................... 745
 culture in Transvaal.................... 545
 fertilizer experiments, Fla.............. 649
 fertilizer experiments, P.R............. 43
 frost damage in transit................. 649
 fumigation.............................. 634
 improvement, U.S.D.A.................. 144
 insects affecting....................... 255
 irrigation, U.S.D.A.................... 319
 irrigation experiments.................. 186
 lightning injury, Fla.................... 656
 nitrogen nutrition, U.S.D.A........... 318,353
 spraying................................ 460
 (*See also* Oranges, Lemons, *etc.*)
Cladosporium—
 citri, notes............................ 556
 cucumerinum, virulence................. 840
 gramium, notes........................ 553
 syringæ n.sp., description............. 550
Cladostephus verticellatus, analyses, Conn.
 State.................................. 814
Clasterosporium—
 degenerans, notes...................... 652
 maydicum n.sp., notes................. 148
Clemson College, notes.................... 300
Climate—
 as a factor in pollination of grasses and
 legumes............................... 735
 changes in.............................. 15
 effect on composition of plant oils....... 418
 effect on composition of wheat, Colo..... 38
 effect on plant growth................ 15,725
 effect on tree growth............... 450,837
 relation to agriculture, Colo........... 209
 (*See also* Meteorology.)
Climatological data. (*See* Meteorological observations.)
Climatology. (*See* Meteorology.)
Clitocybe thvilensis n.sp., notes............ 630
Clivia, greenhouse disease of.............. 353
Clonal varieties, inheritance in........... 240
Clover—
 alsike, for wet lands, Minn............. 229
 and grass mixtures, tests.............. 230
 beetle, European, in California......... 568
 bird-foot, in grass mixtures........... 735
 bur, as a pasture crop, Tex........... 533
 bur, digestibility, Tex................ 168
 crimson, as a cover crop for orchards... 833
 crimson, as a green manure, Md........ 320
 crimson, improvement.................. 136
 crimson, liming experiments........... 428
 crimson nitrogen residue of roots and
 stubble, Ga........................... 29
 culture experiments, Hawaii........... 131
 culture experiments, Idaho............ 30
 culture experiments, La............... 529
 culture experiments, Minn............ 227
 culture in India....................... 232
 fertilizer experiments, Ohio........... 126
 fertilizing value, Ind................. 214
 flowering habits and anatomical structure 535
 irrigation experiments, Idaho......... 639
 Japan, as a pasture crop, Tex........ 533
 leaf weevil, lesser, notes, Mont....... 255

Clover—Continued. Page.
    nectar secretion............................ 633
    nitrogenous fertilizers for................ 133
    pasture for pigs, Minn.................... 270
    pollination experiments.................. 735
    pollination studies, Iowa................. 30
    Pseudopeziza leaf spots.................. 751
    red, behavior in acid soils................ 422
    red, improvement......................... 136
    red, irrigation experiments, Nev........ 435
    rust, æcial stage.......................... 752
    seed, boiling.............................. 829
    seed, bushel weights..................... 889
    seed, determination of origin............ 141
    seed, scarifying experiments, Iowa...... 30
    silage for dairy cows, Wash.............. 75
    sweet. (See Sweet clover.)
    weevil in Iowa............................ 562
Clubroot, studies, N.Y.Cornell............... 454
    (See also Cabbage clubroot.)
Cluster fly, studies, N.J..................... 665
Coal, spontaneous combustion, Iowa......... 788
Coat color. (See Color.)
Cocain, effect on coagulation of blood......... 177
Coccidæ—
    new chalcidoid parasites................. 467
    of Porto Rico............................ 158
Coccidia—
    in sparrows, relation to blackhead in tur-
      keys.................................. 284
    of intestines of birds..................... 280
Coccidiosis—
    in chicks, Cal........................... 182
    in liver of dogs.......................... 280
Coccinellidæ of California, life history and
    feeding records......................... 18
Coccobacillus acridiorum, destruction of locusts
    by............................. 461, 561, 760, 849
Coccomyces hiemalis, studies................. 755
Coccophagus—
    acanthoscelis n.sp., description........... 162
    avæ n.sp., description................... 19
Coccus citricola and C. hesperidum, comparison 663
Cockchafer, remedies........................ 467
Cockerels, fattening test, Minn.............. 268
Cockroaches, notes.......................... 156
Cocoa, alkalinity............................ 414
Coconut—
    beetle, notes............................ 54
    bleeding disease, notes.................. 349
    bud rot, notes................. 252, 453, 839
    cake, sugar content..................... 208
    diseases in West Indies................. 452
    meal, analyses, Conn. State 268
    oil, determination....................... 618
    oil, extraction in Philippines........... 806
    poonac, analyses....................... 814
Coconuts—
    culture................................. 245
    culture experiments.................... 144
    for pigs, Guam......................... 768
    grated for chicks, Guam................ 768
    origin and dispersal.................... 845
Codling moth—
    larvæ, resistance to cold................ 355
    notes................................... 460
    remedies................................ 259
    remedies, Idaho........................ 57

Codling moth—Continued. Page.
    remedies, Ill............................ 242
    remedies, Oreg......................... 54
    studies................................. 463
    studies, N.Mex......................... 57
Coffee—
    aphis, notes............................ 662
    culture experiments.................... 144
    culture in Belgian Kongo............... 545
    diseases and other enemies, notes...... 545
    fruit disease, notes..................... 838
    industry in Abyssinia.................. 835
    industry in French Indo-China.......... 545
    ingestion, effect on uric acid excretion 470
    insects affecting........................ 560
    leaf disease, notes.................. 551, 833
    leaf disease, treatment................. 453
    root diseases in Lesser Antilles......... 454
    soils of Porto Rico, P.R................ 43
    transplanting experiments, P.R........ 649
    varieties................................ 835
Cold—
    frames, construction and management,
      Colo................................. 41
    storage, effect on keeping quality of sugar,
      La................................... 510
    storage laws in California............... 63
    waves at Tampa, Florida, U.S.D.A...... 513
    (See also Temperature, low.)
Coleophora limosipennella, notes, Conn.State.. 255
Coleoptera of British India.................. 765
Coleosporium—
    ribicola, æcial stage.................... 354
    spp., æcial stages.............. 844, 845
Coleus, somatic variations in................ 27
Collard diseases, notes, Ga.................. 45
Colletotrichum—
    anthurii, notes......................... 550
    camelliæ, notes......................... 252
    cinnamoni n.sp., description............ 748
    circinans, studies...................... 841
    citri, notes............................. 353
    coffeæ (?), notes....................... 833
    falcatum, notes.............. 452, 551, 553
    glœosporioides, notes................... 453
    glœosporioides, treatment.............. 352
    gossypii, notes......................... 452
    heveæ, notes........................... 253
    higginseanum n.sp., description, U.S.D.A. 751
    lindemuthianum, notes................. 550
    lindemuthianum, treatment, Colo....... 243
Colloidal—
    mixture for studying protoplasmic ac-
      tion............................ 325, 821
    solutions, monograph.................. 501
Colloids, effect on electrical conductivity of
    salts................................... 520
Color—
    inheritance in mammals................ 863
    numerical expression for............... 110
Colorado—
    River, silt determinations.............. 486
    Station, report......................... 599
Colorimetry, new apparatus for............. 803
Coloring matter, detection in milk........... 113
Colostrum—
    as affected by parturition.............. 172
    proteins of............................. 6

Page.

Columbine leaf miner, notes.................. 255
Colza—
    oil, determination in mixtures........... 312
    seed cake, microscopic examination...... 416
Community school building at Wheaton,
    Minnesota.................................. 793
Complement fixation as affected by temper-
    ature...................................... 688
Compsilura concinnata, notes.............. 459, 764
Comstockiella sabilis in California............ 563
Conarachin, chemistry of.................. 8, 501
Concanavalin, chemistry of.................. 8
Concrete—
    culverts, cost data....................... 885
    expansion and contraction, U.S.D.A.... 884
    strength as affected by water............ 490
    treatise.................................. 590
    use in irrigation......................... 281
    use in the garden........................ 746
Congochrysosoma n.g. and n.sp., description.. 359
Coniferous seedlings, damping off........... 46
Conifers—
    of North America, leaf characters........ 147
    structure of bordered pits............... 128
Coniophora cerebella, notes.................. 253
Coniosporium oryzinum n.sp., notes.......... 148
Coniothecium chomatosporum, studies........ 842
Coniothyrium—
    n.spp., descriptions...................... 748
    pæoniæ n.sp., description................. 550
    sacchari, notes........................... 553
Connecticut—
    College, notes.................... 97, 496, 896
    State Station, notes.............. 196, 700, 896
    Storrs Station, notes............... 496, 896
Conorhinus rubrofasciatus, relation to kala-
    azar...................................... 358
Conotelus mexicanus, notes.................. 847
Conotrachelus nenuphar. (See Plum curculio.)
Conservation law in New York.............. 244
Cooking—
    army, manual............................. 166
    book...................................... 894
    laboratory manual........................ 94
Copper—
    compounds of organic acids, toxicity for
        protozoa.............................. 375
    compounds, protein of.................... 8
    in flora of copper-tailing region.......... 432
    in fresh tomatoes........................ 263
    in soils and water, effect on crops........ 527
    sulphate, antiseptic and germicidal value. 176
    sulphate, production in 1915-16.......... 524
Corn—
    and cowpeas, associated growth, Mo..... 731
    and peanuts as a mixed crop............. 734
    and the westward migration, treatise.... 94
    as a dry-land crop, U.S.D.A.............. 637
    as a supplement for wheat in bread mak-
        ing................................... 263
    assimilation of nitrogen by............... 223
    bacterial disease, new, Ky............... 48
    barren stalks, Ark....................... 536
    billbug, southern, studies, N.C.......... 666
    bread, recipes, U.S.D.A.................. 364

Page.

Corn—Continued.
    breeding experiments..................... 827
    breeding experiments, Minn.............. 226
    bushel weights........................... 889
    chop, digestibility, Ark................. 678
    chop, digestibility and productive value,
        Tex................................... 865
    correlation of aleurone and chlorophyll
        factors............................... 526
    cost of production, W.Va................. 191
    cracked, analyses, Conn.State........... 268
    culture, N.J............................. 642
    culture, Ohio............................ 396
    culture experiments................... 436, 734
    culture experiments, La................. 529
    culture experiments, Minn.............. 226
    culture experiments, Mo................ 730
    culture experiments, N.Mex............ 32
    culture experiments, Tex............... 329
    culture experiments, Va................ 535
    culture in Egypt........................ 233
    culture in Northwest.................... 437
    culture in Tucuman..................... 134
    culture under dry farming, N.Mex...... 329
    dietary properties.............. 164, 264, 767
    digestibility, U.S.D.A.................. 672
    disease in Porto Rico.................. 839
    diseases in West Indies................ 452
    drying.................................. 509
    ear characters in relation to yield...... 136
    ear worm, remedies, Mo................ 760
    effect on soil bacteria, U.S.D.A....... 421
    embryo, morphology..................... 127
    fall irrigation, U.S.D.A................ 822
    feed meal, analyses, Wis............... 471
    fertilizer experiments................. 436
    fertilizer experiments, Ga............. 28
    fertilizer experiments, Minn.......... 229
    fertilizer experiments, Mo............ 731
    fertilizer experiments, Pa............ 627
    fertilizer experiments, Utah.......... 440
    for silage, time of cutting............ 99
    for silage, varieties, Nev............. 435
    for silage, yields, Minn.............. 228
    germinability in relation to temperature
        and humidity.......................... 736
    gluten feed and meal, analyses, Conn.
        State................................. 268
    ground, digestibility, Ill............. 677
    hogging down, Nebr.................... 679
    huskers and shredders, specifications.... 886
    insects affecting........................ 460
    irrigation experiments, Oreg........... 85
    irrigation experiments, Utah........... 440
    leaf-hopper, parasites of.......... 163, 847
    leaves, variation of water and dry matter
        in, D.S.D.A............................ 637
    lobed leaves in.......................... 136
    meal as a flour substitute, Ohio........ 895
    oil meal, analyses, Wis................ 471
    oil, production and use, U.S.D.A....... 511
    pedigreed, yields in Wisconsin......... 438
    Peronospora disease.................... 552
    plant, factors affecting development, Mo. 732
    planting dates, U.S.D.A................ 316

Corn—Continued. Page.

pollination experiments................... 137
protein and ash for growing animals..... 164
removal of plant food by, Conn.State.... 23z
rust, notes............................... 453
seed, selection experiments.............. 830
seeding experiments...................... 734
seeding experiments, Minn............... 226
seeding experiments, Ohio................ 232
seedlings, translocation of seed protein
  reserves in............................ 24
selection experiments.................... 732
selection experiments, N.C.............. 636
selection experiments, Nev.............. 32
self-pollination, determination........... 537
shucks, digestibility, Tex................ 168
silage. (*See* Silage.)
smut, investigations..................... 750
soft or flour............................ 799
soils in United States................... 799
v. oats for work horses, Ohio............. 195
variegated pericarp in.................... 737
varieties...................... 233, 334, 436, 824
varieties, Ark........................... 536
varieties, Ga............................ 35
varieties, Guam.......................... 728
varieties, Idaho......................... 29
varieties, La............................ 529
varieties, Minn.................... 227, 228, 229
varieties, Mo............................ 730
varieties, N.C........................... 636
varieties, N.Mex...................... 32, 329
varieties, Nev........................... 32
varieties, Ohio.......................... 232
varieties, Oreg.......................... 531
varieties, Tex.................... 329, 330, 823
white flint, development, La............ 529
Cornell University, notes........... 98, 498, 600, 898
Cornstalk borer—
lesser, studies, U.S.D.A................ 551
notes.................................... 847
Cornstarch, gelatinization temperature...... 410
Correlation—
coefficient, limitations and applicability. 621
in farm survey data, U.S.D.A........... 209
Corticium—
salmonicolor, studies.................... 52, 452
sp. on rubber......................... 253, 249
vagum, investigations.................... 155
Corynespora melonis, notes............... 248
Coryneum spp. on trees and shrubs.......... 250
Corythuca pura n.sp., description............ 849
Cosmopolites sordida, notes................ 161
Cossus larvæ, resistance to cold.............. 356
Cost of living—
in Massachusetts..................... 469
in New York City..................... 670
in United States..................... 670
on farms, Mo......................... 789
Cotoneaster acutifolia as a hedge plant, Minn. 241
Cottage cheese—
as a food, U.S.D.A..................... 669
manufacture, U.S.D.A.................. 686
Cotton—
angular leaf spot, studies, U.S.D.A...... 49
boll disease, notes....................... 652
boll weevil, control...................... 359

Cotton—Continued. Page.

boll weevil in Georgia................... 847
bollworm, Egyptian, studies............. 55
bollworm, pink, control by flooding..... 762
bollworm, pink, in Mexico and Brazil... 358
bollworm, pink, in United States........ 762
bollworm, pink, parasites of............. 569
bollworm, pink, rate of increase........ 762
bollworm, pink, studies, U.S.D.A....... 564
bollworm, remedies, Guam.............. 729
bollworm, scavenger, U.S.D.A.......... 564
crinkled dwarf rogues.................. 224, 732
culture, U.S.D.A....................... 36
culture experiments.................... 734
culture experiments, Fla............... 635
culture experiments, Miss.............. 334
culture experiments, Tex............... 330
culture in Argentina................. 738, 823
culture in Belgian Kongo.............. 830
culture in Brazil....................... 441
culture in California. U.S.D.A......... 335
culture in French colonies............. 830
culture in Guam, Guam................ 728
culture in various countries........... 891
culture under boll-weevil conditions..... 359
culture under dry farming, N.Mex...... 329
disease, new, in India................. 454
diseases in West Indies................ 452
fertilizer experiments............... 215, 732
fertilizer experiments, Ga............. 29
fertilizer experiments, Mo............. 731
fiber, water absorption capacity........ 736
ginning reports, weather factor, U.S.D.A 114
green manuring experiments............ 734
handling and marketing in Imperial
  Valley, U.S.D.A..................... 37
inheritance of bract teeth.............. 732
insects affecting....................... 460, 560
leaves, nectar glands.................. 727
marketing in North Carolina. U.S.D.A... 36
planter, lister attachment for, U.S.D.A.. 90
prices and movement in 1916............ 492
production in United States, 1915-16..... 441
resistance to leaf blister mite.......... 732
selection experiments.................. 732
selection experiments, Miss............ 335
selection experiments, N.C............ 636
shedding............................... 224, 553
spacing experiments.................... 734
stainer, notes.................... 460, 550, 847
thinning experiments, Ga.............. 29
upland, classification, U.S.D.A........ 830
varieties............................... 824, 825
varieties, Ark.......................... 642
varieties, Ga........................... 35
varieties, Guam........................ 728
varieties, Miss......................... 335
varieties, Mo........................... 731
varieties, N.C.......................... 636
varieties, N.Mex....................... 329
varieties, Tex.......................... 823
varieties in Brazil..................... 441
varieties in Italian Somaliland.......... 336
warehouses, accounts for, U.S.D.A...... 591
water requirements, Ga................ 29
weather conditions for, U.S.D.A........ 116

Cottonseed—	Page.
as human food	60
cake, analyses	873
calculator	137
deterioration at public gin, Miss.	335
digestibility and productive value, Tex..	865
feed, analyses, Wis	471
germination as affected by green manures. Ga	29
meal, analyses	220
meal, analyses, Conn.State	268
meal, analyses, R.I	767
meal, analyses, Wis	471
meal as a top-dressing for grains, Ga	29
meal, digestibility, Ark	678
meal, digestibility, Ga	65
meal, fertilizing value, Mo	731
meal, fertilizing value, Tex	823
meal for breeding ewes, N.C	676
meal for calves, N.C	675, 682
meal for hens, N.C	682
meal for horses and mules, N.C	681
meal, low-grade, analyses, Ohio	768
meal, phosphorus compounds in, Ark	502
meal, sugar content	208
meal, toxicity	60
meal, toxicity, N.C	689
meal, toxicity, neutralizing, N.C	680
oil, detection	13
oil, production and use, U.S.D.A	511
products, effect on composition and properties of butter, Mo	72
Coulee cricket, notes, Wash	54
Country—	
planning, problems in	189
v. city	593
Countryside and Nation	593
County farm bureau, Cal	888
Cover crops—	
for orchards	833
for orchards, Wash	41
Cow manure, storage experiments, Me	628
Cow-testing associations—	
benefits, Wash	96
formation and operation, Ill	474
Cowhage and related species	328
Cowpea—	
hay, digestibility, Tex	168
pod weevil, notes, Fla	659
weevil, injurious to cotton	560
weevil, remedies	262
Cowpeas—	
and corn, associated growth, Mo	731
as a forage crop, Idaho	640
as a green manure, Hawaii	320
as a green manure, N.J	425
culture experiments, Tex	329
culture in Illinois, Ill	438
culture in Tucuman	134
culture under dry farming, N.Mex	329
effect on following wheat crop, Mo	732
inoculation experiments, Guam	729
seed color variation in	334
varieties, Conn.State	235
varieties, Fla	635
varieties, Ill	439
varieties, N.Mex	329
varieties, Tex	329, 330, 331

Cows—	Page.
dairy, efficiency table	775
feeding experiments	171, 372, 872
feeding experiments, Fla	683
feeding experiments, N.C	682
feeding experiments, N.Mex	75
feeding experiments, Ohio	169
feeding experiments, U.S.D.A	766
feeding experiments, Wash	75
forage crops for, Wash	599
Kerry and Dexter, milk and fat records..	172
mineral metabolism, Ohio	169
pasturing experiments, Minn	271
pasturing v. stable feeding, Can	574
poisoning with box elder	80
protection from flies	260
rations for, Conn.Storrs	684
rations for, N.J	684
rations for, Ohio	195
records. (See Dairy herd records.)	
score card for	172
sterility in	379
utilization of feed for development of fetus, Mo	71
Crab apples, varieties, S.Dak	142
Crambid moths, trap lights for	259
Crambids, new, from United States	564
Cranberries—	
acid content	714
fertilizer experiments	745
insects affecting	53
spoilage after picking	745
Craponius inæqualis. (See Grape curculio.)	
Cream—	
cooling tanks, construction, Nebr	591
fat content, factors affecting, Can	576
grading and improvement, Nebr	592
pasteurization, S.Dak	476
pasteurized, for butter making, Can	576
production and grading, Kans	373
production under spring conditions, Ill..	273
separators, operation, Can	576
testing, methods	618
Creameries—	
accounting system for, U.S.D.A	875
in Minnesota	777
Creamery records, proposed system, Idaho...	75
Creosote—	
as a timber preservative	886
from hardwood tar	114
toxicity to wood-destroying fungi	502
Cricket, coulee, notes, Wash	54
Crickets—	
in South America	157
injurious to potatoes, Wash	157
Crimson clover. (See Clover, crimson.)	
Cristatithorax latiscapus n.sp., description	59
Cronartium—	
comptoniæ, notes	845
pyriforme, pycnia of	558
ribicola, control in New York	846
ribicola, mycelium of	757
ribicola, overwintering	845, 846
Crop—	
reports, U.S.D.A	92, 191, 392, 697, 891
reports in Nebraska	291
rotations. (See Rotation of crops.)	
statistics on reclamation projects	92
yields as affected by late spring, U.S.D.A.	316
yields in Illinois, Ill	214

Crops—	Page.
cost of production, Can	790
cost of production, Ohio	595
cost of production, W.Va	190
cost of production in California	890
culture at high altitude	437
culture in California	890
effect on soil bacteria, U.S.D.A	421
for Arizona, Ariz	209
growing without potash	218
insurance against fire	888
toxic effect of copper on	527

Crossties—

industry in Canada	245
industry in 1915, U.S.D.A	838
preservation	748

Crotalaria as a green manure, Hawaii	320
Crotalaria candicans, culture experiments, Hawaii	131
Crowfoot, habits and eradication	542
Crown gall, relation to cancer	245

Crucifer—

bacterial wilt, notes	150
Phoma disease, notes	248

Crude fiber. (See Cellulose.)

Cryptorhynchus—

batatæ, notes	256
lapathi, studies, N.Y.Cornell	464
Crystallization, colloidal bags or containers in	409

Cucumber—

anthracnose, dissemination	840
beetle, striped, notes, Fla	659
beetle, striped, notes, Ohio	261
beetle, striped, remedies, Conn.State	254
beetles injurious to potatoes, Wash	157
diseases, notes, N.J	653
leaf scorch, notes	248
leaf spots, notes	840
mildew, notes	453
mosaic diseases, notes	752

Cucumbers—

culture experiments, Guam	742
culture in greenhouses	41
fertilizer experiments	41
fertilizer experiments, Guam	742
Cucurbit bacterial wilt, notes	150
Cucurbitaria pithyophila, studies	353
Culex pipiens, migration, N.J	664
Culicidæ. (See Mosquitoes.)	

Cultivation—

animal v. motor power	591
mechanical, in Europe	490
Culture media from blood	220

Culverts—

concrete v. cast-iron, for roads	885
corrugated metal, tests	288

Curculionidæ—

in bamboo stems	359
new neotropical	765
of British India	765

Currant—

aphis, migratory habits	562
dieback, notes	251
fruit fly, dark, in California	566
worm, notes, Ohio	599

Currants—

acid content	714
Alpine, as a hedge plant, Minn	241

Currants—Continued.	Page.
aphids affecting, U.S.D.A	358
black, nematodes affecting	843
drying	114, 509
red, history and development	833
varieties, Oreg	243

Cuscuta—

americana, notes	452
sp. on chayote	755

Cutworms—

army, notes, Mont	255
injurious to potatoes, Wash	157
notes, Ohio	195
Cyanid gas as a cause of fruit pitting	634
Cyanuric acid, isolation from soils, U.S.D.A	612

Cyclamen mite—

notes	765
studies, U.S.D.A	857
Cylas formicarius, notes	256
Cylichnostomum n.spp., descriptions	280

Cylindrosporium—

vaccarianum n.sp., notes	630
yuccæ n. sp., description	550
Cyllene robiniæ, notes, Okla	563
Cynodon dactylon for shifting sands	333
Cyrtogaster javensis n.sp., description	667
Cysticercus pisiformis in kittens	693
Cystopus sp. on sweet potatoes	452

Cytospora—

leucostoma, studies	554
sacchari, notes	553
(Dacus) Bactrocera cucurbitæ, studies, U.S.D.A.	565
Dacus spp. in India, Burma, and Ceylon	160
Daffodils, improvement	836
Daincha as a green manure for rice	824

Dairy—

barns as a factor in sanitary milk production, Ill	681
barns, construction	872
barns, construction, Ill	695
buildings, plans	90
chemistry, progress in	373
education in Great Britain	893
education in United States	893
efficiency table	775
farm plant, construction, Wash	591
farming in blue-grass region of Kentucky, U.S.D.A	873
farming, textbook	94, 172
herd records, Can	574
herd records, Fla	684
herds, improvement, Minn	271
industry in Argentina	271
industry, woman's part in	893
inspection in Massachusetts	165
inspection in Minnesota	166
laboratory manual and notebook	872
laws in Michigan	63
laws in Wisconsin	875
products, acidity	373
products, analyses	114, 165
products, handling	777
rations, formulating, Conn.Storrs	684
rations, formulating, N.J	684
score cards, survey	175
sires, selection, Utah	473
statistics in Minnesota	777
wastes, disposal	588

	Page.
Dairying—	
community, U.S.D.A	573
in Denmark	172
notes	872
textbook	894
Dams for prevention of soil erosion	286
Danæa roots, mycorrhiza of	631
Dandelions, nectar secretion	633
Danthonia in New Zealand	537
Dasheens—	
culture and use, U.S.D.A	537
culture experiments, Tex	329
nematodes affecting	841
Dasyprocta punctata n.subsp., descriptions.	757
Dasyscypha subtilissima, studies	354
Datana integerrima, notes, Conn. State	255
Datura—	
breeding experiments	546
for classroom work in genetics	831
Deer Flat bird reservation, Idaho	355
Delaware College and Station, notes	397, 600
Delphastus catalinæ, parasitic on white flies...	58
Dendroctonus micans. (*See* Spruce beetle, European.)	
Dendropemon sp., notes	453
Dendrophoma saccharicola, notes	553
Department of agriculture of Finland, report.	295
Dermacentor venustus, notes	459
Dermanyssus gallinæ—	
life history and habits, U.S.D.A	859
notes	861
Deserts, precipitation-evaporation factor in..	525
Desiccation of Africa, U.S.D.A	607
Desiccator, description	110
Desmodium hirtum, culture experiments, Hawaii	131
Desmosomus longipes, notes	359
Dew, ammonia in, U.S.D.A	116
Dewberries, varieties, Oreg	243
Dewberry diseases, notes	52
Dextrinase, bacterial, preparation	411
Dextrose, determination in muscular tissue..	617
Diabetes, metabolism in	267
Diabrotica—	
graminea, studies	256
spp. injurious to potatoes, Wash	157
vittata. (*See* Cucumber beetle, striped.)	
Diachasma spp., parasitic on fruit fly	856
Diacrisia virginica, control by parasites	760
Diamond-back moth—	
life history, Me	663
life history, U.S.D.A	663
Diaprepes n.sp. and n.subsp., description	765
Diapus furtivus, life history	854
Diarrhea, bacillary white—	
in chicks	82, 280
in chicks, Cal	182
in chicks, Conn.Storrs	383
Diaspis pentagona in Argentina	460
Diatræa—	
saccharalis. (*See* Sugar-cane borer.)	
zeacolella, notes	847
Diatrypella barleriæ n. sp., notes	148
Dibromoorthocresolsulfonphthalein, use in milk cultures, U.S.D.A	686
Dicyphus n.spp., descriptions	561
Didelphis marsupialis particeps n.subsp., description	775

	Page.
Diet—	
and body condition, relation to energy production	469
effect on heat production during mechanical work	671
from vegetable sources	264
lists, compilation	469
of children	671
relation to glycogen content of liver	64
summary and digest of data	571
(*See also* Food.)	
Dietetics, essentials in	164
Digestion—	
apparatus, fumeless, description	503
crate for pigs, description, Ark	678
salivary, in horses	681, 771
Digitalis, action in pneumonia	375
Dilophia graminis, notes	247
Dilophospora graminis on wheat	247
Dimerosporium mangiferum, notes	839
Dioctophyme renale in abdominal cavity	281
Diospilus polydrusi n.sp., description, N. Y. State	359
Diphosphate, fertilizing value	323
Diplodia—	
cacaoicola, notes	349
crebra n.sp., notes	148
natalensis, relation to citrus gummosis, Fla	656
Diplodia on tea roots	52
Diplodina degenerans n.sp., notes	148
Dipping vats, construction	477
Diprion simile, notes	255, 261, 568
Diptera—	
head capsule and mouth parts	159
of District of Columbia	57
Dipylidium caninum, life history	163
Discothecium bakeri n.g. and n.sp., notes	148
Diseases of animals. (*See* Animal diseases.)	
Diseases of plants. (*See* Plant diseases.)	
Disinfectants, bacteriological examination....	711
Distemper, canine. (*See* Dog distemper.)	
Distillation, colloidal bags or containers in...	409
Distillers' grains—	
analyses, Wis	471
dried, analyses, Conn.State	268
dried, analyses, R.I	767
Diversinervus silvestrii n.sp., description	162
Divining rod, use, U.S.D.A	807
Dog—	
diseases, handbook	778
distemper, treatment	584
Dogfish, food value	63
Dogs—	
parasites of	483
treatise	769
Dolichos lablab hay, digestibility and productive value, Tex	865
Dolichurus greenei n.sp., description	569
Dothichiza populea in United States	354
Dothidella—	
ulei, notes	253
vacciniicola n.sp., description	748
Dourine—	
eradication	477
in horses	692
in United States	274

Drainage—   Page.
  districts, organization and administration,
    U.S.D.A................................ 883
  in Egypt................................ 693
  in Hawaii............................... 384
  in Ontario.............................. 385
  in Virginia............................. 384
  law in Washington....................... 281
  of irrigated land.................. 186, 281, 883
  of irrigated land, U.S.D.A............ 86, 587
  tile system, Minn....................... 286
  treatise................................ 587
Draintile. (See Tile.)
Dredgers, suction, manual.................. 555
Dried blood—
  fertilizing value, Ill.................. 449
  fertilizing value, Pa................... 627
  nitrification in semiarid soils, U.S.D.A... 319
  preparation in army slaughterhouses..... 321
Drugs—
  inspection in Connecticut, Conn.State.... 863
  inspection in Indiana................... 63
  inspection in Maine, Me................. 570
  inspection in Massachusetts............. 165
  inspection in Missouri.................. 63
  inspection in North Dakota, N.Dak...... 63,
                                    463, 570, 863
  laws in California...................... 63
  laws in Rhode Island................... 570
Dry farming—
  experiments, Oreg....................... 520
  in central Oregon, U.S.D.A............. 333
  in Colorado, Colo....................... 437
  in eastern New Mexico, N.Mex.......... 328
  in Mexico............................... 134
  papers on............................... 437
Duck disease, new.......................... 483
Durra, varieties, Cal...................... 338
Durum wheat. (See Wheat, durum.)
Dust injury to agriculture and forestry in
  Austria.................................. 528
Dusts, carbonaceous, inflammability....... 109, 410
Duty of water. (See Water, duty.)
Dysdercus—
  albidiventris, notes..................... 847
  suturellus. (See Cotton stainer.)
Ear tick, spinose—
  life history and habits................. 856
  notes, Mont............................. 255
Earias insulana, studies................... 55
Earthquake in Missouri, U.S.D.A.......... 513
East Park bird reservation, California..... 355
Economics, rural. (See Rural economics.)
Ectoedemia spp. in North America.......... 564
Edestin—
  copper compunds of...................... 9
  value for growth or maintenance......... 864
Education, agricultural. (See Agricultural
  education.)
Educational institutions—
  higher, in Iowa......................... 292
  of Washington, survey................... 597
Egg—
  laying contest, Conn.Storrs............. 368
  laying contest at Vineland, N.J......... 71
  production cycles in birds.............. 869
  production, improvement by selection,
    N.J.................................... 871

Egg—Continued.   Page.
  production, studies, Utah.............. 369, 869
  yolk, antineuritic substance from........ 308
  yolk, metabolism during incubation..... 772
  yolk, white and yellow, composition..... 772
Eggplants—
  culture experiments, Guam.............. 742
  fertilizer experiments, Guam........... 742
  Gnomonia on............................ 752
Eggs—
  cost of production, U.S.D.A............. 871
  double, studies, Me.................... 371
  fertility experiments, N.C............. 682
  for hatching, shipping, Can............ 682
  infertile, production, N.J............. 573
  marketing by parcel post and express,
    N.C.................................... 682
  nest, Iowa............................. 70
  preparation for the table.............. 668
  preservation, Ala.College.............. 682
  preservation, Minn..................... 208
  preservation, Utah..................... 473
Eight-spotted forester—
  notes................................... 158
  notes, Conn.State....................... 255
Eimeria—
  arium, morphological study............. 280
  stiedæ, parasitic in liver of dogs...... 280
Eisonyx (Eumononycha) picipes n.sp., description................................ 58
Elæis guineensis, propagation and yields... 835
Elasmopalpus lignosellus, studies, U.S.D.A.. 851
Electric—
  heating, treatise....................... 387
  service, rural, in Wisconsin............ 189
Electrical equipment and transmission,
  treatise................................. 287
Electricity—
  effect on plant growth.................. 336
  for irrigation pumping................. 291, 786
  use on the farm......................... 387
Electrolytes—
  effect on germination of seeds.......... 431
  effect on hydrolysis of starch by malt
    amylase................................ 613
Elephantorrhiza elephantina, culture experiments, Guam............................. 730
Elm case bearer, European, notes, Conn.State 255
Emmer—
  culture experiments, Tex............... 330
  varieties, Ill.......................... 641
  varieties, Md.......................... 332
  varieties, Oreg........................ 530
Emodin-bearing drugs, identification........ 509
Empoasca mali. (See Apple leaf-hopper.)
Empusa muscæ, notes....................... 764
Endocrine glands extracts, effect on milk pro-
  duction.................................. 173
Endophylloides portoricensis n.g. and n.sp.,
  notes.................................... 552
Endophyllum, new combinations........... 552
Endothia—
  havanensis, studies..................... 253
  parasitica, studies..................... 457
Energy production in relation to diet and
  body condition.......................... 469
Engineering courses, disrespect of students
  for....................................... 893
  (See also Agricultural engineering.)

Enteritis—   Page.
  chronic. (*See* Johne's disease.)
  coccidial, in chicks, Cal 182
Enterohepatitis, infectious. (*See* Blackhead.)
Entomological Society of British Columbia,
  proceedings 459
Entomology—
  agricultural, experimental technique 355
  in public schools 459
Enzyms—
  proteolytic, of blood 478
  proteolytic plant, inhibitors 204
Ephestia cautella, notes 156
Epicauta spp. injurious to potatoes, Wash ... 157
Epilachna corrupta, studies, N.Mex 465
Epitetrastichus lecanii n.sp., description 59
Epithelioma, contagious—
  in chickens, Nev 78
  in quail 83
Epitrastichus ibseni n.sp., description 59
Epitrix—
  cucumeris. (*See* Potato flea beetle.)
  nigroænea, notes 765
  spp. injurious to tobacco 256
  subscrinita, notes, Wash 157
Eriococcus azalæ, notes, Conn. State 255
Eriophorum vaginatum as a source of fiber 736
Eriophyes—
  malifoliæ, notes 570
  pyri. (*See* Pear-leaf blister-mite.)
Eriosoma pyricola, studies, U.S.D.A 661
Erysiphe—
  spp., notes 453, 551, 657
  tortilis, notes 550
Erythraspides pygmæus, notes, Conn. State ... 255
Esterases, distribution in animal body 303
Ether—
  effect on permeability 326
  effect on soils 519
Euclemensia bassettella, notes, Conn. State... 255
Eucommia ulmoides as a source of rubber 417
Eumerus strigatus in Canada 565
Eumononycha picipes n.sp., description 58
Euonymus, bud variation in 145
Eupatorium ageratoides as a cause of trembles,
  U.S.D.A 583
Euphorbia spp., root systems 542
Euproctis chrysorrhœa. (*See* Brown-tail
  moth.)
Eupterocalla opazoi n.g. and n.sp., description 460
Euryachora sacchari, notes 553
Eurytoma sp., description 59
Eutettix tenella. (*See* Beet leaf-hopper.)
Euthrips—
  pyri. (*See* Pear thrips.)
  tritici. (*See* Flower thrips.)
  tritici projectus n.var., description 561
Evaporation—
  devices, description 409, 503
  formula 882
  from forest and cultivated soils 418
  from water surfaces and river beds,
   U.S.D.A 785
  in relation to plant succession 725
Evaporator for frozen vegetables, description. 806
Evergreens, leaf persistence 726
Evolution—
  by means of hybridization, treatise 432
  treatise 573

Exoascus—   Page.
  bullatus, notes 550
  cerasi, studies 250, 550
  deformans, biology and treatment 250, 655
  deformans, notes 550
Exobasidium—
  æquale n.sp., notes 630
  unedonis n.sp., description 557
  vezans, notes 252
Exorista spinipennis, notes 764
Exoristoides slossonæ, notes 764
Exosmosis, studies 128
Exosporium—
  durum n.sp., notes 148
  n.spp., descriptions 743
  pulchellum n. sp., notes 148
Experiment stations—
  administration 101
  response to war conditions 1, 605
  (*See also* Alabama, Alaska, *etc.*)
Extension work. (*See* Agricultural exten-
  sion.)
Extraction processes, discontinuous 803
Eye disease, infectious, in cattle 691
Factor, meaning of term in genetic discussion. 526
Fairs, illustrative exhibits 297
Fannia canicularis, studies, N.J 665
Farcy. (*See* Glanders.)
Farm—
  animals. (*See* Live stock *and* Animals.)
  buildings, drawings and photographs 699
  buildings, treatise 90, 789
  bureau, county, Cal 888
  census of New York 491
  equipment for sheep raising, U.S.D.A ... 388
  equipment, minor articles, U.S.D.A 491
  equipment, treatise 388
  grounds, improvement, U.S.D.A 396
  handicraft for rural schools, U.S.D.A 699
  income, factors affecting 491
  laborers. (*See* Agricultural laborers.)
  lands, injury by erosion and floods,
   U.S.D.A 520
  lands, redistribution in France 491
  Loan Act, Federal 91, 492
  loans, rate sheet for 91
  machinery. (*See* Agricultural machinery.)
  management, graduate courses 794
  management in Missouri, Mo 789
  management, papers on 389
  management studies in Knox County,
   Ohio 195
  management, summer courses 794
  management survey data, correlation in,
   U.S.D.A 269
  management survey data, validity,
   U.S.D.A 389
  products. (*See* Agricultural products.)
  survey in Wisconsin 290
  tenancy. (*See* Agricultural tenancy.)
Farmers—
  cooperative purchasing and marketing
   organizations, U.S.D.A 888
  excursions, Wash 895
  institutes, papers on 796
  meeting halfway, U.S.D.A 592
  mutual fire insurance, U.S.D.A 391, 594
  psychology of 401, 592
  "universal military service," Conn. State. 290

Farming—	Page.
in Gallatin Valley, Mont	290
in North Carolina	190
in Wayne County, Ohio	132
plantation, in United States	390
treatise	290
(See also Agriculture.)	
Farms—	
for sale or rent in New York	390
in New Hampshire	790
productivity	290
Fasting, nitrogen elimination in	167
Fat—	
determination, Duclaux method	207, 414
determination in cheese	416
determination in desiccated milk	508
determination in milk and cream	618
determination in milk products	805
determination in milk products, Okla	507
determination of unsaponifiable matter	805
edible, nutritive value	165
rancid, evaluation	114
sulphuric acid or Maumené number	805
Fat-soluble A, separation from milk fat	308
Fatty acids. (See Acids.)	
Fauna of British India	54, 765
Federal—	
Board for Vocational Education	198
Farm Loan Act	291, 492
Food Control Act	399
Food Production Act	301
vocational education law	597
Feeding—	
of farm animals, Tenn	471
of farm animals, treatise	94, 172, 767, 795
(See also Cows, Pigs, etc.)	
Feeding stuffs—	
cooking for pigs	866
cost of digestible nutrients in	767
determination of quality	208
digestibility, Tex	163, 865
digestibility, determination, U.S.D.A.	672
digestibility in mixtures, Ga	65
digestibility in mixtures, Ill	677
inspection and analyses, Conn.State	268
inspection and analyses, R.I.	767
inspection and analyses, Wis	471
inspection in Switzerland	311
law in England	215
law in New Jersey, N.J	767
productive values, Tex	865
rate of passage through steers, U.S.D.A.	673
treatise	767
(See also specific kinds.)	
Feeds. (See Feeding stuffs.)	
Feldspar—	
as a source of potash	427
ground, fertilizing value	522
Fence posts, durability, Ohio	298
Fences, construction	886
Ferments. (See Enzyms.)	
Fern-land, conversion into grass	142
Ferrets, treatise	769
Ferrous sulphate—	
antiseptic and germicidal value	176
effect on soil acidity	23

Fertilizer—	Page.
experiments at Stavropol Caucasian Station	521
experiments in Assam	427
experiments, triangle system	799
(See also special crops.)	
law in England	215
problem, discussion	815
salts, action	624
Fertilizers—	
analyses	24, 114, 127, 219, 220, 429, 630, 818
application	521
application, U.S.D.A.	222
effect on apples, Oreg	41
effect on composition of cereals	827
effect on composition of oranges	649
effect on composition of tobacco ash	541
effect on composition of wheat, Colo	38
effect on lime requirements of soils, Ohio	125
effect on soil acidity	23
effect on solubility of inorganic soil constituents, U.S.D.A.	422
for vegetables, Md	320
handbook	724
inspection and analyses, Ind	724
inspection and analyses, Kans	324
inspection and analyses, Mich	524, 724
inspection and analyses, Mo	428
inspection and analyses, N.J	219
inspection and analyses, W.Va	127
inspection and analyses, Wis	324
inspection in Alabama	219
inspection in Maryland	24, 127
inspection in New Jersey, N.J	219, 429
inspection in North Carolina	220, 630
inspection in Ohio	429
inspection in Pennsylvania	220, 818
inspection in Switzerland	311
international trade	523
long-continued use, Pa	626
loss in industrial wastes	630
nitrogenous. (See Nitrogenous fertilizers.)	
organic nitrogenous compounds	216
phosphatic. (See Phosphates.)	
potash. (See Potash.)	
production and use under war conditions	724
residual value	230
residual value, Ohio	133
sampling	9
supply in England	215
use, Minn	227
use in Canada	425
use on peat soils	134, 720
(See also specific materials.)	
Feterita—	
culture experiments, Guam	730
culture experiments, Hawaii	132
culture experiments, Tex	331
digestibility and productive value, Tex	865
Fiber, crude. (See Cellulose.)	
Fibers of Belgian Kongo	534
Ficus—	
Mexican and Central American species	244
trunk rot, notes	246

Field— Page.
    crops, cost of production, W.Va......... 190
    crops, culture in Dutch East Indies...... 134
    crops for late planting, Nev.............. 436
    crops, Indian names..................... 436
    crops, insects affecting.................. 459
    crops, potash hunger.................... 800
    crops, review of German literature....... 142
    crops, varietal nomenclature............. 437
    (See also special crops.)
    experiments, error in.................. 528, 634
    peas. (See Peas.)
Fig—
    Botrytis disease, notes................... 457
    leaf blight, investigations, Fla.......... 652
    moth, notes............................. 156
    must, fermentation...................... 314
    rust, notes............................. 453
    scale, Mediterranean, in California...... 563
Figs—
    culture in Texas, Tex................... 835
    drying................................. 114
Filaria labiato-papillosa in Philippines....... 277
Filariasis, equine, treatment................. 692
Filbert leaves, symbiosis with fungi......... 327
Filberts—
    culture experiments..................... 243
    culture in Pacific Northwest............. 545
Filter—
    flask, description....................... 711
    paper, reducing matter in............... 409
Fique as a fiber plant....................... 233
Fir—
    Douglas, breakage, defect, and waste.... 651
    Douglas, creosoting...................... 386
    Douglas, for shipbuilding................ 452
    Douglas, needle blight of, U.S.D.A...... 658
    Douglas, oil of.......................... 411
    thinning experiments.................... 147
Fire—
    blight, notes.......................... 554, 652
    blight, transmission by aphids........ 151, 157
    blight, transmission by bees............. 53
    blight, treatment, Ohio................. 195
    insurance, farmers' mutual, U.S.D.A.. 391, 594
Fires—
    due to spontaneous combustion, Iowa... 788
    forest. (See Forest fires.)
Firewood, use on farms, U.S.D.A............. 92
Fireworm, black-head, remedies.............. 56
Fish—
    canning, salting, and smoking.......... 716
    destruction of mosquito larvæ by, N.J.. 260
    fertilizer, tests........................ 321
    food, composition....................... 63
    killed by cold wave in Florida, U.S.D.A. 513
    salt, recipes........................... 670
    scrap, analyses, R.I.................... 767
Flavone derivatives in plants............... 430
Flax—
    anthracnose, studies.................... 47
    blight, notes........................... 248
    culture experiments................... 537, 734
    culture experiments, Minn........... 227, 228
    culture in ancient Egypt................ 537
    culture in Oregon....................... 233
    effect on soil fertility.................. 229

Flax—Continued. Page.
    fall irrigation, U.S.D.A................. 822
    fiber, manufacture...................... 233
    fiber, water absorption capacity........ 736
    green manuring experiments............ 734
    shives, analyses, R.I................... 767
    waste as a source of potash............. 817
Flaxseed—
    bushel weights......................... 889
    ground, for pigs, Minn.................. 268
Flea-beetles injurious to tobacco............ 256
Flea-seed in South Australia................ 542
Fleas injurious to man and domestic animals. 764
Flies—
    biting, relation to trypanosomiasis...... 879
    domestic, of New Jersey, N.J........... 665
    flesh, studies, N.J..................... 665
    house. (See House fly.)
    morphological studies................... 358
    Phorid, from west coast of South America................................ 357
    remedies............... 53, 260, 464, 560, 665
    seasonal abundance in Montana......... 764
    white. (See White flies.)
Flood control for Pecatonica River.......... 186
Floods in California........................ 486
Flora—
    of Colombia and Central America........ 819
    of Sitka, Alaska........................ 526
    of Washington, D.C., and vicinity...... 435
Floriculture, science in..................... 240
Florida Station—
    notes.................................. 196
    report................................. 699
Flour—
    absorption of moisture by, N.Dak....... 362
    analyses, interpretation................. 617
    baking quality, Wash................... 861
    components, effect on baking quality, Wash................................. 862
    mixtures, methods of analysis........... 10
    quality, determination.................. 206
    red dog, analyses, Conn.State........... 268
    red dog, analyses, Wis................. 471
    substitutes, Ohio....................... 895
Flower thrips, studies, Fla.................. 659
Flowers—
    as affected by illuminating gas.......... 726
    monographic studies.................... 239
    nectar secretion........................ 633
    new or noteworthy, tests................ 143
    treatise............................... 145, 746
    varieties............................... 836
    wild, handbook......................... 630
Flue dust as a source of potash.............. 427
Fluids, determination of turbidity........... 14
Flume, Venturi, description and tests, U.S.D.A............................... 282
Fodder plants of Samara.................... 168
Fomes—
    lucidus on tea roots.................. 52, 252
    semitostus, notes..................... 349, 839
    spp. on forest trees, Mo................ 756
Food—
    accessories, notes, N.Dak.............. 468
    analyses............................... 63
    analysis, textbook...................... 503

Food—Continued. Page.
  cereal. (*See* Cereal foods.)
  Control Act, Federal...................... 399
  desire for................................. 166
  digest of data.......................... 469, 571
  economics at Minnesota college.......... 264
  economy in........................... 166, 571
  heated, nutritive value.................. 467
  inspection in Connecticut, Conn.State... 863
  inspection in Indiana.................... 63
  inspection in Maryland.................. 463
  inspection in Massachusetts............. 165
  inspection in Minnesota................. 166
  inspection in Missouri.................. 63
  inspection in North Dakota, N. Dak.... 63,
                         468, 570, 863
  inspection in Pennsylvania.............. 570
  laboratory manual....................... 94
  laws in California....................... 63
  laws in Michigan........................ 63
  laws in Rhode Island.................... 570
  of Labrador Eskimo...................... 264
  physiology of........................... 166
  preparation............................. 670
  preservatives. (*See* Preservatives.)
  Production Act, Federal................. 301
  production, increasing, Ill............. 594
  products, stored, insects affecting, Conn.
    State................................. 848
  selection, U.S.D.A............... 364, 668, 864
  selection and use....................... 469
  substances, isolated, dietary value...... 264
  supply in war time...................... 670
  supply, increasing.............. 290, 390, 890
  supply of Belgium....................... 166
  supply of California, Cal............... 697
  supply of France, Government control... 469
  supply of Germany....................... 166
  supply of New England.................. 890
  supply of New York...................... 166
  supply of Portugal...................... 890
  supply of United Kingdom............ 264, 890
  supply of United States............... 263, 491
  supply of United States, Cal............ 289
  supply of United States, U.S.D.A....... 289
  supply, regulation...................... 571
  textbook................................ 894
  training camps at agricultural fairs...... 400
  war, manual............................. 715
  (*See also* Diet.)
Foodstuffs—
  effect on elimination of uric acid......... 167
  prices and movement in 1916............. 492
  supplemental dietary relationships........ 166
Foot-and-mouth disease—
  control in Great Britain................. 779
  control in Pennsylvania................. 577
  immunization............................ 689
  in Netherlands.......................... 79
  in United States........................ 274
  in Virginia............................. 479
  in Washington........................... 477
  outbreak in Somerset, England.......... 878
  virulence of blood in................... 689
Foot lesions, treatment with sugar........... 82
Forage—
  crop mixtures, tests................... 733, 734
  crops, culture experiments............... 826

Forage—Continued. Page.
  crops, culture experiments, Nev........ 435
  crops, culture experiments, Tex....... 329, 331
  crops, determination of yield........... 439
  crops of Bombay Presidency........... 826
  crops, seeding and harvesting dates...... 135
  crops, varieties........................ 533
  (*See also* special crops.)
  plants of Wallowa National Forest
    U.S.D.A............................. 818
  poisoning, studies.................... 179, 689
Forest—
  administration. (*See* Forestry.)
  ecology in southern Appalachians....... 45
  fires, control...................... 348, 650, 747
  fires, insurance........................ 888
  fires, relation to lightning, U.S.D.A.... 512
  growth, rôle of light in................ 45
  insects, imported in United States...... 559
  insects in British Columbia............. 459
  law in America.......................... 836
  law in Argentina........................ 747
  law in Nebraska......................... 649
  law in New Hampshire.................... 547
  law in New York......................... 244
  plantation margins, notes............... 837
  products of Canada...................... 245
  products of India.................... 245, 548
  products of Quebec...................... 148
  ranger course for Southern Appalachians. 199
  research in America, correlation........ 44
  seeds. (*See* Tree seeds.)
  succession and growth in sphagnum bogs. 837
  succession in central Rocky Mountains... 451
  tracts, mapping......................... 651
  trees. (*See* Trees.)
  workers in Sweden....................... 890
  yields, relation to climate and soils...... 450
Foresters, training........................... 243
Forestry—
  in Algeria........................... 244, 650
  in Australia and New Zealand.......... 244
  in British Columbia.................... 650
  in Canada.......................... 45, 244, 650
  in China............................... 348
  in Hawaii........................... 146, 452
  in India........ 45, 146, 244, 348, 547, 650, 747, 838
  in Indiana............................. 44
  in Maine............................... 243
  in Michigan............................ 348
  in New Jersey........................ 547, 650
  in Ontario............................. 244
  in Patagonia........................... 747
  in Pennsylvania........................ 45
  in Philippines......................... 836
  in South Africa........................ 244
  in Switzerland......................... 650
  in Texas............................ 45, 747
  in the South........................... 450
  in Tunis, Algeria, and Corsica.......... 650
  in West Virginia....................... 747
  working plans, treatise................. 243
Forests—
  coniferous, reproduction in northern New
    England............................. 651
  National, in eastern United States...... 348
  National, nursery practice in, U.S.D.A.. 348
  National, road building, U.S.D.A....... 547

Forests—Continued.　　　　　　　　　Page.

National, stumpage appraisals............ 833

National, volume tables.................. 450

of Colorado, Colo...................... 209

of Java and Madura 346

of Quebec.............................. 147

precipitation-evaporation factor in....... 525

relation to atmospheric and soil moisture- 716

relation to soil erosion,U.S.D.A......... 520

site determination and classification 450

Formaldehyde—

as a fly poison......................... 53

use against mastitis.................... 277

Formalin. (See Formaldehyde.)

Formic acid, effect on plants.............. 224

Foul brood—

control in Kansas....................... 357

notes, Mont............................ 255

treatment.............................. 263

Fowl—

cholera, immunization.................... 83

cholera, immunization, Nev 78, 183

diseases, notes........................ 483

mite, tropical, in Australia 360

typhoid, studies....................... 82

Fowls—

anatomy................................ 772

breeding experiments, Utah 369, 809

cost of feeding, U.S.D.A................ 871

crossing-over in sex chromosome........ 868

egg-laying cycles...................... 869

factors affecting sex ratio............. 868

germ cells as affected by poisons Me.... 370

molting, N.J........................... 774

physiology of reproduction, Me.......... 371

Plymouth Rock, inheritance of color pat-

tern and pigmentation in, Me.......... 370

relation between gonads and soma....... 868

Rhode Island Red, broodiness in 869

selecting and mating for egg production,

N.J.................................. 71

sexual differences in blood............. 773

spring molt, Wash..................... 96

(See also Poultry.)

Fox, silver, raising, U.S.D.A............. 156

Foxgloves, breeding experiments......... 649

Frankliniella tritici projectus, studies, Fla.... 659

Frost, effect on cyanogenetic compounds of

sorghum................................ 109

Fruit—

acid content........................... 714

at Horticultural Gardens, Lucknow..... 646

basket, handling....................... 647

breeding experiments............. 647, 832, 833

buds, development, Mo................. 744

buds, formation 343, 646

buds, freezing, Utah.................. 344

canned, poisoning from, U.S.D.A........ 670

citrus. (See Citrus fruits.)

culture experiments................ 646, 832

culture experiments, Guam............. 743

culture experiments, Minn............. 241

culture experiments, Mo............... 744

culture experiments, Mont............. 241

culture in Chile....................... 544

culture, treatise...................... 41, 544

diseases and insect pests, control, Utah.. 832

Fruit—Continued.　　　　　　　　　Page.

diseases, manual....................... 151

dried, preparation..................... 509

drying............................. 114, 509, 715

drying apparatus for.................. 806

evaporation, Wash.................... 715

Experiment Station, Shillong, report.... 242

fly, Mediterranean, notes.............. 555

fly, Mediterranean, parasites in Hawaii.. 856

fly, parasites of...................... 847

influence of stock on.................. 647

jellies, manufacture.................. 15

juice, pasteurization and biorization 805

lecanium, European, studies........... 662

new, S. Dak........................... 142

new or noteworthy, N.Y.State.......... 343

of Philippines.................... 143, 648

orchard, aphids affecting, U.S.D.A..... 358

picking maturity, U.S.D.A............. 543

protection against frost............... 744

recipes............................... 670

sampling device for................... 711

small, culture, Cal.................... 447

small, treatise.................... 544, 648

small, varieties for Ohio, Ohio......... 241

South American markets................ 345

stone, ripe rot of..................... 151

survey of Mesa County, Colo........... 241

thinning, Ohio........................ 895

tree leaf roller, remedies, Oreg........ 55

trees, oak fungus and wood decay of..... 51

trees, pruning..................... 242, 344

trees, pruning, W.Va.................. 344

varieties......................... 343, 832

varieties, Minn....................... 241

varieties for Maine................... 41

varieties for northern Minnesota, Minn.. 241

varieties for United Kingdom........... 833

washing in canning factories.......... 416

wines, acids of....................... 310

Fucus vesiculosus, analyses, Conn.State...... 814

Fuel oil, larvicidal value, N.J............. 665

Fungi—

causing discoloration in paper......... 630

edible, nutritive value................. 669

growth in plant decoctions............. 728

humidity relations.................... 549

of soils, studies...................... 718

parasitic, specialization.............. 149

physiology..................... 129, 727, 728

Fungicides—

analyses.............................. 114

analyses, N.J......................... 243

tests............................. 47, 247

Fungus beetle, two-banded, notes.......... 567

Funtumia, growth and rubber yielding value 548

Fur farming, notes, U.S.D.A............. 573

Furcræa gigantea as a fiber plant........... 233

Fusarium—

cæruleum, notes....................... 350

conglutinans, control, Ohio........... 150

cubense, generation of aldehydes by...... 843

hevea n.sp , notes.................... 253

lathyri, investigations.............. 155

lycopersici, notes................... 551

solani, notes........................ 551

sp. on beans.......................... 840

Page.

Fusarium—Continued.
sp. on sugar cane........................ 553
spp. on potatoes.................... 652,654
tracheiphilum, studies, U.S.D.A.......... 50
Fusarium diseases as affected by winter covering of cereals............................. 48
Fusicladium—
dendriticum. (*See* Apple scab.)
macrosporum, notes................... 253,838
spp. on orchard fruits................. 550
Gadfly in lambs, prevention, Tex........... 867
Galega officinalis, description and control..... 142
Galerucella cavicollis, studies................. 459
Gall formation in plants..................... 26
Gangrene, gaseous, treatment............... 377
Garbage—
as a source of alcohol.................. 590
tankage, composition and fertilizing value 723
Garden—
crops as affected by asphyxiating gas..... 253
crops, insects affecting.................. 157
crops, insects affecting, Fla.............. 356
crops, manuring, Can.................. 645
furniture and accessories, treatise........ 746
Gardenia, studies........................... 239
Gardening—
back yard, treatise...................... 145
in elementary city schools.............. 395
notes.............................. 342,795
notes, Ill............................. 543
notes, Ky............................ 342
ornamental, manual.............. 145,346,746
treatise................... 94,145,543,645,742
Gardens—
fall vegetable, Ill....................... 645
school. (*See* School gardens.)
vegetable, illustrated lecture, U.S.D.A... 297
vegetable, notes, U.S.D.A.............. 447
Garlic, culture experiments, La.............. 529
Gas—
asphyxiating, effect on vegetation...... 153,253
generator, description.................. 110
illuminating, effect on plants.......... 726,727
injurious to agriculture and forestry in
Austria............................. 528
Gasoline—
carburetion........................... 189
effect on soils......................... 519
Gastroenteritis of sheep and goats........... 380
Gelatin and protoplasm, similarity in behavior.............................. 431
Gelechia gossypiella—
in Mexico and Brazil.................... 358
rate of increase........................ 762
studies, U.S.D.A...................... 564
Gels for studying protoplasmic action....... 425
Gentiobiose derivatives, rotatory powers..... 502
Geococcyx californianus, food habits.......... 155
Geological Survey. (*See* United States Geological Survey.)
Georgia Station, report..................... 95
Geotropism in plants................... 325,821
Geranium leaf spot, studies, Md.............. 856
Germ—
cells as affected by poisons, Me.......... 370
middlings, analyses, Wis................ 471
Ginger, pungent principles................. 612

Page.

Gingerol, notes............................ 612
Gipsy moth—
control, Conn. State..................... 254
control, U.S.D.A.............. 55,452,563
control in Massachusetts................. 646
dispersion by wind..................... 254
in Connecticut......................... 259
parasites in Maine...................... 459
tree bands for......................... 258
Gladiolus, varieties........................ 345
Glanderous serum, reversible precipitation.. 377
Glanders—
control in Austria....................... 781
detection.............................. 79
diagnosis......................... 689,878
in Washington......................... 477
Glaucolepis, new genus, description......... 564
Gliadin, copper compounds of.............. 9
Glœosporium—
alborubrum, notes...................... 253
ampelophagum, notes.............. 52,453
camphorœ n.sp., description............ 844
concentricum, notes................... 551
conviva n.sp., description.............. 557
gossypii, growth in plant decoctions...... 728
heveœ, notes.......................... 253
kaki, notes........................... 656
mangiferœ, notes.................. 755,838
manihotis, notes...................... 551
n.spp., descriptions.................... 748
nervisequum, notes.................... 550
tiliœ, notes.......................... 550
Glœosporium, studies...................... 245
Glomerella—
anthurii n.sp., description.............. 550
gossypii, growth in plant decoctions.... 728
gossypii, nitrogen fixation by............ 129
rufomaculans, investigations............ 155
Glucose, beta, preparation.................. 410
d-Glucose, studies....................... 109
Glue leather as a cattle feed............... 171
Gluten—
absorption of moisture by, N.Dak........ 363
determination......................... 617
feed, analyses, R.I..................... 767
feed, analyses, Wis.................... 471
Glutose, determination.................... 617
Gnomonia—
on cherry leaves........................ 246
on eggplant........................... 752
Goats—
milk production, N.Y.State.............. 575
treatise............................... 709
worms infesting, Guam................. 779
Goat's rue, description and control.......... 142
Goldenrod, western, poisoning of sheep by... 482
Golf courses, turf for...................... 146
Gonatocerus—
bifasciativentris n.sp., description........ 667
mexicanus in Hawaii................... 360
Gongylonema scutatum, life history........... 577
Goniozus cellularis, parasitic on pink bollworm.............................. 667
Gooseberries—
acid content........................... 714
aphids affecting, U.S.D.A.............. 358
varieties, Oreg........................ 243

Gooseberry mildew—　　　　　　　　　Page.
　notes...................................... 550
　treatment.............................. 351
Gopher, pocket—
　life history and control, Cal............ 757
　notes...................................... 355
Gossypium spp.—
　in Italian Somaliland................... 336
　leaf nectaries........................... 727
Gossypol, notes, N.C...................... 689
Gout, metabolism in...................... 167
Grain—
　aphis, spring, outbreak in Kansas....... 561
　bins, concrete, construction.............. 789
　bins, sanitation, Ohio................... 895
　for dry lands of central Oregon, U.S.D.A. 333
　germinated, diastatic activity........... 208
　irrigation experiments, Oreg............. 84
　marketing, U.S.D.A...................... 889
　moth, Angoumois, studies................ 356
　pedigreed, yields in Wisconsin.......... 438
　prices and movement in 1916............ 492
　production in United States............. 595
　smut, investigations, Mo................. 749
　varieties................................. 533
　winter and spring, distribution in United
　　States................................. 533
　(*See also* Cereals *and special crops.*)
Gram—
　as a green manure for rice.............. 824
　culture experiments.................... 734, 825
　green manuring experiments............ 734
　varieties............................. 824, 825
Granulomata, habronemic, in horses........ 279
Grape—
　anthracnose, notes....................... 453
　berry moth, remedies, U.S.D.A......... 852
　cake, fertilizing value................... 426
　court-noué, treatment................... 152
　curculio, notes........................... 58
　disease in California.................... 352
　diseases in northern Italy.............. 52
　diseases, notes.......................... 550
　diseases, relation to fog................ 152
　downy mildew, studies........... 151, 152, 251
　downy mildew, treatment............. 152, 246
　gray rot on figs......................... 457
　gray rot, studies...................... 47, 350
　juice, pasteurization and biorization..... 805
　leaf roll, treatment..................... 246
　powdery mildew, treatment.......... 152, 843
　red scald, notes......................... 555
　root-borer, notes........................ 58
　stocks, root systems of.................. 43
Grapefruit juice, preparation, Fla........... 313
Grapes—
　aphids affecting, U.S.D.A............... 358
　as affected by asphyxiating gas........ 153, 253
　breeding................................. 449
　cambial activity......................... 127
　culture at Paarl viticultural station..... 144
　direct bearer, in relation to disease...... 52
　dust *v.* liquid spraying.............. 532, 843
　hydrofluoric acid injury................. 246
　industry in California................... 144
　muscadine, breeding..................... 544

Grapes—Continued.　　　　　　　　　Page.
　pruning experiments, Iowa.............. 40
　Rotundifolia, inheritance of sex in, N.C... 449
　varieties, Tex............................ 832
　Vinifera, culture experiments, N.Y.State. 544
　winter injury, N.Y.State................ 655
Grapevine—
　sawfly, notes, Conn.State................ 255
　tomato gall, notes, Conn.State........... 255
Graphomyia maculata, studies............... 764
Grass—
　as affected by associated legumes........ 438
　as affected by soil acidity, R.I.......... 446
　embryo, morphology..................... 127
　eradication, Tex......................... 532
　for pasture and hay in Texas............. 827
　for shifting sands....................... 333
　growth under drought conditions......... 437
　in relation to dry farming............... 437
　mixtures, tests...................... 230, 735
　mulch for orchards...................... 833
　pollination experiments................. 734
　seeding on cut-over land, Minn.......... 228
　trees, of South Australia................ 548
　varieties, Hawaii........................ 132
　varieties, Minn......................... 227
　wild fodder, of Poona District, India..... 136
　(*See also specific kinds.*)
Grasshoppers. (*See* Locusts.)
Grasslands—
　composition of herbage................... 230
　liming................................... 230
　precipitation-evaporation factor in....... 525
Gravel—
　for roads.......................... 288, 695
　grading for road construction, U.S.D.A... 788
Grayfish, description and food value......... 63
Green—
　bug. (*See* Grain aphis, spring.)
　manure and manuring in the Tropics,
　　treatise.............................. 28
　manure, effect on soil acidity, Mo........ 718
　manure, effect on soil bacteria, Iowa...... 121
　manure, effect on solubility of inorganic
　　soil constituents, U.S.D.A............. 422
　manure, fertilizing value, N.J............ 425
　manure for semiarid soils, U.S.D.A....... 319
　manure for swamp rice soils............. 425
　manuring experiments, Hawaii.......... 320
　manuring in India....................... 334
Greenhouse—
　crops and soil, injury by gas............. 727
　fumigation experiments, Md............. 660
　leaf tyer, notes, Conn.State.............. 255
Gregarina n.spp., descriptions 558
Gregarines, studies........................ 53
Ground squirrels. (*See* Squirrels, ground)
Groundnuts. (*See* Peanuts.)
Gryllotalpa gryllotalpa, introduction into New
　Jersey................................. 660
Gryllotalpoidea of South America........... 157
Guam—
　grass, digestibility, Tex.................. 168
　Station, report.......................... 796
Guanin, isolation from cows' milk........... 308
Guavas of Hawaii......................... 835

Page.

Guinea—
corn diseases in West Indies............... 452
grass, culture experiments, Guam........ 730
pig serum, anaphylatoxin produced in.... 579
pigs, care and management................. 775
Guizotia abyssinica, culture for seed........... 230
Gymnoconia interstitialis, notes................. 457
Gymnosporangia on Myrica and Comptonia.. 551
Gymnosporangium—
clavariæforme, notes........................ 550
sabinæ, notes............................. 550
Gypsum—
effect on alfalfa, Oreg..................... 33
effect on soil acidity..................... 23
effect on sulfofying power of soils, Iowa... 119
fertilizing value............................ 825
fertilizing value, Pa........................ 626
Habrocytus, North American species........ 162
Habronemiasis, cutaneous, in horses.......... 279
Hackberry—
as a hedge plant, Minn..................... 241
insects affecting........................... 461
Hadrotrichum populi, notes................... 550
Hæmatobia serrata. (*See* Horn-fly.)
Hæmonchus contortus—
in Philippines............................. 277
notes, Guam................................. 779
Hail—
effect on trees............................. 250
in United States, U.S.D.A............... 512
insurance in North Dakota.............. 594
squall in Baltimore, U.S.D.A............ 807
theories, U.S.D.A........................ 512
Hailstorm at Ballinger, Tex., U.S.D.A..... 513
Hakuunboku seed, oil of.................... 109
Halos, notes, U.S.D.A..................... 807
(*Haltica*) *Phyllotreta armoraciæ,* studies,
U.S.D.A................................... 566
Haplographium manihoticola n.sp., description 252
Haplothrips n.sp., description............... 258
Hares, destructive to trees in western Canada. 758
Hawaii—
College, notes................................ 196
Station, report............................. 195
Sugar Planters' Station, notes.......... 497
Hay—
analyses, Cal............................. 236
caps, notes, Wash......................... 699
cost of production, W.Va................. 191
crops for Texas............................. 827
curing in wet weather.................... 189
spontaneous combustion, Iowa.......... 788
(*See also* Alfalfa, Timothy, *etc.*)
Hazel blight, treatment..................... 755
Hazelnuts, varieties, S.Dak................. 143
Heat—
effect on concentration of soil solution.... 719
effect on nutritive value of food.......... 467
(*See also* Temperature.)
Heating by electricity...................... 187
Hedge—
clippings as a source of potash........... 817
plants, tests, Minn....................... 241
Heliothis obsoleta. (*See* Cotton bollworm.)
Heliothrips—
n.sp., description........................ 258
rubrocinctus, notes...................... 357,461

Page.

Helix humboldtiana, notes..................... 755
Helminthosporium—
curoulum n.sp., notes..................... 148
gramineum, treatment.................... 247
theobromæ n.sp., description............. 755
Helminths in cattle and goats in Philippines.. 277
Helopeltis antonii and *H. theivora,* notes...... 55
Hemileia vastatrix, notes............... 349, 453, 551
Hemorrhage, intractable, treatment......... 177
Hemorrhagic septicemia. (*See* Septicemia.)
Hemp—
culture experiments, Minn............... 227
culture in France........................ 830
industry in India........................ 233
industry wastes, fertilizing value........ 219
Hens—
feeding experiments, Guam.............. 768
feeding experiments, Idaho.............. 70, 271
feeding experiments, Iowa................. 70
feeding experiments, Minn............. 268, 271
feeding experiments, Mo................. 774
feeding experiments, N.C................ 682
feeding experiments, Tex................ 871
feeding experiments, U.S.D.A........... 871
selection, Wash............................ 599
selection for egg production, N.J....... 573, 871
Heredity—
in birds.................................. 772
in cattle, Iowa........................... 66
in Coleus................................. 27
in Datura................................. 546
in oats, U.S.D.A.......................... 738
in Œnothera.............................. 724
in poultry, Mo............................ 772
in sunflowers............................. 543
in Zea hybrids, U.S.D.A................. 536
meaning of "factor" in.................... 526
Mendelian factor differences v. reaction
system contrasts......................... 433
of color in mammals..................... 866
of crossability in plants................. 432
of seed color in corn..................... 737
of self-sterility in plants............... 820
of tillering in wheat, Del................ 644
sex-linked, in fowls..................... 771, 868
Hernandia seed, oil of..................... 109
Hessian fly—
dispersion by wind...................... 260
in Kansas............................... 260, 564
studies, Mo.............................. 760
Heterobelyta chilensis n.g. and n.sp., description.................................... 460
Heterodera—
radicicola on sweet peas................. 155
spp. injurious to potatoes, Wash........ 157
Heteropters from west coast of South America 357
Hevea brasiliensis. (*See* Rubber, Para.)
Hibernation, theories...................... 156
Hickory—
gall aphis, notes, Conn.State............ 255
seeds, storage experiments............... 547
Highways. (*See* Roads.)
Histidin, rôle in purin metabolism.......... 265
Hog cholera—
control in Great Britain.................. 779
control in Indiana, Ind................. 882
control in Michigan...................... 274

Hog cholera—Continued.   Page.
  control in Oregon...........................   374
  control in Pennsylvania..................   577
  etiology................................. 382,782
  immunity of suckling pigs to............   881
  immunization, Mo.......................   779
  in Hawaii...............................   374
  in United States........................   274
  notes................................... 477,784
  prevention, Ill.........................   882
  relation to spirochetes of digestive tract..   279
  serum, filtration.......................   881
  serum, separation of active principle, Nev   78
  transmission through infected pork......   691
  virulence of blood in...................   784
Home—
  demonstration work, effect of, U.S.D.A..   598
  grounds, planning and planting......... 44,346
  making schools in New York.............   394
Home economics—
  association in Alabama..................   895
  course for southern schools, U.S.D.A.....   894
  instruction in California................   394
  instruction in Canada...................   699
  instruction in German Switzerland......   793
  instruction in New Hampshire..........   699
  instruction in North Dakota............   193
  instruction in public schools............ 93,494
  instruction in United States.............   393
  instruction in Utah.....................   198
  instruction, papers on.................. 192,596
  textbook............................... 396,894
Hominy feed—
  analyses, Conn.State....................   268
  analyses, R.I...........................   767
  analyses, Wis...........................   471
Homoptera of British India...................   54
Honey—
  analyses and food value.................   570
  eater, new, from Marianne Islands.......   758
  production, relation to weather, Iowa....   854
Honeybees. (See Bees.)
Hookworm, remedies.........................   578
Horizonetta, new genus, erection.............   758
Horn—
  fly, parasites of........................   847
  ground, fertilizing value.................   321
Horse—
  chestnut leaf cast, notes................   658
  diseases, handbook...................... 778,784
  labor, cost, U.S.D.A....................   867
  manure, storage experiments, Me........   628
  racing, plea for.........................   771
  radish flea-beetle, studies, U.S.D.A......   566
  saliva, diastatic action..................   771
Horseflies—
  egg-laying habits and early stages........   853
  in southern Florida.....................   565
Horses—
  breeding, U.S.D.A...................... 368,572
  cost of keeping, U.S.D.A................   867
  diseases of reproductive organs, Okla....   473
  feeding experiments, Guam..............   768
  feeding experiments, Minn..............   269
  feeding experiments, N.C...............   681
  improvement, Guam....................   768
  improvement, value of good sires........   866

Horses—Continued.   Page.
  judging.................................   94
  raising, Kans........................... 368,868
  Percheron, history......................   771
  salivary digestion studies.............. 681,771
  shipping fever of....:...................   182
  Thoroughbred, breeding and racing......   771
  treatise................................   770
Horticultural—
  education in Netherlands................   193
  laws of Washington.....................   342
  societies in Pennsylvania................   888
Hotbeds, construction and management,
  Colo....................................   41
Hothouse milliped, studies, Md..............   667
House fly—
  life history and remedies................ 560,853
  response to foods and their fermentation
    products...........................   159
  seasonal abundance in Montana.........   764
  studies, N.J............................   665
  transmission of typhoid fever by........   854
Household insects, notes....................   459
Housekeeping schools in Norway............   294
Huckleberries—
  acid content............................   715
  drying.................................   509
Humidity—
  and vapor pressure over United States,
    U.S.D.A...........................   314
  effect on insects........................   254
Humogen. (See Peat, bacterized.)
Humus—
  as a guide to soil fertility...............   718
  fertilizing value, judging................   216
  forming materials, effect on soil bacteria,
    Iowa..............................   120
  notes..................................   629
  phosphoric acid of soils................   121
  production from manures................   20
  soluble, effect on soil bacteria...........   517
Hunger, studies............................   166
Hunterellus hookeri, notes...................   360
Hyalopterus arundinis, cat-tail as a summer
  host...................................   461
Hybridization, rôle in evolution.............   432
  (See also Plant breeding.)
Hydraulic development and equipment,
  treatise................................   287
Hydraulics, textbook........................   584
Hydrocampa (Nymphula) nymphæta, notes..   847
Hydrochloric acid—
  effect on plants.........................   224
  effect on rotatory power of sucrose and
    invert sugar........................   802
Hydrochloroplatinic acid, preparation.......   409
Hydrocyanic acid—
  determination in sorghum...............   113
  gas, effect on insects and plants, Md.....   660
  in cassava, Hawaii.....................   168
  in leguminous plants...................   28
Hydrogen—
  determination..........................   803
  ion concentration, determination........   506
  peroxid as an oxidizer..................   409
  sulphid, precipitation under pressure....   712
Hydrometeors, classification, U.S.D.A......   115

Hydrophobia. (*See* Rabies.) .... Page.
Hydrotæa spp., studies...................... 764
Hydroxypyridins, curative forms............ 411
Hygrometer, kite, improved, U.S.D.A...... 513
Hygrometry, improved methods in.......... 16
Hymenochæte noxia—
   on cacao roots............................ 349
   on tea roots.............................. 52
Hymenolepis diminuta and H. nana siebold,
   life history................................. 163
Hymenomycetes—
   association with woody forest plants..... 727
   on fruit trees............................. 47
Hymenoptera—
   leaf oviposition........................... 162
   of British India........................... 765
   of Connecticut............................ 765
   W. M. Giffard collection................. 855
Hypera punctata in Iowa.................... 262
Hypochnus solani, studies................. 47, 350
Hypoderma bovis and H. lineatum, life history 691
Hyponomeuta of Sweden.................... 158
Hypophysis extract, effect on milk produc-
   tion...................................... 173
Ice—
   bacteriological examination.............. 468
   cream, bacteriological examination...... 468
   cream, determination of fat in, Okla..... 507
   cream factories in Minnesota............. 777
   for cream cooling, Nebr.................. 592
Ichneumonidæ of British India.............. 765
Idaho—
   Station, notes............................ 397
   Station, report........................... 95
   University, notes..................... 397, 497
Idiocerus fitchi, notes...................... 157
Illinois—
   Station, report........................... 297
   University and Station, notes........... 700
Immune and anaphylactic reactions, studies 76
Immunity in relation to live-stock diseases.. 688
Immunology, treatise....................... 76
Inbreeding—
   in Jersey cattle........................... 776
   notes.................................... 769
Incubation periods of birds, treatise........ 774
India rubber. (*See* Rubber.)
Indiana Station, notes......... 97, 196, 497, 700, 896
Indicators, quinone-phenolate theory........ 409
Indigo—
   culture in Bihar.......................... 441
   wilt, notes............................... 441
Indigofera anil as a green manure, Hawaii.... 320
Indol, detection........................... 503
Industrial wastes, loss of fertilizers in....... 630
Influenza in United States.................. 774
Inheritance. (*See* Heredity.)
Inoculation experiments, celluloid cylinder.. 549
Inosit-phosphoric acid of cottonseed meal,
   Ark...................................... 502
Insect—
   behavior as a factor in applied entomology 156
   blood cells, growth in vitro............... 759
   photography, apparatus for............... 156
Insecticides—
   analyses.............................. 53, 114
   analyses, N.J............................. 243
   emulsions for............................ 759

Insecticides—Continued. .... Page.
   formulas................................. 460
   tests..................................... 53
   (*See also specific forms.*)
Insects—
   as affected by humidity.................. 254
   as carriers of fire blight.................. 53
   beneficial, in Hawaii..................... 847
   control about abattoirs................... 560
   control by parasites, U.S.D.A............ 559
   determining increase and spread......... 257
   dispersion by wind....................... 254
   economic, of East Africa................. 760
   forest. (*See* Forest insects.)
   imported, losses from in United States... 559
   in British Museum....................... 560
   injurious—
      book................................. 395
      in Arizona........................... 846
      in Bihar and Orissa.................. 357
      in British East Africa............. 54, 460
      in British Guiana.................... 847
      in Colorado.......................... 459
      in Connecticut, Conn.State.......... 254
      in Dutch East Indies................. 246
      in Egypt............................. 54
      in Florida, Fla....................... 659
      in Georgia........................... 847
      in Germany........................... 460
      in Hawaii........................ 459, 847
      in Kansas............................ 357
      in Montana, Mont.................... 255
      in New Jersey........................ 255
      in Oklahoma......................... 157
      in Pennsylvania...................... 459
      in Porto Rico........................ 255
      in Quebec....................... 156, 157
      in St. Vincent........................ 460
      in South America..................... 460
      in Stavropol......................... 760
      in Tasmania.......................... 257
      in Texas............................. 459
      in Uganda............................ 560
      in West Indies....................... 460
      remedies............................. 247
      remedies, Ohio....................... 143
      remedies, Tenn....................... 544
      to apples......................... 847, 848
      to cranberries........................ 53
      to fruits and vegetables, Utah........ 832
      to hackberry......................... 461
      to man and animals in Zanzibar..... 560
      to man, treatise.................. 156, 760
      to meadows and pastures, Ohio...... 847
      to melons and related crops, Mo..... 760
      to nursery stock, Mo................. 760
      to potatoes, Wash.................... 157
      to rice........................... 247, 847
      to stored cereals, remedies, Ohio..... 895
      to stored food products, Conn.State.. 848
      to stored products, remedies......... 459
      to stored wheat...................... 356
      to timber............................ 356
      to tobacco and vegetables............ 256
      to trees............................. 760
      to truck and garden crops, Fla....... 356
      to vegetables, Ohio.................. 895
      to wheat, Md......................... 340

Insects—Continued.   Page.
    longevity in captivity................... 355
    microbial diseases of.................... 76
    of Connecticut........................... 765
    orchard, in British Columbia........... 459
    plant-sucking, studying in situ.......... 53
    polyhedral bodies in.................... 253
    progressive immunity, Wash........... 54
    rearing for experimental work.......... 758
    recognition among....................... 459
    relation to anthrax...................... 170
    relation to precipitation................. 355
    scale. (See Scale insects.)
    transmission of disease by.............. 848
    transmission of Trypanosoma evansi by... 180
    transmission of verruga by............ 356, 358
    underground, method for study......... 254
    wilt disease of.......................... 253
    (See also specific insects.)
Insurance companies, farmers' mutual, U.S.
    D.A...................................... 391
International catalogue—
    of botany................................ 630
    of chemistry............................ 501
Inulase of Aspergillus niger, activity........ 203
Iodoform, antiseptic and germicidal value.... 176
Iowa—
    College, notes..................... 196, 299, 600
    Station, notes......................... 299, 497
    Station, report.......................... 95
Ips typographus killing healthy fir trees....... 465
Iridomyrmex humilis in Silesia............... 766
Iris flowers, abnormalities.................. 130
Iron—
    phosphate, solubility and availability.... 324
    salts, effect on solubility of phosphates.... 323
    sulphid, fungicidal value............... 48
Irrigation—
    canals, cleaning......................... 285
    canals, leakage, prevention.............. 487
    canals, lining........................... 281
    canals, plant growth in............... 281, 285
    distribution systems.................... 185
    economic advisability.................... 184
    engineering, handbook................... 584
    engineering, papers on.................. 281
    fall, U.S.D.A............................ 822
    in Algiers............................... 384
    in Argentina............................ 183
    in Australia............................. 184
    in Bengal............................... 484
    in California......................... 486, 585
    in Egypt................................ 693
    in India........................... 184, 585, 693
    in Italy................................. 183
    in Libia................................ 184
    in New South Wales.................... 585
    in Novouzensk district................. 882
    in Spain................................ 183
    in United States........................ 183
    laws in Washington..................... 693
    pumping for............................ 185
    pumping for, U.S.D.A.................. 585
    pumping plants, Nebr.................. 384
    pumping plants, tests, Mont............ 283
    pumping, power and rates.............. 786
    relation to soil bacteria, Oreg............ 86

Irrigation—Continued.   Page.
    reservoirs, unlined...................... 585
    spray, notes............................ 693
    structures, use of cement in............. 787
    treatise........................... 185, 584, 587
    water. (See Water.)
Isosoma spp., remedies...................... 263
Ives tint photometer, use................... 110
Jack beans—
    as a green manure, Hawaii.............. 320
    culture experiments, Guam............. 729
    digestibility and productive value, Tex.. 865
    proteins of.............................. 8
Jacks—
    in Indiana, Ind......................... 169
    in Oklahoma, Okla...................... 169
    in Utah, Utah.......................... 681
Janus abbreviatus, notes.................... 255
Japanese cane. (See Sugar cane.)
Jassoidea of Missouri....................... 157
Jelly making, notes......................... 715
Johne's disease, studies.................... 479
Johnson grass—
    and Sudan grass seed, distinguishing
      characters, Cal...................... 236
    eradication, La......................... 529
    hay, digestibility, Tex.................. 168
Juniper gall, description.................... 253
Jute—
    fiber, water absorption capacity......... 736
    seed, raffinose in 710
    varieties................................ 825
Kafir corn—
    as a dry-land crop, U.S.D.A............ 637
    culture experiments, Guam............ 730
    culture experiments, Hawaii............ 132
    culture experiments, Tex............... 331
    culture under dry farming, N.Mex...... 329
    digestibility, Ark....................... 678
    digestibility and productive value, Tex.. 865
    fodder, digestibility, Tex................ 168
    leaves, variation of water and dry matter
      in, U.S.D.A......................... 637
    varieties, Cal........................... 338
Kafirin, chemistry of....................... 8
Kainit, destruction of weeds by............. 446
Kakothrips pisivora, notes................... 257
Kala-azar, studies.......................... 357
Kansas—
    College, notes.. .... 196, 497, 700
    Station, notes..................... 196, 299, 497
Kaoliang, varieties, Cal..................... 338
Kedani disease, carrier..................... 858
Kentucky—
    Station, notes...................... 398, 896
    University, notes.................. 398, 497, 896
Keratitis infectiosa in cattle................. 691
Kermes sassceri, notes, Conn.State........... 255
Kerosene, larvicidal value................... 464
Ketchup. (See Catsup.)
Ketohexoses, detection..................... 206
Kidney worm of swine...................... 482
Kikuyu grass, notes, Ga.................... 29
Kuromoji seed, oil of....................... 109
Labor, redistribution........................ 290
Laborers, farm. (See Agricultural laborers.)

	Page.
Lace bugs, remedies	256
Lactalbumin, value for growth	864, 865
Lactic acid—	
decomposition by yeasts	202
effect on baking quality of flour, Wash	861
effect on plants	224
extraction with ether	414
Lactoglobulin, relation to serum proteins	8
Læmophloeus sp., studies	356
Lambs, worm infestation, Wyo	374
(*See also* Sheep.)	
Laminaria spp., analyses, Conn. State	814
Land—	
areas, mapping	651
clearing by-products, Minn	286
grant colleges. (*See* Agricultural colleges.)	
improvement in Province of the Rhine	697
irrigated, drainage, U.S.D.A	86, 587
logged off, clearing, Idaho	87
plaster. (*See* Gypsum.)	
problem and rural welfare	290, 593
settlement in California	190
settlement in Great Britain	190, 390, 791
system of Great Britain, treatise	697
tenure and settlement in New Zealand	791
title registration law in Nebraska	190
title registration law in New York	190
title registration, Torrens system	492, 888
waste, reclamation	214
Landscape gardening, treatise	546, 547
Lantana camara, control by parasites	359
Larch, cambial activity	127
Lard as affected by peanuts, Tex	367
Lasioderma serricorne. (*See* Cigarette beetle.)	
Lasiodiplodia theobromæ, notes	452, 553
Lasioptera vitis, notes, Conn.State	255
Lath—	
industry in Canada	245
production in 1915, U.S.D.A	148
Latheticus oryzæ, studies	356
Laurel psyllid, studies	849
Lavatera, tests, S.Dak	143
Lawns, fertilizer experiments, R.I	446
Lead arsenate—	
analyses, N.J	243
basic, preparation and properties	410
decomposition by water	802
injury to stone fruits	848
insecticidal value, U.S.D.A	759
tests, Nebr	448
Leaf—	
development, studies	324
epidermis, light sensitivity	222
structure as affected by light and shade	747
weevil, new, in New York, N. Y. State	359
Leaf-hoppers, egg parasites	460
Leafy twigs, preservation	837
Leather cuttings as a cattle feed	171
Leaves—	
and seeds, dietary relationship	264
effect on root formation and geotropic curvature	325
plant food constituents	629
symbiosis with fungi	327
winter and summer, comparison	327

	Page.
Lecanium corni, studies	662
Legume—	
bacteria and nonlegume plants, symbiosis, Ill	819
diseases in Switzerland	47
Leguminosæ, economic value, treatise	28
Leguminous plants—	
as green manure, Hawaii	320
culture experiments, Tex	330
effect on associated nonlegumes	438
effect on soil bacteria, Iowa	121
fertilizing value, Ind	214
illustrated lecture on, U.S.D.A	194
irrigation experiments. Idaho	639
nitrogeneous fertilizers for	134
pollination experiments	734
production in Spain	827
root tubercles. (*See* Root tubercles.)	
seed color variation in	334
Leiognathus morsitans, notes	360
Leiomerus granicollis n.sp., description	58
Lemon—	
brown rot, notes, Fla	656
grass oil, production in United States	546
sour rot, description	843
Lemons—	
bud variation	345
optimum soil moisture conditions	834
Lenzites sepiaria—	
enzymatic activity	129
wood decay induced by	727
Lepidoptera—	
Japanese, life history	57
new of North America	564
of Isle of Pines	158
of North America, check-list	563
Lepidosaphes ficus in California	563
Leptinotarsa decemlineata. (*See* Potato beetle, Colorado.)	
Leptobyrsa rhododendri, notes	563
Leptophya distinguenda n.sp., description	563
Leptosphæria—	
cucurbitæ n.sp., description	550
herpotrichoides, notes	248, 653
sacchari, notes	553, 838
Leptospira, new genus, notes	578
Leptotrombidium akamushi—	
n.g. studies	858
relation to *Leptus autumnalis*	859
Leptus autumnalis, notes	859
Lespedeza. (*See* Clover, Japan.)	
Lettuce—	
bacterial diseases, notes. Fla	652
bacterial stem and leaf disease	841
culture, Cal	144
seedlings, damping-off, Fla	651
watering, continuous	543
l-Leucin in sweet clover silage	802
Leucocytozoon anatis, notes	483
Levulose, determination in presence of glucose	507
Lice—	
and their relation to disease	762
destruction on hogs	882
on poultry, U.S.D.A	357
studies	850

Page.

Light—
as a factor in forest growth.............. 45
intensities, measurement................ 821
sensitivity of foliar organs.............. 222
Lightning as a cause of forest fires, U.S.D.A... 512
Ligyrus gibbosus, life history................. 567
Lilies, nectar secretion....................... 633
Lime—
air-slaked, for alfalfa, Oreg.............. 34
analyses.............................. 428, 818
analyses, N.J......................... 219
Barrel Act, Federal...................... 723
effect on soil fertility.................... 219
fertilizing value......................... 733
fertilizing value, Ind.................... 214
fertilizing value, Pa..................... 626
grinding law in Maryland............... 219
insecticidal value...................... 262
inspection in Pennsylvania.......... 220, 818
neutralizer, detection in dairy products,
U.S.D.A........................... 313
niter. (*See* Calcium nitrate.)
nitrogen. (*See* Calcium cyanamid.)
requirements of soils, determination... 212, 622
use in agriculture.............. 218, 219, 629
use on calcareous sugar-cane soils........ 723
use on Iowa soils, Iowa 24
use on Missouri soils, Mo.............. 428
use on peat soils.................... 134, 135
washes, winter application............. 759
Lime kiln, rotary, description.............. 24
Limes—
collar rot of............................. 838
dieback of 556
diseases in West Indies.................. 452
fertilizer experiments.................... 648
root diseases in Lesser Antilles.......... 454
Limestone—
composition, Ohio........................ 195
decomposition and utilization, Ohio..... 219
effect of fineness of subdivision.......... 428
ground, analyses and use, N.Y.State.... 523
ground, for acid silt and clay soils...... 420
ground, use on soils.................... 818
injurious to citrus fruits, Fla............. 656
resources of Michigan.................... 428
resources of Missouri, Mo................ 428
tests, Mo.............................. 428
Lime-sulphur mixture—
analyses, N.J.......................... 243
fungicidal value, Nebr.................... 447
insecticidal value....................... 53
preparation and use, Me................. 544
preparation and use, Wash.............. 143
substitute for, N.J..................... 251
Liming experiments—
Ohio.................................. 124
in Assam.............................. 427
Lindera spp., oils of........................ 109
Linguatulid, new, from Ecuador............ 357
Linguatulida from crocodiles............... 357
Linospora sacchari, notes.................... 553
Linseed—
meal, analyses, Conn.State.............. 268
meal, analyses, R.I...................... 767
meal, analyses, Wis..................... 471
meal, sugar content....................... 208
oil, test for gelatinous matter in......... 13

Page.

Liothrips, North American species.......... 561
Liponyssus bursa, notes...................... 360
Lissorhoptrus simplex, remedies, La.......... 568
Litchi—
culture experiments, Hawaii............ 142
erinose, treatment, Hawaii.............. 142
Lithium—
determination in water.................. 506
nitrate, penetration of trees by.......... 327
Litmus substitute for milk cultures,
U.S.D.A............................. 686
Little peach disease, studies................ 755
Live stock—
breeding in British East Africa.......... 734
breeding, neglected factors in, Me........ 365
classification at county fairs, U.S.D.A... 598
cost of raising, Can...................... 790
feeding, Tenn........................... 471
feeding, treatise......................... 94
function in agriculture, U.S.D.A........ 572
improvement, Guam..................... 768
improvement in Wales.................. 294
in New Zealand......................... 791
in Sweden.............................. 191
industry in Switzerland.................. 769
insects affecting........................ 459
insurance against fire.................... 888
judging, treatise........................ 94
marketing in the South, U.S.D.A........ 390
plants poisonous to...................... 688
prices and movement in 1916........... 492
prices in Ireland........................ 291
products, cost data, Can................. 790
raising in blue-grass region of Kentucky,
U.S.D.A............................. 471
relation to soil fertility.................. 215
statistics in Cuba....................... 892
statistics in Egypt, Spain, Morocco, and
Tunis................................ 292
statistics in France...................... 891
statistics in Rhodesia.................... 492
statistics in Scotland.................... 392
statistics in Sweden.................. 93, 492
types and market classes, textbook...... 194
(*See also* Animals, Cattle, Sheep, *etc.*)
Liver of sulphur, fungicidal value.......... 48
Living conditions in Alabama............... 91
Locust—
bean meal, analyses..................... 873
borer, notes, Okla....................... 566
Locusts—
at sea, U.S.D.A......................... 115
catching machine for.................... 257
control by parasites.................. 357, 760
control in Algeria....................... 461
control in Argentina..................... 849
control in Kansas, Kans................. 560
control in Malay States................. 849
control in South Dakota, S.Dak........ 561
control in Uruguay................... 55, 849
control in various countries............. 848
injurious to potatoes, Wash............. 157
invasions in Egypt...................... 561
life history and remedies, Colo.......... 661
remedies......................... 156, 561
Lonchocarpus spp. in Central America and
Mexico............................... 819

Lophodermium— Page.
macrosporum, notes...................... 550
pinastri, notes........................ 458, 550
Loranthaceæ, osmotic pressure of tissue fluids 47
Loughridge, R. H., biographical sketch...... 496
Louisiana Stations—
notes................................. 196, 700
report................................. 599
Louping-ill, transmission by ticks........... 277
Lucern. (*See* Alfalfa.)
Lulu kernels and oil, analyses.............. 14
Lumber—
industry in Canada...................... 245
production in 1914–15, U.S.D.A.......... 148
storage, U.S.D.A......................... 349
waste as a source of potash.............. 722
(*See also* Timber *and* Wood.)
Lumbermen, conditions among in Sweden... 890
Lungworms, life history and treatment...... 179
Lupines as a cover crop for orchards......... 833
Lygus—
communis novascotiensis, studies......... 462
pratensis. (*See* Tarnished plant bug.)
Lymphangitis—
epizootic, causative organism............ 377
epizootic, in France..................... 692
epizootic, treatment................... 377, 781
ulcerous in horses, immunization........ 583
Lysimeter work, equipment for, N.Y.State.. 521
Macaroni wheat. (*See* Wheat, durum.)
Machinery. (*See* Agricultural machinery.)
Macrophoma trichosanthis n.sp., notes........ 148
Macrophya n.spp., descriptions.............. 667
Macrosiphum solanifolii—
notes, Wash............................ 157
studies, Ohio........................... 850
Macrosporium—
commune, growth in plant decoctions.... 728
commune, nitrogen fixation by........... 129
parasiticum sarcinula, notes.............. 553
solani, notes............................ 249
tomato, notes........................... 150
Magnesium—
carbonate, effect on soil acidity.......... 23
carbonate, effect on sulfofying power of
soils, Iowa............................ 120
determination in water.................. 412
salts, effect on solubility of phosphates. 323, 324
sulphate, antiseptic and germicidal value 176
Magnolia—
oils of................................. 109
powdery mildew, description............. 657
Maine—
Station, abstracts of papers, Me......... 396
Station, notes........................... 497
University notes..................... 97, 497
Maize. (*See* Corn.)
Maladie du coit. (*See* Dourine.)
Malaria—
control in Western Hemisphere.......... 565
equine, in Barbados..................... 483
relation to crop production.............. 57
winter carrier........................... 463
Malate, action on isolated intestine.......... 471
Mallophaga, systematic nomenclature....... 461
Malt—
amylase, action of bromid on............ 614
amylase, action on soluble starch........ 613

Malt—Continued. Page.
sprouts, analyses, Conn.State............ 268
sprouts, analyses, Wis................... 471
Mammals—
color inheritance in..................... 866
new, of North and Middle America...... 757
of North America, treatise.............. 658
wild, of Canada......................... 757
Mammary gland extract, effect on milk production................................ 173
Mammitis, treatment...................... 277
Man, metabolism experiments............... 266
Mandarin brown spot, treatment........... 352
Mandelic nitrile, effect on plant growth...... 632
Manganese—
compounds, solubility in soils........... 18
in leguminous plants.................... 28
occurrence and rôle in plants............ 130
salts, effect on ammonification and nitrification, Iowa......................... 126
salts, effect on solubility of phosphates... 323
sulphate, effect on soil acidity.......... 23
Mange, demodectic, in swine................ 477
Mangel seeds in Denmark................... 742
Mangels—
analyses............................... 233
Barres, history in Denmark............. 736
culture experiments................. 230, 733
culture experiments, Nev............... 435
fertilizer experiments.................. 533
selection experiments, Nev............. 32
varieties, Minn.......................... 228
varieties, Nev........................... 32
Mango—
breeding experiments, Hawaii........... 142
disease in Yucatan...................... 755
diseases and pests in Mysore............ 657
fruit disease, notes...................... 838
history in Florida....................... 745
pollination, U.S.D.A.................... 835
propagating, inarch method, Guam...... 743
Mangrove—
leaf sap osmotic concentration.......... 632
red, ecology and physiology............. 821
Manioc. (*See* Cassava.)
Mannan in gymnosperms.................... 710
Mannite in silage and its use in explosives... 801
d-Mannoketoheptose, chemistry of.......... 9
Mannose, crystalline, preparation and mutarotation................................ 201
Manure—
barnyard. (*See* Barnyard manure.)
disposal in relation to live-stock diseases. 780
effect on composition of cereals.......... 827
effect on corn, Utah..................... 440
effect on lime requirements of soils, Ohio. 125
effect on soil bacteria, Iowa............. 120
effect on solubility of inorganic soil constituents, U.S.D.A.................... 422
fertilizing value........................ 534
fertilizing value, Ind................... 214
fertilizing value, Mo................... 731
for peat soils........................... 720
liquid, as a source of potash............ 817
liquid, fertilizing value................. 730
liquid, mixing with peat dust........... 215
residual effects, Ohio................... 133

	Page.
Manure—Continued.	
sampling device for	711
storage experiments, Me	628
treatise	215
(*See also* Cow, Horse, *etc.*)	
Maple—	
leaves, symbiosis with fungi	327
scale, cottony, notes	358, 459
wood creosote, composition and toxicity.	502
Maples, sterility, Minn	240
Marasmius—	
sacchari, notes	452, 753, 838
sarmentosus, notes	452
spp., on cacao	349
Marattiaceæ, mycorrhiza of	630
Mares—	
and foals, care, Okla	473
artificial insemination, Okla	473
Margarin, nutritive value	165
Margaropus annulatus. (*See* Cattle tick.)	
Marine mud, analyses and fertilizing value, Conn.State	814
Market—	
bureaus, State and Federal	888
survey of Atlanta, Georgia	91
train service, U.S.D.A	594
Marketing—	
and farm credits, book	391
cooperative	391, 796
cooperative, U.S.D.A	888
in Hawaii	391
Marmosa mexicana savannarum n.subsp., description	757
Marmots—	
ectoparasites of	879
relation to plague	180
Marrow mildew, notes	453
Maryland—	
College, notes	97
Station, report	599
Massachusetts—	
College, notes	97, 497
Station, notes	97
Mast, softening effect on pork fat, N.C	680
Mastigosporium album, notes	247
Mastitis. (*See* Mammitis.)	
Mathematics, vocational, textbook	598
Matthiola annua, mutation in	28
Mauritius beans as a green manure, Hawaii..	320
May beetles, destruction by hogs	261
Mayetiola destructor. (*See* Hessian fly.)	
Meadow—	
fescue for muskeg lands, Minn	229
fescue, pollination experiments	735
fescue, yields, Minn	227
foxtail midge, notes	463
foxtail, pollination experiments	735
Meadows—	
culture on peat bogs	826
insects affecting, Ohio	847
irrigation experiments, Oreg	84
liming experiments	733
moorland, botanical composition	135
of Boulder Park region, Colorado	435
(*See also* Grass.)	
Mealy bugs—	
parasites of	563, 847
studies	563

	Page.
Meat—	
ground, determination of added water	414
inspection, handbook	77
inspection in United States, U.S.D.A	577
meal, analyses, Wis	471
preserving	715
prices in Russia	292
scrap, analyses, Conn.State	268
scrap, analyses, R.I	767
scrap, analyses, Wis	471
Mechanic arts schools in New York	394
Mechanical colleges. (*See* Agricultural colleges.)	
Medicagos, improvement	136
Megastigmus aculeatus in New Jersey	856
Melanconium sacchari, notes	452
Melandrium album, root system	542
Melanochelia riparia, studies	764
Meliola heveæ n.sp., notes	253
Meliola in Porto Rico	149
Melittia satyriniformis. (*See* Squash borer.)	
Melolontha spp., remedies	467
Melon fly—	
parasites of	162, 847
studies, U.S.D.A	566
Melons—	
diseases of, N.J	653
insects affecting, Mo	760
sampling device for	711
Melophagus ovinus. (*See* Sheep tick.)	
Memythrus polistiformis. (*See* Grape root-borer.)	
Mendelian—	
characters, models to illustrate segregation and combination	432
class frequency, probable error	432
Meningococcus, food requirements	178
Menthone, inversion	201
Mercury—	
preparations, fungicidal value	247
purification, apparatus for	503
Meromyza americana, notes, U.S.D.A	160
Merulius lacrymans, notes	253
Mesquite, commercial possibilities	747
Metabolism experiments with men	266
Metals, heavy, effect on isolated intestine	266
Metamasius—	
ritchiei n.sp., description	161
sericeus, notes	162
Metastrongylus apri, notes, Guam	779
Meteorological—	
courses for aeronautical engineers, U.S.D.A	807
monthly, Chinese, U.S.D.A	513
observations, Hawaii	116
observations, Idaho	16
observations, Mass	116, 619, 807
observations, Me	314
observations, Minn	210
observations, U.S.D.A	115, 116, 314, 513, 619, 807
observations, Wyo	314
observations in German East Africa	717
observations in Habana	513
observations in New South Wales	513
observations in Paris and vicinity	16
observations on lightships, U.S.D.A	513
(*See also* Climate, Rainfall, Weather, *etc.*)	
service of Colombia, U.S.D.A	115

Page.

Meteorology of Brazil, treatise............... 619
Meteorus versicolor in Maine................. 459
Methi as a fodder crop........................ 137
Methyl—
    alcohol, determination.................... 111
    salicylate, methods of analysis........... 413
    xanthins, action on isolated intestine.... 471
Methylene blue—
    effect on decomposition of pyroracemic
        acid.................................. 202
    effect on formation of carbon dioxid by
        dead yeast............................ 203
    use in chemical analysis.................. 111
Mice—
    development of ascarid larvæ in.......... 374
    field, notes.............................. 156
    new, from Mexico 757
    new, from Wyoming................... 758, 846
Michigan College and Station, notes.......... 197
Microbiology, treatise....................... 76
Microdon n.spp., descriptions................ 766
Microorganisms—
    differentiation........................... 502
    relation to cheese ripening............... 503
    (*See also* Bacteria.)
Microscope, electrically heated slide cham-
    ber...................................... 410
Microscopy, errors in........................ 205
Microsphera alni, investigations............. 155
Microstroma juglandis robustum n.var., de-
    scription................................ 844
Microthyrium sp. on rubber.................. 253
Milk—
    acidity, studies.......................... 373
    and its hygienic relations, treatise....... 174
    as a food, U.S.D.A....................... 669
    as affected by parturition................ 172
    as affected by plane of nutrition......... 272
    bacterial content as affected by factors at
        barn, Ill............................. 684
    bacterial content as affected by gargety
        and high count cows.................. 874
    bacteriological examination.............. 468
    bitter and rancid, studies................ 273
    board of Massachusetts State Depart-
        ment of Health, report............... 372
    certified, abortion bacillus in............ 881
    clarification, N.Y.Cornell................ 475
    clarifier slime, analyses, N.Y.Cornell..... 476
    composition as affected by ingestion of
        placenta............................. 373
    composition as affected by stage of lacta-
        tion.................................. 373
    cost of production, Mich................. 474
    cost of production, Ohio................. 575
    cost of production in Connecticut....... 776
    cultures, litmus substitute for, U.S.D.A. 686
    desiccated, methods of analysis.......... 508
    evaporated, determination of fat in, Okla. 507
    evaporated, determination of total solids. 508
    evaporated, fishiness in, Iowa........... 686
    fat as affected by cottonseed products,
        Mo................................... 72
    fat as affected by parturition............ 172
    fat as affected by temperature........... 373
    fat, buffalo, analyses.................... 272
    fat, changes in during lactation.......... 373

Milk—Continued.
    fat, relation to solids-not-fat............. 113
    fat, separation of "fat-soluble A" from... 308
        (*See also* Fat.)
    for growing chicks, Mo.................. 768
    goat's, composition, N.Y.State.......... 575
    goat's, for infant feeding, N.Y.State... 570, 575
    houses, construction, Nebr.............. 591
    human, composition..................... 273
    onion flavor in, N.C.................... 683
    oxygenation............................. 174
    pasteurization at low temperature...... 777
    pasteurized and raw, differentiation..... 415
    pasteurized, bacterial activity in....... 874
    paying for at cheese factories........... 374
    powders, microscopic appearance....... 415
    production, changes in during lactation.. 373
    production, relation to glands of internal
        secretion......................... 173, 272
    products, determination of fat in........ 805
    products, manual....................... 777
    proteins, studies........................ 8
    records of American and Scotch Ayr-
        shires.............................. 775
    sanitary, production..................... 174
    secretion during process of milking...... 172
    secretion, studies....................... 272
    sickness in animals, Ohio............... 195
    sickness, notes, N.C.................... 690
    sickness, studies, U.S.D.A.............. 583
    significance of colon bacilli in.......... 874
    skimmed. (*See* Skim milk.)
    supply, improvement.................... 777
    supply of Bangalore..................... 175
    supply of cities, treatise............ 174, 874
    supp.y of Massachusetts, report........ 372
    supply of New York..................... 175
    supply, relation to sore throat epidemic.. 273
    testing............................. 618, 875
    transmission of tuberculosis by......... 80
    ultrafiltration.......................... 207
    vetch, toxicity, Wyo.................... 780
    watered, detection.................. 13, 804
Milking machines, tests, Idaho.............. 75
Millet—
    bread, digestibility, U.S.D.A........... 364
    culture and utilization, U.S.D.A........ 37
    culture experiments............. 436, 734, 824
    culture experiments, Guam............. 730
    culture experiments, Minn............. 227
    culture for hay, Nev................... 436
    culture under dry farming, N.Mex...... 329
    digestibility, Tex....................... 168
    fertilizer experiments.................. 436
    for late planting, Nev.................. 436
    green manuring experiments............ 734
    selection experiments, Nev............. 32
    varieties...................... 34, 136, 825
    varieties, N.Mex....................... 329
    varieties, Nev.......................... 32
    varieties, Tex.......................... 331
Milo maize—
    as a dry land crop, U.S.D.A............ 637
    culture experiments, Guam............. 730
    culture experiments, Hawaii........... 132
    culture experiments, Tex.............. 331
    culture under dry farming, N.Mex...... 329
    digestibility and productive value, Tex 658

Milo maize—Continued.　　　　　　　　Page.
　leaves, variation of water and dry matter
　　in, U.S.D.A........................... 637
　recurving, Tex......................... 642
　varieties, Cal.......................... 33S
Mimicry in butterflies, treatise.............. 55
Mineral metabolism of milch cows, Ohio..... 169
Minidoka bird reservation, Idaho............ 355
Minnesota—
　Crookston substation, report............ 297
　Duluth substation, report............... 298
　Morris substation, report.............. 298
　Station, notes............ 197,398,497,600,896
　Station, report........................ 297
　University, notes......... 197,299,398,497,896
Mint rust, notes............................ 457
Miromphalomyia perilampoides n.g. and n.sp.,
　description............................. 162
Mississippi—
　College, notes.......................... 497
　Station, notes......................... 600
Missouri—
　Station, notes....................... 398,897
　Station, report....................... 796
　University, notes.................. 97,398,897
Mistletoe, control in National Forests....... 458
Mites—
　injurious to plants in Sweden............ 163
　new................................. 860
　on poultry, U.S.D.A................... 357
Mitochondria, relation to anthocyanin forma-
　tion.................................. 25
Moisture determinations in entomology..... 355
　(*See also* Water.)
Molasses—
　beet, composition and use.............. 416
　beet pulp. (*See* Beet pulp.)
Mold, prevention on butter.................. 777
Mole—
　cricket, introduction into New Jersey.... 660
　skins, tanning, Wash................... 96
Moles, notes, Wash........................ 699
Molybdenum residues, recovery............. 504
Moniezia expansa, infestation of lambs by,
　Wyo................................. 374
Monilia fructigena, notes................ 151,457
Monobæus hegeli n.sp., description.......... 667
Monodontomerus æreus in Maine............. 459
Montana Station, notes.................. 299,498
Morphin, effect on plant growth............. 632
Mosquito larvæ—
　destruction............................ 464
　development in relation to bacteria and
　　yeasts............................... 763
Mosquitoes—
　anopheline, in California................ 565
　anopheline, infectibility.,.............. 463
　control, Conn.State.................... 255
　control in Connecticut.................. 259
　destruction............................ 86
　fish enemies, N.J...................... 260
　flight of.............................. 853
　life history and control, N. J............ 664
　notes.............................. 57,156
　of Montana, Mont..................... 255
　of mountains of California.............. 564
　of North America and West Indies, hand-
　　book................................ 762

Mosquitoes—Continued.　　　　　　　Page.
　of Peru................................ 357
　relation to salinity of water, N.J........ 259
　relation to swamp fever in horses, Wyo.. 374
Moss—
　as bedding for cattle and horses......... 723
　cleaning from irrigation canals.......... 285
Moth—
　bean hay, digestibility and productive
　　value, Tex........................... 865
　borer, new, on pear trees............... 847
Moths, treatise............................ 358
　(*See also* Lepidoptera.)
Motor plows. (*See* Plows.)
Muck—
　as a source of organic ammoniates....... 815
　fertilizing value, judging............... 216
Mulberry—
　disease in France and Italy............. 655
　leaves, nitrogen in.................... 525
Mules, feeding experiments, N.C........... 681
Muriate of potash. (*See* Potassium chlorid.)
Muridæ, new, of Argentina, Patagonia, and
　Cape Horn........................... 357
Musca domestica. (*See* House fly.)
Muscina—
　spp., studies.......................... 764
　stabulans, studies, N.J................. 665
Muscle, respiratory process in.............. 266
Muscoid Diptera, new, of America.......... 764
Muscovite as a source of potash............ 505
Muscular—
　motion, nature........................ 266
　tissue, function in urea formation....... 802
　tissue, glycolytic properties............. 802
Mushrooms, edible and poisonous, U.S.D.A .. 263
Musk ox, conservation.................... 757
Muskmelons—
　acid content.......................... 714
　culture experiments, Guam............. 742
　fertilizer experiments, Guam............ 742
　varieties, S.Dak...................... 143
Muskrat, parasites of..................... 355
Mustard—
　oil, determination in rapeseed cake...... 416
　white, as a cover crop for orchards....... 833
　wild, eradication in corn................ 342
Musts, separated, analyses................. 806
Mycogone cervina theobromæ n.var., notes.... 148
Mycorrhiza, endotrophic, studies........... 129
Mycosphærella—
　aurea n.sp., description................ 551
　grossulariæ, notes..................... 551
　scutina, notes........................ 550
Mydæa spp. studies...................... 764
Myiasis in man, insect vector.............. 357
Myospila meditabunda, studies............. 764
Myzomela rubratra saffordi n.subsp., descrip-
　tion.................................. 758
Myzus, California species................... 158
Myzus—
　godeliæ n.sp., description.............. 158
　ribifolii n.sp., description............. 562
　ribis. (*See* Currant aphis.)
Næmosphæra chanousiana n.sp., notes....... 630
Napicladium prosopodium n.sp., description. 748
Narcissus diseases, studies................. 47

National—   Page.
  Forest Reservation Commission, report.. 348
  Potato Association...................... 601
  Research Council, work of agriculture
    committee............................   4
Nature study—
  and elementary agriculture in Georgia... 194
  bulletin................................ 598
  course in............................... 395
Nebraska—
  Station, notes.......................... 197, 897
  University, notes.................. 197, 600, 897
Nectar secretion, studies.................... 633
Nectarines, drying........................... 114
Nectria—
  bainati hypoleuca n.var., notes........... 148
  ditissima, mode of attack................ 253
  sp., on sugar cane...................... 553
Nematodes—
  destruction with calcium cyanamid, Fla. 453
  giant, in abdominal cavity.............. 281
  heteroxenous, larval forms.............. 361
  in Philippines.......................... 277
  injurious to black currant.............. 843
  injurious to dasheens................... 841
  injurious to pepper..................... 249
  injurious to pineapples, Fla............ 652
  technique, methods...................... 549
  treatment, Fla.......................... 652
Nematospora lycopersici n.sp., description.... 842
Neotoma cinerea lucida n.subsp., description. 757
Nephelometer-colorimeter, description...... 205
Nephritis, respiratory metabolism in........ 267
Nepticulidæ of North America............... 564
Nest eggs, tests, Iowa........................   70
Nevada—
  Station, notes...................... 97, 498, 897
  Station, report.........................   95
  University, notes....................... 97, 498
New Hampshire College, notes......... 97, 197, 498
New Jersey College and Stations, notes. 98, 197, 498
New Mexico Station, report.................   95
New York—
  Cornell Station, notes............. 98, 498, 600
  Cornell Station, report................. 298
  Produce Exchange, report............... 891
  State Station, notes.............. 197, 299, 797
  State Station, report................... 396
Nezara—
  hilaris, studies, Ohio.................. 258
  viridula, notes.........................   55
Nicotiana hybrids—
  heredity in............................. 433
  sterility in............................. 225
Nicotin—
  determination in tobacco...............   14
  effect on plant growth.................. 632
  emulsion for............................ 760
  solutions, aqueous, concentration and op-
    tical rotatory power..................   14
  sulphate, insecticidal value............ 559
  sulphate, use as a spray, U.S.D.A....... 600
Niger-seed plant, culture for seed........ 230
Nigredo fallens, æcial stage on red clover..... 752
Nipponorthezia, new genus, description...... 358
Nitrate—
  industry of Chile....................... 217
  Norwegian. (See Calcium nitrate.)

Nitrate—Continued.   Page.
  of lime. (See Calcium nitrate.)
  of soda. (See Sodium nitrate.)
  salts, industry in India.................. 722
Nitrates—.
  determination in presence of chlorids.... 504
  determination in soils.................. 111
  determination in water.................. 506
  effect on nodule formation.............. 133
  leaching from pervious soils..............   23
  relation to cultural practices and plant
    growth............................... 813
Nitric—
  acid, effect on plants.................... 224
  nitrogen in country rock, Utah.......... 518
Nitrification—
  as a factor in soil fertility............... 519
  as affected by manganese salts, Iowa..... 126
  in soils................................. 318
  relation to cultural practices and plant
    growth............................... 813
Nitrites—
  accumulation in soils...................   19
  in diseased plants...................... 549
Nitrogen—
  absorption and leaching in soils..........   23
  amino-acid, determination in blood......   14
  amino-acid, in blood of various species... 206
  amino, and anaphylatoxin................ 582
  amino, relation to quality in flour....... 206
  assimilation by corn.................... 223
  atmospheric, fixation by nonlegume
    plants, Ill........................... 819
  atmospheric, industrial fixation....... 321, 815
  compounds of soils and fertilizers....... 216
  compounds, sources in United States.... 217
  determination in alfalfa hay............ 309
  determination in calcium cyanamid..... 413
  determination in fertilizers............. 504
  determination in forage plants.......... 113
  determination in tobacco leaves......... 509
  digestion apparatus, description......... 503
  distribution in soils.................... 517
  fixation and oxygen release in green
    plants...............................   25
  fixation by plants...................... 129
  fixing organisms in Iowa soils........... 517
  fraction, new, in soils.................. 518
  gaseous, in swamp rice soils............. 421
  in mulberry leaves...................... 525
  lime. (See Calcium cyanamid.)
  loss in industrial wastes................ 630
  metabolic, determination, U.S.D.A...... 672
  metabolism of peas.....................   24
  nitrous, in irrigated soils................ 120
  production in United States............. 721
  relation to citrus mottle leaf, U.S.D.A. 353
  removal by corn crop. Conn.State....... 232
  transformation and distribution in citrus
    soils, U.S.D.A........................ 318
Nitrogenous fertilizers—
  comparison...................... 321, 426, 739
  effect on nodule formation.............. 133
  for semiarid soils, U S.D.A............. 319
Nocardia bovis, studies...................... 482
Noctuid, new, form Brazil.................... 564
Nonpartisan League in North Dakota....... 592
North Carolina Station, report.............. 699

North Dakota—

	Page.
College, notes	399
College, survey	596
State engineer, report	84

Nosema—

apis, notes	58
apis, relation to Isle of Wright disease	360
bombycis, structure and life history	361
Nothodiscus antoniæ n.g. and n.sp., notes	630
Notodontoidea, pupæ of, Me	663
β-Nucleoproteins, antigenic properties	77
Nudacotyle novicia n.g. and n.sp., description	355

Nummularia—

bulliardii, notes	246
discreta, notes	151

Nursery—

inspection, Conn.State	254
inspection in Kansas	357
inspection in Massachusetts	646
inspection in Pennsylvania	459
inspection law in Arkansas	544
inspection law in Colorado	544
inspection law in Idaho	544
stock, imported, inspection	257
stock, insects affecting. Mo	760
Nut grass, eradication, Hawaii	132
Nutrients, absorption by roots, U.S.D.A	222
Nutrition, digest of data	469
(See also Digestion, Metabolism, etc.)	
Nuttalliosis in Russian Turkestan	374
Nymphula nymphæta, notes	847
Nymphulinæ, North American, notes	564
Nysius minutus, notes	847

Oak—

mildew, classification and host relationships	155
Oidium in France	756
roots, mycorrhiza on	756
seeds, storage experiments	547
Oaks, hybrid, in United States	820

Oat—

aphis, cat-tail as a summer host	461
crown rust, studies, Mo	749
grass, tall, pollination experiments	735
hay, digestibility, Tex	168
hay, forage poisoning due to	689
kernel, dietary deficiencies	61
middlings, analyses, Wis	471
powdery mildew, studies, Mo	749
smut, inoculation experiments, Mo	750
smut, treatment	750

Oats—

and peas, seeding and harvesting dates	135
and peas, seeding experiments, Idaho	640
as affected by greenhouse temperature	533
breeding experiments	827
breeding experiments, U.S.D.A	738
bushel weights	889
cost of production, W.Va	191
culture, continuous	137
culture experiments	436, 534, 823
culture experiments, La	529
culture experiments, Minn	226
culture experiments, Mo	731
culture experiments, Tex	329
culture for hay, Nev	436
culture under dry farming, N.Mex	329
dietary properties	264

Oats—Continued.

	Page.
digestibility, Ark	678
effect on soil bacteria. U.S.D.A	421
electroculture experiments	336
fertilizer experiments	134, 216, 436, 823
fertilizer experiments, Ga	29
fertilizer experiments, Idaho	30
fertilizer experiments, Me	635
fertilizer experiments, Minn	229
fertilizer experiments, R.I	34
germination tests, Mont	239
ground, analyses, R.I	767
husk percentage in	537
improvement in Canada	831
inheritance in, Wash	332
irrigation experiments, Idaho	640
irrigation experiments, U. S. D. A	822
pedigreed, yields in Wisconsin	438
rolled, as a flour substitute, Ohio	895
seed bed preparation, Ga	29
seeding experiments	537
seeding experiments, Idaho	30
seeding experiments, Me	635
seeding experiments, Minn	226
seeding experiments, Mo	731
seeding experiments, Ohio	134
selection experiments, Minn	226
selection experiments, Nev	32
subsoiling experiments	732
v. corn for work horses, Ohio	195
varieties	134, 135, 436, 438, 537, 823
varieties, Hawaii	132
varieties, Idaho	29, 30, 640
varieties, Ill	641
varieties, Iowa	30
varieties, Md	332
varieties, Me	635
varieties, Minn	227, 228, 229
varieties, Mo	731
varieties, Nev	32
varieties, Oreg	530
varieties, Tex	329, 330
varieties, Wash	33
volume weight and grain characteristics	643
winter, northern limits in United States	533
Obrussa sp., notes	564
Oceanographical research, new instruments for, U.S.D.A	513, 807
Ocypteromima n.g. and n.sp., description	359
Œdionychis sexamaculata, notes, Conn.State	255

Œnothera—

dimorphic mutants	131
mutants with diminutive chromosomes	433
mutations in	328, 724
twin hybrids in	820
variation in	525

Œsophagostomum—

columbianum, notes, Guam	779
spp. in Philippines	277
Ohio State University and Station, notes 98, 498, 797	

Oidium euonymi japonici—

notes	550
treatment	246

Oil—

emulsions, preparation and use, Wash	143
palm, propagation and yields	835
plants of Indo-China	830
seeds of Brazil	511

Oils— Page.
color tests............................... 13
determination of unsaponifiable matter.. 805
fatty, notes............................. 109
rancid, evaluation....................... 114
soluble, insecticidal value.............. 53
spontaneous combustion, Iowa.......... 788
sulphuric acid or Maumené number..... 805
testing.................................. 13
use on roads............................ 490
vegetable, composition in relation to climate.................................. 418
Oklahoma College and Station, notes...... 399,797
Okra, culture experiments, Guam.......... 742
Oleander canker, description.............. 252
Oleoresin of Douglas fir.................. 411
Oligotropus alopecuri, notes............ 463
Olive oil—
index of refraction...................... 508
production and use, U.S.D.A............ 511
Olives—
culture in Crimea 144
culture in Spain......................... 545
oil content.............................. 43
Olpidium brassicæ, notes, N.Y.Cornell... 455
Onchocerca gibsoni, transmission........ 181
Onchocerciasis, bovine, in South America... 80
Oncideres cingulatus, notes, Fla........ 660
Onion—
anthracnose, studies..................... 841
bacterial rot and damping off............ 452
black mold, notes, Ohio.................. 349
mildew, studies.......................... 553
pink root, notes......................... 841
Onions—
breeding experiments, Minn............. 230
culture experiments, Guam.............. 742
culture experiments, Idaho.............. 646
fertilizer experiments................... 215
fertilizer experiments, Guam........... 742
varieties, Idaho......................... 646
Ooencyrtus sp., parasitic on tent caterpillar... 657
Oospora—
citri-aurantii, notes................... 843
oryzetorum n.sp., notes................. 148
piricola n.sp., description............. 250
scabies. (*See* Potato scab.)
Ophiobolus—
graminis, notes........................ 248
herpotrichus, notes.................... 248
oryzinus n.sp., notes.................. 148
Opius—
fletcheri, introduction into Hawaii.... 162
humilis, parasitic on fruit fly........ 856
Opossum, new, from Panama............... 757
Opuntia floccosa, description 454
Orange—
black spot and brown spot, treatment.... 352
juice, preparation, Fla.................. 313
Oranges—
composition as affected by fertilizers...... 649
culture, treatise........................ 835
frost protection......................... 649
June drop................................ 154
maturity standards...................... 745,649
navel, June drop......................... 834
Orchard—
grass, pollination experiments........... 734
inspection. (*See* Nursery inspection.)

Orchards— Page.
clean culture *v.* cover crop, Wash........ 40
cover crops for........................... 833
fertilizer experiments.................... 240
grass mulch for.......................... 833
irrigation................................ 143
spraying experiments..................... 242
Orchid bacterial disease, notes............. 839
Oregon—
College, notes........... 98,197,299,399,499,898
Hood River Branch Station, report....... 96
State Live Stock Sanitary Board, report.. 374
Station, notes.............. 98,299,399,499,898
Organic—
compounds, insecticidal value, determination, U.S.D.A....................... 843
materials, ashing........................ 712
materials, sampling device for........... 711
matter, destruction in animal and vegetable materials........................ 713
matter, determination in water.......... 714
matter, effect on soil acidity, Mo........ 718
matter, effect on solubility of inorganic soil constituents, U.S.D.A.............. 422
matter, showers of, U.S.D.A.............. 808
Oribatoidea, synopsis..................... 858
Ornamental plants, shrubs, or trees. (*See* Plants, Shrubs, *and* Trees.)
Ornithin, detection in plants.............. 201
Ornithodoros megnini—
life history and habits................... 856
notes.................................... 255
Orobanche minor, eradication............. 239
Orokinase, definition..................... 681
Oroya fever, studies...................... 356,377
Orthoptera of Virginia.................... 461
Oryctes monoceros, notes................. 54
Osmotic pressure—
in roots and leaves, relation to water supply.................................. 525
of soil solution, rôle in wheat culture...... 128
table.................................... 630
Otiorhynchus ovatus, notes, Wash......... 54
Otthia sp. on sugar cane................. 553
Ovary extract, effect on milk production..... 173
Oviducal glands, albumin secreted by........ 773
Ox saliva, diastase in..................... 276
Ox warble fly—
larvæ extract, effect on cattle and sheep.. 379
life history.............................. 601
notes................................ 156,464
Oxalic acid, detection in wine............. 207
Oxidase—
action, mechanism....................... 725
activity in plants........... 9,326,429,430
of *Rhus diversiloba*..................... 411
Oxidus gracilis, studies, Md.............. 667
Oxygen, dissolved, in rainwater........... 620
Oysters—
bacteriological examination.............. 405
shucked, cold-storage changes........... 311
Paddy. (*See* Rice.)
Palm—
kernel meal for steers................... 769
nut cake, analyses....................... 873
nut cake for cows........................ 872
nut cake, sugar content.................. 208
oil, detection............................ 13

Page.

Palmetto scale in California.................. 563
Pancreatic vitamin, use in malnutrition..... 65
Panicum miliaceum, botanical studies........ 336
Papaya—
    diseases, treatment..................... 550
    fruit disease, notes........................ 148
Papayas—
    breeding experiments, Hawaii........... 142
    culture................................. 345
Paper—
    as affected by humidity................. 109
    discoloration due to fungi............... 630
    industry in United States............... 748
Para grass—
    digestibility, Tex.......................... 168
    notes, Ga................................. 29
Para rubber. (*See* Rubber.)
Parachrysocharis—
    javensis n.g. and n.sp., description....... 667
    semiflava n.sp., description.............. 570
Paradol, notes............................. 612
Paraffin—
    effect on accumulation of ammonia and
      nitrates in soils, U.S.D.A.............. 812
    emulsions, wetting power................ 759
Parahydroxybenzoic acid, isolation from soil. 709
Paraleptomastix—
    abnormis, studies....................... 569
    notatus n.sp., description............... 467
Paramphistomum sp. in Philippines........ 277
Paramyiocnema, new genus, description...... 569
Paranagrus n.g. and n.spp., descriptions..... 856
Pararabin, effect on horse serum.............. 376
Parasites. (*See* Animal parasites, *etc.*)
Paratrioza cockerelli, studies................. 849
Parhelic circle at Fargo, N.Dak., U.S.D.A.... 115
Paris green, analyses, N.J.................... 243
Partridge peas as a cover crop for orchards.... 833
Paspalum dilatatum—
    as a forage crop, Hawaii................. 132
    culture experiments, Guam.............. 730
Pasture—
    for cows, Minn........................... 271
    grasses for Texas......................... 827
    mixtures, tests, Tex...................... 533
Pastures—
    composition of herbage.................. 230
    improvement............................. 230
    insects affecting, Ohio................... 847
    irrigated, management, Idaho........... 640
    lowland moor, management.............. 333
    peaty, fertilizer experiments............. 134
    permanent, formation................... 826
Patent medicines, examination............... 63
Pavements, cement-concrete, cracks in...... 88
Pea—
    thrips, notes............................. 257
    weevil in British Columbia.............. 459
Peach—
    bacterial spot, treatment, U.S.D.A...... 842
    borer, lesser, studies, Ohio............. 159,396
    borer, notes.......................... 158,159
    diseases, treatment, Oreg................ 51
    leaf curl, studies...................... 250,655
    rust, notes.............................. 453
    scale, West Indian, in Argentina......... 358

Page.

Peach—Continued.
    shipping crates, press for, N.J........... 490
    yellows, studies......................... 735
Peaches—
    acid content............................. 714
    cambial activity......................... 127
    cost of growing.......................... 42
    culture in Mesa County, Colo........... 241
    drying............................... 114,509
    drying, Wash............................ 715
    dust *v.* liquid spraying............... 42,832
    fertilizer experiments, Ga............... 40
    fertilizer experiments, Mo............... 743
    fertilizer experiments, N.Mex.......... 40
    frost injury, Utah....................... 344
    production in West Virginia............. 745
    pruning and training, W.Va............. 344
    spraying, N.J....................... 251,744
    thinning experiments, W.Va........... 448
    varieties, Mont.......................... 241
    varieties, Tex........................... 832
    varieties for Ohio, Ohio................. 241
Peanut—
    cake for steers.......................... 769
    cake, sugar content..................... 208
    diseases in West Indies.................. 452
    hulls and hay, digestibility and produc-
      tive value, Tex........................ 865
    leaf rust, treatment..................... 550
    meal for chicks, N.C..................... 682
    oil, determination in mixtures........... 312
    oil, production and use, U.S.D.A........ 511
    proteins, chemistry of............. 8,468,501
    straw, analyses, Ala.College.............. 234
    wilt, studies; U.S.D.A................... 49
Peanuts—
    as a grazing crop for pigs, N.C........... 679
    culture, Ala.College..................... 234
    culture experiments..................... 734
    culture in cotton belt................... 442
    culture in Egypt........................ 138
    culture in Tucuman..................... 134
    digestibility and productive value, Tex.. 865
    effect on succeeding crops, Ala.College.... 234
    fertilizer experiments................... 825
    fertilizer experiments, Ala.College........ 233
    for hogs, Tex............................ 367
    green manuring experiments............. 734
    softening effect on pork fat, N.C......... 680
    varieties................................. 825
    varieties, Ala.College.................... 233
    varieties, N.Mex........................ 329
    varieties, Tex........................... 330
Pear—
    aphis, woolly, studies, U.S.D.A........ 661
    blight, notes...................... 735,846
    blight, notes, N.Mex.................... 52
    branch blister disease, notes............. 842
    chlorosis, investigations, N.Mex......... 52
    diseases, notes.......................... 51
    diseases, treatment, Oreg................ 51
    leaf blister-mite, alternate form, U.S.D.A. 661
    leaf blister-mite, remedies................ 54
    root aphis, European, U.S.D.A.......... 661
    rust, studies............................. 250
    stocks for apple scions, N.Mex........... 40

Pear—Continued. Page.
thrips, control in British Columbia 55, 462
thrips, studies............................. 257
Pears—
acid content............................. 714
culture in Mesa County, Colo............ 241
culture in Ontario....................... 544
drying.............................. 114, 509
fall v. spring planting, Mo.............. 743
pollination experiments. N. Mex.......... 40
pruning and training, W. Va............. 344
spraying, N. J......................... 744
varieties, Mont......................... 241
varieties for Ohio, Ohio................. 241
Peas—
and oats, seeding experiments. Idaho..... 640
and oats silage for dairy cows, Wash 75
bushel weights......................... 889
culture experiments..................... 825
culture experiments, Idaho.............. 30
culture experiments, La................. 529
culture in Washington. Wash............ 96
drying................................. 509
field, culture, Wash.................... 337
field, culture experiments, Idaho........ 30
field, culture experiments, Minn........ 227
field, culture for hay and seed, Nev...... 436
field, hogging off, Idaho.............. 66, 68
field, irrigation experiments, Idaho....... 640
field, seeding experiments. Idaho........ 30
field, selection experiments. Nev......... 32
field, varieties........................ 135
field, varieties, Idaho.............. 29, 30, 640
field, varieties, Minn................... 228
field, varieties, Nev................... 32
field, varieties, Oreg.................. 530
field, varieties. Wash.............. 33, 337
improvement in Canada.................. 831
nitrogen metabolism.................... 24
seed color variation in................. 334
subsoiling experiments................. 732
varieties.............................. 825
Peat—
as a source of organic ammoniates........ 815
bacterized, fertilizing value..... 426, 629, 719, 814
bogs, converting into meadows.......... 826
digestibility and productive value, Tex... 865
fertilizing value, judging.............. 216
lands or soils. (See Soils, peat.)
Pecan—
catkins, disease of..................... 844
dieback, investigations, Fla............ 652
diseases, notes......................... 756
Pecans—
culture in Maryland.................... 345
varieties, Ga.......................... 44
winterkilling, sun scald, or sour sap...... 755
Pecari angulatus bangsi n. subsp., description. 757
Pecatonica River, flood control.......... 186
Pectic substances of plants.............. 309
Pectin, preparation, Wash............... 715
Pediculus spp., studies................... 850
Pegomya fusciceps, notes................. 854
Pelataclyna pellucida, notes............. 763
Pellagra, relation to sewage disposal........ 694
Pemphigus betæ, notes, Mont............. 255

Penicillium— Page.
expansum, growth in plant decoctions... 728
spp., nitrogen fixation by............... 129
spp., on orchard fruits 550
Pennsylvania—
College and Station, notes....... 98, 197, 499, 898
Institute of Animal Nutrition, notes...... 797
Pentoses, determination.................. 617
Peonies, treatise....................... 145
Pepper—
analyses and standards.................. 112
bacterial diseases, notes, Fla........... 652
black spot, notes....................... 841
cress seeds, germination tests........... 26, 431
culture and diseases in Dutch East
Indies............................. 248, 646
culture experiments, Guam.............. 742
fertilizer experiments............... 215, 343
fertilizer experiments, Guam............ 742
Pepsin—
as a substitute for rennet, Can.......... 576
use in cheese making.......... 175, 373, 778, 875
Peptone anaphylatoxin, studies.......... 581
Peranabrus scabricollis, notes, Wash........ 54
Perchlorates, determination in Chile saltpeter. 111
Percrystallization, notes................. 409
Peridermium—
ribicola, description.................... 354
spp., alternate forms............... 844, 845
strobi in Canada....................... 558
strobi on Swiss pine................... 253
Perilampus hyalinus, leaf oviposition....... 162
Perisierola—
emigrata n. sp., description............. 569
emigrata, parasitic on pink bollworm..... 667
nigrifemur, notes.... 569
Permeability—
of plant tissue, determination.......... 128
studies, tissue tension method.......... 326
Perodipus ordii luteolus n. subsp., description. 757
Peromyscus eremicus papagensis n. subsp., de-
scription............................. 757
Peronospora—
effusa, notes.......................... 550
maydis, studies........................ 552
schleideni, notes....................... 553
Peroxidase, action on chlorophyll.......... 203
Persimmons—
acid content.......................... 714
Japanese, anthracnose of................ 656
Perstillation, notes..................... 409
Peruvian bark, methods of analysis........ 113
Pervaporation, notes................... 409
Pestalozzia palmarum, notes.......... 252, 253, 452
Petroleum fuels, carburetion............. 188
Pezizella ombrophilacea n. sp., notes......... 148
Phacidiella discolor, notes.............. 246
Phacidium infestans, notes.............. 458
Phalonia spartinana, life history.......... 358
Phaonia spp., studies.................. 764
Phorbitis hederacea, fasciation in........... 434
Phaseolus—
aconitifolius, culture experiments, Hawaii 131
mungo for classroom work in genetics.... 831
semierectus as a green manure, Hawaii... 320
Phenol, absorption by barley seeds.......... 25

Page.

Phenological observations in British Isles... 717
Phenolsulphonphthalein, electrical conductivity.. 409
Phenylhydrazids of acids of sugar group.... 201
Philippine College of Agriculture, notes...... 100
Phlebotomus—
   papataci, notes.......................... 460
   verrucarum, transmission of verruga by. 358, 460
Phlegethontius quinque-maculatus. (*See* Tobacco worm.)
Phleospora ptelex n.sp., description.......... 748
Phlxotribus porteri, notes.................... 460
Phlorizin, action on milk secretion........... 272
Phlyctxnia ferrugalis, notes, Conn.State...... 255
Phoma—
   arbuti n.sp., description................. 557
   betx, nitrogen fixation by................ 129
   bumelix n.form, description.............. 748
   citricarpa, treatment.................... 352
   mali, notes............................. 842
   pectinata n.sp., description............. 748
   tabifica, notes.......................... 249
Phomopsis—
   citri, relation to citrus gummosis, Fla.... 656
   palmicola arecx n.var., notes............. 148
Phomotospora migrans n.sp., notes........... 148
Phoradendron sp., notes..................... 453
Phosphate—
   industry in United States................ 217
   precipitated, fertilizing value............ 323
   rock, dissolved. (*See* Superphosphate.)
   rock, fertilizing value, Ind............... 214
   rock, fertilizing value, Minn............. 228
   rock, fertilizing value, Ohio............. 831
   rock, fertilizing value and use........... 723
   rock, mixing with superphosphate....... 816
   rock, production in 1916................. 816
   Thomas, fertilizing value................ 521
Phosphates—
   comparison......................... 23, 521
   comparison, Ohio....................... 831
   comparison, R.I......................... 816
   effect on sulfofying power of soils, Iowa.. 119
   fertilizing value..................... 124, 229
   mineral, solubility.................. 124, 323, 324
   production in 1915-16................... 523
   residual effects......................... 23
   use in Minnesota, Minn................. 217
   (*See also* Superphosphate.)
Phosphatic slag—
   analyses................................ 323
   as a soil neutralizer, R.I................ 815
   availability, determination, R.I......... 816
   fertilizing value...................... 534, 723
   fertilizing value, Ga.................... 29
   fertilizing value, Md.................... 540
   fertilizing value, R.I.................... 815
   mixing with superphosphate............ 816
   residual effects......................... 23
   solubility............................ 323, 723
   use.................................... 723
   use on peat soils........................ 135
Phosphoric acid—
   determination.................. 412, 615, 802
   determination in foodstuffs.............. 618
   effect on decomposition of sugar in soils. 628

Phosphoric acid—Continued.   Page.
   fixation in soils......................... 423
   in humus of soils........................ 121
   loss in industrial wastes...:............ 630
   removal by corn crop, Conn.State........ 232
   solubility in soils........................ 18
Phosphorites, fertilizing value............... 323
Phosphorus—
   compounds of cottonseed meal, Ark...... 502
   effect on alfalfa and other legumes....... 828
   in blood of lactating cows................ 308
   in granitic soils......................... 522
   inorganic, in milk....................... 208
   requirements of barley and oats, R.I..... 34
Photosynthesis, studies...................... 524
Phragmidium—
   rosx-sempervirentis n.sp., description..... 557
   subcorticium, notes..................... 550
Phycitinæ, new, of North America.......... 564
Phyllachora—
   graminis, notes......................... 839
   huberi, notes........................... 253
   texana n.sp., description................ 748
Phyllactinia suffulta, symbiosis with filbert
   leaves.................................. 327
Phyllocoptes schlechtendali, notes........... 570
Phyllophora membranifolia, analyses, Conn.
   State.................................. 814
Phyllosticta—
   bacillaris n.sp., description............. 550
   bacteroides minima n.var., description.... 550
   caryx, treatment....................... 756
   cucurbitacearum, notes................. 550
   euchlxnx n.sp., notes................... 148
   glumarum n.sp., notes.................. 148
   insularum n.sp., notes.................. 148
   italica n.sp., description................ 550
   n.spp., descriptions...................... 748
   solitaria, studies, U.S.D.A.............. 654
   sp. on rubber............................ 253
   sp. on sugar cane........................ 553
Phyllotreta vittula, notes................... 765
Phyllozera caryxcaulis, notes, Conn.State..... 255
Physalospora—
   affinis n.sp., notes...................... 148
   guignardioides n.sp., notes.............. 148
   theobromx n.sp., description............ 755
Physiology, chemical, treatise................ 501
Physokermes picex, studies.................. 662
Phytic acid of wheat kernel.................. 108
Phytomyza aquilegix, notes................. 255
Phytonomus nigrirostris, notes, Mont......... 255
Phytophthora—
   cactorum, notes......................... 550
   colocasix, notes......................... 148
   erythroseptica, notes.................... 350
   faberi, notes................... 148, 349, 452, 458
   infestans. (*See* Potato late blight.)
   nicotianx, studies....................... 553
   parasitica, strain of on *Vinca rosx*........ 844
   sp. on rubber............................ 757
Pig—
   diseases, handbook...................... 778
   diseases, notes.......................... 876
   houses, construction, Iowa.............. 90
   houses, municipal, description........... 388
   manure, storage experiments, Me........ 628

Pigeon peas— Page.
  culture experiments...................... 734
  culture experiments, Guam.............. 729
  green manuring experiments.............. 734
  varieties................................. 825
Pigeons—
  egg-laying cycles.......................... 869
  sex control in.................,.......... 808
Pigments, plant, formation................ 632
Pigs—
  blood and body temperature as affected
    by exercise and sun's heat, U.S.D.A.. 381
  blood, morphology, U.S.D.A.......... 380, 381
  cost of raising, N.C...................... 680
  crude oil for............................ 882
  digestion experiments, Ark.............. 678
  digestion experiments, Ill................ 677
  fall, raising, Minn...................... 270
  feeding experiments...................... 865
  feeding experiments, Guam............... 768
  feeding experiments, Idaho.............. 67
  feeding experiments, Minn......... 268, 269, 270
  feeding experiments, N.C............... 679
  feeding experiments, N.Mex............. 68
  feeding experiments, Nebr.............. 678
  feeding experiments, Tex................ 367
  feeding experiments, Wash............. 69
  grazing experiments, Idaho............. 66, 68
  grazing on irrigated lands, Nebr......... 678
  hairlessness in.......................... 278
  improvement, Guam.................... 768
  improvement, value of good sires........ 866
  judging................................. 94
  marketing in the South, U.S.D.A........ 391
  nutritive requirements.................. 264
  œstrus and ovulation in................. 867
  partial thyroidectomy in................. 278
  raising in Maine, Me.................... 680
  rotation of crops for, La................. 572
  self-feeders for, Mo................... 69, 90
  suckling, immunity to hog cholera....... 881
  treatise................................ 769
  worms infesting, Guam.................. 779
Pine—
  Arizona yellow, growth and density of
    stand................................. 837
  blister rust, control in Massachusetts.... 646
  blister rust, control in New York........ 846
  blister rust in Canada.................... 558
  blister rust in Maine.................... 244
  blister rust in Ontario.................. 155
  blister rust law in New Hampshire..... 547
  blister rust, notes....... 253, 458, 658, 757
  blister rust, overwintering........ 658, 845, 846
  lodgepole, seed behavior................ 244
  needle cast, notes....................... 458
  pitch, characteristics and distribution.... 837
  sawfly, European, in North America.... 568
  seedling disease, notes.................. 458
  tip moth, notes, Conn.State.............. 255
  trees of Rocky Mountain region, U.S.D.A 346
  western yellow, mill tally................ 451
  western yellow, tests, U.S.D.A.......... 89
  white, growth of seedlings............... 837
  yellow, durability....................... 727
Pineapple—
  Kauai wilt, investigations, Hawaii...... 155
  seedlings, growing, Hawaii.............. 142

Pineapple—Continued. Page.
  seeds, germination, Hawaii.............. 142
  weevil, new, in Jamaica.............. 161, 162
  wilt, studies, Fla........................ 652
  wilt, treatment.......................... 550
  yellows, notes, Hawaii................... 155
Pineapples—
  green manure experiments, Hawaii...... 144
  improvement, Hawaii.................... 142
Pinipestis zimmermani, notes, Conn.State.... 255
Pinus tæda belt of Atlantic coastal plain..... 435
Pionnotes capillacea n.sp., notes.............. 148
Piophilidæ, synopsis, Wash.................. 665
Pipes—
  corrugated metal, tests.................... 288
  wood-stave, specifications............... 487
Pipette, automatic suction attachment...... 503
Piricularia oryzæ, notes.................... 838
Piroplasma bigeminum and P. divergens, cross-
  immunization tests...................... 687
Piroplasmosis—
  in Barbados............................. 483
  in Russian Turkestan.................... 374
  status and control....................... 480
  transmission to pigs by ingestion........ 691
Pistachio—
  biology and culture...................... 746
  culture in Crimea....................... 145
  leaf spot, notes......................... 551
Pittosporum tobira variegatum, bud variation. 546
Pituitary extract, effect on milk production.. 272
Placenta, chemical composition.............. 109
Plagiodera versicolora, notes.................. 359
Plague—
  human, vaccine for...................... 378
  transmission among marmots.......... 180, 878
Plant—
  ashes as a source of potash.............. 427
  breeding experiments in Italy........... 827
    (See also Apples, Wheat, etc.)
  cells, acidity........................... 430
  cells, permeability 128, 326, 431, 632
  diseases—
    and pests in German colonies........ 148
    common and scientific names........ 838
    control by seed selection............. 141
    in British East Africa................ 453
    in British Guiana.................... 853
    in Dutch East Indies................. 246
    in Florida, Fla...................... 651
    in Kharkov and vicinity............. 243
    in Mauritius......................... 550
    in New Jersey....................... 652
    in Philippines...................... 148
    in Porto Rico....................... 243
    in Province of Buenos Aires......... 349
    in St. Vincent...................... 652
    in Switzerland.................... 47, 243
    in United States.................... 500
    in West Indies...................... 452
    treatment...................... 247, 453
    treatment, Ohio.................... 143
    treatment, Oreg.................... 51
    treatment, Tenn.................... 544
      (See also different host plants.)
  food, removal by corn crop, Conn.State.. 232
  growth, measurement.................... 223
  growth, relation to climate.............. 15

Plant—Continued.　　　　　　　Page.

inspection. (*See* Nursery inspection.)

introduction gardens, U.S.D.A 542

juices, oxidase activity of 9

lice, effect on pear roots, U.S.D.A 661

lice, notes 460

　　(*See also* Apple aphids, *etc.*)

monstrosities in Buitenzorg 47

parasites, effect on hosts 549

parasitism, physiology 47, 245

pectins, studies 309

peroxidases, mode of action 726

physiology, elementary, experiments 395

physiology for horticulturists, treatise ... 220

products, analyses 114

products, chemistry of, treatise 801

propagation and breeding, textbook 795

protoplasm, acidity 726

succession, monograph 434

succession, notes 526

succession, relation to soil moisture 418, 725

tissues, freezing-point lowering 221

tissues, permeability 128, 326, 431, 632

Plantago psyllium in South Australia 542

Plantain—

bacterial disease, notes 838

ripe rot, treatment 154

Plants—

adaptation 431, 725

anthocyanin pigments 633

as affected by acids 224

as affected by asphyxiating gas 153, 253

as affected by illuminating gas 726, 727

assimilatory apparatus 222

carbohydrate economy 524

copper content 432

correlation between homologous parts ... 630

desert, transpiration in 129

economic, at Horticultural Gardens,

　Lucknow 646

fasciated, development 434

flavone derivatives in 430

growth as affected by organic substances. 632

growth inhibition 324, 632

house, treatise 346

imports, U.S.D.A 819

insect-catching, in southern Georgia 560

leaf injury in relation to cold 224

marine, tolerance to fresh water 431

medicinal, culture and drying 145

monocotyledonous, embryology 127

new or noteworthy, tests 143

nonlegume, symbiosis with nodule bac.

　teria, Ill 819

ornamental, bud variation 546

ornamental, culture experiments, Minn.. 241

ornamental, tests, S.Dak 142

ornamental, treatise 145, 746

oxidase activity 326, 429, 430

poisonous to live stock in Great Britain.. 688

root cuttings, chimeras, and sports 434

seashore, as affected by water supply 27

self-sterile, behavior in intercrosses 820

smoke injury to 130

susceptibility to diseases and pests 245

transpiration in 429

transpiring power, determination 26

transplanting lath for 836

Plants—Continued.　　　　　　Page.

utilization of calcium 631

variation, non-Mendelian 725

watering experiments 325

woodland, emergence of aerial organs 525

woody, anatomy 821

woody, cambial activity 127

woody, pocket guide 746

Plasmodiophora brassicæ. (*See* Cabbage club-

root.)

Plasmopara viticola—

germination of winter spores 252

notes 550

Plaster, land. (*See* Gypsum.)

Plowing experiments, Minn 227

Plowrightia ribesia, notes 251

Plows—

motor, tests 591

specifications 886

Plum—

aphis, cat-tail as a summer host 461

aphis, reddish-brown, notes 562

black knot, notes 555

brown rot, notes 457

curculio, remedies, Ohio 262

dieback, notes 246

leaf spot, studies 755

seed oil, composition 410

Plums—

acid content 714

analyses 42

breeding experiments 833

culture in Europe 42

culture in Maryland, Md 648

culture in Mesa County, Colo 241

dust *v.* liquid spraying 832

planting at different ages 647

pruning and training, W.Va 344

pruning experiments, Minn 240

spraying, N.J 744

sterility, Minn 240

varieties, Mont 241

varieties, S.Dak 143

varieties for Ohio, Ohio 241

wild, recipes, Ala.Tuskegee 364

Plutella maculipennis. (*See* Diamond-back

moth.)

Pneumonia—

action of digitalis in 375

contagious, in donkeys 692

enzootic, in young pigs 477

studies 274

Poa fertilis, pollination experiments 735

Podagrion mantidiphagum n.sp., description. 467

Pœcilanthrax, notes 565

Poisons, effect on germ cells of fowls, Me.. 370

Poles—

industry in Canada 245

preservation 651

Polistes metricus, life history and habits 855

Pollenia rudis, studies, N.J 665

Polychrosis viteana. (*See* Grape berry moth.)

Polydrusus impressifrons, studies, N.Y.State. 359

Polyides rotundus, analyses, Conn.State 814

Polynema reduvioli n.sp., description 856

Polyporus—

lignosus, notes 349

vaporarius, notes 253

Page.

Pomegranate, acid content.................. 715
Pomelos. (*See* Grapefruit.)
Pomology, valuable unpublished work on... 41
Poplar borer, studies, N.Y.Cornell.......... 464
Poria hypolaterita, studies.................... 458
Pork as affected by peanuts, Tex............ 367
Porthetria dispar. (*See* Gipsy moth.)
Porto Rico—
    Federal Station, notes.................... 300
    Insular Station, notes.................... 98
    Insular Station, report.................... 298
Pot culture work, equipment for, N.Y.State. 521
Potash—
    as a cement mill by-product............. 817
    availability in feldspar.................. 522
    availability in New Jersey soils, N.J.... 629
    determination.......................... 504, 712
    extraction from muscovite............... 505
    extraction from silicate rocks............ 427
    fertilizers, comparison.................. 135
    fertilizing value........................ 521
    fertilizing value, Me.................... 636
    from artificial zeolite.................... 322
    from beet sugarhouse waste liquors...... 817
    from biotite and similar silicates........ 321
    from cement materials................... 218
    from incinerator ash.................... 722
    from Nebraska lakes.................... 322
    from wood and plant ashes.............. 427
    industry in America, development....... 818
    loss in industrial wastes................. 630
    removal by corn crop, Conn.State....... 232
    resources and use in New Zealand. 218, 629, 817
    resources of Australia.................. 322
    resources of United States, U.S.D.A..... 522
    salts, analyses and tests................. 322
    salts, production in 1915–16......:........ 523
Potassium—
    aluminum sulphate, fertilizing value..... 527
    chlorid, effect on composition of cereals.. 827
    cyanid, effect on permeability.......... 326
    determination........................... 110
    nitrate, effect on alcoholic fermentation
        by *Sterigmatocystis nigra*............... 223
    permanganate, action with plant peroxi-
        dases.................................. 726
    permanganate, antiseptic and germicidal
        value.................................. 176
    permanganate as an antidote for poison-
        ous plants............................. 688
    requirement of barley and oats, R.I..... 34
    sulphate, effect on soil acidity.......... 23
    sulphate, fertilizing value............. 229, 527
    sulphate, fertilizing value, Guam........ 729
    sulphate, fertilizing value, Ill............ 449
    sulphate, fertilizing value, La........... 529
    sulphid, effect on soil acidity............ 23
Potato—
    aphid, pink and green, studies, Ohio..... 849
    aphis, notes............................. 761
    Association of America.................. 800
    bacterial diseases in Ontario............. 150
    bacterial diseases, notes, Fla............. 652
    beetle, Colorado, control by parasites.... 760
    beetle, Colorado, notes, Ohio............. 599
    bread, recipes, U.S.D.A.................. 364

Page.

Potato—Continued.
    brown streak and blossom abortion...... 549
    canker, treatment 249
    curly dwarf, studies..................... 841
    diseases in Canada....................... 553
    diseases in Dutch East Indies............ 249
    diseases in Germany...................... 150
    diseases in Ireland....................... 350
    diseases in Switzerland.................. 47
    diseases, notes..................... 551, 652
    diseases, notes, Colo.................... 37
    diseases, notes, Me...................... 538
    diseases, notes, Wash................... 150
    early blight, treatment................. 50
    flea-beetle in Colombia.................. 765
    late blight, notes, Ohio................. 895
    late blight, treatment.............. 551, 749
    leaf roll, studies........................ 249
    malnutrition disease, notes............. 752
    material, oxidase activity............... 9
    mosaic disease, effect on yield.......... 752, 842
    mosaic disease, studies................. 47
    powdery scab in Virginia............... 753
    Rhizoctonia disease, notes............. 753
    Rhizoctonia disease, studies, U.S.D.A. 653, 654
    rot, investigations...................... 654
    scab, notes............................. 551
    silage, preparation..................... 800
    starch, farm manufacture............... 800
    tipburn and early blight, treatment,
        Iowa................................ 753
    tubers, frost necrosis................... 842
    Verticillium disease, studies............ 49
    wart disease, notes..................... 753
Potatoes—
    breeding experiments.................... 827
    bushel weights.......................... 889
    cost of production, W.Va............... 191
    culture experiments............... 135, 436, 825
    culture experiments, Idaho............. 30, 37
    culture experiments, Minn............. 228
    culture experiments, N.Mex........... 32
    culture experiments, Ohio............. 338
    culture in Argentina................... 823
    culture in California, Cal.............. 139
    culture in Colorado, Colo............. 37
    culture in Nevada, Nev................ 442
    culture in northern an western States,
        Me.................................. 538
    culture in southwestern Russia......... 338
    culture in Washington, Wash.......... 139
    culture in Wisconsin, Wis............. 442
    culture under glass.................... 643
    culture under irrigation............... 830
    dietary value.......................... 800
    drying.............................. 491, 800
    effect on soil bacteria, U.S.D.A....... 421
    feeding value......................... 800
    fertilizer experiments...... 215, 436, 521, 533, 739
    fertilizer experiments, Me............. 635
    fertilizer experiments, Minn........... 228
    fertilizer experiments, Ohio........... 337
    fertilizer experiments, Va.Truck....... 138
    for late planting, Nev................. 436
    frozen and decayed, utilization......... 806
    immature, for seed..................... 337

Potatoes—Continued. | Page.
importance of clean seed, Wash.......... 96
insects affecting, Wash.................. 157
irrigation experiments, Idaho........... 37
irrigation experiments, Nev............. 30
irrigation experiments, Oreg............ 84
irrigation experiments, U.S.D.A........ 822
irrigation experiments, Utah........... 740
liming experiments...................... 733
planting dates.......................... 732
planting dates, U.S.D.A................. 317
planting experiments.................... 538
potash hunger........................... 800
seed, improvement....................... 823
seed, production..................... 753, 800
selection experiments, Minn......... 228, 240
selection experiments, Nev.............. 32
spraying, Me............................ 538
spraying experiments, Minn.............. 228
subsoiling experiments.................. 732
treatise..................... 533, 543, 645
varieties.............. 135, 138, 436, 825
varieties, Hawaii....................... 131
varieties, Idaho........................ 30
varieties, Md........................... 645
varieties, Minn......................... 227
varieties, N.Mex........................ 329
varieties, Nev....................... 32, 435
varieties, Ohio......................... 333
varieties, Oreg......................... 531
varieties, Wash......................... 41
varieties for Michigan.................. 538
yield as affected by removal of tops...... 138
Poultry—
accounts, Wash.......................... 699
breeding contest, N.J................... 71
breeding experiments, Guam............. 768
diseases, handbook...................... 778
diseases, notes..................... 693, 876
diseases, post-mortem examinations, N.J. 82
experiments, N.C........................ 681
farms, management....................... 872
feeding, Tenn........................... 471
feeding, Wash........................... 699
feeding, textbook....................... 94
feeds, Texas-raised, Tex................ 871
finishing for market, N.J.............. 872
houses and equipment, Tex.............. 887
houses, construction................ 389, 491
houses, construction, Can.............. 696
houses, construction, Minn............. 289
husbandry, collegiate instruction....... 495
husbandry instruction in secondary
　schools............................... 294
husbandry, laboratory instruction....... 295
husbandry work in New Jersey, N.J.... 71
improvement by selection, N.J.......... 871
industry in Connecticut................. 872
inheritance in, Mo...................... 772
inheritance of spangling in............. 771
management on the farm, Kans......... 168
manure production, N.C................. 682
marketing, Can.......................... 682
mites and lice, notes, U.S.D.A......... 357
plant, description, Wash............... 895
preparation for exhibition, N.J........ 71

Poultry—Continued. | Page.
products, marketing..................... 391
rations, balancing, Idaho.............. 271
standards, relation to utility.......... 775
treatise........................... 763, 775
war-time rations, N.J.................. 573
　(See also Chickens, Hens, Turkeys, etc.)
Powdery mildews, relation to hosts, Mo..... 749
Prairie hay, digestibility and productive
　value, Tex........................... 865
Praon, construction of cocoon.......... 856
Precipitates, washing device for.......... 508
Precipitation—
　charts, preparation, U.S.D.A.......... 107
　effect on insects..................... 355
　effect on yield of alfalfa............ 717
　observations, working up, U.S.D.A..... 513
　(See also Rainfall, Snowfall, etc.)
Precipitin reactions, equilibrium in.......... 877
Pregnancy, diagnosis.................... 478
Preservatives, detection in milk........ 113
Preserving, sirups for................. 15
Primrose, evening, rusts of............ 552
Prionomerus calceatus, notes........... 560
Privies, sanitary, description........... 287
Prociphilus—
　approximatus n.sp., description......... 850
　fitchii and P. pyri, synonymy, U.S.D.A.. 661
Prodecatoma sp., description.............. 59
Proso bread, digestibility, U.S.D.A.......... 364
Proteid. (See Protein.)
Protein—
　blood, studies........................ 375
　cleavage products. (See Amino acids.)
　copper compounds...................... 8
　digestibility, determination, U.S.D.A... 673
　digestion, inhibition by adsorbed tin... 470
　foods, selection, U.S.D.A............. 864
　from different sources, comparison...... 864
　intake, effect on creatin excretion....... 469
　of peanuts.................... 8, 468, 501
　of Swede turnips, composition and
　　methods of analysis................. 410
　specific dynamic action............... 266
　substances, synthesis................. 108
　tissue, cleavage by blood serum of other
　　animal species...................... 478
Proteolytic enzyms—
　of blood, origin...................... 478
　of plants, inhibitors for............. 204
Proteose intoxications and injury of body
　protein.............................. 167
Proteus alveicola n.sp., description.......... 360
Protoplasm—
　and gelatin, similarity in behavior....... 431
　physical properties, interpretation....... 325
Protozoa, toxic action of copper compounds
　of amino acids on..................... 375
Protozoan infections of intestinal tract, goblet
　cells in............................. 280
Prune orchards, renovation, Wash.......... 41
Prunes—
　drying............................... 114
　drying, Wash......................... 715
　fertilizer experiments, Wash.......... 41
　frost injury, Utah................... 344

Pruning— Page.
effect on fruit bud formation............. 646
investigations, methods................... 239
notes, W.Va............................. 344
problems in Hood River Valley, Oreg... 41
treatise......................... 41,242,344
Prunus—
crown gall resistance in................... 655
new canker disease of.................... 251
Prussic acid. (See Hydrocyanic acid.)
Pseudococcus citri. (See Citrus mealy bug.)
Pseudoglobulin, transformation into globulin,
U.S.D.A.................................. 77
Pseudomonas—
campestris, notes........................ 550
citri, eradication, U.S.D.A............... 556
citri, inoculation experiments............ 843
citri, notes........................... 556,657
citri, studies, Fla....................... 656
fluorescens in soils, N.Y.State............ 516
phaseoli, notes.......................... 550
phaseoli, treatment, Colo................. 248
sp. on soy beans........................ 842
spp. on vegetables in Ontario............ 150
Pseudopeziza tracheiphila, notes............ 246,555
Pseudotachinomyia webberi n.g. and n.sp.,
description.............................. 763
Pseudotuberculosis—
in guinea pigs........................... 377
in horses................................ 378
in swine................................ 82
Psylla mali, studies....................... 761
Pteris aquilina injurious to horses.......... 182
Pteroptrix australis n.sp., description........ 460
Pterygogramma acuminata n.g. and n.sp.,
description.............................. 855
Puccinia—
chondrillæ, notes........................ 550
coronifera, studies, Mo.................. 749
glumarum, notes......................... 550
graminis, infection through wheat seed.. 751
graminis, new strain..................... 749
maydis, notes............................ 452
menthæ, notes........................... 457
oryzæ, notes............................ 50
pruni-spinosæ, notes.................... 550
purpurea, notes.......................... 452
rubigo-vera, specialization............... 149
spp. in British East Africa............... 453
spp. on Onagraceæ...................... 552
triticina, notes, Mo...................... 749
Pulpwood—
industry in Canada..................... 745,748
of Brazil................................ 452
purchasing.............................. 452
(See also Wood pulp.)
Pulses, breeding experiments.............. 827
Pulvinaria vitis (= innumerabilis). (See Maple-
scale, cottony.)
Pumping for irrigation, Nebr.............. 384
Pumpkins—
breeding experiments.................... 827
culture experiments, Guam.............. 742
drying.................................. 500
fertilizer experiments, Guam............ 742
Pumps—
centrifugal, manual...................... 585
irrigation, U.S.D.A...................... 585

Pumps—Continued. Page.
irrigation, power for..................... 786
irrigation, tests, Mont.................. 283
motor-driven deep-well, maintenance
costs................................. 585
Punga bark, fiber from.................... 535
Purdue University, notes....... 97,196,497,700,896
Pyralids, new, from British Guiana......... 564
Pyraustinæ, North American, notes........ 564
Pyroderces rileyi, description, U.S.D.A...... 564
Pyrogallol, extraction with ether........... 414
Pyroracemic acid, decomposition by dead
plants................................. 201
Pyrox, fungicidal value, Nebr.............. 447
Pythiacystis sp. on avocado............... 555
Pythium debaryanum, notes................ 148
Pyxinia n.spp., descriptions................ 558
Quack grass, eradication, Minn............ 227
Quince diseases, notes.................... 51
Quinces—
acid content............................ 715
drying.................................. 509
pruning and training, W.Va............. 344
spraying, N.J........................... 741
Quinin, methods of analysis................ 113
Quinone-phenolate theory of indicators..... 409
Rabbit serum, anaphylatoxin produced in... 579
Rabbits—
care and management.................... 775
effect on vegetation..................... 758
Rabies—
control............................. 274,577
immunization....................... 480,690
Radish maggot, screening.................. 261
Radishes—
culture experiments, Guam.............. 742
fertilizer experiments, Guam............ 742
varieties, S.Dak........................ 143
watering, continuous.................... 543
Radium—
in honey............................... 570
therapy, effect on metabolism in lymphatic leukemia...................... 267
Raffinose—
occurrence in jute seed.................. 710
physiological behavior.................. 571
Ragweed pollen, composition.............. 612
Rahar, culture experiments................ 826
Rainbows, papers on, U.S.D.A......... 115,513
Rainfall—
and run-off in Oahu, Hawaii, U.S.D.A.. 513
as affected by cannonading....... 418,512,717
in India............................... 716
in Indo-China.......................... 620
in Java................................ 16
in upper Pecos Valley, New Mexico,
U.S.D.A.............................. 808
May and June, U.S.D.A................. 315
minimum, determination................ 315
relation to chestnut blight.............. 557
(See also Precipitation.)
Rainwater, dissolved oxygen in............ 620
Raisins, drying............................ 114
Ramie, culture............................ 830
Ramularia—
n.spp., descriptions.................... 748
violæ, notes............................ 550

Page.

Range—
  lands, reseeding............................ 437
  plants of Wallowa National Forest,
    U.S.D.A.............................. 818
Ranunculus arvensis, habits and eradication. 542
Rape—
  culture experiments, Hawaii............ 132
  dust, fertilizing value..................... 229
  fertilizer experiments.................. 135,533
  varieties................................. 134,135
Rapeseed cake—
  as a feeding stuff......................... 416
  examination.............................. 416
Raspberries—
  acid content.............................. 715
  breeding experiments, Minn.............. 240
  varieties, Oreg........................... 243
Raspberry—
  diseases, notes............................ 52
  orange rust, studies...................... 457
Rat—
  bite fever, causative agent.............. 375
  serum, anaphylatoxin produced in...... 580
Rations—
  balanced from restricted sources,
    U.S.D.A.............................. 766
  for cows, Ohio............................ 195
  mixed, digestibility, Ill.................. 677
Rats—
  development of ascarid larvæ in......... 374
  new, from North America................ 757
  notes..................................... 156
  nutritive requirements................... 264
  use in study of anaphylaxis........:..... 582
Reclamation Service. (*See* United States
  Geological Survey.)
Red—
  clover. (*See* Clover, red.)
  dog flour. (*See* Flour, red dog.)
  rice, eradication, Tex.................... 532
  spider. (*See* Spider, red.)
Redtop—
  as affected by companion crop of clover.. 438
  notes, Ga................................. 29
Reductase—
  animal and vegetable, nonspecificity.... 309
  of plants................................. 203
Reforestation—
  in National Forests, U.S.D.A............ 348
  in Pennsylvania.......................... 45
  of chestnut cut-over land................ 451
  of cut-over pine land in the South....... 836
  rôle of light in........................... 45
Refractometer, description.................. 110
Remedies, new and nonofficial.............. 876
Rennet—
  homemade, preparation.................. 778
  homemade, preparation, Can............ 576
  substitutes for cheese making............ 273
Reproduction—
  physiology of............................. 772
  physiology of, Me 371
Reproductive tissues, variation in composition...................................... 774
Rescue grass, notes, Ga.................... 29
Reseda lutea, root system.................. 542

Page.

Reservoirs, unlined earth, construction...... 585
Respiration in plants as affected by anes-
  thetics.................................... 821
Rhabdospora bernardiana n.sp., notes........ 630
Rhacodineura antiqua, life history and habits. 160
Rhagoletis—
  pomonella. (*See* Apple maggot.)
  ribicola in California...................... 566
Rheumatism, articular, immunization....... 782
Rhinastus pertusus, notes..................... 359
Rhizoctonia—
  microsclerotia n.sp., notes, Fla............ 652
  solani, new strain on potato, U.S.D.A... 654
  solani, studies......................... 47,350
  sp. in seed beds, Fla...................... 651
Rhizoctonia, strains of...................... 753
Rhizopertha dominica, studies................ 356
Rhizopus nigricans on crated strawberries,
  U.S.D.A.................................. 351
Rhode Island—
  College, notes............................ 99
  Station, notes............................ 300
  Station, publications..................... 96
Rhodes grass—
  for hay and pasture, Fla.................. 644
  hay, digestibility and productive value,
    Tex................................. 865
Rhodoxanthin, mitochondrial origin....... 129
Rhodymenia palmata, analyses, Conn.State... 814
Rhopalosiphum nymphex, notes........... 461,562
Rhopobota vacciniana. (*See* Black-head fireworm.)
Rhynchophora—
  of British India.......................... 765
  studies................................... 58
Rice—
  analyses, Tex............................. 363
  blast, notes.............................. 838
  bran, composition and feeding value, Tex. 363
  bran, digestibility, Ark.................. 678
  breeding experiments..................... 827
  by-products, composition, Tex........... 363
  correlation in............................ 141
  culture experiments.............. 823,824,825
  culture experiments, Hawaii............. 131
  culture experiments, Tex................ 532
  culture in Argentina.................. 823,830
  culture in Guam, Guam.................. 729
  culture in New South Wales.............. 442
  culture in Philippines.................... 538
  diet, effect on pigeons.................... 571
  diseases and pests, notes................. 247
  fertilizer experiments...... 338,539,823,824,825
  fertilizer experiments, Guam............. 729
  fertilizer experiments, La............... 529
  fields as a factor in control of malaria.... 565
  germinability in relation to temperature
    and humidity......................... 736
  ground, digestibility and productive val-
    ue, Tex.............................. 865
  hay, digestibility and productive value,
    Tex................................. 865
  hull carbon, use in sugarhouse work..... 806
  hull content, calculating, Tex........... 363
  hulled, volume weight and grain charac-
    teristics............................. 643

Rice—Continued.   Page.
    hulls for chicks, Guam....................   768
    insects affecting.........................   847
    irrigation, Cal...........................   483
    irrigation experiments....................   883
    milling, Tex..............................   363
    new varieties, descriptions...............   831
    polish, composition and feeding value,
        Tex...................................   363
    polish, digestibility, Ark................   678
    red, eradication, Tex.....................   532
    seed selection...................... 538, 539, 824
    seeding experiments.......................   824
    seeding experiments, Tex..................   532
    straw, digestibility, Tex.................   168
    transplanted, morphology and develop-
        ment..................................   643
    transplanting.................... 538, 824, 825
    upland, culture...........................   539
    varieties......................... 824, 825, 826
    varieties, Guam...........................   729
    varieties, Tex............................   532
    water weevil, remedies, La................   568
    weather injuries to, in Italy.............   50
    weevil, studies...........................   356
    yields, determination.....................   634
Rinderpest—
    immunization..............................   480
    in swine..................................   79
River—
    bed materials, evaporation from,
        U.S.D.A...............................   785
    discharge, handbook.......................   484
    measurement. (See Stream measure-
        ment.)
Road—
    dragging contest in Saskatchewan..........   695
    law in New York...........................   590
    laws in Iowa..............................   386
    laws in Maine.............................   289
    materials, specifications.................   386
    materials, tests.................... 386, 695
    regulations in Ontario....................   489
    system, county, engineering cost.........   386
Roadrunner, food habits.......................   156
Roads—
    administration in Baltimore Co., Mary-
        land..................................   787
    administration in Minnesota...............   590
    administration in North Dakota...........   84
    administration in Oklahoma................   585
    administration in Ontario.................   385
    administration in Wisconsin......... 590, 695
    concrete, cracks in.......................   88
    concrete, expansion and contraction,
        U.S.D.A...............................   884
    concrete, grading fine aggregate for,
        U.S.D.A...............................   787
    concrete mixtures for.....................   490
    construction and maintenance.............   89
    construction, Federal aid............. 89, 188
    construction, gravel for..................   288
    construction in Hawaii....................   384
    construction in National Forests, U.S.
        D.A...................................   547
    construction in the Ozarks................   695
    construction in Wayne Co., Michigan......   385
    construction, treatise....................   590

Roads—Continued.   Page.
    improvement, illustrated lecture, U.S.
        D.A...................................   598
    mileage and revenues, U.S.D.A........ 288, 289
    oiling....................................   490
    relation to rural life....................   89
    traffic census data.......................   188
    yearbook..................................   590
Rock phosphate. (See Phosphate.)
Rocks for roads, U.S.D.A......................   386
Rodents, destruction, U.S.D.A.................   558
Roentgen rays, effect on metabolism in
    lymphatic leukemia........................   267
Rœstelia cancellata, studies..................   250
Root—
    crop seeds in Denmark.....................   742
    crops, culture experiments.......... 732, 733
    crops, treatise...........................   645
    crops, varieties.................... 533, 733
    crops, varieties, Minn...................   228
    formation and geotropic curvature of
        stem..................................   325
    hairs, glandular..........................   222
    knot, treatment, Fla......................   453
    maggot injurious to crops in Louisiana...   854
    maggot, studies, Wash............... 566, 599
    tubercles, formation as affected by ni-
        trogeneous salts......................   133
Roots—
    absorption of nutrients by, U.S.D.A......   222
    anatomical structure in different media..   431
    epidermal cells...........................   128
    forest tree, growth.......................   27
    negative geotropism.......................   325
    relation to oxygen........................   525
    sampling device for.......................   711
    secondary, orientation...................   27
Rosa, imperfection of pollen and mutability   328
Rosa rugosa, tests, S.Dak....................   143
Rose—
    diseases, investigations..................   353
    mildew, notes..................... 453, 539
Rosellinia—
    bunodes, notes............................   652
    pepo, notes...............................   452
    spp. in Lesser Antilles...................   454
    spp. on cacao and rubber..................   349
    spp. on limes and citrus trees...........   452
    spp. on tea roots.........................   52
Roses—
    annual....................................   145
    culture......................... 346, 836
    fertilizer experiments, Ill..............   449
Rosin oil, detection..........................   13
Rotation—
    of crops........................... 230, 823
    of crops, Idaho...........................   30
    of crops, Minn.............. 226, 227, 229
    of crops, Mo..............................   731
    of crops, Oreg............................   532
    of crops, Tex.............................   329
    of crops, Wash............................   33
Roundworms in sheep, U.S.D.A.................   277
Rubber—
    canker, studies...........................   458
    coagulants....................... 348, 416
    culture experiments.......................   144
    diseases, notes.................... 252, 349

Rubber—Continued.   Page.
  from *Eucommia ulmoides*................. 417
  Hevea. (*See* Rubber, Para.)
  industry, treatise........................ 347
  inner qualities, factors affecting.......... 347
  latex, natural coagulation................. 806
  leaf disease, notes......................... 838
  Para, black thread disease............... 757
  Para, cortex nodules...................... 727
  Para, latex vessels in..................... 147
  Para, natural accelerator.................. 512
  Para, oil of.............................. 109
  Para, seed selection....................... 837
  Para, tapping during winter.............. 838
  plantation, of Ceylon..................... 347
  quality in relation to age of trees......... 651
  root disease, notes...................... 458, 839
  soils in Fiji.............................. 838
  stem disease, notes....................... 453
  tapping experiments.................. 117, 347
  tapping experiments, probable error in.. 837
  tapping wounds, cicatrization........... 548
Rubus—
  orange rusts, studies..................... 457
  pollen sterility in........................ 131
***Rumex acetosella*, description and eradication,**
  Ind...................................... 239
Rural—
  attitudes, theory of...................... 491
  conditions in Alabama................... 91
  credit. (*See* Agricultural credit.)
  decline in New England.................. 593
  education associations in Saskatchewan.. 394
  education conference at Worcester, Massa-
    chusetts.............................. 892
  electric service in Wisconsin............. 189
  extension schools in Ireland............. 294
  homes, numbering...................... 889
  leadership, development................. 593
  life and education, progress in........... 393
  market conditions in New York........ 790
  migration, causes....................... 390
  sanitation in the Tropics, treatise....... 86
  sanitation notes.................... 592, 695
  schools. (*See* Schools, rural.)
  sociology, teaching................. 93, 794
  surveys in Iowa......................... 592
  surveys, methods........................ 592
Rusts—
  endophyllum-like, o Porto Rico........ 552
  studies, Mo............................. 749
  (*See also* Corn, Wheat, *etc.*)
Rutabagas. (*See* Swedes.)
Rye—
  and wheat hybrid, heredity in........... 432
  as affected by greenhouse temperature... 533
  bran, analyses, Wis...................... 471
  bread, recipes, U.S.D.A................. 364
  breeding experiments.................... 827
  bush weights........................... 889
  culture, Iowa........................... 733
  culture experiments.................. 433, 823
  culture under dry farming, N.Mex....... 229
  fertilizer experiments................. 436, 823
  grass, branching in heads................ 139
  grass, pollination experiments........... 735
  green manuring experiments, N.J....... 425
  middlings, analyses, Conn.State......... 268

Rye—Continued.   Page.
  middlings, analyses, Wis................. 471
  pedigreed, yields in Wisconsin.......... 438
  Rosen................................. 799
  rust, specialization..................... 149
  seeding experiments..................... 733
  seeding experiments, Minn.............. 226
  shorts, analyses, Wis.................... 471
  thrashing injuries....................... 534
  varieties.................. 135, 436, 438, 823
  varieties, Hawaii....................... 132
  varieties, Idaho......................... 29
  varieties, Ill........................... 641
  varieties, Oreg......................... 530
  varieties, Tex.......................... 330
  variety from mountain regions of Italy.. 539
  volume weight and grain characteristics.. 643
Sablefish, food value....................... 165
Saccharin, determination in food products... 804
***Saccharum spontaneum* for shifting sands....** 333
Safflower, culture for seed................... 230
Sailors, land settlement for................. 190
Salad plants, treatise...................... 645
Salix, hybridization experiments........... 432
Salt—
  fertilizing value, Me.................... 636
  glycosuria, mechanism.................. 64
  River national bird reservation.......... 355
  trough for sheep, description, Tex....... 867
Saltpeter—
  Chile. (*See* Sodium nitrate.)
  origin and extraction in India........... 722
Salts—
  antagonism............................. 431
  reactions of ions and molecules.......... 201
Saltusaphis, synopsis..................... 157
Salvarsan, use in dog distemper............ 584
***Salvia nemorosa*, root system..............** 542
Sampling device for organic materials....... 711
San José scale—
  control in Kansas....................... 357
  notes, Tex.............................. 358
  remedies............................... 54
Sand dunes, devastation by................. 720
Sands—
  grading for road construction, U.S.D.A.. 787
  organic impurities, test for............. 490
  shifting, grasses for..................... 333
***Sanninoidea exitiosa.* (*See* Peach borer.)**
Sap—
  ascent in plants, tension hypothesis...... 128
  of desert plants......................... 630
  of plants in mountain and desert habi-
    tats.................................. 525
***Saperda candida.* (*See* Apple-tree borer,**
  round-headed.)
Saponin from *Yucca filamentosa*............ 9
***Sarcocystis tenella*, infestation of lambs by,**
  Wyo.................................... 374
Sarcophaga and allies in North America.... 160
Sarcophaga—
  caridei, parasitic on locusts.............. 357
  hæmorrhoidalis larvæ in human intes-
    tine.................................. 853
Sarcosporidia, zoological position........... 53
Sarcosporidiosis, bovine, in Portugal....... 81
Sauerkraut, fermentation............ 165, 208, 806
Sausage, determination of added water...... 414

Scale insects—	Page.
and their control	55
new, of Japan	358
of Missouri, Mo	760
Schistocerca peregrina, control in Algeria	461
Schizoneura corni, notes	258
Schizophyllum commune (*S. alneum*), notes	553
Schizura ipo ·²æ in Louisiana	564
Schœnobiinæ, North American, notes	564
School—	
building, community, at Wheaton, Minnesota	793
gardens in Canada	93, 293
gardens in Denmark	793
gardens, notes	95, 395, 598, 795
gardens, planning	295, 296
gardens, textbook	295
inspectors and rural science	892
lunches, preparation	64, 796
rooms, humidification, U.S.D.A	807
Schools—	
agricultural. (*See* Agricultural schools.)	
as community centers	593, 793
elementary, agriculture in	194, 295
high, agriculture in	194, 494
high, conference in Illinois	93
public, agriculture in	192, 494, 893
public, entomology in	459
public, home economics in	494
public, in Alaska	393
rural, conveniences for	696
rural, farm handicraft for, U.S.D.A	699
rural, papers on	892
secondary, agriculture in	392
secondary, agriculture in, U.S.D.A	395
secondary, poultry husbandry in	394
sewage disposal for	884
Sciara tritici injurious to Primula seedlings	762
Sciasma frontalis n.sp., description	763
Sclerostome parasites of horses	280
Sclerostomum bidentatum, studies	82
Sclerotinia—	
fructigena, notes	457
libertiana, investigations	155
libertiana, notes	550, 552, 749
libertiana on collards, Ga	48
sclerotiorum, studies	350
Sclerotium—	
rolfsii, studies	247, 250
rolfsii, studies, U.S.D.A	49
sp. on peanuts	452
Scolecotrichum—	
graminis, hosts of	839
heveæ n.sp., notes	253
Scolescosporium coryli n.sp., description	748
Scolytid beetles of Oregon	666
Screenings, analyses, Wis	471
Sea lettuce, analyses, Conn.State	814
Seasonal correlations in Far East, U.S.D.A	807
Seasons, forecasting	619
Seaweeds, analyses and fertilizing value, Conn.State	814
Sedoheptose, notes	502
Seed beds, preparation, Minn	227
Seedlings, damping-off, Fla	651
Seeds—	
absorption of toxic salts by	527
and leaves, dietary relationship	264

Seeds—Continued.	Page.
disinfection with bromin	542
germination in electrolytes	431
germination tests	26
germination tests, tolerance table, Md	541
imports, U.S.D.A	819
improvement in Canada	141, 831
inspection in Argentina	823
inspection in Denmark	742
inspection in Maine, Me	40
inspection in Maryland, Md	541
inspection in Minnesota, Minn	446
inspection in Montana, Mont	238
inspection in New Jersey, N.J	239, 645
inspection in New Zealand	446
longevity in relation to temperatures	725
loss of viability in storage	725
pedigreed, dissemination	437
prices and movement in 1916	492
selective permeability	25
Self-feeders—	
for pigs, Minn	269, 270
for pigs, Mo	90
Separators. (*See* Cream separators.)	
Sepsidæ, synopsis, Wash	665
Septic tank, description	188, 286
Septicemia, hemorrhagic—	
control in Michigan	274
immunization	83, 179, 379
in United States	274
investigations, Nev	78
notes	477
organisms	583
Septoglœum—	
niisimæ n.sp., description	652
ochroleucum n.comb., description	748
Septoria—	
acanthi romana n.var., description	550
ampelina, notes	52
cucurbitæ n.sp., description	550
lycopersici, host limitations	842
n.spp., descriptions	748, 749
ochroleuca, notes	748
perilæ, notes	652
petasitidis n.sp., description	652
petroselina apii, wintering	840
piricola, notes	550
sp., notes	551
spp. on Ribes, life histories	551
spp. on wheat in Australia	149
Sericulture. (*See* Silk.)	
Seriocothrips n.sp., description	258, 849
Serradella as a cover crop for orchards	833
Serum—	
antitoxic, concentration	877
inhibitory action on bacteria staining	478
reactions, mechanism	477
treating with pararabin	376
Sesame—	
cake, sugar content	208
oil, detection	13
Sesbania—	
aculeata as a green manure for rice	824
ægyptiaca as a green manure, Hawaii	320
Sewage—	
aeration	87
disposal for rural schools	696, 884
disposal for village and rural homes	286

Page.

Sewage—Continued.
disposal in institutions.................... 385
disposal on farms, U.S.D.A.............. 589
disposal, relation to pellagra............. 694
filters, notes............................ 488, 489
from packing houses, treatment......... 694
irrigation, notes.......................... 185
methods of examination................. 311
purification............... 286, 483, 694, 787, 789
sludge, utilization....................... 425
Sex determination in birds................. 772, 868
Shallu—
analyses................................. 539
description and culture, U S.D.A....... 740
stover, digestibility and productive value,
Tex.................................... 865
varieties, Cal............................ 338
Shea butter, analyses....................... 14
Sheep—
anaphylactic shock due to ox-warble
extract................................ 379
breeding experiments................. 99, 770
breeding experiments, Idaho............ 66
breeding experiments, N.C.............. 676
breeding experiments, Tex.............. 866
digestion experiments, Tex.............. 168
diseases, handbook...................... 778
diseases, notes......................... 374, 876
farming in British Isles, treatise......... 770
feeding experiments, Idaho.............. 67
feeding experiments, Ind................ 270
feeding experiments, N.C............... 676
feeding experiments, Tex............... 866
improvement, value of good sires........ 866
judging.................................. 94
maggot flies, notes...................... 160
management on farms, Idaho............ 676
manure, storage experiments, Me....... 628
marketing in the South, U.S.D.A....... 391
poisoning by western goldenrod......... 482
raising, equipment for, U.S.D.A........ 388
raising in Argentina..................... 770
raising in Maine, Me.................... 676
selection on basis of family performance,
U.S.D.A.............................. 676
shearing sheds, description, U.S.D.A.... 572
tick, eradication, U.S.D.A............... 357
tick, viability........................... 764
warm water for, Minn................... 268
Shelter belts, notes......................... 837
Shingles—
industry in Canada...................... 245
production in 1915, U.S.D.A............ 148
Shipping fever in horses.................... 182
Shiromoji seed, oil of...................... 109
Shrew, new, from Nova Scotia.............. 753
Shrimp—
analyses and use, U.S.D.A.............. 863
preparation and shipping, U.S.D.A...... 863
waste as a fertilizer, U.S.D.A........... 863
Shrubs—
culture experiments, Minn.............. 241
for eastern Colorado.................... 837
for northern Minnesota, Minn.......... 241
of eastern United States................. 746
ornamental, of Hawaii.................. 546
ornamental, treatise.................... 44

Page.

Sialia n.sp., description.................... 846
Signiphora merceti n.sp., description......... 360
Silage—
and cottonseed meal, associative digestibility, Ga........................... 65
crops, varieties........................ 533
digestibility and productive value, Tex.. 865
effect on melting point of milk fat, Mo... 74
fermentation, heat in, U.S.D.A.......... 612
for dairy cows, N. C................... 682
for dairy cows, Wash.................. 75
forage poisoning due to................. 689
mannite in.............................. 801
measuring, Nebr....................... 887
microorganisms in, Mo.................. 728
palatability, Kans...................... 671
Silicate rocks, extraction of potash from.... 427
Silicic acid, determination in soils.......... 505
Silk production in 1915.................... 463
Silkworm—
development of silk glands.............. 158
genetic studies......................... 158
life history and rearing................. 598
pebrine, studies........................ 361
Silo fillers, specifications.................. 886
Silos—
capacity, Nebr......................... 887
construction................... 591, 696, 789
pit, construction, U.S.D.A.............. 789
pit, semipit, and bank, construction..... 388
wooden-hoop, construction, Wash....... 491
Silpha bituberosa, studies.................. 261
Silt determinations in Colorado River....... 486
Silviculture—
in Canada.............................. 45
in India................................ 547
in southern Appalachians.............. 45
Simulidae of northern Chile................ 460
Sires, value in improvement of herds........ 866
Sirup—
for canning and preserving.............. 15
sources and composition................ 715
Sisal—
culture experiments.................... 734
disease, notes......................... 453
Sitones hispidulus in California.............. 568
Sitotroga cerealella. (See Grain-moth, Angoumois.)
Skim milk—
as a food, U.S.D.A..................... 669
cheese from............................ 576
digestibility, U.S.D.A.................. 673
Skins, subcutaneous matter of, as a cattlefeed 171
Slag. (See Phosphatic slag.)
Slaughterhouses, municipal, construction and
operation.............................. 91
Smelter wastes, effect on barley.............. 526
Smoke—
and daylight intensities, U.S.D.A........ 807
cloud and high haze of 1916, U.S.D.A.... 115
injury in Selby smelter zone............. 634
injury to agriculture and forestry in
Austria............................. 528
pollution, plants as an index............ 301
Smokehouse for fish, construction........... 716
Snakeroot, white—
as a cause of trembles, U.S.D.A.......... 583
toxicity, Ohio.......................... 519

Snowfall— Page.
in New England........................... 16
in New England, U.S.D.A............... 807
relation to water supply, Nev........... 16
Society for Promotion of Agricultural Science.................................. 601, 899
Sodium—
carbonate, effect on blood sugar content.. 64
carbonate, effect on solubility of iron phosphate............................. 324
chlorid. (See Salt.)
nitrate as a top-dressing for grains, Ga.... 29
nitrate as a top-dressing for wheat, Ohio.. 238
nitrate, effect on composition of cereals.. 827
nitrate, effect on nodule formation...... 133
nitrate, effect on soil acidity............. 23
nitrate, effect on wheat.................. 799
nitrate, fertilizing value................ 123
229, 426, 521, 539, 733
nitrate, fertilizing value, Guam.......... 729
nitrate, fertilizing value, Md............. 540
nitrate, fertilizing value, Me............. 635
nitrate, fertilizing value, Pa............. 627
nitrate for alfalfa, Oreg................. 34
nitrate for apples, Oreg.................. 42
nitrate, production in 1915-16............ 723
nitrate, use on peat soils............. 134, 135
salicylate as a fly poison................. 53
salts, antiseptic and germicidal value..... 176
Soil—
acidity as affected by ammonium sulphate 815
acidity as affected by organic matter, Mo. 718
acidity, cause.......................... 623, 624
acidity, effect on availability of ammonium sulphate....................... 521
acidity, effect on grasses, R.I............. 446
acidity, neutralizing with basic slag, R.I.. 815
acidity, studies......................... 118
acidity, studies, Iowa.................... 24
amendments, effect on soil acidity....... 23
bacteria as affected by acids and alkalis... 213
bacteria as affected by humus-forming materials, Iowa........................ 120
bacteria, influence of crops, season, and water on, U.S.D.A.................... 421
bacteria, influence of stable manure on, Ga.................................... 23
bacteria, nitrogen-cycle, as affected by auximones............................. 517
bacteria, nitrogen-fixing, in Iowa soils.... 517
bacteria, notes, Ohio.................... 298
bacteria, oxygen requirements........... 221
bacteria, relation to irrigation, Oreg...... 86
bacteria, studies........................ 19
bacteria, studies, N.Y. State.......... 516, 517
colloids, studies........................ 520
constituents, inhibition of plant toxins by 519
containers, effect of paraffin lining, U.S.D.A............................. 812
depletion, relation to nitrate reduction in plants............................. 549
erosion, prevention...................... 286
erosion, prevention, U.S.D.A........... 87, 520
fatigue, treatment....................... 421
fertility, investigations, Ind............. 214
fertility, maintenance.............. 514, 720, 813
fertility, notes, Ill...................... 214

Soil—Continued. Page.
fertility, notes, Iowa.................... 211
fertility, relation to humus............... 718
fertility, rôle of nitrification in........... 519
fertility, studies, N.C.................... 625
flora, studies, N.Y.State.............. 516, 517
microorganisms, ammonia accumulation 812
moisture and plant succession........... 418
moisture, conservation................. 212, 437
moisture, effect on wheat, Utah........ 340
moisture in forests and cultivated fields... 418
moisture, movement and distribution, U.S.D.A........................... 623, 808
plats, biological variations in........... 719
protozoa, review of investigations....... 213
sampler, description and use............ 811
solution, concentration and composition.. 116
solution, concentration as affected by sterilization......................... 719
solution obtained by oil pressure method.. 717
temperature, surface, measurement....... 520
Soil survey in—
Alabama, Barbour Co., U.S.D.A........ 621
California, Healdsburg area, U.S.D.A.... 810
Delaware, New Castle Co., U.S.D.A.... 211
Georgia, Habersham Co................ 211
Idaho, Latah Co., U.S.D.A............. 21
Illinois, Du Page Co., Ill................ 720
Illinois, Edgar Co., Ill................. 514
Indiana, Wells Co., U.S.D.A............ 21
Indiana, White Co..................... 21
Iowa, Bremer Co....................... 211
Iowa, Clinton Co., U.S.D.A............ 714
Iowa, Van Buren Co., U.S.D.A......... 21
Kansas, Cowley Co., U.S.D.A.......... 419
Maine, Cumberland Co., U.S.D.A...... 810
Mississippi, Chickasaw Co., U.S.D.A.... 621
Missouri, Buchanan Co., U.S.D.A....... 122
Nebraska, Polk Co., U.S.D.A.......... 122
Nebraska, Richardson Co., U.S.D.A.... 211
Nebraska, Washington Co., U.S.D.A.... 22
New Jersey, Camden area, U.S.D.A.... 123
New York, Schoharie Co., U.S.D.A..... 514
North Carolina, Anson Co., U.S.D.A.... 621
North Carolina, Davidson Co., U.S.D.A.. 22
North Carolina, Mecklenburg Co......... 419
North Dakota, Dickey Co., N.Dak...... 720
Ohio, Hamilton Co., U.S.D.A.......... 212
Pennsylvania, Blair Co., U.S.D.A....... 123
Virginia, Fairfax and Alexandria Counties, U.S.D.A...................... 514
West Virginia, Lewis and Gilmer Counties, U.S.D.A...................... 22
Soiling crops—
notes, Wash........................ 96, 895
tests................................. 733
Soils—
absorptive power for water............. 18
Actinomycetes in, N.Y.State........... 517
adsorption by......................... 624
aeration, ecological significance........... 213
alkali, effect on dry farm crops........... 437
alkali, origin, U.S.D.A.................. 809
alkali, reclamation..................... 281
ammonia fixation in, U.S.D.A........... 318
analyses.............................. 114
as affected by organic solvents, U.S.D.A.. 422

Soils—Continued. Page.

biological changes in during storage....... 17
chernozem, of Northern Caucasus........ 516
composition, variation in, U.S.D.A....... 811
determining volume weight.............. 18
disinfection............................ 319,519
effect on forest yields................... 450
fixation of phosphoric acid in............ 423
forest and cultivated, evaporation from.. 418
fungus flora of......................... 718
granitic, phosphorus in................. 522
improvement............................ 813
investigations, botanical method........ 515
investigations, drainage tanks for....... 799
investigations, factors in................. 18
irrigated, drainage...................... 186
irrigated, nitrates in................... 120
lime requirements............ 212,420,622
lime requirements, Ohio................ 124
loess, infertility of subsoils............. 20
nitrification in.......................... 318
nitrogen distribution in................. 517
nitrogen supply, maintenance, N.J..... 425
of Alabama and west Florida............ 810
of Antigua, "gall patches ' in........... 421
of Belgian Kongo, analyses.............. 622
of Hawaii, investigations................ 515
of Kansas, sulphur content.............. 119
of Maryland............................ 514
of New York............................ 317
of New Zealand, lime requirements...... 622
of North Carolina, N.C................. 625
of north Idaho, Idaho.................. 20
of Ohio, southern counties.............. 514
of Quebec, analyses.................... 22
of Southern Rhodesia.................. 212
of Vevey, Switzerland.................. 212
organic matter of........... 20,121,216
organic matter of, maintenance.......... 215
oxidizing power......................... 811
peat, drainage.......................... 135
peat, fertilizers for...................... 720
peat, management....................... 134
peat, of German East Africa............. 317
peat, of Massachusetts.................. 810
peat, of Ohio........................... 212
pervious, loss of nitrates from.......... 23
salt-treated, effect on absorption by seeds. 527
sampling.......................... 719,811
sterilization........... 213,319,421,519,719
sulfofying power, Iowa.................. 119
swamp rice, gases....................... 424
tobacco, of Java........................ 419
toxicity, amelioration................... 519
valuation............................... 18
volcanic, of St. Vincent................. 420
water content........................... 116
water-logged, infertility................. 19
water-retaining capacity and hygroscopic
coefficient, U.S.D.A.................. 117
wheat, of Cape Province................. 622
Solar radiation, variations in............. 417
Soldier bug, green, studies, Ohio........... 258
Soldiers, land settlement for............. 190
Solidago spectabilis, poisoning of sheep by.... 482
Solubility, determination................. 205

Solutions— Page.

evaporating device..................... 503
handling by suction.................... 503
Sordaria oryzeti n.sp., notes.............. 148
Sore throat, septic, transmission by milk.... 273
Sorex fumeus umbrosus n.subsp., description. 758
Sorghum—
as a dry land crop, U.S.D.A............ 637
culture experiments.................... 436
culture experiments, Fla............... 635
culture experiments, La............... 529
culture experiments, Minn............. 227
culture experiments, Tex.............. 329
culture in California, Cal............. 339
culture in Tucuman................... 134
culture under dry farming, N.Mex...... 329
diseases in West Indies............... 452
fertilizer experiments................. 436
grain, analyses....................... 539
grain, bread from..................... 539
hay, digestibility, Tex............. 168,865
hydrocyanic acid in............... 109,113
inheritance of stem characters......... 234
juice, defecation for sirup manufacture... 511
leaves, variation of water and dry matter
in, U.S.D.A....................... 637
seeding experiments, Cal............. 339
seeding experiments, Tex............. 330,331
selection experiments, Nev............ 32
silage and hay, digestibility and productive value, Tex................. 865
silage for cows, Fla................... 683
sirup, notes.......................... 715
varieties............................. 436
varieties, Hawaii..................... 132
varieties, N.Mex................... 32,329
varieties, Nev..................... 32,435
varieties, Tex........................ 331
Sorrel, red, description and eradication, Ind.. 239
South Carolina—
Boll Weevil Commission, report....... 359
Station, notes................. 300,499,600
South Dakota Station—
notes................................ 99
report............................... 195
Southern Forestry Congress, proceedings..... 450
Sows, pregnant, iodin requirement.......... 273
Soy bean—
bacterial blight, studies............... 842
cake, sugar content................... 208
Fusarium blight or wilt disease, U.S.D.A. 50
meal for chicks, N.C.................. 682
Soy beans—
as a forage crop, Idaho................ 640
as a grazing crop for pigs, N.C......... 679
as a green manure, Hawaii............. 320
as a green manure, N.J................ 425
as human and animal food, Ohio........ 236
as human food......................... 164
culture, Conn.State................... 235
culture and use, Md................... 442
culture experiments, Guam............. 729
culture experiments, La............... 529
culture experiments, Minn............. 227
culture experiments, Ohio............. 235
culture in Illinois, Ill................. 433

Soy beans—Continued.   Page.
    effect on succeeding crops, Ohio.........   235
    harvesting, Ohio.........................   895
    seed color variation in..................   334
    seeding experiments, Ill.................   439
    selection experiments, N.C...............   636
    softening effect on pork fat, N.C........   680
    varieties, Conn. State...................   234
    varieties, Ill...........................   439
    varieties, Md............................   442
    varieties, N.C...........................   636
    varieties, Ohio..........................   235
    varieties, Tex...........................   332
Sparrows—
    English, egg-laying cycles...............   869
    relation to blackhead in turkeys.........   384
Spartium junceum seed, chemistry of........   710
Spelt—
    culture experiments, Tex.................   330
    varieties, Md............................   332
    varieties, Oreg..........................   530
Sphacelotheca sorghi—
    inoculation experiments, Mo..............   749
    notes....................................   452
Sphærella—
    fragariæ, treatment......................   246
    sp. on chayote...........................   755
Sphæronema oreophilum n.sp., notes.........   630
Sphæropsis—
    maculans, notes..........................   748
    pseudodiplodia, notes....................   553
Sphærostilbe—
    repens, notes............................   349
    sp. on limes and citrus trees............   452
Sphærotheca—
    mors-uvæ, notes..........................   550
    pannosa, notes...........................   453, 539
Sphagnum—
    bogs, forest growth in...................   837
    moss, use in preparation of bandages.....   736
Sphenophorus callosus, investigations, N.C...   666
Spider, red, notes.............. 460, 461, 847
Spiders, toxins of.............................   461
Spinach carrion beetle, studies...............   261
Spirochæta—
    icterohæmorrhagiæ in American wild rats.   577
    morsus muris n.sp., the cause of rat-bite
        fever................................   375
Spirochetes in digestive tract of swine.......   279
Spiroptera megastoma, splenic abscess due to..   182
Splenic abscess as a secondary infection in
    horses...................................   182
Spondylocladium atrovirens, notes........... 350, 551
Sponge, coarse, analyses, Conn. State........   814
Spongospora subterranea, notes........ 350, 652, 753
Spontaneous combustion as a cause of fires,
    Iowa.....................................   788
Sporobolus phleoides, notes and analyses......   533
Sporodesmium fumagineum n.sp., notes......   630
Sporotrichosis, equine, in Montana..........   82
Sporotrichum globuliferum, notes...........   461
Spotted fever—
    Rocky Mountain, studies..................   560
    tick, control in Montana.................   560
Spraying—
    experiments, Nebr........................   447
    notes....................................   453

Spraying—Continued.   Page.
    notes, N.J...............................   744
    notes, Nebr..............................   544
    notes, Ohio..............................   143
    notes, Wash..............................   95, 699
Sprays—
    dust v. liquid...........................   832
    dust v. liquid, for apples, Ill..........   242
    repellent, effect on bees................   855
Spring of 1917, U.S.D.A.....................   804
Spruce—
    beetle, European, life history and habits..   765
    gall aphid, notes, Conn. State...........   255
    scale, studies...........................   662
    seeding habits...........................   45
Squabs, raising and marketing...............   775
Squash—
    borer, remedies, Conn. State.............   254
    breeding experiments, Minn..............   240
    culture experiments, Guam...............   742
    fertilizer experiments, Guam............   742
Squirrels, ground—
    control in Colorado......................   558
    new race from Wyoming...................   758
Stable fly—
    notes....................................   156
    relation to swamp fever in horses, Wyo..   374
    studies, N.J.............................   665
Stachydrin, isolation from alfalfa hay........   309
Stachylidium theobromæ n.sp., description....   755
Stagonospora convolvuli n.sp., description....   748
Stallions—
    in Indiana, Ind..........................   169
    in Kansas, Kans...................... 270, 863
    in Oklahoma, Okla........................   169
    in Utah, Utah............................   681
    legislation in United States, U.S.D.A....   572
Starch—
    determination of gelatinization tempera-
        ture.................................   410
    effect on soil acidity...................   23
    grains, cleavage in......................   410
    hydrolysis by malt amylase..............   613
Starvation, studies...................... 64, 365
States Relations Service. (See United States
    Department of Agriculture.)
Steers—
    digestion experiments, Ga................   65
    digestion experiments, U.S.D.A..........   673
    fattening, rate and economy of gains, Ill..   471
    feeding experiments......................   760
    feeding experiments, Ill.................   471
    feeding experiments, Ind................   270
    feeding experiments, Iowa...............   66
    feeding experiments, Mo.................   765
    feeding experiments, N.C................   674
    feeding experiments, N.Mex.............   68
    feeding experiments, Pa.................   365
    grazing on Japanese cane, La............   572
Stegomyia fasciata, development in relation to
    bacteria and yeasts.....................   761
Stenopelmatus sp. injurious to potatoes, Wash.   157
Stephanitis pyrioides, studies............... 660, 761
Stephanurus dentatus—
    notes....................................   482
    notes, Guam..............................   773
Sterigmatocystis nigra, notes................ 51, 223

	Page.
Sterility in cows, treatment	379
Stigeosporium marattiacearum n.sp., description	630
Stizolobium spp., studies	328
Stock. (*See* Live stock.)	
Stomach worms—	
in lambs, N.C	691
in sheep	477
Stomatitis—	
contagious, notes	482
infectious, in horses	692
vesicular, in cattle	81
vesicular, in cattle, U.S.D.A	81
vesicular, in horses and mules	182
Stomatoceras pertorvus n.sp., description	569
Stomoxys calcitrans. (*See* Stable fly.)	
Stone—	
grading for road construction, U.S.D.A.	787
road-making qualities	695
Storm at San Diego, Cal., U.S.D.A	513
Stratiomys chamæleon, notes	847
Strawberries—	
composition in relation to soils	648
culture	648
culture, Cal	447
culture experiments, Oreg	243
fertilizer experiments, Mo	743
fertilizer experiments, Tex	832
forcing experiments, Colo	43
marketing and distribution in 1915, U.S.D.A	43
rotting in transit, U.S.D.A	351
selection experiments, Mo	743
sterility, Minn	240
thrips affecting, Fla	659
treatise	42, 648
varieties, Oreg	243
varieties of North America, Va	143
Strawberry—	
root weevil, notes	568
root weevil, notes, Wash	54
weevil, remedies, N.J	466
Stream—	
flow in India	716
gage data, skew frequency curve, U.S.D.A	513
measurements in Alberta and Saskatchewan	187
measurements in North Dakota	84
Streams, self-purification	693
Streptococcus solani n.sp., notes	549
String beans, drying	509
Strongylosis, pulmonary, notes	179
Strontium, determination in water	506
Strychnin, effect on plant growth	632
Stump burner, description	385
Stumps—	
burning, Wash	96
pulling and burning, Idaho	87
Sturnira lilium parvidens n.subsp., description	757
Styrax obassia, oil of	109
Subsoiling—	
experiments	732, 733
experiments, Minn	227
Succinate, action on isolated intestine	471
Succinic acid, extraction with ether	414

	Page.
Sucrose—	
action of acids on	802
determination	506
Sudan grass—	
and Johnson grass seed, distinguishing charaters, Cal	236
as a forage crop, Tex	532
culture	136
culture experiments, Cal	236
culture experiments, La	529
culture experiments, Minn	226, 227
culture experiments, Tex	329, 330
culture for hay, Nev	436
culture for seed, Nev	436
culture under dry farming, N.Mex	329
for late planting, Nev	436
hay, analyses, Cal	236
hay, digestibility and productive value, Tex	865
notes, Ga	29
seeding experiments, N.Mex	32
seeding experiments, Tex	330, 331
silage, preservation and use, Okla	672
Sugar—	
acetyl derivatives	201
aldehyde, determination	714
alpha and beta, rotatory powers	410
analyses and food value	570
as a coagulant for rubber	348
as a wound dressing	82, 876
cold storage experiments, La	510
decomposition in soils	628
defecation precipitate, reducing substances in	13
denatured, for honeybees	647
deterioration, La	509
determination	313
determination in feeding stuffs	208
determination in hay and turnips	618
effect on ammonia accumulation by micro-organisms	812
in floral leaves	246
invert, action of acids on	802
manufacture, treatise	114
maple leaves, plant food constituents	629
maple volume tables, frustum form factor	651
reducing, determination	13
(*See also* Cane sugar.)	
Sugar beet—	
chlorosis, description	249
crown gall, notes	249
curly-top, relation to wild vegetation	847
pulp. (*See* Beet pulp.)	
root louse, notes, Mont	255
seed industry in Russia	443
seed industry in United States, U.S.D.A.	540
sirup, manufacture, U.S.D.A	511
Sugar beets—	
breeding experiments	442
composition in relation to meteorological conditions	539
correlation studies	28, 642
culture experiments	230
culture experiments, Idaho	30
culture experiments, N.Mex	644
culture experiments, Nev	435

Sugar beets—Continued. Page.

culture in California, Cal................ 443
culture in southwestern Russia.......... 339
culture in western South Dakota........ 99
for late planting, Nev.................. 436
irrigation experiments,N. Mex.......... 32
irrigation experiments, Nev............. 30
irrigation experiments, Oreg........... 85
irrigation experiments, U.S.D.A........ 822
irrigation experiments, Utah........... 741
spring v. fall planting, N.Mex.......... 32
treatise................................ 533
variation and correlation in........... 642

Sugar cane—

analyses............................... 826
borer, control by parasites............ 569
borer, effect on composition of sugar cane. 255
breeding experiments................... 236
culture experiments.................... 237,
                   339, 421, 540, 734, 824, 825
culture, fallowing in.................. 443
culture in Hawaii...................... 444
culture in India....................... 139
culture in Tucuman................. 134, 139
diseases in Mauritius.................. 551
diseases in Porto Rico................. 246
diseases in Sao Paulo.................. 553
diseases in West Indies................ 452
dry disease and ring spot, notes....... 838
fertilizer experiments.. 123, 215, 237, 339, 426, 824
fertilizer experiments, La............. 529
green manuring experiments............ 734
insects affecting...................... 255
irrigation experiments................. 824
Japanese, culture experiments, Hawaii.. 132
Japanese, culture experiments, La...... 529
Japanese, culture experiments, Tex..... 140,
                                      329, 532
Japanese, fertilizer experiments, Fla..... 635
Japanese, for steers, La............... 572
Japanese, seeding experiments, Tex..... 533
Japanese, silage from, Fla............. 683
lodging and its prevention......... 443, 444
morphology............................. 443
root disease, notes.................... 753
rotation experiments................... 237
seeding experiments................ 139, 824
thinning experiments................... 139
unloading and conveying machinery..... 90
varieties............... 139, 236, 339, 824, 825, 826
varieties, La.......................... 529
varieties of Dutch East Indies.......... 443
varieties of Java...................... 139
Sulfofication in soils, Iowa............. 119
Sulphate of ammonia. (*See* Ammonium sulphate.)
Sulphid solutions, alkaline, fungicidal value. 47
Sulphites, determination................ 205

Sulphur—

arsenical dusts, use against strawberry
  weevil, N. J.......................... 466
determination in plant material and soils,
  Wash................................. 614
dioxid, determination.................. 205
effect on alfalfa, Oreg................. 33
liver of, emulsion for................. 760
loss in soils.......................... 119
mixtures. (*See* Lime-sulphur mixture.)
production in 1915-16.................. 524

Sulphur—Continued. Page.

soluble and atomic, fungicidal value,
  Nebr................................. 448
Sulphuric acid—

effect on plants....................... 224
larvicidal value, N. J................. 665
Sulphurous acid, preparation........... 205
Sultanas, drying....................... 114
Sumac as a source of tannin............ 548
Sun spots, relation to weather......... 619
Sunflowers—

culture experiments, Guam............. 730
culture experiments, Tex.............. 332
culture for seed...................... 230
silage from........................... 230
variations in......................... 543
varieties............................. 339
Sunn hemp, culture experiments......... 824
Superphosphate—

effect on composition of cereals........ 827
effect on soil acidity................. 23
effect on soil bases, Ohio............. 126
effect on sulfofying power of soils, Iowa.. 119
fertilizing value............ 426, 521, 534
fertilizing value, Ga................. 29
fertilizing value, Guam............... 729
fertilizing value, Ill................ 449
fertilizing value, Ind................ 214
fertilizing value, Md................. 540
fertilizing value, Minn............... 228
fertilizing value, Mo.............. 731, 743
fertilizing value, Ohio............ 535, 831
fertilizing value, Tex................ 823
mixing with basic slag and rock phosphates. 816
preparation........................... 322
residual effects...................... 23
use on peat soils..................... 135
Swamp fever—

in horses, transmission, Wyo.......... 374
in United States...................... 274
Swede seeds in Denmark................. 742
Swedes—

culture experiments................... 733
culture experiments, Minn............. 228
fertilizer experiments, Minn.......... 228
protein of............................ 410
varieties, Minn....................... 228
Sweet clover—

analyses and agricultural value....... 531
as a hay crop, Oreg................... 531
culture, U.S.D.A...................... 540
culture experiments, Minn............. 226
culture experiments, Nev.............. 435
culture experiments, Ohio............. 140
eradication, U.S.D.A.................. 540
seed, germination tests, U.S.D.A...... 540
silage, l-leucin in................... 802
utilization, U.S.D.A.................. 444
yields, Minn.......................... 227
Sweet corn—

culture experiments, Guam............. 742
fertilizer experiments................ 522
fertilizer experiments, Guam.......... 742
Sweet peas—

culture................................ 546
description and culture................ 346
diseases of........................... 155
treatise.............................. 546

Sweet potato—   Page.
 diseases, treatment, Va. Truck 249
 root borer, notes............................ 256
 root disease and white rust..:............ 452
 scarabee, notes............................ 256
 silage for cows, Fla...................... 683
Sweet potatoes—
 culture and storage, U.S.D.A............ 597
 fertilizer experiments, Fla............ 635
 fertilizer experiments, Tex.............. 823
Swine fever, notes............................ 279
Swine. (See Pigs.)
Symbiosis in autumnal leaves................ 527
Symptomatic anthrax. (See Blackleg.)
Synanthedon pictipes, studies, Ohio.......... 159
Synchytrium endobioticum, host plants....... 753
Syntomaspis myrtacearum n.sp., description.. 59
Syrphidæ of District of Columbia............ 57
Systena basalis, notes...................... 256
Tachinidæ of New England.................. 763
Tænia—
 expansa, infestation of lambs, Wyo....... 374
 marginata in liver of swine............ 477
 pisiformis, development in kittens....... 693
Tænioid cestodes of the dog, cat, and related
 carnivores.............................. 82
Tæniothrips pyri, studies.................. 257
Takosis in goats............................ 477
Taliparamba Agricultural Station, report.... 343
Tankage—
 analyses, Conn.State.................... 268
 analyses, R.I........................... 767
 analyses, Wis........................... 471
 fertilizing value, Md.................. 540
Tapeworm in liver of swine.................. 477
Tar fumes, effect on vegetation............ 327
Tarnished plant bug, notes, Conn State...... 255
Tarsonemus—
 pallidus, studies, Md.................. 856
 pallidus, studies, U.S.D.A.............. 858
 sp. on cyclamen......................... 766
Tartaric acid of grape musts and wines...... 310
Tartrate, action on isolated intestine........ 471
"Tarwad" bark as a tanning agent.......... 147
Taurin, use against tuberculosis............ 275
Tea—
 aphis, notes............................ 662
 diseases in northeast India.............. 252
 fermentation, investigations............ 44
 improvement by selection.............. 43
 ingestion, effect on uric acid excretion... 470
 roots and their diseases.................. 52
 seed, germination and selection.......... 835
 seed, oil of............................. 109
 withering, fermentation, and drying..... 619
Teal, Laysan, new generic name for.......... 758
Teff grass, notes, Ga...................... 29
Telenomus coloradensis, parasitic on tent
 caterpillar.............................. 667
Temperature—
 atmospheric, annual variations.......... 417
 changes, world-wide.................... 15
 determinations in entomology.......... 855
 effect on complement fixation rate....... 688
 effect on growth of small grains........ 533
 low, effect on germination of beet seeds.. 829
 relation to chestnut blight............... 657

Tennessee—   Page.
 Station, notes.................. 198,499,600,797
 University, notes.................. 198,300,600
Teosinte—
 culture................................. 136
 culture experiments, La................ 529
Termites injuring shotgun cartridges, Conn.
 State.................................. 255
Terraces, construction, U.S.D.A............ 87
Testis extract, effect on milk production.... 173
Tetanus, treatment.......................... 79
Tethelin, use against tuberculosis............ 880
Tetranychus modestus, notes.................. 847
Tetraphosphate, description.................. 722
Tetrastichus—
 giffardianus, parasitic on fruit fly........ 856
 malacosomæ, parasitic on tent caterpillar. 667
 ovipransus n.sp., description............ 856
Texas—
 College, notes......................... 99,898
 Station, notes...................... 99,600,898
Theileriosis in Russian Turkestan............ 374
Theobromin, determination in cocoa and
 chocolate.............................. 312
Thermobia domestica, notes, Conn.State.... 255
Thielavia basicola—
 investigations.......................... 155
 notes, Wis............................. 58
Thielaviopsis paradoxa—
 notes................................. 452
 notes, Fla............................. 652
Thiobarbituric acid as a qualitative reagent
 for ketohexose......................... 206
Thomas s.ag. (See Phosphatic slag.)
Three-days' fever, notes...................... 460
Thrips n.sp., description.:.................. 258
Thyridaria tarda on tea roots.................. 52
Thyroid gland—
 active constituent of..................... 65
 extract, effect on milk production....... 173
Thysanoptera—
 British, notes........................... 257
 of Plummer's Island, Maryland.......... 561
Thysanosoma actinioides, infestation of lambs
 by, Wyo................................. 574
Tibicen septendecim. (See Cicada, periodical).
Ticks—
 eradication.............................. 477
 eradication, laws and regulations, Ark... 881
 in British Museum...................... 560
 infesting domestic animals in Russian
  Turkestan.......................... 360
 infesting marmots....................... 879
 protozoan parasites transmitted by....... 481
 spotted fever, control in Montana........ 560
 transmission of louping-ill by............ 277
 wood, notes............................ 459
 (See also Cattle tick and Sheep tick.)
Tile—
 drain and sewer, beddings for............ 187
 drain, specifications.................... 587
 drainage system, Minn.................. 286
Tilletia—
 fœtens, inoculation experiments, Mo..... 750
 horrida, notes.......................... 247
 tritici, treatment........................ 247
Timber—
 cut, regulating, Swiss method.......... 451
 decay, prevention, U.S.D.A............. 349

Timber—Continued.   Page.
    dry rot, notes............................   253
    estimating in eastern North Carolina....   747
    estimating in southern Appalachians....   46
    frame structures, design and construction   386
    grading...................................   245
    insects affecting.........................   356
    microscopic identification................   46
    of Canada.................................   245
    of Queensland.............................   650
    preservation..............................   886
    resources of South Dakota.................   790
    resources of Utah.........................   791
    standing, determination of quality..... 243,451
    western, tests, U.S.D.A...................   50
    (See also Lumber and Wood.)
Timothy—
    Arlington, notes, Ohio....................   195
    as affected by companion crop of clover..   438
    culture, Md...............................   540
    fertilizer experiments, Md................   540
    fertilizer experiments, Pa................   627
    flowering habits..........................   140
    hay, effect on melting point of milk fat,
        Mo....................................   73
    pollination experiments...................   735
Tin—
    adsorbed, effect on digestion of proteins..   470
    adsorption by proteins....................   12
    coating on food containers................   715
    determination.............................   110
    solution by canned foods..................   12
Tipula paludosa, biology and economics.....   763
Tissue—
    cells, human, resistance to germicides...   176
    transplantation, negative, cause.........   478
Titration flask, description...................   614
Tobacco—
    artificial drying.........................   417
    ash, composition as affected by fertilizers 541
    biochemistry..............................   509
    black rot, notes..........................   51
    budworm, studies, U.S.D.A.................   663
    cigar wrapper, culture in Philippines....   539
    cost of production, Minn..................   226
    cost of production, W.Va..................   191
    culture, N.C..............................   541
    culture, Wis..............................   37
    culture experiments.......................   734
    culture in Albania........................   445
    culture in Argentina.................. 541,823
    culture in New South Wales................   340
    culture in Philippines....................   791
    culture in Uruguay........................   445
    diseases, descriptions....................   753
    diseases in Dutch East Indies.............   753
    fertilizer experiments................. 315,339
    fertilizer experiments, Guam..............   729
    green manuring experiments................   734
    gummosis, studies.........................   554
    insects affecting...................... 255,256
    lanas disease, studies................. 553,554
    leaves and inflorescence as affected by en-
        vironment.............................   224
    liming experiments.................... 522,523
    mildew, notes.............................   453
    mosaic disease, bacterial origin.,,......   549

Tobacco—Continued.   Page.
    mosaic disease, studies...................   150
    of Java, analyses.........................   419
    press cake, fertilizing value.............   411
    Sclerotium disease, studies...............   249
    seed oil, analyses and use................   411
    shading, Guam.............................   729
    soils, management, Wis....................   37
    variation in..............................   339
    varieties.................................   339
    varieties, Guam...........................   729
    worm injurious to potatoes, Wash..........   157
Toluene, effect on soils.......................   519
Tomaspis tristis injurious to sugar cane......   358
Tomato—
    bacterial diseases, notes, Fla............   652
    blight, studies, Wash.....................   46
    buckeye rot, Fla..........................   652
    diseases in Mauritius.....................   551
    diseases in New Zealand...................   150
    diseases, notes, N.J......................   654
    diseases, studies.........................   842
    late blight, treatment....................   749
    leaf roll, notes..........................   551
    mosaic disease, notes.....................   652
    psyllid, studies..........................   849
Tomatoes—
    breeding experiments......................   827
    breeding experiments, Minn................   240
    copper in.................................   263
    culture, Ohio.............................   143
    culture for canning factory, Ind.........   343
    culture in greenhouses....................   41
    fertilizer experiments....................   41
    fertilizer experiments, Md................   321
    picking maturity, U.S.D.A.................   543
    treatise.................................   645
    varieties, Md.............................   645
Tornadoes, notes, U.S.D.A................. 513, 807
Tortrix viridana, life history.................   57
Toxoptera—
    coffeæ, notes.............................   662
    graminum, outbreak in Kansas.............   561
Tractors—
    specifications........................ 788,886
    tests................................. 387,886
    v. horses, Minn...........................   227
Transpiration—
    in plants, measuring, U.S.D.A.............   420
    in plants, periodicity....................   420
    in steppe plants..........................   120
Tree—
    diseases, notes...........................   760
    diseases, studies, Mo.....................   755
    leaves, effect of sun and shade on........   747
    planting camps............................   243
    rusts and their treatment.................   155
    seedlings, transplanting lath for.........   835
    seeds, depth of covering..................   451
    seeds, storage experiments................   647
Trees—
    as affected by asphyxiating gas...........   153
    broadleaf deciduous, of United State.....   146
    cambial activity..........................   128
    effect on rainfall........................   715
    evergreen, for Iowa, Iowa................   545
    for eastern Colorado......................   887

Trees—Continued.   Page.

for eastern Washington, Wash........... 146
for Idaho, Idaho........................ 244
for northern Minnesota, Minn........... 241
for Rhodesia............................ 746
forest, cryptogamic diseases of........... 53
forest, root growth..................... 27
gas injury.............................. 726
hail injury............................. 250
hardwood, growth data................. 651
insects affecting.................... 459, 760
light and soil requirements.............. 244
of eastern United States................. 746
of Georgia.............................. 650
of Indiana.............................. 44
of Newark, New Jersey.................. 346
of United States, treatise.............. 346
ornamental, for windbreaks, Ohio........ 147
ornamental, of Hawaii.................. 546
ornamental, treatise.................... 44
penetration by solutions................ 327
planting in Texas....................... 452
street and park, for Wisconsin........... 145
toxic atrophy........................... 147
Trefoil, pollination experiments.......... 735
Trematode larva encysted in a crab........ 558
Trembles. (*See* Milk sickness.)
Triænodes bicolor, notes.................. 847
Tribolium castaneum, studies............. 356
Trichina, encysted forms, in polar bear...... 483
Trichinella spiralis—
as affected by radium................... 578
life history............................ 578
Trichinosis, immunization................. 784
Trichogramma—
evanescens, embryonic development...... 855
minuta, studies..................... 460, 569
Trichomonas pullorum, notes............. 785
Trichomoniasis—
in chicks............................... 784
intestinal.............................. 183
Trichuris—
crenata, notes, Guam.................. 779
ovis in Philippines.................... 277
Trioza alacris, notes................. 157, 849
Trombidium akamushi. (*See Leptotrombidium akamushi*.)
Truck crops—
industry in United States, U.S.D.A....... 543
insects affecting..................... 157, 459
insects affecting, Fla.................. 356
Trypanosoma evansi, transmission by insects. 180
Trypanosome anaphylatoxin, studies........ 578
Trypanosomiasis, transmission by flies..... 879
Tryptophan, rôle in purin metabolism....... 265
Tsutsugamushi disease, carrier............. 858
Tuber tonic, fungicidal value, Nebr........ 447
Tubercle bacilli—
determination in sputum................ 180
enzyms of.............................. 275
growth as affected by anilin dyes........ 481
in butter............................... 481
in certified milk....................... 881
in feces of dairy cattle................. 879
longevity in milk....................... 378
staining with carbol fuchsin............. 180
vitality outside the body................ 782

Tubercles, root. (*See* Root tubercles.)   Page.
Tuberculosis—
bovine and porcine, virulence of apparently sound tissue in................ 583
bovine, diagnosis........................ 80
bovine, eradication..................... 379
bovine, in children..................... 782
bovine, in Hawaii...................... 374
bovine, in horses....................... 378
bovine, in man......................... 879
chemotherapy........................... 379
control in Michigan..................... 274
control in Oregon....................... 374
control in Pennsylvania................. 577
delayed or latent infection.............. 378
diagnosis, complement-fixation test.... 180, 481
human and bovine, relationship....... 80, 181
human bone and joint................... 181
immunization........................... 880
in camels.............................. 690
in carnivorous animals................. 880
in goats................................ 481
in horses............................... 880
in swine................................ 82
in United States........................ 274
infection through expired air........... 378
notes.............................. 477, 879
notes, Ind............................. 378
of cervical and axillary glands.......... 378
treatment........................... 275, 880
Tuberculous infection, immune reaction to.. 275
Tubers—
edible. (*See* Root crops.)
sampling device for..................... 711
Tulip poplar, characteristics and value, Ohio. 147
Tulips—
classification.......................... 836
culture experiments.................... 836
Turf—
as bedding for cattle and horses......... 723
for golf courses, treatise............... 146
Turkey industry in United States, U.S.D.A.. 573
Turkeys, raising and marketing, U.S.D.A... 573
Turnip—
aphis, notes, Conn.State............... 254
leaf spot, studies, U.S.D.A............. 753
seeds in Denmark....................... 742
Turnips—
as a catch crop after wheat.............. 136
culture experiments.................... 733
for cattle.............................. 866
subsoiling experiments................. 732
varieties, Minn........................ 228
Twig girdler, notes, Fla................. 660
Tylenchus—
dipsaci, notes......................... 246
tritici in wheat heads................. 840
Tylidæ, erection......................... 846
Typhoid—
fever, transmission by house flies........ 854
fly. (*See* House fly.)
vaccine, effect on tuberculous guinea pigs.................................. 481
Typhus fever organism in lice............. 851
Tyrosinase action, studies............... 110
Udo, culture experiments, Guam........... 742
Ultramicroscope, description............. 711

Ultraviolet rays—　　　　　　　　　　Page.
　action on fig must.......................... 314
　purification of water by.................. 588
Ultuna agricultural institute and farm....... 892
Uncinula aceris, symbiosis with maple leaves. 327
United States Department of Agriculture—
　annual reports............................ 297
　development and activities, U.S.D.A.... 592
　Plant Disease Survey.................... 500
　States Relations Service, notes.......... 500
　war emergency funds.................... 301
　yearbook................................ 599
United States Geological Survey, Reclama-
　tion Service, report........................ 84
Urea, fertilizing value........................ 216
Urease in plants, studies.................... 204
Uredinales—
　of Porto Rico............................ 749
　on Onagraceæ............................ 552
Uredo—
　arachidis, notes.......................... 452, 551
　fici, notes................................ 453
　sp., treatment............................ 550
Uric acid, determination.................... 470
Uromyces—
　appendiculatus, treatment, Colo.......... 248
　betæ, notes.............................. 249
　fallens, life history...................... 752
　spp., notes.............................. 453
Uromyces, short-cycled, of North America... 749
Ustilaginoidea virens, notes.................. 247
Ustilago—
　avenæ and U. levis, inoculation experi-
　　ments, Mo.............................. 750
　sacchari, notes.......................... 551
　tragopogonis, notes...................... 550
　tritici, life history...................... 839
　zeæ, notes.............................. 452, 750
Ustulina zonata, studies.................... 52
Utah—
　College, notes............................ 99, 300
　Station, notes.............. 99, 198, 300, 600, 797
Vaccines, sensitized and nonsensitized, studies 780
Vacuna dryophila, notes.................... 562
Valsa—
　japonica n.sp., studies.................. 251
　paulowniæ n.sp.. description............ 557
Valsaria subtropica, notes.................. 553
Vampyrus spectrum nelsoni n.subsp., descrip-
　tion.................................... 757
Vanillin—
　effect on citrus fruits, Fla.............. 656
　methods of analysis.................... 12
Vapor pressures over United States, U.S.D.A 314
Variety tests, papers on.................... 240
　(See also various crops, fruits, etc.)
Vegetable—
　matter, showers of, U.S.D.A............. 808
　oils. (See Oils.)
　seed production at Vineland, Ontario.... 343
　seeds, longevity in storage, Guam........ 742
Vegetables—
　bacterial diseases of in Ontario.......... 149
　breeding experiments.................... 832
　canned, poisoning from.................. 669
　canned, poisoning from, U.S.D.A....... 670
　culture, Ill.............................. 645
　culture, Ky.............................. 342

Vegetable—Continued.　　　　　　　Page.
　culture experiments...................... 832
　culture experiments, Minn.............. 241
　diseases and insect pests, control, Utah... 832
　dried, cooking.......................... 509
　drying.................................. 509, 715
　drying apparatus for.................... 806
　evaporation, Wash...................... 715
　fertilizer experiments, Can.............. 645
　fertilizer experiments, Md.............. 320
　harvesting and storing, Colo............. 646
　improvement by selection................ 240
　insects affecting........................ 256
　insects affecting, Ohio.................. 895
　picking maturity, U.S.D.A.............. 543
　recipes................................ 670
　varieties................................ 240, 832
　varieties, Md.......................... 645
　varieties, Minn........................ 241
　washing in canning factories............. 416
　(See also specific kinds.)
Vegetation—
　adaptation to climate.................... 725
　in South Africa........................ 526
　native, of Colorado, Colo................ 209
　of Pinus tæda belt of Virginia and the
　　Carolinas............................ 435
　Rocky Mountain, monograph............ 434
　spring, precocity........................ 633
Velvet beans—
　as green manure, Hawaii................ 320
　botanical studies...................... 328
　culture and use, N.C.................... 445
　culture experiments, Guam.............. 729
　culture experiments, La................ 529
　effect on yield of corn, Ga.............. 29
　fertilizer experiments, Fla.............. 635
　selection experiments. N.C.............. 636
　varieties, Fla.......................... 635
　varieties, Guam........................ 729
　varieties, N.C.......................... 636
Venturi flume, description and tests, U.S.
　D.A.................................... 282
Venturia cratægi, pycnidial stage............ 550
Vermicularia—
　sacchari, notes.......................... 553
　xanthosomatis n.sp., notes.............. 148
Vermont—
　Station, notes.......................... 499, 797
　University, notes.............. 99, 499, 700, 797
Verruga—
　and Oroya fever, identity.............. 356, 377
　transmission by insects............ 356, 358, 460
Verticillium alboatrum, studies.............. 49, 350
Vespa—
　crabro, girdling of hardwood twigs by,
　　Conn.State............................ 255
　vulgaris injurious to wheat.............. 667
Vetch—
　as a cover crop for orchards.............. 833
　culture in Washington, Wash............ 96
　hay, digestibility, Tex.................. 168
　milk, toxicity, Wyo.................... 780
　varieties, Oreg......................... 531
　varieties, Tex.......................... 332
Veterinary—
　anatomy, handbook...................... 778
　department of Baluchistan, report....... 274

Veterinary—Continued.   Page.

department of Bengal, report............   780
department of Madras Presidency, report   274
department of Punjab, report...........   78
medicine, handbook................... 176,778
therapeutics, treatise...................   76

Viburnum lantana as a hedge plant, Minn...   241

Vinegar—

cider, volatile reducing substance in.....   112
examination............................   112
grains, analyses, Wis....................   471
investigations..........................   716
manufacture........................... 112,715

Vineland horticultural experiment station,
Ontario, report............................   832

Vines, pruning.............................   242

Vineyards, phylloxera-infested, reconstitution....................................   344

(*See also* Grapes.)

Violets, bud selection experiments...........   240

Virginia—

College, notes............................   300
Station, notes..................... 99,300,500
Truck Station, notes.................. 500,899

Vitamins—

chemical nature..........................   411
notes, N. Dak...........................   468
pancreatic, use in malnutrition..........   65

Viticulture, treatise............................   834

Vocational education—

Federal aid........................ 597,606,798
in California............................   394
in United States........................   192
law in New York.........................   394

Volcanic—

ash, conversion into fertile soil...........   420
eruptions, relation to weather............   619

Wages, farm, in Iowa.......................   91

Walnut —

blight, studies..........................   756
caterpillar, notes, Conn. State...........   255
melaxuma, studies......................   756

Walnuts—

black, varieties, S. Dak.................   143
varieties, Mont.........................   241

Warblers of North America...................   846

War-time dishes, recipes.....................   63

Washington—

Adams Branch Station, report...........   195
College, notes............................   798
Irrigation Institution, proceedings.......   281
Station, notes...................... 99,798
Station, report...........................   96

Wasps injurious to wheat.....................   667

Water—

added, determination in ground meats
and sausage...........................   414
analyses.................... 144,693,883
bacteria in, counting....................   187
continuous application to vegetables.. 325,543
determination in desiccated milk........   508
determination in spices and similar products..................................   414
drinking, purification.....................   488
duty of in irrigation.................. 185,281
effect on composition of wheat, Colo.....   38
effect on strength of concrete............   490

Water—Continued.   Page.

elimination from skin and respiratory
passages................................   267
evaporation formula....................   882
flow through submerged rectangular orifices, U.S.D.A..........................   281
flow through V-notch weirs..............   693
ground, use in irrigation................   185
hemlock, poisoning by, Wash...........   96
irrigation, application...................   281
irrigation, conservation.................   238
irrigation, distribution................. 281,883
irrigation, economic use, Oreg...........   84
irrigation, effect on soil bacteria, U.S.D.A.   421
irrigation in upper Italy.................   586
irrigation, measurement............... 486,883
irrigation, measurement, Colo...........   586
irrigation, measurement, U.S.D.A..... 282,882
irrigation, pumping......................   281
methods of analysis................. 187,311,714
movement in soils.......................   116
movement in soils, U.S.D.A........... 623,808
of Argentina, analyses...................   693
pipes, hot and cold, bursting............   592
pollution, control in Austria.............   528
pollution, test for.......................   587
powers of Alabama......................   84
purification............... 488,588,694,787,884
purification by liquid chlorin and hypochlorite of lime.......................   588
purification by ultraviolet rays..........   588
sphagnum bog, toxicity..................   27
supply for rural schools..................   696
supply of Big Smoky, Clayton, and Alkali
Spring Valleys, Nev....................   484
supply of California.................. 486,585
supply of Denver, Colo..................   286
supply of Fargo, N. Dak.................   488
supply of Hudson Bay and upper Missis-
sippi River basins.....................   84
supply of Indiana........................   883
supply of lower Columbia River and Pa-
cific drainage basins in Oregon.........   384
supply of Missouri River basin..........   84
supply of New Mexico...................   384
supply of north Atlantic drainage basins.   585
supply of Ohio River basin..............   585
supply of Pacific slope basins in California   84
supply of rural district in Hawaii........   187
supply of San Simon Valley, Ariz. and
N. Mex................................   485
supply of Utah...........................   791
supply, treatise..........................   187
supplying continuously to plants...... 325,543
surfaces, evaporation from, U.S.D.A.....   785
turbidity................................   486

Watermelon diseases, notes, U.S.D.A........   554

Watermelons—

acid content.............................   715
culture experiments, Guam..............   742
fertilizer experiments, Guam............   742
fertilizer experiments, Tex..............   832
varieties, S. Dak........................   143

Wattle tanbark industry in Natal...........   748

Waxes, determination of unsaponifiable matter in...................................   805

Weather—   Page.
    effect on honey production, Iowa........   854
    forecasting....................... 417,619,716
    in Argentina, U.S.D.A.................   116
    relation to cotton ginned during certain
        periods, U.S.D.A...................   114
    relation to crops, Ariz................   209
Weeds—
    as a source o potash.................   817
    description, Mont....................   239
    eradication.........................   446
    eradication, Minn....................   226
    eradication, Tex.....................   132
    eradication, Wash....................   895
    eradication from irrigation canals.......   285
    method for study.....................   542
    of Kherson, Russia...................   542
    of Novgorod.........................   239
    root systems........................   542
    (See also specific plants.)
Weevils, studies.........................   58
Weirs—
    construction and use, U.S.D.A.........   582
    flow of water through................   693
    portable, construction................   486
    tests, Colo..........................   586
Wesmaelia spp. in America................   855
West Virginia University and Station, notes.   198
Wheat—
    analyses, Colo.......................   58
    analyses, Idaho......................   39
    and barley hybrid, notes..............   822
    and rye hybrid, heredity in............   432
    as affected by greenhouse temperature...   533
    as affected by osmotic pressure of soil so-
        lution............................   128
    as affected by soil moisture, Utah.......   340
    bran, analyses, Conn.State.............   268
    bran, analyses, R.I...................   767
    bran, analyses, Wis..................   471
    bran, digestibility, Ark...............   678
    bread, recipes, U.S.D.A...............   354
    breeding........................... 799,827
    breeding experiments, Mo.............   731
    bushel weights.......................   889
    classification and grading, U.S.D.A......   860
    correlation in........................   141
    cost of production, W.Va..............   191
    culture, Iowa.........................   736
    culture, Md..........................   340
    culture, continuous...................   445
    culture experiments..................   436,
                          438,534,734,823,824,825
    culture experiments, Idaho.............   30
    culture experiments, Tex..............   330
    culture for hay, Nev..................   436
    culture in England....................   445
    culture under dry farming, N.Mex......   329
    culture under dry farming, Oreg........   829
    destruction by wasps.................   667
    development as affected by heating seeds   742
    dietary properties....................   264
    disease, new, U.S.D.A.................   653
    diseases and insect pests, Md..........   240
    diseases, treatment, Ohio.............   895
    durum, baking quality, U.S.D.A.......   362

Wheat—Continued   Page.
    factors affecting quality, Colo..........   38
    fertilizer experiments.................   215,
                          229,323,436,438,734,822
    fertilizer experiments, Idaho...........   30
    fertilizer experiments, Ind............   214
    fertilizer experiments, Minn...........   229
    fertilizer experiments, Ohio....... 238,337,831
    fertilizer experiments, Pa.............   627
    flour. (See Flour.)
    germinated, baking quality, Wash......   862
    germination and purity tests, Mont.....   238
    gluten, formation, Wash..............   341
    grading, N.Dak......................   863
    green-manuring experiments...........   734
    green-manuring experiments, N.J......   425
    handling in bulk.................... 91,492
    hybrid, new.........................   445
    improvement in Argentina.............   823
    improvement in Canada..............   831
    inheritance in, Wash.................   332
    irrigation experiments.................   238
    irrigation experiments, Idaho..........   640
    irrigation experiments, Nev...........   30
    irrigation experiments, U.S.D.A.......   822
    irrigation experiments, Utah..........   340
    kernel. development, Wash...........   24
    loose smut. life history...............   839
    loose smut, treatment................   247
    manuring in winter, Ohio.............   195
    methods of analysis, Colo.............   11
    middlings, analyses, Conn.State.......   268
    middlings, analyses, R.I..............   767
    middlings, analyses, Wis.............   471
    middlings digestibility. Il............   677
    milling and baking tests, Idaho........   30
    milling and baking tests, N.Dak.......   863
    milling and baking tests, U.S.D.A..... 61,860
    milling qualities, Ohio................   570
    mineral requirement.................   799
    moisture capacity, N.Dak............   362
    Montana-grown, types and quality
        U.S.D.A.........................   361
    of Baluchistan. Khorassan. and Kurram
        Valley............................   446
    of Washington, classific- tion.........   237
    pedigreed, yields in Wisconsin.........   433
    phytic acid and its salts in............   108
    plant, methods of analysis, Colo.......   11
    plant, microchemical studies, Wash....   631
    powdery mildew, studies, Mo.........   749
    products, moisture capacity, N.Dak....   362
    Red Olona, improvement.............   141
    Red Rock............................   799
    rust, infection through seed...........   751
    rust, notes, Mo......................   749
    rusts, notes....................... 247,453
    salvage, analyses, Conn.State..........   263
    seeding experiments, Minn...........   223
    seeding experiments, Mo.............   731
    seeding experiments, Ohio...........   134
    seeding experiments, Oreg...........   530
    seeds, longevity in relation to tempera-
        ture.............................   725
    selection experiments, Minn..........   226
    selection experiments, Nev..........   30

Wheat—Continued   Page.
    Septoria diseases in Australia.............   149
    sheath miner, notes, Mont...............   255
    sheath miner, studies, U.S.D.A..........   160
    shorts, digestibility, Ark...............   673
    shorts, digestibility and productive value,
        Tex....................................   665
    silage for dairy cows, Wash.............   75
    smut, investigations, Wash..............   46
    smut, studies...................... 149, 750
    soils in United States...................   799
    spring, in England and western Europe..   445
    stalk disease, studies.................. 248, 653
    stem sawfly, western, habits.............   855
    stinking smut, inoculation experiments,
        Mo.....................................   750
    stinking smut, overwintering.............   247
    stinking smut, treatment...............   247
    storage and handling in bulk.............   91
    stored, insects affecting................   353
    straw, methods of analysis, Colo.........   11
    stubble, disposal, Oreg..................   531
    subsoiling experiments...................   732
    supplements in bread making............   263
    supply of France....................... 697, 890
    thrashing injuries.......................   534
    tillering, Del...........................   644
    toxic effect on cows, U.S.D.A...........   766
    varieties......... 237, 436, 438, 823, 824, 825, 826
    varieties, Hawaii........................   132
    varieties, Idaho.................... 29, 30, 640
    varieties, Ill...........................   641
    varieties, Iowa..........................   30
    varieties, Md....................... 333, 340
    varieties, Minn..................... 227, 223
    varieties, Mo............................   731
    varieties, Nev...........................   32
    varieties, Oreg..........................   529
    varieties, Tex...........................   330
    varieties, Wash..........................   33
    varieties, classification and registration. 437, 799
    varieties resistant to Hessian fly, Mo.....   760
    volume weight and grain characteristics..   643
    water requirements, Utah...............   340
    water-soaked, milling value, Wash.......   861
    weeding..................................   742
    winter and spring, in United States and
        Canada.................................   533
    winter, protection, Minn...............   226
    yellow-berry, notes, Oreg..............   531
Whey acidity, antiseptic action.............   373
White—
    fly, spiny citrus, notes.................   462
    fly, woolly, notes, Fla..................   659
    grubs, destruction by hogs.............   261
    grubs, notes, Conn.State...............   255
    oak leaves, plant food constituents......   629
Willow—
    borer, studies, N.Y.Cornell.............   464
    galls, aeriferous tissue in.................   26
Willows—
    basket, for Idaho, Idaho.................   244
    cutting from irrigation canals...........   285
Wind—
    avalanche, at Juneau, U.S.D.A..........   513
    rôle in land depletion, U.S.D.A..........   115

Windbreaks—   Page.
    notes, Ohio..............................   147
    notes, U.S.D.A...........................   46
Windmill generating plants, tests..........   387
Windstorms of May 25–June 6, 1917, U.S.D.A.   807
Wine—
    acids of.................................   310
    aldehydes in.............................   805
    analyses............................. 12, 310
    fruit, fermentation......................   509
    making experiments......................   144
    vinegar disease, treatment..............   314
Winter—
    cress, eradication, Mich................   742
    indoor aridity, U.S.D.A..................   807
    of 1916–17, U.S.D.A.................. 513, 807
    of 1916–17 in British Isles..............   418
    stratus, formation, U.S.D.A.   116
Wire fences, construction...................   886
Wireworm—
    common, larval and pupal stages........   765
    injurious to potatoes, Wash.............   157
Wisconsin—
    rivers, profile surveys...................   84
    University and Station, notes........... 99, 198
    Veterinary Medical Association..........   477
Witches' broom, notes.......................   47
Woburn field experiments....................   229
Woman movement in German Switzerland..   793
Women agricultural workers in Germany....   191
Women's institutes in New Brunswick......   895
Wood—
    ashes as a source of potash......... 427, 722, 817
    chemistry of......................... 502, 710
    decay, studies...................... 109, 727
    destroying fungi, new hosts for.........   846
    pipes, specifications....................   487
    pulp industry in United States.........   748
    pulp, manufacture.......................   148
        (See also Pulpwood.)
    seasoning, U.S.D.A......................   886
    specimens in Madras Government
        Museum.................................   748
    tick, notes...............................   459
        (See also Lumber and Timber.)
Woodlot products—
    marketing............................. 548, 833
    marketing, Ohio........................ 195, 895
Woodlots—
    in eastern United States, U.S.D.A.......   245
    in New England, U.S.D.A...............   451
    management, Kans.......................   451
Woods—
    microscopic identification..............   46
    of Queensland............................   548
    of United States, mechanical properties,
        U.S.D.A...............................   885
Wool—
    handling in the West, U.S.D.A.........   572
    textbook.................................   894
    water absorption capacity...............   736
Worm nodules in cattle......................   181
Worms in swine and goats, Guam..........   779
Wounds, treatment.............. 176, 477, 688, 876
Wrens, house, egg-laying cycles.............   869

Wyoming—	Page.
Station, notes......................	198, 300, 899
Station, report.........................	396
University, notes..........	99, 198, 300, 399, 899
Xanthin, action on isolated intestine........	471
Xanthium spp., eradication.................	542
Xanthophyll pigments, formation..........	632
Xanthorrhœa spp. of South America........	548
Xenia in corn.............................	537
Xylaria spp. on apple roots, U.S.D.A.....	457, 754
Xyleborus dispar, notes, Conn.State........	255
Xylomeges eunia, remedies..................	256
Xylose—	
determination...........................	617
preparation from cottonseed hulls.......	410
Xylotrechus aceris n.sp., description........	566
Yackas of South Australia...................	548
Yams, tuber wilt diseases..................	452

Yeast—	Page.
dead, formation of carbon dioxid by.....	203
decomposition of lactic acid by..........	202
development of reproductive organs.....	631
Yellow—	
fever, investigations....................	367
rocket, eradication, Mich................	742
Yucca filamentosa, saponin of................	9
Zacaton, description and culture...........	141
Zea ramosa and *Z. tunicata*, hybrids of,	
U.S.D.A................................	536
Zeolite, artificial, as a source of potash......	329
Zignoella nobilis n.sp., notes...............	148
Zinc chlorid, antiseptic and germicidal value.	176
Zingiberone, isolation and chemical consti-	
tution...................................	612
Zostera marina, analyses, Conn.State........	814
Zygosporium parvnum n.sp., notes...........	253

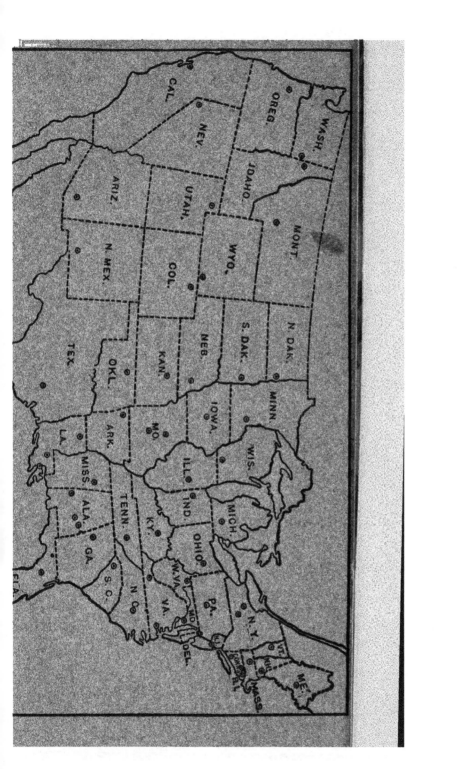

Lightning Source UK Ltd.
Milton Keynes UK
UKHW02f0053260818
327788UK00012BA/727/P